THE HARVARD BIOGRAPHICAL DICTIONARY OF MUSIC

Editorial Board

Edited by DON MICHAEL RANDEL

THE HARVARD BIOGRAPHICAL DICTIONARY OF MUSIC

The Belknap Press of Harvard University Press
Cambridge, Massachusetts, and London, England 1996

n Data

/ edited by Don Michael

1. Music—Bio-bibliography—Dictionaries. I. Randel, Don
Michael.
ML105.H38 1996
780′.92′2—dc20
[B]

96-16456

Preface

The present dictionary, like its companion, *The New Harvard Dictionary of Music,* concerns primarily the history of concert music in the Western tradition. That is, the musicians whose biographies it includes are first and foremost composers of Western concert or art music from the earliest times to the present. But performers of historical importance have a significant presence as well. And a dictionary of musicians produced in America must necessarily include jazz musicians and at least some of the more prominent exponents of popular music.

Many able people have contributed to this effort, and I extend to them profound thanks. The editorial board named in the preceding pages was especially helpful in the early stages of planning the list of entries and in reading early versions of the biographies. The writers of the biographies were Sarah Adams, William Cowdery, Laurel E. Fay, Bettie Jean Harden, Christopher C. Hill, Paul Horsley, Barry Kernfeld, Dennis Libby, Sandra Mangsen, Ronald J. Rabin, Susan Richardson, Alyn Shipton, John Spitzer, Daniel C. Stowe, Carol Traupman, Anna Weesner, Richard J. Will, and Steven D. Zohn. Others contributed to organizing the project, managing the flow of material, updating works lists and bibliographies, and putting everything into proper electronic order. They included Mary Cullen, Carol Randel, Julia Randel, Sally Randel, Cynthia Sedlacek, and Karel Sedlacek. Bettie Jean Harden was particularly helpful in managing the early stages of the project; Ronald J. Rabin was indispensable at the end. James and Nancy Hill gave material and moral support that was essential at a critical moment in between.

The great bulk of the work on this volume was carried out in the Department of Music at Cornell University. Lenore Coral, as head of the Music Library, presides over a collection and a staff without whose strength and generosity this project could not have been accomplished. I am extremely grateful to her and to them. Margaretta Fulton and many others at the Harvard University Press have been not only thoroughly professional and helpful but also patient in the extreme with the progress of this project. Many, many thanks to all.

Don Michael Randel
Ithaca, New York

Abbreviations

General Abbreviations

Middle C is designated c′, the C's below that c, C, C_1, etc. The C's above middle C are designated c″, c‴, etc.

A	alto
ASCAP	American Society of Composers, Authors, and Publishers
B	bass
b.	born
bapt.	baptized
bibl.	bibliography
bk.	book
ca.	circa
cal.	calendar
C.E.	of the common era
cent.	century
chap.	chapter
d.	died
diss.	dissertation
ed.	edition, edited by, editor
facs.	facsimile
fl.	flourished
incl.	inclusive, including
IRCAM	Institut de recherche et de coordination acoustique/musique (Paris)
ISCM	International Society for Contemporary Music
movt.	movement
n.s.	new series
op.	opus
o.s.	old style
p.	page (plural pp.)
perf.	performance, performed
pt.	part
publ.	published by
R:	reprint
rev.	revised, revised by
S	soprano
supp.	supplement
T	tenor
trans.	translation, translated by, translator
vol.	volume
Univ.	University
W.P.A.	Works Projects Administration

Bibliographical Abbreviations

AfMf	*Archiv für Musikforschung* (Leipzig, 1936–43)
AfMw	*Archiv für Musikwissenschaft* (Leipzig, 1918/19–1926; Trossingen, 1952–61; Wiesbaden, 1962–)
AM	*Acta musicologica* (Basel, 1928–)
AMI	*L'arte musicale in Italia,* ed. Luigi Torchi (Milan, Rome: Ricordi, 1897–1908; R: Milan: Ricordi, 1970)

AmZ	*Allgemeine musikalische Zeitung* (Leipzig, 1798–1848, 1863–68)
AMz	*Allgemeine Musikzeitung* (Leipzig, 1874–1943)
AnM	*Anuario musical* (Barcelona, 1946–)
AnMca	*Analecta musicologica* (Cologne, 1963–)
AnnM	*Annales musicologiques* (Neuilly-sur-Seine, 1953–77)
BaJb	*Bach-Jahrbuch* (Leipzig, 1904–)
BBM	*Collezione di trattati e musiche edite in fac-simile* (Milan: Bolletino bibliografico musicale, 1930–ca. 1936)
BMB	*Bibliotheca musica bononiensis* (Bologna: Forni, 1967–)
BzMw	*Beiträge zur Musikwissenschaft* (Berlin, 1959–)
CCT	*Translations,* general ed. Albert Seay (Colorado Springs: Colo Coll Mus, 1967–)
CEKM	*Corpus of Early Keyboard Music* (n.p.: AIM, 1963–)
CM	*Current Musicology* (New York, 1965–)
CMI	*I classici musicali italiani* (Milan: I classici musicali italiani, 1941–43, 1956)
CMM	*Corpus mensurabilis musicae* (n.p.: AIM, 1948–)
CMS	*College Music Symposium* (Madison, Wis., 1961–)
CS	*Scriptorum de musica medii aevi,* ed. Edmond de Coussemaker (Paris, 1864–76; R: Hildesheim: Olms, 1963)
CSM	*Corpus scriptorum de musica* (Rome: AIM, 1950–)
DDT	*Denkmäler deutscher Tonkunst* (Leipzig: Breitkopf & Härtel, 1892–1931; R: Wiesbaden: Breitkopf & Härtel; Graz: Akadem Druck- & V-a, 1957–61)
DM	*Documenta musicologica* (Kassel: Bärenreiter, 1951–)
DTB	*Denkmäler der Tonkunst in Bayern,* Denkmäler deutscher Tonkunst, 2. Folge (Brunswick: H Litolff [etc.], 1900–38; rev. ed., Wiesbaden: Breitkopf & Härtel, 1962)
DTÖ	*Denkmäler der Tonkunst in Österreich* (Vienna: Österreichischer Bundesverlag, 1894–1959; Graz: Akadem Druck- & V-a, 1960–; R: Graz: Akadem Druck- & V-a, 1959)
EDM	*Das Erbe deutscher Musik,* 1. Reihe (Kassel: Nagel; Wiesbaden: Breitkopf & Härtel; Leipzig: Kistner & Siegel, 1935–; R: Kiel: Das Erbe deutscher Musik, 1953–)
EECM	*Early English Church Music* (London: Stainer & Bell, 1963–); suppls. (1972–)
ELS	*The English Lute Songs* (Menston, Eng.: Scolar Pr, 1968–)
EM	*Early Music* (London, 1973–)
EMS	*The English Madrigal School,* ed. Edmond H. Fellowes (London: Stainer & Bell, 1913–24; rev. ed., 1956–)
ESLS	*The English School of Lutenist-Songwriters,* ed. Edmond H. Fellowes, Ser. 1-2 (London: Winthrop Rogers; New York: G Schirmer, 1920–32; rev. ed., London: Stainer & Bell, 1959–)
FAM	*Fontes artis musicae* (Kassel, 1954–)
GS	*Scriptores ecclesiastici de musica sacra,* ed. Martin Gerbert (St. Blasien, 1784; R: Hildesheim: Olms, 1963)
GSJ	*The Galpin Society Journal* (Oxford, 1948–)
HAM	*Historical Anthology of Music,* ed. Willi Apel and Archibald Thompson Davison (Cambridge, Mass.: Harvard U Pr, 1946–50)
IRASM	*International Review of the Aesthetics and Sociology of Music* (Zagreb, 1970–)
JAMIS	*Journal of the American Musical Instrument Society* (Shreveport, La., 1974–)
JAMS	*Journal of the American Musicological Society* (Richmond, 1948–)
JM	*Journal of Musicology* (St. Joseph, Mich., 1982–)

JMT	*Journal of Music Theory* (New Haven, 1957–)
JRBM	*Journal of Renaissance and Baroque Music* (Cambridge, Mass., from no. 2 New Haven, 1946–47; mainly Rome 1948–)
JRMA	*Journal of the Royal Music Association* (London, 1987–)
JRME	*Journal of Research in Musical Education* (Chicago, 1953–)
KmJb	*Kirchenmusikalisches Jahrbuch* (Regensburg, 1886–1911, 1930–38, 1950–)
LSJ	*Lute Society Journal* (London, 1959–)
MAB	*Musica antiqua bohemica* (Prague: Editio Artia, 1943–)
MB	*Musica britannica* (London: Stainer & Bell, 1951–; 2nd ed., 1954–)
MD	*Musica disciplina* (Rome, 1948–)
Mf	*Die Musikforschung* (Kassel, 1948–)
MJb	*Mozart-Jahrbuch* (Salzburg, 1950–)
ML	*Music and Letters* (London, 1920–)
MM	*Modern Music* (New York, 1924–46)
MMC	*Miscellanea musicological* (Prague, 1956–62, 1965–71/3, 1975–)
MME	*Monumentos de la música española* (Barcelona: CSIC, 1941–)
MMFTR	*Monuments de la musique française au temps de la renaissance,* ed. Henry Expert (Paris: Editions M Senart, 1924–29, 1958–; R: New York: Broude Bros, 1952)
MMMA	*Monumenta monodica medii aevii* (Kassel: Bärenreiter, 1956–)
MMML	*Monuments of Music and Music Literature in Facsimile* (New York: Broude Bros, 1965–)
MMN	*Monumenta musicae neerlandicae* (Amsterdam, 1959–)
MMR	*Masters and Monuments of the Renaissance* (New York: Broude Bros, 1980–)
MMRF	*Les maîtres musiciens de la renaissance française,* ed. Henry Expert (Paris: Leduc, 1894–1908; R: New York: Broude Bros, 1952)
MQ	*The Musical Quarterly* (New York, 1915–)
MR	*The Music Review* (Cambridge, Eng., 1940–)
MRM	*Monuments of Renaissance Music* (Chicago: U of Chicago Pr, 1964–)
MSD	*Musicological Studies and Documents* (Rome: AIM, 1951–)
MT	*The Musical Times* (London, 1844–)
NOHM	*The New Oxford History of Music* (London: Oxford U Pr, 1954–)
NRMI	*Nuova rivista musicale italiana* (Turin, 1967–)
NZfM	*Neue Zeitschrift für Musik* (Leipzig, 1834–43, 1950–74, 1979–)
Ömz	*Österreichische Musikzeitschrift* (Vienna, 1953–)
PMFC	*Polyphonic Music of the Fourteenth Century* (Monaco: Oiseau-Lyre, 1956–)
PNM	*Perspectives of New Music* (Princeton, 1962–)
PRMA	*Proceedings of the Royal Musical Association* (London, 1944–), continuation of *PMA*
RBM	*Revue belge de musicologie* (Brussels, 1946–)
RdM	*Revue de musicologie* (Paris, 1917–39, 1945–)
ReM	*La revue musicale* (Paris, 1920–40, 1946–)
RFsC	*Fourscore Classics of Music Literature,* ed. Gustave Reese (New York: Liberal Arts Pr, 1957)
RIM	*Rivista italiana di musicologia* (Florence, 1966–)
RMARC	*Royal Musical Association Research Chronicle* (London, 1961–)
RMFC	*Recherches sur la musique française classique* (Paris, 1960–)
RMI	*Rivista musicale italiana* (Milan, 1894–1932, 1936–43, 1946–55)
RRMBE	*Recent Researches in the Music of the Baroque Era* (Madison, Wis.: A-R Edit, 1964–)

RRMCE	*Recent Researches in the Music of the Classical Era* (Madison, Wis.: A-R Edit, 1975–)
RRMR	*Recent Researches in the Music of the Renaissance* (Madison, Wis.: A-R Edit, 1964–)
SIMG	*Sammelbände der Internationalen Musik-Gesellschaft* (Leipzig, 1899–1914)
SM	*Studia musicologica academiae scientiarum hungaricae* (Budapest, 1961–)
SMw	*Studien zur Musikwissenschaft* (Leipzig and Vienna, 1913–16, 1918–23; Vienna, 1924–34, 1955–56; Graz, Vienna, and Cologne, 1960–66; Tutzing, 1977–)
SMz	*Schweizerische Musikzeitung/Revue musicale suisse* (Berne, 1861–78; Zurich, 1879–)
SR	*Source Readings in Music History,* comp. Oliver Strunk (New York: Norton, 1950)
STMf	*Svensk tidskrift för musikforskning* (Stockholm, 1919–)
SzMw	*Studien zur Musikwissenschaft* (Vienna, 1913–34, 1955–)
TCM	*Tudor Church Music* (London: Oxford U Pr, 1922–29; appendix, 1948; R: New York: Broude Bros, 1963)
TVNM	*Tijdschrift van de Vereniging voor Nederlandse muziekgeschiedenis* (Amsterdam, 1882–)
WE	*The Wellesley Edition* (Wellesley, Mass.: Wellesley College, 1950–)
YTS	*Music Theory Translation Series* (New Haven: Yale U Pr, 1963–)
ZfMw	*Zeitschrift für Musikwissenschaft* (Leipzig, 1918–35)

Illustration Credits

John Adams: photo by Betty Freeman. Marian Anderson: Prints and Photographs Division, Library of Congress. Andrews Sisters, Richard D'Oyly Carte promotional piece, Gian Carlo Menotti's *Amahl and the Night Visitors,* and Arthur Sullivan's *Pirates of Penzance:* courtesy of the Harvard University Theatre Collection. Johann Sebastian Bach and sons: Internationale Bachakademie. Béla Bartók: The New York Times. Amy Beach: University Archives, Special Collections, University of New Hampshire Library, Durham. Alban Berg: courtesy of Lawrence A. Schoenberg and the Arnold Schoenberg Institute. Luciano Berio: photo by Jacqueline Salmon. Hector Berlioz: Collection of Mme. Reboul-Berlioz, Paris. Leonard Bernstein, E. Power Biggs, Mstislav Rostropovich: courtesy of the Harvard University Archives. Georges Bizet, William Byrd, Claude Debussy, Plácido Domingo, Joseph Joachim, Scott Joplin, Fritz Kreisler, Wanda Landowska, Zubin Mehta, Modest Mussorgsky, Birgit Nilsson, Ignacy Paderewski, Leontyne Price, Maurice Ravel, Andrés Segovia, Ravi Shankar, John Philip Sousa, Arturo Toscanini: The Music Division; The New York Public Library for the Performing Arts; Astor, Lenox and Tilden Foundations. Nadia Boulanger: courtesy of Doda Conrad. Johannes Brahms, Robert and Clara Schumann: Gesellschaft der Musikfreunde, Vienna. John Cage: courtesy of John Cage. Enrico Caruso: courtesy of the Metropolitan Opera Association. John Coltrane, Duke Ellington: courtesy of the Institute of Jazz Studies, Rutgers, the State University of New Jersey. Aaron Copland: courtesy of the Fromm Foundation. Guillaume Dufay, Josquin Desprez, Giacomo Meyerbeer, Jacques Offenbach: Bibliothèque Nationale, Paris. Arthur Fiedler: courtesy of the Boston Symphony Orchestra Archives. George and Ira Gershwin: Robert Breen Collection, courtesy of the Jerome Lawrence and Robert E. Lee Theatre Research Institute, The Ohio State University. Christoph Willibald Gluck, Joseph Haydn: Royal College of Music. Benny Goodman, Charles Ives: Yale Music Library, used with permission. George Frideric Handel: courtesy of the Board of Trustees of the Victoria and Albert Museum. Fanny Mendelssohn Hensel, Felix Mendelssohn: Mendelssohn Archive, Staatliche Museen zu Berlin, Preussischer Kulturbesitz. Christopher Hogwood: photo by Donald Dietz, courtesy of the Handel & Haydn Society. Sergey Koussevitzky: photo by Egone, courtesy of the Boston Symphony Orchestra Archives. Orlande de Lassus, Gustav Mahler: Österreichischen Nationalbibliothek, Vienna. Yo-Yo Ma: photo by Walter Scott. Olivier Messiaen: photo by Jean Pierre Leloir. Wolfgang Amadeus Mozart: Mozart Museum, Salzburg. Seiji Ozawa: photo by Akira Kinoshita, courtesy of the Boston Symphony Orchestra Archives. Niccolò Paganini: Musées Nationaux, Paris. Giacomo Puccini: The Bettmann Archive. Cypriano de Rore: Bayerische Staatsbibliothek, Munich. Adolphe Sax instrument: Musée Instrumental, Conservatoire National Supérieur de Musique, Paris. Arnold Schoenberg: Arnold Schoenberg Institute, University of Southern California. Henry E. Steinway: Collection Henry Steinway. Karlheinz Stockhausen: photo by Clive Barda, the Performing Arts Library. Igor Stravinsky: photo by Vera Sudeikina. Guiseppe Verdi: George Eastman House. Richard Wagner: photo by Jules Bonnet, courtesy of the Richard Wagner Museum, Bayreuth. Kurt Weill's *Dreigroschenoper:* Weill-Lenya Research Center, Kurt Weill Foundation for Music, New York.

THE HARVARD BIOGRAPHICAL DICTIONARY OF MUSIC

A

Aaron [Aron], **Pietro** (b. Florence, ca. 1480; d. probably Bergamo, ca. 1550). Theorist. Cantor at the cathedral in Imola from about 1515 until 1522; *maestro da casa* to the Grand Prior in Venice of the Order of St. John of Jerusalem from 1525; entered the monastery of S. Leonardo in Bergamo in 1536. His writings, which were attacked by Gaffurius and defended by Spataro, include an important discussion of the application of the theory of modes to polyphonic compositions; other topics include counterpoint and cadence formation in four voices.

Writings: *Libri tres de institutione harmonica* (Bologna, 1516); facs., *MMML* ser. 2, no. 67 (1976). *Thoscanello de la musica* (Venice, 1523); facs., *MMML* ser. 2, no. 69 (1969); rev. as *Toscanello in musica* (1529); facs., *DM* ser. 1, no. 29 (1970); trans. Eng. Peter Bergquist, *CCT* 4 (1970). *Trattato della natura et cognitione di tutti gli tuoni di canto figurato* (Venice, 1525); facs., *MMML* ser. 2, no. 129 (1979); chaps. 1–7 trans. Eng. in *SR*, pp. 205–18. *Lucidario in musica* (Venice, 1545); facs., *MMML* ser. 2, no. 68 (1978). *Compendiolo di molti dubbi* (Milan, after 1545); facs., *MMML* ser. 2, no. 66 (1974).

Bibl.: Peter Bergquist, "Mode and Polyphony around 1500: Theory and Practice," *Music Forum* 1 (1967): 99–161.

Abaco, Evaristo Felice dall'. See Dall'Abaco, Evaristo Felice.

Abbado, Claudio (b. Milan, 26 June 1933). Conductor. Studied piano at the Milan Conservatory and with Friedrich Gulda in Salzburg; conducting with Hans Swarowsky at the Vienna Academy. Winner of the Koussevitzky Competition at Tanglewood in 1958; of the Mitropoulos Prize in 1963, leading to an association with the New York Philharmonic. Principal conductor at La Scala in Milan from 1968, music director from 1972, and artistic director from 1976 until 1986. Appointed principal conductor of the Vienna Philharmonic in 1971; of the London Symphony, 1979–86. Music director of the Vienna State Opera, 1986–91. Principal guest conductor of the Chicago Symphony from 1982. Chief conductor of the Berlin Philharmonic from 1990. His repertory includes operas of Verdi and Rossini and works of Brahms, Mahler, Berg, and leading contemporary composers.

Abbatini, Antonio Maria (b. Città di Castello, 1609 or 1610; d. there, ca. 1679). Composer, teacher, and theorist. *Maestro di cappella* at St. John Lateran in Rome, 1626–28; at the cathedral in Orvieto in 1633; and at various churches in Rome thereafter, including S. Maria Maggiore (1640–46, 1649–57, 1672–77). Cesti was among his pupils. His *Dal male il bene* (Rome, 1653; libretto by Giulio Rospigliosi; act 2 by Marco Marazzoli) is an important early example of comic opera, employing simple recitative and ensemble finales. Other works include the operas *Ione* (Vienna, 1664) and *La comica del cielo, overo La Baltasara* (Rome, 1668); Latin church music (6 books or more) in both polychoral and few-voiced concertato style; a few secular pieces for solo voice and continuo. He contributed to an edition of Gregorian hymns (1644) and wrote 14 lectures on music.

Bibl.: Galliano Ciliberti, *Antonio Maria Abbatini e la musica del suo tempo (1595–1679): Documenti per una ricostruzione bio-bibliografica* (Perugia, 1986).

Abel, Carl Friedrich (b. Cöthen, 22 Dec. 1723; d. London, 20 June 1787). Composer and viola da gamba player for whose use J. S. Bach's three gamba sonatas may have been composed. He studied with his father, Christian Ferdinand Abel, a viola da gamba player and violinist, and in Leipzig after his father's death in 1737, when he probably joined J. S. Bach's Collegium musicum. A member of the court orchestra in Dresden from 1743 until 1757, he ultimately settled in London, giving his first concert there in April 1759. In February 1764 he gave his first joint concert with J. C. Bach, both serving as chamber musicians to Queen Charlotte from about this time. Together they established the Bach-Abel concerts, series of 10 to 15 concerts given each year from 1765 until 1781. From 1775 these were housed in a room built for the purpose at Hanover Square. The works performed were principally those of Bach and Abel themselves. Performers included Abel on the viola da gamba, of which he was one of the last great exponents, and numerous Continental musicians. After a visit to the Continent beginning in 1782, including a stay at the court of the Crown Prince of

Ticket for a Bach-Abel concert.

Prussia in Potsdam, he returned to London and was prominent in a series of concerts that began in 1785. His works include two dozen symphonies as well as concertos, overtures, and other orchestral works; string quartets, string trios, sonatas, and other chamber music for various combinations; and sonatas and other pieces for viola da gamba.

Bibl.: *Kompositionen* (Cuxhaven, 1958–74). Walter Knape, *Bibliographisch-thematisches Verzeichnis der Kompositionen von Karl Friedrich Abel* (Cuxhaven, 1971). Id., *Karl Friedrich Abel: Leben und Werk eines frühklassischen Komponisten* (Bremen, 1973). Murray R. Charters, "Abel in London," *MT* 114 (1973): 1224.

Abondante, Giulio [Abundante, dal Pestrino, Julio] (fl. 1546–87). Lutenist and composer, perhaps from around Venice, where his three surviving collections of lute music were published between 1546 and 1587 (the last described as the fifth). The collections include intabulations of sacred and secular vocal works by leading composers of the time as well as fantasias and dance pieces such as passamezzos, galliards, pavans, and padoanas.

Abrahmsen, Hans (b. Copenhagen, 23 Dec. 1952). Composer. Studied horn at the Royal Danish Conservatory (1969–71), then at Jutland Academy of Music in Århus, where his teachers included Gudmundsen-Holmgreen and Nørgård. His compositions are almost exclusively instrumental, for both full orchestra and various chamber ensembles. His works make use of Scandinavian elements as well as modern devices. Works include *Winternacht,* flute, clarinet, cornet, horn, piano, violin, cello (1976–78); *Walden,* wind quintet (1978); *Flush,* solo saxophone (1974; rev. 1979); *Canzone,* accordion (1978); *Fantasy Pieces after Hans-Jørgen Nielsen,* flute, horn, cello, piano (1969; rev. 1976); *Universal Birds,* 10 sopranos (1973); 2 symphonies (1974, 1982); *Märchenbilder,* chamber orchestra (1986); a cello concerto (1987).

Abrams, Muhal Richard [Abrahams, Richard] (b. Chicago, 19 Sept. 1930). Jazz pianist and composer. In Chicago he accompanied such soloists as Miles Davis and Sonny Rollins and later played in and wrote for Walter Perkins's hard bop group Modern Jazz Two + Three (1957–60). He formed the Experimental Band, a free jazz big band (1961). He was a founder and the first president of the Association for the Advancement of Creative Musicians (1965). His albums with its members include *Levels and Degrees of Light* as a leader (1967) and *Sightsong* in a duo with the double bass player Malachi Favors (1975). He moved to New York around 1977 and has regularly toured internationally, playing in all jazz styles.

Abravanel, Maurice (de) (b. Thessaloniki, of Sephardic parents, 6 Jan. 1903; d. Salt Lake City, Utah, 22 Sept. 1993). Conductor. Studied in Switzerland from childhood, moving in 1922 to Berlin, where he studied composition with Weill. Conducted in Berlin and elsewhere in Germany until the advent of Hitler, moving to Paris in 1933. Toured Australia in 1934–35. On the staff of the Metropolitan Opera in New York, 1936–38; thereafter conducted Broadway shows (including Weill's *Knickerbocker Holiday* and *Street Scene*). Conductor of the Utah Symphony in Salt Lake City from 1947 until his retirement in 1979, bringing this orchestra to prominence in part through numerous recordings of a wide variety of works. Music director of the Music Academy of the West, 1954–80.

Absil, Jean (b. Bon-Secours, Hainaut, Belgium, 23 Oct. 1893; d. Brussels, 2 Feb. 1974). Composer. After early training in Bon-Secours and Tournai, he studied organ and composition at the Brussels Conservatory beginning in 1913, intending to become an organist. After deciding to pursue composition instead, he studied with Gilson in 1920–22. His First Symphony won the Prix Agniez in 1921, and his cantata *La guerre* won the Belgian second Prix de Rome in 1922, whereupon he was made director of the Etterbeek Music School. The Pro Arte Concerts, established by Paul Collaer in 1921, introduced him to the music of Schoenberg, Berg, Stravinsky, Milhaud, and others, which had a lasting influence on the course of his own development. In 1934 he won the Rubens Prize and founded the concert series La sirène with Souris and Poot for the performance of new music. His *Postulats de la musique contemporaine,* published in 1937, advocated his own brand of polytonality and pointed to its historical roots. In 1938 he helped to found the *Revue internationale de musique.* His First Piano Concerto was commissioned as the compulsory work for finalists in the Ysaÿe Competition of 1938. He began teaching at the Brussels Conservatory in 1930 and was professor of fugue there from 1939 until his retirement in 1959. Although much of his music is rhythmically complex and dissonant, he also composed a number of works deriving from his study of the folk music of Romania and other countries.

Works: the opera *Les voix de la mer* (Brussels, 1954), 3 ballets, and other works for the stage; 5 symphonies; 2 violin concertos, 3 piano concertos, a viola concerto, a guitar concerto, and other works for soloist with orchestra; 2 symphonic poems and other orchestral works; several works for band; 4 string quartets, 2 piano trios, 2 string trios, and other chamber music, including several works with saxophone; cantatas and other choral works, some with orchestra; piano pieces; guitar pieces; songs.

Bibl.: *Jean Absil,* Catalogue des oeuvres de compositeurs belges, 20 (Brussels, 1957). Richard de Guide, *Jean Absil* (Tournai, 1965).

Abt, Franz Wilhelm (b. Eilenburg, 22 Dec. 1819; d. Wiesbaden, 31 Mar. 1885). Composer. Studied at the Thomasschule and the university in Leipzig; a choral conductor in Zurich from 1841; second conductor at the court in Brunswick from 1852 and chief conductor from 1855; traveled widely as a choral conductor and toured America very successfully in 1872. Composed over 3,000 works, including 7 large secular cantatas, numerous choral works (many for male chorus), very many songs ("Wenn di Schwalben heimwärts zieh'n," "Gute Nacht, du mein herziges Kind," "Die stille Wasserrose"), often folklike in character.

Achron, Joseph (b. Lozdzieje, Poland, 13 May 1886; d. Hollywood, 29 Apr. 1943). Violinist and composer. He studied in Warsaw after his family moved there in 1890; in 1898 he entered the St. Petersburg Conservatory, studying violin with Leopold Auer and composition with Lyadov. After graduating in 1904 he went to Berlin, but returned to St. Petersburg in 1907 for further study in composition. In 1911 he joined with other Jewish musicians in the study of Jewish folklore, which played a continuing role in his compositions thereafter. He taught at the conservatory in Kharkov from 1913, served in the Russian army during World War I, and was associated with the Hebrew Chamber Theater in Petrograd in the years 1919–21. After returning to Berlin in 1922, he moved to Palestine in 1924 and emigrated to the U.S. in 1925. He became a U.S. citizen in 1930 and in 1934 settled in Hollywood, where he played violin in film studio orchestras while continuing to compose and to perform as a soloist. His best-known work is *Hebrew Melody* for violin and orchestra (1911). Later works such as *Golem,* a suite for chamber orchestra (1932), employ principles related to those of the music of Schoenberg. Other works include 3 violin concertos; a piano concerto; *Evening Service for the Sabbath* (1930) and other choral works; chamber music; songs.

Bibl.: Philip Moddel, *Joseph Achron* (Tel Aviv, 1966).

Acuff, Roy (Claxton) (b. Maynardville, Tenn., 15 Sept. 1903; d. Nashville, 24 Nov. 1992). Country-and-western singer, fiddler, songwriter, and publisher. After performances in medicine shows and on local radio stations in Tennessee, he became a regular performer in the Grand Ole Opry in Nashville in 1938, appearing with the Smoky Mountain Boys. His performances of "The Wabash Cannon Ball" and "The Great Speckled Bird" were extremely popular, as was his own song "Precious Jewel." He published country music in Nashville in association with Fred Rose.

Adam, Adolphe (Charles) (b. Paris, 24 July 1803; d. there, 3 May 1856). Composer. He studied piano first with his father, Louis, who was a teacher at the Paris Conservatory, and with Henry Lemoine. He then entered the Paris Conservatory, where he studied organ with Benoist, counterpoint with Reicha, and composition with Boieldieu, who was his principal mentor. His friendship with Hérold was also influential. In 1824 he won an honorable mention in the Prix de Rome competition and in 1825 a second prize. Beginning with works for vaudeville theaters in Paris, Adam devoted his career to music for the stage, composing more than 50 operas all told and over a dozen ballets. His first complete works were performed at the Gymnase (where he had served as a chorusmaster) and other Parisian theaters and included the one-act vaudeville *L'oncle d'Amérique* (1826; libretto by Scribe and Mazères) and the one-act comic opera *Le mal du pays, ou La batelière de Brientz* (1827; libretto by Scribe and Mélesville). His first work to be produced at the Opéra-comique, *Pierre et Catherine* (1829), was given on the same program with a work by Auber and ran for 80 performances. One of his greatest successes was the one-act *Le chalet* (1834; libretto by Scribe and Mélesville, after Goethe), which ran for 1,400 performances over the years. Still more successful was the three-act *Le postillon de Lonjumeau,* first produced at the Opéra-comique in 1836, a work that long remained in the international repertory. He is now best known for his ballet *Giselle, ou Les Wilis,* first produced in 1841 with Carlotta Grisi in the title role; the ballet *Le corsaire* (1856) also enjoyed continuing success. A disagreement with the director of the Opéra-comique led to Adam's founding of a new opera house, the Opéra-national, in 1847. After an initial success, the venture failed in the aftermath of the Revolution of 1848, leaving Adam financially broken. He turned to journalism and in 1849 became a professor of composition at the Paris Conservatory, a position he held until the end of his life. His works were again produced at the Opéra-comique, under new management, beginning in 1852 with the opera *Giralda, ou La nouvelle Psyché* (libretto by Scribe); from the same year, *Si j'étais roi* was also successful. He wrote two volumes of memoirs: *Souvenirs d'un musicien* (Paris, 1857) and *Derniers souvenirs d'un musicien* (Paris, 1859). His Christmas carol "Cantique de Noël" ("O Holy Night") is often sung.

Adam, Claus (b. Sumatra, of Austrian parents, 5 Nov. 1917; d. New York, 4 July 1983). Cellist and composer. Studied at the Mozarteum in Salzburg; in the U.S., after his family emigrated in 1929 and settled in Brooklyn, studied cello with Emanuel Feuermann and others, conducting with Leon Barzin, and composition with Stefan Wolpe. Cellist in the Minneapolis Symphony in 1940; of the New Music Quartet, 1948–55; of the Juilliard Quartet, 1955–74. Composed principally chamber music (a string quartet, 1975).

Ádám, Jenő (b. Szigetszentmiklós, 12 Dec. 1896; d. Budapest, 15 May 1982). Composer, conductor, and educator. Studied composition with Kodály in Budapest and conducting with Weingartner in Basel. Conductor and teacher at the Academy of Music in Budapest from 1929 until 1959. Collaborated with Kodály in the reform of music education in Hungary and published teaching materials jointly with him. Hungarian folk music played a prominent part in his work as a teacher and as a composer. Works include 2 operas, orchestral works, choral works (some with orchestra); 2 string quartets and other chamber music; numerous arrangements of folk songs.

Adam de la Halle [Adan le Bossu, Adan le Boscu d'Arras] (b. Arras, 1245–50; d. Naples, 1285–88? or

John Adams, 1993.

England, after 1306?). Trouvère poet and composer. He seems to have returned to Arras around 1270 after studies in Paris. In the late 1270s he went to Italy in the service of Robert II, Count of Artois, and there he entered the service of Robert's uncle Charles of Anjou (d. 1285). A document by a nephew suggests that Adam had died in Italy by 1288, but an English document of 1306 includes a "maistre Adam le Boscu" in a list of musicians who were to perform at the coronation of Edward II in 1307. His works include monophonic chansons and *jeux-partis;* polyphonic rondeaux and motets; and 3 plays, of which one, a pastoral work titled *Le jeu de Robin et de Marion,* makes considerable use of music.

Bibl.: *Oeuvres complètes* (Paris, 1872; R: New York, 1964; Ridgewood, N.J., 1965). *Lyrische Werke, CMM* 44 (1967).

Adamis, Michael (b. Piraeus, Greece, 19 May 1929). Composer and musicologist. Studied Byzantine chant and composition (with Papaioannou) in Greece and then at Brandeis Univ. (1962–65), where he turned increasingly to electronic music. Head of the music department and choral director at Pierce College, Athens, from 1968. Early works employ twelve-tone techniques; more recent ones often draw on Byzantine chant and include a *Byzantine Passion* (1967) and other settings of sacred texts; electronic works include music for classical Greek and other plays.

Adam of St. Victor (d. St. Victor, Paris, late 1140s). Poet and composer. Probably identical with Adam Precentor, canon of the Cathedral of Notre Dame of Paris in the early 12th century; canon of and resident at the Abbey of St. Victor from 1133 or shortly thereafter until his death. Wrote many sequences of a type developed in Paris in the first half of the 12th century and constructed of regular paired strophes of rhymed and rhythmic verse.

Bibl.: Margot E. Fassler, "Who Was Adam of St. Victor?," *JAMS* 37 (1984): 233–69.

Adams, John (Coolidge) (b. Worcester, Mass., 15 Feb. 1947). Composer, clarinetist, and conductor. Studied composition at Harvard with Kirchner, Kim, and Sessions (1965–71). On the faculty of the San Francisco Conservatory and director of the New Music Ensemble there, 1972–82; composer in residence with the San Francisco Symphony, 1982–85. Winner of the 1995 Grawemeyer Award for his violin concerto (1993). Has employed a wide variety of media, including electronics and video, and often makes repetitive use of relatively simple tonal materials. Works include *Shaker Loops, for 7 Strings* (1978); *Common Tones in Simple Time,* orchestra (1979); *Harmonium,* chorus, orchestra (1981); *Grand Pianola Music,* 2 pianos, 2 sopranos, contralto (1982); *Light over Water (Symphony for Brass and Synthesizers)* (1983); *Harmonielehre,* orchestra (1985); *Short Ride in a Fast Machine* (1986); the operas *Nixon in China* (Houston, 1987) and *The Death of Klinghoffer* (Brussels, 1991); *Fearful Symmetries,* orchestra (1988); *Eros Piano,* piano and chamber orchestra (1989); *Chamber Symphony,* fifteen instrumentalists (1992); *El Dorado,* orchestra (1993); *Le livre de Baudelaire,* soprano, orchestra (1994); *Road Movies,* violin, piano (1995); electronic works; piano music.

Adams, Pepper [Park, III] (b. Highland Park, Mich., 8 Oct. 1930; d. Brooklyn, 10 Sept. 1986). Jazz baritone saxophonist. In Detroit he played bop with Barry Harris, Lucky Thompson, Miles Davis, Tommy Flanagan, Thad and Elvin Jones, and Kenny Burrell, among others (1947–51, 1953–55). After moving to New York (1956), he toured with the big bands of Stan Kenton and Maynard Ferguson. He led quintets with Donald Byrd (1958–62), recording the album *At the Half Note Cafe* (1960; released under Byrd's name), and played occasionally with Charles Mingus (1959–63). He played in the Thad Jones–Mel Lewis Orchestra (1965–76), then toured widely as a soloist. A quartet including Flanagan recorded his album *The Master* (1980).

Adam von Fulda (b. Fulda, ca. 1445; d. Wittenberg, 1505). Composer and theorist. At first a Benedictine, he married and entered the service of Frederick the Wise of Saxony in 1490. Wrote a treatise titled *De musica* (1490; ed. in *GS* 3:329–81). Composed a Mass, hymns, antiphons, and other sacred music (ed. in *EDM* ser. 1, 32–33, 1956–60), and 3 secular songs (in the *Liederbuch* of Arnt von Aich of 1519, including "Ach hülf mich leid"), most works being for four voices with cantus firmus.

Adaskin, Murray (b. Toronto, 28 Mar. 1906). Composer and violinist. Studied violin in Paris and with Luigi von Kunits, Kathleen Parlow, and William Primrose; composition with Weinzweig (1944–48) and Milhaud (1949–50, 1953). Member of the Toronto Symphony, 1926–36; head of the music department of the Univ. of Saskatchewan from 1952 and composer in residence there, 1966–72. Works, some of which make use of Eskimo and other folk materials, include a chamber opera, *Grant Warden of the Plains* (Winnipeg, 1967); orchestral works (*Algonquin Symphony,* 1957–58; *Diversion for Orchestra,* 1969; *Qalala and Nilaula of the North,* 1969; *There Is My People Sleeping,* 1970; *Nootka Ritual,* 1974); a violin and a bassoon concerto; chamber music; songs.

Bibl.: Gordana Lazarevich, *The Musical World of Frances James and Murray Adaskin* (Buffalo, 1988).

Adderley, Cannonball [Julian Edwin] (b. Tampa, 15 Sept. 1928; d. Gary, Ind., 8 Aug. 1975). Jazz alto saxophonist and leader of small groups. In 1955 he left a career as a high school music teacher to join Oscar Pettiford's bop group in New York. After leading a quintet (1956–57) with his brother Nat (b. 1931), a cornetist, he joined Miles Davis's sextet (1957–59), recording the albums *Milestones* (1958) and, with Davis's sidemen including John Coltrane, *Cannonball Adderley Quintet in Chicago* (1959). From 1959 to 1975 he led groups with Nat, popularizing soul jazz and also playing in styles ranging from bop to jazz-rock.

Addinsell, Richard (Stewart) (b. London, 13 Jan. 1904; d. there, 14 Nov. 1977). Composer. Studied at the Royal College of Music and in Berlin and Vienna. Commissioned by Eva LeGallienne to compose music for her *Alice in Wonderland* in 1933 and thereafter composed much music for theater and film. His best-known piece is the *Warsaw Concerto,* a work for piano and orchestra from the film *Dangerous Moonlight* (1941, released in the U.S. as *Suicide Squadron*). Other film scores include *Goodbye, Mr. Chips* (1939), *Blithe Spirit* (1945), *A Tale of Two Cities* (1958), *The Roman Spring of Mrs. Stone* (1961), and *The Waltz of the Toreadors* (1962).

Addison, Adele (b. New York, 24 July 1925). Soprano. Studied at the Westminster Choir College, at Tanglewood (with Boris Goldovsky), and with Povla Frijsh. Made her New York debut at Town Hall in 1952, singing thereafter with the New England Opera, the New York City Opera, and major American orchestras. Her repertory has ranged from Bach and Handel to such 20th-century works as Foss's *Time Cycle* (of which she gave the premiere in 1961).

Addison, John (b. Chobham, Surrey, 16 Mar. 1920). Composer. Studied at the Royal College of Music (composition with Gordon Jacob; oboe, Leon Goossens; clarinet, Frederick Thurston) and was a member of its staff from 1951 until 1958, after which he principally composed for theater and films. His more than 60 film scores include *A Taste of Honey* (1961), *Tom Jones* (1963), *The Loved One* (1965), *Torn Curtain* (1966), *The Charge of the Light Brigade* (1968), *Sleuth* (1972), and *The Seven Per Cent Solution* (1976). Other works include a trumpet concerto (1949) and chamber music.

Adler, Guido (b. Eibenschütz [now Ivančice], Moravia, 1 Nov. 1855; d. Vienna, 15 Feb. 1941). Musicologist. Studied at the Vienna conservatory with Bruckner and Dessoff and at the university, earning first a degree in law and then one in music history under Hanslick, whom he succeeded as professor in 1898. Associate of Spitta and Chrysander and influential in the formation of the discipline of musicology. His students included Ficker, Geiringer, Haas, Jeppesen, Kurth, Smijers, Webern, and Wellesz. His many publications include works on Haydn, Brahms, Wagner, and Mahler and a book on the methods of musical scholarship, *Methode der Musikgeschichte* (Leipzig, 1919).

Adler, Kurt Herbert (b. Vienna, 2 Apr. 1905; d. Ross, Calif., 9 Feb. 1988). Conductor and administrator. Studied at the conservatory and the university in Vienna, where he first conducted at the Max Reinhardt Theater and the Volksoper. Conducted in Germany, Italy, and elsewhere; assisted Toscanini in Salzburg in 1936, and then moved to the U.S. Conducted at the Chicago Opera in 1949. At the San Francisco Opera he became chorusmaster in 1943, artistic director in 1953, and general director in 1956, retiring in 1981.

Adler, Larry [Lawrence Cecil] (b. Baltimore, 10 Feb. 1914). Harmonica player. Became the first well-known performer of concert music on the harmonica, appearing in recitals and as a soloist with major orchestras. Composers who have written works for him include Milhaud, Vaughan Williams, and Gordon Jacob. Blacklisted by militant anticommunists, he was effectively forced to reside and perform in England for a number of years beginning in 1949. Wrote an autobiography, *It Ain't Necessarily So* (New York, 1987).

Adler, Peter Herman (b. Jablonec, Czechoslovakia, 2 Dec. 1899; d. Ridgefield, Conn., 2 Oct. 1990). Conductor. Studied at the Prague Conservatory with Fidelio Finke, Vítězslav Novák, and Alexander von Zemlinsky. Opera conductor in Brno from 1923, in Bremen from 1929, and in Kiev from 1932. Returned to Prague in 1937 and emigrated to the U.S. in the face of the Nazi occupation soon thereafter. Artistic director of the NBC Opera Company (where he commissioned Menotti's *Amahl and the Night Visitors*), 1949–59; music director of the Baltimore Symphony, 1959–68; music and artistic director of National Educational Television from 1969 (commissioned and conducted operas by Pasatieri, Henze, and others); director of the American Opera Center at Juilliard, 1973–81.

Adler, Richard (b. New York, 3 Aug. 1921). Composer and producer of musicals. Graduated from the Univ. of North Carolina in 1943. His most successful works were *Pajama Game* (1954) and *Damn Yankees* (1955), both in collaboration with Jerry Ross (1926–55); has also composed for television and produced shows for the White House (1965–69) and on Broadway.

Adler, Samuel (Hans) (b. Mannheim, 4 Mar. 1928). Composer and conductor. In 1939 he emigrated with his family to the U.S., where his father, having been cantor at the synagogue in Mannheim, became music director at a temple in Worcester, Massachusetts. He studied composition in Boston with Herbert Fromm (1943–47); for the B.Mus. at Boston Univ. with Hugo Norden, Karl Geiringer, and Paul Pisk; for the M.A. at Harvard (1948–50) with Piston, Thompson, and Hindemith; at Tanglewood (1949, 1950) with Copland and Koussevitzky. While in the U.S. Army beginning in 1950, he organized and conducted the Seventh Army Symphony Orchestra in Europe. He was director of music at Temple Emanu-El in Dallas from 1953 until 1956 and taught at North Texas State Univ. from 1957 until 1966, when he joined the faculty of the Eastman School. Works include the operas *The Outcasts of Poker Flat* (1959), *The Wrestler* (1972), and *The Lodge of Shadows* (1973); 6 symphonies, concertos for orchestra, for organ, for piano, and for flute, and other orchestral works; several synagogue services and other choral music; much chamber music, including 6 string quartets; songs; an organ fanfare; arrangements; piano pieces. He has published books on choral conducting, sight singing, and orchestration.

Adlgasser, Anton Cajetan (b. Inzell, Bavaria, 1 Oct. 1729; d. Salzburg, 22 Dec. 1777). Composer and organist. Studied with Johann Ernst Eberlin in Salzburg and then succeeded him as court and cathedral organist there in 1750. After his death in 1777 while playing the organ (described in a letter by Leopold Mozart), he was succeeded as cathedral organist by W. A. Mozart, who praised him as a master of counterpoint. He collaborated with Mozart and Michael Haydn on the oratorio *Die Schuldigkeit* (1767). Composed an Italian opera (lost); singspiels; 20 or more German and Latin oratorios (many lost) on sacred and secular subjects; much Latin church music, including 8 Masses and 2 Requiems; perhaps as many as 9 symphonies; keyboard pieces and concertos; and 103 organ versets.

Adlung, Jakob (b. Bindersleben, near Erfurt, 14 Jan. 1699; d. Erfurt, 5 July 1762). Organist and scholar. Studied in Erfurt with Christian Reichardt and at the university in Jena; organist at a Lutheran church in Erfurt from 1727 and teacher of music and languages at the town school there; built 16 keyboard instruments; wrote books on figured bass and on fantasy and fugue, now lost. His *Musica mechanica organoedi* is a detailed treatment of organ building.

Writings: *Musica mechanica organoedi* (Berlin, 1768); facs., *DM* ser. 1, no. 18 (1961). *Anleitung zu der musikalischen Gelahrtheit* (Erfurt, 1758; 2nd ed., 1783); facs., *DM* ser. 1, no. 4 (1953). *Musikalisches Siebengestirn. Das ist: Sieben zu der edlen Tonkunst gehörige Fragen* (Berlin, 1768).

Adolphe, Bruce (b. New York, 31 May 1955). Composer. Attended Juilliard, where he received a B.M. and M.M. (1976). Member of Juilliard faculty beginning 1974; taught at New York Univ. beginning 1983; visiting lecturer in the residential colleges at Yale Univ., 1984–85. Composer-in-residence at Santa Fe Chamber Music Festival (1989), 92nd Street "Y" (New York) School Concert Series (1988–90), Chamber Music Northwest (Portland, Ore., 1992). Has composed the operas *The Tell-Tale Heart,* based on Poe's story (1982), *Mikhoels the Wise* (1982), and *The False Messiah* (1983). Other works include *Chiaroscuro,* chamber orchestra (1984); *Night Journey,* wind quintet (1987); String Quartet no. 1 (1989); *at the stillpoint there the dance is,* clarinet, string quartet (1990); and a brass quintet (1990).

Adorno, Theodor W(iesengrund) [Theodor Ludwig Wiesengrund] (b. Frankfurt am Main, 11 Sept. 1903; d. Visp, Switzerland, 6 Aug. 1969). Philosopher and writer on music. His early training in music included study of piano with Bernhard Sekles in Frankfurt and of composition with Alban Berg in Vienna (1925–27). Returning to Frankfurt in 1927 to study philosophy, he nevertheless wrote extensively about music as editor of *Anbruch* (1928–31). He taught philosophy at the university in Frankfurt from 1931, but was removed by the Nazis and went first to Oxford in 1934 and then, in 1938, to the U.S. at the invitation of Max Horkheimer, who had earlier moved the Institute for Social Research to New York from Frankfurt. After work on Princeton's Radio Research Project (1938–40), he followed Horkheimer and the institute to Southern California in 1941. In 1949 he returned to Frankfurt with Horkheimer to reestablish the institute there, where he ultimately succeeded Horkheimer as director and was appointed to the faculty of the university. As a central figure in the "Frankfurt School," he fashioned an important strand of Marxist thought. He refused to be associated with any practical political program, and his sociology of music championed the music of Schoenberg and related composers while disdaining mass culture.

Writings: *Philosophy of Modern Music* (1949), trans. Anne G. Mitchell and Wesley V. Blomster (New York, 1973). *Prisms: Cultural Criticism and Society* (1955), trans. Samuel and Shierry Weber (London, 1967). *Introduction to the Sociology of Music* (1962), trans. E. B. Ashton (New York, 1976).

Bibl.: Rose Rosengard Subotnik, "The Historical Structure: Adorno's 'French' Model for the Criticism of Nineteenth-Century Music," *19th-Century Music* 2 (1978): 36–60. Otto Kolleritsch, ed., *Adorno und die Musik* (Graz, 1979). Martin Jay, *Adorno* (Cambridge, Mass., 1984).

Adriaenssen, Emanuel (b. Antwerp, ca. 1554; d. there, buried 27 Feb. 1604). Lutenist and composer. Studied in Rome in 1574, then returned to Antwerp to establish a school for lutenists with his brother Gysbrecht. His works were disseminated throughout Europe in three publications: *Pratum musicum* (Antwerp, 1584); a new, revised edition of this work (Antwerp, 1600); and *Novum pratum musicum* (Antwerp,

1592; R: 1977; includes illustrated discussion of methods of intabulation). They include fantasias, dance pieces, and intabulations (published with optional vocal parts) of sacred and secular vocal works by leading composers, all in a highly ornamented style.

Bibl.: Ed. in *Monumenta musicae belgicae,* 10 (1966). Godelieve Spiessens, *Leven en werk van de Antwerpse luitcomponist Emanuel Adriaenssen (ca. 1554–1604)* (Brussels, 1974–76).

Agazzari, Agostino (b. Siena, 2 Dec. 1578; d. there, 10 Apr. 1640). Composer and organist. Worked in Germany; then *maestro di cappella* at the German College in Rome (1602–3) and at the Jesuit Roman Seminary (1606); returned in 1607 to Siena, where he was organist and then *maestro di cappella* at the cathedral until his death. He published an early and widely influential treatise on thoroughbass, *Del sonare sopra 'l basso* (Siena, 1607; facs., *BMB* ser. 2, no. 37, 1969; partial trans. Eng., *SR,* pp. 424–31). Another treatise, *La musica ecclesiastica* (Siena, 1638), discusses church music in light of the Council of Trent. His compositions include a moralizing pastoral drama, *Eumelio* (performed at the Roman Seminary in 1606), largely in recitative style, but with significant use of choruses; much Latin church music, often for one or more voices and basso continuo; and 3 books of secular madrigals (for 5 to 8 voices) and 2 of *madrigaletti* (for 3 voices).

Bibl.: Colleen Reardon, *Agostino Agazzari and Music at Siena Cathedral, 1597–1641* (New York, 1993).

Ager, Milton (b. Chicago, 6 Oct. 1893; d. Inglewood, Calif., 6 May 1979). Composer of popular music. At first, pianist in silent film theaters and in vaudeville; composed music for films and numerous songs, including "Happy Days Are Here Again" (1930), "Ain't She Sweet?" (1927), and "Hard-Hearted Hannah" (1924).

Agnesi, Maria Teresa (b. Milan, 17 Oct. 1720; d. there, 19 Jan. 1795). Composer. Charles de Brosses commented favorably on hearing her play the harpsichord and sing in her home in 1739. She composed several operas (some to her own librettos) that were performed in Milan, Naples, and Venice; arias; keyboard concertos; keyboard pieces. Her sister Maria Gaetana was a mathematician.

Agostini, Paolo (b. Vallerano, ca. 1583; d. Rome, 3 Oct. 1629). Composer and organist. Studied in Rome with Nanino; organist and *maestro di cappella* in Vallerano; returned to Rome as organist at S. Maria in Trastevere and subsequently held appointments at other churches in Rome; *maestro di cappella* of the Cappella Giulia at St. Peter's from 1626 until his death, succeeding Ugolini. An important representative of the Roman school of sacred polyphony and admired for his mastery of counterpoint and canon, he composed much Latin church music, some for elaborate polychoral forces, including Masses, motets, and Psalms.

Agricola, Alexander (b. 1446?; d. Valladolid, Aug. 1506). Composer and singer. Described in his epitaph as Belgian and in Italian documents as "alemanno." After serving Galeazzo Maria Sforza in Milan from 1471 until 1474, he traveled to Florence and the Low Countries and is documented in Cambrai in 1476. Sometime thereafter he joined the French royal chapel, leaving it for Florence, where he was a singer at the cathedral, 1491–92. After a brief stay at the Aragonese court in Naples, he returned to the French court in 1492, where he may have remained until entering in 1500 the service of Philip the Fair, Duke of Burgundy and King of Castile, with whom he traveled through France and, on two occasions, to Spain. His works, in a contrapuntal style reminiscent of Ockeghem, include at least 8 Masses (4 on secular cantus firmi); motets, hymns, Lamentations, and Magnificats; motet-chansons; over 40 French chansons; and textless arrangements of chanson tenors by other well-known composers.

Bibl.: Ed. in *CMM* 22 (1961–70).

Agricola, Johann Friedrich (b. Dobitschen, Saxe-Altenburg, 4 Jan. 1720; d. Berlin, 2 Dec. 1774). Composer, organist, singing teacher, and writer on music. He studied law at the Univ. of Leipzig, 1738–41, simultaneously studying music with J. S. Bach and later with Quantz in Berlin. He became a court composer to Frederick the Great in 1751 and in 1759 succeeded Graun as director of the royal opera. Highly regarded as an organist and as a singing teacher. He published an annotated translation of Tosi's treatise on singing (*Anleitung zur Singekunst,* Berlin, 1757; facs., Celle, 1966), collaborated with C. P. E. Bach on the obituary of J. S. Bach, and helped to prepare the publication of Adlung's work on organs. Other writings include an article on melody (published in the *Magazin der Musik* 2 [1786]), pamphlets taking up the cause of Italian music against Marpurg's advocacy of French taste, and a biography of Graun. His own compositions include 11 Italian operas or other dramatic works produced in Potsdam and Berlin; German sacred oratorios and cantatas; many songs in the style of the First Berlin School; keyboard pieces; chorale preludes for organ.

Agricola, Martin [Martin Sore] (b. Schwiebus, 6 Jan. 1486; d. Magdeburg, 10 June 1556). Theorist and composer. Of peasant origins and self-taught in music, he became a music teacher in Magdeburg in 1519 and choirmaster of the Lutheran Latin school there from 1525 or 1527. He was a friend of Georg Rhau, who published most of his works. His writings include *Ein kurtz deudsche Musica* (Wittenberg, 1528; 3rd ed. as *Musica choralis deudsch,* 1533); *Musica instrumentalis deudsch* (Wittenberg, 1529, and later eds.), written in German verse; *Musica figuralis deudsch* (Wittenberg, 1532); facs. of all three treatises (Hildesheim and New York, 1969). His compositions include Latin motets in the style of Josquin; a book of German Protestant songs for 2 and 3 voices, arranged in the order of the liturgical year; *Instrumentische Gesenge* (Wittenberg, 1561), a collection of over 50 3- and 4-voice instrumental pieces.

Aguiari [Agujari], **Lucrezia** ["La bastardina"] (b. Ferrara, 1743; d. Parma, 18 May 1783). Singer. Allegedly a foundling, she first sang in Florence in 1764. She subsequently sang throughout Italy and, in 1775, in London. In the mid-1760s she settled in Parma, where she met the composer Giuseppe Colla, to whose works she devoted her singing career almost entirely after 1769. A number of contemporaries—most notably Charles Burney and both Leopold and W. A. Mozart—wrote of the remarkable range and flexibility of her voice. She died of tuberculosis only three years after marrying Colla in 1780.

Aguilar Ahumada, Miguel (b. Huara, Chile, 12 Apr. 1931). Composer. He studied piano at the Richard Wagner Conservatory and composition at the Santiago National Conservatory; his teachers were Domingo Santa Cruz and Juan Orrego-Salas. From 1953 he taught at Santiago's Escuela moderna de música, from 1956 in Concepción at the Conservatorio de la Sinfónica, and later at the Escuela superior de música. In 1963–65 he studied conducting with Wolfgang von der Nahmer at the Hochschule in Cologne. His early music indicates influence of Stravinsky and Bartók and of Schoenberg's expressionism. Later he made use of serial, electronic, and aleatoric elements.

Works: *Obertura al teatro integral,* orchestra (1954); a septet, winds, double bass (1954); *Sonatine concertante,* clarinet, piano (1956); *Microscopía,* soprano, piano (1958); *Umbral y ámbito,* chamber ensemble (1962); *Composición sobre tres sonidos,* electronic (1965); *Texturas,* piano, concrete tape sounds (1965); *Torre Eiffel,* soprano, chamber ensemble (1967); *Música aleatórica,* orchestra (1969).

Aguilera de Heredia, Sebastián (b. Zaragoza, bapt. 15 Aug. 1561; d. there, 16 Dec. 1627). Composer. Organist at Huesca Cathedral from 1585 to 1603; then chief organist at the Cathedral of La Seo, Zaragoza, until his death. Wrote only sacred music, for organ and for choir. Some features of his approximately 20 organ works are prominent use of dissonance ("falsas"); *medio registro* technique, through which one voice—here always a lower one—is highlighted as a solo; and contrapuntal elaboration of hymn tunes or fragments. His widely known *Canticum Beatissimae Virginis deiparae Mariae* (Zaragoza, 1618) includes 36 choral settings of the Magnificat, built on the eight church modes; a few are for double chorus.

Aguirre, Julián (b. Buenos Aires, 28 Jan. 1868; d. there, 13 Aug. 1924). Composer and pianist. He spent part of his childhood in Spain, where from 1882 he studied composition with Emilio Arrieta and with Aranguren at the National Conservatory of Madrid. In 1887 he returned to Argentina; during the ensuing decades he lived in rural areas of Argentina in order to study regional folk music. He founded two music schools in Buenos Aires, at the Athenaeum and at the Argentine Music School. His own music, much of it for piano, draws on folk melodies. He is best known for 2 dances for piano, *Gato* and *Huella,* which, in arrangements by Ernest Ansermet (1930), became orchestral standards.

Works: *De mi país,* symphonic poem (1910); *Rapsodia argentina,* violin, piano; songs ("Caminito," "Cueca," "Vidalita"); choral works *(La clase, Emblema);* many piano pieces (*La danza de Belkis, Mazurca española, Aires criollos,* and 4 vols. of *Aires nacionales*).

Ahle, Johann Georg (b. Mühlhausen, bapt. 12 June 1651; d. there, 2 Dec. 1706). Organist, composer, and theorist; son of Johann Rudolf Ahle. At 23 he succeeded his father as organist at St. Balsius, Mühlhausen, where J. S. Bach served as his successor. Emperor Leopold I named him poet laureate in 1680. Among his theoretical treatises were 4 *Gespräche* for the four seasons (e.g., *Johan Georg Ahlens musikalisches Frühlings-Gespräche;* all 4 publ. 1695–1701). He composed sacred and secular choral pieces and authored a number of prose novels, some containing songs or other music.

Ahle, Johann Rudolf (b. Mühlhausen, 24 Dec. 1625; d. there, 9 July 1673). Composer, organist, and theorist. From 1645 he studied theology at the Univ. of Erfurt. Little is known of his musical training, but in 1654 he assumed the post of organist in Mühlhausen. He was also on the town council and in 1673 was elected mayor. He composed many sacred choral works, as well as sacred songs for 1 to 4 solo voices, with or without continuo accompaniment; also instrumental works and more than 60 works for organ.

Bibl.: *Ausgewählte Gesangswerke mit und ohne Begleitung von Instrumenten, DDT* 5 (1901). Carl Georg August von Winterfeld, *Der evangelische Kirchengesang,* 2 (Leipzig, 1843–47; R: Hildesheim, 1966).

Ahrens, Joseph (Johannes Clemens) (b. Sommersell, Westphalia, 17 Apr. 1904). Organist and composer. After early training in organ and choral music he entered the Staatliche Akademie für Kirchen- und Schulmusik in Berlin in 1925 and there studied with Alfred Sittard and Wilhelm Middelschulte. He joined the faculty in 1928. Organist of the Cathedral of St. Hedwig in Berlin from 1934; professor of Catholic church music at the Berlin Hochschule für Musik, serving as deputy director, 1954–58, and chairman of the keyboard department. Noted for his skill as an improviser on the organ, he has composed works that combine strict liturgical forms with modern melodic and harmonic techniques, as in the *Missa dodekaphonica* (1966), where Gregorian chant is interwoven with twelve-tone melodic writing. Other works include numerous compositions for organ and choral settings of sacred texts such as the Passions according to St. Matthew (1950) and St. John (1961).

Aichinger, Gregor (b. Regensburg, 1564–65; d. Augsburg, 20–21 Jan. 1628). Composer. Presented a work in 1577 to the Bavarian court at Munich, where

Lassus headed the court chapel. Enrolled at the Univ. of Ingolstadt in 1578; became the official organist to the Fugger household and hence of the Church of St. Ulrich, Augsburg, in 1584, a position he held until his death. Made two trips to Italy, the first (at some time between 1584 and 1588) including study with Giovanni Gabrieli in Venice and the second (1598–1601) bringing him into contact with the spiritual canzonetta in Rome. By 1603 he was ordained. Sacred vocal works with Latin texts make up the great majority of his compositions, most of which appeared in about 30 published collections, though he also produced a few secular works (before 1601), instrumental pieces, and compositions with vernacular texts. Most of his publications after 1607 include a continuo part.

Airto. See Moreira, Airto.

Aitken, Robert (Morris) (b. Kentville, Nova Scotia, 28 Aug. 1939). Flutist and composer. Studied flute with Nicholas Fiore, Marcel Moyse, and Jean-Pierre Rampal; composition at the Univ. of British Columbia and with John Weinzweig and Myron Schaeffer at the Univ. of Toronto, where he joined the faculty in 1972. Principal flutist of the Vancouver Symphony, 1958–59; of the Toronto Symphony, 1965–70. Active as a soloist, an organizer and director of the New Music Concerts in Toronto (from 1971), and a member of the Lyric Arts Trio. Professor of flute at the Hochschule für Musik in Freiburg, Germany, from 1986. His compositions, frequently scored for unusual instrumental forces including electronics, explore the spatial and coloristic aspects of sound.

Akeroyde, Samuel (b. Yorkshire, ca. 1650; d. London, 1706 or later). Composer and violinist. During the 1680s he was one of the king's musicians. He composed more than 100 songs, many for plays produced on London stages between 1685 and 1706, including D'Urfey's *Commonwealth of Women* (1685) and *Don Quixote III* (1695), and Motteux's *Love's a Jest* (1696). The songs were published in collections such as *The Theater of Music* (1685–87), *The Banquet of Musick* (1688–92), and *Pills to Purge Melancholy* (1699–1720).

Akimenko [Yakimenko], **Fyodor Stepanovich** (b. Kharkov, 20 Feb. 1876; d. Paris, 8 Jan. 1945). Composer, pianist, and writer. Studied at the St. Petersburg Conservatory with Rimsky-Korsakov, Lyadov, and Vitols; professor there from 1919 until 1923, after which he moved to Paris. He was Stravinsky's first composition teacher. Composed an opera; a small number of orchestral works; chamber music; songs; 2 sonata-fantasias and numerous character pieces for piano.

Akiyoshi, Toshiko (b. Dairen, China, 12 Dec. 1929). Jazz composer, pianist, and bandleader of Japanese parentage. After World War II she lived in Japan, where Oscar Peterson set up her first bop recording with his rhythm section (1953). She studied at the Berklee College of Music in Boston (1956–59), then worked with the alto saxophonist Charlie Mariano after their marriage, including periods in Japan (1961, 1963–65); she also joined Charles Mingus's group (1962). With her second husband, Lew Tabackin, she led a big band in Los Angeles (1973–84), composing all its music, drawing on bop, swing, fusion, and Japanese styles (as on the album *Kogun,* 1974). From 1985 she led a big band in New York.

Akses, Necil Kâzim (b. Istanbul, 6 May 1908). Composer. As a boy in Istanbul he learned music theory and cello. He studied composition with Joseph Marx at the Musikakademie in Vienna (1926–31) and with Joseph Suk and Alois Hába at the Prague Conservatory (1931–34). Upon returning to Turkey in 1934 he taught at the Music Teachers College at Ankara. In 1936 he was appointed professor of composition at the conservatory, and in 1948 he was made its director. In 1958–60 he was general director of the Ankara State Opera. His music, while reflecting study with Hindemith (at Ankara) and Hába, also incorporates melodies from the folk and art music of Turkey.

Works: operas (*Mete,* 1933; *Bayönder,* 1934); orchestral works (*Ankara Kalesi* [Ankara Castle], 1942; a symphony, 1966; *Scherzo,* 1972); *Poème,* cello, orchestra (1946); a violin concerto (1972); *Allegro feroce,* saxophone, piano (1931); a sonata (1930) and other piano pieces.

Akutagawa, Yasushi (b. Tokyo, 12 July 1925; d. there, 31 Jan. 1989). Composer. In Tokyo he studied conducting with Kaneko and composition with Hashimoto and Ifukube at the Academy of Music. Upon graduating in 1949, he won first prize in the Japanese radio competition. In 1953 he formed, with Ikuma Dan and Toshiro Mayuzumi, the "Group of Three." His music shows the influence of Soviet composers such as Shostakovich and Khachaturian, with whom he established ties during the 1950s and 1960s.

Works: operas (*Kurai Kagami* [Dark Mirror], 1960; *Hiroshima no Orfe* [Orpheus in Hiroshima], 1967); ballets (*Kumo no ito* [Spider's Web], 1968); orchestral works (*Music for Symphonic Orchestra,* 1950; *Futago no Hoshi* [Twin Stars Symphony], 1957; *Music for Strings,* 1962; *Ostinata sinfonica,* 1967; *Inga,* strings, 1969; *Rhapsody,* 1971); chamber music; piano pieces.

Alain, Jehan (Ariste) (b. St. Germain-en-Laye, 3 Feb. 1911; d. Petits-Puys, near Saumur, 20 June 1940). Composer and organist. Received early organ training from his father, Albert, and studied piano with Augustin Pierson. Entered the Paris Conservatory in 1927, where he studied organ with Dupré and composition with Dukas and Roger-Ducasse. Killed in action in World War II. Works for organ include *Le jardin suspendu* (1934), *Suite* (1934–36), *Intermezzo* (1935), and 2 Fantaisies (1934, 1936); also composed instrumental and choral works, piano pieces, songs.

Alain, Marie-Claire (b. St. Germain-en-Laye, 10 Aug. 1926). Organist. Sister of composer and organist Jehan Alain and of composer, pianist, and musicologist Olivier Alain. Attended Paris Conservatory beginning in 1944; studied there with Duruflé (harmony) and

Dupré (organ). In 1950 she won the organ prize at the Geneva International Competition. She has specialized in music of the 17th and 18th centuries. In addition, she recorded her brother Jehan's complete works, as well as the complete works of Bach.

Alamire, Pierre (b. ca. 1470–75; d. after 1534). Music scribe. Copied much of the surviving Franco-Flemish polyphony of his time. Worked mostly for Margaret of Austria, regent of the Netherlands, and Emperor Charles V; also made manuscripts for numerous other patrons, both political and religious. In addition, sold musical instruments and acted as a spy and a courier for several monarchs, including Henry VIII of England.

Alard, (Jean-) Delphin (b. Bayonne, 8 Mar. 1815; d. Paris, 22 Feb. 1888). Violinist and teacher. From 1827 studied at the Paris Conservatory under Habeneck (violin) and Fétis (composition); active as a soloist and in chamber music (the latter especially through the Société Alard-Franchomme, ca. 1847–ca. 1872); professor at the conservatory, 1843–75, where he taught Sarasate. His *École du violon* (Paris, 1844) was widely used. Composed etudes, concertos and other large works, and opera potpourris.

Albanese, Licia (b. Bari, 22 July 1913). Soprano. Studied voice with Emanuel De Rosa in Bari and Giuseppina Baldassare-Tedeschi in Milan. Operatic debut 10 Dec. 1935 at Parma; both there and in her American debut (New York, 9 Feb. 1940) she played Cio-cio-san in *Madama Butterfly.* Other Puccini roles included Mimi *(La bohème)* and Tosca. Her lyric and spinto roles also included Mozart's Susanna, Donna Anna, and Zerlina; Verdi's Violetta, perhaps her most famous role; Gounod's Marguerite; and Massenet's Manon. Closed her operatic career 10 Nov. 1974 with the New Jersey State Opera.

Albani [Lajeunesse], **(Marie Louise Cécile) Emma** (b. Chambly, near Montreal, 1 Nov. 1847; d. London, 3 Apr. 1930). Soprano. Studied in Paris with Duprez in 1868, then with Lamperti in Milan, and began an opera career in Italy in 1870, taking the name Albani. She sang often in London opera 1872–96 and was equally successful in oratorio and at the various British festivals. She sang widely in Europe and North America and toured India, Australia, and South Africa. Beginning in lighter roles (singing Oscar in *Un ballo in maschera* and Amina in *La sonnambula* her first season), she progressed to heavier dramatic ones, including Eva, Desdemona, and Isolde. She retired in 1911.

Bibl.: Emma Albani, *Forty Years of Song* (London and Toronto, 1911).

Albéniz, Isaac (Manuel Francisco) (b. Camprodón, Lérida, Spain, 29 May 1860; d. Cambô-les-Bains, 18 May 1909). Composer and pianist. A child prodigy on the piano, he gave concerts from the age of 4 and began lessons with Narciso Oliveras in 1865. Two years later his mother took him to Paris to study with Marmontel. In 1869 he entered the Madrid Conservatory but soon ran away, allegedly stowing away aboard a ship bound for the Americas. After a peripatetic youth in South, Central, and North America, Great Britain, and finally Leipzig (where he studied with Reinecke), he returned to Madrid in 1877, at which time Count Morphy, on behalf of Alfonso XII, provided a scholarship for him to study in Brussels. He studied composition there with Gevaert and Dupont and won the conservatory prize in 1879. The following year he studied piano with Liszt, building on an impressive keyboard technique. He traveled to Barcelona in 1883, to Madrid in 1885, and to London in 1890; at this time he quit concertizing and began studying composition with Dukas and d'Indy. In 1891 he started a lucrative operatic collaboration with a London banker and amateur librettist, Francis Money-Coutts; the two produced *The Magic Opal* in 1893 and three more operas during the next four years. In 1898 the composer traveled to Granada, in 1900 to Barcelona, in 1902 to Paris, and the following year to Nice. His best-known works are for the piano and often evoke Spanish scenes through the use of melodic and rhythmic gestures derived from Spanish folklore.

Works: operas (*The Magic Opal,* London, 1893; *Henry Clifford,* Barcelona, 1895; *Pepita Jiménez,* Barcelona, 1896; *King Arthur,* trilogy, not completed); the zarzuela *San Antonio de la Florida* (Madrid, 1894); orchestral works (*Rapsodia cubana* op. 66; *Rapsodia española,* with piano op. 70); a piano concerto in A minor op. 78; numerous works for piano (*Iberia,* 12 pieces publ. in 4 sets of 3, 1906–8, 2 later orchestrated by him and 5 by Enrique Arbós; 5 sonatas; *Suite española* no. 1, 1886, no. 2, 1889; *Suite antigua* nos. 1–3, 1887; *Recuerdos de viaje,* 1887; *España,* 1890; *Cantos de España,* 1896); songs with texts in Spanish, Italian, French, and English.

Bibl.: Henri Collet, *Albéniz et Granados* (Paris, 1926; 2nd ed., 1948). Antonio de las Heras, *Vida de Albéniz* (Barcelona and Madrid, 1940). Angel Sagardia, *Isaac Albéniz* (Plasencia, 1951). Gabriel Laplane, *Albéniz: Sa vie, son oeuvre* [includes works list] (Geneva, 1956). Enrique Franco, "La Suite Iberia di Albéniz," *NRMI* 7 (1973): 51–74. Paul Mast, "Style and Structure in *Iberia* by Isaac Albéniz" (Ph.D. diss., Eastman School of Music, 1974). Pola Baytelman, *Isaac Albéniz: Chronological List and Thematic Catalog of his Piano Works* (Detroit, 1993).

Albéniz, Mateo (Antonio) Pérez de (b. Spanish Basque region, ca. 1755; d. San Sebastián, 23 June 1831). Composer and theorist. Held church posts, primarily in San Sebastián (and, in 1795–1800, Logroño); composed much church music, once performed throughout northern Spain; published *Instrucción metódica, especulativa, y práctica, para enseñar a cantar y tañer la música moderna y antigua* (San Sebastián, 1802). Father of the pianist Pedro Albéniz y Bisanta (1795–1855).

Alberch Vila, Pere (b. Vich, Spain, 1517; d. Barcelona, 16 Nov. 1582). Composer. Widely known also as an organist and organ builder. Organist at Barcelona Cathedral from 1538. Extant works consist of 2 volumes of *odas* (texts in Catalan, Castilian, and Italian; all survive incomplete), 2 *ensaladas,* 2 keyboard *tientos,* and 2 sacred choral works.

Albert, Eugen [Eugène] **(Francis Charles) d'** (b. Glasgow, 10 Apr. 1864; d. Riga, 3 Mar. 1932). Pianist and composer. Studied at the New Music School, London, under Pauer (piano), Prout, Stainer, and Sullivan, arousing much attention with London concerts in 1880–81; went to Vienna in 1881 and studied with Liszt from 1882, coming to consider himself a completely German artist and repudiating his English connections and education. At his peak as a pianist in the 1880s and 1890s before devoting himself so assiduously to composition, he was regarded as one of the principal successors of Liszt. He continued to perform throughout his life and toured widely.

Most of his instrumental music, including concertos, a symphony, and large and small piano works, is early. He composed 21 operas, ranging from Wagnerian music dramas to light comedies. The most successful were the Italianate verismo *Tiefland* (Prague, 1903) and *Die toten Augen* (Dresden, 1916). He became director of the Berlin Hochschule für Musik in 1907.

Bibl.: Wilhelm Raupp, *Eugen d'Albert* (Leipzig, 1930).

Albert, Heinrich (b. Lobenstein, 8 July 1604; d. Königsberg, 6 Oct. 1651). Composer. He was a musician under Schütz in Dresden (1622) and studied law in Leipzig (1623–26); he settled in Königsberg around 1630 and was organist at its cathedral. He is best known for his 170 songs (*Arien;* selection in *DDT* 12–13), most of which appeared in 8 volumes published in Königsberg (1638–50; with important prefaces on continuo playing) and in 3 volumes of *Musicalische Kürbs-Hütte* (1645). He composed dramatic allegories, motets, and many other vocal and instrumental works.

Albert, Stephen (Joel) (b. New York, 6 Feb. 1941; d. Truro, Mass., 27 Dec. 1992). Composer. Studied with Siegmeister (1956–58), Milhaud (1958), Bernard Rogers at the Eastman School of Music (1958–60), Joseph Castaldo at the Philadelphia Music Academy (B.M., 1962), and Rochberg (1963). Held positions at the Philadelphia Music Academy (1968–70), Stanford Univ. (1970–71), Smith College (1974–76), and Julliard (1988–1992). Composer-in-residence with the Seattle Symphony and Seattle Opera (beginning 1985). Early experiments with serialism and the synthesis of traditional and electronic sounds were superseded by a highly expressive, neoromantic idiom for which Mahler was a principal inspiration. Much of his music was inspired by literary sources, especially the works of James Joyce: *To Wake the Dead,* soprano and chamber ensemble (1977–78); *RiverRun,* orchestra (1983–84; Pulitzer Prize, 1985); *Flower of the Mountain,* soprano and orchestra (1985). His second symphony was completed by Sebastian Currier and premiered in 1994. Other works include: *Tribute,* violin, piano (1988); Cello concerto (1990); *Tapioca Pudding,* orchestra (1991); *Wind Canticle,* orchestra (1991); *Ecce Puer,* soprano, oboe, horn, piano (1992).

Bibl.: *Stephen Albert* (Chester, 1993) [incl. catalog of works].

Alberti, Domenico (b. Venice, ca. 1710; d. Rome, 1740). Composer and harpsichordist. A nobleman, he studied counterpoint with Antonio Biffi and Antonio Lotti. On a visit to Spain with the Venetian ambassador in 1736, his singing earned the praise of Farinelli. He is best known for his two-movement keyboard sonatas (14 of some 40 survive), which make use of the familiar arpeggiated accompaniment figure with which his name later became associated (Alberti bass). He also composed 3 operas, arias, and keyboard pieces.

Alberti, Giuseppe Matteo (b. Bologna, 20 Sept. 1685; d. there, 18 Feb. 1751). Composer. In Bologna he was the pupil of Carlo Manzolini and Pietro Minelli (violin) and Floriano Arresti (composition). From 1713 he was a member of the orchestra at S. Petronio and soon after became a member of the Accademia filarmonica; in 1721 he was named president *(principe)* of the latter group. He published 10 *Concerti per chiesa, e per camera* op. 1 (Bologna, 1713), divided equally between violin concertos and ripieno concertos; *Sonate a violino e basso* op. 2 (Bologna, 1721), and other instrumental works, primarily ripieno concertos. He also composed sacred vocal works (including an oratorio, *La vergine annunziata,* 1720).

Bibl.: Michael Talbot, "A Thematic Catalogue of the Orchestral Works of Giuseppe Matteo Alberti (1685–1751)," *RMARC* 13 (1976): 1–26.

Albicastro, Henricus [Weissenburg, Heinrich] (b. probably Switzerland, fl. 1695–1705; d. Netherlands, ca. 1738). Composer. He studied at the Univ. of Leiden from 1681; later he apparently served in the Spanish War of Succession. Around 1700 he was in Amsterdam, where Roger published a number of his virtuosic works for strings, including concertos and more than 50 sonatas for violin (some with viola or cello) and continuo. J. J. Quantz mentions (in his autobiography in Marpurg's *Historisch-kritische Beiträge*) having practiced Albicastro's works as a youth.

Albinoni, Tomaso (Giovanni) (b. Venice, 8 June 1671; d. there, 17 Jan. 1751). Composer. His teachers are not known, though Giovanni Legrenzi is a likely possibility. His family was wealthy and landed, and Tomaso was able to devote himself to the life of a dedicated amateur ("il dilettante veneto," as he was known). He began to attract attention with his op. 2 (*Sinfonie e concerti a cinque,* 1700) and with a prodigious number of operas—first in Venice (*Zenobia,* 1694; *Tigrane,* 1697), then in other Italian cities (*Rodrigo in Algeri,* Naples, 1702; *Griselda,* Florence, 1703). Throughout the first two decades of the 18th century his operas, symphonies, concertos, and cantatas made him widely known, and his works were increasingly performed outside Italy from around 1720. In 1722 he was invited to Munich to conduct his *I veri amici* and *Il trionfo dell'amore* as part of the wedding celebration of Prince-Elect Karl Albert and Maria Amalia. He appears to have stopped composing around 1740, and he spent his last years in Venice. He composed more than 50 works for the theater (other titles include *Vespetta e Pimpinone,* 1708?; *Didone abbandonata,* Venice, 1725); the music for most of these is lost. Other works include some 50 Concerti a cinque (including opp. 5, 7, 9, and 10); 79 solo and ensemble sonatas; *balletti;* solo cantatas (including the 12 cantatas op. 4); a three-voice Mass; and a Magnificat.

Bibl.: *Gesamtausgabe der Instrumentalmusik* (Berg, 1974–). Michael Talbot, *Tomaso Albinoni: The Venetian Composer and His World* (Oxford and New York, 1990).

Alboni, Marietta [Maria Anna Marzia] (b. Città di Castello, 6 Mar. 1823; d. Ville d'Avray, 23 June 1894). Contralto. Studied singing at the Liceo musicale, Bologna, partly with Rossini; made her opera debut in Bologna in 1842; appeared all over Europe in the following years with great success; toured the U.S. in 1852–53; retired in 1863, but after the death of her first husband in 1867 sang occasionally in concert. A true contralto, she had upper notes that allowed her to sing soprano parts.

Bibl.: Arthur Pougin, *Marietta Alboni* (Paris, 1912).

Albrechtsberger, Johann Georg (b. Klosterneuburg, 3 Feb. 1736; d. Vienna, 7 Mar. 1809). Theorist, organist, and prolific composer. As a choirboy he learned counterpoint, figured bass, and organ from the local Augustinians. After study at Melk Abbey (from 1749) and at the Jesuit seminary in Vienna (1754), he was employed as organist at Raab in 1755, at Maria Taferl (from 1757), and at Melk (1759–65). In 1791 he became assistant Kapellmeister at St. Stephen's in Vienna; in 1793 he succeeded Leopold Hofmann as Kapellmeister, a post he held until his death.

A master of counterpoint and of the organ, he is perhaps best known as Beethoven's teacher; his advocacy of strict contrapuntal style exerted a strong influence on the fusion of strict and *galant* styles that characterizes much music of the Viennese classical period. Among his compositions are 300 sacred works, including oratorios and cantatas, and more than 450 instrumental pieces, including symphonies, chamber sonatas, divertimentos, and organ fugues.

Writings: *Gründliche Anweisung zur Composition* (Leipzig, 1790; R: 1968; enl. 3rd ed., 1821). *Kurzgefasste Methode den Generalbass zu erlernen* (Vienna, ca. 1791; enl. 2nd ed., 1792).

Bibl.: *Instrumentalwerke, DTÖ* 33 (1909). Ignaz von Seyfried, ed., *J. G. Albrechtsbergers sämmtliche Schriften* (Vienna, [1826]; 2nd ed., 1837; R: Leipzig, 1975; Eng. ed., 1855). Gustav Nottebohm, *Beethovens Unterricht bei J. Haydn, Albrechtsberger und Salieri,* Beethoven Studien, 1 (Leipzig, 1873; R: Wiesbaden, 1971; rev. in *Beethoveniana,* 1872). Andreas Weissenbäck, "J. G. Albrechtsberger als Kirchenkomponist," *SzMw* 14 (1927): 1–160. Ernst Paul, *Johann Georg Albrechtsberger: Ein Klosterneuburger Meister der Musik und seine Schule* (Klosterneuburg and Vienna, 1976).

Albright, William (Hugh) (b. Gary, Ind., 20 Oct. 1944). Composer, pianist, and organist. Studied at the Univ. of Michigan (1963–70) and the Paris Conservatory; his teachers included Finney, Bassett, Rochberg, and Messiaen in composition and Marilyn Mason on the organ. Has taught beginning 1970 at the Univ. of Michigan and served as associate director of its electronic music studio. His performances and recordings of classical ragtime and his own rag compositions helped spur the revival of the music of Scott Joplin and other ragtime classics. Works include the opera *The Magic City* (1978); theater and mixed media works (*Tic,* two groups of performers, soloist, tape, film, 1967; *Beulahland Rag,* jazz quartet, improvising ensemble, narrator, tape, slides, film, 1967–69; *Seven Deadly Sins,* chamber ensemble and narrator, 1974); music for chamber ensembles (*Sphaera,* 1988) and band; choral music; works for organ (3 *Organbooks,* 1967, 1971, 1978; *The King of Instruments,* with narrator, 1978); many piano pieces (*Pianoagogo,* 1966; *Grand Sonata in Rag,* 1968; *Five Chromatic Dances,* 1976).

Alcock, John (b. London, 11 Apr. 1715; d. Lichfield, 23 Feb. 1806). Organist and composer. After early training under John Stanley he held posts at several smaller parish churches, including St. Andrew's Church, Plymouth (from 1737), and St. Laurence's, Reading (from 1742). In 1750 he took the post of vicar-choral at Lichfield Cathedral. In 1766 he completed a doctorate in music at Oxford. His writings suggest that choir members frequently found his elaborate organ accompaniments distracting. Among his surviving works are 6 services, a number of anthems, chants, and Psalm tunes, and secular catches and glees. His eldest son, John Alcock (1740–91), also a composer and parish organist, published instrumental and sacred choral music.

Alcuin (b. Northumbria, ca. 735; d. Tours, 19 May 804). Writer. Cultural adviser to Charlemagne beginning ca. 780; probably played an important role in the development of the Carolingian liturgy; wrote a number of hymn texts; may have written a work on music, but none survives. *Musica,* a short treatise on church modes, is incorrectly attributed to Alcuin by Gerbert (*GS* 1: 26–27).

Aldrich, Henry (b. Westminster, London, bapt. 22 Jan. 1648; d. Oxford, 14 Dec. 1710). Composer and music scholar. Educated at Westminster School and (from 1662) at Oxford. Traveled to Germany, France, and Italy in the 1670s. Named canon at Christ Church, Oxford, in 1681 and dean of the college in 1689; vice-chancellor of Oxford, 1692–95. He was also an architect, a mathematician, and an expert on printing and engraving techniques. His music collection formed the original basis for the Christ Church library. He composed services, many anthems, 2 Latin motets, and catches; he also adapted (and often translated into English) a number of Italian and Latin works by Byrd, Lassus, Carissimi, Palestrina, and others.

Bibl.: Walter George Hiscock, *Henry Aldrich of Christ Church, 1648–1710* (Oxford, 1960).

Aldrovandini [Aldovrandini], **Giuseppe Antonio Vincenzo** (b. Bologna, 8 June 1671; d. there, 9 Feb. 1707). He studied with G. A. Perti and in 1695 joined the Accademia filarmonica in Bologna; in 1702 he became its president *(principe).* Later he was honorary *maestro di cappella* for the Duke of Mantua. He composed 15 known operas, several in Bolognese dialect (*Amor torna in s'al so',* Bologna, 1698; *Pirro,* Venice, 1704; *L'incoronazione di Dario,* Naples, 1705; *Li tre rivali al soglio,* Bologna, 1711); oratorios (*Giesù nato,* 1698; *La grazia giubilante,* 1704; *Il doppio martire,* 1706); cantatas; string sonatas; trumpet sonatas.

Alessandrescu, Alfred (b. Bucharest, 14 Aug. 1893; d. there, 18 Feb. 1959). Composer and conductor. Studied piano at the Bucharest Conservatory with Saegiu and composition with Castaldi; studied in Paris with d'Indy and Paul Vidal (1913–14 and 1923–24). Conductor at the Romanian Opera, 1921–59; of the Bucharest Philharmonic, 1926–40; of the orchestra of Radio Bucharest, 1933–59. His own music, much of it from his early years, shows the influence of Debussy. He was active as a music critic and wrote a study of Enescu. He composed orchestral works (*Amurg de toamnă* [Twilight of Autumn], 1910; *Didona,* 1911; *Acteon,* 1915; *Fantezie română,* 1913); chamber music (*Pièce pour quatuor à cordes,* 1921; a violin sonata, 1915); many songs ("Nuit d'automne," "Chanson triste," "Berceuse").

Alessandri, Felice (b. Rome, 24 Nov. 1747; d. Casinalbo, 15 Aug. 1798). Composer. He studied music in Naples and composed operas and oratorios for Verona, Venice, Milan, Padua, and other Italian cities. In London from 1768, he composed *La moglie fedele* (1768) and *Il re alla caccia* (1769) for the King's Theatre. He shared direction of the Concert spirituel in Paris in 1777, and during the 1770s and 1780s many of his operas were produced in Italian cities. In 1786 he sought work at the St. Petersburg court, but was named only a singing teacher. He became assistant to Reichardt at the Berlin court opera in 1789, but his works found a cool reception there. He returned to Italy in 1792. His extant works include 19 serious operas, 15 comic operas, and a number of cantatas, ballets, oratorios, and instrumental works.

Alexander, Josef (b. Boston, 15 May 1907; d. Seattle, 23 Dec. 1989). Composer. Studied piano at the New England Conservatory, graduating in 1925; composition with Piston at Harvard Univ. (B.A., 1938; M.A., 1939) and later with Boulanger in Paris and Copland at Tanglewood. Served on the faculty of Brooklyn College from 1943 to 1977. His works include the symphonic poem *The Ancient Mariner* (1938); 4 symphonies; other orchestral music (*Epitaphs,* 1947); much chamber and vocal music; piano pieces.

Alexandrov, Alexander Vasilevich (b. Plakhino, district of Riazan, 13 Apr. 1883; d. Berlin, 8 July 1946). Composer, conductor, and teacher. Studied composition at the St. Petersburg Conservatory with Glazunov and Lyadov and then at the Moscow Conservatory with Vasilenko, graduating in 1913. Taught at the Moscow Conservatory from 1918; choral conductor in Tver (1906–9, 1913–16) and later in Moscow (from 1922). In 1928 founded the Soviet Army Song and Dance Ensemble, which achieved international acclaim and which now bears his name. Composed choral songs, including popular arrangements of folk songs and patriotic music; the song "Holy War" (1941, text by Lebedev-Kumach) became a musical symbol early in World War II. In 1944 his "Hymn of the Bolshevik Party," with a new text, became the Soviet national anthem.

Alfano, Franco (b. Posilippo, Naples, 8 Mar. 1875; d. San Remo, 27 Oct. 1954). Composer. Studied at the Conservatorio di S. Pietro a Maiella; in 1895 moved to Leipzig, where he studied composition with Jadassohn. From 1899 until 1905 was based in Paris but traveled extensively, moving subsequently to Milan and in 1914 to San Remo. From 1916 taught composition at the Liceo musicale, Bologna; 1918–23, director; in 1920 helped found the society Musica nova; 1923–39, director of the Liceo musicale (later Conservatory) of Turin; 1940–42, superintendent of the Teatro massimo, Palermo; 1947–50, acting director of the Liceo musicale, Pesaro. Best known for completing Puccini's last opera, *Turandot* (1925). His greatest international success came with his third opera, *Risurrezione* (1902–3), a work in the tradition of Italian realism. Later operas, including *L'ombra di Don Giovanni* (1913) and *La leggenda di Sakuntala* (1914–20), showed the influence of Debussy and Strauss. Also composed ballets; 3 symphonies (1908–10, rev. 1923, 1953; 1931–32; 1934) and other orchestral music; 3 string quartets and other chamber music; choral music; songs; piano pieces.

Alfvén, Hugo (Emil) (b. Stockholm, 1 May 1872; d. Falun, 8 May 1960). Composer and conductor. After study at the Stockholm Conservatory from 1887 to 1891, he pursued private study of violin (with Lars Zetterquist) and composition (with Johan Lindegren). From 1890 to 1892 he was violinist in the Swedish Royal Opera Orchestra. He studied violin further (1896–99) in Brussels with César Thomson. Partly on the strength of his Second Symphony he won several scholarships for European study, including the Jenny Lind stipend (1900–1903) and a grant in conducting with Kutzschbach in Dresden. After 1904 he directed a number of choirs, including the Siljan Choir (in

Dalarna) and the Orphei Drängar (from 1910). In 1908 he was elected to the Royal Academy of Music, and from 1910 until his academic retirement in 1939 he served as director of music at Uppsala Univ. His own music shows influences from Wagner and Richard Strauss, but also reflects his interest in the folk music of Sweden. *Midsommarvaka* (Midsummer Vigil), for example, his best-known work, embroiders a native melody within an orchestral fabric. The thematic catalog by Rudén lists more than 200 works.

Works: 5 symphonies (no. 1 in F minor, 1897; no. 2 in D major, 1897–98; no. 3 in E major, 1905; no. 4 in C minor, *Från havsbandet* [From the Outskirts of the Archipelago], 1918–19; no. 5 in A minor, 1943–53); 3 Swedish Rhapsodies (*Midsommarvaka,* 1903; *Uppsala-rhapsodi,* 1907; and *Dalarhapsodien,* 1931); ballets (*Bergakungen,* 1916–23; *Den förlorade sonen* [The Prodigal Son], 1957); other orchestral works (*En skärgårdssägen* [A Tale of the Skerries], 1904; *Festspel* op. 25, 1907); incidental music (*Gustav II Adolf* op. 49, 1932); many choral works, including 10 cantatas (*Unge Herr Sten Sture* op. 30, 1912; *Manhem* op. 47, 1928) and the oratorio *Herrans bön* [The Lord's Prayer] op. 15, 1899–1901); chamber works, including a violin sonata op. 1; and more than 50 songs. He published 4 autobiographical vols. (all in Stockholm): *Första satsen* (1946), *Tempo furioso* (1948), *I dur och moll* (1949), and *Final* (1952).

Bibl.: Jan Olof Rudén, *Hugo Alfvéns kompositioner: Käll- och verkförteckning* [thematic catalog] (Stockholm, 1972). Lennart Hedwall, *Hugo Alfvén* (Stockholm, 1972). *Facsimile av originalskissen till Hugo Alfvéns Midsommarvaka,* ed. with intro. by Jan Olof Rudén (Stockholm, 1972). *Musikkultur* 36/4 (1972) [Alfvén issue]. Lennart Hedwall, *Hugo Alfvén: En bildbiografi* (Tirp, 1990).

Algarotti, Francesco (b. Venice, 11 Dec. 1712; d. Pisa, 3 May 1764). Poet and music scholar. After early study of mathematics and philosophy in Bologna and Rome, he went to Paris during the 1730s and became acquainted with Voltaire. From 1740 he was in the service of Frederick II in Berlin, and from 1742 until 1747 he also served Augustus III in Dresden; for both courts he wrote, arranged, and translated opera librettos. Returning to Italy in 1753, he wrote his widely influential *Saggio sopra l'opera in musica* (1755; partial trans., *SR,* pp. 657–72); in it he criticized the elaborate "abuses" of contemporary Italian opera and called for a simpler style in which music was subordinated to poetry; he held up as models the operas of Lully and Quinault.

Ali, Rashied [Patterson, Robert, Jr.] (b. Philadelphia, 1 July 1935). Jazz drummer. From 1963 he played free jazz in New York with Pharoah Sanders and Don Cherry, and Archie Shepp. As a member of John Coltrane's group (1965–67), he recorded *Interstellar Space* (1967), an album of duos with Coltrane. After Coltrane's death he led a group in Copenhagen (1967), studied with Philly Joe Jones in England, then returned to the U.S. to work with Alice Coltrane. He ran Ali's Alley, a New York club (1974–79). Later he played free jazz, bop, funk, and fusions of these styles, touring Europe annually from 1979 and recording with the double bass player Saheb Sarbib (1984).

Alison, Richard (fl. England, 1592–1606). Composer. Wrote sacred and secular instrumental and vocal works. Provided simple harmonizations and, in some cases, optional instrumental accompaniments for a number of Psalm tunes (mostly from the Sternhold and Hopkins psalter); set some secular poetry similarly. Contributed compositions to Thomas Morley's *First Book of Consort Lessons* (London, 1599; 2nd ed., 1611); various other instrumental pieces survive in prints and in manuscript.

Alkan [Morhange], **(Charles-Henri-) Valentin** (b. Paris, 30 Nov. 1813; d. there, 29 Mar. 1888). Composer and pianist. A child prodigy as both composer and pianist (whose four brothers and a sister also adopted the name Alkan when they became musicians), he entered the Paris Conservatory at 6, studying the piano with Zimmermann, winning several first prizes, and beginning to publish piano music in 1828. Apparently of reasonably convivial disposition in his youth (moving in society, a friend of Chopin and other artists, playing in Paris salons and concerts, winning considerable recognition), after 1838 he became increasingly reclusive, giving public concerts only in 1844–45, 1853, and 1870, after which he played regularly in public until his death. His reclusive life made him an obscure and mysterious figure, as reflected in the often repeated but apparently erroneous story that he was crushed to death by a falling bookcase as he reached for the Talmud.

This personal image is reinforced by the idiosyncratic character of much of his music, almost all of it for solo piano, which, after arousing some critical interest in the earlier part of his career, never became widely known, perhaps partly because of the great difficulty of much of it and because he seldom played it in public himself. His earlier works consist largely of pieces related to fashionable salon styles. His later ones, which he continued to publish until about 1873, are more individual, ranging from collections of short pieces and etudes to a Grande Sonata op. 33 (1848) and a long symphony and concerto included in the etudes of op. 39 (1857). In his later years he became interested in and composed for the pedal piano. He also composed a lost symphony, 3 chamber works, and a few vocal pieces. He was remembered after his death primarily as a musical curiosity until the 1960s, when serious interest in him and his music began to develop.

Bibl.: H. H. Bellamann, "The Piano Works of C. V. Alkan," *MQ* 10 (1924): 251–62. Hugh Macdonald, "The Death of Alkan," *MT* 114 (1973): 25. Ronald Smith, *Alkan* (London, 1976). Jacques Arould et al., *Charles Valentin Alkan* (Paris, 1991) [incl. catalog of works].

Allegri, Gregorio (b. Rome, ca. 1582; d. there, 7 Feb. 1652). Composer. Trained as a choirboy in Rome, 1591–96; studied counterpoint with Nanino, 1600–

1607. Tenor soloist at San Luigi dei Francesi from 1604. He sang in cathedrals at Fermo and Tivoli, and in 1629 Urban VIII made him a member of the papal choir. He composed works for this choir and for that of Santa Maria in Vallicella. Five Masses are extant, as well as motets, Lamentations, Magnificats, and solo vocal concertini. He is best known for the nine-voice Psalm setting *Miserere mei Deus,* probably composed in the 1630s and performed regularly during Holy Week at the papal chapel ever since. After hearing this work only once or twice during his stay in Rome in 1770, the 14-year-old Mozart wrote it down from memory, defying an alleged papal ban on its unauthorized dissemination.

Allen, Henry "Red" [Henry James, Jr.] (b. New Orleans, 7 Jan. 1908; d. New York, 17 Apr. 1967). Jazz trumpeter, singer, and bandleader. He joined King Oliver (1927), worked on Mississippi riverboats (1928–29), then joined Luis Russell (1929–32), Fletcher Henderson (1932, 1933–34), the Mills Blue Rhythm Band (1934–37), and Russell again (1937–40). Second only to Louis Armstrong among contemporary jazz trumpeters, he was often cast in the role of accompanist to Armstrong while with Russell in 1929 and 1937–40. His recordings included "Who Stole the Lock" with Jack Bland and his Rhythmakers (1932), "Ride, Red, Ride" with the Mills Blue Rhythm Band (1935), and numerous sessions under his own name, generally in sextets drawn from the Russell and Mills bands. From the 1940s he led traditional and mainstream jazz combos, holding a long engagement at the Metropole in New York with such sidemen as Buster Bailey, Cozy Cole, Vic Dickenson, Coleman Hawkins, J. C. Higginbotham, and Claude Hopkins. He continued recording, including the album *Feelin' Good* (1965), and also toured internationally as a soloist during the 1960s.

Allende (Sarón), Pedro Humberto (b. Santiago, Chile, 29 June 1885; d. there, 16 Aug. 1959). Composer. At the National Conservatory in Santiago he studied violin and composition until 1908. He studied in France and Spain (1908–10), and upon returning home he was elected to the Sociedad de folklore as a result of his studies of native and mestizo folk idioms. He was the first to make recordings of the Mapuche music of Chile's Araucanian Indians. His interest in folk music, both rural and urban, is reflected in his own music; typical is the symphonic poem *La voz de las calles* (1920), incorporating the melodies of city street vendors. His 12 *Tonadas* for piano (1918–22) exhibit the influence of early 20th-century French music. From 1930 to 1950 he taught composition at the National Conservatory. In 1945 he became the first Chilean composer to receive Chile's National Arts Prize, and in the same year *Revista musical chilena* devoted an issue (1/5) to his work.

Works: the opera *La cenicienta* (1948); orchestral works (a symphony in B♭, 1910; *Escenas campesinas,* 1913; 12 *Tonadas,* 1925–36); *Concerto sinfónico,* cello and orchestra (1915), a violin concerto (1940), and a piano concerto (1945); *Paisaje chileno,* chorus and orchestra (1913); *Oda a España,* baritone, chorus, orchestra (1922); a string trio (1920), a string quartet (1930), and other chamber music; several solo vocal works; piano pieces (3 sonatas; *12 tonadas de carácter popular chileno,* 1918–22).

Allende Blin, Juan (b. Santiago, Chile, 24 Feb. 1928). Composer. His father was the composer Adolfo Allende, his mother the pianist and teacher Rebecca Blin. He studied with his parents, with his uncle Pedro Humberto Allende, and in Germany with Messiaen, Bialas, and Thomas Kaufmann. Taught at the National Conservatory, 1954–57. Returned to Germany, working in Frankfurt and Hamburg. Collaborated (1971–72) with Herman Markard, instrument designer and builder, on "Orgelwiese" for the jubilee celebrations at Folkwang Museum in Essen, where he lives. Compositions include music for organ; chamber pieces; ballets *Séquence* (1961) and *Profils* (1964); *Open Air and Water Music* (1972), to be played outdoors; *Tagebuchgesänge,* 2 baritones, chamber ensemble (1986–87).

Alpaerts, Flor (b. Antwerp, 12 Sept. 1876; d. there, 5 Oct. 1954). Composer. At the Flemish School of Music and at Antwerp's Royal Flemish Conservatory he studied violin with J. Coligns and composition with Jan Blockx and Peter Benoit. In 1903 he joined the conservatory's faculty and was its director from 1933 to 1941. He was elected to the Academie royale de Belgique in 1946. His music manifests late romantic lushness and frequently emulates the orchestral color of Debussy. His son Jef (1904–1973) was a conductor and pianist in Antwerp.

Works: an opera, *Shylock* (Antwerp, 1913); orchestral works (*Psyche,* 1899–1901; *Herleving,* 1904; *Pallieter,* 1921–24; *Thijl Uilenspiegel,* 1927); incidental music to 6 plays (Sophocles' *Oedipus Rex,* 1906; Shakespeare's *Cymbeline,* 1938); a violin concerto (1948); a serenade for winds (1915); choral music (a cantata, *Het schoner vaderland,* 1912); 4 string quartets, *3 petites pièces* (piano and violin, 1944), and other chamber music; piano pieces. He also wrote a widely used textbook, *Musieklezen en zingen,* 5 vols. (Antwerp, 1918).

Alsina, Carlos Roque (b. Buenos Aires, 19 Feb. 1941). Composer and pianist. At the National Univ. in Buenos Aires he studied with Kröpfl (1962–64). He was assistant conductor of the Teatro Colón (1960–64) and of the Deutsche Oper, Berlin (1966). He taught at the State Univ. of New York at Buffalo (1966–68) and in 1969 founded, with Vinko Globokar and others, the improvisation chamber group New Phonic Art. He has since lived in Berlin and Paris. His association with Berio left a mark on his music, which also embraces atonality as well as triadic harmonies, and employs aleatory techniques, taped sounds, and extreme instrumental virtuosity (e.g., the *Klavierstücke*).

Works include *Überwindung,* orchestra with soloists (1970); *Klavierstück* no. 1 (1958), no. 2 (1960); a wind quintet (1961); *Textes 1967,* a theater piece for soprano and chamber ensemble (1967); *Jeu de cloches,* 3 or more instruments, tape

(1969); *Fusion,* 2 pianos, 2 percussion (1974); *Omnipotenz,* 2 instruments, chamber orchestra (1972); a cantata for tenor, chorus, and orchestra (1977); *Harmonies* for children's chorus, speakers, vocal soloists, tape, and orchestra (1979); the opera *La muraille* (1981); *Hinterland,* piano, percussion, tape (1982); a piano concerto (1985).

Altenburg, Johann Ernst (b. Weissenfels, 15 June 1734; d. Bitterfeld, 14 May 1801). Trumpet player, organist, and composer. Despite a lengthy apprenticeship on the trumpet—partly under his father, the trumpeter Johann Caspar Altenburg (1689–1761)—he was at first unable to gain a position as a trumpet player. From 1757 he served as field trumpeter in the Seven Years' War. Upon returning home to Weissenfels in 1766, he was organist at nearby Landsberg. He is best known for a treatise on playing trumpet and kettledrums in which he provides important information on trumpet technique and on the social milieu of the court trumpeter: *Versuch einer Anleitung zur heroisch-musikalischen Trompeter- und Pauker-Kunst* (Halle, 1795); trans. Edward H. Tarr as *Essay on an Introduction to the Heroic and Musical Trumpeters' and Kettledrummers' Art* (Nashville, 1974).

Alwyn, William (b. Northampton, 7 Nov. 1905; d. Southwold, 11 Sept. 1985). Composer, flutist, writer, and painter. Studied at the Royal Academy of Music, 1920–23, and taught composition there, 1926–55; flutist with the London Symphony and other orchestras in the intervening years. A founder and chairman three times of the Composers' Guild of Great Britain. Works include the opera *Miss Julie* (to his own libretto, after Strindberg, 1961–76); 5 symphonies (1950, 1954, 1956, 1960, 1973); 3 concerti grossi (1942, 1950, 1964); more than 60 film scores (*Desert Victory,* 1943; *Odd Man Out,* 1947; *The Fallen Idol,* 1949; *Swiss Family Robinson,* 1960; *The Naked Edge,* 1961); a flute divertimento (1939), 2 string quartets (1955, 1976), and other chamber music; piano pieces; songs.

Amadei, Filippo (b. Reggio, ca. 1670; d. Rome?, after 1729). Cellist and composer. Instrumentalist to Cardinal Pietro Ottoboni in Rome, 1690–96, serving under Corelli. After 1700 he was cellist in the Società del centesimo and trumpeter for the Campidoglio. He was in London during the 1720s, where he was known as "Pippo"; from 1720 he was a member of the orchestra of the Royal Academy of Music. In 1721 he composed act 1 of the academy's production of *Muzio Scevola;* acts 2 and 3 were by Bononcini and Handel, respectively. He also composed cantatas (*Il pensiero,* 1709), and various sacred pieces.

Amalar [Amalarius of Metz] (b. "Belgic Gaul," ca. 775; d. Metz?, ca. 850). Writer on the liturgy and liturgical chant. His writings are especially valuable for their accounts of the relationship between Roman and Frankish chant. Extant works are *Liber officialis* and *Liber de ordine antiphonarii.* The latter is a commentary on a lost antiphoner that contained both Roman and Frankish versions of many chants.

Bibl.: Jean Michel Hanssens, ed., *Amalarii episcopi opera liturgica omnia,* Studi e testi, 138–40 (Vatican City, 1948–50).

Amat, Joan Carlos [Carles y Amat, Joan] (b. Monistrol de Montserrat, Catalonia, 1572; d. there, 10 Feb. 1642). Physician, guitarist, and writer on guitar playing, medicine, astrology, and other subjects. In 1596 he published *Guitarra española de cinco ordenes* (numerous editions through 1819), the earliest treatise on the five-string guitar. It includes the earliest discussion of strumming *(rasgueado)* and a method of notating all major and minor chords for the purpose.

Amati, Nicola [Nicolo] (b. Cremona, 3 Dec. 1596; d. there, 12 Apr. 1684). Violin maker. Both his grandfather, Andrea (b. before 1511), and his father, Girolamo (b. 1561), were path-breaking instrument makers; the former had essentially established the form of the modern violin. Nicola was the finest craftsman of the family and assumed control of the business after his father's death from the plague in 1630. After 1640 he produced a large quantity of instruments—mostly violins—and passed on the Cremonese legacy through his illustrious pupils Andrea Guarneri and Antonio Stradivari, and through his own son Girolamo (b. 1649). His best instruments (the "Grand Amatis") were characterized by slightly widened dimensions and by a ready responsiveness.

Ambros, August Wilhelm (b. Mauth [now Vysoké Mýto], 17 Nov. 1816; d. Vienna, 26 June 1876). Music historian. Studied law at Prague Univ. and later worked in the civil service. Wrote *Die Grenzen der Musik und Poesie* (Prague, 1856; R: Hildesheim, 1976; trans. Eng. 1893) in response to Hanslick's aesthetics. His unfinished *Geschichte der Musik,* especially the third volume on Renaissance music (Leipzig, 1868; 2nd ed., rev. Otto Kade, 1893; R: Hildesheim, 1968), was an important step in the evolution of music history in concept and practice. He became professor of music history at Prague in 1869; from 1872 he lectured in Vienna at the conservatory and the university.

Ambrose (b. Trier, ca. 340; d. Milan, 397). Saint. Bishop of Milan from 7 Dec. 374; credited with the establishment of the Milanese or Ambrosian rite and chant. Medieval tradition also assigned to him the introduction of hymns and antiphonal psalmody into the Western church from Eastern models. Four or 6 hymn texts are now generally attributed to him; neither the *Te Deum* nor any melodies can be attributed to him with comparable certainty.

Ameling, Elly [Elisabeth] **(Sara)** (b. Rotterdam, 8 Feb. 1934). Soprano. Studied voice with Jo Bollenkamp in Dresden, Pierre Bernac in Paris. Won the 's Hertogenbosch Competition in 1956 and the Geneva Competition in 1958. She was already known abroad by 1961, the year of her debut recital in Amsterdam. U.S. debut at Lincoln Center, 28 Aug. 1968. Operatic debut at the Amsterdam Opera (as Ilia in *Idomeneo*), 1973. Best known for lieder and concert arias by

Mozart, Schubert, Schumann, and Wolf, cantatas by Bach, oratorios by Handel. She gave several farewell recitals in 1995.

Amirkhanian, Charles (Benjamin) (b. Fresno, Calif., 19 Jan. 1945). Composer. Received M.F.A. (1980) from Mills College, where he studied electronic music and sound recording techniques. Lecturer at San Francisco State Univ., 1977–80. Music director at radio station KPFA (Berkeley) from 1968. Has written articles on contemporary composition. Early works are mostly for percussion and were influenced by Cage and Harrison. After 1970 he turned mostly to tape composition. Works include *Mental Radio,* 9 text-sound compositions (1979–82); *Gold and Spirit,* which uses band cadences, football cheers, and various sports sounds, including bocce and racquetball (1984); works for synthesizer, including *Metropolis San Francisco* (1985–86), *Pas de voix,* "Portrait of Samuel Beckett" (1987).

Ammerbach, Elias Nikolaus (b. Naumburg, ca. 1530; d. Leipzig, buried 29 Jan. 1597). Organist and intabulator of music for keyboard. Organist at the Thomaskirche in Leipzig, 1561–95. Published two collections, *Orgel oder Instrument Tabulatur* (1571; 2nd ed., 1583) and *Ein new künstlich Tabulaturbuch* (1575). The first of these is the first published German organ music and the first example of the so-called new German organ tablature. They contain dances and intabulations of sacred and secular vocal pieces, many by well-known composers of the period, some in a highly ornamented style.

Ammons, Albert (C.) (b. Chicago, 23 Sept. 1907; d. there, 2 Dec. 1949). Boogie-woogie pianist, father of Gene Ammons. He played in bands in Chicago. His Rhythm Kings (1934–38), a swing sextet, recorded *Boogie Woogie Stomp* (1936). A central figure in the popularization of boogie-woogie, he moved to New York in 1938 to perform and record in trios with Pete Johnson and Meade "Lux" Lewis, in duos with Johnson, and as a soloist (including the recording *The Boogie Rocks,* 1944).

Ammons, Gene [Eugene; Jug] (b. Chicago, 14 Apr. 1925; d. there, 6 Aug. 1974). Jazz tenor saxophonist, son of Albert Ammons. He was a principal soloist in Billy Eckstine's bop big band (1944–47). Thereafter, except for a brief period with Woody Herman's big band (1949), he led combos, often together with Sonny Stitt. In these he played bop (including the recording *Blues Up and Down,* 1950) and later, soul jazz (including the album *Boss Tenor,* 1960). From 1958 to 1969 his career was interrupted by two lengthy prison terms for drug offenses.

Amner, John (b. Ely, bapt. 24 Aug. 1579; d. there, buried 24 July 1641). Organist and composer. After some study at Oxford he was made choirmaster at Ely Cathedral in 1610 and remained there until his death. He received a bachelor's degree in music from Oxford in 1613 and from Cambridge in 1640. He composed principally services and full and verse anthems; one set of variations for keyboard also survives.

Amram, David (Werner, III) (b. Philadelphia, 17 Nov. 1930). Composer, horn player, and conductor. Studied horn at the Oberlin Conservatory (1948), then attended George Washington Univ., graduating in 1952. Played in the National Symphony Orchestra, 1951–52; the Seventh Army Symphony Orchestra, 1952–55. In 1955 enrolled at the Manhattan School of Music, where he studied with Mitropoulos, Giannini, and Schuller and performed in the Manhattan Woodwind Quintet. Associated from 1956 with Joseph Papp and the New York Shakespeare Festival; by 1967 he had composed incidental music for 25 productions. Composer in residence with the New York Philharmonic, 1966–67; conductor of the Brooklyn Philharmonia's youth concerts from 1972. His extensive foreign travels sponsored by the State Department and his experience as a performer of jazz have influenced his eclectic tastes. He has written a large number of works ranging from theater and film music to works for orchestra, band, jazz ensemble, and choral and instrumental chamber ensembles.

Bibl.: David Amram, *Vibrations: The Adventures and Musical Times of David Amram* (New York, 1968; R: 1980).

Amy, Gilbert (b. Paris, 29 Aug. 1936). Composer and conductor. Studied at the Paris Conservatory, 1955–60, with Milhaud (composition), Messiaen (analysis), and Loriod (piano and harmony); studied at the Darmstadt summer courses, 1959–61. Met Boulez in 1956 and attended his conducting class in Basel in 1965; succeeded him as conductor of the Domaine musicale in 1967. Musical adviser to the French national radio and television network (ORTF) from 1973. The strict serial orientation of his early music (Piano Sonata, 1957–60), polyphonic rigor, and interest in mobile forms developed to encompass exploration of spatial effects (*Antiphonies* for 2 orchestras, 1960–63), concertante style, and subtlety of tone color. Has composed theater and incidental music; symphonic music (*Triade,* 1965; *Strophe,* soprano and orchestra, 1964–66; *Trajectoires,* violin and orchestra, 1966; *Refrains,* 1972; *D'un espace déployé,* soprano and 2 orchestras, 1972–73; *Orchestrale,* 1985); *Messe,* soprano, alto, tenor, bass, children's chorus, chorus, orchestra (1982–83); *Missa cum iubilo,* soloists, chorus, orchestra (1987); chamber music (*Alpha-Beth,* wind sextet, 1963–64).

Ančerl, Karel (b. Tučapy, Bohemia, 11 Apr. 1908; d. Toronto, 3 July 1973). Conductor. Studied with Vaclav Talich at the Prague Conservatory, then with Hermann Scherchen in Strasbourg. Led the Prague Radio Orchestra from 1933 until 1939, when he was removed by the Nazis, who in 1942 sent him to Theresienstadt and Auschwitz. Led the Prague Opera, 1945–47; Czech Radio Orchestra, 1947–50; Czech Philharmonic, 1950–68. After the Russian invasion of

Czechoslovakia, conductor of the Toronto Symphony from 1968 until his death.

Anchieta, Juan de (b. Urrestilla?, near Azpeitia, Spain, 1462; d. Azpeitia, 30 July 1523). Composer. From 6 Feb. 1489 until 1504 he was a singer in the court chapel of Queen Isabella. After her death he joined the chapel of Isabella's daughter Joanna and Philip the Fair, accompanying them to Flanders and England, along with Pierre de la Rue, Marbriano de Orto, and Alexander Agricola. He held various absentee benefices and church posts, but remained with the royal chapel until being pensioned off by Charles V on 15 Aug. 1519. Surviving works include 2 Masses, 2 Magnificats, several motets, and a few *villancicos.*

Bibl.: Robert Stevenson, *Spanish Music in the Age of Columbus* (The Hague, 1960).

Anda, Géza (b. Budapest, 19 Nov. 1921; d. Zurich, 13 June 1976). Pianist. Studied with Ernst von Dohnányi at the Budapest Acadamy, winning the Liszt Prize. Debut with Budapest Philharmonic, 1939. In 1943 he moved to Switzerland, becoming a citizen in 1955. Best known for his interpretation of Bartók and for a cycle of 25 Mozart concertos with the Salzburg Mozarteum Camerata Academica, recorded 1961–70.

Anderson, Cat [William Alonzo] (b. Greenville, S.C., 12 Sept. 1916; d. Norwalk, Calif., 29 Apr. 1981). Jazz trumpeter. He was trained with other future jazzmen in bands at Jenkins's Orphanage in Charleston. Joined Lionel Hampton (1942, 1944), then Duke Ellington (1944–47, 1950–59, intermittently 1961–71); in the intervals he led bands and worked as a freelance. Best known for high register playing with Ellington, as on the spectacular recording "Trumpet No End," but a growling muted solo on "A Gatherin' in a Clearin'" demonstrates his versatility (both 1946). He also recorded as a leader (1947–79) and with Johnny Hodges (intermittently 1956–67) and Hampton, with whom he toured in the 1970s.

Anderson, Laurie (b. Chicago, 5 June 1947). Composer and performer. She was trained as a violinist. In 1966 she moved to New York, where she studied painting and sculpting, receiving a B.A. from Barnard College and an M.F.A. at Columbia University. She studied privately with minimalist painter Sol LeWitt; wrote art criticism and taught art history. In 1974 started making her own instruments, the most famous of which is a tapebow violin. Performed frequently at the Museum of Modern Art, and at Berlin Festival of 1976. Published *Notebooks* (1977), a collection of scores and photos from her performances. Compositions include the two-evening performance art work *United States* (1983); the song "O Superman (for Massenet)" from this was a commercial success, reaching no. 2 on the British pop charts. Released two albums with Warner Bros., *Big Science* (1982) and *Mister Heartbreak* (1984).

Bibl.: Janet Kardon, ed. *Laurie Anderson: Works from 1969 to 1983* (Philadelphia, 1983).

Marian Anderson.

Anderson, Leroy (b. Cambridge, Mass., 29 June 1908; d. Woodbury, Conn., 18 May 1975). Composer, arranger, and conductor. Studied composition at Harvard Univ. with Piston and Enesco, receiving his M.A. in 1930. Director of the Harvard Univ. Band and an organist and conductor in Boston, 1931–35. Subsequently he worked as an arranger, orchestrator, and member of various boards, including the ASCAP board of review. As a composer he specialized in light music for orchestra; appealing melodies and popular dance rhythms (as in *Belle of the Ball,* 1951; *Blue Tango,* 1952) were often enhanced by striking orchestral effects (as in *The Syncopated Clock,* 1945; *The Typewriter,* 1950; *Sandpaper Ballet,* 1954).

Anderson, Marian (b. Philadelphia, 27 Feb. 1897; d. Portland, Ore., 8 Apr. 1993). Contralto. Studied voice under Giuseppe Boghetti in Philadelphia, Frank La Forge in New York, and several European coaches. Debut recital at Town Hall in New York, 25 Apr. 1924. Soloist with the New York Philharmonic at Lewisohn Stadium, 26 Aug. 1925. Despite favorable notices, her American career was restricted by barriers against black artists. London debut at Wigmore Hall, 1930. Rosenwald Scholarships funded two tours of Scandinavia in 1931 and 1933. These established her career in Europe, where she remained through 1935. The impresario Sol Hurok, hearing her in Paris, undertook to establish her career at home, beginning with a recital at Town Hall, 30 Dec. 1935. In early 1939 she was banned on racial grounds from singing at Constitution Hall in Washington, D.C.; an outpouring of public sympathy led to her Easter concert at the Lincoln Memorial, attended by 75,000 people and broadcast nationally. Operatic debut 7 Jan. 1955 at the Met as Ulrica in *Un ballo in maschera.* She retired in 1965.

Bibl.: Janet Sims, *Marian Anderson: An Annotated Bibliography and Discography* (Westport, Conn., 1981).

Anderson, T(homas) J(efferson, Jr.) (b. Coatesville, Pa., 17 Aug. 1928). Composer. Toured with a jazz or-

The Andrews Sisters, 1941: (from left) Maxene, Patti, and LaVerne.

chestra as a youth before enrolling in West Virginia State College; graduate studies at Pennsylvania State Univ. and with Bezanson and Hervig at the Univ. of Iowa (Ph.D., 1958); studied with Milhaud at Aspen, 1964. Composer-in-residence with the Atlanta Symphony, 1969–71. Professor of music at Tufts Univ. from 1972 (chairman, 1972–80). Collaborated in preparing the premiere of Scott Joplin's opera *Treemonisha* in 1972. Works include an opera, *Soldier Boy, Soldier* (1982); an operetta and other stage music; orchestral works (*Squares,* 1964; *Chamber Symphony,* 1968; *Intervals,* 1971); vocal music (*Variations on a Theme by M. B. Tolson,* soprano and chamber ensemble, 1972; *Horizons '76,* soprano and orchestra, 1976); chamber music; piano pieces.

André, Johann (b. Offenbach, 28 Mar. 1741; d. there, 18 June 1799). Composer and music publisher. Trained in thoroughbass and in his family's silk manufacturing business, which he entered. In the early 1760s he served as a clerk in Frankfurt am Main, where he also translated French opéras comiques. His first original stage work, the singspiel *Der Töpfer* (1773), was much admired by Goethe, whose librettos André later used for *Erwin und Elmire* (1775) and *Claudine von Villa Bella* (1778). In 1774 he gave up the silk business in favor of his own music publishing firm. From 1776 to 1784 he was conductor at Döbbelin's Berlin theater, where he brought many of his own works to the stage. He returned to Offenbach in 1784 to look after his firm, which flourished during the 1780s and 1790s. His known singspiels number 19; he composed at least 13 other stage works and numerous lieder.

Bibl.: Wilhelm Stauder, "Johann André: Ein Beitrag zur Geschichte des deutschen Singspiels" (diss., Univ. of Frankfurt am Main, 1936); extracts in *AfMf* 1 (1936): 318–60. Klaus Hortschansky et al., *Johann André: Musikverlag* (Tutzing, 1973).

André, Johann Anton (b. Offenbach, 6 Oct. 1775; d. there, 6 Apr. 1842). Composer and publisher. Son of Johann André. His music teachers included Ignaz Fränzl and G. J. Vollweiler in Mannheim. On his father's death in 1799, he took charge of the family firm and introduced lithography, and in 1800 bought Mozart's papers from Mozart's widow, Constanze. He devoted much time to cataloguing and publishing Mozart's works. He composed 2 operas, 9 symphonies, concertos, much chamber music, many songs, and keyboard music, some of it didactic. A *Lehrbuch der Tonsetzkunst* was left incomplete.

André, Maurice (b. Alès, France, 21 May 1933). Trumpeter. He was a miner from 1947 to 1951 before studying at the Paris Conservatory. Won the Geneva Competition in 1956; professor of trumpet at the Paris Conservatory from 1967. Made his American debut with the Württemberg Chamber Orchestra, 27 Nov. 1974. A widely recorded proponent of Baroque music, he favors a custom-made four-valved piccolo trumpet in this repertory.

Andreas de Florentia [Andrea degli Organi] (d. ca. 1415). Composer and organist. From 1375 he held various church-related posts in Florence and Pistoia as a member of the Order of the Servi di Maria. With Landini he worked on the building of two organs in Florence. He composed 30 two- and three-voiced *ballate.*

Bibl.: Ed. in *CMM* 8/5 (1964) and W. Thomas Marrocco, ed., *Italian Secular Music,* Polyphonic Music of the Fourteenth Century, 10 (Monaco, 1974).

Andrews, LaVerne (b. Minneapolis, 6 July 1915; d. Brentwood, Calif., 8 May 1967), **Maxene** [Maxine] (b. Minneapolis, 3 Jan. 1918; d. Hyannis, Mass., 23 Oct. 1995), **Patti** [Patricia] (b. Minneapolis, 16 Feb. 1920). Popular vocal trio. After singing in Midwest vaudeville houses, the Andrews Sisters performed in the late 1930s and 1940s on radio and in films and often with the Glenn Miller Orchestra. They recorded with Bing Crosby and Guy Lombardo among others; their songs include "Bei mir bist du schön" (1937), "Boogie-Woogie Bugle Boy" (1941), "Don't Sit under the Apple Tree" (1942), and "Rum and Coca-Cola" (1944).

Andriessen, Hendrik (b. Haarlem, 17 Sept. 1892; d. Heemstede, 12 Apr. 1981). Organist and composer. He studied at the Amsterdam Conservatory until 1916, the year he became organist at St. Joseph's Church, Haarlem. From 1926 he taught music theory and composition at the Amsterdam Conservatory, and from 1937 to 1949 he was director of the Utrecht Conservatory. In 1930 he became *Dozent* in organ at the Nederlands Instituut voor Katholieke Kerkmuziek. In 1934 he was appointed organist of the Cathedral of Utrecht. He was director of the Royal Conservatory, The Hague (1949–57), and professor of musicology at the Catholic Univ. at Nijmegen (1952–63). His musical style is eclectic, a mix of romantic harmony and atonal melody (*Symphonic Etude,* orchestra, 1952), of church modes and polyphony in the style of Notre Dame (*Missa in honorem Sacratissimi Cordis,* 1919), of sonata form and Baroque dances (Third Symphony, 1946). Other works include 2 operas (*Philomela,* 1948; *De spiegel van Venetie,* 1964); 16 Masses; nearly 40 other choral works (a Magnificat, 1936); 4 symphonies (1930, 1937, 1946, 1954); a violin concerto (1969); *Ricercare* (1949) and other orchestral works; chamber music; works for organ and for piano; songs.

Bibl.: Thurston J. Dox, "Hendrik Andriessen: His Life and Works" (diss., Univ. of Rochester, 1969).

Andriessen, Jurriaan (b. Haarlem, 15 Nov. 1925). Composer. At the Utrecht Conservatory he studied composition with his father, Hendrik Andriessen, and conducting with Van Otterloo. He studied in Paris in 1947 and spent 1949–51 in the U.S., studying during two summers at the Berkshire Music Center, where he composed the *Berkshire Symphonies* (1949); from this work George Balanchine produced the ballet *Jones Beach.* The years 1951–53 were spent in Italy and Germany. In 1954 he was made resident composer of The Hague Theater Company, and during ensuing years he composed incidental music for stage and film scores. He has also composed 2 operas (*Kalchas,* 1959; *Het zwarte blondje,* 1954); ballets (*De canapé,* 1953); 8 symphonies and other orchestral works; chamber music (Concertino, bassoon, winds, 1963); keyboard works.

Andriessen, Louis (b. Utrecht, 6 June 1939). Composer. After study with his father, Hendrik Andriessen, at the Utrecht Conservatory (from 1957), he took instruction with Berio in Milan and Berlin (1962–65). A leading Dutch avant-gardist, he employed electronic and collage techniques and jazz idioms. His works include orchestral music (*Ittrospezione 2,* 1963; *Anachrony 1,* "To the Memory of Charles Ives," 1967; and *2,* with oboe soloist, 1969); music for jazz ensemble (*Spectacle,* 1970; *On Jimmy Yancey,* 1973); wind band music (*Symphonieën der Nederlanden,* 1974); *Hoe het is* [What It's Like], electronics and 52 strings (1970); *De Tijd* [Time] (1981); *De Snelheid* [Velocity] (1984); *Die Matiere* [Matter], music theater (1984–88).

Andriessen, Willem (b. Haarlem, 25 Oct. 1887; d. Amsterdam, 29 Mar. 1964). Pianist and composer; brother of Hendrik Andriessen. From 1900 he studied at the Amsterdam Conservatory, receiving the Prix d'excellence upon completion of his studies there in 1908. He taught piano at the conservatories in The Hague (1910–17) and Rotterdam, and in 1937 he became director of the Amsterdam Conservatory. His works include a Mass in F minor (1914–16); other choral works ("Ave Maria," "Exultate"); incidental music (*Lucifer,* 1943); *Hei 't was in de Mei,* Scherzo for Orchestra (1912); a piano concerto (1908); a piano sonata (1938).

Anerio, Felice (b. Rome, ca. 1560; d. there, 26 Sept. 1614). Composer. Brother of Giovanni Francesco Anerio. From 1568 to 1580 he sang in a succession of choirs in Rome, including those of S. Maria Maggiore and the Cappella Giulia, first as a boy and then as a salaried singer. He was *maestro di cappella* of the Collegio degli Inglesi in 1584–85. In 1594 Clement VIII appointed him composer to the papal choir, succeeding Palestrina. He also directed the chapel choir of Duke Giovanni Angelo Altaemps. In 1611–12 he worked with Soriano on a reformation of the Roman Gradual. His works are largely in the tradition of Palestrina and include numerous madrigals and canzonettas (both secular and spiritual, most composed before his appointment to the papal choir), 4 Masses, several Magnificats, motets, hymns, laude, and other sacred works.

Anerio, Giovanni Francesco (b. Rome, ca. 1567; d. Graz, buried 12 June 1630). Composer. Brother of Felice Anerio. During the 1590s Giovanni was apparently organist for services at S. Marcello; he also served at St. John Lateran from around 1600. In 1608 he became *maestro di cappella* at Santo Spirito in Sassia, and from 1609 of the Verona Cathedral as well. In 1611 he settled again in Rome, where he served as *maestro* at S. Maria dei Monti (1613–20). During his last years he directed the choirs for Sigismund III in Poland. Although his sacred music was sometimes in the style of Palestrina, both sacred and secular works include examples of the modern monodic style and the use of basso continuo. He composed some 83 motets; also litanies, Psalm settings, Masses, dramatic dialogues (important works in the development of the oratorio), and secular vocal music (including madrigals and canzonettas).

Anfossi, Pasquale (b. Taggia, 5 April 1727; d. Rome, Feb. 1797). Composer. After violin study in Naples he performed with opera orchestras throughout Italy. During the 1750s and early 1760s he studied composition with Sacchini and Piccinni, and he composed his first opera for Rome, *La serva spirituosa,* in 1763. During the 1770s he composed operas for both Naples and Rome. From 1782 to ca. 1786 he was director of the King's Theatre in London, and in 1792 he was appointed *maestro di cappella* at St. John Lateran in Rome, a post he held for the rest of his life. He composed between 60 and 70 operas, 22 or more oratorios, many cantatas, Masses and other sacred music, and chamber works.

Anhalt, István (b. Budapest, 12 Apr. 1919). Composer, conductor, and pianist. Studied composition under Kodály at the Royal Hungarian Academy, graduating in 1941. Assistant conductor at the Hungarian National Opera in 1945. Moved to Paris in 1946 and continued his studies at the Paris Conservatory and with Boulanger. Emigrated to Canada in 1949 and joined the faculty at McGill Univ., where he founded the electronic music studio. Taught composition at the State Univ. of New York at Buffalo in 1969, and from 1971 until 1984 was head of the music department of Queen's Univ., Kingston, Ontario. His early works (Piano Trio, 1953; Symphony, 1958) were influenced by the dodecaphonic techniques of Schoenberg. His electronic studies (Electronic Composition no. 3, "Birds and Bells," 1960) and works for prepared tape and live media (*Foci,* soprano, 10 instruments, tape, 1969; *La tourangelle,* 3 sopranos, 2 speakers, 15 instrumentalists, tape, 1974) were significant in the development of electronic music in Canada. Other works include *Simulacrum* (1987) and *Sparkskraps* (1988) for orchestra; *Winthrop,* solo voices, boys choir, chorus, orchestra (1986).

Animuccia, Giovanni (b. Florence, ca. 1500; d. Rome, 20 Mar. 1571). Composer. He was in Rome by 1550 and in 1555 became director of the choir of the Cappella Giulia, succeeding Palestrina and remaining there until his death. He was the most prominent and prolific of Palestrina's contemporaries in Rome. His elaborate sacred music, which often reflects the concerns of the Council of Trent, includes one book each of Masses, Magnificats, and motets. Two books of *laude* were composed in simple homophonic style for use in the Oratory of Filippo Neri, a fellow Florentine and an acquaintance since 1551. He also composed four books of madrigals (some spiritual), including extended madrigal cycles, the first such works by a composer from Florence.

Anna Amalia [Amalie] (1) (b. Berlin, 9 Nov. 1723; d. there, 30 Mar. 1787). Composer, patroness of music, and Princess of Prussia. A sister of Frederick II, she studied music with her brother and with Gottlieb Hayne. Around 1735 she established a private library, eventually amassing some 600 compositions (many are autographs) by J. S. and C. P. E. Bach, Handel, Hasse, Telemann, Kirnberger, and many others. Musicians and literati gathered at her soirees in the royal palace. In the 1750s she began instruction in composition with Kirnberger, who in 1771 reproduced part of her setting of *Der Tod Jesu* in his *Kunst des reinen Satzes.* She also composed chorales and chamber music.

Bibl.: Eva Renate Blechschmidt, *Die Amalienbibliothek* [catalog of original collection], Berliner Studien zur Musikwissenschaft, 8 (Berlin, 1965).

Anna Amalia [Amalie] (2) (b. Wolfenbüttel, 24 Oct. 1739; d. Weimar, 10 Apr. 1807). Musician and patroness of music. The daughter of Duke Karl I of Brunswick, she married the Duke of Saxe-Weimar in 1756; she reigned over the duchy from the time of the duke's death two years later until their eldest son, Karl August, succeeded to the throne in 1775. During her reign the Weimar court was an important literary and musical center. The poets Wieland, Herder, and Goethe gathered there; singspiels such as J. A. Hiller's *Die Jagd* (1770) and Wieland and Schweitzer's *Alceste* (1773) received first performances at her court. Goethe wrote singspiel texts for her, including *Erwin und Elmire,* which she set in 1776, and *Das Jahrmarktsfest zu Plundersweilern,* set in 1778. A concerto for 12 instruments and cembalo obbligato is attributed to her.

Ansermet, Ernest (Alexandre) (b. Vevey, 11 Nov. 1883; d. Geneva, 20 Feb. 1969). Conductor. After studies at Lausanne Univ. and the Sorbonne, taught mathematics at the École normale in Geneva (1903–6) and at Lausanne Univ. (1906–9). He studied composition with André Gédalge in Paris (1905–6) and with Ernest Bloch (ca. 1907) in Geneva. In Berlin (1909) he observed the conducting techniques of Nikisch, Richard Strauss, and Weingartner. Debut in Lausanne, 15 Mar. 1910. Conductor, Montreux Kursaal Orchestra, 1912–14; in this capacity he met Stravinsky, who later assisted his appointment as conductor for Diaghilev's Ballets russes (1915–23). His premieres with this company included Satie's *Parade* (1917), Falla's *El sombrero de tres picos* (1919), and Stravinsky's *Les noces* (1923). Founded the Orchestre de la Suisse Romande, leading it from its first concert in Nov. 1918 until his retirement in 1966. A lifelong association with Decca Records began in 1929. His recorded repertory includes the Russian Five, Debussy, Ravel, Roussel, his compatriots Honegger and Martin, and especially Stravinsky, whose music he championed until that composer adopted serial techniques. In 1962 Ansermet published a rejection of such techniques.

Anspach, Elizabeth, Margravine of [Craven, Elizabeth] (b. London, 17 Dec. 1750; d. Naples, 13 Jan. 1828). Composer and playwright. During the 1780s and 1790s she wrote several plays that were performed in London theaters, as well as music for operas such as *The Silver Tankard* (1781) and *The Princess of Georgia* (1794). In 1791, shortly after the death of her first husband, William, 6th Earl of Craven, from whom she had been separated since 1780, she married Margrave Christian Frederick of Anspach; the following year they moved to England. Her only surviving work is a madrigal setting from Shakespeare ("O Mistress Mine").

Antegnati, Costanzo (b. Brescia, bapt. 9 Dec. 1549; d. there, 14 Nov. 1624). Composer and organ builder. Descended from a long line of musicians, most of them directly concerned with the organ. In the treatise *L'arte* *organica* (1608) he lists 144 instruments built under his direction. From 1584 to 1624 he was organist at Brescia Cathedral. He composed Masses, motets, Psalms, madrigals, and organ ricercars.

Antes, John (b. Frederick, Pa., 24 March 1740; d. Bristol, England, 17 Dec. 1811). Composer, instrument maker, and minister. His early training by the Moravians in Pennsylvania was followed by apprenticeship as a watchmaker in Saxony. After missionary service in Egypt during the 1770s, he returned to Saxony. Soon after 1781 he took up residence among the Moravians in Fulneck, England. His compositions include hymn tunes, anthems, songs, and 3 string trios, published in London as op. 3 (1790). He was also an inventor; among his inventions is a mechanism that automatically turns pages on a music stand.

Antheil, George [Georg] **(Johann Carl)** (b. Trenton, N.J., 8 July 1900; d. New York, 12 Feb. 1959). Composer and pianist. Studied piano from age 6; from age 16 studied theory and composition with Constantin von Sternberg in Philadelphia; studied composition with Bloch in New York, 1919–21. Settled in Berlin in 1922 in order to pursue a career as concert pianist. A fascination with machines, time-space theories, and the music of Stravinsky exercised a strong influence on his style in works such as *Airplane Sonata* (1921), noted for its manipulation of rhythmic blocks and ostinato patterns. Became a leading spokesman of the avant-garde on moving to Paris in 1923. The sensational percussion score *Ballet mécanique* (1923–25; rev. 1952–53)—intended for, though never synchronized with, Léger's film—marked the high point of his iconoclastic prestige. In subsequent works (Symphonie en fa, 1925–26; Piano Concerto, 1926) he employed a neoclassic idiom. In 1928 he moved to Vienna. His operatic caricature of American life, *Transatlantic,* with jazz-inspired rhythms and parodies of popular tunes, enjoyed modest success at its premiere in Frankfurt in 1930. In 1933 he returned permanently to the U.S., where he wrote scores for Balanchine and Graham and composed music for films. His Symphony no. 4 "1942" (1942), influenced by Shostakovich, marked a turn to a neoromantic aesthetic and a preoccupation with symphonic form that was pursued in his Symphony no. 5 "Joyous" (1945–46). Among his late works are the Serenade for String Orchestra (1948), Piano Sonata no. 4 (1948), *Songs of Experience* (Blake; 1948), the opera *Volpone* (1949), and *Eight Fragments from Shelley,* chorus and piano (1951).

Writings: *Bad Boy of Music* (Garden City, N.Y., 1945; R: 1981, 1990).

Bibl.: Linda Whitesitt, *The Life and Music of George Antheil, 1900–1959* (Ann Arbor, 1983).

Anthonello de Caserta [Anthonellus, Antonellus Marot de Caserta, A. Marotus de Caserta abbas] (fl. northern Italy?, Naples?, late 14th and early 15th centuries). Composer. His extant Italian music includes 1 madrigal and 6 (or 7) *ballate.* His much more complex French music, written in the style and notation of the *ars subtilior,* includes 5 ballades, 2 rondeaux, and 1 virelay.

Antico [Antiquus, Anticho], **Andrea** (b. Montona, Istria, ca. 1480; d. after 1539). Engraver and publisher. He printed polyphonic music using a single-impression method, in Rome from 1510 to 1518 and later in Venice. He held a privilege to print music in the papal states. Books issued in Rome include collections of frottolas (some arranged for keyboard) and a large folio choirbook of Masses. In 1520–21 in Venice he issued new collections of frottolas (for voice and lute), chansons, motets, and Masses. He engraved several publications for Scotto in the 1530s. Between 1533 and 1539 he was connected with the publication of several books of madrigals (many by Verdelot and Arcadelt, some arranged for voice and lute), chansons, and motets (by Willaert). He composed a few simple frottolas.

Bibl.: Catherine Weeks Chapman, "Andrea Antico" (diss., Harvard Univ., 1964).

Antill, John Henry (b. Sydney, 8 Apr. 1904; d. there, 29 Dec. 1986). Composer. Studied at St. Andrew's Cathedral Choir School in Sydney and later at New South Wales State Conservatorium of Music under Alfred Hill. Became assistant music editor with the Australian Broadcasting Commission in 1936 and in 1947 was appointed supervisor of music; Federal Music Editor for the ABC, 1949–68. His early interest and extensive research in Aboriginal music led to his most successful score, the orchestral suite *Corroboree* (1946), which fostered the notion of a specifically Australian music. Also composed operas, ballets, symphonic works, vocal music.

Antoniou, Theodore (b. Athens, 10 Feb. 1935). Composer and conductor. Studied violin, singing, and composition at the National Conservatory in Athens, 1947–58; composition at the Hellenic Conservatory under Papaioannou, 1956–61, and at the Munich Musikhochschule, 1961–65. Toured the U.S. in 1966 and spent 1968 in Berlin. Has taught at Stanford Univ. (1969–70), the Univ. of Utah (1970), the Philadelphia Musical Academy (1970–77), the Univ. of Pennsylvania (1978), and Boston Univ. (since 1979). Founded a contemporary music group in Athens in 1967 and later founded similar ensembles at Stanford, Philadelphia, and Boston. A prolific composer of works for the stage (including settings of classical Greek theater; the opera *Bacchae,* 1991–92); orchestral music (*Fluxus I,* 1974–75; *Skolion,* 1986; *Paean,* 1989); choral and solo vocal music (*Epigrams,* soprano and chamber orchestra, 1981; *Agape,* mixed choir, flute, brass, percussion, 1990); music for chamber ensembles, and tape music. His style evolved from the early influences of atonality and Greek folklore to explore the abstract relationships of sound and space with modified serial procedures.

ApIvor, Denis (b. Collinstown, near Dublin, of Welsh parentage, 14 Apr. 1916). Composer. After experience as boy chorister at Christ Church, Oxford, he studied privately with Alan Rawsthorne and Patrick Hadley from 1937 to 1939, while studying medicine in London. He has composed operas (*She Stoops to Conquer,* 1943–47, rev. 1976–77; *Ubu Roi,* 1965–66; *Bouvard et Pécuchet,* 1970); 5 ballets (*Blood Wedding,* 1953, after Lorca); choral music (cantata *The Hollow Men,* 1939); 4 symphonies and other orchestral works; several solo concertos; chamber music (*Crystals,* percussion, Hammond organ, guitar, double bass, 1964–65).

Apostel, Hans Erich (b. Karlsruhe, 22 Jan. 1901; d. Vienna, 30 Nov. 1972). Composer. After early music studies at the Munz Conservatory in Karlsruhe, was appointed conductor at the Badisches Landestheater there. Moved to Vienna in 1921 and studied privately with Schoenberg (1921–25) and Berg (1925–35). From 1922 taught piano, theory, and composition privately and later served as an editor at Universal Edition. His early tonal works were withdrawn or revised; a dissonant, expressionistic style and later free use of dodecaphonic procedures (*Variations on a Theme of Joseph Haydn* op. 17, orchestra, 1949) eventually led to a more systematic application of Schoenberg's method of composition with twelve tones (*Rondo ritmico* op. 27, orchestra, 1957; *6 Epigramme* op. 33, string quartet, 1962; *Paralipomena dodekaphonika* op. 44, orchestra, 1970), emphasizing symmetrical structures. Also composed much vocal music, instrumental chamber music, and works for piano.

Appenzeller, Benedictus (b. ca. 1480–88; d. after 1558). Composer. Works published by Attaingnant and Moderne are the chief evidence of his activity until 1536, when he became a singer in the chapel choir of Mary of Hungary in Brussels. He soon became master of choirboys as well. Later he was also active in the choir of the Marian Brotherhood at 's Hertogenbosch. He accompanied Mary to Germany in 1551. His works include chansons and dances, motets, Masses, and Magnificats.

Applebaum, Edward (b. Los Angeles, 28 Sept. 1937). Composer. Studied with Henri Lazarof and Lukas Foss at UCLA (Ph.D., 1966). Also studied with Ingvar Lidholm. Taught at California State Univ., Long Beach, 1968–71. Composer-in-residence, Oakland Symphony Orchestra (1969), Santa Barbara Symphony (1985–87). Professor of music at Univ. of California, Santa Barbara, and from 1989 at Florida State Univ. Works include the one-act opera *The Frieze of Life* (1974); *Foci,* violin and piano (1971); *Montages* (1968); Piano Sonata (1965); and *Shantih,* cello and piano (1969); symphonies (no. 2, 1983); concertos for piano (1986) and for guitar (1987); *The Waltz in Two,* narrator and orchestra (1988).

Appleton, Jon (Howard) (b. Los Angeles, 4 Jan. 1939). Studied at Reed College (B.A., 1961), Univ. of Oregon (M.A., 1965). Studied with Davidovsky, Ussachevsky, and William J. Mitchell at the Columbia–Princeton Electronic Center (1966). Worked as part of the team that developed the Synclavier, a polyphonic digital synthesizer used for live performances. Co-editor of *The Development and Practice of Electronic Music* (Englewood Cliffs, N.J., 1975). Author of *A Special Purpose Digital System for Music* (1970); and *21st-Century Musical Instruments: Hardware and Software* (New York, 1989). Early works include orchestra pieces, instrumental and vocal works; since 1970 almost exclusively electronic compositions.

Araia [Araja], **Francesco** (b. Naples, 25 June 1709; d. Bologna, ca. 1767–70). Composer. He probably received training in music from his father, Angelo Araia; at the age of 14 Francesco directed a performance at the church of S. Maria la Nova in Naples. He is best known for a comic opera in Neapolitan dialect, *Lo matremmonejo pe' vennetta,* performed in 1729. Subsequent serious operas drew the attention of the court of Empress Anne in St. Petersburg, and in 1735 Araia assumed the post of *maestro di cappella* there. Upon Anne's death in 1740 he returned to Italy briefly, only to return to Russia to serve Empress Elizabeth. In 1755 he composed *Cephalus and Procris,* which is known as the first opera on a text in Russian (by Sumarokov). When Catherine had Peter III (Elizabeth's successor) assassinated in 1762, Araia retired and went to Bologna. Fourteen of his operas are known (only 2 survive complete); also cantatas, an oratorio (*S. Andrea Corsini,* 1731), arias, and keyboard works.

Arban, (Joseph) Jean-Baptiste (Laurent) (b. Lyons, 28 Feb. 1825; d. Paris, 9 Apr. 1889). Cornetist, conductor, and teacher. Studied trumpet at the Paris Conservatory under Dauverné, 1841–45; conducted salon orchestras; professor of saxhorn at the École militaire from 1857; taught cornet at the conservatory 1869–74 and, after a period conducting in Russia, again from 1880. He is called the founder of modern trumpet playing and wrote the standard cornet method.

Bibl.: Jean-Pierre Mathez, "Arban (1825–1889)," *Brass Bulletin* 9 (1974): 11–14; 10 (1975): 9–16; 11 (1975): 9–25; 12 (1975): 8–18; 13 (1976): 4–14; 14 (1976): 3–7; 15 (1976): 15–25.

Arbeau, Thoinot [anagram of Tabourot, Jehan] (b. Dijon, 17 Mar. 1520; d. Langres, 23 July 1595). Writer. Studied law at Dijon, Poitiers, and perhaps also Paris. From 1542 active clergyman in Langres and Bar-sur-Aube. His dance manual *Orchésographie* . . . (Langres, 1588; 2nd ed., 1589; reprinted as *Metode et teorie . . . pour apprendre à dancer . . .*, Langres, 1596; R: Geneva, 1972; trans. Eng., New York, 1948, 1967) explains most of the social dances of the time (generally without their more complex variants), in addition to some marching and martial dancing, with the aid of an original dance tablature, correlating the steps with music. Some tunes are included.

Arbós, Enrique Fernández (b. Madrid, 24 Dec. 1863; d. San Sebastián, 2 June 1939). Violinist, conductor, and composer. At the Madrid Conservatory he studied violin with Monasterio; later teachers were Vieuxtemps and Gevaert in Brussels and Joseph Joachim in Berlin. He was concertmaster of the Berlin Philharmonic from 1882 and was appointed professor of violin in Madrid (1884) and at London's Royal College of Music (1894). From 1904 he was conductor of the Madrid Symphony Orchestra and in 1913 assistant conductor of the Boston Symphony. He gave the first performance of Falla's *Noches en los jardines de España* (in 1916) and the Spanish premiere of Stravinsky's *Sacre du printemps* (in 1932). His own works include a comic opera, *Viaje al centro de la tierra* (1895); orchestral works (*Noche de Arabia,* 1905; *Tango,* 1913); and songs.

Arcadelt [Archadelt], **Jacques** (b. 1505?; d. Paris, 14 Oct. 1568). Composer. Although probably French by birth, he lived and worked chiefly in Italy (Florence, Venice, and Rome) from 1532 to 1551. From 1540 to 1551 he was connected with the papal chapel, later becoming a member of the chapel of Charles of Lorraine (remaining until at least 1562) and moving to France. He may also have been in the French royal chapel for a time around 1557. Although his music is predominantly secular, his earliest compositions are motets, of which he eventually wrote about 20. Other sacred music includes 3 Masses, a Magnificat, and several Lamentations settings. Over 200 madrigals (most for four voices) are extant, published in 6 books issued in Venice between 1539 and 1544 and various anthologies dated 1537–59. His 126 extant chansons were produced over a greater span of time (from 1537 on) but were concentrated in the years after he left Italy. The late chansons are almost entirely homophonic, with strong influence from *musique mesurée* in the latest ones. Most are for four, some for three to six voices. He also produced a few secular works with Latin texts.

Bibl.: Ed., *CMM* 31/1–10 (1965–70).

Archer, Violet (Balestreri) (b. Montreal, 24 Apr. 1913). Composer. Studied with Douglas Clarke and Claude Champagne at McGill (B.Mus., 1936), with Bartók in New York (1942), and with Hindemith at Yale (M.M., 1949). Taught at McGill, 1944–47; North Texas State, 1950–53, where she was also composer-in-residence; the Univ. of Oklahoma, 1953–61. Chair of the division of music theory and composition at the Univ. of Alberta, 1962–78. Her works include the operas *Sganarelle* (1973) and *The Meal* (1983); orchestral music (*Fantasy on a Ground,* 1946, rev. 1956; *Fanfare and Passacaglia,* 1948–49); concertos for timpani (1939), piano (1956), violin (1959), clarinet (1971); *Divertimento,* piano, strings (1985); *Evocations,* 2 pianos, orchestra (1987); choral and solo vocal works (*Life in a Prairie Shack,* 1966; *Three Folk Songs from Old Manitoba,* 1966); works for string quartet (1940, 1942, 1948–49, 1949, 1982), 3 trios for winds (1944, 1949, 1949), 2 string trios (1953, 1961), 2 piano trios (1954, 1956–57), and much other chamber music; works for piano (*"Habitant" Sketches,* 1947) and organ.

Bibl.: Linda Bishop Hartig, *Violet Archer: A Bio-Bibliography* (New York, 1991).

Ardévol, José (b. Barcelona, 13 Mar. 1911; d. Havana, 7 Jan. 1981). Composer. He received early instruction in conducting and composition from his father, Fernando, a Barcelona conductor, before emigrating to Cuba in 1930. From 1934 to 1952 he directed the Orquesta de cámara de la Habana. From 1936 to 1951 he taught at universities in Havana and Oriente and at the Havana Municipal Conservatory. In 1942 he formed the Grupo de renovación musical. A supporter of Cuba's revolution, he became the new government's chief musical administrator after 1959. He conducted the orchestra of the new Ministry of Education; from 1965 he taught composition at the Havana Conservatory and from 1968 at the National School of Music. His own varied musical style moves from early neoclassicism to later aleatory and serialism. Works include 3 symphonies and other orchestral music; vocal works (*Cantos de la Revolución,* 1962; a cantata, *Che comandante,* 1968; *Lenin,* 1970); chamber music (6 *Sonate a 3*); 3 piano sonatas; *Tensiones,* piano left-hand.

Arditi, Luigi (b. Crescentino, Piedmont, 16 July 1822; d. Hove, near Brighton, 1 May 1903). Conductor and composer. Studied at the Milan Conservatory. Widely active as an opera conductor, in Havana (from 1846); at Her Majesty's Theatre, London (1858–69); on the Continent; and in Mapleson's U.S. tours (1878–94). He composed several ephemeral operas and much slighter music, including the once very popular song "Il bacio"; published *My Reminiscences* (London, 1896).

Arel, Bülent (b. Constantinople, 23 Apr. 1918; d. Stony Brook, N.Y., 24 Nov. 1990). Composer. Studied composition with Necil Kâzim Akses and Edward Zuckmayer at the Ankara Conservatory, 1941–47; sound engineering in Paris, 1951. Worked at Radio Ankara, 1951–59 and 1963–65; at the Columbia-Princeton Electronic Music Studio, 1959–63. Taught at Yale, 1961–62 and 1965–70. Professor at the State Univ. of New York at Stony Brook from 1971. His early neoclassical style was influenced by Ravel and Stravinsky; has also made use of twelve-tone techniques and free atonality. His electronic music has included works for tape (*Impressions of Wall Street,* 1961), combinations of tape and instruments, dance (*Mimiana I–III,* 1968, 1969, 1973), and video (*Capriccio for TV,* 1969).

Arensky, Anton Stepanovich (b. Novgorod, 12 July 1861; d. Perkiarvi (?), near Terioki, Finland, 25 Feb. 1906). Composer, pianist, and conductor. Studied composition at the St. Petersburg Conservatory under Rimsky-Korsakov. After graduation in 1882, taught theoretical subjects at the Moscow Conservatory until 1895; among his students were Rachmaninoff, Scriabin, and Glier. Directed the concerts of the Russian Choral Society, 1888–95; headed the Russian imperial chapel, 1895–1901. From 1901 concertized widely and successfully as pianist and conductor. An eclectic composer, noted for his lyrical and sometimes sentimental melodic gift, he was influenced by Chopin, Mendelssohn, and, most significantly, Tchaikovsky.

Works: 3 operas (*Rafael,* 1894); a ballet, *Egyptian Nights* (1900, staged Paris 1908); 2 symphonies (1883, 1889), a piano concerto (1882), a violin concerto (1891), and other orchestral music; choral and vocal works; 2 string quartets, 2 piano trios (no. 1 in D minor, 1894) and other chamber music; numerous piano pieces.

Writings: *Kratkoe rukovodstvo k prakticheskomu izucheniiu garmonii* [A Short Guide to the Practical Study of Harmony] (Moscow, 1891; 5th ed., 1929). *Rukovodstvo k izucheniiu form instrumental'noi i vokal'noi muzyki* [A Guide to the Study of Form in Instrumental and Vocal Music] (Moscow, 1893–94; 6th ed., 1930).

Bibl.: G. M. Tsypin, *A. S. Arensky* (Moscow, 1966).

Argenta (Maza), Ataúlfo (b. Castro Urdiales, Spain, 19 Nov. 1913; d. Los Molinos, 21 Jan. 1958). Conductor and pianist. Entered the Royal Conservatory in Madrid in 1927; studied piano with Fernández Alberdi. Awarded the Premio extraordinario, 1930; Kristina Nilsson Prize, 1931. In Germany during the Spanish Civil War, and again 1941–43. Studied conducting with Carl Schuricht; taught piano at the Kassel Conservatory. Debut with Orquesta nacional, 10 Oct. 1945; music director, 1947–58. Recorded late 19th- and early 20th-century music for Decca.

Argento, Dominick (b. York, Pa., 27 Oct. 1927). Composer. He was self-taught in piano and harmony until he went to Peabody Conservatory (B.A., 1951; M.M., 1954), where his teachers included Nicolas Nabokov and Hugo Weisgall. He spent a year in Italy on a Fulbright, where he studied composition with Dallapiccola and piano with Pietro Scarpini. Later he attended Eastman (Ph.D., 1957), where he studied with Hanson, Hovhaness, and Rogers. In 1958 he joined the faculty at the Univ. of Minnesota. In 1964 he wrote *The Masque of Angels* for the Minnesota Opera, of which he was a founder. He won the Pulitzer Prize in 1975 for his song cycle *From the Diary of Virginia Woolf.*

His operas include *Sicilian Limes* (1954); *The Boor* (1957); *Colonel Jonathan the Saint* (1958–61); *Christopher Sly* (1962–63); *The Masque of Angels* (1964); *The Shoemaker's Holiday* (1967); *Postcard from Morocco* (1971); *A Waterbird Talk* (monodrama, 1974); *The Voyage of Edgar Allan Poe* (1975–76); *Miss Havisham's Fire* (1977–78); *Casanova's Homecoming* (1980–84); *The Aspern Papers* (adaptation of the Henry James novella, 1988); *The Dream of Valentino* (1994).

Other works include *The Resurrection of Don Juan* (ballet, 1955); *Royal Invitation* (ballet, 1964); *Volpone* (incidental music, 1964); *The House of Atreus* (incidental music, 1968); *Revelations of St. John the Divine* (tenor, men's chorus, brass, 1966); *A Nation of Cowslips* (chorus, 1968); *Jonathan and the Whale* (oratorio, 1973); *In Memoriam, 1994* (a capella chorus, 1994); *Spirituals and Swedish Chorales* (a capella chorus, 1994); *Song about Spring* (soprano, orchestra, 1950, revised 1954 and 1960); *Ode to the West Wind* (soprano, orchestra, 1956); *The Mask of Night* (soprano, orchestra, 1965); *Bravo Mozart* (oboe, violin, horn, orchestra, 1967); *A Ring of Time* (orchestra and bells, 1972); *In Praise of Music* (7 songs, orchestra, 1977); *Le Tombeau d'Edgar Poe* (orchestra, 1985); *Capriccio: Rossini in Paris* (clarinet, orchestra, 1986); *6 Elizabethan Songs* (high voice, piano, 1958); *Letters from Composers* (tenor, guitar, 1968); *Tria Carmina Paschalia* (women's voices, harp, guitar, 1970); *To Be Sung upon the Water* (high voice, clarinet, piano, 1972); *From the Diary of Virginia Woolf* (mezzo, piano, 1974); a string quartet (1956); *Divertimento* (piano, strings, 1958).

Argerich, Martha (b. Buenos Aires, 5 June 1941). Pianist. Studied with Vincente Scaramuzza, Friedrich Gulda, Madeleine Lipatti, Arturo Benedetti Michelangeli, and Nikita Magaloff. Debut in Buenos Aires, 1946. European tour, 1955; USSR tour, 1961. First prizes at Busoni and Geneva Competitions, 1957; at Chopin Competition in Warsaw, 1965. U.S. debut in New York, 16 Jan. 1966. Well known as a soloist for the earlier Romantics, she also has accompanied (e.g., Rostropovich, Kremer) in this repertory.

Ariosti, Attilio (b. Bologna, 5 Nov. 1666; d. ca. 1730?). Composer. In 1688 he joined the Order of S. Maria de' Servi. Soon after receiving his diaconate (1692) he left the order, and by 1696 he was in the service of the Duke of Mantua. In 1697 he was called by Sophie Charlotte to the court at Berlin, where he served until 1703, contributing a number of dramatic works to the Berlin stage. On his way back to Italy in 1703, he stopped in Vienna and received an appointment from the Austrian court. He remained mostly in Vienna until 1711; in 1712 he returned to his order. During two visits to London (1716–17 and 1723–27) his operas, cantatas, and chamber works brought him much success. Among his known music are 22 stage works (*Tirsi,* Venice, 1696; *Mars und Irene,* Berlin, 1703; *Amor tra nemici,* Vienna, 1708; *Tito Manlio,* London, 1717; *Coriolano,* London, 1723); 5 oratorios; some 45 solo cantatas; and many chamber works, including nearly 60 pieces for viola d'amore with continuo.

Aristides Quintilianus [Aristeidēs Koïntilianos] (fl. ca. 200 C.E.). Theorist. His extensive treatise *On Mu-*

sic, an important source of information about ancient Greek music, is based largely on the works of others, including Aristoxenus, Plato, Damon, and Pythagoras.

Bibl.: *Aristides Quintilianus: De musica libri tres,* ed. Reginald P. Winnington-Ingram (Leipzig, 1963). *Aristides Quintilianus: On Music, in Three Books,* trans. and annotated Thomas J. Mathieson (New Haven, 1983).

Aristoxenus (b. Tarentum, ca. 375–60 B.C.E.; d. Athens?). Theorist. A pupil of Aristotle, he is one of the earliest Greek writers on music and the most important. His extant works, all incomplete, include *Harmonic Elements* (parts of three books on the theory of scales, written at two different times; partial trans. in *SR,* pp. 25–33) and *Elements of Rhythm* (fragments only).

Bibl.: H. S. Macran, ed. and trans., *The Harmonics of Aristoxenus* (Oxford, 1902). Rosetta da Rios, ed. and trans., *Aristoxeni elementa harmonica* (Rome, 1954).

Arizaga, Rodolfo (b. Buenos Aires, 11 July 1926; d. there, 1985). Composer. At the National Conservatory in Buenos Aires he studied composition with Luis Gianneo; at the National Univ. he studied philosophy. In 1950 he toured Spain. In Paris (from 1954) he received instruction from Nadia Boulanger and Olivier Messiaen. He resettled in Argentina in 1960, teaching music at Buenos Aires Univ. and writing music criticism for journals and for daily newspapers such as *Clarín.* Among his writings are *Manuel de Falla* (Buenos Aires, 1961) and an *Enciclopedia de la música argentina* (Buenos Aires, 1971). He has composed cantatas (*Delires,* 1954–57; rev. 1970); orchestral works (*Bailable Real,* 1948; *Música para Cristóbal Colón,* 1966); a piano concerto (1963); 2 string quartets and other chamber music; piano pieces (a sonata, 1946; *Piezas epigramáticas,* 1961); songs.

Arlen, Harold [Arluck, Hyman] (b. Buffalo, 15 Feb. 1905; d. New York, 23 Apr. 1986). Composer of popular songs, musicals, and film scores. After early performances as a pianist and singer in New York, he began to compose songs for the Cotton Club Revue in Harlem in 1929, including "Get Happy" (1929) and "Stormy Weather" (1933). In films he collaborated with lyricists E. Y. Harburg (*Wizard of Oz,* 1939, including "Over the Rainbow") and Ira Gershwin (*A Star Is Born,* 1954), and in musicals with Johnny Mercer (*St. Louis Woman,* 1941) and Truman Capote (*House of Flowers,* 1954). He incorporated melodic elements of the blues and other black idioms into his songs (e.g., "Blues in the Night," 1941) and mixed 12-bar blues and through-composed structures with the standard 32-bar song form.

Armstrong, Louis [Pops; Satchmo] (b. New Orleans, 4 Aug. 1901; d. New York, 6 July 1971). Jazz trumpeter and singer. He replaced King Oliver in Kid Ory's band (1919?) and played with Fate Marable on riverboats based in New Orleans (1918–19) and St. Louis (1919–21). After returning to New Orleans, he left for Chicago, playing second cornet in Oliver's Creole Jazz Band in Chicago (1922–24). In New York he became the featured cornet soloist with Fletcher Henderson's big band (1924–25), then in Chicago, while appearing in cabaret and with Erskine Tate's theater orchestra, made seminal recordings with his Hot Five, Hot Seven, and Savoy Ballroom Five, including Johnny Dodds (1925–27) and Earl Hines (1927–28). By about 1927 he had switched to trumpet. He was accompanied by big bands, notably Luis Russell's, until 1947, when he formed the All Stars, a sextet that initially included Jack Teagarden, Barney Bigard, and Hines, and that toured internationally until 1971. He made a number of films in which he performed as a singer, trumpeter, and popular entertainer.

Armstrong redefined notions of trumpet virtuosity not only for jazz but for all genres. In the 1920s his command of the high register, his fluent technique, his use of special effects, and his melodic inventiveness were unprecedented. He was also the first great jazz singer, often combining lyrics with scat singing. By contrast with his clear trumpet timbre, his voice was gruff. His playing and singing were widely imitated.

Armstrong's recordings include *Heebie Jeebies, Cornet Chop Suey* (both 1926), *Potato Head Blues, S.O.L. Blues, Struttin' with Some Barbecue, Hotter Than That* (all 1927), *West End Blues, Weather Bird* (both 1928), *Black and Blue* (1929), *Rockin' Chair, St. James Infirmary* (1947), the album *Louis Armstrong Plays W. C. Handy* (1954), and *Hello Dolly* (1963).

Bibl.: Max Jones and John Chilton, *Louis: The Louis Armstrong Story, 1900* [sic]*–1971* (London, 1971). James Lincoln Collier, *Louis Armstrong: An American Genius* (New York, 1983). Gary Giddins, *Satchmo* (New York, 1988).

Arne, Michael (b. London, ca. 1740; d. Lambeth, 14 Jan. 1786). Composer and keyboard player. Perhaps the adopted son (or the "natural son," according to Burney) of Thomas Augustine Arne, he was raised by his aunt, Mrs. Cibber. He appeared first as a singer, in 1750, though he soon found a niche as organist and harpsichordist. During the 1750s and 1760s he contributed a large number of songs to stage plays for London theaters. In 1766 he married the singer Elizabeth Wright, who in 1767 sang the lead in her husband's setting of *Cymon.* The composer's interest in alchemy steadily drained his finances during the 1770s and 1780s, and he died in poverty. He had composed 9 operas, collaborated on at least 15 others, and published 7 song collections.

Bibl.: John A. Parkinson, *An Index to the Vocal Works of Thomas and Michael Arne* (Detroit, 1972).

Arne, Thomas Augustine (b. London, 12 Mar. 1710; d. there, 5 Mar. 1778). Composer. After schooling at Eton, he studied violin with Michael Festing. His setting of *Rosamond* (which appeared in 1733 at Lincoln's Inn Fields Theatre) and his masque *Dido and Aeneas* (1734) were the first two in a long series of extraordinary stage successes. From 1734 he was engaged at Drury Lane Theatre, and until well into the 1760s he was England's leading stage composer. He was named D.Mus. in 1759 and thereafter was commonly called simply "Dr. Arne." He composed some 88 works for the stage, including *Comus* (1738); *Don John* (1740); *Alfred* (1740); *Henry and Emma* (1749); *Don Saverio* (1750); *The Sheep-Shearing* (1754); *Eliza* (1754); *Thomas and Sally, or The Sailor's Return* (1760); *Artaxerxes* (1762); *Love in a Village* (1762); and *May-Day* (1755). He also composed many individual songs as well as songs for productions of *The Tempest, As You Like It,* and other Shakespeare plays; oratorios (*Judith,* 1761); odes; cantatas; catches and glees; and chamber works.

Bibl.: John A. Parkinson, *An Index to the Vocal Works of Thomas Augustine Arne and Michael Arne* (Detroit, 1972).

Arnold, Eddy [Richard Edward] (b. Henderson, Tenn., 15 May 1918). Country singer and songwriter. After early performances on radio stations and with the Grand Ole Opry as the "Tennessee Plowboy," in 1943 he began recording for RCA Victor. Successful early songs included "I'll Hold You in My Heart" (1948), "Cattle Call" (1955), and "Anytime" (1958). From 1950 he cultivated a more popular sound and image, and hosted and appeared on national television shows.

Arnold, Malcolm (Henry) (b. Northampton, 21 Oct. 1921). Composer. In 1938–40 he studied in London at the Royal College of Music; his teachers were Gordon Jacob (composition) and Ernest Hall (trumpet). After serving as first trumpet in the London Philharmonic and the BBC Symphony (1942–48), he went to Italy on a Mendelssohn Scholarship. His chief activity subsequently was composing. His music is firmly diatonic, with elements of popular music and of the orchestral lushness of the 19th century.

Works: 2 operas (*The Dancing Master,* 1951; *The Open Window,* 1956); 5 ballets (*Sweeney Todd,* 1959); some 80 film scores (*Bridge on the River Kwai,* 1957, for which he won an Oscar); choral music; many orchestral works (9 symphonies; *A Grand Grand Overture for 3 Vacuum Cleaners, Floor Polisher, 4 Rifles, and Full Orchestra,* 1956; *A Shakespearian Concerto,* 1989); 17 works for solo instrument and orchestra; pieces for brass band; many chamber works (*Trevelyan Suite,* 1968).

Bibl.: Alan Poulton, *Malcolm Arnold: A Catalogue of His Music* (London, 1986). Hugo Cole, *Malcolm Arnold: an Introduction to His Music* (London, 1989).

Arnold, Samuel (b. London, 10 Aug. 1740; d. there, 22 Oct. 1802). Composer, organist, and scholar. He received his first musical training as a choirboy at the Chapel Royal in London. During the 1760s his pastiche operas such as *The Maid of the Mill* were highly successful at Covent Garden, where he was employed as harpsichordist from 1764. In 1773 he was made D.Mus. at Oxford, partly as a result of one of his 5 original oratorios, *The Prodigal Son,* composed for the installation of a university chancellor. He contributed works to London theaters throughout the 1770s, and in 1783 he was made organist of the Chapel Royal. In 1789 he became director of the Academy of Ancient Music and in 1793 organist at Westminster Abbey. His work as a music editor included a 4-volume revision of Boyce's *Cathedral Music* (1790) and 180 parts of a proposed complete edition of Handel's works (1787–97). His own compositions include nearly 100 stage works (many pastiches), oratorios, anthems, hymn tunes, songs, and instrumental works, mostly for keyboard.

Aron, Pietro. See Aaron, Pietro.

Arrau, Claudio (b. Chillán, Chile, 6 Feb. 1903; d. Mürzzuschlag, Austria, 9 June 1991). Pianist. Studied with Bindo Paoli, 1910–12; with Martin Krause at Stern's Conservatory in Berlin, 1912–18. Formal debut 10 Dec. 1914, Kunstlerhaus, Berlin. U.S. debut, Carnegie Hall, 20 Oct. 1923. Won Ibach Prize, 1917; first prize, Concours Genève, 1927. Taught at Stern's Conservatory, 1924–40. Played all of Bach's non-organ keyboard music in 12 recitals in Berlin, 1935; then recital cycles devoted to all of Mozart's and Schubert's solo keyboard music (1930s) and all of Beethoven's sonatas (1953–54). World tours, 1968, 1974–75, and 1981.

Bibl.: Joseph Horowitz, *Conversations with Arrau* (New York, 1982).

Arriaga (y Balzola), Juan Crisóstomo (Jacobo Antonio) de (b. Rigoitia, near Bilbao, 27 Jan. 1806; d. Paris, 17 Jan. 1826). Composer. At 14 he composed his first opera, *Los esclavos felices,* and the following year he entered the Paris Conservatory. He studied counterpoint with Fétis and violin with Baillot; he composed a number of sacred works, including settings of *Et vitam venturi* and *Salve regina* (both lost, but highly praised by Fétis in his biography). He also composed 2 overtures, a symphony in D, and several chamber works, including 3 string quartets that are still performed. His death at age 19 prompted romanticized posthumous assessments of his life and music.

Bibl.: Barbara Rosen, *Arriaga, the Forgotten Genius: The Short Life of a Basque Composer* (Reno, 1988).

Arroyo, Martina (b. New York, 2 Feb. 1936). Soprano. Studied with Marinka Gurewich and Josef Turnau; B.A., Hunter College, 1956. Debut 17 Sept. 1958. Won Metropolitan Opera audition, 1958; Met debut, 14 Mar. 1959. Moved to Europe to establish her career; with Zurich Opera, 1963–68. Major roles at the Met (including several opening nights) after 1965. Covent Garden debut, 1968. Has sung Aida, Tosca, and other standard spinto roles; also Elsa *(Lohengrin),* Donna Anna *(Don Giovanni),* and 20th-century music by Varèse, Stockhausen, Bernstein, and others.

Artemov [Artyomov], **Viacheslav Petrovich** (b. Moscow, 29 June 1940). Composer. Studied with Nikolai Sidelnikov at the Moscow Conservatory, graduating in 1968. Has been particularly interested in musical folklore and improvisational techniques; collaborated with composers Sofia Gubaidulina and Viktor Suslin in the experimental ensemble Astrea (1975–81). Works include *Way to Olympus* (1978–84) and other orchestral music; a Requiem (1986–88) and other music for chorus and orchestra; percussion music; much chamber music, especially for wind instruments; vocal music; piano pieces.

Artusi, Giovanni Maria (b. Bologna ca. 1540; d. there, 18 Aug. 1613). Theorist. In 1562 he entered the Order of S. Salvatore (Bologna), where he spent most of his life. He studied with Zarlino (in Venice), whose views he later defended and amplified in *L'arte del contraponto* (1598), a theoretical work of wide influence. In *L'Artusi, overo delle imperfettioni della moderna musica ragionamenti dui* (Venice, 1600; R: 1969; partial trans. in *SR,* pp. 393–404). and in the *Seconda parte dell'Artusi* (1603), he spoke out against abuses in the "modern" style of an unnamed composer. Claudio Monteverdi, the composer in question, responded in the preface to his fifth book of madrigals (1605) and in a pamphlet, *Ottuso accademico.* Central to the *L'Artusi* volumes is a discourse on the problems in ensemble playing arising from disparate tuning systems.

Bibl.: Claude V. Palisca, "The Artusi–Monteverdi Controversy," in *The Monteverdi Companion,* ed. Denis Arnold and Nigel Fortune (London, 1968), pp. 133–66.

Arutiunian, Alexander Grigorevich (b. Yerevan, 23 Sept. 1920). Composer. Graduated from the Yerevan Conservatory in 1941; continued study in Moscow at the House of Armenian Culture under Litinsky. His graduation work was *The Cantata of the Native Land* (1948), for which he was awarded a State Prize in 1949. From 1954 he served as artistic director of the Armenian Philharmonic Society. His style is influenced by the melodic and rhythmic inflections of Armenian folk music. Works include the opera *Saiat-Nova* (1963–67); cantatas; 2 symphonies and other symphonic music, including concertos for piano (1941), coloratura soprano (1950 and 1959), trumpet (1950), French horn (1962), woodwind quintet (1964), oboe (1979), flute (1980); chamber music; songs; incidental and film music.

Asafiev, Boris Vladimirovich [literary pseud. Igor Glebov] (b. St. Petersburg, 29 July 1884; d. Moscow, 27 Jan. 1949). Musicologist and composer. Received his early music training at the Kronstadt Gymnasium and graduated in history and philology from St. Petersburg Univ. in 1908. Studied with Lyadov (composition) and Rimsky-Korsakov (orchestration) at the St. Petersburg Conservatory, 1904–10. In 1919 helped organize the Petrograd Institute for the History of the Arts and from 1920 directed the music history department. From 1925 to 1943 served as professor of history, theory, and composition at the Leningrad Conservatory. From 1943 taught at the Moscow Conservatory and headed the music section of the USSR Academy of Sciences. In the 1920s he was an active propagandist of contemporary Western and Soviet music; he published the first Russian study of Stravinsky in 1929. Also wrote extensively on 19th-century Russian music, including studies on Mussorgsky's manuscripts. His major theoretical studies, including *Muzykal'naia forma kak protsess* [Musical Form as Process] (Moscow, 1947) formed the cornerstone of the Soviet analytic method. His compositional style in his 11 operas, 28 ballets (*Bakhchisarai fontan,* 1933), 4 symphonies, chamber music, and songs followed in the conservative footsteps of the Russian nationalists.

Writings: *Izbrannye trudy,* ed. T. N. Livanova et al. (Moscow, 1952–57). *Kniga o Stravinskom* [A Book about Stravinsky] (Leningrad, 1929); trans. Richard F. French (Ann Arbor, 1982).

Bibl.: Gordon McQuere, "Boris Asafiev and *Musical Form as Process,*" in *Russian Theoretical Thought in Music* (Ann Arbor, 1983), pp. 217–52. E. Orlova and A. Kriukov, *Akademik Boris Vladimirovich Asaf'ev* (Leningrad, 1984). David Haas, "Boris Asaf'yev and Soviet Symphonic Theory," *MQ* 76 (1992): 410–32.

Ashkenazy, Vladimir (Davidovich) (b. Gorki, 6 July 1937). Pianist and conductor. Studied piano with Anaida Sumbatian (1945–55) and Boris Zemlyianski and Lev Oborin (1955–63); Moscow Conservatory diploma, 1960. U.S. debut 12 Oct. 1958 with the National Symphony. Second prize, Chopin Competition at Warsaw, 1955; first prize, Queen Elisabeth Competition at Brussels, 1956; first prize (shared with John Ogdon), Tchaikovsky Competition at Moscow, 1962. Moved to London, 1963; to Reykjavík, 1968; to Lucerne, 1978. Guest conductor of the London Philharmonic, 1981; principal guest conductor Philharmonia Orchestra, 1982–83; music director Royal Philharmonic, 1987–94; principal guest conductor Cleveland Orchestra from 1987; chief conductor (West) Berlin Radio Orchestra from 1989. His repertory includes Mozart, Beethoven, Chopin, Rachmaninov, Sibelius, and Scriabin.

Ashley, Robert (Reynolds) (b. Ann Arbor, 28 Mar. 1930). Composer. Studied theory, composition, and acoustics at the Univ. of Michigan, 1948–52 and 1957–60; piano and composition at the Manhattan School (M.S., 1953). Among his composition teachers were Riegger, Finney, Bassett, and Gerhard. Active as a composer and performer with Milton Cohen's Space Theater, 1957–64; the ONCE Group, 1958–69; the Sonic Arts Group, 1966–76. From 1969 to 1981 directed the Center for Contemporary Music at Mills College. Interested in the conceptual and theatrical aspects of music, he was a pioneer in the development of mixed-media performance art, turning his attention in the 1970s to televised opera (*Music with Roots in the Aether,* 1976; *Perfect Lives (Private Parts),* 1977–83; *Atalanta,* 1982–89; *Now Eleanor's Idea,* 1986–89; *Gentlemen of the Future,* 1986–90; *Yellow Man with*

Heart with Wings, 1989–90). Has composed extensively for electronic media; films and videotapes; instrumental music.

Asioli, Bonifazio (b. Correggio, 30 Aug. 1769; d. there, 18 May 1832). Composer, theorist, and harpsichordist. After study in Parma around 1780, he composed church works and comic operas. In 1786 he was appointed *maestro di cappella* in Correggio. During the 1780s and 1790s he lived in Turin and Milan; in 1793 his opera *Cinna* was performed at La Scala. In 1808 he became the first director of the Milan Conservatory, where he published the first in a succession of theoretical works, *Principi elementari di musica* (1809). Returning to Correggio in 1814, he established a music school there. Among his compositions are 9 stage works, 10 Masses, an oratorio (*Giuseppe in Galaad,* 1785), cantatas, symphonies, chamber music, and keyboard pieces.

Asola, Giammateo [Giovanni Matteo] (b. Verona, ca. 1532; d. Venice, 1 Oct. 1609). Composer. He was a secular canon from 1546, then a secular priest after 1569, active in various northern Italian cities, including Treviso and Vicenza. He probably studied with Vincenzo Ruffo in Verona. He became a chaplain at S. Severo in Venice in 1588 and remained there until his death. He composed much sacred music in an essentially conservative style and several books of secular and spiritual madrigals.

Bibl.: *Opera omnia* (Bologna, 1963–). *Sixteen Liturgical Works,* Donald M. Fouse, ed., *RRMR* 1 (1964).

Asplmayr [Aspelmayr], **Franz** (b. Linz, bapt. 2 Apr. 1728; d. Vienna, 29 July 1786). Composer. Apart from violin study, he apparently had little formal musical training. Beginning in 1759 he served in the imperial court at Vienna, first in a bureaucratic position and later as composer for the Kärntnertortheater. In the early 1770s he composed ballets for Jean Georges Noverre's troupe, and in 1776 he brought to the stage *Pygmalion* (after J. J. Rousseau), possibly the first German-language melodrama. Subsequently he composed singspiels and incidental music for the Viennese court. His symphonies and chamber works such as the ensemble divertimentos have been cited as important works in the emerging Viennese classical style.

Aston [Ashton], **Hugh** (b. ca. 1485; d. Nov. 1558?). Composer. Received the degree of B.Mus. from Oxford in 1510. May have been in London and associated with the royal court from 1510 to 1525. Master of the choristers at St. Mary Newarke Hospital and College in Leicester from ca. 1525 to 1548, when the institution was closed. Drew a pension in Newarke until 17 Nov. 1558. A few sacred compositions survive along with some keyboard compositions (only one certainly his).

Astorga, Emanuele (Gioacchino Cesare Rincón) d' (b. Augusta, Sicily, 20 Mar. 1680; d. Madrid?, ca. 1757). Composer. Born of Spanish nobility, he moved with his family to Palermo in 1693. He first became known through an opera, *Dafni,* performed in Genoa in 1709; it caught the attention of Charles III, whom the composer apparently followed to Vienna. After a time in Vienna (1712–14) he returned to Italy, married, became a senator of Palermo (1718), and later (1720s) traveled to Sicily, Lisbon, and possibly also to London. The facts of his later years are uncertain; though documentation is scarce, his life was the subject of highly romanticized accounts by Rochlitz and others. He was also the subject of an opera, *Astorga* (1866), by Johann Joseph Abert. He is remembered mainly for a Stabat Mater in C that was popular during the 19th century; he also composed *villancicos,* many solo cantatas, and possibly another opera, *Zenobia* (Vienna, 1712).

Asuar, José Vicente (b. Santiago, Chile, 20 July 1933). Composer. In Santiago he studied music at the National Conservatory and engineering at the Catholic Univ. In Berlin he studied engineering at the Technical Univ. (1959–60) and composition with Blacher at the Hochschule für Musik. From 1958 to 1965 he directed electronic studios in Chile and in Karlsruhe, and in 1965 established the first such studio in Caracas. In Buffalo, N.Y., he studied with Hiller (1970). Since then he has taught acoustics and electronic music at the Univ. of Chile and elsewhere. Among his works are *Heterofonías,* orchestra (1964); *Guararia repano,* Indian instruments, tape (1968); *Formas I* (1970) and *II* (1972), orchestra (computer-generated scores); *Imagen de Caracas,* voices, instruments, tape (1968); many works for tape only (*Catedral,* 1967; *Buffalo 71,* 1971).

Atherton, David (b. Blackpool, 3 Jan. 1944). Conductor. After studies at Cambridge, he founded and was music director (1967–73) of the London Sinfonietta, a group specializing in 20th-century music. Répétiteur, Royal Opera at Covent Garden, 1967–68; resident conductor there, 1968–69. Guest conductor at the San Francisco Opera, 1978; at La Scala, 1976. Principal conductor Royal Liverpool Philharmonic, 1980–83; guest conductor thereafter. Music director San Diego Symphony, 1981–87; Hong Kong Philharmonic from 1989.

Atkins, Chet [Chester Burton] (b. Luttrell, Tenn., 20 June 1924). Country guitarist and record producer. After early work as a backup musician for Red Foley and the Carter Family, he became manager of RCA Victor's Nashville studio in 1957. There he produced and appeared on many country albums that established the popular music–influenced "Nashville Sound." An early proponent of the electric guitar in country music, he recorded many solo albums and some with guitarists Jerry Reed (1972) and Les Paul (1976).

Attaingnant, Pierre (b. ca. 1494; d. Paris, late 1551 or 1552). Printer and publisher. Son-in-law and heir of the printer-engraver Philippe Pigouchet (fl. 1490–1514). Beginning with a collection of chansons dated 4 Apr.

1527/28, he used movable type and a single impression, a method that was probably his invention. Royal privileges protecting his music books were granted or renewed three times, about a year after the first book was printed, in 1531, and in 1537. Eventually he was named *imprimeur et libraire du Roy en musique.* His publications include several books of pieces in lute tablature or keyboard score, 7 books of Masses, 14 books of motets, and over 36 books of chansons, plus numerous re-editions. New music by French composers dominates most of these books, and, in contrast to the usual practice of the times, very little material comes from the publications of his competitors.

Bibl.: Daniel Heartz, *Pierre Attaingnant, Royal Printer of Music* (Berkeley and Los Angeles, 1969).

Atterberg, Kurt (b. Göteborg, 12 Dec. 1887; d. Stockholm, 15 Feb. 1974). Composer, conductor, and critic. Although he studied composition and instrumentation under Andreas Hallén at the Stockholm Conservatory (1910–11) and in Berlin between 1911 and 1915, he was largely self-taught as a composer; he was trained as a civil engineer and made a career from 1912 to 1968 in Sweden's national patent office. He conducted the premiere of his first symphony (1909–11) in 1916 at Göteborg, and from 1916 to 1922 was *kapellmästare* at the Royal Dramatic Theater in Stockholm. A founder and sometime president of both the Swedish Composers' Society and the Swedish Performing Rights Society; music critic of the *Stockholms-tidningen* (1919–57). Composed 5 operas (*Bäckahästen* [The White Horse], 1923–24; *Fanal,* 1929–32); incidental music; 3 ballets (*De fåvitska jungfrurna* [The Foolish Virgins], 1920); 9 symphonies (no. 3, West Coast Pictures, 1914–16) and other orchestral music; choral and chamber music.

Attwood, Thomas (b. London, bapt. 23 Nov. 1765; d. there, 24 Mar. 1838). Composer and organist. From the age of 9 he sang in the choir of the Chapel Royal. The Prince of Wales (later George IV) sponsored his musical study abroad, first in Naples with Gaetano Latilla (1783–85), then in Vienna with W. A. Mozart (1785–87). His valuable compositional studies with Mozart, containing the latter's corrections, have been published with Mozart's works. He returned to England in 1787 and became music instructor for the royal family. In 1796 he was appointed organist at St. Paul's Cathedral and composer for the Chapel Royal. During the 1790s he composed music for nearly 30 comedies and farces for London stages. He was a founding member of the city's Philharmonic Society (1813). After 1800 he composed chiefly sacred music (including 18 anthems, services, hymns, and Psalm tunes) and chamber works (including piano trios and sonatas and pieces for wind choir). In 1821 he was appointed organist of George IV's private chapel, and in 1836 of the Chapel Royal.

Bibl.: *Thomas Attwoods Theorie- und Kompositionsstudien bei Mozart,* ed. Erich Hertzmann et al., in W. A. Mozart, *Neue Ausgabe sämtlicher Werke,* 10/30/1 (Kassel, 1965). Daniel Heartz, "Thomas Attwood's Lessons in Composition with Mozart," *PRMA* 100 (1973–74): 175–83.

Auber, Daniel-François-Esprit (b. Caen, 29 Jan. 1782; d. Paris, 12 or 13 May 1871). Composer. He studied in Paris with the composer Ignaz Ladurner. His father, an art dealer, sent him to London in 1802–3 to learn business, but on returning to Paris he became a musician. An opéra comique by him, performed by amateurs in 1805, led Cherubini to take him as a pupil, and in the following years he composed 4 cello concertos, a violin concerto, chamber music, and a Mass. His first work for the Opéra-comique, *Le séjour militaire* (1813), was a failure, and he gave up composition until forced by his father's bankruptcy in 1819 to try the stage again. Thereafter he produced at least one, and sometimes as many as three, new stage works nearly every year until the early 1850s, when his output became more intermittent. He had a success with his second attempt, *La bergère châtelaine* (1820). From 1823 almost all his stage works were written in collaboration with Scribe (often with other librettists also involved) until Scribe's death in 1861. Their 36 works together included some of the greatest successes in opéra comique of the time, the genre with which Auber was most identified and to which his talent and style were best suited; among these are *Fra Diavolo* (1830), which is still performed, *Le cheval de bronze* (1835), *Le domino noir* (1837), *Les diamants de la couronne* (1841). Their *La muette de Portici* (Opéra, 1828) established the model for French grand opera of the next several decades. *Gustave III* (Opéra, 1833) was on a similar scale. They also wrote several slighter works for the Opéra. Auber was director of the Paris Conservatory, 1842–70. In his last 20 years he composed considerable sacred music.

Bibl.: Herbert Schneider, *Chronologisch-thematisches Verzeichnis sämtlicher Werke von Daniel François Esprit Auber* (Hildesheim, 1994).

Aubert, Jacques ["le vieux"] (b. Paris, 30 Sept. 1689; d. Belleville, nr. Paris, buried 19 May 1753). Composer and violinist. From 1719 he was in the service of the Duke of Bourbon; in 1727 he joined the Vingt-quatre Violons du Roy. He also played with the Académie royale de musique (from 1728), the Opéra (1728–52), and at the Concert spirituel (1729–40). His violin concertos are known as the first published in France (1734). In addition to chamber works, 12 of his stage works are known, including ballets, divertissements, and the comedy *La reine de Pétris* (1725).

Aubert, Louis-François-Marie (b. Paramé, Ille-et-Vilaine, 19 Feb. 1877; d. Paris, 9 Jan. 1968). Composer. Studied composition at the Paris Conservatory with Fauré. His operatic fairy tale *La forêt bleue* scored a success when it was staged in Geneva in 1913 and was subsequently produced in Boston and Paris. Like Debussy and Ravel, with whose music his has similarities, he was attracted to evocative titles (the symphonic suite *Feuilles d'images,* 1931) and Spanish color (the symphonic poem *Habanera,* 1919). Also composed 4 ballets; works for voice or chorus and orchestra; chamber music; songs.

Bibl.: Marcel Landowski and Guy Morançon, *Louis Aubert* (Paris, 1967).

Aubin, Tony (Louis Alexandre) (b. Paris, 8 Dec. 1907; d. there, 21 Sept. 1981). Composer and conductor. Studied composition under Dukas at the Paris Conservatory, 1925–30, and was awarded the Prix de Rome in 1930 for his cantata *Actéon.* Studied conducting with Gaubert in 1934–35. Served as artistic director at the French Radio and Television station Paris mondial, 1937–44; conductor for French radio, 1945–60. Appointed professor at the Paris Conservatory in 1945. His music was influenced in its harmonic and coloristic palette by Ravel and Dukas. Works include an opera; 5 ballets; symphonic music; chamber music; incidental and film scores; songs.

Audran, Edmond (b. Lyons, 11 or 12 Apr. 1840; d. Tierceville, Seine-et-Oise, 17 Aug. 1901). Composer. Studied at the École Niedermeyer until 1859; then worked as a church musician in Marseilles, where his father, the former tenor Marius-Pierre Audran, taught at the conservatory. Produced his first comic operas in Marseilles, including *Le grand Mogol* (1877). In 1879 he began to work for the Bouffes-Parisiens in Paris, and with *La mascotte* (1880) had a worldwide success. He remained one of the genre's leaders through the 1890s with *Gillette de Narbonne* (1882), *Miss Helyett* (1890), and *La poupée* (1896) among his most successful works.

Auer, Leopold (von) (b. Veszprém, Hungary, 7 June 1845; d. Loschwitz, near Dresden, 15 July 1930). Violinist and teacher. Studied with Ridley Kohné at the Budapest Conservatory, 1853–56; with Jakob Dont at the Vienna Conservatory, 1857–58; with Joachim in 1863–64. Concertmaster in Düsseldorf and Hamburg, 1864–68. Court violinist and professor at the St. Petersburg Conservatory, 1868–1917. Pupils there included Mischa Elman, Efrem Zimbalist, Jascha Heifetz. Moved to the U.S., Feb. 1918; U.S. debut 23 Mar. 1918 at Carnegie Hall. In the 1920s taught at the Curtis Institute. The Tchaikovsky violin concerto was written for him, but he declined to perform it. Wrote *Violin Playing As I Teach It* (New York, 1980).

Aufderheide, May (Frances) (b. Indianapolis, 21 May 1888; d. Pasadena, 1 Sept. 1972). Ragtime composer. Her first composition, *Dusty Rag* (1908), published by her father, was popular, and by 1912 she had published 19 works, including *Thriller Rag* (1909). In this brief career she established herself as one of the foremost Indiana composers of rags, and the preeminent woman composer in the genre.

Aurelian of Réôme [Aurelianus Reomensis] (fl. 840–50). Theorist. His *Musica disciplina,* the earliest extant medieval treatise on music, reveals a thorough knowledge of liturgical chant. It includes a nontechnical introduction to music and an extensive discussion of melodic and modal features of antiphonal plainsong.

Bibl.: Lawrence Gushee, ed., *Aurelianus Reomensis: Musica disciplina, CSM* 21 (1975).

Auric, Georges (b. Lodève, 15 Feb. 1899; d. Paris, 23 July 1983). Composer. His first musical studies were at the Montpellier Conservatory. In 1913 he studied with Caussade at the Paris Conservatory. From 1914 to 1916 he studied composition with Vincent d'Indy at the Schola cantorum. His classmates at the conservatory included Milhaud and Honegger, with whom Auric, as well as Durey, Poulenc, and Tailleferre, would eventually form the group first known as "Les nouveaux jeunes," later to be called "Les six." This group of composers grew up around the ideas of Satie, who believed that French music should be free of foreign influence, born of everyday life, and characterized by deliberate simplicity. "Les six" collaborated on a piece called *Les mariés de la tour Eiffel,* with text and choreography by Cocteau, another influential member of their circle. In *Le coq et l'arlequin,* which is dedicated to Auric, Cocteau discussed these ideas for a new kind of music. Auric also had contact with Stravinsky, Diaghilev, and the Ballets russes. He wrote several ballets for Diaghilev, including *Les fâcheux* (1923), *Les matelots* (1924), and *Pastorale* (1925). He was one of the pianists for the premiere of Stravinsky's *Les noces.* He went on to write music for the theater, including *Le mariage de monsieur le Trouhadec* (1925) and *Volpone* (1927). He wrote film scores for Cocteau's *Le sang d'un poète* (1930) and *L'éternel retour* (1943), and for Clair's *À nous la liberté* (1931).

Auric wrote many songs in his early years, including *Trois interludes* on poems of Chalupt (1914) and *8 poèmes* (Cocteau, 1919). His compositional development was marked in 1930–31 by his Piano Sonata in F, a work in which he moved away from the straightforwardness of his earlier style. His later ballets *Le peintre et son modèle* (1948) and *Phèdre* (1949) reflect this stylistic change. *Chemin de lumière,* a ballet of 1951, includes serial writing and the juxtaposition of tonality and atonality. The Partita for Two Pianos (1953–55) is an important example of this late compositional style. Other late works include the ballet *Le bal des voleurs* (1960); *Imaginées I,* flute, piano (1968); *Imaginées II,* cello, piano (1969); *Imaginées III,* clarinet, piano (1971); *Imaginées IV,* viola, piano (1973); *Double-jeux I–III,* 2 pianos (1970–71); and *2 poèmes,* songs (1965).

In addition to composing music, he wrote music criticism for *Paris-soir, Marianne,* and *Nouvelles littéraires.* He was elected president of Société d'auteurs, compositeurs, et editeurs de musique in 1954, a position to which he was reelected in 1968. From 1962 to 1968 he served as director of the Paris Opéra and the Opéra-comique, a position he gave up in order to devote more time to composition.

Bibl.: Georges Auric, *Quand j'étais là* (Paris, 1979). Eveline Hurard-Viltard, *Le groupe des six, ou, Le matin d'un jour de fête* (Paris, 1987).

Austin, Larry (Don) (b. Duncan, Okla., 12 Sept. 1930). Composer. Studied at North Texas State Univ. (B.M., 1951; M.M., 1952) and at Mills College and the Univ. of California, Berkeley (1955–58). Among his teachers were Imbrie, Milhaud, and Shifrin. Taught at the Univ. of California, Davis, 1958–72; the Univ. of South Florida, Tampa, 1972–78; from 1978 at North Texas State Univ. Was instrumental in founding the avant-garde music journal *Source* and served as its first editor, 1966–71. His experience as a modern jazz improviser contributed to the success of *Improvisations for Orchestra and Jazz Soloists* (1961); and later music (*Open Style for Orchestra and Piano Soloist,* 1966) left areas of improvisational choice open to the performer within a controlled context. Open forms and advanced technological and theatrical resources played a role in such works as the children's theater piece *The Magicians* (1968) and in other mixed media and electronic works. Works include *Sinfonia concertante: A Mozartean Episode,* chamber orchestra, computer (1986); *Concertante cybernetica,* performer and Synclavier (1987); *Transmission 2* (1988–89).

Autry, (Orvon) Gene (b. Tioga, Tex., 29 Sept. 1907). Country and popular singer, songwriter, and actor. Through early performances as "Oklahoma's Singing Cowboy" on Radio KVOO in Tulsa and appearances in over 100 western musical films, he popularized the image of the singing cowboy that facilitated the national acceptance of country music. From 1939 to 1956 he hosted the CBS radio show *Melody Ranch.* His many successful recordings included "That Silver-Haired Daddy of Mine" (1931), "You Are My Sunshine" (1941), and "Rudolph the Red-Nosed Reindeer" (1949), which sold over 7 million copies.

Avidom [Mahler-Kalkstein], **Menahem** (b. Stanislav, Ukraine, 6 Jan. 1908). Composer. Emigrated to Palestine in 1925. Studied in Beirut at the American Univ. (1926–28) and in Paris at the conservatory (1928–31). From 1935 he lived in Tel Aviv, where he taught music theory at the conservatory. In 1945 he was made general secretary of the Israel Philharmonic, and in 1955 director of ACUM (the Israeli Performing Rights Society). In 1961 he received the Israel State Prize for the opera *Alexandra ha'Hashmonait.* He has composed 8 other operas (*In Every Generation,* 1955; *The Farewell,* 1971; *The First Sin,* 1980); choral works (*Kantatat t'hilim,* 1955; *12 Hills,* 1976); 10 symphonies (no. 3, *Yam tichonit* [The Mediterranean], 1952); chamber music (a brass quintet, 1969; *Suite on B-A-C-H,* chamber ensemble, 1964).

Avison, Charles (b. Newcastle upon Tyne, bapt. 16 Feb. 1709; d. there, 9 or 10 May 1770). Composer and writer on music. Little is known of his early years or education, though Burney states (*History,* 2) that he traveled to Italy as a youth and later was a pupil of Geminiani. In 1735 he was made organist of St. John's Church, Newcastle, and the following year of St. Nicholas's Church. In 1738 he became director of the town's concert series; he was also an instructor of harpsichord, flute, and violin, and he prepared an edition of Benedetto Marcello's *First Fifty Psalms.* In 1752 he published the treatise for which he is best known, the *Essay on Musical Expression;* Burney called it the first piece of English music criticism. It was apparently a collaboration with other writers. He composed mainly concerti grossi (some 60 in all); also chamber sonatas; a few sacred vocal works; several editions and arrangements.

Bibl.: P. M. Horsley, "Charles Avison: The Man and His Milieu," *ML* 55 (1974): 5–23.

Avni, Tzvi (Jacob) (b. Saarbrücken, 2 Sept. 1927). Composer. In 1935 he emigrated to Palestine; from 1954 to 1958 he studied composition in Tel Aviv with Ehrlich, Seter, and Ben-Haim. In the U.S. (1962–64) he received instruction from Copland and Foss, and he studied electronic music with Ussachevsky at Columbia Univ. and with Myron Schaeffer at the Univ. of Toronto. He began teaching composition at Jerusalem's Rubin Academy in 1971 and was made professor there five years later. Works include ballets (*Requiem for Sounds,* with tape, 1969; *All the King's Women,* 1971; *He and She,* 7 instruments, 1976; *Genesis Reconsidered,* orchestra, 1978); other orchestral and instrumental music (*T'fila,* strings, 1961; *Hirhurim al drama* [Meditations on a Drama], chamber ensemble, 1966; *Al naharot Bavel* [By the Rivers of Babylon], 1971; *Five Pantomimes,* 8 instruments, 1968; *Kaddish,* cello, strings, 1987; *Mashav,* concertino for xylophone, 10 winds, percussion, 1988); works with tape (*Synchromotrask,* 1976; *Of Elephants and Mosquitoes,* 1971).

Bibl.: William Y. Elias, *Tzvi Avni* (Tel Aviv, 1971).

Ax, Emanuel (b. Lvov, Poland, 8 June 1949). Pianist. Moved to Canada, 1959; to the U.S. to attend Juilliard, 1961–66. Studied piano with Mieczyslaw Munz. Concert tour of South America under U.S. State Department auspices, 1969. B.A., Columbia Univ. (in French), 1970. New York debut, Alice Tully Hall, 12 Mar. 1973. Won Artur Rubinstein Competition, 1974; Avery Fisher Award, 1979. Plays the established repertory from Mozart to Ravel plus a few conservative moderns; performs chamber music (with Yo-Yo Ma and others).

Ayala Pérez, Daniel (b. Abalá, Yucatán, 21 July 1906; d. Veracruz, 20 June 1975). Composer and conductor. He studied music first in Mérida, then from 1929 at the conservatory in Mexico City, violin with Silvestre Revueltas and composition with Ponce, Huízar, and Carrillo. During the 1930s he was violinist in the Mexico Symphony, and in 1940 he returned to Yucatán. There he directed a number of ensembles and institutions, including the Mérida Symphony (from 1944) and the Yucatán Conservatory. In 1955 he became director of the Music School at Veracruz. His compositions evoke Mayan music; works include ballets (*El hombre Maya,* 1939; *La gruta diabólica,* 1940); orchestral suites (*Paisaje,* 1935; *Panoramas de México,* 1936; *Mi viaje a Norte América,* 1947); vocal works (*El grillo,* 1933; *U kayil chaac,* soprano, chamber ensemble, Indian instruments, 1934); chamber works (*Vidrios rotos,* oboe, clarinet, bassoon, and piano, 1938); piano works (*Radiogramma,* 1931, in which radio signals are imitated).

Ayler, Albert (b. Cleveland, 13 July 1936; d. New York? between 5 and 25 Nov. 1970). Jazz tenor saxophonist. He played alto saxophone in rhythm-and-blues bands, switching to the tenor while serving in army bands. Stationed in France (1960–61), he remained in Europe, playing with Cecil Taylor in Copenhagen (1962–63). Based in New York from 1963, he led groups which performed and recorded irregularly, owing to the challenging difficulties his music presented listeners. Among the originators of free jazz saxophone playing, Ayler was the most unusual, combining wild swooping lines with rhythm-and-blues honks and squeals, and an old-fashioned wide vibrato (as on the album *Spiritual Unity,* 1964, with Gary Peacock and Sunny Murray).

Aznavour [Aznavurian], **Charles** (b. Paris, 25 May 1924). Popular songwriter, lyricist, singer, and actor. Closely associated with Edith Piaf, who supported his early partnership with composer Pierre Roche. His composition "J'ai bu," sung by Georges Ulmer, won the Grand Prix du Disque in 1947, and in 1955 he achieved success as a singer with "Sur ma vie." In America he was popular in nightclubs with songs such as "On ne sait jamais" and "Ce jour tant attendu." In 1965 he gave an acclaimed recital in Carnegie Hall and had an operetta performed in Paris, *Monsieur Carnaval.*

Azzaiolo, Filippo (b. Bologna; fl. 1557–69). Composer. Perhaps active as a singer in Bologna. He published works in three books of *villotte* printed in Venice; most are four-voiced homophonic settings of popular texts and melodies, with the tune usually in the top voice.

B

Baaren, Kees van (b. Enschede, Netherlands, 22 Oct. 1906; d. Oegstgeest, 2 Sept. 1970). Composer. He studied piano and composition (the latter with Friedrich Koch) at the Berlin Hochschule (1924–29) before returning to his native country to take instruction with Willem Pijper. In 1948 he was made director of the Music Lyceum in Amsterdam, in 1953 of the Utrecht Conservatory, and in 1958 of the Royal Conservatory, The Hague. Much of his music after 1950 employs twelve-tone rows. Works include *Variazioni per orchestra* (1959); *3 Poems of Emily Dickinson,* chorus (1947); *Sonatina in memoriam Willem Pijper,* piano (1948); *The Hollow Men,* soloists, chorus, orchestra (1948; rev. 1955–56); *2 Songs,* chorus (1952); *Sinfonia,* orchestra (1956); the string quartet *Sovraposizioni I* (1962); *Musica,* 72 carillons (1964–68; version of same for 47 carillons, 1964–69); *Musica,* organ (1968–69).

Bibl.: Jos Wouters, "Kees van Baaren," in *Dutch Composers Gallery* (Amsterdam, 1971).

Babbitt, Milton (Byron) (b. Philadelphia, 10 May 1916). Composer and theorist. He was raised in Jackson, Miss.; entered the Univ. of Pennsylvania intending to follow his father's profession of mathematics, but soon replaced mathematics with music at New York Univ. (B.A., 1935, under Bauer and Philip James). Thereafter he studied privately with Sessions and wrote criticism for the *Musical Leader;* went to Princeton to continue studying with Sessions and received his M.F.A. from that university in 1942. In the same year his *Music for the Mass I* (composed 1940) received the Bearns Prize from Columbia; this work and many others composed before 1950 (including a symphony, string trio and quartet, a twelve-tone work for string orchestra, and a film score) were withdrawn by the composer. During the Second World War he taught mathematics at Princeton and did mathematical research in Washington; in 1946 he composed a Broadway musical, *Fabulous Voyage,* which was not successful. He taught music at Princeton from 1948 until 1986; has also taught at Juilliard, the Berkshire Music Center, New England Conservatory, Harvard Univ., the Salzburg Seminars on American Music, and at the summer courses in Darmstadt.

Babbitt has won the New York Music Critics' Circle award (*Composition for 4 Instruments,* 1948; *Philomel,* 1964) and a Pulitzer Prize Special Citation for "a life's work as a distinguished and seminal American composer." He was president of the ISCM American section, 1951–52; has served on the editorial board of *Perspectives of New Music;* and directed the Columbia–Princeton Electronic Music Center beginning in 1959.

He is primarily associated with the extension and rigorous formulation of the twelve-tone method of composition. The analytic vocabulary normally employed today, derived from mathematical set theory, stems from Babbitt; his *3 Compositions for Piano* (1947) was one of the first pieces to extend Schoenberg's method. In addition to pitch class, Babbitt has in an analogous manner serialized register, dynamics, duration, and timbre. In *Relata I* (1965, premiered by Schuller in Cleveland in 1966) the families of orchestral instruments divided into timbral groups are allied to the set structure that controls pitch class; later serial works such as *Arie da Capo* (flute, clarinet and bass clarinet, piano, violin, and cello, 1973–74) employ "weighted aggregates," or transformations of pitch arrays that do not contain unique instances of each pitch class. Even though he relies on extensive precompositional planning, his compositions are not rigidly predetermined in every respect. *Philomel* (soprano and tape, 1964), written on a commission from the Ford Foundation, illustrates the care with which Babbitt attends to text and timbre; in *A Solo Requiem* (soprano and two pianos, 1976–77) he employs a wide range of vocal techniques.

Awarded a Guggenheim Fellowship (1960–61) to study electronic music, Babbitt worked with RCA's newly developed Mark II synthesizer, producing *Composition for Synthesizer* and *Vision and Prayer* (soprano and synthesizer). Electronic composition allows him to require precision, especially in rhythmic events, beyond the capacity of the human performer; yet he has continued to write for live performers, often combining them with tape.

Babbitt sees his system not as a completion of Schoenberg's approach but as a way of experimenting with composition. He believes the university to be the proper home for the serious contemporary composer, just as it is home to other scholars and scientists. In an essay from 1958 (published with a title not of his making, "Who Cares If You Listen?"), he argued that the concertgoing public as consumers of traditional and established music is not the proper audience for the serious composer.

Works: compositions for orchestra (*Relata I,* 1965; *Relata II,* 1968; *Ars combinatoria,* small orchestra, 1981; a piano concerto, 1985; *Transfigured Notes,* string orchestra, 1986); a great deal of instrumental chamber music (*Composition for 4 Instruments,* 1948; *Composition for 12 Instruments,* 1948; 5

string quartets, 1948, 1954, 1969, 1970, 1982; a wind quartet, 1953; *All Set,* jazz ensemble, 1957; *Arie da Capo,* 1973–74; *Paraphrases,* 1979; *The Crowded Air,* 11 instruments, 1988; *Consortini,* 5 instruments, 1989); vocal music (*The Widow's Lament in Springtime,* soprano, piano, 1950; *Du,* soprano, piano, 1951; *Composition for Tenor and 6 Instruments,* 1960; *4 Canons,* women's chorus, 1969; *Phonemena,* soprano, piano, 1970; *A Solo Requiem,* soprano and two pianos, 1976–77); electronic music (*Composition for Synthesizer,* 1961; *Vision and Prayer,* with soprano, 1961; *Philomel,* with soprano, 1964; *Ensembles for Synthesizer,* 1962–64; *Correspondences,* with string orchestra, 1967; *Concerti,* with violin, small orchestra, 1974; *Phonemena,* with soprano, 1975; *Reflections,* with piano, 1975; *Images,* with saxophone, 1979); piano pieces (*3 Compositions for Piano,* 1947; *Partitions,* 1957; *Post-Partitions,* 1966; *Tableaux,* 1973); *Sheer Pluck,* guitar (1984); *None but the Lonely Flute,* solo flute (1993).

Writings: "Some Aspects of Twelve-Tone Composition," *Score and IMA Magazine* 12 (1955): 53. "Twelve-Tone Invariants as Compositional Determinants," *MQ* 46 (1960): 246. "Set Structure as a Compositional Determinant," *JMT* 5 (1961): 72. S. Dembski and J. N. Straus, eds., *Milton Babbitt: Words about Music* (Madison, Wis., 1987).

Bibl.: *PNM* 14/2–15/1 (1976) [including a list of works and writings], and 24/1–25/1 (1987) [special issues on the occasions of Babbitt's 60th and 70th birthdays]. Andrew Washburn Mead, *An Introduction to the Music of Milton Babbit* (Princeton, 1994).

Babcock, Alpheus (b. Dorchester, Mass., 11 Sept. 1785; d. Boston, 3 Apr. 1842). Piano maker. After apprenticing with the instrument maker Benjamin Crehore of Milton, Mass., he worked as a piano maker in Boston and Philadelphia, ending his career in the shop of Jonas Chickering in Boston. His single-cast metal piano frame (patent applied for in 1825) profoundly affected the evolution of the piano.

Bibl.: Keith Grafing, "Alpheus Babcock's Cast-Iron Piano Frames," *GSJ* 27 (1974): 118–24.

Bacewicz, Grażyna (b. Łódź, 5 Feb. 1909; d. Warsaw, 17 Jan. 1969). Composer and violinist. Her early study of violin and piano was at the Kijeska-Dobkiewiczowa Conservatory in Łódź. At the Warsaw Conservatory she studied violin with Jarzębski, piano with Turczyński, and composition with Sikorski. In 1932–34 she studied in Paris with Boulanger. Her successful career as violinist began in 1934, with tours of Europe and prizes from international competitions, and continued after the war. During the 1950s she began devoting herself chiefly to composition. In 1966 she became professor of composition at the Warsaw Conservatory (State Academy of Music). Much of her music is marked by contrapuntal "neoclassicism," though she resisted the term. Works include stage music (the ballet *Z chłopa król* [The Peasant King], 1953–54; the radio opera *Przygoda króla Artura* [The Adventure of King Arthur], 1959); 4 symphonies (1945, 1951, 1952, 1953) and *String Symphony* (1946); 15 concertos (7 for violin, 1937, 1946, 1948, 1951, 1954, 1957, 1965; a concerto for orchestra, 1962); other works for orchestra (*Contradizione,* 1966); chamber works (many for violin: 5 sonatas with piano, 2 solo sonatas, 9 caprices, many dances); preludes, etudes, sonatas, and other works for piano (*Krakowiak koncertowy,* 1949); vocal works (*Kantata olimpijska,* 1948); songs for voice and piano.

Bibl.: Adrian Thomas, *Grażyna Bacewicz: Chamber and Orchestral Music* (Los Angeles, 1985). Sharon Guertin Shafer, *the Contribution of Grażyna Bacewicz (1909–69) to Polish Music* (Lewiston, 1992).

Bach, Carl Philipp Emanuel (b. Weimar, 8 Mar. 1714; d. Hamburg, 14 Dec. 1788). Composer, keyboard player, and writer on music; second son of J. S. and Maria Barbara Bach. His childhood was spent in Cöthen and Leipzig, where his father was his principal teacher. At Leipzig he attended the Thomasschule, and in 1731 he matriculated in law at the Univ. of Leipzig. He switched to the law program at the Univ. of Frankfurt an der Oder in 1734. In 1738 he received a summons from Frederick, then Crown Prince of Prussia, to serve as chamber musician at his court in Rheinsberg. After Frederick's accession to the throne in 1740, when the court moved to Berlin, Bach had frequent contact with J. J. Quantz, the Graun brothers, the Benda brothers, and literary figures such as Ramler and Lessing. Bach published several path-breaking sets of keyboard works during this period, including the Prussian Sonatas Wq. 48 (1743), the Württemberg Sonatas Wq. 49 (1744), and later the Sonatas with Varied Reprises Wq. 50 (1760). Frederick, however, showed little enthusiasm for his music. Bach was severely underpaid at court, and at the end of the Seven Years' War (1763) he began to seek employment elsewhere; in 1767 he was appointed Telemann's replacement in Hamburg. There he assumed posts as music director at five churches and as Kantor at the Johanneum; he remained in the city for the rest of his life. Nearly all of his sacred vocal music dates from these years, including the oratorios *Die Israeliten in der Wüste* (1769), *Die letzten Leiden des Erlösers* (1770), and *Die Auferstehung und Himmelfahrt Jesu* (1777–80). Also from this period are the 10 symphonies Wq. 182–83 and the 6 sonatas, rondos, and fantasies "für Kenner und Liebhaber" Wq. 55–59, 61.

Eugene Helm's thematic catalog includes nearly 900 works; central to the oeuvre is the keyboard. More than 350 works are for solo keyboard: sonatas, fantasies, rondos, variations, fugues. Also included are nearly 100 concertos or sonatinas, about 50 chamber works with obbligato keyboard, 70 trio sonatas, 20 symphonies, about 100 solo songs, and more than 100 choral works. Bach was author of the single most important treatise of the era, *Versuch über die wahre Art das Clavier zu spielen,* 2 vols. (Berlin, 1753–62; facs., Leipzig, 1957); trans. William J. Mitchell as *Essay on the True Art of Playing Keyboard Instruments* (New York, 1948).

Bibl.: Carl Heinrich Bitter, *Carl Philipp Emanuel und Wilhelm Friedemann Bach und deren Brüder,* 2 vols. (Berlin 1868; R: Kassel, 1973). Alfred Wotquenne, ed., *Thematisches Ver-*

zeichnis der Werke von Carl Philipp Emanuel Bach (1714–1788) (Leipzig, 1905; R: Ann Arbor, 1962) [Wq.]. E. Eugene Helm, *Thematic Catalogue of the Works of Carl Philipp Emanuel Bach* (New Haven, 1989). Erich Herbert Beurmann, "Die Klaviersonaten Carl Philipp Emanuel Bachs" (diss., Georg-August Univ., Göttingen, 1952). Ernst Suchalla, *Die Orchestersinfonien Carl Philipp Emanuel Bachs* (Augsburg, 1968). Rachel W. Wade, *The Keyboard Concertos of Carl Philipp Emanuel Bach* (Ann Arbor, 1981). David Schulenberg, *The Instrumental Music of Carl Philipp Emanuel Bach* (Ann Arbor, 1984). Richard Kramer, "The New Modulation of the 1770s: C. P. E. Bach in Theory, Criticism, and Practice," *JAMS* 38 (1985): 551–92. Hans-Günter Ottenberg, *C. P. E. Bach* (New York, 1987). Stephen L. Clark, ed., *C. P. E. Bach Studies* (Oxford and New York, 1988). Carl Philipp Emanuel Bach, *Briefe und Dokumente: Kritische Gesamtausgabe,* ed. Ernst Suchalla (Göttingen, 1994).

Bach, Johann Christian (b. Leipzig, 5 Sept. 1735; d. London, 1 Jan. 1782). Composer; youngest surviving son of J. S. Bach. His early music instruction was with his father and, after 1750, with his half-brother Emanuel, who was 21 years his senior. In 1754 he went to Italy, where his teachers included Padre Martini. In Milan he was made cathedral organist in 1760; that year his first opera seria, *Artaserse* (text by Metastasio), was performed in Turin. It was followed by *Catone in Utica* (Naples, 1761) and *Alessandro nell'Indie* (Naples, 1762). After moving to London, he created pastiches for the King's Theatre late in 1762 and full-scale operas in early 1763. In 1765 he and Carl Friedrich Abel began the Bach–Abel concerts, which helped establish public concerts in London. In 1772 and 1774 he received operatic commissions in Mannheim. He composed *Amadis de Gaule* for the Paris Opéra in 1779. He composed 13 operas, many sacred vocal works, cantatas, serenatas, songs, nearly 50 symphonies, 15 *symphonies concertantes,* some 30 concertos, and much chamber and solo keyboard music.

Bibl.: Fritz Tutenberg, *Die Sinfonik J. C. Bachs* (Wolfenbüttel, 1928). Charles Sanford Terry, *Johann Christian Bach* (London, 1929; rev. 2nd ed., H. C. Robbins Landon, 1967). Ernest Warburton, "A Study of Johann Christian Bach's Operas" (diss., Oxford Univ., 1969). Heinz Gärtner, *John Christian Bach: Mozart's Friend and Mentor,* trans. Reinhard G. Pauly (Portland, 1994).

Bach, Johann Christoph (b. Arnstadt, 3 Dec. 1642; d. Eisenach, 31 Mar. 1703). Composer and organist; first cousin of J. S. Bach's father, Johann Ambrosius Bach. He was educated in music probably by his father, Heinrich Bach (1615–92). He became organist of the Arnstadt court chapel in 1663. Two years later he was appointed organist of the Georgenkirche in Eisenach, where he worked for the rest of his life. From 1700 he was also chamber musician for the Duke of Eisenach. After years of continual quarrels over salary with town authorities, he died a debtor. He composed motets, cantatas and vocal concertos, arias, and organ music (44 chorales with preludes). J. S. Bach, who admired his cousin's music, referred to him (in the so-called *Ursprung,* or family history) as "a profound composer."

Bibl.: Fritz Rollberg, "Johann Christoph Bach: Organist zu Eisenach, 1665–1703," *ZfMw* 11 (1929): 549–61.

Bach, Johann Christoph Friedrich (b. Leipzig, 21 June 1732; d. Bückeburg, 26 Jan. 1795). Composer; eldest surviving son of J. S. and Anna Magdalena Bach. He received early training in music from his father and later enrolled to study law at the Univ. of Leipzig. He gave up his studies in 1750 when he was offered a position as chamber musician at the Bückeburg court of Count Wilhelm of Schaumburg-Lippe; he retained this post until his death. As *Konzertmeister,* beginning in 1759, he directed operas and concerts. The poet Johann Gottfried Herder arrived at the court in 1771, and for the next five years Bach collaborated with him on cantatas and oratorios (*Die Kindheit Jesu* and *Die Auferweckung Lazarus,* ed. in *DDT* 56) and on the opera *Brutus* (music lost). He also composed 20 symphonies, 6 keyboard concertos, solo keyboard music, and many chamber works.

Bibl.: Georg Schünemann, "Johann Christoph Friedrich Bach," *BaJb* 11 (1914): 45–165. Hannsdieter Wohlfahrth, *Johann Christoph Friedrich Bach als Instrumentalkomponist,* Neue Heidelberger Studien zur Musikwissenschaft, 4 (Bern, 1971).

Bach, Johann Sebastian (b. Eisenach, 21 Mar. 1685; d. Leipzig, 28 July 1750). Composer and organist. His father, Johann Ambrosius Bach, served as *Stadtpfeifer* in Arnstadt, as violinist in Erfurt, and (from 1671) as chamber musician in Eisenach. In 1668 Ambrosius married Maria Elisabeth Lämmerhirt (1644–94). Johann Sebastian, the youngest of their four surviving children, was baptized on 23 Mar. in the Georgenkirche at Eisenach. Little is known of his earliest musical experiences. He excelled in singing (as his son Carl Philipp Emanuel later reported), and the organ playing of his father's cousin Johann Christoph Bach (1642–1703) at the Georgenkirche must have made an impression on him.

Probably in 1692 Sebastian entered the local Lateinschule, originally a Dominican school, which boasted such alumni as Martin Luther. Two years later, when Bach's mother, Elisabeth, died, Ambrosius married Barbara Margarete Keul; before three months had passed, however, Ambrosius himself was dead. Sebastian and his brother Johann Jakob were sent to nearby Ohrdruf to live with their eldest brother, Johann Christoph (1671–1721); at the Ohrdruf Lyceum they received a solid foundation in history, science, Lutheran theology, mathematics, classics, and singing. There Bach also met Georg Erdmann, who became a lifelong friend. Emanuel reports that his father's first keyboard studies were with elder brother Johann Christoph, who was organist at St. Michael's, Ohrdruf. Christoph had been a pupil of Pachelbel during the 1680s; it was he who allegedly forbade his youngest brother to copy out a collection of keyboard works,

Portrait by Balthasar Denner (ca. 1730); identified as Johann Sebastian Bach and three of his sons.

thus forcing him to copy the manuscript by night to avoid detection. Sebastian learned much of composition from copying music—probably including, at this period of his life, the music of Froberger and Pachelbel.

In 1700 Sebastian was forced to leave Ohrdruf, probably because his brother's own family (with two young children and a third expected) had grown too large. Sebastian and Erdmann both moved to Lüneberg at about the same time and became members of the Matins chorus of the Michaeliskirche. At the church's school Sebastian continued his general education; he perhaps also took part in the performance of chamber music and took advantage of the school's large collection of musical scores. Although it is not clear that he studied organ there, he probably did have contact with local organists J. J. Löwe, Georg Böhm, and J. A. Reincken of Hamburg.

After a brief period of service in Weimar early in 1703, Sebastian auditioned for and received the post as organist at the Neukirche (previously called Bonifaciuskirche) in Arnstadt. The position represented a professional advance, though Bach's relations with his colleagues and with the town council were stormy: he was reprimanded for insulting the bassoonist Geyersbach; he got along poorly with students under his tutorship; he was accused of overembellishing the hymns and confusing the congregation; he was charged with having invited a young lady into the choir loft (presumably to rehearse). In 1705 he requested a month's leave of absence to enable him to travel to Lübeck, where he hoped to hear Dietrich Buxtehude's famous concert series. He departed Arnstadt in October and did not return until the end of January 1706. His tardy return did not go unremarked, and the council was probably relieved when Bach took another position in 1707, as organist at St. Blasiuskirche in Mühlhausen. There Bach felt financially secure enough to marry: in October 1707 he married Maria Barbara Bach, his second cousin. At Mülhausen Bach composed principally music for organ and clavier, though the cantatas BWV 71, 131, and probably also 4, 106, and 196, were fruits of this period.

In June 1708 Duke Wilhelm Ernst of Weimar, who had heard Bach's organ playing earlier in the year, offered him the position of court organist at his impressive palace. Bach accepted the duke's offer, perhaps realizing that the opposition he had begun to encounter at Mühlhausen would not subside. The Weimar position represented a marked advance in Bach's social and economic standing: at the time of his appointment he earned 150 florins per year (plus substantial incidental fees) and by 1714, 250 florins. As the duke favored the keyboard, it is generally assumed that much of Bach's organ music dates from the Weimar years; his first years at Weimar were occupied chiefly with the performance and composition of keyboard music. It is from this period that his first extensive contact with Italian music dates, and with it his keyboard arrangements of concertos by Vivaldi and others. In 1714 he received the additional post of *Konzertmeister;* from that year he was required to compose "monatlich neue Stücke" (i.e., a new cantata every month), a schedule he maintained until his relations with the duke deteriorated in 1716. Among the 17 or so extant cantatas from this period is the important *Ich hatte viel Bekümmernis* BWV 21. Also during the eight years at Weimar, Maria Barbara bore her husband six children, including Wilhelm Friedemann (b. 1710) and Carl Philipp Emanuel (b. 1714).

Some of Bach's music making at Weimar took place in the nearby palace of Duke Ernst August, nephew of Bach's patron. The two co-regents were on bad terms, and Wilhelm Ernst forbade his musicians involvement in his nephew's court. Bach probably resented the ban, and in 1716 the resentment between patron and composer appears to have grown steadily. In addition, when Kapellmeister Samuel Drese died in 1716, Bach clearly expected to be considered for the position; instead the duke began a search outside the court. Bach began almost immediately to seek a post as Kapellmeister elsewhere. In August 1717 he accepted a position at the court of Prince Leopold in Cöthen. Duke Wilhelm's bitter reluctance to release Bach from duty culminated in a month-long imprisonment of his esteemed organist. Bach was finally released—from prison and from duty—on 2 Dec., and he left Weimar immediately.

Bach's relations with his Cöthen patron were warmer. Leopold was a widely traveled young man whose broad education had included musical studies with Johann David Heinichen. Bach was paid well, and his abilities were esteemed highly. Because the court chapel was Calvinist, Bach composed only secular cantatas in Cöthen, principally for celebrations of the New Year and the prince's birthday. He composed a great deal of chamber music, however, including the sonatas and partitas for violin, the cello suites, several solo concertos, and didactic keyboard music (the inventions and sinfonias, the first book of *Das wohltemperierte Clavier,* the *Clavier-Büchlein* for the 9-year-old Wilhelm Friedemann, and the French Suites for Anna Magdalena). On a trip to Berlin in 1719 he met the Margrave of Brandenburg, to whom he presented, two years later, the 6 Brandenburg Concertos. In 1720 Maria Barbara died of unknown causes; later the same year Bach's elder brother Johann Christoph died as well.

Late in 1721 Bach married Anna Magdalena, a Cöthen court singer who became not only Bach's musical collaborator and copyist but also the mother of 13 of his children (including Johann Christoph Friedrich, b. 1732, and Johann Christian, b. 1735). Also in 1721 Prince Leopold himself married Friderica Henrietta of Anhalt-Bernburg, a 20-year-old who was indifferent to music. The match brought on a cooling between Kapellmeister and patron, and when Johann Kuhnau, Kantor at Leipzig, died in 1722, Bach was among several prominent composers who applied for the post.

The Leipzig authorities first offered the position to Telemann, who was unable to secure release from his employers at Hamburg. But in 1723 Bach accepted the post at which he was to spend his final, most productive years: as Kantor of the Thomasschule (which included academic duties for which he hired an assistant) and as *Director musices* for the town of Leipzig. A large part of his duties involved the Nikolaikirche and the Thomaskirche, though he earned at least half of his salary through supplemental duties (weddings, funerals, official town celebrations). His first, extraordinarily productive years at Leipzig saw the composition of some 200 cantatas, the St. Matthew and St. John Passions, and numerous motets and instrumental works. He produced music for nearby courts as well: on the death in 1733 of Friedrich August I, Elector of Saxony, he composed the Kyrie and Gloria that were later to become part of the B minor Mass.

During the latter 1730s Bach began to show less concern for his duties, which he attempted to delegate in order to create more time for composition. During this decade he composed such works as the Christmas Oratorio, the harpsichord concertos, and the *Clavier-Übung* (much for the Collegium musicum, which he directed 1729–41). His relations with Leipzig authorities were sometimes heated, as indicated by the oft-mentioned power struggle in 1736 over the appointment of prefects. Because his position at Leipzig represented a lower social standing than a court post, he was anxious to retain a courtly title. In 1736 he obtained an appointment as *Hofcompositeur* for the Dresden court.

His final creative years were occupied chiefly with "private" works such as the the Canonic Variations for Organ on *Vom Himmel hoch* BWV 769, the *Musical Offering* (the composition of which was prompted by the composer's celebrated visit to Potsdam in 1747, where his son Carl Philipp Emanuel was chamber musician to Frederick II), and the *Art of Fugue,* which Bach left uncompleted upon his death. In 1749 Bach fell ill, and by early the following year his vision was nearly gone. He died after two unsuccessful operations for a cataract.

Works: *Vocal music.* About 200 known sacred cantatas (representing about three fifths of those he is thought to have composed), including *Wie schön leuchtet der Morgenstern* BWV 1 (1725); *Christ lag in Todes Banden* BWV 4 (1707–8?); *Wär Gott nicht mit uns diese Zeit* BWV 14 (1735); *O Ewigkeit du Donnerwort* BWV 20 (1724); *Ich hatte viel Bekümmernis* BWV 21 (before 1714?); *Wir danken dir, Gott, wir danken dir* BWV 29 (1731); *Freue dich, erlöste Schar* BWV 30 (1738?); *O ewiges Feuer, O Ursprung der Liebe* BWV 34 (ca. 1742); *Jauchzet Gott in allen Landen!* BWV 51 (1730); *Ich will den Kreuzstab gerne tragen* BWV 56 (1726);

Lobe den Herrn, meine Seele BWV 69 (1740s); *Gott ist mein König* BWV 71 (1708); *Die Elenden sollen essen* BWV 75 (1723); *Jesu, der du meine Seele* BWV 78 (1724); *Ein feste Burg ist unser Gott* BWV 80 (1724); *Ich habe genug* BWV 82 (1727); *Gottes Zeit ist die allerbeste Zeit [Actus tragicus]* BWV 106 (1707?); *Sei Lob und Ehr dem höchsten Gut* BWV 117 (ca. 1728–31); *Aus der Tiefen rufe ich, Herr, zu dir* BWV 131 (1707); *Wachet auf, ruft uns die Stimme* BWV 140 (1731); *Herz und Mund und Tat und Leben* BWV 147 (1723); *Sehet, wir gehn hinauf den Jerusalem* BWV 159 (1729); *Leichtgesinnte Flattergeister* BWV 181 (1724); *Mein Herze schwimmt im Blut* BWV 199 (1714).

Secular cantatas include *Der Streit zwischen Phoebus und Pan [Geschwinde, ihr wirbeln den Winde,* "dramma per musica"] BWV 201 (1729); *Weichet nur, betrübte Schatten* [Wedding Cantata] BWV 202 (1718–23?); *Der zufriedengestellte Äolus,* BWV 205 (1725); *Was mir behagt, ist nur die muntre Jagd!* BWV 208 (1740–42); *Schweigt stille, plaudert nicht* [Coffee Cantata] BWV 211 (ca. 1734–35); *Mer hahn en neue Oberkeet* [Peasant Cantata] BWV 212 (1742); *Hercules auf dem Scheidewege* BWV 213 (1733).

Other large-scale sacred vocal works include St. Matthew Passion BWV 244 (1727–29; rev. 1736); St. John Passion BWV 245 (1724–25; rev. 1730s); St. Mark Passion BWV 247 (lost except for nos. used in BWV 54, BWV 198, and BWV 248); Christmas Oratorio BWV 248 (actually 6 separate cantatas, 1734–35); Mass in B minor BWV 232 (1724–47; assembled from separate sections, 1747–49); Magnificat in D BWV 243 (version in E♭ BWV 243a, 1723; rev. ca. 1733); 4 Kyrie-Gloria Masses BWV 233–36; 8 motets, including *Singet dem Herrn ein neues Lied* BWV 225 (1727), *Jesu, meine Freude* BWV 227 (1723), *Lobet den Herrn alle Heiden* BWV 230 (date unknown).

Other vocal works include nearly 200 chorale settings and some 100 sacred songs.

Instrumental music. Orchestral and chamber works include 6 Brandenburg Concertos BWV 1046–51 (ca. 1711–20; nos. 1 and 2 in F, nos. 3 and 4 in G, no. 5 in D, no. 6 in B♭); 4 suites for orchestra BWV 1066–69 (1720s and 1730s); Concerto no. 1 in A minor, violin, orchestra BWV 1041 (1730s); no. 2 in E; Concerto in D minor, 2 violins and orchestra BWV 1043 (1730s); 14 concertos for harpsichord and orchestra BWV 1052–65 (1730s, mostly arrangements of earlier works); 3 sonatas (G minor, A minor, C) and 3 partitas (B minor, D minor, E) for solo violin BWV 1001–6 (1720); 6 sonatas for violin and continuo BWV 1014–19 (1720s); 6 suites for solo cello BWV 1007–12 (G, D minor, C, E♭, C minor, D; ca. 1720); 4 sonatas for flute and harpsichord BWV 1030, 1032, 1034, 1035 (1717–23 and 1730s).

Nearly 250 works for organ: preludes and fugues, toccatas, fantasias, 6 trio sonatas BWV 525–30 (ca. 1727); 6 solo organ concertos BWV 592–97; *Das Orgel-Büchlein* (chorale preludes, ca. 1713–17); 6 chorales after Schübler cantatas BWV 645–50; *Clavier-Übung* 3 (chorale preludes, 1739).

Other keyboard: *Das wohltemperierte Clavier* 1, BWV 846–65 (1722), 2, BWV 879–93 (1738–42); *Clavier-Übung* 4 [Goldberg Variations], BWV 988 (1741); *Italian Concerto* BWV 971 (1735) and *French Overture in B minor* [Partita] BWV 831 (1733?) [these two form *Clavier-Übung* 2]; 15 inventions BWV 772–86 (1723); 15 sinfonias BWV 787–801 (1723); 6 English suites BWV 806–11 (ca. 1715); 6 French suites BWV 812–17; 6 partitas BWV 825–30 [*Clavier-Übung* 1]; 16 concertos for solo clavier [arranged from works by other composers] BWV 972–87; many other fantasias, preludes, fugues, sonatas.

Works for lute include a prelude, fugue, and allegro in E♭ BWV 998. Works for (in part) unspecified performance medium include *Das musikalische Opfer* BWV 1079 (1747) and *Die Kunst der Fuge* BWV 1080 (1742–50).

Bibl.: *Werke,* 47 vols. (Leipzig, 1851–99; R: Ann Arbor, 1947). *Neue Bach-Ausgabe,* ed. Johann-Sebastian-Bach-Institut, Göttingen, and Bach-Archiv, Leipzig, 8 series (Kassel, 1954–). Wolfgang Schmieder, *Thematisch-systematisches Verzeichnis der musikalischen Werke Johann Sebastian Bachs: Bach-Werke-Verzeichnis* [BWV] (Leipzig, 1950; 3rd ed., 1961). Hans-Joachim Schulze and Christoph Wolff, eds., *Bach Compendium: Analytisch-bibliographisches Repertorium der Werke Johann Sebastian Bachs,* 1/1–4, *Vokalwerke* (Leipzig and Frankfurt, 1985–89).

Johann Nikolaus Forkel, *Über Johann Sebastian Bachs Leben, Kunst und Kunstwerke* (Leipzig, 1802; R: Berlin, 1966); trans. Charles Sanford Terry (London, 1920). Philipp Spitta, *Johann Sebastian Bach,* 2 vols. (Leipzig, 1873–80; 5th ed., 1962); trans. Clara Bell and J. A. Fuller Maitland (London; R: New York, 1951). *Bach-Jahrbuch* [*BaJb*] (1904–). André Pirro, *J.-S. Bach* (Paris, 1906); trans. Mervyn Savill (New York, 1957). Albert Schweitzer, *J. S. Bach, le musicien-poète* (Leipzig, 1905); trans. Ernest Newman (Leipzig and New York, 1911). Charles Hubert Hastings Parry, *Johann Sebastian Bach* (London and New York, 1909; rev. ed., 1934; R: Westport, Conn., 1970). Friedrich Rochlitz, *Wege zu Bach* (1832; R. Augsburg, 1926). Charles Sanford Terry, *Bach: A Biography* (London, 1928). Georg Kinsky, *Die Originalausgaben der Werke Johann Sebastian Bachs* (Vienna, 1937; R: New York, 1968). Arnold Schering, *Johann Sebastian Bach und das Musikleben Leipzigs im 18. Jahrhundert,* Musikgeschichte Leipzigs, 3 (Leipzig, 1941). Hans T. David, *J. S. Bach's Musical Offering: History, Interpretation, and Analysis* (New York, 1945; R: New York, 1972). Id. and Arthur Mendel, eds., *The Bach Reader* (New York, 1945; rev. ed., 1966). Karl Geiringer, *The Bach Family: Seven Generations of Creative Genius* (New York, 1954). Georg von Dadelsen, *Beiträge zur Chronologie der Werke Johann Sebastian Bach* (Trossingen, 1958). Erwin Bodky, *The Interpretation of Bach's Keyboard Works* (Cambridge, Mass., 1960). May de Forest McAll, ed., *Melodic Index to the Works of Johann Sebastian Bach,* rev. ed. (New York, 1962). Werner Neumann and Hans-Joachim Schulze, eds., *Bach-Dokumente,* 4 vols. (Kassel, 1963–78). Hermann Keller, *Das Wohltemperierte Klavier von Johann Sebastian Bach: Werk und Wiedergabe* (Kassel, 1965). Karl Geiringer, *Johann Sebastian Bach: The Culmination of an Era* (London, 1966). Ferdinand Zander, "Die Dichter der Kantatentexte Johann Sebastian Bachs: Untersuchungen zu ihrer Bestimmung" (diss., Univ. of Cologne, 1966); excerpts in *BaJb* 54 (1968): 9–64. Martin Geck, *Die Wiederentdeckung der Matthäuspassion im 19. Jahrhundert* (Regensburg, 1967). Christoph Wolff, *Der stile antico in der Musik Johann Sebastian Bachs: Studien zu Bachs Spätwerk* (Wiesbaden, 1968). Percy M. Young, *The Bachs, 1500–1850* (London, 1970). Jacques Chailley, *L'art de la fugue de J.-S. Bach* (Paris, 1971). Alfred Dürr, *Die Kantaten von Johann Sebastian Bach* (Kassel, 1971). Robert L. Marshall, *The Compositional Process of J. S. Bach: A Study of the Autograph Scores of the Vocal Works,* 2 vols. (Princeton, 1972). Alec Robertson, *The Church Cantatas of J. S. Bach* (New York, 1972). Werner Neumann, ed., *Sämtliche von J. S. Bach vertonte Texte* (Leipzig, 1974). Walter Kolneder, *Die Kunst der Fuge: Mythen des 20. Jahrhunderts* (Wilhelmshaven, 1977). Thomas Harmon, *The Registration of J. S. Bach's Organ Works* (Buren, 1978). Werner Neumann, *Aufgaben und Probleme der heutigen Bachforschung* (Berlin, 1979).

Paul Steinitz, *Bach's Passions* (New York, 1978). Peter Williams, *The Organ Music of J. S. Bach* (Cambridge, 1980–83). Joshua Rifkin, "Bach's Chorus: A Preliminary Report," *MT* 123 (1982): 747–54. Robert L. Marshall, "Bach's Chorus: A Reply to Joshua Rifkin," *MT* 124 (1983): 19–22. Denis Arnold, *Bach* (New York, 1983). Lawrence Dreyfus, *Bach's Continuo Group: Players and Practices in His Vocal Works* (Cambridge, Mass., 1987). Robert Marshall, *The Music of Johann Sebastian Bach: The Sources, the Style, the Significance* (New York, 1989). Eric Thomas Chafe, *Tonal Allegory in the Vocal Music of J. S. Bach* (Berkeley, 1991). Christoph Wolff, *Bach: Essays on His Life and Music* (Cambridge, Mass., 1991). Paul Badura-Skoda, *Interpreting Bach at the Keyboard,* trans. Alfred Clayton (Oxford, 1993). Michael Marissen, *The Social and Religious Designs of J. S. Bach's Brandenburg Concertos* (Princeton, 1995).

Bach [Schrotenbach], **Vincent** (b. Baden, Austria, 24 Mar. 1890; d. New York, 8 Jan. 1976). Brass instrument maker and trumpeter. Studied trumpet with Josef Weiss (from 1902), then with Georg Stellwagen (from 1906) while studying engineering (degree, 1910). Coached by Fritz Werner, 1912. Toured Europe and the U.S., 1912–14; first trumpet, Boston Symphony, 1914; Diaghilev Ballet Orchestra, 1915–16. From 1919 to 1962 he combined his talents to design and manufacture brass instruments according to the highest standards. In 1962 he sold his company to the H. & A. Selmer Co., and it was subsequently moved from New York to Elkhart, Ind.

Bach, Wilhelm Friedemann (b. Weimar, 22 Nov. 1710; d. Berlin, 1 July 1784). Composer; eldest son of J. S. and Maria Barbara Bach. As a youth he received the best possible musical education from his father, who composed a *Clavier-Büchlein* and the first volume of the *Well-Tempered Clavier* chiefly for his use. From 1729 to 1733 he studied mathematics and philosophy at Leipzig. In the latter year he accepted a post as organist in Dresden (Sophienkirche), and in 1746 a better position in Halle (Liebfrauenkirche). He accompanied his father on the famous "Musical Offering" visit to Frederick II in 1747. Dissatisfied with employers and salary, Friedemann resigned his Halle post in 1764; he would never again hold a permanent job. After a brief period in Brunswick he moved his family to Berlin in 1774; upon his death he left a destitute widow and child. He composed more than 40 keyboard works, 7 concertos, chamber music, 10 symphonies, 33 sacred cantatas, other vocal works.

Bibl.: Carl Heinrich Bitter, *Carl Philipp Emanuel und Wilhelm Friedemann Bach und deren Brüder,* 2 vols. (Berlin, 1868). Martin Falck, *Wilhelm-Friedemann Bach: Sein Leben und seine Werke* (Leipzig, 1913; R: Hildesheim and New York, 1977). Elena Borysenko, "The Cantatas of Wilhelm Friedemann Bach" (diss., Eastman School of Music, 1982).

Bacharach, Burt (b. Kansas City, Mo., 12 May 1928). Popular composer and pianist. He was educated at the Mannes School and the Music Academy of the West and studied composition with Milhaud, Martinů, and Cowell. From 1957 to 1973 he composed songs with lyricist Hal David (b. 1921), many of which became successful recordings for singer Dionne Warwick ("Walk on By," 1964; "Do You Know the Way to San Jose?" 1968); their score for the film *Butch Cassidy and the Sundance Kid* (1969, including "Raindrops Keep Falling on My Head") won two Academy Awards. In 1981 Bacharach coauthored "Arthur's Theme" for the movie *Arthur,* winning another Oscar, and in 1982 he recorded a symphonic suite with the Houston Symphony.

Bachauer, Gina (b. Athens, 21 May 1913; d. there, 22 Aug. 1976). Pianist. Studied with Ariadne Casasis and Waldemar Freeman at the Athens Conservatory (Gold Medal, 1929); with Alfred Cortot at the École normale in Paris; with Sergei Rachmaninoff privately, 1932–35. Formal debut with the Athens National Symphony, 1935. Paris debut with the Paris Symphony, 1937; London debut, 21 Jan. 1946; U.S. debut at New York's Town Hall, 29 Oct. 1950; toured the U.S. annually thereafter. She was at ease in the virtuoso repertory from Scarlatti to Rachmaninoff, as well as with her favorite composer, J. S. Bach.

Bacheler, Daniel (b. ca. 1574?; d. after 1610). Composer. Wrote lute solos, consort music, and one song, the majority probably between ca. 1600 and ca. 1610. Some works were printed in two volumes edited in 1610 by Robert Dowland; others survive only in manuscript. May have been related to another, slightly earlier composer of the same name. Titles of the consort music suggest some connection with the Sidney and Walsingham families.

Bacilly, Bénigne de (b. Normandy?, ca. 1625?; d. Paris, 27 Sept. 1690). Composer and writer on the voice. He was apparently ordained to the priesthood; little else is known of his life. He lived mostly in Paris, where he was a respected singing master and where he published one of the most significant 17th-century treatises on singing, *Remarques curieuses sur l'art de bien chanter* (1668; R: 1971; 4th ed., 1681); trans. Austin B. Caswell as *A Commentary on the Art of Proper Singing* (Brooklyn, 1968), including the musical examples referred to but not actually printed in the original. He also published some 15 collections of his own sacred and secular songs.

Bäck, Sven-Erik (b. Stockholm, 16 Sept. 1919). Composer. He studied violin with Charles Barkel at the conservatory in Stockholm (from 1938) and composition with Hilding Rosenberg (1940–45). In 1951–52 he studied in Rome with Petrassi; he also took courses at the Schola cantorum in Basel during this period. From 1941 he played violin in the Barkel Quartet. He led the "Kammarorkestern–1953" beginning in 1953, and during the 1950s conducted the youth orchestra of the Swedish radio. In 1959 he became director of the radio's music school near Stockholm. As a composer he began in the late romantic tradition, but subsequently assumed terse, Webern-like serialism and electronic techniques. He maintained an interest in Renaissance and Baroque sacred music. Works include operas (*Tranfjädrarna* [The Crane Feathers], 1956; *Gästabudet* [The Feast], 1958; *Fågeln* [The Birds], 1960); ballets (*Ikaros,* 1963; *Mur och port* [Wall and Gate], 1971); choral and other vocal music (the cantata *Kattresan* [Cat's Journey], 1952, ballet version, 1969; *Humlan,* voices, cello, piano, percussion, 1968; several motets); orchestral works (*Sinfonia da camera,* 1955; *Intrada,* 1964; *O altitudo II,* 1968; *Ekvator,* orchestra and tape, 1988; *Pro musica vitae,* concerto for strings, 1989); many chamber and solo instrumental works, including a sonata for solo flute (1949) and *Time Present* (2 violins, echo-filter, feedback, 1975); also electronic pieces.

Bibl.: *Nutida musik* 10/3–4 (1966–67) [special Bäck issue].

Backer-Grøndahl, Agathe. See Grøndahl, Agathe.

Backhaus, Wilhelm (b. Leipzig, 26 Mar. 1884; d. Villach, Austria, 5 July 1969). Pianist. Studied with A. Reckendorf, 1891–99; with Eugene D'Albert, 1899. Debut in Leipzig, 1892. Taught at the Royal College of Music in Manchester, 1905; won the Rubenstein Prize, Paris, 1905. U.S. debut 5 Jan. 1912 with the New York Symphony. He toured extensively, including visits to the U.S. in 1924, 1925, 1953, and, finally, 1962. He moved to Lugano, Switzerland, in 1930. Chopin, Brahms, and Scriabin were well represented in his repertory; but he was renowned above all for his performances of Beethoven.

Bacon, Ernst (b. Chicago, 26 May 1898; d. Orinda, Calif., 16 Mar. 1990). Composer and pianist. His teachers included Alexander Raab (piano), Goossens (conducting), and Karl Weigl and Bloch (composition; M.A., Univ. of California, 1935). Under Goossens he was assistant conductor of the Rochester Opera Company and taught piano at the Eastman School of Music (1925–28). In California he initiated the Carmel Bach Festival (1935) and a year later organized the WPA Music Project in San Francisco, conducting its symphony orchestra. In 1938 he became dean and professor of piano at Converse College; in 1945 he was appointed director of the School of Music at Syracuse Univ. (retired, 1964). His Symphony in D (1932) was awarded the Pulitzer Prize. He is best known for settings of American texts (Whitman, Dickinson) and arrangements of American folk music (*Along Unpaved Roads,* 1944). He employed nondiatonic scales, but avoided most avant-garde techniques. In addition to an early treatise on harmony, he wrote two other volumes: *Words on Music* (1960) and *Notes on the Piano* (1963).

Works: 3 musical plays (*A Drumlin Legend,* 1949; *Dr. Franklin,* 1976); ballets; 4 symphonies (1932, 1937, 1956, 1963) and other works for orchestra (*Ford's Theatre: Easter Week 1865,* 1943); works for soloist with orchestra; cantatas and works for narrator and orchestra (*From Emily's Diary,* soprano, alto, women's chorus, orchestra, 1945); a piano trio, string quintet with double bass, and other chamber music; various works for piano; other works for chorus; approximately 250 songs.

Badings, Henk (b. Bandung, Java, 17 Jan. 1907; d. Maarheeze, Netherlands, 26 June 1987). Composer. His Dutch parents died when he was young, and in 1915 he was brought to the Netherlands. Apart from violin lessons he had little early formal training in music. At the wish of his guardian he studied engineering at the Technical Univ. in Delft, graduating in 1931. He studied composition with Willem Pijper during the 1930s, and from 1934 to 1937 he lectured on music theory and composition at the Rotterdam Conservatory. During this period he was also active at the Delft Univ. as a paleontologist and geologist. From 1937 he directed the Amsterdam Music Lyceum, and from 1941 to 1945 the State Conservatory at The Hague. During the late 1940s and the 1950s he was occupied almost solely with composing. From 1961 he taught acoustics at Utrecht Univ., and from 1962 to 1972 he was professor of composition at the Hochschule für Musik in Stuttgart. His earlier music was in a post-Romantic style; later Badings employed electronic elements and made use of a 31-note scale. In his melodic construction he often employed a scale consisting of an alternation of tones and semitones.

Works: the operas *De nachtwacht* (1942; first perf., 1950); *Liefde's listen* [Love's Wiles] (1944–45; first perf., 1948); *Orestes,* radio opera (1954); *Asterion,* radio opera (1957); *Salto mortale,* television opera (1959); *Martin Korda, D.P.* (1960); ballet scores (*Orpheus en Euridike,* 1941; *Evolutionen,* tape, 1958; *Jungle,* tape, 1959; *Die Frau von Andros,* tape, 1959; *Genesis,* tape, 1968); oratorios (*Apocalypse,* 1948, first perf., 1959; *Jonah,* 1963; St. Mark Passion, soloists, male chorus, orchestra, tape, 1971); 8 cantatas; 14 symphonies, most programmatic (no. 7, "Louisville," 1954); concertos for a variety of solo instruments; many choral and vocal works (*Psalm 147,* 1959; *Armageddon,* soprano, wind orchestra, tape, 1968); some 100 instrumental works (4 string quartets, 1931, 1936, 1944, 1966; 4 piano sonatas); songs for voice and piano; pieces for tape.

Bibl.: Jos Wouters, *Henk Badings* (Amsterdam, 1971). Id., "Henk Badings," *Sonorum speculum* 32 (1967): 1–23. Paul T. Klemme, *Henk Badings, 1907–87: Catalog of Works* (Warren, Mich., 1993).

Badura-Skoda, Paul (b. Vienna, 6 Oct. 1927). Pianist. Studied with Viola Thern at the Vienna Hochschule für Musik (diploma, 1948) and with Edwin Fischer (1949), whose assistant he became. Won major competitions in Austria (1947), Budapest (1948), and Paris (1949). Concerto soloist with Furtwängler and Karajan, 1949. U.S. debut, 10 Jan. 1953 in New York. Artist-in-residence, Univ. of Wisconsin, 1966–71. Often played his core repertory of Mozart, Beethoven, and Schubert on historic instruments.

Baez, Joan (Chandos) (b. Staten Island, N.Y., 9 Jan. 1941). Folksinger and songwriter. Following successful appearances at the Newport Folk Festival (1959–60), she performed and recorded a repertory of traditional ballads, original songs, and works by other songwriters (such as Bob Dylan). Her performances were often associated with political causes: she was prominent in the movement opposing the war in Vietnam in the 1960s and has worked also for Amnesty International and UNESCO. Her recordings of Robbie Robertson's "The Night They Drove Old Dixie Down" (1971) and of her own "Diamonds and Rust" (1975) were very popular.

Bahr-Mildenburg [née von Mildenburg], **Anna** (b. Vienna, 29 Nov. 1872; d. there, 27 Jan. 1947). Soprano. Studied with Rosa Papier and in 1895 sang Brünnhilde (in *Die Walküre*) in Hamburg under Mahler; followed Mahler to Vienna and sang with the Vienna Opera (1898–1916) in addition to appearances at Bayreuth (1897–1914) and Covent Garden (from 1906). Her repertory included all the leading Wagner roles. After her retirement in 1917 she taught in Munich and Berlin. In 1909 she married the Viennese author Hermann Bahr.

Baïf, Jean-Antoine de (b. Venice, 19 Feb. 1532; d. Paris, Oct. 1589). Poet. Associate of the literary group known as the Pléiade. Beginning in 1567 he developed *vers mesurés à l'antique,* that is, French poetry written in the quantitative meters of classical verse. Music setting such poetry and adhering to related metrical rules was called *musique mesurée.* Such verse and music were cultivated at Baïf's Académie de poésie et de musique (meeting from 1571) and subsequently at the Académie du Palais, established by Henri III and meeting until 1584. Composers who set his poetry in this style included Jacques Mauduit and Claude Le Jeune.

Bibl.: D. P. Walker, "The Aims of Baïf's Académie de poésie et de musique," *JRBM* 1 (1946): 91–100.

Bailey, Buster [William C.] (b. Memphis, 19 July 1902; d. New York, 12 Apr. 1967). Jazz clarinetist. He toured with W. C. Handy (1917–19) before settling in Chicago to join Erskine Tate (1919–23) and King Oliver (1923–24). Moving to New York, he worked with Fletcher Henderson (1924–37), interrupting this affiliation to join Noble Sissle (1929, 1931–32), the Mills Blue Rhythm Band (1934–35), and others. He played with John Kirby (1937–46), the trombonist Wilbur De Paris (1947–49), Henry "Red" Allen (1950–51, 1954–1960s), Wild Bill Davison (1961–63), the Saints and Sinners (including Vic Dickenson; 1963–64), and Louis Armstrong's All Stars (1965–67). "Man with a Horn Goes Berserk," which he recorded as a leader (1938), displays his prodigious technique.

Bailey, Mildred [née Rinker] (b. Tekoa, Wash., 27 Feb. 1907; d. Poughkeepsie, N.Y., 12 Dec. 1951). Jazz singer. She joined Paul Whiteman's orchestra (1929–33), recording "Rockin' Chair" (1932). She sang with Red Norvo (principally 1936–39; they were married, 1933–45) and on radio broadcasts with Benny Goodman (1939). She also recorded extensively in her own right, accompanied by many fine swing musicians, including Bunny Berigan, Johnny Hodges, and Teddy Wilson on "Down-Hearted Blues" (1935) and Roy Eldridge on "Where Are You?" (1937).

Bailey, Pearl (Mae) (b. Newport News, Va., 29 Mar. 1918; d. Philadelphia, 17 Aug. 1990). Jazz and popular singer. In the 1930s and 1940s she performed in New York with the Noble Sissle Band and with Count Basie. She made her Broadway debut in Harold Arlen's *St. Louis Woman* (1941). Among her most successful recordings were "Tired" (1947) and "Takes Two to Tango" (1953). She appeared in films (*Carmen Jones,* 1954; *St. Louis Blues,* 1958; *Porgy and Bess,* 1959), hosted her own television show (1970–71), and performed often with a band led by her husband, Louis Bellson.

Bibl.: Pearl Bailey, *The Raw Pearl* (New York, 1968).

Bainbridge, Simon (Jeremy) (b. London, 30 Aug. 1952). Composer and conductor. Studied at the Royal College of Music, 1969–72; later studied at Tanglewood. Teachers included John Lambert and Gunther Schuller. Has conducted the BBC Symphony, BBC Scottish Symphony, London Sinfonietta, Bournemouth Symphony and Sinfonietta. Ives and Reich have been major influences on his compositional style. Works include a concerto for viola and orchestra (1976); *Concertante in moto perpetuo* (1983); Fantasia for Two Orchestras (1984); *The Devil's Punchbowl,* instrumental ensembles and children (1987); *Trace,* dance score for instruments and electronics (1987); *Metamorphosis,* 13 instruments (1989).

Baird, Tadeusz (b. Grodzisk Mazowiecki, 26 July 1928; d. Warsaw, 2 Sept. 1981). Composer. During World War II he studied composition with Woytowicz and Sikorski; after the war, at the Warsaw Conservatory with Rytel and Perkowski. In 1952 he completed study of musicology at the Univ. of Warsaw. In 1949 he founded the "Group 1949" with composers Kazimierz Serocki and Jan Krenz; its aim was to foster comprehensible music that conformed to official "antiformalist" cultural policies. In 1956 he helped found the "Warsaw Autumn" International Festival of Contemporary Music. His early music was oriented toward uncomplicated neoclassicism. During the late 1950s he became more experimental and began to assimilate elements of the international avant-garde. But his music remained founded on a late romantic tonal language. His works include an opera, *Jutro* [Tomorrow] (1966); much incidental music and film music; vocal music (*4 Love Sonnets,* baritone, chamber ensemble, 1956, rev. for strings and harpsichord, 1969; *Exhortations,* narrator, chorus, orchestra, 1959–60; the cantatas *Ballada o żołnierskim kubku* [Ballad of a Soldier's Cup], 1954, and *Goethe-Briefe,* 1970; the song cycle *Erotyki,* soprano, orchestra, 1961); chamber music (*Play,* string quartet, 1971).

Bibl.: Michel Pazdro, "Dossier: Tadeusz Baird," *Musique*

en jeu 25 (1976): 73–86. B. M. Maciejewski, *Twelve Polish Composers* (London, 1976).

Baker, Chet [Chesney Henry] (b. Yale, Okla., 23 Dec. 1929; d. Amsterdam, 13 May 1988). Jazz trumpeter. In California he worked with Charlie Parker's bop quintet (1952) before joining Gerry Mulligan's pianoless quartet; their cool jazz recordings of "Bernie's Tune" and "My Funny Valentine" (both 1952) exemplify his delicate, lyrical playing. Leaving Mulligan in 1953, he went on to lead groups. Following a European tour (1955–56), addiction to heroin repeatedly disrupted his career, much of which was spent in Europe, especially Italy, after 1959. In 1964 his instrument was stolen in Paris, and he played flugelhorn before returning to the trumpet in 1970. Despite these problems, he recorded scores of albums and in the 1970s and 1980s performed regularly.

Baker, Janet (Abbott) (b. Hatfield, Yorkshire, 21 Aug. 1933). Mezzo-soprano. Studied with Helene Isepp; master classes with Lotte Lehmann in 1956. Won the Kathleen Ferrier Memorial Prize, 1956; the *Daily Mail*'s Queen's Prize, 1959, enabling her to study at the Mozarteum in Salzburg. Joined Britten's English Opera Group, 1962. In 1964 she sang one of her four Britten roles—Hermia in *A Midsummer Night's Dream*—at her Covent Garden debut. U.S. debut in 1968 singing Mahler's *Das Lied von der Erde* with Krips in San Francisco. Baroque operas by Monteverdi, Purcell, Rameau, and especially Handel commanded much of her attention, but her wide repertory also included roles by Gluck, Mozart, Donizetti, Berlioz, Gounod, and Strauss. Retired from the operatic stage July 1982, but continued to be active in recital. President of the Royal Scottish Academy of Music and Dance from 1983; of the London Sinfonia from 1986. Made Dame of the British Empire in 1976.

Baker, Josephine (b. St. Louis, 3 June 1906; d. Paris, 12 Apr. 1975). Entertainer. At 13 she joined a vaudeville troupe, the Dixie Steppers. Settling in New York in 1921, she won attention as a chorus girl in the Sissle and Blake show *Shuffle Along,* leading to main roles in other productions. A starring role in *La revue nègre* in Paris in 1925 won her enormous popularity in Europe, where her blend of the comic and risqué endeared her to society. During the 1930s, 1940s, and 1950s she staged major revues in Paris and New York, made films and recordings, and devoted efforts to wartime and civil rights activities.

Baker, Julius (b. Cleveland, 23 Sept. 1915). Flutist. Studied with William Kincaid at the Curtis Institute. Principal flutist of the Pittsburgh Symphony, 1941–43; of the CBS Symphony, 1943–50; of the Chicago Symphony, 1951–53; of the New York Philharmonic, 1964–83. Member of the Bach Aria Group, 1947–65. Taught at Juilliard from 1954; at the Curtis Institute from 1980.

Bakfark [Greff Bakfark], **Bálint** [Valentin] (b. Brassó, Transylvania, 1507; d. Padua, 15 or 22 Aug. 1576). Composer and lutenist. Educated in Buda at the court of the future King John of Hungary; remained there until 1540. Spent 17 years in Wilna, Poland, at the court of King Sigismund Augustus II beginning in 1549. Lutenist to the imperial court at Vienna, 1566–68. In the service of Prince John Sigismund in Transylvania, 1568–71. Settled thereafter in Padua, where he died of the plague. Traveled widely and was highly esteemed at courts throughout Europe. His works, most published in two collections (Lyon, 1552; Kraków, 1565), are all for lute and include intabulations of motets, chansons, and madrigals, arrangements of dances and Polish songs, and fantasies.

Bibl.: *Opera omnia* (Budapest, 1976–81).

Balada, Leonardo (b. Barcelona, 22 Sept. 1933). Composer and conductor. He studied piano at Barcelona's Conservatorio del Liceo. From 1956 to 1962 he studied in New York, at the New York College of Music, at the Juilliard School (with Persichetti and Dello Joio), and at the Mannes College. He took private lessons in composition with Copland and studied conducting in Paris with Markevitch. In 1970 he joined the faculty of Carnegie-Mellon Univ. in Pittsburgh. His music has manifested Spanish nationalism within a framework of neoclassicism but has also drawn on elements of serialism. Works include music for the stage (*La casa,* ballet, 1967; *Hangman, Hangman!,* chamber opera, first perf. 1982; *Zapata!,* 1983; *Cristóbal Colón,* 1989); choral works (*Maria Sabina,* narrator, chorus, orchestra, 1969; *Ponce de Leon,* 1973); orchestral works (*Música tranquila,* 1960; *Persistencias,* guitar, orchestra, 1972; *Steel Symphony,* 1972; *2 Homages,* 1975; Concerto for 4 Guitars, 1976; *Quasi un pasodoble,* 1982; *Fantasías sonoras,* 1987); chamber music (*Mosaico,* 1970; *Apuntes,* 4 guitars, 1974; *Music,* flute, string quartet, 1988); works for solo guitar; works for keyboard.

Balakauskas, (Jonas-) Osvaldas (b. Miliunai, near Ukmerge, Lithuania, 19 Dec. 1937). Composer. After early studies in choral conducting in Vilnius, attended Kiev Conservatory (1964–69), where he studied composition with Boris Liatoshinsky and Myroslav Skoryk. Worked as editor at Muzychna Ukraïna until 1972; in 1972 returned to Vilnius, where he has served as a consultant to the Lithuanian Union of Composers. Has made use in his music of serial and other advanced techniques as well as melodic and rhythmic ideas inspired by Lithuanian folk sources. Works include 2 symphonies (1973, 1979); concertos for cello (1972) and oboe (1981); the Mountain Sonata, piano and orchestra (1975); *Passio strumentale,* string quartet and orchestra (1980); 2 string quartets (both 1971) and other instrumental chamber music.

Balakirev, Mily Alexeyevich (b. Nizhny-Novgorod, 2 Jan. 1837; d. St. Petersburg, 29 May 1910). Composer.

His first music instruction was with his mother; at 10 he took piano with Alexander Dubuque, continuing his studies with a German musician, Karl Eisrich. He served as Eisrich's assistant for musical evenings at the estate of a wealthy landowner, Alexander Ulïbïshev, where he was exposed to chamber and orchestral music, and began to try his hand at composition. In 1853 Balakirev entered the Univ. of Kazan as a mathematics student, although he continued to perform on the piano and to teach. In 1855 he accompanied Ulïbïshev to St. Petersburg, where he met Glinka; the following year he made his St. Petersburg debut performing the solo part in the first movement of his Piano Concerto in F♯ minor op. 1; the *Overture on a Spanish March Theme* (first version, 1857) and Piano Sonata in B♭ minor op. 5 (1855–56) also date from this time. The overture *King Lear* was performed in 1859, the incidental music completed in 1861 (rev. 1902–5).

Balakirev attracted a number of disciples in the early 1860s, including Mussorgsky, Rimsky-Korsakov, and Borodin; in 1863 he began conducting at the newly opened Free School of Music in St. Petersburg, an important forum both for his own music and for his disciples. After spending several months in the Caucasus he collected Circassian tunes, in addition to Georgian and Persian melodies, an influence evident in a number of his songs. In 1864 he completed the *Second Overture on Russian Themes,* later published as *1000 let* [1,000 Years] to commemorate the millennium of Russia, observed in 1862 (revised and published under the title *Rus'* [Russia] in 1890). A visit to Prague in 1866 to conduct Glinka's operas was cut short by the Austro-Prussian War; he returned the following year to conduct *Ruslan* and *A Life for the Tsar,* and completed his Overture on Czech Themes (1867; rev. 1905). This work appeared on a program given at the Free School, along with compositions by Borodin, Cui, Rimsky-Korsakov, and Mussorgsky; the critic Vladimir Stasov boasted of Russia's "moguchaya kuchka" [mighty little company], often referred to in the West as "The Mighty Five."

In 1867 he succeeded Anton Rubinstein as conductor of the Russian Musical Society concerts, and the following year he was named director of the Free School; the oriental fantasy for piano *Islamey* was completed in 1869 (rev. 1902). In 1872, desperate for money, he took a job with the Warsaw railway, but soon lost the post, and resigned as director of the Free School in 1874; almost no works date from this dark time when Balakirev shunned musical life. In 1881 he resumed his duties with the Free School, and he completed the symphonic poem *Tamara* the following year. In February 1883 he was appointed director of the imperial court chapel, where his duties were primarily administrative; his often stormy relationship with Rimsky-Korsakov was all but severed in 1890. The last decade of his life, spent in retirement, saw the completion of a number of projects, including the Symphony no. 2 in D minor (1908) and a suite on pieces by Chopin (1909); a revision of the Second Piano Concerto in E♭ remained unfinished at his death and was completed by his pupil Lyapunov. An edition of his piano works and songs was published in Moscow.

Balakirev's impact on Russian orchestral and vocal music rivals Glinka's; a generation of composers, most especially Borodin and Rimsky-Korsakov, came under his influence. Of his own compositions, the early overtures, *Tamara,* songs, and a few piano works (*Islamey* and the B♭ minor Sonata) are of greatest interest.

Bibl.: Edward Garden, *Balakirev: A Critical Study of His Life and Works* (New York, 1967). Mikhail Osipovich Zeitlin, *The Five* (New York, 1959).

Balbastre, Claude-Bénigne (b. Dijon, 22 Jan. 1727; d. Paris, 9 May 1799). Composer and organist. As a child in Dijon he studied organ with his father, Bénigne Balbastre, and possibly also with Claude Rameau. In 1750 he went to Paris, where he continued study of the organ with Pierre Février and began instruction in composition under Jean-Philippe Rameau. From 1755 until the 1780s he performed frequently at the Concert spirituel, often his own works. In 1756 he became organist at St. Roch, and in 1760 at Notre Dame Cathedral. Charles Burney writes of meeting him in Paris in 1770. From 1776 he was employed at the French court, where he played organ for the chapel and taught harpsichord to Marie Antoinette. After the Revolution he lived the rest of his life in poverty. He composed chiefly keyboard works, including collections of harpsichord pieces in the style of François Couperin and Rameau, and some sonatas for keyboard accompanied by two violins and cello and two optional horns.

Balfe, Michael William (b. Dublin, 15 May 1808; d. Rowney Abbey, Hertfordshire, 20 Oct. 1870). Composer. Son of a dancing master, who began teaching him the violin, he went to England after his father's death in 1823 as a pupil of the singer and composer Charles Edward Horn. There he played the violin in orchestras and began to sing baritone roles on stage. In 1825 he went to Italy, where he studied singing and composition, after which, through Rossini's influence, he sang for two seasons at the Théâtre des Italiens in Paris. He sang in Italian opera houses (1829–33) and produced three operas in Italy, including one at La Scala. He returned to London in 1833 and had great success with his first English opera, *The Siege of Rochelle* (Drury Lane, 1835), followed by the success of *The Maid of Artois* (Drury Lane, 1836), with Malibran. This led to the commissioning of an Italian opera, *Falstaff* (1838), for Her Majesty's Theatre, an unusual honor for a British composer.

In 1841 he leased the Lyceum Theatre, turning it into the English Opera House, which he inaugurated successfully with his own *Keolanthe,* but then abandoned in 1842. After this he went to Paris, where he collaborated with Scribe on the successful opéra comique *Les puits d'amour* (Opéra-comique, 1843), which was followed by another in 1844 and a work for the Opéra in 1845. He divided his time with London in this period, producing there his best-known work, *The Bohemian Girl* (Drury Lane, 1843), which had a long worldwide popularity. He continued to compose English operas until his retirement in 1864. The most successful of these was *The Rose of Castile* (1857). In 1846–52 he was conductor at Her Majesty's Theatre. His last opera, *The Knight of the Leopard,* left unfinished, was performed in 1874. Some of his approximately 35 solo songs were also popular.

Bibl.: Charles Lamb Kenney, *A Memoir of Michael William Balfe* (London, 1875; R: New York, 1978). William Alexander Barrett, *Balfe: His Life and Work* (London, 1882).

Ballard, Robert (b. Montreuil-sur-Mer, 1525–30?; d. Paris, buried 8 July 1588). Printer. A founder and the business manager of the French printing firm Le Roy & Ballard. After the death of Attaingnant in 1552, the firm became official music printers to the king. The hundreds of books issued before 1600 contained sacred and secular vocal music (nearly 2,000 French chansons alone), instrumental music, instrumental tutors, and two theoretical treatises.

Bibl.: François Lesure and Geneviève Thibault, *Bibliographie des éditions d'Adrian Le Roy et Robert Ballard* (Paris, 1955); supp. *RdM* 40 (1957): 166.

Balsam, Artur (b. Warsaw, 8 Feb. 1906; d. New York, 1 Sept. 1994). Pianist. Studied at the Łódź Conservatory and the Berlin Hochschule für Musik. Won Berlin International Piano Competition, 1930; Mendelssohn Prize, 1931. Emigrated to U.S., 1933, and taught thereafter at Eastman, Boston Univ., and the Manhattan School of Music. Among his many recordings are two complete sets of Mozart's sonatas. He performed and recorded chamber music with Menuhin, Milstein, Oistrakh, and Rostropovich and as a member of the Balsam–Kroll–Heifetz Trio.

Banchieri, Adriano (Tomaso) (b. Bologna, 3 Sept. 1568; d. there, 1634). Composer, organist, and writer on music. He studied organ and composition with Lucio Barbieri and Gioseffo Guami. In 1587 he joined the order of the Olivetans, and he subsequently lived and worked at its monasteries in Lucca, Siena, Bosco, Imola, Gubbo, Venice, and Verona. In 1609 he settled at S. Michele in Bosco, where he lived for the rest of his life. He was named professor in 1613; abbot in 1618. In 1615 in Bologna he founded the Accademia dei Floridi. He was an associate of Monteverdi, and his writings are important works in early Baroque music theory. *L'organo suonarino* (Venice, 1605) describes accompaniment employing figured bass; the multivolume *Cartella* series (Venice, 1601ff.; including *Moderna pratica musicale,* 1613?; *Cartella musicale,* 1614) proposes the recognition of the "variable seventh" degree, outlines the concept of modern barlines, and gives tables of vocal ornaments. He composed vocal *Concerti ecclesiastici,* Masses, Psalm settings, motets, music for Offices, madrigals, and theater works. These last were actually books of madrigals on related texts, using stock comic characters; they were often performed together as madrigal comedies. They include *La pazzia senile* (1598; ed. in *AMI* 4); *Il metamorfosi musicale* (1601); and *Virtuoso ridotto* (1601; also known as *Servizia giovenile*).

Bibl.: *Opera omnia* (Bologna, 1963–). Oscar Mischiati, "Adriano Banchieri: Profilo biografico e bibliografia delle opere," in *Annuario 1965–1970 del Conservatorio di Musica "G. B. Martini" di Bologna* (Bologna, 1971), pp. 39–201.

Banister, John (b. London, ca. 1625; d. there, 3 Oct. 1679). Composer and violinist. He was sent to France in 1661 to observe Louis XIV's Violons du Roy; upon returning to London he directed, for a brief time, a 12-member ensemble extracted from the King's Violins. He remained in the royal service until his death. In 1672 he began a popular series of concerts in his home and in various concert halls; they are often cited as some of the first public concerts in Europe. From 1677 he was apparently music master for Princess Anne. He composed sacred music; songs for plays (Davenant and Dryden's version of Shakespeare's *The Tempest,* 1667; Shadwell's *Epsom Wells,* 1672); and chamber music (some in *Courtly Masquing Ayres,* 1662, and *New Ayres and Dialogues,* 1678). His son John (b. London, date unknown; d. there, 1725?), also a composer and violinist, joined the King's Violins in 1679 and played alongside him; occasionally the two appeared together in the concert series established by John, Sr. The son composed songs for plays and music for violins.

Banks, Don(ald Oscar) (b. South Melbourne, 25 Oct. 1923; d. Sydney, 5 Sept. 1980). Composer. He played several instruments as a youth, often sitting in with his father's jazz band; studied composition in Melbourne. Went to London in 1950, where he studied with Seiber; other teachers included Babbitt, Dallapiccola, and Nono. Supported himself in London as a copyist, arranger, and composer of music for advertising and films until he began to receive commissions in the 1960s. He returned to Australia in 1971, where he became head of composition and electronic music studies at Canberra School of Music (1974); in 1978 he was head of the School of Composition Studies at the Sydney Conservatorium. Banks usually employed serial procedures; several works are influenced by jazz, and others are recognizably Australian in content. He was a founding member of the British Society for Electronic Music. Works include *Assemblies* (1966) and other orchestral music; *Equation* 1–3, jazz group, ensemble, and tape in no. 3 (1963–72), a string quartet (1975), and other chamber and piano music; choral and vocal pieces; electronic music.

Bantock, Granville (b. London, 7 Aug. 1868; d. there, 16 Oct. 1946). Composer. He was educated at the Royal Academy of Music, 1889–92; there he studied with Frederick Corder and won the Macfarren Scholarship. In 1892 his first opera, *Caedmar,* was performed at the Crystal Palace. In 1893 he became editor of the *New Quarterly Musical Review,* and the following year he launched a successful conducting career. In 1897 he was made conductor of "The Tower" orchestra of New Brighton, where he promoted the music of English composers. He was also an early champion in England of the music of Sibelius. From 1901 he directed the music school at Birmingham, and in 1908 he succeeded Edward Elgar as professor of music at the Univ. of Birmingham. The subsequent two decades were occupied chiefly with prodigious compositional activity. During this period he also held posts as choir conductor at the Wolverhampton Festival and as director of the Liverpool Orchestra. In 1930 he was knighted, and shortly afterward he retired from his university post.

His own music shows influences of Berlioz and Brahms in its orchestral palette and of early Wagner in its tonal vocabulary. Works include 4 operas (*The Pearl of Iran,* 1894; *The Seal-Woman,* 1924); incidental music (*Electra,* 1909; *Fairy Gold,* 1938); vocal works with orchestra (*Christus,* 1901; *The Time Spirit,* 1902; *Omar Khayyam,* 1906–9; *The Pilgrim's Progress,* 1928; *The Sphinx,* 1941); works for chorus (the "symphonies for chorus" *Atlanta in Calydon,* 1911; *Vanity of Vanities,* 1913; *A Pageant of Human Life,* 1913); orchestral music (Tone Poems nos. 1–6; *The Pierrot of the Minute,* overture, 1908); chamber music (2 string quartets, 1899 and 1933; 2 cello sonatas, 1940 and 1945; 3 violin sonatas, 1929, 1932, and 1940); some 40 song cycles (*Songs of the East;* several sets of *Songs from the Chinese Poets*).

Bibl.: Peter J. Pirie, "Bantock and His Generation," *MT* 109 (1968): 715–17. Myrrha Bantock, *Granville Bantock: A Personal Portrait* (London, 1972).

Barber, (Donald) Chris(topher) (b. Welwyn Garden City, England, 17 Apr. 1930). English jazz trombonist and bandleader. He studied trombone and double bass at the Guildhall School of Music, London. From 1954 he led a jazz band originally founded by the trumpeter Ken Colyer. It played in the New Orleans style, also pioneering skiffle, and influenced the "trad" jazz movement in Britain. Barber later broadened his repertory to include blues, rhythm and blues, and fusion. He toured in the U.S., recording with his American band (1960), and brought to Europe musicians as diverse as Sonny Terry, Brownie McGhee, Trummy Young, John Lewis, and Dr. John.

Barber, Samuel (b. West Chester, Pa., 9 Mar. 1910; d. New York, 23 Jan. 1981). Composer. Studied piano from childhood; wrote a juvenile opera and many songs; led a high school orchestra and was organist at a local church. His mother was an amateur pianist; her sister, Louise Homer, and Louise's husband, Sidney, were professional musicians. Barber edited a collection of his uncle's songs in 1943. He entered Curtis when it opened (1924), studying composition (Scalero), piano (Boyle, Vengerova), conducting (Reiner), and voice (Emilio de Gogorza); received his B.M. in 1934.

One of the most successful American composers of the 20th century, Barber taught briefly at Curtis (1939–42), but otherwise devoted himself to composition. His early works include a violin sonata (lost; awarded the Bearns Prize from Columbia, 1928) and the Serenade for string quartet or string orchestra. Songs and works for piano, the well-known *Dover Beach* (voice and string quartet, 1931), and the Cello Sonata (1932) were also written during his student years. By the time he left Curtis his works had been performed in New York and Philadelphia (*The School for Scandal,* an overture awarded the Bearns Prize in 1933, premiered by the Philadelphia Orchestra); he had begun his lifelong friendship with Menotti; and he had spent several summers in Europe, where he and Menotti met Toscanini in 1933. The Rome Prize and a Pulitzer Traveling Scholarship enabled him to spend 1935–36 in Rome. During the 1930s his works were performed by major orchestras and soloists, the famous Adagio for Strings (an arrangement of the second movement of his String Quartet, 1936) and the first *Essay for Orchestra* premiered by the NBC Symphony Orchestra under Toscanini in New York (5 Nov. 1938). He served in the U.S. Air Force during the Second World War, composing *Commando March* for band (1943) and his Second Symphony (1944; later revised). Ormandy, Szell, Walter, Koussevitzky, and other well-known conductors programmed his works in the 1940s; Horowitz introduced his piano sonata (commissioned by the League of Composers, funded by Berlin and Rodgers) in Cuba and New York (1949–50). This success continued throughout his life, John Browning introducing his piano concerto in 1962 with the Boston Symphony under Leinsdorf, and Mehta premiering his third *Essay* with the New York Philharmonic (14 Sept. 1978). His songs have been particularly well received, especially *Knoxville: Summer of 1915* (premiered by Eleanor Steber with the Boston Symphony, 9 Apr. 1948) and the *Hermit Songs* on Irish medieval texts (premiered by Leontyne Price accompanied by the composer in Washington, 30 Oct. 1953). He won two Pulitzer Prizes (*Vanessa,* an opera on a libretto by Menotti, 1958; the Piano Concerto, 1962, which also won the New York Critics' Circle Award). Often described as a romanticist in expression and a classicist in his use of form, he wrote in a consistently lyrical vein; in works composed after 1939 his style became more dissonant, and intervals or single pitches replaced traditional keys as tonal foci; his use of canon and fugue is also notable.

Other works include the opera *Antony and Cleopatra* (libretto by Zefirelli, after Shakespeare, 1966); the ballet *Medea* for Martha Graham (1946; first titled *The Serpent Heart,* rev. as *Cave of the Heart,* 1947); 2 symphonies (1936; 1944, rev. 1947, 2nd movt. rev. as *Night Flight,* 1964, other movts. destroyed) and other orchestral music (*Essay for Orchestra* no. 1, 1937, no. 2, 1942, no. 3, 1978; *Capricorn Concerto,* 1944; a violin concerto, 1940; a cello concerto, 1945; a piano concerto, 1962); numerous choral works; chamber music; piano pieces (*Nocturne [Homage to John Field],* 1959); many songs.

Bibl.: D. A. Hennessee, *Samuel Barber: A Bio-Bibliography* (Westport, Conn., 1985). Barbara B. Heyman, *Samuel Barber: the Composer and His Music* (New York, 1992).

Barbieri, Francisco Asenjo (b. Madrid, 3 Aug. 1823; d. there, 17 Feb. 1894). Composer. Studied at the Madrid Conservatory from 1837 (composition with Carnicer); thereafter lived a wandering life at various lowly musical occupations. Returned permanently to Madrid in 1846 and devoted himself to furthering Spanish music, establishing a periodical, *La España musical,* doing extensive research and assembling the best music library in Spain for a history of Spanish music (never written), and helping to organize the society that led to the Teatro de la Zarzuela (1856). His most important scholarly work was an edition, *Cancionero musical de los siglos XV y XVI* (Madrid, 1890; 2nd ed., 1945; facs., Málaga, 1987). He is most widely remembered for his 72 zarzuelas, to which he tried to give a strongly Spanish musical character. His first, *Gloria y peluca* (1850), was successful. *Tramoya* (1850) was widely performed in Spanish-speaking countries. *Pan y toros* (1864), whose hero is the painter Goya, was his greatest and most enduring success. Others still remembered include *Jugar con fuego* (1851) and *El barberillo de Lavapiés* (1874).

Bibl.: Angel Salcedo, *Francisco Asenjo Barbieri: Su vida y sus obras* (Madrid, 1912). Gilbert Chase, "Barbieri and the Spanish Zarzuela," *ML* 20 (1939): 32–39. Augusto Martinez Olmedilla, *El maestro Barbieri y su tiempo* (Madrid, 1941; 2nd ed., 1950).

Barbieri, Gato [Leandro J.] (b. Rosario, Argentina, 28 Nov. 1934). Jazz tenor saxophonist and bandleader. In Buenos Aires he played alto saxophone with Lalo Schifrin. After switching to the tenor, he moved to Rome (1962) and in Paris joined Don Cherry's free jazz group (1964–66), recording the album *Complete Communion* (1965). Beginning in the late 1960s he led groups that combined his free jazz improvising with dance rhythms and simple melodies drawn from Latin American popular music, as on the album *Chapter One: Latin America* (1973). He performed in the movie *Last Tango in Paris* (1972).

Barbireau, Jacques [Jacobus] (b. ca. 1420; d. Antwerp, 8 Aug. 1491). Composer. Choirmaster at Notre Dame Cathedral in Antwerp, where he oversaw a considerable expansion of the choir, from 1448 to his death; was succeeded by Obrecht. His 7 extant works include Masses, a motet, and 3 songs. One song, "Een vroylic wesen," for 3 voices, was internationally famous.

Bibl.: *Opera omnia, CMM* 7 (1954–57).

Barbirolli, John [Giovanni Battista] (b. London, 2 Dec. 1899; d. there, 29 July 1970). Conductor and cellist. Studied cello at the Trinity College of Music and Royal Academy of Music; debut in 1916 at Queens Hall. Active in chamber music before founding the Barbirolli String Orchestra, 1924. Conductor of the Chenil Orchestra, 1925; of the National Opera Company, 1926. Guest conductor of the London Symphony and the Royal Philharmonic, 1927; of the Royal Opera at Covent Garden, 1928. Conductor of the Scottish Orchestra in Glasgow, 1933–36. Guest conductor of the New York Philharmonic, 1936–37; music director, 1937–42. Wartime sentiment lured him back to England in 1942. Permanent conductor of the Hallé Orchestra in Manchester, 1943–58; principal conductor, 1958–68. Conductor-in-chief of the Houston Symphony, 1960–66. Knighted in 1949. His repertory ranged from Bach to Berg, with special sympathy for Elgar and Vaughan Williams.

Barce, Ramón (b. Madrid, 16 Mar. 1928). Composer and critic. At the Univ. of Madrid he studied language and literature; as a composer was chiefly self-taught. He helped found several Spanish new music groups, including the Nueva música (1958), the Aula de música del Ateneo (1959), and the "Zaj" group (1964). As a critic he founded the journal *Sonda* and, from 1971, wrote for the newspaper *Ya* in Madrid. His compositions, which employ serial and nonserial atonality, include an opera, *Los bárbaros* (1965–73); theater music (*Abgrund, Hintergrund,* 1964); choral music (Cantata, soprano, chamber ensemble, 1966); orchestral works (*Las cuatro estaciones,* 1967; *Concierto de Lizara* no. 1, oboe, trumpet, percussion, string orchestra, 1969); chamber music (*Objetos sonoros,* 1966); piano music (*Estudio de sonoridades,* 1962; *Estudio de densidades,* 1965; 48 preludes, 1974–83).

Bardi, Giovanni de' (b. Florence, 5 Feb. 1534; d. Rome, Sept. 1612). Poet and writer on music. Member of a noble family, he was evidently schooled in mathematics, philosophy, and literature. As a youth he served in several military campaigns, including Maximilian II's expulsion of the Turks from Hungary. From 1592 he was a *maestro di camera* at the papal court and an officer in the guard. He helped fund the education of Vincenzo Galilei, Giulio Caccini, and possibly others; during the 1570s and 1580s his home became a gathering place for Florentine composers and poets. This group, which Caccini called "Bardi's camerata" in his preface to *Le nuove musiche* (1601), included Bardi himself, Piero Strozzi, Galilei, and Caccini; its mentor was Girolamo Mei. Bardi's views on music are set forth in a discourse he addressed to Caccini (excerpted in *SR,* pp. 290–301). Bardi criticized complex contrapuntal music and advocated homophonic textures and a declamatory vocal style. He also composed a handful of madrigals.

Bibl.: Claude V. Palisca, *Girolamo Mei (1519–1594): Letters on Ancient and Modern Music to Vincenzo Galilei and*

Giovanni Bardi, MSD 3 (Rome, 1960). Id., "The 'Camerata Fiorentina': A Reappraisal," *Studi musicali* 1 (1972): 203–36.

Barenboim, Daniel (b. Buenos Aires, 15 Nov. 1942). Conductor and pianist. Studied piano with his father from age 5. Buenos Aires debut, 1950. Studied piano with Edwin Fischer and conducting with Igor Markevitch at the Mozarteum in Salzburg, 1952; then violin, theory, and composition at the Santa Cecilia Academy in Rome (diploma, 1956). Won Alfredo Casella Piano Competition, Naples, 1956. U.S. debut with Stokowski, 20 Jan. 1957. Conducting debut with Melbourne and Sydney Symphony Orchestras, 1962. A close association with the English Chamber Orchestra began 1964. Conducted *Don Giovanni* in Edinburgh, 1972. Music director of the Orchestre de Paris from 1975; of the Bastille Opéra in Paris, 1988–89; of the Chicago Symphony from 1991; of the Deutsche Staatsoper in Berlin from 1993. Beethoven Medal, 1958; Beethoven Society Medal, 1982. As a pianist he devoted particular attention to Mozart and Beethoven; his repertory as a conductor extends beyond these composers to Bach and to the late 19th century. He published an autobiography, *Daniel Barenboim: A Life in Music,* ed. Michael Lewin (New York, 1992).

Bargiel, Woldemar (b. Berlin, 3 Oct. 1828; d. there, 23 Feb. 1897). Composer and teacher. The son of Clara Schumann's mother and her second husband, a Berlin music teacher, he was taught by his parents and Dehn (in counterpoint) and then at the Leipzig Conservatory, 1846–50, by Moscheles, Hauptmann, Rietz, and Gade. After establishing himself as a teacher and composer in Berlin, he was made professor of theory at the Cologne Conservatory in 1859 and in 1865–74 was Kapellmeister in Rotterdam and director of its principal music institution, the Association for the Furthering of Music. From 1874 he was professor of composition at the Berlin Hochschule für Musik.

His reputation as a composer was high in his lifetime. Works include a symphony, 3 concert overtures, a string octet, 4 string quartets, 3 piano trios, 4 Psalm settings with orchestra, and many piano works, including sonatas and suites for 2 and 4 hands and numerous collections of short pieces and etudes.

Barkauskas, Vitautas (b. Kaunas, Lithuania, 25 Mar. 1931). Composer. Concurrent with piano studies at the Vilnius Music School, pursued studies in physics and mathematics at the Lithuanian State Pedagogical Institute, graduating in 1953. Studied composition at the Vilnius Conservatory with Antanas Raciunas, 1953–59; beginning 1961 taught theoretical subjects there. His music makes use of serial and aleatoric techniques. Works include an opera (*Legend about Love,* 1975); 3 symphonies (1962, 1971, 1979) and other orchestral music; works for chorus and orchestra (*Hope,* oratorio, 1988); chamber music; works for piano; *The Rebirth of Hope,* organ (1989); incidental and film music.

Barlow, Wayne (Brewster) (b. Elyria, Ohio, 6 Sept. 1912). Composer. As a child he studied piano and violin; he went on to study at the Eastman School (1930–37; Ph.D., 1937) and under Schoenberg at the Univ. of Southern California (1935). He studied electronic music with Schaeffer at the Univ. of Toronto, and then in Belgium and Holland as the recipient of his second Fulbright grant (1963–64). He was associated with the Eastman School after joining its faculty in 1937, becoming chairman of the department of composition (1968–73), director of the electronic music studio (1968–78), and professor emeritus (1978). For much of his teaching career he was an organist and choirmaster in Rochester (1946–78). He is the author of *Foundations of Music* (New York, 1953; R: 1983).

His works, which range from tonal to freely serial to electronic, include ballets; pieces for orchestra (*The Winter's Passed,* oboe and strings, 1938; *Night Song,* 1957; *Soundscapes,* orchestra and tape, 1972); chamber music (Trio, oboe, violin, piano, 1964); works for soloists, chorus, and orchestra or instrumental ensemble, some with tape; choral works; works for piano; works for organ (4 vols. of hymn voluntaries, 1963–80).

Barnet, Charlie [Charles Daly] (b. New York, 26 Oct. 1913; d. 4 Sept. 1991). Jazz bandleader and saxophonist. After playing on cruise ships, he led big bands regularly from 1933 to the 1950s and intermittently thereafter. Billy May's arrangement of *Cherokee,* recorded in 1939, shows off the band's swinging dance riffs. Barnet admired the leading African American bands and especially imitated Duke Ellington's orchestra. He furthered integration in jazz by hiring many prominent African American musicians, including Benny Carter, as early as 1935.

Barnett, John (b. Bedford, 15 July 1802; d. Leckhampton, 16 or 17 Apr. 1890). Composer. The son of a German diamond merchant named Beer, who changed his name on emigrating. Barnett sang on the London stage 1813–18 while studying piano and composition and beginning to compose. In 1826–33 he composed much music for light stage pieces. In 1834 he produced *The Mountain Sylph,* a through-composed English "romantic opera" that remained popular for the rest of the century. Two other large works, but with spoken dialogue (*Fair Rosamond,* 1837, and *Farinelli,* 1839), followed before Barnett, embittered by the theatrical world, moved in 1841 to Cheltenham, where he taught singing. Many of his songs, said to number 2,000, were very popular. He also composed a few instrumental and sacred works and published 2 vocal methods.

Bibl.: Bruce Carr, "The First All-Sung English 19th-Century Opera," *MT* 115 (1974): 125–26.

Barraine, Elsa (b. Paris, 13 Feb. 1910). Composer. She studied with Dukas (composition), Caussade (fugue), and Jean Gallon (harmony) at the Paris Conservatory; won the Prix de Rome in 1929. From 1936 to 1939 she worked as choral director for French Radio; taught at the conservatory, 1954–75. She composed a comic opera (*Le roi bossu,* 1932); *Claudine à l'école* (after Colette, 1950) and several other ballets; incidental music and film scores; 2 symphonies (1931, 1938), *Les jongleurs* (1959), and other orchestral pieces; several works for soloists, chorus, and orchestra (*Christine,* 1959); *Atmosphère* (oboe and 10 instruments, 1966), *Musique rituelle après le Bardo Thödol* (organ, gongs, xylorimba, 1966–67), and other chamber music; several piano and organ works (*La boîte de Pandore,* sight reading exercises for pianists, 1955); a few songs (*3 chansons hébraïques,* 1935).

Barraqué, Jean (b. Puteaux, Seine, 17 Jan. 1928; d. Paris, 17 Aug. 1973). Composer. He studied at the Paris Conservatory with Langlais, and then with Messiaen (1948–51); worked with the Groupe de musique concrète at French Radio (1951–54), where he produced his only electronic piece (*Étude,* 1954). He was not linked to any particular school of composition but employed serial procedures in the service of a lyrical style. In addition to several articles, he wrote a book on the music of Debussy (1962). Early works include the 40-minute Sonata for Piano (1950–52) and *Séquence* (after Nietzsche, soprano and instrumental ensemble, 1950–55). In 1955 he began a large work based on the French translation of Hermann Broch's *The Death of Virgil;* although the project remained unfinished at his death, 3 of the 5 projected parts were completed and performed: . . . *au delà du hasard* (soprano, female chorus, 20 instruments in 4 groups, 1958–59), *Chant après chant* (soprano, piano, 6 percussionists, 1966), and *Le temps restitué* (soprano, choir of 12 voices, 31 instruments, 1957; orchestrated 1968). The *Concerto* (clarinet, vibraphone, 6 groups of 3 instruments, 1968) is not part of the series, but neither is it independent: rather, it is "a work which casts its gaze upon another work."

Bibl.: André Hodeir, "Barraqué," in *Since Debussy: A View of Contemporary Music,* trans. Noel Burch (New York, 1961; R: 1975), pp. 163–210. Rose-Marie Janzen, "A Biographical Chronology of Jean Barraqué," *PNM* 27 (1989): 234–45.

Barraud, Henry (b. Bordeaux, 23 Apr. 1900). Composer. He had composed from his youth, but worked in the family wine trade before finally entering the Paris Conservatory in 1926. He studied with Dukas, Caussade, and Aubert, but was expelled after a brief period, apparently for a string quartet he composed that was considered too innovative. In the early 1930s Pierre Monteux conducted two of his works for orchestra (*Finale of a Symphony* and *Poème*), and in 1933 Barraud cofounded with Rivier the Triton Concerts for performance of contemporary works. He worked in broadcasting for the Resistance during the Second World War, and afterwards joined Radiodiffusion française, from which he retired in 1965. He is the author of a book on Berlioz (1955; 2nd ed., 1966), and 3 other volumes (*La France et la musique occidentale,* 1956; *Pour comprendre les musiques d'aujourd'hui,* 1968; *Les cinq grands opéras,* 1972). His works include operas, ballets, film and radio scores; *Images pour un poète maudit* (after Rimbaud, 1954) and other works for orchestra; a string trio, string quartet, saxophone quartet (1972), and other chamber music; *10 Impromptus* (1941), *Musiques pour les petits mains* (1949), and other piano works; several large-scale vocal works (*Le mystère des Saints Innocents,* solo voices, chorus, and orchestra, 1946–47; *La divine comédie,* 5 solo voices, orchestra, 1972); and songs.

Barrett, Syd [Roger] (b. Cambridge, England, 6 Jan. 1946). Rock singer, songwriter, and guitarist. After early performances as a folksinger in London, he founded the band Pink Floyd with David Gilmour, Roger Waters, Richard Wright, and Nick Mason in 1965. He composed much of their early album *Pipers at the Gates of Dawn* (1967), gaining recognition for his surrealistic and mystical lyrics; the group was also the first in Britain to incorporate light shows and other visual effects into their live performances. After his departure from the band in 1968, his work was released by Harvest Records as *The Madcap Laughs* (1974).

Barry, Gerald Anthony (b. County Clare, Ireland, 28 Apr. 1952). Composer. He studied at Univ. College, Dublin, where he earned a B.Mus. in 1973, an M.A. in 1975, and a Diploma in Music Teaching. He also studied at the Royal Conservatory in The Hague and at the Cologne Hochschule für Musik, where his teachers included Stockhausen and Kagel. He was a founding member of the Association of Irish Composers. Works include *The Intelligence Park,* 3-act opera (1981–87); *Things That Gain By Being Painted,* soprano, speaker, cello, piano (1977); *Ein Klavier Konzert* (1978); *Décolletage,* soprano, actress (1979); *Ø,* 2 pianos (1979); *Sleeping Beauty,* 2 performers, bass drum (1980); *Unkrautgarten,* ballet (1980); the music theater pieces *Cinderella* (1981) and *Snow-White* (1981); *La traviata,* radio play (1981); *Handel's Favorite Song,* clarinet, ensemble (1981); *Sweet Cork,* soprano, bass, recorder, viol, and harpsichord (1985); *Of Queen's Gardens,* chamber orchestra (1986); *Chevaux-de-frise,* orchestra (1988); *Diner,* orchestra (1988); *Cork,* string quartet (1985); *Sweet Punishment,* brass quintet (1987); Oboe Quartet (1988); *Au milieu,* piano (1981); *Sur les pointes,* piano (1981); Five Chorales, 2 pianos (1984).

Barsanti, Francesco (b. Lucca, 1690; d. London, 1772). Composer. He studied science at the Univ. of Padua, and from 1714 played oboe and flute with the Italian opera in London. There he also had his first solo sonatas published (in 1724). By 1735 he was in Edinburgh, where he published his 10 concerti grossi (1742) and 9 overtures (1743). He returned to London in 1743, took a job as orchestral violist, and continued

Béla Bartók, 1936.

to compose. Subsequent publications include 6 *antifoni* (ca. 1750); 6 solo sonatas (op. 6, 1769); several concertos for violin and orchestra; and a number of arrangements of chamber music by his fellow Luccan Geminiani; also sacred music and Latin motets.

Bartók, Béla (b. Nagyszentmiklós, now Sînnicolau Mare, Romania, 25 Mar. 1881; d. New York, 26 Sept. 1945). Composer and ethnomusicologist. His mother was a pianist, and his first lessons on the instrument were from her. His father, a teacher at an agriculture school, died when Bartók was young; after this the family was forced to move frequently. In Nagyszöllös the boy wrote his first pieces; later at Nagyvárad (Oradea, Romania) he studied piano with Ferenc Kersch. In 1894 the family moved to Pozsony (Bratislava), where he studied with László Erkel (piano) and Anton Hyrtl (theory). He entered the Budapest Academy of Music in 1899; there his teachers were Thomán (piano) and Koessler (composition). His pianism had advanced to such a degree that he was able to make his Budapest solo debut in 1901, playing the Liszt B minor Sonata. A growing acquaintance with the works of Wagner and Richard Strauss is apparent in his own works from this period.

Around 1906 he and Zoltán Kodály began collecting folk songs in Hungarian villages (later in Romania, Slovakia, Bulgaria, and Serbo-Croatia). From 1908 he began to assimilate both the spirit and the substance of these melodies in his own music. The year 1910 saw first performances of the String Quartet no. 1 and the Piano Quintet. Bartók's frail health prevented him from serving in World War I, and during this period he composed the Piano Suite and the Second String Quartet; soon after the war he completed the ballet *The Wooden Prince,* which (unlike its predecessor from 1911, the opera *Duke Bluebeard's Castle*) was an immediate success in Budapest. By 1918 he was beginning to achieve international renown. In 1923 he divorced his first wife, Márta (whom he had married in 1909), and married another pupil, Ditta Pásztory; their son Péter was born in 1924. In 1926 Bartók composed, for his own concert tours, a number of large piano works, including the First Piano Concerto, the Sonata, and the *Out of Doors* suite. In 1927–28 he toured the U.S.

The years 1927–33 were prolific ones: dating from this period are the String Quartets nos. 3 and 4, the important *Cantata Profana,* and the Piano Concerto no. 2. In 1934 the Hungarian Academy of Sciences provided a grant for him to publish his work on Hungarian folk song; this collection alone had expanded to 13,000 items. As a reaction to growing fascism, in 1937 he switched publishers, from Universal to London-based Boosey & Hawkes.

Driven out by war and fascism, the Bartóks left Budapest for the last time in 1940. Shortly after arriving in New York, the composer received a stipend from Columbia Univ. to transcribe and classify a collection of Yugoslav folk song recordings housed at Harvard. Despite failing health he continued to compose and give lectures, and he and his wife performed in concerts. During this period he also completed his work on Romanian and Turkish music; both remained in manuscript until after his death. His last compositions were the Concerto for Orchestra, commissioned by Koussevitzky; the Piano Concerto no. 3, written for his wife and completed save for 17 bars; and the Viola Concerto, which was left unorchestrated.

Works: *Stage. A Kékszakállú herceg vára* [Duke Bluebeard's Castle], opera (1911–12; first perf. 1918); *A fából faragott királyfi* [The Wooden Prince], ballet (1914–17); *A csodálatos mandarin* [The Miraculous Mandarin], pantomime (1918–23; rev. 1924–31).

Chorus. Cantata Profana, soloists, chorus, orchestra (1930; first perf. 1934); also many choral settings of folk songs.

Orchestra. Scherzo in B♭ (1902–3); *Kossuth,* symphonic poem (1903); Rhapsody op. 1, piano, orchestra (arr. of Rhapsody for Piano below; 1904); Suite no. 1, op. 3 (1905; rev. 1920); Suite no. 2, op. 4, small orchestra (1905–7; rev. 1920, 1943); 2 violin concertos (no. 1, 1907–8, first perf. 1958, first mvt. rev. as first of 2 Portraits op. 5; no. 2, 1937–38); Four Pieces op. 12 (1912, 1921); *The Wooden Prince,* suite (1921–24); *The Miraculous Mandarin,* suite (1919; 1927); *Táncszvit* [Dance Suite] (1923); 3 piano concertos (1926; 1930–31; 1945); 2 Rhapsodies, violin, orchestra (both 1928; arr. of Rhapsodies, violin, piano, below; no. 2 rev. 1944); *Music for Strings, Percussion, and Celesta* (1936); Divertimento, strings (1939); Concerto, 2 pianos (1940; original version Sonata, 2 pianos, percussion); Concerto for Orchestra (1943; rev. 1945); Viola Concerto (1945; first perf. 1949).

Chamber music. 2 early string quartets (both 1896; both lost); Piano Quartet in C minor (1898); Duo, 2 violins (1902); Piano Quintet (1903–4; rev. 1920); 6 string quartets (no. 1, op. 7, 1908; no. 2, op. 17, 1915–17; no. 3, 1927; no. 4, 1928; no. 5, 1934; no. 6, 1939); 2 sonatas, violin and piano (1921; 1922); 2 rhapsodies, violin and piano (both 1928; arr. as Rhapsodies, violin, orchestra, above); 44 duos, 2 violins (in 4 vols.,

1931); *Contrasts,* violin, clarinet, piano (1938); Sonata, solo violin (1944).

Piano. Many lost and fragmentary early works (1890–ca. 1900); Rhapsody op. 1 (1904); 14 Bagatelles op. 6 (1908); *10 Easy Pieces* (1908); *Gyermekeknek* [For Children] (1908–9; rev. 1945); *7 Sketches* op. 9b (1908–10; rev. 1945); 4 Dirges op. 9a (1909–10); 3 Burlesques op. 8c (1908–11); *Allegro barbaro* (1911); *Romanian Christmas Carols* (1915); Suite op. 14 (1916); *3 Hungarian Folktunes* (1914–18); *15 Hungarian Peasant Songs* (1914–18); 3 Etudes op. 18 (1918); *8 Improvisations on Hungarian Peasant Songs* (1920); Sonata (1926); *Szabadban* [Out of Doors] (1926); *9 Little Pieces* (1926); *Mikrokosmos* (in 6 vols., 1926–39); Suite, 2 pianos (1941).

More than 100 original songs and folk song arrangements.

Writings: With Albert B. Lord, *Serbo-Croatian Folk Songs: Texts and Transcriptions . . .* (New York, 1951). Denijs Dille, ed., *Bartók Béla: Ethnomusikologische Schriften* (Budapest and Mainz, 1965–68). Benjamin Suchoff, ed., *Béla Bartók: Rumanian Folk Music,* texts trans. E. C. Teodorescu, 5 vols. (The Hague, 1967–75). Id., ed., *Béla Bartók: Essays* (London, 1976). Id., ed., *Turkish Folk Music from Asia Minor* (Princeton, 1976). Id., ed., *Yugoslav Folk Music,* 4 vols. (Albany, N.Y., 1978). Id., ed., *The Hungarian Folksong,* trans. M. D. Calvocoressi (Albany, N.Y., 1981).

Bibl.: Denijs Dille, ed., *Thematisches Verzeichnis der Jugendwerke Béla Bartóks* (Kassel and Budapest, 1974). János Demény, ed., *Bartók Béla levelei* [Bartók letters] (Budapest, 1948–71; 2nd ed., 1976); trans. Péter Balabán and István Farkas (London and New York, 1971). Benjamin Suchoff, *Guide to Bartók's Mikrokosmos* (London, 1956; rev. 2nd ed., 1971). Bence Szabolcsi, ed., *Bartók: sa vie et son oeuvre* [with catalog of works and writings] (Budapest, 1956; rev. 2nd ed., 1968; enl. 2nd ed., 1972). József Ujfalussy, ed., *Bartók breviárium: Levelek, írások, dokumentumok* [letters and documents] (Budapest, 1958; rev. 2nd ed., 1974). Victor Bator, *The Béla Bartók Archives: History and Catalogue* (New York, 1963). Denijs Dille, ed., *Documenta bartókiana* (Budapest and Mainz, 1964–70). John W. Downey, *La musique populaire dans l'oeuvre de Béla Bartók* (Paris, 1966). John Vinton, "Bartók on His Music," *JAMS* 19 (1966): 232–43. *Béla Bartók: A Complete Catalogue of His Published Works* [not a thematic catalog] (London and Budapest, 1970). Ernő Lendvai, *Béla Bartók: An Analysis of His Music* (London, 1971). László Vikár, ed., *Ahmed Adnan Saygun: Béla Bartók's Folk Music Research in Turkey* (Budapest, 1976). László Somfai, ed., *Documenta bartókiana* (Budapest, 1977–). Paul Griffiths, *Bartók* (London, 1984). Elliott Antokoletz, *Béla Bartók: A Guide to Research* (New York, 1988). Paul Wilson, *The Music of Béla Bartók* (New Haven, 1992). Halsey Stevens, *The Life and Music of Béla Bartók* (Oxford, 1993). Malcolm Gillies, *The Bartók Companion* (Portland, 1994). László Somfai, *Béla Bartók: Composition, Concepts, and Autograph Sources* (Berkeley, 1996).

Bartolozzi, Bruno (b. Florence, 8 June 1911; d. there, 12 Dec. 1980). Composer and theorist. He studied violin and composition (Fragapane, Dallapiccola) at the Florence Conservatory and at the Accademia Chigiana in Siena. He played violin in the Maggio musicale fiorentino (1941–65). In 1964 he began to teach at the Florence Conservatory, where he directed the orchestra. Edited a series of string and wind methods, the most important of which is a treatise on woodwind techniques that describes the production of chords and of pitches outside the tempered scale (1967; 2nd ed., 1980). In his compositions he employed serialism, aleatoric methods, quarter tones, and speech-song, as well as new playing techniques for most instruments. His works include *Tutto ciò che accade ti riguarda* (mixed media, 1972); orchestral music; chamber music for a variety of instrumental ensembles (*Concertazioni,* 4 flutes, oboe, clarinet, bassoon, 1969), often including guitar; many works for solo instruments, sometimes unspecified (*The Hollow Man,* any woodwind, 1968); a few vocal works.

Basie, Count [William] (b. Red Bank, N.J., 21 Aug. 1904; d. Hollywood, Fla., 26 Apr. 1984). Jazz bandleader and pianist. He toured as a vaudeville pianist (mid-1920s); while in New York he had informal organ lessons with Fats Waller. He joined Walter Page in Oklahoma (1928–29) and Bennie Moten's Kansas City Orchestra (1929–33), led members of Moten's group (1933–35), briefly rejoined Moten (1935), and then in Kansas City formed a 9-piece group that expanded to 14 musicians (including the singer Jimmy Rushing) in 1936. Basie's big band favored a simple repertory of head arrangements that combined swing riffs with strong soloists, including Lester Young, Buck Clayton, Herschel Evans, Harry Edison, the trombonist Benny Morton, Dicky Wells, and Vic Dickenson. Basie, the guitarist Freddie Green, Page, and Jo Jones formed the definitive rhythm section of the swing era. Though fluent in the busy stride piano style, Basie developed the most economical piano style in jazz, supplying sparse accentuations as an accompanist and varying simple motives as a soloist. In the 1940s his band increasingly used formal arrangements. In 1950–52 he led small groups that included Clark Terry and Buddy DeFranco. Re-forming a big band, with Thad Jones, Eddie "Lockjaw" Davis, Frank Foster, Joe Newman, the trombonist Al Grey, and Frank Wess among its soloists and Foster and Neil Hefti among its arrangers of the 1950s and 1960s, he toured internationally into the 1980s. After his death Thad Jones and then Foster assumed the leadership.

Basie's recordings with small groups include "Shoe Shine Boy" (1936) and "Lester Leaps In" (1939); with big bands, "One O'Clock Jump" (1937), "Every Tub," "Doggin' Around," "Jumpin' at the Woodside" (all 1938), "Taxi War Dance" (1939), and the albums *April in Paris* (1955–56) and *The Atomic Mr. Basie* (1957).

Writings: With Albert Murray, *Good Morning Blues: The Autobiography of Count Basie* (New York, 1985).

Bibl.: Stanley Dance, *The World of Count Basie* (New York, 1980). Count Basie, *Good Morning Blues: The Autobiography of Count Basie as Told to Albert Murray* (New York, 1985). Chris Sheridan, *Count Basie: A Bio-Discography* (Westport, Conn., 1986).

Basiron [Baziron], **Philippe** (b. early 15th cent.; d. before 6 Feb. 1497). Composer. Referred to in Guillaume Crétin's *déploration* on the death of Ockeghem (d. 6 Feb. 1497) as having been a singer; mentioned as a "gran musicien" of the 15th century in a book of 1508. Early 16th-century prints include a Mass and two motets under his name. Other extant works are another motet and 5 song settings with French texts. If he is identical with "Philippon," "Philipus," and "Philipus Franc," as some scholars have maintained, he wrote several additional works, including 3 Masses, an Agnus Dei, 3 motets, and 2 songs.

Bassani, Giovanni Battista (b. Padua, ca. 1657; d. Bergamo, 1 Oct. 1716). Composer and violinist. He studied in Venice, possibly with Legrenzi (composition) and Vitali (violin); also with Castrovillari. He was a member of the Accademia della morte in Ferrara (1667) and of the Accademia filarmonica in Bologna from 1677. *Maestro di cappella* at the Confraternità del finale in Modena from 1677; at the court of Duke Alessandro II from 1680; at the Accademia della morte in Ferrara from 1684; and at the cathedral in Ferrara from 1686. In 1712 he went to Bergamo, where he taught music and directed at S. Maria Maggiore. He composed at least 9 operas (all lost except for 10 arias from *Gli amori alla moda,* Ferrara, 1688); some 15 oratorios; madrigals, *ariette,* cantatas; and instrumental works. His sacred works include 13 whole Mass settings and numerous segments; and motets, Psalm settings, and antiphons.

Bibl.: Richard Haselbach, *Giovanni Battista Bassani: Werkkatalog, Biographie und künstlerische Würdigung* (Kassel, 1955).

Bassett, Leslie (Raymond) (b. Hanford, Calif., 22 Jan. 1923). Composer. A pianist and trombone player, he studied with Finney at the Univ. of Michigan and with Honegger and Boulanger (1950–51). Later teachers included Gerhard (1960) and Davidovsky (electronic music, 1964). From 1952 he was on the faculty of the Univ. of Michigan. He received the Pulitzer Prize (1966) for *Variations for Orchestra* (1963). His *Echoes from an Invisible World* was commissioned by the Philadelphia Orchestra (27 Feb. 1976). Both *Variations* and *Echoes* illustrate Bassett's frequent practice of unfolding a lengthy composition from a set of small elements to which the work returns at its close. *Echoes* has been called "romantically impressionistic" as well. He composed a few serial and electronic pieces in the 1960s, but his works are often for conventional instruments and focus on orchestral color. His choral and vocal music usually employs serious or religious texts.

Approximately 20 early works were withdrawn by the composer. After 1961 he composed several pieces for orchestra (*Concerto lirico,* with tuba soloist, 1983) and for band (*Colors and Contours,* 1984); chamber music for strings or strings with piano (*Duo-Inventions,* 2 cellos, 1988); works for various combinations of winds or brass instruments, some with piano (*Dialogues,* oboe, piano, 1987); a work for 5 guitars; choral music and solo vocal music with keyboard or instrumental ensemble; keyboard music (*Liturgies,* organ, 1980).

Bibl.: Ellen S. Johnson, *Leslie Bassett: a Bio-Bibliography* (Westport, 1994).

Bateson, Thomas (b. Cheshire County, 1570–75?; d. Dublin, Mar. 1630). Composer. Organist of Chester Cathedral from 1599; from 1609 organist and vicar-choral at Christ Church Cathedral, Dublin. Received the degrees of B.Mus. and M.A. from Trinity College, Dublin. Extant compositions include one anthem and two books of madrigals, including one piece composed for *The Triumphes of Oriana* (1601) but not published in that collection.

Batten [Battin], **Adrian** (b. Salisbury, bapt. 1 Mar. 1591; d. London, 1637). Composer. As a youth he apparently served at Winchester Cathedral, probably as choirboy; his name is carved on the wall of the chantry (with the date 1608). He moved to London and in 1614 was made lay vicar at Westminster Abbey; there he served until 1624, when he became vicar-choral at St. Paul's Cathedral. He composed many services and anthems and is best known as the scribe of the "Batten-Organbook," a manuscript housed at St. Michael's College, Tenbury. It is one of the largest collections of English church music of the period.

Bibl.: J. Bunker Clark and Maurice Bevan, "New Biographical Facts about Adrian Batten," *JAMS* 23 (1970): 331–33.

Battishill, Jonathan (b. London, May 1738; d. Islington, 10 Dec. 1801). Organist, harpsichordist, and composer. During his service in the choir at St. Paul's (from 1747), he received musical training from William Savage. In the 1750s he appeared as tenor soloist in London concerts and as conductor and harpsichordist at Covent Garden. During the 1760s he became a member of the local Catch Club, for which he composed catches and glees. He assumed positions as organist at St. Clement, Eastcheap (1764), and at Christ Church, Newgate (1767). With Michael Arne he composed an opera, *Almena* (1764); also a pantomime, *The Rites of Hecate,* a number of hymns and anthems, a cantata, *The Shepherd and the Shepherdess,* and short keyboard pieces.

Battistini, Mattia (b. Rome, 27 Feb. 1856; d. Collebaccaro, near Rieti, 7 Nov. 1928). Baritone. Studied singing while a medical student at the Univ. of Rome, making his opera debut as a replacement in *La favorita* at the Teatro Argentina, Rome, in 1878. Appeared in opera houses all over Europe, including seasons from 1893 until 1914 in Russia, where he was a special favorite. He sang 82 roles, primarily in 19th-century Italian and French (also a few German and Russian) works; also a notable Don Giovanni; sang in South America in 1881 and 1882 and again in the summer of 1889; later sang mostly in concert, making his last tour in 1927, with his voice still intact. His many recordings

(1903–25) are still prized as models of 19th-century Italian singing technique and style.

Bibl.: Gino Fracassini, *Mattia Battistini* (Milan, 1914). Franceso Palmegiani, *Mattia Battistini* (Milan, 1949).

Battle, Kathleen (Deanne) (b. Portsmouth, Ohio, 13 Aug. 1948). Soprano. Received M.Ed. in music education, Univ. of Cincinnati, 1971. Studied voice with Franklin Bens, 1972. Invited by Thomas Schippers to sing at Spoleto Festival, 1972, then with Cincinnati Symphony. Coached by James Levine, 1973. Won WGN–Illinois Opera Guild Prize, 1974; Young Artist Award, 1975. New York Broadway debut, 22 Oct. 1975; operatic debut, 8 Sept. 1976; Covent Garden debut, 1985. Roles include Mozart's Susanna and Despina, Rossini's Rosina, Strauss's Zerbinetta, Zdenka, and Sophie.

Baudrier, Yves (Marie) (b. Paris, 11 Feb. 1906; d. there, 9 Nov. 1988). Composer. He was trained in law and mainly self-taught as a composer, although he studied with Georges Loth, organist at Sacré Coeur (1929–33). After 1935 he was associated with Messiaen, Jolivet, and Daniel-Lesur in the group called "La Jeune France," which was opposed to neoclassicism and championed a return to a more lyrical style; his own music reflects his admiration of Debussy. He taught at the Institut des hautes études cinématographiques (1945–60) and made one trip to the U.S. to study techniques of composition for films. Works include many film scores, a ballet, and music for the theater and television; *Le musicien dans la cité* (a "poéme cinématographique" for an imaginary film in 12 continuous movements depicting the nighttime wanderings of a composer in Paris, 1937, rev. 1947, rev. 1964 for a television film), symphonic poems, and other orchestral works; a string quartet (1944); and *Adjuva Domine,* solo voices, boys' choir, chorus, orchestra (1960).

Bauer, Harold (b. Kingston-on-Thames, 28 Apr. 1873; d. Miami, 12 Mar. 1951). Pianist and violinist. Studied violin with his father and Adolf Politzer; debut in London, 1882. Encouraged by Paderewski, he switched to piano, 1892; piano debut in London, Nov. 1892. Based in Paris, 1893–1913. U.S. debut with Boston Symphony, 30 Nov. 1900; New York debut with Kneisel Quartet, 20 Dec. 1900. Moved to the U.S. in 1913; became a citizen in 1917. Helped found Manhattan School of Music; founded Beethoven Association of New York, 1918. His repertory included Beethoven, Brahms, Chopin, and especially Schumann, whose piano works he played devotedly and also edited.

Bauer, Marion (Eugenie) (b. Walla Walla, Wash., 15 Aug. 1887; d. South Hadley, Mass., 9 Aug. 1955). Composer, pianist, teacher, writer on music. Of French parentage, she studied piano first in Portland, then in New York (Huss) and France (Rauol Pugno, 1905–6). She began to compose about 1904 with the encouragement of the New York conductor Rothwell. She was in Berlin (1910–11), and later studied with Campbell-Tipton, Boulanger, and Gédalge in Paris (1923–26). Her compositions are often cast in smaller forms and in an impressionist idiom, sometimes incorporating exotic elements (*Lament on African Themes,* chamber orchestra, 1928). Later works adopted a neoclassical approach (Prelude and Fugue, flute and strings op. 43, 1948). She taught at New York Univ. (1926–51) and at Juilliard (1940–44) and gave lectures at Chatauqua from 1928. Among her students at New York University was Babbitt. A cofounder of the American Music Guild and a board member of the League of Composers from 1926, she was an important advocate for new music in numerous articles for music journals, as New York editor of the *Musical Leader,* and as music critic of the *Evening Mail.* She also wrote several books on music, including *How Music Grew,* with Ethel Peyser (New York, 1925; 2nd rev. ed., 1939), *Twentieth-Century Music* (New York, 1933; 2nd rev. ed., 1947; R: 1978), and *How Opera Grew,* with Ethel Peyser (New York, 1956). She composed works for orchestra (a piano concerto, *American Youth,* 1943; *Symphonic Suite,* strings, 1940); several chamber pieces for strings, winds, some with piano; works for piano, organ; choral music (*A Foreigner Comes to Earth on Boston Common,* 1951); songs; incidental and film music.

Bauldeweyn [Baudoin], **Noel** (b. ca. 1480; d. Antwerp, 1530). Composer. Choirmaster at the Church of St. Rombaut, Mechelen, and later at Notre Dame Cathedral, Antwerp. Although there is no record of his employment after 1517, he evidently remained at the cathedral until his death. His works survive in sources that date from ca. 1510 to ca. 1575 and come from a wide geographical area. These works include 8 Masses, 10 motets, and 2 secular songs.

Bibl.: Edgar H. Sparks, *The Music of Noel Bauldeweyn* (New York, 1972).

Bax, Arnold (Edward Trevor) (b. Streatham, 8 Nov. 1883; d. Cork, 3 Oct. 1953). Composer. After early instruction at the Hampstead Conservatory (beginning in 1898), he enrolled at the Royal Academy of Music in 1900. There he studied composition with Frederick Corder and piano with Tobias Matthay. In 1904 he won the Academy's Charles Lucas Prize for his orchestral *Variations;* the following year he won a gold medal in piano. After completing his studies he traveled to Dresden in 1906 and to Russia in 1910. His frequent visits to Ireland, manifestations of a lifelong fascination with Celtic poetry, culture, and music, made a lasting impression on him. Several important compositions date from this period (the tone poems *In the Faery Hills,* 1909, and *The Garden of Fand,* 1913; a piano quartet, 1915), as do a number of short stories, written under the pseudonymn Dermot O'Byrne. Shortly thereafter Bax began spending most of his time composing; he lived in Ireland from 1911 until the beginning of World War I, when he returned to Hampstead. In 1934 he was awarded an honorary doctorate from Oxford, and in the following year another from Durham Univ. He was knighted in 1937 and in 1941 became Master of the King's Music. His autobiography, *Farewell, My Youth,* was published in London in 1943. His music, firmly founded on the Romantic idiom, includes elements of Irish and folk song and of the tonal palette of early 20th-century France. He was one of the more prolific composers of his generation (some 250 works).

Works: *Stage. Between Dusk and Dawn,* ballet (1917); *The Truth about the Russian Dancers,* incidental music (1920; rev. 1926); film scores (*Oliver Twist,* 1948; *Journey into History,* 1952). *Orchestral.* 7 symphonies (1922–39); 9 symphonic poems (*Christmas Eve on the Mountains,* 1911–12; *November Woods,* 1917; *Tintagel,* 1917; *Summer Music,* 1920); *4 Pieces* (1912–13); *Symphonic Scherzo* (1917; rev. 1933); *Phantasy,* viola, orchestra (1920); *Romantic Overture* (1926); 2 *Northern Ballads* (1927–31, 1934); *Overture to a Picaresque Comedy* (1930); *Winter Legends,* piano, orchestra (1930); *Concertante,* piano left-hand, orchestra (1948–49); *Coronation March* (1953). *Choral and vocal. Fatherland* (1907; rev. 1934); *Mater ora filium* (1921); *This Worldes Joie* (1922); *To Russia,* baritone, chorus, orchestra (1944); *Te Deum* (1944). Also many chamber works (3 string quartets; *An Irish Elegy,* English horn, harp, string quartet, 1916; Legend Sonata, cello, piano, 1943); more than 125 songs; much piano music (6 sonatas, 1898–32).

Bibl.: R. L. E. Foreman, "Bibliography of Writings on Arnold Bax," *CM* 10 (1970): 124–40. Graham Parlett, *Arnold Bax: A Catalogue of His Music* (London, 1972). Colin Scott-Sutherland, *Arnold Bax* (London, 1973). Lewis Foreman, *Bax: A Composer and His Times* (Berkeley, 1983).

Bazelon, Irwin (Allen) (b. Evanston, Ill., 4 June 1922; d. New York, 2 Aug. 1995). Composer. Studied at DePaul Univ. with Leon Stein, with Milhaud at Mills College, and briefly with Hindemith and Bloch. He composed both concert music and music for films. The author of *Knowing the Score* (1975), a book on writing film music, he taught that subject at the School for Visual Arts in New York (1968–73). Often for traditional orchestra with a large percussion section or for brass and percussion, his concert music is usually aggressive in tone and reflects the pace and variety of city life (Symphony no. 2, Testament to a Big City, 1962); its rhythmic force may be compared to that in the music of Bartók or Varèse. In the 1960s he experimented with twelve-tone techniques, employed freely to establish conflicting tonal areas (Symphony no. 5, 1966); some works show the influence of jazz (Chamber Concerto no. 2, Churchill Downs, 1970–71). Other works include chamber music; works for piano; *Propulsions,* a concerto for percussion ensemble (1974); *Motivations,* trombone and orchestra, (1985); *Fourscore + 2,* percussion quartet, orchestra (1988); *Alliances,* cello, piano (1991).

Bazzini, Antonio (b. Brescia, 11 Mar. 1818; d. Milan, 10 Feb. 1897). Violinist, composer, and teacher. He was encouraged by Paganini to become a soloist and toured widely in Europe until 1864, living at times in Germany, France, and Spain. He had already composed much music, including violin concertos and character pieces, such as the still occasionally heard scherzo fantastique *La ronde des lutins,* when he settled in Brescia in 1864 to compose full-time. Thereafter he produced the opera *Turanda* (a failure at La Scala in 1867); concert overtures; choral music, including the symphonic cantata *Sennacheribbo;* and chamber music, including string quartets and 2 string quintets, that made him an important figure in the revival of Italian instrumental music. In 1873 he became professor of composition at the Milan Conservatory and in 1882 its director, having Catalani, Mascagni, and Puccini among his pupils.

Amy Beach, about 1932.

Bibl.: Alceo Toni, *Antonio Bazzini* (Milan, 1946).

Beach, Amy Marcy Cheney (b. Henniker, N.H., 5 Sept. 1867; d. New York, 27 Dec. 1944). Composer and pianist. She was a child prodigy who studied piano with her mother, and then with Perabo and Bärmann in Boston. Except for a year's study of theory with J. W. Hill, she was an autodidact in composition; she examined the standard concert repertory and translated Berlioz's treatise on orchestration. A virtuoso pianist, she often played her own chamber and orchestral music in the U.S. and Europe, premiering her piano concerto with the Boston Symphony Orchestra under Gericke (6 Apr. 1900). During her marriage to Dr. H. H. A. Beach, a Boston physician, she limited her concert career to one or two appearances a year (donating her fees to charity); after his death in 1910 she resumed performing in the U.S. and in Europe, composing during the summers (from 1921 at the MacDowell Colony). She was a prolific composer who favored the rich chromatic textures common to Boston composers of the late 19th century (Chadwicke, Foote, Paine, and Parker), collectively referred to as the Second New England School. The first president of the Association of American Women Composers, she was also a leader in other professional organizations. Most of her music was published during her lifetime. It includes the opera

Cabildo (1932, premiered Athens, Ga., 27 Feb. 1947); 5 orchestral works; chamber music for strings or winds, some with piano; more than 70 piano works; choral music, including the early Mass in E♭ (1890) and Episcopal service music as well as secular works, many for female chorus; about 130 songs, perhaps her best-known works.

Bibl.: A. F. Block, "Why Amy Beach Succeeded as a Composer: The Early Years," *CM* 36 (1983): 41–59. Jeannell Wise Brown, *Amy Beach and Her Chamber Music: Biography, Documents, Style* (Metuchen, N.J., 1994).

Beard, John (b. ca. 1717; d. Hampton, 5 Feb. 1791). Tenor. At the Chapel Royal he studied with Bernard Gates; he first appeared in 1732 as an Israelite priest in Handel's *Esther.* He joined Handel's opera company at Covent Garden in 1734, singing Silvio in *Il pastor fido* in November; during the next quarter century he sang leading parts in nearly all of Handel's English church music, odes, masques, and oratorios (*Judas Maccabaeus, Jephtha, Samson, Semele, Israel in Egypt, Messiah, Alexander's Feast,* and *Esther*) and in a number of the operas (*Ariodante* and *Alcina*). He was also part of the Drury Lane company (from 1737); later he managed Covent Garden. Oxford bestowed the D.Mus. on him in 1759.

Beardslee, Bethany (b. Lansing, Mich., 25 Dec. 1927). Soprano. Received B.Mus. from Michigan State Univ.; diploma from Juilliard. First marriage to Jacques-Louis Monod, with whom she gave many recitals. Second marriage (1956) to composer Godfrey Winham, many of whose works she premiered. Also premiered works by Stravinsky, Berg, Webern, Babbitt, Krenek, Boulez, Dallapiccola, Peter Maxwell Davies, and others. Received Ford Foundation grant (1964) to commission and perform Babbitt's *Philomel.* Taught for one year at Univ. of Calif., Davis, then professor of voice, Univ. of Texas, 1981–82; on the Brooklyn College faculty from 1983.

Beaser, Robert Harry (b. Boston, Mass., 29 May 1954). Composer and conductor. Studied at Yale (B.A., 1976; M.M., 1977; M.M.A., 1980). Teachers included Jacob Druckman and Yehudi Wyner. Studied at the Berkshire Music Center with Betsy Jolas. Won Prix de Rome (American Academy) in 1977; studied there with Gofreddo Petrassi and Arnold Franchetti. Assistant conductor of the Norwalk Symphony, 1975–77. Composer-in-residence, American Composers Orchestra, 1988–93. From 1993 taught composition at Juilliard. Works include *The Seven Deadly Sins* (1979); *Variations* (flute and piano, 1983); *Double chorus* (orchestra, 1990); *The Heavenly Feast* (soprano, orchestra, 1994); *Psalm 150 for Chorus* (1995).

Beaujoyeux [Beaujoyeulx, Belgioioso], **Balthasar de** [Baldassare de; "Baltazarini"] (b. before ca. 1535; d. ca. 1587). Ballet master and violinist. About 1555 left Italy to go to France to serve the royal court. Acted as creator and organizer of and participant in various court entertainments. Especially notable were the elaborate *Magnificences* of 1581. These included the *Balet comique de la Royne,* of which Beaujoyeux was stage manager and choreographer. His only surviving work, it was an influential predecessor of the *ballet de cour* and of French opera.

Bibl.: Carol and L. MacClintock, eds. and trans., *B. de Beaujoyeux: Le balet comique de la Royne, MSD* 30 (Rome, 1971).

Becerra (-Schmidt), Gustavo (b. Temuco, Chile, 26 Aug. 1925). Composer. From 1933 he studied composition with Pedro Allende at Santiago's National Conservatory. In 1946 he graduated from the Univ. of Chile and in 1952 became professor of composition there. After two years in Europe (1954–56) he returned home to hold posts as director of the Extensión musical (1960–62) and of the composition department at the State Conservatory. In 1968 he was named to the Chilean Academy of Arts. His works conform chiefly to classical structures, with the addition of aleatoric and electronic elements. Works include operas (*La muerte de Don Rodrigo,* 1963; *Parsifae,* 1973–); film scores; 4 symphonies (1958, 1958, 1960, 1973–); oratorios, most to texts by Pablo Neruda (*Macchu Picchu,* 1966; *Lord Cochrane,* 1966; *Ode to the Barbed Wire,* 1971); *Missa brevis,* female chorus (1958); 2 guitar concertos (1964, 1968); 7 string quartets; 3 violin sonatas; Saxophone Quartet (1959); *Juegos,* piano, 12 ping-pong balls, brick, tape (1966).

Bibl.: A. Rodrigo Torres, "Notas preliminares y catálogo de la obra musical de Gustavo Becerra-Schmidt," *Revista musical chilena* 164 (1985): 16–51.

Bechet, Sidney (Joseph) (b. New Orleans, 14 May 1897; d. Paris, 14 May 1959). Jazz clarinetist and soprano saxophonist. Moving to Chicago in 1917, he played clarinet with Freddie Keppard and King Oliver. Toured England and France, initially with Will Marion Cook's Southern Syncopated Orchestra (1919); in London acquired a soprano saxophone. In New York he recorded with Louis Armstrong (including "Cake Walking Babies," 1924, as the Red Onion Jazz Babies) and joined Duke Ellington (1924). Toured Europe, including Russia, 1925–30, playing in revues, leading bands, and working with Noble Sissle. In the U.S. he rejoined Sissle (intermittently 1931–38) and with the trumpeter Tommy Ladnier led the New Orleans Feetwarmers (1932–33), recording "Maple Leaf Rag" (1932). From 1939, when he recorded "Summertime," he was active in the New Orleans jazz revival, performing in New York, Boston, and Chicago. He recorded with Jelly Roll Morton (including "High Society," 1939) and the clarinetist Mezz Mezzrow (1945–47); from 1951 lived in France. He played with a wide vibrato and an extremely passionate, powerful sound, his saxophone often competing with or replacing the trumpet in traditional ensembles. Bechet's imaginative, swinging melodies and breaks, though created through improvisation, remained largely preset.

Bibl.: Sidney Bechet, *Treat It Gentle: An Autobiography,* ed. D. Flower (New York, 1960). John Chilton, *Sidney Bechet: The Wizard of Jazz* (New York, 1987).

Bechstein, (Friedrich Wilhelm) Carl (b. Gotha, 1 June 1826; d. Berlin, 6 Mar. 1900). Piano manufacturer. Apprenticed in Berlin and founded his own business there in 1853; made his first grand piano, which was inaugurated by von Bülow, in 1856. The quality and tone of his pianos almost immediately gained them the reputation that the company long maintained, making them the favorite of generations of concert pianists. The company grew rapidly and was carried on by his sons and grandson after his death. In 1974 it became a subsidiary of the Baldwin Co.

Beck, Conrad (b. Lohn, Schaffhausen, Switzerland, 16 June 1901; d. Basel, 31 Oct. 1989). Composer. After training in mechanical engineering, he studied at the Zurich Conservatory and then in Paris and Berlin. He lived in Paris from 1923 to 1932; those years he considered the most artistically stimulating as a result of his association with Boulanger, Ibert, Honegger, and Roussel. His Concerto for String Quartet (1929) won the Coolidge Prize after its performance in Chicago in 1930; *Innominata* (for orchestra) was presented at an international conference in Vienna in 1932 under Ansermet. In that year he moved to Basel, where he eventually became director of Radio Basel (1939); he retired from that position in 1962. His style combines an austere polyphony with clarity of form, later works exhibiting a freedom from tonality and a simplification of texture. His works include a ballet *(Der gosse Bär,* 1936) and incidental music; 7 symphonies (1925–58), several concertos (for piano, violin, viola, cello, string quartet, oboe, flute, and harpsichord), and other orchestral works (*Lichter und Schatten,* 1982; *Nachklänge,* 1983); 5 string quartets (1922–62), a sonata for viola da gamba and organ (1938), and other chamber music; a few piano, organ, and harpsichord works; *Oratorium* (solo voice, chorus, and orchestra, 1934), *Der Tod zu Basle* (speaker, solo voices, chorus, and orchestra, 1952), and other vocal works.

Becker, John J(oseph) (b. Henderson, Ky., 22 Jan. 1886; d. Wilmette, Ill., 21 Jan. 1961). Composer and conductor. He was educated in Ohio, receiving a B.A. from St. Mary's of the Spring in Columbus and simultaneously studying music at the Cincinnati Conservatory; obtained a doctorate in composition from the Wisconsin Conservatory in Milwaukee (1923), where he studied Renaissance polyphony with Wilhelm Middelschulte. Early in his career he taught piano and theory in Texas (1906–ca. 1914); later he taught at Notre Dame (1917–27), the College of St. Thomas (St. Paul, Minn., 1929–33), and Barat College (Lake Forest, Ill., 1943–57). His meeting with Cowell in 1928 effected a radical change in his own composition away from German romanticism toward much greater use of dissonance (*Symphonia Brevis,* 1929). While in Minnesota he was a strong advocate for new music: as conductor of the St. Paul Chamber Orchestra (performing on 25 Mar. 1933 works by Ives, Ruggles, and Riegger and his own *Concerto Arabesque*), by involvement in a series of radio broadcasts of new music, and as associate editor of the *New Music Quarterly* (1936–40). He corresponded with Ives (1931–54) and directed the Federal Music Project in Minnesota between 1935 and 1941. His works include *Abongo: A Primitive Dance* (percussion ensemble, dancers, wordless voices; published 1933; premiered New York, 1963); several multimedia "stageworks" (*A Marriage with Space,* employing large orchestra, dancers, recitations, colors, and lights, Chicago, 1935); works for orchestra, some with chorus or speakers; a ballet, stage and film music; chamber music for piano or small ensembles; choral music, usually on religious texts; over 50 songs.

Bibl.: Don C. Gillespie, "John Becker, Musical Crusader from St. Paul," *MQ* 62 (1976): 195–217.

Beckwith, John (b. Victoria, B.C., 9 Mar. 1927). Composer. He studied at the Toronto Conservatory and the Univ. of Toronto (Mus.B., 1947) and in Paris with Boulanger (1950–52). He worked for CBC Radio (1953–65) hosting programs such as *The World of Music* and wrote music criticism for the *Toronto Star* (1959–66); edited the *Canadian Music Journal* (1956–62); wrote program notes for the Toronto Symphony (1966–71). He was a founding member of the Canadian League of Composers; taught at the Univ. of Toronto (assistant professor, 1961; dean of the faculty, 1970–77). Early works are neoclassical; he began to use serial techniques in 1955; later works often employ collage techniques; some pieces reflect Ontario subjects (*Sharon Fragments,* 1966). Works include operas (*Crazy to Kill,* 1989); a few orchestral works; a string quartet (1977) and other chamber music; piano music; several works for chorus and orchestra (*Place of Meeting,* tenor, blues singer, speaker, chorus, and orchestra, 1966–67); songs; a series of "radio collages" for speakers, solo voices, and instruments (*Canada Dash, Canada Dot,* 1965–67).

Bedford, David (Vickerman) (b. London, 4 Aug. 1937). Composer. He studied at Lancing College in Sussex (1951–55) and at the Royal Academy of Music (1956–60) with Lennox Berkeley; in 1960 he studied with Nono in Venice. After 1963 he taught secondary school in London, and from 1968 taught as well at Queen's College. He is especially interested in working with children and musicians not classically trained. His works often employ indeterminate compositional and improvisatory performance techniques and graphic notation; some are scored for unusual instruments (*100 Kazoos,* 1971), and others employ new instrumental techniques; his music based on small transposable sets of notes employed harmonically and melodically often has a static feeling. Works include *Star's End* (rock instruments and orchestra, 1976),

Pancakes with Butter Maple Syrup and Bacon, and the TV Weatherman (brass quintet, 1973), Symphony no. 2 (symphonic wind band, 1985), and other instrumental music; choral and solo vocal works (*Into Thy Wondrous House,* chorus and orchestra, 1987); many works for children (*The Odyssey,* soprano, girls' voices, instruments, electronics, 1976).

Bédos de Celles, François (b. Caux, 24 Jan. 1709; d. St. Denis, 25 Nov. 1779). Organ builder. He joined the Benedictine order at Toulouse in 1726; later he was secretary at Sainte-Croix (Bordeaux), where he built the organ that is now (in large part) located in the Bordeaux Cathedral. His well-known *L'art du facteur d'orgues* (Paris, 1766–78; R: Paris, 1976; trans. Charles Ferguson, Raleigh, N.C., 1977) is a valuable source of information on French classical organs—their design, specifications, and registration.

Bedyngham [Bedyngeham, Bedingham, Benigun], **Johannes** (d. Westminster?, London, reported between 3 May 1459 and 22 May 1460). Composer. Verger at the chapel of St. Stephen, Westminster, a position generally held by a notable composer. His works, which range from the relatively simple to the rather complex, survive in numerous, widely distributed sources, attesting to his reputation. Although Continental sources rarely include ascriptions to him and he probably spent his entire life in England, his fame seems to have reached as far as Italy. His works (some with conflicting attributions to Dufay, Dunstable, and Frye) include 2 Mass cycles, 2 Mass movements, 3 motets, and 8 songs (with texts in English, French, and Italian).

Beecham, Thomas (b. St. Helens, Lancashire, 29 Apr. 1879; d. London, 8 Mar. 1961). Conductor. He studied at Rossall School and Wadham College, Oxford, and took private composition lessons from Charles Wood (London) and Moszkowski (Paris). He was self-taught as a conductor. In 1909 he founded the Beecham Symphony Orchestra and the following year conducted operas (many of them new to Britain) at Covent Garden, His Majesty's, and Drury Lane. During World War I he conducted the Hallé Orchestra, the London Symphony, and the Royal Philharmonic Society. In 1915 he formed the Beecham Opera Company, which performed in London and the provinces. After withdrawing from musical life to spend a few years putting his financial affairs in order, he returned in 1923 and unsuccessfully attempted to form an Imperial League of Opera. During this time he made several visits abroad. In 1932 he formed the London Philharmonic, with which he subsequently toured to Germany and Paris. Also in that year he returned to Covent Garden as artistic director, remaining there until the theater was closed by the outbreak of war in 1939. From 1940 to 1944 he was in the U.S., conducting the Seattle Symphony, the Metropolitan Opera, and concerts with the New York Philharmonic. Upon his return to Britain in 1944 he again conducted the London Philharmonic, then formed the Royal Philharmonic (1946), with which he toured and made many recordings. Until his retirement in 1960, he continued to conduct operas. He was knighted in 1916.

Bibl.: Alan Jefferson, *Sir Thomas Beecham: A Centenary Tribute* (London, 1979).

Beecroft, Norma (Marian) (b. Oshawa, Ont., 11 Apr. 1934). Composer. She studied flute, piano, and composition (Weinzweig) at the Toronto Conservatory (1950–58); in Rome she studied with Petrassi (1959–61). Other teachers have included Copland and Foss (1958), Maderna (1960 and 1961), Schaeffer (Univ. of Toronto, 1962–63), and Davidovsky (1964). Worked for CBC Radio and Television in various capacities; her documentary *The Computer in Music* (1976) received an award for excellence in broadcasting. Debussy is a major influence on her style, which also reflects the neoclassicism of Hindemith and Stravinsky, interests in electronic music, and twelve-tone methods. Works include music for a puppet show; *From Dreams of Brass* (narrator, soprano, orchestra, tape, 1963–64); *Piece Concertante no. 1* (1966) and other orchestral music; chamber music for traditional ensembles and for ensembles with tape (Brass Quintet, 1975) or live electronics (*Consequences for 5,* 1977); choral music (Requiem Mass, soloists, chorus, orchestra, 1989–90); and vocal pieces.

Beeson, Jack (Hamilton) (b. Muncie, Ind., 15 July 1921). Composer. Studied with Phillips, Rogers, and Hanson at Eastman (B.M., 1942; M.M., 1943), with Bartók in New York (1944–45), and then at Columbia Univ. (musicology, 1945–48), where he also conducted an opera workshop. He began teaching at Columbia in 1945, becoming a full professor in 1965, serving as chairman of the music department (1968–72), as well as supervising the publication of new music by Columbia Univ. Press. A lifelong interest in opera is reflected in stage works including *Lizzie Borden* (1965), *My Heart's in the Highlands* (National Educational Television, 17 Mar. 1970), *Captain Jinks of the Horse Marines* (1975), and *Cyrano* (1990). He has composed other works for orchestra and band; chamber music for piano or instrumental ensemble; choral music (Psalm settings, 1951; *Knots: Jack and Jill for Grown-Ups,* 1979); and songs with piano or string quartet. He has withdrawn 53 works composed before 1950.

Beethoven, Ludwig van (b. Bonn, 15 or 16 Dec., bapt. 17 Dec. 1770; d. Vienna, 26 Mar. 1827). Composer. He was born into a family of musicians who had served at the Bonn court of the Elector of Cologne since 1733. That year his grandfather, Ludwig van Beethoven (1712–73), had come from Mechelen, Belgium, as a bass singer for the court. His son Johann van Beethoven (ca. 1740–92), the composer's father, became a tenor and music teacher at the court. In 1767

Ludwig van Beethoven.
Study by August von Klöber, 1818.

Johann married Maria Magdalena Keverich (1746–87), the daughter of a court cook. The couple's first surviving child was named Ludwig after his grandfather. The young Beethoven studied music first with his father, then with Tobias Pfeifer (piano) and Franz Rovantini (violin), and beginning in 1779 with the court's new opera director, Christian Gottlob Neefe. When Neefe was promoted to court organist in 1781 he began to employ Beethoven as his assistant, allowing him to serve as orchestral cembalist—a position that enabled the youth to become familiar with current operas and with chamber and orchestral music of the day. In 1784 Beethoven was made deputy organist by the new elector Maximilian Franz.

During his first visit to Vienna in the spring of 1787, Beethoven apparently met Mozart and perhaps took a few lessons with him. Shortly after his return to Bonn his mother died of tuberculosis, and when the alcoholic Johann was dismissed from his duties in 1789, Ludwig became a family breadwinner. His first acquaintance with Haydn probably came in December 1790, when Haydn stopped in Bonn on his way to London. Beethoven apparently—according to Wegeler's *Notizen*—showed one of his ambitious Emperor Cantatas (WoO 87 or WoO 88) to the venerated composer at this time, and the two may have discussed the prospect of future lessons.

Beethoven moved to Vienna in November 1792. His lessons with Haydn (initially the principal reason for the move), which began shortly after his arrival, consisted primarily of species counterpoint; upon discovering that the preoccupied Haydn was overlooking errors in the exercises, the pupil employed composer Johann Schenk to aid him further. Beethoven suspected Haydn of intentionally jeopardizing his studies; much has been written of the apparent conflict between the ambitious young composer and the world-famous Haydn. In early 1794 Beethoven began a year of instruction with the Kapellmeister at St. Stephen's, Johann Georg Albrechtsberger; he also studied vocal composition with court composer Antonio Salieri in 1795. During these early Viennese years he began to make himself known as composer and pianist-improviser in the homes of music-loving Viennese aristocrats: Prince Karl Lichnowsky, Prince Franz Joseph Lobkowitz, and the Hungarian Count Nikolaus Zmeskall von Domanovecz. One of his earliest public concerts, a charity benefit in the Burgtheater in March 1795, included a piano concerto in B♭ (probably op. 19). In May of that year the publisher Artaria brought out his op. 1, a set of three brilliant piano trios. His op. 2 piano sonatas, published the following year with a dedication to Haydn, were also received with acclaim.

During 1796 Beethoven embarked on concert tours that included Prague, Dresden, Berlin, and Pressburg (Bratislava). For Berlin he composed two cello sonatas, published in 1797 as op. 5. The years 1797–98 saw the publication chiefly of chamber and keyboard works, including opp. 7, 9, and 10. In 1799 he began work on the op. 18 string quartets, and in April 1800 he gave a concert at the Burgtheater that included his First Symphony. These years saw the onset of several friendships, including those with the Brunsvik family (both Therese and Josephine were his pupils) and their cousin Giulietta Guicciardi, to whom the Moonlight Sonata (op. 27, no. 2) of 1801 was dedicated. Other works dating from around 1800 include the Septet op. 20, 6 String Quartets op. 18, the Pathétique Sonata (op. 13), 2 violin sonatas (opp. 23 and 24), and *Die Geschöpfe des Prometheus.*

Around 1801 Beethoven began to acknowledge to close friends that he was going deaf. Spending the summer and early fall of 1802 in the village of Heiligenstadt (now a Viennese suburb), he completed the Second Symphony and penned the "Heiligenstadt Testament." Ostensibly a letter to his brothers Johann and Caspar, this document was in essence an expression of despondence brought about by the undeniable fact of encroaching deafness. He continued to complete works at a remarkable rate, including the Kreutzer Sonata, the Piano Concerto no. 3, and *Christus am Oelberge.*

The traditional division of Beethoven's works into three style periods generally marks the middle period as beginning about 1802–3. The works from this period do in fact manifest extraordinary structural and textural ambitions, a scope and scale that have been characterized as heroic. Works from this period include the Waldstein Sonata op. 53, the Triple Concerto op. 56, an opera fragment, *Vestas Feuer,* and most important, the Third Symphony *(Eroica),* completed in 1803. (Although the composer retracted the symphony's dedication to Napoleon when the French hero declared himself emperor, the "heroic" subtitle remained.) This middle period culminated in Beethoven's only opera, *Fidelio* (text by Joseph Ferdinand Sonnleithner; the composer preferred its original title, *Leonore*), first performed in Vienna on 20 Nov. 1805 in the midst of an occupation of the city by French troops. The first version failed, achieving only three performances, but the work reappeared in 1806 and again in 1814—each time with substantial revisions by the composer—and in the 1814 version it finally achieved success.

The summer of 1806 found the composer in Martonvásár (Hungary) at the palace of the Brunsvik family; he was in love with the young, recently widowed Josephine, who ultimately rejected his advances. The period following the second version of *Fidelio* was perhaps the composer's most fecund. Among the large, path-breaking works dating from between 1806 and early 1809 are the Symphonies 4, 5, and 6, the Coriolan Overture, the Piano Concerto no. 4, the Violin Concerto, three Razumovsky String Quartets, two Piano Trios op. 70, the Cello Sonata op. 69, and the Mass in C op. 86. His support from noble patrons had continued to increase, and in 1809 the Archduke Johann Joseph Rudolph (who had studied with Beethoven since 1803) and two other patrons, Prince Lobkowitz and Prince Ferdinand Kinsky, signed a contract agreeing to provide the composer with an annuity and, upon his retirement, a pension. Beethoven had also begun to give a great deal of attention to selling his compositions at the highest possible price; his principal publishers during the first decade of the century were, in Vienna, the Bureau des arts et d'industrie and in Leipzig, Hoffmeister & Kühnel and Breitkopf & Härtel.

Rudolph was to remain the composer's favorite benefactor; Beethoven expressed his affection for him in the *Lebewohl* Sonata for piano op. 81a, a work whose three movements depict the archduke's departure from Vienna (in the spring of 1809, when the French again occupied the city), his absence, and his return at the beginning of 1810. Other works dedicated to Rudolph include the Piano Concerto no. 5 and the Piano Trio op. 97 (*Archduke*). In 1811 the ailing Beethoven was ordered by his doctor to visit the baths in Teplitz (Tepliče); there he composed incidental music for two dramas by August von Kotzebue, *König Stephan* and *Die Ruinen von Athen.* Shortly after his return to Vienna he composed the Seventh and Eighth Symphonies in fairly rapid succession. At Teplitz in the summer of 1812 he finally met Goethe, for whose *Egmont* he had composed incidental music two years before. Also during the years 1810–12 Beethoven was charmed by three young and largely unattainable women: Bettina Brentano, Amalie Sebald, and Therese Malfatti. He apparently proposed marriage to Malfatti and was refused.

In July 1812 Beethoven wrote a love confession that has come to be known as the letter to the "unsterbliche Geliebte" (immortal beloved); it was never delivered. Among the names that have been proposed as the intended (unnamed) recipient of the letter, that of Antonie Brentano is perhaps most plausible. The wife of Bettina's half-brother, Antonie not only admired the composer greatly but also was in Vienna, Prague, and Karlsbad (Karlovy Váry) simultaneously with Beethoven during the years 1811–12. The document's significance to the composer's private life can only be a matter of speculation; in it he seems resigned to a permanent state of loneliness. It coincided, in any case, with an all-important event in his daily affairs. In that year his ailing brother Caspar revised his will to make Ludwig sole guardian of young Karl, Caspar's son.

In the traditional division of the composer's works, 1812–13 marks the beginning of a "spiritual" late period; indeed, these years appear to be characterized by a new devotion to Beethoven's only means of self-expression, his music. The first large work of this transcendent period, ironically, was the bombastic *Wellington's Victory,* performed to vigorous acclaim in December 1813. Financial struggles that again arose in 1813–14 were relieved by a new annuity contract with Prince Lobkowitz and with Kinsky's heirs.

The years 1815–17 were relatively unproductive ones for Beethoven. When Caspar died in November 1815, Beethoven discovered to his horror that his brother had changed the will at the last minute to make Ludwig coguardian of Karl with Caspar's wife, Johanna, whom Beethoven deemed morally unfit to raise a child. Only after a rancorous custody battle that lasted nearly five years was the boy ultimately placed in the permanent charge of his overprotective uncle. Early in 1818 Beethoven again began composing large-scale works, beginning with the Hammerklavier Sonata op. 106, a piano work of unprecedented length. The following year he began the *Missa solemnis,* which was initially intended for the installation of Rudolph as Archbishop of Olmütz (Olomouc), scheduled for March 1820; the Mass was not completed until 1823. Also in 1820 the Berlin publisher Schlesinger arranged for him to compose three piano sonatas; op. 109 was completed that year, opp. 110 and 111 during the next two years. The years 1822–23 saw the completion of the Diabelli Variations and *Die Weihe des Hauses.* In 1822 Beethoven also began work on a large symphony with soloists and chorus, employing Schiller's poem *An die Freude;* this Ninth Symphony was performed with great success on 7 May 1824. Around this time the composer also struck an agreement with Schott of Mainz to publish several of the large later works.

Beethoven's final years were characterized by periods of illness and convalescence and by obsessive concern over Karl, whom he had begun to regard as a kind of substitute son. Musically the last four years were devoted entirely to string quartets. At its first performance by the Schuppanzigh Quartet in March 1825, the

E♭ Quartet op. 127 was found "difficult" by the public. Clearly the work—together with the subsequent opp. 130, 131, 132, 133 (*Grosse Fuge,* originally the finale of op. 131), and 135—presented a challenge to audience and players alike. An attempted suicide by Karl in the summer of 1826 dealt a severe emotional blow to his uncle. In December of that year the two returned to Vienna from Gneixendorf; during the ensuing three months Beethoven gradually succumbed to a combination of illnesses, including jaundice and cirrhosis of the liver. He died in March, leaving his whole estate to Karl.

Works: *Orchestra.* Symphonies: no. 1 in C, op. 21 (1799–1800); no. 2 in D, op. 36 (1801–2); no. 3 in E♭, op. 55 (*Eroica,* 1803); no. 4 in B♭, op. 60 (1806); no. 5 in C minor, op. 67 (1807–8); no. 6 in F, op. 68 (*Pastoral,* 1808); no. 7 in A, op. 92 (1811–12), no. 8 in F, op. 93 (1812); no. 9 in D minor, op. 125 (*Choral,* with *Ode to Joy,* 1822–24). Overtures: *Leonore* no. 1, op. 138 (1806–7); *Leonore* no. 2 (for the first version of the opera *Fidelio,* 1805); *Leonore* no. 3 (a revision of no. 2, 1806); *Coriolan,* op. 62 (1807); *Namensfeier,* op. 115 (1815); *Die Weihe des Hauses,* op. 124 (1822); a "Battle symphony" *Wellington's Victory,* op. 91 (1813). Piano Concertos: no. 1 in C, op. 15 (1795); no. 2 in B♭, op. 19 (1795, but begun before 1793); no. 3 in C minor, op. 37 (1803); no. 4 in G, op. 58 (1806); no. 5 in E♭, op. 73 (*Emperor,* 1809). Violin Concerto in D, op. 61 (1806); 2 Romances for violin and orchestra in G, op. 40 (1802), and F, op. 50 (1798?); Triple Concerto op. 56, piano, violin, cello, and orchestra (1804). Much music for wind band.

Chamber music. String quartets: opp. 18 (6, 1798–1800), 59 (3, *Razumovsky,* 1805–6), 74 (*Harp,* 1809), 95 (*Serioso,* 1810), 127 (1823–24), 130 (1825–26), 131 (1826), 132 (1825), 133 (*Grosse Fuge,* 1825–26), and 135 (1826). String Quintet op. 29 (1801); 3 string trios, op. 9 (1797–98); 8 piano trios: WoO 38 (1791?), opp. 1 (3, 1794–95), 11 (1797), 70 (2, 1808), 97 (*Archduke,* 1810–11); 10 violin sonatas: opp. 12 (3, 1797–98), 23 (1800), 24 (*Spring,* 1800–1801), 30 (3, 1801–2), 47 (*Kreutzer,* 1802–3), 96 (1812; rev. 1815?); 5 cello sonatas: opp. 5 (2, 1796), 69 (1807–8), 102 (2, 1815). Octet, winds, op. 103 (1792–93?); Serenade, flute, violin, viola, op. 25 (1801).

Piano. 32 sonatas: opp. 2 (3, 1793–95), 7 (1796–97), 10 (3, 1795–98), 13 (*Pathétique,* 1797–98), 14 (2, 1798–99), 22 (1800), 26 (1800–1801), 27 (2 Sonatas "Quasi una fantasia": no. 1, 1800–1801; no. 2, *Moonlight,* 1801), 28 (*Pastoral,* 1801), 31 (3, 1802; no. 2 *Tempest*), 49 (2, 1795–97), 53 (*Waldstein,* 1803–4), 54 (1804), 57 (*Appassionata,* 1804–5), 78 (1809), 79 (1809), 81a (*Das Lebewohl,* 1809–10), 90 (1814), 101 (1816), 106 (*Hammerklavier,* 1817–18), 109 (1820), 110 (1821–22), 111 (1821–22). Variations: WoO 65, 75, 80; opp. 34, 35 (*Eroica,* 1802), 76, 120 (*Diabelli,* 1819, 1822–23).

Incidental music. Egmont, op. 84 (1809–10); *Die Ruinen von Athen,* op. 113 (1811); *König Stephan,* op. 117 (1811). Ballet: *Die Geschöpfe des Prometheus,* op. 43 (1800–1801).

Vocal music. Opera: *Fidelio oder Die eheliche Liebe (Leonore),* op. 72 (first version, 1804–5; 2nd version, 1805–6; final version, 1814). Choral: Joseph Cantata WoO 87 (1790); Leopold Cantata WoO 88 (1790); *Der glorreiche Augenblick* (cantata), op. 136 (1814); *Christus am Oelberge,* op. 85 (1803–4); Mass in C, op. 86 (1807); *Missa solemnis* in D, op. 123 (1819–23); Choral Fantasy, piano, chorus, orchestra, op. 80 (1808). *Primo amore,* a *scena* and aria, soprano, orchestra, WoO 92 (1790–92). Songs: "Adelaide" op. 46 (1794–95); Six Gellert Songs op. 48 (1802); "An die Hoffnung" op. 32 (1805); Six Songs op. 75 (1809); Three Goethe Songs op. 83 (1810); *An die ferne Geliebte* op. 98 (cycle, 1815–16). Nearly 60 canons and "jokes"; 172 folk song arrangements.

Bibl.: *Ludwig van Beethovens Werke* (Leipzig, 1862–88). *Ludwig van Beethoven: Werke* (Munich, 1961–). Franz Gerhard Wegeler and Ferdinand Ries, *Biographische Notizen über Ludwig van Beethoven* (Koblenz, 1838; suppl. Bonn, 1845; R: 1972). Anton Schindler, *Biographie von Ludwig van Beethoven* (Münster, 1840; rev. 3rd ed., 1860); trans. as *Beethoven as I Knew Him* (Chapel Hill, 1966). Adolf Bernhard Marx, *Ludwig van Beethoven: Leben und Schaffen* (Berlin, 1859; 6th ed., 1908). Hector Berlioz, *A travers chants* (Paris, 1862); trans. Ralph De Sola as *Beethoven: A Critical Appreciation of Beethoven's Nine Symphonies* (Boston, 1975). Gustav Nottebohm, *Ein Skizzenbuch von Beethoven* (Leipzig, 1865; 2nd ed., 1924; R: 1970); id., *Ein Skizzenbuch von Beethoven aus dem Jahre 1803* (Leipzig, 1880; 2nd ed., 1924; R: 1970); both trans. Jonathan Katz as *Two Beethoven Sketchbooks: A Description with Musical Extracts* (London, 1979). Alexander W. Thayer, *Ludwig van Beethovens Leben,* ed. Hermann Dieters, 3 vols. (Berlin, 1866–79); trans. Henry Edward Krehbiel, 3 vols. (New York, 1921); rev. Elliot Forbes as *Thayer's Life of Beethoven,* 2 vols. (Princeton, 1964; 2nd ed., 1967). Gustav Nottebohm, *Beethoveniana* (Leipzig, 1872; 2nd ed., 1925; R: 1970). Id., *Beethovens Studien* (Leipzig, 1873; R: 1970). Romain Rolland, *La vie de Beethoven* (Paris, 1907); trans. B. Constance Hull (London, 1917). Emerich Kastner, ed., *Ludwig van Beethovens sämtliche Briefe* (Leipzig, 1910); rev. 2nd ed. Julius Kapp (Leipzig, 1923; R: Tutzing, 1975). Heinrich Schenker, *Beethovens Neunte Symphonie* (Vienna and Leipzig, 1912; R: 1969). Id., *Beethoven: Fünfte Sinfonie* (Vienna, 1925; R: 1969). Theodore von Frimmel, *Beethoven-Handbuch,* 2 vols. (Leipzig, 1926). Donald Francis Tovey, *A Companion to Beethoven's Pianoforte Sonatas* (London, 1931). Id., *Beethoven* (London, 1944). Georg Kinsky and Hans Halm, *Das Werk Beethovens: Thematisch-bibliographisches Verzeichnis seiner sämtlichen vollendeten Kompositionen* (Munich and Duisburg, 1955). Willy Hess, *Verzeichnis der nicht in der Gesamtausgabe veröffentlichten Werke Ludwig van Beethovens* (Wiesbaden, 1957). Donald W. MacArdle and Ludwig Misch, *New Beethoven Letters* (Norman, Okla., 1957). Emily Anderson, ed. and trans., *The Letters of Beethoven* (New York, 1961). Joseph Kerman, *The Beethoven Quartets* (New York, 1967). Karl-Heinz Köhler et al., eds., *Ludwig van Beethovens Konversationshefte* (Leipzig, 1968–). Joseph Kerman, *Ludwig van Beethoven: Autograph Miscellany from circa 1786 to 1799* (London, 1970). Denis Arnold and Nigel Fortune, eds., *The Beethoven Companion* (London, 1971); publ. in U.S. as *The Beethoven Reader* (New York, 1971). Donald W. MacArdle, *Beethoven Abstracts* (Detroit, 1973). Alan Tyson, ed., *Beethoven Studies,* 1 (New York, 1973; London, 1974); 2 (London, 1977); 3 (Cambridge, 1982). Sieghard Brandenburg, *Beethoven: Kesslersches Skizzenbuch* (Bonn, 1976–78). Maynard Solomon, *Beethoven* (New York, 1977). Kurt Dorfmüller, ed., *Beiträge zur Beethoven-Bibliographie: Studien und Materialen zum Werkverzeichnis von Kinsky-Halm* (Munich, 1978). Douglas Johnson, Alan Tyson, and Robert Winter, *The Beethoven Sketchbooks: History, Reconstruction, Inventory* (Berkeley and Los Angeles, 1985). Maynard Solomon, *Beethoven Essays* (Cambridge, Mass., 1988). Carl Dahlhaus, *Ludwig van Beethoven: Approaches to His Music* (New York, 1991). Lewis Lockwood, *Beethoven: Stud-*

ies in the Creative Process (Cambridge, Mass., 1992). William Kinderman, *Beethoven* (Berkeley, 1995). Scott Burnham, *Beethoven Hero* (Princeton, 1995).

Behrens, Hildegard (b. Varel, West Germany, 9 Feb. 1937). Soprano. Completed studies in law and passed bar examination before studying with Ines Leuwen at the Freiburg Conservatory, 1966–71; coached by Jerome Lo Monaco, 1972. Debut 2 Feb. 1971 with the Deutsche Oper am Rhein in Düsseldorf. In 1975 her Leonore *(Fidelio)* with the Zurich Opera made her famous. U.S. debut, New York, 15 Oct. 1976 in Puccini's *Il tabarro.* Other roles include Mozart's Electra, Weber's Agathe, Strauss's Salome, Janáček's Katya, and Berg's Marie; beginning 1983 especially prized for her Wagner heroines.

Beiderbecke, (Leon Bismarck) Bix (b. Davenport, Iowa, 10 Mar. 1903; d. New York, 6 Aug. 1931). Jazz cornetist. He toured the Midwest with the Wolverines (1923–24). Together with Frankie Trumbauer he played in Jean Goldkette's orchestra (1924, 1926–27); recorded under pseudonyms and Trumbauer's name (1924, 1927–29); and joined Paul Whiteman's orchestra (1927–29). Beiderbecke improvised lyrical, largely diatonic melodies, using expressive timbral effects. He preferred a gentle sound and the cornet's middle register, thus providing an influential alternative to Louis Armstrong's more emphatic approach. His recordings include "Singin' the Blues" and "Riverboat Shuffle" with Trumbauer, "At the Jazz Band Ball" and "Royal Garden Blues" as leader, and "In a Mist" as an unaccompanied pianist (all 1927).

Bibl.: Richard M. Sudhalter and Philip R. Evans, with William Dean-Myatt, *Bix: Man and Legend* (New Rochelle, N.Y., 1974).

Beissel, (Johann) Conrad [Konrad] (b. Eberbach, near Mannheim, 1 Mar. 1691; d. Ephrata, Pa., 6 July 1768). Composer. Apprenticed to a baker; converted to Pietism in 1715; religious intolerance drove him to Pennsylvania, where in 1720 he settled among Baptists. In 1732 he founded the Ephrata Cloister, a monastic community. Benjamin Franklin published three collections of his hymns (1730–36), and in 1739 Christopher Sauer published his *Zionistischer Weyrauchs Hügel.* Eventually the monastic group formed its own press, which in 1747 issued a hymn collection (with texts only) titled *Das Gesang der einsamen und verlassenen Turtel-Taube.* This hymnal contained a preface by Beissel, "Vorrede über die Sing-Arbeit," which outlines his own singing method based on "master" tones (the pitches of the tonic triad) and the remaining "servant" tones. The group's next hymnal, *Paradisisches Wunder-Spiel* (1754), contains both text and music; the hymns are unusual for their curiously random harmonies and lack of regular metric pulse.

Bibl.: Lloyd George Blakely, "Johann Conrad Beisel [sic] and Music of the Ephrata Cloister," *JRMA* 15 (1967): 120–38.

Belafonte, Harry [Harold George, Jr.] (b. New York, 1 Mar. 1927). Popular singer, actor. In the 1950s he made recordings of traditional African, American, and Caribbean music in popular music arrangements; his versions of Trinidadian calypso music, included on the albums *Calypso* (1956) and *Belafonte at Carnegie Hall* (1959), were particularly popular. He studied acting in the 1940s and appeared in films in the 1960s and 1970s.

Belcher, Supply (b. Stoughton, Mass., 29 Mar. 1752; d. Farmington, Maine, 9 June 1836). Composer. After brief stints as salesman (in Boston) and barkeeper (in Stoughton), he moved to what is now Maine and studied at the Hollowell Academy. In 1791 he relocated to Farmington, where he was chief magistrate, schoolteacher, choirmaster, and violinist. A leading figure in the development of American psalmody, in 1794 he published *The Harmony of Maine* (R: *The Harmony of Maine by Supply Belcher,* ed. H. Wiley Hitchcock [New York, 1972]); it is a collection of his own compositions, including hymns, anthems, and fuguing tunes.

Bibl.: E. Owen, "The Life and Music of Supply Belcher" (diss., Southern Baptist Theological Seminary, 1969).

Bellini, Vincenzo (Salvatore Carmelo Francesco) (b. Catania, 3 Nov. 1801; d. Puteaux, near Paris, 23 Sept. 1835). Composer. The son and grandson of professional musicians, both of whom spent their careers in Catania, Bellini had lessons from his grandfather (himself a graduate of one of the Naples conservatories). He had begun to compose sacred and secular vocal works and instrumental pieces before, by means of a subsidy from the Catania city government; became in 1819 (at a rather advanced age for entering) a student at the Naples Conservatory (then called the Real collegio di musica di San Sebastiano). On arriving he was given a scholarship but was assigned to elementary classes because of defects found in the sample compositions he had submitted. Progressing rapidly, he was granted free tuition in 1820; his teachers included Crescentini for vocal style, Furno for figured bass, and Tritto (later Zingarelli) for counterpoint. With his closest friend, Francesco Florimo, he joined the *carbonari,* supporting the constitutionalist unrest of 1820, but escaped retribution in the reaction of 1821. Various student compositions survive, including orchestral pieces, an oboe concerto (1823?), and sacred works. He became a *maestrino* (teaching younger students) and in 1824 *primo maestrino.*

In 1824 Bellini was selected for the honor given the most promising student composers of having an opera performed by other students in the conservatory's little theater. This was *Adelson e Salvini,* an opera semiseria with spoken dialogue and a comic servant in Neapolitan dialect, to an existing libretto by A. L. Tottola. First performed in mid-February 1825, it was successful and was repeated on Sundays throughout the year. It was never produced elsewhere, and Bellini used material from it in five later operas. This success led to a commission for an opera seria for the Teatro San Carlo. *Bianca e Gernando* (libretto by Domenico Gilardoni) was postponed from January 1826 to 30 May, necessitating revisions to accommodate different singers, but was well received.

Through the impresario Barbaja, Bellini was engaged to compose the principal opera for the autumn 1827 season at La Scala, Milan, where he went in April 1827. This began his collaboration with the librettist Felice Romani, who was to write the texts of all his operas until their rupture in 1833. Their *Il pirata,* premiered on 27 Oct. 1827 with Méric-Lalande, Rubini, and Tamburini as its stars, had a success of a magnitude that established Bellini in Italy and internationally as one of the leading opera composers of the day. By 1830 it had been performed in Vienna, Naples, Rome, Dresden, Venice, Trieste, Bologna, Madrid, and London.

With Romani, Bellini then revised his *Bianca e Gernando* as *Bianca e Fernando* for the inauguration of the Teatro Carlo Felice in Genoa on 7 Apr. 1828. Well received, it had a few further productions (La Scala, 1829), but did not enter the repertory. *La straniera* had its premiere, starring Méric-Lalande and Tamburini, on 14 Feb. 1829 at La Scala. A great success and widely performed in Europe and the Americas, the opera marked an important stage in Bellini's freeing himself from Rossinian influences. By this time he had consciously established his pattern of composing fewer operas than most of his contemporaries but more slowly and with greater care, because of which he felt justified in demanding higher fees. Nevertheless, Bellini and Romani both wrote *Zaira* in a hurry for the inauguration of the new Teatro ducale at Parma (16 May 1829); it was a failure, never produced elsewhere. Material from it was used in later operas. For Carnival 1830 Bellini revised *Il pirata* for the company at the Teatro La Fenice, Venice, and again on short notice composed a new opera there, *I Capuleti e i Montecchi,* to an existing libretto by Romani, somewhat revised by him. Premiered on 11 March, it was a great and widespread success. This period marked the onset of the chronic intestinal ailment that was to weaken Bellini and eventually kill him.

After a projected *Ernani,* on Hugo's recent play, was aborted by censorship problems, Bellini and Romani produced the opera semiseria *La sonnambula* for the Teatro Carcano, Milan (6 Mar. 1831). One of Bellini's most enduring successes, it marked the first association with his work of the prima donna Giuditta Pasta, who was also to create Norma and Beatrice di Tenda. *Norma* had its premiere at La Scala on 26 Dec. 1831. After an initially cold reception, it quickly achieved its standing as Bellini's finest work, an opinion shared by the composer himself. In 1832 Bellini visited Naples and Sicily, where he was enthusiastically received. His last opera composed in Italy, *Beatrice di Tenda* (La Fenice, Venice, 16 Mar. 1833), had an unfriendly reception because it had been delayed a month, and the resulting bitterness and recriminations between Bellini and Romani ended their collaboration. Bellini spent April through August 1833 in London directing productions of his operas, featuring Pasta, at the King's Theatre. He then settled in Paris, where at the Théâtre-Italien he produced his last opera, *I puritani* (24 Jan. 1835), to a text by the Italian exile poet Count Carlo Pepoli. Sung by Grisi, Rubini, Tamburini, and Lablache, it was enthusiastically received. A revised version, made for the Teatro San Carlo, Naples, was never performed. Bellini composed almost no nonoperatic music after his student days, apart from many salon romances.

Bibl.: Luisa Cambi, ed., *Vincenzo Bellini: Epistolario* (Milan, 1943). Leslie Orrey, *Bellini* (New York, 1969). Herbert Weinstock, *Vincenzo Bellini: His Life and His Operas* (New York, 1971). Friedrich Lippmann, "Vincenzo Bellini und die italienische Opera seria seiner Zeit," *AnMca* 6 (1969). Pierre Brunel, *Vincenzo Bellini* (Paris, 1981).

Bellson, Louie [Louis Paul; Balassoni, Luigi Paulinho Alfredo Francesco Antonio] (b. Rock Falls, Ill., 6 July 1924). Jazz drummer and bandleader. After playing with Benny Goodman (1942–43, 1946) and Tommy Dorsey (1947–49), he and Charlie Shavers led a sextet. He joined Harry James (1950–51) and Duke Ellington (1951–53). Beginning 1953 he accompanied the singer Pearl Bailey, whom he married in 1952. He toured with Jazz at the Philharmonic (occasionally 1954–1970s). After joining the Dorsey brothers (1955–56), he settled in California. From 1967 he led a big band based in North Hollywood; in the late 1980s he began to lead a big band in New York and combos drawn from both ensembles. Bellson's recordings include his own composition "Skin Deep" on Ellington's album *Seattle Concert* (1954) and, as a leader, the album *Thunderbird* (1963).

Belyayev, Mitrofan Petrovich (b. St. Petersburg, 22 Feb. 1836; d. St. Petersburg, 10 Jan. 1904). Music publisher. Father was a timber merchant, and Belyayev joined his father's business after leaving school. In 1882 he heard Glazunov's Symphony no. 1 and offered to finance publication of the composer's works. Soon after he set up a publishing house in Leipzig (Belaieff) to secure international copyright for Russian composers. Published thousands of works of Russian composers, including Balakirev, Rimsky-Korsakov, Taneyev, Lyadov, Mussorgsky, and others. Financed the Glinka Awards for young composers. Instituted the Russian Symphony Concerts in St. Petersburg in 1885 and did the same at the Paris Exhibition of 1889. The firm moved to Bonn during World War II and later to Frankfurt am Main, where it was eventually taken over by C. F. Peters.

Bemetzrieder, Anton (b. Dauendorf, 1743 or 1748; d. London, ca. 1817). Music theorist and composer. After preparing for the Benedictine order, he abandoned it in 1770 to study with Diderot in Paris. There he established himself as a music teacher, and in 1771 he published *Leçons de clavecin, et principes d'harmonie* (Paris, 1771; R: 1966). After 1781 he lived in London, where he taught and continued to publish treatises. In his writings he systematized and made pragmatic the theories of Rameau and others; he published 13 known theoretical works and several keyboard works.

Bibl.: Robert Niklaus, "Diderot and the *Leçons de clavecin, et principes d'harmonie* par Bemetzrieder (1771)," in *Modern Miscellany Presented to Eugène Vinaver by Pupils, Colleagues, and Friends* (Manchester, 1969), pp. 180–94.

Benda, Franz [František] (b. Staré Benátky [Altbenatek], Bohemia, bapt. 22 Nov. 1709; d. Nowawes, near Potsdam, 7 Mar. 1786). Composer and violin virtuoso. Eldest of five musical children of Jan Jiří [Johann Georg] Benda (1686–1757) and Dorota Brixi. In 1720 he ran away from his position in the choir at St. Nicolas's in Prague; he ended up in Dresden, where he sang in the court chapel choir and began study of violin and viola. In 1723 he returned to Prague, where he was a chorister and seminary student. He received employment in Frederick II's orchestra in 1733, a position he held until his death. In Berlin he had close contact with C. P. E. Bach, Quantz, and the Graun brothers; he has recounted his young years in a valuable autobiography (written 1763). Benda was famous for his cantabile playing; copies of his violin works contain embellished melodic lines that perhaps represent the way he played them. He composed symphonies, concertos, sonatas, and other chamber music.

Bibl.: Franz Benda, autobiography originally in *Neue Berliner Musikzeitung* 10 (1856): 251, 259, 267, 274; trans. Paul Nettl, *Forgotten Musicians* (New York, 1951), pp. 204–45. Franz Lorenz, *Franz Benda und seine Nachkommen* (Berlin, 1967). Douglas A. Lee, *Franz Benda (1709–1786): A Thematic Catalogue of His Works* (New York, 1984). Daniel Heartz, "Coming of Age in Bohemia: The Musical Apprenticeship of Benda and Gluck," *JM* 6 (1988): 510–27.

Benda, Georg (Anton) [Jiří Antonín] (b. Staré Benátky [Altbenatek], Bohemia, bapt. 30 June 1722; d. Köstritz, 6 Nov. 1795). Composer. Early music study was in Kosmonos and Jičín in Bohemia; in 1742 he and his parents moved to Potsdam, where he joined his brother Franz in the court orchestra of Frederick II. In 1750 he became Kapellmeister at Frederick III's ducal chapel at Gotha. Upon the latter's death in 1772, Benda—free from his duties composing sacred works—devoted much effort to theater music. His singspiels such as *Der Jahrmarkt* (1775; publ. as *DDT* 64) and *Romeo und Julie* (1776), and especially the melodramas such as *Ariadne auf Naxos* (1775) and *Medea* (1775), were highly successful. Mozart praised the latter two works, which he heard in Mannheim in 1778 (letter of 12 Nov. 1778). That year Benda moved to Hamburg and shortly thereafter to Vienna, but received no appointment at either court. In all he composed 15 stage works, many sacred cantatas and oratorios, songs, some 30 symphonies, concertos, and many solo keyboard works.

Bibl.: A. H. Fritz Brückner, "Georg Benda und das deutsche Singspiel," *SIMG* 5 (1903–4): 571–621. Karl-Heinz Löbner, "Georg Benda: Sein Leben und sein Werk mit besonderer Berücksichtigung der Sinfonien und Cembalokonzerte" (diss., Univ. of Halle-Wittenberg, 1967). Arthur S. Winsor, "The Melodramas and Singspiels of Georg Benda" (diss., Univ. of Michigan, 1967).

Bendl, Karel (b. Prague, 16 Apr. 1838; d. there, 20 Sept. 1897). Composer. Studied at the Prague Organ School 1855–58 under Pietsch, Blažek, and Zvonař; supported by his wealthy father, he composed for the next 6 years, principally vocal music–songs, duets, and quartets. In 1864–65 he worked as a conductor and chorusmaster in Brussels, Amsterdam, and Paris. Returning to Prague, he conducted the Hlahol Choral Society for 12 years, for which he composed much music. In 1874 he also became assistant conductor at the Provisional Theater, at which his first opera, *Lejla,* had been performed in 1867. In the late 1870s he left Prague, returning in 1881 as a journalist. After holding a post as a church musician beginning in 1886, he succeeded Dvořák as professor of composition at the conservatory in 1894. He composed 9 Czech operas, mostly first performed in Prague, as well as a German opera and one, never performed, in Italian; also a ballet. Several of the stage works use national subjects and, occasionally, folk themes. He also continued in later years to compose songs and choral music. Among the relatively few instrumental works are dances and similar pieces for orchestra, a string quartet, and piano pieces.

Benedict, Julius (b. Stuttgart, 27 Nov. 1804; d. London, 5 June 1885). Composer and conductor. Began studying at 15 with Hummel in Weimar, and in 1821–24 was a pupil of Weber, of whom he published a biography in 1881. From 1825 to 1834 was conductor in Naples at the Teatro San Carlo and Teatro del Fondo, also composing Italian operas for both; moved to Paris in 1834; lived in London from 1835. From 1836 he conducted at the Opera Buffa at the Lyceum Theatre and in 1838–48 at Drury Lane, for which he composed 3 English operas in this period. In 1850–52 he toured the U.S. with Jenny Lind. Became conductor at Her Majesty's Theatre in 1852 and also conducted concerts and oratorios in London and at the British Festivals, especially the Norwich Festival (1845–78), for which he wrote 3 English cantatas (1860–66). An oratorio, *St. Peter,* was given at the Birmingham Festival in 1870. He conducted the Liverpool Philharmonic, 1876–80. His best-known work was the first of his 2 later English operas, *The Lily of Killarney* (Covent Garden, 1862). He was also known as a pianist and piano teacher. He composed 2 piano concertos and much solo piano music, some orchestra pieces, and a string quartet. He also published a book on his friend Mendelssohn (1850) and was knighted in 1871.

Benet [Benett, Bonet], **John** (fl. ca. 1420–50). Composer. May have been master of the choristers at St.

Anthony's Hospital in London from 1443. The majority of his extant compositions are Mass movements (about 18 settings). Some of these can be paired or form part of incomplete cyclic Masses; several carry conflicting attributions to Power or Dunstable. He also composed 3 isorhythmic motets.

Benevoli, Orazio (b. Rome, 19 Apr. 1605; d. there, 17 June 1672). Composer. Son of a French baker, he served as choirboy at S. Luigi dei Francesi in Rome (1617–23) and thereafter assumed posts as *maestro di cappella* at S. Maria in Trastevere (from 1624), at Santo Spirito in Sassia (from 1630), and eventually at his old church, S. Luigi dei Francesi (from 1638). In Vienna he served the Archduke Leopold Wilhelm in 1644–46, but he returned to Rome to serve at S. Maria Maggiore and at the Cappella Giulia (St. Peter's). He composed Masses, motets, Magnificats, and other sacred vocal works. His fame has rested largely on a work that he apparently did not compose: strong external and internal evidence suggests that the 53-part *Missa salisburgensis,* long cited as an example of the "gigantic" Baroque polychoral style, was not the work by Benevoli performed in Salzburg Cathedral in 1628, but dates from later in the 17th century and is probably by H. J. Biber.

Bibl.: *Opera omnia* (Trent, 1966–). Ernst Hintermaier, "The Missa Salisburgensis," *MT* 116 (1975): 965–66.

Ben Haim, Paul (b. Munich, 5 July 1897; d. Tel Aviv, 14 Jan. 1984). Composer and conductor. At Munich's Akademie der Tonkunst he studied conducting and composition with Friedrich Klose and Walter Courvoisier. From 1920 to 1924 he was assistant conductor to Bruno Walter and Hans Knappertsbusch in Munich; subsequently he conducted in Augsberg until 1931. He was forced to leave Germany in 1933; settling in Palestine, he assumed the surname Ben Haim, replacing the original Frankenburger. In Tel Aviv and Jerusalem he taught and conducted at conservatories, and by the 1950s he had established himself as a leading Israeli composer. In 1957 he won the nation's State Prize for *The Sweet Psalmist of Israel,* for harpsichord, harp, and orchestra (first perf., 1956). After the 1940s his music, characterized by a late romantic style, showed influence from Yemenite folk music. Works include 2 symphonies (1940; 1945); Concerto Grosso (1931); *From Israel,* orchestral suite (1952); *To the Chief Musician* (1957–58); *The Eternal Theme* (1965). Choral and other vocal works include *3 Songs without Words* (1952); *Yoram,* soprano, baritone, chorus, orchestra (1963); *Kabbalai Shabbat* [Friday Evening Service], soprano, tenor, chorus, organ, chamber orchestra (1967); and *6 Sephardic Songs,* chorus (1971); also chamber and other instrumental music, including Clarinet Quintet (1941); *Sonatina,* piano, op. 38 (1946); *Serenade,* flute, string trio (1952); *Music,* piano (1957); *3 Pieces,* cello (1973).

Bibl.: Hadassah Guttmann, *The Music of Paul Ben Haim: A Performance Guide* (Metuchen, N.J., 1992).

Benjamin, Arthur (b. Sydney, 18 Sept. 1893; d. London, 10 Apr. 1960). Composer and pianist. From 1911 to 1914 he studied with Charles Stanford (composition) and Frederick Cliffe (piano) at London's Royal College of Music. After service in World War I, he returned to Australia, where from 1919 he taught at the Sydney Conservatory. He resettled in London in 1921 and was made professor at the Royal College of Music in 1926. He is best known for his operas (*The Devil Take Her,* 1931; *The Tale of Two Cities,* 1949–50; *Mañana,* 1956), for the two-piano *Jamaican Rumba* (1938; also in a version for orchestra), and for the Concerto for Oboe and Strings (1942), an arranged pastiche of one-movement keyboard sonatas of Cimarosa. His neoclassical idiom shows influence from dance band and Latin American music. Other works include music for orchestra (*Cotillon,* 9 dance tunes, 1938; *Prelude to Holiday,* 1940; a symphony, 1944–45; *Elegy, Waltz, and Toccata,* viola, piano, orchestra, 1945; *From San Domingo,* 1945); vocal music (*3 Mystical Songs,* 1925); 2 string quartets and other chamber music; many songs; much piano music (*Scherzino,* 1936).

Benjamin, George (b. London, 31 Jan. 1960). Composer. He began piano at 7, started composing at the age of 9. Studied with Peter Gellhorn; at the Paris Conservatory with Messiaen and Yvonne Loriod; at King's College, Cambridge, with Alexander Goehr (1978–82). Has worked with the London Sinfonietta and at the Royal College of Music. His works include a piano sonata (1978) and the orchestral works *Ringed by the Flat Horizon* (1980), *At First Light* (soprano and chamber ensemble, 1982), and *A Mind of Winter* (soprano and orchestra, 1986).

Bennet, John (b. ca. 1575–80?; fl. 1599–1614). Composer. Probably from northwestern England. His works consist of a book of madrigals for 4 voices (London, 1599), 1 madrigal in *The Triumphes of Oriana* (1601), 2 consort songs, 4 Psalm settings and a prayer in Barley's psalter of ca. 1599, a verse anthem, and 6 secular vocal pieces in Ravenscroft's *A Briefe Discourse* (1614). The madrigals include both solemn and lighter works. Many are clearly modeled on the style cultivated by Thomas Morley, but influences from Weelkes, Wilbye, and Dowland are also evident. The consort songs and the anthem show an awareness of earlier English styles.

Bennett, Richard Rodney (b. Broadstairs, Kent, 29 Mar. 1936). Composer and pianist. He studied at the Royal Academy of Music with Lennox Berkeley and Howard Ferguson (1953–56). Upon completing his formal schooling he went to Paris, where he studied privately with Pierre Boulez (1957–58). Later he taught at the Royal Academy (1963–65) and at the Peabody Conservatory in Baltimore (1970–71). His early works employed twelve-tone methods; after the Paris years this was combined with a postromantic lyricism. Some of his music has been compared to that of Berg. He has composed scores for a number of films: *Blind Date* (1955), *Nicholas and Alexandra* (1971), *Murder on the Orient Express* (1973), and *Equus* (1977). Stage works: the operas *The Ledge* (1961), *The Mines of Sulphur* (1963; first perf. 1965), *All the King's Men* (children's opera, 1968), and *Victory* (1970); a ballet score, *Isadora* (1981). Orchestral works: 2 symphonies (1965, 1967); *Journal* (1960); *Nocturnes* (1962–63); Concerto for Orchestra (1973); concertos for oboe (1969–70), viola (1973), violin (1975), double bass (1978), 2 for piano (1968, 1976), saxophone (1988); *Zodiac* (1975–76; written for the U.S. Bicentennial); *Anniversaries* (1982); *Dream Dancing* (1986); *Concerto for Stan Getz,* sax, orchestra (1992); *Celebration,* orchestra (1992); clarinet quintet (1992). Choral works: *The Aviary,* unison voices, piano (1965); *The House of Sleepe,* 6 male voices (1971); *Letters to Lindbergh,* female voices, piano four-hands (1981); *Nonsense,* youth choir (1984). Other vocal works: *Nocturnall upon St. Lucie's Day* (1954); *Soliloquy,* voice, jazz ensemble (1966); *The Music That Her Echo Is* (1967). In addition are some 40 chamber works (4 string quartets, 1952–64; *Sonatina,* solo flute, 1954; *Commedia* I–I); many keyboard works (Sonata, 1954; *Cycle 2 for Paul Jacobs,* 1958; *Scena I,* 1973; *Kandinsky Variations,* 2 pianos, 1977).

Bibl.: Christopher Palmer and Lewis Foreman, "Richard Rodney Bennett," in Lewis Foreman, *British Music Now* (London, 1975). Susan Bradshaw, "Richard Rodney Bennett: The Last Decade," *MT* 123 (1982): 609–11. Stewart R. Craggs, *Richard Rodney Bennett: A Bio-Bibliography* (New York, 1990).

Bennett, Robert Russell (b. Kansas City, Mo., 15 June 1894; d. New York, 18 Aug. 1981). Composer, orchestrator, and conductor. As a child he studied piano with his mother and violin and trumpet with his father; later in Kansas City he studied with Carl Busch. By the age of 16 he was in New York working as a dance band musician and music copyist and in 1919 began orchestrating songs for the publisher T. B. Harms. From 1926 to 1931 he lived in Europe, studying with Boulanger in Paris and holding two successive Guggenheim fellowships (1927–29). From 1937 to 1940 he was president of the American Society of Musical Arrangers and later wrote a book on orchestration (*Instrumentally Speaking,* 1974). By the end of his career he had orchestrated over 200 musicals by all the major Broadway composers: Berlin (*Annie Get Your Gun,* 1946), Friml (*Rose Marie,* 1924), Gershwin (*Of Thee I Sing,* 1931), Kern (*Show Boat,* 1927), Loewe (*My Fair Lady,* 1956; *Camelot,* 1960), Porter (*Anything Goes,* 1934; *Kiss Me, Kate,* 1948), Rodgers (*Oklahoma!,* 1943; *South Pacific,* 1949; *The King and I,* 1951; *The Sound of Music,* 1959), Weill. He worked in Hollywood on more than 30 film scores (1936–40); received an Oscar in 1955 for the film adaptation of *Oklahoma!* Much of his concert music makes use of popular idioms or Americana. Works include 2 operas, a ballet-operetta, 6 symphonies (including *Stephen Collins Foster,* a commemoration symphony for orchestra and chorus, 1959); other works for orchestra, some with soloists (Concerto Grosso, jazz band and orchestra, 1932); a string quartet, a quintet for organ and strings, a piano trio (*Hexapoda,* 1940), and other chamber music; and several works for band or wind ensemble (*Suite of Old American Dances,* 1949).

Bibl.: George Joseph Ferencz, *Robert Russell Bennett: A Bio-Bibliography* (New York, 1990).

Bennett, Tony [Benedetto, Anthony Dominick] (b. New York, 3 Aug. 1926). Popular singer. After singing in American military bands during World War II, he returned to New York, where he came under the tutelage of comedian Bob Hope and Columbia Records' popular music director Mitch Miller. Early recordings included "Cold, Cold, Heart" (1951) and "Rags to Riches" (1953); his greatest success came with the later "I Left My Heart in San Francisco" (1962). He continued to perform with swing bands, popular orchestras, and jazz artists including Bill Evans.

Bennett, William Sterndale (b. Sheffield, 13 Apr. 1816; d. London, 1 Feb. 1875). Composer. From a family of church musicians, he was a choirboy at King's College, Cambridge, 1824–26; then until 1836 studied at the Royal Academy of Music (composition under Crotch and Cipriani Potter). He became a virtuoso pianist and from 1832 began to be known as a composer, especially through his first piano concerto, which aroused much interest, including that of Mendelssohn. The period 1832–38 was the most productive of his life: 5 piano concertos, 5 symphonies, 6 concert overtures; a piano sestet; a piano sonata, Fantaisie, and shorter pieces; and songs. He appeared frequently in concerts as a pianist and visited Germany twice in 1836–37, where he was enthusiastically received by Mendelssohn and Schumann and began to appear with success as a pianist and composer. From 1837 he was very active as a teacher, both privately and from 1837 to 1858 at the Royal Academy. He continued to play in concerts, but his output of music slowed, consisting in the 1840s mainly of piano pieces and songs. In 1849 he founded the Bach Society, which he conducted, giving the English premiere of the St. Matthew Passion; from 1856 to 1866 was conductor of the Philharmonic Society; in 1856 became professor of music at Cambridge and in 1866 principal of the Royal Academy; received knighthood, one of many honors of this period, in 1871. In later years he composed a symphony (1864), a piano sonata (The Maid of Orleans, 1873), cantatas and choral odes, and sacred music.

Bibl.: James Robert Sterndale Bennett, *The Life of William Sterndale Bennett* (Cambridge, 1907). Charles Villiers Stanford, "William Sterndale Bennett, 1816–1875," *MQ* 2 (1916): 628–57. Gerald W. Spink, "Schumann and Sterndale Bennett," *MT* 105 (1964): 419–21. Geoffrey Bush, "Sterndale Bennett: The Solo Piano Works," *PRMA* 91 (1964–65): 85–97. Geoffrey Bush, "Sterndale Bennett: A Note on His Chamber and Piano Music," *MT* 113 (1972): 554–56. Nicholas Temperley, "Sterndale Bennett and the Lied," *MT* 116 (1975): 958–61, 1060–63.

Benoit, Peter (Léonard Léopold) (b. Harlebeke, Belgium, 17 Aug. 1834; d. Antwerp, 8 Mar. 1901). Composer and teacher. Studied at the Brussels Conservatory, 1851–55 (composition with Fétis); was often in great financial need, which led him to take a job as supplementary triangle player at the Théâtre de la Monnaie. In 1856 became conductor at the Park Theater in Brussels and produced his first Flemish opera (with spoken dialogue), *Het dorp in 't gebergte.* In 1857 won the Belgian Prix de Rome, but spent it in Germany in 1858 rather than Italy. From 1859 to 1863 he was frequently in Paris, conducting in 1862–63 at Offenbach's Théâtre des Bouffes-Parisiens. Settling again in Brussels, he was increasingly active in musical life there and as a composer. His growing reputation became fully established with the Brussels premiere of his oratorio *Lucifer* (30 Sept. 1866), which was widely performed. He was increasingly drawn to Flemish musical nationalism, of which he became the central figure and which he furthered through writings (some collected in *Geschriften van Peter Benoit,* ed. August Corbet, Antwerp, 1942), his music, and education. He founded the Flemish Music School in Antwerp in 1867 and headed it until his death; it became the Royal Flemish Conservatory in 1898. He composed several operas and "lyric dramas" that combined rhythmical declamation and music (*Charlotte Corday,* 1876). Admired for his choral writing, he was judged at his best in oratorios (*De schelde,* 1868; *De oorlog,* 1873; *De Rhijn,* 1889) and cantatas (including his best-known work, *De Rubens-cantate,* 1877, and the children's cantata *De Waereld in!,* 1878); also composed sacred music, songs, some instrumental works, and many piano pieces.

Bibl.: Charles van den Borren, *Peter Benoit* (Brussels, 1942). August Corbet, *Peter Benoit: Leven, werk en beteekenis* (Antwerp, 1943). Paul Douliez, *Peter Benoit* (Haarlem, 1954).

Benson, George (b. Pittsburgh, 22 Mar. 1943). Jazz and popular electric guitarist and singer. He played soul jazz with the organist Jack McDuff (1962–65) and recorded with Lee Morgan and Miles Davis (both 1968). From the mid-1960s he led groups. Though renowned for his performances with improvising jazz groups, he increasingly concentrated on relaxed dance rhythms and his singing, especially after the popular success of "This Masquerade" on his album *Breezin'* (1976).

Benson, Warren (Frank) (b. Detroit, 26 Jan. 1924). Composer. Studied theory at the Univ. of Michigan (1943–49; B.M., 1949; M.M., 1951), where he played in and arranged music for a jazz band and was timpanist in the Detroit Symphony (1946). Taught in Greece (1950–52), in North Carolina, at Ithaca College (1953–67), and at the Eastman School (from 1967). At Ithaca he founded the College Percussion Ensemble and developed musicianship courses aided by a Ford Foundation grant (*Creative Projects in Musicianship,* 1967). He is the author of *Compositional Processes and Writing Skills* (Washington, D.C., 1974). Many of his own works reflect interests in timbre and a montage technique that may include quotations. He has composed works for orchestra (Concertino, flute, strings, percussion, 1983); band or wind ensemble (*The Leaves Are Falling,* 1963); percussion and other chamber ensembles (*Pieces,* string quartet, 1987; *Icelandic Songs,* string quartet, 1987; string quartet no. 3, "Cat's Cradle," 1995; *A Gift from Cordoba* (Ruminations on a Chorale by Alfonso Romero), wind band, 1995); piano; choir; and solo voice.

Bentzon, Niels Viggo (b. Copenhagen, 24 Aug. 1919). Composer and pianist; cousin of composer Jørgen (Liebenberg) Bentzon (1897–1951). Early study of the piano was with his mother; later at the Royal Conservatory in Copenhagen he studied composition with Knud Jeppesen (1939–1942). In 1949 he joined the staff of the Copenhagen Conservatory. His music contains elements of Bartók, jazz, nonserialized atonality, and aleatory. (Opus numbers reach into the 400s.) A painter, poet, and critic, he authored books on Beethoven and on twelve-tone composition. Among his operas are *Faust III* (1964) and *Automaten* (1974); ballets include *Metafor* (1950), *Jenny von Westphalen* (1965), *Duell* (1977); orchestral works include 15 numbered symphonies (1942–80; no. 4, Metamorfosen, 1948–49), *Chamber Symphony* (1962), *Sinfonia* (1977), concertos (8 for piano, 4 for violin, 3 for cello, 2 for flute, some 15 others), Overture (chamber orchestra, 1942), Orchestral Sonata (flute, strings, 1943), *Intrada* (1950), *Symphonic Variations* (1953), *5 Mobiles* (1960), *Reflection Suite* (strings, 1972), *Feature Article on René Descartes* (1975), *Variations without a Theme* (piano, orchestra, 1980); choral music includes *Torquilla* (oratorio, 1961), *Bonjour Max Ernst* (cantata, 1961), *Det rustre menageri* (cantata, 1972). Also composed much chamber and solo instrumental music, including 11 string quartets (1940–76); 5 wind quintets; many solo instrumental sonatas, including more than 15 for piano (1940–81); *In the Forest,* solo horn (1968); *Observations* (1974); *Det tempererede Klaver,* 5 sets of 24 preludes and fugues for piano (1964–79).

Bérard, Jean-Antoine (b. Lunel, 1710; d. Paris, 1 Dec. 1772). Singer (*haute-contre,* or high tenor) and writer on the voice. He sang his debut at the Paris Opéra in 1733 as Pélée in Pascal Collasse's *Thétis et Pélée.* After a stint with the Italian troupe in Paris, he returned to the Opéra in 1737 to sing a number of small roles in works of Rameau and others. He played the title role in Boismortier's *Don Quichotte chez la Duchesse* in 1743. From 1762 he played cello at the Comédie italienne. His vocal treatise *L'art du chant* (Paris, 1735), which resembles one by Joseph Blanchet published the following year (Blanchet claimed plagiarism of his manuscript), is a valuable compendium of vocal practice in the middle of the 18th century.

Berardi, Angelo (b. S. Agata, Tuscany, ca. 1636; d. Rome, 9 Apr. 1694). Composer and theorist. He studied with Marco Scacchi from 1650 and served as *maestro di cappella* in several cities, including Tivoli (1673–79), the cathedral in Spoleto (ca. 1681), and at S. Maria in Trastevere in Rome (1690s). He composed Masses (*Missa pro defunctis,* 1663); Psalm settings and other sacred music; secular vocal music (*Musiche diverse variamente concertate per camera,* 2–4 voices, Bologna, 1689). He was one of the leading theorists and pedagogues of his era. His treatises, which deal with contrapuntal composition and harmony, include *Ragionamenti musicali* (before 1681, lost); *Documenti armonici* (Bologna, 1687); *Miscellanea musicale* (Bologna, 1689); *Arcani musicali* (Bologna, 1690); and *Il perchè musicale* (Bologna, 1693). His last writings summarize in several significant ways the musical theory of the 17th century, advocating a coexistence of *prima* and *seconda prattica.*

Berberian, Cathy (b. Attleboro, Mass., 4 July 1925; d. Rome, 6 Mar. 1983). Mezzo-soprano. While soloist with New York's Armenian Folk Group in 1950, she received a Fulbright Scholarship that enabled her to study with Giorgina del Vigo in Italy. Debut in 1957 at a festival of contemporary music in Naples. Her performance of Cage's *Aria with Fontana Mix* the following year established her as a major presence in contemporary vocal music. Stravinsky and Henze wrote for her, as did Berio, her husband from 1950 to 1966. U.S. debut at the Berkshire Festival, 1960. Composed *Stripsody* for solo voice (1966) and *Morsicat(h)y* for piano (1971). In the 1970s she taught at the Univ. of Vancouver and Cologne's Rheinische Musikschule.

Berchem, Jacquet de (b. Berchem-lez-Anvers, near Antwerp, ca. 1505; d. ca. 1565). Composer; often confused with his contemporaries Jacquet of Mantua, Jacques Buus, and Jacques Brunel. He was in Venice by the 1530s and had much music published there beginning in 1538; *maestro di cappella* of Verona Cathedral from 1546 until perhaps 1550; may have visited Ferrara thereafter. Many of his madrigals were published in Rome between 1555 and 1563. He composed about 200 secular pieces, including some early chansons and a great many madrigals. The madrigals, often in cycles, were published in three complete books plus numerous anthologies and played an important role in the history of the genre. The earliest are in a Franco-Flemish contrapuntal style. Later works are more animated, chordal, and syllabic. The last book (1561) contains settings of nearly 100 stanzas from Ariosto's *Orlando furioso,* with the designation "capriccio." He also composed at least 2 Masses and 9 motets.

Berezowski, Nicolai (Tikhonovich) (b. St. Petersburg, 17 May 1900; d. New York, 27 Aug. 1953). Composer and violinist. Studied at the imperial chapel in St. Petersburg (1908–16), then played in opera and theater orchestras. Arriving in the U.S. in 1922, he played in the New York Philharmonic (1923–29) and studied composition and violin (Goldmark, Kochanski) at Juilliard. He became a U.S. citizen in 1928, then spent two years in Europe, where his violin concerto was premiered by Carl Flesch (Dresden, 1930). After his return to the U.S. his compositions were widely performed, especially by Koussevitzky with the Boston Symphony. He played in the Coolidge String Quartet (1935–40) and received a Guggenheim Fellowship in 1948. His works, in a mildly dissonant Russian Romantic idiom, include 4 symphonies, several concertos and other orchestral works, chamber music (string quartet, wind quintet, a brass suite for 7 performers), piano pieces, a cantata (*Gilgamesh,* 1947), and a children's opera, *Babar the Elephant* (premiered in 1953).

Alban Berg. Painting by Arnold Schoenberg.

Berg, Alban (Maria Johannes) (b. Vienna, 9 Feb. 1885; d. there, 24 Dec. 1935). Composer. Berg and Webern were the most prominent students of Schoenberg; the three are collectively referred to as the Second Viennese School. As a teenager Berg had composed songs on Romantic texts; on the basis of these he began to study with Schoenberg without fee in 1904. As Schoenberg's student he wrote the *Seven Early Songs,* which reflect the German lied tradition (1905–8); the Piano Sonata op. 1, generated completely from material exposed in the first few bars (1907–8); the *Four Songs* op. 2, in which tonality is in question and the final song is clearly atonal (completed in 1910); and the String Quartet op. 3 (1910). Berg's devotion to and reliance upon his teacher continued long past the formal termination of his studies in 1911, when Schoenberg moved to Berlin. In the months following his marriage to Helene Nahowski (1911) he worked on several piano reductions for Universal Edition, among them Schoenberg's *Gurrelieder.* He produced as well an analytical guide to that composition and helped to prepare the choruses for the first performance.

Berg's financial situation was improved by his mother's inheritance of substantial Viennese real estate in 1905, but that freedom did not turn him into a prolific composer, in part because the management of the real estate often fell to him. Between 1912 and the onset of the war he produced a set of orchestral songs (a partial performance under Schoenberg in 1913 was disrupted by the audience), *Four Pieces* for clarinet and piano, and *Three Orchestral Pieces,* dedicated to Schoenberg (1914). The songs and clarinet pieces are miniatures (though not so miniature as those of Webern); but in the orchestral pieces Berg attempted to produce a longer work whose structure is based on thematic manipulations rather than on the anchors of tonality. Berg served in the Austrian army for the next three years and apparently found little time for composition, although he did begin to work on *Wozzeck.*

In 1918, discouraged by the lack of appreciation for his own music and that of his followers, Schoenberg and his associates formed the Society for Private Musical Performances in Vienna: Berg wrote the prospectus, which specifies that concerts were by invitation and that works would be adequately rehearsed and could be repeated to give the audience a better chance to appreciate them. At the meetings of the society the press was not welcome, and fees were charged to members on a graduated scale. Berg was heavily involved in the operations of the society: he made piano arrangements, directed rehearsals, and performed other organizational duties in return for a small monthly stipend. Of his few completed works, only the *Altenberg Lieder* were not performed for the society. (They were first performed in Rome in 1952.)

Berg worked on *Wozzeck,* the first of his two operas, from 1917 until 1922. The libretto is his own revision of a drama by Büchner, recast into three acts of five scenes each. Each scene is a self-contained movement (prelude, march, rondo, sonata, scherzo, etc.) and each act a self-contained form, the outer two symmetrically balanced to create a large arch. Berg's combination of Wagnerian leitmotivs with the structure of a number opera was innovatory; his interest in numerology is reflected in the importance of the number 7 in the set of variations that open the third act. In the hope of exciting interest in the work, he published a vocal score with money raised by Alma Mahler; a concert suite was performed in Frankfurt in 1924 under Scherchen; and the entire opera was staged in Berlin on 14 Dec. 1925. Before Berg's death there were productions in Prague, Leningrad, Oldenburg and other small German opera houses, Vienna, Amsterdam, Darmstadt, Philadelphia, New York, and Brussels.

It was during these years that Schoenberg formulated his twelve-tone method, first employed by Berg in his second setting of "Schliesse mir die Augen beide" (1925). The *Lyric Suite* (1923–25) displays various features that distinguish his personal use of the method: a mixture of twelve-tone and freely constructed sections; use of more than one ordered set of twelve pitches; an emphasis on retaining the explicit linear contour of the set; avoidance of the retrograde and retrograde inversions. His treatments are not less systematic than those of his colleagues, merely different. While Schoenberg and Webern were avoiding any implication of tonality in the construction of their rows, the row in Berg's Violin Concerto (1935), consisting of alternate major and minor triads and a fragment of the whole-tone scale, has been called a search for a twelve-tone tonality. Moreover, elements outside the twelve-tone system are of importance: the quotations of the *Tristan* Prelude in the *Lyric Suite* (and of *Wozzeck* and the *Lyric Suite* in *Lulu*); the harmony oriented toward a tonal center but not in a key (e.g., the B pedal in the murder scene in *Wozzeck,* act 3, scene 2); the texture in which melody is ordinarily polarized against another melody, the bass, or an accompaniment layer (compared to the dense or florid counterpoint of Schoenberg and Webern); and Berg's large-scale conception of all his works.

At his death Berg had not completed the orchestration of the last act of *Lulu,* his second opera (after Wedekind). The vocal techniques employed in the opera include normal speech (accompanied or not), rhythmic speech, rhythmic declamation in which pitch is only to be suggested, a "half-sung" rhythmic declamation in which pitch is clearer, and traditional singing. Although fairly complete sketches survived, they remained inaccessible to scholars and performers until the mid-1970s; the first performance of the entire opera was not given until the performance in Paris in 1979 of a version completed by Friedrich Cerha.

Works: 2 operas, *Wozzeck* (1917–22) and *Lulu* (1929–35); *Three Pieces* (orchestra, 1914–15), Violin Concerto (1935), and suites from the operas; String Quartet (1910), *Lyric Suite* (string quartet, 1925–26), Chamber Concerto (violin, piano, and 13 winds, 1923–25), and *Four Pieces* (clarinet and piano, 1913); Piano Sonata (1907–8) and Variations for Piano (1908); *Fünf Orchesterlieder* (after Altenberg, 1912), *Der Wein* (soprano and orchestra, 1929); songs.

Bibl.: Willi Reich, *Alban Berg* [with contributions by Adorno and Krenek] (Vienna, 1937). Hans Redlich, *Alban Berg* (Vienna, 1957); trans., abridged (London, 1957). Willi Reich, *Alban Berg* (Zurich, 1963); trans. (London, 1965).

Mosco Carner, *Alban Berg: The Man and the Work* (London, 1975). George Perle, *Twelve-Tone Tonality* (Berkeley and Los Angeles, 1977). Douglas Jarman, *The Music of Alban Berg* (Berkeley, 1979). George Perle, *The Operas of Alban Berg* (Berkeley and Los Angeles), vol. 1, *Wozzeck* (1980); vol 2., *Lulu* (1984). Douglas Jarman, ed., *The Berg Companion* (Boston, 1990). David Gable and Robert P. Morgan, eds., *Alban Berg: Historical and Analytical Perspectives* (New York, 1991).

Berganza (Vargas), Teresa (b. Madrid, 16 Mar. 1935). Mezzo-soprano. She studied with her father from age 8, then with L. Rodríguez Aragón at the Madrid Conservatory. Won an Isabel la Católica grant in 1957. Following her debut as Mozart's Dorabella at Aachen (1957), her Cherubino (Glyndebourne, 1958), Cenerentola (Glyndebourne, 1959), and Rosina (Covent Garden, 1960) launched an international career. She has sung roles by Monteverdi, Cesti, and Purcell in addition to more standard fare (Mozart, Rossini, Bellini, and Massenet). She has also been heard in popular Spanish songs, excerpts from zarzuelas, and Falla's *La vida breve,* sometimes accompanied by her pianist husband, Felix Lavilla.

Berger, Arthur (Victor) (b. New York, 15 May 1912). Composer and critic. Studied at New York Univ. (B.S., 1934), the Longy School of Music (1935–37), and at Harvard under Piston (M.A., 1936). During the 1930s he met Cowell, Ives, and Varèse; was active in Copland's Young Composers Group; wrote music criticism supporting the avant-garde. He studied analysis with Boulanger (1937–39). Taught at Mills, Brooklyn College, Juilliard, Brandeis, and New England Conservatory. For a decade (from 1943) he was a music critic (*New York Herald Tribune,* 1946–53); was cofounder of *Perspectives of New Music* (1962); wrote a monograph on Copland (1953). After an early interest in twelve-tone procedures ("Two Episodes," piano, 1933) he abandoned composition until his contact with Milhaud at Mills (1939–42), when his interest in Stravinsky's neoclassicism emerged in his own works (*Serenade Concertante,* 1944; rev. 1951). In 1956 he returned to serial procedures (*Chamber Music for 13 Players,* 1956) in a style characterized by Babbitt as "diatonic Webern," in reference to transparent textures and fragmentation of melodic lines by means of registral displacements. After 1966 he employed serial procedures less strictly. He composed works for orchestra, chamber music (string quartet, 1958; piano trio, 1980), piano pieces, songs, and choral pieces.

Bibl.: *PNM* 17 (1978), including a list of his works and writings. Bayan Northcott, "Arthur Berger: An Introduction at 70," *MT* 123 (1982): 323–26.

Bergman, Erik (Valdemar) (b. Uusikaarlepyy, Finland, 24 Nov. 1911). Composer. Studied musicology with Krohn; literature at Helsinki Univ. (1931–33); composition at Helsinki Conservatory (1931–38) with Furuhjelm, Carlsson, and Hannikainen. Studied in Berlin (1937–39), later in Vienna with Joseph Marx; in Switzerland (1944–50) with Wladimir Vogel he learned twelve-tone techniques. Conducted Roman Catholic Church Choir of Helsinki and Akademiska Sångföreningen. Music critic for several Helsinki newspapers. Professor of composition at Helsinki Academy, 1963–76. At the end of the 1960s he abandoned strict serial procedures. Choral works make up the bulk of his compositions, but he also composed the opera *Det sjungande Trädet* [The Singing Tree] (1986–88), several instrumental works, and orchestral pieces (*Aubade,* 1958; a violin concerto, 1982).

Bergonzi, Carlo (1) (b. Cremona?, 1683; d. there, 1747). Violin maker. A leading figure among Cremonese instrument makers, he probably spent his early years in the Guarneri workshop. Not until the 1720s did he put his own labels on his violins; the best of the instruments date from the 1730s. His son Michel Angelo Bergonzi (b. ca. 1722; d. after 1758) carried on the tradition with serviceable violins, as did his sons Nicola (b. after 1746; d. after 1796), Carlo (b. ca. 1758; d. 1838), and Benedetto (1790?–1840).

Bergonzi, Carlo (2) (b. Polisene, near Parma, 13 July 1924). Baritone and tenor. After studies at Parma's Conservatorio di musica Arrigo Boito, he made his debut as baritone singing Rossini's Figaro at Lecce (1948). Three years later he made a second debut as tenor singing Giordano's Andrea Chénier at Bari (12 Jan. 1951). At his La Scala debut (1953) he sang Napoli's Masaniello; the same year he performed Verdi's Alvaro at London's Stoll Theatre. U.S. debut with the Chicago Lyric Opera, 1955. After his debut with New York's Metropolitan Opera, 13 Nov. 1956, singing Verdi's Radames, he remained with that company until 1983. Farewell recital in New York in 1994. His repertory of over 60 operas centers on Rossini, Donizetti, Bellini, Verdi, Massenet, and Puccini.

Bergsma, William (Laurence) (b. Oakland, Calif., 1 Apr. 1921; d. Seattle, 18 Mar. 1994). Composer. Studied violin as a child; composed and conducted while in high school; attended Stanford (1938–40); studied under Hanson and Bernard Rogers at Eastman (1940–44). His early ballet for puppets and solo dancers, *Paul Bunyan,* was staged in San Francisco (22 June 1939). Taught composition at Juilliard (1946–63) and then became director of the School of Music at the Univ. of Washington. Works, consistently tonal and lyrical, include 2 ballets and 2 operas (*The Wife of Martin Guerre,* 1951–56); pieces for orchestra (*A Carol on Twelfth Night,* 1954), some with chorus; chamber and piano music (5 string quartets, 1942–82; *Illegible Canons,* clarinet and percussion, 1969); choral works; songs.

Berigan, Bunny [Rowland Bernart] (b. Hilbert, Wis., 2 Nov. 1908; d. New York, 2 June 1942). Jazz trumpeter and bandleader. He joined Benny Goodman (1935), recording "King Porter Stomp," and Tommy Dorsey (1936–37), recording "Marie" (1937). He

Luciano Berio.

formed a big band (1937–39) known for its driving swing (supported successively by the drummers George Wettling, Dave Tough, and Buddy Rich) and for Berigan's sumptuous reading of the ballad "I Can't Get Started," recorded in 1937. After rejoining Dorsey briefly in 1940 he formed new bands, but his alcoholism impeded further success.

Berio, Luciano (b. Oneglia, Imperia, Italy, 24 Oct. 1925). Composer. The son and grandson of organists, he studied at the conservatory in Milan with Giorgio Ghedini and Giulio Paribeni; worked as accompanist and conductor in provincial opera productions (1948–50); in 1951 studied with Dallapiccola at the Berkshire Music Center. He was acquainted with the earliest electronic compositions of Luening and Ussachevsky, and his subsequent meeting with Maderna, Pousseur, and Stockhausen (1954) resulted in his opening (with Maderna) the Studio di fonologia sponsored by Italian Radio in Milan (1955). He resigned from that position in 1961. From 1963 to 1972 he lived in the U.S., where he taught at Mills, Harvard, and Juilliard; he returned to Italy in 1972. Has been active internationally (e.g., serving on the board of IRCAM, Paris); was Charles Eliot Norton Lecturer at Harvard 1993–94.

Berio's works from before 1962 explore three aspects of contemporary styles: serialism, electronic music, and aleatory procedures in composition and performance. *Serenata I* (flute and 14 instruments, 1958) applied serial procedures to tone color, pitch, and duration, while requiring a virtuosic performance from the flutist. In *Thema (Omaggio a Joyce)* he had Cathy Berberian (to whom he was married in 1950) record an excerpt from Joyce's *Ulysses,* then electronically transformed it to produce a choral-instrumental work. As early as *Sequenza I* (flute, 1958) he used proportional notation to indicate relative durations; in the solo cantata *Epiphanie* (1959–61) 6 instrumental and 5 vocal sections can be performed separately or combined in any order. Later compositions exhibit an even more eclectic and personal style, particularly in the treatment of the voice as pure timbre, the text as "verbal material," and in more and more complex collage and quotation techniques. *Sinfonia* (1968–69) quotes Debussy, Wagner, Mahler, and other composers (including Berio), and treats its texts (ranging from Lévi-Strauss to student slogans) as a gigantic quodlibet intended for performance initially by the Swingle Singers. In *Sinfonia* Berio adopted the "Antonius von Padua" movement of Mahler's Second Symphony as a framework within which to build his composition; his *Chemins* for orchestra treats his own *Sequenza* series as raw material for new works.

Works: Dramatic works including *Opera,* 4 acts, 1970, revised in 3 acts, 1977; *Recital I (for Cathy),* soprano and 17 instruments, 1972; *La vera storia,* opera, 1977–81; *Un re in ascolto,* opera, 1979–84. *Tempi concertati* (flute, violin, 2 pianos, 4 groups, 1958–59), *Entrata* (1980), *Voci* (viola and orchestra, 1984), *Formazioni* (1985–87), a piano concerto (1988), *Festum* (1989), *Rendering,* orchestra (1988–90), *Concerto II (Echoing curves),* orchestra (1990), *Chemins V,* guitar, orchestra (1992), and other orchestral works. The *Sequenza* series for soloists including flute, harp, voice, etc. (1958–), and other chamber music. *Circles* (female voice, harp, 2 percussionists, 1960), *Sinfonia* (8 solo voices, orchestra, 1968; rev. 1959), and other vocal works. *Thema (Omaggio a Joyce)* (1958), *Visage* (1961), and other tape music. Arrangements of folk songs, popular songs, and early Italian instrumental and vocal music.

Bibl.: G. W. Flynn, "Listening to Berio's Music," *MQ* 61 (1975): 388. Luciano Berio, with Rossana Dalmonte and Bálint András Varga, *Luciano Berio* (New York, 1985). David Osmond-Smith, *Playing on Words: A Guide to Luciano Berio's Sinfonia* (London, 1985). Id., *Berio* (New York, 1991).

Bériot, Charles-Auguste de (b. Louvain, 20 Feb. 1802; d. Brussels, 8 Apr. 1870). Violinist and composer. Studied in Louvain until 1821, then for a few months at the Paris Conservatory with Baillot. Began to establish himself with concerts in Paris and Belgium, also teaching; London debut in 1826; in 1828 appeared in concert with his best-known pupil, Henri Vieuxtemps, aged 8. In 1829 began liaison with singer Maria Malibran; their son was the pianist Charles-Wilfrid de Bériot (1833–1914). Their joint concert career (principally in Paris, Italy, and England) continued until her death in 1836. Grief and failing health reduced and in 1841 ended his own concert career; taught at the Brussels Conservatory in 1843–52; became blind in 1858, later partly paralyzed. Published 10 concertos, many opera potpourris, 6 sets of etudes, and a *Méthode du violon* (1857–58).

Berkeley, Lennox (Randall Francis) (b. Boar's Hill, near Oxford, 12 May 1903; d. London, 26 Dec. 1989). Composer. He studied languages at Merton College, Oxford, 1922–26. This was followed by several years' study in Paris (1927–33) with Nadia Boulanger. He returned to London in 1935; during World War II he served as program director for the BBC. In 1946 he was appointed professor at the Royal Academy of Mu-

Hector Berlioz. Sketch attributed to Ingres.

sic. In 1957 he was made Commander of the Order of the British Empire, and in 1970 he received an honorary doctorate from Oxford. Four years later he was knighted. His early music followed the neoclassicism prevalent in France during the 1920s; he apparently destroyed many of his works from this period. He later formed a neoromantic style characterized by lush textures and by a diatonic tonal idiom. His works include 4 operas (*Nelson,* 1951; first complete perf., 1954; *A Dinner Engagement,* 1954; *Ruth,* 1956; *Castaway,* 1967); ballets (*The Judgement of Paris,* 1938); incidental music (*The Tempest,* 1946; *A Winter's Tale,* 1960); film scores; orchestral works (4 symphonies, 1940, 1956–58, 1969, 1976–77; *Mont Juic,* 1937; *Serenade,* string orchestra, 1939; Divertimento in B♭, 1943; *Nocturne,* 1946; a concerto, 2 pianos, orchestra, 1948; *Sinfonietta* op. 34, 1950; a flute concerto, 1952; *Windsor Variations,* chamber orchestra, 1969; *Sinfonia concertante,* oboe, chamber orchestra, 1973); much choral music (*Domini est terra* op. 10, 1937; *Missa brevis* op. 57, 1960; Magnificat op. 71, 1968); numerous chamber and solo instrumental works (3 string quartets, 1935, 1942, 1970; *Introduction and Allegro,* violin, 1946; trio, violin, horn, piano, op. 44, 1954; *Diversions,* 8 instruments, 1964; quartet, oboe, strings, 1967; *Theme and Variations,* guitar, 1970; *In memoriam Igor Stravinsky,* string quartet, 1971); many songs and solo vocal works.

Bibl.: Peter Dickinson, *The Music of Lennox Berkeley* (London, 1988).

Berkeley, Michael (b. London, 29 May 1948). Composer. Son of Lennox Berkeley, with whom he studied. He also studied with George Malcolm and Richard Rodney Bennett at the Royal Academy of Music. He was a chorister at Westminster Cathedral. Associate conductor of Scottish Chamber Orchestra from 1979; composer-in-residence, London College of Music, 1987–88. Political crises in Poland and Afghanistan moved him to write *Uprising: A Symphony in One Movement* (1980). Other works include a string trio (1978), sonata for violin and piano (1979), string quartet (1981), *Meditations* (string orchestra, 1977), Concerto for Oboe and Strings (1977), *Three Moods* (solo oboe, 1979), *Flames* (orchestra, 1981), *Gregorian Variations* (1982), *Or Shall We Die?* (soprano, baritone, chorus, and orchestra, 1982), *Songs of Awakening Love* (soprano, small orchestra, 1986), an organ concerto (1987), *Quartet Study* (string quartet, 1988).

Berlin, Irving [Baline, Israel] (b. Mogilev, 11 May 1888; d. New York, 22 Sept. 1989). Popular songwriter. His family emigrated to New York from Russia in 1893; he worked as a street singer and singing waiter in Chinatown, publishing his first song in 1907 ("Marie from Sunny Italy," music by Nick Nicholson). Hired as a lyricist by Snyder Publishing in 1909, he soon began writing his own music as well; among his most notable early successes was "Alexander's Ragtime Band" (1911). From 1911 he contributed to the Ziegfeld Follies and other Broadway revues; he formed his own publishing company in 1919 and established the Music Box Theatre in 1921. He composed some 1,500 songs that span every major songwriting idiom of the first half of the 20th century; they appeared in musicals (*Watch Your Step,* 1918; *Annie Get Your Gun,* 1946; *Call Me Madam,* 1950), films (*The Cocoanuts,* 1927; *Top Hat,* 1935; *Holiday Inn,* 1942), and on recordings by all important contemporaneous vocal artists. Many of his songs (particularly "Blue Skies," 1927; "God Bless America," 1938; "There's No Business Like Show Business," 1946) have become defining elements of American culture; his "White Christmas" (1942) is perhaps the most commercially successful song of the era of the phonograph.

Bibl.: Alexander Woollcott, *The Story of Irving Berlin* (New York, 1925). Michael Freedland, *Irving Berlin* (New York, 1974). Laurence Bergreen, *As Thousands Cheer: The Life of Irving Berlin* (New York, 1990).

Berlioz, (Louis-) Hector (b. La Côte St.-André, near Grenoble, 11 Dec. 1803; d. Paris, 8 Mar. 1869). Composer. Son of a doctor, he was the eldest of five children, of whom two sisters also reached maturity. He received most of his early education from his father. From 1817 he had music lessons with local teachers, learning to play the guitar and the flute (but never a keyboard instrument), and he began to compose some chamber works and vocal romances, one of which was published in Paris in about 1819. Receiving his bachelor's degree at Grenoble in March 1821, he moved to

Paris in October to study—at his father's insistence—medicine, although he was already impelled toward music. Revolted by the dissecting room, he was intoxicated by the Opéra, where he formed his lifelong devotion to Gluck, whose scores he studied and copied in the Conservatory library. He published six more romances in 1822–23 and late in 1822 began lessons with the composer Lesueur, who encouraged his musical ambitions, to which his parents remained strongly opposed. He did not give up medicine completely until January 1824, but he composed several large works in this period, all of which he later destroyed, though he used parts of them in later compositions. In 1824 he composed a Mass for the Church of St. Roch. The rehearsal on 28 Dec. was a disaster and was taken by his father as a reason to stop his allowance (which was later partly restored); nevertheless, by borrowing money he was able to give a successful performance of the Mass on 10 July 1825. In 1825–26 he composed, to texts by his friend Humbert Ferrand, the *scène héroïque La révolution grecque* and the opera *Les francs-juges,* which he tried unsuccessfully over several years to have staged. He eventually destroyed all of it (partly by absorption into other works) except for the overture, his first surviving orchestral piece. In 1826 he also began his second, the concert overture *Waverley,* after Scott.

In August 1826 he formally enrolled as a student at the Conservatory, whose discipline and pedanticism (personified in his eyes by the director, Cherubini) he found difficult to endure. He lived poorly on his father's allowance (sometimes withheld), also giving lessons and singing for several months, beginning in March 1827, in the chorus of a vaudeville theater. In 1826, even before entering the Conservatory, he had entered the Prix de Rome competition, the first of five successive attempts, but had not survived the preliminary round.

In September 1827 came one of the most significant events of his life, the performance of *Hamlet* and *Romeo and Juliet* by a British company that included Harriet Smithson as leading lady. The effect on him of Shakespeare and the Irish actress was, in combination, overwhelming, although Berlioz then knew no English. To further his pursuit of Smithson, who refused to meet him, he gave on 26 May 1828 a concert consisting of the premieres of his most recent works. It was generally well received and made him better known. Soon after he again competed for the Prix de Rome, winning second prize. That year he also first became acquainted with Beethoven's *Eroica* and Fifth Symphonies through Habeneck's concerts and with Goethe's *Faust* through Nerval's French translation. These were to be artistic influences comparable to his existing idols Gluck, Spontini, Weber, Virgil, and Shakespeare, and his *Huit scènes de Faust* was published in April 1829 as op. 1. In 1829 he discovered Moore's *Irish Melodies,* which resulted in his *Neuf mélodies irlandaises,* published in 1830. On 1 Nov. 1829 he gave his second concert at the Conservatory, the first he himself conducted.

By early 1830 Berlioz's unrequited passion for Smithson had helped precipitate an emotional crisis that found release in the composition, in February–April, of the *Symphonie fantastique,* whose program was in many respects a turning into art of what he perceived as his own situation and state of mind. The previous summer he had competed a fourth time for the Prix de Rome but had lost by alienating the judges with his originality. In 1830 he deliberately set out to write conventionally and won, later destroying his cantata. Before leaving for Italy at the end of Dec. 1830, he gave a concert on 5 Dec., conducted by Habeneck, which included the premiere of the *Symphonie fantastique.* The work aroused considerable interest, its autobiographical significance having been made public knowledge. Berlioz, however, had now found a more accessible object for his passion in the young pianist Camille Moke, to whom he became engaged shortly before his unwilling departure. Finding no letters from his fiancée on reaching Rome, Berlioz, after three anxious weeks, started back to Paris, but learned in Florence that he had been jilted. This news threw him into a rage that lasted until he reached Nice. There he composed the *King Lear Overture* and began his sequel to the *Symphonie fantastique, Lélio, ou Le retour à la vie,* mostly derived from earlier works, and the *Rob Roy Overture.* He returned to Rome, where he remained until May 1832.

After a stay with his family, he returned to Paris in November 1832. In December he gave two concerts, conducted by Habeneck, at which the *Symphonie fantastique* was given with the premiere of *Lélio.* Among the audience was Harriet Smithson, whom Berlioz now met for the first time. Deeply in debt, her career in decline, she responded to his courting and, much against the wishes of both families, they were married in October 1833. Their son Louis was born in August 1834. From 1833 Berlioz regularly wrote music criticism for Paris newspapers, an occupation at which he excelled, and also usually organized three or four concerts of his works every year. After the concert of 22 Dec. 1833 Paganini was moved to commission a work for himself and his Stradivarius viola; in 1834 Berlioz composed *Harold in Italy,* which Paganini never played because the solo part was not sufficiently prominent or brilliant. This was the first of a series of major works over the next few years. The opera *Benvenuto Cellini* was composed in 1836 and produced at the Opéra in 1838. Its failure was one of the major reverses of Berlioz's career and one that he never overcame, operatic success in Paris always eluding him. He composed his Requiem (1837) through a government commission, and a second such commission produced the *Grande symphonie funèbre et triomphale* for the tenth anniversary of the July Revolution in 1840. In 1838 a well-publicized gift of 10,000 francs from Paganini gave Berlioz the freedom to compose his dramatic symphony *Roméo et Juliette* (1839). In 1840–41 he composed the songs of *Les nuits d'été.*

Berlioz may have begun in 1841 his liaison with the singer Marie Recio, whom he married after the death in 1854 of his wife (from whom he had been separated since 1844). In 1842, by this time a virtuoso conductor, he undertook the first of his many foreign concert tours. In 1843 he published his book on orchestration and in 1844 his account of his German tour and of a holiday trip to Nice, *Voyage musical en Allemagne et en Italie.* Other tours included those to Vienna, Prague, Pest, and other cities in 1845–46 and to Russia in 1847. He made the first of his several visits to London in 1847–48, returning there for concert seasons in 1851, 1852, 1853, and 1855. During this period he gave less of his energy to composing. Its major works were *La damnation de Faust,* composed in 1845–46 and coldly received at its premiere in Paris in 1846, the Te Deum (1849), and *L'enfance du Christ* (1850–54). In 1850 he was given the post of librarian at the Conservatory and helped found the Société philharmonique de Paris, which lasted only two seasons. In 1852 Liszt revived *Benvenuto Cellini* at Weimar, but it was a failure at Covent Garden in 1853, and was taken up nowhere else. From 1853 Berlioz spent several summers conducting concerts at Baden-Baden, and this association eventually led to the commissioning of his last opera, *Béatrice et Bénédict,* to his own libretto on Shakespeare's *Much Ado about Nothing;* it had its premiere at Baden-Baden on 9 Aug. 1862. The monumental *Les Troyens* was composed (to his own libretto) in 1856–58 through the persuasiveness of Liszt's mistress, the Princess Sayn-Wittgenstein. After much maneuvering and frustration, its last three acts were performed at the Théâtre-lyrique on 4 Nov. 1863, as *Les Troyens à Carthage.* It was admired by many, but the compromises that had produced such a truncated version of what Berlioz knew to be his greatest work left him much embittered. The royalties allowed him to give up writing criticism, but he also ceased to compose. In ill health, he finished the final section of his memoirs, intended for posthumous publication, in 1865. His second wife had died in 1862, and the death of his son in 1867 was a great blow. He conducted in Vienna and Germany in 1866–67 and in 1867–68 in Russia, from which he returned exhausted; after this his health declined quickly.

Works: *Operas. Benvenuto Cellini* (Paris, Opéra, 10 Sept. 1838); *Béatrice et Bénédict* (Baden-Baden, 9 Aug. 1862); *Les Troyens* (composed 1856–58). *Symphonies. Symphonie fantastique* (1830); *Harold en Italie* (1834); *Roméo et Juliette* (1839); *Grande symphonie funèbre et triomphale* (1840). *Sacred music.* Resurrexit (1824); *Grande messe des morts* (Requiem, 1837); Te Deum (1844); motets. *Other choral and vocal music. La révolution grecque* (1826); *La mort d'Orphée* (1827); *Herminie* (1828); *Cléopâtre* (1829); *Lélio, ou Le retour à la vie* (1831); *Sara la baigneuse* (1834); *Le cinq mars* (1835); *La damnation de Faust* (1846); *Chants des chemins de fer* (1846); *L'enfance du Christ* (1854); *L'impériale* (1854). *Overtures. Les francs-juges* (1828); *Waverley* (1828); *Le roi Lear* (1831); *Rob Roy* (1831); *Le carnaval romain* (1843); *Le corsaire* (1844); *Rêverie et caprice,* violin, orchestra (1841). *Songs.* "La captive" (1831); "Neuf mélodies irlandaises" (1830); "Les nuits d'été" (1841); "Tristia" (1849); "Vox populi" (1849); "Feuillets d'album" (1850); "Fleurs des landes" (1850).

Writings: *Grand traité d'instrumentation et d'orchestration modernes* (Paris, 1843; trans. Eng., 1855). *Les soirées de l'orchestre* (Paris, 1852), ed. Léon Guichard (Paris, 1968); various Eng. trans. *Les grotesques de la musique* (Paris, 1859); ed. Léon Guichard (Paris, 1971). *A travers chants* (Paris, 1862); ed. Léon Guichard (Paris, 1971). *Mémoires* (Paris, 1870); ed. P. Citron (Paris, 1969); trans. David Cairns (London, 1969). Gérard Condé, comp., *Cauchemars et passions* (Paris, 1981) [previously uncollected criticism].

Bibl.: *Werke* (Leipzig, 1900–1907). *New Berlioz Edition* (Kassel, 1967–). Humphrey Searle, trans., *Hector Berlioz: A Selection from His Letters* (London, 1966). Jacques Barzun, *Berlioz and the Romantic Century,* 3rd ed. (New York, 1969). Pierre Citron, ed., *Hector Berlioz: Correspondance générale* (Paris, 1972–). Brian Primmer, *The Berlioz Style* (London, 1973). John Crabbe, *Hector Berlioz: Rational Romantic* (London, 1980). D. Kern Holoman, *The Creative Process in the Autograph Musical Documents of Hector Berlioz, ca. 1818–1840* (Ann Arbor, 1980). Hugh Macdonald, *Berlioz* (London, 1982). Julian Rushton, *The Musical Language of Berlioz* (Cambridge, 1983). David Cairns, *Berlioz: The Making of an Artist, 1803–1832* (London, 1989). D. Kern Holoman, *Berlioz* (Cambridge, Mass., 1989). Peter Bloom, ed., *Berlioz Studies* (Cambridge, 1992).

Bermudo, Juan (b. Ecija, ca. 1510; d. Andalusia, ca. 1565). Theorist. A member of the order of the Observant Minorites; first studied mathematics at the Univ. of Alcalá, then turned to music. Wrote three theoretical treatises; the last, *Declaración de instrumentos musicales* (Osuna, 1555; facs., *DM* ser. 1, 11, 1957), incorporates most of the material of the first two. Subjects treated include plainsong and vocal polyphony; instruments (especially the vihuela); and instrumental performance practice (including tuning and intabulation for keyboard and plucked-string instruments). Nine original compositions for organ appear at the end.

Bibl.: Robert Stevenson, *Juan Bermudo* (The Hague, 1960).

Bernacchi, Antonio Maria (b. Bologna, 23 June 1685; d. there, 13 Mar. 1756). Alto castrato singer. His teachers were A. M. Pistocchi (singing) and Giovanni Antonio Ricieri (composition). He served as soloist at S. Petronio in Bologna and later apparently studied with G. A. Bernabei in Munich. His operatic debut came in 1703 in Genoa. From 1709 he sang in Venice, and subsequently at nearly all major Italian operatic centers. In London (1716–17; 1729–30) he sang in works of Alessandro Scarlatti and Handel at the King's Theatre. In 1721 he sang in the premiere of Scarlatti's *Griselda* in Rome. During the 1720s he often sang in Munich for the Elector of Bavaria.

Bernardi, Stefano (b. Verona, ca. 1585; d. Salzburg?, 1636). Composer. His early music training was at the Verona Cathedral; in 1610 he was *maestro di cappella* at Madonna dei Monti in Rome, but the following year he returned to Verona. Later he served the Archduke Carl Joseph in Breslau (1622–24), after which he moved to Salzburg, where he apparently remained until his death. He composed mostly sacred music (some is edited in *DTÖ* 69), including a Te Deum for 12 choirs (composed for Salzburg). He composed both in the older polyphonic style and also in a Monteverdian concertato style; the *Concerti academici* (1616) and *Salmi concertati* (1637) belong to the latter.

Bernart de Ventadorn (b. Ventadorn, 1130–40?; d. Dordogne?, ca. 1190–1200). Poet and composer. A member of the second generation of troubadours and one of the most important as both poet and musician. Biographical information comes from his *vida;* a small amount can be verified independently, especially through references in his poems to historical personages. Born in the province of Limousin, he spent time in northern France and perhaps even in England in the middle of the 12th century. Forty-five of his poems survive; 19 have melodies extant, 18 complete and 1 fragmentary. Several of these melodies were later used in *contrafacta* (some more than once), with texts in French, Latin, Provençal, and German. The comparatively wide diffusion of his music and his travels to northern Europe together suggest that he may have been instrumental in the spread of the art of the troubadours to the North, prompting the development of the trouvère tradition.

Bibl.: *The Songs of Bernart de Ventadorn* (Chapel Hill, 1962).

Berners (Gerald Hugh Tyrwhitt-Wilson), Lord (b. Arley Park, Shropshire, 18 Sept. 1883; d. Faringdon House, Berkshire, 19 Apr. 1950). Composer and writer. Except for schooling at Eton and casual study of music and art in Vienna and Dresden, he was essentially self-educated. His music is often of a whimsical nature; as a musical satirist he gained some success, as well as the admiration of Stravinsky and others. Works include an opera, *Le carrosse du Saint Sacrement* (1924); ballets (*A Wedding Bouquet,* 1936; *Les sirènes,* 1946); film scores (*Nicholas Nickleby,* 1946); orchestral works (*3 Pieces,* 1919); piano works *(3 petites marches funèbres).* He also authored several novels and 2 autobiographical books, *First Childhood* and *A Distant Prospect.*

Bernhard, Christoph (b. Kolberg, Pomerania [Kolobrzeg, Poland]?, 1 Jan. 1628; d. Dresden, 14 Nov. 1692). Theorist and composer. He apparently studied theology and jurisprudence, as well as music, in Danzig. From 1649 he was in the employ of the Elector of Saxony at Dresden. There he gained the admiration of Heinrich Schütz, from whom he had further instruction. He studied briefly in Rome and soon thereafter was appointed Vice-Kapellmeister at Dresden in 1655. Possibly resentful over the favoring of Italian musicians at the Saxon court, Bernhard procured in 1663 a post as Kantor at St. John's School in Hamburg. In 1670 Schütz commissioned him to compose a funeral piece for him, which was performed at the elder composer's funeral two years later. Though highly regarded by his contemporaries as a composer, principally of sacred vocal works in both German and Latin, Bernhard is remembered today chiefly for his theoretical treatises, especially for the *Tractatus compositionis augmentatus,* widely circulated in manuscript during the second half of the 17th century. In it he divided music into three categories: the *stylus gravis,* the classical polyphony of Palestrina and others; the *stylus luxurians communis,* the style initiated by Monteverdi; and the *stylus luxurians theatralis,* or recitative style.

Bibl.: Walter Hilse, ed. and trans., "The Treatises of Christoph Bernhard," *Music Forum* 3 (1973): 1–196.

Bernier, Nicolas (b. Mantes-la-Jolie, 5 or 6 June 1665; d. Paris, 6 July 1734). Composer and organist. He perhaps studied in Italy and by 1692 was in Paris. He became *maître de musique* at Chartres Cathedral in 1694, at St. Germain l'Auxerrois (Paris) in 1698, and at the Sainte-Chapelle in 1704; he remained at the last until 1726. In 1723 he was appointed, along with André Campra and Charles-Hubert Gervais, to the position of *sous-maître* at the King's Chapel. He composed sacred music, including many motets, a set of *Leçons de Ténèbres* (soprano, continuo), at least one Mass, and a Te Deum; and a number of secular cantatas. He also authored *Principes de composition,* trans. Philip F. Nelson as *Principles of Composition* (Brooklyn, 1964).

Berno of Reichenau (d. Reichenau, 7 June 1048). Theorist. Became Abbot of Reichenau in 1008 and remained in that post until his death. Traveled to Italy three times, twice to Rome for coronations of emperors (Henry II in 1014 and Conrad in 1027) and once between these events, briefly visiting Monte Cassino with Henry. Hermannus Contractus was his pupil. Wrote several treatises on music and liturgy, of which the most important is a tonary with long prologue (*GS* 2:62–91). This conservative and widely disseminated work may have been compiled largely from earlier sources; it includes numerous quotations from other theoretical treatises. Extant manuscripts also incorporate many later interpolations by Berno. His musical compositions include a few hymns and sequences, one trope, and Offices for two saints.

Bibl.: Hans Oesch, *Berno und Hermann von Reichenau als Musiktheoretiker* (Berne, 1961).

Bernstein, Elmer (b. New York, 4 Apr. 1922). Composer and conductor. He received early training on piano at Juilliard, and studied composition with Stefan Wolpe and Roger Sessions. During World War II he arranged American folk songs for performance by military bands, and after the war was commissioned to score radio dramas. He began to compose for film in the 1950s; among his many scores are those for *Sudden*

Fear (1952), *The Man with the Golden Arm* (an early and influential use of jazz, 1955), *Walk on the Wild Side* (1962), *True Grit* (1969), and *Ghostbusters* (1984). Active in advancing the legitimacy of film music, conducting and recording numerous scores; he founded the Film Music Collection in 1974.

Bernstein, Leonard (b. Lawrence, Mass., 25 Aug. 1918; d. New York, 14 Oct. 1990). Composer, conductor, pianist. He conducted, performed as a pianist, and lectured worldwide, as well as on television, was the author of several books, and made signal contributions to musical theater. He studied piano from the age of 10 (Susan Williams, Helen Coates, Heinrich Gebhard). While at Harvard (1935–39) he wrote incidental music for a production of Aristophanes *The Birds* and directed Blitzstein's *The Cradle Will Rock.* After receiving his B.A., he attended Curtis to study piano (Vengerova), conducting (Fritz Reiner), and orchestration (Randall Thompson); from 1940 he was associated with Koussevitzky as student and then assistant at the Berkshire Music Center. In 1943–44 he was assistant conductor of the New York Philharmonic under Rodzinski; his substitution for the ill Bruno Walter in a nationally televised concert (14 Nov. 1943) immediately launched his conducting career. After that broadcast Bernstein was in great demand as a guest conductor in the U.S. and abroad. He conducted the New York City Center Orchestra (1945–58); took over the conducting classes at the Berkshire Center after Koussevitzky's death in 1951; taught at Brandeis Univ. (1951–55). In 1957 he was named codirector of the New York Philharmonic (with Mitropoulos) and was director of that orchestra from 1958 through 1969, retiring as conductor laureate. Under Bernstein the orchestra toured extensively and was nationally prominent as a result of recordings and concerts on television (Young People's Concerts, 1958–73). As a conductor Bernstein premiered more than 40 new works (Copland's *Connotations for Orchestra,* commissioned for the opening of the Lincoln Center, 1962; Berio's *Sinfonia,* 1968; Babbitt's *Relata II,* 1969), but his views of nontonal music did not always please the avant-garde. In the 1970s and 1980s he focused on the standard repertory, recording Wagner's *Tristan und Isolde* in 1983. He worked closely with European orchestras, notably the Vienna Philharmonic, and gave a prominent place in his repertory to the German symphonic tradition from Beethoven through Mahler.

Throughout his career Bernstein continued to perform as a pianist, often conducting from the keyboard. His own Second Symphony (The Age of Anxiety) is a piano concerto (which he premiered with the Boston Symphony under Koussevitzky in 1949). As a composer of concert music, Bernstein contributed to the orchestral, choral, chamber, piano, and solo vocal repertories. His first large orchestral work, *Jeremiah* (1942), won the New York Critics' Circle Award in 1944. During a year's sabbatical from the New York

Leonard Bernstein delivering a Charles Eliot Norton Lecture.

Philharmonic (1964) he explored serial methods of composition but retained his commitment to tonality; he regarded his own music as eclectic, with roots in jazz, Hebrew liturgical music, and the standard concert repertory. During his sabbatical year he wrote "a lot of music, twelve-tone music, and avant-garde music of various kinds" that he discarded, but he also produced his *Chichester Psalms,* "which is simple and tonal and tuneful and pure B-flat . . . Because that was what I honestly wished to write." His use of solo piano, high brass parts, and virtuosic percussion as well as a striking rhythmic language are also characteristic.

He is perhaps best known for dramatic works. *West Side Story* (lyrics by Stephen Sondheim, choreography by Jerome Robbins, 1957) profoundly affected the course of American musical theater. His *Mass: A Theater Piece for Singers, Players, and Dancers,* commissioned for the opening of the Kennedy Center (1971), initially aroused much hostility; but after its first New York performance (1972) Donal Henahan, writing in the *New York Times,* called it "a minor miracle of skillful mixing, mortising together folksy ballads, blues, rock, Broadway style song and dance numbers, Lutheran chorales, plain chant and bits of twelve-tone music." About his own compositions Bernstein said, "I have a deep suspicion that every work I write, for whatever medium, is really theater music in some way."

Works: dramatic works including ballets (*Fancy Free,* with Jerome Robbins, 1944; *Facsimile,* with Robbins, 1946; *Dybbuk,* 1974), musicals (*On the Town,* 1944; *Wonderful Town,* 1953; *West Side Story,* 1957; *1600 Pennsylvania Avenue,* 1976), operas (*Trouble in Tahiti,* 1951, and its sequel, *A Quiet Place,* 1983, rev. 1984; *Candide,* 1956), the theater piece *Mass* (1971), incidental music, and a film score (*On the Waterfront,* 1954); orchestral music, including many suites arranged from the stage works and others (Divertimento, 1980; *Prelude, Fugue, and Riffs,* clarinet and jazz ensemble, 1949); vocal works (Symphony no. 3 [Kaddish], speaker, soprano, chorus, boys' chorus, orchestra, 1963; *Chichester Psalms,* tenor, chorus, orchestra, 1965; *Songfest,* vocal soloists, orchestra, 1977); chamber music; songs.

Writings: *The Joy of Music* (New York, 1959). *Young People's Concerts for Reading and Listening* (New York, 1962). *The Infinite Variety of Music* (New York, 1966). *The Unanswered Question* (Charles Eliot Norton Lectures; Cambridge, Mass., 1976). *Findings* (New York, 1982).

Bibl.: Jack Gottlieb, *Leonard Bernstein: A Complete Catalogue of His Works: Celebrating His 70th Birthday, August 25, 1988* (New York, 1988). Humphrey Burton, *Leonard Bernstein* (New York, 1994). Meryle Secrest, *Leonard Bernstein: A Life* (New York, 1994).

Berry, Chu [Leon Brown] (b. Wheeling, W. Va., 13 Sept. 1908; d. Conneaut, Ohio, 30 Oct. 1941). Jazz tenor saxophonist. He worked in the big bands of Benny Carter (1932; 1933, recording under Spike Hughes's name), Charlie Johnson (1932–33), Teddy Hill (1933–35), Fletcher Henderson (1935–36), and Cab Calloway (1937–41), with whom he recorded "A Ghost of a Chance" the year before his death in an automobile accident. Prolific recordings with others include "Forty-Six West Fifty-Two" as a leader (1938, with Roy Eldridge) and "Sweethearts on Parade" with Lionel Hampton (1939).

Berry, Chuck [Charles Edward Anderson] (b. San Jose, Calif., 15 Jan. 1926). Rock guitarist, singer, and songwriter. During early performances in St. Louis he came to the attention of Muddy Waters, who helped him secure a recording contract with the rock-and-roll label Chess. His 1955 release "Maybelline" was the first rock-and-roll song to reach the top of popular, country, and rhythm-and-blues sales charts, and he achieved similar success with "Roll Over Beethoven" (1956) and "Johnny B. Goode" (1958). He continued to record and tour in the 1970s; the influence of his early work was acknowledged by rock groups including the Beatles and the Rolling Stones. In 1987 he was the subject of a biographical film, *Hail, Hail, Rock and Roll.*

Berti, Giovanni Pietro (d. Venice, 1638). Composer, organist, and singer. From childhood he sang in the choir at St. Mark's in Venice; in 1624 he assumed the position of second organist. He composed over 50 songs, including strophic arias and a number of novel forms: the piece *Dove sei gita* (published in a collection in 1634; see Knud Jeppesen, ed., *La flora,* Copenhagen, 1949) is perhaps the earliest extant example of a da capo aria. His songs are important in the early history of the chamber cantata; most appeared in two collections of *Cantade et arie ad una voce sola con alcune a doi* (Venice, 1624–27).

Bertolli, Francesca (b. Rome; d. Bologna, 9 Jan. 1767). Contralto. She began her career with engagements in Bologna (1728) and for the Duchess of Tuscany. From 1729 to 1733 she sang in London at the King's Theatre with Handel's Royal Academy, an engagement that included appearances in 15 Handel operas. From 1733 she sang with the Opera of the Nobility, then returned to Handel's company for the 1736–37 season. Handel composed 9 roles (both male and female) for her, including Armindo in *Partenope,* Medoro in *Orlando,* and Leocasta in *Giustino.*

Berton, Henri-Montan (b. Paris, 17 Sept. 1767; d. there, 22 Apr. 1844). Composer. Son of Pierre-Montan Berton, conductor and later director of the Paris Opéra, he received a desultory musical education, including some guidance from Sacchini. He began to become known as a composer in Paris in about 1786 with cantatas and, beginning in 1787, with opéras comiques, of which he wrote many. Was appointed harmony professor at the new Paris Conservatory in 1795 and succeeded Méhul as composition professor in 1818. Published *Traité d'harmonie* (Paris, 1815) and other writings, including an attack on Rossini, *De la musique mécanique et de la musique philosophique* (Paris, 1826). His most original and successful opéras comiques were *Montano et Stephanie* (1799), *Le délire* (1799), and *Aline, reine de Golconde* (1803). His popularity in this genre began to fade after about 1810. In 1807–9 he was music director at the Opéra-bouffe and then chorusmaster at the Opéra, where he produced several operas in the 1810s and 1820s, none very successful.

Bertoni, Ferdinando (Gasparo) (b. Salò, 15 Aug. 1725; d. Desenzano, 1 Dec. 1813). Organist and composer. He studied in Brescia, near his birthplace, and during the 1740s in Bologna with Giovanni Battista Martini. His first opera, *La vedova accorta* (Venice, 1745), was a great success throughout Italy. During the next decade he composed opere serie, oratorios, and solo motets, all well received in Venice. In 1785 he was made *maestro di cappella* at St. Mark's (where he had already served as principal organist since 1752); he held this position until his retirement in 1808. His long association with the chapel was twice interrupted by leaves to London, where between 1778 and 1783 he created 14 operas and pastiches for the King's Theatre. He composed approximately 70 stage works (including a setting of *Orfeo ed Euridice* in 1776), more than 50 oratorios (including *David poenitens,* 1775, more than 200 other sacred works, and chamber and orchestral works.

Bertrand, Anthoine [Antoine] **de** (b. Fontanges, Auvergne, 1530–40; d. Toulouse, 1580–July 1582). Composer. He was an associate of humanists and poets in and around Toulouse and evidently had independent means. His 3 books of secular polyphony (1576, 1578, 1578; ed. in *MMFTR* 4–7) include mostly chansons. The texts set in the first 2 are all poems by Ronsard, many of them sonnets from the *Amours.* Bertrand's compositions contain much chromaticism and make some use of microtones. Late in life he composed a number of sacred songs, hymns, and Latin motets.

Berwald, Franz (Adolf) (b. Stockholm, 23 July 1796; d. there, 3 Apr. 1868). Composer. His father, from a family of German musicians, settled in Stockholm as a violinist in the court orchestra. He was taught the violin by his father and joined the court orchestra in 1812, remaining until 1828, with some interruptions, including 1818–20, when he toured Finland and Russia. He began to compose in this period, including instrumental works (theme and variations for violin and orchestra, 1816; orchestral fantasia, 1817; concerto for two violins, 1817; septet, 1817; string quartet, 1818; violin concerto, 1820; symphony, 1820; several works now lost), occasional cantatas, and a serenade for tenor and 6 instruments (1825). He then began an opera, *Gustaf Wasa,* act 1 of which had a concert performance (Stockholm, 1828) but is now lost. In 1828 he left the court orchestra and, with a scholarship, went to Berlin in 1829, where he worked on several operas, only fragments of which survive.

Receiving little encouragement as a composer, in 1835 he opened an orthopedic institute that proved successful; he moved to Vienna in 1841 and back to Stockholm in 1842. In the 1840s he composed most of his surviving music, including his 4 numbered symphonies (the first 3 subtitled *Sérieuse, Capricieuse,* and *Singulière*), other orchestral pieces, 2 string quartets, 3 operas, a cantata, and several large choral works. A concert of his music in Vienna in 1842 was well received, but his reception in Stockholm was mixed; he did not succeed in establishing himself in Swedish opera and was passed over for several vacant Swedish musical posts. In 1850 he became manager, later (until 1859) partner, in a glass factory in northern Sweden, where he also was involved in starting a sawmill in 1853. His opera *Estrella de Soria* was respectfully received at the Royal Theater, Stockholm, in 1862 (composed in the 1840s, but revised for this production). His last important composition apart from some choral pieces, the opera *Drottningen av Golconda* [The Queen of Golconda], was composed in 1864 but not performed until 1968 (Royal Theater, Stockholm). He was finally made composition professor at the Swedish Royal Academy of Music in 1867, but died the next year.

The growth of serious interest in Berwald's music began in Sweden in the early 20th century, but did not spread much farther until after World War II. Other works include 5 piano trios, 2 piano quartets, 2 duos for violin and piano, all from the 1840s and 1850s; a piano concerto, 1855; a concertino for violin and piano, 1859; songs; piano pieces.

Bibl.: *Franz Berwald: Sämtliche Werke,* ed. Nils Castegren et al., in *Monumenta musicae svecicae,* 2nd ser. (Kassel, 1966–). Robert Layton, *Franz Berwald* (London, 1959). Ingvar Andersson, *Franz Berwald* (Stockholm, 1970). Erling Lomnäa et al., eds., *Franz Berwald: Die Dokumente seines Leben* (Kassel, 1979).

Besard, Jean-Baptiste (b. Besançon, ca. 1567; d. Augsburg?, 1625). Composer and lutenist. He studied law in Dôle (until 1587) and medicine and music in Rome (until ca. 1595); in 1597 he was in Hesse, where he perhaps taught lute. He then lived for a period in Cologne, where in 1603 he published a collection for lute, *Thesaurus harmonicus* (R: 1975). It contains mostly arrangements for lute of contemporary instrumental works. Moving to Augsburg, probably around 1610, he continued practicing medicine and law and possibly also teaching the lute. In 1617 he published another collection in Augsburg, *Novus partus, sive Concertationes musicae;* it contains some 60 solo or ensemble pieces, about half by Besard (cf. Sutton).

Bibl.: *Oeuvres pour luth seul de Jean Baptiste Besard,* ed. André Souris and M. Rollin (Paris, 1969). Julia Sutton, "The Music of J. B. Besard's *Novus partus,* 1617," *JAMS* 19 (1966): 182–204.

Bethune (Green), Thomas [Blind Tom] (b. Columbus, Ga., 25 May 1849; d. Hoboken, 13 June 1908). Pianist and composer. Born blind to slave parents, he was bought with his parents in 1850 by General James Bethune of Columbus, whose daughter taught him music when he showed extraordinary abilities. General Bethune began exhibiting him for profit, first locally, then in 1857 throughout Georgia, and in 1860 leased him for $15,000 for 3 years to another entrepreneur, who toured him widely in the slave states. He was exhibited by Bethune in the North immediately after the Civil War, in Europe in 1866–67, and incessantly throughout the U.S. and Canada thereafter, General Bethune having thwarted Emancipation by obtaining legal custody of Tom from his parents, which he retained until 1887, when it was wrested from him by the widow of his son, who continued to exhibit Tom until 1905.

Tom was presented as an idiot and was generally reported to have been one by those who knew him. He could, however, carry on a simple conversation, profit from music lessons, and practice, making the actual extent of his intelligence open to question. His performances, marked by unconventional, seemingly idiotic behavior, included the classics, his own compositions (of which there are over 100) and improvisations (including imitations of natural sounds and machines), songs, recitations, and demonstrations of his extraordinary aural abilities and recall.

Bibl.: Geneva Southall, *Blind Tom: The Post–Civil War Enslavement of a Black Musical Genius* (Minneapolis, 1979).

Bevin, Elway (b. ca. 1554; d. Bristol, buried 19 Oct. 1638). Composer and theorist. Said to have studied with Thomas Tallis; vicar-choral at Wells Cathedral (1579–80), chorusmaster and later organist at Bristol Cathedral (from ca. 1585), and Gentleman Extraordinary at the Chapel Royal (1605). He composed services, anthems, and organ music; his best-known work is the "Dorian" or "Short" Service, in four voices. His primer *A Briefe and Short Instruction in the Art of Music* (London, 1631) was praised by Purcell and Christopher Simpson.

Bianchi, Francesco (b. Cremona, ca. 1752; d. London, 27 Nov. 1810). Theorist and composer, chiefly of operas. At Naples he studied with Jommelli and Cafaro. His first opera, *Giulio Sabino,* was produced in Cremona in 1772; during the next 35 years he composed more than 80 operas, often traveling to Naples, Florence, Venice, or Paris to oversee or conduct performances. From 1785 to 1797 he was an organist at St. Mark's, Venice; there he also helped reorganize the diocesan archive. He composed a few oratorios, cantatas, Masses, and instrumental works. He authored or coauthored five theoretical treatises; all remained in manuscript except for the *Trattato d'armonia teorico pratico,* excerpted (trans. Eng.) in *Quarterly Musical Review* 2 (1820): 22, 172, 296, 434; and 3 (1821): 96.

Biber, Heinrich Ignaz Franz von (b. Wartenburg, Bohemia, bapt. 12 Aug. 1644; d. Salzburg, 3 May 1704). Composer and violinist. Little is known of his musical training. Around 1665 he began his career as a member of the court of Prince-Bishop Karl of Olomouc (Count Liechtenstein-Kastelkorn), at his castle in Kroměříž. In 1670 Biber left the court without permission to join the chapel forces at the Salzburg court of the Archbishop Maximilian Gandolph. He was promoted to Vice-Kapellmeister (possibly from choirmaster) there in 1679, and five years later he was made court Kapellmeister. Emperor Leopold I, who through the years had grown to admire Biber's music and violin playing, bestowed the title of nobility on him in 1690. Biber apparently retired to the country and spent his last years composing sacred and dramatic music for Salzburg. Of his several operas and school dramas the music for only one is extant, *Chi la dura la vince* (1687); his sacred works include motets, vespers, Masses (*Missa S. Henrici,* ed. in *DTÖ* 49), and a Requiem for five voices (ed. in *DTÖ* 59). He has been suggested as the composer of the *Missa salisburgensis,* formerly attributed to Benevoli. He is best known for his violin music, including the Mystery Sonatas and the *Harmonia artificiosa-ariosa* (Nuremberg, 1712; ed. in *DTÖ* 42); many of these works employ *scordatura* tunings.

Bibl.: Elias Dann, "Heinrich Biber and the Seventeenth-Century Violin" (diss., Columbia Univ., 1968). Eric Thomas Chafe, *The Church Music of Heinrich Biber* (Ann Arbor, 1987).

Bigard, Barney [Albany Leon] (b. New Orleans, 3 Mar. 1906; d. Culver City, Calif., 27 June 1980). Jazz clarinetist. As a tenor saxophonist he played with Albert Nicholas in New Orleans (1922–23, 1923–24) before joining King Oliver in Chicago (1924–27), during which time he concentrated on the clarinet. After touring to New York with Oliver (1927), he worked with Charlie Elgar in Milwaukee, then returned to New York, where he played briefly with Luis Russell before joining Duke Ellington (1927?/28?–1942). Recordings with Ellington include "Mood Indigo" (1930) and "Clarinet Lament" (1936). He subsequently performed regularly with Louis Armstrong's All Stars (1947–52, 1953–55, 1960–61).

Bibl.: Barney Bigard, *With Louis and the Duke: The Autobiography of a Jazz Clarinetist* (New York, 1986).

E. Power Biggs.

Biggs, E(dward George) Power (b. Westcliff-on-Sea, Essex, 29 Mar. 1906; d. Boston, 10 Mar. 1977). Organist. Studied at Hurstpierpoint College, 1917–24, then at the Royal Academy of Music, 1924–29. Emigrated to the U.S. in 1930, working a year as organist in Newport, R.I., before moving permanently to Cambridge, Mass. Ten years after his New York debut in 1932 he began for CBS a weekly series of broadcasts that continued until 1958 and made him a household name. He also recorded extensively for Columbia Records. At Harvard and Columbia universities he performed cycles of Bach's complete organ works. He also performed organ works by contemporaries such as Britten, Piston, and Hanson; many of these works he commissioned.

Billings, William (b. Boston, 7 Oct. 1746; d. there, 26 Sept. 1800). The most important American composer of the 18th century. Son of a shopkeeper, he was apprenticed to a tanner. He probably taught himself music, though he may also have attended Boston singing schools. In 1769 he began teaching, first in Boston and later in Providence and in Stoughton, Mass. In 1770 he published his first tune collection, *The New-England Psalm-Singer,* probably the first published collection of the music of a single American composer. His second collection, *The Singing Master's Assistant* (1778; 4th ed., 1786–89), was more pedagogical in intent and was highly successful. This was followed by *Music in Miniature* (1779), *The Psalm-Singer's Amusement* (1781; R: 1974), and *Suffolk Harmony* (1786). They contain chiefly unaccompanied vocal works, mostly for four voices, and include hymns, anthems, Psalm

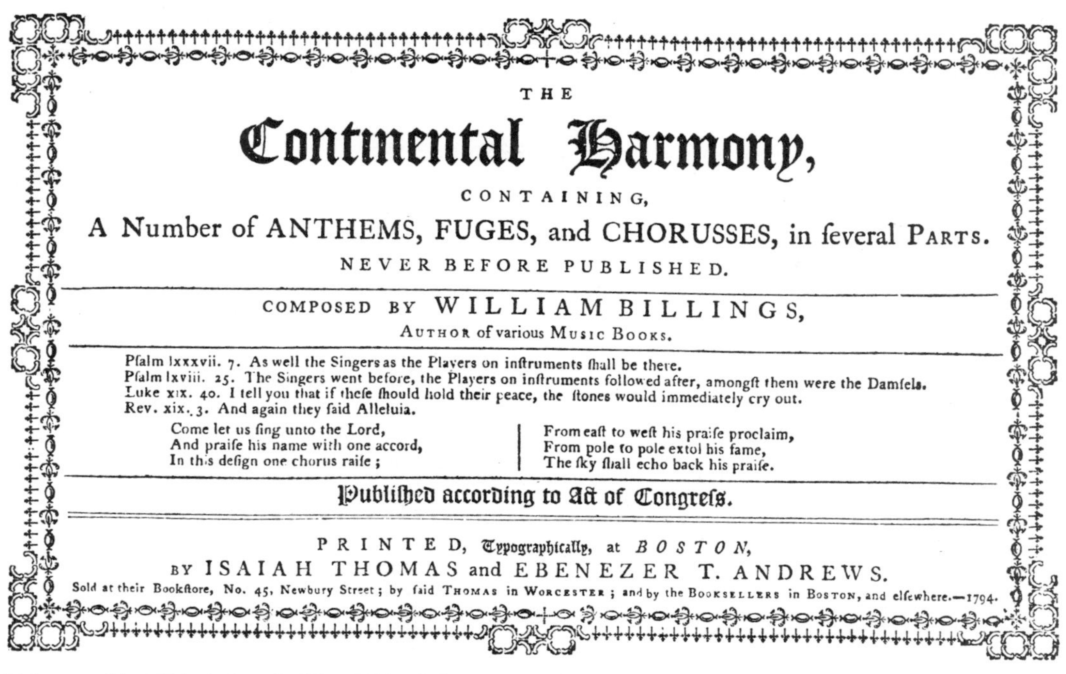
THE

Continental Harmony,

CONTAINING,

A Number of ANTHEMS, FUGES, and CHORUSSES, in ſeveral PARTS.

NEVER BEFORE PUBLISHED.

COMPOSED BY WILLIAM BILLINGS,

AUTHOR of various MUSIC BOOKS.

Pſalm lxxxvii. 7. As well the Singers as the Players on inſtruments ſhall be there.
Pſalm lxviii. 25. The Singers went before, the Players on inſtruments followed after, amongſt them were the Damſels.
Luke xix. 40. I tell you that if theſe ſhould hold their peace, the ſtones would immediately cry out.
Rev. xix. 3. And again they ſaid Alleluia.

Come let us ſing unto the Lord, And praiſe his name with one accord, In this deſign one chorus raiſe;	From eaſt to weſt his praiſe proclaim, From pole to pole extol his fame, The ſky ſhall echo back his praiſe.

Publiſhed according to Act of Congreſs.

PRINTED, Typographically, at BOSTON,
BY ISAIAH THOMAS and EBENEZER T. ANDREWS.
Sold at their Bookſtore, No. 45, Newbury Street; by ſaid THOMAS in WORCESTER; and by the BOOKSELLERS in BOSTON, and elſewhere.—1794.

Title page of the 1794 printing of William Billings' *The Continental Harmony.*

tunes, and fuguing tunes. During the 1770s and early 1780s he held prestigious posts in Boston, as singing master for the Brattle Street Church and the Old South Church. In 1783 he was editor of the *Boston Magazine.* During the latter part of the 1780s his financial situation deteriorated; even his final published collection, *The Continental Harmony* (1794; R: 1961), could not rescue him. Soon he was forced to resume teaching in small schools around Boston and even to accept minor positions such as that of "leather sealer." He died a debtor, leaving nearly 350 compositions; many had been enormously popular in the northeastern U.S. during the 1780s. They demonstrate close attention to the marriage of text and music. Notable are "Lamentation over Boston," "David's Lamentation," "I Am the Rose of Sharon," and "Modern Music."

Bibl.: *The Complete Works of William Billings,* ed. Karl Kroeger and Hans Nathan (Charlottesville, Va., and Boston, 1977–). J. Murray Barbour, *The Church Music of William Billings* (East Lansing, Mich., 1960; R: New York, 1972). H. Wiley Hitchcock, "William Billings and the Yankee Tunesmiths," *HiFi/Stereo Review* 16 (1966): 55–65. David P. McKay and Richard Crawford, *William Billings of Boston: Eighteenth-Century Composer* (Princeton, 1975). Hans Nathan, *William Billings: Data and Documents* (Detroit, 1976). Karl Kroeger, *Catalog of the Musical Works of William Billings* (New York, 1991).

Billington, Elizabeth [née Weichsel] (b. London, 27 Dec. 1765; d. near Venice, 25 Aug. 1818). Soprano. She had singing lessons with J. C. Bach and later with the double bass player James Billington, whom she married in 1783. Her debut was at Dublin's Crow Street Theater in 1784. Subsequent successes were at Covent Garden, at Milan, and at the San Carlo Theater in Naples, where Bianchi, Paisiello, and Paer composed operas for her. She was much admired by Haydn. In the *Memoirs of Mrs. Billington from Her Birth* (London, 1792), an anonymous author, possibly James Ridgway, detailed her allegedly scandalous private life.

Bilson, Malcolm (b. Los Angeles, 24 Oct. 1935). Pianist. Graduated from Bard College in 1957; went to Vienna as a Fulbright scholar; studied with Grete Hinterhofer in Berlin and Reine Gianoli in Paris; earned the D.M.A. after study with Stanley Fletcher and Webster Aitken at the Univ. of Illinois. Joined the faculty of Cornell Univ. in 1968. In 1969 he began to perform on a fortepiano by Philip Belt based on an 18th-century Dulken original. With Sonya Monosoff and John Hsu he founded the Amadé Trio in 1974. A champion of late 18th- and early 19th-century instruments, he has recorded extensively both in solo literature and in chamber music. During the 1980s, together with the English Baroque Soloists led by John Eliot Gardiner, he recorded the complete Mozart keyboard concertos.

Binchois, Gilles de Bins [Binch, Binche] **dit** (b. Mons?, ca. 1400; d. Soignies, 20 Sept. 1460). Composer. He was probably trained as a chorister and organist in Mons, where he was organist at Ste. Waudru from 1419 until his removal to Lille in 1423. In the 1420s he was perhaps in the service of William Pole, Earl of Suffolk, an Englishman resident in France. By about 1427 he joined the Burgundian court chapel, remaining there until retiring in 1453 to Soignies, where he was provost of the Collegiate Church of St. Vincent. He held prebends in absentia at Bruges (from 1430) and Mons (from 1437) despite never having been ordained a priest, and he received payments from the Burgundian court until his death. He is known to have met Dufay at Mons in 1449; the two composers probably had other meetings, the first perhaps as early as 1434.

The 15th-century author Martin le Franc began the tradition that has paired Binchois and Dufay as leading composers of their age and has found the influence of Dunstable in the works of both. Binchois had ample opportunity to become acquainted with English music because of the English occupation of France, and English features in his work extend to the use of specific liturgical melodies and texts. But his music was also widely known, quoted, and cited in its own right; Ockeghem, Bedyngham, Agricola, Josquin, Obrecht, and Isaac, among others, used it as the basis of new works. Laments on his death written by Ockeghem and Dufay further attest to the high regard of his contemporaries.

Binchois is known chiefly for his secular music, about 60 rondeaux and 7 ballades. Almost all of these works are for 3 voices with only the top voice texted. Their range of texts and musical style is in general much more restricted than that of Dufay's secular works. His sacred compositions are almost as numerous and incorporate both more complex and simpler styles. The approximately 20 Mass movements or pairs (no complete cycles survive) are seldom in the simple 3-part texture of the songs. In some pieces chant melodies are paraphrased, but long-note cantus firmi are avoided. There are several large-scale motets, one isorhythmic. The rest of the sacred music—Psalms, hymns, Magnificats, and the like—is very simple in style. Many pieces are in fauxbourdon or a fully written out approximation of fauxbourdon.

Bibl.: Charles van den Borren, ed., *Polyphonia sacra* (Burnham, 1932; 2nd rev. ed., 1962). Jean Marix, ed., *Les musiciens de la cour de Bourgogne au XVe siècle* (Paris, 1937). Wolfgang Rehm, ed., *Die Chansons von Gilles Binchois (1400–1460)* (Mainz, 1957). Sylvia Kenney, *Walter Frye and the "Contenance Angloise"* (New Haven, 1964). A. Parris, "The Sacred Works of Gilles Binchois" (diss, Bryn Mawr College, 1965) [includes ed.]. David Fallows, "Two More Dufay Songs Reconstructed," *EM* 3 (1975): 127. Craig Wright, "Dufay at Cambrai: Discoveries and Revisions," *JAMS* 28 (1975): 175–229. M. Schuler, "Neues zur Biographie von Gilles Binchois," *AfMw* 33 (1976): 68.

Bingham, Seth (Daniels) (b. Bloomfield, N.J., 16 Apr. 1882; d. New York, 21 June 1972). Composer and organist. Studied with Parker at Yale (B.A., 1904; M.A., 1908) and in Paris with d'Indy, Widor, and Guilmant. Taught at Yale (1908–19) and Columbia (1920–54) and lectured at Union Theological Seminary until 1965. Organist and choirmaster at Madison Avenue Presbyterian Church (New York) for most of his career. His compositions are in a conservative and lyrical vein and include an opera; works for organ and orchestra (concerto, 1946); a concerto for bass, snare drum, and organ (1954); chamber music for various ensembles (*Connecticut Suite,* organ and strings, 1953); many liturgical and concert works for organ and for choir (*Wilderness Stone,* narrator, vocal soloists, choir, and orchestra, 1933); songs.

Binkerd, Gordon (Ware) (b. Lynch, Nebr., 22 May 1916). Composer. Educated at South Dakota Wesleyan Univ., Eastman, and Harvard (M.A., 1952, musicology and composition with Piston and Fine). Professor at the Univ. of Illinois, 1949–71. He gave up serial techniques (employed in his sonata for cello and piano, 1952) midway through his first symphony (composed at the MacDowell Colony, 1954) when he experienced "an intense revulsion away from the system. . . [returning] to it only briefly, and in a sense casually." Tonal organization often depends on tritone polarities; motivic development on "backtracking," the relentless reiteration and gradual transformation of minuscule units. Works include symphonies; "The Battle," brass and percussion (1972, based on Frescobaldi's "Capriccio sopra la Battaglia," 1637); chamber music; organ service music; piano works; choral works; many songs.

Birtwistle, Harrison (Paul) (b. Accrington, Lancashire, 15 July 1934). Composer. His initial training was as a clarinetist at the Royal Manchester College (from 1952). At the same time he began studying composition there with Richard Hall. Later he studied clarinet with Reginald Kell at the Royal Academy of Music. He began a career as a clarinetist, but soon composition took precedence. He taught at the Cranborne Chase School (1962–65), was a visiting fellow at Princeton (1966–67), and was a visiting professor at Swarthmore (1973). In 1967 he and Peter Maxwell Davies founded the Pierrot Players; more recently he has composed for the group Matrix. In 1975 he became music director at the South Bank Theatre, London. He was knighted in 1987. His music shows influences from medieval music and from Stravinsky; it is often marked by florid contrapuntal lines and fragmented textures.

Works: *For the stage. Punch and Judy* (1966–67); *Down by the Greenwood Site* (dramatic pastoral, 1969); *Orpheus* (1974–77); *Bow Down* (1977); *The Mask of Orpheus* (1973–84); *Gawain* (1991), *The Second Mrs. Kong* (1994) *Orchestral.* Chorales (1962–63); Three Movements with Fanfares (1964); *Nomos,* amplified flute, clarinet, bassoon, horn, and orchestra (1968); *The Triumph of Time* (1972); *Earth Dances* (1985–86); *Antiphonies,* piano, orchestra (1993); *Panic,* alto sax, drummer, orchestra (1995); *The Cry of Anubis,* tuba, orchestra (1995). *Other ensembles. Grimethorpe Aria,* brass band (1973); *Carmen arcadiae mechanicae perpetuum* (1977); *Aventures des Mercures* (1980). *Choral. Music for Sleep* (1964); *Carmen paschale,* with organ (1965); *The Fields of Sorrow,* 2 sopranos, chorus, instruments (1971). *For soprano with instruments. Entr'actes and Sappho Fragments* (1963–64); *Ring a Dumb Carillon* (1965); *Nenia on the Death of Orpheus* (1970); Five Chorale Preludes (1973); Tenebrae (1992). *Instrumental works. Précis,* piano (1959); *Tragoedia,* chamber ensemble (1965); *Medus,* various combinations of instruments (1969; rev. 1970, 1978); *Chronometer,* 8-track tape (1971); *Tombeau: In memoriam Igor Stravinsky,* chamber ensemble (1972); *For O, for O, the Hobbyhorse is Forgot,* 6 percussionists (1976); *Ritual Fragment,* chamber ensemble (1990); *Three movements for string quartet* (1993).

Bibl.: Michael Hall, *Harrison Birtwistle* (London, 1984).

Bishop, Henry R(owley) (b. London, 18 Nov. 1786; d. there, 30 Apr., 1855). Composer. Son of a London shopkeeper, he was himself running a London music shop with a cousin at age 13. It published his first compositions in 1800–1803. After trying to become a jockey, he studied music with Francesco Bianchi, began to write for the stage in 1804, and produced his first opera, *The Circassian Bride,* successfully at Drury Lane in 1809. Several more operas quickly followed, leading to his appointment as music director at Covent Garden in 1810. During his tenure there until 1824 almost all of his tremendous output of stage music was written for this theater, including operas, ballets, incidental music (both original and arranged), melodramas, and English adaptations of imported operas. He was a founder of the Philharmonic Society (1813) and conducted some of its concerts. In 1824 he became music director at Drury Lane, for which he wrote much music through 1833, including his most substantial opera, *Aladdin* (1826). He was also music director for a time at Vauxhall Gardens. He produced only a few stage works after 1834, the last in 1840. He held the Reid professorship at Edinburgh in 1841–43 and the music chair at Oxford from 1848; he conducted the Antient Concerts, 1840–48. Many of his songs and glees were extremely popular, especially "Home, Sweet Home," which occurs with this text (by John Howard Payne) in the opera *Clari* (1823); also composed several cantatas, an oratorio, and a few orchestral and chamber works. In 1831 he married his second wife, the singer Anna Riviere (1810–84), who in 1839 eloped with the harpist Bochsa. He was knighted in 1842.

Bibl.: Frederick Corder, "The Works of Sir Henry Bishop," *MQ* 4 (1918): 78–97. Richard Northcott, *The Life of Sir Henry R. Bishop* (London, 1920). Trevor Fawcett, "Bishop and Aladdin," *MT* 113 (1972): 1076–77).

Bizet, Georges (Alexandre César Léopold) (b. Paris, 25 Oct. 1838; d. Bougival, near Paris, 3 June 1875). Composer. Bizet's father came from Rouen and was a hairdresser and wigmaker before becoming a singing teacher. His mother's family was of higher social standing and was musically inclined. He entered the Paris Conservatory in 1848, studying piano with Marmontel and taking private counterpoint lessons from Zimmerman (through whom he met Zimmerman's future son-in-law Charles Gounod, early forming a close relationship that was to be an important one for Bizet).

Georges Bizet.

He also studied the organ with Benoist and composition with Halévy. Bizet developed into a brilliant pianist, winning first prize for that as well as for solfège, organ, and fugue. Gounod's musical influence is readily apparent in the most important of Bizet's student compositions, the Symphony in C, written in a month in 1855 and now well known, although not performed until 1935. In 1856 he competed for the Prix de Rome, winning second prize (no first was awarded). He also shared first place in a competition sponsored by Offenbach for a one-act operetta, *Le Docteur Miracle.* Performed 11 times in spring 1857, it attracted little attention. That summer he won the Prix de Rome, leaving for Rome in December.

During his three years in Italy he composed a Te Deum, an opera buffa to an existing Italian libretto, *Don Procopio,* performed only years after his death, and an ode-symphony, *Vasco da Gama.* Returning to Paris in 1860, he began a comic opera and a symphony on Italy, but work was slowed by anxiety over his mother, who died in Sept. 1861. He helped support himself through coaching, teaching, and arranging (especially for the publishers Heugel and Choudens). He assisted Gounod in preparing *La Reine de Saba* for the Opéra in 1862 and did the same for Reyer's *Erostrate* for Baden-Baden that summer. The first version of Bizet's *Ivan IV* may have been begun about this time for Baden-Baden but was never performed there. In 1863 there was a performance of the scherzo, the only movement then completed, from the symphony, and of *Vasco da Gama,* the latter a failure and never revived. An opera for the Théâtre-lyrique, *Les pêcheurs de perles,* was composed quickly, making some use of material from earlier works, and premiered 30 Sept. 1863 with only moderate success. It was given 18 times, arousing criticism of a sort that was to greet much of his later work: that his music was too modern, too difficult, even too Wagnerian. Bizet was now asked to complete *Ivan IV* for the Théâtre-lyrique and did so in summer 1865, but the theater's financial situation prevented its production. Long lost, the score was performed in 1952 (the rediscovered, incomplete score probably represents an early version of the work). In June 1866, however, he contracted with the same theater for *La jolie fille de Perth,* an incompetent libretto based distantly on a novel by Scott. Completed in December, it was not premiered until 26 Dec. 1867. Well received by its first audience and generally by the critics, it still lasted only 18 performances. Bizet had expected a greater success and was considerably disheartened. In 1868–69 he composed *La coupe du roi de Thulé* for a competition at the Opéra, where he was also hoping for a commission. Although he had been assured that he would win the prize, he did not; nor did he receive the expected commission. Only fragments of this score survive. His *Roma* Symphony was performed in 1869 without arousing much interest.

In June 1869 Bizet married Geneviève Halévy, daughter of his former teacher, whose last opera, *Noé,* left unfinished, he now completed. Although his wife brought a sizable dowry, and the marriage was at first happy, producing a son in 1872, Geneviève's emotional instability proved a drain on his energies. After several operatic projects for the Opéra-comique had come to nothing, he was given the one-act *Djamileh,* which he completed quickly in summer 1871, the same year as his *Jeux d'enfants* for piano four-hands, five selections of which were orchestrated as *Petite suite.* Premiered on 22 May 1872, *Djamileh* was a failure, given only 11 times. Daudet's play *L'arlésienne,* for which Bizet wrote incidental music, had the same fate at the Vaudeville on 1 Oct. 1872; the suite of excerpts, however, was well received at a Pasdeloup concert in November and was repeated several times before Bizet's death. He next began to compose *Carmen* for the Opéra-comique, but soon gave preference to a work for the Opéra, *Don Rodrigue,* the story of The Cid, completed in sketch in autumn 1873 but then abandoned because of the burning of the Opéra. *Carmen* was completed in summer 1874 and premiered, after four months of rehearsals, on 3 Mar. 1875. Received with considerable outrage at the earthiness of its subject and not much critical recognition of the quality of its music, it had 48 performances through early 1876 but was not well attended. The opera's rise to universal popularity began with its very successful Vienna production in Oct. 1875, three months after Bizet's death after a short illness.

Other works: the overture *Patrie* (1873); piano pieces; songs (including many derived from unfinished dramatic works).

Bibl.: Edmond Galabert, *Georges Bizet: Souvenirs et correspondance* (Paris, 1877). Hughes Imbert, *Portraits et études: Lettres inédites de Georges Bizet* (Paris, 1894). "Charles Gounod: Lettres à Georges Bizet," *Revue de Paris* 36 (1894): 677–703. Louis Ganderax, ed., Georges Bizet: *Lettres, impressions de Rome (1857–60), la Commune (1871)* (Paris, 1907). Edmond Galabert, ed., *Georges Bizet: Lettres à un ami, 1865–72* (Paris, 1909). Julien Tiersot, "Bizet and Spanish Music," *MQ* 13 (1927): 566–81. Mina Curtiss, *Bizet and His World* (New York, 1958). Howard Shanet, "Bizet's Suppressed Symphony," *MQ* 44 (1958): 461–76. Winton Dean, *Bizet,* rev. ed. (Westport, Conn., 1979). Rebecca Knaust, *The Complete Guide to Carmen* (New York, 1978).

Björling, Jussi [Johan] **(Jonaton)** (b. Stora Tuna, Sweden, 2 Feb. 1911; d. Siarö, near Stockholm, 9 Sept. 1960). Tenor. With his father, Karl David, and his brothers, Olle and Gösta, he toured Europe and the U.S., beginning in 1919, as the Björling Family Quartet. In 1928 he was heard by the director of the Royal Swedish Opera, John Forsell, who took him as a student. Debut with the Royal Swedish Opera 11 July 1930 in a small role from *Manon Lescaut.* By 20 Aug. 1930 he was singing major roles, beginning with Mozart's Don Ottavio. Over the next 5 years he enlarged his repertory to 20 operas. He sang Verdi's Radames in Vienna (1936); Verdi's Rigoletto in Prague and Chicago (1937); Puccini's Rodolfo in New York (1938), after which he was a fixture at the Metropolitan Opera; and Verdi's Manrico at Covent Garden (1939). He remained in Sweden during the Nazi occupation, returning to the Met as the Duke in *Rigoletto* in 1945, and singing with that company in 1947, 1948, and 1950. Waiting in the wings for his second appearance at Covent Garden, he suffered a heart attack that proved fatal.

Bibl: Jack W. Porter and Harald Henrysson, *A Jussi Bjoerling Discography* (Indianapolis, 1982).

Björnsson, Árni (b. Loni i Kelduhverfi, Iceland, 23 Dec. 1905). Composer and pianist. After studying composition and keyboards at the Reykjavík College of Music, he taught and performed in Iceland. Later he studied briefly at the Royal Manchester College. Upon returning to Iceland he joined the faculty of the Reykjavík College, where he taught from 1946 to 1952. His works, largely in a diatonic idiom, include orchestral works (*In the Mountains,* 1939; *A Little Suite,* strings, 1947; *Variations on an Icelandic Song,* 1949); songs and choral works (*Ode to Liberty,* male chorus, 1944); and keyboard music.

Blacher, Boris (b. Niu-chang, China, of German-Russian parents, 19 Jan. 1903; d. Berlin, 30 Jan. 1975). Composer. He played piano and violin as a child. In Berlin from 1922, he studied architecture and mathematics at the Technische Hochschule before turning to composition under Friedrich Ernst Koch at the Hochschule für Musik; studied under Schering, Blume, and von Hornbostel at the Univ. in Berlin (1927–31), supporting himself as a copyist, arranger, and composer of film music. In 1938 he was appointed to teach composition at the Dresden Conservatory but resigned because of conflict with the Nazis; by 1948 he was teaching at the Berlin Hochschule für Musik, which he later directed (1953–70). He taught at the Berkshire Music Center in 1955; was elected to the music section of the West Berlin Academy of Arts in 1955 and served as its president (1968–71).

His works until the late 1940s were tonal and often witty: Satie, Milhaud, and Stravinsky were strong influences, along with jazz idioms. In works of the early 1950s he developed a means of relating varying meters systematically in relation to the twelve-tone idea. In *Ornamente* for piano op. 37 (1950) the changes of meter at each bar correlate with the mathematical series selected to establish the rhythmic row equivalent to a pitch series; the rhythmic designs take precedence over the pitch set. He is noted for extremely apt (but traditional) orchestral scoring and weighty counterpoint (a consequence of his admiration for Hindemith and for the Baroque). The "Amen" section of his Requiem (1958) is a large palindrome.

Many works, especially his operas, contain social criticism. *Die Flut* (chamber opera, 1946) deals with the behavior of people in extreme situations; *Preussisches Märchen* satirizes German character traits. His *Abstrakte Oper no. 1* (libretto by Werner Egk, 1953) abandons narrative and other traditional forms of discourse for the portrayal of fundamental human emotions.

Other works include the ballet *Lysistrata* (1950), the opera *Rosamunde Floris* (1960), and other dramatic works, incidental music, and film scores; about 50 orchestral works including *Orchester-Ornament* (1953) and *Virtuose Musik* (violin, 10 winds, timpani, percussion, harp, 1966); a divertimento for trumpet, trombone, and piano (1948), 5 string quartets, a quintet for flute, oboe, and string trio (1973), and other chamber music; *Ornamente* (7 studies for piano, 1950), 24 Preludes (1924) and other piano music; a Requiem for soprano, baritone, chorus, and orchestra (1958), and other large works for chorus, soloists, and orchestra; songs with ensemble or piano, including *13 Ways of Looking at a Blackbird* (after Stevens, for soprano or tenor and strings, 1957); *Ariadne* (duodrama for 2 speakers and tape, 1971) and other electronic works.

Bibl.: Hans Heinz Stuckenschmidt, *Boris Blacher* (Berlin, 1985).

Blackwell, Ed(ward Joseph) (b. New Orleans, 10 Oct. 1929). Jazz drummer. He played rhythm-and-blues, then in 1951 moved to Los Angeles, where he worked with Ornette Coleman. Later he joined Coleman in New York (1960–61, 1967, 1969, 1970–73), recording the album *Free Jazz* (1960). He played in the quintet of Eric Dolphy and Booker Little (1961), recorded free jazz with Don Cherry (including the album *Complete Communion,* 1965), and joined Randy Weston, touring Africa (1967) and living in Morocco (1968). From 1976 he worked with Cherry, Charlie Haden, and the tenor saxophonist Dewey Redman in Old and New Dreams. He also worked in Cherry's group Nu, and with Anthony Braxton and David Murray.

Blackwood, Easley (b. Indianapolis, 21 Apr. 1933). Composer and pianist. Studied with Messiaen (Berkshire Music Center, 1949), Hindemith (Yale, 1950–54), and Boulanger (Paris, 1954–57). Joined faculty at the Univ. of Chicago in 1958. As a pianist he has actively promoted the contemporary repertory, especially of Ives, Boulez, and the second Viennese School. His works employ polyrhythmic textures and wide-ranging melodic contours; in the 1980s he became interested in equal-tempered tuning systems of more than 12 pitches per octave, resulting in the composition of *12 Mictrotonal Etudes for Electronic Music Media* (1982) and *The Structure of Recognizable Diatonic Tunings* (1986), a rigorous discussion of tuning theory. Works include symphonies; concertos; chamber music including string quartets, sonatas with piano or harpsichord; piano works; vocal music.

Blades, Rubén (b. Panama City, Panama, 16 July 1948). Popular singer, songwriter, and actor. Graduated from the Univ. of Panama in 1974 with a law degree. Went to New York City to pursue a music career, appearing first as a soloist with Ray Barretto's band at Madison Square Garden. Later associated with trombonist and arranger Willie Colón, with whom he recorded (for Fania Records) the very successful song "Siembra" and the politically controversial "Tiburón." His first albums for a major record label (Elektra/Asylum), *Buscando America* (1984) and *Escenas* (1985), continued to explore social and political themes and established him with a wider audience in both the United States and Latin America. Began his career as an actor in the film *Crossover Dreams* (1985), for which he also wrote the music, and appeared in numerous films thereafter. Returned to Panama in 1994.

Bibl.: Dave Marsh, ed., "Ruben Blades: Searching for America," in *The First Rock and Roll Confidential Report* (New York, 1985). Don Michael Randel, "Crossing Over with Rubén Blades," *JAMS* 44 (1991): 301–23.

Blake, Blind (Arthur) (b. Jacksonville, Fla., ca. 1890–95; d. Florida? ca. 1933–35). Blues singer and guitarist. Blake's career is obscure, and his real name and dates of birth and death are subjects of controversy. He made just over 80 recordings as Blind Blake, or under identifiable nicknames (1926–32), and several more as accompanist to other musicians, including Ma Rainey (1926) and Gus Cannon (1927). He was a technically accomplished guitarist, as on *Blind Arthur's Breakdown* or his duet with the pianist Charlie Spand, *Hastings St. (Boogy)* [sic] (both 1929). His repertory included blues, country dance songs, and songster or medicine show pieces, such as *He's in the Jailhouse Now* (1927).

Blake, David (Leonard) (b. London, 2 Sept 1936). Composer. Studied music at Cambridge and composition with Eisler in East Berlin. Beginning 1963 has taught at York Univ. From Eisler he learned twelve-tone composition in the style of Schoenberg; but an interest in Messiaen, chance, and the exotic (in part derived from his having been stationed in Hong Kong in the mid-1950s) have also affected his music. His works include a school musical, *It's a Small War* (1962), and the operas *Toussaint L'Ouverture* (1974–76) and *The Plumber's Gift* (1989); *Metamorphoses* (orchestra, 1970–71) and 2 violin concertos (1976, 1982); string quartets (1961–62, 1973), a nonet for winds (1971), *Scenes* (cello, 1972), and other chamber and instrumental music; *Lumina,* a cantata for soprano, baritone, chorus, and orchestra (after Pound, 1968–69) and several pieces for unaccompanied chorus (*Grandpa,* 1989); the song cycle *In Praise of Krishna* (1973) and other songs; *Alexander's Flight* (1992).

Blake, Eubie [James Hubert] (b. Baltimore, 7 Feb. 1883; d. New York, 12 Feb. 1983). Ragtime and revue pianist and composer. He worked as a pianist, mainly in Baltimore, and claimed to have composed "Sounds of Africa" in 1899 (published as "Charleston Rag," 1919). In partnership with Noble Sissle he wrote for musical revues from 1915. Their hit show *Shuffle Along,* the first African American musical, included the song "I'm Just Wild about Harry" (1921). With Andy Razaf he wrote the popular song "Memories of You," the spiritual "Roll, Jordan," and the novelty song "My Handyman Ain't Handy Any More" for Lew Leslie's Blackbirds (1930). During this period he made records and piano rolls. He retired to study composition at New York Univ. (1946–49). Involved as a performer and lecturer in the first ragtime revival (1950s), he reached his widest audience after recording the album *The Eighty-Six Years of Eubie Blake* (1969). He toured internationally, received honorary degrees in music, and was celebrated in the Broadway show *Eubie* (1978).

Bibl.: William Bolcom and Robert Kimball, *Reminiscing with Sissle and Blake* (New York, 1973).

Blakey, Art [Buhaina, Abdullah ibn] (b. Pittsburgh, 11 Oct. 1919; d. New York, 16 Oct. 1990). Jazz drummer and bandleader. He played with Mary Lou Williams (1942), Fletcher Henderson (1943–44), and Billy Eckstine's bop big band (1944–47). He recorded with Thelonious Monk (intermittently 1947–54), then formed the definitive hard bop combo, the Jazz Messengers, initially sharing leadership with Horace Silver (until 1956). His recordings include *The Jazz Messengers at the Cafe Bohemia* with Kenny Dorham and Hank Mobley (1955), *Art Blakey's Jazz Messengers with Thelonious Monk* and with Johnny Griffin (1957), and *Album of the Year* with Wynton Marsalis (1981). Donald Byrd, Lee Morgan, Wayne Shorter, Freddie Hubbard, JoAnne Brackeen, Woody Shaw, and Branford Marsalis were among other members of his group. He also toured with the Giants of Jazz, including Dizzy Gillespie, Sonny Stitt, and Monk (1971–72).

Bland, James A(llen) (b. Flushing, N.Y., 22 Oct. 1854; d. Philadelphia, 5 May 1911). Minstrel performer and composer. Raised in Washington, D.C., he studied briefly at Howard Univ. but left in favor of a stage career. From 1875 he performed in all-black minstrel groups and composed popular songs, including "Carry Me Back to Old Virginny" (1878) and "Oh, Dem Golden Slippers" (1879). In 1881 he journeyed with Haverly's Genuine Colored Minstrels to England, where he remained until 1890. He returned to the U.S. to find the popularity of the minstrels diminished, and the remainder of his work, including a musical comedy (*The Sporting Girl,* ca. 1900), was unsuccessful. The extent of his compositional output is unknown: although he has been credited with composing several hundred songs, his authorship is verifiable for only the 40 that he copyrighted at the Library of Congress (1879–92).

Blanton, Jimmy [James] (b. Chattanooga, Tenn., Oct. 1918; d. Monrovia, Calif., 30 July 1942). Jazz double bass player. Based in St. Louis, he played in the Jeter–Pillars Orchestra and on riverboats with Fate Marable. He toured with Duke Ellington from 1939 to 1941, when tuberculosis ended his career. In this brief time he became the most important jazz bassist of his era, acclaimed for his full tone, perfect sense of rhythm, harmonically sophisticated walking bass lines, and melodically imaginative solos. Recordings with Ellington include the duos "Plucked Again" (1939), "Pitter Panther Patter," and "Sophisticated Lady," and the big band pieces "Jack the Bear," "Ko-Ko," and "Harlem Air Shaft" (all 1940).

Blavet, Michel (b. Besançon, bapt. 13 Mar. 1700; d. Paris, 28 Oct. 1768). Flutist and composer. A self-taught musician, he moved to Paris in 1723 and became the most admired French flutist of the time, making the first of many public appearances in 1726 at the Concert spirituel; first flute of the Musique du roi in 1738 and at the Opéra in 1740. Works include 3 sets of 6 flute sonatas, opp. 1 (1728), 2 (1732), 3 (1740); one surviving concerto; many arrangements for flute; 4 stage works (1752–53), including one considered the first attempt to imitate Italian simple recitative in setting French.

Bledsoe, Jules [Julius] (b. Waco, Tex., 29 Dec. 1898; d. Hollywood, Calif., 14 July 1943). Baritone. Sang in church as a child; began piano lessons at the age of 8. Graduated from Bishop College (Marshall, Tex.) with B.A. in 1914. Studied at Virginia Union Univ. and Chicago Musical College. After serving briefly in the army he entered Columbia Univ. Medical School in 1919, but took private voice lessons with Claude Warford, Lazar Samoiloff, and Parisolti. Debut recital in 1924 at Aeolian Hall, New York. Performed in Harling's opera *Deep River* (1926). Played Joe in Kern's *Showboat* (1927), and sang the role in the 1929 film version. Traveled to Europe, 1931–32. Sang Amonasro in *Aida;* was the first black to be heard in this role on a first-rate musical stage (Municipal Stadium in Cleveland). Appeared in 1942 film *Drums of the Congo.*

Bibl.: Maud (Cuney-)Hare, *Negro Musicians and Their Music* (Washington, D.C., 1936; R: 1974).

Blegen, Judith (Eyer) (b. Lexington, Ky., 27 Apr. 1940). Lyric soprano. Studied voice and violin at the Curtis Institute (1959–64). Won the 1962 Philadelphia Award, which led to her 1963 debut with the Philadelphia Orchestra. After an apprenticeship at the Santa Fe Opera, she went to Spoleto in 1964 and worked on the Italian repertory with Luigi Ricci. Joined the Nuremberg Opera in 1965, making her professional operatic debut singing Offenbach's Olympia. Success as Mélisande at the 1966 Spoleto Festival led to her debut with the Vienna Staatsoper as Rossini's Rosine. At the Santa Fe premiere of Menotti's *Help! Help! The Globolinks!* (1969) she both sang and played violin as Emily, a role created for her. She debuted as Mozart's Papagena at New York's Metropolitan Opera (19 Jan. 1970); also sang at the Salzburg Festival (1974), Edinburgh Festival (1976), and with the Paris Opera (1977).

Bley, Carla [née Borg] (b. Oakland, Calif., 11 May 1938). Jazz composer, bandleader, and entrepreneur. In the early 1960s she began composing for her first husband, the pianist Paul Bley, who recorded such humorous, miniature free jazz sketches as "Around Again" and "Ida Lupino" on his albums of 1962–66. She also composed "Sing Me Softly of the Blues." With her second husband, the trumpeter Mike Mantler, she formed the Jazz Composers Guild Orchestra (1964), from which grew the Jazz Composers Orchestra Association (1966–), through which in turn developed the New Music Distribution Service (1968–), a principal outlet for independent record labels. She composed *A Genuine Tong Funeral,* recorded by Gary Burton (1967); music for Charlie Haden's Liberation Music Orchestra (recorded in 1969); and the "jazz opera" *Escalator over the Hill* (recorded in 1968–71). From 1976 she played keyboard in and composed eclectic pieces for her own bands; albums include *Dinner Music* (1976) and *Social Studies* (1980).

Bliss, Arthur (Edward Drummond) (b. London, 2 Aug. 1891; d. there, 27 Mar. 1975). Composer. The son of a native New Englander, he was schooled at Rugby and attended Cambridge Univ. until 1913. At the Royal College of Music he studied conducting for a year (1913–14) with Stanford. His works from immediately after World War I show influences of Stravinsky, Ravel, and jazz. In 1921 he became professor of composition at the Royal College of Music; 1923–25 he spent in the U.S., where he fulfilled commissions such as that from Leopold Stokowski's Philadelphia Orchestra (*Introduction and Allegro,* 1926). From 1934 to 1941 he was again in the U.S. and taught at the Univ. of California at Berkeley. Returning to England, he was music director of the BBC (1942–44), was knighted in 1950, and succeeded Bax as Master of the Queen's Music in 1953. In 1970 he published a memoir, *As I Remember.*

Works: operas (*The Olympians,* 1948–49; *Tobias and the Angel,* 1960); ballet scores (*Checkmate,* 1937; *Adam Zero,* 1946; *The Lady of Shallott,* 1958); incidental music; film scores (*Conquest of the Air,* 1937; *Welcome the Queen,* 1954); orchestral music (*Mêlée fantasque,* 1921, rev. 1965; *A Colour Symphony,* 1922, rev. 1932; *Hymn to Apollo,* 1926, rev. 1966; *Music for Strings,* 1935; *The Linburn Air,* military band, 1965; *Metamorphic Variations,* 1972); choral works (*Morning Heroes,* narrator, chorus, orchestra, 1930; *A Prayer to the Infant Jesus,* 1968); other vocal works (*Madame Noy,* soprano, chamber ensemble, 1918; *Rout,* soprano, chamber ensemble, 1920; *Serenade,* baritone, orchestra, 1939; *A Knot of Riddles,* baritone, chamber ensemble, 1963); many songs with piano; chamber and piano works (*Conversations,* 1920; Clarinet Quintet, 1931; *Belmont Variations,* brass, 1963).

Bibl.: Lewis Foreman, *Arthur Bliss: Catalogue of Complete Works* (Kent, 1980). Stewart R. Craggs, *Arthur Bliss: A Bio-Bibliography* (New York, 1988). Arthur Bliss, *Bliss on Music: Selected Writings of Arthur Bliss, 1920–1975* (New York, 1991).

Blitheman, John (b. ca. 1525; d. London, 23 May 1591). Composer and organist. His first name is commonly but incorrectly given as William. Gentleman of the Chapel Royal from sometime between 1553 and 1558 until his death. Received an annuity from Christ Church, Oxford, but had no other connection with this church or with Oxford Univ. Taught John Bull. Composed 2 sacred vocal works (in 4 parts) and about 8 keyboard works, including a set of variations on "Gloria tibi Trinitas" and several liturgical hymn settings.

Blitzstein, Marc (b. Philadelphia, 2 Mar. 1905; d. Fort-de-France, Martinique, 22 Jan. 1964). Composer. Attended the Univ. of Pennsylvania for two years (1921–23), then the Curtis Institute (1924), studying composition with Scalero and continuing piano study in New York with Siloti; from 1926 to 1928 he studied in Paris with Boulanger and in Berlin with Schoenberg. He premiered his own sonata for piano (New York, 1928) and wrote for *Modern Music;* his works from the period 1928–34 were performed in New York, London, and Paris; a one-act opera (*The Harpies,* 1931) parodies his own Parisian neoclassical style. After 1935, influenced by Hanns Eisler and by a meeting with Brecht, he turned to producing dramatic music, often with a leftist political message. *The Cradle Will Rock* (1936–37) was written for the Federal Theater Project, but was rejected just before the scheduled performance; it was produced independently by Orson Welles and John Houseman with neither costumes nor orchestra (Blitzstein accompanied on stage at the piano). During the war he produced 2 works on commission from the Army Air Force: *Freedom Morning* (tone poem, 1943) and *Airborne Symphony* (narrator, soloists, chorus, orchestra, 1943–46). His widest fame came from his translation and adaptation of Brecht and Weill's *Die Dreigroschenoper* as *The Threepenny Opera* (1952). His dramatic works are in an eclectic style, mixing jazz and popular song forms with sophisticated harmonies and the rhythms of American speech. Other works include dramatic works (*No for an Answer,* 1941; *Regina,* after Lillian Hellman's *The Little Foxes,* 1949; *Reuben, Reuben,* 1955; *Juno,* 1959; *Sacco and Vanzetti,* 1959–64, incomplete); orchestral and chamber music; choral and solo vocal works; incidental music; film scores.

Bibl.: Eric Gordon, *Mark the Music: The Life and Work of Marc Blitzstein* (New York, 1989).

Bloch, Ernest (b. Geneva, 24 July 1880; d. Portland, Ore., 15 July 1959). Composer and teacher. In the 1890s he studied violin with Louis Rey and composition with Jaques-Dalcroze in Geneva; then went for further study to Brussels (composition with Rasse, a former pupil of Franck; violin with Ysaÿe), Frankfurt am Main, Munich, and Paris. From ca. 1905 he worked in his father's clock business in Geneva. He lectured on aesthetics at the Geneva Conservatory (1911–15) and conducted concerts in Lausanne (1910–11). Early works are in a German Romantic (the autobiographical Symphony in C# minor, 1901–2) or French impressionist (*Hivers-Printemps,* 1904–5) vein; their modal cast and cyclic construction became consistent features of Bloch's style. In 1916 he emigrated to the U.S., where he taught at the Mannes School (1917–19).

Several works from the period 1911–16 constitute a "Jewish Cycle" (*Schelomo,* a rhapsody for cello and orchestra, 1915–16, as well as Psalm settings). They are large in scale and often on biblical subjects, and they make use of repeated-note patterns and augmented or perfect fourths recalling the shofar employed on High Holy Days in the synagogue. Rhythmic accents on the last or penultimate beat of a bar parallel accents in the Hebrew language; parts for harp and celesta are common.

He became director of the Cleveland Institute of Music in 1920, leaving in 1925 for the San Francisco Conservatory (1925–30); at Cleveland his suggestion for abolishing examinations and textbooks in favor of a return to the study of the great works was not received favorably. His *America: An Epic Rhapsody* (chorus and orchestra) won first prize in the *Musical America* contest of 1927. Dedicated to the memory of Lincoln and Whitman, this work uses indigenous themes (American Indian motifs, spirituals, sea chanteys, patriotic tunes, and car horns) and ends with a chorus in which the audience is expected to join. Most of the works from the 1920s are in a neoclassic style (Concerto Grosso no. 1, 1924–25; the first piano quintet, 1921–23, which uses quarter tones; violin sonatas); more Jewish works appeared as well (*Baal shem,* violin and piano, 1923; *Méditation hébraïque,* cello and piano, 1924).

Bloch had become a U.S. citizen in 1928 but spent the 1930s in Europe and returned to large-scale works, including a violin concerto (1937–38) and a Jewish sacred service (*Avodath hakodesh,* baritone, chorus, and orchestra, 1930–33). He returned to the U.S. to teach at Berkeley (1940–52). Late works range in style from the neoclassic Concerto Grosso no. 2 (1952) to the neoromantic *Concerto symphonique* (piano and orchestra, 1947–48) to the twelve-tone *Sinfonia breve* (1951).

Other works include the opera *Macbeth* (1910); orchestral music, including many works with one or more soloists (cello, viola, piano, violin, trombone, trumpet, flute); chamber music, including 5 string quartets, sonatas, and works for strings and piano; piano pieces and a few organ works; vocal works for soloists or choir, most with orchestra.

Bibl.: David Z. Kushner, *Ernest Bloch and His Music* (Glasgow, 1973). R. Strassburg, *Ernest Bloch, Voice in the Wilderness: A Biographical Study* (Los Angeles, 1977). David Z. Kushner, "Ernest Bloch: A Retrospective on the Centenary of His Birth," *CMS* 20 (1980): 77–86. David Z. Kushner, *Ernest Bloch: A Guide to Research* (New York, 1988).

Blockx, Jan (b. Antwerp, 25 Jan. 1851; d. Kapellenbos, near Antwerp, 26 May 1912). Composer. Studied briefly with Benoit at the Flemish Music School in Antwerp, then with Reinecke at the Leipzig Conservatory. Taught harmony at the Flemish Music School from 1885, succeeding Benoit as director in 1901 (by then the Royal Flemish Conservatory). He composed 7 operas, mostly in Flemish (2 of them in 2 versions), all first performed in Antwerp or Brussels, including *Herbergprinses* (Antwerp, 1896) and *De bruid der zee* (Antwerp, 1901); a ballet and a pantomime; several cantatas and other choral music; a symphony and other orchestral pieces; chamber music; songs; piano pieces.

Bibl: Frank Blockx, *Jan Blockx* (Brussels, 1943).

Blodek, Vilém (b. Prague, 3 Oct. 1834; d. there, 1 May 1874). Composer. Studied with the pianist Dreyschock, and in 1846–52 at the Prague Conservatory with the composer Kittl and the flutist Eiser. Was music teacher to a family in Poland, 1853–55; then teacher, conductor, composer, and pianist in Prague; from 1860 flute teacher at the conservatory. Blodek was committed to an insane asylum temporarily in 1870 and permanently in 1871. He is best known for his one-act Czech folk opera *V studni* [In the Well] (Prague, 1867). A larger opera, *Zitek,* was left unfinished and not performed until 1934. Other works include incidental music to 60 plays, a symphony, 4 concert overtures, flute concerto, flute pieces, a Mass and other sacred choral music, and many part songs.

Blomdahl, Karl-Birger (b. Växjö, 19 Oct. 1916; d. Kungsängen, near Stockholm, 14 June 1968). Composer. At the conservatory in Stockholm he studied composition with Hilding Rosenberg and conducting with Thor Mann; later he studied conducting privately with Mogens Wöldike. He traveled to France and Italy (1946–47) and to the U.S. (Tanglewood, 1954–55;

Princeton, 1959). From 1960 he taught at Stockholm's Royal College of Music; from 1964 he was music director of Swedish Radio. As critic he wrote for *Prisma* and helped edit *Nutida Musik.* In 1965 he won the first Nordiska Rådets Prize for his opera *Aniara* (1957–59). His early music manifests influence of Hindemith and neoclassical experiments; later he explored twelve-tone and electronic techniques. Works include operas (*Herr von Hancken,* 1962–65); ballets (*Sisyfos,* 1954; *Minotaurus,* 1958); incidental music (*Vaknatten* [Wakeful Night], 1945); orchestral works (Concert Overture, 1942; Pastoral Suite, 1948; *Fioriture,* 1960; *Forma ferritonans,* 1961); choral and vocal music (*I speglarnas sal* [In the Hall of Mirrors], oratorio, 1951–52; *Anabase,* baritone, narrator, chorus, orchestra, 1956); tape (*Altisonans,* 1966); chamber music (Chamber Concerto, piano, winds, percussion, 1953).

Bibl.: Gunnar Bucht, *Facetter: av och om Karl-Birger Blomdahl* [with works list] (Stockholm, 1970). R. K. Inglefield, "Karl-Birger Blomdahl: A Portrait," *MQ* 58 (1972): 67.

Blondel de Nesle (fl. 1180–1200). Trouvère. The language of his poetry reveals that he was from Picardy; no other biographical details are available. Two of his songs are dedicated to Conon de Béthune and one to Gace Brulé. Some of his songs survive in an uncommonly large number of sources, and many were used as models for later chansons.

Blow, John (b. Newark, Nottinghamshire, bapt. 23 Feb. 1649; d. Westminster, 1 Oct. 1708). Composer and organist. He probably received early music training at Magnus Song School in Newark; later he was a choirboy at the Chapel Royal. He was appointed organist at Westminster Abbey in 1668 at age 19. In 1674 he became a Gentleman of the Chapel and the same year succeeded Pelham Humfrey as Master of the Children. This position he held for the rest of his life. Among his pupils were William Croft and Henry Purcell. In 1676 he was made one of the Chapel Royal organists; the following year he received the D.Mus. from the Dean of Canterbury. During the next years he composed many of his best-known works, including most of the anthems with string accompaniment and the masque *Venus and Adonis.* He was appointed choirmaster at St. Paul's Cathedral in 1687. In 1695 he was named royal instrument tuner; finally in 1699 or 1700 he became the official Chapel Royal composer, the first to hold such a post. He composed 11 services (edited in William Boyce, *Cathedral Music,* 3 vols., London, 1760–73); some 115 anthems (11 are in Boyce's collection; see also *MB* 7); 10 Latin church works; *Venus and Adonis;* 36 known odes (including several for St. Cecilia's Day; "Great Sir, the joy of all our hearts"; "Ode on the Death of Mr. Henry Purcell"); many songs and catches; pieces for string ensemble; organ works (edited in Watkins Shaw, *Complete Organ Works,* London, 1958; 2nd ed., 1972, titled *Thirty Voluntaries and Verses by John Blow*); harpsichord works. He also authored *Rules for Playing of a Thorough Bass upon Organ and Harpsicon,* ed. in F. T. Arnold, *The Art of Accompaniment from a Thorough-Bass as Practised in the XVIIth and XVIIIth Centuries* (Oxford, 1931; R: 1965).

Blüthner, Julius (Ferdinand) (b. Falkenhain, near Merseburg, 11 Mar. 1824; d. Leipzig, 13 Apr. 1910). Piano manufacturer. After working as a cabinetmaker, he became an apprentice piano maker at 18, working in several firms to increase his knowledge, ending with Breitschneider in Leipzig. He opened his own shop in 1853, employing three men and a boy, but was quickly successful, so that in 1864 he built a large factory with 800 workers and began making upright as well as grand pianos. His improvements to the instrument resulted in several patents and won many prizes. The very large business that resulted (63,000 pianos by 1903) was continued by his sons Max, Robert, and Bruno and resurrected by Bruno's son-in-law Rudolph Blüthner-Haessler after the factory's destruction in World War II.

Boatwright, Helen (Strassburger) (b. Sheboygan, Wis., 17 Nov. 1916). Soprano. Studied with Anna Shram Irving, then at Oberlin College with Marion Simms. Operatic debut as Nicolai's Anna at the Berkshire Music Festival, 1942. New York recital debut at Town Hall, March 1967. From 1964 she taught voice at Syracuse Univ. She performed principally with orchestras and in recital, giving important performances of works by Hindemith and Ives. In 1943 she married the composer and violinist Howard Boatwright, with whom she often performed.

Boatwright, Howard (Leake, Jr.) (b. Newport News, Va., 16 Mar. 1918). Composer and violinist. Studied violin with Israel Feldman in Norfolk and taught violin at the Univ. of Texas (1943–45). Studied composition with Hindemith at Yale (B.M., 1947; M.M., 1948); taught there (1948–64); directed music at St. Thomas's Church in New Haven (1949–64); and was concertmaster of the New Haven Symphony (1950–62). In 1964 he became Dean of the School of Music at Syracuse Univ.; beginning in 1971 taught composition and theory there. He was in India in 1959 and in Romania in 1975. Boatwright authored a music theory textbook (1956), various works on Hindemith, and 2 monographs on Indian music; he edited Ives's writings. In 1943 he married the soprano Helen Boatwright, with whom he often performed. His early choral music is frequently modal and sometimes makes use of Anglo-American folk tunes. His second string quartet (1974) reflects both Hindemith and the twelve-tone techniques he had begun to employ by 1966. Works include a symphony (1976) and other orchestral pieces; chamber music (2 string quartets; a quartet for clarinet and strings, 1958); choral music, including Masses and other church music; cantatas (*The Lament* *of Mary Stuart,* soprano, harpsichord, optional cello, 1968); piano pieces; organ pieces; about 50 songs.

Boccherini, (Ridolfo) Luigi (b. Lucca, 19 Feb. 1743; d. Madrid, 28 May 1805). Composer and cellist; one of the most prolific composers of chamber music of the 18th century. After study in Lucca with Franceso Vanucci and in Rome with Giovanni Battista Costanzi, he received an appointment at the Viennese imperial court theater. During the early 1760s his music began to be noticed in Vienna. In 1766 he joined violinist Filippo Manfredi on a concert tour that took him to Paris, where his first publications appeared in 1767. The tour continued to Madrid in 1768 or 1769, where Boccherini received a post as composer and cellist at the court of the Infante Don Luis. Upon the latter's death in 1785 the composer sought employment at the court of Frederick William of Prussia, who was also a cellist. He sent new works to the prince, such as the op. 22 string quartets and the op. 25 quintet. In 1786 his perseverance was rewarded: he was made chamber musician in the Berlin court of newly crowned King Frederick William. There he produced a large portion of his extant chamber works. After the king's death in 1797 the composer subsisted mostly on a pension from his Madrid appointment and on proceeds from a handful of publications.

Boccherini composed 125 string quintets (nearly all scored for 2 cellos rather than 2 violas), about 100 string quartets, more than 50 string trios, 11 cello concertos, 29 symphonies, other orchestral music, Masses, cantatas, and many secular vocal works. The Gérard thematic catalog (see below) was compiled partly on the basis of a catalog that the composer had prepared of his own works; many of these were lost in 1936 in the Spanish Civil War. His chamber music is of great importance in the history of 18th-century instrumental style.

Bibl.: A. Bonaventura, *Boccherini* (Milan, 1931). Germaine de Rothschild, *Luigi Boccherini: Sa vie, son oeuvre* (Paris, 1962; trans. Eng., rev., 1965). Ellen Iris Amsterdam, "The String Quintets of Luigi Boccherini" (diss., Univ. of California, Berkeley, 1968). Yves Gérard, *Thematic, Bibliographical, and Critical Catalogue of the Works of Luigi Boccherini* (London, 1969). Guido Salvetti, "Luigi Boccherini nell'ambito del quartetto italiano del secondo settecento," *AnMca* 12 (1973): 227–52.

Bochsa, (Robert) Nicholas Charles (b. Montmédi, France, 9 Aug. 1789; d. Sydney, 6 Jan. 1856). Harpist and composer. Studied with his father, a Czech musician who worked in France, and Franz Beck in Bordeaux; from 1806 at the Paris Conservatory, narrowing his precocious talent for many instruments to the harp. He soon became prominent as a harpist and as a prolific composer, especially of harp music but also in 1813–16 of 7 operas for the Opéra-comique. In March 1817 he announced a concert but never appeared, robbing the coatroom while the audience waited and departing Paris for London in a stolen carriage. It was discovered that through forging signatures, including those of prominent musicians and the Duke of Wellington, he had perpetrated swindles amounting to 760,000 francs. In 1818 he was sentenced in absentia to be branded and to 12 years at hard labor, in spite of which he established himself as a leading figure in London music, giving concerts, teaching, moving in society, and holding important positions, including music director at the King's Theatre, 1826–32. He took a second wife, a demimondaine, although his first, the daughter of a marquis, was alive in France. In 1839 he eloped with the brilliant singer Anna Bishop, then wife of the composer Sir Henry Bishop. They toured much of the world (except France), performing together, until his death. He published a *Méthode de harpe* (Paris, n.d.) and much harp music.

Bibl.: A. Pougin, "Un musicien voleur, faussaire et bigame," *Le ménestrel* 73 (1907): 19–20, 36–37, 44, 52–53, 59–61, 67–68, 75–76.

Bock, Jerry [Jerrold Lewis] (b. New Haven, Conn., 23 Nov. 1928). Popular composer. He studied music at the Univ. of Wisconsin (1945–49), then moved to New York City, where he collaborated with lyricist Larry Holofcener on songs for television and Broadway revues and on a full-length musical, *Mr. Wonderful* (1956). Between 1958 and 1970 he composed musicals with lyricist Sheldon Harnick, including *Fiorello!* (1959), which won a Pulitzer Prize for drama, and the immensely popular *Fiddler on the Roof* (1964). After parting with Harnick, Bock ceased to write for Broadway; he produced 2 concept albums, *Album Leaves* (1972) and *Trading Dreams* (1974).

Bo Diddley [McDaniel, Elias] (b. McComb, Miss., 30 Dec. 1928). Rock-and-roll singer. At the age of 5 he moved with his family to Chicago, where he took up violin; later taught himself guitar. First regular job was at the 708 Club in Chicago (1951). Played with several rhythm-and-blues groups in the 1950s. Walked into Chess and Checker Records to audition and was given the name Bo Diddley; the song that was a takeoff on this name reached no. 2 on the R & B charts in 1955. "I'm a Man" was also a Top 10 hit. Other songs include "Bring It to Jerome" and "Diddley Way Diddley." His music had a big influence on pop musicians, including the Yardbirds, the Rolling Stones, and Jimi Hendrix. He continued to record and release through the 1960s, but had no hit singles. Was a regular on *1950s Rock'n'Roll Revival Show* from 1969. One of the first to be inducted into the Rock and Roll Hall of Fame in Cleveland.

Bodley, Seóirse (b. Dublin, 4 Apr. 1933). Composer. He studied at the Royal Irish Academy, at University College, Dublin, and later in Stuttgart with Johann Nepomuk David; he was made lecturer at University College in 1959. His interest in Gaelic folk song is reflected in his own music, which also manifests serial methods. His relatively small musical output includes orchestral music (*Movement for Orchestra,* 1955–56; *Salve Maria virgo,* 1957; Symphony, 1958–59; *Divertimento,* strings, 1961); choral and vocal music (*Cúl an Tí* [The Back of the House], 1956; *An Bás is an Bheatha* [Life and Death], 1959–60; *Trí Aortha* [3 Satires], 1962; *Never To Have Lived Is Best,* soprano, orchestra, 1965); and instrumental music (*Prelude, Toccata, and Epilogue,* piano, 1964; *Scintillae,* 2 harps, 1968; *The Narrow Road to the Deep North,* 2 pianos, 1972).

Boehm, Theobald (b. Munich, 9 Apr. 1794; d. there, 25 Nov. 1881). Flutist and flute designer. The son of a goldsmith, he followed the same craft, teaching himself the flute as a boy and becoming interested in improvements to the instrument; became a virtuoso and received a musical appointment at court in 1818; established a flute factory in 1828. Instruments heard in London while touring in 1831 led to production of a redesigned instrument in 1832 with a new kind of key mechanism. From 1833 to 1846 he worked in the steel industry, but in 1846–47 he studied acoustics and in 1847 produced a new flute, distinguished by a cylindrical bore and holes of a size and placement determined by acoustical considerations, to which his earlier key mechanism was now adapted. In relation to earlier instruments, the Boehm flute is characterized by the strength, purity, and uniformity of its tone. He wrote *Über den Flötenbau und die neuesten Verbesserungen* (Mainz, 1847; trans. Eng., 1882) and *Die Flöte und das Flötenspiel* (Munich, 1871; trans. Eng., 1922).

Boëllmann, Léon (b. Ensisheim, Alsace, 25 Sept. 1862; d. Paris, 11 Oct. 1897). Composer and organist. Studied at the École Niedermeyer, Paris, 1871–81, including the organ with Gigout; became organist at St. Vincent-de-Paul, Paris; married Gigout's niece in 1885 and began teaching at Gigout's new organ school. Highly regarded as an organist and improviser; also a prolific composer. Best known for organ works, especially the *Suite gothique* op. 25 (1895) and *Fantaisie dialoguée* for organ and orchestra op. 35 (1897?); also composed motets, a symphony, *Variations symphoniques* for cello and orchestra, chamber music, songs, and piano pieces.

Bibl.: Paul Locard, "Souvenirs sur Gigout et Boëllmann," *L'orgue* 9 (1937): 71–74.

Boëly, Alexandre-Pierre-François (b. Versailles, 19 Apr. 1785; d. Paris, 27 Dec. 1858). Composer. He had lessons from his father, who was a musician in the royal service, and from I. A. Ladurner. According to Fétis, he studied at the Paris Conservatory until he was 15, but was thereafter largely self-taught, particularly from the German classics. He became a good pianist, and much of his earlier music was for that instrument, including 2 sonatas op. 1 (1810) and many etudes and other short pieces. He was a proponent of the pedal piano and around 1830 devoted himself primarily to the organ, becoming acting organist at St. Gervais in 1834–38 and organist at St. Germain l'Auxerrois from 1840 to 1851, when he was dismissed because his playing was insufficiently showy. Much admired by Saint-Saëns and Franck, on whose music he is thought to have had considerable influence, he composed much organ music in this period, some of it published posthumously.

Bibl.: Amédée Gastoué, "A Great French Organist, Alexandre Boëly, and His Works," *MQ* 30 (1944): 336–44.

Boësset, Antoine de (b. Blois, 1586; d. Paris, 8 Dec. 1643). Composer. At the court of Louis XIII he served as music master for the royal children (from 1613), as the queen's music teacher (from 1615), and in a number of other administrative positions, including finally that of *surintendant de la musique du roy* (from 1623). Best known as a composer of a large number of *airs de cour,* he also composed at least 9 *ballets de cour* and sacred music including Masses and motets. Some of the *airs* were published in the collection *Airs choisis à 1, 2 et 3 voix* (Paris, 1738).

Boethius, Anicius Manlius Severinus (b. Rome, ca. 480; d. ca. 524). Writer. Acted as an adviser to Emperor Theodoric, first through Cassiodorus, then directly from 510 until 523. Soon thereafter was imprisoned and executed for treason. His writings include treatises on logic and theology, the *Consolation of Philosophy,* and texts on what he named the Quadrivium, the four mathematical disciplines: arithmetic, music, geometry, and astronomy. In his works Boethius not only preserved much of Greek tradition but also presented the results of extensive speculative thinking. Much of the music theory of the later Middle Ages is based on ideas set forth in his *De institutione musica,* including the threefold division of music into *musica mundana, musica humana,* and *musica instrumentalis.* This treatise, of which a portion was lost soon after being written, was little known until the 10th century but then was widely copied and disseminated, even being issued in print in the late 15th and 16th centuries.

Böhm, Georg (b. Hohenkirchen, near Ohrdruf, 2 Sept. 1661; d. Lüneburg, 18 May 1733). Composer and organist. He studied with his father, later at the Gymnasium at Gotha, and from 1684 at the Univ. of Jena. He was in Hamburg in 1693; there he may have had contact with Reincken or Buxtehude. In 1698 he assumed the post of organist at the Johanniskirche in Lüneburg, which he filled until his death. He perhaps had contact with J. S. Bach during Bach's years in Lüneburg (1700–1703); C. P. E. Bach later reported to Forkel that his father had studied Böhm's chorales closely. Among Böhm's works are sacred cantatas and motets (including the motet *Nun danket alle gott*); a lost St. Luke Passion; a St. John Passion previously attributed to Handel; and numerous organ chorales and chorale preludes, including "Herr Jesu Christ, dich zu uns wend," "Christ lag in Todesbanden," and "Vater unser im Himmelreich."

Bibl.: *Sämtliche Werke,* ed. Gesa Wolgast and H. Kümmerling (Wiesbaden, 1952–63). Henning Müller-Buscher, *Georg Böhms Choralbearbeitungen für Tasteninstrumente* (Augsburg, 1979).

Böhm, Karl (b. Graz, 28 Aug. 1894; d. Salzburg, 14 Aug. 1981). Conductor. Studied music theory with Eusebius Mandyczewski in Vienna (1913). While a rehearsal pianist with the Graz Opera he made his debut conducting Viktor Nessler's *Der Trompeter von Säckingen* (Graz, 18 Mar. 1917); in 1920 became that company's chief conductor. On the recommendation of Bruno Walter he went to Munich to conduct in 1921 and remained there after Walter's departure; in 1927 he became music director in Darmstadt. Director of the Dresden Staatsoper (1934–42), where he led several premieres, including 2 Strauss operas. Began a lifelong association with the Salzburg Festival in 1938. In 1942 and again in 1954–56 he was director of the Vienna State Opera. Successful London debut, 2 Nov. 1936. He first conducted at La Scala, 4 Feb. 1948; at New York's Metropolitan Opera, 31 Oct. 1957 (U.S. debut with Chicago Symphony, 9 Feb. 1956). He did not conduct at Bayreuth until 1962 or at Covent Garden until 1977. He excelled at Schubert, Wagner, Bruckner, Strauss, and Berg, but was particularly esteemed for his Mozart.

Boieldieu, (François-) Adrien (b. Rouen, 16 Dec. 1775, d. Jarcy, near Paris, 8 Oct. 1834). Composer. Had his musical training at Rouen, where he was a choirboy at the cathedral, principally from the cathedral organist Charles Broche; became organist at a local church in 1791 and also appeared locally as a piano soloist, playing some of his own compositions. His first opéra comique, *La fille coupable,* to a libretto by his father, was successfully performed at the Théâtre des arts, Rouen, in 1793 and followed by another there, with the same librettist, *Rosalie et Myrza,* in 1795. In 1794–95 he began to publish music in Paris—a piano concerto (composed in 1792), 2 sets of piano sonatas, 8 sets of vocal romances—and moved there himself in 1796. He had immediate success with 3 one-act opéras comiques at the Théâtre Feydeau and Salle Favart in 1797, followed by a series of others that established him as one of the leaders of the genre.

In 1798 he became professor of piano at the Conservatory. Unfortunate in his 1802 marriage to a dancer, he left France in 1803 to become director of the French opera at the Russian court, remaining until 1812 and composing 9 opéras comiques for performance there. He reestablished himself on the French stage with *Jean de Paris* (1812), a great success that was, however, not repeated until *Le petit chaperon rouge* (1818). Professor of composition at the Conservatory from 1817 to 1826, he composed little after this, apart from some relatively insignificant collaborations with other composers, until *La dame blanche* (Opéra-comique, 10 Dec. 1825). This work, to a romantically colored libretto by Scribe, had a tremendous and worldwide success and became one of the perennial favorites of the French opera into the 20th century. His last completed opera, *Les deux nuits* (1829), was not a success, although it contains some of his best music. Failing health prevented sustained work in his later years. He also composed a well-known harp concerto (1801) and some chamber music.

Louis Boieldieu (1815–83), his illegitimate son by an Opéra-comique singer, was a minor composer of opéras comiques and songs.

Bibl.: Arthur Pougin, *Boieldieu* (Paris, 1875). Georges Favre, *Boieldieu, sa vie, son oeuvre* (Paris, 1944–45).

Boismortier, Joseph Bodin de (b. Thionville, 23 Dec. 1689; d. Roissy-en-Brie, 28 Oct. 1755). Composer. Around 1700 he moved from his birthplace to Metz; little is known of his musical studies. During the early 1720s he lived in Perpignan, and soon after that he was in Paris, where he spent much of the rest of his life. His op. 1, 6 sonatas for 2 flutes, appeared there in 1724. During the next 20 years he issued more than 100 publications, including both instrumental and vocal works. In 1744 he was orchestral director of the Foire St. Laurent, and the following year at the Foire St. Germain. He has been cited as having composed the first solo concerto in France (in 1729, the Concerto for Cello or Bassoon op. 26). He is remembered today chiefly for his large and varied instrumental output (nearly 500 instrumental pieces), including sonatas and chamber works for fresh combinations of instruments; the flute is of special importance. He also composed 4 stage works (including *Don Quichotte,* ballet-comique, 1743; *Daphnis et Chloé,* pastorale, 1747); sacred vocal works (the grand motet *Exaudiat te Dominus,* 1730); secular vocal music, including 2 books of *cantates françoises* (bk. 1, *Les 4 saisons: Le printemps, L'été,* etc.).

Boito, Arrigo [Enrico Giuseppe Giovanni] (b. Padua, 24 Feb. 1842; d. Milan, 10 June 1918). Librettist and composer. His father, a painter, and his mother, a Polish countess, separated when he was a child. After music lessons from Antonio Buzzolla in Venice he studied at the Milan Conservatory (1853–61), including composition with Mazzucato. He and his close friend and fellow student Franco Faccio collaborated on the music of two student works, for which Boito wrote the texts, the "cantata patria" *Quattro giugno* (1860), on the published score of which he first took the name Arrigo, and the "mistero" *Le sorelle d'Italia* (1861), which aroused considerable attention. Receiving government grants as a result, they went to Paris, where Boito wrote for Verdi the text of the *Inno delle nazioni* for the opening of the London International Exposition in 1862. He also had his first ideas for operas on Faust and Nero; worked on *Amleto,* a libretto for Faccio; began writing musical journalism and criticism; and traveled in England, Belgium, and Germany, also visiting his mother's family in Poland.

On his return to Milan in Nov. 1862 he became a

figure in the leading salons (where his older brother Camille, an architect and teacher at the Brera, had preceded him) and a leader of an artistic movement called the Scapigliatura, a band of youthful rebels against the artistic status quo, which they attacked with violent polemics. Much of Boito's poetry of this period, collected in *Libro dei versi* (Turin, 1877), is in this vein. His ode "All'arte italiana" (1863) was taken personally by Verdi and was to constitute a major obstacle to their later collaboration. The first version of the opera *Mefistofele,* for which Boito wrote text and music, was finished in 1867 and premiered at La Scala on 5 Mar. 1868, conducted by the composer. The premiere was stormy, the result a fiasco. Boito spent much time revising both text and music, and the second version (Bologna, 1875) was a great success, although further revisions preceded the Venice production in 1876. Boito wrote a considerable number of librettos for composers other than Verdi and himself, of which only *La Gioconda* (1876) for Ponchielli is still performed. Another, *Ero e Leandro,* was intended for himself but abandoned (later set by Luigi Mancinelli). His operatic collaboration with Verdi began with the revision of *Simon Boccanegra* (1881), which led to *Otello* (1887) and *Falstaff* (1893) as Verdi's earlier suspicion gradually changed to close friendship. Boito's second opera, *Nerone,* was left unfinished after he had spent decades revising it with obsessive self-criticism. Edited by Toscanini and Vincenzo Tommasini, it was premiered at La Scala in 1924 under Toscanini but never became more than a curiosity. Primarily a man of letters, he composed very little other music.

Bibl.: *Arrigo Boito: Tutti gli scritti,* ed. Piero Nardi (Milan, 1949). Raffaello de Rensis, ed., *Lettere di Arrigo Boito* (Rome, 1932). Piero Nardi, *Vita di Arrigo Boito,* 2nd ed. (Milan, 1944). Mario Medici and Marcello Conati, eds., *Carteggio Verdi-Boito* (Parma, 1978).

Boivin, François (b. ca. 1693; d. Paris, 25 Nov. 1733). Music seller and publisher. Nephew of bass player and composer Montéclair; brother of string instrument maker Claude Boivin. Bought music shop owned by Henry Foucault and formed partnership with his uncle; started publishing music when Foucault died. His widow continued the business when Boivin died. Associated with Amsterdam publisher Le Cène, and composers Boismortier, Philidor, Mouret, and others. Published mostly French music, but some Italian and German.

Bolcom, William (Elden) (b. Seattle, 26 May 1938). Composer and pianist. From age 11 studied piano and composition; attended the Univ. of Washington (1955–58); studied with Milhaud at Mills (1958–61); with Milhaud and Messiaen in France; and with Leland Smith at Stanford (1961–64). Taught at the Univ. of Washington (1965–66); Queens College (1966–68); beginning 1973 taught composition at the Univ. of Michigan. As a performer he has been particularly interested in ragtime and in American popular song of the late 19th and early 20th centuries, which he has widely performed and recorded with the soprano Joan Morris, whom he married in 1975. As a composer he juxtaposes ragtime and electronic music (*Black Host,* organ, percussion, and tape, 1967); popular song, chromatic tonal melody, and *Sprechstimme* (*Open House,* tenor and small orchestra, 1975); microtones, polyrhythm, and pointillism (Piano Quartet, 1976); jazz, blues, serial methods, and Ivesian collages. Other works include 2 cabaret operas (*Dynamite Tonite,* 1963); the operas *Casino Paradise* (1990) and *McTeague* (1992); *Ragomania* for orchestra (1982); 4 symphonies; concertos for piano (1976), violin (1983), and clarinet (1992); choral works (*Songs of Innocence and Experience,* 46 poems of William Blake, soloists, choruses, and orchestra, 1956–81); cello sonata (1990); *A Whitman Triptych,* soprano, orchestra (1995); works for piano and for organ; songs. He is the author, with Robert Kimball, of *Reminiscing with Sissle and Blake* (1973).

Bolden, Buddy [Charles Joseph] (b. New Orleans, 6 Sept. 1877; d. Jackson, La., 4 Nov. 1931). Jazz cornetist and bandleader. He led bands from at least 1895 and by 1901, when he registered as a professional musician, had a sextet of cornet, clarinet, trombone, guitar, double bass, and drums; it became the Eagle Band after he was committed to the State Insane Asylum at Jackson (1907). According to contemporaries Bolden was the first great jazz musician, admired for his powerful sound, his ability to "rag" (to improvise a paraphrase of) a tune, his propulsive sense of rhythm, and his blues playing.

Bibl.: Donald Marquis, *In Search of Buddy Bolden, First Man of Jazz* (Baton Rouge, 1978).

Bolet, Jorge (b. Havana, 15 Nov. 1914; d. Mountain View, Calif., 16 Oct. 1990). Pianist. He made his debut as a prodigy in 1924 and was soloist with the Havana Symphony in 1925. At the Curtis Institute (1925–36) he studied with David Saperton, Leopold Godowsky, and Maurice Rosenthal; afterwards he worked in Vienna with Emil von Sauer. Winner of the Naumburg and the first Josef Hofmann Awards, he made his U.S. debut with the Philadelphia Orchestra, and his New York debut, 28 Feb. 1937. He was Rudolf Serkin's assistant at the Curtis Institute (1939–42). After service in the Cuban army during World War II, he joined the U.S. Army; while musical director of Tokyo's American Quarter, he led the Japanese premiere of the *Mikado.* In 1968 he joined the faculty of Indiana Univ. Bolet consistently performed Beethoven, Chopin, and Reger; his Liszt was especially distinguished.

Bolling, Claude (b. Cannes, France, 10 Apr. 1930). Pianist and composer. He was a child prodigy; later studied with Duruflé. In 1944 won an amateur jazz contest in Paris. After playing with Roy Eldridge, Lionel Hampton, Paul Gonsalves, and others, formed his own orchestra in 1955. Composed some film music. Best known for his semiclassical works, which include Suite for Flute and Jazz Piano Trio (1975); *Toot Suite* (1981); *California Suite* (flute and jazz piano, 1976); Suite for Cello and Jazz Piano Trio (1984).

Bomtempo, João Domingos (b. Lisbon, 28 Dec. 1775; d. there, 18 Aug. 1842). Composer. Had lessons from his father, an Italian oboist in the Portuguese royal chapel; went in 1801 to Paris, where he established himself as a pianist and composer, publishing 2 piano concertos and a sonata there in 1803–5. He became friendly with Clementi, who published most of his later music. Moved to London in 1810, in 1811 to Lisbon, back to London in 1816, settling finally in Lisbon in 1820, In 1822 founded a Philharmonic Society which gave Lisbon's first public concerts, and in 1835 became director of the new conservatory. Works include 2 symphonies, 6 piano concertos; Requiem and other sacred music; cantatas; *Alessandro in Efeso,* an opera not known to have been performed; chamber music; piano sonatas and other pieces; a piano method (London, 1816).

Bibl.: Jean-Paul Sarrautte, *Catálogo de las obras de João Domingos Bomtempo* (Lisbon, 1970).

Bond, Capel (b. Gloucester, bapt. 14 Dec. 1730; d. Coventry, 14 Feb. 1790). Composer and organist. Son of a bookseller, he probably studied music with Daniel Bond, his uncle. From age 12 he was apprentice to the organist at Gloucester Cathedral. He moved to Coventry in 1749, where he held positions at St. Michael's (beginning 1749), All Angels (1749), and Holy Trinity (1752). He composed concerti grossi, concertos for trumpet and bassoon, and anthems. His publications include *Six Concertos in Seven Parts* (London, 1766) and *Six Anthems in Score* (London, 1769).

Bonini, Severo [Luca?] (b. Florence, 23 Dec. 1582; d. there, 5 Dec. 1663). Composer, organist, and writer on music. He took orders at the Benedictine monastery at Vallombrosa in 1598; there he apparently gained instruction in organ and counterpoint. After study at the Univ. of Passignano he served as organist in a number of the order's abbeys in and around Florence (including Santa Trinità, where he may have studied with Caccini, in 1605 and 1609). He later served at S. Merculiale in Forlì (from 1613); at S. Michele in Forcole, Pistoia (from 1615); at S. Martino in Strada (1623–37); and finally as *maestro di cappella* and organist at Santa Trinità in Florence, from 1640 to his death. He wrote a theoretical treatise, *Discorsi e regole sovra la musica et il contrappunto,* in which he praised the monodic style of Caccini and his contemporaries. He composed vocal works in both the *stile antico* and in the modern style. Published works include *Madrigali e canzonette spirituali* (1607), *Il primo libro delle canzonette affettuose in stile moderno* (lost, 1608), *Lamento d'Arianna in stile recitativo* (1613), and *Affetti spirituali* (1615).

Bibl.: Maryann Bonino, "Don Severo Bonini (1582–1663): His 'Discorsi e regole'" [includes trans. of *Discorsi*] (diss., Univ. of Southern Calif., 1971).

Bonno, Giuseppe (b. Vienna, 29 Jan. 1711; d. there, 15 Apr. 1788). Composer. His father was an imperial footman from Brescia. The boy's initial musical instruction was with the Kapellmeister of St. Stephen's, Johann Georg Reinhardt. From 1726 he studied composition with Durante and Leo in Naples. When he returned to Vienna 10 years later, he worked his way up to a post as court composer, which he assumed in 1739. His early successes in the city were the opera *Trajano* (1736) and an oratorio, *Eleazaro* (1739). In 1749 he became Kapellmeister to Joseph Frederick of Sachsen-Hildburghausen, where Gluck and Dittersdorf also served. Upon the death of Florian Gassmann in 1774 he was appointed imperial Kapellmeister. Bonno was active in Viennese musical life until his retirement in 1788; he was well acquainted with the Mozarts, among others. He composed 30 stage works, 4 oratorios, some 30 Masses, and many other sacred vocal works and arias.

Bibl.: Egon Wellesz, "Giuseppe Bonno (1710–1788): Sein Leben und seine dramatischen Werke," *SIMG* 11 (1909–10): 395–442. Alfred Schienerl, "Die kirchlichen Kompositionen des Giuseppe Bonno" (Univ. of Vienna, 1925); extracts in *SzMw* 15 (1928): 62–85.

Bononcini, Antonio Maria (b. Modena, 18 June 1677; d. there, 8 July 1726). Composer and cellist. Like his brother Giovanni, he studied in Bologna with Giovanni Paolo Colonna. He played in the orchestra of Cardinal Pamphili (1690–93), and in 1698 composed an allegory, *La fama eroica,* for Rome. In 1702 he was in Berlin. Later in Vienna he became Kapellmeister for the court of the emperor's brother Charles; there his first true opera, *Tigrane,* was performed in 1710. Antonio accompanied Giovanni to Italy in 1713, where he spent the rest of his life, mostly in Milan, Naples, and (from 1715) Modena. He became *maestro di cappella* in Modena in 1721. He composed some 24 stage works (*Griselda,* 1718; *Merope,* 1721); 40 cantatas, most for solo voice and continuo; sacred vocal works (a Mass in G minor and a *Salve regina*).

Bononcini, Giovanni (b. Modena, 18 July 1670; d. Vienna, 9 July 1747). Composer and cellist. He studied with his father and (from about 1678) in Bologna with Giovanni Paolo Colonna. He entered the Accademia filarmonica in 1685, and two years later he became *maestro di cappella* at S. Giovanni in Monte. During the next few years he fulfilled commissions in Modena and Bologna and published a number of vocal and instrumental pieces. He served as chamber musician for Filippo Colonna and his family in Rome (1692–97); during this period his successful opera *Il trionfo di Camilla* was performed at Naples (in 1696) and later at many other cities. From 1698 he served Leopold I in Vienna; he also served his successor, Joseph (from 1705). From 1714 to 1719 he was in the service of Johann Wenzel in Rome. His string of London successes began in 1720 with *Astarto,* performed at the Haymarket Theatre; subsequent works for the Royal Academy included *Muzio Scevola* (1721), *Crispo* (1722), *Griselda* (1722), *Erminia* (1723), and *Calfurnia* (1724). In spite of cabals against him (and against Italian opera altogether), his works were received with acclaim in London throughout the 1720s and were often in competition with Handel's works. In 1733 he was in Paris, where he composed works for the Concert spirituel; pensioned in Vienna by Maria Theresa, 1741. He was one of the most prominent international musical figures of his day; his output is extremely large and includes some 62 stage works, nearly 300 cantatas for solo voice, and sacred vocal works, including 4 *Messe brevi* (1688), a *Laudate pueri* (5 voices, orchestra, 1733), a Te Deum (1741), and 3 sacred madrigals; instrumental works, including *Trattenimenti da camera a tre* op. 1 (1685), *Concerti da camera a tre* op. 2 (1685), *Sinfonie* in 2–8 parts, opp. 3–6 (1685–87); *Divertimenti da camera* (1722), and *XII Sonatas for the Chamber* (1732).

Bibl.: Anthony Ford, ed., *Giovanni Bononcini: Arias from the Vienna Operas* (London, 1971). Lowell Lindgren, "A Bibliographic Scrutiny of Dramatic Works Set by Giovanni and His Brother Antonio Maria Bononcini" (diss., Harvard Univ., 1972). Anthony Ford, "Music and Drama in the Operas of Giovanni Bononcini," *PRMA* 101 (1974–75): 107–20.

Bononcini, Giovanni Maria (b. Montecorone, near Modena, bapt. 23 Sept. 1642; d. Modena 18 Nov. 1678). Composer and theorist; father of Giovanni and Antonio Maria. He studied counterpoint and composition with Agostino Bendinelli and possibly also with Marco Uccellini in Modena. From 1671 he was court musician for Duchess Laura d'Este and violinist at the Modena Cathedral. In 1673 he published in Bologna a widely used treatise, *Musico prattico* (facs., 1969). He appears to have been a member (from 1672) of Bologna's Accademia filarmonica. He is best known for his chamber and church sonatas. He also composed cantatas, madrigals, arias, and a "dramma da camera," *I primi voli dell'aquila austriaca* (Modena, 1677; lost).

Bibl.: William Klenz, *Giovanni Maria Bononcini of Modena: A Chapter in Baroque Instrumental Music* (Durham, N.C., 1962).

Bonporti, Francesco Antonio (b. Trent, bapt. 11 June 1672; d. Padua, 19 Dec. 1748). Composer. After early studies in Trent and Innsbruck he studied for the priesthood at the Collegium germanicum at Rome (from 1691). Allegedly he took instruction from Corelli (violin) and Ottavio Pitoni (composition). In 1696 he published his 10 trio sonatas op. 1. He was ordained to the priesthood and appointed cleric to the Trent Cathedral in 1697. The bulk of his output was instrumental music: he published at least 12 sets of trio sonatas, *invenzioni,* violin concertos, and other instrumental chamber music. Repeated attempts to gain a post as court musician (at the Viennese court, for example) failed. As a result of a mistaken attribution, 4 "inventions" for violin and continuo from Bonporti's op. 10 (nos. 2, 5, 6, 7) were included in the Bach-Gesellschaft edition of J. S. Bach's works, vol. 45.

Bibl.: Laurence Feininger, *Francesco Antonio Bonporti: Catalogus thematicus operum omnium* (Trent, 1975).

Bontempi [Angelini], **Giovanni Andrea** (b. Perugia, ca. 1624; d. Brufa, Torgiano, 1 July 1705). Composer and writer on music. As a youth Angelini assumed the name of his patron, Cesare Bontempi. In Perugia his teacher was Sozio Sozi (from 1635); later he studied with Virgilo Mazzocchi in Rome, and in 1643 he became a singer at St. Mark's in Venice. From 1650 he served the Saxon Elector Johann Georg I at Dresden; after 1656 he was Kapellmeister (with Schütz). Gradually he turned to nonmusical pursuits: he was stage designer of the court theater (from 1664) and published books on architecture and Saxon history. He returned to Italy (1666–70), was again in Dresden (1671–80), and in 1680 settled again in Perugia. From 1686 he was *maestro di cappella* at the College of S. Maria at nearby Spello. In 1695 he published the *Historia musica,* for which he is best known today. He also composed 3 stage works (*Il Paride in musica,* 1662; *Dafne,* 1671; *Jupiter und Io,* 1673), cantatas, and an oratorio (*Vita e martirio di S. Emiliano,* music lost).

Bonynge, Richard (Alan) (b. Sydney, 29 Sept. 1930). Conductor and pianist. Studied piano with Lindley Evans at the Sydney Conservatory and with Herbert Fryer in London. Debut as a pianist at Wigmore Hall, 1954. Married to Joan Sutherland that year; their careers have been intertwined ever since. Debut as an opera conductor, Vancouver 1963 (Gounod's *Faust*). Conducted opera at San Francisco (1963), Covent Garden (1964), the Metropolitan Opera (1970). Artistic director of the Vancouver Opera, 1974–78. Musical director of the Australian Opera, 1975–86. Expert in bel canto opera, he also conducted the contemporaneous ballet repertory.

Boone, Charles (b. Cleveland, 21 June 1939). Composer. Studied composition under Karl Schiske at the Academy of Music in Vienna (1960–61); attended the Univ. of Southern California (B.M., 1963) and San Francisco State (M.A., 1968); studied also with Krenek and Adolf Weiss. He lived in Berlin, 1975–77. Chaired the San Francisco Composers' Forum (1964–66); directed the Mills College Tape Music Center and Performing Group (1966–68); founded the Bring Your Own Pillow concert series in San Francisco in the early 1970s. His early pointillistic style evolved into what he called "serial music without the aid of the techniques of serialism." Works include a few orchestral pieces (*First Landscapes,* 1971) and much chamber music for winds and percussion (*Raspberries,* 3 percussionists, 1974; *Morphosis,* percussion quartet, 1989–90); *Silence and Light,* string quartet (1989–90); electronic music combined with live performers (*A Cool Glow of*

Radiation, flute and tape, 1966); some pieces have untexted vocal parts.

Boone, Pat [Charles Eugene] (b. Jacksonville, Fla., 1 June 1934). Singer and actor. He became popular for performing country, rock-and-roll (especially cover versions of songs by black artists), and Tin Pan Alley songs in a diluted version of emerging rock-and-roll styles; successful recordings included "Ain't That a Shame" (1955, by Fats Domino), "Long Tall Sally" (1956, by Little Richard), and "Love Letters in the Sand" (1957). His public image was as the overwhelmingly clean-cut alternative to Elvis Presley and others. Beginning in 1957 he acted in 15 movies.

Boosey, Thomas (fl. London, early 19th century). Music publisher. The son of Thomas Boosey, who had opened a bookshop in London by around 1795. Around 1814 or a little after his father started a separate firm publishing and importing music, of which he put his son in charge. It handled music of composers such as Hummel, Mercadante, and Rossini and later published vocal scores of popular operas. From about 1850 it also made wind instruments and in 1868 bought a brass instrument firm. In the later 19th century its publishing was oriented toward popular ballads, and in 1867 John Boosey, son of Thomas Jr., established the London Ballad Concerts. In 1930 the firm merged with Hawkes and Son to become Boosey and Hawkes.

Borden, David (Russell) (b. Boston, 25 Dec. 1938). Composer and keyboard player. Studied with Mennini, Rogers, and Hanson at Eastman (B.M., 1961; M.M., 1962); with Layton, Kirchner, and Thompson at Harvard (M.A., 1965); at the Berkshire Music Center with Fortner (1961) and Schuller (1966); in Berlin with Blacher (1965–66); jazz with Jimmy Giuffre and Jaki Byard and the synthesizer with Robert Moog. He was Ford Foundation composer-in-residence in the Ithaca, N.Y., public schools, then joined the dance department of Cornell Univ. as composer and pianist; joined the Department of Music there in 1987. Has performed with his Mother Mallard's Portable Masterpiece Co. (synthesizers, electronic keyboards, and voices) since 1969. His numerous works for this ensemble often make use of slowly developing, repetitive elements (*The Continuing Story of Counterpoint,* 12 parts, 1976–87). He has also composed works for orchestra and wind ensemble, some with tape, and chamber music for traditional instruments.

Bordoni [Hasse], **Faustina** (b. Venice, ca. 1700; d. there, 4 Nov. 1781). Mezzo-soprano. She was raised in Venice under the protection of the brothers Alessandro and Benedetto Marcello and under the musical tutelage of Michelangelo Gasparini. From 1716 (the year of her debut in Pollarolo's *Ariodante*) to 1723 she sang throughout Italy; her renown spread abroad, and she sang in Munich (1723), Vienna (1725–26), and London (from 1726). In London she created several Handel roles (Alcestis in *Admeto,* 1727; Emira in *Siroe,* 1728). The rivalry between her and soprano Francesca Cuzzoni culminated in 1727 when the two traded blows on stage. Returning to Italy, she married composer Johann Adolf Hasse in Venice in 1730. In 1731 both were engaged at the Saxon court at Dresden; her debut there was in her husband's *Cleofide.* During the next two decades she sang in most of Hasse's operas and appeared frequently in Venice, Naples, and Paris. By 1751 she had retired from the stage. She then lived with Hasse in Vienna (1763–73) and Venice (1773–81). She was one of the great artists of her age and was highly praised for both her singing and her acting.

Boretz, Benjamin (Aaron) (b. New York, 3 Oct. 1934). Composer and theorist. Educated at Brooklyn College (B.A., music and philosophy, 1954); Brandeis (M.F.A., composition, 1957) under Berger and Fine; and Princeton (Ph.D., 1973) under Sessions and Babbitt. During the 1960s he was a music critic for *The Nation;* in 1962 he and Berger founded the journal *Perspectives of New Music,* which he coedited until 1982. Taught at Bard College beginning 1973. His *Group Variations* (version 1 for chamber orchestra, 1964–67; version 2 for computer, 1969–73) exhibits complex formal congruences such that "wholes constantly retrieve and reincarnate the shapes of their component parts"; it was the starting point for his essay "Meta-Variations: Studies in the Foundations of Musical Thought," *PNM* 1969, which explores the possibilities of discourse about music. Other works include a concerto grosso for strings (1954), a violin concerto (1956); pieces for chamber ensemble, piano, guitar, and solo voice, including *Language, as a Music: Six Marginal Pretexts for Composition* (speaker, piano, tape, 1978).

Bořkovec, Pavel (b. Prague, 10 June 1894; d. there, 22 July 1972). Composer. Before World War I he began study of philosophy at Charles Univ.; after the war he studied composition with Joseph Foerster and Jaroslav Křička; later with Joseph Suk at the Prague Conservatory (1925–27). His music from the 1930s shows the influence of Hindemith and Stravinsky. After the Second World War he became professor at the Prague Academy of Music (1946), where he remained until his retirement in 1963. He composed operas (*Satyr,* 1937–38; *Paleček,* 1945–47); orchestral works (3 symphonies; *Stmívání* [Twilight], 1920; *Start,* 1929; *Partita,* 1936; 2 piano concertos; 2 *Symphoniettas,* 1947, 1967); vocal works (*Lidová říkadla,* chorus, 1936; *6 madrigaly o času* [6 Madrigals on Time], chorus, 1957); chamber music (5 string quartets, 1924–61; 2 violin sonatas, 1934, 1956; nonet, 1941–42); *5 Songs* on texts by Pasternak (1935).

Borodin, Alexander Porfir'yevich (b. St. Petersburg, 12 Nov. 1833; d. there, 27 Feb. 1887). Composer. The illegitimate son of the Georgian Prince Luka Stepanovich Gedianov, he was registered as the lawful son of one of Gedianov's serfs, Porfiry Borodin. His mother, who later married an army doctor, gave him an excellent education that included a number of foreign languages and lessons on the flute and piano; he also played through four-hand arrangements of Haydn and Beethoven symphonies with his boyhood friend Mikhail Shchiglev.

In 1850 he entered the Academy of Medicine in St. Petersburg and developed an interest in chemistry; he graduated with honors in 1856 and was appointed an assistant in general pathology and therapy, receiving his doctorate in chemistry two years later. He continued his scientific studies in Europe (1859–62), primarily in Germany (where he met the Russian woman who would become his wife and musical companion, the pianist Ekaterina Sergeyevna Protopopova), and in Pisa, Italy, where he was invited to work by a pair of Italian chemists. A few chamber works date from this time, including the String Sextet in D minor (1860–61, third and fourth movements lost), the Piano Quintet in C minor (1862), and the Cello Sonata in C minor (1860).

In 1862 he returned to St. Petersburg and continued his teaching at the Academy of Medicine in addition to lecturing in chemistry at the Institute of Forestry. He met Balakirev, and under his guidance started working on his Symphony no. 1 in E♭, completed in 1867; he also composed some songs and the opera-farce *Bogatïri* (1867), which was a failure at its first performance. In 1869 he began two new compositions, the Symphony no. 2 and the opera *Prince Igor,* but large-scale works often took him years to complete, and at any rate his lecturing and administrative duties took up considerable time (the symphony was completed in 1876; the opera, which contains the well-known Polovtsian dances, was completed posthumously by Rimsky-Korsakov and Glazunov and was first performed in 1890). An earlier opera project, *The Tsar's Bride,* was abandoned; the String Quartet no. 1 in A, begun in 1874, remained unfinished for five years.

In 1877, during a business trip to Germany, he visited Liszt in Weimar; the well-known musical portrait *V sredney Azii* [In the Steppes of Central Asia] (1880) is dedicated to the Hungarian composer, who championed Borodin's music. (Borodin later wrote about his meetings with Liszt in an essay titled "Liszt in His Weimar Home.") The String Quartet no. 2 in D was completed in 1881; the lyrical third movement (Nocturne) is well known in the West and has been arranged by many composers. His works were performed with increasing frequency in Europe, owing in part to the patronage of the Belgian Countess of Mercy-Argenteau; Borodin was made a member of the French Société des auteurs, compositeurs et editeurs, and heard his works performed in Brussels, Antwerp, Liège, and Paris. A Third Symphony in A minor was begun in 1886 but remained incomplete at his death; the following year, his last, saw the composition of a few more numbers on *Prince Igor.*

One of the "Mighty Five," Borodin is known for only a handful of works: the 2 lyrical string quartets, the colorful Russian orientalism of *In the Steppes of Central Asia,* the 3 symphonies (no. 3 was completed by Glazunov), and above all the rich exoticism of *Prince Igor.*

Bibl.: Marek Bobeth, *Borodin und seine Oper "Fürst Igor": Geschichte, Analyse, Konsequenzen* (Munich, 1982). Gerald Abraham, *Borodin, the Composer and His Music: A Descriptive and Critical Analysis* (New York, 1976). Boris Assafjew et al., *Alexander Borodin: Sein Leben, seine Musik, seine Schriften* (Berlin, 1992).

Borowski, Felix (b. Burton, Westmorland, 10 Mar. 1872; d. Chicago, 6 Sept. 1956). Composer and critic. He studied music in London and Cologne; from 1897 he taught violin and composition at the Chicago Musical College and was its president from 1916 until 1925. From 1937 to 1942 he was professor of musicology at Northwestern Univ. He was on the staff of the Newberry Library until 1956 and was instrumental in bolstering its music collections. He composed ballets (*A Century of the Dance,* 1934); an opera, *Fernando del Nonsensico* (1935); orchestral works (3 symphonies; *Allegro de concert,* 1915; *Le printemps passioné,* 1920; *Semiramis,* 1924); 3 string quartets; keyboard music.

Bortniansky, Dmitry Stepanovich (b. Glukhov, Ukraine, 1751; d. St. Petersburg, 10 Oct. 1825). Composer. From 1759 was a choirboy at the court chapel in St. Petersburg, studying composition with Baldassare Galuppi. From 1769 to 1779 continued his studies in Italy where his operas *Creonte* (Venice, 1776), *Alcide* (Venice, 1778), and *Quinto Fabio* (Modena, 1778) were produced. On his return to St. Petersburg he was appointed Kapellmeister; from 1796, director of vocal music at the court chapel. For his choir he composed more than 50 sacred concerti in 4 parts (some lost), 12 sacred concerti for double choir, and much other choral music, to which he brought a sophisticated command of harmonic and polyphonic development and musical form. Continued also to write secular music, including keyboard sonatas, chamber music, and some patriotic choral music. Wrote operas on French texts for performance at court: *La fête du seigneur* (1786), *Le faucon* (1786), *Le fils-rival* (1787).

Bibl.: M. Rytsareva, *Kompozitor D. Bortnianskii: zhizn' i tvorchestvo* (Leningrad, 1979).

Boschi, Giuseppe Maria (fl. 1698–1744). Bass singer. In Venice he sang operas by Lotti and Francesco Gasparini (ca. 1707). His London debut was in Mancini's *Idaspe fedele* (1710–11); there he also created the role of Argante in Handel's *Rinaldo* (1711); during the next 17 years he sang in many operas by Handel, Bononcini, and Ariosti. He sang in Dresden (1717–20) and in Venice (1728–29), where he was a member of the choir at St. Mark's until at least 1744. His voice was known for its agility in rapid passages.

Bösendorfer, Ignaz (b. Vienna, 27 July 1794; d. there, 14 Apr. 1859). Piano manufacturer. Son of a joiner, he learned piano making under Josef Brodmann, whose business he acquired in 1828, quickly becoming successful and winning prizes and recognition from the court and musicians such as Liszt. After his death his son Ludwig (1835–1919) ran the business until he sold it in 1909, having in 1860 opened the new factory begun under his father. In 1966 the firm was purchased by Kimball.

Boskovich, Alexander Uriah (b. Kolozvár, Hungary [Cluj, Romania], 16 Aug. 1907; d. Tel Aviv, 5 Nov. 1964). Composer. He studied at the Budapest Academy and later in Vienna (1924) and in Paris with Dukas and Boulanger (1925). Afterward he conducted the State Opera in Cluj. He emigrated to Palestine in 1938 and began teaching at the Tel Aviv Academy of Music; from 1955 he was also music critic for the newspaper *Ha'aretz.* His interest in folk music is reflected in his own music, which often integrates a diatonic art-music idiom with Eastern Mediterranean elements. He composed orchestral works (*The Golden Chain,* 1937; *Semitic Suite,* 1946–47, rev. 1959; *Adayim* [Ornaments], flute, orchestra, 1964); vocal music (*Adonai ro'i* [The Lord Is My Shepherd], 1946; *Daughter of Israel,* 1960; *Ha'or haganuz* [The Hidden Light], oratorio, 1964); chamber music (*Psalm,* violin and piano, 1942, rev. 1957; *Kina* [Lament], cello or violin and piano, 1962; *Concerto da camera,* violin, 10 instruments, 1962); piano works.

Bossi, Marco Enrico (b. Salò, Lake Garda, 25 Apr. 1861; d. aboard ship on the Atlantic Ocean, 20 Feb. 1925). Composer, organist, and pianist. He studied organ at first with his father, then in Bologna and Milan with Ponchielli. In 1881 he was appointed organist at the Como Cathedral; from 1890 he taught harmony and organ at the conservatory in Naples; he directed the conservatories in Venice (1895–1902), Bologna (1902–11), and Rome (1916–23). He was an active participant in the revival of nonoperatic composition at the turn of the century in Italy; his own style drew on the late German Romantic tradition; except for an interest in chromaticism similar to that in Reger's organ works, his style remained relatively independent of the more innovative 20th-century trends. Works include 5 operas; an organ concerto (op. 100, 1895), *Intermezzi goldoniani* (op. 127, 1905), and other orchestral works; chamber music; many organ and other keyboard works; several large choral compositions (*Il paradiso perduto,* solo voices, chorus, organ, and orchestra, op. 125, 1902); sacred and secular choral music; songs.

Bossinensis, Franciscus (b. Bosnia?; fl. 1510). Composer. Arranged over 100 frottolas for voice and lute and wrote between 40 and 50 related ricercars for lute solo (ed. Benvenuto Disertori, 1954, 1964). Petrucci printed these works in 2 books dated 1509 and 1511. Most of the frottolas had appeared in earlier prints in 4-part vocal versions. With few exceptions his arrangements follow the original lower 2 parts strictly, and the voice reproduces the top part; the *altus* is omitted.

Bostic, Earl (b. Tulsa, 25 Apr. 1913; d. Rochester, 28 Oct. 1965). Jazz and rhythm-and-blues alto saxophonist and bandleader. After studying music at Xavier Univ. in New Orleans (1933–34), he played on riverboats in the band of Charlie Creath and Fate Marable (1935–36). In New York he played in big bands with Don Redman (1938) and Lionel Hampton (1943–44), led his own bands (1939–42?), and worked with Hot Lips Page (1941, 1943). From 1944 he led groups, achieving considerable popularity with his recording of "Flamingo" (1951). His sidemen included John Coltrane and Stanley Turrentine.

Bottegari, Cosimo (b. Florence, 1554; d. 1620). Composer and performer. From 1570 to 1575 was in the chapel of the Duke of Bavaria, which Lassus directed. Wrote 2 madrigals for a collection published in 1575. Compiled a manuscript collection, dated 1574, of over 100 works for voice and lute, including 8 of his own and one by Caccini (ed. in *WE* 8, 1965). By 1580 he had joined the Medici court at Florence as a singer and lutenist.

Bottesini, Giovanni (b. Crema, 22 Dec. 1821; d. Parma, 7 July 1889). Double bass player, conductor, and composer. Son of a musician, he studied the double bass at the Milan Conservatory, 1835–39; then played in orchestras, eventually becoming a concert soloist and conductor, mostly of opera, throughout Europe and America; chosen by his friend Verdi to conduct the premiere of *Aida* at Cairo in 1871. On Verdi's recommendation he was made director of the Parma Conservatory in 1889. Though not the first double bass soloist (Dragonetti being known as "the Paganini of the double bass" before Bottesini was), he extended its technique and composed several concertos and other solo works for it in addition to studies and a method. Other works include operas, a Requiem and other sacred music, and chamber music.

Bibl.: Cesare Lisei, "Giovanni Bottesini," *Gazzetta musicale di Milano* 41 (1886): 122, 140; also issued separately (Milan, 1886).

Bottrigari [Bottrigaro], **Ercole** (b. Bologna, bapt. 24 Aug. 1531; d. S. Alberto, near Bologna, 30 Sept. 1612). Theorist. During time spent in Ferrara at the court of Alfonso II (1576–86) became interested in music history and theory. Composed a few madrigals; translated many classical writings, including *De musica* by Boethius; and wrote some poetry and several books, 3 on music. Of the books on music, the most important is *Il desiderio overo de' concerti di varij strumenti musicali* (printed in 1594, 1599, and 1601; only the second printing names Bottrigari as the author; facs., Berlin, 1924; ed. and trans. Carol MacClintock, 1962). This book describes the musical life of Alfonso's court in Ferrara and discusses acoustics in reference to problems in tuning instruments.

Boucourechliev, André (b. Sofia, Bulgaria, 28 July 1925). Composer, critic, and musicologist. After studying piano at the Sofia Conservatory (1946–47) he won a national competition; studied at the École normale de musique in Paris (1949–51) and then taught piano there for eight years. He began composing in 1954, attended the Darmstadt summer courses, and worked with Berio and Maderna at the Milan Radio electronic music studio. His compositions explore not only electronic music but also indeterminacy: in *Texte 2* (1960) the second of two tapes may be started at any of several points; *Archipels* (1967–72) incorporates further aspects of indeterminacy that require performers to communicate their decisions verbally; in the last of the series individual parts may be played as solos. He also composed several works for orchestra (*Amers,* 1973). He spent 1963–64 in the U.S. studying the music of the avant-garde. Wrote books on Schumann, Chopin, Beethoven, and Stravinsky as well as articles on Stravinsky, Debussy, Messiaen, and serialism.

Boughton, Rutland (b. Aylesbury, 23 Jan. 1878; d. London, 25 Jan. 1960). Composer. He studied with Charles Stanford and Walford Davies at the Royal College of Music (1898–1901) and taught at the Midland Institute in Birmingham (1905–11). Under the influence of Wagner's ideals he and Reginald Buckley authored *Music Drama of the Future* (1911). Three years after its publication he presented the first Glastonbury Festival; its aim was to provide a forum for his own Wagnerian "choral dramas." He had already completed *The Birth of Arthur* (1909), which became the first of his 5-opera "Arthurian cycle." The festivals proved a success, and *The Immortal Hour,* which opened the 1914 festival, later achieved more than 200 consecutive performances in Birmingham. Around 1930 he retired to Gloucestershire, where he completed the Arthur cycle (in 1945) and mounted festivals at Stroud and Bath. Remaining Arthurian operas were *The Round Table* (1915–16), *The Lily Maid* (1933–34), *Galahad* (1943–44), and *Avalon* (1944–45); other operas include *The Moon Maiden* (1918), *Alkestis* (1920–22), and *The Ever Young* (1928–29). He also composed orchestral, choral, and chamber works.

Boulanger, Lili (b. Paris, 21 Aug. 1893; d. Mézy, 15 Mar. 1918). Composer. Her study of music was at first guided by her sister Nadia, then by Caussade and Vidal at the Paris Conservatory (1912). In 1913 she won the Prix de Rome; despite continuing health problems she wrote prolifically in a style reflecting the mainstream of French music in its subtle chromaticism and contrapuntal character. Works include an opera (left incomplete at her death); the *Poème symphonique* for orchestra (1917) and several works for small orchestra; Nocturne for violin and piano (1911), the Sonata for violin and piano (1916), and other chamber and piano music; *Pour les funérailles d'un soldat,* baritone, chorus, orchestra (1912), large Psalm settings and other works for soloists, chorus, and orchestra; cantatas and songs.

Nadia Boulanger, 1935.

Boulanger, Nadia (b. Paris, 16 Sept. 1887; d. there, 22 Oct. 1979). Teacher, conductor, and composer. She studied organ (Vierne, Guilmant) and composition (Fauré, Widor) and won the second Prix de Rome for her cantata *La sirène,* but she stopped composing before World War I. As a conductor she led performances of and recorded much early music (especially Monteverdi) between the wars; she conducted symphony orchestras in London and in Washington, D.C. (in a notable premiere of Stravinsky's Dumbarton Oaks Concerto). But in the main she is remembered as a teacher. She taught harmony at the École normale in Paris (1920–39) and accompanying at the Paris Conservatory (from 1946); she was associated with the American Conservatory at Fontainebleau from 1921, becoming its director in 1950. Her American students included Copland, Carter, Diamond, Fine, Harris, Piston, Thomson, and many others. During the Second World War she taught at Wellesley, Juilliard, and Radcliffe. Her teaching method consisted of careful analysis of music from various periods combined with a strong emphasis on the writing of counterpoint exercises. Her students often shared and reflected in their own compositions her admiration for Fauré and Stravinsky. She received numerous honors during a very long career.

Bibl.: Léonie Rosenstiel, *Nadia Boulanger: A Life in Music* (New York, 1982).

Boulez, Pierre (b. Montbrison, 26 Mar. 1925). Composer, conductor, and writer on music. As a child he sang in a choir and played the piano; he considered a career in engineering, but instead he entered the Paris Conservatory in 1942. He studied harmony under Messiaen and worked privately at counterpoint with Andrée Vaurabourg-Honegger; later he studied twelve-tone composition under Leibowitz, a disciple of Schoenberg. By the early 1950s Boulez was at the center of the avant-garde, in close touch with Cage, Pousseur, and Stockhausen. He had announced in his famous "Schönberg est mort" (1952) that Webern was the most fertile source of the new approach, one that would serialize other aspects of sound in addition to pitch.

His earliest published compositions already reflected his interest in serialism; its most rigorous early application is in *Polyphonie X* (18 soloists, 1951), premiered at the Donaueschingen Festival. Although the audience hissed and booed during the performance, Strobel (the festival's organizer) commented that "those who knew anything at all knew that this was a very special work, one that in both structure and color opened completely new paths." The electronic pieces *Étude sur un son* and *Étude sur sept sons* (1952, created at Schaeffer's studio for *musique concrète*) represented one route to the precision Boulez demanded; but he did not abandon live performers. *Structures I* (1952), in which pitch, duration, dynamics, and modes of attack are subjected to serial control, was introduced by the composer and Messiaen in Paris. In *Le marteau sans maître* (1952–54) Boulez was in control of a sufficiently well-developed method to write what has become a classic of serialism. The work is scored for contralto, alto flute, viola, guitar, vibraphone, xylophone, and percussion, each of the 9 sections (5 instrumental, 4 setting Char's poetry) calling for different forces. About the form, in which the 3 poems give rise to sets of nonadjacent movements, he remarked: "I was making an effort . . . to create a dimension different from the closed musical form." The exotic instrumentation, whose timbres recall African, Balinese, and Japanese instruments, has been widely imitated.

Boulez has also explored indeterminacy. In his Third Piano Sonata (1955–57) both the order of movements and the routes within movements are open to limited performer choice. In his essay "Alea" Boulez advocated a "controlled chance" that John Cage and David Tudor saw as too limiting. Messiaen claimed that "he never had his heart in aleatory work," but Boulez's interest in combining improvisatory and fixed elements continued in *Pli selon pli* (1957–62), a 5-part portrait of Mallarmé. In *Éclat* (15 instruments, 1965; orchestral version, *Éclat/Multiples,* 1970) the conductor takes over the role of composer.

In other works Boulez combined taped and live sounds and explored the spatial distribution of performers or loudspeakers; in *. . . explosante-fixe . . .* (1971) the forces are not specified, and the form is chosen from a range of possibilities by the performers involved. Although there is no freedom of duration or pitch, there is no regular beat, and "the point is to be irregular . . . to be free." In general, his mature works combine the precision associated with his devotion to an extremely sophisticated serialism with a measure of performer freedom and variable form, often inspired by the text, under the control of composer or conductor.

Boulez's career as a conductor began in 1946 when he became musical director for the Compagnie Renaud–Barrault at the Théâtre Marigny (he stayed with them until 1956). In 1954 he founded the Domaine musical series of concerts in Paris, in which he led many performances of contemporary music. He conducted the Cologne orchestra in several premieres of his own works; in 1963 he led the first French performance of *Wozzeck* at the Opéra; and in 1966 conducted *Parsifal* at Bayreuth. He was guest conductor of the Cleveland Orchestra in 1967, and in 1971 became principal conductor of the BBC Symphony Orchestra and the New York Philharmonic, where he succeeded Bernstein. Although his early conducting activity was confined to contemporary music, he conducted more and more of the standard repertory as his career expanded. He made numerous recordings of his own works, and those of Stravinsky and Bartók. In 1977 he returned to Paris to assume the direction of the Institut de recherche et de coordination acoustique/musique (IRCAM), retiring in 1992. He was appointed principal guest conductor of the Chicago Symphony in 1995.

Other major works include *Le visage nuptial,* vocal soloists and chamber orchestra (1946; rev. for soloists and orchestra, 1950–51); *Livre pour quatuor,* string quartet (1948–49; rev. for orchestra as *Livre pour cordes,* 1968–); 3 piano sonatas (no. 1, 1946; no. 2, 1948, withdrawn; no. 3, 1955–57); *Poésie pour pouvoir,* tape and orchestra (1958); *Structures II,* 2 pianos (1956–61); *Domaines,* clarinet and ensemble (1968); *e. e. cummings ist der Dichter,* 16 voices and 24 instruments (1970–); *Mémoriales,* orchestra (1973–75).

Writings: *Musikdenken heute* [from his Darmstadt lectures, 1963]; trans. as *Boulez on Music Today* (Cambridge, Mass., 1971). *Relevés d'apprenti* (Paris, 1966); trans. as *Notes of an Apprenticeship* (New York, 1968). *Orientations: Collected Writings,* ed. Jean-Jacques Nattiez (Cambridge, Mass., 1986).

Bibl.: M. Fink, "Pierre Boulez: A Selective Bibliography," *CM* 13 (1972): 135. *Par volonté et par hasard: entretiens avec Célestin Deliège* (Paris, 1975); trans. as *Conversations with Célestin Deliège* (London, 1976). Paul Griffiths, *Boulez* (London, 1978). Peter F. Stacey, *Boulez and the Modern Concept* (Aldershot, 1987). Dominique Jameux, *Pierre Boulez* (Cambridge, Mass., 1990). Jean-Jacques Nattiez, ed., *Pierre Boulez and John Cage: Correspondence* (Paris, 1991).

Boult, Adrian (Cedric) (b. Chester, 8 Apr. 1889; d. Tunbridge Wells, 22 Feb. 1983). Conductor. After classes at Westminster School, entered Christ Church, Oxford, in 1908, studying with Hugh Allen. In Leipzig, 1912–13, studied theory with Reger and observed Nikisch's rehearsals. Graduated from Oxford with a doctorate in music, 1914. Conducting debut with an amateur orchestra at West Kirby, 1914. Joined Beecham's staff at Covent Garden the same year. Professional debut as conductor with the Liverpool Philharmonic, 1915. Led London productions by Diaghilev's Ballets russes, 1918–19. Guest conductor with Beecham's Royal Philharmonic, 1919. Conducted the British Symphony and an occasional ensemble, 1919–24, before obtaining his first major post as conductor of the City of Birmingham Orchestra, 1924–30. Assistant music director of Covent Garden, 1926. Created and led the BBC Symphony Orchestra from its first concert in 1930 until his mandatory retirement in 1950. Vienna debut, 1933; U.S. debut with the Boston Symphony, 1935. Guest conductor, New York Philharmonic, 1938–39. Led the London Proms Concerts, 1942–50; the London Philharmonic, 1950–57; the City of Birmingham Orchestra, 1959–60. Toured the USSR in 1956. Taught conducting at London's Royal College of Music, 1919–30, and again 1962–66. Published *The Point of the Stick* (1920; rev. 1968), *Thoughts on Conducting* (1962), and *Boult on Music* (1983). A committed champion of British composers, in 1919 he gave private premieres of Holst's *Planets* and Vaughan Williams's newly revised London Symphony. Thereafter led premieres of major works by Vaughan Williams, Bliss, Howells, and others. Introduced Schoenberg's Variations op. 31 and Berg's *Wozzeck* to English audiences. Knighted in 1937.

Bourgault-Ducoudray, Louis-Albert (b. Nantes, 2 Feb. 1840; d. Vernouillet, Yvelines, 4 July 1910). Composer. Studied law, but after he had an opéra comique performed at Nantes in 1858, he entered the Paris Conservatory, winning the Prix de Rome in 1863; from 1878 taught music history at the Conservatory. He had for his time unusually broad musical interests: in old music (founding an amateur chorus to sing it), in folk music (which he collected and published, including that of Greece, where he worked in 1874, Brittany, and other Celtic regions), and in Russian nationalist composers. He composed prolifically until about 1890, including several operas (especially *Thamara,* Paris Opéra, 1891), choral music, songs, chamber music, and piano pieces, many of them using exotic or folk material.

Bourgeois, Loys [Louis] (b. Paris, ca. 1510–15; d. in or after 1560). Composer and theorist. Between 1545 and 1552 he was active in Calvinist Geneva as a singer and a teacher of choristers. Contributed to the Huguenot Psalter, a collection of unaccompanied tunes, perhaps both by composing new melodies and by adapting existing ones to Clément Marot's French translations of Psalms. Moved to Lyons in 1552, then to Paris by 1560. Of his numerous polyphonic settings of Psalms (the first book published in 1547), most incorporate the Genevan melodies, usually in strict homophony. Some are freer, and a few make no use of these melodies at all. His didactic treatise *Le droict chemin de musique* (Geneva, 1550; facs., *DM* ser. 1, 6 [1954]) deals in a practical and simplified manner with issues involved in singing and sight reading, including solmization.

Bibl.: Pierre Pidoux, *Le Psautier Huguenot du XVIe siècle* (Basel, 1962).

Bourland, Roger (b. Evanston, Ill., 13 Dec. 1952). Composer. He studied with Les Thimmig at the Univ. of Wisconsin (B.M., 1976) and with William Thomas McKinley and Donald Martino at the New England Conservatory (M.M., 1978). Studied with Gunther Schuller at Tanglewood (1978) and John Harbison at M.I.T. (1978–79). Received an M.A. and Ph.D. (1983) from Harvard, where he studied with Earl Kim and Leon Kirchner, and subsequently joined the faculty of UCLA. Works include *Three Magical Places,* solo harp (1979); *Seven Pollock Paintings,* flute, clarinet, soprano sax, bass clarinet, string quartet, and tam-tam (ca. 1980); *Morning Sonata,* organ (ca. 1986); *Three Dark Paintings,* soprano sax, violin, piano (ca. 1989); *Stone Quartet,* soprano sax, viola, cello, piano (1989); and 2 books of *Dickinson Madrigals* (ca. 1987, 1989).

Bouzignac, Guillaume (b. Narbonne, before 1592; d. after 1641). Composer. His early musical training was apparently as a choirboy at the cathedral at Narbonne; he became choirmaster of the Grenoble Cathedral in 1609. For the next two decades he worked as a choirmaster (possibly for the Duke of Montmorency or for the Carcassonne Cathedral), composed a number of works for special persons and occasions (including the motet *Cantate Domino* for Louis XIII), and served in Angoulême at the home of Gabriel de la Charlonye. Later he perhaps held a post at the cathedral at Tours. He composed sacred vocal works (3 Masses; Te Deum; 4 Psalm settings; *Dum silentium;* numerous motets, which survive anonymously but are thought to be by him) and a very few secular vocal works.

Bovicelli, Giovanni Battista (b. Assisi; fl. 1592–94). Theorist. Wrote a manual on vocal ornamentation titled *Regole, passaggi di musica, madrigali et motetti passeggiati* (Venice, 1594; facs., *DM* ser. 1, 12 [1957]). The treatise covers methods of ornamenting various melodic units and also such matters as text underlay, articulation, and techniques of virtuoso singing. Elaborate embellishments are applied to works by Palestrina, Rore, Victoria, and Claudio Correggio.

Bowie [Jones], **David** (b. London, 8 Jan. 1947). Rock singer, songwriter, and actor. From 1972 he released many successful albums (including *The Rise and Fall of Ziggy Stardust and the Spiders from Mars,* 1972; *Young Americans,* 1975, including "Fame"; *Let's Dance,* 1983; *Black Tie White Noise,* 1993), each of which embodied an abrupt stylistic shift between various genres of pop music, including psychedelia, punk, soul, and disco. His tours have included light shows and dramatic staging of songs; he has acted in films (*The Man Who Fell to Earth,* 1976; *Merry Christmas, Mr. Lawrence,* 1983) and on the stage (*The Elephant Man,* 1980).

Bowie, Lester (b. Frederick, Md., 11 Oct. 1941). Jazz trumpeter. He played rhythm-and-blues in St. Louis and Chicago, where he joined the Association for the Advancement of Creative Musicians in 1966. Work with its members led to the formation of the Art Ensemble of Chicago in 1969. He has also led other bands; played in Jack DeJohnette's quartet Directions (ca. 1978–79); and beginning 1986 was a member of the sextet The Leaders. Bowie often manipulates pitch and timbre for humorous effect, as on the title track of his album *The Great Pretender* (1981).

Bowles, Paul (Frederic) (b. Jamaica, N.Y., 30 Dec. 1910). Composer and writer. In the 1930s he studied with Copland, Boulanger, Thomson, and Sessions; and his works were often performed in New York (among them *Scenes d'Anabase,* tenor, oboe, and piano, 1935). He wrote ballets and incidental music for more than 20 plays of Williams (*The Glass Menagerie,* 1945), Welles, Hellman, Saroyan; in 1943 Bernstein conducted his opera *The Wind Remains* in New York. His music reflects his interests in Moroccan folk song (which he recorded and studied beginning in 1959), Mexican music, and jazz. He was music critic for the *New York Herald Tribune* (1942–45); his first novel was published in 1949; his autobiography, *Without Stopping,* appeared in 1972. Other works include ballets; 3 operas; film scores; a few orchestral works, including a concerto for 2 pianos, winds, percussion, and orchestra (1938); chamber music; piano music (Preludes, 1934–45); cantatas; and songs.

Bowman, James (Thomas) (b. Oxford, 6 Nov. 1941). Countertenor. As a boy, sang in the choir at Ely Cathedral. While reading history at New College, Oxford, he developed his voice under F. E. de Rentz and Lucie Manen. An audition with Britten led to his debut with the English Opera Group as Oberon. For him Britten later composed *Canticle IV* and the part of Apollo in *Death in Venice.* His career has naturally centered on the wealth of Baroque operas for which his voice is suited, including works by Monteverdi, Cavalli, Vivaldi, Rameau, and especially Handel; he has also sung early music. Covent Garden debut, 1967; in the U.S. he has sung with opera companies in San Francisco, Santa Fe, and Washington, D.C.

Boyce, William (b. London, bapt. 11 Sept. 1711; d. Kensington, 7 Feb. 1779). Composer and organist. He began as a choirboy at St. Paul's Cathedral; later he studied organ and harmony with Maurice Greene, the cathedral organist. His first position was as organist at the Earl of Oxford's chapel in London; he served there until 1736, when he was appointed both composer to the Chapel Royal and organist at St. Michael's, Cornhill. From 1737 he conducted the Music Meeting. Probably during the late 1730s he composed his first stage work, the masque *Peleus and Thetis.* In 1747 his trio sonatas op. 1 were greeted with wide public acclaim, and in 1749 he received the Bachelor and Doctor of Music degrees from Oxford. Two years after Greene's death in 1755 Boyce was appointed Master of the King's Music in his place; in 1758 he was also named one of the organists of the Chapel Royal. As a result of growing deafness, in 1764 he was dismissed from his duties at All Hallow's Church, and he resigned from St. Michael's in 1768. He spent his last years compiling the 3-volume *Cathedral Music* (publ. 1760, 1768, and 1773), an important collection of music by Purcell, Gibbons, Blow, and others. Boyce composed 17 stage works (most for Drury Lane Theatre); other vocal works, including services, anthems, and odes; instrumental music, including 8 symphonies op. 2 (London, 1760), 12 overtures (London, 1770; ed. in *MB* 13), and the Concerto in D minor (Worcester Overture).

Bibl.: H. Diack Johnstone, "The Genesis of Boyce's 'Cathedral Music,'" *ML* 56 (1975): 26–40.

Boyd, Anne (Elizabeth) (b. Sydney, 18 Apr. 1946). Composer. She studied at the New South Wales Conservatorium, the Univ. of Sydney (1967–69), and in England at York Univ. (D.Phil., 1972). Has taught at the Univ. of Sussex (1975–77) and at the Univ. of Hong Kong (1980–88), pursuing interests in the music of Southeast Asia and in music education. Her compositions include a children's opera (*The Little Mermaid,* 1974) and music theater (*Mrs. Fraser,* 1975); *Bencharong* (strings, 1976–77) and other orchestral works; *The Metamorphosis of the Solitary Female Phoenix* (wind quintet, piano, and percussion, 1971), *As Far as Crawls the Toad* (5 young percussionists, 1969–72), and other piano and chamber works; *The Rose Garden,* a theater piece for mezzo-soprano, chorus, and ensemble (1972); *As I Crossed a Bridge of Dreams* (12 voices, 1975); *Summer Nights* (countertenor, strings, and percussion, 1976).

Boydell, Brian (b. Dublin, 17 Mar. 1917). Composer. He studied science at Cambridge and music in Heidelberg, London, and Dublin (D.Mus., 1959); became a professor of music at the Univ. of Dublin, 1962. He wrote tonal music in conventional forms; his scales are often modal or constructed of alternate tones and semitones. Works include *A Terrible Beauty Is Born* (narrator, solo voices, chorus, orchestra, 1965), written for the 50th anniversary of the Irish Uprising of 1916; *Mors et vita* (solo voices, chorus, orchestra, 1960–61); *The Carlow Cantata or The Female Friend* (1985); a violin concerto (*Megalithic Ritual Dances,* 1956); *Symphonic Inscapes* (orchestra, 1968); string quartets, a quintet for flute, harp, and string trio (1960), *Four Sketches* (2 Irish harps, 1962), and other chamber music; piano works; songs with ensemble, piano, or Irish harp.

Boykan, Martin (b. New York, 12 Apr. 1931). Composer. Studied conducting under Szell at Mannes College (1943) and composition with Piston at Harvard (B.A., 1951); studied composition with Hindemith in

Vienna (1951–52) and at Yale (M.M., 1953); studied further in Vienna (1953–55). From 1957 taught composition at Brandeis. He discarded many early works; later works are in an atonal idiom influenced by Webern and late Stravinsky. In his first mature string quartet (1967) he adopted the serial methods that characterize his later compositions. Works include a concerto for 13 instruments (1972); chamber music (4 string quartets, 1949, 1967, 1974, 1984); a setting of Psalm 128 for chorus; and the *Elegy* for soprano, flute, clarinet, violin, cello, double bass, and piano (in 2 parts, composed in 1979 and 1982).

Brackeen, JoAnne [née Grogan] (b. Ventura, Calif., 26 July 1938). Jazz pianist and composer. She accompanied the saxophonists Teddy Edwards, Harold Land, and Dexter Gordon in Los Angeles in the late 1950s, but then devoted herself to her family, moving to New York in 1965 with her husband (until about 1980), the saxophonist Charles Brackeen. She joined Art Blakey (1969–72), Joe Henderson (1972–75), and Stan Getz (1975–77). Thereafter worked as a leader, principally playing her own compositions in trios, as on the album *Special Identity* with Eddie Gomez and Jack DeJohnette (1981).

Bradbury, William Batchelder (b. York, Maine, 6 Oct. 1816; d. Montclair, N.J., 7 Jan. 1868). Teacher and composer. Mostly educated in Boston, principally with Lowell Mason (with advanced study in Europe, primarily Leipzig, in 1847–49); from 1836 taught singing in Machias, Maine, and St. John's, New Brunswick; from 1840 a church musician in New York, where he organized free singing classes for children in churches on the model of Mason in Boston. As in Boston, these eventually led to music instruction in the public school curriculum. Also organized summer music festivals for children. Published many collections of educational material and music for such purposes, the first in 1841 (like four later ones, in collaboration with Thomas Hastings). Some sold in the hundreds of thousands, making him one of the most influential figures in American musical education. He composed 812 hymns, including "Just As I Am," and much other vocal music, including the once-popular cantata *Esther* (New York, 1856).

Brade, William (b. probably in England, 1560; d. Hamburg, 26 Feb. 1630). Violinist and composer. He left England around 1590 to seek employment at German courts. First he served at the Brandenburg court (until 1594), then at the Copenhagen court of Christian IV (until 1606). From there he went to Bückeburg (1606–8), Hamburg (1608–10 and again in 1613), and Berlin (1619–20). After a number of brief appointments, chiefly as violinist, his career was interrupted by the Thirty Years' War. He died in Hamburg, essentially unemployed. He was an excellent player in the English tradition, especially of divisions over a ground. His surviving works include several published collections of dances for strings in 4 to 6 parts.

Braff, Ruby [Reuben] (b. Boston, 16 Mar. 1927). Jazz cornetist. He worked in Boston with Edmond Hall and Pee Wee Russell before moving in 1953 to New York. There he recorded mainstream jazz as a leader and with Vic Dickenson, the pianist Mel Powell, and Buck Clayton, including the albums *Vic Dickenson Septet* (1953) and *Buck Meets Ruby* (1954). After playing in George Wein's Newport All Stars (1960s), he toured internationally as a soloist. He also led a quartet with the guitarist George Barnes (1973–75).

Braga, (Antônio) Francisco (b. Rio de Janeiro, 15 Apr. 1868; d. there, 14 Mar. 1945). Composer. As a youth he learned to play clarinet, and from 1885 he studied with Moura (clarinet) and Mesquita (composition) at the Rio Conservatory. In 1889 a piece he composed for a contest to choose a national hymn won him a grant to continue study in Europe. (He lost the contest, but the piece, *Hino à bandeira* [Hymn to the Flag], later became the national anthem.) At the Paris Conservatory he studied with Massenet (1890–94); in Germany he composed *Episódo sinfônico* and the symphonic poem *Marabá,* and in Italy the opera *Tupira.* He returned to Rio around 1900, and from 1902 until his retirement in 1938 he was professor at the National Institute of Music. His music manifests a strong influence of Wagner and Massenet. Other compositions include symphonic poems (*Chant d'automne; Fantasie-Ouverture,* 1887); 2 Masses; a Te Deum; chamber and keyboard music.

Braga Santos, (José Manuel) Joly (b. Lisbon, 14 May 1924; d. there, 18 July 1988). Composer and conductor. His chief instructor at the Lisbon Conservatory (1934–43) was Luis de Freitas Branco; later he studied conducting with Scherchen, electronic techniques at the Gravesano Acoustic Studio (1957–58), and composition with Mortari in Rome (1959–60). He also held posts as assistant conductor at Oporto and at the National Radio Symphony. His early music adheres to a late Romantic style; he subsequently assimilated electronic and aleatory techniques. He has composed operas (*Viver ou morrer,* 1952; *Trilogia des barcas,* 1971; ballets (*A nau Catrineta,* 1959; *Encouzilhada,* 1968); orchestral music (3 symphonic overtures; 6 symphonies, including no. 5, *Virtus Lusitaniae,* 1966; *Nocturno,* 1948; *Sinfonietta,* 1963); choral works (*Requiem,* 1964; *8 Madrigals,* 1973); 2 string quartets; songs; keyboard pieces.

Brahms, Johannes (b. Hamburg, 7 May 1833; d. Vienna, 3 Apr. 1897). Composer. His father, Johann Jakob, was of peasant stock in Holstein, became a musician against his family's wishes, and settled in nearby Hamburg, where, playing a variety of instruments (principally the contrabass), he eked out a living. In 1830 he married his landlady, Johanna Nissen, who was 41, plain, lame, and as poor as he. Johannes was the second of their three children (his younger brother, Friedrich, also became a musician) and was brought up in great poverty near the Hamburg waterfront. A local musician, Otto Cossel, began giving him piano lessons in 1840, and in 1846 he began to study music theory with Eduard Marxsen, the leading music teacher in Hamburg, whose thorough technical grounding of Brahms was acknowledged in the dedication of the Second Piano Concerto. At 12 Brahms began giving lessons himself and was soon also playing the piano in waterfront taverns and other low dives, a milieu that has been thought by some to have affected his personality and his later relations with women. He also composed and arranged light music for local publishers and performers. In 1848 he gave his first solo public piano recital. At another in 1849 he played a fantasia of his own.

The first composition that Brahms allowed to survive, the Scherzo for piano op. 4, was composed in 1851, with the three piano sonatas and many songs following in 1852–53. In 1853 came the beginning of his rise to prominence. In April he began a short tour with the Hungarian violinist Eduard Reményi. At Hannover the violinist Joseph Joachim immediately recognized Brahms's abilities and recommended him to Liszt in Weimar and Schumann in Düsseldorf. Brahms and Reményi reached Weimar in July and were cordially welcomed by Liszt, but after a short stay Brahms, attracted neither by Liszt's music nor, apparently, by his admiring circle, left Weimar (and Reményi, who remained there). This has usually been interpreted as a significant moment in Brahms's career, his rejection of the radical wing of contemporary German music. He revisited Joachim, then in Göttingen, with whom he was to have a lifelong though stormy friendship, and in September, after becoming acquainted with a good deal of Schumann's music, of which he had previously known very little, he visited the composer in Düsseldorf. Schumann's resulting enthusiasm led him to the hyperbolic, messianic language with which he announced Brahms's advent in his famous article "Neue Bahnen" in the *Neue Zeitschrift für Musik.*

In December 1853 Brahms visited Leipzig, where, partly through Schumann's influence, the publishers Breitkopf and Härtel and Senff accepted several works for publication and where he gave a recital at the Gewandhaus, heard by both Liszt and Berlioz. He saw the Schumanns once more on a visit in January 1854 to Joachim at Hannover, but in February received news of Robert's insanity and his attempted suicide and went at once to Düsseldorf, where he remained with the Schumann family until Robert's death in 1856. This devotion, while it may have arisen out of pure friendship and gratitude at Schumann's having transformed him nearly overnight from an unknown to one of the principal hopes for the future of German music was sustained by Brahms's growing emotional involvement with Clara Schumann, reflected in the passionate tone of his surviving letters to her. The nature of his attachment to Clara, who was 14 years older and, after the birth of her last child in June 1854, the mother of seven, has been much argued, particularly the question whether they were lovers, the extent to which Clara encouraged or responded to him, and the manner in which this phase of their relationship was transformed, in the period following Schumann's death, into a close but platonic friendship that was to endure until her death. In his later relations with women Brahms, although frequently enamored, was always to draw back before real intimacy or permanency could be established. In at least his Vienna period he sometimes turned to prostitutes.

During this period Brahms had composed a number of works for piano, including the Variations on a Theme by Schumann op. 9 and the Ballades op. 10, as well as the Piano Trio op. 8. He also worked on a symphony, which was to form the basis of the First Piano Concerto, and the first version of the work that was to become the Piano Quartet op. 60, which he later said reflected his suicidal, Wertherian moods of this period.

During 1857–59 Brahms spent the last three or four months of each year at the court of the small principality of Detmold, where he played the piano, gave lessons, directed a chorus, and occasionally conducted the small court orchestra, an experience that seems to have been influential in his composition of the two serenades for small orchestra (although both had their premieres in Hannover in 1860). The major work of this period, the Piano Concerto no. 1, had its premiere on 22 Jan. 1859 at Hannover, with Brahms as soloist and Joachim conducting. It was politely received, but when Brahms played it five days later at Leipzig there was vociferous opposition, perhaps the most emphatic demonstration of this kind that he was ever to experience personally, and to which he reacted with a sort of stolid stoicism that was increasingly to become his way of masking his feelings. The Leipzig audience's response was disapproved in the *Neue Zeitschrift für Musik,* the principal organ of the New German School headed by Liszt, but in 1860 Brahms and Joachim issued a famous manifesto (also signed by two others) denouncing the New German School, mentioning neither Liszt nor Wagner by name, only the *Neue Zeitschrift.* This act defined for Brahms a position as leader (or figurehead) of a classicizing faction in German music and intensified partisanship, with neither of which was he himself ever completely comfortable, never refusing, for example, to grant Wagner what he felt was his considerable due as a composer (although he was much less generous with Liszt and, later, Bruckner).

In 1859 Brahms organized a women's chorus in Hamburg, for which he wrote several works. He was hoping to be made conductor of the Hamburg Philharmonic, and his failure to get the post in 1862 was a bitter blow, which lessened his attachment to his native city. Brahms was making his first visit to Vienna when he suffered this disappointment. Respectfully received

Johannes Brahms (right) with Johann Strauss, 1894.

there as a performer and composer (the premiere of the Second Piano Quartet took place at his concert of 29 Nov. 1862), he was much attracted by the city, the character of its life, and the circle of musicians and friends that he began to form there. In 1863 he was named director of the Vienna Singakademie, but finding the duties too onerous, resigned after one season. He kept returning to Vienna in following years; with his mother's death in 1865 and his father's remarriage soon after, his ties to Hamburg further decreased, especially when he was passed over once more by the Hamburg Philharmonic in 1868, and in that year he settled permanently in Vienna. He was, however, often away touring as a pianist and conductor, mostly in the spring and fall, primarily in central Europe and Germany and as far west as Holland, of which he became very fond. Brahms lived on his earnings as a performer, allowing his income from his compositions to accumulate, so that by his later years he had become moderately wealthy. He spent summers, when he did most of his composing, in various country places and resorts, in his later years mostly at fashionable Ischl near Vienna.

In the earlier part of this period he produced several chamber works, most notably the Piano Quintet op. 34 (1861?–64), and many songs. The most important work of this period was the *Deutsches Requiem,* which, very successful from the first complete performance of the original six movements at Bremen in 1868, clearly showed that Brahms had fulfilled his promise and could be considered a master. The publication of the first two books of Hungarian Dances in 1869 did as much for his general popularity as a composer. The series of large vocal works continued with the cantata *Rinaldo* (1863–68), the *Alto Rhapsody* (1869), the *Schicksalslied* (1868–71), and the *Triumphlied* (1870–71), which celebrated the Prussian victory in the Franco-Prussian War and the ensuing unification of Germany through the genius of Bismarck, whom Brahms idolized and quoted frequently.

In 1872–75 he was conductor of the concerts of the Gesellschaft der Musikfreunde. This was his last regular musical post (he received other offers in later years, including that of conductor of the Hamburg Philharmonic, but always refused them). His tenure was not untroubled: his musical tastes, reflected in his programming, were too serious wholly to please the Viennese public. Brahms's interest in old music, of which he conducted a good deal, was profound; he was of considerable attainment as a scholar and editor, collected manuscripts, and numbered the Beethoven scholar Nottebohm and, later, Mandyczewski, the young librarian of the Gesellschaft der Musikfreunde, among his friends. In the mid-1870s the period of the great vocal and choral works gave way to that of the mature orchestral music, the symphonies, overtures, and later concertos, and much of his chamber music. This began in 1873 with the premieres of the first two string quartets and, at his orchestral concert of Nov. 2, the Variations on a Theme by Haydn, his first orchestral piece in 13 years. On completing the First Symphony, 20 years in the making, Brahms was sufficiently unsure of himself as to prefer having its premiere in relatively small Karlsruhe (4 Nov. 1876) rather than a major center, although he soon took it to Vienna that December and Leipzig in January. The Second Symphony followed quickly in 1877.

While holding his last conducting post, Brahms had toured less than before and did not revive the practice to the same extent on leaving it, although he continued to spend his summers in the country. In summer 1878 he made the first of his eight holiday trips to Italy. It was in this period of his complete acceptance as a great master that Brahms, always pointedly simple in manner and dress, began to become noticeably shabby and unkempt in appearance and often disagreeable in manner. The celebrated beard also appeared. In 1880 Brahms, who had written his Violin Concerto (1878) for Joachim, consulting with him on the violin part, and had gone on concert tours with him in 1879 and earlier in 1880, took the part of Joachim's wife, Amalie, whom he greatly admired as a singer, in the breakup of their marriage. In her divorce proceedings of 1881 Amalie used a letter that Brahms had written her highly critical of Joachim's behavior and character, and Joachim naturally took offense. The relationship was later patched up, partly through the Concerto for Violin and Cello (1887), Brahms's last orchestral work, which served as a conciliatory gesture on his part, but the friendship did not become as close as before. This alienation was somewhat balanced by a new friendship with Hans von Bülow that began in 1881. That autumn Brahms went to Meiningen to try out the new Second Piano Concerto with von Bülow's orchestra there. The work received its official premiere at Budapest in November with Brahms as soloist, and he then toured the concerto through Germany, as well as Vienna, Zurich, and Utrecht, with von Bülow and the Meiningen orchestra. A similar procedure was to be followed with the Fourth Symphony in 1885. Brahms was to visit Meiningen frequently, becoming good friends with the duke and duchess.

Brahms produced three important chamber works in 1886, the Second Cello Sonata, the Second Violin Sonata, and the Third Piano Trio; the Third Violin Sonata, begun that year, was finished and premiered in 1888. After 1888 his output began to decline. He composed relatively little in 1888–89, and in 1890 primarily the Second String Quintet. In 1887 Brahms and Clara Schumann had returned most of their letters to each other at his request, and he immediately destroyed his. The implication that Brahms, although only in his 50s, was bringing a phase of his life to an end was confirmed in 1890 with his decision to retire from composition. He also destroyed many of his papers and unpublished compositions. This retirement was not rigidly adhered to. His enthusiastic reaction to the playing of the Meiningen clarinetist Richard Mühlfeld in 1891 led to the composition that summer of the Clarinet Trio and Clarinet Quintet and in 1894 to the two clarinet sonatas. In 1892–93 he composed, or at least prepared for publication, the four sets of short piano pieces opp. 116–19. The *Vier ernste Gesänge* (1896) were occasioned by the final illness of Clara Schumann, but Brahms may by then have been aware of the first signs of the cancer of the liver that was to take his own life. During his own long final illness he composed at least some of the 11 choral preludes for organ, published in 1902.

Works: *Orchestra.* Symphonies: no. 1 in C minor, op. 68 (1855–76); no. 2 in D major, op. 73 (1877); no. 3 in F major, op. 90 (1883); no. 4 in E minor, op. 98 (1884–85). Piano concertos: no. 1 in D minor, op. 15 (1854–58); no. 2 in B♭ major, op. 83 (1878–81). Violin Concerto in D major, op. 77 (1878); Double Concerto for violin, cello, and orchestra in A minor, op. 102 (1887). Serenades: no. 1 in D major, op. 11 (1857–58); no. 2 in A major, op. 16 (1858–59; rev. 1875). Variations on a Theme by Haydn op. 56a (1873), also for piano 4 hands as op. 56b. *Academic Festival Overture* op. 80 (1880); *Tragic Overture* op. 81 (1880).

Chamber music. String quartets: no. 1 in C minor and no. 2 in A minor, op. 51 (ca. 1865–73); no. 3 in B♭ major, op. 67 (1875). String quintets: no. 1 in F major, op. 88 (1882); no. 2 in G major, op. 111 (1890). String sextets: no. 1 in B♭ major, op. 18 (1859–60); no. 2 in G major, op. 36 (1864–65). Piano trios: no. 1 in B major, op. 8 (1853–54; rev. 1889); no. 2 in C major, op. 87 (1880–82); no. 3 in C minor, op. 101 (1886). Piano quartets: no. 1 in G minor, op. 25 (1855–61); no. 2 in A major, op. 26 (1855–61); no. 3 in C minor, op. 60 (1855–75). Piano Quintet in F minor, op. 3, (1861?–64). Trio for violin, horn or viola, and piano in E♭ major, op. 40 (1865). Trio for violin, clarinet or viola, and piano in A minor, op. 114 (1891). Quintet for clarinet and string quartet in B minor, op. 115 (1891). Violin sonatas: no. 1 in G major, op. 78 (1878–79); no. 2 in A major, op. 100 (1886); no. 3 in D minor, op. 108 (1886–88). Cello sonatas: no. 1 in E minor, op. 38 (1862–65); no. 2 in F major, op. 99 (1886). Clarinet (or viola) sonatas in F minor and E♭ major, op. 120 (1894).

Chorus and solo voices. Ein deutsches Requiem op. 45 (1854–68); *Rinaldo* op. 50 (1863–68); *Alto Rhapsody* op. 53 (1869); *Schicksalslied* op. 54 (1868–71); *Triumphlied* op. 55 (1870–71); *Nänie* op. 82 (1880–81); *Gesang der Parzen* op. 89 (1882); other accompanied motets and choruses; 58 unaccompanied motets and choruses in 12 published collections.

One or more voices with piano. 196 solo songs in 32 published collections, includings Romances from Tieck's *Magelone* op. 33 (1865); *Vier ernste Gesänge* op. 121 (1896). 20 duets in 5 published collections; 60 quartets in 7 published collections, including *Liebeslieder* (33 vocal waltzes) opp. 52 (1868–69) and 65 (1874), also arranged for piano 4 hands as opp. 52a and 65a, and [11] *Zigeunerlieder* op. 103 (1887). 13 vocal canons op. 113. Many folk song arrangements, 1–4 voices.

Piano. Sonatas: no. 1 in C major, op. 1 (1852–53); no. 2 in F♯ minor, op. 2 (1852); no. 3 in F minor, op. 5 (1853). 5 variation sets, including Variations and Fugue on a Theme by Handel op. 24 (1861); Variations on a Theme by Paganini op. 35 (1862–63). Scherzo op. 4 (1851); 34 piano pieces in 7 published sets, including opp. 76 (1878), 79 (1879), 116 (1892), 117 (1892), 118 (1892), 119 (1892). Studies and arrangements. Works for piano 4 hands, including Variations on a Theme by Schumann op. 23 (1861); Waltzes op. 39 (1865); Hungarian Dances (1869–80).

Organ. 11 chorale preludes op. 122 (1896).

Bibl.: *Johannes Brahms: Sämtliche Werke,* ed. H. Gál and E. Mandyczewski (Leipzig, 1926–28). Siegfried Kross, *Brahms Bibliographie* (Tutzing, 1983). Margit L. McCorkle, *Johannes Brahms: Thematisch-bibliographisches Werkverzeichnis* (Munich, 1984). A. Dietrich and J. V. Widmann, *Recollections of Johannes Brahms,* trans. Dora Hecht (London,

1899). *Johannes Brahms: Briefwechsel* (Berlin, 1908–22; R: 1974). Hannah Bryant, trans., *Johannes Brahms: The Herzogenberg Correspondence,* ed. Max Kalbeck (London, 1909; R: 1971). Nora Bickley, ed. and trans., *Letters to and from J. Joachim* (London, 1914). Berthold Litzmann, ed., *Clara Schumann–Johannes Brahms: Briefe aus den Jahren 1853–1896* (Leipzig, 1927; trans. Eng. 1927; R: 1979). Karl Geiringer, *Johannes Brahms* (Vienna, 1935); trans. as *Brahms, His Life and Work,* rev. ed. (New York, 1982). Eric Sams, *Brahms Songs* (London, 1972). P. Dedel, *Johannes Brahms: A Guide to His Autographs in Facsimile* (Ann Arbor, 1978). Jonathan Dunsby, *Structural Ambiguity in Brahms: Analytical Approaches to Four Works* (Ann Arbor, 1981). Siegfried Kross, *Brahms-Bibliographie* (Tutzing, 1983). Walter Frisch, *Brahms and the Principle of Developing Variation* (Berkeley, 1984). Michael Musgrave, *The Music of Brahms* (London, 1985). Walter Frisch, ed., *Brahms and His World* (Princeton, 1990). Malcolm MacDonald, *Brahms* (New York, 1990). George Bozarth, ed., *Brahms Studies: Analytical and Historical Perspectives* (Oxford, 1990). Christian Martin Schmidt, *Johannes Brahms* (Stuttgart, 1994). Reinhold Brinkmann, *Late Idyll: The Second Symphony of Johannes Brahms* (Cambridge, Mass., 1995).

Brailowsky, Alexander (b. Kiev, 16 Feb. 1896; d. New York, 25 Apr. 1976). Pianist. Studied with his father, then with Pukhal'ski at the Kiev Conservatory. In 1911 began study with Leschetizky in Vienna. Spent World War I in Switzerland, where he worked with Busoni. After his debut in Paris in 1919, he toured Europe for several years. In 1924 he gave in Paris a series of six all-Chopin recitals. He gave similar series in the U.S. in 1937–38 and in 1960, Chopin's sesquicentennial. After a triumphant New York debut (Town Hall, 19 Nov. 1924) he made that city his base. Besides Chopin, he played Liszt, Schumann, and Ravel.

Brain, Dennis (b. London, 17 May 1921; d. on the Barnet bypass near Hatfield, 1 Sept. 1957). Horn player. Educated at St. Paul's School, where he studied organ with G. D. Cunningham; then at the Royal Academy of Music, where he studied horn with his father, Aubrey Brain (1893–1955), first horn with Boult's BBC orchestra. Debut 1938 in Bach's Brandenburg Concerto no. 1 with Adolf Busch's chamber orchestra. Drafted into the Royal Air Force Central Band, 1939–46. After demobilization, founded and led the Dennis Brain Wind Ensemble, which in 1955 he enlarged to a chamber orchestra. First horn with Beecham's Royal Philharmonic, then with the Philharmonia Orchestra. Recorded Mozart's 4 horn concertos with that band under Karajan. Died in an automobile accident, returning from the Edinburgh Festival. Brain used the French technique of horn playing, but from 1951 preferred the tone and volume of German instruments. He is considered the founder of the British school of horn playing.

Brand, Dollar. See Ibrahim, Abdullah.

Brand, Max (b. Lvov, 26 Apr. 1896; d. Langenzersdorf, 5 Apr. 1980). Composer. Studied with Schreker in Vienna. Worked with twelve-tone composition in the 1920s. Emigrated to the U.S. in 1940. During the 1960s he experimented with electronic media. His opera *Maschinist Hopkins* (1929) was very successful and received many performances. Other works include the one-act opera *Stormy Interlude* (1955) and the oratorio *The Gate* (1944).

Brant, Henry (Dreyfuss) (b. Montreal, 15 Sept. 1913). Composer. Studied at McGill (1926–29); then in New York at the Institute of Musical Art (1930–34) and Juilliard (1932–34, under Rubin Goldmark); studied composition privately with Riegger, Antheil, and Fritz Mahler. In the 1930s he was active as an orchestrator and arranger in New York; later he also composed and conducted for radio, ballet, and films; taught at Columbia (1945–52), Juilliard (1947–54), and Bennington (1957–80). His longtime interest in timbre is illustrated by his compositions for ensembles limited to one family of instruments (*Angels and Devils,* flute and flute orchestra, 1931; rev. 1956, 1979) and his works for violin family instruments of "true proportions" (*Crossroads,* 1970). After the 1953 *Antiphony I* for 5 orchestral groups, he usually incorporated a spatial element in his music and often presented markedly contrasting styles simultaneously (*Meteor Farm,* orchestra, 2 choruses, 2 percussion groups, jazz orchestra, Javanese gamelan, West African drums and voices, Indian ensemble, and 2 sopranos, 1982). Reflecting concepts advanced by Ives, Brant's ensembles usually proceed independently of one another; he often employs controlled improvisation, specifying register and timbre, but not exact pitch. Others of his many works include pieces for a variety of ensembles (*Orbits,* soprano, organ, and 80 trombones with individual parts, 1979); *Instant Syzygy,* 2 string quartets and whatnot (1987); *Prisons of the Mind,* a spatial symphony (1990); a few early choral works; film scores.

Brassart [Brasart], **Johannes** [Jean] (fl. 1420–45). Composer. Held positions in churches in and near Liège, the papal chapel, the chapel of the Council of Basel, and the chapels of the emperors Sigismund, Albert II, and Frederick III. Wrote only sacred compositions for 3 or, less often, 4 voices, including about 10 Mass movements (one Gloria-Credo pair), 8 Introits, and 14 other pieces. Four motets are isorhythmic; many compositions incorporate fauxbourdon.

Bibl.: *Opera omnia, CMM* 35 (1965–71).

Braunfels, Walter (b. Frankfurt, 19 Dec. 1882; d. Cologne, 19 Mar. 1954). Composer and pianist. He studied piano with Leschetizky in Vienna and with Thuille and Mottl in Munich. In 1925 he established and directed the Cologne Hochschule für Musik, but was forced to resign in 1933. He lived in Switzerland until after the war, when he returned to Cologne to reorganize the Hochschule, from which he retired as professor emeritus in 1950. His works, which belong to the Romantic tradition, were most popular in the 1920s. He wrote 10 operas and other dramatic works; about 15 orchestral works (*Don Juan: eine klassisch-romantis-*

che Phantasmagorie, 1923); chamber music, primarily from his later years (including 4 string quartets from the 1940s); many piano works; an organ toccata; about 17 large works for voices and orchestra (*Passionskantate,* baritone, chorus, and orchestra, 1943); several songs.

Braxton, Anthony (b. Chicago, 4 June 1945). Jazz and avant-garde alto saxophonist, contrabass clarinetist, and composer. Principally as an alto saxophonist he played free jazz in Chicago with members of the Association for the Advancement of Creative Musicians (1966–69), including the trio Creative Construction Company. He lived in Paris (1969–70) and New York (1970) before joining Chick Corea's quartet Circle (1970–71). Having recorded the album *For Alto* (1968), he began giving unaccompanied concerts in 1972. He also led groups, recording bop as a contrabass clarinetist and his own compositions, as on the album *New York Fall 1974.* In 1985 he joined the music faculty of Mills College (California).

Bibl.: Ronald Michael Radano, *New Musical Figurations: Anthony Braxton's Cultural Critique* (Chicago, 1993).

Bream, Julian (Alexander) (b. Battersea, London, 15 July 1933). Guitarist and lutenist. Learned guitar from his father but entered London's Royal College of Music, 1945, to further studies in piano and cello. Hearing recordings by Segovia, he determined to study with that master. After preparatory work with Perrot in 1946 he became Segovia's student in 1947. Debut as a guitarist at Cheltenham the same year; London debut, 1948. After meeting the instrument maker Thomas Goff in 1950, took up the lute. Began a long association with Peter Pears in 1952. Toured internationally during the 1950s and after. Britten, Henze, Walton, Arnold, and other composers wrote works for him. To perform Morley's *Consort Lessons,* formed the Julian Bream Consort in 1961.

Brecker, Michael [Mike] (b. Philadelphia, 29 Mar. 1949). Jazz tenor saxophonist. In 1969 he formed the jazz-rock group Dreams with his brother the trumpeter Randy Brecker (b. 1945) and Billy Cobham. He worked with Horace Silver (1973–74) and Cobham (1974), then with Randy led The Brecker Brothers (1974–77), whose album of the same name (1975) combines jazz and funk. In 1979 he helped form Steps (from 1982, Steps Ahead), a fusion quintet. He toured the U.S. and Japan with Herbie Hancock and recorded the album *Michael Brecker* (both 1987), on which he plays a synthesizer controller, the Electronic Wind Instrument.

Breitkopf, Bernhard Christoph (b. Clausthal, 2 Mar. 1695; d. Leipzig, 23 Mar. 1777). Publisher. After a printing apprenticeship in his hometown, he moved to Leipzig; he married into a printing family and around 1719 began his own firm. Partly as a result of the publication of works of the poet Gottsched, the house flourished. His son Johann Gottlob Immanuel (b. Leipzig, 23 Nov. 1719; d. there, 28 Jan. 1794) assumed control of the firm in 1745. His new printing techniques brought about dramatic improvements in musical typography, and in only a few years he was a leading European publisher. From 1760 to 1787 Breitkopf published catalogs of available stock, complete with thematic incipits of each piece; these catalogs (see Bibl.) are of great value to modern scholars. In 1795 the firm took on partner Gottfried Christoph Härtel (1763–1827), after which the house assumed the name Breitkopf & Härtel.

Bibl.: Rudolf Elvers, *Breitkopf & Härtel, 1719–1969: Ein historischer Überblick zum Jubiläum* (Wiesbaden, 1968). Barry S. Brook, ed., *The Breitkopf Thematic Catalogue: The Six Parts and Sixteen Supplements, 1762–1787* (New York, 1972).

Brel, Jacques (b. Brussels, 8 Apr. 1929; d. Paris, 9 Oct. 1978). Popular singer and songwriter, actor, film director. Began performing in clubs in Paris in 1953; authored and recorded popular songs concerning current social issues, love, and death ("La mort," 1960; "Quand on n'a que l'amour," 1964; "Amsterdam," 1964). Between 1967 and 1973 he appeared in 10 films (*Mon Oncle Benjamin,* 1969), 2 of which he directed (*Frantz,* 1972; *Le Far West,* 1973), and a musical (*L'Homme de la Mancha,* 1968). His music became widely known in America through composer Mort Schuman's retrospective revue *Jacques Brel Is Alive and Well and Living in Paris* (1968; film version, 1977).

Brendel, Alfred (b. Wiesenberg, Moravia, 5 Jan. 1931). Pianist. Studied with Sofija Dezelic in Zagreb, Ludovica von Kaan in Graz, Paul Baumgartner in Basel, and Edwin Fisher in Lucerne. Debut in Graz, 1948; won the Busoni Prize, 1949. Apart from a tour in 1954, much of the next 10 years was spent away from the concert stage. Debut with Vienna Philharmonic at the 1960 Salzburg Festival; debuts in Paris (1962) and New York (21 Feb. 1964 at Hunter College) followed. He twice recorded the 32 sonatas of Beethoven (for Vox and Phillips). His core repertory also includes Mozart (played with great wit), Schubert, and Liszt; also a notable interpreter of Schoenberg. Some of his many essays are collected in *Musical Thoughts and Afterthoughts* (1976).

Brendel, Karl Franz (b. Stolberg, 26 Nov. 1811; d. Leipzig, 25 Nov. 1868). Critic and historian. Studied at the universities of Leipzig, Berlin, and Freiburg until 1840; taught music history at the Leipzig Conservatory from 1846; published a much-read history of European music (1852); an important figure in the New German School through his editorship of the *Neue Zeitschrift für Musik* (1845–68) and his writings, including books on Liszt and *Die Musik der Gegenwart und die Gesamtkunstwerk der Zukunft* (Leipzig, 1854).

Bresnick, Martin (b. New York, 13 Nov. 1946). Composer. Attended Hartt College (B.A., 1967) and Stanford (M.A., 1969; D.M.A., 1972), where he studied with Chowning and Ligeti. In 1969–70 he studied composition in Vienna with Gottfried von Einem and Cerha. He has taught at the San Francisco Conservatory, Stanford, and Yale (from 1976). His compositions are often programmatic and explicitly political; his concern with timbre has led to works for multiples of one instrument treated heterophonically or contrapuntally (*Conspiracies,* 5 flutes, 1979; *B's Garlands,* 8 cellos, 1973). Some pieces incorporate electronic music in which a spatial element is important (*Der Signal,* 3 voices, tape, and chamber ensemble, 1982). Other works include a theater piece (*Ants,* 1976); *Lady Meil's Dumpe,* synthesizer, computer (1987); orchestral (*Pontoosuc,* 1989), chamber (a piano trio, 1988), and piano works (some with tape); vocal music; film music.

Bretón (y Hernández), Tomás (b. Salamanca, 29 Dec. 1850; d. Madrid, 2 Dec. 1923). Composer and conductor. Studied music in Salamanca, where because of extreme poverty he worked as an orchestral violinist from the age of 12; became concertmaster of the Salamanca theater orchestra at 14; from 1865 studied the violin under Juan Diez and composition under Arrieta at the Madrid Conservatory, sharing first prize in composition with Chapí in 1872. The first of his more than 40 zarzuelas was produced in 1874. In 1875 his first opera, *Guzmán el Bueno,* which had been refused by the Royal Theater, was successfully performed at the Teatro Apolo and later was even more favorably received at Barcelona, where his opera *Garín* was premiered in 1892. In 1881 he received a stipend to study in Rome; also visited Vienna (where he composed a symphony), Milan, and Paris, where he worked on his opera *Los amantes de Teruel,* which solidified his standing as a composer when performed at the Royal Theater, Madrid, in 1889. On his return to Spain he conducted concerts in Barcelona and for 8 seasons directed the Madrid Sociedad de conciertos. His most sucessful zarzuela was the one-act *La verbena de la paloma* (Madrid, 1893), which like several others by him was also very popular in South America and has remained so until the present. His most important opera was *La Dolores* (Madrid, 1895). Also composed an oratorio and choral pieces, orchestral works, chamber music, and many songs. In 1901 he began teaching at the Madrid Conservatory and was later its director.

Bibl.: Angel Sánchez Salcedo, *Tomás Bretón: Su vida y sus obras* (Madrid, 1924). J. de Montillana [Gabriel Hernández Gonzáles], *Bretón* (Salamanca, 1952).

Bréval, Jean-Baptiste Sébastien (b. Paris, 6 Nov. 1753; d. Colligis, Aisne, 18 Mar. 1823). Cellist and composer. After study of cello with (Jean-Baptiste?) Cupis, he taught cello in Paris in the early 1770s. In 1775 he published *Six quatuors concertants* op. 1. He was elected a member of the Société académique des enfants d'Apollon in 1776. From 1778 he performed frequently as soloist at the Concert spirituel. He was engaged by several Paris orchestras, including that of the Concert spirituel (1781–91), of the Théâtre Feydeau (1791–1800), and finally of the Opéra (1801–14 intermittently). He composed instrumental music (including 10 *symphonies concertantes* and 7 cello concertos) and an opera, *Inès et Léonore* (1788). He published an influential treatise, *Traité de violoncelle* (Paris, 1804).

Bréville, Pierre (Eugène Onfroy) de (b. Bar-le-Duc, 21 Feb. 1861; d. Paris, 24 Sept. 1949). Composer. Educated to be a diplomat, he turned to music, studying harmony under Dubois at the Paris Conservatory, but then becoming a private pupil and devoted disciple of Franck, of whom he later wrote reminiscences and criticism. Taught counterpoint at the Schola cantorum, 1898–1902; secretary, later president, of the Société nationale de musique; also a longtime journalistic music critic. He composed one opera, *Eros vainqueur,* successfully premiered at Brussels in 1910 but out of date when it reached the Paris Opéra-comique in 1932; much sacred music; many secular choral works (*La tête de Kenwarc'h,* 1890); over 100 songs; orchestral, chamber, and keyboard pieces.

Brian, Havergal (b. Dresden, Staffordshire, 29 Jan. 1876; d. Shoreham, Sussex, 28 Nov. 1972). Composer. Primarily self-taught in music, as a youth he was organist for the church at Meir; early compositions were solo songs and part songs. Around 1907 he began composing the large-scale choral and orchestral works that were to occupy him for the next 65 years. From the 1920s he composed works of increasing scale, almost none of which achieved performance. After World War II his fecundity even increased: he composed 4 operas and 27 large symphonies after age 70. Slowly his music gained recognition, and a Brian Society was formed. His early style showed admiration for Richard Strauss; later he formed an individual style marked by late Romantic tonality and dense textures. Most of the music remains little performed and thus unknown.

Works: *Operas. The Tigers* (1916–30); *Turandot* (Tragikomisches Märchen, 1949?–51); *The Cenci* (1952); *Faust* (1954?–56); *Agamemnon* (1957; London, 1971). *Orchestral works.* 32 symphonies, 1919–68 (no. 1, The Gothic, soloists, 4 choruses, children's chorus, 4 brass bands, large orchestra, 1919–27; no. 4, Das Siegeslied, 1932–33; no. 6, Sinfonia tragica, 1947–48); also *In memoriam* (1911–12); 3 Comedy Overtures; *Elegy* (1954); 5 English Suites. *Large-scale vocal-orchestral works. The Vision of Cleopatra* (1907–8); *Prometheus Unbound* (lyric drama, 1937–44, lost). Numerous smaller choral works; songs; chamber music.

Bibl.: Malcolm MacDonald, *Havergal Brian: Perspective on the Music* (London, 1972). Reginald Nettel, *Havergal Brian and His Music* [with works list] (London, 1976). Malcolm MacDonald, *The Symphonies of Havergal Brian* (New York, 1978).

Bridge, Frank (b. Brighton, 26 Feb. 1879; d. Eastbourne, 10 Jan. 1941). Composer. He studied violin with his father at home and composition with Charles

Stanford at the Royal College of Music (1899–1903). He was violist with the Joachim Quartet and the English Quartet; he also conducted at the Savoy Theatre (1910–11) and at Covent Garden (1913). In 1923 he conducted concerts of his music in the northeastern U.S.; he returned there in 1934 and 1938. During the late 1920s he taught the young Benjamin Britten, who later became a strong advocate of his teacher's music. Bridge's music, characterized by a highly expressive Romantic idiom, later on approached atonality; the influence of Berg and even Schoenberg is apparent.

Works: *Stage works.* An opera, *The Christmas Rose* (1919–29); incidental music (*Threads,* 1921). *Orchestral works.* Suite for String Orchestra (1910); *The Sea* (1911); *Dance Poem* (1913); *Phantasm,* piano and orchestra (1931); *Summer* (1914). *Chamber music. Elegy,* cello and piano (1911); *Pensiero,* viola and piano (1905); 4 string quartets; string sextet (1906–12). Choral and vocal music; Piano Sonata (1926).

Bibl.: Peter J. Pirie, *Frank Bridge* (London, 1971). Paul Hindmarsh, *Frank Bridge: A Thematic Catalogue, 1900–1941* (London, 1983). Karen R. Little, *Frank Bridge: A Bio-Bibliography* (New York, 1991).

Bridgetower, George (Augustus) Polgreen (b. Biala, Poland, 11 Oct. 1778; d. Peckham, Surrey, 29 Feb. 1860). Violinist. Son of a black servant, apparently of West Indian origin, who by about 1780 was a personal page to Prince Esterházy, and a possibly Polish or German mother. His father toured him as a child prodigy, billed as a Haydn pupil: in 1789 at the Concert spirituel, Paris, then in England (where son and father, the latter described as a handsome man with elegant and ingratiating manners, wore "Turkish" costume and were advertised as African princes), playing for the king and queen at Windsor, then in Bath and London. Because of his mistreatment by his father, around 1791 he was taken under the protection of the Prince of Wales, who had him taught by Attwood and Barthélemon; played in London orchestras and as a soloist and from 1795 to 1809 served as first violinist in the prince's private music, becoming a respected figure in English musical life. In 1802–3 he visited his mother in Dresden and in Vienna met Beethoven, with whom he gave a concert on 24 May 1803, including the premiere of Beethoven's Violin Sonata op. 47. Because of a quarrel (over a woman, according to Bridgetower), Beethoven substituted Kreutzer for Bridgetower as the sonata's dedicatee. His life after the mid-1820s is obscure, part of it being spent on the Continent.

Bibl.: F. G. Edwards, "George P. Bridgetower and the Kreutzer Sonata," *MT* 49 (1908): 302–8. B. Matthews, "George Polgreen Bridgetower," *Music Review* 29 (1968): 22–26. J. Wright, "George Polgreen Bridgetower: An African Prodigy in England, 1789–99," *MQ* 66 (1980): 65–82.

Bristow, George Frederick (b. Brooklyn, 19 Dec. 1825; d. New York, 13 Dec. 1898). Composer. Son of an English émigré musician, who was his first teacher; studied theory with Timm and Macfarren; had some violin lessons from Ole Bull. Began playing as a professional violinist at 13, in many orchestras, including the New York Philharmonic Society (1843–79), sometimes as concertmaster. Was a church organist and choirmaster and conducted choral societies, including the New York Harmonic Society (1851–63) and the Mendelssohn Society (1867–71). From 1854 also taught music in New York public schools. Best remembered as a pioneer in the effort to establish a school of American serious music. The Americanness of his music was limited largely to some of its subject matter, as in the opera *Rip van Winkel* (New York, 1855) and the Niagara Symphony op. 62 (1893). He composed 5 symphonies, 4 concert overtures, 2 string quartets, an oratorio, and sacred music.

Britten, (Edward) Benjamin (b. Lowestoft, Suffolk, 22 Nov. 1913; d. Aldeburgh, 4 Dec. 1976). Composer. He attended Gresham's School, Holt, and while still of school age began study of harmony and composition with Frank Bridge and piano with Harold Samuel. Bridge's preparation enabled Britten to win a scholarship to the Royal College of Music, where from 1930 he continued piano studies with Samuel and with Arthur Benjamin and learned composition under Ireland. In 1933 his *Sinfonietta,* composed the previous year, was performed. Perhaps his first popular success was the Variations on a Theme of Frank Bridge (1937). His collaborations with W. H. Auden also began in the 1930s, with works such as the *Ballad of Heroes* (1939).

In 1939, following Auden's lead, Britten emigrated to the U.S. with the tenor Peter Pears. In the U.S. he composed his *Sinfonia da requiem* and the First String Quartet, as well as his first essay into theater music, *Paul Bunyan,* on an Auden text (performed in New York, 1941). During his stay in the U.S. Britten fell ill, and upon recovering he decided to return to England; he arrived home in the spring of 1942.

He and Pears were active giving concerts during the war years; it was Pears, too, who sang the title role of Britten's gripping second opera, *Peter Grimes,* performed by the newly rejuvenated company of Sadler's Wells on 7 June 1945. Its success immediately established Britten's position as one of England's great musical dramatists. *Grimes* was followed by a number of important instrumental works, including *The Young Person's Guide to the Orchestra* and the choral-orchestral Spring Symphony; also by two chamber operas, the *Rape of Lucretia* and *Albert Herring.* In 1948 the first Aldeburgh Festival was mounted; during the subsequent three decades this festival was to be the center of Britten's activities as composer and performer. His first work performed there was the cantata *Saint Nicolas;* other pieces that received première performances at Aldeburgh include the *Lachrymae,* the suites for cello, the Gemini Variations, *Noye's Fludde, Curley River,* and *A Midsummer Night's Dream.*

The 1950s saw a continuation of the stream of major theater works, including *Billy Budd, Gloriana* (written in honor of the coronation of Elizabeth II), and *The Turn of the Screw,* produced for the 1954 Venice Biennale. The 1960s marked new directions in Britten's music, including a thinning of orchestral textures undertaken possibly under the influence of Asian music—especially that of Bali—heard during a tour of the Orient in 1955. With the *War Requiem* the composer again attracted considerable popular acclaim. Early in the 1960s he also met the cellist Rostropovich, for whom he composed a number of works during the subsequent decade; in 1963 and again in 1965 he visited the cellist and his wife in the Soviet Union; there he and Pears gave concerts and were warmly received by audiences. Also in 1965 Britten was awarded the Order of Merit. His next opera, *Owen Wingrave,* was composed for BBC television. *Death in Venice,* his final stage work, was produced in the Aldeburgh Festival's newly enlarged concert hall in 1973. That year Britten underwent surgery to replace a heart valve, and as a result his strength waned during the last three years of his life. He continued composing; works from these years include a tranquil Third String Quartet and several vocal works, including Canticle V, "The Death of Saint Narcissus," for tenor and harp.

Works: *Opera. Peter Grimes* (1944–45; Sadler's Wells, 1945); *Albert Herring* (1947); *Billy Budd* (4 acts, Covent Garden, 1951; two-act version, 1960); *Gloriana* (1953); *The Turn of the Screw* (1954); *Noye's Fludde* (children's opera, 1957; first perf., 1958); *A Midsummer Night's Dream* (1960); *Owen Wingrave* (1971; first staged perf., 1973); *Death in Venice* (1973).

Orchestra. Sinfonietta (1932); *Simple Symphony* (1933–34); *Soirées musicales* (1936); Variations on a Theme of Frank Bridge (1937); Piano Concerto (1938); Violin Concerto (1939; rev. 1958); *Sinfonia da requiem* (1940); *Four Sea Interludes* from *Peter Grimes* (1945); *The Young Person's Guide to the Orchestra,* with narrator (1946); Symphonic Suite (Gloriana), tenor, oboe, orchestra (1954); *Cello Symphony* (1963); *The Building of the House* (1967); *Suite on English Folk Tunes* (1974); incidental music, including *This Way to the Tomb* (1945); the three-act ballet *The Prince of the Pagodas* (1956).

Chorus. A Hymn to the Virgin (1930; rev. 1934); *A Boy Was Born* (1932–33; rev. 1955); *Friday Afternoons,* 12 songs for children's choir (1933–35); Te Deum (1934); *2 Ballads* (1937); *Ballad of Heroes* (1939); *A Ceremony of Carols* (1942); *Rejoice in the Lamb* (1943); *Festival Te Deum* (1944); *St. Nicolas* (1948); *Spring Symphony* (1949); *A Wedding Anthem [Amo ergo sum]* (1949); *Hymn to St. Peter* (1955); *Cantata academica* (1959); *Missa brevis* (1959); *War Requiem* op. 66, soprano, tenor, baritone, boys' choir, chorus, orchestra, chamber orchestra, organ (1961; first perf., 30 May 1962); *Psalm 150* (1962); *Cantata misericordium,* tenor, baritone, chorus, chamber ensemble (1963); *The Golden Vanity,* boys' choir (1967); *Children's Crusade* (1969); *Welcome Ode* (1976).

Solo voice. 5 Canticles (1947–75; no. 2 "Abraham and Isaac," 1952; no. 5 "The Death of Narcissus," 1975); *A Chain of Lullabies* (1948); *Songs from the Chinese* (1957); *The Poet's Echo* (1965); *Phaedra,* mezzo-soprano, chamber ensemble (1975); numerous arrangements of folk songs.

Chamber music. 3 string quartets (1941, 1945, 1975); suites for solo cello (1964, 1967, 1972); *Lachrymae: Reflections on a Song of Dowland,* viola and piano (1950; arranged for viola and orchestra, 1976); Sonata in C, cello and piano (1961); *Nocturnal after John Dowland,* guitar (1963); Gemini Variations, flute, violin, piano 4-hands (1965).

Bibl.: *Benjamin Britten: A Complete Catalogue of His Published Works,* rev. ed. (London, 1973). Eric Walter White, *Benjamin Britten: A Sketch of His Life and Works* (London, 1948); rev. as *Benjamin Britten: His Life and Operas* (London, 1970); 2nd ed. John Evans (Berkeley, 1983). Imogen Holst, *Britten* (London, 1966). Patricia Howard, *The Operas of Benjamin Britten: An Introduction* (New York, 1969; R: 1976). Alan Kendall, *Benjamin Britten* (London, 1973). David Herbert, ed., *The Operas of Benjamin Britten: The Complete Librettos* (London, 1979). Michael Kennedy, *Britten* (London, 1981). Eric Walter White, *Benjamin Britten: His Life and Operas* (Berkeley, 1982). Arnold Whittall, *The Music of Britten and Tippett: Studies in Themes and Techniques* (Cambridge, 1982). Philip Brett, ed., *Benjamin Britten: Peter Grimes* (Cambridge, 1983). Christopher Palmer, ed., *The Britten Companion* (Cambridge, 1984). Donald Mitchell, ed., *Letters from a Life: The Selected Letters and Diaries of Benjamin Britten, 1913–1976* (Berkeley, 1991–). Humphrey Carpenter, *Benjamin Britten: A Biography* (New York, 1992).

Brixi, František [Franz] **Xaver** (b. Prague, bapt. 2 Jan. 1732; d. there, 14 Oct. 1771). Composer. Member of a prominent Bohemian musical family, from 1744 František attended the Piarist Seminary in Kosmonosy; in 1749 he received a post as organist at St. Gallus Church in Prague. He subsequently held a number of other organ positions there, and in 1759 he assumed the top post, that at the Cathedral of St. Vitus. He may also have been choirmaster at the Benedictine monastery of St. George. His oeuvre comprises nearly 500 works, including oratorios, dramatic cantatas, school dramas, symphonies, and many works for keyboard.

Bibl.: Robert Münster, "František Xaver Brixi v Bavorsku" [Brixi in Bavaria], *Hudební veda* 2 (1965): 19–55. Vladimir Novák, Introduction to *Musica antiqua bohemica* 2/6 (1971).

Broadwood, John (b. Cockburnspath, Scotland, Oct. 1732; d. London, 1812). Piano maker. After learning the cabinet making trade he went to London in 1761. There he worked for the harpsichord builder Burkat Shudi, with whom he formed a partnership in 1770. Shudi died in 1773, leaving the firm to Broadwood, who started his own firm. In the early 1780s he produced his first grand pianos, of his own design, using English harpsichord cases and leather-covered hammers. By 1790 he had nearly perfected the triple-strung instrument with greatly increased dynamic range that was to become a favorite of pianists and composers around 1800 (including Haydn, Clementi, and Beethoven, whose instrument was a gift from the firm made in 1817). In 1794 the instrument's range was extended to 6 octaves.

Bibl.: David Wainright, *Broadwood, by Appointment: A History* (London, 1982).

Brod, Max (b. Prague, 27 May 1884; d. Tel Aviv, 20 Dec. 1968). Composer and writer on music. Associated with Kafka and other New School writers in Prague. Studied music at the German Univ., Prague. Translated Janáček's operas into German, promoting international interest in them; also translated Weinberger's *Švanda the Bagpiper.* Wrote the text for Gurlitt's *Nana* (1932). Was music critic for the *Prager Tagblatt.* Emigrated to Palestine in 1939; served as artistic adviser to the Habimah Theatre in Tel Aviv until he died. Composed 38 opuses of music, beginning in 1900 (the works are not numbered chronologically). These include *Zwei Israelische Bauerntänze* for orchestra and *Requiem hebraicum* for baritone and orchestra. Writings include *Die Musik Israels* (Tel Aviv, 1951) and books on Janáček (1924) and Mahler (1961). His autobiography, *Streitbares Leben,* was published in Munich in 1960.

Bibl.: Charles Susskind, *Janáček and Brod* (New Haven, 1985).

Brodsky, Adolph (b. Taganrog, Russia, 2 Apr. [O.S. 21 Mar.] 1851; d. Manchester, England, 22 Jan. 1929). Violinist. Studied under Hellmesberger at the Vienna Conservatory in 1860–63; in 1866–68 played in the Vienna court orchestra; from 1873 studied with Laub at the Moscow Conservatory, succeeding him in 1875. On tour in Vienna in 1881 he premiered Tchaikovsky's Violin Concerto (after Auer pronounced it unplayable), which was dedicated to him. Taught at the Leipzig Conservatory, 1883–91; 1891–94 concertmaster of the New York Symphony; 1894–96 concertmaster of the Hallé orchestra and violin teacher at the Royal Manchester College of Music, succeeding Hallé as principal in 1895. Retired as concert soloist in 1921.

Broman, Sten (b. Uppsala, 25 Mar. 1902; d. Lund, 29 Oct. 1983). Composer and conductor. He studied violin with Henri Marteau and conducting with Zemlinsky at the German Musikakademie in Prague; later studied musicology under Sachs in Berlin and Peter Wagner in Freiburg, Switzerland. During the 1930s he played viola in several string quartets and from 1945 to 1966 conducted the Sydsvenska Filharmoniska Föreningen choir. He was widely active as a conductor and performer, critic for the *Sydsvenska dagbladet* in Malmö (1930–66), and chairman of the Swedish section of the ISCM (1933–62). He composed film music; a ballet, *Malmö dansar för er* [Malmö Dances] (1962); 9 symphonies (1962–74; no. 1 Sinfonia ritmica; no. 5 with soprano; nos. 6–8 with tape; no. 9 with chorus); other orchestral works (*Sententia crevit,* with tape, 1967); choral music (a cantata, 1948; *Musica cathedralis,* 1971); chamber music (4 string quartets, 1928–73; Concerto for Brass, 1970; 3 suites, viola, 1935–42); piano pieces (*Canon,* 1929).

Brookmeyer, Bob [Robert] (b. Kansas City, Mo., 19 Dec. 1929). Jazz valve trombonist, arranger, and pianist. Initially a pianist, he concentrated on trombone after working with big bands. He joined Stan Getz (1952–53), Gerry Mulligan's combos (1953–57, 1962–64, including the album *Paris Concert,* 1954), Jimmy Giuffre's trio (1957–58), and Mulligan's Concert Jazz Band (1960–61). With Clark Terry he led a quintet (1961–66), recording the album *The Power of Positively Swinging* (1964). He played in and arranged for the Thad Jones–Mel Lewis Orchestra (1965–68) and became its music director in the 1980s when Lewis was the sole leader. From 1968 he worked as a studio musician.

Broonzy, Big Bill [William Lee Conley] (b. Scott, Miss., 26 June 1893; d. Chicago, 14 Aug. 1958). Blues singer and guitarist. Although he grew up in Arkansas, Broonzy epitomized Chicago blues and the transition from country to urban styles. He was accomplished in both, recording as a singer and guitarist from ca. 1926 and with jazz band accompaniment from ca. 1937. Identified with the folk blues revival, Broonzy became one of the first blues musicians to tour regularly in Europe (from 1951). His rocking, rhythmic guitar playing and assertive singing were widely imitated, and many of his songs became blues standards, including "Big Bill Blues" (1932), "Keep Your Hands Off Her" (1935), and "Too Many Drivers" (1939).

Bibl.: Yannick Bruynoghe, *Big Bill Blues* (London, 1955).

Broschi, Carlo. See **Farinelli.**

Brossard, Sébastien de (b. Dompierre, Orne, bapt. 12 Sept. 1655; d. Meaux, near Paris, 10 Aug. 1730). Lexicographer, composer, and scholar. He prepared for the priesthood at Caen from 1670, assuming lower orders in 1676. His musical training was chiefly informal, obtained from studying and copying scores amassed for his private music library. From 1678 he spent a decade in Paris, perhaps pursuing formal musical studies. In 1684 he was a priest at Notre Dame; in 1687 at the Strasbourg Cathedral. In 1698 he became *maître de chapelle* at Meaux Cathedral; made a canon in 1709. Among his works are a *Missa quinti toni;* cantatas, oratorios, and motets; a few trio sonatas. He is best known, however, for his *Dictionaire de musique, contenant une explication des termes grecs, latins, italiens et françois* (Paris, 1703; R: Amsterdam, 1964). He wrote other books as well.

Brott, Alexander (b. Montreal, 17 Mar. 1915). Composer, conductor, and violinist. Studied at McGill Conservatorium, 1928–35; joined Montreal Symphony when he graduated. Received Laureat degree from Quebec Academy of Music in 1933. Won a scholarship to Juilliard in 1939, where his teachers included Sascha Jacobsen, Willem Willeke, and Bernard Wagenaar. Won an award to study in England (1939), but World War II prevented him from going there; joined the faculty of McGill University. Concertmaster and assistant conductor of the Montreal Symphony, 1945–58. Compositions include the ballet *Le corriveau* (1966); orchestral works, some with chorus; choral works; works for chamber ensembles, including string quartet and brass quintet. His son Boris (b. 1944) is also a conductor and violinist.

Brouwer, Leo (b. Havana, 1 Mar. 1939). Composer and guitarist. In 1960–61 he studied at Juilliard with Wolpe and Persichetti; later with Isadore Freed at the Hartt College of Music. He has been assistant music director at Radio Havana (1960–61), professor of composition at the Havana Conservatory (1961–67), and music director for the Institute of Arts and Cinematographic Industry (from 1969). In 1969 he helped found the Grupo de experimentaciones sonoras. His early music draws on native popular music; more recently he has employed graphically notated aleatory and electronic sound. Works include *Variantes,* percussion (1962); *Sonogram I,* prepared piano (1963), *II,* orchestra (1964), *III,* 2 pianos (1968); *Homage to Mingus,* jazz ensemble, orchestra (1965); *La tradición se rompe . . . pero cuesta trabajo,* orchestra (1967–69); *Exaedros I–II,* 6 players (1969–70); *La espiral eterna,* guitar (1970); *Sonata pian' e forte,* piano, tape (1970); Guitar Concerto (1972); *El gran zoo* (1972).

Brown, Clifford (b. Wilmington, Del., 30 Oct. 1930; d. Pennsylvania Turnpike, 26 June 1956). Jazz trumpeter. He played bop with Charlie Parker in Philadelphia (1951) and Tadd Dameron in Atlantic City (1953), then toured Europe with Lionel Hampton (1953). After working briefly with Art Blakey, he and Max Roach led a quintet (1954–56) that included Sonny Rollins. He died in an automobile accident. Brown was arguably the greatest bop trumpeter, improvising imaginative lines with the dexterity of a saxophonist and without sacrificing his lustrous tone. Among albums by his quintet are *Clifford Brown and Max Roach* (1954–55, including his compositions "Joy Spring" and "Daahoud"), *Study in Brown* (1955), and *At Basin Street* (1956).

Brown, Earle (Appleton, Jr.) (b. Lunenburg, Mass., 26 Dec. 1926). Composer. He played trumpet as a youth; studied briefly at Northeastern Univ. (mathematics and engineering), but left after returning from army service in 1946; studied at the Schillinger School of Music in New York (1946–50) and taught the Schillinger Method in Denver (1950–52). In the 1950s he was active at the Darmstadt summer courses and worked for Capitol Records; from 1968 to 1973 he taught at Peabody Conservatory; was a visiting professor at Berkeley, Buffalo, Yale, and in Europe; taught at Aspen in 1975 and 1981. His early compositions are organized serially (but not necessarily in groups of twelve tones) and are pointillistic in texture; from the early 1950s he was influenced by the work of Calder and Pollock to produce music in which spontaneity and mobility of form are paramount. In 1952 he became associated with Cage and Tudor; at the same time he began to use his "time notation," a graphic notation in which durations are flexible, and to design pieces in "open form." *Twenty-Five Pages* for 1 to 25 pianos (1953) consists of 25 pages in a graphic notation, each page invertible and the set playable in any sequence; the graphic score for *December 1952* is composed of 31 horizontal or vertical blocks of varying dimensions arranged on a single page, the meaning of which is determined by the performer(s), who also choose the starting point and direction in which the score is to be read. Other works include *Available Forms I,* 18 instruments (1961), *II,* large orchestra, 2 conductors (1962); *Modules I–II,* orchestra (1966); *Sounder Rounds,* orchestra (1982); a string quartet (1965); *Windsor Jambs,* with wordless text, mezzo-soprano, flute, clarinet, piano, percussion, violin, viola, cello (1980); works with tape (*Times Five,* 5 instruments and tape, 1963); *Corroboree,* pianos (1964).

Brown, James (b. Augusta, Ga., 3 May 1928). Soul singer, songwriter, and bandleader. He sang with the vocal gospel group Famous Flames ("Please, Please, Please," 1956), and later toured with a large musical and dance troupe (*Live at the Apollo,* 1963); he was instrumental in popularizing soul (of which he is often described as the godfather) and funk music, and he influenced younger singer/dancer performers such as Michael Jackson. He experienced a resurgence of popularity in the 1980s, in part as a result of his appearance in 2 movies (*Blues Brothers,* 1980; *Rocky IV,* 1985). In 1988 he was sentenced to 6 years in prison for aggravated assault in connection with a high-speed car chase across state lines.

Brown, Lawrence (b. Lawrence, Kans., 3 Aug. 1907; d. Los Angeles, 5 Sept. 1988). Jazz trombonist. He played with Louis Armstrong on the West Coast (1930) before joining Duke Ellington (1932–51, 1960–70). In the interim he worked with Johnny Hodges (1951–55) and as a free-lance and studio musician in New York. With Ellington, Brown's solos display a fluid technique and beautiful tone that contrasted with the growling, muted style of Tricky Sam Nanton; in the 1960s Brown reluctantly utilized both styles. Recordings with Ellington include "The Sheik of Araby" (1932) and "Slippery Horn" (1933).

Brown, Nacio [Ignatio] **Herb** (b. Deming, N.M., 22 Feb. 1896; d. San Francisco, 28 Sept. 1964). Popular songwriter. One of the first composers to work exclusively in the film medium; with lyricist Arthur Freed, composed the first full-length film musical (*The Broadway Melody,* including "You Were Meant for Me," 1929) and songs for many other movies ("Singin' in the Rain," in *Hollywood Revue,* 1929; "All I Do Is Dream of You," in *Sadie McKee,* 1934). In 1952 Freed produced the film *Singin' in the Rain,* a vehicle for their most successful songs.

Brown, Ray(mond Matthews) (b. Pittsburgh, 13 Oct. 1926). Jazz double bass player. He joined Dizzy Gillespie's bop quintet with Charlie Parker, Bud Powell, and Max Roach (1945), then played in Gillespie's big band, recording "One Bass Hit" (1946) and "Two Bass Hit" (1947). From 1948 he accompanied Ella Fitzgerald. He joined Milt Jackson's quartet with Kenny Clarke and John Lewis (1951) and played with Oscar Peterson (1950–66), recording the album *The Oscar Peterson Trio at the Stratford Shakespearean Festival* (1956). In 1966 he became a studio musician in Los Angeles, but continued playing jazz as a free-lance. He recorded duos with Duke Ellington (1972) and helped form the L.A. Four (1974–ca. 1985).

Browne, John (fl. ca. 1490). Composer. Contributed 15 pieces for from 4 to 8 voices to the Eton Choirbook. Seven complete antiphons along with portions of 2 more antiphons and a Magnificat are extant; 2 antiphons and 3 Magnificats are lost. The Fayrfax MS includes 3 carols ascribed to "Browne"; these may be by either John Browne or a contemporary Gentleman of the Chapel Royal named William Browne.

Browning, John (S., Jr.) (b. Denver, 22 May 1933). Pianist. While studying with his mother he made his debut at age 10. Later worked with Lee Pattison at Occidental College and Rosina Lhévinne at Juilliard. After winning the 1954 Steinway Centennial and 1955 Leventritt Awards, he placed second in the 1956 Concours Reine Elisabeth at Brussels. New York debut with the Philharmonic under Mitropoulos the same year. New York recital debut at Town Hall, 6 Nov. 1958. With the Boston Symphony he gave the premiere of Samuel Barber's Concerto (New York, 24 Sept. 1962). He taught at Northwestern Univ., 1975–80, and at the Manhattan School, 1980–85. His repertory includes Mozart, Beethoven, Chopin, Schumann, Debussy, as well as a few conservative contemporary American composers.

Brubeck, Dave [David Warren] (b. Concord, Calif., 6 Dec. 1920). Jazz pianist, composer, and bandleader. While studying with Milhaud at Mills College he led an octet (1946–49). He formed a trio (1949–51), then a quartet including Paul Desmond that recorded the album *Jazz at Oberlin* (1953) and for which Brubeck composed "In Your Own Sweet Way" (ca. 1952) and "The Duke" (ca. 1954). Later, with the drummer Joe Morello (from 1956) and the double bass player Gene Wright (from 1958), it achieved great success with recordings of Desmond's composition "Take Five" (in 5/4 meter) and Brubeck's "Blue Rondo à la Turk" (in 9/8 meter) on the album *Time Out* (1959); the quartet also recorded the album *At Carnegie Hall* (1963). It disbanded in 1967 to allow Brubeck to concentrate on composing, but he soon resumed playing; a new quartet included Gerry Mulligan and the drummer Alan Dawson (–1972). From the mid-1970s one or more of his sons have been among his sidemen. Desmond, Morello, and Wright rejoined for a 25th anniversary tour (1976), and in the 1980s the clarinetist Bill Smith, a colleague from the early octet, joined. As a jazz pianist Brubeck is admired for his continuous experimentation.

Bibl.: Ilse Storb, *Dave Brubeck, Improvisations and Compositions: The Idea of Cultural Exchange,* trans. Bert Thompson (New York, 1994).

Bruch, Max (Christian Friedrich) (b. Cologne, 6 Jan. 1838; d. Friedenau, near Berlin, 2 Oct. 1920). Composer. He had his first music lessons from his mother, a well-known teacher and singer, then studied theory with H. C. Breidenstein in Bonn; he was a prodigy as a composer, having a symphony performed in Cologne at 14. In 1853–57 he studied theory and composition with Ferdinand Hiller in Cologne and the piano with Reinecke (to 1854) and Ferdinand Breunung. After a short stay in Leipzig he spent 1858–61 as a music teacher in Cologne, where in 1858 his first opera, based on Goethe's singspiel *Scherz, List und Rache,* was produced as his op. 1. In 1862–64 he lived in Mannheim, where he produced his second opera, *Die Loreley* (1863), to a libretto by Geibel intended for Mendelssohn, and composed choral works, including the secular cantata *Frithjof,* for soloists, male chorus, and orchestra, which was widely popular and perhaps helped determine the choral genres as a principal sphere of his activity. In 1865–67 he was music director in Koblenz and in 1867–70 court Kapellmeister in Sondershausen. In 1870–73 he lived in Berlin, where his last opera, *Hermione,* based on *A Winter's Tale,* was produced with only mediocre success in 1872; from 1873 to 1878 he was in Bonn. In 1878 he became director of the Sternschen Gesangsverein in Berlin, in 1880–83 conductor of the Liverpool Philharmonic, and after conducting his music in the U.S. in 1883, conductor of the Breslau Orchestra, 1883–90. In 1891 he was made professor at the Hochschule für Musik, Berlin, teaching advanced composition; retired in 1910, having been assistant director of the school from 1907. In his later years he received many academic and official honors.

In his own time Bruch was best known for his choral music, now very rarely heard. Besides *Frithjof,* the most popular works were *Die Birken und die Erlen* op. 8, *Die Flucht der heiligen Familie* op. 20, *Schön Ellen* op. 24, *Normannenzeug* op. 32, *Odysseus* op. 41, the oratorio *Arminius* op. 43, *Das Lied von der Glocke* op. 45, and *Das Feuerkreuz* op. 52, all dating from the 1860s to late 1880s; his later works in this vein were apparently less in touch with popular taste. He published collections of solo songs and part songs for mixed and male voices, some of which were also widely performed. Composed much instrumental music (3 symphonies; Piano Trio op. 5; 2 string quintets) and piano pieces (*Fantasia,* 2 pianos op. 11). Now best remembered for works for soloist and orchestra, especially the first (op. 26, 1867) of his 3 violin concertos and the *Scottish Fantasy* (1880) for violin and orchestra. The *Romance* op. 42 was also often performed at one time. Of several works for cello and orchestra, the *Kol Nidrei* op. 47 (1881) is still often played.

Bibl.: Hans Pfitzner, *Meine Beziehungen zu Max Bruch: Persönliche Erinnerungen* (Munich, 1938). D. Kämper, ed., *Max Bruch-Studien: Zum 50. Todestag des Komponisten* (Cologne, 1970). Karl Gustav Fellerer, *Max Bruch* (Cologne, 1974). Christopher Fifield, *Max Bruch: His Life and Works* (New York, 1988).

Bruck, Arnold von [Pruck, Arnold de; Arnold de Bruges; Arnoldis Brugensis] (b. Bruges, 1500?; d. Linz an der Donau, 6 Feb. 1554). Composer. In the chapel of

Charles V from childhood until about 1519. From 1527 until retirement (1545) Kapellmeister at the court of Archduke Ferdinand I, succeeding Heinrich Finck. After retirement lived in Vienna and finally in Linz. His surviving works include Latin Catholic sacred music (motets ed. in *DTÖ* 99) and German polyphonic songs (sacred ed. in *DDT* 34, secular in *DTÖ* 72). German works predominate, but many Latin works were probably lost along with the libraries of the chapel of Ferdinand I and St. Steven's Cathedral in Vienna.

Bruckner, Anton (Joseph) (b. Ansfelden, near Linz, 4 Sept. 1824; d. Vienna, 11 Oct. 1896). Composer. Son of the village schoolmaster and organist, who gave him his first music lessons; at 11 resident pupil, in nearby Hörsching, of his young cousin and godfather, J. B. Weiss, a competent composer; after a year returned home to substitute for his ailing father. After his father's death in June 1837 became a choirboy at the nearby Augustinian monastery, St. Florian, and later a violinist and substitute organist there. In 1840 began one-year schoolmaster's course in Linz, including music theory with J. A. Dürnberger; then assistant schoolmaster in Windhaag, a menial post requiring work in the fields as well as teaching; there composed a Mass for alto, 2 horns, and organ. In 1842 transferred to Kronstorf near St. Florian; there organized a male quartet, composed a 4-voice Mass and other sacred pieces, and studied music theory with Leopold von Zanetti, choirmaster in Enns. In 1845 appointed first assistant teacher at St. Florian, his 10-year residence there during his early maturity perhaps contributing to the otherworldliness and ingenuousness that were always to characterize him. In 1849 tutor to the choirboys; in 1850 acting organist; his compositions became more numerous (including two Requiems, a Mass, songs for male quartet). In 1854 the prior, Michael Arneth, long his patron, died. His successor was less supportive, and Bruckner seems to have become increasingly dissatisfied and restless.

In 1855 he passed qualifying examinations for high school teachers and in organ playing and improvisation. That summer he was rejected for the post of cathedral organist at Olmütz, but later won the same post at Linz (then a city of 27,000), taking up his duties in December. There he also taught theory and piano and was a member of the leading Liedertafel, the Frohsinn, of which he was music director in 1860 and 1867. In spring 1855 he had been accepted as a pupil by the Viennese pedagogue Simon Sechter. Bruckner pursued these studies zealously, primarily by correspondence, although from 1858 he was allowed 6 to 8 weeks in the summer to spend in Vienna. He did not compose during this period, since Sechter did not allow it.

In November 1861 he was examined at the Vienna Conservatory, made an impressive showing, and received a diploma. He immediately began another course in practical composition with the Linz cellist and conductor Otto Kitzler. In these studies, which lasted to 1863, he composed his first orchestral music: first short pieces, then an Overture in G minor (1862–63), a Symphony in F minor (1863), and that now known as the Symphony "no. 0" (1863–64). He also became acquainted with Wagner's music, which was to be a major but liberating influence, when Kitzler conducted *Tannhäuser* in Linz in 1863 and studied the score with him. He attended the premiere of *Tristan und Isolde* (Munich, 1865), meeting Wagner, and all Wagner premieres thereafter. In 1868 he conducted the final scene of *Die Meistersinger* at a Linz Liedertafel concert two months before the opera's premiere. The Mass in D minor, called no. 1 (Linz, 1864), is often considered his first fully mature work (a maturity thus attained at age 40), and was followed by the Mass no. 2 in E minor (1866) and the Symphony no. 1 (1865–66), which he conducted in Linz in 1868, his first orchestral work performed.

In 1866 his proposal of marriage (a state he was never to give up desiring) to a local 17-year-old was rejected. Overworked and subject to recurrences of depression throughout his life, Bruckner had a nervous breakdown in 1867 and spent three months in a sanatorium at Bad Kreuzen; then composed his last Mass, no. 3 in F minor (1867–68), for the imperial chapel (but not performed there until 1872). After Sechter's death in 1867 he applied for his posts of court organist and professor at the Univ. of Vienna, but was rejected. Through the conductor Herbeck's influence he was eventually appointed acting court organist (for several years without salary) and teacher of harmony and counterpoint at the conservatory, beginning there in October 1868, also giving private lessons and soon adding an organ class at the conservatory. From 1870 he also taught piano at the teachers' college of St. Anna, where he soon got into trouble by addressing a female student as "lieber Schatz," but was saved by the Minister of Education and taught there to 1874. Among his pupils at the conservatory were to be Mottl, Stransky, von Pachmann, and many leading musicians and academics of the next generation. From 1876 to 1894 he lectured at the university (unpaid until 1880). He retired from the court chapel in 1892 (after his first serious illness), having served also as vice archivist from 1875 and acting (later full) singing master of the choirboys. In 1869 he played at the inauguration of the organ of the new cathedral at Nancy, then at Notre Dame, Paris, before an invited audience including many eminent musicians. In 1871 he played on the organ of the new Albert Hall, London, then six times at the Crystal Palace before large audiences.

He composed the first version of his Second Symphony in 1871–72, the Third mostly in 1873, the Fourth in 1874, the Fifth in 1875. Performances of such large works were not easy to obtain, and audience response was mixed. Wagner's acceptance of the dedication of the Third in 1873 gave Bruckner great satisfaction, but resulted in the bitter enmity of the influential Viennese critic Hanslick. The premiere of the Third by the Vienna Philharmonic under Bruckner on 16 Dec. 1877 was a fiasco, with most of the audience leaving the hall before the end. The Fourth was successfully premiered in Vienna in 1881, but the Fifth had its premiere in Graz in 1894, and the Sixth, finished in 1881, was not heard complete until 1899. The balance began to swing in Bruckner's favor with the very successful premiere of the Seventh in Leipzig in 1884 under Nikisch, who became a champion of Bruckner's work.

The problem of what is to be considered the definitive text of some of Bruckner's major works has been much complicated by his letting himself be persuaded by conductors and devoted pupils, principally the brothers Josef and Franz Schalk and Ferdinand Löwe, to cut, rewrite, and reorchestrate, or to allow this to be done by them. Since it is not always clear what he actually wanted and what he only agreed to, arriving at a definitive text is sometimes a matter of interpretation. Bruckner had no intellectual interests apart from music and few other interests of any sort apart from his religion. He died working on his Ninth Symphony, begun in 1887, leaving the finale uncompleted, although voluminously sketched. He was buried at St. Florian.

Works: *Orchestra.* Overture in G minor (1862–63). 2 early symphonies: one in F minor (1863) and "no. 0" (1863–64). 9 numbered symphonies: no. 1 in C minor (1865–66; rev. 1890–91); no. 2 in C minor (1871–72; rev. 1875–76); no. 3 in D minor (1872–77; rev. 1888–89); no. 4 in E♭ (Romantic, 1874; rev. 1878–80, 1887–88); no. 5 in B♭ (1875–76; rev. 1887–88); no. 6 in A (1879–81); no. 7 in E (1881–83); no. 8 in C minor (1884–87; rev. 1887–90); no. 9 in D minor (1887–96, unfinished).

Chorus. 6 early Masses, Requiem, Magnificat, 4 Psalms (ca. 1842–63). 3 Masses: no. 1 in D minor (1864; rev. 1876, 1881–82); no. 2 in E minor (1866; rev. 1876, 1882, 1885, 1896); no. 3 in F minor (1867–68; rev. 1876–77, 1881, 1890–93). Te Deum in C (1881–84); Psalm 40 (1892); many Latin motets; many German part songs.

Other works include a few solo songs; chamber works (String Quintet, 1878–79); a few organ and piano pieces.

Bibl.: *A. Bruckner: Sämtliche Werke,* ed. Robert Haas et al. (Vienna, 1930). *Anton Bruckner: Sämtliche Werke,* ed. Leopold Nowak et al. (Vienna, 1951–). Renate Grasberger, ed., *Werkverzeichnis Anton Bruckners* (Tutzing, 1977). Franz Gräflinger, ed., *Anton Bruckner: Gesammelte Briefe* (Regensburg, 1924). Max Auer, ed., *Anton Bruckner: Gesammelte Briefe,* n.s. (Regensburg, 1924). Erwin Doernberg, *The Life and Symphonies of Anton Bruckner* (London, 1960; R: New York, 1968). Deryck Cooke, "The Bruckner Problem Simplified," *MT* 110 (1969): 20, 142, 362, 479, 828; rev. ed. (New York, 1975). Leopold Nowak, *Anton Bruckner: Musik und Leben* (Linz, 1973). Derek Watson, *Bruckner* (London, 1975). Robert Simpson, *The Essence of Bruckner,* 2nd ed. (London, 1977). Hans Hubert Schönzeler, *Bruckner,* 2nd rev. ed. (London, 1978). Dika Newlin, *Bruckner, Mahler, Schoenberg,* 3rd rev. ed. (New York, 1979). Leopold Nowak, *Über Anton Bruckner: Gesammelte Aufsätze, 1936–1984* (Vienna, 1985). Renate Grasberger, *Bruckner-Bibliographie (bis 1974)* (Graz, 1985).

Brudieu, Joan (b. diocese of Limoges, ca. 1520; d. Urgel, Catalonia, between 22 Apr. and 10 May 1591). Composer. From 1539 until 1577 choirmaster at La Seo de Urgel Cathedral; in 1578 and early 1579 choirmaster and organist at Santa Maria del Mar in Barcelona; then resumed his position at Urgel. A book of madrigals (Barcelona, 1585) contains settings of Spanish and a few Catalan texts. His only other known work is a Requiem Mass, surviving in manuscript at the cathedral in Urgel.

Brueggen, Frans [Franciscus] **(Josef)** (b. Amsterdam, 30 Oct. 1934). Flutist, recorder player, and conductor. Studied transverse flute and recorder with Kees Otten at Amsterdam's Vereniging Muzieklyceum (diploma, 1952); then musicology at the Univ. of Amsterdam (1952–56). Founded the Brueggen-Consort, 1967. Professor of recorder and 18th-century music at Royal Conservatory at The Hague. He prefers instruments that antedate the Boehm flute and is a leader in the performance of 18th-century music on period instruments. Founded the Orchestra of the 18th Century in 1981. He also performs music of the avant garde, however, and has commissioned works such as Berio's *Gesti* (1966).

Bruhns, Nicolaus (b. Schwabstedt, Schleswig-Holstein, during Advent, 1665; d. Husum, 29 Mar. 1697). Composer, organist, and violinist. His grandfather Paul (d. 1655) was a lutenist in and around Lübeck; his father, also named Paul (1640–89?), was organist at Schwabstedt and was the boy's first music teacher. In 1681 Nicolaus and his brother Georg went to study music with their uncle Peter in Lübeck; Nicolaus also studied composition and organ with Buxtehude. He later served as violinist and composer at the Copenhagen court, and in 1689 he was accepted unanimously for the organ post at Husum, where he served only 8 years before his death at age 31. He composed cantatas, chamber music (lost), and organ works (incl. 4 preludes and fugues). Mattheson reported that Bruhns could accompany his own contrapuntal violin improvisations on the organ pedals.

Bibl.: *N. Bruhns: Gesamt-Ausgabe der Werke,* ed. Fritz Stein, *EDM,* 2nd ser., *Schleswig-Holstein und Hansestädte,* 1–2 (1937–39). Martin Geck, *Nicolaus Bruhns: Leben und Werk* (Cologne, 1968).

Brüll, Ignaz (b. Prossnitz, now Prostějov, Moravia, 7 Nov. 1846; d. Vienna, 17 Sept. 1907). Composer. Lived in Vienna from 1850, where he studied the piano with Julius Epstein and composition with Otto Dessoff; toured Germany and beyond as concert pianist; a close friend of Brahms; later mostly active as a composer. Works include 10 operas (*Das goldene Kreuz,* Berlin, 1875); a ballet; a symphony; 3 orchestral serenades; concert overtures; 2 piano concertos; a violin concerto; chamber music; piano pieces; part songs; solo songs.

Bibl.: Hermine Brüll Schwarz, *Ignaz Brüll und sein Freundeskreis* (Vienna, 1922).

Brumel, Antoine [Anton, Anthonius] (b. 1460, perhaps near Chartres; d. after 1520). Composer. Sang at

Chartres Cathedral from 1483; from 1486 until 1492 Master of the Innocents at St. Peter's, Geneva; subsequently a canon at Laon Cathedral; for several years (1498 to late 1500) Master of the Children at Notre Dame in Paris; for one year a singer at the ducal court in Chambéry; and finally *maestro di cappella* at the court of Ferrara from 1506 until 1510, when the chapel was disbanded. He was praised by Gaffurius, Rabelais, Glarean, Zarlino, Morley, and others and was a leading member of his generation. A connection with Ockeghem, suggested by Crétin's mention of him in the *déploration* on Ockeghem's death, has not been independently confirmed.

His works consist chiefly of sacred vocal music with Latin texts, including about 15 complete Masses, half that many isolated Mass movements, and about 35 other sacred pieces of various types, most for 4 voices. His secular compositions (about 5 for voices in 4 parts with French texts and about 10 for instruments in 3 parts) are all certainly or probably settings of preexisting melodies.

Bibl.: *Opera omnia, CMM* 5 (1969–72).

Brün, Herbert (b. Berlin, 9 July 1918). Composer. Studied composition under Wolpe at the Jerusalem Conservatory (1936–38) and at Columbia (1948–49). In Germany and Israel he composed for theatrical productions, radio, and TV; lectured on German radio at Darmstadt and on tours in the U.S.; from 1955 to 1961 he conducted research on electronic music in Paris, Cologne, and Munich; from 1963 taught electronic and computer music at the Univ. of Illinois, where he composed *Gestures for 11* (1964). Other works include ballets; orchestral works; string quartets and other instrumental chamber music (piano, flute, viola); music for live performers and tape (*Soniferous Loops,* 1964); many electronic and computer works (*Dust,* 1976; *More Dust,* 1977; *Destiny,* 1978).

Bruna, Pablo (b. Daroca, Spain, bapt. 22 June 1611; d. there, 26 or 27 June 1679). Blinded in childhood by smallpox, he carried the nickname "El ciego [blind one] de Daroca." In 1631 he became organist at the church of Daroca and in 1647 its choirmaster. His more than 30 surviving works for organ include principally *tientos* in addition to 7 *Pange lingua* settings and pieces titled *gaytilla, batalla,* and *clausula.* They are preserved in manuscripts at Oporto, Barcelona, and in the monastery at El Escorial. Among his pupils was Pablo Nassarre.

Bibl.: Pedro Calahorra Martínez, "Pablo Bruna, 'El Ciego de Daroca,'" *AnM* 22 (1967): 173.

Bruneau, (Louis-Charles-Bonaventure-) Alfred (b. Paris, 3 Mar. 1857; d. there, 15 June 1934). Composer. Son of a musician; studied the cello (under Franchomme), theory (under Savart), and composition (under Massenet) at the Paris Conservatory, 1873–81, winning first prize in cello in 1876 and second Prix de Rome in 1881. He early composed some symphonic works, but after his first opera, *Kérim* (1887), which aroused little attention, he composed mostly for the stage, apart from solo songs. He became famous with *Le rêve* (Opéra-comique, 1891), based on a novel by Zola, to whom he became the analogous musical figure, creator of a style of musical naturalism, deliberately harsh, even brutal. *L'attaque du moulin* (Opéra-comique, 1893) also has a Zola subject, and Zola himself wrote the librettos of *Messidor* (Opéra, 1897) and *L'ouragan* (Opéra-comique, 1901). These 4 operas marked the apex of his critical and popular favor, which suffered from his support of Zola in the Dreyfus affair. His later works, which until 1916 were also based on Zola, were much less successful. He conducted at the Opéra-comique and (his own operas) in other parts of Europe. From 1889 to 1933 he wrote music criticism (3 collections published 1900–1903); also books on Fauré (1925), Zola (1932), and Massenet (1935). Became inspector of music teaching in 1909; elected to the French Academy in 1925.

Bibl.: Arthur Hervey, *Alfred Bruneau* (London, 1907). Adolphe Boschot, *La vie et les oeuvres de Alfred Bruneau* (Paris, 1937).

Brunelli, Antonio (b. Pisa, ca. 1575; d. there, before 1630). Composer and writer on music. Most notable among his several teachers was Giovanni Maria Nanino in Rome. Brunelli was *maestro di cappella* first at S. Miniato Cathedral, near Pisa (ca. 1603–7); then at Prato Cathedral (from ca. 1607); and finally again in Pisa, for the Knights of St. Stephen (from ca. 1613). He remained chiefly in Pisa until his death. Two of his theoretical works were published in Florence, *Regole utilissime* (1606) and *Regole et dichiarationi* (1610); several vocal collections were published in Venice, including *Canoni varii musicali* (1612), *Arie, scherzi, canzonette, madrigali* op. 9 (1613; includes monodies), *Varii esercizii* op. 11 (1614), and *Sacra cantica* op. 13 (1617).

Brunetti, Gaetano (b. Fano?, Italy, 1744; d. Colmenar de Oreja, near Madrid, 16 Dec. 1798). Composer and violinist. As a youth he may have studied with Nardini in Livorno. In 1767 he became violinist in the Madrid court orchestra of Charles III. Upon the succession of Charles IV in 1788, Brunetti was made orchestra director at the court; he remained there until his death. He composed some 450 works, including symphonies, sextets, string quartets, chamber sonatas, 2 operas (*Il Faetón* and *El Jason,* both lost), 6 concert arias, and sacred works.

Bibl.: Alice B. Belgray, "Gaetano Brunetti: An Exploratory Bio-Bibliographical Study" (diss., Univ. of Michigan, 1970).

Bruni, Antonio Bartolomeo (b. Cuneo, Italy, 28 Jan. 1757; d. there, 6 Aug. 1821). Composer and violinist. In Turin he studied with Gaetano Pugnani and in Novara with Speziani. In 1780 he made his debut in Paris as violinist at the Concert spirituel. From 1781 he was a member of the orchestra of the Comédie-italienne. He composed his first opera, *Coradin,* in 1785, and during the 1780s much instrumental music. In 1794 he became a member of the Commission temporaire des arts. He directed the Opéra-comique orchestra (from 1799) and the orchestra of the Opéra-italienne (from 1801). He composed 22 stage works (most are lost), vocal works, 60 string quartets, 36 trios, concertos, duos, and violin sonatas. He also authored pedagogical works, including the *Méthode pour l'alto viola contenant les principes de cet instrument suivis de 25 études* (Paris, ca. 1810).

Brunswick, Mark (b. New York, 6 Jan. 1902; d. London, 26 May 1971). Composer. He left school in 1922 to study with Rubin Goldmark; studied with Sessions and Bloch; and with Boulanger in Paris (1925–29). Living in Vienna in the 1930s, he was influenced by the twelve-tone method, although he continued to favor the tonal music of Bartók and Stravinsky. Returned to the U.S. in 1937 to teach at Greenwich House Music School; taught briefly at Black Mountain College and at Kenyon College; was chairman of the music department at City College of New York (1946–67). His works sometimes recall those of Webern in scale and character; they include an opera (incomplete); a symphony (1945); chamber music (6 bagatelles for piano, 1958); a choral symphony (*Eros and Death,* mezzo-soprano, chorus, and orchestra, 1932–54); choral music and songs (usually settings of classical texts).

Bruson, Renato (b. Este, 13 Jan. 1936). Baritone. Studied on scholarship with Elena Fava Ceriati at Padua's Conservatorio Pollini. Debut as Verdi's Count di Luna at Spoleto, 1961. Sang in provincial Italian houses for several years. A professional liaison with Franco Corelli in Parma in 1967 led to his U.S. debut at the Metropolitan Opera the following season. La Scala and Edinburgh Festival debuts, 1972; Covent Garden debut, 1976. Admired both for his dramatic range and for the depth of his characterizations. His repertory includes over 80 roles in operas by Rossini, Verdi, Puccini, earlier Wagner, and Donizetti (at least 16), among others.

Bryn-Julson, Phyllis (Mae) (b. Bowdon, N.D., 5 Feb. 1945). Soprano. Studied piano at Concordia College (Minn.). There Gunther Schuller heard her sight-read twelve-tone music with great facility and persuaded her to study singing at the Berkshire Music Center, where she worked with Erich Leinsdorf. Studied at Syracuse University with Helen Boatwright. Made her debut with the Boston Symphony in 1966 in Berg's *Lyric Suite.* Gave the American premiere of Sessions's *Montezuma* (Boston, 1976). Has taught at the Univ. of Maryland, at Kirkland-Hamilton College (N.Y.), and at the Peabody Conservatory. Although she is best known for her performances of 20th-century music, her very large repertory includes many earlier works in the concert repertory as well.

Buchner, Hans (b. Ravensburg, 26 Oct. 1483; d. Konstanz?, mid-Feb., 1538). Organist and composer. Studied with Paul Hofhaimer. May have been organist at the court of Emperor Maximilian I for a few years, until being made cathedral organist in Konstanz in 1506, an appointment that became permanent in 1512. In about 1520 he wrote a *Fundamentum,* which treats aspects of playing the organ (including, notably, fingering), arranging vocal works for organ, and adding counterpoint to a cantus firmus. It includes a collection of about 50 (80 in one manuscript) original liturgical pieces illustrating the techniques discussed.

Bibl.: *Sämtliche Orgelwerke,* ed. J. H. Schmidt, *EDM* 54–55 (1974).

Bucht, Gunnar (b. Stocksund, Sweden, 5 Aug. 1927). Composer. From 1947 he studied composition with Blomdahl; in 1953 earned a doctorate in musicology from Uppsala Univ. The following year he studied in Germany with Orff, and from 1954 to 1962 with Petrassi in Rome and with Max Deutsch in Paris. During the 1960s was chairman of the Society of Swedish Composers and of the Swedish section of the ISCM. In 1975 he became professor of composition at the Stockholm Conservatory; director of the Musikhögskolan in Stockholm from 1987. Composed operas (*Jerikos murar* [Walls of Jericho], 1966–67); orchestral music (7 symphonies, 1952–71; *Divertimento,* 1956; *Journées oubliées,* 1976); vocal works (*La fine della diaspora,* 1958; *6 arstidssånger* [Season Songs], 1965; *Eine lutherische Messe,* 1972–73); chamber music (2 string quartets, 1951, 1959; *5 Bagatelles,* string quartet, 1953); piano music (2 sonatas, 1951, 1959); works for tape (*Symphonie pour la musique libérée,* 1969; *Jerikos murar,* 1970, reworking of stage work); *Unter vollem Einsatz,* organ, 5 percussion (1986–87).

Buck, Dudley (b. Hartford, 10 Mar. 1839; d. West Orange, N.J., 6 Oct. 1909). Composer and organist. Son of the owner of a steamship company; educated at Trinity College, Hartford, then as a musician in Leipzig (1858–59), Dresden (1860–61), and Paris (1861–62). Teacher and church organist in Hartford from 1862; in 1869–71 lived in Chicago; in 1872–75 organist in Boston and teacher at the New England Conservatory. Toured extensively as concert organist until the mid-1870s; from 1875 assistant conductor of the Theodore Thomas orchestra, church musician in Brooklyn, and conductor of a male chorus, the Apollo Club, until retirement in 1903; always a very active teacher. His works for organ include 2 sonatas, in E♭ (1866) and G minor (1877); Variations on "The Star Spangled Banner" (1868); many shorter pieces, studies. He also composed sacred cantatas, anthems, sacred songs; 17 secular cantatas, some highly popular (*The Golden Legend,* 1880; *The Light of Asia,* 1886), part songs, solo songs; 2 operas; a lost symphony.

Budd, Harold (b. Los Angeles, 24 May 1936). Composer. Studied at Los Angeles City College (1957–59); composition with Aurelio de la Vega at San Fernando Valley State College (1961–63); and with Dahl at the Univ. of Southern California (1963–66). On faculty at the California Institute of the Arts. Influences on his music include jazz, works of Feldman and Cage, and the minimalists in the graphic arts of the 1960s. His *Coeur d'Orr* (tape, soprano saxophone, and/or voices, 1969) provides 2 triads on separate tape channels, to serve "as a matrix for any number of live, ritual-like performances"; other works include *The Candy Apple Revision* (1970), a D♭ major chord to be produced by any instrument or sound source. Compositions prior to 1970 have been withdrawn; from the 1970s there are works for various small ensembles of traditional instruments and electronic works; beginning 1979 he abandoned notation, composing and modifying electronic works directly in the studio (*Abandoned Cities,* 1984).

Bull, John (b. Old Radnor?, 1562–63?; d. Antwerp, 12–13 March 1628). Composer, virginalist, and organist. Lived and worked in both England and the Low Countries. Most of his career in England was divided between Hereford Cathedral and the royal court in London. Starting in 1573 he was a chorister in both places, organist and master of the choristers in Hereford, and from 1586 a Gentleman of the Chapel Royal, serving the royal household in various capacities (especially as composer and organist) under Elizabeth I and James I. Concurrently he earned the B.Mus. at Oxford and Mus.D. at Cambridge and, from 1597 until being forced to resign in 1607, was a Public Reader in music at Gresham College, London. In 1613 legal difficulties forced him to leave England permanently and precipitously. This flight took him first to Brussels, where Archduke Albert gave him a position in his chapel for a year and then, although obliged to dismiss him because of objections raised by the English king, continued monetary support until 1618. Meanwhile, Bull became assistant organist at Antwerp Cathedral in 1615, then was appointed cathedral organist in 1617. He composed works for keyboard, including plainsong settings and hexachord fantasias for organ and numerous dances, character pieces, and variations for the virginals; sacred vocal works, most with English texts; a small number of compositions for instrumental consort; and over 200 canons, many of considerable intricacy.

Bibl.: *John Bull: Keyboard Music,* ed. Thurston Dart et al., *MB* 14 (1960; rev. 2nd ed., 1967), 19 (1963; rev. 2nd ed., 1970). Walker Cunningham, *The Keyboard Music of John Bull* (Ann Arbor, 1984).

Bull, Ole (Bornemann) (b. Bergen, 5 Feb. 1810; d. Lysøen, near Bergen, 17 Aug. 1880). Violinist. Showed early talent; taught by Bergen musicians until 1827; from 1828 a musician in Christiana (now Oslo). In 1831 went to Paris; won attention with a May 1833 concert featuring his *Souvenirs de Norvège* with folk tunes played on Norwegian peasant fiddle; then toured widely, arousing considerable acclaim: Italy, Britain (1836), northern Europe (including Russia and Scandinavia), the U.S. (first of many tours, 1843–45). The 1848 Revolution stimulated his always strong Norwegian nationalism, and he spent from late 1848 to 1851 there, working for the cause of Norwegian art, principally through his founding in July 1849 of the Norwegian Theater in Bergen, which was to advance the careers of Ibsen and Bjørnson. In 1852 he established a socialistic colony (called Oleona) for Norwegian immigrants in Pennsylvania; it failed in 1853. Having incurred large debts, he began to tour assiduously, continuing until his death.

A charismatic personality of great gifts and wide interests, he is in Norway a national cultural figure. Few of his many compositions were published, and many are lost. The most famous was *Et saeterbesøg* (1848), which includes a beloved Norwegian song, "Saeterjentens Søndag."

Bibl.: Alexander Bull, ed., *Ole Bulls breve i uddrag* (Copenhagen, 1881). Sara Bull, *Ole Bull* (Boston, 1882). Mortimer B. Smith, *The Life of Ole Bull* (New York, 1943; R: Westport, Conn., 1973). Inez Bull, *Ole Bull Returns to Pennsylvania* (New York, 1961).

Bülow, Hans (Guido) von (b. Dresden, 8 Jan. 1830; d. Cairo, 12 Feb. 1894). Conductor and pianist. Studied with Wieck (piano) and Eberwein (harmony) in Dresden, later with Plaidy (piano) and Hauptmann (theory) in Leipzig; gave up law for music in 1850, after meeting Liszt (1849) and Wagner (1850), who helped his beginnings as a conductor. After piano study with Liszt (from 1851) he toured as a pianist; in 1855–64 taught at the Stern Conservatory, Berlin; in 1857 married Liszt's daughter Cosima. His strong support of the New German School probably suggested his appointment by Ludwig II as court pianist and conductor and director of the conservatory in Munich, where he conducted the premieres of *Tristan und Isolde* (1865) and *Die Meistersinger* (1868). In 1869 Cosima left him for Wagner; they divorced in 1870. After a period of seclusion in Florence he resumed touring in 1872, including in 1875–76 and 1889–90 the U.S., where he premiered Tchaikovsky's Piano Concerto no. 1 in Boston in 1875. In 1878–80 conducted at the court theater, Hannover, and in 1880–85 made the court orchestra at Meiningen into one of the finest in Germany, becoming very close to Brahms and encouraging the young Richard Strauss as composer and conductor. He played and conducted (including the Berlin Philharmonic, 1887–93) until his death. Composed symphonic and piano pieces; edited much piano music by classic masters.

Bibl.: Marie von Bülow, ed., *Hans von Bülow: Briefe und Schriften* (Leipzig, 1908). Marie von Bülow, ed., *The Early Correspondence of Hans von Bülow,* trans. C. Bache (London, 1895; R: 1972). Richard du Moulin-Eckart, ed., *Letters of Hans von Bülow,* trans. H. Waller (New York, 1931; R: New York, 1972). W. Schuh and F. Trenner, eds., *Correspondence: Hans von Bülow and Richard Strauss,* trans. A. Gishford (London, 1955; R: Westport, Conn., 1979).

Bumbry, Grace (Melzia Ann) (b. St. Louis, 4 Jan. 1937). Soprano and mezzo-soprano. Studied with Lotte Lehmann at Northwestern Univ. and the Music

Academy of the West, 1955–58. Won a Metropolitan Opera Audition and Marian Anderson Award, 1958. In London with Lehmann she gave a successful debut recital as mezzo-soprano (1959). Operatic debut as Verdi's Amneris with the Paris Opera, 1960; the same year she joined the Basel Opera. Her warm, rich voice together with her assured stage presence propelled her rapidly into the first rank of mezzos. In 1961 she became the first black performer to sing at Bayreuth. Covent Garden debut, 1963; La Scala debut, 1964; Metropolitan Opera debut as Verdi's Princess Eboli, 7 Oct. 1965. In 1970 she appeared for the first time as a soprano, singing Mascagni's Santuzza with the Vienna Staatsoper. Within the year she had sung Strauss's Salome at Covent Garden and Tosca at the Met. As a soprano she also essayed more adventuresome roles, singing Janáček's Jenůfa at La Scala, 1974, and Dukas's Ariane at Paris, 1975.

Buonamente, Giovanni Battista (b. Mantua, late 16th century; d. Assisi, 29 Aug. 1642). Composer and violinist. A Franciscan, he was in the service of the Gonzagas at Mantua until at least 1622. From 1626 to ca. 1630 he served the emperor in Vienna; in 1627 played in the coronation festivities in Prague for Ferdinand III (son of the emperor). In 1632 he became violinist at Parma's Madonna della Steccata church. Finally he was *maestro di cappella* at Assisi from 1633 to his death. Nearly all of his 150 sacred vocal works are lost; he is best known for his violin ensemble music, which cultivates the "new violin style" that Buonamente is credited with having brought to Austria. Collections include *Il quarto libro de varie Sonate, Sinfonie . . .* (Venice, 1626); *Sonate et Canzoni . . .* (Venice 1636); and *Il settimo libro di Sonate, Sinfonie . . .* (Venice, 1637).

Burbank, Albert (b. New Orleans, 25 Mar. 1902; d. there, 15 Aug. 1976). Jazz clarinetist. Although he played regularly from the 1920s, he became widely known only well after the 1940s revival of interest in New Orleans jazz. In 1945 he recorded "Shake It and Break It" with the cornetist Wooden Joe Nicholas. He joined Kid Ory in Los Angeles in 1954, but immediately returned to New Orleans, where he played in clubs and with brass bands. With Kid Thomas he recorded the album *Kid Thomas and His Algiers Stompers* (1961) and later played at Preservation Hall (1969–73) and toured internationally (1971).

Burck [Burgk], **Joachim a** [Moller, Joachim] (b. Burg, near Magdeburg, 1546; d. Mühlhausen, 24 May 1610). Composer. In 1563 settled in Mühlhausen; by 1566 organist of the Protestant church of St. Blasius. Remained there until his death, performing both musical and civic functions. He was self-taught as a musician and considered himself indebted to earlier composers such as Cipriano de Rore, Giaches de Wert, and especially Orlande de Lassus. In the years around 1600 he performed on the organ and was an organ consultant outside Mühlhausen. He composed at least 2 books of polyphonic motets and several choral passions. From the mid-1570s he wrote only homophonic songs and odes, most for 4 voices.

Burge, David (Russell) (b. Evanston, Ill., 25 Mar. 1930). Composer and pianist. Studied at Northwestern Univ. (B.M., 1951; M.M., 1952) and at Eastman (1956). Won a Fulbright to study at the Cherubini Conservatory in Florence (1956–57). Taught at Northwestern Univ. (1949–52), Whitman College (1957–62), and the Univ. of Colorado (1962–75); chairman of the piano department at Eastman beginning 1975. Conducted Boulder Philharmonic Orchestra (1965–72). Compositions include *Sources,* flute and piano (1964); *Sources II,* violin, celeste, and piano (1965); *Sources III,* piano (1969); *that no one knew,* violin, orchestra (1969).

Burgmüller, Johann Friedrich Franz (b. Regensburg, 4 Dec. 1806; d. Beaulieu, near Paris, 13 Feb. 1874). Composer. Son of J. A. F. Burgmüller (1766–1824), musical administrator and composer, and brother of Norbert; settled in Paris around 1832 as pianist, teacher, and composer of salon music for piano and of progressive piano etudes, which remained standard teaching material almost to the present. Also composed a ballet, *La péri* (Paris, 1843), and, with Flotow and Deldevez, the ballet *Lady Henriette* (Paris, 1844), whose subject Flotow then used in *Martha.*

Burgmüller, (August Joseph) Norbert (b. Düsseldorf, 8 Feb. 1810; d. Burtscheid, near Aachen, 7 May 1836). Composer. Brother of J. F. F. Burgmüller; showed great abilities early; studied with Hauptmann and Spohr in Kassel (1828–30); also a good pianist. His musical personality had not fully matured by his early death, which was lamented as a great loss by Schumann and Mendelssohn. Works include 2 symphonies (the 2nd left unfinished, scherzo completed by Schumann); a piano concerto; overture to the unfinished opera *Dionys;* 4 string quartets; a piano sonata; songs.

Bibl.: Heinrich Eckert, *Norbert Burgmüller* (Augsburg, 1932).

Burian, Emil František (b. Plzeň, 11 Apr. 1904; d. Prague, 9 Aug. 1959). Composer and stage director. He was born into a musical family: his father, Emil, was a baritone, his uncle Karl Burian was a tenor, and his mother was a voice teacher. He studied at the Prague Conservatory under Joseph Foerster during the 1920s; while a student he also directed and acted on several local stages, including the Umělecká Beseda [Modern Studio] and the Dada Theater. In 1924 he founded a group for modern music, Přitomnost [Presence], and in 1927 he began the Voice Band, a vocal ensemble that "sang" rhythmic patterns without prescribed pitches. During the 1930s he directed theaters in Brno and Olomouc and performed in a jazz cabaret, Červené eso. In 1933 he established his own theater, D-34. After the war, much of which he spent in a concentration camp, he resumed his theater activities in Brno and Prague. His music shows influences from a variety of sources including jazz, his French contemporaries, Richard Strauss, Janáček, and Czech folk music. He composed the opera *Maryša* (1940); ballets (*The Manège,* 1927); works for "voice band" (Requiem, chorus, jazz band, 1927); orchestral music (Suite, oboe, strings, 1928; *Koktaily* [Cocktails], jazz band, 1926; *Siréha,* suite from film score, 1947); chamber music (6 string quartets; Nonetto).

Burkhard, Willy (b. Evilard-sur-Bienne, 17 Apr. 1900; d. Zurich, 18 June 1955). Composer. Among his teachers in Bern, Leipzig, Munich, and Paris were Robert Teichmüller (piano), and Sigfried Karg-Elert, Walter Courvoisier, and Max d'Ollone (composition). He taught composition, theory, and piano and was active as a conductor in Bern (1924–33); he lived for a few years in the U.S., but returned to Switzerland and taught at the conservatory in Zurich (1942–55). A Willy Burkhard Society was founded in Bern in 1954. He wrote in a contrapuntal and modal style, influenced by Scriabin, Stravinsky, Bartók, and the French impressionists; in his liturgical music he often used Renaissance and Baroque models, including works of Bach and Schütz. His works include a radio score and incidental music; a viola concerto (op. 93, 1953) and other orchestral music; chamber music; piano and organ works; a large amount of choral and vocal music (including Psalm settings, oratorios, part songs, songs, and song cycles).

Burleigh, Harry [Henry] **T(hacker)** (b. Erie, Penn., 2 Dec. 1866; d. Stamford, Conn., 12 Sept. 1949). Baritone and composer. Studied at National Conservatory of Music in New York (1892–95), where Dvořák was the director. Baritone soloist at St. George's Church in New York, 1894–1946. Soloist at Temple Emanu-El, 1900–25. Music editor at Ricordi from 1913 to his death. Wrote over 265 vocal compositions, made 187 choral arrangements of spiritual melodies; published collections of black ministrel melodies. Awarded NAACP Spingarn Medal in 1917.

Bibl.: Eileen Southern, *The Music of Black Americans: A History* (New York, 1971; R: 1983). Anne K. Simpson, *Hard Trials: The Life and Music of Harry T. Burleigh* (Metuchen, N.J., 1990).

Burmeister, Joachim (b. Lüneburg, 5 Mar. 1564; d. Rostock, 5 May 1629). Theorist and composer. He studied presumably with the Kantors Christoph Praetorius and Euricius Dedekind at the Johannisschule in Lüneburg. In 1586 he enrolled at the Univ. of Rostock; three years later he became Kantor at that town's Nikolaikirche, and later at the Marienkirche. He received his Magister degree in 1593. Burmeister is best known for his theoretical writings, especially *Musica autoschediastikē* (1601; pt. 4 also publ. as *Musicae practicae sive artis canendi ratio,* 1601) and *Musica poetica* (1606; facs., 1955). His writings emphasize chords as a basis for the construction of musical textures. Rejecting a notion of affections conveyed by mode, he adopted instead a theory in which melodic "figures" established the affections. His labels for these figures, which he borrowed largely from writings on rhetoric and oratory (Quintilian and others), were widely used and discussed during the 17th century. The musical illustrations of these "figures"—especially in *Hypomnematum musicae poeticae . . .* (1599) and *Musica theorica Henrici Brucaei* (1609)—were derived chiefly from the works of Lassus; Burmeister's compositions also show the influence of that composer.

Bibl.: Martin Ruhnke, *Joachim Burmeister: Ein Beitrag zur Musiklehre um 1600* (Kassel, 1955).

Burney, Charles (b. Shrewsbury, 7 Apr. 1726; d. Chelsea, 12 Apr. 1814). Music historian and composer. Educated at Shrewsbury School and at the Free School, Chester, he was apprenticed to Thomas Arne, 1744–46. In 1749 he became organist at St. Dionis's Backchurch, London, and in 1751 moved to King's Lynn, Norfolk, where he was a teacher and organist. Returning to London in 1760 he taught music to the well-to-do. Meanwhile he cultivated growing interests in science, literature, and history; in 1769 he published a book on comets. The following year he embarked on his brilliantly chronicled travels; although his tours of Italy and France (1770) and of Germany, Austria, and the Netherlands (1772) were made chiefly to gather information for his *General History of Music,* the chronicles themselves are as valuable to scholars as the history. They detail with rare precision and humor the author's personal contacts with figures such as Gluck, Hasse, C. P. E. Bach, Quantz, J. A. Hiller, Galuppi, Padre Martini, Piccinni, Farinelli, Metastasio, Diderot, Rousseau, and Klopstock. In its emphasis on contemporary rather than "ancient" music, the *General History* differs from that by John Hawkins (1776). Burney's writings constitute the most important firsthand account of 18th-century European musical life. In 1806 he was pensioned by the British government.

Principal writings: *The Present State of Music in France and Italy: or, The Journal of a Tour through Those Countries* (London, 1771; 2nd ed. 1773; R: New York, 1969). *The Present State of Music in Germany, the Netherlands, and United Provinces: or, The Journal of a Tour through Those Countries* (London, 1773; 2nd ed., 1775; R: New York, 1969). *A General History of Music from the Earliest Ages to the Present Period* (London, 1776–89; R: London, 1937; 1957). *Account of an Infant Musician* (London, 1779). *An Account of the Musical Performances in Westminster Abbey and the Pantheon* (London, 1785; R: 1964).

Bibl.: Percy A. Scholes, *The Great Dr. Burney* (Oxford, 1948). Id., ed., *Dr. Burney's Musical Tours in Europe,* 2 vols. (Oxford, 1959). Roger Lonsdale, *Dr. Charles Burney: A Literary Biography* (Oxford, 1965). Kerry S. Grant, *Dr. Burney as Critic and Historian of Music* (Ann Arbor, Mich., 1983). Slava Klima et al., eds., *Memoirs of Dr. Charles Burney, 1726–1769* (Lincoln, Nebr., 1988).

Burrell, Kenny [Kenneth Earl] (b. Detroit, 31 July 1931). Jazz guitarist. In Detroit he played in a bop group with Tommy Flanagan, Pepper Adams, Paul Chambers, and Elvin Jones, and also briefly with Dizzy Gillespie (1951). After graduating from Wayne State Univ. (B.M., 1955) he toured with Oscar Peterson, then settled in New York (1956). His prolific recordings included his albums *Kenny Burrell and John Coltrane* (1958) and *Midnight Blue* (1963), as well as sessions with Billie Holiday, Jimmy Smith, and Stanley Turrentine. In 1972 he settled in Los Angeles, where he taught college courses on Duke Ellington. He also worked as a soloist and leader, recorded with Mercer Ellington (1984), and toured with the Philip Morris Superband (1985–86).

Burt, Francis (b. London, 28 Apr. 1926). Composer. After initial study in the natural sciences, he switched to music and studied with Howard Ferguson at the Royal Academy of Music; in 1951 he went to Berlin, where he studied with Blacher. His String Quartet (1951–52) was performed in the 1953 Darmstadt Summer Course. In the 1950s he settled in Vienna; from 1973 professor at the Hochschule für Musik there. His music shows influence of the late Romantics as well as of the African drumming that he heard as a soldier stationed in Nigeria during World War II. Most important are his stage works, including the operas *Volpone* (1952–58; rev. 1960–66) and *Barnstable, or Someone in the Attic* (1967–69) and the ballet *The Golem* (1959–63). He has also composed orchestral music (*Iambics,* 1953; *Espressione orchestrale,* 1958–59) and vocal music (*Bavarian Gentians,* 1956; the cantata *The Skull,* 1956; *Und Gott der Herr sprach,* mezzo, baritone, bass, chorus, orchestra., 1983).

Burtius [Burci, Burzio], **Nicolaus** (b. Parma, ca. 1445; d. there, after Feb. 1518). Theorist. After being ordained in 1472, studied canon law in Bologna. Remained there as rector of the university until 1503, when he returned to Parma, assuming positions first at S. Pietro in Vincula and then at the Cathedral of Parma. His treatise *Musices opusculum* (printed in 1487; facs., *BMB* ser. 2, 4 [1969]) defends Guido's system of hexachords against the attack of Bartolomeo Ramos de Pareia. Among the numerous authorities cited is his teacher Johannes Legrense. Although the book is in large part conservative and based on traditional teachings, it also pays substantial attention to modern trends. The treatise is notable as the first book with musical illustrations, including one complete polyphonic piece, printed from woodblocks.

Burton, Gary (b. Anderson, Ind., 23 Jan. 1943). Jazz vibraphonist and bandleader. In the early 1960s he developed a technique for playing with four mallets; this became standard practice for vibraphonists in all genres. He studied at the Berklee College of Music, then joined George Shearing (1963–64) and Stan Getz (1964–66). From 1967 he has led quartets or quintets that combine jazz with country music, rock, and Latin music in compositions by Carla Bley, Chick Corea, Mike Gibbs, Keith Jarrett, and Steve Swallow. Among his sidemen have been Larry Coryell, Swallow (through the 1980s), Roy Haynes, Pat Metheny, and John Scofield. The group's albums include *Duster* (1967) and *Ring* (1974). Burton also recorded with Stephane Grappelli (1969). Beginning 1971 he regularly worked in a duo with Corea, recording albums including *Crystal Silence* (1972).

Burton, Stephen Douglas (b. Whittier, Calif., 24 Feb. 1943). Composer. Studied at Oberlin (1960–62) with Richard Hoffmann; at the Mozarteum in Salzburg (1962–64) with Hans Werner Henze. Music Director of Munich Kammerspiele, 1963–64. Received M.M. from Peabody Conservatory in 1974. Instructor at Catholic Univ. of America, 1970–74; then on the faculty of George Mason Univ. Wrote *Orchestration* (Englewood Cliffs, N.J., 1982). Compositions include the three-act opera *Duchess of Malfi* (1975) and several one-act operas (*Americana,* 1975; *Dr. Heidegger's Experiment,* 1988).

Busch, Adolf (Georg Wilhelm) (b. Siegen, Westphalia, 8 Aug. 1891; d. Guilford, Vt., 9 June 1952). Violinist, composer, conductor. Brother of Fritz Busch, he studied violin with Willy Hess and Bram Eldering at the Cologne Conservatory. Max Reger, whom he joined in the presentation of chamber music, was from 1907 an important influence in the shaping of his musical character. In 1911 he became concertmaster of Vienna's Konzertverein Orchestra. Within a year of becoming professor of violin at Berlin's Musikhochschule in 1918, he founded the Busch Quartet, one of the preeminent chamber ensembles of its day. When in 1933 the Nazis forbade his concertizing with Rudolf Serkin, a Jew, he moved to Switzerland, then to London, where he founded a chamber orchestra to play 18th-century music and from where he continued to tour widely. In 1939 he moved to the U.S. He established the Marlboro Festival in 1950. He composed symphonic works, concertos, chamber music, and songs.

Busch, Fritz (b. Siegen, Westphalia, 13 Mar. 1890; d. London, 14 Sept. 1951). Conductor and pianist. A child prodigy on the piano, he gave his first concert in 1897. In 1906 entered the Cologne Conservatory, studying conducting with Fritz Steinbach. In 1909 he became conductor at Riga's Deutsches Theater. In 1911–12 Busch toured as a pianist; then served as music director at Aachen until joining the army in 1914. In 1918 became music director of the Stuttgart Opera and in 1922 succeeded Fritz Reiner as general music director of the Dresden Opera. In that capacity he led many first performances, including works by Busoni (1925) and Richard Strauss (1924, 1928, 1933). His opposition to Hitler led to his dismissal, after which he divided his year between Copenhagen, where he frequently led the Danish State Radio Symphony (from 1934); Buenos Aires, where he was associated with the Teatro Colón (1934–36; 1940–47); and Sussex, where he was the first music director of the Glyndebourne Opera (1934–39). He also found time to conduct the Stockholm Philharmonic Orchestra (1937–40). When Germany invaded Denmark and Norway, he went to Buenos Aires. After the war he conducted New York's Metropolitan Opera (1945–49) and the Chicago Symphony (1948–50); he also resumed his work in Copenhagen and Stockholm (1949–51) and Glyndebourne (1950–51).

Bush, Alan (Dudley) (b. Dulwich, South London, 22 Dec. 1900; d. Watford, England, 31 Oct. 1995). Composer. At the Royal Academy of Music he studied composition with Corder (1918–22). Later he took private piano from Artur Schnabel and composition from Ireland (1921–27). In Berlin he studied musicology (1929–31). Beginning in 1925 taught composition at the Royal Academy, and in 1938 was elected fellow of the Academy. He founded the Worker's Music Association in 1936. During the 1950s and 1960s Bush received a number of commissions from East German opera houses and orchestras, including the operas *The Sugar Reapers* (1960–62) and *Joe Hill* (1966–68). His music is marked by a sophisticated but harmonically simple style, which, along with the subjects of his works, reflects his leftist political beliefs. Other works include orchestral music (2 symphonies, 1940, 1949; *Homage to William Sterndale Bennett,* 1946; *Piers Plowman's Day,* suite, 1947; Violin Concerto op. 32, 1948; *Dorian Passacaglia and Fugue,* 1959; *Variations on an English Seasong,* piano, orchestra, 1962; *Festival March of British Youth,* brass band, 1973); the opera *Wat Tyler* (1951); many choral and solo vocal works (*Winter Journey,* soloists, chorus, strings, 1946; *The Dream of Llewelyn ap Gruffydd,* male chorus, 1950; *The Ballad of Freedom's Soldier,* cantata, 1953; *Byron Symphony* op. 53, baritone, chorus, orchestra, 1959–60; *The Tide That Will Never Turn,* speakers, chorus, orchestra, 1961; *Song for Angela Davis,* chorus, 1972); numerous chamber and instrumental works (*Suite of 6,* string quartet, 1975).

Busnois [de Busne], **Antoine** (b. probably Busnes, ca. 1430; d. Bruges, before 6 Nov. 1492). Composer. Texts of some works suggest a connection with Paris in the early part of his life. Before 1467 he was in the service of Charles the Bold. Shortly after Charles became Duke of Burgundy (in 1467), Busnois joined his chapel at Dijon. In 1477 Charles died, and his daughter Mary of Burgundy took Busnois into her chapel, where he remained until her death in 1482. Little is known about what he did thereafter. His contemporaries considered him second only to Ockeghem as a composer. Among those to give special notice to his accomplishments were Tinctoris, Compère, Jean Molinet, and Pietro Aaron.

His sacred compositions comprise 2 complete Masses and about a dozen other works of various types (most for 4 voices). More prominent are his more than 60 chansons. Most are for 3, some for 4 voices; all but 3 pieces have French texts or incipits. They are for the most part in the *formes fixes,* especially the rondeau and the bergerette; some are probably settings of poems by the composer. This music survives in many chansonniers of the late 15th century and in a few prints by Petrucci.

Bibl.: *Trois chansonniers français du XVe siècle,* ed. Eugenie Droz, Yvonne Rokseth, and Genviève Thibault (Paris, 1927). *Der Kopenhagener Chansonnier,* ed. Knud Jeppesen (Copenhagen, 1927; 2nd ed., 1965). *Les musiciens de la cour de Bourgogne au XVe siècle,* ed. Jean Marix (Paris, 1937). Catherine Brooks, "Antoine Busnois, Chanson Composer," *JAMS* 6 (1953): 111.

Busoni, Ferruccio (Dante Michelangiolo Benvenuto) (b. Empoli, near Florence, 1 Apr. 1866; d. Berlin, 27 July 1924). Composer, pianist, writer on music. The son of musicians, he studied piano and began to perform and compose as a young child; he grew up primarily in Austria, and studied composition with Wilhelm Mayer (who composed under the pseudonym A. Remy) for a year or two from 1879; in 1881 he was admitted to the Accademia filarmonica in Bologna; his oratorio *Il sabato del villaggio* was performed there in 1883. Between that time and 1894, when he settled in Berlin, Busoni lived in Vienna, Leipzig, Helsinki, Moscow, Boston, and New York, pursuing his career as a virtuoso pianist and teaching. Except during World War I, when he lived in Switzerland, Berlin remained his home for the rest of his life. In 1913 he made one attempt to return to Italy, as director of the Liceo musicale in Bologna, but it was short-lived.

Busoni's early compositions reflect his familiarity with the music of Bach, Mendelssohn, and Schumann. In 1908 he repudiated some of his youthful works, claiming that he had "first found his way as a composer" in the Second Violin Sonata (1898). Indeed, around the turn of the century he had become interested in the works of such innovatory composers as Schoenberg, Bartók, and Varèse. He pointed especially to the *Elegien* for piano (1907) as an expression of his personal vision of the nature and direction of music. He developed his view of a universal music in the concept of the Young Classicality, by which he meant "the mastering, sifting, and exploitation of all the achievements of preceding experiments" (1920). His arrangements and transcriptions of the music of Bach and others should probably be seen as a part of this quest for perfection in absolute music, in which the piano was a major tool with which to build on past accomplishments. In addition, his commitment to transcription must have been influenced by his admiration of Liszt as composer, transcriber, and virtuoso.

In his compositions Busoni never made as radical a break with the past as did Schoenberg. Yet in *Outline of a New Aesthetic* (1907) and later writings he discussed a whole series of innovatory ideas: microtones, new scales and a new style of polyphony, new machines and instruments, the abolition of consonance and dissonance, and a new system of notation for keyboard. Work on his opera *Doktor Faustus,* in which he hoped to bring to fruition his ideas about the universal music, was frustrated by the war and by his declining health. But his influence on the development of 20th-century music can perhaps be measured by the effect he had on Varèse, who had been in attendance when Schoenberg conducted a private performance of *Pierrot Lunaire* in Busoni's Berlin apartment (1913). About Busoni, Varèse said: "Personally, I know that he crystallized my half-formed ideas, stimulated my imagination, and determined, I believe, the future development of my music."

Works: 5 operas (*Doktor Faust,* 1916–24, completed by Jarnach) and incidental music to Gozzi's *Turandot* (orchestral suite, 1904; the basis of his opera of 1917); violin and piano concertos (*Konzertstück,* 1890), suites, fantasies, *Divertimento* (flute and orchestra, 1920), and other orchestral music; some chamber music, mainly for strings; many works for piano (*Elegien,* 1907; *An die Jugend,* 1909; *Fantasia contrappuntistica,* 4 versions, 1910–22; *Indianisches Tagebuch,* 1915; 6 sonatinas, 1910–20); a few pieces for voice(s) and orchestra; songs; arrangements and editions of works by Bach (*Bach-Busoni gesammelte Ausgabe,* Leipzig, 1920), Beethoven, Brahms, Chopin, and others.

Writings: *Entwurf einer neuen Ästhetik der Tonkunst* (Trieste, 1907); trans. Eng. (1911), reprinted in *Three Classics in the Aesthetic of Music* (New York, 1962). *Gesammelte Aufsätze: von der Einheit der Musik* (Berlin, 1922); trans. Rosamond Ley in *The Essence of Music and Other Papers* (New York, 1957). *Scritti e pensieri sulla musica,* ed. Luigi Dallapiccola and Guido M. Gatti (Florence, 1941).

Bibl.: Edward J. Dent, *Ferruccio Busoni* (London, 1933; 2nd ed., 1974) [includes works list]. H. H. Stuckenschmidt, *Ferruccio Busoni: Chronicle of a European,* trans. Sandra Morris (London, 1970). Jürgen Kindermann, *Thematisch-Chronologisches Verzeichnis der musikalischen Werke von Ferruccio Busoni* (Regensburg, 1980). Antony Beaumont, *Busoni the Composer* (Bloomington, Ind., 1985). Marc-André Roberge, *Ferruccio Busoni: A Bio-Bibliography* (New York, 1991).

Büsser [Busser], **(Paul-) Henri** (b. Toulouse, 16 Jan. 1872; d. Paris, 30 Dec. 1973). Composer, conductor, organist, and writer. The son of an organist, he was trained as a choirboy; lived in Paris from 1885, studying first at the School of Religious Music and then at the Conservatory with Franck, Widor (organ), and Guiraud (composition). In 1892 he was appointed organist at St. Cloud, near Paris; and in 1893 he won the Prix de Rome. After his return to Paris he was active as a conductor of theater orchestras and was appointed conductor at the Opéra in 1905. From 1904 he taught vocal ensembles at the Conservatory, where he was appointed professor of composition in 1931; in 1938 he was elected to the Académie française. He composed prolifically in the French 19th-century tradition, but was also influenced by Debussy, several of whose works he orchestrated. Works include some 10 ballets and operas (*Colomba,* 1921; *Les noces corinthiennes,* 1922); orchestral music; chamber music; piano and organ works (*Marche de fête,* orchestrated 1910); Masses, motets, a Magnificat, and secular choral music; songs; orchestral arrangements of works of Bizet and Rameau. His writings include the volume *Gounod* (Lyons, 1961).

Bussotti, Sylvano (b. Florence, 1 Oct. 1931). Composer. He studied violin from the age of 5; at the Florence Conservatory from 1940 he studied violin, harmony, and piano; his interest in composition was pursued independently (1949–56) and was influenced from the start by his contacts among the Italian avant-garde outside music, especially through his brother and an uncle, both painters. In 1957 he had lessons with Deutsch in Paris; the next year he met Cage in Darmstadt; in 1964–65 he was in the U.S.; in 1972 in Berlin. His first important contribution to contemporary music was the exhibition he organized with Chiari, *Musica e segno* (1962), which toured in Europe and the U.S. From 1971 to 1974 was professor of the history of music drama at L'Aquila Academy of Fine Arts; in 1975 became artistic director of the Teatro La Fenice, Venice. Some early works were serial (*Nottetempo con lo scherzo e una rosa,* voice and chamber orchestra, 1954–57), but *Pièces de chair II* (1958–60; some published as *5 Pieces for David Tudor,* 1959) marks a turn to aleatoric composition, new vocal techniques, and graphic scores. From 1965 was involved with theater, in which he became increasingly responsible not only for music but also for sets, direction, choreography, and costumes in a genre he calls "Bussottioperaballet"; works include *La passion selon Sade* (1965), *Nottetempo* (1976), *Le Racine* (1980; reworked as *Fedra,* 1988), *L'ispirazione* (1988). Orchestral works include *Il catalogo è questo* (1980) and *Timpani* (1987).

Butler, Martin Claines (b. Romsey, Hampshire, 1 Mar. 1960). Composer. Received Mus.B. from Manchester Univ., 1981; attended Royal Northern College of Music, 1978–82; received an M.F.A. from Princeton Univ., 1985; studied at Tanglewood, 1982. Compositions include *Flights of Col* (orchestra, 1983) and *The Siren's Song* (1986).

Butterley, Nigel (Henry) (b. Sydney, 13 May 1935). Composer. He began his musical career as a choirboy in Sydney; from 1952 he studied composition with Noel Nickson and Raymond Hanson at the New South Wales Conservatory. From 1962 he took private composition lessons in London with Priaulx Rainer. Received the Italia Prize in 1966 for *In the Head the Fire,* an oratorio-like work for radio, employing aleatory, tape tracks, and various mystical and religious texts. Also composed ballets (*The Tell-Tale Heart,* 1961); orchestral works (*Canticle of David,* strings, 1959; *Meditations of Thomas Traherne,* 1968; *The Four Elements,* 1971, rev. 1974; a symphony, 1980); chamber and instrumental works (*Sonorities,* carillon, 1968; 3

string quartets, 1965, 1975, 1979; *Watershore,* narrators, chamber ensemble, 1977); vocal works (*Psalm C,* 1961; *Missa Sancti Albani,* chorus, 1961); piano works (*Letter from Hardy's Bay,* 1971).

Butterworth, George (Sainton Kaye) (b. London, 12 July 1885; d. Pozières, 5 Aug. 1916). Composer. He studied organ at Yorkshire and piano at Eton. At Oxford he intended to prepare for a career in law, but soon his musical interests won out: he began writing music criticism for the London *Times* and later attended the Royal College of Music. Around 1910 he befriended Vaughan Williams, whose lost *London Symphony* he helped reconstruct and see through to performance. Upon enlisting in World War I, he destroyed many of his works that he deemed inferior; he died in battle. English folk song—and especially the dances of Oxfordshire and Sussex—played an important role in his music. Many of the melodies he gathered from those regions he employed in a texture of lyrical, late Romantic harmony. Among his works are orchestral pieces (*Cherry Tree,* 1912; *A Shropshire Lad,* rhapsody, 1912; *The Banks of Green Willow,* idyll, 1913–14); vocal music (*Love Blows as the Wind Blows,* baritone, string quartet, 1914); arrangements (*Folk Song from Sussex,* 1912).

Butting, Max (b. Berlin, 6 Oct. 1888; d. there, 13 July 1976). Composer. From 1908 he studied in Munich at the Akademie der Tonkunst and had private composition lessons with Courvoisier. In 1919 he joined his father's firm in Berlin, but also wrote articles on opera, jazz, film music, and Berg for the *Sozialistische Monatshefte.* He was active as well in broadcasting in the 1920s; in 1933 he began to teach composition for radio plays in Berlin; belonged to the Prussian Academy of Fine Arts from 1933, and was until that same year president of the German section of ISCM. During the war he again worked in his father's business, but later became an adviser to the state broadcasting committee of the German Democratic Republic and a founding member of the German Academy of Arts. In his compositional style he was influenced especially by Reger; he wrote elaborate counterpoint and often derived an entire work from a small motivic core. Works include an opera; 10 symphonies and other orchestral music; chamber music, including pieces he called Schul- or Hausmusik (e.g., for 2 recorders and guitar, op. 75, 1950); a few piano works; some 10 large choral works with orchestra; other choral music and a few songs.

Buus, Jacques (b. Ghent? ca. 1500; d. Vienna, between 18 Aug. and 1 Sept. 1565). Composer. He may have begun his career in France and certainly maintained French connections throughout his life. In 1541 he became an organist of St. Mark's, Venice. In 1550 he entered the imperial chapel in Vienna, where he remained until his death. He composed motets, chansons (especially Protestant *chansons spirituelles*), and ricercars.

Bibl.: Howard M. Brown, "The *Chanson spirituelle,* Jacques Buus, and Parody Technique," *JAMS* 15 (1962): 145. Walter Breitner, *Jacob Buus als Motettenkomponist* (Tutzing, 1977).

Buxtehude, Dietrich (b. Helsingborg, Denmark, ca. 1637; d. Lübeck, 9 May 1707). Composer and organist. Details of his early life are uncertain; his first music instructor was probably his father, the organist Johannes Buxtehude (1602–74). Dietrich presumably attended the Lateinschule at Helsingør, where the family lived from about 1641. In 1657 or 1658 he assumed his first post, as organist at Helsingborg; in 1660 he was back in Helsingør as organist for the Marienkirche. When Franz Tunder died in 1667, Buxtehude auditioned for and gained the prestigious post at the Marienkirche in Lübeck. He was appointed in 1668, serving also as *Werkmeister,* a sort of overseer of church musical activities; he remained there for the rest of his life. The *Abendmusik* concerts he gave in Lübeck were famous throughout northern Germany; the young J. S. Bach made a lengthy musical sojourn to Lübeck in 1705–6, doubtless to hear some of these concerts and to make the elder composer's acquaintance. Among Buxtehude's compositions listed in Karstädt's catalogue (abbreviated BuxWV) are 114 sacred vocal works (including cantatas and motets: *Accedite gentes, accurite populi* BuxWV 1; *Erfreue dich, Erde!* BuxWV 26; *Heut triumphieret Gottes Sohn* BuxWV 43; *Ist es recht* BuxWV 54; *Jesu meine Freud und Lust* BuxWV 59; *Jesu, meines Lebens Leben* BuxWV 62; *Membra Jesu nostri* BuxWV 75; *O Gott, wir danken deiner Güt'* BuxWV 86; *Benedicam Dominum,* 6 choirs, BuxWV 113); 10 secular vocal works; 89 organ works including toccatas and fugues, preludes and fugues (Prelude, Fugue, and Chaconne in C BuxWV 137), canzonettas, many chorale preludes ("Ach Herr, mich armen Sünder," Phrygian mode, BuxWV 178; "Ich ruf zu dir, Herr Jesu Christ" BuxWV 196; 2 on "Nun bitten wir den heiligen Geist" BuxWV 208 and 209); also 19 keyboard suites, and chamber works, including trio sonatas opp. 1 and 2. The *Magnificat* BuxWV suppl. 1 (publ. Kassel, 1931, ed. B. Grusnick) is probably not authentic.

Bibl.: *Dietrich Buxtehudes Werke* [vocal works], vols. 1–8, ed. Wilibald Gurlitt (Klecken, Ugrino, Hamburg, 1925–58; R: New York, 1977), vols. 9ff., ed. Kerala J. Snyder (New York, 1987–). *Abendmusiken und Kirchenkantaten,* ed. Max Seiffert, *DDT* 14 (1903; 2nd rev. ed., 1957). *Sonaten für Violine, Gambe und Cembalo,* ed. C. Stiehl, *DDT* 11 (1903; 2nd rev. ed., 1957). *Sämtliche Orgelwerke,* ed. G. Beckmann (Wiesbaden, 1972). Søren Sørensen, *Das Buxtehudebild im Wandel der Zeit* (Lübeck, 1972). Georg Karstädt, ed., *Thematisch-systematisches Verzeichnis der musikalischen Werke von Dietrich Buxtehude: Buxtehude-Werke-Verzeichnis* [BuxWV] (Wiesbaden, 1974; 2nd enl. ed., 1985). Kerala J. Snyder, *Dietrich Buxtehude* (New York, 1987). Hermann Wettstein, *Dietrich Buxtehude (1637–1707): Bibliographie zu seinem Leben und Werk* (Munich, 1989); trans. Eng. (New York, 1989).

Byard, Jaki (John Anthony, Jr.) (b. Worcester, Mass., 15 June 1922). Jazz pianist, saxophonist, bandleader. Born into a musical family, he learned piano and trumpet as a child and later trombone, tenor sax, guitar, and drums. An eclectic stylist noted for versatility and humor, he worked widely as a solo pianist, as sideman with Earl Bostic (pianist, 1949–50), Herb Pomeroy (tenor sax soloist, 1955–57), Maynard Ferguson (pianist, 1962–64 and 1968–70), and with several innovative groups of the 1960s. Beginning in the late 1960s he taught at the New England Conservatory, the Hartt School, and elsewhere. In the late 1970s he formed two big bands in Boston and New York, both named the Apollo Stompers.

Byas, Don [Carlos Wesley] (b. Muskogee, Okla., 21 Oct. 1912; d. Amsterdam, 24 Aug. 1972). Jazz tenor saxophonist. He played alto saxophone in the big bands of Bennie Moten and Walter Page. After switching to the tenor he joined Lionel Hampton (1935), Eddie Barefield, Buck Clayton (1936), Don Redman, Lucky Millinder, Andy Kirk (1939–40), Edgar Hayes, Benny Carter (1940), and Count Basie (1941–43). In New York he began to play with small groups, as a leader and as a sideman with Dizzy Gillespie and Coleman Hawkins; the recording "I Got Rhythm," a duo with Slam Stewart (1945), combines the dexterity of boplike lines with a sound modeled after Hawkins's style. With Redman's band he traveled to Europe in 1946, settling in France, and later in the Netherlands and Denmark. He toured widely and recorded regularly as a soloist in Europe, making the album *Don Byas Meets Ben Webster* in 1968.

Byrd, Donald(son Toussaint L'Ouverture, II) (b. Detroit, 9 Dec. 1932). Jazz trumpeter. After graduating from Wayne State Univ. (B.M., 1954) he studied at the Manhattan School of Music (M.A., music education), during which time he joined Art Blakey (1955) and recorded with many other hard bop groups, playing with John Coltrane on Red Garland's album *All Mornin' Long* (1957). With Pepper Adams he led a quintet (1958–61). After studying composition in Europe (1962–63), he taught at colleges and universities and continued working as a leader, turning to African American dance music upon the success of his album *Black Byrd* (recorded ca. 1972). He earned a law degree (1976) and a doctorate in education (1982).

Byrd, William (b. Lincoln?, 1543; d. Stondon Massey, Essex, 4 July 1623). Composer. A prolific and versatile master of virtually all genres cultivated in England in his time, he enriched English music by incorporating Netherlandish polyphony without diluting specifically English stylistic characteristics. Throughout a difficult era he remained in favor with the (Anglican) royal court, composing both occasional music and music for Protestant worship while also providing music for the liturgy of his own Roman Catholic faith.

Raised in London and taught by Tallis, Byrd was

William Byrd.

first employed, from 1563, as organist and Master of the Choristers at Lincoln Cathedral. In 1570 he became a Gentleman of the Chapel Royal in London, a post that soon included duties as joint organist with Tallis. Some connection with Lincoln continued until 1581; specifically, he was paid to provide compositions for the cathedral from time to time. His activities in London were wide-ranging, including not only composition, performance, and teaching but also publishing and marketing of music and music paper. In 1593 he moved to Stondon Massey, Essex, continuing to compose and to publish, but with an increasingly open bias toward the (outlawed) Catholic church. Ties with London were never completely severed; his death is noted in the Cheque Book of the Chapel Royal, along with a note indicating his unexcelled reputation among his contemporaries as a composer.

Byrd undoubtedly began composing in his teens, but the outlines of his life's work first manifested themselves at Lincoln Cathedral. During these years he produced compositions in a wide variety of genres and for many performance mediums. Inspiration and sometimes specific materials were drawn from pieces by a number of earlier composers, mostly English. This era saw the production of most of his English liturgical music, likely written to fill practical needs at the cathedral; some organ music; some Latin (but not indisputably Catholic) motets; much consort music, including a number of *In nomines* and consort songs; and the beginnings of what would eventually be a large and distinguished body of music for virginals (nearly 100 pieces by the end of his life).

In London after 1570 Byrd produced more songs and consort music, a quantity of virginal music (including the beginnings of his particularly fine series of pavanes and galliards), and additional Latin motets. The earliest of these motets, all with texts that can be construed as suitable for either Anglican or Catholic worship, reveal an understanding of Netherlandish polyphony achieved by no previous English composer. Byrd probably gained his knowledge of this style from Alfonso Ferrabosco, who was at the royal court of England intermittently from 1563 to 1578.

After 1580, still in London, Byrd wrote Latin motets at a greatly increased rate. Although the texts include nothing clearly unacceptable to the Anglican church, they often contain veiled references to the plight of English Catholics. Continuing in favor at the royal court despite his religious sympathies, Byrd provided occasional pieces for Queen Elizabeth as well as remaining active in the Chapel Royal. He also produced a number of consort songs; polyphonic songs; carols; at least one major verse anthem (a genre evidently developed by Byrd from the consort song); and more music for virginals, collected in My Ladye Nevells Booke, which contains both newly written pieces and some much older works.

After moving to Stondon Massey in 1593, Byrd turned his attention to writing Catholic liturgical music for practical use. Simpler, more concise, and less personal expression became the rule. The sacred works of this period include 3 settings of the Mass Ordinary and the *Gradualia,* 2 books of settings of the Propers of the Mass for all major feasts, Marian feasts, and Marian votive masses. Byrd also continued to write consort and polyphonic songs (both sacred and secular, eventually numbering almost 200), full and verse anthems, consort pieces for instruments alone, and keyboard music (mostly pavanes and galliards).

In 1575, having been granted jointly with Tallis a royal patent on publishing part music, Byrd issued a book of Latin motets dedicated to Queen Elizabeth. By 1587 he held the patent alone, Tallis having died, and he became much more active as a publisher. During the next years, even after the patent expired in 1596, he issued several books of English songs, 2 books of Latin motets, his 3 Masses, and the 2 books of *Gradualia.* He also contributed pieces to several other printed or manuscript books, including Watson's *First Sett of Italian Madrigals Englished* (1590), My Ladye Nevells Booke (1591), the Fitzwilliam Virginal Book (1609–19), *Parthenia* (ca. 1612–13), and Leighton's *Tears or Lamentations of a Sorrowful Soul* (1614). Many pieces circulated in manuscript only; some he printed, often with revisions, after manuscript copies had circulated for a number of years.

Bibl.: William Byrd, *The Collected Works,* ed. Edmund H. Fellows (London, 1937–50; rev. 1962–71). *The Byrd Edition,* ed. Philip Brett (London, 1971–). Edmund H. Fellowes, *William Byrd* (London, 1936; 2nd ed., 1948). J. L. Jackman, "Liturgical Aspects of Byrd's *Gradualia,*" *MQ* 49 (1963): 17. H. K. Andrews, *The Technique of Byrd's Vocal Polyphony* (London, 1966). Oliver W. Neighbour, *The Consort and Keyboard Music of William Byrd* (Los Angeles, 1981). Joseph Kerman, *The Masses and Motets of William Byrd* (Berkeley, 1981). Craig Monson, "Authenticity and Chronology in Byrd's Church Anthems," *JAMS* 35 (1982): 280–305. Richard Turbet, *William Byrd: A Guide to Research* (New York, 1987). Alan Brown and Richard Turbet, eds., *Byrd Studies* (New York, 1992).

Byrne, David (b. Dumbarton, Scotland, 14 May 1952). Rock songwriter, singer, and guitarist. In 1974 he formed the Talking Heads with Tina Weymouth and Chris Frantz (Jerry Harrison joined in 1975). Their albums feature his eclectic songwriting, which draws on elements of American minimalism, African polyrhythm (*Remain in Light,* 1980) and country music (*Little Creatures,* 1985). He coproduced their concert film *Stop Making Sense* (1984) and has written for dance (*The Catherine Wheel,* for choreographer Twyla Tharp, 1981) and the stage (for Robert Wilson's *The Knee Plays,* 1984).

C

Caamaño, Roberto (b. Buenos Aires, 7 July 1923). Composer and pianist. Studied piano and composition at the National Conservatory in Buenos Aires; as a concert pianist he toured Latin America and the U.S. In 1955 he became professor of composition and liturgical music at the Catholic Univ., and in 1956 was appointed to the faculty of the Buenos Aires Conservatory. Served as artistic director of the Teatro Colón, 1960–64, and became president of the Argentine Music Council, 1969. Works include orchestral music (*Preludio, Adagio y Fuga,* 1951; *Variaciones americanas,* 1953; a concerto for bandoneon, 1954; *Tripartita,* wind band, 1967); choral music (Magnificat, 1954; *Cantata para la paz,* 1966; *Fábulas,* 1970); chamber music (2 string quartets, 1945, 1946; *5 piezas breves,* string quartet, 1955); songs; piano pieces.

Caballé, Montserrat (b. Barcelona, 12 Apr. 1933). Soprano. From 1942 studied with Napoleone Annovazzi, Eugenie Keminy, and Conchita Badía at Barcelona's Conservatorio del Liceo; won the conservatory's gold medal, 1954. Joined the Basel Opera in 1956, where she made her professional operatic debut as Puccini's Mimi. By the time she moved to the Bremen Opera, 1960–61, she was specializing in bel canto roles. At her U.S. debut with the American Opera Society (20 Apr. 1965) she replaced Marilyn Horne at short notice in Donizetti's *Lucrezia Borgia.* Her success led to engagements the same year at Glyndebourne and the Met (22 December, singing Gounod's Marguerite). In 1972 she was first heard at La Scala (as Bellini's Norma) and Covent Garden (as Verdi's Violetta). Caballé is noted less for her dramatic instincts than for her vocal shadings and melting pianissimos.

Cabanilles [Cavanilles], **Juan Bautista José** [Juan Bautista Josep] (b. Algemesí, near Valencia, 4 Sept. 1644; d. Valencia, 29 Apr. 1712). Composer and organist. He probably began as a chorister at his local church; later he moved to Valencia, where he became second organist in 1665 and first organist the following year. In 1668 he was ordained to the priesthood. His works include sacred vocal works (a 6-voice Mass, a Magnificat, a *Beatus vir,* motets in Spanish) and many organ works, especially *tientos.*

Bibl.: *J. B. Cabanilles: Opera omnia I–IV,* ed. Higini Anglès (Barcelona, 1927–52). *Cabanilles: Obras vocales,* ed. José Climent (Valencia, 1971). Arsenio García Ferreras, *Juan Bautista Cabanilles: Sein Leben und sein Werk (Die Tientos für Orgel)* (Regensburg, 1973). José Climent, "Juan Cabanilles: Puntualizaciones biográficas," *Revista de musicología* 6 (1983): 213–22.

Cabezón [Cabeçón], **Antonio de** (b. Castrillo de Matajudíos, near Burgos, 1510; d. Madrid, 26 Mar. 1566). Composer and organist. Blind from infancy, he was taught music first by local organists, then by the cathedral organist in Palencia. In 1526 he was appointed organist to Queen Isabella. After her death in 1539 he worked for her children, especially Prince Philip, who later became King Philip II and was from 1548 Cabezón's sole employer. He traveled widely in Europe (including England) with the king in the years 1548–56 but settled in Madrid when it became the home of the Spanish royal court, remaining there until his death. His numerous compositions for organ and stringed keyboard instruments include *glosas* (intabulations of polyphonic works by other composers, usually not Spanish, reconceived as keyboard pieces), *diferencias* (variation sets, in which he was a pioneer, most based on melodies from Spanish *cancioneros* and on dances), entirely original *tientos,* and various liturgical pieces such as hymns. Some works were included in Luis Venegas de Henestrosa's *Libro de cifra nueva* (Alcalá de Henares, 1557; ed. in *MME* 2, 1944, 2nd ed., 1965); most were first printed by his son Hernando de Cabezón in *Obras de música para tecla, arpa y vihuela de Antonio de Cabezón* (Madrid, 1578; ed. in *MME* 27–29, 1966). The latter book also includes a general presentation of the composer's teachings on keyboard playing; the discussion of fingering is particularly notable for the progressiveness of the ideas set forth. Only one vocal work, a piece for 5 voices, is known.

Bibl.: Antonio de Cabezón, *Collected Works* (Brooklyn, 1967–). *AnM* 21 (1966) [Cabezón issue]. Macario Santiago Kastner, *Antonio und Hernando de Cabezón: Eine Chronik* (Tutzing, 1977). Id., "Sobre las diferencias de Antonio de Cabezón contenidas en las 'Obras' de 1578," *Revista de musicología* 4 (1981): 213–36.

Caccini, Francesca ["La Cecchina"] (b. Florence, 18 Sept. 1587; d. there? after 1637). Singer and composer. The daughter of Giulio Caccini, she sang as early as 1600 at the wedding of King Henry IV and Maria de' Medici. In 1607 she was officially appointed to the service of the Medicis, chiefly as singer, though she also played harpsichord, wrote poetry, and composed. She wrote the music for the entertainment *Il ballo delle zigane* (1615) and composed the opera *La liberazione di Ruggiero* (1625). *Il primo libro delle musiche* (Florence, 1618), her collection of solo songs, contains early examples of virtuosic vocal ornamentation and figuration.

Bibl.: Carolyn Raney, "Francesca Caccini, Musician to the Medici, and Her *Primo Libro* (1618)" (diss., New York Univ., 1970).

Caccini, Giulio (b. probably Tivoli, 8 Oct. 1551; d. Florence, buried 10 Dec. 1618). Composer and singer. After instruction with Giovanni Animuccia in Rome, he studied with Scipione delle Palle in Florence, under Medici patronage. By 1579 he was singing at the Medici court. His earliest known compositional endeavor came in 1589, when he contributed a song to an *intermedio* for the marriage of Duke Ferdinand I. Initially his fame spread chiefly through his singing: by the 1580s he was singing regularly for Ippolito Aldobrandini in Ferrara and for the Este court there. During the 1570s and 1580s he began a celebrated association with the "camerata" of Florence, and partly under the influence of its members—including Vincenzo Galilei and Bardi—he began composing in a vocal style that, as he declared, more closely approximated speech. After a brief appointment in Rome as Bardi's secretary (1592), Caccini returned to Florence; during the 1590s he served the Medici court, where he became music director in 1600. That year he discussed his new vocal style in the preface (trans. in *SR,* pp. 370–72) to his opera *Euridice.*

In 1602 (1601 old style) Caccini published the epoch-making *Le nuove musiche,* a collection of solo songs with basso continuo; its preface (trans. in *SR,* pp. 377–92) discusses the monodic style in detail, describing the proper way to ornament a song and warning against abuse. The pieces themselves manifest the relatively new practice of writing out implicit embellishments. Beginning about 1610 Caccini frequently took part in chamber concerts for Grand Duke Ferdinando de' Medici; 1610 was also the year in which he was made director of sacred music at S. Nicola.

Works: *Io che dal ciel cader farei la luna* (*intermedio,* first performed Florence, 1589); portions of the opera *Euridice,* largely by Jacopo Peri (libretto by Ottavio Rinuccini; performed Florence, 6 Oct. 1600; publ. Florence, 1600 o.s./1601 n.s.; facs., Rome, 1934); the arias and 2 choruses for the opera *Il rapimento di Cefalo* (libretto by Gabriello Chiabrera; performed Florence, 9 Oct. 1600; some arias published in *Le nuove musiche*); the opera *Euridice* (libretto by Rinuccini; publ. Florence, Dec., 1600, before Peri's work; first performed Florence, 1602; R: Bologna, 1968); 2 collections of accompanied monodies: *Le nuove musiche* (Florence, 1601 o.s./1602 n.s.; facs., Rome, 1934; ed. in *RRMBE* 9, 1970) and *Nuove musiche e nuova maniera di scriverle* (Florence, 1614; ed. in *RRMBE* 28, 1978)

Bibl.: Nino Pirrotta, "Early Opera and Aria," *Grout* (1968): 39–107. H. Wiley Hitchcock, "Vocal Ornamentation in Caccini's *Nove Musiche,*" *MQ* 56 (1970): 389–404. Id., "Caccini's 'Other' *Nuove Musiche,*" *JAMS* 27 (1974): 438–60.

Cadéac, Pierre (b. Cadéac, Gascony?; fl. 1538–56). Composer. Master of the choirboys in Auch in the 1550s. Surviving works, some of which were known as far away as Madrid and Kraków, include 7 Masses, over 30 motets, and other liturgical pieces, most published by Parisian printers; 10 chansons in the "Parisian" style (most published in Paris and Lyons, 1538–41; "Je suis desheritée" was the most widely known and was often the basis of sacred and secular parody works).

Cadman, Charles Wakefield (b. Johnstown, Pa., 24 Dec. 1881; d. Los Angeles, 30 Dec. 1946). Composer. Studied music from the age of 13 (organ, piano, theory, conducting) and was a church organist and accompanist in his 20s in Pittsburgh; critic for the *Pittsburgh Daily Dispatch* (1908–10). An interest in American Indian music and culture led to very popular arrangements of American Indian songs ("From the Land of Sky Blue Water," 1909), visits with various tribes and recordings of their music, and lecture-recitals in the U.S. and Europe with the Indian mezzo-soprano Tsianina Redfeather (1913–23). Although he was best known for his parlor songs ("At Dawning," 1906), he also composed 12 stage works (*Shanewis, or the Robin Woman,* 1918); orchestral works (*Dark Dancers of the Mardi Gras,* 1933); chamber music; and choral music in a conservative style reflecting both Indian and other American traditions.

Bibl.: N. C. Fielder, *Complete Musical Works of C. W. Cadman* [catalog] (Los Angeles, 1951).

Cafaro, Pasquale (b. S. Pietro, near Lecce, 8 Feb. 1716; d. Naples, 25 Oct. 1787). Composer. He studied with Leonardo Leo and with Nicola and Lorenzo Fago at the Naples Conservatory from 1735. In 1745 his oratorio *Il figliuol prodigo ravveduto* was performed in Naples, where he remained for the rest of his life. In 1759 he became *secondo maestro* at the conservatory, and in 1771 he succeeded Giuseppe de Majo as *maestro di cappella* of the royal chapel, after which he composed only sacred music. A 4-voice Stabat Mater from 1784 (publ. 1785) became well known outside of Italy. His operas include settings of Metastasio's librettos *Ipermestra* (1751), *Olimpiade* (1769), and *Antigono* (1770). He also composed oratorios; cantatas; Masses, motets, and other liturgical music.

Caffarelli [Majorano, Gaetano] (b. Bitonto, 12 Apr. 1710; d. Naples, 31 Jan. 1783). Mezzo-soprano castrato singer. He derived his stage name apparently from Domenico Cafarelli, who funded his education and was perhaps also his first teacher. He studied in Naples with Porpora during the early 1720s; in 1726 he made his debut at Rome in Domenico Sarro's *Valdemaro.* His fame spread rapidly throughout Italy during the 1730s; in addition he sang at the King's Theatre, London (1737–38), where he created the role of Handel's *Serse,* and at Madrid (1739), Vienna (1749), Versailles (1754), and Lisbon (1755). After 1756 he sang little, though in 1770 Burney heard him and praised his "expression and grace." He was notorious for his unpredictable behavior, both on and off stage.

Cage, John (b. Los Angeles, 5 Sept. 1912; d. New York, 12 Aug. 1992). Composer and writer on music.

John Cage, 1946.

Cage was one of the most important of contemporary American composers: his explorations of new sounds (e.g., the prepared piano), indeterminacy in composition and in performance, graphic notations, and live electronics and his innovative mixed-media events of the 1960s served as stimuli for like-minded composers. More traditional musicians and audiences, however, often reacted with indifference or hostility. He held few academic positions (Wesleyan Univ., 1960–61; Univ. of Cincinnati, 1967; Univ. of Illinois, 1967–69; Univ. of California at Davis, 1969; gave the Norton Lectures at Harvard, 1988–89), but his influence on contemporary composers (such as Feldman, Young, Cardew, Ichiyanagi, and Wolff) and more generally on musicians and audiences was a significant one, achieved both through his very numerous compositions and through his writings about music.

After graduating from high school, Cage attended Pomona College for two years, then visited Paris, Berlin, and Madrid for his own study of music, art, and architecture; in 1933 he was in New York, studying theory and attending Cowell's classes in non-Western, folk, and contemporary music; in California he studied counterpoint with Schoenberg (1934–35) and theory at UCLA; by 1938 he was in Seattle accompanying a dance group at the Cornish School, where he first met the dancer and choreographer Merce Cunningham, with whom he was often to collaborate. In Seattle he formed a percussion group and continued to compose in a chromatic style, making some use of serial procedures. *Imaginary Landscapes* no. 1 (1939) illustrates his concern with time as a structural unit (it consists of four sections of 3×5 measures separated by interludes) and with timbre (it is scored for two variable-speed turntables, frequency recordings, cymbal, and piano). By 1940 he was in San Francisco, where his first piece for prepared piano (*Bacchanale,* 1940) was occasioned by his need for percussive sounds from one instrument to accompany a dance; most of the dance music from this period employs the prepared piano and is cast in irregular structure appropriate to the choreography; other concert music of the 1940s employs strict rhythmic layouts to produce "nearly stationary" music (*Music for Marcel Duchamp,* prepared piano; *The Seasons,* ballet, both 1947) for which he saw Webern and Satie as models.

National recognition dated from a percussion concert at the Library of Congress in 1943; his Sonatas and Interludes for prepared piano was performed at Carnegie Hall in 1949; Guggenheim and National Institute of Arts and Letters Awards followed. Indeterminacy became important in the compositions of the 1950s, which include the well-known *4′ 33″* (tacet for any instrument or instruments, 1952) as well as *Imaginary Landscape* no. 5 (1952), the score for which is a set of instructions for producing a tape from fragments of recordings from any 42 records; in *Music for Piano* (1952–56) the *I Ching* determined the number of sounds per page, while imperfections in the paper dictated the particular placement of the notes on the staff. The *Concert for Piano and Orchestra* (1957–58), intended for David Tudor, is a compendium of the techniques of composition and graphic notations (including tracings of astronomical charts) that Cage had developed, but in addition implicates performer(s) in the compositional process (e.g., they choose the actual material to be played, draw lines, and define terms in their parts).

In the *Water Music* (1952) Tudor had been required to perform many actions away from the piano (e.g., pouring water from pots, using a radio); in the late 1950s and 1960s such theatrical and multimedia events became more frequent and were combined with indeterminacy. Thus, the performance instruction in *4′ 33″* no. 2 (solo for any player, 1962) is "In a situation provided with maximum amplification (no feedback), perform a disciplined action." In the 1970s Cage became interested in Thoreau (*Renga,* 1976, in which the notation consists of drawings by Thoreau) and in the transformation of literature into music (*Roaratorio, an Irish Circus on Finnegans Wake,* 1979; the score provides the means for translating any book into music; Cage's realization is an electronic piece built from sounds mentioned in the book). *Renga* may be performed together with *Apartment House 1776,* in which the *I Ching* dictates extracts from music of the American Revolution, with vocal interventions reflecting native and immigrant cultures.

Cage's works do not fit easily into traditional genres or categories. When he came closest to achieving his aim of creating a "musical composition the continuity of which is free of individual taste and memory (psychology) and also of the literature and tradition of the art," the response was not always positive: *Atlas eclipticalis* (for any ensemble from 86 instruments, 1961) was not well received by most of the audience nor by the musicians when performed by the New York Philharmonic under Bernstein (1964). Nevertheless, Cage increasingly received honors and commissions from major organizations: in 1968 he was elected to the National Institute of Arts and Letters; in 1978 to the American Academy of Arts and Sciences; in the 1970s he received prestigious commissions from the Boston Symphony (*Renga,* 1976), the Canadian Broadcasting Corporation (*Lecture on the Weather,* 12 instruments or voices, tapes, and films, 1975), and IRCAM (*Roaratorio,* 1979).

Writings: *Silence* (Middletown, Conn., 1961). *A Year from Monday* (Middletown, Conn., 1967). *Notations,* with A. Knowles (New York, 1969). *M* (Middletown, Conn., 1973). *Empty Words* (Middletown, Conn., 1979). *Themes and Variations* (New York, 1982). *I–VI* (Cambridge, Mass., 1990).

Bibl.: R. Dunn, ed., *John Cage* [catalog] (New York, 1962). Michael Nyman, *Experimental Music: Cage and Beyond* (New York, 1974). Paul Griffiths, *Cage* (New York, 1981). Peter Gena and Jonathan Brent, eds., *A John Cage Reader* (New York, 1982). David Revall, *The Roaring Silence: John Cage, a Life* (New York, 1992). Richard Kostelanetz, ed., *Writings About John Cage* (Ann Arbor, 1993). James Pritchett, *The Music of John Cage* (Cambridge, 1993). Marjorie Perloff and Charles Junkerman, eds., *John Cage: Composed in America* (Chicago, 1994).

Cahn, Sammy [Cohen, Samuel] (b. New York, 18 June 1913; d. Los Angeles, 15 Jan. 1993). Lyricist. Wrote for Broadway (*High Button Shoes,* 1947), film (*Three Coins in the Fountain,* 1954), and television, working with composers Saul Chaplin, Jule Styne, and James van Heusen. Well known for his adaptations and parodies of other popular songs ("Bei mir bist du schön," from a Yiddish song, for the Andrews Sisters, 1937). Other songs include "I Should Care" (1945), "Because You're Mine" (1952), and "All the Way" (1957).

Caimo, Gioseppe (b. Milan, ca. 1545; d. there, probably before 31 Oct. 1584). Composer. Organist at S. Ambrogio Maggiore, Milan, from 1564 or earlier, then at Milan Cathedral from 1580; had some contact with the Bavarian court from 1570; knew and was greatly influenced by Vicentino. Composed madrigals, *canzoni napoletane,* and canzonettas, some of which incorporate extensive dissonance and chromaticism.

Caix d'Hervelois, Louis de (b. Amiens, ca. 1680; d. Paris, 1760). Composer and bass viol virtuoso. Though he was one of the leading French viol players of his era, little is known of his origins or of his life. Perhaps related to the musical Caix family, he may have studied with 2 other important viol players in Paris, Sainte-Colombe and Marin Marais. He is known chiefly for 8 published collections of pieces, 6 for 1 and 2 viols with basso continuo and 2 for transverse flute and continuo.

Caldara, Antonio (b. Venice, ca. 1670; d. Vienna, 28 Dec. 1736). Composer. As a chorister at St. Mark's, Venice, he was probably educated in music by *maestro di cappella* Legrenzi. In 1693 and 1699 he published 2 collections of trio sonatas (opp. 1 and 2); also in 1699 he was appointed *maestro di cappella* for Duke Ferdinando Carlo of Mantua. There he composed operas (*L'oracolo in sogno,* 1699; *Opera pastorale,* 1701; *Paride sull'Ida,* 1704) that received lavish productions. During his tenure as *maestro* for Prince Ruspoli in Rome (beginning 1709), he composed 150 solo cantatas (some for Emperor Joseph I and for Cardinal Ottoboni). When Marc'Antonio Ziani, the imperial Kapellmeister, died in 1715, J. J. Fux succeeded him; the following year Caldara was appointed by the new emperor, Charles VI, to assume Fux's former position as Vice-Kapellmeister. This position required Caldara to compose operas and oratorios for a great many court celebrations (name days, birthdays, weddings); in return, the composer demanded of the emperor an ever larger salary. By 1729 he was receiving 3,900 florins, more than Fux's salary. Caldara composed nearly 100 operas, 43 known oratorios, cantatas, Masses, madrigals, and canons.

Bibl.: Ursula Kirkendale, "The War of the Spanish Succession Reflected in the Works of Antonio Caldara," *AM* 36 (1964): 221–33. Id., *Antonio Caldara: Sein Leben und seine venezianisch-römischen Oratorien* (Graz, 1966). Robert Freeman, "The Travels of *Partenope,*" *Strunk,* 1968, pp. 356–85.

Caldwell, Sarah (b. Maryville, Mo., 6 Mar. 1924). Conductor. At the New England Conservatory she studied violin with Richard Burgin and viola with Georges Fourel. While assistant to Boris Goldovsky she staged Vaughan Williams's *Riders to the Sea* at the Berkshire Music Center. Head of Boston Univ. opera workshop, 1952; debut as director in 1953 with Stravinsky's *The Rake's Progress.* Formed Opera Group, 1957, which became Opera Company of Boston, 1965, and of which she has since acted as producer, director, and conductor for most productions, including Sessions's *Montezuma.* Debut conducting a symphony orchestra, 1974, with the American Symphony Orchestra in New York. On 13 Jan. 1976 she became the first woman to conduct New York's Metropolitan Opera (*La traviata*). Named artistic director of the New Opera Company of Israel, 1983.

Calegari, Antonio (b. Padua, 17 Feb. 1757; d. there, 22 or 28 July 1828). Composer and theorist. He studied in Padua and in Venice with Ferdinando Bertoni. In 1801 he was appointed organist at S. Antonio in Padua; in 1814 he became *maestro di cappella.* The following year he published *Gioco pittagorico,* which humorously outlines a method of composition controlled by throws of dice. His methods as pedagogue are outlined in his *Trattato del sistema armonico* (Padua, 1829; 3rd ed., 1878). His *Modi generali del canto* (Milan, 1836, but largely complete in 1809) is an important account of vocal ornamentation of the period. He composed 6 theater works (*Deucalione e Pirra, festa teatrale,* 1781), oratorios (*La risurrezione di Lazzaro,* 1779), cantatas, Masses, antiphons, Psalms, and 6 harpsichord sonatas.

Calestani, Vinzenzo (b. Lucca, 10 Mar. 1589; d. after 1617). Composer. At Pisa he taught music to the wealthy Mastiani family and perhaps also served the Medicis and the Knights of St. Stephen. He published an important collection of pieces for 1 and 2 voices with continuo, *Madrigali et arie* (Venice, 1617; some ed. in *NOHM* 4).

Callas [Kalogeropoulos], **(Cecilia Sophia Anna) Maria** (b. New York, 2 Dec. 1923; d. Paris, 16 Sept. 1977). Soprano. Moved to Greece, 1937. Studied voice with Maria Trivella and at the Athens Conservatory with Elvira de Hidalgo. Sang Mascagni's Santuzza at her student debut, November 1938. After her 1939 professional debut singing a small role in Suppé's *Boccaccio* with the Athens Royal Opera, she joined that company, 1940–45. Debut at the 1947 Verona Festival as Ponchielli's La Gioconda (2 August) launched her international career. For several years she sang dramatic roles such as Puccini's Turandot and Wagner's Brünnhilde and Kundry. Encouraged by the conductor Tullio Serafin, she gradually supplanted these with the bel canto roles for which she is best remembered. She first sang Bellini's Norma, her most acclaimed role, in Florence in 1948; later debuts in this role at Covent Garden (8 Nov. 1952), Chicago (U.S. debut, 1 Nov. 1954), and New York (29 Oct. 1956). La Scala debut as Verdi's Aida, 12 Apr. 1950. She was much praised for her dramatic realizations of Cherubini's Medea (1953) and Donizetti's Lucia (1952) and Anna Bolena (1957). She retired after singing Tosca at Covent Garden, 5 July 1965. Taught at Juilliard, 1971–72. A tour with Giuseppe de Stefano in 1973–74 showed her well past the peak of her powers. She canceled her 1975 engagements and lived in seclusion in a Paris apartment until stricken by a heart attack.

Bibl.: George Jellinek, *Callas: Portrait of a Prima Donna* (New York, 1986). Michael Scott, *Maria Meneghini Callas* (Boston, 1991).

Callcott, John Wall (b. Kensington, 20 Nov. 1766; d. Bristol, 15 May 1821). Theorist and composer of glees. Self-taught in music, from 1784 he contributed glees to the Catch Club competitions, composing some 200 during the subsequent decade. In 1785 he received a Bachelor of Music from Oxford. He assumed positions as organist at St. Paul, Covent Garden (1789), and at the Female Orphan Asylum (1792). In 1806 he taught music at the Royal Institution but suffered a mental collapse the following year. Besides catches and glees, he composed an oratorio (*Elijah,* 1785), a cantata (*Propter Sion non tacebo,* 1800), chamber music, and solo keyboard works. He also authored *An Explanation of the Notes, Marks, Words, &c. Used in Music* (London, 1793) and *A Musical Grammar* (London, 1806); he began a music dictionary (never completed).

Calloway, Cab [Cabell] (b. Rochester, N.Y., 25 Dec. 1907; d. Hockessin, Del., 18 Nov. 1994). Jazz singer and bandleader. He began singing with the Alabamians in Chicago, then joined the Missourians for a successful engagement at the Cotton Club in Harlem (1931–32). From the late 1930s until 1948 he led his own band, which featured several noted jazz instrumentalists, including trumpeter Dizzy Gillespie, drummer Cozy Cole, and bassist Milt Hinton; later he appeared on Broadway, singing Sportin' Life in *Porgy and Bess* (1952–54). His nickname "The Hi-de-ho-Man" derived from his scat singing on songs such as "Minnie the Moocher" (1931).

Calvé (de Roquer), (Rosa-Noémie-) Emma (b. Décazeville, 15 Aug. 1858; d. Millau, Avignon, 6 Jan. 1942). Soprano. Studied with Puget, Marchesi, and, later, Laborde; opera debut, La Monnai, Brussels, 1881; Opéra-comique, Paris, 1885; La Scala, Milan, 1887; then alternated Paris, North America (5 seasons at Metropolitan Opera, 1893–1904, and Manhattan Opera, 1907–8), London, and Italy. First a coloratura soprano, she moved into verismo roles, for which she is best remembered, with Santuzza in *Cavalleria rusticana* in Italy in 1890; a celebrated Carmen. Published memoirs *My Life,* trans. R. Gilder (New York, 1922), and *Sous tous les ciels j'ai chanté* (Paris, 1940).

Bibl.: H. Barnes and W. Moran, "Emma Calvé: A Discography," *Recorded Sound* 59 (1975): 450–52.

Calvisius, Sethus [Kalwitz, Seth] (b. Gorsleben, near Sachsenburg, Thuringia, 21 Feb. 1556; d. Leipzig, 24 Nov. 1615). Theorist. Worked briefly in Leipzig, then for 12 years, beginning in 1582, in Schulpforta. In 1594 became Kantor of the Thomaskirche in Leipzig. Best known for *Melopoeia sive melodiae condendae ratio, quam vulgo musicam poeticam vocant* (Erfurt, 1592), based on Zarlino's *Le istitutioni harmoniche* and including a chapter on poetic and musical figures and their relationship. Discusses modes and the history of music theory in *Exercitationes musicae duae* (Leipzig, 1600; facs., Hildesheim, 1973). Also wrote purely didactic musical treatises. Composed pedagogical works, bicinia and tricinia, 4-part settings of the Psalms and of sacred hymns and songs in Latin and German, and a few motets.

Calzabigi, Raniero [Ranieri] **(Simone Francesco Maria) de** (b. Livorno, 23 Dec. 1714; d. Naples, July 1795). Author and librettist. Educated in Livorno and Pisa. In Paris in the 1750s he collaborated with Metastasio on an edition of the latter's works; his introduction to vol. 1 was the laudatory *Dissertazione su le poesie drammatiche del sig. Abate Pietro Metastasio* (1755). His ideas about opera were to change, however. In Vienna, beginning in 1761, he collaborated with Gluck on operas (especially *Orfeo ed Euridice,* 1762, and *Alceste,* 1767) that became crucial works in the so-called reform of opera, which was in part a reaction against Metastasian music drama. Other librettos include the *dramma giocoso La critica teatrale (L'opera seria)* (set by Gassmann, 1769), *Paride ed Elena* (Gluck, 1770), *L'amor innocente* (Salieri, 1770), *Ipermestra, o Le danaidi* (Salieri, 1784), *Elfrida* (Paisiello, 1792), and *Elvira* (Paisiello, 1794).

Cambert, Robert (b. Paris, ca. 1627; d. London, Feb. or Mar. 1677). Composer and organist. He studied with Chambonnières in Paris, and from 1652 to 1673 he was organist at St. Honoré there. He received the post of *maître de musique* to Anne of Austria, the mother of Louis XIV, in 1662. From the mid-1650s he collaborated with librettist Pierre Perrin on a series of stage works; the earliest extant example is *La pastorale* (perf. 1659; music lost). Others included *Ariane, ou Le mariage de Bacchus* (composed 1659; perf. 1674 in London; lost), and *Pomone,* the inaugural pastoral of the Académie d'opéra established by royal privilege granted to Perrin in 1669 (perf. 1671 at the Salle du Jeu de Paume de la Bouteille). *Pomone,* which survives incomplete, was the first French opera to be staged. His final operatic collaboration was with Gabriel Gilbert in the *pastorale héroïque* of 1671, *Les peines et les plaisirs de l'amour.* In 1672 the royal privilege to stage operas passed from Perrin to Lully. From 1673 Cambert was in London, where in 1674 his *Ariane* was performed at the Theatre Royal. Also among his works are several airs for various combinations of voices, including a collection of *airs à boire* (1665) and the *Trio-bouffe de Cariselli* for a comedy by Brécourt (1666).

Bibl.: P. H. Kennedy, "The First French Opera," *RMFC* 8 (1968): 77.

Cambini, Giuseppe Maria (Gioacchino) (b. Livorno, 13 Feb. 1746; d. Bicêtre, 29 Dec. 1825). Composer and violinist. Little is known of his early life, though he may have studied violin with Manfredini. During the early 1770s he arrived in Paris, where he played solo violin at the Concert spirituel and published his op. 1 string quartets in 1773. In all, some 600 published instrumental works are attributed to him. From 1776 he composed stage works for the Académie royale, the Théâtre Beaujolais, and the Théâtre du Louvois; he held posts as violinist at the latter 2 theaters. He composed some 20 stage works (most are lost); motets and oratorios (*Le sacrifice d'Isaac,* 1774; *Joad,* 1775); secular vocal works, including revolutionary songs; nearly 100 symphonies and *symphonies concertantes;* concertos; over 100 string quintets; nearly 150 string quartets; much other chamber music, including trios, duos, and works for solo instruments. He also authored a *Nouvelle méthode théorique et pratique pour le violon* (Paris, ca. 1795; facs., 1972).

Bibl.: Dieter L. Trimpert, *Die Quatuors concertants von Giuseppe Cambini* (Tutzing, 1967). John Buttry, "New Light on Robert Cambert in London, and His *Ballet et Musique,*" *EM* 23 (1995): 198–220.

Camerloher, Placidus von (b. Murnau, 9 Aug 1718; d. Freising, near Munich, 21 July 1782). Composer. He studied theology at Freising, where he was ordained in 1744. That year he was also made Kapellmeister at Freising and was later appointed Kanonikus at St. Veit (1748) and at St. Andreas (1753). During the 1750s he accompanied Prince-Bishop Johann Theodor on travels throughout Europe, composing symphonies, trio sonatas, and works for solo instruments. His compositions also include church music, singspiels, and school dramas.

Camidge, Matthew (bapt. York, 25 May 1764; d. there, 23 Oct. 1844). Organist and composer. His father, John (1734–1803), was organist at York Minster from 1756 to 1799; Matthew was the sixth child of John and Elizabeth. He assisted his father at the minster and succeeded him in 1799. He compiled the collections *Psalmody for a Single Voice* (1789) and *A Musical Companion to the Psalms Used in the Church of St. Michael-le-Belfrey* (for organ, 1800). Among his own compositions are sacred vocal works, chamber music, secular songs, and *24 Original Psalm and Hymn Tunes* (1823). In 1842 he was succeeded at York by his son John (1790–1859).

Bibl.: Nicholas Temperley, *Jonathan Gray and Church Music in York, 1770–1840* (York, 1977).

Camilleri, Charles (b. Malta, 7 Sept. 1931). Composer. His early career was in London and Toronto (where he studied at the conservatory) as a composer of light music whose melodic style was indebted to Maltese folk music; later works are more indebted to African and Asian folk musics and to his interest in Indian mysticism. Works include *Maltese Dances* (orchestra, 1956) and *Maqam* (orchestra and piano, 1968); *Divertimento 2* (clarinet and piano, 1957), *Abongo* (wind quintet, 1970), and other chamber music; and piano music (*African Drums,* 1967; *Mantra,* 1968).

Campagnoli, Bartolomeo (b. Cento di Ferrara, 10 Sept. 1751; d. Neustrelitz, 6 Nov. 1827). Violinist and composer. After study of violin in Modena, he played in the orchestra either at Cento or at nearby Bologna, and subsequently in Rome. From 1770 to 1775 he studied with Nardini in Florence; from 1776 he was in the service of the Bishop of Freysingen, with whom he toured Poland, Germany, Sweden, and Italy. From 1797 to 1814 he directed the Leipzig Gewandhaus Orchestra. He authored a widely used *Nouvelle méthode de la mécanique progressive du jeu de violon* (Leipzig, 1824; trans. Eng., 1856); compositions include 3 flute concertos, a violin concerto, and chamber works.

Campanini, Cleofonte (b. Parma, 1 Sept. 1860; d. Chicago, 19 Dec. 1919). Conductor. Brother of Italo. From the 1880s a leading conductor, especially of opera, in Europe and the Americas, including the Metropolitan Opera in 1883–84, Hammerstein's Manhattan Opera in 1906–9, the Chicago Opera from 1910 (from

1913 as director); conducted the premiere of Cilèa's *Adriana Lecouvreur* (1902) and of *Madama Butterfly* (1904); American premieres include *Otello* (New York, 1888) and *Pelléas et Mélisande* (New York, 1908).

Campanini, Italo (b. Parma, 30 June 1845; d. Corcagnano, near Parma, 22 Nov. 1896). Tenor. Brother of Cleofonte. Studied at the Parma Conservatory, later with Lamperti in Milan; La Scala debut, 1870; sang *Lohengrin* in its famous Bologna premiere (1871) and at La Scala (1873), and Faust in premiere of second version of *Mefistofele* (Bologna, 1875). Appeared widely in Europe; especially popular in London (debut 1872) and New York; Don José in first London and New York *Carmen* (1878); in opening night of Metropolitan Opera (1883), his voice then in decline; retired in 1894.

Campion [Campian], **Thomas** (b. London, bapt. 12 Feb. 1567; d. London, buried 1 Mar. 1620). Poet and composer. Son of attorney and diplomatic courier John Campion, he was raised in affluence and entered Cambridge in 1581. Leaving three years later, probably without a degree, he joined Gray's Inn, a gentleman's society that engaged in amateur and semi-professional music making. There he composed and performed masques and other music for noble and royal audiences, including Queen Elizabeth. His first published poems appeared in the early 1590s in a collection titled *Astrophel and Stella* edited by Thomas Nash. His first songs to appear in print were in *A Book of Ayres* (1601, ed. Philip Rosseter); the treatise *Observations in the Art of English Poesie* appeared in 1602. He studied medicine abroad, probably in France, and became a physician in 1605. Back in England by 1607, he began a compilation of his theoretical views, which became *A New Way of Making Fowre Parts in Counter-point* (publ. 1614?); it appeared in print again in 1660, revised by Christopher Simpson, as *An Introduction to the Skill of Musick, in Two Books.* Campion published his first *Two Bookes of Ayres* (in 1 vol.; ed. in *ESLS,* 2nd ser., 1–2) around 1613, and later (ca. 1617), *The Third and Fourth Booke of Ayres* (ed. in *ELS,* 2nd ser., 10, and *ESLS,* 2nd ser., 1–2). His oeuvre comprises some 120 songs with lute accompaniment; most are for solo voice, and for all but a few Campion was both poet and composer.

Bibl.: *The Works of Thomas Campion,* ed. Walter R. Davis (London, 1969). Muriel T. Eldridge, *Thomas Campion: His Poetry and Music, 1567–1620: A Study in Relationships* (New York, 1971). Edward Lowbury, Timothy Salter, and Alison Young, *Thomas Campion: Poet, Composer, Physician* (New York, 1970). Stephen Ratcliffe, *Campion: On Song* (London, 1981). Martha Feldman, "In Defense of Campion: A New Look at His Ayres and *Observations,*" *JM* 5 (1987): 226–56. Christopher Wilson, *Words and Notes Coupled Lovingly Together: Thomas Campion: A Critical Study* (New York, 1989).

Campo (y Zabaleta), Conrado del (b. Madrid, 28 Oct. 1879; d. there, 17 Mar. 1953). Composer and conductor. Among his teachers at the Madrid Conservatory were Hierro, Monasterio, and Serrano; later he played in chamber groups and in the orchestra of the Teatro real in Madrid. In 1915 he was made professor at the Madrid Conservatory, where he was an especially influential teacher. His music shows the influence of Beethoven and of folk and popular music of Spain; his stage works show the marks of Wagner and Strauss. He composed operas (*El final de Don Alvaro,* 1910; *Fantochines,* 1922; *El arbol de los ojos,* 1930; *Lola, la piconera,* 1949; *El pájaro de dos colores,* 1951); orchestral tone poems (*Ante las ruinas,* 1899; *Granada,* 1912; *Ariños, aires . . .,* 1916; *Evocación medieval,* 1924; *Ofrenda a los caídos,* 1938); other orchestral works (*Suite madrileña,* 1934; *El viento en Castilla,* 1942; a cello concerto, 1944); film scores; 22 zarzuelas; 3 Masses and other choral music; 12 string quartets (1904–52); songs; keyboard music.

Bibl.: Tomás Borrás y Bermejo, *Conrado del Campo* (Madrid, 1954).

Campos-Parsi, Héctor (b. Ponce, Puerto Rico, 1 Oct. 1922). Composer. He attended the Univ. of Puerto Rico at Río Piedras (1934–44) and the New England Conservatory (1947–50); also studied with Aaron Copland (at Tanglewood, in 1949 and 1956) and in Paris with Nadia Boulanger (1950–53). After returning to Puerto Rico in the mid-1950s, he served as director of musical events for his government's Institute of Puerto Rican Culture and also functioned as a music critic and television commentator. His music has embraced native popular music and neoclassicism, as well as electronic and aleatoric techniques. Works include ballets (*Incidente,* 1949; *Melos,* 1952; *Juan Bobo y las fiestas,* 1957; *Urayoan,* 1958); other orchestral music (*Divertimento,* 1953; *Rapsodia elegiaca,* 1960; *Kolayia,* with percussion and tape, 1963; *Dúo trágico,* with piano, 1964; *Tiempo sereno,* strings, 1983); *Tureyareito,* 1984; *Tissú,* with accordion, small orchestra, 1984); a cantata (*Annunciation,* 1954); chamber music (*Versículos,* viola, 1948; *El secreto,* 1957); keyboard music (Piano Sonata, 1953).

Campra, André (b. Aix-en-Provence, bapt. 4 Dec. 1660; d. Versailles, 29 June 1744). Composer. His younger brother Joseph (1662–1744) was also a musician; some of the latter's works have been wrongly attributed to André. In 1674 Campra entered the choir of the Church of St. Sauveur, where he studied music with Guillaume Poitevin. He took orders for the priesthood in 1678 and was made chaplain three years later. After posts as *maître* in Arles (1681–83) and Toulouse (1683–94), he went to Paris, having received the prestigious post of *maître de musique* at Notre Dame. Around 1695 he may also have served as *maître de musique* at the Collège Louis-le-Grand. During the 1690s a number of patrons employed his theatrical and compositional skills, but because of the moral strictures governing the production of operas during this period, works were often published anonymously: the first editions of Campra's early success *L'Europe galante* (opera-ballet, 1697) appeared with no attribution. In 1700 Campra gave up his post at Notre Dame and assumed theatrical composition full-time. He secured a 12-year printing privilege, with which he published *Iphigénie en Tauride* (first perf. 1704), *Hippodamie* (1708), *Les fêtes vénitiennes* (1710), and *Idomenée* (1712). In 1718 he was pensioned by Louis XV. From 1722 he served the Prince of Conti, Louis-Armand de Bourbon; finally he was appointed *sous-maître,* along with Bernier and Gervais, of the royal chapel, and from 1730 he was also inspector general of the Académie royale de musique. He suffered ill health during his last decade and died only three months after the death of his brother Joseph. In addition to operas he composed more than 20 cantatas, well over 100 motets and *grands motets,* songs and airs, and many other sacred vocal works.

Bibl.: Lionel de La Laurencie, "André Campra, musicien profane," *Année musicale* 3 (1913): 153–205. Maurice Barthélemy, *André Campra: Sa vie et son oeuvre* (Paris, 1957). Conan Jennings Castle, "The Grand Motets of André Campra" (diss., Univ. of Michigan, 1962). James R. Anthony, "The Opera-Ballet of André Campra: A Study of the First Period French Opera-Ballet" (diss., Univ. of Southern California, 1964). Id., "Thematic Repetition in the Opera-Ballets of André Campra," *MQ* 52 (1966): 209–20.

Canis [de Hondt, d'Hondt], **Cornelius** (b. Flanders?, ca. 1510–20; d. Prague, 15 Feb. 1561). Composer. Master of choirboys and later *maître de chapelle* at the court of Emperor Charles V in Brussels from no later than 1542 until about 1555. From 1557 held posts in churches in Courtrai. Died while serving Emperor Ferdinand I. Extant works include 2 Masses, about 30 motets, and about 30 French chansons in both the Parisian and Franco-Flemish styles.

Cannabich, (Johann) Christian (Innocenz Bonaventura) (b. Mannheim, bapt. Dec. 1731; d. Frankfurt am Main, 20 Jan. 1798). Composer and violinist. His father, Martin Friedrich (b. ca. 1690; d. 12 Oct. 1773), was flutist and music teacher at the Mannheim court. As a boy Christian studied violin with Johann Stamitz and began playing in the Mannheim orchestra at age 12 (1744). In the early 1750s he studied in Italy, first with Jommelli in Rome, and later in Stuttgart and Milan. By 1757 he had returned to Mannheim to assume Stamitz's post as first violinist (together with Carl Joseph Toeschi). He visited Paris frequently during the 1760s and 1770s, performing his own works at the Concert spirituel and publishing symphonies and chamber works. In 1774 he became director of instrumental music at Mannheim; 4 years later he moved to Munich with the court. He composed more than 40 ballet scores (10 with Toeschi; many lost), a melodrama, over 75 symphonies, concertos, *symphonies concertantes,* and chamber music. In 1798 his son Carl (1771–1806), who since 1788 had played violin in his father's orchestra, became *Konzertmeister;* in 1800 he was made court music director. Carl Cannabich composed operas, including an *Orfeo* setting (Munich, 1802), symphonies, concertos, and chamber music.

Bibl.: Rudolf Kloiber, *Die dramatischen Ballette von Christian Cannabich* (Munich, 1928). Jean K. Wolf, "Christian Cannabich," in Barry S. Brook et al., eds., *The Symphony, 1720–1840,* ser. C, vol.3, *The Symphony at Mannheim* (New York, 1984), pp. xl–lxxxiii.

Cannon, Gus [Banjo Joe] (b. Red Banks, Miss., 12 Sept. 1883; d. Memphis, 15 Oct. 1979). Blues banjoist, jug player, and singer. An itinerant musician who played country dances and medicine shows throughout Mississippi and Tennessee, Cannon partnered the harmonica player and singer Noah Lewis from about 1916. In the late 1920s the two men were the core of Cannon's Jug Stompers, based in Memphis. Among its recordings are *Money Never Runs Out* (1930) and Cannon's best-known composition, *Walk Right In* (1929). He accompanied other singers, including Blind Blake, and recorded in his own right (including *Can You Blame the Colored Man?* 1927).

Cantelli, Guido (b. Novara, Italy, 27 Apr. 1920; d. Orly Airport, near Paris, 24 Nov. 1956). Conductor. Debut as pianist at age 14. Studied composition and conducting with Arrigo Pedrollo and from 1941 with Ghedini in Milan. Appointed artistic director of Novara's Teatro Coccia, 1943, but was drafted. He refused to fight for fascism and spent 1943–45 at concentration camps in Germany and (after his health collapsed) Stettin, and (after his escape) in Milan under an assumed name. Debut as conductor with Orchestra of La Scala, 27 July 1945. Observed in 1948 by Toscanini, who invited him to conduct the NBC Symphony; U.S. debut with that group, 15 Jan. 1949; guest conductor through April 1954. Also led New York Philharmonic, Boston Symphony, Philharmonia of London. Active at La Scala, 1954–56. Best known for Hindemith, Bartók, Stravinsky, Ravel, and 19th-century Romantics. Died in a plane crash.

Canteloube (de Malaret), (Marie) Joseph (b. Annonay, 21 Oct. 1879; d. Grigny, Seine-et-Oise, 4 Nov. 1957). Composer and writer. He studied at the Schola cantorum with d'Indy from 1901. Most of his music reflects either his interest in depicting his native landscape in the Auvergne region or his activities as a folk song collector and arranger. His writings include a volume on d'Indy (1949) and one on French folk song (*Les chants des provinces françaises,* 1946).

Works: 2 operas (1910–13 and 1930–32; performed at the Opéra, 1929 and 1933, respectively); a symphonic poem (1910–11), *Pièces françaises* (piano and orchestra, 1934–35), and other orchestral pieces; *Dans la montagne* (violin and piano, 1904), *Rustique* (oboe, clarinet, and bassoon, 1946), and other chamber music; songs ("Triptyque," 1914); and choral and solo arrangements of folk songs.

Cape, Safford (b. Denver, 28 June 1906; d. Brussels, 26 Mar. 1973). Conductor. Trained in piano and composition in Denver. Moved in 1925 to Brussels, where he studied musicology under Charles van den Borren, later marrying his teacher's daughter. In 1933 founded the Pro Musica Antiqua to perform medieval and Renaissance music in accordance with the latest scholarship. The ensemble's activities were suspended by war in 1940, but resumed in 1945. Cape composed chamber music and songs.

Capet, Lucien (b. Paris, 8 Jan. 1873; d. there, 18 Dec. 1928). Violinist and composer. At the Paris Conservatory studied violin with J. B. Maurin 1888–93, obtaining first prize. In 1893 founded the Capet Quartet, which did much to promote the Beethoven quartets in France before finally disbanding in 1921. Concertmaster of the Concerts Lamoureux, 1896–99. Taught in Bordeaux, 1899–1903; at the Paris Conservatory, 1907–28, first as professor of chamber music, after 1924 as chief professor of violin. Wrote monographs on the Beethoven quartets and on violin technique. Composed 5 string quartets, other chamber and orchestral music.

Caplet, André (b. Le Havre, 23 Nov. 1878; d. Neuilly-sur-Seine, 22 Apr. 1925). Composer and conductor. He studied piano and played violin in theater orchestras from the age of 14; in 1896 he began study at the Paris Conservatory (composition with Charles Lenepveu), winning a Prix de Rome in 1901 (for the cantata *Myrrha*). He began his conducting career as a substitute for his harmony teacher, Leroux, in 1896. By 1899 he was director of music at the Odéon Theater; he conducted the Boston Opera orchestra (1910–14). His early compositional style is related to that of Debussy and the impressionists; at Debussy's request he orchestrated part of *Le martyre de Saint-Sébastien* and conducted the premiere. Later his compositions became more innovatory: he employed new vocal techniques (*Septet,* 3 voices and string quartet, 1909; *Pain quotidien,* 15 vocalises, 1920) and searched for new instrumental resources. Throughout his career he wrote in a rigorously controlled contrapuntal and melodic style. Works include *Epiphanie* (cello and orchestra, 1923) and other orchestral works; *Conte fantastique* (after Poe, for harp and string quartet, 1919), *2 Divertissements* (solo harp, 1924), and other instrumental music; many religious works for chorus (*Le miroir de Jésus,* for mezzo-soprano, female chorus, harp, and strings, 1923); other choral music and songs.

Caproli, Carlo (b. Rome, ca. 1620; d. Rome? ca. 1695). Composer and violinist. In Rome he may have studied at the German College, where he was organist from 1643. By 1649 he was violinist at S. Luigi dei Francesi, where he played for 20 years. He served Prince Ludovisio Pamphili in Rome until at least 1664. In 1654 he composed an opera for Paris at the request of Cardinal Mazarin, *Le nozze di Peleo e di Theti* (music now lost) and traveled to France to oversee performances of it. From 1659 he was violinist at the Congregazione di S. Cecilia; he served occasionally as *maestro di cappella* at S. Luigi dei Francesi in the 1660s. He is best known as an important composer of cantatas, both sacred and secular; about 125 are known. They follow the model of cantatas by Luigi Rossi: often they are for solo voice, contain an alternation of recitative and arioso sections, and are accompanied by basso continuo.

Capron, Henri (b. France; fl. 1785–95). Cellist, composer, and impresario. From 1785 he appeared as concert organizer and manager in Philadelphia. He also organized concerts in New York from 1788 to 1794, often himself performing on the cello (and occasionally as singer). He played cello in the Old American Company orchestra. In 1794 he resettled in Philadelphia, where he managed a music store. With John Christopher Moller he published a short-lived serial of music scores titled *Moller and Capron's Monthly Number* (1793; only 4 issues published). He composed *New Contredance* and songs such as "Favorite Song (Softly as the Breezes Blowing)," "Delia," "Go Lovely Rose," and "Julia See."

Capuzzi [Capucci], **Giuseppe Antonio** (b. Breno, 1 Aug. 1755; d. Bergamo, 28 Mar. 1818). Violinist and composer. In Venice he studied violin (with A. Nazari) and composition (with F. G. Bertoni). From 1780 he was concertmaster at the Teatro di S. Samuele, and subsequently orchestra director at the Teatro di S. Benedetto. For the latter he composed ballets placed between acts of plays and operas. *La villageoise* (ballet) was performed in London in 1796. In 1805 he took posts at Bergamo as orchestra director at S. Maria Maggiore and as professor at the conservatory. Among his known works are 5 operas, 11 ballets (most lost), 4 violin concertos, 18 string quartets, and other chamber music.

Cara, Marchetto [Marco, Marcus, Marchettus] (b. in or near Verona, ca. 1470; d. Mantua, 1525?). Composer, lutenist, and singer. One of the two foremost composers of frottolas, the other being Bartolomeo Tromboncino. From 1494 or earlier until 1525, served the Gonzaga court in Mantua in various musical capacities. Beginning in 1502, traveled to numerous cities in northern Italy to perform. Aaron and Castiglione mention him as a fine singer and lutenist. His compositions attracted attention from central and southern Italy as well. Many of his more than 100 frottolas were published by Petrucci; others appeared in later anthologies, and some were printed posthumously. Most of the texts are anonymous; in the early works amorous courtly subjects predominate, whereas in the later works (published after 1514) more serious texts often appear. Some of the later settings are in certain respects like the early madrigal. Although Tromboncino also wrote pieces with madrigalian features, Cara eventually became the more important of the two in contributing to this development. He also composed a Salve Regina (probably his earliest work) and 7 *laude.*

Bibl.: William F. Prizer, *Courtly Pastimes: The Frottole of Marchetto Cara* (Ann Arbor, 1980). Id., "Isabella d'Este and

Lucrezia Borgia as Patrons of Music: The Frottola at Mantua and Ferrara," *JAMS* 38 (1985).

Carafa (de Colobrano), Michele (Enrico Francesco Vincenzo Aloisio Paolo) (b. Naples, 17 Nov. 1787; d. Paris, 26 July 1872). Composer. A younger son in one of Naples's great noble families, he was educated for the army, also studying music with Ruggi and later Fenaroli in Naples and in 1806 Cherubini and Kalkbrenner in Paris. From 1806 to 1814 he also served in several military campaigns, distinguishing himself in battle and serving as aide to Murat (King of Naples). After Napoleon's fall he became a professional composer, from 1814 producing several operas, some very successful, in Naples, then elsewhere in Italy, and from 1821 in Paris, where he had success with *La solitaire* (1821) and some later ones, which gradually became exclusively French. His position in Paris was strengthened by his close friendship with Rossini, by whom he was much overshadowed as a composer. He became a French citizen in 1834. Elected to the Académie in 1837; from 1840 was a professor at the Conservatory.

Cardew, Cornelius (b. Winchcombe, Gloucester, 7 May 1936; d. London, 13 Dec. 1981). Composer. His early music training came when he was a choirboy at Canterbury Cathedral; later at the Royal Academy of Music (1953–57) he studied composition with Howard Ferguson and piano with Percy Waller. With a stipend he studied electronic music in Cologne and became an assistant to Stockhausen in 1958. From 1961 he was a graphic artist in England; during this period he also spent two years in Italy working with Petrassi (1963–65) and was made professor at the Royal Academy (1967). His massive Confucian work *The Great Learning* manifested interests in graphic notation, improvisation, electronic music, and indeterminacy. In 1966 he joined the experimental group AMM, and in 1969 formed the Scratch Orchestra, an avant-garde performance and composition ensemble. His turn to socialist thought around 1970 is reflected in writings such as *Stockhausen Serves Imperialism* (London, 1974). Among his works are orchestral pieces (*Movement for Orchestra,* 1962; *Bun Nos. 1 & 2,* 1964–65); chamber and piano music (2 string trios, 1955–56; *3 Winter Potatoes,* piano, 1961–65; Vietnam Sonata, piano, 1976); vocal works (*The Great Learning,* 1968–70; *The Old and the New,* soprano, chorus, orchestra, 1973); and several works for unspecified forces (*The Tiger's Mind,* 1967). His writings also include *Scratch Music* (London, 1972).

Cardoso, Manuel (b. Fronteira, bapt. 11 Dec. 1566; d. Lisbon, 24 Nov. 1650). Composer. As a chorister at the cathedral school in Évora he studied with Manuel Mendes and possibly also with Cosme Delgado. He took vows for the priesthood in 1589 at Lisbon's Convento do Carmo; there he was organist and choral conductor. From 1618 he was in the service of the Duke of Barcelos at the Vila Viçosa. A trip to Madrid in 1631 inspired him to compose a tribute to Philip IV, in the form of the third book of Masses, all based on a motet by Philip himself. Cardoso published 3 books of Masses and 2 collections of motets and other sacred polyphony (ed. in *Portugaliae musica,* ser. A, vols. 5–6, 13, 20, 22, 26).

Carestini, Giovanni (b. Filottrano, Ancona, ca. 1705; d. there? ca. 1760). Alto castrato singer. His musical training was under the auspices of the Cusani family of Milan; his debut (Rome, 1721) came in the role of Costanza in Alessandro Scarlatti's *Griselda.* From 1723 to 1725 he held an appointment at the Viennese imperial theater. During the next decade he established his career with works by Hasse, Vinci, Scarlatti, and Porpora. His London debut was in 1733 in the pasticcio *Semiramide riconosciuta;* between 1733 and 1740 he appeared there on three separate occasions, singing works by Handel and others at Covent Garden and at the New Haymarket Theatre.

Carey, Henry (b. probably Yorkshire, 1687; d. London, 4 Oct. 1743). Poet and composer. He studied in London with Olaus Linnert and (probably from around 1715) with Francesco Geminiani. As a poet he wrote plays, burlesques, and ballad operas; he provided tunes for a number of these operas. *The Contrivances,* an earlier play that was fashioned into a ballad opera in 1729, burlesqued the reigning taste for Italian opera in the city. Other burlesques included the dialogue opera *Chrononhotonthologos* (1734), *The Honest Yorkshireman* (1735), and *Nancy, or The Parting Lovers* (1739; called at various times *The Press Gang* or *True Blue*). His most notable libretto is that for *The Dragon of Wantley,* a highly successful parody of Handel, Farinelli, and the machinery of Italian opera, first performed in the Little Haymarket Theatre in 1737, with music by C. F. Lampe. Carey also published a collection of cantatas and songs, *The Musical Century* (London, 1737–40). His most popular song (for which he composed both words and music) was "Sally in Our Alley."

Bibl.: Frederick T. Wood, *The Poems of Henry Carey* (London, 1930). Harold Gene Moss, "Popular Music and the Ballad Opera," *JAMS* 26 (1973): 365–82.

Carissimi, Giacomo (b. Marini, bapt. 18 Apr. 1605; d. Rome, 12 Jan. 1674). Composer. He is recorded as a singer at Tivoli in 1623; two years later he was organist there. His first appointment as *maestro di cappella* came in 1628, at the S. Rufino Cathedral in Assisi. The following year he was called on by Bernardino Castorio in Rome to fill the post of *maestro* at the German College there, a prestigious post in which Victoria and Agazzari had served earlier. Carissimi spent the rest of his life at the college; he was ordained to the priesthood in 1637. His responsibilities included training the choirs and providing liturgical music for the adjoining S. Apollinare chapel; his official salary of 5 scudi (in 1634) probably reflects only a fraction of his actual income. In 1655–56 he was given the title *maestro di cappella del concerto di camera* by the Queen of Sweden in exile in Rome; also during the 1650s he composed and conducted for the Oratorio del S. Crocifisso. Among his prominent pupils were Marc-Antoine Charpentier, Johann Kaspar Kerll, Christoph Bernhard, and possibly also Johann Philipp Krieger. That he was in a comfortable situation, both financially and professionally, is suggested by his rejection of several opportunities for prestigious employment, including the post at St. Mark's in Venice on Monteverdi's death in 1643 and the position of *maestro* for the emperor's son, Leopold Wilhelm of Brussels. Carissimi chose to remain in Rome, and after 44 years of service to the College he died a rich man.

The first major composer of oratorios, Carissimi helped form the modern notion of the genre. He also composed hundreds of motets and cantatas in addition to Masses and other sacred works. Because no autograph manuscripts survive, problems of attribution in his oeuvre are especially difficult, as are problems of genre, especially in distinguishing between motet and oratorio. Among the oratorios are *Damnatorum lamentatio* (1666), *Jephte* (before 1650), *Jonas,* and *Judicium Salomonis.*

Bibl.: *Giacomo Carissimi: Le opere complete,* ed. Lino Bianchi et al., Pubblicazioni dell'Istituto italiano per la storia della musica, *Monumenti,* 3 (1951–53). Claudio Sartori and Gian Marco Manusardi, *Giacomo Carissimi: Catalogo delle opere attribuite* (Milan, 1975). Günther Massenkeil, "Die oratorische Kunst in den lateinischen Historien und Oratorien Giacomo Carissimis" (diss., Univ. of Mainz, 1952). Gloria Rose, "The Cantatas of Giacomo Carissimi," *MQ* 48 (1962): 204–15. Janet E. Beat, "Two Problems in Carissimi's Oratorio *Jephte,*" *MR* 34 (1973): 339–45. Howard E. Smither, "Carissimi's Latin Oratorios: Their Terminology, Functions, and Position in Oratorio History," *AnMca* 11 (1976): 54–78. Andrew V. Jones, *The Motets of Carissimi* (Ann Arbor, 1982). Graham Dixon, *Carissimi* (New York, 1986).

Carlos, Wendy [formerly Walter] (b. Pawtucket, R.I., 14 Nov. 1939). Composer. Received the A.B. from Brown Univ., under Ron Nelson; then worked with Luening, Ussachevsky, and Beeson at Columbia (M.M., 1965). Aided Moog in improving the synthesizer (1964); Carlos's initial recording, *Switched on Bach,* produced on that synthesizer, was very successful. She has written many film scores (*A Clockwork Orange,* 1971) and other works using synthesizer, digitally synthesized orchestral sounds, or both (*The Shining,* 1978–80). Her album *Digital Moonscapes* (1985) was the first for digitally synthesized orchestra. Other works include an opera (*Noah,* 1964–65), a cello sonata, and other pieces for ensemble, piano, synthesizer, or tape.

Carlton, Richard (b. ca. 1558; d. 1638?). Composer. Received the B.A. from Cambridge in 1577; thereafter vicar of St. Stephen's, Norwich, and master of the choristers at Norwich Cathedral; at Bawsey-cum-Glosthorpe in Norfolk from 1612. Contributed one madrigal to *The Triumphes of Oriana* (1601) and published a complete book of 5-voice madrigals in London in the same year (ed. in *EMS* 27). Other extant compositions are 2 anthems and a pavane for 5 instruments.

Carmichael, Hoagy [Hoagland Howard] (b. Bloomington, Ind., 22 Nov. 1899; d. Rancho Mirage, Calif., 27 Dec. 1981). Popular songwriter. He began performing as a singer and pianist while a law student at Indiana Univ.; after a short stint with a law firm in Florida he returned to Bloomington and around 1930 moved to New York, spending the remainder of his career there and in Hollywood. His songwriting was strongly influenced by experiences with jazz musicians including Bix Beiderbecke, Benny Goodman, Joe Venuti, and Louis Armstrong. He worked with numerous lyricists, including Johnny Mercer, Paul Francis Webster, and Frank Loesser, and wrote songs for films (*To Have and Have Not,* 1944; *Here Comes the Groom,* including "In the Cool, Cool, Cool of the Evening," 1951) and one full-length Broadway musical (*Walk with Music,* Mercer, 1940). His most famous composition was "Stardust" (lyrics by Mitchell Parish, 1929); he also wrote songs for Mildred Bailey ("Georgia on My Mind," 1931) and Frank Sinatra ("The Lamplighter's Serenade," 1942). Other songs include "Lazy River" (1931), "Lazybones" (Mercer, 1933), "Heart and Soul" (Loesser, 1938), "The Nearness of You" (1940), "Skylark" (1942), and "Ole Buttermilk Sky" (1946). He acted in 14 films and wrote 2 autobiographies, *The Stardust Road* (1946) and *Sometimes I Wonder* (1965).

Carney, Harry (Howell) (b. Boston, 1 Apr. 1910; d. New York, 8 Oct. 1974). Jazz baritone saxophonist. He played alto saxophone in Boston, then in 1927 joined Duke Ellington in New York. Soon he specialized on baritone saxophone; he spent his entire career with Ellington, becoming the first great soloist on this instrument. Recordings with Ellington include "Doin' the Voom Voom" (1929), "Lightnin'" (1932), "Harlem Speaks" (1933), "Perdido" (1942), and "Sophisticated Lady" on the album *Duke Ellington's 70th Birthday Concert* (1969).

Carneyro, Cláudio (b. Oporto, 27 Jan. 1895; d. there, 18 Oct. 1963). Composer. He studied at the Oporto Conservatory with Lucien Lambert (composition) and Miguel Alves (violin), and later at the Paris Conservatory with Charles Widor and Paul Dukas. After two years in the U.S. (1928–30) he returned home to teach composition at the Oporto Conservatory, which he directed from 1955 to 1958. His music is in an essentially neo-Romantic idiom and contains some Portuguese folk and native materials. Works include a ballet *Nau Catrineta* (1942–44); orchestral works (*Pregões, Romarias do senhor, Procissões,* 1928; *Dança popular,* 1934; *Variações sobre um tema de Corelli-Kreisler,* 1939; *Catavento,* piano and orchestra, 1942; *Palma a Chopin,* 1949; *Bailadeiras,* 1962); choral works (*Regi-

naldo, 1951; *A estrêla esplendorosa,* 1963; *Avé Maria,* female choir, 1935; *Males de amor,* 1941–43; *Gerinalda,* 1953); chamber and keyboard music.

Carnicer (y Batlle), Ramón (b. Tárrega, near Lérida, 24 Oct. 1789; d. Madrid, 17 Mar. 1855). Composer. Son of a tailor; choirboy at Seo de Urgel Cathedral, 1799–1806; studied in Barcelona with the cathedral choirmaster and the organist, 1806–8. He spent the war years teaching on Minorca; visited London in 1815–16, then recruited an opera company in Italy for Barcelona. From 1818 conductor at the Coliseo theater, Barcelona, also composing 3 Italian operas there in 1819–22; then visited Madrid, Italy, Paris, and London, where he was commissioned to compose the Chilean national anthem. By royal command became director of opera in Madrid, 1827; from 1829 to 1838 had 4 Italian operas performed there (*Cristoforo Colombo,* 1831). From 1831 professor of composition at the new Madrid Conservatory; pupils included Barbieri and Saldoni. Also composed many once-popular Spanish songs, a Mass, 2 Requiems and other sacred works, and a few instrumental pieces.

Bibl.: Vicente Salas Viu, "Ramón Carnicer, músico y liberal," *Revista musical chilena* 48 (1955): 8–14.

Caron, Philippe (fl. 2nd half of 15th century). Composer. His identity and even his first name are uncertain, and all information about his life is conjectural. Tinctoris called him "Firminus Caron" and linked him with Busnois, Regis, and Ockeghem as among the "most excellent" composers he had ever heard. He may have been in the service of Charles the Bold and may have spent time in Italy. He composed about 20 chansons, 2 motets, and 5 Masses (including a *Missa super L'homme armé,* modeled on a chanson by Morton).

Bibl.: *Les oeuvres complètes* (Brooklyn, 1971–76).

Caroso, Fabritio (b. probably in Sermoneta, ca. 1527–35; d. after 1605). Writer. Author of *Il ballarino* (Venice, 1581; facs., *MMML* ser. 2, 46 [1967]) and *Nobiltà di dame* (Venice, 1600; facs., *BMB* ser. 2, 103 [1970]), dance manuals that emphasize elaborate couple dances, especially ballettos, for use in aristocratic society. The later book is a substantially revised and greatly expanded version of the earlier. Rules about basic steps and etiquette, complex choreographies for individual dances, and appropriate music are included. Explicit correlations between the dances and music help today in establishing tempos and details of performance practice.

Carpenter, John Alden (b. Park Ridge, Ill., 28 Feb. 1876; d. Chicago, 26 Apr. 1951). Composer. He entered his father's business on graduation from Harvard (1897) and stayed until his retirement in 1936 while remaining active as a composer. He studied with Paine at Harvard; in Italy with Elgar (1906); in Chicago with Bernhard Ziehn (1908–12). Early works for orchestra were premiered in Chicago (*Adventures in a Perambulator,* 1914; Concertino for Piano and Orchestra, 1915); a song cycle (*Gitanjali,* voice and piano, 1913; orchestrated 1934) was praised by Borowski, a Chicago critic. His ballet *Skyscrapers* (1923–24) was commissioned by Diaghilev for a projected U.S. tour, but was premiered at the Metropolitan Opera (1926); its orchestra included saxophone, tenor banjo, traffic lights, on- and offstage choir; its style incorporated jazz idioms and allusions to popular song. After 1926 he wrote in an impressionist style evident in his tone poems for orchestra (*Sea Drift,* after a poem of Whitman, 1933; and the Spanish-influenced *Danza,* 1937). Other works include ballets (*The Birthday of the Infanta,* 1917; *Krazy Kat,* 1921); orchestral music, including 2 symphonies and concertos for piano, violin, and cello; chamber music for piano and for violin, a string quartet (1927), a piano quintet (1934); works for choir and orchestra (*Songs of Faith,* 1931; *Song of Freedom,* 1941); many songs.

Bibl.: Joan O'Connor, *John Alden Carpenter: A Bio-Bibliography* (Westport, 1994). Howard Pollack, *Skyscraper Lullaby: The Life and Music of John Alden Carpenter* (Washington, 1995).

Carpentras [Genet, Elzéar] (b. Carpentras, ca. 1470; d. Avignon, 14 June 1548). Composer. Active in Rome (1508–?; master of the papal chapel, 1514–21; 1524–26), in the French royal chapel (sometime between 1508 and 1514), and in Avignon (1505–ca. 1508; 1521–24; 1526–48). Upon settling finally in Avignon he became dean of St. Agricole, where he remained until his death. Between 1532 and ca. 1539 he oversaw the publication in Avignon of 4 volumes of his music. These books contain the majority of his extant compositions: 5 Masses, a set of Lamentations, hymns, and Magnificats. Other extant works, some printed in anthologies, are Psalms, another Lamentations setting, almost 20 motets, 4 frottolas, and 2 chansons.

Bibl.: *Collected Works, CMM* 58 (1972–73).

Carr, Benjamin (b. London, 12 Sept. 1768; d. Philadelphia, 24 May 1831). Composer, organist, and publisher. He studied music in London with Samuel Arnold and Charles Wesley. In 1793 he moved to Philadelphia, where he opened a music publishing business; he was the first important American music publisher. From 1800 to 1804 he issued the *Musical Journal for the Piano Forte* and from 1812 until 1825 *Carr's Musical Miscellany in Occasional Numbers.* More than 350 of his works survive, including operas and opera arrangements, incidental music, ballads, overtures for orchestra, chamber music, and keyboard works.

Bibl.: Charles A. Sprenkle, "The Life and Works of Benjamin Carr" (diss., Peabody Conservatory, 1970). Eve R. Meyer, "Benjamin Carr's Musical Miscellany," *Notes* 33 (1976–77): 253–65.

Carr, Leroy (b. Nashville, 27 Mar. 1905; d. Indianapolis, 28 or 29 Apr. 1935). Blues singer and pianist. In the mid-1920s Carr joined the guitarist Scrapper Blackwell (1903–63) to form a duo that made over 150 influential recordings from 1928. Carr's sweet singing voice and rolling piano style were matched with Blackwell's incisive guitar playing. Their poetic songs (mainly written by Blackwell) became part of the repertory, including *How Long How Long Blues* (1928), *Midnight Hour Blues* (1932), and *(In the Evening) When the Sun Goes Down* (1935). Carr's death at an all-night party from alcohol and nephritis spawned a number of songs in his memory.

Carreño, (María) Teresa (b. Caracas, 22 Dec. 1853; d. New York, 12 June 1917). Pianist. From a musically inclined, politically prominent family; studied with Gottschalk, then with Mathias in Paris, later with Anton Rubinstein. Began concert career in 1866; also occasionally sang in opera; with her second husband (1875–85), a baritone, ran opera company in Venezuela. Her tour of Germany in 1889 established her as a preeminent pianist; from then until World War I she lived mostly in Berlin, where she was also very active as a teacher. Married to Eugen d'Albert, 1892–95; gave concerts until her death. Composed piano pieces and other works.

Bibl.: Rosario Marciano, ed., *Selected Works* (New York, 1985). Marta Malinowski, *Teresa Carreño, "By the Grace of God"* (New Haven, 1940).

Carreras, José (b. Barcelona, 5 Dec. 1946). Lyric tenor. Began studies with Jaime Francisco Puig in Barcelona, 1964. Professional debut as Ismaele in Verdi's *Nabucco.* Sang Donizetti's Gennaro with Caballé at Barcelona's Teatro del Liceo, 1970. Award at Verdi Competition in Parma, 1971. Debut in London, 1971, with Caballé in concert version of Donizetti's *Maria Stuarda.* U.S. debut with New York City Opera as Puccini's Pinkerton, 1972. Sang at the San Francisco Opera, 1973; at Covent Garden and at the New York Met, 1974; at La Scala, 1975. In 1976 he sang Verdi's Don Carlo under Karajan at Salzburg. The telecast in 1994 of the second "Three Tenors" concert (with Pavarotti and Domingo) was seen by over a billion people worldwide.

Carrillo (Trujillo), Julián (Antonio) (b. Ahualulco, San Luis Potosí, 28 Jan. 1875; d. San Angél, 9 Sept. 1965). Composer and theorist. At the National Conservatory of Music in Mexico City he studied violin with Pedro Manzano and theory with Melesio Morales. In 1899 he went to Leipzig, where his teachers were Sitt (conducting) and Jadassohn (composition). Around 1900 he began to formulate a theory of microtonality, and he spent much of the rest of his life promoting the theories not only in his compositions but also in short-lived journals and in books. Central to the system was the "sonido 13," an addition to the twelve-note scale (described in his *"Sonido 13": El infinito en las escalas y en los acordes,* Mexico City, 1957). After studying violin at the Ghent Conservatory (1902–4), he returned to Mexico in 1905. The following year he was made professor of music at the National Conservatory, where he later also served as director (1913–14; 1920–24). From 1914 he lived in New York, where he helped found the American Symphony Orchestra. In 1924 he withdrew from official duties, and during the ensuing years he received important commissions, including those from the League of Composers and the Philadelphia Orchestra under Stokowski. In 1930 he formed the "Orquesta sonido 13" in Mexico. His works, about half of which are microtonal, include the operas *México en 1810* (1909) and *Xulitl* (1920; rev. 1947); 3 nonmicrotonal symphonies (1901, 1905, 1948); 3 microtonal symphonies (1924–31); Concertino for piano and orchestra, with 1/3 tones (1950; first perf., 1958); choral works (Requiem op. 1, 1900; *Misa de Santa Catarina,* 1913, rev. 1943; *Pequeño requiem atonal,* 24 vocal parts, 1956); chamber music (16 string quartets, 8 of which are microtonal); works for solo instruments, many in microtones (Sonata, guitar, 1/4 tones, 1960).

Bibl.: Gerald R. Benjamin, "Julián Carrillo and 'sonido trece,'" *Yearbook, Inter-American Institute for Musical Research* 3 (1967): 33–68.

Promotional piece for Richard D'Oyly Carte's productions.

Carte, Richard D'Oyly (b. London, 3 May 1844; d. there, 3 Apr. 1901). Impresario. Son of an instrument manufacturer; studied at University College, London; composed a little, then became an artists' representative and manager; in 1874 began importing French operettas for London staging. In 1875 commissioned Gilbert and Sullivan's *Trial by Jury* as a curtain-raiser; its success led to the formation of a company in 1876 to produce their works. In 1881 he opened the Savoy Theatre, where all of their later works were performed, and which his family continued to run after his death, maintaining the Gilbert and Sullivan tradition.

Carter, Benny [Bennett Lester] (b. New York, 8 Aug. 1907). Jazz alto saxophonist, trumpeter, composer, arranger, and bandleader. He played with and arranged for Fletcher Henderson (1930–31), McKinney's Cotton Pickers (1931–32), and his own big band (1932–34). Moving to Europe in 1935, he arranged for big bands, recording his composition "When Lights Are Low" in Denmark (1936), and recorded with Coleman Hawkins, including "Crazy Rhythm" (1937). Returning to the U.S. in 1938, he led big bands and combos. From the 1930s he also made many recordings playing alto saxophone, trumpet, or clarinet as a free-lance, including "I Can't Believe That You're in Love with Me" by the Chocolate Dandies, with Hawkins and Roy Eldridge (1940). After settling in Los Angeles (1942) he increasingly devoted himself to writing for films (including *Stormy Weather,* 1943) and television. He toured with Jazz at the Philharmonic (intermittently, 1950s and 1960s) and arranged for an all-star group on his album *Further Definitions* (1961). Carter was a leading alto saxophonist of the swing era whose improvisations were characterized by an elegant sound and thoughtful motivic development. His alto playing in the 1970s and 1980s, when he resumed an active performing career, moved forward stylistically from the swing era, as the album *Benny Carter 4: Montreux '77* demonstrates.

Bibl.: Morroe Berger, Edward Berger, and James Patrick, *Benny Carter: A Life in American Music* (Metuchen, N.J., 1982).

Carter, Betty [Jones, Lillie Mae] (b. Flint, Mich., 16 May 1930). Jazz singer. As a teenager in Detroit she sang with Charlie Parker and other bop musicians. She earned the nickname "Betty Bebop" while singing with Lionel Hampton's big band (1948–51). Based in New York, she worked intermittently, touring (1960–63) and recording (1961) with Ray Charles. From 1969 she led groups. Her recordings include *The Audience with Betty Carter* (1979).

Carter, Elliott (Cook) (b. New York, 11 Dec. 1908). Composer and writer on music. In his youth he came to know the music of Stravinsky, Schoenberg, Varèse, Ruggles, Ives, and Copland; he met Ives in 1924. Received B.A. and M.A. from Harvard, where he studied literature before turning to music (1926–32); studied with Boulanger (1932–35). He directed the Ballet Caravan (1935–40); taught at several institutions, including Columbia (1948–56), Yale (1960–62), and Juilliard (from 1967); he also taught at the Dartington and Tanglewood summer courses. His numerous awards and honors include 2 Pulitzer Prizes (String Quartet no. 2, 1960, and String Quartet no. 3, 1973).

His compositions favor large-scale integration of tempo relationships and harmonic material; his conception of structure came to involve superimposition and interpenetration of contrasting material. In a conversation reported by Boretz he characterized his approach: "The idea of my music, if it can be considered apart from its expressive and communicative character (which I doubt), could be said to be a constantly evolving series of shapes, like the patterns of choreography." In the Piano Sonata (1945–46) his conception of meter in terms of steady rhythm combined with a changing pulse is already clear; in the Cello Sonata (1948) this conception led to the technique of metric (or time) modulation, for which he has been most widely known. In the first and second string quartets (1951, 1959) and in the Sonata for Flute, Oboe, Cello, and Harpsichord (1952) the instruments are separately characterized in terms of the intervals, rhythms, and gestures they present; the Double Concerto (1961) separates the piano and harpsichord by means of both musical language and accompanying forces and closely relates rhythmic and harmonic events; in the Third String Quartet (1971) the typical separation of instruments is made more complete by giving each duo entire movements (violin-cello play four slower movements; violin-viola six quicker ones) that are segmented and reordered so that each is eventually heard against the others. Such permutational overlappings of material are also apparent in earlier works: in the Variations for Orchestra (1954–55) two thematic ideas, one presented more slowly and the other more quickly on each reappearance, shift with respect to their relative prominence; in the Concerto for Orchestra (1968–69) four movements are presented often with the sound of the other three in the background.

Other works include early incidental music and ballets (*Pocahontas,* 1936, 1939; *The Minotaur,* 1947); orchestral works (*Remembrance,* with trombone, 1988; *Partita,* 1994; *Adagio Tenebroso,* 1994; suites from his ballets; a Symphony of Three Orchestras, 1976; Oboe Concerto, 1987; Violin Concerto, 1990); chamber music (woodwind quintet, 1948; *Triple Duo,* violin, cello, flute, clarinet, piano, and percussion, 1982–83; *Enchanted Preludes,* flute and cello, premiered in 1988; Quintet, piano and winds, 1991; string quartet no. 5, 1995; *Fragment,* string quartet, 1995); choral music, mainly 1936–46; solo vocal music, including early songs and later song cycles (*A Mirror on Which To Dwell,* soprano and 9 instrumentalists, 1975; *In Sleep, in Thunder,* tenor and 14 instrumentalists, 1981; *Of Challenge and of Love,* soprano, piano, 1995).

Bibl.: Benjamin Boretz, "A Conversation with Elliott Carter," *PNM* 8 (1970): 1–22. E. Stone and K. Stone, eds., *The Writings of Elliott Carter: An American Composer Looks at Modern Music* (Bloomington, Ind., 1977). H. Gleason and W. Becker, "Elliott Carter," in *20th-Century American Compos-*

ers, 2nd rev. ed., Music Literature Outlines, ser. 4 (Bloomington, Ind., 1981). D. Schiff, *The Music of Elliott Carter* (New York, 1983). Charles Rosen, *The Musical Language of Elliott Carter* (Washington, D.C., 1984). David I. H. Harvey, *The Later Music of Elliott Carter: A Study in Music Theory and Analysis* (New York, 1989). William T. Doering, *Elliott Carter: A Bio-Bibliography* (Westport, 1993).

Carter, Mother Maybelle [Maybelle Addington] (b. near Nickelsville, Va., 10 May 1909; d. Madison, Tenn., 23 Oct. 1978). Country singer, guitarist, and autoharpist. Between 1927 and 1943 she worked with her brother-in-law A. P. [Alvin Pleasant] Carter (b. Maces Spring, Va., 15 Dec. 1891; d. there, 7 Nov. 1960) and his wife, Sara Dougherty Carter (b. Flat Woods, Va., 21 July 1898; d. Lodi, Cal., 8 Jan. 1979). As the Carter Family they recorded over 250 traditional American folk and religious songs (mainly collected by A. P.), many of which were later credited as "Carter Family" songs ("Wildwood Flower" and "Foggy Mountain Top," both recorded 1928–29). After their separation, Maybelle formed the Carter Sisters with her daughters Helen (b. 1927), June (b. 1929), and Anita (b. 1933). The Carter Family recordings experienced a resurgence of popularity during the folk revival of the 1960s, and Maybelle and Sara Carter recorded an album at the Newport Folk Festival in 1967 *(An Historic Reunion).*

Carter, Ron [Ronald Levin] (b. Ferndale, Mich., 4 May 1937). Jazz double bass player. After graduating from the Eastman School (B.M., 1959) he joined Chico Hamilton's quintet (1959–60) and studied at the Manhattan School of Music (M.M., 1961). He recorded with Eric Dolphy and Don Ellis (both 1960) and worked with Randy Weston, Jaki Byard, Bobby Timmons, Thelonious Monk, and Cannonball Adderley. As a member of Miles Davis's quintet (1963–68) he recorded the albums *My Funny Valentine* (1964) and *Nefertiti* (1967), and under Herbie Hancock's leadership (with Freddie Hubbard replacing Davis) *Maiden Voyage* (1965). As a free-lance he has recorded numerous jazz and soul albums. He played in the New York Jazz Quartet including Sir Roland Hanna (ca. 1971–76), Hancock's quintet V.S.O.P. (1976–77, 1980s), the Milestone Jazzstars including Sonny Rollins and McCoy Tyner (1978), and duos with Cedar Walton and Jim Hall. He performed in the film *Round Midnight* (1986). In addition, from 1972 he led groups in which he played double bass or piccolo bass.

Carulli, Ferdinando (b. Naples, 20 Feb. 1770; d. Paris, 17 Feb. 1841). Guitarist. Son of a distinguished Neapolitan man of letters; largely self-taught in music; developed his own technique of playing, advanced over earlier ones. He settled in Paris in 1808 and soon became the leading guitarist and teacher there (until the arrival of Sor around 1823). Published a famous *Méthode complète de guitarre ou lyre* (Paris, n.d.), a manual for accompanists, *L'harmonie appliquée à la guitarre* (Paris, 1825), and hundreds of guitar pieces, transcriptions and etudes, and chamber pieces including guitar.

Caruso, Enrico (b. Naples, 25 or 27 Feb. 1873; d. there, 2 Aug. 1921). Lyric and dramatic tenor. Apprenticed to a mechanical engineer at 10, he studied voice with Raffaele de Lutio at the school of Father Giuseppe Bronzetti. Much of his teens he spent manufacturing drinking fountains. In his early teens, his public singing was confined to church; but from the summer of 1891 onward he also sang at seaside cafes, public baths, baptisms, weddings, and birthdays, all the while working as a mechanic. As a result of this public exposure, he was introduced in 1891 to Guglielmo Vergine, with whom he studied for four years. A bad case of nerves postponed his professional debut from the fall of 1894, when he was to sing Wilhelm Meister in Ambroise Thomas's *Mignon,* to 15 Mar. 1895, when he sang the title role in Domenico Morelli's *L'amico Francesco.* His success on this occasion led to a string of engagements in Caserta and Naples. These in turn led to a season in Egypt, where he was able to sing several standard roles. In 1896 coaching in Salerno by Vincenzo Lombardi helped him begin to turn his lyric tenor into a dramatic tenor. In Sicily he first sang the role for which he became best known: Canio in *Pagliacci.* In October and November 1896 the Sicilians presented a special Caruso season. Nicola Daspuro, impresario of the Teatro lirico in Milan, engaged him for the 1897 season, where his creation of Loris in the premiere of Giordano's *Fedora* (17 Nov. 1898) elevated him to the front rank of tenors. Here he also created Federico in *L'Arlesiana* (1897) and Maurizio in *Adriana Lecouvreur* (1902). He toured Russia, South America, and again Russia in 1899, and was invited to sing at Italy's foremost theater, La Scala. Nerves and poor health contributed to a disastrous debut there on 26 Dec. 1900. But he quickly recouped his position and consolidated it.

The youthful Caruso had a limited range; arias had to be transposed. By 1902 he had gained the elusive high notes by doing, as he explained it, the opposite of what he had been taught. The tenor's debuts at Monte Carlo (1 Feb. 1902) and Covent Garden (14 May 1902)—both with Nellie Melba in *Rigoletto*—were dazzling triumphs. He returned to La Scala the world's preeminent star. After his New York debut on 23 Nov. 1903 (as the Duke in *Rigoletto*), he sang every season for the Metropolitan and came to call the U.S. his "stepmother" country. His final performance in Italy was in *Pagliacci* on 23 Sept. 1915. For the duration of the war he sang in North and South America, often appearing at benefits for the Red Cross, etc. His final performance at the Metropolitan was on 24 Dec. 1920 as Eléazar in *La juive.* Caruso's standard repertory encompassed 59 operas, including works by Donizetti (5), Bellini (3), Meyerbeer (3), Verdi (6), Massenet (3), Giordano (3), Mascagni (4), Leoncavallo (2), and Puccini (5). Besides Leoncavallo's Canio *(Pagliacci),* his most requested roles were Verdi's Radames *(Aida),*

Enrico Caruso in *Rigoletto.*

Riccardo *(Un ballo in maschera),* Duke of Mantua *(Rigoletto),* and Alfredo *(La traviata);* Bizet's Don José *(Carmen);* Mascagni's Turiddu *(Cavalleria rusticana);* Ponchielli's Enzo *(La gioconda);* Donizetti's Nemorino *(L'elisir d'amore);* Massenet's Des Grieux *(Manon);* Saint-Saëns's Samson *(Samson et Dalila);* and Puccini's Rodolfo *(La bohème),* Des Grieux *(Manon Lescaut),* Pinkerton *(Madama Butterfly),* Dick Johnson (which he created, *La fanciulla del West*), and Cavaradossi *(Tosca).*

Bibl.: Frances Robinson, *Caruso: A Life in Pictures* (New York, 1957). H. Greensfeld, *Caruso* (New York, 1983). Michael Scott, *The Great Caruso* (New York, 1988). Enrico Caruso, Jr., and Andrew Farkas, *Enrico Caruso: My Father and Family* (Portland, Ore., 1990) [with discography].

Carvalho, João de Sousa (b. Estremoz, Portugal, 22 Feb. 1745; d. Alentejo? 1798). Composer. From 1761 he studied composition in Naples with Cotumacci. His *La Nitteti* was performed in Rome in 1766; he returned to Portugal the following year, where he was appointed professor of composition at the Seminário Patriarcal. He became *mestre de capela* in 1773 and assumed the position of music teacher to the royal family in 1778. Known works include 15 operas, many sacred works, and keyboard music.

Carver, Robert (b. 1487; d. after 1546). Composer. Probably associated with the Scottish royal chapel; sometimes referred to as a canon of Scone. A manuscript anthology often termed the Scone Antiphonary preserves his works: 5 Masses (one on "L'homme armé") and two motets (one for 5 and one for 19 voices).

Bibl.: *Collected Works, CMM* 16 (1959–).

Cary, Tristam (Ogilvie) (b. Oxford, England, 14 May 1925). Composer. Served as a radio operator for the navy in World War II; this spurred his interest in electronic music. Studied at Trinity College of Music (A.Mus., L.Mus, 1949–51). Founded electronic music studio at the Royal College of Music in 1967. Named senior lecturer in 1974; dean of music in 1982 at Univ. of Adelaide. Contributor to *Musical Times, Composer, Electronic Music Review,* and other journals. Compositions include both electronic and nonelectronic works; music for stage, film, and television.

Casadesus, Robert (b. Paris, 7 Apr. 1899; d. there, 19 Sept. 1972). Pianist and composer. His uncle was Francis Casadesus (1870–1954), a conductor, composer, and violinist. His father was Robert-Guillaume Casadesus (1878–1940), an actor, composer, and singer who wrote songs and operettas. His wife, Gaby Casadesus (Gabrielle, née L'Hôte, b. 1901), was a pianist with whom he performed as a piano duo. Robert's formal studies took place at the Paris Conservatory, where he won a prize in piano at age 14, and later a prize in harmony, as well as the Grand Prix Diémer, a prize named for his piano teacher, Louis Diémer. He toured a great deal as a soloist and played under Toscanini in New York in 1935. In addition to the piano duo with his wife, he played in a violin-piano duo with Zino Francescatti. He was a professor, and later director, at the American Conservatory at Fontainebleau. Many of his compositions are unpublished, including 6 symphonies. His published compositions include *6 pièces* (2 pianos, 1938); *24 préludes* (piano, 1924); a string trio (1938); 2 piano sonatas (1947, 1953). He also wrote a concerto for 2 pianos and orchestra (1950) and a concerto for 3 pianos and string orchestra (first performed in New York with his wife and son, Jean, 1965).

Bibl.: Gaby Casadesus, *Mes noces musicales,* conversation with Jacqueline Muller (Paris, 1989) [including works list and discography].

Casals, Pablo [Pau] **(Carlos Salvador Defilló)** (b. Vendrell, Catalonia, 29 Dec. 1876; d. San Juan, Puerto Rico, 22 Oct. 1973). Cellist, conductor, and composer. From 1888 he studied cello with Josep García at Barcelona's Escuela municipal de música; and from 1890 he studied composition with Tomás Bretón and chamber music with Jesús de Monasterio at the Madrid Conservatory, supported by a scholarship from María Christina, Queen Regent of Spain. At the behest of his sponsor, Count Guillermo de Morphy, Casals journeyed to the Brussels Conservatory in 1895. Its director considered him too finished an artist to need conservatory training; and its cello professor, who had not yet heard him play, ridiculed him in class. This persuaded Casals to leave for Paris, where he played in the Opéra's orchestra until the effects of deprivation convinced him to return to Barcelona in 1897. There he got his teacher's old job at the conservatory, where he taught until 1899, the year of his second and successful assault on Paris. An audition with Lamoureux led to a Parisian solo debut and acceptance as one of the era's elect virtuosi. From his base in Paris he launched tours of the U.S. in 1901 and 1904, of South America in 1903, and of Russia in 1905. Beginning in 1905 he also performed frequently in a trio with the violinist Jacques Thibaud and the pianist Alfred Cortot. At the outbreak of war in 1914 he relocated in New York, the home of Susan Metcalfe, whom he married that year. In 1919 he returned to Barcelona, and the following year founded the Orquesta Pau Casals (debut 13 Oct. 1920). Casals composed intermittently. After the Spanish Civil War he settled in the French Catalan village of Prades, refusing to return to Spain so long as Franco remained in power. Here he conducted festivals from 1950 until 1966. He made Puerto Rico his home in 1956, and the annual festivals bearing his name were begun there in 1957. In his later years he promoted peace by conducting his oratorio *El pessebre* (The Manger), in cities throughout Europe and the Americas.

Bibl.: H. L. Kirk, *Pablo Casals: A Biography* (New York, 1974). D. Blum, *Casals and the Art of Interpretation* (London, 1977). Robert Baldock, *Pablo Casals* (Boston, 1993).

Casanovas, Narciso (b. Sabadell, near Barcelona, 17 Feb. 1747; d. Viña Vieja, near Montserrat, 1 Apr. 1799). Composer and organist. In 1763 he became a Benedictine monk at Montserrat; apparently he remained there for most of his life. For keyboard he composed sonatas and fugues (some of the latter called *pasos* or *intentos*); he also composed vocal settings of liturgical texts, including a Benedictus, a Salve Regina in F, and a Mass in D.

Casavant, Joseph (b. St. Hyacinthe, near Montreal, 23 Jan. 1807; d. there, 9 Mar. 1874). Organ builder. A blacksmith in his native village until 1834; then went to school at Ste. Thérèse, where he completed a half-finished organ, which led to an order for a new instrument, completed in 1840. By his retirement in 1866 he had built 17 organs, none of which survives. His sons Joseph-Claver (1855–1933) and Samuel (1859–1929) were taught the trade by his successor, Eusèbe Brodeau, then got further experience in Europe. They returned to start their own firm, Casavant Frères, in 1879, and by the early 20th century they had become the most important organ builders in North America. The firm remains in business on the site of Joseph's workshop.

Casella, Alfredo (b. Turin, 25 July 1883; d. Rome, 5 Mar. 1947). Composer, conductor, pianist, and writer. He made his debut as a pianist in 1894; in 1896, at the age of 12, he went to Paris to study (piano with Louis Diémer, harmony and counterpoint with Leroux, composition with Fauré) and stayed until 1915. By 1902 he had begun his career as a professional pianist, and from 1912 to 1915 he taught a piano class at the Paris Conservatory. He published his first compositions in 1903, and for the next decade his works reflected the influences important in Paris: Fauré and Debussy, Mahler, Strauss, and the Russian nationalists. His associates in Paris included Debussy, Ravel, Enescu, and Falla.

In 1915 Casella returned to Italy to teach at the Liceo musicale di Santa Cecilia in Rome. At this time his own compositional style was changing: he was more receptive to influence from Bartók, Stravinsky, and Schoenberg (*A notte alta* for piano, 1917, is atonal). But by 1920 he was calling himself a neoclassicist and making renewed use of earlier Italian instrumental music and folk song style. He was determined to share his enthusiasms with Italian audiences and to help in "the achievement of a style of our own, which would be based on our great instrumental past but which would also be contemporary in its musical language." Between the wars he was involved in most Italian efforts in contemporary music: he was co-founder (with Castelnuovo-Tedesco, Gui, Malipiero, Pizzetti, Respighi, and Tommasini) of what came to be called the Società italiana di musica moderna (1917–19); in 1922 he co-founded the Corporazione delle nuove musiche, which became the Italian section of the ISCM; in the 1930s he helped to organize the Venice Festival of Contemporary Music. In 1922 he resigned his post at the Liceo in Rome in order to travel as pianist and conductor of contemporary music. In the 1930s, however, he returned to piano teaching, both in a master class at the Accademia di S. Cecilia in Rome and at summer courses that he helped to found at the Accademia Chigiana in Siena.

As composer, performer, conductor, teacher, organizer, and peacemaker his activities were crucial to the development of Italian music in the 20th century. Casella was also the author of books on Beethoven, Stravinsky, Bartók, and Bach; an autobiography (translated as *Music in My Time,* 1955); a book on orchestration (with Mortari, 1950); and numerous articles in music journals.

Works: Operas; ballets (*La giara,* with Pirandello and Chirico, 1924); many orchestral works (*Elegia eroica* op. 29, 1916; *Paganiniana* op. 65, 1942); *Scarlattiana,* piano and small orchestra (1926); some chamber music (Serenade for clarinet, bassoon, trumpet, violin, cello op. 46, 1926); piano works (Sonatina op. 28, 1916; *A notte alta* op. 30, 1917; *11 pezzi infantili* op. 35, 1920; *2 ricercari sul nome B-A-C-H* op. 52, 1932); a Missa solemnis, *Pro pace,* op. 71, soprano, baritone, chorus, and orchestra (1944); solo vocal music; orchestral arrangements of works by Balakirev, Vivaldi, and others and of folk songs.

Bibl.: Fedele D'Amico and Guido M. Gatti, eds., *Alfredo Casella* (Milan, 1958) [with works list and bibl.].

Cash, Johnny [John R.] (b. Kingsland, Ark., 26 Feb. 1932). Country singer and songwriter. After performing on local radio stations in Arkansas, in 1955 he began recording his own songs for Sun Records in

Memphis ("Hey Porter," 1955; "I Walk the Line," 1956). In the 1960s he led a touring country music revue that included the Carter Sisters, the Statler Brothers, and his backup band the Tennessee Three; from 1969 he hosted a television variety show and appeared in movies (*The Gospel Road,* 1971). His album *Johnny Cash at Folsom Prison* (1968) was very popular, as were several duets recorded with June Carter of the Carter Sisters, whom he married in 1968 ("Jackson," 1967).

Bibl.: John L. Smith, *The Johnny Cash Discography* (Westport, Conn., 1985).

Cassadó (Moreu), Gaspar (b. Barcelona, 30 Sept. 1897; d. Madrid, 24 Dec. 1966). Cellist and composer. Son of composer Joaquín Cassadó Valls. Studied with his father before entering Barcelona's Conservatorio Las Mercedes in 1905. His debut in 1907 led to a scholarship that permitted study with Casals in Paris, 1908–14. After 1918 he established a career as soloist. Played with Bauer and Rubinstein; later formed trio with Menuhin and Kentner. U.S. debut, New York, 10 Dec. 1936. Attracted to Italian Fascism, he relocated in Florence. Taught at Siena's Accademia musicale chigiana, 1946–52 and 1955–63. Composed orchestral works, an oratorio, a cello concerto, chamber music.

Cassiodorus, Magnus Aurelianus (b. Scylacium [Scylletium; now Squillace, Calabria], ca. 485; d. Vivarium [now Stalleti], near Scylacium, ca. 580). Writer. He held civic office under Emperor Theodoric from shortly after 500 until between 537 and 540, when Byzantium conquered Italy; then founded and took up residence at the monastery of Vivarium. There he wrote *Institutiones divinarum et humanarum litterarum,* which treats music as one of the seven liberal arts. This treatise, along with that by Boethius (of which Cassiodorus does not make use), was a principal source for medieval music theorists through the 9th century and continued to be quoted as late as the 12th century. He classifies music as *harmonica, rhythmica,* and *metrica* and discusses its power rather than insisting solely on its relationship to mathematics.

Cassuto, Alvaro Leon (b. Oporto, 17 Nov. 1938). Composer and conductor. In Lisbon he studied composition with Lopes Graça, in Hamburg with Klussman, and at Darmstadt (1960–61) with Stockhausen and Ligeti. Back in Lisbon he studied conducting with Freitas Branco and then conducted orchestras in Portugal and the U.S.: the Lisbon Gulbenkian Orchestra (1965–68), the Little Orchestra of New York (1969–70), and the American Symphony (1969–70). At Tanglewood he won the Koussevitzky Prize in 1969. In 1975 he became music director of Lisbon's National Radio Orchestra. He also lectured and conducted at the Univ. of California, Irvine, until 1979. He has written neoclassical, twelve-tone, and aleatory music. Works include *Sinfonia breve* no. 1 (1959), no. 2 (1960); *In memoriam Pedro de Freitas Branco,* orchestra (1963); *Cro(mono)fonia,* 20 strings (1967); *Canticum in tenebris,* soloists, chorus, orchestra (1968); the opera *In the Name of Peace* (1971); *To Love and Peace,* symphonic poem (1973); *Return to the Future,* orchestra (1985); *The Four Seasons,* piano, orchestra (1986).

Castaldo, Joseph (b. New York, 23 Dec. 1927). Composer. In 1947, while stationed in Italy with an army band, he studied at the Accademia di S. Cecilia in Rome; then at the Manhattan School (Giannini) and the Philadelphia Conservatory (Persichetti; B.M., M.M.); taught at the Philadelphia Conservatory and was chair of its department of composition and theory from 1960; retired in 1983. Works include a cello concerto (1984); *Lacrimosa,* strings (1976–77); other chamber music and piano works; a cantata and choral works.

Castelnuovo-Tedesco, Mario (b. Florence, 3 Apr. 1895; d. Beverly Hills, 16 Mar. 1968). Composer and pianist. Studied piano (del Valle, his mother's cousin) and composition (Pizzetti) in Florence. Early orchestral works were performed in Rome (Augusteo Orchestra under Gui) and in Vienna (conducted by Toscanini); these works were impressionistic, depicting his native Tuscany (*Cipressi,* piano, 1920; orchestrated, 1921); his opera *La mandragola* (1920–23) won first prize in the Concorso lirico nazionale in 1925. Neo-Romantic compositions on Jewish themes include a concerto for violin, *The Prophets* (premiered in New York by Heifetz, 1933), *Le danze del Re David* for piano (1921; premiered by Gieseking at the Frankfurt ISCM festival, 1927), and oratorios. In the 1920s he began to employ Shakespearean themes in overtures, settings of sonnets, and finally in operas (*The Merchant of Venice,* 1956, which won first prize in the La Scala competition in 1958). He moved to the U.S. in 1939, where he remained extremely prolific, composing over 100 film scores (*Tortilla Flat,* 1942; *The Day of the Fox,* 1956) as well as more orchestral and chamber music. Several of his later orchestral works exploit American themes; *An American Rhapsody* (1943) uses two folk melodies ("Turkey in the Straw" and "Arkansas Traveler"). He made a significant contribution to the contemporary literature for guitar, much of it commissioned by Segovia.

Bibl.: Nick Rossi, *Catalogue of Works by Mario Castelnuovo-Tedesco* (New York, 1977).

Castiglioni, Niccolò (b. Milan, 17 July 1932). Composer and writer. He studied piano and composition at the Milan Conservatory, then studied composition with Blacher and others in Salzburg at the Mozarteum (1952–53). In 1961 his radio opera *Attraverso lo specchio* won a prize in Italy; between 1966 and 1969 he taught in the U.S. at various universities (Buffalo, Michigan, California at San Diego, and Washington at Seattle). He returned to Italy because of illness, subsequently composing only intermittently. By 1968 he had explored various approaches to composition (neoclassicism, electronic techniques, Cage's indeterminacy). In addition to the radio opera, he wrote orchestral music (*Quodlibet,* piano and orchestra, 1976; a concerto for 3 pianos and orchestra, 1983; *Geistliches Lied,* soprano and orchestra, 1983); chamber and piano music; large works for chorus and orchestra or ensemble (Symphony in C, 1968–69); several works for solo voice and orchestra (*Figure,* 1965); piece for tape (1962).

Castil Blaze [Blaze, François-Henri-Joseph] (b. Cavaillon, Vaucluse, 1 Dec. 1784; d. Paris, 11 Dec. 1857). Writer and critic. Went to Paris in 1799 to study law, also taking lessons at the Conservatory; became a government administrator in the provinces; in 1820 returned to Paris as a writer, publishing that year the first volume of his *De l'opéra en France,* whose provocative views and entertaining style made him a success; became a very influential music critic, writing for the *Journal des débats* (1822–32) and other newspapers and periodicals; other critical and historical books followed. Translated and adapted many foreign operas for the French stage (including works of Mozart, Rossini, Weber, Cimarosa, Donizetti, and Beethoven). His reworking of *Der Freischütz* (as *Robin des bois*) had the greatest success, although criticized by purists. Composed some popular romances and 3 less successful operas.

Castro, Jean de (b. Liège, ca. 1540; d. ca. 1611). Composer. Lived and had works printed in Antwerp, Düsseldorf, and Cologne; also lived in Lyons. His compositions were printed in many other European cities as well. He was exceptionally prolific, and his works were among the most popular of his time. His output filled over 30 volumes (excluding reprints) published between 1569 and 1610. Most pieces are for 2 or 3 voices, although some call for as many as 8. Extant works include 3 parody Masses, 7 books of other sacred music, about 28 books of secular songs (both chansons and madrigals), and sacred and secular pieces in anthologies or manuscript sources.

Castro, Juan Blas de (b. Barrachina, Teruel, ca. 1560; d. Madrid, 6 Aug. 1631). Composer, singer, and guitarist. From the 1590s he was a musician at the court in Salamanca of the Duke of Alba, whom Lope de Vega also served. Castro set Lope's music, and in his poems Lope praised Castro's musical gifts. From around 1600 Castro was in the service of Philip III; later, in the 1620s, he was earning a handsome salary as chamber musician to Philip IV. He composed a large number of polyphonic *canciones* and *romances;* a few appear in Jesús Aroca, ed., *Cancionero musical y poético del siglo XVII recogido por Claudio de la Sablonara* (Madrid, 1916) and in *MME* 32.

Castro, Juan José (b. Avellaneda, near Buenos Aires, 7 Mar. 1895; d. Buenos Aires, 3 Sept. 1968). Composer and conductor. He studied in Buenos Aires with Manuel Posadas (piano, violin) and Eduardo Fornarini (composition). After winning the Europa Prize he studied composition with Vincent d'Indy at the Schola cantorum in Paris. In Buenos Aires he became conductor of the Renacimiento Chamber Orchestra (1928) and of the ballet at the Teatro Colón (1930). From 1947 he conducted the Havana Philharmonic, from 1949 the Sodre Orchestra in Uruguay, from 1952 the Victorian Symphony in Melbourne, and from 1956 to 1960 the National Symphony in Buenos Aires. He directed the Puerto Rico Conservatory until 1964. He composed operas (*La zapatera prodigiosa,* 1943, first perf. 1949; *Proserpina y el extranjero,* 1951, first perf. La Scala, 1952); ballets (*Mekhano,* 1937; *Offenbachiana,* 1940); 5 symphonies (1931, 1932, 1936, 1939, 1956), a piano concerto (1941), *A una madre* (1925), and other orchestral music; choral music (*Martín Fierro,* cantata, baritone, chorus, orchestra, 1944; *Epitafio en ritmos y sonidos,* chorus, orchestra, 1961); sonatas for violin (1914) and cello (1916), a string quartet (1942), and other chamber music; 2 piano sonatas (1917, 1939); *Corales criollos* nos. 1 and 2 for piano (1947), no. 3 for orchestra (1953).

Castro (Herrera), Ricardo (b. Durango, 7 Feb. 1864; d. Mexico City, 27 Nov. 1907). Composer and pianist. Studied at the Mexico City Conservatory, 1877–83; toured the U.S. as pianist, 1885; active as soloist, chamber music player, composer, and teacher in Mexico; played and had his music performed in Europe; director of the Mexico City Conservatory in 1907. Works include 2 symphonies (1883, 1887); a cello concerto (1902); a piano concerto (1904); several operas; many piano pieces.

Castrucci, Pietro (b. Rome, 1679; d. Dublin, 29 Feb. 1752). Violinist and composer. Reportedly a violin student of Corelli, he came to London around 1715, where he was supported by Lord Burlington. Shortly afterward he was made concertmaster of Handel's opera orchestra, a position he maintained until 1737. He was partly responsible for the development of the violalike "violetta marina" (possibly the same as the "English violet"); Handel scored for the instrument in *Sosarme* (1732) and *Orlando* (1733). Castrucci died in poverty, leaving several published works, including 12 violin sonatas op. 2 (London, 1734?) and 12 concerti grossi op. 3 (London, 1736).

Catalani, Alfredo (b. Lucca, 19 June 1854; d. Milan, 7 Aug. 1893). Composer. From a family of musicians; studied to 1872 at the Lucca Conservatory, in 1873–75 at the Milan Conservatory (composition under Bassini, piano under Andreoli). His graduation piece, Boito's one-act *egloga orientale La falce,* which he conducted at the school in July 1875, was published by Giovannina Lucca, who remained his chief supporter until her firm was sold to Ricordi in 1888. His first two operas, *Elda* (Turin, 1880) and *Dejanice* (La Scala, 1883), were not successful, the seriousness of Catalani's music leading to frequent charges of Wagnerism. *Edmea* (La Scala, 27 Feb. 1886) was more successful, and a production at Turin in November, conducted by Toscanini, led to a close friendship and to Toscanini's championing of Catalani's operas. *Loreley,* a revision of *Elda,* was successful at Turin in 1890, but it was *La Wally* (La Scala, 20 Jan. 1892; libretto by Illica) that was to be his most enduring work, although not in the regular repertory. He also composed a symphonic poem, *Ero e Leandro* (1885), piano pieces, and songs. From 1886 he was professor of composition at the Milan Conservatory.

Bibl.: J. W. Klein, "Alfredo Catalani," *MQ* 23 (1937): 287–94. C. Gatti, *Catalani: La vita e le opere* (Milan, 1953). F. Walker, "Verdian Forgeries," *MR* 20 (1959): 28–37. J. W. Klein, "Toscanini and Catalani: A Unique Friendship," *ML* 48 (1967): 213–28. M. Zurletti, *Catalani* (Turin, 1982).

Catalani, Angelica (b. Sinigaglia, 10 May 1780; d. Paris, 12 June 1849). Soprano. Said to have been taught by the castrato Marchesi, the greatest virtuoso of the time, whose technical abilities she eventually rivaled; made her debut with him in Mayr's *Lodoiska* (Venice, 1797). An immediate success, she sang in many leading Italian houses; from 1801 at Lisbon, where in 1804 she married a French diplomat who then managed her career, touring her across Europe; in 1806–13 based in London in opera and concerts, earning huge fees; in 1814–17 director of the Théâtre-Italien, Paris, which was employed as a showcase for her talents. She was often criticized for displaying her immense vocal powers at the expense of good taste and dramatic values; she retired in 1832.

Catel, Charles-Simon (b. Laigle, Normandy, 10 June 1773; d. Paris, 29 Nov. 1830). Composer and theorist. In Paris he studied theory and composition with Gossec (1780s). He taught harmony to the musical corps of the revolutionary army; in 1795 he became professor at the Conservatoire. During the 1790s he composed revolutionary hymns and marches (*Hymne à l'égalité,* 1791; *Ode patriotique,* 1792); after 1800 he concentrated on works for Paris theaters (*Sémiramis, tragédie lyrique,* 1802; *L'Auberge de Bagnères, opéra bouffon,* 1807; *Les bayadères,* opera, 1810; *Wallace, ou Le ménestrel écossais, opéra héroïque,* 1817). Many of his operas look toward the large-scale grand opera of the 19th century. He also composed 3 *symphonies concertantes,* military marches for winds, 6 string quintets, 6 quartets for winds and strings, 6 keyboard sonatas, and a *Recueil de 2 duos bachiques et de 6 canons* (Paris, ca. 1820). His highly popular *Traité d'harmonie* (Paris, 1802) was translated into several languages.

Catlett, Sid(ney) [Big Sid] (b. Evansville, Ind., 17 Jan. 1910; d. Chicago, 25 Mar. 1951). Jazz drummer. His main affiliations were with Benny Carter (1932–33), McKinney's Cotton Pickers (1934–35), Don Redman (1936–38), Louis Armstrong (1938–41), Benny Goodman (1941), and Teddy Wilson (1941–44). He performed in the film *Jammin' the Blues* (1944). After leading a quartet (1944–47), he joined Armstrong's All Stars (1947–49), then worked with Muggsy Spanier and Sidney Bechet at the club Jazz Ltd. in Chicago. Also working as a free-lance throughout his career, Catlett moved fluently among extant jazz styles, recording, for example, "On Katherina" with Eddie Condon's Dixieland septet (1943), "Tuesday at Ten" with Goodman's orchestra (1941), and "Salt Peanuts" with Dizzy Gillespie's bop quintet (1945).

Cato, Diomedes (b. Venice, before 1570; d. after 1607?). Composer and lutenist. In the service of the Polish King Sigismund III from 1588 to 1593 or 1594 and after 1602. Either before 1588 or from 1600 to 1602 worked for Stanisław Kostka, treasurer of Pomerania. Known chiefly for his lute pieces, including dances and intabulations of vocal works as well as free instrumental compositions such as fantasias; also wrote music for keyboard, viol consort, and voices (all secular).

Catoire [Katuar]**, Georgy (L'vovich)** (b. Moscow, 27 Apr. 1861; d. there, 21 May 1926). Composer and musicologist. Studied piano with Klindworth at the Moscow Conservatory. Graduated from the mathematics faculty of Moscow Univ. in 1884. Went to Berlin the following year to study music; continued to work there with Klindworth as well as with Tirsch and Rüfer. Studied briefly with Rimsky-Korsakov and Lyadov. In Moscow he was encouraged by Tchaikovsky, Arensky, and Taneyev. Named professor of composition at Moscow Conservatory, a position he held to his death. Wrote a course in harmony (*Teoretichesky kurs garmonii,* Moscow, 1924–25) and musical form (published posthumously, *Muzïkal'naya forma,* Moscow, 1934–36). Pupils included Abramsky, Kabalevsky, Fere, and others. His works include the cantata *Rusalka* (1888), Symphony in C minor op. 7 (1899), Piano Concerto in A♭ op. 21 (1909), and 2 violin sonatas (1900, 1906).

Caturla, Alejandro García (b. Remedios, Cuba, 7 Mar. 1906; d. there, 12 Nov. 1940). Composer. He studied in Havana with Pedro Sanjuán (1926–27) and in Paris with Nadia Boulanger (1928). In 1932 he founded the Orquesta de conciertos de Caibarién; the same year he was appointed district judge in Remedios. He was shot to death by a criminal whom he had sentenced in his courtroom. His music explores Afro-Cuban rhythms and folk tunes and also employs Cuban popular tunes. Works include a stage work for narrator and marionettes, *Manita en el suelo* (1934–37); orchestral works (*Obertura cubana,* 1927; *3 danzas cubanas,* 1928); choral works (*El caballo blanco,* 1931; *Yamba-ó,* oratorio, 1931; *Canto de cafetales,* 1937); other vocal works (*2 poemas afro-cubanos,* 1929; *La rumba,* 1931; *Sabas,* voice, chamber ensemble, 1937); chamber music (*Bembé,* 14 instruments, 1929; *Primera suite cubana,* piano, winds, 1930); piano pieces (*Berceuse campesina,* 1930).

Caus, Salomon de (b. Dieppe, ca. 1576; d. Paris, buried 28 Feb. 1626). Theorist and mathematician. He spent his life as an engineer and architect for dukes and princes, chiefly in Brussels (from 1605), London (from 1610), and Heidelberg (from 1614). In 1615 he published 2 important treatises dealing with, among other things, the production of sound by musical instruments: *Institution harmonique divisée en deux parties* (Frankfurt, 1615; R: *MMML* 2, vol. 81, New York, 1969; also R: Geneva, 1980) and *Les raisons des forces mouvantes avec diverses machines* (Frankfurt, 1615; 2nd ed., 1624). Part 3 of the latter contains an important early discussion of organ construction.

Caustun [Causton], **Thomas** (b. ca. 1520–25?; d. London, 28 Oct. 1569). Composer. A Gentleman of the Chapel Royal from ca. 1550 until his death. Wrote mostly English cathedral music (anthems and services) published in Day's *Certaine Notes* (London, 1565). Also contributed to Day's *The Whole Psalms in Foure Parts* (London, 1563). His compositions, all for 4 voices, are largely chordal with occasional hints of imitative counterpoint.

Cavaillé-Coll, Aristide (b. Montpellier, 4 Feb. 1811; d. Paris, 13 Oct. 1899). Organ builder. From a family of organ builders active in southern France and Spain; at Rossini's urging settled in Paris in 1833, joined by his father and brother, forming a company that was to build more than 500 organs in western Europe, representing the perfecting of the French romantic organ.

Bibl.: Gilbert Huybens, comp., *Cavaillé-Coll: Complete Theoretical Works* (Buren, 1978) [facs.]. Fenner Douglass, *Cavaillé-Coll and the Musicians: A Documented Account of His First Thirty Years in Organ Building* (Raleigh, N.C., 1980).

Cavalieri, Caterina [Kavalier, Franziska Helena Appolonia] (b. Vienna, 19 Feb. 1760; d. there, 30 June 1801). Soprano. She received early vocal instruction from Salieri in Vienna and made her debut at the Kärntnertortheater in 1775, as the lead in Anfossi's *La finta giardiniera.* When Joseph II's National-Singspiel was founded she became one of its chief sopranos, singing leads in first performances of Umlauf's *Die Bergknappen* (1778), Salieri's *Der Rauchfangkehrer* (1781), and Mozart's *Die Entführung aus dem Serail* (1782; Constanze). She was the first Mlle. Silber in Mozart's *Der Schauspieldirektor* (1786) and the first Viennese Donna Elvira in *Don Giovanni* in 1788; in the latter the composer added the aria "Mi tradì" for her.

Cavalieri, Emilio de' (b. Rome, ca. 1550; d. there, 11 Mar. 1602). Composer, organist, and diplomat. A member of a noble family, young Emilio probably studied music with his father, Tommaso. By 1578 he held a position as organist. Ferdinando de' Medici, upon becoming Grand Duke of Tuscany in 1588, hired him as overseer of musical activities at his court; the duties included sumptuous productions of *intermedi.* During the 1590s Cavalieri became increasingly involved in diplomatic activities, which took him frequently to Rome. In 1600 the musical festivities in Florence surrounding the wedding of Henry IV and Maria de' Medici included Cavalieri's *La contesa fra Giunone e Minerva.* He is best known for his *Rappresentatione di Anima, et di Corpo* (first perf. Rome, 1600; publ. Rome, 1600; facs., 1967), an important early work in the development of the new recitative style and in the history of the oratorio. Although Ottavio Rinuccini claimed in 1600 that he and Peri were the first to use the *stile rappresentativo,* Cavalieri was experimenting with the declamatory style at about the same time. In 1601 Peri reported that it was Cavalieri "before any other" who "enabled us to hear our kind of music upon the stage."

Bibl.: Claude V. Palisca, "The First Performance of 'Euridice,'" in *Queens College,* 1964. Warren Kirkendale, *L'aria di Fiorenza, id est Il ballo del Gran Duca* (Florence, 1972).

Cavalli [Caletti, Caletti-Bruni], **(Pietro)** [Pier] **Francesco** (b. Crema, 14 Feb. 1602; d. Venice, 14 Jan. 1676). Composer and singer. He was the son of Giovanni Battista Caletti, organist and *maestro di cappella* at the cathedral at Crema. As a boy Francesco apparently excelled as a singer in the local choir; Venetian nobleman and governor Federico Cavalli noticed the boy and in 1616 persuaded the elder Caletti to let Francesco accompany him to Venice, where he would see to his musical studies. Young Caletti was immediately taken into the choir of St. Mark's (Monteverdi was *maestro*), where he remained for a decade. From 1620 he was also one of the organists at SS. Giovanni e Paolo. His first known composition appeared in 1625 in a collection of solo motets, *Ghirlanda sacra.* In 1630 his marriage to Maria Sozomeno, member of a wealthy family, provided him with a measure of personal economic stability that enabled him to spend the rest of his life involved in financially insecure operatic ventures.

In 1639, when the post of second organist at St. Mark's became vacant, Cavalli was the unanimous choice for the position. That same year his first opera, *Le nozze di Teti e di Peleo* (libretto by Orazio Persiani), was performed in Venice. It was followed by a number of successes throughout the 1740s: *Gli amori d'Apollo e di Dafne* (1640), with a libretto by Busenello, and *Egisto* (1642) and *Giasone* (1649), both with librettos by Giovanni Faustini. *Egisto* was performed in a great many Italian cities, as well as in Paris and (perhaps) in Vienna. In 1652 Cavalli's wife died, leaving most of her estate to him; during the next eight years he composed operas not only for Venice but also for Naples, Milan, and Florence. In 1656 he published *Musiche sacre,* a collection of concertato Masses, Psalms, and hymns.

In 1659 the French prime minister Cardinal Mazarin invited Cavalli to compose an opera to honor Louis XIV's marriage to Maria Theresia of Spain. Cavalli spent two years in Paris (1660–62) composing *Ercole amante* (libretto by Francesco Buti) for the occasion. When the work was finally performed in 1662 in the lavish, gigantic Tuileries theater built specifically for the event, poor acoustics made the music virtually incoherent. Perhaps embittered by the experience, Cavalli returned to Venice in 1662 and again took up his organ duties at St. Mark's; in 1668 he was made *maestro di cappella.* Of his 6 remaining operas, 2 (*Eliogabalo* and *Massenzio*) were left unperformed, possibly because the music was, by the 1670s, old-fashioned. In 1675 Cavalli brought out his second publication, the 3 *Vesperi.* In addition to 33 verifiable operas and 2 published collections, he also composed cantatas, arias, a Magnificat (1650), and a Cantate Domino (1625).

Bibl.: Henri Prunières, *Cavalli et l'opéra vénitien au dix-septième siècle* (Paris, 1931). Lorenzo Bianconi, "Francesco Cavalli und die Verbreitung der venezianischen Oper in Italien" (diss., Heidelberg, 1974). Ellen Rosand, "Aria as Drama in the Early Operas of Francesco Cavalli," in *Venezia e il melodramma nel seicento,* ed. Maria Teresia Muraro (Florence, 1976). Jane Glover, *Cavalli* (New York, 1978).

Cavazzoni, Girolamo [Hieronimo d'Urbino] (b. Urbino, ca. 1520; d. ca. 1577). Composer. Son of Marco Antonio Cavazzoni. Worked in Mantua from at least 1565 until 1577, supervising the construction of the organ at S. Barbara and then serving as organist there. Wrote mostly for keyboard: ricercars, 2 canzonas (arrangements of chansons by Josquin and Passereau); 3 Masses, 4 Magnificats, and 12 hymns based on chant and designed for *alternatim* performance; also 2 somewhat shorter ensemble ricercars.

Bibl.: *Orgelwerke,* 2 vols., ed. Oskar Mischiati (Mainz, 1959, 1961).

Cavazzoni, Marco Antonio [Marco Antonio da Bologna, Marco Antonio da Urbino] (b. Bologna, ca. 1490; d. Venice, ca. 1570). Composer. Father of Girolamo Cavazzoni. Because of similarity of names and some overlap of jobs, he is often confused with his contemporary Marc'Antonio de Alvise. Spent much of his adult life, from 1517 or perhaps earlier, in or near Venice: as a singer at St. Mark's; perhaps as organist at St. Stephen's and then at Treviso Cathedral; as organist at Chioggia Cathedral. Was in Padua with Pietro Bembo when Girolamo was born. Also lived and worked (usually as an organist) in Urbino, Ferrara, and Rome. Knew Pietro Aaron and Adrian Willaert in Venice. Wrote only keyboard works, all but one ricercar published in Venice in 1523 (facs., *MMML* ser. 1, 12 [1974]; ed. Jeppesen). This publication includes 2 ricercars (the earliest known for keyboard) and intabulations of 4 chansons and 2 motets, for which vocal models are not known.

Bibl.: Knud Jeppesen, *Die italienische Orgelmusik am Anfang des Cinquecento* (Copenhagen, 1943; 2nd rev. ed., 1960).

Cavendish, Michael (b. ca. 1565; d. London, 5 July 1628?). Composer. Little is known of his life. His family included notable patrons of music but no other practicing musicians. He served Prince Charles, son of James I. Wrote a book of lute songs and madrigals published in London in 1598. As described on its title page, the book contains 14 songs with lute accompaniment (in tablature) and also suitable for 2 voices and bass viol, 6 more lute songs with alternate settings for 4 voices, and 8 madrigals for 5 voices. One of these madrigals, substantially recomposed, appears in *The Triumphes of Oriana* (1601). A Psalm setting for 4 voices was published in *The Whole Booke of Psalmes* (London, 1592).

Bibl.: Ed. in *ESLS* 2nd ser., 7 (1926), and *EMS* 36, 2nd ed. (1961).

Cavos, Catterino (b. Venice, 30 Oct. 1775; d. St. Petersburg, 10 May 1840). Composer, conductor, and teacher. Studied with Francesco Bianchi; worked at La Fenice in Venice, where his father was director. His brother Alberto was a dancer and choreographer at La Fenice. His cantata *L'eroe* (1798) celebrated the entrance of the Austrian imperial army into Venice. He went to Russia sometime near the end of the 1790s; named artistic director of the imperial theaters in St. Petersburg; taught at the College of the Order of St. Catherine. He was associated with the Russian Opera in 1804 and began composing his own operas in 1805. These include *Knyaz nevidimka, ili Licharda volshebnik* (1805); *Ilya Bogatïr* (1806), whose story was taken from Russian folklore; and *Ivan Susanin* (1815), his most successful. He conducted many performances of opera throughout his career. Taught singing at the Smolny Institute, 1811–29. Kapellmeister of an Italian opera troupe, 1828–31. His wife was the singer Camilla Baglioni. Their son Alberto (1801–63) was the architect who reconstructed the Moscow Bolshoi Theater after it burned; another son, Giovanni (1805–61), was director of the orchestras of the imperial theaters in St. Petersburg.

Bibl.: Lev Solomonovich, *Istoriya russkoy muzïki v notnïkh obraztsakh* (Moscow, 1969).

Cazden, Norman (b. New York, 23 Sept. 1914; d. Bangor, Maine, 18 Aug. 1980). Composer, pianist, musicologist. Studied at the Institute of Musical Arts in New York (Newstead, C. Seeger) and at the Juilliard Graduate School (1932–39); while working toward his B.S. from City College (1943) he was a composer-pianist for dance groups and taught theory and piano privately; received the Ph.D. in musicology from Harvard in 1948 (composition with Piston and Copland). He taught at the Univ. of Illinois (1950–53) and the Univ. of Maine (1969–80). He wrote strongly contrapuntal and rhythmic music in expanded tonality that often reflects his interest in folk music of the Catskills (*3 Ballads from the Catskills,* orchestra, 1949); as a scholar with a cross-cultural perspective he challenged Helmholtz's theories of consonance and dissonance. Works include a ballet, a "dramatic cantata," and incidental music for Shakespeare; 11 orchestral compositions including a symphony and 2 concertos (clarinet, 1965; viola, 1972); 25 or more chamber pieces; piano pieces; choral music and songs; instrumental music for amateurs; 12 collections of folk music arrangements.

Cazzati, Maurizio (b. Lucera, near Reggio Emilia, ca. 1620; d. Mantua, 1677). Composer. He was ordained to the priesthood and in 1641 received a post as organist and *maestro di cappella* at S. Andrea in Mantua. From ca. 1647 he was *maestro* at Ferrara (Accademia della Morte), and during the 1650s at Bologna—first at S. Maria Maggiore and later (from 1657) at S. Petronio, where he served for nearly 15 years. From 1659 he was engaged in a famous quarrel centering on his *Missa primi toni* (publ. in *Messa e salmi* op. 17, 1655), which was attacked for "musical errors" by Giulio Cesare Arresti. Cazzati responded in *Risposta alle oppositioni fatte dal Sig. Giulio Cesare Arresti nella lettera posta nell'opera sua musicale* (Bologna, 1663). Around 1665 he began his own music publishing shop and presumably published a number of his own works. In 1671 he quit the post at S. Petronio and returned to Mantua; there he spent his remaining years as *maestro* for Anna Isabella Gonzaga. In addition to Masses and Psalm settings, he composed cantatas, oratorios, and instrumental music, including *Correnti e baletti . . . alla francese, e all'itagliana* op. 15 (Venice, 1654); *Sonate a 2, 3, 4, e 5* op. 35 (Bologna, 1665; includes 3 trumpet sonatas); and *Sonate a 2 istromenti* (Bologna, 1670; no. 1 ed. in *HAM* 2).

Bibl.: James F. Armstrong, "The Vesper Psalms and Magnificats of Maurizio Cazzati (ca. 1620–1678)" (diss., Harvard Univ., 1969). Anne Schnoebelen, "Cazzati *vs.* Bologna: 1657–1671," *MQ* 57 (1971): 26–39.

Ceballos [Cevallos, Zavallos, Zaballos], **Rodrigo de** (b. Aracena, ca. 1530; d. Granada, 1591). Composer. From 1556 he was at Córdoba Cathedral, first as assistant to the *maestro de capilla,* then, from 1557, as *maestro.* Appointed to the same post in the Spanish royal court in Granada in 1561; became a royal chaplain in 1572. He composed over 50 motets, 3 Masses, Magnificats, hymns, and a few settings of secular Spanish texts.

Celestin, Papa [Oscar Phillip] (b. Napoleonville, La., 1 Jan. 1884; d. New Orleans, 15 Dec. 1954). Jazz bandleader and trumpeter. From 1910 he began leading a group, initially at the Tuxedo Dance Hall (to 1913). With the trombonist William "Bebe" Ridgley he led the Original Tuxedo Orchestra (1917–25), which functioned as a brass band and a smaller dance orchestra. In 1925 Celestin formed his Tuxedo Jazz Orchestra, which recorded in 1925–28 (including "My Josephine," 1926) and toured until the early 1930s. After playing part-time, he again led a group from 1946, performing for radio, television, and film, and recording "Li'l Liza Jane" (1950).

Celibidache, Sergiu (b. Roman, Romania, 28 June 1912). Conductor, musicologist, composer. Studied philosophy and mathematics at the Univ. of Bucharest; composition (with Heinz Thiessen) and conducting (with Fritz Stein and Walter Gmeindl) at the Berlin Hochschule; dissertation on compositional techniques of Josquin Desprez. As conductor pro tem of the Berlin Philharmonic, 1945–48, rebuilt that orchestra into a world-class ensemble; co-conductor with Furtwängler, 1948–51. Music director, Swedish Radio Symphony, 1964–71. Permanent conductor of the Stuttgart Radio Orchestra, 1971–77; of the Munich Philharmonic, 1979–84, bringing that orchestra into the first rank. On the faculty of the Curtis Institute of Music, 1983–84. U.S. debut, Carnegie Hall, 1984, with Curtis Institute Orchestra. Composer of 4 symphonies and a piano concerto, which he did not want played.

Cererols, Joan (b. Martorell, Catalonia, 9 Sept. 1618; d. Montserrat, 28 Aug. 1676). Composer. His entire life was devoted to the Montserrat Monastery near Barcelona: during the 1620s and early 1630s he was a chorister, and in 1636 he became a novice. Later, as a monk, he studied Latin and theology, and for 40 years he directed the musical activities at the monastery. His extant works include 3 Masses, 11 Psalm settings, hymns, canticles, and secular *villancicos.*

Bibl.: David Pujol, ed., *Joan Cererols,* in *Mestres de l'escolania de Montserrat,* 1–3, 7, 9 (Montserrat, 1930–81).

Cerha, Friedrich (b. Vienna, 17 Feb. 1926). Composer and conductor. In Vienna he studied violin and composition at the academy (with Vasa Přihoda and Alfred Uhl) and philosophy and musicology at the university. With Kurt Schwertsik he founded the chamber ensemble Die Reihe, noted for its performances of contemporary music. From 1960 he taught composition at the Vienna Academy, where he was made professor in 1969 and directed the electronic music studio. At the request of his publisher (Universal) he prepared the third act of Berg's *Lulu* for its premiere at the Paris Opéra in 1979. His own style is concerned with sonority and timbre, as is suggested by his statement that "subtle nuances within one color or timbre have always moved me more than dramatic contrasts." His compositions include an opera, *Baal* (after Brecht, 1973–81); *Exercises,* baritone, speakers, and 17 instruments (for stage or concert performance, 1962–68); *Der Rattenfänger* (for the stage, 1987); orchestral music (*Relazioni fragili,* harpsichord, chamber orchestra, 1957; *Intersecazioni,* 1959–73; *Spiegel,* I–VII, with tape, 1960–68; *Langegger Nachtmusik,* I–II, 1969, 1970; a double concerto for violin, cello, and orchestra, 1975; a double concerto for flute, bassoon, and orchestra, 1982; a flute concerto, 1986); vocal music (*Verzeichnis,* a cappella chorus, 1969; *Keintate,* voice, 11 instruments, 1982–83; the cantata *An die Herrscher der Welt,* 1988); *Elegie,* piano (1963); *Curriculum,* 12 winds and brass (1972–73).

Černohorský, Bohuslav Matěj (b. Nymburk, Bohemia, 16 Feb. 1684; d. Graz, 1 July 1742). Composer and organist. He studied at Prague until 1702, joined the Minorte order the following year, and was ordained to the priesthood in 1708. Soon afterward he became organist in Italy, at Assisi (from 1710) and Padua (from

1715). Returning to Prague in 1720, he was appointed musician at St. Jacob's. During the 1730s he was organist at Padua. Many of his works are lost, and much music has been wrongly attributed to him. He composed mostly sacred vocal music, including *Regina coeli* (soprano, cello, organ) and *Laudetur Jesus Christus sive Offertorium pro omni tempore* (4 voices, chamber orchestra, 1729); these two works are edited in *Česká hudba,* 1918 and 1931, respectively.

Cerone, Pietro (b. Bergamo, 1566; d. Naples, 1625). Theorist and singer. Although Italian by birth, he worked in Spain and (Spanish) Naples from 1592 until his death. He was in the royal chapels of Philip II and Philip III in Madrid. From 1603 he lived in Naples, employed first at the Church of SS. Annunziata, then, from 1610, in the royal chapel. Among his writings is an unusually long treatise in Spanish titled *El melopeo y maestro* (Naples, 1613; facs., *BMB,* ser. 2, 25 [1969]; excerpts trans. in *SR,* pp. 262–73). It reflects very conservative tastes and has sometimes been criticized for borrowings from other writers and for outright misinformation. It remains significant nevertheless, and it strongly influenced Spanish theory during the 17th and 18th centuries.

Certon, Pierre (b. ca. 1510; d. Paris, 23 Feb. 1572). Composer. Worked as a clerk at Notre Dame de Paris from 1529; assumed a similar post at the Sainte-Chapelle in 1532. In 1536 became master of the choristers there, holding this post until his death. Among his close friends was Claudin de Sermisy, whose death in 1562 prompted the composition of a *déploration* modeled on that written by Josquin to honor Ockeghem. Extant sacred works, all published, include 8 Masses, 3 Mass movements, a Magnificat, over 40 motets, and a number of Psalm settings and *chansons spirituelles.* The majority of his compositions, however, are secular chansons: 285 pieces, 100 published in 2 books devoted exclusively to Certon, the rest included in anthologies. The later works contributed substantially to the stylistic transformation of the chanson in the third quarter of the 16th century.

Bibl.: *Pierre Certon: Chansons polyphoniques publiées par Pierre Attaingnant,* ed. Henry Expert and Aimé Agnel, Maîtres anciens de la musique française, 1–3 (Paris, 1967–68).

Cervantes (Kawanag), Ignacio (b. Havana, 31 July 1847; d. there, 29 Apr. 1905). Composer and pianist. Had lessons from Gottschalk and studied for five years with Nicolás Ruiz Espadero in Havana; then in Paris with Alkan and Marmontel at the Conservatory, where he won first prize in piano in 1866 and in accompaniment in 1868. He returned to Havana in 1869 or 1870 but was forced by the government to leave in 1876; gave concerts in the U.S. and lived for a time in Mexico. In January 1899 organized a concert at the Teatro Tacón, Havana, at which his *Himno a Cuba* was played. Considered one of the pioneers of Cuban music, especially for his 21 *Danzas cubanas* for piano (1878–95); also composed 3 operas, a symphony, and much piano music.

Bibl.: Eduardo Sánchez de Fuentes, *Ignacio Cervantes Kawanag* (Havana, 1936).

Cesaris, Johannes (fl. ca. 1385–ca. 1420). Composer. Linked by Martin le Franc with Carmen and Tapissier; perhaps active at Angers Cathedral. Early 15th-century manuscripts transmit the few extant works: a 4-voiced panisorhythmic motet; 2 3-voiced ballades, 1 untexted; and 5 or 6 rondeaux, one for 2 voices, the rest for 3.

Bibl.: *Early Fifteenth-Century Music,* ed. Gilbert Reaney, *CMM* 11/1 (1955).

Cesti, Antonio [Pietro] (b. Arezzo, bapt. 5 Aug. 1623; d. Florence, 14 Oct. 1669). Composer and singer. As a boy Pietro sang in the choir at Arezzo Cathedral (ca. 1630) and at S. Maria della Pieve (1635–37). After joining the Franciscan order (in 1637, at which time he assumed the name Antonio) he was sent to Florence (S. Croce, ca. 1638–40), then back to Arezzo (ca. 1640–43). Apparently he did study in Rome, although his purported study with Carissimi and Antonio Maria Abbatini has not been fully documented. From 1644 Cesti was apparently organist both at the Volterra Cathedral and at S. Croce in Florence; he became *magister musices* at Volterra in 1645. Around 1647 he was ordained to the priesthood. During the late 1640s he also served members of the Medici family, including Cardinal Gian Carlo. His first opera, *Orontea* (libretto G. Cicognini), performed in Venice in 1649, was a sensational success; it was followed by a number of other successes, including *Il Cesare amante* (1651). Meanwhile Cesti was also gaining favor on the stage as a tenor.

In 1652 he was appointed Chor-Kapellmeister at the Innsbruck court of Archbishop Ferdinand Karl, a position he held until 1665. In 1658 he sang at the papal chapel, but upon achieving release from his monastic orders the following year he promptly returned to Innsbruck. (Some have suggested that he sought the papal appointment expressly in order to gain favor to secure this release.) When the archbishop's court disbanded in 1665, Cesti followed it to Vienna, where his *Il Tito* was staged in 1666. The culmination of his career as an opera composer was in his last opera for Vienna, *Il pomo d'oro* (1668), a pinnacle of Baroque opera on the gigantic scale. Cesti reportedly died traveling to Florence the following year. Other known works include the operas *La Dori* (Innsbruck, 1657), *Nettunno e Flora festeggianti* (1666), and *La Semirami* (1667); over 60 cantatas, including *Era la notte e muto, Quante volte* (ed. David Burrows in *Collegium musicum* 2nd ser., 1), and *Vaghi fiori.*

Bibl.: Franco Schlitzer, *Intorno alla 'Dori' di Antonio Cesti* (Florence, 1957). David Burrows, "The Cantatas of Antonio Cesti" (diss., Brandeis Univ., 1961). Id., *Antonio Cesti (1623–1669),* (Wellesley, Mass., 1964) [thematic catalog of cantatas]. William Carl Holmes, "'Orontea': A Study of Change and Development in the Libretto and the Music of Mid-Seventeenth-Century Italian Opera" (diss., Columbia Univ., 1968). Carl B. Schmidt, "The Operas of Antonio Cesti" (diss., Harvard Univ., 1973). Id., "Antonio Cesti's *Il pomo d'oro:* A Reexamination of a Famous Hapsburg Court Spectacle," *JAMS* 29 (1976): 381–412.

Chabrier, (Alexis-) Emmanuel (b. Ambert, Puy-de-Dôme, 18 Jan. 1841; d. Paris, 13 Sept. 1894). Composer. Son of a lawyer; had music lessons from age 6, developing a prodigious talent as a pianist; also began to compose. The family moved to Paris in 1856; he received his law degree in 1861 and became a clerk in the Ministry of the Interior; music lessons from Semet and Hignard (composition) and Edouard Wolff (piano). Duparc and d'Indy were close friends, as were writers such as Verlaine, who wrote librettos for two operettas for him, *Fisch-ton-Kan* (1863–64) and *Vaucochard et fils Ier* (1864), only fragments of which survive, and painters such as Manet, who painted his portrait. (Chabrier also assembled an important collection of the work of contemporary artists, particularly impressionists.) He composed relatively little before the opéra comique *L'étoile* (Paris, Bouffes-Parisiens, 28 Nov. 1877), which made his reputation. It was followed by the somewhat risqué *Une éducation manquée* (Cercle de la Presse, 1879). Already a committed Wagnerian (although capable of twitting Wagnerian pomposity in his *Souvenirs de Munich,* burlesque quadrilles on themes from *Tristan*), upon first hearing *Tristan* in Munich in 1880 he was moved to quit the ministry and become a professional musician. In 1881 he published *10 pièces pittoresques* for piano, a landmark in French music. A visit to Spain in July–Dec. 1882 led to his most popular work, the rhapsody *España,* originally for piano and a tremendous success in its orchestral version on 4 Nov. 1883 at Lamoureux's Nouveaux concerts, which Chabrier had joined at their start in 1881 as secretary and chorusmaster; the *3 valses romantiques* for 2 pianos were premiered by Chabrier and Messager on 15 Dec. 1883. Much of Chabrier's efforts in the 1880s were devoted to the grand tragic opera, an inclination often ascribed to Wagnerian influence and regretted as contrary to his own nature. *Gwendoline,* completed in 1885 and rejected by the Paris Opéra, was given successfully at the Théâtre de la Monnaie, Brussels (10 Apr. 1886), but had only two performances before the management's bankruptcy. The opéra comique *Le roi malgré lui* (Paris, Opéra-comique, 18 May 1887), containing some of his finest music, was doomed by its libretto and by the burning of the opera house after its third performance. Other works: *La sulamite* (1885), *scène lyrique; Joyeuse marche,* piano (1888; later orchestrated); *6 mélodies* (1890); *Ode à la musique* (1890); *Bourrée fantasque,* piano (1891), the last important piece completed before the advance of syphilis left him unable to compose. The grand opera *Briséis,* begun in 1888, was left unfinished.

Bibl.: J. Desaymard, *Emmanuel Chabrier d'après ses lettres* (Paris, 1934). F. Poulenc, *Emmanuel Chabrier* (Paris, 1961), trans. Eng. C. Jolly (London, 1981). R. Delage, "Emmanuel Chabrier in Germany," *MQ* 49 (1963): 75–84. Y. Tiénot, *Chabrier, par lui-même et par ses intimes* (Paris, 1964). Rollo Myers, *Emmanuel Chabrier and His Circle* (London, 1969). Frédéric Tobert, *Emmanuel Chabrier: L'homme et son oeuvre* (Paris, 1969). R. Delage, "Ravel and Chabrier, " *MQ* 61 (1975): 546–52. Roger Delage, *Chabrier* (Geneva, 1982).

Chadwick, George Whitefield (b. Lowell, Mass., 13 Nov. 1854; d. Boston, 4 Apr. 1931). Composer. From a musically inclined family; studied 1872–76 at the New England Conservatory while working in his father's insurance business; in 1876–77 taught music at Olivet College, then, against his father's wishes, studied with Jadassohn at the Leipzig Conservatory (1877–79), where he composed 2 string quartets and conducted his *Rip van Winkle Overture* as his graduation piece; further study with Rheinberger in Munich. Returned to Boston in 1880; worked as an organist and teacher (pupils included Horatio Parker, Sidney Homer, Arthur Whiting); from 1882 taught at the New England Conservatory, from 1897 as director (pupils included Frederick Converse, Henry Hadley, D. G. Mason); published a much-used harmony textbook (1897); established an opera workshop and a student orchestra, which he conducted. Directed the Springfield Music Festival (1889–99) and the Worcester Festival (1898–1901). One of the most important American composers of the late 19th century; his style is based on European models but often has a recognizably American flavor. Works include 3 symphonies (1882, 1885, 1894); *Symphonic Sketches,* suite (1908); Sinfonietta (1904); concert overtures and symphonic poems (*Tam o'Shanter,* 1915); 5 string quartets; a piano quintet; church music; piano pieces; songs. Much interested in dramatic music of very different sorts; works include a burlesque opera, *Tabasco* (Boston, 1894), and a lyric drama, *Judith* (Worcester Festival, 1901). His verismo opera, *The Padrone* (1912), based on Italian immigrant life in Boston, was rejected by the Metropolitan Opera because of its subject matter.

Bibl.: Carl Engel, "George W. Chadwick," *MQ* 10 (1924): 438–57. A. L. Langley, "Chadwick and the New England Conservatory of Music," *MQ* 21 (1935): 39–52. Victor Fell Yellin, *Chadwick, Yankee Composer* (Washington, D.C., 1990).

Chaillou de Pesstain [Chaillou, Raoul] (d. before spring 1336). Writer and perhaps composer. Member of the French royal court. Revised and completed the *Roman de Fauvel,* adding both poetry and music to the work. Much of the music consists of preexisting compositions of the 13th and 14th centuries, adapted as necessary to fit the *roman.* Some pieces are otherwise unknown and may have been written by Chaillou, although his authorship cannot be proved.

Chailly, Riccardo (b. Milan, 20 Feb. 1953). Conductor. Studied composition with his father, Luciano Chailly (artistic director of La Scala, 1968–71), then with Bruno Bettinelli at the Conservatorio Giuseppe

Verdi in Milan. Studied conducting with Piero Guarino at Perugia, Franco Caracciolo in Milan, and Franco Ferrara in Siena. Debut as conductor, Milan, 1970; as opera conductor, at the Teatro nuovo, Milan, 1972. Abbado's assistant at La Scala, 1973–74. U.S. debut with the Chicago Lyric Opera, 1974. Debut with the San Francisco Opera, 1977; at La Scala, 1978; at Covent Garden, 1979; at New York Met, 1982. Principal guest conductor, London Philharmonic, 1980; principal conductor, West Berlin Radio Symphony, 1982–88; artistic director, Teatro communale, Bologna, 1986–89; principal conductor, Amsterdam Concertgebouw, from 1988.

Chaliapin, Feodor (Ivanovich) [Shalyapin, Fyodor Ivanovich] (b. Kazan, Russia, 13 Feb. 1873; d. Paris, 12 Apr. 1938). Bass. After Caruso, the best-known male opera singer of his time. Born to a peasant family, he received little musical training. Joined a touring opera company at Ufa; debut with them as Stolnik (a leading role) in Moniuszko's *Halka,* December 1890. Studied voice with Usatov in Tiflis, 1892; debut there as Gounod's Mephistopheles, 1893. Sang in St. Petersburg, 1894–95. Joined S. I. Marmontov's company in Moscow, 1896–98, singing Ivan in Rimsky-Korsakov's *Pskovityanka* and Mussorgsky's *Boris Godunov.* Sensational debut at Milan, La Scala, 1901 (as Boito's Mefistofele); returned 1904, 1908, 1912, 1929–30, and 1933. Sang nearly every year at the Monte Carlo Opera, 1905–37. His forceful acting did not appeal to audiences at the New York Met, 1907–8, but proved as successful there in 1921–29 as it always had in Europe. London debut, 1913; with Chicago Opera, 1922–24; at Covent Garden, 1926–29. His success in the title role of Massenet's *Don Quichotte* led to a starring nonsinging role in G. W. Pabst's film *Don Quichotte* (1933).

Bibl.: *Chaliapin: An Autobiography as Told to Maxim Gorky* (London, 1968). B. Semeonoff, "Chaliapin's Repertoire and Recordings," *Record Collector,* 20/8–10 (1972): 173 [with discography]. Victor Borovsky, *Chaliapin: A Critical Biography* (New York, 1988).

Challis, Bill [William H.] (b. Wilkes-Barre, Pa., 8 July 1904). Jazz arranger. Associated with groups that included Bix Beiderbecke, he arranged for the orchestras of Jean Goldkette (1926–27) and Paul Whiteman (1927–30) as well as for Frankie Trumbauer's small groups; Trumbauer recorded Challis's arrangement of Hoagy Carmichael's "Riverboat Shuffle" (1927) and Whiteman recorded "San" and "Dardanella" (both 1928). Challis also transcribed Beiderbecke's piano music for publication. As a free-lance he wrote for Fletcher Henderson, the Dorsey brothers, the Casa Loma Orchestra, and Artie Shaw.

Challis, John (b. South Lyon, Mich., 9 Jan. 1907; d. New York, 6 Sept. 1974). Instrument builder. At the Univ. of Michigan he studied organ with Frederick Alexander, who owned a Dolmetsch-Chickering clavichord that Challis tried to duplicate. A Dolmetsch Foundation Scholarship, 1928–30, enabled him to study with Arnold Dolmetsch at Haslemere. Built harpsichords and clavichords in Ypsilanti, Michigan, 1930–46, in Detroit from 1946, and finally in New York. His instruments approximate the tone and touch of 18th-century ones, but increase compass, volume, and reliability by using larger keyboards, up to four sets of strings, aluminum frames, tuning blocks of synthetic materials, pedals in place of hand stops, and other novelties. His shop served as a training ground for several important makers, including William Dowd.

Chaloff, Serge (b. Boston, 24 Nov. 1923; d. there, 16 July 1957). Jazz baritone saxophonist. He played with Boyd Raeburn (1945), the tenor saxophonist Georgie Auld (1945–46, ca. 1947), and Jimmy Dorsey (1946) before joining the saxophone section of Woody Herman's big band (1947–49), the members of which were known as the "Four Brothers." He played in Count Basie's octet (1950), but ill health disrupted his later activities. As a leader of bop combos he recorded "Gabardine and Serge" (1947) and the album *Blue Serge* (1956).

Chambers, Paul (Laurence Dunbar, Jr.) (b. Pittsburgh, 22 Apr. 1935; d. New York, 4 Jan. 1969). Jazz double bass player. In Detroit he played bop with Kenny Burrell, Pepper Adams, Tommy Flanagan, and others (1949–55). He toured to New York with tenor saxophonist Paul Quinichette. After touring the South with the trombonist Bennie Green, he played briefly with Sonny Stitt and J. J. Johnson. He was a member of Miles Davis's quintets and sextets (1955–63), recording the albums *'Round about Midnight* (1955–56) and *Kind of Blue* (1959). He also recorded with Kenny Clarke, Cannonball Adderley, Donald Byrd, Sonny Rollins, Red Garland, Lee Morgan, Art Pepper, Gene Ammons, Johnson, John Coltrane, Kenny Dorham, and Freddie Hubbard. In 1963 he joined Wynton Kelly's trio, which with Wes Montgomery recorded the album *Smokin' at the Half Note* (1965).

Chambonnières, Jacques Champion Sieur de (b. Paris, 1601 or 1602; d. there, Apr. 1672). Composer and harpsichordist. His father, Jacques, and his grandfather Thomas Champion were both distinguished musicians; his maternal grandfather was the source of the title he himself was later to use, Sieur de Chambonnières. (On several occasions during his life he lived at his grandfather's estate.) By 1632 he was a chamber musician—probably harpsichordist—at the Paris court of Louis XIII. His reputation as keyboard virtuoso spread rapidly, and upon his father's death in 1643, he was appointed to the position as court clavecinist. This continued until 1656, when he reverted the post to his brother Nicolas, apparently in anticipation of a position at the Swedish court (an offer he never received). When Nicolas died in 1662, Jacques's old post went to d'Anglebert, and Chambonnières retired. Like Couperin, he spent his final years preparing his own music for publication.

Among his works are *Les pièces de clavessin . . . livre premier,* including suites in A minor, C, D minor, D, F, G minor, and G (Paris, 1670; R: New York, 1967; ed. Thurston Dart, Monaco, 1969); *Les pièces de clavessin . . . livre second,* including suites in C, D minor, D, F, G minor, and G (Paris, 1670; R: New York, 1967; ed. Dart); a large number of keyboard suites in all "white" keys, most in manuscript.

Bibl.: *Oeuvres complètes de Chambonnières,* ed. Paul Brunold and André Tessier (Paris, 1925; R: [with rev. pref.] New York, 1967). M. Le Moel, "Les dernières années de Jacques Champion de Chambonnières (1655–1672)," *RMFC* 1 (1960): 31. David Fuller, "French Harpsichord Playing in the Seventeenth Century: After Le Gallois," *EM* 4 (1976): 22–26. Bruce Gustafson, *The Sources of Seventeenth-Century French Harpsichord Music* (Ann Arbor, Mich., 1979).

Chaminade, Cécile (Louise Stéphanie) (b. Paris, 8 Aug. 1857; d. Monte Carlo, 13 Apr. 1944). Pianist and composer. She composed from childhood and made her debut as a pianist at age 18. Her career as a performer took her on many tours, especially in France and England. Although much of her work has been called drawing room music, her output as a composer was significant. She wrote an opera (unpublished) and a ballet (1890), as well as orchestral works (*Concertstück* op. 40, 1896; *Concertino,* flute and orchestra op. 107, 1902); a Mass for 2 voices and organ or harmonium; 2 piano trios; many works for piano alone; and many songs.

Bibl.: Marcia J. Citron, *Cécile Chaminade: A Bio-Bibliography* (New York, 1988).

Champagne, Claude (Adonai) (b. Montreal, 27 May 1891; d. there, 21 Dec. 1965). Composer. As a youth he studied violin, piano, and saxophone; his composition teacher, Alfred Laliberté, submitted an early symphonic poem to Rachmaninoff, which resulted in Champagne's study in Paris (1920–28) with Gédalge. There he was influenced by Fauré's harmonic language and Debussy's use of whole-tone scales; his interest in French Canadian folk songs was increased when he related their modal language to that of the Renaissance polyphony he sang in the Schola cantorum chorus. He taught at the McGill Conservatory (1930–42) and the École Vincent d'Indy (1930–62); in 1942 helped to found the Montreal Conservatory in imitation of the Parisian model. Trips to Brazil are reflected in a few compositions, but most reflect French Canadian folk elements, his own Irish heritage, and the Canadian landscape. He wrote several impressionistic orchestral works (*Images du Canada français,* 1946; *Altitude* [depicting the Canadian Rockies], 1958–59; both with chorus); chamber music for strings; a few piano works; choral and vocal music.

Chanler, Theodore (Ward) (b. Newport, R.I., 29 Apr. 1902; d. Boston, 27 July 1961). Composer. Studied piano and theory as a youth in Boston and then at the Institute of Musical Art in New York (piano with Buhlig, counterpoint with Goetschius); a meeting with Bloch led to study at the Cleveland Institute (1920–23); then studied at Oxford and with Boulanger in Paris (1924–27). In 1934 he was music critic for the *Boston Herald;* taught briefly at Peabody (1945–47) and at the Longy School in Cambridge, Mass. He is best known for his songs, many of which were recorded; his early "These, My Ophelia" (MacLeish) was written during his study with Boulanger; later settings of texts by De la Mare (*Eight Epitaphs,* 1937; *Three Epitaphs,* 1940; *Four Rhymes from Peacock Pie,* 1940), Blake, and Feeney are sensitively composed in the tradition of Fauré. Other works include a ballet; an opera, *The Pot of Fat* (1955); chamber music; piano works; choral music; about 50 songs.

Chapí (y Lorente), Ruperto (b. Villena, near Alicante, 27 Mar. 1851; d. Madrid, 25 Mar. 1909). Composer. Son of a barber; entered Madrid Conservatory in 1867, studying composition under Arrieta; in 1870 played cornet in a theater orchestra; in 1871 became conductor of a military band; in 1873 his *fantasia morisca La corte de Granada* was played by the Sociedad de conciertos, and the first of his more than 100 zarzuelas was produced. In 1874 he won a three-year scholarship at the Spanish Academy, Rome. He worked in both the large and small zarzuela, among his most popular being *La tempestad* (1882), *La bruja* (1887), *La revoltosa* (1897), *Curro Vargas* (1899).

Bibl.: Angel S. Salcedo, *Ruperto Chapí: Su vida y sus obras* (Cordoba, 1929). J. de D. Aguilar Gómez, *Ruperto Chapí y su obra lírica* (Alicante, 1973) [with works list].

Chardavoine [Chardavoyne], **Jehan** [Jean] (b. Beaufort, Anjou, 2 Feb. 1538; d. ca. 1580). Music editor and perhaps composer. In Paris in 1576 he published a book of *voix de ville.* Monophonic melodies are provided for 190 strophic poems, including both anonymous works and texts by poets such as Ronsard, Baïf, and Du Bellay. Many of the melodies are adapted from polyphonic settings published in the mid-16th century, but some may have been composed by Chardavoine himself.

Charles, Ray [Robinson, Ray Charles] (b. Albany, Ga., 23 Sept. 1930). Rhythm-and-blues and soul singer, pianist, and songwriter. He was blinded by glaucoma as a child in Florida, where he studied music at the St. Augustine School for the Deaf and the Blind. After performances with jazz trios in Seattle in a style influenced by Charles Brown and Nat "King" Cole, he participated in the rising popularity of rhythm-and-blues with recordings of original songs including "I've Got a Woman" (1955) and "What'd I Say" (1959). His vocal style incorporated elements of gospel singing into songs dealing with standard blues topics and themes; his career prepared the success of soul singers such as James Brown and Otis Redding. His repertory is eclectic: he has recorded several albums of country music (*Modern Sounds in Country-and-Western,* vols. 1–2, 1962; *From the Pages of My Mind,* 1986) and Gershwin's *Porgy and Bess* with Cleo Laine (1985).

Bibl.: Ray Charles and D. Ritz, *Brother Ray: Ray Charles' Own Story* (New York, 1978).

Charpentier, Gustave (b. Dieuze, Lorraine, 25 June 1860; d. Paris, 18 Feb. 1956). Composer. Son of a baker with musical inclinations. As a child worked in a spinning mill while also studying the violin; later organized an instrumental ensemble among the factory workers (beginning a lifelong interest in music for the working classes). In 1878, after failing to win a government scholarship to study in Paris, he was given a stipend by the town council to study at the Lille Académie de musique, and after failing again in 1879, an annual one for the Paris Conservatory, where he studied the violin under Massart. In 1887 won the Prix de Rome. He was in Rome from January 1888 to June 1890. In this period he conceived most of his important compositions: the *symphonie-drame La vie du poète* (finished Jan. 1889), the orchestral suite *Impressions d'Italie* (1889–90), and the opera *Louise,* begun in 1889 to his own libretto (said to be based on a love affair he had had with a Paris seamstress in 1882 and in which is manifested his sympathy for working people and his love of Paris), but not completed for several years. Later he produced 4 sets of songs: 2 called *Poèmes chantés* (1894), *Les fleurs du mal* (after Baudelaire, 1895), and *Impressions fausses* (1895). *Sérénade à Watteau* (Verlaine), performed in the Jardin du Luxembourg for the dedication of the Watteau monument (1896), was the first of several festive, usually open-air works, the most important of which was *La couronnement de la muse,* the realization of a festival imagined in *Louise,* featuring the crowning of a working girl. This was performed first at the Nouveau Théâtre in June 1897 and in later years in many French cities under Charpentier's direction. He later added to it the final chorus of *Le chant d'apothéose,* another festival work given in the Place des Vosges for the Victor Hugo centenary (1902). *Louise* was premiered at the Opéra-comique on 2 Feb. 1900 and was a great and continuing success. He produced little new work after it. The opera *Julien,* based on *La vie du poète,* had a succès d'estime at the Opéra-comique in 1913, but was not revived. A symphonic poem, *Munich* (1911), was never published. He founded the Oeuvre de Mimi Pinson, which taught music to working-class women; in 1902 this became the Conservatoire populaire, which lasted until the beginning of World War II.

Bibl.: M. Delmas, *Gustave Charpentier et le lyrisme français* (Paris, 1931). K. Hoover, "Gustave Charpentier," *MQ* 25 (1939): 334–50. F. Andrieux, *Gustave Charpentier: Lettres inédites à ses parents* (Paris, 1984).

Charpentier, Marc-Antoine (b. Paris, 1643; d. there, 24 Feb. 1704). Composer. It was once thought that he came from a family of royal painters; little is actually known of his youth. Apparently he studied with Carissimi in Rome, probably from around 1662; returning to Paris (before 1670), he became *maître de musique* at the residence of Marie de Lorraine, Mademoiselle de Guise. During his years at this post (which lasted until Marie's death in 1688) he composed *La descente d'Orphée aux enfers,* as well as motets, Psalms, and other sacred music. In 1672 he became Molière's musical collaborator when the latter broke with Lully; Charpentier composed prologues, entr'actes, and other music for the poet's *Mariage forcé* (1672) and *Malade imaginaire* (1673), and he continued collaborating with the Comédie-française after Molière's death in 1673. In 1683 Louis XIV, pleased with the composer's theater music, granted him a pension.

During the 1680s Charpentier served as *maître* of the Jesuits' St. Louis church; he was also music teacher to Philippe, Duke of Chartres. When the post of *maître de musique des enfants* opened up at the Sainte Chapelle in 1698, Charpentier won the job over Sébastien de Brossard. The position required him to compose a large number of sacred works and music for special occasions (a Te Deum and the *Judicium Salomonis*). He died leaving few published works (*Médée,* 1694; selections from *Circé,* 1676) but a great many works in manuscript. Among his sacred works are 11 Mass settings, a large number of Psalms, antiphons, sequences, and lessons, and more than 200 motets; he also composed overtures, *symphonies,* and other instrumental works for the church. Nearly 50 of his cantatas and *airs sérieux et à boire* are known. Chief among his works for the stage are *La couronne de fleurs* (pastorale, 1685), *David et Jonathas* (1688), and *Médée* (*tragédie en musique,* 1693). He also wrote 3 treatises, which remain in manuscript.

Bibl.: Claude Crussard, *Un musicien français oublié: Marc-Antoine Charpentier, 1634–1704* (Paris, 1945). H. Wiley Hitchcock, "The Latin Oratorios of Marc-Antoine Charpentier" (diss., Univ. of Michigan, 1954). Id., "The Instrumental Music of Marc-Antoine Charpentier," *MQ* 47 (1961): 58–72. James Platte Dunn, "The 'Grands Motets' of Marc-Antoine Charpentier (1634–1704)" (diss., Iowa State Univ., 1962). H. Wiley Hitchcock, "Marc-Antoine Charpentier and the Comédie-Française," *JAMS* 24 (1971): 255–81. Id., *Les oeuvres de Marc-Antoine Charpentier* (Paris, 1982) [catalogue raisonné]. Id., *Marc-Antoine Charpentier* (New York, 1990).

Chasins, Abram (b. New York, 17 Aug. 1903; d. there, 21 June 1987). Pianist and composer. Studied composition at Juilliard with Rubin Goldmark and piano with Ernest Hutcheson. Later studied with Josef Hoffman at the Curtis Institute; taught piano there, 1926–35. Musical director of WQXR, New York, 1943–65. Musician-in-residence, Univ. of Southern Calif., 1972–77. Composed over 100 works. Best known for 2 concertos (1928, 1931); *Three Chinese Pieces* (piano, 1928; orchestrated, 1929), the first American work conducted by Toscanini.

Chastelain de Couci (b. ca. 1165; d. May or June 1203). Trouvère. Attempts to establish his precise identity have been numerous but unsuccessful. Around

1300 a certain Jakemes wrote the *Roman du Chastelain de Couci et de la Dame de Fayel,* in which the Chastelain is the hero; this work is clearly not biographical, however. It incorporates several of his poems, as do a number of other *romans* of the 13th and 14th centuries, including the *Roman de la rose.* His extant works consist of 16 chansons, of which 3 were used as models for later poems; 8 others may be by him.

Chausson, (Amédée-) Ernest (b. Paris, 20 Jan. 1855; d. Limay, near Mantes, Yvelines, 10 June 1899). Composer. Son of a well-to-do contractor; raised in a highly cultivated milieu, moving in advanced artistic circles, those of painting (being himself talented in drawing) and literature (including the symbolists) as well as music. He became a lawyer in 1876 but never practiced; began to compose, studying at the Conservatory with Massenet in 1879–81 and unofficially with Franck, to whose musical ideals he remained devoted; competed unsuccessfully for the Prix de Rome in 1881; made four Wagnerian pilgrimages to Munich and Bayreuth in 1879–82. He married in 1883 and, enjoying a sizable private income, led a comfortable life devoted to composition and his family. He traveled extensively in Europe, usually spent summers composing in the country, and maintained a Paris salon frequented by leading artistic figures and young artists whose careers he encouraged (including Debussy); from 1886 secretary of the Société nationale de musique. Died in a bicycle accident while summering in the country.

Works: Symphony in B♭ op. 20 (1889–90); 4 symphonic poems (*Poème,* violin and orchestra op. 25, 1896); chamber works (concerto for piano, violin, and string quartet op. 21, 1889–91); several motets; orchestral song cycle, *Poème de l'amour et de la mer* op. 19 (1882–90; rev. 1893); 36 published songs. His magnum opus, the opera *Le roi Arthus* op. 23 (1886–95), to his own libretto, was performed only after his death (Brussels, 1903).

Bibl.: *La revue musicale* (1 Dec. 1925) [special Chausson issue]. J. P. Barricelli and L. Weinstein, *Ernest Chausson: The Composer's Life and Works* (Norman, Okla., 1955). Y. Gérard, "Lettres de Henri Duparc à Ernest Chausson," *Revue de musicologie* 38 (1956): 125–46. F. Lesure, "Dix lettres d'Ernest Chausson à C. Debussy," *Revue de musicologie* 48 (1962): 49–60. Jean Gallois, *Ernest Chausson: L'homme et l'oeuvre* (Paris, 1967). Ralph Scott Grover, *Ernest Chausson: The Man and His Music* (Lewisburg, Pa., 1980). Jean Gallois, *Ernest Chausson* (Paris, 1994).

Chauvin, Louis (b. St. Louis, 13 Mar. 1881; d. Chicago, 26 Mar. 1908). Ragtime pianist and composer. A vaudeville singer, dancer, and pianist, Chauvin concentrated on piano playing from ca. 1903. He wrote songs and a revue with his stage partner Sam Patterson; the song "The Moon Is Shining in the Skies" (1903) survives. Acclaimed as "King of Ragtime Players," he won formal competitions and informal "cutting contests," but was musically illiterate. His sole surviving ragtime composition is "Heliotrope Bouquet," a collaboration with Scott Joplin (1907). He moved from St. Louis to Chicago only five months before his death.

Chávez (y Ramírez), Carlos (Antonio de Padua) (b. Mexico City, 13 June 1899; d. there, 2 Aug. 1978). Composer and conductor. After initial musical training from an older brother, he studied piano with Pedro Luís Orgazón (1915–20) and music theory with Juan Fuentes and Manuel Ponce. In 1921, the year of the installation of Obregón as the new revolutionary president, Chávez's Piano Sextet (1919) became his first publicly performed work. This was also the year that he received a commission from the new Ministry of Education to write a ballet, which became *El fuego,* composed on Aztec themes. Soon after, he traveled to Europe (1922–23), where he spent time in Berlin, Vienna, and Paris; from 1926 to 1928 he lived in New York, where he formed ties with Cowell, Persichetti, and others. In 1928 he helped found the Symphony Orchestra of Mexico (later National Symphony Orchestra) and became its principal conductor. Also in 1928 he was made director of the National Conservatory, and in 1933 he was made fine arts director in the office of the Secretary of Public Education. From 1947 to 1952 he was director of the National Institute of Fine Arts. After 1948, when he resigned his conducting post with the Mexico Symphony, he spent much time concertizing in the U.S. and Europe and received numerous commissions. He was the Charles Eliot Norton Lecturer at Harvard, 1958–59.

His music, while often striving for the simplicity of native Indian tunes, rarely uses actual folk melodies. Works include an opera, *Panfilo and Lauretta* (1953; Spanish version, *El amor propiciado,* 1959; later titled *The Visitors*); ballet scores (*El fuego nuevo,* 1921; *Los cuatro soles,* 1925; *Caballos de vapor,* in U.S. titled *H.P.* or *Horsepower,* first perf., 1926; *La hija de Cólquide,* also titled *Dark Meadows,* 1946; *Pirámide,* 1968); other orchestral works (7 symphonies, 1915–1961, no. 2, Sinfonia india; *Cantos de México,* 1933; a piano concerto, 1938–40; *Resonancias,* 1964; *Clio,* 1969); choral and vocal works (*El sol,* 1934; *Canto a la tierra,* chorus, chamber ensemble, 1946; *Prometheus Bound,* cantata, soloists, chorus, orchestra, 1956; *Lamentaciones,* 1962); much chamber and keyboard music (3 string quartets, 1921, 1932, 1943–44; 6 piano sonatas, 1917–1961); songs.

Writings: *Toward a New Music: Music and Electricity* (New York, 1937). *Musical Thought* (Charles Eliot Norton Lectures; Cambridge, Mass., 1961).

Bibl.: *Carlos Chávez: North American Press, 1936–1950* (New York, 1951). Roberto García Morillo, *Carlos Chávez, vida y obra* (Mexico, 1960). Robert L. Parker, *Carlos Chávez: Mexico's Modern-Day Orpheus* (Boston, 1983). Rodolfo Halffter, ed., *Carlos Chávez: Catálogo completo de sus obras* (Mexico, 1971).

Chaykovsky. See Tchaikovsky.

Cheatham, Doc [Adolphus Anthony] (b. near Nashville, 13 June 1905). Jazz trumpeter. Originally a soprano saxophonist, he also played trumpet and joined the big bands of Chick Webb (1928), Sam Wooding (touring Europe, 1928–30), and Cab Calloway (1933–39). He was a member of Eddie Heywood's sextet (1943–46) and from 1948 played with Latin big bands, touring internationally with these as well as with the trombonist Wilbur De Paris (1957, 1960) and the pianist Sammy Price (1958). He led a band in New York from 1960. He also joined Benny Goodman (1966–67) and toured widely as a free-lance. Known as a lead trumpeter in his early years, he later became a soloist, making his finest recordings in the 1970s and 1980s, including the album *The Fabulous Doc Cheatham* (1983).

Checker, Chubby [Evans, Ernest] (b. Philadelphia, 3 Oct. 1941). Rock-and-roll singer and dancer. His recording "The Twist" in 1960 and performances of the accompanying dance inspired a national craze and spawned numerous imitations; from then until 1965 he recorded other popular songs including another dance number, "Limbo Rock" (1962).

Cherry, Don(ald Eugene) (b. Oklahoma City, 18 Nov. 1936; d. near Malaga, Spain, 19 Oct. 1995). Jazz cornetist and bandleader. He played with Ornette Coleman (1957–61), performing in New York from 1959 and recording the albums *Change of the Century* (1959) and *Free Jazz* (1960). Moving frequently between New York and Europe, he played with Steve Lacy (1961), Sonny Rollins (1962–63), the New York Contemporary Five including Archie Shepp (1963–64), Albert Ayler (1964), and Dollar Brand, then led a group including Gato Barbieri; they recorded the albums *Complete Communion* (1965) and *Symphony for Improvisers* (1966). Traveling widely, he composed and improvised in styles drawn from many cultures, and in addition to the pocket cornet played wooden flutes and the doussn' gouni, and sang. He formed the group Old and New Dreams with Charlie Haden, Ed Blackwell, and the tenor saxophonist Dewey Redman (1976–95) and the trio Codona with Nana Vasconcelos and the sitarist and tablā player Collin Walcott (1976–84). After playing in the all-star sextet The Leaders (1984–86), he formed Nu, including Vasconcelos and the tenor saxophonist Carlos Ward.

Cherubini, Luigi (Carlo Zanobi Salvadore Maria) (b. Florence, 8 or 14 Sept. 1760; d. Paris, 15 Mar. 1842). Composer. First music lessons from his father, the *maestro al cembalo* at Florence's leading opera house, the Pergola; 1778–81 studied with Sarti and began a career as an opera composer; 1784–86 composer to the King's Theatre, London; 1786 settled in Paris. His first French opera, *Démophon* (Opéra, 1788), was not very successful. Music director of an Italian opera company, the Théâtre de Monsieur, 1789–92; his serious opéra comique *Lodoïska* (Théâtre-Feydeau, 1791) was his first big French operatic success, followed at the same theater by *Eliza* (1794), *Médée* (1797; not a great success in Paris, but given in Germany well into the 1800s and revived in recent times), and *Les deux journées* (16 Jan. 1800), his most popular opera, given at the Opéra-comique until 1830 and widely performed in Germany and elsewhere. The seriousness that helped make Cherubini's operas more popular in Germany than in France also made his music unpalatable to Napoleon, and he received little official support under the Empire. After *Faniska* (Vienna, 1805) his opera activity declined, consisting primarily of *Les Abencérages* (Opéra, 1813), which contains some of his best dramatic music, and *Ali-Baba* (Opéra, 1833); both were failures.

Beginning with the Mass in F (1808–9), he turned increasingly to sacred music; his appointment in 1816 as superintendent of the royal chapel (jointly with Le Sueur), which lasted until the chapel was abolished after the 1830 Revolution, led to many Masses and motets (including the Requiem in C minor in memory of Louis XVI, 1816, and the Coronation Mass for Charles X, 1825). His other great Requiem in D minor (1836) was intended for himself. Among his last works were the final 4 of his 6 string quartets (1834–37) and a string quintet (1837). Other works include republican hymns and revolutionary music from the 1790s; a symphony in D, an overture, and a cantata about spring, all commissioned by the London Philharmonic Society in 1815; occasional cantatas from the Empire and Restoration periods.

In 1793 he was appointed to a post, requiring teaching and composing, at the new Institut national de musique, which in 1795 became the Conservatory, and which he served until the Restoration as an inspector; 1822 appointed director of the Conservatory, retiring in February of 1842. His rather rigid nature led him to an emphasis on order, detail, and regularity in his administration that brought him into conflict with freer spirits, most notably Berlioz, who caricatured him in his *Memoirs.* Among didactic works for the Conservatory, his *Cours de contrepoint et de fugue* (Paris, 1835), written with his best-known student, Halévy, was long influential.

Bibl.: E. Bellasis, *Cherubini* (London, 1874; rev. 3rd ed., 1912; R: New York, 1971). Margery Stomne Selden, "Napoleon and Cherubini," *JAMS* 7 (1955): 110–15. Id., "Cherubini and the Italian 'Image,'" *JAMS* 17 (1964): 378–81. Basil Deane, *Cherubini* (London, 1965). Margery Stomne Selden, "Cherubini and England," *MQ* 60 (1974): 421–34.

Chevalier, Maurice (b. Paris, 12 Sept. 1888; d. there, 1 Jan. 1972). Popular singer and actor. He began singing in Parisian cafes and theaters and became popular after World War I for performances in revues at the Casino de Paris, appearances in operettas (*Déclé,* 1921), and recordings of individual songs ("Valentine," 1924). From 1928 he appeared in many American musical films (*Merry Widow,* 1934; Lerner and Loewe's *Gigi,* 1954); in the 1950s and 1960s he toured internationally as a singer.

Chevé, Emile-Joseph-Maurice (b. Douarnenez, Finistère, 31 May 1804; d. Fontenay-le-Comte, 26 Aug. 1864). Writer. A medical doctor who abandoned that profession to work, in company with his wife, Nanine, and his brother-in-law Aimé Paris, on a new method of teaching sight-singing, based on the innovations of Pierre Galin, which came to be known as the Galin-Paris-Chevé method. Chevé became the chief proponent in print of this method, which was much resisted by the French musical establishment but widely used later in the century.

Chevreuille, Raymond (b. Watermael-Boitsfort, Brussels, 17 Nov. 1901; d. Montignies-le-Tilleul, 9 May 1976). Composer. Studied briefly at the Brussels Conservatory, but was essentially self-taught. He was an engineer with Belgian Radio from 1936. He had an extremely large output but destroyed many of his early works. His surviving compositions include 8 symphonies, 3 violin concertos, 3 piano concertos, 2 cello concertos, 6 string quartets, ballets, operas, radio works, and other dramatic works.

Chiari, Giuseppe (b. Florence, 26 Sept. 1926). Composer. He first studied piano and engineering, turning to composition in 1950; in 1961–62 he was involved in the Vita musicale contemporanea in Florence, and in 1962 organized with Bussotti the exhibition Musica e segno, which toured in Europe and the U.S. Member of the Florentine Gruppo 7 and the Fluxus group in New York. His objections to the rituals of art music led him to compose a series of suites in progress, in which musical notation is combined with verbal and graphic instructions to produce "happenings" for any means available; for example, his *Lavoro* (1965) consists of the following direction: "All around the performer are many different things placed in the most complete disorder. He arranges them in the proper order. He follows his own idea of what their proper order is." His work has been performed more in galleries rather than in concert halls. *Lettera* (for voice and orchestra, 1962) and *Per arco* (cello and tape, 1962) are the earliest of his action pieces; later works may contain elements of social criticism (*Suonare la città,* 1972). Also wrote more traditional works for piano.

Chickering, Jonas (b. New Ipswich, N.H., 5 Apr. 1798; d. Boston, 8 Dec. 1853). Piano maker. Trained as a cabinet maker; in 1818 apprenticed to the Boston piano maker John Osborn; in 1823 a founding partner of Stewart and Chickering; in partnership with John Mackay in 1829–41; began making upright pianos in 1830; patented full metal plate for square pianos (1840) and grand pianos (1843). The firm was the leading American piano builder before the establishment of Steinway and Sons in 1853. It was carried on by his descendants until 1908, when it was sold.

Chihara, Paul (Seiko) (b. Seattle, 9 July 1938). Composer. Studied composition with Boulanger (1962–63); D.M.A. in composition from Cornell in 1965 (Palmer); further study with Pepping and Schuller. He taught at UCLA (1966–74) and briefly elsewhere. In 1980 he was composer-in-residence with the San Francisco Ballet. Wrote a series of tone pictures of trees in static textures (including *Branches,* 2 bassoons and percussion, 1968; *Forest Music,* orchestra, 1970) as well as a Ceremony series ("concert meditations on some basic musical objects"). Other works include ballets (*Infernal Machine,* 1975; *Shinju,* 1975); orchestral music, often with solo instruments (Symphony no. 1, [Ceremony V, Symphony in Celebration], 1975; concerto for string quartet and orchestra, 1980; saxophone concerto, 1981; Symphony no. 2 (Birds of Sorrow, 1981); chamber music (*Sequoia,* string quartet and tape, 1984); choral works (*Missa Carminum,* 1976); film and TV scores; arrangements for musicals (Ellington's *Sophisticated Ladies,* 1981).

Chilcot, Thomas (b. Bath? ca. 1700; d. Bath, 24 Nov. 1766). Composer and organist. From 1728 until his death he was organist at the abbey at Bath. He was active in concert life and managed a music shop as well. He published in London *6 Suites of Lessons,* harpsichord (1734); *12 English Songs* (1744); and 2 sets of *6 Concertos* for harpsichord and orchestra (1756, 1765; 2nd ed. in *Musica da camera,* 32–33, London, 1975).

Child, Peter Burlingham (b. Great Yarmouth, England, 6 May 1953). Composer. Won a Bernstein Fellowship to the Berkshire Music Center, where he studied with Jacob Druckman in 1978. He received a Ph.D. from Brandeis Univ. in 1981; his teachers included Arthur Berger, Martin Boykan, and Seymour Shifrin. Has taught at Brandeis and at M.I.T. His works include a piano sonata (1977), duo for flute and percussion (1979), and a wind quintet (1983).

Child, William (b. Bristol, 1606; d. Windsor, 23 Mar. 1697). Organist and composer. His early musical studies were at Bristol Cathedral, where he sang in the choir, and at Oxford, where he completed a degree in 1631. The following year he was made organist at St. George's Chapel, Windsor, where he had served as clerk since 1630. He was expelled from the chapel during the Interregnum; after the Restoration (1660) he was given back his post and was eventually made musician to the chapel royal. He composed some 20 services and 80 anthems, as well as instrumental music.

Bibl.: Edmund H. Fellowes, *Organists and Masters of the Choristers of St. George's Chapel in Windsor Castle* (London, 1939; 2nd rev. ed., 1979).

Childs, Barney (Sanford) (b. Spokane, 13 Feb. 1926). Composer. Studied literature at Oxford (M.A., 1955) and Stanford (Ph.D., 1961). He had studied composition in the 1950s under Ratner, Chávez, Copland, and Carter; continued to compose during his career as professor of literature (1956–69); became composer-in-residence at the Wisconsin College-Conservatory (1970) and then professor of composition at Johnston College, Univ. of the Redlands. He has employed indeterminacy and improvisation (*The Roachville Project,* 1967, in which 4 to 10 performers create an instrument from available materials and improvise on it for at least 30 minutes) and has composed more traditional multisectional pieces whose structures he calls "self-generating." An important advocate for new music as an editor (Genesis West) and writer. His compositions include works for orchestra (2 symphonies, 1954, 1956; a clarinet concerto, 1970; a timpani concerto, 1989) and band; chamber music (for brass, winds, and strings as well as other ensembles; *A Box of Views,* wind quintet and piano, 1988); solo instrumental works (*Mr. T., His Fancy,* double bass, 1967); choral music and songs.

Chilston (fl. early 15th century). Theorist. Wrote three treatises in English (with Latin technical terms) that together describe mathematical proportions as they were used in music of the 15th century. In the single manuscript source, a compilation of 20 treatises by various authors, these works are preceded by a discussion of discant and fauxbourdon. This was for a time erroneously attributed to Chilston, but scholars now refer to its author as Pseudo-Chilston.

Chisholm, Erik (b. Glasgow, 4 Jan. 1904; d. Rondebosch, Cape Town, South Africa, 7 June 1965). Composer and conductor. After early music studies in Glasgow (from 1918 at the Scottish Academy of Music), he took up study of composition with Tovey at Edinburgh Univ., where he earned a Mus.D. in 1934. He conducted the Glasgow Grand Opera (1930–39) and the Anglo-Polish Ballet (1940–43); while touring abroad he founded the Singapore Symphony. From 1946 he was professor of music at the South African College of Music (Univ. of Cape Town). His own music employs relaxed twelve-tone techniques and includes Celtic and Hindu elements. He wrote music criticism and authored a study of Janáček's operas, published in 1971. He composed operas (*The Isle of Youth,* 1941; *Dark Sonnet,* 1952; *The Pardoner's Tale,* 1961); ballets (*The Forsaken Mermaid,* 1942); orchestral works (2 symphonies, 2 piano concertos; concerto for orchestra, 1952); vocal works (*Crabbed Age and Youth,* chorus, 1926).

Chopin, Fryderyk (Franciszek) [Frédéric François] (b. Żelazowa Wola, near Warsaw, 1 Mar. 1810; d. Paris, 17 Oct. 1849). Composer and pianist. His father, Nicolas (1771–1844), was a son of well-to-do peasants in the Vosges region village of Maramville, whose château belonged to a Polish nobleman. When the Polish overseer returned to Poland in 1787, he took Nicolas with him. From the 1790s Nicolas was tutor to a succession of wealthy families and in 1806 married Justyna Krzyzanowska (1780–1861), a poor relation and housekeeper of his current employer, Count Skarbek. Fryderyk was the second of their four children, and the only son. The day of his birth is not certain; the baptismal records give 22 February, but the family always held to 1 March. Six months later they moved to Warsaw, where Nicolas became a French teacher at the high school and later also at a military school.

Chopin's mother, who had had a genteel education, began teaching him the piano as a small child, and his obvious talent led to lessons from a professional

Fryderyk Chopin. Drawing by George Sand, 1841.

teacher, Adalbert Żywny. Since Żywny was primarily a violinist, Chopin developed his own rather individual technique of playing. He early began to compose piano pieces (variations, polonaises, a genre then much cultivated by Warsaw musicians, and other dances), few of which have survived. One of these was privately published in 1817. He began playing at charity concerts in 1818 and was often heard in private salons, becoming a notable figure in Warsaw musical life. He was educated as a gentleman, but also had lessons from Józef Elsner, director of the new Warsaw Conservatory.

In 1824 he played (on the organ) for the czar, then visiting Warsaw. In 1825 he published locally the Rondo in C minor op. 1. In September 1826 he began courses in counterpoint and harmony at the conservatory, and in literature at the university. In 1827–28 he composed several larger works, including the Variations on Mozart's "Là ci darem" op. 2, for piano and orchestra, the Sonata op. 4, the Piano Trio op. 8, and the Fantasy on Polish Airs op. 13, for piano and orchestra. He began to show signs of wanting to move beyond the artistic orbit of Warsaw and the local celebrity that he had achieved there. In 1828 he sent the Variations and Sonata to publishers in Vienna and Leipzig, but without result. In spring 1829, as he was finishing his conservatory course, his father applied for a government grant for him to travel and study in western Europe, but was rejected.

In 1829 Chopin reached a new stage of maturity as a composer, producing works that remain among his most popular (the Nocturnes op. 9, the Piano Concerto in F minor op. 21, and the first of the Etudes op. 10). In July 1829 he made an excursion to Vienna with friends, and on 11 August gave a concert in the Kärntnerthor Theater, whose success led to another on 18 August. Back in Warsaw he gave the premiere of his concerto before an invited audience in the family apartment on 3 March 1830 and repeated it at public concerts at the National Theater on 17 and 22 March to great acclaim. The E-minor Concerto op. 11, completed that summer, was premiered in the same way in private on 22 September, repeated in public on 11 October, Chopin's last public concert in Warsaw, which he left forever on 2 November for Vienna, where he hoped to establish himself as a professional musician. In this he was disappointed. The revolution that broke out in Poland soon after he left was not favorably regarded in Vienna and may have hurt his chances, especially in light of his own nationalist sympathies. He received little encouragement and was not able to arrange a concert of his own, playing only as a guest in two concerts given by singers in April and June 1831, the second shortly before he left Vienna to try Paris, stopping for a month in Munich, where he gave a concert.

In Paris, where he arrived in September 1831, Chopin found a much more hospitable atmosphere both socially and artistically. A large Polish community, including many exiles, gave him the sense of connection with his homeland that he was always to crave. He was to become friendly with many leading musicians, including Liszt and Berlioz, Ferdinand Hiller and the cellist Franchomme, both of whom became very close friends, and the pianist Kalkbrenner, whose playing Chopin greatly admired and who, even though Chopin declined to become his pupil, helped arrange his first Paris concert (Salle Pleyel, 26 Feb. 1832), which was well received. Schumann had already hailed him as a genius in the *Allgemeine musikalische Zeitung* in December 1831.

Chopin seems to have established himself in the forefront of Parisian music with relative ease and on his own terms. He disliked making the tiresome arrangements for his own concerts, and so gave very few, preferring to appear as guest in those of others. In the 1833–34 season he played only in a concert given by Liszt. On 7 December 1834 he played at one of Berlioz's, on 25 December in two duets with Liszt at the Salle Pleyel, and as a guest in three other concerts the next spring. He was more amenable to playing in private salons, but often late at night, after most of the guests had left, when he would sometimes improvise for hours; many, perhaps most, of the ecstatic accounts of Chopin as pianist and improviser are based on having heard him in such intimate surroundings. In this way Chopin's appeal came to reside partly in his exclusivity, both socially and artistically, in contrast to the wider appeal of more public and theatrical virtuosos such as Liszt. He found a larger public primarily through the publication of his music. In 1832 he made an agreement with the publisher Schlesinger for his music past and future, although he also occasionally dealt with other publishers when his interests warranted. Some were to disapprove of Chopin's way of life, seen as that of an aristocratic hanger-on, and of his music, judged excessively mannered and precious, but in general he did not have to struggle for success. Increasingly, from the mid-1830s onwards, his principal obstacle became his health.

The exclusivity of Chopin's image made him one of the most fashionable teachers in Paris, and most of his days were devoted to teaching, his evenings to social events. Much of his composing seems to have been done in the summer, which he spent in the country or on excursions. In spring 1834 he and Hiller went to Aachen for the Lower Rhine Music Festival, organized by Mendelssohn, with whom they spent much time there. In August 1835 he went to Karlsbad for a reunion with his parents. Stopping at Dresden on his return to Paris, he met a young Polish woman, Maria Wodzińska, whom he had known as a girl in Warsaw. He was strongly attracted to her, and they began to correspond. In Leipzig he called upon Mendelssohn and met his great admirer and propagandist Schumann, along with Clara Wieck and her father. In summer 1836 he went to Marienbad to be with Maria Wodzińska and members of her family, then followed them to Dresden, where he proposed marriage. He spent the next year awaiting an answer, which never came, Maria's family's initial concerns over Chopin's health and what they perceived to be his worldly life in Paris hardening into an opposition that caused the possibility of marriage to fade away, bringing Chopin much unhappiness. In July 1837 he made his first visit to London, a pleasure trip made with Pleyel. In February 1838 he took part in a concert given by Alkan, playing in an eight-hand arrangement of Beethoven's Seventh Symphony, and in March in a benefit concert at Rouen for a Polish musician.

He had first met George Sand in October 1836, while still hoping to marry Wodzińska, in the circle of Liszt and his mistress, the Countess d'Agoult. Neither had been impressed by the other, and Sand's unconventional dress, mannerisms (she smoked cigars), and behavior (the freedom of her sex life was well known) were not of a sort likely to attract the elegant and fastidious Chopin. Nevertheless, when they met again in April 1838, she was much taken with him, and he returned her quickly evident passion. Chopin's liaison with Sand, the most intimate and enduring adult relationship of his life, had varied consequences. It gave his life an emotional focus that it otherwise lacked, but Sand had a complex, sometimes self-contradictory personality; she was capable of great generosity and affection, but also at times headstrong, inconsiderate, and self-serving. The injuries, often unintentional, that she did him began almost immediately: in November 1838 she took him and her two children to spend the winter on Majorca without much preparation or prior knowledge of conditions there, a venture ill-considered in light of Chopin's delicate health, which suffered greatly when the Majorcan winter turned out to be less salubrious than they had supposed. The Majorcan doctors' diagnosis of tuberculosis increased their difficulties by causing their eviction from their rented villa.

Chopin reached the mainland in February 1839 hemorrhaging badly, but improved rapidly in Barcelona and then Marseilles. He spent the summer recuperating and composing at Sand's country estate at Nohant, returning to Paris in October. This set a pattern for the rest of his life with Sand. Through 1846 he spent the summer and autumn (until October or November) at Nohant, where he did most of his composing. The rest of the year in Paris, they usually maintained separate but nearby quarters. He seldom played in public after 1838 (Salle Pleyel, 26 Apr. 1841, 21 Feb. 1842), although he was still frequently heard in the salons, which he continued to frequent until about 1845. Gradually the Chopin–Sand liaison became strained. The continued decline of Chopin's strength seems to have caused his always sensitive nature to become at times peevish. It also seems to have brought an early end to their sexual relationship, Sand's attitude toward him becoming increasingly maternal; tiring of this she resumed sexual affairs with other men. The immediate cause of their final break was the circumstances surrounding the marriage in 1847 of Sand's daughter, of whom Chopin was very fond.

On 16 February 1848 Chopin gave his last Paris concert at the Salle Pleyel. In April he went to England at the urging of his rather obsessively devoted pupil Jane Stirling, a Scottish aristocrat. He refused an invitation to play one of his concertos with the London Philharmonic, but was heard at soirees and by Queen Victoria and the Prince Consort. He gave expensive lessons and on 23 June and 7 July private concerts for small audiences. On 28 August, at Manchester, he gave a public concert for an audience of 1200, too large for his playing to be effective. Concerts in Glasgow and Edinburgh followed on 27 September and 4 October. His health continued to deteriorate alarmingly, and he returned to London in late October, where on 16 November, although very weak, he took part in a benefit for Poland. Late that month he returned to Paris and resumed teaching, his health fitfully declining and improving. He composed two mazurkas, having composed almost nothing since his break with Sand. In summer 1849 he moved to Chaillot, where the air was purer, but his illness was entering its final stage. His sister came from Poland to be near him. In September he was moved back to the center of Paris, where he died on 17 October. He was given an impressive funeral in the Madeleine, attended by thousands, with Mozart's Requiem conducted by Habeneck and with Viardot and Lablache among the soloists. He was buried in Père Lachaise cemetery, except for his heart, which he had instructed to be sent to Poland.

Works: *Piano and orchestra.* 2 concertos: no. 1, op. 11 (1830), no. 2, op. 21 (1829–30); Variations on "Là ci darem" op. 2 (1827); Fantasy on Polish Airs op. 13 (1828); Krakowiak, rondo op. 14 (1828); Grand Polonaise op. 22 (1831).

Chamber music. Piano Trio op. 8 (1829); Cello Sonata op. 65 (1846); Introduction and Polonaise, cello and piano, op. 3 (1830); Grand Duo on Themes from *Robert le diable,* cello and piano (1832).

Piano solo. Allegro de concert op. 46 (1841); Andante spianato op. 22 (1834); 4 ballades op. 23 (1835), op. 38 (1839), op. 47 (1841), op. 52 (1843); Barcarolle op. 60 (1846); Berceuse op. 57 (1844); Bolero op. 19 (1833); 27 etudes: 12 op. 10 (1829–32), 12 op. 25 (1832–36), 3 (1839); Fantaisie-impromptu op. 66 (1835); Fantasy op. 49 (1841); 3 impromptus op. 29 (1837), op. 36 (1839), op. 51 (1842); 59 mazurkas: 4 op. 6 (1830), 5 op. 7 (1831), 4 op. 17 (1832–33), 4 op. 24 (1834–35), 4 op. 30 (1836–37), 4 op. 33 (1837–38), 4 op. 41 (1838–40), 3 op. 50 (1842), 3 op. 56 (1843), 3 op. 59 (1845), 3 op. 63 (1846), others posthumous; nocturnes: 3 op. 9 (1830–31), 3 op. 15 (1830–33), 2 op. 27 (1835), 2 op. 32 (1836–37), 2 op. 37 (1838–39), 2 op. 48 (1841), 2 op. 55 (1843), 2 op. 62 (1846), others posthumous; 15 polonaises: 1 (1817), 2 op. 26 (1834–35), 2 op. 40 (1838–39), op. 44 (1841), op. 53 (1842), others posthumous; Polonaise-fantaisie op. 61 (1846); 26 preludes: 24 op. 28 (1839), op. 45 (1841), 1 posthumous; 3 rondos: op. 1 (1825), op. 5 (1826), 1 posthumous; Introduction and Rondo op. 16 (1832); 4 scherzos: op. 20 (1832), op. 31 (1837), op. 39 (1839), op. 54 (1842); 3 sonatas: op. 4 (1828), op. 35 (1839), op. 58 (1844); Tarantelle op. 43 (1841); Introduction and Variations on a Theme by Hérold op. 12 (1833); 2 variation sets, posthumous; 19 waltzes: op. 18 (1831), 3 op. 34 (1831–38), op. 42 (1840), 3 op. 64 (1846–47), others posthumous.

19 Polish songs (1829–47), all posthumous.

Bibl.: I. J. Paderewski et al., eds., *Complete Works* (Warsaw, 1949–61). Maurice Brown, *Chopin: An Index of His Works in Chronological Order,* 2nd rev. ed. (London, 1972). Krystyna Kobylanska, *Frederic Chopin: Thematisch-bibliographisches Werkverzeichnis* (Munich, 1979). K. Michalowski, *Bibliografia Chopinowska, 1849–1969* (Kraków, 1970). G. Sand, *Un hiver à Majorque* (Paris, 1842); trans. Eng. Robert Graves (London, 1956). F. Liszt, *F. Chopin* (Paris, 1852); several Eng. trans. G. Sand, *Histoire de ma vie* (Paris, 1854); trans. Eng. Dan Hofstadter (New York, 1979). H. Opienski, comp., *Chopin's Letters,* trans. and ed. E. L. Voynich (New York, 1931). A. Maurois, *Frederic Chopin,* trans. R. Harris (New York, 1942). A. Gide, *Notes on Chopin,* trans. B. Frechtman (New York, 1949). A. Cortot, *In Search of Chopin,* trans. C. and R. Clarke (New York, 1952; R: Westport, Conn., 1975). Bronislaw Edward Sydow, ed., *Selected Correspondence of Fryderyk Chopin,* trans. A. Hedley (London, 1962; R: New York, 1979). Jean-Jacques Eigeldinger, comp., *Chopin, vu par ses élèves* (Neuchâtel, 1970); trans. Eng. (New York, 1986). Adam Zamoyski, *Chopin: A New Biography* (Garden City, N.Y., 1980). James Methuen-Campbell, *Chopin Playing: From the Composer to the Present Day* (London, 1981). Jim Samson, *The Music of Chopin* (Boston, 1985). Richard Tames, *Fryderyk Chopin* (New York, 1991). Jim Samson, ed., *The Cambridge Companion to Chopin* (Cambridge, 1992). Jeremy Siepmann, *Chopin, the Reluctant Romantic* (Boston, 1995). Jeffrey Kallberg, *Chopin at the Boundaries: Sex, History, and Musical Genre* (Cambridge, Mass., 1996).

Choron, Alexandre(-Étienne) (b. Caen, 21 Oct. 1771; d. Paris, 29 June 1834). Writer. Moved to Paris in the 1790s; published the first of his many books and treatises in 1804; an important French figure in the movement to maintain appropriate styles of church music through the cultivation of older, particularly Renaissance, music and Gregorian chant. Under Louis XVIII he was charged with reforming music in French cathedrals and the royal chapel; in 1817 founded a school, the Institution royale de musique classique et religieuse, which eventually turned into the more influential École Niedermeyer. In 1805 he established a publishing firm that issued editions of early music. He published manuals on various aspects of composition, several drawing heavily on earlier writers (Sala, Marpurg, Albrechtsberger, Martini).

Bibl.: B. R. Simms, "Alexandre Choron (1771–1834) as a Historian and Theorist of Music" (diss., Yale Univ., 1971).

Chou Wen-Chung (b. Chefoo, China, 29 July 1923). Composer. Trained as a civil engineer in China, he came to the U.S. in 1946 and studied composition at the New England Conservatory (Slonimsky) and at Columbia (Luening; M.A., 1954); was a student and associate of Varèse, whose *Nocturnal* he completed. From 1972 he taught at Columbia. His style reflects an interest in the application of Asian concepts to Western music. His *Landscapes* (1949) combines Chinese melodic patterns with Western harmony and orchestration; *Cursive* (flute and piano, 1963) refers to aspects of Chinese calligraphy; in *Pien* (piano, percussion, and winds, 1966) he employed the *I Ching; Yü ko* (9 instruments, 1965) is based on ancient Chinese music for the *qin,* a zither. Most compositions date from before 1970. He composed works for orchestra, and several for winds; chamber music for a variety of ensembles and solo instruments, favoring winds and brass over strings; vocal music and documentary film scores.

Chrétien [Crétien] **de Troyes** (b. Troyes; fl. ca. 1160–90). Trouvère. The earliest known French poet-composer. Also wrote the Arthurian romances *Perceval* and *Lancelot.* After being educated in Troyes, spent time at the court of Henry the Liberal, Count of Champagne. The count's wife, Marie de Champagne, and her "court of love" may have provided the inspiration for Chrétien's lyric poetry. Five chansons, without music, are attributed to him in at least one manuscript source. Of these, only 2 (1 with and 1 without music) are now generally accepted as authentic.

Christian, Charlie [Charles] (b. Bonham, Texas, 29 July 1916; d. New York, 2 Mar. 1942). Jazz guitarist. He played guitar and double bass with Alphonso Trent (1938), then joined Benny Goodman's sextet (1939–41), recording "Seven Come Eleven" (1939) and "Breakfast Feud" (1941) as well as "Solo Flight" with Goodman's big band (1941). His participation in jam sessions during the development of bop included those with Thelonious Monk and Kenny Clarke recorded informally at Minton's Playhouse in New York (1941). He died of tuberculosis. The first great electric guitar soloist, he played with a smooth tone and characteristically juxtaposed running eighth-note lines and swing riffs.

Christoff, Boris (b. Plovdiv, Bulgaria, 18 May 1914; d. Rome, 28 June 1993). Bass. Entered the Gusla Choir at 18. Graduated in law at Sofia. A stipend from Czar Boris III enabled him to study voice with Riccardo Stracciari in Rome, 1942–43. Concert debut, Rome, 1945–46 season. Operatic debut in Reggio Calabria as Colline in *La Bohème.* Debut as Mussorgsky's Boris at Covent Garden, 1949; at La Scala, 1950; at San Francisco (U.S. debut), 1956. Although especially praised as the successor to Chaliapin in the role of Boris, he sang as many as 40 roles, including Verdi's Philippe II (which he was prevented from singing at the New York Met in 1950 because he was barred under the McCarran Act from entering the country), Handel's Giulio Cesare, Wagner's King Marke, and Borodin's Khan Konchak.

Christou, Jani (b. Heliopolis, Egypt, 9 Jan. 1926; d. Athens, 8 Jan. 1970). Composer. Born to Greek parents; in Alexandria he studied at Victoria College; then beginning 1945–48 he studied philosophy with Wittgenstein at Cambridge and had private composition lessons with Hans Redlich in Letchworth. In 1949–50 he studied at the Chigiana in Siena and was briefly a pupil at the Jung Institute in Zurich. He spent the rest of his life in relative isolation, first in Alexandria (from 1950), then in Athens (from 1960). His varied oeuvre embraces serialism, aleatory techniques (often represented in graphic notation), and metaphysical texts; these are often manifested through multimedia combinations of projections, films, choreography, and speakers. Works include much incidental music for classical Greek plays (*Prometheus Bound,* 1963; *The Persians,* 1965; *The Frogs,* 1966; all for chorus, orchestra, and tape); 33 works from the genre he termed *anaparastis* (reenactments), which attempt to re-create primitive rituals for modern uses (*Reconstruction of an Event,* 1966; *Praxis and Metapraxis,* 1968; 120 others remained in sketch form); other orchestral music (2 extant symphonies, 1949–50, 1957–58; a third is lost); oratorios (*Gilgamesh,* 1953–58, lost; *Mysterion,* speaker, actors, choruses, orchestra, tape, 1965–66, first perf. 1974; *Tongues of Fire,* soloists, chorus, orchestra, 1964); chamber and vocal music (*The 12 Keys,* mezzo, chamber ensemble, 1962; *6 Songs,* 1955–57; *Praxis for 12,* 11 strings, pianist, conductor, 1966).

Christy, Edwin Pearce (b. Philadelphia, 28 Nov. 1815; d. New York, 21 May 1862). Entertainer. Usually considered the inventor of the minstrel show; assembled and led the first company in Buffalo in 1842; immediately popular, toured upstate New York, 1843–45; 1846–54, played almost continuously in New York City, also sending touring companies under his name throughout the country and in 1857 to Great Britain, popularizing the genre there; from 1847 introduced many Stephen Foster songs; in 1854–55 took his company to San Francisco, then gave up performing for managing; later became unbalanced and killed himself.

Chrysander, (Karl Franz) Friedrich (b. Lübtheen, Mecklenburg, 8 July 1826; d. Bergedorf, near Hamburg, 3 Sept. 1901). Scholar. Son of a miller, became a schoolteacher but turned to musical scholarship, publishing works on folk song and the oratorio in 1853; doctorate from the Univ. of Rostock, 1855; wrote on a wide variety of musical figures from the Baroque through the early 19th century, principally Handel, of whom his biography (published in part, 1858–67) was never finished. Of his editions by far the most monumental was the Handel complete works, begun in 1858 under the auspices of the Handel Gesellschaft, and continued, at times under considerable financial hardship, until 1894.

Chueca, Federico (b. Madrid, 5 May 1846; d. there, 20 June 1908). Composer. Showed musical talent as a child, but studied medicine at the Univ. of Madrid before abandoning it for music; a cafe pianist and theater orchestra conductor; then began to compose zarzuelas. His talent was mainly melodic; he was aided in other aspects of composition by Joaquín Valverde, who is named as collaborator in many of his 3 dozen works, primarily in the *género chico.* He composed *La canción de la Lola* (1880), his first great success; *La gran vía* (1886), which was translated into French, English, and Italian; *El año pasado por agua* (1889); *Agua, azucarillos y aguardiente* (1897), considered by many his best work and still performed. Also wrote very popular dance music.

Chung, Kyung Wha (b. Seoul, 26 Mar. 1948). Violinist. Began study of violin in 1955. Debut in Seoul, 1957, performing the Mendelssohn concerto. Soloist with the Korean Broadcasting Orchestra, 1958. Studied with Ivan Galamian at Juilliard, 1960–67. Joint winner (with Pinchas Zuckerman) of the Levintritt Competition, 1967. U.S. debut with the New York Philharmonic, 1968. European debut with the London Symphony, 1970. Subsequently performed and recorded 19th- and 20th-century concertos with the world's major orchestras. In the mid-1980s she took leave of the world's stages, married, bore a son, then resumed her career.

Church, John (b. Windsor? 1675; d. London, 6 Jan. 1741). Composer and chorusmaster. After early training as a choirboy at St. John's, Oxford, he was a tenor at the Theatre Royal (from 1695). In 1697 he became lay vicar at Westminster Abbey and Gentleman Extraordinary at the Chapel Royal. As copyist for the chapel he compiled and copied the first surviving set of Chapel Royal Partbooks. He also served as master of the choristers at Westminster Abbey, 1704–40. He published *An Introduction to Psalmody* (1723?), 17 anthems, hymns, songs, catches, and instrumental music. He also compiled *Divine Harmony: A Collection of Anthems Used at Her Majesty's Chapel Royal* (1712).

Ciampi, Vincenzo (Legrenzio) (b. Piacenza, 1719?; d. Venice, 30 Mar. 1762). Composer. May have studied with *maestro di cappella* Rondini in Piacenza and (from ca. 1730) with Francesco Durante and Leonardo Leo in Naples. His first comic opera, *Da un disordine nasce un ordine,* was performed in 1737 at Naples's Fiorentini Theater. After several successful comedies in Naples he composed *Artaserse,* an opera seria, for Palermo (1747). For the Ospedale degli incurabili in Venice, where he was choirmaster from 1747, he composed motets, Masses, and other choral works. During the 1750s he was frequently in London, where his were among the first Italian comic operas performed. His last years were spent in Venice at the Ospedale. In addition to 21 full-length operas and several pasticcios, he composed oratorios (*Betulia liberata,* 1747), a *Missa solemnis* (1758), and instrumental music (24 trio sonatas, 6 harpsichord sonatas, 12 concertos for flute or oboe, 6 overtures).

Ciccolini, Aldo (b. Naples, 15 Aug. 1925). Pianist. Studied with Paolo Denza at the Naples Conservatory; debut Naples, 1941, playing Chopin's Concerto op. 21. Taught at the Naples Conservatory, 1947–49. Moved to Paris after winning the Long–Thibaud Prize, 1949. U.S. debut with New York Philharmonic under Mitropoulos, 2 Nov. 1950. Became French citizen, 1969; professor at the Paris Conservatory from 1971. Among his recordings are the 5 concertos of Saint-Saëns as well as complete piano works by Satie, Massenet, and Déodat de Séverac.

Ciconia, Johannes [Jean] (b. Liège, ca. 1335; d. Padua, between 15 and 24 Dec. 1411). Composer and theorist. Probably the son of another Johannes Ciconia, canon at the church of St.-Jean l'Évangéliste in Liège. In biographical accounts father and son have generally been treated as one person. The composer was a choirboy in Liège in 1385. From at least 1401 until his death, he was associated with the cathedral of Padua. Between these dates he may have spent time in Avignon, encountering the influence of Philipoctus de Caserta, and may have been in the service of Francesco Carrara "il Novello," who was in Avignon in 1389 and in Padua from 1390.

His works are rooted in the musical traditions of northern Italy, but many also incorporate features typical of the French *ars nova* and, especially, the *ars subtilior.* None dates from before ca. 1390. The secular compositions include 4 Italian madrigals and 9 *ballate* (2 incomplete), 2 French virelays, and 1 Latin canon. The sacred works and occasional pieces with Latin text include 10 Mass movements (Glorias and Credos, some paired), 8 motets, and 2 Latin *contrafacta.* These are only the works of undoubted authenticity; there exist a few other compositions in nearly every category that may be by Ciconia. Two theoretical treatises survive: *Nova musica* and *De proportionibus.* The first is a practical work of wide scope presenting both the results of original speculation and the teachings of theorists from Pythagoras to Jehan de Murs and Marchetto da Padova. *De proportionibus* is a later reworking of a portion of *Nova musica.*

Bibl.: Margaret Bent and Anne Hallmark, eds., *The Works of Johannes Ciconia,* Polyphonic Music of the Fourteenth Century, vol. 24 (Monaco, 1985).

Cifra, Antonio (b. near Terracina, 1584; d. Loreto, 2 Oct. 1629). Composer. Began his career as a choirboy and then a director of music at various institutions in Rome. In 1609 became *maestro di cappella* of the Santa Casa, Loreto, holding this post for most of the rest of his life. Briefly (1623–26) *maestro* at St. John Lateran, Rome. He was the most prolific composer of the Roman school in the early 17th century. Produced 8 books of concertato motets, 2 books of Masses, and numerous polychoral motets, Psalms, and litanies. His secular music consists of 6 books of 5-part madrigals, 5 books of scherzi and related pieces for smaller forces, and 2 books of ricercars and *canzoni francese.*

Cikker, Ján (b. Banská Bystrica, Slovakia, 29 July 1911; d. Bratislava, 21 Dec. 1989). He studied composition with Křička and Novák and conducting with Pavel Dědeček at the Prague Conservatory; later he studied conducting with Weingartner at the Vienna Academy (1936–37). From 1938 he was professor at the Bratislava Conservatory, and from 1951 professor of composition at the Bratislava Academy; stage director for the Slovak National Opera (1944–48). From 1973 he served as chairman of the Slovak Music Council. His works are generally diatonic, though during the 1960s he experimented with twelve-tone composition, often within a diatonic context. Stage works: *Juro Jánošík* (1950–53); *Prince Bajazid* (1957); *Mr. Scrooge* (1958–59); *Vzkriesenie* [Resurrection] (1961); *Coriolanus* (1972). Orchestral works: *Leto* [Summer] (1941); *Slovenská suita* (1943); *Spomienky* [Reminiscences], chamber orchestra (1947); *Sinfonietta* (1948); *Blažení sú mŕtvi* [Blessed Are the Dead] (1964); *Hommage à Beethoven* (1969); *Epitaph over an Old Trench* (1973); Symphony "1945" (1974–75). Choral and other vocal works: *Cantus filiorum* (cantata, 1940); *Vojak a matka* [Soldier's Mother] (1943); *O mamičke* [About Mother], song cycle (1949). Piano music: *Tatranské potoky* [Tatia Streams] (1954); *Čo mi deti rozprávali* [What the Children Told Me] (1957).

Cilea, Francesco (b. Palmi, Calabria, 23 July 1866; d. Varazze, near Genoa, 20 Nov. 1950). Composer. Studied at the Naples Conservatory, 1881–89 (composition under Paolo Serrao); his student opera *Gina,* performed at the school in 1889, led to a contract from the publisher Sonzogno that produced the verismo opera *La tilda* (Florence, 1892), also given in Vienna, but not successful. Taught piano for two years at the Naples Conservatory and in 1896–1904 theory and composition at the Florence Conservatory. His next opera, *L'arlesiana,* based on Daudet's play (Milan, Teatro lirico, 1897), was Caruso's first great success, but the opera did not maintain itself without him, although revised in 1898 and 1910. Cilea is remembered only for *Adrianna Lecouvreur* (Milan, Teatro lirico, 6 Nov. 1902), an immediate success and still performed. His last opera, *Gloria* (Milan, La Scala, 1907), was a failure. He was director of the Palermo Conservatory in 1913–16 and of the Naples Conservatory, 1916–35. Also composed orchestral and chamber pieces, songs and piano pieces.

Bibl.: T. d'Amico, *Francesco Cilea* (Milan, 1960).

Cima, Giovanni Paolo (b. Milan, ca. 1570; d. after 1622). Composer and organist. By 1610 he was organist and *maestro di cappella* at S. Celso in Milan; he was a leading musical figure in Milan well into the 17th century. He published sacred collections (motets, 1599; *Concerti ecclesiastici,* 1610, including 6 sonatas for 2–4 instruments with continuo, 2 of which represent the earliest known examples of solo sonatas and 2 of which are early examples of trio sonata texture) and keyboard collections (*Ricercate per l'organo,* 1602; *Partito di ricercari, canzoni alla francese,* 1606, which includes an appendix on tuning the clavichord). He also contributed to Angleria's *Regola del contrapunto* (1622).

Cimarosa, Domenico (b. Aversa, 17 Dec. 1749; d. Venice, 11 Jan. 1801). Composer. He studied in Naples first with a local organist and from 1761 at the Conservatorio di Santa Maria di Loreto, where he developed skills as singer, violinist, keyboard player, and composer of sacred music. In 1772 his first opera, *Le stravaganze del conte,* was performed in Naples, and in 1779 the highly popular *L'italiana in Londra* appeared in Rome. In 1785 he became second organist at King Ferdinand's royal chapel at Naples; during the 1780s he was also appointed music master at the Ospedaletto, one of Venice's schools for orphans. From 1787 he was *maestro di cappella* at Catherine's court at St. Petersburg; he reportedly could not tolerate the climate and returned to Europe after four years. In Vienna, Emperor Leopold II appointed him Kapellmeister in 1791. *Il matrimonio segreto,* performed in the Burgtheater in 1792, became one of the most popular of all 18th-century comic operas; within a few years of its first production it appeared in Berlin, Prague, Leipzig, Dresden, Milan, Siena, Palermo, Barcelona, Madrid, Lisbon, St. Petersburg, and many other operatic centers. He returned to Naples in 1794; two years later he was made first organist at the royal chapel. In 1799 he sided with the antiroyalist factions in Naples that created the Parthenopean Republic, and when the king returned to power later that year he imprisoned the composer. Released in 1800, Cimarosa returned to Venice, where he died the following year.

He composed some 76 operas, chiefly opere buffe. These include, in addition to those mentioned, *Giannina e Bernardone* (Venice, 1781), *I due baroni di Rocca Azzurra* (Rome, 1783), *L'impresario in angustie* (Naples, 1786), *Le astuzie femminili* (Naples, 1794), and *Gli Orazi ed i Curiazi* (*tragedia per musica,* Venice, 1797). He also composed at least 6 oratorios;

18 Masses (*Missa pro defunctis,* G minor) and other sacred works; cantatas (*Cantata pastorale,* ca. 1780; *Angelica e Medora,* 1783; *Il giorno felice,* 1803); intermezzos (*Il maestro di cappella,* ca. 1786–93); a few orchestral pieces, patriotic hymns, some chamber music, and many keyboard sonatas (generally circulated in one movement but, like Scarlatti's, probably intended as multimovement works).

Bibl.: Roberto Vitale, *Domenico Cimarosa, la vita e le opere* (Aversa, 1929). Franco Schlitzer, *Goethe e Cimarosa* (Siena, 1950). Jennifer Elizabeth Johnson, "Domenico Cimarosa, 1749–1801" (diss., Univ. of Wales, Cardiff, 1976). Friedrich Lippmann, "Über Cimarosas Opere serie," *AnMca* 21 (1982): 21–59.

Cinti-Damoreau [née Montalant], **Laure (Cinthie)** (b. Paris, 6 Feb. 1801; d. Chantilly, 25 Feb. 1863). Soprano. Studied at the Paris Conservatory; opera debut at Théâtre-Italien, 1816; took Cinti as stage name; sang in opera mostly in Paris (but also London and Brussels), in 1826–35 at the Opéra. Her specialization in florid, Italianate singing suited the Rossini style then dominating; created leading roles in his *Le siège de Corinthe, Moïse, Le comte Ory, Guillaume Tell,* Auber's *La muette de Portici,* Meyerbeer's *Robert le diable.* Pretty and elegant, she was not strongly dramatic either as singer or actress, and was thus less suited to Meyerbeer's style; therefore moved to the Opéra-comique in 1836, where Auber wrote leading roles for her; retired from the stage in 1843; toured Europe and the U.S., retiring in 1848; taught at the Paris Conservatory, 1833–56.

Bibl.: Austin B. Caswell, "Mme Cinti-Damoreau and the Embellishment of Italian Opera in Paris: 1820–1845," *JAMS* 28 (1975): 459–92.

Clapisson, (Antoine-) Louis (b. Naples, 15 Sept. 1808; d. Paris, 19 Mar. 1866). Composer. Son of a horn player at the Teatro San Carlo, Naples, then at the Grand théâtre, Bordeaux, where Louis became a violinist; from 1830 studied at the Paris Conservatory (the violin under Habeneck, counterpoint under Reicha), also playing the violin at the Théâtre-Italien and, from 1832, the Opéra. His principal gift as a composer was tunefulness, demonstrated first in salon romances, and in 1838–61 in 19 opéras comiques, of which *La perruche* (1840), *La promise* (1854), and *La fanchonnette* (1856) were especially popular and widely performed. Defeated Berlioz for the French Academy in 1854, often interpreted as a sign of the period's prizing of easy mediocrity above genius. Also a noted collector of antique musical instruments, most of which were acquired by the Conservatory, Clapisson serving from 1862 as curator and professor of harmony. Also composed many duets and trios for brass instruments.

Clapp, Philip Greeley (b. Boston, 4 Aug. 1888; d. Iowa City, 9 Apr. 1954). Composer and teacher. Studied at Harvard (Ph.D. 1911; theory and composition with Spalding, Converse, and Hill) and with Max von Schillings in Stuttgart. Carl Muck, a conductor of the Boston Symphony, was his mentor from 1911, arranging for Clapp to conduct two of his symphonies; he taught at Dartmouth (1915–18); after the war became director of music in the School of Fine Arts, Univ. of Iowa. His compositions (primarily symphonic) are in a German Romantic idiom; they are clearly orchestrated with frequent cyclic treatment of thematic material. His works include 2 operas (not produced); 3 symphonic poems and 12 symphonies, a concerto for 2 pianos (1944), and other orchestral works; some chamber music (string quartet, brass sextet, wind quintet, and others); and vocal music (*A Chant of Darkness,* chorus and orchestra, 1919–24; part songs).

Clapton, Eric (b. Ripley, Surrey, 30 Mar. 1945). Rock guitarist, singer, and songwriter. He was a founding member of the Yardbirds (1963) and played with John Mayall's Bluesbreakers (1965–66). His guitar technique was blues-oriented and characterized by extremely clean articulation; this style was exhibited in his work with the bands Cream (1966–68, especially in the song "Crossroads"), Blind Faith (1969), and Derek and the Dominoes (1970–72, especially the album *Layla,* recorded with guitarist Duane Allman). In the 1970s he recorded solo albums that emphasized his songwriting and singing abilities, achieving success with the song "Lay Down Sally" (1977).

Bibl.: Michael Schumacher, *Crossroads: The Life and Music of Eric Clapton* (New York, 1995).

Clarke, Henry Leland (b. Dover, N.H., 9 Mar. 1907). Composer and scholar. In his youth he studied piano, organ, and violin; attended Harvard (a composition course with Gustav Holst; B.A., 1928; Ph.D., 1947); studied with Boulanger (1929–31) and in New York with Weisse and Luening (1932–38). His later teaching career was at UCLA, Vassar, and the Univ. of Washington (1958 until retirement in 1977). He composed in a tonal style, in which line and lyricism outweigh vertical elements; often his works were intended for particular occasions, fulfilling his stated objective of communication and celebration. He used unusual scales (String Quartet no. 3, 1958, uses no semitones) and "wordtones," a strict relation between text and pitch in which the repetition of a word necessitates the repetition of its associated pitch in the same octave (*Lysistrata,* opera, 1968–72; premiered 1984). Works include 2 operas; *Monograph* for orchestra (1952); 3 string quartets and other ensemble and solo pieces; much choral music ("No Man is an Island," 1951); songs on texts of Keats ("Beauty is Truth," 1983), Shelley, Blake, Dickinson, Wilbur, and others.

Clarke [Clark, Clerk], **Jeremiah** (b. London, ca. 1673; d. London, 1 Dec. 1707). Composer. A chorister of the Chapel Royal in London by 1685. Held the post of organist at Winchester College from 1692 until 1695. From 1699 was vicar-choral, then organist, then almoner and Master of the Choristers (succeeding his teacher John Blow in 1704) at St. Paul's Cathedral, London. In addition, from 1700 was a Gentleman Extraordinary of the Chapel Royal and from 1704 until his death (by suicide) organist there (jointly with William Croft). He composed services and anthems (among the latter are *Praise the Lord, O Jerusalem* and *Bow Down Thine Ear*); psalms and hymns; ceremonial odes (*Come, Come Along for a Dance and a Song,* composed in 1695 on Henry Purcell's death); much music for plays and other stage works (*The World in the Moon,* 1697; *The Island Princess,* 1699); and instrumental music (a number of keyboard works in *The Harpsichord Master,* London, 1702). He is best known for a Trumpet Voluntary arranged for trumpet and organ by Henry Wood and attributed by Wood to Purcell. Clarke published it with the title "The Prince of Denmark's March" in a collection of harpsichord pieces in 1700; but Clarke also included it among some pieces for winds.

Bibl.: Thomas Fuller Taylor, *Thematic Catalog of the Works of Jeremiah Clarke* (Detroit, 1977).

Clarke, Kenny [Kenneth Spearman; Klook] (b. Pittsburgh, 9 Jan. 1914; d. Montreuil-sous-Bois, near Paris, 26 Jan. 1985). Jazz drummer and bandleader. In New York he played in big bands from 1935, then helped create the bop style in jam sessions at Minton's Playhouse with Dizzy Gillespie, Thelonious Monk, and Charlie Christian (1940–43); he is among the drummers credited with transferring steady timekeeping to the ride cymbal and thus freeing the bass and snare drums for irregular accentuations. After military service he recorded as a leader, including *Epistrophy* (1946, with Fats Navarro and Bud Powell), which he composed with Monk, and he joined Dizzy Gillespie's big band (1946–48), remaining in Paris after a tour. Returning to the U.S. in 1951, he helped form the Modern Jazz Quartet; he left it in 1955. He recorded the album *Bohemia after Dark,* including Cannonball Adderley (1956), then settled in Paris, where he played with Powell (1959–62). With the Belgian composer and arranger Francy Boland he led an octet and big band (1960–73); their albums include *Volcano,* with Johnny Griffin (1969).

Clarke, Stanley (M.) (b. Philadelphia, 30 June 1951). Jazz electric-bass guitarist. At times playing double bass, he worked with Horace Silver, Joe Henderson (1971), Pharoah Sanders (1971–72?), and Stan Getz (1972), and recorded with Dexter Gordon and Art Blakey (both 1972). He concentrated on the electric instrument with Chick Corea's group Return to Forever; their recordings include the album *Light as a Feather* (1972). After recording his own album *School Days* (1976), he left Corea in 1977 to lead fusion groups, but toured again with Return to Forever in 1983.

Clayton, Buck [Wilbur Dorsey] (b. Parsons, Kans., 12 Nov. 1911; d. 8 Dec. 1991). Jazz trumpeter and arranger. He led a big band in Shanghai (1934–36) and Los Angeles before joining Count Basie (1936–43). He recorded often as a soloist with Basie (including "Topsy," 1937), Billie Holiday (1937–39), and Lester Young (1938–39, 1944). After military service he led groups as a trumpeter (into the early 1970s) and an arranger (through the 1980s) and worked with Jazz at the Philharmonic (from 1946), the pianist Joe Bushkin, Jimmy Rushing, Benny Goodman, Eddie Condon, and Humphrey Lyttelton. His albums include *Buck Meets Ruby* (1954).

Writings: with Nancy Miller Elliott, *Buck Clayton's Jazz World* (London, 1986).

Clemencic, René (b. Vienna, 27 Feb. 1928). Recorder player, composer, and musicologist. Studied recorder with Hans Ulrich Staeps and Johannes Collette; keyboard instruments with Eta Harich-Schneider; musicology and philosophy at Univ. of Vienna, Collège de France, and the Sorbonne. Founded *Musica antiqua,* 1958, known as *Ensemble musica antiqua* from 1959. Professor at the Musikhochschule in Vienna, 1961. Since 1969 his Clemencic Consort, based in Vienna, has performed and recorded music from the Middle Ages through 17th-century Italian operas to the avant garde. Wrote *Alte Musikinstrumente* (Frankfurt am Main, 1970); trans. Eng. (1968).

Clemens (non Papa) [Clement, Jacob] (b. probably in Ieper, ca. 1510; d. Dixmuiden, near Ieper, 1555 or 1556). Composer. His first published work is a chanson issued by Attaingnant in 1536. Bruges Cathedral employed him as succentor, 1544–45. Motet texts suggest a connection with Charles V between 1544 and 1549. Beginning in 1545 Tilman Susato, in Antwerp, published many of his works, of which only 6 chansons had previously appeared in print. Surviving manuscripts indicate some relationship with Leiden. Little else is known of his life.

One of the most prolific composers of the early 16th century, Clemens wrote both sacred and secular music but is chiefly known for the sacred works. These include 15 Masses, 2 Mass fragments, over 230 motets, 2 Magnificats, and 159 *souterliedekens* and *lofzangen* (3-part polyphonic settings of the Psalms in Dutch, all based on preexisting melodies). The secular works include 89 chansons, 8 Dutch songs, and several textless or instrumental pieces.

Bibl.: *Clemens non Papa: Opera omnia, CMM* 4 (1951–76). K. P. Bernet Kempers, "Jacobus Clemens non Papa's Chansons in Their Chronological Order," *MD* 15 (1961): 187. Id., "Bibliography of the Sacred Works of Jacobus Clemens non Papa: A Classified List, with a Notice on His Life," *MD* 18 (1964): 85–150.

Clementi, Aldo (b. Catania, 25 May 1925). Composer. Studied composition with Sangiorgi and Petrassi, and completed piano and composition diplomas at the Santa Cecilia Conservatory (Rome) in 1946 and 1954; attended the Darmstadt summer courses (1955–62); worked under Maderna's guidance at the Milan Radio electronic music studio (1956–57); also explored aleatory methods. His mature compositions are organized around variations in the density of a set of interchangeable events (e.g., *Sette scene,* which won first prize in the Italian section of the ISCM in 1963); in *Blitz* (21 instruments, 1972–73) the order of events is determined by the moves of 8 players engaged in games of chess. Taught composition at the conservatories of both Milan and Bologna. Works include *Collage* (stage, 1961); several orchestral pieces (Violin Concerto, 1977; *O Du Selige,* 1985); pieces for large and small ensembles and for piano (*Adagio,* quintet with prepared piano, 1983; concerto for piano and 11 instruments, 1986); choral and solo vocal music; tape pieces.

Clementi, Muzio [Mutius Philippus Vincentius Franciscus Xaverius] (b. Rome, 23 Jan. 1752; d. Evesham, England, 10 Mar. 1832). Composer, music publisher, and pianist. As a boy he studied counterpoint with Antonio Buroni, organ with Condiceli, and possibly voice with Giuseppe Carpani. An Englishman, Peter Beckford, heard him play in 1766 and paid Clementi's father to allow him to take the boy to his English country estate for intensive musical studies, and to serve as his house musician. For the next seven years Clementi took advantage of the relatively isolated Dorsetshire setting, practicing harpsichord and producing his first compositions, a Mass and an oratorio (both lost), and keyboard sonatas. At the end of this period he moved to London, began concertizing perhaps in 1775, and in 1779 and 1780 published his opp. 2–4 (works for keyboard). Among positions he held during the 1770s was that of keyboard conductor at the King's Theatre, Haymarket. In 1780 he began a concert tour that included Paris (where he allegedly played for Marie Antoinette) and Vienna, where he engaged in the famous keyboard contest with Mozart in 1781. The latter wrote to his father of Clementi's remarkable technique, especially in passages of thirds or octaves. "Otherwise he hasn't a kreutzer's worth of feeling or taste. In a word—a sheer *mechanicus*" (12 Jan. 1782). In addition, Clementi's opp. 7, 9, and 10 were published in Vienna, 1782–83. He returned to London in 1783 by way of Lyons, where his op. 8 was published (3 sonatas for keyboard). After reestablishing London's Hanover Square Concerts in 1783, he returned to Lyons for the sake of an 18-year-old girl, whose disapproving father again drove him off.

During the period 1784 to 1790 he published (as opp. 11–25) some 40 works for keyboard. He settled permanently in London, becoming a successful pianist, pedagogue, and music publisher; he continued to concertize, and his firm (originally called Longman, Clementi, and Co.) thrived. His pupils included Johann Baptist Cramer. When his popularity in London began declining in the 1790s, he concentrated on teaching and publishing. His *Introduction to the Art of Playing on the Piano Forte* appeared in London in 1801 (R: New York, 1974). Nevertheless he continued composing, working steadily during the 1790s on a set of 6 grand symphonies (never completed) that he hoped would secure his place in music history. In 1802 he embarked on another concert tour, to Paris, Vienna, and St. Petersburg, with his pupil John Field. While in Vienna in 1807, Clementi the publisher acquired rights to issue 5 of Beethoven's latest compositions. Back in London, he was appointed director of the Philharmonic Society. During the 1820s he continued directing concerts of his works and made other tours of the Continent. His 3 big piano sonatas op. 50 appeared in 1821 in London, Paris, and Leipzig. The 3 volumes of his highly successful pedagogical work *Gradus ad Parnassum, or The Art of Playing on the Piano Forte* appeared in 1817, 1819, and 1826. He died two years after his retirement from publishing in 1830. His musical legacy includes, in addition to the more than 100 piano sonatas (many accompanied), many works for 4-hand piano, 2 completed symphonies (in B♭ and D), 4 incomplete symphonies (2 completed by Alfredo Casella), a Piano Concerto in C (1796), and many smaller works for piano.

Bibl.: Max Unger, *Muzio Clementis Leben* (Lagensalza, 1914; R: New York, 1971). Adolf Stauch, *Muzio Clementis Klavier-Sonaten im Verhältnis zu den Sonaten von Haydn, Mozart und Beethoven* (Oberkassel bei Bonn, [1931]). Riccardo Allorto, *Le sonate per pianoforte di Muzio Clementi: Studio critico e catalogo tematico* (Florence, 1959). James Donald Kohn, "The Manuscript Piano Sonatas by Muzio Clementi at the Library of Congress: A Comparative Edition with Commentary" (diss., Iowa, 1967). Alan Tyson, *Thematic Catalogue of the Works of Muzio Clementi* (Tutzing, 1967). Pietro Spada, *Le opere sinfoniche complete di Muzio Clementi* (Milan, 1975). Leon Plantinga, *Clementi: His Life and Music* (London, 1977). Sandra P. Rosenblum, "Clementi's Pianoforte Tutor on the Continent," *FAM* 27 (1980): 37–48.

Cleonides [Kleoneidēs] (fl. 2nd cent.). Greek theorist. Wrote *Introduction to Harmonics (Eisagōgē harmonikē),* a treatise based on the theories of Aristoxenus, for whom it remains a valuable source. Because of errors in 16th- and 17th-century editions, the work has sometimes been attributed to Euclid.

Bibl.: Karl von Jan, ed., *Musici scriptores graeci* (Leipzig, 1895; R: Hildesheim, 1962), pp. 167–207.

Clérambault, Louis-Nicolas (b. Paris, 19 Dec. 1676; d. there, 26 Oct. 1749). Composer and organist. His family had served French courts for three centuries; his father, Dominique (1644–1704), had been one of Louis XIV's "Vingt-quatre violons du roi." Louis-Nicolas studied music with André Raison and Jean-Baptiste Moreau, and around 1705 he was appointed *surintendant* for Louis XIV; in this position he organized concerts and composed a number of cantatas. In 1704 he published the *Premier livre de pièces de clavecin;* later (in 1710) he received a 15-year publishing privilege. Soon afterward he assumed the post of organist at St. Sulpice; in 1714 he was also appointed organist at the convent at St. Cyr, and in 1719 at the church in the rue St. Jacques. For the wedding of the Dauphin and the Infanta of Spain, he composed (in 1745) the divertissement *L'Idylle de St. Cyr.* Although his earliest harpsichord pieces are typically French, both vocal and instrumental works thereafter show the increasing presence of Italian elements. Many of his works were published, including some 25 cantatas. Among the known cantatas are *Orphée* (1710), *Médée* (1710), *Le* *triomphe de la paix* (1713), *L'isle de Délos* (1716; ed. in *RRMBE* 27, 1978), *Apollon et Doris* (1720), *Abraham* (1715), and *La muse de l'opéra* (1716; ed. in *RRMBE* 27, 1978). His choral music also includes motets; a Te Deum (1701); and *Le retour du printemps* (1748). His instrumental music includes a collection for harpsichord (1704) and a collection for organ (ca. 1710).

Bibl.: Donald Herbert Foster, "Louis-Nicolas Clérambault and his Cantates françaises" (diss., Univ. of Michigan, 1967).

Cliburn, Van [Lavan, Harvey, Jr.] (b. Shreveport, La., 12 July 1934). Pianist. Studied with his mother, Rilda Bee O'Bryan, a student of Arthur Friedheim, 1938–51. First public performance at Shreveport's Dodd College at age 4. Performed Tchaikovsky's First Piano Concerto op. 23 with the Houston Symphony, 1947. New York debut (as winner of National Music Festival Award), Carnegie Hall, 1948. Entered Juilliard in 1951 and studied with Rosina Lhevinne. Debut with the New York Philharmonic in 1954 as winner of the Leventritt Competition. In politically charged atmosphere won the Tchaikovsky Competition in Moscow in 1958. Returned to the first New York ticker-tape parade for a musician. His subsequent international career includes 4 tours of the USSR, 1960–72. Took a leave of absence from public performance, 1978–89. A U.S. tour in 1994 met with little critical success.

Clicquot, François-Henri (b. Paris, 1732; d. there, 24 May 1790). Member of an important family of organ builders. His grandfather Robert (ca. 1645–1719) of Rheims had built organs at Rouen and Versailles. Robert's sons Jean-Baptiste (1678–1746) and Louis-Alexandre (ca. 1684–1760) both continued in their father's trade. Louis-Alexandre's only surviving son, François-Henri, became one of France's most important organ builders. While still in his teens he trained with his father, and by the time he took over the family shop in 1760 (on the death of Louis-Alexandre), he was in great demand. He completed the organs at St. Roch (Paris) and at Versailles, and subsequently built or rebuilt organs at St. Médard, St. Laurent, St. Sulpice, St. Nicolas-des-Champs (all in Paris), and at Souvigny, Poitiers, and many other places. His organ for Poitiers Cathedral, which survives today virtually intact, was used as the basis for his *Théorie pratique de la facture de l'orgue* (facs., Kassel, 1968), completed after his death by his son Claude François Clicquot (1762–1801).

Bibl.: Jean Albert Villard, *L'oeuvre de François-Henri Clicquot, facteur d'orgues du roi* (Laval, 1973). Norbert Dufourcq, *Les Clicquot, facteurs d'orgues du roi* (Paris, 1990).

Cline, Patsy [Hensley, Virginia Patterson] (b. Winchester, Va., 8 Sept. 1932; d. Camden, Tenn., 5 Mar. 1963). Country singer. She sang in clubs in Winchester and Nashville, and on radio in Washington, D.C., and began recording in 1955. Her first hit was "Walkin' after Midnight" (1957); later, songs such as "Crazy" (1961), "She's Got You" (1962), and "Faded Love" (1963) were successful with both country and popular audiences. She was a major influence on singer Loretta Lynn.

Cliquet-Pleyel, Henri (b. Paris, 12 Mar. 1894; d. there, 9 May 1963). Composer. He studied with Gédalge at the Paris Conservatory and was active between the wars as a performer in concerts devoted to the music of "Les six"; he belonged to the École d'Arcueil, a group founded by Satie in 1923. His own compositions were rarely performed; they include film scores, *La cantique des colonnes* (women's voices and orchestra, 1945); orchestral and chamber music; and piano works (*Hommage à Debussy,* 1962).

Clive, Kitty [née Raftor, Catherine] (b. London, 1711; d. Twickenham, 6 Dec. 1785). Actress and soprano. After vocal instruction from Henry Carey, she was hired by the Drury-Lane Theatre, where she appeared in musical and nonmusical productions. She played in Dublin (1741) and at Covent Garden (1743–44); she was famous for her parts in ballad operas, but also enjoyed success in serious works by Boyce and Arne and in Shakespearean roles. Handel composed for her the part of Delila in *Samson* (1743). Remembered chiefly as an actress; her singing was adequate to the comic servant roles for which she became famous.

Cluytens, André (b. Antwerp, 26 Mar. 1905; d. Neuilly, 3 June 1967). Conductor. At the Conservatoire royal flamand, 1914–22, studied piano with E. Bosquet. Choral coach with the Théâtre royal français d'Anvers (his father, Alphonse, was the music director), 1921–32. Conducting debut with the same company, 1927. Theater conductor in Toulouse, 1932–35; at Lyons, 1935, becoming music director, 1942. Music director of the Opéra-comique, Paris, 1947–53. In 1955 he was the first Frenchman or Belgian to lead at Bayreuth *(Tannhäuser).* U.S. debut with Vienna Philharmonic in Washington, D.C., 4 Nov. 1956. Frequent conductor at Vienna State Opera from 1959. Music director of the Orchestre national de belgique from 1960. Led many premieres; recorded extensively, including integral sets of Beethoven symphonies and Ravel orchestral works.

Coates, Albert (b. St. Petersburg, Russia, of English parents, 23 Apr. 1882; d. Milnerton, South Africa, 11 Dec. 1953). Conductor and composer. Studied organ with his brother while reading science at Liverpool Univ. Entered Leipzig Conservatory, 1902; studied conducting with Nikisch, who made him a coach at the Leipzig Opera. Conductor at the Elberfeld (1906), Dresden (1909), and Mannheim (1910) operas. London debut with the London Symphony, 1910. While music director at the St. Petersburg Opera, 1911–17, became close to Scriabin, whose music and ideas influenced his own. Covent Garden debut, 1913. U.S. debut with New York Symphony, 1920. Led Rochester Philharmonic, 1923–25. Conducted the Paris and Barcelona operas, 1925; Berlin State Opera, 1931; Vienna Philharmonic, 1935. Moved to South Africa in 1946; taught at the Univ. of South Africa at Cape Town and led the Johannesburg Symphony. His compositions include the operas *Samuel Pepys* (Munich, 1929) and *Pickwick* (Covent Garden, 1936) and the symphonic poem *The Eagle* (1925).

Coates, Eric (b. Hucknall, England, 27 Aug. 1886; d. Chichester, 21 Dec. 1957). Composer and violist. He played violin as a child, later taking up viola; studied in Nottingham at age 12. Studied with Hartley Braithwaite (piano), Lionel Tertis (viola), and Frederick Corder (composition) at the Royal Academy of Music, which he entered in 1906. He joined the Hamburg String Quartet in 1908 and toured South Africa with them. Founding member of the Beecham Symphony Orchestra. Played in the Queen's Hall Orchestra, 1910–19. After this he devoted his time to conducting and composition. He concentrated on light music as a composer. Compositions include the ballet suite *Snow White and the Seven Dwarfs* (1930; rev. as *The Enchanted Garden,* 1938); the fantasy *Cinderella* (1929); marches; other orchestral music; and over 100 songs.

Cobham, Billy [William C.] (b. Panama, 16 May 1944). Jazz drummer. Raised in New York, he played with Horace Silver and an early jazz-rock group, Dreams (1969–71), while also recording with Miles Davis. He played in John McLaughlin's Mahavishnu Orchestra (1971–73), recording the album *The Inner Mounting Flame* (1971) and establishing himself as a highly complex and imaginative jazz-rock drummer. After leading jazz-rock groups, some in collaboration with the keyboard player George Duke, he lived in Zurich from 1981, touring widely and working as a leader and a free-lance in many contemporary styles. He joined McLaughlin in a new Mahavishnu Orchestra in 1984.

Cochlaeus [Dobneck, Wendelstein], **Johannes** (b. Wendelstein, 10 Jan. 1479; d. Breslau, 10 Jan. 1552). Theorist. Attended the Univ. of Cologne. In 1510 became rector of St. Lorenz school in Nuremberg. Later studied theology and was ordained; held ecclesiastical posts in various German cities, including Dresden (1528–35), Meissen (1535–39), and Breslau (1545–52). Known chiefly for the treatise *Tetrachordum musices* (Nuremberg, 1511; facs., Hildesheim, 1971; trans. in *MSD* 23, 1970), designed for use as a textbook at St. Lorenz. Much of the work is derivative; its greatest value lies in material written by Cochlaeus himself, including sample compositions and sections on musical instruments.

Coclico, Adrianus Petit (b. Flanders, 1499 or 1500; d. Copenhagen, 1563). Composer. Originally a Flemish Catholic, converted to Protestantism and moved to Germany, first teaching privately at the Univ. of Wittenberg in 1545. Was turned down for the chair in music there in 1546. From late 1547 to 1550, served in the chapel of the Duke of Prussia. Then in Nuremberg in 1552 published a collection of motets entitled *Consolationes piae: musica reservata* and the treatise *Compendium musices* (facs., *DM,* ser. 1, 9, 1954). Both are prominent in their use of the term *musica reservata,* but neither provides the basis for a conclusive definition. Between 1555 and his death Coclico was in Schwerin, Wismar, and finally Copenhagen, where he was a musician at the Danish royal court and then in the service of Marcellus Amersfortius.

Bibl.: Bernhard Meier, "The Musica Reservata of Adrianus Petit Coclico and Its Relationship to Josquin," *MD* 10 (1959): 82.

Codax [Codaz], **Martin** (fl. ca. 1230). Composer and poet. His extant works are 7 poems, 6 with musical settings. The poems are *cantigas d'amigo* and are the only secular medieval Galician–Portuguese lyrics with music that have survived.

Coelho, Rui (b. Alcaçer do Sal, Portugal, 3 Mar. 1891; d. Lisbon, 5 May 1986). Composer and pianist. In Lisbon he studied composition with Tomás Borba and Costa Ferreira, in Berlin with Bruch, Humperdinck, and Schoenberg (1910–13) and in Paris with Paul Vidal. Back in Portugal, he began performing as pianist and writing music criticism for the *Diário de noticias.* His music employs folklike themes and was important in establishing a national style in Portugal. Works include some 20 operas (*Belkiss,* 1924; *Inês de Castro,* 1925; *Tá-mar,* 1926; *Dom João IV,* 1940; *Auto da barca do inferno,* 1950; *Orfeu em Lisboa,* 1963–66; *Auto da barca da glória,* 1970); ballet scores (*A princesa dos sapatos de ferro,* 1912); orchestral works, many on Portugese themes (5 Sinfonias camoneanas, 1912–57; 4 Suites portuguesas, 1925–56; 2 piano concertos, 1909, 1948; *Retábulo português,* 1960; many more); vocal music (*Canções de saudade e amor,* solo voice, piano, 1911–17; *Fátima,* oratorio, 1931; *6 canções populares portuguesas,* voice, orchestra, 1949); chamber works (2 violin sonatas, 1910, 1923).

Coerne, Louis (Adolphe) (b. Newark, N.J., 27 Feb. 1870; d. Boston, 11 Sept. 1922). Composer, conductor, and teacher. Studied violin; attended Harvard (1888–90), studying composition with Paine; studied organ and composition in Munich (1890–93) with Rheinberger, whose Mass in A minor he completed during a second residence in Germany (1899–1902); received the first American Ph.D. in music (Harvard, 1905) with a dissertation on orchestration. He held a variety of church, conducting, and teaching posts; was director of the School of Music at the Univ. of Wisconsin (1910–15) and professor at Connecticut College for Women (1915–22). He left some 500 compositions, of which more than half were published. They include many dramatic works, most unperformed (except *Zenobia* op. 66, performed in Bremen in 1905, the first American opera to be staged in Europe); orchestral overtures and symphonic poems; a violin concerto; a string quartet, violin sonata, and other chamber music; piano pieces; part songs; songs; incidental music.

Coffey, Charles (b. Ireland, late 17th cent.; d. London, 13 May 1745). Author. Wrote many ballad operas, of which about 5 were published with music. The most popular of his plays was *The Devil to Pay* (with music arranged by Seedo). This work was unsuccessful at its premiere in 1731, but after being greatly abbreviated it attained a success surpassed in its century by only *The Beggar's Opera. The Devil to Pay* was a favorite vehicle of the singer Kitty Clive, and in German translation it also achieved currency as a singspiel. Its influence extended to the next century, when it served as the basis for Adolphe Adam's ballet *Le diable à quatre* (1845).

Cohan, George M(ichael) (b. Providence, R.I., 3 July 1878; d. New York, 5 Nov. 1942). Popular songwriter, actor, and producer. He began performing with a family vaudeville group, and in the early 1900s in New York wrote for them several evening-length musical shows that prefigured the Broadway musical comedy (*The Governor's Son,* 1901; *George Washington, Jr.,* 1906). He continued to write, appear in, and produce shows on Broadway, and published music with Sam Harris. His best-known songs were patriotic ("You're a Grand Old Flag," 1906; "Over There," 1917); he was the subject of a biographical movie (*Yankee Doodle Dandy,* 1942) and musical (*George M!,* 1968).

Cohn, Al(vin Gilbert) (b. New York, 24 Nov. 1925; d. East Stroudsburg, Pa., 15 Feb. 1988). Jazz tenor saxophonist and arranger. He played in the big bands of Boyd Raeburn (1946), Buddy Rich (1947), Woody Herman (as a member of the saxophone section known as the "Four Brothers," 1948–49), Artie Shaw (1949–50), and Elliot Lawrence (1952–58). As a leader he recorded the album *The Natural Seven* (1955). Zoot Sims and he led quintets from 1957, when they recorded the album *You 'n Me,* into the early 1980s. He also arranged for big bands and Broadway musicals.

Colbran, Isabella [Isabel] **(Angela)** (b. Madrid, 2 Feb. 1785; d. Castenaso, near Bologna, 7 Oct. 1845). Soprano. Daughter of a court musician; studied in Madrid with Marinelli, later Crescentini; from 1807 a leading prima donna in Italy, possessing a fine voice of wide compass and a majestic beauty well suited to grand tragic roles; 1811–21, a fixture at the San Carlo, Naples, whose impresario, Barbaja, was her lover; from 1815, about the time her voice began to decay, causing her to sing out of tune, Rossini wrote many parts for her there. In 1822 she and Rossini married and took part in a Rossini festival in Vienna. His last role for her was in *Semiramide* (Venice, 1823); by their joint engagement in London, 1824, her voice was so far gone that she had to be replaced, and she retired. She and Rossini separated in 1837.

Cole, Cozy [William Randolph] (b. East Orange, N.J., 17 Oct. 1906; d. Columbus, Ohio, 29 Jan. 1981). Jazz drummer. He recorded with Jelly Roll Morton (1930) and belonged to Benny Carter's big band (1933–34) and Stuff Smith's combo (1936–38) before joining Cab Calloway (1938–42), with whom he recorded "Ratamacue" (1939). He led groups intermittently, recording "Thru' for the Night" (1944), then joined Louis Armstrong's All Stars (1949–53). He toured with Earl Hines and Jack Teagarden (1957) and then as a leader following the success of his recording "Topsy" (1958). He joined Jonah Jones's quintet in 1969 and later toured as a free-lance.

Cole, Nat "King" [Coles, Nathaniel Adams] (b. Montgomery, Ala., 17 March 1917; d. Santa Monica, Calif., 15 Feb. 1965). Singer and pianist. Family moved to Chicago when he was 4; sang in church as a child. Recording debut in 1936 with brother Eddie's band Solid Swingers. Moved to Los Angeles, 1937; formed King Cole Trio with guitar and bass. Hits included "The Christmas Song" (1946), "Straighten Up and Fly Right" (1943), and "Mona Lisa" (1950). Remembered as a singer, but his piano style was very influential, particularly on Errol Garner, Oscar Peterson, Bill Evans, and others.

Bibl.: James Haskins and Kathleen Benson, *Nat King Cole* (New York, 1984).

Coleman, Bill [William Johnson] (b. Centreville, Ky., 4 Aug. 1904; d. Toulouse, France, 24 Aug. 1981). Jazz trumpeter and bandleader. He played in many big bands, including those of Luis Russell (New York, 1929, 1931–32), Willie Lewis (Paris, 1936, 1937–38), and Leon Abbey (Bombay, 1936–37). As a soloist in small groups he recorded with Fats Waller (1934–35) and in Paris with Dicky Wells (1937) and as a leader (including two blistering versions of "After You've Gone," 1936–37, the second with Stephane Grappelli, and a duo with Django Reinhardt, "Bill Coleman Blues," 1937); helped form the Harlem Rhythm Makers in Egypt (1938–40). After playing again in the U.S., he lived in France from 1948 and led groups throughout Europe until 1980, making recordings.

Coleman [Colman], **Charles** (b. ca. 1605; d. London, buried 8 July 1664). Composer. Before and after the years of the English Commonwealth, was associated with the King's Musick as both a performer (instrumentalist and singer) and a composer. During the Commonwealth, was in favor among antiroyalists and remained active as a teacher, performer, and composer, as well as receiving the Mus.D. from Cambridge in 1651. Wrote both songs and, more important, instrumental music. Some of his compositions were published during his lifetime, but many, especially fantasias and dance music, survived in manuscript only.

Coleman, Ornette (b. Fort Worth, 9 Mar. 1930). Jazz alto saxophonist, composer, and bandleader. While in Texas, Natchez, New Orleans, and Los Angeles, he developed a new way of playing from a background of bop and rhythm-and-blues. He played free jazz, in which bop lines and blue notes retained a crucial place. His performances were not encumbered by preset chord progressions, fixed timekeeping, and accompanimental roles for double bass and drums, or a Western conception of pitch. His quartet recorded in Los Angeles (1958–59), the sidemen including Don Cherry, who attended the Lenox (Mass.) School of Jazz with Coleman before beginning a controversial engagement at the Five Spot in New York with Charlie Haden and Billy Higgins (replaced respectively by Scott LaFaro and Ed Blackwell in 1960). Coleman led a trio with double bass player David Izenzon and drummer Charles Moffett (1962, 1965–67) and taught himself trumpet and violin. From 1967 to the mid-1970s his groups included the tenor saxophonist Dewey Redman, Haden, and Blackwell; he also worked with his son Denardo, a drummer, and recorded with Elvin Jones (1968). To play a fusion of free jazz, rock, and funk, in 1975 he formed Prime Time, which by the 1980s had an instrumentation of alto saxophone and two each of electric guitar, electric bass guitar, and drums. He recorded separately on a double album with both Prime Time and colleagues from the early quartets (1987). His albums include *The Shape of Jazz to Come, Change of the Century* (both 1959), *Free Jazz* (1960), *The Ornette Coleman Trio at the Golden Circle* (1965), *New York Is Now* (1968), *Song X* (with Pat Metheny, 1985), *In All Languages* (1987), and *Virgin Beauty* (1988).

Bibl.: David Wild and Michael Cuscuna, *Ornette Coleman, 1958–1979: A Discography* (Ann Arbor, 1980). John Litweiler, *Ornette Coleman: A Harmolodic Life* (New York, 1992).

Coleridge-Taylor, Samuel (b. London, 15 Aug. 1875; d. Croydon, 1 Sept. 1912). Composer. Son of an Englishwoman and an African who returned to Africa, leaving them in England; studied at the Royal College of Music (composition under Stanford) in 1890–97, already composing prolifically (anthems, songs, chamber music, and a symphony performed at the college in 1896). In 1898 he conducted his *Ballade* for orchestra at the Three Choirs Festival and produced the cantata *Hiawatha's Wedding Feast,* which became very popular in England and America and led to other cantatas based on Longfellow's poem, none quite so successful (*Overture to the Song of Hiawatha,* 1899; *The Death of Minnehaha,* 1899; *Hiawatha's Departure,* 1900). Much of his considerable output before his early death from pneumonia was devoted to the cantata and choral genres *(A Tale of Old Japan).* A grand opera, *Thelma* (1907–9), was not performed. In instrumental music he was known primarily for short character pieces, sometimes grouped into suites, although he also composed several large works (*Symphonic Variations on an African Air* op. 63, 1906); also piano pieces (*24 Negro Melodies,* 1908). He was very conscious of his African blood and of having a mission and responsibility as a black artist, often using Negro themes in his music. Also active as a conductor and teacher; visited the U.S. in 1904, 1906, and 1910.

Bibl.: William Sayers, *Samuel Coleridge-Taylor, Musician: His Life and Letters* (Chicago, 1969). W. Tortolano, *Samuel Coleridge-Taylor: Anglo-Black Composer, 1875–1912* (Metuchen, N.J., 1977). Avril Coleridge-Taylor, *The Heritage of Samuel Coleridge-Taylor* (London, 1979). Jewel Taylor Thompson, *Samuel Coleridge-Taylor: The Development of His Compositional Style* (Metuchen, N.J., 1994).

Colgrass, Michael (Charles) (b. Chicago, 22 Apr. 1932). Composer and percussionist. Received his B.Mus. from the Univ. of Illinois (1956); studied composition with Milhaud, Riegger, Weigel, Foss, B. Weber. He was active as a percussionist in New York (1956–66), recording under Stravinsky; from 1967 he was primarily a composer. He received the Pulitzer Prize for his *Déjà Vu,* a concerto for 4 percussionists, in 1978. His earlier works were in an atonal avant-garde idiom; from the mid-1960s his music was more accessible, including multimedia music-theater works (*Best Wishes USA,* solo voices, double chorus, 2 jazz bands, folk instruments, and orchestra, 1976) and featuring the juxtaposition of various musical styles. Moved to Toronto in the early 1970s. His compositions include works for the stage; orchestral works, usually including chorus or soloists (*Demon,* amplified piano, percussion, tape, radio, orchestra, 1984; *Chaconne,* viola and orchestra, 1984); chamber music; many works for percussionists; vocal music with ensemble.

Collasse [Colasse], **Pascal** (b. Rheims, baptized 22 Jan. 1649; d. Versailles, 17 July 1709). Composer. Worked closely with Lully at the Paris Opéra from 1677 until Lully's death in 1687. Continued after that date to act as a composer for the Académie royale de musique. Was a *sous-maître* at the French royal chapel from 1683 until 1704. From 1685 until his death, was variously composer, music director, and *maître des pages* for the royal establishment. In his will Lully left Collasse a pension and a place to live, but the family invalidated these bequests through legal action. Some pieces by Lully did remain in Collasse's library and were used, not always with acknowledgment, in his own compositions. Of some 15 stage works by far the most successful was *Thétis et Pélée,* a *tragédie lyrique.* Other compositions are a number of airs; a setting of Racine's *Cantiques spirituels* for women's voices and orchestra; and many *grands motets* for the royal chapel (most lost).

Colonna, Giovanni Paolo (b. Bologna, 16 June 1637; d. there, 28 Nov. 1695). Composer. Studied composition in Rome. From 1659 was organist at S. Petronio in Bologna (first organist from 1661) and from 1674 until his death *maestro di cappella* there. Was a founding member and a prominent official of the Accademia de filarmonica. In 1685 was involved in a debate by correspondence with Corelli (in Rome) over part-writing. Despite coming out second best in this argument, Colonna was generally recognized in his time as one of the best contemporary Italian composers of church music. His extant works, which are only remnants of what must have been a much larger output, include about 80 sacred pieces, 6 oratorios, and several secular dramatic works (cantatas and operas). Among the sacred works the most notable are polychoral pieces and concerted Masses and Psalm settings for choir(s), soloists, and orchestra.

Colonne, Eduard [Judas] (b. Bordeaux, 23 July 1838; d. Paris, 28 Mar. 1910). Conductor. From a family of musicians; studied at the Paris Conservatory, winning first prize in harmony in 1858 and violin in 1863; played in Paris orchestras; from 1873 conducted the Concert national at the Odéon, then from 1875 the Concerts du Châtelet, later known as the Concerts Colonne. During the 1870s Colonne gradually overtook the initially greater popularity of Pasdeloup's Concerts populaires (reflected in his conducting the official concerts of the Paris Exposition of 1878), using methods similar to Pasdeloup's of featuring new and unfamiliar works by French and foreign composers, as well as Berlioz's large works; 1892–93, conducted at the Opéra; frequent appearances elsewhere in Europe, including London, 1896; conducted the New York Philharmonic, 1905.

Coltrane, John (William) (b. Hamlet, N.C., 23 Sept. 1926; d. Huntington, Long Island, 17 July 1967). Jazz tenor and soprano saxophonist, bandleader, and composer. He played alto or tenor saxophone in various groups before settling on the tenor as a member of Johnny Hodges's septet (1953–54). He played in Miles Davis's quintets and sextets (1955–57, 1958–59) and with Thelonious Monk's quartet (1957), also recording extensively as a leader. Playing ballads (such as his own composition "Naima"), he emphasized tunefulness, romanticism, and a lovely timbre; he improvised over esoteric and fast bop chord progressions (notably his composition "Giant Steps") with great facility and harmonic imagination. After taking up the soprano saxophone in 1960, he formed a quartet that soon included McCoy Tyner (–1965), Elvin Jones (–1966), and Jimmy Garrison (1961–66); Eric Dolphy was an intermittent fifth member (1961–63), and Roy Haynes substituted for Jones. While continuing to play beautiful ballads and spiritual pieces, Coltrane otherwise improvised mainly over slow-moving chordal ostinatos (so-called modal jazz), developing ideas motivically and playing in a freely chromatic manner with seemingly impossible dexterity. In his last years, as the accompanists' role grew freer, the membership changed accordingly; prominent were the pianist Alice Coltrane, Pharoah Sanders, and Rashied Ali. Coltrane was the most influential saxophonist since the 1940s.

With Davis he recorded the albums *'Round about Midnight* (1955–56), *Milestones* (1958), and *Kind of Blue* (1959); as a leader, *Blue Train* (1957), *Giant Steps* (including "Naima," 1959), *My Favorite Things* (1960), *Impressions* (1961, 1963), *A Love Supreme* (1964), *Ascension* (1965), and *Live at the Village Vanguard Again* (1966).

Bibl.: David Anthony Wild, *The Recordings of John Coltrane* (Ann Arbor, 1979). Brian Priestley, *John Coltrane* (London, 1987). Eric Nisenson, *Ascension: John Coltrane and His Quest* (New York, 1993).

John Coltrane.

Comes, Juan Bautista (b. Valencia, 1582; d. there, 5 Jan. 1643). Composer. Choirboy at the Valencia Cathedral from 1594 to 1596 and later choirmaster there (from 1613 to 1618 and from 1632 until his retirement in 1638). Also served as choirmaster or assistant choirmaster at Lérida Cathedral (1605–8), the Colegio del Patriarca in Valencia (1608–13, 1628–32), and the royal chapel in Madrid (1618–28). Wrote about 200 works, some secular (with Spanish texts) but the majority sacred, among which are Masses, Psalms, hymns, motets, Magnificats, and Lamentations. Textures range from accompanied solos to polychoral pieces with specific instruments (in addition to voices) designated for each choir.

Bibl.: José Climent, *Juan Bautista Comes y su tiempo* (Madrid, 1977).

Comissiona, Sergiu (b. Bucharest, 16 June 1928). Conductor. Studied conducting with Constantin Silvestri and Edward Lindenberg at the Romanian Conservatory. Debut with the Romanian Radio Orchestra, 1946. Directed the Romanian State Ensemble, 1948–55. Principal conductor of the Romanian State Opera and frequent guest conductor of the Georges Enesco Philharmonic, 1955–58. Emigrated to Israel, 1958;

naturalized, 1959. Music director of the Haifa Symphony, 1959–64; founder and leader of the Israel Chamber Orchestra, 1960–64. Established his international reputation as frequent guest conductor of the London Philharmonic (1960–63), Stockholm Philharmonic (1964–66), and Berlin Radio Orchestra (1965–67). After three years as guest conductor, chief conductor of the Göteborg Symphony, 1966–72. Music director of the Baltimore Symphony, 1969–84. Became a U.S. citizen, 1976. Artistic director (from 1980), then music director of the Houston Symphony, 1982–87. Chief conductor of the New York City Opera, 1987–88; of the Helsinki Philharmonic from 1990.

Como, Perry [Pierino Ronald] (b. Canonsburg, Pa., 18 May 1912). Popular singer. He began singing with the Ted Weems band and left in 1942 to perform as a soloist. From 1943 he hosted several radio and television shows and made many popular recordings, including "'Till the End of Time" (1945), "Catch a Falling Star" (1958), and "It's Impossible" (1970).

Compère, Loyset (b. Hainaut, ca. 1450; d. St. Quentin, 16 Aug. 1518). Composer. In the chapel of Galeazzo Maria Sforza, Duke of Milan, in the mid-1470s; left Milan in about 1477. By 1486, in the service of the French royal court. Accompanied the king on his invasion of Italy in the 1490s. Held church posts in Cambrai (1498–1500) and Douai (1500–1503 or 1504); motet texts indicate a continued, if intermittent, connection with the royal court even after 1498. During his last years, a canon at the collegiate church in St. Quentin. Among his extant sacred works are about 15 motets, 2 Mass ordinaries, and 3 cycles of *motetti missales.* The finest of the secular works are over 45 chansons, including more than 30 for 3 voices in Burgundian style and about 15 for 4 voices in a style more closely resembling that of the frottola.

Bibl.: *Loyset Compère: Opera omnia, CMM* 15 (1958–72).

Condon, Eddie [Albert Edwin] (b. Goodland, Ind., 16 Nov. 1905; d. New York, 4 Aug. 1973). Jazz guitarist, banjoist, bandleader, and entrepreneur. He recorded "Sugar" and "China Boy" leading McKenzie and Condon's Chicagoans in 1927. He toured with Red Nichols (1929) and the Mound City Blue Blowers (1930–31, 1933) and with the clarinetist Joe Marsala led a band in New York, where he settled and recorded extensively as a rhythm guitarist accompanying prominent jazzmen. He worked with Bobby Hackett, Bud Freeman, and Marsala, promoted concerts at Town Hall (1942–46) and broadcast jazz on television (1942, 1948). He also organized performances mixing traditional and swing musicians at Nick's (1937–44), then at his own club, Eddie Condon's (1945–67), and on international tours. His albums include *Bixieland* (1955).

Writings: with Thomas Sugrue, *We Called It Music: A Generation of Jazz* (New York, 1947; R: 1985).

Cone, Edward T(oner) (b. Greensboro, N.C., 4 May 1917). Composer and writer on music. Studied composition (Sessions) and piano (K. U. Schnabel) at Princeton (B.A., 1939; M.F.A., 1942), where his undergraduate thesis was a string quartet (1938–39); studied musicology (Lang) at Columbia (1939–41), during which time his works were performed at League of Composers concerts in New York. After army service he began to teach at Princeton (1945), an association that remained continuous; lectured widely in the U.S. and Europe and taught for one year at Berkeley. As a composer he employs expanded tonality and often structures harmonic and tonal relations in terms of hexachordal properties (String Sextet, 1966). Especially important as a writer on music concerned with analytical questions of structure and style, meaning in music, analysis and criticism, the relation of narrative modes in literature to musical discourse, and the work of Stravinsky and Schoenberg.

Works: a symphony (1953); Nocturne and Rondo, piano and orchestra (1955–57); concerto for violin and small orchestra (1959); *Music for Strings* (1964); *Variations,* orchestra (1967–68); chamber music (string trio, 1972–73; Serenade, flute, viola, cello, 1975); much piano music; *9 Lyrics from In Memoriam,* baritone and piano (1978), and other songs and vocal music.

Writings: *Musical Form and Musical Performance* (New York, 1968). *The Composer's Voice* (Berkeley, 1974). Edited the writings of Sessions (1979). *Music: A View from Delft: Selected Essays,* ed. Paula Morgan (Chicago, 1989).

Conforti [Conforto], **Giovanni Luca** (b. Mileto, Calabria, ca. 1560; d. after 1607). Theorist and composer. Sang in the papal chapel from 1580 until 1585 and from late 1591. His manual on embellishing vocal music, *Breve et facile maniera d'essercitarsi ad ogni scolaro . . . a far passaggi . . .* (Rome, 1593; facs., *MMML* ser. 2, 115 [1978]), is intended for both singers and composers. Wrote 2 books of elaborately ornamented versions of traditional psalm tones, with continuo accompaniment. In both collections most ornaments are written out; the letters *g* and *t* show where the *groppo* and the *trillo* are to be inserted.

Confrey, Zez [Edward Elezear] (b. Peru, Ill., 3 Apr. 1895; d. Lakewood, N.J., 22 Nov. 1971). Popular composer and pianist. Studied at Chicago Music College; in 1918 his composition "My Pet" (published on piano roll) made popular the style of "novelty piano" playing, which combined elements of contemporary popular and classical musical genres including ragtime and impressionism. This style is sometimes credited with influencing early jazz piano technique; Confrey's other successful pieces include "Kitten on the Keys" (1921) and "Nickel in the Slot" (1923). In 1923 he published a treatise on novelty piano technique.

Conlon, James (b. New York, 18 Mar. 1950). Conductor. Studied at Juilliard (B.M., 1972). Debut as an opera conductor at the Spoleto Festival (1971) with *Boris Godunov;* engagements with the New York Philharmonic (1974) and the Metropolitan Opera (1976). Music director, Cincinnati May Festival, 1979; of the Rotterdam Philharmonic, 1983–91; of the Cologne Opera from 1991.

Conn, Charles Gerard (b. Ontario County, N.Y., 29 Jan. 1844; d. Calif., 1931). Instrument maker. An injury prohibited him from using a conventional cornet mouthpiece; after designing a new one that would suit him, he started making and producing them for other players. Joined by Eugene Dupont in 1875; formed a company in Elkhart, Ind. Eventually produced all brass instruments. Produced the first saxophone made in the U.S., 1888. Company sold to Carl D. Greenleaf in 1915, renamed C. G. Conn, Ltd.

Connolly, Justin (Riveagh) (b. London, 11 Aug. 1933). Composer. Studied at Westminster School; entered the Royal College of Music in 1959; Harkness Fellowship to Yale Univ., 1963. Music of Carter and Babbitt were influential in his development of a new style. Returned to London in 1966 and joined the faculty of the R.C.M. Compositions include: *Triad VI* op. 21, viola, piano, tape (1974); *Regeneration* op. 16/2, chorus and brass (1976); *The Garden of Forking Paths* op. 11a, piano duet (1968); 3 sets of *Poems of Wallace Stevens,* soprano (1967, 1969, 1971); *Fourfold from the Garden Forking Path,* 2 pianos (1983); *Annead, Night Thoughts,* piano (1983); *Nocturnal,* ensemble (1992).

Conon [Quennon, Quenes] **de Béthune** (b. ca. 1160; d. 17 Dec. 1219 or 1220). Trouvère. Was at the French court as a young man. Participated in the Third and Fourth Crusades and in the government of the Latin emperor crowned in Constantinople after its fall in the Fourth Crusade. Poems or their dedications link him with the trouvères Huon d'Oisi, Blondel de Nesle, and Noblet (Guillaume V de Garlande, a friend of Gace Brulé); probably knew the Chastelain de Couci. Of his works 10 poems are extant; most have music in at least one source, although some of the settings are late and clearly not by the poet himself.

Conradi, Johann Georg (d. Oettingen, 22 May 1699). Composer. Between 1671 and 1690 was music director successively at the Protestant courts in Oettingen, Ansbach, and Römhild. For these establishments he wrote much sacred music and organized and maintained orchestras of note. By 1690, had moved to Hamburg as director of the opera. By 1698, was again in Oettingen as Kapellmeister. Little of his music survives. He wrote many occasional pieces for court use and much sacred music (concertos and cantatas for soloists, chorus, and orchestra). Of his 9 operas known to have been performed in Hamburg, there survive only several librettos, a handful of arias in transcription, and one complete work in score (*Die schöne und getreue Ariadne,* 1691, the earliest surviving work for the Hamburg opera). Evidently, Hamburg was first exposed to the French operatic style through these operas.

Bibl.: H. R. Jung, "Johann Georg Conradi," *BzMw* 13 (1971): 31; 14 (1972): 1–62. George J. Buelow, "Die schöne und getreue Ariadne (Hamburg, 1691): A Lost Opera by J. G. Conradi Rediscovered," *AM* 44 (1972): 108.

Consoli, Marc-Antonio (b. Catania, Italy, 19 May 1941). Composer. Came to the U.S. in 1956; studied with Rieti at New York College of Music. Worked with Krenek at Peabody Conservatory, and Schuller and Crumb at the Berkshire Music Center. Received D.M.A. from Yale (1976), where he studied with Alexander Goehr. Founded Musica oggi, 1976; director to 1981. Took over Rinaldo Music Press in 1984. Compositions include *Voci Siculani,* mezzo, instrumental ensemble (1979); *Six Ancient Greek Lyrics,* soprano, cello, flute, piano (1984); *Fantasia Celeste,* soprano, chamber ensemble (1983); a cello concerto (1988); *Greek Lyrics,* soprano, chorus, orchestra (1988).

Constant, Marius (b. Bucharest, 7 Feb. 1925). Composer. At age 20 he came to Paris, studying first with Enescu, then at the Conservatory with Messiaen and Aubin; at the École normale he studied conducting with Fournet; received the Premier Prix from the Conservatory in composition (1949). In 1950 he joined Groupe de recherches musicales studying *musique concrète* at French Radio; in 1953 he was music director of the VHF network and in 1970 music director of ORTF. He won the Italia Prize for the ballet *Le joueur de flûte,* and later won the Koussevitzky Prize (1962) and the Premio Marzotto (1968). He was music director for the ballet company of Roland Petit (1957–63) and led the American tour (1958) of the Paris Ballets. As a composer interested in aleatory music and in timbre, sometimes calling for unusual instruments. Works include several ballets (some for instruments and tape) and operas; *Les Chants de Maldover* (reciter, 23 improvising instrumentalists, 10 cellos with fixed parts, 1962); *Stress* (jazz trio, piano, 5 brass, and percussion, 1977).

Constantinescu, Paul (b. Ploiesti, Romania, 30 June 1909; d. Bucharest, 20 Dec. 1963). Composer. Attended Bucharest Conservatory, 1928–33; studied in Vienna, 1934–35, with Marx and others. He taught harmony, counterpoint, and composition at the Bucharest Academy of Church Music, 1937–41. Named professor of music at the Military Music Lyceum in Bucharest (1941–44). In his teaching he introduced his students to Romanian folk music and to Byzantine chant, two of the many influences at work in his own compositions. His output includes operas, film scores, ballets, many orchestral and instrumental works, and some vocal music.

Bibl.: Vasile Tomescu, *Paul Constantinescu* (Bucharest, 1967).

Contant, (Joseph Pierre) Alexis (b. Montreal, 12 Nov. 1858; d. Montreal, 28 Nov. 1918). Composer. His father was an amateur violinist, mother a pianist. Worked with organist and pianist Joseph Fowler; performed publicly at 13; studied with Calixa Lavallé in 1875. He taught at Collège de l'Assomption, 1880–81. Went to Boston to study, Jan. 1883, returning to Montreal in June. He devoted himself to organ, composition, and teaching. Organist at the church of St. Jean-Baptiste (Montreal), 1885 to his death. Taught at Collège de Montréal, 1883–90; Collège de Mont-St. Louis, 1900–18; Conservatoire nationale, 1905–17. Compositions include orchestral, chamber, and piano works; many vocal and choral compositions, including 8 Masses.

Bibl.: Stephen C. Willis, *Alexis Contant: Catalogue* (Ottawa, 1982).

Conti, Francesco Bartolomeo (b. Florence, 20 Jan. 1681; d. Vienna, 20 July 1732). Composer. From 1701 until 1726, associate theorbist, then principal theorbist at the Habsburg court in Vienna. From 1713, also court composer, succeeding Fux, in which capacity he was responsible for the single most important musical event of the year, the opera for the carnival season. He gave up his position as theorbist in 1726 because of ill health and had gone to Italy by 1729. Returned to Vienna in 1732 and produced 2 new dramatic works before his death in midyear. He composed mostly dramatic works, both operas (including intermezzos; about 30 in all) and oratorios (about 10), to librettos by Pariati (*Galatea vendicata,* 1719; rev. 1724), Zeno (*Griselda,* 1725; the oratorio *David,* 1724), and others; also numerous chamber cantatas; Masses and other sacred works for voices with instruments; a few purely instrumental works, 1 for mandolin solo. Despite Conti's position as a theorbist, his compositions rarely make use of the instrument, even in the continuo ensemble.

Bibl.: Hermine Williams, "Francesco Bartolomeo Conti: His Life and Operas" (diss., Columbia Univ., 1964). Barry S. Brook, ed., *The Symphony, 1720–1840,* ser. B/II, ed. Hermine Williams [with thematic catalog].

Conti, Gioacchino ["Gizziello"] (b. Arpino, 28 Feb. 1714; d. Rome, 25 Oct. 1761). Soprano castrato. Taught in Naples by Domenico Gizzi, from whose name his own nickname was derived. After his operatic debut in 1730 in Rome, sang in Vienna and various Italian cities before going to London in 1736. There performed in many of Handel's operas, some supplied with arias composed or adapted to take advantage of his exceptionally high voice and its wide compass. By 1738 was back in Italy. Went to Lisbon in 1743, but by 1746 was again in Italy, performing most often in Naples. Returned to Lisbon and the court theater in 1752; also performed in Madrid. Retired from the stage after the Lisbon earthquake of 1755.

Converse, Frederick Shepherd (b. Newton, Mass., 5 Jan 1871; d. Westwood, Mass., 8 June 1940). Composer. Studied at Harvard with Paine (B.A., 1893). After a short-lived attempt at a career in business, he resumed study of piano and composition in Boston; then in Munich, where he was instructed in organ and composition by Rheinberger (1896–98). He taught at the New England Conservatory, 1900–1902, and at Harvard, 1903–7; then left teaching to compose more, returning only in 1920 as head of the theory department at New England Conservatory, where he was dean for several years (1931–38). He was president of the Boston Opera Company, 1908–14. Early in his career he favored orchestral tone poems and other descriptive pieces, composed in a German Romantic style (*The Mystic Trumpeter,* a fantasy after Whitman, 1904). *Flivver Ten Million* (1926), subtitled "A Joyous Epic Inspired by the Familiar Legend, 'The Ten-Millionth Ford is Now Serving its Owner,'" requires car horns, wind machine, factory whistles, and anvil with orchestra; other works used American tunes or depicted American scenes (*California,* 1928).

Works: 4 operas, 2 of which were performed in Boston (*The Pipe of Desire,* premiered in Boston, 1906, New York Met, 1910; *The Sacrifice,* Boston, 1911); an oratorio (*Job,* 1906) and other works for voice(s) and orchestra; 5 symphonies, tone poems, and other orchestral works, including piano and violin concertos; 3 string quartets; works for brass and other chamber ensembles; choral music; piano pieces; songs; incidental music and a film score.

Bibl.: Robert Joseph Garofalo, *Frederick Shepherd Converse 1871–1940): His Life and Music* (Metuchen, N.J., 1994).

Conyngham, Barry (b. Sydney, Australia, 27 Aug. 1944). Composer. His early studies were in piano, and many of his early musical experiences were in the world of jazz. In 1964 he composed *Jazz Ballet.* He attended the Univ. of Sydney, where he studied law and later music with Sculthorpe. He composed his cello sonata in 1965 and began taking lessons with Raymond Hanson at the New South Wales Conservatorium. Studied in Japan with Takemitsu (1970) and met Stockhausen and Berio at the Expo there. Taught at the Univ. of New South Wales, later at the Univ. of Western Australia. In 1972 he was awarded a Harkness Fellowship; he studied in California for a year, then at Princeton, where he became interested in electronic music. He moved to France, but returned to Australia in 1975, taking a position at Melbourne Univ.; professor of creative arts, Wollongong Univ., from 1990. His works include the operas *Edward John Eyre* (1971), *Fly* (1984), *The Oath of Bad Brown Bill* (children, 1985), *Bennelong* (puppets, 1988); *Prisms,* 6 violins (1968); *Snowflake,* piano (1973); and *Water . . . Footsteps . . . Time,* piano, harp, electric guitar, tam-tam, orchestra (1970).

Cooder, Ry(land) (b. Los Angeles, 15 Mar. 1947). Rock, jazz, and popular guitarist and singer. Since 1965 he has worked as a studio musician with groups such as the Rolling Stones; from 1970 he released solo albums. His style combines elements of blues bottleneck, Hawaiian, and Bahamian playing; his albums include country, jazz, gospel, and international idioms (*Into the Purple Valley,* 1972; *Bop 'Til You Drop,* 1980). He has also written film scores (*The Long Riders,* 1980; *Paris, Texas,* 1984).

Cook, Will Marion (b. Washington, D.C., 27 Jan. 1869; d. New York, 19 July 1944). Composer, conductor, and violinist. Studied violin at Oberlin and with Joachim in Germany. After a brief career as a violinist, he devoted himself to musical comedy in New York; his *Clorindy, or the Origin of the Cakewalk* was the first Broadway musical composed and directed by blacks (1898). He was composer-in-chief and conductor for the Williams/Walker productions (1900–1908) of black music theater. His "syncopated" symphony orchestra toured Europe and the U.S. (1918–21); his own music draws from black folklore and folk music, couched in a neo-Romantic style. A few of his songs were recorded.

Cooke, Arnold (Atkinson) (b. Gomersal, Yorkshire, 4 Nov. 1906). Composer. Studied with Dent at Cambridge (B.A., Mus.B., 1929; Mus.D., 1948). Went to Berlin, where he studied with Hindemith at the Hochschule für Musik. He taught at the Royal Manchester College of Music, 1933–38; was appointed professor of harmony, counterpoint, and composition at Trinity College of Music (London) in 1947. His works include the opera *Mary Barton* (1949–54); the comic opera *The Invisible Duke* (1975–76); 6 symphonies (1946–47; 1963; 1967–68; 1973–74; 1978–79; 1984); concertos; 2 piano sonatas; a sonata for 2 pianos; orchestral music; organ music; song cycles; songs; and other vocal pieces.

Bibl.: Francis Routh, *Contemporary British Music: The 25 Years from 1945 to 1970* (London, 1972).

Cooke, Benjamin (b. London, 1734; d. there, 14 Sept. 1793). Organist and composer; son of Benjamin Cooke (ca. 1700–1743 or later), a London music publisher. From age 9 he studied music with Pepusch; in 1752 he succeeded his teacher as director of the Academy of Ancient Music. He was appointed Master of the Choristers at Westminster Abbey in 1757, and organist in 1762. Cambridge awarded him a doctoral degree in 1775; Oxford did the same in 1782. Also in 1782 he was appointed organist at St. Martin-in-the-Fields. He composed at least 3 services, 21 anthems, and many glees and catches; best known are the *Morning and Evening Service* (Service in G), *Ode on the Passions* (1784), and the publications *A Collection of Glees, Catches, and Canons* (1775) and *9 Glees and 2 Duets* op. 5 (1795).

Cooke [Cook], **J.** [John] (d. by 25 July 1419?). Composer. Was certainly in the English Chapel Royal in 1402 and from 1413 to 1419. The style of his music is closely related to that of Leonel Power. The Old Hall Manuscript is the unique source for his extant compositions: a Gloria–Credo pair, some single Mass movements, 2 votive antiphons, and an isorhythmic motet.

Cooke [Cook], **Sam(uel)** (b. Chicago, 22 Jan. 1935; d. Los Angeles, 11 Dec. 1964). Popular singer. As a child he sang with his siblings in the gospel group the Singing Children. He joined the Soul Stirrers in 1950. With producer Bumps Blackwell, he made his first secular recording in 1956; he abandoned gospel altogether by 1957. His hits included "You Send Me" (1957), "Only Sixteen" (1959), "Chain Gang" (1960), "Wonderful World" (1960), "Twistin' the Night Away" (1962), and "Another Saturday Night" (1963). He died in a gunfight in a Los Angeles motel. He was extremely influential on Eddie Floyd, Marvin Gaye, Otis Redding, Rod Stewart, and many others.

Cooke, Thomas Simpson (b. Dublin, 1782; d. London, 26 Feb. 1848). Composer and tenor. Son of a theater oboist; studied composition with Tommaso Giordani; at 15 concertmaster at Crow St. Theater, Dublin, also composing music for its productions; ran a music shop, 1806–12. After successfully appearing as a singer in English opera, he moved to London, where he worked at Drury Lane Theatre for 20 years, serving (sometimes simultaneously) as principal tenor, concertmaster, and music director; from 1815 to 1837 he was involved as composer or arranger with more than 50 English operas, plays, burlettas, and adaptations of foreign operas performed there. In 1828–30 a manager at Vauxhall Gardens; sometimes conducted the Philharmonic Society; 1846–48, concertmaster of the Concerts of Ancient Music; a noted singing teacher.

Coolidge, Elizabeth (Penn) Sprague (b. Chicago, 30 Oct. 1864; d. Cambridge, Mass., 4 Nov. 1953). Patron of music and composer. She began her patronage of contemporary composition and performance by founding the Berkshire Festivals of Chamber Music (as the South Mountain Chamber Music Festival) in 1918 in Pittsfield, Mass.; she established a foundation in 1925, the income from its trust to be paid to the Library of Congress for concerts, prizes, and expansion of the resources of the Music Division; made numerous contributions to institutions (e.g., a building at Yale, a pension fund for the Chicago Symphony); in 1932 established a medal for "eminent services to chamber music." She received a number of honorary degrees and honors from foreign governments. Her papers deposited at the Library of Congress are an important source of information on contemporary music; among the many composers of various nationalities who benefited from her commissions are Babbitt, Barber, Copland, Cowell, Crumb, Dallapiccola, Hindemith, Schoenberg, Stravinsky, and Webern. She was trained as a pianist and composed from the 1890s.

Cooper, Kenneth (b. New York, 31 May 1941). Harpsichordist. Studied with Sylvia Marlowe at Mannes College; coached by Fernando Valenti; studied musicology at Columbia Univ. (Ph.D., 1971). Taught at Barnard College, 1967–71; at Brooklyn College, 1971–73; at Mannes College from 1975. Performed and recorded widely in ensembles and as a soloist.

Copland, Aaron (b. Brooklyn, 14 Nov. 1900; d. Westchester, N.Y., 2 Dec. 1990). Composer, conductor, pianist, and writer on music. As a child Copland first studied piano with his elder sister, then with Leon Wolfsohn, Victor Wittgenstein, and Clarence Adler; during and just after his high school years he studied theory with Goldmark; at 20 he went to the American Conservatory at Fontainebleau and began four years of study with Boulanger. Before his return to New York in 1924 he had met Roussel, Prokofiev, Milhaud, and Koussevitzky; heard the music of the modern French and Russian composers in Paris; and been profoundly "affected by the whole rhythmic side of [Stravinsky's] music, also by its dryness, its non-Romanticism." Travels to Austria and Germany enabled him to hear works of Hába, Hindemith, Webern, and Bartók.

On his return to New York he was the first musician to receive Guggenheim Fellowships (1925, 1926); for a decade he lectured at the New School for Social Research (1927–37). During the next few years he made several trips abroad and to Mexico, where Chávez conducted the premiere of his *Short Symphony* in 1934; twice (1941, 1947) he toured Latin America, sponsored by the U.S. Coordinator of Inter-American Affairs and the State Department; taught at Harvard during Piston's leaves (1935, 1944) and was Charles Eliot Norton lecturer (1951–52). One of Copland's most valuable contributions to American musical life was his encouragement of younger composers through his cosponsorship of the Copland–Sessions Concerts (New York, 1928–31), cofounding the Yaddo Festivals and the American Composers Alliance, and his long association with the Berkshire Music Center (1940–65).

Along with other composers in the mid-1920s he had cultivated an interest in jazz in a self-conscious attempt to write recognizably American music (especially in the Piano Concerto, 1926). In the early 1930s he abandoned jazz to explore a more austere style in works such as *Short Symphony* and the Piano Variations; the latter have been viewed as serial (based on a 4-note row), though Copland denied that interpretation. The later Piano Quartet (1950) is clearly based on an 11-note row and employs serial procedures, as do a few other works including *Inscape* (1967). After the mid-1930s he frequently composed in a more immediately accessible style, a conscious attempt to bridge the gap between the "music-loving public and the living composer." In these works he made use of New England hymnody, folk music of North and South America (*El salón México,* 1933–36), and jazz; in the *Lincoln Portrait* (1942) borrowed tunes are blended in an Ivesian fashion. He is perhaps best known for his ballets, especialy *Billy the Kid* (choreography by Eugene Loring, Chicago, 1938), *Rodeo* (Agnes de Mille, New York, 1942), and *Appalachian Spring* (Martha Graham, Washington, D.C., 1944). His "accessible music" continued in the film scores of the 1940s, which raised the standard for that medium in Hollywood. He never worked with electronic music, considering its fixity on tape a disadvantage: "electronic composers are going to be the first ones to get bored with hearing their music without that great advantage of interpretation that we concert composers have."

Copland was active as conductor, lecturer, and pianist on American and British television and on tour. He

Aaron Copland.

served as director or board member for a variety of foundations and arts organizations (the American Music Center, the Charles Ives Society, the Naumburg Foundation). His numerous awards include a Pulitzer Prize (*Appalachian Spring,* 1945) and the Congressional Gold Medal of Honor (1985).

Works: 2 operas (*The Second Hurricane,* 1936; *The Tender Land,* 2 acts, 1952–54; rev. in 3 acts, 1955); 6 ballets (*Billy the Kid,* 1938; *Rodeo,* 1942; *Appalachian Spring,* 13 instruments, 1943–44, orchestral suite, 1945); 8 film scores (*Our Town,* after Wilder, 1940; *The Red Pony,* after Steinbeck, 1948); numerous orchestral works (including the early Symphony for Organ and Orchestra, 1924, composed for Boulanger's first American tour; Piano Concerto, 1926; Short Symphony [Symphony no. 2], 1932–33; *El salón México,* 1933–36; *An Outdoor Overture,* 1938; *Lincoln Portrait,* speaker and orchestra, 1942; *Fanfare for the Common Man,* brass and percussion, 1942; Symphony no. 3, 1944–46; Clarinet Concerto, 1947–48, first performed by Benny Goodman; *Orchestral Variations,* 1957; *Connotations,* 1962; *Inscape,* 1967); the Piano Quartet (1950) and other chamber music; the Piano Variations (1930), other piano works and arrangements from orchestral music; choral music and songs ("As it fell upon a day," soprano, flute, and clarinet, 1923; *12 Poems of Emily Dickinson,* 1944–50).

Writings: *What To Listen for in Music* (New York, 1939; 2nd ed., 1957). *Our New Music* (New York, 1941; 2nd rev. ed., 1968, as *The New Music, 1900–1960*). *Music and Imagination* (Charles Eliot Norton Lectures; Cambridge, Mass., 1952). *Copland on Music* (New York, 1960).

Bibl.: Cole Gagne and Tracy Caras, "Aaron Copland," in *Soundpieces: Interviews with American Composers* (Metuchen, N.J., 1982), pp. 102–16. Aaron Copland and Vivian Perlis, *Copland 1900 through 1942* (New York, 1984). Id., *Copland: Since 1943* (New York, 1989). Neil Butterworth, *The*

Music of Aaron Copland (New York, 1986). JoAnne Skowronski, *Aaron Copland: A Bio-Bibliography* (Westport, Conn., 1985).

Coprario [Coperario, Cooper, Cowper], **John** [Giovanni] (b. ca. 1575; d. London, ca. June 1626). Composer. Born John Cooper but had begun to use the Italianate surname by 1603. Supported until 1621 by various noble patrons, some of whom held high office. From 1622 or earlier, closely associated with Charles, Prince of Wales, who in 1625 became King Charles I. Almost all of his works are secular. Those for voice include songs (mostly lute songs), a few Italian madrigals, and about 20 3-part *villanelle.* Most important, however, are the instrumental works, among which are over 100 fantasias and fantasia-suites for viol ensembles or violin (solo or duet), often with organ; and pieces for 1–3 lyra viols. Before 1617 wrote *Rules how to Compose* (facs., Los Angeles, 1952), a practical manual with original musical examples.

Bibl.: Richard Charteris, "John Coprario (Cooper), c. 1575–1626: A Study and Complete Critical Edition of His Instrumental Music" (diss., Univ. of Canterbury, New Zealand, 1976). Id., *A Thematic Catalogue of the Music of John Coprario with a Biographical Introduction* (New York, 1977).

Corbetta, Francesco [Corbette, Francisque] (b. Pavia, ca. 1615; d. Paris, 1681). Guitarist and composer. Active as a guitar teacher in Italy by 1639. Spent most of his adult life as a teacher and performer at the royal courts in Paris (where he was brought by Mazarin and became the teacher of Louis XIV) and, after the Restoration, in London. A great virtuoso, he wrote exclusively for 5-course guitar. Compositions survive in 5 collections, 3 in Italian style (1639, 1643, 1648) and 2 in French style (written and published much later, in 1671 and 1674). Of the later books, one is dedicated to the English King Charles II and the other to Louis XIV.

Bibl.: R. T. Pinnell, "The Role of Francesco Corbetta (1615–1681) in the History of Music for the Baroque Guitar" (diss., UCLA, 1976) [with ed.].

Corder, Frederick (b. London, 26 Jan. 1852; d. there, 21 Aug. 1932). Composer and teacher. Studied at the Royal Academy of Music, 1873–75, with Hiller in Cologne, 1875–78, and in Milan, 1878–79; conductor at the Brighton Aquarium, 1880–82. With his wife translated all of Wagner's librettos (from *Lohengrin* onwards) into English. Composed, mostly to his own texts, operas (*Nordisa,* 1887), cantatas, melodramas, operettas, part songs, solo songs; also concert overtures, suites, other chamber and orchestral pieces. Corder's Wagnerian aspiration to establish a serious English opera was largely disappointed; he is perhaps more important historically as a teacher; professor of composition at the Royal Academy from 1888; pupils include Bax, Bantock, Holbrook; in 1905, founded Society of British Composers; published pedagogical books and studies of Beethoven, Liszt, Wagner.

Cordero, Roque (b. Panama, 16 Aug. 1917). Composer. He studied in Panama with Máximo Arrates Boza, Herbert de Castro, and Myron Schaeffer. In 1938 he was made conductor of the orchestra that later became the Symphony Orchestra of Panama. In 1943 he traveled to the U.S., where he studied with Krenek at Hamline Univ. in Minneapolis. After graduating he became professor at Panama's National Institute of Music (1950–66), of which he was also director (1953–64); from 1966 he taught at Indiana Univ.; from 1972 at Illinois State Univ. In 1957 his Second Symphony won first prize at the Inter-American Music Festival at Caracas. Works include ballets *(Setatule);* orchestral works (3 symphonies; *Capricho interiorano,* 1939; *8 miniatures,* 1948; *Rapsodia campesina,* 1953; a violin concerto, 1962; *Circunvoluciones y móviles,* 57 instruments, 1967; *5 mensajes breves,* 1959); vocal works (*Salmo 113,* 1944; *Cantata,* 1974); chamber music (2 string quartets; *Paz, Paix, Peace,* strings, 1967; *Variations and Theme for 5,* 1975); piano works (*Sonatina rítmica,* 1943; *9 Preludes,* 1947; *Sonata breve,* 1966).

Cordier, Baude (b. Rheims; fl. early 15th cent.). Composer. His identity is unclear. It has been hypothesized that he was the harpist and organist Baude Fresnel, who served at the court of Philip the Bold from 1384 and died in 1397 or 1398, and that, consequently, his works date from the late 14th century rather than the early 15th. One ballade, 9 rondeaux, and 1 Mass movement are extant. Some employ complex notation and rhythms. The Chantilly Manuscript (*F-CH* 564) includes a piece notated in the form of a heart and another in the form of a circle.

Bibl.: *Early Fifteenth-Century Music,* ed. Gilbert Reaney, *CMM* 11/1 (1955). Craig Wright, "Tapissier and Cordier: New Documents and Conjectures," *MQ* 59 (1973): 177.

Corea, Chick [Armando Anthony, Jr.] (b. Chelsea, Mass., 12 June 1941). Jazz pianist, composer, and bandleader. He played Latin dance music with the percussionists Mongo Santamaria and Willie Bobo (1962–63) and hard bop with the trumpeter Blue Mitchell (1964–66) before joining Stan Getz's group (1967, including the album *Sweet Rain* with his composition "Windows") and Miles Davis's jazz-rock band (1968–70). He led Circle, a free jazz group with Dave Holland and Anthony Braxton (1970–71). In 1971 he recorded 2 unaccompanied albums (both called *Piano Improvisations*), rejoined Getz, then formed Return to Forever: with Stanley Clarke as a constant sideman, it was a delicate Latin jazz group (–1973) that included Airto Moreira and recorded Corea's composition "Spain" on the album *Light as a Feather* (1972); an intense jazz-rock group (1973–76, and a reunion tour in 1983) including Al Di Meola (from 1974); and finally a 13-piece ensemble incorporating brass and a string quartet (–1979). He played in duos with Gary Burton (recording the album *Crystal Silence,* 1972) and Herbie Hancock (world tour, 1978). He led a quartet including Michael Brecker and Eddie Gomez, the group Trio Music with Roy Haynes and the double bass player

Miroslav Vitous (intermittently from 1981), and the Elektric Band, a trio (from 1985).

Corelli, Arcangelo (b. Fusignano, 17 Feb. 1653; d. Rome, 8 Jan. 1713). Composer and violinist. Corelli was the fifth child born to a prosperous family of landowners; his initial musical study was probably with the local clergy, then in nearby Lugo and Faenza, and finally in Bologna, where he went in 1666. His studies there were with Giovanni Benvenuti and Leonardo Brugnoli, the former representing the disciplined style of the Accademia filarmonica (to which Corelli was admitted in 1670), the latter a virtuoso violinist.

By 1675 (and perhaps as early as 1671) Corelli was in Rome; he may have studied composition under Matteo Simonelli, from whom he would have absorbed the styles of Roman polyphony inherited from Palestrina. A trip to France has been postulated during these years, as has a visit to Spain, but neither has been securely documented. In 1675 he is listed as one of the subordinate violinists ("Arcangelo bolognese") in Roman payment documents; by 1679 he had begun to lead Roman orchestras. In 1680 he may have visited Germany; the later dedications of his op. 5 (to Electress Sophie Charlotte of Brandenburg) and op. 6 (to the Elector Palatine Johann Wilhelm) support the idea of direct connections between the composer and German courts.

From 1681 until his death he was in Rome, making only a few trips (one to Naples in 1702 to play in Scarlatti's *Tiberio, imperator d'Oriente,* during which Burney claimed that Corelli was somewhat embarrassed by his own mistakes and surprised by the skill of Neapolitan violinists). His Roman patrons included the dedicatees of three volumes of trio sonatas: Queen Christina of Sweden, Cardinal Benedetto Pamphili, and Cardinal Pietro Ottoboni (op. 3 was dedicated to Francesco II, Duke of Modena). He was active as a performer and leader of small and large instrumental ensembles in Roman homes and churches and at public celebrations. He is known to have directed relatively large orchestras: at an Academy of Music organized by Queen Christina in 1687 he led 150 string players. He composed sinfonias and concertos for these occasions, often as introductions to large concerted works by others; Georg Muffat reported hearing and playing such instrumental music on a visit to Rome in 1682. Two years later Corelli and Alessandro Scarlatti became members of the Congregazione dei Virtuosi di S. Cecilia; Corelli was head of the instrumental section in 1700. In 1706, along with Pasquini and Scarlatti, he was inducted into the Arcadian Academy (taking the name Arcomelo Erimanteo); during that same period he met Handel in engagements at the Pamphili and Ruspoli palaces (he directed the orchestra for performances of *La resurrezione* in 1708). After 1708 he retired from public view.

Compared to other violinist-composers (Marini, Stradella), Corelli eschewed virtuosity. He was firmly in control of the language of tonality, but not all movements are tonally closed. A traditional distinction between sacred and secular pieces is maintained in each collection in terms of the character of most movements and the scoring (in trios for the church, 2 violins, violone or archlute, and organ continuo; for the chamber, 2 violins and violone or harpsichord); but dance movements may appear in church sonatas and fugal movements in chamber works. In fact, there was little precedent in Italian prints for such chamber sonatas as those of Corelli; the precedents are from Germany and England. He published only five volumes during his lifetime.

Arcangelo Corelli.

In the late 17th and 18th centuries Corelli's reputation as a performer and teacher was at least equal to the reputation he achieved as a composer. Italian and foreign students contributed to the dissemination of his works and his style of playing (Gasparini, Geminiani, Somis, Anet, Störl). His sonatas were widely performed and often reprinted, both as ideal practice material for students and as models for composers. For the solo sonatas (op. 5) there are several extant sets of ornaments, some attributed to the composer himself (Walsh, 1710); his works remained especially popular in England, where Ravenscroft imitated the trio sonatas and Geminiani transformed several solo and trio sonatas into concertos.

Works: *Sonate a tre* op. 1 (Rome, 1681); *Sonate da camera a tre* op. 2 (Rome, 1685); *Sonate a tre* op. 3 (Rome, 1689); *Sonate a tre* op. 4 (Rome, 1694); *Sonate a violino e violone o cimbalo* op. 5 (Rome, 1700); Concerti grossi op. 6 (Amsterdam, 1714). Other securely attributed works include a sinfonia for G. L. Lulier's oratorio *S. Beatrice d'Este* (1689); 2 sonatas (G minor, E minor) for 2 violins, violetta, and bass (Amsterdam, 1699); 1 sonata for trumpet, 2 violins, and bass. Some attributions are doubtful.

Bibl.: *Arcangelo Corelli: Historisch-Kritische Gesamtausgabe der musikalischen Werke,* ed. Hans Joachim Marx, 6 vols., 1976– [contains works list]. Hans Joachim Marx, *Arcangelo Corelli: die Überlieferung der Werke,* catalogue raisonné (Cologne, 1980). Marc Pincherle, *Corelli et son temps* (Paris, 1954). M. Rinaldi, *Arcangelo Corelli* (Milan, 1953). Articles in *Studi Corelliani,* ed. A. Cavicchi, Oscar Mischiati, and Pierluigi Petrobelli (Florence, 1972). *Nuovi Studi Corelliani,* ed. G. Giachin (Florence, 1978). *Nuovissimi Studi Corelliani,* ed. Sergio Durante and Pierluigi Petrobelli (Florence 1982). Giovanni Morelli, ed., *L'invenzione del gusto. Corelli e Vivaldi: mutazioni culturali a Roma e Venezia nel periodo post-barocco* (Milan, 1982). Klaus-Jürgen Sachs, "Aspekte der numerischen und tonartlichen Disposition instrumentalmusikalischer Zyklen des ausgehenden 17. und beginnenden 18. Jahrhunderts," *AfMw* 41 (1984): 237–43. John Daverio, "In Search of the Sonata da camera before Corelli," *AM* 57 (1985): 198–214.

Corelli, Franco (Dario) (b. Ancona, 8 Apr. 1921). Dramatic tenor. After courses in naval engineering at the Univ. of Bologna, entered Pesaro Conservatory, 1947; dissatisfied, he developed his vocal technique independently by mimicking recordings. Operatic debut as Don José *(Carmen)* at Spoleto, 1952. La Scala debut, 1954, opening the season with Callas in Spontini's *La vestale.* Debut at Covent Garden, 1957, as Cavaradossi *(Tosca);* at New York Met, 1962, as Manrico *(Il trovatore);* at the Paris Opéra and Vienna Staatsoper, 1970.

Corigliano, John (Paul) (b. New York, 16 Feb. 1938). Composer. The son of a violinist, he studied with Luening at Columbia (B.A., 1959) and with Giannini and Creston. Worked as a music programmer for New York radio stations and as a producer at CBS Television (1959–72). Taught at the Manhattan School (from 1971) and at Lehman College of the City Univ. of New York (from 1974). His early violin sonata (1963) won an award in Spoleto. Compositions are in a relatively conservative, largely tonal, and accessible style, only occasionally employing serial procedures and atonality. His clarinet concerto (1977) was commissioned by the New York Philharmonic; *A Figaro for Antonio* (1984–85) by the Metropolitan Opera. Composer in residence with the Chicago Symphony, 1987–90. Other works include the operas *The Naked Carmen,* mixed media, after Bizet (1970), and *The Ghosts of Versailles* (1991); *Pied Piper Fantasy* (1981) for flute and orchestra, Symphony no. 1 (1989), *To Music* (1995), and other concertos, overtures, and shorter works for orchestra; Scherzo (1975) for oboe and percussion, *Phantasmagoria* (1993) \for cello and piano, *How Like Pellucid Statues, Daddy* (1994) for brass quartet, and other chamber and piano works; choral music, often with orchestra; *The Cloisters* (45 songs for mezzo-soprano and orchestra, 1965) and other works for voice and ensemble; film scores (*Altered States,* 1980).

Cornago, Johannes (fl. ca. 1455–85). Composer. Active chiefly at the Aragonese court of the Kingdom of Naples under Alfonso V of Aragon and Ferdinand I of Naples, but also in Spain in the chapel of Ferdinand V in 1475. His compositions include 4 sacred and 11 (or 12) secular works. Two of the sacred compositions are Masses, one using a Sicilian popular song, "Ayo visto de la mappa mundi," as a cantus firmus. Two secular pieces have Italian texts, the rest Spanish.

Bibl.: Isabel Pope, "The Secular Compositions of Johannes Cornago," *Anglés,* 1958–61, 2:689.

Cornazano [Cornazzano], **Antonio** (b. Piacenza, ca. 1430; d. Ferrara, Dec. 1484). Dance theorist. Studied with Domenico da Piacenza, author of the first dance treatise of the Renaissance. From 1454 until 1466, in the service of Francesco Sforza and taught his children. Spent the next years in military and political pursuits in Venice and Piacenza. From 1479, served Ercole I d'Este in Ferrara. His *Libro dell'arte del danzare* of 1455, most of which is lost, is the second important dance manual of the era. A version written about 1465 survives. The work is clearly based on that of Domenico da Piacenza and gives the same complete dances and dance music (8 *balli* and 3 *bassadanzas*).

Cornelius, (Carl August) Peter (b. Mainz, 24 Dec. 1824; d. there, 26 Oct. 1874). Composer and writer. The son of actors; became an actor and theater orchestra violinist, beginning also to compose, mainly choral pieces and songs; 1844–52, lived in Berlin, moving much in literary circles and beginning to write himself; music lessons from Siegfried Dehn (1844–46); 1852, moved to Weimar and became part of Liszt's circle, serving him as secretary and translator, and through critical articles supportive of the New German School. In 1852–55 he composed 5 Masses, in 1853–62 most of his lieder, many to his own poems, and in 1855–58 his best-known large work, the comic opera *Der Barbier von Baghdad,* to his own libretto. The difficulties accompanying its production under Liszt in Weimar and hostile demonstrations at its premiere (15 Dec. 1858) were factors in Liszt's leaving Weimar in 1861. Cornelius lived in Vienna, 1859–65, as a private music teacher, then in 1865 moved to Munich as part of the Wagnerian circle gathered by Ludwig II. From 1867 he taught music theory and rhetoric at the new conservatory and was one of Wagner's closest associates, although his own music remained relatively free of Wagnerian influences. His second opera, *Der Cid,* to his own libretto, was successfully produced at Weimar in 1865; composed relatively little after 1862, primarily part songs and his third opera, *Gunlöd,* on a subject from the *Edda,* begun in 1866 and left unfinished.

Bibl.: *Literarische Werke* (Leipzig, 1904–5). Max Hasse, ed., *Musikalische Werke* (Leipzig, 1905–6; R: 1971). P. Egert, ed., *Ausgewählte Schriften und Briefe* (Berlin, 1938). H. Federhofer and K. Oehl, eds., *Peter Cornelius als Komponist, Dichter, Kritiker und Essayist* (Regensburg, 1977). Günter

Wagner, *Peter Cornelius: Verzeichnis seiner musikalischen und literarischen Werke* (Tutzing, 1986).

Cornysh, William (d. 1523). Composer, actor, and writer. Active at the English court before late 1493. From 1509 until his death, Master of the Children of the Chapel Royal. Acted in, devised, or wrote many plays and entertainments presented at court. Also supervised the Chapel Royal on 2 trips to France, in 1513 and 1520. Wrote numerous sacred works, of which 6 survive, 1 only as a fragment; copies of all 6 are in the Eton Choirbook (ed. in *MB* 11–12). Also wrote many secular polyphonic pieces, of which 18 survive: 16 part songs and 2 instrumental pieces (some ed. in *MB* 18).

Correa de Arauxo [Correa de Araujo], **Francisco** (b. ca. 1576; d. Segovia, ca. 31 Oct. 1654). Organist and composer. Organist at the Church of S. Salvador in Seville from 1599 until 1636, then at Jaén Cathedral until 1640, finally at Segovia Cathedral until his death. His *Libro de tientos y discursos de música practica, y theorica de organo, intitulado Facultad organica* (Alcalá, 1626; ed. in *MME* 6, 12) contains 62 *tientos* and 7 other pieces, all for organ, introduced by a theoretical treatise and arranged in order of increasing difficulty.

Corrette, Michel (b. Rouen, 1709; d. Paris, 22 Jan. 1795). Composer and author of method books. Worked intermittently as an organist between 1737 and about 1780 and as a teacher. Traveled to England sometime before 1773. A large proportion of his numerous works are arrangements, ranging from simple harmonizations to complete recastings of preexisting material (often popular tunes); they include songs, works for stage, concertos, instrumental chamber works, harpsichord pieces, and sacred vocal works. The nearly 20 methods (for instruments including the violin, cello, bass, flute, recorder, bassoon, harpsichord, harp, and mandolin; a number published in facs. in the 1970s) provide invaluable information on performance practice of the 18th century; among the topics treated are contemporary English music, the differences between French and Italian styles, and the art of accompanying song at the harpsichord. All include numerous musical exercises or complete compositions, of which many are by composers other than Corrette.

Corsi, Jacopo (b. Florence, 17 July 1561; d. there, 29 Dec. 1602). Patron and composer. Sponsored and participated in practical discussions and experiments that led to the beginnings of opera. Giovanni de' Bardi, whose Camerata was more concerned with theoretical and philosophical matters, had moved to Rome in 1592, leaving Corsi the most prominent patron of music in Florence after the Medicis. With Jacopo Peri he composed the musical setting of Ottavio Rinuccini's *Dafne,* first performed in 1598 (only a few excerpts survive, 2 definitely by Corsi). In 1600 he sponsored and played harpsichord in the first performance of Peri's *Euridice.*

Bibl.: William V. Porter, "Peri and Corsi's *Dafne:* Some New Discoveries and Observations," *JAMS* 18 (1965): 170.

Corteccia, (Pier) Francesco (b. Florence, 27 July 1502; d. there, 7 July 1571). Composer. Became a choirboy at S. Giovanni Battista in Florence in 1515; associated with this church until 1522, again from 1527 (as chaplain), from 1535 until 1539 (as organist), and from 1540 until his death (as *maestro di cappella*). Organist at the chapel of the Medici family for a year, beginning in 1531. From 1540 *maestro di cappella* at the court of the Duke of Florence and at Florence Cathedral; these posts were in addition to that held at S. Giovanni. His secular works, some written for festive court occasions, include over 100 madrigals, published in 3 complete books and in many anthologies, and several *intermedi* for voices and specified instruments. The sacred works include 2 early Passions, a cycle of hymns for the church year, 2 books of music for Tenebrae services, and 36 motets for 5 and 6 voices published posthumously in 2 volumes.

Cortés, Ramiro (Jr.) (b. Dallas, 25 Nov. 1938; d. Salt Lake City, 2 July 1984). Composer. He studied with Cowell (1952), at Yale with Donovan (1953–54), and at the Univ. of Southern California with Dahl and Stevens (1954–56). Studied with Petrassi in Rome (1956–58); later with Sessions (1958) and Giannini (1961–62). He worked as a computer programmer, 1963–66, then began teaching: at UCLA (from 1966), at the Univ. of Southern California (1967–72), and at the Univ. of Utah (from 1973). His early music was largely serial; later it became more flexibly chromatic. Works include operas (*Prometheus,* 1960; *The Eternal Return,* 1981); musicals (*The Patriots,* 1975–76; rev. 1978); film and incidental music; orchestral works (*Sinfonia sacra,* 1954; *Xochitl,* 1955; *Meditation,* string orchestra, 1961; *Movements in Variation,* 1972; *Contrasts,* symphonic band, 1979–80); choral and vocal works (*Missa brevis,* female voices, 1954; *De profundis,* song cycle, 1977; *To the Sacred Moon,* soprano, piano, 1980); chamber works (*Homage to Jackson Pollock,* viola, 1968; *Charenton Variations,* 1978).

Cortot, Alfred (Denis) (b. Nyon, Switzerland, 26 Sept. 1877; d. Lausanne, 15 June 1962). Pianist, conductor, and educator. Studied piano with Emil Descombes and Louis Diémer at the Paris Conservatory, winning first prize, 1896. Debut at Concerts Colonne, 1896. Assistant to Mottl and Richter at Bayreuth, 1898–1901. Formed Société des festivals lyriques in 1902 to conduct Wagner's *Tristan* and *Götterdämmerung* (French premiere). Formed Société des concerts Cortot, 1903, to conduct *Parsifal* (French premiere) and recent French music. Led Concerts populaires in Lille, 1904–7. Formed trio with Casals and Thibaud, 1905. Taught piano at the Paris Conservatory, 1907–17. With Adolphe Mangeot founded École normale de musique, 1918; director, 1918–62. His work under the Nazi occupation during World War

II was followed by a restricted role in French musical culture during the last 15 years of his life. Wrote commentaries on music by Chopin, Schumann, Liszt; *Principes rationnels de la technique pianistique* (1928); *La musique française de piano,* 3 vols. (1930–44). Made many recordings, still valued for their interpretations of Chopin especially. Amassed an important collection of manuscripts.

Bibl.: F. F. Clough and G. J. Cuming: "Cortot Discography," *Gramophone Record Review,* new ser., no. 50 (1957): 135. Frank Traficante, "Dispersal of the Cortot Collection: 290 Treatises in Lexington," *Notes* 26 (1969/70).

Coryell, Larry (b. Galveston, Tex., 2 Apr. 1943). Jazz guitarist and bandleader. As an electric guitarist he worked with Chico Hamilton (1966) and then played jazz-rock with the Free Spirits (1966), Gary Burton (1967–68), and his own groups (1969–75); his album *Spaces* (1970) included duets with John McLaughlin. Using the acoustic guitar, he toured in a duo with Philip Catherine (recording the album *Twin House,* 1976) and a trio with McLaughlin and Paco De Lucia. He mainly played the electric instrument in the 1980s.

Costa, Michael (Andrew Agnus) [Michele Andrea Agniello] (b. Naples, 4 Feb. 1808; d. Hove, England, 29 Apr. 1884). Conductor and composer. Son of a musician; studied at the Naples Conservatory under Furno, Tritto (his grandfather), Zingarelli, and Crescentini; had 4 operas performed in Naples, 1826–29; in 1829 settled in London; *maestro al piano* at King's Theatre, 1830; music director there, 1832; conductor, 1833–46, apparently the first to unite that orchestra's direction under a single conductor using a baton, thereby greatly improving the quality of the playing; 1846–54, conductor of the Philharmonic Society; 1847–68, conductor of the Italian Opera, Covent Garden; 1871–81, music director, Her Majesty's Theatre; also conducted choral societies and festivals in London and the provinces (Handel Festival, 1857–80; Sacred Harmonic Society, 1848–82; Birmingham Festival, 1849–82).

Costa's preeminence in London as a conductor made him a leading figure in English musical life, for which he was knighted in 1869. He was less highly regarded as a composer; best known for the oratorios *Eli* (Birmingham, 1855) and *Naaman* (Birmingham, 1864), both widely performed; also sacred music; 6 operas; 4 ballets; 3 symphonies; solo vocal music.

Costeley, Guillaume (b. Fontanges, Auvergne, 1530 or 1531; d. Evreux, 28 Jan. 1606). Composer. His first published works are 2 chansons printed in Paris in 1554. By 1560, had been appointed composer and organist to the court of Charles IX. Closely associated with Baïf and his Académie de poésie et de musique. Settled in Evreux in 1570; retained his position at court, where he spent several months each year, and continued active in musical life, but seems to have stopped composing at this time. Retired from court between 1577 and 1588. Wrote over 100 chansons, 3 motets, and a very brief (perhaps only a fragment) organ fantasy. The chansons, of which he was a leading exponent, include 1 microtonal piece and a number of *airs.* The microtonal chanson reflects the theories of Nicola Vicentino; 2 of the *airs* have something of the metrical freedom of *musique mesurée.* All of the vocal works except 3 early chansons were published by Le Roy and Ballard in a collection called *Musique de Guillaume Costeley* (Paris, 1570; ed. in *MMRF* 3, 18, 19, Paris, 1896–1904; R: New York, 1952).

Bibl.: Kenneth J. Levy, "Costeley's Chromatic Chanson," *AnnM* 3 (1955): 213–63. Carl Dahlhaus, "Zu Costeleys chromatischer Chanson," *Mf* 16 (1963): 253. Irving Godt, "Guillaume Costeley: Life and Works" (diss., New York Univ., 1969).

Costello, Elvis [McManus, Declan Patrick] (b. London, 25 Aug. 1954). Rock singer, songwriter, and guitarist. His first record (*My Aim Is True,* incl. "Alison," 1977) was produced by songwriter Nick Lowe, with whom he remained associated; since 1978 he has released a large number of albums (*Imperial Bedroom,* 1982; *King of America,* 1986; *Spike,* 1989) and toured extensively with his band, The Attractions. Though initially associated with the British New Wave, his music has assimilated many styles, including country, soul, and early rock and roll.

Cosyn, Benjamin (b. ca. 1570; d. London?, after 1652). Composer and organist. Worked as an organist from 1622 until 1643, first for two years at Dulwich College, then at Charterhouse until the post was abolished there. Evidently a virtuoso performer, wrote mostly highly ornamented and difficult keyboard music. Was greatly influenced by John Bull. Copied large numbers of pieces (some his own, some by other composers) into virginal manuscripts, one perhaps begun by Bull and the other (the "Cosyn" Virginal Book) of his own compilation. His extant works not for harpsichord include 2 sacred vocal pieces and 8 organ voluntaries.

Cotton [Cotto, Cottonius], **John** [Johannes]. A name long believed, on the authority of Martin Gerbert, to be that of the author of a treatise written around 1100 and now widely thought to be by Johannes Afflighemensis. All extant manuscript sources give the name "Johannes." The author may, however, be the English monk John Cotton of the abbey of Bec in Normandy.

Coulthard, Jean (b. Vancouver, 10 Feb. 1908). Composer. She studied at the Toronto Conservatory, then at the Royal College of Music in London (1928–30) with Vaughan Williams. In Vancouver she taught at St. Anthony's College, the Queen's Hall School, and the Univ. of British Columbia (1947–73). She pursued composition study with Benjamin (1939), Wagenaar (1945, 1949), and Gordon Jacob (1965–66). In the 1940s she received criticism of her work from Copland, Schoenberg, Bartók, and Milhaud; influenced by Nadia Boulanger during a year spent in Paris (1955). Her compositional style is tonal, lyrical, and contrapuntal; there are some tape pieces and aleatory works. Her early orchestral music established her reputation in Canada, and she received many commissions beginning in the 1960s. Works include 2 ballets; *Song to the Sea* (orchestral overture, 1942); *Music for Saint Cecilia* (organ, tape, strings, 1969); chamber music (*The Birds of Lansdowne,* piano trio and tape, 1972); *The Pines of Emily Carr* (soprano, narrator, and string quartet, 1969); piano music; choral music and songs.

Couperin, Armand-Louis (b. Paris, 25 Feb. 1727; d. there, 2 Feb. 1789). Organist, harpsichordist, and composer. At the age of 21, inherited the position of organist at St. Gervais upon the death of his father, Nicolas Couperin (cousin of François Couperin "le grand"). Eventually held a number of additional posts: at Notre Dame, the Sainte Chapelle, at least three other churches, and the French royal chapel. His wife, three of his children, and some of his students helped him to fulfill the requirements of these jobs. During his life he was regarded as an uncommonly fine organist; his improvisations were especially prized. His relatively few compositions include both secular and sacred pieces for keyboard alone (most for harpsichord, some for two harpsichords, and some for organ); for harpsichord or organ with other instruments, including several sonatas and trio sonatas; and for chorus or chorus and orchestra.

Bibl.: *Selected Works for Keyboard,* ed. David Fuller, *RRMCE* 1–2 (Madison, Wis., 1975).

Couperin, François ["le grand"] (b. Paris, 10 Nov. 1668; d. there, 11 Sept. 1733). Composer, organist, and harpsichordist. His grandfather Charles Couperin (ca. 1595–1654) settled in Chaumes, where he was proprietor of a plot of land and for this privilege held the title Sieur de Crouilly. In 1622 Charles married Marie Andry of Brie. Four of their eight children became prominent musicians: Louis (ca. 1626–61); François (ca. 1631–after 1708; father of musicians Marguerite-Louise and Nicolas); Elisabeth (1636–1705; mother of composer Marc Roger Normand); and Charles (1638–79). In 1662 the last-mentioned—who the year before had succeeded his brother Louis as organist at St. Gervais—married Marie Guérin (d. ca. 1690). Six years later their only child, François, was born, the boy who was to become one of the greatest French composers of the era.

Few details of François's early life are known; it is likely that his early musical instruction came from his father and perhaps also from Louis. When Charles died, the ten-year-old François studied further with the royal organist Jacques Thomelin, and possibly with Charles's successor at St. Gervais, Lalande. In 1685 François assumed Lalande's post at St. Gervais, though he did not receive a full contract of duty until 1689. Also in 1689 he married Marie-Anne Ansault, who bore him two daughters, Marie-Madeleine (b. 1690)

François Couperin.

and Marguerite-Antoinette (b. 1705), and two sons, Nicolas-Louis (b. 1707) and François-Laurent (b. before 1708).

In 1690 François acquired his first royal privilege to print music, which he had planned to use for his first datable composition, the *Pièces d'orgue;* only the engraved title page (attached to a manuscript copy) survives. In 1693 the composer was named one of the four *organistes du roi* for the royal chapel, replacing the recently deceased Thomelin. His salary, at 600 livres, represented an important social and economic advance for Couperin; soon he was also tutoring the royal family in harpsichord, including the Dauphin, the Duke of Burgundy, and others. He was also chamber musician for the court, perhaps filling in for the ailing d'Alembert; it was in this context that works such as the Concerts royaux were first conceived. Already in 1690 the composer was using the noble title Couperin de Crouilly; an offer of purchase of nobility by Louis XIV (in 1696) enabled Couperin to make the title official. During the next two decades Couperin established himself as one of the leading harpsichordists of his day; he also composed church and chamber music during the king's final years. Although official appointments were slow in coming to Couperin (possibly because he did not pursue them with much vigor), in 1717 he was finally appointed to d'Alembert's post as *maître de clavecin du roi.* By that time there was a new king, however—officially, the five-year-old Louis XV. Louis XIV had died in 1715, and Couperin had begun to withdraw from court duties, continuing to edit his music for publication (including *Les goûts-réünis,* the *Nouveaux concerts,* the *Apothéose . . . de l'incomparable monsieur de Lully, Les nations*). Increasing ailments hindered his activities during the 1720s, and in 1730 he passed on his position as royal harpsichordist to his daughter Marguerite-Antoinette. In 1733 he obtained another ten-year printing privilege, but he died before he was able to use it, and none of his family took the initiative to see through to the press his remaining manuscripts. Almost none of the unpublished music survives.

Works: *Vocal music.* Some 40 sacred motets (*Accedo ad te, Festiva laetis* for Ste. Anne, *Laudate pueri Dominum, O Domine quia refugiam, O Jesu amantissime, Quid retribuam tibi Domine, Resonent organa* for St. Cecilia, *Veni sponsa Christi* for St. Suzanne, *Victoria: Christo resurgenti*); secular vocal works, mostly *airs sérieux* (*Qu'on ne me dise,* 1697; *Il faut aimer,* 1711; *Trois vestales champetres et trois Poliçons*); sacred cantatas (lost).

Instrumental music. Concerts royaux nos. 1–4, harpsichord and flute, violin, oboe, viol, or bassoon, in *Troisième livre de pièces de clavecin* (Paris, 1722); *Nouveaux concerts* nos. 5–14, instruments not specified, in *Les goûts-réünis ou Nouveaux concerts* (Paris, 1724); *Le Parnasse, ou l'Apothéose de Corelli,* grande sonade en trio, in *Les goûts-réünis; Concert instrumental sous le titre d'Apothéose composé à la mémoire immortelle de l'incomparable monsieur de Lully* (Paris, 1725); *Les nations: Sonades et suites de simphonies en trio* ("La françoise," "L'espagnole," "L'impériale," "La piemontoise"; Paris, 1926); *Pièces de violes avec la basse chifrée* (Paris, 1928); *La Steinquerque; La superbe; La sultane.*

Harpsichord works. Pièces de clavecin . . . premier livre (Paris, 1713; 1e ordre–5e ordre); *L'art de toucher le clavecin* (allemande and 8 preludes, Paris, 1716; rev. 2nd ed., 1717); *Second livre de pièces de clavecin* (Paris, 1716–17; 6e ordre–12e ordre); *Troisième livre de pièces de clavecin* (Paris, 1722; 13e ordre–19e ordre); *Quatrième livre de pièces de clavecin* (Paris, 1730; 20e–27e ordre).

His theoretical writings include *L'art de toucher le clavecin* (Paris, 1716; rev. 2nd ed., 1717) and *Regle pour l'accompagnement* (both ed. in Cauchie et al., *Oeuvres complètes,* 1).

Bibl.: *Oeuvres complètes de François Couperin,* ed. Maurice Cauchie et al. (Paris, 1932–33). *F. Couperin: Pièces de clavecin,* ed. Kenneth Gilbert, in *Le pupitre,* vols. 21–24 (Paris, 1969–72). *François Couperin: Neuf motets,* ed. Philippe Oboussier, in *Le pupitre,* vol. 45 (Paris, 1972). Charles Bouvet, *Les Couperins: Une dynastie de musiciens français* Paris, 1919; R: as *Une dynastie de musiciens français: Les Couperins, organistes de l'eglise Saint-Gervais,* New York, 1977). André Tessier, *Couperin . . . biographie critique* (Paris, 1926). J. Tiersot, *Les Couperins* (Paris, 1926; R: Paris, 1976). Charles Bouvet, *Nouveaux documents sur les Couperins* (Paris, 1933). Maurice Cauchie, *Thematic Index of the Works of François Couperin* (Monaco, 1949; R: New York, 1976). Wilfred Mellers, *François Couperin and the French Classical Tradition* (London, 1950; R: New York, 1968; rev. 2nd ed., 1987). Pierre Citron, *Couperin* (Bourges, 1956). Shlomo Hofman, *L'oeuvre de clavecin de François Couperin le grand* (Paris, 1961) [with thematic catalog]. *Mélanges François Couperin, publiés à l'occasion du tricentenaire de sa naissance, 1668–1968* (Paris, 1968). Philippe Oboussier, "Couperin Motets at Tenbury," *PRMA* 98 (1971–72): 17–30. James R. Anthony, *French Baroque Music from Beaujoyeulx to Rameau,* 2nd rev. ed. (New York, 1978). Marcel Thomas, *Les premiers Couperin dans la Brie* (Paris, 1978). David Tunley, *Couperin* (London, 1982). Philippe Beaussant, *François Couperin,* trans. Alexandra Land (Portland, 1990).

Couperin, Louis (b. Chaumes, ca. 1626; d. Paris, 29 Aug. 1661). Composer, harpsichordist, and organist. Son of Charles Couperin (ca. 1595–1654) and thus an uncle of the only more distinguished member of the Couperin family, François "le grand." Came to Paris from Chaumes under the sponsorship of Chambonnières by the year 1651. Spent the rest of his short life there, except for visits to Meudon (near Paris) in 1656 and Toulouse in 1659. In 1653 Louis acquired the post of organist at St. Gervais in Paris; this position was held by members of the Couperin family until 1826. He played treble viol and, according to one 18th-century scholar, organ in the French royal chapel, played in the productions of several ballets, and was in contact with many notables of his time, including Froberger.

His known works number slightly over 200. All instrumental, they include about 130 for harpsichord, about 75 for organ, and fewer than 10 for small ensembles. About two thirds of the pieces for harpsichord are dance movements. About 30 other works for harpsichord are conceived on a larger scale: the preludes and the chaconnes and *passacailles.* Of the preludes, about three quarters are unmeasured throughout; several more include a mixture of measured and unmeasured sections.

The organ music is for the most part still unpublished; until about 1955 it was virtually unknown to modern scholars. Couperin was the first composer to conceive some pieces for particular organ registrations or colors. He wrote over 30 fugues or *fantaisies,* nearly as many plainsong versets, a few division basses (imitating the style of bass viol solos), and several more compositions of diverse types.

The pieces for instrumental ensemble include 2 works for 5-part shawm choir, 2 for 5-part string choir, and several for smaller groups (viol duets, or 1 or 2 unspecified instruments plus continuo).

Bibl.: *Oeuvres complètes,* ed. Paul Brunold (Paris, 1936) [not any longer a complete edition]. Bruce Gustafson, "A Performer's Guide to the Music of Louis Couperin," *Diapason* 66/7 (1975): 7.

Courtois, Jean (fl. 1530–45). Composer. *Maître de chapelle* at the cathedral of Cambrai in 1540. Wrote about 15 motets, about 20 chansons, and 2 Masses. The chansons for 4 voices are in the "Parisian" styles of the day; those for 5 and 6 voices are in the more contrapuntal Netherlandish style.

Coussemaker, Charles-Edmond-Henri de (b. Bailleul, Nord, 19 Apr. 1805; d. Bourbourg, near Lille, 10 Jan. 1876). Scholar. Studied law in Paris, 1825–30, also taking music lessons; became lawyer and justice of the peace in Douai and other cities, then from 1845 a judge in Hazebrouck, Dunkirk, and finally Lille; did research in archaeology, history, and almost every aspect of medieval music, publishing studies and editions concerned with chant, liturgical drama, music theory, notation, early polyphony, and folk song. Most of his scholarship is now outmoded, but he is remembered as the discoverer of or first to describe many important manuscript sources and as the first editor of an important body of early music theory (*Scriptorum de musica medii aevi,* Paris, 1864–76; R: 1931, 1968).

Coward, Henry (b. Liverpool, 26 Nov. 1849; d. Sheffield, 10 June 1944). Choral conductor. A worker in the Sheffield cutlery industry from age 9 to 23; then a schoolteacher. In 1876 he founded the Sheffield Tonic Sol-fa Association, which became the Sheffield Musical Union and through his gifts as a trainer of choruses one of the finest choral societies; its reputation spread through the Sheffield Music Festival (founded 1895) and tours. Bachelor of Music, Oxford, 1889; Doctor, 1893; knighted, 1926. Published *Choral Technique and Interpretation* (London, 1914) and *Reminiscences* (London, 1919).

Bibl.: J. A. Rodgers, *Dr. Henry Coward: The Pioneer Chorusmaster* (London, 1911).

Coward, Noël (Pierce) (b. Teddington, Middlesex, 16 Dec. 1899; d. Blue Harbour, Jamaica, 26 Mar. 1973). Songwriter, playwright, and actor. Born into a musical family, he was self-taught in music. He first appeared as an actor at age 11, and his first play was produced in 1920. His light, sophisticated songs had to be dictated to an assistant who notated them. His best-known successes were the comedies *Private Lives* (1930) and *Blithe Spirit* (1942). He also composed operettas and musicals (*Bitter Sweet,* 1929; *Pacific 1860,* 1946; *Ace of Clubs,* 1950; *After the Ball,* 1954) and ballets (*London Morning,* 1959; *The Grand Tour,* 1971). He was also a poet and novelist; he published 2 autobiographical volumes, *Present Indicative* (1937) and *Future Indefinite* (1954), and *The Noël Coward Song Book* (London, 1953), which contains 51 songs. Knighted in 1970.

Cowell, Henry (Dixon) (b. Menlo Park, Calif., 11 Mar. 1897; d. Shady Hill, N.Y., 10 Dec. 1965). Composer, pianist, and writer on music. Cowell was raised in relative poverty after the divorce of his parents in 1903 and educated at home by his mother (d. 1916); his musical talent was recognized in early violin studies (he performed publicly at age 7), which ceased when he was 8 because of a nervous disorder. His contribution to contemporary American music was at least twofold: as a composer who never lost an early curiosity for new approaches and sounds and as an advocate for new music who was an active lecturer, performer, and writer throughout his career.

Cowell first acquired a piano in 1912 and played publicly some of his many compositions in San Francisco (5 Mar. 1914). He studied from 1914 with Samuel Seward (English composition) and Charles Seeger, who encouraged him to write a systematic treatise on his experimental approaches (*New Musical Resources,* 1916–19, publ. 1930); the two quartets written during this period exploit his procedures for relating rhythm and pitch to the overtone series and employ a complex rhythmic language (*Romantic* and *Euphometric,* 1914–15; premiered 1977 and 1964, respectively). In 1916 he studied for one term at the Institute of Musical Art (Damrosch); in 1917 was an assistant at Berkeley; served in the army (1918–19). A concert of his music presented in New York (29 Nov. 1919) launched an international career; he made several European tours as composer-pianist (1923–33) during which he earned the respect of the foremost composers and performers; his formal New York debut was in 1924; in 1929 he was the first American composer invited to the USSR. The piano works he presented in these concerts and lectures employed tone clusters ("The Tides of Manaunaun," 1917?) and new means of sound production on the piano: in "Aeolian Harp" (1923) the performer silently depresses keys with one hand while playing directly on the strings with the other; "Sinister Resonance" (1930) requires playing on the keys with simultaneous stopping and muting of the strings; in the Piano Concerto (1928) objects are placed in the instrument, a technique developed especially by Cage (prepared piano).

Cowell continued to experiment in the 1930s. He collaborated with Lev Termen in 1931 to construct the Rhythmicon, an instrument that could automatically produce complicated rhythmic events in relation to the overtone series (Cowell's *Rhythmicana,* intended for a 1931 Paris performance, was played only in 1971 at Stanford); he employed "elastic form" in dance-related and teaching pieces, in which the performer could assemble composed segments at will (*Mosaic Quartet,* 1935). As a child living near San Francisco's Chinatown he had heard oriental melodies; awarded a Guggenheim Fellowship (1931), he pursued an interest in non-Western music by studying in Berlin with Hornbostel. While continuing to employ approaches that incorporated any and all of his new musical experiences, he also wrote in a more conservative idiom in pieces for students and amateurs. Between 1935 and 1950 he made extensive use of traditional and folk models and in general produced music that was more tonal and rhythmically regular. American music and other traditional elements are evident in works such as the *Hymn and Fuguing Tune* series for various ensembles (1943–64) inspired by his acquaintance with William Walker's *Southern Harmony* and in works drawing on Irish music (*Celtic Set,* 1938; *Gaelic Symphony,* 1942). In 1956–57 a Rockefeller Grant and support from the U.S. State Department enabled him to travel and study a wider range of the world's musics; these new experiences are reflected in several works of the 1950s and later (*Homage to Iran,* violin and piano, 1957; 2 concertos for koto and orchestra, 1961–62 and 1965).

Throughout his career Cowell advocated new American music. In 1927 he founded the *New Musical Quarterly,* a journal that published works of American composers and some Europeans (Ives, Ruggles, Thomson, Varèse, Schoenberg, Webern); in the 1930s he was a cofounder (with Varèse, Salzedo, and Chávez) of the Pan-American Association of Composers. He edited a collection of essays on American composers (*American Composers on American Music,* 1933) for which he wrote several of the articles himself; among his essays were reviews of contemporary music for *The Musical Quarterly* (1947–58); with his wife, Sidney Robertson, whom he married in 1941, he wrote *Charles Ives and His Music* (1955). From 1941 to 1963 he taught courses on non-Western music at the New School for Social Research; he also taught at Peabody (1951–56) and Columbia (1949–65) and lectured in the U.S., Europe, and Asia. Among his well-known pupils were Cage and Harrison. His unfettered curiosity has been attributed in part to his lack of formal education and his unfamiliarity with a large part of the traditional European repertory. Cage called his attitude the "open sesame" for new American music.

He composed dramatic works including an opera, ballets and other dance music, film music, and incidental music; *Synchrony of Dance, Music, Light* (1930), 20 symphonies (no. 20 completed by Harrison, 1965), and numerous other works for orchestra and band; works for soloist and orchestra; a large amount of chamber music and works for piano; choral music; solo vocal works. Lichtenwanger's catalog lists over 900 works, including many unpublished or lost.

Bibl.: Bruce Saylor, *The Writings of Henry Cowell: A Descriptive Bibliography* (New York, 1977). Rita M. Head, *Henry Cowell's New Music, 1925–1936: The Society, the Music Editions, and the Recordings* (Ann Arbor, 1981). M. L. Manion, *Writings about Henry Cowell: An Annotated Bibliography* (New York, 1982). William Lichtenwanger, *The Music of Henry Cowell: A Descriptive Catalog* (New York, 1986).

Cowen, Frederic Hymen [Hymen Frederick] (b. Kingston, Jamaica, 29 Jan. 1852; d. London, 6 Oct. 1935). Conductor and composer. Came to England in 1856; precocious composer and pianist; lessons with Goss and Benedict; 1860–66, studied in Leipzig; 1867, studied conducting at the Stern Conservatory in Berlin; 1868, returned to London, where he established himself as a pianist and composer, producing a First Symphony and Piano Concerto in 1869; an accompanist at Her Majesty's Theatre and elsewhere; 1876, *Pauline,* first of his 4 operas, performed by the Carl Rosa Company; 1880, Scandinavian Symphony, the third of his 6, very successful and much performed; 1881, his oratorio *St. Ursula,* premiered at Norwich Festival; 1888, toured Australia as a conductor; 1888–92, conductor, Philharmonic Society, London (again in 1900–1907); 1896–99, conductor, Hallé Orchestra, Manchester; 1896–1913, conductor, Liverpool Philharmonic; also conducted several choral festivals (Handel Festival, 1903–23); knighted in 1911; other works include many once-popular songs and cantatas (*The Rose Maiden,* 1870; *St. John's Eve,* 1889); published popular biographies of composers and his memoirs, *My Art and My Friends* (London, 1913).

Bibl.: J. E. Potts, "Sir Frederic H. Cowen (1852–1935)," *MT* 94 (1953): 351–53.

Cowie, Edward (b. Birmingham, England, 17 Aug. 1943). Composer. He was educated at Trinity College, Univ. of Southampton, and the Univ. of Leeds and studied with Fricker, Goehr, and Lutosławski. He worked at the Univ. of Wollongong, New South Wales, from 1983; artistic director of the Australian Sinfonietta from 1989. He has pursued studies in music, art, and ornithology, among other areas; also a painter. Works include the opera *Commedia* (1978); Concerto for Orchestra (1982); Concerto no. 2, clarinet, orchestra (1975); Concerto for Orchestra, 1980); Symphony no. 1, *The American* (1981); Symphony no. 2, *The Australian* (1982); Concerto for Harp and Chamber Orchestra (1984); *A Young Person's Guide to the Orchestra* (1986); 4 string quartets (1973, 1977, 1983, 1983); *The Falls of Clyde,* 2 pianos (1980); *Madrigals,* 12 voices (1975).

Cox, Ida [née Prather] (b. Toccoa, Ga., 25 Feb. 1896; d. Knoxville, 10 Nov. 1967). Blues singer. Singing blues and vaudeville songs, she toured theater circuits (1910–44), starring in her own revues from 1929. She often worked with her second husband, the pianist Jesse Crump, from 1925. She recorded 1923–28, including "Ida Cox's Lawdy Lawdy Blues" and "I've Got the Blues for Rampart Street," both accompanied by the pianist Lovie Austin and cornetist Tommy Ladnier (1923). In 1939 she sang in New York at Cafe Society and in the Spirituals to Swing Concert at Carnegie Hall. New recordings (1939–40) with all-star swing groups included "Four Day Creep" (1939).

Craft, Robert (Lawson) (b. Kingston, N.Y., 20 Oct. 1923). Conductor and author. Studied composition and conducting at Juilliard (B.A., 1946). Founded and led New York's Chamber Art Society (1947–50), making his professional debut 26 Nov. 1947 at the Hunter College Playhouse. Conducted the Los Angeles Monday Evening Concerts and Evening-on-the-Roof Series (1950–68). Led premieres of works by Stravinsky (*Agon,* Los Angeles, 1957; *Variations,* Chicago, 1965) and Varèse (*Nocturnal,* New York, 1961). His recording of Webern's complete works was a milestone when released by Columbia in 1957; for the same company he recorded numerous works by Varèse, Schoenberg, and Stravinsky. His meeting with Stravinsky (31 Mar. 1948) led to an extraordinarily intimate creative association. While living in the composer's home from June 1949 until 1971, he helped Stravinsky assimilate serialism and stimulated the composer's production of specific works in a new manner. From 1959 he edited several volumes of "conversations" that portray Stravinsky in a flattering light. The breadth of Craft's culture and sympathies is revealed in *Prejudices in Disguise*

(1974), *Current Convictions* (1977), and *Perspectives* (1984).

Cramer, Johann [John] **Baptist** (b. Mannheim, 24 Feb. 1771; d. London, 16 Apr. 1858). Pianist and composer. Son of the violinist Wilhelm Cramer (1746–99), who from 1772 was an important figure in London concert life. Studied the piano with Schroeter and, for a few months in 1783–84, Clementi and, from 1785, theory with Abel; London concert debut in 1781. A frequent performer from 1783 (including a 2-piano performance with Clementi in 1784 that is the first known); 1788, published his op. 1, 3 sonatas; 1788–90, toured France and Germany; from the 1790s a leading London pianist, keyboard composer, and teacher (noted especially for his legato and the delicacy of his playing); 1799–1800, visited the Netherlands, Germany, and Austria and in 1816–18 the Netherlands and Germany. From 1805 involved in music publishing in a series of firms leading to J. B. Cramer; 1813, a founding member of the London Philharmonic Society; 1823, one of the first teachers at the Royal Academy of Music; retired in 1835 and lived most of the next decade in Paris.

Works: 9 concertos, 1795–ca. 1822; 2 piano quintets; 2 piano quartets; 124 sonatas (many accompanied); many variations, rondos, fantasias, divertimentos, preludes, and other salon pieces; most remembered for his didactic works, including the first systematic course of piano etudes, *Studio per il piano forte,* 84 etudes in 2 vols. (London, 1804–10), followed by several later collections.

Bibl.: Alan Tyson, "A Feud between Clementi and Cramer," *ML* 54 (1973): 281–88. J. C. Graue, "The Clementi-Cramer Dispute Revisited," *ML* 56 (1975): 47–54. Thomas B. Milligan, *Johann Baptist Cramer, 1771–1858: A Thematic Catalogue of His Works* (Stuyvesant, 1994).

Cramer, Wilhelm (b. Mannheim, bapt. 2 June 1746; d. London, 5 Oct. 1799). Violinist. He spent his youth in Mannheim, where his father, Jacob Cramer (1705–70), was violinist in the court orchestra. Johann Baptist Cramer was his eldest son. Wilhelm played violin in the orchestra from 1756, and subsequently at Stuttgart and Paris, where he performed at the Concert spirituel in 1769. In 1772 Wilhelm went to London, where he spent the rest of his life as royal chamber musician and orchestra director.

Crawford (Seeger), Ruth (Porter) (b. East Liverpool, Ohio, 3 July 1901; d. Chevy Chase, Md., 18 Nov. 1953). Composer, teacher, and folk music collector. Studied piano as a child; after high school she taught music to young children and piano in Jacksonville while studying harmony and composition on her own. She received a teacher's certificate after a year's study at the American Conservatory in Chicago (1921), subsequently earning her B.Mus. (1923) and M.Mus. (1929) there. Her early compositions were indebted to Scriabin and Debussy (Preludes for Piano, 1925–28); she also explored polytonality and the use of tone clusters. After a summer at the MacDowell Colony (1929) she studied composition with Charles Seeger, whom she married (1931) after returning from a Guggenheim-sponsored trip to Europe. Her String Quartet (1931) employed twelve-tone procedures. When the family moved to Washington, D.C., she began to transcribe folk music at the Library of Congress, subsequently editing or arranging 8 volumes; she also taught nursery school children during this period. She wrote very little after 1932: *Rissolty, Rissolty,* chamber orchestra (1942), uses folk material; the Suite for Wind Quintet (1952) is more abstract, employing serial procedures.

Other works include the Suite for Orchestra (1926); a violin sonata (1926) and a few other chamber pieces; 2 sets of Preludes (1924–25, 1927–28) and the *Study in Mixed Accents* (1930) for piano; *Adventures of Tom Thumb* (narrator and piano, 1925); choral music; and songs.

Bibl.: Matilda Gaume, *Ruth Crawford Seeger: Memoirs, Memories, Music* (Metuchen, N.J., 1986). Joseph Nathan Straus, *The Music of Ruth Crawford Seeger* (Cambridge, 1995).

Cray, Robert (b. Columbus, Ga., 1954). Blues guitarist and singer. With the electric bass guitarist Robert Cousins he led a blues band in Tacoma, Wash., and Eugene and Portland, Oreg., then accompanied the blues guitarist Albert Collins (1976) and performed at the San Francisco Blues Festival (1977). From around 1980 Cray was the group's singer. He became one of the most popular blues musicians since B. B. King, recording the albums *False Accusations* (1985) and *Strong Persuader* (1986), from which latter came the hit single and television video "Smoking Gun" (1987).

Crecquillon [Créquillon], **Thomas** (b. between ca. 1480 and ca. 1500; d. Béthune? probably early 1557). Composer. In the chapel of Charles V in the 1540s; subsequently a canon in Namur, Termonde (1552–55), and Béthune (1555 until his death). Almost 200 chansons by him, including a handful of *chansons spirituelles,* survive, many also in arrangements for instruments. His sacred works consist of over 100 motets, 12 Masses, and 2 Lamentations cycles.

Bibl.: *Opera omnia, CMM* 63 (1974–). R. M. Trotter, "The Chansons of Thomas Crecquillon: Texts and Form," *RBM* 14 (1960): 56. H. L. Marshall, *The Four-Voice Motets of Thomas Crecquillon,* Musicological Studies, 21 (Brooklyn, 1970–71).

Crespin, Régine (b. Marseilles, 23 Feb. 1927). Soprano. While she was studying in Nîmes to be a pharmacist, her first prize in a vocal contest persuaded her to pursue a career in music. Studied at the Paris Conservatory with Suzanne Cesbron-Viseur and Georges Jouatte. Opera debut as Charlotte *(Werther),* 20 Jan. 1949, at Reims. Sang Elsa *(Lohengrin)* at Mulhouse, 1950. Debut at Opéra-comique, June 1951, as Tosca; at Paris Opéra, August 1951, as Elsa. Created the New Prioress in Poulenc's *Dialogues,* 1957. Sang Kundry *(Parsifal)* at Bayreuth, 1958. New York Met debut, 19 Nov. 1962, as the Marschallin *(Rosenkavalier).* From

1974, sang French operas exclusively. Published her memoirs, *La vie et l'amour d'une femme* (1982) [includes discography].

Creston, Paul [Guttoveggio, Giuseppe] (b. New York, 10 Oct. 1906; d. San Diego, 24 Aug. 1985). Composer and keyboard player. He dropped out of high school to help support his family; studied piano (1921–25) and organ (1925–26); taught himself to compose by studying the works of Bach, Scarlatti, Chopin, Debussy, and others. He played the organ for silent films (1926–29) and later served as a church organist (1934–67). Cowell included his first published composition in the *New Music Quarterly* (*Seven Theses,* piano, 1933). He taught at Swarthmore (1956), the New York College of Music (1963–67), and then at Central Washington State College, where he was appointed professor emeritus upon retirement (1975). He was president of the National Association for American Composers and Conductors (1956–60). His special interest in rhythm is attested by his compositions (also characterized by lush harmonic language and classical forms) and by his 2 published volumes (*Principles of Rhythm,* 1964; *Rational Metric Notation,* 1979).

He composed more than 50 works for orchestra or band, including Symphony no. 6 op. 118 (organ and orchestra, 1981) and many concertos (for marimba, saxophone, piano, violin, accordion) and other works with soloists; the Piano Trio op. 112 (1979), *Ceremonial* op. 103 (percussion ensemble, 1972), and other chamber music; *Rhythmicon,* 10 vols. (1977), and other piano works; Masses and other choral music; solo vocal music.

Bibl.: Monica J. Slomski, *Paul Creston: A Bio-Bibliography* (Westport, 1994).

Crist, Bainbridge (b. Lawrenceburg, Ind., 13 Feb. 1883; d. Barnstable, Mass., 7 Feb. 1969). Composer. Worked for six years in Washington, D.C., as a lawyer, then studied voice, theory, and orchestration in Berlin and London. He taught voice in Boston (1915–21), Washington (1922–23), and Florence (1927–38); then settled on Cape Cod. As a composer he was primarily known for his sensitive treatment of voice and text; his songs were performed and broadcast frequently in the 1940s and 1950s; his book *The Art of Setting Words to Music* was published in 1944. Works include 2 "choreographic dramas" and a Javanese ballet (*Pregiva's Marriage,* 1922); several symphonic poems and other orchestral works (*American Epic 1620,* 1943); many works for voice and orchestra (*Drolleries from an Oriental Doll's House,* 1920); chamber music and piano pieces; choral music; many songs.

Bibl.: J. T. Howard, *Bainbridge Crist* (New York, 1929).

Cristofori, Bartolomeo (b. Padua, 4 May 1655; d. Florence, 27 Jan. 1731). Maker of keyboard instruments. From 1688 he was employed in Florence as a member of the court of Prince Ferdinand de' Medici; custodian of musical instruments at the court after the death of the prince in 1713. He experimented with and constructed many different sorts of instruments, including harpsichords, but is remembered chiefly as the designer and maker of the first piano, developed in the course of work begun in about 1698. An article by Maffei published in 1711 describes and illustrates its action, which was quickly adopted and modified by a number of other instrument makers. A few pianos made by Cristofori still survive.

Croce, Giovanni (b. Chioggia, ca. 1557; d. Venice, 15 May 1609). Composer. Worked for most of his life at the Church of S. Maria Formosa. Assistant *maestro di cappella* at St. Mark's, Venice, from the early 1590s; became *maestro* there in 1603. Wrote both secular and sacred works in conservative styles. The secular compositions include many light madrigals, canzonettas, and the like in a simple diatonic idiom. Some of these pieces were printed in translation in England and were highly influential there. His Masses, motets, and other sacred compositions include some works probably written for a small parish choir and others, including some parody Masses, for double choir. Certain pieces can be classified as early church cantatas, with alternation of soloists (with organ accompaniment) and full choir. Many works were published with organ bass or other instrumental parts.

Crockett, Donald (b. Pasadena, Calif., 18 Feb. 1951). Composer and conductor. He studied at the Univ. of Southern California (B.M., 1974; M.M., 1976), where his teachers included Robert Linn and Halsey Stevens; at the Univ. of California, Santa Barbara (Ph.D. 1981), with Peter Racine Fricker. Composer-in-residence with the Los Angeles Chamber Orchestra, 1991–. Member of the faculty at the Univ. of Southern California and conductor of its Contemporary Music Ensemble; has premiered numerous works as a conductor. His compositions include *Occhi dell'alma mia,* soprano and guitar (1982); *The Pensive Traveller,* voice and piano (1983); *The Tenth Muse,* soprano and orchestra (1986); *Array,* string quartet (1987); and *Roethke Preludes,* orchestra (1994).

Croes, Henri-Jacques de (b. Antwerp, bapt. 19 Sept. 1705; d. Brussels, 16 Aug. 1786). Violinist and composer. In 1723 became first violinist at the Church of St. Jacques, Antwerp. In 1729 acquired a position in the musical establishment of the Prince of Thurn and Taxis, who had residences in Brussels, Frankfurt am Main, and Regensburg. By 1744 was first violinist in the chapel of Charles of Lorraine in Brussels; from 1746 until his death was *maître de chapelle* there. In his compositions Italian and French styles intermingle. The sacred works, often scored for 4 voices and 4 instruments, include Masses, Mass fragments, and a number of cantatalike motets. Chamber works, especially sonatas and concertos, dominate his secular music.

Croft [Crofts], **William** (b. Nether Ettington, Warwickshire, bapt. 30 Dec. 1678; d. Bath, 14 Aug. 1727). Composer. As a chorister in the Chapel Royal was a student of John Blow. From 1700 a Gentleman of the Chapel Royal and from 1704 also organist of the chapel (jointly with Jeremiah Clarke until 1707, then alone). When Blow died in 1708, Croft succeeded him as composer and Master of the Children of the Chapel Royal and organist of Westminster Abbey. Wrote sacred and secular vocal and instrumental music, but concentrated chiefly on sacred compositions (many with some sort of instrumental accompaniment) after the first few years of the 18th century. The sacred music includes morning, Communion, evening, and burial services, numerous anthems (a few full, most verse), and several hymn tunes that are still in use. Of these works, the anthems in particular show a grasp of late Baroque idiom that was new to England. An interest in an older polyphonic choral style is also evident. Perhaps the most substantial of the secular compositions are those written for the degree of D.Mus., received from Oxford in 1713: 2 odes for solo voices, chorus, and orchestra, published in 1715 as *Musicus apparatus academicus.* The 2-volume collection *Musica sacra* consists entirely of Croft's sacred music, engraved in score (a novelty in printed polyphony) and published by the composer in 1724.

Crosby, Bing [Harry Lillis] (b. Tacoma, Wash., 2 May 1901; d. Madrid, 14 Oct. 1977). Popular music singer and actor. Brother of Bob Crosby. He sang and played drums in bands in Spokane; between 1926 and 1930 he and vocalists Al Rinker and Harry Barris performed jazz as the Rhythm Boys with the Paul Whiteman Orchestra. After 1930 he began singing popular music; he hosted radio shows (*Kraft Music Hall,* 1935–46), appeared in over 50 films between 1930 and 1966 (including the *Road* series of musical comedy films with Bob Hope and Dorothy Lamour, 1940–62), and made numerous successful recordings. He was among the first singers to make effective use of the microphone, employing amplification to achieve an intimate, effortless style of delivery that matched his relaxed and friendly stage persona. His most famous recordings were associated with films, including "White Christmas" (in *Holiday Inn,* 1942, music by Irving Berlin) and "Swinging on a Star" (in *Going My Way,* 1944).

Bibl.: Bing Crosby and P. Martin, *Call Me Lucky* (New York, 1953). Ted Crosby, *The Story of Bing Crosby* (Cleveland, 1946). Timothy A. Morgereth, *Bing Crosby: A Discography, Radio Program List, and Filmography* (Jefferson, N.C., 1987).

Crosby, Bob [George Robert] (b. Spokane, 25 Aug. 1913; d. La Jolla, Calif., 9 Mar. 1993). Jazz bandleader. Brother of Bing Crosby. He led a big band under the musical direction of the reed player Gil Rodin (1935–42) which adapted Dixieland jazz to a 13-piece ensemble, as on the double bass player Bob Haggart's arrangement of "South Rampart Street Parade," recorded in 1937. In an octet, the Bob Cats, Crosby presented his soloists, including trumpeter Yank Lawson (later, Billy Butterfield), clarinetist Matty Matlock (later, Irving Fazola), and tenor saxophonist Eddie Miller. Crosby became an actor and singer in movies, radio, and television, and occasionally led big bands or reunions of the Bob Cats.

Bibl.: John Chilton, *Stomp Off, Let's Go! The Story of Bob Crosby's Bob Cats and Big Band* (London, 1983).

Cross, Joan (b. London, 7 Sept. 1900; d. 12 Dec. 1993). Soprano. At Trinity College in London studied violin, then voice with Peter Dawson. Solo debut, 1924, as Cherubino *(Nozze di Figaro)* at Old Vic Theatre. Covent Garden debut as Mimi *(La Bohème),* 1931; returned 1934–35, 1947–54. First soprano of Sadler's Wells Opera, 1931–46. Director there, 1943–45. After creating Ellen Orford in Britten's *Peter Grimes* she developed a close artistic association with the composer; sang in premieres of *The Rape of Lucretia* (1946), *Albert Herring* (1947), *Gloriana* (1953), *The Turn of the Screw* (1954). With Ann Wood founded the National School of Opera, 1948. Retired from the stage in 1955.

Cross, Lowell (Merlin) (b. Kingsville, Tex., 24 June 1938). Composer. Studied English, mathematics, and music at Texas Technicological Univ. (1956–63) and established an electronic music studio there (1961); studied electronic music at the Univ. of Toronto (Schaeffer, Ciamaga). He directed the Mills College Tape Music Center (1968–69) and served as engineer and consulting artist for Experiments in Art and Technology (1968–70); from 1971 taught at the Univ. of Iowa, where he also directed the recording studios in the School of Music. He designed the laser deflection system for Expo 70 in Osaka; often collaborated with Tudor and others on works involving electronic musical and visual devices (*Reunion,* 1968, with Cage, Tudor, and others; *Video III,* with Tudor, for performers, audio system, electronics, television; *Video/Laser I–IV,* with Tudor and others). He compiled *A Bibliography of Electronic Music* (1967; rev. 1968, 1970).

Crosse, Gordon (b. Bury, Lancashire, 1 Dec. 1937). Composer. At Oxford he studied with Wellesz and Rubbra, and in Rome with Petrassi (1962). From 1966 he was professor at Birmingham Univ., from 1969 at the Univ. of Essex, and from 1973 at King's College, Cambridge. His early works follow serialism; more recent works show influence of contemporaries such as Peter Maxwell Davies. His works include operas (*Purgatory,* 1966; *The Grace of Todd,* 1967–68, rev. 1974; *Wheel of the World,* 1969–72; *Potter Thompson,* 1972–73; *Holly from the Bongs,* 1974); orchestral works (*Sinfonia concertante,* 1965, rev. 1975 as Symphony no. 1; Symphony no. 2, 1974–75; *Thel,* concertino for flute, 2 horns, strings, 1974–76; *Playground,* 1978; a cello concerto, 1979; *Young Apollo,* ballet, 1984; *Array,* trumpet and strings, 1986); anthems and hymns (*The Covenant of the Rainbow,* chorus, organ, piano 4-hands, 1968); songs and children's vocal works (*The History of the Flood,* 1970); chamber music (*Three Inventions,* flute, clarinet, 1959; *Wildboy,* clarinet, chamber ensemble, 1978; *Chime,* brass quintet, 1983; a piano trio, 1986).

Bibl.: Andrew Burn, "Gordon Crosse at 50," *MT* 128 (1987): 679–83.

Crotch, William (b. Norwich, 5 July 1775; d. Taunton, 29 Dec. 1847). Composer. Son of a carpenter; a child prodigy, exhibited by his mother on tours of England and Scotland from 1778 to the age of 9; 1785, played his own harpsichord concerto in London; 1786, assistant to the professor of music at Cambridge (mainly playing the organ in churches) and receiving his first regular education; also in 1786 published his first compositions and began composing the oratorio *The Captivity of Judah,* partly performed at Cambridge, 1789. In June 1788 he moved to Oxford to read for the church, but in September 1789 became organist at Christ Church and from about 1792 director of orchestral concerts of the Oxford Music Room; 1794, B.Mus. from Oxford; doctorate in 1799, after having been elected professor of music there in 1797; also named organist at St. John's College, University Church, and the Theatre. In 1798, began lecture course that became a regular feature of Oxford life; 1804, gave first of several lecture courses at the Royal Institution, London; 1805, moved to London, retaining the professorship; lived in London, giving private lessons, playing the organ, conducting (the Philharmonic Society, of which he was a founding member), and offering numerous lecture courses. In 1811 he completed his most important work, the oratorio *Palestine;* 1822, named principal of the new Royal Academy of Music (teaching harmony, counterpoint, and composition, with Bennett his most distinguished pupil), resigning in 1832 after censure for kissing a female student in approval of a harmony exercise; 1834, last important public appearance as organist at the Handel Festival. Published an important historical anthology, *Specimens of Various Styles of Music* (London, 1808). Other works include second setting of *The Captivity of Judah,* performed 1834; many anthems; occasional odes; many glees, canons, rounds; many hymns and chants; 3 organ concertos; orchestral and keyboard pieces. Something of a polymath, he was also a talented artist.

Bibl.: J. Rennert, *William Crotch (1775–1847)* (Lavenham, 1975).

Cruft, Adrian (Francis) (b. Mitcham, Surrey, 10 Feb. 1921). Composer. Attended Westminster Abbey Choir School (1930–35), Westminster School (1935–37), and the Royal College of Music (1938–40; 1946–47), where his teachers included Gordon Jacob and Edmund Rubbra. Won Boult Conducting Scholarship at the R.C.M., 1938. Played double bass in several London orchestras, 1947–49. Professor of theory and composition at the R.C.M. from 1962. Taught at Guildhall School of Music, 1972–75. Contributor to several journals, including *Composer* and *Musical Times.* Compositions include 2 Masses, 4 cantatas, suites, other orchestra works, music for brass band, other sacred music, and vocal works.

Bibl.: Edmund Rubbra, "The Music of Adrian Cruft," *MT* 110 (1969): 822–25.

Crüger, Johannes [Johann] (b. Gross-Breesen, near Guben, Lower Lusatia, 9 Apr. 1598; d. Berlin, 23 Feb. 1662). Composer and theorist. Studied music under Paul Homberger, who may himself have studied with Giovanni Gabrieli. Then traveled widely, finally settling in Berlin, where he first published music in 1619. In 1620 enrolled as a theology student at the Univ. of Wittenberg. Kantor of the Nicolaikirche in Berlin from 1622 until his death. Wrote a few works for conventional choral forces (2–8 voices, usually with continuo), but is remembered chiefly for his work with Lutheran chorales. For several collections, the first published in 1640, he composed some melodies, compiled and arranged many more. The arrangements always include the chorale melody and a figured bass. In publications dated 1649 or later, parts for 3 more voices and 2 or 3 independent instruments (optional) are added. The best known of his chorale books is *Praxis pietatis melica* (for melody and bass only; first published under this title in 1647 and subsequently revised and reissued many times). His various theoretical works are all didactic. They contain little original material but are important for their synthesis of many of the new ideas of the time. Titles include *Synopsis musica* (1630; enl. ed., 1654), *Quaestiones musicae practicae* (1650), and *Musicae practicae . . . Der rechte Weg zur Singekunst* (1660).

Crumb, George (Henry) (b. Charleston, W.Va., 24 Oct. 1929). Composer. The son of two musicians, he studied at the Mason College of Music and Fine Arts in Charleston (B.M., 1950), the Univ. of Illinois (M.Mus., 1953), and the Univ. of Michigan under Finney (D.M.A., 1959); studied with Blacher at the Berkshire Music Center (1955) and in Berlin (1956). He taught at the Univ. of Colorado (1964–69) and SUNY–Buffalo (1964–65) before moving to the Univ. of Pennsylvania. He received the Pulitzer Prize in 1968 for *Echoes of Time and the River.*

Crumb's music is particularly concerned wth sonority and timbre, its effects carefully and often ingeniously notated (although employing some aleatory sections), and deriving from dramatic or symbolic considerations rather than mathematical procedures. His early works reflect acknowledged indebtedness to Bartók and Debussy; in the *Variazioni* for orchestra (1959) he experimented with twelve-tone procedures. Two works from 1970 illustrate elements of Crumb's mature style: in *Ancient Voices of Children* the mezzo-soprano sings phonetic sounds directly into the amplified piano, and exotic instruments such as toy piano, Japanese temple bells, and Tibetan prayer stones are employed; in *Black Angels: 13 Images from the Dark Land* for electric string quartet, Ives-like quotations from Schubert and Saint-Saëns appear. Medieval cosmology and numerology play a part in many of Crumb's designs. He sometimes requires performers to whistle (e.g., an Appalachian hymn in *Makrokosmos II* for amplified piano, 1971); whisper or shout and move around on stage (*Echoes of Time and the River,* subtitled "Four Processionals for Orchestra," 1967); or wear masks (*Lux Aeterna,* for 5 masked musicians including voice and sitar, flute/recorder, and percussion, grouped around a candle on a red-lighted stage, 1971). The search for new sonorities has included covering the piano strings with paper (*Makrokosmos III: Music for a Summer Evening,* 1974) and employing *Sprechstimme,* quarter-tones, and passages marked "senza vibrato" in some of the *Madrigals* (4 books, soprano and ensemble, 1964–69).

Other compositions include *A Haunted Landscape* (1984) and other orchestral works; *An Idyll for the Misbegotten* (string quartet, premiered 1986) and other instrumental chamber music; several works for voice and ensemble (*Songs, Drones, and Refrains of Death,* baritone with guitar, double bass, piano, and harpsichord, all electric, and percussion, 1968); piano music; *Apparition* (after Whitman, soprano and piano, 1979).

Bibl.: Don Gillespie, ed., *George Crumb: Profile of a Composer* (New York, 1985).

Crusell, Bernard Henrik (b. Nystad, Finland, 15 Oct. 1775; d. Stockholm, 28 July 1838). Composer and clarinetist. From a poor family, he was helped to become a musician by a military officer; from age 12 played in a military band, with which he moved to Stockholm in 1792; from 1793, first clarinet in the court orchestra, studying music with the director, G. J. Vogler; from 1798, studied with Tausch in Berlin, becoming one of the best-known clarinet soloists of the time; 1802, gave first known public performance of Mozart's Clarinet Concerto; 1803, studied composition with Berton and Gossec and the clarinet with Lefèvre in Paris; returning to Stockholm, remained in the court service until about 1833–34; from 1818 until his death, music director of 2 regiments of Royal Swedish Grenadiers. Works include 3 clarinet concertos; 3 clarinet quartets; a Swedish opera, *Lilla Slafvinna* (1824); songs.

Bibl.: Sven Wilson, ed., *Bernard Crusell: tonsättare klarinettvirtuos* (Stockholm, 1977).

Cruz, Ivo (b. Corumbá, Brazil, 19 May 1901; d. Lisbon, 8 Sept. 1985). Composer and conductor. At Lisbon he studied music theory (with de Lima and Borba) and piano; at the Univ. of Lisbon he studied law (1919–24). He went to Munich, where he studied composition with Mors and Reuss (1925–30). Returning to Portugal, he founded the Lisbon Philharmonic in 1937 and the following year became director of the Lisbon Conservatory, where he remained until he retired. He was also active as concert manager and music critic, writing for *Revista portuguesa* and *Estudos portugueses.* His works, which are strongly tonal and employ Portuguese folk tunes, include a ballet, *Pastoral* (1942); orchestral works (*Motivos lusitanos,* 1928; *Sinfonia de Amadis,* 1952; *Sinfonia de Quelez,* 1964); songs (*Canções sentimentais,* 1972); chamber works.

Ctesibius [Ktesibios] (fl. Alexandria, 246–221 B.C.E.). Inventor of the hydraulis, an organ whose wind supply was regulated by water pressure. He was widely known for a variety of related inventions, many of them essentially toys.

Cuénod [Cuenod], **Hugues (Adhémar)** (b. Corseaux-sur-Vevey, Switzerland, 26 June 1902). Tenor. Studied as a baritone at the Ribaupierre Institute in Lausanne, the Geneva Conservatory, and the Basel Conservatory, then as a tenor in Vienna with Mme. Singer-Burian. Debut Paris, 1928; opera debut, 1928, in a starring role at the Théâtre Grammont, Paris. To London and the U.S. for Noël Coward's *Bitter Sweet.* Back in Switzerland, 1932–34, he sang modern songs and spirituals as half of the duo Bob and Bobette; concertized with Clara Haskil. Taught at the Geneva Conservatory, 1940–46. Throughout his career he was in demand for Baroque and contemporary parts. He created Sellem in Stravinsky's *The Rake's Progress* (Venice, 1951); thereafter sang premieres of Stravinsky's *Cantata* (1952), *Threni* (1958), and *A Sermon, a Narrative, and a Prayer* (1962). Covent Garden debut, 1954. From 1954 through the 1980s, sang small roles at Glyndebourne. As late as 1982 he sang the Emperor of China (*Turandot*) in London.

Cugat, Xavier (b. Barcelona, 1 Jan 1900; d. there, 26 Oct. 1990). Jazz and popular violinist and bandleader. He was trained as a classical violinist in Cuba and made a formal debut in New York City; from 1928 he led bands that popularized Latin percussion instrumentation and dance rhythms. He worked with singers Dinah Shore, Buddy Clark, and Miguelito Valdés; the bands played for films (*In Caliente,* 1935) and made successful recordings ("Lady in Red," 1935; "Brazil," 1943).

Cui, César [Kyui, Tsezar Antonovich] (b. Vilnius, 18 Jan. 1835; d. Petrograd, 26 Mar. 1918). Composer and critic. His father, an officer in the French Army, married a Lithuanian and taught French at the Gymnasium in Vilnius. There Cui received his early education while studying piano and taking lessons in harmony and counterpoint from Moniuszko. He attended the Engineering School at St. Petersburg, then the Academy of Military Engineering; upon graduating in 1857 he became lecturer and then professor (1878). He became an acknowleged expert in fortifications. Following introductions to Balakirev in 1856 and Dargomïzhsky in 1857, he befriended all the members of the *moguchaya kuchka* (Mighty Handful). Cui's early works were influenced by Balakirev, who in 1857–58 supervised the orchestration of the overture to Cui's first opera, *Kavkazskiy plennik* (A Prisoner in the Caucasus), first given (with a new, central act composed in 1881) at the Mariinsky Theater in 1883. From 1861 to 1868 Cui was occupied with his opera *Vil'yam Ratklif*

(William Ratcliff), given at the Mariinsky in 1869. Reaction to the opera, considered to be his finest dramatic work, was mixed, though it was praised by Rimsky-Korsakov, Stasov, Balakirev, and Mussorgsky. Far from discouraged, Cui embarked on other opera projects, including *The Stone Guest* (1869), the first act of *Mlada* (1872; written in collaboration with Rimsky-Korsakov, Borodin, Mussorgsky, and Minkus), *Anzhelo* (1871–75), *Saratsin* (1896–98), *Pir vo vremya chumï* (A Feast in Time of Plague, 1900), *Mademuazel' Fifi* (1900), *Matteo Falcone* (1901), and *Kapitanskaya dochka* (The Captain's Daughter, 1907–9). Despite his activity as an opera composer, Cui is better known as a miniaturist: the bulk of his output consists of songs ("Ici bas" op. 54, no. 5) and short piano pieces. He also wrote a modest amount of orchestral music, chamber music (*Orientale* from the suite *Kaleidoskop,* 24 pieces for violin and piano, op. 50), and choral music. As a critic Cui contributed to numerous journals and newspapers, including *Sanktpeterburgskiye vedomosti* (1864–77), *Novoye vremya* (1876–80, 1917), *Nedelya* (1884–90), *Novosti i birzhevaya gazeta* (1896–1900), and *Revue et gazette musicale de Paris* (1878–80). In his reviews and his book *La musique en Russie* (Paris, 1880; R: 1974) he championed nationalist ideals.

Bibl.: L. de Ricquet, Comtesse de Mercy-Argenteau, *César Cui* (Paris, 1888). Robert Ridenour, *Nationalism, Modernism, and Personal Rivalry in Nineteenth-Century Russian Music* (Ann Arbor, 1981). Richard Taruskin, *Opera and Drama as Preached and Practiced in the 1860s* (Ann Arbor, 1981).

Curtin, Phyllis (Smith) (b. Clarksburg, W.Va., 3 Dec. 1922). Soprano. After obtaining a B.A. at Wellesley (1943), studied voice with Olga Avierino, Joseph Regneas, and Boris Goldovsky. Stage debut as Tchaikovsky's Lisa *(Queen of Spades),* Boston, 1946. With New York City Opera, 1953–64, where she was featured in New York premieres of Einem's *Der Prozess* (1953), Floyd's *Susannah* (1956), and Walton's *Troilus.* Sang with Vienna Staatsoper, 1959–63; New York Met, 1961–74. Praised for her Salome. Taught voice at Yale School of Music, 1974–83. Appointed Dean, School of the Arts, Boston Univ., 1983. Retired from public singing, 1984.

Curtis, King [Ousley, Curtis] (b. Fort Worth, 7 Feb. 1934; d. New York, 13 Aug. 1971). Rhythm-and-blues tenor saxophonist. After playing with Lionel Hampton's big band he moved to New York in 1952 and became a studio musician, soloing on about 200 hit records by Fats Domino, Bobby Darin, Sam Cooke, Nat King Cole, the Coasters, the Drifters, Ben E. King, Ruth Brown, and Aretha Franklin, among others. He also made 15 hit singles as a leader, including *Soul Twist* (1962). Soon after becoming Franklin's music director, he was murdered outside his home.

Curtis-Smith, Curtis O.(Otto) B.(Bismarck) (b. Walla Walla, Wash., 9 Sept. 1941). Composer. Studied at Whitman College (1960–62) and Northwestern Univ. (B.M., 1964; M.M., 1965), where he studied piano with Gui Mombaerts; attended Berkshire Music Center, 1972. On the faculty of Western Michigan Univ. from 1968. Works include String Quartet no. 3 (commissioned by Kronos Quartet, 1980); *Unisonics,* saxophone, piano (1976); *Music for Handbells* (1977); *Masquerades,* organ (1978); *Ragmala (A Garland of Ragas),* guitar, string quartet (1983); other orchestra (. . . *Float Wild Birds, Sleeping,* 1988), keyboard, vocal works; some music for tape and other instruments.

Curwen, John (b. Heckmondwike, Yorkshire, 14 Nov. 1816; d. Manchester, 26 May 1880). Educator and publisher. A Congregational minister who, with no musical background, became interested in the problems of teaching music in Sunday schools and, by extension, to the lower classes as a means of social uplift. Rejecting generally accepted methods, he based his system on tonic sol-fa; began to publicize this in 1842 in journals and books spread over the rest of his life that developed and improved his methods. From 1844 he published his own writings and sol-fa music; in 1863 founded the firm of J. Curwen & Sons, long devoted to educational music, both sacred and secular.

Bibl.: Bernarr Rainbow, *John Curwen: A Short Biography* (Sevenoaks, 1980).

Curwen, John Spencer (b. Plaistow, 30 Sept. 1847; d. London, 6 Aug. 1916). Publisher. Son of John Curwen; studied at the Royal Academy of Music; on his father's death, succeeded him as leader of the tonic sol-fa movement and head of the publishing firm of J. Curwen & Sons; also principal of the Tonic Sol-Fa College, founded by his father in 1869, and from 1881 editor of the *Tonic Sol-Fa Reporter* (later the *Musical Herald*).

Curzon, Clifford (Michael) (b. London, 18 May 1907; d. there, 1 Sept. 1982). Pianist. Entered the Royal Academy of Music on scholarship in 1919; studied with Charles Reddie and Katherine Goodson, winning McFarren Gold Medal. Debut in Bach's Triple Concerto at Queen's Hall Promenade Concert, 1923. Further studies with Tobias Matthay, Arthur Schnabel, Wanda Landowska, and Nadia Boulanger while teaching at the Royal Academy of Music, 1926–32. Toured Europe with Lionel Tertis, 1936. U.S. debut, 26 Feb. 1939, at New York's Town Hall. At Edinburgh Festival performed in a quartet with Szigeti, Primrose, and Fournier beginning 1952. Renowned for his Mozart. Many recordings, including Brahms solo piano. Knighted, 1977.

Custer, Arthur (b. Manchester, Conn., 21 Apr. 1923). Composer. Studied at the Univ. of Conn. (B.A., 1949); Univ. of Redlands (M.Mus., 1951), with Pisk; Univ. of Iowa (Ph.D., 1959), with Bezanson. Studied with Nadia Boulanger in Paris, 1960–61. Assistant dean of Fine Arts, Univ. of Rhode Island, 1962–65. Dean of Philadelphia Music Academy, 1965–67. Contributed to *Musical Quarterly* and other journals; wrote numerous articles on contemporary American and Spanish music. Director of Arts in Education Project of the Rhode Island Council on the Arts, 1970–73. Compositions include *Interface I,* string quartet, 2 recording engineers (1969); *Interface II,* ensemble, slide projectors, audience (1976); *Colloquy for String Quartet* (1961); and a symphony (1969).

Cutting, Francis (fl. 1583–ca. 1603). Lutenist and composer. He spent at least part of his life in London but was apparently not connected with the court. He composed only instrumental works, most for lute. Eleven of his compositions were published in an anthology of 1596, and one other piece was printed in 1603; over 30 more survive in manuscript only. He may have been related to the younger lutenist Thomas Cutting (fl. 1608–13), who served both the English and Danish royal courts.

Cuvelier, Jo(hannes) [Jean; Jacquemart le Cuvelier] (b. Tournai?; fl. 1372–87). Poet and composer. Served the royal court of France. Of his poetry, 4 ballades survive. One has a musical setting by Hymbert de Salinis; Cuvelier himself wrote polyphonic settings for the other 3. His music is for voice accompanied by 2 instrumental lines and is in the style of the *ars subtilior* (ed. in *CMM* 53/1).

Cuzzoni, Francesca (b. Parma, 2 Apr. 1696; d. Bologna, 1778). Soprano. One of the finest singers of her era and particularly successful for a time in London. Studied with Lanzi; sang in numerous Italian cities between 1716 and 1722. Was a highly successful lead singer in Handel's Royal Academy in London from late 1722 until the academy's closing in 1728. Also participated in many private concerts, most in or near London, during these years. Beginning in 1726, was involved in an intense rivalry with Faustina Bordoni, another great Italian soprano who had joined the academy. After 1728, Cuzzoni performed in Vienna and in Italy for several years. From 1734 to 1736, sang for London's Opera of the Nobility (Handel's competition), but was received less enthusiastically than before. Thereafter performed in many other European cities, with progressively less success. Spent her last years in poverty and obscurity in Bologna.

Cyrille, Andrew (Charles) (b. New York, 10 Nov. 1939). Jazz drummer. He played swing and bop, recording with Coleman Hawkins (1961), then joined Cecil Taylor's free jazz group (1964–75); their albums include *Unit Structures* (1966). He also recorded unaccompanied and with Charlie Haden (both 1969) and gave concerts with the drummers Milford Graves and Rashied Ali, recording duos with Graves (1974). He led the group Maono (1975–1980s). Toured Europe with Carla Bley (1977) and the clarinetist John Carter and worked with Muhal Richard Abrams.

Czerny, Carl (b. Vienna, 20 Feb. 1791; d. there, 15 July 1857). Piano teacher and composer. From a poor family; first music lessons from his father, an ex-soldier turned music teacher; 1800, Vienna concert debut in Mozart's Concerto K. 491. Was early an admirer of Beethoven, whom he met in about 1800 and studied with for about three years; also admired the playing of Hummel and Clementi and studied their techniques. He later wrote that he lacked "the brilliant, calculated charlatanry necessary to touring virtuosos" and never undertook that career. After 1806 gave most of his time to teaching, becoming one of the most fashionable, expensive, and thus, eventually, well-to-do in Vienna; played in public infrequently, apparently mainly in chamber music, although in 1812 he gave the poorly received Vienna premiere of Beethoven's Fifth Concerto. His writings and remarks on the performance of Beethoven's music are of considerable historical importance. He was chosen by Beethoven in 1815 to give lessons to his nephew Karl; 1816–23, held weekly musicales for his students, which Beethoven occasionally attended; visited Baden at the same time as Beethoven in summer 1824 and 1825. His students included Kullak, Heller (briefly), and, most notably, Liszt (1821–23), although he disapproved of the theatricality of Liszt's virtuosity and the direction of his early career. He never married, living with his parents until their deaths in 1827 and 1832, and seems to have had few nonmusical interests. He retired from teaching in 1836, visiting Leipzig that year, Paris and London in 1837, Italy in 1846, but seems to have had occasional later students, such as Leschetizky in the 1840s.

Czerny was self-taught as a composer. He published his op. 1 in 1806, op. 2 in 1819, op. 200 in 1829, op. 500 in 1839, eventually increasing the number to 861; numerous unpublished works. Most of this is ephemeral salon piano music. His serious works, which aroused little attention, include 6 symphonies, 6 overtures, 6 piano concertos, 6 piano concertinos, 8 piano trios, 7 piano quartets, 5 string quartets, much sacred music (11 Masses), 11 published piano sonatas, 28 piano sonatinas. He is best remembered for his didactic works, about 90 in number, including courses for almost every element of piano technique, collections of etudes for 2 or more hands, and treatises on composition (*School of Practical Composition,* London, 1848; probably written by 1837–40) and improvisation. Also edited keyboard music of Bach and Scarlatti; made piano arrangements of many works of Beethoven, Haydn, Mozart, and others.

Bibl.: C. Czerny, "Recollections from My Life," *MQ* 42 (1956): 302–17. D. W. MacArdle, "Beethoven and the Czernys," *MMR* 88 (1958): 124–35. Paul Badura-Skoda, ed., *Carl Czerny: Über den richtigen Vortrag sämtlichen Beethoven'schen Klavierwerke* (Vienna, 1963). Grete Wehmeyer, *Carl Czerny und die Einzelhaft am Klavier* (Kassel, 1983).

D

Dahl, Ingolf (b. Hamburg, 9 June 1912; d. Frutigen, Switzerland, 6 Aug. 1970). Composer, conductor, and pianist. Studied in Cologne and Zurich (1930–36); conducted and coached at the Zurich Opera; moved to the U.S. in 1938, where he composed, conducted, and remained active as a pianist; studied with Boulanger in California in 1944. He taught at the Univ. of Southern California (1945–70); collaborated with Stravinsky, arranging some works for keyboard; taught at the Berkshire Music Center (1952–56). He withdrew his early works, which were in the dissonant, polyphonic style of some German music of the 1920s; after 1940 he composed in a more tonal idiom, often including virtuoso instrumental writing; he began to serialize melodic and harmonic material in the Piano Quartet (1957). Composed works for orchestra (*Aria Sinfonica,* 1965) and wind ensemble (Sinfonietta, 1961); instrumental chamber music for brass, clarinet, flute, and strings; works for piano; *A Noiseless, Patient Spider* (women's voices and piano, 1970); a few songs.

Dalayrac [D'Alayrac], **Nicolas-Marie** (b. Muret, Haute-Garonne, 8 June 1753; d. Paris, 26 Nov. 1809). Composer. His father, Jean d'Alayrac, was an adviser to the king and a member of the nobility. At age 8 Nicolas began attending the college at nearby Toulouse; in 1767 or 1768 he returned to Muret and began playing in the local orchestra. His father was opposed to his son's musical interests, so Nicolas studied law until age 21. In the military-bureaucratic post he obtained at Versailles in 1774 he had informal contacts with highly placed musicians; one of them, the Baron de Bésenval, commissioned Dalayrac in 1781 to compose the stage works *Le petit souper* and *Le chevalier à la mode.* His first big success was *Nina* (1786); it was immediately followed by *Azémia* (1786) and more than 20 other stage works, mostly opéras comiques. His music enjoyed continuous popularity throughout the Revolution. Other works include *Sargines* (1788), *Camille* (1791), *Adolphe et Clara* (1799), *La jeune prude* (1804), *Une heure de mariage* (1804), *Lina* (1807), and *Le poète et le musicien* (1811).

Dalberg, Johann Friedrich Hugo (b. Herrnsheim, near Worms, 17 May 1760; d. Aschaffenburg, 26 July 1812). Pianist, composer, and writer. Born of nobility. His theological studies at Göttingen reflected only one of many interests. In addition to holding several high ecclesiastical offices in Trier, Speyer, and Worms, he became a widely celebrated (and, from the 1770s, widely traveled) concert pianist. He published writings on meteorology, law, and the Orient, and studied counterpoint and composition with Ignaz Holzbauer. Among his musical treatises, which manifest concerns of German Romanticism, are *Blicke eines Tonkünstlers in die Musik der Geister* (Mannheim, 1787; 2nd ed., ca. 1800); *Lieder der Inder und anderer orientalischer Völker* (Erfurt, 1802); and *Die Äolsharfe: Ein allegorischer Traum* (Erfurt, 1801). He composed sacred and secular lieder, chamber works (including 3 violin sonatas op. 1), and keyboard works (including some 14 sonatas).

Dalcroze, Émile Jaques. See Jaques-Dalcroze, Émile.

D'Alembert, Jean le Rond (b. Paris, 16 Nov. 1717; d. there, 29 Oct. 1783). Philosopher and mathematician. An illegitimate child, he was raised by a glazier; his father, an officer, had him admitted to the Collège Mazarin, where he excelled in law, graduating in 1738. He was Diderot's assistant in the initial stages of the *Encyclopédie,* contributing some 30 articles before leaving the project in 1758. Joining the Académie française in 1754, he served as its permanent secretary from 1772. His other writings deal with the Querelle des bouffons and with contemporary questions of theory and aesthetics; his influential *Éléments de musique théorique et pratique suivant les principes de M. Rameau* (1752) was later translated into German by Marpurg.

Dalhart, Vernon [Slaughter, Marion Try] (b. Jefferson, Tex., 6 Apr. 1883; d. Bridgeport, Conn., 14 Sept. 1948). Country singer. Began working in New York as an operatic tenor; his early recordings for Edison included light arias as well as popular songs. In 1924 he recorded two "hillbilly" songs, "The Wreck of the Old '97" and "The Prisoner's Song," which became internationally famous; thereafter he performed country material. He recorded many duets with Carson J. Robison.

Dall'Abaco, Evaristo Felice (b. Verona, 12 July 1675; d. Munich, 12 July 1742). Composer. Perhaps a cello and violin student of Torelli. Went to Modena in 1696 and performed often there alongside Vitali, among others. By 1704 he was cellist at the Bavarian court. He remained in the service of Elector Maximilian II Emmanuel through years of war and hardship that drove the court to Brussels (1704), Mons (1706), and Compiègne (1709), a period nonetheless influential in acquainting the composer with the French style. Maximilian returned to Munich in 1715; Dall'Abaco became *Konzertmeister* and electoral councillor. His influence waned under the new elector, Karl Albrecht (installed 1726); he retired with a pension in 1740. His extant music, contained in 6 printed collections issued between about 1708 and 1735, includes chamber and church sonatas along with concertos (selections ed. in *DTB* 1, 16, and n.s. 1). An indebtedness to Corelli in the earlier works yields later to both French-derived and *galant* elements.

Dallapiccola, Luigi (b. Pisino d'Istria, 3 Feb. 1904; d. Florence, 19 Feb. 1975). Composer and pianist. As a youth he studied piano (from 1912) and composition (from 1914); during the First World War the family was interned at Graz (March 1917–November 1918), where he heard performances of Mozart and Wagner. After they returned to Istria in 1919, he commuted to Trieste to study piano and harmony with Antonio Illersberg; in 1922 he moved to Florence to study piano with Ernesto Consolo and by 1924 had earned a diploma in piano from the conservatory there. He received a diploma in composition (1929–31) under Vito Frazzi, a follower of Pizzetti. During these years he came to know Debussy's music and stopped composing for some time (1921–24) in order to assimilate it; he also became acquainted with some early Italian music (Monteverdi, Gesualdo); in 1924 he heard a performance of Schoenberg's *Pierrot lunaire* organized by Casella. From 1926 he had an active career as a pianist; his duo with the violinist Sandro Materassi endured through 40 years of concerts often devoted to contemporary music. He was appointed professor of "pianoforte complementare" (he taught piano to composition students) at the Florence Conservatory in 1934, a position from which he retired in 1967. For several decades the trips occasioned by recitals enabled him to hear performances of unfamiliar music: in 1930 he heard Mahler's symphonies in Vienna; in 1934 he met Berg and studied the music of Berg, Schoenberg, and Webern; in 1937 he met Milhaud and Poulenc in Paris; in London in 1948 he heard a performance of Webern's "Das Augenlicht" (he had met Webern in Vienna in 1942). During the Second World War he restricted his concerts to Italy, Switzerland, and Hungary.

Dallapiccola was the first Italian composer to adopt the twelve-tone method; in *Liriche greche* (1942–45, a memorial to Webern) he first used the method strictly; in *Job* (1950) he limited himself for the first time to a single series. His use of the dodecaphonic method has been called idiosyncratic; nonetheless, his interest in complex contrapuntal procedures derives from his appreciation of Webern. His arrangements and editions of early Italian music are also reflected in his own compositions, a few of which are recastings of earlier material (*Tartiniana,* violin and orchestra, 1951). His self-quotation, eye music, and word painting are expressive devices in service of his chosen texts (in *Sicut umbra,* 1970, constellations are depicted in the notation of melodic or harmonic events). His experiences during the two world wars (he and his Jewish wife lived in hiding in or near Florence, October 1943–September 1944) help to explain another aspect of his output, the number of works concerned with liberty. *Canti di prigionia* (chorus, 2 pianos, 2 harps, percussion, 1938–41), written after Mussolini's announcement of anti-Semitic policies, uses two twelve-tone rows and fragments of the *Dies Irae* in setting the last words of Mary Stuart, Boethius, and Savonarola.

By 1940 his position as a composer was established in Italy, in part owing to the support he received from Casella; his international reputation developed after the war. He wrote for the publication *Il mondo europeo* beginning in 1945; in the late 1940s his works were widely performed in Europe (especially important was a performance of *Canti di prigionia* at the ISCM in London, 1946); he met Varèse during his trip to teach at the Berkshire Music Center in the summer of 1951 (where Berio was his student); he continued to lecture and perform widely in western Europe and the U.S. until 1972 (Instituto Torcuato di Tella, Buenos Aires, 1964; Dartmouth College and the Aspen Festival, 1969). He was recognized with membership in national academies of arts in several countries including the U.S., France, and England; in 1975 he was posthumously awarded the Albert Schweitzer Prize.

Other works include 3 operas (*Volo di notte,* after Saint-Exupéry, 1937–39; *Il prigioniero,* 1944–48), a ballet, and a sacred drama; 3 film scores; *2 pezzi* (1947, adapted from *2 studi,* violin, piano, 1946–47) and other works for orchestra, some with violin, cello, or piano soloist; chamber music (*Ciaccona, intermezzo, e adagio* for cello, 1945); piano pieces (*Quaderno musicale di Annalibera,* piano, 1952, adapted for orchestra as *Variazioni,* 1954); choral music, some with soloists and orchestra (*Canti di liberazione,* chorus and orchestra, 1951–55); songs (settings of Machado, Jiménez, Sappho, and others, with piano or chamber ensemble).

Writings: *Appunti, incontri, meditazioni* (Milan, 1970; 2nd enl. ed., *Parole e musica,* 1980). *Parole e musica* (Milan, 1980). Rudy Shackelford, ed., *Dallapiccola on Opera: Selected Writings* (London, 1988).

Bibl.: Roman Vlad, *Luigi Dallapiccola,* trans. Eng. (Milan, 1957; new trans. Cynthia Jolly, 1977). Calum MacDonald, ed., "Luigi Dallapiccola, the Complete Works: A Catalogue," *Tempo* (1976): 2–19. F. Nicolodi, ed., *Luigi Dallapiccola: Saggi, testimonianze, carteggio, biografia e bibliografia* (Milan, 1976). Dietrich Kämper, *Gefangenschaft und Freiheit: Leben und Werk des Komponisten Luigi Dallapiccola* (Cologne, 1984). Pierluigi Petrobelli et al., eds., *Studi su Luigi Dallapiccola: Un seminario* (Lucca, 1993).

Dalla Viola [della Viola], **Alfonso** (b. Ferrara, ca. 1508; d. there, ca. 1573). Composer and instrumentalist. Served the Este family for most of his adult life, beginning sometime before 1528; also *maestro di cappella* at the Cathedral of Ferrara from 1563 until 1572. Wrote music for plays performed in Ferrara between about 1541 and 1567 (all but one fragment lost) and a number of madrigals, including 2 books published in Ferrara in 1539 and 1540. He was highly praised as a performer on the viola d'arco.

Dalza, Joan Ambrosio (b. Milan?; fl. 1508). Lutenist and composer. Petrucci's *Intabolatura de lauto libro quarto* (Venice, 1508) consists of original compositions and arrangements by Dalza in a comparatively simple style. In contrast to its predecessors, this book includes only a few intabulations of vocal pieces. It gives valuable information on the grouping of pieces in performance.

Damase, Jean-Michel (b. Bordeaux, 27 Jan. 1928). French composer and pianist. He was precocious as a pianist and composer; at age 12 he studied with Cortot at the École normale, and then with Ferté (piano), Büsser (composition), and Dupré (harmony and counterpoint) at the Paris Conservatory; in 1947 his cantata *Et la belle se réveilla* won the Prix de Rome. His works include the opera *Euridice* (1972) and other stage works; a double concerto for flute, harp or harpsichord, and strings (1974), and other orchestral works; chamber music (a sonata for flute and harp, 1964); choral music and songs.

Dameron, Tadd [Tadley Ewing Peake] (b. Cleveland, 21 Feb. 1917; d. New York, 8 Mar. 1965). Jazz composer, arranger, bandleader, and pianist. He wrote for the big bands of Vido Musso, Harlan Leonard, Jimmy Lunceford, Benny Carter, Teddy Hill, Billy Eckstine, and Georgie Auld, and for Dizzy Gillespie's combo, which recorded "Good Bait" and "Hot House" (both 1945); Count Basie's orchestra later recorded "Good Bait" (1948). After writing for Sarah Vaughan and Gillespie's big band, he played piano, leading a bop group with Fats Navarro (1947–49) that recorded his compositions "Our Delight" (1947) and "Lady Bird" (1948). He played with Miles Davis at the Paris Jazz Fair (1949). Thereafter his career declined owing both to changes in fashionable styles and to his problems with narcotics.

Damoreau, Laure Cinti-. See Cinti-Damoreau, Laure.

Da Motta, José Vianna. See Vianna da Motta, José.

Damrosch, Frank (Heino) (b. Breslau, 22 Jun. 1859; d. New York, 22 Oct. 1937). Studied piano with Jean Vogt and Dionys Pruckner in Europe; with Ferdinand von Inten in the U.S. after his family emigrated in 1871. Studied conducting with his father, Leopold. Led the Denver Choral Club, 1882–85, then became chorusmaster at the New York Met. In the New York area led a variety of orchestral and choral organizations. Supervisor of music for the Denver public schools, 1884–85; director of music in the New York public schools, 1897–1905. In 1905 founded and until 1926 served as dean of the Institute of Musical Art; from 1926 to 1933 dean of the newly merged Institute of Musical Art of the Juilliard Foundation (reorganized in 1945 as the Juilliard School).

Damrosch, Leopold (b. Posen, 22 Oct. 1832; d. New York, 15 Feb. 1885). Conductor. After taking a degree in medicine at the Univ. of Berlin, he became a professional violinist and part of Liszt's Weimar circle; 1858–60, 1862–71, orchestra conductor at Breslau; from 1871 a prominent figure in New York music as choral and later orchestral conductor; 1884–85, director of the Metropolitan Opera, turning it to German opera and introducing Wagner's later works to the U.S. Father of Frank and Walter Damrosch.

Bibl.: George Martin, *The Damrosch Dynasty* (Boston, 1983).

Damrosch, Walter (Johannes) (b. Breslau, 30 Jan. 1862; d. New York, 22 Dec. 1950). Conductor and composer. Studied with his father, Leopold, with the theorist Wilhelm Rischbieter, the composer Anton Urspruch, and with Hans von Bülow before emigrating to the U.S. in 1871. Conductor of the Newark Harmonic Society from 1881. In 1885 inherited his father's post of musical director with the Symphony Society of New York and, also following his father, conducted some German works at the Met. Gave concert performances of *Götterdämmerung* and *Die Walküre* (1894), of *Parsifal* (1896, U.S. premiere). With the Damrosch Opera Company (1895–1900) he brought first-rate productions of German operas—and, after being joined by Nellie Melba in 1898, of Italian and French opera—to many U.S. cities. With the Symphony Society from 1903; led the first European tour by a U.S. orchestra in 1920 and the first radio broadcast of an orchestral concert in 1925. When in 1927 his orchestra merged with the New York Philharmonic Orchestra, he became musical counsel to NBC. Organized the Musicians' Emergency Fund. Wrote *My Musical Life* (New York, 1923). He composed assiduously throughout his adult life, finding particular success with choral and dramatic music. Of his 5 operas, *The Scarlet Letter* was performed by the Damrosch Opera Company (Boston, 1896); *Cyrano de Bergerac* and *The Man without a Country* at the Met in New York (1913 and 1937).

Dan, Ikuma (b. Tokyo, 7 Apr. 1924). Composer. In 1945 he graduated from the Tokyo Music School, where he had studied with Kan'ichi Shimofusa, Kunihiko Hashimoto, and Sabinō Moroi; from 1947 to 1950 he taught composition there. His Symphony no. 1 in A, composed for the Japan radio competition in 1950, launched a successful career; two years later his first opera *Yūzuru* (The Twilight Heron) was also received with wide acclaim both in Japan and abroad. In 1953 he cofounded in Tokyo with Akutagawa and Mayuzumi the Sannin no Kai (Three Men's Club). His music is diatonic, tending toward the lush and exotic. He has composed 5 operas (*Kikimimi zukin,* 1955; *Yō Kihi* [*Yang Kwei-fei*], 1958); choral cantatas (*Kaze ni ikiru,* baritone, chorus, orchestra, 1964); song cycles including *Mino-bito ni* (1950) and *8 Poems of Cocteau* (1962); 5 symphonies (1950–65), *The Silk Road* (1954), and other orchestral works; chamber works (string quartet, 1948).

Danckerts, Ghiselin (b. Tholen, Zeeland, ca. 1510; d. after August 1565). Theorist and composer. Singer in the Sistine Chapel from 1538 until retiring in August 1565. Composed a few motets and madrigals and some puzzle canons. In 1551 he helped to judge a debate between Nicola Vicentino and Vicente Lusitano on the ancient genera and their role in contemporary music. Shortly afterward, perhaps in the same year, the first of three versions of his unpublished theoretical treatise was written.

Bibl.: Lewis Lockwood, "A Dispute on Accidentals in Sixteenth-Century Rome," *AnMca* 2 (1965): 24.

Dancla, (Jean-Baptiste-) Charles (b. Bagnères de Bigorre, Hautes-Pyrénées, 19 Dec. 1817; d. Tunis, 9 or 10 Nov. 1907). Violinist, teacher, composer. Studied at the Paris Conservatory, 1828–40; played in Paris orchestras and as soloist and chamber musician (partly with his two brothers and a sister); 1848–50, small-town postmaster; 1850–56, postal official in Paris; from 1855 taught violin at the Conservatory, professor 1860–92. Composed 14 string quartets; 7 *symphonies concertantes;* violin methods; many etudes and other pieces. Published his memoirs, *Notes et souvenirs* (Paris, 1893; 2nd ed., 1898).

Dandelot, Georges (Édouard) (b. Paris, 2 Dec. 1895; d. St.-Georges-de-Didonne, 17 Aug. 1975). Composer and pianist. His teachers included Diémer, d'Indy, Roussel, Widor, and Dukas; he taught piano at the École normale de musique from 1919 and harmony at the Paris Conservatory from 1942. In addition to didactic works on solfège and harmony he composed operas (*Midas,* 1948) and ballets; a piano concerto (1934), a symphony (1941), and the *Concerto romantique* (violin and orchestra, 1944); an oratorio (*Pax,* 1937); chamber music, including sonatinas for flute (1938), violin (1946), and trumpet (1961) with piano; piano works (*Création du monde,* 1948); choral and vocal music.

Dandrieu, Jean-François (b. Paris ca. 1682; d. there, 17 Jan. 1738). Composer. Both he and his sister Jeanne Françoise were pupils of Moreau; he performed for Mme. Victoire de Bavière before he was 5. Served as unofficial organist at St. Merry from 1704 and was formally installed in 1705; followed his uncle Pierre as organist at St. Barthélemy (so mentioned in a 1710 print, though Pierre formally held the post until 1733); became one of the royal chapel organists in 1721. Highly regarded as a harpsichord composer, he issued several books of suites beginning about 1704 (many of the later pieces are revisions of earlier ones), and also produced trio sonatas, organ noëls (some of which may be the work of his uncle Pierre Dandrieu, d. 1733), and airs.

D'Anglebert, Jean-Henri (b. Paris, 1635; d. there, 23 Apr. 1691). Composer. Served as organist to the Duke of Orléans and to the Jacobins in the rue St. Honoré; appointed *ordinaire de la chambre du Roy pour le clavecin* in 1662, succeeding Chambonnières, and remained in the post until his death, though his son was named as his successor in 1674. His collection *Pièces de clavecin* (Paris, 1689) established him as the major clavecinist before Couperin; it contains 4 suites (each with an unmeasured prelude and with dance movements in the order allemande-courante-sarabande-gigue) along with keyboard arrangements of overtures, airs, and dances by Lully; the publication also includes a short treatise on harmony and the most detailed table of ornaments from the period.

Bibl.: *Jean Henry d'Anglebert: Pièces de clavecin* (New York, 1965) [facs. of 1689 ed.]. Kenneth Gilbert, ed., *Jean-Henri d'Anglebert: Pièces de clavecin* (Paris, 1975). Beverly Scheibert, *Jean-Henry D'Anglebert and the Seventeenth-Century Clavecin School* (Bloomington, Ind., 1986).

Daniel [Danyel], **John** (b. Wellow, near Bath, bapt. 6 Nov. 1564; d. ca. 1626). Lutenist and composer. Brother of the English court poet Samuel Daniel. Received the B.Mus. from Oxford in 1603; known to have been among the royal musicians from 1612 until 1625. Wrote a book of songs for lute, viol, and voice published in 1606 (ed. in *ELS,* 2nd ser., 8) and various pieces for lute(s).

Bibl.: David Scott, "John Danyel: His Life and Songs," *LSJ* 13 (1971): 7.

Daniel-Lesur [Lesur, Daniel Jean Yves] (b. Paris, 19 Nov. 1908). Composer, pianist, and organist. His mother studied composition with Tournemire, who became Daniel-Lesur's first teacher; he attended the Paris Conservatory (1919–29); assisted Tournemire as organist at Ste. Clotilde (1927–37); was organist of the Benedictine abbey in Paris (1937–44). He taught counterpoint at the Schola cantorum from 1935 and was its director, 1957–64. From 1939 he was associated with the French Radio, where he created the series *Nouvelles musicales.* In the 1960s and 1970s he served in various administrative posts in government. He cofounded the Groupe de la jeune France (1936) with Messiaen and others in opposition to the dominant neoclassical style; his own compositions remained rather traditional and often had a modal flavor. His opera *Andrea del Sarto* (1961–68) won the Prix Samuel-Rousseau of the Academy of Fine Arts. Other works include operas and ballets; a symphony (1973) and other orchestral music; *Suite médiévale* (flute, harp, and string trio, 1946) and other chamber music; piano and organ music (2 volumes of organ hymns); a Mass, cantatas, and folk song arrangements for chorus; songs.

Dankworth, John [Johnny] **(Philip William)** (b. London, 20 Sept. 1927). English saxophonist, bandleader, composer, and arranger. He studied at the Royal Academy of Music (1944–46). He led a bop group, The

Johnny Dankworth Seven (1950–53), and a big band from 1953, which recorded his jazz suite *What the Dickens!* (1963). He also wrote film scores, including the soundtracks to *The Servant* (1964) and *Darling* (1965). From 1971 he led a group (generally 10 pieces) to accompany his wife, Cleo Laine (who had sung with him from 1952). They achieved an extraordinary rapport, with Dankworth imitating Laine's complicated improvised lines. From the early 1980s his regular ensemble was a quintet, though he led a big band occasionally. With Laine he formed in 1969 the Wavendon Allmusic Plan near Milton Keynes, England, offering workshops and performances in many genres.

Dannreuther, Edward (George) (b. Strasbourg, 4 Nov. 1844; d. London, 12 Feb. 1905). Pianist and writer. Studied at Leipzig Conservatory (1859–63) with Moscheles, Hauptmann, and Richter; from 1863 a prominent figure in English musical life as pianist (introduced concertos of Liszt, Tchaikovsky, Grieg), chamber musician (1874–93, gave chamber music concerts in his London house), piano teacher (from 1895 at the Royal Academy). One of the foremost English Wagnerians, in 1872 he founded the English Wagner Society; 1873–74, conducted its concerts; 1877, helped organize London Wagner Festival; lecturer, and writer of books on Wagner and on ornamentation.

Bibl.: "Edward Dannreuther," *MT* 39 (1898): 645–54.

Danyel, John. See Daniel, John.

Danzi, Franz (Ignaz) (b. Schwetzingen, 15 June 1763; d. Karlsruhe, 13 Apr. 1826). Composer. From a musical family, his father, Innocenz (d. 1798), having been a cellist in the Mannheim orchestra. Remained in Mannheim when the court moved to Munich in 1778, studying with Abbé Vogler and playing in the orchestra of the National Theater, where his first German opera was produced in 1780; much incidental music also produced through 1783, when he became cellist in the Munich orchestra. In 1790 he married the singer Margarethe Marchand (1768–1800), a pupil of Leopold Mozart, and toured widely with her until 1796, when they settled again in Munich; became deputy Kapellmeister, 1798, resigning after his wife's death; 1807, Kapellmeister at Stuttgart; 1812, Kapellmeister at Karlsruhe. Composed in most theatrical genres. The most widely performed of his many singspiels was *Die Mitternachtsstunde* (Munich, 1788). Other works include symphonies, concertos, much chamber music; an oratorio; sacred music; cantatas; piano pieces; songs.

Da Ponte, Lorenzo (b. Ceneda [Vittorio Veneto], 10 Mar. 1749; d. New York, 17 Aug. 1838). Poet and librettist. He was born Emmanuele Conegliano; when his Jewish father converted to Christianity in 1763 in order to marry Orsola Paietta, Emmanuele, his eldest son by a previous marriage, assumed the name of the Bishop of Ceneda, Lorenzo Da Ponte. The boy's early schooling was at the Ceneda Seminary, and in 1768 he took priestly orders. The following year he moved to Portogruaro, where he taught literature and was ordained a priest in 1770. His early collection of poems *Dittirambo sopra gli odori* was published ca. 1772. In 1774 he became professor of literature at Tiepolo but was dismissed two years later, allegedly for his Rousseau-like views on the laws of man and nature; in 1779 he was banned from the Republic of Venice altogether for adultery. He settled in Gorizia until around 1780, when he began frequently to be present in Vienna. Upon the recommendation of Salieri and the poet Mazzolà, in 1783 he was taken on by Joseph II as imperial court poet for Vienna's Italian theater. There he authored a series of extraordinary texts, including *Le nozze di Figaro* (1786) for Mozart, *Il burbero di buon cuore* and *Una cosa rara* (both 1786) for Martín y Soler, *Don Giovanni* (1787) for Mozart, *Axur, Rè d'Ormus* (1788) for Salieri, *Così fan tutte* (1790) for Mozart, and more than 40 others.

Intrigue drove Da Ponte from the imperial service in 1791; in 1793 he gained a post as librettist for the King's Theatre, London. Deep in debt, he emigrated to New York in 1805; there he taught Italian language and literature at Columbia College, wrote his celebrated *Memorie* (New York, 1823–27; trans. Eng. L. A. Sheppard, London, 1929; ed. A. Livingston and E. Abbot, Philadelphia, 1929; R: 1967), and strove to establish Italian opera in the city. With Manuel Garcia's troupe he brought a highly successful production of *Don Giovanni* to the New York stage in 1825.

Bibl.: Arthur Livingston, *Da Ponte in America* (Philadelphia, 1930). April FitzLyon, *The Libertine Librettist: A Biography of Mozart's Librettist Lorenzo Da Ponte* (London, 1955; R: as *Lorenzo da Ponte,* New York, 1955). Otto Michtner, "Der Fall Abbé Da Ponte," *Mitteilungen des Österreichischen Staatsarchivs* 19 (1966): 170–209.

Daquin, Louis-Claude (b. Paris, 4 July 1694; d. there, 15 June 1772). Composer. Performed for Louis XIV at age 6; pupil of Marchand in organ and Bernier in composition; named organist at Petit St. Antoine in 1706 and was chosen over Rameau as organist at St. Paul in 1727. Took the same post at the Cordeliers in 1732, succeeded Dandrieu as *organiste du Roi* in 1739, and served at Notre Dame beginning in 1755. He was regarded as the best organist of his generation; the *Lettres* of his son give a laudatory account of his life. His extant works are found in 2 prints, the *Premier livre de pièces de clavecin* (1735), containing 4 suites, and the *Nouveau livre de noëls* (ca. 1740), with 12 carol settings for keyboard and other instruments.

Bibl.: Jean-Paul Montagnier, *La vie et l'oeuvre de Louis-Claude Daquin (1694–1772)* (Lyon, 1992).

Darclée, Hariclea [Haricly Hartulary] (b. Braila, 10 June 1860; d. Bucharest, 10 or 12 Jan. 1939). Soprano. Studied in Paris with J. B. Faure; 1888, debut, Paris Opéra in *Faust;* sang much in Italy, Spain, and Russia, and several times in South America; ranged from coloratura to dramatic roles; created title roles in Catalani's *La Wally* (1892) and Puccini's *Tosca* (1900); fine voice and technique but sometimes found lacking in temperament; her voice began to decline around 1905, and she retired in 1918.

Dargomïzhsky, Alexander Sergeyevich (b. Troitskoye, Tula district, 14 Feb. 1813; d. St. Petersburg, 17 Jan. 1869). Composer. The son of a wealthy landowner and a poet, he had early lessons in singing, piano, and violin. He entered government service in 1827, regarding music as a leisure activity. In the winter of 1833–34 he met Glinka, who inspired him to compose his first opera, *Esmeralda* (1841; first perf. 1847). His disappointment over the scant success of this work was tempered by the attentions of his female singing pupils, for whom he wrote a number of songs. In 1843 he resigned from the civil service and went abroad the following year. In Brussels he met Fétis and Auber, and in Paris he met Meyerbeer and Halévy. Upon his return to Russia in 1845 he made studies of Russian folk song and the intonation of Russian speech, the results of which are evident in the opera *Rusalka* (1855). In 1859 he was elected to the committee of the Russian Musical Society; in 1867 he became the society's president. From 1864 to 1865 he visited Warsaw, Leipzig, Paris, London, and Brussels, where his works were enthusiastically received. Upon returning to Russia he resolved to set Pushkin's *The Stone Guest;* the opera lay unfinished at his death, but was completed by Cui and Rimsky-Korsakov. First given in 1872, it never achieved the popularity of *Rusalka.* The influence this opera exerted on the young group of Russian composers known as the *moguchaya Kuchka* ("The Five") has perhaps been overstated. In addition to his operas, Dargomïzhsky wrote several orchestral works, numerous songs, and pieces for piano.

Bibl.: Mikhail Samoilovich Pekelis, *Dargomïzhsky i narodnaya pesnya* [Dargomïzhsky and Folk Song] (Moscow, 1951). Richard Taruskin, "Realism as Preached and Practiced: The Russian Opera Dialogue," *MQ* 56 (1970): 431–54. Jennifer Baker, "Dargomïzhsky, Realism, and *The Stone Guest,*" *MR* 37 (1976): 193–208. Richard Taruskin, "How the Acorn Took Root: A Tale about Russia," *19th-Century Music* 6/3 (1983): 189–212. Corre Berry, "Vocal Duets by Nineteenth-Century Russian Composers," *MR* 45/1 (1984): 1–6. I. Medvedeva, *Dargomïzhsky* (Moscow, 1988).

Darke, Harold (Edwin) (b. London, 29 Oct. 1888; d. Cambridge, 28 Nov. 1976). Organist and composer. At the Royal College of Music he studied organ with Walter Parratt, piano with Herbert Sharpe, and composition with Charles Stanford. He was organist at St. Michael's, Cornhill, in London (1916–69), and taught at the Royal College (1919–69). In 1919 he founded the St. Michael's Singers; in 1924 the City of London Choral Union. During World War II he substituted for organist Boris Ord at the chapel of King's College, Cambridge; from 1945 to 1949 he was a Fellow of the College. He composed *Ye Watchers,* female chorus (1923); the cantata *The Sower* (1929); *A Song of David,* chorus, orchestra (1956); much church music; also orchestral music, chamber music, songs, and organ pieces.

Dart, (Robert) Thurston (b. Kingston, Surrey, 3 Sept. 1921; d. London, 6 Mar. 1971). Musicologist and harpsichordist. Studied music at the Royal College of Music, 1938–39, then mathematics at London University; B.A., 1942. After service in the R.A.F he studied musicology with Charles van den Borren in Brussels. Assistant lecturer in music at Cambridge from 1947; M.A., Cambridge, 1948; full lecturer from 1952. Edited the *Galpin Society Journal,* 1948–58. Wrote an influential book on performance practice, *The Interpretation of Music* (London, 1954), and published numerous articles and editions. Founded 1955 and led through 1959 the Philomusica of London; with them and other artists and as a soloist he recorded much music of the Baroque. Professor of music at Cambridge, 1962–64; professor at King's College, London University, 1964–71.

Daser, Ludwig (b. Munich, ca. 1525; d. Stuttgart, 27 Mar. 1589). Composer. Until 1563, when he was succeeded by Lassus, he was associated with the Bavarian Hofkapelle at Munich, rising gradually from student to Kapellmeister. In 1572 became Kapellmeister of the Protestant court at Stuttgart, remaining there until his death. His works include Latin Masses and motets and German hymns and Psalms, written in a generally conservative style.

Daube, Johann Friedrich (b. Hesse? ca. 1730; d. Vienna, 19 Sept. 1797). Theorist, chamber musician, and composer. He began as a player of the theorbo, first at Frederick II's court in Berlin (from ca. 1740), later at the Prince of Württemberg's court at Stuttgart (1744–65 or later). After 1770 he lived in Vienna, where he was secretary to the Franciscan Academy of Free Arts and Sciences. He authored 3 important treatises on the theory, style, and aesthetics of music: *General-Bass in drey Accorden, gegründet in den Regeln der alt- und neuen Autoren* (Leipzig, 1756); *Der musikalische Dilettant* (1770–73); and *Anleitung zur Erfindung der Melodie und ihrer Fortsetzung* (1797). Of special significance are the instructions in his *Anleitung* for the composition of melodies. He also composed some instrumental music.

Daugherty, Michael (b. Cedar Rapids, Iowa, 28 Apr. 1954). Composer. He earned an M.A. at the Manhattan School of Music in 1976, where he studied with Charles Wuorinen. He also attended Yale, where he earned an M.M.A. in 1982 and a D.M.A. in 1986. His teachers there included Jacob Druckman, Earle Brown, Roger Reynolds, Bernard Rands, and Gil Evans. He studied in Paris at IRCAM from 1978 to 1980, and then with Ligeti at the Hochschule für Musik in Hamburg from 1982 to 1984. From 1986 on the faculty at Oberlin. Orchestral works include *5 Seasons* (1980); *Mxyzptlk,*

2 flute soloists and chamber orchestra (1988); *Oh Lois!* (1989); *Lex* (1990). Chamber works include *Future Music, Part 1* (1984); *Future Funk* (1985); *Piano Plus* (1985); *Re:Percussion* (1986); *Blue Like an Orange* (1987); *SNAP!* (1987); *Celestial Hoops IV* (1987); *Bounce I* (1988); *Lex* (1989).

Dauprat, Louis-François (b. Paris, 24 May 1781; d. there, 16 or 17 July 1868). Horn player, teacher, composer. Studied the horn (1794–98), later theory and composition (1801–5, 1811–14) at the Paris Conservatory; played in military bands, then in theater orchestras (Grand Théâtre, Bordeaux, 1806–8; from 1808, Paris Opéra, in 1817–31 as first horn); 1828, founding member of the Conservatory orchestra; from 1802, adjunct teacher at the Conservatory, professor from 1816; retired 1842. Composed concertos, chamber music, an important horn method, many exercises.

Dauvergne [D'Auvergne], **Antoine** (b. Moulins, 3 Oct. 1713; d. Lyons, 11 Feb. 1797). Composer and violinist. His first employment as violinist was at Clermont-Ferrand; during the 1730s he moved to Paris, where from 1739 he was chamber musician for the royal court. From 1744 he played in the orchestra of the Opéra. In 1752 his first stage work, *Les amours de Tempé* (a ballet), appeared at the height of the Querelle des bouffons; it was the first of a series of Dauvergne successes. During the next two decades he held important posts, including that of court composer (from 1755), *Maître du chambre du roi* (from ca. 1755), director of the Concert spirituel (from 1762) and of the Opéra (from 1769), and finally musical *surintendant* of the court. Among his theater works were *Les troquers* (1753), *Énée et Lavinie* (1758), *Hercule mourant* (1761), and *Le prix de la valeur* (1771). He also composed vocal works, including motets, and instrumental music, including violin sonatas (6 sonatas op. 1; 12 sonatas op. 2).

Bibl.: Lionel de La Laurencie, "Deux imitateurs français des Bouffons: Blavet et Dauvergne," *Année musicale* 2 (1912): 65–125.

David, Félicien (-César) (b. Cadenet, Vaucluse, 13 Apr. 1810; d. St.-Germain-en-Laye, 29 Aug. 1876). Composer. Son of a goldsmith; orphaned as a child; from age 7 a choirboy at St.-Sauveur in Aix, where, after three years at the Jesuit college also in Aix, he was choirmaster, 1828–30. From spring 1830 a small allowance from an uncle let him study a year at the Paris Conservatory (Benoist, Fétis, Reber). He then lived miserably, giving lessons until 1832 when he joined the Saint-Simonian cult, becoming a favorite of its "father," Prosper Enfantine, and withdrawing with the faithful to the cult's community at Ménilmontant outside Paris, where he composed many hymns for cult ceremonies. From March 1833 to June 1835, with other Saint-Simonian "apostles" he visited Istanbul, Smyrna, Jerusalem, Egypt; the exotic musical and cultural impressions of this trip determined his direction as a composer. In 1836 he published 22 *Mélodies orientales* for piano; composed 2 symphonies, 1837–38 (2 more in 1846–49); lived obscurely until he became an overnight celebrity with his ode-symphony *Le désert,* which he conducted in Paris (8 Dec. 1844) to tremendous popular and critical acclaim; 1845, toured France, northern Italy, central Europe, and Germany conducting it; then produced an oratorio *Moïse au Sinai* (1846), the ode-symphony *Christoph Colomb* (1847), and the oratorio *Eden* (1848), of which only the ode-symphony was well received. All had Saint-Simonian implications, less evident in the operas that followed: the moderately successful *La perle de Brésil* (1851); the coldly received grand opera *Herculaneum* (1859); *Lalla Roukh* (Opéra-comique, 1862), his most popular opera; *Le saphir* (1865), a failure; *La captive,* never performed. In 1869 he succeeded Berlioz at the Institute and as librarian of the Paris Conservatory. Other works include *Les quatre saisons* (24 string quintets), chamber music, choral pieces, songs, piano pieces.

Bibl.: Peter Gradenwitz, "Félicien David (1810–1876) and French Romantic Orientalism," *MQ* 62 (1976): 471–506. Dorothy Veinus Hagan, *Félicien David, 1810–1876: A Composer and a Cause* (Syracuse, 1985).

David, Ferdinand (b. Hamburg, 19 Jan. 1810; d. Klosters, Switzerland, 18 July 1873). Violinist, composer, teacher. In 1823 studied in Kassel with Spohr (violin) and Hauptmann (theory); 1823–25, toured with his sister, a pianist; 1826–29, violinist, Königstadt Theater, Berlin; 1829–35, played in a private quartet, Tartu, Estonia; 1836–73, concertmaster, Gewandhaus Orchestra, Leipzig, initially under his close friend Mendelssohn, and at the Stadttheater, also director of Leipzig church music; from 1843, head of the violin department at the new Leipzig Conservatory (pupils include Joachim, Wilhelmj, Wasielewski). He advised Mendelssohn on his Violin Concerto and played its premiere (1845); published widely used *Violinschule* (1863) and etudes; edited much violin music; a prolific composer (including 5 violin concertos and other solo works, chamber music, choral pieces, songs). Neither a great virtuoso nor a highly regarded composer but one of the most generally respected musicians of his time.

Dávid, Gyula (b. Budapest, 6 May 1913; d. there, 14 Mar. 1977). Composer. At the Budapest Academy of Music he studied composition with Kodály (from 1938). After World War II he conducted at the National Theater (1945–49). Professor of wind chamber music at the academy, 1950–60; professor of chamber music at the Budapest Conservatory from 1964 and at the teachers' training college of the academy from 1967. His music reflects the influence of folk song research that he carried out under Kodály's aegis; it also incorporates elements of pre-Baroque music, but does not eschew twelve-tone composition. Works include 4 symphonies (1947–70); concertos for viola (1950), violin (1966), and horn (1971); choral works including

Dob és tánc (1961), *Four Madrigals* (1966); 5 wind quintets (1949–68); 2 string quartets (1962, 1973); *Miniatűrök,* brass sextet (1968); a piano trio (1972); and sonatas for violin, viola, flute, and solo piano.

David, Johann Nepomuk (b. Eferding, Upper Austria, 30 Nov. 1895; d. Stuttgart, 22 Dec. 1977). Composer. He taught primary school before the war and then studied composition with Joseph Marx in Vienna (1920–23); for the next decade he taught school and was organist and choirmaster in Wels. In 1934 he began teaching at the Leipzig Landeskonservatorium (director from 1942); director of the Salzburg Mozarteum (1945–48) and then of the Stuttgart Hochschule für Musik (1948–63). He destroyed works composed before 1927, including much chamber music and songs; many others were lost in the 1943 bombing of Leipzig. Most of his works exhibit an emphasis on craftsmanship and counterpoint similar to that found in the music of Hindemith; he remained committed to conventional methods, but used more and more chromaticism, and even a twelve-tone series in compositions with a strong tonal center (Violin Concerto, 1957); his organ music constitutes a compendium of technique and polyphonic practice after Reger. Extant works include 8 symphonies (1936–65), an organ concerto (1965), and other orchestral music; organ music (including *12 Orgelfugen durch alle Tonarten,* 1968; *Das Choralwerk,* 21 vols., 1932–75); a partita for violin and organ (1975); *Requiem Chorale* (1956), *Komm heiliger Geist* (2 choruses, orchestra, 1972), and other choral music; folk song arrangements for chorus.

Bibl.: Hans Heinz Stuckenschmidt, *Johann Nepomuk David* (Wiesbaden, 1965).

Davïdov, Karl Yul'yevich (b. Goldingen, Courland [now Kuldiga, Latvia], 15 March 1838; d. Moscow, 26 Feb. 1889). Cellist and composer. He studied cello in Moscow with Schmidt and Schuberth while taking a university degree in mathematics. In 1858 he studied composition with Moritz Hauptmann in Leipzig, where he won recognition as a cellist. In 1859 he became principal cellist of the Gewandhaus Orchestra and professor at the Leipzig Conservatory. He returned to Russia in 1862 to take similar posts in the St. Petersburg Opera Orchestra and Conservatory, serving as the conservatory's director, 1876–86. He concertized extensively in Russia and the West. His compositions include 4 concertos and other works for cello and orchestra, chamber music, songs, and a technical method for the cello (1888).

Davïdov [Dawydov], **Stepan Ivanovich** (b. Ukraine? 1777; d. St. Petersburg, 22 May 1825). Composer. As a boy he sang in the court chapel choir at St. Petersburg; there he probably also took music instruction from Giuseppe Sarti. From 1800 he taught singing and acting at the St. Petersburg Drama School, and from 1804 to 1810 he composed stage music for the school. After 1815 he contributed works for the private theater of Count Sheremetev near Moscow. Most of his surviving works are for the stage; they include operas (*Uvenchannaya blagost',* 1801; *Lesta, dneprovskaya rusalka,* 1805; *Rusalka,* 1807); ballets and divertissements (*Torzhestvo pobedï,* 1814–15); a cantata, *Apollon u Admeta* (1817); sacred music (including 13 vocal concertos).

Davidovich, Bella (Muhazhlovna) (b. Baku, Azerbaijan, 16 July 1928). Pianist. Studied with her mother, then at the Moscow Conservatory (1947–54) with Yakov Fliyer and Heinrich Neuhaus. In 1949 shared first prize (with Halina Stefanska-Czerny) in the Chopin Competition, Warsaw. Soloist with the Moscow State Philharmonic, 1957. In 1962 joined the faculty of the Moscow Conservatory. Toured Holland, 1967; Italy, 1971. In 1978 her son, the violinist Dmitri Sitkovetski, emigrated to the U.S.; in 1979 she followed him. Her U.S. debut at Carnegie Hall in 1979 excited much favorable comment and led to an active performing and recording career in the West.

Davidovsky, Mario (b. Buenos Aires, 4 Mar. 1934). Composer and teacher. Studied composition in Buenos Aires with Guillermo Graetzer and others; and with Babbitt (whom he met at the Berkshire Music Center in 1958) at the Columbia–Princeton Electronic Music Center (1960). After several visiting appointments (1964–69), he taught primarily at City College of New York (1968–80), Columbia (1981–95, where he was director of the Electronic Music Center), and Harvard (beginning 1995). He was composer-in-residence at the Berkshire Music Festival, 1981. He is best known for his combination of electronic and traditional instrumental sounds, especially in the series of pieces titled *Synchronism* (1963–74); in 1971 he won the Pulitzer Prize for *Synchronism 6* (piano and tape, 1970). His aim in such combinations was "to integrate all levels of sound—both the electronic media and the conventional instrumental media—into one single coherent musical space." *Synchronism 7* (1973) was premiered by the New York Philharmonic under Boulez. Works for conventional instruments dominated his later output.

Works: *Synchronisms 1–8* (various instrument(s)/voices and tape, 1963–74); *Contrastes* no. 1 (string orchestra and tape, 1960); Divertimento for Cello and Orchestra (1984); *Shulamits' Dreams* (1993); *Inflexions* (chamber ensemble, 1965), *Chacona* (piano trio, 1971), 4 string quartets (1954, 1958, 1976, 1980), string trio (1982), *Capriccio* (2 pianos, 1985), and other chamber music; *Scenes from Shir-ha-Shirim* (soprano, 2 tenors, bass, chorus, and orchestra, 1975); *Romancero* (early Spanish texts for soprano, flute, clarinet, violin, cello, 1983); 3 studies for tape (1960s).

Davies, Dennis Russell (b. Toledo, Ohio, 16 Apr. 1944). Conductor. At Juilliard (1962–72) he studied piano with Lonny Epstein and Sascha Gorodnitzki, conducting with Jorge Mester and Jean Morel; taught at Juilliard, 1968–71; music director of the Norwalk Symphony Orchestra, 1968–72. With Berio he founded the Juilliard Ensemble (later called the Ensemble), leading it, 1968–74. Debut as an opera conductor with the Santa Fe Opera, 1970 (Berio's *Opera*). Conductor of the St. Paul Chamber Orchestra, 1972–80. Led *Pelléas* with the Netherlands Opera, 1974; *Der fliegende Holländer* at Bayreuth, 1978. Music director of the American Composers Orchestra from 1977; music director of the Württemberg State Opera, Stuttgart, from 1980; principal conductor and program director of the Saratoga Performing Arts Center, 1985–88; *Generalmusikdirektor* of the city of Bonn (1987–1995); music director, Brooklyn Academy of Music, and principal conductor, Brooklyn Philharmonic, from 1990.

Davies, Fanny (b. Guernsey, 27 June 1861; d. London, 1 Sept. 1934). Pianist. Studied at the Leipzig Conservatory (1882–83) and at the Frankfurt Conservatory (1883–85) with Clara Schumann, whom she emulated in high seriousness and musicianship. From 1885 prominent in England as soloist and chamber player; from 1887 played much on the Continent. She introduced several Brahms works in England and was a pioneer in the revival of English virginal music.

Davies, Hugh (Seymour) (b. Exmouth, 23 Apr. 1943). Composer. He attended Oxford, 1961–64; worked with Stockhausen as an assistant and member of his electronic music group, 1964–66. In 1967 he became director of the electronic music studio at Goldsmiths' College in London. He constructs his own instruments and sound sculptures, and is interested in improvisation and indeterminacy. In addition to electronic music and music for his own instruments, he has written for traditional instruments.

Works for invented instruments: *Shozyg I, II, I + II* (1968); *Spring Song* (1970); *HD Breadbins* (1972); *Gentle Springs* (1973); *Music for Bowed Diaphragms* (1973); *My Spring Collection* (1975); *Salad* (1977); *The Search for the Music of the Spheres* (1978); *At Home* (1975). Chamber music for traditional and electronic forces: *Contact* (1963); *Vom ertrunkenen Mädchen* (1964); *Quintet* (live electronics, 1967–68); *Interfaces* (tape, live electronics, 1967–68); *Kangaroo* (1968); *Beautiful Seaweeds* (players, dancers, slides, 1972–73); *Raisonnements* (1973); *Wind Trio* (1973–75); *The Musical Educator* (speakers, players, dancers, slides, 1974); *Natural Images* (tape, 1976); *Melodic Gestures* (1978); *Ex una voce* (1979).

Davies, Peter Maxwell (b. Manchester, 8 Sept. 1934). Composer. Studied at the Royal Manchester College of Music (from 1952) and at Manchester Univ., where he wrote a dissertation on Indian music. Upon completing his studies in 1957, he received a scholarship for further study with Petrassi in Rome; his first major orchestral work, *Prolation,* was performed at the ISCM festival there in 1959. That year he returned to England as director of the Cirencester Grammar School. From 1962 to 1964 he was at Princeton on a Harkness Fellowship. His interest in pre-Baroque music found expression in works such as *Veni Sancte Spiritus* (chorus and chamber orchestra, 1963) and the 2 orchestral fantasias (1962 and 1964) on an *In nomine* by John Taverner, and in the opera *Taverner,* completed in 1970. In 1966 he was in Australia, where he was composer-in-residence at the Univ. of Adelaide. Upon returning to England he collaborated with Birtwistle in forming in 1967 the Pierrot Players, a chamber ensemble similar to that required to play Schoenberg's *Pierrot lunaire.* He composed many of his subsequent works for this ensemble (which was reorganized in 1970 as the Fires of London), including theater works *Revelation and Fall* (first perf., 1968), the well-known *Eight Songs for a Mad King* (male singer, chamber ensemble, 1969), *Vesalii icones* (with male dancer, 1969), *L'homme armé* (first perf., 1971), and *Miss Donnithorne's Maggot* (1974); also film scores *The Devils* and *The Boy Friend* (both 1971). He moved to the Orkney Islands in 1971. He was knighted in 1987. Appointed Associate Conductor/Composer of the BBC Philharmonic in Manchester and of the Royal Philharmonic Orchestra in London in 1992.

Other dramatic works include *Blind Man's Bluff* (masque, 1972), *The Martyrdom of St. Magnus* (chamber opera, 1976), *Salome* (ballet, 1978), *The Lighthouse* (chamber opera, 1979), *The Rainbow* (1981), *Resurrection* (one-act opera, 1988). Choral works include *Te lucis ante terminum* (1961), *The Shepherd's Calendar* (1965), *Westerlings* (1976); other vocal works include *Stone Litany* (1973), *Anakreontika* (1976). Orchestral works include *St. Thomas Wake: Foxtrot for Orchestra* (1969), 5 symphonies (1976, 1980, 1984, 1989, 1994), *A Mirror of Whitening Light* (1976–77), *Image, Reflection, Shadow* (1981), *Sinfonia concertante* (1982), *Sinfonietta accademica* (1983), a violin concerto (1986), an oboe concerto (1988), 2 trumpet concertos (1988, 1990), *Cross Lane Fair* (1994), *Strathclyde concerto no. 10* (for orchestra; 1995). Chamber works and pieces for solo instruments, some based on or evoking music of the Middle Ages and Renaissance, include *Ave maris stella* (flute, clarinet, marimba, piano, viola, cello, 1975), *Little Quartet* (string quartet no. 1, 1980; no. 2, 1981), a brass quintet (1981), a piano sonata (1981), an organ sonata (1982).

Bibl.: *Peter Maxwell Davies: The Complete Catalogue of Published Works,* ed. Judy Arnold (London, 1981). Stephan Pruslin, ed., *Peter Maxwell Davies: Studies from Two Decades, Tempo,* booklet 2 (London, 1979). Paul Griffiths, *Peter Maxwell Davies* (London, 1982). Colin Bayliss, ed., *The Music of Sir Peter Maxwell Davies: An Annotated Catalogue* (Beverley, 1991).

Davies, (Henry) Walford (b. Oswestry, Shropshire, 6 Sept. 1869; d. Wrington, Somerset, 11 Mar. 1941). Organist and composer. At St. George's Chapel, Windsor, he studied organ with Parratt and was organist from 1885 to 1890. From 1890 he studied composition on scholarship at the Royal College of Music with Parry and Stanford. From 1891 he was organist at Christ Church, Hampstead; from 1898 at the Temple Church, London; he returned to St. George's Chapel in

1927; taught at the Royal College (from 1895), and at the Univ. of Wales (1919–26). In 1917 he was appointed R.A.F. music director, and in 1934 he was made Master of the King's Musick, succeeding Elgar. He composed an oratorio, *Everyman* (1904); sacred choral and organ music; 2 violin sonatas; part songs. His interest in music education found fruition in a series of BBC broadcasts titled *Music and the Ordinary Listener* (1926–29). He was knighted in 1922.

Davis, Andrew (Frank) (b. Ashridge, Hertfordshire, 2 Feb. 1944). Conductor and organist. Studied organ with Peter Hurford and Piet Kee at the Royal Academy of Music and at Kings College, Cambridge, 1963–67; conducting with Franco Ferrara at the Accademia di S. Cecilia in Rome, 1968. Came to wider attention when he substituted for Inbal and Rozhdestvensky with the BBC Symphony, 1970. Associate conductor of the BBC Scottish Orchestra, 1970–71; of the New Philharmonia, 1973–74. Opera debut at Glyndebourne, 1973, with *Capriccio.* Musical director of the Toronto Symphony, 1975–88; chief conductor of the BBC Symphony from 1988; music director of the Glyndebourne Festival from 1989.

Davis, Anthony (b. Paterson, N.J., 20 Feb. 1951). Jazz and avant-garde pianist and composer. He studied music at Yale University (B.A., 1975) and played free jazz with the trombonist George Lewis (1973) and the trumpeter Leo Smith (1974–77). After moving to New York he joined Leroy Jenkins's trio (1977–79) and worked with James Newton (beginning 1978) in duos, trios, quartets, and Davis's octet Episteme, formed in 1981. The album *Episteme* (ca. 1981) and his unaccompanied album *Past Lives* (1978) suggest the range of his work, from atonal music to pieces based on music for gamelan. *X,* an opera about Malcolm X, was given in Philadelphia (1985) and New York (1986); the opera *Under the Double Moon* was performed in St. Louis in 1989. He wrote music to Kushner's play *Angels in America: Millenium Approaches* (1993). Other works include: Violin sonata (1991); *It Was . . .,* soprano, ensemble (1992); *Tania,* opera (1992); *ESU Variations,* orchestra (1995).

Davis, Colin (Rex) (b. Weybridge, Surrey, 25 Sept. 1927). Conductor. Studied clarinet with Thurston at the Royal College of Music. Like Beecham he was an autodidact in conducting. Began his career in Sweden with the Kalmar Chamber Orchestra, 1949. With the Chelsea Opera Group he led *Don Giovanni,* 1950. Assistant conductor, BBC Scottish Orchestra, 1957–59. He made his operatic mark with Mozart, leading an acclaimed *Die Entführung aus dem Serail* at Sadler's Wells, 1958. With the Philharmonia Orchestra, 1959, substituted for Klemperer in *Don Giovanni;* at Glyndebourne, 1960, substituted for Beecham in *Die Zauberflöte.* U.S. debut with Minneapolis Symphony, 1961. Principal conductor, Sadler's Wells, 1961–64; chief conductor, BBC Symphony, 1967–71. Appointed principal guest conductor of the London Symphony, the Boston Symphony, and the Amsterdam Concertgebouw Orchestra, 1971. Musical director, Covent Garden, 1971–86. Debut at New York Met, 1968, with *Peter Grimes;* at Bayreuth, 1977, with *Tannhauser.* Knighted, 1980. Music director, Bavarian Radio Symphony, from 1983. Appointed music director, London Symphony, 1995. Led the premieres of Henze's *Ariosi* (1964) and *Tristan* (1974), Tippett's *The Knot Garden* (1970) and *The Ice Break* (1978). Closely identified with Berlioz and Sibelius in the concert hall and in recordings.

Davis, Eddie "Lockjaw" (b. New York, 2 Mar. 1922; d. Culver City, Calif., 3 Nov. 1986). Jazz tenor saxophonist. After joining the big bands of Cootie Williams (1942–44), Lucky Millinder (1944), Andy Kirk (1945–46), and Louis Armstrong, he led combos, except for a period as a principal soloist with Count Basie (1952–53, 1957). His group including organist Shirley Scott (1955–60) recorded the soulful albums collectively called *The Eddie Lockjaw Davis Cookbook* (1958). His quintet with Johnny Griffin (1960–62) recorded the album *Tough Tenors* (1960). He rejoined Basie's big band (1964–73), then worked again in combos, sharing leadership with Harry Edison in a quintet (1975–82) that recorded the album *Light and Lovely* (1975).

Davis, Rev(erend) **Gary (D.)** [Blind Gary] (b. Laurens, S.C., 30 Apr. 1896; d. Hammonton, N.J., 5 May 1972). Ragtime guitarist, blues and gospel singer. He played in a string band in Greenville, S.C. (ca. 1912), which pioneered a local blues and ragtime guitar style. A street singer in Asheville (1922) and Durham (from 1926), he drew welfare until moving to New York (1944). He recorded blues (including "Cross and Evil Woman Blues"), preaching songs ("Lord, Stand By Me"), and gospel tunes ("Twelve Gates to The City," all 1935). Ordained in 1933, he generally performed sacred material, until beginning a second career in the 1960s as a blues singer and ragtime guitarist. As a guitarist he translated piano ragtime into a string technique that effectively combined clear melodic and accompanimental lines.

Bibl.: Stefan Grossman, *Rev. Gary Davis: Blues Guitar* (New York, 1974). Bruce Bastin, *Red River Blues* (Urbana, 1986).

Davis, Miles (Dewey, III) (b. Alton, Ill., 25 May 1926; d. Santa Monica, Calif., 28 Sept. 1991). Jazz trumpeter and bandleader. He played bop with Charlie Parker (1945–48) before leading his own bands. His nonet (1949–50) pioneered cool jazz. His hard bop quintet (1955–56) included John Coltrane, Red Garland, Paul Chambers, and Philly Joe Jones. Beginning 1958 his sextets included Coltrane, Cannonball Adderley, Chambers, Jones or Jimmie Cobb, and Garland, Bill Evans, or Wynton Kelly. In addition to hard bop, Davis explored slow-moving harmonies in so-called modal pieces. He also recorded as a trumpeter and flugelhorn soloist with Gil Evans's orchestra, including the albums *Porgy and Bess* (1958) and *Sketches of Spain* (1959–60). In 1963 he formed a quintet with Herbie Hancock, Ron Carter, Tony Williams, and the tenor saxophonist George Coleman, replaced by Sam Rivers and then Wayne Shorter. From 1968 this quintet moved from a repertory of ballads, modal jazz, and extremely fast, nearly atonal hard bop, toward jazz-rock, and Davis's personnel again changed: members included Chick Corea, Joe Zawinul, Keith Jarrett, John McLaughlin, Dave Holland, Jack DeJohnette, Billy Cobham, and Airto Moreira. After a retirement forced by serious ailments (1975–80), he returned to lead jazz-rock groups through the 1980s. Throughout his career Davis's own playing focused on tuneful melody and fine nuances of rhythmic placement and pitch. His dexterity and his control of the high register improved dramatically, but great technical facility was never his interest. A brooding tone, achieved with a stemless harmon mute (from 1954), and his use of the flugelhorn were widely imitated.

Recordings by his own groups include "Move," "Godchild," and "Boplicity" (all 1949) and the albums *'Round about Midnight* (1955–56), *Milestones* (1958), *Kind of Blue* (1959), *My Funny Valentine* (1964), *Nefertiti* (1967), *Bitches Brew* (1969), and *Star People* (1984).

Bibl.: Ian Carr, *Miles Davis: A Critical Biography* (London, 1982). Jack Chambers, *Milestones,* vol. 1 (Toronto, 1983), vol. 2 (Toronto, 1985). Miles Davis with Quincy Troupe, *Miles, the Autobiography* (New York, 1989). Richard Williams, *Miles Davis: The Man in the Green Shirt* (New York, 1993).

Davison, Wild Bill [William Edward] (b. Defiance, Ohio, 5 Jan. 1906; d. Santa Barbara, Calif., 14 Nov. 1989). Jazz cornetist. He worked in Chicago (1927–32), then in Milwaukee following the death of his colleague Frank Teschemacher. He led a group at Nick's in New York in 1941 and in Boston and St. Louis before returning to play with Eddie Condon regularly from 1945; their many recordings together include portions of the album *Bixieland* (1955). After working on the West Coast in the early 1960s, he played as a free-lance, frequently performing in Europe and recording steadily, including his album *Chicago Jazz* (1978).

Davy, John (b. Upton Hellions, Devonshire, 23 Dec. 1763; d. London, 22 Feb. 1824). Composer and violinist. Adopted and raised by a blacksmith, by age 12 he was a pupil of Exeter organist William Jackson. By 1790 he had moved to London, where he was violinist in various theaters, most notably at Covent Garden. After attempting 2 theatrical works for Sadler's Wells, he composed the opera *What a Blunder!* (1800), which had some success at the Little Haymarket Theatre. He contributed music to at least 15 subsequent stage works and composed madrigals, sacred vocal works, and works for harp, including *Divertimentos* op. 6 and Grand Sonata (1805).

Davy, Richard (b. ca. 1465; d. Exeter? ca. 1507). Composer. A musician of this name was a scholar, then *informator choristarum* and an organist at Magdalen College, Oxford, from 1483, and subsequently one of the vicars-choral of Exeter Cathedral from 1497 to 1506. Davy is known to have written about 10 Latin sacred choral works for 4 to 6 parts (including a St. Matthew Passion) and 4 English carols for 2 or 3 parts. Most of the Latin works, plus a note linking the composer with Magdalen College, survive in the Eton Choirbook (ed. in *MB* 10–12).

Dawson, William Levi (b. Anniston, Ala., 23 Sept. 1899; d. Tuskegee, Ala., 2 May 1990). Composer and conductor. He studied at Tuskegee Institute, the Horner Institute of Fine Arts in Kansas City, and the American Conservatory in Chicago (M.Mus.). After a period of teaching and playing trombone in the Chicago Civic Orchestra, he became director of music at Tuskegee; he toured extensively in the U.S. and Europe with the college's choir before retiring in 1955. His style was neo-Romantic and made use of African American song idioms. Works include the *Negro Folk Symphony* (1934), *Out in the Fields* (soprano and orchestra, 1928), a piano trio (1925), a violin sonata (1927); original choral music and arrangements of spirituals for solo voice or choir.

Day, Alfred (b. London, Jan. 1810; d. there, 11 Feb. 1849). Music theorist. Studied medicine in London, Paris, Heidelberg; became a homeopathist in London; music lessons with W. H. Kearns; 1840, music critic for *Musical World.* His *Theory of Harmony* (London, 1845), original and idiosyncratic, especially in its ideas on chord derivation, was severely censured when it appeared, but became influential on English theorists later in the century through the support of Day's close friend G. A. Macfarren, who made a second edition in 1885.

Daza [Daça], **Esteban** (fl. Valladolid, 1575). Composer. Wrote one collection of pieces in vihuela tablature, published in three books as *El Parnasso* (1576). The first book includes original fantasias; the second intabulations of motets, with one voice intended to be sung as well as played; the third similar arrangements of secular songs.

Debain, Alexandre-François (b. Paris, 1809; d. there, 3 Dec. 1877). Instrument maker. Apprentice piano maker at 16, working for Mercier, Pape, and Erard; 1834, started his own factory, specializing in mechanical musical devices; 1840, invented the harmonium, which was immediately successful and widely imitated; 1846, invented the antiphonel (an automatic playing device for keyboards); 1851, invented the harmonicorde.

Debussy, (Achille-) Claude (b. St. Germain-en-Laye, 22 Aug. 1862; d. Paris, 25 Mar. 1918). Composer and writer. Debussy had little formal education; his first piano lessons were with Antoinette Mauté; in 1872 he

Claude Debussy, 1902.

was admitted to the piano (Marmontel) and theory (Lavignac) classes at the Paris Conservatory. In 1880 he joined Guiraud's composition class and four years later won the Prix de Rome (with the cantata *L'enfant prodigue*). He resisted the conservative approach he found at the Conservatory, where his only unqualified success was in Bazille's accompanying class. While still a student he traveled as pianist for Mme. von Meck (Tchaikovsky's patron) to Switzerland, Vienna, and Moscow; the years 1885–87 he spent at the Villa Medici in Rome, often longing for Paris. He returned home early in 1887, visited Bayreuth in 1888 and 1889, and was fascinated by the Javanese gamelan at the Paris Exposition of 1889. Debussy's musical *envois* from Rome, required as a condition of the Rome Prize, had been criticized by the Parisian academics, who encouraged him to "guard against this vague impressionism, which is one of the most dangerous enemies of truth in works of art." One of those works, *La damoiselle élue,* was performed in Paris in April 1893; the *Prélude à l'apres-midi d'un faune* (a response to Mallarmé's poem), in December 1894; but it was the premiere in 1902 of the only opera he completed, *Pelléas et Mélisande,* that brought him significant recognition. By then he had composed several songs (on his own texts and those of Verlaine, Baudelaire, Louÿs, and others); works for orchestra including not only the *Faune* but the *Fantaisie* (with piano) and the *Nocturnes;* several piano works; and what was to be his only string quartet.

He had married Rosalie Texier in 1899, but later divorced her to live with Emma Bardac, with whom he had one child (born in 1905); the break with Texier and her subsequent suicide attempt alienated many of his friends. During the next few years he traveled frequently as conductor and performer of his own music in England, Russia, and throughout Europe; his activities as a critic had begun in 1901 and continued intermittently for the rest of his life in various Parisian publications (in his writing he often invoked the character of M. Croche, the diletante-hater, based on Valéry's M. Teste). Some of these commitments were surely prompted by his difficult financial situation, especially bleak after his wife was disinherited in 1907. Despite the demands of travel and writing he composed several major works during the period 1902–13: *La Mer* and *Images* for orchestra, the ballet *Jeux;* more songs, piano pieces, and chamber music; and *Le martyre de St.-Sébastien* (orchestrated by his friend Caplet). Still, the number of projects begun and put aside was even larger than those completed, particularly among those meant for the stage (he worked especially on two texts of Poe for which he never completed the music, although his libretto for the projected *La chute de la maison Usher* was sent to his publisher in 1916). In 1909 he was appointed to the board of the Conservatory and was the subject of a first biography (Laloy); in 1903 he had received the Légion d'honneur. Unfortunately the riotous reception at the premiere of Stravinsky's *Sacre du printemps* took immediate attention away from *Jeux,* first performed only two weeks earlier. His last trip to England was in 1914, after which he produced the *Études* for piano and three of six sonatas he planned to write for chamber ensembles. His death in 1918 resulted from cancer, which had been apparent since 1910.

Debussy's individual uses of archaic modes and whole-tone or pentatonic scales have long been appreciated; the frequent tonal ambiguity and the subordination of chords to melody rather than to the demands of functional harmonic progressions are well known. His links to the symbolist poets are now seen as more telling than those to the visual arts, although he had M. Croche call both symbolism and impressionism merely "useful terms of abuse." In its 1887 criticsm of *Printemps* the Académie accused Debussy of forgetting "the importance of precise construction and form," yet recent research has shown that many of the composer's works are cast in forms directly related to the Golden Section or to the series of Fibonacci numbers. In the mature songs and in *Pelléas* the declamation of the text is of primary importance, a result of Debussy's intention to remain faithful to the inflections of the French language and of his view that music was too predominant in (especially Wagnerian) opera.

His influence on 20th-century music is unmatched by any of his contemporaries. Bartók, Boulez, Poulenc, Milhaud, Hindemith, and Stravinsky all acknowledged their debt to him. Although his departures may have been radical and his criticism of predecessors and contemporaries quite sharp, Debussy acknowledged his own veneration for his predecessors (especially for Bach, for the French school represented by Rameau and others, for Mussorgsky, and even for Berlioz, Mozart, and Beethoven); but he announced himself against repetition or outright imitation of previous successes. His compositional procedures were not easily discovered or imitated; moreover he resisted any association with a school of disciples. Music was to remain magical, composition to be learned as much from the study of nature as from scores. He wrote in 1903: "Music is a mysterious mathematical process whose elements are a part of Infinity . . . Nothing is more musical than a sunset! For anyone who can be moved by what they see can learn the greatest lessons in development here."

Works: *Dramatic music.* An opera (*Pelléas et Mélisande,* 1893–1902, Opéra-comique, 1902) and several incomplete stage scores; 4 ballets (*Khamma,* 1911–12, orchestration completed by Koechlin, Opéra-comique, 1947; *Jeux,* 1912–13, Paris, 1913; *La boîte à joujoux,* for children, 1913, orchestration completed by Caplet, Paris, 1919; *No-ja-li,* 1913, prelude and first scene extant); incidental music; *Chansons de Bilitis,* to accompany the reading of poetry by Pierre Louÿs (2 flutes, 2 harps, and cello, 1900–1901, lost; cello part reconstructed by Boulez, 1954, and by Hoérée, 1971).

Orchestral music. Symphony (1880); *Intermezzo* (after Heine, for cello and orchestra, 1882); *Triomphe de Bacchus* (after Banville, ca. 1882, lost); Première suite (ca. 1883); *Printemps* (suite for female chorus and orchestra, 1887, lost; arranged for piano 4-hands in 1904, and reorchestrated from that version by Büsser in 1912); *Fantaisie* (piano and orchestra, 1889–90); *Prélude à l'après-midi d'un faune* (after Mallarmé, 1892–94); *Nocturnes* (1897–99); *La mer* (1903–5); *Danse sacrée et danse profane* (chromatic harp and orchestra, 1904); *Images* (1905–12).

Works for voices and orchestra. Daniel (cantata, 3 soloists, 1881, incomplete); *Le printemps* (female chorus, 1882; published as *Salut printemps* in piano arrangement, 1928); *Invocation* (male chorus, 1883); *Le gladiateur* (cantata, 3 soloists, 1883); *Le printemps* (chorus, 1884); *L'enfant prodigue* (scène lyrique, 1884); *Zuleima* (chorus?, 1885–86, lost); *La damoiselle élue* (lyric poem for soprano, female chorus, and orchestra, 1887–88, reorchestrated in 1902); *La saulaie* (1 voice, 1896–1900); *Ode à la France* (soprano and chorus, sketched 1916–17, orchestrated by Gaillard, 1928).

Choral music. "Choeur des brises" (soprano and 3 female voices, sketch, ca. 1882); "Noël pour célébrer Pierre Louÿs" (for all voices including those of the audience, 1903); *Petite cantate* (soprano, baritone, chorus, bells, and piano, 1907); *Trois chansons de Charles d'Orléans* (1898–1908); "Noël" (tenor, chorus, bugles, and piano, 1914).

Chamber music. Premier trio (piano trio, ca. 1879); *Nocturne et scherzo* (cello and piano, 1882); Premier quatuor (string quartet, 1893); *Rapsodie* (alto saxophone and piano, 1901–8); *Première rapsodie* (clarinet and piano, 1909–10); *Petite pièce* (clarinet and piano, 1910); *Syrinx* (flute, 1913, originally incidental music for *Psyché*); Sonata (cello and piano, 1915); Sonata (flute, viola, and harp, 1915); Sonata (violin and piano, 1916).

Piano music. Includes *Rêverie* (1890); *Suite bergamasque* (1890, rev. 1905); *Mazurka* (ca. 1890); *Nocturne* (1892); *Images* (3 pieces, 1894); *Suite: Pour le piano* (1903–4); *D'un cahier d'esquisses* (1903); *Estampes* (1903); *L'isle joyeuse* (1904); *Masques* (1904); *Images* (set 1, 1905); *Sérénade à la poupée* (1906, incorporated in *Children's Corner*); *Children's Corner* (1906–8); *Images* (set 2, 1907); *Hommage à Haydn* (1909); *The Little Nigar* ("cake walk," 1909); *Préludes,* bk. 1 (1910); *La plus que lente* (1910); *Préludes,* bk. 2 (1912–13); *Berceuse heroïque* (1914); *Elégie* (1915); *Études* (1915); *Pièce pour le Vêtement du blessé* (1915). Pieces for piano 4-hands: *Andante* (ca. 1880), *Petite suite* (1886–89); *Marche écossaise sur un thème populaire* (1891); *Six épigraphes antiques* (in part from the *Chansons de Bilitis,* 1914). For 2 pianos: *Lindaraja* (1901); *En blanc et noir* (3 pieces, 1915).

Songs. There are over 80 songs including *Ariettes oubliées* (Verlaine, 1885–88, published together in 1903), *Cinq poèmes de Baudelaire* (1887–89), and *Trois poèmes de Mallarmé* (1913).

Writings: *Debussy on Music,* trans. and ed. Richard Langham Smith (London, 1977); from the original French version, ed. François Lesure (1971). *Debussy Letters,* ed. François Lesure and Roger Nichols (Cambridge, Mass., 1987); from the French version, ed. Lesure (1980). *The Poetic Debussy: A Collection of His Song Texts and Selected Letters,* ed. Margaret G. Cobb (Boston, 1982).

Bibl.: Claude Abravanel, *Claude Debussy: A Bibliography* [regularly updated in *Cahiers Debussy*] (Detroit, 1974). Margaret G. Cobb, *Discographie de l'oeuvre de Claude Debussy* (Geneva, 1975). François Lesure, *Catalogue de l'oeuvre de Claude Debussy* (Geneva, 1977). Edward Lockspeiser, *Debussy: His Life and Mind,* 2 vols. (London, 1962–65). Frank Dawes, *Debussy Piano Music* (London, 1969). David V. Cox, *Debussy Orchestral Music* (London, 1974). François Lesure, *Debussy* (*Iconographie musicale,* vol. 5, 1975). Arthur Wenk, *Debussy and the Poets* (Los Angeles, 1976). Robin Holloway, *Debussy and Wagner* (London, 1979). Robert Orledge, *Debussy and the Theatre* (Cambridge, 1982). Roy Howat, *Debussy in Proportion: A Musical Analysis* (Cambridge, 1983). J. Trillig, *Untersuchungen zur Rezeption Claude Debussys in der zeitgenössischen Musikkritik* (Tutzing, 1983). Arthur Wenk, *Claude Debussy and 20th-Century Music* (Boston, 1983). Richard S. Parks, *The Music of Claude Debussy* (New Haven, 1989). James R. Briscoe, *Claude Debussy: A Guide to Research* (New York, 1990). Gilles Macassar, *Claude Debussy: Le plaisir et la passion* (Paris, 1992). Jean Barraqué, *Debussy* (Paris, 1994). Simon Trezise, *Debussy, La Mer* (Cambridge, 1994).

Deering, Richard. See Dering, Richard.

De Fesch, Willem (b. Alkmaar, Netherlands, 1687; d. London, ca. late 1750s). Composer. Probably a pupil of Rosier, Vice-Kapellmeister at Bonn, whose daughter De Fesch married; active in Amsterdam, 1710–25, performing several times at Antwerp as well; served as *Kapelmeester* at Antwerp Cathedral, 1725–31; moved to London soon thereafter. He gave concerts, also playing violin in Handel's orchestra in 1746 and conducting at Marylebone Gardens in 1748 and 1749; evidently made no public appearances after 1750. Works include the oratorios *Judith* (1733) and *Joseph* (1745), both of which received several performances but are now lost, along with chamber duets, solo and trio sonatas, concertos, and part songs.

DeFranco, Buddy [Boniface Ferdinand Leonardo] (b. Camden, N.J., 17 Feb. 1923). Jazz clarinetist. He played in the big bands of Gene Krupa (1941–42), Charlie Barnet (1943–44), and Tommy Dorsey (1944–48), with whom he recorded "Opus No. 1" (1944). He joined Count Basie's octet (1950), led a bop quartet including Art Blakey and Kenny Drew (1952–53), toured Europe with Billie Holiday (1954), and recorded the album *Art Tatum–Buddy DeFranco Quartet* (1956). He led a bop quartet with the accordionist Tommy Gumina (1960–63) and directed the memorial Glenn Miller Orchestra (1966–74). In the 1980s he led a quintet with the vibraphonist Terry Gibbs.

Bibl.: John Kuehn, *Buddy DeFranco: A Biographical Portrait and Discography* (Metuchen, N.J., 1993).

DeGaetani, Jan (b. Massillon, Ohio, 10 July 1933; d. Rochester, N.Y., 15 Sept. 1989). Mezzo-soprano. Studied voice with Sergius Kagen at Juilliard. After graduation taught theory and solfège there and gave master classes at the Univ. of Wisconsin. Formal debut, New York, 1958. Performed in the New York City area with the Waverly Consort, the Pro Musica Antiqua, and the Abbey Singers. On the faculty of SUNY–Purchase, 1972–73; professor of voice at Eastman from 1973. After the premiere of Crumb's *Ancient Voices of Children* in Washington, D.C., 31 Oct. 1970, she became one of the most sought-after singers of 20th-century scores. New works were written for her by Druckmann, Rochberg, Harbison, and others. At the same time she received plaudits for recordings of Stephen Foster and Hugo Wolf. Despite her theatrical presence she consistently eschewed opera in favor of art song and vocal chamber music.

Dehn, Siegfried (Wilhelm) (b. Altona, 24 or 25 Feb. 1799; d. Berlin, 12 Apr. 1858). Music theorist and teacher. Son of a banker; from 1819, studied law in Leipzig; from 1823, served as a diplomat in Berlin, also studying music with Bernhard Klein; became a music teacher and theorist in 1830 because of his father's bankruptcy; from 1842, music librarian at the Royal Library; 1842–48, edited the journal *Cäcilia;* 1849–58, professor at the Royal Academy of the Arts, where his pupils included Cornelius, Kullak, Glinka, and Anton Rubinstein. His harmony textbook (Berlin, 1840) was much used; counterpoint text published posthumously (1859); edited much old music; especially interested in Lassus, but never completed a projected major study.

DeJohnette, Jack (b. Chicago, 9 Aug. 1942). Jazz drummer, pianist, and bandleader. He played drums with Keith Jarrett in saxophonist Charles Lloyd's quartet (1966–68), with Miles Davis's jazz-rock group (1969–71), later in a trio with Jarrett and Gary Peacock that played standard popular and jazz tunes (1983–), and with Ornette Coleman and Pat Metheny on the free jazz quintet album *Song X* (1984). Beginning in the 1970s he regularly doubled as a drummer and pianist. A member of the guitarist John Abercrombie's trio with Dave Holland (1975–77), he next led the quartet Directions, including Abercrombie and Lester Bowie (ca. 1978–79) and from 1979 Special Edition, which with David Murray recorded *Album Album* (1984).

De Koven, (Henry Louis) Reginald (b. Middletown, Conn., 3 Apr. 1859; d. Chicago, 16 Jan. 1920). Composer, conductor, and critic. In Europe (1872–81) he studied piano and theory in Stuttgart, voice in Florence, and opera in Vienna and Paris; received a degree from Oxford in 1879. From 1882 he was a critic for *Harper's Weekly* and newspapers in New York and Chicago; founded the Washington Symphony (1902–4). He is known for his many operettas staged in New York and elsewhere (*Robin Hood,* Chicago, 1890). He wrote 2 grand operas (*The Canterbury Pilgrims,* New York, 1917; *Rip Van Winkle,* Chicago, 1920); ca. 27 operettas; an orchestral suite; a sonata and other piano works; ca. 400 songs (including "Oh Promise Me").

Delage, Maurice (Charles) (b. Paris, 13 Nov. 1879; d. there, 19 Sept. 1961). Composer. While working as a clerk and serving in the army he taught himself to play the cello and piano; later he was aided in his efforts at composition by Ravel, was influenced by Debussy, and was a close friend of Stravinsky's. Exoticism in his music arose from his travels to India (*Poèmes hindous,* soprano, flute, oboe, clarinet, bassoon, string quartet, and piano, 1913) and Japan (*7 haï-kaï,* voice and ensemble, premiered at the 1929 ISCM). He was not prolific. Other works include an orchestral tone poem, *Conté par la mer* (1908), and *Le bateau ivre* (orchestra, 1954); a string quartet (1948); piano music; and songs (*3 chants de la jungle,* after Kipling, voice and orchestra).

Delalande, Michel-Richard. See Lalande, Michel-Richard de.

Delannoy, Marcel (b. La Ferté-Alais, Seine-et-Oise, 9 July 1898; d. Nantes, 14 Sept. 1962). Composer. Honegger encouraged him to abandon painting and architecture to compose; he sought instruction from Jean Gallon, Gédalge, and Roland-Manuel, but was mainly self-taught. His works illustrate his interest in polytonality, instrumental color, and folklike melodies; the opera *Puck* (1945) employs varying vocal styles, ranging from speech to song. His works include several other operas and ballets; an oratorio; 2 symphonies (1933, 1954), and the *Concerto de mai* (piano and orchestra, 1949–50); a string quartet and other chamber and piano music; songs; incidental and film music.

De Lara [Cohen], **Isidore** (b. London, 9 Aug. 1858; d. Paris, 2 Sept. 1935). Composer. Studied at the Milan Conservatory and with Lalo; composed many operas (*Amy Robsart,* London, 1893; *Messaline,* Monte Carlo, 1899), the last in 1933; also a singer and conductor. Published his memoirs, *Many Tales of Many Cities* (London, 1928).

De Larrocha, Alicia. See Larrocha, Alicia de.

Delden, Lex van (b. Amsterdam, 10 Sept. 1919; d. there, 1 July 1988). Composer. He studied medicine at the Univ. of Amsterdam until the outbreak of World War II; after the war he turned to music, becoming a critic for Amsterdam's daily *Het parool.* In composition he is largely self-taught; his first notable composition was a cantata, *Rubayat,* which won the City of Amsterdam Music Prize in 1947. His works include oratorios (*Anthropolis,* 1962; *Icarus,* radio oratorio, 1968); 8 symphonies (1952–64; no. 1 *De Stroom, Mei 1940*) and other orchestral works (*Musica sinfonica,* 1967); choral works (*Het spoorboekje* [The Railway Timetable], 1952); chamber music (2 string quartets, 1954, 1965; *Musica notturna a 5,* 4 cellos, harp, 1967; *Sestetto,* strings, 1971); songs.

Delgadillo, Luis (Abraham) (b. Managua, 26 Aug. 1887; d. there, 20 Dec. 1961). Composer. After study in Managua and at the Royal Conservatory of Milan, he taught and served as Nicaragua's director general of music culture. Later took teaching posts in Mexico City, then Panama, and also toured widely, conducting a Carnegie Hall concert in 1930. Returning to Nicaragua in 1950, he was named director of the National School of Music and conductor of the Nicaragua Symphony. Works include 12 *sinfonías breves,* chamber music, operas, and other vocal music, Masses, and many piano works.

Bibl.: *Composers of the Americas* 2 (Washington, D.C., 1956), pp. 41–49 [includes works list].

Delibes, (Clément-Philibert-) Léo (b. St. Germain du Val, Sarthe, 21 Feb. 1836; d. Paris, 16 Jan. 1891). Composer. His father, either a postal or stagecoach worker, died when he was 11; his mother, from a family of professional musicians, gave him his first lessons and in 1848 moved to Paris, where he studied at the Conservatory under Benoist (organ), Bazin (harmony), and Adam (composition) while working as a choirboy at the Madeleine and other churches and as a chorister at the Opéra. From 1853 he was accompanist at the Théâtre-lyrique and organist at churches; 1865–72, assistant chorusmaster at the Opéra. He began producing light operas in 1856, 3 in that year and 13 (including 2 collaborative ones) through 1869, most at Offenbach's Bouffes-Parisiens, 2 in 1861–62 at the summer resort of Ems. Several of these proved very popular through Delibes's gift for witty, tuneful melody. His association with the Opéra led to his contributing some music to a ballet, *La source* (1866), clearly showing his affinity for the genre and leading to his most enduring works, *Coppélia* (25 May 1870) and *Sylvia* (14 June 1876). In 1871 he married and gave up his other occupations for composition. He produced 3 substantial opéras comiques at the Opéra-comique: *Le roi l'a dit* (1873), *Jean de Nivelle* (1880), and *Lakmé* (14 Apr. 1883), which alone has maintained a tenuous hold on the repertory as a vehicle for coloratura sopranos. From 1881, professor of composition at the Conservatory; 1884, elected to the Institut. His last opera, *Kassya,* was completed by Massenet (Opéra-comique, 1893). Other works include an occasional cantata, *Alger* (1865); incidental music (including 6 dances for Hugo's *Le roi s'amuse,* 1882); many choruses and songs; grand scena, *La mort d'Orphée,* 1878; sacred music.

Bibl.: H. de Curzon, *Léo Delibes* (Paris, 1926). A. Coquis, *Léo Delibes* (Paris, 1957). W. B. Studwell, *Adolphe Adam and Léo Delibes: A Guide to Research* (New York, 1987).

Delius, Frederick [Fritz] **(Theodor Albert)** (b. Bradford, Yorkshire, 29 Jan. 1862; d. Grez-sur-Loing, near Paris, 10 June 1934). Composer. He was born into a German family of well-to-do merchants; he received his early schooling at the Isleworth International College, and as a boy he learned to play piano and violin. His father, Julius, intended him for the family wool business, and beginning around 1882 he sent Fritz (as friends and family called him) on business trips to Norway, Germany, and France. The young man's efforts as an apprentice merchant were halfhearted; during these travels he apparently spent a great deal of his time in musical and cultural pursuits. In 1884 Delius, aged 22, embarked for the U.S., where for two years he attempted to make his fortune with a Florida orange grove. The venture failed, but during these two years he took formal music instruction for the first time in his life from a well-schooled Jacksonville organist, Thomas Ward. In 1885 he became a music teacher in Danville, Virginia; the following year his father allowed him to enroll at the Leipzig Conservatory, where he studied with Jadassohn, Sitt, and Reinecke. He also became acquainted with Grieg, and in 1888 the elder composer interceded for him, helping to persuade his father to allow Fritz to continue musical studies.

In the summer of 1888 Delius, still partly supported by his father, moved to Paris, where he remained for most of the rest of his life. At first he lived in the Quartier Latin, where he had frequent contact with Strindberg and Gaugin. In 1897 he settled at Grez-sur-Loing, 40 miles from the city, with Jelka Rosen, an artist whom he later married. After this he devoted his energies principally to composition. Fruits of his first musical maturity are the Piano Concerto (1896; rev. 1906) and *Appalachia* for orchestra (1896; rev. for chorus and orchestra, 1898–1903). During the first decade of the century, performances of his works took place chiefly in Germany; not until 1907–8 did Beecham take up the Delius cause in England, performing *A Mass of Life* in 1909, the opera *A Village Romeo and Juliet* in 1910, and concerts of the orchestral music. Delius's final decades were marked by encroaching blindness and paralysis, the effects of a syphilitic infection dating from his American years. In 1928 he began dictating music to Eric Fenby, a young musician who had offered his professional services.

Works: 6 operas or "lyric dramas": *Irmelin* (1890–92; first perf., 1953), *The Magic Fountain* (1893–95), *Koanga* (1895–97; first perf., 1904), *A Village Romeo and Juliet* (1900–1901; first perf., 1907), *Margot la rouge* (1902), and *Fennimore and Gerda* (1909–10; first perf., 1919); incidental music (*Zanoni,* 1888; *Hassan,* 1920–23). Vocal works: *Sea Drift* (after Whitman; baritone, chorus, orchestra, 1903–4); *Songs of Sunset* (1906–7); *Cynara* (1907); *A Song of the High Hills,* chorus, orchestra (1911); *Requiem,* soprano, baritone, chorus, orchestra (1914–16); *Songs of Farewell,* chorus, orchestra (1930); *Idyll,* soprano, baritone, orchestra (1930–32). Orchestral music: *Florida* (suite, 1887–89); Suite, violin, orchestra (1888); *Brigg Fair (An English Rhapsody)* (1907); *North Country Sketches* (1913–15); Violin Concerto (1916); *A Song before Sunrise* (1918); *A Song of Summer* (1929–30); *Caprice and Elegy,* cello, orchestra (1930); *Fantastic Dance* (1931). Chamber music: 3 string quartets (1888, 1893, 1916); 3 violin sonatas (1905–14, 1923, 1930, plus an earlier sonata in B, 1892). Also *5 Pieces,* piano (1922–23); 9 sets of songs (*4 Old English Lyrics,* 1916–19).

Bibl.: Peter Warlock, *Frederick Delius* (London, 1923; rev. 2nd ed., 1952). Thomas Beecham, *Frederick Delius* (London, 1959; 2nd rev. ed., London, 1975). Eric Fenby, *Delius* (London, 1971). Rachel Lowe, *Frederick Delius, 1862–1934: A Catalogue of the Music Archives of the Delius Trust, London* (London, 1974; R: 1986). Lionel Carley, *Delius: The Paris Years* (London, 1975). Robert Threlfall, *A Catalogue of the Compositions of Frederick Delius* (London, 1977). Lionel Carley, ed., *Delius: A Life in Letters* (Cambridge, Mass., 1984). Robert Threlfall, *Frederick Delius: A Supplementary Catalogue* (London, 1986).

Della Casa, Lisa (b. Burgdorf, Switzerland, 2 Feb. 1919). Soprano. After studies with Margarete Haeser in Zurich, made her debut in Solothurn-Biel as Puccini's Butterfly in 1941. Leading roles with the Zurich Stadttheater, 1942–50; with the Vienna Staatsoper from 1947; a *Kammersängerin* from 1953. Sang Strauss's Zdenka at the Salzburg Festival (1947), Strauss's Arabella at Munich (1951), Wagner's Eva at Bayreuth (1952), Mozart's Countess at Glyndebourne (1951) and again with the New York Met (U.S. debut, 20 Nov. 1953). An outstanding interpreter of Strauss, she sang many of his roles from Salome to the Countess in *Capriccio,* being particularly identified with Arabella.

Della Viola, Alfonso. See Dalla Viola, Alfonso.

Deller, Alfred (b. Margate, Kent, 31 May 1912; d. Bologna, 16 July 1979). Countertenor. In adolescence he found that his tenor range lay remarkably high. Unable to find a teacher who could help him capitalize on this tendency, he developed his countertenor autodidactically, chiefly by singing in the alto register; he achieved thereby a rich, almost instrumental timbre. More than anyone else, he stimulated the revival of interest in the countertenor voice and its music. Solo debut recital at Morley College, 1944. In the choir of Canterbury Cathedral, 1940–47; soloist and choir director at St. Paul's Cathedral in London, 1947–61. In 1948 he formed the Deller Consort to undertake performances of music written before 1750, particularly by Englishmen. Through performances and recordings with his Consort he became widely known. On 11 June 1960 he created the part of Oberon at the premiere of Britten's opera *A Midsummer Night's Dream.* His son Mark (b. St. Leonards-on-Sea, 27 Sept. 1938), also a countertenor, joined the Deller Consort in 1962 and became director upon his father's death.

Dello Joio, Norman (b. New York, 24 Jan. 1913). Composer. He studied piano, organ, and theory with his father and godfather (Pietro Yon); in his teens and later he played in jazz bands; studied at City College (1932–34), at Juilliard (Wagenaar, 1939–41), and at Tanglewood and Yale under Hindemith (1941). Taught at Sarah Lawrence (1945–50) and Mannes College (1956–72), and was dean of the School of Fine and Applied Arts at Boston Univ. (1972–78); from 1959 he was associated with the Ford Foundation's Contemporary Music Project for Creativity in Music Education, through which composers placed in high schools wrote new music for student ensembles. His works reflect his interest in Italian opera, Roman Catholic religious music, and jazz (Concertante for Clarinet and Orchestra, 1949, was commissioned by Artie Shaw); they are in a diatonic idiom, characterized by polyphonic textures and clear structure; variation technique is prominent in several works (*Meditations on Ecclesiastes,* composed 1955–56, was awarded the Pulitzer Prize in 1957). He twice won the New York Critics' Circle Award: in 1948 for his *Variations, Chaconne, and Finale* for orchestra (1947) and in 1962 for the opera *The Triumph of St. Joan,* a revision of his earlier *The Trial at Rouen* composed for television in 1955; an earlier opera on the same subject (1949) was withdrawn after its premiere but refashioned as *The Triumph of St. Joan Symphony* (choreographed by Martha Graham as *Seraphic Dialogue,* 1951). His television score *The Louvre* won an Emmy Award in 1965.

His works include operas, ballets, television scores, and incidental music; works for orchestra (*Serenade,* 1948; *New York Profiles,* 1949; *Homage to Haydn,* 1969; *Variants on a Bach Chorale,* 1985); works for band/wind ensemble (*Songs of Abelard,* band with optional voice, 1969); instrumental chamber music; many choral works (including the *Mass in Honor of the Eucharist,* choir, cantor, congregation, brass, and organ, 1975; *Nativity,* soloists, chorus, orchestra, 1987); songs. Many early works have been withdrawn.

Bibl.: Thomas A. Bumbardner, *Norman Dello Joio* (Boston, 1986) [with discography and catalog of works].

Del Monaco, Mario (b. Florence, 27 July 1915; d. Mestre, near Venice, 16 Oct. 1982). Tenor. At 13 sang Massenet's Narcisse at the Teatro B. Gigli in Mondaldo near Pesaro; subsequently won a scholarship to the studium of the Rome Opera, but after a few months decided to learn singing from records alone. In 1939 entered the conservatory at Pesaro and made his debut there as Turridu *(Cavalleria rusticana).* Professional debut at La Scala as Pinkerton *(Madama Butterfly)* 1 Jan. 1941. After war service returned to La Scala. Covent Garden debut, 1946, as Cavaradossi *(Tosca);* U.S. debut with the San Francisco Opera, 1950; from 27 Nov. 1950 one of the most popular artists with the New York Met. Admired for dramatic Verdi roles such as Radames, Alvaro, and Otello.

De los Angeles, Victoria [Gomez Cima, Victoria] (b. Barcelona, 1 Nov. 1923). Soprano. Studied voice and piano at the Barcelona Conservatory, 1940–42. Debut in Barcelona, 1944; professional stage debut at the

Teatro del Liceo as Mozart's Countess, January 1945. First prize at the Concours international de Genève, 1947; sang *La vida breve* on the BBC, 1948. Paris Opéra debut, 1949, as Marguerite in *Faust;* Covent Garden debut, 1950, as Mimi in *La bohème.* U.S. debut at Carnegie Hall, 24 Oct. 1950; New York Met debut, 1951, as Marguerite; remained with the Met through 1961. Among the many successes of her long international career are the title role in *Ariadne auf Naxos* at La Scala, 1951; Elisabeth in *Tannhäuser* at Bayreuth, 1961–62; Carmen with the New York City Opera, 1979. Recordings show her range to good advantage; they include operas by Purcell, Vivaldi, Mozart, Wagner, Verdi, Massenet, Puccini, Mascagni, and Debussy, as well as inimitable renditions of Spanish and Catalonian music.

Del Tredici, David (Walter) (b. Cloverdale, Calif., 16 Mar. 1937). Composer. Studied piano in Berkeley (Bernhard Abramowitch) and New York (Robert Helps); attended Berkeley (B.A., 1959); studied with Sessions and Kim at Princeton (M.F.A., 1963). At 16 he played with the San Francisco Symphony; in 1964, supported by the Fromm Foundation at Tanglewood, his *I Hear an Army* (after Joyce) for soprano and string quartet was performed; his *Syzygy* (Joyce, 1966) was commissioned by the Koussevitzky Foundation; in 1980 he was awarded the Pulitzer Prize for *In Memory of a Summer Day.* Taught at Harvard (1966–72), SUNY-Buffalo (1973), Boston Univ. (1973–84), and City College of the City Univ. of New York (beginning 1984). He was composer-in-residence with the New York Philharmonic (1988–90) before joining the faculty of Manhattan School of Music (1991) and Julliard (1993).

His earlier works (before 1968) employ serial techniques in the tradition of Webern; they are primarily settings of texts by Joyce. Beginning in 1968 he produced a number of "Alice" works on texts of Lewis Carroll and in a richly dissonant tonal style recalling Richard Strauss. These works, especially *Final Alice* (1976), have been warmly received by audiences.

The "Alice" works, all for amplified soprano and orchestra, sometimes with the addition of popular or folk instruments, include *Pop-pourri* (1968; rev. 1973); *An Alice Symphony* (1969); *Adventures Underground* (1971; rev. 1977); *Vintage Alice* (1972); *Final Alice* (1976); *Child Alice* (part 1: *In Memory of a Summer Day,* part 2: *Quaint Events, Happy Voices* and *All in the Golden Afternoon,* 1977–81); *Virtuoso Alice* (1987). Other works include *March to Tonality* (orchestra, 1983–85); *Tattoo* (orchestra, 1988); *The Last Gospel* (text from the Bible; soprano, chorus, rock group, orchestra, 1967; rev. 1984); *Steps* (orchestra, 1990); *Brass symphony,* brass quintet (1992); instrumental chamber music; songs with piano or chamber ensemble.

Bibl.: John Rockwell, *All American Music* (New York, 1983).

De Luca, Giuseppe (b. Rome, 25 Dec. 1876; d. New York, 26 Aug. 1950). Baritone. Studied in Rome with Ottavio Bartolini and at the Accademia di S. Cecilia with Venceslao Persichini and Antonio Cotogni. Debut in Piacenza, 1897, as Valentine in Gounod's *Faust.* Created Michonnet in Cilea's *Adriana Lecouvreur,* 6 Nov. 1902, at the Teatro lirico, Milan; Sharpless in Puccini's *Madama Butterfly,* 17 Feb. 1904, at La Scala, Milan. Besides major Italian theaters, he sang at the Teatro Colón in Buenos Aires, 1906–10; at Covent Garden in London, 1907–10; at the Hofoper in Vienna, 1909. U.S. debut, 25 Nov. 1915, at New York Met as Rossini's Figaro; thereafter sang 52 different roles and gave 928 performances at the Met before retiring in 1946.

De Lucia, Fernando (b. Naples, 11 Oct. 1860; d. there, 21 Feb. 1925). Tenor. Regarded as the best tenor of the generation before Caruso. At the Conservatorio S. Pietro a Majella in Naples he studied bassoon and contrabass, then voice with Benjamino Carelli and Lombardi. Debut 1885 at the Teatro S. Carlo in Naples as Gounod's Faust. Sang in Bologna and Florence, 1886; in Buenos Aires and London, 1887. U.S. debut with the New York Met, 1893, as Don José in *Carmen.* In the 1890s he turned to heavier verismo roles, including Turiddu in *Cavalleria rusticana* and Canio in *Pagliacci.* Created the tenor roles in Macagni's *L'amico Fritz* (1891), and *Silvana* (1898). Retired in 1917, but sang at Caruso's funeral in 1921.

Delvincourt, Claude (b. Paris, 12 Jan. 1888; d. Orbetello, Tuscany, 5 Apr. 1954). Composer. Although he studied music from age 7, he graduated in law before entering the Paris Conservatory in 1908 to study composition with Widor. He won the Prix de Rome (1913, jointly with Lili Boulanger); was badly wounded in the war and withdrew for a time from active musical life; directed the conservatory at Versailles from 1931; and directed the Paris Conservatory from 1941 until his death. He composed in a style drawn from Debussy, Ravel, and earlier French traditions. Works include a musical comedy (1938) and other dramatic works; orchestral music (*Typhaon,* symphonic poem, 1914); *Danceries* (violin and piano, 1935); a string quartet (1953); piano music; *Faust et Hélène* (cantata, 1913); *Pater noster* (chorus and organ, 1944); songs with orchestra or piano.

Demantius, (Johannes) Christoph (b. Reichenberg, Bohemia, 15 Dec. 1567; d. Freiberg, Saxony, 20 Apr. 1643). Composer and theorist. Briefly attended the Univ. of Wittenberg, then moved to Leipzig and published his first book of music there in 1595. Was Kantor of the (Lutheran) cathedral and municipal school in Freiberg from 1604 until his death. Composed *Passion historia* (6 voices, 1631), motets (with Latin and, later, German texts), occasional music, and secular pieces (most choral, a few for instruments alone). Beginning with its eighth edition (1632), his *Isagoge artis musi-*

cae includes an important alphabetical music dictionary in German.

Demessieux, Jeanne (b. Montpellier, 14 Feb. 1921; d. Paris, 11 Nov. 1968). Organist and composer. At the Paris Conservatory she studied harmony with Jean Gallon (first prize, 1937), piano with Magda Tagliaferro (first prize, 1939), fugue with Noël Gallon (first prize, 1939), and organ with Marcel Dupré (first prize, 1941). Organist at the Church of St.-Esprit, 1933–62; at the Church of the Madeleine, 1962–68. After a debut recital (Paris, 1946) she toured Europe as a virtuoso, receiving great acclaim for her improvisations; U.S. tour, 1953. Taught organ at the Conservatoire de Nancy, 1950–53; at the Conservatoire royal de Liège, 1952–68. Her compositions include *Poème* for organ and orchestra (1952), a Te Deum (1965), and numerous pieces for her instrument.

Demus, Jörg (Wolfgang) (b. St. Pölten, Austria, 2 Dec. 1928). Pianist. Studied at the Vienna Academy, 1940–45: piano with Kerschbaumer, organ with Walter, conducting with Swarowsky and Krips, composition with Marx. He worked with Yves Nat in Paris, 1951–53; with Walter Gieseking in Saarbrücken, 1953; briefly with Edwin Fischer, Wilhelm Kempff, and Arturo Benedetti-Michelangeli. Public debut, Vienna, 1943, with the Gesellschaft der Musikfreunde; London debut, 1950; Paris debut, 1953; U.S. debut, New York, 1955. First prize in the Busoni Competition, 1956; won the Harriet Cohen Golden Bach Medal, 1958. While maintaining his career as a soloist he also became well known as an accompanist to Fischer-Dieskau and duo pianist with Badura-Skoda. Author of *Abenteuer der Interpretation* (Wiesbaden, 1967).

Demuth, Norman (b. South Croydon, London, 15 July 1898; d. Chichester, 21 Apr. 1968). Composer and music critic. At the Royal Academy of Music he studied with Thomas Dunhill and Walter Parratt. In 1917 he returned disabled from two years of war service; from that year he served as organist in several London churches. He taught composition at the Royal Academy from 1930; in 1936 he founded the academy's New Music Society. His works, often reflecting elements of French style, include operas (*Volpone,* 1949; *Rogue Scapin,* 1954); ballet and film scores; choral music; many orchestral works (3 symphonies and 2 "symphonic studies"); concertos for violin (1937), saxophone (1938), piano (1943); and chamber music. Writings include *An Anthology of Musical Criticism* (London, 1947); *César Franck* (London, 1949); *French Piano Music* (London, 1958); *French Opera: Its Development to the Revolution* (Sussex, 1963; R: New York, 1978).

Dencke, Jeremiah (b. Langenbilau, Silesia, 2 Oct. 1725; d. Bethlehem, Pa., 28 May 1795). Composer. Served as organist at Gnadenfrei and, from 1748, at Herrnhut, where in 1758 he was ordained deacon; held other Moravian church posts at Gnadenberg and Zeist, Holland, before emigrating to America in 1761. Settled near Nazareth, Pa.; served as warden at Bethlehem, 1772–84, and thereafter as pastor at Bethlehem, Lititz, Nazareth, and once again at Bethlehem, where he remained until his death. He was apparently the first to compose and perform concerted vocal music in America; he wrote arias as well as anthems, in particular producing music for several love feasts in the 1760s.

Bibl.: Albert G. Rau and Hans T. David, *A Catalogue of Music by American Moravians, 1742–1842* (Bethlehem, Pa., 1938; R: New York, 1970).

Denisov, Edison Vasilevich (b. Tomsk, Siberia, 6 Apr. 1929). Composer and theorist. Began studies in music at the age of 15. While a mathematics student at Tomsk University (1946–51), studied piano at the local music school and received initial instruction in composition. Thereafter sent his compositions to Shostakovich, who encouraged him to pursue a career in music and enter the Moscow Conservatory, where he studied with Vissarion Shebalin, 1951–56; in 1959 completed graduate studies there under Shebalin and Nikolai Peiko. Joined the faculty of Moscow Conservatory in 1959 as instructor of analysis and counterpoint; after 1961 taught orchestration there. He was one of the pioneering Soviet composers of the post-Stalin period, using serial and other experimental techniques to develop a style that is noted for its transparency, motivic interplay, and restrained lyricism. In the 1980s his music exhibited a shift toward a neo-Romantic aesthetic. He published *Sovremennaia muzyka i problemy kompozitorskoi tekhniki* [Contemporary Music and Problems in the Evolution of Compositional Technique] (Moscow, 1986).

Works: operas (*L'écume des jours,* after Boris Vian, 1981; *The Four Girls,* after Picasso, 1986); a ballet; a symphony (1988) and other orchestral music (*Peinture,* 1970); concertos for cello (1972), piano (1974), flute (1975), violin (1977), flute and oboe (1979), bassoon and cello (1982), viola (1986), oboe (1986); much chamber and vocal music (*Sun of the Incas,* soprano and ensemble, 1964); choral music (Requiem, soprano, tenor, chorus, and orchestra, 1980); orchestrations of Mosolov, Mussorgsky, Schubert.

Denner, Johann Christoph (b. Leipzig, 13 Aug. 1655; d. Nuremberg, 20 Apr. 1707). Woodwind instrument maker. His father made game whistles and hunting horns. Johann set up his shop in 1680; he turned in the mid-1680s to construction of French-influenced instruments in three pieces and with increased range. He was granted master draftsman status in 1696, receiving the title of *Gassenhauptmann* in 1699. His extant instruments are of superior quality and include 27 recorders, several types of oboe and bassoon, and a chalumeau. His improvements to the chalumeau led to the development of the clarinet. His sons Jacob (1681–1735) and David (b. 1691) also pursued the craft.

Denza, Luigi (b. Castellammare di Stabia, 24 Feb. 1846; d. London, 26 Jan. 1922). Composer. From 1862 studied at the Naples Conservatory. His opera *Wallen-*

stein (Naples, 1876) was only moderately successful; best known for songs, especially "Funiculì-funiculà," introduced at the Piedigrotta festival, 1880, and so successful that R. Strauss mistook it for a folk song, introducing it into his *Aus Italien* (1886). Later a singing teacher in London, from 1898 at the Royal Academy of Music.

De Peyer, Gervase (Alan) (b. London, 11 Apr. 1926). Clarinetist. Studied with Frederick Thurston at the Royal College of Music and with Louis Cahuzac at the Paris Conservatory. Principal clarinet of the London Symphony, 1955–71. Founding member of the Melos Ensemble. Director of the London Symphony Wind Ensemble; conductor of the Haydn Orchestra of London. Professor at the Royal Academy of Music from 1959.

De Reszke [Mieczislaw], **Édouard** (b. Warsaw, 22 Dec. 1853; d. Garnek, Poland, 25 May 1917). Bass. Studied in Warsaw, Italy, Paris; 1876, debut as Amonasro in Paris premiere of *Aida;* 1879, La Scala debut; 1880, Covent Garden; 1885, Paris Opéra. Full recognition as a great singer dates from his 1887 engagement with his brother Jean in London; they appeared frequently together thereafter. U.S. debut, Chicago, 1891; Metropolitan Opera debut, 1891; retired from opera in 1903; later taught. Celebrated roles were Mephistopheles, Sachs, Hagen, Leporello.

Bibl.: H. Klein, "Édouard de Reszke: The Career of a Famous Basso," *MT* 58 (1917): 301–2.

De Reszke [Mieczislaw], **Jean** [Jan] (b. Warsaw, 14 Jan. 1850; d. Nice, 3 Apr. 1925). Tenor. He made operatic appearances as a baritone in 1874–76; then studied with Sbriglia in Paris and became a tenor (debut, Madrid, 1879, in *Robert le diable,* but no further operatic appearances until 1884). Quickly became the leading tenor of his time; Drury Lane, 1887; Covent Garden, 1888–1900; Metropolitan Opera, 1891–1901. Renowned in French roles (Faust, Roméo, Des Grieux, Raoul) and from around 1895 the heavier Wagner roles (Tristan, Siegfried); retired in 1902, then taught.

Bibl.: Clara Leiser, *Jean de Reszke and the Great Days of Opera* (London, 1933). P. G. Hurst, *The Operatic Age of Jean de Reszke* (New York, 1959).

Dering [Deering, Dearing], **Richard** (b. Kent, ca. 1580; d. London, buried 22 Mar. 1630). Composer. Took the degree of B.Mus. at Oxford in 1610. May have been in Italy by 1612, converting to Catholicism around this time, and by 1617 was certainly an organist in Brussels. In 1625 became organist to Queen Henrietta Maria, wife of Charles I, and served as a royal musician for the rest of his life. The majority of his works are Latin (Catholic) motets and Italian madrigals and canzonettas, which display a familiarity with contemporary Italian music. Also wrote some English music, including pieces for viol consort, *City Cries* and *Country Cries* (for 1 voice and viols), 2 madrigals, and Anglican church music (ed. in *MB* 22, 25; *Early English Church Music,* 15).

Dernesch, Helga (b. Vienna, 3 or 13 Feb. 1939). Soprano, mezzo-soprano. Studied at the conservatory in Vienna (1951–57), then sang in oratorios and cantatas before joining the Bern Opera (1961), singing Marina *(Boris Godunov)* at her stage debut. With the Wiesbaden Opera (1963–66) and the Cologne Opera (1966–70) she sang Wagner. Summers at the Bayreuth Festival she sang Wellgunde (1965–67), Elisabeth (1967), Freia and Gutrune (1968–69), and Eva (1969). After her debut at the Salzburg Festival in 1969, von Karajan invited her to sing Brünnhilde and Isolde on stage and for his recordings. By 1978 such roles had overtaxed her voice; debut as a mezzo-soprano, 1979. Sang Erda (1984), Fricka (1985), and Waltraute (1985) in the *Ring.* U.S. debut, 1973, with the Chicago Symphony in New York. Sang Herodias *(Salome)* with San Francisco Opera, 1982. She created several roles, including Hekabe in Aribert Reimann's *Troades* (1986).

De Rogatis, Pascual (b. Teora, Italy, 17 May 1880; d. Buenos Aires, 2 Apr. 1980). Composer. Studied from childhood at the Conservatory of Music in Buenos Aires with Pietto Melani and Rafael Albertini on violin and Alberto Williams in composition; active as professor of chamber music at the conservatory, as a member of the National Commission of Fine Arts, and as a jury member and performer. His opera *Huémac* (1916) was performed throughout Latin America and in Europe; other works include songs, piano pieces, and the tone poem *Atipac* (1928), along with other orchestral music.

Bibl.: *Composers of the Americas* 12 (Washington, D.C., 1966), pp. 131–35 [includes works list].

De Sabata, Victor (b. Trieste, 10 Apr. 1892; d. Santa Margherita Ligure, 11 Dec. 1967). Conductor and composer. A virtuoso pianist and virtuoso violinist up to his last days, he concentrated on conducting and composition at the Milan Conservatory; won the gold medal upon graduation in 1911. His first opera, *Il macigno,* was produced at La Scala in 1917; his symphonic poems *Juventus* (1919), *La notte di Platon* (1924), and *Gethsemani* (1925) entered the repertories of Toscanini and other conductors during the 1920s, and more recently Maazel's. Later works include a second opera, *Lisistrata* (1920), a ballet, *Mille e una notte* (1931), and chamber music. Conductor at the Monte Carlo Opera (1918–29), where he led the premiere of *L'enfant et les sortilèges* (1925). U.S. debut, 1927, with the Cincinnati Symphony. In 1929 began an affiliation with La Scala that lasted to the end of his career. Also conducted in Florence (1933–42), Vienna (1936–37), and Bayreuth (1939). Presented all Beethoven's symphonies with the London Philharmonic, 1947. After the war his style of conducting was deemed eccentric by many. Disheartened especially by his U.S. reception, he retired unexpectedly in 1953.

Artistic superintendent at La Scala, 1954–61. His recording of *Tosca* (1953) is very highly regarded.

De Silva, Andreas (b. ca. 1475–80). Composer. Pope Leo X employed him as a singer and composer in 1519 and 1520; he left Rome in 1522 to take a post in Mantua. He composed principally Masses and motets.

Bibl.: *Opera omnia, CMM* 49 (1970–77).

Des Marais, Paul (Emile) (b. Menominee, Mich., 23 June 1920). Composer. Studied at Harvard (B.A., 1949; M.A., 1953) and in Paris with Boulanger (1949–51); taught at UCLA from 1960. His early compositions were in the neoclassical style; later works have employed serial techniques but remained relatively diatonic. He is the author of a textbook (*Harmony,* 1962). Works include the chamber opera *Epiphanies* (1964–68); the theater piece *Orpheus* (narrator and instruments, 1987); incidental music; music for dance (*Triplum,* organ and percussion, 1981; *Touch,* 2 pianos, 1984); keyboard and chamber pieces (*Baroque Isles: The Voyage Out,* 2 keyboard percussionists, 1986); choral music (*Brief Mass,* chorus, organ, and percussion, 1973; *Seasons of the Mind,* chorus, piano 4-hands, celesta, 1980–81); songs.

Desmarets, Henry (b. Paris, Feb. 1661; d. Lunéville, 7 Sept. 1741). Composer. Sang in the king's chapel until 1678; perhaps studied with Lully. An attempt to become *sous-maître* at the chapel in 1683 was unsuccessful, though his trial composition was much praised; his operas *Endymion* (1682) and *Didone* (1693) were performed at court. Driven into exile by a liaison with a student (whom he later married), he served King Philip V of Spain from 1701 until named *surintendant de la musique* under Leopold I, Duke of Lorraine, at Lunéville in 1707. Although he was pardoned, his efforts to succeed Lalande at the chapel of Louis XV proved fruitless. He wrote ballets, divertissements, and other stage music, along with cantatas, airs, and many *grands motets.*

Desmond, Paul [Breitenfeld, Paul Emil] (b. San Francisco, 25 Nov. 1924; d. New York, 30 May 1977). Jazz alto saxophonist. Most of his career parallels that of Dave Brubeck, including rehearsal groups from 1946, the quartet of 1951–67, and subsequent reunions in duos and combos. Apart from Brubeck, as a leader Desmond recorded with Gerry Mulligan or Jim Hall, including the album *Paul Desmond and Friends* (1959), and he performed in New York with Hall (1974) and in Toronto (1974–75). He had the gentlest of jazz alto saxophone timbres.

Désormière, Roger (b. Vichy, 13 Sept. 1898; d. Paris 25 Oct. 1963). Conductor. Studied with Koechlin at the Paris Conservatory. Conducted the Swedish Ballet in Paris, 1924–25; the Ballets russes, 1925–29; the Opéra-comique, 1936–44; the Grand Opéra, 1945; the BBC Symphony, 1946–47. An admirer of Satie in his youth, he remained attentive to new music, leading, e.g., the premiere of Boulez's *Le soleil des eaux* in 1948. An interest in preclassical music was manifest in his work as director of the Société de la musique d'autrefois (from 1930) and in his many recordings of French Baroque repertory. In 1950 a sudden onset of aphasia forced his retirement.

Desprez, Josquin. See Josquin Desprez.

Dessau, Paul (b. Hamburg, 19 Dec. 1894; d. East Berlin, 27 June 1979). Composer. He was a precocious violin student, but turned to piano and composition in his teens. By 1914 he was an experienced conductor of theater orchestras, and just after the war he was appointed music director and composer of the Hamburg Kammerspiele Theater. He coached and conducted at the operas in Cologne and Mainz before being appointed principal conductor at the Berlin Städtische Oper in 1925. In the 1920s he also composed and conducted for films and had performances of his concert music. He studied twelve-tone music in Paris in the mid-1930s; in 1939 he moved to the U.S., where he met Brecht, with whom he had a long series of collaborations (including *Mutter Courage und ihre Kinder,* 1946). After living in Hollywood, where he also wrote music for films, he returned with Brecht to East Berlin in 1948; Dessau was a member of the German Academy of Arts from 1952 and directed music in a local upper school from 1960. In his prewar compositions interests in twelve-tone method and Jewish folk music are evident; later works are often filled with political commentary, for which he regarded opera as the most powerful vehicle; thus, *Einstein* (opera, 1971–73) deals with the scientist's responsibility for his inventions.

Works include operas and other dramatic works (*Die Verurteilung des Lukullus,* Brecht, 1949; premiered Berlin Staatsoper, 1951); incidental music for the theater; film scores; *Requiem for Lumumba* (Mickel, soprano, baritone, speaker, chorus, and instruments, 1963), *Appell der Arbeiterklasse* (Brecht and others, alto, tenor, chorus, and orchestra, 1961), and other choral and vocal music; 2 symphonies and other orchestral works; chamber music; piano pieces.

Bibl.: Fritz Hennenberg, *Paul Dessau* (Leipzig, 1965) [with works list].

Dessoff, Margarethe (b. Vienna, 11 June 1874; d. Locarno, 19 Nov. 1944). Choral conductor. Daughter of the conductor Felix Otto Dessoff, she studied singing with Jenny Hahn at the Frankfurt Conservatory, then founded the Dessoffsche Frauenchor, the Frankfurter Madrigal-Vereinigung, and the Bachgemeinde. Taught at the Frankfurt Conservatory, 1912–17. Moved to New York City, 1922, where she was chorus director at the Institute of Musical Art. Founded the Adesdi Chorus, 1924, and the A Cappella Singers, 1928; these were united in 1930 as the Dessoff Choirs, and after her retirement to Switzerland in 1936 it continued to flourish under the leadership of Paul Boepple.

Destinn, Emmy [Kittlová, Emilie Pavlína; Destinnová, Ema] (b. Prague, 26 Feb. 1878; d. České Budějovice [Budweis], 28 Jan. 1930). Soprano. In Prague she studied voice beginning in 1892 with Marie Loewe-Destinn, who gave her permission to use the stage name Emmy Destinn. Debut at the Dresden Hofoper, 1897, as Santuzza *(Cavalleria rusticana);* she essayed the same role at Kroll's Opera House and with the Berlin Hofoper (1898), where she remained five years. Sang the first Bayreuth Senta in 1901. Covent Garden debut in 1904 as Donna Anna; U.S. debut (also Toscanini's), 16 Nov. 1908 at the New York Met as Aida. Sang every season at Covent Garden until 1914; at the New York Met until 1916, when her government interned her. Returned to the Met in 1919 as Ema Destinnová. She retired in 1926. During much of her career she was frequently cast opposite Caruso. Created many roles, including Puccini's Minnie (*La fanciulla del West,* 1910); introduced many more major roles to England, Germany, and the U.S. She had a voice of exceptional beauty and evenness and was considered a fine tragic actress.

Destouches, André Cardinal (bapt. Paris, 6 Apr. 1672; d. there, 7 Feb. 1749). Composer. Born to a wealthy family; received a Jesuit education; traveled to Siam in 1687–88; first showed musical skill in the King's Musketeers, playing guitar and composing songs. Leaving the army in 1694, he probably studied with Campra, for whose opera-ballet *L'Europe galante* (1697) he wrote airs. His *pastorale-heroïque Issy* was performed before French and English royalty the same year. He was named inspector general of the Académie royale de musique in 1713; became *surintendant de la musique de chambre* in 1718, succeeding Lalande as *maître de la musique de chambre* in 1727; took the directorship of the Académie royale in 1728, leaving the post in 1730. Began a series of *concerts spirituels* for the queen at Versailles in 1725, presiding over them until 1745. His music is noted for bold harmonic gestures, while his arioso recitative passages were praised by contemporaries.

Bibl.: Renée P.-M. Masson, "André Cardinal Destouches, Surintendant de la musique du roi, directeur de l'Opera," *RdM* 43 (1959): 81–98.

Dett, R(obert) Nathaniel (b. Drummondsville, Ontario, 11 Oct. 1882; d. Battle Creek, Mich., 2 Oct. 1943). Composer, pianist, and conductor. Studied piano and worked as a pianist in Niagara Falls after the family's move to the U.S.; had published several piano rags ("After the Cakewalk," 1900) before attending Oberlin (B.Mus., 1908); in later years he studied at Columbia (1915), with Boulanger in Paris (1929), at Harvard (1920), and at Eastman (M.Mus., 1932). He taught at various institutions, including Hampton Institute (1913–31), whose choir he conducted on European and U.S. tours (1930–31); his last position was as musical adviser to the United Service Organizations. He cofounded the National Association of Negro Musicians (1919) and served as its president (1924–26). He is noted for his piano suites and rags and was an important advocate for African American music, which he employed in most of his own compositions. Works include 3 oratorios; orchestral and instrumental chamber music; 8 suites for piano (*In the Bottoms,* 1913); choral music ("Listen to the Lambs," 1914); songs; arrangements of spirituals.

Bibl.: D. de Lerma and V. McBrier, eds., *The Collected Piano Works of R. Nathaniel Dett* (Evanston, 1973). Anne K. Simpson, *Follow Me: The Life and Music of R. Nathaniel Dett* (Metuchen, N.J., 1993).

Devienne, François (b. Joinville, 31 Jan. 1759; d. Paris, 5 Sept. 1803). Composer and chamber musician. After early study of music with his brother François Memmie, his first professional position was as bassoonist in the orchestra of the Paris Opéra in 1779. During the 1780s he appeared frequently at the Concert spirituel, as bassoonist, flutist, and composer. Later he served in the military band of the Paris Guard and in the orchestra of the Théâtre Feydeau. From 1790 he composed a number of opéras comiques, including *Le mariage clandestin* (1790), *Les précieuses ridicules* (1791), *Le congrès des rois* (1794), and *Les comédiens ambulans* (1798); he also composed songs, orchestral works (including 7 symphonies concertantes, 18 flute concertos, 4 bassoon concertos); and many chamber works. He wrote an influential flute treatise, the *Nouvelle méthode théorique et pratique pour la flûte* ([Paris?], 1794; facs., Florence, 1984).

Bibl.: William Montgomery, "The Life and Works of François Devienne, 1759–1803" (diss., Catholic Univ. of America, 1975).

De Waart, Edo (b. Amsterdam, 1 June 1941). Oboist and conductor. At the Music Lyceum in Amsterdam studied oboe with Haakon Stotijn, conducting with Jaap Spaanderman. Principal oboe with the Concertgebouw Orchestra beginning in 1963. Debut as conductor with Netherlands Radio Philharmonic, 1964. As a result of winning the Mitropoulos Competition in New York, assistant conductor of the New York Philharmonic, 1965–66. Founding conductor of the Netherlands Wind Ensemble, 1966–71. Conductor of the Rotterdam Philharmonic, 1966–73; its artistic director, 1973–79. Principal guest conductor of the San Francisco Symphony, 1974–77; music director, 1977–85. Music director of the Minnesota Orchestra (1986–1995). Chief conductor and artistic director of the Sydney Symphony beginning in 1995. He first conducted opera in 1970 with the Netherlands Opera. Led *Lohengrin* at Bayreuth, 1979; a complete *Ring* with the San Francisco Opera, 1985. In recordings he is often heard in 20th-century works.

Dezède, Nicolas (b. Slovenia?, ca. 1740–45; d. Paris, 11 Sept. 1792). Composer. Born probably of a noble family, as a youth he learned music from an abbé and later continued studies in Paris. His first opéra comique, *Julie,* became an immediate success in Paris in 1772 at the Comédie-italienne. He subsequently composed more than 20 opéras, opéras comiques, and comédies, among them the highly popular *Blaise et Babet* (1783). From 1785 he was occasionally in the service of Duke Maximilian of Zweibrücken (later the King of Bavaria). Other operas include *Les trois fermiers* (1777), *Cécile* (1780), *Alexis et Justine* (1785), and his last, *La fête de la cinquantaine* (1796).

Diabelli, Anton (b. Mattsee, near Salzburg, 5 or 6 Sept. 1781; d. Vienna, 7 or 8 Apr. 1858). Publisher, composer. At age 7 a choirboy at Michaelbeuern monastery; at age 9 at Salzburg cathedral, where he had lessons from Michael Haydn; from 1796 studied for the priesthood at Munich Latin School, also composing sacred music; 1800–1803, at Raitenhaslach monastery, then settled in Vienna as music teacher, composer, and music publisher's proofreader. In 1818 he was a founding partner in the publishing firm of Cappi & Diabelli, which became Diabelli & Cie. in 1824. He retired from the business in 1851. The firm published great quantities of light music, much of it composed or arranged by Diabelli himself; the first published works of Schubert; and several works by Beethoven, including the Diabelli Variations op. 120, based on a waltz by Diabelli. His own compositions include Masses; singspiels; cantatas; dances; songs; piano pieces.

Diaghilev, Sergei (Pavlovich) (b. Gruzino, Novgorod district, 31 Mar. 1872 [o.s. 19 Mar.]; d. Venice, 19 Aug. 1929). Impresario. After studying law he founded the journal *Mir iskusstva* (The World of Art) in 1899. The success of an exhibition of Russian historical portraits that he organized in St. Petersburg in 1905 led him to mount one of modern Russian artists in Paris in 1906. The next year he introduced Paris and the rest of the world outside Russia to *Boris Godunov.* His exceptional discernment in matters artistic and musical allowed him to bring leading innovators together into fruitful collaborations. The vehicle for his ambitions was the Ballets russes, which made its debut in Paris on 18 May 1909. After testing the waters with proven material, he encouraged his choreographer, Fokine, and scenic designer, Bakst, to strike out on new paths with a bold and savage version of *Prince Igor.* For subsequent seasons he commissioned new music by Stravinsky, Debussy, Richard Strauss, Satie, Falla, Prokofiev, Poulenc, and Auric, among others. For the scenic design he drew on the talents of Bakst, Benois, Picasso, Matisse, Rouault, Utrillo, and Chirico. Above all, he stimulated and supported Fokine, Nijinsky, Massine, and Balanchine in their efforts to revolutionize ballet choreography. He was also the first to revive intact (1921) the original choreography by Marius Petipa for *Sleeping Beauty.*

Diamond, David (Leo) (b. Rochester, N.Y., 9 July 1915). Composer. His talent was noted early, when he received violin lessons in public school in Rochester and from André de Ribaupierre in Cleveland; he attended Eastman's preparatory division and had composed some 100 works (withdrawn) on his graduation from high school. After a year at Eastman (composition with Rogers) he studied with Paul Boepple and Sessions in New York (1934–36), then with Boulanger in France (1938). He taught in Rome in 1951 and lived in Florence, 1953–65; he also taught or lectured at various schools and festivals (Salzburg, Aspen, Harvard, SUNY–Buffalo, Manhattan School, Juilliard from 1973). A prolific composer in the classical tradition; his *Sinfonietta* (1935) and *Psalm* (orchestra, 1937) won prizes early in his career; later recognition includes two New York Critics' Circle Awards (*Rounds,* string orchestra, 1944; String Quartet no. 3, 1946); in 1985 he received the William Schuman Award.

Works: operas, ballets, incidental music (*Romeo and Juliet,* 1947; rev. 1950), and film scores; 11 symphonies (1941–93) and other works for orchestra (*Heroic Piece,* 1995); 10 string quartets (1940–68) and other chamber music (*Night Music,* accordion and string quartet, 1961); piano works (*Prelude, Fantasy, and Fugue,* 1983); choral music; songs, including 8 cycles; also a substantial corpus of music for the young; many juvenile and other works withdrawn.

Bibl.: Victoria J. Kimberling, *David Diamond: A Bio-Bibliography* (Metuchen, N.J., 1987).

Diamond, Neil (b. Brooklyn, 24 Jan. 1941). Popular songwriter and singer. He wrote songs in New York City, including "I'm a Believer" (1966) for the Monkees, and moved to Los Angeles in 1966 to record his own material. His successes included "Cherry, Cherry" (1966), "Cracklin' Rosie" (1970), "Song Sung Blue" (1972), and "Love on the Rocks" (1980); he also wrote film scores (*The Jazz Singer,* 1980).

Dianda, Hilda (b. Córdoba, Argentina, 13 Apr. 1925). Composer. Studied in Europe under Scherchen and Malipiero; lived there, 1958–62, working with electronic and concrete music in the studios of the French and Italian broadcasting concerns and attending the *Ferienkurse* at Darmstadt in 1960–61. Returning to Argentina, she became involved in publicizing contemporary music, organizing concerts, and contributing to journals. Composed chamber and orchestral music as well as ballets, vocal pieces, and electronic compositions.

Bibl.: *Composers of the Americas* 9 (Washington, D.C., 1963), pp. 51–56 [includes works list].

Dibdin, Charles (b. Southampton, bapt. 15 Mar. 1745; d. London, 25 July 1814). Composer, singer, playwright, poet, and writer on the theater. He sang in the Winchester Cathedral choir from age 11 and later studied organ there. From 1760 he sang in the Covent Garden chorus, and in 1764 his operetta *The Shepherd's Artifice* was performed there. With librettist Isaac Bickerstaffe he collaborated on successful operas such as *Love in the City* (1767). From 1768 he was engaged at Drury Lane; he also composed for the Little Haymarket and Ranelagh theaters. In 1776 he was forced to go to France to avoid debtor's prison; there he remained until 1778. He was the first manager of the Royal Circus Theatre (1782–84); immediately after being fired from the position for poor financial management he was imprisoned for debt. Near the end of his career he finally began to earn profitably from one-man stage revues. After 1785 he devoted much time to memoirs, novels, and even a *History of the English Stage.* He composed over 60 operas, pantomimes, and "dialogues," including *The Captive* (1769) and *The Seraglio* (1776); among them are adaptations from Dryden, Sedaine, Molière, and Goldoni (*The Wedding Ring,* 1773). He also composed "table entertainments" and hundreds of songs, catches, and glees.

Bibl.: George Hogarth, *The Songs of Charles Dibdin* (London, 1844). Edmund Rimbault Dibdin, *A Charles Dibdin Bibliography* (Liverpool, 1937). H. G. Sear, "Charles Dibdin: 1745–1814," *ML* 26 (1945): 61–65. E. P. Holmes, "Charles Dibdin" (diss., Univ. of Southampton, 1974).

Dickenson, Vic(tor) (b. Xenia, Ohio, 6 Aug. 1906; d. New York, 16 Nov. 1984). Jazz trombonist. He played in the big bands of Claude Hopkins (1936–39), Benny Carter (1939, 1941), and Count Basie (1940), then played with the trumpeter Frankie Newton (1941, 1942–43) and the pianist Eddie Heywood (1943–46). He worked with Newton, Edmond Hall, Sidney Bechet, Pee Wee Russell, and others in Boston (early 1950s) and in New York recorded the swing album *The Vic Dickenson Septet* with Hall and Ruby Braff (1953–54). He joined Henry "Red" Allen (1958). With the pianist Red Richards he led the Saints and Sinners (1960–68) while also working with Wild Bill Davison (1961–62) and Eddie Condon (1964). With Bobby Hackett he led a quintet (1968–70). He joined the World's Greatest Jazz Band (early 1970s), then worked as a free-lance.

Dickinson, Peter (b. Lytham St. Annes, Lancashire, 15 Nov. 1934). Composer, pianist, and organist. His schooling was at the Leys School and at Queens' College, Cambridge; at the latter he studied composition with Philip Radcliffe. From 1958 to 1960 he studied with Wagenaar at Juilliard. He met Cage and Varèse and showed great interest in their music. Returning to England, in 1962 he was made lecturer at the College of St. Mark and St. John, Chelsea, and in 1966 at Birmingham Univ. Beginning in 1974 he taught music at Keele University, where he has cultivated an educational program strong in the study of American music. His own music combines elements of serialism with improvisation. Works include *The Judas Tree,* a theater work for actors, soloists, and orchestra (1965); choral works (*Outcry,* alto, chorus, orchestra, 1968); vocal music (*A Dylan Thomas Cycle,* baritone, piano, 1959); orchestral works (*Transformations: Homage to Satie,* 1970; concerto for strings, percussion, electronic organ, 1971; a piano concerto, 1984; a violin concerto, 1986); chamber music (2 string quartets, 1958 and 1975, the second with tape and/or piano; *Hymns, Blues, and Improvisations,* piano quintet and tape, 1973; *London Rags,* brass quintet, 1986); keyboard music (*Variations,* piano, 1957; *Paraphrase 1,* organ, *Paraphrase 2,* piano, both 1967).

Diddley, Bo. See Bo Diddley.

Diderot, Denis (b. Langres, 5 Oct. 1713; d. Paris, 31 July 1784). Philosopher and critic. As the principal figure behind the *Encyclopédie,* he was central in shaping the intellectual climate of his era; wrote copiously on music, championing the music of Rameau (despite his attacks on the *Encyclopédie*), supporting operatic reform of the type later undertaken by Gluck, and voicing aesthetic views that were ahead of their time. Had contact with many leading musical personages, including C. P. E. Bach and Burney, to the latter of whom he gave a number of his manuscripts, now lost.

Didymus [Didymos ho mousikos]. Theorist. Probably a resident of Rome, younger than the similarly named Alexandrian grammarian of the 2nd half of the first century B.C.E. Fragments quoted by Porphyry and Ptolemy are all that survive of his works. Unlike his predecessors, Didymus recognized a distinction between major and minor whole tones; the difference between these is the syntonic comma, also known as the comma of Didymus.

Diémer, Louis (-Joseph) (b. Paris, 14 Feb. 1843; d. there, 21 Dec. 1919). Pianist. Student at the Paris Conservatory, 1853–61, winning several first prizes; became pianist and teacher; from 1887, professor of piano at the Conservatory (pupils include Cortot and R. Casadesus); 1889, great success of harpsichord recitals at Universal Exhibition led to founding of Société des instruments anciens and to his specialization in early music. His works include a piano method; concerto; chamber music; many piano pieces; songs.

Diepenbrock, Alphons (Johannes Maria) (b. Amsterdam, 2 Sept. 1862; d. there, 5 Apr. 1921). Composer. As a child he learned to play piano and violin. He graduated from the Univ. of Amsterdam in 1888 with a degree in classics; he subsequently taught that subject at a secondary school. In 1894 he moved to Amsterdam, where he gave private lessons in Greek and Latin and devoted himself to music, specifically to an acquaintance with the music of the Renaissance, as well as that of Beethoven, Wagner, and Debussy. His large output consists almost exclusively of choral and solo vocal music; it is characterized by Wagnerian harmony and Debussian modality. Choral works include *Fünf Gesänge nach Goethe* (1884), *Missa in Die festo* (1891), *Te Deum* (1897), *Hymne aan Rembrandt* (1906); other vocal music includes *Ave Maria* (1889), *Zwei Hymnen an die Nacht* (1899), *Bruiloftslied* (1912); incidental music (*Marsyas,* 1910; *The Birds,* 1917; *Faust,* 1918); and more than 30 songs.

Dieren, Bernard van (b. Rotterdam, 27 Dec. 1887; d. London, 24 Apr. 1936). Composer and writer on music. As a youth he learned to play the violin. At age 20 he began serious study of composition in Germany and in his native country, though he was essentially self-taught in music. In 1909 he resettled in the Netherlands, where he was music correspondent for the *Nieuwe Rotterdamsche Courant.* From 1910 he devoted himself chiefly to composition; his music is characterized by polyphonic complexity. Works include a comic opera, *The Tailor* (1917); choral works (*Balsazar,* 1908; *Chinese Symphony,* soloists, chorus, orchestra, 1914; *Les propous des beuveurs,* 1921); orchestral works (*Beatrice Cenci,* 1909; *Serenade,* small orchestra, 1923?; *Anjou,* 1935); numerous solo vocal works including some 70 songs. His chamber and solo instrumental works include 6 string quartets (1912–28); solo sonatas for cello (1929) and violin (1935); and works for piano, including a Toccata (1912). He authored a collection of essays, *Down Among the Dead Men* (London, 1935; R: Freeport, N.Y., 1967).

Dietrich, Marlene [Maria Magdalene] (b. Weimar, 27 Dec. 1901; d. Paris, 6 May 1992). Popular singer and actress. Studied at the Berlin Hochschule für Musik and at the drama school of Max Reinhardt; achieved international fame with her performance of several Friedrich Hollaender songs in the film *Der Blaue Engel* (1930, including "Ich bin von Kopf bis Fuß auf Liebe eingestellt"). She moved to the U. S., appearing in films (*Judgment at Nuremberg,* 1961; *Schöner Gigolo-Armer Gigolo,* 1978) and recording a repertory of Tin Pan Alley, art, and folk songs. In 1984 she was the subject of a documentary by Maximilian Schell.

Dietrich [Dieterich], **Sixt** [Sixtus] (b. Augsburg, ca. 1493; d. St. Gall, 21 Oct. 1548). Composer. Spent most of his life in Konstanz, for years associated with the cathedral choir there, as a choirboy (1504–8), a teacher (from 1517), and a priest (from 1522). From 1508 until 1517 he was in Freiburg, at first as a university student. In 1527 pressure stemming from the Reformation caused the Catholic clergy to leave the city, but Dietrich remained and became a Protestant. His output includes secular songs (from before 1518 and after 1527) but consists chiefly of church music, both Catholic (from 1518) and Protestant (from 1527). He ranks among the most important early Protestant composers.

Dieupart, Charles [François?] (b. ca. 1670; d. ca. 1740). Violinist, harpsichordist, and composer. Although he is known as Charles in most English accounts, other evidence indicates his name was François. Active in London from the early 1700s on, working with Haym and Clayton on *Arsinoe* (1705), the first London venture in Italian-style opera, and also with Haym on Bonocini and Scarlatti operas (1706, 1708), and with Matteux on other stage works. Hawkins states that he later devoted himself to teaching harpsichord. His print *Six suittes* (Amsterdam, 1701) was issued in versions both for keyboard and for cello and treble instrument; Bach and Walter copied out certain of his compositions. His other works include sonatas and songs.

Dilling, Mildred (b. Marion, Ind., 23 Feb. 1894; d. New York, 30 Dec. 1982). Harpist. Studied with Louise Schellschmidt-Koehne; in Paris with Henriette Renié. Debut in Paris, 1911; U.S. debut, 1913. Accompanied Alma Gluck and other singers. The comic actor Harpo Marx was a pupil. She gave recitals in the U.S., South America, Europe, Middle East, and Far East. Edited the widely used pedagogical collections *Old Tunes for New Harpists* (1934) and *Thirty Little Classics for the Harp* (1938). Helped found the American Harp Society (1962).

Dillon, James (b. Glasgow, 29 Oct. 1950). Composer. He attended the Glasgow School of Art (1967–68), Polytechnic of Central London (1972–73), and Polytechnic of North London (1973–76). He was guest composer at Darmstadt in 1982, 1984, and 1986; guest lecturer at the universities of Keele, London, New York, Nottingham, and Oxford. Works include *Spleen* (piano, 1980); *Once upon a Time* (10 instruments, 1980); *Come Live with Me* (mezzo and 4 instruments, 1981); *Parjanya-Vata* (cello, 1981); *East 11th Street NY 10003* (6 percussionists, 1982); String Quartet (1983); *Le rivage* (wind quintet, 1984); *Sgothan* (flute, 1984); *Diffraction* (1984); *Windows and Canopies* (1985); *Überschreiten* (1986); *La coupure* (1986); *Helle Nacht* (1987).

Di Meola, Al (b. Jersey City, N.J., 22 July 1954). Jazz guitarist. He played jazz-rock with the keyboard player Barry Miles (1972–74), Chick Corea's Return to Forever (1974–76, including the album *Where Have I Known You Before?* 1974), and his own groups (beginning 1976). In the early 1980s he formed a trio with John McLaughlin and Paco de Lucia, all playing acoustic guitar, as on the album *Passion, Grace, and Fire* (1983). His later groups combined acoustic and electric jazz fusion.

D'India, Sigismondo. See India, Sigismondo d'.

D'Indy, Vincent. See Indy, Vincent d'.

Diruta, Girolamo (b. Deruta?, near Perugia, ca. 1554; d. after 1610). Organist and writer. His teachers included Zarlino, Porta, and Merulo. Active as an organist from about 1572, he held posts in Venice, where he went in about 1580, Chioggia (by 1593), and Gubbio (by 1609). His principal work is *Il transilvano,* a treatise on organ playing; written in the form of a dialogue and published in two parts (Venice, 1593 and 1609; facs., *BMB* ser. 2, 132, 1969; ed. and trans. Eng., Henryville, Pa., 1984), it contains discussions of a wide range of topics (fingering, ornamentation, diminution, counterpoint) and numerous compositions and intabulations, some original.

Di Stefano, Giuseppe (b. Motta Santa Anastasia, near Catania, 24 July 1921). Tenor. Studied with Luigi Montesanto in Milan. Stage debut at the Teatro municipale, Milan, 1946, as Des Grieux *(Manon Lescaut).* Barcelona debut at the Teatro del Liceo, 1946; Rome debut, 1947; Milan La Scala debut, 1948; New York

Met debut, 1948, as the Duke *(Rigoletto).* Sang 112 times with the New York Met between 1948 and 1968; but his greatest successes occurred at La Scala beginning in 1951. From 1954 he added heavier dramatic roles to his repertory (Don José, Radames, Alvaro), leading to a loss in vocal quality. Often cast with Callas in the 1950s, he joined her in 1973–74 for her final tour. Considered the outstanding Italian lyric tenor of the 1950s.

Distler, Hugo (b. Nuremberg, 24 June 1908; d. Berlin, 1 Nov. 1942). Composer, organist, and choral conductor. He studied piano, then turned to organ and composition on the advice of his teachers at the Leipzig Conservatory; organist at the Jacobikirche in Lübeck (1931–36); in 1937 began teaching at the Württemberg Hochschule für Musik in Stuttgart. His work was considered "degenerate art" by the Nazis, but his colleagues supported him, and sections of his *Möricke Chorlieder Buch* were performed at the Festival of German Choral Music in Graz (1939). In 1940 he was appointed teacher of composition, organ, and choral conducting at the Staatliche Akademische Hochschule für Musik in Charlottenberg, Berlin, and was director of the Berlin State and Cathedral Choir in 1942. He took his own life in 1942. His knowledge of the German choral and organ traditions formed the basis of his harmonically bold style, which draws especially on models from Bach and Schütz. Works include some orchestral and chamber music; piano works; many organ pieces (including suites, trio sonatas, and *30 Spielstücke für Kleinorgel,* 1938); *Kleine Adventsmusik* (speaker, children's choir, flute, oboe, violin, organ/harpsichord, and cello, 1931), *Der Jahrkreis* (52 motets for choir and instruments, 1932–33); *Geistliche Konzerte* (soprano/tenor and organ/harpsichord, 1937). The *Johannespassion* and an oratorio, *Die Weltalter,* were never finished. He published several articles on organ playing (especially on registration for Bach's works) and on church music, as well as a harmony text (1941).

Bibl.: H. Grabner et al., *Hugo Distler* (Tutzing, 1990).

Ditson, Oliver (b. Boston, 20 Oct. 1811; d. there, 21 Dec. 1888). Music publisher. He began working in the Boston book trade in 1823; 1835, started a music publishing firm, in 1836–40 in partnership with S. H. Parker; 1857, founded Oliver Ditson & Co. in partnership with John C. Haynes (1830–1907). By 1890 the firm was the largest music publisher in the U.S., with several branch companies; from 1907 it was headed by his son C. H. Ditson (1845–1929); in 1931 it was acquired by Theodore Presser.

Dittersdorf, Carl [Karl] **Ditters von** (b. Vienna, 2 Nov. 1739; d. Červená Lhotta, Bohemia, 24 Oct. 1799). Composer and violin virtuoso; born Carl Ditters. Through service in Karl VI's army, his father had gained a position as costume designer in the imperial theater. In 1750 the boy Carl obtained a post as violinist in Vienna's Schottenkirche orchestra. Prince Joseph Friedrich von Sachsen-Hildburghausen noticed him and hired him for his court orchestra. There he studied violin with Francesco Trani and composition with Giuseppe Bonno; during this period he also became acquainted with Haydn and Gluck. In 1761 he was made violinist for the imperial court theater, and in 1763 he traveled to Bologna with Gluck.

After a salary dispute with the imperial theater in 1764, Ditters took a post as Kapellmeister for the court of Adam Patachich, Hungarian nobleman and Bishop of Grosswardein (Oradea, Romania). There he composed mostly church music and *Schuldramen;* he lost his job in 1769 when Empress Maria Theresa denounced the bishop. The following year he met Schaffgotsch, Prince-Bishop of Breslau, who wished to start a musical establishment at his court at Johannisberg (near Javorník, Czechoslovakia). In 1770 or 1771 Ditters accepted the post as court composer; this employment formed the center of his creative activities for the next 20 years. He composed symphonies, chamber music, and opere buffe. In 1773 the prince made Ditters *Amtshauptmann* of nearby Freiwaldau, one of several measures to help entice the cosmopolitan composer to remain at the isolated Johannisberg; since this new post required a noble title, Ditters was sent to Vienna to become, for a fee, von Dittersdorf.

From the early 1780s Dittersdorf began making frequent appearances in Vienna: in 1784 or 1785 6 of his 12 programmatic "Ovid" symphonies were performed in the imperial Augarten, and in 1786 his oratorio *Hiob* was performed at a benefit for the Tonkünstlersozietät. His breakthrough came in 1786, when his comic opera *Der Apotheker und der Doktor* became a huge success in Vienna and quickly traveled to nearly every major theater in Europe. In the wake of its success he composed 8 more German comic operas during the next 5 years, 4 of which achieved international fame. In 1789 he traveled to Berlin, where Friedrich Wilhelm had him mount extravagant performances of *Hiob* and *Apotheker.*

In 1794 Dittersdorf began composing comic operas for a small Silesian court theater at Oels (now Olésnica, Poland), which were mounted by the Weimar-based Waeser troupe. At the same time he experienced a falling-out with Schaffgotsch, who finally expelled him from his palace; the composer was spared from utmost poverty by an offer in 1795 from Baron Ignaz von Stillfried to live at his spare castle in southern Bohemia. His final decade was occupied with overseeing operatic productions and with compiling and editing his own music for publication.

He composed some 45 operas *(Il finto pazzo per amore, Betrug durch Aberglauben, Die Liebe im Narrenhause, Das rothe Käppchen),* sacred vocal music, at least 120 symphonies, chamber music (including string quartets), and keyboard music. His florid autobiography (*Lebenbeschreibung,* Leipzig, 1801; ed. Norbert Miller, Munich, 1967) provides a valuable glimpse of the life of an 18th-century court musician.

Bibl.: Karl Krebs, *Dittersdorfiana* (Berlin, 1900; R: New

York, 1972). Margaret Grupp, "First-Movement Form as a Measure of Dittersdorf's Symphonic Development" (diss., New York Univ., 1977). Paul J. Horsley, "Dittersdorf and the Ensemble Finale in Late-18th-Century German Comic Opera" (diss., Cornell Univ., 1988).

Dittrich, Paul-Heinz (b. Gornsdorf, Erzgebirge, 4 Dec. 1930). Composer. He studied at the Musikhochschule in Leipzig (1951–56); was a choirmaster in Weimar (1956–58); studied at the German Academy of the Arts in Berlin (1958–60); conducted a Berlin folk ensemble (1960–63); and lectured at the Berlin Hochschule für Musik. His early style was traditional, but later works involved a mixture of tones, noises, and speech to produce what has been termed a phonetic-instrumental poetry. Works include *Golgotha* (oratorio, solo voices, chorus, and orchestra, 1967); *Memento vitae* (after Sophocles, Brecht; baritone, 12 solo voices, 4 choruses, 5 voices, 9 percussionists, 1971); *Vokalblätter* (texts from the Bible, Joyce, Brecht, and Goethe; soprano, 12 solo voices, flute, oboe, and tape, 1972–73); an oboe concerto (oboe, jazz group, and chamber orchestra, 1973); *Collagen* (oboe, cello, piano, and tape, 1973); *Cantus II: Unum necessarium* (soprano and orchestra, 1977); *Hohes Lied* (soprano, violin, chorus, 1984); *Concert avec plusieurs instruments no. VI* (1986).

Divitis [(de) Rycke, Le Riche], **Antonius** [Anthoine] (b. Louvain, ca. 1475; d. after 1526). Composer. Choirmaster in Bruges from 1501 and in Mechelen from 1504, then a singer in the chapel of Philip the Handsome (1505–6) and, later, the French royal court (from sometime before 1515). His surviving works include 3 parody Masses (important early examples of pieces using this technique), 1 or 2 other Masses and 2 Mass sections, 3 Magnificats, 7 motets, and 1 chanson.

Dixon, (Charles) Dean (b. New York, 10 Jan. 1915; d. Zurich, 3 Nov. 1976). Conductor. While working for the M.A. degree at Teachers College, Columbia Univ. (1936–39), he studied conducting with Albert Stoessel at Juilliard. Debut in 1937 with the chamber orchestra of the League of Music Lovers. Founded the New York Chamber Orchestra (1938); the American Youth Orchestra (1944). On 10 Aug. 1941 he became the first African American to lead the New York Philharmonic; subsequently he conducted the Boston Symphony, the NBC Orchestra, and the Philadelphia Orchestra. Conducted the Israel Philharmonic (1950–51); the Göteborg Symphony (1953–60). Principal conductor of the Hesse Radio Symphony at Frankfurt am Main (1961–70); of the Sydney Symphony (1964–67). He introduced many American works to European and Australian audiences. In the summer of 1970 he conducted the Pittsburgh Symphony, the St. Louis Symphony, and a series of concerts with the New York Philharmonic.

Dixon, Willie (James) (b. Vicksburg, Miss., 1 July 1915). Blues songwriter, double bass player, and singer. After working in Chicago as a bassist (1937–49) he became a writer, producer, and performer for Chess, the principal blues recording company (1952–early 1970s). Through recordings by Muddy Waters and Howlin' Wolf and Dixon's performances accompanying Memphis Slim (notably in Europe, 1960–62), his songs were taken up by John Mayall's Bluesbreakers *(I'm Your Hoochie Coochie Man),* Cream (*Spoonful*), the Rolling Stones *(Little Red Rooster),* the Doors *(Back Door Man),* and Led Zeppelin (*You Need Love,* retitled *Whole Lotta Love*). Dixon moved in 1983 to California, where he continued writing and performing.

Dlugoszewski, Lucia (b. Detroit, 16 June 1934). Composer. She was a premedical student at Wayne State Univ. (1949–52); then studied piano (Sultan, 1952–55) and composition (Varèse) in New York. Beginning in 1951 she composed for "timbre piano," using bows and plectra of various materials directly on the strings; invented some 100 percussion instruments prominent in works from the 1950s (*Eight Clear Places,* 1958–60); wrote on commission for Erick Hawkins Dance Company (from 1952). Her early work attracted the attention of New York artists such as Robert Motherwell and David Smith; thereafter she became more prominent in established musical circles (*Abyss and Caress,* premiered by the New York Philharmonic under Boulez, 1975); she is the first woman to have won the Koussevitzky Record Award (1980 for *Fire Fragile Flight,* orchestra, 1973–74). Her work often employs a technique of "leaping" structures based on surprise and speed (*Strange Tenderness of Naked Leaping,* orchestra, 1977); other concepts include "elusivity" and "tilt" (*Wilderness Elegant Tilt,* concerto for 11 instruments and orchestra, 1981–84). Works include some 14 dance scores, incidental music for plays, film scores; about 25 works for orchestra or for invented percussion instruments; chamber music (*Space Is a Diamond,* trumpet, 1970; *Quidditas,* string quartet, 1984).

Dmitriev, Georgy Petrovich (b. Krasnodar, 29 Oct. 1942). Composer. Studied composition at the Moscow Conservatory under Dmitri Kabalevsky, graduating in 1966; in 1968 completed graduate studies there. Elected chairman of the Moscow branch of the Union of Composers in 1988. His music demonstrates familiarity with a wide range of traditional and contemporary techniques that, especially in the large-scale works, are put in the service of programmatic expression. Works include an opera; symphonic music (2nd Symphony, On the Kulikovo Field, 1979; *Kiev,* symphonic chronicle, 1981; *Ice Congealing, Ice Floating,* musical fantasia inspired by V. I. Lenin, 1983); vocal-symphonic works (*Cosmic Russia,* oratorio, 1985); chamber music; choral and vocal music; music for children.

Dobiáš, Václav (b. Radčice, Bohemia, 22 Sept. 1909; d. Prague, 18 May 1978). Composer. He studied first with Foerster and then at the Prague Conservatory with Novák. His early music (the first 3 string quartets, 1931, 1936, 1938; nonet, 1938; the violin and cello sonatas, 1936, 1939) was influenced by folk music. He later became interested in quarter-tone writing as a result of his study with Hába (Suite, piano, 1939; Concertino, violin, 1941). He worked in the Czech Ministry of Information and then became professor of music at the Prague Academy of Music. His First Symphony (1943) was written in response to the German invasion. His cantatas *Stalingrad* (1945) and *Buduj vlast, posílíš mír* (Build Your Country, Strengthen Peace, 1950) reflect the ideology of the Communist party. Other works include *Lento,* 3 harps (1940), a fourth string quartet (1942); *Sinfonietta* (1946); Symphony no. 2 (1956–57); *Festive Overture* (1966).

Dobrowen, Issay (Alexandrovich) [Barabeichik, Ishok Israelevich] (b. Nizhni-Novgorod, 27 Feb. 1891; d. Oslo, 9 Dec. 1953). Conductor. Studied piano with Igumnov at the Moscow Conservatory, with Godowsky in Vienna. Obtained a post at the Moscow Conservatory, 1917; conducting debut at the Bolshoi, 1919. Gave the German premiere of *Boris Godunov* with the Dresden Opera, 1922; co-conductor with Fritz Busch, 1923–24. Led the Vienna Volksoper, 1924–27; the Royal Opera at Sofia, 1927–28. Conductor of the Oslo Philharmonic, 1927–31; associate conductor of the New York Philharmonic, 1932–33; conductor of the San Francisco Symphony, 1933–35. Made Oslo his base while conductor of the Budapest Opera, 1936–39; of the Palestine Symphony beginning in 1937. During the Nazi occupation of Norway he was conductor of the Göteborg Symphony, 1939–41; of the Stockholm Opera, 1941–45. After World War II he conducted opera at major houses throughout Europe, sometimes also acting as stage director.

Dobrowolski, Andrzej (b. Lvov, 9 Sept. 1921; d. Graz, 8 Aug. 1990). Composer. At the State College of Music at Kraków he studied composition with Artur Malawski. Later he taught at the college (1947–51) and at the Warsaw State College of Music (from 1954). In 1976 he joined the faculty of the Hochschule für Musik at Graz. He composed orchestral music (*Symphonic Variations,* 1949; *Popular Overture,* 1954; Symphony no. 1, 1955; *Music for Strings and Four Groups of Winds,* 1965; *Music for Orchestra* nos. 1–5, 1968–79); vocal works (*Folk Suite,* 1950; *Three Folk Songs,* 1950); instrumental and chamber music (Piano Sonata, 1949; *Music for Tuba Solo,* 1972; *Music for Three Accordions, Harmonica, and Percussion,* 1977); music for tape (*Passacaglia,* 1960).

Dobrzyski, Ignacy (Feliks) (b. Romanów, Volkynia, 15 or 25 Feb. 1807; d. Warsaw, 9 or 10 Oct. 1867). Composer. Son of a musician; from 1825, studied with Elsner at the Warsaw Conservatory; fellow student and friend of Chopin; became a prominent figure in Warsaw musical life as pianist, composer, critic, and teacher; 1845–47, toured Germany as pianist; 1852–53, conductor, Warsaw Opera; 1856, founded symphony orchestra, which collapsed for lack of money; from 1861, teacher at the new Music Institute. Works include 2 symphonies; an opera and incidental music; chamber music; a piano method. Some mazurkas, nocturnes, and other piano pieces had some circulation in western Europe.

Bibl.: William Smialek, *Ignacy Feliks Dobrzyńsky and Musical Life in Nineteenth-Century Poland* (Lewiston, N.Y., 1991).

Dodd, John (b. London? 1752; d. Richmond, Surrey, 1839). Bow maker. His father, Edward Dodd (1705–1810), long said to have made many of the extant 18th-century bows, may not have been a bow maker at all. John worked as a gunlock fitter before he began making bows around 1780. He was known both for the "hammer-head" and for the curved "swan-head" bow types. The popularity of his violin bows waned as the Tourte bow became more widespread during the early 19th century. His cello bows, however, are still favored.

Dodds, Baby [Warren] (b. New Orleans, 24 Dec. 1898; d. Chicago, 14 Feb. 1959). Jazz drummer; brother of Johnny Dodds. After playing on Mississippi riverboats with Fate Marable (1918–21), he joined King Oliver in San Francisco (1922). In Chicago he became a leading jazz drummer. He worked with Oliver (1922–23), Freddie Keppard (1924), and Johnny (1924, 1927–29, intermittently 1930–40) and also recorded with Louis Armstrong and Jelly Roll Morton. Active in the revival of New Orleans jazz in Chicago, New Orleans, and New York, he worked with Jimmie Noone (1940–41), Bunk Johnson (1944–45), and Sidney Bechet, whose recordings include Dodds's solo on "China Boy" (1946). He played at the jazz festival in Nice in 1948.

Writings: with Larry Gara, *The Baby Dodds Story* (Los Angeles, 1959).

Dodds, Johnny [John M.] (b. New Orleans, 12 Apr. 1892; d. Chicago, 8 Aug. 1940). Jazz clarinetist; brother of Baby Dodds. He played with Kid Ory in New Orleans (intermittently ca. 1912–17, 1919) and King Oliver in Chicago (1920–21, 1922–23) and California (1921–22). One of the finest blues soloists among clarinetists, he led the band at Kelly's Stables in Chicago (1924–29) while also recording with Louis Armstrong (including "S. O. L. Blues," 1927), Jelly Roll Morton, ad hoc small groups (Chicago Footwarmers, New Orleans Bootblacks, New Orleans Wanderers, etc.), and as a leader (including "Weary Blues," 1927).

Bibl.: G. E. Lambert, *Johnny Dodds* (New York, 1962; R: in *Kings of Jazz,* ed. S. Green, New York, 1978).

Dodge, Charles (Malcolm) (b. Ames, Iowa, 5 June 1942). Composer. Studied at the Univ. of Iowa (B.A., 1964), Columbia (with Chou and Luening; M.A., 1966; D.M.A., 1970), and Princeton (with Winham, 1969–70); has taught at Columbia (1970–77) and at Brooklyn College (from 1977), directing the Center for Computer Music. He wrote some works for traditional performers (*Folia,* 9 performers, 1965; *Distribu-*

tion, Redistribution, clarinet, violin, and piano, 1982), but his main interest has been in computer music (*Earth's Magnetic Field,* 1970; *The Voice of Binky,* 1989), some with live performers (*Cascando,* radio play by Beckett; actor and tape, 1978; *Wedding Music,* with violin, 1988) and often involving synthesized voices (*In Celebration,* 1975; *He Met Her in the Park,* 1983). With T. A. Jerse he wrote *Computer Music: Synthesis, Composition, and Performance* (New York, 1985).

Dodgson, Stephen [Cuthbert Vivian] (b. London, 17 March 1924). Composer. He studied at the Royal College of Music in London with R. O. Morris and then taught there from 1964 to 1982. A frequent broadcaster on the BBC. Wrote many works for solo guitar as well as 2 concertos for guitar and chamber orchestra (1959, 1972) and a quintet for guitar and strings. Other works include *Margaret Catchpole,* an opera (1979); 5 operas for children; concertos for bassoon (1969), clarinet (1983), and trombone (1986); Magnificat, soloists, orchestra (1975); *Sir John,* cantata, chorus, horn trio (1980); *Cadilly,* entertainment for 4 singers, wind quintet (1968); *Epigrams from a Garden,* contralto, clarinet choir (1977); 2 string trios (1951, 1964); a string quartet (1986); 2 piano trios (1967, 1973); Quintet in C, piano and strings (1966); Suite, wind quintet (1965); 3 piano sonatas (1959, 1975, 1983).

Dohnányi, Christoph von (b. Berlin, 8 Sept. 1929). Conductor. Grandson of Ernst von Dohnányi, he studied at the Berlin Hochschule für Musik and at Munich, where he won the Strauss Prize for conducting in 1951. Chorusmaster, then conductor at the Frankfurt Opera, 1952–56. Conductor of the Lübeck Orchestra, 1957–63; of the Kassel Orchestra, 1963–64; of the West German Radio Orchestra at Cologne, 1964–68. Chief conductor of the Frankfurt Opera, 1968–77. Musical director of the Hamburg Opera, 1977–83; of the Cleveland Symphony, 1984–. His commitment to new music is evident both in concert and in recordings. He led the premieres of Henze's *Der junge Lord* (1956) and *Die Bassariden* (1966) and of Cerha's *Baal* (1981).

Dohnányi, Ernő [Ernst von] (b. Pozsony [Bratislava], 27 July 1877; d. New York, 9 Feb. 1960). Composer, pianist, and conductor. He received early piano and violin lessons from his father, then studied harmony and composition in Pozsony with Karl Forster. In 1894 he entered the Budapest Royal Academy, having already composed a Mass, a string sextet, 3 string quartets, and several songs and piano pieces. There he studied piano with István Thomán and composition with Hans Koessler. In 1895 Brahms recommended Dohnányi's Piano Quintet in E minor op. 1 for performance in the concerts of the Wiener Tonkünstlerverein.

After receiving his diploma from the Royal Academy in 1897, he studied piano briefly with Eugen d'Albert in Berlin, then during the next decade he concertized extensively in Europe and the U.S. From 1908 to 1915 he was professor of piano at the Berlin Hochschule für Musik, after which he returned to Budapest, where from 1918 to 1920 he directed the Royal Academy. During the 1920s he served as conductor of the Budapest Philharmonic (from 1921), as guest lecturer and conductor at American universities (1925–27), and as director of piano and composition at the newly renamed Franz Liszt Royal Academy in Budapest. From 1931 he was also music director of Hungarian Radio, and from 1934 again director of the Liszt Academy; he also conducted the Budapest Philharmonic. In 1941 he resigned as director of the academy, and in 1944—deep in conflict with the Nazi-installed government—he left his conducting post. Late in 1944 he went to Austria, where he lived for a short time in the American Occupied Zone. When Hungary fell to the Russians, the new regime immediately accused him of complicity with the previous government. The accusations appeared in the American press and haunted the composer well into his old age, despite the fact that in 1945 the American Occupation powers had exonerated him of all charges of collaboration.

Dohnányi embarked for America in 1948, settling first in Tucumán, Argentina. In 1949 he accepted a teaching post at Florida State Univ. in Tallahassee; there he spent his last years, becoming an American citizen in 1955. Once called the "last of the Romantics," Dohnányi forged a Brahmsian style that reflected little interest in the folk music that inspired his younger contemporary Bartók.

Works include operas (*Tante Simona,* 1911–12; *Der Tenor,* 1920–27); orchestral works including 2 symphonies (no. 1 in D minor, 1900–1901; no. 2 in E, 1943–44), 2 piano concertos (no. 1 in E minor, 1897–98; no. 2 in B minor, 1946–47), 2 violin concertos (no. 1 in D minor, 1914–15; no. 2 in C minor, 1949–50), *Konzertstück* in D (cello and orchestra, 1903–4), Suite in F♯ minor (1908–9), *Variationen über ein Kinderlied* (piano and orchestra, 1914; perhaps his most popular work), *Ruralia hungarica* (various performing media, 1923–24), *American Rhapsody* (1953); choral works (*Cantus vitae,* 1939–41; *Stabat mater,* 1952–54); songs; chamber music including 2 piano quintets (no. 1 in C minor, 1895; no. 2 in E♭ minor, 1914), 3 string quartets (no. 1 in A, 1899; no. 2 in D♭, 1906; no. 3 in A minor, 1926); piano works (*Suite im alten Stil,* 1913; *Variations on a Hungarian Folksong,* 1917; *Six Pieces,* 1945).

Bibl.: Ernst von Dohnányi, *Message to Posterity from Ernst von Dohnányi* (Jacksonville, Fla., 1960). L. Podhradszky, "The Works of Ernő Dohnányi," *SM* 6 (1964): 357. Bálint Vázsonyi, *Dohnányi Ernő* (Budapest, 1971).

Doles, Johann Friedrich (b. Steinbach-Hallenberg, Thuringia, 23 Apr. 1715; d. Leipzig, 8 Feb. 1797). Composer. He was schooled at Schmalkalden and (from 1737) at the Gymnasium at Schleusingen; at the latter he served as deputy organist and composed chamber music and a number of sacred works. He enrolled at the Univ. of Leipzig in 1739 and during his studies directed the city's Grosses Konzert, the institution that later became the Gewandhaus Orchestra. He

Plácido Domingo in title role of Gounod's *Faust.*

also studied with Bach. From 1744 he was Kantor in Freiberg, but a famous conflict with rector J. G. Biedermann over the role of music in education drove him to seek another appointment in 1755—as Kantor of the Thomaskirche in Leipzig. His resignation from the latter, at the age of 74, again probably resulted from continual struggles between cantor and rector. He composed many sacred works, including some 175 cantatas, 35 motets, 8 Passions, 5 Masses, sacred lieder, more than 200 4-part chorales, and chorale preludes.

Bibl.: Helmut Banning, *Johann Friedrich Doles: Leben und Werk* (Leipzig, 1939).

Dolmetsch, (Eugène) Arnold (b. Le Mans, 24 Feb. 1858; d. Haslemere, 28 Feb. 1940). Performer and historian of early music. Studied violin with Vieuxtemps in Brussels (1881–83), with Henry Holmes at the Royal College of Music (1883–85). While teaching at Dulwich (1885–89) collected, repaired, and played old instruments. Public debut, June 1890, playing viols and harpsichord. Founded the Dolmetsch Trio and devoted himself to performances on original instruments. Built his first lute in 1893, his first clavichord in 1894, his first harpsichord in 1895–96, the first modern recorder to Baroque standards in 1905. Toured the U.S. in 1902. Settled in Boston (1904–11), where he concertized and supervised the building of virginals and harpsichords at Chickering & Sons; similarly in Paris (1911–14) for Gaveau. Published *The Interpretation of the Music of the 17th and 18th Centuries* (London, 1915; 2nd ed., 1946; R: 1969), a pioneering text. Moved to Haslemere in 1917. From 1928 the Dolmetsch Fund supported him and the spread of his teaching. His third wife, Mabel (b. London, 6 Aug. 1874; d. Haslemere, 12 Aug. 1963), played bass viol and researched courtly dance. His daughter Nathalie (b. Chicago, 31 July 1905) was a gambist. His son Rudolph (b. Cambridge, 8 Nov. 1906; d. at sea, 6 or 7 Dec. 1942) played gamba and harpsichord but was primarily a composer, conductor, and author of *The Art of Orchestral Conducting* (London, 1942). His son Carl Frederick (b. Fontenay-sous-Bois, 23 Aug. 1911), made his debut as a recorder player at the first Haslemere Festival in 1925; gave annual recitals at Wigmore Hall beginning in 1946; director Haslemere Festival beginning in 1940; chairman of Arnold Dolmetsch Fund, 1963–78; of Dolmetsch Musical Institutes beginning in 1980.

Bibl.: Margaret Campbell, *Dolmetsch: The Man and His Work* (London, 1975).

Dolphy, Eric (Allan) (b. Los Angeles, 20 June 1928; d. Berlin, 29 June 1964). Jazz alto saxophonist, bass clarinetist, and flutist. He joined Chico Hamilton (1958–59) and Charles Mingus (1959–60, including on the album *Charles Mingus Presents Charles Mingus,* 1960), played on Ornette Coleman's album *Free Jazz* (1960), and with the trumpeter Booker Little led a quintet (1961). He played intermittently with John Coltrane (1961–63), Mingus, and as a leader, recording his album *Out to Lunch* in 1964. Diabetes caused his premature death. Dolphy's music ranged from bop to free jazz. As an alto saxophonist he made startling use of dissonance and wide intervallic leaps, which had a great influence on free jazz saxophonists. He singlehandedly established the bass clarinet as a convincing vehicle for jazz improvisation.

Bibl.: Vladimir Simosko and Barry Tepperman, *Eric Dolphy: A Musical Biography and Discography* (New York, 1979).

Domenico da Piacenza [Ferrara] (b. Piacenza, late 14th cent.; d. Ferrara? ca. 1470). Dance theorist and composer. From 1456 until 1470, except for occasional short absences, he was at the Este court. His students included Guglielmo Ebreo da Pesaro and Antonio Cornazano. He wrote *De arte saltandi e choreas ducendii* (ca. 1420), in which the theory of dancing and the details of many particular dances are discussed.

Domingo, Plácido (b. Madrid, 21 Jan. 1941). Tenor and conductor. His parents, zarzuela performers, moved to Mexico in 1949. At the Mexico City Conservatory he studied conducting, piano, and voice. Debut as a baritone in the zarzuela *Gigantes y cabezudos* by Fernández Caballero. Studies with Carlo Morelli developed his tenor range. Debut as a tenor in the role of Alfredo *(La traviata)* with the Monterrey Opera in

1960. U.S. debut with the Dallas Opera in 1960, singing with Joan Sutherland. Sang 12 operas, most in Hebrew, with the Hebrew Opera in Tel Aviv, 1962–65. Debut with the New York City Opera, 17 Oct. 1965, as Pinkerton *(Madama Butterfly);* with the New York Met (at Lewisohn Stadium), 9 Aug. 1966. Considered one of the two or three best lyric and bel canto tenors of his generation. Has also sung dramatic roles such as Otello. Debut as conductor with the New York City Opera, 7 Oct. 1983 *(La traviata);* led *La bohème* at the New York Met in 1984. An autobiography, *My First 40 Years,* appeared 1983. The 1994 telecast of the second "Three Tenors" concert (with Pavarotti and Carreras) was seen by over a billion people worldwide. Appointed artistic director of the Washington Opera in 1994.

Domino, Fats [Antoine] (b. New Orleans, 26 Feb. 1928). Rock-and-roll singer and pianist. He began playing rhythm-and-blues and worked in the band of trumpeter Dave Bartholomew. Between 1950 and 1960 he released several singles that helped establish rock-and-roll with white audiences, including "Fat Man" (1950), "Ain't That a Shame" (1955), "Blueberry Hill" (1956), and "Walking to New Orleans" (1960). After a decline in popularity he began to tour again in the late 1970s.

Donato, Anthony (b. Prague, Nebr., 8 Mar. 1909). Composer and violinist. After childhood study of violin and composition he attended Eastman (composition with Rogers and Hanson; violin with Tinlot; conducting with Goossens; B.M., 1931; M.M., 1937; Ph.D., 1947). He taught at Drake Univ., Iowa State Teachers College, the Univ. of Texas, and Northwestern (1947–76). He wrote *Preparing Music Manuscript* (Englewood Cliffs, N.J., 1963). His *Centennial Ode* (1967) was commissioned for the Omaha Symphony in honor of the Nebraska Centennial. Other works include an opera; about 20 orchestral works; chamber and piano music including some 20 teaching pieces; choral music; songs.

Donato [Donati], **Baldassare** [Baldiserra] (b. Venice, ca. 1527; d. there, ca. June 1603). Composer. A singer at St. Mark's, Venice, from 1550, succeeding Zarlino as *maestro di cappella* in 1590. He wrote sacred pieces (chiefly motets), serious madrigals, and, most important, popular and influential villanellas.

Donatoni, Franco (b. Verona, 9 June 1927). Composer. Studied at the Milan (1946–47) and Bologna conservatories (1948–51); further composition study with Pizetti in Siena. In 1952 he met Maderna, and the next year he attended the Darmstadt lectures; both experiences were factors in his adoption of serialism after 1955. He taught at conservatories in Bologna, Turin, and Milan, as well as at the Univ. of Bologna (from 1971) and the Accademia Chigiana summer courses in Venice. His early works are indebted to Bartók; *3 improvvisazioni* (piano, 1957) and other serial works from the late 1950s were influenced by Webern, Boulez, and Stockhausen. Beginning 1961 (*Puppenspiel,* orchestra) he employed aleatory procedures and constructed permutable forms in which neither the composer nor the performer controls the course of the music. Examples include *Quartetto IV* (string quartet, 1963) and *Black and White* (37 strings, 1964). In works of the late 1960s he continued to search for new instrumental effects, and reintroduced traditional notation. More recent works include *Ecco* (chamber orchestra, 1986), *Bok* (bass clarinet, marimba, 1990), *Cloches III* (two pianos, two percussionists, 1991), *Aahiel* (mezzo) soprano, clarinet, vibraphone/marimba, piano, 1992), *Feria II* (organ, 1992).

Doni, Antonfrancesco [Antonio Francesco] (b. Florence, 16 May 1513; d. Monselice, Sept. 1574). Writer. After leaving a monastery in Florence ca. 1540 he wandered throughout northern Italy, with extended stays in Piacenza, Venice, Florence (again), and finally Padua. Always closely associated with musicians and music academies; active briefly as a music printer in Florence in the 1540s. Of his writings the most important dealing directly with music are the *Dialogo della musica* (Venice, 1544; ed. Vienna, 1965), which presents tales and conversations with musical insertions, and a portion of *La libraria* (Venice, 1550–51) that lists all printed music books known to the author.

Bibl.: James Haar, "The *Libraria* of Antonfrancesco Doni," *MD* 24 (1970): 101.

Doni, Giovanni Battista (bapt. Florence, 13 Mar. 1595; d. there, 1 Dec. 1647). Theorist. Studied in Bologna, at the Jesuit College in Rome, and later law at Bourges and Pisa. Visited Paris in the service of the papal legate to the King of France in 1621; went there again in 1625 and 1627, and to Madrid in 1626, as secretary to Cardinal Francesco Barberini, making humanist and scholarly contacts on all these journeys. Named secretary to the College of Cardinals in 1629; in 1633 he turned to the study and promulgation of Greek music, devising new modal usages and designing several instruments to this end. He classified types of monody and urged operatic reform along the lines of Greek drama.

Donizetti, (Domenico) Gaetano (Maria) (b. Bergamo, 29 Nov. 1797; d. there, 8 Apr. 1848). Composer. From a poor family, he studied music, 1806–14, at the school of J. S. Mayr, whom he revered throughout life; he sang solo roles in school productions and local concerts and began to compose. In 1815–17, with financial support arranged by Mayr, he studied counterpoint and fugue with Mattei at the Bologna Conservatory. He set a libretto by his friend Bartolomeo Merelli in 1818 and got it performed at the Teatro San Luca, Venice, without arousing any attention. A few more operas followed before the opera seria *Zoraide di Granata* (Rome, 1822) became his first big success and established his career.

From 1822 he worked much in Naples, producing

both comic and serious operas there; but an opera buffa for Rome (*L'ajo nell'imbarazzo,* 1824) was his first work to be widely performed in Italy and beyond. From April 1825 to February 1826 he was music director of a rather shabby and poorly received opera season at the Teatro Carolino in Palermo. Early in 1827 he contracted with the impresario Barbaja to compose 12 operas for the three principal theaters of Naples and to be music director at the Nuovo, giving him a regular income that enabled him to marry in 1828. The following year he was named music director of the royal theaters of Naples. His large Neapolitan output in 1827–32 (3 operas at the Teatro Nuovo, 1827; 4 at the Teatro del Fondo, 1828–31; 8 at the San Carlo, 1828–32) covered all the genres from one-act *farsa* to full-length comic, semiserious, serious, and sacred operas. In these years he produced only 3 new operas outside Naples: the very widely performed comic *Olivo e Pasquale* (Rome, 1827); an opera seria for the inaugural season of the Teatro Carlo Felice, Genoa (1828); and *Anna Bolena* (Milan, Teatro Carcano, 26 Dec. 1830; libretto by Romani), the magnitude of whose critical and popular success moved him into the front rank of Italian composers and put him in demand everywhere.

He now began to concentrate on opera seria (although his next great success was the comic *L'elisir d'amore,* Milan, 12 May 1832). In 1833 he produced two operas in Rome, one in Florence, and one in Milan, all successful; in 1834, one in Florence and one in Milan. He made his first visit to Paris in 1835 for *Marino Faliero* (Théâtre-Italien, 12 Mar.), but this was less successful than Bellini's *I puritani,* which preceded it. In 1836–38 he composed one opera a year for Venice. During this period he produced only four new operas at the San Carlo, but these included three of his most important (*Maria Stuarda,* which was banned by the censor and thus given with a new libretto as *Buondelmonte,* 18 Oct. 1834, the original then performed at La Scala in Milan, 30 Dec. 1835; *Lucia di Lammermoor,* 26 Sept. 1835; *Roberto Devereux,* 29 Oct. 1837).

From 1834 he was counterpoint and composition professor at the Naples Conservatory, and in May 1837 he was named acting director, following Zingarelli's death. On 30 July 1837 Virginia Donizetti died, a month after her third lying-in (none of the infants survived). Donizetti's grief was great; by spring 1838 he was also aware that he would not be named permanent director of the conservatory, as he had expected.

After his next opera for the San Carlo, *Poliuto,* was rejected by the censors, he left Naples in October 1838 for Paris. There his *La fille du régiment* (Opéra-comique, 11 Feb. 1840) became highly popular; a grand opera, *Les martyrs* (Opéra, 10 Apr. 1840), based on the unperformed *Poliuto,* was moderately successful, but *La favorite* (Opéra, 2 Dec. 1840) became very popular. In 1841 one new opera was produced at Rome and one at Milan. Then in 1842 he was invited to Vienna by Merelli, now an important impresario, to compose the opera semiseria *Linda di Chamounix* (19 May), whose great success was followed by his appointment as *maestro di cappella e di camera e compositore* at the imperial court with six months' leave each year.

Donizetti had long suffered blinding headaches, and by 1842 his health was visibly failing. Nevertheless, in 1843 he produced his greatest comic opera, *Don Pasquale* (Paris, Théâtre-Italien, 3 Jan.), the opera seria *Maria di Rohan* (Vienna, 5 June), and his last French grand opera, *Dom Sébastien* (Opéra, 13 Nov.). The last opera premiered in his lifetime was *Caterina Cornaro* (Naples, San Carlo, 12 Jan. 1844), at which he was not present. He prepared *Dom Sébastien* and Verdi's *Ernani* for their Vienna premieres early in 1845; thereafter his physical and mental abilities rapidly deteriorated, presumably owing to the late stages of syphilis. Early in 1846 he was placed in a mental institution at Ivry; in Sept. 1847 he was moved to Bergamo, where he died the following year.

Besides the 60 operas performed in his lifetime (and several brought to light after), he composed much sacred music, much of it student and early work; Requiems for Bellini (1835) and Zingarelli (1837); a Miserere, performed in 1843, the most important of several works composed or revised for the imperial chapel; cantatas and other occasional works, mostly vocal; many songs and duets. Instrumental works include several sinfonie, mostly early, 1 on themes by Bellini (1836); an English horn concerto, 1816; a clarinet concerto; a concerto for violin and cello; 19 string quartets, mostly early; other chamber works; piano pieces.

Bibl.: G. Zavadini, *Donizetti: Vita, musiche, epistolario* (Bergamo, 1948). Herbert Weinstock, *Donizetti* (New York, 1963). *The Donizetti Society Journal* (1974–). John Allitt, *Donizetti and the Tradition of Romantic Love* (London, 1975). William Ashbrook, *Donizetti and His Operas* (Cambridge, 1982). Philip Gossett, *Anna Bolena and the Artistic Maturity of Gaetano Donizetti* (Oxford, 1985).

Donostia, José Antonio de (b. San Sebastián, 10 Jan. 1886; d. Lecároz, Navarra, 30 Aug. 1956). Composer. A Franciscan priest, he studied composition with Eugene Cools and Roussel in Paris and spent time in both Latin America and France. He was a charter member of the Instituto español de musicología in Barcelona, founded in 1943. His compositions encompass sacred works, such as staged cantatas and a Requiem Mass (1945), as well as solo and chamber music, including the 4 volumes of *Preludios vascos* for piano, published 1912–23; he also made important contributions to Basque folk music scholarship, including *La música popular vasca* (1918) and *Euskel eres-sorta* (1922), in the latter of which 493 transcribed Basque folk tunes are published.

Donovan, Richard Frank (b. New Haven, 29 Nov. 1891; d. Middletown, Conn., 22 Aug. 1970). Composer and organist. As a youth he played the piano in dance bands and theater orchestras; studied at Yale and at the Institute of Musical Art in New York; studied in Paris with Widor. Taught at Smith College, in New York, and at Yale (1928–60), where he was professor of theory from 1947. In New Haven he conducted the symphony (1936–51) and was organist and choirmaster at Christ Church (1928–65). He composed works for orchestra (*Design for Radio,* 1945; *Passacaglia on Vermont Folk Tunes,* 1949; *Epos,* 1963); chamber and piano music; organ works (*Antiphon and Chorale,* 1955); a Mass, Magnificat, and other choral works; songs (*Five Elizabethan Lyrics,* 1963).

Dopper, Cornelis (b. Stadskanaal, 7 Feb. 1870; d. Amsterdam, 18 Sept. 1939). Composer and conductor. From 1877 to 1890 he studied at the Leipzig Conservatory with Karl Wendling (piano), Jadassohn (theory), and Reinecke (composition). After returning to Amsterdam, he conducted the Netherlands Opera from 1896. In 1903–4 he toured the U.S. with the Savage Opera Co. He was appointed assistant conductor (to Willem Mengelberg) of the Concertgebouw Orchestra in 1908; he remained in this post until 1931. His compositions manifest a late-Romantic outlook, with special care for details of orchestration. Works include 4 completed operas (*Het blinde meisje von Castel Cuillé,* 1892; *Fritjof,* 1895; *Willem Ratcliff,* 1901; *Het eerekruis,* 1904); choral works *(De wilgen);* 8 symphonies (no. 3, Rembrandt Symphony; no. 5, *Symphonia epica*); 5 orchestral suites; *Ciaconna gotica,* symphonic variations (1920–21, his best known work); a concerto for trumpet and 3 kettledrums; a cello concerto; a string quartet (1914); sonata for violin and piano.

Doppler, (Albert) Franz [Ferenc] (b. Lemberg [now Lvov], 16 Oct. 1821; d. Baden, near Vienna, 27 July 1883). Flutist and composer. Son and pupil of a musician; toured as a flutist, sometimes with his brother Karl; from 1838, first flutist at the German Theater in Pest, and from 1841 at the Hungarian National Theater, where he had 4 Hungarian operas produced with considerable success in 1847–53; from 1858, first flutist at the Vienna Opera, where he was also assistant (later chief) conductor of the ballet, writing much ballet music; from 1865 he taught at the Vienna Conservatory. Other works include a German opera; instrumental and choral pieces; songs.

Doppler, Karl [Karoly] (b. Lemberg [now Lvov], 12 Sept. 1825; d. Stuttgart, 10 Mar. 1900). Flutist and composer. Brother of Franz, with whom he often toured; 1843–46, flutist at the German Theater in Pest, also composing music for productions; 1846–62, flutist and assistant conductor, Hungarian National Theater; his Hungarian singspiel *A gránátos tábor* (The Grenadier Camp) was successful there in 1853; 1865–98, court music director, Stuttgart. He also composed piano pieces and songs.

Dorati, Antal (b. Budapest, 9 Apr. 1906; d. Gerzensee, near Bern, 13 Nov. 1988). Conductor and composer. Studied with Léo Weiner, Bartók, and Kodály at the Franz Liszt Academy, graduating in 1924. From his first appointment (as répétiteur and conductor at the Budapest Opera, 1924–28) until 1945 he was principally engaged as a conductor of opera and ballet. Assistant conductor at the Dresden Opera (1928–29); musical director and conductor at the Münster Opera (1930–32); conductor of the Ballet russe de Monte Carlo (1933–38) and musical director (1938–41); musical director, American Ballet Theater (1941–45); director of New Opera Company in New York (1941–42). U.S. debut with the National Symphony in 1937. After World War II he worked with a series of orchestras, beginning with the Dallas Symphony (musical director, 1945–49). Conductor of the Minneapolis Symphony (1949–54; musical director, 1954–60); chief conductor of the BBC Symphony (1962–66); principal conductor of the Stockholm Philharmonic (1966–70); musical director of the National Symphony (1970–77); senior conductor of the Royal Philharmonic, London (1975–78); musical director of the Detroit Symphony (1977–81). All the while he continued to compose in large forms, e.g., a symphony, a ballet, piano and cello concertos, a cantata, numerous chamber works. Of his more than 500 recordings the most significant are probably his integral cycle of Haydn symphonies, made with the Philharmonia Hungarica (1971–74), and his series of Haydn operas, begun in 1976.

Doret, Gustave (b. Aigle, Vaud, Switzerland, 20 Sept. 1866; d. Lausanne, 19 Apr. 1943). Composer and conductor. He studied with Joachim in Berlin (1885–87) and then with Dubois and Massenet in Paris; began an active conducting career in Paris and in 1894 (when he also led the first performance of Debussy's *Faun*) was appointed director of the Opéra-comique; established the Théâtre du Jorat in Mezières (near Lausanne), for which he wrote many lighter stage works with René Morax. His 2 serious operas (*Les armaillis,* 1906, and *La tisseuse d'orties,* 1927) were performed in Paris; his light works were popular not only in France but also in Switzerland and Belgium. His style shows the influence of both his friend Debussy and his teacher Massenet. He returned to Switzerland in 1914 in order to study Swiss popular music and to aid in the diffusion of Swiss musical culture. He wrote mainly vocal music, including operas, popular musical theater, an oratorio, choral works, and some 300 songs. His instrumental music was limited to 2 orchestral works, a string quartet, and a piano quintet. He acted as musical correspondent for 2 Swiss newspapers and published a volume of memoirs (*Temps et contretemps,* 1942).

Dorham, Kenny [McKinley Howard] (b. near Fairfield, Tex., 30 Aug. 1924; d. New York, 5 Dec. 1972). Jazz trumpeter. He played in the bop big bands of Dizzy Gillespie and Billy Eckstine before joining Charlie Parker's quintet (1948–49). He was a founding member of Art Blakey's and Horace Silver's hard bop quintet (1954) and recorded the album *The Jazz Messengers at the Café Bohemia* under Blakey's leadership (1955). He joined Max Roach's quintet (1956–58) and led groups, including a quintet with Joe Henderson (1962–64).

Dorn, Heinrich (Ludwig Egmont) (b. Königsberg, 14 Nov. 1800 or 1804; d. Berlin, 10 Jan. 1892). Conductor, composer, and teacher. Studied law in Berlin, but also had lessons with Berger (piano) and Zelter and Klein (composition) and produced an opera there (1826). From 1828, theater conductor, Königsberg; 1829–32, music director and theater conductor, Leipzig, where Schumann and Clara Wieck studied with him; 1832, conductor, Hamburg; 1832–42, music director, St. Peter's cathedral, Riga, where he met Wagner and formed the basis for his later opposition to him and his music; 1843, music director and theater conductor, Cologne; 1844–47, directed Lower Rhine Music Festival; 1845, founded Rheinische Musikschule, which in 1850 became the Cologne Conservatory; 1849–69, conductor, Berlin Opera. Taught and wrote, publishing a 7-volume collection of memoirs and opinions, *Aus meinem Leben* (Berlin, 1870–86). He composed several operas (a *Nibelungen* opera, 1854, before Wagner's); concert overtures; chamber music; piano pieces; songs.

Dorsey, Jimmy [James] (b. Shenandoah, Pa., 29 Feb. 1904; d. New York, 12 June 1957). Jazz and popular clarinetist, alto saxophonist, and bandleader. Brother of Tommy Dorsey. He played dixieland jazz with Red Nichols; their recordings (intermittently 1926–32) include "That's No Bargain" (1926), showing his control of special effects on the saxophone. He formed the Dorsey Brothers Orchestra (1934), taking over sole leadership after a dispute with Tommy (1935–53); the band's greatest hit record was "Green Eyes" (1941). The Dorsey Brothers Orchestra re-formed in 1953, with Jimmy briefly assuming control of the big band after Tommy's death (1956).

Dorsey, Thomas A(ndrew) [Georgia Tom; Barrelhouse Tommy] (b. Villa Rica, Ga. 1 July 1899; d. Chicago, 23 Jan. 1993). Blues and gospel pianist, singer, and songwriter. After coming to Chicago (ca. 1918), he accompanied Ma Rainey (1924–28), and then made influential recordings with many blues players, especially guitarist Tampa Red (1928–32), under several names including The Hokum Boys ("Beedle Um Bum," 1928). He contributed numerous blues songs to the standard repertory before turning exclusively to gospel music (ca. 1932). He organized gospel choirs, a publishing company, and a national gospel choral convention (from 1933), and composed many gospel songs, including "Precious Lord, Take My Hand" (1932).

Dorsey, Tommy [Thomas] (b. Shenandoah, Pa., 19 Nov. 1905; d. Greenwich, Conn., 26 Nov. 1956). Jazz and popular trombonist and bandleader; brother of Jimmy Dorsey. After an argument with Jimmy, he left the Dorsey Brothers big band (1934–35) to form his own, which at times included Bunny Berigan, Buddy Rich, and Frank Sinatra. Among its recordings are a fine example of his ballad playing, "I'm Gettin' Sentimental over You" (1935), as well as "Song of India" (1937), and "Everything Happens to Me" (1941). He again led a big band with Jimmy from 1953.

Dowd, William (Richmond) (b. Newark, N.J., 28 Feb. 1922). Harpsichord maker. He studied English at Harvard (A.B., 1948). In 1949 he and Frank Hubbard established a harpsichord workshop in Boston. Dowd created a design based on the two-manual harpsichords of Pascal Taskin that quickly became popular with performers. After the firm dissolved in 1958, Dowd established his own workshop in Cambridge, Mass. In 1971 he established a Paris workshop with Reinhard von Nagel.

Dowland, John (b. London? 1563; d. there, buried 20 Feb. 1626). Composer and lutenist. Spent much of his adult life outside of England but always maintained ties with his native land. Was in Paris from 1580 until about 1584, in the service of the English ambassador to the French royal court. Earned the B.Mus. from Oxford in 1588. Although his compositions began to be known at the English royal court in 1590, his first attempt to gain a post as a court lutenist, in 1594, was unsuccessful. This attempt was followed immediately by a trip abroad, first to two German noble courts, then to Italy, then back to Germany. Returning to England in late 1596 or early 1597, he made another futile attempt to gain a position at court. Early in 1598 the Landgrave of Hesse, who had previously befriended the composer, invited him to take up a court post in Kassel; it is not known whether he accepted. Late that year he became a court lutenist for Christian IV of Denmark, a post he retained until 1606, with an interruption of one year (spent in England) beginning in the middle of 1603. In 1606 an English nobleman with connections at court, Theophilus Howard, Lord Walden, gave him a position, and in 1612 he finally won a post at the English royal court.

During his stay in Paris in the 1580s, Dowland converted to Catholicism. Contrary to the composer's own complaints, this fact seems to have had no effect on his musical career. It is clear that his compositions were widely known and popular both in England and on the Continent. His music is present in many prints and manuscripts of the age, and it was often arranged and musical material borrowed by other composers; also, many literary works, especially plays, include references to particular compositions.

Dowland's works include about 15 settings of Psalms or sacred songs (most for 4 voices) and about twice as many pieces for instrumental consort, most prominent among them being the *Lachrimae or Seven Teares* for consort of 5 viols or violins and lute (London, 1604; ed. P. Warlock, London, 1927). Far more numerous are the works for solo lute (ed. D. Poulton and B. Lam, London, 1974), which include dances, arrangements of songs and popular tunes, and free compositions (particularly fantasias). Most important and most numerous are the secular lute songs or airs, the majority for 1 voice and lute or 4 voices (ed. in *MB* 6; *EL* 1st ser., 1–2, 5–6, 10–11, 12, 14; *EL* 2nd ser., 20); many were first published in London in 3 numbered books (1597, 1600, and 1603) and *A Pilgrim's Solace* (1612). He also published a translation of Ornithoparcus' *Musicae activae micrologus* of 1517 as *Andreas Ornithoparcus his Micrologus* (London, 1609).

Bibl.: Ian Spink, *English Song: Dowland to Purcell* (London, 1974). Diana Poulton, *John Dowland* (Berkeley, 1972; 2nd ed., 1982). John Ward, "A Dowland Miscellany," *Journal of the Lute Society of America* 10 (1977) [Dowland issue].

Dowland, Robert (b. London, 1591; d. there, 28 Nov. 1641). Lutenist and composer. Son of John Dowland. Published 2 anthologies of monodies and lute music, *A Varietie of Lute-Lessons* and *A Musicall Banquet,* both in 1610; played in a masque of Chapman in 1613; traveled in Europe with an acting troupe in the 1620s; succeeded his father as one of the King's Lutes in 1626. Only 3 works are firmly ascribed to him—2 lute pieces in the *Varietie* and 1 in the Margaret Board Lutebook.

Downes, Edward (Thomas) (b. Aston, 17 June 1924). Conductor. Studied horn, theory, and composition at the Royal College of Music (1944–46). A Carnegie Scholarship in 1948 enabled him to study in Zurich with Hermann Scherchen. Returning to London, he obtained a post as coach with the Carl Rosa Opera Company (1950–51), with the Royal Opera at Covent Garden (1951–53). After conducting *La bohème* during a tour of Rhodesia in 1953 he was appointed staff conductor at Covent Garden; by 1969, when he resigned, he had led almost every work in the repertory. In 1967 he became the first English conductor since Beecham to lead a complete *Ring.* Musical director of the Australian Opera at Sydney (1972–76); of the BBC Northern Symphony (1980). Premieres include Davies's *Taverner* (1972); translated the libretti of operas by Mussorgsky, Prokofiev, and Shostakovich.

Draeseke, Felix (August Bernhard) (b. Coburg, 7 Oct. 1835; d. Dresden, 26 Feb. 1913). Composer. From an ecclesiastical family; at 17 he entered the Leipzig Conservatory, but, dissatisfied there, from 1855 he studied privately with Rietz and became a firm adherent of the New German School, meeting Liszt in 1857 and Wagner in 1861. He composed long symphonic poems and an opera, *König Sigurd* (1853–57), which interested Liszt but was never performed. In 1862, discouraged by lack of success (and subject to depression), he moved to Lausanne, where he radically changed his musical direction, turning to classical forms and achieving profound mastery of counterpoint, canon, and fugue. After various disappointments—failing hearing (eventually deafness), a broken engagement, bad investments, failure to receive a hoped-for post at the Geneva Conservatory in 1875—he moved to Dresden in 1876, increasingly attracting composition pupils; from 1884, composition professor, Dresden Conservatory; from 1892, Univ. of Berlin. A prolific composer; his magnum opus, the oratorio tetralogy *Christus* (1895–99; like many of his works, to his own text), intended as a counterpart to Wagner's *Ring,* had only one complete production (Berlin and Dresden, 1912). Other works include 5 symphonies; 5 operas; violin and piano concertos; chamber music; much sacred music; choral works; songs; books on music theory and one attacking modern music.

Bibl.: Erich Roeder, *Felix Draeseke* (Dresden and Berlin, 1932–37).

Draghi, Antonio (b. Rimini, ca. 1634; d. Vienna, 16 Jan. 1700). Composer and librettist. Perhaps served in the court orchestra at Mantua; possibly also studied at Venice, where he appeared as a bass singer in 1657. He served the Viennese court from 1658 to his death, first as a member of the dowager Empress Eleonora's Kapelle; took over over as her Kapellmeister in 1669; became director of dramatic music for the imperial court in 1673 and imperial Kapellmeister in 1682, retaining the latter post for the rest of his life. In addition to 124 stage works and 50 vocal chamber pieces, he produced over a dozen oratorios, some 30 *sepolcri* (staged sacred dramas for Holy Week), and a variety of other sacred works, as well as many libretti.

Draghi, Giovanni Battista (b. Italy, ca. 1640; d. London, 1708). Keyboardist and composer. Brought to England in the 1660s by King Charles II; became organist at the queen's Catholic chapel, Somerset House, in 1673, supplanting Locke; named organist at the chapel of James II in 1687. He composed many songs for inclusion in plays and published collections along with suites and other keyboard music, and provided the setting for Dryden's *Ode for St. Cecilia's Day* in 1687.

Drăgoi, Sabin V(asile) (b. Selişte, Arad, Romania, 18 June 1894; d. Bucharest, 31 Dec. 1968). Composer. After early study at the conservatory at Cluj (1919–20), where his teachers were Augustin Bena and Hermann Klee, he enrolled at the Prague Conservatory, where he was a student of Novák. At the conservatory at Timisoara he taught theory and composition (1924–42 and 1946–50). Later he held posts as director of the Folklore Institute at Bucharest (1950–64) and as a member of the International Folk Music Council. His works include the operas *Năpasta* (1927; rev. 1958; first perf., 1961), *Kir Ianulea* (1937; first perf., 1939), and Păcală (1956; first perf., 1962); cantatas (*Mai multă lumină,* 1951; *Cununa,* 1959); film scores (*Ciocîrlia,* 1954); orchestral music (*Three Symphonic Tableaus,* 1922; a piano concerto, 1941; *Seven Popular Dances,* 1960); chamber and instrumental works (a string quartet, 1952; *Fifty Colinde,* piano, 1957); songs and other vocal music.

Dragonetti, Domenico (Carlo Maria) (b. Venice, 7 Apr. 1763; d. London, 16 Apr. 1846). Double bassist and composer. Mostly self-taught, he become a phenomenal virtuoso; from 13 played in Venetian opera orchestras, from 1782 in the San Marco cappella; from 1794 a leading figure in London music, as first double bassist in many orchestras (Italian Opera, many concert societies, and provincial festivals); 1845, led double basses at the unveiling of the Beethoven monument in Bonn; also noted for his eccentricities, which included keeping his dog by him in orchestras; composed concertos and much chamber music for bass, almost none of it published until recent times.

Dragoni, Giovanni Andrea (b. Meldola, near Forlì, ca. 1540; d. Rome, Dec. 1598). Composer. Studied with Palestrina; worked chiefly in Rome. *Maestro di cappella* at St. John Lateran from 1576, he wrote much sacred music, all but one book of motets preserved only in manuscript and most now lost, and many secular works, particularly madrigals and villanelle, published in 7 complete books and numerous anthologies.

Drdla, František [Franz] Alois (b. Žďár nad Sázavou, Moravia, 28 Nov. 1869; d. Bad Gastein, Austria, 3 Sept. 1944). Composer and violinist. He studied at the Prague Conservatory (1880–82) with Foerster (composition) and Bennewitz (violin) and then at the Vienna Conservatory (1882–88) with Hellmesberger (violin) and Krenn and Bruckner (composition). He was a violinist in the Viennese Royal Opera (1890–93) and then concertmaster of the orchestra at the Theater an der Wien (1894–99). He toured Europe and the U.S. His lighter compositions achieved great popularity, especially Serenade no. 1 in A (1901), and *Souvenir in D* (1904). Other works include the operettas *Zlatá síť* [The Golden Net] (Leipzig, 1916) and *Komtesa z prodejny* [The Shop Countess] (Brno, 1917); a violin concerto (1931); works for violin and piano.

Drechsler, Joseph (b. Wällisch-Birken, Bohemia, 26 May 1782; d. Vienna, 27 Feb. 1852). Composer, conductor, and organist. From 1815, organist or choirmaster at various Viennese churches and a highly regarded teacher (pupils include J. Strauss II); from 1821, conductor at the Josefstadttheater; 1824–30, chief conductor at the Leopoldstadttheater; from 1844, choirmaster at St. Stephen's Cathedral. Composed over 50 singspiels and other stage works; much sacred music; chamber, piano, organ pieces; pedagogical works.

Dresden, Sem (b. Amsterdam, 20 Apr. 1881; d. The Hague, 30 July 1957). Composer. Born of a family of merchants, he began musical study with Bernard Zweers in Amsterdam, then from 1903 studied with Pfitzner in Berlin. He returned to the Netherlands to begin a career as a conductor, chiefly of choral music. From 1919 he taught composition at the Amsterdam Conservatory, of which he was appointed director in 1924. Later he directed the Royal Conservatory, The Hague (1937–41; 1945–49). After his retirement from teaching in 1949 he was prolific, producing several of his best works as a septuagenarian, including the orchestral suite *Dansflitsen* (1951), perhaps his best-known work. He also wrote music criticism for the Amsterdam daily *De Telegraaf* and authored two books on new music. His chiefly Romantic musical idiom is often infused with impressionistic sonorities. He composed operas (*Toto,* 1945; *François Villon,* 1956–57, orchestrated by Jan Mul; first perf., 1958); choral and vocal works (*Chorus tragicus,* with brass and percussion, 1927; *O Kerstnacht,* 1939; *Assumpta est Maria,* 1943; *Saint Antoine,* oratorio, 1953; *Rembrandt's Saul en David,* soprano, orchestra, 1956); orchestral works (*Theme and Variations,* 1913; *Symphonietta,* clarinet, orchestra, 1938; concertos for oboe, piano, flute, organ, and 2 for violin, 1936 and 1942); chamber works (3 suites for piano and winds, 1911–20; sonata for solo violin, 1943; suite for solo cello, 1943–47); *Hor ai dolor,* piano (1950).

Dresher, Paul Joseph (b. Los Angeles, 8 Jan. 1951). Composer. He earned a B.A. in Music at the Univ. of California at Berkeley in 1977 and an M.A. in composition at the Univ. of California at San Diego in 1979, where his teachers included Robert Erickson, Roger Reynolds, and Pauline Oliveros. He studied North Indian music with Nikhil Banerjee (1974–77), Ghanaian drumming with C. K. and Kobla Ladzekpo (1975–79), and Javanese and Balinese gamelan. In 1984 he started the Paul Dresher Ensemble. He has written many theater pieces in collaboration with George Coates. Works include the operas *The Way of How* (1981), *ave ave* (1983), *See Hear* (1984), *Slow Fire* (1985–86), *Power Failure* (1989), *Pioneers* (1989–90). Other works include *Loose the Thread* (violin, piano, percussion, 1988); *Rhythmia* (tape piece for dance, 1987); *Shelflife* (dance piece, 1987); *The Tempest* (theater score, 1987); *Figaro Gets a Divorce* (theater score, 1986); *re:act:ion* (orchestra, 1984).

Dressler, Gallus (b. Nebra, Thuringia, 16 Oct. 1533; d. Zerbst, Anhalt, between 1580 and 1589). Composer. In 1557 enrolled in the academy in Jena, perhaps after having studied with Clemens non Papa in the Netherlands. In 1558 succeeded Martin Agricola as Kantor of the grammar school at Magdeburg, remaining there until about 1570, when he took a degree at Wittenberg Univ. Most of his compositions date from the years in Magdeburg. The largest number are contrapuntal settings of Latin texts; the more influential are early examples of the German-language motet. He wrote 3 treatises: *Practica modorum explicatio* (Jena, 1561), *Praecepta musicae poeticae* (unpublished, 1563), and *Musicae practicae elementa in usum scholae Magdeburgensis edita* (Magdeburg, 1571).

Driessler, Johannes (b. Friedrichsthal, Saarland, 26 Jan. 1921). Composer and organist. Studied organ and composition at the Hochschule für Musik in Cologne

(1939–40). From 1946 taught at the Northwest German Academy of Music in Detmold; director from 1960. He wrote 4 dramatic works (1952–58); several concertos and symphonies (Symphony no. 3, op. 63, strings and percussion, 1969; a sinfonia da camera, *Ikarus,* 2 soloists, chorus, and orchestra, 1960); chamber and piano music; works for organ (*20 choralsonaten* op. 30, 1955); and vocal music (*Altenberger Messe* op. 33, 7 voices and 10 winds, 1955).

Drigo, Riccardo (b. Padua, 30 June 1846; d. there, 1 Oct. 1930). Conductor and composer. Studied at the Venice Conservatory, 1860–64; from 1869 gradually became known as an opera conductor in northern Italy and on tour; 1878–79, conductor at the Teatro Manzoni, Milan; 1879–86, conductor at the Italian Opera, St. Petersburg; 1886–1919, at the Imperial Ballet, conducting the premieres of *Sleeping Beauty* and *Nutcracker;* composed much additional and substitute music for ballets and several complete ones (including *Arlekinada,* 1900, whose *Serenade* and *Valse bluette* became widely popular as light music); spent 1914–16 in Italy; retired to Padua in 1920.

Bibl.: S. Travaglia, *Riccardo Drigo: L'uomo e l'artista* (Padua, 1929). R. J. Wiley, trans., "Memoirs of R. E. Drigo," *Dancing Times* 72 (1981–82): 577–78, 661–62.

D'Rivera, Paquito (b. Havana, 4 June 1948). Jazz alto saxophonist. In 1967 he helped form a jazz, pop, and salsa group which for political reasons took the name Orquesta cubana de música moderna. Several members remained together in the band Irakere (from ca. 1973), which began touring internationally. While in Spain, D'Rivera defected and moved to New York (1980). After playing with Dizzy Gillespie and McCoy Tyner, he formed his own Afro-Cuban jazz combo. His albums include *Paquito Blowin'* (1981) and *Live at Keystone Korner* (1983).

Drouet, Louis (-François-Philippe) (b. Amsterdam, 14 Apr. 1792; d. Bern, 30 Sept. 1873). Flutist. Child prodigy, largely self-taught; at 15, soloist to the King of Holland; 1811, invited to Paris by Napoleon and given a court appointment, making successful solo appearances; at the restoration, made first flutist of royal chapel; toured widely in Europe; 1817–18, played in England and started flute manufacture; 1840–54, Kapellmeister at Coburg; 1854, visited U.S. Composition lessons from Méhul and Reicha. Composer of 10 flute concertos and much other flute music, a flute *Méthode* (1827), and collections of études (including *100 études* op. 126); arranger of the song "Partant pour la Syrie," attributed to Queen Hortense, which became the anthem of the Second Empire.

Druckman, Jacob (Raphael) (b. Philadelphia, 26 June 1928). Composer. As a youth he studied piano and violin and played trumpet in jazz ensembles; studied composition with Copland at the Berkshire Music Center (1949); attended Juilliard (B.S., 1954; M.S., 1956; composition with Wagenaar, Mennin, and Persichetti); studied at the École normale in Paris (1954). Taught at Bard College (1961–67), Brooklyn College (1972–76), and Yale (from 1976), where he directed the electronic music studio. His *Windows* (orchestra, 1972) won the Pulitzer Prize. He was composer-in-residence to the New York Philharmonic, 1982–87.

Having explored serialism (String Quartet no. 2, 1966), in the mid-1960s he began to combine recorded electronic music and live performers, often with elements of theater. The clarinetist in *Animus III* (with tape, 1969) must speak and mumble into his instrument; "When it's done properly, there's a projection of complete insanity on the part of the performer." *Synapse* (1971), a purely electronic piece, is meant to be performed as a prelude to *Valentine* (double bass and tape, 1969). *Windows* (1972) demonstrates Druckman's role in the New Romanticists' revival of the orchestra and employs elements of chance. Several works from the 1970s incorporate preexistent material; *Prism* (1980) quotes a different opera (Charpentier, Cavalli, Cherubini) in each of its 3 movements.

Other works include an opera (*Medea,* commissioned by the Metropolitan Opera in 1982); works for orchestra (*Chiaroscuro,* 1977; a viola concerto, 1978; *Brangle,* 1989; *Nor Spell Nor Charm,* 1990; *Summer Lightning,* 1991; *Demos,* 1992); works for performers and tape (*Delizie contente che l'alme beate,* after Cavalli, wind quintet and tape, 1973; *Animus I–IV,* 1966–77); *Incenters* (13 instruments, 1968), 3 string quartets (1948, 1966, 1981), *Tromba marina* (4 double basses, 1981), and other chamber music; piano works; choral and vocal music, some with ensemble or orchestra (*Counterpoise,* soprano, orchestra, 1994).

Bibl.: *Jacob Druckman: A Complete Catalogue of His Works* (New York, 1981).

Dubensky, Arcady (b. Viatka, Russia, 15 Oct. 1890; d. Tenafly, N.J., 14 Oct. 1966). Composer and violinist. From the age of 13 he played violin in a local theater orchestra; trained at the Moscow Conservatory (diploma, 1909); played in the Moscow Imperial Opera Orchestra (1910–19); left Russia in 1919; arrived in New York in 1921, where he played in the New York Symphony (later Philharmonic) Orchestra (1922–53). His compositions, in a diatonic style drawn from Russian Romanticism, were performed by orchestras in Boston, New York, Philadelphia, and elsewhere during his career with the New York Philharmonic.

Dubois, (François-Clément-) Théodore (b. Rosnay, Marne, 24 Aug. 1837; d. Paris, 11 June 1924). Composer and teacher. Studied with the choirmaster at Rheims, then at the Paris Conservatory, winning the Prix de Rome in 1861. Organist at Ste.-Clotilde, then, 1869–77, choirmaster at the Madeleine and organist there from 1877. Also taught at the Conservatory: from 1871, harmony; from 1891, composition; 1896–1905, director; 1894, elected to the Académie. A prolific composer, he is best known for his organ music (88 solo pieces; *Fantaisie triomphale,* organ and orchestra) and religious vocal music (5 oratorios, cantatas, Masses, 71 motets). Other works include operas; a ballet, *La farandole* (Opéra, 1883); orchestral and chamber music; piano pieces; songs; textbooks on harmony, counterpoint, solfège.

Du Caurroy, (François-) Eustache (b. Gerberoy or Beauvais, bapt. 4 Feb. 1549; d. Paris, 7 Aug. 1609). Composer. From about 1570 he was associated with the French royal court, first as singer, then composer; later also held ecclesiastical posts in provincial churches. His *Meslanges de musique* (Paris, 1610; ed. in *MMRF* 17), a collection of Psalms, noëls, and chansons, includes examples of *musique mesurée à l'antique.* A Requiem composed in 1606 was performed at the funeral in 1610 of Henry IV and at funerals of all French kings for some time thereafter. He also wrote many motets and other sacred music and 3 instrumental fantasias.

Bibl.: *Les oeuvres complètes* (Brooklyn, 1975–).

Du Chemin, Nicolas (b. Sens, ca. 1515; d. Paris, 1576). Printer. Issued books of various sorts from 1541, but concentrated on music after being granted a royal privilege in 1548. Claude Goudimel and other musicians served as his editors. He published about 100 books of sacred and secular vocal music, 4 collections of instrumental dances, and 1 of lute music.

Bibl.: François Lesure and Genviève Thibault, "Bibliographie des éditions musicales publiées par Nicolas du Chemin," *AnnM* 1 (1953): 269–373; 4 (1956): 251; 6 (1958–63): 403.

Ducis [Herzog], **Benedictus** [Benedikt] (b. near Konstanz, ca. 1490; d. Schalckstetten, near Ulm, 1544). Composer and Protestant pastor. His musical style, the sources transmitting his works, and certain biographical details suggest that he had some connection, perhaps indirect, with the musicians at the court of the Emperor Maximilian, particularly Isaac and Senfl. His compositions consist chiefly of sacred music with Latin or German texts. Most of the liturgical works are lost. The secular music includes Latin odes and German lieder. Because of the identity of the first names of Ducis, Benedictus de Opitiis, and Benedictus Appenzeller, many attributions have been uncertain.

Dufallo, Richard (John) (b. E. Chicago, Ind., 30 Jan. 1933). Conductor. Studied clarinet at the American Conservatory of Music in Chicago; composition at UCLA with Foss; joined Foss's Improvisation Chamber Ensemble in 1957. Associate conductor, Buffalo Philharmonic (1962–67), during Foss's tenure; taught at SUNY-Buffalo (1963–67). After participating in European performances of Stockhausen's *Carré* (1972) he was in demand as a conductor of music by Xenakis, Druckman, Davies, and others. Music director of the 20th-century music series at Juilliard (1972–79).

Dufay, Guillaume (b. ca. 1400; d. Cambrai, 27 Nov. 1474). Composer. His contemporaries regarded him as the greatest composer of their age. Most of his life was spent in association with Cambrai Cathedral, beginning with several years as a choirboy from 1409 to 1414. His movements for the next few years are unclear, but he seems in this time to have established connections with Italy and with the Malatesta family; documents, compositions, and circumstantial evidence suggest that he may have been in Constance (at the Council of Constance), Rimini (where one branch of the Malatesta family was based), and Laon, returning in 1426 or 1427 to Cambrai. From late 1428 until 1433 he was in Rome as a member of the papal chapel, which had close ties with Cambrai. From 1433 until 1435 the court of Savoy employed him, then for several more years the papal chapel, which at that time was temporarily in Florence and later in Bologna. From no later than 1439 until his death, Dufay resided in Cambrai, except for part of the 1450s, when he was in Savoy for seven years, a stay preceded by a brief visit to Turin and followed by another to Besançon. From at least 1433 he had some contact with the Este family in Ferrara. In the last decades of his life he was visited or contacted by many prominent personages, including Binchois, Morton, Hayne van Ghizeghem, Ockeghem, Tinctoris, Antonio Squarcialupi, and Pierre VII de Ranchicourt, Bishop of Arras. Busnois, Ockeghem, and Héniart composed lamentations on his death.

Guillaume Dufay with Binchois.

His sacred music can be divided into three broad categories. The first, which encompasses hymns, antiphons, many independent Mass movements, and some motets, consists of pieces in a simple, often treble-dominated style. In many cases the melody on which the piece is based is a plainchant, which may be lightly or more elaborately ornamented and which usually appears in the top of three voices; many such pieces are written in fauxbourdon. The second category consists of musically complex motets, most in four parts. Many of these pieces are isorhythmic, polytextual, or both, and they were usually written for specific occasions and used only then. The third category consists of

Mass pairs, three-section sets of Mass movements, and Mass cycles. Early compositions in this group are only loosely unified, by mode, mensuration, head motifs, perhaps vague similarities in melodic material, and may have either three or four voices. The later compositions are all tenor Masses in four voices. Dufay's most conspicuous innovation in this category is his use in some instances of a secular *cantus prius factus.* A few additional independent Mass movements lie outside these categories.

The secular songs are, with only a few exceptions, in three parts, and almost all have French texts. The rondeau predominates. Usually one voice is texted and the others untexted, but sometimes texts are provided for two or even all three voices.

Works: 9 Masses, including *Missa Ave regina caelorum, Missa Caput* (of doubtful authenticity), *Missa L'homme armé, Missa Se la face ay pale;* nearly 30 Mass movements or sets of movements, including *Gloria ad modum tube;* about 20 other Mass compositions; 15 antiphons; almost 30 hymns; over 30 motets (13 isorhythmic), including *Ecclesie militantis, Flos florum, Nuper rosarum flores;* almost 90 secular songs; many more works with doubtful or conflicting attributions.

Bibl.: Guillaume Dufay, *Opera omnia, CMM* 1 (1947–49, 1951–66). Charles E. Hamm, *A Chronology of the Works of Guillaume Dufay Based on a Study of Mensural Practice* (Princeton, 1964). Craig Wright, "Dufay at Cambrai: Discoveries and Revisions," *JAMS* 28 (1975): 175. Allan W. Atlas, ed., *Papers Read at the Dufay Quincentenary Conference, Brooklyn College, December 6–7, 1974* (Brooklyn, 1976). David Fallows, *Dufay* (New York, 1988). Don Michael Randel, "Dufay the Reader," in *Studies in the History of Music* 1 (New York, 1983), pp. 38–78. Alejandro Enrique Planchart, "The Early Career of Guillaume Du Fay," *JAMS* 46 (1993): 341–68. Craig Wright," Dufay's *Nuper rosarum flores,* King Solomon's Temple, and the Veneration of the Virgin," *JAMS* 47 (1994): 395–441.

Dugger, Edwin (b. Poplar Bluff, Mo., 21 March 1940). Composer. He studied at Oberlin Conservatory and at Princeton, where his teachers included Roger Sessions, Earl Kim, and Milton Babbitt. He taught at Oberlin from 1967 to 1969, and then at the Univ. of California at Berkeley. Works include *Divisions of Time* (woodwind quartet, piano, percussion, 1962); *Intermezzi* (12 performers, 1969); *Fantasy* (piano, 1977); *Duo* (flute, viola, 1979); *Variations and Adagio* (9 performers, 1979); *Music for Synthesizer and 6 Instruments* (1966); *Abwesenheiten und Wiedersehen* (11 performers and tape, 1971).

Dukas, Paul (Abraham) (b. Paris, 1 Oct. 1865; d. there, 17 May 1935). Composer and critic. Studied harmony and piano at the Paris Conservatory from age 16, and in 1883 was a member of Guiraud's composition class. He later taught orchestration (1910–13) and composition (from 1928) there. In between those two teaching appointments he served as inspector of music education in the provincial conservatories. He was appointed to the Académie des beaux arts in 1934. By the 1890s he had begun writing criticism for several publications *(Revue hebdomadaire, Gazette des beaux-arts, Chronique des arts et de la curiosité).* He was friendly with d'Indy and with Debussy, in whose memory he wrote "La plainte, sur loin, du faune," piano (1920). With Saint-Saëns he collaborated on the orchestration of Guiraud's *Frédégonde* and in editions of works by Rameau; he also arranged or edited works by Couperin, Scarlatti, Beethoven, Wagner, and Saint-Saëns. Relatively few works survive; many others were merely projected or were completed and destroyed (including operas, ballets, orchestral works, and a violin sonata). He is particularly admired for his skilled orchestration; and some of his harmonic practices (use of whole-tone scales and symmetrical harmonies) anticipated works of Debussy. Surviving works include an opera (*Ariane et Barbe-bleue,* after Maeterlinck, Paris, Opéra-comique, 1907) and a ballet (*La péri,* 1912); *L'apprenti sorcier* (symphonic scherzo after Goethe, 1897) and the Symphony in C (1895–96); a few piano works (*Variations, interlude, et final sur un thème de Rameau,* ca. 1899–1902); 2 cantatas and other vocal music.

Duke, Vernon [Dukelsky, Vladimir Alexandrovich] (b. Parfianovka, near Pskov, Russia, 10 Oct. 1903; d. Santa Monica, Calif., 16 Jan. 1969). Composer and violinist. He studied at the Kiev Conservatory (1916–19); fled Russia for Constantinople (1920–21) and then New York (1922); he lived in Paris (1924–25), where Diaghilev commissioned a ballet *(Zephyr et Flore)* for which the composer was praised as successor to Stravinsky in expressing "the new tendency in Russian music." Thereafter he went to London (ca. 1926–29) and composed stage music; after his return to New York he studied orchestration with Schillinger (1934–35) and became a U.S. citizen. He was best known for the stage music he wrote between 1932 and 1952 under the pseudonym Vernon Duke, adopted for this purpose at the suggestion of George Gershwin. As Dukelsky he continued to write serious music and Russian poetry; Koussevitzky in particular supported his compositions; 2 operas were produced in California (1958, 1963). He wrote an autobiography (*Passport to Paris,* 1955) and *Listen Here!: A Critical Essay on Music Depreciation* (1963).

Works include at least 12 musicals and revues (*Walk a Little Faster,* 1932, including "April in Paris"; *Ziegfeld Follies of 1936,* with Ira Gershwin; *Cabin in the Sky,* 1940, including "Takin' a Chance on Love"), most for New York; 2 operas; ballets, incidental music, and 3 film scores (*April in Paris,* 1952); 3 symphonies and other orchestral music (*Variations on Old Russian Chant,* oboe and strings, 1958); a string quartet (ca. 1956), violin sonata (1960), and other chamber music; many piano works (including *Souvenir de Venise,* 1955; *Serenade to San Francisco,* 1956); choral music and songs ("Autumn in New York," 1935).

Du Mont [de Thier], **Henri** (b. Villers-L'Évêcque, near Liège, 1610; d. Paris, 8 May 1684). Composer. Enrolled in the choir school at Maastricht in 1621 and served as organist there, 1630–32. Later studied with Du Hodemont at Liège, returning to Maastricht from

1636 until 1638, when he left for Paris; he became organist at St. Paul in 1640, holding the post until his death. Named keyboardist to the Duke of Anjou in 1652 and harpsichordist to the queen in 1660; became one of the four *maîtres* of the royal chapel in 1663, receiving the titles of *compositeur de la chapelle du roi* in 1672 and *maître de la musique de la reine* and Abbot of Notre Dame de Silly in 1673. He composed airs, keyboard dances, and sacred music and was central to the rise of the *grand motet.*

Dunayevsky, Isaak Iosifovich (b. Lokhvitsa, province of Poltava, 30 Jan. 1900; d. Moscow, 25 July 1955). Composer. He studied violin with Akhron at the Kharkov Music School (1910–15) and composition with Bogatïryov at the Kharkov Conservatory (1915–19). He was music director of the Ermitazh and Korsh theaters in Moscow (1924–29), for which he composed ballets, and composer of the Moscow Theater of Satire (1926–29). His operetta *Zheniki* (The Bridegrooms, 1927) helped breathe new life into Russian musical comedy. From 1929 to 1941 he was music director of the Leningrad Music Hall, where he attempted an adaptation of jazz styles to Soviet popular music. His film scores assured his success as a songwriter in Russia. He also directed the ensemble of the Leningrad House of Culture of Railwaymen (1938–48).

Dunhill, Thomas (Frederick) (b. London, 1 Feb. 1877; d. Scunthorpe, 13 Mar. 1946). Composer. In 1893 he enrolled in the Royal College of Music, where he studied composition with Charles Stanford and piano with Franklin Taylor. From 1899 he was assistant to music master Charles Lloyd at Eton College; he also taught theory and counterpoint at the Royal College (from 1905). He published books on chamber music, on Elgar, and on Mozart's chamber music. Among his compositions are operas (*The Enchanted Garden,* 1928; *Tantivy Towers,* 1931); ballet scores (*Gallimaufry,* 1937); orchestral works (*Elegiac Variations on an Original Theme,* 1922; Symphony in A minor); children's cantatas; and songs. He is perhaps best known as a composer of chamber music, including Piano Quintet in C minor, String Quartet in B minor, and 2 violin sonatas.

Duni, Egidio [Romualdo] (b. Matera, 9 Feb. 1709; d. Paris, 11 June 1775). Composer. His father was *maestro di cappella* at Matera. His opera *Nerone* (Rome, 1735) eclipsed Pergolesi's *Olimpiade,* which it followed on the stage; others were presented at Rome, London, Milan, and Florence between 1736 and 1743; his last opera seria was *Olimpiade* (Parma, 1755). Served as *maestro di cappella* at S. Nicola di Bari in Naples and at the court in Parma. He was the first to set Goldoni's *La buona figuola* (Parma, 1757); after his *Le peintre amoureux de son modèle* (Paris, 1757) established him in France, he moved to Paris and was important in the development of the opéra comique, many of his settings of Anseaume and Favart librettos having lasting popularity. Some of his sacred and instrumental music also survives.

Bibl.: Kent M. Smith, "Egidio Duni and the Development of the Opéra-comique from 1753 to 1770" (diss., Cornell Univ., 1980).

Dunn, Thomas (Burt) (b. Aberdeen, S.D., 21 Dec. 1925). Conductor. After obtaining a B.S. from Johns Hopkins Univ., studied choral conducting with G. Wallace Woodworth at Harvard (M.A., 1948), orchestral conducting with Anton Van der Horst at the Amsterdam Conservatory. Taught at Swarthmore College, 1949–51; at the Univ. of Pennsylvania, 1955–60; music director at the Church of the Incarnation, New York, beginning in 1957; of the Cantata Singers, 1958–65. Founded and led the Festival Orchestra of New York, 1959–69. Led Bach concerts at Carnegie Hall (1961–62) that tried to replicate Bach's performing forces. Taught at Union Theological Seminary, 1961–69. Music director of the Handel and Haydn Society, Boston, 1967–86; director of choral activities, Boston University, from 1977.

Dunstable [Dunstaple], **John** (b. ca. 1390; d. 24 Dec. 1453). Composer, mathematician, and astronomer. It has been conjectured on slender evidence that he was in the service of the Duke of Bedford, perhaps accompanying the duke to France during his regency in the years 1422–35. Otherwise, nothing is known of his career. His contemporaries and successors both in England and on the Continent recognized him as the foremost English composer of the 15th century. The considerable influence of his music and of the English style in general on the works of such composers as Dufay, Binchois, Ockeghem, and Busnois was noted in his own era by Martin le Franc (who termed this style the *contenance angloise*) and Tinctoris, among others.

Most of Dunstable's works are for 3 voices, though most of his isorhythmic motets are for 4. The smallest part of Dunstable's output is secular songs. Three songs survive with attributions to him; but of these only one, a French-texted rondeau, *Puisque m'amour,* is certainly his. Twelve isorhythmic motets, one untexted, the rest sacred, survive complete. Almost 30 more pieces are nonisorhythmic settings of liturgical texts outside the Mass Ordinary. Many are melodically free, while others allude to, paraphrase, or strictly state chant melodies. Among these compositions are antiphons, a hymn, a trope, sequences, and Magnificats. About 20 Mass cycles and Mass movements are known. Several are based on plainsong in some respect. One cycle is isorhythmic; 2 others are unified by a single melody used in the tenor in all movements. Dunstable's works are known chiefly through Continental manuscripts.

Bibl.: *John Dunstable: Complete Works, MB* 8 (London, 1953; 2nd rev. ed., 1970). Margaret Bent, *Dunstaple* (New York, 1981).

Duparc, Elisabeth (d. ca. late 1770s). Soprano. Studied in Italy; came to London in 1736, singing for the royal family and in several operas. She sang another operatic season in 1737–38, and thereafter was closely identified with Handel's music, appearing in his oratorios throughout the 1740s, taking the title roles in *Esther* (1740), *Semele* (1744), and *Deborah* (1744), along with many other parts. Burney commented on her "larklike execution."

Duparc [Fouques Duparc], **(Marie Eugène) Henri** (b. Paris, 21 Jan. 1848; d. Mont-de-Marsan, 12 Feb. 1933). Composer. While a piano student of Franck at the Jesuit College of Vaugirard in Paris, he also studied law and composed. Beginning in 1869 he made a series of trips to Germany specifically to see productions of Wagner's operas; in 1872 he was among the founders of the Société nationale de musique and served as its secretary from 1876; in 1878 he founded the Concerts de musique moderne, which were directed by d'Indy. His affliction with an illness that eventually left him blind and paralyzed led him to abandon composition almost completely in 1885 and to live in retirement. He destroyed many of his compositions, as well as his correspondence with Wagner and others; in 1885 he acknowledged only 13 songs composed between 1868 and 1884.

Altogether 16 songs survive, of which 1 was initially intended for soprano and orchestra ("La vague et la cloche," 1871); 7 others were written for voice and piano and orchestrated only later. He set texts by Théophile Gautier ("Lamento," 1883; "Au pays oû se fait la guerre," orchestrated ca. 1876, rev. ca. 1911–13), Baudelaire ("L'invitation au voyage," ca. 1870, orch. ca. 1892–95; "La vie antérieure," 1884, orch. 1911–13), and other important French poets. Other works include fragments of an opera *(Roussalka);* a few orchestral works, including *Suite de valses* (composed by 1874); a sonata for cello and piano (1867); a few piano and organ works (in manuscript); a motet (1882) and a vocal duet ("La fuite," 1871); and keyboard transcriptions of works by Bach and Franck.

Duport, Jean-Louis (b. Paris, 4 Oct. 1749; d. Paris, 7 Sept. 1819). Cellist and composer. His first cello teacher was his elder brother, Jean-Pierre Duport, whose virtuosity he ultimately outstripped. After playing his Concert spirituel debut at age 19 (1768), Jean-Louis was inducted into the Société Olympique. At the onset of the Revolution he followed his brother to Potsdam, returning to France in 1806 to take up service in the court of the exiled Charles IV of Spain (at Marseilles). He taught cello at the Paris Conservatory (1813–16); it was in his role as pedagogue that he left his most valuable legacy: the *Essai sur le doigté du violoncelle et sur la conduite de l'archet* (Paris, [1813?]), the most comprehensive cello method of its day.

Duport, Jean-Pierre (b. Paris, 27 Nov. 1741; d. Berlin, 31 Dec. 1818). Cellist and composer. He made a successful debut at the Concert spirituel in 1761; from 1769 he was engaged at the court of the Prince of Conti. After concert tours throughout Europe he was invited to Berlin in 1773 by Frederick the Great. Engaged first as chapel cellist and then (from 1778) as chamber musician, Duport remained in Berlin for the rest of his life. Beethoven probably composed his two op. 5 cello sonatas (dedicated to Duport's patron-pupil Friedrich Wilhelm II) with Duport in mind.

Dupré, Desmond (John) (b. London, 19 Dec. 1916; d. Tunbridge, 16 Aug. 1974). Lutenist and gambist. Studied with Ivor Jame and Herbert Howells at the Royal College of Music. Played cello in the Boyd Neel Orchestra, 1948–49. As a guitarist accompanied Alfred Deller on record in 1950. As a gambist concertized and recorded with Thurston Dart. During the 1950s and 1960s played with many prominent early music ensembles, including the Deller Consort, the Morley Consort, the Jaye Consort of viols, and Musica Reservata.

Du Pré, Jacqueline (b. Oxford, 26 Jan. 1945; d. London, 19 Oct. 1987). Cellist. Studied with William Pleeth, Tortelier, Casals, and Rostropovich. First played publicly in 1952. Debut recital at Wigmore Hall in 1961. At Festival Hall in 1962 and again at U.S. debut with New York Philharmonic 14 May 1965 she played the Elgar Concerto. Married Daniel Barenboim in 1967; concertized with him as a duo and in trio with Pinchas Zukerman. Gave the premiere of Goehr's *Romance* for cello and orchestra, 1968. Her career was cut short in 1972 by the effects of multiple sclerosis.

Dupré, Marcel (b. Rouen, 3 May 1886; d. Meudon, 30 May 1971). Organist and composer. Studied organ with his father, Albert; debut at age 10. At age 12 he was appointed organist at St. Vivien in Rouen and began study with Guilmant. At the Paris Conservatory beginning in 1904 he studied piano with Diémer (first prize, 1905), organ with Guilmant and Vierne (first prize, 1907), and fugue with Widor (first prize, 1909). Assistant to Widor at St. Sulpice from 1906; succeeded his master in 1934. Performed all J. S. Bach's organ works from memory in 10 concerts in 1922, then made the first of several concert tours in England and the U.S. Made a world tour in 1939. He was a celebrated improviser. As a composer he won the Prix de Rome in 1914. Among his compositions are 2 symphonies, the cantata *Psyché,* a violin sonata, *Fantaisie* for piano and orchestra, and a wealth of solo and ensemble music for organ.

Durand, (Marie-) Auguste (b. Paris, 18 July 1830; d. there, 31 May 1909). Music publisher. Studied at the Paris Conservatory; 1849–74, organist at various Paris churches; composed sacred music and several very popular piano pieces; 30 Dec. 1869, formed a music publishing firm in partnership with Schoenewerk (who retired in 1891), leading to A. Durand & fils with his son Jacques (1865–1928), who studied at the Conservatory and succeeded to the business, also publishing his memoirs (*Quelques souvenirs d'un éditeur de musique,* Paris, 1924–25) and a collection of Debussy's letters to him. The firm published the work of Debussy, Ravel, and many other French composers of the time.

Durante, Francesco (b. Frattamaggiore, 31 Mar. 1684; d. Naples, 30 Sept. 1755). Composer. Tutored in music by his uncle, a priest and composer; also a violin pupil of Francone, and possibly later of Pitoni and Pasquini. Studied at S. Onofrio, Naples, 1702–5; perhaps later went to Rome, but taught at S. Onofrio in 1610–11; his name appears as *maestro* of the Accademia S. Cecilia, Rome, in 1718; a sacred drama of his was given at Naples in 1719. Served as *primo maestro* of the conservatory Poveri del Gesù Cristo, Naples, 1728–38, where Pergolesi studied with him. Took the same post at S. Maria di Loreto in 1742, remaining for the rest of his life; Anfossi and Traetta were among his pupils. Succeeded Leo as *primo maestro* at S. Onofrio in 1744, but de Majo was chosen over him for Leo's post as *maestro* of the royal chapel. Though he wrote many dramas and secular vocal and instrumental works, his fame rests on his church music (Masses, motets, Psalms, Magnificats, and other liturgical pieces) and on his considerable reputation as a teacher.

Durastini, Margherita (fl. 1700–1734). Soprano. Appeared in Venice in 1700; served Prince Ruspoli in Rome from 1707, performing several of Handel's cantatas. Sang at Venice (1709–12), Parma (1714), and Naples (1716), and was very highly paid for appearances at Dresden (1719), Munich (1721), and London (1720–21, 1722–24, 1733–34). She sang in premieres of operas by Caldara, Lotti, and Scarlatti, and created roles in Handel's *Agrippa* (1709), *Radamisto* (1720), and *Giulio Cesare* (1724), among others.

Durazzo, Giacomo (b. Genoa, 27 Apr. 1717; d. Venice, 15 Oct. 1794). Diplomat and operatic impresario. Born of a noble family in Genoa, he was made ambassador to Vienna in 1749; by 1754 he was in charge of the imperial theaters. In his position as *Generalspektakeldirektor* he improved the standards both at the Burgtheater and at the Kärntnertortheater. He was a key figure in the Gluckian reform of opera, as he was largely responsible for bringing together Calzabigi and Gluck in 1761 for their epoch-making operatic collaborations. He is also credited with fostering comic opera in Vienna, employing composers such as Giuseppe Scarlatti and Florian Leopold Gassmann to compose opere buffe. In 1764 he resigned from his Viennese posts amid conflict and intrigue. Shortly afterward he was appointed Viennese ambassador to Venice, a post he held until 1784.

Bibl.: Robert M. Haas, *Gluck und Durazzo im Burgtheater* (Vienna and Zurich, 1925).

Durey, Louis (Edmond) (b. Paris, 27 May 1888; d. St. Tropez, 3 July 1979). Composer. Studied at the Schola cantorum in Paris with Léon Saint-Requier until 1914; as an orchestrator he was self-taught. He was a member of "Les six" from 1919, but dissociated himself from that group in 1921. His early song cycle *L'offrande lyrique* (1914) is indebted to Schoenberg, but Satie's ideas about simplicity, and Stravinsky's polytonality were more influential in later works. From the 1930s to the 1960s Durey was the most important French communist musician: he served as an officer in the Fédération musicale populaire and other organizations, made arrangements of popular songs, and wrote music with overt political content (*La longue marche,* Mao, for chorus and orchestra, 1949; *10 choeurs de métiers,* 1957). He wrote reviews for various publications (including *L'humanité* and *Musique soviétique*) and edited chansons of Janequin and other 16th-century composers.

He composed a few dramatic works, radio and film scores, incidental music; *Mouvement symphonique* (piano and strings, 1963) and 5 other orchestral works, as well as orchestrations of piano pieces; string quartets and trios, a wind quintet, and other chamber music; piano music, including preludes, sonatinas, and inventions; 5 large-scale works for soloists, chorus, and orchestra; choral and vocal music, including song cycles and individual songs for voice with piano, ensemble, or orchestra (*Trois poèmes de Petronne,* 1918).

Durkó, Zsolt (b. Szeged, 10 Apr. 1934). He studied composition with Ferenc Farkas at the Budapest Academy; after graduating in 1960, he studied in Rome with Petrassi (until 1963), afterward returning to Hungary. He has won the Atri Prize (1963, for *Episodi sul tema B-A-C-H*) and the Erkel Prize (1968, for his First String Quartet). Though his harmonic idiom is atonal, his music uses fragments of Hungarian folk tunes, and its instrumentation is often reminiscent of native music. Works include an opera, *Moses* (1977); other vocal music, including Dartmouth Concerto (soprano, chamber orchestra, 1966), *Altimara* (chorus and orchestra, 1967–68), the oratorio *Halotti beszéd* (1972), *Colloïdes* (3 contraltos, flute, chamber ensemble, 1975), *Ilmarinen* (choir, 1989); orchestral music (*Fioriture,* 1966; a concerto for 12 flutes, orchestra, 1970); chamber music (*Improvisations,* wind quintet, 1965; 2 *Iconographies,* 1970, 1971; *Turner Illustrations,* solo violin, 14 instruments, 1976; an octet for winds, 1988).

Durón, Sebastián (bapt. Brihuega, 19 Apr. 1660; d. Cambó, 3 Aug. 1716). Composer. Organ pupil of de Sola, whom he served as assistant at Zaragoza in 1679; named second organist at Seville Cathedral in 1680; became organist at Burgo de Osma Cathedral in 1685, moving to Palencia Cathedral in the following year. Succeeded Sanz as Capilla real organist at Madrid in 1691, becoming *maestro de capilla* and choir school rector in 1702. Exiled in 1706 as a result of the War of the Spanish Succession, he lived mainly in France for the rest of his life. His considerable output includes zarzuelas and operas, songs, sacred and secular *villancicos,* church music, and organ works.

Duruflé, Maurice (b. Louviers, 11 Jan. 1902; d. Paris, 16 June 1986). Organist and composer. At the Paris

Conservatory he studied organ with Tournemire and Vierne, composition with Dukas, winning first prizes in organ, harmony, and composition. Appointed organist at the church of St-Étienne-du-Mont in Paris, 1930. Gave the premiere of Poulenc's Organ Concerto in 1941. Assisted Dupré at the Paris Conservatory in 1942 and became professor of harmony there in 1943. His organ compositions are typified by *Prélude, adagio et choral varié sur le "Veni Creator"* (1931) and *Prélude et fugue sur le nom d'Alain* (1943). A large-scale Requiem was published in 1947, a Mass in 1967.

Dušek [Dussek], **František Xaver** (b. Chotěborky, Bohemia, baptized 8 Dec. 1731; d. Prague, 12 Feb. 1799). Composer and pianist. Born of the servant class, he was educated at a Jesuit school through the patronage of Count Johann Sporck. Turning to music, he studied in Prague and later with Wagenseil in Vienna. Around 1765 he settled in Prague, where for three decades he was a popular keyboard player and an influential teacher. His Prague home and his Bertramka summer villa were centers of local musical activity; Mozart completed *Don Giovanni* at the latter in 1787. A leading composer of *galant* style instrumental music, Dušek composed some 40 symphonies, keyboard concertos, 20 string quartets, wind chamber music, and keyboard sonatas.

Dushkin, Samuel (b. Suwalki, Russian Poland, 13 Dec. 1891; d. New York, 24 June 1976). Violinist. Emigrated to the U.S. as a child. Studied violin at the Music School Settlement in New York, with Rémy at the Paris Conservatory, and with Auer and Kreisler in New York. Toured Europe in 1918, the U.S. in 1924. A champion of contemporary music, he gave the first performances of Ravel's *Tzigane* (1926) and of Stravinsky's Violin Concerto (1931) and *Duo concertant* (1932). Revised the violin part of Martinů's *Suite concertante* with the composer's blessing; first performance in 1943 with piano and in St. Louis in 1945 with orchestra. He composed in small forms and, like Kreisler, attributed some of his own works to 18th-century composers.

Dussek [Dusík], **Jan Ladislav** [Johann Ludwig] (b. Čáslav, Bohemia, 12 Feb. 1760; d. St.-Germain-en-Laye, 20 Mar. 1812). Composer and keyboard virtuoso. Son of organist and teacher Jan Dussek (1738–1818), he received his early music training as a choirboy at Jihlava (Iglau) and at the Jesuit school at Kutná Hora; at the latter he was also chapel organist. After giving up his intention of becoming a Cistercian monk, he studied in Prague through the patronage of a Count Männer (1776–78). During the 1780s he performed as pianist in the Netherlands, St. Petersburg, Berlin, Kassel, Mainz, Frankfurt, and in Hamburg, where he met C. P. E. Bach. He moved to Paris in 1786, but soon after had to flee the Revolution; settling in London, he gained popularity as a piano virtuoso throughout the 1790s, performing frequently with Salomon and occasionally with Haydn. During this period he was composing works for the English-made Broadwood piano, whose extended range spanned 6 octaves by the late 1790s. Around 1790 he entered into a publishing venture with his father-in-law, Domenico Corri; when the business failed in 1799, Dussek fled to Hamburg to escape debt. After brief residence in Hamburg and Bohemia, in 1804 he entered the service of Prince Louis Ferdinand of Prussia. The latter's death in 1806 inspired the composer's famous *Élégie harmonique.* In 1807 Dussek returned to Paris, where for his remaining years he was *maître du chapelle* for Prince Talleyrand.

Dussek is recognized as a pioneer of the colorful, virtuosic sonorities of early 19th-century piano music. Chief among his works are more than 40 piano sonatas (and numerous other keyboard pieces); 18 piano concertos (Military Concerto in B♭ op. 40); nearly 90 accompanied keyboard sonatas; chamber music (a piano quintet in E♭ op. 56; 3 string quartets op. 60; several works with harp). He also composed vocal works, including an opera (*The Captive of Spillberg,* 1798) and a Solemn Mass (1811). In addition he authored *Instructions on the Art of Playing the Piano Forte or Harpsichord* (London, 1796; many later eds.).

Bibl.: Leo Schiffer, *Johann Ladislaus Dussek: Seine Sonaten und seine Konzerte* (Leipzig, 1914; R: New York, 1972). Howard Allen Craw, "A Biography and Thematic Catalog of the Works of J. L. Dussek (1760–1812)" (diss., Univ. of Southern Calif., 1964). Alexander L. Ringer, "Beethoven and the London Pianoforte School," *MQ* 56 (1970): 742–58. Luca Palazzolo, *Il tocco cantante: Jan Ladislav Dussek, compositore e virtuoso tra Mozart e Clementi* (Bologna, 1992).

Dutilleux, Henri (b. Angers, 22 Jan. 1916). Composer. He studied at the Paris Conservatory (1933–38), where his composition teacher was Büsser; won the Prix de Rome in 1938; in 1967 he was awarded the Grand prix national de la musique. After a year as director of singing at the Paris Opéra (1942), he joined the French Radio, where from 1945 to 1963 he was director of music productions. In 1961 he was appointed professor of composition at the École normale; in 1970 he began to teach at the Conservatory. He worked with the French section of the ISCM, and was on the executive committee of the UNESCO International Music Council. Since he destroyed most works composed before 1945, his own early development as a composer cannot be traced, but his postwar style derives from the tradition of Ravel, Debussy, and Roussel. His own assessment of his works refers to an emphasis on economy of means, a predilection for the spirit of variation, and the avoidance of any program or message; his treatment of the orchestra as a collection of soloists (Symphony no. 1) has been noted, as has his relative independence from established conventions, either academic or avant-garde. He composed a ballet (*Le loup,* 1953); several works for orchestra (*Metaboles,* premiered by the Cleveland Orchestra under Szell, 1964; *Timbres, espaces, mouvement* or *La nuit étoilée,* 1978; and a concerto for violin, 1982); chamber music (*Ainsi la* *nuit,* string quartet, 1975–76; *3 strophes sur le nom* SACHER, solo cello, 1982); piano music; 4 sets of songs with orchestra or piano; incidental and film music.

Dutoit, Charles (Edouard) (b. Lausanne, 7 Oct. 1936). Conductor. Studied violin at the Lausanne Conservatory (diploma, 1954); conducting with von Karajan in Lucerne (1955), with Samuel Baud-Bory at the Geneva Academy of Music (first prize, 1958), with Munch at the Berkshire Festival (1959). Professional debut 8 Nov. 1962 with the Bern Symphony Orchestra. Assistant to von Karajan at the Vienna Opera, 1964; to Paul Kletzki with the Bern Symphony Orchestra, 1963–67. Music director, Zurich Radio Orchestra, 1964–66; of the Bern Symphony Orchestra, 1967–77. U.S. debut 31 Aug. 1972 at the Hollywood Bowl. Music director of the National Orchestra of Mexico, 1974–76; of the Göteborg Symphony Orchestra, 1975–78; of the Montreal Symphony Orchestra beginning in 1977; chief conductor of the Orchestre national de France beginning in 1990; principal conductor of the NHK Orchestra in Tokyo beginning in 1996. His first orchestral recording in Montreal, *Daphnis and Chloë* (1980), was a worldwide success; further recordings and annual tours beginning in 1981 of Europe, the Americas, and Asia brought the orchestra into the first rank, especially in French repertory.

Dvořák, Antonín (Leopold) (b. Nelahozeves, near Kralupy, 8 Sept. 1841; d. Prague, 1 May 1904). Composer. His parents ran a village inn; his father was also a butcher. He had violin lessons and played for village occasions as a child. In 1854–56 he was a butcher's apprentice in Zlonice, where he also had music lessons with the town organist, beginning to learn harmony and keyboard instruments; then in 1856–57 he studied German in Česká Kamenice while continuing music lessons. Eventually his father let him become a musician, and in 1857–59 he studied at the Prague Organ School. He was poor, shy but sensitive, not initially fluent in German, and his talent was not immediately recognized at the school. He graduated with a second prize and then supported himself as violist in a small orchestra playing in restaurants and at dances. In 1862 this orchestra became the basis of a larger, regular one at the Prozatímní (Interim) Theater, with Dvořák as principal violist until 1871, from 1866 under Smetana. He also worked as organist and teacher, his pupils including Josefina Čermáková, with whom he fell in love, and her younger sister Anna, whom he married in 1873.

His earliest known large compositions, the String Quartet op. 1 and String Quintet op. 2, date from 1861–62. In 1865 he composed his first two symphonies and a song cycle inspired by Josefina; in 1870 his first opera, *Alfred* (to a German text; not performed until 1938). His music began to be heard locally; his first great success was the first version of his patriotic *Hymnus* op. 30 for mixed chorus and orchestra (and an early manifestation of his strong national feelings), premiered by the Hlahol Choral Society under his close friend Karel Bendl (9 Mar. 1873). The first version of his second opera, *King and Charcoal Burner* (to a Czech text, like all later ones), composed in 1871, had been rejected by the Prague Theater; Dvořák reset the libretto in 1874 and it was premiered on 24 Nov. 1874. He composed a third symphony in 1873 (conducted by Smetana in 1874), a fourth in 1874, and a fifth in 1875.

In 1874–77 he was organist of St. Adalbert's church, Prague. In 1874 he was awarded a government grant for poor, young artists, having submitted 15 compositions. The judges were Hanslick, Herbeck, and Brahms; he won again in 1876 and 1877. In 1877 Brahms recommended Dvořák's music to his own publisher, Simrock in Berlin, who in 1878–79 brought out several works, soon followed by the firms of Bote & Bock and Schlesinger. This led to performances, and several works, especially the Slavonic Dances and Rhapsodies, began to be widely popular. (In gratitude, Dvořák dedicated his String Quartet op. 34, composed in 1877, to Brahms and always regarded him reverently.)

This opening of wider musical horizons may have diverted Dvořák's course as a composer away from what seemed to be becoming a concentration on Czech opera. He had composed the one-act *The Stubborn Lovers* in 1874 (premiere Prague, 1881), the serious five-act *Vanda* in 1875 (premiere Prague, 1876) and the comic two-act *The Cunning Peasant* (or *The Peasant a Rogue*) in 1877 (premiere Prague, 1878). In the next 20 years he composed only two completely new operas: *Dmitrij* (premiere Prague, 1882) and *Jakobin* (Prague, 1889). His life quickly became that of a major creative figure, traveling to Vienna and German cities for important performances, negotiating with Simrock, who remained his principal publisher in spite of occasional rifts over money and matters such as Dvořák's nationalist insistence that the titles of his works be printed in Czech as well as German. There were setbacks. Joachim never played the Violin Concerto op. 53 (1879–80), written for and dedicated to him. The Sixth Symphony op. 60 (1880) was premiered not by Richter and the Vienna Philharmonic as Dvořák had hoped but in Prague. His operas aroused some interest abroad (*The Peasant a Rogue* was given at Dresden in 1882, later in Hamburg and Vienna), but no lasting acceptance.

In the 1880s English enthusiasm for his music was perhaps the most important factor in Dvořák's recognition as a major figure. His popularity had been founded there in the early 1880s by Richter and others. Dvořák made the first of nine visits in March 1884, invited by the London Philharmonic to conduct his music (his first engagement to do so outside his homeland). He conducted three concerts (including his Stabat Mater, which became very popular) and returned in September for the Three Choirs Festival at Worcester. He was enthusiastically received on both visits and given several important commissions (Symphony no. 7, *St. Ludmilla*), through which he was able to buy a country house at Vysoká, where he thereafter spent much of his time and did most of his composing. In April and May 1885 he visited London, conducting the new symphony; August 1885, the Birmingham Festival; October and November 1886, the Leeds Festival, conducting the successful premiere of *St. Ludmilla,* repeating it twice in London.

His great facility as a composer was at its height in these years, resulting in a stream of new works in all genres. He began to conduct more widely, although not frequently (Mar. 1888, Budapest; Mar. 1889, Dresden; Mar. 1890, Moscow and St. Petersburg, a trip arranged partly by Tchaikovsky, whom Dvořák had met at Prague in 1888; Nov. 1890, Frankfurt am Main). In 1890 he conducted the premiere of his Symphony no. 8 in Prague, repeating it in London, and was awarded an honorary doctorate by Prague University. Although initially reluctant, he accepted the post of professor of composition and orchestration at the Prague Conservatory. His duties began in January 1891 and obligated him to seven or eight months a year. Among his first pupils was his future son-in-law Josef Suk. In June 1891 he received an honorary doctorate from Cambridge Univ.; in October 1891 he made his eighth visit to England, conducting the premiere of his Requiem at the Birmingham Festival.

Although because of his strong attachment to his homeland and his sense of himself as a Czech artist he never accepted the advice of Brahms and others that he move to Vienna, he spent September 1892 through May 1895 in the U.S. as composition teacher and titular director of the National Conservatory of Music in New York. The reason seems to have been the high salary offered by the conservatory's founder (and administrator) Mrs. Jeannette Thurber, which he saw as ensuring his family's financial security. Mrs. Thurber was at least partly motivated by the hope that Dvořák would help stimulate the development of a native American music. Beginning on October 21 with the Boston Symphony, he made concert appearances that were part of his contractual obligation. His music was frequently performed; he and it were enthusiastically received. In January through May 1893 he composed his last symphony, "From the New World," which was given its very successful premiere in New York under Seidl on December 16. Dvořák and his family (the four older children having come to spend the second year with the rest of the family in the U.S.) summered (June–Sept. 1893) in the Czech community of Spillville, Iowa, where Dvořák composed the American String Quartet op. 96 and the String Quintet op. 97. He conducted his music at Czech Day (Aug. 12) at the Chicago Exposition; also visited Omaha and St. Paul, and stopped at Niagara Falls on his return to New York. The family returned to Europe for the summer holiday in 1894. Dvořák had renewed his two-year contract for 1894–96, but after the 1894–95 academic year, during which only his youngest child had been with him and his wife in New York, perhaps increasing his homesickness, he decided during his 1895 summer holiday in Europe that he could not complete his contract and resigned, resuming his post at the Prague Conservatory in November 1895.

The death of his sister-in-law Josefina in 1895 led him to recompose the end of his Cello Concerto, composed in New York in 1894–95, giving it its present melancholy conclusion. He made his last visit to England in March 1896 for its premiere. He completed his last chamber works at the end of 1895 and his last orchestral (and instrumental) works, five symphonic poems, in 1896–97. The rest of his life (with, for him, long intervals of creative inactivity) was devoted to opera. He produced the fairy-tale comic opera *Kate and the Devil* (Prague, 1899), which was successful; the tragic fairy-tale opera *Russalka* (Prague, 1901), perhaps the most successful of his operas within and outside his homeland; and *Armida* (Prague, 1904), which was not a success. He was taken ill at its premiere and died five weeks later. He had begun sketches for another opera, *Horymir.* In 1901 he was named director of the Prague Conservatory, a largely honorary post.

Works: *Vocal.* 11 operas, several revised at least once; Stabat Mater (1877); Requiem (1890); Psalm 149 (1879); Mass (1887); *St. Ludmilla,* oratorio (1886); cantatas (*The Specter's Bride,* 1884); part songs, choruses; many duets and songs.

Orchestral. 9 symphonies (no. 7 in D minor, op. 70, 1884–85, first publ. as no. 2; no. 8 in G, op. 88, 1889, first publ. as no. 4; no. 9 in E minor, op. 95, "From the New World," 1893, first publ. as no. 5); Piano Concerto in G minor op. 33 (1876); Violin Concerto in A minor op. 53 (1879–80); Cello Concerto in B minor op. 104 (1894–95); 8 concert overtures (Carnival Overture op. 92, 1891); 6 symphonic poems; Slavonic Dances, 2 ser., op. 46 (1878), op. 72 (1886–87), originally for piano duet; 3 Slavonic Rhapsodies op. 45 (1878); Symphonic Variations op. 78 (1877); 2 serenades (op. 22 in E for strings, 1875; op. 44 in D minor for winds, cello, double bass, 1878); other orchestral pieces.

Chamber. 14 string quartets (no. 12 in F, op. 96, *American,* 1893); 3 string quintets; 4 piano trios (Dumky Trio op. 90, 1890–91); 2 piano quartets; 2 piano quintets (op. 81 in A, 1887); String Sextet in A op. 48 (1878) ; Violin Sonata in F op. 57 (1880); Violin Sonatina in G op. 100 (1893); other chamber pieces; piano pieces for 2 and 4 hands.

Bibl.: O. Šourek et al., eds., *Souborné vydání* [Complete Works] (Prague, 1955–). Jarmil Burghauser, *Antonín Dvořák: Thematisches Werkverzeichnis* (Prague, 1960). Otakar Šourek, *Antonín Dvořák: Letters and Reminiscences,* trans. Robert Simpson (Prague, 1954; R: New York, 1985). Antonín Hořejš, *Antonín Dvořák: The Composer's Life and Work in Pictures,* trans. Jean Layton (Prague, 1955). John Clapham, *Dvořák* (New York, 1975). Neil Butterworth, *Dvořák: His Life and Times* (Speldhurst, 1980). John Clapham, "Dvořák on the American Scene," *19th-Century Music* 5 (1981): 16–23. Hans Hubert Schönzeler, *Dvořák* (New York, 1984). Michael Beckermann, *Dvořák and His World* (Princeton, 1993). Klaus Döge and Peter Jost, eds., *Dvořák-Studien* (Mainz, 1994).

Dykes, John Bacchus (b. Hull, 10 Mar. 1823; d. Ticehurst, Sussex, 22 Jan. 1876). Composer. Earned a classics degree from Cambridge, 1847; 1849–62, minor canon and precentor, Durham Cathedral; composed many favorite Victorian hymn tunes (*Nicaea,* sung to "Holy, Holy, Holy"; *Saint Agnes,* "Come, Holy Spirit, heavenly dove"; *Horbury,* "Nearer my God to Thee"), 60 of which were included in *Hymns Ancient and Modern* (1861); also more extended church works. From 1862 vicar of St. Oswald, Durham, where a running battle with his bishop (a low-churchman opposed to Dykes's high-church principles) eventually led to his mental breakdown; died in an asylum.

Bibl.: J. T. Fowler, *The Life and Letters of John Bacchus Dykes* (London, 1897).

Dylan, Bob [Zimmerman, Robert] (b. Duluth, 24 May 1941). Folk and rock songwriter and singer. From 1961 performed folk songs, protest songs, and "talking blues" by Woody Guthrie and himself in New York; began recording in 1962. From 1965 played rock-oriented music, recording albums with electric instrumentation (*Bringing It All Back Home,* 1965; *Highway 61 Revisited,* 1965; *Blonde on Blonde,* 1966) and performing with members of the rock group The Band (*The Basement Tapes,* 1975); in the 1970s toured with folk singers Joan Baez and Jack Elliot in the Rolling Thunder Revue. Between 1979 and 1981 became a fundamentalist Christian and recorded religious songs; in 1983 worked with reggae musicians *(Infidels).* He was a central figure to both folk and rock music in the 1960s and early 1970s: his song "Blowin' in the Wind" (1963) became an anthem of the civil rights movement, while other pieces were recorded by rock musicians including The Byrds ("Mr. Tambourine Man," 1965) and Jimi Hendrix ("All Along the Watchtower," 1968). His own recordings were also popular (including "Like a Rolling Stone," 1965; "Lay Lady Lay," 1969).

Bibl.: Bob Dylan, *Lyrics: 1962–1985* (New York, 1985). Elizabeth Thomson and David Gutman, eds., *The Dylan Companion* (London, 1990). William McKeen, *Bob Dylan: A Bio-Bibliography* (Westport, 1993).

Dyson, George (b. Halifax, Yorkshire, 28 May 1883; d. Winchester, 28 Sept. 1964). Composer and writer on music. He studied at Oxford and at the Royal College of Music (1900–1904); then he received a Mendelssohn Scholarship for study in Italy and Germany (1904–8). After 1908 he held several teaching posts (at Osborne, Marlborough, Rugby). Returning from war duty in 1921, he became director of music at Wellington College. Later he also taught at the Royal College, which he directed from 1938 to 1952. He was knighted in 1941. He composed choral music (the cantatas *The Canterbury Pilgrims,* 1931, and *Nebuchadnezzar,* 1935; *Quo vadis I,* 1938, and *II,* 1948); orchestral works (*Suite for Little Orchestra,* 1930; *Preludium, Fantasie, and Chaconne,* cello and chamber orchestra, 1936; Symphony in G, 1937; Concerto for Violin in E♭, 1942; *At the Tabard Inn,* overture, arranged from *The Canterbury Pilgrims*).

Dzerzhinsky, Ivan Ivanovich (b. Tambov, 9 Apr. 1909; d. Leningrad, 18 Jan. 1978). Composer. He studied piano with Yavorsky at the First Music Tekhnikum in Moscow (1925–29) and composition with Mikhail Gnesin at the Gnesin School (1929–30). He then studied with Gavriil Popov and P. B. Ryazanov at the Leningrad Central Music Tekhnikum (1930–32) and with Asaf'yev at the Leningrad Conservatory (1932–34). His early works were influenced by Grieg, Rachmaninoff, and early Ravel. By the early 1930s he had come under the influence of Shostakovich, with whom he consulted while writing his opera *Tikhiy Don* (Quiet Flows the Don), a tribute to the Don cossacks. After seeing it performed in 1936, Stalin immediately recognized its worth as propaganda. The opera was soon held up as a model of Soviet realism in music and won a Stalin Prize. Although written in an undistinguished musical style, it had 200 performances by May 1938. None of his later operas made their way into the Soviet repertory. He held important posts in the Union of Soviet Composers from 1936, and in 1948 was appointed to the central committee of the union. Besides his 11 operas and comedies, he wrote piano concertos, symphonic poems, songs and romances, piano music, incidental music, and film scores.

E

Eames, Emma (Hayden) (b. Shanghai, 13 Aug. 1865; d. New York, 13 June 1952). Soprano. Studied in Boston and from 1886 in Paris with Marchesi; Paris Opéra, 1889–91, debut as Juliette; sang then primarily at Covent Garden (1891–1901) and the Metropolitan (1891–1909); retired 1912; beautiful appearance and fine voice, though sometimes judged cold in temperament; noted for Marguérite, Micaëla, Desdemona, Aida, Tosca, and several Mozart and light Wagner roles. Memoirs: *Some Memories and Reflections* (New York, 1927; R: 1977).

Easdale, Brian (b. Manchester, 10 Aug. 1909; d. 30 Oct. 1995). Composer. His musical study was at the Westminster Abbey Choir School and at the Royal College of Music. At age 18 he wrote his first opera, *Rapunzel;* it was followed by *The Corn King* (1935) and *The Sleeping Children* (1951). After 1936 he composed chiefly incidental music and film scores; best known of the latter is the music for *The Red Shoes* (1948). During the war he served as director of Information Films in India (1942–45) and, after returning to England in 1946, of the Archer Film Unit. He composed *Missa Coventriensis* (1962); orchestral music including *Dead March* (1931); a piano concerto (1937); chamber music; songs.

East, Michael (b. ca. 1580; d. Lichfield, 1648). Composer. Provided a madrigal to *The Triumphs of Oriana* (1601); took a B.Mus. at Cambridge in 1606; perhaps served the Hatton family for a time; cited as a clerk at Ely Cathedral, 1609–14. He was master of the choristers at Lichfield by 1618; supplied an anthem for St. John's College, Oxford, in 1620. He issued 7 publications: 2 madrigal books (1604, 1606; ed. *EMS* 29, 30); 2 varied collections of madrigals, consort songs, and anthems, the earlier print also containing a series of viol fancies (1610, 1618; ed. *EMS* 31); 2 books exclusively for viol (1618–38); and a collection of anthems and consort songs. Service music and other anthems remain in manuscript.

East [Easte, Este], **Thomas** (b. London, ca. 1535; d. there, Jan. 1608). Printer and publisher. Active in England from 1565; greatly successful from 1588, when he started to print music. His publications include most of the works of Byrd and Morley; many books of songs or ayres, English madrigals, and lute songs by various composers; a book of music by Lassus; Yonge's *Musica transalpina* (1588, 1597), *The Triumphs of Oriana* (1601), and *The Whole Booke of Psalmes* (1592 and later eds.), the first such collection to be printed in score rather than partbooks.

Easton, Florence (b. Middlesborough-on-Tees, Yorkshire, 25 Oct. 1882; d. New York, 13 Aug. 1955). Soprano. Raised in Canada; returned to England in 1898; studied voice with Agnes Larkcom at the Royal Academy of Music and with Elliot Haslam in Paris. Debut in 1903 at Newcastle-on-Tyne as the Shepherd *(Tannhäuser)* with the Moody–Manners Company. U.S. debut in 1905 at Baltimore as Gilda *(Rigoletto)* with the touring Savage English Grand Opera Company. Joined the Berlin Royal Opera (1907–13), singing Strauss's Elektra, 1909; moved to the Hamburg Opera, 1913; to the Chicago Opera Company, 1915, making her debut as Sieglinde; to the New York Met, 1917. Considered a leading artist there after singing the title role in Liszt's *St. Elisabeth,* 3 Jan. 1918. At the Met she created Lauretta in *Gianni Schicchi,* 1918. After appearances in England she returned to the Met as Brünnhilde, 1936. Her repertory comprised some 150 roles in 4 languages.

Eaton, John (Charles) (b. Bryn Mawr, Pa., 30 Mar. 1935). Composer and keyboard player. Studied at Princeton (1953–59, B.A., M.F.A.) under Babbitt, Cone, and Sessions; his early career was as a jazz pianist. From 1971 he taught at Indiana Univ., where he directed the Center for Electronic and Computer Music; he was composer-in-residence at the American Academy in Rome (1975–76). He has performed on and composed especially for the Syn-ket, a synthesizer designed by Paolo Ketoff (1964) with pressure-sensitive keys, and for synthesizers designed and built by Robert Moog. Works include *Concert Piece, for Syn-ket and Symphony Orchestra* (1966); *Blind Man's Cry* (soprano, various synthesizers, and 2 tape recorders, 1968); a Mass (soprano, clarinet, and an orchestra of synthesizers, 1969); *Remembering Rome* (sinfonietta for strings, 1987). Other concert music has explored microtones (*Microtonal Fantasy,* 2 pianos tuned a quarter-tone apart, 1966; *Vibrations,* 1967, one for flute and 2 oboes, another for 2 clarinets, the instruments to be tuned a quarter-tone apart) and interesting sonorities (*Sonority Movements,* flute and 9 harps, 1971). Eaton has also written a number of operas, including *Heracles,* performed at the opening of the opera house at Indiana Univ. (1972); *Myshkin,* commissioned by Public Television (after Dostoyevsky, 1973); *Danton and Robespierre* (1978); *The Cry of Clytemnestra* (1980); *The Tempest,* commissioned by the

Santa Fe Opera (Andrew Porter, after Shakespeare, 1985); *The Reverend Jim Jones* (1989). He is the author of *Involvement with Music: New Music since 1950* (1976).

Ebeling, Johann Georg (b. Lüneburg, 8 July 1637; d. Stettin, 4 Dec. 1676). Composer. Studied for 13 years at the St. Johanneum, Lüneburg, under Kantor Michael Jacobi. Began theological studies at the Univ. of Helmstedt in 1658; in 1660 took over the Hamburg Collegium musicum founded in 1659 by Weckmann; succeeded Crüger as Kantor at St. Nicholas, Berlin, working alongside the poet Paul Gerhardt. Turned down an offer from his hometown in 1663; in 1667 moved to Stettin as a teacher of music and Greek. In 1666–67 he published a collection of 120 of Gerhardt's hymns, for 112 of which he had written the melody and harmonization. Additional works include devotional songs and a history of music.

Eben, Petr (b. Žamberk, 22 Jan. 1929). Composer. He was raised in Český Krumlov, where he studied organ, cello, and piano; after the war he studied at the Academy of Musical Arts in Prague (1948–54) with Friedrich Rauch (piano) and Pavel Bořkovec (composition). In 1955 he was appointed professor of music theory at Charles Univ. in Prague; he also concertized extensively as pianist. A prominent music educator, he published a number of folk song arrangements for school use. His works include orchestral music (an organ concerto, *Symphonia gregoriana,* 1954; a piano concerto, 1961; *Vox clamantis,* 3 trumpets, orchestra, 1970); choral music (*Hořká hlina,* cantata, 1959; *Apologia Sokrates,* soloists, chorus, orchestra, 1961–67; *Slavíček rajský,* 1970); chamber and solo instrumental music (Oboe Sonata, 1950; Piano Sonata, 1950; *Suite baladica,* cello, piano, 1955; *Sonatina semplice,* violin/flute, piano, 1957; *Variations on a Chorale,* brass quintet, 1969; *Okna,* trumpet, organ, 1976).

Eberl, Anton (Franz Josef) (b. Vienna, 13 June 1765; d. there, 11 Mar. 1807). Composer and pianist. He began studying music, possibly with Mozart, when his law studies went aground. In 1784 he gave his first public piano recitals in the Vienna Burgtheater. The first of his stage works, a comedy *Die Marchande des Modes,* was produced in 1787 at the Leopoldstädtertheater. Others include *Graf Balduin von Flandern* (1788), *Die Zigeuner* (1793), and *Die Königin der schwarzen Inseln* (1801); most of the music for these is lost. From 1795 to 1802 he made concert tours as pianist and conductor in Germany and Russia. After 1798, the year his op. 1 keyboard sonata was published, several of his works were repeatedly attributed to Mozart. Among his compositions are a cantata, *Bey Mozarts Grab* (1791); many keyboard pieces (including 12 variations on "Bei Männern welche Liebe fühlen," 1792); at least 5 symphonies; 4 piano concertos; chamber music (3 string quartets op. 13); songs.

Eberlin, Johann Ernst (bapt. Jettingen, Bavaria, 27 Mar. 1702; d. Salzburg, 19 June 1762). Composer. Attended Augsburg Gymnasium, performing in school plays; went to Salzburg in 1721, becoming fourth organist at the cathedral in 1724 and succeeding Gugl as court and cathedral organist in 1729. He served five archbishops, becoming Kapellmeister in 1749. Leopold Mozart, first his student, then a musician under him, praised him in his contribution to Marpurg's *Kritischer Beiträgen* (1757). Some works long thought to have been by Bach and W. A. Mozart are actually his; the latter offered a low opinion of Eberlin's keyboard fugues, however. Other music includes stage and dramatic works (many lost), church music, and keyboard pieces.

Eberwein, (Franz) Carl (Adalbert) (b. Weimar, 10 Nov. 1786; d. there, 2 Mar. 1868). Composer and violinist. From a family of musicians; brother of Traugott; studied with his father, a Weimar court musician, and became a court musician himself in 1803; from 1807 also private music director for Goethe (who helped him study with Zelter in Berlin, 1808–9). Set many Goethe texts, from songs to singspiels, the monodrama *Proserpine,* and incidental music for *Faust.* From 1810, musician of the Weimar city church, director there from 1818, and singing teacher at the seminary; 1826–49, Weimar court Kapellmeister and opera conductor. He composed operas, cantatas, incidental music, instrumental pieces, many songs.

Eberwein, Traugott (Maximilian) (b. Weimar, 27 Oct. 1775; d. there, 2 Dec. 1831). Violinist and composer. Brother of Carl; 1793–94, toured Germany, France, and Italy as a violinist; from 1797, court musician in Rudolstadt; from 1810 chamber musician and from 1817 Kapellmeister there. Like his brother, he belonged to Goethe's circle; 2 of his 12 operas are set to Goethe singspiels. Other works include incidental music, cantatas, a Mass, 3 symphonies, chamber music, songs.

Eccard, Johannes (b. Mühlhausen, 1553; d. Berlin, 1611). Composer. Probably studied in Mühlhausen with Joachim a Burck, with whom he later published works jointly; sang in the chapel of the Weimar court from 1567 to 1571, then until late 1573 in the Bavarian Hofkapelle in Munich, where he was a pupil of Lassus. After serving in the musical household of Jakob Fugger in Augsburg in 1577 and 1578, he became Vice-Kapellmeister (from 1579), later Kapellmeister (acting from 1586, officially from 1604), of the Prussian Hofkapelle in Königsberg. From 1608 he was Kapellmeister to the Elector in Berlin. He composed simple 5-part chorale harmonizations with the melody in the top voice, designed for congregational participation, as well as more elaborate chorale motets, of which he was a leading exponent.

Eccles, John (b. probably London, ca. 1668; d. Hampton Wick, 12 Jan. 1735). Composer. Issued a number of songs in 1691; joined the United Companies of Drury Lane as theater composer in 1693; when some actors split off to form a new troupe at Lincoln's Inn

Fields in 1695, he became their music director. Produced many songs and masques along with incidental music for both theaters; active also at court, he served as musician-in-ordinary to the king and composed many court odes. He took part in a composing contest on Congreve's *The Judgement of Paris* in 1701 and composed *Semele,* an opera on a Congreve libretto (completed in 1707 but never performed). He retired from the theater soon thereafter, but continued to compose for the court.

Eckard, Johann Gottfried (b. Augsburg, 21 Jan. 1735; d. Paris, 24 July 1809). Composer and pianist. Trained as a painter and engraver, he taught himself to play the keyboard, reportedly through the use of Emanuel Bach's *Versuch.* In 1758 he traveled to Paris with a friend and fellow Augsburger Johann Andreas Stein, the piano manufacturer. Throughout the 1760s and 1770s he was acclaimed in the city both as pianist and as composer. He has been cited as the first composer in France to write sonatas specifically for fortepiano. His keyboard sonatas were admired by the young Mozart, who transcribed the op. 1, no. 4 sonata for his own K. 40 piano concerto. Eckard's published works include 6 keyboard sonatas op. 1 (1763) and 2 sonatas op. 2 (1764).

Bibl.: Eduard Reeser, ed., *J. G. Eckard: Oeuvres complètes* (Kassel, 1956). Id., *Ein Augsburger Musiker in Paris: Johann Gottfried Eckard (1735–1809)* (Augsburg, 1984).

Eckhard, Jacob (b. Eschwege, Hessen, 24 Nov. 1757; d. Charleston, S.C., 10 Nov. 1833). Organist and composer. He came to North America in 1776, settling in Richmond, Va.; he may have been organist at St. John's Episcopal Church. In 1786 he received the post of schoolmaster and organist at St. John's Lutheran Church in Charleston, and in 1809 moved to St. Michael's Episcopal Church. As choirmaster of the latter he compiled an important collection of Episcopal Psalms and tunes (facs. of manuscript published in 1971) and also published a *Choral-Book* (Boston, 1816).

Bibl.: George W. Williams, "Jacob Eckhard and His Choirmaster's Book," *JAMS* 7 (1954): 41–47.

Eckhardt-Gramatté, S(ophie)-C(armen) (b. Moscow, 6 Jan. 1899; d. Stuttgart, 2 Dec. 1974). Violinist, pianist, and composer. She became a Canadian citizen in 1958. From 1904 she studied with her mother and later (from 1909) at the Paris Conservatory; she composed from 1905, and a career as a virtuoso performer on both piano and violin began in 1911 in Berlin. From the 1930s she devoted more time to composition, studying with Max Trapp in Berlin (1936–38); in Vienna from 1945, she helped to establish the Austrian branch of the ISCM. She lived in Canada from 1957, when her second husband became director of the Winnipeg Art Gallery. Confined to instrumental genres, her compositions from the 1920s and 1930s reflect in their virtuosity her own remarkable skills as a performer; in the 1940s she wrote in a neoclassic style; in the 1950s she explored serialism and the metric innovations of Blacher and Messiaen.

Eckstine, Billy [William Clarence; Mr. B.] (b. Pittsburgh, 8 July 1914; d. Pittsburgh, 8 Mar. 1993). Popular singer and jazz bandleader. He sang with Earl Hines's big band (1939–43), recording "Jelly, Jelly" (1940) and "Skylark" (1942). He formed the first bop big band, with Charlie Parker, Dizzy Gillespie, Sarah Vaughan, Gene Ammons, Fats Navarro, Miles Davis, Dexter Gordon, Sonny Stitt, and Art Blakey among its members (1944–47); Eckstine himself, a smooth-voiced baritone, sang ballads. After recording "Everything I Have Is Yours" (1947) he briefly became the most popular singer in the U.S. (1949–50). From the 1950s on he toured as a nightclub entertainer.

Eddy, Nelson (b. Providence, R.I., 29 June 1901; d. Miami Beach, 6 Mar. 1967). Baritone. After obtaining a B.A. from UCLA, studied voice with William Vilonat in New York and David Bispham in Philadelphia. With Philadelphia Civic Opera, 1924–30; professional debut there as Tonio *(Pagliacci);* later roles included Escamillo *(Carmen),* Count Almaviva *(Le nozze di Figaro),* and Mercutio *(Roméo et Juliette).* Auditioned for Fritz Busch at the Dresden Opera, 1927; was offered a contract as leading baritone there, but returned to the U.S. Sang in U.S. premieres of Strauss's *Feuersnot* (1927), Strauss's *Ariadne auf Naxos* (1928), Berg's *Wozzeck* (1931), and Respighi's *Maria Egiziaca* (1932). In 1933 appeared in *From Broadway to Hollywood,* the first of 18 operettas and musicals filmed by M.G.M. Achieved great popularity as partner to Jeanette MacDonald in 8 of these, from *Naughty Marietta* (1935) to *I Married an Angel* (1942); to Ilona Massey in 3 films (1937–48); to Risë Stevens in *The Chocolate Soldier* (1941).

Edelmann, Jean-Frédéric [Johann Friedrich] (b. Strasbourg, 5 May 1749; d. Paris, 17 July 1794). Composer and keyboard player. After studying law in Strasbourg under the patronage of a Baron de Dietrich, he took up residence in Paris around 1773. There he gained a reputation as composer, pianist, and keyboard instructor. In 1789 he returned to Strasbourg and was given an administrative post in the lower Rhine region. As a result of his own bureaucratic and political entanglements, he was executed at the guillotine. He composed the dramatic works *La bergère des Alpes* (1781), *Ariane dans l'isle de Naxos* (1782), *Diane e l'amour* (1802); an oratorio, *Esther* (1781); symphonies; chamber music; keyboard works.

Eder, Helmut (b. Linz, 26 Dec. 1916). Composer. He studied at the Linz Conservatory until 1948, and then in Stuttgart (with Johann Nepomuk David) and Munich (with Orff); subsequently taught at the Linz Conservatory, where he became professor in 1962. He conducted the Singakadamie in Linz (1953–60) and founded the first electronic studio there in 1959. In 1967 he was appointed professor of composition at the Salzburg Mozarteum. Works include several operas, ballets, and radio and television scores; symphonies; the *Concerto semiserio* (2 pianos and orchestra, 1962), *Concertino für Orchester* (1986), and other concertos for violin, oboe, bassoon, and organ (on "L'homme armé"); *Metamorphosen über ein Fragment von Mozart* (flute, oboe, string quartet, and orchestra, 1970); . . . *Missa est* (soloists, 2 choruses, 3 orchestras, 1986); chamber music (String quartet no. 3, 1986); organ works; choral music; and songs.

Edison, Harry "Sweets" (b. Columbus, Ohio, 10 Oct. 1915). Jazz trumpeter. He joined Count Basie's big band (1938–50), recording solos regularly (including "Every Tub," 1938). He performed in the film *Jammin' the Blues* (1944). He toured with Jazz at the Philharmonic from 1950, joined Buddy Rich intermittently (1951–53), became a principal soloist accompanying Frank Sinatra (from ca. 1952 on and off to at least 1978), worked as a studio musician, and played again with Basie intermittently (1966–81). Throughout this period he also led groups, including a quintet with Eddie "Lockjaw" Davis (1975–82). His albums include *Jazz at the Haig* (1953) and the duo *Oscar Peterson & Harry Edison* (1974).

Edmunds [St. Edmunds], **John (Charles Sterling)** (b. San Francisco, 10 June 1913; d. Berkeley, 9 Dec. 1986). Composer. Studied composition with Scalero at Curtis, then at Columbia and Harvard; taught at Syracuse Univ. and Berkeley; was in charge of Americana at the New York Public Library (1957–61); lived in England (1968–76), where he worked with Dart on 17th-century English song, of which he published many transcriptions and arrangements. As a composer he was best known for his songs (Yeats, Housman, Dryden, Shakespeare, Middle English texts); the collection *Hesperides* (1935–60) and his *Psalms of David* (1960) employ ground basses, a technique common to Baroque song. Other works include a masque in Middle English, ballets, oratorios, hymns and carols, many songs, and folk song arrangements.

Edwards, George (Harrison) (b. Boston, 11 May 1943). Composer. He studied at Oberlin College (B.A., 1965) and Princeton (M.F.A., 1967). In 1968 he joined the theory faculty at the New England Conservatory. In 1976 he began teaching at Columbia Univ. Compositions include *Parallel Convergences* (1989), *A Mirth but Open'd* (1986), *Suave Mari Magno* (1984), *Moneta's Mourn* (1983), String Quartet no. 2 (1982), *Northern Spy* (1980), *Veined Variety* (1978), *Gyromancy* (1977), *Draconian Measures* (1976), *Exchange Misere* (1974), *Giro* (1974), *Monopoly* (1972), *Kreuz und Quer* (1971), String Quartet (1967).

Edwards, Richard (b. Somerset, 1524; d. London, 31 Oct. 1566). Poet, dramatist, and composer. He attended Oxford in the 1540s, then joined the Chapel Royal, becoming Master of the Children in 1561. His writings include a well-known collection of poems suitable for use as song texts and several plays (only one survives) for choirboys. Two sacred choral pieces and 6 secular songs survive with attributions to him. Three of the songs are known in keyboard arrangement only; the others are for one voice with accompaniment of lute or viols.

Edwards, Ross (b. Sydney, 23 Dec. 1943). Composer. After studies at the New South Wales State Conservatory (1959–62) and at Sydney Univ. (1963), and with Richard Meale and Peter Sculthorpe, in 1966 he won a scholarship to study with Sándor Veress and Peter Maxwell Davies at the Univ. of Adelaide. His music, like that of Davies, employs elements of medieval and Renaissance styles. Works include vocal music (*Quem quaeritis: A Play of the Nativity,* soloists, chorus, chamber ensemble, 1967; *Kan-Touk,* female voice, chamber ensemble, tape, 1973; *Antiphon,* chorus, chamber ensemble, 1973); orchestral music (Chamber Symphony, 1962; Sonata, chamber orchestra, 1967; Etude for Orchestra, 1969; *Choros,* piano, orchestra, 1971); chamber music (Sextet, 1966; 3 string quartets, 1968–72; *Music,* flute, tape, 1965).

Effinger, Cecil (b. Colorado Springs, 22 July 1914; d. Boulder, 22 Dec. 1990). Composer, oboist, inventor. Studied and briefly taught mathematics before turning to composition with Wagenaar (1938) and Boulanger (1939). Taught music at Colorado College (1936–41, 1946–48), the American Univ. (Biarritz, 1945–46), and the Univ. of Colorado, where he was appointed professor emeritus and composer-in-residence upon retirement (1981). In the 1930s he played first oboe in the Colorado Springs Symphony and the Denver Symphony; led an army band during the war. He invented the Music Writer, a typewriterlike machine for producing musical notation. Works include *Paul of Tarsus* (chorus, strings, and organ, 1968) and other oratorios, operas, musical theater, and incidental music; 5 symphonies, a piano concerto, and other orchestral works; 6 string quartets and other ensemble and piano works; many choral works (*2 Sonnets from the Portuguese,* 1985).

Egge, Klaus (b. Gransherad, 19 July 1906; d. Oslo, 7 Mar. 1979). Composer. At the Oslo Conservatory he was a pupil of A. Sandvold (organ), Nils Larsen (piano), and Fartein Valen (composition); later he studied in Berlin with W. Gmeindl. He was vocal coach in Oslo from 1932 to 1945; he also edited the music journal *Tonekunst* and was music critic for the *Arbeiderbladet* in Oslo. From 1946 to 1948 he presided over the *Nordisk Komponistråd.* His music is characterized by harmony based on fourths and fifths, with shifting tonal centers, and melodies employing all 12 notes serially or nonserially. Works include 5 symphonies (no. 1, *Sounds of Destiny,* 1945; no. 4, *Sinfonia seriale sopra B.A.C.H.—E.G.G.E.,* 1968); 3 piano concertos (1938–74); concertos for violin (1953) and cello (1966); choral works (*Sveinung Vreim,* chorus, orchestra, 1938; *Noreg-songen,* 1941); a violin sonata (1932), a string quartet (1933), 2 piano sonatas (1933, 1955), Sonatina (harp, 1974), and other chamber music.

Eggen, Arne (b. Trondheim, 28 Aug. 1881; d. Baerum, near Oslo, 26 Oct. 1955). Composer and organist. He studied at the Oslo Conservatory, then in 1906 went to Leipzig, where he was a pupil of Karl Straube (organ) and Stephan Krehl (composition). He held organ posts at Bragernes (1908–24) and later at Bryn and Tanum (in Akershus, near Oslo). From 1927 to 1945 he was president of the Norwegian Composers' Association. His music is in the post-Romantic nationalist style of Grieg. He composed 2 operas (*Olav Liljekrans,* first perf., 1940; *Cymbelin,* first perf., 1948); an oratorio, *Kong Olav* (1930); Symphony in G minor (1920); *Ciaconna* (organ, 1917?; also an orchestrated version); a piano trio, 2 violin sonatas, and other chamber music; songs.

Egidius de Murino (fl. mid-14th cent.). Theorist. Author of a short practical treatise on motets called *De motettis componendis* (*CS* 3:124–28), which discusses chiefly the rhythmic organization of the tenor and, in 4-part works, the contratenor. Some mention is made of text underlay and, in a brief final section, the forms of ballades, rondeaux, and virelays. Although he may have been active as a composer, no music can be firmly attributed to him.

Egidius [Aegidius] **de Zamora** (fl. ca. 1260–80). Theorist. His *Ars musica* (ed. and trans. French, *CSM* 20 [1974]), was written in Spain at the court of Alfonso X the Wise in about 1270. It is highly conservative, heavily dependent on earlier authorities, and conventional in the subjects covered. A long section concentrating on instruments, however, includes more original material. That the church makes use of the organ ("organa") but excludes all other instruments is also mentioned.

Bibl.: Don M. Randel, "La teoría musical en la época de Alfonso X el Sabio," *Revista de musicología* 10 (1987): 39–51.

Egk [Mayer], **Werner** (b. Auchsesheim, near Donauwörth, 17 May 1901; d. Inning, Bavaria, 10 July 1983). Composer and writer. He studied in Augsburg at the Gymnasium, and in Frankfurt and Munich with Orff; lived briefly in Italy (1925–27) and Berlin (1928), and then in Munich (1929–36), where he wrote music for radio plays and a radio opera (*Columbus,* 1932, staged in Frankfurt in 1942). He was guest conductor at the Berlin Staatsoper from 1937 to 1941, and after the war was director of the Berlin Hochschule für Musik (1950–53). In later years he continued to write successfully for the stage, providing his own librettos; belonged to the Academy of Fine Arts in Bavaria (1951) and East Berlin (1966) and was president of the German Society of Authors and Publishers (1950). His works were influenced primarily by the French impressionist and neoclassical traditions, especially by Stravinsky. His writings include essays in German and Austrian periodicals *(Melos, Das Orchester)* and 2 volumes of essays: *Musik, Wort, Bild* (1960) and *Die Zeit wartet nicht: Künsterlisches, Zeitgeschichtliches, Privates aus meinem Leben* (1981). He also provided the libretto for Blacher's *Abstrakte Oper no. 1,* and wrote a stage play *(Das Zauberbett).*

Works: at least 7 operas (*Die Zaubergeige,* after Pocci, Frankfurt, 1935; *Der Revisor,* after Gogol, Schwetzingen, 1957; *Die Verlobung in San Domingo,* after Kleist, Munich, 1963); some 5 ballets (*Casanova in London,* Munich, 1969); *Orchestersonate* 1 and 2 (1948, 1969), suites from his dramatic works, *Nachtanz über ein Thema aus dem 16 Jahrhundert* (1983), *Canzona* (cello and orchestra, 1982), and other orchestral music; a sonata for piano (1947); an oratorio (*Furchtlosigkeit und Wohlwollen,* tenor, chorus, and orchestra, 1931; rev. 1959), *Mein Vaterland* (Klopstock, hymn for unison chorus and orchestra or organ, 1937), and other choral music; *Nachtgefühl* (cantata for soprano and orchestra, 1976) and other vocal music.

Ehrlich, Abel (b. Cranz, near Königsberg, 3 Sept. 1915). Composer. He studied in Germany, then at Zagreb with Václav Huml. Settling in Jerusalem in 1939, he studied composition further with Shelomo Rosovsky at the Jerusalem Academy of Music; from 1940 he taught music at local schools. From 1959 he took part in several Darmstadt summer courses. Beginning in 1964 he taught at the Israel Academy (which two years later became part of Tel Aviv Univ.), and from 1972 was professor of theory and composition there. Starting in the 1950s he employed, under the influence of Darmstadt colleagues Stockhausen and Nono, serialism and other more recent techniques. He has composed vocal music (*Ha-bayit ha-zeh,* oratorio, 1967; *Immanuel Haromi,* "musical spectacle," 1971; *Job 7: 11–16,* baritone, chorus, orchestra, 1971; *A Vision of God,* voices, chamber orchestra, 1975; *Tevicah,* soloists, chorus, orchestra, 1974; *Giordano Bruno,* semi-oratorio, 1986); chamber music (4 wind quintets; *Improvisations with a Game in Hell,* string trio, 1970; *Because You Are My Kinsman,* soprano, cello, piano, 1989).

Ehrling, Sixten (Evert) (b. Malmö, 3 Apr. 1918). Conductor and pianist. Studied conducting with T. Mann at the Stockholm Conservatory, 1936–40; with Karl Böhm in Dresden, 1941. Toured Europe as a concert pianist during the 1940s. Coach at the Royal Opera House in Stockholm, 1940; conductor, 1944; artistic director, 1953–60. Led the Detroit Symphony, 1963–73; the Göteborg Symphony, 1973–75. Taught conducting at the Salzburg Mozarteum, 1954; at Juilliard beginning in 1973. Led a complete *Ring* at the New York Met, 1975. Principal guest conductor of the Denver Symphony, 1978–85; artistic adviser, San Antonio Symphony, 1985–88.

Eichner, Ernst (Dietrich Adolph) (b. Arolsen, Hessen, 9 Feb. 1740; d. Potsdam, 1777). Composer and bassoon virtuoso. He probably received his first instruction from his father, Johann Andreas Eichner

(1694–1768), a chamber musician at the court of Waldeck. In 1762 Ernst was appointed violinist and in 1769 Konzertmeister at the court of Christian IV in Zweibrücken; he remained there until 1772, gathering a reputation as a bassoonist. In 1772–73 he appeared in London in the Bach–Abel concert series; after 1773 he served under Friedrich Wilhelm II at Potsdam, where he spent most of his remaining years. He composed some 30 symphonies; also solo concertos, chamber works, and sonatas.

Eimert, (Eugen Otto) Herbert (b. Bad Kreuznach, 8 Apr. 1897; d. Cologne, 15 Dec. 1972). Composer and critic. He studied in Cologne, where he received the doctorate in musicology (1931); worked for German Radio there (1927–33; 1945–65) and founded the electronic music studio, 1951; was professor of electronic music at the Musikhochschule in Cologne (1965–71). He wrote criticism for and edited the *Kölnische Zeitung* (1936–45) and founded the periodical *Die Reihe* in 1955. An important essay (*Atonale Musiklehre,* 1924) contained the first systematic discussion of twelve-tone technique; other writings include *Lehrbuch der Zwölftontechnik* (1950), *Grundlagen der musikalischen Reihentechnik* (1963), and *Das Lexikon der elektronischen Musik* (with H. U. Humpert, 1973). Works include a ballet (*Der weisse Schwan,* saxophone, flute, and mechanical instruments, 1926), music for the radio play *Cain* (Byron, 1948); orchestral, chamber, and choral pieces; electronic works (Requiem, speaker, harmonica, and tape, 1957).

Einem, Gottfried von (b. Bern, of Austrian parents, 24 Jan. 1918). Composer. Educated in Austria and England, he was a vocal coach at the Berlin State Opera and the Bayreuth Festspielhaus from 1938. He studied composition with Blacher in Berlin (1941–43) when Blacher's works had been officially declared degenerate. His ballet *Prinzessin Turandot* was staged in Dresden in 1944 and led to a position as musical adviser to the Dresden Opera; *Dantons Tod,* his first opera, was staged at the Salzburg Festival in 1947, where he was chairman of the board, 1948–51. During the war he actively helped escapees from Germany; his arrest and interrogation by the Gestapo served as the basis for his opera *Der Prozess* (after Kafka, 1950–52). He was director of the Vienna Festival, 1960–64, and was appointed professor of composition at the Vienna Hochschule für Musik in 1965. From 1965 to 1970 he was president of the Austrian Society of Authors, Composers, and Music Publishers.

His compositional style is conservative and eclectic, reflecting expressionist, neoclassic, and jazz elements, rhythmic innovations of Stravinsky and Blacher, and the primitivism of Egk and Orff; Blacher provided the librettos for 4 of his operas. Compositions include operas (*Der Besuch der alten Dame,* 1971; *Prinz Chocolat,* 1982; *Tulifant,* 1990), several ballets, and incidental music; many orchestral works (*Münchner Symphonie,* 1984–85; Symphony no. 4, 1988); chamber music (Trio for Strings, 1985); large works for soloists, chorus, and orchestra; piano and organ works; other choral and vocal music.

Eisler, Hanns (Johannes) (b. Leipzig, 6 July 1898; d. Berlin, 6 Sept. 1962). Composer. He attended the Staatsgymnasium in Vienna (1908–15) and learned music on his own. After service in the First World War he studied composition at the Vienna Conservatory under Weigl and worked as a proofreader for Universal Edition. From 1919 to 1923 Schoenberg and Webern taught him without fee; *Palmström* (op. 6, voice and ensemble, 1924) reflects that study by employing *Sprechstimme* and a twelve-tone series. In Berlin from 1925 he began to compose in a sparser texture; he broke with Schoenberg in 1926, the year he joined the German Communist party. Subsequent works reflect his leftist political stance and his collaborations with Brecht and Ernst Busch. His music was banned by Hitler in 1933; during and immediately after the war he lived in the U.S. (1938–48), teaching at the New School in New York and at the Univ. of Southern California, writing film music, and again collaborating with Brecht. Anticommunist pressure in the U.S. led to his return to Berlin, where he devoted himself to "applied music" for theater, film, television, cabaret, and public events. He taught at the Hochschule für Musik in East Berlin and belonged to the German Academy of Arts. His output was enormous (but often involved reuse of old material); the melodies in his songs mix modal, jazz, and modern elements, supported by a triadic but nonfunctional harmony; in other music his style was more dissonant and chromatic, and he continued to employ twelve-tone methods in a manner that has been called tonal serialism.

Works: 38 stage works (*Galileo Galilei,* Brecht, Los Angeles, 1947); 42 film scores; 15 orchestral works, many related to his stage music; 8 works for chorus and orchestra (*Deutsche Sinfonie,* Brecht, 1935–39); many sets of unaccompanied choral pieces; chamber and piano music; some 80 works for voice and orchestra, instrumental ensemble, or piano ("Auferstanden aus Ruinen," the national anthem of the German Democratic Republic, 1949).

Writings: With Theodor Adorno, *Composing for the Films* (London, 1947). *Reden und Aufsätze* (Berlin, 1959). *Materialen zu einer Dialektik der Musik* (Berlin, 1973). *Musik und Politik,* ed. Guenter Mayer (Berlin, 1973).

Bibl.: Albrecht Betz, *Hanns Eisler: Political Musician* (Cambridge, 1982). Eberhardt Klemm, "Chronologisches Verzeichnis der Kompositionen Hanns Eislers," *BzMw* 15 (1973): 93–115; shorter version of this catalogue in *Hanns Eisler* (Berlin, 1973). Manfred Grabs, *Hanns Eisler: Kompositionen, Schriften, Literatur: Ein Handbuch* (Leipzig, 1984).

Eisma, Will (b. Singailiat, Indonesia, of Dutch parents, 13 May 1929). Violinist and composer. At the Amsterdam Conservatory (1948–53) he studied with Jewsey Wulf and Oskar Back (violin), and with George Stam and Kees van Baaren (theory, composition). Later he was a pupil of Petrassi in Rome and from 1961 of Koenig in Utrecht (electronic music). As violinist he has played with the Società Corelli, the Rotterdam Philharmonic (from 1953), and the Netherlands Radio Chamber Orchestra (from 1961). Compositions include orchestral music (*Concert-Piece,* violin, orchestra, 1958; *Le choix de costume est libre,* string trio, chamber orchestra, 1974); chamber music (*Rugiada,* mezzo-soprano, piano, 1967; *La gibet,* baritone, chamber ensemble, electronic sound, 1971; *This Light of the Cold, Still Moon,* cello, piano, 1972; *Kalos,* string quartet, piano, 1987); works for tape only (*Elaborated Relaxation,* 1968).

Eklund, Hans (b. Sandviken, 1 July 1927). Composer. He studied at the Stockholm Conservatory (1947–52), then with Lars-Erik Larssen, and finally with Ernst Pepping in Berlin. From 1964 he taught at the Stockholm Conservatory. His music shows the influence of Hindemith and manifests an interest in Baroque and classical formal procedures. Compositions include "radio opera," *Moder Svea* (1971); 8 symphonies (1958–85); 6 sets of *Musica da camera* (1955–70); *Variations for Strings* (1952); *Symphonic Dances* (1954); *Music for Orchestra* (1960); *Variazioni brevi* (1962); *Introduction and Allegro* (harpsichord, string orchestra, 1972); *Due pezzi* (orchestra, 1988); chamber music; *Pezzo spansivo,* piano (1967).

El-Dabh, Halim (Abdul Messieh) (b. Cairo, 4 Mar. 1921). Composer. He composed (from 1940) while studying agricultural engineering; having developed his skill in playing Egyptian instruments, he studied piano and Western music at Cairo Univ. (1941–44), and then with Copland and Fine at the Berkshire Music Center (1950); finally at New England Conservatory and Brandeis. He has taught in Ethiopia (1962–64), at Howard Univ. (1966–69), and at Kent State, where he directed the Center for the Study of World Musics. Some of his compositions blend Egyptian and Western styles. He became a U.S. citizen in 1961. Works include operas or opera-pageants (*Drink of Eternity,* 1981) many of which draw on Egyptian history and mythology; ballets (*Clytemnestra,* an epic dance drama for Martha Graham, 1958); symphonies and other orchestral works (Concerto for Darabukka, Clarinet, and String Orchestra, 1981; *Rhapsodia egyptico-brasileira,* 1985); chamber and piano music; choral works and pieces for solo voice and ensemble; some electronic music.

Eldridge, (David) Roy [Little Jazz] (b. Pittsburgh, 30 Jan. 1911; d. Valley Stream, N.Y., 26 Feb. 1989). Jazz trumpeter. He was a soloist in the big bands of Teddy Hill (1935), Fletcher Henderson (1935–36), Gene Krupa (1941–43), with whom he recorded "Rockin' Chair" (1941), and Artie Shaw (1944–45). From 1935 he also led combos and big bands, recording "Wabash Stomp" (1937) and, as a free-lance with Chu Berry's sextet, "Sittin' In" (1938). From 1949 he toured with Jazz at the Philharmonic, interrupting this association to tour with Benny Goodman to Paris, where he remained in 1950–51. He led groups, including an intermittent one with Coleman Hawkins (from 1952) that recorded the album *At the Opera House* (1957). He also recorded in studio groups with many prominent jazzmen. He accompanied Ella Fitzgerald (1963–65), briefly joined Count Basie (1966), then resumed leading groups, playing traditional jazz and swing at Jimmy Ryan's club in New York from 1970 through 1980; in the late 1970s, no longer up to the demands of the trumpet, he played drums or piano. Eldridge was the stylistic link between Louis Armstrong and Dizzy Gillespie. He favored an extroverted, fiery, joyful style, used expressive variations in timbre (e.g., growls and rasps), and in that decade set new standards for facility in the instrument's upper range.

Elgar, Edward (William) (b. Broadheath, near Worcester, 2 June 1857; d. Worcester, 23 Feb. 1934). Composer. His father was a piano tuner and music salesman and played organ at St. George's Catholic Church in Worcester. Edward was raised mostly in Worcester, where he attended school at Catholic academies and at Littleton House. His earliest formal music lessons were with a violin teacher in Worcester and with London violinist Adolf Pollitzer. He worked in a solicitor's office and in his father's music shop until the 1870s, when he began to take on musical posts; in 1878 he was violinist in the Three Choirs Festival Orchestra, and the following year worked as band director at the county mental asylum. During the 1880s his works began to be performed in London: *Sevilliana* was presented in 1884 at the Crystal Palace, and *Salut d'amour* became popular during the late 1880s.

In 1889 he married Alice Roberts; the following year the couple moved to London. He was unable to find sufficient interest for his music in the city, however, and was forced to return to Worcester in 1891. Nevertheless, his renown continued to grow during the 1890s; the relative success of the *Imperial March* of 1897 led to other commissions, including one from the Leeds Festival for the cantata *Caractacus.* The large choral works of this period (including *Scenes from the Saga of King Olaf* and *Scenes from the Bavarian Highlands,* both 1896) had already gained him recognition around Worcester, but it remained for the *Enigma Variations* of 1899 to win him genuine popularity in London. Partly in recognition of this inventive piece, he received an honorary doctorate from Cambridge Univ. in 1900. Later that year his cantata *The Dream of Gerontius,* possibly his crowning achievement, was received somewhat coolly at its underrehearsed first performance under Hans Richter; subsequent performances in Düsseldorf revealed it to be a remarkable piece and launched a new period of recognition for Elgar's music in the rest of Europe.

Gerontius and the *Variations* were followed immediately by such important (and well-received) works as the *Coronation Ode, The Apostles,* and the first of the

Pomp and Circumstance marches. He was knighted in 1904. In 1905 he was appointed professor of music at Birmingham Univ.—though he was loath to take on academic posts—and the Elgars moved to a large house in Hereford. The next years were among the composer's most productive, and in addition he was appointed conductor of the London Symphony for the 1911–12 season; the period was capped by the couple's move back to London in 1912. Wartime works included *Carillon, Polonia,* and the ballet *The Sanguine Fan.* Elgar continued to compose until Alice's death in 1920, when he lost much of his will to compose. His last years were occupied largely with arranging earlier pieces and with recording his own works. Doctors found a tumor in 1933, and the ailing Elgar returned to the town of his boyhood to die; as a lifelong Catholic he was refused burial at Westminster Abbey and was interred instead at St. Wulstan's Church in Little Malvern.

Works: *Stage. The Crown of India* op. 66 (masque, 1911–12); *The Sanguine Fan* op. 81 (ballet, 1917); songs for a collaborative opera *The Spanish Lady.* Incidental music, including *Grania and Diarmid* op. 42 (1901); *The Starlight Express* op. 78 (1915); *Arthur* (1923); and *Beau Brummel* (1928).

Chorus and orchestra. The Light of Life (Lux Christi) op. 29 (1896); *Scenes from the Saga of King Olaf* op. 30 (1894–96); *Te Deum* op. 34 (1897); *Caractacus* op. 35 (1897–98); *The Dream of Gerontius* op. 38 (1899–1900); *Coronation Ode* op. 44 (1902); *The Apostles* op. 49 (1902–3); *Give unto the Lord* op. 74 (1914); *The Spirit of England* op. 80 (1915–17).

Chorus. A Christmas Greeting op. 52 (1907); *Angelus* op. 56 (1909); *Great Is the Lord* op. 67 (1910–12; verse with orchestra, 1913); *Spanish Serenade* op. 23 (1892); *From the Bavarian Highlands* op. 27 (1895); *The Reveille* op. 54 (1907); *Go, Song of Mine* op. 57 (1909); *Death on the Hills* op. 72 (1914); *The Prince of Sleep* (1925).

Orchestra. Sursum corda (Elevation) op. 11 (1894); *Imperial March* op. 32 (1897); *Variations on an Original Theme* op. 36 (*Enigma Variations,* 1898–99); *Pomp and Circumstance* op. 39 (5 marches: 1901, 1901, 1904, 1907, 1930); *Cockaigne (In London Town)* op. 40 (1900–1901); *Introduction and Allegro* op. 47 (1904–5); 2 symphonies: no. 1 in A♭, op. 55 (1907–8), no. 2 in E♭, op. 63 (1903–11); *Elegy,* strings, op. 58 (1909); Violin Concerto in B minor, op. 61 (1909–10); *Romance,* bassoon, orchestra, op. 62 (1909); *Coronation March* op. 65 (1911); *Falstaff* op. 68 (1902–13); *Polonia* op. 76 (1915); Cello Concerto in E minor, op. 85 (1919).

Solo voice with orchestra. Sea Pictures op. 37 (1897–99); *Pleading* op. 48 (1908); *Carillon* op. 75 (1914); *Une voix dans le désert* op. 77 (1915); *Le drapeau belge* op. 79 (1917).

Romance, Violin and piano, op. 1 (1878); *Salut d'amour,* piano, op. 12 (1888); *Études caractéristiques,* violin, op. 24 (1892); Sonata for Violin and Piano in E minor, op. 82 (1918); String Quartet in E minor, op. 83 (1918); Piano Quintet in A minor, op. 84 (1918–19); some 40 songs for voice and piano; a number of arrangements of works by Bach, Handel, Beethoven, Chopin, Schumann, Wagner, and others.

Bibl.: Ernest Newman, *Elgar* (London, 1906; 3rd ed., 1922; R: of 3rd ed., New York, 1976). William H. Reed, *Elgar* (London, 1939; 2nd ed., 1943; rev. 3rd ed., 1949). Percy M. Young, *Elgar O.M.: A Study of a Musician* (London, 1955; rev. 2nd ed., London, New York, 1973). Id., ed., *Letters of Edward Elgar, and Other Writings* (London, 1956). Herbert Arthur Chambers, ed., *Edward Elgar Centenary Sketches* (London, 1957). Michael Kennedy, *Portrait of Elgar* (London, 1968; 2nd ed., 1973; New York, 1987). John Knowles, *Elgar's Interpreters on Record: An Elgar Discography* (Malvern, 1977; 2nd ed., London, 1985). Michael De-la-Noy, *Elgar, the Man* (London, 1983). Christopher Redwood, ed., *An Elgar Companion* (Ashbourne, Derbyshire, 1982). Jerrold Northrop Moore, *Edward Elgar: A Creative Life* (London, 1984). Id., ed. *Edward Elgar: Letters of a Lifetime* (New York, 1990). Robert Anderson, *Elgar* (New York, 1993). Christopher Kent, *Edward Elgar: A Guide to Research* (New York, 1993).

Elías, Alfonso de (b. Cuernavaca, 30 Aug. 1902; d. Mexico City, 19 Aug. 1984). Composer. Studied at the National Conservatory, 1915–27; in addition to activities as a pianist, composer, and private teacher, he joined the piano faculty at the Universidad autónoma of Mexico in 1958 and became professor of harmony at the National Conservatory in 1964. His music, Romantic and tonal in character, includes orchestral works, chamber compositions, keyboard music, and songs.

Bibl.: *Composers of the Americas* 18 (1972): 21–28 [includes works list].

Elias, Brian (b. Bombay, of English parents, 1948). Composer. He studied with Bernard Stevens and Humphrey Searle at the Royal College of Music and later with Elizabeth Lutyens. Works include *La Chevelure* (soprano, chamber orchestra, 1967); *ELM* (soprano, tenor, piano, 1969); *Proverbs of Hell* (chorus a cappella, 1975); *Tzigane* (violin, 1978); *Somnia* (tenor, orchestra, 1979); *Edge of Time* (tenor, piano, 1982); *L'Eylah* (orchestra, 1984); a violin concerto (1984); *Five Songs to Poems by Irina Ratushinskaya* (chorus, 1989); piano pieces (*Five Pieces for Right Hand,* 1969).

Elías, José (fl. 1715–51). Composer. Born in Cataluña; perhaps a student of Cabanilles, hundreds of whose works he knew. After serving as organist at the Church of SS. Justo y Pastor, Barcelona, 1715–25, he went to Madrid and was named *capellán de su Majestad* and organist at the Convento de las Descalzas Reales. Widely admired by his contemporaries; his known works consist entirely of organ music: tientos, *pasos, tocatas,* and similar types, along with versets for alternatim use in the liturgy.

Bibl.: *Obras completas* (Barcelona, 1971–).

Elías, Manuel Jorge de (b. Mexico City, 5 June 1939). Composer. Son of Alfonso de Elías, from whom he received initial instruction. Continued his training, 1959–62, at the Universidad autónoma and at the National Conservatory; later attended lectures by Stockhausen, among others. In 1968 he was named assistant conductor of the National Symphony of Mexico; after additional study in the U.S. and Europe he founded the Institute of Music at the Univ. of Veracruz in 1976. His music combines traditional and experimental timbres and uses aleatory procedures; works include orchestral music, choral and solo vocal pieces, and an extensive output of chamber music.

Bibl.: *Composers of the Americas* 15 (1969): 68–77 [includes works list].

Elizalde, Federico [Fred] (b. Manila, 12 Dec. 1908; d. there, 16 Jan. 1979). Composer and conductor. Born of Spanish parents, he went to Spain in 1917, studied piano with Manuel Cendoya in San Sebastián and with Pérez Casas at the Madrid Conservatory. Moved to California in 1923 and studied conducting with Alfred Hertz (debut leading the San Francisco Symphony, 1923), composition with Ernest Bloch. Moved to England in 1927, thence to Paris, where he studied composition with Ernesto Halffter. Returned to the Philippines in 1930 to become conductor of the Manila Symphony. In France during the Japanese Occupation. President of the Manila Broadcast Company beginning in 1948. Among his works are music for García Lorca's *Los títeres de Cachiporra* (1935); *Sinfonia concertante* (1936); Violin Concerto (1943); Piano Concerto (1947); an opera, *Paul Gauguin* (1948).

Elkan, Henri (b. Antwerp, 23 Nov. 1897; d. Philadelphia, 12 June 1980). Music publisher. Studied at the conservatories of Antwerp and Amsterdam, 1914–17. Settled in the U.S. in 1920. Violist with the Philadelphia Orchestra, 1920–28. Conductor of the Philadelphia Ballet Company, 1926–39; of the Philadelphia Grand Opera Company, 1928–36; of the Trenton Civic Orchestra, 1933. Founded Henri Elkan Music Publishing Company, 1926; with Adolphe Vogel, a cellist, cofounded Elkan–Vogel Music Publishing Company, which flourished after obtaining distribution rights to several important French catalogues; he dissociated himself from it 1952 and in 1960 revived the Henri Elkan Music Publishing Company, which published American and Latin American music.

Elkus, Albert (Israel) (b. Sacramento, 30 Apr. 1884; d. Oakland, 19 Feb. 1962). Composer and pianist. Studied at Berkeley (M.Litt., 1907) but was trained from childhood as a pianist; studied composition with Kaun in Berlin (1907–8) and then in San Francisco with Weil; spent 1912–13 in Paris, Berlin, and Vienna studying piano, composition, and conducting. On his return, gave piano recitals and taught in the Bay area, and then at San Francisco Conservatory (1923–25, 1930–37; director, 1951–57), at Mills College (1929–44), and at Berkeley (1931–59). He employed chromatic harmony and wrote in a style drawn from Brahms. He composed 3 works for orchestra (*Impressions from a Greek Tragedy,* 1917); 2 string quartets and a violin sonata; piano music (*Klavierstücke,* 1906); choruses and songs; co-edited *The Letters and Papers of Oscar Weil* (1923).

Eller, Heino (b. Yur'yev [Tartu], Estonia, 7 Mar. 1887; d. Tallinn, 16 June 1970). Composer. Before World War I he studied law at St. Petersburg Univ. (1908–12); after 1920 he took up music, studying composition

Duke Ellington.

with Kalafati at the Petrograd Conservatory. During his student years he also worked as an orchestral violinist. From 1920 he taught theory and composition at the Higher Music School in Tartu; in 1940 he was appointed professor of music at Tallinn Conservatory, where he spent his remaining years. During his half century as a teacher, he had great influence on Estonian composers, including his pupils Eduard Tubin, Boris Korver, and Arvo Pärt. Grounded in folk music, his own style contains elements from late Romantic northern Europeans such as Grieg and Sibelius, and from Russian composers, especially Scriabin. Works include 3 symphonies (1936–61); orchestral tone poems (*Zarya* [Dawn], 1918; *Öö hüded* [Night Sound], 1920, rev. 1960); *Fantasy* (violin, orchestra, 1916; rev. 1963); *Sinfonietta* (strings, 1965); chamber music (5 string quartets, 1925–59; 2 violin sonatas, 1922, 1946); and 4 piano sonatas (1920–58).

Ellington, Duke [Edward Kennedy] (b. Washington, D.C., 29 Apr. 1899; d. New York, 24 May 1974). Jazz bandleader, pianist, and composer. From 1923 he led the Washingtonians, which by 1927 had performed at the Hollywood and Kentucky clubs in New York and expanded to 10 players, among them Sonny Greer, Bubber Miley, Tricky Sam Nanton, and Harry Carney. As a 12-piece band at the Cotton Club (1927–31) it included Johnny Hodges, Barney Bigard, and Cootie Williams (who replaced Miley). During this period Ellington's band played "jungle music," involving growling muted brass, tom-tom drum rhythms, and unusual voicings of harmonies. In 1932 the group began a lifetime of touring; its 14 players included Rex

Stewart, Lawrence Brown, and Juan Tizol. Later additions were Jimmy Blanton (with whom Ellington also recorded duos), Ben Webster, and Billy Strayhorn (from 1939); Ray Nance, Oscar Pettiford, Jimmy Hamilton, Cat Anderson (1940s); Paul Gonsalves, Clark Terry, Louie Bellson (1950s). With few exceptions Ellington's compositions were tailored to the duration of a 78-rpm disc until the mid-1940s, some involving themes borrowed from, or developed in collaboration with, his sidemen. Ellington displayed an unrivaled gift for jazz orchestration, harmonization, and miniature form to compose a body of the finest big band recordings in jazz. From 1943 to 1948 he gave concerts at Carnegie Hall. This coincided with a change in his orientation as a composer. He concentrated on suites, tone poems, ballets, and (from the mid-1960s) sacred music, with pretentions toward European art music. He also wrote soundtracks for the films *Anatomy of a Murder* (in which he acted, 1959) and *Paris Blues* (1961) and in 1962 recorded in small groups with Charles Mingus and Max Roach, Coleman Hawkins, and John Coltrane. His recordings include "East St. Louis Toodle-o" (1926), "Black and Tan Fantasy" (1927), "The Mooche" (1928), "Old Man Blues," "Mood Indigo" (both 1930), "It Don't Mean a Thing" (1932), "Sophisticated Lady" (1933), "Diminuendo in Blue/Crescendo in Blue" (1937), "Ko-Ko," "Concerto for Cootie," "Harlem Air Shaft," "In a Mellotone" (all 1940), "Take the 'A' Train" (1941), "Trumpets No End" (1946), and the albums *Ellington at Newport* (1956), *Money Jungle, Duke Ellington Meets Coleman Hawkins* (both 1962), *Concert of Sacred Music* (1965), and *The New Orleans Suite* (1970).

Writings: *Music Is My Mistress* (Garden City, N.Y., 1973; rev. 2nd ed., 1982).

Bibl.: Stanley Dance, *The World of Duke Ellington* (London, 1970; R: 1981). Derek Jewell, *Duke: A Portrait of Duke Ellington* (London, 1977). Mercer Ellington and Stanley Dance, *Duke Ellington in Person: An Intimate Memoir* (Boston, 1978). James Lincoln Collier, *Duke Ellington* (New York, 1987). Ken Rattenbury, *Duke Ellington, Jazz Composer* (New Haven, 1990). Mark Tucker, *Ellington: The Early Years* (Urbana, Ill., 1991). Id., ed., *The Duke Ellington Reader* (New York, 1993).

Ellis, David (b. Liverpool, 1933). Composer. He studied at the Royal Manchester College of Music from 1953 to 1957. In 1964 he was appointed to the Manchester staff of the BBC; he became music director for BBC North in 1978. His compositions include an opera, *Crito* (1963); orchestral works (*Dance Rhapsody,* 1963; *Elegy,* 1966; Symphony no. 1, 1973; concertos for violin, 1958, and piano, 1962; *Solus,* string orchestra, 1973; *February Music,* cello and chamber orchestra, 1977; *Circles,* 1979); choral music (*Sequentia in tempore natalis sacri,* 1964; *Sequentia IV (Visions),* 1972); chamber music (String Trio, 1954; Wind Quintet, 1956; Double Bass Sonata, 1977; Piano Sonata, 1956).

Ellis, Don(ald Johnson) (b. Los Angeles, 25 July 1934; d. Hollywood, 17 Dec. 1978). Jazz trumpeter, composer, and bandleader. He studied composition at Boston Univ. (B.M., 1956), then played in big bands, including Maynard Ferguson's (1959). He recorded the quartet album *How Time Passes* (1960) and worked with George Russell (1961–62). His Hindustani Jazz Sextet (actually a septet) incorporated Indian instruments and rhythms. From 1966 he led a big band that explored odd meters and rock music; as its principal soloist, Ellis used a 4-valve instrument to play quarter tones, modifying it with electronic devices to alter timbre and to produce echo effects (as on the album *Electric Bath,* 1967). A 21-piece band, utilizing a woodwind quartet, a brass quintet, and an amplified string quartet, is preserved on the album *Tears of Joy* (1971). In 1972 Ellis won a Grammy Award for his arrangement of the theme of the film *The French Connection.*

Elman, Mischa [Mikhail Saulovitch] (b. Talnoy, 20 Jan. 1891; d. New York, 5 Apr. 1967). Violinist. Studied violin with Alexandre Fidelmann in Odessa, 1897–1901; with Leopold Auer in St. Petersburg, 1901–4. Debut in 1899, playing de Bériot's Seventh Concerto. His professional debut in Berlin on 14 Oct. 1904 was followed by tours of Germany (1904) and England (1905). U.S. debut on 10 Dec. 1908 in New York, playing the Tchaikovsky concerto. Passionate in temperament and prodigious in technique, he, together with Heifetz and Zimbalist, brought to Auer's Russian school an unsurpassed prestige. Became a U.S. citizen in 1923. Ysaÿe wrote *Extase* for him, Martinů the Second Concerto. A composition student of Cui in his youth, Elman himself wrote *La Gondola, Romance,* and other character pieces for violin.

Elmendorff, Karl [Carl] **Eduard Maria** (b. Düsseldorf, 25 Oct. 1891; d. Hofheim, 21 Oct. 1962). Conductor. Studied with Fritz Steinbach and Hermann Abendroth at the Cologne Conservatory beginning in 1913. His first posts as conductor were in Düsseldorf (1916), Mainz, and Hagen. Conductor at the Berlin and Munich State Operas, 1925–32; at Bayreuth, 1927–42. General music director of the Hesse State Theater at Kassel-Wiesbaden, 1932. Musical director of the Mannheim National Theater, 1935; of the Dresden State Opera from 1942 until the city was firebombed in 1944. Led first performance of Sonata for 13 Wind Instruments by Strauss, 1944. Conducted in Kassel-Wiesbaden, 1948–56.

Eloy, Jean-Claude (b. Mont-St.-Aignan, near Rouen, 15 June 1938). Composer. He studied piano with Descaves and composition with Milhaud at the Paris Conservatory (1953–61); attended summer courses in Darmstadt under Scherchen and Pousseur; and studied with Boulez in Basel (1961–62). He was at first known as a disciple of Boulez, who conducted *Étude III* (winds, celesta, harp, piano, and percussion) and other early works in 1963 and 1964. Eloy lived in the U.S.

(1966–70) and taught for two years at Berkeley, after which his interest in Middle Eastern and Hindu musics began to be reflected in his own compositions, as in *Kamakala* (3 choral and orchestral groups, 1971). At Stockhausen's invitation he worked at the Cologne studio (1972), where he completed *Shanti* (6 voices, instruments, and electronics). Some works are structured with reference to scientific or philosophical principles (*Faisceaux-diffractions,* 1970). He wrote music for 2 films by Rivette (*La religieuse* and *L'amour fou*).

Elsner, Józef (Antoni Franciszek) [Joseph Anton Franciskus; Józef Ksawery; Joseph Xaver] (b. Gródkow, Silesia, 1 June 1769; d. Elsnerowo, near Warsaw, 18 Apr. 1854). Composer and teacher. He studied at the Gymnasium and University in Breslau, 1781–88; in 1789 began to study medicine in Vienna, but became a musician; 1791–92, first violinist, Brno theater; 1792–99, theater conductor in L'vov, also composing symphonies, chamber music, and his first operas (German, later Polish); 1799, settled in Warsaw, becoming a central figure in its musical life as conductor at the Opera (1799–1824), where he had many works produced through 1821. He was also a music publisher (from 1802), music critic (1802–25), and teacher, founding several schools, including the conservatory (1821–30) where Chopin, his most celebrated pupil, studied. Other works include much sacred music; oratorios, cantatas; 8 symphonies; 6 string quartets and other chamber pieces; piano pieces (21 polonaises). His memoirs, written in German, were published in Polish translation (Warsaw, 1855; new ed., Kraków, 1957).

Elwell, Herbert (b. Minneapolis, 10 May 1898; d. Cleveland, 17 Apr. 1974). Composer and critic. Trained in piano and theory, he went to New York to study composition with Bloch (1919–21); studied with Boulanger in Paris (1921–24), after which he was at the American Academy in Rome (1924–27). He taught at the Cleveland Institute (1928–45) and at Eastman and Oberlin summer sessions (from the 1940s); wrote program notes for the Cleveland Symphony (1930–36) and criticism for the *Cleveland Plain Dealer* (1932–65). Works include a ballet, *The Happy Hypocrite* (1925); *Concert Suite* (violin and orchestra, 1957), and 4 other orchestral pieces; chamber music for strings and piano; a few choral works; many songs (*Blue Symphony,* a song cycle for soprano and string quartet, 1944).

Elwes, Gervase (Cary) (b. Billing Hall, Northampton, 15 Nov. 1866; d. near Boston, 12 Jan. 1921). Tenor. Educated for the diplomatic service, he worked at the British embassy in Vienna, 1891–95. Studied voice with Désiré Demest at Brussels Conservatory, with Henry Russell and Victor Beigel in London, with Jules Bouhay in Paris. Best known as a singer in oratorios and cantatas. Professional debut in 1903 at the Westmoreland Festival as Kendal in Humperdinck's *Die Wallfahrt nach Kevelaar* (London debut, Oct. 1903). Sang in Elgar's *Dream of Gerontius* over 150 times, beginning in 1904. Also admired as the Evangelist in Bach's St. Matthew Passion. Toured Germany with Fannie Davies, 1907. Sang the premiere of Vaughan Williams's *On Wenlock Edge,* 1909. U.S. debut in Boston, 1909; returned to the U.S. on tour, 1920–21. Died under a moving train.

Emerson, Keith (b. Todmorden, West Yorkshire, 1 Nov. 1948). Rock keyboardist, songwriter, and arranger. Trained as a classical pianist; began playing rock music with The Nice; formed Emerson, Lake, and Palmer with bassist-singer Greg Lake (b. 1948) and drummer Carl Palmer (b. 1951) in 1970. They were the most classically oriented of the art rock bands: Emerson arranged Mussorgsky (*Pictures at an Exhibition,* 1972) and produced large-scale original compositions (*Brain Salad Surgery,* 1973). They disbanded in 1980; Emerson wrote for films and played with various reincarnations of the group.

Emmanuel, (Marie François) Maurice (b. Bar-sur-Aube, 2 May 1862; d. Paris, 14 Dec. 1938). Composer and musicologist. He grew up in Beaune, where he sang in the church choir. In 1880 he studied composition with Delibes at the Paris Conservatory; other teachers there included Savant (solfège), Dubois (harmony), and Bourgault-Ducoudray (history). He also studied classics, poetics, philology, and history of art at the Sorbonne and the École du Louvre. His *Overture pour un conte gai* (orchestra, 1890) made use of medieval modes and a free approach to rhythm, and was criticized by Delibes, who forbade his entry for the Prix de Rome.

In 1896 he earned a doctorate for a thesis on ancient Greek dance. He taught art history at the Lycée Racine and Lycée Lamartine until 1904, when he was appointed *maître de chapelle* at Ste. Clotilde. In 1909 he succeeded Bourgault-Ducoudray at the Paris Conservatory, where he pursued his interest in folk song and the ancient modes. He taught there until 1936; his students included Casadesus, Migot, and Messiaen.

He destroyed all but 30 works composed up to 1938. His 3 major stage works, *Prométhée enchaîné* (opera, after Aeschylus, 1916–18), *Salamine* (opera, after Aeschylus, 1921–23, 1927–28), and *Amphitryon* (incidental music, 1936), all reflect his knowledge of ancient Greek civilization. His Fourth Piano Sonatina is based on Indian modes and was the result of a conversation with Busoni. Other works include 2 symphonies (1919, 1930–31), *Suite française* (orchestra, 1934–35), and *Le poème du Rhône* (symphonic poem after F. Mistral, 1938). Writings include *Histoire de la langue musicale* (Paris, 1911; new ed., 1928); *Traité de l'accompagnement modal des psaumes* (Lyons, 1913); *La Polyphonie sacrée* (with R. Moissenet, Oullins, 1923); *Pelléas et Mélisande de Claude Debussy* (Paris, 1926; new ed., 1950); *César Franck* (Paris, 1930); *Anton Reicha* (Paris, 1936).

Emmett, Dan(iel Decatur) (b. Mt. Vernon, Ohio, 29 Oct. 1815; d. there, 28 June 1904). Minstrel show musician and composer. Taught himself the fiddle; 1834–35, played fife and drum in the U.S. Army; 1835–42, a blackface singer and banjoist in touring circuses. In 1842 he was half of a blackface fiddle-and-bones duo in New York; in 1843 two more performers were added to form one of the earliest minstrel companies, the Virginia Minstrels; they toured Great Britain, 1843–44. From 1844 he worked as a minstrel performer, sometimes heading his own company, later more often as a member of others' troupes, until the 1870s, when he lost his voice and was reduced to fiddling in saloons. From 1867 he was based mostly in Chicago; in 1888 he retired to Mt. Vernon. He published collections of minstrel songs (not all original) in 1843–44 and many individual songs of his own thereafter to 1865, the best known being "Dixie," first performed in New York in 1859 and published in 1860.

Bibl.: Hans Nathan, *Dan Emmett and the Rise of Negro Minstrelsy* (Norman, Okla., 1962; R: 1977).

Encina [Enzina], **Juan del** [Fermoselle, Juan de] (b. Salamanca, 12 July 1468; d. León, late 1529 or early 1530). Writer and composer. Spent the first three decades of his life in or near Salamanca, as a singer in the cathedral choir from 1484, then from 1492 in the service of Fadrique, the second Duke of Alba, for whom he wrote most of his plays and music. From 1498 until 1521 he lived chiefly in Rome but retained connections with Spain, even spending part of his time from late 1508 until 1519 at Málaga Cathedral. Upon Encina's ordination as a priest in 1519, the pope appointed him prior of León Cathedral, where he was resident from 1521 until his death. His writings include poems (some specifically intended as song texts), sacred and secular plays with music, and numerous other works showing ecclesiastical and humanistic learning, including a treatise on Spanish metrics. He was a central figure in the emergence of Spanish theater. His compositions, which number slightly more than 60, are all secular and polyphonic; most are *villancicos* for 3 or 4 voices and are contained in the *Cancionero musical de Palacio* (ed. in *MME* 5, 10, 14).

Bibl.: *Juan del Encina: L'opera musicale,* Pubblicazione dell'istituto ispanico (Messina, 1974). Miguel Querol Gavaldá, "La producción musical de Juan del Encina (1469–1529)," *AnM* 24 (1969): 121.

Enescu, George [Enesco, Georges] (b. Liveni-Vîrnav [now George Enescu], Romania, 19 Aug. 1881; d. Paris, 4 May 1955). Composer, conductor, and violinist. He studied in Vienna from age 7, with Joseph Hellmesberger, Robert Fuchs, and Sigismund Bachrich at the Gesellschaft der Musikfreunde. In 1889 he made his concert debut as violinist at Slănic (Moldavia). Upon completing his studies in Vienna he went to Paris in 1894, where he took further instruction in violin (from M. P. J. Marsick), and in theory and composition (from Thomas, Dubois, Massenet, and Fauré). A concert of his works in Paris in 1897 included a string quintet, a piano suite, a violin sonata, and songs. During the next two decades he became prominent as conductor and violinist, not only in Paris but also in his native country; he established the Enescu Prize for composition in Bucharest in 1912 and the George Enescu Symphony Orchestra in Jassy in 1917. He taught courses at the Accademia Chigiana in Siena and at the American Conservatory in Fontainebleau, and from 1928 was an instructor of violin and composition at the École normale de musique. During the 1920s and 1930s he toured the U.S. and Europe as violinist and conductor. He spent the war years on his farm in Sinaia (near Bucharest); in 1946 he went to New York, where he taught at the Mannes School of Music. In 1954 he suffered a stroke that disabled him for his remaining years.

As a violinist Enescu was known especially for his Bach interpretations. His compositions include stage works (*Oedipe,* 1931; first perf., 1936); 5 symphonies (1906, 1915, 1918, 1934, 1941; also 3 earlier, unnumbered symphonies); 3 orchestral suites (1903, 1915, 1937–38); a violin concerto (1896); *Fantaisie* (piano and orchestra, 1896); a piano concerto (1897); 2 Rumanian Rhapsodies (1901, 1902); *Symphonie concertante* (cello, orchestra, 1901); *Symphonie de chambre* (1954); *Vox maris* (soprano, tenor, voices, orchestra, 1955); *Chamber Symphony* op. 33 (1954); 2 piano quintets; 2 piano quartets; 2 string quartets (1916–20, 1950–53); 2 piano trios; 3 suites for piano op. 3; 2 piano sonatas (1924, 1933–35); *Andante religioso* (2 cellos, organ, 1900).

Bibl.: George Balan, *George Enescu* (Bucharest, 1963). Romeo Draghici, *George Enescu: Biografie documentarua* (Bacau, 1973). Mircea Voicana, ed., *Enesciana,* 3 vols. (Bucharest, 1976–81). Clemansa Liliana Firca, *Catalogul tematico al criatiei lui George Enescu* (Bucharest, 1985). Noel Malcolm, *George Enescu: His Life and Music* (London, 1990).

Engel, (A.) Lehman (b. Jackson, Miss., 14 Sept. 1910; d. New York, 29 Aug. 1982). Composer and conductor. Studied at the Cincinnati College–Conservatory, at Juilliard with Goldmark, and privately with Sessions. In the 1930s he founded the Lehman Engel Singers and the Madrigal Singers; was active as a composer from the 1920s through the 1950s; in the later years he turned away from his early atonal style to compose in a diatonic idiom marked by sharp rhythms. Among the many works he conducted in New York were Copland's *The Second Hurricane* (1937), Menotti's *The Consul* (1950), Bernstein's *Wonderful Town* (1953), and a number of musical comedies. He wrote several books including *The Making of a Musical* (New York, 1977) and *Words with Music* (New York, 1972). Works include *The Soldier* (New York, 1956) and other operas and musical comedies; several ballets, often for Martha Graham; 2 symphonies, *Overture for the End of the World* (1945), and a viola concerto; *The Creation* (narrator and orchestra, 1945); chamber music for strings; piano works; a cantata; choral works; incidental music and film scores.

Engelmann, Hans Ulrich (b. Darmstadt, 8 Sept. 1921). Composer and theorist. At first he intended a career in architecture but turned to music in 1945, studying composition with Fortner, Leibowitz, and Krenek, then musicology at the University of Frankfurt (D.Phil., 1952). He lived in Iceland (1953–54); was musical adviser and composer for the Landestheater in Darmstadt (from 1954); lived in Rome (1960–67); was appointed in 1969 to teach harmony at the Hochschule für Musik in Frankfurt. His compositional style ranges from atonality to twelve-tone and serial music, and in later music to the use of chance, graphic notation, and live electronics. Works include several operas and ballets; orchestral music; *Modelle I oder "I love you, Bäbi"* (electronic ensemble, 1970), *Assonanzen* (2 pianos, 1983), and other instrumental music; *Commedia humana* (double choir, cello, and tape, 1972), *Stele für Georg Büchner* (chorus, orchestra, 1986), and other choral music.

Englund, (Sven) Einar (b. Ljugarn, Gotland, Sweden, 17 June 1916). Composer. Among his teachers at the Helsinki Academy were Palmgren (composition) and Paavola (piano). During the 1940s and 1950s he frequently supported himself as a jazz pianist. From 1949 he studied with Copland at Tanglewood; he then traveled in Europe and the Soviet Union. Returning to Finland, he took a position as music critic for the Helsinki daily *Hufvudstadsbladet* and in 1958 began teaching theory and composition at the Sibelius Academy in Helsinki. His music shows the influence of jazz, neoclassicism, and Shostakovich. Works include 7 symphonies (1946–88); *Chaconne* (chorus, trombone, double bass, 1969); *Odysseus* (ballet, 1959); film scores and incidental music (*The Great Wall of China,* music for Frisch's play, 1949); *The White Reindeer* (film score, 1954); concertos for cello (1954), violin (1981), and 2 for piano (1955, 1974); *Odeion* (overture, 1987); concerto for 12 solo cellos (1980); piano quintet (1941).

Enna, August (Emil) (b. Nakskov, Denmark, 13 May 1859; d. Copenhagen, 3 Aug. 1939). Composer. He began in his father's shoemaking trade before taking up violin and piano; by his twenties he was playing in orchestras in Finland, including the one in Björneborg. In 1884 he returned to Denmark, where he was to spend most of the rest of his life; that year he composed his first opera, *Agleia. Heksen* [The Witch], perhaps his best-known opera, was composed on a grant in 1888–89; it was performed in Copenhagen in 1892. After its success he composed 14 more operas, including *Ung elskov* [Young Love] (1902); *Princessen på aerten* [The Princess on the Pea] (after Andersen, 1910); and *Børnene fra Santa Fé* [The Children from Santa Fe] (1918). He also composed choral works; orchestral works (2 symphonies, 1886, 1908; a violin concerto, 1897; the "festival overture" *Hans Christian Andersen,* 1905). His music manifests influences from Wagner, Richard Strauss, and Puccini.

Enríquez (Salazar), Manuel (b. Ocotlán, Jalisco, Mexico, 17 June 1926; d. Mexico City, 26 Apr. 1994). Composer. Received early training from his father; served as concertmaster of the Guadalajara Symphony, 1949–55; attended Juilliard, 1955–57, studying with Galamian, Mennin, and Primrose. Wolpe was also an important teacher in this period. He taught at the Music School of the National Univ. and at the National Conservatory in Mexico. His music contains many serial as well as aleatory elements; he was active in new music circles in Mexico as well as in the U.S. and in Europe. His output is predominantly instrumental, with works for both orchestra (*Ixamatl,* 1969; a piano concerto, 1970; *Encuentros,* 1971; *El y ellos,* violin and orchestra, 1972) and chamber ensembles (*Móvil II,* violin, tape, 1969).

Bibl.: *Composers of the Americas* 15 (1969): 96–100 [includes works list].

Epstein, David M(ayer) (b. New York, 3 Oct. 1930). Composer, conductor, and theorist. As a youth he studied piano and played jazz (clarinet, saxophone); attended Antioch (B.A., 1951) and New England Conservatory; studied at Brandeis and with Babbitt and Sessions at Princeton (Ph.D., 1968); with Milhaud at Aspen (1955–56). He taught at Antioch (1957–62); was music director for the Educational Broadcasting Corporation in New York (1962–64); taught at M.I.T. from 1965. In 1984 he became music director of the New Orchestra of Boston, having previously conducted orchestras in Harrisburg and Worcester. His style, related to the serialism of Webern, is concise and complex; he is the author of several theoretical articles and of *Beyond Orpheus: Studies in Musical Structure* (1979). Works include *Night Voices* (narrator, children's chorus, and orchestra, 1974; commissioned by the Boston Symphony) and other orchestral works; *Ven-tures* (large wind ensemble, 1970); chamber and piano music; a song cycle (*The Seasons,* Dickinson, 1955); other choral and vocal works.

Epstein, Julius (b. Agram, Croatia, 7 Aug. 1832; d. Vienna, 1 Mar. 1926). Pianist and pedagogue. In Agram studied piano with Ignaz Lichtenegger; in Vienna piano with Anton Halm, composition with Johann Rufinatscha. While a professor of piano at the Vienna Conservatory, 1867–1901, performed frequently with the Vienna Philharmonic. Edited Schubert's piano music, which he also performed frequently, for the Breitkopf & Härtel edition. His son Richard (1869–1919) also taught piano at the Vienna Conservatory before becoming a well-known accompanist in London (1904–14) and New York (1914–19).

Érard, Sébastien (b. Strasbourg, 5 Apr. 1752; d. La Muette, near Paris, 5 Aug. 1831). Instrument maker. The son of a cabinetmaker, he was apprenticed to a

Paris harpsichord maker in 1768. His invention of a *clavecin mécanique* won him the patronage of the Duchess of Villeroy. In 1777 he made the first French piano and in 1780, with brother Jean-Baptiste (d. 1826), began to manufacture pianos. He spent 1786–96 mostly in London, learning English methods and opening a branch there, run first by his brother, then by his nephew Pierre (ca. 1796–1855). In 1796 he made his first French grand piano in the English style. Through his inventiveness (single-action harp, 1794; double-action harp, 1811; improvements in piano design) the Érard firm, carried on by Pierre, was one of the most successful in Europe in the first half of the 19th century; it failed to keep up with technical advances in the second, however.

Erb, Donald (James) (b. Youngstown, Ohio, 17 Jan. 1927). Composer. Studied at Kent State Univ. (B.S., 1950), then worked as a jazz trumpeter; he worked briefly under Boulanger in Paris (1953), but her antipathy to the serialism he favored presented an obstacle; studied composition with Marcel Dick at the Cleveland Institute (M.M., 1953) and with Bernard Heiden at Indiana Univ. (D.Mus., 1964). Taught at the Cleveland Institute and Case Western Reserve (beginning in 1965), Southern Methodist Univ. (1981–84), and Indiana Univ. (from 1984). He was composer-in-residence with the St. Louis Symphony, 1988–90. His compositional style has reflected jazz, neoclassicism, and serialism; nevertheless, he destroyed works from before 1958 that exhibited "a direct influence of jazz and serial methods" and later claimed to write more intuitively: "I write . . . on an instinctual level for climax, coloration, melody, ways of creating contrast, and so on." He is best known for his orchestral compositions, many written on commission, and for concertos (piano, 1958; percussion, 1966; trombone, 1976; cello, 1976; keyboards, 1978; trumpet, 1980; clarinet, 1984; contrabassoon, 1984). He has often combined electronically synthesized sound with traditional instruments (*The Devil's Quick Step,* winds, piano, percussion, strings, and tape, 1983); some pieces employ live electronics.

Works: *Souvenir* (instruments, tape, lighting, 1970) and *Fission* (soprano saxophone, piano, tape, dancers, lighting, 1968); *Christmasmusic* (1967), *The Purple-Roofed Ethical Suicide Parlor* (winds, tape, 1972), *Autumnmusic* (orchestra, tape, 1973), *Prismatic Variations* (1983), a concerto for brass and orchestra (1986), *Evensong* (1994), and other orchestral works; *Klangfarbenfunk I* (rock band, orchestra, tape, 1970) and other works for band, many with solo instruments or tape; *Phantasma* (flute, oboe, harpsichord, double bass, 1964), *Fantasy for Cellist and Friends* (cello, 2–4 harmonicas, 4–8 percussionists, 1983), string quartet no. 2 (1990), Violin Sonata (1994), and other chamber music; choral works (*Fallout,* chorus, narrator, string quartet, piano, 1964; *Kyrie,* chorus, piano, percussion, tape, 1965).

Erb, Karl (b. Ravensburg, 13 July 1877; d. there, 13 July 1958). Tenor. Self-taught, he was discovered while singing in the chorus of the Stuttgart Opera; debut there in 1907 in *Der Evangelimann* by Kienzl. Sang with the Lübeck Opera, 1908–10; with the Stuttgart Opera, 1910–12; with the Munich Opera, 1913–25. His vocal timbre and stage presence suited him for roles such as Parsifal, which he sang at the Munich premiere in 1914; Pfitzner's Palestrina, which he created in 1917; and the Evangelist in Bach's Passions. Two accidents in the 1920s cut short his theatrical career, but he continued to sing recitals and perform as the Evangelist until after World War II. His last recording, of Schubert songs, was made in 1951. Married to soprano Maria Ivogün, 1920–31. He was the model for the tenor, Erbe, in Thomas Mann's *Doktor Faust.*

Erbach, Christian (b. Gaualgesheim, near Mainz, ca. 1568–73; d. Augsburg, ca. June–Sept. 1635). Composer. His first published work appeared in a collection of 1596, around which time he was employed by Marcus Fugger in Augsburg; became organist at St. Moritz Church and Augsburg city organist in 1602; the latter appointment was renewed in 1609, 1614, and 1620. He moved to Augsburg Cathedral as second organist in 1614 and was promoted to the principal post in 1625; he built a reputation as a teacher and as an evaluator of organs. As a result of the Thirty Years' War, his post was suspended in 1635 for lack of funds. His output includes organ music and sacred vocal works, all showing Italian influence.

Bibl.: *Ausgewählte geistliche Chorwerke,* ed. A. Gottron (Mainz, 1943). *Collected Keyboard Compositions, CEKM* 36.

Erbse, Heimo (b. Rudolstadt, 27 Feb. 1924). Composer. He studied in Weimar, was active as a theatrical producer (1947–50), and then went to Berlin for further study with Blacher (1950); settled in Salzburg in the early 1950s. Wrote dramatic music for the stage (the ballet *Ruth,* 1959), incidental and film music; several orchestral works (2 symphonies, 1964, 1970); works for piano and orchestra (*6 Miniaturen,* piano, strings, percussion, 1951; Piano Concerto, 1963; Triple Concerto, piano, violin, cello, orchestra, 1973). Other compositions include chamber (String Quartet no. 2, 1987) and piano music and vocal works (*5 Orchestergesänge nach G. Trakl,* baritone, orchestra, 1969).

Erickson, Robert (b. Marquette, Mich., 7 Mar. 1917). Composer. Studied composition with May Strong, La Violette, Krenek, and Sessions; taught at the College of St. Catherine in St. Paul (1953–54), Berkeley (1956–58), the San Francisco Conservatory (1957–66), and then at the Univ. of California at San Diego; directed the Pacifica Foundation in Berkeley (1954–63). Wrote two books (*The Structure of Music,* 1955, rev. 1977; *Sound Structures in Music,* 1975). His early works were serial and contrapuntal; later works more concerned with timbre and texture (in *General Speech,* 1969, the trombonist must speak into the instrument, change the shape of his mouth cavity, and swallow air to affect the timbre produced). Wrote a one-act monodrama; orchestral works (*East of the Beach,* 1980; *Auroras,* 1982; *Taffytime,* 1983; *Corona,* 1986); string quartets (*Solstice,* 1985; *Corfu,* 1986), pieces for tube drums (the composer's invention), and other chamber music (*Night Music,* trumpet, ensemble, 1978); piano works; choral and solo vocal music (*The Idea of Order at Key West,* after Stevens, soprano, ensemble, 1979; *Sierra,* tenor or baritone, chamber orchestra, 1984); electronic music, usually with live performers.

Bibl.: John MacKay, "On the Music of Robert Erickson: A Survey and Some Selected Analyses," *PNM* 26/2 (1988): 56–85.

Erkel, Ferenc [Franz] (b. Gyula, Hungary, 7 Nov. 1810; d. Budapest, 15 June 1893). Composer and conductor. Son of a schoolmaster and choirmaster; 1822–25, student at Pozsony Gymnasium; 1827–34, lived mostly in Kolozsvár as musician and piano teacher; 1834, debut as opera conductor at the local theater; 1835, conductor at new Hungarian Theater, Buda; Nov. 1836–Jan. 1838, conductor, German Theater, Pest; then at new Hungarian National Theater, Pest; also the capital's leading pianist until Liszt's appearances in 1839–40 discouraged him. His early compositions (first published, *Duo brillant en forme de fantaisie sur des airs hongrois,* 1837) use Hungarian themes. He founded Hungarian opera with *Bátori Mária* (1840), followed by his two greatest successes (although none of his operas aroused much interest outside Hungary), *Hunyadi László* (1844) and *Bánk Bán* (1861), the latter orchestrated with the help of two of his sons, four of whom became professional musicians. His later operas, all composed in collaboration with his sons (all four in the case of *Névtelen Nósök,* 1880), were less successful. In 1844 he composed the Hungarian national anthem. He also composed incidental music and songs for many popular Hungarian plays and made the National Theater orchestra one of the finest in Europe, retiring in 1874. Between 1853 and 1874 he founded and conducted Philharmonic Concerts; 1868–71, principal conductor, National Association of Choral Societies, composing male-voice works for its festivals; first director, Budapest Academy of Music, 1875–87, also teaching the piano there. In his later years he was revered as a great national figure; his statue was placed in front of the new Hungarian Opera House in 1884.

Erlanger, Camille (b. Paris, 25 May 1863; d. there, 24 Apr. 1919). Composer. Of Alsatian descent, she studied at the Paris Conservatory (composition under Delibes), 1881–89, winning the Prix de Rome. She produced her first opera in 1897. Her first great and widespread success came in 1900 with *Le juif polonais* (Opéra-comique), set in Alsace; this success was repeated with *Aphrodite* (Opéra-comique, 1906), with Mary Garden; later operas (including *Bacchus triomphant,* Bordeaux, open-air, 1909, for the city's millenium) were less successful. She also composed a French Requiem; symphonic poems and other orchestral pieces; chamber and piano pieces.

Erlebach, Philipp Heinrich (baptized Esens, Ostfriesland, Lower Saxony, 25 July 1657; d. Rudolstadt 17 Apr. 1714). Composer. Perhaps schooled at the local court of Ostfriesland; sent to the court of Count Albert Anthon von Schwartzburg-Rudolstadt in 1678, where he served as valet and musician before becoming Kapellmeister in 1681. He visited several of the surrounding courts, becoming friendly with J. P. Krieger at Weissenfels and accompanying Albert Anthon to Mühlhausen for performance of one of his ceremonial works. J. C. Vogler was among his pupils. His extant works include dozens of cantatas along with 2 collections of arias (*Harmonische Freude, musicalischer Freunde,* Nuremberg, 1697 and 1710) and collections of overtures (Nuremberg, 1693) and sonatas (Nuremberg, 1694). Much of his music, including 6 cantata cycles, biblical *historiae,* Masses, and several operas and serenades, was lost in a fire in 1735 and appears only in 2 Rudolstadt catalogues.

Ernst, Heinrich Wilhelm (b. Brno, 6 May 1814; d. Nice, 8 Oct. 1865). Violinist and composer. From 1825, studied at the Vienna Conservatory. In 1828 he heard Paganini and began to follow his tours, absorbing his technique; he became a great virtuoso, but also a highly expressive and musicianly player. Paris debut, 1831; London debut, 1843; toured Europe continuously, visiting Russia in 1847; also a fine chamber player; 1859, member Beethoven Society String Quartet. Works include *Elégie* op. 10; Variations on "Le carnaval de Venise" op. 18; Concerto in F♯ minor op. 23.

Escher, Rudolf (George) (b. Amsterdam, 8 Jan. 1912; d. De Koog, Texel, 17 Mar. 1980). From 1931 he studied violin and piano at the conservatory at Rotterdam and took lessons in composition from Pijper (1934–37). After World War II he lived mostly in Amsterdam; later he worked at electronic studios in Delft and Utrecht (1959–61) and taught at the Amsterdam Conservatory (1960–61) and Utrecht Univ. (1964–75). His music shows influences from Debussy and Ravel, but also from more recent French composers such as Boulez. Orchestral works include *Musique pour l'esprit en deuil* (1943); 2 symphonies (no. 1, 1953–54; no. 2, 1958–64); *Sinfonian* (10 instruments, 1973–76); *Summer Rites at Noon* (2 orchestras, 1962–68). Vocal music includes *Nostalgies* (1951); *Le vrai visage de la paix* (1953); *Songs of Love and Eternity* (1955); *Ciel, air et vents* (chorus, 1957); *Univers de Rimbaud* (1970); *Three Poems of W. H. Auden* (chorus, 1975). Chamber music includes *Le tombeau de Ravel* (1952) and a string trio (1959).

Escobar, Luis Antonio (b. Villapinzón, Colombia, 14 July 1925). Composer. Received early training at the National Conservatory in Bogotá; enrolled in 1947 at the Peabody Conservatory as a pupil of Nicolás

Nabuko; studied later at Columbia Univ. and in Salzburg and Berlin. After returning to Colombia in 1953 he held a variety of posts, including professor at the National Conservatory and director of music programming for the national television network, and served in the Education Ministry. Works include music for orchestra, chamber ensemble, chorus, solo voice, and piano, as well as the ballet *Avirama* (1955) and the opera *La princesa y la arveja* (1957).

Bibl.: *Composers of the Americas* 8 (1962): 65–70 [includes works list].

Escobar, Pedro de [Pedro do Porto?] (b. Oporto, ca. 1465; d. Évora, after 1535). Composer. The Spanish chapel of Isabella I employed him as a singer from 1489 to 1499. In 1507 he was recalled from his native Portugal to become *maestro de capilla* at Seville Cathedral, staying there until 1514. In 1521 Pedro do Porto (probably identical with Escobar) was chapelmaster to Cardinal Dom Affonso, son of the Spanish king Manuel I. By 1535 Escobar was living in Évora, no longer active as a musician. His compositions include sacred vocal works, particularly Masses (some ed. in *MME* 1) and motets, and *villancicos* (ed. in *MME* 5, 10).

Escobedo, Bartolomé de (b. diocese of Zamora, ca. 1500; d. between 21 Mar. and 11 Aug. 1563). Composer. Singer at the cathedral in Salamanca until becoming a member of the papal choir in Rome, where he served from 1536 until 1541 and again from 1545 to 1554. His erudition earned him a position as a judge in the debate over the Greek modes between Vicentino and Lusitano in 1551. In 1554 he retired to Spain, holding a nonresident benefice at Segovia Cathedral. Two Masses and several motets by him survive.

Escot, Pozzi (Olga) (b. Lima, 1 Oct. 1933). Composer and theorist. She first studied music at the Sas-Rosay Academy of Music in Lima, and then at Juilliard and the Hamburg Hochschule für Musik. Taught at New England Conservatory beginning 1964 and concurrently at Wheaton College beginning 1972. Her vocal music is marked by an interest in unusual combinations of voices and instruments. Works include 5 symphonies; 5 string quartets (fifth premiered in New York Mar. 1996), *Lamentos* (soprano, 2 violins, 2 cellos, piano, and percussion, 1962), *Visione* (soprano, speaker, flute, alto saxophone, and double bass, 1964), and other chamber music; pieces for piano and other solo instruments. She and her husband, composer and theorist Robert Cogan, wrote *Sonic Design: The Nature of Sound and Music* (Englewood Cliffs, N.J., 1976).

Escribano, Juan [Scribanus, Iohannes] (b. Salamanca?, ca. 1478; d. Spain, Oct. 1557). Singer and composer. Belonged to the choir of Salamanca Cathedral from 1498 until joining the papal choir in Rome in 1502. Numerous honors and offices both within and outside the choir were granted him in the succeeding years. In 1539 he retired to Salamanca. Of his works, a Magnificat, a set of Lamentations, 2 other sacred compositions, and 2 Italian secular vocal pieces survive.

Eshpai, Andrei Iakovlevich (b. Kozmodemiansk, Mari ASSR., USSR., 15 May 1925). Composer. Attended the Moscow Conservatory, 1948–53, where he studied piano with Vladimir Sofronitsky and composition with Nikolai Rakov, Nikolai Miaskovsky, and Evgeny Golubev; 1953–56, pursued graduate studies there under Aram Khachaturian. A prominent figure in Soviet musical life, he received numerous awards (State Prize, 1976; Lenin Prize, 1986) and honors (Peoples' Artist of the USSR, 1981; Order of Lenin, 1985). His music incorporates the influences of Mari folklore and jazz into a highly melodic, accessible idiom. Works include ballets (*Angara,* 1975); music for the theater; 5 symphonies (1959, 1962, 1964, 1981, 1985); concertos for piano (1954, 1972), violin (1956, 1977), orchestra with solo trumpet, piano, vibraphone, and double bass (1966), oboe (1982), soprano saxophone (1987), viola (1987); choral music; chamber music; works for piano; much film and popular music.

Bibl.: A. Bogdanova, *Andrei Eshpai* (Moscow, 1986). *Andrei Eshpai: besedy, stat'i, materialy, ocherki* (Moscow, 1988). Nina Sladkova, *Composer Andrei Eshpai: Complete Catalogue of Works* (Moscow, 1990).

Eslava (y Elizondo), (Miguel) Hilarión (b. Burlada, near Pamplona, 21 Oct. 1807; d. Madrid, 23 July 1878). Composer. From age 9 a choirboy at the Pamplona Cathedral; from 17 a violinist there. In 1827 studied composition in Calahorra; 1828, choirmaster at Burgo de Osma; 1832, at Seville Cathedral, where he became a priest. In 1844 he was made director of the Royal Chapel, Madrid; 1854, composition professor, Madrid Conservatory, and from 1866 its director. He produced 3 Italian operas (1841–43), but he is best known for sacred music and his 10-volume anthology of Spanish sacred music, *Lira sacro-hispana* (Madrid, 1869). His Spanish textbooks in harmony and counterpoint were long used.

Bibl.: Gilbert Chase, "Miguel Hilarion Eslava," *MQ* 24 (1938): 74–83.

Espinosa, Juan de (fl. 1479–1520). Theorist and composer. Held various ecclesiastical posts in Spain, especially in Toledo and Burgos. His fame is due chiefly to a controversy in which he defended traditional teachings against the innovations of the theorist Gonzalo Martínez de Bizcargui, *maestro de capilla* of Burgos Cathedral. As a composer he is known only by 2 *villancicos* in the *Cancionero musical de Palacio.*

Esplá (y Triay), Oscar (b. Alicante, 5 Aug. 1886; d. Madrid, 6 Jan. 1976). Composer. Studied engineering and philosophy at the Univ. of Barcelona (1903–11). The Vienna National Music Society International Prize in 1911 for his *Suite levantina* spurred him to devote himself to music; he studied at Munich and Meiningen with Reger in 1912 and at Paris with Saint-Saëns in

1913. Joined the faculty at the Madrid Conservatory in 1930, serving as director, 1936–39; appointed music director of the Laboratoire musical scientifique, Brussels, in 1948; served UNESCO in various capacities; succeeded del Campo at the San Fernando Academy in 1953, and Honegger at the Institut de France in 1955; became director of the Oscar Esplá Academy in his native city in 1958. As a composer he was most influenced by Debussy and Stravinsky, integrating materials from the popular music of Spain's Mediterranean coast into some compositions as well. He also published many writings on music.

Works: the operas *La bella durmiente del bosque* (1909, rev. 1943 as *La forêt perdue*), *La balteira* (1935), *Plumas al viento* (1941), and *El pirata cautivo* (1974); choral-orchestral works, including *Nochebuena del diablo* (1923), *Sinfonía coral* (1942), *Oratorio profano* (1947), *Requiem* (1949), and *De profundis* (1966); orchestral works, including *El sueño de Eros* (1905), *Don Quijote velando las armas* (1924), 2 *Suites folklóricas* (1924, 1934), *Concierto de cámara* (1937), and *Sinfonia aitana* (1964); ballets; chamber music, including 2 string quartets (1920, 1943) and *Lírica española* (1952–54); piano pieces; songs; and orchestral transcriptions of works by Albéniz.

Bibl.: Antonio Iglesias, *Oscar Esplá* (Madrid, 1973).

Esser, (Karl?) Michael, Ritter von (b. Aachen, bapt. 3? Apr. 1737; d. ca. 1795). Violinist and composer. From 1756 he was solo violinist in the chapel orchestra at the Hessen-Kassel court; in 1761 he became the orchestra's director. He left the court without permission to embark on a successful concert tour throughout Europe, performing as soloist both on violin and on viola d'amore. Mozart, who heard Esser play in Munich in 1780, praised his playing while criticizing his overladen manner of ornamentation. Among his compositions is an opera, *Die drei Pächter* (1783, lost); symphonies; chamber music; and several works for solo violin.

Esswood, Paul (Lawrence Vincent) (b. West Bridgford, Nottinghamshire, 6 June 1942). Countertenor. Studied at the Royal College of Music, 1961–64. Lay vicar at Westminster Abbey, 1964–71. His international career was established by a recording of *Messiah* under Mackerras in 1965. Sang in Cavalli's *Erismena* at Berkeley, Calif., 1968, and Brussels, 1974. In Vienna beginning in 1968 he collaborated frequently with the Concentus musicus Wien under Harnoncourt, particularly in works by J. S. Bach. Participated in the 1979 premiere of Penderecki's *Paradise Lost* and created the title role of Philip Glass's *Akhnaton* in Stuttgart in 1984.

Estrada, Carlos (b. Montevideo, 15 Sept. 1909; d. there, 7 May 1970). Composer. After early training in his home city, studied in Paris with Roger-Ducasse and Büsser, among others. Founded the Montevideo Chamber Orchestra in 1936; served as director of the National Conservatory until 1968 and as music adviser of the national broadcasting service (SODRE), 1948–54; founded the Municipal Symphony in 1959, acting as its principal conductor until his death; appeared as guest conductor of orchestras throughout Latin America and Europe. Works include the oratoio *Daniel* (1942), stage music, orchestral pieces, chamber and piano music, and vocal works.

Bibl.: *Composers of the Americas* 16 (1970): 72–81 [includes works list].

Etler, Alvin (Derald) (b. Battle Creek, Iowa, 19 Feb. 1913; d. Northampton, Mass., 13 June 1973). Composer and oboist. Studied composition with Arthur Shepherd at Case Western Reserve (1931–36) and with Hindemith while teaching woodwinds and conducting the band at Yale (1942–46). He played first oboe in the Indiana Symphony (1936–38) and toured with the North American Woodwind Quintet (1941); taught at Cornell Univ. (1946–47), the Univ. of Illinois (1947–49), and Smith College (1949–73). He employed serial techniques but usually established a tonal center; some jazz influence is evident. Orchestral works include 2 symphoniettas (1940–41, withdrawn), a symphony (1951), Concerto in 1 Movement (1957), Concerto for Woodwind Quintet and Orchestra (1960), *Convivialities* (1967), Concerto for String Quartet and Orchestra (1968). Other works include chamber music (often for brass or woodwinds) and choral music, usually on his own texts (*Onomatopoesis,* male voices, brass, winds, and percussion, 1965).

Europe, James Reese (b. Mobile, 22 Feb. 1881; d. Boston, 10 May 1919). Bandmaster. He formed the Clef Club, an agency for and union of African American musicians (1910), and the 100- to 150-piece Clef Club symphony orchestras, which brought together African American and European traditions of performance practice and instrumentation in concerts at Carnegie Hall (1912–14). His Society Orchestra toured, accompanying the dancers Irene and Vernon Castle (1914–17), for whom he is said to have written the first foxtrot. In World War I he led the 369th Infantry Band, giving concerts in France and the U.S. He was the first African American bandleader to record (from 1913, including a jazz version of "Memphis Blues," 1919).

Eustachio Romano (fl. first quarter of the 16th cent.). Composer. Contemporary sources indicate that he was a Roman. Several frottolas, published in 2 of Petrucci's books, and 45 instrumental duets in imitative style constitute his known works. The duets, published in Rome in 1521 (ed. *MRM* 6 [1974]), are the earliest instrumental ensemble music to have been printed.

Evangelisti, Franco (b. Rome, 21 Jan. 1926; d. there, 28 Jan. 1980). Composer. He was at first an engineering student, then studied music in Rome (D. Paris, 1948–53), Freiburg (Genzmer, 1953–56), and Darmstadt (Eimert, Stockhausen). In 1961 he founded Nuova consonanza, an ensemble devoted to contemporary music and, from 1964, to group improvisation. He lived in Berlin for two years (1966–68), after which he taught electronic music at the Accademia di S. Cecilia (1968–72), the Conservatorio dell'Aquila (1969–75), and the Conservatorio di S. Cecilia in Rome (1974–80). In an effort to avoid "making something academic of the avant garde" he composed little after 1962; his writings include the volume *Dal silenzio ad una nuova musica* (1967). Works include *Die Schachtel* (pantomime, 1962–63); 6 orchestral pieces (*Random or Not Random,* 1962); chamber and piano music (*Proiezioni sonore,* piano and tape, 1956); and *Campi integrati* (1959, 1979), in which he applied aleatory procedures to electronic music.

Evans, Bill [William John] (b. Plainfield, N.J., 16 Aug. 1929; d. New York, 15 Sept. 1980). Jazz pianist. In 1956 he began recording as a leader (the album *New Jazz Conceptions,* including his composition "Waltz for Debby"). He came to prominence as a member of Miles Davis's sextet (1958–59) and composed "Blue in Green" for Davis's album *Kind of Blue* (1959). He also recorded in a duo with Jim Hall in 1959 and from that year made his principal contribution as a leader of trios, in which he developed a remarkable interplay with his bassists, especially Scott LaFaro (as on the album *Sunday at the Village Vanguard,* 1961), and then Chuck Israels, Gary Peacock, and Eddie Gomez. Founded in bop traditions, his original, influential piano playing involved a sensitive touch, a keen sense of voice leading, and an unusual approach to chordal substitution and the voicing of chords. He should not be confused with Yusef Lateef, who initially worked under his given name Bill Evans, or with the saxophonist Bill Evans (b. 1958), who also worked with Davis (1980–84).

Evans, Geraint (Llewellyn) (b. Pontypridd, South Wales, 16 Feb. 1922; d. Aberystwyth, 19 Sept. 1992). Baritone. Studied voice at Cardiff; after World War II with Theo Hermann in Hamburg while working for the British Forces Radio Network; with Fernando Carpi in Geneva; with Walter Hyde in London. Stage debut as the Nightwatchman *(Die Meistersinger)* at Covent Garden, 1948; sang Mozart's Figaro there (1949) and later with great success at La Scala (1960), the Vienna Staatsoper (1961), the Salzburg Festival (1962). New York Met debut as Falstaff in 1964. Sang in premieres of Vaughan Williams's *Pilgrim's Progress* (1951); Britten's *Billy Budd* (1951) and *Gloriana* (1953); Walton's *Troilus and Cressida* (1954); Hoddinott's *The Beach of Falesá* (1974) and *Murder the Magician* (1976). Knighted in 1971; retired from opera in 1983.

Evans, Gil [Green, Ian Ernest Gilmore] (b. Toronto, 13 May 1912; d. Cuernavaca, Mexico, 20 Mar. 1988). Jazz arranger and bandleader. As a member of Claude Thornhill's big band (1941–43, 1946–48) he arranged the bop tunes "Anthropology," "Donna Lee," and "Yardbird Suite" (all recorded in 1947). He arranged "Boplicity" for Miles Davis's cool jazz nonet (recorded in 1949), and later Davis recorded with Evans's orchestra; their albums *Miles Ahead* (1957), *Porgy and Bess* (1958), and *Sketches of Spain* (1959–60) offer the finest examples of the integration of French horns, tuba, and orchestral woodwinds into big band jazz. From the mid-1960s his orchestra turned toward rock music. From 1983 it held a residency in New York clubs, playing on Monday nights at either Sweet Basil or Seventh Avenue South.

Evans, Herschel (b. Denton, Tex., 1901; d. New York, 9 Feb. 1939). Jazz tenor saxophonist. He played with Bennie Moten (1933–35), then briefly with Hot Lips Page, Lionel Hampton, and Buck Clayton. Soloist with Count Basie (1936–39), his emotive, hard-driving approach, based on Coleman Hawkins's, contrasting with Lester Young's delicate manner, as on the recording "John's Idea" (1937). Other recordings with Basie include "One O'Clock Jump" (1937), the ballad "Blue and Sentimental," "Texas Shuffle," and—as a clarinet soloist—"Jumpin' at the Woodside" (all 1938).

Everly, Don (b. Brownie, Ky., 1 Feb. 1937) and **Phil** (b. Brownie, Ky., 19 Jan. 1939). Rock-and-roll singers. They began singing in their parents' country music shows in Iowa, and from 1957 made numerous recordings as the Everly Brothers. Performing a repertoire of songs by Boudleaux and Felice Bryant ("Bye, Bye, Love" and "Wake Up, Little Susie," both 1957), and themselves ("Cathy's Clown," 1960), they created a unique sound by singing country-style vocal harmony over a rock-and-roll instrumental background. After separating in 1973 each pursued a solo career; they reunited for a concert in 1983.

Evett, Robert (b. Loveland, Colo., 30 Nov. 1922; d. Tacoma Park, Md., 3 Feb. 1975). Composer and critic. Studied with Roy Harris at Colorado Springs (1941–47) and with Persichetti at Juilliard (1951–52); chaired the music department at the Washington Institute of Contemporary Arts (1947–50). He was book editor and music critic for the *New Republic* (1952–68) and editor of the "Arts and Letters" section of the *Atlantic Monthly* (1968–69); wrote criticism for the *Washington Star* (1961–75). As a composer he employed a mildly dissonant style; many compositions were commissioned by ensembles in the Washington, D.C., area. Works include several concertos and 3 symphonies; 2 piano quintets and sonatas for clarinet, violin, viola, cello, oboe; keyboard works; a Mass (S.A.T. B. and organ); other songs and liturgical music.

Ewing, Maria (Louise) (b. Detroit, 27 Mar. 1950). Mezzo-soprano. Studied with Eleanor Steber at the Cleveland Institute; with Jennie Tourel at Juilliard. Debut in 1973 at the Ravinia Festival under James Levine. Debut at the New York Met as Cherubino *(Le nozze di Figaro),* 1976; at La Scala as Genevieve *(Pelléas),* 1976; at the Paris Opéra as the Composer in *Ariadne auf Naxos,* 1981. Broadening her repertory, she sang Poulenc's Blanche *(Dialogue des Carmelites)* at the

Met in 1981, and Monteverdi's Nero *(L'incoronazione di Poppea)* at the Glyndebourne Festival in 1984. With the encouragement of her husband, the director Sir Peter Hall, her acting matured in the 1980s, and she scored her greatest success to date as Carmen at the Met in 1985. Covent Garden debut as Salome, 1988.

Eximeno (y Pujades), Antonio (b. Valencia, 26 Sept. 1729; d. Rome, 9 June 1808). Theorist and essayist on music. He attended seminary in Valencia and joined the Jesuits in 1745. His early specialty was mathematics, which he taught in Segovia around 1765. He moved to Rome in 1767 and studied music with Felice Masi, *maestro di cappella* at the Church of the Holy Apostles. During the 1770s he achieved notoriety with 3 treatises published (first in Italian in Rome) to refute writings on music (such as those by Tartini, Rameau, and Padre Martini) that used mathematics and strict rules to explain musical principles.

Eybler, Joseph (Leopold) [von] (b. Schwechat, near Vienna, 8 Feb. 1765; d. Vienna, 24 July 1846). Composer. Son of a village schoolmaster and choirmaster; 1771–82, choirboy at St. Stephen's, Vienna, also studying with Albrechtsberger, 1776–79; from 1782 a professional musician (as organist and player of several other instruments) and composer (op. 1, 3 string quartets, dedicated to his distant relative Haydn) in Vienna; assisted in rehearsals of *Così fan tutte.* Close to Mozart in his last days, he was given Mozart's Requiem to complete, but felt unable to do so. Kapellmeister at the Carmelite Church from 1792; at the Schottenkloster from 1796. He was patronized by the empress and became music teacher to the imperial family in 1801. He became assistant court composer in 1804 and succeeded Salieri as court Kapellmeister in 1824. He retired in 1833 after a stroke while conducting Mozart's Requiem, and was ennobled in 1835. Works include an opera; a famous Requiem (1803); 32 Masses and much other sacred music; the oratorio *Die vier letzten Dinge* (1811); orchestral, chamber, piano works.

Bibl.: Hildegard Herrmann, *Thematisches Werkverzeichnis der Werke von Joseph Eybler* (Munich and Salzburg, 1976).

Eysler, Edmund (b. Vienna, 12 Mar. 1874; d. there, 4 Oct. 1949). Composer. He studied composition with Johann Nepomuk Fuchs, then taught piano and conducted theater orchestras. His operetta *Bruder Straubinger* (1903) was extremely successful (with over 100 performances in the year of its premiere); later works were somewhat less popular, but altogether he wrote more than 50 operettas, most before the First World War and performed in Vienna. Other works include a ballet, 2 operas (*Der Hexenspiegel,* 1900; *Hochzeitspräludium,* 1946), songs, dances, and piano works.

F

Faber, Heinrich [Lichtenfels, Hainrich] (b. Lichtenfels, before 1500; d. Ölsnitz, Saxony, 26 Feb. 1552). Theorist. Active perhaps as a singer at the Danish royal court, then as a student at the Univ. of Wittenberg, a teacher, and a rector. He wrote *Compendiolum musicae* (Brunswick, 1548), a very popular textbook that includes a number of his own *bicinia; Ad musicam practicam introductio* (Nuremberg, 1550), which relies heavily on Gaffurius' *Practica musicae;* and the more speculative *Musica poetica* (1548), in which improvised and composed music are compared.

Fabini, Eduardo (b. Solis de Mataojo, Uruguay, 18 May 1882; d. Montevideo, 17 May 1950). Composer and violinist. After initial instruction in Uruguay, he attended the Royal Conservatory in Brussels, receiving a prize for his violin playing. He returned permanently to Uruguay in 1907. His tone poem *Campo* premiered in Montevideo in 1922; it was performed under Richard Strauss in Buenos Aires in 1923 and recorded in the U.S. in 1927. He last performed in 1933, and his final piece appeared in 1937. Works include orchestral concert music, 2 ballets, vocal music with and without instruments, and pieces for piano, guitar, and violin.

Bibl.: *Composers of the Americas* 2 (1956): 53–57 [includes works list].

Fabri, Annibale Pio (b. Bologna, 1697; d. Lisbon, 12 Aug. 1760). Tenor and composer. Studied with the castrato Pistocchi; appeared in 1710–11 in two Caldara operas in Rome; accepted into the Accademia filarmonica in 1719; sang during the 1720s in operas throughout Italy. Handel brought him to London in 1729; there he performed in *Giulio Cesare* (in the role of Sextus), *Scipione* (the title role), and *Rinaldo* (Goffredo), among others; Handel wrote roles expressly for him in *Partenope* and *Poro.* Burney owned a book of his vocal exercises, "by which we may judge his taste and knowledge." Named virtuoso to Emperor Charles VI in 1732. From 1735–48 he sang often in Italy, appearing also in several Hasse operas at Madrid (1738–39). Upon retiring he served in the Royal Chapel at Lisbon.

Fabricius, Werner (b. Itzehoe, Holstein, 10 Apr. 1633; d. Leipzig, 9 Jan. 1679). Organist and composer. Studied with Selle and Scheidemann in Hamburg; later attended the Univ. of Leipzig, eventually practicing law there and serving as organist at the Nicolaikirche and director of music at the Paulinerkirche. Works include instrumental suites, sacred songs for 2–8 voices, and organ preludes, as well as writings on organ building and realizing figured bass.

Faccio, Franco [Francesco Antonio] (b. Verona, 8 Mar. 1840; d. Monza, 21 July 1891). Conductor. Son of an innkeeper; 1855–60, student at Milan Conservatory; aroused attention through two collaborations with fellow student and close friend Boito, but his aspirations to be a progressive force in Italian music foundered on the lack of success of his two operas, *I profughi fiamminghi* (La Scala, 1863) and *Amleto* (libretto by Boito; Genoa, 1865; a fiasco at La Scala, 1871). From 1866 found his vocation as a conductor; 1866–68, conducted in northern Europe; from 1868 in Milan, first at the Teatro Carcano, then from 1869 assistant conductor at La Scala and from 1871 chief conductor there, directing many important productions (premiere of *Otello,* 1887; also London premiere, 1889). In 1879 founded the Società orchestrale della Scala for public concerts; 1868–78, professor of composition, Milan Conservatory. In 1890 advanced syphilis caused his resignation from La Scala; then briefly director, Parma Conservatory.

Bibl.: R. de Rensis, *Franco Faccio e Verdi: Carteggi e documenti* (Milan, 1934).

Fagan, Gideon (b. Somerset West, South Africa, 3 Nov. 1904; d. Cape Town, 21 Mar. 1980). Composer and conductor. His early musical studies were at the South African College of Music in Cape Town (1916–22); from 1922 he studied at the Royal College of Music with Adrian Boult and Malcolm Sargent (conducting) and with Vaughan Williams. In London he conducted for theater companies and, from 1939 to 1942, the BBC Northern Symphony. In 1949 he assumed the post of conductor for the Johannesburg City Orchestra; he also taught conducting, theory, and composition at the Univ. of Cape Town (1967–73). Among his compositions are vocal works (*Tears,* symphonic poem, baritone, and chamber ensemble, 1970); orchestral works (*Ilala,* tone poem, 1941; *South African Folktune Suite,* 1942; *Unitate vires,* symphonic sketches, 1970; *Serenade,* strings, 1974); film scores.

Fago, (Francesco) Nicola (b. Taranto, 26 Feb. 1677; d. Naples, 18 Feb. 1745). Composer. Studied at the Conservatorio della Pietà dei Turchini in Naples, 1693–97; *primo maestro* there, 1705–40, and at S. Onofrio, 1704–8; served also as *maestro di cappella* at the Tesoro di S. Gennaro of Naples Cathedral, 1709–31, where his son succeeded him, and at S. Giacomo dei Spagnuoli from 1736 to his death. Works include several operas, secular cantatas and arias, and much sacred music.

Fairchild, Blair (b. Belmont, Mass., 23 June 1877; d. Paris, 23 Apr. 1933). Composer. Studied at Harvard under Paine and Spalding; then studied piano in Florence with G. Buonamici. He was in business and in the diplomatic service in Turkey and Persia (1901–3); from 1905 until his death he lived in Paris, where he studied with Widor and others. His ballet pantomime *Dame Libellule* (1919) was the first American work performed at the Paris Opéra (1921). Orchestral works often reflect his interest in the Near East; also wrote chamber, piano, choral, and vocal music.

Fairlamb, James Remington (b. Philadelphia, 23 Jan. 1838; d. Ingleside, N.Y., 16 Apr. 1908). Composer. In his teens, church organist in Philadelphia and published first of his many songs; 1858–65, mostly in Europe, studying at Paris Conservatory and in Florence; then U.S. consul, Zurich; later organist and composer in Washington, Philadelphia, New Jersey; from 1898 music teacher, DeWitt Clinton High School, New York. Published much sacred choral music and 2 chamber operas.

Falconieri, Andrea (b. Naples, 1585 or 1586; d. there, 19 or 29 July 1656). Composer and lutenist. At the court of Parma from 1604 until 1614, then elsewhere in northern Italy, at Rome, and late in life at Naples; travels in Spain and France from 1621 until 1628; from 1639 lutenist, from 1647 *maestro di cappella* at the royal chapel at Naples. Compositions include songs and instrumental music.

Falkner, (Donald) Keith (b. Sawston, Cambridgeshire, 1 Mar. 1900). Bass. Studied voice with Plunkett Greene at the Royal College of Music (1920–25), with Theodor Lierhammer in Vienna, with Dossert in Paris. Assistant vicar at Westminster Abbey, 1920–21; at St. Paul's Cathedral, 1921–26. Debut at the Promenade Concerts, 1925; then soloist in oratorios and recital through 1940, touring Europe, South Africa, New Zealand, and the U.S., where he also appeared in 3 Warner Brothers musicals. Professor at Cornell Univ., 1950–60; director of the Royal College of Music, 1960–74; knighted, 1967.

Fall, Leo(pold) (b. Olomouc, Moravia, 2 Feb. 1873; d. Vienna, 16 Sept. 1925). Composer and conductor. After study at the Vienna Conservatory with Robert and Johann Nepomuk Fuchs, he played in and directed theater orchestras and wrote stage music in Berlin, Hamburg, and Cologne. In 1906 he returned to Vienna, where his subsequent operettas had considerable success. His father and two brothers were also active in stage and cabaret music as conductors or composers. Works include 3 operas, more than 20 operettas for Vienna (*Die Dollarprinzessin,* 1907), Mannheim, London, and Berlin (*Die Rose von Stambul,* 1916). He also composed overtures, waltzes, and songs.

Falla (y Matheu), Manuel (María) de (los Dolores) (b. Cádiz, 23 Nov. 1876; d. Alta Gracia, Argentina, 14 Nov. 1946). Composer. His mother was Catalan, his father Valencian; the family was relatively well off during Falla's youth. Falla's mother gave him his first music lessons; he later studied under Alejandro Odero and Enrique Broca and participated in chamber music evenings at the house of Salvador Viniegra (a friend of Saint-Saëns). Concerts given by a newly formed orchestra in 1893 decisively turned him from literary pursuits toward music.

Falla had for a time been traveling between Cádiz and Madrid to study piano under José Tragó when his family, beset by economic hardship, moved to the capital in 1896. Entering the conservatory, he completed his studies in 1899, winning first prize, and subsequently pursued zarzuela composition. Of five he composed (two in collaboration with Amadeo Vives, later to gain renown in the genre), only one, *Los amores de la Inés,* was performed. He also came into contact around this time with Felipe Pedrell, who introduced him to Spain's musical heritage and apprised him of current European developments, and was also influenced by Louis Lucas's *L'acoustique nouvelle* (1854), which, among other things, dealt sympathetically with folk music.

He won two competitions in 1904, the first in composition sponsored by the San Fernando Academy (for his opera *La vida breve,* which, however, was not performed as expected), the second in piano organized by a Madrid piano firm. Falla had already resolved to visit France; he became pianist for a touring mime company and by 1907 had arrived in Paris. He remained there until 1914, acquainting himself with Dukas, Ravel, Debussy, and Stravinsky, as well as with fellow Spaniard Albéniz. His four *Pièces espagnoles* for piano were published there in 1909, and the *Trois mélodies* appeared the next year; in addition, he finally brought *La vida breve* (as *La vie brève*) to the stage, first in Nice (Apr. 1913), then at the Opéra-comique (Jan. 1914). An acclaimed Madrid performance followed in December 1914. Living in Madrid in 1914–20, he produced some of his best-known works, including the Gypsy ballet *El amor brujo* (1915), *Noches en los jardines de España,* piano and orchestra (1916), and *El sombrero de tres picos* (1917; rev. 1919; composed for Diaghilev's Ballets russes). The *Fantasía bética* for piano (1919), dedicated to Artur Rubenstein in gratitude for financial assistance, dates also from this period, as do two aborted projects, the comic opera *Fuego fatuo,* based on the music of Chopin, and incidental music for the play *Don Juan de España.*

Falla visited Granada in 1919; he and his sister María del Carmen (who remained his companion throughout his life) moved there in 1920. Among his neighbors were Lorca, with whom he collaborated on occasion, as in the offerings of Lorca's private puppet theater, or with the *cante jondo* competition for traditional Andalusian singers in 1922 . The puppet theater piece *El retablo de maese Pedro* (1923, after Cervantes), though commissioned by the Princesse de Polignac, also grew out of the Falla–Lorca experiences. He traveled often during these years, to London and Paris as well as to various ISCM festivals. Contact with Wanda Landowska spurred him to write his Harpsichord Concerto (1923–26), the only major Falla composition with an abstract title. In 1926 he also began the massive "scenic cantata" *Atlántida,* with a macaronic text (Catalán, Castilian, and Latin) that fused Christian themes with the myth of the great lost city. The work remained unfinished at his death and was completed only in 1976 by Ernesto Halffter.

Many difficulties soon closed in upon him. He was always a pious, even ascetic man; his will of 1932 stipulated that his stage music must be performed following Christian guidelines, and he repeatedly submitted the *Atlántida* text for Jesuit censorship. The antichurch policy of the Republican government that ruled Spain from 1931 until 1936 disturbed him deeply. Periodic depression aggravated his already severe health problems; Falla was never a prolific composer, and his output now fell even further. He made two long visits to Mallorca in 1933 and 1934, writing the *Balada de Mallorca* (based on Chopin's F major Ballade op. 38, also composed on the island) for a local choir and making several transcriptions. His last Spanish public appearance came in 1936 at Barcelona; the same year his friend Lorca was arrested and shot and the Civil War began.

With these repeated emotional setbacks, the only work he completed after 1935 was the suite *Homenajes,* four movements in memory of the Spanish conductor Arbós, of Debussy and Dukas (the music for both drawn from earlier *Tombeaux* in their memory), and of Pedrell. It was premiered in Buenos Aires, where he was invited in 1938 as a guest of the Spanish Cultural Institute. After two final conducting appearances with a radio orchestra, he spent his last days in isolation with his sister in the Argentinian province of Córdoba. Falla drew upon the entire range of his musical inheritance, from the Cántigas of Alfonso X to Iberian folk song; although his music is evocative of the French milieu in which he came of age as a composer, it nonetheless is viewed as the embodiment of Spanish nationalism.

Bibl.: Federico Sopeña, *Atlántida: Introducción a Manuel de Falla* (Madrid, 1962). Ronald Crichton, *Manuel de Falla: Descriptive Catalogue of His Works* (London, 1976). Suzanne Demarquez, *Manuel de Falla,* trans. Salvator Attanasio (Paris, 1963; Philadelphia, 1968). Ronald Crichton, *Falla* (London, 1982). Gilbert Chase and Andrew Budwig, *Manuel de Falla: A Bibliography and Research Guide* (New York, 1986). Federico Sopeña, *Vida y obra de Manuel de Falla* (Madrid, 1988). Jean-Charles Hoffelé, *Manuel de Falla* (Paris, 1992).

Farberman, Harold (b. New York, 2 Nov. 1929). Composer, conductor, percussionist. Studied percussion with Sol Goodman at Juilliard (B.S., 1951) and then played in the Boston Symphony (1951–63) and conducted the Boston New Arts Orchestra (1957–61). From 1954 he studied at New England Conservatory with Jud Cooke and at the Berkshire Music Center with Copland, Babbitt, Berio, and Foss. He conducted the Colorado Springs Symphony (1967–70) and the Oakland Symphony (1971–79). Compositions employ twelve-tone methods; has often written for percussion and has included jazz elements, especially in mixed-media works. His compositions include operas, ballets, film scores; orchestral works; *Alea* for 6 percussionists (1976) and other chamber music; vocal works with percussion or orchestra (*New York Times,* mezzo-soprano, piano, percussion, 1964).

Farina, Carlo (b. Mantua, ca. 1600; d. ca. 1640). Violinist and composer. Began his career in Mantua; was *Konzertmeister* at the court of Dresden, 1626–29, alongside Schütz; surfaces only once again, at Danzig in 1637. His music, all of which was published in Dresden, shows great virtuosity and is important in establishing an idiomatic violin style. Works include dance movements, programmatic pieces, and sonatas, all for 2–4 parts and continuo.

Fariñas, Carlos (b. Cienfuegos, Cuba, 28 Nov. 1934). Composer. Attended the Havana Conservatory; visited Tanglewood in 1956, studying with Copland and Eleazar de Carvalho; received further training, 1961–63, at the Moscow Conservatory. Works include orchestral compositions (*El bosque la echado a andar,* 1976, in memory of Ché Guevara), chamber and guitar music, and *Tiento I* and *II* for piano and percussion.

Farinelli [Broschi, Carlo] (b. Andria, Apulia, 24 Jan. 1705; d. Bologna, 15 July 1782). Soprano castrato. Probably received early musical training from his father; became a student of Porpora after castration. After his debut in Porpora's serenata *Angelica e Medoro* (Naples, 1720; the libretto was Metastasio's first printed poetry), he scored successes at Naples and Rome in operas of Porpora, Hasse, and others (1722–24), and later in northern Italy, Vienna, and Munich (1724–32). Porpora drew him to London in 1734, where his triumphs made him wealthy and hastened Handel's withdrawal from operatic composition. He performed in Paris and London in 1736–37, then went to Spain, where he was a prized court performer and confidant to Philip V (until 1746) and Ferdinand VI (1746–59). Dismissed by Charles III in 1759, he retired to a sumptuous villa near Bologna, where he remained until his death; his visitors included Padre Martini, Gluck, Burney, and the young Mozart.

Farkas, Ferenc (b. Nagykanizsa, 15 Dec. 1905). Composer. He studied piano as a youth, then from 1922 studied composition at the Budapest Academy with Albert Siklós and Leo Weiner. During a brief tenure as assistant director of choruses at the Municipal Theater in Budapest (1927–29) he came into contact with Diaghilev's company; later he studied with Respighi in Rome (1929–31). During the 1930s and

1940s he composed nearly 100 scores for stage and films, in Vienna, Budapest, and Copenhagen. He held academic posts at the Higher Music School in Budapest (1935–41), at the Koloszvár Conservatory (1941–46; director from 1943), and at the Budapest Academy (1949–75). Works include operas (*The Magic Cupboard,* 1938–42; *Vidróczki,* 1964; *Story of Noszty Junior with Mari Tóth,* "musical comedy," 1971; *A Gentleman from Venice,* 1980); orchestral works (*Rhapsodia Carpathiana,* 1940; *Lavotta,* 1951; Symphony, 1952; *Ouverture philharmonique,* 1989; Concertino for Trumpet and Strings, 1984); vocal works (*Cantus Pannonicus,* 1959); chamber works (*Szenen aus Ungarn,* 4 clarinets); songs; piano works.

Farkas, Philip (Francis) (b. Chicago, 5 Mar. 1914; d. Bloomington, Ind., 21 Dec. 1992). Horn player. Studied horn with Louis Dufrasne in Chicago. Began his professional career as first horn with the Kansas City Philharmonic, 1933–36. First chair in the Chicago Symphony, 1936–41 and 1947–60; in the Cleveland Orchestra, 1941–45 and 1946–47; in the Boston Symphony, 1945–56. Taught horn at Northeastern Univ., 1953–60; at Indiana Univ. from 1960. Wrote several books, including *The Art of French Horn Playing* (1956), *The Art of Brass Playing* (1962), and *The Art of Musicianship* (1976).

Farlow, Tal(madge Holt) (b. Greensboro, N.C., 7 June 1921). Jazz guitarist. He played in Red Norvo's trio (1949–53, 1954–55; initially with Charles Mingus) and Artie Shaw's Gramercy Five (1954) and recorded as a leader (1953–59), including the album *The Interpretations of Tal Farlow* (1955). After working more often as a sign painter than a musician, he recorded the album *A Sign of the Times* (1976) and then began performing regularly again in the 1980s, including a reunion with Norvo. He is the subject of the documentary film *Talmadge Farlow* (1981). The fleetest of bop guitarists, he favored a more tuneful approach in his later years.

Farmer, Art(thur Stewart) (b. Council Bluffs, Iowa, 21 Aug. 1928). Jazz flugelhorn player and trumpeter. He played trumpet in Lionel Hampton's big band (1952–53), then worked with Horace Silver, Gerry Mulligan, and George Russell. In 1959 he and Benny Golson founded the Jazztet, a hard bop sextet that recorded the album *Meet the Jazztet* (1960). Favoring a lyrical style, a warm tone, and melodies in the middle and low registers, he began concentrating on flugelhorn. From 1962 he led groups. He settled in Vienna (1968), working in a radio big band and the Clarke–Boland Big Band. In 1977 he resumed regular international touring, notably with the Jazztet, re-formed in 1982.

Farmer, John (b. ca. 1570; fl. 1591–1601). Composer. Little is known about his life. From 1595 he was a musician and teacher at Christ Church Cathedral, Dublin, but was living in London in 1599. His best-known works are English madrigals, of which he wrote a complete volume (1599) and a single piece published in *The Triumphes of Oriana* (1601). He also composed a book of 2-part canons (1591) and about 20 pieces published in East's psalter of 1592.

Farnaby, Giles (b. ca. 1563; d. London, buried 25 Nov. 1640). Composer. Received the B.Mus. from Oxford in 1592; then lived in a village near Lincoln; by 1611 or shortly thereafter had moved to London. His works include over 50 keyboard pieces (most preserved only in the Fitzwilliam Virginal Book), Psalms (a large unpublished collection, of which only one partbook survives, and 9 settings in East's psalter of 1592), and a book of canzonets for 4 voices.

Farrant, Richard (b. ca. 1525–30?; d. London, 30 Nov. 1580). Composer. Gentleman of the Chapel Royal from ca. 1550 until 1564, then Master of the Choristers at St. George's Chapel, Windsor, and, from 1569, also at the Chapel Royal. From 1567 until 1579 his choirboys, working as a dramatic company, put on a number of his plays, of which nothing is known but some titles and two songs. His few extant liturgical compositions include one of the first verse anthems.

Farrar, Ernest Bristow (b. Blackheath, London, 7 July 1885; d. in action in France, 18 Sept. 1918). Organist and composer. Studied organ with Parratt and composition with Stanford at the Royal College of Music from 1905. Organist at the English church in Dresden; then in Yorkshire at St. Hilda, South Shields (from 1910), and at Christ Church, Harrogate (from 1912). Composed orchestral works (*The Forsaken Merman,* symphonic poem; *English Pastoral Impressions,* 1921); choral works (*Out of Doors,* 1923; *A Song of St. Francis,* 1919); part songs; solo songs; chamber music (*Celtic Suite,* violin, piano, 1920); keyboard works.

Farrar, Geraldine (b. Melrose, Mass., 28 Feb. 1882; d. Ridgefield, Conn., 11 Mar. 1967). Soprano. She studied with Emma Thursby in New York (1897–98) and with Trabadelo in Paris (1899–1900). Debut 15 Oct. 1901 at the Berlin Opera as Marguerite *(Faust)*; coached there, 1901–6, by Lilli Lehmann. U.S. debut in 1906 at the Metropolitan Opera as Gounod's Juliette. Sang Cio-Cio-San opposite Caruso at the Met premiere of *Madama Butterfly* in 1907. From 1914 she was closely identified with the part of Carmen. Among the roles she created for the Met were Humperdinck's Goose Girl (*Königskinder,* 1910), Wolf-Ferrari's Susanna (1911), and Puccini's Suor Angelica (1918). Her farewell performance in 1922 was as Leoncavallo's Zazà. Published *The Story of an American Singer* (1916; 2nd ed., New York, 1938, retitled *Such Sweet Compulsion*).

Farrell, Eileen (b. Willimantic, Conn., 13 Feb. 1920). Soprano. Her parents were in vaudeville. She studied voice with her mother, with Merle Alcock, and with

Eleanor McLellan. Debut as "The Voice of Rosa Ponselle" on a movie newsreel, *The March of Time,* 1939. Performed in the CBS radio chorus, then hosted her own show, *Eileen Farrell Presents,* 1941–46. Concert debut, 1947. In New York her appearance as Marie in a concert performance of *Wozzeck* and her recital on 24 Oct. 1950 led to an invitation from Toscanini to sing and record with him. Stage debut as Santuzza *(Cavalleria rusticana)* in Tampa, Fla., 1956. Debut with the San Francisco Opera as Leonora *(Il trovatore),* 1956; with the Chicago Lyric Opera as La Gioconda, 1957; with the New York Met as Gluck's Alceste, 1960. Remained at the Met until 1966. Many concert performances thereafter, often in Wagnerian roles. Beginning in the 1980s, sang and recorded much popular music. Taught voice at Indiana Univ., 1971–80; at the Univ. of Maine at Orono, 1980–84.

Farrenc [née Dumont], **(Jeanne-) Louise** (b. Paris, 31 May 1804; d. there, 15 Sept. 1875). Composer, teacher. From a family of artists; studied with Reicha from age 15; 1821, married the flutist and publisher Aristide Farrenc (1794–1865) and traveled with him; 1825, settled in Paris, resuming lessons with Reicha and beginning to publish piano music in the salon genres and several sets of etudes; from the 1830s produced considerable chamber music (mostly with piano), 2 concert overtures, 3 symphonies; 1842–73, professor of piano, Paris Conservatory; with her husband, began editing the historical anthology *Le trésor des pianistes* (Paris, 1861–74; R: 1977), continuing it alone after his death.

Bibl.: Bea Friedland, "Louise Farrenc (1804–1875): Composer, Performer, Scholar," *MQ* 60 (1974): 257–74.

Farwell, Arthur (b. St. Paul, Minn., 23 Apr. 1872; d. New York, 20 Jan. 1952). Composer, critic, and editor. After training in electrical engineering (B.S., 1893), he studied composition with Norris and Chadwick in Boston and with Humperdinck, Pfitzner, and Guilmant in Europe; returned to the U.S. in 1899 and taught at Cornell (1899–1901); chaired the music department at Berkeley (1918–19); taught at Michigan State (East Lansing, 1927–39), after which he returned to New York and taught privately (among his students was Roy Harris). In 1901 he founded the Wa-Wan Press (its catalogue was taken over by G. Schirmer in 1912), which published his own music and that of 36 other American composers; he wrote introductions and designed the covers for many of its publications. He intended the press to encourage the development of a characteristically American music using "ragtime, Negro songs, Indian songs, Cowboy songs, and . . . new and daring expressions of our own composers." From 1904 to 1907 he toured the U.S. giving lecture recitals on American music; was chief music critic of *Musical America* (1909–14) and supervisor of municipal music for New York City (1910–13); he founded the New York Community Chorus (1916). He is remembered primarily as an Indianist; early works are Wagnerian in their harmonic language; later works are very chromatic.

Works: 30–35 pageants and other stage music (*Cartoon, or Once Upon a Time Recently,* 1948, an operatic fantasy); some 17 orchestral works (several symphonic poems and a series of "Symbolist Studies"); chamber music (Piano Quintet op. 103, 1937, inspired by his early visits to the West); piano works (*From Mesa and Plain* op. 20, 1905, and *Polytonal Studies* op. 109, 1940–52); choral music; some 100 arrangements of Indian melodies and original songs.

Bibl.: Brice Farwell, *A Guide to the Music of Arthur Farwell and to the Microfilm Collection of His Work* (New York, 1972). Evelyn Davis Culbertson, *He Heard America Singing: Arthur Farwell, Composer and Crusading Music Educator* (Metuchen, N.J., 1992).

Fasano, Renato (b. Naples, 21 Aug. 1902; d. Rome, 3 Aug. 1979). Conductor and composer. Studied piano and composition at the Naples Conservatory. Through the early 1940s best known as a composer (*Isola eroica,* symphonic poem, 1942). Wrote a general history of music in 1949; later edited Vivaldi. Director of the Cagliari Conservatory, 1931–39; of the St. Cecilia Academy in Rome, 1944–47, and its president, 1972–76; of the Rome Conservatory, 1960–72. In 1948 founded the Collegium musicum italicum; their repertory was limited to 18th-century Italian composers plus J. S. Bach; as I virtuosi di Roma (from 1952) they became widely known through recordings.

Fasch, Carl Friedrich Christian (b. Zerbst, 18 Nov. 1736; d. Berlin, 3 Aug. 1800). Composer. Received initial instruction from his father, Johann Friedrich; appointed second harpsichordist (after C. P. E. Bach) at the court of Frederick the Great in 1755; taught privately as well. He was promoted after Bach's departure for Hamburg in 1767, and directed the royal opera, 1774–76. In his later years he devoted much time to choral music, founding the Berlin Singakademie in 1789; Zelter, his successor, wrote his biography in 1801.

Fasch, Johann Friedrich (b. Buttstädt bei Weimar, 15 Apr. 1688; d. Zerbst, 5 Dec. 1758). Composer. Sang as a boy in Weissenfels under J. P. Krieger; studied with Kuhnau in Leipzig; early works show Telemann's influence. In 1712 he visited many cities and courts en route to Darmstadt, where he studied under Graupner and Grünewald; he worked in Bayreuth and Lukavec before accepting in 1724 the post of Kapellmeister in Zerbst, where he remained for the rest of his life. An autobiographical sketch appeared in Marpurg's *Historisch-kritisch Beyträge* in 1757. None of his music was printed in his lifetime; much of it, including 4 operas and 12 cantata *Jahrgänge,* is lost. Fasch's modern reputation rests on his overtures, symphonies, concertos, and chamber music; manuscript copies by Bach and others show their broad circulation, while scholars see him as an important link between the Baroque and classical styles.

Bibl.: David A. Sheldon, "Johann Friedrich Fasch: Problems in Style Classification," *MQ* 58 (1976): 92–116. Rüdiger Pfeiffer, *Verzeichnis der Werke von Johann Friedrich Fasch (FWV): kleine Ausgabe* (Magdeburg, 1988).

Fassbaender, Brigitte (b. Berlin, 3 July 1939). Mezzo-soprano. Studied voice with her father, Willy Domgraf-Fassbänder, at the Nuremberg Conservatory, 1957–61. Debut in 1961 with the Bavarian State Opera in Munich as Nicklausse *(Les contes d'Hoffmann)*. Debut at the San Francisco Opera, 1970, as Carmen; at Covent Garden, 1971, as Octavian *(Rosenkavalier);* at the Paris Opéra, 1972, as Brangäne *(Tristan);* at Salzburg, 1972, as Dorabella *(Così fan tutte);* at the New York Metropolitan Opera, 1976, as Octavian. Sang in the 1976 premiere of Gottfried von Einem's *Kabale und Liebe* at the Vienna Staatsoper. Praised for her Countess Geschwitz *(Lulu)* and for her solos in Bach Passions.

Faugues, Guillaume (fl. ca. 1460). Composer. Nothing is known of his life. His name is included in a list of composers in the text of a motet by Compère and is mentioned in treatises by Tinctoris. Otherwise he is known only through 4 cantus firmus Masses, 2 of which incorporate something like parody technique.

Bibl.: *The Collected Works of Faugues* (Brooklyn, 1960).

Fauré, Gabriel (Urbain) (b. Pamiers, 12 May 1845; d. Paris, 4 Nov. 1924). Composer. His father was a schoolteacher and later principal of a teachers' college at Montgauzy, where Fauré, the youngest of six children, spent 1849–54. His musical talent, largely self-developed, was sufficient to get him a scholarship at the École Niedermeyer in Paris, newly established to train organists and choirmasters. There from 1854 to 1865 he studied under Loret (organ), Wackerthaler (counterpoint, fugue), Dietsch (harmony), and Niedermeyer (singing, piano, plainsong). The instruction, with its emphasis on plainsong, established Fauré's penchant for modality; acquaintance with contemporary music came through Saint-Saëns, who became his piano teacher after Niedermeyer's death in 1861 and who remained a close friend and furthered Fauré's career. He won prizes in almost every area of study and composed his first songs and piano pieces and the choral *Cantique de Jean Racine* op. 11, still one of his most popular works.

From January 1866 until March 1870 he led a dreary provincial life as organist at St. Sauveur in Rennes. He then returned to Paris as assistant organist at Notre Dame Clignancourt, but in August became an infantryman in the war against Germany. He mustered out early in 1871 and left Paris during the Commune, spending the summer in Switzerland, where the École Niedermeyer had taken refuge. He taught its composition class, one of his students being André Messager, who became a close friend and his roommate (1877–83) and with whom he made several visits to Germany (1878–84) and London (1882) to attend Wagner operas. From October 1871 he was assistant organist to Widor at St. Sulpice and from 1874 filled in at the Madeleine for Saint-Saëns when the latter, who introduced him to Paris musical society, was away. He became choirmaster at the Madeleine in 1877.

In 1883 he married Marie Fremiet, daughter of a distinguished sculptor (two sons, born 1883 and 1889). He led an arduous life of church work and private teaching to support this family, causing periods of depression. He had again begun to compose songs after his return to Paris. From about 1875 he also produced regularly in his two other favorite genres, piano pieces and chamber music. In 1871 he was a founder of the Société nationale de musique for the furtherance of contemporary French music, becoming its secretary in 1874; most of his chamber music was first heard in its concerts (including the 2 violin sonatas opp. 13, 108; 2 piano quartets opp. 15, 45; 2 cello sonatas opp. 109, 117; the Second Piano Quintet op. 115; the Piano Trio op. 120), and its existence probably stimulated his emphasis on this genre. In 1887 he began the Requiem, the most important of his sacred works (first performed in 1888 but revised later).

He spent a holiday in Venice in 1891 with and at the expense of a patroness, an American heiress, the Princesse de Scey-Montbéliard (better known later as the Princesse Edmond de Polignac), to whom he was strongly attached. Emma Bardac, later Debussy's wife, was the inspiration for his most important song cycle, *La bonne chanson* op. 61 (1892–94). Marguérite Hasselmans, a young pianist, was his mistress in his last 20 years. Nevertheless, he also remained a strong family man in the conventional manner.

Increasing recognition came in the 1890s: 1892–1905, inspector of provincial conservatories, a post that allowed him to give up private teaching but required considerable travel; 1896, succeeded Massenet as professor of composition at the Paris Conservatory (pupils included Ravel, Koechlin, Schmitt, Roger-Ducasse, Nadia Boulanger) and became organist at the Madeleine. From 1894 he made several visits to England, where he had influential supporters, leading to the most important of his several attempts at incidental music, that for Maeterlinck's *Pelléas et Mélisande* (London, 1898); this was followed by *Prométhée,* an outdoor spectacle, part opera, part spoken tragedy (Béziers, 1900). In general he became not a widely popular composer but one appealing primarily to connoisseurs, a condition that his music has never entirely escaped.

In 1901 he became professor of composition at the École Niedermeyer. From 1903 he was afflicted with growing deafness and the distortion of musical sounds; in spite of this he served as music critic of *Le Figaro,* 1903–21. In 1905, as part of the "Ravel affair," the controversy aroused by the extremely reactionary attitude of the Conservatory in five times rejecting Fauré's former pupil Ravel (of whom he remained a strong supporter) for the Prix de Rome, Fauré was appointed director of the Conservatory, reforming admissions policy, the faculty, and curriculum. In 1909 he became the first president of the Société musicale indépendente, founded in reaction against the conservatism of the Société nationale de musique, dominated by D'Indy. He was elected to the Institut in 1909 and president of the Société nationale in 1916. His composing was restricted to summer holidays, spent in Switzerland, the South of France, and elsewhere; those of 1907–12 were devoted primarily to his only opera and magnum opus, *Pénélope* (1913, Monte Carlo, then Paris), which never succeeded in entering the repertory, although much admired by musicians.

He visited England (1908, 1914), Germany (1908), and Russia (1910). In 1920 he resigned from the Conservatory because of deafness and age. He continued to compose, although increasingly feeble in his last two years with respiratory ailments, the result of heavy smoking. His last work, the String Quartet op. 121, was performed posthumously (1925). Other works: nearly 100 songs; piano pieces, including 13 nocturnes, 13 barcarolles, 5 impromptus, 4 valse-caprices, *Thème et variations* op. 73, *Dolly Suite,* 4-hands; works for piano and orchestra (Ballade op. 19; Fantaisie op. 111).

Bibl.: Robert Orledge, *Gabriel Fauré* (London, 1979). Jean-Michel Nectoux, ed., *Gabriel Fauré: Correspondence* (Paris, 1980); trans. J. A. Underwood as *Gabriel Fauré: His Life through Letters* (London and New York, 1984). Robin Tait, *The Musical Language of Gabriel Fauré* (New York, 1989). Jean-Michel Nectoux, *Gabriel Fauré: A Musical Life* trans. Roger Nichols (Cambridge, 1991).

Favart, Charles-Simon (b. Paris, 13 Nov. 1710; d. Belleville [Paris], 12 May 1792). Playwright and librettist. Studied at the Collège Louis-le-Grand; worked at various times both for the Opéra-comique and the Théâtre-Italien. Influential in the rise of opéra comique; he wrote libretti for Monsigny, F. A. Philidor, and Grétry. His works, in German adaptations by Durazzo and Gluck (and also in Mozart's *Bastien und Bastienne*), are part of the singspiel heritage as well.

Fayrfax, Robert (b. Deeping Gate, Lincolnshire, 25 Apr. 1464; d. St. Albans?, Hertfordshire, 24 Oct. 1521). Composer. Gentleman of the Chapel Royal by 6 Dec. 1497, remaining in service to the English royal family until his death; received Mus.B. (1501) and Mus.D. (1504) from Cambridge, Mus.D. (1511) from Oxford. His numerous surviving works include Masses, Magnificats, motets, secular part songs, and a few instrumental compositions. The Masses, most based on single cantus firmi throughout, constitute his most important body of work.

Bibl.: *Collected Works, CMM* 17 (1959–66). Edwin Brady Warren, *Life and Works of Robert Fayrfax, 1464–1521, MSD* 22 (1969).

Felciano, Richard (James) (b. Santa Rosa, Calif., 7 Dec. 1930). Composer. Studied with Milhaud at Mills College and in Paris, at the Univ. of Iowa (Ph.D., 1959), and with Dallapiccola in Italy. He chaired the music department at Lone Mountain College (1959–67) and then taught at Berkeley; composer-in-residence for the National Center for Experiments in Television in San Francisco (1967–71) and for the City of Boston (1971–73). Aleatoric, electronic, and dramatic elements are common in his music; he was among the first to use electronic music in a liturgical context (*Glossolalia,* baritone, organ, percussion, and tape, 1967). Works include a chamber opera and theater piece; orchestral pieces; *Salvador Allende* (string quartet, clarinet, percussion, 1983) and other chamber music; organ and piano works (*In Celebration of the Golden Rain,* gamelan and organ, 1977; Organ Concerto, 1986); choral music.

Feld, Jindřich (b. Prague, 19 Feb. 1925). Composer. He studied violin with his father, Jindřich (1883–1953), who was a professor of violin at the Prague Conservatory; after high school he studied composition with E. Hlobil (from 1945) and later with J. Řídký at the Academy of Music in Prague. From 1948 he studied musicology and philosophy at Charles Univ., earning a Ph.D. in 1952. During the 1950s and 1960s he worked as a free-lance violinist and composer; in 1968–69 he was guest professor at the Univ. of Adelaide in Australia. After 1972 he taught at the Prague Conservatory. The neoclassicism of his early music gave way in later works to more freedom in the use of serialism and aleatory. Works include operas (*Pohádka o Budulínkovi,* 1955; *Poštácká pohádka,* 1958); orchestral works (Concerto for Orchestra, 1951; a violin concerto, 1958; *Koncertní hudba,* oboe, bassoon, orchestra, 1964; *Dramaticka fantasie "Srpnové dny,"* 1969); many chamber works (5 string quartets; Chamber Suite, 1960; *Elegy,* saxophone, piano, 1981).

Feldman, Morton (b. New York, 12 Jan. 1926; d. Buffalo, 3 Sept. 1987). Composer. Studied piano from the age of 12, and composition with Riegger and Wolpe in his teens; in 1950 he met Cage and became associated with Tudor, Wolff, and Brown in New York. Taught at SUNY–Buffalo from 1972.

Feldman's music is characterized by soft dynamics and understated gestures (especially *In Search of an Orchestration,* 1967, primarily concerned with changing timbres undisturbed by sharp attacks); he used aleatoric devices and graphic notation as well as conventional notation believing that "notation . . . determines the style of the piece." One aim was to use sound as painters (Jackson Pollock, Philip Guston, and others) use color. Precise pitch is sometimes left to performer choice (e.g., *Projections,* 1950–51, in which only the register is indicated and rectangles enclosing a numeral define the relative length of an event and the number of notes to be included); after 1957 he controlled pitch and direction of a line more precisely by employing "free duration notation." In *Piece for Four Pianos* (1957) a single part is played by the performers independently, resulting in a polyphonic texture with much repetition; the conductor of *Out of Last Pieces*

(1958) can gather any combination from 38 precisely notated events, in which each performer can enter each box of the notation at will. He reverted to conventional notation again in *On Time and the Instrumental Factor* (1969) for orchestra: the consonance and repetition in that work align it with minimalism, but the choice of pitches follows no systematic plan. Late in his career he produced some very long pieces (String Quartet no. 1, 1979, lasts for an hour and 40 minutes; the Second String Quartet, 1983, lasts for 6 hours), reflecting his view that after Stravinsky, the movement form became outmoded.

Works: a monodrama (*Neither,* after Beckett, soprano and orchestra, 1977); film scores; works for orchestra (*Orchestra,* 1976; *The Turfan Fragments,* 1980; *Coptic Light,* 1986); a wide variety of chamber music (*False Relationships and the Extended Ending,* trombone, tubular bells, 3 pianos, violin, and cello, 1968; *For John Cage,* violin and piano, 1982; 2 string quartets, 1979, 1983, and *Structures,* string quartet, 1987); works for voice(s) and ensemble; a few songs.

Bibl.: Cole Gagne and Tracy Caras, "Morton Feldman," in *Soundpieces: Interviews with American Composers* (Metuchen, N.J., 1982), pp. 164–177. Morton Feldman, *Morton Feldman* (Munich, 1986).

Fenby, Eric (William) (b. Scarborough, Yorkshire, 22 Apr. 1906). Composer. Studied organ with Claude Keeton. From 1928 to 1934 he served as amanuensis to Delius in France, a period he wrote about in his book *Delius as I Knew Him* (London, 1936; 4th ed., 1981). From 1935 to 1939 he was music adviser to Boosey & Hawkes, and from 1948 to 1962 was director of music at North Riding Training College. In 1964 he became professor of composition at the Royal Academy of Music. His overture *Rossini on Ilkley Moor* is his best-known piece.

Bibl.: Christopher Redwood, ed., *A Delius Companion: A 70th Birthday Tribute to Eric Fenby* (London, 1976).

Fender, (Clarence) Leo (b. Anaheim, Calif., 1909). Electric guitar maker. In 1944 he and Clayton Orr ("Doc") Kauffman established the K & F Company, which made electric steel guitars. When the partnership broke up in 1946, Fender formed the Fender Electric Instruments Company in Fullerton, Calif. With George Fullerton he developed in 1948 the first commercially produced solid-bodied electric guitar, the Fender Broadcaster (renamed Telecaster in 1950; a new model named the Stratocaster was introduced in 1954). In 1951 Fender invented and marketed the Fender Precision Bass, the first electric bass guitar. He sold the company to CBS in 1965 but was active in the design of the Fender–Rhodes electric piano and other projects until 1970, when he left to form new ventures. CBS sold the company bearing his name to a group of investors in 1985.

Fennell, Frederick (b. Cleveland, 2 July 1914). Conductor. Studied at the Eastman School (1933–37, 1938–39); at the Mozarteum Academy (1938). Conducted the Eastman Symphonic Band, 1935–62. Music director of the Eastman Opera Theater, 1953–60. Founding conductor of the Eastman Chamber Orchestra and the Eastman Wind Ensemble, 1953–62. With the latter group he became widely known through 24 albums. Associate conductor of the Minnesota Symphony, 1962–63. Conductor of the Univ. of Miami Symphony, 1965–80. Principal guest conductor at the Interlochen Arts Academy, 1980–83. Music director of the Tokyo Kosei Wind Ensemble from 1984.

Fennelly, Brian (b. Kingston, N.Y., 14 Aug. 1937). Composer and theorist. Studied at Yale (1963–68) with Mel Powell (composition) and at N.Y.U. Uses twelve-tone procedures (Wind Quintet, 1967) as well as a freely atonal idiom (*Canzona and Dance,* clarinet, piano, violin, and cello, 1982–83), usually exhibiting instrumental virtuosity and rhythmic complexity. In later works particular pitch sequences are chosen from harmonic fields dependent on tone rows. His works include *Quintuplo* (brass quintet and orchestra, 1977–78), *Tropes and Echoes* (clarinet and orchestra, 1981), a concerto for saxophone and string orchestra (1984); *Evanescences* (alto flute, clarinet, violin, cello, and tape, 1969), *Prelude and Elegy* (brass quintet, 1969), *Sonata Seria* (piano, 1976), a brass quintet (1987), and other chamber music; SUNYATA (tape, 1970); choral works; *Songs with Improvisations* (after e. e. cummings, mezzo-soprano, clarinet, and piano, 1964).

Feo, Francesco (b. Naples, 1691; d. there, 28 Jan. 1761). Composer. Studied with Basso and Fago, perhaps also in Rome with Pitoni. Served as *maestro* of the Conservatorio di S. Onofrio, 1723–39, with Jommelli among his students; as *maestro* of the Conservatorio dei Poveri di Gesù Cristo, 1739–43; and as *maestro di cappella* at the church of the Annunziata, 1726–45, where he was succeeded by his nephew, Gennaro Manna. A portrait of him, seated alongside theory books of Zarlino, Fux, and Scorpione, is in the Civico Museo bibliografico musicale, Bologna.

Works: several operas, including *L'amore tirannico* (Naples, 1713), *Siface* (Naples, 1723; Metastasio's first *dramma per musica*), *Andromaca* (Rome, 1730; libretto by Zeno), and *Alsace* (Turin, 1740; libretto by Salvi); intermezzi; arias and duets; oratorios; sacred dialogues, cantatas, and motets; Masses and Mass sections; the *Passio secundum Joannem* (1744); other sacred works.

Ferencsik, János (b. Budapest, 18 Jan. 1907; d. there, 12 June 1984). Conductor. Studied conducting with Anton Fleischer at the Budapest Conservatory. Joined the Budapest State Opera as a répétiteur in 1927, becoming a conductor in 1930. Worked as a musical assistant at Bayreuth, 1930–31. Guest-conducted at the Vienna State Opera, 1948–50, 1964. Music director of the Hungarian State Symphony from 1952; of the Budapest State Opera, 1957–74; of the Budapest Symphony, 1960–68; of the Danish Radio Symphony, 1966–68. U.S. debut in 1962; toured the U.S., 1972; Japan and Australia, 1974. Considered one of his generation's outstanding interpreters of Bartók and Kodály.

Ferguson, Howard (b. Belfast, 21 Oct. 1908). Composer. He was educated at Westminster School and (from 1925) at the Royal College of Music, meanwhile studying piano privately with Harold Samuel. During the 1940s he concertized and helped Myra Hess organize the "Lunchtime Concerts" at the London National Gallery. From 1948 to 1963 he taught composition at the Royal College. In 1959, having composed only a handful of works, he decided to stop composing; from that time he devoted himself to editing and writing about music. Among his compositions are choral works (*Amore langueo,* tenor, chorus, orchestra, 1955–56; *The Dream of the Rood,* tenor, chorus, orchestra, 1958–59); orchestral works (*Partita,* 1935–36; *Chaunteclee*r, ballet, 1948; Concerto, piano, strings, 1950–51; *Overture for an Occasion,* 1952–53); piano music; songs. He edited several music anthologies, including *Style and Interpretation,* 4 vols. (London, 1963–71); *W. Croft: Complete Harpsichord Works,* 2 vols. (London, 1974).

Ferguson, Maynard (b. Verdun, Canada, 4 May 1928). Jazz trumpeter and bandleader. He joined the big bands of Boyd Raeburn, Charlie Barnet, Jimmy Dorsey, and, in 1950–53, Stan Kenton. After working as a studio musician in California he led bands from 1956, recording the album *A Message from Newport* (1958). His band turned toward rock during his years in England (ca. 1967–71) and later, in the U.S., toward disco; its biggest hit was "Gonna Fly Now" (1978), the theme song of the film *Rocky.* From the mid-1980s he led a 10-piece band, and then a combo. Known for his extraordinary control of the trumpet's highest register.

Fernández Caballero, Manuel (b. Murcia, 14 Mar. 1835; d. Madrid, 20 or 26 Feb. 1906). Composer. Musically precocious; 1850–53, studied at the Madrid Conservatory (under Albéniz, Eslava), also working as orchestral violinist at the Teatro real; from 1853, conducted theater orchestras, also beginning to compose zarzuelas and other theater music. From 1864 to 1870, he conducted at a Cuban zarzuela theater. Returning to Madrid, he became a prolific zarzuela composer; some were very popular (including the 3-act *El salto del pasiego,* 1878, and many in *género chico: La viejecita,* 1897; *Gigantes y cabuzados,* 1898). Also wrote much sacred music. From 1882, conductor of concerts of the Unión artístico-musical.

Ferneyhough, Brian (b. Coventry, 16 Jan. 1943). Composer. After initial study at the Birmingham School of Music (from 1961), he studied composition with Lennox Berkeley and conducting with Maurice Miles at the Royal Academy of Music. With a Mendelssohn Prize (1968) he studied for a year in Amsterdam under Ton de Leeuw; later he also took instruction with Klaus Huber in Basel (1969–71). He has taught at the Hochschule in Freiburg, Germany (from 1971), at the Darmstadt summer courses (1976, 1978, 1980), and at the Univ. of California at San Diego (from 1985). His music employs the total serialism and dense textures common to Boulez; more recent music shows the influence of Stockhausen and other Darmstadt figures. Choral/orchestral works: *Missa brevis,* 12 voices (1971); *Transit,* 6 voices, chamber orchestra (1972–75); *La Terre est un homme* (1976–79); chamber works, including 3 string quartets; Sonata for Two Pianos (1966); *Carceri d'invenzione I–III,* various chamber ensembles (1982, 1984, 1986); *Mnemosyne* (bass flute, tape, 1986).

Ferrabosco, Alfonso (1) (b. Bologna, bapt. 18 Jan. 1543; d. there, 12 Aug. 1588). Composer. By 1562 was in England at the court of Queen Elizabeth I, where he served in the 1560s and 1570s, with frequent and often extended interruptions for professional and personal visits to Rome, Paris, and Bologna; from no later than 1582 (perhaps as early as 1578) until his death, was in Turin at the court of the Duke of Savoy. His extant works include nearly 80 sacred pieces, mostly motets and Lamentations; over 100 madrigals, the majority settings of somber texts in Italian; and an important body of solo lute music, which has sometimes been erroneously attributed to his son Alfonso (2).

Bibl.: Richard Charteris, *Alfonso Ferrabosco the Elder (1543–1588): A Thematic Catalogue of His Music with a Biographical Calendar* (New York, 1984).

Ferrabosco, Alfonso (2) (b. Greenwich?, before 1578; d. there, buried 11 Mar. 1628). Composer. Son of Alfonso Ferrabosco (1), born and employed until his death in England. From 1592 he was associated with the royal court as a musician and teacher. Between 1605 and 1622 several court masques by Ben Jonson with Ferrabosco's music were produced at Whitehall or Greenwich. His other compositions include about 15 Latin motets; some English anthems; songs and lute songs; short settings for 4 voices of light Italian verse; a quantity of music for viol consort, including fantasias, *In nomine*s, and dances; and nearly 70 technically demanding lessons (single pieces or pairs of dances) for lyra viol.

Ferrabosco, Domenico Maria (b. Bologna, 14 Feb. 1513; d. there, Feb. 1574). Composer. Father of Alfonso Ferrabosco (1). Singer and later *maestro di cappella* at San Petronio; *magister puerorum* at the Cappella Giulia in Rome in 1546 and a singer in the papal chapel, 1551–55. His most important compositions are Italian madrigals, most for 4, some for 5 voices, published between 1542 and 1600.

Ferrari, Benedetto (b. Reggio Emilia, 1597–1604; d. Modena, 22 Oct. 1681). Composer and librettist. Studied in Rome, 1617–18; worked at Parma, 1619–23, and perhaps at Modena sometime between 1623 and 1637. Produced music and libretti in Venice and Bologna, 1637–44; his *Andromeda,* with music by Manelli, was the first Venetian opera performed in a public theater (1637). Went to Vienna in 1651; upon returning to Modena in 1653 he was appointed court choirmaster. His post was eliminated in 1662 but reinstated in 1674, after which he served until his death. Many accounts mention his virtuosity on the theorbo. None of his operatic music survives; extant works include libretti, an oratorio, and 3 books of monodies.

Ferrari, Luc (b. Paris, 5 Feb. 1929). Composer. He studied with Cortot, Honegger, and Messiaen (1951–54); taught in Cologne (1964–66) and Montreal (1966–67, 1969). His early works were atonal; in 1958 he joined the Groupe de recherches musicales at French Radio; employed aleatory principles (*Spontanés,* 1962, requires collective improvisation from 8 to 11 instrumentalists). His works include stage, film, and radio music; orchestral (*Symphonie inachevée,* 1963–66), chamber, and piano music; multimedia pieces (*Allo, ici la terre,* 1972); choral works; and electronic music for tape alone or with live performers (*Musique socialiste?,* harpsichord and tape, 1972).

Ferras, Christian (b. Le Touquet, 14 June 1933; d. Paris, 15 Sept. 1982). Violinist. Studied violin with his father, 1940–41; with Charles Bistesi at the Conservatoire de Nice, 1941–44 (first prize in violin, 1944); with René Benedetti at the Conservatoire de Paris, 1944–46 (first prize in violin, 1946); with Georges Enescu privately, 1949. Public debut in 1942 playing with an orchestra in Nice. He recorded the complete Beethoven violin sonatas, 1960; much of the standard concerto literature with von Karajan after 1964. Introduced numerous works, including Honegger's *Solo Sonata* (1948). He owned two Stradivarius violins: the Président (1721) and the Minaloto (1728).

Ferretti, Giovanni (b. ca. 1540; d. after 1609). Composer. From 1575 until 1603, *maestro di cappella* at various Italian churches, beginning with Ancona Cathedral; resident in Rome by 1609. His most important works are *napolitane,* 5 books for 5 voices and 2 books for 6 voices; many were widely reprinted and exerted considerable influence, as, for instance, on the works of Thomas Morley. Also extant are a Mass and a number of other sacred compositions.

Ferrier, Kathleen (b. Higher Walton, 22 Apr. 1912; d. London, 8 Oct. 1953). Contralto. Originally a pianist; while accompanying vocalists at a competition in 1931 she decided she "could make nicer noises than those." Studied voice with Thomas Duerden of St. John's Parish; with J. H. Hutchinson and Roy Henderson in London. Sang with the Bach Choir of London during World War II. Created Lucretia in Britten's *The Rape of Lucretia* for her opera debut at Glyndebourne in 1946. Sang Gluck's Orpheus at Glyndebourne, 1946, and at Covent Garden, 1953. Soloist in Mahler's *Das Lied von der Erde* under Bruno Walter at the Edinburgh Festival, 1947, and at Salzburg, 1949. For her voice Britten wrote the alto part of his *Second Canticle;* Bliss wrote *The Enchantress.* Her career was cut short by cancer.

Festa, Costanzo (b. ca. 1490; d. Rome, 10 Apr. 1545). Composer. A few years at the French royal court may have preceded his entry into the papal choir in 1517, where he remained for the rest of his life. Both Italian and French writers of the 16th century praise his works, which were printed and reprinted until as late as 1596; many were included in manuscript anthologies made throughout Europe. The sacred works hold a prominent position in manuscripts of the Vatican Library. He wrote several Masses and Mass movements, as well as many motets and vesper hymns and a few other sacred compositions. His numerous madrigals are among the first of this genre and include the earliest pieces so titled. He has been called the first native Italian madrigalist.

Bibl.: *Opera omnia, CMM* 25 (1962–77). David Crawford, "A Review of Festa's Biography," *JAMS* 28 (1975): 102. James Haar and Ian Fenlon, "Fonti e cronologia dei madrigali di Costanzo Festa," *RIM* 13 (1978): 212–42.

Festing, Michael Christian (d. London, 24 July 1772). Violinist and composer. Studied with Richard Jones and Geminiani; his own pupils included Thomas Arne. First played publicly in 1724; first published works appeared in 1730; named Master of the King's Musick in 1735. He was active in several musical societies, playing in subscription concerts and garden performances, and was cofounder of the charitable Society of Musicians. His works include violin solos and concertos, cantatas, and songs.

Fétis, François-Joseph (b. Mons, near Liège, 25 Mar. 1784; d. Brussels, 26 Mar. 1871). Writer and teacher. From a family of musicians; student at the Paris Conservatory from 1800 (second prize in composition, 1807); 1806, married a rich woman, allowing him to pursue historical studies and a revision of Gregorian chant (a 30-year project); 1811, lost this fortune and became a music teacher in the provinces. In 1818 he returned to Paris, establishing himself as composer (6 opéras comiques, 1820–32), teacher (1821, teacher of counterpoint and fugue at the Conservatory; librarian there, 1826–30) and journalistic critic, also founding and editing the *Revue musicale* (1827–33). From 1833 he was director of the new Brussels Conservatory; also music director to King Leopold I. He published many didactic, critical, and historical writings, most important the encyclopedic *Biographie universelle des musiciens et bibliographie générale de musique* (Brussels, 1835–44; 2nd ed., 1860–65; R: 1963).

Bibl.: R. Wangermée, *François-Joseph Fétis, musicologue et compositeur* (Brussels, 1951). B. Huys et al., *François-Joseph Fétis et la vie musicale de son temps* (Brussels, 1972).

Feuermann, Emanuel (b. Kolomea, Galicia [now Ukraine], 22 Nov. 1902; d. New York, 25 May 1942). Cellist. His family moved to Vienna in 1908; debut there in 1913. Studied with his father, then with Friedrich Buxbaum and Anton Walter. Further studies with Julius Klengel in Leipzig, 1917–19, led to his appointment to the faculty of the Gürzenich Conservatory in Cologne in 1919; of the Berlin Hochschule in 1929. Returned to Vienna when Hitler came to power in 1933; moved to the U.S. with the annexation of Austria in 1938. U.S. debut 6 Dec. 1934 with the Chicago Symphony. Taught at the Curtis Institute, 1941–42. Formed famous trios with Szymon Goldberg and Paul Hindemith, with Artur Schnabel and Bronisław Huberman, and with Artur Rubinstein and Jascha Heifetz.

Févin, Antoine de (b. Arras?, ca. 1470; d. Blois, late 1511 or early 1512). Composer. Associated with the French royal court from no later than 1507. Various written documents (including mentions by Glarean and Rabelais) and editions of his works by Petrucci and Antico attest to his fame among his contemporaries. Surviving compositions include a number of Masses and motets and a few other sacred pieces, plus some 3-voice French chansons (usually based on a monophonic popular melody).

Bibl.: Howard Mayer Brown, ed., *Theatrical Chansons of the Fifteenth and Early Sixteenth Centuries* (Cambridge, Mass., 1963). Edward H. Clinkscale, "The Complete Works of Antoine de Févin," (diss., New York Univ., 1965).

Fiala, Joseph (b. Lochovice, Bohemia, 3 Feb. 1748?; d. Donaueschingen, 31 July 1816). Composer, oboist, gambist, and cellist. Born into the service of Countess Netolická, he studied oboe and cello in Prague and in Lochovice. Later he served at Prince Kraft Ernst's court at Oettingen-Wallerstein (1774–77) and at the Munich court of Maximilian Joseph (1777–78); at the latter he encountered the Mozarts, father and son, and became a lifelong friend of the family. In 1778 W. A. Mozart secured Fiala a position in the orchestra at Salzburg, and apparently again in 1785 in Vienna, where Fiala received a post in Prince Esterházy's regiment. After a period of service in the court at St. Petersburg (1786–90?), he concertized in Berlin and Breslau for Friedrich Wilhelm II of Prussia. He spent his last years at the court of Prince Fürstenberg in Donaueschingen, where he composed much music for wind band. Works include a *Missa solemnis,* symphonies, a *sinfonia concertante,* at least 12 string quartets (6 quartets op. 1, publ. 1777; 3 quartets op. 3, 1785), trios, duos, works for keyboard.

Fibich, Zdeněk [Zdenko] **(Antonín Václav)** (b. Všebořice, Bohemia, 21 Dec. 1850; d. Prague, 15 Oct. 1900). Composer. From a family of foresters, but his mother was an educated Viennese who gave him piano lessons; attended schools in Vienna (1859–63) and Prague (1863–65), where in 1864–65 he also studied at Kolešovsky's music school; composed much from 1862, beginning to publish in 1865; 1865–67, studied at Leipzig (Moscheles, Richter, Jadassohn); 1868–69, 8 months in Paris; 1869–70, studied with the conductor Vincenz Lachner, Mannheim; then lived with his parents in Žáky (1870–71) and Prague (1871–73), composing his first extant opera, *Bukovín* (Prague, 1874). In 1873 he married and became a choral director in Vilnius; 1874, returned to Prague, where his wife died (twin children died in infancy); 1875, married her sister, a leading contralto, by whom he had a son; 1875–78, assistant conductor and chorusmaster, Provisional Theater; 1878–81, choirmaster, Russian Orthodox Church; then a private composer and teacher until 1899–1900, when he was dramaturg at the National Theater. In the 1890s he formed a passionate liaison with his pupil Anežka Schulzová, chronicled in a musical "diary" of 376 piano pieces, published as opp. 41, 44, 47, 57 (including the much-anthologized *Poème* op. 41, no. 6); she was the librettist of his last 3 operas (*Hedy,* 1896; *Šárka,* 1897, perhaps his most successful; *Pád Arkuna,* 1898–1900); he left his wife in 1897.

Works: 7 operas; concert and theatrical melodramas; incidental music; 3 symphonies; much program music, including concert overtures, symphonic poems; chamber works; much piano music; choral works. He destroyed most of his church music and about half of his 200 songs.

Bibl.: *Souborné vydáni* [Complete Works] (Prague, 1950–67). Gerald Abraham, "An Erotic Diary for Piano," in *Slavonic and Romantic Music* (New York, 1968). Id., "The Operas of Zdeněk Fibich," *19th Century Music* 9 (1985): 136–44.

Ficher, Jacobo (b. Odessa, Russia, 15 Jan. 1896; d. Buenos Aires, 9 Sept. 1978). Composer and violinist. After early training on the violin he entered the Imperial Conservatory, St. Petersburg, in 1912, remaining until 1917; in 1919 he became first violinist for the State Opera there. After emigrating to Argentina in 1923, he was important in the founding of the composers' society Grupo renovación and was a charter member of the Argentinian Composers' League, established in 1947. He was also active as a teacher at the Univ. of La Plata and at the Municipal and National Conservatories in Buenos Aires. Compositions include symphonies, tone poems, and other orchestral music; chamber operas and ballets; chamber and piano music; and vocal works.

Bibl.: *Composers of the Americas* 2 (Washington, D.C., 1956): 60–68 [includes works list].

Fiedler, Arthur (b. Boston, 17 Dec. 1894; d. Brookline, Mass., 10 July 1979). Conductor. His father, Emanuel, was a founding member of the Kneisel Quartet and also played among the first violins of the Boston Symphony. Arthur studied violin with his father, then with Willy Hess at the Royal Academy in Berlin, 1911–14. Joined the second violins of the Boston Symphony, 1915; after service in the army, 1918, he rejoined the orchestra as a violist. Founding conductor of the Boston Sinfonietta, 1924; as the Fiedler Sinfonietta it recorded Corelli, Handel, Mozart, and Hindemith's *Der Schwanendreher* with the composer as soloist. Also active as a choral conductor with the Cecilia Society and the Boston Male Choir. Organized a season of open-air concerts in 1929 with such popu-

Arthur Fiedler.

lar success that he was appointed music director of the Boston Pops in 1930. His skillful amalgamation of light classics, American popular music, and commissioned works (notably by Leroy Anderson) became the model for other musical organizations. After their recording of Jacob Gade's *Jalousie,* the first orchestral record to sell over one million copies, Fiedler and the Boston Pops assumed the status of a national institution. Also led annual concerts with the San Francisco Symphony, 1951–78.

Field, John (b. Dublin, 16 or 26 July 1782; d. Moscow, 23 Jan. 1837). Composer and pianist. From a family of musicians; studied with Tommaso Giordani from age 9; 1793, the family moved to London and Field apprenticed for 7 years to Clementi; from 1798 began to make a name in London concert life; 1799, played his first concerto; 1801, published 3 sonatas op. 1, dedicated to Clementi; also taught (pupils included Charles Neate). In 1802 Clementi took him to Paris and Vienna, intending to leave him there to study with Albrechtsberger, but Field insisted on accompanying him to St. Petersburg, where their relations deteriorated, Clementi treating Field harshly and earning his hatred; 1803, Clementi left Russia and Field remained, soon creating a vogue as pianist and teacher; made much money but lived prodigally; composed sporadically, usually to provide material for upcoming concerts. A penchant for drink advanced to alcoholism; he lived much of 1807–12 and all of 1821–31 in Moscow; 1810, married a Frenchwoman, his pupil (and probably his mistress) since 1807; separated in 1821; illegitimate son Leon Charpentier (b. 1815) became a Russian opera singer. In 1815 Field contracted with Breitkopf and Härtel to publish his music, making it known in the West, but virtually stopped composing in about 1822; illness was a principal reason for his return in 1831 to London, where he had surgery, gave concerts, and taught, also resuming composition.

Field's playing had become legendary in western Europe, but by the time he was heard there again, it was somewhat outmoded by more advanced virtuosos; in 1833, toured France, Switzerland, and Italy, where he collapsed, spending 9 months in a Naples hospital; 1835, returned to Russia, but never completely recovered. Especially remembered for his piano nocturnes, whose style is a compositional equivalent of his elegant, expressive playing. Also composed piano rondos, variations, dances, etudes; 7 concertos; some duets, chamber works.

Bibl.: Cecil Hopkinson, *A Bibliographical Thematic Catalogue of the Works of John Field* (London, 1961). Patrick Piggott, *The Life and Music of John Field, 1782–1837* (London, 1973).

Fillmore, (James) Henry (Jr.) (b. Cincinnati, 3 Dec. 1881; d. Miami, 7 Dec. 1956). Composer and conductor. He came from a family of musicians active in 19th-century Ohio; his father (1849–1936) headed the family publishing house (founded in the 1870s), which was primarily devoted to religious music until Henry's successful efforts to convert it to a publisher of band music. He had left home as a youth to play with a circus band and later became widely known as a band conductor. When he retired to Miami in 1938 he encouraged the growth of school bands and served as president of the American Bandmasters Association (1941–46). He wrote over 250 pieces and arranged another 774 works under his own name and 7 pseudonyms.

Fils [Filtz, Filz], **(Johann) Anton** (b. Eichstätt, bapt. 22 Sept. 1733; d. Mannheim, buried 14 Mar. 1760). Composer and cellist. His father was apparently a cellist at Eichstätt and probably was his first music instructor. In 1754 Johann gained a position as second cellist in Germany's finest orchestra, that at Mannheim; there he studied further (probably counterpoint and harmony) with Johann Stamitz. He remained at Mannheim until his death at age 26. Most of his published works appeared after his death, when his music experienced a vogue in Paris and elsewhere. He composed more than 40 symphonies (*6 simphonies à 4 parties* op. 1); Masses; concertos; trio sonatas.

Bibl.: Ed. in *DTB* vols. 4, 13, and 27; thematic catalog of his works in vol. 28. Walter Lebermann, "Biographische Notizen über J. A. Fils, Johann Anton Stamitz, Carl Joseph und Johann Baptist Toeschi," *Mf* 19 (1966): 40–41.

Finck, Heinrich (b. Bamberg?, 1444 or 1445; d. Vienna, 9 June 1527). Composer. From boyhood until perhaps as late as 1510 he lived chiefly in Poland, often serving in the royal court. After 1510 his places of residence included Stuttgart, Salzburg, and Vienna. Of his sizable output relatively little survives; at least portions of over 100 sacred and secular pieces are extant. Many Masses and motets are missing parts. In contrast, most of his hymns and songs written after 1500 have survived intact. These include nearly 30 German Tenorlieder.

Bibl.: *Ausgewählte Werke, EDM* ser. 1. Lothar Hermann-Berbrecht, *Henricus Finck, musicus excellentissimus (1445–1527)* (Cologne, 1982).

Finck, Hermann (b. Pirna, 21 Mar. 1527; d. Wittenberg, 29 Dec. 1558). Theorist and composer. Great-nephew of Heinrich Finck; lived in Wittenberg from 1545; composed mostly motets, several for important weddings. His *Practica musica* (Wittenberg, 1556; 2nd ed. enl., 1556; R: 1969) is his major work; this large theoretical treatise on the rudiments of music is illustrated with nearly 100 compositions by some of the best modern composers and includes discussion of certain historical topics and of contemporary performance practice.

Fine, Irving (Gifford) (b. Boston, 3 Dec. 1914; d. there, 23 Aug. 1962). Composer and conductor. Studied piano as a youth; attended Harvard, where he studied with E. B. Hill and Piston (M.M., 1938); studied composition with Boulanger in Cambridge, Mass., and Paris and conducting with Koussevitzky at the Berkshire Music Center. He taught at Harvard (1939–50) and then at Brandeis; directed the Salzburg Music Seminar for American Studies (summer 1950). He wrote criticism for *Modern Music, Notes, Musical America,* and the *New York Times.* Early works were in a neoclassical mold derived from Stravinsky and Hindemith; with the String Quartet of 1952 he began to employ the twelve-tone procedures that he regarded as secondary to matters of tonality, harmonic rhythm, and form. Works include 5 orchestral works (Symphony, 1962); a violin sonata (1946) and other chamber music; choral music; songs (*Childhood Fables for Grown-ups,* medium voice and piano, 1954–55).

Fine, Vivian (b. Chicago, 28 Sept. 1913). Composer and pianist. Studied piano with Djane Lavoie-Herz (a pupil of Scriabin); studied composition with Ruth Crawford (1925–28) and Adolf Weidig (1930–31). She had dropped out of high school in order to concentrate on composition at age 16, and received much early encouragement and important performances in New York, Chicago, and Germany; Cowell had introduced her work in Chicago (1929–31), and Copland was an important supporter after her arrival in New York (1931), where she launched a career as a professional pianist; she continued her studies at the Dalcroze School (1935–36) and with Sessions (composition, 1934–42), Szell (orchestration, 1942), and Whiteside (piano, 1937–45). She taught at New York Univ. (1945–48), Juilliard (1948), SUNY–Potsdam (1951), the Connecticut College School of Dance (1963–64), and then at Bennington; she also composed and accompanied for various dance groups and co-founded the American Composers' Alliance. Commissions include *Alcestis* (for Martha Graham, 1960) and *Drama for Orchestra* (San Francisco Symphony, 1982). Although she employed serial techniques to produce a dissonant counterpoint, after 1937 her style became more diatonic. Works include ballets; an opera (*The Women in the Garden,* San Francisco, 1978); other works for orchestra; chamber music; piano works (*Momenti,* 1978); choral music (*Paean,* narrator, women's chorus, and brass ensemble, 1969); works for solo voice(s) and orchestra or ensemble; songs.

Finger, Gottfried (b. Olomouc, Moravia, ca. 1660; buried Mannheim, 31 Aug. 1730). Composer. Went to London in 1685 as part of the Catholic chapel of James II; the chapel was dissolved in 1688, but he stayed in England, writing masque music as well as an *Ode for St. Cecilia's Day,* 1693. After a composing contest in 1700, in which he was apparently slighted, he left England, first serving Queen Sophie-Charlotte of Prussia, then Duke Karl Philipp of Pfalz-Neuburg, whom he eventually followed to Innsbruck, Düsseldorf, Heidelberg, and Mannheim, where he last appears in the Hofkapelle register in 1723. Aside from his stage and vocal music, he published many chamber suites and sonatas.

Finke, Fidelio Friedrich (Fritz) (b. Josefstal, near Gablonz, Bohemia, 22 Oct. 1891; d. Dresden, 12 June 1968). Composer. He came from a family of musicians who taught him before he entered the Prague Conservatory to study with Novák (1908–11). He taught piano and theory at the conservatory (1915–26), then taught composition at the German Academy in Prague (1927–45); directed the Academy for Music and Theater in Dresden (1946–51); professor of composition at the Leipzig Musikhochschule (1951–59). Early works drew on Czech folk music and German Romanticism; in the mid-1920s he wrote expressionist pieces indebted to Schoenberg (*Der zerstörte Tasso,* soprano and string quartet, uses *Sprechstimme*); after 1927 he wrote neoclassical (or neo-Baroque) works. Compositions include 4 operas; 8 suites for orchestra (no. 8 is for 5 winds, 2 pianos, and strings, 1961); chamber, keyboard, choral, and solo vocal music (some of the keyboard and vocal music draws on folk songs).

Finney, Ross Lee (b. Wells, Minn., 23 Dec. 1906). Composer. As a youth he studied piano and cello; he studied composition with Donald Ferguson at the Univ. of Minnesota and at Carleton College, where he also taught cello and piano; studied with Boulanger (1927–28), Berg (1931–32), Sessions (1935), and Malipiero (1937). He supported his studies in part by playing in a jazz band. He taught at Smith (1929–48) and then became professor and composer-in-residence at the Univ. of Michigan (1949–73), where his students included Albright and Crumb. He won the Pulitzer Prize for his First String Quartet (1935).

His study with Berg came to fruition only after 1950, when he began to combine serial and tonal approaches: in his Third Symphony (written in 1960, when he was composer-in-residence at the American Academy in Rome) the row was constructed and manipulated to encourage tonal relations and to avoid excessive dissonance. In the Second Symphony (1959) both durations and pitches were derived from serial procedures.

Some earlier works exploit American themes: *Hymn, Fuguing, and Holiday* (hommage to Billings, orchestra, 1943); *Poor Richard* (B. Franklin, song cycle with string quartet, 1946). In the 1950s and 1960s Finney sang American folk songs with guitar in Greece, Germany, Poland, Austria, and England for the U.S. Information Agency. Orchestral compositions from the 1970s combined aleatoric procedures with quotes from folk songs (*Summer in Valley City,* 1969; *Landscapes Remembered,* 1971).

Works: dramatic works including an opera (*Weep Torn Land,* Finney, 1984) and 2 ballets; a setting of Chaucer's *Nun's Priest's Tale;* 4 symphonies, 2 piano concertos, 2 violin concertos, and other orchestral works; 8 string quartets and other chamber music; piano works; choral music (the trilogy *Earthrise,* soloists, chorus, orchestra, and tape, 1962–78); song cycles.

Bibl.: Frederic Goossen, ed., *Thinking about Music: The Collected Writings of Ross Lee Finney* (Tuscaloosa, Ala., 1991). Ross Lee Finney, *Profile of a Lifetime: A Musical Autobiography* (New York, 1992).

Finnissy, Michael (b. London, 17 Mar. 1946). Composer. Among his teachers at the Royal College of Music were Bernard Stevens and Humphrey Searle; later he studied privately in Rome with Roman Vlad. From 1968 he taught at the London School of Contemporary Dance, creating a music department there the following year. His avant-garde music often employs aleatory and dense counterpoint. Works include stage music (*Mysteries,* 8 parts to biblical texts, 1972–79; *Orfeo,* soloists, instrumental ensemble, 1974–75; *Medea,* 1973–76; *The Undivine Comedy,* opera with 5 singers and small ensemble, 1988); vocal music (*World,* soloists, chorus, orchestra, 1968–72; *Cipriano,* 10 voices, 1975; *Tom Fool's Wooing,* 14 voices, 1975–78; *Jeanne d'arc,* soloists, cello, chamber orchestra, 1967–71; *Goro,* tenor, chamber ensemble, 1978); instrumental music (5 concertos for piano and chamber ensemble, 1975–80; *Offshore,* 1975–76; *Alongside,* chamber orchestra, 1979; *Alice,* double bass, 1970–75; *Sea and Sky,* orchestra, 1980; *Red Earth,* orchestra, 1988); piano music (*Grainger,* 1979; *Boogie-Woogie,* 1980; *Nancarrow,* 1980).

Finzi, Gerald (b. London, 14 July 1901; d. Oxford, 27 Sept. 1956). Composer. He studied music privately with Ernest Farrar (1915–16), Edward Bairstow (1917–22), and R. O. Morris (1925). Settling in London, he began teaching at the Royal Academy of Music in 1930; during the 1930s he composed his first important works, including the Interlude in A minor op. 21 (1933–36) and *Seven Part Songs* for chorus op. 17 (1934–37). He moved first to Aldbourne, Wiltshire, then to Ashmansworth. In 1939 he formed a chamber orchestra, the Newbury String Players, for which he composed a number of works. During the war he was employed by the Ministry of War Transport; after 1945 he immersed himself in composition and in the creation of scholarly editions of the works of Boyce (*MB* 13 [1957]) and others. In 1951 his leukemia was diagnosed; during his last five years he continued to compose (Cello Concerto op. 40, 1951–55), and he also revised many of his earlier works. Other principal compositions include orchestral works: Introit in F major, violin and orchestra (1925; rev. 1935 and 1942); Clarinet Concerto in C minor (1948–49); *Grand Fantasia* (1928); Toccata in D minor, piano and orchestra (1953); *Romance,* strings (1928); choral works: *For St. Cecilia,* tenor, chorus, orchestra, op. 30 (1947); *Magnificat* op. 36 (1952); *White-Flowering Days* op. 37 (1953); solo vocal: *Dies natalis,* 5 songs, soprano or tenor, string orchestra, op. 8 (1926–39); *Two Sonnets,* soprano or tenor, chamber orchestra, op. 12 (ca. 1928); more than 60 songs with piano; chamber music.

Firkušný, Rudolf (b. Napajedla, 11 Feb. 1912; d. Straatsburg, N.Y., 19 July 1994). Pianist. Studied music with Leos Janáček from 1917; made his public debut in Prague in 1922 while studying piano with Růzena Kurzová at the Brno Conservatory, 1920–27. He studied piano with Vilém Kurz (1927–31), composition with Josef Suk (1929–30). After the premiere of his Piano Concerto in 1930 he toured Europe. Studied with Artur Schnabel in Tremezzo (1932) and again in New York (1938). U.S. debut 13 Jan. 1938 in New York while on tour. Settled in the U.S. after the German annexation of Czechloslovakia, September 1938. Played premieres of piano concertos by Menotti (Boston, 1945), Hanson (Boston, 1948), and Martinů (3rd in Dallas, 1949; 4th in New York, 1956). Concertized internationally after World War II, usually including Czech music in his programs. Taught at the Juilliard School from 1965. Composed chamber music, song cycles, piano pieces.

Firsova, Elena Olegovna (b. Leningrad, 21 Mar. 1950). Composer. Studied with Alexander Pirumov (composition) and Yuri Kholopov (analysis) at the Moscow Conservatory, 1970–75; also credits Edison Denisov as a significant influence on her compositional development. Her works include symphonic scores; chamber concertos for flute (1978), cello (1982), piano (1985), horn (1987); 2 violin concertos (1976, 1983); chamber music (*Misterioso,* string quartet, 1980). The poetry of Mandelstam has inspired many of her vocal scores: the cantatas *Tristia* (1979), *The Stone* (1983), *Earthly Life* (1984), and *Forest Walks* for soprano and ensemble (1987).

Fischer, Carl (b. Buttstädt, Thuringia, 7 Dec. 1849; d. New York, 14 Feb. 1923). Publisher. Studied music in Gotha; then partnered with a brother to make musical instruments. In 1872 he emigrated to New York, opening a musical instrument shop; also started to provide music for bands, schools, and other such purposes through importing and copying and then through his own publishing house, which became one of the most important in these fields and was continued by his son Walter (1882–1946) and by Walter's son-in-law Frank Connor (1903–77).

Fischer, Edwin (b. Basel, 6 Oct. 1886; d. Zurich, 24 Jan. 1960). Pianist and conductor. Studied piano with Hans Huber at the Basel Conservatory, 1896–1904; with Martin Krause at the Stern Conservatory in Berlin, 1904–5. Taught piano there, 1905–14; at the Berlin Hochschule from 1931. As a pianist he played new music (Scriabin, Reger, Schoenberg) through 1924, but was most influential for the depth and purity of his interpretations of Bach and Mozart; his was the first integral recording of Well-Tempered Clavier. As a conductor he explored neglected 18th-century pieces with the Lübeck Musikverein, 1926–28; with the Munich Bachverein, 1928–31; and from 1932 with his own chamber orchestras in Berlin and Basel. Moved to Hertenstein on Lake Lucerne, 1942; founded a famous trio with Georg Kulenkampff (later Wolfgang Schneiderhan) and Enrico Mainardi. Author of books on Bach and Beethoven. Composer of Sonatina in C for piano (1916/38), *Das Donnerwetter* for chamber orchestra (1938, an arrangement of Mozart's contradance K. 534), songs.

Fischer, Irwin (b. Iowa City, Iowa, 5 July 1903; d. Wilmette, Ill., 7 May 1977). Composer, conductor, and organist. After an arts degree at the Univ. of Chicago, he studied at the American Conservatory with Robyn (piano), Middelschulte (organ), and Weidig (composition); then with Boulanger and Kodály, and at the Salzburg Mozarteum. He taught at the American Conservatory from 1928, becoming dean in 1974; conducted orchestras and played the organ in Chicago. He wrote in a conservative style, but explored polytonality in the 1930s and used serial procedures in his Piano Sonata (1960). He completed some 18 orchestral works (*Hungarian Set,* 1938; *Overture on an Exuberant Tone Row,* 1964; several concertos); string quartets and other chamber music; piano and organ works (including chorale preludes and transcriptions); choral and vocal music.

Fischer, Johann Caspar Ferdinand (b. ca. 1665–70; d. Rastatt, 27 Mar. 1746). Composer. Details of early life unknown; first clear documentation of him is the title page of his *Le journal du printems* (1695), listing him as Hofkapellmeister to Margrave Ludwig Wilhelm of Baden, in residence at Schlackenwerth at this time. The court moved to Rastatt in 1716, Fischer presumably accompanying it. In addition to providing sacred music for the court chapel, he wrote music (now lost) for a singspiel for the wedding of the Margrave's son, Ludwig Georg, in 1721. It seems that Fischer remained linked to the Baden court until his death. He led in establishing the French style of Lully in Germany, both for 5-part string ensemble *(Le journal)* and in the keyboard idiom (*Les pièces de clavessin,* 1696; *Musicalischer Parnassus,* 1738). A cycle of preludes and fugues in various keys (*Ariadne,* 1702) prefigures J. S. Bach's work.

Editions: *Sämtliche Werke für Klavier und Orgel,* ed. E. von Werra (Leipzig, 1901; R: 1965). Rudolf Walter, *Johann Caspar Ferdinand Fischer, Hofkapellmeister der Markgrafen von Baden* (Frankfurt am Main and New York, 1990).

Fischer, Johann Christian (b. Freiburg, 1733; d. London, 29? Apr. 1820). Oboist and composer. He was oboist at the court in Dresden from the early 1760s; in 1764 he was a member of the court orchestra of Frederick the Great. After 1765 he traveled frequently, performing at The Hague (1765), Mannheim and Paris (1766–68), and in London, where from 1768 he performed in the Bach-Abel concerts. In 1780 he married the daughter of the artist Gainsborough, who painted a striking portrait of the composer. Also in 1780 Fischer became a chamber musician for the queen. Among his compositions are 11 oboe concertos, divertimentos for 2 flutes, and 10 sonatas for flute and continuo. He also authored *The Compleat Tutor for the Hautboy* (London, ca. 1790).

Fischer-Dieskau, Dietrich (b. Berlin, 28 May 1925). Baritone and conductor. Studied with Georg A. Walter privately, 1942–43; with Hermann Weissenborn at the Berlin Musikhochschule, 1943; coached privately by Weissenborn, 1947–59. Public debut, January 1943, in Berlin. Performed regularly as a prisoner of war in Italy, 1945–47. Professional debut in 1947 as soloist in the Brahms *Requiem.* Active in opera from the late 1940s. Sang Schubert's *Winterreise* on the radio in 1947. Eventually recorded much of the lieder repertory, including extensive collections of Schubert, Mendelssohn, Brahms, Schumann, and Wolf; also collections of Loewe, Liszt, Tchaikovsky, Ives. Stage debut as Rodrigo *(Don Carlos)* at the West Berlin Opera, 1948. Sang at Bayreuth from 1954, at the Vienna State Opera from 1957. New York debut in concert, 2 May 1955. Acclaimed Covent Garden debut in 1965 as Mandryka *(Arabella).* Created Mittenhofer in Henze's *Elegie für junge Liebende,* 1961; soloist in the premiere of Britten's *War Requiem,* 1962; created Lear in Aribert Reimann's opera, 1978. Sang first performances of works by Busoni, Blacher, Dallapiccola, Fortner, Krenek, Hermann Reutter, Stravinsky, Tippett, and others. Debut as conductor in 1973 with the English Chamber Orchestra; recordings include symphonies by Schubert, Berlioz, Schumann, Brahms. Retired from performing in 1993. Published *Auf den Spuren der Schubert-Lieder* (1971); *Wagner und Nietzsche* (1974); *Nachklang* (his memoirs, 1987).

Fišer, Luboš (b. Prague, 20 Sept. 1935). Composer. He studied at the Prague Conservatory (1952–56), with Pavel Bořkovec, and at the Prague Academy (1956–60), with Emil Hlobil and then further with Bořkovec. During the 1960s he came to prominence in Prague; the traditional style of the stage musical *The Good Soldier Schweik* (1962) gave way to more experimentalism during the late 1960s. In 1971 he emigrated to the U.S. Works include operas (*Lancelot,* 1959–60); orchestral works (2 symphonies, 1956; 1958–60; *Fifteen Prints after Dürer's Apocalypse,* 1965; *Lament,* 1972); choral works (*Caprichos,* 1967; *Requiem,* 1968; *Lament for the Destruction of the City of Ur,* 1971; *The Rose,* 1977; *Per Vittoria Colonna,* 1979; *Znameni,* 1981); chamber works (string quartet, 1955; *Pietà,* chamber ensemble, 1967); piano music (6 sonatas, 1955–78).

Fisk, Charles Brenton (b. Washington, D.C., 7 Feb. 1925; d. Boston, 16 Dec. 1983). Organ builder. He studied at Harvard and Stanford, then apprenticed to John Swinford and the elder Walter Holtkamp. In 1955 he cofounded the firm of Andover (Methuen, Mass.) with Thomas W. Byers. Sole owner of the firm from 1958, he became the first modern maker in the U.S. to build organs with mechanical key action. The firm was renamed C. B. Fisk (Gloucester, Mass.) in 1961. He built important organs throughout the U.S.

Fisk, Eliot (Hamilton) (b. Philadelphia, 10 Aug. 1954). Guitarist. Studied guitar with Oscar Ghiglia at Aspen, 1970–76; harpsichord with Ralph Kirkpatrick and Albert Fuller at Yale, 1972–77 (M.M.A., 1977). After his professional debut in New York in 1976, he founded the guitar department at Yale in 1977 and taught there until 1982; at Mannes College in New York, 1978–82; at the Cologne Hochschule für Musik from 1982.

Fitelberg, Jerzy (b. Warsaw, 20 May 1903; d. New York, 25 Apr. 1951). Composer. His first music teacher was his father, composer and conductor Gregor Fitelberg (1879–1953). From 1922 to 1926 he studied with Walther Gmeindl and Franz Schreker at the Musikhochschule in Berlin. After six years in Paris (1933–39) he moved to New York in 1940, and he remained in the U.S. until his death. His music contains elements of the neoclassicism of the 1920s and 1930s and also of late Romantic expressiveness. Orchestral works include 3 suites (1925, 1928, 1930); Concerto for Strings (1930); *Konzertstück* (1937); concertos: 2 for violin (1928, 1935), 2 for piano (1929, 1934), for cello (1931), for clarinet (1948); chamber works (5 string quartets; Sonata for Two Violins and Piano, 1938; *Twelve Studies,* 3 clarinets, 1948); 3 sonatas for piano.

Fitzgerald, Ella (b. Newport News, Va., 25 Apr. 1918). Jazz and popular singer. She sang with Chick Webb's big band (1935), giving it a hit song with her swing version of the nursery rhyme "A-tisket, A-tasket" (1938). After Webb's death she took over the band (1939–41). Thereafter she worked through the 1980s as a soloist in varied settings, accompanied by her trio (whose members included Ray Brown, Hank Jones, and Tommy Flanagan), the all-star cast of Jazz at the Philharmonic (with which she toured from 1948 to the 1970s), big bands, and orchestras. Her work ranges from infectiously cheerful swing, to bop scat singing ("How High the Moon," 1947), to the "song books," definitive versions of American popular songs recorded mainly with studio orchestras, including Nelson Riddle's (*Ella Fitzgerald Sings the George and Ira Gershwin Song Book,* 1959).

Bibl.: Sid Colin, *Ella: The Life and Times of Ella Fitzgerald* (London, 1986).

Fizdale, Robert (b. Chicago, 12 Apr. 1920; d. New York, 6 Dec. 1995). Duo pianist. While studying with Ernest Hutcheson at Juilliard, he met pianist Arthur Gold and formed a duo. Joint debut at the New School for Social Research in 1944 in a path-breaking recital of music by John Cage. Their reputations in the standard repertory were established with a Town Hall recital in 1946. With Gold he made numerous tours of Europe and the Americas before retiring in 1982. The duo commissioned works for 2 keyboards by Barber, Rorem, Dello Joio, and many others.

Flagello, Nicolas (b. New York, 15 Mar. 1928; d. New Rochelle, N.Y., 16 Mar. 1994). Composer, conductor, and pianist. Raised in a musical family of Italian singers (including a brother Ezio, a bass, b. New York, 28 Jan. 1931), composers, and conductors, he studied piano, violin, and oboe from childhood; studied composition with Giannini at the Manhattan School (M.M., 1950); conducting with Mitropolous; and at the Accademia di S. Cecilia (Rome). He was active as a professional accompanist (1947–58) and taught at the Manhattan School (1950–77); conducted and recorded operas in Rome, Salerno, Chicago, and New York. Works include 7 operas (1953–83) and an oratorio; *Concerto sinfonico* (saxophone quartet and orchestra, 1985), the Concerto for Strings (1959), and other orchestral works; *Prisma* (7 horns, 1974), Concertino (piano, brass, timpani, 1963), and other chamber music; choral and vocal music with orchestra or piano (*Contemplazioni,* after Michelangelo, soprano and orchestra, 1964).

Flagg, Josiah (b. Woburn, Mass., 28 May 1737; d. Boston? 1795?). Psalmodist, bandmaster, and engraver. By the 1760s he had settled in Boston, where he was a prominent musical figure. His two compilations of psalm tunes number among the most important tune-book publications before Billings. *A Collection of the Best Psalm-Tunes . . .* (1764) was engraved by Paul Revere; *Sixteen Anthems . . .* was published in 1766 in the wake of the first collection's success. A military band he organized gave a concert in 1769; two years later he put on a concert of works by Handel and J. C. Bach. During the 1770s he moved to Providence, where he apparently served as lieutenant-colonel in the revolutionary army.

Flagstad, Kirsten (Marie) (b. Hamar, Norway, 12 July 1895; d. Oslo, 7 Dec. 1962). Soprano. Daughter of conductor Michael Flagstad and Marie Flagstad-Johnsrud, a répétiteur at the Oslo opera. Studied voice, 1911–18, in Oslo with her mother, Ellen Schytte-Jacobsen, and Albert Westwang; in Stockholm with Gillis Bratt. Debut at the Oslo opera in 1913 as Nuri *(Tiefland).* Sang operetta and opera, 1919–32, with the Mayol Theater and National Theater in Oslo and with the Storn Theater in Göteborg. Toured France in 1921, Finland in 1928. Engaged at Bayreuth in 1933 for two minor roles; returned in 1934 in two major roles, Sieglinde *(Die Walküre)* and Gutrune *(Götterdämmerung).* For the rest of her career she was widely regarded as the foremost Wagnerian soprano of her generation. Debut at the New York Met, 2 Feb. 1935, as Sieglinde; based there, 1935–41. Debut at Covent Carden and the Vienna Staatsoper, 1936. Toured Australia, 1938. Returned to Norway, 1941–45, to be with her husband, who was associated with the Quisling government. Cleared of collaboration charges in 1946, she nevertheless aroused controversy when she returned to the U.S., 1947–48. Based at Covent Garden, 1948–51; gave the first performance of Strauss's *Vier letzte Gesänge,* 1950. Sang Purcell's Dido at the Mermaid Theatre in London, 1951; returned to the Met in 1951; sang Gluck's Alceste there, 1952. Farewell tour, 1955, but continued to record. Director of the Oslo opera, 1958–60.

Flanagan, Tommy (Lee) (b. Detroit, 16 Mar. 1930). Jazz pianist. In Detroit he joined the tenor saxophonist Billy Mitchell's bop quintet (with Thad and Elvin Jones) and Kenny Burrell, with whom he moved to New York in 1956. He worked with Oscar Pettiford, J. J. Johnson (1956–58), Miles Davis (1956–57), and Coleman Hawkins (1960, 1962), and recorded with Sonny Rollins (the album *Saxophone Colossus,* 1956) and John Coltrane (1959). He accompanied Ella Fitzgerald (1956, 1963–65, 1968–78) and Tony Bennett (1966). From 1978 he worked as a soloist, mainly leading trios, as on the album *Super-Session* (1980) with Elvin Jones and Red Mitchell.

Flanagan, William (Jr.) (b. Detroit, 14 Aug. 1923; d. New York, 31 Aug. or 1 Sept. 1969). Composer and critic. He first studied journalism, then turned to music in 1945 at Eastman (under Bernard Rogers and Burrill Phillips); at the Berkshire Music Center (1947–48) he worked under Barber, Honegger, and Copland; in New York he studied with David Diamond. He wrote music criticism for the *New York Herald Tribune* (1957–60), for the *Musical Quarterly,* and for *Stereo Review.* As a composer he focused on small vocal forms, in which he set texts of Melville, Whitman, Stein, and others. Works include 2 operas (*The Ice Age,* incomplete; commissioned by the New York City Opera); 5 orchestral works (*A Concert Ode,* 1951); a string quartet, *Chaconne* (violin and piano, 1948), and other chamber music and piano works; *Chapter from Ecclesiastes* (S. A. T. B., string quartet, 1962) and other choral music; songs and cycles (*The Lady of Tearful Regret,* Albee, soprano, baritone, flute, clarinet, string quartet, and piano; 1959); incidental music.

Flatt, Lester (Raymond) (b. Overton County, Tenn., 28 June 1914; d. Nashville, 11 May 1979). Bluegrass singer and guitarist. After early performances in hillbilly groups, in 1944 he joined Bill Monroe's Bluegrass Boys, where he met banjo player Earl Scruggs. They left in 1948 to form the Foggy Mountain Boys, which became one of the first bluegrass bands to attract popular and rock as well as country audiences. Their versions of "The Ballad of Jed Clampett" (for the television series *The Beverly Hillbillies,* 1962) and Scruggs's "Foggy Mountain Breakdown" (1949) were very popular. After the group separated in 1969, Flatt led a bluegrass band called the Nashville Grass.

Flecha, Mateo (1) (b. Prades, near Tarragona, 1481; d. Poblet, Tarragona, 1553). Composer. Singer, then *maestro de capilla* at Lérida Cathedral until 1525; 1525–43, served in Spanish ducal courts; 1543–48, *maestro de capilla* at the court at Arévalo of the princesses of Spain. He wrote chiefly *ensaladas* (often macaronic).

Flecha, Mateo (2) (b. Prades, near Tarragona, ca. 1530; d. monastery of Portella, Lérida, 20 Feb. 1604). Composer. Nephew of Mateo Flecha (1). Chorister at Arévalo in the court chapel directed by his uncle; from 1552 a Carmelite in Valencia; from 1564 a member of the imperial chapel in Vienna; from 1599 abbot of the (Benedictine) monastery of Portella in Spain. His works include a volume of Italian madrigals (Venice, 1568), 3 *ensaladas* published in 1581 along with those of Mateo Flecha (1), and several sacred pieces.

Fleisher, Leon (b. San Francisco, 23 July 1928). Pianist and conductor. Studied piano from age 4; first public recital, 1935. Studied with Artur Schnabel, 1938–48; professional debut in 1942 playing the Liszt A major Concerto with the San Francisco Symphony. Won the Queen Elisabeth of Belgium Competition in 1952. In the 1960s carpal tunnel syndrome disabled his right hand; his ailment was diagnosed and treated in the early 1980s, but while making several attempts at two-handed performance, he continued to refer to himself as a left-handed pianist. Joined the faculty of the Peabody Conservatory in 1959. Debut as conductor with the New York Chamber Orchestra, 1970. Associate conductor of the Baltimore Symphony, 1973–74; conductor, 1974–78. Director of the Walter W. Naumburg Foundation from 1965. Founding codirector of the Theatre Chamber Players in Washington, D.C., from 1968. Artistic director of the Tanglewood Music Center from 1985. Joined the piano faculty at the Curtis Institute in 1986 and Juilliard in 1993.

Fleming, Robert (b. Prince Albert, Saskatchewan, 12 Nov. 1921; d. Ottawa, 28 Nov. 1976). Composer. He studied at the Royal College of Music in London with Howells (composition) and Arthur Benjamin (piano) from 1937; returned to Saskatoon to teach piano and perform; studied with Willan at the Toronto Conservatory (1941–45). He worked for the National Film Board as a staff composer (1946–58) and musical director (1958–70); in addition he held organ-choirmaster positions for brief periods in Saskatoon, Montreal, and Ottawa. His style was at first heavily influenced by British music and later incorporated Canadian folk song and jazz elements; he remained committed to tonal music throughout his career. His ballet *Shadow on the Prairie* (Winnipeg, 1952) and a song cycle for Maureen Forrester (*The Confession Stone,* 1967) are his best-known works; others include some 50 pieces for orchestra or band (the jazz-influenced *Ballet Introduction,* 1961); chamber music; works for piano or organ; hymns, carols, and Anglican service music; some 50 songs.

Flentrop, Dirk (Andries) (b. Zaandam, Netherlands, 1 May 1910). Organ builder. Trained as an organist, in 1940 he took over the Flentrop firm (Zaandam), which had been founded by his father in 1903. From the 1930s he and his father restored 17th- and 18th-century organs, which served as models for his own instruments. From 1950 he built and restored important organs in the Netherlands, the U.S., and other countries.

Bibl.: John T. Fesperman, *Flentrop in America* (Raleigh, N.C., 1981).

Flesch, Carl (b. Wieselburg, Hungary, 9 Oct. 1873; d. Lucerne, 14 Nov. 1944). Violinist and pedagogue. Studied with Jakob Grün at the Vienna Conservatory, 1886–90; with Martin Marsick at the Paris Conservatory, 1890–94; first prize in violin, 1894 (his competition included Enesco, Kreisler, and Thibaud). Debut in Vienna, 1895. Taught violin at conservatories in Bucharest (1897–1902), Amsterdam (1903–8), Berlin (1908–23), Philadelphia (1924–34), Baden-Baden (1928–34). Taught in London, 1934–43; finally at the Lucerne Conservatory, 1943–44. Played in a trio with Artur Schnabel and Hugo Becker. Edited violin music by Mozart, Kreutzer, Beethoven, Paganini, Brahms, Tchaikovsky, and others. Published *Die Kunst des Violinspiels,* 2 vols. (Berlin, 1923, 1927; trans. Eng., 1924, 1930), which became a standard work.

Fletcher, (Horace) Grant (b. Hartsburg, Ill., 15 Oct. 1913). Composer and conductor. Studied at Illinois Wesleyan, with Krenek at the Univ. of Michigan, at Eastman (Ph.D., 1951; with Hanson, Rogers), and with Elwell in Cleveland; later studied conducting with Szell and Thor Johnson. He taught at Illinois Wesleyan (1938–41) before joining the staff of Arizona State Univ. in 1956. His style is varied, with melody always primary; wrote for professionals and amateurs, using some aleatoric procedures, some electronic composition; later work reflects aspects of southwestern U.S. Indian and Spanish cultures (*Seven Cities of Cibola,* orchestra, 1971). Works include operas, ballets; orchestral and many chamber works; piano music; choral and solo vocal works; film scores and incidental music.

Fleury, André (Édouard Antoine Marie) (b. Neuilly-sur-Seine, 25 July 1903; d. 6 Aug. 1995). Organist and composer. His father (a student of D'Indy and Vidal) gave him his first instruction; entered the Paris Conservatory in 1915 to study composition with Gigout and Dupré; studied organ with Marchal and Vierne and composition with Vidal. He held a long series of organ positions: assistant to Gigout at St. Augustin and to Tournemire at St. Clotilde; organist at St. Augustin (1930); at Dijon Cathedral (1949); and in Paris at St. Eustache (1971). He taught organ at the École normale de musique. As a recitalist he introduced Messiaen in London (1937). Composed in a tonal idiom; works include chamber and piano music, songs, and pieces for the organ (liturgical and concert).

Florio, Caryl [William James Robjohn] (b. Tavistock, Devonshire, 3 Nov. 1843; d. Morganton, N.C., 21 Nov. 1920). Composer. At 14 emigrated with his family to New York; 1858–60, boy soloist, Trinity Church; 1861–67, an actor; then a professional musician (changing his name in 1870 because of family opposition). Widely active in New York, Baltimore, and Indianapolis as organist, accompanist, and conductor of choruses and opera (Havana, 1878); 1886, organized Palestrina Choir for early music; 1889–91, music director, Wells College; 1896–1901, music director, Vanderbilt estate, Asheville, N.C.; from 1903, teacher and church musician, Asheville. Published cantatas, Sunday school songs, piano pieces. An opera on *Uncle Tom's Cabin* was unsuccessful (Philadelphia, 1882); also composed 2 symphonies, piano concerto, chamber music.

Flothuis, Marius (b. Amsterdam, 30 Oct. 1914). Composer and musicologist. As a youth he took piano lessons with his uncle and with Arend Koole; later he studied classics and musicology at Amsterdam and Utrecht. From 1937 he was an assistant manager of the Concertgebouw Orchestra; he was dismissed (his wife was Jewish) and spent the latter part of the war in concentration camps. He returned to his job with the orchestra in 1953; after nearly 20 years as its artistic director (1955–74), he became professor of musicology at Utrecht. Wrote about Mozart and edited works of Haydn and Mozart. His own compositions include orchestral works (concerto, piano, small orchestra, 1948; *Symphonische muziek,* 1957; *Per sonare ed ascoltare,* flute, orchestra, 1971); vocal works (*Cantata silesiana,* women's voices, chamber ensemble, 1946); songs and other solo vocal works; and many chamber works.

Flotow, Friedrich (Adolf Ferdinand) Freiherr von (b. Teutendorf, Mecklenburg-Schwerin, 27 Apr. 1812; d.

Darmstadt, 24 Jan. 1883). Composer. From an aristocratic, landowning family; early showed musical talent, and his father, a Prussian officer, allowed him to study at the Paris Conservatory from 1828 (under Pixis, piano; Reicha, composition); began an opera, but left Paris because of the 1830 Revolution. His first opera was given in German at Ludwigslust and Schwerin, 1835; in the later 1830s he lived mostly in Paris and composed several operas, given in noble houses. He reached the public theaters by collaborating on two opéras comiques with Albert Grisar at the Théâtre de la Renaissance, both successful, especially *L'eau merveilleuse* (1839); also had a success there with *Le naufrage de la Méduse* (1839), composed with Pilati, but did not produce an opera all his own until the one-act *L'esclave de Camoëns* (Opéra-comique, 1843). His next, *Alessandro Stradella* (Hamburg, 1844), was one of his two great successes, but limited mostly to German-speaking regions; the other, *Martha* (Vienna Opera, 25 Nov. 1847), its plot based on a ballet, *Lady Harriette* (Paris Opéra, 1844), of which Flotow composed one act, was a greater and worldwide success and is still occasionally performed. Some of his later operas, especially *Indra* (1852, based on *L'esclave de Camoëns*), *La veuve Grapin* (Paris, 1859), and *L'ombre* (Paris, 1870) had some shorter-lived success. In 1853–63 intendant, Schwerin court theater, for which he composed operas, ballets, and other theater music. He produced little new after 1870. Published memoirs, "Erinnerungen aus meinem Leben," in *Vor den Coulissen,* ed. J. Lewisky (Berlin, 1882). Also composed a few orchestral works, chamber music, songs.

Floyd, Carlisle (b. Latta, S.C., 11 June 1926). Composer. Studied with Bacon at Converse College and Syracuse Univ. (M.A., 1949). Taught piano at Florida State Univ. from 1947, where he developed a course on music and text coordination in opera for composers and librettists. He began to compose operas in 1949, writing or adapting his own librettos; his third opera, *Susannah,* an adaptation of the biblical story in two acts (1953–54), was premiered in Tallahassee (2 Feb. 1955) and won the New York Critics' Circle Award after its New York performance at City Opera (27 Sept. 1956); later it represented American opera at the Brussels World's Fair. By 1981 he had written 7 other operas, most with American settings and in a conservative style, including *Wuthering Heights* (1958), heavily revised after its intial performance in Santa Fe, and *Willie Stark* (Houston, 1981). The latter is based on Robert Penn Warren's *All the King's Men.* From 1976 Floyd taught at the Univ. of Houston and directed the Houston Opera Studio. Other works include a monodrama for soprano and orchestra (*Flower and Hawk,* 1972); a few orchestral works (*In Celebration,* overture, 1971); piano pieces; songs and song cycles (*Citizen of Paradise,* Emily Dickinson, mezzo-soprano and piano, 1983); and pedagogical works.

Foerster, Josef Bohuslav (b. Prague, 30 Dec. 1859; d. Nový Vestec, Bohemia, 29 May 1951). Composer and writer on music. A member of an important musical family, he studied first at the Prague Organ School, where his father taught. In 1882 he received a post as organist at St. Vojtěch, succeeding Dvořák, and in 1889 he was made choirmaster at Panna Maria Sněžná. His wife was an opera singer, and in 1893 he moved with her to Hamburg, where he wrote music criticism and was engaged eventually as professor at the conservatory (from 1901). In 1903 he moved to Vienna, where he taught at the New Conservatory; his friend Mahler secured a place at the court opera for his wife. Returning to Bohemia in 1918, Foerster taught first at the Prague Conservatory and later at the Univ. of Prague (1920–36). His legacy includes a number of prominent students, including Pavel Bořkovec and Emil František Burian. He composed 6 operas (*Debora,* Prague, 1893; *Eva,* Prague, 1899; *Srdce,* 1902–4; *Bloud,* 1935–36); Masses and other large-scale choral works (*Svatý Václav,* oratorio, 1928; *Mše ke cti sv. Vojtěcha,* 1947; *Máj,* cantata, 1936); 5 symphonies (1887–88; 1892–93; 1894; 1905; 1929); symphonic poems (*Mé mládí,* 1900); 2 violin concertos, a cello concerto; *Jičínská suita,* 1923; more than 15 pieces for chorus a cappella; chamber music; songs. He published several books, including *Der Pilger: Erinnerungen eines Musikers* (Prague, 1955).

Bibl.: František Pala, *Josef Bohuslav Foerster* (Prague, 1962).

Fogerty, John (b. Berkeley, Calif., 28 May 1945). Rock singer, songwriter, and guitarist. From 1959 performed with brother Tom Fogerty (b. 1941), bassist Stu Cook (b. 1945), and drummer Doug Clifford (b. 1945); from 1967 they were known as Creedence Clearwater Revival and made numerous successful recordings, including "Proud Mary" (1969), "Bad Moon Rising" (1969), and "Have You Ever Seen the Rain" (1971). After releasing solo albums in the early 1970s, Fogerty ceased recording until the mid-1980s, when his albums *Centerfield* (1985, including "The Old Man Down the Road") and *Eye of the Zombie* (1986) were very popular.

Fogliani [Fogliano], **Lodovico** [Ludovico] (b. Modena, late 15th cent.; d. ca. 1539). Theorist and composer. Brother of Giacomo Fogliano. Served at the Cathedral of Modena from 1503; in 1513–14 at the Capella Giulia in Rome; then again at Modena. Surviving compositions include frottole published by Petrucci and one Mass. His *Musica theorica* (Venice, 1529; facs., *BMB* sec. 2, 13 [1970]) accepts Ptolemy's tetrachord of greater and lesser tones and a diatonic semitone.

Fogliano [Fogliani], **Giacomo** [Jacopo] (b. Modena, 1468; d. there, 10 Apr. 1548). Composer. Brother of Lodovico Fogliani. Organist at the Cathedral of Modena from 1479 to 1497 and from 1504 to 1548; his duties there included singing, teaching, and composing as well as playing the organ. Among his works are a few motets and *laude,* a number of frottole, many frottolalike madrigals, and 4 keyboard ricercars.

Fomin, Evstigney Ipatovich (b. St. Petersburg, 16 Aug. 1761; d. there, 27 Apr. 1800). Composer. As a child he was accepted for study at the Academy of Fine Arts in St. Petersburg; he began as a full student there in 1776, studying with Matteo Buini and Blasius Sartori. In 1782 he went to Bologna to study with Padre Martini and Stanislao Mattei; three years later he was accepted into the Accademia filarmonica. Returning to St. Petersburg in 1785, he taught at the theatrical school and composed operas. From 1797 he was répétiteur for the imperial theater under Paul I. His operas include *Yamshchiki na podstave* [The Coachmen] (1787); *Vecherinki* [Soirees] (1788); *Orfey i Evridika* (1792); *Amerikantsï* [Americans], comic opera (1800); and *Zolotoye yabloko* [The Golden Apple] (perf. 1803).

Fonesca, Julio (b. San José, Costa Rica, 22 May 1885; d. there, 22 June 1950). Composer. Studied in his home city, producing several early works, before entering the Lyceum of the Arts and the Royal Conservatory in Milan; also studied later in Brussels. Returned to Costa Rica in 1906 and pursued conducting and teaching; he visited New York in 1914. Joined the faculty at the Colegio superior de señoritas in 1927; moved to the National Conservatory in 1942; founded the Academia Euterpe in 1934, directing it until 1939. His output includes works in most genres, notably orchestral music, choral compositions, and piano pieces; he was also active in the collection and study of folk music.

Bibl.: *Composers of the Americas* 2 (Washington, D.C., 1956), pp. 73–76 [includes works list].

Fontaine, Pierre (b. 1390–95?; d. ca. 1450). Composer. Belonged to the Burgundian chapel from at least 1403 (perhaps starting as a choirboy) until his death, with an interruption for service in the papal chapel from 1420 until sometime between 1428 and 1430. Although his contemporary fame was considerable, only a few French chansons by him have survived (1 ballade and 6 rondeaux, all in 3 voices).

Fontana, Giovanni Battista (b. Brescia; d. Padua, ca. 1630). Violinist and composer. The preface to his posthumous *Sonate a 1.2.3. per il violino, o cornetto, fagotto, chitarone, violoncino o simile altro istromento* (Venice, 1641), which contains all of his extant works, provides the only known details of his life: a Brescian, he worked also in Rome, Venice, and Padua. The Brescian Cesario Gussago dedicated a sonata of 1608 to him.

Fontanelli, Alfonso (b. Reggio Emilia, 15 Feb. 1557; d. Rome, 11 Feb. 1622). Composer. Served various members of the Este family from no later than 1586 until 1620, with occasional short interruptions and much traveling; then took holy orders; lived in Ferrara, Modena, Rome, and Florence. The style of his madrigals, most published in 2 complete books (1595 and 1604), reflects his friendship with Gesualdo and his long association with the Ferrarese court.

Foote, Arthur William (b. Salem, Mass., 5 Mar. 1853; d. Boston, 8 Apr. 1937). Composer, organist, pianist. Studied piano with Fanny Paine from age 12; attended Harvard, where he worked with John Knowles Paine and directed the Glee Club; after graduation he began organ lessons with Benjamin Lang and returned to Harvard to receive the first M.A. in music granted in the U.S. (1875). His entire career was spent in Boston: teaching piano, organ, and composition privately; performing as a pianist until 1895; serving as organist and choirmaster at the Church of the Disciples (1876–77) and at the First Unitarian Church (1878–1910); sponsoring and actively participating in a chamber music series. He taught piano at the New England Conservatory (1921–37). His compositions reflect his admiration for Brahms and Wagner and his training in the U.S. by German or German-influenced teachers; most of his large output was published (by Arthur P. Schmidt, Boston), and his orchestral works were performed by major orchestras, often by the Boston Symphony with himself as pianist. Works include 8 orchestral pieces (Suite in E for strings op. 63, 1907); at least 3 string quartets, 2 piano trios, and other chamber works; piano and organ works; ca. 52 part songs; ca. 35 anthems; ca. 100 songs.

Forbes, Sebastian (b. Amersham, Buckinghamshire, 22 May 1941). Composer and organist; of Scottish parentage. At the Royal Academy of Music he was a pupil of Howard Ferguson (from 1958), and at Cambridge he studied with Philip Radcliffe and Thurston Dart (1960–64). He founded the Aeolian Singers in 1965 and was their director until 1969. He held posts as producer for BBC London, as organist for churches in London and Cambridge, and as lecturer at the universities at Bangor (from 1968) and Surrey (from 1972). He composed an opera, *Tom Cree* (1970–71); orchestral works (*Pageant of St. Paul,* 1964; *Chaconne,* 1967; *Essay,* clarinet, orchestra, 1970; *Symphony in Two Movements,* 1972); choral music (*Sequence of Carols I–III,* 1967, 1968, 1971); and chamber music (Piano Quintet, 1961; 2 string quartets; *Fantasy,* solo cello, 1974).

Ford, Thomas (buried London, 17 Nov. 1648). Composer. Named one of the musicians to Prince Henry in 1611; later became a lutenist and singer to Prince Charles. His *Musick of Sundrie Kindes* (London, 1607) contains many well-known ayres, including "Faire sweet cruell," "Since first I saw your face," and "There is a ladie, sweet and kind," as well as dances "for two Basse-viols, the Liera way." Other works include anthems for 3–6 voices, part songs, and 5-part viol fantasies.

Forkel, Johann Nicolaus (b. Meeder, Lower Franconia, 22 Feb. 1749; d. Göttingen, 20 Mar. 1818). Music historian and bibliographer. He held choral positions in Lüneburg (1766) and in Schwerin (1767) before a patron enabled him to study law at the Univ. of Göttingen (1769). There he was university chapel organist, taught music theory, and eventually (ca. 1779) became director of concerts; in 1787 the university elevated him to professorial status. He is recognized as one of the founders of musicology. Of chief value are his bibliographies *Musikalisch-kritische Bibliothek* (Gotha, 1778–79; R: Hildesheim, 1964) and *Allgemeine Litteratur der Musik* (Leipzig, 1792; R: Hildesheim, 1962), and his *Allgemeine Geschichte der Musik* (Leipzig, 1788–1801; R: Graz, 1967). He also published, in 1802, the first biography of J. S. Bach.

Forqueray, Antoine (b. Paris, 1672; d. Mantes, 28 June 1745). Viol player and composer. At 5 years of age he played for Louis XIV, who brought him into the court musical establishment and named him royal chamber musician in 1689. A favorite at court, where he was an associate of François Couperin and Robert de Visée, he had many noble pupils and was a famed performer on the bass viol, as was his son Jean-Baptiste. His Italianate style contrasted with that of his contemporary and rival Marin Marais, a student of Lully. He retired to Mantes in the 1720s. Some of his works are included in the *Pièces de viol . . . composée par Mr Forqueray le père,* published by his son in 1747.

Forrester, Maureen (Katherine Stewart) (b. Montreal, 25 July 1930). Contralto. Studied voice in Toronto with Sally Martin, Frank Rowe, and Bernard Diamant. Debut with the Montreal Elgar Choir, 1951; operatic debut with the Operatic Guild of Montreal, 1953; Paris recital debut, 1955. Became widely known in 1957 after a performance of Mahler's Symphony no. 2 with Bruno Walter in New York followed by a well-received recital there. For many her vocal timbre and interpretive depth recalled Kathleen Ferrier's; her first operatic leading role, Gluck's Orfeo (Toronto, 1961), was closely associated with Ferrier. Sang Handel's Cornelia *(Giulio Cesare)* at the New York City Opera theater, Lincoln Center, 1966. Debut with the San Francisco Opera in 1967 as La Cieca *(La Gioconda);* with the Metropolitan Opera in 1974 as Erda *(Ring).* Taught at the Philadelphia Academy of Music, 1966–71; at the Univ. of Toronto from 1971.

Forster, Georg (b. Amberg, ca. 1510; d. Nuremberg, 12 Nov. 1568). Editor and composer. A chorister at the electoral court in Heidelberg by about 1521, where he also began to compose and to collect songs; from 1531 chiefly active as a doctor of medicine in various German cities. His most important musical work is *Frische teutsche Liedlein,* a 5-volume collection of Tenorlieder by various composers, including himself, spanning the late 15th to mid-16th centuries.

Fortner, Wolfgang (b. Leipzig, 12 Oct. 1907; d. Heidelberg, 5 Sept. 1987). Composer. He attended the conservatory in Leipzig (studying composition with Grabner and organ with Straube) and studied musicology at the university. He taught composition and theory at the Heidelberg Institute of Church Music from 1931; taught at Darmstadt from 1946; professor of composition at the Northwest German Music Academy in Detmold (1954–56) and then at the conservatory in Freiburg (1957–72). His pupils included Günter Becker, Engelmann, and Henze. In 1935 he founded the Heidelberg Chamber Orchestra, with which he toured extensively, and later the Musica Viva concerts (1947), which he directed from 1964 to 1978. He was president of the German section of ISCM (1957) and belonged to both the Berlin Academy of Arts and the Bavarian Academy of Fine Arts.

During the 1930s and early 1940s he wrote in a neoclassical style influenced by Hindemith's counterpoint and Stravinsky's rhythmic language; his attention to the suite, toccata, capriccio, and fugue testify to his interest in Baroque forms. From the mid-1940s he began to compose according to twelve-tone and, later, serial principles; his individual serial procedures involved free transpositions of segments of a row. The Symphony of 1947 was atonal, and the Third String Quartet (1948) was composed in the twelve-tone style; *Phantasie über die Tonfolge B-A-C-H* (1950) reflects his continuing interest in Baroque counterpoint and a radical implementation of serial principles. His *Immagini* (1967) and *Prismen* (1974) employ aleatoric methods. He has often employed mirror forms and other symmetrical arrangements or isorhythmic devices in compositions that cover a wide variety of genres: opera, ballet; Mass and oratorio; choral cantata; symphonic and chamber music.

Works: operas (including *Die Bluthochzeit,* after García Lorca, 1957; *Elisabeth Tudor,* 1972), ballets, and other dramatic music; *Phantasie über B-A-C-H* (9 solo instruments, 2 pianos, and orchestra, 1945), *Prismen* (flute, oboe, clarinet, harp, percussion, and orchestra, 1974), several concertos, and other orchestral music; chamber, piano, and organ works; *Die Pfingstgeschichte* (tenor, chorus, instrumental ensemble, and organ, 1963) and other choral music; cantatas and other solo vocal music (*Machaut-Balladen,* tenor and orchestra, 1973; *That Time,* scenic cantata for mezzo-soprano, baritone, actor, speaker, guitar, harpsichord, piano, electronics, 1977).

Foss, Lukas (b. Berlin, 15 Aug. 1922). Composer, conductor, and pianist. He studied in Berlin and Paris until 1937; then attended the Curtis Institute, studying piano (Vengerova), composition (Scalero, Thompson), and conducting (Reiner); he studied with Koussevitzky at the Berkshire Music Center (1939–43) and with Hindemith at Yale (1939–40). He was pianist for the Boston Symphony (1944–50); spent two years in Rome; then succeeded Schoenberg at UCLA, where in 1957 he founded the Improvisation Chamber Ensemble (clarinet, piano, cello, and percussion); taught at SUNY–Buffalo (1963–70) and conducted the Buffalo

Philharmonic; directed the Brooklyn Philharmonic from 1971; conducted the Kol Israel Orchestra in Jerusalem (1972–76); was music director of the Milwaukee Symphony (1981–86). In 1979 he received the ASCAP award for adventurous programming.

His cantata *The Prairie,* (after Sandburg, S. A. T. B. soloists, chorus, and orchestra, 1944) won the New York Critics' Circle Award in 1944. The revised version of his Second Piano Concerto (1953) won the Critics' Circle Award in 1954. *Time Cycle* (1959–60), premiered by Bernstein and the New York Philharmonic, won the New York Critics' Circle Award in 1961.

Most of Foss's earlier works are related to the neoclassicism of Hindemith and Stravinsky, often tinged with the Americanism of Copland (*The Jumping Frog of Calaveras County,* his first opera, premiered in 1950, is based on Mark Twain and uses a cowboy tune). By the mid-1960s Foss had moved firmly into the experimental realm. He explored a serialism in which composer and performers choose at will from material generated by the row (*Echoi,* 1961–63); minimalism (String Quartet no. 3, 1975); compositions based on recomposition of preexisting works (*Baroque Variations,* 1967). Some pieces involve competition between players or players and tapes (*MAP,* a musical game for 4 instrumentalists competing against their own tapes, 1973).

Works include operas (*Griffelkin,* 1993), ballets, and incidental music; many orchestral compositions (*Geod* for 4 orchestral groups, 1969; *Exeunt,* 1982; *Celebration,* 1990); instrumental chamber music; choral music (*Fragments of Archilochos,* countertenor, male and female speakers, 4 small choruses, large chorus ad libitum, mandolin, guitar, and percussion, 1965); and songs.

Bibl.: Cole Gagne and Tracy Caras, "Lukas Foss," in *Soundpieces: Interviews with American Composers* (Metuchen, N.J., 1982), pp. 195–208. Karen L. Perone, *Lukas Foss: A Bio-Bibliography* (New York, 1991).

Foster, Frank (Benjamin, III) (b. Cincinnati, 23 Sept. 1928). Jazz tenor saxophonist, flutist, arranger, composer, and bandleader. He joined Count Basie's big band (1953–64), for which he composed and arranged "Shiny Stockings" on the album *April in Paris* (1955–56). He led a big band intermittently from 1964, joined Elvin Jones (late 1960s to mid-1970s), toured with the Thad Jones–Mel Lewis Orchestra (mid-1970s), and with Frank Wess led a hard bop quintet (1980s) that recorded the album *Two for the Blues* (1983). In 1986 he assumed the leadership of the memorial Count Basie orchestra.

Foster, Pops [George Murphy] (b. McCall, La., 18 May 1892; d. San Francisco, 30 Oct. 1969). Jazz double bass player. He played on riverboats with Fate Marable (1918–21), with whom he doubled on tuba; joined Kid Ory in California (ca. 1923). As a member of Luis Russell's big band (1929–40), which accompanied Louis Armstrong in 1929 and again from 1935, he recorded frequently, his propulsive contribution to the rhythm section being exemplified by "Swing That Music" (1936). During the revival of traditional jazz he worked with Sidney Bechet (1945) and performed on the radio series *This Is Jazz* (1947). He toured Europe with the pianist Sammy Price (1955–56), then settled in San Francisco, where he free-lanced, including work with Earl Hines, until the early 1960s. With Tom Stoddard and Ross Russell he wrote *Pops Foster: The Autobiobraphy of a New Orleans Jazzman* (Berkeley, 1971).

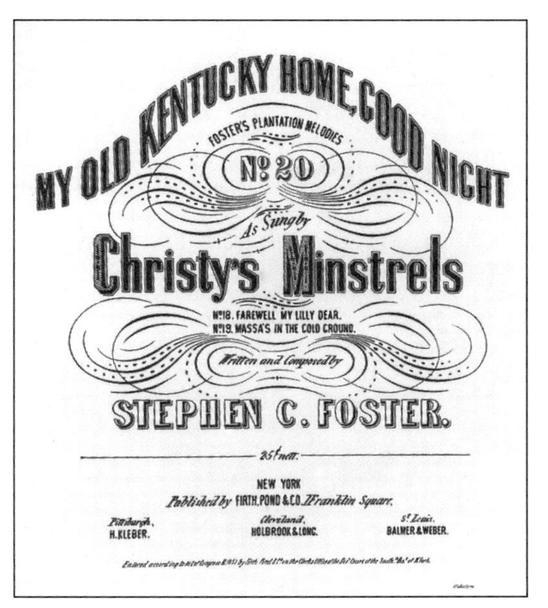

Sheet music for a song by Stephen Foster.

Foster, Stephen Collins (b. Lawrenceville [now in Pittsburgh], 4 July 1826; d. New York, 13 Jan. 1864). Composer. The ninth of 10 children of a prosperous Pittsburgh family whose fortunes became more erratic from the late 1830s, he was largely self-taught in music, learning to play the flute and piano and compositional technique sufficient to compose songs, of which he published his first in 1844. From 1846 he worked as a clerk in Cincinnati, also publishing several songs there; it was, however, the tremendous success of his "Oh! Susanna" and "Uncle Ned," both published in New York in 1848 without his knowledge or name, that determined him in 1850 to become a full-time songwriter. He returned to Pittsburgh to live and married Jane McDowell, a doctor's daughter (one daughter, Marion, born 1851).

In 1850 he agreed with E. P. Christy of Christy's Minstrels in New York to introduce and have the rights to his minstrel show songs. His 1851 hit "Old Folks at Home" was published with Christy as author, although Foster's authorship was generally known. Other hits of the period included "Nelly Bly," "Camptown Races" (1850); "Massa's in de Cold Ground," "Old Dog Tray" (1852); "My Old Kentucky Home" (1853). In 1853 he moved to New York, the center of the music business, and made an exclusive contract with the firm of Firth and Pond, which had published some of his songs since 1849 and which now began to advertise his work intensively, describing him in 1854 as the most popular songwriter of the day. This marked the zenith of his career. Most of his hits had appeared by 1855 (including, in 1855, "Come Where My Love Lies Dreaming," "Hard Times Come Again No More"; thereafter only "Old Black Joe," 1860; "Beautiful Dreamer," 1864, his last song). He ended the exclusive contract with Firth and Pond in 1854 (although they continued to publish some of his work) and returned with his family to the Pittsburgh region, where he lived until 1860, apparently in declining circumstances. He published fewer songs in 1855–58, but more thereafter.

From at least the mid-1850s his drinking seems to have turned into chronic alcoholism. In 1860 he moved again to New York, where his wife left him (they had separated briefly in 1853). He composed several Civil War songs, none popular; in 1863 he contributed 20 songs to a church and Sunday school collection. He died poor and obscure after falling in his hotel room while ill, but by the end of the century he had achieved legendary status as America's best-loved songwriter.

Bibl.: William Austin, *"Susanna," "Jeanie," and "The Old Folks at Home": The Songs of Stephen C. Foster from His Time to Ours* (New York, 1975). Calvin Elliker, *Stephen Collins Foster: A Guide to Research* (New York, 1988). Steven Saunders and Deane L. Roots, eds., *The Music of Stephen C. Foster: A Critical Edition* (Washington, 1990).

Foulds, John (Herbert) (b. Manchester, 2 Nov. 1880; d. Calcutta, 24 Apr. 1939). Composer and conductor. After early experience as cellist in a Manchester theater orchestra, in 1900 he joined the city's Hallé orchestra; later he studied with conductor Hans Richter. After 1910 he devoted himself to composing; moving to London, he became music director of the central YMCA there in 1918. He went to India in 1935, where from 1937 he directed programs of European music for All-India Radio in Delhi and Calcutta. He formed an Indo-European orchestra employing both indigenous and European instruments and composed works that attempted to fuse Eastern and Western styles. His compositions include 2 lost opera scores (*Cleopatra,* 1909; *Avatara,* 1930); choral works (*The Vision of Dante,* 1905–8; *A World Requiem,* 1919–21); orchestral works (*Epithalamium,* 1906; *Apotheosis,* violin, orchestra, 1908–9; *Indian Suite,* 1932–35; *Symphony of East and West,* 1937–38; music lost); chamber works; and piano music *(Dichterliebe).*

Bibl.: Malcolm MacDonald, *John Foulds and His Music: An Introduction: With a Catalog of the Composer's Works and a Brief Miscellany of His Writings* (White Plains, 1989).

Fountain, Primous, III (b. St. Petersburg, Fla., 1 Aug. 1949). Composer. Studied trumpet and double bass in Chicago, where his family had moved by 1951; during high school and college there he played and arranged jazz; he cites Stravinsky and Miles Davis as primary influences on his neoclassical style; Quincy Jones acted as a patron for a period of over two years. In 1970 he settled in Madison, Wisconsin. Orchestral works include *Manifestation* (1969; later performed as a ballet by the Arthur Mitchell Dance Theater of Harlem) and *Grudges* (1972) as well as a cello concerto (1976); chamber works include a piano trio, *Ricia* (1980).

Fournier, Pierre (Léon Marie) (b. Paris, 24 June 1906; d. there, 8 Jan. 1986). Cellist. Began musical studies as a pianist, but changed to cello after being stricken with polio at age 9. Studied with Paul Bazelaire and André Hekking at the Paris Conservatory; first prize for cello, 1923. After playing in theater orchestras he made his debut in Paris in 1928, then pursued an international career as soloist with most major European orchestras and conductors. Taught at the École normale de musique, 1937–39; at the Paris Conservatory, 1939–49. Martin, Martinon, and Martinů dedicated concertos to him; Honegger and Poulenc sonatas. Concertized with Szigeti, Schnabel, and Primrose. Moved to Switzerland, 1973.

Fox, Virgil (Keel) (b. Princeton, Ill., 3 May 1912; d. West Palm Beach, 25 Oct. 1980). Organist. Studied with Wilhelm Middelschulte in Chicago, 1928–29; with Louis Robert at the Peabody Conservatory, 1929–32; with Marcel Dupré in Paris, 1932–33. Debut in Cincinnati, 1927; debuts in New York (Carnegie Hall) and London (Kingsway Hall), 1932. Professor of organ at Peabody Conservatory, 1938–42. As organist at Riverside Church in New York, 1946–65, he became a tourist attraction. During the late 1960s his penchant for flamboyant showmanship and oratory enabled him to reach out to a new generation, touring with an electronic organ and a psychedelic light show.

Frackenpohl, Arthur (Roland) (b. Irvington, N.J., 23 Apr. 1924). Composer. Studied with Bernard Rogers at Eastman (M.A., 1949) and with Milhaud at the Berkshire Music Center (1948); with Boulanger (1950); and at McGill (D.M.A., 1957). Taught at SUNY-Potsdam from 1949; composing in an eclectic style, was quite prolific. He was composer-in-residence in the Hempstead, N.Y., public schools (1959–60) and produced many works for high school band; a few works use graphic notation. He is the author of a textbook, *Harmonization at the Keyboard* (1962; 4th ed., 1981). Works include an opera (1964), pieces for orchestra and band (*Cantilena,* recorded 1969; *American Folk Song Suite,* 1973); a string quartet, brass quintet, and other chamber music; *Rag* (4 pianos, 16-hands) and other keyboard pieces; choral music; songs.

Frager, Malcolm (b. Clayton, Mo., 15 Jan. 1935; d. Lenox, Mass., 20 June 1991). Pianist. Studied with Carl Madlinger in St. Louis, 1942–49; with Carl Friedberg (a student of Clara Schumann) in New York, 1949–55. Soloist with the St. Louis Symphony, 1945.

Studied at the American Conservatory in Fontainebleau, 1952. Won the Geneva International Competition, 1955. B.A. in Russian, Columbia Univ., 1957. Won the Leventritt Competition in New York, 1959; the Queen Elisabeth of Belgium Competition in Brussels, 1960. First tour of the U.S. and Europe, 1959. One of the earliest modern exponents of the fortepiano for performances of Haydn and Mozart. His scholarly interests led him to perform little-known versions of works such as the original one-movement version of the Schumann concerto (1968).

Françaix, Jean René (b. Le Mans, 23 May 1912). Composer and pianist. His father directed the conservatory in Le Mans, where his mother taught singing; he studied there and then at the Paris Conservatory, where he obtained a first prize in piano (1932); he studied composition with Nadia Boulanger. He had composed from the age of 6, and throughout his career he continued to write with great facility, in a style influenced most by that of Ravel. As a pianist he toured in Europe and the U.S.; he and his daughter premiered his concerto for 2 pianos (1964). His oratorio *L'apocalypse selon St. Jean* (1939) employs choral psalmody and full orchestra, with a second instrumental group that includes saxophones, accordion, mandolin, and guitar (depicting Hell); the work was performed at the ISCM in Vienna (1932) and Palermo (1949).

Works: 5 operas (*La princesse de Clèves,* 1965), 16 ballets, film scores, and incidental music; some 50 orchestral works (piano concertino, 1932; guitar concerto, 1983) and large-scale works for chorus or soloists and orchestra; *Quasi improvisando* (11 winds, 1975), *11 Variations on a Theme of Haydn* (double bass and 9 winds, 1982), 2 wind quintets (1948, 1987), and other chamber music; piano and organ works; *La grenouille qui veut se faire aussi grosse que le boeuf* (after La Fontaine; soprano or tenor, male chorus, and piano, 1965) and other choral music; songs.

Francescatti, Zino [René] (b. Marseilles, 9 Aug. 1905; d. La Ciotat, France, 18 Sept. 1991). Violinist. Studied with his father (whose own teacher, Sivori, was a disciple of Paganini). Perfomed Beethoven's concerto at age 5. After further studies with Jacques Thibaud, made his Paris debut in 1925; toured England with Ravel, 1926. The best-known French violinist of his generation, he toured Europe (1928–38) and South America (1928, 1947, 1952), and made his U.S. debut with the New York Philharmonic (1 Nov. 1939). Began playing with Robert Casadesus in 1942; their joint recordings include the complete Beethoven sonatas. Gave the premiere of Milhaud's *Suite anglaise* (1945). Retired in 1975. Composed *Préludes* for piano; *Aria, Polka,* and *Berceuse sur le nom de Ravel* for violin.

Francesco Canova da Milano [Francesco da Milano] (b. Monza, 18 Aug. 1497; d. Milan, 15 Apr. 1543). Composer and lutenist. His contemporaries and successors ranked him among the finest of lutenists. Various popes and cardinals employed him in Rome (1516–39, with brief interruptions). His compositions survive in many manuscripts and in numerous prints issued throughout Europe between 1536 and 1603. They include ricercars, fantasias, and intabulations of vocal pieces.

Bibl.: *The Lute Music of Francesco Canova da Milano,* ed. Arthur J. Ness (Cambridge, Mass., 1970). *Opere complete per liuto,* ed. Ruggero Chiesa (Milan, 1971).

Franchetti, Alberto (b. Turin, 18 Sept. 1860; d. Viareggio, 4 Aug. 1942). Composer. He studied in Turin and Venice and in Germany with Draeseke and Rheinberger; he directed the Florence Conservatory (1926–28). Verdi recommended him to compose *Cristoforo Colombo* (1892) on the basis of his first opera, *Asrael* (1888), but after these successes his reputation declined. He was influenced by Meyerbeer and Wagner and was particularly adept at creating monumental scenes. Nine operas were performed in Italy (1888–1922), and a few others were incomplete or unperformed. In addition to operas he wrote some orchestral music; *Inno* (soloists, chorus, and orchestra, 1888); chamber music; songs.

Franchomme, Auguste (Joseph) (b. Lille, 10 Apr. 1808; d. Paris, 21 Jan. 1884). Cellist. Studied at the Paris Conservatory (first prize, 1825); prominent in Paris musical life as orchestral and chamber player and soloist; from 1846, professor at the Conservatory; close friend of Chopin and dedicatee and first performer of his cello sonata. Composed cello pieces, including 12 Caprices op. 7, 12 Etudes op. 35.

Franck, César (-Auguste-Jean-Guillaume-Hubert) (b. Liège, 10 Dec. 1822; d. Paris, 8 Nov. 1890). Composer. He and a brother, Joseph (who also became a professional musician), early showed musical talent; 1830–35, studied at the Liège Conservatory; spring 1835, his father toured him through Belgium, hoping to make him a fashionable virtuoso, a dream that lasted 10 years in spite of César's unsuitability for the role. In summer 1835 the family moved to Paris, where César studied with Zimmermann (piano) and Reicha (composition); 1837–42, studied at the Paris Conservatory with Zimmermann, Leborne (counterpoint, composition), Habeneck (violin), and Benoist (organ), winning first prizes in piano and composition, second in organ (1841). In 1843–45, his father again tried to start him on a concert career, with little success and growing repugnance in Franck himself.

He had composed much piano music from an early age, but it was 3 piano trios, published as op. 1 in 1843, that first brought him favorable attention. The oratorio *Ruth* (Conservatory, 1846), however, was unsuccessful, and a symphonic poem, *Ce que l'on entend sur la montagne,* was not performed. In 1847 he broke free of his father's control and in 1848 married the daughter of actors, settling into an obscure life as a church organist (Notre Dame de Lorette; from 1853, St. Jean-St. François du Marais) and teacher. He composed little; the only significant work of this period, an opéra comique, *Le valet de ferme* (1851–53), was never performed. In 1853 he suffered a nervous breakdown and went to recuperate in Switzerland.

A major turning point was his appointment in 1858 as organist and precentor at the new Basilica of Ste. Clotilde, with its grand Cavaillé-Coll organ. This post, which he held until his death, brought him considerable notice, especially for his improvisation; he was a Cavaillé-Coll consultant but also tried out other organs as well. In his early years there he composed some sacred works (Mass, 1860) and organ pieces (*Six pièces,* 1860–62), but little in the later 1860s, when, however, he began to attract the circle of pupils and devotees (initially Duparc, then Lekeu, de Castillon, D'Indy, Holmès, de Bréville, de Wailly, de Serres, Cahen, Chausson, Coquard, Dukas, Ropartz, Pierné) that in the 1870s and 1880s was to propagandize in his favor, provide occasions for his music to be heard, especially through the Société nationale de musique, of which Franck became president in 1886, and promote his posthumous acceptance as a great composer.

From his appointment in 1872 as professor of organ at the Conservatory, this class became the center of his circle, less concerned with organ playing than with improvisation and composition. This support probably stimulated the considerable fecundity of Franck's final 20 years. Major works of the 1870s were the oratorios *Les béatitudes* (composed 1869–79) and *La rédemption* (1871–72). The first, considered by Franck his magnum opus, was not given a complete public performance in his lifetime, and neither has found acceptance by public or critics. The same is true of the operas *Hulda* and *Ghiselle,* to which he devoted much of his energies in the 1880s; both were posthumously performed at Monte Carlo (1894, 1896) and then forgotten. It was the orchestral works (4 symphonic poems; Symphonic Variations, piano and orchestra, 1885; Symphony, 1886–88), chamber music (Piano Quintet, 1878–79; Violin Sonata, 1886; String Quartet, 1889), and solo keyboard works (*Prélude, choral et fugue,* 1884, and *Prélude, aria et final,* 1886–87, both for piano; *Trois piéces,* 1878, and *Trois chorals,* 1890, both for organ) that were the basis of his growing fame in the years immediately after his death (from pleurisy, possibly as a complication of having been hit by a streetcar a few months earlier).

Bibl.: Vincent D'Indy, *César Franck* (Paris, 1906); trans. Rosa Newmarch (London, 1910, R: New York, 1965). Laurence Davies, *César Franck and His Circle* (London, 1970).

Franck, Melchior (b. Zittau, ca. 1579; d. Coburg, 1 June 1639). Composer. Possibly a student of Demantius and Gumpelzhaimer. Worked in Nuremberg, 1601–3; there he was influenced by Hassler and, through him, by Lechner and the Gabrielis. Became Kapellmeister in Coburg in 1603, where he remained until his death. He issued dozens of publications; among his works are hundreds of German sacred works (many based on chorales), secular pieces, and instrumental dances.

Franck, Salomo [Salomon] (bapt. Weimar, 6 Mar. 1659; buried there, 14 June 1725). Poet and court official. Studied law, and possibly theology, in Jena; worked as administrator at the courts of Arnstadt and Zwickau before receiving a similar post at Weimar in 1701, where he was also court poet. His first published poetry appeared in 1685. Most of J. S. Bach's Weimar cantatas were set to his texts, as were a few from Leipzig; his work was also included in many poetic anthologies of the era.

Franco, Hernando [Fernando] (b. Galizuela, near Alcántara in Extremadura, 1532; d. Mexico City, 28 Nov. 1585). Composer. A chorister at Segovia Cathedral from 1542 to 1549; probably went to the New World in 1554; *maestro de capilla* at Guatemala Cathedral by 1573; *maestro* at the cathedral at Mexico City from 1575. His compositions include 16 Magnificats, a Lamentations setting, and 20 motets.

Franco, Johan (b. Zaandam, Netherlands, 12 July 1908; d. Virginia Beach, Va., 14 Apr. 1988). Composer. Studied composition with Willem Pijper while a law student in Amsterdam; moved to the U.S. in 1934; a Town Hall concert of his works was presented on 15 Mar. 1938; became an American citizen in 1942. He favored a polymodal harmonic language and cyclical formal structures; composed over 100 works for carillon (*As the Prophets Foretold,* soprano, tenor, bass, and carillon, publ. 1955; *Cranbrook Nocturne,* recorded 1975). Other works include 5 symphonies (1933–58), concertos, and other works for orchestra and band; 6 string quartets and other chamber music; piano music; electronic music; choral works; solo songs; and incidental music.

Franco of Cologne (fl. 13th cent.). Theorist. He is described as a papal chaplain and preceptor of the Knights Hospitallers of St. John of Jerusalem at Cologne, and he may have worked at the Univ. of Paris. He wrote *Ars cantus mensurabilis* (*GS* 3:1–16; *CS* 1:117–36; trans., *SR,* pp. 139–59), in which a notational system for rhythm is proposed that in its essentials remained in use for two centuries. His work is closely associated with the polyphonic music developed in Paris in the 13th century. The treatise also discusses issues such as consonances and dissonances and their use in composition, and various genres, particularly those in discant style (in which all voices are in measured rhythm).

Bibl.: Fritz Reckow, *Der Musiktraktat des Anonymus 4* (Wiesbaden, 1967).

Francoeur, François ("le cadet") (b. Paris, 21 Sept. 1698; d. there, 5 Aug. 1787). Composer. He joined the Paris Opéra as a *dessus de violin* at age 15, then became a member of the Musique de la Chambre du Roi. In 1723 he and François Rebel traveled to Vienna and Prague in the retinue of General Bonneval. From 1726 the two composers collaborated on over 20 dramatic works; from 1757 to 1767 they directed the Opéra. In 1727 Francoeur became *compositeur de la chambre du* *roi,* and in 1744 became *surintendant de la musique de la chambre.* Besides operas, he wrote chamber music, including 2 books of violin sonatas.

Frank, Claude (b. Nuremberg, 24 Dec. 1925). Pianist. His family moved to Paris in 1937; he studied there with Louise Wacksmann-Field from 1938. His family then moved to New York in 1940, where he studied with Artur Schnabel (1941–44, 1946–48, 1951). Debut in New York, 1947. On the faculty at Bennington College, 1948–55; at Mannes School from 1963; also at the Aspen Music School from 1970 and the Yale School of Music from 1972. Among his recordings are the 32 Beethoven sonatas.

Frankel, Benjamin (b. London, 31 Jan. 1906; d. there, 12 Feb. 1973). Composer. Largely self-taught in music, he began as a watchmaker's apprentice; in 1922 he studied piano with Victor Benham in Germany. He supported himself playing jazz violin and piano in London nightclubs. By the 1930s he was contributing music for plays, musicals, and eventually films. From 1946 he taught at London's Guildhall School of Music and Drama. He composed more than 100 film scores, including that for the Alec Guinness classic *The Man in the White Suit* (1952). He also continued composing concert music, including 8 symphonies (1958–71); *Serenata concertante* (1960); *Pezzi melodici* (1972); chamber music; songs ("The Aftermath," tenor, chamber ensemble, 1947).

Franklin, Aretha (b. Memphis, Tenn., 25 Mar. 1942). Soul and gospel singer. She performed in her father's Baptist church in Detroit and in his traveling evangelical shows. From 1966 she made recordings of rhythm-and-blues and popular songs, including "I Never Loved a Man (The Way I Love You)" (1967) and "Jump to It" (1982). She recorded gospel music as well, including the albums *Amazing Grace* (with James Cleveland, 1972) and *One Lord, One Faith, One Baptism* (1987).

Franz [Knauth], **Robert** (b. Halle, 28 June 1815; d. there, 24 Oct. 1892). Composer. His father changed the family surname from Knauth for business reasons. Little encouraged by his family toward a musical career, he had music lessons in Halle, then (1835–37) studied theory with J. C. Friedrich Schneider in Dessau; thereafter self-taught. From 1841 he worked as a musician in Halle, as church organist and from 1841 as conductor of the Halle choral society, greatly improving it and organizing choral festivals. In 1843 a set of 12 lieder, which he had sent to Schumann, was published on Schumann's recommendation as his op. 1; 1848, married a daughter of the philosopher Friedrich Hinrichs (one of Franz's formative intellectual influences), fathering three children; from 1851 taught at the university in Halle. He early began to become deaf and was totally so by 1867, when he had to resign his various posts; he also suffered periodically from a nervous disorder. These circumstances made his later years somewhat isolated and needy.

He received some official honors, public recognition—the admiration of contemporary musicians is reflected in Liszt's book *Robert Franz* (Leipzig, 1872)—and financial support (including a government annuity), although his music did not achieve the degree of popularity or acclaim of that of some of his contemporaries, partly because of its limited scope, consisting entirely of vocal works. Principal among them are the 279 songs (published 1843–84) on which his reputation mainly rests, many still part of the lieder repertory; also part songs and a few sacred works (including a Lutheran service). He made many arrangements of older music (especially many works of Bach and Handel), much used in his day and later, but criticized and now largely abandoned because of his realizations of continuo parts and elaborations of textures in a manner, though tasteful, contrary to the trend toward fidelity to the original text and authentic performance practice.

Bibl.: Robert Bethge, ed., *Robert Franz: Gesammelte Schriften über die wiederbelebung Bach'scher und Händel'scher Werke* (Leipzig, 1910). D. Loë, ed., *Robert Franz–Brevier* (Leipzig, 1915). Joseph Boonin, *An Index to the Solo Songs of Robert Franz* (Hackensack, N.J., 1970). Bernhard Hartmann, *Das Verhältnis von Sprache und Musik in den Liedern von Robert Franz* (New York, 1991).

Frasi, Giulia (fl. 1742–72). Soprano. Went to London from Milan in 1742; studied with G. F. Brivio in Milan and with Burney in England. Sang in operas of Galuppi, Porpora, Hasse, and others; appeared extensively in Handel's operas and oratorios as well, with several parts written for her. Burney commented on her "sweet and clear voice" but also referred to her lack of "application and diligence." She went into debt and died in poverty.

Frauenlob [Heinrich von Meissen] (b. in or near Meissen?, between 1250 and 1260; d. Mainz, 29 Nov. 1318). Minnesinger. Many courts in northern and eastern Germany and a number of persons of high secular or ecclesiastical rank played a part in his life, though little biographical detail survives. His works include melodies in a traditional rather than innovative style and examples of the late courtly *Spruch.* The Meistersinger regarded him as one of their most important predecessors.

Frederick II of Prussia [Frederick the Great] (b. Berlin, 24 Jan. 1712; d. Sanssouci, Potsdam, 17 Aug. 1786). Monarch, flutist, and composer. Despite a very stern upbringing, he managed as a boy to study the flute and thoroughbass; while at Dresden in 1728 he saw his first opera, Hasse's *Cleofilde,* and first heard his future court flutist and chamber composer Quantz perform. His father forbade music in 1730; he tried to escape to England but was captured and imprisoned. He received command of a regiment soon thereafter and balanced duties of state with musical pursuits, receiving intermittent lessons from Quantz and maintaining an orchestra. He ascended the throne on 31 May 1740; within two months he had moved to found the Berlin opera. C. P. E. Bach was hired as first harpsichordist in the same year, with Quantz arriving in 1741. From 1742 until 1756, as Frederick pursued an aggressive foreign policy to expand the Prussian state, two major operas were produced each year, with C. H. Graun and Hasse the most prominent composers; in addition, chamber concerts featured both the music and performances of the king. His preoccupation with the Seven Years' War and his hardening personality soon caused the musical environment at court to sour. Bach left in 1767; the opera house was dark from 1756 until 1764, and offerings thereafter were mainly revivals. Frederick's works show considerable skill, even if only sketched (the inner parts were generally filled in by his musicians), and his flute playing was accomplished; he also wrote several operatic plots and libretti.

Bibl.: Eugene E. Helm, *Music at the Court of Frederick the Great* (Norman, Okla., 1960).

Freed, Isadore (b. Belorussia, 26 Mar. 1900; d. New York, 10 Nov. 1960). Composer. Spent his childhood in Philadelphia and attended the Univ. of Pennsylvania; studied with Bloch and Josef Hoffman; and in Europe with d'Indy and Vierne. On his return he taught at Temple Univ. (1937–46) and at the Hartt School of Music (1947–60). He wrote *Harmonizing the Jewish Modes* (1958) and was known primarily for his Jewish sacred music composed in a diatonic, neoclassical style. Works include 2 operas, an oratorio, and a ballet; concertos for violin and cello and other orchestral pieces (*Improvisation and Scherzo,* horn, oboe, strings, 1960); 3 string quartets and other chamber, piano, and organ music; Sabbath services; sacred songs and choruses; secular songs.

Freedman, Harry (b. Łódź, Poland, 5 Apr. 1922). Composer and performer. Raised in Canada, he studied painting in Winnipeg; his interest in jazz led to clarinet lessons when he was 18. At the Toronto Conservatory (1945–51) he studied oboe with Perry Bauman and composition with Weinzweig; in 1949 he had composition lessons from Messiaen at Tanglewood. Freedman played English horn in the Toronto Symphony for 25 years; his skill at orchestration may be attributed in part to that experience. His study with Weinzweig led to some use of twelve-tone procedures, but he has also employed aleatory and theatrical effects. Some works stem from Freedman's interest in art, for example, the orchestral piece *Klee Wyck* (1970), inspired by the paintings of Emily Carr. His works include ballets and film music; many orchestral pieces (*Scenario,* alto saxophone, electric bass guitar, orchestra, 1970); chamber and vocal music (*Epitaph for Igor Stravinsky,* tenor, 4 trombones, string quartet, 1978). The Canada Council named him Composer of the Year in 1980.

Freeman, Bud [Lawrence] (b. Chicago, 13 Apr. 1906; d. there, 15 Mar. 1991). Jazz tenor saxophonist. His definitive recordings of Chicago jazz with McKenzie and Condon's Chicagoans (1927) initiated an affiliation with Eddie Condon that extended into the 1960s and included the recording "The Eel" (1933). He joined Ben Pollack (1927–28), Red Nichols (1929), Tommy Dorsey (1936–38), and Benny Goodman (1938) before leading the Summa cum Laude Orchestra, an octet that combined swing and Dixieland (1939–40). He briefly led a big band, but over the next 50 years mainly toured internationally as a soloist in small groups. He also was a member of the World's Greatest Jazz Band (1969–71) and recorded the duo album *Bucky and Bud* with the guitarist Bucky Pizzarelli (ca. 1975).

Writings: *You Don't Look like a Musician* (Detroit, 1974). *If You Know of a Better Life, Please Tell Me* (Dublin, 1976). *Crazeology* (Urbana, Ill., 1989).

Freeman, Harry Lawrence (b. Cleveland, 9 Oct. 1869; d. New York, 21 Mar. 1954). Composer and conductor. He studied piano with Edwin Schonert and composition with Johann Beck; played the organ in churches from the age of 10. In the 1890s he played the piano and composed pieces and marches in Denver; taught at Wilberforce Univ. (1902–4) and was active as a theater-orchestra conductor in Chicago (Pekin Theatre Stock Company) and New York (Red Moon Company) until 1910; then established the Freeman School of Music in New York. He conducted the Negro Choral Society and the Negro Grand Opera Company, which performed his *Voodoo* (1914) and *Vendetta* (1923) in the 1920s; his first opera (*The Martyr,* 1893) was performed in concert version in Carnegie Hall in 1947; others were heard on the radio. Works include 14 operas, 2 ballets; *The Slave,* a symphonic poem for chorus and orchestra (1925); dances and marches; cantatas; songs.

Freer, Eleanor Everest (b. Philadelphia, 14 May 1864; d. Chicago, 13 Dec. 1942). Composer. She studied voice and piano from childhood; studied voice (Mathilde Marchesi) and composition (Benjamin Godard) in Paris (1883–86); taught piano in Philadelphia before marrying and moving to Chicago in 1891, where she studied theory with Bernard Ziehn (1902–7). She was a founding member of the American Opera Society. Works include 11 operas (most performed in Chicago; *Massimiliano, the Court Jester, or the Love of a Caliban,* 1932); over 150 songs (a cycle of *44 Sonnets from the Portuguese,* after E. B. Browning); piano pieces.

Freitas (Branco), Frederico (Guedes) de (b. Lisbon, 15 Nov. 1902; d. there, 12 Jan. 1980). Composer. Studied at the National Conservatory, winning the National Composition Prize in 1926 for his *Nocturno* for cello and piano. Served as conductor of the Portuguese Broadcasting Company's chamber orchestra, and as assistant director of its symphony; in 1940 created the Lisbon Choral Society, and from 1949–53 led the Oporto Symphony. His music ranges from polytonal to nationalist and pictorial in character; works include a radio opera, ballets, and many other orchestral compositions in addition to vocal and chamber music and piano pieces.

Freitas Branco, Luis de (b. Lisbon, 12 Oct. 1890; d. there, 27 Nov. 1955). Composer. Studied with Borba, Pacques, and Mancinelli in Lisbon, and also with Humperdinck in Berlin and Grovlez in Paris; joined the National Conservatory faculty upon returning to Lisbon in 1916, serving later as assistant director and in other posts until withdrawing from public life in 1939 under official pressure. He played a major role in introducing then-current European musical styles into Portugal, not only as a composer but also as a critic for several journals and as a reformer of the conservatory curriculum. In addition to writing biographies of Beethoven and King João IV and investigating Portuguese polyphony and theater music, he contributed to the discovery of the first Spanish opera, *Celos a un del ayre matan.* His earlier music is impressionist in nature, with his work after the mid-1920s often showing neoclassical features.

Works: *Manfredo* and *Noemi,* soloists, chorus, orchestra (1905, 1937); 4 symphonies (1924, 1926, 1943, 1952); symphonic poems (*Antero do Quental,* 1908; *Os paraísos artificiais,* 1910; *Vathek,* 1913; *Viriato,* 1916; *Solemnia verba,* 1952); *Suite alentejana* nos. 1, 2 (1919, 1927); *Balada,* piano, orchestra, and *Cena lírica,* cello, orchestra (1917); film scores; chamber music (2 violin sonatas, 1907, 1928; a string quartet, 1911); vocal music.

Fremstad, Olive (b. Stockholm, 14 Mar. 1871; d. Irvington-on-Hudson, N.Y., 21 Apr. 1951). Soprano. An illegitimate child, she was adopted by an evangelist. Played harmonium and sang at revival meetings as a small child. In her early teens she emigrated with her family to Minnesota, where she played organ in church and dreamed of becoming a concert pianist. Studied voice with F. E. Bristol in New York, 1891–92. Stage debut as Lady Saphir *(Patience)* with the Boston Ideals. Studied with Lilli Lehmann in Berlin from 1893. Grand opera debut as Azucena (*Il trovatore;* a mezzo role) with the Cologne Opera, 1895. Sang small mezzo parts at Bayreuth, 1896; London debut, 1897. With the Munich Opera (1900–1903) she developed her high range; New York Metropolitan Opera debut as Sieglinde *(Die Walküre),* 23 Nov. 1903. She remained there 11 seasons, singing the major Wagnerian roles as well as Carmen (from 1906), Salome (1907), Tosca (1910), and Armide (1910). At the time of her last Met performance (1914) she had already sung several seasons with the Chicago Opera, with which she gave her final stage performance in 1918. Sang in concert until 1920.

French, Jacob (b. Stoughton, Mass., 15 July 1754; d. Simsbury, Conn., May 1817). Composer and singing master. In 1774 he attended William Billings's singing school in Stoughton; after his war service (ca. 1775–81) he taught music and served as singing master in Uxbridge, Mass., and in Providence, R.I. He is best known for 3 published tunebooks that appeared during his lifetime: *The New American Melody* (1789), *The Psalmodist's Companion* (1793), and *The Harmony of Harmony* (1802); they contain more than 100 of his own compositions as well as works by his contemporaries.

Freni, Mirella [Fregni] (b. Modena, 27 Feb. 1935). Soprano. Studied voice from 1951 with her uncle, Dante Arcelli, in Bologna, then with Ettore Campogalliani in Mantua. Debut in 1955 at the Teatro comunale in Modena as Micaëla *(Carmen).* Sang at the Amsterdam Opera (1957); at the Glyndebourne Festival (1960) as Zerlina *(Don Giovanni);* at Covent Garden (1961) as Nannetta *(Falstaff);* at La Scala (1963) as Mimi *(La bohème)* in a production that was filmed. Debut at the New York Metropolitan Opera as Mimi on 29 Sept. 1965. Sang annually at Salzburg beginning 1968. Ill health interrupted her career in the 1970s; she returned as Liù *(Turandot).* Traveled with the Paris Opéra on its first American tour, 1976.

Frescobaldi, Girolamo (b. Ferrara, mid-Sept. 1583; d. Rome, 1 Mar. 1643). Keyboardist and composer. His father was a musician and a prominent Ferrarese citizen; he studied with the Ferrarese court organist Luzzaschi (a debt he often acknowledged in dedications), from whom he received training on Vicentino's chromatic *archicembalo* as well. He was named organist at the Accademia della Morte in 1597 at the age of 14. At some point he came under the patronage of Guido Bentivoglio, a cleric and member of a powerful Ferrarese family. The duchy of Ferrara reverted to the papacy upon Alfonso's death in 1597; the principal Vatican figure in the affair, Cardinal Pietro Aldobrandini, promised a post at the papal court to Guido, who soon went to Rome, taking Frescobaldi with him. Girolamo was admitted to the Accademia di S. Cecilia in 1604 and became organist at S. Maria in Trastevere in 1607. He accompanied Guido to Flanders in 1607–8, where a set of his 5-part madrigals was published. He was summoned back to Rome by Guido's brother Enzo, a Vatican official, and was appointed organist of the Cappella Giulia, St. Peter's, upon his return; he worked also as a member of Enzo's household *musica,* though he was less than diligent in that post. He married in 1612 after fathering two illegitimate children by his future wife; by 1615 he seems to have left the service of the Bentivoglio family for that of Cardinal Aldobrandini, while the court of Mantua made an abortive effort to engage him in that same year.

The next 13 years were his most fruitful in terms of output, with the 2 books of toccatas, sets of ricercars, canzonas, and capriccios, and a collection of ensemble canzonas appearing during this time. In addition, his fame as a keyboardist continued to grow; he took various engagements while keeping his posts at the Vatican and with the Aldobrandini family. He was in the employ of the Medici in Florence, 1628–34; his only works from this period are the 2 books of *Arie musi-*

cali, encompassing strophic songs, through-composed madrigals, and works in *stile recitativo.* Returning again to Rome, he resumed playing at St. Peter's, in addition taking a post with Cardinal Francesco Barberini and appearing at the celebrated Oratorio del Crocifisso during Lent; the French viol player Andrè Maugars commented in 1639 on his masterly improvisations at these Lenten performances. His international reputation brought Froberger to study with him in 1637–41. He took ill and died amidst the chaos of the final years of the Barberini papacy of Urban VII.

Frescobaldi's compositions were central to keyboard study until well into the next century; Gasparini was among those commending them, and J. S. Bach copied out the *Fiori musicali* (1635), a publication of liturgical organ music. Revised versions of earlier toccatas and ensemble canzonas show him to be concerned with the final state of his work.

Bibl.: *Opere complete* (Milan, 1975–). *Orgel- und Klavierwerke,* ed. Pierre Pidoux, 5 vols. (Kassel, 1957–63). Frederick Hammond, *Girolamo Frescobaldi* (Cambridge, Mass., 1983). Id., *Girolamo Frescobaldi: A Guide to Research* (New York, 1988). Alexander Silbiger, ed., *Frescobaldi Studies* (Durham, N.C., 1987).

Freund, Marya [Maria] (b. Breslau, 12 Dec. 1876; d. Paris, 21 May 1966). Soprano. She studied violin with Pablo de Sarasate and with Florian Zajic in Berlin; voice with Julius von Stockhausen in Frankfurt and Raimund von Zur Mühlen in London. Debut in Berlin in 1909 as soloist in Rubinstein's *Christus.* Toured Europe and the U.S. from 1910; appeared with most major orchestras and conductors as a sensitive singer of the standard repertory. Sang Mahler's *Kindertotenlieder* (1912); Schoenberg's *Pierrot lunaire* in Berlin (1912); Schoenberg's Wood Dove at the premiere of *Gurrelieder* (1913); later one of the first to sing dodecaphonic vocal music. Her many premieres included works by Satie, Bloch, Kodály, Malipiero, Prokofiev, Poulenc, Szymanowski.

Frick, Gottlob (b. Ölbronn, Germany, 28 July 1906; d. Pforzheim, 18 Aug. 1994). Bass. Youngest of a forester's 13 children, he studied with Fritz Windgassen as an extramural student at the Stuttgart Conservatory, then with the baritone Neudörfer-Opitz. After singing in the choruses at the Stuttgart Opera and at Bayreuth, made his solo debut in 1934 at Coburg as Daland *(Der fliegende Holländer).* Sang Wagnerian and other bass roles (Osmin, Sarastro, Rocco, Philippe II) at the Dresden State Opera, 1938–52; at the Berlin State Opera from 1947. Sang at Covent Garden, 1951, 1957–67, 1971. Appeared with the Vienna State Opera every year from 1953; with the Munich Opera every year for 20 years. Sang Pogner *(Meistersinger)* at Bayreuth, 1960–64.

Fricker, Peter Racine (b. London, 5 Sept. 1920; d. Santa Barbara, Calif., 1 Feb. 1990). Composer. At the Royal College of Music his instructors were Reginald Morris (theory) and Sir Ernest Bullock (organ). He met Michael Tippett in 1939 at Morley College, and after his war service he returned to Morley to study with Mátyás Seiber (1946–48). In 1952 he joined the faculty there; later he also taught at the Royal College (1955–64). He taught composition at the Univ. of California, Santa Barbara, 1964–84; chairman of its music department, 1970–82. His musical style, which grew from that of Bartók and Hindemith, occasionally employs twelve-note melodies and partial serialism. His oeuvre is large: stage works include incidental music to *King John* (1961); 7 film scores (*The White Continent,* 1951); radio operas (*My Brother Died,* 1952–54; *The Death of Vivien,* 1955–56); orchestral works (5 symphonies, 1948–76; 4 *Concertantes; Rapsodia concertante,* 1953–54; *Litany,* 1955; *Nocturne,* chamber orchestra, 1971; *Sinfonia,* winds, 1976–77; *Laudi concertati,* organ and orchestra, 1979); choral music (*Rollant et Oliver,* 1949; *The Vision of Judgement,* oratorio, 1957–58; *Ave maris stella,* 1967; *Magnificat,* 1968); he also composed solo vocal music (*Night Landscape,* soprano, string trio, 1947); many songs; chamber works (4 string quartets, 1947, 1953, 1974, 1976; 5 serenades; an octet for winds and strings, 1957–58; *The Groves of Dodona,* 6 flutes, 1973); piano music (*Variations,* 1958; *Episode I,* 1968; *II,* 1969); organ works (*Toccata "Gladius Domini,"* 1968; *Five Short Pieces,* 1980).

Fricsay, Ferenc (b. Budapest, 9 Aug. 1914; d. Basel, 20 Feb. 1963). Conductor. Studied with his father at the Budapest Academy from 1921, then with Kodály and Bartók. At 15 replaced his father at the head of a military orchestra. In Szeged conducted the symphony and opera, 1934–44. As musical director reorganized the National Philharmonic of Hungary in 1945. Though he conducted at the Vienna State Opera in 1945, his international reputation dates from 1947, when he replaced Klemperer at Salzburg for the premiere of an opera by Gottfried von Einem; engaged there to conduct new operas by Frank Martin (1948) and Carl Orff (1949). Conductor at the Berlin State Opera, 1948–52; of the Berlin Radio Symphony, 1948–54; of the Houston Symphony, 1954–55. Music director of the Munich State Opera, 1955–59; of the West Berlin Opera, 1961–63.

Frid, Géza (b. Máramarossziget, Hungary, 25 Jan. 1904; d. Beverwijk, the Netherlands, 13 Sept. 1989). Composer and pianist. A child prodigy pianist, he began his formal musical studies in 1912 at the Budapest Academy. His piano teacher was Bartók, his composition instructor Kodály; after completing his studies in 1924 he toured Europe and the Far East, occasionally with violinist Zoltán Székely. Settling in the Netherlands in 1929, he established himself as concert pianist and accompanist; among those with whom he toured was the soprano Erna Spoorenberg. In 1964 he was made professor of chamber music at the Utrecht Conservatory. He was a prolific composer; works include an opera, *De zwarte bruid* (1959); orchestral works

(*Suite,* 1929; a violin concerto, 1930; a symphony, 1933; *Fête champêtre,* string orchestra, 1951; *Études symphoniques,* 1954; *Sinfonietta,* string orchestra, 1963); choral music (Schopenhauer Cantata, 1944; *Hymne aan de Arbeid,* male chorus, orchestra, 1951; *Das Sklavenschiff,* 1956; *Houdt den Tijd!,* male chorus, percussion, 1971); chamber music (4 string quartets; *Twelve Metamophoses,* winds and piano, 1963; *Sous roumains,* chamber ensemble, 1975); songs; choruses; music for keyboard.

Fried, Oskar (b. Berlin, 1 Aug. 1871; d. Moscow, 5 July 1941). Composer and conductor. After playing in the opera orchestra in Berlin, he studied briefly in Munich; was prominent as a conductor of contemporary music in the early 1900s (especially in works of Mahler, Strauss, and Stravinsky); in Berlin he conducted the Neuen Konzerte (1905) and the Gesellschaft der Musikfreunde (1907). By 1913, when he stopped composing, he had written an opera and several works for orchestra (*Praeludium und Doppelfuge* op. 10, 1902) as well as music for women's voices and songs; in addition he wrote pieces for voices and orchestra (*Verklärte Nacht,* mezzo-soprano and tenor, 1901). From 1934 he conducted opera in Tbilisi.

Friedheim, Arthur (b. St. Petersburg, 26 Oct. 1859; d. New York, 19 Oct. 1932). Pianist, conductor, and composer. Studied piano with Carl Siecke, 1865–74 (concert debut, 1869); with Anton Rubinstein, 1874–78. In 1879–80 conducted at the Court Theater of Schwarzburg-Rudolstadt. Student and companion of Liszt, 1880–86; respected thereafter as Liszt's most persuasive interpreter. Based in New York, 1891–97; in England, 1897–1908. Conducted in Munich, 1908–10. Toured North America and Europe, 1910–14; then accompanied silent films and played vaudeville in the U.S. Taught at the New York School of Music and Arts, 1917–32; at the Canadian Academy in Toronto, 1922–24. His memoirs, *Life and Liszt,* were edited by a pupil, Theodore Bullock, in 1961. He composed several operas, 2 piano concertos, some orchestral music.

Friedhofer, Hugo (William) (b. San Francisco, 3 May 1901; d. Los Angeles, 17 May 1981). Composer and cellist. Supported himself as a cellist while studying composition with Domenico Brescia and Schoenberg; later studied with Toch, Boulanger, and Ernest Kamitz. Arranged and sometimes composed music for silent films; from 1935 he worked as an orchestrator for Warner Bros.; beginning in 1938 he composed the music for some 70 films, including *The Adventures of Marco Polo* (1938), *The Best Years of Our Lives* (Academy Award, 1946), *Joan of Arc* (1948), *The Sun Also Rises* (1957), and *Geronimo* (1962).

Friedman, Ignaz [Freudmann] (b. Podgorze, near Kraków, 14 Feb. 1882; d. Sydney, 26 Jan. 1948). Pianist and composer. Studied piano with his father in Kraków; theory with Hugo Riemann in Leipzig; piano with Theodor Leschetizky and musicology with Guido Adler in Vienna. From 1904 toured Europe, the U.S., and Australia, giving in all about 2,800 concerts, and winning particular praise for his interpretations of Chopin. Based in Berlin from 1904; in Copenhagen from 1914; in the U.S. from 1920 (chiefly Tacoma, Wash.); in Sydney from 1941. With Pablo Casals and Bronislaw Hubermann, he performed the complete piano trios of Beethoven in Vienna. Edited works of Chopin, Schumann, and Liszt. Wrote many piano pieces, chamber music, songs.

Friml, (Charles) Rudolf (b. Prague, 7 Dec. 1879; d. Los Angeles, 12 Nov. 1972). Composer and pianist. Studied piano with Josef Jiránek and composition with Dvořák, to whose style his own works are closely related. He was active as an accompanist; after tours with the violinist Jan Kubelík, he emigrated to the U.S. (1906). He performed his Piano Concerto no. 1 with the New York Symphony Orchestra under Damrosch and remained active as a pianist throughout his career. As a composer, he wrote serious and lighter music, the latter often under the pseudonym Roderick Freeman; his career as a composer of operettas was launched with *The Firefly* (1912), in which he substituted for Victor Herbert; other successes were *High Jinks* (1913), *Rose Marie* (1924; in collaboration with Stothart, Harbach, and Oscar Hammerstein II), *The Vagabond King* (1925), and *The Three Musketeers* (1928). After 1929, when his shows became less successful, he was more active as a pianist. In addition to operettas he composed 3 film scores; a symphony *(Round the World),* a symphonic poem (*Escape to Hong Kong,* ca. 1961), 2 piano concertos, and orchestral suites; dances, character pieces (*5 Mood Pictures* op. 79), etudes, and suites (*Bohemian Suite* op. 60) for piano; many songs ("I Want the World To Know," 1937; "Two Lovely Lying Eyes," 1921).

Frizzell, Lefty [William Orville] (b. Corsicana, Tex., 31 Mar. 1928; d. Nashville, 19 July 1975). Country singer and songwriter. He began singing in bars in West Texas and New Mexico, then moved to Nashville, where he made recordings of original and borrowed material. His own "If You've Got the Money, Honey, I've Got the Time" (1950) was popular, as were his renditions of "Long Black Veil" (1959) and "Saginaw, Michigan" (1964). His vocal style, inspired by Jimmy Rodgers's recordings, has influenced many later artists including Merle Haggard.

Froberger, Johann Jacob (bapt. Stuttgart, 19 May 1616; d. Héricourt, near Belfort, France, 6 or 7 May 1667). Keyboardist and composer. Probably studied with his father, Kapellmeister at Stuttgart, and possibly also with local organists Steigleder and Eckhardt. Became a court organist at Vienna in 1637; studied with Frescobaldi in Rome at imperial expense, 1637–41; returned to Vienna as organist, 1641–45. He perhaps visited Italy again in 1649, making contact with Carissimi at Rome and performing in Florence and Mantua;

back in Vienna, a presentation manuscript of his keyboard works dedicated to Emperor Ferdinand III is dated 29 Sept. 1649. He evidently was in Brussels in 1650, in France in 1652 (where he performed successfully and met Chambonnières, Louis Couperin, and Denis Gaultier), and also in England around this time. Mattheson refers to a competition with Weckmann (whom Froberger later befriended) in Dresden. He was reinstated as Viennese court organist in 1653 but dismissed in 1658; his final position was as tutor to Princess Sibylla of Württemberg-Montbéliard at Héricourt, where he died suddenly during a vespers service.

Though little of his music was published in his lifetime, he was very influential through posthumous prints and manuscript copies; his fusion of Frescobaldi's Italianate idiom with the French style of the era served as a model for many later German keyboard composers. His frequent designation as creator of the standardized suite must be questioned, however; the autograph manuscripts of his suites generally make the sarabande the last dance, with the gigue taking this position only in prints dating from the 1690s. His works, almost all for keyboard, reflect his mixed musical heritage: his partitas, capriccios, ricercars, and toccatas (some *alla levatione* for use in the liturgy) are in a style close to Frescobaldi's, while his suites and programmatic works (including several moving *tombeaux*) are based on the French usage.

Bibl.: *Orgel- und Klavierwerke,* ed. Guido Adler, *DTÖ* 8, 4/1 (1897); 10, 6/2 (1899); 21, 10/2 (1903). *Oeuvres complètes pour clavecin,* ed. Howard Schott (Paris, 1979–). H. Siedentopf, *Johann Jakob Froberger: Leben und Werk* (Stuttgart, 1977).

Frumerie, (Per) Gunnar (Fredrik) de (b. Nacka, Sweden, 20 July 1908; d. Mörby, 9 Sept. 1987). Composer and pianist. He studied piano with his mother and then with L. Lundberg; attended the Stockholm Conservatory (1923–28) and later continued his piano studies in Vienna with Emil von Sauer and then in Paris with Alfred Cortot. From 1945 to 1974 he was a piano teacher at the Stockholm Musikhögskolan. His opera *Singoalla* (1937–40) won him distinction as a composer of music drama. He is also known for his vocal music. Works include 2 piano concertos (1929, 1935); concertos for violin (1936), 2 pianos (1953), clarinet (1958), trumpet (1959), oboe (1961), flute (1969), horn (1972), and cello (1984, orchestration of Sonata no. 2 for cello and piano, 1947; also orchestrated as a trombone concerto, 1986). He also wrote choral and chamber music.

Fry, William Henry (b. Philadelphia, 10 or 19 Aug. 1813; d. Santa Cruz, Virgin Islands, 21 Dec. 1864). Composer. Son of a newspaper publisher; educated in Philadelphia (studying music there with Leopold Meignen) and at St. Mary's College, Maryland; began to compose in his teens. His *Leonora* is usually considered the first American grand opera to be staged (Philadelphia, 4 June 1845); followed by *Notre Dame de Paris* (Philadelphia, 1864), both to librettos by his brother. In 1846–52 he was European correspondent for various American newspapers; from 1852, editorial writer and music critic, *New York Tribune,* championing the development of a native American music; 1861, secretary of legation, Turin. Other works include concert overtures, program symphonies; Mass; oratorio.

Bibl.: W. T. Upton, *William Henry Fry: American Journalist and Composer–Critic* (New York, 1954; R: 1974).

Frye, Walter (fl. ca. 1450–75). Composer. Although most of his music survives in Continental manuscripts only, he probably never worked outside his native England. The extant compositions include three Mass cycles (all based on cantus firmi), a handful of motets and other short sacred compositions, and a few secular songs.

Bibl.: *Opera omnia, CMM* 19 (1960). Sylvia W. Kenney, *Walter Frye and the Contenance angloise* (New Haven, Conn., 1964).

Fuchs, Joseph (Philip) (b. New York, 26 Apr. 1900). Violinist. Brother of Lillian; studied violin with Franz Kneisel at the Institute of Musical Art, New York (diploma, 1918). Debut at Aeolian Hall in 1920; concertmaster of the Cleveland Orchestra, 1926–40, and leader of the first Cleveland Quartet, 1930–34. Established career as soloist in 1943. Joined faculty of the Juilliard School in 1946. Toured widely; gave premieres of concertos by Ben Weber (1959), Walter Piston (1960), and others.

Fuchs, Lillian (b. New York, 18 Nov. 1903; d. Englewood, N.J., 5 Oct. 1995). Violist. Sister of Joseph. At the Institute of Musical Art, studied violin with Louis Svečenski and Franz Kneisel and composition with Percy Goetschius. Founding violist with the Perolé Quartet, 1925–45. Solo debut (as a violinist) in New York, 1926. Taught at the Manhattan School of Music from 1962; also at Juilliard from 1971. Gave premieres of viola works by Martinů, Quincy Porter, and Rieti. Composed numerous works for her instrument, including *12 Capricci* (1950), *Sonata Pastorale* (1956), and *Fantasy Etudes* (1961).

Fuchs, Robert (b. Frauenthal, Styria, 15 Feb. 1847; d. Vienna, 19 Feb. 1927). Composer and teacher. Studied at the Vienna Conservatory (composition under Dessoff); 1875–1912, professor there (harmony, theory), his pupils including Mahler, Wolf, Schreker, Sibelius, Zemlinsky, Franz Schmidt. From 1875, conductor of the concerts of the Gesellschaft der Musikfreunde; 1894–1905, court organist. His compositions include operas, 5 symphonies, 5 orchestral serenades, chamber music, choral works, songs, organ and piano pieces. Brother of Johann Nepomuk Fuchs (1842–99), opera conductor and director of the Vienna Conservatory.

Bibl.: Anton Mayr, *Erinnerungen an Robert Fuchs* (Graz, 1934). R. Pascall, "Robert Fuchs," *MT* 118 (1977): 115–17.

Fuenllana, Miguel de (b. Navalcarnero, near Madrid, early 16th cent.; d. after 1568). Vihuelist and composer. Employed in Spanish royal and noble courts, including those of Philip II and of his third wife, Elisabeth de Valois. His *Orphénica lyra* (Seville, 1554) presents numerous intabulations for vihuela of works by other composers and nearly 70 original pieces, of which over 50 are fantasias. The preface gives information on performance practice.

Fukushima, Kazuo (b. Tokyo, 11 Apr. 1930). Composer. Largely self-taught in music, he joined Jikken Kōbō in 1953, a group of experimental composers that included among its members Toru Takemitsu. He began to claim recognition during the late 1950s; Stravinsky reportedly admired his *Ekagura* (1958) for flute and piano. In 1961 he lectured at the Darmstadt Summer Course, and in 1963 he won a fellowship to study in New York. From 1964 he taught in Tokyo at the Ueno Gakuen Academy. His music mixes elements of traditional Japanese musical styles and of Western avant-garde virtuosic styles. Works include *Kadha hihaku* [Flying Spirit], chamber orchestra (1959); *Tsukishiro* [Moon-Spirit], string orchestra, piano, percussion (1965); *Shizu-uta,* soprano, female chorus, flutes, harp (1961); *Requiem,* flute (1956); *Three Pieces from Chu-u,* flute, piano (1958); *Mizu no wa* [A Ring of the Wind], piano (1968); *Shun-san* [Hymn to Spring], flute (1969).

Fuleihan, Anis (b. Kyrenia, Cyprus, 2 Apr. 1900; d. Stanford, Calif., 11 Oct. 1970). Composer, conductor, and pianist. He came to the U.S. in 1915 and made his New York debut as a pianist in November, 1919. He was self-taught as a composer, but studied piano with Alberto Jonas and theory with Harold Milligan and Louis Loth. In the 1920s he toured in the U.S. and the Near East as a pianist; spent two years in Cairo studying folk music; in the next decade he was active as a radio conductor and worked for G. Schirmer. He taught at Indiana Univ. (1947–53) and was director of the Beirut Conservatory (1953–60); he founded and conducted the Orchestre Classique in Tunis (1962–65), sponsored by the U.S. State Department. Dissonance was more pronounced in his earlier compositions; many show Eastern influences. Works include an opera and ballets; 2 symphonies, many concertos, symphonic poems (*The Pyramids of Giza,* 1952), and other orchestral works; 5 string quartets (1940–65) and other chamber music for winds and brass; piano music; choral music and songs.

Fulkerson, James Orville (b. Manville, Ill., 2 July 1945). Composer and trombonist. Studied trombone and composition at Illinois Wesleyan Univ. (B.A., 1966) and then at Univ. of Illinois (Martirano, Gaburo, Hiller, and Brün); after periods in Buffalo, Germany, and Australia, he settled at Dartington College (England) in 1981. He has written more than 150 works, some minimalist and many using graphic notation or live electronics. His compositions include mixed media, theater pieces, dance, incidental music, television scores (*Put Your Foot Down Charlie,* 3 dancers, speaker, electric guitar and piano, amplified saxophone, electric trombone, 1982); some 15 orchestral works; instrumental chamber music; electronic music and live electronics (*Elective Affinities,* amplified cello and trombone, tape, and live electronic ensemble, 1980).

Fuller, Albert (b. Washington, D.C., 21 July 1926). Harpsichordist. Studied organ with Paul Callaway at the National Cathedral; with Ernest White at the Peabody Conservatory; with Ralph Kirkpatrick at Yale (M.Mus., 1954). New York recital debut, 1957; European debut, 1959. Taught at Catholic Univ. of America, 1949–51; at Juilliard from 1964. Founding music director, 1972–83, of Aston Magna, a touring ensemble and a summer institute in Great Barrington, Mass., dedicated to the performance of Baroque and early classical music on authentic instruments; of the similar Helicon Foundation, 1984, which was limited to private symposiums until the debut of the Helicon Ensemble in 1989.

Fuller, Blind Boy [Allen, Fulton] (b. Wadesboro, N.C., ca. 1909; d. Durham, N.C., 13 Feb. 1941). Blues guitarist and singer. A leading player of the "Piedmont" style of blues developed by Blind Blake, he made numerous recordings in the 1930s, including "Rag Mama Rag" (1935) and "Pistol Slapper Blues" (1938). He worked with Blind Gary Davis and Brownie McGhee and Sonny Terry.

Furtwängler, (Gustav Heinrich Ernst Martin) Wilhelm (b. Berlin, 25 Jan. 1886; d. Baden-Baden, 30 Nov. 1954). Conductor and composer. Studied theory and composition privately with Anton Beer-Walbrunn (1898), Josef Rheinberger (1900), and Max von Schillings (1902). His uncle, Georg Dohrn, conducted in Breslau; there Furtwängler heard his *Te Deum* premiered in 1904 and obtained his first post in 1905 as a répétiteur. Répétiteur, then assistant conductor at the Zürich Municipal Theater, 1906–8. Conducting debut in Munich in 1906, leading his own Adagio in B minor and Bruckner's Ninth Symphony. Répétiteur at the Munich Opera, 1908–9. Assistant conductor there under Felix Mottl, 1909–10; at the Strasbourg Opera under Pfitzner, 1910–11. A revision of the *Te Deum* in 1910 established his reputation as a composer. Conductor of the Lübeck Philharmonic, 1911–15. Music director of the Mannheim Opera, 1915–20. Guest conductor of the Berlin Philharmonic, 1917; an influential review spoke of "the Furtwängler miracle." Succeeded Strauss in 1920 as conductor of symphony concerts at the Berlin State Opera; succeeded Nikisch in 1922 as conductor of the Leipzig Gewandhaus Orchestra and the Berlin Philharmonic. Stayed with Leipzig until 1928; with Berlin the rest of his life. Acclaimed U.S. debut with the New York Philharmonic on 3 Jan. 1925; returned in 1926, 1927; declined its music directorship in 1927. Conducted at Bayreuth, 1931–32. Director of the Berlin State Opera, 1933. He incurred disapprobation in Nazi Germany by continuing to hire Jewish musicians and to program new works by Schoenberg,

Stravinsky, Bartók, Prokofiev, and Hindemith; when officials forbade the premiere of Hindemith's *Mathis der Mahler* in 1934, Furtwängler published a defense of the work and the next month resigned all his posts; eventually he returned to the Berlin Philharmonic and Opera. Placed under continual surveillance from 1937; after the failure of a plot to kill Hitler in 1944 he fled with his family to Switzerland. Tried as a Nazi collaborator in 1946; acquitted in 1947 and allowed to conduct again. His compositions include a piano quartet (1934), 2 violin sonatas (1935, 1938), a piano concerto (1936/37), and 3 symphonies (1937–43, 1943–46, 1954).

Fussell, Charles (Clement) (b. Winston-Salem, N.C., 14 Feb. 1938). Composer. He earned a B.M. in 1960 from Eastman, where his teachers included Thomas Canning, Wayne Barlow, and Bernard Rogers. In 1962 he studied with Boris Blacher at the Berlin Hochschule für Musik. In 1963 he attended Friedelind Wagner's Bayreuth Festival Master Class in opera production and conducting. He returned to Eastman for an M.M. in 1964 and became a theory and composition teacher at the Univ. of Massachusetts in Amherst in 1966, where he founded Pro Musica Moderna. He later taught at the North Carolina School of the Arts and at Boston Univ. Works include *Caligula* (opera, 1962); 3 symphonies (1963, 1964–67, 1978–81); 3 Processionals (1972–73); *Northern Lights* (chamber orchestra, 1977–79); *4 Fairy Tales* (1980–81); *Three Portraits* (chamber orchestra, 1986); chamber and vocal music.

Fux, Johann Joseph (b. Hirtenfield, near St. Marein, Styria, 1660; d. Vienna, 16 Feb. 1741). Theorist and composer. Little is known of his early years. He was admitted to the Jesuit Univ. in Graz in 1680 and by 1683 was enrolled in a similar school at Ingolstadt, where he was also organist at St. Moritz in 1685–88. He may have served the Hungarian bishop Count von Kollnitsch after this time and perhaps traveled to Italy. His later posts included organist at the Schottenkirche in Vienna (by 1696–1702), court composer (from 16 Apr. 1698), Vice-Kapellmeister at St. Stephen's (from 1 Oct. 1705), and Kapellmeister at the same cathedral (1712–15). Charles VI appointed him principal court Kapellmeister, the most prestigious musical position in the land, in 1715; he remained in this post the rest of his life. His students included Wagenseil and Gottlieb Muffat. The main body of his work consists of church music (motets, 3 Requiems, oratorios, a double-choir Te Deum, dozens of Masses, and other liturgical pieces), but also includes some 20 operas, the most acclaimed perhaps being *Costanza e Fortezza* (Prague, 1723), as well as partitas, church sonatas, overtures, and keyboard works. His *Gradus ad Parnassum* (1725; German translation with commentary by L. C. Mizler, Leipzig, 1742) is the most influential book of its type, with masters such as Mozart, Haydn, Beethoven, and Brahms, not to mention countless students to the present day, indebted to it as a tutor for species counterpoint.

Bibl.: *Sämtliche Werke,* ed. Hellmut Federhofer and Othmar Wessely (Graz and Kassel, 1959–). L. W. von Köchel, *Johann Joseph Fux* (Vienna, 1874; R: 1974). Andreas Liess, *Fuxiana* (Vienna, 1958). Egon Wellesz, *Fux* (London, 1965). Hellmut Federhofer, "25 Jahre Johann Joseph Fux–Forschung," *AM* 52 (1980): 155–94. Harry White, ed. *Johann Joseph Fux and the Music of the Austro-Italian Baroque* (Aldershot, 1992).

G

Gabriel, Peter (b. London, 13 May 1950). Rock songwriter, singer, keyboardist, and guitarist. From 1969 to 1975 he was lead singer for the art rock band Genesis; many of their recordings were popular ("The Musical Box," 1971; *The Lamb Lies Down on Broadway,* 1974), as were Gabriel's live appearances, which incorporated elements of performance art. Composed the score for Martin Scorcese's *Last Temptation of Christ.* Later he released solo albums, achieving success with *Security* (1982, including "Shock the Monkey") and *So* (1986, including "Sledgehammer"). Genesis continued to record independently, led by drummer/singer Phil Collins (b. 1951).

Gabrieli, Andrea [Andrea di Cannaregio] (b. Venice, ca. 1510; d. there, late 1586). Organist and composer. Uncle of Giovanni Gabrieli. Almost nothing is known of his life before 1557, when he first tried (unsuccessfully) to become organist at St. Mark's, Venice. A lasting friendship with Lassus began during a trip to Germany in the early 1560s. The position of organist at St. Mark's was his from 1566 until his death. His influence in the later 16th century was considerable, especially in Italy but also in Germany. His works are among the first by a native Venetian to escape the dominance of the Netherlandish style. Innovative techniques are found particularly in the ceremonial music composed after he took up his post at St. Mark's. Such music tends to be homophonic, largely syllabic, perhaps polychoral, and above all sonorous. His many compositions, in nearly every genre known at the time, include sacred vocal pieces (Masses, Psalms, motets, concerti); madrigals (8 books and many independent pieces); other secular vocal works of various types; and many instrumental compositions (canzonas, ricercars, *intonationi,* and toccatas), most for keyboard. Many of his works were first published posthumously, edited by Giovanni Gabrieli.

Bibl.: *Ricercari für Orgel, I, II,* ed. Pierre Pidoux (Kassel, 1936; 2nd ed., 1952). *Musica di chiesa,* ed. G. d'Alessi, *CMI* 5 (1941). *Intonazionen für Orgel,* ed. Pierre Pidoux (Kassel, 1941; 2nd ed., 1967).

Gabrieli, Giovanni (b. Venice, ca. 1553–56; d. there, Aug. 1612). Composer. Nephew and pupil of Andrea Gabrieli. Court musician in Munich from 1575 or earlier until 1579, then an organist at St. Mark's, Venice, from 1584 until his death. After 1586 his duties included composition. His works are mostly sacred or instrumental, except for a few madrigals and canzonettas written in the 16th century.

Of his sacred vocal works all but the earliest are for two or more choirs and reveal a penchant for full, homophonic textures. Even in pieces from before 1600 some parts, especially lower ones, seem to be conceived for instruments, although none is explicitly so designated. His later works show an interest in more modern techniques. Although multiple performing groups are still called for, these tend to differ in nature—choral, soloistic, or instrumental (now frequently marked as such)—and in idiom. Organ (basso continuo) or instrumental ensembles may accompany solo vocal lines. This modernity is clear not only in his own works but also in pieces composed by certain of his students, such as Heinrich Schütz.

Purely instrumental music is unusually prominent in Gabrieli's output. Of his many works for keyboard solo, the ricercars are the most distinguished. More important, however, are the ensemble pieces, commonly named canzonas or sonatas. The majority of these are for multiple "choirs," with some florid voices for particular instruments, especially violins and cornets.

Relatively little of Gabrieli's work was published during his lifetime. The most substantial collection by far is his *Sacrae symphoniae* of 1597, which contains both motets and instrumental pieces. Much more came out shortly after his death, particularly the *Symphoniae sacrae . . . liber secundus* and the *Canzoni et sonate,* both of 1615. This music had little influence in Italy but greatly affected musical developments in Germanic lands.

Bibl.: *Opera omnia, CMM* 12 (1956–69). Egon Kenton, *Life and Works of Giovanni Gabrieli, MSD* 16 (1967) [includes list of early prints and manuscripts and a thematic catalog]. Denis Arnold, *Giovanni Gabrieli and the Music of the Venetian High Renaissance* (London, 1979). Richard Charteris, "Newly Discovered Works by Giovanni Gabrieli," *ML* 68 (1987): 343–62.

Gabrielli, Caterina (b. Rome, 12 Nov. 1730; d. there, 16? Feb. 1796). Soprano. Daughter of a cook in the kitchen of a nobleman, she carried the nickname "La cochetta" or "Coghetta." She perhaps studied with Porpora in Venice for a short period around 1745; later with castrato Gaetano Guadagni. Her Vienna debut in 1755 gained her a contract with the Imperial Theater; there she studied declamation with Metastasio and grew into one of the most prominent singers in all of Europe. She created roles in works by Gluck, Traetta, and many others. From 1771 she was engaged at Milan, from 1772 at St. Petersburg, and in 1775–76 in London.

Gabrielli, Domenico (b. Bologna, 15 Apr. 1651; d. there, 10 July 1696). Cellist and composer. Student of Legrenzi in Venice, of Franceschini in Bologna; succeeded the latter in 1680 as cellist at S. Petronio; admitted into the Accademia filarmonica in 1676, serving as president in 1683. Dismissed from S. Petronio in 1687, he was soon reinstated, serving in the interim at the Este court in Modena, where he had performed previously. His operas, dating from the 1680s, were staged at Venice, Bologna, Modena, and Turin; other works include a collection of dances published in 1684, ricercars for solo cello and for chamber ensemble, trio sonatas, trumpet sonatas (popular in Bologna at the time), and secular and sacred vocal music.

Gabrilowitsch, Ossip (Salomonovich) (b. St. Petersburg, 7 Feb. 1878; d. Detroit, 14 Sept. 1936). Conductor and pianist. At the St. Petersburg Conservatory (1888–94) studied piano with Victor Tolstov and Anton Rubinstein, composition with Liadov and Glazunov; studied theory with Navratil and piano with Leschetizky in Vienna (1894–95). Debut as pianist in Berlin in 1896; toured Europe and Russia to 1900. Based in the U.S., 1900–1910. Married the mezzo Clara Clemens, daughter of Mark Twain, in 1909; they gave frequent joint recitals. Conducted the Leipzig Gewandhaus Orchestra, 1905; the Munich Konzertverein, 1910–14; the Detroit Symphony, 1918–36. Guest conductor with the Philadelphia Orchestra and New York Philharmonic. He composed *Ouverture rhapsodie* for orchestra; piano pieces.

Gaburo, Kenneth (Louis) (b. Somerville, N.J., 5 July 1926; d. Iowa City, Iowa, 26 Jan. 1993). Composer. Studied composition with Bernard Rogers at Eastman (M.M., 1949), with Petrassi at the Accademia di S. Cecilia in Rome (1954–55), and at the Univ. of Illinois (D.Mus., 1962); taught primarily at the Univ. of Illinois (1955–68) and the Univ. of California at San Diego (1968–75). He was founder/conductor of the New Music Choral Ensemble (1962–75); in 1975 he established Lingua Press. His style varies from tonal, to serial (1954–59), to more experimental approaches incorporating theater and electronics. In 1959 he began his own serious study of linguistics, which led him to a "compositional linguistics" in which texts may be fragmented or clearly stated, voices live or electronically processed. Works include an opera, mixed media (*Antiphony VI: Cogito,* 1972, in which the string quartet plays, hums, whistles, etc. while a poem is read, slides of quartet members are shown, and a tape is played), and theater pieces, and incidental music; orchestral, chamber, and piano music; electronic pieces; various linguistic works (*Lingua II: Maledetto,* 7 virtuoso speakers); choral music and songs.

Gabussi, Vincenzo (b. Bologna, ca. 1800; d. London, 12 Sept. 1846). Composer. Studied under Padre Mattei, Bologna Conservatory; 3 operas produced in Italy and Paris without great success; best known as prolific composer of salon romances and duets and as a fashionable singing teacher in London, where he mostly lived from about 1825. His younger sister Rita was a well-known opera singer ca. 1830–51.

Gace Brulé (b. ca. 1160; d. after 1213). Trouvère. Little biographical information is known except that suggested in his poetry. He was evidently active at several French noble courts, such as that of Marie de France, knew many of the earliest trouvères, and may have participated in one or two Crusades. His exceptionally numerous poems and melodies achieved a wide popularity, being often quoted in literary works, imitated by later trouvères and minnesingers, and used as the basis for Latin *contrafacta.*

Bibl.: Ed. in *MMMA* 11 (1977). H. P. Dyggve, *Gace Brulé: Trouvère champenois* (Helsinki, 1951).

Gade, Niels (Wilhelm) (b. Copenhagen, 22 Feb. 1817; d. there, 21 Dec. 1890). Composer. Son of a cabinetmaker who turned to making violins and guitars; studied the violin and from 1834 was a student member of the Royal Orchestra; composed without much success until 1840, when his concert overture *Efterklange af Ossian* op. 1 won a prize from the Copenhagen Musical Society. In 1841–42 composed First Symphony op. 5, which, when it was rejected for performance in Copenhagen, he sent to Mendelssohn, who was enthusiastic, conducting it in Leipzig in 1843; Gade visited Leipzig, became Mendelssohn's friend, conducted some concerts, and in 1844 was named assistant conductor of the orchestra and a teacher at the conservatory. In 1847 he succeeded Mendelssohn as conductor, but the war over Schleswig-Holstein (1848) caused him to return to Copenhagen. In 1849 he became director of the Copenhagen Musical Society, which he remained until his death, establishing a new orchestra and chorus. This post, along with his international standing as a composer, made him a dominating figure in Danish (and, more broadly, Scandinavian) musical life. Also active as an organist; from 1866, joint director with Paulli and Hartmann of the new Copenhagen Conservatory, teaching composition and music history; 1852, married J. P. E. Hartmann's daughter (d. 1855); remarried 1857.

Works: 8 symphonies (1842–71); incidental music and ballets (2 for Bournonville); concert overtures; a violin concerto (1880); chamber music (Octet for Strings op. 17, 1848; *Novelletter,* piano trio, op. 29, 1863; a piano trio op. 42; 3 violin sonatas); piano pieces (*Aquarellen* op. 19, 1850); songs. His choral cantatas (especially *Comala* op. 12, 1846; *Elverskud* op. 30, 1853; *Die heilige Nacht* op. 40, 1862; *Die Kreuzfahrer* op. 50, 1873) were widely popular. His *Optegnelser og breve* were edited by his daughter Dagmar Gade (Copenhagen, 1892; trans. Ger., 1893). His son Axel Willy Gade (1860–1920) was a composer, conductor, and teacher in Copenhagen.

Bibl.: Dan Fog, *N. W. Gade-katalog: en fortegnelse over Niels W. Gades trykte kompositioner* (Copenhagen, 1986).

Gadski, Johanna (Emilia Agnes) (b. Anclam, Pomerania, 15 June 1872; d. Berlin, 22 Feb. 1932). Soprano.

Studied voice with Schröder-Chaloupka at Stettin. Debut at age 17 with the Kroll Opera in Berlin. U.S. debut 1 Mar. 1895 with the Damrosch Opera Company as Elsa *(Lohengrin)*. U.S. Metropolitan Opera debut (on tour), 28 Dec. 1899. Sang at the Met, 1900–1904; in Munich and Salzburg, 1905–6; again at the Met, 1907–17. Although she sang Countess Almaviva *(Nozze di Figaro),* Elvira *(Don Giovanni),* Leonora *(Trovatore),* and even Santuzza *(Cavalleria rusticana),* she was best known at the Met for her portrayals of Wagner's heroines, especially Isolde and Brünnhilde. Returned to Germany when the U.S. entered World War I. In 1928 she founded the German Opera Company and appeared in the U.S., 1929–31. Returned to Germany, where she died after an auto accident.

Gaffurius [Gafurio, Gaforio, Gafori], **Franchinus** [Franchino] (b. Lodi, 14 Jan. 1451; d. Milan, 25 June 1522). Theorist and composer. Recognized by contemporaries as one of the foremost musicians of his era; active in many Italian cities from 1473, particularly Naples and Milan (*maestro di cappella* of the cathedral from 1484); knew much of the music written in his time and many composers and theorists, including Tinctoris. Composed mostly Masses and motets, some madrigals; wrote treatises that together cover all aspects of speculative and practical theory.

Writings: *Theorica musicae* (Milan, 1492; facs., Rome, 1934; trans. ed. Claude W. Palisca, *The Theory of Music,* New Haven, 1993). *Practica musicae* (Milan, 1496; facs., Farnborough, 1967; trans. Irwin Young, *The Practica Musicae,* Madison, Wis., 1969). *De harmonia musicorum instrumentorum opus* (Milan, 1518; facs., *MMML* ser. 2, 97, 1979; trans., *MSD* 33, 1977).

Bibl.: *Opera omnia, CMM* 10 (1955–60). Clement A. Miller, "Gaffurius's *Practica musicae:* Origin and Contents," *MD* 22 (1968): 105.

Gagliano. Family of violin makers active in Naples over many generations from ca. 1700. Alessandro, the patriarch (ca. 1660–ca. 1730), was taught by an unknown maker, though some accounts suggest his teachers included Amati and Stradivari. His sons Nicola (1675–1763) and especially Gennaro (1690–1771) are regarded the best makers in the family, working primarily from the Stradivari model and using a different varnish than did their father, harder and with a yellow-orange rather than a deep red tint. Other makers in the family included Ferdinand (1706–84), Antonio (1728–1805), Giuseppe (1726–93), and Giovanni (ca. 1740–1806), all presumably sons of Nicola. Giovanni's sons continued the trade.

Gagliano, Marco da (b. Florence, 1 May 1582; d. there, 25 Feb. 1643). Composer. Student of Bati; became his assistant at S. Lorenzo, Florence, in 1602. At an early age he was admitted to the Compagnia dell'Arcangelo Raffaello (Compagnia della Natività), a musically active lay confraternity; he became *maestro* there in 1607. His contact with the Gonzagas of Mantua began in that year, leading to an acclaimed performance of his opera *Dafne* (libretto by Rinuccini) at Carnival, 1608 (publ. Florence, 1608; facs., 1970). He staged several others of his works at Mantua that year before returning to Florence. Bati died on 25 October; Gagliano took his post as *maestro di cappella* at S. Lorenzo, becoming *maestro* at the Medici court as well in 1609 and retaining these positions until his death. He later added important clerical posts to his list of appointments; he formed the musical Accademia degli Elevati in 1607, with the most prominent Florentine musicians among its members. His duties for the Medici included presentation of ballets, operas, and other entertainments at court, and of sacred music at S. Maria del Fiore. His large output encompasses stage works (many lost); 6 books of madrigals published 1602–17; a print, *Musiche a 1, 2, e 3 voci,* containing monodies (1615), the complete *Ballo di donne turche,* and sacred pieces; several publications of Masses, motets, responsories, and spiritual madrigals issued 1607–30; and much sacred music still in manuscript.

Gagnebin, Henri (b. Liège, 13 Mar. 1886; d. Geneva, 2 June 1977). Composer and organist. He studied in Lausanne, Berlin, and Paris (with d'Indy); taught music history and organ in Lausanne, Neuchâtel, and Geneva (from 1916); directed the Geneva Conservatory (1925–28). In 1938 he founded (and directed until 1959) the Geneva International Competition for Musical Performance; in 1961 he was awarded the Prize of the City of Geneva. His works are in the style of Franck and d'Indy, but also show the influence of Stravinsky. Among his compositions are works for orchestra (3 symphonies; *2 Suites sur les psaumes huguenots,* 1950 and 1966); 3 string quartets and other chamber music; piano and organ works; oratorios, cantatas, Psalm settings (*Psalm 104,* soloists, choir, and orchestra, 1962), and other choral music (*Messe de concert,* choir and organ, 1973); songs with ensemble or piano. He wrote 4 books on music, including *Orgue, musette et bourdon* (1975).

Gál, Hans (b. Brunn, near Vienna, 5 Aug. 1890; d. Edinburgh, 4 Oct. 1987). Composer and musicologist. He studied with Mandyczewski in Vienna (1908–13) and won the State Prize for Composition; lectured at the university in Vienna (1919–29); directed the Hochschule für Musik and the conservatory in Mainz (1929–33); and was active as a conductor in Vienna before he was forced out by the Nazis. He taught at the Univ. of Edinburgh from 1945. He published more than 100 works, all in tonal idioms similar to those of Brahms and Strauss. He wrote 5 operas (all before 1933); orchestral music including several concertos and concertini (for violin, cello, piano, and organ), and 4 symphonies (1928, 1949, 1952, 1975); a concertino for recorder and string quartet (1961), 4 string quartets, and other chamber music; piano and organ music; oratorios and part songs for chorus. His writings include volumes on Brahms, Wagner, and Schubert as well as *The Golden Age of Vienna* (1948).

Galamian, Ivan (Alexander) (b. Tabriz, Persia, 5 Feb. 1903 [23 Jan. o.s.]; d. New York, 14 Apr. 1981). Violinist and teacher. His parents settled in Russia in 1904. Studied violin with Konstantin Mostras and Georgy Konius in Moscow, 1916–22; with Lucien Capet in Paris, 1922–23. Debut in Paris, 1923. Taught in Paris at the Russian Conservatory, 1925–39; at the École normale, 1936–39; in New York at the Henry Street Settlement School, 1939–44; in Philadelphia at the Curtis Institute, 1944–46; in New York at the Juilliard School, 1946–81. Students included Pinchas Zuckermann, Itzhak Perlman, Kyung-Wha Chung, Paul Zukovsky, Jaime Laredo. Published *Principles of Violin Playing and Teaching* (1962); *Contemporary Violin Technique* (1966).

Galán, Cristóbal (b. ca. 1630; d. Madrid, 24 Sept. 1684). Composer. Sang at Teruel and Morella; visited Corsica and Sardinia before appearing at Madrid in 1659. He was choirmaster at Segovia Cathedral (1664–67), serving sometime thereafter as director of music at the Real Convento de Señoras Descalzas in Madrid; in 1680 he was appointed *maestro* of the royal chapel. His music is mainly sacred (Masses, responses, a Passion, pieces with occasional texts), but also includes secular vocal works and incidental music for court plays. It enjoyed wide manuscript circulation in Spain and the New World.

Galeazzi, Francesco (b. Turin, 1758; d. Rome, Jan. 1819). Theorist and writer on music. He was educated in Turin and moved to Rome, possibly around 1780. There he taught violin and directed the orchestra of the Teatro Valle. Later he moved to Ascoli, where he was aided by a patron, Tommaso Balucanti. In 1791 and 1796 he published in Rome the 2 volumes of his *Elementi teorico-pratici di musica con un saggio sopra l'arte di suonare il violino,* one of the most significant and influential treatises of the 18th century. It comprises both a violin method and a comprehensive theory of music, including an important early description of sonata form.

Bibl.: Bathia Churgin, "Francesco Galeazzi's Description (1796) of Sonata Form," *JAMS* 21 (1968): 181–99.

Galilei, Vincenzo (b. S. Maria a Monte, near Florence, probably late 1520s; d. Florence, buried 2 July 1591). Theorist, lutenist, and composer. Father of the astronomer Galileo Galilei. Studied with Zarlino in Venice around 1563; settled in Florence in 1572. His best-known theoretical writings deal with lute intabulation *(Fronimo)* and with the modern application of principles of ancient music (the *Dialogo* and *Discorso*). Among the ideas discussed in the *Dialogo,* which derives in part from correspondence with Girolamo Mei, is the notion that monody might achieve effects similar to those of ancient Greek music. He composed many lute pieces (both intabulations and original works), some madrigals, and for the Camerata of his patron Giovanni de' Bardi in Florence some monodies (now lost).

Writings: *Fronimo* (Venice, 1568 and 1584; facs., *BMB* 2:22, 1969). *Dialogo della musica antica et della moderna* (Florence, 1581; facs., Rome, 1934; *MMML* ser. 2, 20, 1967). *Discorso intorno all'opere di Messer Gioseffo Zarlino* (Florence, 1589; facs., *BBM,* 1933).

Bibl.: Claude V. Palisca, "Vincenzo Galilei and Some Links between 'Pseudo-Monody' and Monody," *MQ* 46 (1960): 344. D. P. Walker, "Some Aspects of the Musical Theory of Vincenzo Galilei and Galileo Galilei," *PRMA* 100 (1973–74): 33.

Galin, Pierre (b. Samatan, near Toulouse, 1786; d. Bordeaux, 31 Aug. 1821). Mathematician and music pedagogue. He attended the École polytéchnique in Bordeaux; later he became a teacher at the town's lycée. While teaching science and mathematics, he experimented with new methods for teaching sight-singing. The published result of his experiment was *Exposition d'une nouvelle méthode pour l'enseignement de la musique* (Paris, 1818; trans. as *Rationale for a New Way of Teaching Music,* Kilkenny, Ireland, 1983); with modifications, it became known as the Galin-Paris-Chevé method.

Galindo Dimas, Blas (b. San Gabriel, Jalisco, Mexico, 3 Feb. 1910; d. 19 Apr. 1993). Composer. Pupil of Chávez, Rolón, and Huízar, among others, at the National Conservatory in Mexico City, where he studied, with some interruptions, 1931–44. In 1934 he and three colleagues (Ayala Pérez, Contreras, and Moncayo) formed the Grupo de los Cuatro, aiming to develop a contemporary musical idiom using indigenous materials. His *Sones de mariachi* was played at New York in 1940; he was a student of Copland at the Berkshire Music Center in 1941 and 1942. After three years as an instructor at the conservatory he was named director there in 1947, serving until 1961; in 1947 he also became director of the music department at the National Institute of Fine Arts. He served as music director of the Symphony of the Mexican Institute of Social Security from 1960 to 1965, when he decided to focus on composition. His works embrace a wide variety of styles and include orchestral music, concertos, ballets, chamber music, and vocal compositions with and without instruments.

Bibl.: *Composers of the Americas* 11 (Washington, D.C., 1965): 35–46 [includes works list].

Galli, Caterina (b. ca. 1723; d. Chelsea, 1804). Mezzo-soprano. Forkel mentions a "Catterina Gallo" from Cremona; otherwise, she is first heard from in Italian opera at London in 1742. Handel enlisted her for the Covent Garden oratorio season of 1747; she sang in the *Occasional Oratorio, Jepthe,* and *Judas Maccabeus.* Parts in *Joshua* and *Susanna* as well as the title role of *Solomon* were composed for her. After singing in Italy she returned to England, performing occasionally from 1773 into the 1790s.

Galliard, John Ernest [Johann Ernst] (b. Celle, ca. 1685; d. London, 1749). Composer. Studied flute and oboe with Maréchal, composition with Steffani. Went to London in 1706. His English operas failed; his music for the pantomimes of John Rich was more successful. His important English translation of Tosi's singing manual appeared in 1742. Handel knew and admired him; Burney liked him but thought little of his music. Works include vocal music plus sonatas and concertos for oboe and bassoon.

Galliculus [Hennel], **Johannes** (fl. first half of 16th cent.). Composer and theorist. His *Isagoge de compositione* (Leipzig, 1520; 6th ed., Wittenberg, 1553) is an introductory text on counterpoint. He composed liturgical works for the Lutheran church, using Latin texts that sometimes incorporate texts or melodies of German *Leisen.*

Bibl.: *Gesamtausgabe der Werke* (Brooklyn, 1975–).

Galli-Curci, Amelita (b. Milan, 18 Nov. 1882; d. La Jolla, Calif., 26 Nov. 1963). Soprano. Studied piano with Vincenzo Appiani at the Milan Conservatory, obtaining first prize in 1903. Developed her voice by listening to recordings of herself. Pietro Mascagni discovered her vocal talents. Vocal debut as Gilda *(Rigoletto)* at the Trani Municipal Theater, 1906; she sang the same role at her Rome debut in 1909 and her sensational U.S. debut on 18 Nov. 1916 with the Chicago Opera. At her New York debut, 28 Jan. 1917, as Meyerbeer's Dinorah, she was recalled 60 times. Sang with the Chicago Opera, 1916–18; with the Met, 1921–31. In 1936, while still at the peak of her powers, she required an operation on her throat. A subsequent performance as Mimi *(La bohème)* in Chicago showed that her voice had been compromised, and she retired. Probably the greatest Italian coloratura of her time.

Gallus, Jacobus. See Handl, Jacob.

Gallus, Joannes (fl. mid-16th cent.). Composer(s). The name most likely applies to a person also known as Lecocq whose works appear in prints made in the Lowlands and Germany between 1542 and 1555. The Venetian publisher Scotto probably erred in saying on one title page that Gallus was Maistre Jhan. The published works by Gallus/Lecocq are 9 Latin motets and 22 French chansons.

Galpin, Francis W(illiam) (b. Dorchester, Dorset, 25 Dec. 1858; d. Richmond, Surrey, 30 Dec. 1945). Writer on old musical instruments. He received his education at King's School, Sherborne, and Trinity College, Cambridge (1877–83), where he studied organ with J. R. Sterndale Bennett. Following his ordination in 1883 he was curate at St. Giles in the Fields, London (1887–91); vicar of Hatfield Regis (1891–1915); vicar of Witham (1915–21); and rector of Faulkbourne (1921–33). In 1916 he sold his collection of between 500 and 600 instruments to the Museum of Fine Arts, Boston. In addition to various articles, he wrote *Old English Instruments of Music* (1910) and a *Textbook of European Musical Instruments* (1937). From 1938 to 1943 he was president of the [Royal] Musical Association. The Galpin Society, devoted to organological studies, was formed in 1946.

Galuppi, Baldassare (b. Burano, near Venice, 18 Oct. 1706; d. Venice, 3 Jan. 1785). Composer. His early music training was from his father, a barber and amateur violinist. Benedetto Marcello supposedly recommended him as a pupil to Antonio Lotti; with the latter the youth studied counterpoint, harmony, and keyboard playing. Possibly his first professional appointment was in Florence, where by 1726 he was a theater harpsichordist. From 1728 he was composing operas, collaborating with Giovanni Battista Pescetti. In 1740 he became *maestro di musica* at the Ospedale dei mendicanti. After two years in London (1741–43), where he composed serious operas for the Haymarket Theatre, he returned to Venice, where he began composing Neapolitan-style opere buffe, mostly to librettos by Carlo Goldoni. In 1748 he received the post of *vicemaestro* at St. Mark's; in 1762 he became *maestro,* and the same year he was appointed director of the Ospedale degli incurabili. He spent three years at Catherine the Great's court in St. Petersburg (1765–68), where he composed sacred works on Russian texts. On returning to Venice in 1768 he was made choirmaster at the Ospedale. He composed more than 100 stage works; the most popular were *Il conte Caramella* (1749), *Il mondo della luna* (1750), *Il filosofo di campagna* (1754), *L'amante di tutte* (1760), and *Il marchese villano* (1762). He also composed 19 known cantatas, nearly 30 oratorios, many liturgical works, and some 90 keyboard sonatas.

Bibl.: Daniel Heartz, "Hasse, Galuppi, and Metastasio," *Venezia e il melodramma nel Settecento* (Florence, 1978), pp. 309–39.

Galway, James (b. Belfast, 8 Dec. 1939). Flutist. Studied flute with John Francis at the Royal College of Music in London, 1956–59; with Geoffrey Gilbert at the Guildhall School of Music and Drama, 1959–60; with Gaston Crunelle and Jean Pierre Rampal at the Paris Conservatory, 1960–61; with Marcel Moyse privately. Played in the orchestra of the Royal Shakespeare Theatre, at Sadler's Wells and Covent Garden, in the BBC and London symphonies. After winning the Birmingham International Competition in 1966, became principal flute in the Royal Philharmonic, 1966–69; in the Berlin Philharmonic, 1969–75. Taught at the Eastman School, 1975–76. Thereafter marketed himself successfully as a soloist in light classical and popular repertories. Published *James Galway: An Autobiography* (1979); *Flute* (1982).

Ganassi dal Fontego, Sylvestro di (b. Fontego, near Venice, 1492; d. mid-16th cent.). Writer. Was an instrumentalist for the Signoria of Venice by 1535; wrote 2 treatises on instrumental performance. *Opera intitulata Fontegara* (Venice, 1535; facs., *BMB* 2:18, 1969; trans. Eng., Berlin-Lichterfelde, 1959) concerns the playing of wind instruments, particularly the recorder, and treats ornamentation at length. The viola da gamba is the subject of *Regola rubertina* (2nd vol., *Lettione seconda;* Venice, 1542 and 1543; facs., *BMB* sec. 2, 18a and b, 1970; trans. *Journal of the Viola da Gamba*

Society of America 18 [Dec. 1981]: 14–66; 19 [Dec. 1982]: 99–163).

Gandini, Gerardo (b. Buenos Aires, 16 Oct. 1932). Composer and pianist. Studied composition in his native city with Ginastera, and later in the U.S. and Italy. Back in Argentina, he founded the Grupo de experimentacion musical, a contemporary ensemble. He has held several teaching positions in Buenos Aires; in 1970 he returned to the U.S. as an instructor at the Juilliard School. He also appeared widely as a pianist. Works include *Contrastes* (1968); *Concertinos I, II,* and *III,* various chamber ensembles (1962–63); *Fantasie-impromptu,* "an imaginary portrait of Chopin," piano and orchestra (1970); a guitar concerto (1975).

Ganz, Rudolph (b. Zurich, 24 Feb. 1877; d. Chicago, 2 Aug. 1972). Pianist, conductor, and composer. Studied cello with his great-uncle, Carl Eschmann-Dumour, in Lausanne; piano with F. Blumer at the Strasbourg Conservatory; piano with Robert Freund at the Zurich Conservatory beginning 1889; piano with Busoni and composition with Heinrich Urban in Berlin from 1899. Debut as a pianist in 1899 with the Berlin Philharmonic. Conducted his Symphony op. 1 with the Berlin Philharmonic, 1900. Taught piano at the Chicago College of Music, 1901–5. Toured the U.S., Canada, Europe, and Cuba, 1906–15. Conductor of the St. Louis Symphony, 1921–27; of the New York Philharmonic's Young People's Concerts, 1938–49. Returned to the Chicago College as vice president, 1928; director, 1929; president, 1934–54. Dedicatee of Ravel's *Scarbo,* of Busoni's Sonatine no. 1, of Griffes's *White Peacock.* A champion of contemporary composers in general and of American composers in particular; his own works, written in a conservative style, include Piano Concerto op. 32 (1940) and the overture *Laughter—Yet Love* (1950).

Bibl.: Jeanne Colette Collester, *Rudolph Ganz: A Musical Pioneer* (Metuchen, N.J., 1995).

Garant, (Albert Antonio) Serge (b. Quebec City, 22 Sept. 1929; d. Sherbrooke, Quebec, 1 Nov. 1986). Composer, conductor, pianist, and critic. As a youth in Sherbrooke he played clarinet in the symphony and saxophone in jazz ensembles; studied in Montreal with Claude Champagne (composition) and Yvonne Hubert (piano) and in Paris with Messiaen and Andrée Vaurabourg-Honegger (1951–52). By 1950 he was performing piano works of Schoenberg; this early interest in twelve-tone and serial composition was later extended to include works of Webern, Stockhausen, and Boulez. Many of his own compositions employ serial techniques; other works allow controlled improvisation and leave the order of movements up to performers. After a brief period as a jazz pianist in Sherbrooke, Garant became active as a performer and conductor of contemporary music in Montreal; he was instrumental in organizing the series Musique de notre temps (1956–57) and then the Société de musique contemporaine du Québec, whose concerts he conducted from the first season in 1966 until shortly before his death. He also conducted the Montreal Symphony Orchestra in performances of contemporary music (for example, in his *Phrases II,* for 2 orchestras each with its own conductor, premiered in 1968) and orchestras in other Canadian cities. He studied with Boulez in 1969 and in the same year began to teach composition at the Univ. of Montreal. His works include some 15 pieces for large ensembles or orchestra and 8 for chamber ensembles; piano pieces; compositions for voice and ensemble (*Rivages,* baritone, 1978); and a few songs.

Garbousova, Raya (b. Tbilisi, 25 Sept. 1905 [12 Sept. o.s.]). Cellist. She studied cello at the Tbilisi Conservatory (diploma, 1923). Debut in 1923 in Moscow. Studied in Berlin with Hermann Becker, 1926; in New York with Felix Salmond, 1927; in London with Pablo Casals. Concertized extensively in Europe. U.S. debut 4 Dec. 1934 in New York. Settled in the U.S. in 1939. Introduced the Barber Cello Concerto, 1946; the Martinů Third Sonata, 1952; the Rieti Cello Concerto, 1960. Taught at the Hartt College of Music from 1970.

Garcia, Jerry [Jerome John] (b. San Francisco, 1 Aug. 1942; d. Forest Knolls, Calif., 9 Aug. 1995). Rock songwriter, singer, and guitarist. In the mid-1960s he formed The Grateful Dead, which included singer Ron "Pigpen" McKernan (1945–73) and guitarist Bob Weir (b. 1947); they were the leading band of the San Francisco psychedelic era. They produced studio albums (*American Beauty,* 1970) but were best known for live performances, which are preserved on several live albums and numerous band-sanctioned bootleg tapes; their most famous songs ("Truckin'," 1970; "Sugaree," 1971) are by Garcia and lyricist Robert Hunter. They achieved new popularity in 1987 with the album *In the Dark,* which yielded their first Top-Ten single ("Touch of Grey"). Shortly after Garcia's death, the remaining members of The Grateful Dead announced they were dissolving the band.

Garcia, José Maurício Nunes. See Maurício, José.

García, Manuel (Patricio Rodríguez) (b. Madrid, 17 Mar. 1805; d. London, 1 July 1906). Singing teacher. Son of Manuel Garcia; remained in Madrid to 1815, when he joined his parents in Naples; singing pupil of his father, making opera debut in his New York company, 1825, but, lacking a good voice, left the stage in 1829; 1830, took part in French invasion of Algiers and later connected with military hospitals, where he began the scientific study of the voice, of which he was a pioneer (invented laryngoscope, 1855); his *Traité complet de l'art du chant* (Paris, 1840; trans. Eng., 1870) was perhaps the most important singing treatise of the 19th century, and he the most celebrated teacher; professor of singing, Paris Conservatory, 1847; Royal Academy of Music, London, 1848–95, with pupils including Lind, Frezzolini, M. Marchesi.

Bibl.: Malcom Sterling Mackinlay, *Garcia: The Centenarian and His Times* (Edinburgh and London, 1908; R: New York, 1976).

García [del Popolo], **Manuel (Vicente Rodríguez)** (b. Seville, 21 or 22 Jan. 1775; d. Paris, 2 or 9 June 1832). Tenor. García was his stepfather's name. From 1798 to 1807, singer in Spanish musical theaters, debut in Cadiz but mostly in Madrid; 1808, Paris, Théâtre-Italien, an immediate success; 1809–16, sang in leading Italian houses, mainly in opera seria but also buffa (1816, created Almaviva in Rossini's *Barbiere*); 1817–25, sang mainly at Théâtre-Italien, Paris, and the Italian opera, London; 1825–26, headed the first Italian opera company in the New World, in New York and Mexico; after returning to the Théâtre-Italien, gave up the stage for teaching. Children included Maria Malibran, Pauline Viardot, Manuel García. Composed over 40 operas and operettas in French, Spanish, Italian.

Bibl.: Gladys Malvern, *The Great Garcías* (New York, 1958).

García Morillo, Roberto (b. Buenos Aires, 22 Jan. 1911). Composer. Studied under Ugarte, André, and others at the National Conservatory, and later under Nat in Paris. Became a music critic for the Buenos Aires newspaper *La nación* in 1938; wrote extensively for other journals, and published several books. Named to the faculty of both the municipal and national conservatories in 1942, and in 1952 researched the Italian lyric theater. Compositions include the pantomime drama *Usher* (1942), symphonies and other orchestral works, concertos, stage pieces of various types, film music, cantatas, chamber music, and piano works.

Bibl.: *Composers of the Americas* 8 (Washington, D.C., 1962), pp. 77–85 [includes works list].

Gardane [Gardano], **Antonio** (b. southern France, 1509; d. Venice, 28 Oct. 1569). Printer and composer. He began printing music in Venice in 1538 using movable type and a single impression, as did Attaingnant. He and his rival Girolamo Scotto between them virtually monopolized Italian music printing for three decades. His publications include works of many types, particularly madrigals and a smaller number of Masses and motets, by composers from Italy, the Netherlands, France, Spain, Germany, and the imperial court. Among his own compositions, most printed by Moderne and Le Roy & Ballard, are nearly 70 chansons, 2 Masses, and 7 motets. His sons Alessandro and Angelo were also music printers.

Gardelli, Lamberto (b. Venice, 8 Nov. 1915). Conductor and composer. Studied piano in Pesaro at the Liceo musicale Rossini; composition with Petrassi in Rome at the Conservatorio di S. Cecilia. Vocal coach and assistant to Tulio Serafin at the Rome Opera, 1935–43. Composed the operas *Alba novella* (1932); *L'etrusco* (1938); *Il sogno* (1942). Conducting debut in Rome, 1941, with *La traviata.* Called to the Royal Swedish Opera, 1943; permanent conductor there, 1946–55. Led the Danish Radio Symphony, 1955–61. Guest conductor at the Budapest Opera, 1961–65. U.S. debut, 1964, with Bellini's *Les Capulets* at Carnegie Hall. Metropolitan Opera debut, 1966, with *Andrea Chénier;* conducted there regularly to 1968. Named music director of the Bern Theater, 1968; of the Royal Opera at Copenhagen, 1973; of the Munich Radio Orchestra, 1982. Other compositions include a symphony, a Requiem, triple concertos for trombone, cornet, bassoon and for oboe, clarinet, trumpet.

Garden, Mary (b. Aberdeen, 20 Feb. 1874; d. there, 3 Jan. 1967). Soprano. Her family emigrated to U.S. in 1880. Studied in Chicago with Mrs. Robinson Duff; in Paris from 1896 with Jacques Bouhy, Mathilde Marchesi, Lucien Fugère, and Jules Chevalier. Triumphant debut in 1900 at the Opéra-comique replacing an indisposed Marthe Rioton in midperformance as Charpentier's Louise. She remained with the Opéra-comique through 1906, creating title roles in several French operas, most notably Debussy's *Pelléas et Mélisande,* 30 Apr. 1902. With Hammerstein's Manhattan Opera she sang U.S. premieres of Massenet's *Thaïs* (1907), Debussy's *Pelléas* (1908), and created a sensation as Strauss's Salome in 1909. Prima donna with the Chicago-Philadelphia Opera, 1910–31; her season as the company's director, 1921–22, was artistically adventurous (she staged Prokofiev's *Love for Three Oranges*) but financially problematic. Her later U.S. premieres included Alfano's *Risurrezione* (1925) and Honegger's *Judith* (1927). She continued to sing in Europe through 1934; her final operatic appearance was at the Cincinnati Zoo as Carmen in 1935. Her most important recordings were made with Debussy at the piano in 1903.

Gardiner, Henry Balfour (b. London, 7 Nov. 1877; d. Salisbury, 28 June 1950). He studied at the Charterhouse School, London (from 1891); at the Musikhochschule in Frankfurt (from 1894); and at New College, Oxford (from 1897). In 1903 his String Quintet in C minor was performed in London. In 1907 he served a brief appointment on the faculty of Winchester College. Before World War I he spent time collecting English folk tunes. His own compositions manifest this research, as well as an interest in the music of Vaughan Williams. Among his works are pieces for orchestra (*Overture to a Comedy,* 1906?; a lost Symphony in D, 1908); choral-orchestral works (*News from Wydah,* 1912; *April,* 1912–13; *Philomela,* 1923); works for chorus a cappella; songs; chamber works; piano music.

Gardiner, John Eliot (b. Springhead, Dorset, 20 Apr. 1943). Conductor; great-nephew of composer Henry Balfour Gardiner. Read history and Arabic at King's College, Cambridge, 1961–65. At the same time studied conducting under George Hurst with the BBC Northern Symphony; formed the Monteverdi Choir in 1964. Studied two years in Paris with Nadia Boulanger; in London with Thurston Dart. Debut leading the Monteverdi Choir, London, 1966. Attracted widespread attention in 1967 with a performance of his own edition of Monteverdi's *Vespro della Beata Vergine* at Ely Cathedral. Debut as orchestral conductor at the Promenade Concerts, 1968; as an opera conductor at Sadler's Wells, 1969. Founder of the Monteverdi Choir and the English Baroque Soloists. Led his own editions of Rameau operas in London, 1973–75. Conductor of the CBC Radio Orchestra in Vancouver, 1980–81; music director of the Lyons Opéra, 1983–88; chief conductor of the North German Radio Symphony from 1991. Numerous recordings with historical instruments of instrumental and vocal works of the 17th, 18th, and early 19th centuries.

Gardner, John Linton (b. Manchester, 2 Mar. 1917). Composer. His studies were at Wellington College (from 1930) and at Oxford, where from 1933 he studied on an organ scholarship with Ernest Walker, Hugh Allen, and Thomas Armstrong. During World War II he served as bandleader and navigator for the Royal Air Force. In 1946 he was appointed assistant director at Covent Garden; when he resigned in 1952 he taught at Morley College, and in 1965 he became director of its music program. He also taught at the Royal Academy of Music from 1956. He composed operas (*The Moon and Sixpence,* 1954–57; *The Entertainment of the Senses,* 1974); Symphony in D minor (1946); and many choral works (*Herrick Cantata,* 1961; *Cantata for Christmas,* 1966; *Cantata for Easter,* 1970); also chamber and instrumental works.

Gardner, Samuel (b. Elisavetgrad [now Kirovograd], 25 Aug. 1891; d. New York, 23 Jan. 1984). Violinist and composer. His family moved to Providence, R.I., in 1892. Studied violin there with Felix Wendelschaefer, 1897–1902; in Boston with C. M. Loeffler and Felix Winternitz, 1902–8. At the Institute of Musical Art in New York he studied composition with Percy Goetschius and violin with Franz Kneisel, 1911–13. Member of the Kneisel Quartet, 1914–15; of the Chicago Symphony, 1915–16. His tone poem *New Russia* won the Loeb Prize in 1918; his String Quartet no. 1 the Pulitzer Prize in 1918. Other compositions include the tone poem *Broadway* (1924), a piano quintet (1925), a violin concerto, String Quartet no. 2 (1944), and *Country Moods* for string orchestra (1946). Taught at the Institute of Musical Art (which became the Juilliard School in 1926), 1924–41.

Garland, Red [William McKinley] (b. Dallas, 13 May 1923; d. there, 23 Apr. 1984). Jazz pianist. He joined Billy Eckstine's bop big band (1945–46), accompanied bop soloists at the Down Beat club in Philadelphia (1947–49), toured with Coleman Hawkins and Roy Eldridge (early 1950s), and led a trio in Boston. With Paul Chambers and Philly Joe Jones he formed the fiery rhythm section of Miles Davis's quintets and sextets (1955–58), while also recording his own albums *All Mornin' Long* and *Soul Junction* with Donald Byrd and John Coltrane (1957). He led hard bop trios and combos to about 1963 and again from 1977.

Garlandia, Johannes de. See Johannes de Garlandia.

Garner, Erroll (Louis) (b. Pittsburgh, 15 June 1921; d. Los Angeles, 2 Jan. 1977). Jazz pianist. In New York he substituted for Art Tatum and stayed with the trio under Slam Stewart's leadership (1945). He recorded with Charlie Parker (1947), but otherwise spent his career leading trios and playing alone. Characteristic of his style were unpredictable introductions to popular songs, involving improvised counterpoint and flexible tempos; within the songs themselves, tension between a steady chordal "four-beat" in his left hand and rhythmically freer melodies in his right. His recordings include "Fantasy on Frankie and Johnny" (1947), "Laura" (1951), his composition "Misty" (1954), and the album *Concert by the Sea* (1956).

Bibl.: James M. Doran, *Erroll Garner: The Most Happy Piano* (Metuchen, N.J., 1985).

Garrido, Pablo (b. Valparaiso, Chile, 26 Mar. 1905; d. Santiago, 14 Sept. 1982). Composer. Studied several instruments as well as composition and the humanities in his native city; founded an orchestra and string quartet in Antofagasta in 1929. Did folkloric research throughout South America and in Spain, 1930–32, after which he moved to Santiago to pursue an interest in jazz. A prolific writer, he contributed to various journals as well as to Chilean newspapers. His *Biografía de la cueca chilena* (1943) is the standard scholarly reference on that Chilean dance; a visiting professorship at the Univ. of Puerto Rico (1949–51) resulted in a study of that country's popular music. His own music often draws on folk material; works include an opera, orchestral and chamber music, vocal pieces, and piano music.

Bibl.: *Composers of the Americas* 9 (Washington, D.C., 1963), pp. 67–73 [includes works list].

Garrido Lecca, Celso (b. Piura, Peru, 9 Mar. 1926). Composer. Studied under Sas and Holzmann at the National Conservatory, Lima; subsequently attended the Univ. of Chile, Santiago, where he also composed theater music; he joined the faculty at the Univ. of Chile in 1967. He integrated both international and indigenous elements into his music, the latter approach exemplified by his *Elegía a Machu Picchu* (1965) and the setting of the Quechua poem *Apu Inc Atahualpaman* (1971); both are large-scale works. Also composed chamber and piano music, as well as songs and some music with tape.

Gascongne, Mathieu (fl. first half of 16th cent.?). Composer. May have been associated with Cambrai but more likely served in the French royal court. Prints, manuscripts, and references to his name and to his music suggest that he was highly regarded in his time. Works attributed to him in all sources include nearly 10

Masses, about 20 motets, 2 Magnificats, and over 15 chansons (many using popular tunes as cantus firmi).

Gasparini, Francesco (b. Camaiore, near Lucca, 5 Mar. 1668; d. Rome, 22 Mar. 1727). Composer. Possibly a student of Legrenzi; joined the Accademia S. Cecilia, Rome, in 1689; perhaps studied with Corelli and Pasquini as well. Named *maestro di coro* at the Ospedale della pietà, Venice, in 1701; he composed operas for Venice at the rate of several per year, while his important thoroughbass manual *L'armonico pratico al cimbalo* appeared there in 1709. He left Venice in 1713 and eventually became *maestro di cappella* at S. Lorenzo in Lucina, Rome. In addition to over 60 operas, he cultivated other secular and sacred vocal genres and was an influential teacher, with Marcello, Quantz, and Domenico Scarlatti among his pupils.

Gasparo da Salò [Bertolotti] (b. Salò, bapt. 20 May 1540; d. 14 Apr. 1609). Instrument maker. Among the finest makers of bowed stringed instruments, active in Brescia from 1562. His output consisted chiefly of viols of all sizes and various members of the violin family. His best work was in double basses and, particularly, tenor violas. These instruments remain in demand today, despite the considerable alterations many have undergone since their making.

Gassmann, Florian Leopold (b. Brüx, Bohemia, 3 May 1729; d. Vienna, 20 Jan. 1774). Composer. After early music training with the choirmaster at Brüx, he went to Italy; in 1757 his *Merope* was produced in Venice. Following several more successes in that city, in 1763 he was appointed ballet composer to the Viennese imperial court, succeeding Gluck. Back in Venice in 1766, he met the 16-year-old Salieri and brought the youth to Vienna with him. The following year his popular *L'amore artigiano* was performed at the Burgtheater. In 1768 he married Barbara Damm, who bore two daughters, Maria Anna (1771–1858) and Therese (1774–1837); both became well-known singers. In 1770, during the meeting of Joseph II and Frederick II, Gassmann composed *La contessina,* which became his best-known work (ed. in *DTÖ* 42–44); partly in the wake of its success he was appointed court Kapellmeister in 1772. He immediately set about reorganizing the chapel's administration. One of Vienna's most important 18th-century musicians, he composed at least 22 operas; vocal works including the oratorio *La Betulia liberata* (1772); sacred choral works; secular cantatas (*Amore e Venere,* 1768; *L'amor timido*); instrumental works, including more than 30 symphonies; and chamber works, including 8 string quintets (publ. 1772) and 37 string quartets.

Bibl.: George Robert Hill, *A Thematic Catalog of the Instrumental Music of Florian Leopold Gassmann* (Hackensack, N.J., 1976).

Gastoldi, Giovanni Giacomo (b. Caravaggio, 1550s?; d. 1622?). Composer. Was in the chapel of the Gonzaga family in Mantua, eventually as *maestro di cappella* (succeeding Giaches de Wert) from 1572 until 1608; then probably moved to Milan. Among his compositions are madrigals, a variety of sacred vocal music, and a small amount of instrumental music. Most prominent and influential, however, are his 2 sets of *balletti,* strophic vocal dance-songs with passages of nonsense syllables. These were often reprinted, widely known, and much imitated, especially outside Italy (e.g., by Thomas Morley).

Gatti-Casazza, Giulio (b. Udine, Italy, 3 Feb. 1869; d. Ferrara, 2 Sept. 1940). Impresario. After studying naval engineering at the Univ. of Genoa, he took over the Teatro comunale in Ferrara from his father in 1893. Boito selected him to head La Scala in 1898. With Toscanini on the podium he established a high artistic standard there. Backed by Otto Kahn, the two migrated to the Metropolitan Opera in New York in 1908. Toscanini left in 1916; Gatti-Casazza remained until 1935. Under his regime most of the important singers of the day sang at the Met.

Gaultier, Denis (b. 1603; d. Paris, 1672). Lutenist and composer. He was a cousin of Ennemond Gaultier, with whom he was closely connected (Denis was called "Gaultier le jeune" to separate him from Ennemond, but nonetheless publications often misattributed works between them or printed only their last name); perhaps also a student of Charles Racquet, whose death he commemorated with a *tombeau.* He held no court position, but gained fame through salon playing; his works consist mainly of dance suites for the lute. Three published collections of his music appeared later in his life: *La rhétorique des dieux* (1652), containing suites arranged into the 12 modes; *Pièces de luth sur trois différens modes nouveaux* (ca. 1670), whose title page designates the contents as wholly his own; and *Livre de tablature . . . de Mr. Gaultier Sr. de Nève et de Mr. Gaultier son cousin* (ca. 1672).

Gaultier, Ennemond (b. Villette, Dauphiné, 1575; d. Nèves, near Villette, 11 Dec. 1651). Lutenist and composer. Called "le vieux Gaultier" to distinguish him from his younger cousin Denis. Served as page to the Duchess of Montmorency in Languedoc, then as valet de chambre to Maria de' Medici, Henri IV's queen, from 1600; upon her exile in 1631 he left Paris. Though his works (with those of his cousin) constitute a corpus of music influencing both other lutenists and later *clavecinistes,* they were not published during his lifetime; Denis brought out some of them in 1672.

Bibl.: André Souris and Monique Rollin, eds., *Oeuvres du vieux Gaultier* (Paris, 1965).

Gauthier, (Ida Joséphine Phoebe) Eva (b. Ottawa, 20 Sept. 1885; d. New York, 26 Dec. 1958). Mezzo-soprano. Studied voice with Frank Buels in Ottawa beginning 1899. At the Paris Conservatory beginning 1902 studied voice with Auguste-Jean Dubulle, declamation with Sarah Bernhardt. After an operation on her vocal cords, studied in Paris, London, Berlin, and Milan. Toured England in 1905; Canada in 1906. Stage debut in Pavia in 1909 as Micaela *(Carmen).* In 1910 Debussy chose her to sing Mélisande in the English premiere of *Pelléas,* but the opera was postponed. Settled in New York in 1916; by the time of her retrospective recitals there in 1936 she had introduced over 700 new works, including pieces by Ravel, Stravinsky, Bartók, Hindemith, Schoenberg, Satie, Honegger, and Poulenc. In 1923 she gave a recital of songs by Kern, Berlin, and Gershwin, accompanied by Gershwin.

Gautier de Coincy (b. Coincy-l'Abbaye, 1177 or 1178; d. Soissons, 25 Sept. 1236). Trouvère. Author of the long verse narrative *Miracles de Nostre-Dame,* which includes many songs with music, and of a number of independent songs. The texts and some of the melodies are new, but most of the music is drawn from earlier sources. His importance lies chiefly in his emphasis on sacred (especially Marian) texts, unusual in a trouvère of his time.

Gavazzeni, Gianandrea (b. Bergamo, 27 July 1909). Composer, conductor, pianist, and writer on music. He studied piano in Rome and composition with Pizzetti in Milan. After early success as a pianist, he became a prominent opera conductor; he conducted regularly at La Scala from the 1950s and later was musical director (1965–68) and conducted in England, the U.S., and Russia. He composed an opera, a ballet, several orchestral works, and a significant body of chamber and vocal music; in 1949 he stopped composing and discouraged performance of his works. He wrote criticism for the national newspaper *Il corriere della sera* and produced many books, among them studies of Donizetti, Bellini, Pizzetti, Mussorgsky; in 1974 his *Non eseguire Beethoven e altri scritti* won the Viareggio Prize for musical criticism.

Gaveaux, Pierre (b. Béziers, 9 Oct. 1760; d. Charenton, near Paris, 5 Feb. 1825). Composer and singer. At the Béziers Cathedral he was a chorister from age 7; he studied organ with Abbé Combès. He later moved to Bordeaux, where his teacher was the local *maître* François Beck. He prepared for the clergy, but around 1780 he abandoned his studies for a life in the theater. He sang at Montpellier and was first tenor at the Théâtre de Bordeaux. In 1789 he began singing at the Théâtre de Monsieur in Paris. He composed several opéras comiques; best known is his setting of *Léonore, ou L'amour conjugal* (1798), based on the same Bouilly libretto that Beethoven used for *Fidelio.* His operas number more than 30; he also composed sacred vocal works, revolutionary songs, and instrumental music.

Gaviniès, Pierre (b. Bordeaux, 11 May 1728; d. Paris, 8 Sept. 1800). Violinist and composer. He began to concertize as a boy of 11, and played at the Concert spirituel in 1741. As a result of an illicit love affair he was imprisoned during the 1750s, but afterward returned to prominence at the Concert spirituel, becoming its director in 1773. After the Revolution he played in theater orchestras, and in 1795 he was made professor of violin at the newly founded Paris Conservatory. Among his works is the opéra comique *Le prétendu* (1760), orchestral and chamber works, and solo vocal music.

Gay, John (bapt. Barnstaple, 16 Sept. 1685; d. London, 4 Dec. 1732). Poet and dramatist. Wrote the libretto to Handel's *Acis and Galatea* (1718), but is best known for the phenomenally successful *Beggar's Opera,* the first so-called ballad opera, which with its popular tunes and lowly characters satirized Italian opera and contemporary politics. He wrote 2 other ballad operas, *Polly* (a sequel to the first, banned and not staged until 1779) and *Achilles* (Covent Garden, 10 Feb. 1733).

Gaye [Gay], **Marvin** (b. Washington, D.C., 2 Apr. 1939; d. Los Angeles, 1 Apr. 1984). Soul singer and songwriter. Early performances in his father's church and with touring rhythm-and-blues bands; from 1961 recorded for the Motown label, becoming popular with both black and white audiences for songs such as "How Sweet It Is To Be Loved by You" (1964) and "I Heard It through the Grapevine" (1968). He remained popular into the 1980s, achieving great success with the song "Sexual Healing" (1982).

Gaztambide (y Garbayo), Joaquín (Romualdo) (b. Tudela, Navarre, 7 Feb. 1822; d. Madrid, 18 Mar. 1870). Composer. An orphan; became a choirboy in Tudela, then studied music in Pamplona and from 1842 at the Madrid Conservatory; from 1848 prominent as theater conductor in Madrid, including the Teatro real; from 1862, director of the orchestra concerts of the conservatory; 1869, began zarzuela tour of Central and South America, cut short in Mexico by his last illness; 1848–68, produced 44 zarzuelas in Madrid, including *Catalina* (1854), the most successful; *El valle de Andorra* (1852), *Los Magyares* (1857), *El juramento* (1858) also widely performed.

Gazzaniga, Giuseppe (b. Verona, 5 Oct. 1743; d. Crema, 1 Feb. 1818). Composer. From 1760 he studied in Venice and Naples, with Nicola Porpora and at the Naples Conservatorio di Sant'Onofrio. During his subsequent studies (from 1767–70) with Niccolò Piccinni, his first stage work, *Il barone di Trocchia* (intermezzo, 1768) was performed in Naples. During the 1770s he composed operas for theaters in Dresden and Vienna and throughout Italy. In 1786 his *Il finto cieco,* with a libretto by Lorenzo da Ponte, was performed to great acclaim at the Burgtheater in Vienna. The work for which he is best remembered appeared in Venice in 1787: *Don Giovanni Tenorio o sia Il convitato di pietra.* The one-act opera buffa, with text by Giovanni Bertati, is generally recognized as a prototype (in some notable details) for Da Ponte's and Mozart's *Don Giovanni* of later that year. In 1791 Gazzaniga was appointed *maestro di cappella* at the cathedral at Crema. He composed 47 known operas; liturgical and other sacred music.

Bibl.: Stefan Kunze, *Don Giovanni vor Mozart: Die Tradition der Don-Giovanni-Opern im italienischen Buffo-Theater des 18. Jahrhunderts* (Munich, 1972).

Gazzelloni, Severino (b. Roccasecca Frosinone, 5 Jan. 1919; d. Cassino, 21 Nov. 1992). Flutist. Studied flute from 1926 with Giambattista Creati; 1939–42 with Arrigo Tassinari at the Conservatorio di S. Cecilia in Rome. First chair in the Belgrade Symphony, then in the Orchestra sinfonica della RAI in Rome. Began playing and teaching at the Darmstadt Festival in 1952; he quickly became known as an able exponent of the avant garde; over 150 works were written for him, including pieces by Messiaen, Boulez, Stockhausen, Berio, Nono, and others.

Gédalge, André (b. Paris, 27 Dec. 1856; d. Chessy, 5 Feb. 1926). Composer. He entered the Paris Conservatory at age 28 after a career as a bookseller; studied composition with Guiraud and won the second Prix de Rome in 1885. His *Traité de la fugue* (1901) and his work as assistant to Guiraud and Massenet led to an appointment at the Conservatory as a teacher of counterpoint (among his students were Ravel, Honegger, and Milhaud); other didactic works include collections of solfège melodies, harmony lessons, and *L'enseignement de la musique par l'éducation de l'oreille* (1920); in 1906 he was made inspector of the provincial conservatories. His compositions were in the style of Saint-Saëns and Lalo, and he remained relatively untouched by the influence of impressionism; his Third Symphony (1910) is marked "sans littérature ni peinture." In addition to 6 dramatic works, he wrote 4 symphonies (the last is incomplete) and a piano concerto; a string quartet and 2 violin sonatas; piano music and songs.

Gedda [Ustinoff], **Nicolai (Harry Gustaf)** (b. Stockholm, 11 July 1925). Tenor. His father, Mikhail, sang bass in a Don Cossack choir and was cantor in a Russian Orthodox church. Nicolai adopted his mother's maiden name for professional purposes. He studied voice with his father; with Carl Martin Öhmann in Stockholm from 1934; with Paola Novikova in New York. Debut at the Stockholm Royal Opera in 1952 as Chapelou (Adam's *Postillon*); at La Scala, 1953, as Don Ottavio *(Don Giovanni);* at the Paris Opéra, 1954, as Hüon *(Oberon);* at Covent Garden, 1954, as the Duke of Mantua *(Rigoletto)*. Debut at the Metropolitan Opera, 1957, as Gounod's Faust; sang 28 roles there over the next 26 years, including Barber's Anatole *(Vanessa)* at the first performance. Of his more than 60 roles, the best known were in French and Russian operas from Rameau's *Platée* to Shostakovich's *Lady Macbeth;* he also sang Gluck, Mozart, Bellini, Verdi, and Puccini frequently and with distinction.

Gehlhaar, Rolf (Rainer) (b. Breslau, 30 Dec. 1943). Composer. He moved to the U.S. in 1953; studied philosophy at Yale (B.A., 1965) and composition at Berkeley (1965–67); became Stockhausen's assistant in Cologne (1967–70); cofounded Feedback Studio Verlag in 1970 as a performance center and publishing company; has lectured at the Darmstadt summer courses and at Dartington College of the Arts. He has written orchestral pieces (*Prototypen,* 4 orchestral groups, 1973; *Tokamak,* piano and orchestra, 1982); instrumental music (*Strangeness, Charm, and Colour,* piano and 3 brass instruments, 1978); piano music; works for amplified instruments or instruments and tape (*Polymorph,* bass clarinet and tape delay, 1978); and electronic and computer music (*Copernic Opera F6,* 1987).

Gehot, Joseph [or Jean?] (b. Brussels, 8 Apr. 1756; d. U.S., ca. 1820). Violinist and composer. As a violinist he reportedly toured the Continent before settling in London around 1780. During the next decade he published treatises on music theory and instrumental playing. He was possibly a member of Johann Peter Salomon's orchestra organized for Haydn's London visit of 1791. In 1792 he emigrated to the U.S. with several of his musical colleagues; settling in Philadelphia, he played in and conducted the city orchestra. During the late 1790s he was violinist in the orchestra of Philadelphia's New Theatre.

Geissler, Fritz (b. Wurzen, near Leipzig, 16 Sept. 1921; d. Bad Saarow-Pieskow, Frankfurt on the Oder, 11 Jan. 1984). Composer. After a career as a composer of light music, he studied in Leipzig and Berlin (with Blacher and others); taught theory and composition in Leipzig and Dresden (1959–78) and then devoted himself to composition. He employed dodecaphonic techniques and explored various other modern approaches (including aleatory music and variable meters), but retained links to the past in his emphasis on the symphony. Works include 4 theater pieces, 3 ballets, and 2 oratorios; 10 symphonies and other orchestral music; chamber music; organ and piano works; and songs.

Gelbrun, Artur (b. Warsaw, 11 July 1913; d. Tel Aviv, 24 Dec. 1985). Composer and conductor. He studied at the Warsaw State Conservatory, then in Italy with Bernardo Molinari (conducting) and Alfred Casella (composition), and finally in Switzerland with Hermann Scherchen and Willy Burkhard. He was also an orchestral violinist in Warsaw and Switzerland. He emigrated to Israel in 1949; four years later he accepted a post as professor of conducting and composition at the Rubin Academy of Music in Tel Aviv. Works include *Esquisses,* narrator, flute, harp, orchestra (1946); *Hedra,* ballet (1951); *Variations,* piano, orchestra (1955); *Prologue symphonique* (1956); a cello concerto (1962); *Miadoux,* ballet (1967–68); Concertino, chamber orchestra (1974); *Song of the River,* soprano, orchestra (1959); *Salmo e Allelujah,* soprano, orchestra (1965); String Trio (1945); Sonatina, solo violin (1957); Partita, solo clarinet (1969); Piano Trio (1977); solo piano music.

Gelinek, Joseph (b. Sedlec, Bohemia, 3 Dec. 1758; d. Vienna, 13 Apr. 1825). Composer and pianist. He attended the university in Prague and took private lessons in counterpoint and organ from J. N. Seger. Later he attended seminary in Prague, receiving his orders in 1786. Around 1790 he traveled to Vienna to become personal chaplain and musical tutor for Count Philipp Kinsky and his family. Later (from ca. 1805) he was chaplain for Prince Nikolaus (II) Esterházy. Throughout his years in Vienna he maintained ties with Mozart and with the young Beethoven. In addition to chamber works and songs, he composed at least 120 sets of variations for piano, on themes ranging from operas by Gluck to the Seventh Symphony of Beethoven (6 variations, 1816). He also published numerous piano arrangements of works by Beethoven, Haydn, Mozart, Romberg, and others.

Gellman, Steven (b. Toronto, 16 Sept. 1947). Composer. At 16 he was soloist in his own piano concerto with the CBC Symphony. He studied at the Royal Conservatory of Music in Toronto, then at Juilliard with Berio, Sessions, and Persichetti, and, during the summers of 1965 and 1966, with Milhaud at Aspen. From 1974 to 1976 he studied with Messiaen at the Paris Conservatory. Member of the faculty of the Univ. of Ottawa from 1976. Orchestral works include *Chori* (1976); *Anima, animus* (1976); *Odyssey* (1971); *Overture for Ottawa* (1972); Symphony in Two Movements (1971); Symphony no. 2 (1972); *Awakening* (1982); *The Bride's Reception* (1983); Universe Symphony (large orchestra and 3 polyphonic synthesizers, 1984–85). Other works include 2 piano sonatas (1964, 1973); *Mythos ll* (flute, string quintet, 1968); *Soliloquy* (cello, 1966); *Wind Music* (brass quintet, 1978); *Deux Tapisseries* (1978); *Dialogue* (horn, 1978); *Transformation* (1980); *Keyboard Triptych* (1986); *Chiaroscuro* (flute, clarinet, violin, viola, cello, piano, percussion, 1988).

Geminiani, Francesco (bapt. Lucca, 5 Dec. 1687; d. Dublin, 17 Sept. 1762). Violinist, composer, and theorist. Probably a pupil of Lonati, Alessandro Scarlatti, and Corelli. He served the court at Lucca, 1707–10, and evidently led a theater orchestra in Naples, 1711. He arrived in England in 1714, performing at court in 1716 with Handel at the harpsichord. In 1726 he released concerto grosso arrangements and embellished versions of Corelli's op. 5 sonatas. He played in a cycle of 20 subscription concerts beginning on 9 Dec. 1731; other public appearances were rare, however, his income deriving from royal patronage and teaching, with Festing, Dubourg, and Avison among his pupils. He visited Ireland several times; on the first, in 1733, and on subsequent visits, he gave concerts at the Spring Garden. In 1739 he received a 14-year exclusive privilege for publication of his music in Britain, and in 1741 was granted the same for 12 years in France; among his offerings in the 1740s were a set of keyboard arrangements of his violin solos (Paris, 1743) and a collection of concerti grossi op. 5. His *The Inchanted Forest* was staged as a ballet-pantomime at Paris in 1754. The treatises on which his modern reputation rests appeared between 1748 and 1760; they include *A Treatise on the Art of Good Taste in Music* (London, 1749), *The Art of Accompaniment* (London, ca. 1754), and the famous *The Art of Playing on the Violin* (London, 1754; facs. ed. with intro. by David D. Boyden, London, 1952). His final years were divided between England and Ireland, with his last documented public appearance on 3 Mar. 1760; an observer praised the 72-year-old violinist's "fine and elegant taste, and the perfection of time and tune."

Bibl.: Enrico Careri, *Francesco Geminiani, 1687–1762* (Oxford, 1993).

Generali, Pietro (b. Masserano, 23 Oct. 1773; d. Novara, 3 Nov. 1832). Composer. At an early age he moved to Rome with his family; after early study there (with Giovanni Masi), he studied briefly in Naples at the Conservatorio di S. Pietro a Maiella. He began his career in Rome as a composer of sacred works; after 1800 he composed mostly operas. Among his approximately 50 stage works are *Pamela nubile* (Venice, 1804); *Le lagrime di una vedova* (Venice, 1808); *Adelina* (Venice, 1810); and *Il servo padrone* (Parma, 1818). In later years he served as music director of the opera at Palermo (ca. 1823–25) and as *maestro di cappella* at the Novara Cathedral (from 1827). In addition to operas, he composed Masses, cantatas, a Requiem, and other sacred music (including an oratorio, *Il voto di Jefte,* 1827).

Genzmer, Harald (b. Blumenthal, near Bremen, 9 Feb. 1909). Composer. After studying with Hindemith at the Berlin Hochschule für Musik (1928–34), he served as rehearsal director for the Breslau Opera chorus; taught theory and ensemble playing at the Volksmusikschule in Berlin-Neukölln (1938–40), where he began to compose music for amateurs; was professor of composition at the Musikhochschule in Freiburg (1946–57) and then in Munich. Before the war he had begun to experiment with electronic instruments, especially with the trautonium, for which he wrote 2 concertos (1940, 1952). He has written several ballets; orchestral music (3 symphonies, 1957, 1958, 1986; concertos for various instruments, including one for cello and contrabass, 1985; *Hölderlin,* 1979); chamber music (*Concertino piccolo,* recorder and percussion, 1978); works for piano (5 sonatas) and organ (2 concertos); works for solo voices or chorus and orchestra (*Oswald von Wolkenstein,* soprano, baritone, and orchestra, 1977); other choral music and songs.

George, Earl (b. Milwaukee, 1 May 1924). Composer and conductor. All of his academic training was at the Eastman School (M.M., 1947; Ph.D., 1958); taught at the Univ. of Minnesota (1948–55); was a visting lecturer at the Univ. of Oslo (1955–56); taught at Syracuse Univ. (from 1959). In Syracuse he wrote criticism and program notes and conducted and performed (as pianist) with the Syracuse Symphony. His compositional style is neoclassical and often features American themes. Works include 2 operas; *A Currier* *and Ives Set* (1953) and other orchestral pieces; instrumental music for strings and piano; many choral works (*Hum-Drum Heaven,* soprano, narrator, chorus, percussion, and piano, 1978); song cycles.

Gerber, Ernst Ludwig (b. Sondershausen, 29 Sept. 1746; d. there, 30 June 1819). Organist, composer, and writer on music. His first music teacher was his father, the composer and organist Heinrich Nikolaus Gerber, a student of J. S. Bach. In 1765 Ernst went to Leipzig to study law at the university; meanwhile he also became a proficient cellist and chamber musician. Having completed his studies, he returned home in 1775 to succeed his father as court organist to the Prince of Schwarzburg-Sondershausen. During the 1780s he compiled a biographical dictionary of music, which was published in Leipzig in 1790–92 as *Historisch-biographisches Lexicon der Tonkünstler.* It and its sequel, the greatly expanded *Neues historisch-biographisches Lexicon der Tonkünstler* (4 vols., Leipzig, 1812–14), together form an invaluable resource for the study of 18th-century music and are still drawn upon by scholars. (Both were reprinted in 4 volumes, including a volume of changes compiled by Ottmar Wessely, Graz, 1966–69.) Gerber also authored articles on style, harmony, and concert life; most appeared in the *Allgemeine musikalische Zeitung.*

Gerbert, Martin (b. Horb am Neckar, 12 Aug. 1720; d. St. Blasien, 13 May 1793). Scholar and writer on music. He attended Jesuit schools in Freiburg im Breisgau and in Klingenau; in 1744 he was ordained in the Benedictine abbey at St. Blasien, where he had lived from 1736. Soon he was director of the abbey library, later professor of philosophy and theology. He traveled through Europe, collecting manuscripts of music and works on music. In 1764 he was named Prince-Abbot at St. Blasien, and the following year he published the first fruits of his research, a catalog of medieval codices. His most important publications are the *De cantu et musica sacra a prima ecclesiae aetate usque ad praesens tempus* (St. Blasius, 1774; R: 2 vols., Graz, 1968), and the *Scriptores ecclesiastici de musica sacra potissimum* (St. Blasien, 1784; R: 3 vols., Hildesheim, 1963). The latter, an edition of nearly 50 medieval music treatises, formed the basis for Coussemaker's 19th-century *Scriptorum de musica medii aevi nova series.*

Gerhard, Roberto (b. Valls, Catalonia, 25 Sept. 1896; d. Cambridge, 5 Jan. 1970). Composer. Of Swiss parentage, he began his studies in the Lausanne École de commerce, but broke them off to study music. After brief study with Courvoisier in Munich (1914), he returned to Spain to take instruction in Barcelona, with Felipe Pedrell (composition) and Enrique Granados (piano). In 1923 he began five years of study in Schoenberg's master classes in Vienna and later in Berlin. In 1931 he was made professor of music at Barcelona's Ecola normal de la Generalitat. Throughout the 1930s he was active in the Catalan political movement. He edited music by Catalan composers (such as Soler and de Milán) and served in bureaucratic posts of the Catalan government, including adviser to the Ministry of Fine Arts. After the defeat of the Catalan Republicans in 1939, he settled briefly in Paris before emigrating to England, where he lived in Cambridge and took British citizenship. Around 1950 he began to receive belated attention in the form of commissions—from the Koussevitzky Foundation, the Fromm Foundation, and many others. His works were performed at ISCM festivals (in 1947 and 1951) and on BBC broadcasts. He was visiting professor twice in the U.S., at the Univ. of Michigan (1960) and at Tanglewood (1962). In 1967 he was made Commander of the British Empire, and he received an honorary doctorate from Cambridge the following year. His works are characterized by the harmony and orchestral color of Debussy and Ravel; his melodic material often follows twelve-tone technique.

Works: *Ariel* (ballet, 1934); *Don Quixote* (ballet, 1940–41); *Alegrías* (ballet, 1943–44); *The Duenna* (opera, 1945–47). For orchestra: Symphony "Homenaje a Predrell" (1941); concertos for violin (1942–43), piano (1951), harpsichord (1955–56); Concerto for Orchestra (1965); 5 symphonies (1952–53, 1957–59, 1960, 1967, 1969); *Epitalamion* (1966); also incidental music for films, plays, radio, and television. Vocal works: *Cancionero de Pedrell* (1941); *The Akond of Swat,* mezzo or baritone and 2 percussionists (1954); *Cantares* (1956); *The Plague,* speaker, chorus, orchestra (1963–64). Chamber and tape music: Wind Quintet (1928); Chaconne, violin (1959); 2 string quartets; *Concert for Eight,* chamber ensemble (1962); *Libra,* chamber ensemble (1968); *Leo,* chamber ensemble (1969); *Lament for the Death of a Bullfighter,* speaker, tape (1959); *Sculptures I–V,* tape (1963).

Gericke, Wilhelm (b. Schwanberg, near Graz, 18 Apr. 1845; d. Vienna, 27 Oct. 1925). Conductor. In 1862–65 he was a student at the Vienna Conservatory (composition under Dessoff). Opera conductor, 1868–74, at Linz; 1874–84, assistant conductor, Vienna Opera; 1880–83, 1890–95, conductor of concerts of the Gesellschaft der Musikfreunde; 1884–89, 1898–1906, conductor, Boston Symphony. He also composed chamber, choral, piano works; an operetta; songs.

Gerle, Hans (b. Nuremberg, ca. 1500; d. there, 1570). Compiler and arranger, especially of music for lute. The music in his 3 books consists of intabulations, arrangements, and reprints of works by others. The earliest also contains music for ensembles of bowed strings and introductory essays on playing technique and on musical notation.

German, Edward [Jones, German Edward] (b. Whitechurch, Shropshire, 17 Feb. 1862; d. London, 11 Nov. 1936). Composer. Became known as J. E. German at the Royal Academy to avoid confusion with another Edward Jones. His father was an organist at the local Congregational church. He studied piano and organ from the age of 5 and taught himself to play the violin. He studied with Walter Hay at Shrewsbury until 1880, when he entered the Royal Academy of Music, where he studied organ with Charles Steggall, violin with Alfred Burnett, theory with Barrister, and composition and orchestration with Prout. In 1888 he became conductor at the Globe Theatre, where his music for *Richard III* brought him public recognition. In 1892 Sir Henry Irving commissioned him to write music for *Henry VIII.* He also wrote a score for Anthony Hope's *English Nell.* After Sullivan's death in 1900, he was commissioned to complete *The Emerald Isle;* his own comic operas *Merrie England* (1902) and *Tom Jones* (1907) were quite successful. He wrote many songs; *Glorious Devon* (1904) and his settings of Kipling's *Just So Stories* (1903) were most successful. He was knighted in 1928. Other works include 2 symphonies, 3 orchestral suites, and chamber and piano music.

Bibl.: Brian Rees, *A Musical Peacemaker: The Life and Work of Sir Edward German* (Buckinghamshire, 1986).

Gero [Ghero], **Jhan** [Jan, Jehan] (fl. 1540–55). Composer. Active in Venice but probably of northern origin. Wrote or arranged many madrigals and chansons for the printers Antonio Gardane and Girolamo Scotto. His works for 2 or 3 parts were particularly popular in Germany and Italy, some being reprinted repeatedly for over a century. Two collections of *note nere* madrigals for 4 voices appeared in 1549 and 2 books of 5-part motets in 1555.

Gerschefski, Edwin (b. Meriden, Conn., 19 June 1909). Composer and pianist. He studied composition at Yale (1926–31); went to England to study piano, then to Como to study with Schnabel (1935); returned to New York to study composition with Schillinger (1936–38). He taught at Converse College from 1940 (dean of the music school there, 1945–59); briefly at the Univ. of New Mexico; and then at the Univ. of Georgia (1960–80). He set "informal" texts such as news stories (e.g., *Border Raid* op. 57, 1966) and business letters. His output includes a symphony, piano and violin concertos and other orchestral works; much chamber and piano music (*Poem* op. 75, cello and piano, 1973); choral and vocal music; incidental music and 9 film scores.

Gershwin, George (b. Brooklyn, 26 Sept. 1898; d. Hollywood, 11 July 1937). Composer, pianist, and conductor. He grew up in Manhattan and studied piano with neighborhood teachers; in 1914 he dropped out of high school to work for the Tin Pan Alley publisher Jerome H. Remick as a "song plugger," playing and singing newly published works to encourage sales; his first song was published in 1916, and a year after he left Remick (1917), he was under contract to T. B. Harms as a songwriter. He worked as a rehearsal pianist on Broadway and began to contribute songs to other composers' shows. His first musical was successfully produced in 1919 (*La La Lucille,* 104 performances); in 1920 Al Jolson recorded his first hit song, "Swanee." Gershwin continued to have successful shows in both New York and London in the early 1920s, but during that period he also launched a career in concert music. He accompanied the Canadian soprano Eva Gauthier at Aeolian Hall (November 1923) in a concert of popular and art song; his performance of his *Rhapsody in Blue* early in 1924 with the Paul Whiteman Band made him famous as a composer and performer who managed to insert jazz, a distinctively American music, into the concert hall.

These successes with stage and concert works made him financially secure; in his remaining years he continued to compose in both popular and serious realms, although his Broadway shows began to appear at a slower rate. In an effort to increase his technical mastery, he studied with various teachers in the 1920s (Goldmark, Riegger, Cowell) and later with Schillinger (1932–36). Concert works received performances by major orchestras, often with the composer as pianist: the New York Symphony Orchestra under Damrosch (Concerto in F, 1925); the New York Philharmonic (*An American in Paris,* 1928; *Cuban Overture,* 1932); the Boston Symphony under Koussevitzky (*Second Rhapsody,* 1932); the Philadelphia Orchestra (*Catfish Row,* a suite from *Porgy and Bess,* 1936). This career in concert music was carried on simultaneously with his continued success on Broadway and in film. His first collaboration with his brother Ira, who was to provide almost all subsequent lyrics, was in *Lady, Be Good!* (opened 1 Dec. 1924), a show that helped to launch Fred Astaire's long career; among its famous songs is "Fascinating Rhythm." *Of Thee I Sing,* a musical satire on American politics, opened in December 1931 to run for 441 performances; it received the Pulitzer Prize for drama and included such well-known songs as "Love Is Sweeping the Country." *Shall We Dance,* a film starring Fred Astaire and Ginger Rogers, was released in May 1937 ("Let's Call the Whole Thing Off," "They Can't Take That Away from Me"). Other late songs include "Nice Work If You Can Get It" and "Love Walked In," both from film scores.

Gershwin's musical style is essentially the same in popular and serious works. The harmonic language ranges from diatonic to chromatic and avoids extreme dissonances; unprepared tonal shifts (especially from the tonic to neighboring keys) are common. The parallel sixths and tenths, blue notes, syncopations, and oom-pah accompaniments of jazz and dance bands are employed frequently in concert works. The songs have been categorized as rhythmic and declamatory ("Love Is Sweeping the Country"), balladlike ("Someone To Watch Over Me"), or relaxed and swinging ("They Can't Take That Away from Me"). His larger works can often be viewed as extended songs, consisting of attractive tunes that are restated immediately, and filler; regular 4-bar phrases and AABA designs are common. The 12-bar blues progression serves as the basis for much of *An American in Paris.*

Porgy and Bess, a synthesis of opera and American

George (left) and Ira (right) Gershwin with DuBose Heyward, 1935.

popular music, opened on Broadway in 1935; it was revived in San Francisco and Los Angeles (1938), in New York (1942), elsewhere in the U.S., Latin America, Europe, the Middle East, and the USSR (1952–56), and at the Vienna Volksoper (1965). These revivals often substituted spoken dialogue for recitatives and made substantial cuts; in the mid-1970s concert and staged versions of the original were presented in Cleveland and Houston. Gershwin's popular songs have been published, performed, and recorded in a wide variety of arrangements by singers, pianists, swing bands, and jazz performers; his harmonic progressions often served as the bases for new jazz improvisations.

Works: *Operas. Blue Monday Blues* (1922); *Porgy and Bess* (after Dubose Heyward and Ira Gershwin, 1935). *Operetta. Song of the Flame* (after Oscar Hammerstein II and Otto Harbach, 1925).

Musical comedies. La La Lucille (1919); *Lady, Be Good!* (1924; "Fascinating Rhythm," "Oh, Lady, Be Good!"); *Strike Up the Band* (1927; "The Man I Love," "Strike Up the Band"; 2nd version, 1930); *Funny Face* (1927; "Funny Face," "'S Wonderful"); *Girl Crazy* (1930; "But Not for Me," "Embraceable You," "I Got Rhythm"); *Of Thee I Sing* (1931); *Pardon My English* (1933); *Let 'em Eat Cake* (1933).

Films with songs. Shall We Dance (1937; "Let's Call the Whole Thing Off," "They All Laughed," "They Can't Take That Away from Me"); *A Damsel in Distress* (1937; "A Foggy Day," "Nice Work If You Can Get It"); *The Goldwyn Follies* (1938; "Love Is Here To Stay," "Love Walked In").

Orchestral works. Rhapsody in Blue (piano and jazz band, orchestrated by Ferde Grofé, 1924; orchestrated for full orchestra by Grofé, 1926); *Concerto in F* (piano and orchestra, 1925); *An American in Paris* (tone poem, 1928); *Second Rhapsody for Piano and Orchestra* (1931); *Cuban Overture* (1932); *"I Got Rhythm" Variations* (1934); *Catfish Row: Suite from Porgy and Bess* (1935–36).

Lullaby for string quartet (1919–20); piano pieces (including Preludes for Piano, ca. 1923–26, and *George Gershwin's Song Book,* 1931).

Bibl.: Edward Jablonski, *Gershwin* (New York, 1987). Walter Rimler, *A Gershwin Companion: A Critical Inventory and Discography, 1916–1984* (Ann Arbor, 1991). Joan Peyser, *The Memory of All That: The Life of George Gershwin* (New York, 1993).

Gershwin, Ira [Gershvin, Israel] (b. New York, 6 Dec. 1896; d. Beverly Hills, Calif., 17 Aug. 1983). Lyricist. As a student he wrote verse for newspapers and periodicals. Later he joined his brother George Gershwin to write songs. From 1924 *(Lady, Be Good!)* to George's death in 1937 they formed a close partnership. They wrote more than a dozen Broadway shows, the first musical comedy to win a Pulitzer Prize for drama (*Of Thee I Sing,* 1931), and songs for films. Ira later worked with a number of other composers, including Weill (*Lady in the Dark,* 1941), Kern (*Cover Girl,* 1944), Arthur Schwartz (*Park Avenue,* 1946), and Arlen (*A Star Is Born,* 1953).

Gervaise, Claude (fl. Paris, 1540–60). Composer, editor, and arranger. Worked for the printer Pierre Attaingnant and his widow, most notably as editor of 3 volumes of the *Danceries;* composed the contents of the sixth and last volume of this collection of ensemble dances; of chansons, intabulated 10 for viol, composed 20, and arranged about 25 others.

Gesualdo, Carlo, Prince of Venosa, Count of Conza (b. Naples?, ca. 1561; d. Gesualdo, Avellino, 8 Sept. 1613). Composer. Known mostly for polyphonic madrigals for 5 or more voices in a highly mannered style that includes extreme chromatism. His family was ennobled in 1560 but the title died with the composer, who had no surviving heirs. He was married twice, first to the unfaithful Maria d'Avalos, then to Leonora d'Este of Ferrara. His first marriage ended in 1590 with the murder, at his instigation, of his wife and her lover. The resulting notoriety caused the composer to withdraw permanently from Naples to his estate at Gesualdo, but it also drew attention to his music. His second marriage, solemnized in Ferrara in 1594, provided the occasion for establishing connections with many musicians active in that region (especially Luzzacho Luzzaschi) and for much musical activity.

His first two books of madrigals were originally published under a pseudonym. Beginning with his third book (Ferrara, 1595), he adopted a complex, chromatic, often dissonant polyphonic idiom rooted in the precepts of the *seconda prattica,* with great emphasis on text expression. His madrigals display melodic extravagance, an unusually wide variation in rhythm, musical fragmentation of poetic lines, frequent emphatic pauses, and for purposes of emphasis much repetition of words and their music (usually varied rather than exact). Six books were published during his lifetime and one posthumously. None of his printed works employs monody or any instrumental accompaniment. A similar style is used in his sacred works, mostly motets and responsories. The many pieces written for private use at the composer's estate show virtually the same musical characteristics as the madrigals. Those meant for public consumption, however, are in a much more conventional vein.

Although Gesualdo's music has been the focus of much attention in the 20th century, its influence on his successors was limited. It was often praised. Some was published in score in 1613 for instructional use. But other styles formed the basis of the music of the 17th century.

Bibl.: *Sämtliche Werke* (Hamburg, 1957–67). Cecil Gray and Philip Heseltine, *Carlo Gesualdo, Prince of Venosa, Musician and Murderer* (London, New York, 1926; R: Westport, Conn., 1971). Glenn E. Watkins, *Gesualdo: The Man and His Music* (London, 1973). Carl Dahlhaus, "Gesualdos manieristische Dissonanztechnik," in *Convivium musicorum: Festschrift Wolfgang Boetticher* (Berlin, 1974). Denis Arnold, *Gesualdo* (London, 1984).

Getz, Stan [Stanley] (b. Philadelphia, 2 Feb. 1927; d. Malibu, Calif., 6 June 1991). Jazz tenor saxophonist and bandleader. He played in the big bands of Jack Teagarden (1943), Stan Kenton (1944–45), Benny Goodman (1945–46), and Woody Herman (1947–48), with whom as a member of the saxophone section known as the "Four Brothers" he recorded the ballad solo "Early Autumn" (1948). Thereafter, except for a tour with Jazz at the Philharmonic (1957–58), he led small groups, helping establish the careers of Horace Silver, Jimmy Raney, Bob Brookmeyer (early 1950s), Gary Burton, Steve Swallow, Chick Corea (mid-1960s), and JoAnne Brackeen (mid-1970s). Although based most often in New York, he spent periods in Los Angeles (ca. 1953–57), Scandinavia (1958–61), Spain (1969–71), and the San Francisco Bay area, where from ca. 1985 he was an artist-in-residence at Stanford Univ. Getz's most innovative albums were *Focus* (1961), an unusually successful union of saxophone solos with Eddie Sauter's arrangements for string orchestra, and *Jazz Samba* (1962), which initiated the craze for bossa nova. Other albums include *West Coast Jazz* (1955), *Sweet Rain* (1967), *Captain Marvel* (1972), *The Dolphin* (1981), and *Voyage* (1986).

Gevaert, François-Auguste (b. Huysse, Belgium, 31 July 1828; d. Brussels, 24 Dec. 1908). Scholar, composer, and teacher. He studied at the Ghent Conservatory, 1841–47; 1847, won Belgian Prix de Rome, enabling him to travel in Europe in 1849–52; then settled in Paris, producing 8 opéras comiques there (1853–64) and 1 in Baden (1861); 1867–70, director, Paris Opéra, leaving because of the war; 1871–1908, director, Brussels Conservatory, greatly increasing its reputation and conducting its concerts. Also composed cantatas, songs, sacred music, instrumental pieces; published once-influential pedagogical works on plainchant, instrumentation, solfège, organ playing, harmony; also important historical works on the music of antiquity and the early church (*La mélopée antique dans le chant de l'Église latine,* Ghent, 1895–96; R: 1967). Created a baronet in 1907 for composing a national anthem for the Belgian Congo.

Ghedini, Giorgio Federico (b. Cuneo, 11 July 1892; d. Nervi, near Genoa, 25 Mar. 1965). Composer. He studied the cello at the Liceo musicale in Turin, composition privately with Giovanni Cravero, and briefly with Marco Enrico Bossi at the Liceo musicale in Bologna; he taught in Turin, Parma, and Milan, where he was director of the conservatory (1951–62). He was active in the promotion of contemporary music as an organizer of the Settimane musicale senesi and the Italian branch of the ISCM. He was a prolific composer, whose early works remain unpublished and relatively unknown. Like Casella, he was interested in early Italian music; he arranged several of Frescobaldi's canzonas for orchestra (1931) and edited works of the Gabrielis and Monteverdi. Many works reflect this interest by adopting Baroque forms or imitating the rhythm and texture of Baroque music (*Partita,* orchestra, 1926; *Concerto funebre per Duccio Galimberti,* 1948). Works such as *Architetture* (orchestra, 1940), constructed as a series of "edifici sonori," show the influence of Stravinsky. Although he remained very productive in his later years, he was not associated with avant-garde developments in postwar Italy. He composed 6 operas, a ballet, film and incidental music; many orchestral pieces (*Contrappunti,* string trio and orchestra, 1962); chamber and piano music; several works for voices and orchestra (*Missa monodica in honorem Sancti Gregori Magni,* unison voices and optional organ or harmonium, 1932); choral music; songs.

Ghent, Emmanuel (Robert) (b. Montreal, 15 May 1925). Composer and psychoanalyst. He studied medicine at McGill; completed a diploma in psychoanalysis in New York (1956), where he maintained a part-time practice and taught at N.Y.U. As a student he had composed chamber music; studied further with Shapey (1961–63); from 1963 he used "intervallic groupings as the basis for pitch structure both melodically and vertically." Works include *Hex* (trumpet, 11 instruments, and 4-track tape, 1966); works for dancers with computer-generated lighting, electronic and computer music, and live performers (*Phosphones,* 1971).

Gherardello da Firenze (b. ca. 1320–25; d. Florence, 1362 or 1363). Composer. Associated with various churches in Florence from at least 1343. His contemporaries knew him chiefly as a composer of liturgical pieces, but more secular works survive, all in Tuscan manuscripts, including the Squarcialupi Codex. Among the extant works of this member of the first generation of Florentine trecento composers are monophonic *ballate,* a *caccia*, and 2-voiced madrigals and Mass movements.

Bibl.: Nino Pirrotta, ed., *The Music of Fourteenth-Century Italy, CMM* 8/1 (1964) [edition].

Ghiaurov, Nicolai (b. Lydjene, near Velingrad, Bulgaria, 13 Sept. 1929). Bass. Studied with Cristo Brambarov at the Sofia Conservatory, 1949–50, then on scholarship at the Leningrad and Moscow conservatories, 1950–55. Debut with the Sofia Opera in 1955 as Basilio *(Barbiere).* Won the Paris International Competition, 1955. Debut at the Vienna State Opera in 1957 as Ramfis *(Aida);* at the Bolshoi Opera in 1958 as Pimen *(Boris);* at La Scala in 1959 as Varlaam *(Boris);* at Covent Garden in 1962 as Padre Guardiano *(Forza);* at Chicago in 1963 and the Metropolitan Opera in 1965 as Mephistophélès *(Faust);* at Salzburg in 1965–66 as Boris. Other major roles included Philippe II *(Don Carlos),* Boito's Mefistofele, and Massenet's Don Quichotte.

Ghiglia, Oscar (Alberto) (b. Livorno, 13 Aug. 1938). Guitarist. Originally self-taught on the guitar, he studied solfeggio and basic theory at the Conservatorio di S. Cecilia in Rome; guitar with Andrés Segovia at the Accademia Chigiana in Siena and at Santiago de Compostela, 1958–63; assistant to Segovia at Siena and at the Univ. of California at Berkeley, 1964. Debut at the Spoleto Festival in 1961. Studied musicology with Jacques Chailley in Paris, 1963–64. New York and London debuts in 1966.

Ghiselin [Verbonnet], **Johannes** (fl. early 16th cent.). Composer. An esteemed contemporary and associate of Josquin and Obrecht; probably of Flemish origin, but active chiefly in Ferrara and at the French royal court. His works include 8 Masses (most based on secular chansons), about a dozen motets, and around 20 chansons, the majority with French or Flemish titles or texts.

Bibl.: *Opera omnia, CMM* 23 (1961–68).

Ghislanzoni, Antonio (b. Lecco, 25 Nov. 1824; d. Caprino Bergamasco, 16 July 1893). Librettist. After a varied and unsettled early life as seminarian, medical student, operatic baritone (1846–55), he became a writer and journalist, publishing poetry, novels (his novel of theatrical life *Gli artisti da teatro,* Milan, 1865, was republished into the 20th century), and about 85 librettos (for Ponchielli, Catalani, Gomes, Petrella, among others); best remembered for collaborating with Verdi on the revision of *La forza del destino* and on *Aida.*

Giacomelli, Geminiano (b. Piacenza, ca. 1692; d. Loreto, 25 Jan. 1740). Composer. Pupil of Capelli; *maestro di cappella* at Parma cathedral; supposed study with Alessandro Scarlatti is questionable. Served together with Capelli as *maestro* at the Parmesan court, and also at the Chiesa della Steccata (1717–27); later took a similar post at the Church of S. Giovanni in Piacenza (1727–32), but returned to Parma (1732–37) before becoming *maestro di cappella* at the Santa Casa in Loreto, where he remained until his death. He wrote some 19 operas, including *Cesare in Egitto* (Milan, 1735; revived at Graz, 1737) and settings of libretti by Zeno and Metastasio. His output includes arias, intermezzi, oratorios, and other sacred pieces.

Giacosa, Giuseppe (b. Colleretto Parella, near Turin, 21 Oct. 1847; d. there, 2 Sept. 1906). Librettist. A lawyer like his father, but became a writer (*Impressioni d'America,* Milan, 1898) and a highly successful dramatist. He was engaged by Ricordi to collaborate with Luigi Illica on librettos for Puccini *(La bohème, Tosca, Madama Butterfly).*

Bibl.: P. Nardi, *Vita e tempo di Giuseppe Giacosa* (Milan, 1949). A. Barsotti, *Giuseppe Giacosa* (Florence, 1973).

Giannini, Vittorio (b. Philadelphia, 19 Oct. 1903; d. New York, 28 Nov. 1966). Composer. He studied the violin with his mother; studied at the Milan Conservatory on scholarship (1913–17), and later at Juilliard with Hans Letz (violin) and Rubin Goldmark (composition). In the 1930s he had numerous European performances and won the first of 3 Rome prizes; he taught at Juilliard, the Manhattan School, the Curtis Institute (from 1956), and was appointed director of the North Carolina School of the Arts shortly before his death. He has been called a modern Romantic, who combined Italian lyricism and Wagnerian chromaticism; his opera *The Taming of the Shrew,* premiered on NBC television, won the New York Critics' Circle Award (1954) and was revived in Houston (1979). Works include 10 operas; several symphonies (*In Memoriam Theodore Roosevelt,* 1935), concertos, and other orchestral and band works; chamber music; piano works; sacred and secular choral music; vocal music with orchestra or piano.

Giardini [Degiardino], **Felice (de)** (b. Turin, 12 Apr. 1716; d. Moscow, 8 June 1796). Violinist and composer. In Milan he was a choirboy in the cathedral; later he studied music in Turin, and during the early 1730s began playing violin in theater orchestras, first in Rome, then in Naples. At the Teatro S. Carlo, where he was deputy violinist, the composer Jommelli is reported to have slapped him for embellishing excessively the violin lines of his operas. During the 1750s Giardini toured Europe as a violinist, scoring successes in Paris, Berlin, and England. In London he played at the Bach–Abel concerts and at the Three Choirs Festival, and he served as music master for the Duke of Gloucester. After attempting to start an opera troupe in Italy, he went to Russia in 1796, where he fell ill and died. He composed operas (*Enea e Lavinia,* 1764); parts of an oratorio, *Ruth* (1763–68); catches and glees; chamber and solo instrumental works; tutorial works for clavier, violin, and cello.

Gibbons, Christopher (bapt. Westminster, London, 22 Aug. 1615; d. there, 20 Oct. 1676). Organist and composer. Second son of Orlando Gibbons, he sang as a boy in the Chapel Royal under Giles; probably also studied with his father, after whose death in 1625 he went to live with an uncle in Exeter. Succeeded Thomas Holmes as organist at Winchester Cathedral in 1638; the Civil War, and subsequent suppression of church music, terminated this post in 1642. He lived and taught in London, 1651–60; collaborated with Locke on the masque *Cupid and Death* in 1653 and was heard on the organ at Oxford in 1654. He became organist at the Chapel Royal and to King Charles II upon the Restoration in 1660, later also serving at Westminster Abbey until his death. A bribery scandal involving construction of an organ did not diminish his stature with the king, who nominated him for an Oxford doctorate in 1663. Known in his time primarily as a performer. His compositions include sacred works along with consort and keyboard music. Blow was among his pupils.

Bibl.: Clare G. and Sheila F. Rayner, "Christopher Gibbons," *MD* 24 (1970): 151–71.

Gibbons, Orlando (bapt. Oxford, 25 Dec. 1583; d. Canterbury, 5 June 1625). Composer and organist. His father, William, was a civic musician at Oxford, his brother Edward an organist at Exeter. Orlando joined the King's College choir in 1596, enrolling there as a student in 1599; he received payment from the college on two occasions in 1602–3 for special music on feast days. He is first listed in the Chapel Royal Cheque Book in 1603; two years later he succeeded Cock as chapel organist, a post he held for the rest of his life. A court favorite throughout his tenure, he received a royal gift of £150 in 1615, and became one of the king's private virginalists in 1619; in 1623 he was appointed organist of Westminster Abbey. He received two degrees, the B.Mus. at Cambridge in 1606 and the D.Mus. at Oxford in 1622, and was perhaps the most illustrious organist in England when he died suddenly of apoplexy. His sacred works, which circulated widely but were not printed in his lifetime, include full anthems with impressively managed imitative counterpoint (as in the 6-part *Hosanna to the Son of David* and the 8-voice *All People Clap Your Hands*) along with verse anthems in which organ, soloist, chorus, and occasionally viol consort alternate in a through-composed format. He also composed a madrigal collection (London, 1612), fantasias and dances for consort or keyboard, and consort songs.

Bibl.: Edmund H. Fellowes, *Orlando Gibbons and His Family* (London, 1925; 2nd ed., 1951; R: 1970).

Gibbs, Cecil Armstrong (b. Great Baddon, Essex, 10 Aug. 1889; d. Chelmsford, 12 May 1960). Composer. At Trinity College, Cambridge, he was a student of Edward Dent and Charles Wood (organ); later (1919–20) he studied with Vaughan Williams and Adrian Boult at the Royal College of Music, and he stayed on there after 1920 as instructor of music theory and composition. After settling in Danbury in Essex during the 1920s, he continued to compose an enormous amount of music. He served as vice president of the British Federation of Music Festivals (1937–52). He is best known for *Dusk,* a waltz for piano solo that was popular during the 1940s; among his other compositions are stage works (*The Oresteia,* 1921; *The Blue Peter,* 1923; *The Sting of Love,* 1926; *When One Isn't There,* 1927; *Twelfth Night,* 1946–47); orchestral works (3 symphonies; *The Enchanted Wood,* 1919; *A Spring Garland,* strings, 1937); cantatas (*La belle dame sans merci);* chamber music; some 200 choral works; 100 songs.

Gibson, Jon Charles (b. Los Angeles, 11 Mar. 1940). Composer. He studied saxophone, flute, jazz, and composition; graduated from San Francisco State (B.A., 1964); associated with the Philip Glass Ensemble from its inception (1968). His own style involves jazz and minimalism; his skill as a visual artist has led him to include drawings in some musical performances; he has written for dancers (Merce Cunningham, Lucinda Childs). Works include an opera (*Voyage of the Beagle,* 1982), instrumental music (*Multiples,* any melody instruments, 1972; *Relative Calm,* a dance score for small ensemble and tape, 1981); and videotapes such as *Interval* (1985), which includes performance of his *30's* (any instruments, 1970) with its graphic score.

Gibson, Orville H. (b. Chateaugay, N.Y., 1856; d. Ogdensburg, N.Y., 19 Aug. 1918). Instrument maker. Began making fretted instruments, primarily mandolins and guitars, in Kalamazoo, Mich., in the 1870s, contributing importantly to the evolution of both. He left the firm that bears his name in 1909; it has continued as a leading manufacturer of fretted (now mostly electrically amplified) instruments.

Gideon, Miriam (b. Greeley, Colo., 23 Oct. 1906). Composer. M.A. in musicology at Columbia (1946); D.S.M. in composition from the Jewish Theological Seminary (1970); additional study with Lazare Saminsky (1931–34) and Sessions (1935–43). She taught at Brooklyn College (1944–54), the City College of New York (1947–55; 1971–76), the Jewish Theological Seminary (from 1955), and the Manhattan School (from 1967). An interesting aspect of her freely atonal style is the frequent incorporation of a poem and its translation in the same work (e.g., *The Condemned Playground,* 1963). Elsewhere she employed Spanish, Javanese, Irish, and Hebrew themes. She composed an opera; *Symphonia brevis* (1953) and 3 early orchestral works; chamber music (*Fantasy on Irish Folk Motives,* oboe, bassoon, viola, percussion, 1975) and piano works; Jewish sacred music for choir, soloists, and instruments (including a Sabbath service, 1970); works for voice(s) and orchestra (*Songs of Youth and Madness,* high voice and orchestra, 1977); songs with piano or ensemble (*Creature to Creature,* medium voice, flute, and harp, 1985).

Gielen, Michael (Andreas) (b. Dresden, 20 July 1927). Conductor and composer. His father, Josef, directed opera at the Teatro Colón in Buenos Aires from 1939. Michael studied piano there with Erwin Leuchter, 1942–49. Debut as pianist in 1949 playing the complete works of Schoenberg. Répétiteur at the Teatro Colón. Studied composition in Vienna with J. Polnauer, 1950–53. Assistant conductor at the Vienna State Opera, 1951–60. Conductor at the Stockholm Royal Opera, 1960–65. Created Zimmermann's *Die Soldaten* at the Cologne Opera, 1965. Music director of the Belgian National Orchestra in Brussels, 1968–72. U.S. debut with the New York Philharmonic, 1971. Chief conductor of the Netherlands National Opera, 1972–77. Music director of the Frankfurt Opera, 1977–80; of the Cincinnati Symphony, 1980–86; of the South-West Radio Symphony in Baden-Baden from 1986. In Europe he premiered numerous works by Stockhausen, Ligeti, and others. His own compositions take the music of the Second Vienna School as their point of departure; they include *Variations for 40 Instruments* (1959), *Pentaphonie* (1960–63), *Les cloches sont sur une fausse voie* (1967–69), *Quelques difficultés dans l'acte de surmonter l'angoisse* (1972), *Pflicht und Neigung* (22 players, 1988).

Gieseking, Walter (b. Lyons, of German parents, 5 Nov. 1895; d. London, 26 Oct. 1956). Pianist and composer. While still a baby he moved with his family to Naples; there he did not attend school but studied flute, violin, and piano privately. Studied piano with Karl Leimer at the Hannover Conservatory, 1911–16. During World War I played violin, drums, and popular piano for the German army. After the war he developed his powers of memory and concentration to an unusual degree. First European tour, 1921; U.S. debut, New York, 22 Feb. 1926. Quickly became one of the most respected pianists of his generation. In 1947 led a master class at the Saarbrücken Conservatory. Tried and acquitted of Nazi collaboration in 1949. His playing of Debussy won special admiration. Compositions include Concerto-Sonatina for cello and piano; a wind quintet; Serenade for string quartet. Published *Modernes Klavierspiel* (Mainz, 1930; trans. Eng., 1932); *So wurde ich Pianist* (Wiesbaden, 1963).

Gifford, Gene [Harold Eugene] (b. Americus, Ga., 31 May 1908; d. Memphis, 12 Nov. 1970). Jazz arranger. As a guitarist, banjoist, and writer, he joined the Orange Blossoms (1928), which became the Casa Loma Orchestra (1929). He continued playing until 1933, but concentrated on writing fast, intricate, showy arrangements such as "Casa Loma Stomp" (1930) and "White Jazz" (1931), and lush ballads such as "Smoke Rings" (1932; all his own compositions). After leaving the group in 1939, he worked as a free-lance arranger, a radio engineer and recording consultant, and a music teacher.

Gigault, Nicolas (b. Paris, ca. 1627; d. there, 20 Aug. 1707). Organist and composer, perhaps also a violinist. Born into poverty, he had by 1662 acquired a broad collection of keyboard and stringed instruments. Held posts as organist at St. Honoré (1646–52), St. Nicolas-des-Champs (1652 to his death), St. Martin-des-Champs (from 1673), and the Hôpital du Saint Esprit (from 1685). He is listed as a "Maitre de 1ere classe" in a tax roll of 1695, and was perhaps a teacher of Lully. His extant works are included in publications of 1683 and 1685. The first consists primarily of variations on French noëls; the second of "plus de 180 pièces" encompassing plainsong settings, *récits,* dialogues, preludes, and short fugues, generally arranged by church mode and often using pervasive dotted rhythms.

Edition: A. Pirro and A. Guilmant, eds., *Livre de musique pour l'orgue par Nicolas Gigault* (Paris, 1904; R: 1972).

Gigli, Beniamino (b. Recanati, 20 Mar. 1890; d. Rome, 30 Nov. 1957). Tenor. In Rome he studied with Agnese Bonucci privately, with Antonio Cotogni and then Enrico Rosati at the Liceo musicale. Won the

Parma International Competition in 1914. Debut at the Teatro sociale in Rovigo in 1914 as Enzo *(La gioconda).* As Boito's Faust he made his debut at the Metropolitan Opera in New York on 26 Nov. 1920. Remained with the Met 13 seasons, singing 29 roles. Covent Garden debut in 1930 as Giordano's Andrea Chénier. Settled in Rome in 1932, where his willingness to serve as a musical ambassador for the Fascist government led to difficulties after World War II. Beginning in 1947 he favored recitals when away from Rome and Naples. Official retirement in Rovigo in 1954; farewell U.S. tour in 1955. For four decades his golden tone and artful mezza voce made him the natural heir to Caruso's lyric repertory. He appeared in 6 films, including *Mamma.*

Gigout, Eugène (b. Nancy, 23 Mar. 1844; d. Paris, 9 Dec. 1925). Organist and composer. Studied at the École Niedermeyer (teachers included Saint-Saëns), marrying Niedermeyer's daughter and, on graduating, becoming a teacher there (1863–85, 1900–1905). From 1863 to 1925 he was organist at St. Augustin; 1885, established a state-supported school of organ playing and improvisation (being himself a noted improviser); from 1911, professor of organ, Paris Conservatory. He performed throughout Europe. Many organ compositions, especially the collections *Pièces breves* (1889), *Album grégorien* (1895), *L'orgue d'église* (1904).

Bibl.: Gabriel Fauré, *Hommage à Eugène Gigout* (Paris, 1923).

Gilbert, Anthony (b. London, 26 July 1934). Composer. After studying piano at Trinity College of Music until 1955, he went to Morley College, where he studied theory with Anthony Milner and composition with Walter Goehr (1959). In 1960 he studied with Matyas Seiber as well. In 1969 he began his teaching career in London at Goldsmiths' College. Subsequently he taught at Lancaster College (1971–73) and at Morley College (from 1971); he also worked as a music editor for Schott's. His musical style is fundamentally lyrical and tonally based; works include an opera *The Scene-Machine* (first perf. 1971); orchestral works (*Sinfonia,* chamber orchestra, 1965; *Peal II,* jazz or school orchestra, 1968; a symphony, 1973; *Ghost and Dream Dancing,* 1974; *Welkin,* 1976); vocal works (Missa brevis, 1964–65; *Shepherd Masque,* children's choir, chamber ensemble, 1968; *Inscapes,* soprano, narrator, 2 clarinets, percussion, 1975); chamber music (*Mother,* chamber ensemble, 1969; *A Treatment of Silence,* violin and tape, 1970; *String Quartet with Piano Pieces,* 1972; *Long White Moonlight,* soprano, double bass, 1980).

Gilbert, Henry F(ranklin Belknap) (b. Somerville, Mass., 26 Sept. 1868; d. Cambridge, Mass., 19 May 1928). Composer. From a family of musicians, he learned to play violin, piano, and various wind instruments as a youth; studied composition with MacDowell (1889–92). Having played the violin in small orchestras and worked from time to time in his uncle's printing company in order to support himself, he decided to concentrate on composition only after a trip to Paris in 1901 to hear Charpentier's *Louise.* His acquaintance with the nationalism of European and Russian music led him to strive for an equivalent American music (he compared himself to Grieg); in 1902 he helped Farwell establish the Wa-Wan Press. He was interested in a wide variety of exotic and folk musics, drawing on spirituals, ragtime, and jazz in his own works; edited a volume of folk songs (Boston, 1910); transcribed Indian songs and wrote music for Edward Curtis's lectures on Indian life (*The Intimate Story of Indian Tribal Life,* orchestra, 1911). His style remained diatonic and tonal, his forms standard; his orchestration, however, was varied and colorful.

Works: 2 operas (*Uncle Remus,* incomplete, ca. 1906) and a ballet (*The Dance in Place Congo,* ca. 1908; rev. 1916; premiered New York Metropolitan Opera, 1918); incidental music and a film score; orchestral works (*Comedy Overture on Negro Themes,* ca. 1906); 8 string quartets, the *Tempo di Rag* (flute, oboe, cornet, piano, 2 violins, cello, ca. 1906–17), and other chamber and piano music; works for chorus and orchestra; many songs ("The Pirate Song," 1902).

Gilbert, Kenneth (b. Montreal, 16 Dec. 1931). Harpsichordist, organist, and musicologist. He studied at the Montreal Conservatory; after winning the 1953 Prix d'Europe for organ, he studied with Nadia Boulanger (composition), Maurice Duruflé (organ), and Gustav Leonhardt (harpsichord). He was an organist in Montreal, 1952–67, and an exponent of historical organ building in Canada. In 1965 he began a series of critical editions of early keyboard music; subsequently pursued a European-based concert career as harpsichordist and recorded extensively. From 1988 he taught at the Salzburg Mozarteum and as professor at the Paris Conservatory. Edited the complete keyboard works of François Couperin, Rameau, D'Anglebert, Dieupart, and Domenico Scarlatti.

Gilbert, William Schwenck (b. London, 18 Nov. 1836; d. Harrow Weald, Middlesex, 29 May 1911). Librettist. Educated at King's College, London; 1857–61, government clerk; 1863–67, unsuccessful barrister; 1860s, wrote humorous pieces and criticism for London magazines, then a steady stream of theatrical works of various sorts, beginning in 1870s to collaborate with Sullivan; the tremendous success of their *H.M.S. Pinafore* (1878) led to concentration on joint works in the 1880s (including *The Pirates of Penzance,* 1879; *Patience,* 1881; *Iolanthe,* 1882; *The Mikado,* 1885; *The Gondoliers,* 1889). In 1890 this collaboration interrupted, partly because of Gilbert's contentiousness; resumed with less success in 1893–96. Thereafter he produced sporadically for the stage until his death.

Gilboa, Jacob (b. Košice, 2 May 1920). Composer. After spending his youth in Vienna, he went to Palestine in 1938. There he studied architecture in Haifa and music at the Jerusalem Music Teachers Seminary (with Josef Tal and Paul Ben-Haim); he graduated from the latter in 1947. Attending courses in Germany with Stockhausen and others during the 1960s, he began to assimilate quarter tones, aleatory, and other newer techniques into his formerly "Mediterranean" style. Works include *Wild Flowers,* voice, chamber orchestra (1957); *The Twelve Jerusalem Glass Windows by Chagall,* soprano, voices, chamber ensemble (1966); *Crystals,* chamber ensemble (1967); *Horizons in Violet and Blue,* chamber ensemble (1970); *Fourteen Epigrams for Oscar Wilde,* voice, piano, tape (1973); *Lament of Klonimos,* orchestra (1974); *Five Red Sea Impressions,* chamber ensemble (1976).

Gilchrist, William Wallace (b. Jersey City, 8 Jan. 1846; d. Easton, Pa., 20 Dec. 1916). Composer. From 1865 studied music with H. A. Clarke at the Univ. of Pennsylvania; then active as church musician, conductor, and singing teacher in and around Philadelphia; edited the official Presbyterian hymnal, 1895; collaborated on a series of music readers for schools, 1903–6. Composed 2 symphonies, chamber music, piano pieces, songs; best known for choral music, both secular and sacred, including *A Christmas Idyll* (Boston, 1898), Psalm 46 (New York, 1882), *The Rose* (New York, 1887), *The Lamb of God,* Passion oratorio (New York, 1909).

Bibl.: Martha Furman Schleifer, *William Wallace Gilchrist* (Metuchen, 1985).

Gilels, Emil (Grigor'evich) (b. Odessa, 19 Oct. 1916; d. Moscow, 14 Oct. 1985). Pianist. Studied with Yakov Tkatch and Berthe Ringold at the Odessa Institute of Music, 1923–29; with N. M. Reingbald at the Odessa Conservatory, 1929–35; with Heinrich Neuhaus at the Moscow Conservatory, 1935–38. Public debut in 1929 in Odessa. Won the Moscow All-Union Competition, 1933; second prize at the Vienna Competition, 1936; first prize at the Ysaÿe Competition in Brussels, 1938. Won the Stalin Prize in 1946, the Lenin Prize in 1962. He began touring Europe in 1947. U.S. debut 11 Oct. 1955; over a dozen tours thereafter. Taught at the Moscow Conservatory from 1938; professor from 1951. Best known for Mozart, Beethoven, Schubert, Schumann, and his Russian contemporaries.

Giles, Nathaniel (b. Worcester, ca. 1558; d. Windsor, 24 Jan. 1634). Organist and composer. Probably a student of John Colden, whom he succeeded at Worcester Cathedral. Received the B.Mus. from Oxford in 1585 and the D.Mus. in 1622; became organist and Master of the Children at St. George's Chapel in Windsor in 1585, taking a similar post at the Chapel Royal in 1597 and holding both positions until his death. Works include anthems, services, motets, and madrigals.

Gilles, Jean (b. Tarascon, 8 Jan. 1668; d. Toulouse, 5 Feb. 1705). Composer. Student and successor of Poitevin as *maître de musique* at the Cathedral of St. Saveur in Aix-en-Provence. Named to the same post at Agde Cathedral in 1675, then at St. Étienne in Toulouse in 1697, where he remained until his death despite an appointment at Avignon. His *Messe des morts* was widely performed, including as late as 1764 at Rameau's funeral, and in 1774 at that of Louis XV. Other works include a Mass and motets for various vocal and instrumental forces.

Gillespie, Dizzy [John Birks] (b. Cheraw, S.C., 21 Oct. 1917; d. Englewood, N.J., 6 Jan. 1993). Jazz trumpeter, composer, and bandleader. He joined Teddy Hill's big band, touring Europe (1937). While working with Cab Calloway (1939–41) he contributed to the development of bop in jam sessions with Charlie Parker, Thelonious Monk, and Kenny Clarke. With Oscar Pettiford he led a combo (1943–44). He joined Billy Eckstine's bop big band (1944–45), led his own, and with Parker led a quintet that made the first mature bop recordings (1945). His second big band (1946–50) established Afro-Cuban jazz. Its sidemen included Chano Pozo, J. J. Johnson, Sonny Stitt, James Moody, Jimmy Heath, Paul Gonsalves, John Coltrane, John Lewis, Milt Jackson, Ray Brown, and Clarke. Later he led big bands when finances allowed, as on tours of the Near East and South America (1956), but mainly led combos; he also toured with the Giants of Jazz, a sextet including Monk, Stitt, and Art Blakey (1971–72). Gillespie's widely influential bop playing was marked by unprecedented dexterity. Also a hilarious scat singer, he used a collection of nonsense syllables that capture the sound of bop. Among his recordings of his compositions are "Groovin' High" (1945), "A Night in Tunisia" (1946), "Woody 'n' You," "Manteca" (both 1947), and "Con Alma," in which the elusive tonality summarizes his skill with harmony (on the album *Duets with Sonny Rollins and Sonny Stitt,* 1957). Other recordings as a leader include "Salt Peanuts," "I Can't Get Started," "Hot House" (all 1945), "Oop-bop-sh'bam" (1946), and "Oop-pop-a-dah" (1947). An all-star group with Parker, Bud Powell, Charles Mingus, and Max Roach recorded the album *Jazz at Massey Hall: Quintet of the Year* (1953).

Writings: with Al Fraser, *To Be, or Not . . . to Bop: Memoirs* (Garden City, N.Y., 1979).

Bibl.: Michael James, *Dizzy Gillespie* (London, 1959; R: in *Kings of Jazz,* ed. S. Green, South Brunswick, N.J., 1978). Raymond Horricks, *Dizzy Gillespie and the Be-Bop Revolution* (New York, 1984). Jürgen Wölfer, *Dizzy Gillespie: Sein Leben, seine Musik, seine Schallplatten* (Waaskirchen, 1987).

Gillier, Jean-Claude (b. Paris, 1667; d. there, 31 May 1737). Composer. Student of Jean Mignon at the Notre Dame choir school. Became contrabassist in the orchestra of the Comédie-Française in 1693, also supplying music for many of the theater's offerings, including plays by Regnard and especially Dancourt. From 1713 he was associated with the Théâtres de la Foire, collaborating on some 70 productions. His duties ranged from finding suitable tunes for new lyrics to composing music for added preludes and divertissements. Some of his music was published and performed in England; he may have visited there on several occasions. His son succeeded him at the Comédie-Française, and was also active as a composer.

Gillis, Don (b. Cameron, Mo., 17 June 1912; d. Columbia, S.C., 10 Jan. 1978). Composer. He studied at Texas Christian Univ. and later at North Texas State Univ. (M.M., 1943); was trombonist for a radio station in Fort Worth, and directed various instrumental ensembles in Texas; produced Toscanini's NBC radio broadcasts (1944–54), after which he was executive vice president of Interlochen Music Camp (1958–61); chaired the arts department at Dallas Baptist College (1968–72) and was composer-in-residence and chairman of the Institute of Media Arts at the Univ. of South Carolina from 1973. He wrote 2 books, *The Unfinished Symphony Conductor* (1967) and *The Art of Media Instruction* (1973). His composition style is conservative but often witty, drawing on American sources such as jazz. He wrote 7 operas, several oratorios and ballets; 10 symphonies, tone poems (*Tulsa, a Symphonic Portrait in Oil,* 1950), and other orchestral and band pieces; chamber music; vocal music (*This Is Our America,* baritone and orchestra, 1945).

Gilmore, Patrick S(arsfield) (b. Ballygar, Galway, 25 Dec. 1829; d. St. Louis, 24 Sept. 1892). Bandmaster. From 15 a cornettist in a regimental band. Emigrated at 19, settling in Boston in 1849 and winning increasing recognition over the next decade as director of a series of local bands and as cornettist; 1858, founded Gilmore's Band; on outbreak of the Civil War, attached his band to the 24th Massachusetts Volunteers; charged with organizing Massachusetts army bands; made bandmaster general of occupied Louisiana; 1864, organized monster band concert in New Orleans, forerunner of his gigantic Peace Jubilees (Boston, 1869, 1872). From 1873 he directed the New York 22nd Regiment Band, giving hundreds of concerts at the Hippodrome and elsewhere in the city and (in summer) Manhattan Beach; toured the U.S., Canada, and (in 1878) Europe. Composed songs and marches, including "When Johnny Comes Marching Home," published under a pseudonym.

Bibl.: Margaret Darlington, *Irish Orpheus: The Life of Patrick Gilmore* (Philadelphia, 1950).

Gilson, Paul (b. Brussels, 15 June 1865; d. there, 3 Apr. 1942). Composer. Mainly self-taught until he studied composition with Gevaert at the Brussels Conservatory (1887–89). In 1889 he won the Belgian Prix de Rome for his cantata *Sinaï.* He became professor of harmony at the Brussels Conservatory in 1899 and also at Antwerp in 1904. He resigned these two posts in 1909 when he became inspector of music education.

Most of his music has some literary basis. His most successful piece, *La mer* (orchestra, 1892), is a set of symphonic sketches on a poem by Eddy Levis. His oratorio *Francesca da Rimini* (1892) is based on Dante. *Prinses Zonneschijn* (opera, 1901) was written in the Wagnerian tradition; he had attended a performance of *Der Ring des Nibelungen* by the Bayreuth cast in 1883. He also wrote on music, especially after 1905, when he began to compose less. His respect for traditional harmony and form is in evidence in *Le tutti orchestral* (Brussels, 1913) and *Traité d'harmonie* (Brussels, 1919). In 1925 some of his students formed Synthétistes, a group loyal to Gilson's ideas. The same students founded the Revue musicale belge, of which Gilson was artistic director. He was active as a music critic and wrote booklets for Belgian radio. His memoirs, *Notes de musique et souvenirs,* were published in 1942.

Other works include 4 operas, 2 ballets, some 50 pieces for orchestra, 6 cantatas, 70 pieces for wind or brass band, chamber music, and solo piano music.

Bibl.: Gaston Brenta, *Paul Gilson* (Brussels, 1965).

Giménez (Jiménez) (y Bellido), Jerónimo (b. Seville, 10 Oct. 1854; d. Madrid, 19 Feb. 1923). Composer. Admitted at age 12 to the orchestra of the Teatro principal, Seville; appointed opera director at age 17. Later a pupil of Savard, Alard, and Thomas at the Paris Conservatory. After an Italian sojourn, he was named director at the Teatro Apolo in 1885, later moving to the Teatro de la Zarzuela, where he led the Spanish premiere of Bizet's *Carmen.* He also served as director of the Musical Artistic Union and the Madrid Concert Society. As a composer he is best known for his 60-odd zarzuelas, mostly of the one-act variety *(género chico)* and often drawing on Spanish folk material; titles include *De vuelta de vivero* (1895), *La tempranica* (1900), and *La boda de Luis Alonso* (1897).

Ginastera, Alberto (b. Buenos Aires, 11 Apr. 1916; d. Geneva, 25 June 1983). Composer. Enrolled at age 12 in the Williams Conservatory, graduating in 1935; attended the National Conservatory, 1935–38, studying with André, Gil, and Palma. First work of his recognized was the ballet *Panambí* (concert premiere 1937; staged in 1940). Another ballet, *Estancia,* followed in 1941 (concert premiere 1943; staged in 1952); that year he joined the National Conservatory faculty and married the pianist Mercedes de Toro. Visited the U.S., 1945–47, studying with Copland and hearing performances of his music. Back in Argentina he formed the local chapter of the ISCM and became director of the Buenos Aires Provincial Conservatory in La Plata. Attended several European ISCM festivals in the 1950s where his music was featured; removed from his La Plata post by Perón in 1952, he was reinstated in 1956. Became dean at the Argentine Catholic University in 1958, also taking a post at the Univ. of La Plata; the same year his Second String Quartet was premiered in Washington, D.C., solidifying his international reputation; 1961 saw the premieres of his *Cantata para América mágica* and the First Piano Concerto, also in Washington. In 1962–69 he directed the Torcuato di

Tella Institute; many of Latin America's best young composers took part in two-year programs conducted by Ginastera and his invited guests (Copland, Messiaen, Malipiero, and others). The operas *Don Rodrigo* (Buenos Aires, 1964) and *Bomarzo* (Washington, D.C., 1967) date from this period; his final opera, *Beatrix Cenci,* followed in 1971. Ginastera spent his last years in Geneva with his second wife, cellist Aurora Nátola, for whom he wrote a sonata (1979) and the Second Concerto (1981). He grouped his music into three periods: "objective nationalism" (to 1954), "subjective nationalism" (to 1958), and "neo-Expressionism" (post-1958). The first segment uses Argentine folk material overtly; the second suggests a national character; the third uses serialism with a powerful expressive element and some contemporary timbres and techniques within traditional forms.

Other compositions include stage music; orchestral works (*Obertura para el "Fausto" criollo,* 1943; *Ollantay,* 1947; *Pampeana núm. 3,* 1954; concertos for harp, 1956, piano, 1961, 1972, violin, 1963, and cello, 1968, 1981; *Iubilum,* 1980); chamber music (3 string quartets, 1948, 1958, 1973; piano quintet, 1963; *Pampeanas núm. 1 y 2,* violin/cello with piano, 1947/1950); vocal music (3 *Cantatas dramáticas,* 1961, 1964, 1971; *Turbae ad passionem gregorianam,* 1973); solo music for piano, organ, and guitar.

Bibl.: Gilbert Chase, "Alberto Ginastera: Argentinian Composer," *MQ* 43 (1957): 439–60. Eduardo Storni, *Alberto Ginastera* (Madrid, 1983). *Alberto Ginastera: A Complete Catalogue* (London, 1986).

Gingold, Josef (b. Brest-Litovsk, 28 Oct. 1909; d. Bloomington, Ind., 11 Jan. 1995). Violinist and teacher. His family emigrated to the U.S. in 1920. Studied violin with Vladimir Graffman in New York, 1922–27; with Eugene Ysaÿe in Brussels, 1927–30. Debut in New York in 1926. Concertized in northern Europe, then joined the first violins of the NBC Symphony Orchestra under Toscanini, 1937–43. Concertmaster with the Detroit Symphony, 1943–47; with the Cleveland Orchestra, 1947–60. Taught violin at Case–Western Reserve Univ. in Cleveland, 1950–60; at Indiana Univ. from 1960; at the Manhattan School of Music, 1980–81.

Giordani, Giuseppe (b. Naples, ca. 1750; d. Fermo, 4 Jan. 1798). Composer. He studied composition in Naples with Fedele Fenaroli at the Conservatorio S. Maria di Loreto. During the 1770s he began composing operas for Italian stages; his first notable success was *Epponina,* performed in Florence in 1779. In 1791 he was appointed *maestro di cappella* at Fermo, where he remained until his death. Among his 30 or more stage works are *Tito Manlio* (Genoa, 1784); *Ifigenia in Aulide* (Rome, 1786); *La vestale* (Mantua, 1786); *I tre fratelli ridicoli* (Rome, 1788); *La disfatta di Dario* (Milan, 1789); *Don Mitrillo contrastato* (Venice, 1791?).

Giordani, Tommaso (b. Naples, ca. 1730; d. Dublin, Feb. 1806). Composer. His entire family, including father, Giuseppe (not the above), were members of a traveling theater troupe that performed in Graz, Frankfurt, and Amsterdam ca. 1750. Settling in London, from 1753 they performed frequently at Covent Garden; Tommaso's first opera, *La comediante fatta cantatrice,* was performed at that theater in 1756. By 1765 the company had moved to Dublin; from 1769 Tommaso was also conducting at the King's Theatre, London. Around 1783 he settled in Dublin, where he continued to compose operas and pasticcios; he was music director in several local theaters and also taught piano. Among his theater works are *The Maid of the Mill* (1765), *L'eroe cinese* (1766), *Il padre e il figlio rivali* (1770), *The Happy Disguise* (1784), *Perseverance* (1789), *The Cottage Festival* (1796); numerous adaptations; many songs for pasticcios. He also published 35 instrumental collections, mostly chamber music.

Giordano, Umberto (b. Foggia, 28 Aug. 1867; d. Milan, 12 Nov. 1948). Composer. Despite the opposition of his parents, he studied intermittently at the conservatory in Naples, 1880–90. A student opera, which failed to win a competition, led to a commission for his *Mala vita* (Rome, 1892); an example of verismo (its main character is a laborer who vows to reform a prostitute if only the Virgin Mary will cure his own tuberculosis), this opera aroused strong reactions wherever it was staged. In 1894 he moved to Milan, where later operas had great success; *Fedora* (Milan, 1898) was conducted in Vienna by Mahler; it has been called the unique example of a "giallo musicale," that is, melodramatic popular literature transformed into opera. *Andrea Chenier* (1896) has been compared to works of Massenet in its emphasis on grand scenes; *Siberia* (Milan, 1903) entered the repertory at the Paris Opera as a result of the admiration of Fauré and Lalo. With Franchetti he composed *Giove a Pompeii* (Rome, 1921; Giordano's contribution was finished by 1901); in *La cena delle beffe* (Milan, 1924) he began to compose longer musical sections than were standard in his earlier verismo efforts. In addition to 13 operas he wrote a ballet and incidental music; 5 orchestral works; chamber music; piano pieces; choral music and songs.

Bibl.: Pierluigi Alverà, *Giordano* (New York, 1986).

Giornovichi [Jarnovi], **Giovanni Mane** (b. Palermo? or Ragusa?, ca. 1740; d. St. Petersburg, 23 Nov. 1804). Violinist and composer. Possibly of Croatian parentage; details of his education are not known. In 1773 he made his debut as violinist at the Paris Concert spirituel. From 1779 to 1782 he traveled to Berlin, Frankfurt, and Warsaw; subsequently spent four years in Catherine II's service. After further successes as soloist in Vienna, Moscow, Hamburg, and the British Isles, he retired to St. Petersburg in 1802, where he again was given a position in the court orchestra. He composed chiefly chamber music, but in addition more than 20 violin concertos.

Giovannelli, Ruggiero (b. Velletri, near Rome, ca. 1560; d. Rome, 7 Jan. 1625). Composer. Active in Rome from at least 1583; *maestro di cappella* of the Cappella Giulia at St. Peter's (1594–99, succeeding Palestrina) and singer at the Sistine Chapel (1599–1624); played a small role in the reform of the Gradual. He wrote both secular and sacred pieces: light madrigals, canzonettas, and the like (6 books and over 30 works in anthologies), a few Masses, and numerous motets (2 books plus about 50 independent compositions).

Giovanni da Cascia [Johannes de Florentia, Giovanni da Firenze] (fl. northern Italy, 1340–50). Composer. A contemporary of Jacopo da Bologna and of Maestro Piero, members of the first generation of trecento composers and evidently his colleagues at courts in Verona and Milan. His extant works are 16 2-voiced madrigals and 3 3-voiced cacce. His greatest contribution was in consolidating the style of the madrigal.

Bibl.: Nino Pirotta, ed., *The Music of Fourteenth-Century Italy, CMM* 8/1 (1954). W. Thomas Marrocco, ed., *Italian Secular Music,* Polyphonic Music of the Fourteenth Century, 6 (1967).

Giovanni da Firenze. See Giovanni da Cascia.

Gipps, Ruth (b. Bexhill-on-Sea, Sussex, 20 Feb. 1921). Composer, pianist, and conductor. After studying composition with R. O. Morris, Gordon Jacob, and Vaughan Williams at the Royal College of Music, and with Kendall Taylor (piano) and Leon Goossens (oboe), she won the Caird Traveling Scholarship. She was choirmaster of the City of Birmingham Choir (1948–50) and also conducted the London Repertory Orchestra. In 1961 she founded the Chanticleer Orchestra, and in 1967 she became professor at the Royal College and chairperson of the Composers' Guild of Great Britain. Works include 5 symphonies (1942–80); concertos for violin (1943), piano (1948), violin and viola (1957), and horn (1968); choral works (*The Cat,* soloists, chorus, orchestra, 1947; *Goblin Market,* 1953; *Gloria in excelsis,* 1974); chamber music.

Giraldus Cambrensis [Gerald of Wales] (b. ca. 1146; d. Lincoln?, ca. 1223). Writer. Several of his books include descriptions of everyday life in Ireland and Wales. *Topographia hibernica* (ca. 1187) and *Descriptio Cambriae* (1194) mention music (both ed. and trans. W. L. Williams, London, 1908). One passage talks about group singing in Wales. This singing was clearly not in unison; it may have been in a sort of popular polyphony or, more probably, in heterophony.

Giraut [Guiraut] **de Bornelh** [de Borneill] (b. Excideuil, near Périgeux, ca. 1140; d. ca. 1200). Troubadour. Extant poems and his *vida* indicate that he traveled widely in southern France and northern Spain and probably took part in one Crusade. Almost 80 poems, 4 with music (including the famous "Reis glorios"), are ascribed to him.

Giuffre, Jimmy [James Peter] (b. Dallas, 26 Apr. 1921). Jazz clarinetist, saxophonist, and composer. He wrote "Four Brothers" for Woody Herman (1947) and played in the big bands of Boyd Raeburn, Jimmy Dorsey, Buddy Rich, and in 1949 Herman. He played West Coast jazz with Howard Rumsey (1951–53) and Shorty Rogers (1952–56), experimenting with expanded and free forms on his own album *Tangents in Jazz* (1955). His trio of 1956–59 with Jim Hall and a double bass player (later replaced by trombonist Bob Brookmeyer) turned toward folk influences, as on the album *The Jimmy Giuffre Three* (1956); that of ca. 1961–62, with Steve Swallow and pianist Paul Bley, played free jazz. After exploring Eastern and African influences, he turned to the bop tradition in the 1980s. From 1978 he taught at the New England Conservatory of Music.

Giuliani, Mauro (Giuseppe Sergio Pantaleo) (b. Bisceglie, near Bari, 27 July 1781; d. Naples, 8 May 1829). Guitarist and composer. From 1806 to 1819 he lived primarily in Vienna as the leading guitarist and guitar teacher and composer, recognized as one of the principal figures in Europe; then, heavily in debt, he returned to Italy, living in Rome until 1823 and thereafter in Naples, where he was patronized by court and aristocracy; known also for playing the lyre-guitar. His guitar compositions, including 3 concertos, chamber music, and many solo pieces, ranging from sonatas to etudes, variations, and dances, were highly popular, being published in Germany, Paris, and London as well as Vienna.

Giulini, Carlo Maria (b. Barletta, Italy, 9 May 1914). Conductor. Studied viola and composition at the Accademia S. Cecilia in Rome; conducting with Bernardino Molinara. Played viola in the Rome Augusteo Orchestra. Conducting debut with the same in 1944. Conductor of the RAI Symphony in Milan, 1946–50. Operatic debut leading *Traviata* in Bergamo, 1950. Assistant to De Sabata at La Scala, 1951–53; principal conductor, 1953–56; Covent Garden debut, 1958, leading *Don Carlos.* Frustrated by lack of rehearsal time, he left the pit for the podium in 1967. Principal guest conductor of the Chicago Symphony, 1968–78; conductor of the Vienna Philharmonic, 1973–76; of the Los Angeles Philharmonic, 1978–86.

Giunta [Junta]. Family of printers and booksellers. Their activity spanned the late 15th to the 17th century in Florence, Venice, Rome, Lyons, and Spain (Burgos, Salamanca, Madrid). Liturgical books were emphasized. The firm began in Florence but never printed music there. Its books produced in Lyons had some plainchant. In Spain it printed much chant and a little polyphony (ca. 1598–ca. 1624). In Venice, however, a branch founded by Luc'Antonio Giunta (1457–1538) produced many excellent music books, some with chant, a number with polyphony, printed in collaboration with Antico. The Roman branch produced yet more polyphony, both by itself and along with other printers, including Antico.

Glanville-Hicks, Peggy (b. Melbourne, 29 Dec. 1912; d. Sydney, 25 June 1990). Composer. In her youth she studied at the Melbourne Conservatory. From 1931 she studied on scholarship at the Royal College in London; among her instructors there were Arthur Benjamin (piano), Malcolm Sargent (conducting), and R. O. Morris and Vaughan Williams (composition). Later she was a pupil of Nadia Boulanger in Paris (1936–38) and studied ethnomusicology with Egon Wellesz in Vienna. In 1942 she settled in the U.S., where she remained until 1959. During this period she was music critic for the *New York Herald Tribune* (1948–58), was active in the League of Composers Committee (1943–44), and organized concerts of new music for the Metropolitan Museum and for the Museum of Modern Art. During the 1960s she was engaged in musical research in the Aegean and in the Middle and Far East. In 1969 she went blind, and she returned to Australia in 1976. Her works combine elements of Eastern musics with traditional Western idioms, especially theatrical idioms. Her works include operas (*The Transposed Heads,* 1953); ballet scores (*The Masque of the Wild Man,* 1958); film scores; vocal works (*Profiles from China,* tenor, chamber orchestra, 1945; *Thomsoniana,* soloists, chamber ensemble, 1949; *Letters from Morocco,* songs, tenor, chamber orchestra, 1952); instrumental music (*Sinfonia da Pacifica,* 1953).

Bibl.: Deborah Hayes, *Peggy Glanville-Hicks: A Bio-Bibliography* (New York, 1990).

Glarean, Heinrich [Glareanus, Heinricus; Loriti] (b. Mollis, canton of Glarus, June 1488; d. Freiburg, 28 Mar. 1563). Theorist and writer. His widely humanistic education, concentrating particularly on philosophy, theology, mathematics, and music, began in Bern and Rottweil; from 1506 he attended the Univ. of Cologne. Public recognition (for poetry) came first in 1512. From 1514 until 1529 he spent most of his time in Basel, where he came to know Erasmus. Extended trips to Pavia, Milan, and Paris (where he met the composer Mouton) occupied 1516 and 1517. A firm opposition to the Reformation motivated a move in 1529 from Basel to Freiburg im Breisgau. There he taught poetry and theology at the university and pursued his own studies of and writings on music, mathematics, and ancient Greek and Roman literature, as well as undertaking other activities concerned with education.

Of his treatises on music, the best known today and the most influential in his time is the *Dodecachordon* (Basel, 1547; facs., *MMML* ser. 2, 65, 1967; trans. *MSD* 6, 1965), in which a system of 12 modes (rather than 8) is advocated and its application to both monophony and polyphony discussed. His much earlier *Isagoge in musicen* (Basel, 1516; ed. and trans., *JMT* 3 [1959]: 97–139) treats the elements of music, solmization, and the 8 modes.

Glass, Philip (b. Baltimore, 31 Jan. 1937). Composer. Studied flute as a child; attended the Univ. of Chicago (B.A. in music, 1956); then studied composition at Juilliard (Bergsma, Persichetti; M.A., 1961); other composition teachers included Milhaud (Aspen Music Festival, 1960) and Boulanger (Paris, 1963–65); before going to France he was composer-in-residence in the Pittsburgh public schools in a program sponsored by the Ford Foundation. In Paris Glass was hired by Ravi Shankar to notate his Eastern music for the French musicians playing for the film *Chappaqua.* This exposure to Indian music and his study of tabla caused him to change his own compositional style radically, by adopting the rhythmic language and additive/repetitive construction of Indian music.

According to the composer, the term minimalist suits his music from the decade after 1965, but the feature that most clearly differentiates his works both from traditional concert music and from most avant-garde music is not the limitation to a small pitch and rhythm set hypnotically repeated but the nonnarrative structure he favors. They are not "story symphonies and story concertos"; they thus require a new mode of listening "in which neither memory nor anticipation . . . [has] a place in sustaining the texture, quality, or reality of the musical experience." Even the operas are independent of the tradition of "literary theater," related instead to "a theater that comes from the worlds of painting and dance." Since the 1976 Metropolitan Opera performance of his first opera, *Einstein on the Beach* (collaboration with Robert Wilson), Glass has been successful in attracting large audiences and selling records to supporters of both art and popular musics. For performance of his works he founded an ensemble in 1968 consisting of amplified flutes and saxophones, electric organs, and synthesizers.

Works: Operas (*Einstein on the Beach,* 1975; *Satyagraha,* 1980; *Akhnaten,* 1983; *The Juniper Tree,* 1985; *The Making of the Representative for Planet 8,* 1988; *The Fall of the House of Usher,* 1988; *The Voyage,* commissioned by the Metropolitan Opera, 1992) and other theatrical pieces (*The Civil Wars,* 1983; *1000 Airplanes on the Roof,* 1987; *Hydrogen Jukebox,* 1990); dance music and incidental music; film and television scores; ensemble music for the Philip Glass Ensemble (*Music in 12 Parts,* 1971–74; *Glassworks,* 1981); other instrumental music (*Strung Out,* amplified violin, 1967; *Modern Love Waltz,* piano, 1977; String quartet no. 5, 1992; *Low Symphony,* 1993; Symphony no. 2, 1994); works composed before 1965 have been withdrawn.

Bibl.: Philip Glass, *Music by Philip Glass,* ed. with supp. material by Robert T. Jones (New York, 1987). Id., *Orphée—the Making of an Opera: Eine Collage* (Düsseldorf, 1993).

Glazunov, Alexander Konstantinovich (b. St. Petersburg, 10 Aug. 1865; d. Paris, 21 Mar. 1936). Composer. He studied piano from the age of 9 and composed from the age of 11. In 1879 Balakirev suggested he study composition with Rimsky-Korsakov; the lessons lasted less than two years, as Glazunov made rapid progress. In 1882 both his First Symphony and First String

Quartet were performed. He soon became a prominent member of the "Belyayev Circle," a group of young Russian composers supported by the wealthy art patron Mitrofan Belyayev. During a trip to western Europe with Belyayev in 1884, he met Liszt in Weimar. Following Borodin's death in 1887, Glazunov and Rimsky-Korsakov completed and revised his unfinished compositions. The following year Glazunov made his debut as a conductor. The 1890s were a productive decade: he wrote 4 symphonies, 2 string quartets, and the ballets *Raymonda* (1896–97), *Baryshnia-Sluzhanka* (*Les ruses d'amour,* 1898), and *Vremena goda* (The Seasons, 1899). In 1899 he became professor of orchestration and composition at the St. Petersburg Conservatory; from 1905 to 1930 he was the conservatory's director. During this time Glazunov wrote many of his best works, including the Violin Concerto and the Eighth Symphony, although his productivity suffered as a result of his work at the conservatory. In 1907 he conducted in Paris and received the honorary D.Mus. from Oxford and Cambridge. Despite the hardships of World War I, he remained active as a composer and conductor. In 1928 he went to Vienna and Paris, and from 1929 to 1931 conducted in Portugal, Spain, France, England, Czechoslovakia, Poland, Holland, and the U.S. When his health declined in 1932 he settled in Paris. In addition to symphonies and concertos, Glazunov wrote a number of other orchestral works, incidental music, choral music, string quartets and other chamber music, piano pieces, and songs.

Bibl.: M.A. Ganina, ed., *Aleksandr Glazunov: Pis'ma, stat'i, vospominaniya* [Glazunov: Letters, Articles, Recollections] (Moscow, 1958). M.O. Iankovskii, ed., *Glazunov: Issledovaniya, materialï, publikatisii, pis'ma* [Glazunov: Research, Materials, Publications, Letters] (Leningrad, 1959–60). M. Ganina, *A. Glazunov: zhizn'i tvorchestvo* [Glazunov: Life and Works] (Leningrad, 1961). Gerald Abraham, "Glazunov and the String Quartet," in *Slavonic and Romantic Music* (New York, 1968), pp. 218–24. A. Kryukov, *A. Glazunov* (Moscow, 1984). Donald J. Venturini, *Alexander Glazunov: His Life and Works* (Delphos, Ohio, 1992).

Gleason, Frederick Grant (b. Middletown, Conn., 17 or 18 Dec. 1848; d. Chicago, 6 Dec. 1903). Composer. Studied with Dudley Buck; 1869–75, in Europe, studying at the Leipzig Conservatory, then in Berlin and London. Returned to the U.S. in 1875 and began to publish, chiefly songs, piano pieces, sacred choral music; 1875–76, organist in Hartford and New Britain; from 1877 lived in Chicago, becoming a leading figure there as teacher (Hershey School of Music, then the Chicago Conservatory, from 1891 as head of theory department, from 1900 director), critic (*Chicago Tribune,* 1884–89; editor of *The Music Review,* 1891–94), and composer. His major work, the opera *Otho Visconti* (composed 1876–77, to his own libretto), was performed in Chicago in 1907 (excerpts published 1877–90). A second, *Montezuma* (completed 1885), was not performed complete. Also wrote cantatas, piano concerto, a symphonic poem *Edris* (performed Chicago, 1896).

Glier, Ryngol'd Moritsevich [Glière, Reinhold] (b. Kiev, 11 Jan. 1875; d. Moscow, 23 June 1956). Composer. He studied at the Moscow Conservatory, where he had violin lessons from Hřímalý and studied theory and composition with Taneyev, Arensky, Konyus, and Ippolitov-Ivanov. He was professor of composition at the conservatory (1920–41) and chairman of the organizing committee of the USSR Composers' Union (1938–48). He earned a doctorate in art criticism and won numerous official honors. His compositions include operas (*Shakh-Senem,* 1923; *Gyul'sara,* 1936; *Leyli i Mejnun,* 1940), symphonies (Third Symphony, *Il'ya Muromets,* 1909–11), concertos (for harp, 1938), symphonic poems, overtures, ballets (*Krasnïy tsvetok* [The Red Flower], 1949; *Mednïy vsadnik* [The Bronze Horseman], 1948–49), chamber music, and songs.

Bibl.: B. S. Yagolim, *R. M. Glier: notograficheskiy spravochnik* [Glier: Catalogue of Works] (Moscow, 1964). V. M. Bogdanov-Berezovsky, ed., *R. M. Glier: stat'i, vospominaniya, materialï* [Glier: Articles, Reminiscences, Materials] (Leningrad, 1965–67).

Glinka, Mikhail Ivanovich (b. Novospasskoye, Smolensk district, 1 June 1804; d. Berlin, 15 Feb. 1857). Composer. While in the custody of his paternal grandmother, he was exposed to folk music and church bell music. Passing into the care of his parents in 1810, he became exposed to Western music. In 1817 he went to school in St. Petersburg, where he studied languages and the natural sciences and received an unsystematic musical education. Upon graduating in 1822, he frequented the salons of St. Petersburg as a dilettante musician. From 1824 to 1828 he was an undersecretary in the office of the Council of Communications; during this time he associated with many important figures in the Russian literary world. He also composed, taking as his early models the operas of Rossini and the French school and selected works by Haydn, Mozart, and Beethoven. In 1830 he went to Italy with the tenor Nikolay Ivanov. In Milan he met Bellini, Donizetti, and Mendelssohn and established himself as a pianist. In Rome he met Berlioz. He went to Berlin in 1833 and took five months of composition lessons with Siegfried Dehn. The results of this study, his only thorough training in composition, was a Capriccio on Russian Themes for piano duet and an unfinished Symphony on Two Russian Themes.

Following his father's death in 1834, Glinka returned to Russia. During the next two years he was occupied with the composition of *Ivan Susanin,* to a libretto by Georgy Rosen. Shortly before the 1836 premiere, the tsar suggested that the opera should be renamed *Zhizn'za tsarya* (A Life for the Tsar). The work was enthusiastically received. He began almost immediately on his next opera, a setting of Valerian Shirkov's libretto based on Pushkin's poem *Ruslan and Lyudmila.* In early 1837 he was appointed Kapellmeister of the imperial chapel. During the next few years various projects interrupted work on the opera. In 1838 he set a number of Pushkin's poems, including

Gde nasha roza? (Where is our rose?) and *Ya pomnyu chudnoye mgnoven'ye* (I recall a wonderful moment). A set of 12 songs followed in 1840, as well as incidental music to the play *Knyaz' Kholmsky* (Prince Kholmsky). *Ruslan and Lyudmila* was first given on 9 Dec. 1842 and received a lukewarm reception. Disappointed by this, Glinka remained inactive for the next year. In June 1844 he went to Paris, where he met with Berlioz and studied the French composer's works. The following year he went to Spain and studied Spanish music for two years. While in Madrid he composed his First Spanish Overture. After returning to Russia for a time, he spent much of the next few years in Warsaw, where he composed *Recuerdos de Castilla* (expanded in 1851 into *Souvenir d'une nuit d'été à Madrid,* also known as the Second Spanish Overture) and *Kamarinskaya,* both for orchestra. During this time he also wrote songs, many of which were influenced by Chopin's style (*Adel'* [Adèle], *Zazdravniÿ kubok* [The Toasting Cup], *Finskiy zaliv* [The Gulf of Finland]). He returned to St. Petersburg in September 1851, but spent nearly two years in Paris from June 1852. During his final years Glinka worked on several projects: the assembling of his memoirs, initial work on his Ukrainian Symphony and a third opera, *Dvumuzhnitsa* (The Bigamist), and the orchestration of some of his songs. In 1856 he traveled to Berlin to study Western contrapuntal techniques with Dehn. There he had contact with Meyerbeer, who conducted the Trio from *A Life for the Tsar.* He died in Berlin a few weeks after catching a cold.

Bibl.: E. Kann-Novikova, *M. I. Glinka: noviÿe materialï i dokumentï* [New Material and Documents], 3 vols. (Moscow, 1950–55). A. S. Lyapunov, ed., *M. I. Glinka: literaturniÿe proizvedeniya i perepiska* [Writings and Correspondence] (Moscow, 1973–77). D. Brown, *Glinka: A Biographical and Critical Study* (London, 1974). Richard Taruskin, "Glinka's Ambiguous Legacy and the Birth Pangs of Russian Opera," *19th-Century Music* 1 (1977–78): 142–62. W. Wasina Grossmann, *Glinka* (Berlin, 1982). Richard Taruskin, "How the Acorn Took Root: A Tale of Russia," *19th-Century Music* 6/3 (1983): 189–212. O. Levashyova, *M. I. Glinka,* vol. 1 (Moscow, 1987). M. Woodside, "Western Models for a Russian Opera: Glinka's 'Ruslan and Ludmilla'" (diss., Univ. of Chicago, 1987). Aleksandra Orlova, *Glinka's Life in Music: A Chronicle,* trans. R. Hoops (Ann Arbor, 1988).

Globokar, Vinko (b. Anderny, Meurthe-et-Moselle, 7 July 1934). Composer and virtuoso trombonist. Of Slovene ancestry, Globokar left France in 1947 to study music at the conservatory in Ljubljana; graduating in 1954, he went to Paris to continue his studies with René Leibowitz (1959–63). In 1965 he was a pupil of Luciano Berio in Berlin, and after a brief term as professor of composition at SUNY–Buffalo (1965–66) he became trombone instructor at the Hochschule für Musik in Cologne. In 1972 he formed New Phonic Art, a new-music performing ensemble. His music followed the developments of the European avant-garde, incorporating serialism and aleatory. Compositions include vocal works (*Voie,* narrator, chorus, orchestra, 1965–66; *Accord,* soprano, chamber ensemble, 1966; *Traumdeutung,* 4 choruses, chamber ensemble, 1967; Concerto grosso, chamber ensemble, chorus, orchestra, 1969–70; *Miserere,* voices, orchestra, 1982); orchestral works (*Material zur Diskussion eines historischen Instruments,* 1974); chamber works (*Plan,* zarb [Persian drum], 4 instruments, 1965; *Fluide,* chamber ensemble, 1967; *Discours I–IV,* various instrumental groupings, 1967–74; *Dos a dos,* 2 performers, 1988). He has also written articles on improvisation and interpretation.

Bibl.: Wolfgang König, *Vinko Globokar: Komposition und Improvisation* (Wiesbaden, 1977).

Glover, Jane (Alison) (b. Helmsley, Yorkshire, 13 May 1949). Conductor and musicologist. Studied at St. Hugh's College, Oxford (Ph.D., 1975, with a dissertation on Cavalli). Debut at the Wexford Festival in 1975 conducting Cavalli's *Eritrea.* Music director of the Glyndebourne Festival from 1981; of the London Choral Society from 1983; of the London Mozart Players from 1984.

Gluck, Alma [Reba Fiersohn] (b. Bucharest, 11 May 1884; d. New York, 27 Oct. 1938). Soprano. She was taken to the U.S. as a child. Attended Union College in Schenectady, N.Y., then worked as a stenographer until she married Bernard Gluck. Studied voice, 1906–9, with Arturo Buzzi-Peccia, who provided an introduction to Gatti-Casazza, manager of the Metropolitan Opera. Debut, 16 Nov. 1909, at the Met as Sophie *(Werther).* Sang 11 roles her first season, including Mimi, Marguérite; added 9 more by 1912. That year Gatti-Casazza offered her, in the wake of a divorce, a generous stipend to go to Europe, ostensibly to prepare herself for the "profession of prima donna." In the event she studied with Marcella Sembrich in Berlin, 1912–13, but never returned to the Met. Instead she became a recording star, the only female vocalist to rival Caruso and John McCormack in popularity. Of her nearly 120 recordings, "Carry Me Back to Old Virginny" sold the most—more than 1 million copies. Her version of Rameau's "Rossignol amoureux" *(Hippolyte et Aricie)* captured her artistry and voice at its best. Many of her records featured obbligato violin solos by her second husband, Efrem Zimbalist.

Gluck, Christoph Willibald (b. Erasbach, 2 July 1714; d. Vienna, 15 Nov. 1787). Composer. His father, Hans Adam, was hunting and forest master for the Lobkowitz family in the Upper Palatinate, later in northern Bohemia. The family relocated several times during Christoph's young years, and little is known of the boy's schooling or of his first music instructors. Gluck's early attempts to practice musical instruments were reportedly thwarted by his father, who had his son assist him in the hunt. By 1731 (though probably earlier) the boy had left home and escaped to Prague, where he continued his musical studies and supported himself partly as organist at the Týn Church. He matriculated at the Univ. of Prague, but apparently nothing came of his studies there. In music he remained

Christoph Willibald Gluck. Bust by Jean-Antoine Houdon.

essentially self-taught. After a few years in Prague he went to Vienna (probably 1735), where at the Lobkowitz Palace he met the Milanese Antonio Maria Prince Melzi; in 1736 or early 1737 Gluck moved to Milan, having been hired as chamber musician for Melzi's household. There he played violin in the prince's court orchestra and probably also studied counterpoint and composition with the city's leading musician, Giovanni Battista Sammartini. Four years passed before Gluck's first opera, *Artaserse,* was produced at Milan in 1741; its success brought commissions, and during the next four years Gluck composed seven more operas, for Milan, Venice, Crema, and Turin. In 1745 he went to London and composed two Italian operas for the King's Theatre at the Haymarket. Thereafter he traveled to Dresden and Bohemia and possibly also to Hamburg; by 1748 he was in Vienna, where he had been commissioned to set Metastasio's *Semiramide riconosciuta* for the opening of the newly reconstructed Burgtheater.

In 1750 Gluck married Maria Anna Bergin, daughter of a merchant with close ties to the imperial court. From 1752 until the 1770s he lived mostly in Vienna, where his first employment was as *Konzertmeister* in the court of the imperial field marshal Prince Joseph Friedrich Wilhelm of Saxe-Hildburghausen; there he came into contact with Kapellmeister Giuseppe Bonno and with the young Carl Ditters (later von Dittersdorf). In 1754 Count Durazzo, imperial theater director, began hiring Gluck to adapt French opéras comiques to the Viennese stage; from 1758 Gluck composed several successful opéras comiques of his own for the Burgtheater, including *La fausse esclave* (1758). When Italian opera made a comeback on the Viennese stage around 1760 (partly the result of the marriage of the heir apparent, Joseph, to Isabella of Parma), Durazzo introduced Gluck to librettist Raniero Calzabigi, and in 1761 the two collaborated on their first big success, *Don Juan.* Their even more important *Orfeo ed Euridice* was performed in 1762; it became a decisive work in operatic quarrels of the period and remains one of the most rewarding of all 18th-century operas. In 1767 the two collaborated again on *Alceste.* Gluck contributed a famous preface to the 1769 publication of the opera (trans. in *SR,* pp. 673–75); in it he expounded on his ideals of opera, stating that in *Alceste* he had attempted to avoid the "disfiguring abuses" of Italian opera and "to restrict music to its true office of serving poetry by means of expression." He spoke against the florid vocal display of the Italian style, ostensibly aligning himself with "musical dramatists" through the ages.

A number of Gluck's Italian operas from this period were revised for the Paris stage. During the 1770s the composer won further acclaim there with *Iphigénie en Aulide* (1774), *Armide* (1777), and *Iphigénie en Tauride* (1779). The 1770s also saw his health failing; he suffered an apparent stroke during preparations for his last opera, *Echo et Narcisse.* He returned to Vienna, and after a few years of marginal health (during which he prepared an important German version of *Iphigénie en Tauride*), he finally succumbed to two more strokes. He was buried in Matzleinsdorf Cemetery (near Vienna); his body was later transferred to the city's main cemetery.

Other theater works include *Demofoonte* (1743); *Le nozze d'Ercole e d'Ebe* (1747); *Ezio* (1750); *Le cinesi* (1754); *L'innocenza giustificata* (1755); *Le diable à quatre* (1759); *L'ivrogne corrigé* (*Der bekehrte Trunkenbold,* 1760); *Le cadi dupé* (1761); *Il trionfo di Clelia* (1763); *La rencontre imprévue* (1764); *Telemaco* (1765); *Paride ed Elena* (1770). He also composed sacred vocal works, including *De profundis* (performed at Gluck's funeral, 1787); secular vocal music, including songs and odes; and instrumental works, including at least 18 symphonies and a set of 6 published trio sonatas (London, 1746).

Bibl.: *Sämtliche Werke,* ed. Staatliches Institut für Musikforschung, Berlin (Kassel, New York, 1951–). Alfred Wotquenne, *Catalogue thématique des oeuvres de Chr. W. v. Gluck* (New York, 1904; R: New York, Hildesheim, 1967); trans. Ger. (Leipzig, 1904; additions, 1911). *The Collected Correspondence and Papers of Christoph Willibald Gluck,* ed. Hedwig and E. H. Mueller von Asow; trans. Stewart Thomson (New York, 1963). Alfred Einstein, *Gluck* (London, 1936; R: 1964); trans. Eric Blom (New York, 1962). Cecil Hopkinson, *A Bibliography of the Printed Works of C. W. von Gluck, 1714–1787* (London, 1959; 2nd rev. ed., New York, 1967). Patricia Howard, *Gluck and the Birth of Modern Opera* (London, 1963). Walter Vetter, *Christoph Willibald Gluck: Ein Essay* (Leipzig, 1964). Joseph Müller-Blattau, *Gluck und die Sprache der europäischen Musiknationen: Von der Vielfalt der Musik* (Freiburg, 1966). Paolo Gallarati, *Gluck e Mozart* (Turin, 1975). Patricia Howard, *Christoph Willibald Gluck: A Guide to Research* (New York, 1987). Klaus Hortschansky, ed., *Christoph Willibald Gluck und die Opernreform* (Darmstadt, 1989). Bruce Alan Brown, *Gluck and the French Theatre in Vienna* (New York, 1991).

Gnattali, Radamés (b. Pôrto Alegre, Brazil, 27 Jan. 1906). Composer and conductor. Attended the Fine Arts Institute of Rio Grande do Sul from 1920, winning the gold medal in piano in 1924, then moved on to the Escola nacional de música in Rio de Janeiro. After a period of concert appearances as pianist and violist he was named permanent conductor of the Radio nacional orchestra, gaining fame through his popular arrangements and radio-play incidental music. His concert compositions are retrospectively Romantic in style, often with an infusion of Brazilian elements; works include *Rapsódia brazileira* (1931); 10 *Brasilianas* for piano solo or with orchestra (1944–62); the folk ballet *Negrinho do pastoreio* (1959); concertos for piano, guitar, and harmonica; chamber music; and songs.

Bibl.: *Composers of the Americas* 16 (Washington, D.C., 1970): 90–96 [includes works list].

Gnazzo, Anthony J(oseph) (b. Plainville, Conn., 21 Apr. 1936). Composer. Studied music theory (B.A., 1957) and mathematics (B.A., 1963) at the Univ. of Hartford; then worked under Krenek, Berger, and Shapiro at Brandeis (M.F.A., 1969). He directed the Tape Music Center at Mills College and worked in association with other electronic music studios at Stanford, Berkeley, Univ. of York, and Univ. of California at Haywood. His graphic scores have been exhibited in Italy and in California (Oakland, 1984) and have been included in anthologies of avant-garde music. He has written "text-sound" pieces to read or to look at (*Hisnia and Hernia,* S. A. T. B., 1975); mathematically constructed works (*Prime Source 1–23,* solo voice[s], chorus, or chorus and tape, 1971–79); and mixed-media performance pieces (*Lontano,* narrator, tape, and slides, 1982). Other works include dance scores, film and TV music, incidental music; environmental works; instrumental music (*Music for Piano and Percussion,* 1971); electronic and computer-generated music; choral and solo vocal music.

Gnecchi, Vittorio (b. Milan, 17 July 1876; d. there, 5 Feb. 1954). Composer. His composition teachers included M. Saladino and Gaetano Coronaro at the Milan Conservatory. His operas include *Virtù d'amore* (Como, 1896); *Cassandra* (Bologna, 1905); *La Rosiera* (Gera, 1927); and *Giuditta* (Salzburg, 1953). *Cassandra* (revived in Ferrara, 1909) became the subject of international polemics when Giovanni Tebaldini claimed that Strauss had borrowed extensively from the Italian work in composing *Elektra* (1909); neither composer joined the debate. In addition to operas, Gnecchi composed a ballet (*Atalanta,* 1929); orchestral music (*Poemo eroico,* 1932); and sacred choral music.

Gnesin, Mikhail Fabianovich (b. Rostov-na-Donu, 2 Feb. 1883; d. Moscow, 5 May 1957). Composer. He studied at the Rostov Technical Institute (1892–99) and took music lessons, then studied composition with Rimsky-Korsakov (1901–9) and Lyadov at the St. Petersburg Conservatory. He traveled to Germany and France (1911), and to Palestine (1914, 1921). An organizer of the Society of Jewish Folk Music in St. Petersburg (1908–11), he was professor of composition at Moscow Conservatory (1925–36); he held the same position at the Gnesin Academy from 1923. From 1935 to 1944 he was professor at the Leningrad Conservatory (1935–44), then was principal of the reestablished Gnesin State Institute for Musical Education, Moscow (1944–51). Among his pupils were Khachaturian and Khrennikov. His compositions, over 50 of which have Jewish subjects, include works for the stage, orchestral music, chamber music, piano pieces, film scores, choral music, and songs.

Gobbi, Tito (b. Bassano del Grappa, 24 Oct. 1913; d. Rome, 5 Mar. 1984). Baritone. Studied law at the Univ. of Padua, then voice with Giulio Crimi in Rome. Semiprofessional debut in Gubbio in 1935 as Rodolfo *(Sonnambula).* After winning first prize in the Vienna International Competition of 1936, made his official debut at the Teatro Adriano in Rome, 1937, as Germont *(Traviata),* then joined the Rome Opera. He soon was recognized as the leading Italian baritone of his generation. Debuts at La Scala, 1942, as Belcore *(L'Elisir);* in San Francisco, 1948, as Figaro *(Barbiere);* at Covent Garden, 1951, as Belcore; at the Metropolitan Opera, 1956, as Scarpia *(Tosca).* Sang with the Chicago Lyric Opera, 1954–73; at the Met through 1976. Staged *Simon Boccanegra* in 1965 in Chicago and at Covent Garden; staged *Tosca* in 1978 at the Met. Among his ca. 100 roles was the first Wozzeck heard in Italy (Rome, 1942). An exceptional actor, he also appeared from 1937 in 26 films. Published his memoirs, *My Life* (1979).

Godard, Benjamin (Louis Paul) (b. Paris, 18 Aug. 1849; d. Cannes, 10 Jan. 1895). Composer. Studied at the Paris Conservatory (composition under Reber); prolific composer of salon and concert music (including descriptive symphonies; a dramatic symphony with voices, *Le Tasse,* 1878; 2 piano and 2 violin concertos; much chamber music; many piano pieces and songs) which appealed to French taste in the 1870s and 1880s and brought him great, though ephemeral, popularity. He was less successful in the theater, most of the several operas he produced after 1880 having to hold premieres outside Paris; only the once much-anthologized "Berceuse" from *Jocelyn* (Brussels, 1888) long survived him.

Bibl.: M. Clerjot, *Benjamin Godard* (Paris, 1902?).

Godowsky, Leopold (b. Soshly, Russian Poland, 13 Feb. 1870; d. New York, 21 Nov. 1938). Pianist and composer. Debut in 1879 at Vilnius, Poland. Briefly studied composition with Woldemar Bargiel, piano with Ernst Rudorff at the Berlin Musikhochschule, 1884. Toured the U.S., 1884–85. Protégé of Saint-Saëns in Paris, 1887–90. Taught in New York, 1890–94 (naturalized 1891); in Philadelphia, 1894–95; at the Chicago Conservatory, 1894–1900. Based in Berlin,

1900–1909. In Vienna, 1909–14, he took over Busoni's master class. Toured the U.S. (1912–13, 1913–14); settled in New York at the outbreak of war. A stroke suffered during a recording session in 1930 ended his concert career. Aside from a group of *Impressions* for violin or cello (1916), he wrote exclusively for piano, including *53 Studies on Chopin's Études* (1893–1914), Sonata in E minor (1911), *Triakontameron* (1920) [includes *Alt Wien*], *Phonoramas* (Java Suite, 1925), *Passacaglia* (1928).

Goeb, Roger (John) (b. Cherokee, Iowa, 9 Oct. 1914). Composer. Studied chemistry and agriculture at the Univ. of Wisconsin (B.S., 1936), after which he worked in factories and played jazz for two years to afford study in Paris with assistants of Boulanger; on his return he studied with Luening and at the Cleveland Institute with Elwell; he received the Ph.D. from the Univ. of Iowa in 1945. He taught at Bard College (1945–47). He completed his Third Symphony in 1950–51; it was premiered on CBS Radio by Stokowski. He wrote little during the prolonged illnesses of his wife and son (d. 1967 and 1974), but in 1979 returned to composition. Works include at least 6 symphonies and other orchestral music (*Fantasia,* 1983); 4 woodwind quintets and other chamber music; a few vocal pieces.

Goehr, (Peter) Alexander (b. Berlin, 10 Aug. 1932). Composer. His father was Walter Goehr (1903–60), a composer and conductor who had studied with Schoenberg and was actively involved in the performance of new British music, especially that of Tippett. The Goehr family moved from Germany to England in 1933. Alexander studied at the Royal Manchester College (1952–55) and in France with Messiaen and Loriod (1955–56). He then worked in London as a copyist and translator until 1960. From 1960 to 1968 he was a producer of orchestral concerts for the BBC. In 1964 he organized the Wardour Castle Summer School of Music with Davies and Birtwistle, who had been his classmates at Royal Manchester College. He was composer-in-residence at New England Conservatory, 1968–69, and assistant professor at Yale, 1969–70. During the following year he was a visiting lecturer at Southampton Univ. He joined the faculty at Leeds Univ. in 1971 and then at Cambridge in 1976.

The 1959 premiere of *The Deluge* (after Da Vinci, soprano, alto, chamber ensemble, 1957–58) brought Goehr recognition and commissions. His Violin Concerto op. 13 (1961–62) explores combinatorial serialism. Two substantial and important chamber works, the Piano Trio op. 20 (1966) and String Quartet no. 2 op. 23 (1967), make use of variation form.

Works: Dramatic. *La belle dame sans merci* (ballet, 1958); *Arden Must Die* (opera, 1966; first perf. in German as *Arden muss sterben*); *Naboth's Vineyard* (dramatic madrigal, 1968); *Shadowplay-2* (music theater, 1970); *Sonata about Jerusalem* (music theater, 1970); *Bauern, Bomben und Bonzen* (film score, 1973); *Behold the Sun* (opera, 1985; first perf. in German as *Die Wiedertäufer*); *Arianna* (opera, 1994–95).

Orchestra. *Fantasia* (1954; rev. 1958); *Hecuba's Lament* (1959–61); Violin Concerto (1961–62); *Little Symphony* (1963); *Little Music* (1963); *Pastorals* (1965); *Three Pieces from Arden Must Die* (1967); *Romanza* (1968); *Konzertstücke* (1969); *Symphony in One Movement* (1969–70); Piano Concerto (1971–72); *Metamorphosis/Dance* (1973–74); *Chaconne* (1974); *Fugue on Psalm iv* (1976); *Romanza on Ps. iv* (1976); *Sinfonia* (1980); *2 Etudes* (1981); *Symphony with Chaconne* (1987); *Colossos or Panic* (1993).

Voice. *The Deluge* (2 soloists and ensemble, 1957–58); *Four Songs from the Japanese* (soloist and orchestra or piano, 1959); *Sutter's Gold* (bass, chorus, orchestra, 1959–60); *A Little Cantata of Proverbs* (chorus and piano, 1962); *Two Choruses* (1962); *Virtutes: Songs and Melodramas* (chorus, piano, percussion, 1963); *Five Poems and an Epigram of William Blake* (chorus and trumpet, 1964); *Warngedichte* (alto or bass and piano, 1967); *Psalm iv* (soloists with organ, 1976); *Babylon the Great Is Fallen* (chorus and orchestra, 1979); *Das Gesetz der Quadrille* (baritone and piano, 1979); *Eve Dreams in Paradise* (2 soloists with orchestra, 1989).

Chamber music and piano pieces. Piano Sonata (1951–52); *Fantasias* (clarinet and piano, 1954); String Quartet no. 1 (1956–57); *Capriccio* (piano, 1957); *Variations* (flute and piano, 1959); *Suite* (ensemble, 1961); *Three Pieces* (piano, 1964); Piano Trio (1966); String Quartet no. 2 (1967); *Concerto for Eleven* (1970); *Lyric Pieces* (wind quintet and brass, 1974); String Quartet no. 3 (1975–76); Prelude and Fugue (3 clarinets, 1978); *In Real Time II–IV.* (piano, 1992).

Bibl.: Bayan Northcott, ed., *The Music of Alexander Goehr: Interviews and Articles* (London, 1980).

Goehr, Walter (b. Berlin, 28 May 1903; d. Sheffield, 4 Dec. 1960). Conductor and composer. Father of Alexander; studied with Arnold Schoenberg at the Prussian Academy of Arts in Berlin. Conducted the Berlin Radio Orchestra, 1925–31; composed *Malpopita,* an early radio opera. Settled in England in 1933. Music director for the H.M.V. and Columbia Recording Companies. Conducted the Morley College Concerts, 1943–60; the BBC Theatre Orchestra, 1945–48. Led the premiere of Tippett's *A Child of Our Time;* of Britten's *Serenade for Tenor, Horn, Strings.* Composed symphonic, chamber, and film music, including the score of the movie *Great Expectations.* During the 1950s he made many recordings of 17th-, 18th-, 19th-, and 20th-century music.

Goetz, Hermann (b. Königsberg, 7 Dec. 1840; d. Hottingen, near Zurich, 3 Dec. 1876). Composer. While studying math and physics (1858–59), he was active as a conductor of amateur orchestras and as a pianist; he studied conducting, piano, organ, and composition (with Hugo Ulrich) in Berlin (1860–62); in 1863 became organist and choirmaster in Winterthur, where he was active as a pianist, conducted opera and oratorio performances, and founded the choral society. In 1870 he moved to Hottingen and began to write music criticism for various publications (*Allgemeine musikalisches Zeitung* and the *Zürcher Zeitung*). His comic opera *Die Widerspenstigen Zähnung* (1868–72; staged Mannheim, 1875) was successful; it was heavily influenced by his familiarity with the operas of Mozart, avoiding Wagnerian continuity in favor of closed numbers. Other works include 2 symphonies, concertos and *Frühlings-Ouverture* (orchestra, 1864); 2 string quartets and other chamber music; piano works; choral music with orchestra (*Nenie,* 1874); unaccompanied choral works and songs.

Goeyvaerts, Karel (August) (b. Antwerp, 8 June 1923; d. there, 3 Feb. 1993). Composer. He first studied at the Antwerp Conservatory (1942–47) and then at the Paris Conservatory (1947–50), where his teachers included Messiaen and Milhaud. He won the Lili Boulanger Prize in 1949. His Sonata for Two Pianos (1951) attracted the attention of Stockhausen at the Darmstadt summer course. His work with electronic music began when he was invited to work in the West German Radio electronic studio. *Composition no. 4 aux sons mort* (1953) and *Composition no. 5 aux sons purs* (1954), both for tape, are from this period. Instrumental sounds were added to electronic sounds in *Opus 6 for 180 Sound Objects* (1954).

He taught music history at the Antwerp Conservatory, 1950–57. In 1958 he took a position as translator and editor for the Belgian airline Sabena, but continued to compose, returning to conventional instruments, as in *Improperia,* a cantata on the Good Friday liturgy scored for alto, double chorus, and 6 instruments (1959), *Zomerspelen* for 3 orchestral groups (1961), and *De Passie* for orchestra (1962). His *Pièce pour piano* (1964) is for live piano and transformed piano sounds on tape.

In 1967 he began to give seminars in composition at the Antwerp Conservatory. In 1970 he left his post at Sabena to work at the Ghent Institute for Psycho-Acoustics and Electronic Music. His works of this period make use of performers' improvisation (*Van uit de kern,* 2 players, 1969; *Catch à quatre,* 4 players, 1969). Later works include a piano quartet with tape (1972); pieces for mixed media; choral music; a ballet; and 2 works for chamber ensemble (*Zum Wassermann,* 1984; *De Heilige Stad,* 1986).

Goffriller, Matteo (b. Bressanone, ca. 1659; d. Venice, 23 Feb. 1742). String instrument maker. Arriving in Venice in 1685, he probably worked under Martin Kaiser, marrying one of Kaiser's daughters and, by 1690, taking over his business. He is most renowned for his cellos, with Pablo Casals and Janos Starker two famous players of his instruments; his violins and violas are also highly regarded. A son, Francesco, seems to have pursued the same craft.

Goicoechea Errasti, Vicente (b. Ibarra de Aramayona, Alava, 5 Apr. 1854; d. Valladolid, 9 Apr. 1916). Composer. Studied for the priesthood in Valladolid, where from 1890 he was music director at the cathedral. His later church music became the leading Spanish model for the reforms ordered by the papal bull of 1903 and thus of great influence on Spanish church music.

Gold, Arthur (b. Toronto, 6 Feb. 1917; d. New York, 3 Jan. 1990). Duo pianist. While studying with Rosina Lhévinne at Juilliard, he met pianist Robert Fizdale and in 1944 formed a duo that survived until their retirement in 1982. Gold and Fizdale revived the Mendelssohn 2-piano concertos and significantly expanded the repertory by commissioning large works from Milhaud, Poulenc, Rieti, Berio, and many other composers.

Goldberg, Johann Gottlieb (bapt. Danzig, 14 Mar. 1727; buried Dresden, 15 Apr. 1756). Organist, harpsichordist, and composer. A student of J. S. and/or W. F. Bach, brought to Dresden by Count Keyserlingk, and the central figure in Forkel's story concerning the Goldberg Variations of Bach. He served Count Heinrich von Brühl from 1751 to his death. Several accounts attest to his amazing keyboard skills; his compositions range from cantatas written for Leipzig during Bach's tenure to trio sonatas, *galant* works, and progressive concertos intended for Brühl's orchestra. His sister Constantia was a noted pianist.

Goldberg, Szymon (b. Włoclavek, 1909; d. northwestern Japan, 19 July 1993). Violinist and conductor. Studied violin with Carl Flesch in Berlin. Concertmaster of the Dresden Philharmonic, 1926–30; of the Berlin Philharmonic, 1930–34, also playing in a trio with Hindemith and Feuermann, and in duo with Lili Kraus. While touring Indonesia he was taken prisoner by the Japanese, 1942–45. Conducted the Netherlands Chamber Orchestra from 1955 and the New Japan Philharmonic from 1990; taught at Yale, Juilliard, and Curtis; made many recordings.

Goldman, Edwin Franko (b. Louisville, Ky., 1 Jan. 1878; d. New York, 21 Feb. 1956). Bandmaster and composer. At 8 he enrolled in the National Conservatory and studied composition with its director, Dvořák. He took up the cornet, studying in 1895 with Jules Levy, and played solo cornet for the Metropolitan Opera, 1899–1909. In 1911 he founded the New York Military Band; in 1918 he renamed it the Goldman Band and began a series of outdoor concerts on the Green at Columbia Univ., later on the Mall in Central Park, and at other New York venues. The band set standards of excellence for performance and repertoire. Goldman composed over 100 marches ("On the Mall," 1923) and other band works. He wrote technical methods and studies for the cornet and other winds, and for band (*Band Betterment,* 1934; *The Goldman Band System,* 1936).

Goldman, Richard Franko (b. New York, 7 Dec. 1910; d. Baltimore, 19 Jan. 1980). Composer, bandmaster, and writer on music. Son of bandmaster Edwin Franko Goldman. After attending Columbia University (1930) and studying composition in Paris with Nadia

Boulanger, he became assistant conductor to his father with the Goldman Band, succeeding him in 1956 until 1979, when he retired and the group disbanded. He taught at Juilliard (1947–60) and was a visiting professor at Princeton (1952–56). He became director of the Peabody Conservatory in 1968. From 1948 to 1968 he was New York critic for the *Musical Quarterly.* Works include *The Lee Rigg* (orchestra); *A Sentimental Journey* (band, 1941); Sonatina, 2 clarinets (1945); Duo for Tubas (1948); Violin Sonata (1952); many pieces and arrangements for band. Writings include *Landmarks of Early American Music* (New York, 1943; R: 1974); *The Wind Band: Its Literature and Technique* (Boston, 1961; R: 1974); and *Richard Franko Goldman: Selected Essays and Reviews, 1948–1968,* ed. Dorothy Klotzman (New York, 1980).

Goldmark, Karl [Karoly] (b. Keszthely, Hungary, 18 May 1830; d. Vienna, 2 Jan. 1915). Composer. From a large Jewish family, not very supportive of his musical aspirations. He received some instruction in Vienna, 1844–48, partly at the conservatory, but was largely self-taught, evolving an eclectic personal style, comprising Hungarian, Jewish, and Wagnerian elements (his Wagnerism was to create obstacles in Vienna). Early worked as a theater violinist (from 1851 in Vienna) and teacher. His first compositions were not well received; success began with his String Quartet op. 8 (1860), followed by *Sakuntala* Overture op. 13 (1865) and other orchestral, chamber, and choral works. The first of his 6 operas, *Die Königin von Saba* (Vienna, 1875), achieved considerable contemporary success. The "Rustic Wedding" Symphony op. 26 and Violin Concerto op. 28 are still occasionally performed. Memoirs: *Erinnerungen aus meinem Leben* (Vienna, 1927); trans. as *Notes from the Life of a Viennese Composer* (1927).

Goldmark, Rubin (b. New York, 15 Aug. 1872; d. there, 6 Mar. 1936). Composer and teacher. He studied at the Vienna Conservatory (composition with Robert Fuchs; piano with Anton Door); then in New York with Dvořák and Joseffy. He directed the conservatory in Colorado Springs (1895–1901), after which he established himself in New York as a private teacher of composition (Copland and Gershwin were among his students); from 1924 he headed the composition department at the Juilliard Graduate School. He composed in a conservative style based on the European Romantic tradition, sometimes tinged with Indian or African American themes. His Piano Quintet won the Paderewski Prize (1909); other works include *The Call of the Plains* (orchestra, 1925), chamber and orchestral music, songs, and part songs.

Goldoni, Carlo (b. Venice, 25 Feb. 1707; d. Paris, 6 or 7 Feb. 1793). Librettist and playwright. Wrote a great deal for Venetian theaters, 1734–43 and 1748–62, spending the interim period as a lawyer in Tuscany. From 1762 he was associated with the Comédie italienne in Paris; he later retired with a government pension. He is recognized as the leading Italian dramatist of the 18th century; his achievements in opera were also great. After initial efforts in opera seria, he created the *dramma giocoso,* an opera buffa in which seria and buffa characters are combined; he contributed to the development of the ensemble finale as well. His libretti were set by Galuppi, Piccinni, and Haydn, among others.

Goldovsky, Boris (b. Moscow, 7 June 1908). Pianist, conductor, and opera producer. Studied piano in Moscow with his uncle Pierre Luboshutz; in Berlin with Kreutzer and Artur Schnabel; in Budapest with Ernő Dohnányi. Soloist with the Berlin Philharmonic, 1921; director of the Berkshire Music Center Opera Workshop; founding director of the New England Opera Company, 1946. Moderator for broadcasts of the Metropolitan Opera and frequent lecturer on musical subjects.

Goldschmidt, Berthold (b. Hamburg, 18 Jan. 1903). Conductor and composer. He attended the St. George's School (Hamburg) and studied at the universities in Hamburg and Berlin. Later he studied composition (with Franz Schreker) and conducting (with Krasselt) at the Prussian State Academy, Berlin. He conducted the Berlin Staatsoper (1926) and the Darmstadt Opera (1927–29), and during the early 1930s was artistic adviser to the Städtische Oper, Berlin. After his emigration to England in 1935, he conducted at Glyndebourne (1947) and at the Edinburgh Festival. His music contains elements of the styles of Busoni and Weill. Works include operas (*Der gewaltige Hahnrei,* 1930–31; *Beatrice Cenci,* 1949–50); ballets (*Chronica,* 1938; *Cambridge,* 1939); other orchestral works (a symphony, 1944; *Passacaglia,* 1925; a violin concerto, 1933; *Sinfonietta,* 1945; a clarinet concerto, 1954).

Goldschmidt, Otto (Moritz David) (b. Hamburg, 21 Aug. 1829; d. London, 24 Feb. 1907). Conductor. From 1843 a student at Leipzig Conservatory; from 1848 based in London; best known as husband (from 1852) of Jenny Lind, frequently accompanying and touring with her; also church organist, conductor, teacher; founder and first conductor, London Bach Choir (1875–85); also composed, most notably the sacred pastoral *Ruth* (1867).

Goldsmith, Jerry [Jerrald] (b. Los Angeles, 10 Feb. 1929). Composer and conductor. He studied film music with Rozsa at the Univ. of Southern California. Beginning in the 1950s he wrote and conducted music for CBS radio series and for television, including programs such as *Gunsmoke, Perry Mason,* and *The Waltons;* produced nearly 100 film scores, including *Lonely Are the Brave* (1961), *Planet of the Apes* (1967), *Chinatown* (1974), *Star Trek* (1979), *Poltergeist* (1982), and *Rambo* (1985). His style is eclectic.

Goleminov, Marin (b. Kyustendil, near Sofia, 28 Sept. 1908). Composer. Son of an attorney, he began study of law before switching to music; he attended the Sofia State Academy, then (from 1934) the Schola cantorum in Paris, where he was a pupil of d'Indy. After spending time in Bulgaria as conductor and music teacher, he went to Munich (1938–39) to study with Joseph Haas and Alfred Lorenz; in 1943 he became lecturer in composition and conducting at the Sofia State Academy, and four years later professor. He also conducted the National Opera (1965–67). Works include stage music (*Nestinarka,* ballet, 1938–40; *Ivaylo,* 1958–59; *Zlatnata ptitsa,* 1960–61; *Dasterjata na Kalojana,* 1974); cantatas (*Father Paissy,* 1966); orchestral works (3 symphonies, 1963–71; *Nacht,* 1933; *Variations on a Theme by Dobri Christov,* 1943; *Prelude, Aria, and Toccata,* piano and orchestra, 1947; Cello Concerto, 1950; *Aquarelles,* string orchestra, 1973; Piano Concerto, 1975); chamber music (7 string quartets; 2 wind quintets); songs; choral music.

Golestan, Stan (b. Vaslui, Moldavia, 7 June 1875; d. Paris, 21 Apr. 1956). Music critic and composer. After 1895 he was in Paris, where he studied at the Schola cantorum (1897–1903); his instructors were Roussel, d'Indy, and Dukas. After 1900 he wrote for French and Romanian periodicals, and eventually for *Le Figaro,* where for two decades he was music critic. He also taught composition at the Paris École normale de musique. Among his many prizes was the 1915 Enescu Prize, awarded for his *Première rapsodie roumaine.* His works incorporate Gypsy and other native Romanian folk idioms; they include orchestral works (*La Dembovitza,* 1902; Symphony in G minor, 1910; *Concerto roumain,* violin, orchestra, 1933); chamber works (2 string quartets, 1927 and ca. 1936; Sonata in E♭, violin, piano, 1908; *Arioso et allegro de concert,* viola, piano, 1932; Sonatina, flute, 1932); songs; piano works (*Poèmes et paysages,* 1932).

Golschmann, Vladimir (b. Paris, 16 Dec. 1893; d. New York, 1 Mar. 1972). Conductor. Studied violin at the Schola cantorum, Paris. Began his professional career as violinist under Lucien Caplet in the Concerts rouges. In 1919 established and for five seasons conducted the Concerts Golschmann, which featured regular premieres of music by "Les six," Ibert, Prokofiev, and Falla. Conducted the Sorbonne orchestra from 1920. Invited by Diaghilev in 1920 to lead *Le sacre* with the Ballets russes—the company's first reprise of the score since 1913. Conductor of the Bilbao Symphony, 1923–28; of the Scottish Orchestra, 1928–30. U.S. debut with the New York Symphony, 1924. Conductor of the St. Louis Symphony, 1931–58; of the Denver Symphony, 1964–70. Naturalized in 1947.

Golson, Benny (b. Philadelphia, 26 Jan. 1929). Jazz tenor saxophonist and composer. He joined Lionel Hampton (1953), Earl Bostic (1954–56), and Dizzy Gillespie (1956–57), and composed the hard bop theme "Stablemates" and the ballad "I Remember Clifford" (after Clifford Brown's death in 1956). As a member of Art Blakey's Jazz Messengers (1958–59) he wrote "Whisper Not" and "Blues March." With Art Farmer he led the Jazztet (1959–62). He concentrated on writing for jazz-related ensembles and for films and television, then resumed playing, touring with the reformed Jazztet from 1982.

Golyshev [Golishev, Golyscheff], **Yefim** (b. Kherson, Ukraine, 20 Sept. 1887; d. Paris, 25 Sept. 1970). Composer. He studied violin with Auer in Odessa, gaining a reputation as a prodigy. In 1909, to avoid persecution as a Jew, he moved to Berlin, where he became a friend of Busoni and studied at the Stern Conservatory. In 1933 he fled Nazi persecution and took refuge in Portugal and Spain, losing many of his compositions in the process. During the Spanish Civil War he moved to France. There he was eventually captured and imprisoned by the Vichy government. In 1956 he settled in São Paulo, Brazil, and worked as a chemist and acoustician. From 1966 he worked as a painter in Paris. Among his compositions are the String Trio (1925), perhaps the first piece in which both pitch and time are serialized; the symphonic poem *Das eisige Lied* (1920); and the "Anti-Symphony" *Musical Circular Guillotine.*

Gomberg, Harold (b. Malden, Mass., 30 Nov. 1916; d. Capri, 7 Sept. 1985). Oboist. Brother of Ralph. Entered the Curtis Institute in 1928 as a pupil of Tabuteau. Occupied first chairs in the National Symphony (1934–38), the Toronto Symphony (1938–39), the St. Louis Symphony (1939–43), and the New York Philharmonic (1943–77). Taught at Juilliard, 1948–77.

Gomberg, Ralph (b. Boston, 18 June 1921). Oboist. Brother of Harold. Entered the Curtis Institute in 1935 as a pupil of Tabuteau; played first oboe in the All-American Youth Orchestra under Stokowski. Occupied first chairs in the Baltimore Symphony, 1945–49, and the Boston Symphony, 1949–85. Taught at the Peabody Conservatory, 1945–49; at Boston University, 1949–86.

Gombert, Nicolas (b. ca. 1495; d. ca. 1560). Composer. The imperial chapel of Charles V employed him from 1526 as a singer, from 1529 as *maître des enfants,* and for about a decade unofficially as court composer. This employment ended by 1540, apparently because of sexual abuse of a boy, for which he was exiled to the galleys. A pardon from the emperor allowed him eventually to retire, perhaps to Tournai. His compositions are most often in a dense style in which pervading imitation is the rule. This technique was widely adopted by his successors, who ranked Gombert among the greatest composers of his era. Pieces are commonly for 5 or 6 voices, less frequently for 4. His extant works include 10 complete Masses (most based on motets or chansons), 8 Magnificats, over 160 motets, and over 70 chansons.

Bibl.: *Opera omnia, CMM* 6 (1951–75).

Gomes, (Antônio) Carlos (b. Campenas, Brazil, 11 July 1836; d. Belém, 16 Sept. 1896). Composer. From a family of musicians, his father a bandmaster; had already composed several modinhas and a *Hinc acadêmico* performed in São Paulo in 1859, before entering the conservatory at Rio de Janeiro that year (composition under Joaquin Giannini). He had 2 modinhas and 2 piano pieces published in 1859–60, and 2 cantatas heard there in 1860 attracted attention and gave him the opportunity to produce his first opera, the genre in which he was thereafter primarily active. *A noite do castelo* (1861) was followed by *Joana de Flandres* (1863), which resulted in a government scholarship to study at the Milan Conservatory (from 1864; composition under Lauro Rossi). His first 2 Italian operas were light comedies, *Se sa minga* (Milan, Teatro Fossati, 1867) and *Nella luna* (Milan, 1868), both well received. With *Il Guarany* (La Scala, 19 Mar. 1870), on a Brazilian subject, he achieved a great and widespread success, not equaled by his later operas, *Fosca* (La Scala, 1873), a failure; *Salvator Rosa* (Genoa, 1874), a success; *Maria Tudor* (Milan, 1879); and *Lo schiavo* (Rio de Janeiro, 1889; La Scala, 1891), also on a Brazilian subject. Also composed an ode, *Il saluto del Brasile,* for the Philadelphia Exposition (1876) and a large cantata, *Colombo* (Rio de Janeiro, 1892). Shortly before his death he became director of the Belém Conservatory.

Bibl.: I. Gomes Vaz de Carvalho, *A vida de Carlos Gomes* (Rio de Janeiro, 1935; 3rd ed., 1946). G. Nello Vetro, ed., *Antonio Carlos Gomes: Carteggi italiani* (Milan, 1976?).

Gomez, Eddie [Edgar] (b. San Juan, Puerto Rico, 4 Nov. 1944). Jazz double bass player. Raised in New York, he worked with Jim Hall, Marian McPartland, the pianist Paul Bley, and Gerry Mulligan in the mid-1960s, playing bop or free jazz. He joined Bill Evans's trio (1966–77) and also recorded the duo album *Intuition* with Evans (1974). He concentrated on studio work, but also played with Jack DeJohnette (from 1978), Hank Jones (from 1980), JoAnne Brackeen (with whom he recorded the album *Special Identity,* 1981), and Chick Corea. With Michael Brecker and others he founded the fusion group Steps (later, Steps Ahead) in 1979, remaining until 1985.

Gomólka, Mikołaj [Nicolas] (b. Sandomierz?, ca. 1535; d. Jazłowiec, western Ukraine, in or after 1591). Composer. Chorister, then wind player, at the Polish royal court, 1545–63; civic official in Sandomierz, 1566–78; subsequently a musician for various high-ranking persons in Kraków and perhaps Jazłowiec; wrote *Melodie na Psalterz polski* (Kraków, 1580; ed. *Wydawnictwo dawnej muzyki polskiej* 47–49, Kraków, 1963–66), a book of 150 4-part settings of Psalms in Polish.

Gonsalves, Paul [Mex] (b. Boston, 12 July 1920; d. London, 15 May 1974). Jazz tenor saxophonist. After playing in the big bands of Count Basie (1946–49) and Dizzy Gillespie (1949–50) he joined Duke Ellington's, where he remained. Although renowned for his raucous rhythm-and-blues solo on "Diminuendo and Crescendo in Blue" (recorded in performance on the album *Ellington at Newport,* 1956), he was a sophisticated ballad and swing soloist, as demonstrated on "Happy Reunion" on Ellington's album *Newport 1958* and the album he recorded with Sonny Stitt, *Salt and Pepper* (1963).

Goodall, Reginald (b. Lincoln, 13 July 1905; d. Canterbury, 5 May 1990). Conductor. At the Royal Academy of Music in London studied piano with Arthur Benjamin, violin with W. H. Reed. Organist and choir director at St. Albans Cathedral at Holborn. Assistant conductor under Albert Coates at Covent Garden, 1936–39; under Furtwängler with the Berlin Philharmonic. Joined the Sadler's Wells Opera in 1944; led the premiere of *Peter Grimes* there in 1945; the *Rape of Lucretia* (with Ansermet) at Glyndebourne in 1946. Staff conductor at Covent Garden, 1946–60; reduced to répétiteur under Solti, 1961–71. Conducted and recorded Wagner to great acclaim with the Sadler's Wells Opera (*Meistersinger,* 1968; *Ring,* 1973), and the Welsh National Opera (*Tristan,* 1979), using Andrew Porter's English texts. Knighted in 1985.

Goode, Richard (b. New York, 1 June 1943). Pianist. Studied with Claude Frank and Nadia Rosenberg at Mannes College, with Elvira Szigeti and Rudolf Serkin at the Curtis Institute. Participated in the Marlboro Festival, 1957–63; in the Spoleto Festival, 1964–66. Debut, New York, 1961. Won the Clara Haskil International Competition at Montreux-Vevey, 1973; the Avery Fisher Prize, 1980. With Charles Treger gave the premiere of Carlos Chávez's Variations for Violin and Piano; premieres of works by George Perle. Numerous recordings, including the complete Beethoven sonatas.

Goodman, Benny [Benjamin David] (b. Chicago, 30 May 1909; d. New York, 13 June 1986). Jazz and classical clarinetist and jazz bandleader. He joined Ben Pollack (1925–29) and recorded as a leader and with Red Nichols (1929–31) and Joe Venuti and Eddie Lang (1931). In 1934 he formed a big band including Gene Krupa and later Harry James. The sensational reception of its performances in California in 1935 is often chosen to mark the beginning of the swing era and the merger of jazz and popular music. From 1935 he also led a racially integrated combo including Teddy Wilson, Krupa, and later Lionel Hampton, Charlie Christian, and Cootie Williams. His big band of 1940–42 was known for playing adventurous arrangements by Eddie Sauter, but in his subsequent jazz work Goodman returned to swing, apart from a band oriented toward bop (1947–49). From the 1950s he played jazz intermittently. His most important engagements were overseas, including a tour of the USSR (1962). Goodman could be an intense and imaginative improviser, as in his solo on Mel Powell's recording "The World Is Waiting for the Sunrise" (1942), but in countless per-

Benny Goodman (right) with Leonard Bernstein, 1963.

formances he concentrated on playing melodies beautifully with perfect intonation and technique and a round timbre. He brought these inclinations to bear upon a parallel career in classical music. Having commissioned and performed major works by Bartók (1939), Hindemith, and Copland (both 1947), he devoted himself as much to art music as to swing after disbanding his group. Playing concerts into the 1980s, he worked with all leading American orchestras and made recordings of the Mozart Clarinet Concerto, Stravinsky's *Ebony Concerto,* and other works in the classical repertory. His jazz recordings as a leader include "Clarinetitis" (1928), "King Porter," "After You've Gone" (both 1935), "Lady Be Good," "Moonglow," "Stompin' at the Savoy" (all 1936), "Sing, Sing, Sing" (1937), the album *Carnegie Hall Concert,* "Don't Be That Way" (both 1938), "Benny Rides Again" (1940), and the album *Benny Goodman Today* (1970).

Writings: with Irving Kolodin, *The Kingdom of Swing* (New York, 1939). *Benny, King of Swing: A Pictorial Biography Based on Benny Goodman's Personal Archives* (London, 1979).

Bibl.: D. Russell Connor, *Benny Goodman: Listen to His Legacy* (Metuchen, N.J., 1988) [with discography]. James Lincoln Collier, *Benny Goodman and the Swing Era* (New York, 1989).

Goodrich, (John) Wallace (b. Newton, Mass., 27 May 1871; d. Boston, 6 June 1952). Organist, conductor, and educator. In Boston at the New England Conservatory, 1888–92, he studied organ with Henry Dunham and composition with Chadwick. In Europe, 1894–97, studied organ with Rheinberger in Munich, with Widor in Paris. On the faculty of the New England Conservatory, 1897–42; dean from 1907; director from 1931. In Boston organist at the Church of the Messiah, 1900–1902; at Trinity Church, 1902–9. Founding conductor of the Choral Art Society, 1901–7; conductor of the Cecilia Society, 1907–10; of the Boston Opera Company, 1909–12. Translated Pirro's study of Bach; published 2 books on the organ (1899, 1917).

Goodrich, William Marcellus (b. Templeton, Mass., 21 July 1777; d. E. Cambridge, 15 Sept. 1833). Organ builder. First organ builder in Boston (first chamber organ, 1804; first church organ, 1805–6); trained most of the Boston builders of the next generation; 1809, built an orchestrion on Maelzel's model, exhibited throughout Massachusetts. His brother Ebenezer (1782–1841) was for a time associated with him.

Bibl.: Barbara Owen, *The Organ in New England* (Raleigh, N.C., 1979).

Goossens, (Aynsley) Eugene (b. London, 26 May 1893; d. Hillingdon, Middlesex, 13 June 1962). Conductor and composer. His Belgian-born grandfather Eugène (1845–1906) was an important conductor in London and Liverpool during the latter part of the 19th century; among his posts was that as conductor of the Carl Rosa Opera Company. Eugene's father, also named Eugène (1867–1958), conducted and played violin for the Carl Rosa Company around the turn of the century. Young Eugene was first sent to Belgium for his education, then in 1904 he returned to England to study at the Liverpool College of Music. Later (beginning around 1907) he attended the Royal College; his instructors there were Rivarde (violin), Dykes (piano), Charles Wood (harmony), and Charles Standford (composition). From 1912 he was violinist for the Haymarket Theatre and for the Queen's Hall Orchestra. After World War I his reputation as conductor began to grow; in 1921 he conducted the highly successful first English concert performances of *Le sacre du printemps.* The Goossens Orchestra, as his own ensemble was called, survived only a few concerts; after 1922 he conducted frequently at Covent Garden and at the British National Opera. In 1923 he traveled to the U.S. to become conductor, first of the Rochester Philharmonic, then (from 1931) of the Cincinnati Symphony (until 1946). Subsequently in Australia he directed the New South Wales Conservatory (1947–56) and conducted the Sydney Symphony. He was knighted in 1955 and returned to England in 1956.

He also built a considerable reputation as a composer; his music looks toward that of Debussy and Strauss. Works include operas (*Judith,* 1929; *Don Juan de Mañara,* 1937); incidental music (*East of Suez,* 1922; *Autumn Crocus,* 1931); orchestral works (*Perseus,* symphonic poem, 1914; *Ossian,* symphonic prelude, 1915; 2 symphonies, 1940, 1942–44; Oboe Concerto, 1927; *Concertino,* double string orchestra/string octet, 1928; *Cowboy Fantasy,* 1942–44; *Variation on a Theme by Eugene Goossens,* 1946); choral and other vocal works (*The Apocalypse,* oratorio, 1953; *Persian Idylls,* 1916); chamber works (*Phantasy Quartet,* 1915; 2 string quartets, 1915, 1940; 2 sonatas, violin and piano, 1918, 1930; *Islamite Dance,* oboe and piano, 1962); piano music.

Goossens, Leon (Jean) (b. Liverpool, 12 June 1897; d. Tunbridge Wells, 12 Feb. 1988). Oboist; brother of Eugene. Studied with Charles Reynolds from age 8; with William Malsch at the Royal College of Music in London, 1911–14. Principal oboe with the Queen's Hall Orchestra, 1914–15, and again, 1918–24, after war service, during which he was wounded. First chair in the Covent Garden Orchestra and Royal Philharmonic, 1924–32; in the London Philharmonic, 1932–39. Taught at the Royal Academy of Music, 1924–35; at the Royal College of Music, 1924–39. U.S. debut in 1927 during his first international tour.

Gordon, Dexter (Keith) (b. Los Angeles, 27 Feb. 1923; d. Philadelphia, 25 Apr. 1990). Jazz tenor saxophonist. He played in the big bands of Lionel Hampton (1940–43), Louis Armstrong (1944), and Billy Eckstine (1944–46), recording "Blowin' the Blues Away" as a soloist with Eckstine (1944). Recordings with Dizzy Gillespie (1945) and as a leader (including "Long Tall Dexter," 1946) marked his emergence as a leading bop soloist. A celebrated improvisatory duel with Wardell Gray, recorded as "The Chase" (1947), resulted in their leading a group intermittently to 1952. Drug addiction impeded his career until 1960, when he acted and played in, and composed for, the play *The Connection.* His soulful ballad playing was exemplified by "You've Changed," on his album *Doin' Allright* (1961). He settled in Copenhagen (1962–77), until an acclaimed tour and album, *Homecoming* (1976), resulted in his moving back to the U.S. In 1986 he starred in the film *'Round Midnight.*

Gordy, Berry, Jr. (b. Detroit, 28 Nov. 1929). Soul songwriter, record producer, and record company executive. In 1960 he founded Motown Records and was instrumental in developing its characteristic sound, which mixed black idioms such as gospel and rhythm-and-blues with white popular styles; it was the definitive "soul" sound throughout the 1960s and 1970s. Motown was immensely successful in bringing black artists before a large white audience. The artists associated with Motown include Smokey Robinson, Diana Ross and the Supremes, the Jackson Five, the Temptations, Marvin Gaye, Stevie Wonder, and many others.

Górecki, Henryk (Mikołaj) (b. Czernica, Poland, 6 Dec. 1933). Composer. His early studies were at the Higher School of Music in Rybnik. From 1951 to 1953 he was a schoolteacher; in 1955–60 he studied with B. Szabelski at Katowice. After studying in Paris in the early 1960s, where he took lessons from Messiaen, he joined the teaching staff of the Katowice Conservatory in 1968. His early, chiefly serial works show the influence of Webern; he later tended toward a more flexible formal design, with a tonal language akin to that of Messiaen. Orchestral works: 3 symphonies (no. 1, "1959"; no. 2, Kopernikowska, with soloists and chorus, 1972; no. 3, with soprano, 1976); *Scontri* (1960); *Chôros I,* 53 strings (1964); *Refren* [Refrain] (1965); *Muzyka staropolska* (1969); *Canticum graduum* (1960); Concerto-cantata, flute, orchestra (1992). Choral music: *Monologhi,* soprano, 3 instrumental ensembles (1960); *Do matki,* soprano, chorus, orchestra (1972); *Euntes ibant et flebant* (1974); *Beatus vir,* baritone, chorus, orchestra, 1979; 3 *Monodrammas,* soprano, chamber ensemble (1963). Chamber music: Concerto, chamber ensemble (1957); 2 *Canti strumentali,* chamber ensemble (1962); *Elementi,* string trio (1962); *Muzyczka I–IV,* various instrumental ensembles (1967–70); *Already It Is Dusk,* string quartet (1988); *Quasi Una Fantasia,* string quartet no. 2 (1990–91); *Kleines Requiem für eine Polka,* piano, 13 instruments (1993).

Gorr, Rita [Marguerite Geimaert] (b. Zelzaete, Belgium, 18 Feb. 1926). Mezzo-soprano. Studied in Brussels, winning the Verviers Competition in 1946. Stage debut at Antwerp in 1949 as Fricka *(Walküre).* At Strasbourg, 1949–52, she progressed to major roles; participated in the French premiere of *Mathis der Mahler.* In 1958 created Mère Marie in the French premiere of Poulenc's *Dialogues des Carmelites.* Sang at Bayreuth as Fricka (1959) and Ortrud (1960); at Covent Garden as Amneris (1959); at La Scala as Kundry (*Parsifal,* 1960); at the Metropolitan Opera as Amneris, 17 Oct. 1962. With the Met four seasons before personal problems curtailed her career. In 1981 she returned to the stage.

Goss, John (b. Fareham, England, 27 Dec. 1800; d. London, 10 May 1880). Composer. Son of the local organist; choirboy in Chapel Royal; later studied with Attwood; church organist from 1813 at St. Paul's Cathedral; also a teacher (Sullivan, Cowen, Frederick Bridge). Noted for glees and church music. Knighted in 1872.

Gossec, François-Joseph (b. Vergnies, Belgium, 17 Jan. 1734; d. Passy, near Paris, 16 Feb. 1829). Composer. As a child he studied music in chapels in Walcourt and Maubeuge, and at Notre Dame Cathedral in Antwerp, where he was an organ and violin pupil of André-Joseph Blavier. In 1751 he went to Paris, where Rameau helped him procure a position as violinist and bass player in the house orchestra of the wealthy music lover Le Riche de La Pouplinière. There he came into contact with Johann Stamitz; he also began publishing his own works during this period, including *Trois grandes symphonies* op. 8 (publ. 1765) and *Six simphonies à grande orchestre* (1769). His initial attempt at composing for the stage was *Le périgourdin* (intermezzo, 1761); it was followed by some 22 other works, including *Le faux lord* (opéra comique, 1765); *Les pêcheurs* (opéra comique, 1766); *Sabinus* (tragédie lyrique, 1733); *Mirza* (ballet, 1779); *Thésée* (tragédie lyrique, 1782); *Rosine* (opera, 1786); *Les sabots et le cerisier* (opera, 1803). In 1769 he founded the Concerts des amateurs; in 1773 he resigned to become director of the Concert spirituel. Two years later he was also *maître de musique* at the Opéra. From around 1790 he published a number of Revolutionary hymns and tunes. After 1799 he was primarily a professor of composition at the Conservatory; in 1804 he was made Chevalier of the Légion d'Honneur. When Louis XVIII closed the Conservatory in 1816, Gossec was left to die in penury. In addition to the works listed above, he composed many symphonies (some 50 of which were published); *symphonies concertantes;* chamber works; more than 50 Revolutionary songs; and sacred vocal music including Masses (*Missa pro defunctis,* called *Messe des morts,* publ. 1780) and oratorios.

Gotovac, Jakov (b. Split, 11 Oct. 1895; d. Zagreb, 16 Oct. 1982). Composer. At the universities in Zagreb and Graz he studied law; in Zagreb he also studied music with Antun Dobronić. Around 1920 he attended Joseph Marx's composition master classes in Vienna. In 1923 he was appointed music director of the Croatian National Opera in Zagreb. He also conducted choirs in Šibenik (in 1922) and in Zagreb. Drawing much from Croatian folk melody, his music employs the tonal vernacular of late Romanticism. He composed theater works (*Dubravka,* 1928; *Morana,* 1930; *Ero s onoga svijeta* [Ero from the World Beyond], 1935; *Mila Gojsalića,* 1952; *Stanac,* 1959; *Dalmaro,* 1964; *Petar Svačić,* composed 1969, not performed); orchestral music (*Orači,* 1937; *Pjesme i ples za Balkana,* 1939; *Guslar,* 1940); vocal works (*Koleda,* 1925; *Rizvan-aga,* baritone, orchestra, 1938; *Pjesme vječnog jada* [Songs of Eternal Sorrow], 1939).

Gottlieb, Jack S. (b. New Rochelle, N.Y., 12 Oct. 1930). Composer. He studied with Karol Rathaus at Queens College; Irving Fine at Brandeis, and Burrill Phillips and Robert Palmer at the Univ. of Illinois (D.M.A., 1964); at the Berkshire Music Center he worked with Copland and Blacher (summers 1954–55). He assisted Bernstein at the New York Philharmonic (1958–66); was music director at Temple Israel in St. Louis (1970–73); and taught at Hebrew Union College. He set Jewish religious texts in a solemn style, and wrote some secular works with humorous texts in which he adapted popular styles (*Downtown Blues for Uptown Halls,* soprano, clarinet, and piano, 1967). Works include operas; orchestral, chamber, and piano works; sacred choral music; songs; a film score and 2 "lecture-entertainments" (1972, 1981).

Gottschalk, Louis Moreau (b. New Orleans, 8 May 1829; d. Tijuca, Brazil, 18 Dec. 1869). Composer and pianist. His father was a London-born merchant, apparently of Jewish origin, who settled in New Orleans in the 1820s, marrying a genteel Creole whose family had fled the slave uprising in Santo Domingo in the 1790s. A child prodigy as a pianist, he was taught by François Letellier, music director of the cathedral, and appeared in concerts. In May 1842 he was sent to Paris for study (piano with Halle, later Stamaty, composition with Maleden); 1845, gave well-received recital at the Salle Pleyel; 1849, began professional concert career, having already won popularity with piano compositions, especially the exotic genre pieces *Bamboula, La savane, Le bananier,* which introduced a new idiom to European music; toured Switzerland and France (summer 1850) and Spain (1851–52), where he was especially successful; January 1853, began U.S. concert career in New York. His father's death in October 1853 made him the main support of a large family, causing him to tour incessantly and to publish more piano pieces, having a tremendous success with *The Last Hope* (1855), one of the most popular parlor pieces of the time. He spent February 1854–February 1855 in Cuba; returned there in 1857 and toured much of the Caribbean region and parts of Central and South America, activities including organizing "monster" concerts, perhaps inspired by French models (one in Havana in 1861 included 40 pianists, military bands, all the amateur singers in Havana, and African drums). From 1862 he toured the Union states of the U.S., giving approximately 1,100 concerts in the next 4 years, including some in the Far West. Here in September 1865 his involvement with a girl attending the Oakland Female Seminary created a widely reported scandal that resulted in his going to Panama and then to Peru, Chile, Uruguay, and Rio de Janeiro, where he organized several monster concerts and, weak from yellow fever, collapsed while playing his own lamentation *Morte!!* at a concert on 25 November. His highly entertaining *Notes of a Pianist* (Philadelphia, 1881; ed. J. Behrend, New York, 1964) is an English translation of a lost French journal intermittently kept, 1857–68.

Bibl.: V. B. Lawrence, ed., *The Piano Works of Louis Moreau Gottschalk* (New York, 1969). R. Offergeld, *The Centennial Catalogue of the Published and Unpublished Compositions of Louis Moreau Gottschalk* (New York, 1970). John G. Doyle, *Louis Moreau Gottschalk, 1829–1869: A Bibliographical Study and Catalog of Works* (Detroit, 1983). William E. Korf, *The Orchestral Music of Louis Moreau Gottschalk* (Henryville, Pa., 1983). Louis Moreau Gottschalk, *Les voyages extraordinaires de L. Moreau Gottschalk, pianiste et aventurier* (Lausanne, 1985).

Goudimel, Claude (b. Besançon, 1514–20; d. Lyons, 28–31 Aug. 1572). Composer. A university student in Paris by 1549 and later an associate of the publisher Nicolas du Chemin; lived in Metz for about 10 years beginning in 1557; then moved to Lyons, where he died in the St. Bartholomew's Day massacres. His works, most written between 1551 and 1558, include nearly 20 sacred Latin pieces, about 70 chansons (some setting poetry by Ronsard), odes on texts by Horace (all lost), and especially Psalms in French.

Bibl.: *Oeuvres complètes* (Brooklyn, 1967–83).

Gould, Glenn (Herbert) (b. Toronto, 25 Sept. 1932; d. there, 4 Oct. 1982). Pianist. At the Toronto Conservatory studied organ with Frederick C. Silvester (1942–49), piano with Alberto Guerrero (1943–52). Debut recital as an organist, Toronto, 1945. Played Beethoven's Concerto no. 4 with the Toronto Symphony, 1947. First of many broadcast recitals on CBC, 1950. Toured Western Canada, 1951, but determined to compose rather than concertize. The success of his U.S. debut in Washington, D.C., 31 Jan. 1955, of his New York debut eight days later, and especially of his recording of Bach's Goldberg Variations in June 1955 caused him to modify his plans. European debut with the Moscow Philharmonic, 1957. London debut in 1959 playing all five Beethoven concertos. He acquired a reputation in musical circles for brilliant but idiosyncratic musicianship. In 1964 he retired from the concert stage, preferring to communicate through recordings. From 1967 he wrote and produced experimental radio scripts for CBC. By 1982 he had published about 50 articles and monographs on musical topics.

Bibl.: Tim Page, ed., *The Glenn Gould Reader* (New York, 1984). Elizabeth Angilette, *Philosopher at the Keyboard, Glenn Gould* (Metuchen, N.J., 1992). Michael Stegemann, *Glenn Gould: Leben und Werk* (Munich, 1992).

Gould, Morton (b. New York, 10 Dec. 1913; d. Orlando, 21 Feb. 1996). Composer and conductor. As a child he studied at the Institute of Musical Art in New York, and then with Abby Whiteside (piano) and Vincent Jones (theory and composition); in recitals he gave as a teenager he included improvisations on themes suggested by the audience, his own compositions, and the standard piano repertory. He left high school to help support his family by playing in theater orchestras and jazz bands; worked as staff pianist at Radio City Music Hall (1931–32). Associated with radio since 1933 as a pianist; from 1935 to 1942 he was composer, arranger, and conductor for WOR in New York (Mutual Broadcasting System); from 1942 to 1945 was responsible for *The Chrysler Hour* and other programs at CBS; some of his own orchestral works were introduced on these programs (*American Concertette,* piano and orchestra, 1943; later incorporated in *Interplay,* choreographed by Jerome Robbins, 1945). Early in his career his works were performed by major orchestras in Philadelphia (*Chorale Fugue in Jazz,* 2 pianos and orchestra, Stokowski, 1936), Chicago, Pittsburgh (*Stephen Foster Gallery,* 1940), and Cleveland. In 1945 he conducted the Boston Symphony in a program of his own works; in 1965 he received a Grammy Award for his recording of the works of Charles Ives with the Chicago Symphony. Early works tended to draw from vernacular styles (*Derivations,* clarinet and jazz band, was written for Benny Goodman; *Fall River Legend,* a ballet for Agnes De Mille, draws on American folk song in portraying Lizzie Borden); but in the 1950s Gould employed serial techniques (*Jekyll and Hyde Variations,* 1955), drawing away somewhat from his more popular sources while retaining "at least the residue of these influences." He was president of ASCAP 1986–94. He was awarded a Pulitzer Prize for *Stringmusic* (orchestra, 1994). Works include ballets (*I'm Old Fashioned,* Robbins, 1983), musicals, film and television scores (*Holocaust,* 1978); many works for orchestra (*Venice,* 2 orchestras, 1967); pieces for symphonic band (*Global Greeting,* 1994); chamber and piano music (*Concerto Concertante,* violin, piano, and woodwind quintet, 1983); and choral music (*Quotations,* 2 choruses and orchestra, 1984).

Gounod, Charles (François) (b. Paris, 18 June 1818; d. St. Cloud, 18 Oct. 1893). Composer. His father (d. 1823) was a painter; his mother, to whom he remained passionately devoted, a good pianist who gave him lessons. He graduated from Lycée St.-Louis; music lessons from Reicha (d. 1836); 1836, entered Paris Conservatory (counterpoint under Halévy; composition, Lesueur; piano, Zimmermann); 1837, co-winner, second Prix de Rome; 1839, won Prix de Rome. His early compositions were mostly sacred; had Masses performed in Paris, then in Rome during his stay there (1839–42), where he also immersed himself in the Palestrina style, and two in Vienna during his subsequent (1842–43) tour of Austria and Germany, where he visited Mendelssohn and came to know Schumann's music.

Back in Paris, his life was strongly oriented toward the church, as he became organist of the Missions étrangères and in 1846–48 studied for the priesthood; composed relatively little, publishing a Mass as op. 1 (1846) and a Holy Week Office as op. 2. Then, encouraged by the singer Pauline Viardot, he turned to the theater, composing his first opera, *Sapho* (Opéra, 1851), in which she sang the title role, and incidental music for the tragedy *Ulisse* (Comédie-Française, 1852), in a sober style contrary to the tendency of the time and with little success. He married Zimmermann's daughter, but continued to be susceptible to other women, and this, together with his religiosity and at times a certain lack of scruple in his professional dealings, has led his character to be portrayed by biographers as somewhat lubricious, even morally weak. He acquired a Scribe libretto, *La nonne sanglante,* on which Berlioz had worked without completing it, and with which Gounod apparently hoped to appeal to popular taste, but again unsuccessfully (Opéra, 1854). From the early 1850s he became a prolific composer and in the period through the 1860s produced his most important, popular, and long-lived work. Having become conductor of the male-voice chorus, the Orphéon de la ville de Paris, in 1852, he composed much choral music, including his best-known Mass, the *Messe solennelle de Ste. Cécile* (1855), Latin motets, and other sacred and secular choruses; also many solo songs; and 2 symphonies.

Theatrical work continued with incidental music for *Le bourgeois gentilhomme* (Comédie-Française, 1857), and his first opera for the Théâtre lyrique, a comedy based on Moliere's *Le médecin malgré lui* (1859); but it was his second opera there, *Faust* (19 Mar. 1859), that became one of the most popular and widely performed operas of the 19th century and made him an international celebrity. He then produced 2 small works, *Philémon et Baucis* (Théâtre lyrique, 1860) and *La colombe* (Baden-Baden, 1860), and another relatively unsuccessful grand opera, *La reine de Saba* (Opéra, 1862). His last 2 operas for the Théâtre lyrique, *Mireille* (1864) and *Roméo et Juliette* (1867), had considerable and long-lived success, without equaling that of *Faust*.

In September 1870 Gounod fled to London from the Franco-Prussian War. The rest of his family returned to Paris in May 1871, but he made London his base until 1874, at first to capitalize on the great appeal of his music to English taste (1871–72, conductor, Royal Albert Hall Choral Society; composed many choral pieces and solo songs in English); then through his fascination with Mrs. Georgina Weldon, an English amateur singer and a personality of extraordinary energy and forcefulness but capricious behavior, whom he met in 1871, coming to live with her (and her husband). In addition to the havoc that this relationship wreaked on Gounod's nerves and personal life, its inevitable rupture was equally injurious to his reputation because of Mrs. Weldon's practice of publishing lengthy self-justifications of her actions. He continued to compose prolifically but less successfully in this period, most notably the opera *Polyeucte,* in which his deliberately simple late style is apparent, but which was a failure (Opéra, 1878), as was *Cinq Mars* (Opéra-comique, 1877) and his last opera, *Le tribut de Zamora* (Opéra, 1881).

In his later years his focus as composer shifted back to sacred music. The oratorios *Rédemption* (Birmingham Festival, 1881) and *Mors et vita* (Birmingham Festival, 1885) aroused considerable attention, reflecting Gounod's prestige, but proved to have no staying power. In his last 23 years he also composed 12 Masses and a posthumous Requiem, completed by Busser.

Bibl.: *Mémoires d'un artiste* (Paris, 1896); trans. Eng., 1896. J. G. Prod'homme and A. Dandelot, *Gounod (1818–1893): Sa vie et ses oeuvres d'après des documents inédits* (Paris, 1911; R: 1973). J. Tiersot, "Gounod's Letters," *MQ* 5 (1919): 40–61. T. Marix-Spire, "Gounod and His First Interpreter, Pauline Viardot," *MQ* 31 (1945): 193–211, 299–317. J. Harding, *Gounod* (Briarcliff, N.Y., 1973). Steven Huebner, *The Operas of Charles Gounod* (Oxford, 1990).

Graener, Paul (b. Berlin, 11 Jan. 1872; d. Salzburg, 13 Nov. 1944). Composer and conductor. He had been a boy soprano in Berlin, but was largely self-taught as a composer; moved to London in 1896, where he briefly conducted the orchestra at the Haymarket Theatre and taught privately; in 1908 he taught at the New Conservatory in Vienna, then worked in various German cities; he was professor of composition at the Leipzig Conservatory in 1920 but resigned in 1925 in order to compose; later held the same position at the Reichsmusikkammer (1935–41). His compositions belong to the German tradition of Strauss and Reger. In addition to orchestral, chamber, and piano works, he wrote at least 10 operas (*Friedemann Bach,* 1931), which were staged in Germany and Vienna, and some 130 songs.

Graffman, Gary (b. New York, 14 Oct. 1928). Pianist. Son of violinist Vladimir Graffman; studied piano with Isabelle Vengerova, 1936–46, first privately, then at the Curtis Institute. Recital debut at New York's Town Hall in 1939. Won the Rachmaninoff Fund Special Award in 1946, leading to three appearances with the Philadelphia Orchestra beginning in 1947. Won the Leventritt Award in 1949. After a season in Europe, 1950–51, on a Fulbright Scholarship, studied with Vladimir Horowitz in New York and Rudolf Serkin at Marlboro. In the 1960s and 1970s he frequently joined the Guarneri and Juilliard Quartets as well as Leonard Rose and Henryk Szeryng to perform chamber music. In 1979 his right hand became disabled by carpal tunnel syndrome. He continued his concert career playing the solo and concerto literature for left hand. Taught at the Curtis Institute from 1980; artistic director from 1986. Published *I Really Should Be Practicing,* a literate memoir (1981).

Grainger, (George) Percy (Aldrige) (b. Melbourne, Australia, 8 July 1882; d. White Plains, N.Y., 20 Feb. 1961). Composer, pianist, folk song collector, and musical inventor. During his childhood in Melbourne he studied piano with his mother and with Louis Pabst. Traveling to Frankfurt in 1894, he began studies at the Hoch Conservatory; his piano teacher was James Kwast, his instructor in composition was Iwan Knorr. In 1901 he moved to London, and during the next decade he played piano recitals throughout England and the rest of Europe, as well as in Australia and New Zealand. During this period he also began collecting the folk songs that he later published in collections such as *British Folk-Music Settings.* Around 1906 Grainger established a friendship with Grieg, becoming an important early proponent of the latter's piano concerto.

Emigrating to the U.S. in 1914, he settled first in New York, where he held a position (1917–19) as director, oboist, and saxophonist in the U.S. Army Band. Subsequently he taught summer sessions in piano at the Chicago Musical College (from 1918), he collected folk songs in Jutland (1925–27), and he chaired the music department of New York Univ. (1932–33). Around 1935 he began preparations for the Grainger Museum, to be established in Melbourne to house his manuscripts and inventions and to serve as a center for research on folk music; it opened in 1938. By the 1940s he had all but stopped composing, but was engaged instead in revising earlier works and in perfecting his system of "free music," which would be characterized by increasing discordance, smaller intervals, "gliding tones," an informality of musical form, and irregular rhythms. He invented and constructed a series of electronic composition machines in order to produce free music.

For many years after his death he was remembered largely for short piano pieces such as *Country Gardens* and *Molly on the Shore* (1918) or the piano transcription *Flower Waltz* (1904) from Tchaikovsky's *Nutcracker.* More recently his more unusual works such as *Free Music* (1936), for a quartet of theremins, have received attention for their innovation. Several early works illustrate his departures from European tradition: irregular meters; nonsense syllables as text; polytonality; new sonorities (whistlers, mandolins, ukeleles); indeterminacy ("Random Round," 1912–15, in which performers enter at will). *The Warriors* (orchestra, 3 pianos, tuneful percussion ad libitum, 1912–16) requires 3 conductors and glockenspiel, handbells, marimbas, and xylophone. His output was huge and includes not only choral, orchestral, chamber, and keyboard music but also 400–500 folk song settings, arranged for various instrumental or vocal combinations. In these his aim was to be faithful to the songs themselves. He did not incorporate folk songs into his original works. He was also active as a music editor, producing editions of works as diverse as Grieg's A minor Piano Concerto and the *Dolmetsch Collection of English Consorts.*

Original works: *Orchestral music. Colonial Song,* harp and orchestra (1905–12); *Mock Morris* (1911); *The Warriors* (1912–16); *Suite "In a Nutshell"* [4 pieces], orchestra, tuned percussion instruments, piano (1916); *The Power of Rome and the Christian Heart* (1918–43); *To a Nordic Princess* (1927–28); *Handel in the Strand* (1932); *The Immovable Do* (1939).

Choral music. The Beaches of Lukannon (1898, 1941); *Hunting-Song of the Seonee Pack* (1899; rev. 1922); *Love Verses from "The Song of Solomon"* (2 versions, 1899–1901 and 1911); *We Have Fed Our Seas* (1900–1904; rev. 1911); *The Peora Hunt* (1901–6); *Mowgli's Song against the People* (1903; rev. 1907 and 1923); *Morning Song in the Jungle* (1905); *Tiger, Tiger!* (1905); *The Bride's Tragedy* (1908; rev. 1909–13); *Tribute to Foster* (1913–16); *The Merry Wedding* (1916).

Chamber music. Walking Tune, wind quintet (1900–1905); *Hill Song,* various instruments, I (2 versions, 1901–2 and 1921–23) and II (1907; rev. 1911 and 1940–46); *Harvest Hymn,* various scoring possibilities (1905–6); *Echo-Song Trials,* chamber ensemble (1945).

Band music. Colonial Song (1918); *The Lads of Wamphray March* (1906–7; rev. 1937–38).

Keyboard works. Versions of several works listed above *(Colonial Song; Handel in the Strand; Harvest Hymn; Hill Songs I–II; Mock Morris; The Immovable Do; To a Nordic Princess; Walking Tune);* also *Random Round,* 2 pianos, 12-hands (1943); *English Waltz,* 2 pianos, 4-hands (1947).

Bibl.: Teresa Balough, *A Complete Catalogue of the Works of Percy Grainger* (Nedlands, Western Australia, 1975). Robert Simon, *Percy Grainger: The Pictorial Biography* (Troy, N.Y., 1983). John Blacking, *"A Commonsense View of All Music": Reflections on Percy Grainger's Contributions to Ethnomusicology and Music Education* (New York, 1987). Wilfried Howard Mellers, *Percy Grainger* (Oxford, 1992).

Gram, Hans (b. Copenhagen, 20 May 1754; d. Boston, 28 Apr. 1804). Composer, organist, and writer on music. After receiving a diploma in philosophy from the Univ. of Copenhagen (1772) and studying music privately, he emigrated to the New World: first to the West Indies (1781) and later to Massachusetts (1785). He played organ at the Brattle Street Church in Boston and wrote articles on music for *Massachusetts Magazine.* He also composed and arranged anthems, hymns, and psalmody, and apparently helped edit the *Massachusetts Compiler* (Boston, 1795), a collection of psalm tunes and other sacred music. Gram is thought to have penned its introduction, an important theoretical treatise on psalmody.

Gramm [Grambsch], **Donald (John)** (b. Milwaukee, 26 Feb. 1927; d. New York, 2 June 1983). Bass-baritone. Studied piano and organ at the Wisconsin College-Conservatory, 1935–44; voice with George Graham at the Chicago Music College, 1944–49, with Martial Singher at the Music Academy of the West in Santa Barbara, with Ruth Streiter in Boston. Sang at the New York City Opera, 1952–66 (debut as Colline in *Bohème*); at the Santa Fe Opera, 1960–77; at the Metropolitan Opera, 1964–83 (debut as Truffaldin in *Ariadne*). His U.S. premieres included Wolf's *Der Corregidor* (New York, 1952), Dr. Schön in Berg's *Lulu* (Santa Fe, 1963), Diaz in Sessions's *Montezuma* (Boston, 1966). Among his 20 roles at the Met were Leporello, Papageno, Don Alfonso, Balstrode *(Peter Grimes),* the Doctor *(Wozzeck),* and Schoenberg's Moses.

Granados, Enrique (b. Lérida, Spain, 25 July 1867; d. at sea, English Channel, 24 Mar. 1916). Composer and pianist. Studied piano with Jurnet and Pujol and composition with Pedrell in Barcelona (1883–87), and piano with Bériot in Paris (1887–89). Returning to Barcelona, he made his recital debut and made a living as a pianist; performed as soloist in the Grieg piano concerto on a Perez Cabrero Orchestra program of 1892 that included some of his *Danzas españolas.* His zarzuela *Maria del Carmen* (1898) was warmly received, though 4 later such works (*Picarol,* 1901; *Follet,* 1903; *Gaziel,* 1906; *Liliana,* 1911) were not as successful. He founded a concert society in 1900, and his Academia Grandados in 1901; virtuosi such as Pablo Casals, Ivan Manén, and Camille Saint-Saëns collaborated with him in recitals as he spent the decade composing, teaching, and performing. He premiered the *Goyescas,* widely considered his greatest work, in 1914; a performance of the work on 4 Apr. 1914 at the Salle Pleyel, Paris, was a huge success, and he soon was named to the Legion of Honor. He adapted the *Goyescas* into an opera, to be performed in Paris; wartime difficulties and the Opéra's indecision caused him to offer it to the Metropolitan Opera in New York, where it was given to acclaim on 28 Jan. 1916. He played at the White House at the request of President Wilson, then left for Europe. While en route from Folkestone to Dieppe, his ship (the *Sussex*) was torpedoed by a German U-boat; he dove out of a lifeboat in an attempt to save his wife, but both were drowned.

Granados's musical influences were many. His early operas place him in the zarzuela tradition, while other works show his affinity for the Spanish *tonadillas* of the 18th century. His piano music draws on his Spanish heritage in both program and content, notably in the *Danzas españolas* (1892–1900), but echoes of the French tradition are heard in the Chopinesque roulades and slippery chromaticism of the *Goyescas* (1911; the Berceuse and Mazurka movements of the 6 *Escenas románticas* give additional evidence of the connection). Unlike most of his contemporaries, he did not often draw from his local heritage, that of Catalonia. Granados was also a fine writer and painter, with Goya as his favorite artist; he owned several of Goya's paintings and fittingly chose to memorialize the painter in his musical masterpiece.

In addition to works mentioned, he composed tone poems (*Divina commedia,* 1908; *Elisenda,* piano and orchestra, 1912); chamber music (a piano quintet, 1898; 3 preludes and a sonata, violin and piano); piano music *(Escenas poéticas, Estudios expresivos, Valses poéticos);* songs *(Colleción de tonadillas escritas en estilo antiguo).*

Bibl.: José Subirá, *Enrique Granados* (Madrid, 1926). Antonio Fernández-Cid, *Granados* (Madrid, 1956). Carol A. Hess, *Enrique Granados: A Bio-Bibliography* (New York, 1991).

Grandi, Alessandro (b. ca. 1575–80; d. Bergamo, 1630). Composer. Possibly a student of G. Gabrieli. Named *maestro di cappella* of the Accademia della morte at Ferrara in 1597; moved to the Accademia dello Spirito Santo in 1610, and finally to the Ferrara Cathedral (1615–17). Sang at St. Mark's, Venice, from 1617, becoming vice-*maestro* under Monteverdi in 1620. Appointed *maestro* of S. Maria Maggiore in Bergamo in 1627 without an audition; he died in the plague of 1630. His publications appeared regularly from 1610 to his death; the print *Il primo libro de motetti* . . . (1610) shows Gabrieli's influence, while his later works, primarily small-scale motets, identify him as a major exponent of the concertato style. In the 1620s he turned to the solo motet with obbligato instrumental accompaniment, producing 3 volumes of *Motetti . . . con sinfonie* (1621, 1625, 1629). Other works include Masses and Psalms along with secular cantatas, arias, and concertato madrigals.

Grandjany, Marcel (George Lucien) (b. Paris, 3 Sept. 1891; d. New York, 24 Feb. 1975). Harpist. Studied harp with Henriette Renié at the Paris Conservatory; first prize for harp, 1905; for harmony, 1909. He was already harpist with the Concerts Lamoureux at the time of his debut recital at age 17. Organist at Sacré-Coeur, 1915–18. Debut as solo harpist in London, 1922; in New York, 1924. Taught harp at the American School at Fontainebleau, 1921–35. Moved to New York in 1936 and taught at the Juilliard School, 1938–75; at the Montreal Conservatory, 1943–63; at the Manhattan School of Music, 1956–66. Became a U.S. citizen in 1945. Founded the American Harp Society in 1961. Composed songs and several dozen works for harp, including *Poème symphonique* (harp, horn, orchestra, 1911), *Rhapsodia* (1921), *Fantasie on a Theme of Haydn* (1953), *Petite suite classique* (1968).

Grappelli [Grappelly], **Stéphane** (b. Paris, 26 Jan. 1908). Jazz violinist. With Django Reinhardt he was the central figure in the swing group the Quintette du Hot Club de France, developing a fluid improvisatory style that influenced American jazz violinists; the group's recordings include "Dinah" and "Tiger Rag" (both 1934). He often doubled as a pianist during this period. He moved to England in 1939, playing frequently with George Shearing. He was reunited with Reinhardt (1946–49) and returned to France. A new career of international festival appearances began with the recording of the album *Violin Summit* with Svend Asmussen, Jean-Luc Ponty, and Stuff Smith (1966). His free-lancing included work with Joe Venuti, Gary Burton, Earl Hines, Ponty, and Shearing. Among many albums is the *Stephane Grappelli–Oscar Peterson Quartet* with Niels Henning Ørsted-Pederson and Kenny Clarke (1973).

Bibl.: Geoffrey Smith, *Stephane Grappelli: A Biography* (London, 1987).

Graun, Carl Heinrich (b. Wahrenbrück, 1703–4; d. Berlin, 8 Aug. 1759). Composer. Sang in the Dresden Kreuzschule under Grundig; later attended Leipzig Univ. Studied with Benisch, Pezold, and J. C. Schmidt; participated as chorus member in Dresden's opera; visited Prague for the coronation festival in 1723. He was appointed tenor in the opera of the Duchy of Braunschweig in 1725, soon becoming Vice-Kapellmeister, and wrote 6 operas for the court. Crown Prince Frederick of Prussia had wanted to engage him as early as 1733, but was unable to do so until the death of Duke Ludwig Rudolph in 1735. As part of Frederick's musical retinue he wrote and performed cantatas, directed the chamber music, and instructed both the prince and Franz Benda. Upon Frederick's ascent to the throne in 1740, Graun was sent to Italy to recruit singers for the Berlin Opera; from 1741 on he was the principal stage composer in Berlin, producing 26 operas. These works show the imprint of the king's personality in many ways: Frederick wrote several of his librettos, including *Montezuma* (1755), while Graun was often obliged to rewrite music or use particular forms to please the monarch. As representative examples of opera seria, they generally consist of an alternation between recitative and florid aria (though in a letter to Telemann he stated that in arias "one must make no unnatural difficulties without considerable cause"). Later pupils of his included Nichelmann and Kirnberger. In addition to operas, he produced sacred and secular vocal music, concertos, trio sonatas, and other chamber pieces. Apart from a Te Deum written to commemorate Frederick's victory at the Battle of Prague in 1756, his best-known work (and acknowledged masterpiece) is the Passion oratorio *Der Tod Jesu* (1755, libretto by Rammler), performed repeatedly in Germany well into the 19th century and cited by Marpurg, Hiller, and Koch as both a popular and worthy composition.

Graun, Johann Gottlieb (b. Wahrenbrück, ca. 1702–3; d. Berlin, 27 Oct. 1771). Violinist and composer. Student of Pisendel; like his brother Carl Heinrich, he sang at the Kreuzschule, enrolled in Leipzig Univ., and traveled to Prague in 1723, where he studied with Tartini. Became *Konzertmeister* in Meresburg around 1726; J. S. Bach sent his eldest son to him as a pupil. Performed at court at Berlin in 1728; served Prince von Waldek at Arolsen before joining the orchestra of Crown Prince Frederick of Prussia in Ruppin in 1732, moving with it to Rheinsburg in 1736 and finally to Berlin in 1740 when Frederick became king. He led the violins in the opera orchestra and was also a chamber musician at court, remaining at Berlin until his death. His works include a great many sinfonias, overtures, concertos, and trio sonatas, very few of them printed, along with sacred and secular concerted music.

Graupner, (Johann) Christoph (b. Kirchberg, Saxony, 13 Jan. 1683; d. Darmstadt, 10 May 1760). Composer. First teachers were Mylius and the organist Küster, whom Graupner followed to Reichenbach in 1694. He entered the Leipzig Thomasschule in 1696, where Heinichen was a fellow student; studied under Schelle and Kuhnau and befriended Telemann and his future colleague Gottfried Grünewald during his 9 years in the city. Leaving Leipzig in 1706, he went to Hamburg, replacing Schieferdecker at the harpsichord of the Oper am Gänsemarkt in June 1707; he composed his first 5 operas there, perhaps also collaborating with Keiser on 3 others. In 1709 he became Vice-Kapellmeister at the court of Ernst Ludwig, Landgrave of Hessen-Darmstadt, succeeding Briegel as Kapellmeister in 1712; Grünewald replaced him as Vice-Kapellmeister, and J. F. Fasch came to study with him in the same year. He wrote many operas up to 1719, when he turned to sacred and instrumental composition. In 1722–23 he was chosen to succeed Kuhnau as *Thomaskantor* when Telemann declined the post; the Landgrave rejected his resignation, the vacant position went to J. S. Bach, and Graupner never again sought to leave Darmstadt. Though blind later in life, he produced immense amounts of music, including 1,418 sacred cantatas (many grouped in *Jahrgänge* in alternation with those of Grünewald; some ed. in *DDT* 51–52), 24 secular cantatas, 113 symphonies, some 50 concertos, 80 suites, 36 chamber sonatas, and keyboard music, in addition to his operas. He also copied out many works of other composers, a custom he first cultivated as Kuhnau's student; his scores were said by Mattheson to be "so neatly written that they compete favorably with one engraved in copper."

Bibl.: Friedrich Noack, *Christoph Graupner als Kirchenkomponist, DDT* 51–52, suppl. 1 (1926). Andrew D. McCredie, "Christoph Graupner as Opera Composer," *Miscellanea musicologica* 1 (1966): 74–116.

Graupner, (Johann Christian) Gottlieb (b. Verden, Lower Saxony, 6 Oct. 1767; d. Boston, 16 Apr. 1836). Oboist, conductor, and composer. His father, Johann Georg, was oboist in Saxon courts, and Johann Christian himself joined a regimental band in Hannover (as oboist) at an early age. Upon leaving the band in 1788 he went to London, where he possibly played in Salomon's orchestra assembled for Haydn's London visit of 1791–92. During the mid-1790s he went to North America, landing first at Prince Edward Island in Canada. By 1795 he was in Charleston, S.C., where he performed concerts and (in 1796) married an English-born singer, Catherine Hillier, who was later to be an important presence in the musical life of Boston. After settling in Boston around 1797, in 1801 Graupner co-founded the American Conservatorio, chiefly a music publishing venture. In 1810 he also founded the Boston Philharmonic Society, and five years later was a cofounder of what later became the Handel and Haydn Society. He published a widely used *Rudiments of the Art of Playing on the Piano-Forte* (Boston, 1806; 2nd ed., 1819), as well as instructional books for the clarinet and flute.

Gray, Wardell (b. Oklahoma City, 1921; d. Las Vegas, 25 May 1955). Jazz tenor saxophonist. He played with Earl Hines (1943–45). Jam sessions in Los Angeles with Dexter Gordon led to their recording "The Chase" (1947) and subsequently forming a group (intermittently until 1952). He also recorded with Charlie Parker's bop group (1947). In 1948 he joined Benny Goodman, Count Basie, and Tadd Dameron, with whom he recorded "Lady Bird" (1948). He rejoined Goodman (1948–49) and Basie (1950–51), then worked as a free-lance.

Grechaninov, Alexandr Tikhonovich (b. Moscow, 25 Oct. 1864; d. New York, 4 Jan. 1956). Composer. He studied piano from age 14, then attended the Moscow Conservatory (1881–90), where he studied with Kashkin (piano), Gubert, Larosh, Arensky (counterpoint and theory), Taneyev (form), and Safonov (piano). From 1890 to 1893 he studied with Rimsky-Korsakov at the St. Petersburg Conservatory. In 1894 his String Quartet op. 2 won a prize in a composition organized by Belyayev. The following year Rimsky-Korsakov conducted his First Symphony. During this time he worked as a piano teacher in St. Petersburg and Moscow. Between 1896 and 1901 he wrote an opera, *Dobrïnya Nikitich,* to his own libretto, and supplied incidental music in Moscow. He also arranged songs and wrote music for children. In 1906 he was appointed to teaching positions at the Gnesin Institute and the Moscow Conservatory. In 1910 he was granted a pension of 2,000 rubles for his liturgical music, which was banned after he began using instruments. Having lost his pension after the Revolution, he visited western Europe and soon settled in Paris (1925). In 1939 he moved to the U.S., settling in New York the following year. His compositions include works for the stage, orchestral music, incidental music, sacred choral music, songs, chamber music, and piano pieces.

Green [Greene], **Al** (b. Forrest City, Ark., 13 Apr. 1946). Soul singer and songwriter. He began performing in gospel groups with family members; from 1969 to 1977 he made successful recordings of soul, popular, and rhythm-and-blues songs, including "Let's Stay Together" (1971). In the late 1970s he entered the clergy and limited his performances and recordings to religious music.

Green, Ray (Burns) (b. Cavendish, Mo., 13 Sept. 1908). Composer and publisher. He studied with Bloch at the San Francisco Conservatory (1927–33) and Berkeley; studied composition and conducting with Milhaud and Monteux in Paris (1935–37). He returned to work on federally funded music projects in San Francisco (1938–41); was chief of music for the Veterans' Administration (1946–48); and secretary of the American Music Center in New York (1948–61). He was the first president of the National Association for Music Therapy (1950) and in 1951 founded American Music Editions. Wrote for orchestra (*Sunday Sing Symphony,* flute, clarinet, bassoon, orchestra, 1939–40), chamber ensembles, and piano; drew on shape-note hymnody and fuguing tunes (*Festival Fugues, An American Toccata,* 1934–35). Other works include choral music; songs; incidental music.

Greenberg, Noah (b. New York, 9 Apr. 1919; d. there, 9 Jan. 1966). Conductor and musicologist. After service as a seaman in the Merchant Marine, 1944–49, he conducted the choir at St. Luke's, Greenwich Village. In 1952 with Bernard Krainis he founded the Pro musica antiqua, named and inspired by Safford Cape's ensemble in Brussels; later renamed the New York Pro Musica. With the Pro Musica he researched, performed, and recorded Renaissance and medieval music, demonstrating to Americans the artistic and even commercial viability of these repertories. His realizations of *The Play of Daniel* (1958) and *The Play of Herod* (1963) were particularly influential; with them he toured Europe in 1960 and 1963; the USSR in 1964. The New York Pro Musica disbanded in 1973.

Greene, Maurice (b. London, 12 Aug. 1696; d. there, 1 Dec. 1755). Organist and composer. Sang under Jeremiah Clarke in the choir of St. Paul's; studied with Richard Brind, cathedral organist; received his first organ post in 1714 and succeeded Brind at St. Paul's in 1718. He climbed quickly to the top of England's musical hierarchy, becoming organist and composer of the Chapel Royal in 1727 and Master of the King's Musick in 1735. He was also active in various amateur and charitable societies. A project to compile an edition of music for England's churches remained unfinished at his death. His works include services, oratorios, and dozens of anthems, along with secular vocal music and keyboard works.

Greenfield, Elizabeth Taylor (b. Natchez, 1817? or 1819?; d. Philadelphia, 31 Mar. 1876). Singer. Born a slave; raised from age 1 by a wealthy Quaker, Mrs. Greenfield, in Philadelphia, where she became locally known as a soloist. Began concert career at Buffalo in 1851, causing a sensation because of her race and an extraordinary voice of wide range and powerful lower register, becoming known as the Black Swan; 1853–54, sang in England, including a command performance at Buckingham Palace; later taught in Philadelphia, continuing to sing occasionally in the U.S. and Canada into the 1860s.

Bibl.: A. LaBrew, *The Black Swan: Elizabeth T. Greenfield* (Detroit, 1969).

Greer, Sonny [William Alexander] (b. Long Branch, N.J., 13 Dec. ca. 1895; d. New York, 23 Mar. 1982). Jazz drummer. As a member of Duke Ellington's band (1920–51) he used a conventional drum set (as on "Ko-Ko," "Cotton Tail," and "Harlem Air Shaft," all recorded 1940), but from time to time adopted a full complement of orchestral percussion instruments (heard on recordings of "Ring Dem Bells," 1930, and the "Liberian Suite," 1947). He joined Johnny Hodges (1951) and Henry "Red" Allen (1952–53) and worked as a free-lance. In the 1970s he joined the trio of Brooks Kerr, a pianist devoted to Ellington's music.

Gregory the Great [Gregory I] (b. Rome, ca. 540; d. there, 12 Mar. 604). Pope. Rome's ambassador to Constantinople from 579; in Rome, adviser to the pope from 585 or 586, pope from 590; extended the influence of the Roman church; added elements from Byzantine practice to the Roman liturgy; probably either founded or reorganized the Schola cantorum. His predecessors began and immediate successors completed a reform of the entire liturgy. Gregory's part in this is unclear. Although tradition has maintained that he edited or even composed the "Gregorian" melodies, this notion first arose only in the 8th century. Evidence from his own time suggests that his interest in liturgy centered more on the texts than on the music.

Greiter, Matthias [Matthaeus] (b. Aichach, ca. 1495; d. Strasbourg, 20 Dec. 1550). Composer. From 1510 a university student in Freiburg; by 1520 Kantor at Strasbourg Minster, a post he kept after converting to Protestantism in 1524; from 1538 also taught music at a local Gymnasium; lost these posts in 1546 but soon regained that at the Gymnasium; in 1549 became Catholic again and in 1550 was reinstated as Kantor at the Minster; died of the plague within the year. His works include a handful of polyphonic Psalms and motets; about a dozen hymn tunes and liturgical melodies for early Protestant books; 15 Tenorlieder (most for 4 voices); and a short treatise on musical rudiments, *Elemantale musicum* (Strasbourg, 1544).

Grenon, Nicolas (b. ca. 1380; d. 1456). Composer. Spent various periods of time from no later than 1403 until 1427 at the cathedrals of Laon and Cambrai and in the Burgundian and papal chapels, usually as master of the choirboys. From 1427 until his death he was again at Cambrai. His extant works include 1 Mass movement, 4 panisorhythmic motets, and 5 secular songs with French texts (1 ballade, 3 rondeaux, and 1 virelay).

Grétry, André-Ernest-Modeste (b. Liège, 8 Feb. 1741; d. Montmorency, Paris, 24 Sept. 1813). Composer, chiefly of operas. His father, François-Pascal Grétry, was violinist at the Church of St. Denis in Liège, and young André was a chorister there from 1750; later he also became second violinist at the chapel. He studied harpsichord and harmony with the organist at St. Pierre in Liège. In 1761 he began formal music study at the Collège de Liège in Rome, where he had obtained a scholarship. There he began composing church music under the tutelage of G. B. Casali; in Rome he also developed further his interest in opera buffa. In 1765 his first stage works, a pair of intermezzi called *La vendemmiatrice,* were performed in Rome. The following year he taught music in Geneva and set some songs from a Favart libretto, *Isabelle et Gertrude.* Partly on the advice of Voltaire, whom the composer had met in Geneva, Grétry went to Paris in 1767 and began composing comic operas; the first, *Les mariages samnites* (1768), was a failure, but it was immediately followed by *Le huron* (Comédie italienne, 1768), the first in a series of highly popular theater works. His most prominent successes during the next decade were *Silvain* (1770), *L'amitié à l'épreuve* (1770), *Zémire et Azor* (1771), *Le magnifique* (1773), *Le jugement de Midas* (1778), and *Les événements imprévus* (1779).

Partly because of the resounding success of *Colinette à la cour* (1783), Grétry received a pension from the Opéra that year. In 1783 his *La caravane du Caire* became one of the composer's most durable successes. In 1780 Grétry had resumed his collaborations with Sedaine; they included the popular *Richard Coeur-de-lion* (1784), *Amphitryon* (1786), *Le comte d'Albert* (1786), and *Guillaume Tell* (1791). By the early 1790s Grétry's pension, which had grown considerably as a result of his fame, had been revoked as a result of the Revolution. Falling into financial difficulties, he published literary works, including *Mémoires, ou Essais sur la musique* (1789–1801), *De la vérité, ce que nous fûmes, ce que nous sommes . . .* (1801), and *Méthode simple pour apprendre à préluder* (1803). In his last years he was elected to the Institut de France and received the Légion d'honneur.

Grétry was one of the founders of the opéra comique on the French stage. In general he sided with the "Gluckists" in the dispute against the "Piccinnists" over operatic excesses; his own music shows great concern for careful declamation and spare texture. In all he composed some 70 works for the stage, 40 of them opéras comiques. Later titles included *La rosière républicaine* (1794), *Elisca, ou L'amour maternel* (1799), and *Le casque et les colombes* (1801).

Bibl.: *Collection complète des oeuvres* (Leipzig, 1884–1936). Felix van Hulst, *Grétry* (Liège, 1842). Ernest Closson, *André-Modest Grétry* (Turnhout and Brussels, 1920). Heinz Wichmann, *Grétry und das musikalische Theater in Frankreich* (Halle, 1929). Justin Sauvenier, *André Grétry* (Brussels, 1934). Suzanne Clercx, *Grétry, 1741–1813* (Brussels, 1944; R: New York, 1978). Georges de Froidcourt, ed., *La correspondance générale de Grétry* (Brussels, 1962). José Quitin, *Les maîtres de chant et la maîtrise de la collégiale Saint-Denis à Liège, au temps de Grétry* (Brussels, 1964). Robert DeRoy Jobe, "The Operas of André-Ernest-Modeste Grétry" (diss., Univ. of Michigan, 1965). Karin Pendel, "The Opéras Comiques of Grétry and Marmontel," *MQ* 62 (1976): 409–34.

Grieg, Edvard (Hagerup) (b. Bergen, 15 June 1843; d. there, 4 Sept. 1907). Composer. From a prosperous mercantile family of Scottish origin, he received piano lessons from his mother and early began to compose piano pieces. In October 1858 at Ole Bull's urging he entered the Leipzig Conservatory (piano under Plaidy and Moscheles; theory under Hauptmann; composition under Richter and Reinecke), where he later claimed to have learned nothing, blaming it for his difficulty in handling large forms. His talent was recognized by his teachers; he became a good pianist, playing from his four piano pieces op. 1 and his songs op. 2 in the graduation concert in spring 1862. His brother John, a cellist, also studied there but became a businessman. In 1860 a serious illness left him weak in the chest and his later health was always precarious.

He returned to Bergen in 1862, taking part in local music, but in spring 1863 settled in Copenhagen, the center of Scandinavian cultural life. On Gade's advice he composed a symphony, but later suppressed it (arranging two movements for piano duet as op. 14). In July 1864 he became engaged to his cousin Nina Hagerup, who, although not a highly trained singer, became a great interpreter of his songs, of which he wrote many during this engagement. They frequently shared concerts after their marriage in 1867.

In autumn 1864 he met the young Norwegian composer Rikard Nordraak, whose intense nationalism is thought to have influenced Grieg; in 1865 they were among the founders of Euterpe, a society to promote Scandinavian music. This year, highly productive for Grieg (Piano Sonata op. 7; First Violin Sonata op. 8), ended with Grieg and Nordraak leaving to spend the winter in Italy. Nordraak fell ill in Berlin, Grieg leaving him there to die (for which he has sometimes been blamed). In Italy he composed the 4-hand Fantasy op. 11 (revised and orchestrated, 1887, as the overture *In Autumn*).

In 1866 he settled in Christiana (now Oslo) as a private teacher; became conductor of the Harmonic Society, an amateur orchestra (replaced in 1871 by the Music Society, which he also conducted, along with Svendsen); 1867, completed the Second Violin Sonata op. 13 and helped found a Norwegian Academy of Music; 1868, became father of a daughter, who lived a year; on summer holiday in Denmark, composed the Piano Concerto op. 15, revised throughout his life; summer 1869, became acquainted with Lindeman's published collection of Norwegian folk tunes, 25 of which he arranged for piano as op. 17; he was to use such tunes frequently in the future. Having received a government grant, he spent the winter of 1870 in Rome, meeting Liszt, who encouraged him.

His growing stature as a composer is reflected by his collaboration in the 1870s with the great Norwegian writers Bjørnson and Ibsen; he set 4 Bjørnson lyrics as op. 21 (1870–72), other texts as cantatas op. 20 and 31, and the melodrama *Bergliot* op. 45; in 1872 composed incidental music for his *Sigurd Jorsalfar.* Bjørnson also seemed about to fulfill Grieg's dream of composing a Norwegian opera, but after 3 scenes of the libretto *Olav Trygvason* (1873) he failed to write more, partly because of Grieg's collaboration with Ibsen on *Peer Gynt* (1874–75; premiere, Christiana, 28 Feb. 1876). In 1876 Grieg composed 6 songs to poems by Ibsen as op. 26. The great popularity of the 2 suites from *Peer Gynt* opp. 46 and 55 greatly increased his international reputation.

In 1876 he attended the first complete *Ring* at Bayreuth, sending reports to a Bergen newspaper (also attended first Bayreuth *Parsifal,* 1883). He admired Wagner's music but was not an unqualified Wagnerian. Summer 1877–autumn 1878 was spent mostly in the mountainous Hardanger region, where he came closer to living folk music (as opposed to published collections) and where he composed the String Quartet op. 27, a conscious attempt to master large abstract forms (unsuccessful in the sense that he was to complete only 2 further such works, the Cello Sonata op. 36 and the Third Violin Sonata op. 45), his output continuing to consist mainly of songs and short piano pieces (especially the 10 collections of *Lyric Pieces,* 1867–1901); 1880–82, conductor of the Bergen Harmonic Society; thereafter freed from such posts by an annual subvention from his publisher and the earnings from usually annual concert tours; 1885, built Troldhaugen, his house near Bergen, where he spent summers (with frequent excursions to the rural and mountainous parts of Norway).

From the 1880s he was a celebrated international figure, especially popular in Scandinavia, Germany, Holland, and Britain; 1889, first concert in Paris, very well received; 1899, protested Dreyfus affair by canceling Paris concert, causing a furor, but returned in 1903, occasioning a well-known critique by Debussy. He died suddenly on the eve of an English tour. Important later works include *Old Norwegian Romance with Variations,* 2 pianos, op. 51 (1891); *Symphonic Dances,* orchestra, op. 64 (1896–97); *Slåtter* (arrangements of fiddle dances), piano, op. 72 (1903–5); his last composition was *Four Norwegian Psalms,* baritone and chorus, op. 74 (1906).

Bibl.: *Samlede verker* [Collected Works] (New York, 1977–). Dan Fog, *Grieg-Katalog* (Copenhagen, 1980). Percy Grainger, "Personal Recollections of Grieg," *MT* 48 (1907): 720. H. T. Finck, *Grieg and His Music* (New York, 1909; 2nd ed., New York, 1929). Julius Röntgen, *Grieg* (The Hague, 1930). Elsa von Zschinsky-Troxler, ed., *Edvard Grieg: Briefe an die Verleger der Edition Peters, 1866–1907* (Leipzig, 1932). David Monrad-Johansen, *Edvard Grieg* (Oslo, 1934); trans. Eng. (1938; 2nd ed., New York, 1945). Gerald Abraham, ed., *Grieg: A Symposium* (London, 1948). Dag Schjelderup-Ebbe, *Edvard Grieg, 1858–1867* (Oslo and London, 1964). John Horton, *Grieg* (London, 1974). Bjarne Kortsen, ed., *Grieg, the Writer* (Bergen, 1972–) [writing and letters, mostly in Eng. trans.]. Finn Benestad and Dag Schjelderup-Ebbe, *Edvard Grieg: The Man and the Artist* (Lincoln, Nebr., 1988).

Griffes, Charles T(omlinson) (b. Elmira, N.Y., 17 Sept. 1884; d. New York, 8 Apr. 1920). Composer and pianist. He studied piano with his elder sister and then with Mary Selena Broughton, who later financed his studies in Berlin (1903–7) with Philippe Rüfer and Engelbert Humperdinck. After leaving the conservatory in 1905, he taught piano and harmony privately and performed. He was director of music at the Hackley School (Tarrytown, N.Y.) from his return to the U.S. until his death; he spent most summers in New York composing and promoting his own music. His earlier style reflects his training in the German Romantic tradition of Brahms and Strauss. From about 1911, influenced by the music of Debussy and Ravel, he began to use whole tone-scales, augmented triads, parallel chords, shifting tonal centers, and irregular meters within pieces in free forms (e.g., *The Pleasure Dome of Kubla Khan,* piano, 1912). In his last years an interest in the East asserted itself (e.g., in the songs *Five Poems of Ancient China and Japan,* 1917); at the same time he was abandoning his impressionist approach in favor of absolute music in which he returned to traditional forms and wrote in a more dissonant harmonic language, sometimes employing polymeters and polytonality. The Piano Sonata of 1917–18 employs diminished and augmented triads that Griffes found appealing in Scriabin's piano works. His Three Preludes for Piano (1919) were miniatures; the incomplete *Salut au Monde,* a festival drama after Whitman (flute, clarinet, 2 horns, trumpet, 2 trombones, timpani, 2 harps, piano, 1919) employs a choral speech-song in which rhythm and inflection are carefully notated, while each voice is expected to seek its natural pitch.

Griffes was not a prolific composer, and several of his orchestral works were arrangements of piano pieces requested by conductors such as Stokowski in Philadelphia and Monteux, who conducted the Boston Symphony in the orchestral version of *The Pleasure Dome of Kubla Khan* (1919). He was most appreciated in his lifetime as a pianist-composer and successor to MacDowell. At the time of his death, however, he was regarded as a major composer and was poised to contribute to the avant-garde.

Works include a festival drama (incomplete) and 3 ballets; 2 tone poems and arrangements of piano works for orchestra; *Poem,* solo flute, orchestra (1919); *Ko mori uta, Noge no yama* (flute, oboe, clarinet, harp, 2 violins, cello, double bass, Chinese drum, ca. 1917) and 3 string quartets; piano music (*Three Tone Pictures* op. 5, 1910–12; *Roman Sketches for Piano* op. 7, 1915–16); an organ chorale; 4 choral works; songs to German, English, and French texts (*Three Poems of Fiona Macleod,* 1918).

Bibl.: Edward Maisel, *Charles T. Griffes: The Life of an American Composer* (New York, 1984). Donna K. Anderson, *The Works of Charles T. Griffes: A Descriptive Catalogue* (Ann Arbor, 1984). Id. *Charles T. Griffes: A Life in Music* (Washington, 1993).

Griffin, Johnny [John Arnold, III; Little Giant] (b. Chicago, 24 Apr. 1928). Jazz tenor saxophonist. He toured with Lionel Hampton's big band (1945–47), played hard bop with Art Blakey's Jazz Messengers (1957), and joined Thelonious Monk's quartet (1958). With Eddie "Lockjaw" Davis he led a quintet (1960–62) which recorded the album *Tough Tenors* (1960). Moving to Europe in 1963, he worked in combos with Kenny Clarke and Kenny Drew, and he was the principal soloist in the Clarke–Boland Big Band (1967–69). He began touring internationally in the 1970s and recorded a succession of fine albums, including *Return of the Griffin* (1978).

Grigny, Nicolas de (bapt. Rheims, 8 Sept. 1672; d. there, 30 Nov. 1703). Organist and composer. Served at St. Denis, Paris, 1693–95; returned to Rheims in 1696 and soon became cathedral organist, a post he kept until his death. His *Premier livre d'orgue* (Paris, 1699), copied out by J. S. Bach around 1710, contains music for liturgical use in the familiar pattern of *récits,* duos, trios, and dialogues of the French classical organ school and is marked by rich contrapuntal textures, a wide variety of tone colors, and extensive pedal work.

Editions: A. Pirro and A. Guilmant, eds., *Livre d'orgue . . . par N. de Grigny* (Paris, 1903; R: 1972). Norbert Dufourcq and Noelie Pierront, eds., *Premier livre d'orgue de Nicolas Grigny* (Paris, 1953).

Grillo, Frank Raul. See Machito.

Grisar, Albert (b. Antwerp, 26 Dec. 1808; d. Asnières, 15 June 1869). Composer. Studied music in Antwerp, then in Paris under Reicha; achieved success as opéra comique composer in Brussels (1833) and Paris (1836–40), especially in collaboration with Flotow (*L'eau merveilleuse,* 1839) and Louis Boieldieu (*L'opéra à la cour,* 1840); then several years in Italy, studying in Naples with Mercadante; resumed producing opéras comiques in Paris in 1848, achieving considerable popularity in the next few years (especially *Gille ravisseur,* 1848; *Les porcherons,* 1850; *Bonsoir, Monsieur Pantalon,* 1851; *Le carillonneur de Bruges,* 1852; *Le chien du jardinier,* 1853; *Les amours du diable,* 1853).

Bibl.: A. Pougin, *Albert Grisar* (Paris, 1870).

Grisi, Giulia (b. Milan, 22 May 1811; d. Berlin, 29 Nov. 1869). Soprano. After studying in Milan and Bologna, sang in Italian opera houses, 1828–32; 1832, debut at Théâtre-Italien, Paris, becoming a principal factor in the Golden Age of Italian opera there in the 1830s and 1840s (premieres include Elvira in *I puritani,* 1835, and Norina in *Don Pasquale,* 1843); also a fixture of London summer seasons at the King's Theatre (later Her Majesty's) (1834–46) and Covent Garden (1847–61). In 1839 began long liaison (being already married) and artistic partnership with the tenor Rubini, with whom she also visited St. Petersburg (1849), New York (1854, then somewhat past her prime), and Madrid (1859); retired 1861.

Grocheo, Johannes de. See Johannes de Grocheo.

Grofé, Ferde [Ferdinand Rudolph von] (b. New York, 27 Mar. 1892; d. Santa Monica, Calif., 3 Apr. 1972). Composer, arranger, and pianist. His mother was a cellist, and two uncles had long careers in the string section of the Los Angeles Philharmonic, in which Grofé played viola for a decade (1909–19). He played a variety of other instruments in commercial bands and arranged Gershwin's *Rhapsody in Blue* for the Paul Whiteman band, with which he was associated, 1917–33. In 1937 he conducted a concert of his own works at Carnegie Hall; taught composition and arranging at Juilliard (1939–42); won an Academy Award for his film score *Minstrel Man* (1944). Drawing from the traditions of European concert music and from jazz, he wrote more than 20 orchestral tone poems (*Grand Canyon Suite,* 1931); other works include 2 ballets, film scores, original pieces for jazz and brass band, piano and chamber music, and songs; some works employ unusual sound sources (cable car bells, typewriters, sirens) to achieve programmatic effects.

Grøndahl [née Backer], **Agathe (Ursula)** (b. Holmestrand, Norway, 1 Dec. 1847; d. Oslo, 4 June 1907). Composer and pianist. Studied the piano and composition in Christiana (now Oslo), then continued piano study at Kullak's school in Berlin (1865–67) and (1871–72) with von Bülow and Liszt; became a prominent concert pianist in Norway and toured Scandinavia, Germany, and Britain. As a composer she was best known for some 190 Norwegian art songs and her piano pieces and etudes; also Norwegian folk song arrangements for piano.

Bibl.: I. Hoegsbro Christensen, *Biography of the Late Agathe Backer-Grøndahl* (New York, 1913).

Grove, George (b. Clapham, now in London, 13 Aug. 1820; d. Sydenham, 28 May 1900). Editor and writer. Son of a fishmonger; became a civil engineer; 1852–73, secretary of the Crystal Palace, writing program notes for its concerts until near his death. A voluminous writer on many subjects for newspapers and periodicals (musical specialties: Beethoven, Schubert, Mendelssohn); 1868–83, editor of *Macmillan's Magazine;* 1873, began editing his *Dictionary of Music and Musicians* for Macmillan (1st ed., 1879–80); 1882, raised money to establish the Royal College of Music; 1882–94, its first director. Knighted in 1883.

Bibl.: Charles L. Graves, *The Life and Letters of Sir George Grove* (London, 1904; R: 1978). Percy Young, *George Grove, 1820–1900* (London, 1980).

Grové, Stefans (b. Bethlehem, Orange Free State, 23 July 1922). Composer. As a boy he studied piano with his mother and later with an uncle, David J. Roode. From 1945 he took instruction in composition with William Bell and studied piano with Cameron Taylor and Eric Chisholm at the South African College of Music in Cape Town. In 1951 his *Three Inventions for Piano* were performed in Salzburg at the ISCM Festival, and in 1953 he won a Fulbright Fellowship to study with Walter Piston at Harvard. During his American years he also was a pupil of Copland at Tanglewood (1954), received an M.M. from Bard College (1955), and became instructor of composition at the Peabody Conservatory (1957). In 1972 he assumed a lectureship at the South African College of Music and later also at the Univ. of Pretoria (1973). After breaking out of an essentially Debussian model, Grové began composing music with the linear clarity of Piston and the contrapuntalism of Hindemith. Among his orchestral works are *Elegy* (1948); *Symphonia concertante* (1956); Violin Concerto (1959); Symphony (1962); and *Partita* (1964). Ballet scores include *Die dieper Reg* (1950); *Alice in Wonderland* (1959); and *Warata* (1976). His chamber music includes a piano trio (1952); a sonata for flute and piano (1955); *Twelve Different Pieces for Piano in the Nature of an Experiment* (1971); *For a Winter Day,* bassoon, piano (1977); *Rendezvous,* piccolo and tuba (1978).

Groven, Eivind (b. Lårdal, Telemark, 8 Oct. 1901; d. Oslo, 8 Feb. 1977). Composer and musicologist. After completing his schooling in 1923, he attended the Oslo Conservatory for one term in 1925. From 1931 he was folk music consultant for Norwegian Radio, and from 1940 received a pension (as a composer) from the government. An ambitious collector of folk songs, he amassed a compilation of nearly 2,000 tunes, including a large number of pieces for the Norwegian Hardanger fiddle. His own compositions incorporate both the substance and the spirit of these folk tunes. Groven also experimented with microtonal instruments and helped develop an organ with 43 pitches in an octave. Works include 2 symphonies (no. 1, Innover viddene [Toward the Mountains], 1937, rev. 1951; no. 2, Midnattstimen [Midnight Hour], 1946); symphonic poems (*Renessanse,* 1935; *Historiske Syner* [Historical Visions], 1936; *Felltonar* [Mountain Tunes], 1938; *Bryllup i skogen* [Wedding in the Forest], 1939); a piano concerto (1950); *Faldafeykir* (1967); choral works (*Brudgommen* [Bridegroom], soloists, orchestra, 1928–33; *Naturens tempel,* 1945; *Margjit Hjukse,* chorus, Hardanger fiddle, 1963); solo vocal songs, many with orchestral accompaniment; chamber and instrumental music (*Solstemning* [Sun Mood], flute, piano, 1946); works for 1 or more Hardanger fiddles.

Groves, Charles (b. London, 10 Mar. 1915; d. there, 20 June 1992). Conductor. Entered the Choir School of St. Paul's Cathedral in 1923. Studied piano and organ at the Royal College of Music. Hired in 1938 as a chorusmaster for the BBC; promoted to conductor of the BBC Theatre Orchestra, 1942–43; the BBC Revue Orchestra, 1943–44; and the BBC Northern Symphony Orchestra, 1944–51. Conductor of the Bournemouth Symphony, 1951–61. Music director of the Welsh National Opera, 1961–63; of the Royal Liverpool Philharmonic, 1963–77. Associate conductor of the Royal Philharmonic Orchestra, 1967. Music director of the English National Opera, 1978–79. Knighted 1973.

Grovlez, Gabriel (Marie) (b. Lille, 4 Apr. 1879; d. Paris, 20 Oct. 1944). Composer, conductor, and pianist. He studied at the Paris Conservatory with Gédalge, Fauré, and others; was active as a performer and taught piano at the Schola cantorum (1899–1909); was rehearsal pianist and choirmaster at the Opéra-comique and then music director at the Théâtre des arts; he assumed musical direction of the Paris Opéra in 1914. In 1939 he became professor of chamber music at the Paris Conservatory. His style derives from that of his teacher Fauré. He wrote operas and ballets (*Le vrai arbre de Robinson,* New York, 1922); orchestral, chamber, and piano music; choral and solo vocal works. His writings include *De l'initiative à l'orchestration* (Paris, 1946).

Grua, Carlo Luigi Pietro (b. Florence, ca. 1665). Composer. A member of the Hofkapelle in Dresden from 1691; appointed Vice-Kapellmeister in 1693. Took the same post in the Hofkapelle at Düsseldorf in 1694, evidently remaining there until the court transferred in 1718 to Heidelberg, where his presence is recorded at a baptism in that year. A serenade given the same year at Heidelberg is probably his, as are operas staged at Venice in 1721–22; other works include operas performed at these courts in 1693 and 1697, chamber duets, and sacred music.

Grua, Carlo (Alisio) Pietro (b. Milan?, ca. 1695–1700; d. Mannheim, 11 Apr. 1773). Composer. Little is known of his early years. By 1734 he was serving as Kapellmeister at the Mannheim court, a position he maintained until his death. He is best known for 2 operas (both lost), *Meride,* composed in 1742 to honor the marriage of the future elector Carl Theodor, and *La clemenza di Tito,* first performed in 1748. He also composed 5 oratorios (*La conversione di Sant'Ignazio,* 1740; *Il figliuolo prodigo,* 1742) and numerous sacred works. His son Franz Paul Grua later became one of his successors as Kapellmeister.

Grua, Franz Paul [Paolo; Francesco da Paula] (b. Mannheim, 1 Feb. 1753; d. Munich, 5 July 1833). Composer and violinist. Son of Carlo (Alisio) Pietro Grua. After early composition studies with Ignaz Holzbauer (who was in Mannheim from 1753) and violin instruction with Iganz Fränzl, in 1776 he became deputy violinist to the concertmaster at the Mannheim Palatine court. In 1777 he studied with Padre Martini in Bologna and possibly also with Traetta. When the court moved to Munich in 1778 he was among the orchestra members to move there; the following year he was named Vice-Kapellmeister, and in 1784 Kapellmeister at Munich. He composed an opera (*Telemaco,* Munich, 1780), 31 known Masses, and many other sacred works.

Gruber, Franz Xaver (b. Unterweizburg, Austria, 25 Nov. 1787; d. Hallein, near Salzburg, 7 June 1863). Composer. Son of a weaver; became a village schoolmaster and church musician. On Christmas Eve 1818, while Kantor and organist at St. Nicholas's church, Oberndorf (1816–29), he composed the Christmas hymn "Stille Nacht" (Silent Night), which soon became a quasi–folk song. Also composed several Latin church works.

Gruber, H(einz) K(arl) (b. Vienna, 3 Jan. 1943). Composer and double bass player. He sang in the Vienna Boys Choir (1953–57) and studied at the Vienna Hochschule für Musik from 1963 (where his teachers included Jelinek and von Einem). From 1961 he was a double bass player in the Tonkünstler Orchestra (Vienna) and a member of the new music ensemble Die Reihe; in 1969 he joined the Austrian Radio Symphony. His works in the 1960s were serial and electronic, but his links to tonality were never entirely abandoned. His melodrama *Die Vertreibung aus dem Paradies* (Richard Bletschacher, 1966) employs techniques of collage and quotation and elements of cabaret and music theater; *Konjugationen* (tape, 1963) includes jazz elements. The Violin Concerto (1977) and the earlier Concerto for Orchestra (1960) are indebted to Stravinsky and Blacher.

In 1967 he co-founded the MOBart & tonART ensemble (with Zykan and Schwertsik), which for three years gave a series of "Salon Concerts" aimed at making contemporary music more accessible; often included were "verbal compositions," or scenes designed according to musical principles. The MOBart & tonART ensemble adopted an improvisatory style, and many of Gruber's compositions exist in several versions. *Revue* (1968) is a 6-movement work for chamber orchestra that surveys Gruber's range from serious to lighter music; the first (and most serious) movement was extracted and published separately as *Vergrösserung* (Augmentation 1970). His opera *Gomorra* (Vienna Festival, 1976) won the Austrian State Prize. Other works include *Frankenstein!!* (baritone and orchestra on a text by H. C. Artmann, 1977); *Phantom-Bilder* (10 players or small orchestra, 1977–78), a series of meditations on a theme of Bartók; *Rough Music* (concerto for percussion and orchestra, 1983); a cello concerto (1989); *Gloria: A Pigtale* (music theater, Munich, 1995).

Gruberová, Edita (b. Bratislava, 23 Dec. 1946). Soprano. Studied at the Prague Conservatory beginning in 1962 with Maria Medvecká; later in Vienna with Ruthilde Boesch. Debut as Rosina *(Barbiere)* in Bratislava, 1968. Engaged at the Vienna Staatsoper from 1972. Sang the Queen of the Night *(Zauberflöte)* in Vienna, 1970; at Glyndebourne, 1973; at Salzburg from 1974; at the Metropolitan Opera beginning 5 Jan. 1977. Her Zerbinetta *(Ariadne)* brought her particular acclaim; other roles include Gilda *(Rigoletto),* Violetta *(Traviata),* and bel canto roles by Rossini, Bellini, and Donizetti.

Gruenberg, Louis (b. near Brest-Litovsk, 3 Aug. 1884; d. Beverly Hills, 10 June 1964). Composer and pianist. He was raised in the U.S.; studied piano and composition in Berlin with Busoni and Friedrich E. Koch and made his debut as a pianist under Busoni with the Berlin Philharmonic (1912). Thereafter he toured as a pianist in the U.S. and Europe; taught at the Vienna Conservatory. By 1920, when he came permanently to the U.S., he had written operas, a piano concerto (1915), and the first of several symphonies; his tone poem *The Hill of Dreams* (1920) won the Fagler Prize after its performance under Damrosch in New York. He cofounded the League of Composers (1923); won various awards in the 1920s and 1930s (including the Elizabeth Sprague Coolidge Medal, 1930, for his string quartet *Four Diversions* and the RCA Victor Prize for the revised version of his First Symphony, premiered by Koussevitzky in Boston in 1934); won three Academy Awards for film scores (1940–42). His compositions reflect his training in Romantic and impressionist styles, but he also drew on jazz and Negro spirituals in an effort to write distinctively American music; the final aria of his opera *The Emperor Jones* (premiered at the Metropolitan Opera in 1931) is based on the spiritual "Standin' in the Need of Prayer." The Violin Concerto (premiered by Heifetz with the Philadelphia Orchestra, 1944) uses two other spirituals in its middle movement; the final movement employs jazz and an American folk song, "The Arkansas Traveler."

Works: 17 dramatic works including operas, operettas, musicals; 10 film scores (*All the King's Men,* 1949); an oratorio; 6 symphonies, symphonic poems, concertos (violin, cello, 2 for piano), the *Jazz-Suite* (1925), and other works for orchestra; chamber music for strings and piano; piano and choral music; vocal music with orchestra, ensemble, or piano (*The Daniel Jazz,* tenor, clarinet, trumpet, string quartet, 1924).

Grumiaux, Arthur (b. Villers-Perwin, Belgium, 21 Mar. 1921; d. Brussels, 16 Oct. 1986). Violinist. At the Charleroi Conservatory studied violin and piano with Fernand Quinet (first prizes in both); at the Brussels Conservatory studied violin with Alfred Dubois, fugue with Jean Absil (first prizes in both); in Paris studied with Georges Enescu. Won the Vieuxtemps and Prume prizes in 1939. War interrupted his career. In 1945 he performed for newly arrived Allied forces; thereafter he toured Europe and quickly gained an eminent position among violinists. Taught at the Brussels Conservatory from 1949. Met Clara Haskil at the Prades Festival in 1950; with her he frequently performed and later recorded the complete Beethoven violin sonatas. In 1967 he founded the Grumiaux Trio with Georges Janzer and Eve Czako. Made a baron by King Baudouin in 1973.

Grützmacher, Friedrich (Wilhelm Ludwig) (b. Dessau, 1 Mar. 1832; d. Dresden, 23 Feb. 1903). Cellist. Studied with Drechsler (cello) and Schneider (theory); from 1849, solo cellist in Leipzig Gewandhaus Orchestra and teacher at the conservatory; from 1860 Dresden court orchestra, solo cellist from 1864; toured frequently throughout Europe; also a prominent teacher; composed cello concertos, solo works, and etudes; compiled (and partly composed) the so-called Boccherini B♭ Cello Concerto. His brother Leopold (1835–1900) was also a prominent cellist, as was Leopold's son Friedrich (1866–1919).

Guadagni, Gaetano (b. Vicenza or Lodi, ca. 1725; d. Padua, Nov. 1792). Castrato. Sang at the Basilica del Santo in Padua and at the Teatro S. Moisè, Venice, in 1746; joined a *burletta* troupe in London in 1748; Handel later used him in *Messiah, Samson,* and *Theodora.* He later performed in operas throughout Europe, creating the title role in Gluck's *Orfeo* in 1762 and singing for Frederick the Great. Burney describes him as a "well-toned countertenor," adding that "as an actor he had no equal on any stage in Europe."

Guadagnini. Family of violin makers. Lorenzo (b. late 17th century; d. 1748) called himself a student of Antonio Stradivari; he may have been active at Cremona at some time, but several of his labels indicate he worked at Piacenza, and his son Giovanni Baptista (b. Piacenza, ca. 1711; d. 18 Sept. 1786) described himself as "Placentius." The elder maker's work more resembles that of Guarneri than that of Stradivari. Giovanni, whose violins are the best in the family, was active in many cities, including Piacenza (1740–49), Milan (1749–58), Parma (1759–71), and Turin (from 1771). His early instruments follow his father's example; he later embraced the technique of Antonio Stradivari, following models acquired by his Turin patron Count Cozio di Salabue, while these labels are inscribed both "Cremonensis" and "Alumnus A. Stradivari." Later members of the family worked into the 20th century.

Bibl.: Ernest N. Doring, *The Guadagnini Family of Violin Makers* (Chicago, 1949).

Guami, Francesco (b. Lucca, ca. 1544; d. there, 30 Jan. 1602). Composer and trombonist. Brother of Gioseffo Guami. Served as an instrumentalist in the Bavarian court chapel from no later than 1568 until 1580, then as chapel master in Baden-Baden, Venice, and finally Lucca. His extant compositions include a motet, a book of ricercars (bicinia), and many madrigals (most published in 3 numbered volumes) in a style typical of Venetian music of his time. A book of Masses is lost.

Guami, Gioseffo [Giuseppe] (b. Lucca, ca. 1540; d. there, 1611). Organist and composer. Brother of Francesco Guami. His varied career encompassed service at St. Mark's, Venice (twice, the second time as first organist, 1588–91), the Bavarian court chapel (organist, 1568–79), the court in Genoa (*maestro di cappella* by 1585), and Lucca (3 times, the last as organist at the cathedral from 1591). Extant works include many madrigals, including 4 complete books; a number of motets; a parody Mass; instrumental canzonas and 1 organ toccata. His pieces often make use of modern features such as chromatic subjects, *basso continuo* and *basso seguente, coro spezzato* effects, and ornamental *passaggi.*

Guarneri. Family of stringed instrument makers. The patriarch, Andrea (b. Cremona, ca. 1626; d. there, 7 Dec. 1698), was an apprentice of Nicola Amati in 1641–46, returning 1650–54; he married in 1652, moving to his father-in-law's house (later called Casa Guarneri) in 1654. His violins are often marked by a lack of symmetry, but many examples are highly prized; he also made violas and cellos. In his later years he often worked together with two of his sons, Pietro Giovanni "de Mantova" (b. Cremona, 18 Feb. 1655; d. Mantua, 26 Mar. 1720) and Giuseppe Giovanni Battista (b. Cremona, 25 Nov. 1666; d. there, ca. 1739–40). Pietro started in the trade around 1670; he married in 1677, and by 1683 had moved to Mantua, working as violin maker and court musician. He apparently made few instruments, one of which was played by Szigeti; a cello of his also survives. Giuseppe began as his father's assistant, eventually inheriting the house and business in 1698, with his work prominent there after about 1680. Recognized today as one of the great builders, in his life he labored in the shadow of Antonio Stradivari; in addition to violins, he produced many fine cellos. After about 1715 his own sons Pietro "da Venezia" (b. Cremona, 14 Apr. 1695; d. there, 7 Apr. 1762) and Bartolomeo Giuseppe "del Gesù" (b. Cremona, 21 Aug. 1698; d. there, 17 Oct. 1744) were active in the shop; his output all but ceased after 1720. Pietro left home in 1718, perhaps finding work in a shop in Venice; his first Venetian labels date from about 1730, with his production peaking in the next decade and declining after 1750. Giuseppe "del Gesù" (so named because of the cipher on his labels) ranks as one of the two greatest makers in history. He left his father's house in 1722 or 1723; after initial influence from both Stradivari and his father, his violins become distinct from either tradition and legendary for their full tone. Later examples show extraordinary, if uneven, woodworking as well. Paganini played one of his instruments; 20th-century devotees include Grumiaux, Heifetz, Stern, and Zuckerman.

Bibl.: William H., Arthur F., and Alfred E. Hill, *The Violin-Makers of the Guarneri Family* (London, 1931; R: 1965; New York, 1989).

Guarnieri, (Mozart) Camargo (b. Tietê, São Paulo, 1 Feb. 1907; d. São Paulo, 13 Jan. 1993). Composer. Studied with Baldi, Andrade, and de Sá Pereira; received a piano appointment at the São Paulo Conservatory in 1927; directed one of Brazil's first contemporary concerts in 1931; took over conducting duties for the newly established São Paulo Department of Culture in 1935. Studied with Koechlin and Ruhlmann in Paris in 1938, also meeting Boulanger and receiving hearings of his music. Returned to Brazil at the outset of the war; visited the U.S. in 1942, conducting his works in New York, Boston, Washington, and other cities, and in 1946 leading the Boston Symphony in his First Symphony. Later became permanent conductor of the São Paulo Symphony, also acting as director of the conservatory (from 1960) and as teacher at Santos Conservatory (from 1964). Brazilian nationalism is a common thread in his work, from the *Dança Brasileira* for piano (1928) onward.

Works: *Pedro Malazarte* (comic opera, 1932, premiered 1952); 3 symphonies (1944, 1944, 1952); 2 piano concertos (1931, 1946) and 2 for violin (1940, 1953); orchestral suites *Brasiliana, IV centenario,* and *Vila Rica* (1950, 1954, 1958); works for solo voice and orchestra; orchestral dances; 2 string quartets (1930, 1934), 6 violin sonatas (1930–65), *Homenajem a Villa-Lobos,* winds (1966), and other chamber music; piano music (*Ponteios,* 5 vols., 1931–59); songs.

Bibl.: *Composers of the Americas* 1 (Washington, D.C., 1955): 28–49 [includes works list].

Gubaidulina, Sofia Asgatovna (b. Chistopol, Tatar ASSR, 24 Oct. 1931). Composer. Studied piano and composition at the Kazan Conservatory, 1949–54; composition with Nikolai Peiko at the Moscow Conservatory, 1954–59; graduate work there with Vissarion Shebalin, 1959–63. In 1987 awarded the Prix de Monaco in recognition of her lifetime achievement. Along with other composers of the post-Stalin generation, she rejected the proscriptions of socialist realism, embracing the full panorama of contemporary musical discourse. Interested in the symbolic potential of musical instruments, religious imagery, and differing perceptions of musical time. Works include 2 symphonies (*Stimmen . . . verstummen . . .,* 1986; *Pro et Contra,* 1989); concertos for bassoon and low strings (1975), piano and chamber orchestra (*Introitus,* 1978), violin (*Offertorium,* 1980; rev. 1982, 1986); vocal-symphonic works (the cantata *Rubaiat,* 1969; *Hour of the Soul,* 1976; rev. 1988); 4 string quartets (1971, 1987, 1987, 1994) and other chamber music; music for percussion; vocal works; film music.

Bibl.: Enzo Restagno, ed. *Gubajdulina* (Turin, 1991).

Gudmundsen-Holmgreen, Pelle (b. Copenhagen, 21 Nov. 1932). Composer. After taking private composition instruction with Finn Høffding (1951), he studied with Svend Westergaard (theory), and further with Høffding at the Copenhagen Conservatory (1953–58). From 1959 he was an assistant at the Royal Theater in Copenhagen, and from 1967 to 1973 he taught composition at the Jutland Academy of Music in Århus. During the 1960s he followed the movement known as "Den ny Enkelhed" (The New Simplicity). His early music reflects the influence of Bartók; later he explored aleatory and total serialism. Orchestral music: *Chronos* (1962); *Mester Jakob* (1964); Symphony (1962–65); *Signals* (1966); *Kadence,* band (1969); *Tricolore IV* (1969). Vocal works: *Vandringen* (1956); *Je ne me tairai jamais. Jamais!,* 12 voices, chamber ensemble (1966); *Three Songs,* alto, chamber ensemble (1967). Instrumental music: 4 string quartets (1958–67); *Pictures at an Exposition,* piano (1968); *Plateau pour deux* (1970); *Recall,* chamber ensemble (1975).

Gueden, Hilde (b. Vienna, 15 Sept. 1917; d. Klosterneuburg, 17 Sept. 1988). Soprano. Studied voice with Wetzelberger at the Vienna Conservatory. Operetta debut in Robert Stolz's *Servus, Servus,* 1939; opera debut several months later at the Zurich Opera as Cherubino *(Nozze).* Sang with the Munich Opera, 1941–47, and again from 1967; with the Rome Opera, 1942–46; with the (West) Berlin Stadtische Oper from 1946; with the Vienna Staatsoper, 1947–73; with the New York Metropolitan Opera, 1951–60. Created Julia in Blacher's *Romeo und Julia* (1947); Anne Truelove in the U.S. premiere of Stravinsky's *The Rake's Progress,* 1953. Although in Vienna she sang Mozart, Bellini, and Verdi, abroad she was usually seen in German operas, especially those by Strauss. Greatly praised for her Zerbinetta *(Ariadne),* 1954; created Zdenka *(Arabella),* 1955; sang Aminta *(Die schweigsame Frau)* at Salzburg in 1959, Sophie *(Rosenkavelier)* at the opening of the new theater there in 1960; acclaimed as Daphne, 1964.

Guédron, Pierre (b. province of Beauce, Normandy, ca. 1570; d. Paris (?), 1619–20). Singer and composer. First mentioned as a member of the choir of Cardinal de Guise, Louis II of Lorraine, in 1585; moved to the royal chapel in 1588 and was made a secular court musician two years later, first as *maître des chanteurs,* then in 1601 upon the death of Le Jeune as *compositeur de la chambre du Roi.* He yielded these posts in 1613 to his son-in-law Antoine Boesset, becoming *intendant des musiques de la chambre;* he also was a singing teacher. His many publications of *airs de cour* (1602–20) show his importance in the genre; many of these airs were performed as part of court ballets. "Est-ce que Mars" (1613) circulated throughout Europe; Scheidt and Sweelinck composed variations on it. Some airs show traces of *musique mesurée,* while others are more freely declamatory and shaped to text rhythms.

Bibl.: Don L. Royster, "Pierre Guédron and the Air de cour, 1600–1620" (diss., Yale Univ., 1972).

Guerra Peixe, César (b. Retrópolis, Brazil, 18 Mar. 1914; d. Rio de Janeiro, 23 Nov. 1993). Composer. Studied violin first in his home city, then after moving to Rio de Janeiro in 1934 continued under Paulino d'Ambrosiano at the Escola nacional de musica. Around 1938 he received instruction in harmony and counterpoint with Newton Pádua, later enrolling at the Brazilian Conservatory and studying with H. J. Koellreutter. During this time he embraced twelve-tone composition, joining Koellreutter's Grupo de música viva in 1945; his turn toward a nationalist approach in about 1950 coincided with an awakened interest in folk music, on which he published several articles. He also appeared as conductor with several orchestras, and in 1963 became a member of the National Symphony. Most of his twelve-tone music consists of chamber or piano works; later compositions include many orchestral pieces as well.

Bibl.: *Composers of the Americas* 16 (Washington, D.C., 1970): 110–21 [includes works list].

Guerrero, Francisco (b. Seville, 4 Oct.? 1528; d. there, 8 Nov. 1599). Composer. Brother and pupil of Pedro Guerrero and, briefly, a pupil of Morales. During most of his life he was a musician at Seville Cathedral: a singer from 1542, associate *maestro de capilla* from 1551, and finally *maestro* from 1574. This work was punctuated by a short period as *maestro* at Jaén Cathedral (1546–49) and by trips to other Spanish cities, Portugal, Rome, Venice, and the Holy Land. He wrote 18 Masses, about 150 motets and other liturgical works, and a number of secular songs, many published as sacred *contrafacta.* Some of his sacred music remained popular for two centuries. Over 20 of his pieces were printed in his lifetime in intabulations for vihuela.

Bibl.: *Opera omnia, MME* 16, 19 (1949–57).

Guerrero, Pedro (b. Seville, ca. 1520). Composer. Brother and teacher of Francisco Guerrero; may have been a chorister at the cathedral in Seville; was a singer at S. Maria Maggiore in Rome around 1560. His known compositions include a half dozen motets and about 10 secular pieces with Spanish texts. The secular music survives only in intabulations for vihuela.

Guézec, Jean-Pierre (b. Dijon, 29 Aug. 1934; d. Paris, 10 Mar. 1971). Composer. He studied with Milhaud and Messiaen at the Paris Conservatory (1955–63); adopted an "aesthetic of precision" affecting form and notation of his compositions; many works are related to the visual arts (as in *Suite pour Mondrian,* orchestra, 1962). From 1969 he taught at the Paris Conservatory. Works include *Textures enchainées* (12 winds, harp, and 3 percussionists, 1967) and the series *Couleurs juxtaposées* (various chamber groups), in which texts consist of phonemes selected to treat vocal colors in a manner parallel to instrumental timbres.

Guglielmi, Pietro (Alessandro) (b. Massa, 9 Dec. 1728; d. Rome, 19 Nov. 1804). Composer, principally of operas. His father Jacopo (d. 1731?) was *maestro di cappella* for the Duke of Massa; Pietro studied music in Naples from around 1745, at the Conservatory S. Maria di Loreto. He also was a pupil of Durante and became *primo maestrino* around 1750. His first known opera buffa was *La solachianello 'mbroglione,* a Neapolitan dialect comedy first performed in 1757. In 1763 his first opera seria, *Tito Manlio,* was staged in Rome. After 1764 he traveled extensively to operatic centers in northern Italy; possibly he settled in Venice for a period. During the years 1767–72 he lived mostly in London and composed 8 operas for the Haymarket Theatre. After four years of travel (1772–76) he settled again in Naples, where during the next two decades he composed some 40 new stage works, in both serious and comic genres. In 1793 he was made *maestro di cappella* at St. Peter's, Rome; he remained there until his death, composing a large number of sacred works. He was one of the most significant operatic composers of his era; in all he composed more than 100 stage works. Among the most important are *Li rivali placati* (Venice, 1764); *Il ratto della sposa* (Venice, 1765); *La sposa fedele* (Venice, 1767?); *La contadina superba* (Rome, 1774); *La Quakera spirituosa* (Naples?, 1783?); *La virtuosa di Mergellina* (Naples, 1785); *L'inganno amoroso* (Naples, 1786); *La pastorella nobile* (Naples, 1788); *La bella pescatrice* (Naples, 1789); *La serva innamorata* (Naples, 1790); *La lanterna di Diogene* (Venice, 1793); *La morte di Cleopatra* (Naples, 1796).

Guglielmi, Pietro Carlo (b. Rome? or Naples?, ca. 1763; d. Naples, 21 Feb. 1817). Composer. The eldest son of Pietro Alessandro Guglielmi, he perhaps studied at the Loreto Conservatory from around 1782. His first stage work, *Demetrio,* was performed in 1794 in Madrid. After operatic successes in Lisbon and Florence he settled in Naples, where he built a reputation as an opera composer, with productions also taking place in Venice, Rome, Milan, and London. In 1814 he assumed the post of *maestro di cappella* for Beatrice, the Duchess of Massa and Carrara; he composed operas there until his death. Works include *Dorval e Virginia* (Lisbon, 1795); *I raggiri amorosi* (Lisbon, 1799); *Due nozze e un sol marito* (Florence, 1800); *La distruzione di Gerusalemme* (*dramma sacro,* Naples, 1803); *La serva bizzarra* (Naples, 1803); *L'equivoco degli sposi* (Naples, 1805); *La scelta dello sposo* (Venice, 1805); *Le nozze in campagna* (Naples, 1811).

Gui, Vittorio (b. Rome, 14 Sept. 1885; d. Florence, 17 Oct. 1975). Composer and conductor. His conducting career began in 1907 when he substituted on short notice to conduct *La gioconda;* in Florence he founded the Orchestra Stabile (1928) and organized the Maggio musicale festival, where he conducted operas. In addition to opera, he often conducted the music of Brahms in Italy; his later career took him to Berlin, Vienna, Japan, England, and Scotland. He wrote 2 operas, the symphonic poem *Giuletta e Romeo* (with voices, 1902), cantatas, and songs; made arrangements of operas by Mozart, Gluck, and Carissimi; translated several librettos into Italian (including Purcell's *Dido and Aeneas,* Handel's *Acis and Galatea*); wrote many articles, collected in *Battute d'aspetto* (1944).

Guido of Arezzo [Guido d'Arezzo, Guido Aretinus] (b. ca. 991–92; d. after 1033). Theorist. He is best known for the invention of staff notation and the codification of a method of sight-singing using solmization syllables. The notation is explained in *Aliae regulae* (*GS* 2:34–42) and *Regulae rhythmicae* (*GS*

2:25–34), both prefaces or guides to a lost antiphoner compiled at the Benedictine abbey of Pomposa, near Ferrara, his residence until about 1025. *Epistola de ignoto cantu* (*GS* 2:43–50; trans. *SR*, pp. 121–25), a letter written shortly after visiting Pope John XIX in about 1028, discusses the sight-reading method. The *Micrologus* (*GS* 2:2–24; ed. *CSM* 4 [1955]; trans. *YTS* 3 [1978]: 49–83), a comprehensive work widely known and used throughout the Middle Ages, was written between 1026 and 1033, while he lived in Arezzo under the protection of Theodaldus, bishop of the city. None of the extant works mentions the "Guidonian" hand or the hard, soft, and natural hexachords.

Guillaume de Machaut. See Machaut, Guillaume de.

Guillaume li Vinier (b. Arras, ca. 1190; d. 1245). Trouvère. A relatively prolific and, to judge from the number of poems dedicated to him, well-regarded writer of the Arras circle. Twenty-six songs by him alone survive, as do 8 *jeux-partis,* written in conjunction with individuals such as Gille li Vinier (his brother), Adam de Givenci, and Andrieu Contredit. His works vary widely in genre, poetic form, and musical construction.

Guillelmus Monachus (fl. late 15th cent.). Theorist. His *De preceptis artis musicae* (ed. *CSM* 11 [1965]), a compilation touching on many matters, includes rules for improvised counterpoint, particularly several sorts of gymel and of fauxbourdon. He clearly considered English styles to be foreign and novel to his readers but styles resembling Continental fauxbourdon and Italian *falsobordone* to be familiar.

Guillemain, Louis-Gabriel (b. 15 Nov. 1705; d. Chaville, near Paris, 1 Oct. 1770). Violinist and composer. Studied violin in Italy with Giovanni Battista Somis. Named first violinist of the Dijon Academy of Music ca. 1730; became *musicien ordinaire du Roy* (Louis XV) in 1737. He often performed as a soloist, but never at the Concert spirituel, though his own music was played there. His output is wholly instrumental, with 18 publications encompassing concertos, trio symphonies, quartets, trio sonatas, and violin solos and duets both unaccompanied and with keyboard; he also composed music for the ballet-pantomime *L'opérateur chinois* (Paris, 1748).

Guillou, Jean (b. Angers, 18 Apr. 1930). Organist and composer. He studied with Dupré, Duruflé, and Messiaen at the Paris Conservatory from 1945; taught organ in Lisbon and toured as an organist in the U.S., Canada, and Europe; in 1963 he became organist at St. Eustache in Paris. Some works are transcriptions of the organ improvisations for which he is noted (*Sagas* 2, 4, and 6); in general his style is atonal and makes frequent use of ostinatos and conflicting rhythms. He has written several pieces for orchestra, including organ concertos (no. 3, 1971); *Colloques 1–4* (for various ensembles) and other chamber music; an oratorio and other vocal works with organ or orchestra; many original organ works and transcriptions of Bach's *Musical Offering* and *Goldberg Variations* and of Prokofiev's *Toccata.*

Guilmant, (Félix) Alexandre (b. Boulogne-sur-mer, 12 Mar. 1837; d. Meudon, 29 Mar. 1911). Organist and composer. From a family of organists and organ builders; his first lessons were from his father, whom he succeeded in 1857 as organist at St. Nicolas, Boulogne, but he was largely self-taught. He became a well-known soloist in Paris, also touring Europe and North America (1893–97); 1863, organist at St. Sulpice; 1868, at Notre Dame; 1870–1901, at Ste. Trinité, Paris. In 1894 he was one of the founders of the Schola cantorum and became an organ teacher there; in 1896 he succeeded Widor as professor at the Paris Conservatory (pupils included Bonnet, Nadia Boulanger, Jacob, Dupré). He composed much organ music, including 8 sonatas (1874–1909); Symphony for Organ and Orchestra op. 42; numerous collections of pieces; also edited much older organ music.

Guiraud, Ernest (b. New Orleans, 23 June 1837; d. Paris, 6 May 1892). Composer and teacher. Son of a French musician and Prix de Rome winner who emigrated to New Orleans. At 12 he went to Paris, where he studied at the Paris Conservatory under Marmontel and Halévy, winning first prize in piano (1858) and Prix de Rome (1859). He was a fellow student and close friend of Bizet, and is best remembered for composing the recitatives still usually performed with *Carmen* (1875); also arranged the second *L'arlésienne* suite and orchestrated Offenbach's *Contes d'Hoffmann.* From 1876 he was professor of harmony at the Paris Conservatory; from 1880, professor of composition (pupils included Debussy, Dukas). He composed 6 opéras comiques (performed Paris, 1864–82); the grand opera *Frédégonde,* completed by Dukas (1895); orchestral pieces, piano pieces, songs.

Gulda, Friedrich (b. Vienna, 16 May 1930). Pianist and composer. At the Vienna Hochschule für Musik studied piano with Bruno Seidlhofer, theory and composition with Josef Marx. Debut in 1944. Won first prize in the Geneva International Piano Competition in 1946. First tour of Europe, 1947–48; of the U.S., 1950. In the 1940s and 1950s he played several cycles of Beethoven's 32 sonatas. From 1956 he also played jazz, including engagements at Birdland in New York and the Newport Jazz Festival; performed on baritone saxophone and flute as well as keyboards. Founded the Eurojazz Orchestra in 1960. In 1968 he opened a school for improvisation, the International Musikforum at Ossiach. Compositions include *Galgenliedern,* baritone and 2 pianos (1954); *The Veiled Old Land,* jazz orchestra (1964); *Blues Fantasy,* piano (1971); *Concerto for Myself,* piano and orchestra (1986). Published *Worte zur Musik* (1971).

Gumpelzhaimer [Gumpeltzhaimer], **Adam** (b. Trostberg, 1559; d. Augsburg, 3 Nov. 1625). Composer. His education included musical instruction from Jodocus Entzenmüller. From 1581 his life was devoted to the direction of extensive and well-regarded musical activity at the (Lutheran) school and church of St. Anna in Augsburg. His *Compendium musicae,* a treatise on musical rudiments that includes well over 100 compositions, many his own, was widely known in Germany for nearly a century and was repeatedly re-edited. He also wrote numerous books of polyphonic German sacred songs (mostly strophic and chordal) and some Latin motets, particularly 2 books called *Sacri concentus* (1601 and 1614) for double choir.

Gungl, Joseph [József] (b. Zsámbék, Hungary, 1 Dec. 1810; d. Weimar, 1 Feb. 1889). Composer. A bandsman (oboist) and then bandmaster in the Austrian army; later toured Europe and (in 1849) the U.S. with bands or dance orchestras; from 1836 published much once-popular march and dance music.

Guridi (Bidaloa), Jesús (b. Vitoria, Alava, 25 Sept. 1886; d. Madrid, 7 Apr. 1961). Composer and organist. A descendant of many musicians, he was a child prodigy. Received early training in Bilbao; attended the Schola cantorum, Paris, from 1904, studying under Decaux and d'Indy, among others; also received instruction from Jongen at Liège in 1906 and from Neitzel at Cologne in 1908. Served long terms as organist at Santos Juanes and the Basílica del Señor Santiago in Bilbao, also directing the Bilbao Choral Society, 1911–26. Most of his choral music, often based on Basque song, dates from this period. He later had much success with operas such as *Mirentxu* (1915) and *Amaya* (1920) and the zarzuela *El caserío* (1926), as well as with his symphonic *Una aventura de Don Quixote.* Academic appointments included those in composition and organ at the Biscay Conservatory (1922) and the Madrid Conservatory (1944).

Gurlitt, Manfred (b. Berlin, 6 Sept. 1890; d. Tokyo, 29 Apr. 1973). Composer and conductor. He studied in Berlin with Humperdinck and began his career in opera as a rehearsal pianist and coach in 1908; was assistant conductor at Bayreuth (1911) and director of the opera in Bremen (1914), where he founded the Contemporary Music Society. In 1924 he became music director of the State Opera in Berlin and taught at the Hochschule für Musik. Just before the war he moved to Japan to teach and conduct opera; he formed his own opera company there in 1953. He himself composed several operas as well as works for orchestra (*Wozzeck,* 1928; *3 politische Reden,* male chorus, 1944; concertos for piano, violin, and cello); chamber and piano music; and songs.

Gurney, Ivor (Bertie) (b. Gloucester, 28 Aug. 1890; d. Dartford, near London, 26 Dec. 1937). Composer. His earliest training in music was as a choirboy (from 1900) at Gloucester Cathedral. Subsequently he studied on scholarship at the Royal College of Music; he studied composition with Stanford. His war service (from 1915) left him with physical and emotional injuries from which he never fully recovered; after the war he returned to the Royal College, however, to study with Vaughan Williams. Between 1917 and 1922 he composed a number of excellent solo songs, many of which were settings of his own texts. Among the more than 200 songs are *Five Elizabethan Songs* (1913), *Ludlow and Teme* (7 songs, 1919), 4 volumes of 10 songs each (1917–22), and *Six Songs* (1918–25). He also composed instrumental works (*The Apple Orchard,* violin and piano, 1919; *Five Preludes,* piano, 1919–20; *Western Watercolor,* piano, 1920).

Bibl.: Michael Hurd, *The Ordeal of Ivor Gurney* (Oxford, 1978).

Gutchë, Gene [Gutsche, Romeo Maximilian Eugene Ludwig] (b. Berlin, 3 July 1907). Composer. He was educated in business and economics in Europe, but had also studied piano with Busoni; came to the U.S. in 1925 and supported himself alternately in business and in musical activities. He returned to formal study of music in the 1950s, eventually focusing on composition with Philip Greeley Clapp (M.A., Univ. of Minnesota, 1950; Ph.D., Univ. of Iowa, 1953); from 1953 lived in Minneapolis, devoting himself to composition, publishing some of his own works; also wrote 2 books, *Music of the People* (1968) and *Come Prima* (1970). He composed in a neo-Romantic and often programmatic style, but explored polytonality, microtones, and serialism (*Holofernes,* orchestral overture, 1958). Works include 6 symphonies, *Genghis Khan* (winds and double basses, 1964), *Akhenaten (Eidetic Images)* (1978), and other orchestral music; 4 string quartets and other chamber music; a few choral works. Early compositions were withdrawn.

Guthrie, Woody [Woodrow Wilson] (b. Okemah, Okla., 14 July 1912; d. New York, 3 Oct. 1967). Folksinger and songwriter. Traveled extensively in the West, South, and Southwest during the Great Depression; many of his over 1,000 folk songs concern his experiences in that period. In 1937 he worked in radio in Los Angeles; in 1940 he moved to the East Coast, where he recorded much of his repertory with ethnomusicologist Alan Lomax at the Library of Congress and met and performed with folksingers Pete Seeger, Leadbelly, and Cisco Houston. Many of his songs have entered American oral tradition, including "This Land Is Your Land," "So Long, It's Been Good To Know Ya'," "Hard Travelin'," and "Union Maid." His son Arlo Guthrie (b. Brooklyn, 10 July 1947) is a folk and rock singer, songwriter, and guitarist.

Gutiérrez, Horacio (Tomás) (b. Havana, 28 Aug. 1948). Pianist. Soloist with the Havana Symphony at age 11. Moved to Los Angeles in 1962; naturalized in 1967. Twice soloist in Los Angeles Philharmonic Youth Concerts; chosen by Bernstein for a New York Young People's Concert. Won first prize in the San Francisco Symphony auditions, 1967. Studied with

Sergei Tarnovsky and Adele Marcus at Juilliard; diploma, 1970. Won the silver medal in the 1970 Tchaikovsky Competition in Moscow. Toured Russia in 1971. Won the Avery Fisher Award in 1982.

Gutiérrez (y) Espinosa, Felipe (b. San Juan, Puerto Rico, 26 May 1825; d. there, 27 Nov. 1899). Composer. Largely self-taught; became an army musician; 1858–98, choirmaster of San Juan Cathedral, also conducting at Teatro Tapia; composed several operas, of which only *Macías* survives. He ran a free music school, for which he published a textbook. Also composed much sacred music, an oratorio, 2 Passions.

Gutiérrez Heras, Joaquín (b. Tehuacán, Mexico, 28 Sept. 1927). Composer. After initial architectural study at the Univ. of Mexico, attended the National Conservatory (1950–52) as a composition pupil of Blas Galindo and Rodolfo Halffter. Studied at the Paris Conservatory (1952–53) with Messiaen, among others, and also at Juilliard (1960–61) with Bergsma and Persichetti. A cofounder in 1957 of the ensemble Nueva música de México, he also served as director of Radio Universidad de México (1966–70), delivering radio lectures. Works include *Divertimento* (piano and orchestra, 1949), *Chamber Cantata* (soprano, 2 flutes, harp, and strings, 1961), the symphonic scene *Los cazadores* (1962), and *Night and Day Music* (wind ensemble, 1973), as well as theater and film scores.

Guy, Barry (John) (b. London, 22 Apr. 1947). Composer and double bass player. He studied jazz style with Graham Collier (from 1964) and composition and counterpoint with Stanley Glasser (from 1965). At the Guildhall School in London his composition instructors were Buxton Orr and Patric Standford, and his bass instructor was J. Edward Merrett. In 1971 he formed the London Jazz Composers' Orchestra, a group for which he has composed several of his best works, including a series of *Statements* for jazz orchestra (1971–75). His music amalgamates western European instrumental timbres with jazz rhythms, tonal schemes, and structures. Works include *Incontri* (cello and orchestra, 1968–69); *Anna* (double bass and orchestra, 1974); *Ode* (jazz orchestra, 1971); *Patterns and Time Passing* (1973); string quartets and other chamber works (*Games [for All Ages],* 1973; *Play,* 1976); *After the Rain* (orchestra, 1992).

Gyrowetz, Adalbert [Jírovec, Vojtěch Matyáš] (b. česke Budějovice, 20 Feb. 1763; d. Vienna, 19 Mar. 1850). Composer. He received his earliest music lessons from his father, a local music master. Later he studied philosophy and law in Prague and, breaking off his studies because of illness, became a violinist at the court of Count Franz von Fünfkirchen. One of the 6 symphonies that he composed for the count was performed in 1785 by Mozart in his subscription concerts in Vienna. He then traveled to Venice, where he became secretary and music teacher for the family of Prince Ruspoli. Subsequently he traveled to Florence, Rome, Bologna, Naples, Paris, and London; in London he had frequent contacts with Haydn during Haydn's visit to the city in 1791–92. After a short period in the employ of Count von Sickingen (in Munich and Schwetzingen), in 1804 he received a post in Vienna as imperial composer and Kapellmeister. There he composed operas and ballets for nearly three decades; after his retirement in 1831 he lived his last years in penury. He wrote an autobiography. Works include stage music (*Das zugemauerte Fenster,* Vienna, 1810; *Federica ed Adolfo,* Vienna, 1812; *Robert,* 1815; *Il finto Stanislao,* 1818; *Das Ständchen,* 1823; *Der Geburtstag,* 1828; *Hans Sachs im vorgerückten Alter,* 1834); over 40 symphonies and other orchestral works; much chamber music; secular songs; 11 Masses, 2 vespers, and other sacred vocal works.

H

Haas, Joseph (b. Maihingen, 19 Mar. 1879; d. Munich, 30 Mar. 1960). Composer. He was a pupil of Reger (from 1904) and composition teacher at the conservatory in Stuttgart (from 1911); named professor there in 1916. He cofounded the Donaueschingen Festival in 1921 and directed the Musikhochschule in Munich (1945–50). His compositions are in the late Romantic idiom of Reger; he was particularly associated with the use of folk music in a series of "folk oratorios." His compositions include 3 operas, 6 Mass settings, a Te Deum (soloists, choir, and orchestra, 1945), and 6 folk oratorios (*Die Seligen* op. 106); *Variationen Suite über ein altes Rokokothema* (1924) and other works for orchestra; chamber, piano, and organ music (including a set of organ preludes); sacred and secular choral music and songs.

Hába, Alois (b. Vizovice, Moravia, 21 June 1893; d. Prague, 18 Nov. 1973). Composer. Brother of Karel Hába. He studied music education in Kroměříž (1908–12), then composition with Novák at the Prague Conservatory (1914–15) and with Schreker in Vienna and Berlin (1918–22). Returning to Prague in 1923, he taught at the National Conservatory (1924–51). His lifetime interest in tempered microtonal music manifested itself in 1917 in a suite for strings. During the 1920s he designed and had built a piano and clarinet for playing tempered microtonal music; later he had a trumpet, a guitar, and two harmoniums adapted for the same purpose. Although he wrote for all media, the focus of his compositional output was on chamber music. He wrote 3 operas (2 to his own librettos), but only one was mounted (in Munich, 1931) before the German annexation of Czechoslovakia, during which his music was banned. After the war he founded and led the Smetana Theater Opera (1945–49). In 1951 his Department of Microtonal Music at the conservatory was dissolved by Communist authorities. Although Hába's subsequent music tended to become simpler, this was probably the result of his personal evolution rather than politics; he never abandoned composition with microtonal scales. Hába's fame as the foremost European advocate of tempered microtonal music sometimes obscured the fact that he had never stopped writing music that uses the tempered chromatic scale. His works in all scales have their roots in folk music, but abandon themes per se in favor of other means of articulating form (rhythms, textures, harmonic complexes, timbres).

Works include the operas *Matka* [The Mother] op. 35 (1927–29, 1/4 tone), *Nová země* [The New Land] op. 47 (1934–36), *Přijď království Tvé* [Thy Kingdom Come] op. 50 (1932–42, 1/6 tone); *Symfonická fantazie* op. 8 (piano, orchestra, 1921); Cesta života [The Way of Life] op. 46 (orchestra, 1933); Violin Concerto op. 83 (1955); Viola Concerto op. 86 (1957); 4 *Fantazie*s (nonets, 1931–63); 16 string quartets (1920–67); Sonata op. 1 (violin, piano, 1915); Suite op. 24 (1/4-tone clarinet, 1/4-tone piano, 1925); Six Pieces op. 37 (1/6-tone harmonium, 1928); Sonata op. 54 (guitar, 1943); Suite op. 56 (1/4-tone trumpet, trombone, 1944); Suite op. 63 (1/4-tone guitar, 1946); Suite op. 72 (4 1/4-tone trombones, 1950); Suite op. 91 (cimbalom, 1960); Suite op. 103 (violin, piano, 1972); 11 piano sonatas (1918–58).

Bibl.: Alois Hába, *Neue Harmonielehre des diatonischen, chromatischen, Viertel, Drittel, Sechstel-, und Zwölftel-Tonsystems,* 2 vols. (Leipzig, 1927). Geoffrey Whitman, "Alois Hába: Seminal Works of Quarter-Tone Music," *Tempo* 80 (1967): 11. Jiří Vizloužil, "Hába's Idea of Quarter-Tone Music," *Hudebni věda* 5 (1968): 466. Alois Hába, *Mein Weg zur Viertel- und Sechstel-Tonmusik* (Düsseldorf, 1971).

Hába, Karel (b. Vizovice, Moravia, 21 May 1898; d. Prague, 21 Nov. 1972). Composer and violinist. Brother of Alois Hába. Studied violin with Karel Hoffmann and Jan Mařák, composition with Novák at the Prague Conservatory. Joined his brother's classes in tempered microtonal music, 1925–27. During that time he visited Paris, Frankfurt, and other cities as a quarter-tone violin virtuoso and also wrote one quarter-tone work each year (but none thereafter). He played violin with the Prague Radio Orchestra (1929–36), then was made head of the radio music education department. From 1951 until his retirement he lectured on music education at the Prague Institute of Education. His music was performed at ISCM Festivals of 1928, 1929, 1934. He composed 4 operas, including *Janošík* (1929–32) and *Kalibův Zločin* (1957–61); concertos for violin (1927) and cello (1935); 2 symphonies (1948, 1954); Suite for Orchestra (1963); 4 string quartets (1922–69); Septet (1929); Piano Sonata (1942).

Habeneck, François Antoine (b. Mézières, 22 Jan. 1781; d. Paris, 8 Feb. 1849). Conductor. Son of a military bandsman; two brothers became orchestral violinists in Paris. Largely self-taught until he entered the Paris Conservatory, ca. 1800, studying with Baillot; in 1804 won premier prix. From 1806 to 1815 he was conductor of the student orchestra at the Conservatory; 1818–21, conductor of the Concert spirituel at the Opéra; 1821–24, director of the Opéra; 1824–26, joint and then sole chief conductor there, conducting many significant premieres. In 1828 he organized the Société des Concerts du Conservatoire, conducting it until his death. He also taught violin at the Conservatory, as adjunct violin teacher, 1808–16, and professor, 1825–48. The most important French conductor of his day, he was influential in the introduction of Beethoven's orchestral music into France; he was much less sympathetic to newer music, including Berlioz's (although he conducted premieres of works such as the *Symphonie fantastique* and the Requiem).

Hackett, Bobby [Robert Leo] (b. Providence, 31 Jan. 1915; d. Chatham, Mass., 7 June 1976). Jazz cornetist. While working at Nick's in New York he performed tunes associated with Bix Beiderbecke at Benny Goodman's Carnegie Hall concert (1938) and began recording with Eddie Condon's groups (1938–62). He doubled on guitar (his first instrument as a professional) with Glenn Miller's big band (1940–41), recording the cornet solo on "String of Pearls" (1941). While working as a studio musician he accompanied Louis Armstrong at Town Hall, New York (1947), and Jackie Gleason on a series of romantic albums with string sections (early 1950s). He recorded the albums *Coast Concert* (1955) and *Jazz Ultimate* (1957) with Jack Teagarden and led an unusual octet (including alto horn, baritone saxophone, vibraphone, and tuba) at the Henry Hudson Hotel in New York (1956–58). He joined Goodman (1962–63) and with Vic Dickenson led a quintet (1968–70). Hackett was a consistently lyrical cornet soloist.

Haden, Charlie [Charles Edward] (b. Shenandoah, Iowa, 6 Aug. 1937). Jazz double bass player. As a member of Ornette Coleman's first quartet (1959–60) he defined the role of the free-jazz bassist: to combine supportive drones and walking lines with stimulating melodic improvisation, played pizzicato or arco, as on the album *Change of the Century* (1959). He worked with Archie Shepp (1966), Keith Jarrett (ca. 1967–76), and Coleman (intermittently from 1966, including the album *Soapsuds,* 1977). As a leader he recorded an album of revolutionary and freedom songs, *Liberation Music Orchestra* (1969). With Don Cherry, Dewey Redman, and Ed Blackwell he formed Old and New Dreams, devoted to Coleman's music (from 1976). He re-formed the Liberation Music Orchestra (from 1982).

Hadjidakis, Manos (b. Xanthi, Macedonia, 23 Oct. 1925; d. Athens, 15 June 1994). Composer. He was entirely self-taught in music; his leanings toward folk and popular idioms found early expression in his reworkings of the urban folk idiom *rebétiko* beginning in the early 1940s. After the war he was a central musical figure in Greece, and in a series of lectures in 1953 he encouraged interest in American composers such as Copland. He helped establish and encourage a Greek avant-garde through such activities as his "ATI-Hadjidakis" composition contest (founded in Athens in 1962) and the Athens Experimental Orchestra (which he founded in 1964). From 1967 to 1972 he lived in New York; upon his return to Athens he was made director general of the National State Opera (1974) and of the Athens State Orchestra (1976). His music incorporates elements as disparate as Greek folk music and Baroque styles. He won an Oscar in 1960 for the title song for the film *Never on Sunday.* Other works include music for the stage (ballets *Marsyas,* 1949, and *Erimia,* 1957; the "folk opera" *Rinaldos kai Armída,* 1962; a revue, *Odos Oneiron,* 1962); film and incidental music (*Kaesar kai Kleopatra,* after Shaw, 1962); many song cycles (*Mythology,* 1965–66; *The Return,* 1969; *The Legends of Our Time,* 1970; *Liturgica I,* 1971; *Amorgos,* 1972; *Athanassia,* 1976); instrumental music (*Rhythmology,* piano, 1969–71).

Hadley, Henry (Kimball) (b. Somerville, Mass., 20 Dec. 1871; d. New York, 6 Sept. 1937). Composer and conductor. His father taught him piano, violin, and conducting; studied harmony, counterpoint, and composition with Emery and Chadwick; studied in Vienna with Mandyczewski (1894–95) and in Munich with Ludwig Thuille (1905–7). The influence of Chadwick and of Richard Strauss (whom he met in London, 1905) was critical to his development as a composer. He succeeded Horatio Parker as a teacher at St. Paul's School (Garden City, N.Y., 1895–1902); conducted in the U.S., Europe, South America (1927), and Japan (1930); held a number of permanent conducting posts including Mainz Stadttheater (1907–9), the Seattle Symphony (1909–11), the San Francisco Symphony (founder-conductor, 1911–15), the New York Philharmonic (associate conductor, 1920–27), and the Manhattan Symphony (1929–32). He founded the National Association of American Composers and Conductors (1933) and the Berkshire Music Festival (1934). His works, composed in a late Romantic style, were popular during his lifetime. Compositions include 14 operas (*Cleopatra's Night,* Metropolitan Opera, 1920) and other dramatic works; at least 5 symphonies, the tone poem *Salome* (1905–6), *Scherzo diabolique* (1934), and other orchestral works; a piano quintet (1919) and other chamber music for strings; piano music; oratorios, cantatas, anthems, and other choral pieces; over 200 songs.

Hadley, Patrick (Arthur Sheldon) (b. Cambridge, 5 Mar. 1899; d. King's Lynn, Norfolk, 17 Dec. 1973). Composer. After his war service he studied at Cambridge and at the Royal College of Music (1922–25); at the latter he was a pupil of Vaughan Williams and was awarded the Sullivan Prize for composition. From 1925 to 1938 he taught at the Royal College. In 1938 he was awarded a Mus.D. and became lecturer in music at Cambridge; in 1946 he was made professor. His music, essentially tonal and lyrical, shows influences from Delius and from folk music. Choral works include *The Trees So High* (1931), *The Hills* (cantata,

1944), *Fen and Flood* (1954), and *A Cantata for Lent* (1962); he also composed vocal works (*Mariana,* mezzo-soprano, orchestra, 1937) and orchestral works (*One Morning in Spring,* 1942).

Haeffner, Johann Christian Friedrich (b. Oberschönau, Thuringia, 2 Mar. 1759; d. Uppsala, 28 May 1833). Composer and organist. In the town of Schmalkalden he studied organ and counterpoint with J. G. Vierling; by 1776 he was in Leipzig, where he was employed as a proofreader by Breitkopf and possibly studied at the Univ. of Leipzig. Around 1780 he traveled to Stockholm; he spent the rest of his life in Sweden, engaged mostly at the royal court. By 1781 he was organist at the German church, St. Gertrud; he was also appointed singing master at the Royal Opera. In 1793, after several of his operas had been performed at court, he became conductor of the Royal Orchestra, succeeding Joseph Martin Kraus. In 1808 he moved to Uppsala, where he was music director at the Music Academy and served as organist at the cathedral. Works include the operas *Electra* (Stockholm, 1787) and *Renaud* (Stockholm, 1801); sacred oratorios; orchestral works (3 overtures); and keyboard works.

Haefliger, Ernst (b. Davos, Switzerland, 6 July 1919). Tenor. After attending the Wettingen Conservatory, studied voice with Fernando Carpi in Genf and Julius Patzak in Vienna. Debut in 1942 as a concert singer. Engaged by the Zurich Stadttheater, 1943–52; by the Berlin Deutsche Oper, 1952–74. First performed his acclaimed Evangelist in Bach's St. Matthew Passion, 1943. At the Salzburg Festival in 1949 he created Tiresias in Orff's *Antigone.* Other premieres include *Le vin herbé, Golgotha,* and *In terra pax* by Frank Martin. From 1971, professor at the Munich Musikhochschule. Published a pedagogical treatise, *Die Singstimme* (1984).

Hagegård, Håkan (b. Karlstad, Sweden, 25 Nov. 1945). Baritone. Studied voice with Helga Görlin at the Royal Academy, Stockholm; with Tito Gobbi in Rome; with Gerald Moore in London; with Erik Werba in Vienna. Debut in 1968 as Papageno *(Zauberflöte)* at the Royal Opera, Stockholm. He sang that role in Ingmar Bergman's film of the opera and at La Scala in 1985. Sang regularly at the Drottningham Festival from 1970. At Glyndebourne sang Strauss's Count *(Capriccio)* in 1973, Mozart's Count *(Figaro)* in 1974, Guglielmo *(Così)* in 1978. Joined Janet Baker for a concert performance of *Dido and Aeneas,* London, 1977. After his New York Metropolitan debut in 1978 as Malatesta *(Pasquale),* he returned as Rossini's Figaro, Wagner's Wolfram (the role of his Covent Garden debut, 1987), Berg's Eisenstein, and Corigliano's Beaumarchais (*The Ghosts of Versailles,* 1991).

Hageman, Richard (b. Leeuwarden, Holland, 9 July 1882; d. Beverly Hills, 6 Mar. 1966). Composer, conductor, and pianist. Studied with his father, Maurits, then with Gevaert and Arthur de Greef at the Brussels Conservatory. Worked as répétiteur and assistant conductor at the Royal Opera in Amsterdam (1899–1903). From 1904 he accompanied Mathilde Marchesi and later Yvette Guilbert in Paris; with Guilbert he came to New York in 1906. Conducted at the Metropolitan Opera, 1908–22 and 1936; at the Chicago Civic Opera, 1922–23; at the Los Angeles Grand Opera, 1923. He was also head of the opera department at the Curtis Institute in Philadelphia. His opera *Caponsacchi,* completed 1931, was given by the Freiburg opera in 1932 (as *Tragödie in Arezzo*), by the Met in 1937. He collaborated with Max Steiner on the score to John Ford's *The Informer* (1934; screen credits list him as an arranger), then moved to Hollywood in 1938, where he provided music for Paramount Studio films directed by John Ford *(Stagecoach, The Long Voyage Home, The Fugitive, Fort Apache, Three Godfathers, She Wore a Yellow Ribbon, Wagon Master),* Frank Lloyd *(If I Were King, Rulers of the Sea, The Howards of Virginia),* Josef von Sternberg *(The Shanghai Gesture),* and others (including *Angel and the Badman, Mourning Becomes Electra*). Among his many songs, "Do Not Go, My Love" (1917), "At the Well" (1919), "The Night Has a Thousand Eyes" (1935), and "Christmas Eve" (1936) were especially popular.

Hagen, Francis Florentine (b. Salem, N.C., 30 Oct. 1815; d. Lititz, Pa., 7 July 1907). Composer. Son of a tailor, a former Moravian missionary; educated in Moravian schools; learned to play the organ, violin, and other instruments; 1835–44, teacher in Moravian schools. Ordained in 1844, he served churches in North Carolina (1844–55), then in Pennsylvania, around New York City, and in Iowa. He wrote on Moravian church history. Composed 17 anthems, 6 choral pieces, a Christmas cantata (incompletely preserved), Overture in F for orchestra, songs, organ pieces and hymn arrangements, piano pieces; best known for the carol "Morning Star" (1836), traditionally sung by child soloist and chorus in the Moravian Christmas service.

Bibl.: James Boeringer, *Morning Star: The Life and Work of Francis Florentine Hagen* (Winston-Salem, 1986).

Hagen, Peter Albrecht von [van], **Sr.** (b. Netherlands, 1755; d. Boston, 20 Aug. 1803). Composer, violinist, and music publisher. In 1774 he and his wife emigrated to the U.S., settling first in Charleston, S.C. He moved to New York around 1789, and to Boston by 1796; in both cities he supported his family as music teacher, concert manager, and publisher. In Boston he composed and published some of his own songs; from 1798 he was organist at King's Chapel; he also conducted his own theater orchestra. His wife, Elizabeth, taught keyboard at Salem and in Boston. The attribution of works between him and his son (see below) is virtually impossible to determine.

Hagen, Peter Albrecht von [van], **Jr.** (b. Charleston?, S.C., ca. 1780; d. Boston, 12 Sept. 1837). Composer and violinist. Like his father (see above), he taught music in New York and Boston; from 1800 he played organ in Boston at Trinity Church, and he led bands there and in Virginia. After his father died in 1803, he lost control over the family publishing firm, which was sold the following year. Little record remains of his later life, except that he was a violist in the orchestra of Boston's Tremont Theatre during the 1830s. Published works of father and son include an overture, 12 songs, and works for keyboard.

Haggard, Merle (Ronald) (b. Bakersfield, Calif., 6 Apr. 1937). Country singer and songwriter. After performances in clubs on the West Coast, he began recording in 1962; from 1965 with his band The Strangers. His most famous song was "Okie from Muskogee" (1969), a humorous rejection of 1960s radicalism; other songs have dealt with a wide variety of social and personal issues ("Mama Tried," 1968; "If We Make It through December," 1973).

Hahn, Reynaldo (b. Caracas, 9 Aug. 1874; d. Paris, 28 Jan. 1947). Composer and conductor. He was raised in Paris and studied composition with Massenet; he had begun writing songs by the age of 13 ("Si mes vers avaient des ailes," after Hugo, was the first one published), which he played and sang at Paris salons and concerts. The elegant songs for which he is now best known set texts of Hugo, Verlaine, Daudet, Heine, and Lecomte de Lisle. In 1898 his first opera, *L'île du rêve,* was staged at the Opéra-comique; later *Le marchand de Venise* was staged at the Paris Opéra (1935). He also wrote operettas (*Ciboulette,* 1923) and musical comedies (*Mozart,* 1925). In 1945 he conducted several works at the Paris Opéra. From 1934 he wrote musical criticism for *Le Figaro.* He was also one of the editors of the complete works of Rameau.

Works include 4 serious operas and 9 operettas, musical comedies, or comic operas; 6 ballets and other stage works; concertos for violin and piano and other orchestral music; *Prométhée triomphant* (soloists, chorus, orchestra, 1908); string quartets and other chamber music; piano and organ works; 7 sets of songs (publ. 1893–1947). Writings include *Du Chant* (1920), *La grande Sarah* (1930), *L'oreille au guet* (1937), and *Thèmes variés* (1946).

Haieff, Alexei (Vasilievich) (b. Blagoveshchensk, Siberia, 25 Aug. 1914; d. Rome 1 Mar. 1994). Composer. Moved to China in 1920 and then to the U.S. in 1932, becoming an American citizen in 1939. He studied with Jacobi and Goldmark at Juilliard (1934–38), and with Boulanger (1938–39); served as composer-in-residence at the American Academy in Rome (1952–53, 1958–59); taught at SUNY–Buffalo (1962, 1964–65), the Carnegie Institute of Technology (1962–63), Brandeis (1965–66), and the Univ. of Utah (composer-in-residence, 1967–70). His music is often described as neoclassical; some jazz influence is also evident. Works include ballets (*Zondilda and Her Entourage,* 1946; *Beauty and the Beast,* 1947); orchestral works (3 symphonies, 1942, 1957, 1961; Divertimento, small orchestra, 1944; a violin concerto, 1948; Piano Concerto no. 1, 1949–50; *Caligula,* baritone, orchestra, 1971; Piano Concerto no. 2, 1976); chamber music (Serenade, oboe, clarinet, bassoon, piano, 1942; *Eclogue,* cello, piano, 1947; Sonata, piano, 1955; *Éloge,* 9 instruments, 1967); other piano works; vocal music.

Haig, Al(lan Warren) (b. Newark, 22 July 1924; d. New York, 16 Nov. 1982). Jazz pianist. As a member of Dizzy Gillespie's bop combo (1945–46) he recorded "Salt Peanuts" and "Shaw 'Nuff" (both 1945). He joined Jimmy Dorsey's big band (1947), then played bop with Charlie Parker (1948–50) and Stan Getz (1949–51). He also recorded with Ben Webster (1946), Eddie "Lockjaw" Davis (1947), Wardell Gray, Coleman Hawkins (both 1948–49), and Miles Davis's cool jazz nonet (1949). After working steadily but in increasing obscurity for 20 years, he came to prominence with the bop revival of the 1970s, playing in New York clubs and recording about 20 albums, including *Chelsea Bridge* (1975).

Hailstork, Adolphus Cunningham (b. Rochester, N.Y., 17 Apr. 1941). Composer. Studied with Mark Fax at Howard University (B.Mus., 1963), where his musical *A Race for Space* was performed; with Nadia Boulanger at Fontainebleau (summer 1963); with Ludmila Uleha, Nicholas Flagello, Vittorio Giannini, and David Diamond at the Manhattan School of Music (M.Mus., 1966). In 1966 his *Statement, Variations, and Fugue* was performed by the Baltimore Symphony. He completed his formal studies at Michigan State Univ. (with H. Owen Reed; Ph.D., 1971), and at a summer workshop by the Electronic Music Institute at Dartmouth College (1972). He has taught at Youngstown State Univ. in Ohio (1971–76) and Norfolk State Univ. in Virginia (from 1976). Composed works for orchestra (*Bellevue,* 1974; *Celebration,* 1975; *Epitaph: For a Man Who Dreamed,* 1979; Symphony no. 1, 1988); for band (Bagatelles for Brass, 1974; *American Landscape no. 1,* 1976; no. 3, 1982); choral works; chamber music; guitar pieces; 2 sonatas (1980, 1989) and other piano pieces.

Haitink, Bernard (Johann Herman) (b. Amsterdam, 4 Mar. 1929). Conductor. Studied violin from age 9; violin and conducting with Felix Hupka at the Amsterdam Conservatory. Joined the Netherlands Radio Philharmonic as violinist; after studying conducting with Ferdinand Leitner at Hilversum, became its assistant conductor in 1955; principal conductor in 1957. First conducted Concertgebouw Orchestra in 1956; toured Britain with them, 1959. Named joint permanent conductor (with Eugen Jochum) in 1961; sole permanent conductor and artistic director, 1964. Principal conductor of the London Philharmonic, 1967; artistic director, 1969. Quit this post in 1978 to turn his attention to opera. Debut at Glyndebourne in 1972 conducting *Die Entführung;* music director there, 1977–87. Music director of the Royal Opera from 1987. New York

Metropolitan debut in 1982 leading *Fidelio.* His recorded legacy with the Concertgebouw Orchestra, which he left in 1988, includes performances of Brahms, Bruckner, Mahler, and Strauss. In the theater he concentrated early on Mozart, but also gave much-admired performances of Stravinsky, Britten, Borodin, and Wagner.

Hakim, Talib Rasul [Chambers, Stephen Alexander] (b. Asheville, N.C., 8 Feb. 1940; d. New Haven, Conn., 31 Mar. 1988). Composer. Studied clarinet and piano at the Manhattan School of Music, 1959–63; composition at the New School for Social Research, 1963–65. Teachers included Robert Starer, William Sydeman, Hall Overton, Morton Feldman, Chou Wen-Chung, and Ornette Coleman. Began composing in 1963. During the 1960s he attracted wide attention through performances in the Music in Our Time concert series (New York). Taught at Pace College (1970–72) and Nassau Community College (1972–88); also at Morgan State Univ. (1978–79). Works include *Shapes,* chamber orchestra (1965); *Sound Gone,* piano (1967); *Placements,* 5 percussionists and piano (1970); *Re/Currences,* orchestra (1975); *Concepts,* orchestra (1976); *Arkan-5,* tape and orchestra (1980); *Quote-Unquote,* tenor, oboe, trumpet, percussion (1983); concert works for jazz ensembles; vocal works; works for chamber ensembles.

Halévy, (Jacques François) Fromental (Elie) (b. Paris, 27 May 1799; d. Nice, 17 Mar. 1862). Composer. From a Jewish family, whose name until 1807 was Levy; his father, of German origin, was a noted Hebraic scholar. In 1809 he entered the solfège class at the Paris Conservatory, his talent coming to the attention of Cherubini, of whom he was a favorite pupil (1811–16); also studied with Berton (harmony) and Lambert (piano); 1816–17, répétiteur in solfège; from 1818, adjunct professor; 1816–17, second Prix de Rome; 1819, Prix de Rome. Because of his mother's death he deferred his Italian sojourn (Rome and Naples) until 1820–22, visiting Vienna on his return; resumed Conservatory post, becoming professor of harmony, 1827.

In 1826 he succeeded Hérold as *maestro al cembalo* and chief vocal coach at the Théâtre-Italien. He had by then composed several unperformed operas; he reached the stage with a one-act work for the Opéra-comique in 1827, attracting attention with an Italian opera for Malibran, *Clari* (Théâtre-Italien, 1828). His first sizable success came with the one-act *Le dilettante d'Avignon* (Opéra-comique, 1829). He was chief vocal coach, 1829–40, at the Opéra; in 1830, a ballet, *Manon,* was given there and in 1832 an opéra-ballet, *La tentation;* meanwhile he continued to produce opéras comiques. In 1833 he succeeded Fétis as professor of counterpoint and fugue at the Conservatory; 1840, professor of composition.

He attained the pinnacle of his opera career in 1835 with his two greatest successes, *La juive* (Opéra) and *L'éclair* (Opéra-comique); composed 5 more grand operas in 5 acts (*Guido et Ginevra,* 1838; *La reine de Chypre,* 1841; *Charles VI,* 1843; *Le juif errant,* 1852; *La magicienne,* 1858, all at the Opéra), as well as smaller works there and 11 more opéras comiques, including some considerable but not enduring successes. In 1850 he was invited to London to compose an Italian opera, *La tempestà* (after Shakespeare) for Her Majesty's Theatre. His marriage in 1842 to the daughter of a wealthy banking family allowed him to live a luxurious, highly social life. Among his pupils were many who achieved fame (including Bizet, who married one of his daughters in 1869 and completed his last opera, *Noé*); most found him a sympathetic but lax and neglectful teacher; some (Saint-Saëns, Lecocq) did not remember him fondly. From 1844 he published historical and critical essays on music (including an unfinished biography of Cherubini, 1845), collected in *Souvenirs et portraits* (1861) and the posthumous *Derniers souvenirs et portraits* (1863). This literary inclination probably contributed to his election (1854) to the prestigious post of permanent secretary of the Académie des Beaux-Arts.

Bibl.: M. Curtiss, "Fromental Halévy," *MQ* 39 (1953): 196–214. J. W. Klein, "Jacques Fromental Halévy (1799–1862)," *MR* 23 (1962): 13–19.

Haley, Bill [William John Clifton, Jr.] (b. Highland Park, Mich., 6 July 1925; d. Harlingen, Tex., 9 Feb. 1981). Rock-and-roll singer, songwriter, and bandleader. He began as a country artist and recorded rhythm-and-blues songs in the early 1950s. In 1954 he released 2 songs, "Shake, Rattle, and Roll" and "Rock around the Clock," whose success initiated the rise of rock-and-roll to widespread popularity. He continued to record with his band the Comets, further successes including "See You Later, Alligator" (1955), but he was soon eclipsed by other performers such as Elvis Presley and Chuck Berry.

Halffter (Jiménez), Cristóbal (b. Madrid, 24 Mar. 1930). Composer. Nephew of Ernesto and Rodolfo Halffter. Studied at the Madrid Conservatory under del Campo (1947–51) and in Paris with Alexandre Tansman; took a job with Spanish radio in 1952 and taught at the Madrid Conservatory from 1960 until 1967, serving as director, 1964–66. As a conductor he led the Orquesta Manuel de Falla, 1955–63, making guest appearances in Europe and the Americas as well; he also was music director of the Madrid Radio Symphony in 1965–66. His early music includes works such as *Dos movimientos* for timpani and string orchestra (1956), in which a debt to both Stravinsky and Bartók is clear. Later works use a wide variety of contemporary techniques, with some twelve-tone organization as well as exploration of new timbres, aleatory procedures, contrasting blocks of sonority, and electronic media; examples include *Variaciones sobre la resonancia de un grito* (instruments, tape, and live electronic transformation, 1977), the Violin Concerto (1980), and the *Sinfonía para tres grupos instrumentales* (1963). He has composed other orchestral works (*Tres poemas de* *la lírica española,* baritone and orchestra, 1984–86; Double Concerto for Violin and Viola, 1986; *Dortmunder Variationen,* 1987) as well as music for chorus (both sacred and secular), chamber ensemble, and solo instruments, and the opera *Don Quichotte* (1970).

Bibl.: Emilio Casares, *Cristóbal Halffter* (Oviedo, 1980).

Halffter (Escriche), Ernesto (b. Madrid, 16 Jan. 1905; d. there, 5 July 1989). Composer. Brother of Rodolfo Halffter; uncle of Cristóbal Halffter. He had composed several pieces by his mid-teens; after study first with his mother and then with Francisco Esbrí and Fernando Ember, he came to the attention of the influential critic Adolfo Salazar, who sent a score of his to Falla; as a result, Halffter studied with Falla for several years, traveling to Granada for lessons. Works from this period include *Dos canciones de Rafael Alberti* (1923), the *Sinfonietta* (the Spanish National Prize recipient for 1925), and the ballet *Sonatina* (1928). Halffter also drew on the styles of Stravinsky and Ravel, actually studying with Ravel in Paris during 1936. At Falla's behest, Halffter was named conductor of the Orquesta bética de cámara in 1924; in 1934–36 he conducted the orchestra of the Seville Conservatory, an institution he founded in 1931. His marriage in 1928 to the Portuguese pianist Alicia Cámara Santos drew him to Lisbon, where he resided until returning to Spain in 1960. While in Lisbon, he taught at the Instituto español (1942–52); back in Madrid, he served as musical adviser to the Spanish Television Network (from 1966). He was elected to the Spanish Academy of Fine Arts in 1973.

Halffter's close association with Falla continued after the latter moved to Argentina in 1939. Halffter introduced Falla's *Homenajes* to Europe. In addition, after Falla's death Halffter undertook to complete the unfinished scenic cantata *Atlántida,* a project that began in 1954 but was completed only in 1976, though an earlier version was given at La Scala in 1962. Several of Halffter's own works for chorus and orchestras in the 1960s seem to have grown out of the work on *Atlántida;* these include the memorials for Pope John XXIII and Prince Pierre de Polignac (1964, 1966), the *Dominus pastor meus* and the settings of Psalms 23 and 114 (all 1967), and the *Gozos de Nuestra Señora* (1970). His compositions, which might be either adventurous in their modernism or evocative of the past, are usually firmly grounded tonally. He produced works in nearly every genre except opera, with several ballets and some incidental music; film scores; several orchestral works suggestive of Iberian topics (*Amanecer en los jardines de España,* clearly modeled on Falla, 1937; *Rapsodia portuguesa,* 1940, rev. 1951); various collections of songs; chamber music; and keyboard works.

Halffter (Escriche), Rodolfo (b. Madrid, 30 Oct. 1900; d. Mexico City, 14 Oct. 1987). Composer. Brother of Ernesto Halffter; uncle of Cristóbal Halffter. He was a self-schooled musician, though he received some guidance from Falla in 1929 while a member of the Grupo de los ocho. He wrote criticism for *La voz* and *El sol* in 1934–36, but as a result of his holding important posts in the Loyalist government, he was obliged to flee the country after the Fascist victory in 1939. He went first to France, then to Mexico, where he became a citizen and a very influential musical figure; he taught at the National Conservatory from 1940, founded the journal *Nuestra música* in 1946, editing it until 1953, and managed the Ediciones mexicanas de música from 1946. He later held appointments at the National Institute of Fine Arts (from 1959) and served as director of the Mexican ballet group La paloma azul; he joined the Mexican Academy of Fine Arts in 1969 and the Instituto de cultura hispánica, Madrid, in 1970. His music is generally tonal in conception, though with some injections of parallel dissonance and polytonality; works include a lost opera, several ballets (some of which exist also in concert versions), and a few other orchestral compositions; works for chorus, including the Easter piece *Pregón para una pascua pobre,* with its use of the *Victimae paschali laudes* sequence text; chamber music; works for both piano and guitar. He compiled a catalog of the works of Carlos Chávez (1971).

Bibl.: *Composers of the Americas* 2 (Washington, D.C., 1956): 83–89 [includes works list].

Halíř, Karel [Karl] (b. Hohenelbe [now Vrchlabi], Bohemia, 1 Feb. 1859; d. Berlin, 21 Dec. 1909). Violinist. Studied with Bennewitz (Prague Conservatory, 1867–73) and Joachim (Berlin, 1874–76); then played in and conducted orchestras; from 1884, concertmaster, Weimar orchestra; 1893–1907, concertmaster, Berlin Opera orchestra; also taught at Berlin Hochschule für Musik. In 1896–97 he toured the U.S.; 1897, second violin, Joachim Quartet; later led his own quartet; published scale studies for violin (Berlin, 1896).

Hall, Edmond (b. New Orleans, 15 May 1901; d. Boston, 11 Feb. 1967). Jazz clarinetist. He worked with Buddy Petit in New Orleans (1921–23). After joining the big bands of Claude Hopkins (1929–35) and Lucky Millinder (1936, 1937), he played in the swing combos of Zutty Singleton (1939), Joe Sullivan (1939–40), Henry "Red" Allen (1940–41), and Teddy Wilson (1941–44). He recorded "Profoundly Blue" as a leader (1941), led groups in New York and Boston (1944–50), recorded with Eddie Condon from 1945 (including the album *Bixieland,* 1955), and in 1950–55 worked at Condon's club. He joined Louis Armstrong's All Stars (1955–58). Favoring a gruff, vocalized timbre, he played with a fierce drive. His brother Herb(ie) [Herbert L.] Hall (b. Reserve, La., 28 Mar. 1907), also a clarinetist, occasionally crossed paths with Edmond during a long career in jazz; Herb joined Condon in the late 1950s.

Hall, Jim [James Stanley] (b. Buffalo, 4 Dec. 1930).

Jazz guitarist. He studied at the Cleveland Institute of Music (B.M., 1955); joined Chico Hamilton (1955–56), Jimmy Giuffre (1956–59), Lee Konitz (1960–61), Sonny Rollins (1961–62, 1964), and Art Farmer (1963–64). He recorded with Paul Desmond (1959–65) and in duos with Bill Evans (1959, 1966) and Ron Carter (1972), with whom he later performed in New York (1984–85). From the mid-1960s he also worked unaccompanied and leading trios, as on the album *Jim Hall Live!* (1975).

Hall, Richard (b. York, 16 Sept. 1903; d. Horsham, 24 May 1982). Composer. He studied organ at Peterhouse, Cambridge, then held an organ post at Leeds before becoming professor of composition at the Royal Manchester College of Music (1938–56); director of music at Dartington (1956–67). His music is adventurous in its chromatic counterpoint. Works for orchestra: 5 symphonies (1941–64), Piano Concerto (1949), *Fantasy for String Orchestra* (1951); for chorus: *Bread of the World* (anthem, 1931), *Three Carols* (1964); for chamber groups: String Quartet no. 1 (1946) and no. 2 (1973), Suite, violin, viola (1953), *5 Epigrams,* cello, piano (1953), *2 Diversions,* flute, bassoon (1961); for organ: *3 Cathedral Voluntaries* (1936), Toccata, Intermezzo, and Fugue (1943), *Pastorale du Nord* (1944); for piano: *4 Pieces* (1944), *3 Lyric Pieces* (1948); Suite (1971).

Hallé, Charles [Carl] (b. Hagen, Westphalia, 11 Apr. 1819; d. Manchester, 25 Oct. 1895). Pianist and conductor. Son of a church organist; early learned several instruments; conducted opera at 11; 1835, studied at Darmstadt with Rinck and Weber; from 1835, piano pupil of George Osborne, Paris, becoming a figure in Paris musical life as pianist (championing Beethoven's sonatas), chamber player, and teacher. In 1849 he settled in Manchester, organizing concerts, founding the St. Cecilia Society (1850), conducting the orchestra (from 1849), founding the Hallé Concerts (1858), and working for the establishment of the Royal Manchester College of Music (1893), of which he was the first principal and piano teacher. He was also active as pianist and conductor in London, Edinburgh, Liverpool, Bristol Festival. Knighted in 1888. He toured with his second wife (from 1888), the violinist Wilma Norman-Neruda (1839–1911), visiting Australia (1890–91) and South Africa (1895).

Bibl.: C. E. and M. Hallé, *Life and Letters of Sir Charles Hallé* (London, 1896; R: 1975). M. Kennedy, ed., *The Autobiography of Charles Hallé* (London, 1972).

Hallén, (Johannes) Andreas (b. Göteborg, 22 Dec. 1846; d. Stockholm, 11 Mar. 1925). Composer and conductor. From 1866 to 1871 he studied in Leipzig (Reinecke), Munich (Rheinberger), Dresden (Rietz); 1872–78, 1883–84, conductor, Göteborg Musical Society; 1879–83, critic and singing teacher, Berlin; 1885–95, conductor, Stockholm Philharmonic; 1892–97, conductor, Royal Opera; 1902–7, founder and conductor, Southern Swedish Philharmonic, Malmö; 1909–19, professor of composition, Stockholm Conservatory. He was an admirer of Liszt and Wagner, whose influence is strong in his own music, which includes 3 operas, incidental music, choral works, *Missa solemnis,* 3 symphonic poems, 2 rhapsodies, songs, chamber music. He published a collection of essays and criticism, *Musikaliska kåserier* (Stockholm, 1894).

Hallström, Ivar (Christian) (b. Stockholm, 5 June 1826; d. there, 11 Apr. 1901). Composer and pianist. His early piano studies were with E. Passy. He studied law at the Univ. of Uppsala, taking a degree in 1849. During this period he was a close friend of Prince Gustaf, with whom he composed his first opera, *Hvita frun på Drottningholm* (The White Woman from Drottningholm; Stockholm, 1848). From 1850 he was court librarian (for Oscar II) and from 1861 to 1872 director of the Lindblad School of Music. After 1881 he was also a vocal coach at the Royal Opera. His music shows the influence of Gounod; it consists chiefly of stage works: operas (*Duke Magnus,* 1867; *The Enchanted Cat,* 1869; *The Bewitched One,* 1874); ballets; incidental music (*Stolts Elisif,* 1870); also nearly 100 songs; piano works (including folk song settings and *Variations on a Swedish Folksong "Sven i Rosengård"*).

Hambraeus, Bengt (b. Stockholm, 29 Jan. 1928). Composer, organist, and music scholar. As a composer he was chiefly self-trained; he studied organ with Alf Linder (1944–48) and, at the Univ. of Uppsala, musicology with Carl Allan Moberg; he also studied art history and theology. At the university he taught and served as librarian. He came into contact with Krenek and Messiaen at the Darmstadt summer courses, 1951–55. From 1957 he was on the staff of the Swedish Broadcasting Corporation, and in 1969 he became its production director. In 1972 he moved to Montreal, becoming professor of music at McGill Univ. A central figure in European electronic music, he worked at nearly every major electronic studio. Works include the operas *Experiment X* (Stockholm, 1971) and *Se människan* (Ecce homo; Stockholm, 1971); choral/instrumental works (*Triptychon,* 1950; *Responsorien,* tenor, chorus, ensemble, 1964; *Motetum archangeli Michaelis,* 1967; *Symphonia sacra,* soloists, chorus, winds, percussion, 1986; *Echoes of Loneliness,* 4 choirs, viola, percussion, 1988); orchestral works (*Rota,* 3 orchestras, tape, 1956–62; *Transfiguration,* 1963; *Rencontres,* 1971; *Pianissimo in due tempi,* 1972; *Ricordanza,* 1976; *Quodlibet re BACH,* 1984); solo vocal works; chamber music; works for organ and for piano; tape music (*Doppelrohr,* 1955; *Transit I,* 1963; *Tetragon,* 1965; *Tides,* 1974; *Intrada,* 1975). He authored a book on notation, *Om notskrifter: paleografi-tradition-förnyelse* (Stockholm, 1970).

Hamerik [Hammerich], **Asger** (b. Fredericksberg,

Denmark, 8 Apr. 1843; d. there, 13 July 1923). Composer. Brother of musicologist Angul Hammerich (1848–1931); father of Ebbe Hamerik. Son of a university professor who opposed a musical career for him; early began to compose, encouraged by Gade and Hartmann; 1862–64, studied in Berlin with Wüerst (theory) and Bülow (piano, conducting); then in Paris with Berlioz (his only pupil); excerpts from 2 operas were heard there in 1865; in 1870 an Italian opera, *La vendetta,* was performed privately in Milan; 1871–98, director of the Peabody Conservatory, Baltimore, also teaching theory and conducting the school orchestra, which premiered much of his music. Undertook a conducting tour in 1899 (Berlin, Venice, Dresden, Paris, Milan); then retired to Copenhagen, where his music, in spite of a Scandinavian flavor, was and remains little known. He composed 7 numbered symphonies (and 1 unnumbered), 5 Nordic Suites, a Requiem, and many other choral works and cantatas.

Hamerik, Ebbe (b. Copenhagen, 5 Sept. 1898; d. there, 11 Aug. 1951). Composer, conductor. Son of Asger Hammerik. He studied conducting with Franz van der Stucken, 1916–19, then became assistant conductor at the Royal Theater, Copenhagen, 1919. He conducted both in Denmark and on tour throughout Europe during the 1920s. After 1930 he devoted himself to composition. His works include the operas *Stepan* (1924), *Leonardo da Vinci* (1930–32), *Marie Grubbe* (1940), *Rejsekammeraten* (1946), *Drommerne* (1950, book by Isak Dinesen); 5 symphonies (*Cantus Firmus I–V,* 1936, 1947, 1948, 1949, 1949), 2 string quartets. He drowned in the river Kattegat during a storm.

Hamilton, Chico [Foreststorn] (b. Los Angeles, 21 Sept. 1921). Jazz drummer and bandleader. He accompanied Lena Horne (1948–55) and worked intermittently with Gerry Mulligan's cool jazz quartet and "tentette" (1952–54), showing an ability to generate intense swing at low volumes. He led a popular West Coast jazz combo of winds, cello, guitar, double bass, and drums, as on the album *The Chico Hamilton Quintet with Buddy Collette* (1955). Sidemen included Jim Hall and later Ron Carter and Eric Dolphy, but then from 1960 Hamilton turned toward hard bop, replacing the cello with a trumpet. From 1966 he worked in advertising while continuing to lead groups occasionally.

Hamilton, Iain (Ellis) (b. Glasgow, 6 June 1922). Composer. He trained as an engineer before entering the Royal Academy of Music on a scholarship in 1947. His first major works appeared the following year. In his works of the early 1950s, tonality and chromaticism intersect. In 1953 he began writing for the voice and, at first, made more traditional uses of tonality, but occasionally drew on serial technique. By 1958 he was writing large-scale works that use serial techniques. Hamilton moved to New York in 1961. He was composer-in-residence at Tanglewood in 1962, then Mary Duke Biddle Professor of Music at Duke University until 1981. From 1967 Hamilton began devoting much of his attention to opera. The first to be produced, *The Royal Hunt of the Sun,* is as much a theater piece as an opera in the traditional sense. *The Cataline Conspiracy* marks a partial return to tonal means and to opera as drama. With *Tamburlaine,* and especially *Anna Karenina,* Hamilton embraced not only the musical diction but also the formal divisions of late Romantic opera. In these operas and others he acted as his own librettist, basing his dramas, however, on texts by others.

Works for the stage: *Agamemnon* (1967–69); *The Royal Hunt of the Sun* (1967–69); *Pharsalia* (1968); *The Cataline Conspiracy* (1972–73); *Tamburlaine* (radio version, 1976; stage version, 1979); *Anna Karenina* (1981); *Raleigh's Dream* (1984); *Lancelot* (1985). Vocal: Cantata, 4 soloists, piano (1954); *The Bermudas,* baritone, chorus, orchestra (1956); *A Testament of War,* baritone, ensemble (1961); *Epitaph for This World and Time* (1970), 3 choirs and organs; Te Deum, soprano, alto, tenor, bass, orchestra (1973–74); Mass in A, chorus (1982); *The Morning Watch,* chorus, 10 winds (1982); St. Mark's Passion, 4 soloists, chorus, orchestra (1983); Requiem, chorus; *Prometheus,* 4 soloists, chorus, orchestra. Orchestral: Symphony no. 1 (1948), 2 (1950–51), 3 (1980), 4 (1981); Symphonic Variations (1953); Sinfonia, 2 orchestras (1958); Violin Concerto no. 1 (1952), 2 (1971); Jazz Trumpet Concerto, 1957; Piano Concerto no. 1 (1959–60; rev. 1967), 2 (1989); *Voyage,* horn, chorus, orchestra (1970). Chamber: String Quartet no. 1 (1948), 2 (1965), 3 (1987); octets (1954–55, 1984); Quintet for Brass (1964); Piano Sonata no. 1 (1951; rev. 1971), 2 (1973), 3 (1981).

Hamilton, Jimmy [James] (b. Dillon, S.C., 25 May 1917; d. St. Croix, Virgin Islands, 20 Sept. 1994). Jazz clarinetist. He was a member of the swing sextets of Teddy Wilson (1940–42) and Eddie Heywood before joining Duke Ellington's big band as a fluid clarinet soloist and (less often) a raucous tenor saxophonist (1943–68). Recordings with Ellington include "The Tattooed Bride" on the album *Masterpieces* (1950). After playing and teaching in the Virgin Islands, he worked in the U.S. with Mercer Ellington (1980s) and with John Carter's clarinet quartet, which recorded swing tunes on the two-volume album *Clarinet Summit* (1981, 1985).

Hamilton, Scott (b. Providence, 12 Sept. 1954). Jazz tenor saxophonist and bandleader. He led groups in New York from 1976, often in association with the cornetist Warren Vaché, Jr. They also worked as sidemen with Benny Goodman (1977 to mid-1980s), Rosemary Clooney (from 1978), and Woody Herman (1980s); Hamilton sometimes teamed with Ruby Braff rather than Vaché (from 1982). His playing is firmly rooted in swing. His albums include *Skyscrapers* (1979) and, with Braff, *A First* (1985).

Hammerschmidt, Andreas (b. Brüx, 1611 or 1612; d. Zittau, 8 Nov. 1675). Composer. Moved with his family to Freiberg, Saxony, in 1626; no details of his education are available. He perhaps knew Demantius,

Kantor at Freiberg; befriended Stephan Otto, with whom he served Count Rudolf von Bünau at Weesenstein, Saxony, and for whom he wrote dedicatory verses for a print of 1648; perhaps studied with Christoph Schreiber, whom he succeeded as organist at St. Petri, Freiberg (1635–39) and at St. Johannis, Zittau (1639 to his death). At Zittau Hammerschmidt also taught and was later named village and forest administrator, becoming wealthy in the process. The bulk of his output consists of German sacred concertos for a variety of vocal forces and continuo, sometimes with instrumental participation; other works include dances, secular vocal pieces, and occasional music.

Hammerstein, Oscar (Greeley Clendenning), II (b. New York, 12 July 1895; d. Doylestown, Pa., 23 Aug. 1960). Lyricist and librettist. He began writing for college revues at Columbia Univ. and worked in musical comedy production for his uncle, Arthur Hammerstein (1917–19). After an attempt at spoken drama (*The Light,* 1919), from 1920 he collaborated with librettist Otto Harbach. He produced musicals with composers Herbert Stothart, Vincent Youmans, Rudolf Friml (*Rose-Marie,* 1924), Sigmund Romberg (*The Desert Song,* 1926), George Gershwin, and Jerome Kern. Then, in 1943, he formed a partnership with composer Richard Rodgers. Several of his works, including *Showboat* (1927, music by Kern) and the musicals with Rodgers (including *Oklahoma!,* 1943; *Carousel,* 1945; *South Pacific,* 1949; *Sound of Music,* 1959), were central to the development of the American musical theater, using novel subject matter and dramatic structure. He wrote for television and film (*State Fair,* 1945), and in 1943 he adapted Bizet's *Carmen* for Broadway as *Carmen Jones.*

Hammond, Laurens (b. Evanston, Ill., 11 Jan. 1895; d. Cornwall, Conn., 1 July 1973). Inventor and entrepreneur. He studied engineering at Cornell, worked in Detroit on the synchronization of electrical impulses in motors, then founded the Hammond Clock Company in Chicago, 1928. In 1934 he and fellow engineer John Hanert obtained a patent for an electronic instrument in which sound is produced by rotating tone wheels driven by a synchronous motor. In 1935 the company began manufacturing the Hammond Organ, Model A, an instrument that coupled 91 of the tone wheels to 2 5-octave manuals and a 2-octave pedal. Model A was an immediate commercial success. At first Hammond marketed it by claiming complete fidelity to the sound of a pipe organ; a lawsuit stopped this but fell short of denying him use of the word organ. Later, musicians such as Jimmy Smith developed musical idioms that capitalize on the unique timbre of Hammond's instrument.

Hampel, Anton Joseph (b. Prague, ca. 1710; d. Dresden, 30 Mar. 1771). Horn player and inventor. During the early 1730s he was appointed horn player in the Dresden court orchestra. He subsequently became a well-known master of the instrument and is said to have been the first to hand-stop the horn to produce chromatic tones. Later he collaborated on the invention of a horn with crooks in the body (as in the modern horn) instead of in the mouthpiece. He authored a horn primer, edited by Giovanni Punto as *Seule et vrai méthode pour apprendre facilement les éléments des premier et second cors* (Paris, ca. 1795). He also composed concertos for horn.

Hampton, Lionel (b. Louisville, Ky., 20 Apr. 1909). Jazz vibraphonist, drummer, and bandleader. While working as a drummer in the Los Angeles area, he began playing vibraphone during a recording session with Louis Armstrong (1930). He became the first important vibraphone soloist in jazz. He joined Benny Goodman's quartet (1936–40); their recordings include "Moonglow" (1936) and "The Blues in Your Flat" (1938). During this period he led all-star swing groups for recordings, including "Hot Mallets" (1939). On some of these he played drums, sang, and played piano, adopting a two-fingered style similar to the use of mallets on vibraphone. He formed a big band (1940) that remained active through the 1980s. Known for extroverted, emotive performances, the group helped establish the rhythm-and-blues style, but also included strong swing and bop soloists. Among Hampton's sidemen were Illinois Jacquet, Cat Anderson, Charles Mingus, Clifford Brown, and Art Farmer; Dinah Washington, Joe Williams, and Betty Carter sang with the band.

Hanboys [Hamboys], **John** (fl. 1470). Theorist. Widely known and highly regarded in his native England; held Mus.D.; his one extant treatise (ed. *CS* 1:403–48) discusses the development of notation and mensuration from the time of Franco of Cologne (13th cent.) until the "modern" era (late 15th cent.), with particular attention to methods of writing values smaller than Franco's *semibrevis* and to variant forms of certain notational symbols.

Hancock, Herbie [Herbert Jeffrey] (b. Chicago, 12 Apr. 1940). Jazz and popular keyboard player, composer, and bandleader. He studied music at Grinnell College, Iowa, graduating in 1960. As a jazz pianist he recorded the album *Takin' Off* (1962), including his widely performed composition "Watermelon Man." With Miles Davis (1963–68) he joined Ron Carter and Tony Williams in a rhythm section renowned for its flexible treatment of bop and modal jazz. Under Hancock's leadership, with Freddie Hubbard replacing Davis, the quintet made the album *Maiden Voyage* including his compositions "Dolphin Dance" and the title track (1965). He led a jazz sextet (1970–73) that explored African and Indian musics, unusual meters, electric instruments, and dance rhythms. He formed a funk band that remained popular through the 1970s after the success of his recording "Chameleon" on the album *Headhunters* (1973). While concentrating on a disco style, he also led Hubbard, Carter, Williams, and Wayne Shorter on recordings and tours (1976–77) and played piano duos with Chick Corea (1978). His dual career continued into the 1990s. In jazz he led combos including Carter, Williams, Wynton and Branford Marsalis, and Michael Brecker. He wrote the Oscar-winning score for the film *'Round Midnight* (1986), in which he acted and played. In pop music his performance of "Rockit" won numerous awards in 1983 for single and video of the year.

Handel, George Frideric (b. Halle, 23 Feb. 1685; d. London, 14 Apr. 1759). Composer. Son of a barber-surgeon who was 63 years old at the time of his son's birth. Most of the material on Handel's early life is drawn from the *Memoirs of the Life of the Late George Frederic Handel* by John Mainwaring (London, 1760; R: London, 1964, 1967). During a visit to the court of Saxe-Weissenfels, where Handel's father was court physician, the boy's organ playing aroused the interest of the duke, who persuaded the father to allow musical studies. Back in Halle, Handel began study with Liebfrauenkirche organist Zachow, who had a large library of German and Italian music; a collection of Handel's manuscript copies, dated 1698 but lost by the 19th century, included works by Froberger, Kerll, Krieger, and Zachow himself. Handel studied harmony, counterpoint, keyboard, and violin in these years, also probably serving as Zachow's assistant.

Handel enrolled at the Univ. of Halle on 10 Feb. 1702 and replaced Johann Leporin as organist at the Calvinist Cathedral on 13 March. During these years he also cultivated a friendship with Telemann, then studying at Leipzig; the two corresponded and visited each other. Leaving the university, he moved to Hamburg in 1703; he played ripieno violin and later harpsichord in the opera orchestra during Reinhard Keiser's tenure, studying the art and business of the theater. He was befriended by Johann Mattheson, four years his senior, with whom he traveled to Lübeck in August 1703. Their relationship was briefly clouded by an incident at the opera in December 1704 when, during a performance of Mattheson's *Cleopatra,* the two dueled at the exit of the theater. Handel kept in contact with Mattheson and his music after leaving Hamburg, but declined to supply an autobiography for the latter's *Ehrenpforte.*

Although Handel claims to have "written like the Devil" during these years, only the opera *Almira* (Hamburg, 1705) survives complete. His *Nero* was staged the same year, while *Florindo* and *Daphne* were produced in 1708, after his departure for Italy. Mainwaring reports that Handel "made a considerable number of Sonatas" at Hamburg, and Mattheson refers to many vocal works; none of these survives, though they were perhaps incorporated into later works.

While still in Hamburg, Handel was invited to Florence by Prince Ferdinando de' Medici, but instead "resolved to go to Italy on his own bottom" (Mainwaring), probably arriving at Florence by autumn 1706.

Statue of George Frideric Handel in Vauxhall Gardens.

Soon thereafter he went to Rome. Among his patrons there were the cardinals Colonna, Pamphili, and Ottoboni and the lay prince Francesco Ruspoli. Pamphili wrote the libretto for Handel's first oratorio, *Il trionfo del tempo e del disinganno* (probably May 1707). Ottoboni employed Rome's finest musicians, including Corelli, and it was at Ottoboni's palace where the famous keyboard competition between Handel and Domenico Scarlatti took place. Most of Handel's Roman works were intended for Ruspoli's household, however; he worked there for at least three periods, each of several months' duration, in 1707–9, producing weekly secular cantatas. He also composed the three Psalms *Dixit Dominus, Laudate pueri,* and *Nisi Dominus* in mid-1707 at Rome, all perhaps intended for the feast of the Madonna del Carmine on 16 July.

Handel also served Prince Ferdinand in Florence annually during the autumn season. In 1707 the opera *Rodrigo* was given, after which he continued to Venice for the winter. His sacred drama *La Resurrezione* was given on Easter 1708 at Ruspoli's palace with an orchestra (led by Corelli) of over 45 players. From May through July of 1708 he was in Naples; returning to Rome, he wrote cantatas for Ruspoli and the Accademia degli Arcadi. His greatest Italian success came in Venice during Carnival 1709–10, when his *Agrippina* received 27 performances. The score combines the reworked music of Mattheson, Keiser, and Handel himself with five new arias; his lifelong penchant for borrowing had asserted itself by this time. Musical contacts in Italy included the Scarlattis, Corelli, Caldara, Pasquini, and perhaps Steffani in Rome, and

Lotti and Gasparini as well as Vivaldi and Albinoni in Venice; he also met representatives of the Hannoverian and English courts, his two most important future employers.

In February 1710 he headed northward. He was greeted warmly in Hannover by Steffani and named Kapellmeister in June. The terms of employment were flexible; Handel was allowed an immediate 12-month leave. He went to Düsseldorf, where he played before the Elector and offered advice about a harpsichord purchase. He arrived in London late in 1710. His music had preceded him; selections from *Rodrigo* had been used as incidental music for a revival of Jonson's *The Alchemist* in 1710. He remained until at least June 1711, gaining success with the opera *Rinaldo* at the Queen's Theatre, Haymarket, also giving concerts at court and in the home of coal trader Thomas Britten. He returned via Düsseldorf to Hannover, where he wrote several vocal duets for Princess Caroline; his request in 1712 for leave was granted, provided he "return within a reasonable time," but he apparently remained in London until 1716, producing theater works (*Il pastor fido,* 1712, revised with dances in 1734 as *Terpsichore; Teseo,* 1713; *Silla,* 1713; *Amadigi,* 1715) and occasional music (the Utrecht *Te Deum* and *Jubilate* as well as a Birthday Ode for Queen Anne, from whom he received a £200 pension; all 1713). He spent three years at the mansion of Lord Burlington, leading musical gatherings there and at the Queen's Arms Tavern, and on occasion played organ at St. Paul's after evening services.

Upon Queen Anne's death on 1 Aug. 1714, Handel's official employer, the Elector of Hannover, became George I of England. Though delinquent in his duties at Hannover, Handel was probably never out of favor with the king, despite anecdotes to the contrary; Handel's annuity was doubled, and he was engaged as teacher for the princesses. Handel accompanied the king to Hannover in 1716, visiting Halle and an old friend, Johann Christoph Schmidt, who became (as John C. Smith) the composer's secretary and copyist; Smith was Mainwaring's principal source for his biography. Handel's setting of the Brockes Passion may date from this trip, though the first documented performance took place only in 1719.

In 1717 Handel composed his *Water Music* for a royal boat trip on the Thames; the score was later issued in various forms, making the original order and content of the work uncertain. The same year he joined the service of the Duke of Chandos at Cannons, probably residing there until February 1719. His music from this period includes the 11 Chandos Anthems, a Te Deum, and *Acis and Galatea* and *Esther,* two masques from whose revival in 1732 the oratorio tradition in part grew. Handel later indicated his satisfaction with the Chandos music by borrowing heavily from it for other works.

In 1719 several nobles launched an operatic venture, the Royal Academy of Music, choosing Handel as musical director. He left for Germany in May, visiting Dresden, where he heard Lotti's *Teofane* and engaged several of its singers (Senesino, Berselli, Durastanti, and Boschi) for the London academy; this journey is known also for its supposed near-miss with Bach. *Radamisto* made the inaugural academy season a great success, but financial difficulties soon ensued (hastened by the huge South Sea fraud), and after internal squabbles and declining public support, the company folded in 1728. Among the operas Handel contributed were *Floridante* (premiere Dec. 1721), *Ottone* (Jan. 1723), *Flavio* (May 1724), *Giulio Cesare* (Feb. 1724), *Tamerlano* (Oct. 1724), *Rodelinda* (Feb. 1725), *Scipione* (Mar. 1726), *Alessandro* (May 1726), *Admeto* (Jan. 1727), and *Siroe* (Feb. 1728). His principal librettists were Rolli and Haym; several later works have two prima donna parts, to accommodate both Cuzzoni and the newly hired Bordoni. Bononcini and Amadei also wrote music for the academy, with each of the three composers supplying one act for the composite *Muzio Scevola* (Apr. 1721). Apart from opera, Handel published his *Suites de pièces pour le clavecin* in 1720; the anthems for the coronation of George II in 1727 also fall in the academy period. He had moved to his permanent home in Brook Street by 1723 and in 1727 took English citizenship.

After the dissolution of the Royal Academy in 1728, Handel was hired to produce operas at the King's Theatre, with Heidegger, an impresario long active in London, as manager. New operas included *Lotario* (Dec. 1729), *Partenope* (Feb. 1730), *Poro* (Feb. 1731), and *Ezio* (Jan. 1732), while *Rinaldo, Rodelinda,* and *Giulio Cesare* were revived. In response to a pirate performance, Handel revived *Esther* in May 1732 with new material in a quasi-concert setting (scenic decoration but no action; Burney relates that the Bishop of London forbade sacred drama in the theater); *Acis and Galatea* was presented under similar circumstances. Though cobbled together on short notice (*Acis* being sung in both Italian and English), both productions were great successes and foreshadowed Handel's future triumphs with oratorio.

Handel's Italian operas of 1732–33 faltered in the face of competition from the short-lived English Opera at Lincoln's Inn Fields; he refused to attempt an English opera, despite pleas from associates, but rather responded with *Orlando* (Jan. 1733). Although Burney and Hawkins dismissed *Orlando,* along with all of Handel's Italian offerings of the 1730s, as inferior, modern critics find it one of his greatest operas. His oratorio *Deborah* made an unsuccessful debut in March 1733, with the composer's doubled admission prices prompting attacks on him by his opponents; in July, however, his oratorio *Athalia* received its premiere successfully (and profitably) at Oxford.

Arianna in Creta was his only new opera for the 1733–34 season, his last with Heidegger. That season several of Handel's former singers, led by the castrato Senesino, had defected to a new company, the Opera of the Nobility, with Porpora initially serving as musical director and several nobles, including the Prince of

Wales, providing support. Heidegger rented the Haymarket to the Nobility for 1734–35; the company then engaged the famous Farinelli. Handel moved to Covent Garden and produced *Ariodante* and *Alcina,* the latter of which was one of his greatest public operatic triumphs. The same season he revived *Esther, Deborah,* and *Athalia,* initiating his famous habit of playing organ concertos during the intermissions. The setting of Dryden's *Alexander's Feast* (Feb. 1736) was a success; *Atalanta* followed in May, but interest in both Handel's enterprise and that of the Nobility was declining. Handel wrote three new operas and thoroughly revised his *Il trionfo* of 1707 for 1736–37, to no avail. He suffered a physical breakdown and temporary paralysis in April 1737, and in June both companies folded, deeply in debt.

Handel spent six weeks in fall 1737 at the baths of Aix-la-Chapelle regaining his health. He prepared a pasticcio for the town of Elbing in October, then returned to London, where Heidegger hired him at £1,000 for a season at the King's Theatre in 1737–38. *Farabundo* (Jan. 1738) and *Serse* (April) were far outdrawn by Lampe's Italian operatic parody *The Dragons of Wantley,* but Handel's benefit concert on 28 March was a success. In 1738 a statue of him was commissioned from Roubiliac for Vauxhall Gardens, an indication of his towering position in English musical life, despite his critics. After Heidegger canceled plans for a 1738–39 season, Handel began the oratorio *Saul,* on a libretto by Charles Jennens given to him in 1735, composing it and *Israel and Egypt* in close succession. Both received premieres during a 12-night King's Theatre run in January 1739; *Saul* was by far the more successful. The op. 6 concertos date from October 1739 and were immediately issued in subscription; they were played along with *L'Allegro, il Penseroso ed il Moderato* (libretto by Jennens, after Milton) and other revivals at Lincoln's Inn Fields during the 1739–40 season.

Handel's last two operas, *Imeneo* and *Deidamia,* were prepared for the 1740–41 season; both failed, and oratorio revivals fared little better. A rumor of Handel's impending departure from England later proved to be untrue, perhaps because of an invitation from the Lord Lieutenant of Dublin to present a series of concerts there. For this Handel composed *Messiah* on scriptural passages as arranged by Jennens, finishing the score in 24 days. The series began with *L'Allegro* on 23 Dec. 1742, to general acclaim; *Messiah* was first performed on 13 April and given again at his last Dublin concert on 3 June. He returned to London in August, soon thereafter contracting for the first of the annual Lenten concert series that he presented until his death. *Samson* was first performed on 18 Feb. 1743, followed by the failed London debut of *Messiah* on 23 March. He fell ill in April, but soon recovered, writing *Semele* (Feb. 1744), the *Dettingen Te Deum* and *Anthem* (Nov. 1743), and *Joseph and His Brethren* (Mar. 1744) in succession during his normal summer period of composition.

Handel planned a more ambitious King's Theatre season for 1745, with 24 performances, among them the premieres of *Hercules* and *Belshazzar.* In January, however, he suspended operations after only six dates because of low attendance and offered partial subscription refunds; renewed support allowed him to continue with a shortened schedule. The Second Jacobite Rebellion of 1745–46 called forth patriotic sentiment, and for the following seasons Handel responded with the *Occasional Oratorio* (Feb. 1746), *Judas Maccabaeus* (Apr. 1747), *Joshua* (Mar. 1748), and *Alexander Balus* (Mar. 1748), all with martial overtones. He produced *Susanna* and *Solomon* during the 1749 Lenten season, and in April of that year his *Music for the Royal Fireworks* in Vauxhall Gardens celebrated the Treaty of Aix-la-Chapelle (some 12,000 people attended the rehearsal, but the affair itself six days later was a pyrotechnic disaster). Handel's first association with the Foundling Hospital also dates from 1749, when he presented a charity concert in May; he later was named a governor, and from 1750 *Messiah* was given annually in the Hospital Chapel as a benefit, with the composer taking an active role through at least 1754.

Theodora was the only new offering for the 1750 Lenten concerts, which were ill-attended because of an earthquake scare; the ensuing exodus from London also victimized a production of Smollett's *Alceste* for which Handel had provided incidental music. He wrote no new oratorios for Lent 1751, presenting instead revivals, new organ concertos, and an "additional New Act" for *Alexander's Feast,* titled *The Choice of Hercules* (the music was reused from *Alceste*).

On 13 Feb. 1751, while composing the chorus "How dark, O Lord, are thy decrees" from his last oratorio, *Jepthe,* he was struck with blindness in his left eye; he did not finish the work until 30 August. He led *Jepthe*'s premiere in February 1752, but his eyesight continued to deteriorate, until by January 1753 he was blind. Very few works date from after 1752; still, he played organ concertos until his final days, performing from memory or extempore while the other players waited for his cue. Upon his death he left an estate of some £20,000, bequeathing in addition a score and set of parts of *Messiah* to the Foundling Hospital. Although he asked for burial in Westminster Abbey "in a private manner," over 3,000 people attended the interment on 20 Apr. 1759.

Works: *Vocal Music.* 45 operas (some with new music for revivals), including pasticci with music by Handel (*Oreste,* Dec. 1734; *Alessandro Severo,* Feb. 1738); 9 adapted pasticci from Vinci, Hasse, and others; 31 oratorios and odes; sacred music, including several motets written for Italy, 11 Chandos Anthems, 4 Coronation Anthems, 5 Te Deums, 2 Jubilates, and several other occasional pieces; over 100 cantatas composed in Italy, 1707–9; some 20 continuo duets and trios; English songs, many with new texts adapted to Handel's music (authentic songs include "Love's But the Frailty of the Mind," 1740, and "Stand Round My Brave Boys," 1745); French songs, including several from a "Cantate françoise" (1707); German songs, including 9 arias on Brockes texts (1724–27).

Instrumental Music. Orchestral concertos, including 6 Concerti grossi op. 3 (1734) and *12 Grand Concertos in 7 Parts* op. 6 (1740); organ, harp, and harpsichord concertos, including *6 Concertos* op. 4 (1738), *A Second Set of 6 Concertos* (keyboard only, 1740), *A Third Set of 6 Concertos* op. 7 (posthumous, 1761); *Concerti a due cori* (performed with 1748 oratorios); suites, including *Water Music* (1717, published later), *Music for the Royal Fireworks* (1749, originally for winds; strings added in published parts); several overtures; minuets, marches, and other movements (some dance-related) for orchestra and wind ensemble; chamber music, including 12 *Sonates* (ca. 1730; rev. ed. ca. 1732), *VI Sonates* op. 2 (ca. 1730; rev. ed. ca. 1732–33), and *7 Sonatas or Trios* op. 5 (1739) for 2 treble instruments and continuo, and several solo sonatas (original works and reworkings); and over 250 movements for keyboard solo, including some 25 suites along with sonatas ("lessons"), preludes, airs, allegros, chaconnes, sonatinas, and fugues.

Bibl.: Friedrich Chrysander, ed., *G. F. Händels Werke: Ausgabe der Deutschen Händelgesellschaft,* 1–48, 50–96, supps. 1–6 (Leipzig and Bergedorf bei Hamburg, 1858–94, 1902; R: 1965). *Hallische Händel-Ausgabe im Auftrage der Georg Friedrich Händel-Gesellschaft* (Kassel, 1955–). Walter and Margret Eisen, eds., *Händel Handbuch,* 4 vols. (Kassel, 1978); chronology by Siegfried Flesch, thematic catalogue by Bernd Baselt. Bernd Baselt, *Verzeichnis der Werke Georg Friedrich Händels* (Leipzig, 1986). Edward J. Dent, *Handel* (London, 1934). Otto Erich Deutsch, *Handel: A Documentary Biography* (London, 1955; R: 1974). Winton Dean, *Handel's Dramatic Oratorios and Masques* (London, 1959; New York, 1990). Paul Henry Lang, *George Frideric Handel* (New York, 1966; R: 1977). Ellen T. Harris, *Handel and the Pastoral Tradition* (New York, 1980). Christopher Hogwood, *Handel* (London, 1984). H. C. Robbins Landon, *Handel and His World* (London, 1985). Winton Dean and J. Merrill Knapp, *Handel's Operas, 1704–26* (New York, 1987). Mary Ann Parker-Hale, *G. F. Handel: A Guide to Research* (New York, 1988). Donald Burrows, *Handel* (New York, 1994). Donald Burrows and Martha J. Ronish, *A Catalogue of Handel's Musical Autographs* (Oxford, 1994). Ruth Smith, *Handel's Oratorios and Eighteenth-Century Thought* (Cambridge, 1995).

Handl, Jacob [Gallus, Jacobus] (b. probably at Ribniča, between 15 Apr. and 31 July 1550; d. Prague, 18 July 1591). Composer. Resident in Austria and neighboring areas from the mid-1560s; a singer in the imperial chapel in Vienna from no later than 1574 until 1575; 1579 or 1580–85, choirmaster to the Bishop of Olomouc; thereafter Kantor of St. Jan na Brzehu in Prague. All but a handful of his works have Latin texts. He wrote 20 Masses (parodies of motets or secular songs), about 450 motets, and 3 Passions, as well as several books of secular Latin songs. Most of the motets were published in the *Opus musicum* (4 books; Prague, 1586–91). The Latin secular songs appeared as *Harmoniae morales* (3 books; Prague, 1589–90) and *Moralia* (Prague, 1596).

Handy, W(illiam) C(hristopher) (b. Florence, Ala., 16 Nov. 1873; d. New York, 28 Mar. 1958). Blues composer. After playing cornet in brass bands and his own ragtime and minstrel bands, he formed the Pace–Handy music publishing company in Memphis with Harry Pace (1908–20; from 1918 in New York), issuing his compositions "Mr. Crump" (1909; revised as "Memphis Blues," 1912), "St. Louis Blues" (1914), and "Beale Street Blues" (1916). After splitting with Pace, he formed his own publishing company. Although Handy recorded with his blues- and jazz-oriented Memphis Orchestra in New York (1917–23), the finest of countless versions of his music is the album *Louis Armstrong Plays W. C. Handy* (1954). Handy staged concerts presenting a wide spectrum of African American music, notably at Carnegie Hall (1928) and in Chicago, New York, and San Francisco (throughout the 1930s). Although best known as a collector, organizer, and popularizer of blues, he also wrote spirituals, popular songs, stage songs, and art songs. He wrote *Father of the Blues: An Autobiography* (New York, 1941; R: 1991).

Hanff, Johann Nicolaus (b. Wechmar, Thuringia, 1665; d. Schleswig, winter 1711–12). Composer. Mattheson studied with him in Hamburg in 1688–92; by 1696 he was organist to the Prince-Bishop of Lübeck at Eutin. This position was terminated in 1705; he was named cathedral organist in Schleswig in 1706, but the post did not open up until 1711. After spending the interim in Hamburg, he was able to serve only a few months before he died. Extant works include 3 cantatas and several organ chorale preludes.

Hanlon, Kevin (Francis) (b. South Bend, Ind., 1 Jan. 1953). Composer, singer, and conductor. He studied at the Univ. of Indiana (South Bend), the Eastman School, and the Univ. of Texas at Austin (D.M.A., 1983); teachers included Barton McLean, Samuel Adler, Warren Benson, and Mario Davidovsky (Berkshire Music Center). His works include *Cumulus nimbus* (1977) and other orchestral pieces; chamber and keyboard music (*Centered,* chamber ensemble and tape, 1983; *Ostinato Suite,* harpsichord, 1982); choral and vocal music.

Hanna, Roland (P.) (b. Detroit, Mich., 10 Feb. 1932). Jazz pianist. He studied at the Eastman School (1953–54) and Juilliard (B.M., 1960) while also working with Benny Goodman (1958) and Charles Mingus (1959–60). He accompanied Sarah Vaughan (1960), toured with Coleman Hawkins (ca. 1963), then joined the Thad Jones–Mel Lewis Orchestra (1966–74). After raising large sums for education through concerts in Liberia, he was knighted there in 1970. In 1971 he formed the New York Jazz Quartet, and he has worked as a free-lance, recording the unaccompanied album *Perugia: Live at Montreux* (1974). Based in the bop style, his eclectic playing ranges from earthy blues to classically oriented compositions.

Hannay, Roger (Durham) (b. Plattsburgh, N.Y., 22 Sept. 1930). Composer. Studied composition at Syracuse Univ., Boston Univ., and the Eastman School (Ph.D., 1956) under Hanson; other teachers have included Foss (Berkshire Music Center), Sessions, and Carter. Beginning 1966 he taught at the Univ. of North

Carolina at Chapel Hill; in 1982 he was resident at the MacDowell Colony. His style ranges from freely atonal or serial, through experimentation with electronic and percussion music, to a new lyricism and recomposition of music of the past; his third symphony, *The Great American Novel* (1966–67), is based on 19th- and 20th-century American orchestral music; several mixed-media theater works are laden with social and political comment. Works include an opera and other stage works; at least 4 symphonies and other orchestral music, some with tape; chamber and keyboard music (including string quartets and *Dream Sequence,* piano and tape, 1980; *Scarlatti on Tour,* harpsichord, 1989); songs and choral music (*Emerging Voices,* soprano, alto, tenor, bass, 1984).

Hanslick, Eduard (b. Prague, 11 Sept. 1825; d. Baden, near Vienna, 6 Aug. 1904). Critic. His father, of a Catholic peasant family, became a musician and library cataloguer; his mother, daughter of a Jewish banker, converted in 1823 (Hanslick was to deny his Jewish ancestry when Wagner used it against him). Studied music with his father and 4 years with Tomášek; also law at Prague University; 1844, began to write music criticism in Prague. His progressive views found favor with Schumann, who invited him to Dresden, where he heard *Tannhäuser,* of which his laudatory review (1846) began his long career as music critic in Vienna; 1849, law degree, Univ. of Vienna; became civil servant until 1861; 1854, published his most famous book, *Vom Musikalisch-Schönen* (trans. as *On the Beautiful in Music*), which proposed an aesthetic resulting from his growing antipathy to Wagner, Liszt, Berlioz, and, later, any adherent of Wagnerism (such as Bruckner). This was balanced by his championing of Brahms, a close friend from 1862. His views were highly influential through his commanding position in Viennese musical life, reflected in Wagner's attack on him by identifying him with Beckmesser in *Die Meistersinger.* From 1856, lectured at Univ. of Vienna (professor from 1870); 1876, married 19-year-old singer, Sophie Wohlmut; published many collections of his criticism and memoirs, *Aus meinem Leben* (Berlin, 1894; R: 1971).

Bibl.: Henry Pleasants, ed., *Vienna's Golden Years of Music, 1850–1900: Eduard Hanslick* (New York, 1950).

Hanson, Howard (Harold) (b. Wahoo, Nebr., 28 Oct. 1896; d. Rochester, N.Y., 26 Feb. 1981). Composer, conductor, and teacher. Having studied piano and cello as a child, he attended Luther College in Wahoo; studied with Percy Goetschius at the Institute of Musical Art in New York (1914) and then with Arne Oldberg at Northwestern Univ. (B.A., 1916). In 1916 he began his career as a teacher at the College of the Pacific in San José, becoming dean in 1919; in 1921 he was awarded the Rome Prize and spent the next 3 years in Italy studying with Respighi; on his return he was appointed director of the Eastman School, a position he held for 40 years. When he retired from Eastman, he remained in Rochester to found the Institute of American Music, devoted to research on and publication of American music. He was instrumental in transforming the Eastman School into an important center for music education; in 1961–62 he toured with its orchestra in the USSR, Europe, and North Africa, sponsored by the U.S. State Department.

As a conductor he made his American debut in 1924, at the invitation of Damrosch leading the New York Symphony Orchestra in his symphonic poem *North and West* (orchestra and textless chorus). He often conducted the Boston Symphony, which commissioned his Second Symphony (1929); he composed the *Elegy in Memory of Serge Koussevitzky* (1955) for that orchestra. At Eastman he founded the American Composers Concerts as annual festivals of American music, at which he had conducted over 1,500 new compositions before his retirement. He often conducted American music elsewhere in the U.S. and abroad. His numerous honors include a Pulitzer Prize (1944, for his Fourth Symphony), membership in the Royal Swedish Academy (1938; his parents were Swedish immigrants), membership in the National Institute of Arts and Letters (1935), the Oliver Ditson Award (1945, for outstanding contribution to American music), and the George Foster Peabody Award (1946, for his radio broadcasts).

Hanson composed in a neo-Romantic style, primarily as a symphonist; his use of northern folk styles without actual quotation (his First Symphony is entitled the *Nordic*), subtle dissonances, and orchestration often favoring low registers have led to comparison with the music of Sibelius. His study of earlier music, especially that of Palestrina, is evident in the careful construction of his works; he made frequent use of chorale melodies and of Gregorian chant. His 7 symphonies overtly reflect extramusical ideas: the Third (1937–38) portrays the epic qualities of Swedish settlers in the Delaware Valley in 1638; the Fourth (1943) is a Requiem inspired by the death of his own father; the Fifth (1954), *Sinfonia Sacra,* deals with the Crucifixion and Resurrection according to St. John and was designed "to invoke some of the atmosphere of tragedy and triumph, mysticism and affirmation of the story which is the essential symbol of the Christian faith"; the last, *A Sea Symphony* (1977), is based on a text of Whitman. He remained committed to composing music that was "a direct expression of my own emotional reactions." This neo-Romantic stance did not inhibit his profound interest in theoretical problems, reflected in his book *Harmonic Materials of Modern Music: Resources of the Tempered Scale* (1960), articles for professional journals, and criticism in the *Rochester Times-Union.*

Works: an opera (*Merry Mount,* commissioned by the Metropolitan Opera, 1934) and 2 ballets; 7 symphonies, tone poems, concertos and other orchestral works with soloists (Piano Concerto op. 36, 1948); a few works for band (including *Variations on an Ancient Hymn,* 1977); chamber music (*Pastorale,* oboe and piano, 1949; arranged for oboe, harp, and strings, 1949); works for piano (*Scandinavian Suite* op. 13, 1918–19); many large-scale choral works (*Song of Democracy,* Whitman, solo voices, chorus, and orchestra, op. 44, 1957); other choral music and songs.

Bibl.: Ruth T. Watanabe, *Music of Howard Hanson* (Rochester, 1966). James E. Perone, *Howard Hanson: A Bio-Bibliography* (Westport, 1993).

Harbison, John (b. Orange, N.J., 20 Dec. 1938). Composer and conductor. As a child he had instruction in piano, violin, and viola; played in jazz ensembles as a teenager; won the B.M.I. Award (1954) for his Capriccio for trumpet and piano. He studied with Piston at Harvard (B.A., 1960); in Berlin with Boris Blacher; and at Princeton with Sessions and Earl Kim (M.F.A., 1963). Thereafter he held two successive fellowships from the Society of Fellows at Harvard (1963–68); on the faculty at M.I.T. from 1969. He has been composer-in-residence at Reed College (1968–69), the Pittsburgh Symphony (1982–84), the Berkshire Music Center (1984), and the Los Angeles Philharmonic (1985). He has conducted both Baroque (the Cantata Singers) and contemporary ensembles (Collage, from its founding in 1984); he has guest-conducted the Boston and the San Francisco symphonies. In 1987 he was awarded the Pulitzer Prize for his cantata *The Flight into Egypt.*

His style has been influenced by his experience in jazz improvisation. Early works employed twelve-tone procedures (*Confinement,* flute, oboe, clarinet, trumpet, trombone, alto saxophone, piano, percussion, and string quartet, 1965); later works exhibit his approach to thematic materials in a context of developing variation, in which a single "formal impulse is generating and ordering everything."

Works: 2 operas (*A Winter's Tale,* 1974; *Full Moon in March,* 1977), ballets, and incidental music; 3 symphonies (1981, 1987, 1991), violin (1980), viola (1990), oboe (1991), cello (1993), and flute (1993) concertos, and other orchestral works (*Four Hymns,* 1987; *The Most Often Used Chords,* 1993); *Deep Potomac Bells* (250 tubas, 1983); *Bermuda Triangle* (amplified cello, tenor saxophone, and electric organ; 1970), string quartets (1985, 1987, 1993), and other chamber and piano music; choral and vocal music (*The Flower-Fed Buffaloes,* cantata, baritone, chorus, and instrumental ensemble, 1976); *Three City Blocks,* band (1991).

Harburg, E(dgar) Y. [Yip; Hochberg, Isidore] (b. New York, 8 Apr. 1898; d. Los Angeles, 5 Mar. 1981). Popular lyricist and librettist. From 1929 he wrote songs for revues with composer Jay Gorney ("Brother, Can You Spare a Dime," 1932) and for musicals and films with Vernon Duke and Burton Lane. His most famous work was with Harold Arlen, with whom he wrote many films, including *The Wizard of Oz* (1939).

Hardelot, Guy d' [Mrs. W. I. Rhodes, née Helen Guy] (b. Château Hardelot, near Boulogne, ca. 1858; d. London, 7 Jan. 1936). Composer. Daughter of Helen Guy, a professional singer; at 15 entered the Paris Conservatory. In her 20s published a very popular setting of "Sans toi" (Victor Hugo), followed by over 300 other songs, some also very popular ("Because"), especially in the 1890s and early 1900s and sung by Melba, Maurel, Calvé (whom she served as accompanist on a U.S. tour in 1896), and others. Later a singing teacher in London.

Harline, Leigh (b. Salt Lake City, 26 Mar. 1907; d. Long Beach, Calif., 10 Dec. 1969). Composer and conductor. After working for radio stations in Salt Lake City, Los Angeles, and San Francisco, he wrote music for more than 120 films, many for Walt Disney Studios (1932–41). Among his best-known film scores are *Snow White* (1937) and *Pinocchio* (1940), including the song "When You Wish upon a Star," which won an Academy Award. He also wrote the *Centennial Suite* for the Utah centennial (1947) and one other orchestral work.

Harman, Carter (b. Brooklyn, 14 June 1918). Composer and critic. Studied composition with Sessions (Princeton, B.A., 1940) and Luening (Columbia, M.A., 1949). He taught at Princeton (1940–42); was music critic for the *New York Times* (1947–52) and for *Time* (1952–57); by 1967 he was associated with Composers Recording Incorporated and served as its executive director (1976–84) until his retirement. His own compositions are lyrical and expressive; contact with Babbitt led him to experiment with tape composition. Works include a ballet, a children's opera, and a staged "musical fantasy"; 2 orchestral pieces; chamber music (*Variations,* string quartet, 1950); piano music; electronic compositions (*Alex and the Singing Synthesizer,* 1974); choral and vocal music including many children's songs (1947–52).

Harney, Ben(jamin) R(obertson) (b. Middletown, Ky., 6 Mar. 1871; d. Philadelphia, 11 Mar. 1938). Ragtime songwriter, pianist, and singer. He worked in Louisville from 1889, and in New York from 1897; published probably the first ragtime songs (including "You've Been a Good Old Wagon but You Done Broke Down," 1895; "Mr. Johnson, Turn Me Loose," 1896), and the first ragtime instruction manual (1897), which included traditional songs and hymns arranged in ragtime version for piano.

Harnick, Sheldon (Mayer) (b. Chicago, 30 Apr. 1924). Lyricist and songwriter. Wrote for collegiate shows while attending Northwestern Univ.; moved to New York around 1950 and contributed songs to revues. From 1956 worked exclusively as a lyricist; from 1958 to 1970 collaborated with composer Jerry Bock on 7 musicals, including *Fiorello!* (1959, Pulitzer Prize for Drama) and *Fiddler on the Roof* (1964).

Harnoncourt, Nikolaus (b. Berlin, 6 Dec. 1929). Conductor and cellist. Studied cello with Paul Grümmer in Graz and Emanuel Brabec in Vienna. Played in the Vienna Symphony, 1952–69. As a student he began collecting historical instruments. In 1953, together with colleagues in the symphony, he founded the Concentus musicus, dedicated to performances of Renaissance and Baroque music on original instruments or copies of them. His wife, Alice, served as first violin. After four years of rehearsals the ensemble made its debut in 1957. In 1960 they began to tour and in 1962 gained international recognition through a recording of Bach's Brandenburg Concertos. Further recordings of Bach, Rameau, and masters of the Italian Baroque followed in the 1960s, 1970s, and 1980s, capped by a recording of the extant Bach cantatas, the leadership alternating between Harnoncourt and Gustav Leonhardt. In the meantime he began conducting and recording with the Amsterdam Concertgebouw Orchestra in 1981. Taught at the Mozarteum from 1972.

Harreld, Kemper (b. Muncie, Ind., 31 Jan. 1884; d. Detroit, 23 Feb. 1972). Violinist and music educator. Studied violin in Chicago with Felix Borowski and at the Frederickson Violin School; in Berlin with Siegfried Eberhardt, 1914. Developed a music department at Atlanta Baptist (later Morehouse) College from 1911, also leading the orchestra and glee club there. Helped organize the National Association of Negro Musicians in 1919 (president, 1937–39). Recorded for the Black Swan label in the early 1920s. Without leaving Morehouse, became chairman of the music department at Spelman College from 1927. Founded a string quartet in 1937.

Harrell, Lynn (b. New York, 30 Jan. 1944). Cellist. He studied with Leonard Rose at Juilliard, with Orlando Cole at the Curtis Institute; master classes with Casals and Piatigorsky. Debut with the New York Philharmonic, 1960; New York recital debut, 1971. Principal cellist with Cleveland Orchestra, 1965–71. Taught at Cincinnati College-Conservatory, 1971–76; at Juilliard from 1976; at the Univ. of Southern California from 1986. Co-winner of first (1975) Avery Fisher Prize. London debut, 1975. Appointed director of the Royal Academy of Music, 1993.

Harris, Barry (Doyle) (b. Detroit, 15 Dec. 1929). Jazz pianist. He accompanied leading swing and bop musicians who visited Detroit, which he left briefly to join Max Roach's quintet (1956). After touring with Cannonball Adderley (1960) he settled in New York and later accompanied Coleman Hawkins (1965–69). One of the finest bop pianists and a renowned teacher within the bop community, he nonetheless worked intermittently. Albums with his own trio include *At the Jazz Workshop* (1960) and *Live in Tokyo* (1976).

Harris, Bill [Willard Palmer] (b. Philadelphia, 28 Oct. 1916; d. Hallandale, Fla., 21 Aug. 1973). Jazz trombonist. He joined Benny Goodman (1943–44) before becoming a principal soloist with Woody Herman's big band (1944–46, 1948–50, 1956–58, 1959), with which he recorded "Goosey Gander" and "Bijou" (both 1945). He toured with Jazz at the Philharmonic from 1950, led combos and big bands (recording "Bill Not Phil," 1952), worked with Oscar Pettiford (1952), and rejoined Goodman (1959). Later he mainly played in Florida. His playing was often humorous, juxtaposing raucous outbursts and delicate passages.

Harris, Charles K(assel) (b. Poughkeepsie, N.Y., 1865 or 1867; d. New York, 22 Dec. 1930). Popular songwriter and music publisher. Began performing and composing in Milwaukee; from 1892 wrote numerous famous songs (including "After the Ball," 1892; "Break the News to Mother," 1897; "Always in the Way," 1903). He was an early proponent of composers' rights in publication: he published all of his own works, lobbied for the passage of the copyright act of 1909, and served as an officer of the newly founded ASCAP (1914). His autobiography, *After the Ball: Forty Years of Melody* (1926), is a valuable source for early Tin Pan Alley history.

Harris, Donald (b. St. Paul, Minn., 7 Apr. 1931). Composer. He studied piano and saxophone and anticipated a career in jazz arranging; his teachers included Paul Wilkinson, Finney, Homer Keller, Blacher, and Foss in the U.S.; Boulanger, Jolivet, and Max Deutsch in Europe (from 1956). He returned from Europe in 1967 and taught at the New England Conservatory until 1977; at Hartt College until 1988; dean of the College of the Arts at Ohio State Univ. from 1988. His style fuses his French experience (Milhaud, Poulenc) with an idiosyncratic employment of serialist procedures. Works include the opera *The Little Mermaid* (1985–90); incidental music to *Twelfth Night* (1989); pieces for orchestra; *Ludus I* (10 instruments, 1966) and other chamber and keyboard music; and *Of Hartford in a Purple Light* (for the centenary of Wallace Stevens, soprano and piano, 1979).

Harris, Roy [LeRoy] **(Ellsworth)** (b. near Chandler, Okla., 12 Feb. 1898; d. Santa Monica, 1 Oct. 1979). Composer. His parents farmed in Oklahoma and then in California, where Harris studied piano and clarinet as a child. After high school he farmed, then drove a truck for a dairy company while studying organ and theory; after service in the army, he studied philosophy and economics at Berkeley (1919–20), had lessons in organ (Charles Desmarets) and piano (Fannie Charles Dillon), and wrote his first large piece for chorus and orchestra; in 1924–25 Harris studied composition with Farwell. In 1926 his *Andante* for strings was conducted by Hanson in Rochester; in New York for another performance of the *Andante,* Harris met Copland, at whose suggestion he went to Paris for study with Boulanger. His Paris trip was supported by private funds and two Guggenheim Fellowships (1927, 1929). He returned to the West Coast in 1929 to convalesce after a spinal injury. His Concerto for String Quartet, Piano, and Clarinet had been performed in Paris by Boulanger, and was heard on national radio in 1933 in the U.S. In that year Koussevitzky commissioned a work for the Boston Symphony Orchestra (performed

1934), which he called "the first tragic symphony by an American." Farwell had already called him a genius on the basis of an early piano sonata (1928), and Copland too was enthusiastic; but Cowell judged Harris's music only "mildly interesting." His Third Symphony was particularly popular; the Boston Symphony performed it in 10 cities in 1939; it had 33 performances in 1941 and 1942. After the premiere a critic for *Modern Music* remarked, "It can find no peer in the musical art of America." Indeed, polls of New York Philharmonic listeners in 1935 and 1937 had rated Harris the best American composer.

For Harris, musical nationalism had the force of moral conviction. He wrote the orchestral overture *When Johnny Comes Marching Home* (1934) "to express a gamut of emotions particularly American and in an American manner." His Fourth Symphony (*Folksong Symphony,* 1939), which combines five choral sections with two instrumental interludes, uses fiddle and cowboy tunes; the composer's stated intention was "to bring about a cultural cooperation and understanding between the high school, college, and community choruses of our cities and their symphonic orchestras." Other American themes in orchestral works include the Gettysburg Address, the life of Lincoln, the preamble to the Constitution, and the voyages of Father Marquette in North America.

There are original aspects to Harris's style. Four of his symphonies are thematically unified constructions in one movement (3, 7, 8, 11). His melodies are indebted to Anglo-American folk song, early hymnody, and monophonic chant; often they are deployed in what Harris called a polytonal adaptation of the church modes. His harmonic language is based on his classification of chords according to the degree to which upper pitches are reinforced by overtones of lower pitches within a sonority. He often treated the orchestra as a set of discrete choirs, made increasingly lush in the 1940s by divisi scoring. Asymmetrical rhythms he saw as peculiarly American in comparison with a European focus on the symmetrical; somewhat unorthodox fugues and canons were favored devices (String Quartet no. 3 consists of four preludes and fugues). He explored twelve-tone procedures in Symphony no. 7 (1952; rev. 1955).

Harris taught at many institutions, including the Juilliard School (summers, 1932–40), Westminster Choir School (1934–38), Cornell Univ., Colorado College (1943–48), the Pennsylvania College for Women (where he organized the Pittsburgh Festival of Contemporary Music in 1952), UCLA (1961–73), and California State Univ. in Los Angeles (1973). In 1958 he was a Cultural Ambassador to the USSR, sponsored by the U.S. State Department; he won a third Guggenheim Fellowship in 1975.

Works: 4 ballets, a film score, incidental music; numerous orchestral works including symphonies, pieces with descriptive titles (*Epilogue to Profiles in Courage JFK,* 1964), and concertante works (mainly for piano or organ); pieces for band; chamber music, much of it for strings; some piano music (*American Ballads,* 2 sets, 1942–45); choral music with orchestra or other instrumental accompaniment, and unaccompanied; cantatas (*Abraham Lincoln Walks at Midnight,* 1953) and songs ("Fog," Sandburg, 1945).

Bibl.: Dan Stehman, *Roy Harris: An American Musical Pioneer* (Boston, 1984). Id., *Roy Harris: A Bio-Bibliography* (New York, 1991).

Harris, William (Henry) (b. London, 28 Mar. 1883; d. Petersfield, Hampshire, 6 Sept. 1973). Composer and organist. From 1899 he studied with Walter Parratt (organ) and with Walford Davies (composition) at the Royal College of Music. He held organ positions at New College, Oxford (from 1919), at Christ Church Cathedral (from 1929), and at St. George's, Windsor (from 1933). From 1923 he also taught organ at the Royal College, and he conducted the Oxford Bach Choir (1926–33). Later (1956–61) he was director of the music department of the Royal School of Church Music. He composed mostly sacred choral music, including anthems and motets (*Faire Is the Heaven,* 1925; *Bring Us, O Lord,* 1959; *Michelangelo's Confession of Faith,* 1935); also *The Hound of Heaven* (baritone, chorus, orchestra, 1919) and a number of organ works. Knighted in 1954.

Harrison, George (b. Wavertree, Liverpool, 25 Feb. 1943). Rock guitarist, sitarist, singer, and songwriter. From 1956 he played in groups with John Lennon and Paul McCartney in Liverpool, and from 1962 to 1970 served as lead guitarist and backup vocalist for the Beatles. His songwriting contributions to their albums included "Taxman" (*Revolver,* 1966) and "While My Guitar Gently Weeps" (*The Beatles,* 1968); he introduced the sitar into songs including "Within You, Without You" (*Sgt. Pepper's Lonely Hearts Club Band,* 1967). After their separation he released solo albums (including *All Things Must Pass,* 1970; *Living in the Material World,* 1973; *Cloud Nine,* 1987) and formed the record company Dark Horse (1974); in 1971 he organized a benefit concert for the hungry of Bangladesh, which subsequently yielded an album and a film. He wrote a memorial song following John Lennon's murder in 1981 ("All Those Years Ago") and in 1994 he reunited with the other surviving Beatles to record some new music (based on tapes made by John Lennon before he was killed).

Harrison, Guy (Fraser) (b. Guilford, Surrey, 6 Nov. 1894; d. San Miguel de Allende, Mexico, 20 Feb. 1986). Conductor and organist. Studied piano, organ, and theory with Basil Allchin at Oxford, 1904–11; organ with Walter Parrott and conducting with Walford Davies at the Royal Academy of Music in London, 1911–14. Organist at the Cathedral of St. Mary and St. John in Manila, 1914–20; at St. Paul's Episcopal Church in Rochester, N.Y., 1920–23. Conductor of the Rochester Civic Orchestra from 1929; associate conductor of the Rochester Philharmonic from 1930. Conductor of the Oklahoma City Orchestra, 1951–53; music director, 1953–73.

Harrison, Jimmy [James Henry] (b. Louisville, Ky., 17 Oct. 1900; d. New York, 23 July 1931). Jazz trombonist. In New York he joined big bands, including those of Fletcher Henderson (intermittently, 1927–31) and Charlie Johnson (1928). In this brief career, ended by cancer, he was widely influential. He helped develop jazz trombone by playing fluid, fast, high-pitched solos, as on Henderson's recording "I'm Coming Virginia" (1927) and Johnson's "Walk That Thing" (1928).

Harrison, Lou (b. Portland, Oreg., 14 May 1917). Composer. He studied at San Francisco State College, learning to play several instruments as well as singing in a madrigal group and accompanying dancers. Under Cowell he learned of the music of Ives and was exposed to microtonal composition and music for percussion ensembles. He met Cage while teaching at Mills College (1936–39), then attended Schoenberg's seminars at Univ. of Southern California (1941), working as accompanist in the dance department. In New York in the 1940s he met Thomson, worked as a copyist and dance composer, and wrote criticism for the *New York Herald Tribune, New Music Quarterly,* and other publications. In 1947 he conducted the premiere of Ives's Third Symphony; later, with Ives's approval, he reconstructed and edited other works. In 1949 he taught at Reed College; from 1951 to 1953 at Black Mountain College, where he composed mainly for dancers (Merce Cunningham and others). In 1952 and 1954 he won Guggenheim Fellowships, the second of which enabled him to travel to Rome for the premiere of his opera *Rapunzel,* which won an international competition.

By 1954 he had settled in Aptos, Calif.; over the next several years he managed to visit the Far East (1961–62), teach at the East–West Center of the Univ. of Hawaii, and spend a year in Mexico. In 1967 he taught at San Jose State, and later was visiting professor at various California institutions; in 1980 he began teaching at Mills College and in 1983 was a Senior Fulbright Scholar in New Zealand. Whereas earlier works had often employed a twelve-tone idiom or imitated Ives or Copland, depending on the requirements of the particular commission, his compositional style began in these years to reflect his interests in just intonation and Eastern culture. In the 1960s he had begun to design and build instruments; ca. 1973 he and William Colvig built an American gamelan tuned in just intonation. In addition to composing, Harrison wrote plays and poetry, and painted.

Works: several ballets, operas (*Young Caesar,* puppets, 1971), incidental music and film scores; Symphony on G (1948–61), Symphony no. 3 (1937–82), a piano concerto (1985), *A Parade* (1995) and other orchestral music, some requiring both Eastern and Western instruments (*Pacifika rondo,* chamber orchestra, 1963); many pieces for gamelan (including the Double Concerto for violin, cello, and gamelan, 1981–82); instrumental music for various ensembles or soloists, including much for percussion (*Summerfield Set,* piano, 1988); choral and solo vocal music (including *4 Strict Songs,* 8 baritones and orchestra, text in Esperanto, 1955).

Bibl.: Peter Garland, ed., *A Lou Harrison Reader* (Santa Fe, 1987).

Harsányi, Tibor (b. Magyarkanisza, 27 June 1898; d. Paris, 19 Sept. 1954). Composer and pianist. He attended the Budapest Academy of Music from 1908, a pupil of Kodály (composition) and Sándor Kovács (piano). After completing his studies he concertized (on piano) in Vienna and the Netherlands before settling in Paris in 1923. He became a central figure in that city's musical life and in the École de Paris; in 1924 he co-founded a group for new music, the Société Triton. In 1932 his *Nonette* was performed in Vienna at the ISCM festival; it received high acclaim, as did the opera *Les invités,* performed in Paris in 1937. His compositional idiom derives from Hungarian folk music and from a lyrical Romanticism. Other works include a radio opera, *Illusion* (1948); ballet scores (*Les pantins,* 1938, and *Chota roustaveli,* 1945); orchestral works (*Suite hongroise,* 1935); Violin Concerto (1941); *Divertimento,* trumpet, strings (1943); chamber works (a string trio, 1934, and a viola sonata, 1954); piano works (*La semaine,* 1924; *Trois pièces de danse,* 1928; Bagatelles, 1930).

Hart, Fritz (Bennicke) (b. Greenwich, 11 Feb. 1874; d. Honolulu, 9 July 1949). Conductor and composer. He studied at the Royal College of Music (1893–96); in 1908 he settled in Australia and was named director of the Melbourne Conservatory (1915) and artistic director of the Melbourne Symphony (1928). After a number of guest appearances with the Honolulu Symphony he moved to Honolulu in 1936, where he conducted the orchestra and taught at the Univ. of Hawaii. Although his compositions include orchestral and chamber music, he is best known for his vocal works, which include over 500 songs and 22 operas. He was also a prolific painter and writer.

Hart, Lorenz (Milton) (b. New York, 2 May 1895; d. there, 22 Nov. 1943). Lyricist and librettist. He began collaborating with composer Richard Rodgers on collegiate shows while both were students at Columbia Univ. Their song "Any Old Place with You" was included in the revue *A Lonely Romeo* (1919); they composed their first complete Broadway musical in 1925 *(Dearest Enemy).* From then until 1943 they wrote many musicals (including *A Connecticut Yankee,* 1927; *Babes in Arms,* 1937; *I Married an Angel,* 1942; *The Boys from Syracuse,* 1938; *Pal Joey,* 1940), as well as songs for films (beginning with *The Hot Heiress,* 1931).

Hartke, Stephen (Paul) (b. Orange, N.J., 6 July 1952). Composer. He studied at Yale (B.A., 1973), the Univ. of Pennsylvania (M.A., 1976), and the Univ. of

California at Santa Barbara (Ph.D., 1982); his teachers have included James Drew, George Rochberg, and Edward Applebaum. Hartke has taught at the Univ. of São Paulo, Brazil (1984–85) and the Univ. of Southern California (from 1987), and became composer-in-residence with the Los Angeles Chamber Orchestra in 1988; his compositions include *Caoine, Iglesia Abandonada, Oh Them Rats Is Mean in My Kitchen.*

Hartley, Walter S(inclair) (b. Washington, D.C., 21 Feb. 1927). Composer. He studied with Bernard Rogers and Howard Hanson at Eastman (B.M., 1950) and continued his studies at the Univ. of Rochester (M.M., 1951; Ph.D., 1953); taught at the National Music Camp at Interlochen (1956–60), at Davis Elkins College, and the State Univ. College at Fredonia, N.Y. Works include Concerto for 23 winds (1957); Concerto, alto sax, tuba, wind octet (1969); Octet for saxophones (1975); Concerto, tuba, percussion, orchestra (1976); Concerto no. 2, alto sax and small orchestra (1989); a series of sinfonias and other works for band; Concerto, tuba and 6 percussionists, 1974; *Sonata euphonia,* euphonium, piano (1979); *Mediation,* horn, piano (1980); other chamber music, especially for winds and brass.

Hartmann, Johan Peter Emilius (b. Copenhagen, 14 May 1805; d. there, 10 Mar. 1900). Composer. Son of a musician (and grandson of Johann Ernst Hartmann); his mother was a governess to the royal family, leading to his childhood friendship with the future king. He learned the piano, organ, and violin from his father, whom he succeeded at 19 as a church organist; studied law at Copenhagen Univ.; 1828–70, a lawyer in government service; active as a musician throughout his life, as composer, teacher, organist, becoming a leading figure in Danish and Scandinavian music, although little known farther abroad. In 1836, a founder of the Copenhagen Musical Society; its chairman, 1868–1900; 1867, a founder and co-director of Copenhagen Conservatory, teaching there until his death.

Works: 3 operas (*Liden Kirsten,* 1846); ballets; incidental music; 2 symphonies; concert overtures; chamber music; many cantatas and choruses; church music; songs; much piano music.

Hartmann, Johann Ernst (b. Glogau, Silesia, 24 Dec. 1726; d. Copenhagen, 21 Oct. 1793). Violinist and composer. In 1754 he received a post as violinist in the orchestra of the Prince-Bishop of Breslau. After holding orchestral posts in Rudolstadt and Plön in Holstein, in 1762 he went to Copenhagen to serve at the Danish court. In 1766 he settled there permanently, becoming director of the royal chapel in 1768. Of his ample musical output only a small amount remains; the rest was destroyed in a palace fire in 1794. Most significant are his singspiels, especially *Balders død* (Balder's Death; Copenhagen, 1779) and *Fiskerne* (The Fishermen; Copenhagen, 1780). The latter contains a melody that is now part of the Danish national anthem; long thought to be by Hartmann, the tune—which in any case does not appear in the earliest source of the work—may in fact have been derived from a Danish folk melody. Other extant works are 2 cantatas, Symphony in D, a violin concerto (1780?), and trio sonatas. He also authored a *Violin-Schule* (1777), which remained in manuscript.

Hartmann, Karl Amadeus (b. Munich, 2 Aug. 1905; d. there, 5 Dec. 1963). Composer. He was a pupil of Haas at the Munich Academy (1924–27) and then studied with Scherchen; under the Nazis he withdrew from German musical life, although his works continued to be performed elsewhere (for example, the *Miserae,* for orchestra, at the Prague ISCM meeting in 1935); he destroyed many of these early works; in 1941 and 1942 he studied with Webern. After the war he founded the concert series Musica viva, was elected to the Berlin Academy of Arts and the Bavarian Academy of Fine Arts, and was awarded the ISCM Schoenberg Medal (1954). The influences on his compositional style include works of Mahler and Bruckner, the Second Viennese School, Bartók, Stravinsky, and Blacher; he was particularly important as a composer who revitalized the German symphonic tradition and composed works organized in large spans.

Works: an opera (*Simplicius Simplicissimus,* 1934–35; staged Munich, 1948) and oratorios; symphonies (no. 8, 1963), concertos (piano, winds, and percussion, 1953; viola, piano, winds, and percussion, 1955) and other orchestral music; string quartets (1933, 1945–46) and other chamber music; piano music; *Ghetto* (alto, baritone, and small orchestra, 1960) and other vocal music.

Bibl.: Andrew D. McCredie, *Karl Amadeus Hartmann, sein Leben u. Werk* (Wilhelmshaven, 1980). Id., *Karl Amadeus Hartmann: A Thematic Catalogue of His Works* (New York, 1982).

Harty, (Herbert) Hamilton (b. Hillsborough, County Down, Ireland, 4 Dec. 1879; d. Brighton, 19 Feb. 1941). Composer, conductor, and pianist. He learned piano and counterpoint from his organist father; from age 12 he held organ posts, first at Magheracoll Church in Ireland's Antrim County, then at Belfast and Bray (near Dublin). He also played viola in a Dublin orchestra. He may have studied privately with Michele Esposito, professor at the Royal Irish Academy. He moved to London around the turn of the century and made a name as piano accompanist; he also began publishing and performing his own works. His Keats setting *Ode to a Nightingale* was performed to high acclaim at the Cardiff Festival in 1907. In 1920 he also took on a post as conductor of the Hallé Orchestra, which he formed into one of the country's finest orchestras. In 1924 he was named a fellow of the Royal College of Music; the next year he was knighted.

Works include *The Mystic Trumpeter* (baritone, chorus, orchestra, 1913); *Comedy Overture* (1906); Violin Concerto (1908–9); *An Irish Symphony* (1924); *The Children of Lir* (symphonic poem, 1939); chamber music (Piano Quintet, 1904; *Irish Fantasy,* violin and piano, 1912; Suite, cello and piano, 1928); many songs; arrangements of orchestral classics (e.g., Handel's *Royal Fireworks Music*).

Bibl.: David Greer, ed., *Hamilton Harty: His Life and Music* (New York, 1980).

Harvey, Jonathan (Dean) (b. Sutton Coldfield, Warwick, near Birmingham, 3 May 1939). Composer. After early musical experience as choirboy at St. Michael's College, Tenbury, and as cellist in the National Youth Orchestra, he attended Cambridge, studying music privately with Hans Keller and Erwin Stein. Later studied at the Univ. of Glasgow (Ph.D., 1964); with Babbitt on a Harkness Fellowship to Princeton (1969–70). Lecturer at Sussex University from 1977. He has composed large choral/instrumental works (*Cantata VI: On Faith,* chorus, strings, 1970; *Cantata VII: On Vision,* chorus, orchestra, and tape, 1971; *Cantata X: Spirit Music,* 1976; *Passion and Resurrection,* a "church opera," 1979; *Resurrection,* 2 choruses, organ, 1981); other vocal music (*Four Songs of Yeats,* 1965; *Spirit Music,* 1975); orchestral works (a symphony, 1966; *Persephone's Dream,* 1972; *Inner Light,* 1976; *Madonna of Winter and Spring,* with synthesizers, 1986; *Timepieces,* 1987; *Lightness and Weight,* tuba and orchestra, 1987); works for tape (*Time-Points,* 1970; *Veils and Melodies,* 1978; *Vivos voco,* 1980; Toccata, organ and tape, 1980); 2 string quartets (1977, 1988) and other chamber music. He also authored a book on Stockhausen.

Harwood, Basil (b. Woodhouse, Gloucester, 11 Apr. 1859; d. London, 3 Apr. 1949). Composer and organist. After private study of piano with J. L. Roekel and organ with George Riseley, he studied theory and composition briefly at the Leipzig Conservatory under Reinecke and Jadassohn. He held a succession of important organ posts, including at Ely Cathedral (1887–92) and at Christ Church, Oxford (1892–1909); at Oxford he conducted the orchestral society and (1896–1900) the Bach Choir. He composed chiefly sacred choral works (*Inclina domine,* 1898; *Ode on May Morning,* 1913; many other anthems) and organ music (2 organ sonatas; a concerto, 1910; *Dithyramb; Christmastide*). He also edited the 1908 edition of the *Oxford Hymn Book.*

Haskil, Clara (b. Bucharest, 7 Jan. 1895; d. Brussels, 7 Dec. 1960). Pianist. Entered the Bucharest Conservatory in 1901. With a stipend from Queen Elisabeth of Romania, studied piano with Richard Robert in Vienna, 1902–5; also studied violin. In Paris studied with Morpain, 1905–7; with Alfred Cortot at the Conservatoire, 1907–10. As a violinist won the Concours de l'Union française de la jeunesse, 1909; obtained first prize in piano at the Conservatoire, 1910. Coached by Busoni and Paderewski, 1912; performed in recitals with Ysaÿe and Casals. The onset of a muscular disorder thwarted her career until 1920, when a remission made possible piano recitals in Switzerland, Belgium, and the U.S. For several decades her art was scarcely appreciated outside of Switzerland. After a triumph at Casals's first Prades Festival (1950) and an equally successful Paris recital (1951) she was recognized internationally, especially for performances of Mozart, Beethoven, and Schubert.

Haslinger, Tobias (b. Zell, Upper Austria, 1 Mar. 1787; d. Vienna, 18 June 1842). Music publisher. After receiving musical training as chorister at the cathedral at Linz, he worked in a music and book shop there; in 1810 he moved to Vienna. In 1814 he became acquainted with Sigmund Anton Steiner, whose publishing firm had received the imperial privilege initially bestowed upon Senefelder. In 1815 Steiner and Haslinger became partners; 1815–26, the firm published Beethoven's opp. 90–101, 112–118, and 136–138. In 1826 Haslinger became sole proprietor; in 1830 he was made art and music dealer of the imperial court. Under his guidance the firm embarked on a complete Beethoven edition (begun in 1828) and published editions of works by Schubert (opp. 77–83), Chopin, Handel, Schumann, J. S. Bach, and others.

Hasse, Johann Adolf (bapt. Bergedorf, near Hamburg, 25 Mar. 1699; d. Venice, 16 Dec. 1783). Composer. His great-grandfather, grandfather, father, and brother were musicians, active in Lübeck and Bergedorf. He studied voice in Hamburg from 1714 until joining the local opera as a tenor in 1718, moving to Braunschweig-Wolfenbüttel in 1721, where his first opera, *Antioco,* was performed. Traveled to Italy in 1722, spending time in a number of cities before settling in Naples, where he studied briefly with Porpora, then with Alessandro Scarlatti; during 1726–33 over 20 of his stage works were produced for the Neapolitan court.

A lifelong association with Venice began with his first documented visit in 1730 for the staging of *Artaserse,* his first opera on a libretto by Metastasio. During his stay there he married the famed soprano Faustina Bordoni and was engaged as *maestro di cappella* at the electoral court in Dresden (the libretto to *Artaserse* identifies him as such). The couple arrived in Dresden in July 1731. Hasse's first opera for the court was *Cleofide* (adapted from Metastasio's *Alessandro nell'Indie* by Bocardi), first performed in September, with J. S. and W. F. Bach probably in attendance. He was in Italy from October 1731 to February 1734, and from November 1734 to January 1737; he wrote operas for Naples, Rome, Turin, Pesaro, Bologna, and Venice and produced a sizable body of sacred music for the Ospedale degli incurabili in Venice as well (he had probably contributed music to this institution since 1730, but is first named as its *maestro di cappella* in 1736 in the libretto to *Alessandro nell'Indie*). Five Hasse operas with libretti by court poet Pallavicino were premiered in Dresden between February 1737 and May 1738; after a sojourn in Venice he returned to

Dresden, writing new operas and mounting revivals in 1740–42.

In January 1742 Frederick the Great heard *Lucio Papirio;* Hasse soon became his favorite composer, and Hasse operas were given in Berlin until the king's death in 1786. Hasse's friendship with Metastasio also began around this time; the two worked closely together on many operas. The next 15 years were divided between Saxony and Italy, with Hasse presenting new works in both places; he also visited Paris. The Seven Years' War forced the Elector's court to remain in Warsaw from 1756 until 1762; Hasse probably visited Poland, but spent most of his time in the South. His last commercial opera production was *Nitteti,* given in Venice at Carnival 1758; he produced operas for the Neapolitan court, 1758–60, and for the court in Vienna, 1760–63. After a short stay in Dresden following the court's return, he was dismissed in 1764 and returned to Vienna, where he lived until 1772, continuing to compose and traveling periodically to Venice or Turin. His final 10 years were spent in Venice; some sacred music, including 3 Masses and a Requiem, dates from this time. Despite his towering reputation only a few years before, he died in obscurity, receiving a gravestone only in 1820.

Works: about 80 operas, intermezzi, and other theater works, including *La Contadina* (Naples, 1728), *Artaserse* (Venice, 1730), *Alessandro nell'Indie* (also *Cleofide;* Dresden, 1731), *Cajo Fabrizio* (Rome, 1732), *Demetrio* (Venice, 1732), *Siroe* (Bologna, 1733), *La clemenza di Tito* (2 versions: Pesaro, 1735; Naples, 1759), *Didone abbandonata* (Hubertusburg, 1742), *Lucio Papirio* (Dresden, 1742), *Antigono* (Hubertusburg, 1743), *Semiramide* (Venice, 1744), *Demofoonte* (Dresden, 1748), *Solimano* (Dresden, 1753), *Il Rè pastore* (Hubertusburg, 1755), *Nitteti* (Venice, 1758), *Zenobia* (Warsaw, 1761), *Piramo e Tisbe* (Vienna, 1768), and *Ruggiero* (Milan, 1771); arias for revivals and pasticci; cantatas; church music, including Masses, motets, and antiphons.

Bibl.: Sven Hansell, *Works for Solo Voice of Johann Adolf Hasse (1699–1783)* (Detroit, 1968). Fredrick L. Millner, *The Operas of Johann Adolf Hasse* (Ann Arbor, 1979). Friedrich Lippmann, ed., *Colloquium "Johann Adolf Hasse und die Musik seiner Zeit" (1983: Siena)* (Laaber, 1987).

Hassell, Jon (b. Memphis, 22 Mar. 1937). Composer and trumpeter. Studied in Cologne with Stockhausen and Pousseur (1965–67), then with Rogers at the Eastman School (M.M., 1970). He performed in minimalist ensembles of Riley and Young; in 1972 he began to study Indian classical music with the singer Pandit Pran Nath and imitates some aspects of that music in his trumpet playing. In his own compositions he combines minimalism, electronic techniques, and various non-Western musical styles to produce what he calls "Fourth World Music." Between 1977 and 1983, 5 recordings were released, some as a result of collaboration with Brian Eno, a rock musician (*Vernal Equinox,* employing concrete sounds, percussion, and electronics, 1977). He also wrote for the stage (*Sulla Strada,* a collaboration with M. Criminali based on Kerouac's *On the Road,* 1982); earlier works include *Solid State* (2 synthesizers, 1969), *Superball* (for 4 players with hand-held magnetic tape heads, 1969), mixed-media pieces.

Hassler, Hans Leo (b. Nuremberg, bapt. 26 Oct. 1564; d. Frankfurt am Main, 8 June 1612). Composer. Born into a family of organists; received initial musical instruction from his father; 1584–85, study in Venice with Andrea Gabrieli; 1586–ca. 1600, chamber organist to the Fugger family of Augsburg; 1601–4, director of town music in Nuremberg; 1604, moved to Ulm; from 1608, chamber organist and eventually Kapellmeister to the Saxon electoral chapel in Dresden; died during a visit of this chapel to Frankfurt am Main. Despite the nature of his musical employment and his outstanding reputation in his own time as an organist, the majority (and the best) of his works are choral or polychoral, most with Latin texts. The sacred pieces include Masses, motets, Psalms, and spiritual songs. The earlier ones are for Catholic, the later for Lutheran use. The secular compositions include Italian madrigals, German part songs, dance songs, and instrumental works for ensembles or for keyboard.

Bibl.: *Sämtliche Werke* (Wiesbaden, 1961–).

Hässler, Johann Wilhelm (b. Erfurt, 29 Mar. 1747; d. Moscow, 29 Mar. 1822). Pianist, organist, and composer. His first musical study was with his uncle Johann Christian Kittel, organist at Erfurt; around 1762 he assumed the post of organist at the local Barfüsserkirche. After his father's death in 1769 he managed the family fur business. During the early 1770s he made concert tours of Germany. He concertized during the 1780s and 1790s, making important contacts with Forkel, Hiller, Benda, and C. P. E. Bach. After two years in London (1790–92) he moved to Russia, settling first in St. Petersburg, then (in 1794) in Moscow, where he was a prominent composer and pedagogue. He published many keyboard works, including sonatas, fantasies, and preludes; also a Grand concert op. 50; a cantata; chamber works; and songs. Best known of his piano works is the *Grand gigue* in D minor op. 31.

Hastings, Thomas (b. Washington, Conn., 15 Oct. 1784; d. New York, 15 May 1872). Composer and educator. At 12 moved with his family to Clinton, N.Y.; became church choirmaster; winter 1806–7, established his first singing school; published *Musica sacra* (Utica, 1815), a collection of original tunes, joined to the anthology *Springfield Collection* in 1816 and much republished; published didactic *Musical Reader* (Utica, 1817), a collection of *Flute Melodies* (Utica, 1822), and a pioneering *Dissertation on Musical Taste* (Albany, 1822; enlarged 2nd ed., 1853). Lived in Utica (1823–32) as editor of *Western Reader,* a religious weekly, in which he expounded ideas for the improvement of church music; moved to New York City (1832), where he was invited to put these ideas into practice in leading churches; also choirmaster,

Bleecker Street Presbyterian Church; a leading figure there and throughout the country in musical education, recognized by an honorary degree from New York Univ. (1858). He published many collections of hymns, Sunday school songs, and other church music, either alone or in collaboration; composed over 1,000 hymns, including "Rock of Ages."

Bibl.: M. B. Scanlon, "Thomas Hastings," *MQ* 32 (1946): 265–77. M. Teal, "Letters of Thomas Hastings," *Notes* 34 (1977–78): 303–18.

Haubenstock-Ramati, Roman (b. Kraków, 27 Feb. 1919; d. Vienna, 3 Mar. 1994). Composer. From 1934 to 1938, while still in secondary school, he studied theory and counterpoint with Artur Malawski at the Kraków Conservatory. From 1939 he was a pupil of Józef Koffler at the Lwów Academy, and he later studied philosophy at the Univ. of Kraków. After the war he served as music director at Kraków Radio, secretary of ISCM, and editor of the music journal *Ruch Muzyczny.* He spent six years in Israel (1950–56), where he taught at the Academy of Music and directed the State Music Library in Tel Aviv. In 1957, after working briefly in Paris at the Studio des recherches de musique concrète, he settled in Vienna. Works such as his series of "Mobiles" (e.g., *Interpolation,* 1958) were important and influential experiments in aleatoric musical structure. Many of his works are characterized by variable form and unspecified instrumentation. In 1959 he organized an exhibition of musical scores employing graphic notation.

Stage works: *Amerika* (1962–64, after Kafka's novel); *Divertimento,* 2 actors, dancer, 2 percussionists (1968); and *La comédie,* 3 soloists and 3 percussionists (1969; German version as *Spiel*). Vocal works: *Blessings,* soprano, chamber ensemble (1951; rev. 1978); *Mobile for Shakespeare,* voice, 6 instruments (1960); *Prosa Texte* (1962); *Madrigal,* 16 vocal parts (1970); *Sonans* (1974). Orchestral: *Les symphonies de timbres* (1956); *Séquences,* violin, orchestra (1958); *Tableaux,* orchestra, I–III (1967–71); *Concerto per archi* (1977); *Symphonien* (1977); *Sotto voce,* chamber orchestra (1986); *Imaginaire* (1989). Other instrumental works: *Ricercare,* string trio, (1948; rev. 1978); *Liaisons,* "mobile," vibraphone and marimbaphone (1958); *Credentials* (1960); *Multiples,* various instruments, I–VI (all 1969); 2 string quartets; *Shapes,* I (organ, tape, 1973); II (organ, piano, harpsichord, celesta, 1973); *Self,* bass clarinet, 3 tapes (1978).

Haubiel [Pratt], **Charles (Trowbridge)** (b. Delta, Ohio, 30 Jan. 1892; d. Los Angeles, 26 Aug. 1978). Composer and pianist. He studied piano with Wilhelm Ganz in Europe, returning to the U.S. in 1913 to tour with a Czech violinist. He taught in Oklahoma City until 1917, served in the army, then returned to New York to study at Mannes College (1919–24; composition with Scalero, orchestration with Modest Altschuler). He continued his piano study with Josef and Rosina Lhévinne and taught piano at the Institute of Musical Art (1920–30). From 1923 to 1947 he taught composition and theory at New York Univ.; in 1935 he founded the Composer's Press (taken over by Southern Music in 1966). He moved to California in the mid-1960s. A prolific composer; his style was tinged with a deliberate Americanism in works such as *Pioneers* (a symphonic saga of Ohio, 1946; rev. 1956) and *Metamorphoses* (1926, piano or orchestra), a set of variations on "Swanee River" in styles ranging from his conception of the medieval to that of Gershwin.

Works include 7 operas; incidental music; *Portraits* (1935) and other pieces for orchestra, many transcribed from piano or other instrumental works; 5 piano trios, *Cryptics* (cello and piano, 1973), *In the French Manner* (flute, cello, and piano, 1942), and other chamber music; piano music; a choral song cycle, part songs, works for chorus and orchestra; 3 cantatas, song cycles, some 25 songs.

Hauer, Josef Matthias (b. Wiener Neustadt, 19 Mar. 1883; d. Vienna, 22 Sept. 1959). Composer. He taught elementary school until an illness forced him to retire (1919); in addition he studied organ, cello, voice, and conducting. At 28 he began to compose songs and piano pieces similar to the minatures of Schoenberg and Webern, and in 1919 began to systematize his "law of twelve notes." Although he and Schoenberg contemplated a joint formulation, it never appeared, and Hauer claimed precedence for his own theory, though he dedicated his treatise *Vom Melos zur Pauke* (1925) to Schoenberg. Hauer's formulation is in terms of 44 unordered hexachords (which he called tropes) rather than ordered sets of 12 pitch classes. He regarded twelve-tone music not as "an art in the classical, romantic, or modern sense but [as] a cosmic game with the twelve tempered half-steps." He wrote 92 works with opus numbers and more than 100 without. In the 1920s his works were performed at Donaueschingen and ISCM; he won the Vienna Artist's Prize in 1927. He had many ties to the artistic community in Vienna and served as the model for the composer in novels by Hesse, Stoessel, and Werfel. More performances occurred after the war, and he received the Major Austrian State Prize in 1955.

He composed an opera and a singspiel (1932, perf. Vienna, 1966); 8 orchestral suites, violin and piano concertos, and other orchestral music; string quartets and other chamber music; choral and vocal music (*Wandlungen,* 6 solo voices, chorus, orchestra, 1927; perf. Baden-Baden, 1928); many twelve-tone works without opus number (1939–59).

Bibl.: Johann Sengstschmidt, *Zwischen Trope und Zwölfstonspiel: J. M. Hauers Zwölftontechnik in ausgewählten Beispielen* (Regensburg, 1980).

Hauk, Minnie [Amalia Mignon Hauck] (b. New York, 16 Nov. 1851; d. Triebschen, near Lucerne, 6 Feb. 1929). Singer. Studied in New Orleans and New York; opera debut, Brooklyn Academy of Music, 1866 *(La sonnambula);* 1867, U.S. premiere, Gounod's *Roméo* *et Juliette;* very successful in Paris (Théâtre-Italien, 1868), London (Covent Garden, 1868), Russia (1869–70), Vienna (1870–74), Berlin (1874–77), Budapest (1876). Sang over 100 roles, soprano and mezzo, light and dramatic; best known for her *Carmen* (first at Brussels, 1877; London and New York premieres, 1878); active in Europe and the U.S. through the mid-1890s. Ghost-written memoirs, *Memories of a Singer* (London, 1925).

Hauptmann, Moritz (b. Dresden, 13 Oct. 1792; d. Leipzig, 3 Jan. 1868). Theorist, teacher. Studied music in Dresden; 1811, lessons (violin, composition) in Gotha from Spohr, one of the principal influences in his life; 1812–15, violinist, Dresden orchestra; 1815–20, music teacher in service of the Russian military governor of Dresden, Prince Repnin. From 1822 to 1842 he was violinist in the Kassel orchestra under Spohr, also teaching theory and composition; 1842–68, Kantor, Thomasschule, Leipzig; 1843–68, taught theory, Leipzig Conservatory. Much interested in early music, he was one of the founders (1850) and first president of the Bach Gesellschaft, also editing its first 3 volumes. He composed much sacred music, an opera, instrumental pieces, and songs, but is best known as a teacher and for his theoretical works, especially *Die Natur der Harmonik und Metrik* (Leipzig, 1853; 2nd ed. 1873; trans. Eng. 1880).

Hausegger, Siegmund von (b. Graz, 16 Aug. 1872; d. Munich, 10 Oct. 1948). Conductor and composer. Studied music with his father, Friedrich, a critic in the Wagner camp. While attending Graz Univ. he continued extracurricular musical studies with E. W. Degner, K. Pohling, and M. Plüdemann. Conducting debut with the Graz Opera, 1895. Conductor of the Kaim Orchestra, Munich, 1898–1903; of the Frankfurt Museum Concerts, 1903–6; of the Scottish Orchestra in Glasgow, 1906–10; of the Hamburg Philharmonic and the Blüthner Orchestra in Berlin, 1910–20. As chief conductor of the Munich Philharmonic, 1920–38, he was one of the first to perform Bruckner's symphonies from the Haas editions.

Hausmann, Robert (b. Rottleberode, Harz, 13 Aug. 1852; d. Vienna, 18 Jan. 1909). Cellist. Studied at Berlin Hochschule, 1869–71, then with Piatti. Cellist with Hochberg Quartet, Dresden, 1872–76; then taught at Berlin Hochschule; 1879–1907, cellist, Joachim Quartet. He premiered Brahms's Cello Sonata no. 2 and (with Joachim) his Double Concerto.

Haussermann, John (William, Jr.) (b. Manila, 21 Aug. 1909; d. Denver, 5 May 1986). Composer. He was raised in Ohio from 1915 and studied at Cincinnati Conservatory (1924–27) and Colorado College; studied organ (Dupré) and composition (Paul Le Flem) in Paris (1930–34). He spent most of his active career in Cincinnati. Although cerebral palsy forced him to dictate his compositions note by note, he made occasional appearances as an organist performing his own works and improvisations. In New York in 1940 he cofounded the American Colorlight Music Society, which espoused the theories of Scriabin and Lászlo. He retired to San Francisco in 1967, but in 1981 returned to Cincinnati and began to compose again. His impressionist style reflects his French training and his friendship with Ravel. Works include a concerto for organ and strings (1985) and other orchestral pieces; chamber music for strings (2 quartets) and other ensembles; keyboard music; choral and solo vocal music.

Haussmann, Valentin (b. Gerbstedt, near Eisleben, about 1565; d. in or before 1614). Composer. Student of Rasdius at the Gymnasium poeticum, Regensburg, until 1589; during the next decade he was in Nuremberg, Wolfenbüttel, Hannover, Halberstadt, and Königsberg, and later also at Hamburg, Magdeburg, and Gerbstedt. He produced several volumes of German secular vocal music along with sacred and occasional works and dances; as a poet he translated or adapted madrigal texts for the many anthologies of Italian music he produced, featuring composers such as Vecchi, Gastoldi, and Marenzio. Many of his own works were also included in contemporary collections.

Hawes, William (b. London, 21 June 1785; d. there, 18 Feb. 1846). Composer. Choirboy, 1795–1801, Chapel Royal; 1803, deputy lay vicar, Westminster Abbey; 1817–20, lay vicar there; 1805, gentleman of the Chapel Royal; 1812–46, master of the choristers, St. Paul's; 1817–46, master of the children, Chapel Royal. He was also active as singing teacher, conductor (Madrigal Society), organist (Lutheran Chapel of the Savoy), founding member Philharmonic Society (1813), music publisher, and concert organizer. He adapted many Continental operas for the English stage, especially at the English Opera House (Lyceum); also composed light operas, glees, church music, and other works.

Hawkins, Coleman (Randolph) [Bean; Hawk] (b. St. Joseph, Mo., 21 Nov. 1904; d. New York, 19 May 1969). Jazz tenor saxophonist. After touring with Mamie Smith (1921–23), he became the first important jazz tenor saxophone soloist as a member of Fletcher Henderson's big band (1924–34), which recorded "The Stampede" (1926). He worked as a freelance in Europe (1934–39), recording "Crazy Rhythm" with Benny Carter and Django Reinhardt among his sidemen (1937). Returning to the U.S., he reasserted his preeminence in jam sessions and with a famous improvisation on "Body and Soul," recorded in 1939. He led a big band (1939–41), then small groups, while also touring intermittently with Jazz at the Philharmonic (1946–67). From the mid-1940s he, unlike other major players of his generation, embraced bop, altering his approach to soloing and using sidemen such as Dizzy Gillespie, Max Roach, Thelonious Monk, and Miles Davis. Having previously concentrated on popular song forms, he made powerful interpretations of blues in the 1950s. Later he recorded the album *Duke Ellington Meets Coleman Hawkins* (1962).

Bibl.: Albert McCarthy, *Coleman Hawkins* (London, 1963; R: in *Kings of Jazz,* ed. S. Green, South Brunswick, N.J., 1978). John Chilton, *The Song of the Hawk: The Life and Recordings of Coleman Hawkins* (Ann Arbor, 1990).

Hawkins, John (b. London, 29 Mar. 1719; d. there, 21 May 1789). Writer on music. Studied architecture under Edward Hoppins, law and literature with John Scott; began a practice as an attorney in 1742. He was involved in a number of music clubs, including the Academy of Ancient Music (1743) and the Madrigal Society (1748), supplied texts for vocal works by Boyce and John Stanley, and was acquainted with Handel. He left his law practice upon receipt of a sizable inheritance in 1759 and built a large collection of music in print and manuscript. His *General History of Music,* issued in 1776, was the result of years of research; though the initial response to it was positive, it soon became the target of attacks by the associates of Burney, who had published his history a few months before. He was knighted in 1772.

Bibl.: Percy A. Scholes, *The Life and Activities of Sir John Hawkins* (London, 1953).

Hawthorne, Alice. See Winner, Septimus.

Hayasaka, Fumio (b. Sendai City, 19 Aug. 1914; d. Tokyo, 15 Oct. 1955). Composer. In Sapporo, where he was raised, he met Akira Ifukube; in 1933 the two were among the founders of Shin Ongaku Renmei (New Music League). Two years later Hayasaka's work *Futatsu no sanka e no zensōkyoku* won the Japanese Radio Competition Prize; in 1938 he won the Weingartner Prize for *Kodai no bukyoku.* In 1939 he moved to Tokyo, where he composed (among other things) nearly 100 scores for films. His score for Kurosawa's *Rashōmon* (1951) won first prize at the 1952 Venice International Festival. Other works include a piano concerto (1946); *Metamorphosis,* orchestra (1953); *Yūkara,* orchestra (1955); chamber music (including a string quartet, 1950).

Hayashi, Hikaru (b. Tokyo, 22 Oct. 1931). Composer. His music studies began in 1941; after the war he resumed instruction with Hisatada Otaka and Tomojirō Ikenouchi at the National Univ. of Fine Arts in Tokyo. In 1953 he cofounded the new-music group Yagi no Kai. Among his awards are the Art Festival Award (1953, for the Symphony in G) and the Otaka Prize (1956, for *Variations for Orchestra*). At the Moscow Film Festival he was recognized with a prize for the score to the film *The Naked Island.* He has composed operas (*Esugata nyōbō* [The Beautiful Wife], 1961; *Okonjōruri,* 1975; *Sero-hiki no Gshu* [Gorsh the Cellist], 1986; *Shiroi kemono no densetsu* [Legend of a White Beast], 1987); orchestral music (*Music for Orchestra,* 1965; *Winds,* 1974); many choral works (Requiem, 1960; *The Gold Rush,* 1960; *Kojiki no uta* [Beggar's Song], 1962; *Japan,* 1970; *Genbaku shōkei* [A Little Landscape of the Bomb], 1971; *Hi no yoru* [Flaming Night], 1972); chamber music (Piano Sonata, 1965; *Winter on 72nd St.,* violin, piano, 1968); solo vocal works.

Haydn, (Franz) Joseph (b. Rohrau, 31 Mar. 1732; d. Vienna, 31 May 1809). Composer. He was one of six children born to Mathias Haydn (a wheelwright and civil servant) and Anna Maria Koller in Lower Austria. His parents, wanting to prepare him for the priesthood, sent him in 1738 to a church school in nearby Hainburg. There Haydn took his first formal instruction in music. When Georg Reutter, the newly installed music director at St. Stephen's Cathedral, Vienna, came recruiting, the young Haydn was recommended for the choir. Upon reaching the choir's minimum age of 8, Haydn was invited to Vienna.

At St. Stephen's Haydn received instruction in voice, violin, and keyboard, but little general education except for a smattering of Latin. In 1745 he was joined there by his brother Michael, and almost immediately the gifted younger sibling assumed the elder's position as soloist. Passing out of the limelight probably encouraged Haydn in his natural bent for composition, but he received little help: Reutter, himself a professional composer, gave the youngster only two lessons. As Haydn's voice changed, his position as a chorister became increasingly untenable. In late 1749 he was dismissed peremptorily over a practical joke.

Taking an attic room next door to St. Michael's Church, he made ends meet by giving violin and keyboard lessons, working as a free-lance musician in churches, and performing in (and sometimes composing for) groups playing the open-air evening serenades so popular in Vienna. At the same time he began an intensive study of counterpoint (using the writings of Fux) and figured bass (using Mattheson). The results of his industry were clearly evident by 1751, when Pietro Metastasio, the renowned poet and architect of opera seria, engaged Haydn to tutor a gifted girl, Marianna Martines. Haydn's earliest extant composition, perhaps the first that he did not discard as apprentice work, was a *Missa brevis,* written by 1753. That same year Martines began vocal studies with Nicola Porpora; through her and Metastasio, Haydn gained an entree to that famous opera composer.

Haydn proposed to serve as Porpora's factotum in return for instruction; although this arrangement was undertaken for no more than three months, Haydn later credited Porpora with teaching him "the true fundamentals of composition"; he also learned much about setting Italian texts. Haydn's interest in writing for the theater received a further boost at this time. One of his open-air serenades was heard by the manager of the Kärtnerthortheater; the result was a collaboration mounted there in 1753—and again, with some revisions, in 1758—*Der krumme Teufel;* neither version survives. Two scores dated 1756 do survive, an organ

Sketch of Joseph Haydn made during his stay in England.

concerto and a Salve Regina, the first and possibly the second written for the ceremony during which Haydn's first great love, Therese Keller, took the vows of a nun.

During this period keyboard pieces by Haydn began circulating in Vienna. Countess Philippine Aloysia Thun liked one of them so much that she sought out Haydn to teach her keyboard technique and singing. To have such a student certainly added luster to Haydn's name, but it was probably the attractiveness and originality of his music that ultimately gained him his first patron, Freiherr Karl Joseph von Fürnberg, an amateur violinist at whose country house in Weinzierl musicians gathered. There Haydn produced his first string quartets to great acclaim. In 1759 Fürnberg recommended Haydn to Count Karl von Morzin, whereupon the count made the composer his music director; as such Haydn spent at least one summer at the count's estate at Lukavec, Bohemia. For Fürnberg and Morzin, and probably for concerts in Vienna, Haydn began the imposing series of symphonies and string quartets for which he is best known. A collection of manuscripts once owned by the Fürnbergs (currently housed at the Helikon Library in Keszthély) shows that from the start Haydn saw these genres as ones in which to explore and experiment.

In November 1760 Haydn, now confident of modest financial security, married Therese Keller's elder sister, Maria Anna. He had hardly done so when Count Morzin, early in 1761, decided to disband his costly orchestra. Apparent disaster turned into a stroke of luck when Prince Paul Anton Esterházy, himself a sometime composer and one of Europe's most lavish patrons of music, heard that Haydn was available and invited him to become the assistant music director at his lodgings in Vienna and Eisenstadt (which he knew by the Hungarian name Kismarton). Haydn officially reported to work (in Vienna) on 1 May 1761; by that time, however, he had already spent some six weeks recruiting musicians for the prince's band.

Haydn had worked scarcely a year when the prince died on 18 March 1762. If Haydn was once again plunged into uncertainty about his future, his fears would have been dispelled quickly, for Nikolaus, brother and successor to Paul Anton, possessed an appetite for music that was, if anything, even keener than his predecessor's. Haydn's original contract stipulated that he report to the prince in the morning and again in the afternoon to see if music making was wanted. This arrangement probably continued with Nikolaus, whose evenings were given over to theater and music theater. Daily music making often meant accompanying the prince in divertimentos for his favored instrument, the baryton, typically in concert with viola and cello (Haydn created a repertory of at least 126 such works in the years 1765–76); it sometimes meant playing solo keyboard works. Twice a week, orchestral "academies" were held; for these Haydn could probably count on assembling, before 1776, two oboes, two horns, one bassoon, and nine strings (disposed 3–3–1–1–1), with himself the leader; trumpets and drums were added on festive occasions. There is no evidence that Haydn (or anyone else) played continuo in instrumental music.

In 1766 Prince Nikolaus moved his entourage into a palace, Esterháza, that he was building in Hungary. About the same time, or perhaps slightly earlier, Haydn first encountered keyboard music by Carl Philipp Emanuel Bach. In later years Haydn saw these two events as having been decisive for his development: isolation at Esterháza forced him to be original; the keyboard music of Emanuel Bach inspired him to forge a musical idiom that went beyond the pleasantries of the *galant* style. There is probably a grain of truth in both assertions, even though inventories made in 1759 and 1803 show a wealth of contemporary music in the princely library and an emphatically international bias to the collection, and even though Haydn by the mid-1760s was already too assured and original a composer to imitate Bach's music directly. Haydn's remarkable musical development both before and after 1766 can be seen, above all, in the symphonies and keyboard sonatas. In his chamber music, written for the daily pleasure of his prince, one finds a more conventional idiom that remains anchored in the aesthetic framework of the divertimento. But beginning with his opus 9 string quartets of 1769, Haydn began writing some of his most challenging and original music for chamber groups as well.

For Prince Nikolaus, more music lover than musician, Haydn's increasingly complex musical style seems to have brought challenges that were not always welcome. Haydn's letters reveal that the prince did not hesitate to recommend (i.e., command) specific musical revisions in the baryton works; but Nikolaus did not stop there: a surviving autograph for Symphony no. 42 (1771) shows the prince censoring a musically audacious passage.

During his years at Eisenstadt and Esterháza, Haydn did not neglect dramatic music. By the time of the move to Esterháza he had written for Prince Nikolaus five one-act operas and a two-act intermezzo. At Esterháza a 400-seat theater and a smaller marionette theater were built. Haydn wrote for both, including, for the opening of the former in 1768, his first full-length opera, *Lo speziale.* During the same period he also composed a series of liturgical works for the prince's chapel. That Haydn set great store by his vocal music was only natural: vocal genres had always carried more prestige than instrumental ones. It was not until Haydn's later years, when the impact of his own music (together with the best of his contemporaries') had been absorbed by the musical public, that larger instrumental forms began to assume the same prestige as vocal music.

In an autobiographical sketch of 1776 (trans. Landon, 1977, 2:397–99), Haydn emphasized his connection with Porpora and named a Stabat Mater (1767), an oratorio, *Il ritorno di Tobia,* and three of his recent operas as his most important works to date. Haydn's contemporaries recognized his flair for theatrical music. In 1775 Viennese critics received Haydn's oratorio warmly, being particularly impressed by the power of his choral writing, which they likened to Handel's. The following year he was commissioned to write an opera for the imperial court. Prince Nikolaus, who had always hired professionals from Vienna to run his opera, now turned this responsibility over to Haydn. In 1779 Haydn brought his opera buffa *La vera costanza* to Vienna. But instead of being produced, his opera—like that of many another composer—was sunk by backstage intrigues. This unhappy experience probably had some bearing on Haydn's subsequent reluctance to write an opera for theaters (as in Prague) where he was not well connected.

In his contract of 1761 it was stipulated that Haydn "neither communicate [his] compositions to any other person, nor allow them to be copied . . . and not compose for any other person without the knowledge and permission of His Highness." This injunction did little to slow the dissemination of Haydn's works abroad. Between 1764 and 1780, 51 authentic chamber works and 43 authentic symphonies had their first publications in unauthorized editions in Paris, Amsterdam, and London. These 94 works are but the tip of an iceberg that includes pirated republications, a large number of circulating manuscript copies, and many spurious works. The extent of Haydn's complicity in this dissemination is not known, but he cannot have been pleased to go without recompense for his labors. From this flagrant piracy two results ensued. First, in 1779 Haydn obtained from Prince Nikolaus the freedom to write for and publish with whomever he pleased. Second, by the early 1780s Haydn had become one of the best-known and most sought after composers in Europe. For Lisbon he revised his oratorio; for Cadíz he wrote *Die sieben letzten Wörte unseres Erlösers am Kreuze;* for the King of Naples he penned several concertos; for Paris he revised *La vera costanza* (as *Laurette*) and composed six symphonies.

Attempts to get Haydn to England began with the Earl of Abingdon's invitation in 1782; throughout the decade the popular papers kept a running account of these efforts. During the 1780s Haydn composed operas, symphonies, and quartets that further expanded the horizons of those genres. When in Vienna he met and kept in touch with Mozart, whose music impressed him profoundly. In September 1790 Prince Nikolaus died. His son and successor, Anton, immediately disbanded the orchestra and opera at Esterháza. Haydn was given a stipend and permission to leave. He had scarcely done so when the English entrepreneur Johann Peter Salomon convinced him to visit London. On his way to London in December 1790 he stopped at Bonn, where Beethoven may have met him. Either then or when Haydn passed through Bonn on his return in 1792, he was shown one of Beethoven's cantatas; Haydn was sufficiently impressed to accept the young man as a student. In England Haydn wrote his last opera and his best-known symphonies, trios, and sonatas. All his London concerts were well received, but the public seems to have especially liked the symphony Hob. I:94 with its unexpected timpani outburst in the slow movement; the work was soon heard again at a benefit concert, christened "the Surprise" by the organizer of that occasion.

Haydn returned to Vienna in July 1792 only to set out for England again in January 1794. The second visit was, if possible, even more successful than the first, and King George III asked Haydn to move to London permanently. This Haydn felt unable to do, and he returned to Austria in August 1795. In the meantime Prince Anton had died. A new Prince Nikolaus pressed Haydn back into limited service to provide an annual Mass for the Esterházy chapel. As it happened, Haydn's own thoughts had centered on choral music ever since he had attended the Handel commemoration at Westminster Abbey. In the last eight years of his creative life Haydn produced an unbroken series of masterpieces that constitute his most public and his most private utterances: on the one hand, two large-scale oratorios and six Masses in which Austrian choral tradition is fused with the classical symphony; on the other the eight and one-half quartets of opp. 76, 77, and 103.

After 1803 he found it impossible to compose. But by then he had become an institution of sorts. Five medals were struck in his honor. Breitkopf & Härtel issued a putative *Oeuvres complètes* in 12 volumes (1801–6), an honor previously reserved for the dead;

Pleyel published a *Collection complette des quatuors* (1801).

Works: *Operas* (ca. 24; in following selected list no. of acts indicated before date). *Acide* (1, 1762; rev. 1773), *La cantarina* (1, 1766), *Lo speziale* (3, 1768), *Le pescatrici* (3, 1769), *L'infedeltà delusa* (2, 1773), *L'incontro improvviso* (3, 1775), *Il mondo della luna* (3, 1777), *La vera costanza* (3, 1779; rev. 1785), *La fedeltà premiata* (3, 1780), *Orlando paladino* (3, 1782), *Armida* (3, 1783), *L'anima del filosofo* (5, 1791).

Oratorios. Il ritorno di Tobia (1774–75; rev. 1784), *Die Schöpfung* (1796–98), *Die Jahreszeiten* (1799–1801).

Masses (15). *Missa brevis* (1753 or 1749?), *Missa Cellensis in honorem Beatae Virginis Maria* (1766), *Missa Sunt bona mixta malis* (1767–69?), *Missa in honorem Beatae Virginis Maria* (1768–69?), *Missa Sancti Nicolai* (1772), *Missa brevis Sancti Johannis de Deo* (1775?), *Missa Cellensis* (1782), *Missa in tempore belli (Paukenmesse)* (1796), *Missa Sancti Bernardi von Offida* (1796), Missa (*Nelsonmesse,* 1798), Missa (*Theresienmesse,* 1799), Missa (*Schöpfungsmesse,* 1801), Missa (*Harmoniemesse,* 1802).

Symphonies (107; Hob. I numbers in approximate order of composition, following Gerlach, 1969–70, and Larsen, 1988). 1758: 37; 1759: 1; by 1760: 106, 107, 2, 4, 5, 10, 11, 15, 18, 27, 32, 33; 1760–61: 17, 19, 25, 108; 1761: 6 (Le matin), 7 (Le midi); 1761–62: 3, 8 (Le soir); 1761–63: 14, 16; 1762: 9; 1763: 12, 13, 40; 1763–65: 34, 36, 72; 1764: 21, 22, 23, 24; 1765: 29, 30, 31 (Hornsignal), 28; 1767: 35; 1767–68: 58; 1767–69: 38, 59; 1768: 49 (La passione); 1768–70: 26, 41; 1769?: 48; 1770: 20, 39; 1770–71: 43, 44 (Trauersinfonie), 52; 1771: 42; 1771–72: 65; 1772: 45 (Farewell), 46, 47; 1773: 50, 51, 64; 1774: 54, 55, 56, 57, 60; 1774–75: 68; 1775–76: 67, 69 (Laudon), 66; 1776: 61; 1779: 75, 63 (La Roxelane), 70; 1780: 53, 71, 62, 74; 1781–82: 76; 1782: 73 (La chasse), 77, 78; 1783–84: 79, 80, 81; 1785: 83 (La poule), 85 (La reine), 87; 1786: 82 (L'ours), 84, 86; 1786–87: 88; 1787: 89; 1788: 90, 91; 1789: 92 (Oxford); (nos. 93–104, London Symphonies) 1791: 93, 94 (Surprise), 95, 96 (Miracle); 1792: 97, 98; 1793: 99; 1793–94: 100 (Military), 101 (Clock); 1794: 102; 1795: 103 (Drumroll), 104 (London).

String quartets (in sets of 6, except as noted; publication date, then approximate composition date). "Op. 0," 1 (1765, ca. 1757–59); op. 1, 1–4, 6 (1762, ca. 1757–59; 5 = Sym. 107 arr.); op. 2, 1–2, 4, 6 (1765–66; ca. 1760–62; 3, 5 = Divert. arr.); op. 9 (1771, ca. 1769–70); op. 17 (1772, 1771); op. 20 (Sun Quartets, 1774, 1772); op. 33 (Russian Quartets, 1782, 1781); op. 42, no. 1 (1786, 1785); op. 50 (Prussian Quartets, 1787, 1787); op. 51 (*Die 7 letzten Worte,* 1787, 1787); op. 54, 1–3 (Tost Quartets, 1789, 1788); op. 55, 1–3 (Tost Quartets, 1790, 1788); op. 64 (Tost Quartets, no. 5 *Lark,* 1791, 1790); op. 71 (1795–96, 1793); op. 76 (Erdödy Quartets, no. 2 Fifths, no. 3 Emperor, no. 4 Sunrise, 1799, 1797); op. 77, 1–2 (1802, 1799); op. 103 (2 movts.; 1806, 1803).

Keyboard trios (42; Hob. XV numbers in approximate order of composition). 1784: 5, 6; 1785: 7–10; 1788: 11; 1788–89: 12; 1789: 13; 1789–90: 14; 1790: 15–17; 1794: 18–20, 32; 1794–95: 26, 21–23; 1795: 24, 25, 31; 1795–97: 27–29; 1796: 30.

Keyboard sonatas (58; Hob. XVI numbers, except where noted, in approximate order of composition, following Brown, 1986). 1750–55: 16, 5, Es2, Es3; 1750s: G1, 1, XVII:D1, 1, 7, 9, 10, 12; ca. 1760: 2, 6, 8, 13; 1761/62–67: 3, 4, 14; ca. 1765: 47/2–4; 1766: 45, XVIIa:1 (4 hd.), XVIIa:2 (4 hd.); 1767: 19; 1767–68: 46, 5, 18; late 1760s: 27; ca. 1770: 44; 1771: 20; 1773: 21–26; 1774: 29; 1774–76: 28, 30–32; 1774–78: 36, 38, 33, 43; 1777–1780: 34, 35, 37, 39; 1784: 40–42; 1789: 48; 1789–90: 49; 1791–96: 51; 1793: XVII:6; 1793–94: 50/2; 1794: 52; 1795: 50/1, 3.

Bibl.: *Joseph Haydn Werke,* Jens Peter Larsen and Georg Feder, gen. eds. (Monaco-Duisburg, 1958–). Anthony van Hoboken, *Joseph Haydn: Thematisch-bibliographisches Werkverzeichnis,* 3 vols. (Magonza, 1957, 1971, 1978). *Haydn Jahrbuch* (1962–). *Haydn-Studien* (1965–).

G. A. Griesinger, "Biographische Notizen über Joseph Haydn," *Allgemeine musikalische Zeitung* (1809); trans. Eng. in Gottwals, 1963. A. C. Dies, *Biographische Nachrichten von Joseph Haydn* (Vienna, 1810); trans. Eng. in Gottwals, 1963. C. F. Pohl, *Joseph Haydn,* 3 vols. (Leipzig, 1875, 1882, 1927). H. C. Robbins Landon, *The Symphonies of Joseph Haydn* (London, 1955; suppl. 1961). Dénes Bartha and László Somfai, *Haydn als Opernkapellmeister* (Budapest, 1961). H. C. Robbins Landon, *Haydn: Chronicle and Works,* 5 vols. (Bloomington, Ind., 1976–80). Jens Peter Larsen, *Three Haydn Catalogues: Second Facsimile Edition with a Survey of Haydn's Oeuvre* (New York, 1979). Steven C. Bryant, and G. W. Chapman, *A Melodic Index to Haydn's Instrumental Music: A Thematic Locator for Hoboken's Thematisch-bibliographisches Werkverzeichnis* (New York, 1982). A. Peter Brown, *Joseph Haydn's Keyboard Music: Sources and Style* (Bloomington, Ind., 1986). Jens Peter Larsen, *Handel, Haydn, and the Viennese Classical Style* (Ann Arbor, 1988). Floyd K. Grave and Margaret G. Grave, *Franz Joseph Haydn: A Guide to Research* (New York, 1990). James Webster, *Haydn's "Farewell" Symphony and the Idea of Classical Style* (Cambridge, 1991). Gretchen A. Wheelock, *Haydn's "Ingenious Jesting with Art": Contexts of Musical Wit and Humor* (New York, 1992). Elaine R. Sisman, *Haydn and the Classical Variation* (Cambridge, Mass., 1993).

Haydn, (Johann) Michael (b. Rohrau, Lower Austria, bapt. 14 Sept. 1737; d. Salzburg, 10 Aug. 1806). Composer. Brother of Franz Joseph. Around 1745 he went to Vienna as chorister at St. Stephen's, where he also learned violin, clavier, and counterpoint through the use of Fux's *Gradus ad Parnassum.* Like his older brother Joseph before him, when his voice broke he remained in Vienna for several lean years; this period ended in 1757, when he received a post at the court of the Bishop of Grosswardein (now northern Romania). In 1763 he assumed duties as *Konzertmeister* to Archbishop Schrattenbach in Salzburg; in 1768 he married a singer in the court chapel there, Maria Lipp. In Salzburg Haydn held several important organ posts, including that at the Dreifaltigkeitskirche (from 1777), and as Mozart's successor as court and cathedral organist. He remained in the latter position for the rest of his life, despite the death of Schrattenbach in 1771. From 1787 he was violin instructor for the court (succeeding Leopold Mozart), and after 1798 he visited Vienna several times. In 1800 Archbishop Colloredo was forced out of his position, a development that caused Haydn great financial hardship. Nevertheless, when he was offered (during his visit to his brother in Vienna and Eisenstadt in 1801–2) a post as Vice-Kapellmeister for the Esterházy court, he turned it down in favor of his position at Salzburg. In 1804 he was inducted into the Royal Swedish Academy of Music.

Michael Haydn composed more than 400 sacred works. He also composed stage works (*Die Wahrheit der Natur,* 1769; *Der englische Patriot,* ca. 1779; *Die Ährenleserin,* 1788; incidental music to Voltaire's *Zayre,* 1777); oratorios (including a lost collaboration with W. A. Mozart and Adlgasser, *Die Schuldigkeit des ersten Gebots; Der Kampf der Busse und Bekehrung,* 1768; *Oratorium de Passione Domini nostri Jesu Christi,* ca. 1775) and cantatas (*Ninfe in belli,* 1765; *Die Jubelfeyer,* 1787); some 40 symphonies (Symphony in G, P16, formerly attributed to Mozart as K. 444); concertos; divertimentos and other ensemble works (*cassatios*, serenades, etc.); chamber music (12 string quartets, string sonatas).

Bibl.: *Michael Haydn: Instrumentalwerke,* ed. Lothar Herbert Perger, *DTÖ* 29 (14/2; Vienna, 1907; R: Graz, 1959). *Michael Haydn: Kirchenwerke,* ed. Anton Maria Klafsky, *DTÖ* 62 (32/1; Vienna, 1925; R: Graz, 1960). Gerhard Croll and Kurt Vössing, *Johann Michael Haydn: Sein Leben, sein Schaffen, seine Zeit* (Vienna, 1987). Charles H. Sherman and T. Donley Thomas, *Johann Michael Haydn (1737–1806): A Chronological Thematic Catalogue of His Works* (Stuyvesant, 1993).

Hayes, Roland (b. Curryville, Ga., 3 June 1887; d. Boston, 1 Jan. 1977). Tenor. Son of a slave, he moved to Chattanooga in 1900 after his father's death. Studied voice with A. Calhoun there, then with Jennie Robinson in Nashville, 1901–5; with Arthur J. Hubbard in Boston, 1906–14. His debut recital in Boston (1915), his concert at Symphony Hall (1917), and his tour of the U.S. (1919) were poorly received, but in London in 1920 he achieved a triumph and renown. Remaining there, he studied with Sir George Henschel through 1922, then toured the Continent, 1922–23, singing in Budapest, Prague, Leipzig, Munich, Amsterdam, Madrid, and Copenhagen. There followed a New York debut at Carnegie Hall (1923), and an extended second U.S. tour (1924). Settled in Brookline, Massachusetts, 1926; visited Italy, 1927, Russia, 1928. In later years he taught at Boston Univ. His recitals were noteworthy for their inclusion of spirituals arranged as solo songs. A volume of these, *My Songs,* was published in 1948.

Hayes, William (bapt. Gloucester, 26 Jan. 1708; d. Oxford, 27 July 1777). Composer. Sang under Hine at Gloucester Cathedral; named organist at St. Mary's, Shrewsbury, in 1729, and at Worcester Cathedral in 1731; became organist and choirmaster at Magdalen College, Oxford, in 1734, assuming a professorship there in 1742. He often participated in music festivals and was a devotee of Handel's music, whose style influenced his own. Works include oratorios, anthems, secular cantatas, masques, concertos, and trio sonatas.

Haym, Nicola Francesco (b. Rome, 6 July 1678; d. London, 11 Aug. 1729). Cellist, librettist, and composer. Played under Corelli in Cardinal Ottoboni's orchestra in Rome (1694–1700), also composing vocal music at the time. Served the second Duke of Bedford in London, 1701–11, later working for the Duke of Chandos. He was an important figure in London's Italian opera, playing cello for Clayton's *Arsinoe* (1706), the first full-length Italian-style opera to be staged there; later he wrote substitution arias for Bononcini's *Camilla* and *Etearco* (1706, 1708), Scarlatti's *Pirro e Demetrio* (1708), and various pasticcios, and adapted many libretti for Handel, including *Giulio Cesare* (1724), *Tamerlano* (1724), and *Rodelinda* (1725). He also performed chamber music, was active as a teacher, edited Italian literature, and produced catalogs of Greek and Roman coins and rare Italian books. His works include sacred and secular vocal music as well as sonatas.

Hayne van Ghizeghem (b. ca. 1445; d. between 1472 and 1497). Composer. Was perhaps born in a village near Ghent; served Charles the Bold of Burgundy as a musician from boyhood (while Charles was still a count) until at least the middle of 1472, the date of the siege of Beauvais; perhaps died at or soon after that siege, or more likely, in light of the style and sources of his compositions, spent some years thereafter at the French royal court. Late 15th- and early 16th-century manuscripts and prints ascribe to him 20 chansons. Of these slightly over half are surely his. All but one doubtful work are 3-voice rondeaux. His "Allez regrets" and "De tous biens plaine" were made the basis of works by several other composers.

Bibl.: *Opera omnia, CMM* 74 (1977).

Haynes, Roy (Owen) (b. Roxbury, Mass., 13 Mar. 1926). Jazz drummer. After joining Luis Russell's big band (1945–47), he worked in small combo idioms ranging from swing to jazz-rock under such leaders as Lester Young (1947–49), Charlie Parker (1949–52), Sarah Vaughan (1953–58), Thelonious Monk (1958), Eric Dolphy (1960), John Coltrane (1961–65, including the album *Selflessness,* 1963), Stan Getz, Gary Burton (both 1960s–1980s), Dizzy Gillespie (1979), and Chick Corea (including the album *Trio Music,* 1981). From 1960 he also led groups, playing hard bop, turning toward jazz-rock (as the Hip Ensemble), then returning to bop styles in the 1980s.

Hays, Doris (Ernestine) (b. Memphis, 6 Aug. 1941). Composer and pianist. She studied at the Univ. of Chattanooga, the Munich Hochschule (harpsichord and piano, 1966), and the universities of Wisconsin (M.M., 1968) and Iowa; teachers have included Paul Badura-Skoda, Hilde Somer, and Richard Hervig. In 1971 she won first prize in the International Competition for Interpretation of New Music (Rotterdam). She has taught at Queens College, City Univ. of N.Y. (1974–75) and has been active in organizations for women composers. Her mixed-media composition *Sens Events* (1970–77) in its realization for Lincoln Center involved dancers, tape, chamber ensemble, sound sculpture, and computerized lighting. Many works reflect her southern origins (*Southern Voices,* orchestra and soprano, 1981). Other works include mixed-media pieces; film scores; works for children; music for instrument(s), many for winds, often with tape; piano pieces; and music for voices (including *Something (To Do) Doing,* Stein and Hays, 16 chanters and tape; 1984).

Hays, Will(iam) S(hakespeare) (b. Louisville, Ky., 19 July 1837; d. there, 23 July 1907). Songwriter. Attended colleges but mostly self-taught in music; 1857, published first of more than 300 songs, said to have sold over 20 million copies, including sentimental ballads ("Evangeline"), Irish songs ("Mollie Darling," "Nora O'Neal"), Civil War songs ("Drummer Boy of Shiloh"), pseudo-spirituals, and minstrel songs. During the Civil War he commanded a river transport boat; for 4 years thereafter worked on Ohio and Mississippi River steamboats; then worked as marine reporter for the Louisville *Courier-Journal.* He also wrote much poetry.

Healey, Derek (b. Wargrave, Eng., 2 May 1936). Composer. Studied composition (with Howells) and organ at Durham Univ. (B.Mus., 1961); in Italy, 1961–66, composition with Petrassi, Porena, and Berio. Taught at the Univ. of Victoria, British Columbia (1969–71); Univ. of Toronto (1971–72); Univ. of Guelph (1972–78); Univ. of Oregon (from 1979). Made use of serial procedures, electronic music, aleatory, and musical materials of Native Americans in Canada and the U.S. Works include the opera *Seabird Island* (after Native American legend from the Pacific Northwest, 1977); the children's opera *Mr. Punch* (1969); orchestral works (Symphony no. 3, *Music for a Small Planet,* 1984); chamber music; music for piano and for organ; songs.

Hebenstreit, Pantaleon (b. Eisleben, 1667; d. Dresden, 15 Nov. 1750). Instrumentalist. Perhaps played violin and taught dance and keyboard in Leipzig before being forced to flee because of debt. While living with a pastor near Merseburg he developed the pantaleon (a large dulcimer), which Kuhnau heard him play as early as 1697. He was appointed dancing master at Weissenfels in 1698, visited Paris in 1705, and was engaged at Eisenach in 1708, where Telemann praised his pantaleon and violin skills and his aptitude for the French style. After acclaimed concert tours, he became a chamber musician at Dresden at a very high salary; he was also active as a teacher. Poor eyesight ended his performing career in 1730, and he was granted a pension.

Heckel, Johann Adam (b. Adorf, Saxony, 14 July 1812; d. Biebrich, near Wiesbaden, 13 Apr. 1877). Instrument maker. Working for Schott (1829), he met the bassoonist Carl Almenraeder (1786–1843), with whom he worked to improve the bassoon, leading to the Heckel-Almenraeder bassoon, manufactured by their own firm (founded 1831). This work was carried on by his son Wilhelm (1856–1909), who further improved the bassoon and contrabassoon and introduced the heckelphone and other new or hybrid instruments.

Hefti, Neal (b. Hastings, Nebr., 29 Oct. 1922). Jazz, film, and television composer and arranger. He played trumpet with Charlie Barnet (ca. 1943) and Woody Herman (1944–45). After Herman recorded his compositions "The Good Earth" and "Wild Root" (both 1945), he concentrated on writing as a free-lance, leader, and studio musician. From 1950 he composed and arranged for Count Basie, supplying "Li'l Darlin'" and "Whirlybird" for the album *The Atomic Mr. Basie* (1957). Later he composed television and film soundtracks, including *Batman* (1965–68), *Lord Love a Duck* (1965), *Barefoot in the Park,* and *The Odd Couple* (both 1967).

Hegar, Friedrich (b. Basel, 11 Oct. 1841; d. Zurich, 2 June 1927). Composer. From a family of musicians, son of a music engraver; 1857–59, student at the Leipzig Conservatory under Hauptmann, Rietz, and David and also a violinist in the Gewandhaus Orchestra; 1860–61, violinist and conductor in Warsaw and Gebweiler, Alsace; from 1862 a major figure in the musical life of Zurich; 1862–65, concertmaster, Tonhalle Orchestra, 1865–1906, its conductor; also conductor of the mixed chorus, 1865–1901, and several other choruses; 1876–1914, director of the Music School (later Conservatory). His oratorio *Manasse* (1885; rev. 1888) was widely performed, but he is historically important for his male choruses, marking a stage in that genre's development.

Bibl.: Adolf Steiner, *Friedrich Hegar: Sein Leben und Wirken* (Zurich, 1928). Fritz Müller, ed., *Friedrich Hegar: Sein Leben und Wirken in Briefen* (Zurich, 1987).

Heiden, Bernhard (b. Frankfurt am Main, 24 Aug. 1910). Composer. Studied with Hindemith at the Berlin Hochschule für Musik (1929–33); moved to Detroit in 1935, where he conducted the Detroit Chamber Orchestra and taught at the Art Center Music School; during the war he served as an assistant band master in the army; then studied musicology under Grout at Cornell Univ. (1945–46). Thereafter he taught at Indiana Univ., retiring as professor emeritus in 1981. His early works show Hindemith's influence in their neoclassicism; later his primary concern was sonority, in terms of texture, color, and register. He composed an opera, music for dance and for Shakespearean plays, and a film score; 2 symphonies, concertos (for recorder and chamber orchestra, 1987), and other orchestral works (*Partita,* 1970); much chamber music including string quartets, a woodwind quintet, sonatas for various instruments, and the *Variations* for solo tuba and 9 horns (1974); choral and solo vocal music.

Heifetz, Jascha (b. Vilna, Lithuania, 2 Feb [20 Jan. Julian cal.] 1899; d. Los Angeles, 10 Dec. 1987). Violinist. Studied with his father, Ruvin (a theater orchestra violinist), from age 5; with Elias Malkin at the Vilna Conservatory, 1906–10. Played the Mendelssohn concerto in Kovno, 1907. Ignoring a law that forbade Jews to reside in St. Petersburg, he studied with J. Nalbandian and Leopold Auer at the conservatory there, 1909–14. In 1914 went to Berlin, making his debut under Nikisch. Emigrated to the U.S. in 1917 (naturalized 1925). From his first New York recital (27 Oct. 1917) to the end of his career, an aristocratic élan and perfect technique made him both a violinist's violinist and a public favorite. With Godowsky he founded the Hebrew Music Conservatory in Palestine in 1926. In 1928 he married movie actress Florence Vidor. In 1939 he appeared in the film *They Shall Have Music.* A world tour in 1934 included his last concert in Russia. Played and recorded chamber music in trio with Rubinstein and Piatigorsky. From 1959 taught at the Univ. of Southern California. After a concert to benefit U.S.C. in 1972, he retired from the stage. Commissioned and played concertos by Walton, Korngold, Rozsa, and others. Gave the U.S. premiere of Prokofiev's Second Concerto. Encouraged by Kreisler, he published more than 100 transcriptions, of which the most celebrated is the *Hora staccato.* His popular songs were published under the name Jim Hoyl. Cofounder (with Lawrence Tibbett) of the American Guild of Musical Artists.

Heinichen, Johann David (b. Krössuln, near Weissenfels, 17 Apr. 1683; d. Dresden, 16 July 1729). Theorist and composer. Keyboard student and assistant of Kuhnau at the Leipzig Thomasschule; enrolled in Leipzig Univ. in 1702, earning a law degree in 1706; began a practice in Weissenfels, where he had contact with Kapellmeister J. P. Krieger and his assistant Grünewald. Moved back to Leipzig in 1709 as opera director, also leading a collegium musicum; journeyed to Italy in 1710, where he enjoyed acclaim as an opera composer in Venice and taught Prince Leopold of Anhalt-Cöthen in Rome. In 1717, while still in Italy, he was appointed Kapellmeister in Dresden, a post he held until his death. Although his output includes a great variety of sacred and secular vocal music and instrumental works, he is best known for his treatise *Der Generalbass in der Composition* (1728, partially reworked from a publication of 1711), an exhaustive account not only of continuo practice but also of the technical and aesthetic aspects of composition.

Bibl.: George Buelow, *Thoroughbass Accompaniment According to Johann David Heinichen* (Berkeley and Los Angeles, 1966; 2nd ed., 1986). Melvin P. Unger, *The German Choral Church Compositions of Johann David Heinichen, 1683–1729* (New York, 1990).

Heininen, Paavo (b. Helsinki, 13 Jan. 1938). Composer. He studied privately with Usko Meriläinen, then (1956–60) at the Sibelius Academy in Helsinki with Aarre Merikanto, Joonas Kokkonen, and Sven Einar Eglund. From 1957 he studied musicology at Helsinki Univ., from 1960 composition at the Hochschule in Cologne, and from 1961 with Vincent Persichetti at Juilliard. He later taught composition and theory at the Helsinki Sibelius Academy (1962–63), at the Turku Music Academy (1963–66), and, beginning 1966, again at the Sibelius Academy. His early music adopted twelve-tone composition; he later explored aleatory and improvisational styles. Works include operas (*The Silken Drum,* 1976; *Veitsi* [The Knife], 1985–88); orchestral music, including 4 symphonies (no. 2, *Petite symphonie joyeuse,* 1962), 2 piano concertos (1964, 1966), a cello concerto (1985); *Soggetto* op. 11 (1963); *Arioso,* strings (1967); vocal music (*Canto di natale,* soprano, piano, 1961; *Cantico delle creature* op. 17, baritone, keyboard or orchestra, 1968; *Love's Philosophy* op. 19, tenor, piano, 1968–73; *Schatten der Erde,* mezzo-soprano, piano op. 30, 1973; other songs); chamber and instrumental music (a string quartet, 1975; *Discantus* I–III, 1965–76; *Cantilena* I–II, both 1970; *Sonata,* violin and piano, 1970; *Poésie des pensées,* solo cello, 1970; *Préludes—Études—Poèmes,* piano, 1974).

Heinrich, Anthony Philip (b. Schönbüchel [now Krásný Búk], Bohemia, 11 Mar. 1781; d. New York, 3 May 1861). Composer. Adopted by a wealthy uncle whose property he inherited in 1800. His business failing, he emigrated to the U.S. by 1810. He turned to music as violinist, pianist, and teacher for his livelihood; lived in Philadelphia (1816–17), then went to Kentucky. In 1817 he organized a concert in Lexington that gave the first known U.S. performance of a Beethoven symphony. In 1818, after a serious illness, living in a log cabin near Bardstown he had the quasi-mystical experience that caused him to begin to compose to express the feelings aroused in him by the American wilderness. He produced songs and piano pieces published in his collections *The Dawning of Music in Kentucky* op. 1 (Philadelphia, 1820), *The Western Minstrel* op. 2 (Philadelphia, 1820), and *The Sylviad* op. 3 (Boston, 1823–26). A Boston review (1822) called him "the Beethoven of America," an appellation that stuck and that he took seriously. He was in London, 1826–31, as an orchestral violinist, failing to win success as a composer. From 1837 to 1861 he lived mostly in New York, primarily through teaching, continuing to compose the large orchestral works that he had begun to produce in 1831, mostly on programmatic or descriptive American subjects; some of these he heard incompetently performed in concerts he organized (1842, 1846, 1853). He visited Prague, 1857–59, and had some of his music performed there.

In spite of decades of neglect of his work, Heinrich had an unwavering devotion to his art that won him friends and in old age a personal veneration (reflected in his nickname, "Father" Heinrich). He also manifested a boundless self-confidence in his works which made him bitter at his lack of success and quick to take offense at real or imagined slights.

Bibl.: W. T. Upton, *Anthony Philip Heinrich* (New York, 1939; R: 1969). B. E. Chmaj, "Father Heinrich as Kindred Spirit: or, How the Log-House Composer Became the

Beethoven of America," *American Studies* 24/2 (1983): 35–57.

Heiss, John C. (b. New York, 23 Oct. 1938). Composer and flutist. Studied mathematics at Lehigh University (B.A., 1960), then studied composition at Columbia (Luening, Westergaard) and at Princeton (M.F.A., 1967; Babbitt, Cone, Kim). Other teachers have included Milhaud (Aspen), Cowell, and Beeson. He taught at Columbia, Barnard, and M.I.T.; began teaching at the New England Conservatory in 1967. For several years (1969–74) he played principal flute in the Boston Musica Viva ensemble. Among his compositions are orchestral works (Concerto for Flute, 1977), a series of *Mosaics* (no. 1, "for very large array of flutists," 1986; no. 2, large cello choir, 1987; no. 3, trombone choir, 1990), chamber music, much of it involving flute (*Capriccio,* flute, clarinet, and percussion, 1976); choral music; piano pieces; songs.

Hellendaal, Pieter (b. Rotterdam, bapt. 1 Apr. 1721; d. Cambridge, 19 Apr. 1799). Composer, organist, and violinist. In 1732 he was appointed organist at the St. Nicolas Church in Utrecht; he then went to Italy to study with Tartini (1737–43). Returning to Amsterdam, he issued his first publication in 1744 or 1745, 6 violin sonatas. In 1749 he enrolled at the Univ. of Leiden, where he remained for two years. He traveled to London in 1751, where he established himself as a prominent musician; in 1754 he participated in a performance of Handel's *Acis and Galatea,* and four years later he published his *Six Grand Concertos,* for strings in 8 parts (ed. in *MMN* 1). After 1762 he lived chiefly in Cambridge, where he gave concerts and was appointed organist at Peterhouse Chapel in 1777. Other works include *Three Grand Lessons,* keyboard, violin, and continuo (ca. 1790); vocal works (including canons, catches, and glees).

Heller, Stephen [István] (b. Pest, 15 May 1813; d. Paris, 14 Jan. 1888). Composer. Studied the piano in Vienna with August Halm (Czerny having proved too expensive). In 1827–28 he played in Viennese concerts; a concert tour in 1828–30 through central Europe and Germany ended with his breakdown from exhaustion in Augsburg, where he remained, patronized by the local gentry, teaching the piano and studying composition with Hippolyte Chelard. His early work was reviewed enthusiastically by Schumann, who considered him a kindred spirit (the two corresponded but never met). In 1838 he moved to Paris to study with Kalkbrenner, from whom he soon parted, establishing himself as teacher, composer, and pianist and writing criticism for the *Gazette musicale.* He was a friend of Hiller, Hallé, and Berlioz. Around 1883 his sight began to fail; needy in his last years, he was partly supported through donations organized by Hallé. He composed almost exclusively for the piano, publishing over 150 works from 1829 through about 1880, ranging from 4 sonatas to many collections of character pieces and dances as well as variations, opera potpourris, etc.; best known for etudes, widely used and long republished, especially *L'art du phraser* op. 16 (1840?) and opp. 45, 46, 47 (1844?).

Bibl.: J. J. Eigeldinger, ed., *Stephen Heller: Lettres d'un musicien romantique à Paris* (Paris, 1981). Ursula Müller-Kersten, *Stephen Heller, ein Klaviermeister der Romantik: Biographische und stilkritische Studien* (New York, 1986).

Hellermann, William (b. Milwaukee, 15 July 1939). Composer and guitarist. After completing a degree in mechanical engineering in Wisconsin, he studied at Juilliard (1963–65) and then at Columbia with Luening, Chou Wen-chung, and Ussachevsky (D.M.A., 1969); studied composition privately with Wolpe (1964–66). He taught at Columbia from his student days until 1972, when he won the Prix de Rome; was executive director of the Composers Forum (1968–80) and editor of the *Calendar for New Music* in New York; composer-in-residence at SUNY–Buffalo, 1977. Performed as a guitar soloist and in new music ensembles. His "Eyescores" (visually oriented works) have been exhibited in galleries; from the mid-1970s he devoted himself to performance art (*Squeak,* chair, 1977; *Progress in Music Demands Daily Drill,* tape and sculpture, 1982). Wrote for orchestra, for variable ensembles (*Frozen Music Is Not Melted Architecture,* 1975), for guitar, piano, and voices; many works involve tape and mixed media.

Hellinck, Lupus [Wulfaert] (b. ca. 1496; d. Bruges, ca. 14 Jan. 1541). Composer. Choirboy at St. Donatian, Bruges, 1506–11; verger, then cleric and singer there, 1513–15 and 1519–21; choirmaster at Notre Dame, Bruges, 1521–23; choirmaster at St. Donatian, 1523 to his death. He wrote under a half dozen French chansons and fewer Flemish songs. The rest of his works are sacred: 11 German chorales, about 15 motets, and, his most important compositions, 13 parody Masses.

Hellmesberger, Georg (b. Vienna, 24 Apr. 1800; d. Neuwaldegg, near Vienna, 16 Aug. 1873). Violinist. Choirboy in the court chapel; studied the violin with Joseph Böhm, Vienna Conservatory, where he became a teacher, 1821–67, professor from 1826; 1819, began concert career; 1830, concertmaster, court opera orchestra; 1842, conductor of new Philharmonic Orchestra.

Hellmesberger, Joseph (b. Vienna, 3 Nov. 1828; d. there, 24 Oct. 1893). Violinist. Son and pupil of Georg Hellmesberger. Leader of his own string quartet, 1849–91, the most prominent in Vienna; 1851–93, director of the conservatory, violin teacher there (to 1877), and conductor of its concerts (to 1859); 1855–77, concertmaster, Philharmonic Orchestra; from 1860, concertmaster, Vienna Opera Orchestra; from 1877, court Kapellmeister.

Helm, Everett (Burton) (b. Minneapolis, 17 July 1913). Composer and writer on music. He attended

Harvard (M.A., 1936; Ph.D., 1939), but studied composition and musicology in Europe (1936–38). He taught in the U.S. for a decade (1940–50) after which he moved to Europe, returning to the U.S. only for two years to serve as editor of *Musical America* (1961–63). Authored several books, including German volumes on Liszt (1972) and Bartók (1965); writings in English include *Composer, Performer, Public* (1970) and *Music and Tomorrow's Public* (1981); his volume on Bartók appeared in English in 1971. His compositions include operas (*Adam and Eve,* 1951; *The Siege of Tottenburg,* 1956); 2 piano concertos (1951, 1956) and other orchestral works; chamber music and songs.

Helmholtz, Hermann (Ludwig Ferdinand) von (b. Potsdam, 31 Aug. 1821; d. Berlin, 8 Sept. 1894). Scientist. Studied medicine in Berlin, 1838–42. He quickly established a reputation in physiological optics and acoustics; 1855, professor of anatomy and physiology, Bonn Univ.; 1858, professor of physiology, Heidelberg. After 1866 he worked primarily in physics, and in 1871 became professor of physics, Berlin. His work included research on physiological acoustics and overtones; this is found primarily in his book *Die Lehre von den Tonempfindungen als physiologische Grundlage für die Theorie der Musik* (Brunswick, 1863; trans. Eng., 1875, R: 1954).

Bibl.: Leo Koenigsberger, *Hermann von Helmholtz* (Brunswick, 1902–3; trans. Eng., 1906, R: 1965).

Helps, Robert (Eugene) (b. Passaic, N.J., 23 Sept. 1928). Composer and pianist. He studied at Columbia (1947–49) and Berkeley (1949–51); in addition he studied piano with Abby Whiteside and composition with Sessions. He taught piano in California (1968–70), at New England Conservatory (1970–72), and at the Manhattan School and Princeton (1972–78). In 1980 he joined the faculty of the Univ. of South Florida at Tampa. As a pianist, noted as an interpreter of contemporary music. His own works employ twelve-tone procedures; they include a symphony (1957) and other orchestral and chamber music; many piano works; and songs (*Gossamer Noons,* soprano and orchestra, 1977).

Hemel, Oscar van (b. Antwerp, 3 Aug. 1892; d. Hilversum, 7 July 1981). Composer. Of Dutch parentage. At the Antwerp Conservatory he studied with Lodewijk Mortelmans and August de Boeck. He moved to the Netherlands in 1914 and became violinist in the Amsterdam Opera Orchestra; four years later he settled in Bergen op Zoom. He studied privately with Willem Pijper in Rotterdam, 1931–33, and in 1938 he won the Queen Elisabeth Prize for his Piano Quartet. His musical style rarely strayed far from a late Romantic idiom. He composed stage works (*Viviane,* 1950); many orchestral works: 5 symphonies (1935, 1948, 1952, 1962, 1963–64); concertos for piano (1941–42), 2 for violin (1946, 1968), viola (1951), oboe (1955), wind instruments (1960), cello (1963), 2 violins (1974); *Divertimento,* piano and orchestra; vocal works including *Maria Magdalena,* cantata (1941), *Hart van Nederland* [Heart of the Netherlands], male choir, winds (1952), *Te Deum* (1958); 6 string quartets and other chamber music; piano works.

Hempel, Frieda (b. Leipzig, 26 June 1885; d. Berlin, 7 Oct. 1955). Soprano. At Leipzig Conservatory studied piano; at Stern Conservatory in Berlin studied voice with Selma Nicklass-Kempner, 1902–5. Debut as Nikolai's Frau Fluth at the Berlin Court Opera, 1905. With the Schwerin Opera, 1905–7, she built her repertoire. Sang Woglinde at Bayreuth, 1905, Mozart roles at Munich and Salzburg, 1906. At the Berlin Court Opera, 1907–12, she specialized in coloratura roles, but also sang the Marschallin *(Rosenkavalier)* there in 1911 and was renowned for her Mozart heroines. At the New York Metropolitan Opera, 1912–19, she debuted as Meyerbeer's Marguérite *(Huguenots).* Her popularity with New York opera audiences, though great, was eclipsed by that of Terazzini and Galli-Curci; in 1920 she began a second career as a recitalist. Her memoirs, *Mein Leben dem Gesang,* were published in 1955.

Henderson, Fletcher (Hamilton, Jr.) [Smack] (b. Cuthbert, Ga., 18 Dec. 1897; d. New York, 29 Dec. 1952). Jazz bandleader, arranger, and pianist. Earned a degree in chemistry and mathematics at Atlanta Univ. He toured with Ethel Waters (1921–22) and began recording accompaniments for blues singers. From 1924 he led a group at the Roseland Ballroom in New York which became the first important jazz big band, known for its soloists and arrangers. His sidemen included in the mid-1920s Louis Armstrong, Buster Bailey, Coleman Hawkins, Don Redman; in the late 1920s Benny Carter, Jimmy Harrison, Rex Stewart; in the mid-1930s Henry "Red" Allen, Chu Berry, Roy Eldridge, J. C. Higginbotham, John Kirby, Ben Webster. Henderson's arrangements, including "King Porter Stomp," contributed greatly to the success of Benny Goodman's band in 1935. He became a staff arranger for Goodman (1939–41), then resumed bandleading (to 1950). His recordings include "Copenhagen," "Shanghai Shuffle" (both 1924), "Sugar Foot Stomp" (1925), "The Stampede" (1926), "King Porter's Stomp" [sic] (1933), "Wrappin' It Up" (1934), and "Christopher Columbus" (1936; arranged by his brother, the pianist Horace Henderson, b. Cuthbert, Ga., 22 Nov. 1904).

Bibl.: Walter C. Allen, *Hendersonia: The Music of Fletcher Henderson and His Musicians: A Bio-Discography* (Highland Park, N.J., 1973).

Henderson, Joe [Joseph A.] (b. Lima, Ohio, 24 Apr. 1937). Jazz tenor saxophonist. He studied music at Kentucky State College and Wayne State Univ. (1956–60). With Kenny Dorham he led a quintet (1962–64), while also recording the album *The Sidewinder* with Lee Morgan (1963). As a member of Horace Silver's hard bop quintet (1964–66) he recorded the album *Song for My Father* (1964). He joined Herbie Hancock

(1969–70), then mainly led groups based in San Francisco. He also worked intermittently with Freddie Hubbard in the 1980s. In 1992 he led a quintet including Wynton Marsalis in a recording, titled *Lush Life,* of works by Billy Strayhorn.

Henderson, Skitch [Lyle Russell Cedric] (b. Birmingham, England, 27 Jan. 1918). Conductor and bandleader. Before World War II worked as a pianist in dance bands and theater orchestras; moved to Hollywood, accompanied Judy Garland on tour. After serving in the Army Air Force returned to Hollywood to serve as music director for Bing Crosby's radio show and work on the music staff at MGM. In 1949 went to NBC, where he achieved his widest recognition as leader of the *Tonight Show* band with Steve Allen, 1954–56, and Johnny Carson, 1962–66. After a period as guest conductor, he became in 1973 conductor of the Tulsa Symphony. This affiliation ended abruptly in 1975. In 1982 he founded the New York Pops; debut concert, 1983. During the late 1980s he also served as pops director with the Florida Orchestra and as principal pops conductor with the Virginia Symphony.

Hendrix, Jimi [James Marshall] (b. Seattle, Wash., 27 Nov. 1942; d. London, 18 Sept. 1970). Guitarist and singer. He played for Little Richard, the Isley Brothers, and Joey Dee and the Starlighters, and in New York in 1964 led Jimmy James and the Blue Flames; in 1966 he formed the Jimi Hendrix Experience in London. His guitar technique, which pioneered the use of electronic sound modification through distortion devices and feedback, strongly influenced rock musicians of the 1970s, as did his performances, which included guitar tricks (playing with the teeth and behind the back), use of the guitar as a dramatic (primarily sexual) prop, and destruction of equipment. His most popular recordings were those of Bob Dylan's "All Along the Watchtower" (1968) and his own "Purple Haze" (1967); he made famous appearances at the Monterey Pop Festival in 1967 and at Woodstock in 1969.

Henkemans, Hans (b. The Hague, 23 Dec. 1913). Composer and pianist. Early piano studies with Bernard van den Sigtenhorst Meyer were followed by medical studies at the Univ. of Utrecht (from 1933), where he was also a composition pupil of Willem Pijper. He first came to public attention in 1932 in his premiere as soloist in his own Concerto for Piano and Strings. From 1945 he was active as both composer and piano soloist; after 1969 he devoted himself chiefly to composition and to his psychiatric practice. His music shows the influence of Debussy. Works include orchestral music (2 piano concertos, 1932, 1936; *Ballade d'Orléans,* 1936; concertos for violin, 1948, for viola, 1954, for harp, 1956; *Dona montana,* 1964; *Élégies,* 4 flutes and orchestra, 1967; *Riflessioni,* strings, 1986); vocal works (*Driehonderd waren wij,* chorus and orchestra, 1940; *Bericht aan de levenden,* 1964; *Villonerie,* baritone, orchestra, 1965; *Canzoni amorose,* soprano, baritone, orchestra, 1973); chamber music (2 wind quintets, 1934 and 1962; a sonata for violin and piano, 1944).

Henrici, Christian Friedrich [Picander] (b. Stolpen, Saxony, 14 Jan. 1700; d. Leipzig, 10 May 1764). Poet. After initial schooling in Stolpen he studied law at Wittenberg in 1719; moving to Leipzig in 1720, he worked as a tutor, later taking a variety of administrative posts. Early on in Leipzig he penned satires and occasional poetry; he later produced devotional verse, cantata texts, and plays. As J. S. Bach's most important librettist, he wrote the texts for the Passions according to St. Matthew and St. Mark, and for many cantatas.

Henry, Pierre (b. Paris, 9 Dec. 1927). Composer. At the Paris Conservatory he was a pupil of Boulanger (piano), Félix Passerone (percussion), and Messiaen (composition); joined Schaeffer at the electronic music studios of French Radio in 1949, where he led the Groupe de recherche de musique concrète (1950–58); in works composed during the 1950s he combined live performers in dialogue with their own electronically altered sounds; combined recorded and synthesized sounds; wrote the first electronic work for the stage (*Orphée,* Donaueschingen, 1953); and began his long collaboration with the choreographer Béjart (works for Béjart include *Nijinsky, clown de Dieu,* 1971). In 1960 he cofounded his own electronic studio (Apsone-Cabasse), where large-scale works such as *L'apocalypse de Jean* (1968) have been realized. His *Mise en musique du corticolart* (1971) attempted to transform brain waves into sound and lighting. He continued to explore the possibilities of electronic music, for example, with *Pierre réfléchies* (1982).

Henry VIII (b. Greenwich, 28 June 1491; d. Windsor, 28 Jan. 1547). King of England, 1509–47. In his reign music was unusually prominent at court. The numbers of royal musicians increased greatly, and the king made a vast collection of instruments. He enjoyed playing, singing, dancing, and listening to fine performances. Of his (mostly quite short) compositions, 34 survive, all but one secular (secular pieces ed. in *MB* 18 [1962]).

Henschel, (Isidor) George [Georg] (b. Breslau, 18 Feb. 1850; d. Aviemore, Scotland, 10 Sept. 1934). Singer and conductor. He studied at the Leipzig Conservatory, 1867–70, then at the Berlin Hochschule für Musik. Baritone soloist; debut in 1877 in London, where he mostly lived thereafter. Conductor, 1881–84, Boston Symphony; 1881, married an American singer, Lillian Bailey (1860–1901), with whom he thereafter often appeared in joint recitals. In 1907 retired to Scotland, making occasional concert appearances. Knighted in 1914. He wrote *Personal Recollections of Johannes Brahms* (Boston, 1907) and *Musings and Memories of a Musician* (London, 1918; R: 1979). Composed operas, sacred music, songs, instrumental pieces.

Bibl.: Helen Henschel, *When Soft Voices Die* (London, 1944).

Henschel, Lillian June [née Bailey] (b. Columbus, Ohio, 17 Jan. 1860; d. London, 4 Nov. 1901). Soprano. Studied in Boston; professional debut there in 1876; 1878, studied with Pauline Viardot in Paris; 1879, English debut, London Philharmonic, in a Handel duet with George Henschel, whom she married in 1881. In 1884 they settled in London, frequently appearing in joint recitals.

Hensel, Fanny (Cäcilie) Mendelssohn (Bartholdy) (b. Hamburg, 14 Nov. 1805; d. Berlin, 14 May 1847). Composer. Elder sister of Felix Mendelssohn. In 1811 the family moved to Berlin; she studied there with Ludwig Berger (piano) and Zelter (composition); considered equal in musical talent to Felix, but her father (and later Felix) objected to a public career for her as unsuitable to her sex. Felix included 6 of her songs, unacknowledged, in his own opp. 8, 9, but discouraged her from publishing under her own name. She composed (choral music, piano pieces, chamber music, songs) and played (in private musicales) throughout her life. In 1829 she married the painter Wilhelm Hensel, who encouraged her musical pursuits. Her diary is a principal source of information on the Mendelssohn family.

Bibl.: Marcia J. Citron, "The Lieder of Fanny Mendelssohn Hensel," *MQ* 69 (1983): 570–94. Id., ed., *The Letters of Fanny Hensel to Felix Mendelssohn* (Stuyvesant, N.Y., 1987). Françoise Tillard, *Fanny Mendelssohn* (Paris, 1992).

Fanny Mendelssohn Hensel. Drawing by her husband, Wilhelm Hensel, 1829.

Henselt, (Georg Martin) Adolf von (b. Schwabach, near Nuremberg, 9 May 1814; d. Bad Warmbrunn [now Cieplice], Silesia, 10 Oct. 1889). Composer and pianist. Grew up in Munich, his talent as pianist winning him a royal grant for eight months of study with Hummel in Weimar (1831); then two years of theory with Sechter in Vienna; 1834–38, toured Europe, but his health and temperament kept him from a career as a virtuoso. In 1838 he settled in St. Petersburg, becoming a fashionable teacher, pianist to the empress, and later inspector of music at girls' schools. Ennobled, 1840. He rarely played in public but achieved a legendary reputation. Works include a once-popular Piano Concerto op. 16; *12 études de concert* op. 2 (no. 6, "Si oiseau j'étais"), *12 études de salon* op. 5, and other piano pieces.

Henze, Hans Werner (b. Gütersloh, Westphalia, 1 July 1926). Composer and conductor. Studied at the State Music School in Brunswick (1942–44), and started to compose as a teenager. In 1946 he began to study composition with Wolfgang Fortner at the Institute for Church Music in Heidelberg; he attended the Darmstadt summer courses from 1946, and studied privately with René Leibowitz from 1948. From 1948 to 1949 he served as musical director of the German Theater in Constance, and then music artistic director and ballet conductor in the State Theater in Wiesbaden. In 1953 he left Germany for Italy. In the early 1960s he became director of the master classes in composition at the Salzburg Mozarteum; increasingly active as a conductor, especially of his own works.

Henze credited his study with Fortner for his secure grounding in traditional counterpoint and form; early works reflect the styles of Hindemith, Fortner, and Stravinsky. His association with Darmstadt and Leibowitz can be seen in his use of twelve-tone methods, beginning with the Violin Concerto (1947) and Piano Variations (1949). The opera *Boulevard Solitude* (1951) makes use, within the serial method, of tonal, atonal, and polytonal structures and of blues and jazz progressions. In the early 1950s Henze moved away from the styles encouraged at Darmstadt. In the decade after his move to Italy he continued to compose prolifically, now more widely influenced by the music of Mahler, 19th-century Italian opera, and classical formal procedures. The Fourth Symphony (1955), for example, is a one-movement work that incorporates five traditional movements: overture, sonata, variations, scherzo, and rondo. Two works of the early 1970s illustrate both his view that "everything turns toward the theater and returns again from it," by reducing the gap between concert and theater music, and his continuing interest in the use of soloists with orchestra: the Second Violin Concerto (1971) and *Tristan* (1974), both of which include taped sounds as well as live performers.

When Henze broke with the Darmstadt composers in the early 1950s, his reasons went beyond the purely musical. His Marxist political orientation called for an "engaged music." He continued to regard music as inevitably political; he collaborated with Blacher, Dessau, Hartmann, and Wagner-Régeny in the collective composition *Aufstand: A Jewish Chronicle,* in response to an apparent resurgence of the Nazis (performed 1966). His founding of and five-year association with the Montepulciano Cantieri (1976–80) was an attempt to effect a cultural reawakening in a small Italian community. The premiere there in 1980 of *Pollicino* he saw as evidence of the success of his view that "art has to go right among the people . . . [and] play a vital role in the shaping of a new and better society."

Works: operas and music theater (*Boulevard Solitude,* 1952; *König Hirsch,* 1956, rev. 1962 as *Il re cervo; Der Prinz von Homburg,* 1960; *Elegy for Young Lovers,* 1961; *Der junge Lord,* 1965; *The Bassarids,* 1966; *We Come to the River,* 1976; *The English Cat,* 1983; *Das verratene Meer,* 1990); ballets (*Ondine,* 1957; *Orpheus,* 1978); film scores and incidental music; numerous orchestral pieces (including suites arranged from his dramatic works as well as 8 symphonies (no. 8, 1993); *Sieben Liebeslieder,* cello and orchestra, 1985; *Allegro brillante,* 1989); 5 string quartets (1947–77), *Canzona* (1982, wind quintet), and other chamber music; a few works for piano or harpsichord; several works for chorus and instrumental ensemble or orchestra (*Chor gefangener Trojer,* 1948, rev. 1964; *Jephte,* after Carissimi, soloists, chorus, instruments, 1976); solo vocal music (*Apollo et Hyazinthus,* alto, instruments, 1948; 5 Neapolitan songs, baritone and orchestra, 1956; *3 Auden Pieces,* voice and piano, 1983).

Writings: *Undine: Tagebuch eines Balletts* (Munich, 1959). *Essays* (Mainz, 1964). *Musik und Politik: Schriften und Gespräche, 1955–1975* (Munich, 1976); trans. and enlarged as *Music and Politics: Collected Writings, 1953–81* (Ithaca, N.Y., 1982). *Die englische Katze: Arbeitstagebuch, 1979–82* (Frankfurt, 1988).

Bibl.: Klaus Geitel, *Hans Werner Henze* (Berlin, 1968). Dieter Rexroth, ed., *Der Komponist Hans Werner Henze* (Mainz, 1986). P. Peterson, *Hans Werner Henze, ein politischer Musiker: zwölf Vorlesungen* (Hamburg, 1988).

Herbert, Victor (August) (b. Dublin, 1 Feb. 1859; d. New York, 26 May 1924). Composer, conductor, and cellist. After the death of his father and his mother's marriage to a German physician, he was raised in Stuttgart, where he studied at the conservatory from 1876 with Max Seifriz; he played in the court orchestra and performed as a soloist; in 1885 he began to teach at a new music school in the city. The next year he and his wife (Therese Foerster, a soprano) went to New York to work at the Metropolitan Opera. Herbert made a career as cellist (performing his second Cello Concerto with the New York Philharmonic Society in 1894) and as conductor of the Pittsburgh Symphony (1898–1904), after which he founded his own orchestra. In addition to a substantial amount of concert music, he wrote over 40 operettas between 1894 and 1924 (among the more well known are *Babes in Toyland,* 1903, *Naughty Marietta,* 1910, and *Sweethearts,* 1913). He wrote as well some of the first through-composed scores for feature films (*The Fall of a Nation,* 1916; *Indian Summer,* 1919). He was a skilled melodist whose ability at orchestration had evolved during his own long experience as performer and conductor. He wrote two serious operas drawing on the traditions of Wagner and Strauss: *Natoma,* staged in Philadelphia (1900), and *Madeleine,* staged in New York (1914). He was a cofounder of the American Society of Composers, Authors, and Publishers (ASCAP), serving as vice president for a decade.

Works: 2 operas, over 40 operettas, scenes for Ziegfeld's Follies, film and incidental music; 2 cello concertos (1884, 1894), *Irish Rhapsody* (1892), *Columbus* (1903), and other orchestral music; *The Captive* (a symphonic poem for solo voices, chorus, and orchestra, 1891); ca. 22 chamber works; ca. 25 piano pieces; choral music; ca. 80 songs.

Bibl.: Edward N. Waters, *Victor Herbert: A Life in Music* (New York, 1955).

Herbig, Günther (b. Osti nad Labem, Czechoslovakia, 30 Nov. 1931). Conductor. Studied conducting with Hermann Abendroth at the Franz Liszt Hochschule in Weimar; later coached by Hermann Scherchen and Herbert von Karajan. His first conducting post was at the Erfurt Civic Theater, 1956–57. He then led the Weimar National Theater, 1957–62; was music director at the Hans Otto Theater in Pottsdam, 1962–66; conducted the East Berlin Symphony, 1966–72; was music director of the Dresden Philharmonic beginning 1970; and was chief conductor of the East Berlin Symphony, 1977–78. Guest conductor of the Dallas Symphony, 1979–81; music director of the Detroit Symphony, 1984–90; music director of the Toronto Symphony from 1990.

Herbst, Johann Andreas (bapt. Nuremburg, 9 June 1588; d. Frankfurt am Main, 24 Jan. 1666). Theorist and composer. Became Kapellmeister to Landgrave Philipp V von Butzbach in 1614; took the same post under Landgrave Ludwig V at Darmstadt in 1619, and in 1623 moved to a similar position at Frankfurt. He returned to Nuremberg in 1636, leading the music at the Frauenkirche, but left again for Frankfurt in 1644. He apparently wrote only vocal music, chiefly sacred and in styles ranging from late Renaissance polyphony to polychoral works and concertato settings; his treatises *Musica practica* (Nuremberg, 1642), a singing manual for the Italian style, and *Musica poetica* (Nuremberg, 1643), a composition handbook, both circulated widely.

Herbst, Johannes (b. Kempten, Swabia, 23 July 1735; d. Salem, N.C., 15 Jan. 1812). Composer. He was trained as a minister in Saxony and served in several Moravian congregations (in nonclerical posts) in Germany and England. In 1774 he was ordained and became director of the Moravians in Neudietendorf and Gnadenfrey. In 1786 he fled to America with his wife, settling first in Pennsylvania, where he was pastor of the Moravian congregation in Lancaster. In 1791 he was named pastor at Lititz; in 1811 he moved to Salem, N.C., upon being appointed a bishop in the Moravian church. His extensive personal library of manuscripts, consisting of European and American music (much of it copied by Herbst himself), forms one of the most important early American music collections; it is now housed at the archives of the Moravian Music Foundation in Winston-Salem. It contains nearly 1,000 songs and anthems, 50 large-scale vocal/choral works by C. P. E. Bach, Haydn, Mozart, and others; and 6 volumes of keyboard music. Among his own works are nearly 200 anthems and 150 solo songs.

Bibl.: Marilyn P. Gombosi, *Catalog of the Johannes Herbst Collection* (Chapel Hill, N.C., 1970). Joan O. Falconer, "Bishop Johannes Herbst" (diss., Columbia Univ., 1969).

Herman, Woody [Woodrow Charles] (b. Milwaukee, 16 May 1913; d. Los Angeles, 29 Oct. 1987). Jazz bandleader, clarinetist, alto saxophonist, and singer. For 50 years from 1936 he led big bands (from 1944, his "Herd"), beginning with a repertory of swing music (mostly blues) and moving into newer styles. Among his sidemen were Bill Harris, Dave Tough, Stan Getz, Zoot Sims, Serge Chaloff (these last three in Herman's first saxophone section of tenors and baritone, known as the "Four Brothers"), Al Cohn, Gene Ammons, and Sal Nistico. His recordings include "Woodchopper's Ball" (1939), "Caldonia" (1945), "Summer Sequence" (1946–47, composed by Ralph Burns), "Four Brothers" (1947, by Jimmy Giuffre), "Early Autumn" (1948, by Burns), and the album *Woody's Winners* (1965). Stravinsky composed the *Ebony Concerto* for Herman's First Herd (1945).

Bibl.: Steve Voce, *Woody Herman* (London, 1986). Dexter Morrill, *Woody Herman: A Guide to the Big Band Recordings, 1936–1987* (New York, 1990).

Hermannus Contractus [Hermann von Reichenau] (b. Swabia, 18 July 1013; d. Reichenau, 24 Sept. 1054). Writer. Author of works on many subjects. Music is mentioned in a world chronicle that covers the years from the time of Christ until 1054 and is the focus of his *Musica* (ed. Leipzig, 1884; ed. and trans. Eng., Rochester, N.Y., 1936), which is concerned with species of perfect intervals and their connection with the church modes. An interval notation using Greek and Latin letters and two associated didactic songs appear outside this treatise. Although it is clear that he composed, very few pieces can be attributed to him with any certainty.

Hernando (y Palomar), Rafael (José María) (b. Madrid, 31 May 1822; d. there, 10 July 1888). Composer. Student, 1837–43, at the Madrid Conservatory (under Carnicer, Albéniz, Saldoni) and, 1843–48, at the Paris Conservatory (Galli, García, Auber). His opera *Romilda,* accepted by the Théâtre-Italien, was not performed because of the Revolution. He returned to Madrid, beginning to produce zarzuelas there in 1848 and having great success with *Colegiales y soldados* (1849) and *El duende* (1848); several others proving less successful in 1850–54, he retired from the stage. He wrote on musical matters, composed sacred music; in 1852 became secretary, later professor of harmony, Madrid Conservatory.

Hérold, (Louis Joseph) Ferdinand (b. Paris, 28 Jan. 1791; d. there, 19 Jan. 1833). Composer. Son of a piano teacher and composer of Alsatian origin. From 1806 a student at the Paris Conservatory (Adam, piano; Kreutzer, violin; Catel, harmony; Méhul, whose favorite pupil he became, composition). In 1812 he won the Prix de Rome; because of poor health (probably the tuberculosis that later killed him) he spent September 1813 to February 1815 in Naples, where he became music teacher to the two daughters of the king (Murat) and had an Italian opera semiseria produced (1815). He returned to Paris via Vienna and Munich, becoming maestro al cembalo at the Théâtre-Italien. His chance to begin an opera career came from Boieldieu, who invited him to compose an act of *Charles de France* (Opéra-comique, 1816), leading to further commissions there in 1817–20, the later of which were unsuccessful. In 1823 he resumed opera production with the successful one-act *Le muletier* (Opéra-comique); this was followed by 9 more there, including his 3 most important and successful works: *Marie* (1825), *Zampa* (1831; 682 performances at the Opéra-comique to 1895), *Le pré aux clercs* (1832; 1,589 performances there through 1898). From 1826 he was chief vocal coach at the Opéra; 1827–29, 5 ballets given there. His last opera, *Ludovic,* was completed by Halévy. Other works: 2 symphonies, 4 piano concertos, 10 piano sonatas, much piano music, including many opera potpourris.

Herrmann, Bernard (b. New York, 29 June 1911; d. Los Angeles, 24 Dec. 1975). Composer and conductor. He studied at New York Univ. (Grainger, Philip James) and at Juilliard (Wagenaar, Stoessel). He worked at CBS Radio (1934–40) as arranger and conductor, and composed new music for some 125 programs (including Welles's *The War of the Worlds,* 1938). The first of his 61 film scores was *Citizen Kane* (1941); others include several for Hitchcock (*Vertigo,* 1958; *Psycho,* 1960) and Truffaut's *Farenheit 451* (1966). He won an Oscar for *All That Money Can Buy* (1941), which quotes New Hampshire folk songs; in *Anna and the King of Siam* (1946) he used Western instruments to imitate Siamese scales and rhythms. In addition he wrote the music for several television series *(The Alfred Hitchcock Hour, Twilight Zone).* Throughout his career he remained active as composer and conductor of concert music. He founded and led the New Chamber Orchestra (1931); conducted the CBS Symphony (1940–45); and guest-conducted the New York Philharmonic. He introduced many American works (especially Ives) in England and British works in the U.S. His own concert music includes ballets, 3 operas (2 for television, including *A Christmas Carol,* 1954); a musical; a symphony (1937–40), suites based on his film scores *(The Devil and Daniel Webster),* and other orchestral and chamber music; 2 cantatas and a song cycle for 4 soloists, chorus, and orchestra.

Bibl.: Steven C. Smith, *A Heart at Fire's Center: The Life and Music of Bernard Herrmann* (Berkeley, 1991).

Herschel, William [Friedrich Wilhelm] (b. Hannover, 15 Nov. 1738; d. Slough, near Windsor, 25 Aug. 1822). Musician and astronomer. His early music lessons were with his father, a member of the infantry band in Hannover. In 1753 he joined the Hannover guard band (as oboist), and two years later he traveled to Durham with the regiment during the Seven Years' War. After a brief return to Germany, he moved to London and became a music copyist for various publishers there. In the 1760s he established a reputation in England as violinist and conductor; from 1766 he played organ at the Octagon Chapel in Bath. During the 1770s he devoted himself to music and to astronomy. In 1780 he was accepted into the Bath Literary and Philosophical Society, and the following year, using a telescope he had partially designed and constructed himself, he discovered the planet Uranus. He was knighted in 1817. Among his works are 24 symphonies; concertos; trio sonatas; capriccios for solo violin; keyboard pieces *(Variations upon the Ascending Scale of the Treble).*

Hertel, Johann Wilhelm (b. Eisenach, 9 Oct. 1727; d. Schwerin, 14 June 1789). Composer, organist, and violinist. His grandfather Jakob Christian was Kapellmeister at Oettingen and Merseberg; his father, Johann Christian (1699–1754), was *Konzertmeister* at Eisenach. Johann Wilhelm studied music at Eisenach under Heil, a pupil of J. S. Bach, and later took instruction from Karl Höckh. In 1744 he received a post as violinist at the Strelitz court; through his travels to Berlin he maintained close contacts with C. P. E. Bach and the Benda brothers, and he continued study of composition with Carl Heinrich Graun. In 1752 he took his father's place at the Mecklenburg-Strelitz court for a brief time before the court was dissolved. He became court composer at Schwerin in 1754 and remained there until his death, giving violin and keyboard lessons to the royal family. He composed sacred choral music, cantatas, lieder, symphonies, concertos, chamber music, and solo keyboard pieces.

Hertz, Alfred (b. Frankfurt am Main, 15 July 1872; d. San Francisco, 17 April 1942). Conductor. Studied with Anton Urspruch at the Raff Conservatory, then conducted opera at the Halle State Theater, 1891–92; at Altenburg, 1892–95; at Bermen-Elberfeld, 1895–99; and at Breslau, 1899–1902. In 1902 he was employed by the New York Metropolitan Opera and in 1903 led there, without approval from Bayreuth, the first American performance of *Parsifal.* As a result he was blacklisted by the powerful Wagner organization for future performances of Wagner in Germany and Austria. He remained with the Metropolitan until 1915, leading first U.S. performances of *Salome, Rosenkavelier,* and the premiere of Humperdinck's *Königskinder.* He built the fledgling San Francisco Symphony into a major ensemble, 1915–30, and inaugurated the Hollywood Bowl Concerts in 1922.

Hervé [Florimond Ronger] (b. Houdain, Pas de Calais, 30 June 1825; d. Paris, 3 Nov. 1892). Composer. Left fatherless in 1835, he became a choirboy at St. Roch, Paris; educated there, and also had lessons from Elwart and Auber. He became an organist, but gravitated to the theater, taking the name Hervé. In 1848 he began to compose (often both words and music) light musical comedies, often singing (as a tenor) and acting in them; in 1849 he became music director at the Odéon. He ran his own theater, 1854–56, the Folies-concertantes (renamed Folies-nouvelles, 1855), producing a flood of small comedies. In 1867 he began a series of more substantial three-act operettas, some produced throughout Europe and in America (especially *L'oeil crevé,* 1867; *Chilpéric,* 1868; *Mam'zelle Nitouche,* 1883, his most popular). He also worked in London, 1870–71 and 1886–92.

Bibl.: Louis Schneider, *Les maîtres de l'opérette française: Hervé. Charles Lecocq* (Paris, 1924). Renée Cariven-Galharret and Dominique Ghesquiere, *Hervé: Un musicien paradoxal, 1825–1892* (Paris, 1992).

Herz, Henri (b. Vienna, 6 Jan. 1803; d. Paris, 5 Jan. 1888). Pianist. In 1816 he entered the Paris Conservatory (Pradher, piano; Reicha, composition), winning first prize in piano in 1818; his manner of playing was much influenced by Moscheles (1821). He became a popular virtuoso, touring Europe from the 1830s, also North and South America (1845–51), resulting in his book *Mes voyages en Amérique* (Paris, 1866; trans. Eng., 1963). He also became a successful piano manufacturer in Paris; and with brother Jacques Simon Herz (1794–1880) founded École spéciale de piano, Paris, which also housed a leading Paris concert hall. Professor of piano, 1842–74, Paris Conservatory. Published over 200 works of piano salon music; also 8 concertos; a sonata; a piano trio; a much-used collection of scales and exercises; piano method.

Herzogenberg, (Leopold) Heinrich (Picot de Peccaduc), Freiherr von (b. Graz, 10 June 1843; d. Wiesbaden, 9 Oct. 1900). Composer. Well educated, including composition with Dessoff at the Vienna Conservatory, 1862–64. In 1868 he married Brahms's close friend Elisabeth von Stockhausen (1847–92). Lived in Graz, 1868–72, composing. He was in Leipzig, where for ten years he conducted the Bach Society; from 1885 he taught composition at the Berlin Hochschule für Musik, with interruptions because of poor health and the death of his wife. He composed much sacred music, oratorios, cantatas, part songs, solo songs, 3 symphonies, much chamber and piano music. Brahms respected his seriousness as a composer but did not value his music, which never became widely performed.

Bibl.: Max Kalbeck, ed., *Johannes Brahms: The Herzogenberg Correspondence* (New York, 1905; R: 1987).

Heseltine, Philip. See Warlock, Peter.

Hess, Myra (b. London, 25 Feb. 1890; d. there 25 Nov. 1965). Pianist. Studied with Julian Pascal, Orlando

Morgan, and Tobias Matthay. Debut 1907 in London, playing Beethoven's Fourth Concerto under Beecham. After many tours, including her first to the U.S. in 1922, she joined her cousin Irene Scharrer to concertize as a duo pianist. During World War II she gave a famous series of Lunchtime Concerts. In 1941 she was made a Dame. After the war she excised many Baroque and contemporary pieces from her repertory, retaining Bach (often in her own transcriptions), Scarlatti, and the standard composers from Mozart to Brahms.

Heuberger, Richard (Franz Joseph) (b. Graz, 18 June 1850; d. Vienna, 28 Oct. 1914). Composer. Trained as an engineer. In 1876 he turned to music. From 1878 he conducted various Viennese choruses; from 1881 he was also a Vienna music critic; and, from 1902, professor at the Vienna Conservatory. Composed operas, a ballet, choral and orchestral pieces. He is best known for the first of his 7 operettas, *Der Opernball* (Vienna, 1898), which was very successful and widely performed.

Heugel, Jacques Léopold (b. La Rochelle, 1 Mar. 1815; d. Paris, 12 Nov. 1883). Publisher. In 1839 he became a partner in the music publishing firm of Meissonnier and in 1842 sole owner. It grew to be one of the most important firms in Paris, publishing much theater music. Meissonnier acquired the journal *Le ménestrel* in 1839 (ceased publication in 1940). The business was carried on by his son Henri Georges (1844–1916), then by descendants.

Hewitt, James (b. Dartmoor? 4 June 1770; d. Boston, 2 Aug. 1827). Composer, publisher, and conductor. Little is known of his early life in England; apparently he played violin in Astley's circus orchestra in London, and possibly also in the court orchestra. In 1792 he moved to New York, where he was active in that city's concert life, particularly as conductor of the orchestra of the Park Street Theater. He gave music lessons and sold musical instruments. Moving to Boston in 1811, he continued to teach and compose, and he took the post of organist at Trinity Church. From 1816 he lived in New York, Boston, Charleston, Augusta, Ga., and several other cities. As a publisher he issued some 650 compositions, including works by Mozart, Haydn, and others; many were in his own arrangements, and more than 150 were his original compositions. His works included some 15 stage works (*The Tars from Tripoli,* 1806–7); ballets; orchestral overtures (*The Fourth of July,* 1801; *Yankee Doodle with Variations,* 1807–10; *Lafayette's Quick Step,* ca. 1824); sacred hymns and anthems; and many songs. Hewitt's daughter and sons also pursued musical professions: Sophia Henrietta Hewitt Ostinelli (1799–1845) was a singer and keyboard player, and from 1819 the organist for the Handel and Haydn Society; John Hill Hewitt (1801–90) was a composer, poet, and journalist in Augusta, Boston, and Baltimore, and composed several popular Confederate songs; James Lang Hewitt (1803–53) was a prolific music publisher in Boston. George Washington [Thomas] Hewitt (1811–93) was a music teacher and arranger.

Bibl.: John W. Wagner, "James Hewitt, 1770–1827," *MQ* 58 (1972): 259–76.

Hewitt, John Hill (b. New York, 12 July 1801; d. Baltimore, 7 Oct. 1890). Composer. Eldest son of James Hewitt; attended public schools in Boston; apprenticed to a sign painter but ran away; West Point cadet, 1818–22, studying music with the bandmaster. In 1823 he accompanied his father on a theatrical tour, remaining in Augusta, Ga., as a music teacher. Journalism and music were to remain his primary occupations. He lived in various southern cities, but mostly in Baltimore; composed dance music, marches, the oratorio *Jepthah,* theater music, sentimental songs, some of which were popular, Civil War songs (as an adherent of the South, where he spent the war years). He also wrote plays, stories, poetry, and his memoirs, *Shadows on the Wall* (Baltimore, 1877; R: 1971).

Bibl.: J. T. Howard, "The Hewitt Family in American Music," *MQ* 17 (1931): 25–39. Frank W. Hoogerwerf, *John Hill Hewitt: Sources and Bibliography* (Atlanta, 1982).

Heyden [Haiden], **Sebald** (b. Bruck, near Erlangen, 8 Dec. 1499; d. Nuremberg, 9 July 1561). Theorist. Father and grandfather of musicians; from 1521 Kantor and school rector at the Spitalkirche in Nuremberg; from 1525 rector of the school of St. Sebald there. His three didactic treatises concentrate on practice and avoid strictly theoretical questions. *Musicae stoicheiōsis* (1532) treats the essentials of mensural notation and of polyphony. *Musicae* (1537) covers a broader range of subjects and includes many practical examples drawn from works of great contemporary composers. A much expanded version was published as *De arte canendi* (1540; R: *MMML* 2nd ser., 139 [1969]; trans. Eng., *MSD* 26 [1972]).

Hidalgo, Juan (b. Madrid, 1612–16; d. there, 30 Mar. 1685). Composer. Entered the royal chapel around 1631 as harpist and harpsichordist; he remained there for the rest of his life. He was the most important musical figure at court; his music enjoyed wide popularity throughout Iberia and Latin America, to judge from surviving copies. He composed the earliest extant Spanish opera, *Celos aun del aire matan* (Madrid, 1660); the libretto, as is the case with many of his stage works, is by Pedro Calderón de la Barca. His other music includes 2 Masses (1 with continuo), motets, and over 100 secular *villancicos* and *tonos humanos.*

Higginbotham, J(ay) C. (b. Social Circle, Ga., 11 May 1906; d. New York, 26 May 1973). Jazz trombonist. He was a soloist with Luis Russell's big band (1928–31), recording "Case on Dawn (Ease on Down)" and, as a leader, "Higginbotham Blues" (both 1930). After working with Chick Webb, Fletcher Henderson, Benny Carter, and the Mills Blue Rhythm

Band, he rejoined Russell, whose band was then accompanying Louis Armstrong (1937–40). He joined Henry "Red" Allen's swing combo (1940–47), then worked as a free-lance mainly in New York, rejoining Allen and recording the album *The Big Reunion* (1957) with Henderson's sidemen under Rex Stewart's leadership.

Higgins, Billy (b. Los Angeles, 11 Oct. 1936). Jazz drummer. He was a member of Ornette Coleman's free jazz quartet during its controversial debut in New York (1959–60) and recorded the album *Change of the Century* (1959). He toured with Thelonious Monk (1960) and Sonny Rollins (1962–63) and began recording extensively, most often with hard bop musicians, including Lee Morgan's album *The Sidewinder* (1963). He worked intermittently with the pianist Cedar Walton from 1966 and occasionally rejoined Coleman (1977, 1987). From 1981 a member of the Timeless All Stars, a sextet including Bobby Hutcherson, Walton, and the tenor saxophonist Harold Land. He performed in the film *'Round Midnight* (1986).

Higgins, Dick [Richard Carter] (b. Cambridge, England, 15 Mar. 1938). Composer, performer, writer, artist, and publisher. He studied composition with Harry Levenson (1953), then with Cowell (Columbia, B.S., 1960) and Cage. He was associated with the earliest "happenings" in New York in the late 1950s; collaborated in intermedia events with Cage, Cowell, Tenney, and others. He taught at the California Institute of the Arts (1970–71) and SUNY–Purchase (from 1983); wrote several books and articles on theater, visual arts, architecture, and music (*Horizons: The Poetics and Theory of the Intermedia,* 1983); active as novelist and poet, and in film, stage, and radio productions. His music relies on improvisation and often uses graphic notation. Works include an opera (1965), *26 Mountains for Viewing the Sunset From* (singers, dancers, and chamber orchestra, 1980); orchestral and chamber music, often for variable instrumentation *(Danger Music);* performance pieces; a sonata for prepared piano (1981); many vocal works; film scores.

Hildegard of [von] **Bingen** (b. Bemersheim, near Alzey, Rheinhessen, 1098; d. Rupertsberg, near Bingen, 17 Sept. 1179). Abbess, mystic, writer, and composer. Born into the German nobility but early entrusted to the church: a novice at age 8, a nun at 15, a mother superior from 1136, founder of a monastery (Rupertsberg) near Bingen between 1147 and 1150 and of a daughter house nearby, ca. 1165. Temporal and spiritual leaders of all ranks consulted her on religious, political, and diplomatic matters. Despite inquiries conducted under 4 popes, she was never canonized but does have a feast day in the Roman calendar. Her writings include 2 lives of saints, treatises on natural history and medicine, and extensive records of her visions. A liturgical cycle of 77 lyric poems with monophonic music also survives, as does her *Ordo virtutum*

Hildegard of Bingen receiving a vision.

(ed. Audrey E. Davidson, Kalamazoo, Mich., 1985), a morality play in verse with 82 melodies.

Bibl.: Audrey Ekdahl Davidson, ed., *The "Ordo virtutum" of Hildegard of Bingen: Critical Studies* (Kalamazoo, 1992).

Hill, Alfred (Francis) (b. Melbourne, 16 Nov. 1870; d. Sydney, 30 Oct. 1960). Composer. He was first employed as a violinist in traveling theater orchestras. He then studied at the Leipzig Conservatory (1887–91). Thereafter he was active as a conductor in both New Zealand and Australia. Many of his compositions are based on Maori legend or make use of Australian aboriginal materials, including *Hinemoa* (cantata, 1895) and *Tapu* (opera, 1902). He wrote over 500 works, including 9 operas (some on European topics, some on Maori legend), 13 symphonies (all but Symphony no. 1, *Maori,* 1896–1900, are transcriptions of chamber music), 8 string quartets, choral music, and other chamber music. His many songs include Maori settings. He taught at the Austral Orchestral College in Sydney and published *Harmony and Melody* (London, 1927).

Hill, Edward Burlingame (b. Cambridge, Mass., 9 Sept. 1872; d. Francestown, N.H., 9 July 1960). Composer. He studied with Paine at Harvard, receiving his B.A. in 1894; then spent two years in New York studying piano with B. J. Lang and Arthur Whiting. He returned to Boston to teach piano and harmony, studied briefly in Paris with Widor, and took a course in orchestration from Chadwick. He was on the faculty at Harvard from 1908 until his retirement in 1940; his many students included Bernstein, Thomson, Finney, and Carter. His own style remained conservative, although in later years he moved away from his earlier programmatic pieces toward more abstract music.

Many of his orchestral works were introduced by Koussevitzky with the Boston Symphony; the earliest were premiered by Damrosch in New York.

Works: 3 symphonies (1927–36), a concerto for violin (1933–34), *Stevensonian Suites I and II* (1916–17, 1921–22), *Ode* for the 50th anniversary of the Boston Symphony (chorus and orchestra, 1930), *Prelude* (1953) and other orchestral works; chamber and piano music (*Jazz Studies,* 1924 and 1935); a cantata for female voices and orchestra (1907).

Bibl.: Linda L. Tyler, *Edward Burlingame Hill: A Bio-Bibliography* (New York, 1989).

Hillemacher, Paul (Joseph Guillaume) (b. Paris, 29 Nov. 1852; d. Versailles, 13 Aug. 1933), and **Lucien (Joseph) Edouard Hillemacher** (b. Paris, 10 June 1860; d. there, 2 June 1909). Composers. Sons of a painter; both studied at the Paris Conservatory, winning the Prix de Rome in 1876 and 1880; began collaborating in 1879, from 1881 signing their work Paul-Lucien Hillemacher. Composed much for the stage, including operas, especially *Orsola* (Opéra, 1902) and *Circé* (Opéra-comique, 1907), both unsuccessful; incidental music, and an English pantomime; 2 oratorios and other choral works; many songs; an orchestral suite; chamber music; piano pieces; also a joint biography of Gounod (1906). Paul produced a few works of his own after his brother's death.

Hiller, Ferdinand (von) (b. Frankfurt am Main, 24 Oct. 1811; d. Cologne, 11 May 1885). Conductor, pianist, and composer. His musical talent early aroused much interest; pupil of Hummel, 1825–27, in Weimar. He was in Paris, 1828–36, as pianist giving concerts of his own music; a friend of Chopin and Berlioz. In Italy, 1836–39 and 1840–42, producing an unsuccessful Italian opera in Milan, 1839. Conductor, 1843–44, of the Gewandhaus concerts, Leipzig; 1844–47, conducted Dresden concerts; 1847–50, municipal conductor, Düsseldorf. Beginning 1850 he was music director of Cologne (also conducting widely in Europe); he reorganized the music school into the Cologne Conservatory and became its director; also directed the Lower Rhine Music Festival 11 times (1853–83). He was a commanding figure in German musical life, partly through his many books, representing a conservative, anti-Wagnerian position. His early promise as a composer was never fulfilled, although he produced prolifically in most genres.

Hiller, Johann Adam (b. Wendisch-Ossig, near Görlitz, 25 Dec. 1728; d. Leipzig, 16 June 1804). Composer and writer on music. He studied keyboard, counterpoint, and continuo at the Dresden Kreuzschule with G. A. Homilius (from 1746), and quickly became active in that city's musical life. In 1751 he matriculated at the Univ. of Leipzig, where he studied law, languages, and philosophy. In 1754 he became Hofmeister to Count Brühl in Dresden; but in 1758 he traveled back to Leipzig with the count. Leipzig's principal orchestral society, the Grosses Konzert, was reopened at the end of the Seven Years' War (1763), with Hiller as director; during the next eight years he brought its concerts to a standard of almost unmatched variety and technical excellence. He also edited the periodical *Wöchentliche Nachrichten* (1766–70), which remains a vital source of information on German musical life of the period.

With the poet Christian Felix Weisse, Hiller established the first full-blown German singspiel; their first collaboration, *Die verwandelten Weiber oder Der Teufel ist los* (Leipzig, 1766), contained songs by Standfuss and Hiller. Other successes followed: *Lisuart and Dariolette* (1766), *Die Jagd* (1770), *Der Dorfbalbier* (1771), *Der Aerndtekranz* (1771), and *Das Grab des Mufti* (1779). He also composed sacred vocal works and secular cantatas; published song collections; and authored a number of central musical treatises, including *Anweisung zum musikalisch-zierlichen Gesange* (Leipzig, 1780), *Lebensbeschreibungen berühmter Musikgelehrten und Tonkünstler,* 1 (Leipzig, 1784) [includes Hiller's autobiography, *Über Metastasio und seine Werke,* Leipzig, 1786].

Hiller, Lejaren A(rthur, Jr.) (b. New York, 23 Feb. 1924; d. Buffalo, 26 Jan. 1994). Composer. He studied piano, clarinet, and saxophone as a youth; was trained in chemistry (Princeton, Ph.D., 1947); worked in industry (1947–52); taught chemistry at the Univ. of Illinois (1952–58). While at Princeton he had studied oboe and composition (Babbitt, Sessions). In 1957 he collaborated with Leonard Isaacson on the *Illiac Suite* (String Quartet no. 4), composed on the computer at the Univ. of Illinois; later he wrote *Experimental Music* (1959), dealing with the techniques of computer composition. For a decade he taught in the music department at Illinois; in 1968 he became Slee Professor of composition at SUNY–Buffalo, where he initially co-directed with Foss the Center for Creative and Performing Arts. He wrote music in a variety of styles: twelve-tone and serial, microtonal, aleatory, electronic, and computer assisted; some works make use of American themes (*Jesse James,* vocal quartet and piano, 1950). His aleatoric *HPSCHD* (1967–69), a collaboration with Cage, employs 1–7 harpsichords and 1–51 tapes.

Other works include *An Avalanche,* narrator, soprano, percussion, player piano, and tape (1968); *The Birds,* a musical (1958); *Blues Is the Antecedent of It,* an electronic theater fantasy (1959); *John Italus,* opera (1989); 2 symphonies and other orchestral works; 7 string quartets and other chamber music (*The Fox Trots Again,* 1985); *Twelve-Tone Variations* (1954), several sonatas, and other works for piano; electronic music; a few songs.

Hillis, Margaret (Eleanor) (b. Kokomo, Ind., 1 Oct. 1921). Conductor. After graduating from Indiana Univ. (B.A., 1947) she studied choral conducting at Juilliard, then privately with Robert Shaw. Taught choral conducting at Union Theological Seminary, 1950–60; at Juilliard, 1951–53. Formed the American Choral Foundation, 1954. Chorusmaster of the American Opera Society, 1952–68. Founded the Chicago Symphony Chorus, 1957. Choral director of the Cleveland Orchestra, 1969–71; of the San Francisco Orchestra, 1982–83. Music Director of the Kenosha Civic Orchestra, 1961–68.

Hilton, John (1) (d. Cambridge, before 20 Mar. 1608). Composer. Singer and probably deputy organist at Lincoln Cathedral, where he was active from at least 1584 until early 1594; then organist at Trinity College, Cambridge. Morley's *The Triumphes of Oriana* (London, 1601) contains his one known secular piece, a madrigal. Most of the liturgical music (services and anthems) attributed to "John Hilton" may be by either him or his son, John Hilton (2).

Hilton, John (2) (b. Cambridge? 1599; buried Westminster, 21 Mar. 1657). Composer. Received the Mus.B. from Trinity College, Cambridge, in 1626; became organist at St. Margaret's, Westminster, in 1628. Publications include *Ayres or Fa-las for three voyces* (1627) and *Catch as Catch Can* (1652); his songs and rounds turn up in other prints as well. Other works, some of which may be confused with those of his father, include services, a Te Deum, verse and full anthems, and music for viols.

Himmel, Friedrich Heinrich (b. Treuenbrietzen, 20 Nov. 1765; d. Berlin, 8 June 1814). Composer. After early study in his hometown, he entered the Univ. of Halle to study theology, though apparently his chief interest was music. When Friedrich Wilhelm II heard him play the clavier in Potsdam in 1786, he agreed to send him to Dresden for study with Johann Gottlieb Naumann. Himmel returned to Berlin in 1791 to mount performances of a cantata, *La danza,* and an oratorio, *Isacco figura del redentore;* he was appointed chamber composer in 1792; soon after this he embarked on a musical tour of Italy, during which his opera *Semiramide* was performed in Naples. Returning to Berlin, in 1795 he replaced J. F. Reichardt as Kapellmeister. During the next two decades he made extensive tours of Russia, Scandinavia, Italy, and central Europe, where his operas were performed; the most successful was *Fanchon das Leyermädchen* (Berlin, 1804). He composed 8 known works for the stage (*Vasco da Gama,* Berlin, 1801; *Frohsinn und Schwärmerey,* Berlin, 1801); many oratorios and cantatas; nearly 200 songs; a Sinfonia in F (lost); concertos and chamber works; clavier music (including *12 variations sur un air connu*).

Hindemith, Paul (b. Hanau, near Frankfurt am Main, 16 Nov. 1895; d. Frankfurt, 28 Dec. 1963). Composer, theorist, violist, and conductor. Hindemith's musical abilities were recognized early by his violin teachers in Frankfurt; he had begun lessons at the age of 6, and in 1907 began to work under teachers from the conservatory (Anna Hegner, then Adolf Rebner). He was a scholarship student at the conservatory until 1917, studying composition with Arnold Mendelssohn and Bernard Sekles; in addition to the violin and viola, he became a skilled performer on clarinet and piano. By 1915 he was playing second violin in Rebner's string quartet, and was concertmaster of the Frankfurt Opera Orchestra conducted by his future father-in-law, Ludwig Rottenberg. He served in the army (playing in a band and in a string quartet that gave private performances for the commanding officer) from 1917 to 1919; after the war he returned to the quartet as a violist and to the opera orchestra. During those years his works were performed at the Donaueschingen Festival (1921, 1922), the administrative committee of which he joined in 1923. From 1921 to 1929 he played viola in the Amar–Hindemith Quartet, which was especially noted for its performances of contemporary music and was well regarded throughout Europe. The demands of his solo and ensemble career led him to resign from the Frankfurt opera position in 1923. In 1927 he was appointed to teach composition at the Berlin Hochschule für Musik. From 1929 until 1934 he played in a string trio with colleagues at the Hochschule, Josef Wolfsthal and Emanuel Feuermann.

In Berlin he taught not only at the Hochschule but also an evening class for amateurs at the Volksmusikschule Neu-Kölln. His experiences with amateurs contributed to his growing sense "of the danger of an esoteric isolationism in music" and his advocacy of music composed with a specific purpose, *Gebrauchsmusik.* That term dogged him for the rest of his career, especially in the U.S. It is nonetheless true that among his works are significant examples of *Hausmusik* and sonatas for nearly every imaginable instrument, all motivated by his desire to reduce the distance separating performing amateurs and professional musicians.

When the Nazis came to power, Hindemith came under increasing pressure because of his Jewish wife, his association with Jewish musicians, and his "degenerate" compositions. The official boycott of performances of his music announced in November 1934 so angered Furtwängler that he wrote an article in the *Deutsche allgemeine Zeitung* in Hindemith's defense, which resulted in the loss of his own conducting and administrative posts. In 1935 Hindemith was made to take a leave of absence from his teaching position at the Hochschule; he emigrated to Switzerland in 1938, and to New York in 1940.

In his first year in the U.S. Hindemith taught and lectured at Buffalo, Yale, and Cornell universities, Wells College (Aurora, N.Y.), and the Berkshire Music Center (1940–41). For over a decade he taught composition, harmony, and theory at Yale (1940–53); in addition he directed the Yale Collegium Musicum, whose concerts were presented in both New Haven and New York. He returned to Europe in 1947 to conduct and lecture; and in 1949–50 held the Charles Eliot Norton chair at Harvard (lectures published as *A Composer's World,* 1952). In 1951 he began to divide his time between the Univ. of Zurich and Yale and in 1953 moved permanently to Switzerland; he gave up the Zurich appointment in 1955 and devoted his last years to composing and conducting (in Europe, the U.S., Japan, and South America).

Hindemith was initially regarded as a radical who explored in turn Brahmsian late Romanticism, Impressionism, Expressionism (in the operas *Mörder, Hoffnung der Frauen,* and *Sancta Susanna,* 1919–21, and the Second String Quartet, 1921), and "anti-Romanticism" (in the puppet play *Das Nusch-Nuschi* with its parody of *Tristan und Isolde*), before arriving at the mature neoclassicial language for which he is best known. With the performance in 1922 of his *Kammermusik 1* (for small orchestra) at Donaueschingen he had become a central figure in German musical life, not only as a performer but also as a composer. The works from his middle period (1924–33) exploit a variety of neo-Baroque elements: Baroque rhythms, ritornellos, linear contrapuntal textures, clear formal divisions marked by triadic chordal progressions that contrast markedly with his dissonant counterpoint; 6 concertos from the mid-1920s *(Kammermusik 2–7)* focus on soloists in the manner of Bach's Brandenburg Concertos. The 3 concertos from 1930 (*Konzertmusik,* viola, piano, and brass) herald an increasing preoccupation with lyrical melody, fully developed in the opera *Mathis der Maler* (1934–35). In this and other works from the last three decades of his life, Hindemith cultivated a more tonal idiom, drawing on classical sonata forms and conventions, and combining a fundamentally contrapuntal texture with passages of accompanied melody and a parallelism indebted to Debussy. Two more operas and a Mass were among the works composed in the final decade of his life.

In *Unterweisung im Tonsatz* (3 vols.; 1937, 1939, 1970) Hindemith presented what he saw as a general method of composition, valid for all styles and periods. He revised many of his earlier compositions to accord with his theories of a broadened tonality in which each of the twelve chromatic pitches stands at a defined distance from the tonic (dependent upon its position in the overtone series) and a sixfold classification of chords and intervals (by means of which he could regulate the tension of a harmonic progression independent of the conventions of functional tonality). No "Hindemith school" of composers resulted from his teaching or his writings; but his ideas on *Gebrauchsmusik* did have a certain influence on composers (Copland and Britten, for example). His *Elementary Training for Musicians* is still widely used as a textbook in general musicianship.

Works: 7 operas (*Cardillac,* 1926; *Mathis der Maler,* 1934–35; *Die Harmonie der Welt,* 1956–57; *The Long Christmas Dinner,* 1960), ballets, film and radio scores, and other stage works; some 40 orchestral works, including concertos (for violin, viola, cello, viola d'amore, piano, organ, horn, clarinet), Concerto for Orchestra (1925), symphonies, and other pieces; chamber music for solo instruments, duets (including many sonatas with piano), 6 string quartets, a septet for winds (1948), and other pieces; *Ludus tonalis* (1942), 3 sonatas (1936), and other piano music; 3 sonatas for organ (1938–40); *Das Unaufhörliche* (oratorio, 1931) and other accompanied choral music; *Zwölfe Madrigale* (à 5, 1958), *Messe* (1963), and other unaccompanied choral music; *Das Marienleben* (1922–23) and other vocal music with ensemble or orchestra; songs with piano.

Writings: *Unterweisung im Tonsatz,* 3 vols. (1937; 1939; 1970), the first 2 vols. trans. as *The Craft of Musical Composition* (1941–45). *A Concentrated Course in Traditional Harmony,* 2 vols. (1943, 1948). *Elementary Training for Musicians* (1946). *A Composer's World* (1952). *Johann Sebastian Bach: Ein verpflichtendes Erbe* (1979; trans. Eng., New Haven, 1952).

Bibl.: Ian Kemp, *Hindemith* (London, 1970). *Hindemith Jahrbuch* (1971–). Geoffrey Skelton, *Paul Hindemith: The Man behind the Music* (New York, 1975). Andres Briner, *Paul Hindemith* (Zurich, 1978). Giselher Schubert, *Hindemith* (Reinbek bei Hamburg, 1981). Clifford Taylor, "The Hindemith Theories: A Revaluation of Premise and Purpose," *MR* 44 (1983): 246–62. Eberhard Preussner, *Paul Hindemith, ein Lebensbild* (Innsbruck, 1984). David Neumayer, *The Music of Paul Hindemith* (New Haven, 1986). Luther Noss, *Paul Hindemith in the United States* (Urbana, Ill., 1989).

Hines, Earl (Kenneth) [Fatha] (b. Duquesne, Pa., 28 Dec. 1903; d. Oakland, Calif., 22 Apr. 1983). Jazz pianist and bandleader. In Chicago he worked in changing associations with Louis Armstrong (1926–28) and joined Jimmie Noone's small group (1927–28). In 1928 he recorded Noone's "Apex Blues" and staked a claim among jazz soloists as the principal rival to Armstrong in a series of recordings with Armstrong's small groups, as well as their duo "Weather Bird"; Hines's "trumpet style" improvisations helped move jazz piano playing away from approaches based on ragtime. That same year he formed a big band that was resident at the Grand Terrace through the 1930s. In the early 1940s, when Billy Eckstine and Sarah Vaughan were his singers, the group turned toward bop, with Charlie Parker and Dizzy Gillespie among Hines's sidemen. After a later group disbanded, he joined Armstrong's All Stars (1948–51). He led swing and Dixieland groups mainly in the San Francisco Bay area (to 1983), but also toured Europe as a co-leader with Jack Teagarden (1957). Beginning with concerts in New York he performed alone, as on the album *Quintessential 1974.*

Bibl.: Stanley Dance, *The World of Earl Hines* (New York, 1983).

Hingeston [Hingston, Hinkson], **John** (b. early 17th cent.; buried London, 17 Dec. 1688). Composer. Choir member at York Minster in 1618; perhaps served Charles I; honored by Playford in his *Musicall Banquet* (London, 1651); organist and musician to Cromwell, 1654–58; named viol player and instrument repairer at court upon the Restoration in 1660. Later became a member of the Chapel Royal and a deputy marshal of London. Blow was his pupil, Purcell his apprentice. His music, much of which is lost, includes works for viols, organ, and chorus.

Hinton, Milt(on John) [the Judge] (b. Vicksburg, Miss., 23 June 1910). Jazz double bass player. He worked with the violinist Eddie South and Zutty Singleton in Chicago, then joined Cab Calloway (1936–

51), with whom he recorded "Ebony Silhouette" (1941). Apart from brief periods with Count Basie and Louis Armstrong, from 1951 he recorded prolifically as a free-lance in New York, including the trumpeter Joe Newman's album *All I Wanna Do Is Swing* (1955), performing in local clubs and at international festivals. He is also known for his photographs of jazz musicians.

Writings: with David G. Berger, *Bass Lines: The Stories and Photographs of Milt Hinton* (Philadelphia, 1988).

Hirao, Kishio (b. Tokyo, 8 July 1907; d. there, 15 Dec. 1953). Composer. He studied music theory with Ryūtaro Hirota while a student of medicine at Keiō Univ. After graduating in 1930, he went to Paris to study at the Schola cantorum and the École César Franck. During the years following his return to Japan in 1936, he won several prizes, including that of the New Symphony (twice, in 1937 and 1938) and the prize of the Japan Composers' League (1940, for his String Quartet). From 1947 he was professor of composition at the Kunitachi Music College in Tokyo. His music shows traces of early 20th-century French style; works include *Sumida-gawa* (1936); incidental music to *Wanasa otome monogatari* [Tale of Wanasa Maiden] (1943); orchestral works (*Heiwa* [Peace], 1950); chamber music (Flute Sonata, 1940; Wind Quintet, 1950).

Hirose, Ryōhei (b. Hakodate [Hokkaido], 17 July 1930). Composer. After studying piano and theory with Hidetake Tsutsui, he enrolled in the Tokyo Univ. of Arts (from 1955), where his instructors were Tomojirō Ikenouchi and Akio Yashirō. He traveled to India in the early 1970s; the resulting influences are manifested in works using ragas. He employed native Japanese instruments (koto, shakuhachi) in works such as *Yume jūya* [Dreams for Ten Nights] (1973). Other works include a string quartet (1958); several works for shakuhachi and strings (including *Heki,* 1964; *Ryoh,* 1966; *Hi,* 1969; *Shuh,* 1969); works for koto (including *Yoh,* 1972; *Hanashizume,* 1973); also *Krima,* orchestra (1976).

Hoddinott, Alun (b. Bargoed, Wales, 11 Aug. 1929). Composer. At University College in Cardiff he studied music until 1949, and in London he took private instruction from Arthur Benjamin. He taught at Welsh College of Music and Drama (from 1951) and at University College in Cardiff (1959–87). At the latter he received a doctorate in 1960 and became professor in 1967. A great deal of his huge output is characterized by a highly chromatic, late Romantic tonal language, with large gestures and big climaxes. Among his works are 5 operas (*The Beach of Falesá,* Cardiff, 1974; *What the Old Man Does Is Always Right,* Fishguard, 1977; *The Rajah's Diamond,* TV performance, 1979; *The Trumpet Major,* Manchester, 1981); choral works (*Sinfonia Fidei,* soprano, tenor, chorus, orchestra, 1977); orchestral works, including 7 symphonies (1955–89), 4 sinfoniettas (1968–71), many concertos (clarinet, 1950; oboe, 1955; harp, 1957; viola, 1958; 3 for piano, 1960–66; violin, 1961), Concertino (trumpet, horn, orchestra, 1971), *Star Child* (1989), *Noctis Equi* (scena for cello and orchestra, 1989).

Bibl.: Basil Dean, *Alun Hoddinott* (Cardiff, 1978). Stewart R. Craggs, *Alun Hoddinott: A Bio-Bibliography* (Westport, 1993).

Hodges, Johnny [Hodge, Cornelius; Jeep; Rabbit] (b. Cambridge, Mass., 25 July 1907; d. New York, 11 May 1970). Jazz alto saxophonist. After working in New York with Willie "the Lion" Smith (ca. 1924), Sidney Bechet (1925), and Chick Webb (1926–27), he joined Duke Ellington in 1928, remaining for most of his career and contributing to the special identity of the band with his broad tone, strong blues soloing, and graceful use of slow glissandos in interpreting ballads (including "Warm Valley," recorded in 1940). Into the 1940s he doubled as a soprano saxophonist. Members of the groups, among them Ellington himself, recorded under Hodges's name from 1937 (including "Jeep's Blues," 1938, and "Passion Flower," 1941). He left Ellington, 1951–55, to lead a small group with Lawrence Brown and John Coltrane among his sidemen.

Hodkinson, Sydney (Phillip) (b. Winnipeg, 17 Jan. 1934). Composer, conductor, and clarinetist. He studied with Rogers and Louis Mennini at the Eastman School (M.M., 1958); Carter, Sessions, and Babbitt at Princeton; and Bassett, Castiglioni, and Finney at the Univ. of Michigan (D.M.A., 1968). While a student at Eastman he taught woodwinds in New York State schools, then taught at the Univ. of Virginia (1958–63), Ohio Univ. (1963–66), and the Univ. of Michigan (1968–73), where he directed the Rockefeller Foundation New Music Project; beginning in 1973 he chaired the departments of conducting and ensembles at Eastman. His compositional styles are diverse, ranging from jazz-influenced to electronic. His orchestral compositions include *Frescoe* (Symphony no. 1, 1968), *The Edge of the Olde One* (electric English horn, strings, and percussion, 1976), and Symphony no. 6, 1995. Other works include 4 operas (*The Wall,* 1980; *The Catsman,* 1985) and an oratorio; piano trios, brass and woodwind quintets, works for percussion ensemble, and other chamber music (string quartet no. 3, 1995); organ, vocal, and choral music.

Høffding, (Niels) Finn (b. Copenhagen, 10 Mar. 1899). Composer. After private study of composition with Knud Jeppesen and Thomas Laub, he went to Vienna, where in 1921–22 he was a pupil of Joseph Marx. During the 1920s he came to prominence in Denmark with works such as *Karlsvognen* (chorus and orchestra, 1924). Around 1930 his interest turned to folk music and musical pedagogy; in 1931 he cofounded the Copenhagen School of Folk Music, the first of a number of such schools throughout Denmark. He also began teaching composition at the Copenhagen Conservatory in 1931, and by 1949 he was full professor; in 1954 he was appointed director of the Copenhagen Conservatory. He won the Nielsen Prize in 1956 and 1958. His later music tends toward dense, chromatic one-movement forms. He composed 2 operas; choral works (*Christofer Columbus,* 1937; *Kantate til Det kongelige danske Musikkonservatoriums årsfest,* 1948; *Giordano Bruno,* 1968); orchestral works (Symphony no. 1, Sinfonia impetuosa, 1923; no. 2, Il canto deliberato, 1924; no. 3, 1928; no. 4, Sinfonia concertante, 1934; *Fantasia concertante,* 1965); chamber works (2 string quartets, 1920 and 1925; a wind quintet, 1940). He also wrote pedagogical theory treatises.

Bibl.: Svend Bruhns and Dan Fog, *Finn Høffdings kompositioner* (Copenhagen, 1969).

Hoffman, Richard (b. Manchester, England, 24 May 1831; d. Mt. Kisco, N.Y., 17 Aug. 1909). Pianist and composer. Studied with his father, a musician; also a few piano lessons in London with Leopold de Meyer; 1847, emigrated to New York, where, after tours with the violinist Joseph Burke and (1850–52) Jenny Lind, he spent his life as pianist, organist, teacher, and composer, celebrating a 50th anniversary concert at Chickering Hall in 1897. Played in many New York Philharmonic concerts, 1847–92; played with Gottschalk in his New York debut in 1853 and several times thereafter. Works include piano salon music (*La gazelle,* 1858?, especially popular), sacred anthems, songs. Memoirs: *Some Musical Recollections of Fifty Years* (New York, 1910; R: 1976).

Hoffmann, E(rnst) T(heodore) A(madeus) (b. Königsberg, 24 Jan. 1776; d. Berlin, 25 June 1822). Composer, author, conductor, and music critic. Son of an attorney in Königsberg, he took early instruction in clavier from his uncle Otto Wilhelm Doerffer and from Carl Gottlieb Richter; he also learned counterpoint from cathedral organist Christian Wilhelm Podbielski. In 1792 he enrolled to study law at the Univ. of Königsberg, and after completing his studies in 1795 he was employed as junior attorney at Glogau (1796) and Berlin (from 1798). In Berlin he studied composition with Johann Friedrich Reichardt (1798–1800) and composed his first singspiel, *Die Maske* (no known performances). After serving in bureaucratic positions in Poznán and Płock, he moved to Warsaw in 1804; there his first staged opera appeared *(Die lustigen Musikanten).* When Napoleon's troops marched on Prussia in 1806, Hoffmann lost his legal position and applied instead for music posts; in 1808 he was accepted as conductor of the Bamberg Opera. In 1814 he was appointed conductor of the theatrical company of Joseph Seconda, which performed in both Dresden and Leipzig. Leaving the post in 1814, he again was appointed judge in Berlin; there his magnum opus, the "Zauberoper" *Undine,* was performed in 1816 to great acclaim. His fantastic tales have inspired many musical interpretations (such as those in Schumann's *Kreisleriana* and in Offenbach's *Les contes d'Hoffmann*), and his essays on contemporary music, such as that on Beethoven's Fifth Symphony (*AmZ* 12, 1809–10; R: *SR,* pp. 775–81) are still admired for their insight. His operas *Aurora* (1811–12) and *Undine* are remembered as precursors of Weberian Romantic opera. He composed some 20 stage works; sacred music (including a Miserere in B♭ minor, 1809); secular vocal works; orchestral works including a Symphony in E♭ (1805–6); and chamber and piano music. Among his literary works are *Fantasiestücke in Callots Manier; Nachtstücke;* and *Die Serapions-Brüder.*

Bibl.: *E. T. A. Hoffmann: Ausgewählte musikalische Werke,* ed. Georg von Dadelsen et al. (Mainz, 1970–). Friedrich Schnapp, *Der Musiker E. T. A. Hoffmann: Ein Dokumentenband* (Hildesheim, 1981). Werner Keil, *E. T. A. Hoffmann als Komponist* (Wiesbaden, 1986). Judith Rohr, *E. T. A. Hoffmanns Theorie des musikalischen Dramas* (Baden-Baden, 1985). David Charlton, ed. *E. T. A. Hoffmann's Musical Writings: "Kreisleriana," "The Poet and the Composer," Music Criticism* (Cambridge, 1989)

Hoffmeister, Franz Anton (b. Rothenburg am Neckar, 12 May 1754; d. Vienna, 9 Feb. 1812). Publisher and composer. He went to Vienna in 1768; after completing his study of law he turned to music, and in 1783 began publishing his own series of symphony publications. His business flourished during the late 1780s, with publication of works by Haydn, Mozart, Ordoñez, Pleyel, and Vanhal. During the 1790s he worked toward improving the technical quality of type and paper. In 1800 he moved to Leipzig, where together with Ambrosius Kühnel he established the Bureau de musique, later to become C. F. Peters. They produced complete editions of Bach, Haydn, and Mozart. In 1805 he returned to Vienna and devoted his last years to composition. His Viennese firm left a legacy that includes first editions of works by Haydn, Beethoven (Piano Sonata op. 13), and Mozart (String Quartets K. 478 and 499). His own huge oeuvre includes 10 stage works (*Liebe macht kurzen Prozess,* 1801); nearly 70 symphonies; 75 concertos; some 500 chamber works (57 string quartets).

Bibl.: Alexander Weinmann, *Die Wiener Verlagswerke von F. A. Hoffmeister* (Vienna, 1964).

Hoffstetter, Roman (b. Laudenbach, 24 Apr. 1742; d. Miltenberg am Main, 21 May 1815). Composer. In 1763 he took vows as a Benedictine in Amorbach (near Würzburg). He was ordained in 1766 and became director of the choir; when the monastery was dissolved in 1803 he moved to Miltenberg. He is best known as the composer of 6 string quartets "op. 3," previously attributed to Joseph Haydn. By his own admission he was a great admirer of the latter's music, and a number of his works, including his op. 1 string quartets, have been misattributed to Haydn. Further confusion arises from the fact that his brother Johann Urban Alois (1742–ca. 1810) was also a composer.

Bibl.: Alan Tyson and H. C. Robbins Landon, "Who Composed Haydn's Op. 3?" *MT* 105 (1964): 506–8.

Hofhaimer, Paul (b. Radstadt, 25 Jan. 1459; d. Salzburg, 1537). Composer and organist. His contemporaries considered him the finest organist of his time, particularly as an improviser, a teacher, and an expert on organ building. From 1478 he was active in Innsbruck at the court of Duke Sigmund of Tyrol, assuming in 1489 an additional post of organist to Maximilian I. His ties with Maximilian, though at times quite loose, remained unbroken until Maximilian's death in 1519. His last years were spent in Salzburg as organist at the cathedral and to the archbishop. Only a fraction of his output as a composer survives: a book of chordal settings of classical odes, over 24 songs (mostly Tenorlieder), and a few instrumental pieces, including only 2 liturgical organ compositions.

Bibl.: H. J. Moser, *Paul Hofhaimer* (Stuttgart and Berlin, 1929; R: 1966).

Hofmann, Heinrich (Karl Johann) (b. Berlin, 13 Jan. 1842; d. Gross-Tabarz, Thuringia, 16 July 1902). Composer. At 9 a choirboy, Berlin Cathedral; from 1857 a student at Kullak's school, Berlin. He became a concert pianist, but after success with a one-act comic opera, *Cartouche* (Berlin, 1869), composed prolifically; his music was highly popular in Germany in the 1870s and 1880s. Works include 5 operas (*Ännchen von Tharau,* Hamburg, 1878); orchestral works (*Frithjof Symphony* op. 22); chamber music (Piano Trio op. 18); choral works (*Das Märchen von der schönen Melusine* op. 30; *Aschenbrödel* op. 45); piano pieces (*Italienische Liebesnovelle* op. 19, 4-hands); songs. Judged lacking in individuality even when popular, his music had become passé before his death.

Hofmann, Josef (Casimir) [Józef Kazimierz] (b. Podgorze, Poland, 20 Jan. 1876; d. Los Angeles, 16 Feb. 1957). Pianist and composer. Studied piano with his sister and aunt from 1879. Debut in Ciechnocinek, 1882; first European tour as pianist and composer, 1883. His New York debut, 29 Nov. 1887, was enormously successful. He studied privately, 1892–94, with Anton Rubinstein, whose influence proved decisive on his music making. Subsequently he toured as one of the greatest Romantic pianists. First Russian tour 1896. Rachmaninoff dedicated his Third Concerto to him 1909. Published *Piano-Playing with Piano-Questions Answered* (1915). Naturalized U.S. citizen, 1926. Director of the Curtis Institute in Philadelphia, 1926–38. He played his farewell concert in New York, 19 Jan. 1946. Many of his over 100 compositions, which include symphonic and concerted works, were published under the name Michel Dvorsky.

Hofmann, Leopold (b. Vienna, 14 Aug. 1738; d. there, 17 Mar. 1793). Composer. As a boy he served as chorister under František Tuma; later he studied clavier and counterpoint with Wagenseil. By 1764 he was choral director at St. Peter's, Vienna, and by 1766 Kapellmeister. In 1769 he became teacher to the royal family; he was later passed up for the post of court Kapellmeister, which went to Giuseppe Bonno instead. He composed a large number of vocal works, including Masses, motets, vespers, and litanies; numerous symphonies and chamber works (some of which have occasionally been misattributed to Haydn); and clavier sonatas and variations.

Christopher Hogwood.

Hofmannsthal, Hugo von (b. Vienna, 1 Feb. 1874; d. there, 15 July 1929). Poet, dramatist, and librettist. He transformed his play *Elektra* into a libretto for Richard Strauss, thus beginning one of the most exceptional composer-librettist collaborations in music history; many aspects of the compositional process are preserved in their correspondence. Librettos for Strauss: *Elektra* (1909); *Der Rosenkavalier* (1909–10); *Ariadne auf Naxos* (1912; 2nd version, 1915–16); *Die Frau ohne Schatten* (1914–18); *Die ägyptische Helena* (1924–27); *Arabella* (1930–32); *Die Liebe der Danae* (Gregor, after Hofmannsthal, 1938–40).

Hofmeister, Friedrich (b. Strehla, 24 Jan. 1782; d. Reudnitz, near Leipzig, 30 Sept. 1864). Publisher. In 1797 apprenticed with Breitkopf und Härtel, Leipzig; employed by Hoffmeister and Kühnel's Bureau de musique in 1801. In 1807 he opened his own music shop, soon expanding to publishing; from 1819, also published periodical works of music bibliography. When he retired in 1852 the business passed to his sons.

Hogwood, Christopher (Jarvis Haley) (b. Nottingham, 10 Sept. 1941). Conductor and harpsichordist. Studied under Raymond Leppard and Thurston Dart at Cambridge, graduating in 1964; then studied harpsichord with Rafael Puyana in Spain. Harpsichordist in the Academy of St. Martins-in-the-Fields from 1966. With David Munrow founded the Early Music Consort of London in 1967. With Peter Woodland formed the

Academy of Ancient Music in 1973 to record the orchestral music of Arne on period instruments. Success led to the recording of Mozart's symphonies, which established his reputation internationally. Artistic director of the Handel and Haydn Society of Boston from 1986; music director of the St. Paul Chamber Orchestra from 1988.

Hoiby, Lee (b. Madison, Wis., 17 Feb. 1926). Composer and pianist. As a youth he studied piano with Gunnar Johansen (1941–46); he attended the Univ. of Wisconsin (B.A., 1947); went to the Curtis Institute, where he studied composition with Menotti (1948–51); then to Mills College (M.M., 1952) as a composition student of Milhaud and piano student of Egon Petri (whose master classes he had attended earlier). Menotti encouraged him to attempt an opera; *The Scarf,* performed while he was at Curtis, led to many subsequent opera commissions, all completed in a Romantic, tonal style. His rather late formal debut as a pianist (New York, 1978) was met with critical acclaim. Works include operas (*The Scarf,* 1958; *Natalia Petrovna,* 1964, rev. as *A Month in the Country,* 1981; *Summer and Smoke,* 1972; *The Tempest,* 1986); ballets (*After Eden,* 1966); incidental music; an oratorio (*Galileo Galilei,* soloists, chorus, and orchestra, 1975); 2 piano concertos (1958, 1980), suites from his stage works, and other orchestral music; chamber music (a violin sonata; a woodwind quintet; Serenade, violin and piano, 1988); piano music; choral music (*Psalm 93,* large chorus, organ, brass, percussion, 1985); songs.

Holborne, Antony [Anthony] (fl. from 1584?; d. between 29 Nov. and 1 Dec. 1602). Composer. Little about his life except his nationality (English) is known with any certainty. His music was widely popular for a time. His compositions appeared in print, both in English and Continental anthologies and in books devoted entirely to him, from at least 1597 until about a decade after his death. In a book of 1600 Dowland referred to him as "most famous." Of his roughly 150 compositions virtually all are for instruments alone, and the great majority (over 100) are dances. An unusual number survive in multiple distinct versions.

Bibl.: Anthony Holborne, *The Complete Works* (Cambridge, Mass., 1967–73). Brian Jeffery, "Antony Holborne," *MD* 22 (1968): 129–205 [includes thematic index].

Holbrooke, Joseph [Josef Charles] (b. Croydon, 5 July 1878; d. London, 5 Aug. 1958). Composer. He studied composition with Frederick Corder at the Royal Academy of Music, and piano privately with Frederick Westlake. He then worked as pianist and conductor; beginning in 1900 with his Poe setting *The Raven,* his works began to gain prominence and notoriety, especially for their length and complexity of texture. His biggest work, inspired by Wagner's *Ring,* was a trilogy, *The Cauldron of Annwyn,* based on a Welsh epic poem; its three parts are *The Children of Don* (first performed 1912); *Dylan* (1914); and *Bronwen* (1929). His huge oeuvre recalls that of his contemporary Havergall Brian; and like that of Brian, much of the music remains unpublished or out of print. Other works include operas *(The Sailor's Arms);* choral works (*The Bells,* 1903; *Byron,* 1906; *Homage to E. A. Poe,* Dramatic Choral Symphony, 1908); orchestral music (*The Viking,* 1904, and other symphonic poems; 8 symphonies; 2 concertos for piano, concertos for violin and for cello); works for military brass band; chamber and piano music.

Bibl.: George Lowe, *Josef Holbrooke and His Work* (London, 1920).

Holden, Oliver (b. Shirley, Mass., 18 Sept. 1765; d. Charlestown, Mass., 4 Sept. 1844). Composer and minister. He was an apprentice to a cabinetmaker in Grafton, Mass., then served in the navy during the Revolutionary War. Afterward he settled in Charlestown, where he was a carpenter and, from ca. 1790, owned a music store. He founded a church, taught in singing schools, and compiled anthologies of anthems and hymns, some his own. Among his compositions are more than 200 works; he compiled *American Harmony* (Boston, 1792); *Union Harmony* (Boston, 1793; 2nd ed., 1801); 3 editions of the *Worcester Collection* (Worcester, Mass., 1797–1803); *Charlestown Collection* (Boston, 1803); and others. He also coauthored the *Massachusetts Compiler of Theoretical Principles* (Boston, 1795).

Holiday, Billie [Fagan, Eleanora; Lady Day] (b. Baltimore, 7 Apr. 1915; d. New York, 17 July 1959). Jazz singer. From 1935 to 1942 she recorded with Teddy Wilson and under her own name, accompanied by some of the finest swing musicians, including Lester Young. In this unsurpassed collection of jazz singing Holiday reinterpreted popular melodies with great freedom and in her blues-inflected delivery brought an emotional depth to ostensibly simple lyrics. Examples include "These Foolish Things" (1936, under Wilson's leadership), "He's Funny That Way" (1937), "Them There Eyes" (1939), "All of Me," and "God Bless the Child" (both 1941). After controversial stays in the big bands of Count Basie (1937–38) and Artie Shaw (1938), she sang with small groups, at first mainly in New York, but later touring widely. Although the physical effects of drug addiction and alcoholism had caused her voice to decline by the 1950s, she retained her ability to interpret material poignantly.

Writings: with William Dufty, *Lady Sings the Blues* (Garden City, N.Y., 1956; R: 1984).

Bibl.: John Chilton, *Billie's Blues: A Survey of Billie Holiday's Career, 1933–1959* (London, 1975). Bud Kliment, *Billie Holiday* (New York, 1990). Donald Clarke, *Wishing on the Moon: The Life and Times of Billie Holiday* (New York, 1994).

Holland, Dave [David] (b. Wolverhampton, 1 Oct. 1946). Double bass player. He played free jazz and hard bop with leading English jazzmen while studying at the Guildhall School of Music and Drama in London

(1964–68), then moved to the U.S. to join Miles Davis's jazz-rock group (1968–70). After playing in Chick Corea's free-jazz group Circle (1970–71), he continued working with fellow sideman Anthony Braxton (to 1976); with Sam Rivers they recorded Holland's album *Conference of the Birds* (1972). He also joined Stan Getz (1973–75) and the guitarist John Abercrombie's trio with Jack DeJohnette (1975–77). He worked with Rivers (1976–80), then formed a quintet (1982–), which recorded the album *Seeds of Time* (1984). In 1987 he began teaching at the New England Conservatory.

Höller, York (b. Leverkusen, 11 Jan. 1944). Composer. He attended the Musikhochschule in Cologne, where he studied electronic music with Eimert and composition with Zimmermann; studied at Darmstadt in the summer of 1965 under Boulez. Lectured on music theory at the Leverkusen Staatliches Pädagogisches Fachinstitut (1969–71). Member of the Cologne ensemble Gruppe 8. In 1990 he succeeded Stockhausen as director of the WDR Electronic Studio in Cologne. Works include the opera *Der Meister und Margarita* (1989); *Aura* (1991–92) and other orchestral music (a piano concerto, 1984; *Umbra,* with tape, 1980; *Resonance,* with computer sounds, 1981; *Traumspiel,* with soprano and electronic sounds, 1983); *Décollage,* 2 speaking choruses, 3 amplified instruments, live feedback, and tape (1972); *Tangens,* cello, guitar, piano, and 2 synthesizers (1974), *Improvisation sur le nom de Pierre Boulez,* 17 instruments (1985), and other works for small ensemble (*Pas de Deux,* cello, piano, 1993); *Horizont,* tape, realized at the German Radio Studios in Cologne (1971–72).

Holliger, Heinz (b. Langenthal, Switzerland, 21 May 1939). Oboist and composer. Studied at the Bern and Basel conservatories, 1955–59. Won the Geneva International Competition, 1959, then played first oboe in the Basel Symphony, 1959–64. Won the Munich Competition, 1961. At the Paris Conservatory, 1962–63, he studied oboe with Émile Passagnaud and Pierre Pierlot; privately he studied composition with Pierre Boulez. Professor of oboe at the Staatliche Musikhochschule in Freiburg from 1965. His oboe repertory spanned the Baroque and the avant-garde. For him—often with his wife, Ursula, a harpist—works were written by Jolivet, Denisov, Martin, Henze, Lutoslawski, Berio, Stockhausen, and others. Many of his own compositions feature oboe and harp (*Sequenzen über Johannes I,32,* harp, 1959; *Mobile,* oboe and harp, 1962; *Studie II,* oboe, 1982; *Ballad,* harp, orchestra, 1985; *Präludium, Arioso und Passacaglia,* harp, 1987). Other works include *Der magische Tänzer* (2 dancers, 2 actors, chorus, orchestra, tape, 1965), *Come and Go* (chamber opera, after Beckett, 1978), *NOT I,* monodrama for female voice and live electronics, 1980), *What Where* (chamber opera, after Beckett, 1989); orchestral works (*Tonscherben,* 1985; *Zwei Liszt-Transcriptionen,* 1986; *Gesänge der Frühe,* with choir and tape, 1987); vocal works (*Variazioni su nulla,* 4 voices, 1988); chamber music (a string quartet, 1973; *Vier Stücke,* violin, piano, 1984); piano pieces; organ pieces.

Holloway, Robin (Greville) (b. Leamington Spa, 19 Oct. 1943). Composer. His first musical training came during the years spent as choirboy at St. Paul's, London (1952–57); he also studied with Alexander Goehr. From 1965 to 1969 did doctoral research at Oxford and Cambridge, receiving a doctorate in 1972. In 1974 appointed lecturer in music at Cambridge. His works include the opera *Clarissa* (1976; staged 1990); *The Blackbird and the Snail* (melodrama, voice, piano, 1995); *Cantata on the Death of God,* 1973; *The Spacious Firmament* (chorus, orchestra, 1990; orchestral works: *Domination of Black,* 1974; Concerto for Orchestra no. 2, 1979; *Second Idyll,* 1983; a viola concerto, 1984; a double concerto for clarinet, saxophone, 2 chamber orchestras, 1988; a violin concerto, 1990); chamber music (*Winter Music: Concertino no. 6,* mixed sextet, 1993); songs and song cycles.

Holly, Buddy [Holley, Charles Hardin] (b. Lubbock, Tex., 7 Sept. 1938; d. near Clear Lake, Iowa, 3 Feb. 1959). Rock-and-roll singer, songwriter, and guitarist. Played country music in bands in high school; began recording original country and rock-and-roll songs in 1956 with his band The Three Tunes ("Changing All Those Changes"). From 1957 to 1959 he recorded in New Mexico with producer Norman Petty and toured extensively with his renamed band, the Crickets. His songs were among the most popular rock-and-roll recordings of the late 1950s and early 1960s, particularly "That'll Be the Day," "Oh, Boy," and "Peggy Sue" (all 1957); he has been credited with expanding the musical and emotional scope of rock and roll, addressing complicated personal issues in his lyrics and anticipating rock musical styles of the 1960s. His music has been recorded by artists including the Rolling Stones and Linda Ronstadt, and in 1978 he was the subject of a biographical film, *The Buddy Holly Story.* His complete recordings were reissued as *The Complete Buddy Holly* (Coral/MCA, 1978, with liner notes by J. Beecher and M. Jones).

Bibl.: Ellis Amburn, *Buddy Holly: A Biography* (New York, 1995).

Holmboe, Vagn (b. Horsens, eastern Jutland, 20 Dec. 1909). Composer. From 1926 he studied at the Royal Conservatory of Music in Copenhagen; his teachers were Finn Høffding and Knud Jeppesen. Later he studied with Ernst Toch in Berlin (1930–33), and in 1933 he embarked on a tour of Romania to study folk music. Returning to Denmark, from 1940 to 1944 he taught at the Institute for the Blind, and from 1947 he wrote music criticism for the Copenhagen *Politiken.* As a composer he began to rise in prominence during the 1940s, and in 1950 he was appointed to the staff of the Copenhagen Conservatory, becoming professor in

1955. He received a lifetime grant from the Danish government. His music recalls that of Nielsen, but also shows equally strong influences from Hindemith and Stravinsky.

Works include theater music (*Fanden og borgmesteren,* 1940; *Lave og Jon,* 1948); choral works (*Requiem,* 1931; 5 books of *Liber canticorum,* 1951–67; *Requiem for Nietzsche,* 1963–64); 11 numbered symphonies (no. 3, *Sinfonia rustica,* 1941; no. 8, *Sinfonia boreale,* 1951–52; in addition to 11 unnumbered symphonies); *Kairos* (4 sinfonias, string orchestra, 1957–62); 3 chamber symphonies (1951–70); 13 chamber concertos; ballets; other orchestral works (*Epitaph,* 1956; *Epilogue,* 1961–62; *Diafora,* strings, 1973; concertos for violin (1938), recorder (1974), and tuba (1976); 14 string quartets and other chamber works (3 violin sonatas; solo sonatas for flute, oboe, double bass, cello); piano works (*Choral-Fantasy,* 1929); organ music (*Fabula* I, 1972; *Contrasti,* 1972).

Bibl.: Paul Rapoport, *Vagn Holmboe: A Catalogue of His Music; Discography, Bibliography, Essays* (London, 1974; rev. 2nd ed., Copenhagen, 1979). Id., "Vagn Holmboe's Symphonic Metamorphoses" (diss., Univ. of Illinois, 1975).

Holmès, Augusta (Mary Anne) (b. Paris, 16 Dec. 1847; d. there, 28 Jan. 1903). Composer. Her father was Irish, a retired officer settled in France; her Scottish-Irish mother published poetry and had literary friends (De Vigny was possibly her actual father); raised in Versailles; a devoted Wagnerite from age 13 and an experienced if largely self-taught composer (having had a Psalm performed at a Paris concert in 1873 and an opera auditioned, though not accepted, at the Théâtre Châtelet in 1874) before becoming a pupil of Franck in 1875. Her beauty, charm, and talent made her a figure of the salons. Saint-Saëns is said to have proposed marriage and Franck to have composed his Piano Quintet under her spell. She composed 11 symphonic poems and dramatic symphonies, including *Les Argonautes* (1881); 4 operas (to her librettos), only *La montagne noire* produced (Opéra, 1895) but a failure; over 100 songs, some very popular.

Bibl.: Ethyl Smyth, "Augusta Holmès, Pioneer," in *A Final Burning of Boats Etc* (London, 1928), pp. 126–36. Rollo Myers, "Augusta Holmès: A Meteoric Career," *MQ* 53 (1967): 365–76.

Holst, Gustav(us, Theodore von) (b. Cheltenham, 21 Sept. 1874; d. London, 25 May 1934). Composer. His father, Adolphus, an organist and pianist, was his first music teacher; while attending Cheltenham Grammar School, Gustav began conducting local orchestras. In 1892 he played organ at Wyck Rissington, Gloucestershire. After studying counterpoint briefly at Oxford, he went to London to begin study with Charles Stanford; in 1893 he enrolled in the Royal College of Music, where two years later he won a scholarship. In addition to his studies with Stanford he took piano instruction with Herbert Sharpei; in 1895 he met Vaughan Williams, a fellow student who was to become a lifelong friend. His first professional position after he left the Royal College in 1898 was as trombonist with the Carl Rosa Opera Company. He gave this up in 1903 when offered his first teaching post, at James Allen's School, Dulwich; from 1905 he taught at St. Paul's Girls School in Hammersmith. Two years later he became director of the music department at Morley College. Though physically too frail for combat, in 1918 he was sent to Greece and Turkey to organize amateur concerts for the troops there. He returned to serve on the faculty at Reading College, and also (finally) at the Royal College of Music. After a collapse from nervous exhaustion in 1923, he gave up most of his teaching duties; his last years were occupied wholly with composing. In 1932 he was invited to be visiting professor at Harvard, but he fell ill and had to return home after only a few months. His orchestral suite *The Planets* (1914–16; first performed, London, 1918) consists of seven movements, one for each of the planets known at that time; it remains one of the enduring standards of the orchestral literature.

Works: *Stage works. Sita* (opera, 1900–1906); *The Vision of Dame Christian* (masque, 1909); *The Perfect Fool* (opera, Covent Garden, 1923); *At the Boar's Head* (opera, Manchester, 1925); *The Golden Goose* (ballet, 1926); *The Morning of the Year* (ballet, 1926–27); *The Coming of Christ* (incidental music, after Masefield, 1927); *The Wandering Scholar* (chamber opera, 1929–30; Liverpool, 1934). *Choral/orchestral works. Choral Hymns from the Rig Veda* (4 groups, 1908–12); *Christmas Day* (1910); *Hecuba's Lament* (1911); *Hymn to Dionysus* (1913); *Three Carols* (1916–17); *Three Festival Choruses* (1916); *The Hymn of Jesus* (1917; first performance, 1920); *Ode to Death* (1919); *First Choral Symphony* (1923–24); *Seven Partsongs* (1925–26); *A Choral Fantasia* (1939). For chorus alone: *Ave Maria* (1900); *Five Partsongs* (1902–3); *Songs from The Princess* (1905); *This Have I Done for My True Love* (1916); *Six Choral Folk Songs* (1916); *The Evening Watch* (1924). Orchestral works: Symphony, *The Cotswolds* (1899–1900); *The Mystic Trumpeter* (1904; rev. 1912); *Songs of the West* (1906–7); 2 suites for military band, no. 1 in E♭, no. 2 in F (1909–11); *St. Paul's Suite* (strings, 1912–13); *The Planets* (1914–16); *Japanese Suite* (1915); *A Fugal Overture* (1922); *A Fugal Concerto* (flute, oboe, strings, 1923); *Egdon Heath* (1927); Double Concerto (1929); *Hammersmith* (suite, 1930; 2nd version 1931); *Jazz-Band Piece* (1932); *Lyric Movement* (viola, chamber orchestra, 1933). Chamber and instrumental music includes Quintet in A minor (piano and ensemble, 1896); Wind Quintet in A♭ major (1903); Toccata (piano, 1924); many songs and smaller vocal works. He also edited works by Purcell, J. S. Bach, and others.

Bibl.: *Gustav Holst: Collected Facsimile Edition of Autograph Manuscripts of the Published Works,* ed. Imogen Holst and Colin Matthews, 4 vols. (London, 1974–83). Imogen Holst, *A Thematic Catalogue of Gustav Holst's Music* (London, 1974). Id., *Gustav Holst: A Biography* (London, 1938; 2nd ed., 1969). Edmund Rubbra, *Gustav Holst* (Monaco, 1947). Imogen Holst, *The Music of Gustav Holst* (London, 1951; rev. 3rd ed. published with *Holst's Music Reconsidered,* Oxford, 1986). Edmund Rubbra, *Collected Essays on Gustav Holst* (London, 1974). Michael Short, ed., *Gustav Holst (1874–1934): A Centenary Documentation* (London, 1974). Michael Kennedy, *Elgar, Delius, and Holst* (Oxford, 1984). John C. Mitchell, *From Kneller Hall to Hammersmith: The*

Band Works of Gustav Holst (Tutzing, 1990). Michael Short, *Gustav Holst: The Man and His Music* (New York, 1990). Richard Greene, *Holst, the Planets* (New York, 1995).

Holst, Imogen (Clare) (b. Richmond, Surrey, 12 Apr. 1907; d. Aldeburgh, 9 Mar. 1984). Writer on music and conductor. Daughter of Gustav Holst. She attended the Royal College of Music; served on the Arts Council of Great Britain and as director of music at the Arts Centre, Dartington Hall, 1943–51. She became an assistant to Britten at the Aldeburgh festival and later was named artistic director, 1956–77; founded and conducted the Purcell Singers, 1953–67. She wrote a number of books about her father.

Holtkamp, Walter Henry, Sr. (b. St. Mary's, Ohio, 1894; d. Cleveland, 1962). Organ builder. His father, Henry Holtkamp, was manager of the Votteler–Holtkamp–Sparling Organ Company; Walter assumed leadership of the firm upon his father's death and brought it to prominence. Considered one of the principal builders in the early organ revival in the U.S.; his innovations included bringing organ pipework out of chambers, first used in the *Rückpositiv* of the organ at the Cleveland Museum of Art (1933); other organs include those at the Crouse Auditorium in Syracuse, N.Y. (1950); M.I.T. (1957); the Univ. of New Mexico, Albuquerque (1967). In 1951 the firm was renamed the Holtkamp Organ Company, and its leadership was assumed by Walter Henry Holtkamp, Jr. (b. 1929), on his father's death.

Bibl.: John Allen Ferguson, *Walter Holtkamp: American Organ Builder* (Kent, 1979).

Holton, Frank (b. Allegan, Mich., 10 Mar. 1858; d. Elkhorn, Wis., 17 Apr. 1942). Trombonist and brass instrument maker. He studied cornet and played trombone with the Hi Henry Minstrels; performed with Ellis Brooks and played duets with Herbert L. Clarke; in 1893 he joined Sousa's first band. He opened a music store in Chicago, introducing his own trombone and cornet models and a widely used valve oil; the firm was successful and expanded several times before moving in 1918 to Elkhorn, where it became a subsidiary of G. Leblanc in 1964.

Holyoke, Samuel (Adams) (b. Boxford, Mass., 15 Oct. 1762; d. East Concord, N.H., 7 Feb. 1820). Composer and singing master. He had no formal training in music, though apparently he helped organize the orchestras that played for the Harvard commencement in 1787. Two years afterward he graduated from Harvard, and in 1792 he received a master's degree. During the 1790s he taught school at Groton, Mass., and organized singing-school concerts. In 1797 he founded the Essex Musical Association. He composed prodigiously and published numerous collections of his nearly 900 works. Chief among the collections of his own music are *Harmonia americana* (Boston, 1791), *The Columbian Repository* (Exeter, N.H., 1803), and *The Christian Harmonist* (Salem, 1804). He also edited collections of works by other composers, and he contributed to *The Massachusetts Compiler of Theoretical Principles* (Boston, 1795).

Bibl.: James Laurence Willhide, "Samuel Holyoke, American Music Educator" (diss., Univ. of Southern Calif., 1954).

Holzbauer, Ignaz (Jakob) (b. Vienna, 17 Sept. 1711; d. Mannheim, 7 Apr. 1783). Composer. Against the wishes of his father, who wanted him to study law, he took instruction in singing, violin, clavier, and in Fux's Gradus from members of the St. Stephen's choir in Vienna. Fux reportedly examined his counterpoint exercises and recommended that Holzbauer study further in Italy. Around 1730 he traveled to Venice, but returned to Vienna after a short time. He received a post as Kapellmeister for Count Rottal of Holešov in Moravia. Little is known of his activities during the late 1730s; apparently he was engaged at the Viennese Imperial Theater around 1740, then traveled briefly to Milan and Venice. In 1751 he was appointed Kapellmeister in Stuttgart. Two years later, after the successful performance of his opera *Il figlio delle selve* (Schwetzingen, 1753), he was called to the Mannheim court as Kapellmeister to Karl Theodor, in whose service he remained for 25 years. There his operas, oratorios, and symphonies exerted a substantial influence on that court's already flourishing musical life. When the court moved to Munich in 1778, Holzbauer, nearly 70, remained in Mannheim, where he continued teaching and composing until his death. Among his stage works is the German opera *Günther von Schwarzburg* (Mannheim, 1777; ed. *DDT* 8–9, 1902); others included *Don Chisciotte,* "opera semi-ridicola" (Schwetzingen, 1755); *La clemenza di Tito* (Mannheim, 1757); and *Alessandro nell'Indie* (Milan, 1759). Other works include sacred oratorios (*La Betulia liberata,* 1760); Masses and motets; ballet scores; some 70 symphonies; chamber and instrumental music (string quartets, notturni, sonate da camera, etc.).

Homer, Louise (Beatty) (b. Shadyside, Pa., 30 Apr. 1871; d. Winter Park, Fla., 6 May 1947). Contralto. Studied in Philadelphia and Boston. In 1895 married her harmony teacher, Sidney Homer, then traveled with him to Paris, where she studied singing with Fidèle Koenig. Debut in Vichy, 1898, as Léonor *(Favorite).* U.S. debut, San Francisco, 1900, as Amneris *(Aïda)* with a touring Met troupe. Hers was a major career: in New York, 1900–19; Chicago, 1920–25; San Francisco, 1926; and again New York, 1927–29. She commanded a broad repertoire of Italian, French, and Wagnerian contralto roles, including Gluck's Orfeo; Gounod's Siebel *(Faust);* Verdi's Azucena and Maddelena; Ponchielli's Laura *(La gioconda);* Wagner's Brangäne, Fricka, and Ortrud; and Humperdinck's Witch *(Königskinder).* She was a maternal aunt of Samuel Barber.

Homer, Sydney (b. Boston, 9 Dec. 1864; d. Winter Park, Fla., 10 July 1953). Composer. He studied in

Boston with Chadwick and in Munich and Leipzig with Rheinberger and others. From 1888 to 1895 he taught theory in Boston, after which he began to travel with his wife, the contralto Louise Beatty. From 1900 they lived in New York, retiring to Florida in 1940. Homer wrote over 100 songs in a conservative diatonic style, a collection of which was edited by his nephew, Samuel Barber, in 1943. In his later years he wrote some chamber music (including a piano trio and string quartet, both 1937); he also wrote an autobiography, *My Wife and I* (New York, 1939; R: 1978).

Homilius, Gottfried August (b. Rosenthal, Saxony, 2 Feb. 1714; d. Dresden, 2 June 1785). Composer and organist. Son of a Lutheran pastor, he was a pupil at St. Anne's School, Dresden; in 1735 he began the study of law at the Univ. of Leipzig. There he also studied organ with Johann Schneider and counterpoint with J. S. Bach. In 1742 he received a post as organist for the Frauenkirche in Dresden; from 1755 he held the position of Kantor at the Kreuzkirche and with it the concomitant posts as music director at the Kreuzkirche, the Sophienkirche, and the Frauenkirche. He remained in these positions for the rest of his life. His large output includes a *Markuspassion,* a *Messias,* and other passion works; more than 200 cantatas; some 60 motets; oratorios *(Die Freude der Hirten über die Geburt Jesu);* 8 Magnificats; many organ works, including chorale arrangements and chorale preludes. He is recognized as one of the most important Protestant church composers of the generation after J. S. Bach.

Homs (Oller), Joaquín (b. Barcelona, 22 Aug. 1906). Composer. Played the cello as a youth, but studied engineering at the Univ. of Barcelona (1922–29), after which he returned to music under the tutelage of Roberto Gerhard, as a result of whose influence he gravitated toward serialism. His compositions were featured at ISCM festivals in 1937, 1939, and 1956; his piano work *Présences* received a municipal award from Barcelona in 1967. He has written works in most standard genres except for stage music, with a focus on chamber ensemble and Catalan vocal compositions.

Honegger, Arthur (b. Le Havre, 10 Mar. 1892; d. Paris, 27 Nov. 1955). Composer. Having studied violin and harmony as a child, he entered the Zurich Conservatory (1909–11) and then studied with Gédalge, Widor, d'Indy (conducting), and Capet (violin) at the Paris Conservatory. After World War I he was associated with the group of composers known as "Les six," of whom he was the most individualistic. His *Le roi David* (staged at Mézières, Switzerland, 1921) brought international recognition and remains one of his most frequently performed pieces (although it is usually presented as an oratorio rather than in its original conception as incidental music for a stage work). Performances of his cello concerto (at ISCM) and his Concertino for piano and orchestra (in Paris), the latter strongly influenced by jazz, took place in 1925. In 1927 he married the pianist Andrée Vaurabourg, who later performed much of his music for piano. In the 1930s he was active as lecturer and conductor; in the 1940s he taught at the École normale in Paris and wrote music criticism; in 1947 he toured the U.S. and South America.

He wrote over 200 works, of which the large choral works are particularly notable. Among the influences obvious in Honegger's music are his Swiss Protestant heritage, Gregorian chant, impressionism, jazz, and the French and German symphonic and operatic traditions. Composers whom he acknowledged as influences were Wagner, Strauss, Reger, Debussy, Fauré, Stravinsky, Schoenberg, Milhaud. His use of chorales was in part a result of his admiration for and early exposure to the music of Bach.

Melodic and rhythmic relationships he considered of more importance than tonality in shaping his works. Some compositions refer to a literary or visual pretext, for example, his *Pacific 231* (1923), a programmatic description of a locomotive. His admiration of Wagner shows in the drama of *Le roi David,* which nonetheless is cast in the form of a Baroque oratorio in separate numbers. In several large-scale works he made innovative use of the voice, integrating singing and speech. His overall aim was "to write music which would be comprehensible to the great mass of listeners and at the same time sufficiently free of banality to interest genuine music lovers." He claimed success when *Jeanne d'Arc* both moved the people of Orléans and interested the specialists at its first performance.

Works: 4 operas (*Antigone,* Cocteau, after Sophocles, 1924–27, staged Brussels, 1927; *Charles le téméraire,* Morax, 1943–44, Mézières, 1944), 2 operettas, and 7 other dramatic works (*Le roi David,* dramatic Psalm, Morax, Mézières, 1921; *Jeanne d'Arc au bûcher,* Claudel, 1934–35, Basel, 1938); 14 ballets; incidental music for some 25 plays, 44 film scores, and 8 radio scores; 5 symphonies (1930–51), 3 *Mouvements symphoniques* (no. 1, *Pacific 231,* 1923; no. 2, *Rugby,* 1928), Concerto da camera (flute, English horn, and strings, 1949), *Jour de fête suisse* (suite, 1943), *Suite archaique* (1952), and other orchestral works; 3 sonatas for violin and piano (1916–18, 1919, 1940), 3 string quartets (1916–17, 1934–36, 1936), sonatas with piano for viola (1920), cello (1920), clarinet (1921–22), *3 Contrepoints* (flute, English horn, violin, and cello, 1923), *Prelude et blues* (harp quintet, 1925), and other chamber music; piano pieces (*Le cahier romand,* 1921–23; Partita, 2 pianos, 1930; *Prélude, arioso et fughetta sur le nom de Bach,* 1932); other keyboard works (*Fugue et choral,* organ, 1917; *Sortilèges,* ondes martenot, 1946); several works for voice(s) and orchestra (*Cantique de Pâques,* solo voices and female chorus, 1918; *La danse des morts,* Claudel, 1938; *Une cantate de Noël,* baritone, chorus, children's chorus, organ, 1953); some 50 songs.

Writings: *Incantation aux fossiles* (Lausanne, 1948). *Je suis compositeur* (Paris, 1951; trans. Wilson O. Clough (1966). *Écrits* (Paris, 1992).

Bibl.: Jacques Feschotte, *Arthur Honegger, l'homme et son oeuvre* (Paris, 1966). Pierre Meylan, *René Morax et Arthur Honegger au Théâtre du Jorat* (Lausanne, 1966). Pierre Meylan, *Arthur Honegger, Humanitäre Botschaft der Musik*

(Frauenfeld, Switzerland, 1970). Jean Maillard et Jacques Nahoum, *Les symphonies d'Arthur Honegger* (Paris, 1974). H. D. Voss, *Arthur Honeggers "Le Roi David:" Ein Beitrag zur Geschichte des Oratoriums im 20. Jahrhundert* (Munich and Salzburg, 1983). Geoffrey K. Spratt, *Catalogue des oeuvres de Arthur Honegger* (Geneva, 1986). Id., *The Music of Arthur Honegger* (Dublin, 1987). Harry Halbreich, *Arthur Honegger: Un musicien dans la cité des hommes* (Paris, 1992).

Hook, James (b. Norwich, 3? June 1746; d. Boulogne, 1827). Organist and composer. A child prodigy at the keyboard, he studied with Garland, the cathedral organist in Norwich, and possibly also with Charles Burney. At 8 he composed his first ballad opera; he spent his youth concertizing and teaching music in Norwich. Around 1763 he went to London, where he held several organ posts (including at St. John's, Horsleydown) and began composing stage works. He contributed more than 30 theater works to Covent Garden, Drury Lane, the Haymarket, and Vauxhall Gardens (including *The Lady of the Manor,* 1778; *The Fair Peruvian,* 1786; *The Soldier's Return,* 1805; *Tekeli,* 1806; *The Fortress,* 1807). In addition he composed cantatas and odes; songs, catches, and canons; concertos and chamber works. He also authored a treatise, *Guida di musica* (1785–94).

Hooker, John Lee (b. Clarksdale, Miss., 22 Aug. 1917). Blues singer, guitarist, and songwriter. After playing blues and gospel music in Memphis and Cincinnati, he moved to Detroit in the mid-1940s. He recorded regularly from 1948 (including "Boogie Chillen'") and wrote many blues standards, among them "Hobo Blues," "Crawling King Snake," and "Birmingham Blues." His chordal boogie-woogie style pulse, incisive single-string guitar runs, and varied vocal techniques influenced many rock groups, notably the Rolling Stones and the Animals, who adopted his 1961 hit "Boom Boom Boom Boom" and other songs. He recorded unaccompanied, with blues and jazz groups, and with rock musicians including Canned Heat (1970, 1980) and Van Morrison (1971).

Hope-Jones, Robert (b. Hooton Grange, Cheshire, 9 Feb. 1859; d. Rochester, N.Y., 13 Sept. 1914). Organ builder. An engineer and telephone company electrician and a church organist, he became interested in electric organs. In 1889 he founded a firm with innovative ideas and important commissions (Worcester Cathedral, 1894–96) but criticized for musical insensitivity. In 1899 the firm went into receivership, and in 1903 Hope-Jones emigrated to the U.S. to escape litigation. In 1907 he founded a U.S. firm, but sold it to Wurlitzer after financial difficulties (1910), remaining as an employee; subsequent problems with Wurlitzer contributed to his suicide.

Bibl.: M. Sayer, "New Light on Hope-Jones," *The Organ* 60 (1980–81): 20–38.

Hopkins, Claude (Driskett) (b. Alexandria, Va., 24 Aug. 1903; d. New York, 19 Feb. 1984). Jazz bandleader and pianist. He toured Europe as the music director of the Revue nègre, which launched the career of Josephine Baker; Sidney Bechet was among his sidemen (1925–26). He led a big band (1930–40) that was resident at the Savoy and Roseland ballrooms and the Cotton Club in New York before touring the U.S. It recorded "I Would Do Anything for You" (1932) and broadcast nationally with Edmond Hall, Vic Dickenson, and Jabbo Smith as soloists. Later he led lesser-known bands, worked with Dickenson in Boston (ca. 1951–53) and Henry "Red" Allen in New York (from 1954), and joined Wild Bill Davison in the Jazz Giants (1968–ca. 1969).

Hopkins, (Charles) Jerome (b. Burlington, 4 Apr. 1836; d. Athenia [now Clinton], N.J., 4 Nov. 1898). Composer. Attended Univ. of Vermont and (briefly) medical school; from 1853, organist and choirmaster, New York. He was a strong proponent of American music and music education. In 1861 he founded Orpheon Free Schools to teach music to poor children; 1864, began concerts to promote the schools and *Orpheonist and Philharmonic Journal* (1864–80); from 1871 toured East and Midwest (and in 1889–90, England) giving lecture–piano recitals. He composed operas, especially a children's opera, *Taffy and Old Munch* (1880); the oratorio *Samuel;* church music; the symphony *Life;* Serenade in E, orchestra; a piano concerto; chamber music; songs. Edited *A Collection of Sacred Song* (New York, 1859) and other sacred anthologies.

Bibl.: Nicolas Slonimsky, "The Flamboyant Pioneer," in *A Thing or Two about Music* (New York, 1947), pp. 250–61.

Hopkins, Lightnin' (Sam) (b. Centerville, Tex., 15 Mar. 1912; d. Houston, 30 Jan. 1982). Blues singer, guitarist, and songwriter. His nickname came from playing on the West Coast with pianist Wilson "Thunder" Smith (1946–47). Otherwise, almost all his career was spent in and around Houston, where he consolidated the influences of Blind Lemon Jefferson and Texas Alexander (possibly his cousin) into a semiautobiographical repertory of country blues songs, usually accompanying himself on guitar. These included "Short Haired Woman" and "Penitentiary Blues." From the mid-1960s, he traveled widely, playing clubs and festivals in the U.S. and Europe.

Hopkinson, Francis (b. Philadelphia, 21 Sept. 1737; d. there, 9 May 1791). Musician, statesman, and inventor. He studied at the College of Philadelphia, graduating in 1757, and studied law until passing the bar exam in 1761. From his youth he was interested in music; he played harpsichord and, around 1770, served as organist for Christ Church, Philadelphia. He was a delegate of the Continental Congress and signed the Declaration of Independence; he was also a judge in Philadelphia (from 1779). He arranged and compiled texts for a political oratorio, *America Independent, or The Temple of Minerva.* He also compiled *Collection of Psalm*

Tunes (1763) and *The Psalms of David* (1767). Among his own compositions are *Seven* [actually 8] *Songs for the Harpsichord or Forte Piano* (1788). One of his songs, "My Days Have Been So Wondrous Free," dated 1759, has been cited as the earliest surviving American secular composition.

Bibl.: George Everett Hastings, *The Life and Works of Francis Hopkinson* (Chicago, 1926; R: New York, 1968). Gillian B. Anderson, "'The Temple of Minerva' and Francis Hopkinson: A Reappraisal of America's First Poet-Composer," *Proceedings of the American Philosophical Society* 120 (1976): 166–77.

Horenstein, Jascha (b. Kiev, 6 May 1898; d. London, 2 Apr. 1973). Conductor. When he was 6 his family moved to Königsberg, where he studied with Max Brode. In 1911 they removed to Vienna. At the Academy of Music he studied composition with Franz Schreker, then followed him to the Berlin Musikhochschule in 1920. In Berlin he conducted the Schubert Choir and served as an assistant to Furtwängler. Debut with the Vienna Symphony, 1924. Conducted the Blüthner Concerts in Berlin, 1924–28; guest conductor with the Berlin Philharmonic, 1925–28. While music director of the Düsseldorf Opera, 1929–33, he mounted *Wozzeck* and also led the premiere of Berg's *Lyrische Suite,* 1929. After the Nazis forced his departure, he traveled to Australasia, then settled in the U.S. in 1941. U.S. debut with the Works Projects Administration Symphony, 1942. Settled in Lausanne after the war. Conducted the Paris premieres of *Wozzeck,* 1950, and Janaček's *House of the Dead,* 1951, and the New York premiere of Busoni's *Doktor Faust,* 1964. Throughout his career he championed symphonic scores of Bruckner, Mahler, Nielsen, and other composers whose international popularity grew after the introduction of the long-playing record.

Horn, Charles Edward (b. London, 21 June 1786; d. Boston, 21 Oct. 1849). Composer. Son of Karl Friedrich Horn; taught by his father (singing by Rauzzini); double bassist and cellist in London theater orchestras; 1809–10, a singer (combined baritone-tenor range, but of poor quality) in English opera; 1814, returned to the stage after study with Thomas Welsh. In 1810 he began prolific output of English operas, musical comedies, and pasticcios, some very successful (*The Boarding House,* 1811; *The Devil's Bridge,* 1812; *The Woodman's Hut,* 1814); also many popular songs and ballads ("Cherry Ripe," "I've Been Roaming"). From 1827 he lived mostly in the U.S. (but 1830–32 and 1843–47 in London), as singer, composer, teacher, music publisher. His oratorio *The Remission of Sin* (New York, 1835) is said to be the first composed in the U.S. He was conductor of the Handel and Haydn Society, Boston, 1847–49.

Horn, Karl Friedrich (b. Nordhausen, Saxony, 13 Apr. 1762; d. Windsor, 5 Aug. 1830). Organist, composer, and theorist. He studied in Nordhausen with Christoph Gottlieb Schröter, then went to London in 1782 to become music master to the court. In 1823 he was appointed organist at St. George's Chapel, Windsor. He was a central figure in the revival of interest in the music of J. S. Bach in Britain; he helped prepare the first English editions of *Das wohltemperierte Klavier* (1810–13), of the organ trio sonatas (1809–10), and of the first English version of Forkel's Bach biography (1820).

Horne, Lena (Calhoun) (b. Brooklyn, N.Y., 30 June 1917). Popular singer and actress. She began singing and dancing at the Cotton Club in Harlem, and toured with the bands of Noble Sissle and Charlie Barnet. From 1939 she appeared on Broadway (including *Blackbirds,* 1939; *Jamaica,* 1957) and from 1942 in films (*Panama Hattie,* 1942; *Ziegfeld Follies,* 1946); she also recorded extensively. Her version of "Stormy Weather" (from a film of the same title, 1943) was especially popular and in 1993 she released an album *(We'll Be Together Again).*

Horne, Marilyn (b. Bradford, Pa., 16 Jan. 1934). Mezzo-soprano. Studied voice with William Vennard and Lotte Lehmann in California. After touring Europe with the Roger Wagner Chorale, she made her stage debut in Los Angeles in Smetana's *Bartered Bride.* Dubbed Dorothy Dandridge's songs in the film *Carmen Jones,* 1954, then went to Europe, where she was engaged, 1957–60, by the Gelsenkirchen Stadttheater. Appeared in *Wozzeck* in San Francisco and Chicago, 1960. In New York, 1962, sang Bellini's Agnes *(Beatrice di Tenda)* in the first of many performances (this first one in concert) with Joan Sutherland, continuing the restoration of bel canto to the active repertoire that Callas began. Covent Garden debut, 1965; La Scala debut, 1969. Member of the New York Metropolitan Opera from 1970. She played an important role in the revival of Handelian opera seria and the works of Rossini.

Horowitz, Vladimir (b. Berdichev, 1 Oct. 1903; d. New York, 5 Nov. 1989). Pianist. Studied with his mother, a graduate of the Kiev Conservatory, 1911–13; with Sergei Tarnovsky from 1913; later at the Kiev Conservatory with Felix Blumenfeld. Debut, Kiev, 1921. In 1923 he gave 70 concerts in Russia. U.S. debut, 12 Jan. 1928, with the New York Philharmonic under Beecham. Married Wanda Toscanini, daughter of Arturo, in 1933. Between 1928 and 1936 he gave over 100 U.S. recitals each year, in addition to his European schedule. He stopped concertizing in 1936. After a concert in Zurich in 1938 and one in Paris in 1939, he moved to the U.S. and began touring once again. After a recital in Carnegie Hall in 1953 he again ceased to give public performances, though he continued to record. His return to the concert stage in 1965 (Carnegie Hall, 9 May) was a momentous event, superseded only by his return to Russia for concerts in 1986. Throughout his career he was for many the personification of the virtuoso. He was especially associated with the Third Piano Concerto of Rachmaninoff (with whom he enjoyed a close friendship), the concertos of Tchaikovsky, and works of Chopin, Schumann, and Liszt.

Horst, Louis (b. Kansas City, Mo., 12 Jan. 1884; d. New York, 23 Jan. 1964). Composer. He studied piano and violin as a youth in San Francisco; in his 20s he was music director of the Denishawn Dance Company (1915–25), then studied composition in Vienna with Richard Stöhr and in New York with Riegger and Max Persin. From 1926 to 1948 he was music director of Martha Graham's dance company, for which he provided numerous scores. He founded the *Dance Observer* (1934) and wrote for other dance journals; his view that music should be composed to suit an already choreographed dance was innovative in the 1930s. He taught at Bennington (1934–45), Columbia University Teachers College (1938–41), and the Juilliard School (1958–63). He was the author of 2 books on dance: *Pre-Classic Dance Forms* (1940) and, with Carroll Russel, *Modern Dance Forms* (1961).

Bibl.: Janet Mansfield Soares, *Louis Horst: Musician in a Dancer's World* (Durham, N.C., 1992).

Horszowski, Mieczysław (b. Lemberg [now Lvov, Ukraine], 23 June 1892; d. Philadelphia, 22 May 1993). Pianist. He studied with Henryk Melcer at the Lwów Conservatory and with Theodor Leschetizky, making his Carnegie Hall debut in 1906. In 1957 he gave a 12-concert cycle of Beethoven's complete solo piano works, and in 1961 performed at the White House with Schneider and Casals. He was active at the Casals Festival. He joined the faculty of the Curtis Institute in 1942. He continued to concertize and record until he was nearly 100, and he regularly took part in chamber music.

Hothby [Ottobi], **John** (b. ca. 1410; d. 1487). Theorist and composer. Left his native England after 1435, having studied and taught at Oxford; then lived on the Continent, mostly in Italy. Composed 6 sacred Latin works, 3 secular Italian songs (ed. in *CMM* 33 [1964]). Wrote over 15 conservative theoretical treatises: many didactic works (ed. *CS* 3:328–34; *CSM* 26 [1977]; *CSM* 31 [1983]); speculative treatises (*Calliopea legale,* ed. and trans. Fr., Edmond de Coussemaker, *Histoire de l'harmonie au moyen âge* [Paris, 1852; R: 1966], pp. 295–349); and rebuttals of contemporary innovative ideas, especially those of Ramos de Pareja (*Excitatio, Epistola,* and *Dialogus Johannis Ottobi Anglici in arte musica;* all ed. *CSM* 10 [1964]).

Hotter, Hans (b. Offenbach am Main, 19 Jan. 1909). Bass-baritone. Studied at the Munich Musikhochschule, originally with a view to becoming an organist and choral conductor. His voice was developed under Matthäus Roemer. Concert debut in Munich, 1929, singing a solo in Handel's *Messiah.* Stage debut with the Troppau Stadttheater, 1930. Sang with the German Theater in Prague, 1932–34; with the Hamburg Staatsoper, 1934–37. With the Munich Staatsoper, 1937–42, he created Strauss's Kommandant (*Friedenstag,* 1938) and Olivier (*Capriccio,* 1942). His creation of Strauss's Jupiter *(Liebe der Danaë)* proceeded as far as dress rehearsal before wartime conditions aborted the opera's premiere. After the war he was heard regularly at Bayreuth (especially as Wotan), at Covent Garden (1947–67), and at the New York Metropolitan Opera (1950–54). After retiring from his major roles, he was active as a director, and he continued to appear as Schigolch *(Lulu)* and the speaker in *Gurrelieder.*

Hotteterre, Jacques(-Martin) ["Le Romain"] (b. Paris, 29 Sept. 1674; d. there, 16 July 1763). Woodwind player and maker, theorist, and composer. Admitted to the Grands Hautbois sometime between 1692 and 1707; by 1708 he was playing bassoon in the ensemble, and was identified as "flute of the King's chamber" in a publication of his compositions from the same year. He was also active as an instrument maker and as a teacher. His *Principes de la flûte traversière* (1707) was Europe's first flute manual and circulated widely; other writings include a treatise on improvising flute preludes and a didactic work for the musette. His music consists of suites, duets, and sonatas for any of a number of treble instruments and continuo.

Numerous other members of the Hotteterre family were reputed to have been fine woodwind players; some also had a decisive impact on woodwind instrument construction. Jacques's grandfather Jean (ca. 1605 to 1690–92) was noted for his playing and innovative building and may have been influential in certain developments in such instruments around this time. Jean and Jacques's father, Martin (ca. 1640–1712), were responsible for important advances in musette making.

Bibl.: Jacques Hotteterre le Romain, *Principles of the Flute, Recorder, and Oboe,* trans. with intro. by David Lasocki (London, 1968). Jane M. Bowers, "The French Flute School from 1700 to 1760" (diss., Univ. of California, Berkeley, 1971). Tula Giannini, "Jacques Hotteterre le Romain and His Father, Martin: A Re-examination Based on Recently Found Documents," *EM* 21 (1993): 377–95.

House, Son [Eddie James, Jr.] (b. near Clarksdale, Miss., 21 Mar. 1902; d. Detroit, 19 Oct. 1988). Blues singer and guitarist. He took up guitar in the late 1920s. His first recordings, from 1930, "Preachin' the Blues," "Dry Spell Blues," and "My Black Mama," show a fully formed style: a strongly sung vocal line contrasts with sliding bottleneck guitar figures. Representative of the Delta blues, he played with Charley Patton (late 1920s) and Willie Brown (1930s). He recorded for the Library of Congress (1941–42) and continued to perform into his 70s, despite a long absence from music (mid-1940s–1964).

Hovhaness [Hovaness], **Alan** [Chakmakjian, Alan Hovhaness] (b. Somerville, Mass., 8 Mar. 1911). Composer. An extremely prolific composer whose over 400 works merge Eastern and Western influences. He studied piano (from 1929 with Heinrich Gebhard) and composed as a child; he attended Tufts, then transferred to New England Conservatory, where he studied composition with Converse (1932–34). His early works reflect his interest in Renaissance music and employ the harmonic language of the late 19th century. From 1940 to 1947 he lived in Boston; teaching, accompanying, and a position as organist at St. James Armenian Church were his means of support. During these years he studied Armenian music, the music of India, and Eastern philosophy. Most compositions from before 1940 were withdrawn as his works began to reflect these Armenian and Eastern influences; in 1943 he studied with Martinů at the Berkshire Music Center and had some contact with Copland and Bernstein. By 1945 he had produced many Armenian compositions, including *Lousadzak,* a concerto for piano and orchestra, in which aleatory procedures were used for the first time and Western instruments imitated the sounds of Eastern music; a flute concerto (*Elibris,* 1944) uses Hindu ragas.

From 1948 to 1951 he taught at Boston Conservatory of Music; a National Institute of Arts and Letters Grant in 1951 permitted him to move to New York. He wrote incidental and dance music (*The Flowering Peach,* Clifford Odets, 1954; *Ardent Song,* for Martha Graham, London, 1954) and traveled widely, supported by three Guggenheim Fellowships (1953, 1954, 1958) and a Fulbright Fellowship (1959); the latter took him to India and Japan for study and performances. In 1961 his music was performed in France and Germany; a year later he went to Japan and Korea (supported by the Rockefeller Foundation) to study their ancient court musics (Gagaku and Ah-ak). Works from the 1960s show increasing indebtedness to Eastern musics (Symphony no. 16, 1962, uses Western and Ah-ak instruments). His oratorio *Revelations of St. Paul* (op. 343, 1981) reflects both the religious cast of most of his music and the uncluttered textures of his later compositions; its simple instrumental motives are played off against a vocal material reminiscent of the church modes.

Works: Operas (*Lady of Light,* opera-oratorio, 1969; *The Frog Man,* chamber opera, 1987); ballets; over 60 symphonies (no. 2, *The Mysterious Mountain,* 1955; no. 63, *Loon Lake,* 1988) and other orchestral works (*And God Created Great Whales,* taped whale sounds and orchestra, 1970; *3 Armenian Rhapsodies,* 1944); a large corpus of chamber music (*Koke no niwa,* English horn, harp, and percussion, 1954); piano works (the sonata *Fred the Cat,* 1977); religious choral music; solo vocal music.

Hovland, Egil (b. Mysen, near Oslo, 18 Oct. 1924). Composer. At the Oslo Conservatory he studied composition and organ with Per Steenberg and Arild Sandvold (1946–49); later he studied privately with Vagn Holmboe in Copenhagen (1954), with Aaron Copland at Tanglewood (1957), and with Luigi Dallapiccola in Florence (1959). In 1949 he was made organist at the Glemmen Church in Fredrikstad. His music moved from neoclassicism during the 1950s to the use of serial techniques beginning in the mid-1960s. Works include *Missa vigilate* (soloists, dancers, chorus, organ, tape, 1967); *Brunnen* ("church opera," 1972); Masses (*All Saints' Mass,* 1970); many other sacred choral works; 3 symphonies (1952–70), concertos for trombone (1972), violin (1974), piano (no. 1, 1976–77), and other orchestral works; chamber and instrumental music (*Cantus,* I–IV, for various ensembles, 1964–79; a string quartet, 1981); organ works (5 "Koralpartitaer," 1947–67; *Elementa,* 1965).

Howarth, Elgar (b. Cannock, Staffordshire, 4 Nov. 1935). Conductor, trumpeter, and composer. He studied at Manchester Univ. and at the Royal Manchester College of Music; then played trumpet in the London Brass Soloists and the Philip Jones Brass Ensemble. He was principal trumpeter of the Royal Philharmonic Orchestra, 1963–68; music director of the London Sinfonietta from 1973; Covent Garden debut, 1985; principal guest conductor for Opera North, 1985–88. As a conductor he toured extensively, primarily with the BBC Symphony and the London Symphony. His own compositions comprise chiefly instrumental music, especially solo and ensemble music for brass.

Howe, Mary (b. Richmond, Va., 4 Apr. 1882; d. Washington, D.C., 14 Sept. 1964). Composer and pianist. She studied piano in Germany (Richard Burmeister) and at Peabody Conservatory, where she completed a diploma in composition in 1922 (under Strube). She studied briefly with Boulanger in Paris. From 1920 to 1935 she performed as part of a piano duo with Ann Hull. She composed in a late 19th-century, tonal style; many works have a programmatic or literary cast (*Castellana,* 2 pianos and orchestra, 1930, was based on Spanish folk songs; *Three Pieces after Emily Dickinson,* string quartet, 1941). She was a founding member of the Association of American Women Composers (1926) and served on the boards of many other organizations; a program of her orchestral works was presented by the National Symphony (21 Dec. 1952). She wrote 2 ballets, over 20 orchestral works, and more than 50 pieces of chamber music, as well as choral and vocal music.

Howells, Herbert (Norman) (b. Lydney, Gloucestershire, 17 Oct. 1892; d. Oxford, 24 Feb. 1983). Composer. At the Royal College of Music he was a pupil of Charles Stanford in composition and Charles Wood in counterpoint and harmony. In 1920 he began teaching at the Royal College; he also taught at St. Paul's Girls' School, Hammersmith, 1936–62, and was professor of music at the Univ. of London, 1950–64. His lush, frankly Romantic style recalls the music of Elgar and Vaughan Williams. He composed a large amount of sacred vocal music, including *Requiem* (unaccompanied chorus, 1936); *Hymnus Paradisi* (1938); *Missa Sabrinensis* (1954); *A Sequence for St. Michael* (1961); *Stabat Mater* (1963); *Take Him, Earth, for*

Cherishing (1964); *The Coventry Mass* (choir and organ, 1968); *Winchester Canticles* (1968); *Exultate Deo* (1974); *Sweetest of Sweets* (1976). He is also recognized for his many songs (*Peacock Pie,* 6 songs, 1919); among his other works are 2 piano concertos (1913, 1924), *Pageantry* (band, 1934), Suite for Strings (1944), *Triptych* (band, 1960), chamber music (a piano quartet, 1916; 3 sonatas for violin and piano, 1918–23), piano works (*Country Pageant,* 1928), and many organ works (2 sonatas, 1911, 1933; *Prelude—De profundis,* 1958; *Partita,* 1971).

Bibl.: Robert Spearing, *H. H.: A Tribute to Herbert Howells on His Eightieth Birthday* (London, 1972). Christopher Palmer, *Herbert Howells: A Study* (Sevenoaks, 1978). Id., *Herbert Howells: A Centenary Celebration* (London, 1992).

Howlin' Wolf [Burnett, Chester Arthur] (b. West Point, Miss., 10 June 1910; d. Hines, Ill., 10 Jan. 1976). Blues singer, harmonica player, and guitarist. After working in Mississippi and Arkansas he moved to Chicago in 1952 to perform in clubs and record for the the Chess label. His aggressive, gravelly singing defined the rough side of Chicago blues and greatly influenced rock music through performances in Europe (1961–64) and recordings such as "Smoke Stack Lightning" (1956), "Sitting on Top of the World" (1957), "Back Door Man," "Spoonful" (both 1960), "The Red Rooster," and "I Ain't Superstitious" (both 1961). He continued performing, most often in Chicago, until 1975.

Hrabovsky [Grabovsky], **Leonid Alexandrovich** (b. Kiev, 28 Jan. 1935). Composer. After graduating from Kiev Univ. in 1956 with a degree in economics, entered the Kiev Conservatory, where he studied composition with Lev Revutsky and Boris Liatoshinsky. He graduated in 1959, received a graduate diploma in 1962, and after 1966 taught theory and composition there. He moved to Moscow in 1981. In the 1960s, along with a small group of Ukrainian composers, he experimented widely with modern techniques and styles, becoming a pioneer of the Soviet avant garde. He later sought a complex stylistic synthesis in his music. His works include symphonic scores (*Homeomorphia IV*, 1970); vocal-symphonic scores (*La Mer*, melodrama for narrator, chorus, and orchestra, 1970); works for chamber orchestra; vocal and choral music; much chamber music.

Hrisanidis [Hrisanide], **Alexandre** (b. Petrila, Romania, 15 June 1936). Composer and pianist. From 1953 he studied at the Bucharest Conservatory; among his teachers were Paul Constantinescu and Zeno Vancea. From 1959 he taught at the Bucharest Academy, and from 1962 at the conservatory. He went to Fontainebleau in 1965 to study with Nadia Boulanger; for two summers (1966–67) he also studied at Darmstadt. After emigrating in 1972 he taught briefly at the Univ. of Oregon (1972–74), then settled in the Netherlands. Among his works are cantatas (*Les lumières de la patrie,* 1965); orchestral works (*Passacaglia,* 1959; *Vers antiqua,* 1960; *Sonnets,* concerto for harpsichord, 1973); chamber works (3 flute sonatas; *Directions,* wind quintet, 1967–69); several works with tape; 3 piano sonatas (1955–64); "Piano Pieces" nos. 1–13 (1955–64).

Hsu, John (Tseng-Hsin) (b. Shantou, 21 Apr. 1931). Viol player, barytonist, and cellist. Studied cello in Shanghai with Johann Kraus and Walter Joachim; at Carroll College, 1949–50, with Joseph Schroetter; at the New England Conservatory, 1950–55, with Alfred Zighera and Samuel Mayes. Cellist in the Rhode Island Philharmonic and Springfield Symphony, 1950–53; in the orchestras of the Handel and Haydn Society and New England Opera, 1953–55. Taught at Cornell from 1955. There, encouraged by Donald Grout, he took up the viola da gamba about 1960. Recorded the viol music of Marin Marais, 1977. Published *A Handbook of French Baroque Viol Technique* (1981); edited the *Instrumental Works of Marin Marais,* 7 vols. (1980–). Founding cellist of the Cornell University Trio, 1956, which evolved into the Amadé Trio, 1975–85, a period instrument group including pianist Malcolm Bilson and violinist Sonya Monosoff. Member of the Aston Magna Foundation from 1973; artistic director, 1985–91. Cofounder of the Haydn Baryton Trio, 1981.

Hubay [Huber], **Jenő** (b. Budapest, 15 Sept. 1858; d. there, 12 Mar. 1937). Violinist and composer. His father, Karl Hubay, professor of violin at the Budapest Conservatory, was his first violin instructor. The boy made his debut at age 11. Subsequently he studied with Joseph Joachim in Berlin (1871–76) and with Henri Vieuxtemps in Paris (from 1878); in 1878 he made a highly successful Paris debut. Later he taught violin at the Brussels Conservatory (1882–86) and at the Budapest Conservatory (1886–1919). At the latter he was director after 1919; his violin pupils there included Franz Vecsey, Jelly d'Aranyi, and Joseph Szigeti. His own works are in a strongly Romantic style; he composed 8 operas (*A falu rossza* [The Village Vagabond], Budapest, 1894; *Moharózsa* [The Moss Rose], Budapest, 1903; *Anna Karenina,* Budapest, 1915; *Az álarc* [The Mask], Budapest, 1931); 4 symphonies (no. 3, *Vita nuova* [Dante Symphony], 1921; no. 4, [Petőfi Symphony], soloists, chorus, orchestra, 1925); 4 violin concertos (no. 1, Dramatique; no. 4, All'antica, 1908); solo violin pieces.

Hubbard, Frank (Twombly) (b. New York, 15 May 1920; d. Newton, Mass., 25 Feb. 1976). Harpsichord maker. He studied at Harvard (B.A., 1942; M.A., 1947); went to London and worked with Hugh Gough, then returned to the U.S. and set up a harpsichord workshop in Boston with William Dowd (1949–58), subsequently establishing his own firm. His experience as a restorer for many museums and private collections led to the publication of his books *Harpsichord Regulating and Repairing* (Boston, 1963) and *Three Centu-*

ries of Harpsichord Making (Cambridge, Mass., 1967).

Hubbard, Freddie [Frederick Dewayne] (b. Indianapolis, 7 Apr. 1938). Jazz trumpeter, flugelhorn player, and bandleader. He toured Europe with Quincy Jones's big band (1960–61), joined Art Blakey's Jazz Messengers (1961–64), and then began leading groups, initially playing in hard bop and modal jazz styles, but turning to simpler danceable styles after the success of his albums *Red Clay* (1970) and *First Light* (1971). His sidemen have included the pianist Kenny Barron and, with his return to a bop basis in the 1980s, Joe Henderson. He also recorded the album *Maiden Voyage* in 1965 with Herbie Hancock's quintet, with which he was reunited in 1976–77.

Huber, Hans (b. Eppenburg, Solothurn, Switzerland, 28 June 1852; d. Locarno, 25 Dec. 1921). Composer and pianist. He was a choirboy in Solothurn and active as a pianist and organist; spent four years at the conservatory in Leipzig (1870–73), then taught music privately in Alsace, and was organist in a local church (1875–77); in 1877 he went to Basel, where he taught, performed, and composed; began to teach at the music school there in 1889 and directed it from 1896 until 1918. He also directed the Choral Society (1899–1902) and remained active as an accompanist. As a composer he wrote in many genres, employing a Romantic style; works include opera and oratorio; 9 symphonies, 4 piano concertos; chamber music for strings, winds, and piano; choral works; and songs.

Huber, Klaus (b. Bern, 30 Nov. 1924). Composer. After working as a schoolteacher, he attended the Zurich Conservatory (1947–49), studying composition with Burkhard; later studied in Berlin with Blacher (1955–56). In the 1950s he taught violin at the Zurich Conservatory; 1960–63, taught music history at the Lucerne Conservatory and then took over theory and composition classes at the Music Academy in Basel. His works employ serial procedures and often deal with spiritual subjects; his metric and rhythmic structures are frequently based on mystical or allegorical numerical relations. *Des Engels Anredung an die Seele* (tenor and ensemble, 1958) won first prize at ISCM in Rome (1959). His many works include the opera *Jot, oder Wann kommt der Herr zurück* (1973); pieces for orchestra, some with tape (*Protuberanzen,* 1986; *Orchesterstücke mit Sängern und Sprechern,* 1987); *Cantiones de circulo gyrante* (soloists, chorus, and 15 instruments, after Hildegard von Bingen and Heinrich Böll, 1985); *Spes contra spem* (voice, narrator, orchestra, 1988); *Von Zeit zu Zeit* (string quartet, 1985) and other chamber and keyboard music; choral and vocal music.

Huberman, Bronisław (b. Częstochowa, 19 Dec. 1882; d. Corsier-sur-Vevey, 15 June 1947). Violinist. He studied with Michałowicz and with Isidor Lotto; went to Berlin in 1892, continuing his studies with Charles Grigorovich, Hugo Heermann in Frankfurt, and Martin Marsick in Paris. He performed in many European cities before he reached his teens; in 1895 his performance of the Mendelssohn concerto at Adelina Patti's farewell concert in Vienna created a sensation, and an 1896 performance of the Brahms violin concerto was warmly received by the composer himself. He toured widely, including the U.S. (1896–97, 1937); in 1936 he helped organize the Palestine Symphony (later Israel Philharmonic).

Hucbald (b. at or near Tournai, ca. 840; d. St. Amand, 20 June 930). Monk and theorist. Studied and taught at various monastic schools; in some cases designed or revised curricula. His one treatise, *De harmonica institutione* (*GS* 1:104–25; trans. *YTS* 3 [1978]: 3–46), is a practical work aimed toward the teaching of chant; it is the earliest known systematic explanation of Western music theory. Although the author's familiarity with the works of Boethius and other early writers on music is evident, the treatise is original and advances some notions that were to be highly influential. Attributions of the "Enchiriadis" treatises, among others, to Hucbald, are erroneous.

Huízar (García de la Cadena), Candelario (b. Jérez, Zacatecas, Mexico, 2 Feb. 1883; d. Mexico City, 3 May 1970). Composer. Studied at the National Conservatory from 1918; worked as a free-lance hornist and copyist until 1929, when he joined the Mexico Symphony under Chávez, playing the horn until 1937 and serving as librarian until 1948. The *Imágenes* for orchestra (1929) is indebted to Debussy, while later works, especially the 4 symphonies (1931, 1936, 1938, and 1942), show a nationalist character, with actual indigenous melodies appearing alongside invented ones. The symphonic poem *Pueblerinas* (1931) is his best-known work. Other compositions include a sonata for clarinet and bassoon (1931), a string quartet (1938), and vocal music.

Hullah, John (Pyke) (b. Worcester, 27 June 1812; d. London, 21 Feb. 1884). Educator. Studied music with Horsley (1829), singing with Crivelli (1833); from 1837 a church organist (1858–84 at the Charterhouse); 1836–38, produced 3 English operas; from 1840, after studying Wilhem's methods of teaching singing in Paris, taught similar methods in London (from 1841 at Exeter Hall; 1849–60 at St. Martin's Hall) and throughout Britain. Government support made him very influential in this field, but his fixed-do system was eventually supplanted by movable-do. Active as lecturer, conductor, writer of textbooks and music history, editor of musical anthologies, composer of songs ("O That We Two Were Maying," "The Three Fishers"). From 1844 to 1874 he taught singing at King's College, later at Queen's College, Bedford College.

Bibl.: [F. Hullah], *Life of John Hullah* (London, 1886).

Humble, Leslie (Keith) (b. Geelong, Victoria, Australia, 6 Sept. 1927). Composer. After studying piano with

Roy Shepherd at the Melbourne Conservatorium (from 1947) he traveled to London, where in 1950–51 he was a composition pupil of Howard Ferguson's at the Royal Academy. He spent the next 15 years in Paris, first as a student at the École normale de musique (1952–54) and as a private pupil of René Leibowitz (from 1953), then as music director of the Center of American Studies (1960–66). He returned to Melbourne in 1966 and was appointed lecturer in composition; made frequent visits to the U.S. since 1969, including periods as visiting professor at the Univ. of California at San Diego. His music employs avant-garde techniques, including *musique concrète,* aleatory, "sound collages," and multimedia events. He has composed stage works, including *Oeuvres mechantes* nos. 1–4 (1965), *La légende* (1970), and *In Five* (1972); other works include *L'armée des saluts* (actors, singers, instruments, 1965), *Nunque* I–VI, *The Seasons* (4 choruses, 1971), *Music for Monuments* (bassoon, tape, 1967), *Moto perpetuo* (tape, 1968), *Arcade I* (organ, tape, percussion), *II* (piano), *III* (flute, tape), *IV* (guitar, percussion), *V* (orchestra; all 1969); Trio no. 3 (flute, percussion, piano, 1985).

Hume, Tobias (b. ca. 1560s; d. London, 16 Apr. 1645). Viol player and composer. Served as a soldier for Sweden and Russia; in his *First Part of Ayres* (1605) he wrote, "My Profession being, as my Education hath beene, Armes." He published two collections of music, mainly for lyra viol: the 1605 print and *Captaine Hume's Poeticall Musicke* (1607), both containing dances, programmatic pieces, and accompanied songs. He was admitted to an almshouse in 1629, where he later died.

Bibl.: F. W. Sternfield, ed., *English Lute Songs, 1597–1632: A Collection of Facsimile Reprints* (Menston, England, 1969) [contains both the 1605 and 1607 prints]. Colette Harris, "Tobias Hume: A Short Biography," *Chelys* 3 (1971): 16–23.

Humel, Gerald (b. Cleveland, 7 Nov. 1931). Composer and conductor. He studied at Hofstra (B.A., 1954) with Elie Siegmeister, at the Royal College of Music (ARCM, 1956), Oberlin (M.M., 1958), and the Univ. of Michigan (1958–60) with Ross Lee Finney and Roberto Gerhard; also worked with Boris Blacher and Rufer. He wrote a number of ballets, including *Herodias* (1967), *Lilith* (1973), *Othello und Desdemona* (1984), *Zwei Giraffen Tanzen Tango* (1980); other works include a flute concerto (1964); served as conductor of the Gruppe Neue Musik in Berlin.

Humes, Helen (b. Louisville, Ky., 23 June 1913; d. Santa Monica, Calif., 13 Sept. 1981). Jazz and blues singer. She sang with Count Basie (1938–41), then worked mainly in New York and California, including concerts with Jazz at the Philharmonic, and made two rhythm-and-blues hit records: "Be-ba-ba-le-ba" (1945) and "Million Dollar Secret" (1950). After working with Red Norvo and in rhythm-and-blues tours, she retired in 1967. A performance at the Newport Jazz Festival in New York (1973) led to new recordings, including the album *Helen Comes Back* (Paris, 1973), and a residency at the Cookery in New York (to 1973).

Humfrey, Pelham (b. 1647; d. Windsor, 14 July 1674). Composer. Sang under Cooke in the Chapel Royal, where some of his anthems were performed (1660–64); he then traveled to France and Italy. He was named court lutenist and Gentleman of the Chapel Royal while on his journey. He arrived back in England during October 1667; according to Pepys, certain of his anthems were sung immediately upon his return. He was elected Assistant for the Corporation of Music in 1670, became a Warden in 1672, and in the same year was appointed Master of the Children of the Chapel Royal, where Purcell was among his pupils. He soon took ill and died at the age of 27. Although his output includes songs, court odes, and masque music, he focused mainly on sacred works; 19 verse anthems survive, 17 of which integrate instrumental ritornelli.

Bibl.: *Complete Church Music, MB* 34–35 (1972). Peter Dennison, "Pelham Humfrey, 1647–74: A Tercentenary Survey," *MT* 115 (1974): 553–55. Id., *Pelham Humfrey* (New York, 1986).

Hummel, Johann Nepomuk (b. Pressburg [now Bratislava], 14 Nov. 1778; d. Weimar, 17 Oct. 1837). Composer and pianist. Son of a musician; a child prodigy. At 8 he moved with his family to Vienna, where his father was conductor at the Theater auf der Wieden. He was a pupil of Mozart's until 1788, when he began a tour managed by his father through Germany to Copenhagen, Scotland, and London (1790–92), where he was much admired; 1791–92, published his first piano and chamber music there; played in Holland and Germany on his return to Vienna. He spent the next decade in Vienna, first studying with Albrechtsberger and Salieri, and having a few organ lessons from Haydn in 1795; he played little in public, earning his living through a heavy schedule of piano teaching, and producing a few compositions, primarily chamber. His position in Vienna's musical life was shaken by the emergence of Beethoven, whose abilities somewhat overawed him and with whom his personal relations were sometimes difficult. (Nevertheless, he came from Weimar in 1827 to visit Beethoven on his deathbed and was a pallbearer at his funeral.)

In 1804 he became concertmaster to Prince Esterházy at Eisenstadt, thus de facto music director there (Haydn remaining titular Kapellmeister until his death in 1809). In this post he composed most of his sacred music (including 5 masses, a Te Deum, motets) and was very active in the Esterháza theater as conductor and composer while keeping up contacts with Vienna, for which he composed much dance music and other works, and where he published some piano and chamber works. His tenure in the Esterháza post was not entirely smooth. For unknown reasons he was dismissed in 1808, soon reinstated, and finally dismissed in May 1811. He returned to Vienna; he had produced an opera there in 1810 and continued to compose a good deal for its theaters through 1814, when his wife (since 1813), the singer Elisabeth Röckel, persuaded him to resume his public career as a pianist. This he did with great success, soon winning an international reputation; in 1816 he successfully toured Germany. He was court Kapellmeister in Stuttgart, 1816–18, but disliked the post because of difficulties with the theater management, and in 1819 moved to Weimar as court Kapellmeister under very favorable terms. He conducted the opera but composed little theater music, and as a Catholic at a Protestant court was exempted from composing sacred music. This left him free to make piano arrangements for foreign publishers (causing him to become an important figure in the evolution of relations between composers and publishers and in the fight for copyright protection) and to compose piano music for his tours, which an annual three-month leave allowed him to make nearly every year (1821, Berlin and Holland; 1822, Russia; 1825, Paris; 1826, Germany; 1827, Vienna; 1828, Germany and Warsaw; 1830, Paris and London). He was known for the elegance and expressiveness of his playing and equally for his polished improvisations. After 1830 changing musical fashions, especially through the rise of flashier virtuosos, made him increasingly passé. His visit to London in 1831 was a failure because of the presence there of Paganini. He returned in 1833, primarily as conductor of a season of German opera, which was not successful. In 1834 he visited Vienna, after which he ceased to tour, his health also failing. He died rich.

His theater music aroused scant attention beyond its immediate purpose, and he composed little for orchestra apart from dance music. He composed considerable chamber music, mostly with piano, including piano trios and the celebrated Septet in D minor op. 74 (ca. 1816). Of his piano concertos, those in A minor op. 85 (ca. 1816), B minor op. 89 (1819), E major op. 110 (1814), and A♭ major op. 113 (1827) were the best known. His piano music included sonatas and much salon music (rondos, variations, fantasies, etc.); 24 etudes op. 125 (1833); 2 Sonatas for 4-hands opp. 51, 92. Also songs, choruses.

Bibl.: D. Zimmerschied, *Thematisches Verzeichnis der Werke von Johann Nepomuk Hummel* (Hofheim, 1971). Joel Sachs, "A Checklist of the Works of Johann Nepomuk Hummel," *Notes* 30 (1973–74): 732–54. Id., *Kapellmeister Hummel in England and France* (Detroit, 1977).

Humperdinck, Engelbert (b. Siegburg, 1 Sept. 1854; d. Neustrelitz, 27 Sept. 1921). Composer. He attended the Cologne Conservatory, 1872–77, studying piano, organ, cello, and composition with Hiller; won Mozart Prize (1876); summer 1877, studied with Franz Lachner; 1877–79, Munich Music School, studying counterpoint with Rheinberger. *Die Wallfahrt nach Kevelaar* for chorus and orchestra, performed at a school concert (July 1878), won the Mendelssohn Prize (a year in Italy). At Naples (winter 1879–80) he met Wagner and, after a tour of Sicily, became a member of his circle, invited to Bayreuth to assist in the preparation of *Parsifal.* Arriving there in January 1881, he copied the full score, then coached roles and chorus, also getting conducting experience as director of the Bayreuth Music Society. In August 1882 (having won the Meyerbeer Prize in 1881) he went to Italy, then Paris, where, through Liszt, he met Saint-Saëns, Pauline Viardot, and others. In November 1883 he was appointed assistant conductor, Cologne Theater, a post whose drudgery made him restive, but attempts to get other posts fell through because of his Wagnerism; 1885–86, an unhappy academic year teaching at Barcelona Conservatory; 1886–88, Cologne Conservatory; 1888–90, editor, Schott publishing house, Mainz, also writing newspaper music criticism. From 1890 to 1897 he lived in Frankfurt as critic and from 1891 as teacher at the Hoch Conservatory (professor from 1896).

Hailed by some as Wagner's chosen successor, he composed little in the period 1880–90. In 1890–92 he composed *Hänsel und Gretel* (to a libretto by his sister, the outgrowth of some children's songs to her poems). Premiered on 23 Dec. 1893 at Weimar under Richard Strauss, it was produced in more than 50 theaters within a year, making Humperdinck rich and famous. In 1895–96 he composed music to *Königskinder* (Munich, 1897), a Märchenspiel; this began as incidental music but became a through-composed melodrama, the climactic parts set in a kind of *Sprechgesang.* It was widely performed without approaching the success of *Hänsel und Gretel.* From 1900 to 1920 he taught composition at the Berlin Hochschule für Musik, from 1910 as chairman of the theory and composition department. Of his 4 later operas, only *Königskinder* (Metropolitan Opera, 1910), based on the earlier melodrama, was a considerable (though not enduring) success; but his incidental music for Max Reinhard's productions of Shakespeare and other dramas (Berlin, 1905–12) was widely used. Also wrote music for a pantomime, *The Miracle* (London, 1911); songs; 3 string quartets.

Bibl.: H. J. Irmen, ed., *Engelbert Humperdinck: Briefe und Tagebücher (1863–1880)* (Cologne, 1975).

Hunt, Jerry (Edward) (b. Waco, Tex., 30 Nov. 1943; d. Canton, Tex., Nov. 1994). Composer. He studied piano and composition at North Texas State Univ. (1960–61) and has performed in concerts of contemporary music. He was artist-in-residence at the Video Research Center in Dallas (1974–77), where most of his multimedia and computer-assisted projects were realized. Most works are theatrical, involving performer interaction not only with instruments but also with elements of the performing space; *Voltage (One Shot Coverage 2)* involves computer-assisted response to sounds generated by one vocal soloist. Other works include *Helix* (1 or more instruments, 1964); *Sur Dr. John Dee* (for 0–11 performers, 1963); *Parallel Helix* (tape, 1970); and *Quaquaversal Transmission 5* (telephony, television monitors, on-site decoders, 1982).

Hünten, Franz (b. Coblenz, 26 Dec. 1793; d. there, 22 Feb. 1878). Composer. Son and pupil of the Coblenz court organist; student, 1819–21, at the Paris Conservatory (Pradher, piano; Reicha and Cherubini, composition); then a fashionable teacher and very popular salon composer in Paris; returned to Coblenz, 1835–39, and retired there in 1848. Composed over 250 piano pieces, including variations, opera potpourris and fantasies, rondos, dances (including *Les bords du Rhin,* grande valse brillante, op. 120, one of his most popular); also a widely used *Méthode de piano* op. 60 (1833); etudes opp. 80, 81, 114; 4 piano trios.

Hunter, Alberta (b. Memphis, 1 Apr. 1895; d. New York, 17 Oct. 1984). Blues and cabaret singer. She sang in Chicago and, from 1921, New York, where she began recording, accompanied by Fletcher Henderson, Louis Armstrong, Fats Waller, Sidney Bechet, and other leading jazzmen. Her composition "Downhearted Blues" (1922) became Bessie Smith's first recording (1923). From 1927 to 1938 she worked mainly in Europe, starring in the musical *Showboat* with Paul Robeson in London (1928–29). She toured, entertaining U.S. servicemen (1944–53), then left music for nursing. She resumed her musical career in 1977, singing at the Cookery in New York until 1984.

Hurford, Peter (John) (b. Minehead, Somerset, 22 Nov. 1930). Organist. He attended Jesus College, Cambridge; studied with Harold Darke, and with André Marchal in Paris. He served as Master of the Music at St. Albans Abbey (1958–78), and in 1963 founded the International Organ Festival there. As a performer and recording artist he specialized in the music of Bach and 18th-century French music; served as visiting professor at the Univ. of Cincinnati (1967–68) and the Univ. of Western Ontario (1976–77).

Hurt, Mississippi John (b. Teoc, Miss., 3 July 1893; d. Grenada, Miss., 2 or 3 Nov. 1966). Blues singer and guitarist. He recorded 20 sides in Memphis and New York in 1928, then worked on farms and railroads until 1963. Rediscovered, he recorded that year for the Library of Congress, performing folk and country blues songs with nimble finger-picking guitar work in a style unchanged since the 1920s. After a brief career of club and festival appearances he returned to Mississippi. His style is demonstrated by his 1920s and 1960s recordings of songs such as "Casey Jones," "Nobody's Dirty Business," and "Candy Man."

Husa, Karel (b. Prague, 7 Aug. 1921). Composer and conductor. He studied violin and piano as a youth; composition and conducting at the Prague Conservatory (1940–45) and at the Academy of Music (1945–46); teachers included Jaroslav Rídký, Pavel Dedecek, and Vaclav Tálich. Two student orchestral works (Overture, 1944; Sinfonietta, 1946) were performed by the Prague Symphony under the composer; the Sinfonietta won a prize from the Czech Academy of Arts and Science (1948). A French government fellowship enabled him to study in Paris (1946–51; composition with Honegger and Boulanger; conducting with Jean Fournet, Eugène Bigot, and André Cluytens). In 1954, Husa joined the faculty at Cornell Univ., retiring in 1992. He won the 1993 Grawemeyer Award for his cello concerto (1989).

Whereas early works were neoclassical in form and modal in their harmonic-melodic language, his compositional style since the Second String Quartet (1953) embraced twelve-tone (*Poem,* viola and orchestra, 1959) and serial methods (*Mosaïques,* orchestra, 1961), quarter-tones, and new string techniques (String Quartet no. 3, 1968; awarded the Pulitzer Prize). In *Music for Prague* (1968) serial techniques are applied to the sounds allotted to the 3 percussionists, bells portray Prague's churches, a piccolo produces bird calls symbolic of liberty, and a Hussite religious song represents resistance to tyranny; in *Apotheosis of This Earth* (chorus and band/orchestra, 1970) the chorus members hum, howl, speak, whisper, stamp their feet, and clap to depict contemporary problems of man and environment; both of those works employ aleatory procedures. A Bicentennial work (*An American Te Deum,* baritone, band, and chorus, 1976) makes programmatic use of Indian songs, music of Dvořák, and a Swedish emigrant ballad.

Other works include the ballet *The Trojan Women* (1980), 2 symphonies (1954, 1983), and other works for orchestra (*Serenade,* woodwind quintet and orchestra/piano, 1963; Concerto for Orchestra, 1986; a trumpet concerto, 1988; an organ concerto, 1987; *Cayuga Lake (Memories),* 1992); music for wind ensemble (*Al fresco,* 1975; *Five Poems,* 1994); chamber music (String Quartet no. 4, 1989; *Landscapes,* brass quintet and piano, 1977; *Sonata a tre,* clarinet, violin, and piano, 1981); several choral works; a few songs.

Bibl.: Lawrence W. Hartzell, "Karel Husa: The Man and the Music," *MQ* 51 (1976): 87–104. Susan Hayes Hitchens, *Karel Husa: A Bio-Bibliography* (New York, 1991).

Huss, Henry Holden (b. Newark, N.J., 21 June 1862; d. New York, 17 Sept. 1953). Pianist and composer. He studied with his father, George John Huss, and with Otis B. Boise; attended the Munich Conservatory, where his teachers were Joseph Rheinberger and Josef Giehrl (1882–85). He had a successful career as a concert pianist, frequently performing his Rhapsody (op. 3, piano, orchestra, 1885) and Piano Concerto (op. 10) with a number of American orchestras. In 1904 he married the soprano Hildegard Hoffmann; the two often performed together. Huss taught at Hunter College (1930–38) and was the co-author, with his father, of *Condensed Piano-Technics* (1904). Other compositions include the symphonic poem *Life's Conflicts* (1921); vocal music; chamber music.

Huston, (Thomas) Scott (Jr.) (b. Tacoma, Wash., 10 Oct. 1916). Composer. He studied music at the Eastman School (1938–42; 1950–52) under Rogers, Hanson, and Burill Phillips. He taught on the West Coast and at Kearney State College in Nebraska (1947–50) before returning to Eastman to complete his Ph.D.; a member of the faculty of the Cincinnati College–Conservatory, 1952–88 (dean of the conservatory when it merged with the Cincinnati College of Music in 1955–56). His later compositions employed some atonality and exhibited a special concern with timbre (*Four Phantasms,* orchestra, 1964, has no fixed tonality); earlier works were in a tonal idiom within forms reminiscent of Brahms. Works include the opera *The Blind Girl* (1982) and an oratorio; at least 6 symphonies (*The Human Condition,* 1981) and other orchestral works; chamber music for winds, strings, and brass (*For Our Times,* 6 brass instruments, 1974); liturgical and other choral music (*An Ecumenical Mosaic of Cincinnati,* 1988); songs.

Hutcherson, Bobby [Robert] (b. Los Angeles, 27 Jan. 1941). Jazz vibraphonist and marimba player. With Al Grey and Billy Mitchell's sextet he came to New York (1961), where he later worked with Jackie McLean, Archie Shepp, Hank Mobley, Herbie Hancock, and Eric Dolphy, with whom he recorded the album *Out to Lunch* (1964). In Los Angeles he and the tenor saxophonist Harold Land led a hard bop combo (1967–71). From the 1970s he worked in San Francisco. Beginning 1981 he also toured with the Timeless All Stars, a sextet including Land. In 1984 he recorded the bop album *Good Bait,* with Branford Marsalis and Philly Joe Jones among his sidemen.

Hutchinson Family. Performers. In 1841, 4 of the 11 sons and 1 of the 2 daughters of a Milford, N.H., farmer began to tour, singing and playing; the 5 were soon reduced to a quartet: Judson (1817–59), John (1821–1908), Asa (1823–84), and Abby (1829–92). They wrote much of their material and, raised in an abolitionist milieu, from the beginning espoused progressive social causes: abolition, temperance, and, later, women's rights. Quickly becoming popular, their tour expanded from New England to New York City (1843), Philadelphia and Washington (1844), England and Ireland (1844–45). Abby's withdrawal after marriage (1849) to a Wall Street financier ended the period of their greatest popularity, but the remaining 3 continued to tour widely; in 1855 they founded the town of Hutchinson, Minnesota, moving their families there. In 1858 they split up. Judson, mentally ill, hanged himself in 1859; Asa and John toured separately with members of their own families up to the 1870s and 1880s, respectively.

Bibl.: Carol Brink, *Harps in the Wind: The Story of the Singing Hutchinsons* (New York, 1947). Dale Cockrell, *Excelsior: Journals of the Hutchinson Family Singers, 1842–1846* (New York, 1989).

Hüttenbrenner, Anselm (b. Graz, 13 Oct. 1794; d. Ober-Andritz, near Graz, 5 June 1868). Composer. In 1811 began two and a half years as novice in a Cistercian monastery; then studied law in Graz and from 1815 in Vienna, where he also studied music with Salieri, along with Schubert, who became a close friend; published a few songs, piano pieces, string quartets there. In 1821, after military service, returned to Graz, married, and, on his father's death, managed the family property; 1825–29 and 1831–39, was conductor at the Steiermärkischer Musikverein. He composed much music, largely unpublished and of primarily regional renown, including several operas performed in Graz; much church music; symphonies; chamber music; male part songs; songs; piano and organ pieces; 1854, wrote his somewhat unreliable recollections of Schubert, edited by O. E. Deutsch in the *Jahrbuch der Grillparzer Gesellschaft* 16 (1906): 99–163.

Huygens, Constantin (b. The Hague, 4 Sept. 1596; d. there, 28 Mar. 1687). Composer and writer on music, also a diplomat and scientist. Schooled by tutors and at the Univ. of Leiden; served the House of Orange from 1625 to his death. Heard Monteverdi in Venice; met Chambonnières in Paris; carried on correspondence with many other theorists and musicians. Composed over 800 works for lute, harpsichord, viola da gamba, guitar, and theorbo, virtually all of which are lost; his treatises support the use of organ in Psalm recitation and advocate certain changes in the Genevan Psalter. His son Christian (1629–95) was a talented musician as well as an important scientist; he developed a tuning method whereby the octave may be divided into 31 equal intervals.

Hyla, Lee (b. Niagara Falls, N.Y., 31 Aug. 1952). Composer. He grew up in Greencastle, Indiana; studied with Malcolm Peyton and John Heiss at the New England Conservatory of Music, and with David Lewin at SUNY–Stony Brook. Taught at St. John's Univ. from 1982. Works include String Trio (1980–81); *Revisible Light* (piano, 1978); *Pre-Amnesia* (solo alto saxophone, 1980); *The Dream of Innocent III* (cello, piano, percussion, 1987); *Amnesia* (6 instruments, 1980).

I

Iannaccone, Anthony (Joseph) (b. Brooklyn, 14 Oct. 1943). Composer. He studied violin and piano as a child, then attended the Manhattan School, where his teachers included Ludmila Ulehla, Giannini, Diamond, and Flagello (1961–68); earned Ph.D. at the Eastman School under Samuel Adler and Warren Benson (1968–71). From 1971 taught at Eastern Michigan Univ., directing the electronic music studio and the collegium musicum. His works from before 1975 are serial; later works show increasing concern with timbre and often include virtuosic material for winds. He has written orchestral music (symphonies and the Variations for violin and orchestra, 1969; *Sinfonia concertante,* flute, violin, viola, cello, piano, orchestra, 1988, rev. 1989; *Whispers of Heavenly Death,* 1989); music for wind ensemble and band; much chamber music (*3 Mythical Sketches,* brass quartet, 1971; *Parodies,* wind quintet, 1974; *Rituals,* violin and piano, 1973; *Mobiles,* 3 brass, 2 percussion, 1988) and piano music; vocal works (*Whitman Madrigals,* soprano, alto, tenor, bass, piano, 1984; *The Prince of Peace,* vocal soloists, chorus, and orchestra, 1970) and a few songs.

Ibert, Jacques (François Antoine) (b. Paris, 15 Aug. 1890; d. there, 5 Feb. 1962). Composer. After a period as a drama student, he studied at the Paris Conservatory with Gédalge (counterpoint), and with Fauré and Paul Vidal (composition), 1911–14 and after the war; won the Prix de Rome (1919) for the cantata *Le poète et la fée.* He later returned to Rome as director of the French Academy (1937–40, 1946–60); 1955–56, director of the Réunion des théâtres lyriques nationaux (encompassing both the Paris Opéra and the Opéra-comique).

Related to "Les six" in style and temperament, but not officially associated with them, Ibert contributed to most genres. He collaborated with Honegger on two operas. Some works are impressionistic (*Escales,* a description of three Mediterranean ports), and many works carry descriptive titles, in harmony with the composer's view that music should be "the expression of an interior adventure." He adopted classical forms, but used them freely; his incidental music for *A Midsummer Night's Dream* is actually based on the work of four earlier English composers. His style was eclectic, and his composition was closely linked to expression in the other arts. He avoided exclusive association with any particular school, and considered that "all systems are valid." Some of his works have been compared to those of Milhaud and Poulenc, for their wit (especially the Wind Quintet, *3 pièces brèves,* 1930).

Works: 7 operas (*Angélique,* a farce in one act, 1926; 2 collaborations with Honegger, *L'aiglon,* 1937, and *Les petites cardinal,* 1939); 7 ballets (*Valse,* 1927, a collaboration with 9 contemporaries; *Le chevalier errant,* after *Don Quixote,* 1935); incidental and film music, radio scores; 25 works for orchestra or large ensemble (*Escales,* 1922; Concertino da camera, alto saxophone and 11 instruments, 1935; *Bacchanale,* scherzo, 1956; and *Hommage à Mozart,* rondo, 1957; many others are suites drawn from his stage and film scores); a string quartet (1937–42), pieces for winds or strings; solo works for organ, harp, guitar, flute, cello, and violin; piano music (*Le vent dans les ruines,* 1915); accompanied and unaccompanied works for small vocal ensemble or chorus; songs; arrangements of orchestral works, and cadenzas for Mozart bassoon and clarinet concertos.

Bibl.: Gerard Michel, *Jacques Ibert, l'homme et son oeuvre* (Paris, 1968) [includes catalog].

Ibrahim, Abdullah [Dollar Brand; Adolph Johannes Brand] (b. Cape Town, 9 Oct. 1934). Jazz pianist and composer. He led the Jazz Epistles, the first black group to record in South Africa (1960), then in 1962 moved to Zurich. After recording the album *Duke Ellington Presents the Dollar Brand Trio* (1963), he divided his time between Europe and the U.S., returning also to South Africa until 1976, from which time he used his Muslim name. He concentrated on free jazz in the mid-1960s, working with Elvin Jones, Don Cherry, and Gato Barbieri, but later drew upon many jazz and African styles. He has worked alone and leading small groups, including the septet Ekaya (from 1983).

Ichiyanagi, Toshi (b. Kobe, 4 Feb. 1933). Composer. He studied composition privately with Tomojirō Ikenouchi, and piano with Chieko Hara. In 1952 he went to New York, where he studied at the Juilliard School and met John Cage, who exerted a profound influence on his music and ideas. Returning to Japan in 1961, he spent the next years organizing concerts of new music; in 1963 he founded the New Directions Group, and three years later organized the Orchestral Space Festival. Works include *Appearance,* 3 instruments and 5 electronic devices (1967); *Extended Voices,* chorus (1967); *Activities,* electronic ensemble and orchestra (1967); *Up-to-Date Applause* (1968); *Music for Living Space,* chorus, computer (1969); *Theatre Music,* tape (1969); *Music for Living Process,* 2 dancers, chamber ensemble (1973); *Time Sequence,* piano (1976); a piano concerto (1988).

Ifukube, Akira (b. Kushiro, Hokkaidō, 7 Mar. 1914). Composer. He studied forestry at Hokkaidō Univ. and was a forester until World War II. During the 1930s he began studying music; for a short time he took lessons from Alexander Tcherepnin, and in 1935 he won the Tcherepnin Prize for his work *Nihon kyōsō-kyoku* [Japanese Rhapsody]. After the war he composed chiefly orchestral and ballet scores; his music contains elements of pentatonic "oriental" melody and the sharp, percussive rhythms of Prokofiev and Bartók. Among his ballet scores are *Bon odori* [Bon Dance] (1936?), *Nihon no taiko* [Drums of Japan] (1951), *Ningen Shaka* [Buddha] (1953), and *Nihon nijūroku seijin* (1972); other orchestral works include *Ballata sinfonica* (1943); a violin concerto (1948), *Sinfonia Tapkaara* (1954), *Ritmica ostinata* (piano, orchestra, 1961), *Eclogue symphonique* (Japanese instruments, orchestra, 1982); also guitar works (*Kugo-ka,* 1969).

Ikebe, Shin-Ichiro (b. Tokyo, 15 Sept. 1943). Composer. Studied at Tokyo Univ. of Arts and Music (with Tomojirō Ikenouchi and Akio Yashirō); graduated in 1967. In 1971 his opera *The Death Goddess* won the Salzburg Opera Prize. He has composed works for Western instruments and for traditional Japanese instruments such as the koto. Orchestral music: *Movements* (1965); *Construction* (1966); Piano Concerto (1966–67); 3 symphonies (1967, 1979, 1984); *Petite symphonie pour enfants* (1969); *Dimorphism,* organ and orchestra (1974); *Quadrants,* Japanese instruments, orchestra (1974). Chamber works: *Raccontino,* violin, piano (1967); *Energia,* 60 players (1970); *Trivalence,* I and II (1971, 1973). Also *Kusabi,* dancers, female chorus, and 11 players (1972); *Oedipus' Pilgrimage,* joruri, male chorus, 10 players.

Ikenouchi, Tomojirō (b. Tokyo, 21 Oct. 1906). Composer. After beginning his studies at Keiō Univ., in 1927 he went to Paris to study at the conservatory. His instructors were Henri-Paul Büsser (composition) and Paul Fauchey (harmony). He returned to Japan in 1933 and then again went to Paris (1934–36) to complete his studies. From 1936 he taught composition at Nihon Univ. Later, as a professor at the National Univ. of Fine Arts (from 1947), he became an influential teacher; most of the Japanese composers of the postwar generation studied with him. In 1955 he helped found the Shinshin Kai, a new-music group. His music reflects the French influence of his training; works include *Tanshō Kumikyoku,* orchestra (1937); *Shiki* [The Four Seasons], orchestra (1938); *Symphony in Two Movements* (1951); vocal music (*Yuya,* soprano, chamber orchestra, 1942; *Koi no omoni,* baritone, chorus, timpani, 1974); chamber and instrumental works include 3 string quartets (1937, 1945, 1946); *Fantasy on a Japanese Folksong,* violin and piano (1940); Flute Sonata (1946); 3 "Sonatines," cello (1946); piano (1954); violin (1956).

Ileborgh, Adam (fl. ca. 1448). Composer. The Ileborgh Tablature (ed. *CEKM* 1 [1963]), a very early German organ tablature consisting of only a few folios, is the one extant source of his 8 known pieces. These works (preludes and settings of a secular cantus firmus) probably reflect average improvisational practices in organ music of the mid-15th century in Germany.

Iliev, Konstantin (b. Sofia, 9 Mar. 1924; d. there, 6 Mar. 1988). Composer and conductor. At the Sofia State Music Academy he was a student (1942–46) of Pantcho Vladigerov (composition) and Marin Goleminov (conducting). After World War II he went to Prague for further study with Jaroslav Řídký and Alois Hába. He conducted the Bulgarian State Opera in Sofia, 1947–56; the Varna Symphony, 1956–72; the Sofia Philharmonic, 1978–85. Taught at the Bulgarian State Conservatory, 1964–85; in 1970 he was made professor of conducting. His own compositions employ Bulgarian folk elements in a context of twelve-tone and aleatoric techniques. Works include the operas *Bojanskiyat maĭstor* [Master of Boyana] (1960–62; Sofia, 1962) and *Elenovo zarstvo* [Kingdom of the Deer] (1975); vocal/choral music (*Chudnoto choro* [The Miraculous Dance], children's chorus, piano, wind quintet, 1956; *Eulogy to Constantin the Philosopher,* oratorio, 1971); 5 symphonies (1947, 1951, 1954, 1958, 1959), Concerto grosso (piano, strings, percussion, 1949), *Symphonic variations* (1951), *Tempo concertato I* (1967), *II* (1969), Violin Concerto (1971) and other orchestral works; chamber music (4 string quartets, 1948–56; Cello Sonata, 1957; *Neues Stück für 10 Instrumente,* 1988); piano pieces (*Movimenti,* 1964).

Illica, Luigi (b. Castell'Arquato, near Piacenza, 9 May 1857; d. Colombarone, 16 Dec. 1919). Librettist. Left school and went to sea for four years, also fighting the Turks; then a journalist. In 1882 he published his first books; 1883, first of several plays, some highly successful, often satirical; 1886, first libretto, *Il vassallo di Szigeth* (in collaboration with Pozza, set by Smareglia; Vienna, 1889). From 1890 to 1911 he was primarily a librettist. He wrote librettos for Catalani's *Wally* (1892), Giordano's *Andrea Chenier* (1896), Mascagni's *Iris* (1898), among others; most notable was his collaboration with Giocosa on Puccini's *Bohème* (1896), *Tosca* (1900), and *Madama Butterfly* (1904).

Imbrie, Andrew (Welsh) (b. New York, 6 Apr. 1921). Composer and pianist. He studied piano with Leo Ornstein in Philadelphia (1930–42) and performed Saint-Saëns's *Carnival of the Animals* with the Philadelphia Orchestra in 1933. He studied composition with Sessions, 1938–48 (privately, at Princeton, and at Berkeley). His First String Quartet, produced when he was a senior at Princeton, won the New York Music Critics Circle Award (1944) and was recorded by the Juilliard Quartet; his Third String Quartet (1957) makes use of twelve-tone procedures. He was appointed an instructor at Berkeley after completing his master's degree, but delayed teaching for the two years that he spent at the American Academy in Rome (1947–49); he became a full professor in 1960.

Works: 2 operas; 3 symphonies and concertos for violin, cello, flute, and piano as well as other orchestral music; a large number of chamber pieces (including string quartets; *Dandelion Wine,* oboe, clarinet, string quartet, and piano, 1967; *Pilgrimage,* flute, clarinet, violin, cello, piano, and percussion, 1983); some piano music (Sonata, 1947; *Short Story,* 1982); an anthem, "Let All the World" (soprano, alto, tenor, bass, brass, percussion, and organ, 1971), a Requiem (in memoriam John H. Imbrie, soprano, chorus, and orchestra, 1984), and other choral music; a few songs.

India, Sigismondo d' (b. Palermo, ca. 1582; d. Modena?, before 19 Apr. 1629). Composer. Traveled among various Italian courts for about a decade before settling in Turin in 1611 as director of chamber music at the ducal court of Savoy; remained there until 1623; from 1626 held a post at the Este court in Modena. His sacred works include one Mass and one sacred drama (both lost) and many motets (most contained in 3 books published in Venice, 1610–27). Better known, however, are his secular compositions, all vocal: books of polyphonic madrigals (some with continuo) and of villanellas, one opera (*Zalizura,* incomplete), and, most important, many monodies and a number of duets (nearly all with continuo).

Bibl.: *Sigismondo d'India,* Musiche rinascimentali siciliane, 9, 10 . . . (1980–).

Indy, (Paul Marie Théodore) Vincent d' (b. Paris, 27 Mar. 1851; d. there, 2 Dec. 1931). Composer. From an old Cévénol family, ennobled (Vincent was a vicomte, later comte, but used neither title) under Charles X, to whose line it remained loyal after the 1830 Revolution. His mother dying at his birth, he was raised by his fiercely devoted but tyrannical paternal grandmother, who imbued him with uncompromising principles of high seriousness, but also a narrowness and dogmaticism in his views. From 1864 he had piano lessons from Louis Diémer; 1865–73, studied harmony, later counterpoint, orchestration with Albert Lavignac, beginning to compose songs (one published 1870) and piano pieces; 1869–72, worked on a grand opera, never completed, on Hugo's *Les burgraves.* He greatly admired Wagner and visited Munich and Bayreuth frequently for performances; also made friends with Liszt at Weimar, 1873. A long admiration for Beethoven's music eventually culminated in a book in 1911. From September 1870 to March 1871 he served in the National Guard, defending Paris, publishing a book on his battalion's experiences (1872). In 1871–73 he studied law to please his family, but was increasingly drawn to music. Parts of a symphony were tried out by the Pasdeloup orchestra in 1871–73; in 1871 he became the youngest member of the new Société nationale de musique, which was to be a major force in French music in the following decades. The death of his grandmother in February 1872 removed the principal restraint on his doing as he pleased (although his father's opposition kept him from marrying his cousin until 1875). Urged by his friend Duparc, he began studying fugue privately with Franck in fall 1872, also becoming an auditor in Franck's organ class at the conservatory and a regular conservatory student in 1874–75. (He was to revere Franck and his musical principles throughout life.) He also increased his musical skills as percussionist in orchestras, church organist, piano accompanist, choral director, eventually also becoming a good orchestra conductor.

By the late 1870s d'Indy began to emerge as a major figure in French music. He composed large, serious works. In 1880 he conducted the premiere of his *Wallenstein* (3 concert overtures after Schiller); in 1884 *Le chant de la cloche,* a dramatic symphony with voices (after Schiller), won the Prix de Paris; 1887, premiere of *Symphonie sur un thème montagnard,* op. 25, his only work still performed frequently. In 1886 he led a takeover of the Société nationale, ousting Saint-Saëns (thereafter his enemy) and installing Franck as figurehead president.

The decade beginning in the mid-1890s was perhaps the apex of his career. This is the period of the first 2 of his 3 major operas (all to his own librettos): *Fervaal,* composed 1887–95 (Brussels, 1897; Paris, Opéra-comique, 1898); *L'étranger* (Brussels and Paris Opéra, 1903); also the *Istar* Variations (1897), Second Symphony (1902–3), *Jour de l'été à la montagne* (1906). From 1897 he taught composition at the Schola cantorum (this eventually resulted in his *Traité de composition,* Paris, 1903–33); his pupils included Roussel and Séverac. After a financial crisis in 1904, he was made director, the school increasingly becoming an embodiment of his personality and ideals. He also taught orchestration (1912–19) and conducting (1914–29) at the conservatory; appeared widely in western Europe as a conductor, also visiting Russia (1904, 1907, 1908) and the U.S. (1905, 1921–22). The Dreyfus Affair exacerbated d'Indy's conservative social and political beliefs, which ultimately found expression in his third major opera, *Le légende de Saint Christophe,* which he described as a "drame antijuif." Composed in 1908–15, it was produced only once (Paris Opéra, 1920). Increasingly out of step with contemporary trends, and increasingly subject to attack, first from Debussyist critics (especially Émile Vuillermoz), later from "Les six," he remained uncompromisingly loyal to his artistic ideals and active as musician and composer until the end of his life.

Other works: symphonic poems, Concerto for flute and cello, op. 89; 3 string quartets, String Sextet, 2 piano trios, Piano Quintet op. 81, Piano Quartet, violin and cello sonatas; choral music, songs; many piano pieces. Also an editor of early music (Destouches, Monteverdi, Gluck, Rameau). From the mid-1890s he was a prolific writer of criticism, essays, polemics.

Bibl.: Leon Vallas, *Vincent d'Indy* (Paris, 1946–50). G. B. Paul, "Rameau, d'Indy, and French Nationalism," *MQ* 58 (1972): 46.

Infantas, Fernando de las (b. Córdoba, 1534; d. ca. 1610). Composer and theologian. He went to Rome in 1571 or 1572, supported by a pension from Philip II, and remained there until about 1597. Many of his compositions, all written before his ordination in 1584, are based on Gregorian melodies. They include a set of 101 counterpoints on a single brief Gregorian melody and a large number of motets, most published in 3 numbered books.

Ingegneri, Marc'Antonio [Marco Antonio, Marc Antonio, Marcantonio] (b. Verona, ca. 1547; d. Cremona, 1 July 1592). Composer. Probably a student of Vincenzo Ruffo while a choirboy at Verona Cathedral. Moved to Cremona well before 1572, where he was prefect of music (by 1578) and later *maestro di cappella* (by 1579) at the cathedral. His works are generally conservative in style and include Masses, motets (many based on plainsong melodies), 27 responsories for Holy Week (long attributed to Palestrina), and numerous books of madrigals. Monteverdi was his pupil.

Inghelbrecht, Désiré Émile (b. Paris, 17 Sept. 1880; d. there, 14 Feb. 1965). Composer and conductor. The child of musicians, he studied violin but was expelled from the Paris Conservatory; played in theater orchestras from 1896. He conducted at the Théâtre des arts from 1908 and was appointed director of music at the Théâtre Champs Elysées in 1913; in 1934 he founded the French National Radio Orchestra; and from 1945 to 1950 he conducted at the Paris Opéra. He composed in the styles of Fauré and Debussy, whose friendship and support he enjoyed; some works employ folk songs. He wrote operas, operettas, and ballets; orchestral music (*Pour le jour de la première neige au vieux Japon,* 1908; *Iberiana,* with solo violin, 1949); a Requiem (soloists, chorus, and orchestra, 1941); chamber music; piano pieces (*La Nursery,* 5 vols., 1905–11); choral music and songs.

Insanguine, Giacomo (Antonio Francesco Paolo Michele) (b. Monopoli, near Bari, 22 Mar. 1728; d. Naples, 1 Feb. 1795). Composer. He studied at the Conservatorio dei Poveri di Gesù Cristo (1743) and with Girolamo Abos and Francesco Durante at the Conservatorio di S. Onofrio (1743–55). His first opera, *Lo funnaco revotato,* was performed in Naples in 1756; it was followed by at least 20 more stage works, including *L'osteria di Marechiaro* (Naples, 1768); *La finta semplice* (Naples, 1769); *La Didone abbandonata* (Naples, 1770); *La dama bizzarra* (Naples, 1770); *Merope* (Venice, 1772); *Medonte* (Naples, 1779); and *Calipso* (Naples, 1782). In 1767 he became a teacher at S. Onofrio, in 1774 second *maestro.* He was made *maestro di cappella* at the Tesoro di S. Genuaro in 1781, and in 1785 S. Onofrio placed him in the position of *primo maestro.* He also composed sacred music (including 6 known Masses); a cantata, *La speranza;* and numerous "insertion arias" for operas by other composers.

Ioannidis, Yannis (b. Athens, 8 June 1930). Composer. He studied at the Odeon Conservatory in Athens (1946–54), then in Vienna at the Academy of Music, with Karl Walter (organ) and Otto Siegl (composition). From 1963 to 1968 he directed the music program at Pierce College in Athens. In 1968 he settled in Caracas, where he was professor of composition at the Instituto nacional de cultura y bellas artes (from 1969), and directed its chamber orchestra. In 1971 he founded the Orquesta de camera de Caracas; the same year he was named professor at the Universidad metropolitana and organ instructor at the Caracas Conservatory. He returned to Athens in 1976. His early music manifested serial techniques; this later gave way to "free atonality." Works include choral music (*Europa Cantat III,* 1967); orchestral music (*Symphonic Triptych,* 1963; *Tropic,* 1968; *Transitions,* 1971); chamber and instrumental music (*Peristrofi,* 8 strings, 1965; *Arioso,* 9 strings, 1967; *Versi,* clarinet, 1967; *Actinia,* wind quintet, 1969; *Seven Greek Folk Melodies,* recorders, 1970; *Nocturne,* piano, 1972).

Ippolitov-Ivanov [Ivanov], **Mikhail Mikhaylovich** (b. Gatchina, 19 Nov. 1859; d. Moscow, 28 Jan. 1935). Composer and conductor. He entered the St. Petersburg Conservatory in 1875; moved to Tbilisi in 1882, where he conducted the opera and directed the music school. In 1893 he became a professor at the Moscow Conservatory, where he remained until his death; he also served as director there (1905–22). He had a distinguished conducting career, directing the Russian Choral Society (1895–1901), the Mamontov Opera (1898–1906), the Zimin Opera, and the Bolshoi Theater (from 1925). His musical style, which changed little during his long life, shows the influence of oriental folk song; he is best known outside Russia for his *Caucasian Sketches;* his students included Vasilenko and Glier.

Works: operas (*Ruf'* [Ruth] op. 6, 1887; *Asya* op. 30, 1900; *Izmena* [Treachery] op. 43, 1910; *Olye iz Nordlanda* [Ole from Nordland], 1916; *Zhenit'ba* [The Marriage] op. 70, completion of opera by Mussorgsky, 1931; *Poslednyaya barrikada* [The Last Barricade], 1933); orchestral works (*Yar-khmel'* op. 1, "spring overture," 1882; *Kavkazskiye eskizï* [Caucasian Sketches] op. 10, 1894; *Iveriya* op. 42, 1896; Symphony in E minor op. 46, 1908; *Armyanskaya rapsodiya* [Armenian Rhapsody] op. 48, 1895; *Mtsïri* op. 54, 1929; *Iz pesen Ossiana* [From Ossian's Songs] op. 56, 1925; *Tyurkskiye fragmentï* [Turkish Fragments] op. 62, 1930; *V stepyakh Turmenistana* [On the Steppes of Turkmenistan] op. 65 (1935); *Muzïkal'nïye kartinki Uzbeskistana* [Musical Pictures of Uzbekistan] op. 69); choral works (*Gimn trudu* [Hymn to Labor], chorus, orchestra, brass band, op. 59, 1934); chamber music; songs.

Iradier [Yradier], **Sebastián** (b. Sauciego, Álava, Spain, 20 Jan. 1809; d. Vitoria, Spain, 6 Dec. 1865). Composer. Worked in Madrid, publishing songs there in the 1840s; said to have been professor of solfège at the conservatory and to have visited Cuba, which may have left traces in his songs; in the 1850s, lived in Paris; said to have been singing master to the Empress

Eugénie. In the early 1860s Heugel published collections of his Spanish songs, some of which were extremely popular (especially "La paloma," called a *canción americana,* and "Ay Chiquita!") and republished in Germany, the U.S., etc. Bizet based Carmen's Habanera on Iradier's "El arreglito," apparently thinking it a folk song.

Bibl.: Dionisio Preciado, "Sebastián de Iradier (1809–1865), organista y 'sacristán mayor' en Salvatierra de Álava," *Revista de musicología* 7 (1984): 125–70.

Ireland, John (Nicholson) (b. Bowdoin, Cheshire, 13 Aug. 1879; d. Rock Mill, Washington, Sussex, 12 June 1962). Composer and pianist. He studied at the Royal College of Music (1893–1901) with Charles Stanford (composition) and Frederick Cliffe (piano). During the next two decades he was organist and choirmaster at several churches, chiefly at St. Luke's Church in Chelsea, where he served from 1904 to 1926. In 1905 he received a B.Mus. from Durham Univ., and in 1932, a D.Mus. from the same institution. Among his pupils at the Royal College of Music, where he taught composition from 1923, were Ernest Moeran and Benjamin Britten. His principal works date from the period 1915–40, and include the Second Violin Sonata (1917), the Cello Sonata (1923); the Sonatina for piano (1927); the Piano Concerto in E♭ (1930); *Legend,* piano and orchestra (1933); and the choral *These Things Shall Be* (1936–37). When he retired around 1940, he moved first to Guernsey, then Sussex. He stopped composing shortly after World War II; his last work was the score to the film *The Overlanders* (1947).

Other works include choral music (*Greater Love Hath No Man,* motet, soloists, chorus, organ, 1912–24); many services (*Morning Service,* 1907–20); part songs; song cycles (*Songs of a Wayfarer,* 1903–5; *The Land of Lost Content,* 1920–21; *We'll to the Woods No More,* 1926–27); orchestral works (*The Forgotten Rite,* 1913; *Mai-Dun,* "symphonic rhapsody," 1921; *A Downland Suite,* brass instruments, 1932; *A London Overture,* 1936; *Concertino Pastorale,* strings, 1939; *Satyricon,* 1946). His chamber music includes 2 string quartets (1895; 1897); 3 piano trios (no. 1, *Phantasie Trio,* A minor, 1906; no. 2 in E, 1917; no. 3 in E, 1938); 2 sonatas for violin and piano (no. 1, 1919; rev. 1927 and 1944; no. 2, 1917); *Fantasy-Sonata,* clarinet and piano (1943); organ music; piano works, including the Sonata (1920) and some 40 "lyric pieces."

Bibl.: Ernest Chapman, *John Ireland: A Catalogue of Published Works and Recordings* (London, 1968). Nigel Townshend, "The Achievement of John Ireland," *ML* 24 (1943): 65–74. John Longmire, *John Ireland: Portrait of a Friend* (London, 1969). Vernon L. Yenne, "Three Twentieth-Century English Song Composers: Peter Warlock, E. J. Moeran, and John Ireland" (diss., Univ. of Illinois, 1969). Muriel V. Searle, *John Ireland: The Man and His Music* (Tunbridge Wells, 1979).

Irino, Yoshirō (b. Vladivostok, 13 Nov. 1921; d. Tokyo, 28 June 1980). Composer. He played the clarinet and studied composition privately with Saburō Moroi at the same time that he studied economics at Tokyo Univ. (1941–43). He was employed by the Bank of Tokyo and spent time in the navy before 1946, when he made music his profession. He worked as a music editor (1949–54) and then as a teacher at the Tōhō Gaknen School of Music, where he was appointed director in 1960. In 1973 he became professor of composition at the Tokyo Music College. He organized the Institute of Twentieth-Century Music in 1957.

He is known as the first Japanese composer for whom twelve-tone technique figured prominently. String Sextet (1950) and *Sinfonietta* for small orchestra (1953) are among his early serial works. He wrote music for traditional Japanese instruments (*Music for 2 Koto,* 1957) and for less conventional ensembles (*Quintet,* clarinet, alto saxophone, trumpet, piano, and cello, 1958). *Wandlungen* (2 shakuhachi and orchestra, 1973) was commissioned by the Koussevitzky Foundation and attempts to combine traditional Japanese music with serial music. Other works include an opera (*Aya no Tsuzumi,* 1975); an operetta (*The Man in Fear of God,* 1954); 4 radio dramas; a television opera; 3 dance dramas; 8 choral pieces; 16 orchestral/ensemble pieces (2 symphonies, 1948 and 1964; *Music for Harpsichord, Percussion, and 19 Strings,* 1963; *Strömung,* flute, harp, percussion, 1973; *Klänge,* percussion, 1976); many pieces for a variety of chamber ensembles (*Duo concertante,* alto saxophone, koto, 1979).

Irving, Robert (Augustine) (b. Winchester, England, 28 Aug. 1913; d. there, 13 Sept. 1991). Conductor. He studied at Winchester College, at New College, Oxford (B.Mus., 1935), and with Sir Malcolm Sargent and Constant Lambert at the Royal College of Music. He was named associate conductor of the BBC Scottish Orchestra (1946–49) and music director of the Sadler's Wells Ballet (1949–58). Conductor of the New York City Ballet from 1958; was regarded as one of the leading ballet conductors of his day.

Isaac [Ysaac, Isaak], **Heinrich** [Henricus] [Arrigo il Tedesco] (b. Flanders, ca. 1450; d. Florence, 26 Mar. 1517). Composer. Although the majority of his professional life was spent in Italy, particularly Florence, his influence was greatest in Germanic lands, where he lived intermittently from 1497, when he became court composer to Maximilian I. Of his students, the most notable was Ludwig Senfl.

His long association with Italy began when he entered the service of the Medici in Florence around 1485 as a singer in the Cantori di S. Giovanni, a group that supplied polyphonic music for the cathedral and other local churches. His work for Maximilian I, from 1497 until his death, did not require continuous residence at the court but allowed stays of considerable length in various German cities, in northern Italy, and in Florence. Nevertheless, his position as imperial court composer and the many pieces he wrote for the Hofkapelle brought the Netherlandish style of music to German-speaking areas.

Among his works are about 40 Mass Ordinaries, half cyclic (in the Netherlandish tradition), half based on liturgically appropriate plainsong melodies (in the German tradition); almost 100 cycles of the Proper of the Mass (following Germanic liturgical custom; most published posthumously in the 3-volume *Choralis constantinus*); over 50 independent motets; and nearly 100 secular songs, including French chansons, a few Italian frottole, and a large number of German Tenorlieder.

Bibl.: *Opera omnia, CMM* 65 (1974–). Martin Staehelin, *Die Messen Heinrich Isaacs* (Bern, 1978). Martin Picker, *Henricus Isaac: A Guide to Research* (New York, 1991).

Isamitt, Carlos (b. Rengo, Colchagua, Chile, 13 Mar. 1887; d. Santiago, 2 July 1974). Composer. Studied composition at the National Conservatory, violin privately, and painting at the Santiago School of Fine Arts; studied in Europe during 1924–27, returning as director of the School of Fine Arts, 1927–28. Later served as an official in the Education Ministry, taught at the National Conservatory, and was president of the Association of Chilean Composers. Pursued ethnomusicological research among the Araucanian Indians, whose musical style he partially incorporated into his own work; he also used twelve-tone techniques. He was an award-winning painter as well as composer and contributed many articles on the arts to journals throughout the Americas. Works include a ballet and other symphonic music, a violin concerto, chamber music, many piano pieces, and songs.

Bibl.: *Composers of the Americas* 13 (Washington, D.C., 1967): 62–71 [includes works list].

Ishii, Kan (b. Tokyo, 30 Mar. 1921). Composer. Son of dancer and ballet promoter Bac Ishii. At the Musashino School of Music in Tokyo he studied piano and composition (1939–43), the latter with Taijiro Goh and Tomojirō Ikenouchi. After World War II he was pianist in his father's dance company; in 1952 he went to Munich to study with Carl Orff at the Hochschule für Musik. Returning to Japan in 1954, he was appointed professor of composition at the Tōhō Gakuen School of Music, and in 1966 at the Aichi Prefectural Arts Univ. in Nagoya. From 1964 to 1970 he was president of the Japan Composers' Federation. His music shows the influence of the works of Orff and Debussy; of chief importance are his ballet scores, including *Kami to bayādere* (Tokyo, 1950); *Ketsueki* [Blood] (Tokyo, 1951); *Ningen tanjō* [Birth of a Human Being] (1954); and *Hakai* [Sin against Buddha] (1965). He has also composed operas (*Kaguya-hime* [Princess Kaguya], 1963; *Kesa to Moritō,* 1968; *Kantomi,* 1981; *Aojishi* [The Blue Lion], operetta, 1989); orchestral works (*Prelude,* 1949; *Yama,* 1953); film scores; choral/vocal music (*Ōinaru Akita* [Akita the Great], soprano, chorus, orchestra, 1974); instrumental music (Piano Sonata, 1948; Viola Sonata, 1960).

Ishii, Maki (b. Tokyo, 28 May 1936). Composer. Son of dancer Bac Ishii and brother of Kan Ishii. After private study with Akira Ifukube and Tomojirō Ikenouchi (1952–58), he went to Berlin, where he was a student at the Hochschule (1958–61) under Boris Blacher and Josef Rufer. Back in Japan, from 1962 to 1965 he was an important figure in encouraging new-music activities in Japan; he was also active in the N.H.K. electronic studio. He returned to Berlin in 1966–67. His music attempts to fuse elements of Western and Japanese musical traditions. Orchestral works include *Expression* (string orchestra, 1967), *Kyō-ō* (piano, orchestra, tape, 1968), *Kyō-sō* (percussion, orchestra, 1969), *Dipol* (1971), Violin Concerto (1978), *Translucent Vision* (1982), *Gioh* (Japanese flute, orchestra, 1984), *Gedatsu* (version 1, Japanese flute, orchestra; version 2, recorder, orchestra; 1985), *Intrada* (1986); chamber music (*Nucleus,* biwa, harp, shakukachi, flute, 1973; *Anime amare,* harp, percussion, tape, 1974; *Concertante,* marimba, 6 percussionists; *13 Drums,* solo percussion, 1986); tape works including the ballets *Samsara* (1968) and *Yukionna* (1971); many works for Japanese instruments alone (*Musik für Shakuhachi,* 1970).

Ishiketa, Mareo (b. Wakayama, 26 Nov. 1916). Composer. His composition teacher was Kan'ichi Shimofusa; in 1939 he graduated from the Tokyo School of Music. He became an instructor at the school in 1946, and in 1952 professor of composition at the National Univ. of Fine Arts in Tokyo. In 1947 he joined the new-music group Shinsei Kai; his works include operas (*Sotoba Komachi,* Tokyo, 1960; *Kakekomi,* Tokyo, 1968); choral/vocal works (*Sen no koe, sen no kokoro* [Thousand Voices, Thousand Hearts], 1962); *Futasu no hanashi,* 1963); orchestral works (2 symphonies, 1956 and 1965; *Concerto for Koto,* 1969); and chamber music (String Quartet, 1947; 2 cello sonatas, 1946 and 1964; *Mue no uta,* ensemble of Japanese instruments, 1969).

Isidore of Seville (b. Cartagena?, ca. 559; d. Seville, 4 Apr. 636). Cleric and encyclopedist. Archbishop of Seville from about 599. Of his numerous writings, those touching on music are his *Etymologiarum sive Originum libri xx* (ed. Wallace M. Lindsay, Oxford, 1911; partial trans., *SR,* pp. 93–100; *CCT* 12 [1980]: 11–20) and *De ecclesiasticis officiis.* The *Etymologiarum* treats music as number, largely following Cassiodorus and St. Augustine; both books discuss music in the Divine Office.

Ísólfsson, Páll (b. Stokkseyri, Iceland, 12 Oct. 1893; d. Reykjavík, 23 Nov. 1974). Composer and organist. His father was also a composer and organist; from 1913 Páll studied organ in Leipzig with Karl Straube. Eventually he was made assistant organist at the Thomaskirche. Later he studied further with Joseph Bonnet in Paris. From 1930 he was director of the Reykjavík College of Music and of the music department of Icelandic Radio; from 1939 to 1968 he was also organist at Reykjavík Cathedral. His musical style is closely allied to that of the late Romantics. Works include the *Althing Festival Cantata,* soloists, chorus, and orchestra (1930); *Skálholtsljódh Cantata* (1956); *Lyric Suite,* orchestra; many organ works (*Introduction and Passacaglia,* 1938; *Chaconne,* 1948); songs, piano works.

Bibl.: Amanda M. Burt, *Iceland's Twentieth-Century Composers and a Listing of Their Works* (Annandale, Va., 1977).

Isouard, Nicolas [Nicolò] (b. Malta, 6 Dec. 1775; d. Paris, 23 Mar. 1818). Composer. His father was a merchant from Marseilles; young Nicolas was sent to school in Paris, where he studied mathematics, Latin, and music. Fleeing France and the Revolution in 1789, he returned to Malta, where he worked for his father; there he continued to pursue musical studies with Maltese musicians. Later he studied in Palermo with Nicolas of Amendola, and in Naples with Nicola Sala. After his first opera, *L'avviso ai maritati,* was performed in Florence in 1794, he began devoting most of his energy to music. During the next 20 years he composed some 40 opere serie, opere buffe, and opéras comiques. Around 1795 he was given the post of organist at St. John of Jerusalem, Malta; he remained there until 1798, when the French invaded Malta. Later he returned to Paris, where he remained for most of the rest of his life. In 1802 he cofounded, with Méhul, Cherubini, Boieldieu, and others, Le magasin de musique, a publishing venture. He is remembered chiefly as one of the most successful composers of the mature opéra comique; his best works were *Le petit page* (Paris, 1800), *La statue* (1802), *Le baiser et la quittance* (1803), *Cendrillon* (1810), *Le billet de loterie* (1811), *Joconde* (1814), and *Les deux Maris* (1816). He also composed sacred music; cantatas (*La paix,* 1802?); solo vocal music, and vocal chamber music.

Istomin, Eugene (George) (b. New York, 26 Nov. 1925). Pianist. He studied with Kiriena Siloti and at Curtis Institute with Rudolf Serkin and Mieczysław Horszowski; in 1943 he made his orchestral debut with the Philadelphia Orchestra, and won the Leventritt Award the same year, leading to a performance with the New York Philharmonic. He performed with the Adolf Busch Chamber Players and embarked on a successful concert career; in 1961 he formed a trio with Isaac Stern and Leonard Rose.

Ištvan, Miloslav (b. Olomouc, 2 Sept. 1928; d. Brno, 20 Jan. 1990). Composer. From 1948 to 1952 he studied with Jaroslav Kvapil at the Janáček Music Academy in Brno; from 1956 he was assistant lecturer in music there and, from 1966, full lecturer. In 1963 he joined the experimental Tvůrčí Skupina A (Composers' Group A). His early music took its impetus from folk music; by the 1960s he was employing serial, aleatoric, and electronic techniques. Works include orchestral music: Concerto for horn, piano, and strings (1949); *Československá suita* (1951); Symphony (1952); Concerto-Symphony, piano and orchestra (1958); *Balada o jihu* [Ballad of the South] (1960); *Concertino,* violin, chamber orchestra (1961); *Shakespearean Variations* (1975). Choral/vocal works: *Zaklínání času* [Conjuration of Time], speakers, orchestra (1967); *Já, Jákob,* chamber cantata (1968); *Lásky horlivé toužení* (1974). Chamber/instrumental works: *6 Studies,* chamber ensemble (1964); String Quartet (1962–63); *Dodekameron,* 12 instruments (1964); trio for clarinet, violin, and cello (1985); 2 piano sonatas; *Odyssea lidického dítěte,* piano (1963); organ music; works for tape (*Avete morituri,* 1970).

Ito, Ryūta (b. Kure City, 4 Mar. 1922). Composer. He attended medical school at the Univ. of Tokyo; after receiving his medical degree in 1955 he began studying music in earnest, with Tomojirō Ikenouchi, Shiro Fukai, and Saburō Moroi. He then taught pharmacology at Toho Univ. and became an active composer. In 1952 he joined the Japanese Society for Contemporary Music. Much of his music combines Eastern and Western elements and instruments; compositions include theater music (*The Court of Judgment,* chamber opera, 1954); orchestral works (*Two Moments,* 1947; *Divertissement,* 1950; *Ostinato concertanto,* piano, orchestra, 1957; Concerto, Japanese flute and orchestra, 1958; *Suzuka,* suite, 1959); vocal music (*Les cloches,* Japanese instruments, male chorus, chamber ensemble, 1971; *Abrasion of a Life,* mixed chorus, 1984); *Duets 1 and 2,* shakuhachi, juschichi-gen (1988).

Iturbi, José (b. Valencia, Spain, 28 Nov. 1895; d. Hollywood, Calif., 28 June 1980). Pianist and conductor. He studied at the Valencia Conservatory and the Paris Conservatory; taught at the Geneva Conservatory (1919–23) and toured Europe, South America, and the U.S., where he eventually settled. He appeared in a number of films; his performances of Spanish music were especially noteworthy. Iturbi was appointed conductor of the Rochester Philharmonic (1936–44); he often appeared with his sister Amparo, also a pianist.

Iturriaga, Enrique (b. Lima, 3 Apr. 1918). Composer. Studied at the Sas-Rosay Academy, Lima, and under Rodolfo Holzmann at the National Conservatory; received instruction from Honegger in Paris in 1950. He has served as composition instructor at the Lima Conservatory, where he became director in 1973, and has taught composition and ethnomusicology at the Univ. of San Marcos. An interest in music education spurred him to study the U.S. system and attend various international conferences on the topic. As a composer he has integrated European and indigenous elements; works include *Preludio y danza* (1954), *Vivencias* (1965), and *Homenaje a Stravinsky* (1972), all for orchestra, as well as other vocal and chamber music.

Ivanovs, Jānis (b. Preili, Latvia, 9 Oct. 1906; d. Riga, 27 Mar. 1983). Composer. His musical studies took place at the Riga Conservatory; from 1931 he worked for Latvian Radio, and in 1944 he received a post at the Latvian Conservatory. He was appointed professor of composition there in 1955. In 1950–51 he was president of the Soviet Latvian Composers' Union. He composed some 20 symphonies (no. 4, Atlantida, 1941; no.

6, Latgales simfonija, 1949; no. 10, ca. 1963; no. 12, Sinfonia energica, 1967; no. 15, Sinfonia da camera, 1971; no. 17, 1976); several symphonic poems and suites (*Zilie ezeri* [The Blue Lakes], 1935; *Rāzna,* band, 1940; *Salna pavasarā* [Frost in Spring], 1955; *Poema luttuoso,* strings, 1966; a cello concerto, 1938; a violin concerto, 1951; chamber music (3 string quartets, 1933–61); piano works (*Sonata brevis,* 1962; *24 Sketches,* 1967–72).

Ives, Charles (Edward) (b. Danbury, Conn., 20 Oct. 1874; d. New York, 19 May 1954). Composer. He grew up in Danbury, where his father, George E. Ives (1845–94), directed bands, choirs, and orchestras and taught theory and a number of instruments. Ives's father had an intense curiosity about aspects of music such as microtones, bitonality, and acoustics that he shared with Charles and his brother J. Moss (1876–1939), who became a lawyer. Ear-training exercises such as singing in one key while being accompanied in another were commonplace in the Ives household. In addition to his experimental outlook, Charles Ives received from his father a grounding in Bach's music and an appreciation of American vernacular musics. He held a salaried position as an organist at age 14 and had begun to compose and play percussion in his father's bands even earlier; the earliest of his Psalm settings were composed before 1894. That year was Ives's first at Yale, where he took music courses with Parker; throughout his Yale years he was organist at Center Church (New Haven), where the choirmaster was Cornelius Griggs, whose support of his compositional efforts Ives particularly valued after his father died in November 1894. Under Parker's guidance Ives wrote the First Symphony as well as numerous contrapuntal exercises and resettings of well-known song texts. While a Yale student he also composed his First String Quartet, over 40 songs, and several marches, overtures, anthems, part songs, and organ pieces.

After graduation from Yale Ives lived in New York, sharing a Manhattan apartment with several classmates and working in the actuarial department of the Mutual Insurance Company. In 1899 he met Julian Myrick (1880–1969), with whom he was to found his own insurance company in 1906; he retired from the business in 1930. For the first few years after he left Yale he had continued as an organist (at First Presbyterian Church, Bloomfield, N.J., 1898–1900; then at Central Presbyterian Church, New York, until June 1902). After relinquishing his organ position, Ives gained a little more time for composition, always confined to nights and weekends. Although his failure to compose after 1926 is surely in part attributable to his health problems (he had a severe heart attack in 1918), there are indications that he had run out of creative energy as well as physical stamina: Mrs. Ives (Harmony Twitchell, whom he married in 1909) reported that in 1926 he had "said he couldn't seem to compose any more—nothing went well—nothing sounded right." In 1947 Ives received the Pulitzer Prize for his Third Symphony.

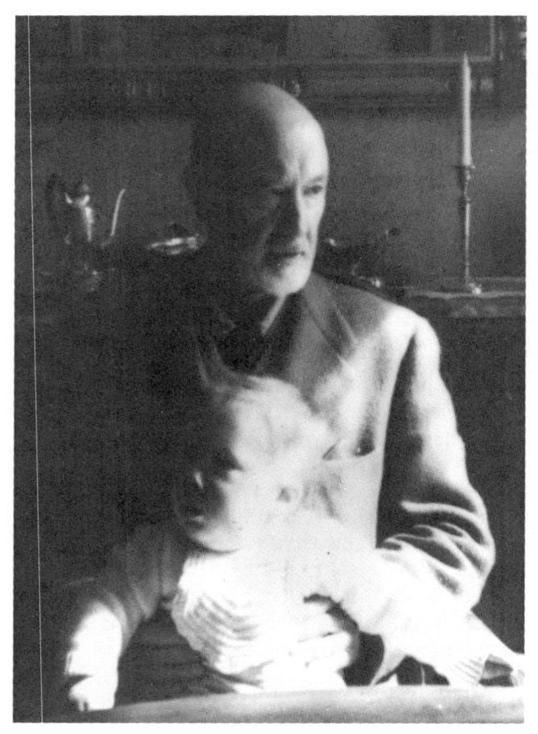

Charles Ives with his grandson, 1946.

Ives's independent explorations of atonality and serial procedures, polymetric and polyrhythmic constructions, experiments with quarter-tones, use of space as an important compositional element, and his layered polyphony and multidimensionality all constitute evidence of a curiosity and independence of thought. His collage techniques have descendants in the works of Berio and others. His frequent quotation of American tunes (hymn tunes, marches, songs of Stephen Foster) shows how immersed he was in his own culture and illustrates his "citizen" approach to musical material. An improvisational attitude is said to affect all of his mature work; his own changes to works in performance and in successive manuscript versions are reported by many musicians who performed or edited his music; but many experienced performers and editors have concluded that Ives's notation, while complex, is ordinarily very precise.

Ives's works were rarely performed in his lifetime, nor were they often published; but his supposed indifference to public appreciation may be doubted. He published and distributed not only the *Essays before a Sonata* but also the collection of *114 Songs* and the Concord Sonata. He is known to have sent his music willingly to those he thought were truly interested and able (e.g., Lou Harrison) and to have taken some trouble over the few early performances (inviting percussion players to his home for coaching in the case of a partial performance of the Fourth Symphony in 1927 under Goossens). In any event, he made considerable anonymous financial contributions to Cowell's publishing and performance activities from the 1930s until his death and thus is known to have been concerned about the need for public presentation of new music.

His music is not unrelated to 19th-century American composition: both he and Foster, for example, wrote songs characterized by disjunct melodic lines, optional instruments and choruses, parallel fifths, odd chord spacings, unusual dissonances, and variable accompaniment patterns. Ives may have been a radical innovator, but his subject matter was often a nostalgic reflection on the New England of his boyhood. The complicated state of his manuscripts, incorporating many undatable revisions (which often add dissonances) makes any final judgment on his supposed innovations difficult.

Works: 4 symphonies (1895–98, 1900–1902, 1904, 1910–16), *The Unanswered Question* and *Central Park in the Dark* (1906), and many other works for orchestra and band; string quartets, violin sonatas, and other chamber music mainly for strings; organ and piano works (including the Second Piano Sonata "Concord, Mass., 1840–60," 1910–15, and 3 Quarter-Tone Pieces, 2 pianos, 1923–24); choral music and some 150 songs.

Writings: *Essays before a Sonata and Other Writings*, ed. Howard Boatwright (New York, 1962). *Memos*, ed. John Kirkpatrick (New York, 1972).

Bibl.: Henry Cowell and Sidney Cowell, *Charles Ives and His Music* (New York, 1955; 2nd ed., 1969). Dominique-René de Lerma, *Charles Ives, 1874–1954: A Bibliography of His Music* (Kent, Ohio, 1970). Richard Warren, *Charles E. Ives: Discography* (New Haven, 1972). H. Wiley Hitchcock, *Ives* (London, 1977; R: 1983). H. Wiley Hitchcock and Vivian Perlis, eds., *An Ives Celebration: Papers and Panels of the Charles Ives Centennial Festival Conference* (New Haven, 1977). J. Peter Burkholder, *Charles Ives: The Ideas behind the Music* (New Haven, 1985). Vivian Perlis, *Charles Ives Papers* (New Haven, 1983). Maynard Solomon, "Charles Ives: Some Questions of Veracity," *JAMS* 50 (1987): 443–70. Geoffrey Holden Block, *Charles Ives: A Bio-Bibliography* (New York, 1988). Stuart Feder, *Charles Ives, "My Father's Song": A Psychoanalytic Biography* (New Haven, 1992). Larry Starr, *A Union of Diversities: Style in the Music of Charles Ives* (New York, 1992).

Ivey, Jean Eichelberger (b. Washington, D.C., 3 July 1923). Composer and pianist. She was educated at Trinity College, Peabody Conservatory (M.M. in piano, 1946), the Eastman School (M.M. in composition, 1956), and the Univ. of Toronto (D.Mus. in composition, 1972). She taught at Peabody throughout her career and founded the electronic music studio there in 1969; performed widely in Europe, Mexico, and the U.S.; and wrote articles on electronic music. Her early compositions were tonal and neoclassical, drawing especially on the styles of Bartók and Ravel; in the 1960s she began to explore the serial and electronic procedures that remained important in her later compositions. She wrote much vocal music, often setting her own texts.

Works: *Birthmark* (opera in 1 act, Ivey after Hawthorne, 1980–82) and incidental music for 2 plays; *Forms in Motion* (1972), *Sea-Change* (with tape, 1979), a concerto for cello (1983–85), and other works for orchestra; a septet for winds (1953), String Quartet (1960), *Aldebaren* (viola and tape, 1972), *Ariel in Flight* (violin and tape, 1983), and other chamber music; concert and teaching pieces for piano; *Terminus* (mezzo-soprano and tape, 1970), *Hera Hung from the Sky* (mezzo-soprano, 7 woodwinds, 3 percussionists, piano, and tape, 1973), and other vocal music; electronic music; 2 film scores.

J

Jacchini, Giuseppe Maria (b. Bologna, ca. 1660–65; d. there, 2 May 1727). Cellist and composer. Cello student of Domenico Gabrielli, composition pupil of Perti. Served as cleric at S. Petronio, named cellist there in 1689; dismissed in 1695 when the *cappella* was disbanded, but reinstated in 1701, and served there for the rest of his life, working also in the Collegio dei Nobili and as *maestro di cappella* at S. Luigi. Admitted to the Accademia filarmonica in 1688. His cello playing was praised by contemporaries and by Padre Martini; he composed only instrumental music, with sonatas, concertos, and sinfonias (some with cello and trumpet obbligato parts) among his works.

Jackson, George K(nowil) (b. Oxford, bapt. 15 Apr. 1757; d. Boston, 18 Nov. 1822). Composer and organist. The family moved to London in 1766, where George possibly received music lessons from James Nares of the Chapel Royal. Later he served as organist of St. Alban's Church (1774–90) and attended St. Andrews Univ. He emigrated to the U.S. around 1796; in 1797 he was teaching music in New Brunswick, N.J., and giving concerts that drew the attention of New Yorkers. From 1802 he was organist at St. George's Church, New York, and in 1805–6 was concertizing in Hartford, Conn. Moving to Boston in 1812, he became a central figure in the city's musical culture, as teacher, performer, and music editor. Among his compilations are *The Choral Companion* (Boston, 1814), *A Choice Collection of Chants in Four Voices* (Boston, 1816), and *The Boston Handel and Haydn Society Collection of Church Music* (Boston, 1820). He composed more than 100 works, including sacred vocal music (anthems, psalm tunes, a Te Deum); secular choral and solo vocal music (*Dr. Watts's Divine Songs Set to Music,* London, 1791?); and keyboard works.

Jackson, Mahalia (b. New Orleans, 26 Oct. 1911; d. Chicago, 27 Jan. 1972). Gospel singer. She sang in Chicago churches and after 1932 toured with the Johnson Gospel Singers; she began recording in 1937. Her repertory included many songs by the Rev. Thomas A. Dorsey ("Precious Lord"); among her most popular recordings were "God's Gonna Separate the Wheat from the Tares" (1937) and "Move on Up a Little Higher" (1947). She hosted radio and television shows in the 1950s and made famous appearances at the inauguration of John F. Kennedy (1961) and at the funeral of Martin Luther King, Jr. (1968); her work was central to the international dissemination and acceptance of gospel music.

Jackson, Michael (Joseph) (b. Gary, Ind., 29 Aug. 1958). Popular singer and songwriter. He began singing in a vocal group with his brothers, the Jackson Five (later The Jacksons), and served as lead vocalist for their first success, "I Want You Back" (1969). They continued to perform throughout the 1970s; Michael had a concurrent solo career beginning in 1971. After 1976 he released several extremely popular albums of his own songs, including *Off the Wall* (1979), *Thriller* (1982, including "Billie Jean," "The Girl Is Mine"), and *Bad* (1987). He was a pioneer in the use of music videos for creative and promotional purposes; in 1984 he reunited with his brothers for an album *(Victory)* and tour. Recent albums include: *Dangerous* (1991) and *HIStory: Past, Present and Future, Book I* (1995).

Bibl.: Carol D. Terry, *Sequins and Shades: The Michael Jackson Reference Guide* (Ann Arbor, 1987).

Jackson, Milt(on) [Bags] (b. Detroit, 1 Jan. 1923). Jazz vibraphonist. He joined Dizzy Gillespie's bop sextet (1945–46) and big band (1946–48), then worked briefly with Howard McGhee, Thelonious Monk (recording "Misterioso" in 1948), Charlie Parker, and Woody Herman. While again with Gillespie (1950–52), he began recording as the leader of the group which became the Modern Jazz Quartet (1952–74, 1981). He also recorded extensively with other prominent jazzmen, including his composition "Bags' Groove" on the album *Miles Davis All Stars* (with Monk, 1954) and an album with John Coltrane, *Bags and Trane* (1959). From 1974 he toured widely as a leader and a free-lance apart from the MJQ. The greatest of bop vibraphonists, he slowed the instrument's normal vibrato; this effect, coupled with his sense of swing and soulful melody, is especially telling on blues and ballads.

Jackson, Papa Charlie (b. New Orleans, 1880s; d. Chicago, early 1938). Blues and folk singer and banjoist. Having played in medicine and tent shows prior to 1920, Jackson moved to Chicago and became one of the earliest songsters or blues singers to record (1924). Singing traditional songs and his own compositions, including "Salty Dog (Blues)" (1924, and, with Freddy Keppard, 1926) and "Shake That Thing" (1925), he influenced blues, vaudeville, and jazz performers. He worked in Chicago clubs and continued to record (including sessions with Ida Cox, 1925, and Ma Rainey, 1928) until 1935.

Jacob, Gordon (Percival Septimus) (b. London, 5 July 1895; d. Saffron Walden, 8 June 1984). Composer. He attended Dulwich College before World War I; after the war he studied at the Royal College of Music with Charles Stanford and Herbert Howells. In 1924 he was named deputy professor at the Royal College, and in 1926, professor of composition and orchestration. He received a D.Mus. in 1935, and a John Collard Fellowship (1943–46); he retired from the Royal College in 1954 in order to devote himself wholly to composition. His compositions include orchestral music (2 symphonies; *Variations on an Original Theme,* 1936; 3 suites, 1941–49); many instrumental concertos (2 for viola, 1925, 1979; 2 for piano, 1927, 1957; oboe and strings, 1933; bassoon, strings, and percussion, 1947; horn and strings, 1951; flute, 1951; trombone, 1952; piano duet, 1969; Concerto for Band, 1970); songs; choral works; chamber music (String Quartet in C, 1928; Suite for Bassoon and String Quartet, 1969; Suite for Four Trombones, 1968; Sonata for Viola and Piano, 1978).

Jacob, Maxime [Clément] (b. Bordeaux, 13 Jan. 1906; d. Tarn, 26 Feb. 1977). Composer and organist. He studied with Gédalge at the Paris Conservatory; belonged to the École d'Acueil with other supporters of Satie; in 1929 converted to Catholicism and became a Benedictine monk; later studied organ (with Duruflé) and Gregorian chant. He composed orchestral music (Piano Concerto, 1961); 8 string quartets and other chamber music; piano sonatas and miscellaneous pieces; a *Livre d'orgue* (1967) and other organ music; liturgical choral music (*Les psaumes pour tous les temps,* solo voices and chorus, 1966); and over 400 songs for the stage. He wrote 2 books, *L'art et la grâce* (1939) and *Souvenirs à deux voix* (1969).

Jacob de Senleches [Jacomi] (fl. 1378–95). Composer. Associated with a number of courts in his native France and in Spain, including the papal court at Avignon. His surviving works (3 ballades and 3 virelays, one written in the shape of a harp) contain some of the most extreme musical and notational complexities of the *ars subtilior.*

Bibl.: Willi Apel, ed., *French Secular Compositions of the Fourteenth Century, CMM* 53/1 (1970), nos. 88–93.

Jacob of Liège. See Jacques de Liège.

Jacobi, Frederick (b. San Francisco, 4 May 1891; d. New York, 24 Oct. 1952). Composer and conductor. He studied piano (Gallico, Joseffy) and composition (Goldmark, Bloch) in New York; studied composition in Berlin with Juon. From 1913 to 1917 was assistant conductor of the Metropolitan Opera, after which he lived in the western U.S. for several years and studied music of the Pueblo Indians. He returned to New York in 1924 to teach harmony at the Master School of United Arts; from 1936 he taught composition at the Juilliard School; was executive director of ISCM and served on the board of the League of Composers; wrote articles for *Modern Music.* He included Indian and Hebrew material in some compositions, but wrote more abstract music as well; Koussevitzky introduced his *Indian Dances* with the Boston Symphony in 1928. Works include an opera; 2 symphonies, a violin concerto (1936–37), *Two Pieces in a Sabbath Mood* (1946), and other orchestral music; string quartets, a woodwind quintet, other chamber music; works for piano and organ; a few songs.

Jacobs, Paul (b. New York, 22 June 1930; d. there, 25 Sept. 1983). Pianist and harpsichordist. He studied with Ernest Hutcheson and at Juilliard; made his debut in New York in 1951, then worked in Europe for almost a decade with the Domaine musical, for ISCM in Italy and Austria, and at Darmstadt; in 1956 he performed a complete cycle of Schoenberg's piano music in Paris. He returned to the U.S., where he taught at Mannes, the Manhattan School, the Berkshire Music Center, and Brooklyn College; he was appointed pianist (1962) and harpsichordist (1974) with the New York Philharmonic. Best known for his performances and recordings of the 20th-century repertory.

Jacopo da Bologna [Jacobus de Bononia] (fl. northern Italy, 1340–60?). Composer. A member of the first generation of Italian trecento musicians, directly associated with Maestro Piero and Giovanni da Cascia, active at courts in Verona and Milan, and acquainted with Petrarch. His 34 surviving works include many madrigals (most for 2 voices, a few for 3), a handful of *cacce,* a *lauda-ballata,* and a motet.

Bibl.: W. Thomas Marrocco, ed., *The Music of Jacopo da Bologna* (Berkeley and Los Angeles, 1954). Nino Pirrotta, ed., *The Music of Fourteenth-Century Italy, CMM* 8/2 (1960) and 8/4 (1963). W. Thomas Marrocco, ed., *Italian Secular Music by Magister Piero, Giovanni da Firenze, and Jacopo da Bologna,* Polyphonic Music of the Fourteenth Century, 6 (Monaco, 1967).

Jacopone da Todi [Jacobus de Benedictis] (b. Todi, between 1228 and 1236; d. Collazzone, 25 Dec. 1306). Poet. From 1278 a member of the *spirituali,* the most zealous branch of the Franciscan order. Among his works are 92 *laude,* some of which survive with melodies. He has sometimes, probably incorrectly, been credited with writing the text of the sequence *Stabat Mater dolorosa.*

Jacotin (fl. first half of the 16th cent.). Composer(s). Perhaps identical with Jacotin Le Bel, a member of the French royal chapel from 1532 to 1555. Among his sacred compositions are a few Magnificats and motets. More notable are his secular chansons, of which Attaingnant published over 30, usually for 4 voices and most often incorporating preexisting material in superius or tenor.

Jacques de Liège [Iacobus Leodiensis, Jacob of Liège] (b. Liège, ca. 1260; d. there, after 1330). Theorist. His encyclopedic and highly conservative treatise *Speculum musicae* (ed. *CSM* 3, 1955–73 [complete]; *CS* 2:193–433 [partial]; partial trans., *SR,* pp. 180–90; summary, *RFsC,* pp. 27–28) covers in 7 long books both speculative and practical music theory of the *ars antiqua,* refuting in the last book (on measured music) the teachings of the *ars nova.* Statements of both ancient and more recent authorities (e.g., Boethius, Isidore, Guido, Johannes de Garlandia, Franco) are accepted. This longest of medieval treatises on music was for a time incorrectly attributed to Jehan des Murs.

Jacquet, (Jean Baptiste) Illinois (b. Broussard, near Lafayette, La., 31 Oct. 1922). Jazz tenor saxophonist and bandleader. As a principal soloist in Lionel Hampton's big band (1941–42) he recorded a widely imitated, aggressive, rifflike, bluesy improvisation on "Flying Home" (1942). He joined Cab Calloway (1943–44) and Count Basie (1945–46), performed in the film *Jammin' the Blues* (1944), worked with Jazz at the Philharmonic (1944, tours from 1950), and led groups, recording the album *Genius at Work* in 1971. From 1984 he led a big band.

Jacquet de La Guerre, Élisabeth-Claude (b. ca. 1666–67; d. Paris, 27 June 1729). Harpsichordist and composer. One of several musicians in her family and a prodigy, she had been performing for several years in Paris by the age of 10. Louis XIV supported her, attending her performances and consenting to the dedication of her works to him. She married organist Marin de La Guerre in 1684; after his death and that of her son by 1704, she gave enthusiastically received concerts at her home until her retirement in 1717. A commemorative medal was minted for her after her death. Her works include an opera, a ballet, cantatas, songs, a lost Te Deum performed for Louis XV in 1721, sonatas, and keyboard suites.

Bibl.: Carol Henry Bates, ed., *Élisabeth-Claude Jacquet de La Guerre: Pièces de Clavecin* (Paris, 1986; contains publications from 1687 and 1707). Edith Boroff, *An Introduction to Élisabeth-Claude Jacquet de La Guerre* (Brooklyn, 1966).

Jacquet [Jaquet, Jachet] **of Mantua** [Colebault, Jacques] (b. Vitré, 1483; d. Mantua, 2 Oct. 1559). Composer. Born in France, he had moved to Italy by 1519 and lived in Mantua from about 1526, as titular *maestro di cappella* of the Cathedral of SS. Peter and Paul from 1534; in this capacity he was directly responsible only to the Bishop of Mantua, Ercole Cardinal Gonzaga. The most significant of his works, almost all sacred, appeared between 1520 and 1540. Particularly prominent are his nearly 25 Masses, most parodies, and 5 books of motets, including a small number of occasional or purely secular pieces. His skill and influence in these genres were unmatched in the time between Josquin and Palestrina.

Bibl.: *Collected Works, CMM* 54 (1971–82).

Jaffee, Michael (b. Brooklyn, 21 Apr. 1938). Lutenist, guitarist, and musicologist. He studied with Gustave Reese at New York Univ. (B.A., 1952; M.A., 1963), and in 1964 founded the Waverly Consort with his wife, Kay; he served as artistic director and made many recordings with the ensemble. Jaffee also appeared with the Bach Aria Group, the Fine Arts Quartet, Clarion Concerts, and the New York City Orchestra.

Jaffee, Stephen (Abram) (b. 30 Dec. 1954). Composer. He attended the Univ. of Pennsylvania (A.B., 1976; A.M., 1978) and the Geneva Conservatory; his teachers include George Crumb, George Rochberg, and Richard Wernick; taught at Swarthmore (1980–81) and Duke Univ. (from 1981). Compositions include *Three Yiddish Songs,* soprano, chamber orchestra (1978); *Centering,* violin duo (1978); *Four Images,* orchestra (1982–83); *Arch,* flute, clarinet, bass clarinet, violin, viola, cello, piano, celesta (1981); *Three Figures and a Ground,* flute, piano (1988); Double Sonata, 2 pianos (1989); *Pedal Point,* cycle of four songs (1994).

Jagger, Mick [Michael Philip] (b. Dartford, Kent, 26 July 1944). Rock singer and songwriter. In 1962 he helped form the Rolling Stones, whose other members were Keith Richard, Brian Jones (1962–69), Charlie Watts, Bill Wyman, Mick Taylor (1969–74), and Ron Wood (from 1974). The only rock group to rival the popularity of the Beatles, they were the most prominent of the very few bands to survive the social and musical changes of the end of the 1960s, and became established in the 1970s as rock music's first durable institution. Their most successful songs were authored by Jagger and Richard, including "Satisfaction" (1965), "19th Nervous Breakdown" (1966), "Jumpin' Jack Flash" (1969), and "Honky Tonk Woman" (1969). The 1981 album *Tattoo You* and subsequent concert tour of the U.S. seemed to mark their dissolution. Jagger later released solo albums (*She's the Boss,* 1985; *Primitive Cool,* 1987; *Wandering Spirit,* 1993).

Bibl.: Felix Aeppli, *Heart of Stone: The Definitive Rolling Stones Discography, 1962–83* (Ann Arbor, 1985). Christopher Sandford, *Mick Jagger: Primitive Cool* (London, 1993).

Jamal, Ahmad [Fritz Jones] (b. Pittsburgh, 2 July 1930). Jazz pianist. From 1951 he led groups, usually trios. An unkind reception by critics was more than balanced by the success of the album *Ahmad Jamal at the Pershing* (1958), which remained on the best-selling charts for 108 weeks, and by the support of Miles Davis, who admired Jamal's approach and adopted several of his arrangements. He played in both fusion and bop-oriented styles.

James, Harry (Hagg) (b. Albany, Ga., 15 Mar. 1916; d. Las Vegas, 5 July 1983). Jazz and popular trumpeter and bandleader. After working with Ben Pollack (1935–36), he gained fame for his fiery solos with Benny Goodman's big band (1937–38), including "Ridin' High" (1937). He formed his own big band, playing conventional swing (Frank Sinatra sang with the group in 1939) before turning to novelty songs ("Flight of the Bumble Bee," 1940) and sentimental ballads, which James played with a full-bodied tone and sweet and wide vibrato ("You Made Me Love You," 1941). From 1937 he acted and performed in films, including *The Benny Goodman Story* (1955). He turned back from popular music toward swing after 1946, leading groups mainly in Las Vegas from the 1960s until his death.

James, Philip (Frederick Wright) (b. Jersey City, 17 May 1890; d. Southampton, N.Y., 1 Nov. 1975). Composer, organist, and conductor. He graduated from the City Univ. of New York (1910) and studied composition privately with Goldmark, Scalero, Herbert, and others; in 1910 he was made a fellow of the American Guild of Organists. He taught at New York Univ. (1923–55) and at Columbia (1931–33). He conducted theater orchestras (1915–16; 1919–22) and an army band (1918–19); founded the New Jersey Symphony (1922–29); was elected to the National Institute of Arts and Letters in 1933. His compositions in a late Romantic style won several awards, including first prize in an NBC Radio contest for a satirical piece about broadcasting (*Station WGZBX,* orchestral suite, 1931). Other works include 2 symphonies and other pieces for orchestra; band music; a string quartet, woodwind quintet, and other chamber music; organ and piano works; several cantatas (*General William Booth Enters into Heaven,* male chorus, trumpet, trombone, percussion, and 2 pianos, 1932), liturgical vocal music, part songs; a few songs.

Bibl.: Helga James, *A Catalog of the Musical Works of Philip James (1890–1975)* (n.p., 1984).

Janáček, Leoš [Leo Eugen] (b. Hukvaldy, Moravia, 3 July 1854; d. Moravská Ostrava, 12 Aug. 1928). Composer. He was the son of Jiří Janáček (1815–66), cantor and Kapellmeister in Moravia. Leoš's musical training began at age 11, in the choir of the Augustinian monastery in Brno. He studied at the Czech Teachers' Training Institute (1869–72), and for two years subsequently taught music at the institute's school; from 1872 he also directed the choir at the monastery. He went to Prague in 1874 and became an organ pupil of František Skuherský at the Organ School; after a year he returned to Brno, and during the 1870s conducted various choral groups there. In 1879–80 he traveled to Leipzig to study composition with Oskar Paul and Leo Grill at the conservatory and with Franz Krenn in Vienna. During the 1880s he taught at the institute and continued to develop the Beseda Choir, which he had directed since the 1870s. In 1881 he helped found the Brno Organ School, which later became the Brno Conservatory; in 1884 he began editing the Beseda's journal, *Hudební listy.* Around 1887, after his marriage to Zdenka Schulzova had failed, he began composing his first opera, *Šárka,* which was not performed until 1925. He spent much of 1888 collecting folk songs in northern Moravia with František Bartoš; this collecting was to have a marked effect on his future musical style, which until that point had followed closely the path of late 19th-century Romanticism. After composing a short opera, *Počátek románu* (The Beginning of a Romance), Janáček spent nearly a decade (1894–1903) composing his first major opera, *Jenůfa,* which was warmly received in Brno in 1904.

That year the composer retired from teaching at the institute, and began to expand the activities of the Organ School. For the next 20 years he was occupied almost wholly with composing operas and seeing them through production; he also continued composing symphonic works, chamber music, and works for male chorus. In 1916 *Jenůfa* was finally performed in Prague; before then his works had been known primarily in Moravia. During the last decade of his life he composed three masterpieces, *Kát'a Kabanová, Příhody Lišky Bystroušky* (The Cunning Little Vixen), and *Věc Makropulos* (The Makropulos Affair); he also taught composition at the Prague Conservatory (from 1920) and saw all his major works receive Prague performances. In 1925 he received an honorary doctorate from Masaryk Univ. in Brno. During the 1920s knowledge of Janáček's music began to spread through Europe and to the U.S. as well; his 1926 *Sinfonietta* received performances in New York in 1927. He became an important authority on folk music, publishing a great many editions and collections of folk tunes, as well as writings on the subject. Janáček's musical style can be said to show manifold influences, including those of Russians such as Mussorgsky (particularly in his method of "speech-melody"), of French impressionists (especially in the orchestration of the late operas), and of Moravian folk song, which pervades his music after 1890.

Works: Stage works: *Šárka* (opera, 1887–88; rev. 1918–25; perf. Brno, 11 Nov. 1925); *Rákos Rákoczy* (ballet, 1891); *Počátek románu* [The Beginning of a Romance] (opera, 1891; perf. Brno, 10 Feb. 1894); *Její pastorkyňa* [Her Foster Daughter], generally known under Ger. title *Jenůfa* (opera, 1894–1903; rev. early 20th cent.; perf. Brno, 21 Jan. 1904); *Osud* [Fate] (opera, 1903–5; rev. 1906–7; perf. Brno radio, 1934); *Výlet pana Broučka do měsíce* [Mr. Brouček's Excursion to the Moon] (opera, 1908–17; perf. Prague, 1920); *Výlet pana Broučka do XV. století* [Mr. Brouček's Excursion to the 15th Century] (opera, 1917; perf. Prague, 1920); *Kát'a Kabanová* (opera, 1919–21; perf. Brno, 1921); *Příhody Lišky Bystroušky* [The Adventures of the Vixen Bystrouška; The Cunning Little Vixen] (opera, 1921–23; perf. Brno, 1924); *Věc Makropulos* [The Makropulos Affair] (opera, 1923–25; perf. Brno 1926); *Z mrtvého domu* [From the House of the Dead] (opera, 1927–28; perf. Brno, 1930); several other planned operas and ballets. Sacred choral music, including *Hospodine!* (1896); Mass in E♭ (1907–8); *Veni sancte spiritus* (1910); many secular choruses, including *Mužské sbory* (ca. 1880); *Sbor při kladení základního kamene Masarykovy university v Brně* (1928). Cantatas: *Glagolská mše* [Glagolitic Mass] (1926). Orchestral: *Šumařovo dítě,* symphonic poem (1912); *Taras Bulba,* rhapsody (1915–18); *Balada blanická* [The Ballad of Blaník] (1920); *Sinfonietta* (1926); *Dunaj* [Danube], symphonic poem, fragment completed by O. Chlubna (1923–28). Chamber works: Violin Sonata (1914–21); String Quartet no. 1 (1923); no. 2, "Listy důvěrné" [Intimate Letters] (1928); *Mládí* [Youth] (1924); Concertino, chamber ensemble (1925); *Capriccio "Vzdor"* [Defiance], ensemble (1926). Piano works include *Sonata 1.X.1905, "Z ulice"* [From the Street] (1905; third mvt. lost). Also organ works; folk song settings and compilations; arrangements of Liszt, Grieg, and others.

Bibl.: Bohumir Štědroň, *Dílo Leoše Janáčka: abecední seznam Janáčkových skladeb a úprav* [An Alphabetical Catalogue of Janáček's Compositions and Arrangements] (Prague, 1959); trans. as *The Work of Leoš Janáček* (1959). *L. Janáček: Souborné kritické vydání,* ed. Jiří Vysloužil et al. (Prague, 1978–). Max Brod, *Leoš Janáček: život a dílo* [Life and Works] (Prague, 1924; Ger. orig., 1925; rev. 2nd ed., 1956). Janáčkův archiv, ed., *Korespondence Leoše Janáčka* (Prague, 1934–). Bohumir Štědroň, ed. *Janáček ve vzpomínkách a dopisech* (Prague, 1946); trans. as *Leoš Janáček: Letters and Reminiscences* (1955). Horst Richter, *Leoš Janáček* (Leipzig, 1958). Jaroslav Vogel, *Leoš Janáček: Leben und Werk* (Kassel, 1958); trans. Eng. (London, 1962; rev. 2nd ed., 1981). Erik Chisholm, *The Operas of Leoš Janáček* (Oxford, 1971). Michael Ewans, *Janáček's Tragic Operas* (London, 1977). Vilem and Margaret Tausky, eds., *Janáček: Leaves from His Life* (New York, 1982). Charles Susskind, *Janáček and Brod* (New Haven, 1985). John Tyrrell, *Leoš Janáček: Kát'a Kabanová* (Cambridge, 1982). Id., *Czech Opera* (Cambridge, 1988). Id., *Janáček's Operas: A Documentary Account* (London, 1992). Michael Brim Beckerman, *Janáček as Theorist* (New York, 1994).

Janequin [Jannequin], **Clément** (b. Châtellerault, ca. 1485; d. Paris, 1558). Composer. His career consisted of a series of minor posts in various French cities, including Angers, where he spent his most productive years as a composer (the 1530s in particular). For a short time before his death in Paris, he held the titles of *chantre,* then *compositeur ordinaire du roi.* The majority of his works are chansons, of which over 250 survive. He is best known for his programmatic (or descriptive) and narrative pieces ("Le chant des oiseaux"; "Les cris de Paris"; "La chasse"; "La bataille de Marignan" ["La guerre"]; "Chantons, sonnons, trompettes"; "Ce moys de may"; "Il estoit une fillette"). In his last years he wrote about 150 French Psalms and *chansons spirituelles,* whose tenors may consist of unadorned traditional Calvinist tunes. Other works include 2 Masses, both closely based on his own chansons, at least one motet, and an Italian secular song.

Bibl.: *C. Janequin (c. 1485–1558): Chansons polyphoniques,* ed. A. Tilman Merritt and François Lesure (Monaco, 1965–71).

Janiewicz, Feliks [Felix Yaniewicz] (b. Vilnius, 1762; d. Edinburgh, 21 May 1848). Composer and violinist. He played violin in the orchestra of the Warsaw royal chapel (beginning 1777), then traveled to Vienna, where he possibly studied with Haydn, and to Italy, where he met Pugnani in Turin and gave concerts on violin in Milan. In 1787 he made his Paris debut at the Concert spirituel; later he was chapel violinist for the Duke of Orleans. He moved to England in 1792, playing concerts in London, Liverpool, Bath, and Ireland. In 1813 he was among the founders of the Philharmonic Society in London, and in 1815 he played in the first Edinburgh Festival. His compositions are chiefly instrumental music, including 5 violin concertos; violin sonatas; piano works (including several Rondos); also songs ("The Battle of Freedom," Philadelphia, 1805).

Janigro, Antonio (b. Milan, 21 Jan. 1918; d. there, 1 May 1989). Cellist and conductor. He studied cello with Gilberto Crepax at the Milan Conservatory, then with Alexanian and Casals at the École normale de musique. Following his debut in 1933, he made a number of international concert tours. He was professor at the Zagreb (1939–53) and Düsseldorf (from 1965) conservatories. He conducted the Zagreb Radio Symphony (1954–64), the Orchestra dell'Angelicum in Milan (1965–67), and the Saar Radio Chamber Orchestra (from 1968). In 1954 he formed the Solisti di Zagreb.

Janis [Yanks, Yankelevitch], **Byron** (b. McKeesport, Pa., 24 Mar. 1928). Pianist. He studied in New York with the Lhévinnes and Adele Marcus; debuted in 1943 with the NBC Symphony in Rachmaninoff's 2nd Piano Concerto, and performed the same work the following year with the Pittsburgh Symphony. Horowitz heard him on the latter occasion and offered to teach him; their lessons continued for a number of years. Janis gave his Carnegie Hall debut in 1948 and embarked on a number of tours, including one of the Soviet Union in 1960. His career suffered a number of setbacks owing to illness, including arthritis.

Janitsch, Johann Gottlieb (b. Schweidnitz, Silesia, 19 June 1708; d. Berlin, ca. 1763). Composer. Attended the Dreifaltigkeitsschule in his hometown; moved to Breslau to complete his musical education; enrolled in law studies at Frankfurt an der Oder in 1729, where he directed his works before Friedrich Wilhelm I and Crown Prince Frederick. Took a Prussian state post in 1733, but joined Frederick's orchestra at Ruppin in 1736, moving with it to Rheinsberg in the same year and to Berlin as "Contraviolonist" upon Frederick's coronation in 1740. There he led the renowned chamber concerts of his "Friday Academy," also writing dance music for Carnival balls and receiving other commissions. His works include quartets and sonatas for various instruments, sacred and secular vocal music, sinfonias, and keyboard music.

Jannaconi, Giuseppe (b. Rome, 1741; d. Rome, 16 Mar. 1816). Composer. He may have studied with Gaetano Carpani in Rome; later he became a pupil of and assistant to Pasquale Pisari, a supernumerary at the Sistine Chapel. From Pisari, whom Padre Martini dubbed the "Palestrina of the 18th century," he received solid training in the strict style of Rome. In 1811 he was appointed *maestro di cappella* at St. Peter's. His own compositions reflect the purity of style of his training. Known works include more than 30 Masses; motets, Psalms, and antiphons; also a Passion oratorio (*L'agonia di Gesù Cristo,* for 2 tenors and a bass); and many canons.

Janssen, Werner (b. New York, 1 June 1899; d. Stony Brook, N.Y., 19 Sept. 1990). Composer and conductor. Studied at Dartmouth (D.Mus., 1935) and at New England Conservatory; in Europe he studied conducting with Weingartner (1920–21) and Scherchen (1921–25) and orchestration with Respighi (1930–33). He conducted the New York Philharmonic (1934–35) and the Baltimore Symphony (1937–39); founded the Janssen Symphony in Los Angeles (1940–52) to perform contemporary music; and led orchestras in Utah, Oregon, and California. His own style incorporates jazz and descriptive effects (e.g., *New Year's Eve in New York,* orchestra and jazz band, 1928). He composed more than 50 film scores, orchestral and chamber music, including the Quintet for 10 instruments (6 winds and string quartet, 1968), piano music, and songs.

Jaques-Dalcroze, Émile (b. Vienna, 6 July 1865; d. Geneva, 1 July 1950). Composer and pedagogue. After attending the Univ. of Geneva he traveled to Vienna, where he studied with Robert Fuchs and Anton Bruckner; later he was a pupil in composition of Léo Delibes and Gabriel Fauré in Paris. In 1892 he was appointed theory instructor at the conservatory in Geneva. Around the turn of the century he began his experiments with new methods of teaching music, especially rhythm, through carefully coordinated body motions (whole pieces are transferred to movement, with different limbs indicating separate musical elements or voices). In 1910 he founded, in Hellerau (near Dresden), the first institute designed to teach these techniques, which came to be known as "rhythmic gymnastics" or "Eurythmics"; his ideas gained currency in pedagogical circles during World War I, with the founding of the London School of Dalcroze Eurythmics (1913), the Institut Jaques-Dalcroze in Vienna (1914), and a number of schools throughout Europe, Russia, and the U.S. Jaques-Dalcroze also disseminated the results of his experiments through his early writings, including *La respiration et l'innervation musculaire* (Paris, 1906) and *Méthode Jaques-Dalcroze* (Paris, 1906–17). Eventually the techniques were molded to conform to the requirements of operatic productions. Though they gradually fell out of fashion, Dalcroze's techniques left an indelible mark on subsequent generations of music educators. He also composed prolifically; his works show strong influence from Swiss folk song. Works include operas (*Janie,* Geneva, 1894; *Sancho Panza,* Geneva, 1897; *Les Jumeaux de Bergame,* Brussels, 1908; *Fête de la jeunesse et de la joie,* Geneva, 1932); orchestral works (a violin concerto, 1902; *Nocturne,* violin and orchestra; *Dance Suite*); chamber music (a string quartet; *Rondeaux,* piano, 1933); also many song collections. Among his major writings are *La rhythmique* (Lausanne, 1916–17); *La portée musicale* (Lausanne, n.d.); *Le rhythme, la musique et l'éducation* (Paris, 1919; 2nd ed., 1965); trans. Eng. (1921; 2nd ed., 1967).

Bibl.: Ann Driver, *Music and Movement* (Oxford, 1936). A. C. van Deventer, *Dalcroze* (Amsterdam, 1965). Frank Martin et al., eds., *Émile Jaques-Dalcroze: L'homme, le compositeur, le createur de la rythmique* (Neuchâtel, 1965). Irwin Spector, *Rhythm and Life: The Work of Émile Jaques-Dalcroze* (Stuyvesant, N.Y., 1990).

Járdányi, Pál (b. Budapest, 30 Jan. 1920; d. there, 29 July 1966). Composer and music critic. At the Budapest Academy of Music he studied composition with Zoltan Kodály and Albert Siklós (1938–42); he was also a pupil at Budapest Univ. and received a doctorate in 1943, with a dissertation on Hungarian folklore. He worked as music critic from 1943 to 1949, and from 1946 to 1959 he was an instructor at the Liszt Academy of Music in Budapest. He won the Bartók Prize in 1948 (for the String Quartet no. 1) and the Erkel Prize in 1952 and 1953. His music shows the strong effects of the music of Bartók and Kodály. Works include orchestral music (a sinfonietta, 1940; *Divertimento concertante,* 1949; Symphony "Vörösmarty," 1952; Violin Concertino, 1964); vocal works (*Missa brevis,* 2-voice chorus, 1940; *Savaria,* chorus, 1963); chamber and instrumental music (Duos, 2 violins, 1937; 3 sonatinas for piano, 1940–58; a sonata, violin and piano, 1944; a string trio, 1963).

Jarnach, Philipp (b. Noisy, France, 26 July 1892; d. Bornsen, 17 Dec. 1982). Composer. Of Spanish and Flemish origin. From 1907 he studied with A. Lavignac in Paris; before the war he had published songs and orchestral and chamber music influenced by the music of Debussy and Ravel. He spent the war years in Switzerland, where he became a close friend of Busoni; from 1918 to 1921 he taught at the conservatory in Zurich; in 1921 he moved to Berlin, where he completed Busoni's opera *Dr. Faustus* after the composer's death in 1924. He became a German citizen in 1931; taught composition at the Hochschule für Musik in Cologne (1927–49); then directed the Hochschule in Hamburg (1949–59), where he continued to teach composition until 1970. Kurt Weill was among his many students. He was elected to the Berlin Academy of Art (1955) and (with Blacher) received the Bach Prize from the city of Hamburg in 1957. He wrote tonal music in a neoclassical style; *Musik mit Mozart* (orchestra, 1935) consists of variations on themes of Mozart. Works include orchestral and chamber music; piano and organ works; choral music; and a few songs with orchestra or piano.

Järnefelt, (Edvard) Armas (b. Viipuri [Vyborg, Finland], 14 Aug. 1869; d. Stockholm, 23 June 1958). Conductor and composer. He studied at the Helsinki Conservatory with Busoni and Martin Wegelius (from 1887), in Berlin with Albert Becker (1890), and finally in Paris with Jules Massenet (1893–94). He then held posts as opera conductor in Magdeburg, Düsseldorf, and Vyborg. In 1906 he was appointed director of the Helsinki Institute of Music; a year later he was made conductor of the Royal Opera in Stockholm and, in 1923, that company's principal conductor. Although he obtained Swedish citizenship, he returned to Finland often: in 1932, to direct the National Opera for four years, and in 1942, to direct the Helsinki Philharmonic. His own compositions include choral/orchestral works (*Päivänpoika* [Son of Day], 1939; *Temppelinrakentajat* [The Temple Builders], chorus, orchestra, 1940); and orchestral music (*Berceuse,* 1904).

Jarre, Maurice (b. Lyons, 13 Sept. 1924). Composer. He studied composition with Honegger and percussion with Félix Passerone at the Paris Conservatory; played percussion under Boulez from 1946 at the Renaud–Barrault Theater Company, and then at the Théâtre populaire. His concert works employ serial techniques, but after moving to Hollywood he concentrated on film music, receiving Oscars for *Lawrence of Arabia* (1963) and "Lara's Song" in *Doctor Zhivago* (1965). He wrote ballets and radio operas; orchestral music (*Cantate pour une démente,* soprano, chorus, viola, and orchestra, 1963); incidental music; and many film scores.

Jarreau, Al (b. Milwaukee, 12 Mar. 1940). Popular and jazz singer. He sang in clubs while working as a psychological counselor in San Francisco. He moved to Los Angeles in 1968 and in the mid-1970s emerged as one of the finest jazz scat singers, especially for his improvisation on "Take Five" on his album *Look to the Rainbow* (1977). Thereafter he concentrated on urbane, soulful, popular music, achieving many hit recordings, including the album *Jarreau* (1983) and the song "L Is for Lover" (1986).

Jarrett, Keith (b. Allentown, Pa., 8 May 1945). Jazz pianist and bandleader. He joined Art Blakey's Jazz Messengers (1965–66), Charles Lloyd's quartet (1966–69, recording the album *Forest Flower* in 1966), and Miles Davis's jazz-rock group (1970–71), in which he played electric keyboards. Concurrently, from 1966 he led a trio with Charlie Haden and the drummer Paul Motian; it became a quartet with the saxophonist Dewey Redman (1971–76). From 1971 he began improvising unaccompanied (as on the album *Solo-Concerts Bremen Lausanne,* 1973) and through this work became one of the most popular jazz musicians of the day. He also led a European quartet with the saxophonist Jan Garbarek (1974–79, recording the album *Belonging* in 1974) and from 1983 a trio with Gary Peacock and Jack DeJohnette that played the central repertory of jazz, recording the albums *Standards* I and II (1983).

Bibl.: Ian Carr, *Keith Jarrett: The Man and His Music* (London, 1991).

Järvi, Neeme (b. Tallinn, Estonia, 7 June 1937). Conductor. Studied at Leningrad Conservatory. Conductor of the Estonian Opera from 1963. Won the Santa Cecilia Competition, 1971. New York Metropolitan debut, 1979, conducting *Eugen Onegin.* Music director of the Scottish National Orchestra, 1984–88; of the Detroit Symphony from 1990. He made numerous recordings of unfamiliar repertory of the 19th and 20th centuries.

Jaubert, Maurice (b. Nice, 3 Jan. 1900; d. Azerailles, Meurthe-et-Moselle, 19 June 1940). Composer. Received a Premier Prix in piano from the Nice Conservatory; after two years as a lawyer, he returned to music, studying with Albert Groz in Paris. In 1925 he became music director for Pleyela recordings and in 1930 for Pathé Cinéma discs; directed the orchestra at the Paris Exposition in 1937. He wrote orchestral music (a concerto for violin and cello, 1936); ballets; chamber and piano music; choral music and songs; over 40 film scores (Vigo's *L'Atalante,* 1934); and works for the theater (some in association with Giraudoux). He died in battle in World War II.

Jefferson, Blind Lemon (b. Couchman, Tex., July 1897; d. Chicago, Dec. 1929). Blues singer and guitarist. Partially sighted from birth, he traveled Texas as a street singer. He moved to Chicago in the mid-1920s, beginning an influential series of recordings (including gospel material under the name Deacon L. J. Bates) in December 1925. Before his death from exposure on the streets of Chicago, he had recorded more than 100 sides, including "Long Lonesome Blues" (1926), and "Black Snake Moan" and "Match Box Blues" (1927, the latter recorded both in Atlanta and Chicago).

Jeffreys, George (b. ca. 1610; d. Weldon, Northamptonshire, 1 July 1685). Composer. Perhaps a member of the Chapel Royal early in life; became joint organist (with John Wilson) to Charles I at Oxford in 1643; served as steward to Lord Hatton in Northhamptonshire from the siege of Oxford (1646) to his death, though links to the Hatton family date from at least 1631, when he set several poems written by Sir Richard Hatton. Some 250 letters to his patron survive; autograph copies of over 100 works by composers such as Carissimi, Marini, Reggio, and Grandi indicate Italian influence. The bulk of his output is sacred and for private devotional use; he also wrote masque music, viol fantasias, and secular cantatas and dialogues.

Bibl.: Peter Aston, "George Jeffreys," *MT* 110 (1969): 772–76.

Jehan des Murs [Johannes de Muris] (b. diocese of Lisieux, ca. 1300; d. ca. 1350). Astronomer and music theorist. Work in Paris and elsewhere never led him entirely to sever his ties with his native Normandy, especially Évreux. His most important musical works are *Notitia artis musicae* (or *Ars nove musicae, GS* 3:312, 256–57, 313–15, 292–301; *CSM* 17 [1972]; *SR,* pp. 172–79) and *Musica speculativa secundum Boetium* (*GS* 3:249–83). Of ideas of the *ars nova,* with which he is traditionally identified, these treatises contain no more than an argument that relationships between note values are fundamentally binary, not ternary. Only the mid-14th-century *Libellus cantus mensurabilis* (*CS* 3:46–48), which is probably not by des Murs but merely conveys his late teachings, transmits any account of *ars nova* notation. His work and thought strongly influenced the vast majority of music theorists of the 14th and 15th centuries.

Jehannot de l'Escurel [Jehan de Lescurel] (d. Paris, 23 May 1304). Composer. Little is known of his life except that he was hanged for debauchery while a young cleric in Paris. A copy of the *Roman de Fauvel* includes his only extant compositions, one 3-voiced rondeau and 33 monophonic ballades, rondeaux, virelays, and *diz entés* (2 very long poems with music for the refrains only).

Bibl.: *Works, CMM* 30 (1966).

Jelinek [Elin], **Hanns** (b. Vienna, 5 Dec. 1901; d. there, 27 Jan. 1969). Composer. He had some lessons in harmony and counterpoint with Schoenberg and at the Vienna Music Academy; under the pseudonym Elin he supported himself as a bar pianist, bandleader, and composer of film scores. From 1952 to 1958 he worked on a study of twelve-tone methods, *Anleitung zur Zwölftonkomposition;* earlier he had written a series of piano and chamber works to demonstrate those methods (*Zwölftonwerk* op. 15, 1947–52). In 1958 he was appointed to teach composition at the Vienna Musikhochschule and was subsequently named professor there. Received the Austrian State Prize for music (1966). His output was large and varied: from tonal to serial, and encompassing film scores, jazz, popular, electronic, and traditional concert and stage music. He wrote an operetta (*Bubi Caligula,* 1947–53); orchestral and chamber music; piano works (*Zwölftonfibel* op. 21, 1953–54); *Prometheus* (after Goethe, baritone and orchestra, 1936) and other vocal music.

Jemnitz, Sándor [Alexander] (b. Budapest, 9 Aug. 1890; d. Balatonföldvár, 8 Aug. 1963). Composer, conductor, and critic. He studied with Koessler at the Budapest Academy of Music (1906–8), and with Reger (composition) and Nikisch (conducting) at the Leipzig Conservatory; later attended Schoenberg's classes in Berlin (1921–24). Wrote for a number of newspapers in Germany and Hungary, then became a regular music critic for the Hungarian paper *Népszava* (1924–50); served as editor-in-chief of *Éneklő munkás* and as editor of *Éneklő nép,* and taught at the Budapest Conservatory. Toward the end of his life he published a number of popular books on famous composers. His compositions, mostly instrumental, show the influence of both Reger and Schoenberg; they include orchestral works (*7 miniatűr,* 1947); chamber music (trio, flute, violin, viola, 1923; 2 string trios: op. 21, 1924; op. 24 *Serenade,* 1927); keyboard (5 sonatas: op. 8, 1914; op. 23 *Tanzsonate,* 1927; op. 26, 1929; op. 30, 1933; op. 64, 1954).

Jenkins, Florence Foster (b. New York, 1868; d. there 26 Nov. 1944). Singer. Gave annual soirées at the Ritz-Carlton Hotel. On these occasions she appeared extravagantly costumed, sometimes with angel wings, singing only the most difficult coloratura arias and songs with an ineptitude that reduced many in her audience to tears. For the Verdi Club she organized an annual ball; for the Euterpe Club various tableaux vivants. The high point of her activities came six weeks before her death, when she performed her annual concert for a larger public at Carnegie Hall. Her private recordings were much sought after as humorous records and were later commercially published by RCA.

Jenkins, John (b. Maidstone, 1592; d. Kimberley, Norfolk, 27 Oct. 1678). Composer. Little is known of his early years; his patrons included the Dereham family of Norfolk and the L'Estrange family of Hunstanton, but he probably never had official ties to these houses. His father bequeathed a bandora to him in 1617; he played lyra viol before Charles I and in 1634 took part in Shirley's masque *The Triumph of Peace.* He seems to have moved among many houses during the Commonwealth, visiting that of Lord Dudley North from the late 1650s and serving as tutor there to Roger and Montagu, 1660–66. Roger North's writings supply much information about Jenkins, who was named theorbo player in the King's Musick in 1660 but probably spent little time at court. He passed his final years at the home of Sir Philip Wodehouse at Norfolk. Famed as a lutenist and viol player, he was a major exponent of the English 17th-century viol fantasia; he also wrote vocal music.

Bibl.: Carolyn Coxon, "A Handlist of the Sources of John Jenkins' Vocal and Instrumental Music," *RMARC* 9 (1971): 73–89 [with list of editions]. Andrew Ashbee, Introduction to *John Jenkins: Consort Music of Four Parts, MB* 26. Id., "John Jenkins, 1592–1678, and the Lyra Viol," *MT* 119 (1978): 840–43.

Jenkins, Leroy (b. Chicago, 11 Mar. 1932). Jazz violinist. From 1965 he played free jazz in Chicago with members of the Association for the Advancement of Creative Musicians, including the Creative Construction Company with Anthony Braxton (1967–71), which was based in Paris, 1969–70. In New York he founded a cooperative trio, the Revolutionary Ensemble (1971–77, recording an album under that title, 1977). He led a trio with Andrew Cyrille and Anthony Davis (1977–79, recording the album *The Legend of Ali Glatson,* 1978) and a quintet (1982–83), and played with Cecil Taylor (1987).

Jennens, Charles (b. 1700; d. 20 Nov. 1773). Librettist. Born into a rich family, he entered but did not graduate from Balliol College. He befriended Handel, who often visited and corresponded with him (nine of Handel's letters are extant); he was Handel's most talented oratorio librettist, providing texts for *Saul, L'Allegro, Messiah,* and *Belshazzar.* Late in his life he also issued editions of 5 of Shakespeare's tragedies.

Bibl.: Ruth Smith, "The Achievements of Charles Jennens (1700–1773)," *ML* 70 (1989): 161–90.

Jennings, Terry (b. Eagle Rock, Calif., 19 July 1940; d. San Pablo, Calif., 11 Dec. 1981). Composer and performer. He played jazz (piano, clarinet, and alto and soprano saxophone) in Los Angeles with La Monte Young (ca. 1953) and composed in Young's minimalist style, employing sustained tones and long time periods. His works were performed by Young in New York (1960), and Jennings was active there as a performer of avant-garde works in association with Riley and Young; he composed for the James Waring Dance Company (1962). His *Winter Trees* and *Winter Sun* (both for piano, 1965) incorporate aleatory procedures in the performer's repetition of phrases in a specified order, at will. A few late works were composed in a neo-Romantic idiom.

Jennings, Waylon (Arnold) (b. Littlefield, Tex., 15 June 1937). Country singer, guitarist, and songwriter. He worked as a singer and radio announcer in Texas and New Mexico and played in Buddy Holly's Crickets (1958–59). He began recording with his band, the Waylors, in 1965; successful songs include "That's What You Get for Loving Me" (1966) and "Good Ol' Boys" (1980). Incorporating many elements of rock into his work, with Willie Nelson he has cultivated the image of an outsider to the Nashville country music establishment; he has recorded with Nelson and Jessi Colter (including *Wanted: The Outlaws,* 1976).

Jensen, Adolf (b. Königsberg, 12 Jan. 1837; d. Baden-Baden, 23 Jan. 1879). Composer. From a family of musicians; studied with Ehlert, Köhler, Marpurg (1849–52); active as pianist and teacher (1856, Brest-Litovsk; 1858–60, Copenhagen; 1861–62, Königsberg; 1866, Tausig's school, Berlin); 1857–58, theater conductor. A fortunate marriage (1863) allowed him to spend his last years comfortably after consumption curtailed his activities (1868–70, lived in Dresden; 1870–75, Graz; 1875–79, Baden-Baden). Works include an unperformed opera and choral works; he is best known for many piano pieces and songs, published from 1859 on.

Jeremiáš, Otakar (b. Písek, 17 Oct. 1892; d. Prague, 5 March 1962). Conductor, composer, and cellist. From 1907 he was a student at the Prague Conservatory, and he studied privately with Burian (cello) and Novák (composition). Cellist in the Czech Philharmonic, 1911–13. In 1918 he moved to České Budějovice to assume directorship of the music school that his father, composer and conductor Bohuslav Jeremiáš, had founded there. In 1929 he was made conductor of the newly formed Prague Radio Orchestra, and in 1945 director of the National Theater in Prague. His works include 2 operas (*Bratři Karamazovi* [The Brothers Karamazov], Prague, 1928; and *Enšpígl* [Till Eulenspiegel], Prague, 1949); incidental music (including that to plays of Goethe, Schiller, and Čapek); choral/orchestral works (*Fantasie,* 1915; *Tvůrci Fausta* [To the Creator of Faust], 1932); songs; chamber and instrumental music.

Jerger, Alfred (b. Brünn, Moravia [Brno, Czechoslovakia], 9 June 1889; d. Vienna, 18 Nov. 1976). Bass-baritone. After studies at the Vienna Academy of Music, conducted opera in Passau (1913), Winterthur (1914), and Zurich (1915). There his voice was discovered, and he made his debut in 1917 as Lothario *(Mignon).* Engaged by Strauss for the Munich Opera in 1919, he went in 1921 to Vienna, where he sang with the Staatsoper until his retirement in 1964. Sang in the premieres of Schoenberg's *Die glückliche Hand* (1924) and Wellesz's *Die Bakchantinnen* (1931). Created Strauss's Mandryka *(Arabella)* in Dresden (1933). Professor at the Vienna Academy of Music from 1947.

Jeritza [Jedlitzková, Jedlitzka], **Maria** [Mimi, Marie] (b. Brünn, Moravia [Brno, Czechoslovakia], 6 Oct. 1887; d. Orange, N.J., 10 July 1982). Soprano. Studied with Auspitz in Prague, with Marcella Sembrich in New York. Debut in 1910 with the Olmütz Opera as Elsa *(Lohengrin).* With the Vienna Volksoper (1911) she sang in the premiere of *Der Kuhreigen* by Wilhelm Kienzl. At the request of Emperor Franz Josef, engaged by the Court Opera (1912–35). She created Strauss's Ariadne (Stuttgart, 1912) and Kaiserin (Vienna, 1919), and Korngold's Marietta (1921). She repeated the last role at her New York Metropolitan Opera debut in 1921. Dividing her time between Vienna and New York, she became the Met's leading soprano until her retirement, introducing Jenůfa and Turandot to U.S. audiences. She was the recipient of Strauss's last work, the lied "Malven." Her memoirs, *Sunlight and Song,* were published in 1924.

Jerome of [Hieronymus de] **Moravia** (fl. 1272–1304). Theorist. His encyclopedic *Tractatus de musica* (*CS* 1:1–94; Simon M. Cserba, ed., *Hieronymus de Moravia,* Regensburg, 1935) covers many aspects of music but is designed chiefly for teaching ecclesiastics about chant. Passages from many other writers are quoted and identified, as are 4 complete discant treatises: *Discantus positio vulgaris,* and works by Johannes de Garlandia, Franco of Cologne, and Petrus de Picardia. Tunings of the vielle and rebec are mentioned briefly.

Jessel, Léon (b. Stettin, 22 Jan. 1871; d. Berlin, 4 Jan. 1942). Composer. In Stettin he studied at the Marienstiftsgymnasium; from 1894 he was theater conductor in Freiberg, Paderborn, Chemnitz, and several other cities. In 1911 he settled in Berlin, where he composed popular operettas in the Strauss and Léhar tradition; most notable was *Schwarzwaldmädel* (Berlin, 1917), which received nearly 1,000 performances in Berlin alone. He is best known for the piano piece *Parade der Zinnsoldaten* (Parade of the Tin Soldiers) from 1905. In 1934 his works were banned in Germany, and he was imprisoned by the Nazis. At age 70 he died in prison.

Jiménez Mabarak, Carlos (b. Tacuba, Mexico, 31 Jan. 1916). Composer. Studied piano in Guatemala and the humanities in Chile before attending the Institute of Advanced Musical Studies and the Royal Conservatory in Brussels (1933–36). Back in Mexico, he studied conducting with Revueltas in 1937, later teaching at the National Conservatory in Mexico City (1942–65) and at the School of Arts in Villahermosa (to 1968). A 1956 UNESCO grant allowed him to study in Europe under René Leibowitz. He composed in a variety of idioms, from folk-derived to serialist; works include several ballets, operas (*Misa de seis,* 1961; *La güera,* 1982), concertos, and other orchestral music, along with chamber and piano music, choral pieces, and songs.

Bibl.: *Composers of the Americas* 8 (Washington, D.C., 1962), pp. 96–101 [includes works list].

Jirák, Karel Boleslav (b. Prague, 28 Jan. 1891; d. Chicago, 30 Jan. 1972). Composer and conductor. At the university in Prague he studied law and philosophy and took private lessons with Vítěslav Novák (from 1909) and Joseph Bohuslav Foerster (from 1911). He conducted the Hamburg Opera (1915–18) and later was director of the opera companies at Brno and Ostrava (1918–20). He was second conductor of the Czech Philharmonic (1920–21), professor at the Prague Conservatory (1920–30), and finally music director of Czech Radio (1930–45). In 1947 he settled in Chicago, where he taught at Roosevelt College until his death. His later music follows the Czech late Romantic style. Works include an opera, *Žena a bůh* [The Woman and the God] (1912–13; perf. Brno, 1928); orchestral works (6 symphonies; *Rhapsody,* violin, orchestra, 1942; Piano Concerto, 1946; *Legenda,* 1954; Concertino, violin, small orchestra, 1957); choral works (Requiem, soloists, chorus, orchestra, 1952; *In memoriam,* 1971); chamber works (7 string quartets); piano works (2 sonatas, 1926, 1950).

Bibl.: Alice Tischler, *Karel Boleslav Jirák: A Catalog of His Works* (Detroit, 1975).

Joachim, Joseph (b. Kittsee [now Köpcsény] near Poszony, 28 June 1831; d. Berlin, 15 Aug. 1907). Violinist. In 1831 the family moved to Pest, where he began violin study; 1839–43, studied at the Vienna Conservatory (Hellmesberger, Böhm); 1843, the Leipzig Conservatory (with David, but was very close to Mendelssohn), also beginning to tour. Debut 1844, in London, where he became a favorite. In 1850, concertmaster at Weimar under Liszt, with whom he was artistically incompatible; Joachim aligned himself with Schumann and Brahms. In 1852, violinist to the King of Hannover, also leading his own string quartet, which became one of the most admired in Europe. From 1868 to 1905, director of the new Berlin Hochschule für Musik, which under him became one of Germany's great music schools. He toured annually and also composed. His works include 3 concertos (especially the Hungarian Concerto op. 11, 1857); 5 concert overtures; violin and viola pieces. His cadenzas (for concertos by Mozart, Beethoven, Brahms) have been much used.

Bibl.: A. Moser, *Joseph Joachim: Ein Lebensbild* (Berlin, 1898; 2nd ed., 1908–10); trans. Eng. (1901). J. A. Fuller-Maitland, *Joseph Joachim* (London, 1905). Nora Bickley, trans., *Letters from and to Joseph Joachim* (London, 1914). Boris Schwarz, "Joseph Joachim and the Genesis of Brahms' Violin Concerto," *MQ* 69 (1983): 503–23.

Joseph Joachim, 1888.

Joachim, Otto (b. Düsseldorf, 13 Oct. 1910). Composer and violinist. He studied in Cologne (1916–31), then worked in China (1934–49) before emigrating to Montreal, where he taught at McGill Univ. and at the conservatory. He was active as a performer and was a founder of both the Montreal Consort of Ancient Instruments and the Société de musique de notre temps. He employed twelve-tone methods as well as aleatory procedures, sometimes in the same work (*Contrastes,* orchestra, 1967). Several works use mixed media and are characterized by open form (*Mankind,* 4 speakers, organ, timpani, synthesizers, slides, lighting, incense, 1972; *Mobile für J. S. Bach,* oboe, clarinet, bassoon, string quartet, celesta, organ, tape, Vocoder, 1985). *Katimavik* (tape) was commissioned for the Canadian Pavilion at the Exposition in Montreal (1967). In addition to chamber and keyboard music, he wrote many twelve-tone works for children, and some vocal and choral music.

Jochum, Eugen (b. Babenhausen, 1 Nov. 1902; d. Munich, 26 Mar. 1987). One of three conducting brothers, he studied organ and piano at the Augsburg Benedictine Gymnasium (1914–22), conducting with Siegmund von Hausegger at the Munich Academy of Music (1922–24). After working as répétiteur at the Munich and Kiel operas (1924–25; 1926–27), he was named conductor at Kiel and leader of the Lübeck Symphony (1927–29); of the Mannheim Orchestra (1929–30). Two years as music director at Duisburg led to extended tenures (1934–49) in three major posts:

the Berlin Radio Orchestra, Berlin Civic Opera, and Hamburg Philharmonic. Founding conductor of the Bavarian Radio Orchestra in Munich (1949–60); conductor of the Amsterdam Concertgebouw Orchestra (1961–64) and of the Bamberg Symphony (1969–71); laureate conductor of the London Symphony (1975–78). Best known as a champion of Bruckner's Masses and symphonies, which he performed from the Nowak editions.

Joel, Billy [William Martin] (b. New York, 9 May 1949). Popular singer, songwriter, and pianist. He played in rock groups in the 1960s, including the Echoes and Attila; began recording in 1972. From 1973 he produced several albums of original songs, among the most popular of which were "Piano Man" (1973), "Just the Way You Are" (1977), and "It's Still Rock and Roll to Me" (1980). In 1987 he toured the Soviet Union and subsequently issued a live album.

Johannes Afflighemensis (fl. ca. 1100). Theorist. A monk of Affligem, near Brussels; his widely known practical and didactic treatise with tonary called *De musica* (*GS* 2:230–65; *CSM* 1 [1950]; trans., *YTS* 3 [1978]: 87–190) was once attributed to an Englishman named John Cotton. Among the contents of the work, which is modeled on Guido's *Micrologus,* is the earliest known description of organum as it was practiced after Guido's time.

Johannes de Florentia. See Giovanni da Cascia.

Johannes de Garlandia [Johannes Gallicus] (fl. ca. 1240). Theorist. His two treatises are, with the work of Franco of Cologne, the most important and influential writings on music from the 13th century. *De plana musica* survives in 3 versions, one of which introduces Philippe de Vitry's *Ars nova* (*CSM* 8 [1964], chaps. 1–13, ed. and trans. Fr.). *De mensurabili musica* (ed. Rudolf Rasch, IMM Musicological Studies 20, New York, 1969; Erich Reimer, *AfMw,* Beihefte 10–11 [1972]; trans. *CCT* 9 [1978]) treats the polyphony of the Notre Dame era, its rhythm, notation, consonances, and dissonances, and the 3 species discant, copula, and organum. A revision of *De mensurabili musica* appears in the *Tractatus de musica* of Jerome of Moravia.

Johannes de Grocheo (fl. ca. 1300). Theorist. His *Ars musice* or *Theoria* describes musical practice in Paris around 1300. The treatise is especially important for its treatment of secular monophony and of the poetic and social functions of various sorts of music. Several types of *cantus* (e.g., *cantus coronatus*) and cantilena (e.g., *stantipes* and *ductia,* each in both vocal and instrumental forms) are described, sometimes with musical examples. Unfortunately, the descriptions are not always clear or congruent with extant compositions.

Bibl.: Facs., ed., trans. Ger., Ernst Rohloff, *Die Quellenhandschriften zum Musiktraktat des Johannes de Grocheio* (Leipzig, 1972); trans. Eng., *CCT* 1 (1967).

Johannes de Muris. See Jehan des Murs.

Johannesen, Grant (b. Salt Lake City, 30 July 1921). Pianist. Studied with Robert Casadesus at Princeton (1941–46). Debut, New York, 1944. After further studies with Egon Petri at Cornell, won the Ostend International Competition (1949), then made his first European tour. He toured Europe again with the New York Philharmonic under Mitropoulos (1956–57); toured the USSR with the Cleveland Orchestra under Szell (1968). On the faculty of the Aspen School in Colorado (1960–66). Music director of the Cleveland Institute of Music from 1974; president, 1977–84. Throughout his career he consistently programmed French works, especially by Poulenc, Debussy, and Roussel. Married to the cellist Zara Nelsova (1963–73).

Johansen, David Monrad (b. Vefsn, Norway, 8 Nov. 1888; d. Sandvika, 20 Feb. 1974). Composer. In Oslo he studied piano with Winge and Johnson (1904–9), theory with Catharinus Elling and Iver Holter (1909–15); later he studied in Berlin with Engelbert Humperdinck (1915–16) and in Leipzig with Hermann Grabner (1933–35). His debut as composer came in 1915, with a concert of his works in Oslo. From 1916 he was editor and music critic for the *Norsk musikerblad,* and in 1925 he was awarded a state artist's stipend. His music often employs folk melodies in a context of late Romantic style. Works include choral music (*Voluspaa,* soloists, chorus, orchestra, 1926; *Gryningens flicka,* chorus, 1965); orchestral works (Suite op. 4, 1916; *Symfoniske variasjoner,* 1944–46; Piano Concerto, 1954); songs (*Nordlands trompet,* 1925; *6 strofiske sanger,* 1964); chamber works (String Quartet, 1969); works for piano (Suite no. 3, "Prillar-Guri," 1924).

John [João] **IV, King of Portugal** (b. Villa Viçosa, 19 Mar. 1604; d. Lisbon, 6 Nov. 1656). Writer on music, collector, and composer. A pupil of Tornar. After becoming king upon breaking away from Spanish rule in 1640, he assembled a great library of music and treatises; although the collection was destroyed in the earthquake and fire of 1755, a partial catalog issued in 1649 survives. A treatise by him listed in the library catalog is lost, but two others are extant; one defends the modal structure in a Palestrina Mass, while the other sides for the music of Palestrina, Victoria, and others against that of the Ancients. Two of his compositions also survive; both are 4-part *stile antico* motets.

John, Elton [Reginald Kenneth Dwight] (b. Pinner, Middlesex, 25 Mar. 1947). Rock singer, songwriter, and pianist. Studied music at the Royal Academy; played in groups in London including Bluesology (1966–68); from 1970 to 1976 collaborated with lyricist Bernie Taupin on several albums, successful songs including "Your Song" (1970), "Honky Cat" (1972), "Goodbye, Yellow Brick Road" (1973), and "Benny and the Jets" (1973). He continued to record and perform, working with other lyricists; in 1980 his "Little Jeannie" was very popular.

John Damascene [John of Damascus] (b. Damascus, ca. 675; d. St. Sabas, near Jerusalem, ca. 749). Theologian and hymnographer. Tradition maintains that he organized the Byzantine system of 8 modes and wrote the entire *Oktoēchos,* a liturgical book of Office hymns. This is certainly an exaggeration. His contribution to the work was nevertheless significant, encompassing at the least many hymn texts and melodies.

Johns, (Paul) Emile (b. Kraków, ca. 1798; d. Paris, 10 Aug. 1860). Pianist and merchant. Perhaps spent early years in Vienna; settled in New Orleans by 1818 (often visiting Europe) as pianist and teacher; 1819, soloist in first known U.S. performance of a Beethoven piano concerto; ca. 1831–34, published *Album Louisiannais* (his only known work: 6 songs, 2 piano pieces); 1830–46, owned music shop, importing Pleyel pianos; later a cotton merchant; best remembered as dedicatee of Chopin's Mazurkas op. 7.

Johnson, Blind Willie (b. Marlin, Tex., ca. 1902; d. Beaumont, Tex., ca. 1950). Gospel singer and guitarist. Blinded by his stepmother at the age of 7, he spent his life as an itinerant street musician. He performed with his wife, Angeline, a singer, from about 1927, when he began a brief period of recording (–1930). The timbre of his bass voice was sometimes clear, but often he sang with powerful growling and rasping. ("If I Had My Way I'd Tear That Building Down," 1927), humming and moaning ("Dark Was the Night, Cold Was the Ground," 1927); the latter also exemplifies his bluesy guitar technique, in which a bass drone supported a sliding melody; alternatively, he played lightly brushed chords above the bass.

Johnson, Bunk [Willie; William Geary] (b. New Orleans, 27 Dec. 1889; d. New Iberia, La., 7 July 1949). Jazz trumpeter and bandleader. He claimed to have worked with Buddy Bolden and certainly worked later with Bolden's former group, the Eagle Band, around 1910. He worked with lesser-known groups until dental problems forced him to stop around 1934. From 1942 he became the central figure in the revival of New Orleans jazz, leading groups in New Orleans, San Francisco, New York, and Chicago, and sharing a stormy engagement with Sidney Bechet in Boston. His recordings include "Dusty Rag" (1942) and, in one of the earliest sessions by a jazz brass band, "Over in the Gloryland" (1945). His style was ragtime oriented.

Bibl.: Christopher Hillman, *Bunk Johnson* (Tunbridge Wells, England, 1988).

Johnson, Edward (b. Guelph, Ontario, 22 Aug. 1878; d. there, 20 Apr. 1959). Tenor and manager. After graduating from the Univ. of Toronto, studied voice with Von Feilitsch in New York and sang in Broadway operettas. Further studies with Vincenzo Lombardi in Florence led to his debut in 1912 in Padua as André Chenier. In 1914 he introduced Parsifal to La Scala and there created the leads in Pizzetti's *Fedra* (1915) and Montemezzi's *Nave* (1918). In 1919 he created Puccini's Gianni Schicchi in Rome. He joined the Chicago Opera (1919–22), then the New York Metropolitan Opera, creating leads in operas by Taylor and Hanson before retiring from the stage in 1935 to become general manager. Under his administration (1935–50) the Met increased the number of American singers invited to sing (in part because of the effects of the depression and the Second World War), and the Metropolitan Opera Association purchased the opera house from its box holders (1940). After retiring from the Met, he helped organize an opera school at his alma mater.

Johnson, Frank [Francis] (b. Martinique?, ca. 1792; d. Philadelphia, 6 Apr. 1844). Dance and military bandmaster. Settled in Philadelphia, ca. 1809; from ca. 1818, increasing local, later national recognition as military bandmaster, his band often serving white military units; also a popular dance conductor and music teacher; 1837–38, played in London with 4 members of his band, all on a variety of instruments; returning to Philadelphia (after a U.S. tour as far west as Detroit), very successfully introduced the new European fashion for promenade concerts in December 1838. His band survived until the Civil War. Composed dances, marches, songs, piano pieces.

Bibl.: Eileen Southern, "Frank Johnson and His Promenade Concerts," *Black Perspective in Music* 5 (1977): 3–29.

Johnson, Hunter (b. Benson, N.C., 14 Apr. 1906). Composer. He studied at the Univ. of North Carolina (1924–26) and at Eastman (1929); taught at the Univ. of Michigan (1929–33), the Univ. of Manitoba (1944–47), Cornell (1948–53), the Univ. of Illinois (1959–65), and the Univ. of Texas (1966–71). His compositional style shows the influence of jazz idioms. Works include 2 ballets commisioned by Martha Graham (*Letter to the World,* 1940; *The Scarlet Letter,* 1975) and other orchestral works (Symphony no. 1, 1913; Concerto, piano, chamber orchestra, 1935–36; *For an Unknown Soldier,* flute, strings, 1938; *Deaths and Entrances,* ballet, 1943; *Music for String Orchestra,* 1949–54; *North State,* 1963; *Past the Evening Sun,* 1964); instrumental music (*Scherzo from the South,* piano, 1928; Piano Sonata, 1933–34, rev. 1936 and 1947–48; *Elegy for Hart Crane,* clarinet quintet, 1936; Serenade, flute, clarinet, 1937; *In Time of Armament,* ballet, 2 pianos, 1939; Trio, flute, oboe, piano, 1954); songs (2 Songs, 1932; 3 Songs, 1956–59).

Johnson, James P(rice) (b. New Brunswick, N.J., 1 Feb. 1894; d. New York, 17 Nov. 1955). Pianist and composer. In jazz he was the foremost exponent of the stride piano style, and his composition "Carolina Shout," recorded in 1921, became the test piece for younger musicians. From 1921 he accompanied blues singers, including recordings (1927–30) and the film *St. Louis Blues* (1929) with Bessie Smith. In musical theater, Cecil Mack and he wrote "Runnin' Wild," and their hit song "The Charleston" started that dance craze (1923). He wrote numerous other stage shows, including *Keep Shufflin'* with Fats Waller (1928), *The Kitchen Mechanics Revue* (1930), and *Sugar Hill* (1931). Among his many songs were "If I Could Be With You One Hour Tonight" (1926) and "A Porter's Love Song to a Chambermaid" (1930); among piano compositions, "Snowy Morning Blues" (1927) and "Riffs" (1929). From 1927 he also began composing orchestral works drawing on jazz and classical sources, including *Yamekraw* for piano and orchestra (1927). From the late 1930s he was active as a soloist, leader, and sideman in the revival of traditional jazz, including broadcasts on the radio series *This Is Jazz* (1947).

Bibl.: Scott E. Brown, *James P. Johnson: A Case of Mistaken Identity* (Metuchen, N.J., 1986); discography by Robert Hilbert, Jr.

Johnson, James Weldon [William] (b. Jacksonville, Fla., 17 June 1871; d. Wiscasset, Maine, 26 June 1938). Writer and lyricist. He was an educator and a lawyer in Florida. Moved to New York in 1899 to produce an operetta written with his brother J. Rosamund Johnson; they subsequently collaborated with lyricist and composer Bob Cole on many songs for musical comedies ("Under the Bamboo Tree," 1902; "The Congo Love Song," 1903). His brother's setting of his poem "Lift Every Voice and Sing" (1901) became known as the "Negro National Anthem"; he authored 2 valuable sources for early 20th-century black musical society, *Autobiography of an Ex-Colored Man* (1912) and *Black Manhattan* (1930), and with his brother compiled 2 collections of Negro spirituals (1925–26).

Johnson, J. J. [James Louis] (b. Indianapolis, 22 Jan. 1924). Jazz trombonist. He joined the big bands of Benny Carter (1942–45) and Count Basie (1945–46). Moving to New York in 1946, he played trombone with a previously unimagined dexterity (as on his recording *Mad Bebop,* 1946) and began working mainly with the leading bop musicians, but also with Illinois Jacquet (1947–49). Kai Winding and he led a quintet (1954–56, 1958, 1960, including the album *The Great Kai and J. J.,* 1960). Johnson also led his own groups (1956–64) and joined Miles Davis (1961–62). Having written big band arrangements and bop themes, in 1956 he began composing extended jazz compositions and a decade later largely abandoned jazz performance for a career writing for films and television. He resumed regular playing in 1987.

Johnson, J(ohn) Rosamund (b. Jacksonville, Fla., 11 Aug. 1873; d. New York, 11 Nov. 1954). Popular songwriter, lyricist, and singer. He studied music at the New England Conservatory; from 1899 he composed songs for musicals in collaboration with his brother, James Weldon Johnson, and Bob Cole; he produced 2 full-length works, *The Shoo-Fly Regiment* (1907) and *The Red Moon* (1909). He directed and performed in musicals in New York and London, and published 4 collections of black music, including 2 volumes of spirituals compiled with his brother (1925–26), as well as *Shout Songs* (1936), and *Rolling Along in Song* (1937).

Johnson, John (fl. 1579–94). Composer. English lutenist appointed to the royal court in 1579. Most of his works, nearly all for lute or lute duet, are pavanes, galliards, or settings of popular tunes. His greatest contribution lies in the duets.

Bibl.: Lyle Nordstrom, "The Lute Duets of John Johnson," *Journal of the Lute Society of America* 9 (1976): 30–42.

Johnson, Lonnie [Alonzo] (b. New Orleans, 8 Feb. 1889; d. Toronto, 16 June 1970). Jazz and blues guitarist and singer. He worked in Mississippi riverboat orchestras, in TOBA theaters, and clubs in St. Louis and New Orleans. He recorded prolifically in St. Louis, New York, and Chicago, making equally assertive contributions to blues and jazz. As a blues singer his best early work is with his multi-instrumentalist brother James 'Steady Roll' Johnson. As a jazz guitarist he recorded with Louis Armstrong (1927, including "Hotter Than That," and 1929) and Duke Ellington (1928). His solo guitar tour-de-force "To Do This You Gotta Know How" (1926) is rivaled only by his duets with Eddie Lang (1928–29). Later he recorded mainly as a blues singer for 40 years, adopting a hard-edged urban style, though often accompanied by major jazz musicians.

Johnson, Pete(r) (b. Kansas City, Mo., 25 Mar. 1904; d. Buffalo, 23 Mar. 1967). Boogie-woogie pianist. He accompanied Joe Turner at the Sunset Cafe in Kansas City. Moving to New York, he played at the Famous Door club, recorded "Roll 'em Pete" with Turner (1938), and formed the Boogie Woogie Trio with Albert Ammons and Meade "Lux" Lewis for the Spirituals to Swing concert at Carnegie Hall (1938) and subsequent work at Cafe Society (1939). In the 1940s he worked as a soloist and in duos with Ammons or Lewis. He played mainly in Buffalo from 1950 until suffering a stroke in 1958.

Johnson, Robert (1) (b. ca. 1583; d. London, before 26 Nov. 1633). Lutenist and composer. Entered the service of Lord Chamberlain Sir George Carey as "allowes of covenant servaunt, for seven years" beginning in 1596; became lutenist to King James I in 1604, serving in the same post under Charles I and adding the title of composer for "lute and voices" in 1628. A successor was appointed on 26 Nov. 1633. He was deeply involved in stage productions (Sir George Carey was patron of the King's Men Players), writing songs for plays by Shakespeare *(The Tempest),* Webster, Beaumont and Fletcher; also collaborated with Jonson, Chapman, and Campion in the staging of court masques. Other music includes anthems, dances, and works for lute.

Johnson, Robert (2) (b. Hazelhurst, Miss., 8 May 1911; d. Greenwood, Miss., 16 Aug. 1938). Blues singer and guitarist. Second-hand accounts describe a wild life as a musical hobo in the South. His contemporaries regarded him as among the finest blues musicians, a claim supported by three dozen recordings (1936–37). He treated the blues with rhythmic flexibility, yet also created driving steady rhythmic patterns which later reappeared in urban blues and rock ("Walking Blues"). His lyrics focused on love life ("Terraplane Blues"), but also presented haunting images ("Hellhound on My Trail") and addressed social issues ("Crossroads Blues"). His singing, generally high-pitched, nasal, and piercing, incorporated growls, soft-spoken asides, and falsetto swoops. He was murdered in 1938.

Johnson, Robert Sherlaw (b. Sunderland, Durham, 21 May 1932). Composer. After studying at Durham Univ. (1950–53), he attended the Royal Academy (1953–57), and from 1957 took instruction from Nadia Boulanger, Olivier Messiaen, and Jacques Février in France. He was appointed lecturer in music in 1961 at the Univ. of Leeds; later he taught at Bradford Grammar School (from 1963), at the Univ. of York (1965–70), and at Oxford (from 1970). His music shows the strong influence of Messiaen, with a nod to the serialism of Boulez. Works include an opera, *The Lambton Worm* (1976–77); choral/orchestral works (*A Liturgy of the Nativity,* 1962; *Veni Sancte Spiritus,* chorus, percussion, 1965; *Congregational Mass,* 1967; *Incarnatio,* chorus, 1970; *Christus resurgens,* chorus, 1972); solo vocal (*Green Whispers of Gold,* soprano, piano, tape, 1971; *Where the Wild Things Are,* soprano, tape, 1974); chamber/instrumental music (*In Nomine for Edmund Rubbra,* piano, 1971; 3 piano sonatas, 1963, 1967, 1976; 2 string quartets, 1966, 1969; Piano Quintet, 1974).

Johnson, Tom (b. Greeley, Colo., 18 Nov. 1939). Composer and critic. He studied English and music at Yale (M.M., 1967) and composition privately with Feldman (late 1960s). From 1971 to 1983 he served as contemporary music critic for the *Village Voice;* in 1983 he moved to Paris. His compositions include minimalist operas (*The Four-Note Opera,* 1972; *Réservé aux sopranes,* 1984; *Riemannoper,* 1986; *200 ANS,* 1989); theater pieces (*Self Portrait,* for actor/box mover and instrumental ensemble, 1983); *Nine Bells* (for a performer wandering among suspended fire alarm bells, 1979); *The Towers of Hanoi* (gamelan, 1982), *Elegy* (string quartet, 1982), *Risks for Unrehearsed Performers* (one or more instruments, 1977), *An Hour for Piano* (1971), and other instrumental music; some vocal and choral music.

Johnston, Ben(jamin Burwell, Jr.) (b. Macon, Ga., 15 Mar. 1926). Composer and theorist. He was educated at Catholic Univ. and the College of William and Mary (1945–49), then at the Cincinnati Conservatory (M.M., 1950); he studied privately with Partch (1950–51), on whose music he has lectured and written. From 1951 he taught at the Univ. of Illinois, retiring in 1983. In 1959 he studied at the Columbia–Princeton Center for Electronic Music with Luening and Ussachevsky; he also studied privately with Cage. He composed in a variety of styles (serial, electronic, aleatory, microtonal) but is especially associated with works in just intonation. Works include a rock chamber opera (*Carmilla,* 1970), theater pieces, ballets, and incidental music; *Quintet for Groups* (orchestra, 1966); several string quartets, *12 Partials* (flute and retuned piano, 1981), Sonata for microtonal piano (1965), and other instrumental music; choral music and songs; music for films and exhibitions.

Bibl.: Heidi von Gunden, *The Music of Ben Johnston* (Metuchen, N.J., 1985).

Jolas [Illouz], **Betsy** (b. Paris, 5 Aug. 1926). Composer and conductor. Moved to the U.S. in 1940 and studied music at Bennington (B.A., 1946) under Boepple (composition), Helen Schnabel (piano), and Weinrich (organ); she returned to Paris to study with Milhaud, Messiaen, and Simone Plé-Caussade. She won an international conducting competition at Besançon (1953); taught at the Paris Conservatory from 1971 (at first at Messiaen's request, from 1975 as a member of the regular faculty); in the U.S. she was active at Mills, the Berkshire Music Center, Yale, and the Univ. of Southern California. Her music is in a lyrical style, sometimes employing serial procedures. Compositions include a chamber opera (1975) and the operas *Le cyclope* (after Euripides, 1986) and *Schliemann* (1988–89); works for orchestra (*Stances,* piano and orchestra, 1978); many pieces for ensembles of 10–20 players (*Points d'Aube,* viola and 13 winds, 1968); works for smaller ensembles (*Quatuor III,* 9 etudes for string quartet, 1973; a piano trio, 1989); choral and solo vocal music.

Jolivet, André (b. Paris, 8 Aug. 1905; d. there, 20 Dec. 1974). Composer. As a child Jolivet studied piano, cello, harmony, and organ, and began to compose; at 15 he trained as a teacher and taught in Paris schools from 1927. His study of harmony, counterpoint, and classical forms continued with Le Flem (1928–33) and with Varèse (1930–33). His pieces for piano, *Mana* (1935), caused Messiaen to write an enthusiastic article in support of the young composer, and subsequently Jolivet joined with Yves Baudrier, Daniel Lesur, and Messiaen in forming the group Jeune France, whose first concert was presented in 1936.

Pieces composed during World War II were more conventional than his prewar work, but some of the innovatory techniques were reappropriated and integrated with the more traditional in pieces from 1945 on. He remained interested in exoticism. The concertos of the 1950s and 1960s emphasize virtuosity of the soloists.

He served as director of music at the Comédie-

Française (1943–59); was a technical consultant to the Direction générale des arts et lettres (1959–62); was a founder of the Centre français d'humanisme musical at Aix-en-Provence (1959); taught composition at the Paris Conservatory (1966–70).

Works: ballets and other dramatic works; *Cosmogenie* (1938) and *5 danses rituelles* (1939), both for piano or orchestra, and other orchestral works (including several concertos and 3 symphonies); *Cérémonial, hommage à Varèse* (6 percussionists, 1968), *Rapsodie à 7* (clarinet, bassoon, cornet, trombone, percussion, violin, double bass, 1957), and other chamber music; *La vérité de Jeanne* (oratorio, 6 solo voices, reciter, chorus, orchestra, 1956) and other large-scale choral works; *Cinq incantations* (flute, 1936) and other solo works for guitar, violin, viola, cello, harp; piano and organ works (*Étude sur des modes antiques,* piano, 1944); songs with piano, ensemble, or orchestra; didactic works; and incidental music.

Bibl.: Serge Gut, *Le groupe Jeune-France: Y. Baudrier, D. Lesur, André Jolivet, O. Messiaen* (Paris, 1977). Hilda Jolivet, *Avec André Jolivet* (Paris, 1978).

Jolson, Al [Yoelson, Asa] (b. Srednike [now Seredzius], Lithuania, 26 May 1886; d. San Francisco, 23 Oct. 1950). Popular singer, actor. He was raised in Washington, D.C., and began appearing in vaudeville and minstrel shows there and in New York; from 1911 he sang in revues at the Shubert Brothers' Winter Garden Theatre. There he became famous for stepping out of character and establishing direct rapport with the audience; in later shows he dispensed with dramatic situations and featured only his singing. In 1927 he appeared in the first successful sound film, *The Jazz Singer,* performing songs from the Shubert revues including "My Mammy" (from *Sinbad,* 1918) and "Toot, Toot, Tootsie" (from *Bombo,* 1921). He continued to appear in films and made many popular recordings ("Swanee," first recorded in 1920; "Sonny Boy," 1928); in 1946 he was the subject of a biographical film, *The Jolson Story.*

Bibl.: Larry F. Kiner, *The Al Jolson Discography* (Westport, Conn., 1983).

Jommelli, Niccolò [Nicolò] (b. Aversa, near Naples, 10 Sept. 1714; d. Naples, 25 Aug. 1774). Composer. From 1725 to 1728 he studied at the Conservatorio S. Onofrio in Naples, with Ignazio Prota and Francesco Feo; then he took further instruction at the Conservatorio Pietà dei Turchini, under Fago, Basso, and Sarconi. He composed his first opera, *L'errore amoroso,* for Naples in 1737; it was followed by other successes, most notably *Ricimero rè dei Goti* (Rome, 1740). In 1741 he moved to Bologna to oversee the production of his *Ezio;* there he met Padre Martini, with whom he probably studied counterpoint, and was elected to membership in the Accademia filarmonica in Bologna. In Venice he served for three years (1743–46) as director of the Ospedale degli incurabili. He moved to Rome in 1747, and two years later he was appointed *maestro coadiutore* of the papal chapel; during this period he continued to compose operas, in addition to the sacred music required of him at the chapel. He spent 1749–50 in Vienna, where he helped to mount performances of two of his opere serie, *Achille in Sciro* and *Didone abbandonata.* In 1754 he was called to Stuttgart, where he remained as court opera composer until 1768; he composed some of his finest operas for the court's Ludwigsburg Palace (*Fetonte,* 1768), and also contributed operas for the court theater of José I of Portugal. In 1769 he negotiated a contract with José that allowed him to compose operas for Lisbon without having to travel there; in the same year he returned to Italy. His final years were occupied chiefly with the composition of operas and sacred music for Lisbon and Naples. Overworked and plagued by gout, he suffered a stroke in 1771; continuing to work in spite of paralysis, he completed his final opera seria, *Il trionfo di Clelia,* months before his death. In all some 220 theater works are known, including more than 60 opere serie; titles not mentioned include *Demetrio* (Parma, 1749); *Ciro riconosciuto* (Venice, 1749); *Attilio Regolo* (Rome, 1753); *L'Olimpiade* (Stuttgart, 1761); *Demofoonte* (Stuttgart, 1764); and *Temistocle* (Ludwigsburg, 1765). He also composed comic operas (*La critica,* Ludwigsburg, 1766; *La schiava liberata,* Ludwigsburg, 1768); serenatas and pasticcios; oratorios, cantatas, and hundreds of other sacred works (including some 20 Masses); chamber works and concertos.

Bibl.: Hermann Abert, *Niccolò Jommelli als Opernkomponist* (Halle, 1908). Rudolf Kraus, *Das Stuttgarter Hoftheater* (Stuttgart, 1908). Robert R. Pattengale, "The Cantatas of Niccolò Jommelli" (diss., Univ. of Michigan, 1973). Jon Olof Carlson, "Selected Masses of Niccolò Jommelli" (diss., Univ. of Illinois, 1974). Audrey Lyn Tolkoff, "The Stuttgart Operas of Niccolò Jommelli" (diss., Yale Univ., 1974). Marita McClymonds, *Niccolò Jommelli: The Last Years* (Ann Arbor, 1980). Wolfgang Hochstein, *Die Kirchenmusik von Niccolò Jommelli (1714–1774)* (New York, 1984).

Jones, Charles (b. Tamworth, Ont., 21 June 1910). Composer. He studied violin at the Institute of Musical Art in New York (1928–32) and composition with Wagenaar at Juilliard (1939). Taught at Mills College (1939–44), the Music Academy of the West (Santa Barbara, 1949–50), the Aspen Festival (from 1951), Juilliard (1954–60, 1973), and Mannes College (from 1972). In the course of his career, his early diatonic and neoclassical style developed increasing chromaticism and complexity.

Works: an oratorio (*Piers the Plowman,* 1963); *Allegory* (divided orchestra, 1970) and other orchestral music; 8 string quartets (1936–80), *Meditation* (bass clarinet and piano, 1982), and other chamber music; several piano sonatas, pieces for 2 pianos and piano 4-hands, children's pieces, and other piano works; choral music; a cantata and several song cycles.

Jones, Daniel (Jenkyn) (b. Pembroke, Wales, 7 Dec. 1912; d. 1993). Composer. He attended Swansea Univ. College (1931–34) and studied composition (with Harry Farjeon) and conducting (with Henry Wood) at the Royal Academy of Music (1935–38). He received the Mendelssohn Scholarship in 1935 and a D.Mus. from the Univ. of Wales in 1951. He was a boyhood friend of Dylan Thomas, whose poetry he edited in 1971. His music embraces Welsh folk music, "oriental" sonorities, and complex polyrhythms; works include operas (*The Knife,* 1963; *Orestes,* 1967); cantatas (*The Country Beyond the Stars,* 1958); oratorios (*St. Peter,* 1962); other choral works (*Triptych,* 1969; *The Witnesses,* 1971); 9 symphonies (no. 4, In Memory of Dylan Thomas, 1954); Violin Concerto (1966); chamber/instrumental music (8 string quartets; *Suite,* viola and cello, 1949; string trios; a sonata for cello and piano, 1972). His dissertation at Swansea Univ. was "Elizabethan Lyric Poetry and Its Relations with Elizabethan Music" (1939).

Jones, Elvin (Ray) (b. Pontiac, Mich., 9 Sept. 1927). Jazz drummer and bandleader. Brother of Hank and Thad Jones. He joined the saxophonist Billy Mitchell's bop quintet in Detroit (ca. 1950–53). After moving to New York, he worked with Charles Mingus, Bud Powell, J. J. Johnson, Pepper Adams and Donald Byrd, and Harry Edison. As a member of John Coltrane's quartet (1960–66), he created a complex, constantly changing, yet clearly articulated flow of overlapping rhythms; their recordings include the albums *Coltrane* (1962), *A Love Supreme* (1964), and *Ascension* (1965). From 1966 through the 1980s he led groups. The film *Different Drummer: Elvin Jones* (1979) surveys his career.

Jones, George (b. Saratoga, Tex., 12 Sept. 1931). Country singer and songwriter. After early performances in honky-tonks and on radio in Texas, he joined the "Louisiana Hayride" and the Grand Ole Opry in 1956. He began recording in 1954; popular songs included "White Lightning" (1958), "The Race Is On" (1964), and "Walk Through This World with Me" (1967). He also recorded duets with Tammy Wynette (including "We're Gonna Hold On," 1973, and the album *Together Again,* 1980).

Jones, Hank [Henry] (b. Vicksburg, Miss., 31 July 1918). Jazz pianist. He joined Hot Lips Page in New York (1944), then worked with John Kirby, Coleman Hawkins, Andy Kirk, and Billy Eckstine. While touring with Ella Fitzgerald and Jazz at the Philharmonic (1947–53), he recorded with Charlie Parker, including "Star Eyes" (1950). He joined Artie Shaw and began a long intermittent association with Benny Goodman before joining the staff of CBS (1959–ca. 1976). He played in and conducted the show *Ain't Misbehavin'* (late 1970s–early 1980s) and led the Great Jazz Trio from 1976. Throughout his career he recorded prolifically, including the album *Solo Piano* (ca. 1980).

Jones, Jo(nathan) (b. Chicago, 7 Oct. 1911; d. New York, 3 Sept. 1985). Jazz drummer. He joined Count Basie (1934–44, 1946–48), forming a part of one of the finest swing rhythm sections, as on recordings such as "One O'Clock Jump" (1937) and "Jumpin' at the Woodside" (1938). He performed in the film *Jammin' the Blues* (1944); toured with Jazz at the Philharmonic intermittently from 1947; joined Illinois Jacquet, Lester Young, and Teddy Wilson; led groups; and worked as a free-lance, including a featured role in the television show *The Sound of Jazz* (1957). On the album *The Drums* (1973) he demonstrates jazz drumming, including the variety and subtlety of his hi-hat cymbal playing.

Jones, Jonah [Robert Elliott] (b. Louisville, Ky., 31 Dec. 1909). Jazz trumpeter and bandleader. He joined Stuff Smith (1932–34, 1936–40), recording "After You've Gone" in 1936. He played in the big bands of Benny Carter (1940), Fletcher Henderson (1941), and Cab Calloway (1941–52, including the recording "Jonah Joins the Cab," 1941). After working with Earl Hines (1952–53) and as a free-lance, he formed a swing quartet which became popular while working at the Embers club in New York (1955 to mid-1960s), and continued into the 1980s touring internationally. The quartet's albums include *Muted Jazz* (1957).

Jones, Philip (b. Bath, 12 Mar. 1928). Trumpeter. He studied with Ernest Hall at the Royal College of Music, subsequently served as first trumpet with most of the leading London orchestras, including the Royal Philharmonic (1956–60), the Philharmonia (1960–64), the London Philharmonic (1964–65), the New Philharmonia (1965–67), and the BBC Symphony (1968–71). In 1951 he formed the Philip Jones Brass Ensemble, which enjoyed considerable success in recital and in many recordings. From 1983 he taught at the Guildhall School of Music.

Jones, Philly Joe [Joseph Rudolph] (b. Philadelphia, 15 July 1923; d. there, 30 Aug. 1985). Jazz drummer. After occasionally performing (from 1952) and recording (from 1953) with Miles Davis, he joined Davis's hard bop quintet and sextet (1955–58), recording the albums *'Round about Midnight* (1955–56) and *Milestones* (1958). He also recorded often as a free-lance, including John Coltrane's album *Blue Train* (1957). He led a group (1959–62), briefly rejoined Davis (1962), then played and taught in Japan, the U.S. (including a period with Bill Evans, 1967), England, and France. He led a jazz-rock group in Philadelphia from 1972, rejoined Evans (1976), toured with Red Garland, and formed Dameronia, a nonet devoted to Tadd Dameron's music (1981–85).

Jones, Quincy (Delight, Jr.) (b. Chicago, 14 Mar. 1933). Composer, arranger, conductor, producer, and bandleader. He played trumpet in Lionel Hampton's big band (1951–53), touring Europe, and began arranging for jazz groups. He directed Dizzy Gillespie's big band on international tours (1956), composed music for his own album *This Is How I Feel about Jazz* (1956), studied composition while working for Barclay Records in Paris, and returned to Europe directing his own all-star big band in the show *Free and Easy* (1959–60). While working as an executive for the Mercury and A&M record companies, he began writing for films and television, including soundtracks for *The Pawnbroker* (1965), *In the Heat of the Night, In Cold Blood* (both 1967), and *The Color Purple* (1985), and themes for two Bill Cosby series. In the 1980s he produced and directed albums for Michael Jackson

(*Thriller,* 1982) and Frank Sinatra (1984), as well as the song "We Are the World" (1986), which raised substantial funds for the Ethiopian famine relief effort.

Bibl.: Raymond Horricks, *Quincy Jones* (Tunbridge Wells, England, 1986).

Jones, Robert (fl. 1597–1615). Composer. Received the B.Mus. at Oxford in 1597; published 5 lute song collections beginning in 1600, and a single book of madrigals in 1607, also writing a madrigal for *The Triumphs of Orianna* (1601). In 1610–15 he was one of 4 leaders of an ensemble of children called Children of the Revells of the Queene. The technical failings in some of his compositions have come under criticism from both his contemporaries and modern writers.

Jones, (James) Sydney (b. London, 17 June 1861; d. there, 29 Jan. 1946). Composer. Son of a musician; played the clarinet in bands and orchestras conducted by his father; later a theater conductor (Prince of Wales Theatre, London; from 1905, Empire Theatre). Between 1893 and 1916 he composed many English musical comedies produced in London, including *The Geisha* (1896), one of the most successful and widely performed of the period.

Jones [née Joyner], **(Matilda) Sissieretta** (b. Portsmouth, Va., 5 Jan. 1869; d. Providence, 24 June 1933). Soprano. Studied singing at Providence Academy of Music and New England Conservatory; 1888, began to tour widely with black concert companies (U.S., West Indies, Canada, eventually Europe) or (occasionally) minstrel troupes, quickly becoming a star, billed as the "Black Patti." Sang at the White House in 1892. Toured with her own vaudeville company, 1896–1915, Black Patti's Troubadours. Her repertory ranged from opera arias to popular songs.

Bibl.: Eileen Southern and J. Wright, "Sissieretta Jones," *Black Perspective in Music* 4 (1976): 191–201.

Jones, Thad(deus Joseph) (b. Pontiac, Mich., 28 Mar. 1923; d. Copenhagen, 20 Aug. 1986). Jazz trumpeter, cornetist, flugelhorn player, composer, and bandleader; brother of Elvin and Hank Jones. Together with Elvin, he worked in the saxophonist Billy Mitchell's quintet in Detroit, accompanying leading bop musicians (1950–53). He worked with Charles Mingus, recording the album *The Fabulous Thad Jones* (1954), and joined Count Basie's big band (1954–63). With Mel Lewis he led a big band of studio musicians (1965–79), mainly playing at the Village Vanguard in New York, but also touring. Jones's compositions for it include *The Big Dipper* and the title track on the album *Central Park North* (1969). Having led groups in Denmark from 1977, he settled there in 1979, then returned to the U.S. to direct the memorial Basie orchestra (1984–86).

Jongen, Joseph (Marie Alphonse Nicolas) (b. Liège, 14 Dec. 1873; d. Sart-lez-Spa, province of Liège, 12 July 1953). Composer. Brother of composer and pianist Léon Jongen. His musical training began at age 7, when he entered the Liège Conservatory, where he later won prizes in fugue (1891), piano (1892), and organ (1896). In 1894 his String Quartet op. 3 won the Belgian Royal Academy competition. In 1897 his cantata *Comala* won the Belgian Prix de Rome, after which he was able to study first in Berlin, where he was influenced by Strauss, then in Munich, where he became interested in Wagner, and finally in Paris (1899), where he met d'Indy and Fauré. The Piano Quartet (1902) is dedicated to d'Indy. He returned to Belgium in 1902 to become a professor at the Liège Conservatory.

In 1914, at the start of World War I, he went to England, where he founded a piano quartet, the Belgian Quartet, that performed some of his music. In 1920 he was elected to the Belgian Royal Academy and joined the faculty of the Brussels Conservatory in counterpoint and fugue; he became its director in 1925. His brother Léon succeeded him in this post in 1939. He was also conductor of a musical society known as the Concerts spirituels, with whom he premiered Belgian contemporary works. His music of the early 1920s shows the influence of Debussy and Ravel. His *Symphonie concertante* (1926) contains atonal passages. He wrote numerous pieces for orchestra and for chamber ensembles. Toward the end of his life Jongen reevaluated his catalog of works and withdrew all but 137 of his compositions. The Centre belge de documentation musicale published a catalog of his works in 1954.

Jongen, Léon (Marie Victor Justin) (b. Liège, 2 Mar. 1884; d. Brussels, 18 Nov. 1969). Composer. Brother of composer and organist Joseph Jongen. He studied at the conservatory in Liège, where he was also organist at St. Jacques from 1898 to 1904. He won the Belgian Prix de Rome in 1913 with his cantata *Les fiancés de noël.* After a period of concertizing as a pianist he was conductor of the Tonkin Opera in Hanoi (1927–29). Then he became professor of fugue at the Brussels Conservatory, where he succeeded his brother Joseph as director from 1939 to 1949. He was elected to the Belgian Royal Academy in 1945. His Violin Concerto (1962) was the compulsory piece for the 1963 Queen Elisabeth Instrumental Competition. Works include 2 operas (*L'ardennaise,* 1909; *Thomas l'Agnelet,* 1922–23); 2 ballets; *Ouverture pour Oedipe roi* (orchestra, 1908), *Malaisie* (orchestra, 1935), *Prélude, divertissement et finale* (piano, orchestra, 1937), *Fantaisie* (piano, orchestra, 1938), *Rhapsodia belgica* (violin, orchestra, 1948), *4 miniatures* (orchestra, 1949); *Improvisation en mode lyrique* (after Lassus, orchestra, 1955); 4 works for chorus and orchestra; chamber music, songs, film music, and pieces for brass band.

Joplin, Janis (Lyn) (b. Port Arthur, Tex., 19 Jan. 1943; d. Hollywood, 4 Oct. 1970). Blues and rock singer. Began performing in bars in Texas and California; in 1966 joined Big Brother and the Holding Company in

Scott Joplin.

San Francisco; later led the Kozmic Blues Band and the Full Tilt Boogie Band. A leading figure of the San Francisco psychedelic era, she was one of the first women to establish an independent image in rock music, becoming famous for her highly emotional, blues-oriented interpretations. Her recordings included "Women Is Losers" (1968), "Me and Bobby McGee" (1971), and "Get It While You Can" (1971).

Joplin, Scott (b. near Marshall, Tex., or Shreveport, La., 24 Nov. 1868; d. New York, 1 Apr. 1917). Composer, pianist. He grew up in Texarkana, Tex., in a large musical family: his father, a former slave, had been a plantation fiddler, his mother a singer. He learned several instruments as a child and taught himself to play a used piano his parents bought for him; he later had classical piano training from a local German immigrant. In his early teens he sang, played, and taught professionally; he organized a touring vocal group. In about 1894 he left home, settling in St. Louis, where he played piano in brothels and cafes. He traveled widely, notably to the 1893 Chicago World's Fair, as a bandleader playing cornet and piano. In 1895 he toured a vaudeville circuit singing in his own eight-voice Texas Medley Quartette; he issued his first publications, two waltz songs, in Syracuse, N.Y.

In 1896 Joplin resettled in Sedalia, Mo., to study music at George R. Smith College for Negroes. He also taught, played at a prominent black dance hall, the Maple Leaf Club, and published piano pieces with a Kansas City firm. With a local publisher, John Stark, he issued his first wholly original ragtime piece, the *Maple Leaf Rag.* This piece brought enormous success to Joplin and Stark, engendering a stream of some 40 piano rags, marches, and waltzes from Joplin's pen that spanned the rest of his career and ensured his financial stability.

Success fired his ambitions; he produced a ragtime ballet, *The Ragtime Dance,* in 1899, but to little notice. He married, moved back to St. Louis, and in 1903 produced a ragtime opera, *The Guest of Honor* (lost), which achieved only modest recognition. Living in Chicago in 1906–7 he began his last major work, the ragtime opera *Treemonisha.* His health failing from syphilis, he separated from his wife. In 1907 he moved to New York following Stark; he remarried and continued to teach and compose. In 1911 he published *Treemonisha* at his own expense, and in 1915 staged a concert performance of it. Although critical interest was aroused, no producer came forth. He claimed to have finished other New York projects—a vaudeville sketch, a musical comedy, and a ragtime symphony—but the scores are unknown. Late in 1916 his sanity waned, and he was hospitalized until his death. A rebirth of recognition came over half a century later with extensive recording of his rags and a successful premiere of *Treemonisha* in Atlanta in 1972.

Bibl.: Edward A. Berlin, *King of Ragtime: Scott Joplin and His Era* (New York, 1994). Susan Curtis, *Dancing to a Black Man's Tune: A Life of Scott Joplin* (Columbia, 1994).

Jora, Mihail (b. Roman, Romania, 14 Aug. 1891; d. Bucharest, 10 May 1971). Composer. He studied at the Iaşi Conservatory (1909–11), and with Reger at the Leipzig Conservatory (1912–14); later he was a pupil of Florent Schmitt in Paris (from 1919). He founded and chaired the Romanian Composers' Society (beginning 1920), and was music director at Romanian Radio (1928–33). From 1929 he taught theory and composition at the Bucharest Conservatory, and from 1941 to 1947 was its rector. His music employs elements of late Romantic German style as well as early 20th-century French impressionism. Works include the ballet scores *La piaţţă* [At the Marketplace] (1928), *Curtea veche* [The Old Court] (1948), *Cînd strugurii se coc* [When the Grapes Ripen] (1958), and *Hanul Dulcinea* [Dulcinea's Inn] (1966); the orchestral works *Suita* (1915), *Poveste indică* [Hindu Tale] (1920), Symphony in C (1937), *Burlesca* (1949); many songs; chamber works (*Poze şi pozne* [Pictures and Tricks], piano; a violin sonata, 1951, a viola sonata, 1962).

Jordan, Louis (b. Brinkley, Ark., 8 July 1908; d. Los Angeles, 4 Feb. 1975). Rhythm-and-blues saxophonist, singer, and bandleader. After playing in Chick Webb's big band (1936–38), he formed the Tympany Five, which perhaps more than any other combo established the rhythm-and-blues style during the 1940s. Hit songs included "Five Guys Named Moe" (1943), "Is You Is, or Is You Ain't (Ma' Baby?)" (1945), "Choo Choo Ch'Boogie" (1946), and "Saturday Night Fish

Fry" (1949); films included *Caldonia* (1945). Jordan led his Tympany Five regularly through the 1950s and intermittently into the 1970s.

Jordan, Stanley (b. Chicago, 31 July 1959). Jazz guitarist. He graduated in music from Princeton (1981). Exploiting the amplification of the electric guitar, he developed a technique that allowed him to stop and sound strings independently with each hand, separating melody and chords, or producing 2 independent solo lines. After acclaimed performances at jazz festivals in 1984–85, he recorded the albums *Magic Touch* (1985) and *Standards* (ca. 1986). He tours widely as an unaccompanied soloist.

Joseffy, Rafael (b. Hunfalu, Hungary, 3 July 1852; d. New York, 25 June 1915). Pianist. Student at the Leipzig Conservatory, 1866–68; his principal teacher was Tausig in Berlin, 1868–70; also had lessons from Liszt at Weimar (summer 1870, 1871). From 1870 he toured Europe, from 1879 America, settling in New York; later turned increasingly to teaching (1888–1906, at the National Conservatory, New York), writing studies (*School of Advanced Piano Playing,* New York, 1902), and editing Chopin and other piano classics.

Bibl.: E. Hughes, "Rafael Joseffy's Contribution to Piano Technic," *MQ* 2 (1916): 349–64.

Josephs, Wilfred (b. Newcastle upon Tyne, 24 July 1927). Composer. After studying and practicing dentistry until the early 1950s, in 1954 he enrolled in the Guildhall School of Music on a scholarship; there he studied composition with Alfred Nieman. Subsequently he took instruction in Paris from Max Deutsch. He won first prize at the 1963 International Competition of La Scala and the City of Milan, for composition of a Requiem on the text of the Kaddish. Since then he devoted his time chiefly to music. Works include theater music (*The Nottingham Captain,* 1962; *Pathelin,* "opera-entertainment," 1963; *Adam and Eve,* 1967; *The Appointment,* television opera, 1968); the opera *Rebecca* (1981–83); 2 children's operas after Lewis Carroll (*Through the Looking Glass,* 1977–78; *Alice in Wonderland,* 1985–88); ballets (*La répétition de Phèdre,* 1964–67); orchestral music (9 symphonies, 1955–80; 2 piano concertos, 1965, 1971; a cello concerto, 1962; concerto for 2 violins and chamber orchestra, 1969; *Aeolian Dances,* 1961; *Monkchester Dances,* 1961; *Canzonas on a Theme of Rameau,* strings, 1965; *Polemic,* strings, 1967; *Rail,* 1967; *Saratoga Concerto,* guitar, harp, harpsichord, chamber orchestra, 1972; *Four Horsemen of the Apocalypse,* 1973–74; *The Brontës,* overture, 1981; a percussion concerto, 1982; a viola concerto, 1983; *Requiem,* baritone, 2 choruses, string quintet, orchestra, 1963; *Mortales,* soloists, chorus, orchestra, 1967–69; *Death of a Young Man,* baritone, orchestra, 1970); 4 string quartets (1954–81); 2 sonatas for violin and piano (1965, 1975); a string quintet (1971); a piano quintet (1977); a piano sonata (1963).

Josquin Desprez [Juschino; Jodocus Pratensis; Joducus a Prato] (b. Picardy?, northern France, ca. 1440; d. Condé-sur-Escaut, Hainaut, 27 Aug. 1521). Composer. Although his association with Condé may extend back to before 1477, a document found there indicates that he registered with the authorities as an alien shortly before his death, and thus was born in France. Nothing is known of his early training; a 17th-century source names him as a choirboy at St. Quentin in Picardy, without providing documentation. The *déplorations* for Ockeghem written by Molinet and Crétin suggest an association between Josquin and the older composer, but the earliest evidence of his life is a 1459 notice listing him as a singer ("biscantor," presumably not a choirboy) at Milan Cathedral. He remained at that post until December 1472. In July 1474 he appears among the 22 chapel singers of Duke Galeazzo Maria Sforza, alongside Compère, Martini, and Weerbecke; upon the duke's assassination in December 1476, Josquin apparently entered the service of King René of Anjou, where in 1477 he was named as a singer in the chapel and in March 1478 was granted a prebend in the king's duchy of Bar.

He was back in Milan in 1479, where he was granted a travel pass for a pilgrimage; in 1483 he visited Condé, a payment record indicating that this was Josquin's "first return after the French wars" begun in 1477. Lowinsky (1976) suggested that the years 1479–86 were spent in the employ of Cardinal Ascanio Sforza, but for a portion of this time he was clearly occupied elsewhere; a sonnet by Serafino, titled "Ad Juschino, suo compagno musico d'Ascanio," dates from this period, but implies that the composer had trouble securing a regular position. Macey (1991) argues for a term of service to Louis XI between 1481 and 1483, and assigns to these years the anecdote, passed on by Glarean, regarding a piece with a "regis vox" consisting of a single repeated note. (Glarean identified the monarch in question as Louis XII, but an early 16th-century songbook specifies Louis XI.) Josquin's name appears in the rolls of the papal chapel in Rome between 1486 and 1494, with periods of absence in 1487 and 1489; the records for 1495–1500 are missing, and when they resume in 1501 he is no longer listed. Letters from the Ferrarese ambassador to France to his sovereign Duke Ercole I from 1501 and 1503 indicate that Josquin was at the court of Louis XII, but the circumstances are unclear; they also reveal that he apparently made a recruiting trip to Flanders on behalf of Ercole. Other correspondence details the manner in which Josquin himself was engaged at the Ferrarese court, where he served as *maestro di cappella* (at the exorbitant salary of 200 ducats) between April 1503 and April 1504. A "Josse Deprés" appears in the records of Notre Dame at Condé in May 1504. In 1508 he was serving as provost at Notre Dame, and was "in very good health," according to a letter from that institution to Margaret of Austria; the ambiguous tone of the correspondence makes any affiliation between her court and the composer conjectural. A singer from

Josquin Desprez.

Condé "called Joskin" received a 1520 disbursement from the court of Charles V, though Herbert Kellmann notes that such a laconic entry could scarcely refer to someone of Josquin's musical renown and church rank.

Upon his death Josquin left his house and grounds to Notre Dame and requested that his motets *Pater noster* and *Ave Maria* be sung before his house during processions. His posthumous reputation eclipsed that of any other composer before him. His music circulated widely throughout the 16th century, serving as models for parody composition and transcription; Spataro, Lanfranco, and Glarean extolled it, as did Coclico, who also supplied what he contended was a description of the master's teaching methods.

Problems of chronology and authenticity continue to occupy Josquin scholars. Music printing developed only near the end of his life; early editions of his music, such as the Mass collections issued by Petrucci, are thus likely to be retrospective surveys of his output. Many works attributed to him survive only in posthumous publications that undoubtedly place spurious works alongside authentic ones. Several researchers have attempted to devise stylistic criteria for authenticity and dating. Helmut Osthoff postulated a three-period chronology for the composer's works, though his conclusions are in dispute. Richard Sherr places the motet *Illibata Dei Virgo nutrix* in Josquin's Roman period; Patrick Macey associates *Misericordias Domini* with Louis XI. Texts can also help in the case of individual works: Herbert Kellmann gives a date of about 1 January 1508 for Jean Lemaire's poem *Plus nuls regrets,* while Molinet's *déploration, Nymphes des bois,* laments Ockeghem's death in 1497.

In all, some 20 Masses are believed to be by him, along with another dozen of questionable authenticity; about 110 motets, with another 85 doubtful or spurious examples; and some 75 secular works (out of 120 that bear some attribution to him), primarily French chansons but with a handful of instrumental pieces and 3 Italian-texted compositions.

Bibl.: *Werken,* ed. Albert Smijers et al. (Amsterdam, 1921–69). Willem Elders and Howard M. Brown, eds., *New Edition of the Collected Works* (30 vols. projected; Utrecht, 1987–). Edmond vander Straeten, *La musique aux Pays-Bas avant le XIXe siècle* (Brussels, 1867–88; R: 1969). Helmut Osthoff, *Josquin Desprez,* 2 vols. (Tutzing, 1962–65). Martin Picker, *The Chanson Albums of Marguerite of Austria* (Los Angeles, 1965). Edward Lowinsky, ed., *Josquin des Pres: Proceedings of the International Josquin Festival Conference* (London, New York, and Toronto, 1976). Sydney Robinson Charles, *Josquin des Pres: A Guide to Research* (New York, 1983). Willem Elders, ed., "Proceedings of the Josquin Symposium, Cologne, 11–15 July 1984," *TVNM* 35/1–2 (1985). Richard Sherr, "*Illibata Dei Virgo nutrix* and Josquin's Roman Style," *JAMS* 41 (1988): 434–64. Michael Long, "Symbol and Ritual in Josquin's *Missa di Dadi,*" *JAMS* 42 (1989): 1–22. Willem Elders, "Authenticity Problems in Josquin and the Editions of Petrucci—A Preliminary Study," *FAM* 36/2 (1989): 108–15. Anthony Cummings, "The Transmission of Some Josquin Motets," *PRMA* 115/1 (1990): 1–32. Patrick Macey, "Josquin's *Misericordias Domini* and Louis XI," *Early Music* 19/2 (1991): 163–77; Willem Elders and Frits de Haen, eds., *Proceedings of the International Josquin Symposium, Utrecht, 1986* (Utrecht, 1991).

Josten, Werner (Erich) (b. Elberfeld, Wuppertal, Germany, 12 June 1885; d. New York, 6 Feb. 1963). Composer and conductor. After a brief career in business, he studied music with Rudolf Siegel (Munich) and Jaques-Dalcroze (Geneva). He was assistant conductor of the Munich Opera during the First World War; in 1920 he traveled to the U.S. as an accompanist for song recitals; he remained to teach at Smith College (1923–49) and became a U.S. citizen in 1933. In 1938 a Composers' Forum concert in New York was devoted to his works; another was held at the New York World's Fair (1939). He composed in a neoclassic style, employing mild dissonance and some bitonality. Works include 3 ballets; *Jungle* (1928), Symphony in F (1936), and other orchestral works; a string quartet, piano trio, the *Canzona seria: A Hamlet Monologue* (flute, oboe, clarinet, bassoon, and piano, 1957), and other chamber music; piano music; *Ode for St. Cecilia's Day* (1925) and other choral music; many songs.

Joubert, John (Pierre Herman) (b. Cape Town, 20 Mar. 1927). Composer. He studied at the South African College of Music in Cape Town, then (from 1946) at the Royal Academy of Music; at the latter his instructors were Theodore Holland and Howard Ferguson. In 1950 he received a B.Mus. from Durham Univ., and in 1953 his Sonata for Viola and Piano was performed at the ISCM Festival in Oslo. He taught music at the Univ. of Hull (from 1950 to 1962) and at Birmingham Univ. His music, with diatonic sonorities and airy textures, emulates that of British contemporaries such as Britten. Compositions include the stage works *Antigone* (radio opera, 1954), *In the Drought* (1956), *Silas Marner* (1961), *The Quarry* (1965), *Un-*

der Western Eyes (1969), *The Prisoner* (school opera, 1973), *The Wayfarers* (opera for young people, 1983); cantatas including *The Martyrdom of St. Alban* (1969) and choral music (*The Holy Mountain,* 1963; many anthems, hymns, and carols); symphonies (1956, 1971), concertos (violin, 1954; piano, 1958; bassoon, 1973), *Temps perdu* (string orchestra, 1984), and other orchestral works; chamber music (2 string quartets, 1950, 1977; a string trio, 1960).

Judenkünig, Hans (b. Schwäbisch Gmünd, ca. 1450; d. Vienna, Mar. 1526). Lutenist and composer. Each of his 2 lute manuals includes both original compositions and arrangements. *Utilis et compendiaria introductio* (Vienna, ca. 1515–19) provides basic information. *Ain schone kunstliche Underweisung . . . zu lernen auff der Lautten und Geygen* (Vienna, 1523; ed. H. Mönkemeyer, *Die Tabulatur* 10, Hofheim am Taunus, 1970) discusses fingering and, more briefly, the principles of intabulation.

Jullien, Louis (b. Sisteron, 23 Apr. 1812; d. Paris, 14 Mar. 1860). Conductor. Son of a provincial bandmaster; served in the army, then studied at the Paris Conservatory until 1836; became a popular conductor of dance music in Paris; in 1838 he settled in London, from 1840 establishing himself as a leading conductor of inexpensive popular concerts; also toured the provinces, the U.S. (1853–54, managed by Barnum), and Holland (1857). His shrewd mixture of high and low elements in his programs, his showmanship, and his sense of novelty made him an important figure in the development of techniques of popularizing "serious" music among mass audiences. He was not always financially successful (a season of grand opera at Drury Lane in 1847–48, for which he engaged Berlioz as conductor, failed). In 1859 he returned to Paris, but, arrested for debt, went insane and was institutionalized.

Bibl.: Adam Carse, *The Life of Jullien* (Cambridge, 1951).

Juon [Yuon], **Paul** [Pavel Fedorovich] (b. Moscow, 6 Mar. 1872; d. Vevey, Switzerland, 21 Aug. 1940). Composer. He was raised in Moscow, studying violin and composition at the Imperial Conservatory; he studied in Berlin (1894–95), settling there in 1897 after a brief period of teaching in Russia. From 1906 he taught composition at the Hochschule, where he became professor in 1911; in 1919 he was elected to the Prussian Academy of Arts. He retired to Switzerland because of ill health. His chamber music has led to comparison with Brahms, but there are elements of Russian folk song in much of his music, combined with the German tradition he admired. He wrote harmony texts and a biography of Tchaikovsky and counted S. Wolpe and Jarnach among his students. He wrote 3 violin concertos, *Sinfonietta Capricciosa* (1940), *Psyche* (tenor, chorus, and orchestra, 1906), and other orchestral music; chamber music for winds, strings, and piano; piano works; choral music and songs.

Jurinac, Sena [Srebrenka] (b. Travnik, Yugoslavia, 24 Oct. 1921). Soprano. After studies at the Zagreb Academy of Music and with Milka Kostrenćić, she appeared with the Zagreb Opera in 1942 as Mimi *(Bohème).* She joined the Vienna Staatsoper in 1944 and made her debut there in 1945 singing Cherubino *(Figaro).* She sang Dorabella *(Così)* at Salzburg in 1947 and Glyndebourne in 1949. At La Scala in Milan, the Teatro Colón in Buenos Aires, and the San Francisco Opera she achieved great success singing Mozart and Strauss heroines. She was also distinguished for her Elisabeth *(Don Carlos)* and Butterfly. Her farewell performance was as the Marschallin *(Rosenkavalier)* at the Vienna Staatsoper, 1983.

Juzeliūnas, Julius (b. Čepolė, 20 Feb. 1916). Composer. He studied with Gruodis at the Kaunas Conservatory, graduating in 1948; later worked with Voloshinov at the Leningrad Conservatory. His earliest works are in a neo-Romantic style; in the 1960s he began working with serial and cell techniques. Works include opera (*Sukilėliai* [The Rebels], 1957; *Avarie,* 1968; *Žaìsmas* [The Game], 1967–68); ballet (*Ant marių kranto* [On the Seashore], 1953); orchestral music (3 symphonies, 1948, 1949, 1965; *Afrikietiški eskizai* [African Sketches], 1961; Concerto grosso, 1966); instrumental chamber music (4 string quartets, 1962, 1966, 1969, 1980; sonata, violin, cello, 1977; *Radamalika,* woodwind quintet, 1982; *Flobo-Clavio,* flute, oboe, harpsichord, cello, 1987; 2 piano sonatas, 1947, 1986); vocal works (*Milika,* voice, organ, 1973; *The Voices of Flowers,* voice, organ, 1985).

K

Kabalevsky, Dmitri Borisovich (b. St. Petersburg, 30 Dec. 1904; d. Moscow, 14 Feb. 1987). Composer, pianist, and writer on music. In 1918 the family moved to Moscow, where he studied painting and took piano with Selyanov at the Scriabin Institute (1919–25); entered the Moscow Conservatory in 1925, studying composition with Catoire and Myaskovsky, and piano with Gol'denveyzer. In the late 1920s Kabalevsky began contributing articles to the journal *Sovremennaya musïka;* he later became editor (1940–46). He was involved in the organization of the Moscow branch of the Union of Soviet Composers in 1932 and held a number of high administrative posts; also worked as an editor at a music publishing house. In 1932 he was appointed instructor in composition at the Moscow Conservatory, becoming full professor in 1939. He joined the Communist party in 1940, and wrote a number of large-scale patriotic works during the war; turned to vocal music later in his career, including cantata-oratorios, solo songs, and the operettas *Vesna poyot* and *Sestrï*. But he is best known outside of Russia for his instrumental music, including various concertos, the *Comedians* suite, and piano music. His association with *Sovremennaya musïka* made him an important party spokesman.

Works: *Dramatic. Colas Breugnon* op. 24 (1936–38; rev. 1953, 1969); *V ogne* [Into the Fire] op. 37 (1942); *Sem'ya Tarasa* [The Taras Family] op. 47 (1947; rev. 1950, 1967); *Nikita Vershinin* op. 53 (1954–55); *Vesna poyot* [Spring Sings] op. 58 (1957); *V skazochnom lesu* [In the Magic Forest] op. 62 (1958); *Sestrï* [The Sisters] op. 83, operetta (1967).

Orchestral. Symphonies: no. 1 in C♯ minor op. 18 (1932); no. 2 in C minor op. 19 (1934); no. 3 in B♭ minor op. 22, chorus, orchestra (1933); no. 4 in C minor op. 54 (1954). *Romeo and Juliet,* suite from incidental music (1956); *Komediantï* [The Comedians] op. 26, suite (1940); *Rodina velikaya* [The Mighty Homeland] op. 35, cantata (1941–42); *Narodnïye mstiteli* [The People's Avengers] op. 36, suite, chorus, orchestra (1942); *Pis'mo v XXX bek* [Letter to the 30th Century] op. 93, oratorio (1972). Piano concertos: no. 1 in A minor op. 9 (1928); no. 2 in G minor op. 23 (1935); no. 3 in D major op. 50 (1952); *Rhapsody* op. 75, piano, orchestra (1963); Violin Concerto in C major op. 48 (1948); Cello Concerto no. 1 in G minor op. 49 (1948–49); Cello Concerto no. 2 in C major op. 77 (1964).

Chamber. 2 pieces op. 2, cello, piano (1927); String Quartet no. 1 in A minor op. 8 (1928); *Improvisation* op. 21, violin, piano (1934); String Quartet no. 2 in G minor op. 44 (1945); *Rondo* op. 69, violin, piano (1961); Sonata in B♭ major op. 71, cello, piano (1962).

For piano: 3 sonatas op. 6 (1927, 1945), op. 46 (1946); 2 sonatinas (1930, 1933); 24 preludes (1943–44); 6 preludes and fugues (1958–59). Also choral works; songs; incidental music for plays; film scores.

Kabeláč, Miloslav (b. Prague, 1 Aug. 1908; d. there, 17 Sept. 1979). Composer. He studied composition with Jirák and conducting with Dědeček at the Prague Conservatory (1928–34). In 1932 he was appointed conductor and director of music productions for Czech Radio; became head of the Prague Radio music department in 1945, then served as professor of composition at the Prague Conservatory (1958–62). His compositions reflect a wide range of interests including early music, Chinese, Japanese, and Indian music, as well as more recent techniques such as electronic sounds; he gave an important series of seminars on electronic music at the Czech Radio studios (1968–70). From 1966 he chaired the committee for non-European music of the Oriental Society, part of the Czech Academy of Sciences. Works include 8 symphonies (no. 3, 1957), other orchestral compositions; works for instrumental ensemble (a wind sextet, 1940; *Osm invenci,* 6 percussion instruments, 1963); tape (*E fontibus bohemicis,* 1972); vocal works.

Kadosa, Pál (b. Léva [now Levice, Czech Republic], 6 Sept. 1903; d. Budapest, 30 Mar. 1983). Composer and pianist. He studied at the Budapest Academy of Music, taking piano with Arnold Székely and composition with Kodály (1921–27); taught piano at the Fodor Conservatory (1927–43) and the Goldmark School of Music in Budapest (1943–44), and was appointed professor of piano at the Budapest Academy in 1945. A joint founder of the Society of Modern Hungarian Musicians in 1928, he later served as vice president of the Hungarian Arts Council (1945–49) and became a committee member of the Union of Hungarian Composers (1949). His early compositions reflect the influence of Bartók and Stravinsky, with clashing harmonies and driven rhythmic movement; after a brief period of longer melodic lines and greater lyricism in his works (ca. 1950), Kadosa returned to more complex idioms, including free twelve-tone elements. As a pianist he was known for his performances of Bartók. Works include 2 comic operas (*Irren ist staatlich,* 1931; *A huszti kaland* [Adventure at Huszt], 1949–50); 8 symphonies (no. 4, 1958–59; no. 8, 1968); other orchestral works (divertimenti, a serenade and sinfonietta); 4 piano concertos (no. 1, 1931); concertos for violin, viola; cantatas (*Folksong Cantata,* 1939; *Március fia* [Son of March], 1952); songs; string quartets, other chamber music; various piano works.

Kagel, Mauricio (Raúl) (b. Buenos Aires, 24 Dec. 1931). Composer. Studied with Paz and Schiuma in his home city, also studying philosophy and literature at the Univ. of Buenos Aires. Began an association with the Agrupación nueva música in 1949, and helped found the Cinémathèque argentine in 1950. Worked as chorusmaster at the Teatro Colón in 1949–56, becoming director of the Colón Chamber Opera and the Teatro itself in 1955. Visited Cologne in 1957, eventually settling there permanently; led new music concerts of the Rhineland Chamber Orchestra (1957–61) and lectured at the Darmstadt summer courses (1960–66). Toured the U.S. in 1961–63 and taught at SUNY–Buffalo during 1965; lectured also at Berlin in 1967 and at Göteborg, Sweden, in 1968. He was named director of the Institute of New Music at the Rhenische Musikschule, Cologne, in 1969, and in 1974 joined the faculty at the Cologne Musikhochschule; he was also a cofounder of the Cologne Ensemble for New Music. Apart from music, Kagel is known for his films and plays, riding the crest of the avant-garde in all three areas. His music often incorporates theatrical elements, mixing actors and musicians or requiring action of the musicians themselves; as in Cage, it often satirizes the performance act itself. In addition to exploring new instrumental timbres, he has delved into *musique concrète* (*Der Schall,* 1968; *Unter Strom,* 1969), new vocal techniques (*Anagrama,* 1958; *Hallelujah,* 1968), and electronic composition (*Música para la torre,* 1952; *Transición I–II,* 1958–60; *Acústica I–III,* 1968–70; *Atem,* 1970). He has also based works on the music of Beethoven (*Ludwig Van,* 1968; made into a film in 1969) and Brahms (*Variationen ohne Fuge,* 1972) in the interest of new perceptual effects. His radio plays include *Ein Aufnahmezustand* (1969) and *Guten Morgen!* (1971). Other works include the operas *Die Erschöpfung der Welt* (1980) and *Aus Deutschland* (1977–80); *Sankt-Bach-Passion* (1985); *Musik für Tasteninstrumente und Orchester* (1989). He has also written extensively on new music.

Bibl.: Dieter Schnebel, *Maurice Kagel: Musik, Theater, Film* (Cologne, 1970). Werner Klüppelholz, *Mauricio Kagel, 1970–1980* (Köln, 1981).

Kahn, Erich Itor (b. Rimbach, Germany, 23 July 1905; d. New York, 5 Mar. 1956). Composer and pianist. He studied at the conservatory in Frankfurt and then directed music at the State Radio (1928–33); from 1933 he lived in Paris and was active as a chamber musician and accompanist; he toured Europe and North Africa with Casals in 1938–39. In 1941 he settled in New York, where he formed the Albeneri Trio with Alexander Schneider and Benar Heifetz (1944); he received the Coolidge Medal for service to chamber music (1948). Among his relatively few compositions are works for orchestra (*Symphonies bretonnes,* 1955); *Actus tragicus* (10 instruments, 1946) and chamber music for strings; piano pieces (*Ciaccona dei tempi di guerra,* 1943); and songs.

Kahn, Robert (b. Mannheim, 21 July 1865; d. Biddenden, Kent, 29 May 1951). Composer. Studied at Berlin Hochschule für Musik (1882–85) and at the Munich Academy of Music with Rheinberger (1885–86); lived briefly in Vienna, then, after military service, in Leipzig, as coach at the opera and conductor of women's chorus (1890–93); teacher (1894–1930), Berlin Hochschule, first piano, then theory, later (1912) composition (professor from 1903). In 1937 he emigrated to England to escape the Nazis. A respected conservative composer, especially of chamber music, choral music, songs, piano pieces. Brother of the American banker and patron of the arts Otto Kahn (1867–1934).

Kajanus, Robert (b. Helsinki, 2 Dec. 1856; d. there, 6 July 1933). Conductor. Studied at the Helsinki Conservatory, at the Leipzig Conservatory (1877–79), with Svendsen in Paris (1879–80), and in Dresden and Leipzig (1880–82). The principal mover, through his forceful, somewhat authoritarian personality, in modernizing musical life in Helsinki through the creation and leadership of various musical institutions: 1882, founded the Helsinki Orchestral Society, conducting it (under various names) until his death and bringing it to a high degree of excellence; 1888–1911, founder and conductor, Helsinki Symphony Choir; 1897–1926, music director at the university (professor from 1908). He composed considerable music, often on Finnish subjects, but yielded in this area to Sibelius, whose genius he early recognized and encouraged.

Kalabis, Viktor (b. Červený Kostelec, Bohemia, 27 Feb. 1923). Composer. He studied with Hlobil at the Prague Conservatory (1945–48) and with Řídký at the Academy of Music (1948–52); served as programmer for Czech Radio in Prague (1953–72). His early works reflect his interest in cellular techniques (and admiration for Brahms); later compositions use modified serial techniques. Works include symphonies (no. 1, 1957; no. 2, *Sinfonia pacis,* 1960); concertos (Piano Concerto, 1955; Violin Concerto, 1959; Concerto for Orchestra, 1966); *Diptych for Strings* (1987); chamber music (6 string quartets, 1949, 1962, 1977, 1984, 1984, 1987; *Chamber Music,* strings, 1963; *Duettino,* violin, cello, 1987; *Meantatioas,* 13 winds, 1988); vocal works; piano works.

Kalafati, Vasily Pavovlich (b. Evpatoriya, Crimea, 10 Feb. 1869; d. Leningrad, 30 Jan. 1942). Composer. He graduated in 1899 from the St. Petersburg Conservatory, where he studied with Rimsky-Korsakov; joined the teaching staff there in 1907, serving as professor of composition from 1914 to 1929. His pupils included Stravinsky, Prokofiev, Bogatïryov, and Slonimsky. Kalafati's compositions are in the traditions of the Russian National School; they include the opera *Zygany* [The Gypsies] (1939–41), a symphony, an overture, 2 string quartets, and a number of piano pieces and choral works.

Kalinnikov, Vasily Sergeyevich (b. Voina, Oryol district, 13 Jan. 1866; d. Yalta, 11 Jan. 1901). Composer. He studied for a short time at the Moscow Conservatory but had to withdraw owing to lack of funds; subsequently was awarded a scholarship as a bassoonist to the Moscow Philharmonic Society Music School, where his teachers included Kruglikov (harmony), Il'yinsky (counterpoint), and Blaramberg (composition). Tchaikovsky recommended him for a position as assistant conductor of the Maliy Theater (1893); tuberculosis forced him to spend the remainder of his life in southern France and the Crimea. Kalinnikov is best known for his Symphony no. 1 in G minor (1894–95), which was successful not only in Kiev and Moscow but also in subsequent performances in Vienna, Berlin, Paris, and London; the work bears resemblances to Tchaikovsky and Borodin in its use of folk-like melodies. Other important works include the Symphony no. 2 in A (1895–97); *Tsar Boris* (incidental music, 1899); *Kedr i pal'ma* [The Cedar and the Palm] (orchestra, 1897–98); *Grustnaya pesenka* [Chanson Triste] (piano, 1892–93).

Kalish, Gilbert (b. Brooklyn, 2 July 1935). Pianist. While obtaining degrees from Columbia (B.A., 1956; M.A., 1958) he studied privately with Julius Hereford, Isabelle Vengerova, and Leonard Shure. After his New York debut in 1962 he became one of the most versatile pianists of his generation, promoting new works by American composers while receiving acclaim as an outstanding performer in the standard repertoire, most notably in the works of Haydn. Appeared with the Juilliard String Quartet and other chamber ensembles and with mezzo Jan De Gaetani and cellist Joel Krosnick. Taught at Rutgers (1965–67), Swarthmore (1966–72), and SUNY–Stony Brook (from 1970).

Kalkbrenner, Friedrich Wilhelm (Michael) (b. near Kassel, between 2 and 8 Nov. 1785; d. Enghien-les-Bains, 10 June 1849). Pianist and composer. Son of the composer Christian Kalkbrenner (1755–1801); student, Paris Conservatory (premier prix: piano, harmony, 1801); 1803–4, studied with Albrechtsberger, Vienna; 1804–5, toured Germany as pianist; on his return to Paris, where he was active mainly as piano teacher and composer, published his op. 1 (1807). Very popular in London as pianist, teacher, and composer, 1814–24; toured much from early 1820s to mid-1830s, establishing a great international reputation; noted for the elegance of his playing, admired by Chopin among others; from 1824, based in Paris. Part-owner of the Pleyel firm, whose pianos he promoted. From the mid-1830s the rise of flashier virtuosos and poor health dimmed his reputation; he died of cholera.

Works: 13 sonatas; much salon music; etudes; 4 concertos; a 2-piano concerto; chamber music; a much republished *Méthode* op. 108 (1831); a *Traité* on piano improvisation op. 185 (1849).

Kalliwoda, Johann Wenzel [Kaliwoda, Jan Křtitel Václav] (b. Prague, 21 Feb. 1801; d. Karlsruhe, 3 Dec. 1866). Composer. Student, 1811–16, at the Prague Conservatory; 1816–21, violinist, Prague Theater orchestra; 1821, toured as solo violinist. From 1822 he was Kapellmeister of Prince von Fürstenberg, Donaueschingen, continuing to tour as a solo violinist. Musical activity at Donaueschingen was much curtailed after the 1848 Revolution. Kalliwoda moved to Karlsruhe, but resumed his duties on a reduced scale, 1857–66. A prolific composer (2 operas, 7 symphonies, 18 overtures, chamber music, 10 Masses, piano pieces, songs) and one of the most frequently performed of the second quarter of the century. His son Wilhelm (1827–93) was a conductor and pianist.

Kallman, Chester (b. Brooklyn, 7 Jan. 1921; d. Athens, 18 Jan. 1975). Poet, librettist, and translator. He collaborated with his friend W. H. Auden on the libretto for Stravinsky's *The Rake's Progress;* they also worked together on 2 librettos for Henze, *Elegy for Young Lovers* and *The Bassarids,* and on a number of libretto translations. Kallman's independent works include the libretto *The Tuscan Players* for Chávez and translations of Monteverdi's *Poppea* and Verdi's *Falstaff.*

Kallstenius, Edvin (b. Filipstad, Sweden, 29 Aug. 1881; d. Danderyd, 22 Nov. 1967). Composer. He studied science at Lund University (1898–1903) and music at the Leipzig Conservatory (1904–7); served as music critic of the *Svenska Dagbladet* and music librarian to Radio Sweden (1928–46). His later compositions use an adapted twelve-tone method. Works include tone poems (*Sista striden* [The Last Battle], 1908; *En serenad i sommarnatten* [A Serenade in the Summer Night], 1918); 5 symphonies (*Sinfonia su temi 12-tonici,* 1960); Piano Concerto, 1922; choral music (*När vi dö* [When We Are Dying], requiem, 1919); chamber music (8 string quartets; clarinet quintet, 1930); solo vocal music.

Kálmán, Imre [Emmerich] (b. Siófok, Hungary, 24 Oct. 1882; d. Paris, 30 Oct. 1953). Composer. He joined Koessler's composition class at the Budapest Academy of Music in 1900, where his fellow students included Bartók and Kodály; served as music critic for the *Pesti napló* (1904–8). The enormous success of his first operetta, *Tatárjárás* [The Gay Hussars] (1908), especially in Vienna, prompted him to settle in that city, where he spent his most productive years until the Anschluss; moved to Paris in 1939 and finally to the U.S. His librettos often have a Hungarian subject. His most popular operettas include *Gold gab ich für Eisen* (Vienna, 1914); *Zsuzsi kisasszony* [Miss Springtime] (Budapest, 1915); *Die Csárdásfürstin* [Riviera Girl] (Vienna, 1915); *Gräfin Mariza* (Vienna, 1924).

Bibl.: Rudolf Oesterreicher, *Emmerich Kálmán: Das Leben eines Operettenfürsten* (Vienna, 1988).

Kalomiris, Manolis (b. Smyrna, Turkey, 14 Dec. 1883; d. Athens, 3 Apr. 1962). Composer. He went to school in Athens (1894–99) and Constantinople (1899–1900) and attended the Gesellschaft der Musikfreunde in Vienna, where he took piano with Bauch and Sturm, composition with Grädener, and history with Mandyczewski. He taught piano at the Obolensky Lyceum in Russia (1906–10) before returning to Athens and teaching piano and counterpoint at the Athens Conservatory (1911–19). Kalomiris founded and directed both the Hellenic Conservatory in Athens (1919–26) and the National Conservatory (1926–48); he served as president of the Union of Greek Composers and was made honorary president in 1958. From 1944 to 1945 he was director of the National Opera in Athens, later becoming chairman of the board (1950–52); he also served as critic for *Ethnos* until 1957. A champion of Greek nationalism; his compositions reflect his love of Greek folk song as well as his contact with German music (particularly Wagner) and the Russian school of composition. Works include opera (*O protomastoras* [The Master Builder], 1915, rev. 1929, 1940; *To dachtylidi tis manas* [The Mother's Ring], 1917, rev. 1939; *Anatoli* [Sunrise], 1945, rev. 1948); vocal works (*I elia* [The Olive Tree], female chorus, orchestra, 1907–9; rev. 1944); orchestral works (*Romeiki,* suite, 1907; rev. 1910, 1936); other instrumental works and concertos, rhapsodies; many songs and arrangements of folk songs.

Bibl.: F. Anoyanakis, *Catalogue of the Works of Manolis Kalomiris, 1883–1962* (Athens, 1964).

Kamieński, Mathias [Maciej] (b. Sopron? [Ödenburg], 13 Oct. 1734; d. Warsaw, 25 Jan. 1821). Composer. He spent his youth in Sopron at the court of Count Karl Henckel von Donnersmarck; in 1760 he moved to Vienna, and in 1770 he settled in Warsaw, where he taught keyboard and singing. Later he began composing operas; his *Nędza uszczęśliwiona* [Poverty Made Happy], performed in Warsaw in 1778, was probably the first publicly performed Polish opera. Other stage works, all performed in Warsaw, include *Zośka czyli Wiejskie zaloty* [Sophie, or Country Courtship] (1779, lost); *Słowik czyli Kasia z Hanka na wydaniu* [The Nightingale, or Kasia and Hanka, Two Maidens] (1790). He also composed a cantata for the unveiling of the Sobieski memorial; Masses, offertories, etc.; works for harpsichord.

Kaminski, Heinrich (b. Tiengen, near Waldshut, 4 July 1886; d. Ried near Benediktbeuren, 21 June 1946). Composer. He studied composition briefly with Juon and Kaun in Berlin (from 1909), but was largely self-taught. By 1914 he had retired to Ried, where he lived in the house of Franz Marc and taught privately; among his students was Carl Orff. In 1930 he taught the master class in composition at the Prussian Academy of Arts in Berlin, but resigned that and other appointments in 1933; performances of his works were discouraged under the Nazis. His music has an introspective, broadly religious cast; his reliance on contrapuntal textures reflects an interest in Baroque models. Works include 2 operas (performed 1929 and 1946), 5 orchestral pieces (*Orchesterkonzert mit Clavier,* 1936); 2 string quartets; *Musik* (2 violins, harpsichord, 1931); piano and organ works; a Magnificat (soprano, chorus, viola, orchestra, 1925) and other choral music; songs with organ or instrumental ensemble.

Bibl.: Hans Hartog, *Heinrich Kaminski: Leben und Werk* (Tutzing, 1987).

Kaminski, Joseph (b. Odessa, 17 Nov. 1903; d. Tel Aviv, 14 Oct. 1972). Composer and violinist. Raised in Warsaw; studied later in Berlin and Vienna. He was concertmaster of the Warsaw Radio Orchestra and formed the Warsaw String Quartet; joined the Palestine Orchestra (eventually the Israeli Philharmonic) in 1937, serving as concertmaster until 1969. His compositions include *Israeli Sketches* (1955) and *Symphonic Overture* (1960) for orchestra, a trumpet concertino (1941), a violin concerto (1948, premiered 1954), and a string quartet (1945).

Kaminsky, Max (b. Brockton, Mass., 7 Sept. 1908; d. Castle Point, N.Y., 6 Sept. 1994). Jazz trumpeter. He frequently worked in Eddie Condon's Chicago-style Dixieland groups, 1933–45, recording "Tennessee Twilight" (1933), "Nobody's Sweetheart" (1939), and "Fidgety Feet" (1942). He joined the big bands of Tommy Dorsey (1936, 1938) and Artie Shaw (1938, 1941–43), also playing with Dixieland and traditional groups. He toured Europe with the Jack Teagarden and Earl Hines All Stars (1957), then often worked at Jimmy Ryan's club in New York (late 1960s–1983).

Kancheli, Giia [Giya] **(Alexandrovich)** (b. Tbilisi, 10 Aug. 1935). Composer. Studied composition under I. I. Tuskiia at the Tbilisi Conservatory, 1959–63; after 1972 taught orchestration there. Beginning in 1971, directed musical activities at the Rustaveli Dramatic Theater, contributing scores to a number of productions by Robert Sturua and creating with him the opera *Music for the Living* (1984), a probing contemplation of the destructive force of war. Won numerous official state awards. His music, almost all composed for symphony orchestra, is noted for the dynamic juxtaposition of meditative stasis with cataclysmic outbursts. Works include 7 symphonies (1967; 1970; 1973; 1975, In Memoriam Michelangelo; 1977, In Memory of My Parents; 1980; 1986, Epilogue), *Bright Sorrow* (2 boy soloists, boys' choir, orchestra, 1985), *Mourned by the Wind* (solo viola, orchestra, 1987).

Kapell, William (b. New York, 20 Sept. 1922; d. King's Mountain, Calif., 29 Oct. 1953). Pianist. Studied with Olga Samaroff at the Philadelphia Conservatory and the Juilliard School. New York debut 1941. In 1941 he won the Philadelphia Orchestra Competition and the Naumburg Award. He made his New York debut the same year. After the war his international career developed quickly. A champion of contemporary composers, he frequently played the Khachaturian and Shostakovich (First) piano concertos. Copland's *Piano Fantasy* was dedicated to Kapell after his death in a plane crash.

Kapp, Artur (b. Suure-Jaani, Estonia, 16 Feb. 1878; d. there, 14 Jan. 1952). Composer. He studied composition at the St. Petersburg Conservatory with Rimsky-Korsakov and Lyadov, graduating in 1900; directed the music school in Astrakhan (1903–20), then went to Tallinn, where he taught composition at the conservatory (1924–43) and conducted the Estonia Theater (1920–24). Kapp founded the "Tallinn School" and taught a generation of Estonian musicians. Compositions include the oratorio *Hiob* (1929), 5 symphonies, and over 100 songs.

Kapp, Eugen (Arturovich) (b. Astrakhan, 13 May 1908). Composer. Studied with his father, Artur Kapp; graduated from the Tallinn Conservatory in 1931 and joined the faculty in 1935 as a composition instructor. He was appointed professor at the Estonian Conservatory in 1947 and served as chairman of the Estonian Composers' Union (1948–65). Kapp's compositions are characterized by simple harmonies and march rhythms. Works include operas (*Tasuleegid* [Fire of Revenge], 1945; *Vabaduse laulik* [Bard of Freedom], 1950; *Enneolematu ime* [An Unseen Wonder], children's opera, 1983); the ballet *Kalevipoeg* (1952); symphonies and other orchestral works (*Theme and Variations on Ukrainian Folk Music,* string orchestra, 1982); vocal music.

Kapr, Jan (b. Prague, 12 Mar. 1914; d. there, 29 Apr. 1988). Composer. He studied at the Prague Conservatory with Řídký and J. Křička (1933–40); served as music producer for Czech Radio (1939–46) and critic for *Lidove noviny,* and was appointed professor of composition at the Janáček Academy of Music (1961–70). During the war he experimented with the folk song idiom, though his later works utilize serial procedures; Kapr is perhaps best known for his large-scale symphonies. Works include opera (*Muzikantská pohádka* [Musical Fairy Tale], 1961); orchestral music (8 symphonies, 1942–77; *Marathon,* symphony scherzo, 1939; Piano concerto no. 1, 1938); chamber music (String Quartet no. 1, 1937); cantatas; film music.

Kapsberger, Johann Hieronymous [Giovanni Girolamo] (b. Venice, ca. 1580; d. Rome, 1651). Composer. After 20 or 25 years in Venice, went to Rome, where his contacts included poets, academy people, and members of the papal Barberini family. Renowned as a player on the lute and related instruments, his music for which contains many virtuoso effects. He also composed several books of vocal *villanelle* and *passeggiate* along with sacred music; an opera and a chittarone manual are lost.

Karaev [Karayev], **Kara Abdulfaz-ogly** (b. Baku, 5 Feb. 1918; d. Moscow, 13 May 1982). Composer. After early lessons in piano, pursued studies in composition and Azerbaijani folk music at the Baku Conservatory, 1935–38. From 1938 to 1941, studied at the Moscow Conservatory under A. N. Alexandrov (composition) and S. N. Vasilenko (orchestration); 1943–46, continued composition studies with Shostakovich. In addition to his role as composer, he took an active role in the expansion of professional musical life in Azerbaijan. Served as artistic director of the Baku Philharmonic, 1941–42; director of the music section of the Institute of Azerbaijani Art, 1949–51. Taught at Baku Conservatory, 1946–82, also serving as rector, 1949–53. Held major positions in the Composers Union of the USSR; 1956–82, chairman of the Azerbaijani branch. Recipient of numerous official state awards and prizes. His music is noted for its assimilation of national traits within the classical tradition. Works include operas; ballets (*Seven Beauties,* 1952; *The Path of Thunder,* 1957); other dramatic works; 3 symphonies (1943, 1946, 1965); suites, concertos, and other orchestral music; cantatas and choral music; chamber music; songs.

Writings: *Kara Karaev: nauchno-publitsisticheskoe nasledie* (Baku, 1988).

Bibl.: *Kara Karaev: stat'i, pis'ma, vyskaziyvaniia* (Moscow, 1978).

Karajan, Herbert von (b. Salzburg, 5 Apr. 1908; d. Anif, Austria, 16 July 1989). Conductor. Attended the Mozarteum in his home city, then studied conducting with Franz Schalk at the Vienna Music Academy and music history at Vienna Univ. He made his conducting debut with a student orchestra in 1928 and served as staff conductor at Ulm from 1929 to 1934. He joined a Vienna chapter of the Nazi party in 1933, then joined again at Aachen the following year, when he took a post there as general music director; he made debuts at Vienna in 1936, at Berlin in 1937, and at La Scala, Milan, in 1938. He appeared at the Berlin State Opera from 1938 until 1945, when he was banned by the Allies. After two years of forced retirement at Salzburg, he recorded with the Vienna Philharmonic; he would eventually make over 800 recordings. He appeared in London in 1947 with the Philharmonia Orchestra and held posts at Vienna from 1948; he also conducted and produced operas at La Scala from 1948 and appeared at Bayreuth from 1951. His U.S. debut took place in 1955, amid protests of his wartime activities; the same year he succeeded Furtwängler as music director for life of the Berlin Philharmonic. He led the Salzburg Festival from 1956 to 1960 and again from 1964 onward, founding the Salzburg Easter Festival in 1967. He also led the Vienna Opera from 1957 until resigning in 1964. Prolonged friction between him and the Berlin authorities led to his resignation there in April 1989.

Bibl.: Roger Vaughan, *Herbert von Karajan: A Biographical Portrait* (London, 1986). Herbert von Karajan, *Mein Lebensbericht* (Vienna, 1988). Richard Osborne, ed., *Conversations with von Karajan* (New York, 1989).

Karel, Rudolf (b. Plzeň, Czechoslovakia, 9 Nov. 1880; d. Terezín, 6 Mar. 1945). Composer. He attended the Prague Conservatory, where he was Dvořák's last pupil; went to Russia and taught at the Taganrog Music

School and Rostov Conservatory. In 1923 he was appointed professor of composition at the Prague Conservatory but was forced to give up the post in 1941; he was arrested by the Gestapo in 1943 and died in the Terezin concentration camp. His early works show the influence of Dvořák and Tchaikovsky; later compositions are more complex, with irregular rhythms and modal-based progressions. Works include operas (*Ilseino srdce* [Ilsa's Heart], 1909); orchestral music (*Jarní symfonie* [Spring Symphony], 1938); cantatas.

Karg-Elert [Karg], **Sigfrid** (b. Oberndorf-am-Neckar, 21 Nov. 1877; d. Leipzig, 9 Apr. 1933). Composer, theorist, and organist. He was a boy soprano in Leipzig; trained as a teacher; later attended the Leipzig Conservatory, where Wendling and Reinecke were among his teachers. Rejecting a career as a pianist, he taught briefly at Magdeburg Conservatory, and with the financial support of Grieg focused on composition. After army service he taught theory and composition at the conservatory as Reger's successor (1919); toured the U.S. as an organist (1931–32) but never held an organ post in Leipzig. The composers he admired included Schoenberg, Debussy, Scriabin, and Bach; his renewed use of the chorale as the basis for polyphonic works is an important element of the German organ tradition after Reger. Works include a few orchestral pieces; chamber music; over 100 pieces for harmonium; some 250 works for organ (*66 Chorale-Improvisationen,* 1908–10); piano pieces (*24 Preludes,* 1918) and didactic works; choral and vocal music. He wrote volumes on the harmonium, the organ, and music theory.

Bibl.: Sonja Gerlach, *Sigfrid Karg-Elert: Verzeichnis sämtlicher Werke* (Frankfurt, 1984).

Karkoff, Maurice (Ingvar) (b. Stockholm, 17 Mar. 1927). Composer. Studied at the Stockholm Musikhögskolan (1945, 1948–53); his teachers included Larsson, Blomdahl, and Erland von Koch. He served as music critic of the *Stockholms-tidningen* (1962–66) and *Hi-Fi Music* (from 1976) and in 1965 was appointed to a teaching post at the Stockholm Municipal Institute. His compositions are noted for their lyricism and have been described as Romantic modernism; they also show the influence of oriental harmonies and rhythms. Works include a chamber opera (*Gränskibbutzen* [The Border Kibbutz], 1972–73); orchestral works (8 symphonies, 1955–80; Variations, 1961); cantatas (*Sju rosor senare* [7 roses later], 1964–65); chamber music (*Epitafium,* 1968; *Ballata quasi una fantasia,* baritone saxophone, piano, 1988); solo vocal music.

Karkoschka, Erhard (b. Mährisch Ostrau, 6 Mar. 1923). Composer. Studied at the Stuttgart Musikhochschule (1946–53) and at the Univ. of Tübingen, where he wrote a dissertation on early compositional techniques of Webern. In 1958 he was appointed lecturer in Stuttgart and, in 1964, professor; he founded the Ensemble Neue Musik (1963) and directed an electronic music studio. His works include *Versuch für alle* (23 instruments, 8 solo voices, audience, 1960); *Geburtztaxtextelein* (word-music score, 1989); pieces for improvising orchestra (*Kollektives Improvisieren,* 1973); chamber music, some with tape (*Bläsergedichte,* woodwind quintet, 1987); organ pieces (*Tryptichon über BACH,* 1966); *Im Zonen* (3 choruses, instruments, audience, 1972); solo vocal music (*Omnia ad majorem Dei gloriam,* tenor, 12 instruments, 1963); electronic works (*Zeitmosaik I,* 1985; *Skulpturmusik,* 1985).

Karlins, M(artin) William (b. New York, 25 Feb. 1932). Composer. He attended the Manhattan School (studying under Giannini, until 1961) and the Univ. of Iowa (Ph.D., 1965). Taught at the Univ. of Illinois (1965–67) and Northwestern University (from 1967). His works, which have been described as chromatic and lyrical, include several orchestral pieces (*Concert Music 1–5,* no. 2 with chorus; Symphony, 1979–80; a concerto for saxophone and orchestra, 1981–82); *Fanfare with Fugato* (amplified cello, 2 trumpets, 2 trombones, 1981); *Variations on "Obiter dictum"* (1965), a string quartet, and other chamber music; pieces for solo organ, clarinet, cello, and flute.

Karłowicz, Mieczysław (b. Wiszniewe, 11 Dec. 1876; d. near Zakopane, Galicia, 8 Feb. 1909). Composer. Son of the scholar Jan Karłowicz (1836–1903), who gave him a broad cultural background and independent financial means; studied the violin and theory in Warsaw, composition in Berlin with Heinrich Urban (1895–1901); then took an active part in Warsaw musical life as composer, writer, and organizer (especially through the Warsaw Music Society, of which he was executive director, 1904–6). In 1906 he studied conducting with Nikisch in Leipzig. An avid mountaineer and skier, he died in an avalanche. Considered one of the most significant members of "Young Poland," a group of progressive composers that he joined in 1906. His music, especially his symphonic poems and songs, is still known in Poland.

Karr, Gary (Michael) (b. Los Angeles, 20 Nov. 1941). Double bass virtuoso and educator. Studied with Herman Reinshagen, Warren Benfield, Leonard Rose (at the Juilliard School; B.Mus., 1965), and Stuart Sankey. He became widely known when featured by Leonard Bernstein in a televised concert in 1962. Subsequently performed as soloist with major orchestras in the U.S., Canada, and Europe. Cofounded the Karr–Lewis Duo with Harmon Lewis, 1971. Taught at a number of schools including the New England Conservatory and Indiana Univ. before settling in 1976 at the Hartt School of Music in Connecticut.

Kasemets, Udo (b. Tallinn, Estonia, 16 Nov. 1919). Composer. After study in Stuttgart and Darmstadt (his teachers included Scherchen and Krenek), he emigrated to Canada (1951) and taught piano, theory, composition, and conducting at Hamilton Conservatory (1951–57). He wrote music criticism for the Toronto *Daily Star* (1959–63); taught at the Brodie School of Music and Modern Dance (1963–67); and joined the staff of the Ontario College of Art in 1970 to lecture on mixed-media presentations. He was active as a concert organizer and conductor, directing among others the Toronto Bach Society (1957), the Isaacs Gallery Mixed Media Ensemble (1965–67), and the 1968 festival Sightsoundsystems. His works from the 1950s and earlier are neoclassical in orientation, but in the 1960s he adopted chance mixed-media procedures similar to those of Cage. Many of his works invite active audience participation, as in *Tt,* a tribute to Buckminster Fuller, Marshall McLuhan, and John Cage (1968), in which the audience selects frequency, amplitude, color, and intensity on computer cards, the results of which are projected as graphs for use by performers; other works aim at awakening senses other than hearing, as in *Colourwalk* (1971). Pre-1960 works include a violin concerto (1956); *Visions* (dancer, narrator, orchestra, 1953); and other orchestral, chamber, and vocal music. Most post-1960 works are for indeterminate ensemble and involve multipurpose scores, for example, *Music of the Eighth Moon of the Year of the Dragon* (recordings, tapes, mixers, reader, transparencies, 1976), *Vertical Music: In Remembrance of Morton Feldman* (any 7 instruments, 1987), *Portrait: Music of the 12 Moons of the I Ching,* (various instruments, 1988).

Kassern, Tadeusz Zygfryd (b. Lwów, Poland, 19 Mar. 1904; d. New York, 2 May 1957). Composer. He studied composition with Soltys and piano with Lalewicz at the Lwów Conservatory, later studying at the Poznań Conservatory with Brzostowski and Opieński (1922–26). He went to Paris in 1931, then to New York in 1948 as cultural attaché to the Polish consulate and later as a Polish cultural delegate to the United Nations; became an American citizen in 1956. He first gained recognition with his Concerto for Soprano (1928); many of his compositions are based on Polish folk music. Works include operas (*The Anointed,* 1949–51; *Sun-Up,* 1952); orchestral music (Concertino, oboe, strings, 1936–37; rev. 1946); vocal works (*Suita orawska,* male chorus, 1938); works for piano.

Kastal'sky, Alexandr Dmitriyevich (b. Moscow, 28 Nov. 1856; d. there, 17 Dec. 1926). Composer and musicologist. He entered the Moscow Conservatory in 1875, studying with Tchaikovsky, Taneyev, and Gubert; in 1887 became an instructor at the Moscow Synodal Academy and served as director of the Synodal Choir (1910–23), touring Europe with them in 1911. In 1923, when the academy merged with the Moscow Conservatory, Kastal'sky became a faculty member there. His compositional output consists almost entirely of choral music; he was also a scholar of old Russian chant.

Bibl.: Alexandr Kastal'sky, "My Musical Career and My Thoughts on Church Music," *MQ* 11 (1925): 231–47.

Kastner, Jean-Georges [Johann Georg] (b. Strasbourg, 9 Mar. 1810; d. Paris, 19 Dec. 1867). Writer. After abandoning theology, studied at his father's wish, he became locally known as a musician in Strasbourg; an opera given there in 1835 led the city council to send him to the Paris Conservatory. Marriage to a wealthy pupil enabled him to devote himself to composition (operas, mostly unperformed; choral music; songs) and didactic and theoretical writings, which won more attention, ranging from methods for voice and many instruments to instrumentation and military-music treatises and what he called *livres-partitions,* 9 historical or speculative essays on various musical subjects, published with related musical compositions.

Katchen, Julius (b. Long Branch, N.J., 15 Aug. 1926; d. Paris, 29 Apr. 1969). Pianist. Appeared with the New York Philharmonic and the Philadelphia Orchestra at age 11; graduated from Haverford College at 19; later studied in Paris, performing there and throughout Europe; eventually settled in France. He formed a trio in 1967 with Suk and Starker. He cultivated a wide repertory, from the classics to Slavic music and contemporary works, achieving particular distinction with his Brahms readings.

Kauer, Ferdinand (b. Klein-Tajax, Znaim [now Znojmo], near Brno, bapt. 18 Jan. 1751; d. Vienna, 13 Apr. 1831). Composer. He studied classics and philosophy with the Jesuits in Znaim and Tyrnau (Trnava) and played organ at churches in both cities. Around 1777 he went to Vienna, where he was organist and played the violin in the orchestra of the Leopoldstadt Theater (ca. 1781–82). From ca. 1790 he began composing operas for that theater, and in a little more than 20 years he produced some 200 stage works, including such highly popular pieces as *Das Faustrecht in Thüringen* (1796), *Die Löwenritter* (1799), and especially *Das Donauweibchen* (1798), which became one of the most popular German operas of the first half of the 19th century. After a year in Graz (1810), he was engaged at the Josefstadt Theater (from 1814); he lost this post in 1818 and died in poverty shortly after the Danube flood of 1830 destroyed all of his possessions. In addition to stage works, he composed church music, some 30 symphonies, and chamber and keyboard music.

Kaufman, George S(imon) (b. Pittsburgh, 14 Nov. 1889; d. New York, 2 June 1961). Librettist and director. After a stint as a journalist, collaborated with Marc Connelly on the libretto *Helen of Troy, New York* (music by Kalmar and Ruby, 1923); subsequently wrote the librettos for the Gershwin musicals *Of Thee I Sing* (with Ryskind, 1931), which won a Pulitzer, and *Let 'em Eat Cake* (1933). He wrote the librettos and lyrics for *Hollywood Pinafore* (1945) and directed Loesser's

Guys and Dolls (1950) as well as some of his own productions.

Kaun, Hugo (b. Berlin, 21 Mar. 1863; d. there, 2 Apr. 1932). Composer and choral conductor. He studied at the Berlin Hochschule für Musik (1879–80) and the Prussian Academy of Arts (under Friedrich Kiel); taught piano, composed, and conducted a chorus in Berlin; moved to Milwaukee in 1886 where he pursued a similar career; returned to Germany in 1902. He was elected to the Academy of Arts in 1912, and taught composition at the Berlin Conservatory from 1922. His works were heavily influenced by Wagnerian operatic and harmonic procedures. He composed at least 3 operas; 3 symphonies, 3 piano concertos, and other orchestral music; 4 string quartets, a piano quintet, and other chamber music; some 230 choral pieces; over 100 piano works; some 170 songs.

Kay, Hershy (b. Philadelphia, 17 Nov. 1919; d. Danbury, Conn., 2 Dec. 1981). Composer. He studied cello and orchestration (with Randall Thompson) at the Curtis Institute (1936–40). Among the many Broadway musicals he orchestrated are Bernstein's *On the Town* (1944), Webber's *Evita* (1978), and works by Blitzstein and Rodgers. For Bernstein he also orchestrated the *Mass* (1971) and *1600 Pennsylvania Avenue* (1976). He composed many ballets, often for Balanchine, such as *L'inconnue* (1965, after Poulenc) and *Stars and Stripes* (1958, after Sousa); other composers whose works served as the bases for his ballets include Weber, Gottschalk, Chopin, and Gershwin. *The Clowns* (1968) is an original ballet employing serial methods. He taught orchestration at Columbia for one year (1972) and composed film scores.

Kay, Ulysses (Simpson) (b. Tucson, 7 Jan. 1917; d. Englewood, N.J., 20 May 1995). Composer. He was raised in a musically active family (the nephew of King Oliver); studied piano, violin, and saxophone as a child; then attended the Univ. of Arizona and the Eastman School (M.A.), the Berkshire Music Center, and Yale (where he worked with Hindemith). During the Second World War he played flute, saxophone, and piccolo in the navy band, and piano in a jazz orchestra. Later study at Columbia was followed by a period in Europe supported by Fulbright and Rosenwald awards and a Rome Prize. From 1968 to 1988 a professor at Lehman College, CUNY (in 1972 he became Distinguished Professor of Music there). His works are in a neoclassical idiom.

Works: 5 operas (*Frederick Douglass,* 1983), a ballet, film and television scores; *Sinfonia* (1950), *Umbrian Scene* (1963), *Fantasy Variations* (1963), *String Triptych* (string orchestra, 1987), and other orchestral music; a brass quartet (1950), *Five Portraits* (violin, piano, 1972), a wind quintet (1984), and other chamber music; several large-scale works for voices and orchestra or ensemble (*Phoebus Arise,* cantata, soprano, baritone, chorus, orchestra, 1959; *The Western Paradise,* narrator, orchestra, 1975); piano (*2 Impromptus,* 1986) and organ music; choral music for mixed, treble, or low voices, accompanied and unaccompanied ("What's in a Name," mixed choir, piano, 1954; *Festival Psalms,* baritone, mixed choir, piano, 1983); *3 Pieces after Blake* (soprano, orchestra, 1952) and other songs with piano.

Bibl.: Constance Tibbs Hobson, *Ulysses Kay: A Bio-Bibliography* (Westport, 1994).

Keats, Donald (Howard) (b. New York, 27 May 1929). Composer. He studied with Quincy Porter and Hindemith at Yale, and with Luening and Cowell at Columbia (M.A., 1951); received a Fulbright Fellowship to study with Jarnach in Hamburg (1954–56) and then studied at the Univ. of Minnesota (Ph.D., 1961). He taught at Antioch College (1957–75) and then at the Lamont School of Music of the Univ. of Denver. With the Second String Quartet his works became less tonal, but his use of serial procedures is occasional and rather free; lyricism is the dominant characteristic of his style. His works include 2 symphonies (1955–57, 1960–62), a piano concerto (1981–85), and other orchestral music; 2 string quartets (1951, 1964–65), *Musica Instrumentalis I* (10 instruments, 1980); piano and choral music; *Tierras del alma* (song cycle for soprano, flute, guitar, 1979) and songs.

Keene, Christopher (b. Berkeley, Calif., 21 Dec. 1946; d. New York, 8 Oct. 1995). Conductor. While studying at the Univ. of California, Berkeley, he staged operas. In 1968 he began an association with Menotti's Spoleto Festival, of which he became the general director in 1973 and the music director in 1976. In the meantime he had served as music director of the American Ballet Company (1969–70) and had made his orchestral debut with the Rochester Philharmonic (1973). Music director at ArtPark, 1975–89; of the Syracuse Symphony, 1976–87. Founding conductor of the Long Island Philharmonic, 1979–89. In 1983 he began conducting at the New York City Opera; in March 1989 he assumed its directorship.

Keilberth, Joseph (b. Karlsruhe, 19 Apr. 1908; d. Munich, 20 July 1968). Conductor. After studies in Karlsruhe he worked at the opera, begining as répétiteur and eventually becoming general music director (1935–40). He served as conductor at the Prague Opera (1940–45) and as music director at the Dresden Opera (1945–51). Founding conductor of the Bamberg Symphony (1950–68). During the same period he conducted regularly at Bayreuth and was appointed chief conductor (1951–59) and music director (1959–68) at the Munich Opera.

Keiser, Reinhard (b. Teuchern, 10 or 11 Jan. 1674; d. Hamburg, 12 Sept. 1739). Composer. Entered the Leipzig Thomasschule in 1685 for a seven-year program, studying under Thomaskantor Schelle and possibly with Thomaskirche organist Kuhnau; the dates of his departure from Leipzig and his engagement at the Brunswick court are unknown. His first stage work, *Der königliche Schäfer,* was performed at Braunschweig between 1692 and 1694; he was appointed chamber composer there in 1694. He soon moved to Hamburg, supplying several operas (mostly to librettos by Postel) to the Oper am Gänsemarkt during G. Schott's time as director (1695–1702). Schott's widow passed the opera directorship to Keiser in 1702; he teamed with the writer Drüsicke to manage the theater until 1707, during which time many operas of his own were given along with those of Handel, Mattheson, and Gottfried Grünewald. After relinquishing the theater (which had gone into debt) in 1707, he served several Holstein nobles during the next year; his opera *Der Karneval von Venedig* (1707), with substitute arias by Graupner and other songs in local Hamburg dialect, met with great success, playing for over a year. He wrote at least 25 operas for the Oper am Gänsemarkt between 1708 and 1718; his 1712 setting of Brockes's Passion-oratorio text was the first of a string of settings by several composers, including Handel, and was central to the development of the genre. All of Keiser's oratorios date from roughly this period, as do several collaborative efforts with Mattheson.

He was in Stuttgart in 1719–20 but failed to secure a permanent court position. He returned to Hamburg in August 1721, but Telemann's newly established dominance there caused him to seek a post at Copenhagen; this too ultimately proved fruitless, though he staged three of his operas there in 1722. He spent his last years back in Hamburg, writing several operas as well as church music; in 1728 was named to succeed Mattheson as *Canonicus minor* and cantor at the cathedral. Mattheson and Telemann paid him high tribute in obituaries upon his death, while Scheibe and Hasse acknowledged his great talent and influence many years later (the latter comparing him favorably with Scarlatti); Burney wrote that his works showed "all the vigor of a fertile invention, and correctness of study and experience." He numbered his operas at over 100, but this probably includes pasticcios and smaller works.

Bibl.: Klaus Zelm, *Die Opern Reinhard Keisers* (Munich, 1975).

Kelemen, Milko (b. Podravska Slatina, Croatia, 30 Mar. 1924). Composer. He took composition with Sulek at the Zagreb Academy of Music (1945–52), continuing his studies at the Paris Conservatory with Messiaen and Aubin (1954–55) and at the Freiburg Musikhochschule with Fortner (1958–60). He taught at the Zagreb Academy of Music and the Düsseldorf Conservatory (1970–72); in 1973 he was appointed professor of composition at the Stuttgart Musikhochschule. Kelemen founded the Zagreb Biennale in 1961 and became its first president. His early compositions were influenced by folk music, but his works since the late 1950s adopted serial and electronic sound techniques. Works include music for the stage (*Le Héros et son miroir,* 1960; *Der Belagerungszustand,* 1970; *Apocalyptica,* ballet, 1983); orchestral music (*Koncertantne improvizacije,* 1955; *Sonabile,* piano, ring modulator, orchestra, 1972; *Phantasmes,* viola, orchestra, 1985; *Antiphonie,* organ, orchestra, 1985; *Drammatico,* cello, orchestra, 1984; *Archetypon,* 1986); chamber music (String Quartet no. 4, *Landschaftsbilder,* 1986); film scores.

Kéler, Béla [Keler, Adalbert Paul von] (b. Bártfa, Hungary [now Bardejov, Czech Republic], 13 Feb. 1820; d. Wiesbaden, 20 Nov. 1882). Violinist and composer. Theater violinist, from 1845 in Vienna; 1854–55, dance orchestra conductor; 1856–60, Austrian military bandmaster; later conducted at Wiesbaden (1863–70) and Bad Spa (from 1870); also toured widely. One of the leading figures in light music of his day, he published very popular dances and marches; also 12 overtures (*Lustspiel-Ouverture* op. 73; *Ungarische Lustspiel-Ouverture* op. 108).

Kell, Reginald (Clifford) (b. York, 8 June 1906; d. Frankfort, Ky., 5 Aug. 1981). Clarinetist. Studied with Haydn Draper at the Royal Academy of Music in London. Appointed first clarinet with the London Philharmonic in 1932, of the London Symphony in 1937. He also taught at the Royal Academy of Music beginning 1935. In 1948 he emigrated to the U.S., where he worked as a soloist and as a chamber partner to ensembles such as the Fine Arts Quartet.

Kelley, Edgar Stillman [Stillman-Kelley, Edgar] (b. Sparta, Wis., 14 Apr. 1857; d. New York, 12 Nov. 1944). Organist, composer, and writer on music. He studied piano in Wisconsin and Chicago; in 1876 went to Stuttgart to study composition (with Max Seifritz), organ, and piano. Upon his return to the U.S. in 1880 he taught, composed, and performed in San Francisco and studied the music of the Chinese community; from 1886 to 1892 he lived in New York as a composer-arranger, conductor of light opera, and teacher of piano and theory. In 1898 he was elected to the National Institute of Arts and Letters; taught at Yale (1901–2); lived in Berlin (1902–10) teaching piano and composition; taught at Western College for Women (Oxford, Ohio) and the Cincinnati Conservatory (1911–34). Many of his works are programmatic and reflect American nationalism; he was seen by some as a successor to MacDowell. He wrote operettas and other stage music (*The Pilgrim's Progress,* a musical miracle play after Bunyan, Boston, 1917) and one film score (*Corianton,* ca. 1930, not released); *Aladdin: A Chinese Suite* (1887–93; published 1915), Symphony no. 2, "New England" (op. 33, 1913), and other orchestral music; chamber and piano music; works for chorus and orchestra ("O Captain! My Captain!," after Whitman, op. 19, n.d.; *America's Creed* op. 40, 1919) and other choral music; *A California Idyll* (soprano, orchestra, op. 38, 1918) and other songs with piano.

Kellogg, Clara Louise (b. Sumterville, S.C., 9 or 12 July 1842; d. New Hartford, Conn., 13 May 1916). Soprano. From 1857, studied singing in New York; 1861, opera debut as Gilda (New York Academy of

Music); 1863, Marguérite in American premiere of *Faust* (her best-known role); 1867, European debut, London. Until retirement in 1887 she sang widely in Europe and the U.S. (1873–76, toured the U.S. with her own opera company). She published *Memoirs of an American Prima Donna* (New York and London, 1913; R: 1978).

Kelly, Bryan (George) (b. Oxford, 3 Jan. 1934). Composer. He studied composition with Howells and Jacob at the Royal College of Music (1951–55), then with Boulanger in Paris; was appointed professor of theory and composition at the Royal College of Music in 1962. The style of "Les six" is evident in his lighter works. He collaborated frequently with the poet John Fuller in his compositions for children. Works include children's operas (*Herod Do Your Worst,* 1968; *The Spider Monkey Uncle King,* 1971; *The Queen in the Golden Tree,* 1973); children's cantatas (*Half a Fortnight,* 1972; *Foxtrot,* 1972; *Adam's Apple,* 1974); orchestral music (*Latin Quarter,* overture, 1954; Sinfonia Concertante, 1968); choral music (*Canticum Festivum,* 1964; Stabat Mater, 1970); brass band; chamber music; organ music.

Kelly, Michael (b. Dublin, 25 Dec. 1762; d. Margate [Kent], 9 Oct. 1826). Tenor, composer, and theater manager. In Dublin he studied voice with Passerini and Rauzzini and clavier with Michael Arne. As a youth he sang in comic operas in Dublin. He went to Italy in 1779; in Naples he studied with Finaroli and Aprile. From 1783 he was engaged as a singer at the imperial theater in Vienna; among the roles he created during the next four years was that of Don Basilio in *Figaro.* He moved to London in 1787, where he was the leading tenor at Drury Lane, and where for three decades his activities as director and composer were centered. His *Reminiscences* (London, 1826; R: New York, 1968; ed. Roger Fiske, London, 1975) are a lively source of information on Viennese and London musical life; they were dictated to Theodore Hook from Kelly's notes. He composed more than 60 stage works, including the popular *Blue Beard* (1798).

Bibl.: Stewart M. Ellis, *The Life of Michael Kelly, Musician, Actor, and Bon Viveur* (London, 1930).

Kelly, Wynton (b. Jamaica, 2 Dec. 1931; d. Toronto, 12 Apr. 1971). Jazz pianist. He accompanied Dinah Washington on and off through the 1950s, while also working with Lester Young (ca. 1952), Charles Mingus (1956–57), and Dizzy Gillespie (1957), and leading a trio from 1957. He joined Miles Davis (1959–63, including on the album *Someday My Prince Will Come,* 1961), then resumed leading trios, initially with Paul Chambers and the drummer Jimmy Cobb as his sidemen. Working as a quartet with Wes Montgomery, they recorded the album *Smokin' at the Half Note* (1965).

Kelterborn, Rudolf (b. Basel, 3 Sept. 1931). Composer and conductor. He studied piano, conducting, and theory as a youth and at the Basel Music Academy; further study with Blacher in Salzburg (1953) and with Fortner and Bialas in Detmold (1955). He taught at the Music Academy in Basel, the Darmstadt summer courses (1956–60), the Northwest German Music Academy in Detmold (1960–68), and in Zurich at the Musikhochschule (1968–75). From 1975 to 1979 he directed the music section of Radio Beromünster; in 1980 he was appointed to teach composition and theory at the Hochschule für Musik in Karlsruhe. His style includes neo-Baroque as well as serial and aleatory features; pictorialism is common. He has written a harmony textbook and a volume on contemporary music.

Works: 7 operas (*Ophelia,* 1984; *Julia,* chamber opera, 1991) and a ballet; symphonies (no. 4, 1987), *Kammersinfonie I* (violin, 10 winds, harp, percussion, low strings, 1960), *Kommunikationen* (6 groups of instruments, 1971–72), *Musica luminosa* (1985), and other orchestral music; an oratorio, *Die Flut* (solo voices, speaker, chorus, orchestra, 1963–64), *Gesänge zur Nacht* (soprano, chamber orchestra, 1978), and other large works for voices and orchestra; 4 string quartets (1954, 1956, 1961–62, 1970) and other chamber music; organ, piano, and harpsichord pieces; choral music and songs.

Bibl.: Andres Briner et al., eds., *Rudolf Kelterborn: Komponist, Musikdenker, Vermittler* (Zurich, 1993).

Kempe, Rudolf (b. Niederpoyritz, 14 June 1910; d. Zurich, 11 May 1976). Conductor. Studied oboe at the Orchestra School of the Saxon State Orchestra in Dresden. First oboist with the Dortmund Opera Orchestra, 1929; oboist with the Leipzig Opera, 1929. Became a répétiteur in Leipzig, 1933; made his debut as conductor there, 1935. After service in the German army he conducted opera at Chemnitz, 1943–48. Thereafter his career became international in scope; his appointments included music director of the Bavarian State Opera, 1952–54; conductor of the Royal Philharmonic, 1961–75; of the Munich Philharmonic 1967–76; of the BBC Symphony, 1975–76. He conducted at the New York Metropolitan Opera, 1954–56.

Kempen, Paul Van (b. Zoeterwoude, 16 May 1893; d. Hilversum, 8 Dec. 1955). Conductor. Studied violin at the Amsterdam Conservatory. He joined the Concertgebouw at age 17 as concertmaster. From 1916 he assumed the same function at Posen and Bad Nauheim. Music director at Oberhausen, 1932–34; of the Dresden Philharmonic, 1934–42; at Aachen, 1942–44. From 1949 to 1955 he taught conducting at the Accademia Chigiana in Siena and conducted the Hilversum Radio Philharmonic. He was the first in Germany to conduct Bruckner's symphonies as they were written rather than from Schalk's recomposed versions.

Kempff, Wilhelm (b. Jüterbog, 25 Nov. 1895; d. Positano, Italy, 23 May 1991). Pianist and composer. At the Berlin Hochschule he studied piano with K. H. Barth and Ida Schmidt-Schlesicke; composition with Robert Kahn. After serving as director of the Stuttgart Musikhochschule, 1924–29, he embarked on a performing career. He thrice recorded Beethoven's 5 concertos, twice recorded Beethoven's 32 piano sonatas and 10 violin sonatas (with Schneiderhan and Menuhin), and produced integral versions of the trios (with Szeryng and Fournier) and the cello sonatas (with Fournier). Later in life he performed Schubert's piano sonatas with increasing regularity. His own compositions include 4 operas (1928–37), a ballet (1947), concertos for piano (1927, 1931) and violin (1936), 2 symphonies (1923, 1926), a tone poem (1961), and chamber music. His transcription of Bach's *Siciliana* became widely known through a recording by Lipatti.

Kendricks, Eddie (b. Birmingham, Ala., 17 Dec. 1939). Soul singer. He sang in vocal groups with Melvin Franklin and Otis and Paul Williams; from 1963 they were known as The Temptations. The group was among the earliest successes for Motown records, and despite numerous personnel changes (Kendricks left in 1974), remained popular through the 1970s. Their hits were produced mainly by Smokey Robinson ("My Girl," 1965) and David Whitfield ("Papa Was a Rolling Stone," 1972); original members of the group (including Kendricks) rejoined in 1982 for an album and tour.

Kennan, Kent (Wheeler) (b. Milwaukee, 18 Apr. 1913). Composer. He studied at the Univ. of Michigan and at the Eastman School (under Hanson, 1932–36); spent three years in Italy after receiving the Rome Prize. In 1939 he began a teaching career at Kent State Univ.; subsequently taught at the Univ. of Texas, served in the army as a bandmaster, taught at Ohio State Univ. (1947–49), and then returned to the Univ. of Texas at Austin. Early influences included Romanticism, impressionism, and jazz; later the predominant element in his style was neoclassicism similar to that of Hindemith. His writings include an orchestration textbook (1952; 2nd ed., 1970) and *Counterpoint* (1959; 2nd ed., 1972). He also wrote several orchestral works (Concerto for Piano, 1946); chamber music (*Scherzo, Aria, and Fugato,* oboe, piano, 1948; *Sea Sonata,* violin, piano, 1939); piano music; *Blessed Are They That Mourn* (chorus, orchestra, 1939) and *The Unknown Warrior Speaks* (male chorus, 1944).

Kentner, Louis [Lajos Philip] (b. Karvin, Silesia, 19 July 1905; d. London, 21 Sept. 1987). Pianist and educator. At the Royal Academy in Budapest, 1911–22, he studied piano with Arnold Székely and Leo Weiner, composition with Hans Koessler and Zoltán Kodály. Recital debut in 1918; toured Europe in 1920. In 1933 he gave the premiere of Bartók's Concerto no. 2 for piano. Two years later he settled in London. There he gave complete cycles of sonatas by Beethoven and Schubert and of Bach's *Well-Tempered Clavier.* In 1946 he played the European premiere of Bartók's Concerto no. 3. He performed frequently with his brother-in-law Yehudi Menuhin.

Kenton, Stan(ley Newcomb) (b. Wichita, Kans., 15 Dec. 1911; d. Los Angeles, 25 Aug. 1979). Jazz bandleader, pianist, and arranger. From 1941 he led big bands, the first of which recorded "Eager Beaver" and "Artistry in Rhythm" (1943). For a decade culminating in his 20-piece Progressive Jazz Orchestra (1949) and 43-piece Innovations in Modern Music Orchestra (1950–51), he attempted to bring contemporary classical devices into jazz. His jazz soloists included Stan Getz, Anita O'Day, Kai Winding, Art Pepper, Maynard Ferguson, and Shelly Manne; among his arrangers were Pete Rugolo, Shorty Rogers, Bill Russo, Bill Holman, and Gerry Mulligan. From the time of Lee Konitz's joining in 1952 and the album *New Concepts of Artistry in Rhythm* (recorded that year), Kenton's bands were more firmly grounded in swing and bop traditions, although he led the Los Angeles Neophonic Orchestra in 1965–66 and used rock rhythms in his band of the 1970s. From 1959 he directed college workshops ("jazz clinics"), contributing greatly to the popularization of jazz in American education, although with an emphasis on arrangement, big bands, and white jazz traditions.

Bibl.: William F. Lee, *Stan Kenton: Artistry in Rhythm* (Los Angeles, 1980). Lillian Arganian, *Stan Kenton: The Man and His Music* (East Lansing, Mich., 1989).

Keppard, Freddie (b. New Orleans, 27 Feb. 1890; d. Chicago, 15 July 1933). Jazz cornetist. He led the Olympia Orchestra, a dance band (ca. 1906–12), and left New Orleans to join the Original Creole Band, touring the U.S. (1914–17) and perhaps rejoining in Chicago (1918), where he settled. His early work as a pioneer of jazz cornet playing went unrecorded. In his later years, in poor health, he made impressive recordings under his own name ("Stock Yards Strut," 1926) and with Doc Cook (1924–26), in whose orchestra he was the principal hot cornet soloist.

Kerker, Gustave A(dolph) (b. Hereford, Westphalia, 28 Feb. 1857; d. New York, 29 June 1923). Composer. From a family of musicians that emigrated to Louisville, Ky., in 1867. He composed a musical comedy in 1879 that toured the South; then went to New York, becoming a theater orchestra conductor, from 1889 at the Casino Theater, where many of the musical comedies that he produced almost yearly from 1888 to 1912 were performed; best known was *The Belle of New York* (1897).

Kerle, Jacobus de (b. Ieper [Ypres], 1531 or 1532; d. Prague, 7 Jan. 1591). Composer and organist. From 1555 he is known to have been active in various Italian and German cities. More long-lasting than any individual post was his connection with Cardinal Otto, Lord High Steward of Waldburg and Bishop of Augsburg, who met him in 1561; commissioned him to compose the *Preces speciales,* prayers sung at the Council of Trent and embodying the council's declarations on clarity in the setting of liturgical texts; employed him as director of his private chapel, 1562–65; and later gave him a position at Augsburg Cathedral, where

Kerle remained for six years (1568–74). His surviving works, nearly all sacred, include Masses, motets, and other liturgical genres.

Kerll [Kerl, Gherl], **Johann Kaspar** (b. Adorf, Saxony, 9 Apr. 1627; d. Munich, 13 Feb. 1693). Composer and organist. Perhaps studied with his father, an organist, then at Vienna with Valentini, and in Rome with Carissimi and possibly Frescobaldi. Served his patron, Archduke Leopold Wilhelm, in Brussels until 1656, when he moved to Munich as Vice-Kapellmeister, becoming Kapellmeister later that year. Resigned in 1673, returning to Vienna; served as organist at St. Stephen's, 1674–77, with Pachelbel as his assistant, and as imperial organist from 1677 to his death. He was widely admired as a composer, organist, and teacher; his output consists of Masses and other sacred pieces, dramatic works (including 11 lost Munich operas), and keyboard and chamber music.

Kern, Jerome (David) (b. New York, 27 Jan. 1885; d. there, 11 Nov. 1945). Popular songwriter. He studied music at the New York College of Music (1902) and in Europe; his early activity as a composer was linked with work as a song plugger for the firms of Lyceum and Harms. He published his first song in 1902 ("At the Casino") and in the following years produced works for interpolation into revues in London and New York; his first American success came in 1905 ("How'd You Like To Spoon with Me?" for *Earl and the Girl*). From 1911 he wrote full-length musical shows whose combination of the dramatic structure of European operetta with American subject matter fundamentally influenced the subsequent development of the American musical theater. The most important of these were several works done in collaboration with book writer Guy Bolton and lyricist P. G. Wodehouse (including *Very Good Eddie,* 1915; *Oh Boy!,* 1917) and particularly *Show Boat* with Oscar Hammerstein II (1927, including "Ol' Man River," "Why Do I Love You?"). After 1935 he wrote primarily for film ("The Way You Look Tonight," in *Swing Time,* 1936; "The Last Time I Saw Paris," *Lady Be Good,* 1941); in 1946 he was the subject of a biographical film *(Till the Clouds Roll By).*

Bibl.: Michael Freedland, *Jerome Kern* (New York, 1978). Gerald Bordman, *Jerome Kern* (New York, 1980). Andrew Lamb, *Jerome Kern in Edwardian London* (Littlehampton, 1981; 2nd ed., 1985).

Kerr, Harrison (b. Cleveland, 13 Oct. 1897; d. Norman, Okla., 15 Aug. 1978). Composer. He studied in Cleveland and in Paris (with Boulanger, 1921); taught in Cleveland, West Virginia, and at the Chase School in Brooklyn (from 1928 until after World War II); and taught at the Univ. of Oklahoma (1949–68; serving as dean of the College of Fine Arts until 1959). In New York he was actively involved in the American Music Center and on the editorial board of New Music Editions. His compositions include an opera (1958–60) and a ballet; 3 symphonies, a concerto for violin (1950–51), and other orchestral pieces; 2 string quartets (1935, 1937) and other chamber and piano music; choral music and songs.

Kertész, István (b. Budapest, 28 Aug. 1929; d. Kfar Saba, Israel, 16 Apr. 1973). Conductor. After studies at the Franz Liszt Academy he was appointed conductor of the Györ Philharmonic, 1953–55; of the Budapest Opera, 1955–56. After the 1956 uprising he moved to Germany; there he served as general music director at Augsburg, 1958–63, and at the Cologne Opera, 1964–73. He made his U.S. debut in 1961 with the Detroit Symphony. Principal conductor of the London Symphony, 1965–68; of the Gürzenich Orchestra at Cologne, 1971–73. Drowned while swimming in the Mediterranean.

Kes, Willem (b. Dordrecht, Netherlands, 16 Feb. 1856; d. Munich, 21 Feb. 1934). Conductor. Studied violin, 1871–75, with David in Leipzig, Wieniawski in Brussels, Joachim in Berlin; 1877–88, conductor and teacher in Dordrecht; 1888–95, first conductor, Concertgebouw Orchestra, Amsterdam; 1895–98, conductor, Scottish Orchestra, Glasgow; 1898–1905, conductor, Moscow Philharmonic (from 1901 also director of its music school); 1905–26, conductor, Koblenz, and director of the conservatory. He also composed.

Kessel, Barney (b. Muskogee, Okla., 17 Oct. 1923). Jazz guitarist. He performed in the film *Jammin' the Blues* (1944) and joined Artie Shaw (1945) before beginning a career as a studio musician in Los Angeles. He also recorded with Charlie Parker's bop group (1947), toured with Oscar Peterson's trio (1952–53), then recorded widely as a free-lance with jazz groups, including his own album *To Swing or Not To Swing* (1955). In 1968 he abandoned studio work to play and teach jazz. He toured internationally, performing as a soloist and leading groups, including Great Guitars with Charlie Byrd and Herb Ellis, beginning in 1973.

Ketèlbey, Albert W(illiam) [Vodorinski, Anton] (b. Birmingham, 9 Aug. 1875; d. Cowes, Isle of Wight, 26 Nov. 1959). Composer and conductor. At the age of 13 he won the Queen Victoria Scholarship for composition at Trinity College, London; became organist of St. John, Wimbledon, at 16, then was appointed music director of the Vaudeville Theatre at 22. Early compositions include songs and some piano works published under the name Anton Vodorinski; became famous through a series of light narrative works for orchestra, beginning with *In a Monastery Garden* (1915). Works include orchestral music (*In the Moonlight,* 1919; *In a Chinese Temple Garden,* 1923; *In the Mystic Land of Egypt,* 1931); songs; anthems; solo instrumental works; music to accompany silent films.

Ketting, Otto (b. Amsterdam, 3 Sept. 1935). Composer and trumpeter. Studied composition with his father, Piet Ketting, and at the Hague Conservatory; played trumpet with The Hague Philharmonic (1955–60), and taught at the conservatories in Rotterdam (1967–71) and The Hague (1971–74). Ketting has composed scores for stage and cinema and worked with a number of choreographers including Jaap Flier, Richard Glasstone, and Job Sanders. Works include operas (*Dummies,* 1974; *O, Thou Rhinoceros,* 1977; *Ithaka,* 1986); ballets (*Het laatste bericht* [The Last Message], 1962; *The Golden Key,* 1964); orchestral music (*Due canzoni,* 1957; *In Memoriam Igor Stravinsky,* 1971); chamber music; piano music; *Minimal Music,* 28 toy instruments, 1970.

Ketting, Piet (b. Haarlem, 29 Nov. 1905; d. Rotterdam, 25 May 1984). Composer. He studied with Willem Pijper (1926–32) and formed a chamber ensemble with Johan Feltkamp and Jaap Stotijn that toured throughout the world. He taught choral conducting and composition at the Rotterdam Conservatory (1930–56), directed the Amsterdam Music Lyceum (1946–49), and conducted the Rotterdam Chamber Choir and Orchestra. Ketting's early compositions followed the late Romantics and Debussy, but later works utilize driving rhythms and extremes of instrumental register. Works include orchestral music (Symphony no. 1, 1929; Symphony no. 2, cello, orchestra, 1963); instrumental pieces (3 string quartets); choruses and other vocal music (3 Shakespeare sonnets, voice, piano, 1938).

Khachaturian, Aram Il'yich (b. Tbilisi, 6 June 1903; d. Moscow, 1 May 1978). Composer. He moved to Moscow in 1921 and enrolled in the Gnesin Music Academy (1922–29), where he studied with Sergei Bychkov (cello) and Gnesin (composition), in addition to lessons with Glier. He continued his studies at the Moscow Conservatory (1929–34), where he worked with Miaskovsky; the *Dance Suite,* First Symphony, and trio for clarinet, violin, and piano all date from this time. The success of the piano concerto (1936) was repeated with the concertos for violin (1940) and cello (1946); they are often considered a kind of grand cycle. The ballet *Gayane* (1942, including the favorite "Sabre Dance") and the Second Symphony (1943) were also successful and were warmly praised by Shostakovich. In 1948 Khachaturian was one of the prominent Soviet composers, along with Prokofiev and Shostakovich, who came under attack for "following an antipopular, formalistic trend"; he traveled to Armenia, where he wrote folk songs; also composed film music. Beginning in 1950 he taught composition at the Gnesin School, and later at the Moscow Conservatory; also began work on his ballet *Spartacus* and appeared as a conductor of his own works. His later works include the concerto-rhapsodies for violin, cello, and piano (1960s) and the solo sonatas for unaccompanied cello, violin, and viola (1970s), considered his second and third instrumental trilogies.

Works: The ballets *Shchast'ye* [Happiness] (1939); *Gayane* (1942; rev. 1957); *Spartak* [Spartacus] (1954; rev. 1968). Incidental music: *Macbeth* (1934, 1955); *The Widow of Valencia* (1940); *Masquerade* (1941); *King Lear* (1958); others.

Orchestral. Symphonies: no. 1 (1935), no. 2 (1943), no. 3, Simfoniya-poema (1947); *Dance Suite* (1933); Piano Concerto (1936); Violin Concerto (1940); *Gayane,* 3 suites (1943); *Masquerade,* suite (1944); Cello Concerto (1946); *Traurnaya oda pamyati Vladimira Il'yicha Lenina* [Funeral Ode in Memory of Lenin] (1949); *The Battle for Stalingrad,* suite (1952); *The Widow of Valencia,* suite (1953); *Concert Waltz* (1955); *Spartak,* suites nos. 1–3 (1955–7); suite no. 4 (1967); *Kontsert-rapsodiya,* violin, orchestra (1961–2); *Kontsert-rapsodiya,* cello, orchestra (1963); *Kontsert-rapsodiya,* piano, orchestra (1965). *Song of Stalin,* chorus, orchestra (1937), expanded as *Poema o Staline* (1938); *Oda radosti* [Ode of Joy], chorus, orchestra (1956).

Chamber. Tants, violin, piano (1926); *Pesnya-poema* [Song-Poem], violin, piano (1929); Suite, viola, piano (1930); Sonata, violin, piano (1932); Trio, clarinet, violin, piano (1932); Double Fugue, string quartet (1923; rev. as Recitative and Fugue, 1967); *Sonata-Monologue,* cello (1974); *Sonata-Fantasia,* violin (1975); Sonata, viola (1977). For piano: *Poema* (1927); *Tants* (1927); Toccata (1932); *Album of Children's Pieces,* 2 vols (1946, 1964); Sonatina (1959); Sonata (1961).

Bibl.: Victor Yuzefovich, *Aram Khachaturyan,* trans. Nicholas Kournokoff and Vladimir Bobrov (New York, 1985). Maria Biesold, *Aram Chatschaturjan: Komponist zwischen Kaukasus und Moskau* (Wittmund, 1989).

Khachaturian, Karen Surenovich (b. Moscow, 19 Sept. 1920). Composer. Nephew of Aram Khachaturian. Began study of music at the age of 8; in 1941 he entered the Moscow Conservatory but shortly afterward was called up for military service. Resumed studies at the conservatory in 1945 under Shebalin, Miaskovsky, and Shostakovich; completed postgraduate course in 1953 and was appointed lecturer in orchestration. An active figure in the Union of Composers. Works include an operetta, a ballet (*Chippolino,* 1973); 3 symphonies (1955, 1968, 1982), a cello concerto (1983), and other orchestra music; cantatas and choral music; chamber music; incidental and film music; music for children.

Bibl.: Nina Sladkova, *Composer Karen Khachaturyan: Complete Catalogue of Works* (n.p., 1985).

Khaikin, Boris Emmanuilovich (b. Minsk, 26 Oct. 1904; d. Moscow, 10 May 1978). Conductor. At the Moscow Conservatory he studied piano with Alexander Gedike, conducting with Nicolai Malko and Konstantin Saradiev. After obtaining his diploma in 1928 he was continuously engaged as a conductor in Soviet theaters: at the Stanislavski Theater (1928–35); at the Mali and Kirov Theaters in Leningrad (1936–43, 1943–54); and finally at the Bolshoi Theater in Moscow (1954–78). At the same time he educated a generation of Soviet conductors at the Moscow Conservatory (1925–28, 1930–36, and 1954–78) and the Leningrad Conservatory (1939–40, 1946–55).

Khan, Ali Akbar (b. Shibpur, Bengal, 14 Apr. 1922). Sarod player and composer. Studied with his father, Ustad Allauddin Khan, the leading musical figure of his generation; Ravi Shankar was a fellow pupil. After years of training on various instruments, he first performed on sarod at age 14, later serving the court of the Maharaja of Johdpur. With the support of Yehudi Menuhin, he made his U.S. debut in 1955 at New York and the same year appeared on U.S. television and released the first Western recording of Indian art music; he subsequently built a worldwide following. In 1956 he established the Ali Akbar School of Music at Calcutta. Also founded a school at San Rafael, California. His compositions include several ragas, many talas, and music for ballet, theater, and film.

Khrennikov, Tikhon Nikolaevich (b. Elets, Russia, 10 June 1913). Composer and pianist. Began piano lessons at the age of 9 and composing at 13. In 1929, enrolled at the Gnesin Music School in Moscow; 1932–36, studied composition with Shebalin at the Moscow Conservatory. Achieved early success with his First Piano Concerto (1933) and First Symphony (1935); his first opera, *Into the Storm* (1939), became a prototype for the melodious, patriotic, folk-based "song opera" favored by Stalin. In 1948, came to political prominence when he took an active role in the condemnation of Shostakovich, Prokofiev, Miaskovsky, and other leading composers, and was elected leader of the Union of Composers, a post he retained for more than 40 years. His style remained rooted in a tuneful, highly accessible idiom. Works include operas and comic operas (*Much Ado about Hearts,* 1972; *Dorothea,* 1983; *The Golden Calf,* 1984; *The Naked King,* 1988); operettas; ballets (*Love for Love,* 1976); 3 symphonies (1935; 1942, rev. 1944; 1974); concertos, suites, and other orchestral music; choral music and songs; incidental and film music.

Bibl.: I. Shekhonina, *Tvorchestvo T. N. Khrennikova* (Moscow, 1985). I. I. Martynov, *Tikhon Nikolaevich Khrennikov* (Moscow, 1987).

Kienzl, Wilhelm (b. Waizenkirchen, Austria, 17 Jan. 1857; d. Vienna, 3 Oct. 1941). Composer. Studied at Prague Univ. (1876); Leipzig Univ. (1877); Ph.D., Vienna Univ. (1879), publishing his dissertation, *Die musikalische Deklamation* (Leipzig, 1880). Traveled as accompanist, conductor, and lecturer; lived in Graz, 1886–90, as director of the Steiermärkischer Musikverein; 1890–92, conductor of the Hamburg Opera; 1892–94, conductor of the Munich Opera; then based in Graz, and from 1917 in Vienna. Between 1884 and 1926 he produced 10 musical stage works, *Der Evangelimann* (Berlin, 1895) the most successful; also much choral music, many songs, piano pieces, a few chamber pieces. He was one of the leading Austrian composers of his day, but his music began to fade before his death; stopped composing in 1936 because of ill health. Published collections of his essays and criticism and a book on Wagner, to whom he had a lifelong devotion.

Kilar, Wojciech (b. Lwów, 17 July 1932). Composer. He studied piano and composition with Woytowicz at the Katowice State Music School (1950–55), continuing with Woytowicz at the Krakow Conservatory (1955–58); also studied privately with Boulanger in Paris (1959–60). Best known in Poland for his film scores; some of his works (e.g. *Diphthongos*) make use of unusual methods of vocal production. Works include ballet (*Maska czarnej śmierci* [The Mask of the Black Death], 1961); orchestral music (Symphony no. 1, 1955; 2 piano concertos, 1958; *Riff 62,* 1962); vocal works (*Diphthongos,* chorus, percussion, 2 pianos, strings, 1964; *Upstairs-Downstairs,* 2 girls'/boys' choruses, orchestra, 1971; *Angelus,* soprano, chorus, orchestra, 1984); instrumental pieces (*Training 68,* clarinet, trombone, cello, piano, 1968; *Orawa,* 15 string instruments, 1986); film scores.

Kilpatrick, Jack Frederick (b. Stillwater, Okla., 23 Sept. 1915; d. Muskogee, Okla., 22 Feb. 1967). Composer. He studied at the Univ. of Redlands in California and at the Catholic Univ. of America; much of his music is based on Indian folklore, and the pentatonic scale is often prevalent. Works include music dramas (*Unto These Hills,* 1950; *The Golden Crucible,* 1959; *The Blessed Wilderness,* 1959); symphonies (no. 5, 1957; no. 6, 1957; no. 7, "The Republic of Texas," 1957; no. 8, "Oklahoma," narrator, dancers, orchestra, 1957).

Kilpinen, Yryö (Henrik) (b. Helsinki, 4 Feb. 1892; d. there, 2 May 1959). Composer. He studied with Furuhjelm at the Helsinki Music Institute, with Hofmann and Heuberger in Vienna (1910–11), and with Juon and Taubmann (1913–14) in Berlin; was elected to the Finnish Academy in 1948. Kilpinen's songs (over 700 in number) to German, Finnish, and Swedish words achieved considerable popularity during his lifetime; the works eschew modern techniques in favor of simple melodies and ostinato accompaniments, often favoring a single interval. Song cycles include *Reflexer* [Reflections] (1922); *Fantasi och verklighet* [Fantasy and Reality] (1922); *Lieder der Liebe I–II* (1928); *Hochgebirgswinter* (1954).

Kim, Earl [Eul] (b. Dinuba, Calif., 6 Jan. 1920). Composer. He studied composition and theory with Schoenberg at UCLA (1939), with Bloch at Berkeley; after service in the war he returned to Berkeley to study with Sessions (M.M., 1952). Taught conducting, composition, and piano at Princeton (1952–67) and then at Harvard. His sung and spoken vocal parts use silence effectively to separate blocks of material, reflecting his view that "statements are made when nothing is being said." Works include *Footfalls* (orchestra, 1983); a concerto for violin (1979); *Caprices* (violin and piano, 1980); piano music and other chamber music; several large works for instruments, singers, actors, dancers, films, television, and lighting (*Narratives: Monologues, Melodrama 1, Lines, Eh Joe, Melodrama 2, Duet, Earthlight,* 1973–78); *Where Grief Slumbers* (7 songs after Apollinaire and Rimbaud, soprano, harp, strings, 1982), *The 11th Dream* (soprano, baritone, violin, cello, piano, 1988), *3 Poems in French* (soprano, string quartet, 1989), and other vocal music.

Kimball, Jacob (b. Topsfield, Mass., 15 Feb. 1761; d. there, 24 July 1826). Composer and tunebook editor. He played in militia bands at the battles of Lexington and Bunker Hill. He attended Harvard College (1776–80) and became a schoolteacher, first in Ipswich (from 1781), then in Topsfield (from 1792). He also taught at singing schools and compiled tunebooks, including *The Rural Harmony* (Boston, 1793), *The Essex Harmony* (Exeter, N.H., 1800), and *The Village Harmony* (Exeter, 4th ed., 1798). More than 100 of the pieces they contain are his own compositions.

Kincaid, William (b. Minneapolis, 26 Apr. 1895; d. Philadelphia, 27 Mar. 1967). Flutist. Studied with Georges Barrère at the Institute of Musical Art in New York, 1911–14. Played in the New York Symphony, 1914–18; with the New York Chamber Music Society, 1919–21. While first chair in the Philadelphia Orchestra, 1921–60, he also taught at the Curtis Institute.

Kindermann, Johann Erasmus (b. Nuremberg, 29 Mar. 1618; d. there, 14 Apr. 1655). Composer. Pupil of Staden; sang and played violin at the Sunday afternoon Frauenkirche concerts while in his teens; visited Italy at city council expense in 1635; returned in 1636 to become second organist at the Frauenkirche; served as organist at Schwäbisch Hall in 1640, but soon returned to his home city as organist in the Egidienkirche, remaining there until his death. Wecker, Schwemmer, and J. Agricola were among his pupils. He issued 13 publications at Nuremberg between 1639 and 1653; his music shows some idiomatic conception, with organ works using obbligato pedal and violin music calling for scordatura. Contrasting solo and choral movements in his cantatas and recitative passages in his dialogues are progressive traits, while his concertato pieces reflect his Italian training and are suggestive of Schütz's work. Other music includes arias, sonatas, and suites.

Bibl.: Harold E. Samuel, *The Cantata in Nuremberg during the Seventeenth Century* (Ann Arbor, 1982).

King, B. B. [Riley B.] (b. Itta Bena, Miss., 16 Sept. 1925). Blues singer, guitarist, and bandleader. He moved to Memphis in 1947, performing and then working as a disc jockey on radio station WDIA (1949–53). From 1953 he led urban blues groups. He reached vast international audiences from the 1960s, when he was championed by leading rock guitarists (especially Eric Clapton) as the principal influence on their style. His full-bodied, tuneful singing and playing and command of blues effects are evident on his album *Live at the Cook County Jail* (1970).

Bibl.: Charles Sawyer, *B. B. King: The Authorized Biography* (Poole, England, 1980).

King [Klein], **Carole** (b. Brooklyn, N.Y., 9 Feb. 1942). Popular songwriter and singer. With collaborator Gerry Goffin she composed songs in various styles for a wide range of artists: "Will You Still Love Me," for The Shirelles (1961); "A Natural Fool," Aretha Franklin (1967); "Hi-De-Ho," Blood, Sweat, and Tears (1970). From 1962 she made recordings of her own material, including "It Might As Well Rain until September" (1962) and the extremely successful album *Tapestry* (1971, including "It's Too Late").

King, E(lisha) J. (b. Wilkinson County, Ga., ca. 1821; d. near Talbotton, Ga., 31 Aug. 1844). Composer. A singing-school teacher; remembered as joint compiler (with B. F. White) of *The Sacred Harp* (1844), the most widely used and long-lived collection of sacred songs in shape-note notation, of which he contributed the largest number. His brothers Joel and Elias were also musicians.

King, Karl L(awrence) (b. Paintersville, Ohio, 21 Feb. 1891; d. Fort Dodge, Iowa, 31 Mar. 1971). Bandmaster and composer of band music. He played baritone in a number of town bands and with circuses, including Barnum & Bailey (1913) and Barnum & Bailey's Greatest Show on Earth (1917–18), for which he wrote his most famous march, *Barnum & Bailey's Favorite* (1913); also composed marches for universities, including Northwestern, Illinois, and Minnesota, and many other band works. From 1920 to 1958 he was leader of the Fort Dodge Military Band; toured widely with them, playing at many county fairs, in addition to guest-conducting other bands and serving as a band judge. King was one of the founders of the American Bandmasters Association, serving as president (1939) and later named honorary lifetime president (1967); the musical *The Music Man* was inspired partly by King's music.

King, Robert (fl. London, 1676–1728). Composer. Succeeded Banister in the private music of Charles II in 1680, serving several monarchs up to 1728; named composer-in-ordinary to William and Mary in 1689; appeared often in public between 1689 (when he was given a license to stage concerts) and at least 1702, also selling music during this period. His works consist of songs (some for plays) along with sonatas, suites, and other chamber music.

King, William (b. Winchester, 1624; d. Oxford, 17 Nov. 1680). Composer. Son of Winchester Cathedral organist George King; received B.A. from Magdalen College, Oxford, 1649; served Charles I at Oxford during the Civil War and later held posts at Magdalen College (1652–54) and All Souls College (1654–64) before becoming organist at New College in 1664. Works include anthems and service music along with the 1668 print *Songs and Ayres* for solo voice and continuo.

Kipnis, Alexander (b. Zhitomir, Ukraine, 13 [o.s. 1] Feb. 1891; d. Westport, Conn., 14 May 1978). Bass. Studied conducting at the Warsaw Conservatory and served briefly as a bandmaster before training his voice with Ernst Grenzebach in Berlin, 1912–14. After his debut at the Hamburg opera in 1915, he sang at the Wiesbaden Court Theater from 1916 until in 1917 interned as a Russian. After the war he rejoined the Wiesbaden Theater, then sang at the Berlin Charlottenburg Oper, 1919–29, and at the Staatsoper, 1930–35. In the meantime he developed an international reputation as guest artist at Milan, Paris, Buenos Aires, Covent Garden, Bayreuth, Vienna, and Chicago. He joined the Vienna Staatsoper, 1934–38. In 1940 he made his New York Metropolitan debut as Gurnemanz and remained with the company to 1946, when he retired. Particularly admired for Sarastro, Baron Ochs, Boris Godunov, Hagen, and Philip II.

Kipnis, Igor (b. Berlin, 27 Sept. 1930). Harpsichordist. Son of Alexander Kipnis. Attended the Westport School of Music and Harvard; worked in the record industry, in radio, and as a critic before launching a performing career in 1959. Toured Europe, the Americas, and Australia, playing the fortepiano and clavichord as well as harpsichord; taught at Fairfield Univ., Conn. (1971–77), and the Royal Northern College of Music, Manchester (from 1982); from 1974 was associated with the Festival Music Society in Indianapolis; also lectured and wrote on Renaissance and Baroque music and was active as an editor.

Kirby, John (b. Baltimore, 31 Dec. 1908; d. Hollywood, 14 June 1952). Jazz double bass player and bandleader. He played tuba, switching to double bass during his first tenure with Fletcher Henderson (1930–33). After further work in the big bands of Chick Webb (1933–35), Henderson (1935–36), and others, he led a swing sextet from 1937, often working with the singer Maxine Sullivan. Unusually for that time, the sextet emphasized complex arrangements (many by its trumpeter Charlie Shavers) more than improvisation, typified by recordings such as "Undecided" (1938) and "Opus 5" (1939). From 1942 the group's stability was disrupted by illness and army draft calls, and it disbanded in 1946.

Kirbye, George (d. Bury St. Edmunds, buried 6 Oct. 1634). Composer. A resident musician in various great houses near Bury St. Edmunds; probably acquainted with the similarly employed English madrigalist John Wilbye, and certainly familiar with the Italian music of the late Renaissance. Most notable among his known compositions are a number of madrigals (including a volume published in 1597 and one piece in *The Triumphes of Oriana* [1601]) and several sacred vocal works, especially 19 Psalm settings for East's *The Whole Booke of Psalmes* (1592).

Kircher, Athanasius (b. Geisa, near Fulda, 2 May 1601; d. Rome, 27 Nov. 1680). Scholar and theorist. Educated by the Jesuits at Fulda and Paderborn until 1622, when he went to Cologne; taught at Heiligenstatt, near Göttingen, until 1623; ordained in 1628 after four years of theological study at Mainz; was then called to Würzberg as professor of mathematics, philosophy, and oriental languages. Driven by war to France in 1631, he taught at Avignon until named mathematician to Emperor Ferdinand III in 1633; he intended only to visit Rome en route to Vienna, but upon his arrival was made a professor at the Collegio Romano, and remained there until his death. His principal work on music, *Musurgia universalis* (Rome, 1650), was influential well into the next century.

Kirchgässner [Kirchgessner], **Marianne (Antonia)** (b. Bruchsal, 5 June 1769; d. Schaffhausen, 9 Dec. 1808). Glass harmonica player. Blind from age 4, she was first trained on the piano; later in Karlsruhe she learned to play glass harmonica under the instruction of J. A. Schmittbauer. In 1791 she began concert tours on the instrument; Mozart heard her in Vienna in May of that year and composed for her the Quintet in C major K. 617 for glass harmonica, flute, oboe, viola, and cello. She also played for Friedrich Wilhelm II in Berlin, for Salomon's concerts in London (1794–96), and in St. Petersburg (1798).

Bibl.: Hermann Josef Ullrich, *Die blinde Glassharmonikavirtuosin Mariane [sic] Kirchgessner und Wien: Eine Künstlerin der empfindsamer Zeit* (Tutzing, 1971).

Kirchner, Leon (b. Brooklyn, 24 Jan. 1919). Composer, pianist, and conductor. He studied with Toch at Los Angeles City College, Schoenberg at UCLA, Bloch at Berkeley, and Sessions in New York. After service in the army, he returned to Berkeley (M.A., 1949), where he was appointed a lecturer. Taught at Univ. of Southern California (1950–54), Mills College, and Harvard (from 1961). He was active as a pianist and conductor of classical works (especially Mozart and Schubert) and his own compositions. His first 2 string quartets received New York Critics Circle Awards, and the third (with tape, 1966) was awarded a Pulitzer Prize. *Music for Cello and Orchestra* (1992) was awarded first prize in the 1994 Friedheim Awards competition. His works are primarily influenced by the aesthetic of the Second Viennese School. They include an opera (*Lily,* 1973–76, after Saul Bellow's *Henderson, the Rain King*); 2 piano concertos (1949, 1963), Toccata (strings, winds, percussion, 1955), *Orchestra Piece* (Music for Orchestra II, 1990), *Toccata* (orchestra, 1995), and other orchestral music; *Music for 12* (1985) and other chamber music; piano and choral music (*Trio II,* piano trio, 1993); *The Twilight Stood* (song cycle, after Dickinson, soprano and piano, 1983) and other songs.

Kirchner, Theodor Fürchtegott (b. Neukirchen, Saxony, 10 Oct. or Dec. 1823; d. Hamburg, 18 Sept. 1903). Composer. Studied in Leipzig from 1838, briefly in Dresden (1842); 1843–62, organist and teacher in Winterthur; also toured; 1862–72, in Zurich as conductor, pianist, organist; 1873–75, director of the Wurzburg Conservatory; 1883–90, taught at the Dresden Conservatory. As a composer he is best known for his many character pieces for piano.

Bibl.: Peter Schneider, ed., *Theodor Kirchner: Briefe aus den Jahren 1860–68* (Zurich, 1949).

Kirckmann, Jacob (b. Bischweiler, 4 Mar. 1710; buried Greenwich, 9 June 1792). Keyboard instrument builder. Worked in the London shop of Hermann Tabel in the 1730s; he married Tabel's widow in 1738, "by which prudent measure he became possessed of all Tabel's seasoned wood, tools, and stock-in-trade" (Burney). With Shudi, he controlled much of the English harpsichord market; naturalized in 1755, he entered a partnership with his nephew Abraham in 1770. He built an enharmonic harpsichord about 1757 and also constructed claviorgana, spinets, and pianos. His firm, passing through Abraham's sons, built pianos until bought out by Collard in 1898.

Bibl.: Donald H. Boalch, *Makers of the Harpsichord and Clavichord, 1440–1840* (Oxford, 1974).

Kirk, Andy [Andrew Dewey] (b. Newport, Ky., 28 May 1898). Jazz bandleader, saxophonist, and tuba and double bass player. In Dallas he joined Terrence Holder's Dark Clouds of Joy (1925). He assumed leadership of the Clouds of Joy in 1929, moving its base to Kansas City. The band's soloists included Mary Lou Williams (who also composed and arranged for it until 1942), the singer Pha Terrell (on the band's hit recording "Until the Real Thing Comes Along," 1936), and the tenor saxophonist Dick Wilson (on "Lotta Sax Appeal," 1936). Before it disbanded in 1948, other soloists included Don Byas, Howard McGhee, and Fats Navarro. Kirk then worked for the American Federation of Musicians and occasionally led bands into the 1980s.

Writings: *Twenty Years on Wheels,* ed. Amy Lee (Ann Arbor, 1989).

Kirk, (Rahsaan) Roland (b. Columbus, Ohio, 7 Aug. 1936; d. Bloomington, Ind., 5 Dec. 1977). Jazz saxophonist, flutist, and bandleader. By the age of 20 he was proficient at playing 3 instruments at once: tenor saxophone, stritch (a modified alto saxophone), and manzello (a modified soprano saxophone). These, his vocalized flute playing, and auxiliary sirens and whistles are all on his album *We Free Kings* (1961). Apart from a period as a soloist with Charles Mingus's soul jazz group (1961, including the album *Oh Yeah!*), he led groups. His performances were founded in bop styles, but ranged from early jazz to jazz-rock. He achieved modest commercial success with his speech-song *Bright Moments* (1973).

Kirkby, (Carolyn) Emma (b. Camberley, 26 Feb. 1949). Soprano. She read Classics at Oxford before training her voice. After her London debut in 1974 she rose quickly to the first rank of English sopranos. Toured the U.S. in 1978, New Zealand in 1980, the Middle East in 1981 and 1983. She specializes in Renaissance and Baroque music: solo songs (often accompanied on lute by Anthony Rooley), madrigals (with the Madrigal Ensemble), as well as operas, cantatas, and other concerted genres (with the Academy of Ancient Music, Taverner Players, and other groups).

Kirkpatrick, John (b. New York, 18 March 1905; d. Ithaca, N.Y., 8 Nov. 1991). Pianist and scholar. After studies at Princeton he journeyed to France, where he worked with Nadia Boulanger (1925–28) and Louta Nouneberg (1928–31). Back in the U.S. he befriended Charles Ives and in 1939 gave the first public performance of Ives's *Concord Sonata.* He taught at Monticello College (1942–43), Mount Holyoke College (1943–46), and Cornell Univ. (1949–68). He became curator of the Ives Collection at Yale Univ. in 1968. In 1955 Harmony Ives asked him to catalog her husband's manuscripts; his catalog was published in 1960, his annotated edition of Ives's 1932 *Memos* in 1973. He recorded infrequently, but his renderings of Ives are authoritative and those of other Americans such as MacDowell noteworthy.

Kirkpatrick, Ralph (Leonard) (b. Leominster, Mass., 10 June 1911; d. Guilford, Conn., 13 April 1984). Harpsichordist and scholar. After discovering the harpsichord while a student at Harvard (B.A., 1931) he made his debut in 1930, then worked with Wanda Landowska in Paris, 1931–32, later with Arnold Dolmetsch at Haslemere and with Heinz Tiessen in Berlin. A Guggenheim Fellowship in 1937 enabled him to return to Europe to study old instruments and manuscripts. In 1940 he joined the faculty of Yale Univ., where he compiled the first chronological catalog of the works of Domenico Scarlatti; in 1953 he also published a monograph on the composer. He promoted a contemporary literature for harpsichord by introducing new works such as Milhaud's Sonata for violin and harpsichord and Carter's Double Concerto, which is dedicated to him. Before his retirement in 1976 he recorded the complete keyboard works of Bach.

Kirkpatrick, William J(ames) (b. Duncannon, Pa., 27 Feb. 1838; d. Germantown, Pa., 20 Sept. 1921). Hymn book compiler. Son of a schoolteacher and musician; 1854, moved to Philadelphia to learn carpentry; 1858, began to publish music and to collect and edit camp meeting songs; from 1865, music director of Methodist churches. In 1880 he published the first of about 50 gospel song collections in collaboration with John R. Sweeney, selling millions of copies; issued many more after Sweeney's death in 1899.

Kirnberger, Johann Philipp (bapt. Saalfeld, 24 Apr. 1721; d. Berlin, 26 or 27 July 1783). Theorist and composer. Studied violin with Kellner and organ with H. N. Gerber, and from 1739 to 1741 composition under J. S. Bach at Leipzig. Worked for a number of Polish nobles, 1741–51, serving also at the Benedictine convent of Reusch-Lemburg; studied violin at Dresden for a short time before joining the royal chapel at Berlin as violinist. In 1754 he moved to the chapel of Prince Heinrich of Prussia and from 1758 to his death served Princess Anna Amalie. He is known chiefly for voluminous writings, most important his 4-volume *Die Kunst des reinen Satzes in der Musik* (1771–79; R: Hildesheim, 1968; trans. David Beach and Jurgen Thym, New Haven, 1982), and for his articles in J. G. Sulzer's *Allgemeine Theorie der schönen Kunste*

(1773). Kirnberger viewed J. S. Bach as the greatest of teachers and worked to propagate Bach's methods; his compositions, many written to complement his treatises, include lieder, motets, cantatas, sonatas, and keyboard works.

Kistler, Cyrill (b. Grossaitingen, near Augsburg, 12 Mar. 1848; d. Bad Kissingen, 1 Jan. 1907). Composer and writer. He studied with Rheinberger, Wüllner, and Franz Lachner at the Royal School of Music in Munich (1876–80); taught theory at the Sondershausen Conservatory (1883–85), then lived in Bad Kissingen as principal of a music school and free-lance composer. He was the editor of the pro-German periodical *Musikalische Tagesfragen* and authored a number of pedagogical books; his 10 operas are unsuccessful attempts to emulate Wagner.

Kitt, Eartha (b. North, S.C., 26 Jan. 1928). Popular singer, actress, dancer. She attended the High School for the Performing Arts in New York and joined Katherine Dunham's dance troupe in 1944. She began singing in cabarets and nightclubs in Paris (1950) and New York (1952); her cosmopolitan style and multilingual repertoire were very popular. She appeared in films (*Time Runs,* 1950), musicals (*New Faces of 1952,* including "Monotonous"), and on television, and made many recordings.

Kittel, Johann Christian (b. Erfurt, 18 Feb. 1732; d. there, 17 Apr. 1809). Organist and composer. An organ pupil first of Jakob Adlung and in 1748–50 of J. S. Bach, he served as organist at Langensalza (beginning 1751) and at Erfurt (Barfüsserkirche, 1756–62; Predigerkirche, from 1762). He was also a prominent teacher; his principles of keyboard instruction (which he characterized as Bach-influenced) are compiled in a treatise, *Der angehende praktische Organist* (1801–8). He also compiled chorale books (*Vierstimmige Choräle mit Vorspielen,* 1803) and composed chorale preludes in a style that incorporates Baroque and classical elements.

Kittl, Jan Bedřich [Johann Friedrich] (b. Orlík nad Vltavou, 8 May 1806; d. Lissa, Prussia [now Leszno, Poland], 20 July 1868). Composer. Began to compose at 16; studied law and music (with Tomášek) in Prague; held a government post to 1842; gave a well-received concert of his music in 1836 and had wide success with his Second Symphony (The Hunt) in 1837. Director, Prague Conservatory, 1843–65, resigning because of financial difficulties; thereafter a piano teacher. Perhaps the leading Czech Romantic composer before Smetana. His opera *Bianca und Giuseppe* (Prague, 1848; libretto by Wagner) was successful; also 4 symphonies, 3 concert overtures, choral and chamber music; songs; piano pieces.

Kiyōse, Yasuji (b. Yokkaichi, Ōita prefecture, Japan, 13 Jan. 1900; d. Tokyo, 14 Sept. 1981). Composer. He studied composition with Kōsaku Yamada and Kōsuke Komatsu; helped organize the society which later became the Japanese section of the ISCM. His compositions combine Romanticism and impressionism with Japanese folk song; Kiyose's most famous pupil is Toru Takemitsu. Works include choral (*Hebi-matsuri kōshin* [March of the Snake Festival], 1954; *Itaziki-yama no yoru* [A Night at Mount Itaziki], 1957; *Yoso kara kita shōjo* [A Foreign Girl], 1972); chamber music (3 violin sonatas, 1941–50; Shakuhachi Trio, 1964); songs (*Mannyō kak-yoku-shū* [Songs from Mannyō], 1942); orchestral works.

Kjerulf, Halfdan (b. Christiania [now Oslo], 15 or 17 Sept. 1815; d. Grefsen, near Christiania, 11 Aug. 1868). Composer. Studied law at his father's wish, but his inclinations were to music; in 1840, after the death of his father, brother, and sister, became a journalist to support his remaining family. In 1841 he published his op. 1, 6 songs; also taught the piano and conducted a male students' chorus (1845–49); studied composition with Carl Arnold (1848–49), then received a scholarship to study with Gade in Copenhagen (1849–50) and at the Leipzig Conservatory (1850–51); then a piano teacher in Oslo, increasingly in poor health. One of the principal Norwegian composers before Grieg, he was also interested in folk song; best known for his songs (about 130), male part songs (about 40 original, 50 arrangements), and piano pieces, some of which had considerable international popularity in the 1880s and 1890s (especially the song "Laengsel," the part song "Brudefaerden," and the piano pieces op. 4 no. 3, *Vuggevise* [Cradle Song], and op. 7 no. 5).

Klami, Uuno (Kalervo) (b. Virolahti, Finland, 20 Sept. 1900; d. there, 29 May 1961). Composer. He studied at the Helsinki College of Music, then continued his studies in Paris with Ravel (1924–25) and in Vienna with Willner (1928–29). He served as music critic for *Helsingin sanomat* (1932–59) and received a state pension from the Finnish government (1938–59); in 1959 he was appointed to the Finnish Academy. Klami's early works reflect his admiration for impressionism and for Ravel in particular. In 1927 he composed the *Karjalainen rapsodia* [Karelian Rhapsody], a work in which Finnish folk tunes are utilized for their distinctive sound; this was followed by a number of similar works, especially the *Fantaisie tschérémisse* for cello and orchestra (1931). Klami's most famous work is the *Kalevala sarja* [Kalevala Suite] (orchestra, 1933; rev. 1943), based on episodes from the *Kalevala.*

Klebe, Giselher (Wolfgang) (b. Mannheim, 28 June 1925). Composer. He studied in Berlin with Kurt von Wolfurt (1941–43), Rufer (1946), and Blacher (1946–51); from 1946 to 1949 he worked for Radio Berlin and in 1957 was appointed to teach composition at the Northwest German Music Academy in Detmold. His familiarity with the works of the Second Viennese School, gained through his study with Rufer and Blacher, provided the basis for his style; the dark and weighty manner of many compositions is reminiscent of Berg. He gained early recognition when his orchestral work *Die Zwitschermaschine* (inspired by a Klee painting) was performed at the first postwar Donaueschingen Festival (1950). Works include 12 operas (*Die Räuber,* 1957; *Die Fastnachtsbeichte,* 1983) and other stage music; orchestral music (5 symphonies; *Herschläge: Furcht, Bitte, und Hoffnung,* symphonic scenes for rock group and orchestra, 1969; *Begrüssung-Salutations,* 1981; *Notturno,* 1988; a harp concerto, 1988); *Quasi una fantasia* (piano quintet, 1967), *Nenia* (solo cello, 1975), and other chamber music; piano and organ music; 3 Mass settings and other choral works; *Roskolnikows Traum* (dramatic scene after Dostoyevski, soprano, clarinet, and orchestra, 1956) and other vocal music.

Kleber, Leonhard (b. Göppingen, ca. 1495; d. Pforzheim, 4 Mar. 1556). Organist. A student at Heidelberg Univ. from 1512, vicar-choral and organist in Horb (1516–17) and Esslingen (1517–21), organist in Pforzheim from 1521. Between 1521 and 1524 he compiled a large organ tablature consisting chiefly of arrangements of vocal works by composers such as Josquin, Isaac, Obrecht, and Senfl, as well as several lesser-known figures.

Kleiber, Carlos (b. Berlin, 3 July 1930). Conductor. Son of Erich Kleiber. He studied chemistry at Zurich but chose music as his vocation. Worked in Munich as a répétiteur at the Gärtnerplatz Theater, then made his conducting debut with the opera in Potsdam. After appointments at Düsseldorf (1956), Zurich (1964), Stuttgart (1966), and Munich (1968) he limited himself to guest-conducting, almost exclusively inside Germany. He appeared at Bayreuth in 1974. Metropolitan Opera debut, 1989.

Kleiber, Erich (b. Vienna, 5 Aug. 1890; d. Zurich, 27 Jan. 1956). Conductor and composer. Studied at the Prague Conservatory. While working as chorusmaster at the German Theater in Prague he made his conducting debut in 1911. He subsequently served as conductor at the Darmstadt Opera (1912–18), at Barmen-Elberfeld (1919–21), at Mannheim (1921–22), and at Düsseldorf (1922–23) before becoming general music director at the Berlin Staatsoper (1923–34). In Berlin he produced Janáček's *Jenůfa,* Berg's *Wozzeck* (1925), Milhaud's *Christophe Colomb* (1930), and other contemporary works. When in 1934 the German government forbade him to premiere Berg's *Lulu,* he resigned, being careful to introduce Berg's Five Symphonic Pieces from *Lulu* at his last concert. After relocating to Argentina in 1936 (naturalized 1938), he led the German Opera at the Teatro Colón in Buenos Aires (1937–49) and was conductor of the Havana Philharmonic (1944–47). In 1951 he was named chief conductor at the Deutsche Staatsoper in East Berlin, but quit in 1955 to protest political interference in the artistic domain. His compositions include concertos for piano and violin, orchestral works, much chamber music, and songs.

Klein, Bernhard (Joseph) (b. Cologne, 6 Mar. 1793; d. Berlin, 9 Sept. 1832). Composer. A mostly self-taught musician. From 1818 he lived in Berlin as teacher (Institute for Church Music) and composer (2 operas, church music, piano pieces, songs); studied the Palestrina style in Rome (1824). Never widely popular; his reputation was much furthered by the writings of his pupil Ludwig Rellstab.

Klein, Lothar (b. Hannover, 27 Jan. 1932). Composer. While still young went to England (1939) and to the U.S. (1941); studied with Paul Fetler at the Univ. of Minnesota (Ph.D., 1961), with Dorati, and with Josef Rufer and Boris Blacher in Berlin; taught at the Univ. of Minnesota (1962–64), the Univ. of Texas at Austin (1964–68), and the Univ. of Toronto (from 1968). His early works were essentially tonal; he later worked with serial and collage techniques. Compositions include stage works (*Canadiana,* 1980; *Lost Love,* 1950–56; *Orpheus,* 1976); orchestral music (*Appassionata for Orchestra,* 1958; *The Bluebird,* 1952; *Charivari: Music for an Imaginary Comedy,* 1966; Symphony no. 1, 1955; Symphony no. 2, 1966; *Concerto sacro,* viola and orchestra, 1984); chamber music (wind quintet, 1952; piano quintet, 1953; piano sonata, 1968); cantatas; choral works; songs.

Kleinsinger, George (b. San Bernardino, Calif., 13 Feb. 1914; d. New York, 28 July 1982). Composer. He studied at New York Univ. (with Bauer, Haubiel, and James) and at Juilliard (1938–40, with Jacobi and Wagenaar). His cantata *I Hear America Singing* (Whitman, 1940) and *Tubby the Tuba* (P. Tripp, narrator and orchestra, 1942; subsequently a film for which he received an Oscar nomination) are his best-known works. He composed several other melodramas (*The Tree That Found Christmas,* 1955) and a chamber opera (*Shinbone Alley,* after Don Marquis's *Archy and Mehitabel,* 1954); a symphony, and concertos for cello (1946), harmonica (1947), and violin (1953); chamber music; cantatas.

Klemperer, Otto (b. Breslau, 14 May 1885; d. Zurich, 6 July 1973). Conductor and composer. He studied piano with James Kwast and theory with Ivan Knorr at the Frankfurt Conservatory, composition and conducting with Hans Pfitzner at the Klindworth–Schwarenda Conservatory in Berlin. His meeting with Mahler in 1905 began a relationship that proved decisive. After his 1906 debut he was appointed on Mahler's recommendation chorusmaster at the German Opera in Prague (1907); later he became permanent conductor there. In 1910 he obtained on Mahler's recommendation the post of chief conductor at the Hamburg Opera. He conducted at Barmen (1913–14), at Strasbourg (1914–17), and at Cologne (1917–24), where he created Korngold's *Die tote Stadt.* He was music director at Wiesbaden (1924–27), and at the Kroll Opera in

Berlin (1927–31) he introduced Stravinsky's *Oedipus Rex,* Schoenberg's *Erwartung,* Janáček's *From the House of the Dead,* and other outstanding works. He was conducting at the Berlin Staatsoper (1931–33) when the advent of the Nazi regime necessitated his emigration. In the U.S. he studied composition with Schoenberg during tenures with the Los Angeles and Pittsburgh Philharmonics (1933–39; 1937–38). Removal of a brain tumor in 1939 resulted in partial paralysis and an interruption of his career. He served as musical director of the Budapest Opera (1947–50); after a fall at the Montreal airport in 1951 he often sat when conducting. During the 1950s he began to work regularly with Walter Legge's Philharmonia Orchestra and was named conductor for life in 1955; with them he recorded a broad repertory.

Bibl.: Peter Heyworth, *Otto Klemperer: His Life and Times,* vol. 1 (Cambridge, 1983).

Klenau, Paul (August) von (b. Copenhagen, 11 Feb. 1883; d. there, 31 Aug. 1946). Composer and conductor. He studied composition with Malling and violin with Hillmer in Copenhagen, continuing his studies at the Berlin Hochschule für Musik with Bruch (composition) and Halíř (violin). He studied in Munich with Thuille (1904) and in 1907 was appointed Kapellmeister to the Freiburg Opera; took a post with the Hofoper in Stuttgart (1909), then returned to the Freiburg Opera in 1913. After World War I he studied with Schoenberg and conducted the Danish Philharmonic (1920–26) and the Vienna Konzerthausgesellschaft (1922–30). Works include operas (*Sulamith,* 1913; *Rembrandt van Rijn,* 1937; *Elisabeth von England,* 1939); ballet (*Klein Idas Blumen,* 1916); orchestral and vocal music; piano pieces.

Klengel, August (Stephan) Alexander (b. Dresden, 29 Jan. or June 1783; d. there, 22 Nov. 1852). Composer. From 1803 a pupil of Clementi, traveling with him, remaining behind in St. Petersburg (1805–11); then toured Europe as a pianist, living in Paris (1811–13), Italy (1813–14), Dresden (1814), London (1815–16). He published much piano salon music; other works include 2 concertos, 7 sonatas, a piano trio. From 1817, organist at the Dresden court chapel. He later turned to Bach and strict composition and is best known for his 48 canons and fugues (Leipzig, 1854).

Klengel, Julius (b. Leipzig, 24 or 29 Sept. 1859; d. there, 26 or 27 Oct. 1933). Cellist. From a family of musicians, brother of conductor Paul Klengel (1854–1935); studied music in Leipzig; member of the Gewandhaus Orchestra from age 15, principal cellist, 1881–1924; toured Europe as soloist and cellist of the Gewandhaus Quartet; 1881–1933, teacher (professor from 1899), Leipzig Conservatory (pupils included Feuermann, Piatigorsky); also composed and edited, especially for cello.

Klenovsky, Nikolay Semyonovich (b. Odessa, 1857; d. Petrograd, 6 July 1915). Conductor and composer. He studied with Tchaikovsky (harmony) and Ivan Hřimalý (violin) at the Moscow Conservatory, graduating in 1879; served as conductor of the Bolshoi Theater in Moscow (1883–93), director of the music school at Tbilisi (1893–1902), and deputy director of the imperial chapel in St. Petersburg (1902–6). As a composer Klenovsky is best known for his 3 ballets: *Prelesti gashisha* [The Delights of Hashish] (1885), *Svetlana* (1886), and *Salanga* (1900).

Kletzki, Paul [Pavel Klecki] (b. Łódź, 21 Mar. 1900; d. Liverpool, 5 Mar. 1973). Conductor and composer. He studied violin in Łódź with Emil Młynarsky (1914–19), then in Berlin with Fr. E. Koch from 1921. Debut as a conductor in 1923. He taught composition at Venice and at the Milan Conservatory (1935–38). Conducted the Kharkov Philharmonic (1937–38), then settled in Switzerland, where he taught at the Lausanne Conservatory (1944–45). After ten years as a guest conductor, named head conductor of the Royal Liverpool Orchestra (1954–55), of the Dallas Symphony (1958–61), the Bern Symphony (1964–66), and the Orchestre de la Suisse Romande (1967–70). His compositions include 3 symphonies, concertos for piano and violin, and 4 quartets.

Klindworth, Karl (b. Hannover, 25 Sept. 1830; d. Stolpe, near Potsdam, 27 July 1916). Pianist and teacher. A musician from an early age (active as a theater conductor from 1847); from 1852, a Liszt pupil at Weimar; 1854–68, pianist, conductor, teacher in London, but not entirely successful there; 1868–71, piano professor, Moscow Conservatory; then worked in Berlin as pianist, conductor, teacher (headed his own piano school, 1884–93); toured as pianist (England, U.S., 1887–88); retired in 1910. Best known for his piano reductions of all the operas of Wagner (a friend from 1855) from *Rienzi* to *Parsifal.* Edited and arranged much piano music.

Klose, Friedrich (b. Karlsruhe, 29 Nov. 1862; d. Ruvigliana, Lugano, 24 Dec. 1942). Composer. Studied in Karlsruhe with V. Lachner, then law at the Univ. of Geneva; 1886–89, studied in Vienna with Bruckner, recalled in his *Meine Lehrjahre bei Bruckner* (Regensburg, 1927); then taught at various schools and privately in Switzerland (of which he became a citizen in 1886), Austria, Germany; 1907–19, taught at the Munich Academy of Music (professor from 1910); thereafter lived in Switzerland. Became known as a composer from the 1880s with a Mass in D minor op. 6 (1889), the symphonic poems *Elfenreigen* (1892) and *Das Leben ein Traum* (1896), and the opera (called a "dramatic symphony") *Ilsebill* (1903). His reputation held through the first quarter of the century, then declined. Also composed an oratorio, chamber music, songs.

Klosé, Hyacinthe Eléonore (b. Corfu, 11 Oct. 1808; d. Paris, 29 Aug. 1880). Clarinetist. Migrated to Paris and played in military bands from about 1823, becoming a bandmaster around 1831; from 1831 studied at the Paris Conservatory under Berr, whom he succeeded as clarinet professor (1839–68); collaborated with the instrument maker L. A. Buffet on a Boehm-style key-ring clarinet (patented 1844), for which he wrote a still-used *Méthode complète* (1844); also clarinet etudes and exercises, saxophone method and exercises.

Klusák, Jan (b. Prague, 18 Apr. 1934). Composer. Studied composition with Řídký and Bořkovec at the Prague Academy (1953–57). The tonal neoclassicism of his earlier works gave way to lyrical twelve-tone serialism. Works include operas (*Proces,* after Kafka, 1966; *Viola,* 1984–85); the ballet *Stories from Tapestries* (1988); orchestral works (3 symphonies, 1956–60; *Invention I,* chamber orchestra, 1961; *Invention III,* strings, 1962; *Invention IV,* 1964; *6 Small Preludes,* 1984); chamber music (*Hudba k vodotrysku* [Music for a Fountain], wind quintet, 1954; *Invention V,* wind quintet, 1965; *Invention VI,* nonet, 1969; String Quartet no. 4, 1990); choral works; songs; piano pieces.

Klyuzner, Boris Lazarevich (b. Astrakhan, 1 June 1909). Composer. He studied with Gnesin at the Leningrad Conservatory (1936–41) and worked as a choir director; served in the Leningrad branch of the Soviet Composers Union (1955–61). His works are noted for their contrapuntal mastery and Russian folklike melodies. Compositions include orchestral music (piano concerto, 1939; violin concerto, 1950; 3 overtures, 1951, 1952, 1953; Symphony no. 1, 1955; Symphony no. 2, 1963; concerto, 2 violins, 1969); vocal works (*Poema o Lenine,* baritone, chorus, orchestra, 1960; *Vremena goda* [The Seasons], soprano, baritone, orchestra, 1935–68; Symphony no. 4, vocalist, chorus, orchestra, 1972; 14 songs); instrumental music (2 piano sonatas, 1935, 1966).

Knab, Armin (b. Neuschleichach, Lower Franconia, 19 Feb. 1881; d. Bad Wörishafen, 23 June 1951). Composer and writer on music. He studied law at the Univ. of Würzburg (until 1904) and piano at the conservatory there (1897–1902); while composing and writing on music, he pursued a career as a lawyer and judge until 1934, when he was appointed to teach at the Berlin Academy of Music Education and Church Music. He won the Max Reger Prize in 1940, and in 1943 retired to southern Germany. He composed an oratorio (*Das gesegnete Jahr,* soprano, bass, chorus, orchestra, 1935–43) and music for the theater and radio; orchestral works; chamber and piano music; the cantatas *Vanitas mundi* (1946) and *Engelsgruss* (1950) and other vocal music; many choral arrangements of folk and popular songs. His writings, most concerned with the German youth movement, are collected in *Denken und Tun,* edited by Hans Wegener (1959).

Knabe, (Valentin) William [Wilhelm] **(Ludwig)** (b. Kreuzberg, Prussia, 3 June 1803; d. Baltimore, 21 May 1864). Piano manufacturer. Trained as piano maker in Gotha; 1833, emigrated to Baltimore, working for Henry Hartje; 1839, opened his own firm (in partnership with Henry Gaehle, 1839–54). His business dominated the piano market in the South and was therefore damaged by the Civil War. It was reinvigorated by his sons Ernest (1827–94) and William (1841–89). The firm moved to East Rochester, N.Y., in 1929 and in 1932 became a subsidiary of Aeolian American Corporation, which ultimately entered bankruptcy in 1985. The name Knabe was subsequently acquired by Falconi of Massachusetts.

Knaifel, Alexander Aronovich (b. Tashkent, 28 Nov. 1943). Composer. In 1944, returned with his family to Leningrad from evacuation. From 1950 to 1961, studied cello at the preparatory school of the Leningrad Conservatory; 1961–63, pursued cello studies with Rostropovich at the Moscow Conservatory. In 1964, began composition studies at the Leningrad Conservatory under Boris Arapov, graduating in 1967. Has worked as an editor and a teacher. A member of the Soviet musical avant-garde, he has been drawn to micro-intervallic, mathematical, and symbolic qualities of sound in his scores. Works include an opera, *The Canterville Ghost* (1966); ballets (*Medea,* 1968); numerous works for nonstandard ensembles (*Jeanne,* Passion for 13 instrumental groups of 56 soloists, 1978); chamber music (*Agnus Dei,* 4 instrumentalists, 1985); choral and vocal music (*A Silly Horse,* singer and piano, 1981); film music.

Knappertsbusch, Hans (b. Elberfeld, 12 Mar. 1888; d. Munich, 25 Oct. 1965). Conductor. Studied philosophy at Bonn, then music with Fritz Steinbach and Otto Lohse at the Cologne Conservatory (1908–12). Conductor with the Mülheim Orchestra (1910–12). Assisted at Bayreuth in the summers. Permanent conductor at the Elberfeld Opera (1913–18), at Leipzig (1918–19), at Dessau (1919–22). His career breakthrough occurred when he succeeded Bruno Walter as general music director at Munich (1922–36). From there he went to Vienna to conduct both the Philharmonic and the opera (1937–45). From 1951 he conducted at the Bayreuth Festivals. Although he was known as a committed champion of Bruckner symphonies, he clung to the Schalk recompositions of them.

Knecht, Justin Heinrich (b. Biberach, 30 Sept. 1752; d. there, 1 Dec. 1817). Organist, composer, and music theorist. Little is known of his youth; apparently he was self-taught in music. He was organist and music director in Biberach for most of his life; from 1806 he served two years as *Konzertmeister* at the Stuttgart court. Among his theoretical works, which manifest the influence of Abbé Vogler, are the *Erklärung einiger . . . missverstandener Grundsätze aus der Voglerschen Theorie* (Ulm, 1785) and the *Gemeinnütziges Elementarwerk der Harmonie und des Generalbasses* (Augsburg, 1792–98). He composed a number of

Hiller-like singspiels, sacred vocal works, programmatic symphonies, and chamber music.

Kneisel, Franz (b. Bucharest, 26 Jan. 1865; d. New York, 26 Mar. 1926). Violinist. After graduating from the Bucharest Conservatory in 1879, he studied in Vienna with Jacob Grün and Joseph Hellmesberger, making his debut there in 1882. He served as concertmaster of the Bilse Symphony in Berlin (1884–85), then emigrated to the U.S. to occupy the same chair in the Boston Symphony (1885–1903). In 1886 he founded a quartet that made excellent performances of European chamber music a normal part of musical life in Boston and New York. Through its commitment to American composers, his quartet was also responsible in large part for the flowering of native chamber music in the U.S. From 1905 he taught in New York at the Institute of Musical Art.

Knight, Gladys (M.) (b. Atlanta, 28 May 1944). Soul singer. After early performances of gospel music with church choirs in the South, in 1952 she formed the vocal group The Pips with family members. As a quartet (with Merald Knight, William Guest, and Edward Patten), The Pips achieved great success with many recordings of the 1960s and 1970s ("Every Beat of My Heart," 1961; "I Heard It through the Grapevine," 1967; *Imagination,* 1973); they continued to record and perform into the 1980s (*About Love,* 1980; *Life,* 1985).

Knipper, Lev Konstantinovich (b. Tbilisi, 3 Dec. 1898; d. Moscow, 30 July 1974). Composer. He studied with Glier and Zhilyayev (composition) and Gnesina (piano) at the Gnesin School of Music in Moscow; continued his studies with Jarnach in Berlin and Julius Weissmann in Freiburg. He held various posts in the music division of the Red Army and was a member of the Association of Contemporary Music in Moscow. Beginning in the 1930s Knipper moved away from the style of *The North Wind,* which the authorities attacked as modernist, and began to compose more in line with "socialist realism" aesthetics. Of his many symphonies the most famous was the Fourth (1933–34), part of which became popular in the U.S. under the title *Meadowland.* Works include operas (*Severnïy veter* [The North Wind], 1929–30; *Marya,* 1936–38; *Aktrisa* [The Actress], 1942; *Na Baykale* [On Lake Baikal], 1946–48; *Koren' zhizni* [The Source of Life], 1948–49); ballets (*Istochnik schast'ya* [The Source of Happiness], 1949); orchestral music (14 symphonies, 1929–54; *Saga,* cello, chorus, orchestra, 1963); chamber music (string quartet, 1942; *Concerto Scherzo,* violin, piano, 1964).

Knorr, Ernst-Lothar von (b. Eitorf, 2 Jan. 1896; d. Heidelberg, 30 Oct. 1973). Composer. He studied at the Cologne Conservatory (violin, conducting, and harmony). After World War I he taught violin at the Heidelberg Conservatory and the Mannheim Musikhochschule; was a founder of the Heidelberg Chamber Orchestra. From 1925 until 1969 he served successively as the principal of music academies in Berlin, Frankfurt, Trossingen, Hannover, and Heidelberg. Many of his manuscripts were destroyed in the bombing of Frankfurt; surviving works include a concerto for piano, chorus, and orchestra and a serenade for strings (1973); 4 string quartets (1929–70) and other chamber music; piano, organ, and harpsichord works; cantatas (2 for children); choral music; some 70 songs.

Knorr, Iwan (Otto Armand) (b. Mewe, West Prussia, 3 Jan. 1853; d. Frankfurt am Main, 22 Jan. 1916). Composer and teacher. Grandson of a church musician, his first teacher; his family lived in southern Russia, 1857–67. Beginning in 1868, a student at the Leipzig Conservatory; 1874–83, taught the piano and theory in Kharkov; from 1883, taught the piano and theory, later composition at the Hoch Conservatory, Frankfurt (professor from 1895, director from 1908). His pupils include Scott, Pfitzner, Toch. Composed 3 operas; orchestral, chamber, choral, piano pieces; songs. Also wrote books on Tchaikovsky (whom he knew), harmony, fugue.

Knorr, Julius (b. Leipzig, 22 Sept. 1807; d. there, 17 June 1861). Piano teacher. Studied philology but became a pianist, a close friend of Schumann (member of the Davidsbündler as "Julius"), an editor of the *Neue Zeitschrift für Musik* in its first year (1834); a piano teacher in Leipzig; best known for his collections of progressive exercises and other didactic works (published 1835–61).

Knüpfer, Sebastian (b. Asch, 6 Sept. 1633; d. Leipzig, 10 Oct. 1676). Composer. Attended the Gymnasium Poeticum, Regensburg, 1646–54, perhaps studying with Kradenthaler; moving to Leipzig, he sang bass and gave lessons, and in 1657 was named successor to Michael as Thomaskantor over A. Krieger and three others. Broadly versed in humanistic studies, he was active in the academic as well as musical life of the city. He visited Halle in 1664–65 and 1675 to present some of his music. Except for *Lustige Madrigalien und Canzonetten* (1663), intended for his Thomasschule students, his extant music consists exclusively of sacred vocal works in Latin and German, the latter often using chorales.

Knussen, (Stuart) Oliver (b. Glasgow, 12 June 1952). Composer and conductor. He attended the Central Tutorial School for Young Musicians; studied with John Lambert (1963–69) and Gunther Schuller (1970–73). A precocious talent, Knussen was 15 when he directed the London Symphony in a performance of his own First Symphony. From 1983 artistic director of the Aldeburgh Festival; from 1986 coordinator of contemporary music at Tanglewood. In the early 1990s he was composer-in-residence to the Chamber Music Society of Lincoln Center. Works include orchestral compositions (Symphony no. 1, op. 1, 1966–67; Concerto for Orchestra, op. 5, 1968–70, rev. 1976; Symphony no. 2, soprano, orchestra, op. 7, 1970–71; Symphony no. 3, op. 18, 1973–79); other instrumental works (*Masks* op. 3, flute, 1969; *Océan de terre* op. 10, flute, clarinet, violin, cello, double bass, percussion, piano, 1972–73; rev. 1976); Cantata, op. 15, oboe, string trio (1977); a children's opera (*Max and the Maximonsters,* 1980); with Maurice Sendak, 2 one-act operas, *Where the Wild Things Are* (1979–83) and *Higglety Pigglety Pop!* (1984–90).

Kobelius, Johann Augustin (b. Waehlitz, 21 Feb. 1674; d. Weissenfels, 17 Aug. 1731). Composer. Studied organ with Brause and Schieferdecker, and composition with J. P. Krieger; traveled to Venice, among other places; became a chamber musician at Weissenfels, then took a post as organist in Sangerhausen in 1702, becoming *director chori musici* in 1703 and serving also in the town of Querfurt. Went to Weissenfels after Krieger's death as *Landrentmeister* in 1725; he had been composing for that court since at least 1712. His music, all lost, seems to have consisted principally of German operas written for Weissenfels; over 20 of his works premiered there between 1715 and 1729.

Koch, (Sigurd Christian) Erland von (b. Stockholm, 26 Apr. 1910). Composer. Studied music with his father, Sigurd von Koch, continuing his studies at the Stockholm Conservatory (1931–35) and in Germany and France with Höffer (composition), Kraus and Gmeindl (conducting), and Arrau (piano). Koch taught at Wohlfart's Music School in Stockholm (1939–53), then started teaching harmony at the Stockholm Musikhögskolan and was appointed professor there in 1968; he also served as chairman of Fylkingen (1946–48). One of the most popular Swedish composers; Koch's works effectively combine folk melodies with twelve-tone techniques. Works include operas (*Lasse Lucidor,* 1943; *Pelle Svanslös* [Tailless Peter], for children, 1948); orchestral music (4 symphonies; *Dans* no. 2, 1938, arr. strings, 1966; *Impulsi-trilogen: Impulsi,* 1964, *Echi,* 1965, *Ritmi,* 1966; *Festmarsch,* 1974; *Midvinterblot-Sommarsolstånd,* 1987); choral works; chamber music (6 string quartets, 1934–63); songs.

Koch, Heinrich Christoph (b. Rudolstadt, 10 Oct. 1749; d. there, 19 Mar. 1816). Theorist, composer, and violinist. He studied composition and violin in Rudolstadt with Christoph Scheinpflug and Karl Göpfert; later he studied in Berlin, Dresden, and Hamburg, and became chamber musician at the Rudolstadt court in 1772. From the 1780s he was active as a writer, and in 1795 he edited the short-lived *Journal der Tonkunst* (publ. Erfurt). He is best known for his *Versuch einer Anleitung zur Composition* (Rudolstadt and Leipzig, 1782–93; R: Hildesheim, 1969; partial trans. Nancy Kovaleff Baker, New Haven, 1983) and his *Musikalisches Lexikon* (Frankfurt, 1802; R: Hildesheim, 1964; 2nd ed., 1817; later edited as *Kurzgefasstes Handwörterbuch der Musik,* Leipzig, 1807). They are two of the most influential theoretical sources of the 18th century. The *Versuch* is a comprehensive treatment of classical-period harmonic principles, counterpoint, and forms; its discussion of melodic construction (vol. 2) formed the basis for subsequent discussions of "periodic" phrase structures. The *Lexikon* contains clear, precise definitions of terms such as *sonata, rondo,* etc., as they were viewed during the last quarter of the 18th century.

Bibl.: Jane R. Stevens, "An 18th-Century Description of Concerto First-Movement Form," *JAMS* 24 (1971): 85–95. Elaine R. Sisman, "Small and Expanded Forms: Koch's Model and Haydn's Music," *MQ* 68 (1982: 444–75.

Köchel, Ludwig (Alois Ferdinand) von (b. Stein, near Krems, 14 Jan. 1800; d. Vienna, 3 June 1877). Scholar. Law graduate, Vienna Univ. From 1823 a tutor to distinguished families; 1827–42, with the children of Archduke Carl. Traveled, 1842–47, doing botany; 1850–63, lived in Salzburg (on whose minerals he published a book in 1859) researching his thematic catalog of Mozart's music (1862; later editions prepared by others); from 1863, lived in Vienna and published several works on its music history and an edition of letters of Beethoven.

Kocsis, Zoltán (b. Budapest, 30 May 1952). Pianist. Studied piano and composition at the Bartók Conservatory (1963–68), then with Pál Kadosa, Ferenc Rados, and György Kurtág at the Liszt Conservatory. Debut in Budapest in 1970; the same year he won the Hungarian Radio Beethoven Competition. In 1973 he received the Liszt Prize and the Kossuth Prize. Taught at the Liszt Academy from 1976. Toured the U.S. in 1971 and 1982.

Kocžwara, František (b. Prague? ca. 1750; d. London, 2 Sept. 1791). Composer. Little is known of his young years; publications of his music first began to appear in London in 1775. During the 1780s he was in Ireland, where his *The Battle of Prague* was published (Dublin, 1788); it became one of the most popular programmatic piano pieces of its day. In 1791 he is cited as a participant in the Handel Commemoration and as a string player at the King's Theatre. (Fétis reports having played keyboard for him as a boy in Mons, mistakenly placing the date as 1792.) He composed chiefly chamber music, including trio sonatas, string quartets, and solo keyboard music.

Kodály, Zoltán (b. Kecskemét, Hungary, 16 Dec. 1882; d. Budapest, 6 Mar. 1967). Composer and ethnomusicologist. He came from a musical family—his father played violin and his mother piano—and Zoltán learned to play the piano, violin, viola, and cello, and sang in the church choir. He also tried his hand at composition at a young age, working on a Mass at the age of 15 and a string trio at 16. He enrolled at Budapest Univ., concurrently studying composition at the Academy of Music with Koessler; received diplomas in composition (1904), teaching (1905), and a Ph.D. in

Hungarian folk song (1906). He became associated with Bartók in compiling, organizing, and editing the vast body of Hungarian folk song; the two became close friends, their first joint project being the publication of *Magyar népdalok* (Hungarian Folk Songs) in 1906. In December 1906 Kodály went to Berlin, then to Paris the following April, where he encountered the music of Debussy. Upon his return to Budapest he was appointed professor at the Academy of Music, teaching theory and eventually composition. A concert of his music was given in Budapest on 17 March 1910; the same year also saw his marriage to Emma Sándor. The First World War curtailed Kodály's fieldwork in collecting folk song, and beginning in 1917 he worked as a music critic for *Nyugat* and *Pesti napló,* writing about folk music and analyzing some of Bartók's compositions. Appointed assistant director (under Dohnányi) of the Academy of Music in 1919, he was relieved of this post for political reasons, though he resumed teaching in 1922. In 1921 Universal Edition began publishing his scores. His commissioned oratorio *Psalmus hungaricus* premiered in Budapest in 1923 to considerable acclaim and was followed by numerous performances of the work throughout Europe and in the U.S.

Kodály gained further fame with his national opera *Háry János* (1926) and the orchestral suite drawn from it; the suite quickly entered the concert repertory and remains a popular favorite. He scored another success with the suite of folk dances entitled *Marosszéki táncok* (Dances of Marosszék, 1927); the folk ballad *Székely fonó* (The Transylvanian Spinning-Room) was first performed in Budapest in 1932 and enjoyed considerable success at La Scala the following year. Kodály published a 10-volume collection of folk songs for voice and piano under the title *Magyar népzene* (Hungarian Folk Music, 1924–32) and composed some large-scale works in response to commissions. From 1930 he lectured on folk music at the Univ. of Budapest and at the Free Univ.; during the Second World War he remained in Budapest, continuing to compose. In the postwar years he received a considerable number of honors: election as chairman of the board of directors of the Academy of Music, president of the Hungarian Art Council, and honorary membership in the Academy of Sciences, where he also served as president (1946–49). After 1946 Kodály embarked on a series of concert tours, conducting his own works in the U.S., the United Kingdom, the Soviet Union, and western Europe. He continued to write in his later years, completing some important compositions including the *Zrinyi szózata* (Hymn of Zrinyi) for baritone and chorus (1954) and the *Laudes organi* for chorus and organ (1966); he also received additional academic honors, including honorary doctorates from the universities at Budapest (1957), Oxford (1960), and East Berlin (1964) as well as honorary membership in the Moscow Conservatory (1963) and the American Academy of Arts and Sciences (1963).

In addition to his importance as a composer and ethnomusicologist, Kodály is noted for his role as music educator; toward this end he penned numerous singing and reading exercises, presided at many conferences on music education, and from 1964 until his death served as honorary president of the International Society for Music Education.

Works: Incidental music to stage works (all first performances in Budapest): *Notre Dame de Paris* (1902); *Le Cid* (1903); *A nagybácsi* [The Uncle] (1904); *Pacsirtaszó* [Lark Song] (1917). Singspiels/plays: *Háry János* (1926); *Székely fonó* [The Transylvanian Spinning-Room] (1932); *Czinka Panna* (1948).

Orchestral music: *Nyári este* [Summer Evening] (1906; rev. 1929–30); *Háry János,* suite (1927); *Marosszéki táncok* [Dances of Marosszék] (1930); *Galántai táncok* [Dances of Galánta] (1933); *Variations on a Hungarian Folk Song 'Felszállott a páva'* [The Peacock] (1938–39); *Concerto for Orchestra* (1939–40); *Minuetto serio* [from *Cinka Panna*] (1948–53); Symphony in C (1930s–61).

Vocal works: *Stabat Mater* (1898); *Magyar népdalok* [20 Hungarian Folk Songs] (with Bartók, 1906); *Psalmus hungaricus* (1923); *Budavári Te Deum* (1936); *Missa brevis* (1944); *Vértanúk sírjánál* [At the Martyr's Grave]; *Kállai kettös* [Kálló's Double Dance] (1950); unaccompanied choral works; songs and choruses for music students and children.

Chamber music: *Romance lyrique,* cello and piano (1898); Trio in E♭, 2 violins and viola (1899); 2 string quartets (1908–9, 1916–18; Sonata op. 4, cello and piano (1909–10); Duo op. 7, violin and cello (1914); Sonata op. 8, cello (1915); *Capriccio,* cello (1915); *Magyar Rondo,* cello, piano (1917); Serenade op. 12, 2 violins, viola (1919–20); Sonatina, cello, piano (1921–22); *Hivogató tábortűhöz* [Calling to Campfire], clarinet (1930). Piano works include *Meditation* (1907), *Gyermektáncok* [Children's Dances] (1945).

Bibl.: *The Selected Writings of Zoltán Kodály,* trans. Lili Halápy and Fred Macnicol (London, 1974). Lászlo Eősze, *Zoltán Kodály: His Life and Work* (London, 1962). Percy M. Young, *Zoltán Kodály: A Hungarian Musician* (London, 1964). György Ránki, ed., *Bartók and Kodály Revisited,* Indiana Univ. Studies on Hungary, 2 (Budapest, 1987). János Breuer, *A Guide to Kodály,* trans. Maria Steiner (Budapest, 1990).

Koechlin, Charles (Louis Eugène) (b. Paris, 27 Nov. 1867; d. Le Canadel, Var, 31 Dec. 1950). Composer and writer on music. Began to study music seriously when he was in Algeria convalescing from tuberculosis (1889); attended the Paris Conservatory (from 1890). His composition teachers included Massenet and (after his resignation in 1896) Fauré; studied counterpoint with Gédalge. He began to write criticism in 1909 (for the *Chronique des Arts*) and works on music theory in 1915. In 1909, with the backing of Fauré, he helped to found the Société musicale indépendante in opposition to d'Indy's more conservative Société nationale and Schola cantorum. His works were popular in Paris in the 1920s, but much remained unpublished and unperformed despite the efforts of Paul Collaer to arrange performances in the 1940s. Although he remained attached to the genre of symphonic poem and the large orchestra longer than most of his contemporaries, his mature style rested on polytonality; extramusical content is obvious in many works. Among his students were Poulenc, Tailleferre, and Milhaud. Koechlin made three lecture tours in the U.S. (1918, 1928, 1937); was president of the French section of the ISCM; in the 1930s his leftist sympathies became apparent in his "music for the people" and his membership on the Committée Association France–URSS. His writings include many articles and books on counterpoint, harmony, theory, fugue, Fauré, Debussy, woodwind instruments, and orchestration.

Works: 4 ballets and other stage music; some 16 symphonic poems (4 that make up the *Jungle Book Suite,* 1926–40, after Kipling), some 16 chorales for orchestra, *Introduction et 4 interludes de style atonal-sériel* (orchestration incomplete, 1947), and other orchestral and band music; 3 string quartets, *Sonata à 7* (flute, oboe, harpsichord or harp, and string quartet, 1949), and other chamber music; many piano and organ works including those for students; choral music (*Quelques chorales sur les fêtes populaires*); songs; orchestrations.

Bibl.: Henri Sauguet, ed., *Oeuvres de Charles Koechlin* (Paris, 1975) [catalog]. Robert Orledge, *Charles Koechlin (1867–1950): His Life and Works* (New York, 1989).

Koellreutter, Hans Joachim (b. Freiburg im Breisgau, 2 Sept. 1915). Composer. Studied flute, piano, and composition at the Berlin Conservatory under Hindemith, among others (1934–36), and flute at Geneva under Moyse (1936–37). Moving to Brazil, he taught at the Brazilian Conservatory, Rio de Janeiro (1937–52), and the São Paulo Institute of Music (1942–44), and directed the São Paulo Free Academy of Music (1952–55). Later led the Bahia Univ. music department (1952–62), also conducting the Bahia Symphony. From 1963 he worked for the Goethe Institute in Munich, New Delhi, and Tokyo, before returning to Brazil in the 1970s. Much of his music uses twelve-tone techniques; his extended stays in Brazil, India, and Japan are reflected in the use of indigenous instruments in his compositions; later he applied aleatory methods. Works include orchestral music (*Música,* 1947; *Mutações,* 1953; *Advaita,* sitar and orchestra, 1968); and vocal and chamber music.

Koenig, Gottfried Michael (b. Magdeburg, 5 Oct. 1926). Composer. Studied at the State Music School in Brunswick (1946–47), at the Northwest German Music Academy in Detmold (1947–50), and in Cologne. From 1954 to 1964 he worked in Cologne at the Electronic Music Studio of the West German Radio, composing and realizing works of others (including Hambraeus, Kagel, Ligeti, and Pousseur); he has taught at the Musikhochschule in Cologne (1962–64), the Darmstadt summer courses, and the Cologne New Music courses. In 1964 he became director of the Instituut voor Sonologie at Utrecht Univ., where he has been especially interested in interactive computer music influenced by composers and audiences in real time. He has published many articles in *Die Reihe* and elsewhere; has written works for traditional instruments (*Orchesterstück 1–3,* 1960–63; *Beitrag,* orchestra, 1986) and tape music (*Funktion Grün,* 1967).

Koetsier, Jan (b. Amsterdam, 14 Aug. 1911). Composer and conductor. He studied at the Berlin Hochschule für Musik (1927–34); conducted in Lübeck and Berlin before returning to the Netherlands, where he conducted the Hague Philharmonic and served as second conductor of the Concertgebouw (1942–48). Koetsier became principal conductor for Bavarian Radio (1950–66) and joined the faculty of the Munich Hochschule für Musik as a professor of conducting (1966–76). Works include orchestral music (Suite, 1937; 3 symphonies, 1945–54; *Concerto capriccioso,* piano, orchestra, 1975; Concertino, trombone, strings, 1984; *Burg-Serenade,* orchestra, 1987; *Petit concert pour violon et contrebass,* 1987); vocal music (*Der Mann Lot,* oratorio, 1940, rev. 1962; *Frans Hals,* opera, 1951); chamber music (horn sonatina, 1972); ballets; songs; piano and organ pieces.

Koffler, Józef (b. Stryj, Poland, 28 Nov. 1896; d. Wieliczka, 1943). Composer. He studied in Vienna with Graedener (1914–16), Schoenberg (1920–24), and Adler (1920–24), receiving his doctorate from the Univ. of Vienna in 1925; taught composition at the Lvov Conservatory (1929–41) and served as music critic of the *Ekspres wieczorny.* He was killed in a roundup of Jews near Kraków. The first Polish composer to use twelve-tone serialism, Koffler combined this technique with folk material and his natural gift for instrumental color; many of his most accomplished compositions are in variation form. Works include orchestral music (Symphony no. 3, winds, harp, percussion, 1938; *Wariacje na temat serii dwunastotonowej* [Variations on a Twelve-Tone Series], strings, 1933); chamber music (string trio, 1929); piano pieces (*Variations sur une valse de Johan Strauss,* 1936); vocal works.

Kogan, Leonid (Borisovich) (b. Dnepropetrovsk, 14 Nov. 1924; d. Mytishcha, 17 Dec. 1982). Violinist. Studied violin with his father, then with Abram Yampolsky at the Moscow Conservatory, graduating in 1948. Won the Queen Elisabeth of Belgium Competition in 1951. Appointed to the faculty of the Moscow Conservatory in 1952, becoming a full professor in 1963. Formed a trio with his brother-in-law Emil Gilels and Rostropovitch. U.S. debut in Boston, 1958. Received the Lenin Prize, 1965.

Köhler, (Christian) Louis (Heinrich) (b. Brunswick, 5 Sept. 1820; d. Königsberg, 16 Feb. 1886). Teacher. Studied in Vienna (1839–43) and began to compose prolifically. From 1845 he lived in Königsberg, first as conductor, then (1847) as piano teacher and writer of didactic and critical books and articles. His output reached op. 314, primarily piano pieces; his exercises and studies were long and widely used.

Kohn, Karl (George) (b. Vienna, 1 Aug. 1926). Composer, pianist, and conductor. He emigrated to the U.S. in 1939, studying with Werschinger and Prüwer at the New York College of Music (1940–44); continued his studies with Piston, Ballantine, Irving Fine, and Randall Thompson at Harvard (B.A., 1950; M.A., 1955). He became a professor of music at Pomona College and Claremont Graduate School in 1950. As a pianist he specialized in modern music, often performing music for 2 pianos with his wife, Margaret Kohn. Early works show the influence of Hindemith and Bartók and of serial procedures. Some of his pieces use borrowed fragments from other works or rework them in some way; thus, *Introductions and Parodies* borrows from Mendelssohn's Violin Concerto, and *The Prophet Bird* from Schumann's *Bird of Paradise.* Others combine more general stylistic techniques of earlier music with Kohn's own idiom. Works include orchestral music (*Concerto mutabile,* piano, orchestra, 1962; *Interludes,* 1964; *Episodes,* piano, orchestra, 1964; *Centone,* 1973; *Time Irretrievable,* 1983); *Introductions and Parodies,* clarinet, horn, bassoon, string quartet, piano (1967); *Paronyms,* flute, piano (1974); *Innocent Psaltery,* wind orchestra (1975); *The Prophet Bird,* chamber orchestra (1976); *Serenade II,* concert band (1977); *Son of Prophet Bird,* harp (1977); *Prophet Bird II,* piano, chamber ensemble (1980); *Concert Music IV,* wind quintet (1990); keyboard works; vocal works (*Lions on a Banner,* 7 Sufi texts for soprano, chorus, orchestra, 1988).

Kohoutek, Ctirad (b. Zábřeh, Czechoslovakia, 18 Mar. 1929). Composer. He studied composition with Kvapil at the Brno Academy of Music, joining the faculty there after graduation as an instructor of theory and composition; also taught at the Janáček Academy in Brno (1965–80) and the Academy of Music Arts, Prague (from 1980). Artistic director of the Czech Philharmonic, 1980–87. After an initial interest in folk song during the 1950s, Kohoutek began to utilize twelve-tone techniques in his chamber music; Hindemith was another important influence on his compositions of the late 1950s and early 1960s. Works include the opera *O Kohoutkovi a Slepičce* [About the Cock and the Hen] (1989); orchestral music (a violin concerto, 1958; *Velký přelom* [The Great Turning Point], 1959–60; *Memento 1967,* winds, percussion, 1966; *Slavností světla* [Festivals of Light], 1974–75; *Pocta životu* [Homage to Life], 1989); chamber music (suite, viola, piano, 1957; suite, wind quintet, 1958–59; string quartet, 1959; *Rapsodia eroica,* organ, 1963; *Inventions,* piano, 1965; *Panychida,* 2 violas, ensemble, tape, 1968); vocal works (*Od jara do zimy* [From Spring to Winter], children's chorus, 1962; *Janek a Kača,* cantata, 1973).

Kohs, Ellis (Bonoff) (b. Chicago, 12 May 1916). Composer. He studied at the San Francisco Conservatory, the Univ. of Chicago (1933–38), the Juilliard School (with Wagenaar, 1938–39), and Harvard (with Piston, Apel, and Leichtentritt, 1939–41). After service as an Army Air Force bandmaster, he taught (1946–50) at Kansas City Conservatory, Wesleyan Univ., the College of the Pacific, and Stanford Univ.; from 1950 until 1985 he taught at the Univ. of Southern California, chairing the theory department until 1973. Wrote 3 textbooks (*Music Theory,* 1961; *Musical Form,* 1976; *Musical Composition,* 1980). His 2 symphonies were commissioned by Monteux (1950) and the Fromm Foundation (1957). Other works include an opera (*Amerika,* Kohs, after Kafka, 1966–69) and incidental music; a violin concerto (1981) and other orchestral works; 2 string quartets, a sonata for snare drum and piano (1966), and other chamber music; pieces for piano, organ, and harpsichord (*Variations on l'homme armé,* piano, 1947; and suite for 2 pianos, 1980); *Psalm 23* (4 solo voices and chorus, 1957), *Lord of the Ascendant* (D. Allen, after the epic of Gilgamesh, 7 solo voices, chorus, orchestra, and 8 dancers, 1955), and other choral music; songs with piano or orchestra.

Kokkonen, Joonas (b. Iisalmi, Finland, 13 Nov. 1921). Composer. In 1949 he graduated from the Sibelius Academy, where he studied with Palmgren and Ranta; also studied musicology under Krohn at Helsinki Univ. He taught at the Sibelius Academy as a lecturer (1950–59) and professor of composition (1959–63) and chaired the board of the Sibelius Academy (from 1966) and the Society of Finnish Composers (1965–70). A symphonic composer, Kokkonen was inevitably influenced by Sibelius; with the *Music for Strings* he began to experiment with twelve-tone serialism, though this soon gave way to chromatic works within a more tonal context. He has composed works for the stage (*Viimeiset kiusaukset* [The Last Temptations], 1973–75); orchestral works (*Music for strings,* 1956–57; 4 symphonies, 1958–71; *Il paesaggio,* chamber orchestra, 1987); chamber music (3 string quartets, 1958–76); choral works.

Kolb, Barbara (b. Hartford, 10 Feb. 1939). Composer and clarinetist. She attended the Hartt College of Music in Hartford to study clarinet and composition (with Franchetti); at the Berkshire Music Center in 1964 and 1968 she studied with Foss and Schuller. She played clarinet in the Hartford Symphony (1960–66); was the first American woman to win the Rome Prize (1969–71). She taught at Brooklyn College (1973–75) and at Temple Univ. (1978); in 1979 she became artistic director of the series "Music New to New York" at the Third Street Music School Settlement. Her works range from the diatonic to the nontonal; employ serial and chance procedures, quotation, and combine live performers and taped or computer-generated sounds. Her works include a film score (*Cantico,* 1982); a ballet score *(New York Moonglow, 1995); Trobar Clus* (1970), *Soundings* (orchestra and tape, 1971–72; rev. for orchestra and 2 conductors, 1975), *Yet That Things Go Round* (chamber orchestra, 1987), *All in Good Time* (orchestra, 1993), and other orchestral music; *Millefoglie* (ensemble and computer-generated sound, 1984–85), *Homage to Keith Jarrett and Gary Burton* (flute and vibraphone, 1976), *Spring River Flowers Moon Night* (2 pianos, percussion, tape, 1974–75), *Ex-*

tremes (flute, cello, 1989), and other instrumental music; *Chromatic Fantasy* (Stern; amplified narrator, amplified alto flute, oboe, saxophone, trumpet, electric guitar, and vibraphone; 1979), *Chansons bas* (song cycle, Mallarmé, soprano, harp, and percussion, 1966) and other vocal music.

Kolisch, Rudolf (b. Klamm, 20 July 1896; d. Watertown, Mass., 1 Aug. 1978). Violinist. He studied with Otakar Ševčík at the Vienna Academy, obtaining his diploma in 1913. Unlike most violinists, he held the instrument with his right hand and bowed with his left. After compositional studies with Arnold Schoenberg, 1919–21, he determined to make his mark playing chamber music rather than the solo literature. In 1922 he founded a quartet to promote new music. He emigrated to the U.S. in 1935; became first violin in the Pro Arte Quartet in 1942. Taught at the Univ. of Wisconsin (1944–67), then at the New England Conservatory in Boston. From the early 1950s his summers were spent teaching at Darmstadt.

Kollmann, Augustus Frederic Christopher (b. Engelbostel, Hanover, 21 Mar. 1756; d. London, 19 Apr. 1829). Composer and theorist. He studied organ in Hanover with Johann Christian Büttner and was appointed to the organ post at the Lüne Monastery in 1781. The following year he emigrated to England, taking a position as organist at the Royal German Chapel in London. He lived there for the rest of his life. He composed a piano concerto (published 1804), chamber and solo instrumental music, and songs. He is recognized chiefly for his theoretical treatises, including *An Essay on Musical Harmony* (London, 1796; 2nd ed., 1817) and *An Essay on Practical Musical Composition* (London, 1799; R: New York, 1973; 2nd ed., 1812). His harmonic theories, which expand upon those of J. P. Kirnberger (and refute those of Rameau), use the music of J. S. Bach as a basis; Kollmann also apparently wrote at least part of the first English translation of Forkel's biography of Bach (London, 1820).

Komeda [Trzciński], **Krzysztof** (b. Poznań, 27 Apr. 1931; d. Warsaw, 23 Apr. 1969). Film and jazz composer, and jazz pianist. He led groups that combined swing, bop, and (in the 1960s) free jazz with elements of Polish folk and avant-garde music. He gained an international reputation, composing the soundtracks to about 40 films, including *Le départ* (1966), and, under Roman Polanski's direction, *Noz w Wodzie* [*Knife in the Water*] (1962) and *Rosemary's Baby* (1968). From 1967 to 1969 he worked in Hollywood.

Komitas [Gomidas; Soghomonian, Soghomon] (b. Kyotaya, Turkey, 8 Oct. 1869; d. Paris, 22 Oct. 1935). Composer and ethnomusicologist. Orphaned at the age of 12, he was sent to a seminary in Vagharshapat (now Edjmiadsin), where he came into contact with folk song and recorded and harmonized the songs of the Ararat Valley peasants. In 1894 he published research on Armenian church melodies and took the name Komitas from a 7th-century Armenian hymn writer. He went to Berlin in 1896, studying under Schmidt, Fleischer, Bellermann, and Friedlaender; collected material pertaining to Armenian folk music, publishing numerous papers on the subject as well as composing works based on folk and sacred melodies. In 1910 he moved to Constantinople; he spent his last years in Paris. His vocal compositions make use of Armenian modes to add polyphony to mostly monodic folk music.

Komorous, Rudolf (b. Prague, 8 Dec. 1931). Composer and bassoonist. He attended the Prague Conservatory (1946–52) and Academy of Music (1952–56), taking bassoon with Pivoň and composition with Bořkovec; taught bassoon and chamber music at the Peking Conservatory (1959–61). He returned to Prague and helped organize the Musica viva pragensis ensemble; in 1971 he became professor of composition at the Univ. of Victoria, British Columbia. Heavily influenced by the visual arts, particularly the Šmidrové group of the 1950s, Komorous often used graphic notation. Works include *Glücklicher Augenblick* (1957); *Sladká královna* [The Sweet Queen], harmonica, ensemble (1964); *Gone,* tape (1969); *The Gentle Touch,* 5 flutes, 4 violas, 3 cellos, piano (1977); the opera *No No Miya* (1988).

Kondracki, Michal (b. Połtawa, Ukraine, 5 Oct. 1902). Composer. He studied with Szymanowski at the Warsaw Conservatory and with Dukas and Boulanger at the École normale in Paris. After returning to Warsaw he moved to Rio de Janeiro in 1940, eventually settling in New York in 1943. His early compositions often combined Polish folk themes with rich harmony influenced by Ravel and Prokofiev; later works employ simpler textures. Works include the ballet *Metropolis* (1929), the *Mała symfonia góralska* [Little Highlander Symphony] (1930), and a piano concerto (1935).

Kondrashin, Kirill (Petrovich) (b. Moscow, 6 Mar. 1914; d. Amsterdam, 7 Mar. 1981). Conductor. Attended the Moscow Conservatory until 1937, studying conducting under Khaikin. Directed the Children's Theater (1931–34) and the Nemirovich-Dantichenko Theater (1934–37) in Moscow before moving to the Malyi Opera Theater in Leningrad (1937–42); conducted at the Bolshoi Theater from 1943 to 1956. He was the first postwar Soviet conductor to perform in the U.S. (in 1958), making several subsequent visits; directed the Moscow Philharmonic between 1960 and 1975 and also taught at the Moscow Conservatory (1950–53, 1972–75). Emigrating in 1978, he led the Concertgebouw Orchestra, Amsterdam, from 1979 to his death.

Königsperger, Marianus [Johann Erhard] (b. Rodling, 4 Dec. 1708; d. Prüfening, 9 Oct. 1769). Composer. Sang as a boy at the Benedictine abbey at Prüfening and was eventually named organist and music director there in 1734, holding the post until his death. His Masses and other sacred works, published at Augsburg, were profitable for the abbey and popular in parish churches throughout South Germany. Some instrumental music survives, though his singspiels are lost.

Konitz, Lee (b. Chicago, 13 Oct. 1927). Jazz alto saxophonist. After studying with Lennie Tristano in Chicago, he joined Claude Thornhill's big band (1947). He was a member of the two definitive cool jazz groups, Miles Davis's nonet (1948–50) and Tristano's combo, which recorded "Subconscious-Lee" (1949); Konitz's smooth-toned, quietly accentuated, streaming improvised lines played a major role. He was the lead alto saxophonist in Stan Kenton's big band (1952–53). He then worked as a free-lance, later co-leading a group with the tenor saxophonist Warne Marsh in Europe (1975–76), leading a nonet (from 1975), and playing in duos, including one with Martial Solal (from 1974).

Bibl.: Michael Frohne, *Subconscious-Lee: 35 Years of Records and Tapes: The Lee Konitz Discography, 1947–82* (Freiburg, 1983).

Konjović, Petar (b. Čurug, 5 May 1883; d. Belgrade, 1 Oct. 1970). Composer. He studied under Stecker at the Prague Conservatory and worked as a choral director and teacher in Zemun and Belgrade. In 1917 he moved to Zagreb, where his first opera, *Ženidba Miloša Obilića,* had its premiere; wrote for various Yugoslav periodicals, and served as director of the Zagreb Opera (1921–26). He settled in Belgrade in 1939 and served as professor and rector at the academy of music there. His studies in Prague and interest in folk music are clearly evident in his works; they include operas (*Ženidba Miloša Obilića* [The Marriage of Miloš Obilić], 1917, rev. 1922; *Koštana,* 1931, rev. 1940 and 1948; *Otadžbina* [The Fatherland], 1960); orchestral music (*Makar Čudra,* 1946); vocal works (100 folk song arrangements under the title *Moja zemlja* [My Country]); chamber music (3 string quartets).

Konrad von Würzburg (b. Würzburg, between 1220 and 1230; d. Basle, 31 Aug. 1287). Minnesinger. A prolific and versatile poet whom the Meistersinger named one of their 12 *alte Meister.* His output includes lyric, epic, and allegorical poetry, in which substantial knowledge of Latin, law, and theology is evident. Only one of the many melodies attributed to him is in an early source and is apparently genuine. Many more appear first in a 15th-century manuscript and are probably not his.

Kontarsky, Alfons (b. Iserlohn, 9 Oct. 1932). Pianist. Like his brother Aloys, studied with Else Schmitz-Gohr and Eduard Erdmann. With his brother he won the 1955 Bavarian Radio Competition for piano duo; they subsequently went on a worldwide tour. He led classes at the Darmstadt summer courses in 1962–69; joined the faculty at Cologne in 1967. He introduced the works of many contemporary composers.

Kontarsky, Aloys (b. Iserlohn, 14 May 1931). Pianist. Brother of Alfons Kontarsky. At the Cologne Conservatory (1952–55) studied piano with Else Schmitz-Gohr, chamber music with M. Franck; at the Hamburg Conservatory (1955–57) piano with Eduard Erdmann. In addition to performing frequently with Alfons, he was affiliated with the International Festival Series, Darmstadt, from 1960, and also appeared with cellist Siegfried Palm.

Kontski [Kątski], **Antoine de** (b. Kraków, 27 Oct. 1817; d. Ivanichy, Novgorod district, 7 Dec. 1899). Pianist. Son of a civil servant in Kraków, who from 1822 presented his children in concert; they studied in Warsaw; 1827–30, toured to Russia, where Antoine had lessons from Field; 1832, the family began tour of central and western Europe, arousing much attention. Antoine later toured widely, living in Paris, St. Petersburg (1854–67), London, and the U.S. (1883–96); round-the-world tour, 1896–98. He composed large works, but is known for salon music, especially *Le réveil du lion, caprice hëroique,* op. 115. His brothers Charles (1815–67) and Apollinaire (1825–79) were violinists, Stanislas (b. 1820) a pianist.

Konwitschny, Franz (b. Fulnek, Moravia, 14 Aug. 1901; d. Belgrade 28 July 1962). Conductor. Studied at the German Music Society School in Brno (1921–23), at the Leipzig Conservatory (1923–25). Played viola in the Leipzig Gewandhaus Orchestra under Furtwängler. Began at the Stuttgart Opera as a répétiteur in 1927; rose to director, 1930–33. Music director of the opera at Freiburg im Breisgau (1933–38), at Frankfurt am Main (1938–45), at Hannover (1946–49). Conductor of the Leipzig Gewandhaus Orchestra (1949–62). Director of the Dresden Staatskapelle (1953–55), of the Berlin Staatsoper (1955–62).

Kopelent, Marek (b. Prague, 28 Apr. 1932). Composer. He studied with Jaroslav Řídký at the Prague Academy (1951–55), then worked as an editor of contemporary music scores for the Supraphon publishing house (1956–69). Member of the Prague New Music Group; also served as director of the ensemble Musica viva pragensis. Webern's influence can be detected in his compositions after 1960; he also experimented with techniques such as sound texture and chance elements. Works include vocal music (*Matka* [Mother], chorus, flute, 1964; *Snehah,* soprano, jazz alto, ensemble, tape, 1967; *Messaggio della povertà,* soprano, baritone, children's chorus, chorus, orchestra, 1988); instrumental music (5 string quartets, 1954, 1955, 1963, 1967, 1980; *Zátiší* [Still Life], viola, ensemble, 1968).

Koppel, Herman D(avid) (b. Copenhagen, 1 Oct. 1908). Composer and pianist. He studied at the Copenhagen Conservatory (1926–29) under Bangert (theory), Hansen (orchestration), and Simonsen (piano), and was befriended by Nielsen, at that time the conservatory's director. In 1930 he made his debut as a concert pianist, toured widely, and was appointed music instructor at the Royal Institute for the Blind (1940–49); in 1949 he joined the piano staff of the Copenhagen Conservatory. Koppel's compositions reveal the influence of Nielsen, Bartók, and Stravinsky, as well as an interest in jazz. His experience as a fugitive in Sweden during the last years of World War II is evident in works such as the *Tre-Davids-salmer* op. 48 for chorus and orchestra, inspired by the plight of Jewish prisoners under the Nazis. Other works include the opera *Macbeth* (1970); 7 symphonies (1929–61); numerous concertos; chamber music; choral works; songs; film scores.

Korbay, Ferencz [Francis Alexander] (b. Budapest, 8 May 1846; d. London, 9 Mar. 1913). Teacher. Studied with Volkmann, singing with Gustave Roger; 1865–68, a tenor at the Budapest Opera, but, after straining his voice, toured Europe as pianist (1869–71), settling in New York in 1871 as pianist and teacher. Recovering his voice, he gave recitals accompanying himself; 1895–1903, taught singing, Royal Academy of Music, London. He published piano pieces and songs; best known for his *Hungarian Melodies* (1891), arrangements of Hungarian songs.

Korchmaryov, Klimenty Arkad'yevich (b. Verkhnedneprovsk, 3 July 1899; d. Moscow, 7 Apr. 1958). Composer and pianist. He studied with Biber and Malïshevsky at the Odessa Conservatory, graduating in 1919; lived in Moscow and then in Turkmenia. As a composer he often used revolutionary themes; he also collected Turkmenian folk songs. Works include operas (*Ivan-Soldat,* 1925–7; *Desyat'dney, kotorïye potryasili mir* [Ten Days That Shook the World], 1929–31; *Ditya radosti* [Child of Joy], 1953; *Bagttlï yashlïk* [Happy Youth]); orchestral music (*Ivan-Soldat,* suite, 1928; *Raznokharakternaya syuita* [Suite in Different Characters], 1947); vocal symphonies (*Oktyabr* [October], 1931; *Narodï sovetskoy stranï* [Peoples of the Soviet Land], 1935); chamber music (sonata, viola, double bass, piano, 1926; string quartet, 1935; *Pieces,* flute, piano, 1949; *Pieces on Turkmenian Themes,* clarinet, piano, 1949); vocal music (*Levïy marsh* [Left March], chorus, piano, 1923); ballets; piano works; film scores.

Korn, Peter Jona (b. Berlin, 30 Mar. 1922). Composer, conductor, and writer on music. He studied in Berlin (1932–33), London (with Rubbra, 1934–36), and at the Jerusalem Conservatory (with Wolpe, 1936–38). In 1941 he moved to the U.S., where he continued his studies with Schoenberg and later with Toch and Eisler. He became an American citizen in 1944. Korn founded and conducted the New Orchestra of Los Angeles (1948–56); taught composition at the Trapp Conservatory in Munich (1960–61) and at UCLA (1964–65); became director of the Strauss Conservatory in Munich in 1967. He wrote music criticism for *Die Welt* and other newspapers. His works include an opera (*Heidi,* 1963); *Eine kleine Popmusik* (1972), *Concerto classico* (harpsichord, orchestra, 1988), and other orchestral pieces; the cantata *Der Psalm von Mut* (baritone, chorus, orchestra, 1985); chamber music (mainly for brass and winds); piano and organ works; choral music and songs. Published writings include *Musikalische Umweltverschmutzung* (1975).

Bibl.: N. Düchtel, et al., *Peter Jona Korn* (Tutzing, 1989) [incl. works list].

Kornauth, Egon (b. Olmütz, 14 May 1891; d. Vienna, 28 Oct. 1959). Composer and pianist. He studied flute, clarinet, cello, organ, and piano as a child, making his piano debut at age 15; studied musicology with Adler at the Univ. of Vienna, where he wrote a dissertation on Haydn string quartets. In the 1920s he was active as a pianist; led an orchestra in Sumatra (1926–27); and in the next decade made a tour of Brazil (1933–35). In 1940 he was appointed to teach at the Musikhochschule in Vienna and in 1945 at the Mozarteum in Salzburg. Works include suites and other orchestral music; chamber music, primarily for strings; and piano pieces.

Korngold, Erich Wolfgang (b. Brno, 29 May 1897; d. Hollywood, 29 Nov. 1957). Composer. The son of Julius Korngold, Hanslick's successor as music critic, he was considered by Mahler and Schnabel to be a child prodigy on the basis of a cantata (*Gold,* 1907) and a sonata for piano (before 1910). Other early works include an orchestral overture (*Schauspiel,* 1911), a ballet (*Der Schneemann,* performed at the Vienna Court Opera, 1910), and an opera (*Violanta,* 1916). His reputation as a mature composer was confirmed by performances in Hamburg and Cologne of the opera *Die Tote Stadt* (1920). In the 1920s he taught at the Vienna State Academy; in 1934 he went to Hollywood, where he wrote 19 film scores over the next two decades, receiving two Oscars (for *Robin Hood* and *Anthony Adverse*). He became an American citizen in 1943. From 1942 to 1944 he directed the New York Opera Company in performances of operettas of Strauss and Offenbach. He wrote in a Romantic idiom.

Works: 5 operas and other dramatic works; 19 film scores; orchestral music (*Tomorrow* op. 33, symphonic poem for chorus and orchestra, 1942; a concerto for violin op. 37, 1946; and a symphony op. 40, 1951–52); chamber music (a piano trio op. 1, 1909; Sextet for strings op. 10; and String Quartet no. 2 op. 26, 1935); piano music (3 sonatas; *Don Quixote,* 1908); song cycles and songs.

Korte, Karl (Richard) (b. Ossining, N.Y., 25 Aug. 1928). Composer. He studied at Juilliard (B.S., 1952; M.S., 1956) under Copland, Mennin, Luening, Persichetti, and Petrassi; taught at Arizona State Univ. (1963–64), SUNY–Binghamton (1964–70), and the Univ. of Texas at Austin (from 1971). His style is influenced by serialism, jazz, computer procedures, and neo-tonality. Works include an oratorio (*Pale Is This Good Prince,* 1973); symphonies, a concerto for piano and winds (1977), and other orchestral and band music; *Matrix* (wind quintet, saxophone, percussion, piano, 1968), a piano trio (1979; rev. 1982), and other chamber music; *Hill Country Birds* (slides and tape, 1982); choral and vocal music.

Kósa, György (b. Budapest, 24 Apr. 1897; d. there, 16 Aug. 1984). Composer and pianist. At the age of 7 he began studying piano with Bartók; entered the Budapest Academy of Music in 1908, where he took composition with Herzfeld and Kodály, later continuing his piano studies with Dohnányi (1915–16). Between 1917 and 1920 he went on concert tours in Germany, Austria, Italy, and Africa; conducted at the Theatre Tripolis (1920–21), then settled in Budapest, serving as professor of piano at the music academy (1927–60). His compositions can be characterized as expressionist and reveal Mahler's influence; Kósa remained relatively indifferent to serialism and folk music. Works include operas (*A király palástja* [The King's Cloak], 1926; *Tartuffe,* 1951; *Kocsonya Mihály házassága* [The Marriage of Mihály Kocsonya], 1971); orchestral works (9 symphonies, 1920–69; *6 Pieces for Orchestra,* 1919); chamber (8 string quartets, 1920–1965; wind quintet, 1960); oratorios; cantatas; piano works; songs.

Köselitz, (Johann) Heinrich [pen name: Peter Gast] (b. Annaberg, Germany, 10 Jan. 1854; d. there, 15 Aug. 1918). Composer. Student, 1872–75, Leipzig Conservatory; 1875, went to Univ. of Basel to be near Nietzsche, to whom he became devoted, serving for a time as secretary, later as literary executor and editor. From 1878 he lived in Venice; from 1891 in Annaberg. He organized the Nietzsche Archive in Weimar, 1900–1908. His compositions (5 operas, instrumental works, songs) received some attention because of their attempt to embody Nietzschean, anti-Wagnerian principles, but were never much performed.

Kostelanetz, André (b. St. Petersburg, 22 Dec. 1901; d. Port-au-Prince, 13 Jan. 1980). Conductor. Studied at the St. Petersburg Conservatory (1920–22); emigrated to the U.S. in 1922 and was active as a pianist with the Metropolitan and Chicago opera companies. He was hired by CBS Radio in 1930, where he gained fame for his broadcasts mixing the standard orchestral repertory with popular arrangements. He also made frequent guest appearances with U.S. orchestras. He commissioned works by Copland, Schuman, Thomson, Hovhaness, and others and initiated the Promenade Concerts of the New York Philharmonic in 1962. More than 50 million of his recordings have been sold.

Kotík, Petr (b. Prague, 27 Jan. 1942). Composer and flutist. He studied in Prague and Vienna, where his teachers included Karl Schieske and Jelinek; active as a performer in Prague, Vienna, and Warsaw in the 1960s; in residence at the Center for Creative and Performing Arts at SUNY–Buffalo (1969–74), where he founded the S.E.M. ensemble; active in the 1970s and 1980s in presenting works of Marcel Duchamp and of Cage. He became an American citizen in 1977. His own compositions include works for live electronics, tape, and conventional instruments (*Solos and Incidental Harmonies,* flute, violin, 2 percussionists, 1983; rev. 1984); many settings of texts of Gertrude Stein (*There Is Singularly Nothing,* 21 instrumental and vocal solos that may be performed simultaneously, 1971–73); *Integrated Solo,* flute, tambourine, trumpet, keyboard (1988); *Letters to Olga,* 5 voices, flute, trumpet, 3 guitars (1989).

Kotoński, Włodzimierz (b. Warsaw, 23 Aug. 1925). Composer. He studied at the Warsaw Conservatory (1945–51) with Piotr Rytel, took lessons from Szeligowski in Poznań (1950–51), and attended Darmstadt summer courses (1959–60); in 1959 he went to Paris and became acquainted with Pierre Schaeffer and Olivier Messiaen. He served as music adviser to the Warsaw Documentary Film Center (1956–58), worked at electronic music studios in Cologne and Warsaw, and from 1967 taught electronic music at the Warsaw Conservatory; in 1978 he lectured at SUNY–Buffalo. Kotoński published a study on Polish folk music and incorporated folk tunes into some of his compositions. After attending Darmstadt he began to experiment with atonality and serial techniques in his works, as well as electronic sounds and complex rhythms. Works include orchestral music (*Poemat,* 1949; *Tańce góralskie* [Highlander Dances], 1950; *Szkice baletowe* [Ballet Sketches], 1951; Prelude and Passacaglia, 1953; *Muzyka kameralna,* 1958; *Musique en relief,* 1959; *Music for 16 Cymbals and Strings,* 1969; *Wind Rose,* 1976; *Terra incognita,* 1984); chamber music (wind quintet, 1964; *Spring Music,* flute, oboe, violin, synthesizer, 1978; *Birds,* 8 pieces for clarinet, cello, piano, 1988); electronic music (*Etiuda na jedno uderzenie w talerz* [Study on a Cymbal Stroke], tape, 1959; *Klangspiele,* electronic music on tape, 1967; *Textures,* computer, 1984); piano pieces (Sonata, 1948; 4 preludes, 1952).

Kotter, Hans [Johannes] (b. Strasbourg, ca. 1485; d. Bern, 1541). Organist and composer. A student of Paul Hofhaimer from 1498 until about 1500; then court organist in Torgau until 1508; organist of the collegiate church of St. Nikolaus in Fribourg, Switzerland, from 1514 until 1530; and finally a schoolmaster in Bern from no later than 1534. Most of his original compositions and many arrangements by him of vocal pieces by Hofhaimer, Isaac, Sermisy, and others survive in 3 organ tablatures that belonged to Bonifacius Amerbach (1495–1562) of Basel. Kotter's role in the compilation and copying of these manuscripts was substantial, perhaps reflecting a connection with the Amerbach family that dated from shortly after his leaving Torgau.

Kotzwara, Franz. See Koczwara, František.

Koukouzeles, Johannes (b. Dyrrachium [Durrës], Albania, ca. 1280; d. Great Laura?, Mount Athos, 1360–

75?). Composer. The Byzantine emperor sponsored his education at the imperial court in Constantinople, where his singing brought him great fame. Eventually, however, the monastic life attracted him permanently to Mount Athos. His compositions include one didactic piece and many liturgical chants. The chants are highly innovative, expanding in every way the traditional manner of presenting texts and music and confirming his reputation as the finest of Byzantine composers of his time.

Kounadis, Arghyris (b. Constantinople, 14 Feb. 1924). Composer. He studied piano with Farandatos at the Athens Conservatory, graduating in 1952; took composition with Papaïoannou at the Hellenic Conservatory (1953–55) and with Fortner at the Staatliche Hochschule für Musik in Freiburg (1958–61), and in 1963 was appointed assistant professor to Fortner and director of the Musica viva program. Early compositions showed the influence of Bartók and Stravinsky, his later works utilized serial and aleatoric techniques. In 1960 his orchestral composition *Chorikon* (1958) became the first Greek work to be performed at an ISCM festival.

Koussevitzky, Sergey (Alexandrovich) (b. Vyshni-Volochek, Russia, 26 July 1974; d. Boston, 4 June 1951). Conductor. Received initial training from his father, and began double bass study at the Moscow Philharmonic School at 14; he played in the Bolshoi Opera from 1894 and began a solo career in 1896, composing some of his own music. Turning to conducting around 1905, he first led a Berlin Hochschule ensemble, then in 1908 his father-in-law underwrote his debut concert with the Berlin Philharmonic; that same year he also appeared with the London Symphony. In 1909 he led concert series in both Moscow and St. Petersburg and formed a publishing concern. The following year he established his own orchestra, performing in Russian cities and touring the Volga by riverboat. He directed the Russian State Orchestra from 1917 until 1920, when he left the newly founded Soviet Union. After several years in Paris (during which time the Concerts Koussevitzky became fixtures) he was engaged as permanent conductor by the Boston Symphony, where he remained until 1949. Throughout his career he had been a champion of new music; in Boston he programmed over 100 premieres, commissioning a great many of them. He conducted summer concerts at Tanglewood from 1936, forming the Berkshire Music Center there in 1940, where his eventual successor, Leonard Bernstein, was among the first students. In 1942 he established the Koussevitzky Music Foundation in memory of his wife.

Sergey Koussevitzky.

Koutzen, Boris (b. Uman, near Kiev, 1 Apr. 1901; d. Mount Kisco, N.Y., 10 Dec. 1966). Composer and violinist. He studied violin with his father, and violin and composition at the Moscow Conservatory (from 1918); he was playing professionally in Moscow at the age of 17. In 1923 he joined the Philadelphia Orchestra; directed the violin department of the Philadelphia Conservatory (1925–62); taught and conducted at Vassar College (1944–66); and played in the NBC Symphony Orchestra under Toscanini (1937–45). His compositions, in a Romantic style, include 2 operas; *Valley Forge* (symphonic poem, 1931) and other orchestral works; 3 string quartets and other chamber music; piano and organ pieces; a concerto for chorus and orchestra (1966) and other choral music and songs; arrangements, didactic works, and cadenzas.

Kovařovic, Karel (b. Prague, 9 Dec. 1862; d. there, 6 Dec. 1920). Conductor. Studied clarinet, harp, and piano, 1873–79, at the Prague Conservatory, singing and composition privately with Fibich. Then active in Prague and, occasionally, elsewhere as harpist (National Theater orchestra, 1879–85); piano accompanist; teacher (Pivoda's singing school, 1880–1900); conductor. From 1900 to 1920 he was one of the leading figures in Czech musical life as conductor at the National Theater, bringing orchestral playing and dramaturgy there to a high degree of excellence. Also composed 6 Czech operas, ballets, orchestral, chamber, and choral music, songs.

Kowalski, Henri (b. Paris, 1841; d. Bordeaux, 8 July 1916). Pianist and composer. From 1853, student at the Paris Conservatory; from 1858 toured as a pianist, including North America (1869, 1876), resulting in his book *À travers l'Amérique* (Paris, 1872), and Australia (1880–82), where he settled in 1885, becoming a leading figure in musical life as conductor (Sydney Philharmonic, 1886–89), pianist, and teacher. He published much piano music, especially *Marche hongroise,* op. 13 (1864); also composed several operas.

Kowalski, Max (b. Kowal, Poland, 10 Aug. 1882; d. London, 4 June 1956). Composer. He was raised in Germany; took a doctorate in law at the Univ. of Marburg; then studied voice (with Alexander Heinemann) and composition (with Sekles) in Berlin and Frankfurt am Main. He was imprisoned at Buchenwald, but released in 1939. He went to London, where he supported himself by tuning pianos, teaching voice, and singing in a synagogue. His compositions are almost entirely in the genre of the Romantic lied, with German texts, and include settings of the *Pierrot lunaire* texts contemporary to those of Schoenberg. In addition he wrote a few piano works.

Kox, Hans (b. Arnhem, Netherlands, 19 May 1930). Composer. He attended Utrecht Conservatory, later studying composition privately with Henk Badings; from 1956 until 1971 he served as director of the Doetinchem Music School. His first large orchestral work, *Concertante muziek,* was written in 1956 in response to a commission from the Concertgebouw Orchestra. His Symphony no. 2 (1966) ended a period of works influenced by Berg and Mahler; compositions after the late 1960s include aleatoric elements. Some of his works utilize the scale of 31 equal intervals invented by the physicist Fokker. Works include opera (*Dorian Gray,* 1973; rev. 1975); choral works with orchestra (*In Those Days,* 1969; *Requiem for Europe,* 1971); orchestral music (Symphony no. 1, 1959; piano concerto, 1962; violin concerto, 1963; Symphony no. 3, 1985; *Le songe du vergier,* cello, orchestra, 1986); chamber music (string quartet, 1955; 3 pieces, violin in 31st-tones, 1958; 4 pieces, string quartet in 31st-tones; *Capriccio,* 2 violins, piano, 1974; piano trio, 1976); *Cyclophony* nos. 1–12 (orchestral or chamber music, 1964–79); solo vocal works.

Kozeluch [Koželuh], **Johann Antonin** [Jan Evangelista Antonín Tomáš] (b. Velvary [Welwarn, Bohemia], 14 Dec. 1738; d. Prague, 3 Feb. 1814). Composer. He attended school at Velvary and sang in the chapel choir in Březnice; later he was a pupil of Josef Seeger in Prague. Around 1763 he went to Vienna to study with Hasse, Florian Gassmann, and Gluck; he returned to Prague to serve as Kapellmeister, first at St. Francis' Church, then (from 1784) at St. Vitus' Cathedral. During the 1780s and 1790s he was an influential teacher; his cousin Leopold Kozeluch was among his pupils. Among his works are 2 operas, *Alessandro nell' Indie* (1769) and *Il Demofoonte* (1771); sacred music (oratorios, cantatas, nearly 50 Masses, 30 motets, many other works); symphonies and concertos. As a contrapuntist he was almost without peer among late 18th-century composers.

Kozeluch [Koželuh], **Leopold** [Jan Antonín] (b. Velvary [Bohemia], 26 June 1747; d. Vienna, 7 May 1818). Composer, pianist, and music publisher. After schooling in Velvary he studied in Prague with his cousin Johann Antonin and with Dušek. During the 1770s he composed ballets and other stage works for Prague; settling in Vienna in 1778, he became a prosperous teacher and (from 1784) a music publisher. In 1792 he succeeded Mozart as *Hofmusik Compositor* for the imperial court. As a composer he was an important early pioneer in aspects of keyboard style and technique idiomatic to the fortepiano. Both Mozart and Beethoven wrote disparagingly of his keyboard playing, but his large number of published compositions had broad influence. In addition to some 30 symphonies, more than 20 piano concertos, chamber music with piano, and 50 piano sonatas, he also composed several operas (of which only *Gustav Wasa* survives), cantatas, oratorios (*Moisè in Egitto,* 1787), numerous sacred works.

Kraft, Anton (b. Rokycany, Bohemia, 30 Dec. 1749; d. Vienna, 28 Aug. 1820). Cellist and composer. His father was an amateur cellist who gave the boy his first cello lessons. After beginning, but abandoning, his university studies, Anton went to Vienna; in 1778 he became first cellist at Prince Nikolaus Esterházy's chapel orchestra, and later he joined the court orchestras of Prince Antal Grassalkovich de Gyarak in Bratislava (1790) and of Prince Lobkowitz in Vienna (from 1796). He was possibly the most prominent cellist in Vienna during the 1780s and 1790s; Haydn's D major Cello Concerto was composed for him (not by him, as was once held), as was the cello part for Beethoven's Triple Concerto op. 56. He performed in the first performance of Mozart's Divertimento K. 563. His own compositions include cello concertos and chamber works with cello. His son Nikolaus Kraft (1778–1853) was also an important cellist in Vienna.

Kraft, Leo (Abraham) (b. Brooklyn, 24 July 1922). Composer. He studied at Queens College and at Princeton (with Randall Thompson); later studied in Paris with Boulanger (1954–55); taught at Queens from 1947 until 1989; composer-in-residence at New York Univ. from 1989. Active in organizations promoting contemporary music; was president of the American Music Center (1976–78); wrote several music theory and ear-training texts. His earlier compositions were diatonic, but with his Second String Quartet (1959) he adopted a freely atonal style. His works include a concerto for cello, winds, and percussion (1969), *Pacific Bridges* (clarinet, string orchestra, 1989), and other pieces for orchestra and band; *Antiphonies* (piano 4-hands and tape, 1972), *Tableaux* (10 winds, piano, 1989), and other chamber and piano music; choral and solo vocal music (*Spring in the Harbor,* soprano, flute, cello, and piano, 1970).

Kraft, Nikolaus (b. Esterháza, Hungary, 14 Dec. 1778; d. Cheb, Czechoslovakia, 18 May 1853). Cellist. Son and pupil of the cellist Anton Kraft (1749–1820); toured with him as a child; 1792–95, schooling in Vienna; from 1796, cellist (with his father) in Prince Lobkowitz's orchestra. While in Lobkowitz's service also studied with Duport in Berlin (1801–2), toured Germany (1802), was cellist in the Schuppanzigh Quartet, and first cellist in the court opera orchestra (from 1809); 1814, chamber musician at the Stuttgart court, also touring. In 1824 he injured his hand, which gradually grew worse; 1834, retired. Composed much cello music.

Kraft, William (b. Chicago, 6 Sept. 1923). Composer. He studied at Columbia (M.A., 1954) with Luening, Ussachevsky, Beeson, Brant, and Cowell. From 1955 to 1981 he was percussionist with the Los Angeles Philharmonic. In 1981 he became director of the new music group within that orchestra and served as composer-in-residence for the next four years. He founded the Los Angeles Percussion Ensemble and Chamber Players in 1956. Visiting professor at UCLA, 1988–90. Most of his works are constructed on a large scale, for orchestra and percussion.

Works: *Interplay* (1984), Concerto for Tuba (1977, revision of *Andirivieni,* 1976), *A Kennedy Portrait* (narrator, orchestra, 1988), *Vintage Renaissance* (1989), *Vintage 1990–91* (1990), and other orchestral music; *Configurations* (4 percussionists and jazz ensemble, 1966), *Doppio Trio* (piano, prepared piano, guitar, tuba, 2 percussionists, 1966), *Encounters II–X* (*Encounters V. Hommage to Scriabin,* is for cello and percussion, 1975), and other chamber music; *Ombra* (piano, 1975, renamed *Translucences,* 1979); *Games: Collage II* (32 voices and winds, 1970) and *The Innocents* (32 voices, percussion, harmonium, and celesta, 1970); *Kandinsky Variations* (1 or more instruments, slide, 1981); 3 film scores.

Krainis, Bernard (b. New Brunswick, N.J., 28 Dec. 1924). Recorder player. After playing trombone in high school, began study of the recorder at Denver Univ. (1946–48). Studied musicology at New York Univ. (1948–50). Cofounded the New York Pro Musica with Noah Greenberg (1952); founded the Krainis Baroque Trio (1961). Taught at Kirkland College (1969–71), at Smith College (1977–81), and at Mannes College (beginning 1981).

Kramer, A(rthur) Walter (b. New York, 23 Sept. 1890; d. there, 8 Apr. 1969). Composer, critic, editor, and publisher. He studied violin with his father and others; wrote for *Musical America* (1910–22) and later served as editor-in-chief (1929–36). He spent five years in Europe, studying and writing music and prose; returned to become music supervisor for CBS Radio (1927–28); later he became managing director of Galaxy Music Corporation (1936–56). Kramer was a founding member (1919) and later president (1934–40) of the Society for Publication of American Music, and served on the Board of Directors of ASCAP (1941–56). Over 300 of his compositions were published, including orchestral and chamber works; piano and organ music; vocal music; and transcriptions.

Kramer, Jonathan D. (b. Hartford, 7 Dec. 1942). Composer and theorist. He studied at Harvard and Berkeley (Ph.D., 1969) under Imbrie, Sessions, and others; he also studied briefly with Stockhausen and Chowning. Taught at Berkeley, Oberlin, Yale (1971–78), the Cincinnati College-Conservatory (1978–90), and Columbia (from 1988); composer-in-residence with the Cincinnati Orchestra from 1988. His music employs serialism and various experimental approaches. Compositions include *No Beginning, No End* (chorus and orchestra, 1983); *Musica pro musica* (orchestra, 1987); *About Face* (orchestra, 1989); *Renascence* (clarinet, tape delay system, and prerecorded tape, 1974; rev. 1977) and other instrumental and tape works; mixed-media and conceptual works (*Higher Education,* teacher with office, 1971; *En noir et blanc,* 2 actor-pianists, actor-dancer, 1988). His writings include *The Time of Music: New Meanings, New Temporalities, New Listening Strategies* (New York, 1988).

Krasner, Louis (b. Cherkassi, Russia, 21 June 1903; d. Brookline, Mass., 4 May 1995). Violinist. While still a child, emigrated with his family to the U.S. Studied violin with Eugene Gruenberg at the New England Conservatory in Boston (diploma, 1923), then with Carl Flesch, Lucien Capet, and Otakar Ševčik in Europe. He commissioned and in 1936 gave the premiere of Berg's Violin Concerto. He also introduced the violin concertos of Schoenberg (Philadelphia, 1940) and Sessions (Minneapolis, 1946). From 1944 to 1949 he was concertmaster of the Minneapolis Symphony. He taught at Syracuse Univ. (1949–72) and at the New England Conservatory (from 1974).

Kraus (Trujillo), Alfredo (b. Las Palmas, Canary Islands, 24 Sept. 1927). Tenor. Studied with Mercedes Llopart in Barcelona, then in Milan. Debut in 1956 in Cairo as the Duke of Mantua *(Rigoletto);* the same year sang Verdi's Alfredo at Turin. London debut as Alfredo in 1957; New York Metropolitan debut as the Duke in 1966. He had special success in bel canto roles such as Donizetti's Edgardo *(Lucia)* and Gennaro *(Lucrezia),* Rossini's Count Almaviva *(Il barbiere);* on several occasions sang opposite Joan Sutherland.

Kraus, Joseph Martin (b. Miltenberg am Main, 20 June 1756; d. Stockholm, 15 Dec. 1792). Composer. After early schooling in Mannheim, he studied law in Mainz, Erfurt, and Göttingen (1773–78). In 1778 he traveled to Sweden; by 1782 he was a chamber musician at King Gustavus III's court. After an important trip through England, Austria, Germany, France, and Italy (1782–87), during which he met Gluck and Haydn, he returned to Sweden to assume the duties of Kapellmeister at the court. He composed a number of operas, including the celebrated *Aeneas i Carthago*

(Dido och Aeneas), first performed at the Stockholm Royal Opera in 1799; others include *Soliman II* (1789) and *Fiskarena* (1789). He also composed much ballet and incidental music; cantatas (*Begravningskantata,* for Gustavus III, 1792); sacred choral works (*Der Tod Jesu,* oratorio, 1777); also Masses, motets, etc.; symphonies (*Wiener Sinfonie,* ca. 1783; *Pariser Sinfonie,* 1784); chamber works (6 string quartets); solo piano music (2 sonatas; *Scherzo con Variazioni*). He authored a *Versuch von Schäfergedichten* (Mainz, 1773) and *Etwas von und über Musik für's Jahr 1777* (Frankfurt, 1778).

Bibl.: Bertil H. Van Boer, *Die Werke von Joseph Martin Kraus: systematisch-thematisches Werkverzeichnis* (Stockholm, 1988).

Kraus, Lili (b. Budapest, 4 March 1905; d. Burnsville, N.C., 6 Nov. 1986). Pianist. Studied with Bartók and Kodály at the Royal Academy of Music (1913–22), then with Artur Schnabel and Eduard Steuermann at the Vienna Academy. Taught at the Vienna Academy (1925–31), then toured as a pianist. Touring in Java in 1942 she was interned by the Japanese army for three years. After the war she settled in New Zealand, then in the U.S. She focused particularly on Mozart; performed a cycle of his complete concertos (1966–67), his complete sonatas several times during the 1967–68 season (also recording them). In 1968 she was appointed artist-in-residence at Texas Christian Univ. in Fort Worth.

Krauss, Clemens (Heinrich) (b. Vienna, 31 Mar. 1893; d. Mexico City, 16 May 1954). Conductor. Studied with Grädener and Heuberger at the Vienna Conservatory. Chorusmaster at the Brno Opera (1912–13); conducting debut there with Lortzing's *Zar und Zimmerman;* conductor of the German Theater in Riga (1913–14), at Nuremberg (1915–16), Stettin (1916–21), and Graz (1921), and the Vienna Opera (1922–24). There began an enduring friendship with Richard Strauss; he gave premieres of *Arabella* (1933), *Friedenstag* and *Daphne* (1938), *Die Liebe der Danäe* (1952), and *Capriccio* (1942), for which he wrote a libretto after sketches by Stefan Zweig. Conducted at the Frankfurt Opera (1924–29) and at the Berlin Staatsoper (1934–36); was music director of the Munich Opera (1937–40); in 1944–45 he led Viennese broadcast concerts. He tainted his career by compliance during the Nazi era. He resumed conducting in 1947 in Vienna and made guest appearances elsewhere.

Krauze, Zygmunt (b. Warsaw, 19 Sept. 1938). Composer and pianist. He studied piano with Maria Wilkomirska and composition with Sikorski at the Warsaw Conservatory, receiving his M.A. in 1964; continued his studies with Boulanger in Paris (1966–67). He founded the Warsztat Muzyczny (Music Workshop) ensemble during the mid-1960s, and taught piano at Cleveland State Univ. (1970–71) and composition at Yale (1982). A respected performer of new music, especially aleatoric works; Krauze's own compositions utilize a wide variety of techniques, including electronic sounds and folk instruments. Works include *Space Music Composition,* tape (1968); *Folk Music,* 36 instruments (1971–72); *One Piano and Eight Hands* (1973); *Idyll,* folk instruments (1974); *Ballade,* piano (1978); *Die Kleider,* chamber opera (1982); *Symphonie parisienne* (1986).

Krebs, Johann Ludwig (bapt. Butterstedt, Weimar, 12 Oct. 1713; d. Altenburg, 1 Jan. 1780). Composer. Son of Johann Tobias Krebs, an organist who was a student of J. G. Walther and J. S. Bach in about 1714. Received early lessons from his father; entered the Leipzig Thomasschule in 1726, where he studied lute, violin, and keyboard, and was a private pupil of J. S. Bach, whom he served also as a copyist. Bach gave him a glowing recommendation in 1735; he attended Leipzig Univ. in 1735–37, also playing in Bach's collegium musicum. Served as organist at the Marienkirche, Zwickau (1737–44), at Zeitz (1744–56; he applied unsuccessfully for Bach's Thomaskantor post during this time), and at the court of Altenburg-Gotha (1756 to his death). A renowned organist; his output includes keyboard works, sinfonias, and church and chamber music.

Krebs, Karl August (b. Nuremberg, 16 Jan. 1804; d. Dresden, 16 May 1880). Conductor. Son of actors named Miedke; adopted by his godfather, composer-singer J. B. Krebs (1774–1851); precocious pianist and composer; 1825, studied in Vienna (Seyfried) and began conducting career there as second assistant conductor at the Kärntnertor Theater (1826); 1827–50, city Kapellmeister, Hamburg; 1850–72, succeeded Wagner as court Kapellmeister, Dresden; from 1872, music director of Dresden's Catholic church. Composed operas, church music, songs and part songs (his greatest successes), piano pieces.

Krein [Krayn, Kreyn], **Aleksandr Abramovich** (b. Nizhni-Novgorod, 20 Oct. 1883; d. Staraya Ruza, near Moscow, 21 Apr. 1951). Composer. He graduated in 1908 from the Moscow Conservatory, where he studied with A. Glehn (cello) and Yavorsky (composition); taught at the People's Conservatory of Moscow (1912–17). His father collected folk songs, including Jewish melodies, and they had considerable impact on his compositions (*Hebrew Sketches,* clarinet quintet, 1909–10; Piano Sonata op. 34, 1922), as did oriental folk songs; other influences include the music of Scriabin and Debussy. He wrote music for many Jewish plays. Other works include the First Symphony (1925), the opera *Zagmuk* (1930), and *Threnody in Memory of Lenin* (chorus, orchestra, 1925).

Krein [Krayn, Kreyn], **Grigory Abramovich** (b. Nizhni-Novgorod, 18 Mar. 1879; d. Komarovo, near Leningrad, 6 Jan. 1955). Composer. Brother of Aleksandr Krein. He studied at the Moscow Conservatory (1900–1905) with Hřímalý (violin), and Glier and

Juon (composition); continued his studies in Leipzig with Reger (1907–8). His compositions show the influence of Scriabin and the French impressionists; many are on Jewish themes. Works include a symphonic cycle on Lenin's life (1937), a symphony (1946), a violin concerto (1934), 2 piano sonatas (1906, 1924), and a *Hebrew Rhapsody* (clarinet, orchestra, 1926).

Krein, Julian Grigor'yevich (b. Moscow, 5 Mar. 1913). Composer. Son of Grigory Krein. He studied with his father, and then in Paris at the École normale de musique, where he worked with Dukas (1928–32). Returned to the Soviet Union and taught at the Moscow Conservatory (1934–37). His compositions were influenced by Scriabin and the French impressionsists, but he has made less use of Jewish folk song than either his father or his uncle. Works include *Five Preludes,* orchestra (1927); a cello concerto, 1931; piano pieces; songs.

Kreisler, Fritz [Friedrich] (b. Vienna, 2 Feb. 1875; d. New York, 29 Jan. 1962). Violinist and composer. Entered the Vienna Conservatory at age 7, taking the gold medal at 10; also attended the Paris Conservatory, ending all his violin study by age 12. At 14 he toured the U.S., after which he returned to Vienna for premedical study and military service. Returning to the violin, he first failed an audition for the Vienna Opera Orchestra, but successes with the Vienna Philharmonic (1898) and Berlin Philharmonic (1899) established his reputation as a virtuoso. He subsequently toured Europe and the U.S. In 1910 he premiered Elgar's Violin Concerto. He was wounded while serving in the Austrian army early in World War I; he spent the remainder of the war in the U.S., but did not perform there owing to strong anti-German sentiment. He resumed his career in 1919, and from 1924 to 1934 resided in Berlin. In 1935 he admitted that many pieces he identified as written by composers such as Vivaldi, Couperin, and Martini were really his own, a ruse for which several critics (including Ernest Newman) lambasted him. A serious accident in 1941 left him in a coma, but after recovering he continued to perform until 1950. Apart from his forgeries, he composed a string quartet; *Caprice viennois, Tambourin chinois, Liebesfreud, Schön Rosmarin,* and many other popular violin pieces; and cadenzas for the Beethoven and Brahms concertos.

Bibl.: Louis Paul Lochner, *Fritz Kreisler* (New York, 1950).

Krejčí, Iša (František) (b. Prague, 10 July 1904; d. there, 6 Mar. 1968). Composer and conductor. He studied composition with Jirák and Novák and conducting with Talich at the Prague Conservatory (1923–29). He served as conductor of the Bratislava Opera (1928–32) and music director of Radio Prague (1934–45); during 1945–58 he was artistic director of the Olomouc Opera, and from 1957 until his death served the Prague National Theater in the same capacity. Krejčí's compositions combine a neoclassical style with a love of folk song; his works are often compared to those of "Les six." Works include the operas *Antigona* (1933–34; rev. 1963) and *Pozdvižení v Efesu* [Revolt in Ephesus] (1943); orchestral music (4 symphonies, 1954–66; Serenade, 1949); chamber music (*Kasace* [Cassation], flute, clarinet, bassoon, trumpet, 1925; 3 string quartets, 1928, 1953, 1960); songs; choral works.

Fritz Kreisler (left) with Thomas Beecham.

Kremer, Gidon (b. Riga, 27 Feb. 1947). Violinist. Studied with V. Sturestep at the Riga School of Music, with David Oistrakh and P. Bondarenko at the Moscow Conservatory (1965–73). In 1967 he won the bronze medal at the Queen Elisabeth of Belgium Competition in Brussels; he took first prize at the 1970 Tchaikovsky Competition.

Krenek [Křenek], **Ernst** (b. Vienna, 23 Aug. 1900; d. Palm Springs, Calif., 22 Dec. 1991). Composer and writer. He studied composition with Schreker in Vienna from 1916 and then in Berlin (1920–23). His reputation as a radical innovator was established with his atonal Second Symphony (1923), but a visit to Paris in 1924 (when he became acquainted with the work of "Les six" and Cocteau) led him to write music that was more "useful, entertaining, and practical," as in the neoclassic Concerto grosso no. 2 (1924–25). From 1925 to 1927 he was Bekker's assistant at the State Opera Houses in Kassel and Wiesbaden; his opera *Jonny spielt auf* (1925–26) was widely produced, enabling Krenek to devote himself to composition for some time after his return to Vienna in 1928. The music of Schubert served as the model for his neo-Romantic period (1926–31), partly as a result of his friendship with the pianist and modernist composer Eduard Erdmann, a devotee of Schubert's music. Other influences came from contact with Adorno and with the satirist Karl Kraus, whom Krenek revered as a writer. His works were banned in Germany when the Nazis came to power in 1933, and in the following year the premiere of *Karl V* was canceled as a result of pressure from Nazi sympathizers at the Vienna State Opera (where it was performed only in 1984; the premiere had taken place in Prague in 1938). After visiting the U.S. in 1937, Krenek emigrated and taught at the Malkin Conservatory (Boston), Vassar (1939–42), and Hamline College in St. Paul, Minnesota (from 1942); during summer sessions he taught at the universities of Wisconsin and Michigan. He became an American citizen in 1945 and settled in Los Angeles two years later, moving in 1966 to Palm Springs.

His adoption of the twelve-tone system in the opera *Karl V* (1930–33) he saw as an alternative to giving up composition entirely; he had been writing for the *Frankfurter Zeitung* and had seriously considered a literary career. He acquired knowledge of the twelve-tone method on his own, since "the practitioners of the technique whom I knew, Alban Berg and Anton Webern, were quite reticent about what they were doing." An idiosyncratic aspect of his approach to dodecaphony is the "principle of rotation" in which a single row can generate several derivative rows by means of a systematic exchange of adjacent pitches (thus, a series 1–2–3–4–5–6 becomes 6–1–5–2–4–3, 3–6–4–1–2–5, etc., in successive rotations). This principle was applied to *Lamentatio Jeremiae Prophetae* (1941–42). In 1957, when many other composers had already abandoned it, Krenek turned toward the serialism that continued to interest him. He used serial and even computer-generated materials (in *They Knew What They Wanted,* narrator, oboe, piano, percussion, and computer, 1976–77), but overtly political messages remained important as well, for example, in his opera *Pallas Athene weint* (Hamburg, 1955), which reflects contemporary McCarthyism via the metaphor for Sparta's destruction of Athenian democracy. His preoccupation with the philosophical problems of predetermination and chance led him "to deliberately open the door to unpremeditated sound combinations" (for example, in *Horizon Circled* and *Fibonacci Mobile*); but he regarded such a deliberate exploration of inevitable surprises in totally predetermined musical processes as essentially "different from chance as a result of hazard, such as tossing coins or rolling dice."

His works have had greater success in Europe than in the U.S. He wrote over 230 compositions as well as literary works including prose, poetry, musicological studies, and many of the libretti for his own operas.

Works: 20 operas (*Jonny spielt auf,* 1925; *Karl V,* 1933; *Der goldene Bock,* 1963), ballets, and a film score (*Jedermann,* 1961); symphonies (no. 5, op. 119, 1949); concertos for piano (1923, 1937, 1946, 1950), violin (1924, 1954), cello (1953, 1982), harp (1951), 2 pianos (1951), organ (1979, 1982), a concerto grosso (1924), concertino (flute, violin, and harpsichord, 1924), and *Little Concerto* (organ, harpsichord, 1940); other orchestral music (*Horizon Circled,* 1967); 8 string quartets (1921–44, 1981), *Fibonacci Mobile* (string quartet and piano 4-hands, 1964), Wind Quintet (1951), *Alpbach Quintet* (wind quintet and percussion, 1962), and other chamber music; organ and piano music (*Orga-nastro,* organ and tape, 1971; 7 piano sonatas; *20 Miniatures,* piano, 1954) and other solo instrumental music; some 40 choral works (*Gib uns den Frieden,* Mass for solo voices, chorus, and instruments, 1970; *Feiertags-Kantate,* Krenek, mezzo-soprano, baritone, speaker, chorus, and orchestra, 1974–75; *O Holy Ghost,* Donne, 1964; *Opus sine nomine,* oratorio, 1990); solo vocal music (*Spiritus intelligentiae, sanctus,* oratorio, 2 voices and tape, 1955; *Sestina,* Krenek, soprano and 10 instruments, 1957; and songs with piano); 2 pieces for tape.

Writings: 15 books including *Music Here and Now* (New York, 1939; revision of *Über neue Musik: sechs Vorlesungen zur Einführung in die theoretischen Grundlagen,* Vienna, 1937). *Musik im goldenen Westen* (Vienna, 1949). *Johannes Okeghem* (New York, 1953). *Tonal Counterpoint in the Style of the 18th Century* (New York, 1958). *Modal Counterpoint in the Style of the 16th Century* (New York, 1959). *Exploring Music* (London, 1966). *Horizons Circled: Reflections on My Music* (Berkeley, 1974). *Das musikdramatische Werk* (Vienna, 1974–82). *Im Zweifelsfalle: Aufsätze über Musik* (Vienna, 1984). Also many articles and an autobiographical manuscript in the Library of Congress to be accessible 15 years after Krenek's death.

Bibl.: Theodor W. Adorno, *Theodor W. Adorno und Ernst Krenek: Briefwechsel* (Frankfurt am Main, 1974). Garrett H. Bowles, *Ernst Krenek: A Bio-Bibliography* (New York, 1989). John L. Stewart, *Ernst Krenek: The Man and His Music* (Berkeley, 1991).

Krenz, Jan (b. Włocławek, Poland, 14 July 1926). Conductor and composer. He studied at the State Academy of Music in Łódź with Wilkomirski and Górzyński (conducting), Sikorski (composition), and Drzewiecki (piano). In 1948 he became conductor of the Poznań Philharmonic and Opera; named assistant conductor of the Polish Radio Symphony, he later served as principal conductor (1953–68) before taking a similar post with the Warsaw Opera (1967–73). From 1979 until 1982 he worked in Bonn as *Generalmusikdirektor.* His compositions include a symphony (1950) and the cantata *Dwa miasta* [Dialogue between Two Towns] (1950); from 1952 he employed serial and aleatoric techniques, as in *Capriccio,* 24 instruments (1962).

Kreutzer, Conradin [Conrad] (b. Messkirch, Baden, 22 Nov. 1780; d. Riga, 14 Dec. 1849). Composer. Choirboy in Messkirch, and from 1789 at two Austrian monasteries; 1799?–1800, law student, Freiburg; then a musician in Switzerland (1801–4) and Vienna (1804–10), having some lessons from Albrechtsberger and first stage success with Goethe's *Jery und Bätely* (1810); 1810–12, toured as performer on the panmelodicon. A successful opera at Stuttgart led to appointment as court Kapellmeister there (1812–16); court Kapellmeister at Donaueschingen (1818–22). Music director (1822–40) of the Vienna court opera at the Kärntnertor Theater, except for 1827–29, spent in Paris, where he produced an unsuccessful opéra comique, and 1833–35, spent as music director of the Josefstadt Theater, Vienna, where he produced his two most successful and long-lived stage works: the opera *Das Nachtlager in Granada* and incidental music to Raimund's play *Der Verschwender* (both 1834). Civic Kapellmeister, 1840–42, Cologne. A few of his more than 30 operas were very successful; other works include an oratorio, church music, chamber and piano pieces, some very popular male choruses and songs.

Kreutzer, Rodolphe (b. Versailles, 16 Nov. 1766; d. Geneva, 6 Jan. 1831). Violin virtuoso and composer. His father was a member of the Swiss Guard and played violin at Versailles; from 1778 Rodolphe studied composition and violin with Anton Stamitz. In 1780, aged 13, he performed at the Concert spirituel in Paris, playing a concerto by Stamitz. From 1785 he was a member of the French court orchestra, where he served until 1792. He composed his first opera in 1790 *(Jeanne d'Arc);* it was the first of a long series of successful stage works. In 1796 he toured Italy, and two years later he was in Vienna, where Beethoven reportedly heard him play; the composer was later to dedicate his op. 47 violin sonata (the Kreutzer) to him. In 1801 Kreutzer joined the orchestra of the Opéra, and from 1804 that of the Tuileries Chapel. From 1802 he was a cofounder (with Méhul, Cherubini, and others) of the Magasin de musique. In 1815 he was made *maître de la chapelle du roi;* two years later he was finally appointed chief conductor of the Opéra and was its music director from 1824 until 1826. He was one of the most significant violin virtuosos of his age. He was also a prolific composer; among his 46 extant stage works (all first performed in Paris) are *Lodoiska* (1791); *Le siège de Lille* (1792); *Le déserteur* (1793); *Imogène* (1796); and *Le camp de Sobieski* (1813). He also composed 19 violin concertos; numerous *symphonies concertantes;* 15 string quartets; string trios; duets; violin sonatas; and *42 études ou caprices* (Paris, 1796).

Křička, Jaroslav (b. Kelč, Moravia, 27 Aug. 1882; d. Prague, 23 Jan. 1969). Composer. He studied at the Prague Conservatory (1902–5) and served as an associate to Novák; continued his studies in Berlin (1905–6) and taught music in Ekaterinoslav, Russia (1906–9), becoming friendly with Glazunov. After his return to Prague in 1909 he conducted the Prague Glagol choir and joined the faculty of Prague Conservatory as a professor of composition (1918), later serving as rector of the institution. His compositions show the influence of Dvořák and Mussorgsky. Works include operas (*Hyppolita,* 1916; *Orgari,* 1918; *King Lavra,* 1939; *Circus Humberto,* 1955); orchestral music (*Idyllic Scherzo,* 1909; *Adventus,* 1912; *Sinfonietta semplice,* 1962); choral music (*Temptation in the Desert,* 1922; Requiem, 1949; Masses); chamber music; songs.

Krieger, Adam (b. Driesen, 7 Jan. 1634; d. Dresden, 30 June 1666). Composer. Resident at Leipzig from 1650 or 1651 as part-time student and prominent musical figure within student circles, perhaps also studying organ with Scheidt at Halle; succeeded Rosenmüller as Nicolaikirche organist in 1655, leading figural music and composing various occasional works as well. His *Arien von einer, zwey, und drei Vocal-Stimmen* appeared in 1657; the same year he was named keyboard teacher to the daughter of Elector Johann Georg II at Dresden and attempted unsuccessfully to become Thomaskantor. He became chamber and court organist at Dresden in 1658, holding the post until his death; a second publication, *Neue Arien* (Dresden, 1667, enlarged 1676), was assembled after his death by court poet D. Schirmer and composer J. W. Furchheim, the latter writing several ritornellos for the second edition. His influence through these collections continued into the 18th century.

Krieger, Armando (b. Buenos Aires, 7 May 1940). Composer and pianist. Studied composition with Ginastera at the Municipal Conservatory, Buenos Aires, and with Copland, Dallapiccola, Messiaen, and Malipiero at the Di Tella Institute. Concertized widely as a pianist, playing both new music and standard repertory. Appointed permanent conductor of the Teatro Colón and established the Solistas de música contemporánea de Buenos Aires. His music has been heard at many international festivals. Works include a string symphony (1959); a 2-piano concerto (1963); *Aleatoria I–II,* winds (1961); *Metamorphose d'aprés une lecture de Kafka,* piano and 15 instruments (1968); *Angst* (1970); cantatas and solo vocal works.

Krieger, Edino (b. Brusque, Santa Catarina, Brazil, 17 Mar. 1928). Composer. Received early training in violin from his father; studied violin with Reis and composition with Koellreutter in Rio de Janeiro, 1944–48, also participating in the latter's Música viva organization. Attended the Berkshire Music Center in 1948, studying with Copland; studied later with Mennin in New York (leading the New York Philharmonic in a concert in 1949) and with Lenox Berkeley in London in 1955. Residing in Rio, he worked as critic and as musical director of the National Symphony; he later served at Radio Jornal do Brazil (1963–73), and taught at the Curitiba summer program (1964–68) and at the Instituto Villa-Lobos (1968). He was president of the Brazilian Society of Contemporary Music in 1971–73. His first works show a free impressionism; after a serial period in the late 1940s he embraced a more neoclassical posture, with some nationalist elements. Works include the oratorio *Rio de Janeiro* (1965), various orchestral pieces, chamber and piano music, and songs.

Bibl.: *Composers of the Americas* 13 (Washington, D.C., 1967), pp. 81–88 [includes works list].

Krieger, Johann (b. Nuremberg, 28 Dec. 1651; d. Zittau, 18 July 1735). Composer. A pupil of Schwemmer, according to Mattheson; studied keyboard with Wecker, 1661–68, and perhaps composition with his brother Johann Philipp at Zeitz in 1671; took over as organist at Bayreuth in 1672, a post his brother had vacated soon before; worked as organist at Greiz (1678–80) and Eisenberg (1680–82) before becoming cantor at St. Johannis in Zittau, where he stayed for the rest of his life. Praised by Mattheson and Handel for his contrapuntal skill, he published keyboard collections in 1697 and 1698 containing suites and a variety of other types of pieces; he also wrote church music.

Krieger, Johann Philipp (b. Nuremberg, 25 Feb. 1649; d. Weissenfels, 6 Feb. 1725). Composer. Studied as a boy with Drechsel and G. Schütz in Nuremberg, and in Copenhagen for about five years in his teens as a pupil of Schröder and Förster. Served as organist at Bayreuth and possibly Zeitz upon his return, while the Nuremberg Council promised him the first available position. Traveled to Italy in 1673, studying in Venice with Rosenmüller and Volpe and in Rome with Abbatini and Pasquini; played before Leopold I at Vienna, who ennobled him in 1675. After a short time in Bayreuth he visited Frankfurt and Kassel, refusing offers in both places; named chamber musician and organist at Halle in 1677, he became Vice-Kapellmeister in 1678 and Kapellmeister when the court moved to Weissenfels in 1680. The court musical establishment soon became among the best in Germany; a catalog of vocal works performed there lists over 2,000 of Krieger's compositions along with hundreds more by his brother Johann and other German and Italian composers. He also wrote keyboard music, trio sonatas, and operas.

Bibl.: Harold E. Samuel, *The Cantata in Nuremberg during the Seventeenth Century* (Ann Arbor, 1982).

Krips, Josef (b. Vienna, 8 Apr. 1902; d. Geneva, 13 Oct. 1974). Conductor. Studied under Weingartner and Mandyczewski; was active as violinist, coach, and choir director at the Vienna Volksoper from 1918 to 1924, from 1921 conducting on occasion as well; served as music director of theaters at Aussig (1924), Dortmund (1925–26), and Karlsruhe (1926–33) before moving to the Vienna State Opera. He lost his job in the 1938 Anschluss, and after a year in Belgrade he conducted no more until 1945, when he returned to the Vienna post. After a successful international tour he became principal conductor of the London Symphony in 1950, later holding the same post in Buffalo (1954–63) and San Francisco (1963–70) before assuming control of the Vienna Symphony.

Křížkovský, Pavel [Karel Krischkowsky] (b. Kreuzendorf, Silesia, 9 Jan. 1820; d. Brno, 8 May 1885). Choral composer and choirmaster. He was trained as a chorister in the monastery of Opava (then Troppau) and studied philosophy in Olomouc and Brno. He entered the Old Brno Augustinian monastery in 1845, taking the name Pavel; he became choirmaster there in 1848. He also became central in the musical life of Brno as concert conductor, chamber music performer, and founder and director of two choral societies. He championed Moravian, Czech, and pan-Slavic cultural nationalism. In the 1860s he won the admiration of Smetana, and taught the young Janáček among his choristers. In the 1870s, responding to Cecilian reforms, he left the secular sphere to direct the cathedral choir of Olomouc. He retired in ill health in 1877, returning to Brno in 1883. His compositions include choral folk song settings and sacred choral works.

Krombholc, Jaroslav (b. Prague, 30 Jan. 1918; d. there, 16 July 1983). Conductor. Studied under Novák and Talich at the Prague Conservatory and the Master School, also attending Prague Univ. (1937–42); worked at the Prague National Theater from 1940, conducting the premiere of Bořkovec's *Satyr* in 1942. After short tours with the Czech Philharmonic and Ostrava Opera, he became director of the National Theater in 1945 and of the Czech Radio Symphony in 1973; he also made numerous guest appearances in Western Europe and the USSR.

Krommer, Franz (Vinzenz) [Kramář, František Vincenc] (b. Kamenice [Kamenitz], 27 Nov. 1759; d. Vienna, 8 Jan. 1831). Composer and violinist. In nearby Tuřan he studied organ and violin with his uncle, Anton Matthias Krommer. He settled in Vienna in 1785 and received a post as violinist in the court orchestra of the Duke of Styrum (in Simontornya; now in Hungary); later (from 1790) he was Kapellmeister of the Pécs Cathedral. He also served at other small courts in the region. He returned to Vienna in 1795 and from 1798 was Kapellmeister for Duke Ignaz Fuchs; later he became ballet master for the Hoftheater (1810), and eventually imperial court composer and Kapellmeister (from 1818). He composed symphonies, concertos, chamber music (including string quartets); sacred works (Masses; an Ave Maria).

Krosnick, Joel (b. New Haven, Conn., 3 Apr. 1941). Cellist. Student of Claus Adam, William D'Amato, Jens Nygard, and Luigi Silva; attended Columbia, forming a contemporary ensemble there; taught at the Univ. of Iowa (1963–66), the Univ. of Massachusetts (1966–70), and the California Institute of the Arts (1970–74) before joining the Juilliard Quartet and taking a faculty post at Juilliard. He has also toured as soloist and with the New York Chamber Soloists.

Krueger, Karl (Adalbert) (b. Atchison, Kans., 19 Jan. 1894; d. Elgin, Ill., 21 July 1979). Conductor. Studied at the Univ. of Kansas, at the New England Conservatory, and from 1920 to 1922 in Vienna and Heidelberg with Felix Weingartner, Robert Fuchs, and Franz Schalk. Directed the Seattle Symphony (1925–32), the Kansas City Philharmonic (1933–43), and the Detroit Symphony (1943–49).

Krumpholtz, Jean-Baptiste [Johann Baptist, Jan Křtitel] (b. Budenice, near Zlonice, 3 or 8 May 1742; d. Paris, 19 Feb. 1790). Harpist and composer. He learned music from his father while growing up in Paris; in

1773 he played a successful harp concert in the Burgtheater in Vienna. After serving three years in Count Nicolas Esterházy's court orchestra (1773–76), during which he apparently took counterpoint lessons with Joseph Haydn, he embarked on a successful concert tour of Europe. In Paris and Metz he worked with manufacturers toward improving the construction of the harp. He drowned himself in the Seine after his wife, Anne-Marie Krumpholtz (1755–1824), also a virtuoso harpist, eloped to London with the pianist Jan Ladislav Dussek. He composed concertos and sonatas for harp and various chamber music.

Krumpholtz, Wenzel [Václav] (b. Budenice?, ca. 1750; d. Vienna, 2 May 1817). Violinist. Brother of Jean-Baptiste Krumpholtz, he also played briefly in the Esterházy orchestra and later in that of Prince Kinsky in Vienna. From 1796 he was a member of the imperial opera orchestra. He was one of Beethoven's few close friends and may even have given him violin lessons (this according to Beethoven biographer Ferdinand Ries). Upon the violinist's death, Beethoven dedicated his 3-voice *Gesang der Mönche* (WoO 104) to his memory.

Krupa, Gene (b. Chicago, 15 Jan. 1909; d. Yonkers, N.Y., 16 Oct. 1973). Jazz drummer and bandleader. He recorded with McKenzie and Condon's Chicagoans (1927) and Red Nichols (1929–31). He joined Benny Goodman in 1934, becoming a soloist in the big band and small groups. Epitomized by the unrelenting tom-tom drum rhythm on Goodman's "Sing, Sing, Sing" (first recorded in 1937), Krupa's soloing did much to popularize the jazz drummer, and jazz itself. He formed his own big bands (1938–51), recording "Let Me Off Uptown" with Anita O'Day and Roy Eldridge (1941) and "Leave Us Leap" (1945). He often hired bop soloists, but his own playing remained firmly grounded in swing. From 1951 he toured with Jazz at the Philharmonic, led small groups, and taught.

Bibl.: Bruce Crowther, *Gene Krupa* (Tunbridge Wells, England, 1987).

Kubelík, Jan (b. Michle, Czechoslovakia, 5 July 1880; d. Prague, 5 Dec. 1940). Violinist and composer. He studied under Ševčík at the Prague Conservatory, first appearing professionally in 1898; made his London debut in 1900 and U.S. debut in 1902, eventually playing concerts on six continents. He married a Hungarian countess in 1903 and became a citizen of that country in 1904. He focused on composition during World War I, resuming his concert career in 1921. Although he was initially hailed as an equal of Paganini, his playing declined in later years; still, he continued to play in public up to the year of his death. At one time he was quite wealthy, able to provide financial assistance to the Czech Philharmonic with the millions he earned in concert, but by 1932 he was bankrupt. His compositions include a symphony, 6 violin concertos (1916–24), chamber music, and cadenzas for works of other composers.

Kubelík, Rafael (Jeronym) (b. Býchory, Czechoslovakia, 29 June 1914). Conductor and composer. Son of Jan Kubelík. He attended the Prague Conservatory and made his conducting debut with the Prague Philharmonic in 1934; he led the ensemble from 1936 to 1938 and again from 1941 to 1948, conducting at some of his father's last concerts. In the interim, he conducted opera at Brno. Leaving Czechoslovakia in 1948, he was initially engaged by the Glyndebourne Opera; he later conducted the Chicago Symphony (1950–53), the Covent Garden Opera (1955–58), and the Bavarian Radio Symphony in Munich (1961–79), appearing also at the Metropolitan Opera (serving briefly as music director there, 1973–74) and as guest conductor of numerous orchestras. His own compositions include 5 operas (*Veronika,* 1947; *Cornelia,* 1972); 2 symphonies; *Orphikon* for orchestra (1981); concertos for violin and cello; several Requiems; 6 string quartets; music for piano and violin; and songs.

Kubik, Gail (Thompson) (b. South Coffeyville, Okla., 5 Sept. 1914; d. Claremont, Calif., 20 July 1984). Composer. He studied violin and composition at Eastman (with Rogers and Edward Royce, 1930–34), the American Conservatory in Chicago (with Sowerby), Harvard (with Piston, 1937–38), and had contacts with Boulanger from 1937. He worked as staff composer and adviser for NBC (1940–41), and then for the Office of War Information and the U.S. Army, composing and directing music for films (1942–46). In 1969 he was composer-in-residence at Kansas State Univ., and in 1970 at Gettysburg College; from 1970 to 1980 he was at Scripps College. He won a Pulitzer Prize in 1952 for the *Symphony concertante* (piano, viola, trumpet, and orchestra). Most of his music is neoclassical in style; he was a melodist with talent for dramatic music, and composed a large number of scores for radio, television, and film (*Gerald McBoing-Boing,* 1950; arranged in a concert version for narrator, 9 instruments, and percussion, 1950). Works include operas and other dramatic works; orchestral music (3 symphonies and a piano concerto, 1982–83); works for chorus and orchestra (*Magic, Magic, Magic!,* alto, chamber chorus, chamber orchestra, 1976); chamber and piano music; *Scholastica* and other choral pieces and songs.

Kučera, Václav (b. Prague, 29 Apr. 1929). Composer and musicologist. He entered Prague Univ. in 1948, then went to Moscow in 1951, where he studied composition with Shebalin and musicology with Gruber and Cukkerman. After returning to Prague he worked as head of foreign music at Czech Radio (1956–59) and served at the Institute for Musicology of the Czechoslovak Academy of Sciences (1962–69); in 1972 he was appointed to the music department of the Academy of Arts in Prague. Beginning in the mid-

1960s many of his works made use of electronic sounds. Works include orchestral music (Symphony, 1962; *Obraz* [Picture], piano, orchestra, 1970); instrumental works (*Invariant,* bass clarinet, piano, tape, 1969; *Argot,* brass quintet, 1970; *Spring Manifesto,* flute, bass clarinet, piano, percussion, 1974; *Listening Time,* voice and percussion, 1981); tape (*Labyrinth,* 1968; *Kinechromie,* 1969).

Kuerti, Anton (Emil) (b. Vienna, 21 July 1938). Pianist and composer. He studied with Edward Goldman in Boston; professional debut with the Boston Pops playing Grieg's concerto at age 9. Studied piano with Erwin Bodky and Gregory Tucker at the Longy School (1948–52), with Erno Balogh at the Peabody Institute (1952–53), with Arthur Loesser at the Cleveland Institute (1953–55), and with Rudolf Serkin at the Curtis Institute (1955–58). At the same time he studied composition with Arthur Shepherd, Henry Cowell, and Marcel Dick. Taught from 1965 at the Univ. of Toronto. His recordings include an integral set of Beethoven sonatas. His compositions include a symphony, string quartets and other chamber music, piano pieces.

Kuhlau, (Daniel) Friedrich (Rudolph) (b. Uelzen, near Hannover, 11 Sept. 1786; d. Copenhagen, 12 March 1832). Composer and pianist. In his youth he studied in Hamburg with Schwenke; soon he became prominent in that city as a concert pianist. He fled to Copenhagen in 1810 when Napoleon marched into Hamburg; by 1813 he was court *Kammermusiker,* and by 1816 chorusmaster of the Royal Theater. During the 1820s he made successful concert tours through Scandinavia, Germany, and Austria. He is best known for his piano music, which includes some 20 sonatas; also sonatinas, variations, rondos, airs, fantasies, and numerous works for piano 4-hands. He also composed operas (*Elisa,* 1820; *Lulu,* 1824; *William Shakespeare,* 1826; *Hugo og Adelheid,* 1827; all Copenhagen); a piano concerto in C major (1810); a concertino in F minor, 2 horns, orchestra (1821); chamber music (a string quartet; 3 piano quartets); chamber works with flute.

Bibl.: Dan Fog, ed., *Kompositionen von Fridr. Kuhlau: thematisch-bibliographischer Katalog* (Copenhagen, 1977). Arndt Mehring, *Friedrich Kuhlau im Spiegel seiner Flötenwerke* (Frankfurt, 1992).

Kuhnau [Kuhn], **Johann** (b. Geising, 6 Apr. 1660; d. Leipzig, 5 June 1722). Composer. Studied as a boy in Dresden with Kittel and Krügner, becoming a member of the Kreuzschule choir (alongside his brother Andreas) in 1771; returned to Geising during an outbreak of the plague in 1680, then went to the Johanneum, Zittau, later in the year at the invitation of Kantor Titius, whose death (along with that of Edelmann, the organist) enabled Kuhnau temporarily to fill both posts; he also wrote music for the school dramas of Weise. Enrolled in law studies at Leipzig Univ. in 1682; became Thomaskirche organist in 1684; upon graduation in 1688 he set up a thriving law practice. His important keyboard collections of suites and sonatas, *Neue Clavier-Übung* (1689, 1692), *Frische Clavier-Früchte* (1696), and *Musicalischer Vorstellung einiger Biblischer Historien* (1700), soon appeared; he also studied Hebrew and Greek and wrote the satirical novel *Der musicalische Quack-Salber* (Dresden, 1700). He succeeded Schelle as Thomaskantor in 1701. His later years in the post were beset by falling quality of students, competition from the Leipzig Opera, and rival musical ventures initiated by Telemann, Hoffmann, and J. F. Fasch; nonetheless, he was praised by Scheibe and Mattheson as one of the major musical and intellectual figures of his day. Some 50 cantatas are extant, along with other church music, though his dramatic music and some treatises are lost.

Kulenkampff, Georg (b. Bremen, 23 Jan. 1898; d. Schlaffhausen, 4 Oct. 1948). Violinist. Studied under Willy Hess at the Berlin Hochschule (1912–15), teaching there himself from 1923 to 1926; taught at the Lucerne Conservatory from 1943; formed a trio with Edwin Fischer and Enrico Mainardi. His memoirs, *Geigerische Betrachtungen,* were published in 1952.

Kullak, Theodor (b. Krotoszyn, Poland, 12 Sept. 1818; d. Berlin, 1 Mar. 1882). Piano teacher. Musical talent brought him the patronage of Prince Anton Radziwill; from 1837, studied medicine, law, and music in Berlin; 1842, received a grant for a year's study in Vienna (Czerny, Sechter, Nicolai); then became a piano teacher in Berlin, quickly winning the patronage of the rich, aristocracy, and royalty (court pianist from 1846). In 1850 he founded a conservatory with Stern and Marx, but withdrew after disagreements. In 1855 he founded his own school, specializing in the piano; it became one of the largest in Europe, with many noted pupils.

Works: a piano concerto, 2 sonatas, salon and character pieces (especially *Kinderleben* opp. 62, 81); best known for exercises (especially *Die Schule des Oktavenspiels* op. 48, 1848); edited much piano music. His son Franz (1844–1913) was also a noted teacher.

Kullman, Charles [Kullmann] (b. New Haven, Conn., 13 Jan. 1903; d. there, 8 Feb. 1983). Tenor. Studied with Marcosano in New Haven, with Anna Eugénie Schön-René and Thomas Salignac in New York. Appeared in student productions of Monteverdi's *Orfeo* (U.S. stage premiere) and in Handel's *Xerxes* while at Smith College. Professional debut, 1929, with the touring American Opera Company as Pinkerton *(Madama Butterfly).* At Salzburg beginning in 1934 he sang both Italian and German roles, including Fernando *(Così fan tutti)* and Walther *(Meistersinger).* At his New York Metropolitan debut in 1935 he sang a French role, Gounod's Faust. He remained with the company through 1960. Sang under Bruno Walter in the first recorded performance of Mahler's *Das Lied von der*

Erde, recorded live in Vienna in 1936. In 1947 he appeared in a filmed fantasy about Rimsky-Korsakov, *Song of Scheherazade.*

Kummer, Friedrich August (b. Meiningen, 5 Aug. 1797; d. Dresden, 22 Aug. 1879). Cellist. From a family of wind musicians; his father an oboist, from 1805 at the Dresden court; studied the cello there with Dotzauer after 1811; from 1814, in the Dresden orchestra first as oboist, then (1817) as cellist; 1852–64, first cellist; also a noted chamber player and a distinguished teacher at the conservatory and privately. He composed much cello music and many studies, some still used.

Kunzel, Erich (b. New York, 21 March 1935). Conductor. Holds degrees from Dartmouth and Brown, and taught at Brown from 1958 to 1965; served as assistant conductor of the Rhode Island Philharmonic from 1963 to 1965; moved on to the Cincinnati Symphony, where he scored major successes with pops concerts and recordings with the Cincinnati Symphony and Pops Orchestras. He also conducted the Philharmonia Orchestra (1967–71) and the New Haven Symphony (1974–77). Active with the San Francisco Arts Commission Pops concerts beginning 1981.

Kupferman, Meyer (b. New York, 3 July 1926). Composer and clarinetist. He studied in New York at the High School of Music and Art and at Queens College; as a composer he was self-taught. Taught at Sarah Lawrence College from 1951 and remained active as a performer. A prolific composer. *Cycle of Infinities* (begun in 1961) includes more than 30 pieces for various ensembles based on a single twelve-tone set and incorporating jazz and chance elements; *Infinities 5* includes the material for a solo cello concert, with tape, jazz band, and voices. Other works include 9 operas (*Prometheus Condemned,* 1975; *The Proscenium,* chamber opera, 1991), 9 ballets, 17 film scores, and other stage music; 11 symphonies (1950–83), concerto for cello, tape, and orchestra (1974), and some 30 other orchestral works (*Savage Landscape,* 1989); over 170 chamber and instrumental pieces (*Infinities 34,* organ, 1983); choral and solo vocal music.

Kuri-Aldana, Mario (b. Tampico, Mexico, 15 Aug. 1931). Composer. Studied piano at the Academia J. S. Bach (1948–51) and composition at the Escuela nacional de música of the Univ. of Mexico (1952–60), during which time he also received instruction in conducting at the National Institute of Fine Arts. Later he studied composition with Herrera de la Fuenta and Rodolfo Halffter (1961–62); with Ginastera, Malipiero, Messiaen, Dallapiccola, and Copland at the Di Tella Institute (1963–64); and with Stockhausen at the National Conservatory (1968). He directed the Symphonic Band of the Secretariat of Public Education (1968–73) and the chamber orchestra of the Lebanese Center (from 1971). An active folklorist, from 1972 he served as professor of music at the Academy of Mexican Dance of the National Institute of Fine Arts. Works include orchestral, choral, chamber, and solo vocal music in a variety of styles.

Kurka, Robert (Frank) (b. Cicero, Ill., 22 Dec. 1921; d. New York, 12 Dec. 1957). Composer. He studied briefly with Luening and Milhaud, but was primarily self-taught. He taught at Queens College and Dartmouth. His best-known work is the opera *The Good Soldier Schweik* (1957, orchestration completed by Hershy Kay), based on a satirical antiwar novel by Hasek (staged at the New York City Opera, 1958). It is often compared to the operas of Weill for its irony, tonal language, and reference to popular styles. Other works include at least 2 symphonies, 5 string quartets, 6 violin sonatas, piano music, songs, and choral music.

Kurpiński, Karol (Kazimierz) (b. Włoszakowice, Poland, 6 Mar. 1785; d. Warsaw, 18 Sept. 1857). Composer. Son of an organist; himself a church organist at Sarnów at 12; from 1800, violinist and piano teacher in Moscow. Beginning 1810, violinist, and 1824–40, chief conductor, Warsaw Theater orchestra. A leading figure in Warsaw musical life, also as teacher and composer. Works include 11 Polish operas, 18 ballets, sacred music, orchestral, chamber, piano pieces, songs.

Kurtág, György (b. Lugoj, Romania, 19 Feb. 1926). Composer. He studied composition with Veress and Farkas and piano with Kadosa at the Budapest Academy of Music, receiving his diploma in 1953. He went to Paris in 1957, where he worked with Milhaud and Messiaen at the Conservatory; in 1967 he was appointed to the faculty of the Budapest Academy of Music, teaching first piano, then chamber music. Kurtág's early compositions, such as the viola concerto (1954) and various works for chamber ensemble, show the influence of Bartók and Kodály; with the publication of his String Quartet no. 1, Kurtág began using serial techniques and concentration of form reminiscent of Webern. Other works include the concerto for soprano and piano, *Bornemisza Péter mondásai* [The Sayings of Péter Bornemisza] (1963–68); *Kafka Fragments* (soprano, violin, 1986); *Quasi una fantasia* (chamber orchestra, 1988); *Samuel Beckett: What is the Word . . .* (voices, ensemble, 1991).

Kurz, Selma (b. Bielitz, 15 Nov. 1874; d. Vienna, 10 May 1933). Soprano. Discovered by the cantor Ignatz Goldmann; moved to Vienna, where she studied under Johann Ress after being rejected as untalented by Joseph Gänzbacher. After her debut in 1896 with the Frankfurt Opera as Elisabeth *(Tannhäuser),* she joined the Hamburg Opera in 1895. Engaged by Mahler in 1899 to sing Thomas's Mignon with the Vienna Staatsoper, she became a favorite there and stayed 25 years. She specialized in coloratura roles, her trill being especially prized. Sang at Covent Garden, 1904–7, when intrigues by Melba prevented further appearances until 1924. Created Zerbinetta in Strauss's revised *Ariadne auf Naxos* (1916).

Kusser [Cousser], **Johann Sigismund** (bapt. Pressburg [now Bratislava], 13 Feb. 1660; d. Dublin, Nov. 1727). Composer. Studied for six years in Paris under Lully, according to Walther; served the court at Ansbach, tutoring violinists in the French style, 1682–83. Surfaces next as opera Kapellmeister at Brunswick in 1690, perhaps traveling extensively in the interim; went to Hamburg in 1694, where his opera *Porus* was staged to broad acclaim. Founded an opera company in 1696, taking it throughout Germany; served as Oberkapellmeister in Stuttgart, 1700–1704; finished his career in Britain and Ireland, taking posts at Trinity College, Dublin, in 1711 and with the Crown in Ireland in 1716. He was respected for his mastery of the French and Italian styles; most of his music is lost, but orchestral suites and arias from his operas *Erindo* and *Ariadne* survive.

Kuula, Toivo (Timoteus) (b. Vaasa, Finland, 7 July 1883; d. Viipuri, 18 May 1918). Composer and conductor. He studied under Nováček, Wegelius, and Järnefelt at the Helsinki Music Institute (1906–8); continued his studies in Bologna, Leipzig, Paris, and Berlin. He worked as a conductor in Vaasa (1903–5), Oulu (1910–11), and Helsinki (1914–16) and conducted the orchestra of the Viipuri friends of music (1916–18). His compositions reveal his indebtedness to Finnish folk song in addition to a few impressionist elements. Works include orchestral music (*Eteläpohjalainen sarja* [South Ostrobothnian Suite] no. 1, 1906–9; no. 2, 1912–14); choral music (*Meren virsi* [The Song of the Sea], chorus, orchestra, 1909; *Kuolemattomuden toivo* [Hope of Immortality], baritone, chorus, orchestra, 1910); songs; instrumental works.

Kvandal [Johansen], **(David) Johan** (b. Oslo, 8 Sept. 1919). Composer. He studied conducting and organ at the Oslo Conservatory; took composition from Marx at the Hochschule für Musik, Vienna, and from Boulanger in Paris. He served as music critic for the Oslo newspapers *Morgenposten* and *Aftenposten,* and as organist of the Vålerengen Church in Oslo. Many of his compositions utilize folk elements. Works include orchestral music (Divertimento, strings, 1942; Symphony no. 1, 1958; *Visions norvégiennes,* 1985); choral music (*Våkn op!* [Wake Up!], chorus, 1951; 3 motets, 1971); chamber music (3 string quartets, 1954, 1966, 1983; *Duo concertante,* 2 pianos, 1974); solo vocal works; piano; organ.

Kvapil, Jaroslav (b. Fryšták, Czechoslovakia, 21 April 1892; d. Brno, 18 Feb. 1959). Composer. He studied under Janáček at the Brno School of Organists and with Reger at the Leipzig Conservatory (1911–13); taught at the school of organists and at the Janáček Academy of Music in Brno (1947–57), and served as conductor and choirmaster of the Brno Beseda (1919–47). Works include orchestral music (4 symphonies, 1914, 1921, 1927, 1943; piano concerto, 1954); vocal music (*Píseň o čase, který umírá* [Song of the Dying], cantata, 1924; *Lví srdce* [The Lionheart], oratorio, 1931; *Pohádka máje* [A May Fairy Tale], opera, 1943); instrumental pieces (String Quartet no. 4, 1945; no. 5, 1956).

Kyr, Robert (Harry) (b. Cleveland, 20 Apr. 1952). Composer. He attended Yale (B.A., 1974), the Univ. of Pennsylvania (M.A., 1978), and Harvard (Ph.D., 1989). He also studied at the Royal College of Music in London (1974–76). Composer-in-residence with the New England Philharmonic, 1985–89. Taught at Yale, UCLA, Hartt School of Music, Longy School of Music, and Aspen; at Univ. of Oregon 1990–, chair of composition 1995–. Works include five symphonies (1986–90); music for chorus and orchestra (*There Is a River,* 1985; *Unseen Rain,* 1991; *The Passion according to Four Evangelists,* 1995; *The Inner Dawning,* 1996); vocal chamber music (*Songs of the Shining Wind,* 1992; *Threefold Vision,* 1993); music for chamber orchestra (*Vanished Lightning,* 1992; *Infinity's Edge,* 1996; *On the Nature of Love,* 1996); two string quartets (1990, 1991); *Maelstrom,* 1981; *The Lover's Almanac* (1989).

L

La Barbara, Joan (Linda) [née Lotz] (b. Philadelphia, 8 June 1947). Composer, vocal performer. She studied voice with Helen Boatwright at Syracuse Univ. (B.S., 1970), with Curtin at the Berkshire Music Center, and with Marion Szekely Freschl at Juilliard. She performed as a founding member of the New Wilderness Preservation Band and in ensembles of Glass and Reich in the 1970s; toured in the U.S. and Europe, presenting works of Cage and her own compositions and teaching workshops on extended vocal techniques (such as circular breathing and the production of multiphonics, throat clicks, and flutter). She spent 1979 as composer-in-residence in West Berlin. From 1981 she taught composition and voice at the California Institute of the Arts. Among her many vocal works are *Loose Tongues* (8 solo voices, tape, 1985); *The Solar Wind: I–III* (*I,* 1 or 2 voices, 8 instruments, tape, and percussionist, 1983; *II,* 16 voices, 2 percussionists, flute, and electronic keyboard, 1983; *III,* voice and chamber orchestra, 1984); *Vlissingen Harbor* (voice, flute and piccolo, clarinet, trumpet, harp, piano and celesta, cello, and percussion, 1982); *October Music: Star Showers and Extra Terrestrials* (amplified voice and tape, 1980).

La Barre, Michel de (b. Paris, ca. 1675; d. there, 15 Mar. 1745). Flutist and composer. A set of his suites was issued in 1694, and *Le triomphe des arts* was staged in 1700. Became a member of the Musettes et hautbois de Poitou in 1704, resigning in 1730; he was also a member of the royal chamber music by 1705. He released a dozen or more books of suites between 1700 and 1725, including several for 2 unaccompanied flutes, and also wrote airs and a *comédie-ballet.*

Labarre, Théodore (François Joseph) (b. Paris, 5 Mar. 1805; d. there, 9 Mar. 1870). Harpist. Studied privately with Cousineau (1812–14), Bochsa (1814–16), Naderman (1816–20), and also at Paris Conservatory (1817–23); then toured Europe as a harpist. He was especially popular in Britain, where he lived for long periods. Conductor, 1847–49, of the Opéra-comique; from 1852, inspector of the imperial chapel and director of the emperor's private music; also a teacher (from 1867, professor at the Conservatory) and composer.

L'abbé *le fils* [Joseph-Barnabé Saint-Sévin] (b. Agen, 11 June 1727; d. Paris, 25 July 1803). Composer. Became a violinist in the Comédie-Française orchestra in 1738; studied with Leclair, 1740–42; played in the Paris Opéra orchestra, 1742–62, while also performing frequently at the Concert spirituel. He was obliged to join the orchestra at the Théâtre de la République et des arts during the Revolution in order to earn a living, and died penniless. Works include several chamber music collections issued between 1748 and 1763, along with a number of symphonies. His *Principes du violon* (Paris, 1761) gives important information on the violin technique of the period.

Labey, Marcel (b. Le Vesinet, Yvelines, 6 Aug. 1875; d. Nancy, 25 Nov. 1968). Composer and conductor. After a career in law, he studied at the Schola cantorum with d'Indy and others and taught there from 1903 to 1913. After d'Indy's death Labey became director of the school (1931). In 1901 he was secretary-general of the Société nationale de musique. He wrote an opera, 4 symphonies, a string quartet (1911), and other instrumental and vocal works in a Romantic style.

Lablache, Luigi (b. Naples, 6 Dec. 1794; d. there, 23 Jan. 1858). Bass. His parents were French and Irish immigrants; studied at the Naples conservatories from 1806, but was expelled for misbehavior; began his stage career in miserable circumstances, but from 1812 at the Teatro San Carlino his reputation quickly grew. By the 1820s he was a star all over Italy, including La Scala (1821–23), San Carlo (1823–30), and in Vienna (1823, 1825); from 1830 to the early 1850s a principal figure in the golden age of Italian opera at the Théâtre italien, Paris (winter seasons to 1851), and Covent Garden, London (summer seasons to 1856); 1852–53, St. Petersburg. He sang serious roles but was best known in comic roles, creating many, including Don Pasquale. Published a much-used singing *Méthode* (1840).

La Borde [Laborde], **Jean-Benjamin (-François) de** (b. Paris, 5 Sept. 1734; d. there, 22 July 1794). Composer and writer. After studying composition with Rameau and violin with Dauvergne, he entered the service of Louis XV in 1762; he later became the king's confidant and a *premier valet de chambre.* He fled Paris during the Revolution but was arrested and executed. Many of his operas achieved success; he collaborated in writing several librettos and set many of his own chanson texts. His interest in old music led to the 4-volume *Essai sur la musique ancienne et moderne* (1780), publications of trouvère songs, and a design for a keyboard with 21 notes to the octave. His many attacks on Rousseau's views led to retaliation from Rousseau's disciples.

Labroca, Mario (b. Rome, 22 Nov. 1896; d. there, 1 July 1973). Composer and critic. He studied at the conservatory in Parma with Respighi and Malipiero;

helped to found the Corporazione delle nuove musiche (1923) and was active throughout his career in promoting new music. He worked in the Ministry of Popular Culture, managed the Teatro Comunale (Florence), and was artistic director of the Teatro alla Scala (Milan). He directed the music department of Italian Radio (1949–58); from 1959 lived in Venice, where he helped to organize its music festivals. He wrote criticism for the newspapers (1923–36). His works, most composed before 1940, include 2 children's operas, ballets, film scores; orchestral and chamber music; *Stabat Mater* (soprano, chorus, orchestra, 1933) and other vocal music. Among his books are volumes on Malipiero and Toscanini.

Labunski [Łabuński], **Feliks Roderyk** (b. Ksawerynów, Poland, 27 Dec. 1892; d. Cincinnati, 28 Apr. 1979). Composer. He studied at the conservatory in Warsaw, and then in Paris with Dukas and Boulanger at the École normale (1924–34). Director of classical music for Polish Radio in Warsaw (1934–36), but then emigrated to the U.S. (became a citizen in 1941). Taught at Marymount College (Tarrytown, N.Y., 1940–41), and at the Cincinnati College of Music (from 1945); was active as a pianist and critic throughout his career. His works, in a Romantic style, include *Music* (piano and orchestra, 1968) and *Canti di aspirazione* (orchestra, 1963); a ballet (*God's Man,* 1937); string quartets, a brass quartet, and other chamber, organ, and piano music; choral works and songs.

Labunski, Wiktor (b. St. Petersburg, 14 Apr. 1895; d. Kansas City, Mo., 26 Jan. 1974). Composer and pianist. Brother of the composer Feliks Labunski. He studied in St. Petersburg and Poland; directed the piano department of the Kraków Conservatory (1919–28); made his U.S. debut in Carnegie Hall (1928) and remained to teach at the Nashville Conservatory, the Memphis College of Music, and the Kansas City Conservatory (1937–71, director from 1941). He was an active performer and lecture-recitalist and composed in a Romantic style. Works include a symphony (1936), pieces for piano and orchestra, a concerto for 2 pianos and orchestra (1951); piano music and songs.

Lacerda, Osvaldo (Costa de) (b. São Paulo, 23 Mar. 1927). Composer. Studied composition under Guarnieri; took degrees from both the Carlos Gomez Conservatory (1960) and the São Paulo Univ. Law School (1961); studied with Copland and Giannini in the U.S. in 1963. Taught both privately and at the São Paulo Mozarteum Academy (from 1966) and municipal music school (from 1969), serving also on various state and federal commissions. His music draws on both Western and native elements; works include the orchestral suite *Piratininga* (1962) along with other symphonic music, chamber pieces, choral works, songs, and piano compositions.

Bibl.: *Composers of the Americas* 15 (Washington, D.C., 1969), pp. 129–41 [includes works list].

Lachenmann, Helmut (b. Stuttgart, 27 Nov. 1935). Composer. He studied piano with Jürgen Uhde and composition with Johann Nepomuk David at Stuttgart; later composition and analysis with Luigi Nono in Venice. After working in electronic music at the Univ. of Ghent, he held teaching positions at the Hochschule für Musik in Stuttgart (1966–70), the Ludwigsburg Pädagogische Hochschule (1970–76), and the Hochschule für Musik in Hannover (from 1976). His works include *Souvenir,* 41 instruments (1959); *Introversion I* and *II,* 6 instrumentalists (1964–66); String Trio (1966); *Consolation I–IV,* solo voices and instruments (1967–73); *Kontrakadenz,* orchestra (1970); *Fassade,* orchestra (1973); *Accanto,* clarinet and orchestra (1975); *Harmonica,* tuba, large orchestra, (1983); *Staub,* orchestra (1987); *Toccatine für Violine* (1988).

Bibl.: Heinz-Klaus Metzger and Rainer Riehn, eds., *Helmut Lachenmann* (Munich, 1988).

Lachner, Franz Paul (b. Rain am Lech, Upper Bavaria, 2 Apr. 1803; d. Munich, 20 Jan. 1890). Conductor and composer. Son and pupil of the town watchmaker and organist; in 1822 went to Munich, 1823 to Vienna, where he was organist at the Lutheran church, studied with Sechter and Stadler, and became Schubert's friend. Assistant conductor, 1827, Vienna Opera; 1829–34, chief conductor; 1834–36, Kapellmeister, Mannheim; from 1836, conductor (opera, concerts, royal chapel), Munich (*Generalmusikdirektor* from 1852). On Wagner's arrival in 1864 he was shunted aside (inactive from 1865; pensioned in 1868). A prolific composer of operas, oratorios, 8 symphonies, 7 orchestral suites; chamber, piano, organ pieces; songs.

Lachner, Ignaz (b. Rain am Lech, Upper Bavaria, 11 Sept. 1807; d. Hannover, 24 Feb. 1895). Conductor and composer. Studied with Molique in Munich and from 1824 with his brother Franz in Vienna, succeeding him as Lutheran church organist and assistant conductor at the opera; 1831, assistant conductor, Stuttgart Opera; 1842–53, assistant conductor (under his brother), Munich Opera; from 1853, conductor, Hamburg Municipal Theater; from 1858, court Kapellmeister, Stockholm; 1861–75, chief conductor, Frankfurt. Composed opera, including the one-act, folk-oriented *Alpenszenen;* church music; orchestral works, including *Kinder-Sinfonie* op. 85; chamber and piano pieces; songs, some much sung.

Lachner, Vinzenz (b. Rain am Lech, Upper Bavaria, 19 July 1811; d. Karlsruhe, 22 Jan. 1893). Conductor. Went to school in Augsburg; then (1830–33) a private tutor in Posen; 1834, succeeded his brother Franz as conductor, Vienna Opera, and in 1836–73 as Kapellmeister at Mannheim; retired to Karlsruhe, teaching at the conservatory there from 1884; also a composer, especially known for his male part songs.

Lachnith [Lachnitt], **Ludwig Wenzel** (b. Prague, 7 July 1746; d. Paris, 3 Oct. 1820). Composer and horn player. He studied violin and horn in Prague, then served in the orchestra of the Duke of Zweibrücken from 1768. Around 1780 he moved to Paris, where he studied composition with F. A. Philidor and horn with Rodolphe. He spent the rest of his life in Paris, except for a period of exile during the Revolution. From 1806 to 1816 he was *instructeur* at the Opéra; there he composed stage works and adapted works by other composers to suit French tastes. The most notorious of these was *Les mystères d'Isis,* a pastiche-arrangement of *The Magic Flute,* incorporating music from other works by Mozart and Haydn. Other stage works included *L'heureuse réconciliation* (1785) and *Eugénie et Linval* (1798).

Lacombe, Louis (Trouillon) (b. Bourges, 26 Nov. 1818; d. St-Vaast-la-Hougue, Manche, 30 Sept. 1884). Pianist and composer. Student, 1829–32, Paris Conservatory (first prize, piano, 1831); toured Europe as pianist, studying in Vienna in 1834 with Czerny, Sechter, and Seyfried, and beginning to compose. He settled in Paris ca. 1840, married a well-to-do woman, and concentrated on composition and writing criticism and essays, some collected in *Philosophie et musique* (Paris, 1896). Composed operas, all but one performed posthumously; dramatic symphonies with voices; sacred, orchestral, chamber works; many songs and piano pieces.

Lacombe, Paul (b. Carcassonne, 11 July 1837; d. there, 5 June 1927). Composer. Studied with a local organist, otherwise self-taught; from 1866, a correspondent and close friend of Bizet; traveled frequently abroad and to Paris, where much of his music was performed. Composed prolifically: 3 symphonies, concert overtures; sacred and chamber music; many piano pieces and songs.

Lacy, Steve [Lackritz, Steven Norman] (b. New York, 23 July 1934). Jazz soprano saxophonist, composer, and bandleader. He played Dixieland jazz, joined Cecil Taylor's incipient free jazz group (1955–57), and began to work with Gil Evans (1957–1980s). After working with Thelonious Monk (1960), Lacy and Roswell Rudd formed a quartet devoted to Monk's music (1961–64). Lacy played with free jazz musicians in Europe, South America, and New York and with the group Musica elettronica viva in Rome from 1967, then settled in Paris in 1970. Gave many unaccompanied performances (including his album *Solo,* 1972) and also led a group, often playing his own compositions, including the album *The Tao Suite* (1979).

Bibl.: Heinrich-Lucas Lindenmaier, *25 Years of Fish Horn Recording: The Steve Lacy Discography, 1954–1979* (Freiburg, 1982).

Laderman, Ezra (b. Brooklyn, 29 June 1924). Composer. He studied composition with Wolpe (1946–49), with Miriam Gideon at Brooklyn College, and with Luening and Douglas Moore at Columbia (M.A., 1952). Taught at Sarah Lawrence College (1960–61, 1965–66) and was composer-in-residence at SUNY–Binghamton (1971–82); served as president of the American Music Center (1973–76) and directed the music programs of the National Endowment for the Arts (1979–82); dean of the Yale School of Music from 1989. His works combine lyrical, atonal, twelve-tone, and aleatory approaches. He has composed operas (*Galileo Galilei,* 1978; *Marilyn,* 1993) and other dramatic music (including several dance scores, film and television scores, incidental music); 8 symphonies (1964–94), *Stanzas* (21 solo instruments, 1959), several concertos (flute, 1985; violin and cello, 1987; clarinet, 1994), and other works for orchestra (*Pentimento,* 1986; *Citadels,* 1990) or large ensemble; 8 string quartets (1959–85), *A Single Voice* (flute, string quartet, 1991), and other chamber music; a few piano and organ works; *A Mass for Cain* (solo voices, chorus, and orchestra, 1983) and other choral and vocal works.

Ladmirault, Paul (Émile) (b. Nantes, 8 Dec. 1877; d. Kerbili en Kamoel, St. Nagoire, 30 Oct. 1944). Composer and critic. His first opera was staged in Nantes in 1893 *(Gilles de Retz);* in 1895 he began to study in Paris with Fauré and Gédalge. Professor and then director of the conservatory in Nantes; wrote criticism for local and Paris publications (including *Courrier musical*). Works include ballets, another opera (incomplete), and incidental music; orchestral and band music (including a symphony and several symphonic poems); chamber music; piano music; *Messe brève* (chorus and organ) and other sacred music; some 20 songs, including arrangements of Breton folk songs.

Laet, Jean [Jan] **de** (b. Stabroeck, ca. 1525; d. Antwerp, ca. 1567). Printer. His professional activity, begun in Antwerp in 1545, encompassed at first the production of Bibles, histories, and classical and Spanish texts. In 1554 music books, some published in conjunction with Hubert Waelrant, were added. In 1556 Laet issued one of the first editions of Lassus's works, a book of motets.

LaFaro, Scott (b. Newark, N.J., 3 Apr. 1936; d. Geneva, N.Y., 6 July 1961). Jazz double bass player. He accompanied Chet Baker (1956–57), Sonny Rollins (1958), Barney Kessel, and Benny Goodman (1959), but then redefined the role of the jazz bassist while working in Bill Evans's trio (1959–61). On albums such as *Sunday at the Village Vanguard* and *Waltz for Debby* (both 1961) he moves freely between timekeeping and engaging in contrapuntal dialogues with Evans. He also recorded with Ornette Coleman (1960–61) and worked with Stan Getz shortly before his death in an automobile accident.

L'Affilard, Michel (b. ca. 1656; d. Versailles?, 1708). Theorist and composer. Sang at the Sainte-Chapelle, Paris, from 1679; perhaps a member of the royal chapel at Versailles from 1683, and certainly from 1696, when he obtained a coat of arms; he was replaced by Santoni in 1708. L'Affilard is best known for his *Principes très-faciles pour bien apprendre la mu-*

sique (Paris, 1701; revised and/or reprinted several times up to 1747). Essentially a singing tutor, the fifth edition (1705) includes dance songs to which are appended "metronome" markings based on the pendulum system of Saveur; other valuable information in the treatise concerns *agréments* and *notes inégales.*

Lafont, Charles Philippe (b. Paris, 1 Dec. 1781; d. near Tarbes, 14 or 23 Aug. 1839). Violinist. Studied with his uncle, the violinist Isidore Bertheaume, with whom he toured in the 1790s, later in Paris with Kreutzer and, briefly, Rode. Toured Europe, 1801–8; solo violinist to the czar at St. Petersburg, 1808–14; from 1815, solo violinist to Louis XVIII. Composed 7 concertos and other violin pieces, over 200 vocal romances.

La Grotte, Nicolas de (b. 1530; d. ca. 1600). Composer. A keyboard player connected with the court of Navarre from no later than 1557 until 1562 and with the musical establishment of Henri de Valois, Duke of Anjou (who in 1574 became Henri III of France) from 1562 until retiring in 1587. Although his contemporary reputation was based chiefly on his skill as an organist, only one keyboard work, a fantasia, is extant. Yet nearly 50 chansons certainly by him and 50 others likely to be his survive. These were first published in partbooks but are clearly monodic in conception; some were also published for voice with lute accompaniment. A few are *chansons mesurées* or have texts by poets of the Pléiade.

La Guerre, Elisabeth-Claude Jacquet de. See Jacquet de la Guerre, Elisabeth-Claude.

La Guerre, Michel de (b. Paris, 1605–6; buried there, 13 Nov. 1679). Composer. Named organist at St. Leu, Paris, at age 14; served in the same capacity at the Sainte-Chapelle from 1633 until succeeded by his son Jérôme in 1675; he was elsewhere referred to as *organiste du roi.* His "pastorale en musique" *Le triomphe de l'Amour sur des bergers et bergères* premiered in late 1654, was given in the presence of the king in 1655, and was revived with scenery in 1657; it was likely the first attempt at French opera.

Laine, Cleo [Dankworth (née Campbell), Clementina Dinah] (b. Southall, Middlesex, 28 Oct. 1927). Singer. From 1952 a jazz singer with Johnny Dankworth, although after their marriage in 1958 she pursued a stage career from time to time, including performances in Weill's *The Seven Deadly Sins, Show Boat* (1971), and *The Mystery of Edwin Drood* (1985–86). She also performed *Pierrot lunaire* (1974) and (as a soloist and with Dankworth) maintained a successful career in popular music, winning awards for several albums, including *Best Friends* with John Williams (1977). Her contralto voice extended upwards into a high soprano range; an accomplished scat singer, especially effective in duets with Dankworth. A prime mover in the Wavendon Allmusic Plan near Milton Keynes, England, presenting workshops and performances.

Laine, Frankie [LoVecchio, Frank Paul] (b. Chicago, 30 Mar. 1913). Popular singer. After performances in nightclubs and on radio in Chicago and New York, in the mid-1940s he moved to Los Angeles to work with Hoagy Carmichael. From 1947 he released a series of highly popular jazz-influenced recordings, including "That's My Desire" (1947), "Mule Train" (1949), and "Moonlight Gambler" (1957).

Lajtha, László (b. Budapest, 30 June 1892; d. there, 16 Feb. 1963). Composer. He studied under Victor Herzfeld (composition) and Árpád Szendy (piano) at the Academy of Music in Budapest. Became associated with Kodály and Bartók in collecting folk songs; met many important musicians on his travels to Leipzig (1910), Geneva (1910–11), and Paris (1911–13). Appointed to the ethnographical department of the Hungarian National Museum, 1913; taught composition and chamber music at the National Conservatory in Budapest (1919–49), and from 1952 served as professor of musical folklore research at the Budapest Academy. Lajtha also was appointed director of the music department in the Hungarian Broadcasting Service in 1945, and received the Kossuth Prize in 1951 for his work on Hungarian folk music. His compositions combine folk material with mastery of contrapuntal procedures. Works include ballets (*Lysistrata,* 1933; *Le bosquet des quatre dieux,* 1943; *Capriccio,* 1944); film scores (*Hortobágy,* 1935; *Murder in the Cathedral,* 1948); Symphonies (no. 1, 1936; no. 2, 1938; no. 3, 1948; no. 4, Le printemps, 1951; no. 5, 1952; no. 6, 1955; no. 7, 1957; no. 8, 1959; no. 9, 1961); other orchestral works (cello concerto, 1940; Suite no. 3, 1952); choral works (*Missa in tono phrygio,* chorus, orchestra, 1950; Magnificat, female voices, organ, 1954); chamber music (10 string quartets; 3 string trios); piano works; solo vocal works.

Lakner, Yehoshua (b. Bratislava, Czechoslovakia, 24 Apr. 1924). Composer. He moved to Palestine in 1941, taking composition with Partos and Boskovich and piano with Pelleg; graduated from the Tel Aviv Academy, then studied with Copland at Tanglewood in 1952. In 1959–60 he continued his studies in Cologne under Zimmermann at the Hochschule für Musik and under Koenig, Kagel, and Stockhausen at the Westdeutscher Rundfunk; also attended several Darmstadt summer courses. Lakner moved to Zurich in 1973 and joined the faculty of the conservatory there the following year. From 1965 he wrote a number of electronic music scores to accompany plays at the Theater an der Winkelwiese, in addition to film and television music.

Lalande, Michel-Richard de (b. Paris, 15 Dec. 1657; d. Versailles, 18 June 1726). Composer. Joined the choir at St. Germain l'Auxerrois, Paris, in 1666; served as harpsichord tutor for certain nobles and as organist for several Paris churches until 1691. Competed successfully for one of the four posts as *sous-maître* at the royal chapel in 1683, and by 1714 had become the sole holder of all four appointments; similarly, he became one of the chamber composers in 1685, but by 1709 had complete control of the office. Named *surintendant de la musique de la chambre* in 1689, and *maître* of the same in 1695. Active also as a teacher; his pupils Destouches, Blamont, and La Porte later assumed many of his court duties. In 1722 he relinquished three quarters of his chapel responsibilities and was given the title of Chevalier of the Order of St. Michel. He was the most influential composer of *grands motets,* writing over 70 such works; greatly expanded in scope compared to those of his predecessors, they remained staples of the Concert spirituel repertory until the Revolution. His later reworkings of early motets provide the chance to examine evolution in style and taste. Instrumental music includes *Symphonies de noëls* (carol settings) and *Sinfonies pour les soupers du Roi* (varied types of movements, some dance-related); he also wrote ballets, airs, and a variety of sacred works.

Bibl.: Norbert Dufourcq, *Notes et références pour servir à une histoire de Michel-Richard Delalande* (Paris, 1957).

Lalo, Édouard (Victoire Antoine) (b. Lille, 27 Jan. 1823; d. Paris, 22 Apr. 1892). Composer. Studied the violin and cello at the Lille Conservatory. His father opposing a musical career, he left for Paris at 16, where he studied and later worked as violinist and teacher. From 1848 published vocal romances, violin pieces, and in the 1850s chamber music (2 piano trios, violin sonata, string quartet), but these last aroused little interest and he gave up composing such works; also a founding member (violinist; from 1861, second violinist) of the Armingaud Quartet (1856–67). In 1865 he married one of his pupils, Julie de Maligny, a contralto, for whom he wrote songs. Their son Pierre (1866–1943) became a noted critic. In 1866 composed a grand opera, *Fiesque,* for a competition by the Théâter-lyrique; it received third place and was never performed; he published the vocal score at his own expense. In the more serious musical atmosphere of Paris in the 1870s, he began again to compose large instrumental works: Violin Concerto op. 20 (1873), played by Sarasate; *Symphonie espagnole,* violin and orchestra, op. 22 (1874), also played by Sarasate, Lalo's most enduring work; Cello Concerto (1877); *Fantaisie norvégienne,* violin and orchestra (1878); Symphony in G minor (1886); Piano Concerto (1889). These brought him a recognition that he had not had before. A ballet for the Opéra, *Namouna* (1882), was a failure, although its music was admired. He capped his career with the opera *Le roi d'Ys,* mostly composed in 1875–81, but which he was unable to get performed until 1888 (Opéra-comique), when it had a great success.

Bibl.: *Correspondence* (Paris, 1989).

Lamb, Joseph F(rancis) (b. Montclair, N.J., 6 Dec. 1887; d. Brooklyn, 3 Sept. 1960). Ragtime composer. He spent most of his life in the textile trade and wrote his most famous rags by 1919; was rediscovered in 1949 and resumed composing rags; also wrote songs for Tin Pan Alley. Along with Scott Joplin and James Scott, one of the greatest of ragtime composers; works include "Sensation" (1908), "Excelsior Rag" (1909), "Champagne Rag" (1910), "American Beauty Rag" (1913), "Contentment Rag" (1915), "The Ragtime Nightingale" (1915), "Top Liner Rag" (1916), "Bohemia Rag" (1919), and "Alaskan Rag" (published posthumously).

Bibl.: *Ragtime Treasures: Piano Solos by Joseph F. Lamb* (New York, 1964).

Lambert, (Leonard) Constant (b. London, 23 Aug. 1905; d. there, 21 Aug. 1951). Composer and conductor. He won a scholarship to the Royal College of Music, where his teachers included Vaughan Williams and Morris. He met the Sitwells, Walton, and Diaghilev; Diaghilev commissioned a score from him for the Ballets russes (*Romeo and Juliet,* Monte Carlo, 1926), soon followed by a second ballet for the choreographer Nizhinska (*Pomona,* Buenos Aires, 1927). Lambert became increasingly interested in jazz, especially the music of Duke Ellington; with the BBC broadcast in 1928 of *The Rio Grande* for piano, chorus, and orchestra to a poem of Sacheverell Sitwell, Lambert was hailed (along with Walton) as one of the leading English composers of his generation. He was also acclaimed as a conductor: he led the Vic-Wells (later Sadler's Wells) Ballet (1931–47; artistic director, 1948), appeared as a guest conductor with the Hallé and Scottish orchestras after 1947, and conducted opera (Purcell and Puccini) at Sadler's Wells and Covent Garden. A provocative writer; Lambert's musical thoughts appeared in *Nation and Athenaeum* and the *Sunday Referee;* his book *Music ho!* was published in 1934. Among the many composers he championed (sometimes unfashionably so) were Puccini, Boyce, Chabrier, and Liszt. Compositions include other ballets (*Horoscope,* 1937; *Tiresias,* 1950–51; arrangements of Scarlatti, Schubert, Meyerbeer, Liszt, Boyce, etc.); orchestral works (*Elegiac Blues,* 1927; Music for Orchestra, 1927; a piano concerto, 1930–31; *Aubade héroïque,* 1942); choral works (*Summer's Last Will and Testament,* baritone, chorus, orchestra, 1932–35; Dirge from *Cymbeline,* tenor, baritone, male chorus, strings, 1940); songs (8 poems of Li-Po, voice and instruments, 1926–29); incidental music; film scores; arrangements.

Bibl.: Andrew Motion, *The Lamberts: George, Constant, and Kent* (London, 1986). Richard Shead, *Constant Lambert* (London, 1973).

Lambert, Michel (b. Champigny-sur-Veude, 1610; d. Paris, 29 June 1696). Composer. Sang as a boy at Champigny; served Gaston d'Orléans as a page in Paris, and Gaston's daughter as singer and member of her "six violons" until at least 1652. Danced and sang in ballets at court during the 1650s; served as *Maître de la musique de la chambre du Roy* from 1661 until his death and had a substantial reputation as a singing teacher. Hundreds of his airs are extant, as is some stage music produced in collaboration with Lully, along with a set of *leçons de ténèbres* from 1689, though most of his collections of airs printed under royal privilege are lost.

Lambertus, Magister [Pseudo-Aristotle] (fl. 1270). Theorist. His *Tractatus de musica* (late 1260s or early 1270s; ed. *CS* 1:251–81; ed. and trans. with commentary, M. Ralph, diss., New York University) ranks with the treatises of Johannes de Garlandia and Franco of Cologne as one of the most important 13th-century documents on music. Its teachings are mentioned in the writings of several other late medieval theorists. The work is most notable for its treatment of measured music and rhythmic notation.

La Montaine, John (b. Chicago, 17 Mar. 1920). Composer. He studied at Eastman with Rogers and Hanson (1938–42), at Juilliard with Wagenaar, and at Fontainebleau with Boulanger. He was pianist with the NBC Symphony Orchestra (1950–54), then taught at Eastman (1964–65). Won the Pulitzer Prize in 1959 for a piano concerto commissioned by the Ford Foundation. Influences on his work include serialism, medieval music, folk song, and jazz. Works include 5 operas (1957–74; 3 are Christmas pageants based on medieval texts); orchestral music, and music for jazz band; *Conversations* (clarinet, flute, tuba, violin, viola, or marimba, with piano, op. 42) and other chamber music; choral and vocal music.

Lamotte, Franz (b. 1751?; d. The Hague?, 1781?). Violinist and composer. Apparently his only violin teacher was Felice Giardini, with whom he studied in London. In 1766 he performed for the imperial court at Vienna, and the following year Emperor Franz I financed his first European tour, which included Prague, Leipzig, Paris, Padua, Naples, and Venice. Leopold Mozart reported on his appearance in Naples in 1770. Around 1772 he returned to Vienna to become violinist in the court orchestra. He also played at the Paris Concert spirituel several times during the 1770s. Later he was in London (1776–80).

Lamoureux, Charles (b. Bordeaux, 28 Sept. 1834; d. Paris, 21 Dec. 1899). Conductor. From 1850 a student of Girard at the Paris Conservatory (first prize, 1854); also played in theater orchestras, eventually at the Opéra; 1860, helped form a chamber music society. Marriage to a woman of means enabled him to realize his aim of concert organizations in Paris on English and German models; 1873–74, underwrote and conducted the Société de l'harmonie sacrée, which gave large sacred works; 1876, conductor, Opéra-comique; 1877–79, conductor, Opéra; 1881–97, conducted his Concerts Lamoureux, which introduced Paris to much native and foreign instrumental music; conducted Paris premiere of *Lohengrin* (1887) and *Tristan* (1899).

Lampadarios [Klada], **Joannes** (fl. ca. 1400). Composer. Along with his predecessor Joannes Koukouzeles, one of the foremost composers of Byzantine chant in the 14th and 15th centuries. His works, most of which date from the first half of the 15th century, are scattered throughout the liturgy and continue the trend of the time toward expanded proportions, incorporating, for instance, increased range, melodic repetition and sequence, and extensive troping of texts.

Lampadius, Auctor (b. Brunswick, ca. 1500; d. Halberstadt, 1559). Theorist. His career as schoolmaster and pastor included a few years as cantor of a school in Lüneburg, where he wrote *Compendium musices tam figurati quam plani cantus* (Berne, 1537). This treatise includes both traditional didactic material and an original discussion of 16th-century composition, particularly the music of Josquin.

Lampe, John Frederick (b. Saxony, ca. 1703; d. Edinburgh, 25 July 1751). Composer. Possibly attended St. Catherine's School, Braunschweig; studied law at Helmstedt, 1718–20; probably visited Hamburg before going to London in about 1725. Played bassoon in a theater band; composed 4 English operas, 1722–23, all of which failed; continued to write pantomimes and burlesques into the 1740s, of which *The Dragon of Wantley* (1737), a satire on Italian opera, was best received. Married Arne's sister-in-law, a successful singer, in 1738, and later befriended Wesley, many of whose hymns appear in a 1746 print set to Lampe's music. In addition to other isolated instrumental and vocal works, he wrote manuals on thoroughbass and harmony.

Bibl.: Dennis Martin, *The Operas and Operatic Style of John Frederick Lampe* (Detroit, 1985).

Lamperti, Francesco (b. Savona, 11 Mar. 1811; d. Cernobbio, near Como, 1 May 1892). Singing teacher. Studied at the Milan Conservatory, where he taught singing, 1850–75; one of the most sought-after teachers of the day, with many distinguished pupils. His *Arte del canto* (Milan, 1883) was much read and translated. His son Giovanni Battista (1839–1910) was also a famous singing teacher in Milan, Dresden, and Berlin.

Lampugnani, Giovanni Battista (b. Milan, 1706; d. there, after late 1786). Composer. Probably educated in Milan, where several of his operas were premiered between 1732 and 1738; his works were also given at Rome, Vicenza, and Padua. Presented *Rossane* (perhaps a pasticcio), *Alceste,* and *Alfonso* at the King's Theater, London, 1743–44; Walsh printed a set of his sonatas around this time. Worked in Italy, 1746–51; his operas were later staged at Barcelona (1753) and in London (1756). He was based in Milan from 1758 to his death, writing operas for other Italian cities as well (some to Goldoni librettos), and played harpsichord at the Milan opera, participating in the performance there of Mozart's *Mitridate* (1770). In addition to over 30 stage works, he composed arias and many sonatas and sinfonias.

Landi, Stefano (b. Rome, ca. 1586–87; d. there, 28 Oct. 1639). Composer. Enrolled as a soprano in the Collegio germanico, Rome, in 1595; received low orders in 1599; entered the Seminario romano in 1602, graduating in 1697. Served as organist at S. Maria in Trastevere during 1610 and as singer at the Oratorio del SS. Crocifisso in 1611; a 3-voice motet of his was published in 1616. By 1618 he was *maestro di cappella* to the Bishop of Padua; his opera *La morte d'Orfeo* (1619) dates from this time. The dedication of his first book of arias (1620) places him in Rome, where he probably succeeded Anerio as *maestro di cappella* at S. Maria di Monte, composing for other Roman institutions as well. He issued a Psalm collection in 1624 and a second book of arias in 1627, and was also active as a teacher; his noble patrons included the papal Barberini family. He joined the papal choir in 1629; a document of 1630 there lists his age as 43. His influential sacred opera *Il Sant'Alessio* (libretto by Rospigliosi), given at the Barberini Palace in 1632, was the first historical opera, combining comic scenes and lofty moralizing, and includes important early examples of the operatic overture. His last years saw the publication of several additional books of arias; other works include church music in both *stile antico* and *stile moderno,* madrigals, and dialogues.

Bibl.: Silke Leopold, *Stefano Landi: Beiträge zur Biographie: Untersuchungen zur weltlichen und geistlichen Vokalmusik* (Hamburg, 1976). Gerda Panofsky-Soergel, "Nachträge zu Stefano Landis Biographie," *AnMca* 22 (1984): 69–130.

Landini [Landino], **Francesco** [Francesco degli organi] (b. Fiesole? or Florence, ca. 1325; d. Florence, 2 Sept. 1397). Composer and organist. His study of music began after a childhood bout with smallpox, which left him blind. Instrumental performance, especially on the organ, was his first area of proficiency. Subsequent years saw activity also in singing, organ tuning and building, and instrument making, as well as the writing of poetry. By 1361 he was organist at the monastery of Santa Trinità; from 1365 *cappellanus* at the Church of SS. Annunziata in Florence. His work as an organ tuner and builder continued in the 1370s and 1380s.

His over 150 compositions constitute about a quarter of the extant music from the Italian trecento. Most copies are in Italian sources, including the Squarcialupi Codex. The works surely by him include one French virelay, 1 *caccia,* about 10 madrigals, and 140 *ballate,* a form hardly known in Florence previously. The style of his compositions ranges from the clearly Italian (some of the 2-voiced pieces) to a synthesis of Italian and French idioms (especially the 3-voiced pieces with text in 1 voice only).

Bibl.: Leonard Ellinwood, ed., *Works of Francesco Landini* (Cambridge, Mass., 1939; 2nd ed. 1945). Leo Schrade, ed., *Polyphonic Music of the Fourteenth Century,* 4 (Monaco, 1958). Leonard Ellinwood, "Francesco Landini and His Music," *MQ* 22 (1936): 190–216. Kurt von Fischer, "On the Technique, Origin, and Evolution of Italian Trecento Music," *MQ* 47 (1961): 41. Id., "Ein Versuch zur Chronologie von Landinis Werken," *MD* 20 (1966): 31.

Landowska, Wanda [Alexandra] (b. Warsaw, 5 July 1879; d. Lakeville, Conn., 16 Aug. 1959). Harpsichordist and pianist. Studied piano with J. Kleczynski and A. Michalowski from 1883. Studied composition with Heinrich Urban in Berlin, then moved to

Wanda Landowska.

Paris; at the Schola cantorum she took courses with Henri Lew, whom she married. She commissioned a harpsichord from the Maison Pleyel and performed on it at the Breslau Bach Festival in 1912. Taught at the Berlin Conservatory, 1913–19; at the École normale in Paris; then (summers 1925–40) at a school founded by Alfred Cortot and herself at Saint-Leu-la-Forêt. Also taught at the Curtis Institute in Philadelphia, 1925–28. Moved to New York in 1941. Gave summer courses at her home in Lakeville from 1950. She first recorded in 1923; made the first recording of Bach's Goldberg Variations; gave the first performances of Falla's Harpsichord Concerto and Poulenc's *Concert champêtre,* both of which she commissioned.

Bibl.: Denise Restout, ed. and trans., *Landowska on Music* (New York, 1964).

Landowski, Marcel (b. Pont l'Abbé, Finistère, 18 Feb. 1915). Composer and writer on music. He studied at the Paris Conservatory with Büsser and others from 1934. Director of the conservatory in Boulogne-sur-Seine, where he lived after World War II (1959 to 1962); directed music at the Comédie-Française (1962–65); then served as inspector general for music education and director of the music division of the Ministry of Cultural Affairs. Honegger, whose advice he received early in his career, had a major influence on his style; Landowski's book on the composer, *Honegger,* appeared in 1957. With Aubert he wrote *L'orchestre* (1951); with G. Morançon *Louis Aubert: Musicien français* (1967). He composed several operas and ballets, film and incidental music; symphonies, symphonic poems, concertos, and other orchestral music; chamber and piano works; and vocal music including several large works for soloists, choir, and/or orchestra.

Landré, Guillaume (Louis Frédéric) (b. The Hague, 24 Feb. 1905; d. Amsterdam, 6 Nov. 1968). Composer.

He studied with his father, Guillaume Landré, and with Pijper and Zagewijn; also studied law at Utrecht Univ. He taught law and served as a music critic in Amsterdam, then became chairman of the Dutch section of the ISCM and the Society of Dutch Composers (1950–62). After some early works influenced by Pijper, Landré's compositions started utilizing longer, more lyrical melodies; he also experimented with serial techniques and jazz-influenced rhythms. Works include opera (*De snoek,* 1938; *Jean Lévecq,* 1963; *La symphonie pastorale,* 1968); orchestral music (Symphony no. 1, 1932; Suite, strings, piano, 1936; violin concerto, 1940; Symphony no. 2, 1942; *Permutazioni simfoniche,* 1957); vocal works (*Piae memoriae pro patria mortuorum,* chorus, orchestra, 1942); chamber music (4 string quartets, 1927, 1943, 1950, 1966; sextet, flute, clarinet, string quartet, 1959).

Lane, Burton [Morris Hyman Kushner] (b. New York, 2 Feb. 1912). Popular songwriter. Worked as a pianist for Remick Music House in New York; authored songs for revues (including *The Third Little Show,* 1931; *New Americana,* 1932) and films (including "How about You," in *Babes on Broadway,* 1941). From 1940 wrote musicals, including *Finian's Rainbow* (1947, including "Old Devil Moon," "Look to the Rainbow") and *On a Clear Day You Can See Forever* (1965); he worked with lyricists Alan Jay Lerner, Sammy Cahn, and E. Y. Harburg.

Lanfranco, Giovanni Maria (b. Terenzio, near Parma, ca. 1490; d. Parma, late Nov. 1545). Theorist. Maestro di cappella in Brescia (from 1528), Verona (1536–38), and Parma (from 1540). The most notable of his several theoretical treatises is *Scintille di musica* (Brescia, 1533; trans. B. Lee, diss., Cornell Univ., 1961), a textbook for beginners. It includes an explanation of *tactus* and the earliest known set of rules for text underlay, as well as a list of the writers from whom material or ideas have been borrowed.

Bibl.: Don Harrán, "New Light on the Question of Text Underlay Prior to Zarlino," *AM* 45 (1973): 24–56.

Lang, B(enjamin) J(ohnson) (b. Salem, Mass., 28 Dec. 1837; d. Boston, 3 or 4 Apr. 1909). Pianist, organist, conductor, composer. Son of a Salem piano teacher; a church organist from 1850 (from 1852 in Boston); 1855–58, studied music in Germany (piano with Alfred Jaëll); from 1858 prominent in Boston musical life as pianist in chamber music and as soloist (including appearances with the Boston Symphony), organist (from 1862, Old South Church; from 1885, King's Chapel), conductor, especially of choral societies (1868–1901, Apollo Club; 1874–1907, Caecilia; 1895–97, Handel and Haydn Society, having been its organist in 1859–95), teacher (pupils included Nevin, Foote), and composer. Conducted premiere of Tchaikovsky's First Piano Concerto.

Lang, David (b. Los Angeles, 8 Jan. 1957). Composer. He studied at Stanford (A.B., 1978) with Lou Harrison, Martin Bresnick, and Leland Smith; at the Univ. of Iowa (M.M., 1980) with Richard Hervig, Donald Jenni, and William Hibbard; and at Yale (D.M.A., 1989) with Bresnick, Jacob Druckman, Roger Reynolds, and Morton Subotnick. He has also studied with Hans Werner Henze. He won the Rome Prize in 1990. Along with Michael Gordon and Julia Wolfe he founded the Bang on a Can Festival in New York. Works include *Judith and Holofernes* (puppet opera, 1989); *Modern Painters* (opera, 1994); orchestral music (*Eating Living Monkeys,* 1985, rev. 1987; *International Business Machine,* 1990; *Bonehead,* 1990; *Concerto on Orpheus,* two pianos and orchestra, 1994); works for chamber orchestra (*Spud,* 1986; *Are You Experienced?* 1988; *Dance/Drop,* 1989); and chamber music (*Orpheus Over and Under,* 2 pianos, 1989; *The Anvil Chorus,* percussion, 1990).

Lang, Eddie [Massaro, Salvatore; Dunn, Blind Willie] (b. Philadelphia, 25 Oct. 1902; d. New York, 26 Mar. 1933). Jazz guitarist. He often played with Joe Venuti, a childhood friend. He joined the Mound City Blue Blowers (1924) and moved to New York. While performing with Venuti (1926, 1928), Roger Wolfe Kahn (1926–27), Adrian Rollini (1927), and Paul Whiteman (1929–30), he made numerous recordings that established the guitar as a solo instrument in jazz. Among these are sessions with Red Nichols, Frankie Trumbauer (and Bix Beiderbecke), Venuti (including the duo "Stringing the Blues," 1926), Lonnie Johnson (including a trio with King Oliver), Louis Armstrong, and as a leader (including "Eddie's Twister," 1927). While working as an accompanist to Bing Crosby (from 1932), he died of complications following a tonsillectomy.

Láng, István (b. Budapest, 1 Mar. 1933). Composer. He studied with Viski and Szabó at the Budapest Academy of Music (1950–58); in 1966 he was appointed director of the Hungarian Marionette Theater and later became lecturer at the Budapest Academy. His compositions utilize a variety of modern techniques including free twelve-tone writing, aleatoric elements, and proportions based on numbers such as the Fibonacci series. Láng's stage works include *Mario és a varázsló* [Mario and the Magician] (1962), *Hiperbola* (1963), *A gyáva* [The Coward] (1964–68), *Csillagra-törők* [Starfighters] (1971); other works include *Pezzo lirico* (oboe, orchestra, 1985), an organ concerto (1987), *Interpolations* (bassoon, 1988).

Lang, Josephine (Caroline) (b. Munich, 14 Mar. 1815; d. Tübingen, 2 Dec. 1880). Composer. Daughter of Munich Kapellmeister Theobald Lang (1783–1834) and singer Regina Hitzelberger (1788–1827); had some lessons (1830–31) from Mendelssohn; became a music teacher and sang in the court chapel (1835), also composed songs and piano pieces; 1841, married Christian Reinhold Köstlin (1813–56), a lawyer. They settled in Tübingen, their house becoming a center of musical life. She bore 6 children and had little time to compose until her husband's death forced her to return to teaching and composition to support her family. Published 52 opuses of songs and piano pieces.

Lang, Margaret Ruthven (b. Boston, 27 Nov. 1867; d. there, 29 May 1972). Composer. Daughter of B. J. Lang, with whom she studied, beginning to compose at 12; 1886–87, music student in Munich; back in Boston, studied with Chadwick and MacDowell; best known for about 200 songs, some quite popular; also published choral music, some of it premiered by her father's choruses; piano pieces; also composed large orchestral works, now lost. She was the first U.S. woman to have a work performed by a major orchestra (Dramatic Overture op. 12, played by the Boston Symphony under Nikisch, 1893); stopped composing in about 1917.

Lange-Müller, Peter Erasmus (b. Frederiksborg, Denmark, 1 Dec. 1850; d. Copenhagen, 26 Feb. 1926). Composer. From 1870 studied law at Copenhagen Univ., from 1871 also music at the conservatory, but his health forced him to withdraw; restricted his activities thereafter; 1879–83, assistant conductor of a concert society that he had helped found, the only public post he ever held. Largely self-taught as a composer, he was highly regarded in Denmark for his ca. 200 songs and his part songs; also composed 4 operas (*Vikingeblod,* 1900, not successful) and other stage music; 2 symphonies; 2 orchestral suites; a violin concerto; chamber music. Composed little after 1900, nothing after 1910.

Langgard, Rued [Rud] **(Immanuel)** (b. Copenhagen, 28 July 1893; d. Ribe, Denmark, 10 July 1952). Composer and organist. He began his musical training with his parents, subsequently studying with Gustav Helsted (organ), Christian Petersen (violin), and C. F. E. Horneman (theory); made his debut as organist in 1905. His early compositions were influenced by Liszt and Bruckner; an experimental atonal phase (1916–24) was followed by a return to a more purely Romantic style, reminiscent of Gade and Wagner. An outcast in official music circles, Langgard was eventually appointed cathedral organist in the small town of Ribe (1940), where he continued to compose. Works include the biblical opera *Antikrist* (1921–39, Danish Radio, 1980), compositions for chorus and orchestra, 16 symphonies (1908–51), 8 string quartets (1914–31).

Bibl.: Bendt Viinholt Nielsen, *Rued Langgaards Kompositioner,* annotated catalogue of works (Odense, 1991).

Langlais, Jean (b. La Fontenelle, 15 Feb. 1907; d. Paris, 8 May 1991). Composer and organist. At the Paris Conservatory he studied organ under Dupré (Premier Prix, 1930) and composition under Dukas (Premier Prix, 1932); he also had organ and improvisation lessons with Tournemire, whom he succeeded in 1945 as organist at Ste. Clotilde. He composed ca. 240 works, of which ca. 100 are for organ (including 3 concertos). He played and taught widely in Europe and the U.S.; his *Prélude Gregorien* (1979) was written for the dedication of the tracker organ at Catholic Univ. in Washington, D.C., where he was awarded an honorary doctorate. Other works include 12 for orchestra; ca. 20 chamber works; and over 100 vocal and choral pieces.

Bibl.: Kathleen Thomerson, *Jean Langlais: A Bio-Bibliography* (New York, 1988).

Langlé, Honoré (François Marie) (b. Monaco, 1741; d. Villiers-le-Bel, near Paris, 20 Sept. 1807). Composer and theorist. Between 1756 and 1764 he studied in Naples at the Conservatorio della Pietà dei Turchini. He spent three years in Genoa as theater director (beginning 1765), and finally settled in Paris in 1768. From 1784 he was a voice teacher at the École royale de chant, and he continued to teach there after the Revolution, when the school was reorganized as the Paris Conservatoire. Most significant are his theoretical works, including *Traité d'harmonie et de modulation* (Paris, 1795); *Nouvelle méthode pour chiffrer les accords* (Paris, 1801); and *Traité de la fugue* (Paris, 1805). He composed operas (*Corisandre,* 1791), symphonies, and chamber works.

Langlotz, Karl A. (b. Saxe-Meiningen, 20 June 1834; d. Trenton, N.J., 25 Nov. 1915). Songwriter. Son of a Saxe-Meiningen court musician; then in Weimar (played in the orchestra under Liszt at the *Lohengrin* premiere, 1850); 1853, emigrated to the U.S., becoming a music teacher in Philadelphia; 1857–68, taught German at Princeton, composing the school song "Old Nassau" (1859); 1868–71, studied at the Princeton Theological Seminary; from 1874, a music teacher in Trenton.

Lanier, Nicholas (bapt. London, 10 Sept. 1588; buried there, 24 Feb. 1666). Composer. Member of a musical family, he served the Earl of Salisbury (to 1607) and the Cecil family (between 1605 and 1613). Performed in a Campion masque in 1613; joined the King's Musick as lutenist in 1616; collaborated with Jonson on several masques; named Master of the Musick of Prince Charles in 1618, becoming de facto master of the king's music upon Charles's accession in 1625. Took several trips to Italy as art agent for the king, buying paintings. Went into exile during the Commonwealth, spending time both in the Netherlands and in Paris, being active as an artist in the latter. His extant music includes many songs, a genre of which he was a major 17th-century English exponent, along with a few instrumental works; much else is certainly lost.

Bibl.: *English Songs, 1625–1660,* ed. Ian Spink, *MB* 33 (1971). Michael I. Wilson, *Nicholas Lanier: Master of the King's Musick* (Aldershot, 1994).

Lanier, Sidney (Clopton) (b. Macon, Ga., 3 Feb. 1842; d. Lynn, N.C., 7 Sept. 1881). Poet and musician. Largely self-taught as a musician, learning several instruments and mastering the flute; 1857–60, student at Oglethorpe Univ.; 1861–64, served in Confederate

Army; then worked as a hotel clerk, teacher, and in his father's law office; also began to write in earnest. In 1873, tubercular and realizing his life would be short, decided to devote the remainder to literature and music. He moved to Baltimore, where he lectured on both at Johns Hopkins (from 1879), and was first flutist in the Peabody Orchestra. His *The Science of English Verse* (1880) investigates the relations between poetry and music; other essays collected in *Music and Poetry* (1899; R: 1969). Composed flute pieces and songs, of interest mainly because of his standing as a poet.

Lanner, Joseph (Franz Karl) (b. Vienna, 12 Apr. 1801; d. Oberdöbling, near Vienna, 14 Apr. 1843). Composer and dance orchestra conductor. Mostly self-taught in music; from 1813, violinist (with Strauss, Sr.) in Michael Pamer's dance orchestra; 1818, member of a trio that by 1824 grew to a full dance orchestra with Lanner as violinist-conductor; quickly popular, leading in 1825 to division into two orchestras, the other headed by Strauss, Sr. Quarrels soon led to their complete separation. In 1829, music director of the Redoutensäle; 1832, gave first promenade concerts in Vienna; died of typhus. Published over 200 works, mostly dances, over half of these waltzes, widely popular in Europe and America in the 1830s and 1840s.

Bibl.: E. Kremser, ed., *Gesamtausgabe* (Leipzig, 1889–91: R: 1973). Herbert Krenn, *"Lenz-Blüthen." Joseph Lanner: Sein Leben, sein Werk* (Vienna, 1994).

Lansky, Paul (b. New York, 18 June 1944). Composer. He studied with Perle and Weisgall at Queens College and at Princeton with Babbitt, Cone, and Kim (Ph.D., 1969). Taught at Princeton from 1969. His systematization of Perle's theory of twelve-tone tonality serves as the basis for his own works, which combine conventional instruments and computer-generated sounds. In 1956 he became associate editor of *Perspectives of New Music.* Works include a string quartet (1971, rev. 1977), *Cross Works* (piano, flute, clarinet, violin, and cello, 1974–75), *Modal Fantasy* (piano, 1970), *Six Fantasies on a Poem by Thomas Campion* (computer, 1978–79), and *As If* (string trio, computer, 1982).

Lantins, Arnold de (fl. ca. 1430). Composer. The region of Liège was probably the birthplace of this highly esteemed musician, who is known today chiefly from music in north Italian manuscripts. For a few months beginning in late 1431, he sang with Dufay in the papal choir. His one cyclic Mass and several Mass pairs are unified by *finalis* and head motifs. Other works include 3 movements of a composite Mass (completed by Ciconia), motets, ballades, and over a dozen rondeaux.

Lantins, Hugo de (fl. 1420–30). Composer. Possibly related to Arnold de Lantins. The works of the two men appear in the same sources, and many are of the same genres. Hugo de Lantins was connected with Venice and the Malatesta family and with Dufay. His music, which, exceptionally for its time, makes extensive use of imitation, includes several Mass movements, one Gloria-Credo pair, 5 motets, 4 Italian secular songs, and over a dozen French rondeaux.

Lanza, Alcides (b. Rosario, Argentina, 2 June 1929). Composer. Composition student of Bautista and Ginastera; later teachers included Copland, Messiaen, Malipiero, Loriod, Maderna, and Ussachevsky at the Di Tella Institute (1963–64) and elsewhere during the 1960s. Served on the staff of the Teatro Colón, Buenos Aires, 1959–65; visited the U.S. in 1965, remaining until 1971, composing and teaching at the Electronic Music Center of Columbia and Princeton. Named to the faculty of McGill Univ., Montreal, in 1971; resident composer of the Deutsche Akademischer Austauschdienst, Berlin, in 1972–73. Toured widely as both lecturer and pianist, as well as conductor of the New York–based Composers/Performers Group. His early works use traditional media, often notated graphically; much of his later music is electronic, sometimes calling for instruments as well.

Bibl.: *Composers of the Americas* 17 (Washington, D.C., 1971), pp. 84–88 [includes works list].

Lanza, Mario [Cocozza, Alfred Arnold]. (b. Philadelphia, 31 Jan. 1921; d. Rome, 7 Oct. 1959). Tenor. Developed his voice in his spare time before being discovered by Sergey Koussevitzky, who encouraged him to study at the New England Conservatory with Enrico Rosati. In 1947 he, George London, and Frances Yeend formed the Bel Canto Trio, which took its repertory from musicals and light opera. In Hollywood he assumed the mantle of Nelson Eddy in films such as *Louisiana Fisherman, Old Heidelberg, Serenade,* and above all *The Great Caruso* (1951). In 1956 he moved to Rome, succumbing to cardiac arrest there three years later.

Laparra, Raoul (b. Bordeaux, 13 May 1876; d. Suresnes, 4 Apr. 1943). Composer and critic. He was a student at the Paris Conservatory (1890–1903), where his teachers included Gédalge, Fauré, Lavignac, and Diémer. In 1903 he won the Prix de Rome, after which he pursued a career as a music critic until 1937 for *Le matin.* His works include at least 4 operas (*Le joueur de viole,* 1926) as well as *Un dimanche basque* (piano and orchestra) and other instrumental works. Many compositions reflect his interest in Spanish and Basque folk music.

Lara, Agustín (b. Tlacotalpán, Mexico, 30 Oct. 1900; d. Mexico City, 6 Nov. 1970). Popular songwriter. He authored over 600 songs, including "Mujer," "Maria Bonita," and "Rosa"; among his most popular works were those on Spanish topics (including "Madrid," "Granada").

Larrocha (y de la Calle), Alicia de (b. Barcelona, 23 May 1923). Pianist. Studied in Barcelona with Frank Marshall; made her orchestral debut at age 12 with the

Madrid Symphony under Fernández Arbós. Began touring outside Spain in 1947; made her British debut in 1953 and her American debut in 1955. Concertized with cellist Gaspar Cassadó from 1956, and in 1959 became director of the Marshall Academy in Barcelona. She served as a juror at several international piano competitions during the 1960s; in 1961 she received the Paderewski Memorial Medal in London. Her interpretations of classical and Romantic works have earned her high esteem; several of her recordings of works by Granados and Albéniz have won international prizes.

Larsson, Lars-Erik (Vilner) (b. Äkarp, Skåne, Sweden, 15 May 1908; d. Hälsingborg, 27 Dec. 1986). Composer. He studied at the Stockholm Conservatory (1925–29) with Ernest Ellberg (composition) and Olallo Morales (conducting); went to Vienna and Leipzig on a grant, studying with Berg and Fritz Reuter (1929–30). Upon his return to Sweden he served as choirmaster to the Royal Theater in Stockholm (1930–31); became composer and conductor for Swedish radio (1937–53) in addition to serving as professor of composition at Stockholm Conservatory (1947–59) and music director at Uppsala Univ. (1961–66). Larsson experimented with a number of modern techniques in his compositions, including neoclassicism, polytonality, and a personally devised twelve-tone method.

La Rue, Pierre de (b. probably Tournai, c. 1460; d. Courtrai [Kortrijk], 20 Nov. 1518). Composer. He spent formative years in Italy (he sang at Siena Cathedral during parts of 1482–85), then returned to the Netherlands. From 1489 he sang at s'Hertogenbosch Cathedral; he began to compose about that time. In 1492 he entered the Burgundian *grande chappelle* in Brussels, serving Archduke Maximilian and later his son Philip the Fair (after Maximilian became emperor in 1493). His associates at the court included Agricola, Orto, and Weerbeke; on travels through Europe with Philip the Fair he came to know Isaac, Fevin, and probably Josquin.

On Philip's death in Spain in 1506, La Rue remained briefly there in his widow's service. In 1508 he returned north to enter the Malines court of Philip's sister Margaret of Austria, regent of the Netherlands; an avid musical patron, she held La Rue in high esteem. In 1514 he joined the chapel of her son (later Emperor Charles V). In 1516 he retired as an abbot at Courtrai, where he had maintained lodgings since 1501.

Contemporaries regarded La Rue's music as a model of excellence, along with that of Josquin, Isaac, and Obrecht. Rich in canonic and imitative procedures, it also possesses exceptional melodic fluidity. His works include 30 Masses and a Requiem, several Ordinary sections, about 30 motets (including 7 Magnificats, 6 Salve reginas, and a Lamentations), and about 30 chansons. Petrucci and others published his music extensively in its own time. His name appeared variously translated as Petrus de Vico, Petrus Platensis, Peteren van Straeten, etc., and in diminutives Pierchon, Pierrazon, etc.

Orlande de Lassus.

Laserna, Blas de (b. Corella [Navarre], 4 Feb. 1751; d. Madrid, 8 Aug. 1816). Composer. Little is known of his youth or training; around 1768 he traveled to Madrid, and by 1776 was already a leading composer of tonadillas and zarzuelas. He composed some 700 of the former, in addition to *sainetes, melólogos,* and incidental music for stage works. In 1778 he was appointed *compositor de compañía* for the two theaters in Madrid. In 1790 he became conductor at the Teatro de la Cruz. Among his works are *El majo y la italiana fingida* (1778), *La gitana por amor* (1791), *Idomeneo* (1792).

Bibl.: José Luis de Arrese et al., *El músico Blas de Laserna* (Corella, 1952).

Lassen, Eduard (b. Copenhagen, 13 Apr. 1830; d. Weimar, 15 Jan. 1904). Conductor. His family moved to Brussels when he was a child; studied at the Brussels Conservatory; 1851, won Belgian Prix de Rome, meeting Liszt in Weimar on his travels. In 1857 Liszt conducted his opera *Landgraf Ludwigs Brautfahrt* at Weimar with some success; 1858, he succeeded Liszt as Kapellmeister there, becoming a respected figure in German musical life. He composed 2 other operas, much incidental music, a ballet; orchestral works. Some of his songs were popular in his day.

Lassus, Orlande de [Orlando (di) Lasso, Orlandus Lassus, Roland Delattre] (b. Mons, Hainaut, 1532; d. Munich, 14 June 1594). Composer. Legend holds that as a choirboy with an uncommonly beautiful voice he was thrice kidnapped from his birthplace for service elsewhere. It is not certain, however, that he was ever a chorister in Mons. His first known position was in the service of Ferrante Gonzaga, who passed through the Low Countries in 1544 on his way to Italy. Lassus spent the next decade in Italy, at first with Gonzaga, later in the service of Constantino Castrioto of Naples. By 1553 he was choirmaster at St. John Lateran in Rome, remaining there for a year, then returning to his homeland and settling briefly in Antwerp. His career from 1556 was centered in Munich at the court chapel of Duke Albrecht V of Bavaria, as *maestro di cappella* from 1563, with duties that included some travel in Germany, Flanders, France, and Italy. While employed at Munich, he came to know both Gabrielis, each of whom spent time in the musical establishment he directed. His accomplishments brought formal recognition from Emperor Maximilian II, the French king Charles IX, and Pope Gregory XIII.

Lassus's production of over 2,000 works in nearly every Latin, French, Italian, and German vocal genre known in his time places him among the most prolific and versatile composers of the era. A close connection between text and music, in both small- and large-scale respects, is perhaps the single most prominent characteristic of his output.

His approximately 530 exceptionally fine motets include many religious works, humorous and ceremonial pieces, didactic compositions (bicinia and tricinia), and settings of classical or humanistic texts, such as the *Prophetiae Sibyllarum.* This cyclic work was probably composed at an early date in Italy and exhibits an extreme chromaticism not elsewhere to be found in Lassus's output. It was preserved in a manuscript of 1560 but was printed only in 1600, after the composer's death. Similarly, his *Seven Penitential Psalms* were written around 1560 and copied into a lavish manuscript in Munich but were printed only in 1584. Belated publication was not usual, however. Some of Lassus's motets were printed as early as 1555, and the peak of both composition and printing of his works in this genre came in about 1568–73.

Almost 60 Masses of undoubted attribution survive complete. Few predate the Munich years. Most are parodies, modeled usually on his own sacred motets or, more often, other composers' secular works (until 1570 French, afterwards Italian). Yet one widely popular Mass is a parody of his own chanson *Susanne un jour.* Three fairly late works are for double choir; of the rest, the majority are for 4–6 voices. Among his other liturgical compositions are hymns, canticles (including over 100 Magnificats), responsories for Holy Week, Passions, Lamentations, and some independent pieces for major feasts.

The compositions in the vernacular include about 175 Italian madrigals and villanellas, roughly 150 French chansons, and around 90 sacred and secular German lieder. Production of the Italian works spans his entire adult life but was concentrated in the early years (until the end of his first decade in Munich); a return visit to Italy in 1585 prompted renewed efforts, with the result that some of his latest works have Italian texts. The French chansons likewise span his productive life, but few were written in his later years. Most were composed in Munich but published in Paris (Le Roy & Ballard, Du Chemin) and the Low Countries (Phalèse, Susato, Laet). Their style evolved with the times. His *Une puce* was the first example of *musique mesurée* to be printed (1576). His output of German lieder began comparatively late; the first were published in 1567. The earliest and the secular lieder incorporate a madrigal-like musical style rather than the traditional methods of the Tenorlied. Closer adherence to German musical custom, including some strict use of borrowed melodies, is usual from his second book of lieder on, especially in the sacred pieces.

Lassus's influence was extensive. His compositions were frequently reprinted both during and after his lifetime. Many were intabulated for lute, keyboard, or cittern. The Latin works especially were widely used in Germany in the 16th and 17th centuries as models or source material; such use was encouraged particularly by his pupils Leonhard Lechner and Johannes Eccard. The collection *Magnum opus musicum* (1604), a republication of most of his motets, shows the high regard of his contemporaries, for he is the earliest composer to be honored immediately after his death by such a work of preservation. In general, his prodigious production of finely crafted pieces, cosmopolitan style, creation of hybrid forms (Latin chanson, double-choir drinking song, etc.), and personal connections with Italy (and the Gabrielis) helped to bring Germany into the mainstream of European music. Not only were German composers strongly influenced by his work, but also his widely disseminated output, often published in multilingual volumes or books not limited to a single genre, increasingly drew the attention of other Europeans to his adopted country as a possible source of music fully as well-written, sophisticated, and individual as any produced elsewhere.

Bibl.: *Sämtliche Werke* (Leipzig, 1894–1926; R: New York, 1974); *Sämtliche Werke, neue Reihe* (Kassel, 1956–). *RBM* 39–40 (1985–86). Jerome Roche, *Lassus* (New York, 1982). James Erb, *Orlando di Lasso: A Guide to Research* (New York, 1990). David Crook, *Orlando di Lasso's Imitation Magnificats for Counter-Reformation Munich* (Princeton, 1994).

Lateef, Yusef [Evans, Bill (William)] (b. Chattanooga, Tenn., 9 Oct. 1920). Jazz tenor saxophonist, flutist, and bandleader. Raised in Detroit, he moved to New York in 1946 and worked with big bands, including Dizzy Gillespie's (1949–50). Returning to Detroit, he took his Muslim name while studying flute and composition at Wayne State Univ. He led a quintet that played hard bop and also adapted Asian and Middle Eastern music to jazz. Again in New York, he joined Charles Mingus (1960, 1961) and Cannonball Adderley (1962–64), and led groups. His albums include *Eastern Sounds* (1961) and *Live at Pep's* (1964). By this time he also played oboe, bassoon, and non-Western reeds and flutes. His playing moved toward free jazz (mid-1960s) and disco (late 1970s). In the 1980s he taught in Nigeria.

Lateiner, Jacob (b. Havana, Cuba, 31 May 1928). Pianist. Studied with Jascha Fischermann in Havana, 1934–40; public debut there at age 10. In 1940 won a scholarship to Curtis, where he studied with Isabelle Vengerova. Won the Philadelphia Youth Competition in 1945, then made his professional debut with the Philadelphia Orchestra. Performed at Tanglewood in 1947. Thereafter he maintained a full recital schedule. Also studied composition with Schoenberg in 1950. Played Heifetz–Piatigorsky concerts from 1962. Commissioned Elliott Carter's Piano Concerto, premiered with Boston Symphony in 1967. Introduced Sessions's Third Sonata in 1968. His accounts of late Beethoven highly praised. Beginning 1966 on the faculty of the Juilliard School.

Latham, William P(eters) (b. Shreveport, La., 4 Jan. 1917). Composer. He studied with Goosens at the Cincinnati Conservatory and with Elwell and Hanson at the Eastman School (Ph.D., 1951); taught at Iowa State College (1946–65) and then at North Texas State Univ. until 1984. His works include the opera *Orpheus in Pecan Springs* (1980), 2 symphonies (1950, 1953); several concertos (2 saxophones and orchestra, 1960); orchestral music (*Supernovae,* 1983); works for band (*Revolution!,* 1975; *Dodecaphonic Set,* 1966); *The Music Makers* (wind band, rock group, and guru, 1972); chamber and piano music; Psalm settings, *Music for the Eucharist* (1977), and other choral music; *River to the Sea* (baritone and orchestra, 1942) and songs.

Latilla, Gaetano (b. Bari, 12 Jan. 1711; d. Naples, 15 Jan. 1788). Composer. He was a choirboy at the Bari Cathedral, then from 1726 he studied at the Conservatorio S. Maria di Loreto in Naples. From 1738 he composed comic operas for theaters in Italy. After periods of service at S. Maria Maggiore, Rome (1738–41), and at the Conservatorio della Pietà, Venice (1753–66), he was made second *maestro di cappella* at St. Mark's, Venice. He returned to Naples ca. 1772, possibly to escape the law, where he remained for the rest of his life. In addition to sacred music and instrumental works he composed many operas, including *Li marite a forza* (Naples, 1732), *Gismondo* (Naples, 1737), *Zenobia* (Turin, 1742), *Ezio* (Naples, 1758), and *Antigono* (Naples, 1775).

La Tombelle, (Antoine Louis Joseph Gueyrand) Fernand (Fouant) de (b. Paris, 3 Aug. 1854; d. Château de Fayrac, Dordogne, 13 Aug. 1928). Organist and composer. Studied at the Paris Conservatory (organ, Guilmant; composition, Dubois); an organist in Paris (1885–98, assistant organist, Madeleine), also toured; 1896–1904, professor, later inspector, of harmony, Schola cantorum. Composed 2 operettas, orchestral works, songs, piano pieces; later primarily church music: Masses, oratorios, motets, organ pieces, settings of chant.

Laub, Ferdinand (b. Prague, 19 Jan. 1832; d. Bozen-Gries, near Bolzano, 18 Mar. 1875). Violinist. A child prodigy; 1843–46, student at the Prague Conservatory, winning the notice of Ernst and Berlioz; 1846–47, toured Austria and Germany; 1848–50, solo violinist, Theater an der Wien, Vienna, also studying theory with Sechter. He toured widely in Europe in the 1850s and 1860s as soloist, also appearing frequently in chamber music; concertmaster at Weimar (from 1853) and teacher at the Stern Conservatory, Berlin (1855–57); 1866–73, professor at the Moscow Conservatory, resigning because of consumption.

Laurenti, Bartolomeo Girolamo (b. Bologna, 1644; d. 18 Jan. 1726). Composer. Violin pupil of Gaibara; founding member of the Accademia filarmonica in 1666; violinist at S. Petronio, for a time alongside Torelli, retiring with full pay in 1706; performed elsewhere in Bologna and played concerts throughout Italy. Sonatas and concertos of his were published, though only the sonatas survive. Many other members of the Laurenti family contributed to Italian music in the Baroque era.

Lauri-Volpi, Giacomo (b. Lanuvio, 11 Dec. 1892; d. Valencia, 17 Mar. 1979). Tenor. Studied with Antonio Cotogni and Enrico Rosati at the Accademia di Santa Cecilia in Rome. Debut in Viterbo, 1919 (under the name Giacomo Rubini), as Arturo *(Puritani).* After appearances in Rome (1920) and Florence (1921), Toscanini invited him to sing the Duke of Mantua *(Rigoletto)* at La Scala; he subsequently sang at La Scala through 1940. He also appeared at the New York Metropolitan Opera (1923–33), creating Calaf *(Turandot)* and Rodolfo *(Luisa Miller)* for the U.S. In Rome (1928) he created the title role in Boito's *Nerone.* He published an autobiography in 1939 and 3 works of fiction (1948, 1953, 1955).

Lavallée, Calixa (b. Verchères, Quebec, 28 Dec. 1842; d. Boston, 21 Jan. 1891). Composer. Learned the piano, violin, organ, cornet, studying in Montreal from 1855; from 1857 traveled through Latin America and the U.S.; 1861–62, bandsman in a U.S. army regiment; 1863–65, returned to Canada, then in the U.S. (partly in Boston and New York); 1873–75, studied at the Paris Conservatory, where he composed his concert etude *Le papillon* op. 18, which had some currency. He returned to Canada, and in 1880 composed *O Canada,* now the national anthem; then, beginning to suffer from consumption, moved to Boston as teacher, choirmaster, pianist. Produced a comic opera, *The Widow* (ca. 1881), and a music comedy, *Tiq* (1883). Much of his unpublished music, including large orchestral and vocal works, is lost.

Bibl.: Eugène Lapierre, *Calixa Lavallée,* 2nd rev. ed. (Montreal, 1945; R: 1966).

La Violette, Wesley (b. St. James, Minn., 4 Jan. 1894; d. Escondido, Calif., 29 July 1978). Composer and music educator. He studied at Northwestern Univ., served in the army, and returned to music study at the Chicago Music College (D.Mus., 1925), where he later served as dean. He taught at DePaul (1933–34); was president of the Chicago section of ISCM; and helped organize the first Yaddo festival. On the West Coast he taught privately and at Los Angeles Conservatory, and lectured on philosophy, religion, and the arts; he wrote *Music and Its Makers* (1938), and books on religious mysticism *(The Crown of Wisdom).* His musical compositions (most before 1940) are atonal and contrapuntal but somewhat conservative. They include 2 operas and a ballet; 3 symphonies (1936, 1939, 1952), 4 concertos and other orchestral music; 3 string quartets and other chamber music; ca. 10 vocal and choral works.

Lavista, Mario (b. Mexico City, 3 Apr. 1943). Composer. Student of Roberto Halffter and Héctor Quintanar; later participated in symposia at Darmstadt and Cologne given by Ligeti, Stockhausen, and Xenakis. Founded the contemporary ensemble Quanta in 1970 at Mexico City. His music combines traditional timbres and media with avant-garde elements; works include *5 Pieces* and *Diacronia,* string quartet (1967, 1969); *Game,* solo flute (1970); *Cluster,* piano (1973); *Antifonia,* flute, 2 bassoons, and percussion (1974); *Espejos,* piano, 4-hands (1975); and a piano trio (1976), as well as pieces employing radios, alarm clocks, prepared instruments, and electronic equipment.

Lavry, Marc (b. Riga, 22 Dec. 1903; d. Haifa, 24 Mar. 1967). He studied at the Leipzig Conservatory with Teichmüller, and also privately with Glazunov; did some conducting in Germany and Sweden before emigrating to Palestine in 1935. He achieved popularity there with his symphonic poem *Emek* [The Valley] (1937), followed by a number of works influenced by Jewish cantillation, such as *Shir ha'shirim* [The Song of Songs] and *Tamar and Judah* (1958); Lavry received some commissions from the U.S., which he visited in the mid-1960s. Other works include the folk opera *Dan ha'shomer* [Dan the Guard] (1945), piano concertos, chamber music, etc.

Law, Andrew (b. Milford, Conn., 21 Mar. 1749; d. Cheshire, Conn., 13 July 1821). Composer, singing master, and tunebook compiler. He attended Rhode Island College until 1775, and soon afterward received an M.A. (1778). He then studied theology and in 1787 was ordained a minister. He began compiling tunebooks, and from 1783 he did much traveling, founding singing schools in Philadelphia, New York, Boston, Charleston, and other cities; in several of these he also served as minister. Around 1802–3 he formulated a new form of staffless shape notation, which first employed 4 shapes, later 7. He published tunebooks using these methods, which never became widely popular. Among compilations he published are *Select Harmony* (Cheshire, Conn., 1779); *A Collection of Hymns for Social Worship* (Cheshire, 1782); *The Rudiments of Music* (Cheshire, 1783; 4th ed., 1794); *The Art of Singing* (Cheshire, 1792–93); *The Harmonic Companion and Guide to Social Worship* (Philadelphia, 1807).

Bibl.: Richard Crawford, *Andrew Law, American Psalmodist* (New York, 1981).

Lawes, Henry (b. Dinton, 5 Jan. 1596; d. London, 21 Oct. 1662). Composer, brother of William Lawes. Tutored the daughters of the Earl of Bridgewater, to whom he dedicated his first book of *Ayres and Dialogues* (London, 1653); named Gentleman of the Chapel Royal in 1626 and a member of the King's Musick in 1631; composed music for some court entertainments during the 1630s, coming into contact with poets such as Milton, Carew, and Herrick, all of whose verse he set. Taught during the Commonwealth, also hosting musical evenings at his home; took his old court posts again upon the Restoration. A champion of English music, he spoke out against the pervasiveness of the Italian style. His output includes over 400 vocal compositions preserved in 3 collections (1653, 1655, 1658), many anthologies (including one containing 43 of his works, issued by Playford in 1669), and an autograph manuscript consisting of 325 songs; he also produced a collection of *Choice Psaumes* (1648), several anthems, and instrumental works.

Lawes, William (bapt. Salisbury, 1 May 1602; d. Chester, 24 Sept. 1645). Composer, brother of Henry Lawes. Probably sang at Salisbury Cathedral, where his father was lay vicar; studied with Coprario at the expense of the Earl of Hertford; became a musician to Prince Charles (another pupil of Coprario), continuing in his service after he took the throne in 1625. Accompanied Charles to Oxford in 1642 as part of his private retinue, and was slain in the Civil War battle at Chester in 1645. As the most prominent composer at court from the 1630s onward, he supplied vocal and instrumental music for many masques and plays, along with much church music (principally for 3 voices); he also composed chamber music, keyboard works, and suites for viol consorts. His music remained popular up to the time of Purcell.

Bibl.: Murray Lefkowitz, ed., *William Lawes: Select Consort Music* (London, 1963). Id., *William Lawes* (London, 1960).

Lawrence, Marjorie (b. Dean's March, Australia, 17 Feb. 1909; d. Little Rock, Ark., 13 Jan 1979). Soprano. Studied with Ivor Boustead in Melbourne and Cécile Gilly in Paris. Her successful debut in Monte Carlo (1932) as Elisabeth *(Tannhäuser)* led to a three-year contract at the Paris Opéra. Sang German roles at the New York Metropolitan Opera for eight seasons beginning 1935. In 1941 poliomyelitis left her paralyzed from the waist down. She nevertheless carried on with her career through 1946; later wrote her memoirs, *Interrupted Melody.*

Laws, Hubert (b. Houston, 10 Nov. 1939). Jazz flutist. After graduating from the Juilliard School in 1963, he began recording as a leader. Albums such as *The Laws of Jazz* (1964, with Chick Corea) helped establish the flute as a jazz instrument. While playing in the Metropolitan Opera Orchestra (1968–73) he recorded jazz-rock and jazz versions of classical works. He also gave concerts with Jean-Pierre Rampal.

Layolle, Francesco de (b. Florence, 4 Mar. 1492; d. Lyons, ca. 1540). Composer. Florence was his home until 1518. In 1521 he took up permanent residence in Lyons, working as a composer and music editor for various printers, particularly Moderne. Most of his sacred music is lost; his secular music, which survives in greater quantity, includes many Italian madrigals (most in 2 books published by Moderne in 1540) and about a dozen French chansons.

Bibl.: *Collected Works, CMM* 32/3–6 (1969–73).

Layton, Billy Jim (b. Corsicana, Tex., 14 Nov. 1924). Composer. Having played saxophone and clarinet in school orchestras and dance bands before the war, he studied with Quincy Porter, Gombosi, and Piston at the New England Conservatory, Yale, and Harvard (where he wrote a dissertation on medieval Mass settings under Pirrotta); he spent three years in Rome after winning the Rome Prize in 1954. He taught at Harvard until 1966, when he became professor and chairman of the music department at SUNY–Stony Brook. In an essay in 1965 he proposed a new liberalism in opposition to the constructivism of Boulez and to aleatory procedures; his own works are influenced by jazz and popular idioms, as well as by his knowledge of medieval music. Works include orchestral pieces; *Divertimento* (clarinet, bassoon, trombone, harpsichord, percussion, violin, and cello, 1958–60); *5 Studies* (violin and piano) and other instrumental music; a setting of Dylan Thomas poems for choir and brass.

Lazarof, Henri (b. Sofia, Bulgaria, 12 Apr. 1932). Composer. He studied at the Sofia Academy until 1948, and then at the New Conservatory in Jerusalem, with Petrassi in Rome (1955–57), and at Brandeis (1957–59). Taught at UCLA from 1962 until 1987. He employs serial procedures; some works are scored for instrumentalists and tape. Works include a ballet (*Mirrors, mirrors . . . ,* 1980); *Spectrum* (trumpet, orchestra, and tape, 1972–73), concertos (orchestra, 1977; violin, 1985; clarinet, 1989 and 1991), Choral symphony (symphony no. 3, 1994), Three piece for orchestra (1995), and other orchestral music; string quartets (1956, 1962, 1980), *Cadence VI* (tuba and tape, 1973), *Concertazioni* (trumpet, 6 instruments, and tape, 1973), Trio (winds, 1981), and other chamber music; *Intonazioni e variazioni* (organ, 1980) and other keyboard works; and *Canti* (chorus, 1971).

Lazzari, Sylvio (b. Belzano, Austria, 30 Dec. 1857; d. Suresnes, Paris, 10 June 1944). Composer. He studied law in Austria and Germany, turning to music only in 1882, when he began to work under Guiraud and Franck in Paris. In 1894 he was president of the Wagnerian League in Paris. In its use of cyclic structures his chamber and orchestral music reflects his study with Franck; his operas are Wagnerian; Breton folklore was also a significant influence on his style. Works include 6 operas (*La lépreuse,* composed 1899, staged in Paris, 1912) and a pantomime; incidental music; *Harmonie du soir* (1925) and many other orchestral pieces; chamber and piano music (some for 4-hands); 5 sets of songs, and a piece for women's voices.

Leadbelly. See Ledbetter, Huddie.

Lear, Evelyn (Shulman) (b. Brooklyn, 8 Jan. 1926). Soprano. Studied with John Yard in Washington, D.C., Sergius Kagen at the Juilliard School in New York, and (on a Fulbright Scholarship) Maria Ivogün at the Berlin Musikhochschule. Debut at the Städtische Oper in Berlin (1957) singing the Composer *(Ariadne auf Naxos).* London debut in 1959 singing the *4 Last Songs* of Strauss. She sang Berg's Lulu at the Vienna Staatsoper in 1962 and created the heroine in Werner Egk's *Die Verlobung in San Domingo* in Munich in 1963. After her New York Metropolitan Opera debut in 1967 as Lavinia in Marvin Levy's *Mourning Becomes Electra,* she sang leading roles with that company for 13 seasons, usually in works by Mozart, Strauss, and Berg.

Lebègue, Nicolas-Antoine (b. Laon, ca. 1630; d. Paris, 6 July 1702). Composer. The first certain mention of him is as organist at St. Merry (1664 to his death), though he presumably was established in Paris earlier. A 1666 document at Troyes lists him as "fameux organiste de Paris"; named one of the *organistes du Roy* in 1678; Grigny was his pupil. He produced much keyboard music; his organ music is particularly significant, with several types of sacred and secular compositions and an equally wide range of technical requirements represented.

Bibl.: *Oeuvres complètes d'orgue,* ed. André Pirro (Mainz, 1909).

Lebrun [née Danzi], **Franziska** [Francesca] **(Dorothea)** (b. Mannheim, bapt. 24 March 1756; d. Berlin, 14 May 1791). Soprano. Sister of composer Franz Danzi. She made her debut in 1772 in Schwetzingen in *La contadina in corte* by Sacchini; shortly afterward she was made principal soprano at the Mannheim court, where she created lead roles in Holzbauer's *Günther von Schwarzburg* (1777) and Schweitzer's *Rosamunde* (1780). In 1778 she married the oboist Ludwig August Lebrun. She also sang in Salieri's *Europa riconosciuta* in Milan (1778) and at the Concert spirituel in Paris (1779). Burney praised her ability to copy with perfect accuracy the tone of her husband's oboe sound.

Lebrun, Ludwig August (b. Mannheim, bapt. 2 May 1752; d. Berlin, 16 Dec. 1790). Oboist and composer. His father, possibly Belgian, was oboist at the Mannheim court from at least 1747. By 1764 the 12-year-old Ludwig August, who had been studying oboe with his father, was already playing with the court orchestra on occasion; he became a full member in 1767. After Ludwig's marriage to the soprano Franziska Danzi, the couple toured extensively: Milan, Paris, London, Vienna, Prague, Naples, and Berlin. He was praised for his sweet tone and is reported to have extended the upper range of the instrument beyond the standard of the day. He composed incidental music; concertos and chamber works with oboe.

Lechner, Leonhard [Lechnerus, Leonardus Athesinus] (b. valley of Adige, Austrian Tirol, ca. 1553; d. Stuttgart, 9 Sept. 1606). Composer. The foremost German writer of choral music in the late 16th century. His experiences included being a chorister in Munich under Lassus (ca. 1564–68), a teacher and musician in Nuremberg (by 1575), and a court musician and eventually Kapellmeister in Stuttgart (from 1585). Both Netherlandish and Italian traits are evident in all of his compositions, probably reflecting both his early training and a visit to Italy in the early 1570s. Among his sacred works are 5 books of Latin motets and liturgical pieces, and a German motet-Passion. His numerous vernacular songs and song-motets, mostly secular German works, were inspired by Italian villanellas and madrigals but incorporate complex contrapuntal and textual devices to create entirely new forms and genres.

Bibl.: *Werke,* ed. K. Amelm et al. (Kassel, 1954–).

Leclair, Jean Marie [*l'aîné*] (b. Lyons, 10 May 1697; d. Paris, 22 Oct. 1764). Violinist and composer. Danced at the Lyons opera; traveled to Turin in 1722, perhaps studying violin under Somis; went to Paris the following year, publishing his op. 1 sonatas and gaining the support of the Bonnier family. Quantz relates that Leclair was in Turin as a pupil of Somis in 1726; returning to Paris in 1728, he issued his op. 2 sonatas, made an acclaimed debut at the Concert spirituel, journeyed to London to arrange Walsh's publication of his sonatas, and appeared with Locatelli before the court at Kassel. In 1730 he married the engraver Louise Roussel, who prepared for printing all of his works from op. 2 on. Named *ordinaire de la musique* by Louis XV in 1733, he resigned in 1737 after a clash with Guidon over control of the *musique du Roy;* he was engaged by Princess Anne of Orange, a fine harpsichordist and former student of Handel, and from 1738 until 1743 served three months annually at her court, working in The Hague as a private maestro di cappella for the remainder of the year. Returned to Paris in 1743; his only opera, *Scylla et Glaucus,* premiered in 1746. From 1740 to his murder in 1764 he served the Duke of Gramont. Leclair was renowned as a violinist and as a composer; he successfully drew upon all of Europe's national styles; many suites, sonatas, and concertos survive along with his opera, while some vocal works, ballets, and other stage music is lost.

Bibl.: Neal Zaslaw, "Materials for the Life and Works of Jean-Marie Leclair l'aîné" (diss., Columbia Univ., 1970).

Leclair, Jean-Marie [*le cadet*] (b. Lyons, 23 Sept. 1703; d. there, 30 Nov. 1777). Composer. Brother of Jean-Marie *l'aîné.* Left Lyons to direct the Académie de musique at Besançon in 1732, but returned the following year as violin teacher and leader of the Académie des Beaux-Arts, where he distinguished himself. He held a substantial reputation in France as a violinist; his compositions include 2 books of sonatas and several lost vocal and instrumental works.

Lecocq, (Alexandre) Charles (b. Paris, 3 June 1832; d. there, 24 Oct. 1918). Composer. A good student at the Conservatory, 1849–54, he had to leave to support his family as pianist and teacher; 1856, shared first prize with Bizet in an operetta contest sponsored by Offenbach, but began to produce regularly only in 1864 with one-act works for small theaters. *Fleur-de-thé* (1868) was his first large success, establishing his international reputation. Because of the war he moved to Brussels (1870–74) and had great success there with *Les cent vierges* (1872), *La fille de Madame Angot* (1872), which had an extraordinary international vogue, and *Giroflé-Girofla* (1874). Back in Paris he had a string of successes through the early 1880s; his popularity gradually waned thereafter, and he produced relatively little after 1890.

Bibl.: L. Schneider, *Les maîtres de l'opérette française: Hervé, Charles Lecocq* (Paris, 1924).

Lecuona, Ernesto (b. Guanabacoa, Cuba, 7 Aug. 1896; d. Sta. Cruz de Tenerife, 29 Nov. 1963). Composer. He played piano at a very young age and wrote his first song at 11. He attended the National Conservatory in Havana and continued his studies with Joaquín Nin; formed a dance band, Lecuona's Cuban Boys, which became quite popular when the group toured South America and the U.S. Lecuona's most famous melodies include "Malagueña," "Andalucía," "Siboney," and "Rosa la china."

Ledbetter, Huddie "Leadbelly" (b. Mooringsport, La., 21 Jan. 1885 [or 1888, 1889]; d. New York, 6 Dec. 1949). Folk and blues singer, guitarist, songwriter. Born of black and Cherokee descent, he grew up in the Caddo Lake area, Louisiana, and in Leigh, Texas. He learned concertina from his uncle and guitar on his own. He became a traveling musician in his teens and styled himelf "King of the Twelve-String Guitar." About 1912 he teamed briefly with Blind Lemon Jefferson in Dallas. He was prodigiously strong and prone to violence; he served several jail terms, notably in 1918–25 for murder, and in 1930–34 for attempted murder.

During the latter imprisonment he was discovered by John Lomax of the Library of Congress's Archive of American Folksong; impressed by Leadbelly's skill and enormous folk repertory, Lomax recorded dozens of items and secured his release. Following Lomax to New York, Leadbelly entered a new career, performing largely for white intellectual audiences as a voice of traditions past. He was championed by folklorists Woody Guthrie and Pete Seeger. His music combined skillful guitar work with primitively powerful singing. He toured and recorded extensively; his best known songs include "Goodnight, Irene" and "Rock Island Line."

Ledger, Philip (Stevens) (b. Bexhill-on-Sea, Sussex, 12 Dec. 1937). Organist and conductor. Studied at King's College, Cambridge, and at the Royal College of Music. Was Master of the Music at Chelmsford Cathedral (1961–65), director of music at the Univ. of East Anglia, Norwich (1965–73), artistic director of the Aldeburgh Festival from 1968, director of music and organist at King's College, Cambridge (1974–82), and principal of the Royal Scottish Academy of Music and Drama from 1982.

Leduc, Alphonse (b. Nantes, 9 Mar. 1804; d. Paris, 17 June 1868). Music publisher and composer. From a family of musicians; student at the Paris Conservatory (piano, flute, guitar) to 1826, then returned to Nantes; 1841, founded a music publishing firm in Paris, which was carried on by his descendants. Prolific composer of salon music and didactic works for piano; songs; flute, guitar pieces.

Leduc, Pierre (b. Paris, 1755; d. Netherlands, Oct. 1816). Violinist and music publisher. He was the younger brother of Simon Leduc, with whom he took violin lessons. After his Concert spirituel debut in 1770, he took an interest in music publishing; from 1775 he issued chamber music and symphonies. The house flourished during the 1780s, then waned somewhat during the succeeding decade. In 1803 Pierre passed on the operation to his son August (1779–1823), whose success as a publisher was less complete than his father's.

Leduc, Simon [*l'aîné*] (b. Paris, 15 Jan. 1742; d. there, 20 Jan. 1777). Composer and violinist. He studied with Gaviniès and made his solo debut in 1763 at the Concert spirituel. There he played frequently for the rest of his life, serving in its orchestra from 1763. From 1768 he held a privilege to publish several of his chamber and orchestral works; from 1773 he was co-director of the Concert spirituel. Among his published works are symphonies, *symphonies concertantes,* concertos, and trio sonatas.

Bibl.: Barry S. Brook, "Simon Le Duc *l'aîné,* a French Symphonist at the Time of Mozart," *MQ* 48 (1962): 498–513.

Lee, Brenda [Tarpley, Brenda Mae] (b. Lithonia, Ga., 11 Dec. 1944). Popular singer. She was associated with Red Foley and performed with him and on the television shows of Ed Sullivan and Bob Hope; from 1957 she released popular and rock recordings including "I'm Sorry" (1960), "Fool #1" (1961), and "Losing You" (1963). In the 1970s she began recording country material, achieving success with songs such as "Big Four Poster Bed" (1974) and "The Cowgirl and the Daddy" (1980).

Lee, Dai-Keong (b. Honolulu, 2 Sept. 1915). Composer. He prepared for a medical career at the Univ. of Hawaii, but then studied music with Sessions and Jacobi at Juilliard (1938–41), with Copland at the Berkshire Music Center (1941), and with Luening at Columbia (M.A., 1951). Some of his compositions use Polynesian elements such as tetratonic scales, certain percussion instruments, Hawaiian chants, and native dances. He has written stage works (including opera and musical plays, ballet, and incidental music) and film scores; orchestral music includes *Polynesian Suite,* composed in 1958 in celebration of Hawaii's statehood; other works include chamber and piano music, songs, and *Meleolili* (Joyful Songs based on Hawaiian chants; soloists, chorus, and orchestra, 1960).

Lee, Noël (b. Nanking, of American parents, 25 Dec. 1924). Composer and pianist. He studied at Harvard and the Boston Conservatory, and with Boulanger in Paris. Taught piano in the U.S., Belgium, France, and England, and recorded more than 100 discs, including complete works of Debussy, Ravel, Stravinsky, and Copland. His compositions include a ballet (1953), chamber music for woodwinds and strings, much of it with piano or harpsichord (*Convergences,* flute and harpsichord, 1972); piano music (including *3 Préludes néoclassiques,* 1951); *Devouring Time* (after Shakespeare, chorus and piano, 1957), *Five Songs* (after Lorca, soprano, flute, and guitar, 1955), and other vocal music.

Lee, Peggy [Egstrom, Norma Dolores] (b. Jamestown, N.D., 26 May 1920). Popular singer and actress. From 1936 toured with dance bands including Will Osborne's; began recording popular songs in swing styles (including "Why Don't You Do Right?" with Benny Goodman, 1942; "Mañana," 1947). Many of her songs were associated with films (including "Bali Ha'i," *South Pacific,* 1949; "Lover," *Love Me Tonight,* 1952); acting appearances included *The Jazz Singer* (1953).

Leedy, Douglas (b. Portland, Oreg., 3 Mar. 1938). Composer. He studied at Pomona College, Berkeley (M.A., 1962), and at the Berkshire Music Center (1958). From 1960 to 1965 he played French horn in the Oakland Symphony; then studied contemporary music in Poland; studied with K. V. Narayanaswamy in Madras (1979–80). Taught at UCLA (1967–70), the Centro Simón Bolivar (Caracas), Reed College, and the Univ. of Southern California. In the 1970s he abandoned equal temperament. From 1980 active as a conductor and editor of early music (conducting the Portland Baroque Orchestra, 1984–85). Works include a chamber opera (*Sebastian,* after J. S. Bach documents,

1971–74), *Entropical Paradise: 6 Sonic Environments* (electronic instruments, 1969); *Symphoniae Sacrae* (soprano, viola da gamba, harpsichord, 1976), *Music for Meantone Organ* (1984) and music for harpsichord; *4 Hymns* (Rigveda, chorus and gamelan, 1982–83); *Pastorale* (solo voices, chorus, retuned piano, 1987).

Lees [Lysniansky], **Benjamin** (b. Harbin, Manchuria, 8 Jan. 1924). Composer. His parents were Russian, but he was brought to the U.S. at an early age. After service during the Second World War he studied at the Univ. of Southern California with Dahl, Antheil, and others (1945–48). He lived abroad (in France, Austria, and Finland) from 1954 to 1961, and then taught at Peabody Conservatory (1962–64 and 1966–68), Queens College (1964–66), the Manhattan School (1972–74), and Juilliard (1976–77). His style is not defined by any particular school, but involves expanded tonality and clear formal designs. He has written 3 operas and a ballet; *The Trumpet of the Swan* (after E. B. White, narrator and orchestra, 1972); 5 symphonies (no. 5, 1988), *Borealis* (1993), and several concertos (for orchestra, chamber orchestra, violin, string quartet, oboe, wind quintet, brass choir, French horn, cello and piano, and 2 for piano), *Echoes of Normandy* (tenor, tape, organ, orchestra, 1994) and other orchestral music; *Soliloquy Music for King Lear* (flute, 1975), sonatas for violin and piano (1953, 1973,1991), and for cello and piano (1981), *Fantasy Variations* (piano, 1984), and other instrumental music; choral music and songs.

Leeuw, Ton [Antonius Wilhelmus Adrianus] **de** (b. Rotterdam, 16 Nov. 1926). Composer. He took piano and composition with Toebosch and Badings (1947–49), then worked with Messiaen and Hartmann in Paris (1949–50); also studied ethnomusicology with Jaap Kunst (1950–54). He was employed as a music producer for Dutch Radio from 1954 until 1960, and taught composition and contemporary music at the conservatories in Utrecht and Amsterdam (from 1960) as well as at Amsterdam Univ. (from 1963). His earliest works were heavily influenced by Pijper's germ-cell principle; during the late 1950s and early 1960s he experimented with "static" music, as well as serial methods (sometimes extended to dynamics and duration, as in the First String Quartet), aleatoric, and mathematical techniques. In 1961 he traveled to India and became fascinated with both the "objectivity" of Eastern music and its sophisticated use of rhythm; shortly afterward he devised his own system of proportional rhythmic notation, first used in his *Symphonies of Winds* (1963). From 1965 he experimented with spatial relations in his compositions, sometimes having the musicians move about during the performance. He composed dramatic works (*Alceste,* television opera, 1963; *De droom* [The Dream], opera, 1963; *Hiob* [Job], radio oratorio, 1956; *Antigone,* opera, 1991); orchestral works (Concerto grosso, strings, 1946; *Treurmuziek in memoriam Willem Pijper,* 1946; Symphony, strings, percussion, 1950; Symphony, strings, 1951; *Mouvements rétrogrades,* 1957; *Ombres,* 1961; *Symphonies of Winds,* 1963; *Spatial Music I,* 1966; *Spatial Music V,* 1971; *Résonances,* 1985); instrumental music (String Trio, 1948; String Quartet no. 1, 1958; *Antiphony,* wind quintet, tape, 1960; *Spatial Music II,* percussion ensemble, 1967; *Rime,* flute, harp, 1974); songs; piano music.

LeFanu, Nicola (Frances) (b. Wickham Bishops, Essex, 28 Apr. 1947). Composer. Daughter of composer Elizabeth Maconchy. She attended St. Hilda's College, Oxford, and the Royal College of Music; studied composition with Petrassi in Siena and Davies at Dartington. Taught at Morley College in London (1970–75) and at King's College, London, from 1977. Compositions include the operas *The Story of Mary O'Neill* (radio, 1989), *The Green Children* (1990), *Blood Wedding* (1992); other theatrical works (*Antiworld,* dancer, ensemble, 1972; *The Last Laugh,* 1973; *Dawnpath,* soprano, baritone, dancer, ensemble, 1977); orchestral works (*Preludio,* chamber orchestra, 1968; *The Hidden Landscape,* 1973; *Wind among the Pines,* soprano, orchestra, 1987); chamber music (Variations, oboe quartet, 1968; *Omega,* organ, 1972; String Quartet, 1988); choral works; solo vocal music.

Lefébure-Wély, Louis James Alfred (b. Paris, 13 Nov. 1817; d. there, 31 Dec. 1869). Organist and composer. Son of the organist at St. Roch, Paris, for whom he substituted from 1825, and succeeded (through the queen's influence) in 1831–47; 1832, student of Benoist at the Paris Conservatory (first prize, piano, organ, 1835); 1847–58, organist at the Madeleine; from 1863 at St. Sulpice. One of the most fashionable Parisian organists of the day, he was a celebrated improviser. Noted for salon music for piano, especially the nocturne *Les cloches du monastère* op. 54, and the concert fantasy *Titania,* and organ music, including the collections *L'organiste moderne* and *L'office catholique.*

Lefebvre, Charles Édouard (b. Paris, 19 June 1843; d. Aix-les-Bains, 8 Sept. 1917). Composer. Earned a law degree; then a student at the Paris Conservatory. Co-winner of the Prix de Rome in 1870; returned from Rome in 1873 after touring Greece and the Near East; winner, Prix Chartier (1884, 1891); from 1895, professor of the ensemble class, Paris Conservatory. Composed much instrumental music, especially the wind suites opp. 57, 122; operas, especially the sacred drama *Judith* (1874) and *Djelma* (Opéra, 1894); cantatas; sacred music; choruses; 35 songs.

Lefèvre, (Jean) Xavier (b. Lausanne, 6 Mar. 1763; d. Paris, 9 Nov. 1829). Clarinetist. Studied the clarinet in Paris with Yost; 1778, joined the band of Gardes françaises; 1791–1817, played in the Opéra orchestra; 1795–1825, taught at the Conservatory, producing its official *Méthode de clarinette* (1802, R: 1974); 1807–29, member of the imperial (later royal) chapel. He composed 7 concertos, chamber music with clarinet; used a sixth key, but not the first to do so, as is sometimes claimed.

Le Flem, Paul (b. Lézardrieux, Côtes-du-Nord, 18 Mar. 1881; d. Trégastel, 31 July 1984). Composer and critic. He studied at the Paris Conservatory with Lavignac (1899); traveled in Russia; then continued his studies in philosophy at the Sorbonne and music at the Schola cantorum (1904). He succeeded Roussel as counterpoint teacher at the Schola (1923–39); conducted the choir of St. Gervais; and was chorusmaster at the Opéra-comique. He composed tonal music in conventional forms and genres, but his criticism for *Comoedia* (1921–37) was consistently open-minded. Works include 4 operas, a ballet, the choral fable *Aucassin et Nicolette* (1908), radio and film scores; 3 symphonies (1907, 1956, 1971) and other orchestral and instrumental music; choral music (including settings of Breton folk songs); and several early songs.

Bibl.: Geneviève Bernard-Krauss, *Hundert Jahre französischer Musikgeschichte in Leben und Werk Paul Le Flems* (Frankfurt am Main, 1993).

Leginska [Liggins], **Ethel** (b. Hull, England, 13 April 1886; d. Los Angeles, 26 Feb. 1970). Pianist, composer, and conductor. Studied at the Hoch Conservatory in Frankfurt; later in Vienna and in Berlin. Made her debut in London at age 16, then made concert tours in Europe before coming to the U.S. in 1913. Began composing in 1914; studied with Bloch in 1918. Her works include songs, chamber music, symphonic poems, and 2 operas. Nervous disorders forced her to retire as a pianist in 1926. She studied conducting, then directed major orchestras in Europe before conducting the Boston Philharmonic (1926–27), the Boston Woman's Symphony (1926–30), and the Woman's Symphony of Chicago (1927–29). She moved to Los Angeles in 1940 and taught piano into the 1950s.

Legley, Vic(tor) (b. Hazebrouck, 18 June 1915). Composer. He studied viola and composition at the Brussels Conservatory (1934–37); and after the war studied composition with Absil. He won the Belgian second Rome Prize (1943). From 1936 to 1948 he played viola in the Belgian Symphony; in the latter year he became music producer for the Flemish section of Belgian Radio, and in 1962 was head of serious music. He taught at the Brussels Conservatory (harmony from 1949; composition from 1959) and at the Chapelle musicale Reine Elisabeth (from 1950); was elected to the Belgian Royal Academy in 1965 (and served as president in 1972). Works include an opera (*La farces des deux nues,* H. Closson, 1939–63) and a radio drama (1950); 6 symphonies (1942–76), several concertos (violin, piano, harp, viola, alto saxophone, and cello; a concerto grosso for violin, alto saxophone, and strings, 1976), and other orchestral music; 4 string quartets (1941–63), *Middagmuziek* (flute, clarinet, bassoon, horn, string quartet, and double bass, 1948), and other chamber music; piano music; a few songs and choral works (*Mijn gegeven woord,* tenor and piano, 1976).

Legrand, Michel (b. Paris, 24 Feb. 1932). Popular composer and arranger. He studied at the Paris Conservatory (1943–50) and became known as an orchestrator through an engagement with Maurice Chevalier in 1954–55; subsequently he worked with Henri Salvador and Claude Nougans. Several of his film scores earned Oscars (including *Les parapluies de Cherbourg,* 1965; *Summer of 42,* 1971); his songs "La valse des lilas" and "Comme elle est longue" were also popular.

Legrant [Lemacherier], **Guillaume** (fl. 1418–56). Composer. Sang in the papal chapel from 1418 until at least 1421, and held church benefices in the region of Rouen until 1449. He may have belonged to the chapel of Duke Charles of Orléans in the mid-1450s. His 3 extant Mass movements, exceptionally for polyphony of their time, distinguish soloistic from choral sections. Three virelays also survive.

Legrenzi, Giovanni (bapt. Clusone, 12 Aug. 1626; d. Venice, 27 May 1690). Composer. Named organist at S. Maria Maggiore, Bergamo, in 1645, becoming chaplain there in 1651; appointed *maestro di cappella* at the Accademia dello Spirito Santo, Ferrara, in 1656, remaining until about 1665 and coming under the influential patronage of Hippolito Bentivoglio there; his first dramatic works date from this period. He failed in attempts to gain posts at Vienna (1665), Milan (1669), Parma (1670), and Bologna (1671), and was forced to turn down an offer from the court of France because of illness. Resident in Venice from about 1671, he served first at the Conservatorio dei mendicanti, then at the Oratorio S. Maria della Fava; after an initially unsuccessful effort to become maestro at St. Mark's, he was named vice-maestro there in 1681, and was promoted to maestro in 1685. His Venetian years also included spans of operatic activity, with several such works of his presented in the periods 1675–78 and 1681–84. In addition to his dramatic works, he produced church music, several collections of sonatas, and secular vocal works; the counterpoint, thematic design, formal structure, and rhythmic profile of his instrumental music in particular point toward the late Baroque style of Vivaldi and others.

Bibl.: Stephen Bonta, "The Sonatas of Giovanni Legrenzi" (diss., Harvard Univ., 1964).

Lehár, Franz [Ferencz] **(Christian)** (b. Komáron, Hungary, 30 Apr. 1870; d. Bad Ischl, 24 Oct. 1948). Composer and conductor. He was the leading operetta composer of the early 20th century, whose most successful work was *Die lustige Witwe* (The Merry Widow; Theater an der Wien, 30 Dec. 1905). His father was a horn player and military bandmaster who sent his son to study violin at the Prague Conservatory at the age of 12. From 1888 he played violin in theater orchestras. In the 1890s he was active as a military bandmaster; by 1899 he was in Vienna, where his many waltzes and marches were increasingly popular. He left the military bands in 1901 to conduct theater orchestras in Vienna and to compose. His opera *Kukuska* (Leipzig, 1896) and early operettas were not particularly successful, but when he was called in as a substitute composer for *Die lustige Witwe,* his reputation for stage music was established. In the 1920s he wrote many successful operettas for the tenor Tauber; but after *Giuditta* (Vienna Staatsoper, 20 Jan. 1934) he wrote no more new stage works. In 1935 he founded the publishing house Glocken Verlag, which acquired the rights to most of his works. He is credited with raising the standards of operetta composition through his skill as a melodist and orchestrator, his careful counterpoint, and his use of more serious subjects; many later works are revisions of earlier operettas. He used an expanded tonal framework similar to that of Puccini, who was a close friend.

Works: an opera, ca. 30 operettas (*Die Graf von Luxembourg,* Vienna, 1909; and *Das Land des Lächelns,* Berlin, 1929, a revision of *Die gelbe Jacke,* 1923), and 5 film scores (*Une nuit à Vienne,* 1937); 3 symphonic poems, 2 violin concertos and other orchestral works; some 65 waltzes ("Gold und Silber" op. 79), marches, and dances; piano music; some 90 songs.

Bibl.: Stan Czech, *Franz Lehár: Sein Leben und Sein Werk* (Vienna, 1940; R: 1957). Bernard Green, *Gold und Silver: The Life and Times of Franz Lehár* (London, 1970). Max Schönherr, *Franz Lehár: Bibliographie zu Leben und Werk* (Vienna, 1970). Christian Marten, *Die Operette als Spiegel der Gesellschaft: Franz Lehárs "Die lustige Witwe": Versuch einer sozialen Theorie der Operette* (New York, 1988).

Lehmann, Hans Ulrich (b. Biel, canton of Bern, 4 May 1937). Composer and cellist. He studied with Boulez and Stockhausen in master classes in composition at the Basel Academy of Music (1960–63); taught cello and theory at the Academy (1964–72), musicology at the Univ. of Zurich (from 1969) and composition and theory at the Musikhochschule in Zurich (from 1972). His works employ serial procedures, but the approach became freer in the later 1960s. Works include *Streuungen* (3 choruses and 2 orchestras, 1975–76); *Homage à Mozart* (chamber orchestra, 1978–79), *Aphorismus* (chamber orchestra, 1985), and other orchestral music; *Structures transparentes* (clarinet, viola, and piano, 1960), *Stroiking* (percussion ensemble, 1982), and other instrumental music; *Bringen um zukommen* (soprano and 5 instruments, 1972) and a few other vocal pieces.

Lehmann, Lilli (b. Würzburg, 24 Nov. 1848; d. Berlin, 16 May 1929). Soprano. She grew up in Prague, where her mother taught voice. Made her debut at the Prague Landestheater in 1867 as Mozart's First Lady *(Magic Flute).* In 1868 she was engaged by the Danzig Municipal Theater, in 1869 by the Leipzig Opera. Invited to Berlin in 1870 to sing Queen Marguerite *(Les Huguenots),* she stayed with that company as a coloratura soprano until 1886, when she broke her contract to sing at the New York Metropolitan Opera. By the time she left New York in 1891 she had sung over 170 roles there, given recitals, and married the tenor Paul Kalisch. Back in Berlin she was not welcomed into the Staatsoper company until Emperor Wilhelm II intervened. Afterwards she quickly regained her public as an outstanding Wagnerian heroine. She was later considered exceptional for her way with Mozart roles. She wrote several books, including *Meine Gesangskunst* (1902) and *Mein Weg* (1913).

Lehmann, Liza [Elizabeth] **(Nina Mary Frederica)** (b. London, 11 July 1862; d. Pinner, Middlesex, 19 Sept. 1918). Composer. Studied singing and composition on the Continent and in London; 1885–94, a concert singer in England; began to publish songs by the late 1880s, and had great success with her cycle for 4 voices *In a Persian Garden* (1896). Also composed stage works, including the musical comedy *Sergeant Brue* (London, 1904; New York, 1905) and *Everyman,* produced by Beecham in 1916; cantatas, piano pieces. Memoirs: *The Life of Liza Lehmann, by Herself* (London, 1919).

Lehmann, Lotte (b. Perleberg, 27 Feb. 1888; d. Santa Barbara, Calif., 26 Aug. 1976). Soprano. Studied with Erna Tiedke and Eva Reinhold at the Berlin Musikhochschule, later with Mathilde Mallinger. Sang German roles at the Hamburg Opera from 1910, at the Vienna Staatsoper from 1914. Created Strauss's Composer (*Ariadne,* 1916), Dyer's Wife (*Frau,* 1919), and Christine (*Intermezzo,* 1924) at the composer's request. U.S. debut in 1930 as Sieglinde *(Die Walküre)* with the Chicago Civic Opera. Emigrated to the U.S. in 1933; naturalized in 1938. Sang with the New York Metropolitan Opera, 1934–45. In later years she turned more to song. Gave her farewell recital in 1951. Wrote a novel, *Orplid, mein Land* (1937); two books of memoirs, *Anfang und Aufstieg* (1937), *My Many Lives* (1948); and a book on the interpretation of song, *More Than Singing* (1945).

Leibowitz, René (b. Warsaw, 17 Feb. 1913; d. Paris, 29 Aug. 1972). Musicologist, composer, and conductor. From 1930 to 1933 he studied with Schoenberg and Webern in Berlin and Vienna; in 1933 he had lessons from Ravel in orchestration. He was active as a conductor from 1937; in 1945 he moved to Paris, where he founded the International Festival of Chamber Music, at which many Paris premieres of works of Schoenberg and others were presented. In the 1930s he was known as an authority on the twelve-tone method, when information about it was still scarce; among his students were Boulez and Henze. His first two volumes on that method were well received (*Schönberg et son école,* 1946; *Instruction à la musique de douze sons,* 1949), but later writings were more controversial. His compositions are similar to those of Schoenberg and Berg; his last opera (*Les espagnols à Venise,* Grenoble, 1970) combines expressionism with the twelve-tone method. He wrote 5 operas; *Träume vom Tod und vom Leben* (symphonie funèbre, soloists and orchestra, 1955); a symphony, 3 piano concertos and other works for orchestra; 4 string quartets, *Humoresque* (percussion, 1958), and much other chamber music; piano music; choral and solo vocal music. Writings include *L'artiste et sa conscience* (1950), *L'évolution de la musique, de Bach à Schönberg* (1952), *Histoire de l'Opéra* (1957), *Schönberg* (1962), *Le compositeur et son double* (1971), and *Les fantômes de l'opéra* (1973).

Leider, Frida (b. Berlin, 18 Apr. 1888; d. there, 4 June 1975). Soprano. Studied privately with Otto Schwartz in Berlin. Debut in Halle in 1915 as Venus *(Tannhäuser).* After engagements in Rostock, Königsberg, and Hamburg, she joined the Berlin Staatsoper as a dramatic soprano (1923–40). There and at Covent Garden (1924–38), Bayreuth (1928–38), Chicago (1928–32), and the Metropolitan Opera (1933–34) she was celebrated for her portrayals of Wagner heroines (Elsa, Isolde, Fricka, Sieglinde, Brünnhilde, Kundry), as Leonore *(Fidelio),* and as the Marschallin *(Rosenkavalier).* As a teacher she headed the Studio of the Berlin Staatsoper (1945–52) and taught at the Musikhochschule in Berlin-Charlottenburg. Her memoirs, *Das war mein Teil,* appeared in 1959.

Leifs, Jón (b. Sólheimer Farm, Iceland, 1 May 1899; d. Reykjavík, 30 July 1968). Composer and conductor. He studied at the Reykjavík College of Music, and then in Leipzig (1916–22) with Szendrei, Scherchen, Lohse, Graener, and Teichmüller. He remained in Germany for several decades, conducting concerts in various towns. He founded the Union of Icelandic Artists (1928) and the Icelandic Composers' Society (1945), and served as adviser to Icelandic Radio (1934–37). His compositions, descended from the German Romantic tradition, occasionally make use of Icelandic folk music. Works include orchestral music (*Galdra-Loftur Suite* op. 6; *Baldur* op. 34; *Iceland Ouvertüre* op. 9, 1926); string quartets; sacred works; piano music.

Leigh, Walter (b. London, 22 June 1905; d. near Tobruk, Libya, 12 June 1942). Composer. He won an organ scholarship to Christ's College, Cambridge; studied there under Edward Dent and graduated in 1926. He continued his studies under Hindemith at the Berlin Hochschule für Musik (1927–29), and from 1931 to 1932 served as musical director at the Festival Theater in Cambridge; he was killed in action during World War II. Leigh was particularly known for his stage music, which included the 2 light operas *The Pride of the Regiment, or Cashiered for His Country* (Midhurst, 1931) and *The Jolly Roger, or The Admiral's Daughter* (Manchester, 1933).

Leighton, Kenneth (b. Wakefield, Yorkshire, 2 Oct. 1929; d. Edinburgh, 24 Aug. 1988). Composer. He studied composition with Rose at Queen's College, Oxford (B.Mus., 1951), continuing his studies in Rome with Petrassi. He served as a lecturer in composition at Edinburgh Univ. (1956–68), lecturer in music at Worcester College, Oxford (1968–70), and in 1970 was appointed professor of music at Edinburgh. Leighton's compositions employ lyrical melodies and virtuosic solo writing; some works make use of serial techniques. Compositions include opera (*Columba,* 1978); vocal works (*The Birds,* soprano, tenor, chorus, strings, piano, 1954; *The Light Invisible,* tenor, chorus, orchestra, 1958; *Missa brevis,* soprano, alto, tenor, bass, 1967; Mass, treble voices, organ, 1979); orchestral works (Symphony, 1949; Piano Concerto no. 1, 1951; Violin Concerto, 1952; Piano Concerto no. 2, 1960; no. 3, Estivo, 1969; Symphony no. 2, Sinfonia mistica, soprano, chorus, orchestra, 1974; Symphony no. 3, 1986); instrumental music (*Fantasia on the Name BACH,* viola, piano, 1955; String Quartet no. 2, 1957); piano pieces (Sonata no. 1, 1948; no. 2, 1953; *Fantasia contrappuntistica,* 1956; Sonata, 1972); organ music; other vocal music including motets and anthems.

Leinsdorf [Landauer], **Erich** (b. Vienna, 4 Feb. 1912; d. Zurich, 11 Sept. 1993). Conductor. Studied piano, cello, and composition at the Vienna Staatsakademie, 1931–33. Assistant to Bruno Walter (1934) and Toscanini (1935–37) at Salzburg; assistant conductor at the New York Metropolitan Opera, 1937; second conductor, 1938–43. Music director of the Cleveland Orchestra, 1943; served in the military, then as music director of the Rochester Philharmonic, 1947–56. After a brief tenure in 1956 as director of the New York City Opera, he conducted at the New York Metropolitan, 1957–62. Music director of the Boston Symphony Orchestra, 1962–69. Thereafter he was much in demand as guest conductor. His memoirs, *Cadenza,* appeared in 1976; a widely praised essay on conducting, *The Composer's Advocate,* in 1981.

Le Jeune, Claude [Claudin] (b. Valenciennes, 1528–30; d. Paris, buried 26 Sept. 1600). Composer. His large and varied output reflects in its style both his Netherlandish roots and his adult life in Paris: Flemish contrapuntal techniques and concern with sonority as well as the comparatively lighter idiom of Paris are both evident. His Protestant faith influenced both the nature of his sacred compositions (mostly Psalm settings, ranging from simple harmonizations of Genevan melodies to elaborate Psalm-motets) and the course of his career, pursued from 1560 under the protection of French Huguenot nobles and often at Huguenot courts. His works of all sorts show a concern with text-music relationships, including but not limited to rhythms determined according to the precepts of Baïf's Académie de poésie et de musique, to which he belonged from its inception in 1570. Such rhythms are manifested most clearly in his many *chansons mesurées,* a genre of which he was one of the chief advocates. Certain pieces encompass chromaticisms resulting from experiments with the Greek genera as understood in the Académie. Among his compositions are also Latin sacred music, sacred and secular chansons *non mesurées,* and Italian madrigals. Most of his music remained in manuscript until after his death but, once printed, was widely popular and influential.

Lekeu, Guillaume (Jean Joseph Nicolas) (b. Heusy, near Verviers, Belgium, 20 Jan. 1870; d. Angers, 21 Jan. 1894). Composer. In 1879 his family moved to Poitiers and in 1888 to Paris so that he could study there; in 1889 he visited Bayreuth. He had music lessons from Franck and advice from d'Indy; composed prolifically from 15, including String Quartet (1887), Cello Sonata (1888), Piano Sonata (1891), Violin Sonata (1892, his best-known work, commissioned by Ysaÿe), *Fantaisie symphonique sur deux airs populaires angevins* (1892). In 1891 he shared second prize, Belgian Prix de Rome. He died of typhus. His last works were completed by d'Indy.

Le Maire, Jean (b. Chaumont-en-Bassigny, ca. 1581; d. ca. 1650). Mathematician and inventor. Active in Toulouse and Paris; named *Gentilhomme de la chambre du Roi* by Louis XIII. His interests included architecture and typography; in music he created an even-tempered scale of 8 scale degrees and invented a lute called an *almérie,* along with a new notational system for it. Mersenne was an ardent supporter, but his idea failed to gain wide acceptance.

Le Maistre, Mattheus [Matthaeus] (b. near Liège, ca. 1505; d. Dresden, before Apr. 1577). Composer. Kapellmeister at the court at Dresden from 1554, succeeding Johann Walter, until his retirement in 1568. His works reflect his Protestantism and his strong conservative bent. Among them are Masses and motets in Latin and sacred and secular songs in either German or Latin.

Lemare, Edwin (Henry) (b. Ventnor, Isle of Wight, 9 Sept. 1865; d. Hollywood, 24 Sept. 1934). Organist and composer. He studied at the Royal Academy of Music and taught there from 1892. He was very prominent as a recitalist and held various organ positions in Cardiff and London; toured the U.S. and Canada in 1900; taught organ at Carnegie Institute in Pittsburgh (1902–5). He played at the San Francisco Exhibition (1915) and was municipal organist there in 1917; he also held positions in Portland, Maine, and in Chattanooga. He composed some 200 works for organ, choir, or solo voice and made organ transcriptions of 600–800 works. *Organs I Have Met: The Autobiography of Edwin H. Lemare, 1866–1934, together with Reminiscences by His Wife and Friends* (1956) contains a list of works.

Lemmens, Jacques Nicolas (b. Zoerle-Parwijs, near Antwerp, 3 Jan. 1823; d. Zemst, near Malines, 30 Jan. 1881). Organist and composer. Son and pupil of a church organist; 1839 and 1841–45, star pupil, Brussels Conservatory; organ professor there, 1849–69, doing much to raise the level of playing in Belgium, and spreading Bach's organ music there and in France. His own compositions aimed at creating a Catholic music based on plainchant. His *École d'orgue basée sur le plain-chant romain* (1862) was widely used, and some of his organ works are still played. In 1879 he established a school at Malines for church musicians.

Lemoyne, Jean-Baptiste (b. Eymet, 3 Apr. 1751; d. Paris, 30 Dec. 1796). Composer. Student at Berlin from 1770 under J. G. Graun, Kirnberger, and J. A. P. Schulz; worked in Warsaw, then returned to France, where his opera *Electre* was given at Paris in 1782; though it failed, his next effort, *Phèdre* (1786), was a success. Journeyed to Italy in 1787; several more of his dramatic works were performed in Paris during the 1790s; some had Revolutionary themes, but none was very popular. His son Gabriel (1772–1815), a pianist and composer, wrote songs, chamber works, 2 piano concertos, and solo piano pieces.

Lendvai, Erwin (b. Budapest, 4 June 1882; d. Epsom, Surrey, 31 Mar. 1949). Composer and conductor. He studied with Koessler and in Milan with Puccini; taught composition at the conservatory in Frankfurt and at the Klindworth–Scharwenka conservatory in Berlin (1919–22). Lendvai also taught at the Hamburg Volksmusikschule (1923–25) and served as a choral conductor in Munich, Erfurt (Switzerland), and ultimately London. His compositions include the opera *Elga* (Mannheim, 1916), a symphony (1909), the choral suite *Nippon;* chamber music.

Lenepveu, Charles (Ferdinand) (b. Rouen, 4 Oct. 1840; d. Paris, 16 Aug. 1910). Composer. Studied law in Paris at his father's wish, secretly studying music; 1863–65, student at the Paris Conservatory (Prix de Rome, 1865). His opera *Le florentin* won a government competition (1869) but failed at the Opéra-comique (1874), and he was unable to get his grand opera *Velléda* performed in Paris (London, 1882, with Patti). Also composed a sacred opera, *Judith* (Rouen, 1886), and 2 one-act opéras comiques. Taught harmony, 1880–94, Paris Conservatory (professor from 1891, professor of composition from 1894). He composed relatively little after the 1890s.

Leng, Alfonso (b. Santiago, Chile, 11 Feb. 1884; d. there, 7 Nov. 1974). Composer. A dentist by profession, he studied music under Enrique Soro, though was basically self-taught. He was active in the humanities circle Group of Ten, a significant force for artistic modernism in Chile. His music has a Romantic, often impressionistic character, rich in dissonance. Works include the symphonic poem *La muerte de Alsino* (1921); several *Doloras* for both piano (1901–14) and orchestra (1920); *Fantasía,* piano and orchestra (1936); and *Salmo 77,* chorus and orchestra (1941), in addition to many piano pieces (some of which he transcribed for orchestra) and songs. The August–September 1957 issue of *Revista música chilena* was dedicated to him and his compositions.

Lennon, John [Winston] (b. Liverpool, 9 Oct. 1940; d. New York, 8 Dec. 1980). Rock singer, songwriter, pianist, and guitarist. He began working with Paul

McCartney and George Harrison in 1957; they were known first as the Quarrymen and later the Beatles (Ringo Starr joined in 1962); Lennon and McCartney collaborated on the majority of their songs. Their early recordings revived American rock-and-roll and rhythm-and-blues of the 1950s (*Meet the Beatles,* 1964, including "I Want To Hold Your Hand"; *Hard Day's Night,* 1964); later they experimented with non-Western musics, contemporary classical music, and San Francisco psychedelic rock (*Rubber Soul,* 1965; *Sgt. Pepper's Lonely Hearts Club Band,* 1967). They ceased performing in 1966, and their last albums explore advanced studio recording techniques (*The Beatles* ["The White Album"], 1968; *Abbey Road,* 1969); they also made several movies. They were the most important rock band of the 1960s; their unprecedented popularity and stylistic derivation from American, predominantly black styles revolutionized popular music in both England and the U.S.

After the group's dissolution in 1970 Lennon pursued a solo career in the U.S., mainly in collaboration with his wife, Yoko Ono. While his albums met with uneven success (*John Lennon/Plastic Ono Band,* 1970; *Imagine,* 1971; *Double Fantasy,* 1980), he remained the most prominent cultural figure from the Beatles era, and his murder in 1980 inspired an international outcry.

Bibl.: Walter J. Podrazik and Harry Castleman, *All Together Now* (Ann Arbor, 1975) [includes discography]. Elizabeth Thompson and David Gutman, eds., *The Lennon Companion* (New York, 1987). Bruce W. Concord, *John Lennon* (New York, 1994).

Lennon, John Anthony (b. Greensboro, N.C., 14 Jan. 1950). Composer. He studied at the Univ. of San Francisco (B.A.) and the Univ. of Michigan (M.Mus., D.M.A.). He won the Rome Prize in 1980. Compositions include *Metapictures* (small orchestra); *Symphonic Rhapsody* (alto saxophone, orchestra); *Distances within Me* (saxophone, piano, 1979); *Death Angel* (piano, 1981); *Another's Fandango* (guitar, 1981); *Voices* (string quartet, 1982); *Ghostfires* (soprano, flute, guitar, harp, 1983).

Lenormand, René (b. Elbeuf, Normandy, 5 Aug. 1846; d. Paris, 3 Dec. 1932). Composer. He abandoned a business career in 1868 to devote himself to music, studying with Damke, a friend of Berlioz, in 1870. He was especially interested in song and founded the Société "Du lied en tous pays" in Paris. He composed dramatic works (*Le cachet rouge,* Le Havre, 1925); a piano concerto (1903), *Le Lahn de Mabed* (violin and orchestra, on an old Arabic theme), and other orchestral works; a string quartet and other chamber music for strings and piano; piano music; and some 150 songs. His writings include *Étude sur l'harmonie moderne* (Paris, 1912).

Lentz, Daniel K(irkland) (b. Latrobe, Pa., 10 Mar. 1942). Composer. He studied at St. Vincent College, Ohio Univ., and Brandeis (1965–67) under Berger, Alvin Lucier, Harold Shapero, and others; in 1966 he had lessons from Sessions and Rochberg at the Berkshire Music Center. Taught at the Univ. of California, Santa Barbara (1968–70), and at Antioch College (1973). Earlier works were often theatrical or multimedia events; later works are more lyrical and consonant but often involve unusual sound sources and the use of an echo delay system to create rich polyphony from the simple actions of a few players. From the mid-1980s directed his own ensemble in Los Angeles. Works include *Lascaux* (16 wine glasses, 1984) and *On the Leopard Altar* (1 voice, 2 keyboards, 1983).

Lenya, Lotte [Blamauer, Karoline Wilhelmine] (b. Vienna, 18 Oct. 1898; d. New York, 27 Nov. 1981). Actress and singer. In 1914–20 she studied dance in Zurich and later worked in Berlin; in 1926 she married composer Kurt Weill. She became famous in Europe and (after 1935) the U.S. for her interpretations of Weill's music; she created Jenny in the *Mahagonny Songspiel* (1927), Jenny in *Die Dreigroschenoper* (1928; trans. *The Threepenny Opera,* 1952), and Anna in *Die Sieben Todsünden* (1933). After Weill's death in 1950 she continued to record and perform his music.

Leo, Leonardo [Lionardo] **(Ortensio Salvatore de)** (b. S. Vito degli Schiavi, 5 Aug. 1694; d. Naples, 31 Oct. 1744). Composer. Pupil of Fago at the Conservatorio S. Maria della Pietà dei Turchini, Naples, from 1709; became *maestro di cappella* to the Marchese Stella and an organist at the viceroyal chapel in 1713, succeeding A. Scarlatti as the viceroy's first organist in 1725. Active as an opera composer from at least 1714, he wrote dramatic music for Naples, Venice, Rome, and other cities, and from 1723 was also a major figure in comic opera. Though temporarily eclipsed in the late 1720s by Hasse and Vinci, he soon regained his preeminent position, succeeding Vinci at the royal chapel in 1730, becoming vice-maestro there in 1737 and *maestro di cappella* shortly before his death; important also as a teacher, he served as *primo maestro* at both the Conservatorio S. Onofrio (succeeding Feo in 1739) and the Conservatorio dei Turchini (replacing Fago in 1741), with Piccinni and Jommelli among his pupils. In addition to some 30 serious operas (many later examples of which are set to Metastasian libretti) and 20 comic operas, he produced serenatas and other shorter dramatic works, secular vocal music, oratorios, church music, and instrumental compositions, along with several didactic manuals.

Léonard, Hubert (b. Bellaire, near Liège, 7 Apr. 1819; d. Paris, 6 May 1890). Violinist. Studied in Liège, then at the Paris Conservatory (1836–39). He toured Europe as soloist, later with his wife (from 1849), the Spanish singer Antonia Stiches de Mendi; taught at the Brussels Conservatory (1849–51, 1853–66), then in Paris (except 1870–72, Liège); in later years primarily a chamber player, retiring in 1881. He composed and edited much violin music; also wrote a method and etudes.

Leoncavallo, Ruggero (b. Naples, 23 Apr. 1857; d. Montecatini, 9 Aug. 1919). Composer. Student, 1866–74, Naples Conservatory (under Cesi, piano; Ruta and Rossi, composition); 1877–78, student of Carducci, Bologna Univ., receiving his doctorate in literature there. He composed a first opera, *Chatterton* (to his own libretto, like all his operas through 1904), which was to be produced in Bologna (1878), but the impresario disappeared with the money. Subsequently toured the Near East as a pianist, ending in Egypt, where an uncle was a government official; gave recitals, receiving official support and employment, but the Anglo-Egyptian war (1882) caused him to flee the country, first to Marseilles, then Paris, where he eked out a living as a café pianist, songwriter, teacher, and vocal accompanist, meeting in this way Victor Maurel, who recommended him to Giulio Ricordi. He returned to Italy in 1887.

Ricordi took options on *Chatterton* and *I Medici,* the first opera in a Renaissance trilogy *(Crepusculum),* but saw Leoncavallo's potential primarily as a librettist, putting him to work on *Manon Lescaut* for Puccini, who had him replaced. When Ricordi disliked the completed *I Medici,* the angry Leoncavallo composed *I pagliacci* for Ricordi's rival Sanzogno, who had it produced at the Teatro dal Verme, Milan, on 21 May 1892, under Toscanini (and with Maurel as Tonio). Its great success made him a celebrity. Sanzogno also arranged the premieres of *I Medici* (Milan, 1893), which was initially successful but damned by the critics and had few further productions, and the revised *Chatterton* (Rome, 1896), also a failure (as was a later revision, Nice, 1905). Leoncavallo had announced a *La bohème* in 1893 at the same time as Puccini, who reached the stage first (1896). Leoncavallo's version (Venice, 1897) was a success at first, receiving numerous productions until about 1901, but then succumbed to Puccini's setting. His only other considerable success, although far smaller than that of *I pagliacci,* was *Zazà* (Milan, 1900), a vehicle for several sopranos of the period. The Kaiser's admiration for *I Medici* had led to the commissioning of a German opera, *Der Roland von Berlin* (Berlin, 1904), on which Leoncavallo labored for years; it had a succès d'estime in Berlin and nowhere else. His later operas *Maià* (Rome, 1910), *Zingari* (London, 1912), and the posthumous *Edipo re* (Chicago, 1920) aroused little attention. From 1906 he produced 7 operettas and musical comedies, 2 more posthumously. He traveled much (including to the U.S. in 1906 and 1913–14), conducting his music. After the assassination of King Umberto (1900), he received a government commission for a Requiem, but his work could not be performed in church because of its use of female voices. Also composed songs, especially the very popular *Mattinata* (1904), written to be recorded by Caruso; also occasional works, piano pieces, etc. He was in poor health in his later years, suffering from nephritis and near-blindness.

Bibl.: Jürgen Maehder and Lorenza Guiot, eds., *Ruggero Leoncavallo nel suo tempo: Atti del I Convegno internazionale di studi su Ruggero Leoncavallo* (Milan, 1993).

Leonhardt, Gustav (Maria) (b. Graveland, Netherlands, 30 May 1928). Harpsichordist, organist, and conductor. Studied at the Schola cantorum in Basel, and made his debut in Vienna in 1950 playing Bach's *Die Kunst der Fuge* on the harpsichord; in 1952 he published a study on this work. He was professor of harpsichord at the Vienna Academy of Music (1952–55) and at the Amsterdam Conservatory from 1954. He performed and recorded extensively on antique harpsichords and was associated with several period instrument ensembles including the Leonhardt Consort, which he founded in 1955. His conducting of Baroque choral and operatic music won him high praise. Also edited keyboard music of Sweelinck for the complete critical edition.

Leoni, Franco (b. Milan, 24 Oct. 1864; d. London, 8 Feb. 1949). Composer. Studied with Ponchielli at the Milan Conservatory; produced his first opera in Milan, 1890; ca. 1891 to ca. 1917, lived in London, producing oratorios, English operas, cantatas, many English songs; also a singing teacher and conductor. He produced several later operas in France and Italy, but is remembered only for his one-act *L'oracolo* (Covent Garden, 1905), which long served as a vehicle for Antonio Scotti; later lived in France and Italy, returning to England in old age.

Leoni, Leone (b. Verona, ca. 1560; d. Vicenza, 24 June 1627). Composer. Musical studies in his native Verona preceded his appointment in 1588 as *maestro di cappella* at Vicenza Cathedral, where he remained until his death. Nearly 90 madrigals and close to 150 motets survive.

Léonin [Leonius, Leo, Leoninus] (b. Paris, ca. 1135; d. there, in or shortly after 1201). Musician, canon, and poet. A canon in Paris at the Church of St. Benoît and later the Cathedral of Notre Dame; author of a lengthy versification of part of the Old Testament. According to the 13th-century music theorist Anonymous IV, he was creator of the *Magnus liber organi,* originally a book of 2-voiced organal settings of certain Mass and Office chants. Various revised, updated, and supplemented forms of this collection survive in 13th-century manuscripts.

Bibl.: Craig Wright, "Leoninus, Poet and Musician," *JAMS* 39 (1986): 1–35.

Leopold I (b. Vienna, 9 June 1640; d. there, 5 May 1705). Holy Roman Emperor and composer. Recipient of a Jesuit education, he studied music with Bertali and M. and W. Ebner. Becoming successor to the throne when his elder brother died, he was crowned emperor in 1658. He was both an active patron and a composer, despite many hardships during his reign. Dramatic music flourished, with the production of Cesti's *Il pomo d'oro* in 1666, a particularly opulent example; a deeply religious man, he focused attention on oratorios and *sepolcri* as well. Many of his musicians were Italians, though he also supported talented Germans such as Kerll and Fux. His own compositions, primarily vocal, include sacred and secular dramatic works along with liturgical music, and demonstrate his considerable skill.

Bibl.: Guido Adler, ed., *Musikalische Werke der Kaiser Ferdinand III, Leopold I, und Joseph I* (Vienna, 1892–93).

Leppard, Raymond (John) (b. London, 11 Aug. 1927). Conductor, harpsichordist, and editor. Studied at the Univ. of Cambridge and made his debut as a conductor in London in 1952; he soon became an exponent of 17th- and 18th-century music. Taught at Trinity College, Cambridge (1957–67). Appeared at Covent Garden in 1959, Glyndebourne in 1964, Sadler's Wells in 1965, the Metropolitan Opera in New York in 1978. A frequent conductor of orchestral concerts, especially with the English Chamber Orchestra; principal conductor of the BBC Northern Symphony, 1973–80; principal guest conductor of the St. Louis Symphony, 1984–90; music director of the Indianapolis Symphony from 1987. He revived many 17th- and 18th-century Italian operas, several of which he recorded; some of his editions have been published. He also published a book on performance practice, *The Real Authenticity* (London, 1988).

Lerdahl, Fred [Alfred] **(Whitford)** (b. Madison, Wis., 10 Mar. 1943). Composer and theorist. A graduate of Lawrence Univ. and of Princeton (M.F.A., 1968), he also studied with Fortner in Freiburg (1968–69). Composer-in-residence at IRCAM in Paris in 1981–82. Taught at Berkeley, Harvard (1970–79), Columbia (1979–85), and the Univ. of Michigan (from 1985). In 1983 he published an important theoretical treatise in collaboration with the linguist Ray Jackendoff *(A Generative Theory of Tonal Music).* His own works employ traditional tonal elements in novel ways and are cast in strict forms. In *Eros,* a set of 21 variations, both text and music are subjected to variation processes; the 2 string quartets constitute a series of "expanding variations," each 50 percent longer than its predecessor. His works include *Chords* (orchestra, 1974; rev. 1983); *Beyond the Realm of Birds* (Dickinson; soprano and chamber orchestra, 1981–84); *Crosscurrents* (orchestra, 1987); *Waves* (chamber orchestra, 1988); 2 string quartets (1978, 1982); *Episodes and Refrains* (wind quintet, 1982); a string trio (1965–66); *Wake* (fragments from *Finnegan's Wake;* mezzo-soprano, violin, viola, cello, harp, and percussion ensemble, 1968); *Eros* (Pound; mezzo-soprano, alto flute, viola, harp, piano, electric guitar, electric double bass, and percussion, 1975).

Lerner, Alan Jay (b. New York, 31 Aug. 1918; d. there, 14 June 1986). Popular lyricist and librettist. He graduated from Harvard in 1940; from 1942 he worked with composer Frederick Loewe, writing musicals (*Brigadoon,* 1947; *Paint Your Wagon,* 1951; *My Fair Lady,* 1956; *Camelot,* 1960) and films (*Gigi,* 1958). While his biggest successes came with Loewe, he also worked with Kurt Weill, Burton Lane, and Leonard Bernstein.

Le Roux, Maurice (b. Paris, 6 Feb. 1923). Composer and conductor. He studied with Messiaen and Leibowitz and received a Premier prix in orchestral conducting at the Paris Conservatory (1952). He conducted the Orchestre nationale of the French Radio (1960–68), making recordings of works of Messiaen and Xenakis, and toured widely. He was artistic adviser to the Paris Opéra (1969–73) and in 1973 was appointed *Inspecteur générale de la musique.* Most of his compositions are serial and date from before 1955 (they include the ballet *Le petit Prince,* 1950); a more recent work is *Un koan* (orchestra, 1973); his film music includes scores for *The Red Balloon* and *A View from the Bridge.* His writing includes music criticism and 2 books, *Introduction à la musique contemporaine* (1947) and *Claudio Monteverdi* (1951).

Leroux, Xavier (Henry Napoléon) (b. Velletri, Italy, 11 Oct. 1863; d. Paris, 2 Feb. 1919). Composer. Son of a military bandmaster; student, Paris Conservatory (Prix de Rome, 1885). Best known as an opera composer, beginning with *Evangeline* (1895), followed by the moderately successful *Astarté* (Opéra, 1901) and the comic operas *La reine Fiammette* (Opéra-comique, 1903) and *Le chemineau* (Opéra-comique, 1907). From 1896, professor of harmony, Paris Conservatory. Also composed songs, piano pieces.

Le Roy, Adrian (b. Montreuil-sur-mer, ca. 1520; d. Paris, 1598). Music printer, composer, and writer. Artistic director of the firm Le Roy & Ballard, active under Le Roy's name and virtually without competition in France from 1551 until 1598; friend of many composers, including Lassus, most of whose works he printed; author of long-popular pedagogical books for plucked-string instruments; composer of chansons, accompanied songs, and pieces for cittern, lute, and guitar.

Bibl.: *Oeuvres* (Paris, 1961–78).

Leschetizky, Theodor (b. Łańcut, near Lwów, 22 June 1830; d. Dresden, 14 Nov. 1915). Piano teacher. Son and pupil of a musician; a child prodigy; 1840, his family moved to Vienna, where he studied with Czerny and Sechter; 1844, already a popular teacher himself; 1845–48, studied philosophy, Vienna Univ.; 1852–78, a fashionable piano teacher, St. Petersburg (from 1862, head of the piano department at the conservatory), also touring as pianist and conductor; spent the rest of his life in Vienna, one of the most sought-after teachers of the time. His pupils included Paderewski, Schnabel, Gabrilovich, Friedman, Moisewich. Composed 2 operas, piano pieces.

L'Escurel, Jehannot de. See Jehannot de l'Escurel.

Lessard, John (Ayres) (b. San Francisco, 3 July 1920). Composer, pianist, and conductor. He studied piano and trumpet as a child; from 1937 to 1940 studied with Boulanger, Dandelot, Cortot, and others at the École normale in Paris. He taught at SUNY–Stony Brook, 1962–90. Works include *Sinfonietta Concertante* (1961) and other orchestral music; Octet for Winds (1952), *Drift, Follow, Persist* (horn, piano, percussion, 1988), and other chamber music; piano and harpsichord pieces; *Don Quixote and the Sheep* (baritone, bass, orchestra, 1955), *Fragments from the Cantos of Ezra Pound* (baritone and chamber ensemble, 1969), *The Pond in a Bowl* (soprano, piano, marimba, vibraphone, 1984), and some 35 songs for voice and piano.

Le Sueur [Lesueur], **Jean-François** (b. Drucat-Plessiel, near Abbeville, 15 Feb. 1760; d. Paris, 6 Oct. 1837). Composer. After early schooling in Abbeville and nearby Amiens, from 1776 he was choirmaster at several small churches, including that in Séez. During this time he went to Paris for a brief period of study of counterpoint with Abbé Roze; he was also Roze's assistant at Holy Innocents' Church. In 1781 he was appointed *maître de musique* at Dijon, and he served subsequently in Le Mans (1783) and Tours (1784). He returned to Paris upon receiving the post of *maître de chapelle* at Notre Dame in 1786, but after a year he was forced out because of his controversial directorial style. A polemic ensued in which he defended his aims of a "theatrical" church music, complete with large choir and orchestra. He turned to opera instead, and in 1793 his first stage work, *La caverne,* was performed in Paris to great acclaim; other successes followed. In 1795 he became an inspector (a directorial position) at the newly formed Paris Conservatory. In 1804 his most spectacular success, *Ossian,* was performed in Paris. From 1804 he was *maître* at the chapel at the Tuileries, a position he later shared with Cherubini. As a professor at the Conservatory (from 1818), he taught Gounod and Berlioz. His other stage works include *Paul et Virginie* (*drame lyrique,* 1794); *Télémaque* (1796); *Le triomphe de Trajan* (1807); *La mort d'Adam* (1809); sacred music (including Masses, motets, oratorios, cantatas, etc.); songs. He also authored an *Exposé d'une musique une, imitative et particulière à chaque solemnité* (Paris, 1787), defending his church style.

Bibl.: Jean Mondgrédien, *J. F. Le Sueur: A Thematic Catalogue of His Complete Works* (New York, 1980).

Lesur, Daniel Jean Yves. See Daniel-Lesur.

Letelier (Llona), Alfonso (b. Santiago, Chile, 4 Oct. 1912). Composer. Student of Hügel and Allende at the National Conservatory (1930–35); later studied in Europe under del Campo. Cofounded the Escuela moderna de música in 1940; named professor of the National Conservatory in 1946, dean of music at the Univ. of Chile in 1953, and president of the National Association of Chilean Composers (1950–56); served also as a university administrator (to 1962) and as an official in the Ministry of Education (from 1969). His early compositions draw on indigenous Chilean music, impressionism, and modality, while later works move closer to serialism. Works include incidental music, the opera/oratorio *La historia de Tobías y Sara* (1955), film scores, and other orchestral works (some with chorus); choral and chamber music; and several piano works.

Bibl.: Luis Merino, ed., "Catálogo de la obra musical de Alfonso Letelier Llona," *Revista musical chilena* 153–55 (1981): 97–116.

Leutgeb [Leitgeb], **Joseph** [Ignaz] (b. Salzburg?, ca. 1745; d. Vienna, 27 Feb. 1811). Horn player. During the late 1760s he was first hornist at Salzburg; in 1770 he made his debut at the Concert spirituel in Paris, and in the ensuing years he traveled to Vienna and Italy. In 1777 he settled in Vienna, where he ran a cheese shop and became a friend of Mozart, who composed the horn concertos K. 417, K. 447, and K. 495 for him, and several other works as well, including the Quintet K. 407.

Leveridge, Richard (b. 1670–71; d. London, 22 Mar. 1758). Bass and composer. Sang in H. Purcell's *The Indian Queen* (1695) and in other works by D. Purcell, Clarke, and Leveridge himself around this time; the latter three collaborated on *The Island Princess* (1698). Went to Dublin in 1699, returning in 1702; sang in several early Italian-style operas, including Clayton's *Arsinoe* (1705), and in Handel's *Il pastor fido* and *Teseo* in 1713. Joined Rich's company at Lincoln's Inn Fields in 1714, appearing in its popular pantomimes and remaining with it until his retirement in 1751. In addition to his dramatic efforts, he issued several books of songs between 1697 and 1730; others of his songs were inserted in plays and included in anthologies.

Levi, Hermann (b. Giessen, Upper Hesse, 7 Nov. 1839; d. Munich, 13 May 1900). Conductor. Went to school in Mannheim, studying there with V. Lachner (1852–55), then at the Leipzig Conservatory (1855–58); conducted at Saarbrücken (1859–61), Mannheim (1861), Rotterdam (1861–64); 1864–72, court Kapellmeister, Karlsruhe; from 1872, Kapellmeister (from 1894 Generalmusikdirektor), Munich, retiring because of health in 1896. He achieved a great international reputation. His relationship with Brahms, whose music he had championed, was damaged by his later association with Wagner. Despite being Jewish, which caused difficulties with both Wagner and Cosima, Levi became a leading figure at Bayreuth, conducting the premiere and later performances through 1894 (except 1888) of *Parsifal.*

Levidis, Dimitrios (b. Athens, 8 April 1885 or 1886; d. Palaeon Phaleron, near Athens, 29 May 1951). Composer. He studied at the Athens Conservatory (1898–1905) with Boemer, Mancini, Lavrangas, and Choisy;

also at the Lausanne Conservatory with Denéréaz and at the Munich Academy (1907–8) under Mottl (orchestration) and Strauss (composition). He settled in France in 1910, becoming a French citizen; returned to Athens in the early 1930s to teach at the Music Lyceum and the Hellenic Conservatory, and served as president of the Union of Greek Composers (1946–47). Some of his compositions were written for new or unusual instruments, such as the ondes martenot and the chromatic harp.

Levine, James [Lawrence] (b. Cincinnati, 23 June 1943). Conductor and pianist. Debut as pianist in 1953 with the Cincinnati Symphony. At the Juilliard School studied piano with Rosina Lhévinne, conducting with John Morel. As a participant in the Ford Foundation's American Conductors Project, he studied with Alfred Wallenstein, Max Rudolf, and Fausto Cleva. Assistant conductor of the Cleveland Orchestra, 1964–70. Led *Tosca* at the San Francisco Opera in 1970, at the New York Metropolitan Opera in 1971. In 1973 became the first principal conductor of the Met, in 1975 music director, in 1986 artistic director. Director of the Ravinia Festival, 1973–93. In 1982 and subsequently he conducted *Parsifal* at Bayreuth; also active at the Salzburg Festival.

Levy, Alexandre (b. São Paulo, 10 Nov. 1864; d. there, 17 Jan. 1892). Composer. Son of an emigrant from France who in 1860 founded Casa Levy, which became the city's leading music store and a center of musical life; 1880–82, had piano pieces published in Europe; 1883–87, helped organize the Haydn Club, conducting some of its concerts; May–Oct. 1887, in Milan and Paris, studying and hearing music; on return conducted, wrote criticism, composed; 1891, with brother Luis (1861–1935), also a musician, took over Casa Levy. He is remembered as a pioneer of Brazilian art music and for his use of popular tunes in it. Works include *Suite brasileiro* for orchestra (1890); piano pieces, including *Tango brasileiro* (1890).

Lévy, Ernst (b. Basel, 18 Nov. 1895; d. Morges, Switzerland, 19 Apr. 1981). Composer and pianist. He studied in Basel and Paris; from 1917 to 1921 directed the piano master class at the Univ. of Basel; in 1928 founded the Choeur philharmonique in Paris. He taught at several schools in the U.S. between 1941 and 1966 (Bennington, New England Conservatory, Univ. of Chicago, M.I.T., and Brooklyn College), but returned to Switzerland when he retired. He made recordings of piano works of Beethoven and Liszt, and wrote 4 books on music (*A Theory of Harmony,* 1985; 2 collaborations with S. Levarie). As a composer he remained committed to tonality. Works include an operetta; some 15 symphonies and other orchestral music; 4 string quartets, other chamber and keyboard music; choral Psalm settings, motets, cantatas, and songs.

Levy, Marvin David (b. Passaic, N.J., 2 Aug. 1932). Composer. He studied with Philip James at New York Univ., with Luening at Columbia, and in Europe. His opera *Mourning Becomes Elektra* (after Eugene O'Neill) was commissioned by the Metropolitan Opera in New York (1967). His style is atonal and characterized by a rhythmic flexibility; many works are theatrical. Works include 4 operas (1955–78); *The Balcony* (after Jean Genet, 1978); *Arrows of Time* (1988) and other orchestral music; *Canto de los Marranos* (soprano, orchestra, 1977); *Christmas Oratorio* (1959), *Sacred Service* (1964), *Massada* (oratorio, narrator, tenor, chorus, and orchestra, 1973; rev. 1987), and other choral music; some chamber music (*Chassidic Suite,* horn, piano, 1956); songs; incidental music and film scores.

Lewis, Anthony (Carey) (b. Bermuda, 2 Mar. 1915; d. Haslemere, 5 June 1983). Scholar, conductor, composer. Educated at Cambridge, he became professor at the Univ. of Birmingham in 1947. He founded and was general editor of Musica Britannica, to which series he contributed *John Blow, Coronation Anthems.* Other publications include Handel's songs and cantatas. As a conductor he led the first commercial recordings of Monteverdi's *Vespers,* Purcell's *Fairy Queen* and *King Arthur,* and Rameau's complete *Hippolyte et Aricie.* His own compositions include a trumpet concerto (1947) and a horn concerto (1956). Knighted in 1972.

Lewis, George (1) [Zeno(n), George Joseph Francois Louis] (b. New Orleans, 13 July 1900; d. there, 31 Dec. 1968). Jazz clarinetist and bandleader. Having worked in New Orleans bands, including Buddy Petit's from around 1920, he became involved in the traditional jazz revival with Bunk Johnson's band (1942–46). He also worked as a leader, recording his own "Burgundy Street Blues" (1944). A central figure in the movement following Johnson's death in 1949, he toured internationally from the late 1950s. His numerous albums include *Concert!* (1954).

Bibl.: Tom Bethell, *George Lewis: A Jazzman from New Orleans* (Berkley, 1977).

Lewis, George (2) (b. Chicago, 14 July 1952). Composer and trombonist. After professional experience as a jazz trombonist, he studied at Yale (B.A., 1974), where he belonged to the Association for the Advancement of Creative Musicians (devoted to contemporary jazz); he established himself securely as a member of the jazz avant-garde with his *Solo Trombone Record* (1977). From 1980 to 1982 he was director of the Kitchen, a New York avant-garde cultural center. His style incorporates free improvisation, electronic and computer music, and other contemporary styles; early works were often scored for jazz ensembles, but in later pieces he was less likely to specify exact instrumentation; many works include both tape and live performers. In *Audio Tick* (1983) computers linked to digital synthesizers respond to sounds made by the performers. Other works include *Homage to Charles Parker* (alto saxophone, electronic keyboard, synthesizer, percussion, electronics, 1978); *Carthera* (trombone and piano, 1981); and *Rainbow Family* (one or more instruments and interactive computer, 1984).

Lewis, Jerry Lee (b. Ferriday, La., 29 Sept. 1935). Rock-and-roll and country singer and pianist. He began playing piano and drums in clubs in Ferriday and Natchez, Mississippi; his recordings for Sun Records in Memphis played an important role in the rock-and-roll movement ("Crazy Arms," 1956; "Whole Lotta Shakin' Goin' On," "Great Balls of Fire," both 1957), as did his performances, which featured his athletic piano style. Although his career was interrupted several times by personal difficulties, he remained popular in the 1960s and 1970s, recording country music ("To Make Love Sweeter for You," 1968), and country-rock ("Chantilly Lace," 1972).

Lewis, John (Aaron) (b. LaGrange, Ill., 3 May 1920). Jazz pianist and composer. He joined Dizzy Gillespie's bop big band (1946–48) and recorded with Charlie Parker (1948) while studying at the Manhattan School of Music (M.M., 1953). He recorded with the Milt Jackson Quartet (1951–52); it became the Modern Jazz Quartet (1952–74, from 1981), in which Lewis was the music director and for which he composed *Versailles* (1956), *Three Windows* (1957), *Vendome, Django* (both 1960), and the ballet suite *The Comedy* (1962). Apart from this central activity, he was music director of the Monterey Jazz Festival (1958–82) and a founder of the third-stream big band Orchestra U.S.A. (1962–65) and the American Jazz Orchestra (from 1985). He also appeared as a soloist.

Lewis, Meade (Anderson) "Lux" (b. Chicago, 4 Sept. 1905; d. Minneapolis, 7 June 1964). Boogie-woogie pianist. He recorded "Honky Tonk Train Blues" (1927), as a result of which he later became the object of a search by the producer John Hammond. Rediscovered in 1935, Lewis again recorded "Honky Tonk Train Blues" and thereby initiated a national craze for boogie-woogie. He formed a trio with Albert Ammons and Pete Johnson (1938–39) but otherwise worked as a soloist. From 1941 he was based in Los Angeles.

Lewis, Mel [Sokoloff, Melvin] (b. Buffalo, 10 May 1929; d. New York, 3 Feb. 1990). Jazz drummer and bandleader. His career has centered around membership in big bands, including Boyd Raeburn (1948), Stan Kenton (1954–57), Gerry Mulligan (1960–63), and Benny Goodman (1962), and work as a studio musician in Los Angeles (from 1957) and New York (from 1963). He cofounded the Thad Jones–Mel Lewis Orchestra (1965–79), which then continued under Lewis's leadership, with Bob Brookmeyer as the music director. His albums include *Thad Jones–Mel Lewis Live at the Village Vanguard* (1967).

Lewis, Richard [Thomas, Thomas] (b. Manchester, 10 May 1914; d. Eastbourne, 13 Nov. 1990). Tenor. Studied at the Royal Manchester College of Music and at the Royal Academy of Music. Concertized in Denmark and Norway in 1946, then made his British concert debut at Brighton in 1947; also sang at Glyndebourne, Sadler's Wells, and Covent Garden. During the 1954–55 season at Covent Garden he sang in the premieres of Walton's *Troilus and Cressida* and Tippett's *The Midsummer Marriage.* Was a notable Aaron in Schoenberg's *Moses und Aron* at Covent Garden, Paris, and in the U.S. Made his U.S. debut at San Francisco in 1953. In 1956 he took part in the world premiere of Stravinsky's *Canticum sacrum* at Venice. He also had a successful concert career singing oratorios.

Lewis, Robert Hall (b. Portland, Oreg., 22 Apr. 1926). Composer, conductor, and trumpet player. He studied at Eastman with Rogers and Hanson (Ph.D., 1964), with Boulanger and Eugène Bigot in Paris (1952–53), and in Vienna with Krenek and others (1955–57). Taught at the Peabody Conservatory (from 1958) and at Johns Hopkins (1969–80). Early works are serial; in the 1970s he began to explore spatial effects, electronic music, quotations, and aleatory techniques. Works include 4 symphonies (no. 4, 1990), *Destini* (strings and winds, 1985), *3 Movements on Scenes of Hieronymous Bosch* (1989), and other orchestral music; the series *Combinazioni* for various ensembles (*II* is for 8 percussionists and piano, 1974; *V* for 4 violas, 1982), *Monophony I–IX* (solo winds, 1966–77), *Dimensioni* (clarinet, violin, cello, piano, 1988), 4 string quartets, Scena for string ensemble (1995), and other chamber music; *Serenades I* (piano, 1970); *Monophony X* (soprano, 1983), *Three Prayers for Jane Austen* (small chorus, piano, and percussion, 1977), and other vocal music.

Lewkovitch, Bernhard (b. Copenhagen, 28 May 1927). Composer. He attended the Royal Danish Conservatory (1946–50), studying organ and theory; took composition and orchestration with Schierbeck and Jersild. He served as organist at St. Ansgar (1947–63) in Copenhagen, and founded and directed the Schola cantorum and the all-male Schola gregoriana to perform his own works as well as sacred music of the Middle Ages and Renaissance. Lewkovitch's early compositions are closely linked to the Roman Catholic liturgy and Gregorian chant; during the mid-1950s he became influenced by the sacred music of Stravinsky, employing bi- and polytonality in his works in addition to twelve-tone techniques.

Ley, Henry George (b. Chagford, 30 Dec. 1887; d. near Ottery St. Mary, 24 Aug. 1962). Organist and composer. He studied organ with Walter Parratt at the Royal College of Music, then won an organ scholarship to Keble College, Oxford; in 1909 he became organist of Christ Church, Oxford. He later taught organ at the Royal College of Music and was music director at Eton College (1926–45). His works include

Variations on a Theme by Handel for orchestra as well as chamber music and organ pieces.

Ley, Salvador (b. Guatemala City, 2 Jan. 1907; d. there, 21 Mar. 1985). Composer. Studied piano and composition in Berlin from age 15; became director of the National Conservatory upon his return to Guatemala in 1934, serving until 1937, when he moved to the U.S. Held his old post at the conservatory again from 1944 to 1953, but then returned to the U.S. to settle permanently. He concertized frequently, both in Germany and later in Latin America and the U.S., and was a faculty member at the Westchester Conservatory, 1963–70. Works include orchestral pieces; chamber music (including several compositions for piano and various solo instruments); piano music; and many songs set to Spanish, German, and English poetry.

Bibl.: *Composers of the Americas* 12 (Washington, D.C., 1966), pp. 92–98 [includes works list].

Lhéritier, Jean [Johannes] (b. ca. 1480; d. after 1552). Composer. His activities, of which few specifics are known, alternated between his native France and Italy. Stylistic evidence and a contemporary reference suggest some contact with composers at the French royal court around 1501. He held posts in Ferrara (1506–8) and Rome (1521–22, at St. Louis-des-Français) and several benefices in the region of Avignon, may have had connections with Florence, and perhaps lived in the region of Venice in the 1550s. His most important compositions are his nearly 50 motets; also wrote a Mass, Magnificats, a chanson.

Bibl.: *Opera omnia, CMM* 48 (1969).

Lhévinne, Josef (b. Orel, near Moscow, 13 Dec. 1874; d. New York, 2 Dec. 1944). Pianist. Studied with Safonov at the Moscow Conservatory, where his fellow students were Rachmaninoff and Scriabin. Made his debut in Moscow in 1889 and began traveling abroad, but was recalled to Russia to serve in the military. In 1898 he married the pianist Rosina Bessie. Taught in Tiflis (1900–1902) and at the Moscow Conservatory (1902–6). Made his U.S. debut in New York in 1906 with the Russian Symphony under Safonov. He lived mostly in Berlin from 1907 to 1919, in internment during World War I; after the war he moved to New York, where he joined the staff of the Juilliard School in 1922. His performances and recordings displayed a formidable technique and a mastery of tone and phrasing.

Lhévinne, Rosina (Bessie) (b. Kiev, 29 March 1880; d. Glendale, Calif., 9 Nov. 1976). Pianist and educator. Studied with Remesov and Vasily Safonov at the Moscow Conservatory, graduating in 1898 with a gold medal. At the Juilliard School, 1924–76, she taught John Browning, Van Cliburn, and others who went on to establish major careers. After marrying Josef Lhévinne, she subordinated her career to his. In 1945 she reappeared as a soloist; at 95 she gave a full-length recital.

Lhotka, Fran (b. Mladá Vožice, Budejovice, Czechoslovakia, 25 Dec. 1883; d. Zagreb, 26 Jan. 1962). Composer. He studied composition and horn playing under Stecker, Klička, and Dvořák in Prague, later settling in Zagreb, where he joined the opera orchestra in 1909. He directed the Zagreb Chorus Lisinski (1912–20) and served as professor at the Zagreb Academy of Music (1920–61). Lhotka is best known for his stage works, including the ballets *Đavo u selu* [The Devil in the Village] (Zurich, 1935) and *Luk* [The Arc] (Munich, 1939) and the opera *Minka* (Zagreb, 1918).

Lhotka-Kalinski, Ivo (Zagreb, 30 July 1913; d. there, 29 Jan. 1987). Composer. Son of Fran Lhotka; he studied music with his father and at the Zagreb Academy of Music, continuing his composition studies in 1937 with Pizzetti in Rome; after World War II he taught singing at the Zagreb Academy, becoming regional director there in 1967. Lhotka-Kalinski gradually discarded the influence of folk song in his early compositions in favor of twelve-tone and atonal techniques. He is best known for his radio and television operas, which include *Analfabeta* [The Illiterate] (1954); *Putovanje* [The Journey] (1956); *Dugme* [The Button] (1957); *Vlast* [Political Power] (1958); *Svijetleći grad* [The Shining City] (1967).

Liadov, Anatol Konstantinovich. See Lyadov, Anatol Konstantinovich.

Liberace, (Walter) [Wladziu Valentino] (b. West Allis, Wis., 16 May 1919; d. Palm Springs, Calif. 4 Feb. 1987). Pianist. After studying in Milwaukee, he made his debut with the Chicago Symphony in 1940; he began performing in New York as Walter Busterkeys. His repertory included principally lighter works and arrangements of classical works (including a conflation of Beethoven's Moonlight Sonata and Rachmaninoff's C# minor Prelude with portions of Rachmaninoff's Paganini Rhapsody as "Story of Three Loves," 1953); his ornate pianos and flamboyant personal appearance were widely known through numerous television appearances and concert tours.

Lidholm, Ingvar (Natanael) (b. Jönköping, Sweden, 24 Feb. 1921). Composer and conductor. He entered the Stockholm Music High School in 1940, studying with Barkel (violin), Brandel (piano), and Mann (conducting), and played viola in the Stockholm opera orchestra; later studied composition with Rosenberg, becoming associated with the Monday Group; took additional composition lessons in England with Seiber (1954). He conducted the Örebro Orchestra (1947–56), directed chamber music for Swedish Radio (1956–65), and taught at the Stockholm Music High School (from 1965). His compositions reveal the influence of Nielsen and Stravinsky; many use serial practices. Works include dramatic works (*Riter,* ballet, orchestra, tape, 1960); orchestral works (*Toccata e canto,* chamber orchestra, 1944; *Ritornell,* 1955; *Poesis,* 1963; *Greetings from an Old World,* 1976);

vocal music (*Laudi,* chorus, 1947; *A cappella-bok,* 1956–; . . . *a riveder le stelle,* voice, chorus, 1971–73; *De profundis,* chorus, 1983); chamber music (*Klavierstück,* 1949; 4 pieces, cello, piano, 1955; *Tre elegier-Epilog,* string quartet, 1982–86).

Lie, Sigurd (b. Drammen, Norway, 23 May 1871; d. Vestre Aker, 30 Sept. 1904). Composer. Studied music in Norway, then at the Leipzig Conservatory (1891–93) and composition with Urban in Berlin (1894–95). He worked as a teacher, composer, and conductor in Bergen and Christiania; composed considerable music in spite of poor health (he spent part of 1902–3 in a sanatorium), including orchestral and chamber music and piano pieces; best known for choral music and some of his ca. 80 songs, especially *Sne* [Snow].

Liebermann, Rolf (b. Zurich, 14 Sept. 1910). Composer and administrator. He studied law at the Univ. of Zurich and music at the José Berr Conservatory there; his main composition teacher was Scherchen, for whom he acted as assistant and secretary, 1937–38. He established himself as a critic in Switzerland and studied twelve-tone music with Vogel; he was a producer at Swiss Radio in Zurich, 1945–50; manager of the Beromünster Radio Orchestra, 1950–57; music director of North German Radio in Hamburg, 1957–59; general manager of the Staatsoper in Hamburg, 1959–73, 1985–87; of the Paris Opéra, 1973–80. His compositions include operas (*La forêt,* 1987), radio and incidental music; a concerto for jazz band and orchestra (1954); *Concert des échanges* (machines and performers, 1964); *Cosmopolitan Greetings* (music theater for jazz singers and symphony orchestra, 1988).

Lieberson, Goddard (b. Hanley, Staffordshire, 5 Apr. 1911; d. New York, 29 May 1977). Composer and recording executive. He was raised in Seattle; studied at the Univ. of Washington and at Eastman (with Rogers); worked as a critic and teacher in Rochester. In 1936 he worked in New York as a critic (sometimes under the pseudonym John Sebastian). In 1939 he became associated with Columbia Records, where he supervised the first recording of Berg's Violin Concerto and was responsible for recording much American contemporary music. His compositions include a ballet and incidental music; a symphony; a string quartet (1938) and other chamber music; *Songs without Mendelssohn* (recorded 1964) and other piano music; and choral music. He also wrote a novel, *Three for Bedroom C* (1947).

Lieberson, Peter (b. New York, 25 Oct. 1946). Composer. Son of Goddard Lieberson. He graduated in English literature from New York Univ., and then studied composition with Babbitt and at Columbia with Wuorinen and Sollberger (M.A., 1974). In 1972 he was assistant to Bernstein and assistant producer of the CBS Young People's Concerts. He was a founder of the Composers' Ensemble and of the New Structures Ensemble. From 1976 to 1981 he studied Tibetan Buddhism; then undertook doctoral studies at Brandeis. His Variations for Solo Flute (1971) led to commissions from Boulez, the Berkshire Music Center, and other groups. His works include orchestral music (a piano concerto, 1983; *Drala,* 1986; *Gesar Legend,* 1988); chamber music (*Wind Messengers,* 13 instruments, 1990); piano music; *3 Songs,* soprano and chamber orchestra (1982).

Liebling, Emil (b. Pless [now Pszczyna, Poland], 12 Apr. 1851; d. Chicago, 20 Jan. 1914). Composer. Studied music in Berlin (piano with Kullak, at whose school he taught in 1874–76; composition with Dorn), also some lessons from Liszt; spent most of his life (1872–74; after 1876) in Chicago as pianist and teacher; published piano pieces and exercises.

Lieurance, Thurlow (Weed) (b. Oskaloosa, Iowa, 21 Mar. 1878; d. Boulder, 9 Oct. 1963). Composer. A bandmaster during the Spanish-American War, he studied harmony and singing at the Cincinnati College of Music; sang in an opera company for two seasons; then settled in Kansas as a teacher of piano and voice (1901). His interest in Native American music and culture led him to begin making field recordings in 1911; his collection is now in the Library of Congress Archive of Folk Culture. He toured as a performer of Indian melodies (1917–26) and tried to develop an indigenous music based on Indian musical styles. His compositions include a stage work (lost); *Queen Esther* (oratorio, 1897); orchestral music; many chamber works (flute, violin, piano); choral music and songs and many arrangements of Indian melodies (*By the Waters of Minnetonka,* 1917).

Ligeti, György (Sándor) (b. Dicsöszentmárton, Transylvania, 28 May 1923). Composer. His family moved to Kolozsvár shortly after he was born; he began his composition studies at the conservatory there with Farkas (1941–43) and with Kadosa in Budapest (1942, 1943). Ligeti continued his studies with Farkas at the Budapest Academy in 1945, also working with Veress and Járdányi; after graduating he was appointed to the faculty as a professor of harmony and counterpoint (1950–56). At the end of 1956 he went to Vienna, where he met Stockhausen, Eimert, Koenig, and other leading figures, and began to work at the West German Radio electronic studios in Cologne. He lectured at the Darmstadt summer courses, taught at the Academy of Music in Stockholm, and in 1973 was appointed professor of composition at the Hamburg Musikhochschule.

Ligeti gained considerable recognition when his orchestral composition *Apparitions* (1958–59) was performed at the ISCM Festival in 1960. In this work, along with *Atmosphères* (1961) and the organ piece *Volumina* (1961–62), Ligeti furthered the concept of *Klangflächenkomposition* (composition with planes of sound); the clear articulation of melody, harmony, and rhythm are abandoned (although still notated precisely) in favor of the timbre and texture of the sound itself. The vocal works from this time, *Aventures* (1962) and

Nouvelles aventures (1962–65), later arranged for the stage, use an invented language of phonetic sounds and inflections and hence resemble the electronic *Artikulation* for 4-track tape (1958). The seemingly contradictory styles embodied in *Atmosphères* and *Aventures* are combined to some extent in the *Requiem* (1963–65). Some of Ligeti's later compositions use microtones (String Quartet no. 2, 1968; Double Concerto, 1972); *Ramifications* (1968–69) is scored for 2 string ensembles tuned a quarter tone apart. The success of Ligeti's opera *Le grand macabre,* first given at Stockholm in 1978, was evident through subsequent performances of the work within a short time in Hamburg, Saarbrücken, Bologna, Paris, and London.

Works include *Artikulation,* 4-track tape (1958); *Apparitions* [rev. of *Víziók,* 1956–57], orchestra (1958–59); *Atmosphères,* orchestra (1961); *Fragment,* chamber orchestra (1961; rev. 1964); *Poème symphonique,* 100 metronomes (1962); *Aventures,* 3 solo voices, 7 instruments (1962; arr. stage, 1966); *Nouvelles aventures,* 3 solo voices, 7 instruments (1962–65; arr. stage, 1966); Requiem, soprano, mezzo, 2 choruses, orchestra (1963–65); a cello concerto (1966); *Lux aeterna,* 16-part chorus (1966); String Quartet no. 2 (1968); Ten Pieces, wind quintet (1968); *Ramifications,* 12 solo strings, string orchestra (1968–69); *Melodien,* orchestra, chamber orchestra (1971); *Clocks and Clouds,* female chorus, orchestra (1972–73); *Le grand macabre,* music theater (Stockholm, 1978); a piano concerto (1986); *Loop,* solo viola (1991); Violin concerto (1993).

Bibl.: György Ligeti, *Complete List of Published Works up to January 1989* (New York, 1989). Herman Sabbe, *György Ligeti: Studien zur kompositorischen Phänomenologie* (Munich, 1987). *György Ligeti in Conversation,* ed. Péter Várnai et al. (London, 1983). Robert W. Richart, *György Ligeti: A Bio-Bibliography* (New York, 1990). Wolfgang Burde, *György Ligeti: Eine Monographie* (Zurich, 1993).

Lightfoot, Gordon (b. Orillia, Ont., 17 Nov. 1938). Folksinger and guitarist. He studied briefly at Westlake College in California; his songs became famous in the folk movement through recordings by Ian and Sylvia ("For Lovin' Me," 1965) and Peter, Paul, and Mary ("Early Morning Rain," 1965). From 1966 he issued his own recordings in the U.S. (including "If You Could Read My Mind," 1970; "Sundown," 1973; "The Wreck of the *Edmund Fitzgerald,*" 1976).

Lilburn, Douglas (Gordon) (b. Wanganui, New Zealand, 2 Nov. 1915). He studied at Canterbury Univ. College (1934–36) and at the Royal College of Music (1937–40) under Vaughan Williams; in 1947 he became lecturer at Victoria Univ. of Wellington, becoming full professor and director of the electronic music studio there in 1970. Lilburn's earlier works were influenced by Vaughan Williams, Stravinsky, and the Second Viennese School; from the early 1960s he worked extensively with electronic music. Many of his compositions were inspired by other art forms, such as poetry and painting.

Jenny Lind, 1846.

Lili'uokalani [Kamaka'eha Paki, Lydia] (b. Honolulu, 2 Sept. 1838; d. there, 11 Nov. 1917). Queen, songwriter. Daughter and adopted daughter of high court dignitaries; educated by missionaries, becoming a pianist, organist, choir director. In 1877 she was designated heir apparent by her brother; her reign (January 1891–January 1893) was stormy through antagonism of American interests, which finally overthrew her. She lived on to become a venerated elder figure; published her memoirs; also a few Hawaiian songs, of which "Aloha'oe" (1878) became extremely popular.

Lind, Jenny [Johanna] **(Maria)** (b. Stockholm, 6 Oct. 1820; d. Wynds Point, Herefordshire, 2 Nov. 1887). Soprano. From 1830 a pupil at the Royal Opera School, Stockholm; from 1838 a prima donna there (debut as Agathe in *Der Freischütz*); 1841, her voice showing strain, she studied ten months in Paris with Garcia, then resumed her career in Stockholm. In 1844–45 she sang at the Berlin Opera (including Meyerbeer's *Ein Feldlager in Schlesien,* composed for her) and elsewhere in Germany; 1846–47, great success in Vienna (debut as Norma) and in Germany; 1847, sensational London debut (as Alice in *Robert le diable*), singing there much and throughout the country through 1849, when she gave up opera; 1847, created Amalia in Verdi's *I Masnadieri* at Covent Garden. Her great European reputation led to P. T. Barnum's arrangement with her for an American tour, which he made a milestone in the development of modern publicity, resulting in unparalleled public interest. She broke with Barnum in 1851, continuing her concerts through that year; returned to Europe after three farewell concerts in New York in May 1852. She settled in Dresden, later in England, continuing to sing in concerts and oratorios; from 1883 taught singing at the Royal College of Music. Her great popularity was based as much on her personal qualities as on her voice—her charity and her embodiment to a seemingly superhuman degree of Victorian notions of female virtue, propriety, and gentility.

Bibl.: Jenny Maude, *The Life of Jenny Lind* (London, 1926; R: 1979). E. Wagenknecht, *Jenny Lind* (Boston, 1931; R: 1980). W. P. Ware, trans. and ed., *The Lost Letters of Jenny Lind* (London, 1966). W. P. Ware and T. C. Lockard, Jr., *P. T. Barnum Presents Jenny Lind* (Baton Rouge, 1980).

Lindley, Robert (b. Rotherham, Yorkshire, 4 Mar. 1776; d. London, 13 June 1855). Cellist. From 1792, student of James Cervetto, who took him to Brighton, then London. From 1794 he was principal cellist, Royal Opera, London; also played with the principal concert societies, festivals, and eventually the Philharmonic, usually teamed with the contrabassist Dragonetti. From 1822 he taught at the Royal Academy; retired 1851. He composed cello music, especially duos. His son William (1802–69) was also a cellist.

Linley, Thomas, Jr. (b. Bath, 5 May 1756; d. Grimsthorpe, 5 Aug. 1778). Composer and violinist. He was a child prodigy on the violin, and in 1763 he played a concerto in a concert at Bristol. After studying composition with William Boyce (1763–68), he went to Florence for instruction with Nardini on the violin (from 1768). During his travels he met Mozart and Burney. After returning briefly to Bath, he moved to London with his family. He composed theater and choral works, including an oratorio, *The Song of Moses;* he also collaborated with his father, Thomas Linley, Sr., on the comic opera *The Duenna* (1775). He died in a boating accident.

Linley, Thomas, Sr. (b. Badminton, 17 Jan. 1733; d. London, 19 Nov. 1795). Composer and harpsichordist. He studied music with organist Thomas Chilcot in Bath; later he organized and directed concerts there. In 1767 his opera *The Royal Merchant* was produced in London. He was appointed director of the Drury Lane Theatre in 1774, and two years later he moved from Bath, settling in London. For the next two decades he composed and arranged operas, pastiches, pantomimes, and incidental music for London theaters. A number of his 12 children pursued musical careers, including Thomas, Jr. The father composed *Selima and Azor* (1776); *The Gentle Shepherd* (1781); *Love in the East* (1788).

Lipatti, Dinu [Constantin] (b. Bucharest, 19 Mar. 1917; d. Geneva, 2 Dec. 1950). Pianist and composer. At 4 he gave a concert for charity and began composing. At the Bucharest Conservatory in 1928–32 he studied piano with Florica Musicescu and composition with Mihail Jora. In 1933 he completed a symphonic poem and violin sonatina. When in 1934 he obtained only second prize at the Vienna International Competition, Alfred Cortot, a member of the jury, quit in protest. Lipatti then settled in Paris for private studies in piano with Cortot and Yvonne Lefébure; in conducting with Charles Munch; in composition with Dukas, Boulanger, and Stravinsky. In 1936 he wrote his *Concertino in the Classic Style* and made his first tour of Germany and Italy; began recording for Walter Legge after World War II. His largest works, the Symphonie Concertante and 2-piano *Suite,* were completed 1938. Returned to Romania in 1939–43, concertizing and recording with his godfather, Georges Enescu, as well as with Mengelberg. Settled in Switzerland in 1943; began teaching at the Geneva Conservatory. His classicism, both as composer and pianist, was not unlike the mature Busoni's.

Lipiński, Karol [Carl] **Józef** (b. Radzyń, Poland, 30 Oct. or 4 Nov. 1790; d. Urłów, near Lwów, 16 Dec. 1861). Violinist. Son and pupil of a musician; from 1799 played in a Lwów orchestra conducted by his father; 1809, first violin, later (1812) conductor of a theater orchestra there. In 1814 he met Spohr in Vienna, leading him to concentrate on improving his playing; 1817–18, made concert tours through Europe, playing twice with Paganini in Italy (1818); 1819–28, played widely in Poland, Germany, Russia; 1835–37, toured western Europe; 1838–39, toured Russia. From 1839 he was concertmaster at Dresden, also led a string quartet there and taught; 1861, retired to Urłów. Composed operas and much violin music, especially his Military Concerto op. 21.

Lipkin, Malcolm (Leyland) (b. Liverpool, 2 May 1932). Composer. He studied piano with Gordon Green (1944–48) and continued his education at the Royal College of Music (1949–53) with Stevens and later with Boris Blacher and Seiber (1954–57). Lectured at the Department of External Studies at Oxford (1965–75) and at the Univ. of Kent (from 1975). Works include 3 symphonies (no. 1, *Sinfonia da Roma,* 1958–65; no. 2, *The Pursuit,* 1975–77; no. 3, *Sun,* 1979–86) and other orchestral music (*Variations,* 1971; 2 violin concertos; a piano concerto; an oboe concerto, 1989); choral music (Psalm 96, soprano, alto, tenor, bass, chamber orchestra, 1969; 2 Psalms, 92 and 121, soprano, alto, tenor, bass, 1972–73); chamber music (string quartet, 1951; wind quintet, 1985; piano trio, 1988); 5 piano sonatas and other works for keyboard (*Metamorphosis,* harpsichord, 1974); songs.

Lippius, Johannes (b. Strasbourg, 24 June 1585; d. Speyer, 24 Sept. 1612). Theorist. Studied at Strasbourg Gymnasium, afterward traveling throughout Germany and studying with Calvisius at Leipzig; took a Master's degree at Wittenberg and a doctorate at Giessen, after which he was offered a post as professor of theology at Strasbourg, but died before he could return to the city. His *Synopsis musicae novae* (1612; ed. and trans. Benito V. Rivera, Colorado Springs, 1977) labels the bass a "fundamental melody" that supports triads (symbolic representations of the Trinity) above it, thus mirroring the actual continuo practice of the time; theorists such as Printz and J. G. Walther are indebted to his work.

Bibl.: Benito Rivera, *German Music Theory in the Early 17th Century: The Treatises of Johannes Lippius* (Ann Arbor, 1980).

Lisinski, Vatroslav [Fuchs, Ignacije] (b. Zagreb, 8 July 1819; d. there, 31 May 1854). Composer. Studied law and philosophy in Zagreb, also music, working as a clerk; became an adherent of Croatian nationalism, composing nationalistic songs and piano pieces, eventually the first Croatian opera, *Ljubav i zloba* [Love and Malice] (his vocal score was orchestrated by his teacher, Wisner von Morgenstern); 1847, went to Prague to enter the conservatory, but being too old, studied privately with Pitsch and Kittl; 1848, returned to Zagreb, legalizing the Croatian form of his name; tried to make a living as a musician and teacher, but in 1853 was forced to become a clerk again, virtually abandoning composition; died of dropsy. Composed a second opera, *Porin* (1848–51), not performed until 1897; 7 concert overtures.

Lissenko, Nikolai Vitalievich. See Lysenko, Nikolay Vitalyevich.

List, Garrett (b. Phoenix, 10 Sept. 1943). Composer and trombonist. He studied at California State Univ. at Long Beach and at Juilliard (M.M., 1969); was active as a performer of contemporary music (in the ensemble Music Elettronica Viva from 1971; in 1977 he was a founding member of the A-1 Band, devoted to jazz fusion); music director of The Kitchen (1975–77), an avant-garde cultural center in New York. Beginning 1980 he taught at the Liège Conservatory. Many of his compositions contain strong political messages (*Elegy to the People of Chile,* one or more instruments, 1973). *American Images* (1972) are settings of "found texts" for voice and one or more instruments. Other works include *Fear and Understanding* (jazz band, 1981) and 4 film scores (*The Man Ray Cycles,* 1983).

Listenius, Nikolaus (b. Hamburg, ca. 1510). Theorist. Studies at Wittenberg Univ., begun in 1529, led to the Master of Arts degree in 1531. His treatise *Rudimenta musicae* was published in 1533; in revised form, retitled *Musica,* it went through dozens of printings in 16th-century Germany and Austria. The work presents simple rules with plentiful musical examples and was widely used as a schoolbook for teaching singing.

Liszt, Franz [Franciscus] (b. Raiding, Hungary [now Austria], 22 Oct. 1811; d. Bayreuth, 31 July 1886). Pianist and composer. His father, Adam (1776–1827), had been for two years a Franciscan novice, an inclination that is thought to have influenced his son's religious leanings as well as his name; he also had musical abilities (having played in the Esterházy orchestra, 1805–9) and some training as a composer. From 1809 he was in charge of the Esterházy sheep at Raiding, 30 miles from Eisenstadt. Liszt's mother, (Maria) Anna Lager (1788–1866), had been a chambermaid in Vienna, marrying in 1811. Franz was their only child, a delicate boy of a religious, mystical nature, who early showed musical abilities and had his first piano lessons from his father, who in August 1819 took him to Vienna, where he played for Czerny. Czerny recognized his talent in spite of his lack of disciplined training and offered to teach him. That year he also played for Prince Esterházy, who promised help, but not to the extent that Adam Liszt had hoped for, making him (and later his son) resentful. Franz gave his first public concerts in Oedenburg in 1820, then in Pressburg during a sitting of the Hungarian Diet. A group of nobles agreed to finance his studies for six years. In the spring of 1822 he began to study with Czerny and Salieri in Vienna. That year Liszt contributed a variation to the composite set sponsored by Diabelli, his first published composition. Then on 1 Dec. he gave his first Vienna concert; others given through April 1823 made him a well-known local figure. In May he played five concerts in Pest.

In September 1823 Liszt left Vienna with his father for Paris, where he was quickly successful in the salons. Since the Conservatory would not admit foreign pianists, he studied privately with Reicha and Paer. He played in England in May 1824, June 1825, and June 1827, and in early 1826 toured the French provinces and Switzerland. His one-act opera *Don Sanche* was given at the Opéra (17 Oct. 1825) with moderate success, but his most significant work of the period was the *Étude en douze exercices* (1826), which included early versions of material reworked in the *Transcendental Etudes.* When Adam Liszt died of typhus in August 1828, Franz's mother came from Austria to look after him.

In the next two years he underwent a crisis. He largely gave up playing in public and composing; his depression was intensified by his first great love affair (1828), with one of his aristocratic pupils, whose father discovered it and broke it off. He again thought of entering the priesthood, but it was in the priestly function of the artist that he was to find his calling. This was defined for him through his attraction to Saint-Simonism in 1830–31, an association (never formalized by membership in the cult) that he later found embarrassing and tried to play down, but whose ideas remained central to his thinking, as did those of his next great intellectual enthusiasm, the Abbé de Lamennais, whom he began to read in 1833 and to whom he was personally close in 1834–36. From 1830 he was a friend of Berlioz, often playing his arrangement of the *Symphonie fantastique* (1833) and performing Berlioz's music at Weimar in the 1850s. In 1832 he met Chopin, with whom he played in Paris concerts. Chopin's attitude toward Liszt was equivocal; Liszt's admiration is manifested in his book *F. Chopin* (1852).

Liszt's most important musical influence in this period was Paganini, whom he heard in Paris in April 1832 and who became the model for his development

Franz Liszt at the piano with Berlioz, Czerny, and Ernst, 1846.

of a comparable piano virtuosity. This finding of his true direction also energized him as a composer, resulting in the *Malédiction* for piano and orchestra (1833), the *Album d'un voyageur* (1835–38), *Transcendental Etudes* (1837), *Grand galop chromatique* (1838), *Paganini Etudes* (1838–39), and the first plans for what were to become his two piano concertos and his two symphonies.

He spent the winter of 1832–33 in Switzerland with his mistress, Countess Adèle Laprimarède; in January 1833 he met Countess Marie d'Agoult, who was to dominate his life for over a decade. A complex figure who has been interpreted in nearly as diverse ways as Liszt himself, she was rich, beautiful, idealistic, artistically talented, and was to reinforce Liszt's aspirations to become a serious creative artist. She was, however, also emotionally unstable, self-centered, and jealous (not without reason). She and Liszt were immediately attracted and soon became lovers. After a separation in 1834 during her grief over the death of a child, in May 1835 Marie deserted her husband and joined Liszt in Switzerland for 13 months, where in December their daughter Blandine was born. Liszt taught a little at the new Geneva Conservatory, but mostly composed and wrote (he began to publish essays on music in 1834; the extent to which Liszt's writings were coauthored by Marie and later the Princess of Sayn-Wittgenstein is still debated). In summer 1836 the couple toured Chamonix with George Sand and in October returned to Paris, where they led a lively social life. Liszt resumed giving concerts there, and in 1837 had a pianistic duel with Thalberg, which ended inconclusively but brought both much publicity. April–July 1837 the couple spent at George Sand's country estate, then went to Italy, where Liszt gave some concerts. Their daughter Cosima was born at Como on 24 Dec. 1837. In the spring of 1838 Liszt gave eight benefit concerts in Vienna to aid victims of Hungarian floods, leaving Marie, who felt ill and abandoned, in Venice. When he returned they quarreled, initiating the disintegration of their relationship. They remained in Italy until summer 1839, their son Daniel being born at Rome in May. That autumn Liszt volunteered to raise funds for the proposed Beethoven monument in Bonn. The countess, who regarded his concert giving as self-degradation, returned to Paris. Since Liszt was to tour incessantly from 1839 to 1847, this marked another stage of their declining relationship. On 4 Jan. 1840 Liszt gave his first concert in Pest since 1823, resulting in a tremendous outpouring of national feeling (bolstering

Liszt's own nationalism, reawakened the previous year), manifested in unbridled idolatry of the greatest living Hungarian and setting a standard for the Lisztomania of his touring years. Much taken with the Gypsy music that he heard in Hungary, he composed the first versions of some of the pieces later called Hungarian Rhapsodies.

The idolatry of Liszt was to be repellent to some (his relations with both Schumann and Chopin suffered) and damaged his standing as a serious musician. In 1840 he played his first concerts in Prague, Dresden, and Leipzig (where he was not well received because of a conservatism that later made Leipzig a center of anti-Liszt sentiment). Three tours of England in 1840–41 were well received by audiences but not critically or financially successful. In October 1841 he began a tour of Germany, including his first visit to Weimar, where on returning in 1842 he accepted the post of Kapellmeister extraordinaire, and to Berlin, where he was hysterically received, giving 21 concerts in 10 weeks. In 1842 he was on to Warsaw and St. Petersburg, where he gave 6 concerts in April–May with huge success. He returned to Russia in 1843 (making his first appearances in Moscow) and 1847, but with less éclat.

He spent the summers of 1841–43 on a deserted island in the Rhine near Bonn with the countess. In April 1844 she ended their liaison (Liszt had been linked with other women on his tours, including the infamous Lola Montez). The countess had been making a name for herself (as Daniel Stern) as a professional writer since 1841 and had already begun her novel *Nélida,* a thinly veiled account of Liszt's character and of their relationship from her own point of view. Published in 1846, it aroused much attention, although Liszt always refused to acknowledge its relevance to himself. In 1845 they began to quarrel over the custody of their children, to whom neither seems previously to have paid much attention. Liszt as acknowledged father had legality on his side, and the children were raised away from their mother, mainly by their grandmother Liszt and in boarding schools. Liszt wrote to them but did not visit them again until 1853. In October 1844–April 1845 he made his one, tremendously successful tour of Spain and Portugal. In the summer of 1845 he unsuccessfully proposed marriage to Countess Valentine de Cessiat, Lamartine's niece and mistress. In August 1845 he played a prominent role in the unveiling of the Beethoven monument, which he had largely financed, in Bonn, his Festival Cantata being heard. He played in Vienna, Prague, Pest, and elsewhere in central Europe in the spring and summer of 1846, then in September began his longest tour, through Hungary, Transylvania, Romania, and southern Russia to Istanbul, where in June–July 1847 he played twice for the sultan, returning then to southern Russia, where he gave his last public recital for personal profit at Elisabetgrad in September.

Liszt had long intended to give up concert tours; his health had suffered, and he drank too much as a means of enduring their discomforts, but a decisive factor in his doing so was probably his meeting the other dominating female figure in his life. Princess Carolyne von Sayn-Wittgenstein (1819–1887) heard his concert at Kiev on 2 Feb. 1847. The owner of large estates in the Ukraine, estranged from her husband, she had no particular beauty and no distinction of dress or manner; some found her conversation bizarre or pretentious, others brilliant. Intensely devout, with her own personal Catholicism, she was interested in art but was unmusical. Liszt spent ten days at her house in February and returned there for a lengthy stay in the fall after his last concert. In February 1848 he settled in Weimar, becoming Kapellmeister in earnest. In April the princess left Russia with her daughter, also leaving behind respectability and much of her wealth. She rented the Villa Altenburg in Weimar, where Liszt lived with her, although their liaison was not recognized by the court or local society, by which she was ostracized, and their initial hopes of her obtaining a divorce so that they could marry were frustrated.

Liszt's work of the next decade represented his bid to be taken seriously as a major composer in the great tradition. It includes his principal large-scale instrumental works: the Faust and Dante symphonies, the first 12 symphonic poems, and the B-minor Piano Sonata. With Wagner in exile (he had sought Liszt's help in May 1849 after fleeing Dresden; Liszt himself took no active part in the revolutionary events of 1848), Liszt became the center of the radical wing of German music, known as the New German School, attracting a coterie of pupils and admirers including Raff (who until 1856 helped Liszt with the orchestration of his music), Cornelius, von Bülow (who married Cosima Liszt in 1857). Others, including Joachim (Weimar concertmaster in 1850–52) and Brahms, who visited in 1853, were repelled by Liszt's artistic ideals, his suave, urbane personality, and the adulation with which he was surrounded. In spite of limited resources, he made Weimar a center for the performance of new music, including Berlioz, Wagner (especially the productions of *Tannhäuser,* February 1849, and *Lohengrin,* August 1850), and aspiring young composers. It was the adverse audience reaction at the premiere of Cornelius's *Der Barbier von Bagdad* (1858) that led to his resignation. Further personal blows included the death of his son Daniel in 1859 (his daughter Blandine was to die after childbirth in 1862).

He settled in Rome in 1861, expecting the imminent annulment of the princess's marriage (she had moved there in 1860), but it never happened, and their desire for legal union seems to have faded. They did not marry even after the prince's death in 1864, although they remained on close (but apparently not intimate) terms. In 1861–69 Liszt's life was centered in Rome (he made trips to Germany in 1864 and 1867, Paris in 1866), and his religious inclinations took the ascendancy. From 1863 he lived much in a small cell at the Oratorio della Madonna dĭ Rosario; in 1867 he moved to the Santa Francesca Roma monastery, also maintaining quarters at the Villa d'Este outside Rome. (He did not become hermetic but had extensive social contacts.) On 25 Apr. 1865 he took the four minor orders of the church, receiving the tonsure, thereafter wearing a cassock and wishing to be known as Abbé Liszt. This move caused considerable comment, much of it uncomprehending or doubtful of Liszt's sincerity. Liszt's compositional interests turned away from the large instrumental works of the Weimar period to sacred music, including his oratorios *Die Legende von der heiligen Elisabeth,* begun in Weimar (premiere, Pest, 1865) and *Christus* (mostly composed in 1862–66; premiere, Weimar, 1873), Masses and motets; other works included the two *Légendes* for piano (1863). In 1869, tired of Rome (it has been suggested that he was disappointed at not having his efforts in sacred music recognized by a papal appointment), he began to spend part of the year (usually the summer) teaching in Weimar, and from 1872 the first three or four months of the year in Budapest, teaching and helping found the National Academy of Music, of which he was the first president (1875), and in whose affairs he took an active part. From 1867 he was disturbed by Cosima's affair with Wagner and her treatment of von Bülow and did not attend her wedding in 1870, although he never wavered in his devotion to Wagner's music (Cosima, resentful of her illegitimacy and of Liszt's remoteness in her childhood, never displayed much warmth toward her father). Their relations were restored in 1872. Liszt thereafter visited the couple at Bayreuth, resisting Wagner's urging to settle there. Wagner dedicated *Parsifal* to him. After 1870 Liszt's own creative energies were less focused, although his output remained extensive, including sacred works, the last symphonic poem (*Von der Wiege bis zum Grabe,* 1881–82), the third book of the *Années de pèlerinage* (1867–77), and the experimental piano pieces of his last years that show his musical intellect still active in ways that have aroused much interest among later theorists and historians. He continued to travel frequently, almost restlessly, especially to attend, sometimes to conduct, performances of his works throughout Europe, though in his last years he reduced his public charitable appearances as a pianist, pleading lack of practice. He did not visit Rome in 1882–83, but returned in 1884 and 1885, leaving the princess for the last time in January 1886. Although ailing and failing in his sight, he traversed much of Europe from Budapest to London in 1886, attending concerts of his music. He died from pneumonia, attended (none too graciously) by Cosima.

An overview of Liszt's music is complicated by the long gestation of some of it and the existence of many works in more than one version or in arrangements for various performing forces. An important part of his output consists of piano transcriptions of music not by himself, although a dividing line between original music and transcription is hard to draw in his work, ranging as it does from the 19 Hungarian Rhapsodies, original compositions based on borrowed melodies, through the operatic potpourris, which often interpret the material in an original way, to the transcriptions of symphonies of Berlioz and Beethoven and songs by Schubert, Franz, and Schumann, which were influential in familiarizing his audiences with these works, but in which, through the way they are adapted to the piano, Liszt himself is also strongly present.

Bibl.: *Musikalische Werke* (Leipzig, 1901–36). Imre Sulyok and Imre Mĕzo, eds., *New Liszt Edition* (Budapest, 1970–). Francis Hueffer, trans., *Correspondence of Wagner and Liszt* (London, 1888). La Mara, ed., *Franz Liszts Briefe* (Leipzig, 1893–1905; trans. Eng., 2 vols. (New York, 1894; R: 1968). Howard Eppens Hugo, ed. and trans., *The Letters of Franz Liszt to Marie zu Sayn-Wittgenstein* (Cambridge, Mass., 1953). Alan Walker, *Franz Liszt: The Virtuoso Years, 1811–1847,* 2nd rev. ed. (Ithaca, N.Y., 1987). Ernst Burger, *Franz Liszt: A Chronicle of His Life in Pictures and Documents* (Princeton, 1989). Derek Watson, *Liszt* (London and New York, 1989). Michael Benton Saffle, *Franz Liszt: A Guide to Research* (New York, 1991).

Litaize, Gaston (Gilbert) (b. Ménil-sur-Belvitte, Vosges, 11 Aug. 1909). Organist and composer. He studied organ with Dupré and composition with Büsser; received the Premier Prix in organ, fugue, and composition at the Paris Conservatory. He had studied initially at the National School for the Blind and later taught there; from 1946 was organist at St. François Xavier, Paris. His recording of Couperin's *Messe pour les Paroisses* won the Grand Prix du Disque in 1955. Works include a symphony for organ and orchestra (1943) and other piano and organ pieces as well as sacred choral music.

Literes Carrión, Antonio (b. Artá, Majorca, 18 June 1673?; d. Madrid, 18 Jan. 1747). Composer. He was listed as a bass viol player at the royal choir school, Madrid, in 1688; he moved to the Capilla real in 1693. His contemporaries praised his talents in both sacred and secular composition. Three of his dramatic works written for the Spanish court are extant; he also provided the Lisbon cathedral with an oratorio based on St. Vicente's life (1720, lost), composed three Masses along with vespers music for the Portuguese court to replace the repertory lost in the 1734 fire, and produced sacred and secular cantatas.

Litinsky, Genrikh Il'ich (b. Lipovets [now Vinnitsa district], 3 Apr. 1901; d. Moscow, 26 July 1985). Composer. He studied composition with Glier at the Moscow Conservatory; subsequently taught there (1928–43). He later taught at the Gnesin Institute (from 1947) and at the Kazan Conservatory (1949–64). In 1945 he went to Yakutsk and collaborated on the first Yakut operas; he also wrote 3 Yakut ballets. Other works include *Dagfestan Suite,* orchestra (1931); Trumpet Concerto (1934); *Festive Rhapsody,* orchestra (1966); 12 string quartets; various other chamber music; and vocal cycles. He published 2 textbooks on polyphony (1965–67, 1970).

Litolff, Henry Charles (b. London, 6 Feb. or 7 Aug. 1818; d. Bois-Colombes, near Paris, 5 or 6 Aug. 1891). Composer and pianist. Son of an Alsatian musician settled in London and a Scotswoman; 1830–35, piano lessons from Moscheles; professional debut in 1832; largely self-taught in composition. In 1835 he eloped with a young woman, settling near Paris, where he appeared as pianist; 1839–41, in Brussels; fleeing for debt, he seems to have wandered through Europe, appearing as pianist and conductor. In 1845 he returned to London, hoping to divorce his wife; her family had him imprisoned, but he escaped to the Continent. In Vienna during the 1848 Revolution he became involved and had to flee. In 1849 he settled in Brunswick; 1851, married the widow of a music publisher there, gave the firm his own name, and specialized in cheap popular editions of classical works (1860, gave the business to his adopted son); from 1855, court Kapellmeister, Saxe-Coburg-Gotha. In 1858 his second wife demanded divorce (he had abandoned her), and he settled in Paris. A prolific composer (operas, oratorios, orchestral and piano pieces); best known for his 5 piano concertos (1 lost), all called Concerto Symphonique, especially no. 4, op. 102 (ca. 1852).

Little Richard [Penniman, Richard] (b. Macon, Ga., 25 Dec. 1935). Rock-and-roll singer, songwriter, and pianist. He began performing and recording in Macon, Atlanta, and Houston, and became a central figure in the mid-1950s rock-and-roll movement; his recordings showcased a virtuosic vocal style involving vocalizations and falsetto techniques ("Tutti Frutti," 1956; "Keep a Knockin'," 1957; "Good Golly, Miss Molly," 1958). Beginning in the late 1950s his career alternated between music and work as a Seventh-Day Adventist minister; also recorded gospel and soul music.

Little Walter [Jacobs, Marion Walter] (b. Marksville, La., 1 May 1930; d. Chicago, 15 Feb. 1968). Blues harmonica player. He joined Muddy Waters's band in Chicago in 1948 and developed a rough amplified harmonica style heard on Waters's recording "Long Distance Call" (1951). He regularly played with Waters at sessions until 1956, but mainly led his own groups after the success of his recording "Juke" (1952).

Llobet, Miguel (b. Barcelona, 18 Oct. 1878; d. there, 22 Feb. 1938). Guitarist. Studied with Francisco Tárrega. Played recitals and at soirées at the Paris Exhibition in 1900; later toured Europe, Argentina (1910), Chile (1912), and the U.S. (1915–17). Formed a duo with María Luisa Anido in Buenos Aires. Made many solo transcriptions and arrangements for 2 guitars of classical and Romantic works. Falla wrote *Homenaje,* a tribute to Debussy, for Llobet.

Lloyd, Charles Harford (b. Thornbury, Gloucestershire, 16 Oct. 1849; d. Slough, near London, 16 Oct. 1919). Organist and composer. Student, 1868–75, Magdalen Hall, Oxford (M.A.; later, 1893, D.Mus.). Organist, 1876–82, Gloucester Cathedral, conducting the Three Choirs Festival there in 1877 and 1880; 1882–86, organist, Christ Church, Oxford; 1887–92, taught organ and composition, Royal College of Music; 1892–1914, preceptor and music teacher, Eton; from 1914, organist, Chapel Royal St. James's. Composed much Anglican church music; secular cantatas; part songs; chamber music; an organ concerto; organ sonata; organ and piano pieces.

Lloyd, George (Walter Selwyn) (b. St Ives, Cornwall, 28 June 1913). Composer. He studied composition with Farjeon and counterpoint with Kitson; made his debut conducting the Bournemouth Symphony in his own Symphony no. 1 in 1933. Principal guest conductor and music adviser to the Albany, N.Y., Symphony, from 1989. Best known for his 3 operas on medieval or legendary Britain, *Iernin* (1933–34), *The Serf* (1936–38), *John Socman* (1951), all to librettos by his father, William Lloyd; also composed 12 symphonies (1932–89) and 4 piano concertos (no. 4, 1984).

Lloyd, Jonathan (b. London, 30 Sept. 1948). Composer. He studied composition with Emile Spira (1963–65) prior to his enrollment at the Royal College of Music (1965–69), where his teachers included Edwin Roxburgh and John Lambert (composition) and Tristram Cary (electronic music); in 1973 he worked with Ligeti at Tanglewood, where he received the Koussevitzky Prize for his music theatre piece *Scattered Ruins* (1973); served as composer-in-residence at the Dartington College theater department in Devon (1978–79). Lloyd's music often relies on pastiche techniques, incorporating episodes of jazz and popular music. Works include a viola concerto (1981), 5 symphonies (1983–89), chamber music (*Won't It Ever Be Morning,* chamber ensemble, 1980), vocal music.

Lloyd, Norman (b. Pottsville, Pa., 8 Nov. 1909; d. Greenwich, Conn., 31 July 1980). Composer. He studied at New York Univ. (M.S., 1936); then taught at Sarah Lawrence until 1945, spending summers at Bennington College. Having written many dance scores for Martha Graham and others, he established the dance department at Juilliard, where he was director of education, 1946–1949. In 1963 he was dean of the Oberlin College Conservatory, and in 1965 director of arts programming for the Rockefeller Foundation; he retired in 1972. Works include band, choral, and piano music as well as many dance and film scores. He edited *The Golden Encyclopedia of Music* (1968) and several collections of folk songs.

Lloyd-Jones, David (Mathias) (b. London, 19 Nov. 1934). Conductor. Studied German and Russian at Oxford, and music privately with Iain Hamilton. Became chorusmaster and assistant conductor of the New Opera Company in 1960; in 1963 he began guest-conducting orchestras and opera companies including the BBC Welsh Orchestra, the Welsh National Opera, and Covent Garden. Assistant musical director at Sadler's Wells from 1972; musical director of the English National Opera North, Leeds, 1977–81, and artistic director, 1981–90. Translated the librettos of *Boris Godunov* and *Eugene Onegin;* published a critical edition of *Boris Godunov.*

Lloyd Webber, Andrew (b. London, 22 Mar. 1948). Composer. He received his earliest musical instruction from his mother, a piano teacher, and his father, director of the London College of Music. He subsequently attended Westminster School in London, Magdalen College in Oxford, and the Royal College of Music. While in college he wrote his first musical, *The Likes of Us.* In 1967 he composed *Joseph and the Amazing Technicolor Dreamcoat* (lyrics by Tim Rice), which achieved great success in England and the U.S., where it was seen on television in 1972. His next work, *Jesus Christ Superstar* (Rice, 1970), a "rock opera," was first released as a record album, eventually selling 3 million copies. The musical opened on Broadway in October 1971 amid protests by religious groups and won 7 Tony awards; it opened in London the following year and ran for 3,357 performances. *Evita* (Rice, 1976; stage version, 1978) opened in London in 1978. *Cats,* inspired by T. S. Eliot's *Old Possum's Book of Practical Cats,* was produced in London in May 1981 and enjoyed great success in New York following its opening there in October 1982. *Phantom of the Opera* (Richard Stilgoe and Charles Hart, 1986) was also very successful. Other works include *Jeeves* (Alan Ayckbourn, 1975); *Tell Me on a Sunday* (Don Black, 1980); *Starlight Express* (Stilgoe, 1984); Requiem (1985); *Variations on a Theme of Paganini,* orchestra (1986); *Aspects of Love* (1989); *Sunset Boulevard* (1993).

Bibl.: Kurt Gänzl, *The Music of Andrew Lloyd Webber* (London, 1989). Michael Walsh, *Andrew Lloyd Webber: His Life and Works* (New York, 1989).

Lloyd Webber, Julian (b. London, 14 Apr. 1951). Cellist. Studied at the Royal College of Music in London, 1968–72, then privately with Pierre Fournier, 1973. After his debut in London in 1972 he appeared as soloist with major English, Continental, and American orchestras. He was particularly resourceful in finding and recording little-known works by Haydn, Arthur Sullivan, Vaughan Williams, Holst, Bridge, and others. He is the brother of the composer Andrew Lloyd Webber.

Lobe, Johann Christian (b. Weimar, 30 May 1797; d. Leipzig, 27 July 1881). Writer and composer. Son of a book illustrator; largely self-taught in music, learning the flute and violin; 1811–42, flutist, later violist, Weimar court orchestra, also composing 5 operas there and other music; a member of Goethe's circle; 1846, moved to Leipzig; 1846–48, editor, *Allgemeine musikalische Zeitung.* He is best known for his writing, especially the 4-volume *Lehrbuch der musikalischen Komposition* (Leipzig, 1850–67), one of the most highly regarded texts of the day. His musical catechisms (1851, 1872) were widely used and translated; essays collected in *Gesammelte Schriften: Consonanzen und Dissonanzen* (Leipzig, 1869); memoirs: *Aus dem Leben eines Musikers* (Leipzig, 1859).

Lobkowitz, Joseph Franz Maximilian (b. Roudnice nad Labem, 7 Dec. 1772; d. Třeboň, 15 Dec. 1816). Singer and patron of the arts. Descended from an important line of Bohemian nobility, he spent much of his life in Vienna. He often performed in that city as a bass singer, and also played cello and violin. From ca. 1810 until 1814 he was director of the Viennese court theaters. He cofounded the Gesellschaft der Musikfreunde in Vienna and the institution that was later to become the Prague Conservatory. He was a benefactor of Haydn (whose op. 77 he commissioned) and especially of Beethoven, who dedicated to him the Third, Fifth, and Sixth symphonies, the Triple Concerto, the String Quartet op. 74, and other works. He was one of the three noblemen who put up an annuity for Beethoven's financial support.

Lobo [Lobo de Borja], **Alonso** (b. Osuna, ca. 1555; d. Seville, 5 Apr. 1617). Composer. A choirboy at Seville Cathedral; from 1591 assistant to Guerrero, *maestro de capilla* there; from 1593 maestro at Toledo Cathedral; from 1604 maestro in Seville. His compositions include 6 Masses, 7 motets, and assorted other sacred choral works, many for 2 choirs. Victoria and other contemporaries and successors held him in the highest regard.

Lobo, Duarte [Lupus, Eduardus] (b. Alcáçovas, 1565?; d. Lisbon, 24 Sept. 1646). Composer. Musical studies and employment in Évora and Lisbon led by 1594 to the position of *maestro de capilla* at Lisbon Cathedral. His considerable compositional skill earned the respect of his contemporaries and recognition from the Portuguese royal court. Most of his works were published in 6 volumes of liturgical music, some for multiple choirs.

Locatelli, Pietro Antonio (b. Bergamo, 3 Sept. 1695; d. Amsterdam, 30 Mar. 1764). Composer. Played violin as a boy at S. Maria Maggiore, Bergamo; received leave in 1611 to travel to Rome, where he perhaps studied with Valentini (though probably not with Corelli). Appeared often at S. Lorenzo in Damaso between 1717 and 1723; named *virtuoso da camera* at Mantua in 1725, but freely pursued other engagements, including performances at Venice (1725), Bavaria (1727), and Berlin and Kassel (1728), appearing with Leclair *l'aîné* in Kassel. Moved to Amsterdam in 1729, where he lived for the rest of his life, leading a group of amateur musicians and teaching. He released in 1721 a corrected version of his concerti grossi in 1729; two years later he received a 15-year exclusive privilege for the printing of his music in the Netherlands, renewing it in 1747; from 1741 he sold imported Italian violin strings as well. Though his playing was highly praised, some observers found it too brilliant;

likewise, the originality of his works was admired, while others criticized a lack of technique and invention. As a composer he focused on the sonata and concerto, achieving a fusion of sorts between the Roman and Venetian styles; his caprices for solo violin in *L'arte del violino* (Amsterdam, 1733) at one time earned him the title "Paganini of the 18th century." An extensive art collection, along with a library featuring books on history, philosophy, and science in addition to music, testify to his breadth of learning.

Bibl.: Albert Dunning, *P. A. Locatelli: Der Virtuose und seiner Welt* (Buren, 1981). Arend Koole, "P. A. Locatelli," *Chigiana* 21 (1964): 29–46.

Locke, Matthew (b. Exeter, 1621–22; d. London, Aug. 1677). Composer. Sang at Exeter Cathedral under Edward Gibbons. Traveled to the Netherlands in the 1640s, perhaps with exiled royalists; returned to England by 1651, possibly living near Hereford; collaborated with Christopher Gibbons on *Cupid and Death* (1653; rev. 1659), supplied music to several of Davenant's dramas, and was associated with figures such as Playford, H. Lawes, and Simpson. Became royal composer-in-ordinary and composer for wind and violin music upon the Restoration in 1660; provided music for the coronation of Charles II in 1661, and was named organist to the queen in 1662. A difficult and vindictive personality, he was embroiled in many controversies in his later years; nonetheless, among his intimates was Purcell, who succeeded him as composer-in-ordinary and whom he influenced substantially. His extensive oeuvre includes anthems, motets, and services along with songs, dramatic works, and dance music.

Lockwood, Annea [Anna] **(Ferguson)** (b. Christchurch, New Zealand, 29 July 1939). Composer. She graduated from the Univ. of Canterbury, New Zealand (B.Mus., 1961), and attended the Royal College of Music, London (1961–63), working with Fricker (composition) and Taylor (piano); continued her studies of composition in Darmstadt (1961–62) and with Koenig at the Staatliche Hochschule für Musik in Cologne (1963–64), and studied psychoacoustics at the Institute of Sound and Vibration Research at Southampton Univ. (1969–72). Taught composition and electronic music at various American universities, including Hunter College and Queens College of the City Univ. of New York and Vassar College (1973–83). Lockwood's experiments in total sensory art (such as burning or drowning a piano), mixed media, and environmental sound reflect her interest in avant-garde theater and performance. Works include *Glass Concert,* sheets of plate glass, spotlight bulbs, wine glasses, milk bottles, etc. (1966); *Humm,* 70 or more hummers (1971); *Conversations with the Ancestors,* mixed-media installation (1979); *Sound Map of the Hudson River,* tape installation (1982); *Nautilus,* didgeridoo, conch shells, percussion (1989).

Lockwood, Normand (b. New York, 19 Mar. 1906). Composer. His father and uncle taught piano and violin, respectively, at the Univ. of Michigan, where Lockwood studied piano and composition. In 1924 he went to Europe to study with Respighi (1924) and Boulanger (1925–28); a fellow at the American Academy in Rome from 1929 to 1932. He taught at Oberlin College Conservatory (1932–43), Columbia and Union Theological Seminary (1945–53), Trinity Univ., San Antonio (1953–55), and elsewhere; in 1961 he was appointed professor of composition and composer-in-residence at the Univ. of Denver, retiring as professor emeritus in 1975. His style is accessible and concise, often involving quotation. Works include 5 operas (1945–64); 2 symphonies (1943, 1979), concertos for organ and brass (1951, 1978), and other orchestral music; 7 string quartets (1933–50), *Valley Suite* (violin and piano, 1976), and other instrumental music; many choral (*A Child's Christmas in Wales,* children's voices and piano, 1984) and solo vocal works.

Bibl.: Kay Norton, *Normand Lockwood: His Life and Music* (Metuchen, N.J., 1993).

Loeffler, Charles Martin (b. Mulhouse, Alsace, 30 Jan. 1861; d. Medfield, Mass., 19 May 1935). Composer. Son of an expert on agriculture and horses (both interests shared by his son), who also published plays, novels, and humorous works and who ran afoul of the Prussian government for his opinions and died in prison, ca. 1884–85, a traumatic and embittering experience for his son (who, it has been suggested may have denied German birth because of it; school records list Schöneberg near Berlin as his birthplace). After early childhood in Alsace, his father's work took the family to a village near Kiev, where Loeffler had violin lessons in summer from a vacationing member of the imperial orchestra of St. Petersburg, then for several years to Debrecen, Hungary, and two years in Switzerland. In 1874 or 1875–77 he was a student at the Berlin Hochschule für Musik (violin under Rappoldi, then Joachim); later in Paris with Massart and Guiraud; violinist in Pasdeloup's orchestra for a season; 1879–81, in the private orchestra of Paul de Derwies, a very rich Russian nobleman who had winter and summer homes in Nice and Lugano. In 1881 he emigrated to the U.S., a citizen from 1887; 1881–82, violinist in Leopold Damrosch's orchestra, New York; 1882–1903, assistant concertmaster, Boston Symphony, also appearing as soloist in works by himself and others (a brother, Erich, was a cellist in this orchestra; a sister, Helen, was a harpist in Frankfurt); 1884, further study with Hubert Léonard in Paris. After leaving the Boston Symphony he spent a year in Paris (1904–5), then lived on his farm in Medfield, near Boston, where he had a studio for teaching.

Loeffler developed slowly as a composer and was intensely self-critical. A string quartet (1889) was his first important work to be heard, *Nights in the Ukraine* (Boston Symphony, 1891) his first orchestral work. His early orchestral music tends to feature a solo instrument, usually the violin. In *La mort de Tintagiles* op. 6 (1897–1900), for 2 violas d'amore (later rev. for 1), both the choice of solo instruments and subject matter reflect the antiquarian and mystical interests that flavor much of his music. His musical tastes were broad, ranging from Gregorian chant to (in his later years) jazz. His best-known work was the orchestral version of *A Pagan Poem* op. 14 (1906), originally for chamber ensemble. He published almost nothing until after he left the Boston Symphony, and even then much remained in manuscript. He was a highly respected composer in the U.S. in his time, although, because of the personal character of his music, not an influential one.

Bibl.: Walter Damrosch, *Charles Martin Loeffler* (New York, 1936). Ellen E. Knight, *Charles Martin Loeffler: A Life Apart in American Music* (Urbana, Ill., 1993).

Loeillet, Jacques [Jacob] (bapt. Ghent, 7 July 1685; d. there, 28 Nov. 1748). Composer. Brother of Jean Baptiste [John] Loeillet. Served as oboist to the Elector of Bavaria during his exile in the Netherlands, joining the same court at Munich in 1726; later was chamber musician to Louis XV at Versailles, returning to Ghent in 1746. Surviving works include 6 duets and 6 solo sonatas (opp. 4, 5; opp. 1–3 are lost), along with 2 concertos.

Loeillet, Jean-Baptiste [John] (bapt. Ghent, 18 Nov. 1680; d. London, 19 July 1730). Composer. Brother of Jacques Loeillet. Moved to London around 1705; played in the Drury Lane orchestra by 1707, and was oboist and flutist in that of the Queen's Theatre soon thereafter; initiated a series of concerts at his home in 1710 and built a reputation as a harpsichord player and teacher. He was reputedly pivotal to the acceptance of the transverse flute in England. His extant compositions, wholly instrumental, consist of 5 prints issued between about 1712 and 1729 and include suites of lessons for harpsichord and both trio and solo sonatas for various combinations of flute, recorder, oboe, and violin.

Loeillet [Loeillet de Gant], **Jean-Baptiste** (bapt. Ghent, 6 July 1688; d. Lyons, ca. 1720). Composer. Cousin of Jacques and Jean-Baptiste [John] Loeillet. Served the Archbishop of Lyons and presumably died young. His works, published in Amsterdam and reissued in London, consist of 4 books of solo sonatas for recorder (Amsterdam, ca. 1710, 1714, 1715, 1716) and a collection of trio sonatas (1717).

Loesser, Frank (b. New York, 29 June 1910; d. there, 26 July 1969). Popular songwriter, lyricist, and librettist. He wrote lyrics for Feist and R.K.O. in the early 1930s and published his first song in 1931 ("In Love with a Memory of You," music by William Schuman). From 1936 he worked in Hollywood, writing lyrics for films with Hoagy Carmichael ("Small Fry," "Two Sleepy People," both 1938), Burton Lane ("Says My Heart," 1938) and Jimmy McHugh ("Can't Get Out of This Mood," 1942). He began writing his own music during World War II, scoring success with several patriotic songs ("Praise the Lord and Pass the Ammunition," 1942), and after the war produced musicals on Broadway for which he wrote score, lyrics, and book. The most popular of these were *Where's Charley?* (1948), *Guys and Dolls* (1950, including "A Bushel and a Peck," "I've Never Been in Love Before," and "Sit Down, You're Rocking the Boat"), *Most Happy Fella* (1956, including "Big 'D'"), and *How To Succeed in Business without Really Trying* (1961, including "I Believe in You"), which won a Pulitzer Prize in drama.

Loewe, (Johann) Carl (Gottfried) (b. Löbejün, near Halle, 30 Nov. 1796; d. Kiel, 20 Apr. 1869). Composer. Son and pupil of a village school- and choirmaster; choirboy at Cöthen; 1807, went to school at Halle, studying music with Türk; given a stipend by King Jerome, who was impressed by his singing; after 1813 private sponsors supported his studies, from 1817 at Halle Univ. (theology). He began to compose early, publishing a song in 1813, his specialty becoming dramatic and narrative ballads, including his early *Erlkönig* (1818); also acquired a reputation as a singer (baritone) of them. Toured Germany 1819–20; in January 1820 he settled in Stettin as teacher at the gymnasium and seminary, also taking the posts of cantor and organist at St. Jacobus (from November 1820) and city music director (from February 1821). He was married twice, from 1826 to Auguste Lange, a singer of his songs. His reputation from his own performances, which combined expressive intensity with emotive gifts, spread through North Germany and later more widely through his concert visits to Vienna (1844), London (1847), Sweden and Norway (1851), and Paris (1857). In 1864 he suffered a stroke from which he did not completely recover; he retired in 1866 to Kiel.

Composed 6 operas, but only the comic singspiel *Die drei Wünsche* was performed, and only at Berlin (1834) and Weimar; more successful with some of his ca. 16 oratorios, especially *Die Zerstörung Jerusalems* (Berlin, 1832). Also cantatas, part songs; 4 string quartets, a piano trio, other chamber works; piano sonatas, piano tone poems; but best known for his ballads and other lieder, which he published copiously from 1824 to about 1860. Also wrote memoirs, published posthumously as *Selbstbiographie,* ed. by C. H. Bitter (Berlin, 1870).

Bibl.: M. Runze, ed., *Carl Loewes Werke: Gesamtausgabe der Balladen, Legenden, Lieder und Gesänge* (Leipzig, 1899–1904; R: 1970). Reinhold Dusella, *Die Oratorien Carl Loewes* (Bonn, 1991).

Loewe, Frederick (b. Berlin, 10 June 1901; d. Palm Springs, Calif., 14 Feb. 1988). Popular composer. He studied piano (with Busoni) and composition in Berlin, and emigrated to the U.S. in 1924. Son of an operetta tenor; his first works were in Viennese style (including "Love Tiptoed through My Heart," 1935; and the show *Great Lady,* 1938); his entrance into the genre of the American musical came with his collaboration with

Alan Jay Lerner, with whom he worked exclusively after 1947. They wrote the musicals *Brigadoon* (1947, including "The Heather on the Hill," "Almost Like Being in Love"), *Paint Your Wagon* (1951, including "They Call the Wind Maria"), *My Fair Lady* (1956, including "With a Little Bit of Luck," "Rain in Spain," "I Could Have Danced All Night," "On the Street Where You Live," and "I've Grown Accustomed to Her Face"), and *Camelot* (1960), and the film *Gigi* (1958). Loewe was notable for his ability to write imaginatively for technically inexperienced singers (including Rex Harrison and Richard Burton); he retired after the failure of the film *The Little Prince* (1974).

Lofton, Cripple Clarence (b. Kingsport, Tenn., 28 Mar. 1887; d. Chicago, 9 Jan. 1957). Boogie-woogie pianist and singer. From 1917 he lived in Chicago, working into the 1940s mainly as a soloist. Known for his energetic performances, as on the recording "Strut That Thing" (1935), he had an undisciplined technique that, paradoxically, brought vitality to the often rigidly interpreted boogie-woogie form. "Blue Boogie" (c. 1939), for example, is an 11-bar blues containing striking dissonances.

Logier, Johann Bernhard (b. Kassel, 9 Feb. 1777; d. Dublin, 27 July 1846). Teacher. Son and pupil of a musician of Huguenot descent; learned keyboard and flute; 1791, emigrated to England; 1794–1807, flutist in a regimental band in Ireland, then a musician in Westport, Kilkenny, and Dublin (1809), where he opened a music shop and taught. In 1814 he patented the chiroplast, a device for guiding the hands of piano students; from 1816, published explanations of the chiroplast and of his teaching methods, which, although controversial, proved influential in Britain and Germany; 1822–26, taught his methods in Berlin; 1826–29, in London, then returned to Dublin as teacher and music seller. Also published books on figured bass and composition and composed.

Logothetis, Anestis (b. Pyrgos, Greece, 27 Oct. 1921). Composer. He went to Vienna in 1942 as a mechanical engineering student but entered the Music Academy in 1945 to study for six years with Alfred Uhl and Erwin Ratz; later attended courses in Rome and Darmstadt and in 1957 worked in the electronic music studios in Cologne. Thereafter he taught piano privately and worked for Universal Edition (1955–64), Edition Modern (1962–67), and Edition Gerig (1965–68). After 1969 he devoted himself to composition. Works composed before 1960 employed twelve-tone and serial methods; he later explored graphic notations, and often left the instrumentation and other aspects of performance up to the performers (as in *5 Porträte der Liebe,* ballet, 1960). Works include musical plays and other stage music (*Das Urteil des Paris in Paris,* actor and piano, 1968), radio operas, and ballets; *Koordination* (5 instrumental groups, 1960) and other orchestral music; *Integrationen 51* (violin, 1951) and other instrumental music; *Textures* (1957) and other piano music; some choral and solo vocal music; many works for unspecified instrument(s) in graphic notation (*Reversible Bi-Junction,* 1965). His writings include *Notation mit Graphischen Elementen* (Salzburg, 1967) and many articles.

Logroscino, Nicola (bapt. Bitonto, 22 Oct. 1698; d. Palermo, after 1765). Composer. Attended the Conservatorio S. Maria di Loreto, Naples, 1714–27; served as organist at Conza (Avellino), 1728–31; after perhaps turning out comic operas in Naples the preceding seven years, he presented his opera *Il Quinto Fabio* in Rome in 1738; he later taught at the Ospedale dei figliuoli dispersi, Palermo. He was the most important figure in Neapolitan comic opera between the death of Leo and the ascent of Piccinni, though earlier assertions of his role as creator of comic opera or of the ensemble finale have been discounted. In addition to his serious and comic operas (*Il governatore* is the only example of the latter that survives intact), he wrote a small amount of church music.

Löhlein [Lelei], **Georg Simon** (b. Neustadt an der Heide, near Coburg, bapt. 16 July 1725; d. Danzig, 16 Dec. 1781). Composer and theorist. His father, Johann Michael Löhlein, was organist at Neustadt and probably also his first teacher. After serving in the Prussian Guard from age 16, during which period he was wounded, he studied at the Univ. of Jena, then (from 1763) at the Univ. of Leipzig, where he played in J. A. Hiller's ensembles. He composed a singspiel, *Zemire und Azor* (Leipzig, 1775), concertos, and chamber music. He taught music in Leipzig, and the fruit of this experience was the *Clavier-Schule, oder Kurze und gründliche Anweisung zur Melodie und Harmonie* (Leipzig and Züllichau, 1765); its second volume (1781) was subtitled *Worinnen eine vollständige Anweisung zur Begleitung der unbezifferten Bass . . . gegeben wird.* Derived from C. P. E. Bach, it was widely influential into the 19th century. In 1781 Löhlein moved to Danzig to take a position as organist at St. Mary's Church.

Löhner, Johann (bapt. Nuremberg, 21 Nov. 1645; d. there 2 Apr. 1705). Composer. A student of his brother-in-law, J. C. Wecker; served as singer and organist in several Nuremberg churches, St. Lorenz and the Spitalkirche among them. Works include over 300 songs for private devotion (mostly strophic, but through-composed in the case of *Auserlesene Kirch-und-Tafel-Musik,* 1682) and several operas, of which only a few arias survive.

Bibl.: Harold E. Samuel, *The Cantata in Nuremberg during the Seventeenth Century* (Ann Arbor, 1982).

Lohse, Otto (b. Dresden, 21 Sept. 1858; d. Baden-Baden, 5 May 1925). Conductor. Student at the Dresden Conservatory; 1882–93, conductor (rising to chief), Riga; 1893–95, assistant conductor, under Mahler, Hamburg Opera. In 1893 he married the prima donna Katarina Klafsky; 1895–96, both were in Damrosch's company in New York and on tour; then opera conductor at Strasbourg (1897–1904); Royal Opera, London (1901–4); Cologne (1904–11); Brussels (1911–12); Leipzig (1912–23).

Lolli, Antonio (b. Bergamo, ca. 1725; d. Palermo, 10 Aug. 1802). Violinist and composer. Engaged as solo violinist by the Württenburg court at Stuttgart in 1758 on the recommendation of Padre Martini and Jommelli. He made several concert tours during his Stuttgart tenure, appearing throughout Europe. Difficulties at court curtailed these activities in the late 1760s, and he went heavily into debt, despite the handsome salaries he and his wife (a dancer) received. More concert tours followed in the early 1770s; he came into contact with the Mozarts in Italy in 1771 and called on Dittersdorf as well. While he was on tour in 1774, his position at Stuttgart was eliminated. He soon entered the service of Catherine the Great, but his pattern of frequent absences continued. His Russian tenure ended in 1783; a visit to England followed in 1785, and another in 1791, noted by Haydn in his first London notebook. His son by now had become a skillful cellist and performed with him. He may have served the King of Naples during the 1790s; he died poor in Palermo. Though his reputation stood upon his playing, by all accounts superb, he also wrote music for his own use and for publication. As a composer he was self-taught; hoped-for lessons with Padre Martini never materialized. Works include violin concertos (op. 2, 1764; op. 4, 1766; op. 5, 1768) and sonatas (op. 1, ca. 1760; op. 3, 1767; op. 9, 2 violins, 1785).

Lombardo, Guy [Gaetano] **(Alberto)** (b. London, Ont., 19 June 1902; d. Houston, 5 Nov. 1977). Popular bandleader. He formed his first band in 1917 and from 1923 performed in the U.S. as Guy Lombardo and his Royal Canadians. Made up partly of family members (including songwriter Carmen), this band maintained a stability and popularity rivaled by few other big bands. From 1929 until 1962 they performed at the Roosevelt Grill in New York; their New Year's Eve broadcasts from there and the Waldorf Astoria were very popular. They made numerous successful recordings, including "Charmaine" (1927), "It Looks Like Rain on Cherry Blossom Lane" (1937), and "Third Man Theme" (1950).

Lonati, Carlo Ambrogio [Giovanni Ambrogio Leinati] (b. Milan?, ca. 1645; d. probably Milan, ca. 1710). Violinist and composer. Played at the Royal Chapel of Naples from 1665 until 1667, singing also in a Cavalli opera there. Active in Rome from 1668 until 1677, serving as orchestra leader for Queen Christina of Sweden (hence the nickname "the Queen's Hunchback"), playing also at various oratorios and kindling a friendship with Stradella. Scandals drove them to Genoa, where Stradella was killed in 1682; Lonati later was engaged as virtuoso at Mantua, also composing operas for Modena, Genoa, and Milan and perhaps visiting England with the castrato Siface as well. He probably spent his final years in Milan; Geminiani's first lessons are said to have been with him there around 1700. Works include operas, secular cantatas, and solo and trio sonatas; other attributions to him have been discounted.

London, Edwin (b. Philadelphia, 16 Mar. 1929). Composer. He studied at Oberlin College Conservatory and the Univ. of Iowa (Ph.D., 1961) and briefly with Schuller, Dallapiccola, and Milhaud; taught at Smith College (1960–68), the Univ. of California at San Diego (1972–73), and the Univ. of Illinois (from 1973). In 1978 he became chairman of the music department at Cleveland State Univ. His works include *Metaphysical Vegas* (solo voices, dancers, instruments, 1981) and other dramatic music; instrumental music for large and small ensembles; electronic music; Psalm settings and other choral and solo vocal music.

London [Burnstein], **George** (b. Montreal, 30 May 1920; d. Armonk, N.Y., 24 Mar. 1985). Bass-baritone. His family moved to Los Angeles in 1935. He studied there with Richard Lert, Hugo Strelitzer, and Nathan Stewart. Shortly after his first public concert performance, he made his stage debut at the Hollywood Bowl in 1941 (under the name George Burnson) as Dr. Grenvil *(La traviata)*. Studied in New York with Enrico Rosati and Paola Novikova while singing in musical comedies. In 1947 became part of the Bel Canto Trio with Mario Lanza and Frances Yeend. Attracted attention in 1949 when he sang Amonastro *(Aïda)* at the Vienna Staatsoper without rehearsal. Sang Mozart's Figaro at Glyndebourne in 1950, Amfortas at Bayreuth in 1951, Count Almaviva at Salzburg in 1952. Invited in 1951 to the New York Metropolitan Opera, he was heard there in 22 leading roles through 1966. In 1960 he became the first non-Russian to sing Boris Godunov at the Bolshoi Theater. In 1967 his stage career was cut short when his vocal cords became partially paralyzed. He became artistic director of the Kennedy Center in Washington, D.C., 1968–71, then directed the Opera Society of Washington, D.C., 1975–80. He produced the first English-language *Ring* in the U.S. (Seattle, 1975).

Long, Marguerite [Marie-Charlotte] (b. Nîmes, 13 Nov. 1874; d. Paris, 13 Feb. 1966). Pianist. After preparation in her native city, she entered the Paris Conservatory in 1887 as a student of Tissot and Marmontel. After her public debut in 1893 she did not perform publicly again until 1903. As a professor at the Conservatory from 1906 she developed a method of teaching that she published in 1963. A friend of Debussy, later of Ravel, and a colleague of Fauré, she introduced major works by all three, as well as pieces by Satie, Poulenc, and Deodat de Séverac. In 1941 she opened the École Marguerite Long–Jacques Thibaud and began a similarly named competition that quickly became one of the world's most prestigious.

Bibl.: *Cecilia Dunoyer, Marguerite Long: A Life in French Music* (Bloomington, 1993).

Longo, Alessandro (b. Amantea, 30 Dec. 1864; d. Naples, 3 Nov. 1945). Editor, pianist, and composer. At the Naples Conservatory studied piano with Beniamino Cesi, composition with Paolo Serrao. Taught there beginning 1887. Founded the Cercolo Scarlatti in 1892 and edited most of Domenico Scarlatti's extant harpsichord works in 11 volumes; his numbering system was superseded by Kirkpatrick's. His more than 300 compositions include music for piano and for strings, and suites for various instruments.

Longueval [Longaval], **Antoine de** [Jo. à la Venture] (b. Longueval-sur-Somme?; fl. 1507–22). Composer. Singer by 1507, *maître* by 1517, at the French royal chapel; mentioned in the texts of a few compositions of his time. The best known of his own works is a 4-part motet-Passion in a simple, mostly chordal style; also extant are 2 motets and a chanson.

Longy, (Gustave-) Georges (-Leopold) (b. Abbeville, 28 Aug. 1868; d. Moreuil, France, 29 Mar. 1930). Oboist, conductor, and educator. Studied oboe at the Paris Conservatory, winning a premier prix in 1886. Played with several orchestras in Paris, then was first oboist of the Boston Symphony (1898–1925). In Boston he founded the Longy Club to give concerts of chamber music in 1900, and the Longy School of Music (in Cambridge) in 1911, which he and his daughter directed. He conducted the Boston Orchestral Club (1899–1913), the MacDowell Club (1915–25), and the Cecilia Society chorus; he also led the Boston Musical Association (1919–21). He resigned from the Boston Symphony during Koussevitzky's first season and returned to France.

Loomis, Clarence (b. Sioux Falls, S.D., 13 Dec. 1889; d. Aptos, Calif., 3 July 1965). Composer. He studied piano and composition at Dakota Wesleyan Univ. and the American Conservatory in Chicago, where he later taught (1914–29); in 1918 he studied with Schreker in Vienna. Later teaching included positions at the Arthur Jordan Conservatory (Indianapolis, 1930–36) and the New Mexico Highlands Univ. (Las Vegas, 1945–55). His music is tonal, chromatic, and not particularly virtuosic; he often employed American themes and texts. He composed 6 operas and other stage music (*The Fall of the House of Usher,* after Poe, performed 1941); *Fantasy,* piano and orchestra (1954), and other orchestral music; 3 string quartets; piano and organ music; a few choral pieces and song cycles.

Loomis, Harvey Worthington (b. Brooklyn, 5 Feb. 1865; d. Boston, 25 Dec. 1930). Composer. He held a three-year scholarship to study composition with Dvořák at the National Conservatory in New York; during a long career he composed more than 500 works, many of which were never published (manuscripts are in the Library of Congress). He was one of the many composers of his time fascinated by Native American melodies, which he published in piano arrangements (for example, *Lyrics of the Red Man,* Wa-Wan Press). He was also a successful composer of pantomimes, which consist of dances combined with dramatic recitations to musical backgrounds (for example, *Her Revenge,* libretto by Edwin Starr Belknap). He also wrote 4 comic operas; incidental music; a violin sonata, piano works *(Norland Epic),* and songs (some with violin and piano).

Lopatnikoff, Nicolai (Lvovich) (b. Reval, Estonia, 16 Mar. 1903; d. Pittsburgh, 7 Oct. 1976). Composer and pianist. His studies of piano and theory were at the conservatories in St. Petersburg and Helsinki (1917–20); for the next seven years he studied civil engineering at the Technische Hochschule in Karlsruhe; he studied composition privately with Toch. Early orchestral works (2 piano concertos and a symphony) received attention in the U.S. (in part as a result of the premieres conducted by Koussevitzky) and Europe (1925–30); the Second Piano Concerto was performed at the ISCM in 1932. His style was tonal and linear. He was active as a pianist during this period, living in Berlin (1929–33) and London (1933–39); in 1939 he moved to the U.S. to teach at Hartt College and Westchester Conservatory (1939–45) and then at the Carnegie Institute of Technology (1945–69). Between 1929 and 1937 Lopatnikoff wrote many articles for the periodical *Modern Music.* His works include an opera (*Danton,* 1930–32) and a ballet (*Melting Pot,* 1975); 4 symphonies (1928–70), *Variazioni Concertanti* (1958), a violin concerto (1942), and other orchestral music; *Variations and Epilogue* (cello and piano, 1946) and other chamber music; and 2 pieces for mechanical piano (1927).

Lopes-Graça, Fernando (b. Tomar, Portugal, 17 Dec. 1906). Composer, musicologist, and pianist. He studied at the Lisbon Conservatory (1924–31) with Merea and da Mota (piano), Freitas Branco (theory and musicology), and Borba (composition), concurrently attending Lisbon Univ.; taught at the Coimbra Academy of Music (1932–36), and in 1937 worked with Paul-Marie Masson (musicology) and Koechlin (composition) at the Sorbonne. With the outbreak of World War II he returned to Lisbon and taught at the Academia de amadores de música (1941–54), also working as a journalist and musicologist; he established the Sonata concert company for performances of contemporary music. Lopes-Graça published numerous books on music, including biographies of Mozart, Chopin, and Bartók. Early compositions reveal the influence of Stravinsky, Schoenberg, and Bartók as well as folk song; in his works after the 1960s folk idioms are present but are less overt. Compositions include stage works (*La fièvre du temps,* revue-ballet, 1938; *Don Duardos e Flérida,* cantata-melodrama, 1964–69; *Dançares,* choreographic suite, 1984), orchestral music (*Poemeto,* strings, 1928; *Prelúdio, Pastoral e*

Dança, 1929; 2 piano concertos, 1940, 1942; *3 danças portuguesas,* 1941; *Sinfonia,* 1944; *5 estelas funerárias,* 1948; *Scherzo heróico,* 1949; *Suite rústica no. 1,* 1950–51; *Concerto da camera,* with cello obbligato, 1967; *Homenagem a Haydn,* 1980; *Em louvor da paz,* 1986), chamber music (2 sonatinas, violin, piano, 1931; piano quartet, 1939, rev. 1963; string quartet, 1964; *Suite rústica no. 2,* string quartet, 1965; *Homenagem a Beethoven-Tres Equali,* double-bass quartet, 1986; *Geórgicas,* oboe, viola, double bass, piano, 1989), piano music (6 sonatas, 1934, 1939 rev. 1956, 1952, 1961, 1977, 1981; 24 preludes, 1950–55), guitar music, and vocal music, including settings of nearly all the major Portuguese poets.

López, Miguel (b. Villarroya de la Sierra, Aragon, 1 Feb. 1669; d. Saragossa, 1723). Composer. A choirboy at the Escolanía of Montserrat from 1678, he took Benedictine vows there in 1686; served as organist at S. Martín, Madrid (1687–96), and at S. Benito, Valladolid (1705–15), and as choirmaster at Montserrat (1696–1705 and 1715–18). Extant music includes sacred vocal music, both concerted or with continuo alone, *villancicos,* secular cantatas, and organ compositions, all transmitted in the autograph manuscript *Miscellanea musicae* prepared near the end of his life. He also wrote a history of the Montserrat monastery and a lost theoretical tract.

Bibl.: Ireneu Segarra and Gregori Estrada, eds., *Miguel López: Obres completes* (Monastir de Montserrat, 1970–).

López Capillas, Francisco (b. Andalusia?, ca. 1615; d. Mexico City, 18 Jan. or 7 Feb. 1673). Composer. Appointed organist at Puebla (Mexico) Cathedral on 17 Dec. 1641, also playing bassoon; succeeded Fabián Ximeno as *maestro de capilla* at Mexico City Cathedral, serving as organist until 1668 as well. Works are filled with skilled contrapuntal artifice and include Masses (several based on his own compositions as well as on those of composers such as Janequin and Palestrina), motets, Magnificats, and a setting of the St. Matthew Passion. A sumptuously illustrated choirbook of his compositions prepared for the Spanish court is now in the Biblioteca nacional, Madrid.

López-Chavarri y Marco, Eduardo (b. Valencia, 29 Jan. 1871; d. there, 28 Oct. 1970). Composer, conductor, and musicologist. He was mainly self-taught, although he studied composition with Pedrell and had piano lessons. From 1897 he was music critic for the Valencian daily *Las provincias.* In 1903 he founded and directed the Valencian Chamber Orchestra, championing the Valencian school of contemporary Spanish music; in 1906 he conducted the orchestra of the Teatro principal. He taught music history at the Valencia Conservatory (1910–21) and was musical adviser for the Sección femenina (from 1943). He wrote orchestral music, chamber music, piano pieces, and songs. His writings include translations, *Música popular española* (1927), and *Historia de la música* (1930).

López Cobos, Jesús (b. Toro, 25 Feb. 1940). Conductor. After taking a degree in philosophy, he studied composition at the Madrid Conservatory (diploma, 1966), conducting at the Vienna State Academy (diploma, 1969). Won the Besançon Conducting Competition and made his debut leading the Prague Symphony in 1969. After conducting opera at La Fenice in Venice, he was appointed general music director of the Deutsche Oper in East Berlin, 1981–90. Director of the Spanish National Orchestra, 1984–89, of the Cincinnati Orchestra, 1986–90; principal guest conductor of the London Philharmonic, 1981–86; music director of the Lausanne Chamber Orchestra from 1990.

Loqueville, Richard (d. Cambrai, 1418). Composer. In his last years, his principal occupation was the teaching of music (from 1413 at Cambrai Cathedral). His extant compositions include both sacred and secular works: several Mass movements, 2 motets (1 isorhythmic), 1 ballade, and 4 rondeaux.

Bibl.: *Early Fifteenth-Century Music,* ed. Gilbert Reaney, *CMM* 11/3 (1966).

Lorentzen, Bent (b. Stenvad, Denmark, 11 Feb. 1935). Composer. He studied musicology at Århus Univ. and attended the Royal Academy of Music, Copenhagen, taking composition with Jersild; also attended Darmstadt summer classes and studied electronic music at the EMS studio in Stockholm. Lorentzen taught theory at the Jutland Conservatory and was associated with the Danmarks Laererhøjskole in 1972–73; his experience with electronic sounds is evident in his instrumental music, which sometimes exploit timbral effects.

Lorenzani, Paolo (b. Rome, 1640; d. there, 28 Nov. 1713). Composer. Sang under Benevoli at the Cappella Giulia in the Vatican, 1651–54; named *maestro di cappella* at the Seminario romano in 1675. Fled to Paris in 1678, where he had some success in reintroducing Italian music despite the dominant presence of Lully. With the support of several noble patrons his motets and Psalms were performed before Louis XIV, and the pastorale *Nicandro e Fileno* met with success in 1681. His position later deteriorated; he returned to Italy in 1694 as maestro at the Cappella Giulia, where he remained until his death. Other works include a Mass and Magnificat, various airs and cantatas, and the opera *Orontée* (1688); influences range from that of the "colossal" Roman Baroque to that of Carissimi and the *grand motet.*

Lorenzo da Firenze [Laurentius de Florentia, Lorenzo Masini] (d. Florence, Dec. 1372 or Jan. 1373). Composer. In time and place his career overlapped partly with that of Landini, who may have been his pupil. His works include monophonic *ballate,* 10 madrigals in highly melismatic polyphony, 1 *caccia,* 1 or 2 Mass movements, and a monophonic pedagogical piece called *Antefana.*

Bibl.: *The Music of Fourteenth-Century Italy,* ed. Nino Pirrotta, *CMM* 8/3 (1962).

Lorenzo Fernândez, Oscar (b. Rio de Janeiro, 4 Nov. 1897; d. there, 27 Aug. 1948). Composer. Studied piano and composition at the National Music Institute, succeeding his harmony teacher Nascimiento as professor there; founded the Brazilian Conservatory in 1936, directing it until his death. As a composer he moved from impressionism to the nationalism of works such as the *Suite sinfônica sôbre 3 temas populares brasileiros* (1925) and the Amerindian tone poem *Imbapara* (1928); other music includes the opera *Malazarte* (1931–33), 2 symphonies (1945, 1947), violin and piano concertos (1941), chamber music, piano works, and songs. The finale ("Batuque") of the *Reisado do pastoreio* (1930) is now a staple for Brazilian orchestras.

Bibl.: *Composers of the Americas* 7 (Washington, D.C., 1961), pp. 9–16 [includes works list].

Loriod, Yvonne (b. Houilles, Seine-et-Oise, 20 Jan. 1924). Pianist. Studied piano with Lazare Lévy at the Paris Conservatory. After marrying her composition professor, Olivier Messiaen, she introduced many piano works by her classmates and compatriots, including the Concerto (1945) of Nigg, the Sonata no. 2 (1950) and *Structures* (1962) of Boulez, the Sonata (1957) of Barraqué, and the Sonata no. 2 (1959) of Jolivet. She gave first French performances of concertos by Bartók and Schoenberg. Above all, she inspired and premiered many solo and concerted piano works by Messiaen. She taught at the Paris Conservatory from 1967.

Lortzing, (Gustav) Albert (b. Berlin, 23 Oct. 1801; d. there, 21 Jan. 1851). Composer. Son of a leather dealer with theatrical inclinations who in 1811 gave up his business and with his wife became professional actor-singers, working, often close to destitution, in Breslau (1812), Coburg, Bamberg (1813), Strasbourg (1814), and Freiburg, where Albert first appeared in child roles. From 1817 the family belonged to De Rossi's company, which made a circuit of five German cities, and from 1822 to Ringelhardt's company, based in Cologne and Aachen. By 1820 Albert was in young-lover roles, singing tenor and baritone parts. He had had music lessons in Berlin and continued studying largely on his own, early beginning to compose music, now lost, including incidental music and theater songs. In 1824 he married the *première amoureuse* of the company, who was to bear him 11 children, some of whom joined the family profession. Also in 1824 he had his first singspiel produced, apparently winning little notice. From 1824 the couple belonged to the Detmold Theater. He studied orchestration and had an oratorio performed (*Die Himmelfahrt Jesu Christi,* Münster, 1828). In 1830 he made a new version of Hiller's old singspiel *Die Jagd;* 1832, he wrote the texts and compiled the music (mostly borrowed but partly original) for 2 one-act vaudevilles and 2 one-act singspiels.

Wishing a more settled life with less touring, in 1833 Lortzing moved to the Leipzig Stadttheater. In 1835 he composed his first full-length comic opera, *Die beiden Schützen* (Leipzig, 1837), which was widely successful and initiated a sustained production of operas, mostly comic and to his own librettos. It was followed by his most successful and enduring work, *Zar und Zimmermann* (Leipzig, 22 Dec. 1837), still performed in Germany. There followed, with varying success, *Caramo* (1839), *Hans Sachs* (1840), *Casanova* (1841), *Der Wildschütz* (1842). In 1844 he gave up acting, becoming music director of the Leipzig Theater, also beginning to conduct his operas elsewhere. His Romantic opera *Undine* (Magdeburg, 1845) was a change of genre; it was long performed in Germany. In 1845 he was dismissed from his Leipzig post, but engaged in 1846–48 at the Theater an der Wien, Vienna, because of the success there of his *Der Waffenschmied* (30 May 1846). He was not, however, a great success there, feeling Viennese taste to be unsympathetic to his work. A new opera, *Rolands Knappen,* was very successful at Leipzig in 1849, but a promised reinstatement in his old post there fell through. In need, he returned to being a touring actor, which he hated. In May 1850 he found a poorly paid post as conductor at the new Friedrich Wilhelmstädtischen Theater, Berlin; he died unexpectedly of a stroke. Apart from theater music, he composed a few occasional pieces, instrumental and vocal, and many part songs for male or mixed voices.

Bibl.: G. R. Kruse, *Albert Lortzing* (Berlin, 1899). Id., ed., *Albert Lortzing: Gesammelte Briefe* (Regensburg, 1913). H. C. Worbs, *Albert Lortzing in Selbstzeugnissen und Bilddokumenten* (Reinbek bei Hamburg, 1980). Irmlind Capelle, *Chronologisch-thematisches Verzeichnis der Werke von Gustav Albert Lortzing* (Cologne, 1994).

Los Angeles, Victoria de. See De los Angeles, Victoria.

Lotti, Antonio (b. Venice?, ca. 1667; d. there, 5 Jan. 1740). Composer. His father was Kapellmeister at Hannover. Studied with Legrenzi from at least 1683; made a career at St. Mark's, singing alto from 1689 and serving as second organist's assistant (1690–92), second organist (1692–1704), first organist (1704–36), and *maestro di cappella* (from 1736). He produced sacred music both for St. Mark's and for the Ospedale degli incurabili, where he was active prior to Porpora's appointment in 1726. He also composed some 30 stage works between 1692 and 1719, including *Porsenna* (1712), *Polidoro* (1714), and *Alessandro Severo* (1716, the first setting of Zeno's libretto); several others were written for Dresden, where Lotti spent the years 1717–19, and for Vienna. He also was a noted teacher, with Galuppi and Marcello among his pupils; his wife, Santa Stella, was a renowned soprano. Burney reported being moved to tears by Lotti's music during a visit to Venice in 1770. Other works include many secular cantatas along with instrumental pieces, 6 sinfonias and 6 solo sonatas among them.

Loucheur, Raymond (b. Tourcoing, 1 Jan. 1899; d. Nogent-sur-Marne, 14 Sept. 1979). Composer. He studied with d'Indy and Boulanger; won the Rome Prize (1928) and later the Georges Bizet Prize (1935). In 1940 he was appointed chief inspector of musical education in Paris and in 1947 became inspector general of state education. From 1956 until 1962 he was director of the Paris Conservatory. His compositions include a ballet (*Hop-Frog,* 1953); 3 symphonies (1932, 1944, 1970) and several concertos; a string quartet (1930), *Rencontres* (oboe and cello, 1972), and other chamber music; choral music and songs.

Loudermilk, Ira (b. Rainsville, Ala., 21 Apr. 1924; d. near Jefferson City, Mo., 20 June 1965), and **Charlie** (b. Rainesville, Ala., 7 July 1927). Country duo known as the Louvin Brothers. They began performing on radio in West Virginia and Tennessee (joining the Grand Ole Opry in 1955) and made their first recordings in 1949. Their first success was with gospel music ("The Family Who Prays," 1952); later they sang secular music (including "When I Stop Dreaming," 1955; "My Baby's Gone," 1958) but remained strongly traditional performers. The duo disbanded in 1963, but Charlie continued to perform and record.

Loudová, Ivana (b. Chlumec nad Cidlinou, Czechoslovakia, 8 Mar. 1941). Composer. She studied composition at the Prague Conservatory under Kabeláč (1958–61) and under Hlobil at the Prague Academy of Arts and Music (1961–66); in addition to assisting Kabeláč's composition classes she received a six-month grant for study in Paris, where she worked with Messiaen and Jolivet (1971). Her compositions employ a variety of modern techniques including serialism, aleatoric elements, and timbral effects. Works include orchestral music (a concerto for chamber orchestra, 1962; 2 symphonies, 1964, 1965; *Rhapsody in Black,* ballet, 1966; a double concerto for violin, percussion, strings, 1989); vocal music (*Meeting with Love,* male chorus, flute, piano, 1966; *Stabat mater,* male chorus, 1966); instrumental music (string quartet, 1964; *Solo for King David,* harp, 1972; *Hukvaldy Suite,* string quartet, 1984; *Don Giovanni's Dream,* wind octet, 1989).

Louis Ferdinand [Friedrich Christian Ludwig], Prince of Prussia (b. Friedrichsfelde, near Berlin, 18 Nov. 1772; d. Saalfeld, 13 Oct. 1806). Composer and amateur keyboard player. Frederick the Great's nephew; he learned to play keyboard instruments in the court orchestra of his father, Prince Ferdinand of Prussia. He had a distinguished military career, including great heroism in the Franco-Prussian War (1792–95). He studied composition with Jan Ladislav Dussek, who was in his royal entourage for many years. In 1804 he met Beethoven, who had earlier praised his pianism; later Beethoven dedicated his Third Piano Concerto to him. He composed a number of pieces, including concertos and chamber works. Died in battle.

Loulié, Étienne (b. Paris?, ca. 1655; d. there, ca. 1707). Writer. Sang at the Sainte-Chapelle, Paris, under Géhénault and Ouvrard from around 1663 until 1673; later served Mlle. de Guise, but evidently held no official appointment. A close friend of Brossard, he is known for his *chronomètre* and *sonomètre,* the first an instrument for determining tempos, the second an aid in tuning keyboards. Quantz refers to the metronomic device but reports that "the almost universal oblivion into which it has fallen arouses a suspicion as to its adequacy and soundness." Theoretical works include *Éléments ou principes de musique* (Paris, 1696); ed. and trans. Albert Cohen (New York, 1965).

Lourié, Arthur Vincent (b. St. Petersburg, 14 May 1892; d. Princeton, N.J., 12 Oct. 1966). Composer. After studying at the conservatory in St. Petersburg, he began to experiment with twelve-tone and serial composition (for example, in the 3 Sonatinas for piano, 1915). In 1918 he was appointed music commissar; in 1921 moved to Berlin, where he knew Busoni; in 1924 to Paris, where he was in contact with Stravinsky; in 1941 he settled in the U.S. In later works he favored free atonality and sometimes employed quarter tones; a few works are scored for unusual forces (for example, the cantata *Birth of Beauty,* soprano soloist, 12 soprano voices, and 4 instruments, 1937). Works include an opera (*Blackamoor of Peter the Great,* 1961) and an opera-ballet; 2 symphonies and other orchestral music; 3 string quartets, *Funeral Games in Honor of Chronos* (flute, piano, and cymbals, 1964), and other chamber music; piano music; *Sonata liturgica* (alto voices and chamber orchestra) and other choral and solo vocal music.

Bibl.: Detlef Gojowy, *Arthur Lourié und der russische Futurismus* (Laaber, 1993).

Löwe, Ferdinand (b. Vienna, 19 Feb. 1865; d. there, 6 Jan. 1925). Conductor. Student, 1879, Vienna Conservatory (theory under Bruckner); 1884–97, taught piano and choral music there; became a leading conductor in Vienna, Munich, and elsewhere; 1918–22, director, Vienna Staatsakademie für Musik. He was a leading proponent of Bruckner's works but much criticized in later times for his revisions of them.

Lowry, Robert (b. Philadelphia, 12 Mar. 1826; d. Plainfield, N.J., 25 Nov. 1899). Hymn writer. About 1848–54 he attended Lewisburg Univ., becoming a Baptist minister, serving churches in West Chester, Pa. (1854–58), New York (1859–61), Brooklyn (1861–69), Lewisburg, Pa. (1869–75, also serving as professor of belles-lettres at his old university), and finally in Plainfield, N.J. He composed (usually both words and music) many hymns and gospel songs, including "Shall We Gather at the River?" (1865), "I Need Thee Every Hour" (1872, words by Annie S. Hawkes), "All the Way My Savior Leads Me" (1875, words by Fanny J. Crosby), "Low in the Grave He Lay" (1875), "Where Is My Wandering Boy Tonight?" (1877); also compiled, often in collaboration with William Doane, many much-used collections.

Bibl.: J. F. Zellner III, "Robert Lowry, Early American Hymn Writer," *The Hymn* 26 (1975): 117–24; 27 (1976): 15–21.

Lualdi, Adriano (b. Larino, Campobasso, 22 Mar. 1885; d. Milan, 8 Jan. 1971). Composer, conductor, and writer on music. Until 1907 he studied in Rome and Venice; in the 1930s he led orchestras in South America, Germany, and the USSR, as well as in Italy. His musical criticism was written between 1923 and 1942; he produced 17 books (1927–69) including *Viaggio musicale in Italia* (1927), which provides a rich description of musical activity in Italy after the First World War. Lualdi was elected to Parliament in 1929 as a representative of the Sindacato nazionale dei musicisti; with Casella he organized the first Venice festivals of contemporary music (1930–34); directed the conservatories in Naples (1936–44) and Florence (1947–56), the latter after a period of enforced retirement as a result of his Fascist sympathies. He composed *Euridikes Diatheke: Il Testamento di Euridice* (radio opera, 1963) and other operas and incidental music; 5 works for chorus and orchestra; symphonic poems and other orchestral music; some instrumental chamber music; choral pieces and songs.

Lübeck, Vincent (b. Paddingbüttel, Land Wursten, Sept. 1654; d. Hamburg, 9 Feb. 1740). Organist and composer. Tutored in music by his father; named organist at SS. Cosmos and Damian, Stade, in 1675; served as organist at St. Nicolai, Hamburg, from 1702 to his death. By all accounts an excellent player, he was also in demand as a teacher and as a judge of organs. His preludes and fugues for organ parallel in style and form those of Buxtehude, though often making far greater technical demands; other extant works include chorale preludes, a 1728 print of keyboard dances, and 3 sacred vocal compositions.

Lucca, Pauline (b. Vienna, 25 Apr. 1841; d. there, 28 Feb. 1908). Soprano. Rose from the chorus to leading roles in Olmütz (1859) and Prague (1860); 1861–72, Berlin Opera, also guesting elsewhere (Covent Garden from 1863; Russia, 1868–69; Paris, 1872); 1872–74, U.S. and Havana; 1874–89, one of the greatest stars of the Vienna Opera, retiring to teach in Gmunden. She sang a wide range of roles, but mainly a dramatic soprano; noted for her handsome stage presence and her stormy offstage life.

Lucchesi, Andrea (b. Motta di Livenza, near Treviso, 23 May 1741; d. Bonn, 21 March 1801). Composer. He studied in Venice with Domenico Gallo and Gioacchino Cocchi; in 1765 he composed his first opera there, *L'isola della fortuna* (1765). He composed operas and sacred works for Venice during the late 1760s; in 1771 he moved to Bonn, where he directed a traveling theater troupe for several years. In 1774 he received the post as court Kapellmeister there, beating out Beethoven's father, Johann. He traveled to Italy during the 1780s; in 1794 the court moved from Bonn, and he stayed on with nearly no income. He died in poverty. His works include operas (*Il matrimonio per astuzia,* Venice, 1771); cantatas (*Il natale di Giove,* 1772); *La Passione di Gesù Cristo;* other sacred works; orchestral and chamber music.

Lucier, Alvin (Augustus, Jr.) (b. Nashua, N.H., 14 May 1931). Composer. His composition teachers included Berger, Fine, and Shapero at Yale and Brandeis (M.F.A., 1960), Copland and Foss at the Berkshire Music Center (1958–59), and Quincy Porter. In the early 1960s he held a Fulbright Award for study in Rome; in 1963 he began to teach at Brandeis and in 1969 moved to a position at Wesleyan Univ., where he was appointed chair of the world music department in 1979. His compositional style owes much to the thought and work of Cage; many pieces explore the resonant properties of performing spaces (*Vespers,* performers and echo-location devices, 1967), or the possibilities inherent in unusual sound sources (*Music on a Long Thin Wire,* electronic monochord and audio oscillators, 1977). He cofounded the Sonic Arts Union, an electronic music performing ensemble; like Cage he fulfilled many commissions for dance scores from choreographers such as Merce Cunningham; from 1972 to 1977 he was music director of the Viola Farber Dance Company. Wrote many articles on contemporary music and in 1981 edited (with Douglas Simon) a collection of his music and interviews (*Chambers*). Other works include *Music for Solo Performer* (enormously amplified brain waves and percussion, 1965); *I Am Sitting in a Room* (speakers and tape, 1970); *Memory Space* (1970) and a few other orchestral pieces; *Intervals* (voices and sound-sensitive lights, 1983); *Navigations* (string quartet, 1991); *Amplifier and Reflector I* (open umbrella, ticking clock, glass oven dish, 1991); incidental music, film music, and television scores.

Luders, Gustav (Carl) (b. Bremen, 13 Dec. 1865; d. New York, 24 Jan. 1913). Composer. Studied music with the violinist Henri Petri; 1888, emigrated to Milwaukee, conducting in theaters and light music; 1889, moved to Chicago; from 1899, composed musical comedies, mostly to books by Frank Pixley, premiered in Chicago or New York. Most successful was *The Prince of Pilsen* (New York, 1903). He died of a stroke, thought to have been caused by harsh reviews of his last show, *Somewhere Else.*

Ludford, Nicholas (b. ca. 1485; d. Westminster?, in or after 1557). Composer. Worked at the Church of St. Stephens, Westminster, until its dissolution in 1547. His post as verger there entitled him to a pension, which was paid until at least 1557. His music, most written by about 1530, is dominated by Masses of clearly English style: several large-scale works for 5 or 6 voices and 7 3-voiced *alternatim* Lady Masses. Also extant are a 6-voiced Magnificat based on one of the Masses, and 5 incompletely preserved motets. Plainsong and "squares" appear as both solo melodies and cantus firmi.

Bibl.: *Opera omnia, CMM* 27 (1963–).

Ludwig, Christa (b. Berlin, 16 Mar. 1928). Mezzo-soprano. Studied with her mother, Eugenia Besalla, in Frankfurt with Felicie Hüm-Mihacsek. Debut in Frankfurt in 1946 as Orlovsky *(Fledermaus).* Member of the Darmstadt Opera (1952–54), of the Hannover Opera (1954–55). Following her success in 1955 as Cherubino *(Nozze di Figaro)* at the Salzburg Festival, she was engaged by the Vienna Staatsoper. Sang leading roles at the New York Metropolitan Opera from 1959, at Bayreuth from 1966, at Covent Garden from 1969. As her voice matured she moved from lyric and spinto to dramatic roles. Her vast repertory included Bizet's Carmen, Strauss's Marschallin, Verdi's Ulrica, Beethoven's Leonore, Monteverdi's Octavia, Berlioz's Dido, Wagner's Kundry, and contemporary roles by von Einem and Orff. She also ventured briefly into the soprano repertory with performances of Verdi's Lady Macbeth and Strauss's Dyer's Wife, and was much sought after as a singer of Mahler. She gave a series of farewell recitals in many cities in 1993–94.

Ludwig, William F., Sr. (b. Nenderoth, Germany, 15 July 1879; d. Chicago, 14 June 1973). Maker of percussion instruments. In 1909 he founded Ludwig and Ludwig with his younger brother Theobald; he designed and patented various types of pedal timpani. In 1936, several years after the company merged with C. G. Conn, he resigned and established the W. F. L. Drum Company in Chicago, which produced a variety of percussion instruments; the corporation, eventually known as Ludwig Industries, was acquired by Selmer in 1982.

Luening, Otto (Clarence) (b. Milwaukee, 15 June 1900). Composer, conductor, and flutist. He had piano lessons from his father (a conductor and pianist) from age 6; studied at the Staatliche Hochschule für Musik in Munich (1915–17), where his family had moved in 1912; then at the conservatory and university in Zurich; and privately with Jarnach and Busoni. He had made his debut as a flutist in Munich (1916) and in Zurich played flute in the Tonhalle Orchestra and the Municipal Opera Orchestra; he conducted a Viennese operetta in Zurich (1917) as well as a performance of Grieg's Piano Concerto by Ernst Weilemann and the Tonhalle Orchestra; in the same year some of his works were performed at the conservatory. For one season he was also an actor and stage manager in Joyce's English Players Company.

In 1920 Luening returned to the U.S., settling in Chicago, where he conducted opera for the American Grand Opera Company, taught theory, played flute in a theater orchestra and in chamber ensembles. He also wrote music for silent films and arranged gospel hymns. He was executive director of the opera department of the Eastman School (1925–28), lived for a year in Cologne, then conducted opera and other concerts in New York. Two Guggenheim Fellowships (1930–32) enabled him to write both text and music of the opera *Evangeline* (produced at Columbia in 1948). In subsequent years Luening taught at the Univ. of Arizona in Tucson (1932–34); Bennington College (1934–44), where he was named a Hadley Fellow in 1975; Barnard College (1944–64); Columbia (1944–68), where he was director of the School of the Arts (1968–70); and the Juilliard School (1971–73). He participated in the Vermont Chamber Music Composers' conferences from 1941 in Bennington and Middlebury; served as an officer in many organizations devoted to the promotion of American music; cofounded the American Composers Alliance (1938; president 1945–51), the American Music Center (1939, chairing its board until 1960), and Composers Recordings, Inc. (1954).

Luening was a prolific composer, writing over 275 works in every medium. Early works were aggressively modern, polytonal and atonal; in parts of the Trio for soprano, flute, and violin (1924), duration and timing of entrances are left to the performers and only pitch is notated. In 1928 he formulated a theory of "acoustic harmony" concerned with the manipulation and reinforcement of overtones, a theory that remains relevant to later compositions. He is most noted for his pioneering efforts in electronic music, beginning in 1952 with *Fantasy in Space* (based on his own recorded flute sounds). Shortly thereafter he collaborated with Ussachevsky on *Rhapsodic Variations* for orchestra and tape (1953–54), one of the earliest pieces to combine live and recorded sounds. He collaborated with Ussachevsky on several other electronic pieces (including concert works, a ballet, television scores, and incidental music); together with Babbitt they founded the Columbia-Princeton Electronic Music Center. Luening continued to compose music for traditional instrumental and vocal forces, often for specific performers and occasions. He was an extremely important teacher whose own catholicity served to foster a wide range of approaches among his students, including Carlos, Chou Wen-chung, Davidovsky, and Wuorinen.

Works: *Evangeline* (Luening, after Longfellow, 1930–32; rev., 1947–48; New York, 1948) and other stage works; *Symphonic Fantasia I–IX* (1924–88), *Symphonic Interlude* no. 3 (1975), no. 5 (1987), and other orchestral music; string quartets (1919–20, 1923, 1928), suites for solo flute (1947, 1953, 1961), and much other chamber music; *Sonata in memoriam Ferruccio Busoni* (1955), *Sonority Forms I and II* (1982–84), and other piano music; choral music and songs (*Lines from The First Book of Urizen and Vala, or a Dream of 9 Nights,* Blake, solo voices and chorus, 1983); and electronic music.

Writings: *Music Materials and the Public Library* (1949). *Electronic Tape Music, 1952: The First Compositions* (with Ussachevsky, 1977). *The Odyssey of an American Composer: The Autobiography of Otto Luening* (New York, 1980).

Bibl.: Ralph Hartsock, *Otto Luening: A Bio-Bibliography* (New York, 1991).

Luigini, Alexandre (Clément Léon Joseph) (b. Lyons, 9 Mar. 1850; d. Paris, 29 July 1906). Composer. Son of an Italian theater conductor (Toulouse, Lyons, Paris) and composer naturalized in France; student at the Paris Conservatory (second prize, violin, 1869); from 1869 concertmaster, Grand Théâtre, Lyons, under his father; conductor there from 1877, also teaching at the Lyons Conservatory; from 1897, conductor, Opéra-comique, Paris (except 1903, Théâtre-lyrique). He is best known for ballets, especially the extremely popular *Ballet égyptien* (Lyons, 1875), which seems to have led to other exotic subjects (*Fête arabe* op. 49; *Carnaval turc,* symphonic poem, op. 51); also 3 comic operas, instrumental pieces, songs.

Lully, Jean-Baptiste [Giovanni Battista Lulli] (b. Florence, bapt. 29 Nov. 1632; d. Paris, 22 Mar. 1687). Composer. The son of a miller, he likely was entrusted to the care of a local court after the death of his mother, and was taken to France by the Chevalier de Guise in March 1646 to serve as *garçon de chambre* and Italian conversationist in the household of Mlle. de Montpensier. At some point he was tutored in guitar and violin as well as dance; the March 1687 edition of *Mercure de France* lauds his skill as a violinist, also quoting him as having learned by age 17 everything about music he was ever to know. He studied keyboard with Gigault and Roberday, and cultivated a relationship with Michel Lambert, a highly sought-after singer and *air de cour* composer who served Lully's patron among other nobles and whose daughter Lully later married.

Perhaps partly as a result of Lambert's guidance, Lully quickly gained prestige at court. Mlle. de Montpensier released him from his post in October 1652, after her exile for her participation in the Frondes. He danced several roles in the *Ballet de la nuit* on 23 February 1653 and succeeded Lazarini as composer of the king's instrumental music on 16 March. From 1652 he was active at court as a dancer and composer and from 1657 onward was responsible for most of the *ballets de cour,* with the poet Benserade as chief collaborator. Around this time he also took control of the 16-member "petits violons," who played for the king's meals and traveled in his entourage; contrary to general belief, the group evidently predated Lully's leadership, under which they first performed in *La galanterie du temps* in 1656.

Cardinal Mazarin died on 6 March 1661, and Louis XIV took de facto power. On 16 May the king named Lully *surintendant de musique et compositeur de la musique de chambre;* he became a naturalized French citizen in December of that year. On 3 July 1662 he was appointed *maître de la musique de la famille royale* and on July 24 married Madeleine Lambert, with the king and other high officials attending the service. He composed entrées for a revival of Corneille's *Oedipe* in 1664 and between 1664 and 1671 worked with Molière on machine plays and *comédies-ballets,* including *Le mariage forcé* (1664), *Le sicilen* (1667), and *Le bourgeois gentilhomme* (1670). Lully's contributions to Molière's works included dances, vocal music, and entire scene complexes, musical structures of the type that he would later use in his *tragédies lyriques.*

Lully soon gained the sole privilege of presenting operas. In 1669 Pierre Perrin succeeded in getting permission to form an Académie de poesie et de musique. His production of *Pomone* in 1671 was a success, but he was subsequently jailed for debts. While in jail, Perrin promised the rights to various people involved in the undertaking; Lully intervened, pledging to pay off Perrin's debts and grant him a pension in exchange for the privilege. Perrin agreed, and despite legal action brought by the disenfranchised partners, Lully prevailed, forming the Académie royale de musique in March 1672. Other restrictive patents followed, until by April 1673 any production not affiliated with the Académie royale was limited to two singers and six players.

Lully then embarked on the production of *tragédies lyriques,* aided by the librettist Quinault and, initially, the machinist Vigarini. The Académie royale took over the Palais Royal Theater after Molière's death in 1673. A cabal attempted to dislodge Quinault in 1674, and the poet was banished from 1677 until 1680 for an ungracious portrayal of the king's mistress, Mme. de Montespan, in *Isis* (1677); still, Lully considered Quinault the "only poet with whom he could work" (*Mercure galant,* March 1687). Lully himself was the target both of attacks by La Fontaine and Boileau and of criticism in the *Mercure galant* and was involved in legal proceedings in 1675–77 over an alleged murder conspiracy led by Guichard. His position at court never waned, however; the king became godfather of his eldest son in a ceremony on 9 September 1677, the stage works after 1678 were granted royal privilege to be printed, and Lully gained the extremely powerful post of *secrétaire du Roi* in 1681.

Louis XIV became ill in late 1686; to mark his recovery, Lully on 6 January 1687 led a performance of his *Te Deum,* during which he struck his foot with the large conducting stick. He refused to have his toe amputated; eventually fatal gangrene set in, but before his death he took care to arrange the details of his huge estate.

The *tragédie lyrique* held the stage of the Opéra until the late 18th century; their airs circulated throughout Europe in printed collections. Details of Lully's activities are provided by Le Cerf de La Viéville in *Comparaison de la musique italienne et de la musique françoise* (Brussels, 1704–6; R: Paris, 1972), acting on the information of Brunet, Lully's former page. He relates that the composer generally wrote only the outer voices of the five-part instrumental music, leaving the inner parts to secretaries, and details Lully's firm discipline as a conductor. Lully's pupils included Pelham Humfrey, Georg Muffat, J. S. Kusser, and J. K. F. Fischer, who carried the French orchestral style to England, Germany, and the rest of Europe.

Works: 13 *tragédies lyriques: Cadmus et Hermione* (1673), *Alceste* (1674), *Thésée* (1675), *Atys* (1676), *Isis* (1677), *Psyché* (1678), *Bellérophon* (1679), *Proserpine* (1680), *Persée* (1682), *Phaëton* (1683), *Amadis* (1684), *Roland* (1685), and *Armide* (1686); some 30 ballets and *intermèdes,* including *L'amour malade* (1657), *Ballet des saisons* (1661), *Ballet des arts* (1663), *Ballet des muses* (1666), *Le triomphe de l'amour* (1681), and *Le temple de la paix* (1685); incidental music; motets; instrumental marches and dances; and airs.

Bibl.: Henry Prunières, ed., *J.-B. Lully: Les oeuvres complètes* (Paris, 1930–39). *J.-B. Lully: Complete Works* (New York, 1986–). Herbert Schneider, *Chronologisch-thematisches Verzeichnis sämtlicher Werke von Jean-Baptiste Lully* (Tutzing, 1981). Bruce Gustafson with Matthew Leshinskie, *A Thematic Locator for the Works of Jean-Baptiste Lully: Coordinated with Herbert Schneider's Chronologisch-thematisches Verzeichnis . . .* (New York, 1989). J. Eppelsheim, *Das Orchester in den Werken Jean-Baptiste Lullys* (Tutzing, 1961). H. M. Ellis, "The Dances of J. B. Lully" (diss., Stanford Univ., 1967). James Anthony, *French Baroque Music from Beaujoyeulx to Rameau* (London, 1973; rev. ed., 1978). Joyce Newman, *Jean-Baptiste Lully and His Tragèdies Lyriques* (Ann Arbor, 1979). John Hajdu Heyer, ed., *Jean Baptiste Lully and the French Baroque: Essays in Honor of James Anthony* (Cambridge, 1989). Emmanuel Haymann, *Lulli* (Paris, 1991). Philippe Beausant, *Lully* (Paris, 1992). Manuel Couvreur, *Jean Baptiste Lully: Musique et dramaturgie au service du Prince* (Brussels, 1992).

Lumbye, Hans Christian (b. Copenhagen, 2 May 1810; d. there, 20 Mar. 1874). Conductor and composer. A trumpet player in military bands; from 1840, violinist-conductor of his own light-music orchestra, playing in theaters and other places of entertainment. He was music director of Tivoli Gardens, 1843–72 (resigning because of deafness); 1844–60, made several tours of Europe; known as "the Strauss of the North." He composed many dances and other light music. Two sons, Carl (1841–1911) and Georg (1843–1922), carried on the tradition.

Lumsdaine, David (Newton) (b. Sydney, 31 Oct. 1931). Composer. After studying at Sydney Univ. and the New South Wales Conservatorium he moved to London in 1952 and enrolled at the Royal Academy of Music, taking composition with Seiber; in 1970 he became lecturer in music at Durham Univ., subsequently establishing an electronic music studio there. A variety of modern techniques and varied sound sources is evident in his compositions, including serial theory, birdsong, aleatoric elements, and electronic distortion. Works include a Missa brevis (1964), the cantata *Annotations from Auschwitz* (1964), *Flights* (2 pianos, 1967), *Episodes* (orchestra, 1968), *Babel* (tape), *Looking Glass Music* (brass quintet and tape, 1970), *Mandala V* (orchestra, 1988), and *Round Dance* (sitar, tabla, flute, cello, keyboard, 1989).

Lunceford, Jimmie [Jimmy; James Melvin] (b. Fulton, Mo., 6 June 1902; d. Seaside, Oreg., 12 July 1947). Jazz bandleader. He studied at Fisk Univ. (B.Mus., 1926). In Memphis he formed a student band that began working professionally in 1929. It was a leading big band of the swing era from 1934, when it began recording regularly and performed at the Cotton Club in New York until Lunceford's death. The group's strengths were precise ensemble playing, flamboyant showmanship, and challenging original arrangements, particularly those by Sy Oliver, including "Organ Grinder's Swing" (recorded in 1936) and "For Dancers Only" (recorded in 1937).

Lunetta, Stanley (b. Sacramento, 5 June 1937). Composer and percussionist. He attended Sacramento State College and the Univ. of California at Davis; later teachers included Tudor, Cage, and Stockhausen. He was a founder of the New Music Ensemble (1963) and edited *Source: Music of the Avant Garde* (1971–77). Many of his works incorporate slides, dance, theater, electronic devices, and sculpture; beginning 1967 he built several sound sculptures activated by changes in light, wind, heat, or other aspects of the environment. Compositions include *Many Things* (orchestra, 1966); *A Day in the Life of the Moosack Machines* (1972); and *The Unseen Force* (orchestra, chamber ensemble, percussion, electronics, sound sculptures, narrators, and dancers, 1976).

Lupi, Johannes [Leleu, Jehan] (b. ca. 1506; d. Cambrai, 20 Dec. 1539). Composer. A choirboy in Cambrai from 1514 to 1522; university student in Louvain from 1522; from 1526 vicar, then subdeacon, and master of the choirboys at Cambrai. His compositions include 2 Masses, nearly 40 motets (most for 5 or 6 voices), and about 30 chansons.

Bibl.: *Opera omnia, CMM* 84 (1980).

Lupo, Thomas (d. London, Jan. 1628). Composer. Born in England of an Italian family of musicians active at the English court from 1540 until about a century later. His musical relatives were his uncles Ambrose and Peter; father, Joseph; brother Horatio; a cousin also named Thomas; and son Theophilus. Thomas was at court from 1591, a player of either viol or violin and from 1621 officially "composer to the violins," later also "composer to the lutes and voices." His works include a few sacred and secular vocal pieces but more instrumental music, especially fantasias and dances. The fantasias, for 3 to 6 voices, are among the first compositions written for broken consort.

Lupus (fl. 1518–30). Composer. One of a group of Renaissance musicians of confusingly similar names. His works and their sources suggest that he was of northern origin but worked mainly in Italy. Of his few compositions (Masses, Lamentations, and motets), some are rather poorly written, but others are much better made and seem to have enjoyed considerable popularity.

Bibl.: Bonnie J. Blackburn, "The Lupus Problem" (diss., Univ. of Chicago, 1970).

Luscinius [Nachtgall], **Othmar** (b. Strasbourg, between ca. 1478 and 1480; d. Freiburg, 5 Sept. 1537). Theorist. Wide-ranging studies in a number of cities led to a career as an organist (until 1520), a preacher, and a prominent humanist scholar. Among his many works are 2 music treatises, *Musicae institutiones* (Strasbourg, 1515) and *Musurgia seu praxis musicae* (completed in 1518 but first published in 1536). The latter contains Virdung's *Musica getutscht,* freely translated, and an original discussion of contemporary compositional techniques.

Lusitano, Vicente (b. Olivença; d. Rome?). Theorist and composer. His career as a performer began in his native Portugal but by 1550 had led him to the papal choir. His few motets and one madrigal, published in Italy, are far overshadowed in importance by his theoretical work, especially the ideas he successfully espoused in a debate in Rome in 1551 with the more radical Nicola Vicentino over the role of the diatonic, chromatic, and enharmonic genera in music of the mid-16th century. These ideas appear in his brief *Introdutione facilissima et novissima de canto fermo* (Rome, 1553; later editions, Venice, 1558 and 1561), which also covers rudiments of music and, particularly, improvised counterpoint.

Lusse, (Charles) de (b. early 1720s; d. after 1774). Composer and flutist. Gerber places him at the Opéra-comique around 1760, but neither this nor any connection to the Delusse family of instrument makers can be authenticated. Works include collections of flute sonatas and trios published during the 1750s, along with the comic opera *L'amant statue* (1759), and songs and romances; in addition, he contributed to Diderot's *Dictionnaire* and produced a treatise *L'art de la flûte traversière* (1760; facs., Greta Moens-Hansen, Buren, 1980) containing 20 caprices also usable as cadenzas for concertos.

Lutkin, Peter Christian (b. Thompsonville, Wis., 27 Mar. 1858; d. Evanston, Ill., 27 Dec. 1931). Composer, conductor, and organist. He taught piano at Northwestern Univ. and then studied in Europe (1881–84); in Chicago he held organ posts at St. Clement's and St. James's (1884–97). He was founder and first dean of the School of Music at Northwestern (1895–1928); cofounder of the American Guild of Organists; founder and choral conductor of Chicago's North Shore Festival (1909–30). Most of his works were for the church; writings include *Music in the Church* (1910) and *Hymn-Singing and Hymn-Playing* (1930).

Lutosławski, Witold (b. Warsaw, 25 Jan. 1913; d. Warsaw, 7 Feb. 1994). Composer. He studied piano privately with Śmidowicz (1924–25) and with Lefeld at the Warsaw Conservatory (1932–36); took violin with Kmitowa (1926–32) and composition with Maliszewski (from 1928), receiving diplomas in these areas from the Warsaw Conservatory in 1936 and 1937. After a year of service in the Polish army he completed the Symphonic Variations (1938), a work whose use of polychords reveals the influence of the early Stravinsky ballets. During the war Lutosławski formed a piano duo with his old classmate Andrzej Panufnik and performed in various cafés in Warsaw; one of his best-known works (though it is an arrangement rather than an original composition), *Wariacje na temat Paganiniego* [Variations on a theme of Paganini] (1941), was written for this purpose. With the end of the war he began composing various functional pieces for Polish Radio, an association that would last some 15 years and provide his principal source of income; he also completed his first symphony (1941–47): a lengthy work, it continued Lutosławski's period of experimentation with "weakened" tonality within classical forms and brought him some recognition when it was premiered in 1948. During the early postwar years Lutosławski composed numerous children's songs and scores for radio dramas, many using folk material; two important orchestral works for Polish Radio (*Mała suita* [Little Suite] and *Tryptyk śląski* [Silesian Triptych], soprano and orchestra) date from this time as well. With the highly successful premiere of Lutosławski's Concerto for Orchestra (1950–54), the composer's reputation was firmly established with the public and within musical circles. Like Bartók's work of the same name, the Concerto for Orchestra utilizes a significant amount of folk material, but in Lutosławski's composition the folk tunes are broken into motivic fragments, continuously transformed, and combined contrapuntally.

During the late 1950s Lutosławski began to experiment with a new tonal style in which the primary musical interest is centered on the use of twelve-tone chords; toward this end rhythm becomes rather static and texture on the whole more homophonic. This new style, first employed in the *5 Songs* (voice and piano, 1956–57), led in the following year to *Muzyka żałobna* [Funeral Music] (1958) for strings, whose success in the U.S. and throughout Europe quickly gained Lutosławski international recognition. After encountering Cage's music in the early 1960s Lutosławski developed (some have credited him with originating) a technique of limited aleatory that gives the performer a greater interpretive role and adds rhythmic complexity to the work; the first composition to employ this technique was *Gry weneckie* [Venetian Games] (1961), and it was used to some degree in all his subsequent works. Having established a distinctive harmonic style, Lutosławski experimented with questions of form in his compositions from the early 1960s; this included an end-oriented, two-movement plan (String Quartet; Second Symphony) as well as other novel forms (*Livre pour orchestre,* Preludes and Fugue).

Lutosławski lectured on composition at Tanglewood, the Stockholm Academy, the Folkwang Hochschule für Musik in Essen, Dartmouth College, and Texas State Univ.; he also conducted a number of his own works.

Works: For orchestra. Symphonic Variations (1938); Symphony no. 1 (1947); Overture, strings (1949); *Mała suita* [Little Suite] (1951); Concerto for Orchestra (1954); *Preludia taneczne* [Dance Preludes], clarinet, harp, piano, percussion, strings (1955); *Muzyka żałobna* [Funeral Music], strings (1958); 3 postludia (1958–60); *Gry weneckie* [Venetian Games], chamber orchestra (1961); Symphony no. 2 (1966–67); *Livre pour orchestre* (1968); Cello Concerto (1970); *Preludes and Fugue,* strings (1972); *Mi-parti* (1976); *Novelette* (1978–79); *Partita,* violin, piano, orchestra (1985); Piano Concerto (1988); Symphony no. 4 (1993).

Vocal works. *Tryptyk śląski* [Silesian Triptych], soprano, orchestra (1951); 5 Songs, female voice, instruments (1958); *3 poematy Henri Michaux,* 20 voices, orchestra (1963); *Paroles tissées,* tenor, chamber orchestra (1965); *Les espaces du sommeil,* baritone, orchestra (1975); *20 kolęd polskich* [20 Polish Christmas Carols], voice, piano (1946); *Spóźniony słowik, Pan Tralaliński* [Belated Nightingale and Mr. Tralala], children's songs, voice, piano (1949); 5 songs, female voice, piano (1956–57).

Chamber and piano music. Trio, oboe, clarinet, bassoon (1945); *Preludia taneczne* [Dance Preludes], clarinet, piano (1954); String Quartet (1964); *Sacher Variation,* cello (1975); *Epitaph,* oboe, piano (1979). For piano: *2 etiudy* (1941); *Wariacje na temat Paganiniego,* 2 pianos (1941); *Melodie ludowe* [Folk Melodies] (1945); *Bukoliki* (1952).

Bibl.: Tadeusz Kaczyński, *Conversations with Witold Lutosławski,* trans. Eng. Yolanta May (London, 1984). Steven Stucky, *Lutosławski and His Music* (Cambridge, 1981). Charles Bodman Rae, *The Music of Lutosławski* (London, 1994).

Lutyens, (Agnes) Elisabeth (b. London, 6 July 1906; d. there, 14 Apr. 1983). Composer. A daughter of the architect Sir Edwin Lutyens, she studied at the École normale de musique in Paris (1922–23) and at the Royal College of Music (1926–30) with Darke (composition) and Tomlinson (viola); in 1942 she married the conductor Edward Clark. Lutyens's earliest music is highly chromatic and dissonant; with the Chamber Concerto no. 1 for nine instruments (1939–40) she began using serial techniques. Inevitable comparisons with Webern's op. 24, written in 1934 for the same nine instruments, resulted, but Lutyens traced the origins of her serialism to English tradition, especially the linear counterpoint and equal part writing of Purcell's fantasias. An important milestone was her setting of Rimbaud's poem "O Saisons! O Châteaux!" (1946), which demonstrated her mastery of twelve-tone technique. Serialism was anathema in England during the 1950s, but the quality of her best works—including the Chamber Concerto no. 1, *And Suddenly It's Evening, Requiescat, Essence of Our Happinesses, Quincunx, Driving Out the Death*—eventually brought recognition, and she was made a C.B.E. in 1969.

Works for the stage and radio include *The Pit* (London, 1947); *Infidelio* (1954; London, 1973); *The Numbered* (1965–67); *Time Off?—Not a Ghost of a Chance!* (1967–68; London, 1972); *Isis and Osiris* (1969–70; London, 1976); *The Linnet from the Leaf* (1972; BBC radio, 1979); *The Waiting Game* (1973); *One and the Same* (1973; York, 1976); *The Goldfish Bowl* (1975); *Like a Widow* (BBC radio, 1977).

She also composed much vocal music; orchestral music including *3 Pieces* (1939), 5 chamber concertos for various forces (1939, 1940–41, 1945, 1946, 1946), *3 Symphonic Preludes* (1942), a viola concerto (1947), *Music for Orchestra I* (1954), *II* (1962), *III* (1964), *IV* (1981), *Music* (piano, orchestra, 1964), *The Winter of the World* (2 orchestras, 1974), *Wild Decembers* (1980); 13 string quartets (1938–82) and much other chamber music; piano pieces; organ pieces; guitar pieces; music for film.

Bibl.: Elisabeth Lutyens, *A Goldfish Bowl* (London, 1972) [autobiography]. Meirion and Susie Harries, *A Pilgrim Soul: The Life and Work of Elisabeth Lutyens* (London, 1989) [includes list of works].

Luzzaschi, Luzzasco (b. Ferrara, 1545?; d. there, 10 Sept. 1607). Composer. After early studies with Cipriano de Rore came service at the Este court in Ferrara as a singer (from 1561), then first organist (from 1564), director of a court orchestra, composer, teacher, and from 1570 director of Duke Alfonso II's *musica da camera.* His considerable contemporary fame rested largely on his excellent keyboard playing, both at the court and in his capacity as organist at the Cathedral of Ferrara and the Accademia della Morte. He wrote and published much keyboard music; little survives, however. The majority of his extant compositions are madrigals, including 7 books for 5 voices and 1 book for 1–3 virtuoso sopranos with keyboard accompaniment. At least some of the madrigals in the latter were composed for the duke's private musical establishment, which included several highly skilled female singers.

Bibl.: Edmond Strainchamps, "Luzzasco Luzzaschi and His Five-Part Madrigals" (diss., Columbia Univ., 1960).

L'vov [Lvoff], **Aleksey Fyodorovich** (b. Reval [now Tallinn], Estonia, 5 June 1798; d. near Korno [now Kaunas], Lithuania, 28 Dec. 1870). Composer and violinist. After military service he succeeded his father as director of the imperial court chapel choir (1837–61). As a violinist he was praised by Schumann and performed Mendelssohn's Violin Concerto in the Leipzig Gewandhaus, with the composer conducting. In 1833 he composed a Russian national anthem at the request of the tsar; this hymn, *Bozhe, tsarya khrani* [God Save the Tsar], served as the Russian national anthem until the 1917 Revolution. He wrote several operas; violin music (caprices and a concerto), *Le duel* for violin and cello; sacred music (hymns and a Stabat mater); and secular songs.

Lyadov [Liadov], **Anatol** [Anatoly] **Konstantinovich** (b. St. Petersburg, 11 May 1855; d. Polïnovka, Novgorod district, 28 Aug. 1914). Composer. He studied with his father before entering the St. Petersburg Conservatory in 1870. There he soon abandoned his study of piano and violin in order to study counterpoint with Johannsen and composition with Rimsky-Korsakov. He was expelled from the conservatory in 1876 for failing to attend the latter's classes but was allowed to take his final examinations in 1878. Later that year he became an instructor of theory at the conservatory; from 1901 he taught advanced counterpoint and, from 1906, composition. His ideas on teaching harmony are reflected in Rimsky-Korsakov's theory textbook (1886); among his students were Prokofiev, Asafiev, and Myaskovsky. In the 1870s he became associated with the Moguchaya Kuchka ("The Five"). During the 1890s he often conducted the Imperial Russian Music Society concerts. He never completed any large-scale works. His failure to write a ballet score for Diaghilev in 1910 forced the impresario to turn to Stravinsky. Among his orchestral music, the 3 pieces based on Russian fairy tales, *Baba-Yaga* (1891?–1904), *Volshebnoye ozero* [The Enchanted Lake] (1909), and *Kikimora* (1909) are the most successful and popular. His miniatures for piano include the popular *Muzïkalnaya tabakerka* [A Musical Snuffbox] (1893) and a number of preludes, etudes, and intermezzi. He also made numerous arrangements and harmonizations of Russian folk songs.

Bibl.: Gerald Abraham, "Random Notes on Lyadov," *Slavonic and Romantic Music* (New York, 1968). Dorothee Eberlein, *Anatolij K. Ljadov: Leben-Werk-Musikanschaung* (Cologne, 1978). Vasiliï Vasil'evich Yastrebtsev, *Reminiscences of Rimsky-Korsakov,* 2 vols. (London, 1959, 1960); ed. and trans. Florence Jonas (New York, 1985).

Lyadov [Liadov], **Konstantin (Nikolayevich)** (b. St. Petersburg, 10 May 1820; d. there, 19 Dec. 1868). Violinist, conductor, and composer. He studied at the St. Petersburg Theatrical School, then played violin in the Imperial Opera Orchestra and conducted the Russian Opera in St. Petersburg (from 1850). He premiered Dargomïzhsky's *Rusalka,* Serov's *Judith* and *Rogneda,* and Gulak-Artemovsky's *A Cossack beyond the Danube.* From 1862 he taught at the St. Petersburg Conservatory. His works include a ballet, music for vaudevilles, choral works, and piano pieces.

Lyapunov, Sergey (Mikhaylovich) (b. Yaroslavl, Russia, 30 Nov. 1895; d. Paris, 8 Nov. 1924). Pianist, composer, and conductor. He studied piano with his mother, continuing his lessons at the Moscow Conservatory (1878–83) with Klindworth, Pabst, and Wilborg (piano), and Hubert, Tchaikovsky, and Taneyev (composition). In 1884 he went to St. Petersburg and studied with Balakirev; served as assistant director of the imperial chapel (1894–1902), inspector of music at St. Helen's Institute (1902–10), and director of the Free Music School (1905–11); taught piano and music theory at the St. Petersburg Conservatory (1910–17) and lectured at the State Institute of Art (1919). Beginning in 1923 he ran a music school in Paris. His works reveal the influence of Balakirev; he is best known for his piano compositions, including *12 études d'exécution transcendante* (1900–1905).

Lyatoshinsky, Boris (Nikolayevich) (b. Zhitomir, Ukraine, 3 Jan. 1895; d. Kiev, 15 April, 1968). Composer. He studied law at Kiev Univ. and composition with Glier at the Kiev Conservatory; following graduation he was appointed to a teaching post at the conservatory (1919–35), later becoming a professor (1935–68); he also taught orchestration at the Moscow Conservatory (1935–38, 1941–44). A prolific composer in many genres; Lyatoshinsky's compositions reveal the influence of Ukrainian folk melodies and motifs; he is also known for his orchestrations and editions of Glier's music. Works include 2 operas (*The Golden Ring,* Odessa, 1930; *Shchors,* Kiev, 1938; rev. 1970), 5 symphonies (1918–66), 4 string quartets (1915–43), many folk song arrangements.

Lybbert, Donald (b. Cresco, Iowa, 19 Feb. 1923; d. Norwalk, Conn., 26 July 1981). Composer. He studied with Wagenaar at the Univ. of Iowa; Carter and Luening at Columbia; and in Paris with Boulanger. He taught at Juilliard (1948–49) and later at Hunter College (1954–80). His works are freely atonal and cast in well-defined formal structures; in 1969 he collaborated with Ferdinand Davis on *The Essentials of Counterpoint.* He wrote 2 operas (*The Scarlet Letter,* 1965); *Zap* (chorus, 4 instrumental ensembles, and rock group, 1970) and other orchestral music; a concerto for piano and tape (n.d.); *Lines for the Fallen* (soprano, 2 quarter tone–tuned pianos, ca. 1967).

Lynes, Frank (b. Cambridge, Mass., 16 May 1858; d. Bristol, N.H., 24 June 1913). Composer. Studied at the New England Conservatory, also with Lang and Paine; 1883–85, Leipzig Conservatory. Then a church organist (1888–90, First Parish Church, Cambridge; 1891–1913, Church of the Disciples, Boston), piano teacher, choral conductor (Cantabrigia Ladies' Chorus). He composed anthems, part songs, songs, organ and piano pieces (including Bagatelles: 10 Melodious Sketches op. 14, 1890).

Bibl.: Olin Downes, *Frank Lynes* (Boston, 1914).

Lynn [née Webb], **Loretta** (b. Butcher Hollow, Ky., 14 Apr. 1932). Country singer and songwriter. In 1948 she moved to Washington state, where she sang in country clubs and on radio; she made her first recording in 1960 ("Honky Tonk Girl"). From 1962 she performed at the Grand Ole Opry in Nashville and released many popular records, including "Success" (1962), "Coal Miner's Daughter" (1970), "Somebody Somewhere" (1976), and several duets with Conway Twitty. She cultivated an image of a "sincere" country artist in the tradition of Patsy Cline: this was strengthened by her autobiography (*Coal Miner's Daughter,* 1976), which details her rural upbringing and subsequent career. It was the subject of a film in 1980.

Lyon, George Washburn (b. Northbury, Mass., 15 Jan. 1833; d. after 1889, before 1905). Merchant. Studied the violin and, especially, the harp; from 15 worked as a clerk in Boston music shops, eventually along with Patrick Joseph Healy (b. Burnfort, County. Cork, 17 Mar. 1840; d. Chicago, 3 Apr. 1905), who emigrated to Boston in 1850 and became a clerk in 1854. In 1864 the pair, bankrolled by Oliver Ditson, opened Lyon &

Healy in Chicago, which became the world's largest manufacturer of musical instruments. Lyon focused on the mechanical side of the business, receiving several patents for improvements in instruments; Healy, who had no musical inclinations, handled the business side. In 1889 they introduced the celebrated Lyon & Healy harp, which the company, much reduced in other respects, continues to manufacture. In October 1889 Healy bought out Lyon after disagreements.

Lyon, James (b. Newark, N.J., 1 July 1735; d. Machias, Maine, 12 Oct. 1794). Composer and tune collector. He graduated from the College of New Jersey (which later became Princeton) and was then pastor of a church in Nova Scotia (beginning 1764). From 1774 he was pastor at Machias, where he remained until his death. He was best known for his landmark tunebook *Urania,* published in Philadelphia in 1761 (R: New York, 1974); it was the largest of its kind and was used as a model for many subsequent tune compilations. It was the first tunebook to include British fuging tunes.

Lysenko [Lissenko], **Nikolay (Vitalyevich)** (b. Grinki, near Kremenchug, Ukraine, 22 Mar. 1842; d. Kiev, 6 Nov. 1912). Composer, pianist, and folk song collector. He was taught piano by his mother before attending the Univ. of Kiev (1860–64), where he studied the natural sciences; continued his musical studies at the Leipzig Conservatory (to 1869) with Richter (theory), Reinecke (piano), and Papperitz (organ); returned to Russia and studied composition and orchestration with Rimsky-Korsakov at the St. Petersburg Conservatory (1874–76). In 1876 he settled in Kiev and in 1904 founded a Ukrainian School of Music; the following year he composed the choral work *Vechny revolyutsioner* [The Eternal Revolutionary] to celebrate the Revolution. An ardent nationalist, Lysenko set to music a great number of poems by the Ukrainian poet Shevchenko; he also published some 600 folk songs, and wrote treatises on Ukrainian folk music. Works include opera (*Taras Bulba,* 1880–90, Kiev, 1903; *Natalka Poltavka,* 1889), orchestral works, choruses, chamber music, songs, and piano pieces. A collected edition of his works was published in Kiev (1950–59).

Lyttelton, Humphrey (b. Eton, England, 23 May 1921). Jazz bandleader, trumpeter, clarinetist, author, and radio commentator. The son of an Eton College housemaster, he collected jazz records from an early age; he gained playing experience at Eton and with the Grenadier Guards during World War II. In 1947 he joined George Webb's Dixielanders; the next year he started his own band in the Louis Armstrong revival fashion. Finding rapid success, he increasingly embraced mainstream styles; he toured, collaborated, and recorded extensively. His autobiography of 1954 led to further books, essays, columns, and reviews in the 1960s. This in turn led to radio broadcasting activities, including many years as host of the BBC series *The Best of Jazz.* In the 1980s he established his own recording label.

M

Ma, Yo-Yo (b. Paris, 7 Oct. 1955). Cellist. Studied cello with his father from age 4 and gave his first recital at Univ. of Paris two years later. In 1962 he began studies with Janos Scholz and Leonard Rose at the Juilliard School in New York; attended Harvard (1972–76) before embarking on a career as soloist; awarded the Avery Fisher Prize in 1978. Ma has appeared frequently with major orchestras in the U.S. and Europe; his numerous recordings include the Beethoven cello sonatas with pianist Emanuel Ax, a frequent collaborator.

Yo-Yo Ma.

Maag, (Ernst) Peter (Johannes) (b. St. Gall, 10 May 1919). Conductor. He attended the universities of Zurich, Basel, and Geneva, studying theory and piano under Czeslaw Marek and conducting under Franz von Hoesslin and Ernest Ansermet. He was appointed first conductor at Düsseldorf in 1952 and principal conductor at the Vienna Volksoper (1964–68); also served as *Generalmusikdirektor* at Bonn (1954–59), subsequently artistic director of the Teatro Regio in Parma and Teatro Regio in Turin. Maag made his British and American conducting debuts in 1959 and first appeared at the Metropolitan Opera in 1972.

Maayani, Ami (b. Ramat-Gan, 13 Jan. 1936). Composer and conductor. He studied at the New Jerusalem Academy of Music (1951–53), privately with Ben-Haim (1956–60), and at Columbia (electronic music with Ussachevsky, 1961–62, 1964–65). He studied architecture at the Israel Institute of Technology and Columbia, and philosophy at Tel Aviv Univ. Taught at the Jerusalem Academy (1972–73) and was appointed conductor of the Israeli National Youth Orchestra in 1971. His music combines Near Eastern elements with European forms and French impressionist orchestration. Among his works are pieces for orchestra (Symphony no. 3, *Hebrew Requiem,* mezzo, chorus, orchestra, 1977; a concertino for harp and strings, 1980; Symphony no. 4, *Sinfonietta on Popular Hebraic Themes,* chamber orchestra, 1982; *Scherzo Mediterranean,* 1983); chamber music, songs, and electronic music. His music for harp is well known among harpists.

Maazel, Lorin (Varencove) (b. Neuilly, 6 Mar. 1930). Conductor and violinist. He was raised in Los Angeles and Pittsburgh; studied conducting with Vladimir Bakaleinikoff, in addition to violin and piano lessons. He conducted the New York Philharmonic at the 1939 World's Fair; began to conduct complete programs from the age of 11 with various orchestras, including the NBC Symphony. Made his debut on the violin in 1945 in Pittsburgh, where he entered the university and joined the Pittsburgh Symphony as violinist (1948) and apprentice conductor (1949–51). In 1960 he became the first American to conduct at the Bayreuth Festival *(Lohengrin);* has served as music director of the Berlin Deutsche Oper (1965–71) and Radio Symphony (1965–75), and associate principal conductor of the New Philharmonia Orchestra in London (1971–72). He was appointed music director of the Cleveland Orchestra (1972–82) and the Orchestre national de France (1977–82), and artistic director and general manager of the Vienna State Opera (1982–84); beginning 1984 he served as adviser to the Pittsburgh Symphony and was music director from 1988 until 1996.

Mabellini, Teodulo (b. Pistoia, 2 Apr. 1817; d. Florence, 10 Mar. 1897). Conductor, composer. Studied at the Florence Conservatory (1833–37). In 1836 his first opera was produced in Florence, causing the grand duke to send him to Novara to study with Mercadante. His second opera, *Rolla* (Turin, 1840), was his most successful; there were 7 more through 1857. Beginning 1843, he was conductor of the Società filarmonica concerts in Florence; from 1847, court *maestro di cappella;* from 1848, conductor at the Pergola Theater. He taught composition at the Florence Conservatory from 1860 until 1887. Other works include oratorios, cantatas, much sacred music, orchestral pieces, songs.

McBride, Robert (Guyn) (b. Tucson, 20 Feb. 1911). Composer. He played clarinet, oboe, saxophone, and piano in jazz and school bands; then studied with Luening at the Univ. of Arizona, where he later taught (1957–76). Earlier he had taught at Bennington College (1935–46); performed with the League of Composers Woodwind Quintet (1941); worked as a composer and arranger for Triumph Films in New York (1945–47). His compositions, many of which involve jazz or theater, include the ballet *Punch and the Judy* (for Martha Graham, 1941) and 4 other ballets; *Swing Stuff* (clarinet and orchestra, 1940), *Panorama of Mexico* (orchestra, 1960); *Way Out, But Not Too Far* (euphonium and piano, 1970); songs and choral music.

McCabe, John (b. Huyton, 21 Apr. 1939). Composer. As a child he suffered from poor health, but became acquainted with music through recordings and the piano. He had written 13 symphonies by the time he entered the Liverpool Institute at age 11. He later studied composition with Proctor Gregg at Manchester Univ. and with Pitfield at the Royal Manchester College of Music, where he studied piano with Greene. In 1964 he entered the Munich Hochschule to study composition with Genzmer. He was resident pianist at Cardiff Univ. (1965–68) before moving to London, where he was active as a recital pianist and as soloist in his own concertos with orchestras. From 1983 until 1990 he was principal of the London College of Music. His dramatic works include *The Lion, the Witch, and the Wardrobe* (children's opera, 1968); *This Town's a Corporation Full of Crooked Streets* (entertainment, 1969); *The Teachings of Don Juan* (ballet, 1973); *The Play of Mother Courage* (chamber opera, 1974); and *Mary Queen of Scots* (ballet, 1975). Among his orchestral works are 2 violin concertos (1963, 1979); 3 symphonies (1965, 1971, 1978); 3 piano concertos (1966, 1970, 1976); *Metamorphoses,* harpsichord and orchestra (1968); *Notturni ed Alba,* soprano and orchestra (1970); *The Chagall Windows* (1974); Concerto for Orchestra (1984); *Rainforest I* (1984); and *Fire at Durilgai* (1989). He has also written choral and vocal works, chamber music (5 string quartets), music for piano, and music for organ.

Bibl.: Stewart R. Craggs, *John McCabe: A Bio-Bibliography* (New York, 1991).

McCartney, (John) Paul (b. Liverpool, 18 June 1942). Rock singer, songwriter, bass guitarist, and keyboardist. One of the four Beatles; with John Lennon he was a principal songwriter for them. When the group broke up he made recordings with his wife, Linda McCartney (including *McCartney,* 1970; *Ram,* 1971), and in 1971 they assembled the band Wings, which made several successful albums (including *Band on the Run,* 1974; *Wings over America,* 1976). From 1980 he worked as a solo artist again, producing the albums *McCartney II* (1980), *Tug of War* (1982), and *Flowers in the Dirt* (1989); he also recorded a duet with Stevie Wonder, "Ebony and Ivory" (1982). In 1994 he reunited with the other surviving Beatles to record some new music based on tapes made by John Lennon before he was murdered.

Bibl.: Geoffrey Giuliano, *Blackbird: The Life and Times of Paul McCartney* (New York, 1991).

McCormack, John (b. Athlone, 14 June 1884; d. Dublin, 16 Sept. 1945). Tenor. Graduated from Sligo College with honors in 1902, then went to Dublin to join the civil service. There his voice was discovered and trained by Vincent O'Brien. Further training under Sabatini in Milan led to his stage debut in 1906 at Savona *(L'amico Fritz).* After his successful London debut in 1907 (at a Sunday League concert) he was invited to Covent Garden; debut there as Turiddù *(Cavalleria).* Debuts at the Teatro San Carlo in Naples and as Alfredo *(Traviata)* with Hammerstein's Manhattan Opera in 1909. Sang Italian roles with the Boston Opera in 1910–11, with the Philadelphia and Chicago Operas in 1912–14. After guest appearances at the New York Metropolitan Opera and elsewhere he turned in 1918 to recitals and recordings, adding to his repertory both German lieder and popular songs. He concertized throughout North America, Europe, South Africa, Australia, and Japan. He retired in 1938, returning to Ireland.

Bibl.: Paul W. Worth and Jim Cartwright, *John McCormack: A Comprehensive Discography* (New York, 1986).

McCracken, James (John Eugene) (b. Gary, Ind., 16 Dec. 1926; d. New York, 29 Apr. 1988). Tenor. Attended Columbia and studied singing with Ezekiel, making his professional debut as Rodolfo in *Bohème* in Colorado (1952) and his Metropolitan Opera debut as Parpignol in the same opera (1953). In 1957 he went to Europe for further training, including studies with Marcello Conati in Milan. Sang Otello with the Washington Opera in 1960; this became his most celebrated role, which he subsequently performed at the Zurich Festival (1960), San Francisco Opera (1962), the Metropolitan (1963), and Covent Garden (1964). He remained with the Met through the 1977–78 season, returning on a few occasions in the mid-1980s, and sang at most of the world's leading houses.

MacCunn, Hamish (James) (b. Greenoch, Scotland, 22 Mar. 1868; d. London, 2 Aug. 1916). Composer, conductor. Lived in London from 1883, studying with Parry and Stanford at the Royal College of Music (1883–87). He early aroused attention with works on Scottish subjects, especially the concert overture *Land of the Mountains and the Flood* (1887) and 5 cantatas produced in 1888–92 (all but the first premiered in Scotland). He composed 2 Scottish operas, *Jeanie Deane* (after Scott, 1894), which was successful and held the stage for a time, and *Diarmid* (1897), as well as other stage works and many songs. Professor of harmony at the Royal Academy of Music (1888–94); later primarily active as conductor of opera and light opera in London and on tour.

McCurdy, Alexander (b. Eureka, Calif., 18 Aug. 1905; d. Philadelphia, 1 June 1983). Organist. He studied with Lynnwood Farnam (1924–27), made his debut in 1926 in Town Hall, New York, and graduated from the Curtis Institute in 1934. He served as organist and choirmaster at Second Presbyterian Church in Philadelphia (1927–71) and headed the organ departments at Curtis (1935–72) and Westminster Choir College in Princeton (1940–65).

McDonald, Harl (b. Boulder, Colo. 27 July 1899; d. Princeton, N.J., 30 Mar. 1955). Composer, pianist, and conductor. He studied at the Univ. of Southern California and in Leipzig; toured the U.S. as a piano recitalist and accompanist; taught at the Philadelphia Music Academy (1924–26) and at the Univ. of Pennsylvania (1926–46). His research in acoustics led to the book *New Methods of Measuring Sound,* with O. H. Schenck (1935). He was general manager of the Philadelphia Orchestra (1939–55). His style was eclectic. Compositions include many orchestral works (a violin concerto, 1943; a tone poem, *My Country at War,* 1945); some chamber music; a large amount of piano and choral music.

MacDonald, Jeannette (b. Philadelphia, 18 June 1903; d. Houston, 14 Jan. 1965). Soprano and film actress. Toured with a children's revue beginning 1912. In New York studied voice with Ottavia Torriani, Grace Adele Newell, and Lotte Lehmann. Began as a chorus girl on Broadway in 1921, graduating to ingenue roles by the mid-1920s. Following a concert tour abroad she appeared in a musical film, *The Love Parade;* its success led to major roles in other films, culminating in 1935–42 in 8 popular musicals with Nelson Eddy (*Naughty Marietta,* 1935; *Rose Marie,* 1936; *Sweethearts,* 1939). Sang Gounod's Juliette 10 times in Canada in 1943. U.S. opera debut with the Chicago Civic Opera in 1944 as Juliette and also Gounod's Marguerite. Concert tour of the U.S. in 1939, of England in 1946.

MacDowell, Edward (Alexander) (b. New York, 18 Dec. 1860; d. there, 23 Jan. 1908). Composer. (He changed the spelling of his name from McDowell in the late 1870s.) At 8 began piano lessons with a friend of Teresa Carreño, who also taught him occasionally; from April 1876, studied the piano in Paris with Marmontel, first privately and from February 1877 at the Conservatory. Dissatisfied, in late 1878 he went to Germany and studied theory and composition with Louis Ehlert in Wiesbaden. In May 1879 he entered the Hoch Conservatory, Frankfurt, studying with the pianist Carl Heymann and the director, Raff, both of whom recognized his talent and with whom he continued studying privately after leaving the conservatory in July 1880. In 1880 he composed *Modern Suite,* piano, op. 10, the first work he considered worthy of preservation, and a *Second Modern Suite* op. 14 in 1881, partly while commuting to Darmstadt, where he taught piano at the conservatory in March 1881–March 1882. The composition of his First Piano Concerto was suggested by Raff, who was so impressed by it that he recommended MacDowell to Liszt (who had already heard him play). Liszt approved the work (which MacDowell and D'Albert played for him at Weimar in spring 1882) and had him play his first Suite at the July 1882 meeting of the Allgemeiner Deutsche Verein at Zurich, where he was very well received. His music began to be regularly performed and (initially through Liszt's influence) published. In the next two years he produced mainly piano pieces, including the once-popular *Hexentanz* op. 17, no. 2, and songs. In summer 1884 he returned to the U.S. to marry his pupil Marian Nevins (1857–1956). They settled in Frankfurt. Unsuccessful in attempts to get a regular teaching post (Würzburg Conservatory, 1884; Royal Academy, Edinburgh, 1885), he taught privately, but gave most of his time to composition. In autumn 1885 MacDowell and his wife moved to Wiesbaden, in spring 1887 to a secluded cottage on its outskirts. In this period he composed his symphonic poems *Hamlet and Ophelia* op. 22, *Lancelot and Elaine* op. 25, and *Lamia* op. 29, the 2 orchestral pieces op. 30, the Romance for cello and orchestra op. 35, his best-known large work, the Second Concerto op. 23, and many piano pieces and songs.

In September 1888, primarily to improve his financial situation, MacDowell moved to Boston, where he became a busy teacher (pupils including Henry Gilbert, Ethelbert Nevin, Margaret Lang). In Boston he composed his first 2 sonatas (Tragica op. 45; Eroica op. 50), 2 orchestral suites, the second of which (Indian op. 48) was his best-known purely orchestral work, songs and piano pieces, including the once extremely popular *Woodland Sketches* op. 51. In autumn 1896 he became the first professor of music at Columbia Univ., organizing the new department. Some of his lectures were published as *Critical and Historical Essays,* ed. W. J. Baltzell (Boston, 1912; R: 1969). He also conducted the Mendelssohn Glee Club (1896–98), a male chorus for which he composed several part songs, and was president of the new Society of American Musicians and Composers (1899–1900). His late compositions include the third and fourth sonatas (Norse op. 57; Keltic op. 59), songs, part songs, and piano pieces, especially *Sea Pieces* op. 55. During his sabbatical year 1902–3 he made a concert tour through the U.S. and Canada, ending in London in May 1903, where he played his Second Concerto. On returning to Columbia he clashed with its new president Nicholas Murray Butler over educational matters. Their disputes became public, and he left Columbia at the end of that academic year, remaining in New York as a private teacher. But he soon began showing signs of a mental illness that became completely disabling.

After MacDowell's death, in fulfillment of an idea of his, his wife turned their farm in Peterborough, New Hampshire, into an artists' colony.

Bibl.: L. Gilman, *Edward MacDowell: A Study* (New York, 1908; R: 1969). J. Erskine, "MacDowell at Columbia: Some Recollections," *MQ* 28 (1942): 395–405. M. MacDowell,

Random Notes on Edward MacDowell and His Music (Boston, 1950).

McDowell, John Herbert (b. Washington, D.C., 21 Dec. 1926; d. Scarsdale, 3 Sept. 1985). Composer and choreographer. He graduated from Colgate in English literature (1948) and then studied music at Columbia and at the Bennington Summer Conferences with Luening, Beeson, and others. He taught at several institutions including the New School for Social Research, Hunter College, the Pratt Institute, and the American Dance Festival; he was music director of the Gulbenkian Dance School at the Univ. of Surrey (1976–82) and also served as music director for Paul Taylor and other dance companies. He composed over 400 works, including about 140 dance scores (for orchestra, chamber ensemble, or tape) commissioned by American and European companies; over 60 theatrical works (*Tumescent lingam,* oboe, chorus, tape, 101 performers, dog, infant, visual effects, 1971); *The Parlor Trick with Ferns* (concertino for violin, bassoon, cello, and orchestra, 1960) and other orchestral music; chamber music; a few vocal works.

Mace, Thomas (b. Cambridge?, 1612 or 1613; d. there?, ca. 1706). Writer, singer, and lutenist. In 1635 he joined the choir of Trinity College, Cambridge; he remained in Cambridge (except for an interval during the Civil War) for the rest of his life. Mace's compositions include a verse anthem and works for viol, but he is principally known as the author of *Musick's Monument* (London, 1676; facs., Paris, 1958). Written between 1671 and 1675, it is a defense of traditional English music against the French style that Charles II favored; the work also contains valuable information about performance practice, including ornamentation and continuo playing.

Macero, Teo [Allitio Joseph] (b. Glens Falls, N.Y., 30 Oct. 1925). Composer, conductor, and saxophonist. He studied at Juilliard (1949–53), where Brant was among his teachers; taught privately; was a producer for Columbia Records (1957–75), where he specialized in jazz; then founded his own recording company (Teo Productions). He composed many works for jazz ensembles (*A Jazz Presence,* narrator and jazz ensemble, 1980); several operas and over 80 dance scores (*Jamboree,* for the Joffrey Ballet, 1984); *Time Plus 7* (chamber orchestra, 1963), *Theme for the Uncommon Man* (brass and percussion, 1981), and other orchestral music; *Butter and a Big Horn* (tuba and tape, 1977); many documentary film scores (for which he won Emmy Awards in 1977 and 1979) and television scores.

McEwen, John (Blackwood) (b. Hawick, 13 Apr. 1868; d. London, 14 June 1948). Composer. He studied at Glasgow Univ. before becoming choirmaster of St. James's Free Church and then of Lanark Parish Church. He later studied with Prout, Corder, and Matthay at the Royal Academy of Music (1893–95), then returned to Scotland, where he was choirmaster of South Parish Church, Greenock, and teacher of piano and composition at the Athenaeum School of Music, Glasgow (now the Royal Scottish Academy of Music). He returned to the Royal Academy of Music as professor of harmony and composition in 1898, becoming principal in 1924. He received an honorary Mus.D. at Oxford in 1926, and was knighted in 1931. Among his works are several orchestral suites (1893–1941); *Three Border Ballades: Coronach, Grey Galloway, The Demon Lover* (1905–8); a symphony ("Solway," 1911); 7 Bagatelles ("Nugae," strings, 1912); 17 string quartets (1893–1947); 7 violin sonatas (1913–29); piano pieces; songs.

Macfarren, George Alexander (b. London, 2 Mar. 1813; d. there, 31 Oct. 1887). Composer and teacher. Son of the playwright and theater manager George Macfarren (1788–1843), who wrote librettos for some of his operas. Studied music in 1827–29 with Charles Lucas; 1829–36 at the Royal Academy of Music (composition with Potter), having much music (symphonies, overtures, a piano concerto, musical comedies) performed while still a student. Professor of harmony and composition at the Royal Academy, 1837–47, resigning because of faculty opposition to his teaching Day's system of harmony, which he championed throughout his life; reinstated in 1851. From 1875 principal of the Royal Academy and professor at Cambridge. Knighted, 1883. Failing eyesight troubled him from childhood, and he went blind in 1860.

Of his English operas *King Charles II* (1849) and, especially, *Robin Hood* (1860) were the most successful. After 1870 he devoted himself mainly to oratorios for the provincial festivals, of which *St. John the Baptist* (Bristol, 1873) was the most successful. Also composed cantatas, especially *May Day* (1857), 9 symphonies and other orchestral works, much chamber music, Anglican church music, many songs. He was perhaps best known for his part songs. He lectured frequently, published textbooks, edited old music, and conducted (before his blindness).

Bibl.: H. C. Banister, *George Alexander Macfarren* (London, 1891).

McFerrin, Bobby (b. New York, 11 March 1950). Jazz and popular singer. Trained as a pianist, he concentrated on singing from 1977, working mainly unaccompanied from 1983. He regularly juxtaposes in a single concert soul music, rock and roll, jazz ballads, scat singing, children's nursery rhymes, excerpts from musical theater, and reggae. An astonishing control and breadth of timbre and register enable him to create complex polyphonic solo textures. His recordings include the albums *The Voice* (1984) and *Spontaneous Inventions* (1985) and the hit song "Don't Worry, Be Happy" (1988); he has also recorded with Yo-Yo Ma. He made his conducting debut with the San Francisco Symphony in a performance of Beethoven's Seventh Symphony.

McFerrin, Robert (b. Marianna, Ariz., 19 Mar. 1921). Baritone. Studied at Fisk Univ., with George Graham at Chicago Musical College (B.M., 1948), and at the Kathryn Turney Long School in New York. Sang with the New York City Opera in 1949 and joined the New England Opera Company the following year. In 1953 won the Metropolitan Opera Auditions of the Air and became the first male black singer to join the Met, making his debut in 1955 as Amonasro; other roles included Rigoletto and Valentin. In 1959 he sang the role of Porgy on the *Porgy and Bess* film soundtrack; toured widely as a recitalist.

McGhee, Brownie (Walter) (b. Knoxville, Tenn., 30 Nov. 1915; d. Oakland, Calif., 16 Feb. 1996). Blues guitarist, singer, and songwriter. Best known for his long partnership (1939–79) with blues harmonica player Sonny Terry. The two performed together at many blues and folk music festivals; their albums include *Life Is a Gamble, Tell Me Why, Blues Had a Baby (And I Called It Rock and Roll), Walk On, Hole in the Wall,* and *Rainy Day.*

McGhee, Howard (B.) [Maggie] (b. Tulsa, 6 Mar., 1918; d. New York, 17 July 1987). Jazz trumpeter. His work in big bands included two periods with Andy Kirk (1941–42, 1943–44), for whom he wrote his own solo feature "McGhee Special," recorded in 1942. That same year he played in early bop jam sessions in New York. Later, in Los Angeles, he recorded as a leader ("Bebop," 1946) and with Charlie Parker ("Relaxin' at Camarillo," 1947). He toured with Jazz at the Philharmonic and his own bop groups (late 1940s), but then drug addiction impeded his career. After 1960 he resumed playing regularly.

McGlaughlin, William (b. Philadelphia, 3 Oct. 1943). Conductor and trombonist. He studied at Temple University (B.M., 1967; M.M., 1969); became assistant principal trombonist with the Philadelphia Orchestra, later co-principal with the Pittsburgh Symphony. He founded and conducted the Pittsburgh Symphony Players and the Pittsburgh Camerata in 1973, and worked with the St. Paul Chamber Orchestra from 1975 to 1978. In 1980 he became music director and presenter of the National Public Radio program *St. Paul Sunday Morning;* music director of the Eugene (Oregon) (1981–85) and Tucson (1983–87) Symphonies; music director of the San Francisco Chamber Orchestra (1986–1988); and of the Kansas City, Mo., Symphony from 1986.

Mácha, Otmar (b. Ostrava, 2 Oct. 1922). Composer. He studied with Řídký at the Prague Conservatory (1945–48) and was music adviser to Czech Radio in Prague (1945–55) before serving as secretary of the Czech Composers' Union. From 1969 he worked at Czech Radio. Works include 4 operas: *Polapená nevěra* [Infidelity Unmasked] (1956–57), *Jezero Ukereve* [Lake Ukereve] (1960–63), *Svatba na oko* [Feigned Wedding] (1974–76), and *Metamorphoses Promethei* (1981); the symphonic poem *Noc a naděje* [Night and Hope] (1959); *Variations on a Theme by Jan Rychlík* (orchestra, 1964); *Janinka zpívá* [Janinka Sings] (soprano and orchestra, 1969); and *Symfonietta* I and II (1971, 1982); 2 string quartets (1943, 1982); 2 violin sonatas (1948, 1987); choruses; songs.

Machaut [Machault], **Guillaume de** (b. ca. 1300; d. Rheims?, 13 Apr. 1377). Composer and poet. In both arts the foremost figure of 14th-century France. Contemporary documents refer to him as *maître,* implying possession of the university degree of *magister;* however, no direct record of his studies survives. From about 1323 until about 1340, he traveled widely throughout Europe as secretary to John of Luxembourg, King of Bohemia. From about 1340 Rheims was his home, left only for occasional trips to visit the French court. Among his protectors and patrons after this date were members of the French royal house and other nobles, including Bonne of Luxembourg; Charles of Normandy (later King Charles V of France); Jean, Duc de Berry; Charles of Navarre; Amadée of Savoy; and Pierre de Lusignan, King of Cyprus.

His artistic output began probably about the time he entered John of Luxembourg's service and continued until almost the end of his life. Certain of his long poems were written specifically for particular patrons, as were some manuscript copies of his works, including at least one of the "complete works" manuscripts with music. His poetry itself provides little, if any, biographical information that is not readily available otherwise; even the ostensibly autobiographical late work *Le livre du voir dit* is now thought to be a purely literary creation without basis in historical fact, although it, like many other poems, incorporates names of historical personages and references to historical events (such as the Black Death).

His poetic output was extensive and varied: 10 long and 4 shorter narrative poems, a poetic *Prologue* (in both shorter and longer versions) to his complete works, and about 400 lyric poems independent of the narratives and a great many more incorporated into them. The musical compositions, too, are numerous: 19 *lais,* 1 *complainte,* 1 *chanson royale,* 42 ballades, 21 rondeaux, 33 virelays, 24 motets (all double-texted), 1 Mass, and 1 hocket. Machaut wrote the words—usually French, sometimes Latin—as well as the music for all of his works except the hocket, which is not texted, and the Mass. The long poems *Remède de Fortune* and *Voir dit* include a few of these pieces as lyrical interludes.

His works, both poetic and musical, are preserved in a number of manuscripts made during the 14th century. Those devoted exclusively to his artistic output and containing more or less everything he had written up until the making of the copy are known as "complete works" manuscripts. About 6 such copies including the music survive, along with an immense number of less complete or text-only manuscripts and some "repertory" manuscripts that transmit works by Machaut alongside works by other authors or composers.

Bibl.: *Musikalische Werke,* ed. Friedrich Ludwig and Heinrich Besseler (Leipzig, 1926–29, 1943; R: 1954). Leo Schrade, ed., *Polyphonic Music of the Fourteenth Century,* vols. 2–3 and commentary vol. (Monaco, 1956; R: 1977). Paulin Paris, ed., *Le Livre du voir-dit* (Paris, 1875). *Oeuvres,* ed. Ernest Hoepffner (Paris, 1908–21) [the bulk of the narrative poetry]. *Oeuvres lyriques,* ed. Vladimir Chichmaref (Paris, 1909) [lyric poetry]. *Le jugement du roy de Behaigne; and, Remede de Fortune,* ed. and trans. James I. Wimsatt, William W. Kibler, and Rebecca Baltzer, Chaucer Library (Athens, Ga., 1988) [2 narrative poems and associated music]. Siegmund Levarie, *Guillaume de Machaut* (New York, 1954; R: 1969). Armand Machabey, *Guillaume de Machaut, 130?–1377: La vie et l'oeuvre musicale* (Paris, 1955). Daniel Poirion, *Le poète et le prince: L'évolution du lyrisme courtois de Guillaume de Machaut à Charles d'Orléans* (Paris, 1965). Gilbert Reaney, *Guillaume de Machaut* (London, 1971). Daniel Leech-Wilkinson, *Machaut's Mass: An Introduction* (Oxford, 1990).

Mâche, François Bernard (b. Clermont-Ferrand, 4 Apr. 1935). Composer and theorist. He studied with Messiaen at the Paris Conservatory, but was also strongly influenced by Varèse. From 1958 he taught literature at the École normale supérieure; then taught music at the Sibelius Academy in Helsinki. He received a doctorate in music from the Sorbonne and in 1983 was appointed director of the Institute of Musicology at the Univ. of Strasbourg. Published numerous articles on contemporary music. Composed works for the stage (*Temboctou,* a theater piece, 1982); orchestral music (*Andromède,* with chorus and three pianos, 1980); instrumental music, some with tape (*Sopiana,* flute and tape, 1981; *Lethe,* 2 pianos, 1985); vocal music.

Machito [Grillo, Frank Raul] (b. Tampa, Fla., 16 Feb. 1912; d. London, 15 Apr. 1984). Jazz and salsa bandleader, singer, and maraca player. Raised in Cuba, where he began working professionally, he returned to the U.S. in 1937. In 1940 he formed his Afro-Cubans, a big band that soon moved toward jazz under the musical direction of the trumpeter Mario Bauza. The group's recordings included "Cubop City" (1949), "Okiedoke" (with Charlie Parker as soloist, 1949), and the album *Kenya* (1957). Machito's popularity continued through crazes for the mambo and salsa and into the 1980s. He is the subject of the documentary film *Machito: A Latin Jazz Legacy* (1987).

Machover, Tod (b. New York, 24 Nov. 1953). Composer, conductor, and cellist. He studied at Juilliard, Columbia, and elsewhere (1971–77), principally with Dallapiccola, Sessions, and Carter; first cellist in the National Opera Orchestra in Toronto (1975–76); composer-in-residence and then director of musical research at IRCAM in Paris (1978–84); in 1985 began teaching at M.I.T. His works employ both acoustic and electronic instruments, as well as the computer, in a style that is often vocally inspired and dramatic. They include the opera *Valis* (1987); *Desires* (orchestra, 1983–84); *Spectres parisiens* (flute, horn, cello, synthesizer, 18 instruments, computer, 1983–84); *Soft Morning, City!* (after Joyce, soprano, double bass, computer-generated tape, 1980); *Flora* (computer tape, 1989); *Epithalamion* (vocal soloists, 25 players, live and recorded computer-generated sounds, 1990); *Song of Penance* (computer-enhanced viola, chamber ensemble, 1992).

McHugh, Jimmy [James] **(Francis)** (b. Boston, 10 July 1894; d. Beverly Hills, 23 May 1969). Popular songwriter, pianist, and music publisher. He worked as a song plugger in Boston (from 1916) and New York (1921), and wrote songs for Cotton Club revues. From 1938 he collaborated with Dorothy Fields on songs for films, including "One More Waltz" (in *Love in the Rough,* 1930) and "I'm in the Mood for Love" (in *Every Night at Eight,* 1935); in 1939 he returned to Broadway, writing a musical (*As the Girls Go,* 1948) and several popular songs ("Comin' in on a Wing and a Prayer," 1943; "Too Young to Go Steady," 1955, both with words by Harold Adamson). He also toured performing his own songs; after 1959 he was active in music publishing.

McKenna, Dave [David J.] (b. Woonsocket, R.I., 30 May 1930). Jazz pianist. He began playing in his teens in the Boston area. In 1949–53 he worked with big bands of Charlie Ventura and Woody Herman, and in 1953–67 with smaller ensembles of Gene Krupa, Stan Getz, Eddie Condon, Zoot Sims, Bobby Hackett, Al Cohn, and others. In the late 1960s and 1970s he lived on Cape Cod working as soloist in local venues and in Boston. From the late 1970s he was associated with the Concord label, playing and recording with other Concord artists.

Mackenzie, Alexander (Campbell) (b. Edinburgh, 22 Aug. 1847; d. London, 28 Apr. 1935). Composer, conductor, and educator. At the age of 10 he was sent to Germany to attend the Realschule in Schwarzburg-Sondershausen (1857–62), where his teachers included Ulrich (violin) and Stein (theory); he went to London in 1862 and studied at the Royal Academy of Music with Sainton (violin), Lucas (harmony and counterpoint), and Jewson (piano). In 1865 he returned to Edinburgh, where he performed as a violinist and served as precentor of St. George's Church (from 1870) and conductor of the Scottish Vocal Musical Association (from 1873). Between 1879 and 1885 Mackenzie lived in Florence and devoted himself to composition; works from this time include the cantata *The Bride* (1881), the opera *Colomba* (London, 1883), and the oratorio *The Rose of Sharon* (1884). The success of *The Rose of Sharon* led to his appointment, in 1885, as conductor of the Novello Oratorio Concerts in London. In 1888 he was elected principal of the Royal Academy of Music; during his 36 years in office he continued to compose and conduct, serving as permanent conductor of the Philharmonic Society's concerts (1892–99). He was knighted in 1895. Mackenzie's compositions reveal the influence of Schumann, Wagner, and Liszt; his *Pibroch Suite* for violin and orchestra, performed by Sarasate at the Leeds Festival (1889), achieved considerable popularity.

Mackerras, (Alan) Charles (MacLaurin) (b. Schenectady, N.Y., 17 Nov. 1925). Conductor and oboist. His family emigrated from the U.S. to Australia in 1927. Studied there at the New South Wales Conservatorium. Principal oboe in the Sydney Symphony, 1943–46. On a British Council scholarship studied conducting with Václav Talich in Prague, 1948. Conductor at Sadler's Wells, 1948–53; of the BBC Concert Orchestra, 1954–56. During the 1950s he was one of the first conductors to study and revive authentic performance practice of 18th-century vocal music. His recording of Handel's *Messiah* in 1967 was influential in its use of Baroque ornamentation, bowing, and phrasing. In later repertory, his productions and recordings based on his own editions of Janáček's works did much to spread that composer's popularity in English-speaking countries. Musical director of the English National Opera, 1970–77. Principal conductor of the Sydney Symphony, 1980–85. Musical director of the Welsh National Opera, 1987–92. He was knighted in 1979.

Mackey, Steven (b. Frankfurt, 1956). Composer. He attended the Univ. of California, SUNY–Stony Brook, and Brandeis Univ. He has held teaching positions at the Univ. of California at Davis, Northeastern Univ., the College of William and Mary, and Princeton Univ. Works include a string quartet (1983), *3 Rhondo Variations* (solo cello, 1983); *TILT* (orchestra, 1992); *Eating Greens* (orchestra, 1993); *Banana/Dump Truck* (cello, orchestra, 1995); *Deal* (electric guitar, drum set, chamber ensemble, 1995).

McKinley, Carl (b. Yarmouth, Maine, 9 Oct. 1895; d. Boston, 24 July 1966). Composer and organist. He studied composition with Goldmark in New York; other training was at the Conservatory in Galesburg, Illinois, and at Harvard with Hill and Boulanger. For some years he was organist at Center Church in Hartford, Conn. In 1928 he conducted at the Munich Opera; for most of his career he taught organ, composition, and history at the New England Conservatory. He composed works for orchestra (*The Blue Flower,* symphonic poem, 1921; the oratorio *The Man of Galilea,* 1916); a string quartet (1941) and other chamber music; piano and organ music; songs.

McKinley, William Thomas (b. New Kensington, Pa., 9 Dec. 1938). Composer and jazz pianist. After study at Carnegie-Mellon Univ. and Yale (with Schuller, Powell, Wyner, and Moss) he taught at the Univ. of Chicago (1969–73) and then at New England Conservatory. His earlier works were influenced by expressionism (as in the Clarinet Concerto of 1977, inspired by Schoenberg's monodrama, *Erwartung*); his later style, reflected in the Symphony for 13 players (1983), is more accessible; many compositions borrow from jazz styles. His works include an oratorio, *Deliverance Amen* (chorus, chamber ensemble, and organ, 1982–83), symphonies (no. 5, 1988), and several concertos (trumpet, 1987; flute, 1987); *Scarlet* (jazz band, 1983) and other works for large ensembles; string quartets (no. 7, 1988), *Double Concerto* (double bass, bass clarinet, and ensemble, 1984), and other chamber music; piano and choral music; songs.

Bibl.: Jeffrey S. Sposato, *William Thomas McKinley: a Bio-Bibliography* (Westport, Conn., 1995).

McKinney, Baylus Benjamin (b. Heflin, La., 22 July 1886; d. Bryson City, N.C., 7 Sept. 1952). Composer of hymns and church music administrator. After attending Louisiana College, he studied and then taught (1919–32) at Southern Baptist Theological Seminary; was music editor for the firm of Robert H. Coleman in Dallas (1918–35); assistant pastor of a Baptist church in Fort Worth (1931–35); and music editor for the Baptist Sunday School Board in Nashville (from 1935). He wrote words and music for about 150 hymns and provided the musical setting for 115 other hymn texts.

McKuen, Rod (Marvin) (b. Oakland, 29 Apr. 1933). Composer, poet, and singer. Having left home several years earlier, he returned to Oakland as the host of a radio show at age 17; two years of army service followed, after which he began an active career as a performer; in 1959 he settled in New York, but spent the years 1963 and 1964 in Paris, where he was influenced by the style of Jacques Brel. Wrote more than 1,000 songs and about 10 film scores (*A Boy Named Charlie Brown,* 1970). Other works include about 20 ballets and a musical; 4 symphonies and concertos for harpsichords, guitar, piano, and cello; *I Hear America Singing* (soprano, narrator, and orchestra, 1973); piano and chamber music.

McLaughlin, John [Mahavishnu] (b. Yorkshire, England, 4 Jan. 1942). Guitarist and bandleader. He moved to New York in 1969 to join Tony Williams's group Lifetime and immediately began recording with Miles Davis's jazz-rock groups, including the album *Bitches Brew* (1969). After recording his album *My Goal's Beyond* (1970), he formed the Mahavishnu Orchestra. Its first manifestation was a quintet including Billy Cobham (1971–73); the group's albums include *The Inner Mounting Flame* (1971). He led a less successful Mahavishnu Orchestra (1974–75) and formed Shakti, in which, playing acoustic guitar, he explored a fusion of jazz and Indian improvisatory methods (1973–77). He also played the acoustic instrument in guitar duos and trios, including one with Paco de Lucia and Al Di Meola which recorded the album *Passion, Grace, and Fire* (1983). In 1984 he toured with a new Mahavishnu Orchestra. Beginning 1975 he lived in France, where he acted and played in the film *Round Midnight* (1986).

McLean, Jackie [John Lenwood, Jr.; Abdul Kareem, Omar Ahmed] (b. New York, 17 May 1932). Jazz alto saxophonist. He worked with Sonny Rollins (1948–49), Miles Davis (1951–52), Charles Mingus (1956, 1958–59), and Art Blakey (1956–58). He acted and performed in the play *The Connection* in New York, London, and Paris (1959–61, 1963). As a leader he recorded the hard bop album *Bluesnik* (1961) and in the mid-1960s took up some devices of free jazz playing. In 1968 he began teaching at the Hartt School of Music while performing during the summer. He is the subject of the documentary film *Jackie McLean on Mars* (early 1980s).

Bibl.: A. B. Spellman, *Four Lives in the Bebop Business* (New York, 1966; R: as *Black Music: Four Lives,* 1970).

MacMillan, Ernest (Alexander Campbell) (b. Mimico, Ont., 18 Aug. 1893; d. Toronto, 6 May 1973). Conductor, composer, and organist. He studied organ from the age of 8 in Toronto and Edinburgh; was organist at Knox Church, Toronto (1908–10); in 1911 he was awarded a B.Mus. from Oxford. He studied history at the Univ. of Toronto (1911–14) while serving as an organist in nearby Hamilton; in 1914 he went to Paris to study piano, but was interned at the start of the war while on a visit to Bayreuth; during this internment he composed and conducted, was awarded a B.A. in absentia from the Univ. of Toronto, and earned a D.Mus. from Oxford. From 1919 to 1925 he was organist at Timothy Eaton Memorial Church (Toronto); was principal of the Toronto Conservatory (1926–42) and dean of the Faculty of Music of the university (1927–52). MacMillan conducted the Toronto Symphony (1931–56) and the Mendelssohn Choir (1942–57); he also conducted in the U.S., Brazil, and Australia. He was knighted in 1935; received the Canada Council Medal (1964) and the Canadian Music Council Medal (posthumously, 1973). His works include a ballad opera (1933); several pieces for orchestra; chamber and piano music; a Te Deum (vocal soloists, chorus, and orchestra, 1936); original songs and arrangements of folk songs.

MacNeil, Cornell (Hill) (b. Minneapolis, 24 Sep. 1922). Baritone. He studied voice with Friedrich Schorr at the Hartt School of Music (1944–45) and with Virgilio Lazzari, Dick Marzollo, and Otto Guth in New York. Debut in Philadelphia in 1950 as John Sorel *(The Consul).* With the New York City Opera, 1952–55. Debuts at the San Francisco Opera in 1955 as Wagneers Heerrufer *(Lohengrin),* at La Scala in Milan in 1958 as Carlo *(Ernani).* Performed at the New York Metropolitan Opera, 1959–87, making his debut as Rigoletto, later gaining particular acclaim for his Nabucco. Guest at the Vienna Staatsoper, at the Teatro Colón in Buenos Aires, at Covent Garden in London. President of the American Guild of Musical Artists, 1971–77.

Macon, Uncle Dave [David Harrison] (b. Smart Station, Tenn., 7 Oct. 1870; d. Murfreesboro, Tenn., 22 Mar. 1952). Country singer and banjo player. He was raised in Nashville, where he learned vaudeville and folk music from tenants at his parents' boarding house; from 1900 he performed as an amateur while operating a drayage company. He played professionally from 1918, made recordings from 1924, and appeared on the W.S.M. Barn Dance (later the Grand Ole Opry) from 1925 until his death. He was instrumental in introducing minstrel, vaudeville, and early Tin Pan Alley material to the growing country movement. Among his popular recordings were "Keep My Skillet Good and Greasy" (1924) and "Wreck of the Tennessee Gravy Train" (1930).

Maconchy, Elizabeth (b. Broxbourne, Hertfordshire, 19 March 1907; d. Norwich, 11 Nov. 1994). Composer. She was of Irish descent and grew up in rural Ireland. She studied at the Royal College of Music, London, with Charles Wood and Ralph Vaughan Williams, in Prague with Karel Jirák, and in Vienna and Paris. In 1930 her first major works were performed in Prague and London, and she married Irish literary scholar William LeFanu. In 1932 she suffered a severe setback from tuberculosis. She continued to work while raising a family through the war years, gaining wide recognition for her individuality and versatility. Her chamber works have won greatest acclaim, especially a series of string quartets that span the 1930s to the 1980s. She fulfilled many commissions, notably from operatic and choral groups of both professional and amateur standing. In 1987 she was made Dame of the British Empire. She is the mother of composer Nicola LeFanu.

Her works include 7 operas; 3 ballets; over 25 orchestral works, including concertos and concertante pieces for solo piano, violin, viola, cello, clarinet, oboe, and bassoon; over 20 choral works, some with orchestra (many for women's voices); over 15 songs and song cycles, some with orchestra; 14 string quartets; over 25 duos, trios, quartets, and quintets for various instruments; solo pieces for piano, harpsichord, harp, violin, viola, cello, and bassoon.

Maconie, Robin (John) (b. Auckland, 22 Oct. 1942). Composer and writer. He studied composition with Page at Victoria Univ., Wellington (1960–63), with Messiaen at the Paris Conservatory (1963–64), and with Zimmermann and Eimert at the Cologne Musikhochschule (1964–65). At the Kurse für Neue Musik in Cologne he studied with Stockhausen, Heike (acoustics), and Schernus (conducting). In New Zealand he worked as a film composer (1961–63, 1965–67), a composer of electronic incidental music for the NZBC Drama Unit, and a lecturer at Auckland Univ. (1967–68). He moved to England in 1969, where he concentrated on criticism and research into the phenomenology of music. His compositions include *Māui* (television ballet for speaker, mime, 6 male dancers, and orchestra, 1967–72); *Music for a Masque* (string orchestra, 1962); *Canzona* (chamber orchestra, 1962); Sonata (string quartet, 1968); String Quartet (1970); a sonata for clarinet and piano (1961); *A:B:A* (harp, 1964); *A:D:C* (piano, 1965); the song cycle *Basia Memoranda* (voice and string quartet, 1962); *Ex evangelio Sancti Marci* (chorus, 1964); and the modified soundtrack *Limina* (1975). His writings include *The Works of Karlheinz Stockhausen* (London, 1976; 2nd ed., 1990); *Stockhausen on Music: Lectures and Interviews* (London, 1989); and *The Concept of Music* (Oxford, 1990).

McPartland, Jimmy [James Dougald] (b. Chicago, 15 Mar. 1907; d. Port Washington, N.Y., 13 Mar. 1991). Jazz cornetist. He replaced Bix Beiderbecke in the Wolverines (1924–25). While working with Ben Pollack (1927–29), he played on the definitive Chicago jazz recording session by McKenzie and Condon's Chicagoans, including "Sugar" and "China Boy" (1927). Continuing to play Dixieland and traditional jazz, for 60 years he worked mainly as a free-lance and a leader in New York and Chicago. His albums include *Shades of Bix* (1953). Military service brought him to Europe, where he married Marian Turner in 1945; though later divorced, they worked together occasionally.

McPartland [née Turner], **Marian (Margaret)** [Page, Marian] (b. Windsor, England, 20 Mar. 1920). Pianist. She came to the U.S. in 1946 after marrying Jimmy McPartland. She led trios, notable for an engagement at the Hickory House in New York (1952–60). Her sidemen included Joe Morello and later Eddie Gomez. Among her albums were *Jazz at the Hickory House* (1952–53) and *From this Moment On* (1978). From about 1978 and into the 1990s she hosted the nationally syndicated radio show *Piano Jazz.* She also wrote on jazz, mainly for *Down Beat* magazine, and published *All in Good Time* (New York, 1987).

McPhatter, Clyde (b. Durham, N.C., 15 Nov. 1933; d. New York 13 June 1972). Popular singer. He joined the vocal group the Dominoes in 1950, singing their hit "Sixty Minute Man" (1951), and in 1953 formed the Drifters, whose successes included "Money Honey" (1953) and "Whatcha Gonna Do" (1955); both groups were early exponents of rhythm-and-blues and soul. He subsequently made successful recordings as a solo artist, including "A Lover's Question" (1958) and "Lover Please" (1959). Later incarnations of the Drifters continued to record into the 1970s.

McPhee, Colin (Carhart) (b. Montreal, 15 Mar. 1900; d. Los Angeles, 7 Jan. 1964). Composer and writer on music. He studied at the Peabody Conservatory until 1921 and then returned to Canada as a piano student of Arthur Friedheim; in 1924 he was a piano soloist with the Toronto Symphony. He also studied composition in Paris with Le Flem and had lessons in New York with Varèse. He spent the years 1934–39 in Southeast Asia, becoming an authority on the music of Java and Bali; his writings on this music include *A House in Bali* (1946), *A Club of Small Men* (1948), *Music in Bali* (1966), and many articles. In his last years he taught harmony, orchestration, composition, and ethnomusicology at UCLA (1958–64). His own compositions are heavily indebted to his study of Balinese and Javanese gamelan styles. His compositions include *Tabu-tabuhan* (2 pianos and orchestra, 1936) and 3 symphonies; a concerto for piano and 8 woodwinds (1929); *Balinese Ceremonial Music* (2 pianos, 1940); *From the Revelation of St. John the Divine* (male voices, 3 trumpets, 2 pianos, timpani, 1935).

Bibl.: Carol J. Oja, *Colin McPhee: A Composer in Two Worlds* (Washington, D.C., 1990).

Macque, Giovanni [Jean] de (b. Valenciennes, 1548–50?; d. Naples, Sept. 1614). Composer. Of Flemish birth; a choirboy in Vienna; student of Philippe de Monte; by 1574 resident in Rome as an organist and composer; in Naples from 1585, first in service to the father of the composer Carlo Gesualdo, then as an organist, joining in 1594 the Spanish viceregal chapel, of which he eventually became *maestro di cappella.* His compositional style evolved from a conservatism typical of Rome in his day to a more experimental idiom, some late works incorporating considerable chromaticism and dissonance. Works include many madrigals; sacred vocal pieces, such as motets and *laude;* instrumental compositions, many for keyboard.

McRae, Carmen (b. New York, 8 Apr. 1922; d. Beverly Hills, Calif., 10 Nov. 1994). Jazz singer. After singing with Benny Carter (1944) and Mercer Ellington (1946–47), she played piano and sang in New York clubs. After recording as a leader in 1954, she mainly sang, accompanied by a bop-oriented trio with which she worked through the 1980s, including tours of Europe and Japan. Her albums include *By Special Request* (1955), *Lover Man* (1961), and *Live at Bubba's* (1981). Her voice had a smoky timbre, and biting articulation gave her work an intense rhythmic quality, both in scat singing and in poignant interpretations of popular songs.

McShann, Jay [James Columbus; Hootie] (b. Muskogee, Okla., 12 Jan. 1916). Jazz pianist and bandleader. In 1939 he formed a swing big band in Kansas City. Its recordings include "Hootie Blues" and "Confessin' the Blues" (both 1941). Among its soloists was Charlie Parker, who came with the band to New York in 1942. After military service (1943–44) McShann formed a new big band, and then led small groups, playing blues, boogie-woogie, and swing. The year 1969 marked his return to prominence: he began recording regularly in Europe, and he continued to perform through the 1980s. His albums include *The Man from Muskogee* (1972). He is the subject of the film *Hootie's Blues* (1978) and a central figure in the film *The Last of the Blue Devils* (1979).

McTell, Blind Willie (b. Thomson, Ga., ca. 1898; d. Milledgeville, Ga., 19 Aug. 1959). Blues singer, guitarist, and songwriter. Blind from birth, he grew up in

Statesboro, Ga.; he became a traveling musician early in life. In his late teens he attended schools for the blind in Macon, Ga., and New York, thereafter settling in the Atlanta area. He developed a very personal blues style akin to Piedmont traditions; he also possessed exceptional skills on the twelve-string guitar. He recorded for major labels and for the Library of Congress, performing a broad range of blues, folk tunes, ballads, dances, rags, and increasingly gospel and sacred songs. His songs include "Statesboro Blues" and "Atlanta Rag."

Maddy, Joe [Joseph] **(Edgar)** (b. Wellington, Kans., 14 Oct. 1891; d. Traverse City, Mich., 18 Apr. 1966). Music educator and conductor. Studied violin, clarinet, and viola; played with the symphonies in Minneapolis (1909–14) and St. Paul (1914–18). Served as supervisor of music instruction in the public schools of Rochester, N.Y. (1918–20) and Richmond, Ind. (1920–24), and was appointed professor of music education at the Univ. of Michigan (from 1924). In 1926 he founded and conducted the National High School Orchestra, and he was one of the founders of the National Music Camp at Interlochen, Mich., which opened in 1928.

Maderna, Bruno (b. Venice, 21 Apr. 1920; d. Darmstadt, 13 Nov. 1973). Composer and conductor. Maderna was a child prodigy as violinist and conductor; studied composition with Alessandro Bustini in Rome (1940) and with Gian Francesco Malipiero in Venice (1942–43); conducting with Antonio Guarnieri (Siena, 1941) and with Scherchen (Venice, 1948); made his conducting debut in Munich (1950). He taught at the conservatory in Venice (1948–52); from 1954 at the summer courses in Darmstadt; the conservatory in Milan (1957–58); the summer courses at Dartington College (Devon, 1960–62); the conservatory in Rotterdam (1967–68); the Mozarteum in Salzburg (1960–70); and the Berkshire Music Center (1971–72). In 1955 he and Berio founded the Electronic Music Studio at Milan Radio, and he organized a series of "Incontri musicali" to promote new music in Milan (1956–60); in 1961 he founded and conducted the Darmstadt International Chamber Ensemble; ten years later he was appointed conductor of the Milan Radio Orchestra.

His early works are neoclassic and influenced by the music of Bartók and Stravinsky, but he soon turned to twelve-tone and serial procedures and to electronic music. His *Musica su due dimensioni* (1951, rev. 1957 and 1963) was one of the earliest works to combine live and taped sounds; the version published in 1957 consists of 5 pieces (2 for solo flute, 3 with tape) in which both flutist and technician make decisions with respect to ad libitum repetitions, interpolated improvisations, and particular combinations of electronic and live sounds. Later electronic works included not only live performers but also stage action: *Hyperion,* first presented (Venice, 1964) as a "lirica in forma di spettacolo" of Maderna and Virginio Puecher with a text by Friedrich Hölderlin, phonemes by Hans Helms, requires the flutist to spend 10 minutes unpacking flutes of various sizes, only to be confronted by fortissimo taped sounds (single vowels or consonants or phonemes elaborated by Helms from sounds recorded in several languages) when he attempts to begin his solos. Maderna was among the most important of the post-Webern serialists.

Works: *Don Perlimplin* (radio opera, 1962) and other dramatic music; *Quadrivium* (4 percussionists and 4 orchestral groups, 1969), 3 oboe concertos (1962, 1967, 1973), and other orchestral music; *Divertimento in due tempi* (flute and piano, 1953) and other chamber music; vocal music (*Venetian Journal,* tenor, orchestra, and tape, 1972); film scores; many transcriptions of Italian Baroque and other early music; arrangements of light music, jazz, and songs of Kurt Weill.

Bibl.: Massimo Mila, *Maderna musicista europeo* (Turin, 1976). Mario Baroni and Rossana Dalmonte, eds., *Bruno Maderna: Documenti* (Milan, 1985). Mario Baroni and Rossana Dalmonte, eds., *Studi su Bruno Maderna* (Milan, 1989). Raymond Fearn, *Bruno Maderna* (New York, 1990).

Madetoja, Leevi (Antti) (b. Oulu, 17 Feb. 1887; d. Helsinki, 6 Oct. 1947). Composer. In Helsinki he studied at the university and at the music institute under Sibelius (1906–10). He then studied with d'Indy in Paris (1910–11), with Fuchs in Vienna, and in Berlin (1911–12). Returning to Finland, he was the conductor of the Helsinki Philharmonic Society (1912–14) and of the orchestra of Viipuri (1914–16), where he also directed the orchestra school. In Helsinki he taught at the music institute (later academy) (1916–39) and served as music critic of the *Helsingin sanomat* (1916–32). He spent time in France during the 1920s and 1930s. A leading member of the Finnish national school of composition, which followed Sibelius, he made extensive use of Finnish folk tunes. He was particularly skilled at orchestration; his music displays great clarity of texture. His works include 2 operas: *Pohjalaisia* [The Ostrobothnians] (1923) and *Juhu* (1934); *Symphonic Suite* (1910); *Tanssinäky* [Dance Vision] (1910); 3 symphonies (1915–16, 1917–18, 1926); *Huvinäytelmäalku* [Comedy Overture] (1923); the ballet *Okon Fuoko* (1930); Piano Trio (1910); *Lyric Suite* (cello and piano, 1921–22); *Kuoleman puvtarha* [The Garden of Death] (piano, 1918–19); over 50 pieces for chorus; cantatas; about 50 solo songs; violin music; incidental music for plays; and film music.

Madonna [Ciccone, Madonna Louise] (b. Bay City, Mich., 16 Aug. 1958). Popular singer and songwriter. She moved to New York in 1978, where she worked briefly in dance (with Alvin Ailey), acted, and modeled; since 1983 she has recorded original and co-written popular songs. Her albums include *Madonna* (1983, including "Lucky Star"), *Like a Virgin* (1984, including "Material Girl"), *Like a Prayer* (1989), *Erotica* (1992), and *Bedtime Stories* (1994). She was among the first artists to make extensive use of music videos for promotion; she has also appeared in films (*Desperately Seeking Susan,* 1985; *Dick Tracy,* 1990).

Madonna has been an unusually prominent figure in American popular culture, often challenging the conventions of female behavior.

Maegaard, Jan (Carl Christian) (b. Copenhagen, 14 Apr. 1926). Composer and musicologist. He studied at the Copenhagen Conservatory with Schierbeck (composition), Jeppesen (counterpoint), Jersild (orchestration), and Hjelmborg (theory), earning a teacher's diploma in 1953; continued his training with Robert Nelson at UCLA (1958–59) and with Larsen and Schiørring (musicology) at the Univ. of Copenhagen, where he earned his Ph.D. in 1972 with a dissertation on Schoenberg. In 1971 he was appointed professor of music at the Univ. of Copenhagen; he lectured as a visiting professor at SUNY–Stony Brook (1974) and at UCLA (1978–81). Maegaard's early compositions are in a diatonic style reminiscent of Nielsen (Chamber Concerto no. 1, 1949; a trio for oboe, clarinet, bassoon, 1950). Subsequent works employed twelve-tone techniques (*Five Preludes,* violin, 1957; trio serenade "O alter Duft aus Märchenzeit," piano trio, 1960), and total serialism (*Due tempi,* orchestra, 1961), sometimes combined with aleatoric elements (Chamber Concerto no. 2, 1961); he also experimented with tonally oriented music, including the use of nine-tone scales (*Triptykon,* violin, string orchestra, 1984). Maegaard is the author of numerous studies of Schoenberg, including *Praeludier til musik af Schönberg* (Copenhagen, 1976).

Maelzel, Johann[es] Nepomuk (b. Regensburg, 15 Aug. 1772; d. in the harbor of La Guiara, Venezuela, 21 July 1838). Inventor. In 1792 settled in Vienna, where his first successful invention was the Panharmonicon, which contained a number of instruments that played through mechanical means. From 1808 he was a court "mechanician" at Vienna; Beethoven showed interest not only in his ear trumpet but also in his invention of a musical chronometer, forerunner of the metronome. In 1813 Beethoven composed a "battle-piece" for the Panharmonicon, which he later orchestrated as *Wellington's Victory.* Maelzel is best known for the metronome that he began manufacturing in 1816 in Paris.

Maessens [Maessins], **Pieter** [Massenus Moderatus, Petrus] (b. Ghent, ca. 1505; d. Vienna, Oct. 1563). Composer. A choirboy in the chapel of Margaret of Austria; a mercenary soldier in the imperial and Spanish armies until becoming a priest in 1539; chapelmaster at Notre Dame in Courtrai from 1540 until 1543; subsequently assistant Kapellmeister, then Kapellmeister of the Viennese court chapel. The majority of his compositions are sacred or secular Latin motets.

Maggini, Gio(vanni) Paolo (b. Brescia, Italy, bapt. 29 Nov. 1579; d. there, ca. 1631). String instrument maker. He started out as a pupil in the workshop of Gasparo da Salò, then opened up his own shop after his marriage in 1615. As Maggini and Gasparo worked together closely until the latter's death in 1609, it is difficult to know which to credit as the inventor of the contralto viola. Approximately 50 Maggini violins and 20 violas and cellos survive; they reveal, in comparison to Amati instruments, a compact outline later adopted by Guarnieri. His labels (never dated) read Gio. Paolo Maggini, Brescia.

Gustav Mahler.

Magnard, (Lucien Denis Gabriel) Albéric (b. Paris, 9 June 1865; d. Oise, 3 Sept. 1914). Composer. Took a law degree in 1887, but studied in 1886–88 at the conservatory and also four years with d'Indy, who greatly influenced him, composing a symphony, an orchestral suite, and songs during this period. His first opera, *Yolande,* was a failure (Brussels, 1892). Best known for the opera *Bérénice* (Opéra-comique, 1911); also composed 2 later symphonies and other orchestral music, chamber works, songs; wrote his own librettos and some essays on music. In his operas he uses leitmotivs in the manner of Wagner.

Mahler, Gustav (b. Kalischt [Kaliště], Bohemia, 7 July 1860; d. Vienna, 18 May 1911). Composer and conductor. His childhood is usually described as unhappy, partly because of his parents' incompatibility and quarreling, but they lived in reasonable comfort, from 1860 in Iglau (Jihlava), and his musical talent, which was apparent early, was encouraged by both. In 1870 he appeared as a pianist in a local concert and thereafter took part in local musical activity. In 1875–78 he was a student at the Vienna Conservatory, studying piano with Julius Epstein (1875–77), who recognized and encouraged his talent (his arrogance and resentment of schoolwork did not make him a popular student), harmony with Fuchs (1875–76), composition with Krenn (1875–78). He won the piano prize in 1876 and 1877 but then abandoned the piano for composition. In September 1876 he gave a concert in Iglau, playing the piano and having some of his work performed (almost none of his student compositions survives). In 1877–78 and spring 1880, he attended lectures at the Univ. of Vienna, possibly including some of Bruckner's; he later denied that Bruckner had been his teacher, but the two were rather close in the 1870s, Mahler making part of the four-hand piano score of Bruckner's Third Symphony (1880). In 1878 he won the conservatory composition prize with the scherzo of a lost piano quintet.

After graduating from the conservatory he eked out a bare living in Vienna by giving lessons and with a small allowance from his father. A passionate Wagnerian, he in this period embraced Wagner's vegetarianism and teetotalism and was attracted to socialism. In 1878–80 Mahler composed text and music for his first large surviving work, the cantata *Das klagende Lied,* which in 1881 he unsuccessfully entered for the Beethoven Prize of the Gesellschaft der Musikfreunde. (The judges included Brahms, who was later to admire Mahler's conducting; Mahler's opinion of Brahms's music remained highly equivocal.)

In 1880, deciding to attempt a career as a conductor, Mahler signed a ten-year contract with an agent. The summer of 1880 brought his first engagement, conducting operettas in a tiny summer theater in the Upper Austrian spa, Hall; he was then again in Vienna until engaged from September 1881 to April 1882 at the Laibach (Ljubljana) theater, where he was very successful. In January 1883 he was suddenly called as a replacement to the Olmütz (Olomouc) theater, where he found working conditions frustrating; here he already evinced the idealistic pursuit of artistic perfection, carried on with great energy and a tyrannical disregard for the opinions and feelings of others that was to characterize his career as conductor and administrator. After serving as chorusmaster for a season (March–May 1883) of Italian opera at the Carl-Theater, Vienna, he was engaged for three years as assistant to the Kapellmeister at Kassel. In Kassel he became infatuated with the singer Johanna Richter, the dedicatee of the *Lieder eines fahrenden Gesellen,* composed to his own poems and under her spell, mostly in 1884. He was engaged for the intervening year, August 1885–July 1886, as chief conductor at Prague. This marked an important step in his career, since it was here that, supported by the impresario Angelo Neumann, he first conducted an important part of the opera repertory, works of Mozart and the Prague premieres of *Rheingold* and *Walküre.* Journalistic criticism of his Prague conducting announces themes that recur throughout his career, often recognizing his high artistic aims but frequently censuring his tempos, which tended toward extremes.

On 20 April 1886 Betty Frank sang three of his lieder at a Prague concert, the first public performance of any of his mature music. In 1887 Mahler was asked by Weber's grandson to complete Weber's sketches for the comic opera *Die drei Pintos.* Becoming enthusiastic for the work (as well as for the grandson's wife, with whom he had an affair), he completed the opera, which, through the interest it aroused in Germany after its Leipzig premiere on 20 January 1888, did much to make his name known and to help his finances. This was a highly creative period in which he composed much of the music for what was to be his First Symphony (completing the first version early in 1888), the first movement of the Second Symphony, and late in 1887 sketches of the first settings of poems from *Des Knaben Wunderhorn,* which was to be his almost exclusive source of song texts through 1900.

In September 1888 Mahler became director of the Budapest Opera, a highly prestigious appointment, although the opera was in artistic and administrative decline and subject to nationalistic tensions. He announced an ambitious program of strengthening the repertory and company with Hungarian singers. He had some notable successes, but in his second season his budget was reduced, and in the third a hostile and nationalistic new intendant was appointed, limiting Mahler's power. In March 1891 he moved to Hamburg as chief conductor at the theater, a post that did not have the artistic control of Budapest but did give him a first-rate company of singers to work with (joined in 1895 by the soprano Anna von Mildenburg, whom he shaped into a leading artist and with whom he had a love affair). He was at first respectfully received, but the critics eventually turned hostile; however, his conducting won the admiration of Hans von Bülow, one of the few conductors that Mahler himself admired, and he began to gain experience as a symphonic conductor by deputizing for the ailing Bülow. (Bülow's attitude toward Mahler's own music, however, was entirely negative.)

Mahler's First Symphony (still called a symphonic poem) was premiered in Budapest on 20 November 1889 by Bülow, who repeated it in Hamburg in 1893; it was given in Weimar in 1894 by Richard Strauss (whom he had met in 1887; relations between the two were respectful but not cordial, reflecting Strauss's lukewarm regard for Mahler's music). Mahler spent part of summer 1892 conducting a well-received Wagner season at Covent Garden. He finished several lieder in winter 1891–92 and more in 1893 and revised *Das klagende Lied* (1892–93). He worked on the Second Symphony at Steinbach (where he summered from 1893 to 1898), conducting it without the finale in Berlin in March 1895 and complete there on 13 December 1895, with considerable success. In summer 1895 he visited Bayreuth at Cosima Wagner's invitation, but was never invited to conduct there, partly because he was Jewish. In the summers of 1895 and 1896 he composed the Third Symphony (premiere, Krefeld, 9 June 1902).

After lengthy negotiations and with the support of Brahms and Hanslick and after conversion to Catholicism in February 1897, Mahler was appointed conductor (April 1897) and director (September 1897) at the Vienna Opera, one of the supreme posts in the German-speaking world—although then undergoing a decline—making his conducting debut there with *Lohengrin* (10 May 1897). In 1898 he succeeded Richter as conductor of the Vienna Philharmonic, taking it to Paris in summer 1900; but he alienated the players and resigned in 1901. His direction of the Vienna Opera was characterized by emphasis on productions as integrated artistic ensembles rather than as showcases for star singers. As usual, his administration was highly controversial and he suffered from increasingly virulent press criticism, much of it strongly anti-Semitic. One source of criticism was Mahler's absences for guest-conducting, particularly his own works, opportunities for which increased considerably in this period, although his music did not become a concert staple.

Mahler continued to compose mainly in the summer in the country (from 1900 at Maiernigg in Carinthia, where in 1901 he built a house). In summer 1898 he wrote only two *Wunderhorn* songs. By the end of summer 1899 he had only composed one additional *Wunderhorn* setting, "Revelge," when he began working feverishly on the Fourth Symphony, which was essentially completed the following year (premiere, Munich, 25 November 1901; the finale, "Das himmlische Leben," had already been completed in 1892). In summer 1901 he composed five *Rückert Lieder,* three *Kindertotenlieder,* and two movements of the Fifth Symphony, completed in 1902 (premiere, Cologne, 18 October 1904). The Sixth was composed in summers 1903–4 (premiere, Essen, 27 May 1906), the Seventh in 1904–5 (premiere, Prague, 19 September 1908), the Eighth in 1906. In November 1901 Mahler met a young Viennese, Alma Schindler (1879–1964), daughter of a prominent painter and herself a talented musician, beautiful and clever, moving in artistic and intellectual circles. They were married in March 1902; daughters were born in November 1902 and June 1904.

In June 1907 Mahler resolved his Vienna difficulties by accepting a very remunerative four-year contract to conduct part of each season at the Metropolitan Opera. In June his elder and favorite daughter died of scarlet fever. Moving to the Tirol, the sorrowing Mahler began *Das Lied von der Erde;* he was himself diagnosed as having a weak heart and was ordered to lead a restricted life. On 1 January 1908 he made his Metropolitan debut with *Tristan.* In summer 1908, at Toblach, Mahler worked on *Das Lied von der Erde* and began his Ninth Symphony. In his second season at the Metropolitan, Gatti-Casazza became manager, bringing with him Toscanini, who took over some of Mahler's repertory. Mahler responded by accepting an offer to become conductor of the New York Philharmonic in the 1909–10 season; in the summer of 1909 he had completed *Das Lied von der Erde* and the Ninth Symphony. Returning from New York in April 1910, he conducted his Second Symphony in Paris, during which Debussy, Fauré, and Dukas walked out. His Eighth Symphony had perhaps the most successful premiere of all his works, in Munich on 12 September 1910 (the last he was to conduct himself).

Mahler's insistence that their marriage should focus almost exclusively on his needs seems to have put considerable strain on Alma, who became subject to recurring nervous and physical ailments leading to frequent cures at various spas. At one of these in summer 1910 she met the young architect Walter Gropius, who eventually asked Mahler, apparently without her prior knowledge, to give her up to him. Although Alma decided not to leave him, Mahler was greatly disturbed; some of his passion and anguish are expressed in comments in the sketches of the Tenth Symphony, on which he worked that summer (he also consulted Freud). Returning to New York in October, he was troubled by disagreements with the orchestra's board. In January 1911 he became ill; he returned to Vienna, pausing in Paris for further futile treatment, and he died in May, leaving his Tenth Symphony unfinished.

Bibl.: Natalie Bauer-Lechner, *Erinnerungen an Gustav Mahler* (Vienna, 1923); trans. Eng. (1980). Alma Mahler, ed., *Gustav Mahler: Briefe, 1879–1911* (Vienna, 1924); trans. Eng. (1979). Alma Mahler, *Gustav Mahler: Erinnerungen und Briefe* (Amsterdam, 1940); abridged Eng. trans. (New York, 1946); new ed. Donald Mitchell (London, 1968). Donald Mitchell, *Gustav Mahler: The Early Years* (Berkeley, 1980). Id., *Gustav Mahler: Songs and Symphonies of Life and Death: Interpretations and Annotations* (Berkeley, 1986). Deryck Cooke, *Gustav Mahler: An Introduction to His Music* (New York, 1988). Karl-Josef Müller, *Mahler: Leben, Werke, Dokumente* (Mainz, 1988). Susan M. Filler, *Gustav and Alma Mahler: A Guide to Research* (New York, 1989). Kurt Blaukopf, *Gustav Mahler, oder, Der Zeitgenosse der Zukunft* (Kassel, 1989). Hermann Danuser, *Gustav Mahler und seine Zeit* (Laaber, 1991). Michael Kennedy, *Mahler* (New York, 1991). Peter Franklin, *Mahler, Symphony no. 3* (Cambridge, 1991). Theodor W. Adorno, *Mahler,* trans. Edmund Jephcott (Chicago, 1992). Kurt Blaukopf and Herta Blaukopf, eds., *Mahler: His Life, Work, and World* (New York, 1992). Carl E. Schorske, *Gustav Mahler: Formation and Transformation* (New York, 1992). Hermann Danuser, ed., *Gustav Mahler* (Darmstadt, 1992). Frank Berger, *Gustav Mahler: Vision und Mythos* (Stuttgart, 1993). Constantin Floros, *Gustav Mahler: The Symphonies,* trans. Vernon Wicker (Portland, 1993). Norman Lebrecht, *Gustav Mahler: Erinnerungen seiner Zeitgenossen* (Mainz, 1993). Henry-Louis de La Grange, *Gustav Mahler* (Oxford, 1995–).

Maillard, Jean (fl. ca. 1538–70). Composer. Publishing history, texts, and dedications of his works suggest a career in Paris and some association with the French royal court. He composed Masses, dozens of motets, and nearly 60 chansons.

Maillart, Aimé [Louis] (b. Montpellier, 24 Mar. 1817; d. Moulins-sur-Allier, 26 May 1871). Composer. Son of a provincial actor who later ran a theatrical agency in Paris; from 1833 a student at the Paris Conservatory (1841, Prix de Rome). He produced 6 comic operas in

Paris, 1847–64, some very successful, especially *Les dragons de Villars* (1856). Also composed cantatas.

Maillart, Pierre (b. Valenciennes, 1550; d. Tournai, 16 Aug. 1622). Theorist. A member of the Flemish chapel in Madrid from 1563 until returning to his native country in 1570; by no later than 1581, active at the Cathedral of Tournai. His treatise *Les tons ou discours sur les modes de musique et les tons de l'église, et la distinction entre iceux* (Tournai, 1610; facs., 1972) was influential throughout the 17th century.

Mailman, Martin (b. New York, 30 June 1932). Composer. He studied at Eastman with Barlow, Rogers, and Hanson (Ph.D., 1960); held a Ford Foundation grant as composer-in-residence in Jacksonville (1959–61); and taught at the Brevard (N.C.) Music Center, West Virginia Univ., East Carolina College, and North Texas State Univ. (from 1966). He has also led workshops in comprehensive musicianship for the Contemporary Music Workshop (1959–72). Composed in a neoclassical and lyrical style, his works include an opera; 3 symphonies (1969–83), a violin concerto (1982), *Mirror Music* (1987), and other orchestral music; chamber and piano music; *Generations 3: Messengers* (solo voice, children's choruses, band, 1977) and other choral and vocal music; *Toward the Second Century* (1989) and other works for band; incidental music and television scores.

Mainardi, Enrico (b. Milan, 19 May 1897; d. Munich, 10 Apr. 1976). Cellist. He graduated from the Milan Conservatory in 1920, continuing his studies in Berlin with Hugo Becker (cello) and Giacomo Orefice (composition). In 1913 he performed Reger's Fourth Sonata op. 116 with the composer; formed duos with Dohnányi and Edwin Fischer, and a trio with Fischer and Kulenkampff (later replaced by Schneiderhan). He taught cello at the Accademia di S. Cecilia, Rome (from 1930), and in Berlin, Lucerne, and Salzburg; in 1933 he was invited to collaborate with Strauss on a recording of *Don Quixote.* Mainardi's compositions include 4 cello concertos.

Maio [Mayo, Majo], **Giovan Tomaso di** (b. Naples?, ca. 1500; d. there, 1 Feb. 1563). Composer. *Maestro di cappella* at the church of SS. Annunziata, Naples, from 1548. His known compositions include 9 pieces printed in 1519 in a Neapolitan anthology called *Fioretti di frottole* and a collection of 30 *villanesche* in Neapolitan dialect printed in Venice in 1546.

Maistre Jhan [Gian, Jehan] (b. ca. 1485; d. ca. 1545). Composer. Of French origin but known chiefly through service at the court of Ferrara (by 1512 until 1543; *maestro di cappella* from at least 1537). His compositions include a Mass, 2 Mass movements, nearly 90 motets (some occasional or political), a French chanson, and over 20 Italian madrigals.

Majo, Gian Francesco (de) (b. Naples, 24 Mar. 1732; d. there, 17 Nov. 1770). Composer. His father, Giuseppe de Majo (1697–1771), was *maestro di cappella* at the Naples court chapel; Gian Francesco studied first with him, then with Gennaro Manno and Francesco Feo. As a youth he served as chapel harpsichordist at Naples and as supernumerary organist; in 1758 he was made second organist. Also in 1758 his first opera, *Ricimero re dei Goti,* was a great success in Parma. During the 1760s he traveled to northern Italy, where he studied briefly with Padre Martini (1761–63), and to Vienna, where in 1764 he composed the opera *Alcide negli orti Esperidi* for the coronation of Joseph II. The same year he composed *Ifigenia in Tauride* for the Mannheim court. He returned to Naples during his last years, resuming his post as second organist; he finally succumbed to tuberculosis. Among his 20 known serious operas are *Astrea placata* and *Cajo Fabricio* (both Naples, 1760); *Catone in Utica* (Turin, 1762); *Alessandro nell'Indie* (Mannheim, 1766); *Antigono* (Venice, 1767); *Didone abbandonata* (Venice, 1769); *Eumene* (Naples, 1771; completed by others). He also composed oratorios, cantatas, Masses, and other sacred works.

Majo [Maio], **Giuseppe de** (b. Naples, 5 Dec. 1697; d. there, 18 Nov. 1771). Composer. The father of Gian Francesco de Majo. He studied under Nicola Fago at the Turchini Conservatory in Naples. After several appointments and promotions in the royal chapel, he succeeded Leo as *primo maestro* in 1745. The bulk of his output consists of sacred music. His serenata *Il sogno d'Olimpia* (1747) was well received, but his few attempts at serious and comic opera never met with much success.

Major [Mayer], (Jakab) Gyula [Julius] (b. Kassa, Hungary [now Košice, Slovakia], 13 Dec. 1858; d. Budapest, 30 Jan. 1925). Composer and pianist. He studied at the Buda Conservatory and at the Academy of Music in Budapest (1877–81), where his teachers included Volkmann (composition), Erkel and Liszt (piano); taught at the Budapest Music Society, and in 1889 cofounded the Hungarian Music School; also toured Germany as a concert pianist. Major's works combine the traditional German school of composition with nationalistic elements, including folk tunes. Works include opera (*Erzsike,* Budapest, 1901; *Mila,* Bratislava, 1913), 6 symphonies (no. 2, Hungarian, n.d.), chamber music, piano sonatas (2 Hungarian sonatas, 1896), songs.

Makeba, Miriam (b. Prospect, South Africa, 4 Mar. 1932). Folk and popular singer. She rose to prominence in 1959 for her role in the opera *King Kong* in London; subsequently moved to the U.S. and performed a repertory of primarily African popular and folk musics. Active in political causes since the 1960s, she was particularly critical of apartheid; in 1986 she participated in Paul Simon's *Graceland* tour (1986), which included the South African group Ladysmith Black Mambazo.

Maklakiewicz, Jan Adam (b. Chojnata, Mazuria, Poland, 24 Nov. 1899; d. Warsaw, 7 Feb. 1954). Composer. He studied at the Chopin Music School with Biernacki (harmony), Binental (violin), and Szopski (counterpoint), and took composition from Statkowski at the Warsaw Conservatory (1922–25); also studied with Dukas in Paris. He returned to Poland and taught at the conservatories of Łódź (1927–29) and Warsaw (from 1929); later taught at Kraków Conservatory (from 1947), and directed the Kraków Philharmonic (1945–47) and the Warsaw Philharmonic (1947–48). Maklakiewicz's compositions from the late 1920s and early 1930s (Cello concerto, 1930; Symphony no. 2, with baritone, chorus, *Święty Boże* [O Holy Lord], 1928) are experimental and often dissonant; his works after World War II make use of extremely simplified textures.

Maksymiuk, Jerzy (b. Grodno, Poland, 9 April 1936). Conductor, composer, and pianist. He studied at the Warsaw Conservatory with Perkowski (composition), Madey (conducting), and Kirjacka and Lefeld (piano); conducted the Warsaw Teatr Wielki (1970–72), and in 1972 founded the Polish Chamber Orchestra and served as music director. Maksymiuk also conducted the Polish Radio National Symphony in Katowice (1975–77), and the BBC Scottish Symphony in Glasgow (1983–93); in 1991 he made his debut at the English National Opera conducting *Don Giovanni.* His compositions include ballets, orchestral music, and choral works.

Malawski, Artur (b. Przemyśl, Poland, 4 July 1904; d. Kraków, 26 Dec. 1957). Composer, violinist and conductor. He studied violin with Chmielewski at the Kraków Conservatory, and taught violin and theory there after graduating (1928–1936). In 1936 he attended the Warsaw Conservatory, where his teachers included Sikorski (composition) and Bierdiajew (conducting); he taught conducting and composition in Kraków (1945–57), and conducting in Katowice (1950–54); his students included Penderecki and Schäffer. Malawski's early works (*Allegro capriccioso,* orchestra, 1929; cantata *Wyspa gorgon* [Gorgon's Island], 1939) demonstrate the influence of Debussy; with the Symphony no. 1 (1938–43) and the String quartet no. 2 (1941–43) he forged a more individual style. Malawski's best works include the *Etiudy symfoniczne* (piano, orchestra, 1947) and the ballet-pantomine *Wierchy* [The Peaks] (soprano, tenor, baritone, chorus, orchestra, 1942; rev. 1950–52).

Maldere, Pierre van (b. Brussels, 16 Oct. 1729; d. there, 1 Nov. 1768). Composer and violinist. In 1746 he was playing in the royal chapel of Brussels as a second violinist, and was promoted to first violin in 1749. Prince Charles of Lorraine, Governor-General of the Netherlands and brother-in-law of Empress Maria Theresa, took a personal interest in van Maldere, allowing him to perform in Dublin (1751–53), Paris (1754), and Austria and Bohemia (1757–58). In 1758 Charles appointed van Maldere his *valet de chambre;* he was director, 1762–67, of the Grand-théâtre in Brussels. Works include symphonies and violin sonatas, many published during his lifetime; most of his attempts at opéra comique have been lost.

Malengreau [de Maleingreau], **Paul (Eugène)** (b. Trélon, Nord, France, 23 Nov. 1887; d. Brussels, 9 Jan. 1959). Composer and organist. He studied at the Brussels Conservatory (1905–12), taught there from 1913, and was professor of organ (1929–53). He wrote liturgical music and sacred concert music in the manner of Franck. Works include an oratorio (*La légende de St. Augustin,* 1934); *Symphonie de la Passion* for orchestra; chamber and piano music; organ symphonies, preludes, and other organ music; Masses, motets, and songs.

Maler, Wilhelm (b. Heidelberg, 21 June 1902; d. Hamburg, 29 Apr. 1976). Composer. His teachers included Haas (Munich), Jarnach (Berlin), and Grabner (Heidelberg). He taught in Cologne from 1925 and was made professor at the Musikhochschule there in 1936; taught theory at the Univ. of Bonn (1931–44); after the war was made deputy director of the Music and Theater School in Hamburg and director of the Northwest German Academy at Detmold; from 1959 until 1971 he held similar positions in Hamburg. His works, most composed before the war, are contrapuntal and influenced by Hindemith's contrapuntal style, Reger, Busoni, and by interests in folk song and impressionism. His harmony textbook was widely used (*Beitrag zur durmolltonalen Harmonienlehre,* 1931; 4th ed., 1957).

Malfitano, Catherine (b. New York, 18 Apr. 1948). Soprano. She studied at the Manhattan School of Music and with Frank Corsaro. Made her professional debut at the Central City Opera in 1972, then sang with the Minnesota Opera (1972–73) and the New York City Opera (1973–79). Made her European debut at the Holland Festival in 1974, her Metropolitan Opera debut in 1979, and her Vienna Staatsoper debut in 1982; filmed *Tosca* with Domingo in 1992; has performed with most major American opera companies and in Salzburg, Florence, and Munich.

Malgoire, Jean-Claude (b. Avignon, 25 Nov. 1940). Conductor and oboist. Studied music at the Avignon Conservatory before entering the Paris Conservatory in 1956. Studied with Pierre Bajeux, Roland Lamorlette, and Étienne Baudo, obtaining first prizes in oboe and chamber music in 1960. In 1968 won first prize as oboist at the Geneva International Competition. Upon its foundation in 1967 joined the Orchestre de Paris as its English horn. The same year he founded La grande écurie et la chambre du roy, dedicated to bringing to performance rarely heard Baroque music in its original timbres. For performances of medieval and Renaissance music he established the Florilegium musicum de Paris in 1970. From 1981 he was director of the Atelier lyrique de Tourcoing. He also developed projects in which the Écurie cooperated with the Opéra du nord.

Malibran [née García], **María (Felicia)** (b. Paris, 24 Mar. 1808; d. Manchester, 23 Sept. 1836). Singer. Daughter of Manuel García; sister of Manuel García II and Pauline Viardot. In 1816 she returned with her family from Italy to Paris, where she had lessons from her father, Hérold, and Panseron. Her voice was not a naturally good one, and her father trained her with great severity. Opera debut, London, 1825, in *Il barbiere di Siviglia;* then went to New York with her father's company. Probably to escape her father, she married a French merchant 30 years older, Eugène Malibran, who, his business failing, tried to exploit her as a singer. In 1827 she returned to Europe alone. From 1828 to 1832 she sang mainly in London and Paris, then more widely, including many Italian houses (Rome, Naples, Milan, Venice). From ca. 1830 she had a liaison with the violinist Bériot, bearing a son, Charles Wilfride Bériot (1833–1914). She died from neglecting the effects of a fall from a horse. Her voice was said to have been naturally a contralto, which had been extended into the soprano register, but was flawed by weak or uneven notes. She sang and acted with great intensity. Her romantic life and early death made her the subject of a considerable literature. Composed some songs.

Bibl.: Howard Bushnell, *Maria Malibran: A Biography of the Singer* (University Park, Pa., 1979).

Malipiero, Gian Francesco (b. Venice, 18 Mar. 1882; d. Treviso, 1 Aug. 1973). Composer and musicologist. His grandfather (Francesco, 1824–87) was a noted opera composer and pianist; his father (Luigi, 1853–1918) was active in both Germany and Austria as pianist and conductor. He studied harmony at the Vienna Conservatory (1898–99); having returned to Venice with his father, he studied counterpoint with Bossi at the Liceo musicale, where he also began to learn bassoon. He received his diploma in fugue in 1902, and in composition after further study with Bossi at the Liceo musicale in Bologna (1904). He composed in Venice until 1913, with brief trips to Berlin, where he had contact with Bruch. In that year he spent time in Paris in touch with Ravel, made the acquaintance of Casella and of d'Annunzio, and heard Stravinsky's *Sacre du printemps.* He returned to Italy to live in Venice and Asolo, but in 1917 moved his family to Rome; in 1921 he was appointed to teach composition at the conservatory in Parma; in 1924 he refused a position at the conservatory in Florence and reestablished his family in Asolo. He taught a course in composition at the Liceo musicale in Venice (1932–40), in 1936 was appointed to the chair in music history at the Univ. of Padua, and in 1938–39 directed the local Music Institute. In 1939 he resigned from those duties to assume the direction of the Liceo in Venice, a post he held until 1952. From 1947 he also headed the Italian Vivaldi Institute.

Malipiero was one of the most important of that group of composers (including Casella, Respighi, and Pizetti) who were to effect a definitive break with 19th-century Italian music. In *Impressioni dal vero* (orchestra, 1910) his harmonic language reflects that of the French impressionists; his *Pause del silenzio* (7 "impressioni sinfonici," 1917) brought international recognition of Malipiero's revolution in Italian music. That revolution encompassed a liberation not only from the domination of musical life in Italy by the conventions of 19th-century opera, but also from the formal schemes employed by the German Romantics. Influenced by French impressionism, German expressionism, and a devotion to the music of 17th- and 18th-century Italy, Malipiero had by the 1920s evolved a personal style that depended less on traditional thematic construction, academic counterpoint, and singable melodies than on development by means of "free conversation" producing cumulative formal structures unique to each work. The works of the 1920s are dissonant, those of the 1930s and 1940s modal and diatonic; later works moved toward atonality via increased dissonance and chromaticism, but he remained independent of any formalized approaches to atonality via dodecaphony or serialism. The 11 symphonies in particular demonstrate the progression from a clear diatonicism to an atonal expressionism.

His 40-odd theatrical works departed early from the conventions of 19th-century Italian melodrama by avoiding vocal display and closed forms, and giving a greater dramatic role to the orchestra. The *Sette canzoni* (7 "espressioni dramatiche," 1919) consist of seven scenes for a single character, without recitative, on texts drawn by Malipiero from earlier Italian poetry; influenced by expressionist monodrama and by Busoni's conception of music and theater, this work was the first of several to stand apart from theatrical and operatic realism. But a few works of this period (*Tre commedie goldoniane,* 1920–22) have a more realistic content, and include spoken recitative to advance the plot. In both operatic and instrumental works of the period, Malipiero often borrows from procedures of the 17th and 18th centuries; in the string quartet *Stornelli e ballate* (1923) one theme ("quasi ritornello") connects a large number of independent sections.

His interest in Italian Baroque music began early in his career, when he "went frequently to the Marciana Library to study the music of old composers who were practically unknown to my fellow students and teachers. I copied not only Monteverdi's works, but also many by Stradella, Galuppi, Nasco, Tartini, and others. From the very start I reacted instinctively against musical conditions in an Italy that was suffocated by the tyranny of 19th-century opera." He edited the complete works of Monteverdi, 350 sonatas and concertos of Vivaldi, as well as selected works of Bassani, Cavalieri, Galuppi, Jommelli, Leo, Luzzaschi, Marcello, Stradella, Tartini, and other early Italian composers. His writings include studies of Scarlatti (1927), Monteverdi (1930), Stravinsky (1945), Doni (1946), and Vivaldi (1958).

Works: *L'Orfeide,* (trilogy, Malipiero, after early Italian poetry: *La morte delle maschere,* 1922; *Sette canzoni,* 1919; *Orfeo, ovvero l'ottava canzone,* 1920; Düsseldorf, 1925), *Venere prigionera* (Malipiero, after Gonzales; Florence, 1957), and over 30 other dramatic works and 5 ballets; 11 symphonies (1933–69), 8 *Dialoghi* for solo instruments and orchestra, several concertos, and other orchestral music (*Notturno di canti e balli,* 1951); oratorios and cantatas for soloists and/or chorus, with orchestra; 8 string quartets (1920–64), *Sonata a tre* (violin, cello, and piano, 1927), and *Serenata* (bassoon and 11 instruments, 1961), and other chamber music; works for 1 or 2 pianos; works for solo voice or chorus and instrumental ensemble; unaccompanied choral music and songs; transcriptions and arrangements of works by Monteverdi, Vivaldi, Corelli, and others.

Writings: In addition to those mentioned, *L'orchestra* (1920); *Teatro* (1920), *I Profeti di Babilonia* (1924); *Così va lo mondo* (1946); *L'armonioso laberinto* (1946); *Il filo di Arianna* (1966); *Maschere della commedia dell'arte* (1969); and other volumes of recollections and thoughts; many articles and much musical criticism.

Bibl.: Mario Labroca, *Malipiero Musicista Veneziano,* (Venice, n.d.) [catalogue compiled by Biancamaria Borri]. John C. G. Waterhouse, *La musica di Gian Francesco Malipiero* (Turin and Rome, 1990).

Malipiero, Riccardo, Jr. (b. Milan, 24 July 1914). Composer, critic, and pianist. Son of the cellist Riccardo (1886–1975) and nephew of Gian Francesco. He studied piano and composition in the conservatories in Milan and Turin (1930–37) and composition with his uncle in Venice (1937–39). He was active as a pianist and wrote criticism for *Il popolo* and *Corriere lombardo* (1945–66); lectured in the U.S. (1954, 1959, 1969) and in Buenos Aires (1963); and from 1969 to 1984 directed the Liceo musicale di Varèse. His earliest mature works followed Dallapiccola into atonality (*Minnie la candida,* opera, 1942); by 1945 he had adopted the twelve-tone method and was organizer of the first international conference devoted to that topic (Milan, 1949). His many compositions include dramatic works; *Requiem* (prompted by the death of Dallapiccola, 1975); *Notturno* (cello and orchestra, 1984) and other orchestral music; *Diario d'agosto* (piano, clarinet, and cello, 1986) and other chamber music; a few piano pieces; *Go Placidly* (cantata for baritone and chamber orchestra, 1974–75) and other accompanied vocal and choral music.

Malko, Nikolay (Andreyevich) (b. Brailov, 4 May 1883; d. Sydney, 23 June, 1961). Conductor. He studied with Rimsky-Korsakov, Lyadov, Glazunov, and Tcherepnin at the St. Petersburg Conservatory, and with Mottl in Munich. Beginning in 1908 he conducted ballet and opera at St. Petersburg and taught at the Moscow (1918–25) and Leningrad (1925–29) conservatories; also served as principal conductor of the Leningrad Philharmonic (1926–29). He left the country in 1928, conducted a number of orchestras in Europe, and was appointed permanent guest conductor of the Danish State Radio Orchestra (1928–32). He settled in Chicago in 1940, became an American citizen in 1946, and guest-conducted in the U.S.; subsequently conducted the Yorkshire Symphony in England (1954–55) and the Sydney Symphony (from 1957). Malko published a conducting textbook titled *The Conductor and His Baton* (Copenhagen, 1950).

Malvezzi, Cristofano (b. Lucca, bapt. 28 June 1547; d. Florence, 22 Jan. 1599). Composer. Under the patronage of the Medici, a canon at S. Lorenzo from 1562; later organist there and in several other Florentine churches; from 1573 *maestro di cappella* at S. Giovanni Battista and at the Cathedral of Florence. His known compositions include keyboard and ensemble ricercars, madrigals, sinfonias and polychoral works for *intermedi,* and 2 motets.

Mamangakis, Nicos (b. Rethymnon, Crete, 3 Mar. 1929). Composer. He studied at the Hellenic Conservatory in Athens (1947–53) and composition with Orff and Genzmer at the Munich Musikhochschule (1957–64); he also attended the Darmstadt summer courses and studied with Riedl at the Siemens electronic studios (1961–62). Settled in 1965 in Athens. Much of his music uses whole-number relationships as a means to organize pitch, rhythm, density, dynamics, and timbre; within a given work, blocks of such music alternate with sections incorporating wide intervals and microtones. In addition to works for stage, vocal music, orchestral music, and chamber music, his compositions include a number of lighter works with social or political content.

Mamiya, Michio (b. Asahikawa, 29 June 1929). Composer. Although he began to compose at age 6, he received formal training only after World War II. From 1947 he studied piano with Hiroshi Tamura and composition with Ikenouchi. He then studied at the National Univ. of Fine Arts and Music in Tokyo (1948–52). Around 1952 he became interested in Japanese folk music, incorporating tunes in works such as the Three Movements for 2 pianos (1952) and the Violin Sonata (1953). This interest led to his founding the group Yagi no Kai with Hayashi and Toyama in 1953, and collaborating with the singer Ruriko Uchida in field studies of folk songs starting in 1955. In 1957 he wrote his first works using traditional Japanese instruments: *Music for Four Koto* and the Concerto for 8 koto and chamber orchestra. In his series *Composition for Chorus* (1958–72), he quoted fragments from vocal and instrumental folk music. His interest in African music and jazz is reflected in works such as the First String Quartet (1963) and the *Deux tableaux pour orchestre '65.* Among his other works are *Mukashibanashi hitokai Tarobei* [Tale of Tarobei the Slave-Dealer] (radio opera, 1959); *Gion-matsun* [Gion Festival] (ballet, 1963); *Elmer no bōken* [Elmer's Adventure] (musical, 1967); 2 piano concertos (1954, 1970); Double Concerto Grosso (1966); Serenade (1974); Concerto for Orchestra (1978); chamber music; choral music; solo vocal music; incidental music; and film scores.

Mamlok, Ursula (b. Berlin, 1 Feb. 1928). Composer. She studied piano and violin as a child; moved with her family to Ecuador about 1940 and then to the U.S. (1941). She became an American citizen in 1945. Her musical studies in the U.S. were at the Mannes College of Music (with Szell, 1942–46), the Manhattan School (with Giannini; M.M., 1958), and privately with Wolpe, Sessions, and others. She was most influenced by the works of Schoenberg. Her works include a concerto for oboe (1976); *Phanta Phei* (Time in Flux; violin, cello, and piano, 1981); *Haiku Settings* (soprano and flute, 1967); electronic music and teaching pieces.

Mana Zucca [Zuckermann, Augusta; Zuckerman, Gussie] (b. New York, 25 Dec. 1885; d. Miami, 8 Mar. 1981). Composer and pianist. She made a European tour in 1907 and played her piano concerto with the Los Angeles Symphony in 1919. Her catalog lists some 390 published works (beginning in 1915), but she claimed to have published and written many more. Works include 2 operas, a violin concerto (1955), chamber and choral music, and some 172 songs. Her songs were widely performed between 1920 and 1940; papers and manuscripts are at the Univ. of Miami.

Manchicourt, Pierre de (b. Béthune, ca. 1510; d. Madrid, 5 Oct. 1564). Composer. From 1525 perhaps a choirboy at Arras Cathedral; later held posts at the cathedrals of Tours and Tournai, returning to Arras as a canon by 1556; in Madrid from 1559 led Philip II's Flemish chapel and perhaps also his Spanish chapel. His compositions include about 20 Masses; over 60 motets; 9 Psalms; a Magnificat; and over 50 chansons, the majority Flemish but a few Parisian in style.

Bibl.: *Opera omnia, CMM* 55 (1971–82).

Mancinelli, Luigi (b. Orvieto, 6 Feb. 1848; d. Rome, 2 Feb. 1921). Conductor and composer. Became an orchestral cellist, then in the 1870s quickly rose to prominence as a leading opera and concert conductor in Rome and elsewhere; 1881–86, director, Bologna Conservatory and music director at S. Petronio; one of the principal conductors at the Madrid Opera (1887–93; from 1891 also conducting the Sociedad de conciertos), Covent Garden (1888–1905), Metropolitan Opera (1893–1903), S. Carlos, Lisbon (1901–20); guest-conducted elsewhere. Three operas by him were performed, none lastingly successful; also composed incidental and film music, orchestral pieces, sacred works, songs.

Mancini, Francesco (b. Naples, 16 Jan. 1672; d. there, 22 Sept. 1737). Composer. He studied organ at the Conservatorio della pietà dei turchini in Naples, and served as director of the royal chapel in Alessandro Scarlatti's absence (1707–8) and after Scarlatti's death in 1725. Mancini also was director of the Conservatory of S. Maria di Loreto (1720–35). Works include cantatas, oratorios, and liturgical works, but he was best known during his lifetime as the composer of over 20 operas, most receiving their first performance in Naples.

Mancini, Henry (b. Cleveland, 16 Apr. 1924; d. Los Angeles, 14 June 1994). Popular composer, pianist, and arranger. After service in World War II he worked in Los Angeles, and in 1952–58 was a staff composer at Universal Studios. His film and television scores, many of which have become popular as separately released recordings, won several Oscar and Grammy awards: they include *Peter Gunn* (1958), *The Pink Panther* (1964), and *Victor/Victoria* (1982). He is credited with introducing the style of "cool jazz" to film writing.

Bibl.: Henry Mancini, with Gene Lees, *Did They Mention the Music?* (Chicago, 1989).

Mandelbaum, (Mayer) Joel (b. New York, 12 Oct. 1932). Composer. He studied at Harvard, Brandeis, and Indiana universities, the Berkshire Music Center, and the Berlin Hochschule für Musik; composition teachers included Blacher, Dallapiccola, Irving Fine, Piston, and Shapero. In 1961 he began teaching at Queens College, CUNY. He is noted particularly for his exploration of microtonal tunings, especially those based on 19- and 31-note divisions of the octave. Works include 3 operas; orchestral music; *Xenophony no. 2* (violin, cello, double bass, woodwind quintet, and organ, 1979) and other chamber music; keyboard music; choral and vocal works (*Light and Shade,* soprano, oboe, and piano, 1983).

Manelli, Francesco (b. Tivoli, Sept. 1594; d. Parma, July 1667). Composer and singer. Started out as a chorister at Tivoli Cathedral (1605); later served there as chapel singer (1609–24) and eventually choirmaster (1627–29). He collaborated with the librettist Ferrari on *L'Andromeda* (1637), which inaugurated the first public opera house in Venice, the Teatro San Cassiano; the work's success prompted the pair to produce *La maga fulminata* the following year. In 1640 he served as an impresario in Bologna; from 1645 until his death he was in the service of the Duke of Parma. All of Manelli's operatic scores have been lost.

Manén, Juan (b. Barcelona, 14 Mar. 1883; d. there, 26 June 1971). Composer. Showed early talent on both piano and violin; became famous as a virtuoso on violin, circling the globe several times. Resided much of his life in Germany. He was also active as a conductor and writer, penning several articles for French and Spanish journals as well as an autobiography (1944; rev. 1964) and several of his own libretti. Works include the operas *Juana de Nápoles* (1903) and *Soledad* (1952); several orchestral works, among them violin showpieces, the symphony *Nova Catalonia* op. 17, and the *Sinfonía ibérica* (1966); chamber music; piano pieces; various vocal works; and many arrangements for violin.

Manfredini, Francesco (Onofrio) (b. Pistoia, bapt. 22 June 1684; d. there, 6 Oct. 1762). Composer and violinist. Studied music in Bologna, taking violin with Torelli and counterpoint with Petri. He left for Ferrara around 1700, becoming first violinist of the Church of the Holy Spirit; returned to Bologna in 1704 and took an orchestral post. His whereabouts from 1711 to 1726 remain unclear: perhaps he served Prince Antoine I at the court of Monaco. From 1727 until his death Manfredini was *maestro di cappella* at St. Philip's Cathedral in Pistoia. Most of his compositions show the strong influence of Torelli. Published works include Concertini per camera op. 1 (Bologna, 1704); Sinfonie da chiesa op. 2 (Bologna, 1709); Concerti op. 3 (Bologna, 1718); Six Sonatas (London, ca. 1764).

Manfredini, Vincenzo (b. Pistoia, 22 Oct. 1737; d. St. Petersburg, 16 Aug. 1799). Composer. Son of Francesco Manfredini. He studied music in Pistoia with his father, and later in Bologna (with Giacomo Perti) and Milan (with Giovanni Fioroni). He traveled to Moscow with his brother Giuseppe in 1758; both were probably members of Locatelli's theater troupe. Soon afterward he went to St. Petersburg to become *maestro di cappella*. In 1762 he was made director of the opera company, and he composed operas and ballets there until his return to Bologna in 1769. He is perhaps best known for his *Regole armoniche, o sieno Precetti ragionati* (Venice, 1775; 2nd ed., 1797), which contains instructions for singing and keyboard accompaniment. His operas include *Semiramide* (St. Petersburg, 1760), *Olimpiade* (Moscow, 1762), and *Armida* (Bologna, 1770); he also composed ballets, cantatas, sacred music (including a Requiem), chamber music, and keyboard works.

Mangelsdorff, Albert (b. Frankfurt am Main, 5 Sept. 1928). Jazz trombonist and bandleader. After playing mainly cool jazz and hard bop (1950s), he recorded the album *Animal Dance* with John Lewis (1962). An Asian tour in 1964 led him to incorporate Eastern music into his playing and then to move to a free jazz style. Mastering the technique of multiphonics (producing several notes simultaneously), he returned in the 1970s to chordally based pieces but with a wholly unconventional approach, as in his interpretation of "Mood Indigo" on the album *The Wide Point* (1975). Apart from concerts as a leader and an unaccompanied soloist, he was a member of Alex Schlippenbach's Globe Unity Orchestra (1967–1980s), the United Jazz & Rock Ensemble (1975–1980s), and other groups.

Mangione, Chuck [Charles Frank] (b. Rochester, N.Y., 29 Nov. 1940). Jazz flugelhorn player and bandleader. He studied music education at the Eastman School (B.S., 1963) while leading a hard bop group, the Jazz Brothers, with his brother Gap, a pianist. He joined Woody Herman (1965), Maynard Ferguson (1965), and Art Blakey (1965–67). He switched from trumpet to flugelhorn after forming his own quartet in 1968. The group reached wide audiences throughout the 1970s, performing alone and in collaboration with orchestras and symphonic wind sections. Among his hit recordings were "Land of Make Believe" on the album *The Chuck Mangione Quartet* (1972) and the title track of the album *Feels So Good* (1977). He also headed the jazz program at the Eastman School, 1968–72.

Manilow, Barry (b. New York, 17 June 1946). Popular singer, songwriter, and arranger. He began composing and arranging for radio and television; his success as a singer came after 1974 with songs such as "Mandy" (1974), "I Write the Songs" (1975), and "Looks Like We Made It" (1977). His album *2:00 A.M.: Paradise Café* (1984) featured jazz artists Shelley Manne and Sarah Vaughan.

Mann, Elias (b. Canton, Mass., 8 May 1750; d. Northampton, Mass., 12 May 1825). Composer. He worked as a house carpenter and taught singing in Massachusetts. He contributed tunes to Isaiah Thomas's *The Worcester Collection* (1786), then aided Thomas in later editions of the work (1792, 1794). In 1795 he moved to Northampton and became the town's leading musician until he left in about 1802; there he taught singing, directed a choir, and published the sacred tunebook *The Northampton Collection* (1797). In 1805 he settled in Boston, where he was a founding member of the Massachusetts Musical Society (1807–10) and published *The Massachusetts Collection of Sacred Harmony* (1807). He composed 4 secular songs, including "The Grasshopper" (1790).

Mann, Herbie (b. New York, 16 Apr. 1930). Jazz flutist. He studied at the Manhattan School of Music. In the 1950s he carved a largely unprecedented niche for the flute in the mainstream jazz world. In 1959 he founded the Afro-Jazz Sextet and progressively incorporated elements of African, Latin, and Middle Eastern styles; he pioneered bossa nova in the U.S. From 1970 he produced his own recording label, Embryo. In the 1970s and 1980s his group Family of Mann fused jazz with rock, funk, disco, and reggae. He appeared widely as soloist with pop orchestras and remained among the foremost jazz flutists.

Mann, Robert (Nathaniel) (b. Portland, Oreg., 19 July 1920). Violinist and composer. He studied with Edouard Déthier at Juilliard, also receiving instruction from Betti, Salmond, and Hans Letz. In 1941 he won the Naumburg Competition, and he joined the Juilliard faculty in 1946 after army service. He was a founding member, in 1948, of the Juilliard Quartet, playing first violin; also founded the Mann Duo with his violinist son Nicholas in 1980. In addition to his performances in chamber music, he appeared as violin soloist and conducted a number of contemporary works; his own compositions include both orchestral and chamber works. In 1971 Mann became president of the Naumburg Foundation.

Manne, Shelly [Sheldon] (b. New York, 11 June 1920; d. Los Angeles, 26 Sept. 1984). Jazz drummer and bandleader. From 1942 he mainly worked in big bands, including Stan Kenton's (intermittently, 1946–52), but also recorded "The Man I Love" with Coleman Hawkins (1943), played with Bill Harris, and toured with Jazz at the Philharmonic (both 1948–49). After settling in Los Angeles, he led small groups from 1955 through the 1970s, formed the trio the Poll-Winners with Barney Kessel and Ray Brown (1957–60), and with André Previn recorded the album *My Fair Lady* (1956), which started a fashion for jazz interpretations of musicals. He ran a nightclub, Shelly's Manne Hole (1960–74), and formed the L.A. Four, again with Brown (1974–77). His albums as a leader include *At the Black Hawk* (1959).

Mannes, David (b. New York, 16 Feb. 1866; d. there, 25 Apr. 1959). Educator, violinist, and conductor. Studied violin in New York with August Zeiss and C. R. Nicolai, and in Brussels with Ysaÿe. In 1895 he was invited by Damrosch to join the New York Symphony Society, later serving as concertmaster (1903–12); he married Clara Damrosch in 1898. Concerned with the musical education of the young and underprivileged, Mannes founded the Music School Settlement in 1894 and the Music School Settlement for Colored Children in Harlem in 1912. In 1916 he and his wife founded the David Mannes Music School (from 1953 the Mannes College of Music).

Mannes, Leopold Damrosch (b. New York, 26 Dec. 1899; d. Martha's Vineyard, Mass., 11 Aug. 1964). Educator, pianist, and composer. The son of David and Clara Damrosch Mannes, he studied piano with Elizabeth Quaile, Guy Maier, Berthe Bert, and Alfred Cortot, and composition with Schreyer, Goetschius, and Scalero. Taught theory and composition at the Mannes School, later serving as director (1940–48), co-director (1948–52), and president (1950–64). From 1931 to 1939 he worked as a research chemist at Eastman Kodak in Rochester; there he and Leopold Godowsky, Jr., invented and developed the Kodachrome process of color photography.

Mannino, Franco (b. Palermo, 25 Apr. 1924). Composer, pianist, and conductor. He studied piano and composition in Rome and began an active international career as a pianist in the early 1940s, winning the Columbus Prize in the U.S. (1950). From 1952 he conducted in major opera houses; was director of Teatro San Carlo in Naples (1969–70) and of the National Arts Center Orchestra in Ottawa (1982–86). Head of the Academia filarmonica in Bologna from 1990. He won the Diaghilev Prize in France (1956) for *Mario e il mago,* one of his 14 dramatic works. Other works include Symphony no. 5 (*Rideau Lake,* 1985), a concerto for 6 violins and 2 pianos (1980); chamber music (*Turbamento,* oboe, 1985); piano and vocal music; film scores; and transcriptions of works by Monteverdi, Brahms, and others.

Manns, August (Friedrich) (b. Stolzenberg, near Stettin, 12 Mar. 1825; d. Norwood, London, 1 Mar. 1907). Conductor. Learned the violin, clarinet, flute; played in military bands; 1849–51, conducted a Berlin beer garden orchestra; then military bands in Königsberg and Cologne. Emigrated to London in 1854, becoming assistant conductor, Crystal Palace; 1855, chief conductor, enlarging the orchestra to a full one and instituting the famous Saturday Concerts (1855–1901), designed to bring concert music to the masses. Knighted in 1903.

Mansurian, Tigran (b. Beirut, 27 Jan. 1939). Composer. Moved to Armenia in 1947. Studied composition with E. Bagdassarian, 1956–60. Attended Yerevan Conservatory (1960–65), where he studied composition with L. Sarian; in 1967, completed graduate studies there and joined the faculty. Recipient of awards including the Armenian State Prize (1981). In early works he infused a neoclassical idiom with Armenian folk traditions; later works were influenced by the music of Webern and Boulez. Compositions include symphonic music (*Night Music,* 1980); concerti; chamber music (*Tovem,* chamber ensemble, 1979); vocal works.

Mantia, Simone (b. near Palermo, 6 Feb. 1873; d. Flushing, N.Y., 25 June 1951). Euphonium player and trombonist. He came to the U.S. as a child and studied with euphonium soloist Joseph Raffayolo. In 1896 Mantia succeeded his teacher as soloist with the Sousa Band, then left the organization with Arthur Pryor in 1903 to become soloist and conductor with Pryor's own band. In 1909 he began a 35-year tenure as first trombonist of the Metropolitan Opera; conducted his own orchestra in Asbury Park, N.J. (1921–25), and later appeared with Paul Lavalle's Band of America.

Mantovani [Annunzio Paolo] (b. Venice, 15 Nov. 1905; d. Tunbridge Wells, England, 29 Mar. 1980). Popular violinist and orchestra leader. Trained as a classical violinist in Italy, he led string orchestras in London from the 1930s. His elaborate arrangements became popular primarily through albums of film music (*Film Encores,* 1957; *Exodus and Other Great Themes,* 1960) as well as other collections (*Gems Forever,* 1958; *Italia mia,* 1961).

Manzoni, Giacomo (b. Milan, 26 Sept. 1932). Composer and critic. He studied in Messina and then in Milan (until 1956; diplomas in piano and in German language and literature). From 1958 until 1966 he was music critic for the newspaper *L'unità;* taught at the conservatory in Milan and at the Univ. of Bologna; won the Unesco Prize in 1973 for his *Parole da Beckett* (2 choruses, 3 instrumental groups, and tape, 1970–71). Other works include several for the stage (*Doktor Faustus,* opera, 1984–88); *Omaggio a E. Varèse* (piano and orchestra, 1977); *Ombre* (alla memoria di Che Guevara, chorus and orchestra, 1968); and *Omaggio a*

Josquin (soprano, horn, 2 violins, and 2 cellos, 1985). He translated writings of Schoenberg and Adorno; wrote *Guida all'ascolto della musica sinfonica* (1967), *A. Schönberg: l'uomo, l'opera, i testi musicali* (1975), and many articles.

Manzuoli, Giovanni (b. Florence, ca. 1720; d. there, 1782). Castrato. He performed in operas in Florence and Verona in the 1730s and sang at San Carlo in the mid-1740s; later appeared in Madrid (1749–52) and Parma (1754). His performances in Vienna (1760) and London (1764–65) were highly successful; he met the Mozart family in London, and Wolfgang encountered him again in 1770 in Florence. Manzuoli ended his public career in 1771 performing in Mozart's *Ascanio in Alba* K. 111.

Mara [née Schmeling], **Gertrud Elisabeth** (b. Kassel, 23 Feb. 1749; d. Reval [Tallinn], 20 Jan. 1833). Soprano. As a child she studied violin; later she took vocal coaching with Paradisi in London, then in 1765 she returned to Germany to sing under J. A. Hiller in Leipzig. Her operatic debut was in 1767 in Dresden; in 1771–79 she was engaged by Frederick II at Berlin. She spent the next three decades performing in concerts and operas in Germany, the Netherlands, Vienna, Paris, Italy, and especially in London, where she became a local favorite. She settled in Moscow and later in Reval (ca. 1813). A childhood illness affected her stage appearance, but her voice was known for its wide range and excellent tone.

Marais, Marin (b. Paris, 31 May 1656; d. there, 15 Aug. 1728). Composer and bass viol player. He studied bass viol with Sainte-Colombe and composition with Lully, joining the royal orchestra in 1676; spent his entire life in Paris as a famous virtuoso on the instrument, retiring from royal service in 1725. Lully's influence can be seen in Marais's 4 operas (*Alcide,* 1693; *Ariane et Baccus,* 1696; *Alcione,* 1706; *Sémélé,* 1709), which were quite successful during his lifetime. Marais's most important compositions, however, are the 5 collections of music for 1–3 bass viols with figured bass published between 1686 and 1725. These include typical dance movements as well as fantaisies, rondeaux, tombeaux, and a number of works with descriptive titles (Marais called them "pièces de caractère") like the famous *Le tableau de l'opération de la taille* that depicts an operation to remove a stone in the bladder. Marais's *Pièces en trio pour les flûtes, violon, et dessus de viole* (Paris, 1692) are regarded as the first appearance of the trio sonata in France.

Bibl.: *Instrumental Works,* ed. John Hsu (New York, 1980–). Sylvette Milliot, *Marin Marais* (France, 1991).

Marazzoli, Marco (b. Parma, between 1602 and 1608; d. Rome, 26 Jan. 1662). Composer. He accompanied his patron, Cardinal Antonio Barberini, to Urbino in 1631; moved to Rome in 1637, where he entered the cardinal's service as a musician and sang tenor in the papal chapel. He collaborated with Mazzocchi on one of the first comic operas, *Chi soffre speri* (1639; facs., New York, 1982), a revision of *Il falcone* (1637); some Latin oratorios were probably written during this time as well. Marazzoli traveled from 1640 to 1642 to supervise productions of his operas *L'Armida* (Ferrara, 1641) and *Gli amori di Giasone e d'Issifile* (Venice, 1642, not extant). At the end of 1643 he was engaged by Cardinal Mazarin to produce a theatrical work for Paris, possibly *Il capriccio.* He returned to Rome in 1645, continuing his service at the papal chapel and composing principally sacred music and cantatas during the Barberini family's exile in France (1645–53); nearly 400 cantatas and oratorios survive. His opera *La vita humana* (1656) was dedicated to Queen Christina of Sweden (who held her court in Rome); in his last years Marazzoli's name was associated with Fabio Chigi, Pope Alexander VII, and his family. Other operas include *Le pretensioni del Tebro e del Po* (Ferrara, 1642); *Dal male il bene* (with Abbatini, Rome, 1653); *Le armi e gli amori* (Rome, 1654).

Marbeck, John. See Merbecke, John.

Marcabru (b. Gascony, 1100–1110?; fl. 1128–50). Troubadour. His lyric poems (in Provençal) provide the only reliable information about his life, indicating that he spent some years at the court of Guillaume X of Aquitaine, was later in the service of Alfonso VII of Castile, and returned in 1144 to France. Of his 43 known chansons, 4 survive with melodies.

Marcello, Alessandro (b. Venice, 1684; d. there, 1750). Composer. Older brother of Benedetto Marcello. He took violin lessons with his father; his studies included painting, poetry, and mathematics. Not a prolific composer, he published under the pseudonym Eterio Stinfalico. His best-known work is the Oboe Concerto in D minor that was transcribed for keyboard by J. S. Bach (BWV 974); the concerto was formerly attributed to his brother.

Marcello, Benedetto (b. Venice, 24 July or 1 Aug. 1686; d. Brescia, 24 or 25 July 1739). Composer. Brother of Alessandro Marcello. He studied violin with his father and singing and counterpoint with Gasparini and Lotti. Marcello held a number of important political posts, including a 14-year membership in the Council of Forty and an appointment as papal chamberlain at Brescia (1738–39). He achieved great fame through his settings of Giustiniani's Italian paraphrases of the first 50 Psalms, published in 8 volumes (*Estro poetico-armonico, parafrasi sopra i cinquanta primi salmi,* Venice, 1724–26; facs., London, 1967). Secular and sacred vocal music constitute the bulk of his output, including over 400 secular cantatas. Marcello's writings include *Il teatro alla moda* (Venice, ca. 1720; trans. Eng. Reinhard Pauly in *MQ* 34 [1948] and 35 [1949]), a satire on operatic manners that spoofed Vivaldi and other contemporaries.

Bibl.: William S. Newman, "The Keyboard Sonatas of Benedetto Marcello," *AM* 29 (1957): 28–41; "Postscript," *AM* 31 (1959): 192–96. Claudio Madricardo and Franco Rossi, eds., *Benedetto Marcello: La sua opera e il suo tempo* (Florence, 1988). Eleanor Selfridge-Field, *The Music of Benedetto and Alessandro Marcello: A Thematic Catalogue with Commentary on the Composers, Repertory, and Sources* (Oxford and New York, 1990).

Marchal, André (Louis) (b. Paris, 6 Feb. 1894; d. St. Jean-de-Luz, 27 Aug. 1980). Organist. Blind from birth, he studied at the Institution nationale des jeunes aveugles; then at the Paris Conservatory with Eugène Gigout, obtaining first prize in 1913; first prize in counterpoint in 1917. Organist at St. Germain des Prés 1915–45; at St. Eustache 1945–63. Acclaimed for his improvisations and for his performances of Bach and French masters of the 17th and 18th centuries, he was a significant force in the return to performance of Baroque music on Baroque-style instruments.

Marchand, Louis (b. Lyons, 2 Feb. 1669; d. Paris, 17 Feb. 1732). Organist and composer. Sometime before 1689 he moved to Paris, and by 1691 he was organist of the Jesuit church in rue St. Jacques; he also held posts at St. Benoît and the Cordeliers. In 1708 he became an *organiste du roi,* and he undertook an extensive performing tour of Germany in 1713. A contest between J. S. Bach and Marchand was scheduled for September 1717 in Dresden, but Marchand failed to appear and Bach won by default. His most important compositions are for keyboard, most dating from before 1700.

Bibl.: *Pièces de clavecin,* ed. Thurston Dart (Monaco, 1960). *L'oeuvre d'orgue édition intégrale,* ed. Jean Bonfils (Paris, 1972–).

Marchesi, Blanche (b. Paris, 4 Apr. 1863; d. London, 15 Dec. 1940). Soprano, daughter of Salvatore and Mathilde Marchesi. She studied with her mother, making her London debut in 1896 and her operatic debut in Prague in 1900 as Brünnhilde in *Die Walküre.* Following several seasons with the Moody–Manners company in London, she performed a number of Wagnerian roles at Covent Garden, including Elisabeth in *Tannhäuser,* Elsa in *Lohengrin,* and Isolde. She was a highly regarded teacher in London during her later years and published her memoirs, *A Singer's Pilgrimage* (London, 1923).

Marchesi, Luigi [Marchesini] (b. Milan, 8 Aug. 1755; d. Inzago, near Milan, ca. 15 Dec. 1829). Castrato singer and composer. He studied singing with Albuzzi and Caironi; from 1765 he was a chorister at the Milan Cathedral, and he studied music with director Giovanni Fioroni. His debut was in Rome in 1773; in 1776 he was appointed to sing at the Munich opera and two years later at the Teatro S. Carlo in Naples. He appeared in Vienna (1785), St. Petersburg (1785–87), and London (1788–90); after 1790 he lived chiefly in Italy. He was one of the greatest of the castratos; his vocal range was g–d'''. He also composed songs and arias.

Marchesi (de Castrone) [née Graumann] **Mathilde** (b. Frankfurt am Main, 24 Mar. 1821; d. London, 17 Nov. 1913). Singing teacher. Studied with Ronconi and Nicolai (1843–45), making her concert debut as a mezzo-soprano in 1844, then with García in Paris and London. García discovered her gift for teaching, to which she mainly devoted herself from 1854 at the conservatories of Vienna (1854–61; 1868–78) and Cologne (1875–78) and privately in Vienna and Paris. In 1852 she married the baritone Salvatore de Castrone Marchesi. Their daughter Blanche (1863–1940) was also a distinguished singing teacher. Her students (mostly female) include Gerster, Klafsky, Nevada, Adama, Calvé, Eames, Garden, Melba, Sanderson. She published *L'art du chant* (Paris, 1886) and her memoirs (1877); enl. and trans. as *Marchesi and Music* (New York, 1897).

Marchesi de Castrone, Salvatore (b. Palermo, 15 Jan. 1822; d. Paris, 20 Feb. 1908). Baritone and singing teacher. From a noble Sicilian family (title: Marchese della Rajata); studied singing with Raimondi in Palermo and (1846) Lamperti in Milan; had to leave Italy for taking part in the 1848 Revolution. Opera debut, New York (as Carlo in *Ernani*); after further study with García, had a career primarily in concerts, sometimes with his wife (from 1852), Mathilde. From 1854 they were primarily active as teachers in Vienna (1854–61, 1868–78), Cologne (1865–68), and Paris (1861–63, 1888–1908). He published singing exercises, songs.

Marchetti, Filippo (b. Bolognola, Macerata, 26 Feb. 1831; d. Rome, 18 Jan. 1902). Composer. Student, 1850–54, at the Naples Conservatory. Produced a successful first opera (Turin, 1856), but his second (also Turin, 1856) had only four performances, and he was unable to get his third staged; settled in Rome as a singing teacher and song composer; 1862, moved to Milan, where he composed *Romeo e Giulietta* (Trieste, 1865), which had some success, especially at Milan in 1867. His *Ruy Blas* (La Scala, 3 Apr. 1869) was one of the most successful Italian operas of its time, performed all over Europe and abroad. His last 2 operas (1875, 1880) were not successful. From 1881 to 1886, president of the Accademia di S. Cecilia, Rome; 1886–1901, director of its conservatory.

Marchetto da Padova [Marchettus de Padua] (b. Padua, 1274?; fl. 1305–26). Theorist. From 1305 to 1307 *maestro di canto* at the Cathedral of Padua; from 1308 resident in various other Italian cities, including Cesena and Verona. His principal theoretical works are *Lucidarium* (*GS* 3:65–121; ed. Jan W. Herlinger, Chicago, 1985) and *Pomerium* (*GS* 3:121–87; *CSM* 6 [1961]; *SR,* pp. 160–71). These treatises provide the most complete known 14th-century explanation of Italian trecento theory. The *Lucidarium,* which covers the basics of traditional music theory and of plainchant, includes an original and highly influential section setting forth a division of the whole tone into five parts. The *Pomerium* deals with mensural music, emphasizing notation in the Italian manner. Both were widely known and were claimed as authorities, quoted, or argued against, by many later writers.

Marco, Tomás (b. Madrid, 12 Sept. 1942). Composer. Studied violin, composition, and law at the Univ. of Madrid (1959–64). Attended the summer courses in Darmstadt in 1962, 1965, 1966, and 1967, studying composition and conducting with Stockhausen, Boulez, and Ligeti, and electronic music with Kagel, Maderna, and Koenig; in the 1967 session he attended the sociology lectures of Adorno and participated in Stockhausen's four-hour collective composition *Ensemble.* During this period he traveled widely, attending conferences and coming into contact with Cage and Lutosławski, among others. He began an association with Spanish Radio in 1966, taking over the concert music department in 1970. His *Vitral* for organ and strings won the National Prize for Music in 1969. In 1973 he gave a course with Cristóbal Halffter and Bernaola at the Royal Conservatory on new compositional techniques; active as a teacher elsewhere as well. He published several books and monographs; his critical writings appeared in many newspapers and journals. In 1967 he founded the new music journal *Sonda,* serving also as editor. Various media and theatrical elements are put to use in his music, which is often a study in the psychological process of musical perception. Works include *Voz* (reciter and 13 instruments, 1963); *Piraña* (piano, 1965); *Schwann* (6 instruments, 1966); *Jabberwocky* (actress, 4 percussionists, 6 radios, piano, tenor saxophone, and slides, 1967); *Tea-Party* (4 singers and 4 instruments, 1973); *Escorial* (orchestra, 1973); *Concierto austral* (oboe, orchestra, 1982); *Espacio sagrado* (piano, 2 choruses, orchestra, 1982); Symphony no. 3 (1986).

Bibl.: Carlos Gomez Amat, *Tomás Marco* (Madrid, 1974).

Maréchal, (Charles) Henri (b. Paris, 22 Jan. 1842; d. there, 12 May 1924). Composer. From 1866, a student at the Paris Conservatory (1870, joint winner, with Massé, Prix de Rome); in Rome composed a cantata, *La nativité,* performed in 1875; 1876, had a well-received one-act opéra comique performed at the Opéra-comique, followed by others. He also composed orchestral and sacred works, incidental music, a ballet, oratorio, songs. Published 3 volumes of memoirs.

Marenco, Romualdo (b. Novi Ligure, 1 Mar. 1841; d. Milan, 9 Oct. 1907). Composer. A theater-orchestra violinist in Genoa when he composed his first ballet. Assistant concertmaster and director of ballet music, La Scala, 1873–80. He composed many ballets, collaborating with noted choreographers, including Manzotti (1878–97), especially the celebrated *Excelsior* (1881), and Pratesi (1868–1905); also 2 operas and some operettas.

Marenzio, Luca (b. Coccaglio, near Brescia, 1553 or 1554; d. Rome, 22 Aug. 1599). Composer. One of the so-called virtuoso madrigalists of the late Renaissance in Italy. His reputation is based chiefly, if somewhat misleadingly, on his numerous earlier madrigals, those published in the first half of the 1580s. His output is far from uniform, however; it includes a great variety of vocal compositions with many sorts of texts, most secular but some sacred. A progression from the light to the more serious in both music and text is evident over the course of his career.

Marenzio may have studied with Giovanni Contino of Brescia, who was in the service of the Gonzaga family in Mantua. Around 1574 he moved to Rome, serving first Cardinal Cristoforo Madruzzo and later (1578–86) Cardinal Luigi d'Este, under whose patronage the majority of his madrigals (those on which his reputation has been based) and one book of motets were written and musical connections with Ferrara were established. In early 1588, after about a year of travel in Italy, Marenzio assumed a position in Florence in the service of the Grand Duke Ferdinando de' Medici, where he remained until late 1589. His last decade was spent in looser associations with various cardinals in Rome and in an extended trip to Poland.

Among Marenzio's works are nearly 25 books of madrigals and related pieces. The later works are more serious and make prominent use of affective devices such as chromatic alteration, dissonance, or sudden harmonic shifts to reflect verbal meanings. Many of the late madrigals are in cycles. Some music composed for 2 *intermedi* also survives. The sacred music certainly by Marenzio, most published posthumously if at all, comprises about 75 motets, many polychoral; a few Masses may be his. Marenzio's works were often reprinted and quickly came to be known throughout Europe. Some appeared in English translation in Yonge's *Musica transalpina* (1588), and they had an especially strong influence on the English madrigal.

Bibl.: *Sämtliche Werke* (Leipzig, 1929–31, R: 1967). *Opera omnia, CMM* 72 (1976–). James Chater, *Luca Marenzio and the Italian Madrigal, 1577–1593* (Ann Arbor, 1981). Bernhard Janz, *Die Petrarca-Vertonungen von Luca Marenzio: Dichtung und Musik im späten Cinquecento-Madrigal* (Tutzing, 1992).

Mareš [Maresch], **Jan Antonín** [Johann Anton] (b. Chotěboř, Bohemia, 1719; d. St. Petersburg, 30 May 1794). Horn player and music director. He studied horn and cello in Dresden and Berlin; in 1748 he received a post in St. Petersburg as horn player for Count Bestuzhev-Ryumin. In 1757 he was appointed director of the royal hunting band. He also served in the court orchestra (1752–74), first as horn player and then as cellist. His hunting-horn bands consisted of groups of single-note horns (as many as 36) arranged chromatically. He composed and arranged many pieces for these ensembles, including symphonic works. The music of such groups later came to be known as Russian horn music; its popularity waned in the late 19th century.

Bibl.: Robert Ricks, "Russian Horn Bands," *MQ* 55 (1969): 364–71.

Mariani, Angelo (Maurizio Gaspare) (b. Ravenna, 11 or 12 Oct. 1821; d. Genoa, 13 June 1873). Conductor. Studied music in Ravenna, then Bologna; quickly established himself as an opera conductor, working up from small places to larger ones (Messina, 1844–45) and becoming a leading conductor at the court theater in Copenhagen. He then took part in the 1848 Revolution, after which he absented himself in Constantinople (1848–51). Returning to Italy in 1852 he settled in Genoa as conductor at the Teatro Carlo Felice (1852–73), beginning there a lifelong liaison with the Marchesa Teresa Sauli Pallaviamo; 1860–73, also conductor at the Teatro comunale, Bologna, including the first Italian *Don Carlo* (1867) and the famous productions of *Lohengrin* (1871) and *Tannhäuser* (1872). He was an important figure in the Italian evolution to modern conducting, making the shift from violin bow to baton.

Marini, Biagio (b. Brescia, ca. 1587; d. Venice, 20 Mar. 1665). Composer and violinist. He played violin at St. Mark's, Venice, under Monteverdi (1615–18), returning to Brescia in 1620 as music director of the Accademia degli erranti. After serving as violinist at the Farnese court in Parma (1621), was employed as Kapellmeister at the Wittelsbach court at Neuburg (1623–49), though he was absent for long periods, traveling to Brussels, Düsseldorf, Brescia, Padua, and elsewhere. In 1649 he was *maestro di cappella* at S. Maria della Scala in Milan and was later appointed director of the Accademia della morte in Ferrara (1652–53). Marini is principally known today as a composer of instrumental music. His *Affetti musicali* op. 1 (Venice, 1617; facs., Florence 1978) contains some of the earliest examples of the Italian solo violin sonata, while op. 8, *Sonate, symphonie* (Venice, 1629), includes some of the first musically significant examples of the genre. Marini also employed double stopping, scordatura, and tremolos in his string writing.

Bibl.: Thomas D. Dunn, "The Instrumental Music of Biagio Marini" (diss., Yale Univ., 1969). Willene B. Clark, "The Vocal Music of Biagio Marini (ca. 1598–1665)" (diss., Yale Univ., 1969). Fabio Fano, "Biagio Marini violinista in Italia e all'estero," *Chigiana* 22 (1965): 47–57. Dora Julia Iselin, *Biagio Marini: Sein Leben und seine Instrumentalwerke* (Hildburghausen, 1930).

Mario, Giovanni Matteo, Cavaliere de Candia (b. Cagliari, Italy, 17 Oct. 1810; d. Rome, 11 Dec. 1883). Tenor. Clashes with his father (who rose to general and governor of Nice) and his liberal politics led to his moving to Paris, where he lived poorly until (on Meyerbeer's advice) he studied singing, making a very successful debut at the Opéra in 1838 in *Robert le diable* (under the stage name Mario). From 1839 he had a romantic and artistic liaison with Giulia Grisi (who was already married). They alternated between the Théâtre-Italien, Paris, and Her Majesty's, London (from 1847 Covent Garden), also appearing (after her retirement, alone) in St. Petersburg, Madrid, and on a much-publicized U.S. tour (1854–55; he returned in 1872–73 with Patti). The 1840s was the couple's heyday; both voices were in decline by the mid-1850s, although Mario remained active until the 1870s, retiring then to Rome (he never sang in Italy). He created Ernesto in *Don Pasquale* (1843).

Markevitch, Igor (b. Kiev, 27 July 1912; d. Antibes, 7 Mar. 1983). Composer and conductor. He studied music in Vevey, Switzerland, where his family had settled in 1914; and then in Paris with Cortot and Boulanger (from 1926); he studied conducting with Scherchen and made his debut in Amsterdam (1930). With Diaghilev's encouragement he wrote and premiered a piano concerto (1929) and the ballet *Rébus* (1930); after the war he rebuilt the Orchestra del Maggio musicale in Florence and conducted major orchestras in Europe and America (in London, Stockholm, Montreal, Havana, Madrid, Monaco, and Rome). He taught in Salzburg (1948–56), Mexico (1957–58), and at the Moscow Conservatory (1963); from 1957 to 1961 he directed the Concerts Lamoureux (Paris). His works (most composed by 1940) include 2 ballets; an oratorio (*Le paradis perdu,* Cocteau after Milton, 1936); orchestral music; chamber and piano works; songs; and transcriptions of *The Musical Offering* (Bach) and other works.

Marley, Bob [Robert Nesta] (b. Rhoden Hall, St. Ann, Jamaica, 6 Feb. 1945; d. Miami, 11 May 1981). Reggae singer, songwriter, and guitarist. In 1961 he formed the Rudeboys with future reggae star Peter Tosh; they later became the Wailers and were prominent in the Kingston reggae scene with songs such as "Summer Down" (1964). In the 1970s he toured internationally, becoming the most popular exponent of reggae in the U.S. through the albums *Rastaman Vibrations* (including "Roots, Reggae, Rock," 1976), *Burnin'* (1973), and *Babylon by Bus* (1978); his reputation grew after his death with the issue of previously unreleased material. Rastafarianism and Jamaican social ills were the main topics of his lyrics. The reggae group The Melody Makers, formed by son David "Ziggy" Marley, became popular in the late 1980s.

Marliani, Marco Aurelio, Count (b. Milan, Aug. 1805; d. Bologna, 8 May 1849). Composer. Studied at the College of Siena, but in about 1830 had to leave Italy because of his liberalism, to which he also sacrificed his money, so that he had to eke out his living in Paris as a singing teacher (pupils included Grisi); later Spanish consul general. Encouraged by Rossini, produced a successful and widely performed first opera, *Il bravo* (1834); best known for one-act *La xacarilla* (Opéra, 1839). He died from wounds suffered while fighting for Italian independence against Austria. Also composed songs, piano pieces.

Marlowe [Sapira], **Sylvia** (b. New York, 26 Sept. 1908; d. there, 10 Dec. 1981). Harpsichordist. Studied piano and organ at the École normale in Paris and took composition with Nadia Boulanger; later studied harpsichord with Wanda Landowska. Achieved fame through a number of radio broadcasts, which included contemporary music and jazz in addition to Renaissance and Baroque works; toured extensively in Europe, North and South America, and the Far East. Marlowe founded the Harpsichord Music Society in 1957, an organization that commissions new works for the instrument; she was appointed to the faculty of Mannes College in 1948.

Marmontel, Antoine François (b. Clermont-Ferrand, 18 July 1816; d. Paris, 16 or 17 Jan. 1898). Teacher. Student, 1827–37, Paris Conservatory (piano, Zimmermann; first prize, 1832); then a piano teacher, succeeding Zimmermann at the Conservatory (1848–87), becoming one of the most illustrious of his day, with many distinguished pupils. He published piano pieces, etudes, exercises. A noted art collector, he wrote a book on aesthetics (1884) and a *Histoire du piano* (Paris, 1885) but is best remembered for his biographical and critical essays, originally in *Le ménestrel,* collected in *Les pianistes célèbres* (Paris, 1878; many reissues), *Symphonistes et virtuoses* (Paris, 1881), and *Virtuoses contemporains* (Paris, 1882).

Maros, Rudolf (b. Stachy, 19 Jan. 1917; d. Budapest, 2 Aug. 1982). Composer. He attended the teachers' training college in Györ and studied with Kodály (composition) and Temesváry (viola) at the Budapest Academy of Music (1939–42). From 1942 he taught in Pécs, and in 1949 studied composition in Hába's master class in Prague; during this time he played viola in the Budapest Concert Orchestra. He was on the faculty of the Budapest Academy (1949–78). His early music was heavily influenced by Kodály; after a brief adoption of serial technique he turned to the exploitation of shifts in timbre and register. His works include ballets; orchestral music (*Ricercare,* 1959); *Eufonia I-III,* 1963–65; *Monumentum,* 1969); chamber music; and vocal music.

Marpurg, Friedrich Wilhelm (b. Seehof, Brandenburg, 21 Nov. 1718; d. Berlin, 22 May 1795). Theorist and writer on music. As a youth he attended university (probably in Berlin) and came into close contact with Lessing and Winckelmann. In 1746 he received a position in Paris as private secretary to a Prussian general, probably Friedrich Rudolph Graf von Rothenburg. In Paris he made the acquaintance of Voltaire, Rameau, and others. In 1749 he began his first music journal, *Der critische Musicus an der Spree* (1749–50); from this point onward he devoted himself chiefly to music criticism and to theoretical writings. His other serials were *Historisch-kritische Beyträge zur Aufnahme der Musik* (1754–62; 1778) and *Kritische Briefe über die Tonkunst* (1760–64). He authored a number of important early assessments of the music of J. S. Bach, including the preface to the second Leipzig edition of *Die Kunst der Fuge* (1752). He also assimilated the theories of Rameau and propagated them in his German translation of D'Alembert's 1752 *Elémens de musique* (*Systematische Einleitung in die musikalische Setzkunst, nach den Lehrsätzen des Herrn Rameau,* Leipzig, 1757). His most important treatise is the *Abhandlung von der Fuge nach den Grundsätzen der besten deutschen und ausländischen Meister* (Berlin, 1753–54; R: 1970), the best and most systematic treatment of fugal practices of its day. Other important treatises were the *Handbuch bey dem Generalbasse und der Composition* (3 vols., Berlin, 1755–58; R: 1971) and the *Anleitung zur Musik überhaupt und zur Singkunst besonders* (Berlin 1763; R: 1975).

Bibl.: Howard Serwer, "Friedrich Wilhelm Marpurg (1718–1795)" (diss., Yale Univ., 1969). Joyce Mekeel, "The Harmonic Theories of Kirnberger and Marpurg," *JMT* 4 (1960): 169–93. David A. Sheldon, *F. W. Marpurg's Thoroughbass and Composition Handbook: A Critical Study and Translation* (New York, 1989).

Marqués y García, Pedro Miguel (b. Palma de Mallorca, 20 May 1843; d. there 25 Feb. 1918). Composer. Studied in Paris, privately (including orchestration lessons from Berlioz) and at the Conservatory; from 1867, at the Madrid Conservatory under Monasterio. Violinist in the orchestra of the Sociedad de conciertos, which in 1869 played the first of his 6 symphonies. He composed other orchestral works, but is best known for his many zarzuelas, especially *El anillo de hierro* (1878), *El reloj de Lucerna* (1884), *El monaguillo* (1891).

Marriner, Neville (b. Lincoln, England, 15 Apr. 1924). Conductor and violinist. Studied violin with Albert Sammons at the Royal College of Music in London, 1939–42 and 1945–46; with René Benedetti at the Paris Conservatory, 1946–47. Taught at Eton College, 1948–49; at the Royal College of Music, 1949–59. With Thurston Dart formed the Jacobean Ensemble, 1952. Played in the Martin String Quartet, 1946–53; in the London Philharmonic, 1952–56; in the London Symphony, 1956–68; in the Philomusica of London beginning 1957. In 1959 formed the Academy of St. Martin-in-the-Fields as a string orchestra. Attended Pierre Monteux's conducting class in Maine. Founding conductor of the Los Angeles Chamber Orchestra, 1969–77. Associate conductor of the Northern Sinfonia, 1971–73. Music director of the Minnesota Orchestra, 1979–86; of the Stuttgart Radio Orchestra, 1983–89. Knighted in 1985.

Marsalis, Branford (b. Breaux Bridge, La., 1960). Jazz tenor and soprano saxophonist. Brother of Wynton Marsalis. He toured with Art Blakey's hard bop group (1981–82), Wynton's quintet (1982–84), Clark Terry's big band, Herbie Hancock's quintet VSOP (1983), Miles Davis's jazz-rock group (1984–85), and the rock guitarist Sting (1985–88). In addition to appearing as a soloist in videos with Sting, including "Bring on the Night" (ca. 1986), he had his own video hit with a bop rendition of the traditional jazz tune "Royal Garden Blues" (1987). In 1994 he released an album with DJ Premier entitled *Buckshot LeFonque.*

Marsalis, Wynton (b. New Orleans, 18 Oct. 1961). Jazz and classical trumpeter, jazz bandleader. Brother of Branford Marsalis. While studying at the Juilliard School he joined Art Blakey's hard bop group (1980–82). Toured with Herbie Hancock (1981, 1983) and, after recording his first album (1981), began leading groups. Having concurrently pursued a career as a classical trumpeter, he became in 1984 the first musician to win Grammy awards in jazz and classical music, for the albums *Think of One* (1982) and *Haydn, Hummel, Leopold Mozart* (1983). His compact disc *The Majesty of the Blues* (ca. 1989) pays homage to blues and New Orleans jazz. His first work for big band, *Blood on the Fields,* was premiered in 1994.

Marschner, Heinrich August (b. Zittau, 16 Aug. 1795; d. Hannover, 14 Dec. 1861). Composer. Went to school in Zittau; 1808, a choirboy in Bautzen, returning to school in Zittau when his voice changed; began to compose and studied music (from ca. 1811) with Karl Gottlieb Hering; 1813, went to Prague to avoid being drafted into the Prussian army, studying music there with Tomasek, but soon went to Leipzig, ostensibly to study law as his father had wished, but increasingly drawn to music, studying it there with Schicht. He composed piano and guitar pieces and songs, which he began publishing by 1814; also began appearing locally as a pianist and in 1815 more widely, incuding at Karlsbad. From 1816 he was music teacher in the family of Count Zichy in Bratislava, where he studied with Heinrich Klein and composed piano pieces, a Mass, a singspiel (*Der Kyffhäuserberg,* 1816), privately performed there and taken up by some small theaters.

A turning point in Marschner's career was Weber's acceptance of his opera *Heinrich der Vierte und d'Aubigné,* composed in 1817–18, for Dresden (another opera, *Saidar und Zulima,* was given in Bratislava in 1818 and nowhere else). The Dresden production (1820) was not a great success, but in 1821 Marschner moved to Dresden, eking out a living by teaching, giving concerts, and composing (including incidental music for three plays, 1821–23). His initially warm relationship with Weber cooled. (The difficulties that beset Marschner's career were probably due in large part to his personality: he was quick to anger.) In November 1823 he was appointed, over Weber's opposition, Weber's assistant at the Dresden court, with the title of music director. His duties, which included conducting at the theater, soon became arduous when he was called upon to substitute (because of illness) for both Weber and Morlacchi. During this period he produced only one new opera, a one-act singspiel *Der Holzdieb* (1825), which was quite widely performed.

In 1826 he married a moderately well known singer, Marianne Wohlbrück (1806–54). On Weber's death in 1826 Marschner applied for his post and, on being denied it, resigned and traveled with his wife on her singing engagements to Berlin, Breslau, Danzig (where he was also for six months music director at the theater, producing an unsuccessful opera there in January 1827), Magdeburg, and elsewhere, augmenting his income by publishing piano sonatas, chamber music, part songs, solo songs. He was then appointed music director at the Leipzig theater, where took place the premieres of *Der Vampyr* (29 March 1828) and *Der Templer und die Jüdin* (22 December 1829). The great and widespread success of both made him a leading figure in German music and led to his appointment as music director at the Hannover court theater beginning in January 1831. The comic opera *Des Falkners Braut* (Leipzig, 1832) was unsuccessful, but *Hans Heiling* (Berlin, 24 May 1833) remained a German favorite through the rest of the century. None of his five later operas was lastingly successful, and he had increasing difficulty in getting them performed, especially his last, *Hiarne,* composed in 1857–58; he twice visited Paris unsuccessfully seeking a production of it at the Opéra. He was appointed Hannover court Kapellmeister in 1852, but his position there was never secure, and he was forced to retire in 1859. In his later years he traveled much to conduct his earlier operas (visiting England in 1857) but was increasingly embittered by the neglect of his later ones.

Bibl.: A. Dean Palmer, *Heinrich August Marschner, 1795–1861: His Life and Stage Works* (Ann Arbor, 1980). Thomas Lippert, *Die Klavierlieder Heinrich Marschners* (Wiesbaden, 1989).

Marsh, Roger (Michael) (b. Bournemouth, 10 Dec. 1949). Composer. He studied at the Univ. of York (1972–76) before becoming director of the Clap Music Theater Group (1972–75). Has held teaching positions at the Univ. of Keele (1978–88) and the Univ. of York (from 1988). His compositions include *CASS* (music theater, 1971); *DUM* (music theater, 1973); *Three Hale Mairies* (3 sopranos and ensemble, 1976); *Not a Soul but Ourselves* (amplified voices, 1977); *Still* (orchestra, 1980); *Samson* (music theater, 1984); *Three Biblical Songs* (baritone, soprano, chorus, and ensemble, 1985); *Music for Piano and Wind Instruments* (1986); *Dying For It* (ensemble, 1987); *Trio: Ferry Music* (1988); and *The Big Bang* (music theater, 1989).

Marshall, Ingram D(ouglass) (b. Mount Vernon, N.Y., 10 May 1942). Composer. He attended Lake Forest College; studied with Paul Henry Lang and Ussachevsky at Columbia (1964–66), then with Subotnik at New York Univ. and at the California Institute of the Arts (1969–71). After travel to Indonesia (1971), he taught at the California Institute, then held a Fulbright Award in Stockholm (1975). His music often reflects his travels by means of concrete sounds, slides, and narration; most performances combine composed works, improvisation (singing or playing the gambuh, a Balinese flute), and live electronics (*Fog Tropes,* 6 brass instruments, tape, and live electronics, 1982); but his notated works illustrate his high regard for the traditions of Western music (*Spiritus,* 6 strings, harpsichord, vibraphone, 1981). Other pieces include *Wood-*

stone (gamelan, 1982) and *Voces resonae* (string quartet, 1984).

Marteau, Henri (b. Rheims, 31 Mar. 1874; d. Lichtenberg, 3 Oct. 1934). Violinist, composer, and conductor. Took lessons with Léonard; performed as soloist in Vienna at the age of 10 and in London at 14. Entered Garcin's class at the Paris Conservatory in 1891, where he won a premier prix; became a professor of violin at the Geneva Conservatory in 1900 and succeeded Joachim at the Hochschule für Musik in Berlin in 1908. Went to Sweden in 1915; later taught in Prague (1921–24), at the Leipzig Conservatory (1926–28), and at the Dresden Conservatory (1928–34). Reger, a personal friend, wrote a violin concerto for him. Marteau's own compositions include a cantata, *Les voix de Jeanne d'Arc;* an opera, *Meister Schwalbe;* 2 violin concertos.

Bibl.: Klaus Bangerter, *Henri Marteau als Komponist im Spiegel der Kritik: eine Studie zum Begriff der "Einheit" in der Musikkritik um 1900* (Tutzing, 1991).

Martelli, Henri (b. Santa Fe, Argentina, 25 Feb. 1895; d. Paris, 15 July 1980). Composer. He studied at the Paris Conservatory with Widor and Caussade (1912–24). From 1940 to 1944 he was responsible for chamber and orchestral programming on French Radio and was president of the French section of the ISCM (1953–73). His works, tonal or polytonal, are in a neoclassical style with much attention to counterpoint. He wrote dramatic works; 3 symphonies, several concertos, and other orchestral music; a trio for piano, cello, and harp (1976), and other chamber and piano music; a few choral works; songs; radio and theater scores.

Martenot, Maurice (Louis Eugène) (b. Paris, 14 Oct. 1898; d. there, 10 Oct. 1980). Musician and inventor. He studied cello and composition at the Paris Conservatory, then taught at the École normale de musique in Paris and directed the École d'art Martenot at Neuilly. In 1928 he demonstrated his electronic musical instrument, the ondes martenot, a significant improvement on existing electronic instruments. Milhaud, Messiaen, Jolivet, Ibert, Honegger, and others have written for the instrument.

Martín, Edgardo (b. Cienfuegos, Cuba, 6 Oct. 1915). Composer. Student of Ardévol at the Municipal Conservatory in Havana (1939–46); received a pedagogy doctorate in 1941 from the Univ. of Havana, where he served as professor of music, 1945–68. He was an important critic and cultural figure in the early days of the Castro regime, participating in education reforms and in 1968 forming the national Composers' Collective. His music is lyric, tonally oriented; works include *Soneras* and *Cuadros de Ismaelillo* for orchestra as well as chamber music, choral pieces, and songs, the vocal works often political in nature.

Martin, Frank (b. Geneva, 15 Sept. 1890; d. Naarden, Netherlands, 21 Nov. 1974). Composer. He studied mathematics and science (1908–10) before embarking on a career in music. He had studied piano and violin as a child and was composing by the age of 8; with Joseph Lauber (also a Swiss through whom Martin was introduced to both German and French traditions) he studied piano, harmony, and composition; he had no other formal instruction, but was influenced by his study of works of Strauss, Mahler, Debussy, and Schoenberg. In 1910 three orchestral songs for baritone were presented at the Festival of Swiss Composers in Vevey; he spent the years 1916–1922 in Zurich and Rome; Ernest Ansermet's performance of his cantata *Les Dithyrambes* (solo voices, children's choir, mixed choir, and orchestra, 1918) in Lausanne was the start of that conductor's lifelong support for Martin's work. After a period in Paris (1925) he settled in Geneva, where he studied with Emil Jaques-Dalcroze (1926–27) and then taught at the Dalcroze Institute (1928–38). He was active as pianist and harpsichordist; lectured at the conservatory and was appointed professor there in 1939; in addition was director (1933–39) of the Technicum moderne de musique, a private music school founded by a Russian couple in Geneva. In 1946, having married for the third time, he moved to his wife's native city of Amsterdam; from 1950 to 1957 he commuted from there to Cologne, where he held the chair of composition at the Musikhochschule; Stockhausen was among his pupils in Cologne. During his final two decades his works became widely known and performed; he received the Swiss Composer's Prize in 1947; became a member of the Academy of Saint Cecilia in Rome (1955), the Roman Accademia filarmonica (1962), and the Vienna Academy of Music (1965).

Martin had been inspired by a performance in 1900 of Bach's *St. Matthew Passion,* and the influence of Bach's harmonic language is clear not only in the Piano Quintet (1919) but also in the much later oratorio *Golgotha* (1945–48). Other important influences include Chopin, Schumann, Ravel, and especially the harmonic language of Franck (in the Sonata for Violin and Piano, 1913). *Le vin herbé* (a chamber oratorio for 12 voices, 7 strings, and piano) was first performed in Zurich in 1940, but staged and performed in its complete version in Salzburg eight years later; that work reflects Martin's investigations of Schoenberg's twelve-tone method as well as a refinement in harmonic and melodic language and in orchestration that are consistent aspects of Martin's style reminiscent of Debussy. He found the techniques of twelve-tone composition useful, but never abandoned his commitment to an extended tonality in which movements rarely begin and end in the same key.

Works: *Monsieur de Pourceaugnac* (opera, 1961–62; conducted by Ansermet, Geneva, 1963), several ballets and incidental music; oratorios (*In terra pax,* soloists, 2 choruses, orchestra, 1944; *Golgotha,* soloists, chorus, orchestra, and organ, 1945–48); *Petite symphonie concertante* (harp, harpsichord, piano, 2 string orchestras, 1945), *Trois danses* (oboe, harp, and strings, 1970), Piano Concerto no. 2 (1948–49), and other orchestral music; a string quartet (1967), *Trio sur les mélodies populaires irlandaises* (piano trio, 1925), and other chamber music; *8 Preludes* (1948) and a few other piano works; cantatas and other choral music (*Ode à la musique,* Machaut; baritone, chorus, 6 brass instruments, double bass, and piano, 1961); solo vocal music (*Poèmes de la mort,* Villon; tenor, baritone, bass, and 3 electric guitars, 1970).

Writings: *Responsabilité du compositeur* (Geneva, 1966). *Un compositeur médite sur son art,* ed. M. Martin (Neuchâtel, 1977). Many articles.

Bibl.: Bernard Billeter, *Frank Martin: Ein Aussenseiter der neuen Musik* (Frauenfeld, 1970). "Dokumente," *Schweizerische Musikzeitung* 116 (1976): 378ff. [includes works list, writings, bibliography]. Charles W. King, *Frank Martin: A Bio-Bibliography* (New York, 1990). Dietrich Kämper, ed., *Frank Martin: das kompositorische Werk: 13 Studien* (Mainz, 1993).

Martinelli, Giovanni (b. Montagnana, 22 Oct. 1885; d. New York, 2 Feb. 1969). Tenor. Played clarinet in a military band, then studied voice with Mandolini in Milan. Stage debut in 1908 as the Messenger in *Aïda.* Appeared as Ernani at the Teatro dal Verme in Milan in 1910. Puccini heard him and cast him as Dick Johnson in the European premiere of *La fanciulla del West* (Rome, 1911). La Scala debut in the same role, 1912. Covent Garden debut as Wolf-Ferrari's Gennaro, 1912. New York Metropolitan debut in 1913 as Rodolfo *(Bohème).* He remained with the Met as first tenor until his retirement in 1946, often as partner to Rosa Ponselle. Sang Tristan with the Chicago Lyric Opera in 1939. From 1946 taught in New York. In 1967 sang the Emperor in Puccini's *Turandot* in Seattle. His most important roles were Radames, Canio, Eléazar *(La juive),* and Otello.

Martinet, Jean-Louis (b. Ste. Bazeille, Lot-et-Garonne, 8 Nov. 1912). Composer and conductor. He studied with Ducasse and Münch at the Schola cantorum and the Paris Conservatory, and after the war with Leibowitz, Desormière, and Messiaen; he spent 1949 in Vienna studying the music of Webern. Won the Grand prix musicale of Paris in 1952, was a member of the French section of the ISCM, and taught at the conservatory in Montreal from 1971. Works include *Le triomphe de la mort* (symphonie dramatique, 1973) and 7 other orchestral pieces; Variations (string quartet, 1946) and *Pièce* (clarinet and piano, 1954); choral and solo vocal music (*Sept poèmes de René Char,* 4 solo voices and orchestra, 1952).

Martinez, Marianne [Anna Katharina] **von** (b. Vienna, 4 May 1744; d. Vienna, 13 Dec. 1812). Singer and composer. Through the influence of Metastasio, a family friend, Marianne studied singing with Porpora, keyboard with Haydn, and composition with Giuseppe Bonno. As a singer, keyboard player, and composer she became a favorite in the courts of Vienna. Burney spoke of her perfectly trained voice; Metastasio praised her slightly archaic compositions. She composed oratorios (*Isacco,* Vienna, 1782); cantatas (*Amore timido; La tempestà,* soprano, orchestra, 1778); *Orgoglioso fiumicello,* soprano, orchestra, 1786); sacred works; a symphony; concertos; sonatas.

Martínez, Odaline de la (b. Matanzas, Cuba, 31 Oct. 1949). Composer and conductor. She moved to the U.S. in 1961, then attended Tulane (1968–72) before studying composition with Paul Patterson at the Royal Academy of Music (1972–76) and with Reginald Smith Brindle (1975–77) at the Univ. of Surrey. She became the conductor of Lontano, a London-based chamber ensemble devoted to contemporary music, which she helped found in 1976. In 1982 she founded, also conducting, the London Contemporary Chamber Orchestra. Her works show the influence of Crumb, electronic music, minimalism, and her Latin American heritage. Among them are the opera *Sister Aimee* (1978–83); *Phasing* (chamber orchestra, 1975); *2 American Madrigals,* (chorus, 1979); a string quartet (1985); *Cantos de amor* (soprano, piano, string trio, 1985).

Martínez de Bizcargui, Gonzalo (b. Azcoita; d. after 1538). Theorist. His *Arte de canto llano* (Saragossa, 1508; ed. Albert Seay, Colorado College Music Press Critical Texts 9, 1979) went through numerous editions and revisions before the middle of the 16th century. This exceptionally well known didactic treatise on plainsong follows in some details the theories of Ramos de Pareja—considered heretical by some writers—but is overall traditional and conservative.

Martini, Giovanni Battista ["Padre Martini"] (b. Bologna, 24 Apr. 1706; d. there, 3 Aug. 1784). Writer on music, pedagogue, and composer. As a youth he studied music with his father, Antonio Maria, and later, in Bologna, singing under Angelo Predieri and Giovanni Ricieri and harmony and composition under Giacomo Perti. In 1721 he took orders at the Franciscan monastery in Lugo di Romagna. Returning to Bologna, in 1725 he was appointed *maestro di cappella* at the Church of S. Francesco, a position he occupied for the rest of his life. He was ordained in 1729. His first published work was the *Litaniae atque antiphonae finales, BVM,* for voices, organ, and instruments (Bologna, 1734); during the next three decades he established himself as a teacher and scholar. In 1758 he was elected to Bologna's Accademia dell'Istituto delle scienze, and to the Accademia dei filarmonici di Bologna. Among his numerous pupils were Jommelli, Grétry, J. C. Bach, Gluck, and Mozart. He composed prolifically, and although he received many offers of important positions (including that as *maestro* at the Vatican), he chose to remain in Bologna. He authored important books and treatises, including *Storia della musica* (3 vols., Bologna, [1761]–81; R: Graz, 1967) and especially the influential *Esemplare o sia saggio fondamentale pratico di contrappunto sopra il canto fermo* (2 vols., Bologna, 1774–75; R: Ridgewood, N.J., 1965). Among his compositions are oratorios; nearly 40 Masses; some 1,000 canons; sinfonias; concertos; sonatas for various ensembles and solo instruments; liturgical organ works.

Bibl.: Howard Brofsky, "The Instrumental Music of Padre

Martini" (diss., New York Univ., 1963). Bernhard Wiechens, *Die Kompositionstheorie und das kirchenmusikalische Schaffen Padre Martinis* (Regensburg, 1968).

Martini [Schwarzendorf], **Johann Paul Aegidius** (b. Freystadt, Palatinate, bapt. 31 Aug. 1741; d. Paris, 10 Feb. 1816). Organist and composer. He studied at the Jesuit seminary at Neuberg an der Donau, where he was made organist, and later at the Univ. of Freiburg. In 1760 he settled in Nancy. In 1761 he joined the court at Lunéville of Stanislaus Leszcynski, Duke of Lorraine. Moving to Paris around 1766, he composed military music and eventually joined the Hussars; later he served as orchestral director at the Théâtre Feydeau. In 1792 he fled to Lyons, returning to Paris for his final years. He was appointed director of the royal court orchestra in 1814. He is remembered especially for the popular *L'amoureux de quinze ans* (1771); other operas included *Henry IV* (1774), *L'amant sylphe* (1783), and *Sappho* (1794). He also composed sacred vocal music, secular cantatas (including a cantata, 1810, for the marriage of Napoleon and Marie-Louise), and chamber music.

Martini, Johannes [Zohane; Giovanni] (b. Brabant, ca. 1440; d. Ferrara, late 1497 or early 1498). Composer. Of Flemish origin but active in Italy; from 1473 until his death a member of the ducal chapel in Ferrara, with a brief interruption in 1474 for service in the Sforza chapel in Milan. Isabella d'Este may have been his pupil at some time before 1490, when she married and moved from Ferrara to Mantua. Most of his works survive in Italian manuscripts, including a chanson collection honoring Isabella's marriage to Francesco Gonzaga; but a few sacred pieces are known only from a compilation made in Innsbruck. His output includes 10 Masses; almost 70 Psalms; about 20 hymns, Magnificats, and motets; and slightly over 30 secular pieces, most settings of French texts.

Martino, Donald (James) (b. Plainfield, N.J., 16 May 1931). Composer. He studied composition with Bacon at Syracuse Univ., with Sessions and Babbitt at Princeton, and with Dallapiccola in Florence (1954–56). He taught at the Third Street Settlement School in New York, at Princeton, and at Yale before his appointment in 1969 as chairman of the composition department at the New England Conservatory; on the faculty at Harvard beginning 1983. In 1973 he won the Naumburg Chamber Music Award for *Notturno* (piccolo, flute, and alto flute; clarinet and bass clarinet; violin and viola; cello; piano; and percussion) and a year later received the Pulitzer Prize for the same work. Along with his use of serial procedures, he has been especially interested in the development of exact notation for fingerings, bowings, and articulations; but within his carefully notated scores the performer is often given some flexibility. Works include the Triple Concerto (clarinet, bass clarinet, contrabass clarinet, and orchestra, 1977); *The White Island* (after Robert Herrick, chorus and instrumental ensemble, commissioned by the Boston Symphony, 1987); *Paradiso Choruses* (solo voices, chorus, orchestra, and tape, 1974); a concerto for alto saxophone and orchestra (1987); chamber and piano music (String Quartet no. 4, 1983; *Fantasies and Impromptus,* piano, 1981; *From the Other Side,* divertimento for flute, cello, percussion, piano, 1988); *Seven Pious Pieces* (after Herrick, chorus, 1971) and other choral and vocal music; a few film scores, popular songs, and jazz arrangements.

Martinon, Jean (b. Lyons, 10 Jan. 1910; d. Paris, 1 Mar. 1976). Composer and conductor. After receiving a premier prix in violin at the Paris Conservatory (1928), he studied composition with Roussel and conducting with Münch and Desormière. While a prisoner during the war he wrote several works including *Stalag IX* (Musique d'exil for jazz orchestra, 1941) and *Chants des captifs* (soprano, tenor, speaker, chorus, and orchestra, 1945), which received the Paris Composition Prize in 1946. Upon his release he began to conduct the concerts of the Paris Conservatory and the Bordeaux Symphony (1946); was associate conductor of the London Philharmonic (1947–48); conducted the Concerts Lamoureux in Paris (1951–57); and made his North American debut with the Boston Symphony in 1957. He held other conducting positions with the French Radio Orchestra and with orchestras in Israel, Düsseldorf, Chicago, and The Hague; his repertory ranged from classical to contemporary music and included works of French composers, Bartók, and Prokofiev, as well as his own compositions. His Fourth Symphony (*Altitudes,* 1965) was written for the 75th anniversary of the Chicago Symphony while he was its conductor (1963–69). His own compositions include an opera (*Hécube,* Serge Moreux after Euripides, 1949–54, Strasbourg, 1956) and a ballet (1946); 4 symphonies, a concerto for flute (1970–71), and other orchestral music; 2 string quartets (1946, 1967) and other instrumental music; piano pieces; songs.

Martinů, Bohuslav (Jan) (b. Polička, east Bohemia, 8 Dec. 1890; d. Liestal, Switzerland, 28 Aug. 1959). Composer. He took violin lessons from a local tailor and started composing at the age of 10. In 1906 he entered the Prague Conservatory to study violin; he transferred to the Prague Organ School in 1909 but neglected his studies and was expelled the following year. During World War I he worked as a music teacher in Polička to avoid conscription; after the war he joined the Czech Philharmonic as a violinist (1918–23) and took a few lessons with Suk. In 1923 Martinů went off to Paris, where he had some lessons with Roussel and quickly made a name for himself through repeated performances of his ballets and orchestral and chamber works; the Second Quartet (1925) was played at the 1927 Baden-Baden Festival and at the 1928 ISCM Festival, and the String Sextet (1927) was awarded the 1932 Coolidge Prize. His residence in Paris led to imitations of Stravinsky (*Half-Time,* 1924), experimentation with jazz and ragtime idioms (the ballet *Kuchyňská revue* [Kitchen Revue], 1927; *Jazz Suite,* 1928), exploration of Baroque formal principles (Concerto for string quartet and orchestra, 1931; Concerto grosso, 1937) and motivically developmental works (*Invence,* 1934; Double Concerto, 1938).

In 1940 Martinů fled Paris and went to Lisbon, eventually entering the U.S. with his wife in March 1941. Between 1942 and 1946 he composed five symphonies, a number of concertos, and much chamber music, as well as the *Memorial to Lidice,* a tribute to the victims of the Nazi massacre in that Czech town. In 1946 he was invited to teach composition at the Prague Conservatory, but the political situation there made a return impossible. He took a summer teaching post at Tanglewood, and in 1948 he became chair of composition at Princeton, where he remained for three years; works from this time include the *Sinfonia concertante* (1949), the Second Piano Trio (1950), and the Sixth Symphony, *Fantaisies symphoniques* (1951–53). He lived for a time in Nice (1953–55) and returned to the U.S. in 1955 to teach at the Curtis Institute, but left the following year to become a professor at the American Academy in Rome. The last two years of his life were spent in Switzerland.

Matinuů's large, diverse, and uneven output defies easy classification. He is often regarded as a successor to Janáček. The influence of Czech folk music is most evident in the songs and cantatas but pervades the instrumental music as well; the instrumental dances *Les rondes* (1930) are based on Moravian folk song, while the ballet *Špalíček* (1931) draws on Czech folk texts and customs. The symphonies, especially the *Fantaisies symphoniques,* demonstrate Martinů's mastery of developmental techniques, while the works written after 1953 show a return to his Czech roots.

Works: *Operas. Voják a tanečnice* [The Soldier and the Dancer] (Brno, 1928); *Les larmes du couteau* (1928; Brno, 1968); *Tři přání* [The Three Wishes] (1929; Brno, 1971); *Hry o Marii* [The Miracles of Mary] (Brno, 1935); *Hlas lesa* [The Voice of the Forest] (Czech radio, 1935); *Veselohra na mostě* [Comedy on the Bridge] (Czech radio, 1937); *Divadlo za bránou* [Theater behind the Gate] (Brno, 1936); *Juliette* (Prague, 1938); *Čím člověk žije* [What Men Live By] (television opera; New York, 1953); *Mirandolina* (Prague, 1959); *Ariadne* (Gelsenkirchen, 1961); *Řecké pašije* [The Greek Passion] (Zurich, 1961).

Ballets. Istar (Prague, 1924); *Kdo je na světě nejmocnější* [Who Is the Most Powerful in the World] (Brno, 1925); *Vzpoura* [Revolt] (Brno, 1928); *Kuchyňská revue* [Kitchen Revue] (Prague, 1927); *Špalíček* (Prague, 1933); *Uškrcovač* [The Strangler] (New London, Conn., 1948).

Vocal music. Polní mše [Field Mass] (baritone, male voices, wind, brass, percussion, 1939); *Otvírání studánek* [The Opening of the Wells] (chamber cantata, 1955); *Romance z pampelišek* [The Romance of the Dandelions] (1957).

Orchestra. Half-time (1924); Piano Concerto no. 1 (1925); *La bagarre* (1926); Concertino (piano left-hand, chamber orchestra, 1926); *Le jazz* (1928); *Jazz Suite* (1928); Cello Concerto no. 1 (1930, rev. 1955); Serenade (chamber orchestra, 1930); Concerto (string quartet, orchestra, 1931); Partita (Suite no. 1) (strings, 1931); *Sinfonia concertante* (2 orchestras, 1932); *Invence* (1934); Piano Concerto no. 2 (1934); Concerto grosso (1937); Three Ricercari (1938); Double Concerto (2 string orchestras, piano, timpani, 1938); *Concerto da camera* (violin, orchestra, 1941); Symphony no. 1 (1942); Symphony no. 2 (1943); *Památník Lidicím* [Memorial to Lidice] (1943); Double Piano Concerto (1943); Violin Concerto (1943); Cello Concerto no. 2 (1944–45); Symphony no. 3 (1944); Symphony no. 4 (1945); Symphony no. 5 (1946); *Concerto da camera* (1947); Piano Concerto no. 3 (1948); *Sinfonia concertante* (oboe, bassoon, violin, cello, orchestra, 1949); *Intermezzo* (1950); *Fantaisies symphoniques* (Symphony no. 6, 1951–53); Oboe Concerto (1955); Piano Concerto no. 4, (Incantations, 1955–66); Piano Concerto no. 5, (Fantasia concertante, 1957); *Skála* [The Rock] (1957); *Paraboly* [The Parables] (1957–58); *3 estampes* (1958).

Chamber music. Piano Quintet (1911); 7 string quartets (1918; 1925; 1929; 1937; 1938; 1946; 1947, *Concerto da camera*); Quartet (clarinet, horn, side drum, cello, 1924); Sextet (flute, oboe, clarinet, 2 bassoons, piano, 1929); Piano Trios nos. 1–3 (1930, 1950, 1951); *Les rondes* (oboe, clarinet, bassoon, trumpet, 2 violins, piano, 1930); String Sextet (1932); Piano Quartet (1942); Quartet (oboe, piano trio, 1947).

Keyboard. Black Bottom (1929); *La fantaisie* (2 pianos, 1929); *Fantasie a toccata* (1940); *Three Czech Dances* (2 pianos, 1949); Sonata (1954).

Bibl.: Miloš Šafránek, *Bohuslav Martinů: His Life and Works,* trans. Roberta Finlayson-Samsourová (London, 1962). Harr Halbreich, *Bohuslav Martinů: Werkverzeichnis, Dokumentation und Biographie* (Zurich, 1968) [includes detailed works list]. Brian Large, *Martinů* (London, 1975). Guy Erismann, *Martinů: Un musicien à l'éveil des sources* (Arles, 1990). Jitka Brabcová, ed., *Bohuslav Martinů Anno 1981: Papers from an International Musicological Conference, Prague, 26–28 May 1981* (Prague, 1990).

Martín y Soler, (Anastasio Martín Ignacio) Vicente (Tadeo Francisco Pellegrin) [lo Spagnuolo] (b. Valencia, 2 May 1754; d. St. Petersburg, 10 Feb. 1806). Composer. His father, Francisco Xavier Martín, was a tenor at the cathedral in Valencia; as a youth Vicente was a chorister there. He moved to Madrid probably around 1775, and later he studied with Padre Martini in Bologna. After 1776 he composed Italian operas, both comic and serious, which were performed throughout Italy. Around 1780 he was appointed court composer for the Infante, later Charles IV of Spain. Among his early operas were *Ifigenia in Aulide* (Naples, 1779); *L'amor geloso* (Naples, 1782); and *Vologeso* (Turin, 1783). He moved to Vienna in 1785 and was soon composing highly successful opere buffe for Joseph II's imperial theater, including *Il burbero di buon cuore* (1786); *Una cosa rara* (1786); and *L'arbore di Diana* (1787). In 1788 he went to St. Petersburg to serve as composer and singing instructor in Catherine's court. He traveled to London in 1795, remaining for only one season before returning to St. Petersburg; he served as inspector for the Italian opera there until shortly before his death. He is remembered today chiefly for the melody from *Una cosa rara* quoted in the dining scene of Mozart's *Don Giovanni.*

Martirano, Salvatore (b. Yonkers, N.Y., 12 Jan. 1927). Composer. He studied with Elwell at Oberlin (1947–51), with Rogers at Eastman, and with Dallapiccola in Florence (1952–54); was a Fellow of the American Academy in Rome (1956–59). On the faculty at the Univ. of Illinois beginning 1963. Early works employed the twelve-tone method; in 1958 he began to include popular elements in his works (*O, O, O, O, That Shakespeherian Rag,* chorus and ensemble, 1958). In 1968 he began to develop the Sal-Mar Construction (1971), an instrument that permits simultaneous creation and performance of improvisatory compositions. In 1983 Martirano held an IRCAM grant to develop computer algorithms to mimic the processes of the Sal-Mar Construction. Some works of the 1970s and later employ standard notation, but many have significant electronic components (*In memoriam Luigi Dallapiccola,* 2-track tape, 1978). Others are mixed-media presentations; one of those with significant political content is *L's G. A.* (Lincoln's Gettysburg Address; for gas-masked politico, 2-track tape, helium bomb, 3 16-mm films, 1967–68) performed at the New York Electric Circus and elsewhere. *L's G. A. Update* (video) was created in 1985. Early works include a chamber opera (*The Magic Stone,* after Boccaccio, 1951); *Piece* (orchestra, 1952); String Quartet (1951); a Mass (double choir, 1952–55); and *Chansons innocentes* (soprano and piano, 1957). More recent works include *Dance/Players I and II* (video pieces, 1986); *3 not 2* (variable forms piece, 1987); *Phleu* (amplified flute, synthetic orchestra, 1988); *LON/dons* (chamber orchestra, 1989).

Marttinen, Tauno (b. Helsinki, 27 Sept. 1912). Composer. Studied composition from 1935 to 1937 with Palmgren at the Viipuri (Vyborg) Institute of Music and the Sibelius Academy in Helsinki. He also studied piano and conducting during this time, as well as composition with Vogel in Switzerland. From 1949 to 1959 he conducted the city orchestra of Hameenlinna; he served as director of the Music School, 1950–75. His early works were within a conservative nationalistic tradition. His later works, in which he adopted twelve-tone techniques, were more eclectic and international in style. His greatest strength lay in musical drama; he composed principally operas (*Päällysviitta* [The Cloak], television opera after Gogol's story, 1960; *Poltettu oranssi* [Burnt Orange], television, 1971, stage, 1975; *Häät* [The Wedding], 1986) and ballets (*Dorian Grayn muotokuva* [Portrait of Dorian Gray], ballet after Oscar Wilde, 1969). Other works include 7 symphonies (1957–77), concertos (*Dalai Lama,* cello and orchestra, 1964–66; bassoon, 1966–68; violin, 1958–62), chamber music, choral works, film music, and songs for solo voice and orchestra (*Tumma maa* [Dark Land], alto and orchestra, 1962).

Martucci, Giuseppe (b. Capua, 6 Jan. 1856; d. Naples, 1 June 1909). Composer. Son of a trumpeter and bandmaster; from 1867 to 1871 or 1872, student, Naples Conservatory, leaving at his father's insistence to tour as concert pianist, which he did with some success until 1880, visiting Britain (1875), Germany, France. He is best known for his later career as academic, composer, and conductor and as an important figure in the attempt to absorb the German tradition into Italian musical life and to revive instrumental genres in Italian composition. Piano teacher, 1880–86, Naples Conservatory, also conducting orchestral concerts; 1886–1902, director, Bologna Conservatory; 1902–9, director, Naples Conservatory, continuing to conduct until 1908 (including the Italian premiere of *Tristan,* Bologna, 1888). His early works were mostly salon piano genres, but from the late 1870s he produced orchestral works (including 2 piano concertos, especially no. 2 in B♭ minor, op. 66, 1885, and 2 symphonies, especially no. 2 in F, op. 81, 1904); chamber music; also shorter pieces (his *Notturno* op. 70, no. 1, and *Novelletta* op. 82, no. 2, were for a long period light concert favorites), songs; an oratorio. His music did not receive much attention outside Italy, but there he is regarded as an important historical figure and is still occasionally performed.

Bibl.: F. Fano, *Giuseppe Martucci* (Naples, 1950).

Marvin, Frederick (b. Los Angeles, 11 Jun. 1923). Pianist and musicologist. He studied with Maurice Zam and Milan Blanchet in Los Angeles, with Rudolf Serkin at the Curtis Institute (1939–40), and with Claudio Arrau (1950–54). He received a Carnegie Hall award for his New York debut in 1948; often performed lesser-known works, including compositions of Moscheles and Dussek. Marvin also unearthed a large number of manuscripts by the Spanish composer Antonio Soler and edited and recorded a number of Soler's keyboard sonatas.

Marx, Adolf Bernhard (b. Halle, 15 May 1795; d. Berlin, 17 May 1866). Writer and composer. Became a lawyer, also having music lessons with Türk in Halle, but then turned to music in Berlin as editor of the *Berliner allgemeine musikalische Zeitung* (1824–30), critic, and teacher. He had some lessons from Zelter, whom he alienated by criticizing the Singakademie in his periodical (1824–27); 1828, doctorate from Univ. of Marburg; 1830, professor, Univ. of Berlin; 1832, choir director there; 1850, founded with Kullak and Stern the school that after his withdrawal in 1856 became the Stern Conservatory; continued to teach privately. He was close to Mendelssohn in the latter's youth, but jealousy of Mendelssohn's success as a composer seems to have undermined their relations, since Marx's own music aroused little interest; their friendship ended over Mendelssohn's refusal to perform Marx's oratorio *Moses* (1841) at Leipzig (because of his low opinion of it). Marx's works are mostly vocal, sacred and secular, choral and solo. He contributed to the Berlin revival of J. S. Bach. Remembered mainly as a writer of criticism (some collected in *Musikalische Schriften über Tondichter und Tonkunst,* ed. L. Hirschberg, Hildburghausen, 1912–22), books on Beethoven (1859; many later editions) and Gluck (1863), and memoirs, *Erinnerungen: Aus meinem Leben* (Berlin, 1865), but especially for his theoretical-didactic works, notably the 4-volume *Die Lehre von der* *musikalischen Komposition* (Leipzig, 1837–47), an outgrowth of his teaching, which is a principal source of the standard 19th- and 20th-century concept of sonata form.

Marx, Joseph (b. Graz, 11 May 1882; d. there, 3 Sept. 1964). Composer and critic. He completed a doctorate at the Univ. of Graz before turning to composition at the age of 26; he wrote some 120 songs between 1908 and 1912. In 1914 he began to teach theory at the Music Academy in Vienna (later Hochschule für Musik) and became its director in 1922; from 1931 to 1938 he was music critic for the *Neue Wiener Journal;* after the war he held the same position at the *Wiener Zeitung.* He composed in a conservative style, concentrating in the 1920s and early 1930s on orchestral music and later on chamber music. He wrote textbooks on harmony and counterpoint as well as 2 volumes of essays (1947, 1964). His works include *Idylle* (1926) and other orchestral music; *Quartetto in modo cromatico* (1937), *Quartetto in modo antico* (1940), *Quartetto in modo classico* (1942); *Lieder und Gesange,* 3 vols. (1910–17); *Verklärtes Jahr* (song cycle for mezzo-soprano or baritone and orchestra, 1935–36).

Marx, Karl (b. Munich, 12 Nov. 1897; d. Stuttgart, 8 May 1985). Composer. He had a few lessons from Orff while a prisoner during the war (1917–19), then studied at the Munich Academy of Music (1920–24). He taught there and led the Bach Society Choir (from 1928); taught at the Graz Hochschule für Musikerziehung, becoming a professor in 1944; taught at the Stuttgart Hochschule für Musik (from 1946), of which he was director from 1955. He won the Munich Music Prize in 1932. Works include orchestral music (concertos for piano, violin, viola, flute, strings, and 2 violins); chamber music for winds and strings; organ works; *Und endet doch alles mit Frieden* (solo voices, chorus, and orchestra, 1953) and a large amount of unaccompanied choral music; several collections of songs.

Marxsen, Eduard (b. Nienstädten, near Altona, 23 July 1806; d. Altona, 18 Nov. 1887). Teacher. Son of an organist; studied with him in Hamburg; from 1830, studied in Vienna with Seyfried; from 1833 a highly respected teacher and pianist in Hamburg; also composed; best known as teacher (1843–53) of Brahms, who expressed his gratitude with the dedication of the Second Piano Concerto (but who also recognized Marxsen's intellectual and musical limitations).

Mascagni, Pietro (b. Livorno, 7 Dec. 1863; d. Rome, 2 Aug. 1945). Composer. From 1876 studied theory and composition in Livorno with Alfredo Soffredini, beginning to compose while very young; then through the generosity of a local nobleman entered the Milan Conservatory in October 1882, where he studied with Ponchielli and Saladino and was a fellow student of Puccini, at one time sharing a room with him, but proved incompatible with regular study and in 1884 was expelled. He became conductor of a succession of touring operetta companies, composing an operetta himself; also worked on an opera, *Guglielmo Ratcliff,* begun in 1882. When his wife became pregnant, he abandoned touring in Cerignola in Puglia, where he conducted the local orchestra and at the theater, gave piano lessons, and composed a Mass and songs. To enter one of the publisher Sonzogno's contests for a one-act opera, he composed *Cavalleria rusticana* and was one of three winners. The success of the premiere was extraordinary (Rome, 17 May 1890), and it soon spread over Italy and the rest of the world (Mascagni did not fare so well with the critics, who attacked the work for its verismo violence and supposed musical and dramatic crudeness and vulgarity). *L'amico Fritz,* a romantic comedy composed hurriedly to capitalize on this success, was also successful (Rome, 1891, with Calvé) and is still occasionally performed.

The more violent *I Rantzau* (Florence, 1892) was a failure, and *Guglielmo Ratcliff* (La Scala, 1893) did not sustain itself, while the verismo *Silvano* (La Scala, 1893), which Mascagni had planned as a companion piece to *Cavalleria rusticana,* was an absolute failure. Masagni was director, 1895–1903, of the Pesaro Conservatory, presenting there in 1896 a one-act "idyll" *Zanetto,* also given at La Scala but not lastingly successful. The Japanese opera *Iris* (Rome, 1898) somewhat restored his flagging reputation, but the public relations ploy of having the comedy *Le maschere* premiered simultaneously in six leading Italian theaters (17 Jan. 1901) backfired, only the Rome premiere, conducted by Mascagni himself, proving at all successful. In 1902–3 he toured the U.S. conducting his own works, a financial disaster that also cost him his Pesaro post because of his long absence. Conducting his works became a prime occupation of his later years as his output slowed: *Amica* (Monte Carlo, 1905); *Isabeau* (Buenos Aires, 1911, whose premiere he combined with a successful conducting tour of South America); *Parisiana* (libretto by D'Annunzio, La Scala, 1913), a failure; *Lodoletta* (Rome, 1917); the operetta *Si* (Rome, 1919); *Il piccolo Marat* (Rome, 1921), a considerable but not lasting success; his rediscovered student opera *Pinotta* (San Remo, 1932); finally *Nerone* (La Scala, 1935).

An admirer of Mussolini, he replaced the anti-fascist Toscanini as director of La Scala in 1929; 1940, made a 50th anniversary tour of Italy with *Cavalleria rusticana* and recorded it. Other works include *Rapsodia satanica* for the film *Alfa* (1915), a symphonic poem, *Contemplando la S. Teresa del Bernini* (1923), occasional works, songs.

Bibl.: D. Stivender, ed. and trans., *The Autobiography of Pietro Mascagni* (New York, 1975). Piero e Nandi Ostali, eds., *Cavalleria rusticana, 1890–1990: Cento anni di un capolavoro* (Milan, 1990). Giovanni Gelati, *Il vate e il capobanda: D'Annunzio e Mascagni* (Livorno, 1992).

Maschera, Florentio [Fiorenzo] (b. Brescia?, ca. 1540?; d. there, ca. 1584). Composer and organist.

Studied with Claudio Merulo, whom he succeeded as organist at the cathedral in Brescia from 22 Aug. 1557, after a period of service in Venice. His 23 4-part canzonas are among the first such pieces originally written for instrumental ensemble.

Mascheroni, Edoardo (b. Milan, 4 Sept. 1852; d. Ghirla, 4 Mar. 1941). Conductor. Studied music in Milan with Boucheron; from 1880 established himself as an opera and symphony conductor, especially at Rome, where he worked in all the major theaters; 1891–97, conductor at La Scala; also conducted in Spain and South America, retiring in 1925. Greatly admired by Verdi, he conducted the premiere of *Falstaff* (La Scala, 1893), also introducing it elsewhere in Italy and in central Europe.

Masnelli, Paolo (b. Verona; fl. 1578–1609). Composer. Active as an organist for a few years (1585–92) in Mantua but mostly in Verona, where he was associated with the Accademia filarmonica as well as the cathedral. All of his known compositions are Italian madrigals, including 2 books for 5 voices, 1 book for 4 voices, and a number of pieces first published in anthologies in Italy and Germany.

Mason, Daniel Gregory (b. Brookline, Mass., 20 Nov. 1873; d. Greenwich, Conn., 4 Dec. 1953). Composer. The grandson of Lowell Mason (1792–1872); his father, Henry, co-founded the piano firm of Mason & Hamlin. He studied at Harvard (1891–95) and undertook further work in composition with Goetschius and Chadwick; his *Birthday Waltzes* for piano were published in 1894 as opus 1. In 1905 he began to teach at Columbia, the institution with which he was associated throughout his long career; he became MacDowell Professor in 1929 and retired as head of the Music Department in 1942. He was a pioneer in the area of music appreciation and published the first of his many books in this field *(From Grieg to Brahms)* in 1902; other books include volumes on Beethoven, Brahms, and Romantic composers, as well as more general guides to music and volumes of reminiscences. In 1913 he spent a year in Paris studying with d'Indy; his compositional style remained conservative and Germanic, but he advocated an eclectic approach for American composers and even attempted to color some of his own works with American elements (*String Quartet on Negro Themes* op. 19, 1918–19).

Works: *Chanticleer* (festival overture, 1926), 3 symphonies (no. 3, *A Lincoln Symphony* op. 35, 1933–36), and other orchestral music including incidental music for the stage and transcriptions; Divertimento (wind quintet op. 26b, 1926), *Fanny Blau, Folksong Fantasy* (string quartet op. 28, 1927), and other chamber music for winds and strings; piano and organ music (*2 Choral Preludes on Lowell Mason's Tunes* op. 39, 1941); choral music and many songs.

Writings: *Beethoven and His Forerunners* (1904). With T. W. Surette, *The Appreciation of Music* (1907). *The Orchestral Instruments* (1908). *A Guide to Music* (1909). *A Neglected Sense in Piano Playing* (1912). *Artistic Ideals* (1925). *The Dilemma of American Music and Other Essays* (1928). *Music in My Time and Other Reminiscences* (1938).

Mason, Henry (b. Brookline, Mass., 10 Oct. 1831; d. Boston, 15 May 1890). Instrument manufacturer. Son of Lowell Mason; educated in Boston schools, then at Göttingen, Paris, Prague; worked in Pond's music shop in New York, also as church organist. In 1854, in partnership with Emmons Hamlin (b. Rome, N.Y., 16 Nov. 1821; d. Boston, 8 Apr. 1885), who had, while working at the Prince melodeon factory in Buffalo, made improvements in the voicing of reeds, he set up a melodeon factory in Boston (from 1861 also making parlor organs). Through their improved instruments (first prize, Paris Exposition, 1876) the firm quickly proved internationally successful; from 1883 they also made pianos. The business was carried on by his sons.

Mason, Lowell (Medford, Mass., 8 Jan. 1792; d. Orange, N.J., 11 Aug. 1872). Educator and composer. At 13 attended a singing school taught by Amos Albee; also studied with Oliver Shaw; learned several instruments; choir director and bandmaster in Medfield. In 1812 he composed an anthem (with Albee's help) for a minister's installation. In 1812 he went to Savannah in the dry goods business; later a bank clerk; active in church music there, a singing-school teacher and church organist; also studied harmony and counterpoint in a more traditional European way with a German immigrant musician, Frederick Abel (in Savannah from 1817).

In 1818 he and Abel began compiling a hymn collection, whose sources in the European classical composers reflect his growing European orientation. It was published (Boston, 1822) as *The Boston Handel and Haydn Society Collection of Church Music* and had great success (early editions without Mason's name as editor). This and his advocacy of "reform" in church music (*Address on Church Music,* Boston, 1826; R: 1965–66) led to his being called to Boston, where he was a choirmaster and organist (1827–51) and director (1827–32) of the Handel and Haydn Society. In 1829 he published *The Juvenile Psalmist,* which he believed to be the first collection of Sunday school music; 1830–31, *The Juvenile Lyre,* for public school use; these were followed by many others. In 1833 he founded the Boston Academy of Music, which sponsored concerts but was most influential through its classes and its courses for singing teachers and from about 1836 its "conventions," an idea that was to become an important part of 19th-century American music and to which Mason was to devote much time in his later years. In 1837 he taught music on a provisional, unpaid basis in Boston public schools, so successfully that in 1838 music was accepted into the curriculum, with Mason in charge of it until 1845 and continuing to teach there until 1851.

He visited Europe in 1837 and 1851–53; on returning based his work in New York, continuing to produce (although less frequently) the collections of hymns (and sometimes part songs, glees, etc.) that through their popularity brought him a large income. He composed or arranged many hymns, some of which remain a staple of American hymnody. His original tunes include "Olivet" ("My faith looks up to thee") and "Bethany" ("Nearer, my God, to thee"). By the late 19th century his work was sometimes denigrated as having propagated a simpleminded, debased version of European music; in the 20th it has sometimes been regretted for having undermined the native tradition of hymnody.

Bibl.: Carol A. Pemberton, *Lowell Mason: A Bio-Bibliography* (New York, 1988). Michael Broyles, ed., *A Yankee Musician in Europe: The 1837 Journals of Lowell Mason* (Ann Arbor, 1990).

Mason, Luther Whiting (b. Turner, Maine, 2 or 3 Apr. 1818; d. Buckfield, Maine, 14 July 1896). Music educator. Inclined to become a missionary, but became a singing-school teacher and choirmaster; studied at Lowell Mason's Boston Academy; taught public school music in Japan (where that kind of music became known as "Mason-song"). He is best known in the U.S. for his widely used National Music Course, a comprehensive series of textbooks and other teaching materials.

Mason, Marilyn (May) (b. Alva, Okla., 29 June 1925). Organist. She studied at Oklahoma State Univ., at the Univ. of Michigan with Palmer Christian, and at Union Theological Seminary in New York; also worked with Nadia Boulanger and Schoenberg. She was appointed to the faculty of the Univ. of Michigan in 1946, later becoming chair of the organ department (1962) and professor (1965). She toured widely and commissioned a number of works.

Mason, William (b. Boston, 24 Jan. 1829; d. New York, 14 July 1908). Pianist and teacher. Third son of Lowell Mason; had piano lessons in Boston but learned more from observing Leopold de Meyer in 1847–48. From 1849 to 1854 he studied with Moscheles in Leipzig (to March 1850), with Dreyschock in Prague, and (1853–54) was one of Liszt's informal pupils in Weimar, as vividly described in his *Memories of a Musical Life* (New York, 1901). He returned to New York and after a concert tour became a leading piano teacher and performer (including the Mason–Thomas chamber music concerts, 1855–68). He published more than 50 piano pieces, some of which had some popularity in the U.S. (e.g. *Silver Spring* op. 6, 1856); also several didactic works, especially *Mason's Fortepiano Techniques* (1878). He was particularly interested in the mechanics and muscular aspects of playing, especially of the touch.

Massart, (Joseph) Lambert (b. Liège, 19 July 1811; d. Paris, 13 Feb. 1892). Violinist. From a family of musicians; 1822, played in a Liège concert; studied in Paris, privately with Kreutzer, Zimmermann, Fétis, then (1829–32) a composition student at the Conservatory. He disliked giving concerts and did so relatively seldom, occasionally appearing with Liszt (last in 1841); more comfortable in chamber music. Violin professor, 1843–90, Paris Conservatory (pupils included Wieniawski, Sarasate, Kreisler). His wife, Louise Aglaé Masson (1827–87), was a pianist and teacher at the Conservatory.

Massé, Victor [Félix Marie] (b. Lorient, 7 Mar. 1822; d. Paris, 5 July 1884). Composer. Star student, 1834–44, Paris Conservatory (first prize: piano, 1839; harmony, 1840; counterpoint, 1843; Prix de Rome, 1844). He first attracted notice with songs; 1849–59, 10 opéras comiques performed in Paris (and a one-act operetta in Baden), some of them very successful, especially *Galathée* (1852) and *Les noces de Jeannette* (1853), which was long and widely popular. From 1860 he was chorusmaster at the Opéra, where his *La mule de Pedro* had little success (1863); this was also the fate of his few other late operas, of which the most important was *Paul et Virginie* (1876). Professor of composition at the Conservatory, 1866–76, but forced to resign because of a nervous complaint that eventually made him a shut-in. Elected to the Académie in 1872.

Masselos, William (b. Niagara Falls, N.Y., 11 Aug. 1920; d. New York, 23 Oct. 1992). Pianist. Studied piano with Carl Friedberg at Juilliard, 1932–44; with David Saperton at the Curtis Institute. Recital debut, New York, 1939. After giving the premiere of Ives's *First Piano Sonata* in 1948, he was known as a skilled champion of contemporary music, including Copland's *Piano Fantasy,* which he introduced 1957. Taught at the Catholic Univ. of America (1965–71), at Georgia State Univ. (1972–75), at Juilliard from 1976. As a soloist he broke with tradition by playing recitals and even concertos from the score rather than from memory.

Massenet, Jules (Émile Frédéric) (b. Montaud, near St. Étienne, 12 May 1842; d. Paris, 13 Aug. 1912). Composer. His family moved in 1847 to Paris, where they lived poorly; from 1851 he was a student at the Paris Conservatory; 1854, the family moved to Savoy; 1855, Massenet ran away, returning to his studies in Paris, supporting himself through piano lessons, playing in cafés and as an orchestra drummer, setting a pattern of hard work that was to be lifelong. Won first prize, 1859, piano; then studied with Reber (harmony), Thomas (composition), Benoist (organ); 1863, Prix de Rome. He composed a Requiem, concert overture, and two orchestra suites in Italy and worked on an opera and oratorios. There proposed marriage to a young French woman, his piano student, but was rejected by her parents. They were married in Paris in 1866 (one child, a daughter, born 1868, to whom Massenet was devoted), as he began to win recognition as a composer through his *10 pièces de genre* op. 10 for piano (1866) and a collection of songs, some of which, especially *Poème d'avril,* had considerable popularity.

He began an opera career with two modest successes at the Opéra-comique in 1867 and 1872; work on two serious operas was stopped by the 1870 war, which he spent in the infantry. It was the enthusiasm of Pauline Viardot for his oratorio *Marie Magdeleine,* causing her to emerge from semi-retirement to sing its title part in 1873, that ensured his success, which he followed up with the well-received orchestral *Scènes pittoresques* (his fourth suite) in 1873, the overture to *Phèdre* in 1874, and the oratorio *Eve* in 1875. These successes gave him entrance to the Opéra, where *Le roi de Lahore* was one of the last triumphs of French grand opera (27 Apr. 1877). It was widely performed, and Massenet himself supervised its staging in several Italian houses, reflecting his intense concern with practical theatrical matters. His resulting position in French music was evidenced in 1878 by his appointment as professor of composition at the Conservatory and his election to the Académie (over Saint-Saëns, who was thereafter an enemy). His personality and manner—ingratiating, impenetrably urbane and suave—and his complete professionalism in calculating his work for maximum audience appeal also alienated those such as d'Indy who had an almost religious view of art. Even so, he was not invariably successful; his next oratorio, *La vierge,* was coolly received when he conducted it at the Opéra in 1880, and he abandoned the genre. The Opéra refused his next opera, *Hérodiade,* but it was very successful at Brussels (1881). His next, *Manon,* was a tremendous success at the Opéra-comique (19 Jan. 1884) and became his most enduring work in France and beyond. His grand opera *Le Cid* had a success of considerably lesser magnitude with the De Reszkes at the Opéra in 1885.

At this time Massenet became infatuated with a young American singer, Sybil Sanderson. He trained her for opera and composed *Esclarmonde* for her, spending the summer of 1888 in Switzerland teaching it to her. She and the opera were a success at the Opéra-comique in 1889, but, tailored so completely to her unusual voice, it was not widely performed. *Le mage* (Opéra, 1891) had only a succès d'estime, but *Werther,* premiered at the Vienna Opera (1892) because the Opéra-comique rejected it, after a slow start became his most enduring opera after *Manon. Thaïs* (Opéra, 1894), another Sanderson vehicle, also established itself slowly but was very popular into the early 20th century. With *La navarraise* (Covent Garden, 1894), composed for Calvé, he attempted with considerable success the then-new verismo genre. *Sapho* (Opéra-comique, 1897), also a vehicle for Calvé, was well-received but did not sustain itself. In 1896 he was offered the directorship of the Conservatory but refused it because the appointment would not be made for life, also resigning his professorship.

In his later years he became even more productive than before (his lifelong regime was to rise every day at 4 A.M. and compose until noon). Most of his later works had initial success, a reflection of his immense prestige and of his celebrated instinct for public taste, but none was to become a permanent repertory piece. They span most of the genres between farce and classical tragedy. His last operas premiered at the Opéra-comique were *Cendrillon* (1899), a fairy-tale opera, and *Grisélidis* (1901). The Opéra-comique's rejection of *Le jongleur de Notre-Dame,* a work with no female roles, led to a long association with the opera at Monte Carlo (1902), including also *Chérubin* (1903), a slightly risqué 18th-century comedy; *Thérèse* (1907), a bourgeois drama; the comedy *Don Quichotte* (1910); the tragic grand opera *Roma* (1912); and the posthumous grand operas *Cléopâtre* (1914) and *Amadis* (1922). He returned to the Paris Opéra after 20 years for two classical grand operas, *Arianne* (1906), which had a succès d'estime (60 performances), and *Bacchus* (1907), one of his few outright failures (6 performances). Prosperine in *Arianne* was sung by Sanderson's successor as the object of Massenet's personal and artistic devotion, the contralto Lucy Arbell. For her he wrote the title part in *Thérèse* and Dulcinea in *Don Quichotte.* (She was to sue his heirs, unsuccessfully, for the right to the female leads in *Cléopâtre* and *Amadis.*)

Other works include much incidental music; orchestral pieces, especially 7 suites, Piano Concerto (1902); some 250 songs; a last oratorio, *La terre promise* (1900), aroused little attention. He wrote his memoirs: *Mes souvenirs* (Paris, 1912); trans. Eng. (1919; R: 1970).

Bibl.: A. Pougin, *Massenet* (Paris, 1914). J. Harding, *Massenet* (London, 1970).

Masson, Diego (b. Tossa, Spain, 21 June 1935). Conductor. He studied percussion and chamber music at the Paris Conservatory (1953–59); took composition with Maderna (1964) and conducting with Boulez (1965). After serving as a percussionist with the Domaine musical, Masson founded his own group, Musique vivante, in 1966; the ensemble premiered a number of compositions and worked closely with Boulez and Stockhausen. Masson was music director of the Marseilles Opera and from 1969 of the Ballet-théâtre contemporain, which ultimately became, along with an opera company under his direction, part of the Théâtre-musical d'Angers. He conducted both opera and concert music elsewhere in France as well as in England, Scotland, and the Netherlands.

Masur, Kurt (b. Brieg, Silesia, 18 July 1927). Conductor. Studied piano and cello at the National Music School in Breslau (1942–44), and conducting, piano, and composition at the Leipzig Conservatory (1946–48); served as conductor of the Erfurt (1951–53) and Leipzig city theaters (1953–55), and as general music director at the Mecklenburg Staatstheater, Schwerin (in 1958). Masur also served as musical director of the Komische Oper, Berlin (1960–64); chief conductor of the Dresden Philharmonic (1955–58, 1967–72); conductor of the Leipzig Gewandhaus Orchestra (1970–98), with which he has a number of recordings; principal guest conductor of the London Philharmonic (from 1988); and music director of the New York Philharmonic (from 1991).

Mata, Eduardo (b. Mexico City, 5 Sept. 1942; d. near Cuernavaca, 4 Jan. 1995). Composer and conductor. Studied composition with Rodolfo Halffter at the National Conservatory (1954–60), and composition and conducting with Carlos Chávez and Julián Orbón (1960–65). Attended Tanglewood in 1964, studying conducting with Schuller and Leinsdorf. Became director of the Guadalajara Symphony in the same year, taking over the orchestra of the National Univ. of Mexico in 1966, and the Phoenix Symphony in 1970. Guest appearances with major orchestras throughout the Americas (principal guest conductor of the Pittsburgh Symphony from 1990) and in Europe followed; music director of the Dallas Symphony, 1977–94, where in addition to the standard repertoire he performed works by Berio, Stockhausen, and other contemporary composers.

Mata's own compositions are similarly divided between traditional and contemporary media. Works include 3 symphonies (no. 1, *Clásica,* 1962; no. 2, *Romántica,* 1963; no. 3, horn and winds, 1967); chamber music, including *Trio a Vaughan Williams* (1957), several *Improvisaciones* (clarinet and piano; string quartet and piano 4-hands; strings and 2 pianos; violin and piano), and cello and violin sonatas (1966, 1967); a piano sonata (1960); *Aires sobre un tema del siglo XVI,* mezzo-soprano and chamber ensemble; and the ballet *Los huesos secos,* a tape composition. Mata died in a plane crash.

Materna (-Friedrich), Amalie (b. St. Georgen, Styria, 10 July 1844; d. Vienna, 18 Jan. 1918). Soprano. Discovered by Suppé; became a chorus singer in Graz theater, then had solo roles in operetta there and in Vienna (1866). Between 1869 and 1894, one of the stars of the Vienna Opera; among the greatest early Wagner singers, prototype of the Wagnerian dramatic soprano; Brünnhilde in the first complete *Ring* (Bayreuth, 1876); created Kundry in *Parsifal* (Bayreuth, 1882, holding the role to 1891). She made several visits to the U.S. (1882–94).

Mather, Bruce (b. Toronto, 9 May 1939). Composer and pianist. Studied in Toronto with Weinzweig, Oskar Morawetz, and Godfrey Ridout (1953–59); and with Messiaen and Milhaud in Paris (1959–61); attended the 1960 summer course at Darmstadt and had further contact with Boulez when he studied conducting at Basel (1969). Taught in Toronto (1964–66) and at McGill (from 1966); performed as a pianist in France, Spain, and North America. After meeting Wyschnegradsky in Paris (1974) he began to explore in his own works some of the harmonic implications of quarter tone music; in addition he recorded some of Wyschnegradsky's music for pianos tuned in quarter and sixth tones. Works include orchestral music (*Scherzo,* 1987; *Dialogue pour trio basso et orchestre,* 1988); chamber music (*Barbaresco,* viola, cello, double bass, 1984); Sonata for 2 pianos (1970) and other piano and organ works; a series of madrigals for 1 or 2 voices and instrumental ensemble, and other choral and vocal music (*Musique pour Champigny,* 3 solo voices, clarinet, horn, harp, piano, percussion, 1979); film scores.

Mathews, Max V(ernon) (b. Columbus, Nebr., 13 Nov. 1926). Computer scientist and composer. After study at California Institute of Technology and M.I.T., he worked at the Bell Telephone Laboratories in New Jersey, where he developed languages for computer sound synthesis and for its control in real time. He also developed "intelligent instruments," such as the Sequential Drum and some electronic violins. James Tenney, Jean-Claude Risset, and Pierre Boulez are among the composers who worked with Mathews at Bell Labs. He subsequently played a leading role at IRCAM in Paris. He wrote several works for computer as well as the volume *The Technology of Computer Music* (1969).

Mathias, William (James) (b. Whitland, Dyfed, Wales, 1 Nov. 1934; d. Menai Bridge, Gwynedd, 29 July 1992). Composer. He studied with Ian Parrott at the Univ. College of Wales, Aberystwyth, then with Peter Katin (piano) and Lennox Berkeley (composition) at the Royal Academy of Music. He became a fellow of the R.A.M. in 1965 and in 1966 received the D.Mus. from the Univ. of Wales. He taught at Univ. College of Wales, Bangor (1959–68 and 1970–88), and the Univ. of Edinburgh (1968–69). In 1972 appointed artistic director of the North Wales Music Festival. His music, influenced by Hindemith, Stravinsky, and Tippett, is essentially tonal in its harmonic language. Works include the opera *The Servants* (1980) and the "musical morality" *Jonah* (1988); 3 piano concertos (1955, 1960, 1968), Concerto for Orchestra (1964), *Litanies* (1967), *Symphony, Vol. I* and *II* (1969, 1983), a harp concerto (1970), *Celtic Dances* (1972), *Requiescat* (1977), *Melos* (1977), *Reflections on a Theme by Tomkins* (1981), a violin concerto (1989), and other orchestral music; *Lux aeterna* (soloists, boys' choir, chorus, large orchestra, 1987); *Three Medieval Lyrics* (chorus, 1966); *Eight Shakespeare Songs* (1978); *Songs of William Blake* (1979); *Let the People Praise Thee O God* for the marriage of the Prince and Princess of Wales (1981); divertimento for flute, oboe, and piano (1964); Wind Quintet (1963); 3 string quartets (1967, 1981, 1986); 2 violin sonatas (1961, 1984); incidental music; and scores for film and television.

Bibl.: Malcolm Boyd, *William Mathias* (Cardiff, 1974).

Mathis, Johnny [John Royce] (b. San Francisco, 30 Sept. 1935). Popular singer. He began singing in nightclubs in San Francisco and New York; in the mid-

1950s he was one of the few Tin Pan Alley–oriented artists to compete successfully with rock-and-roll. Hits included "It's Not for Me To Say" (1957) and "What Will Many Say" (1963); his most popular later recording was a duet with Deniece Williams, "Too Much, Too Little, Too Late" (1978).

Matsudaira, Yoriaki (b. Tokyo, 27 Mar. 1931). Composer. Son of Yoritsune Matsudaira. Studied science at Tokyo Metropolitan Univ. (1948–57); self-taught as a composer. Taught physics and biology at Rikkyō in Tokyo. He pursued composition independently and formed the composing collective Group 20.5. His music uses both traditional Japanese music and contemporary Western music as sources. Most of his music is for chamber ensemble, though he composed an opera (*Sara,* 1960). Also made use of electronic devices (*Alternation,* jazz ensemble, ring modulator, 1967; *Gradation,* violin, viola, oscillator, 1971; *Shift,* tape, dancer, 1976).

Matsudaira, Yoritsune (b. Tokyo, 5 May 1907). Composer. Studied composition privately with Kōsuke Komatsu while studying French literature at Keiō Univ. Also studied composition with Alexander Tcherepnin. He was influenced by early 20th-century French composers and espoused neoclassicism. He became a director of the Nihon Gendai Sakkyokuka Renmei (later the Japanese Society for Contemporary Music) and, after World War II, developed use of twelve-tone technique and total serialism. Throughout his career he pursued his interest in piano and in gagaku. In 1952 he won a prize at an ISCM festival with a piece that incorporated twelve-tone and gagaku influences (*Theme and Variations,* piano, orchestra, 1951). His music is characterized by careful use of woodwind and percussion timbres (*Music for 17 Performers: Tōei [Projection] Henkei [Metamorphosis],* flute, oboe, clarinet, harp, piano, vibraphone, xylophone, 10 percussionists, 1967). Improvisation as a structural as well as an ornamental device is also drawn from Japanese musical traditions. He wrote principally orchestral and chamber instrumental music (*Rhapsody on a Gagaku Theme,* 1983). Vocal works include *Kashin* (female voices, orchestra, 1969) and works for high solo voice and instrumental accompaniment.

Matsumura, Teizō (b. Kyoto, 15 Jan. 1929). Composer. Although he never formally enrolled in a conservatory, in 1949 he studied composition with Kiyose and subsequently worked with Ifukube and Ikenouchi. He taught at the Tokyo Institute Geijutsu Daigaku. Recognition came in 1955 when his work *Josō to Kyōsōteki areguro* won first prize at the National Music Competition. His music is influenced by French composers and uses typically Western ensembles but frequently draws on traditional Japanese culture (*Sorei kitō* [Totem Ritual], orchestra, 1969) and music (*Bonnō no fue* [Flute of Evil Passions], poetic drama in music, orchestra, Japanese flutes, 1966). Other works include *Pneuma* (strings, 1987), a piano trio (1987), *Offrande orchestrale* (1989).

Matsushita, Shin-ichi (b. Osaka, 1 Oct. 1922). Composer. Studied mathematics and music at Kyushu Univ. in Fukuoka. In 1958 he began work in an electronic music studio in Osaka. He taught mathematics and music at the Univ. of Osaka City and at Nara Women's Univ.; member of the Japan Federation of Composers and of the Institute for Music of the 20th Century. In 1965 he studied in Germany and in an electronic music studio in Sweden. His music draws on international rather than traditional Japanese styles, and frequently calls for chamber ensemble utilizing piano and percussion as well as winds and strings (*Correlazioni per 3 Gruppi,* flute, clarinet, alto sax, bass clarinet, violin, viola, cello, bass, piano, claviolini, percussion, 1958). It occasionally uses electronic media (*Musique pour soprano et ensemble de chambre,* soprano solo or ondes martenot, piano, percussion, string quartet, 1962–63). Works also include compositions for keyboard (*Konzentration for Organ,* 1973).

Mattei, Stanislao (b. Bologna, 10 Feb. 1750; d. there, 12 May 1825). Composer and theorist. In 1765 he entered the Franciscan monastery in Bologna; by 1770 he was a pupil of Padre Martini, with whom he remained a close friend and colleague. When Martini died in 1784 Mattei succeeded him as *maestro di cappella* of the Church of S. Francesco, becoming *maestro di cappella* of S. Petronio in 1789. In 1804 he helped found the Liceo filarmonico, where his pupils included Rossini and Donizetti. He composed sacred works, some 60 symphonies, and chamber works; he also authored *Practica d'accompagnamento sopra bassi numerati* (Bologna, ca. 1825).

Matteis, Nicola (b. Naples; d. London?, ca. 1707). Composer. Arrived in England sometime after 1670; his skills as a violinist were praised by Evelyn, North, and Burney, though he never entered royal service. His compositions include 4 books of *Ayrs* (dance suites) for violin (London, 1685; facs., 1966), notable for their careful bowing indications and virtuoso devices; the prefaces to these volumes are a valuable source of information about performance practice. His son, also named Nicola (b. 1670s?; d. 1749?), gave Burney violin and French lessons.

Matteo da Perugia [Matheus de Perusio] (d. in or before Jan. 1418). Composer. A singer at Milan Cathedral, 1402–7 and 1414–16, at first under the patronage of Archbishop Pietro Filargo (later Pope Alexander V), and at the papal court at Bologna (1409–1414). Most of his music is known from unique copies in the Modena Codex (early 15th century). Among the works surely or probably by him are a few Mass movements and motets, over 20 French songs (most in the *formes fixes*), 2 Italian *ballate,* and about 8 single voices for preexisting pieces. These works, the majority in a French style, vary widely in complexity, ranging from extreme examples of the *ars subtilior* (e.g., the ballade "Le greygnour bien") to pieces in much simpler idioms.

Bibl.: Fabio Fano, ed., *La capella musicale del Duomo di Milano,* vol. 1, *Le origini e il primo maestro di cappella: Matteo da Perugia* (Milan, 1956). Willi Apel, ed., *French Secular Compositions of the Fourteenth Century, CMM* 53 (1970–72).

Matthay, Tobias (Augustus) (b. London, 19 Feb. 1858; d. High Marley, near Haslemere, 15 Dec. 1945). Pianist, composer, and teacher. He won a Sterndale Bennett Scholarship and enrolled in the Royal Academy of Music in 1871, studying with Bennett, Macfarren, and Arthur Sullivan; appointed subprofessor there (1876) then full professor (1880–1925). After a brief career as a concert pianist, interest in pedagogy led him in 1900 to the founding of his own piano school in London; published a number of didactic books, the most famous being *The Act of Touch in All Its Diversity* (London, 1903). Matthay's compositions include much piano music.

Mattheson, Johann (b. Hamburg, 28 Sept. 1681; d. there, 17 Apr. 1764). Composer, theorist, and lexicographer. He received a broad liberal arts education at the Johanneum, studying English, French, and Italian and receiving general music instruction from the cantor Joachim Gerstenbüttel. At 6 he took private lessons in keyboard instruments and composition from J. N. Hanff as well as singing and violin lessons from a local musician. By the age of 9 he was a prodigy, singing and playing organ in Hamburg churches as well as performing in the chorus of the Hamburg opera. After graduating from the Johanneum in 1693, he served as a page at the court of Graf von Güldenlöw, then made his solo debut with the Hamburg opera in 1696 in female roles. After his voice changed, he sang tenor for the opera in addition to conducting rehearsals and composing operas (1697–1705). He met Handel in 1703 and the two became friends, journeying together to Lübeck that year to apply for the organist post at the Marienkirche vacated by Buxtehude's retirement; both turned down the position. The two remained close despite a violent argument in 1704 that led to a duel.

In 1704 Mattheson became the tutor of Cyrill Wich, son of the British envoy to Hamburg, Sir John Wich. Sir John appointed Mattheson his personal secretary in 1706, a position of considerable status and salary that he held for most of his life, serving Cyrill when he succeeded his father in 1715. Also in 1715 Mattheson became music director of the Hamburg Cathedral, for which he composed much sacred music, but he gave up the position in 1728 because of deafness. In 1719 he was named Kapellmeister to the Duke of Holstein, later becoming legation secretary (1741) and counsel (1744) to the duke.

Mattheson was a prolific composer up to the 1730s, especially of sacred music and opera, but much of his music has been missing since World War II. His literary writings constitute a large body of work (all published in Hamburg) that comments on nearly every aspect of music making in his day. Of particular interest is *Der vollkommene Capellmeister* (1739; facs., Kassel, 1954; trans. Eng., 1981), containing a wealth of information for the Kapellmeister-in-training, including an attempt to systematize the doctrines of rhetoric as they apply to music. Of great historical importance is *Grundlage einer Ehren-Pforte* (1740; facs., Kassel, 1969), a biographical lexicon of 149 musicians; many of the entries were based on information provided by the subjects themselves. Other important writings include *Das neu-eröffnete Orchestre* (1713); the first German music periodical, *Critica musica* (1722–25); *Der musicalische Patriot* (1728); *Grosse General-Bass-Schule* (1731; facs., Hildesheim, 1968).

Bibl.: Beekman Cox Cannon, *Johann Mattheson, Spectator in Music* (New Haven, 1947; R: 1968). Hans Lenneberg, "Johann Mattheson on Affect and Rhetoric in Music," *JMT* 2 (1958): 47–84, 193–236. *New Mattheson Studies,* ed. George J. Buelow and Hans Joachim Marx (Cambridge, 1983).

Matthews, Colin (b. London, 13 Feb. 1946). Composer. Younger brother of David Matthews. He studied classics at the Univ. of Nottingham, graduating in 1967. He earned an M.Ph. in composition in 1971 and a D.Ph. in 1977 at the Univ. of Sussex. Studied and edited the work of Mahler and Holst, both of whom were influences on his music, as were Reich and Ligeti. With Deryck Cooke he edited *A Performing Version of the Draft of the 10th Symphony* (ca. 1966) and, with Imogen Holst, the *Collected Facsimile Edition* of Holst's works (1974–83). His early music was tonal and lyrical, in a Romantic style, with frequent changes of meter and tempo. More recently he has explored increasing chromaticism, large-scale heterophony, and radical textural changes. Works include orchestral pieces (Sonata no. 5, 1977–81; Divertimento for Double String Orchestra, 1983; *Variation on "Sumer Is Icumen In,"* 1987; *Cortège,* 1988), concertos (cello, 1983–84), and piano works (*Berceuse and Sarabande,* 1978–79; *11 Studies in Velocity,* 1987).

Matthews, David (John) (b. London, 9 Mar. 1943). Composer. Brother of Colin Matthews. He received a B.A. in classics at Nottingham Univ. and studied composition privately with Milner. Edited and wrote about the music of Mahler (*Gustav Mahler: The Early Years,* with Donald Mitchell, 1980) and Tippett (*Michael Tippett,* 1980). Mahler and Tippett both heavily influenced Matthews. He has composed much orchestral music, including *Little Concerto* (1974), 3 symphonies (1975, 1979, 1985), a violin concerto (1982), and *Chiaroscuro* (1990). His chamber music includes 5 string quartets, *Introit* (2 trumpets, strings, 1981), 5 concertinos for wind quintet (1990), and other works. He has also written a variety of vocal works.

Matton, Roger (b. Granby, Quebec, 18 May 1929). Composer and ethnomusicologist. He studied at the Montreal Conservatory with Champagne (1943–48) and in Paris with Boulanger, Messiaen, and Vaurabourg-Honegger. He studied archival procedures for folklore under Marius Barbeau at the National Museum of Canada; wrote background scores for CBC; and from 1956 to 1976 was folklore archivist at Laval Univ., where he also taught composition and ethnomusicology. He transcribed several volumes of Acadian folk songs. His compositions are influenced by his interests in folk music and jazz; many use large percussion forces, and most are for large instrumental groups. Works include *Mouvement symphonique* (commissioned by the Montreal Symphony, 1962) and other orchestral music; chamber and keyboard works.

Maturana, Eduardo (b. Valparaiso, Chile, 14 Apr. 1920). Composer. Studied composition with Allende and viola with Mutschler at the National Conservatory, Santiago (1939–44). Formed the ensemble Agrupación tonus in 1954; became a violist in the Santiago Municipal Philharmonic in 1958, serving as board president, 1966–68. Active in the musicians' union, the Chamber Opera, and the National Association of Chilean Composers. His music uses serial, aleatory, and electronic techniques. Works include the opera *Regreso a la muerte* (1963); *Concertante* (horn and orchestra, 1967), *Elegías* (cello and orchestra, 1970), *Responso para el Ché Guevara* (tape and orchestra, 1968), and other symphonic pieces; chamber compositions; piano pieces; and vocal music for various forces.

Matzenauer, Margarete (b. Temesvár [Timişoara], 1 June 1881; d. Van Nuys, Calif., 19 May 1963). Soprano and contralto. Studied voice in Graz with Georgine von Januschowsky; in Berlin with Antonie Mielke and Franz Emmrich. Sang at the Strasbourg Civic Theater, 1901–4; debut as Puck *(Oberon).* While a member of the Munich Court Opera, 1904–11, was guest artist at theaters in Vienna, Berlin, London, and Paris. Member of the New York Metropolitan Opera, 1911–30; debut with Caruso and Destinn as Amneris *(Aida).* During her last decade at the Met she sang mezzo roles with increasing frequency. Created Eboli in the New York premiere of Verdi's *Don Carlos* (1920), the Sextoness in the U.S. premiere of *Jenůfa* (1924). From 1930 she taught voice in New York, later in California.

Mauceri, John (b. New York, 12 Sept. 1945). Conductor. He studied at Yale (B.A. 1967; M.Phil., 1972), was appointed associate professor there in 1968, and became conductor of the Yale Symphony (1968–74). Widely respected as an opera conductor, he appeared at the Metropolitan, the New York City Opera, and the San Francisco Opera. Mauceri served as music director for the production of Bernstein's *Candide* in 1974 and won a Tony Award for producing (with Roger Stevens) a revival of the musical comedy *On Your Toes* (1982). He was named consultant for music theater at the Kennedy Center (1981) and served as music director of the Washington Opera (1980–82). Music director of the American Symphony, 1984–87; of the Scottish Opera from 1987; of the Hollywood Bowl from 1990.

Mauduit, Jacques (b. Paris, 16 Sept. 1557; d. there, 21 Aug. 1627). Composer. From shortly after 1581 Baïf's Académie de poésie et de musique was the focus of his musical activities. His compositions, including settings of some of Baïf's poems, follow strictly the principles of *musique mesurée.* He often led large forces of both voices and instruments, frequently disposed in the most modern Italian manner. The majority of his large output of sacred and secular vocal and instrumental music is lost. Extant works, some printed by Mersenne, include 1 book of *Chansonettes mesurées* (1586; ed. *MMRF* 10 [1899; R: 1952]); 3 airs for voice and lute; *Psaumes mesurées* and other short sacred pieces, and a section of a Requiem.

Maurel, Victor (b. Marseilles, 17 June 1848; d. New York, 22 Oct. 1923). Tenor. From age 17 studied two years at the Marseilles Conservatory, then at the Paris Conservatory until 1868; opera debut, Marseilles, 1867. He sang at the Paris Opéra, 1868, 1879–94; from 1869 he established himself in Italian houses, then at Covent Garden (1873–79, 1891–95, 1904), in the U.S. (1873–74), and all over Europe. He directed the dying Théâtre-Italien in Paris in 1883–85, with disastrous financial results. Beloved by Verdi, he created the revised Simon Boccanegra (La Scala, 1881), Iago (La Scala, 1887; his Metropolitan debut role, 1894), Falstaff (La Scala, 1893). Discoverer of Leoncavallo, he created Tonio in *I pagliacci* (1892), but seldom sang it after. He retired in 1905; then a singing teacher in Paris and (from 1909) New York. Memoirs: *Dix ans de carrière* (Paris, 1897; R: 1977).

Maurício (Nunes Garcia), José (b. Rio de Janeiro, 20 Sept. 1767; d. there, 18 Apr. 1830). Composer. In 1791 he joined the Brotherhood of São Pedro dos clérigos, and the following year he was ordained. He became *mestre de capela* at the cathedral in Rio de Janeiro in 1798, where he remained for nearly three decades, steadily building his fame and reputation. When Dom João VI arrived in 1808, Maurício became organist and *mestre* for the royal chapel. He composed more than 200 sacred works (Masses, Requiems, hymns, motets, antiphons), as well as a *drama heróico, Ulissea* (1809); also miscellaneous orchestral works.

Bibl.: Cleofe Person de Mattos, *Catálogo temático das obras do Padre José Maurício Nunes Garcia* (Rio de Janeiro, 1970).

Maw, (John) Nicholas (b. Grantham, 5 Nov. 1935). Composer. From 1955 to 1958 he studied at the Royal Academy of Music, composition with Berkeley and harmony and counterpoint with Steinitz. He played piano and clarinet. With a scholarship from the French government and the Lili Boulanger prize, he studied composition in Paris with Nadia Boulanger and Deutsch. From 1966 to 1970 served as resident composer at Trinity College, Cambridge; in 1972 was visiting lecturer in composition at Exeter Univ.

Maw developed an individual musical language that integrated serialism and tonal centrism in various ways and that have been characterized as expressionistic. He composed 2 operas, *One Man Show* (1964) and *The Rising of the Moon* (1970), both of which comment on social and political themes. His orchestral works include Sonata for String Orchestra and 2 Horns (1967), *Oddyssey* (1987), *The World in the Evening* (1988), and *Shahnama* (1992). His vocal works include *Nocturne* (mezzo-soprano and chamber orchestra, 1958), *Scenes and Arias* (3 women's voices and orchestra, 1962), and works for various combinations of voices a cappella. Chamber music includes 3 string quartets (1965, 1982, 1993–94), *Life Studies* (15 solo strings, 1973), and a quartet for flute and strings (1981).

Maxfield, Richard (Vance) (b. Seattle, 2 Feb. 1927; d. Los Angeles, 27 June 1969). Composer. He studied at the Univ. of California, and at Princeton with Sessions and Babbitt (M.F.A., 1955); then with Dallapiccola and Maderna in Italy (1955–57). He taught at the New School for Social Research (1959–62) and at San Francisco State College; his *Five Movements for Orchestra* (1959) won the Gershwin Prize. Before 1959 he composed several works for traditional instruments (*Structures,* 10 winds, 1954; *Composition,* clarinet and piano, 1956); later works usually involve tape, either alone or with live performers (*Pastoral Symphony,* tape, 1959; *Stacked Deck,* opera, D. Higgins, voices and tape, 1960; *Piano Concert for David Tudor,* piano and tape, 1961).

Maxwell Davies, Peter. See Davies, Peter Maxwell.

Mayer, William (Robert) (b. New York, 18 Nov. 1925). Composer. He studied at Yale and at Mannes College (with Salzer, 1949–52); then with Sessions at Juilliard; studied conducting at Aspen under Solomon. He worked with Composers Recordings, Inc., beginning 1972 (chairman, 1977–81); in 1982 his opera *A Death in the Family* was cited as the outstanding new American opera. Bartók, Barber, Stravinsky, and Jerome Kern have been seen as influential on his style. Works include 4 operas and a ballet; *Octagon* (piano, orchestra, 1971), *Inner and Outer Strings* (string quartet, strings, 1982); *Of Rivers and Tains* (orchestra, 1988); *Passage* (song cycle, mezzo-soprano, flute, harp, 1981); *Good King Wenceslas* (narrator, orchestra, 1994); piano pieces; choral music.

Mayfield, Curtis (b. Chicago, Ill., 3 June 1942). Soul singer, songwriter, and guitarist. In 1956 he formed with Jerry Butler the vocal group The Impressions, and from 1961 to 1970 served as their lead singer and principal songwriter; their recordings included "It's All Right" (1963) and "Keep on Pushing" (1965). He also authored several of Butler's solo hits ("He Will Break Your Heart," 1960) and made recordings as a solo artist ("Freddie's Dead," from the movie *Superfly,* 1972). In 1990 an accident during a concert left Mayfield paralyzed. A tribute album, featuring performances of his compositions by various artists, was issued in 1993.

Maynard, John (b. St. Albans, bapt. 5 Jan. 1577; d. between 1614 and 1633). Composer. From late 1599 until 1601 perhaps a singer (as "Johan Meinert") in the court of King Christian IV of Denmark; from 1600 Commissary of Musters in Ireland; later (by 1611 but after 1607) lutenist at the school of St. Julians (near St. Albans). His one publication, *The XII Wonders of the World* (London, 1611), contains 12 songs, 6 duets for lute and bass viol, and 7 pieces for lyra viol with optional bass viol.

Maynor [Mainor], **Dorothy (Leigh)** (b. Norfolk, Va., 3 Sept. 1910). Soprano. Daughter of a preacher, she sang in church. As a student at the Hampton Institute sang in its choir on a tour of Europe in 1924. An anonymous benefactor facilitated study at the Westminster Choir School in Princeton. This was followed by work with the teachers William Klamroth and John Alan Haughton. Having married a preacher, she led a church choir in Brooklyn from 1936. Her solo debut in 1939 at the Berkshire Festival led to an invitation from Koussevitzky to perform and record Handel and Mozart arias with the Boston Symphony. There followed acclaimed debuts in New York in 1939, and with the Philadelphia Orchestra (singing Debussy's *L'enfant prodigue*). She then embarked on successful tours of North America, Europe, and later South America. From 1945 she was director of Bennett College in Greensboro, N.C. Founding director of the Harlem School of the Arts, 1963.

Mayone [Maione], **Ascanio** (b. Naples, ca. 1565; d. there, 9 Mar. 1627). Composer. Organist (from 1593) and later *maestro di cappella* (from 1595, jointly with Camillo Lambardi) until at least 1621 at the Church of the Annunziata in Naples. Also organist at the Spanish viceregal chapel (second from 1602, first from 1614). His few vocal pieces (madrigals, sacred works) are far outweighed in importance by his innovative compositions for keyboard, which in thematic, textural, rhythmic, motivic, and harmonic devices prefigure the works of Frescobaldi.

Mayr, Richard (b. Henndorf, Austria, 18 Nov. 1877; d. Vienna, 1 Dec. 1935). Bass. Trained his voice while studying medicine at Vienna Univ. Mahler invited him to the Vienna Court Opera in 1902; Mayr remained there until his death, journeying to Munich to sing in the premiere of Mahler's Symphony no. 8, to Salzburg for Mozart roles (Figaro, Leporello, Sarastro) and *La serva padrona,* to the New York Metropolitan Opera in 1927–30 for Pogner *(Meistersinger)* and other German roles, and to Covent Garden in 1924–31. He was the foremost Baron Ochs *(Rosenkavalier)* of his day, creating the role at its Vienna and London premieres (1911, 1913). Also sang in the premiere of Strauss's *Die Frau ohne Schatten* (1919) and the Vienna premiere of *Arabella* (1933).

Mayr [Mayer], **(Johannes) Simon** (b. Mendorf, Bavaria, 14 June 1763; d. Bergamo, 2 Dec. 1845). Composer. His earliest musical education, chiefly in keyboard instruments, was from his father; he was also a chorister at the local church. In 1774 he entered the Jesuit school in Ingolstadt, and in 1781 he began theological studies at the university there. He supported himself through a post as organist at Ingolstadt Cathedral. In 1787 he went to Italy for further study; two years later he began lessons in counterpoint and composition with Carlo Lenzi, *maestro di cappella* at Bergamo Cathedral. Later he also studied with Ferdinando Bertoni in Venice; there he composed his first oratorio, *Jacob a Labano fugiens* (1791), and his first opera, *Saffo o sia I riti d'Apollo Leucadio* (1794). During the next two decades he produced nearly 70 operas for Venice, Milan, Naples, Rome, Vienna, Paris, and many other cities. In 1802 he moved to Bergamo upon being appointed Lenzi's successor; he remained until his death, becoming a central figure in the city's cultural life. He was cofounder of the Scuole caritatevoli di musica (1805) and the Pio istituo musicale (1809), and he established a concert series that introduced the music of Beethoven to Bergamo. After 1817 he composed chiefly sacred music, and by the 1820s he was suffering from an eye disease that eventually led to his blindness.

Among his operas were *La Lodoiska* (Venice, 1796); *Un pazzo ne fa cento* (Venice, 1796); *Ginevra di Scozia* (Trieste, 1801); *I virtuosi* (Venice, 1801); *Ercole in Lidia* (Vienna, 1803); *Amor non ha ritegno* (Milan, 1804); *Zamori, ossia L'eroe dell'Indie* (Piacenza, 1804); *L'amor coniugale* (Padua, 1805); *Palmira, o sia Il trionfo della virtù e dell'amore* (Florence, 1806); *Il sacrifizio d'Ifigenia* (Brescia, 1811); *L'amor figliale* (Venice, 1811); *Elena* (Naples, 1814); *La figlia dell'aria* (Naples, 1817); *Lanassa* (Venice, 1818); *Alfredo il grande* (Rome, 1818). Sacred works: *Tobia, o Tobiae matrimonium* (oratorio, 1794); *Il sacrifizio di Iefte* (oratorio, n.d.); *Samuele* (oratorio, 1821); some 56 cantatas including *Ferramondo* (1810) and *Il sogno di Partenope* (1817); Masses, Requiems, vespers, other sacred works. He also composed 2 symphonies (in C and F); *Sinfonia piccola* in D; piano concertos; chamber music (including a harp suite); piano works. He authored a number of historical and theoretical treatises, including *Breve notizie storiche della vita e delle opere di G. Haydn* (Bergamo, 1809).

Bibl.: Arrigo Gazzaniga, *Il fondo musicale Mayr della Biblioteca civica di Bergamo* (Bergamo, 1963). James Freeman, "Johannes Simon Mayr and His *Ifigenia in Aulide*," *MQ* 57 (1971): 187–210. John Allitt, *J. S. Mayr: Father of 19th-Century Italian Music* (Longmead, 1989). Giovanni Simone Mayr, *Passi scelti dallo Zibaldone e altri scritti* (Bergamo, 1993).

Mayuzumi, Toshirō (b. Yokohama, 20 Feb. 1929). Composer. From 1945 to 1951 he studied composition with Ikenouchi and Ifukube at the National Univ. of Fine Arts and Music in Tokyo. He then studied with Aubin at the Paris Conservatory, 1951–52. There he came into contact with the serialism of Messiaen and Boulez and with *musique concrète.* In Tokyo he cofounded one of the most important new music groups of the 1950s, the Saunin no Kai (Group of Three). He also formed Ars Nova Japonica and worked extensively with electronic music. From his earliest works he drew on many sources, including jazz, Middle Eastern music, and Western new music trends. He was at the forefront of exploration with electronic media in Japan; *Shūsaku I* (Study I, 1955) was the first piece to use synthetic electronic music. He was the first Japanese composer to write for prepared piano (*Piece for Prepared Piano and String Quartet,* 1957). Mayuzumi continued to develop a fairly eclectic style through the integration of aleatoric devices, serialism, and electronic media. He experimented with timbres, including electronically generated or altered sounds, as well as the timbres of traditional instruments. From the late 1950s he developed interests in the music and philosophy of Buddhism (*Nehan Kōkyōkyoku* [Nirvana Symphony], 1958) and in traditional Japanese music (*Shōwa Tenpuōraku,* gagaku ensemble, 1970). His music includes an opera (*Kinkakuji* [The Golden Pavilion], 1976); musicals; symphonic works (*Essay for String Orchestra,* 1963; *Perpetuum mobile,* 1989); chamber music; and music for theater productions and films (*Tokyo Olympic,* 1964).

Mazas, Jacques Féréol (b. Lavaur?, 23 Sept. 1782; d. Bordeaux, 25 or 26 Aug. 1849). Violinist. Student of Baillot, 1802–5, at the Paris Conservatory (first prize, violin, 1805). As a concert soloist he toured Europe (1811–12, Spain; 1814, England, Low Countries; 1822–27, Italy, Germany, Russia). In 1829 he settled in Paris but was not successful there as a soloist; 1831, first violin in the orchestra of the Théâtre du Palais Royal; then taught and directed concerts at Orléans and (1837–41) Cambrai. He published much-used violin methods and etudes, especially *Études mélodiques et progressives* op. 36.

Mazzinghi, Joseph (b. London, 25 Dec. 1765; d. Downside, Bath, 15 Jan. 1844). Composer and pianist. His father was a Corsican merchant who lived in London. As a boy Joseph studied clavier with J. C. Bach, and at age 10 he succeeded his father as organist of the Portuguese chapel in London. Later he studied with Antonio Sacchini and Pasquale Anfossi. In 1786 he was appointed director of the King's Theatre, and during the next two decades he composed dramatic works and "pantomime-ballets." He became a tutor to the Princess of Wales, composing some 75 clavier sonatas. Among his stage works are *A Day in Turkey* (Covent Garden, 1795); *Ramah Droog* (in collaboration with William Reeve, 1798); and *Paul and Virginia* (also with Reeve, 1800); he also composed more than 20 ballets, as well as overtures and chamber works.

Mazzocchi, Domenico (b. Veja, near Cività Castellana, bapt. 8 Nov. 1592; d. Rome, 21 Jan. 1665). Composer. He studied at the seminary at Cività Castellana, was ordained in March 1619, and made a Doctor of Laws the same year or slightly earlier. In 1621 he entered the service of Cardinal Ippolito Aldobrandini as a musician, beginning a long association with that family that included works written for the cardinal's brother and niece. In addition to lifelong financial support from the cardinal, Mazzocchi received a benefice from both Pope Urban VIII (Maffeo Barberini) and his successor, Innocent X (Giambattista Pamfili). His output consists primarily of vocal music, both sacred and secular; one opera survives, *La catena d'Adone* (Rome, 1626; facs., Bologna, 1969). In his *Madrigali* (Rome, 1638) he uses the modern-day symbols for crescendo, decrescendo, piano, forte, and trill, all carefully explained in the preface.

Bibl.: Wolfgang Witzenmann, *Domenico Mazzocchi, 1592–1665: Documente und Interpretationen* (Cologne, 1970).

Mazzocchi, Virgilio (b. Cività Castellana, bapt. 22 July 1597; d. there, 3 Oct. 1646). Composer. He studied music in Rome with his brother Domenico, was appointed *maestro di cappella* at the Chiesa del Gesù; served in the same capacity at St. John Lateran (1628–29) and the Cappella Giulia at St. Peter's (1629–46). Mazzocchi composed both sacred and secular vocal music, including motets, madrigals, and oratorios; he collaborated with Marazzoli on the comic opera *Chi soffre speri* (1639; facs., New York, 1982), an important early example of the genre.

Mazzucato, Alberto (b. Udine, 28 July 1813; d. Milan, 31 Dec. 1877). Teacher and composer. Studied in Padua (mathematics, then music); 1834–47, composed several operas with varying success, especially *Esmeralda* (Mantua, 1838). From 1839 he taught singing to women at the Milan Conservatory; 1851, professor of composition; from 1852, also taught music history and aesthetics; 1857, orchestration; 1872–77, director of the conservatory. He was editor of Ricordi's *Gazzetta musicale di Milano* and wrote for various periodicals; 1854–55, director of La Scala; 1858–68, *maestro concertatore* there.

Meale, Richard (Graham) (b. Sydney, 23 Aug. 1932). Composer. He studied piano, harp, and clarinet at the New South Wales Conservatorium from 1947 to 1955, exploring composition on his own. From 1955 he worked for a phonograph company, working concurrently as a pianist and a conductor of 20th-century works. In 1960 he received a Ford Foundation Grant to take courses in Asian music at UCLA. He subsequently spent time in Spain, exploring the music of Lorca. He returned to Sydney and from 1962 to 1969 was program planner for the orchestral concerts of ABC. He became a lecturer in composition at the Univ. of Adelaide and continued to work with contemporary music in both Adelaide and Sydney.

He composed 19 works before 1959, later withdrawn. Around 1960 he developed an interest in the serialism of Messiaen and Boulez. Simultaneously he continued to find inspiration in Spanish literature (*Homage to García Lorca,* 1962–63). His studies in ethnomusicology, and especially the music of Japan, resulted in a series of works (*Images,* 1965) that relate to the Nagauta music drama. Meale was similarly interested in French images, including medieval mysticism, and used Rimbaud as inspiration for his orchestral work *Incredible Floridas* (1971). After the early 1970s his works became more abstract and less clearly related to literary text. His opera *Voss* was first performed in 1986.

Medek, Tilo (b. Jena, 22 Jan. 1940). Composer. He studied musicology and composition (with Wagner-Régeny) at the Univ. of Berlin (1959–67). In 1967 he won the Gaudeamus Prize for *Todesfuge* (soprano, 4 choruses). In many works he quotes and transforms existing music (*Sensible Variationen um ein Schubert-thema,* flute, violin, and cello, 1973). He has written stage works, including *Katharina Blum* (H. Böll, 1985); orchestral music (*Rheinische Sinfonie,* 1986) and concertos for piano (1987), cello (1978, 1984), organ (1979, 1983), and violin (1980); 3 wind quintets and other chamber music; pieces for marimba, guitar, piano, and organ; choral music and songs.

Mediņš, Jānis (b. Riga, 9 Oct. 1890, d. Stockholm, 4 Mar. 1966). Composer. Studied piano, violin, and cello at the First Riga Musical Institute through 1909. From 1913 to 1915 he was a violist and a conductor at the Riga Opera House. He spent time in St. Petersburg working with a piano firm and as a military bandmaster. From 1920 until 1928 he served as conductor of the Latvian National Opera and was head conductor of the Latvian Radio Symphony, 1928–44. He lived in Germany from 1944 to 1948 and in Stockholm after 1948. His musical style was conservative and within the nationalistic tradition. He wrote much dramatic music (5 operas, 1 ballet), orchestral music (*Imanta,* symphonic sketch, 1923), and vocal music.

Medtner, Nicolai. See Metner, Nikolay.

Méfano, Paul (b. Basra, Iraq, 6 Mar. 1937). Composer. He studied in Paris at the École normale and the Conservatory (1960–64) with Dandelot, Messiaen, and Milhaud; in Basel with Boulez, Stockhausen, and Pousseur. In 1971 he was awarded the Unesco Prize and in 1972 founded the Collectif musical international de Champigny 2E2M, which he directed. His early works reflect his study with Boulez; he often combines electronic music and live performers. Works include *À B. Maderna* (12 strings and tape, 1970); *Fragment* (chamber orchestra, 1975); *Micromégas* (solo voices, speakers, chorus, brass, and tape, 1979); and *Traits suspendus* (bass flute, 1980).

Mehta, Zubin (b. Bombay, 29 Apr. 1936). Conductor. Son of the violinist and conductor Mehli Mehta (b. Bombay, 25 Sept. 1908), who founded the Bombay Symphony (1935) but ultimately settled in the U.S. Studied piano and violin as a child and entered the Vienna Academy, where he took conducting with Hans

Zubin Mehta, 1969.

Swarowsky and played double bass. In 1958 he won an international conducting competition organized by the Royal Liverpool Philharmonic and served as musical assistant there for a year, then guest-conducted the Vienna Philharmonic and the Montreal and Los Angeles orchestras. He was appointed music director of the Montreal Symphony (1960–67) and the Los Angeles Philharmonic (1962–78), thus serving in two major conducting posts simultaneously and becoming the youngest to hold such a position with a leading American orchestra. Mehta made his Metropolitan Opera debut in 1965 *(Aïda)* and at Covent Garden in 1977 *(Otello),* and took the Israel Philharmonic on a number of tours of Europe, North and South America, and Australia; he became chief musical adviser to the Israel Philharmonic in 1969 and music director for life in 1981. He served as music director of the Hollywood Bowl Summer Festival (1970–78), and in 1978 succeeded Boulez as music director of the New York Philharmonic, serving until 1991.

Méhul, Étienne-Nicolas (b. Givet, 22 June 1763; d. Paris, 18 Oct. 1817). Composer. His father was the housemaster to the Count of Montmorency. Nicolas received his first instruction in music from the organist at the convent in Givet; allegedly at age 10 he began serving as organist in its chapel. From 1775 he studied with the convent's newly appointed German music director, Wilhelm Hanser. Around 1778 he traveled to Paris to begin study with Jean-Frédéric Edelmann; under the latter's tutelage he presented *Ode sacrée* at the Concert spirituel in 1782, which was well received, and he published a set of keyboard sonatas in 1783. He composed his first opera, *Cora,* by 1785, but it was not performed at the Opéra until 1791, when it was a failure. His first work for the Comédie-Italienne was a success: performances of *Euphrosine* (1790; later *Euphrosine et Coradin*) continued to appear well into the next century, in Paris and abroad. It initiated a series of collaborations with the librettist François-Benoît Hoffman; others included *Stratonice* (1792); *Le jeune sage et le vieux fou* (1793); *Adrien* (1799); *Epicure* (1800); and *Le trésor supposé* (1802). In 1793 Méhul joined the faculty of the newly formed Institut national de musique; two years later when the Paris Conservatory was formed he was made one of its inspectors. About this time he began composing republican songs and hymns; his first was *Hymne à la raison,* first performed in 1793. He received a pension in 1794 from the Comédie-Italienne. His career as a composer of comic operas culminated in *Joseph* (1807), one of the most popular works of the period. It was followed by five first-rate symphonies composed during the next three years. His last successful opera was *La journée aux aventures,* performed at the Opéra-comique in 1816.

Méhul composed prolifically. Other stage works (all performed first in Paris) included *Le congrès des rois* (1794); *Mélidore et Phrosine* (1794); *La prise du pont de Lodi* (1797); *Epicure* (1800); *Héléna* (1803); *Le baiser et la quittance, ou Une aventure de garnison* (1803); *L'heureux malgré lui* (1803); *Les deux aveugles de Tolède* (1806); *Uthal* (1806); *Gabrielle d'Estrées, ou Les amours d'Henri IV* (1806); *Les amazones* (1811); *L'oriflamme* (1814); and *Valentine de Milan* (1822). He also composed many choral works, including a Mass in A♭ (ca. 1804); *Chant national du 14 juillet 1800,* soloists, triple chorus, and triple instrumental ensemble (1800); "Napoleonic" cantatas, including *O doux printemps* (1810); and *Du trône où jusq'à Toi* (1810). Among his instrumental works are symphonies (no. 1 in G minor, 1809; no. 2 in C, 1809; no. 3 in C, 1809?; no. 4 in E, 1810?; no. 5 in A, incomplete; also 2 earlier unnumbered symphonies); Overture in F, wind ensemble (1793); chamber and keyboard music. His operas such as *Ariodant* and *Joseph* point toward early Romantic opera, while his symphonic technique finds echoes in the music of Beethoven and Mendelssohn, both of whom admired Méhul's music.

Bibl.: Pierre Ange Vieillard, *Méhul, sa vie et ses oeuvres* (Paris, 1859). Arthur Pougin, *Méhul: Sa vie, son génie, son caractère* (Paris, 1889; 2nd ed., 1893). Constant Pierre, *Les hymnes et chansons de la Révolution* (Paris, 1904). René Brancour, *Méhul* (Paris, 1912). Heinrich Strobel, "Die Opern von E. N. Méhul," *Zeitschrift für Musikwissenschaft* 6 (1923–24): 362–402. Alexander L. Ringer, "A French Symphonist at the Time of Beethoven: Étienne Nicolas Méhul," *MQ* 37 (1951): 543–65. David Charlton, "Motive and Motif: Méhul before 1791," *ML* 57 (1976): 362–69. M. Elizabeth C. Bartlet, *Étienne Nicolas Méhul and Opera: Source and Archival Studies of Lyric Theatre during the French Revolution, Consulate, and Empire* (Saarbrücken, 1992). Malcolm Boyd, ed., *Music and the French Revolution* (Cambridge, 1992).

Mei, Girolamo (b. Florence, 27 May 1519; d. Rome, July 1594). Writer. Studied ancient Greek music, producing treatises and letters of great influence on the early development of monody and opera. The letters have been edited by Claude V. Palisca as *Girolamo Mei (1519–1594): Letters on Ancient and Modern Music to Vincenzo Galilei and Giovanni Bardi, MSD* 3 (1960; 2nd ed. 1977). Piero Vettori taught him philosophy, Greek, and Latin and allowed him to assist in the editing of classical texts. After leaving Florence he lived in France, Padua, and Rome (from 1559). Concentrated work on Greek music began in 1561. His *De modis musicis antiquorum libri IV* (1567–73) defines the Greek *tonoi,* differentiating them from the church modes, and explains the uses of music in Greek society and Greek drama. Among his other writings are *Discorso sopra la musica antica e moderna* (Venice, 1602; facs. *BMB* ser. 2, 35 [1968]).

Meineke, Christopher (b. Germany, 1782; d. Baltimore, 6 Nov. 1850). Composer. Probably a son of the organist and composer Karl Meineke of Oldenburg; 1800, emigrated to Baltimore, where he worked as an organist; 1817–19 in Vienna. He published *A New Instruction for the Piano/Forte* (Philadelphia, 1823); songs, especially *The Bird at Sea* (1834?); piano variations, dances, marches; a collection of hymns and Psalms, *Music for Church* (Baltimore, 1844), and other church music.

Melartin, Erkki Gustaf (b. Käkisälmi, 7 Feb. 1875, d. Pukinmäki, 14 Feb. 1937). Composer. He studied at the Helsinki Music Institute with Wegelius from 1892 to 1899 and in Vienna with Fuchs from 1899 until 1901. He pursued his interest in art history while traveling across Europe. In 1898 and from 1901 through 1907 he taught theory at the Helsinki Conservatory and, after Wegelius left, served as its director, 1911–36. His musical style was conservative and drew on folk repertory in the nationalist tradition of Sibelius. He wrote an opera and ballet, but concentrated more on orchestral works, including 8 symphonies (1902–24, 2 incomplete), 3 symphonic poems, a violin concerto, and incidental music. He also wrote prolifically for solo piano (over 350 pieces) and for solo voice (over 300 songs).

Melba, Nellie [Mitchell, Helen Porter] (b. Richmond, near Melbourne, 19 May 1861; d. Sydney, 23 Feb. 1931). Soprano. Studied in 1886 in Paris with Marchesi; opera debut, 1887, in Brussels as Gilda; then was heard in most of the major houses: Covent Garden (1888), Paris Opéra (1889), Monte Carlo (1890), St. Petersburg (1890), in Italy (1892–93), in Scandinavia (1893), and at the Metropolitan Opera (1893), becoming one of the great operatic celebrities from the 1890s to World War I, especially in England and the U.S. From 1902 she sang principally at Covent Garden with occasional seasons in New York; toured Australia with her own company in 1902 and 1911; from 1915 taught at the Melbourne Conservatory. In 1926, celebrated Covent Garden farewell (which was recorded); 1928, Australian farewell concerts. Her voice was agile and brilliant, but also rich and powerful; generally considered a poor actress, she was also judged by her detractors to project a cold perfection; her repertory, which was not large, ranged from *Lucia, Traviata, Rigoletto, Faust,* and *Hamlet,* mainstays of her early career, to *Bohème,* perhaps her favorite later role (of which she sang the London and New York premieres), and included the lighter Wagner roles. Her one attempt to sing Brunnhilde in *Siegfried* was a celebrated disaster, requiring her to return to Marchesi to repair the damage. Published memoirs: *Melodies and Memories* (London, 1925; R. 1970, 1980).

Bibl.: J. A. Hetherington, *Melba: A Biography* (New York, 1968). W. R. Moran, ed., *Nellie Melba: A Contemporary Review* (Westport, Conn., 1984).

Melchior, Lauritz [Hommel, Lebrecht] (b. Copenhagen, 20 Mar. 1890; d. Santa Monica, 18 Mar. 1973). Tenor. Studied with Paul Bang at the Royal Opera School, Copenhagen, making his Royal Opera debut in 1913 in *Pagliacci* (as a baritone); after studies with Vilhelm Herold revealed his true vocal nature, he made a second debut (as a tenor) at the same theater in 1918 singing the title role in *Tannhäuser.* Following a further period of study with Beigel, Grenzebach, and Anna Bahr-Mildenburg he made his Covent Garden debut in 1924 as Siegmund; later the same year sang Siegmund and Parsifal at Bayreuth, where he performed regularly until 1931. A mainstay of the Wagnerian repertory at Covent Garden (1926–39), Melchior made his Metropolitan debut in 1926 (as Tannhäuser), and remained with the house until 1950; his status as the outstanding Wagnerian tenor of his day is confirmed by his numerous recordings. In the 1940s and 1950s he appeared in films and operetta. He became a U.S. citizen in 1947.

Melkus, Eduard (b. Baden, near Vienna, 1 Sept. 1928). Violinist. He studied violin with Ernst Moravec (1943–53) and musicology at the Univ. of Vienna with Erich Schenk (1951–53); further violin studies with Firmin Touche, Peter Rybar, and Alexander Schaichet. He was appointed professor of violin and viola at the Vienna Hochschule für Musik in 1958, and in 1965 founded the Vienna Capella Academica, an ensemble whose goal was to perform on instruments dating from the 18th century. He recorded a number of 18th-century sonatas and some dance music.

Mellers, Wilfred (Howard) (b. Leamington, 26 Apr. 1914). Composer and writer. From 1933 to 1938 he studied music and English at Leamington College and at Cambridge Univ., concurrently pursuing composition with Wellesz and Rubbra. He was on the faculty at Dartington Hall (1938–40), at Downing College, Cambridge (1945–48), and at Birmingham Univ. (1948–59). Andrew Mellon Professor of Music at the Univ. of Pittsburgh from 1960 until 1963, when he received a D.M. from Birmingham Univ.; professor of music at the Univ. of York, 1964. The author of numerous books and articles, throughout his career he explored the relationship between music and its social background and the relationship between music and poetic text, especially concentrating on 20th-century English and French composers. As a composer his style is largely tonal, using traditional formal structures (*Sonata,* cello, 1961) and often referring to Baroque genres and titles (*Festival Galliard,* orchestra, 1951). His experience in the U.S. inspired the use of popular elements and avant-garde techniques such as indeterminacy and sound clusters (*Cloud Canticle,* 1969). His works are predominantly vocal and include dramatic works (*Lysistra,* play in music, 1948) and many traditionally sacred forms, sometimes combined with nonreligious text (Missa Brevis, 1962; *Chants and Litanies of Carl Sandburg,* 1960). They include some orchestral (*The Spring of the Year,* double string orchestra, 1985) and chamber works, sometimes for eclectic combinations of instruments (*The Key and the Kingdom,* dancing soprano, improvising flutes, harp or piano, 1974). His books include *Music in a New Found Land* (1964; 2nd ed., 1987), *Caliban Reborn: Renewal in Twentieth-Century Music* (1967), *Twilight of the Gods: The Music of the Beatles* (1973), and *The Masks of Orpheus: Seven Stages in the Story of European Music* (1987).

Mellnäs, Arne (b. Stockholm, 30 Aug. 1933). Composer. Studied composition with Larsson and Blomdahl at the Royal Academy of Music in Stockholm, 1953–63. He later worked with Blacher at the Berlin Hochschule für Musik; also with Deutsch in Paris and with Ligeti in Vienna. He explored electronic music with Koenig and at the San Francisco Tape Music Center and was influenced by Varèse. Served on the faculty at the Stockholm Royal Academy from 1963 to 1972, teaching theory and orchestration. His musical language is eclectic within the western European tradition, bearing the mark of his broad range of influential teachers. He has concentrated on choral and chamber music. The choral music is for various combinations of adult or children's voices with organ or instrumental accompaniment (*Noel,* 2 sopranos, children's voices, chamber orchestra, 1972). His chamber works are for unusual groupings of instruments, frequently involving percussion instruments (*The Mummy and the Humming-Bird,* harpsichord and recorder, 1974; *Gardens,* flute, clarinet, percussion, violin, cello, piano, 1986) or electronics (*Soliloquim IV,* bassoon, electronics, 1976). He also composed the chamber opera *Bed of Roses* (1984) and Symphony no. 1 *Ikaros* (1986).

Memphis Minnie [Douglas, Lizzie] (b. New Orleans, 3 June 1897; d. Memphis, 6 Aug. 1973). Blues singer and guitarist. After touring with the Ringling Brothers Circus (1916–20), she worked in Memphis (to 1930) and Chicago (to 1954). She consecutively worked with and married three blues singer-guitarists, Casey Bill Welson, Kansas Joe McCoy, and Little Son Joe (Ernest Lawlars). With McCoy she recorded "Bumble Bee" (1930) and with Little Son Joe "Me and My Chauffeur Blues" (1941). Upon returning to Memphis in the 1950s she was largely inactive, owing to illness. Her style was that of down-home blues, rather than the vaudeville style of "classic" women blues singers.

Memphis Slim [Chatman, Peter] (b. Memphis, 3 Sept. 1915; d. Paris, 24 Feb. 1988). Blues pianist, singer, songwriter. He traveled as a musician from age 15, modeling his barrelhouse piano and "shout" vocal styles on Roosevelt Sykes, for whom he deputized in 1934. From 1937 to 1961 he lived in Chicago; he worked first as sideman with Big Bill Broonzy and others, later as bandleader and soloist, often teaming with bassist Willie Dixon. This activity culminated in appearances at Carnegie Hall and the Newport Festival in 1959. In 1961 he settled in Paris, devoting himself to popularizing American blues in Europe. He composed and recorded prolifically.

Mendelsohn, Alfred (b. Bucharest, 17 Feb. 1910; d. there, 9 May 1966). Composer. Through 1931 he studied composition in Vienna under Marx, Schmidt, and Wellesz, then went on to work with Jora at the Bucharest Conservatory, 1931–32. He conducted the Romanian Opera in Bucharest, 1946–54, and taught at the Bucharest Conservatory from 1949 until his death. He was also an officer of the Romanian Composers' Union. He was influenced by the late 19th-century German Romantic style; his early works were tonal. Later in his life he explored serialism, though never moving too far from tonal centrism. The late works show a nationalistic tendency. His strength lay in larger dramatic genres, including ballet (*Călin,* 1956) and opera (*Michelangelo,* 1964). He also wrote orchestral works, including 9 symphonies (1944–64), concertos, and symphonic poems; choral works; chamber music (10 string quartets).

Mendelssohn, Arnold (Ludwig) (b. Ratibor [now Racibórz], Silesia, 26 Dec. 1855; d. Darmstadt, 19 Feb. 1933). Composer and teacher. Son of a second cousin of Felix Mendelssohn; studied law, then (1877–80) music at the Institut für Kirchenmusik, Berlin; then held organist or teaching posts in Bonn, Bielefeld, Cologne; 1891–1912, in Darmstadt as director of church music and teacher at the conservatory (professor from 1897); from 1912, taught at Frankfurt Conservatory (pupils included Hindemith). A prolific composer: 3 operas, incidental music, orchestral and chamber works, piano pieces, songs, but best known as a moving force in the "renewal" of Lutheran church music (German Mass, cantatas, motets), an influence disrupted by the suppression of his work in the Nazi period; essays published as *Gott, Welt und Kunst,* ed. Wilhelm Ewald (Wiesbaden, 1949).

Mendelssohn, Fanny. See Hensel, Fanny (Cäcilie) Mendelssohn (Bartholdy).

Mendelssohn (Bartholdy), (Jakob Ludwig) Felix (b. Hamburg, 3 Feb. 1809; d. Leipzig, 4 Nov. 1847). Composer. Second of four children of Abraham Mendelssohn, a Jewish banker; grandson of the noted thinker Moses Mendelssohn. In 1811, because of the French occupation of Hamburg, the family moved to Berlin, where his mother collected intellectual and artistic notables in her salon, creating a milieu in which Felix grew up accustomed to easy intercourse with both wealth and talent. In 1816 his father had his children converted to Christianity, converting himself in 1822, adding the gentile name Bartholdy (borrowed from his wife's brother, who had adopted it on his conversion) to distinguish themselves from unconverted Mendelssohns. Felix was carefully educated by his parents, later by private tutors, with piano lessons from Ludwig Berger, violin lessons from Eduard Rietz (later preferring to play the viola in chamber ensembles); from 1819, studied theory and composition with Zelter, the major formative influence on him as a musician, and attended classes at Zelter's Singakademie.

Mendelssohn began to compose by 1820, developing with astonishing rapidity; in the next few years he produced short comic operas, 13 string symphonies (1821–23), concertos, chamber music, piano pieces, and songs. The sense that a great talent was in formation is manifested in Zelter's taking him in 1821 to Weimar to display him to his friend Goethe, who was impressed (Mendelssohn was to visit Goethe four times more). Zelter declared Mendelssohn at 15 a fully formed musician; this was reflected in his music, which in 1824 included the Symphony no. 1 for full orchestra, his second concerto for two pianos, chamber pieces, and the once-popular *Rondo capriccioso* for piano; nevertheless, his parents were unconvinced of the rightness of his becoming a professional musician, and early in 1825 his father took him to Paris for Cherubini's opinion, which was affirmative. Cherubini was validated by Mendelssohn's composition that year of his first great masterpiece, the Octet in E♭, and in 1826 of the *Midsummer Night's Dream Overture.* In April 1827 the Berlin Opera gave his opera *Die Hochzeit des Camacho,* which was soon forgotten. From May 1827 he took courses (including Hegel's lectures) at Berlin Univ. His compositions of this period include the overture *Meeresstille und glückliche Fahrt* (1828, based on Goethe), String Quartet no. 2 (1827), and two occasional cantatas performed in 1828. On 11 March 1829 he conducted the first revival, much cut, of Bach's St. Matthew Passion with the Singakademie. This has generally been regarded as marking a giant step in the Bach revival; it reflected Mendelssohn's own deep immersion in Bach's music, stimulated by Zelter, although Zelter's initial opposition to these performances, doubting their success, indicates that Mendelssohn had gone beyond him.

In spring 1829 Mendelssohn began a grand tour of Europe, regarded by his father as completing his formation as man and artist. He had already traveled much

Felix Mendelssohn, 1833.

as a boy with his family and spoke French, Italian, and English. He went first to London, appearing as pianist and conducting his First Symphony with the Philharmonic, which made him an honorary member, and twice the *Midsummer Night's Dream Overture* at other concerts. An excursion to the Highlands and Hebrides that summer produced the *Hebrides Overture* (final version, 1832) and the Scottish Symphony, conceived and partly sketched at this time but not completed until 1842. He spent December 1829–May 1830 in Berlin, then began an Italian tour via Weimar (where he saw Goethe for the last time), Munich (where he began a romance with Delphine von Schauroth, a young woman who set her sights on marriage), Salzburg, and Vienna, recording his impressions in letters illustrated with his drawings. In Rome he met Berlioz, of whose music he showed no understanding, and his contempt for Italian music was complete; indeed, he had little taste for any music except that of the tradition of Bach, Handel, Mozart, and Beethoven (just beginning to be conceived of as a tradition), dismissing almost anything that did not have the most serious artistic or at least moral purpose; this attitude drew him to Renaissance church music. He cared little for the contemporary generation of Romantics, admiring Chopin's playing more than his music, and shared none of the Romantic feeling for folk music. Even improvising seems to have made him uncomfortable, since its spontaneity was unwelcome to him in an artistic context—except on the organ, where the Bach tradition seems to have legitimized it for him and where he could display his mastery of counterpoint. After Naples and Pompeii he returned via Switzerland, whose scenery and hiking were to draw him back repeatedly.

In Munich Mendelssohn's romance with Delphine von Schauroth resumed, but her very apparent goal of marriage was opposed by his family and his own inclinations, although she seems to have inspired his First Piano Concerto, which he premiered in Munich. He spent December 1831–April 1832 in Paris, where he was soloist in Beethoven's Fourth Concerto and had his *Midsummer Night's Dream Overture* performed, but was disappointed by the conservatory orchestra's rejection of his Reformation Symphony, composed in 1829–30. The close deaths of Goethe and Zelter were a shock; as a diversion, and to help recover from cholera caught in Paris, he visited London in May 1832, where he was received as a celebrity and had several works performed. This contrasted with his treatment back in Berlin, where, apparently against his better judgment, he became a candidate to succeed Zelter as director of the Singakademie, but was rejected, leaving him with long-lasting animosity against Berlin (he was offered but refused the post of assistant director). In May 1833 he went to London to conduct the very successful premiere of his Italian Symphony. An invitation to conduct the Lower Rhine Music Festival at Düsseldorf that summer (most notable for his highly successful revival of Handel's *Israel in Egypt*) led to his appointment as music director of Düsseldorf from September 1833, giving him the professional base that he (and his father) had wanted.

That Düsseldorf was a largely Catholic city was not entirely congenial to Mendelssohn, who was in charge of church music. Moreover, his unhappy involvement as music director of the theater, under the intendant, the writer K. L. Immermann, whose libretto on *The Tempest* he had earlier rejected, suggests that he was not equipped by nature or experience to deal with the practicalities of the theater world. He began with ambitious plans to raise the level of performance, and Mendelssohn conducted several operas, but this eventually led to a rupture with Immermann and his resignation from Düsseldorf in summer 1835. The most positive aspect of this period was his performance of several Handel oratorios (*Alexander's Feast,* 1833; *Messiah, Judas Maccabaeus,* 1834; *Solomon* at the Lower Rhine Music Festival, 1835), thus providing a background for his major work of the period, the oratorio *St. Paul,* for which Handel and Bach are the obvious models. Its premiere at the Lower Rhine Music Festival of 1836 was a considerable success, and it was soon widely performed, notably in England, where Mendelssohn conducted it at the Birmingham Festival in 1837.

In fall 1835 he became music director in Protestant Leipzig, where he was happier and widely respected (honorary doctorate from Leipzig Univ., 1836). Much of his initial effort was directed to building up the Gewandhaus Orchestra. He had his friend Ferdinand David appointed concertmaster and conducted historically oriented concerts (1837–38) that foreshadow modern, historically varied programming. Substituting for an ailing friend as choral director in Frankfurt in summer 1836, he met his future wife in the chorus. Cécile Jeanrenaud, daughter of a pastor of Huguenot stock, was beautiful and gracious but unintellectual; the marriage, which took place in 1837 and produced a son in 1838, a daughter in 1839, and a second son in 1841, became the stable center of Mendelssohn's life. Major works of this period were the Second Piano Concerto (1837), the string quartets in E minor, E♭, and D (1837–38), the *Ruy Blas Overture* (1839), the First Piano Trio (1839), the *Lobgesang* (or Symphony no. 2) for the Leipzig celebration of the 400th anniversary of the printing press (1840), organ and piano pieces, church music, part songs.

The accession in 1840 of a new Prussian king, Frederick William IV, who had ambitious plans for making Berlin the center of German art, led to Mendelssohn's appointment as royal Kapellmeister with a sizable salary. Because of bureaucratic and other resistance, however, little was accomplished, and the period 1841–44 was one of considerable frustration for Mendelssohn. When it became obvious in 1841 that a new conservatory would not be established, he asked to withdraw, but the king had become interested in Greek tragedy and commissioned incidental music for Sophocles' *Antigone.* Its success at court in October 1841 and in public in 1842 led to a *A Midsummer Night's Dream* (1843), *Oedipus at Colonnus* (1845), and *Athalie* (1845). In autumn 1842 he again tried to resign, but the king offered him the title of *Generalmusikdirektor* and asked him to occupy himself with one of the king's major musical concerns, the improvement of church music, by building a chorus and orchestra to participate in services at the cathedral and in concerts of oratorios. In autumn 1843 he moved his family to Berlin to work with the newly formed male-voice cathedral choir and to conduct a concert series with the royal orchestra; he again experienced obstacles and frustrations, however (opposition from the cathedral authorities is reflected in criticism of his setting of Psalm 98 as profane because of his inclusion of a harp in the orchestra). He left Berlin in April 1844 and that fall asked the king to release him, which the king did, reserving the right to commission special compositions.

In these years he had also kept up other strands of his varied activities, including conducting at the Gewandhaus, except for the 1843–45 seasons, when Ferdinand Hiller took his place (a move that eventually ended their friendship). One of his achievements of the period was the establishment of the Leipzig Conservatory. He persuaded the King of Saxony to use a bequest from a private citizen for this purpose and was largely responsible for determining its structure, curriculum, and faculty, himself teaching the piano and later composition, although he felt no great inclination or talent for teaching. The conservatory, which was soon one of the great European music schools, reflected Mendelssohn's own thinking in its strongly conservative orientation, becoming later in the century almost a symbol of musical reaction.

Although still only in his mid-30s Mendelssohn had engaged in activities sufficient for a lifetime, and his stamina and general health were beginning to show the strain. From 1838 he suffered migraine. He often expressed a wish to withdraw to a quiet creative life but seemed unable to do so except to a limited degree, also seeing his public career as a duty, part of his artist's mission. From mid-1844 to mid-1845 he stayed relatively withdrawn, living near his wife's family in Frankfurt, working on his last orchestral work, the Violin Concerto, completed in September 1844, the six Organ Sonatas op. 65, and other works. In August 1845 he returned to Leipzig to resume conducting the orchestra. A commission from the Birmingham Festival led to the composition, mostly in early 1846, of his oratorio *Elijah,* a subject that he had been considering since the 1830s. The soprano part was conceived for Jenny Lind, with whom he had become very close, but she did not sing its triumphant premiere at Birmingham on 26 August 1846. Mendelssohn then revised the score (also in October 1846 carrying out a commission from the King of Prussia for a Lutheran liturgy), conducting it on his tenth visit to England in April 1847. He had conducted the Lower Rhine Music Festival in summer 1846 and shared the direction of the Gewandhaus Orchestra in his last season, 1846–47, with Gade. The sudden death of his beloved sister Fanny from a stroke in May 1847 was a great blow. A summer holiday in Switzerland, during which he composed his last major work, the String Quartet op. 80, as a reaction to his sister's death, brought some improvement (although only 38 he was said to be stooped and old). At the end of October he began to have what were apparently small strokes, followed early in November by more massive ones, from which he died. He was buried in Berlin. At his death he was working on an opera, *Loreley,* and an oratorio, *Christus.*

Bibl.: J. Rietz, ed., *Werke* (Leipzig, 1875–77). *Leipziger Ausgabe der Werke Felix Mendelssohn Bartholdys* (Leipzig, 1960–). P. and C. Mendelssohn, eds., *Briefe aus den Jahren 1830 bis 1847* (Leipzig, 1861–63); trans. Eng. (1862–63, R: 1970). S. Hensel, *Die Familie Mendelssohn 1729–1847, nach Briefen und Tagebüchern* (Berlin, 1879); trans. Eng. (1882, R: 1969). Rudolf Elvers, ed., *Felix Mendelssohn Bartholdy Briefe* (Frankfurt am Main, 1984). M. F. Schneider, *Felix Mendelssohn in Bildnis* (Basel, 1953). H. E. Jacob, *Felix Mendelssohn und seine Zeit* (Frankfurt, 1959–60); trans. Eng. (1963). Erik Werner, *Mendelssohn: A New Image of the Composer and His Age* (New York, 1963; R: 1978). G. R. Marek, *Gentle Genius: The Story of Felix Mendelssohn* (New York, 1972). R. Larry Todd, ed., *Mendelssohn and His World* (Princeton, 1991). Gregory John Vitercik, *The Early Works of Felix Mendelssohn: A Study in the Romantic Sonata Style* (Philadelphia, 1992). R. Larry Todd, ed., *Mendelssohn Studies* (Cambridge, 1992). Eka Donner, *Felix Mendelssohn Bartholdy: aus der Partitur eines Musikerlebens* (Düsseldorf, 1992). R. Larry Todd, *Mendelssohn, the Hebrides and Other Overtures* (Cambridge, 1993). Arnd Richter, *Mendelssohn: Leben, Werke, Dokumente* (Mainz, 1994).

Mendes, Gilberto (Ambrósio, García) (b. Santos, Brazil, 13 Oct. 1922). Composer. Attended the Santos Conservatory (1941–49); later studied composition with Santoro (1954) and Toni (1958–60), and with Boulez, Pousseur, and Stockhausen at Darmstadt in 1962 and 1968. He taught classes in contemporary music, contributed articles to *O Estado de São Paulo* and *A tribuna,* and organized new music festivals; also active in the Santos Musica nova group. Works include music for orchestra, incidental music, and works for solo instrument and chamber ensemble, as well as a substantial amount of vocal music and avant-garde pieces.

Bibl.: *Composers of the Americas* 19 (Washington, D.C., 1977), pp. 73–84 [includes works list].

Mengelberg, (Josef) Willem (b. Utrecht, 28 Mar. 1871; d. Chur, Switzerland, 21 Mar. 1951). Conductor. He studied in Utrecht and at the Cologne Conservatory with Seiss, Jensen, and Wüllner, and in 1891 became conductor of the municipal orchestra of Lucerne. He was named conductor of the Amsterdam Concertgebouw in 1895, an appointment that would last until the end of his career; during his tenure Mengelberg elevated the orchestra to a position of prominence among European ensembles. In addition to his annual Palm Sunday performances (from 1899), he directed Museum Concerts at Frankfurt am Main (1907–20) and made a number of appearances with the Royal Philharmonic in London (1911–14) and the New York Philharmonic (1921–29). He was especially celebrated for his performances of Mahler and Strauss (Strauss dedicated *Ein Heldenleben* to him), and he organized a complete Mahler cycle in 1920. During World War II he made a number of conducting appearances in Germany, and his (apparent) sympathy for the Nazi cause led to his being barred from professional activities in Holland after 1945; consequently spent his last years in retirement in Switzerland.

Mennin [Mennini], **Peter** (b. Erie, Pa., 17 May 1923; d. New York, 17 June 1983). Composer and educator. He began studying music and composing as a young child; attended the Oberlin Conservatory, where he studied with Norman Lockwood (1941–42), served in the armed forces, and then studied with Rogers and Hanson at the Eastman School (from 1943; Ph.D., 1947). His career as an educator began at Juilliard, where he taught composition from 1947 to 1958; he was then director of the Peabody Conservatory (1958–62); and from 1962 until his death was president of the Juilliard School. At Juilliard he established the Theater Center (1968), the American Opera Center (1970), and the Contemporary Music Festival. Mennin is best known as a composer of large-scale works, having written 9 symphonies between 1941 and 1981; his harmonic language remained tonal, but his emphasis on polyphonic textures results in the impression of harmonic freedom. He wrote for the usual collections of instruments and confined himself to their characteristic ranges; orchestral color often helps to define formal structure (especially in Symphony no. 8, 1973).

Works: 9 symphonies (1941–1981; no. 4, 1948, the Cycle, employs chorus; no. 7, 1963, is subtitled the Variation Symphony), concertos (cello, 1956; piano, 1958; flute, 1983), *Concertato "Moby Dick"* (1952), and other orchestral music; *Canzona* (band, 1951); String Quartet no. 2 (1951), Sonata concertante (violin and piano, 1959); *Cantate de virtute: Pied Piper of Hamelin* (Browning and liturgical texts; narrator, tenor, bass, double choir, children's chorus, orchestra, 1969), *Reflections of Emily* (Dickinson; boys' chorus, harp, piano, and percussion, 1978), and earlier choral music (1941–49); *Voices* (Thoreau, Melville, Whitman, Dickinson; 1 voice, piano, harp, harpsichord, percussion, 1975); a few early songs were withdrawn.

Mennini, Louis (Alfred) (b. Erie, Pa., 18 Nov. 1920). Composer. Brother of Peter Mennin. He studied at Oberlin College (1939–42) and at the Eastman School (1945–49) with Rogers and Hanson. He taught briefly at the Univ. of Texas (Austin) and then at Eastman (1949–65). From 1965 to 1971 he was dean of the School of Music at the North Carolina School of the Arts, and then chaired the music department of Mercyhurst College (Erie, Pa.), retiring in 1983; founder and head of the Virginia School of the Arts, 1983–88. Wrote 2 operas (*The Well,* 1951; *The Rope,* 1955) and a ballet (1948); several works for orchestra (2 symphonies, "da chiesa," 1960, and "da festa," 1963); chamber and piano music; and a *Proper of the Mass* for chorus (1953).

Scene from Gian Carlo Menotti's *Amahl and the Night Visitors.*

Menotti, Gian Carlo (b. Cadegliano, Varese, 7 July 1911). Composer and librettist. He showed musical ability in early childhood and had written his first opera *(La morte di Pierrot)* by age 10, having begun to study piano with his mother and then with teachers brought from Milan. The family lived in Milan for a few years during which Gian Carlo studied at the conservatory (1923–27) and frequented La Scala, where he was impressed by Toscanini's performances. Toscanini advised that the young composer be sent to study at the Curtis Institute in Philadelphia with Scalero (composition) and Vera Resnikoff (piano). Samuel Barber (with whom Menotti shared a home in Mt. Kisco for 30 years) was a fellow student; while students, they spent several summers together in Vienna and in Italy. Menotti taught composition at Curtis for several years (1948–55), but was active primarily as a composer, librettist, and stage director for his own and others' operas. His success as an opera composer began shortly after his graduation in 1933, when his first mature opera *(Amelia al ballo)* was successfully staged in Philadelphia and New York (1937), and then at the Metropolitan Opera (1938). NBC Radio commissioned his second work (*The Old Maid and the Thief,* 1939), which was also successful on stage (1941). But the following serious opera, *The Island God* (1942), was a failure; Menotti had responded to this Metropolitan Opera commission by writing a "big, heavy opera for a big, heavy orchestra." He never published it, and came to consider the music uninspired. In *The Medium* Menotti recaptured a lighter style; he was stage director for its first production at Columbia (1946) and during the subsequent eight-month run on Broadway. European productions followed, and a film was made in 1950 under the composer's direction. In that year *The Consul* was presented on Broadway to rave reviews and received the Drama Critics' Circle Award and the Pulitzer Prize. Again the composer was librettist and stage director. He took the work to Paris and then to Milan; at La Scala many in the audience booed and hissed, and the critics called the work old-fashioned and impotent, but Menotti's success elsewhere was assured. *Amahl and the Night Visitors,* composed for NBC television (Dec. 1951), rapidly became one of the most frequently performed operas in the U.S. *The Saint of Bleeker Street,* commissioned by the City Center for Music and Drama and the Rockefeller Foundation, was premiered on Broadway (1954), where it ran for four months. Its large cast and orchestra precluded commercial success, but it received the Drama Critics' Circle Award, the New York Music Critics' Circle Award, and the Pulitzer Prize (1955). In 1958 Menotti founded the Spoleto Festival of Two Worlds, an enterprise that took much of his attention for several years.

He composed operas commissioned by the Paris Opéra (*Le dernier sauvage,* 1963), NBC (*Labyrinth,* 1963), the Hamburg Opera (*Help, Help, the Globolinks!,* 1971), the New York City Opera (*The Most Important Man,* 1971), the Ninth International Congress of Anthropological and Ethnological Sciences

(*Tamu-Tamu,* 1973), the Opera Company of Philadelphia (*The Hero,* 1976), and the San Diego Opera (*La loca,* 1979). Many of his later works are directed toward children (*Martin's Lie,* children's church opera commissioned by CBS for the Bath Festival, 1964). In 1984 Menotti received a Kennedy Center Honor for his lifetime of achievement in the arts. *Goya,* premiered in November 1987 in Washington, D.C., received mixed reviews. In 1993 he ended his long tenure as artistic director of the Spoleto Festival and became director of the Rome opera.

Menotti's melodic and harmonic language is tonal and diatonic; his operas, which have been termed "small melodramas," make more use of recitativelike passages than of closed aria forms, and the text setting is natural.

Works: Operas other than those mentioned include *The Unicorn, the Gorgon, and the Manticore* (1956); *Maria Golovin* (1958); *The Egg* (1976); *The Trial of the Gypsy* (1978); *Chip and His Dog* (1979); *A Bride from Pluto* (1982); *The Boy Who Grew Too Fast* (1982); *The Singing Child* (1993); ballets (*Sebastian,* 1944; *Errand into the Maze,* 1947); cantatas (*The Death of the Bishop of Brindisi,* 1963; *Landscapes and Remembrances,* 1976; *Muero porque no muero,* 1982; *The Wedding,* 1988); a symphony (The Halcyon, 1976), concertos (2 for piano, 1945, 1982; violin, 1952; double bass, 1983), a triple concerto for 3 trios (piano, harp, and percussion; oboe, clarinet, and bassoon; and violin, viola, and cello; 1970), and *Apocalypse* (1951); *Missa o pulchritudo* (4 soloists, chorus, orchestra, 1979); *Gloria* (tenor, chorus, orchestra, 1995); chamber music (suite, 2 cellos and piano, 1973; *Cantilena scherzo,* harp and string quartet, 1977); piano music (*Poemetti per Maria Rosa,* 12 pieces for children, 1937); *Canti della lontananza* (cycle of 7 songs, soprano and piano) and other choral and vocal music.

Writings: *A Hand of Bridge* (libretto for Barber, 1960). *Introductions and Goodbyes* (libretto for Foss, 1961). *Vanessa* (libretto for Barber, 1964). *The Leper* (play, Tallahassee, 1970). *Gian Carlo Menotti* (New York, 1991).

Bibl.: John Gruen, *Menotti: A Biography* (1978). John Ardoin, *The Stages of Menotti* (1985).

Menuhin, Yehudi (b. New York, 22 Apr. 1916). Violinist. He was taken to San Francisco as a child, where he studied with Sigmund Anker and Louis Persinger; made his debut with the San Francisco Symphony at the age of 7 and received considerable acclaim for his recitals in San Francisco (1925), New York (1926), and Paris (1927). After further study with George Enescu, became an overnight celebrity with his New York performance in 1927 of the Beethoven concerto under Fritz Busch. He embarked on a series of tours throughout the U.S. and Europe, making his London debut in 1929 and performing with the Berlin Philharmonic under Bruno Walter in the same year; completed his first world tour, including performances in Australia, in 1935. Menuhin organized a number of music festivals, including the Gstaad Festival in Switzerland (1956) and, after settling in London, the Bath Festival (1959). He conducted and toured with his own chamber orchestra and devoted much time to musical education. Menuhin's sister Hephzibah (b. San Francisco, 20 May 1920; d. London, 1 Jan. 1981), a pianist, was a frequent collaborator on recital programs.

Bibl.: Yehudi Menuhin, *The Compleat Violinist: Thoughts, Exercises, Reflections of an Itinerant Violinist* (New York, 1986). Tony Palmer, *Menuhin: A Family Portrait* (London, 1991). David Dubal, *Conversations with Menuhin* (New York, 1992).

Merbecke [Marbeck], **John** (b. Windsor, ca. 1510 or earlier; d. ca. 1585). Composer and writer. Organist at St. George's Chapel, Windsor, by 1531 until his death, although not active in this capacity after 1550. By 1543 he had written many theological works with Calvinist leanings, including a concordance of the English Bible, and in that year was arrested for heresy and sentenced to death but was reprieved by Henry VIII. Upon his release from prison, Merbecke wrote another concordance, replacing that confiscated at the time of his arrest, but this was too lengthy for publication. A third concordance, a shorter work, came out in 1550; it was the first such book to be published in English. By this time Edward VI was King of England, and Merbecke's religious views were no longer illegal. He was then asked to write music for the newly mandatory English-language church services. The resulting book, which contains his only published compositions, is *The Booke of Common Praier Noted* (1550), a collection of simple settings often based on plainchant melodies. Because of the revision of the *Book of Common Prayer* in 1552 and subsequent changes in the religious practices of the country, this collection was in use only briefly. Other compositions: 4 polyphonic pieces, including 1 Mass, 2 Latin motets, and 1 English anthem.

Mercadante, (Giuseppe) Saverio (Raffaele) (b. Altamura, near Bari, bapt. 17 Sept. 1795; d. Naples, 17 Dec. 1870). Composer. Moved with his family to Naples in 1806; 1808–20, student, Naples Conservatory (causing later confusion by lying about his age and birthplace to obtain free tuition); studied there with Furno and Tritto, and composition with Zingarelli (1816–20), becoming his favorite pupil; composed much instrumental music as a student, also sacred music, an occasional cantata; came to public notice with three ballets for the Teatro S. Carlo (1818–19) and the Teatro del Fondo (1818), leading to an opera seria commission from the S. Carlo (1819). Achieving success with ease in Naples, he was then invited to work for the principal theaters of Rome (1820), Bologna, and Milan, where his opera semiseria *Elisa e Claudio* was a hit in 1821, also making his name known outside Italy. This, however, was followed by several failures, including his first opera for Venice (1822) and two at La Scala in 1822. His first for Mantua was not well received (1822), but *Didone abbandonata* at Turin (1823) was. He then worked in Naples and Rome before going to Vienna in June 1824 for the local premiere of *Elisa e Claudio.* The new operas that he produced there were all failures and severely criticized.

Late in 1824 he resumed work in Italy, having a notable success with *Caritea, regina di Spagna* (Venice, 1826) before going to Spain and Portugal, where he worked in 1827–31. Returning, he had one of his greatest successes with *I normanni a Parigi* (Turin, 1832). From 1832 to 1840 he was music director at Novara Cathedral, for which he composed much sacred music, also remaining active in opera.

Mercadante went to Paris in 1835 at Rossini's invitation to compose *I briganti* for the Théâtre-Italien. A failure, it was followed at La Scala in 1837 by *I giuramenti,* judged his masterpiece and occasionally revived in recent times. It initiated a change to a more serious and carefully worked style that may reflect his experience of French opera in Paris. It is the work of this period, including *Elena da Feltre* (S. Carlo, 1838), *Il bravo* (La Scala, 1839), and *La vestale* (S. Carlo, 1840), that has been seen as most significant historically, foreshadowing aspects of Verdi. In 1838 he became blind in one eye. In 1839 Rossini offered and he accepted the directorship of the Bologna Conservatory, then rejecting it in 1840 when offered that of the Naples Conservatory (a post that Donizetti had wanted). Thereafter his production of operas gradually slowed: one a year in 1842–46, including *Orazi e Curiazi* (S. Carlo, 1846), one of his most highly regarded works, 5 more in 1848–57. He also composed some sacred works and occasional pieces and other vocal and instrumental works, some even after he became completely blind in 1862, an event apparently commemorated in an orchestral piece, *Il lamento del bardo,* dictated in the same year.

Bibl.: Frank Walker, "Mercadante and Verdi," *ML* 33 (1952): 311–21; 34 (1953): 33–38. Santo Palermo, *Saverio Mercadante: Biografia, epistolario* (Fasano, 1985). T. G. Kaufman, *Verdi and His Major Contemporaries* (New York, 1990).

Mercer, Johnny [John Herndon] (b. Savannah, Ga., 18 Nov. 1909; d. Los Angeles, 25 June 1976). Popular lyricist, songwriter, and singer. He performed in and wrote songs for Broadway revues in the late 1920s; though his performing activities continued, in later years he was known mainly as a lyricist. He wrote musicals (*St. Louis Woman,* music by Harold Arlen, 1946; *Li'l Abner,* music by G. de Paul, 1956) and for many films with collaborators Jerome Kern ("Dearly Beloved," "I'm Old Fashioned," 1942), Hoagy Carmichael ("In the Cool, Cool, Cool of the Evening," 1951), Henry Warren ("On the Atchison, Topeka and the Santa Fe," 1946), and Henry Mancini ("Blue Moon," 1961; "Moon River," 1961; "The Days of Wine and Roses," 1962). Other songs include "Lazybones" (1933) and "Skylark" (1942), both with tunes by Carmichael, and songs for which he composed both music and words, such as "I'm an Old Cowhand" (1936) and "Dream" (1945). His lyrics often address rural southern themes. In 1942 he cofounded Capitol Records, but sold his interest soon after.

Mercer, Mabel (b. Burton-on-Trent, England, 3 Feb. 1900; d. Pittsfield, Mass., 20 Apr. 1984). Popular singer. She sang in family groups and with black touring troupes, and after World War I became famous in nightclubs across Europe, particularly in Paris. In 1938 she moved to the U.S., where her style is thought to have had a large impact on singers such as Frank Sinatra. She made few recordings.

Mercure, Pierre (b. Montreal, 21 Feb. 1927; d. Avallon, France, 29 Jan. 1966). Composer, bassoonist, and administrator. He studied at the Montreal Conservatory (1944–49) with Champagne; thereafter he went to Paris, where he studied conducting with Jean Fournet and orchestration with Arthur Hoérée and Milhaud; he worked briefly with Boulanger; was actively engaged with his contemporaries (including Clermont Pépin) in Paris in collective composition and improvisation. In 1951 he studied twelve-tone composition with Dallapiccola at the Berkshire Music Center, but his mature works do not make use of that method. Returning to Canada in 1950, he wrote background scores for CBC productions and became a CBC television producer (1952–66), responsible for productions of *Wozzeck* and the series *L'heure du concert.* A study trip to Paris (1957–58) enabled him to explore *musique concrète* with Pierre Schaeffer; in 1961 he organized a contemporary music festival in Montreal; in 1962 he made another study trip to Darmstadt, Paris, and Dartington. His *Psaume pour abri* combines live performers and electronic music (narrator, 2 choruses, brass quintet, string quartet, harpsichord, piano, harp, percussion, and tape, 1962). He played bassoon in the Montreal Symphony (1947–52) and was commissioned by the orchestra to write *Lignes et points* (1963), which uses graphic notation. *H_2O for Severino* (1965) is scored for 4–10 flutes or clarinets and has an open form. Other works include ballets (*Incandescence,* tape, 1961) and film scores.

Merighi, Antonia Margherita (fl. 1717–40; d. ca. 1764). Contralto. She received considerable acclaim for her performance in Gasparini's *Sesostri* in Bologna, 1719; appeared in 19 operas in Venice and 14 in Naples, and later sang in Parma, Florence, and Turin, sometimes taking male roles. In 1729 Handel engaged her for London and she performed at the King's Theatre for 2 seasons, appearing in 8 Handel operas; Handel's esteem for her ability is evident through the parts written for her. Her last public appearance was in Munich in 1740.

Merikanto, Aarre (b. Helsinki, June 29, 1893; d. there, 29 Sept. 1958). Composer. Son of Oskar Merikanto. From 1912 through 1914 he studied composition with Reger in Leipzig and from 1916 to 1917 with Vadilenko in Moscow. From 1936 until his death he taught theory and composition at the Sibelius Academy in Helsinki, following Palmgren as head of the department in 1951. His music showed the Germanic and Russian influence of his teachers, and he developed a keen interest in Scriabin. His musical style ranged from tonally romantic to highly chromatic. It was often contrapuntal and drew on Finnish musical traditions. Much of his music remained unperformed until after his death and was revived after 1960. His one opera, *Juha,* was written in 1920–22 but was not given a radio performance until 1958 and its stage premier in Lahti on 28 October 1963. His orchestral works include 3 piano concertos, 3 symphonies, and 4 violin concertos. He wrote pieces for voice and orchestra (*Genesis,* soprano, chorus, orchestra, 1956). His chamber music includes 2 string quartets.

Merikanto, (Frans) Oskar (b. Helsinki, 5 Aug. 1868; d. Hausjärvi-Oiti, 17 Feb. 1924). Composer. Studied composition in Helsinki, Leipzig, and Berlin. He worked in Finland as an organist. From 1911 to 1922 he conducted the Finnish National Opera in Helsinki. He did much to further the performance of opera and was active in the education of church musicians. He wrote 3 operas (1908–20), incorporating Finnish lore (*Elinan surma* [Elina's Death], Helsinki, 17 Nov. 1910). He wrote predominantly popular songs and keyboard works.

Meriläinen, Usko (b. Tampere, 27 Jan. 1930). Composer. He studied at the Sibelius Academy in Helsinki with Aarre Merikanto and Leo Funtek (1951–55), then studied privately with Ernst Krenek in Darmstadt and Wladimir Vogel in Switzerland. He conducted and taught in Kuopio (1956–57), then conducted the theater in Tampere (1957–60), where he subsequently held teaching positions at the music institute (1961–66) and the university (from 1965). His works include the ballet *Arius* (1958–60); 5 symphonies (1952–55, 1964, 1971, 1975, 1976); 2 piano concertos (1955, 1969); *Musique du printemps,* orchestra (1969); a cello concerto (1975); *Mobile,* game for orchestra (1978); *Kinetic Poem,* piano and orchestra (1982); *Visions and Whispers,* orchestra (1985); a flute concerto (1986); *Arabesques,* solo cello (1963); *Divertimento,* wind quintet, harp, viola, and cello (1968); *Concerto,* double bass and percussion (1973); *Aspects of the Ballet "Psyche,"* tape instrumental ensemble (1973); *Kyma,* string quartet (1979); and 4 piano sonatas (1960, 1966, 1972, 1974).

Merkel, Gustav Adolf (b. Oberoderwitz, near Zittau, 12 Nov. 1827; d. Dresden, 30 Oct. 1885). Organist and composer. From 1844 a student at the teachers' college in Bautzen; 1848–53, schoolteacher in Dresden; then taught the piano to support himself while he studied organ with Johann Schneider, piano with Wieck, theory with Otto, and composition with Schumann and Reissiger. From 1858 he was a church organist; 1867–73, directed Dreyssig Singakademie. A popular and prolific organ composer; his sonatas, chorale preludes, fantasies, and trios were much played into the early 20th century. Also composed didactic works (*Organ School* op. 177) and etudes.

Merman [Zimmerman], **Ethel (Agnes)** (b. Astoria, N.Y., 16 Jan. 1908; d. New York, 15 Feb. 1984). Actress and popular singer. From 1930, when she appeared in Gershwin's *Girl Crazy,* she was the preeminent musical comedy heroine of Broadway. Her classic roles included those in Cole Porter's *Anything Goes* (1934) and Irving Berlin's *Annie Get Your Gun* (1946, including her signature tune "There's No Business Like Show Business") and *Call Me Madam* (1950).

Bibl.: George B. Bryan, *Ethel Merman: A Bio-Bibliography* (New York, 1992).

Merola, Gaetano (b. Naples, 4 Jan. 1881; d. San Francisco, 30 Aug. 1953). Conductor and impresario. Studied at the Naples Conservatory, then served as assistant conductor at the Metropolitan Opera (1899); conducted at the Manhattan Opera (1906–10), London Opera (1910–12), and San Carlo Opera in San Francisco (1918–22). In 1923 he founded the San Francisco Opera and became its first general director; during his 30-year tenure the company became one of America's finest. Also served as general director of the Los Angeles Grand Opera (1924–31).

Merrick, Frank (b. Clifton, Bristol, 30 Apr. 1886; d. London, 19 Feb. 1981). Pianist and composer. Studied with his father and with Leschetizky in Vienna, making his London debut in 1903; taught at the Royal Manchester College of Music (1910–29), Royal College of Music (1929–56), and from 1956 at Trinity College of Music. He won the Columbia Gramophone Company's contest in 1928 by "completing" Schubert's Unfinished Symphony; composed a number of piano concertos and edited some music of John Fields.

Merrill, Robert (b. Brooklyn, 4 June 1917). Baritone. Studied with his mother, a concert singer, and with Samuel Margolis; made his Metropolitan debut (as Germont in *La traviata*) in 1945 and remained with the company through the 1974–75 season. Appeared frequently in recital and with most of the major orchestras in the U.S.; his recordings include *Traviata* and *Un ballo in maschera* under Toscanini. Author of *Once More from the Beginning* (1965), *Between Acts* (1976), and *The Divas* (1978).

Merriman, Nan [Katherine-Ann] (b. Pittsburgh, 28 Apr. 1920). Mezzo-soprano. Studied with Alexia Bassian in Los Angeles and sang background music for Hollywood films; made her opera debut at the Cincinnati Summer Opera in 1942 (as La Cieca in *La Gioconda*). Subsequently worked with Toscanini and appeared at Glyndebourne, Edinburgh, and Aix-en-Provence before retiring in 1965. Her roles included Dorabella, Meg *(Falstaff),* Maddalena *(Rigoletto),* Emilia *(Otello),* and Baba the Turk *(The Rake's Progress).*

Merryman, Marjorie (b. 9 June 1951). Composer. She attended Scripps College (B.A., 1972) and Brandeis Univ. (M.F.A., 1975; Ph.D., 1981). Her composition teachers included Seymour Shifrin, Martin Boykan, Gail Kubik, and Betsy Jolas. Taught at M.I.T. (1976–77), Brandeis (1975–79); in 1979 appointed to the faculty of Boston Univ. Works include *Serenade for Six Instruments* (flute, bass clarinet, violin, cello, harp, piano, 1974); *Three Pieces for Piano* (1975); *Laments for Hektor* (2 sopranos, alto, flute, clarinet, horn, violin, cello, percussion, piano, 1977); *Ariel* (soprano, clarinet, cello, percussion, 1978); *The River Song* (soprano, orchestra, 1981).

Mersenne, Marin (b. La Soultière, Maine, 8 Sept. 1588; d. Paris, 1 Sept. 1648). Music theorist and philosopher. He studied at the college of Le Mans, and from 1604 at the Jesuit school at La Flèche, leaving for Paris in 1609 to study at the Collège Royal and the Sorbonne. He joined the Order of Minims in 1611, receiving his holy orders the following year; taught philosophy and theology at the monastery near Nevers (1615–18), returning to Paris in 1619 as conventual of the order.

Mersenne corresponded with the leading thinkers of his day, including Descartes, Hobbes, Galileo, and Doni. In his writings music is treated as a discipline that can be scientifically analyzed and explained. He discerned, through experimentation, that sound was pure motion rather than substance; he formulated rules concerning vibrating strings according to their variable factors, and discussed the relation of partials to a fundamental note. His chief work: *Harmonie universelle* (Paris, 1636–37); trans. Eng. (The Hague, 1957).

Bibl.: Albion Gruber, "Mersenne and Evolving Tonal Theory," *JMT* 14 (1970): 36–67. Fred B. Hyde, "The Position of Marin Mersenne in the History of Music" (diss., Yale Univ., 1954). Hellmut Ludwig, *Marin Mersenne und seine Musiklehre* (Halle and Berlin, 1935).

Merula, Tarquinio (b. Cremona, 1594 or 1595; d. there, 10 Dec. 1665). Composer and organist. In 1616 he was appointed organist of S. Maria Incoronata, Lodi; moved to Poland, probably in 1621, serving as *organista di chiesa e di camera* to the King of Poland, Sigismund III, from at least 1624. Returning to Cremona, Merula was appointed *maestro di cappella* at Laudi della Madonna, a post he held on three different occasions (1627–31, 1633–35, 1646–65); he held positions in Bergamo during intervening years, at both S. Maria Maggiore (1631–32) and the neighboring cathedral (1638–42). He collaborated with five others in composing the opera *La finta savia* (Venice, 1643) and was a member of the Accademia dei filomusi of Bologna. Merula was one of the first composers to write solo motets with string accompaniment; his sacred concertos for small forces resemble Monteverdi's settings in their rich elaboration. His secular monodies and accompanied madrigals include some of the finest work of the period.

Bibl.: *Opere complete,* ed. Adam Sutkowski (Brooklyn, 1974–).

Merulo [Merlotti], **Claudio** (b. Corregio, 8 Apr. 1533; d. Parma, 5 May 1604). Composer, organist, and music publisher. Student of Tuttovale Menon and Girolamo Donato. Organist at Brescia (1556–57); at St. Mark's, Venice (1557–84); and in Parma (from 1586, first at the ducal court, then also at the cathedral; from 1591 for the ducal church La Steccata). His contemporaries considered him the finest organist of his time. His most distinguished works are for organ (especially toccatas, ricercars, organ Masses, and organ canzonas). Most are in some degree based on vocal models, although only a few are simply transcriptions; many more incorporate highly idiomatic ornamentation and figuration and a free treatment of dissonance unusual for the time. Didactic treatises by his students, notably *Il transilvano* by Girolamo Diruta, transmit his contributions to organ technique. His activity as a publisher, though brief (1566–70), encompassed the production of numerous volumes—reprints and new books, collections of his own works and of works by other Italian composers. Volumes edited by him appear up until 1575 and include pieces by composers as Verdelot, Arcadelt, Rore, and Lassus, often substantially changed in underlay, accidentals, and even the musical fabric itself. Other works include sacred and secular vocal music (chiefly Masses, motets, and madrigals); *intermedi* for 2 dramas.

Messager, André (Charles Prosper) (b. Montluçon, France, 30 Dec. 1853; d. Paris, 24 Feb. 1929). Composer and conductor. Student, 1869–74, at the École Niedermeyer, Paris, meeting Fauré when he taught there in 1871. They became close friends, sharing quarters and visiting Bayreuth together (*Parsifal,* 1883). Attracted first notice in 1876 as a composer with a prizewinning symphony, performed (1878) at the Concerts Colonne, but found his true field in light theater music; 1878–79, composed 3 ballets for the Folies-Bergères; 1883, completed an unfinished opera of Bernicat, followed by 10 of his own in 1885–98, including *La béarnaise* (1885), *Les p'tites Michu* (1897), *Véronique* (1898). *Mirette* (1894) was composed in English for the Savoy Theatre, London, where his works were also popular, in collaboration with the Irish composer Dotie Davies (1859–1938; pen name Hope Temple), who became his second wife in 1895. During this period he also produced 2 opéras comiques, including the very successful *La basoche* (Opéra-comique, 1890), several ballets (including the highly regarded *Les deux pigeons* for the Paris Opéra, 1886), and incidental music. After beginning as a church musician, he found his true field of performance as a conductor. From conducting at the Folies-Bergères in the 1870s, he rose to the important posts of music director at the Opéra-comique (1898–1903, 1919–20), where he conducted the premieres of *Louise* (1900) and *Pelléas et Mélisande* (1902), which is dedicated to him; director and conductor at Covent Garden, London (1901–17); co-director and conductor, Paris Opéra (1907–14); he conducted the Ballets Russes in 1924; also a noted symphonic conductor, directing the Concerts Lamoureux (1905) and the Conservatory concerts (1908–19), with which he toured Argentina (1916) and the

Olivier Messiaen (left) with Pierre Boulez, 1987.

U.S. (1918). After 1898 his composing was intermittent, including the opéras comiques *Fortunio* (Opéra-comique, 1907) and *Béatrice* (Monte Carlo, 1914) and 7 operettas and musical comedies, including *Monsieur Beaucaire* in English (Birmingham and London, 1919). Also wrote music criticism for newspapers and periodicals.

Bibl.: Henri Février, *André Messager, mon maître, mon ami* (Paris, 1948). M. Augé-Laribé, *André Messager, musicien de théâtre* (Paris, 1951). John Wagstaff, *André Messager: A Bio-Bibliography* (New York, 1991).

Messiaen, Olivier (Eugène Prosper Charles) (b. Avignon, 10 Dec. 1908; d. Paris, 27 Apr. 1992). Composer and organist. Messiaen's father, an English teacher who translated the works of Shakespeare, and mother, the poet Cécile Sauvage, encouraged his musical career, although he undertook formal instruction only after he had begun to compose at age 8. He entered the Paris Conservatory in 1919, achieving between 1926 and 1930 five Premier Prix in counterpoint and fugue, accompaniment, organ and improvisation, history of music, and composition. His teachers there included Caussade (fugue), Dupré (organ, improvisation), and Dukas (composition and orchestration). In 1931 he became principal organist at l'Église de la Sainte Trinité in Paris, a position he held for over 40 years. In the 1930s he taught at the École normale de musique and at the Schola cantorum; in 1936 he founded the group La jeune France with Jolivet, Daniel-Lesur, and Yves Baudrier, an effort at a musical humanism in reaction to the prevailing French neoclassicist aesthetic. He served in the army and was held for a year as a prisoner of war (1940–41), composing the *Quatuor pour la fin du temps* in the prison camp. Returning to occupied France he taught harmony at the Conservatory and from 1943 to 1947 also gave semiprivate classes in analysis and composition at the home of Guy Bernard-Delapierre that were attended by Boulez and other young composers. In 1944 his book *Technique de mon langage musical* appeared. He was appointed to teach analysis at the Paris Conservatory in 1947; in 1966 he became its teacher of composition, retiring at age 70. His many students included Boulez, Barraqué, Stockhausen, and Goehr. Messiaen also taught in Budapest (1947), the Berkshire Music Center (1949), and Buenos Aires (1964).

Three elements are critical to a comprehension of the works of Messiaen: the theological creed of the Catholic faith, the theme of love, and an interest in nature. The first is reflected in almost all of the organ works and in several large-scale compositions (e.g., the *Transfiguration de notre Seigneur Jésus-Christ,* 100-voice choir, 7 instrumental soloists, and large orchestra, 1965–69; and *Des canyons aux étoiles,* solo piano, full orchestra, a 12-movement cycle of "contemplations on the majesty of God revealed in the depths of the earth, and in the far distances of the heavens," 1971–74). The

Tristan legend finds particular expression in a trilogy of works inspired by Messiaen's devotion to his former student and second wife, Yvonne Loriod (*Harawi,* song cycle, 1945; *Turangalîla-symphonie,* 1946–48; and *Cinq rechants,* chorus, 1948). The composer's interest in bird song was long-standing; he belonged to several ornithological societies and notated the songs of a wide variety of birds; when these were employed in a composition, he often indicated the source in the score. The bird songs are most important in compositions from the mid-1950s (*Le reveil de oiseaux* and *Oiseaux exotiques,* both piano and orchestra, and *Catalogue d'oiseaux,* piano solo), but are found in later works as well.

Influences on his musical style arose from his study of Greek meters, medieval rhythmic procedures, Hindu rhythms, and certain later developments in the rhythmic language of Western music (in works of LeJeune, Mozart, Beethoven, Chopin, Debussy, and Stravinsky). He is particularly associated with the technique of "added value" and the use of nonretrogradable rhythms, rhythmic pedals and canons, and polyrhythmic textures. His "interversions" (changes in the order of individual durations), the progressive transformation of one rhythm into another, extremely long and short durations, and use of irrational durations are also notable. In the area of harmony, his coloristic approach and his modes of limited transposition (sets that can be transposed only a few times before the original series reappears) are critical, as is the association between specific modes and certain colors. In his works color and timbre achieve an importance equal to that of pitch and duration. Several pieces are monumental in conception: *Turangalîla* in 10 movements; *La transfiguration* in 14 parts; the 4 1/2-hour opera; some of the music for piano *(Vingt regards, Catalogue d'oiseaux).*

Though independent of any particular school, Messiaen has had a major influence on contemporary music. His *Modes de valeurs et d'intensités* (1949) was a pioneering exploration of the serial treatment of pitch, duration, mode of attack, and intensity. Boulez derived the twelve-tone set of *Structures* from Messiaen's piece; Stockhausen and Xenakis acknowledged its importance to their very different compositional methods.

Works: an opera, *Saint François d'Assise: Scènes franciscaines* (Paris, 1983); orchestral music (*Turangalîla-symphonie,* piano, ondes martenot, 1946–48; *Chronochromie,* 1959–60; *Et exspecto resurrectionem mortuorum,* 34 winds, 3 percussionists, 1964; *Des canyons aux étoiles,* piano, 23 winds, 7 percussionists, 13 strings, 1971–74); *Quatuor pour la fin du temps* (clarinet, violin, cello, and piano, 1940–41); piano works (*Préludes,* 1928–29; *Vision de l'Amen,* 2 pianos, 1943; *Vingt regards sur l'enfant Jésus,* 1944; *Catalogue d'oiseaux,* 1956–58); organ music (*La nativité du Seigneur: Neuf méditations,* 1935; *Livre d'orgue,* 1951; *Méditations sur le mystère de la Sainte Trinité,* 1969); *O sacrum convivium!* (chorus or soprano and organ, 1937), *Trois petites liturgies de la Présence Divine* (36 female voices, piano, ondes martenot, 5 percussionists, and strings, 1943–44); *Poémes pour Mi* (text by Messiaen; soprano and piano, 1936; arranged for orchestra, 1937), *Chants de terre et de ciel* (text by Messiaen; soprano and piano, 1938); a few unpublished works for ondes martenot; an electronic work for tape, withdrawn.

Bibl.: Carla Huston Bell, *Olivier Messiaen* (Boston, 1984) [includes discography]. Paul Griffiths, *Olivier Messiaen and the Music of Time* (Ithaca, N.Y., 1985). Theo Hirsbrunner, *Olivier Messiaen: Leben und Werk* (Laaber, 1988). Robert Sherlaw Johnson, *Messiaen* (London, 1989). Olivier Messiaen, *Music and Color: Conversations with Claude Samuel,* trans. E. Thomas Glasow (Portland, 1994). Beate Carl, *Olivier Messiaens Orchesterwerk Des canyons aux étoiles: Studien zu Struktur und Konnex* (Kassel, 1994).

Mester, Jorge (b. Mexico City, 10 Apr. 1935). Conductor. Studied conducting at Juilliard with Morel and worked with Bernstein (at the Berkshire Music Center) and with Albert Wolff. Debut in Mexico City in 1955; appeared with most of the major orchestras in the U.S. and with several in London; won the Naumburg Award for conducting (1968). He served as music director of the Louisville Orchestra (1967–79), Aspen Music Festival (from 1970), Kansas City Philharmonic (1971–74), Casals Festival in Puerto Rico (from 1980), and the Pasadena Symphony (from 1984). During his tenure with the Louisville Orchestra Mester conducted nearly 200 first performances and was the first to record many 20th-century works. A member of the Juilliard faculty, 1957–67 and from 1980.

Mestres-Quadreny, Josep María (b. Manresa, Barcelona, 4 Mar. 1929). Composer. Student of Cristófor Taltabull at the Univ. of Barcelona, 1950–56; cofounded the group Música abierta in 1960, later establishing with fellow Catalan composers Xavier Benguerel, Joaquim Homs, and Josep Soler the Conjunt català de música contemporània; began in 1968 an association with the Electronic Music Laboratory of Barcelona. While his first efforts were purely serial in nature, he soon combined serialism and aleatory elements; joined forces with artists in other fields to produce a variety of multimedia works, and explored computer applications to composition. He composed a variety of theater pieces, including *Concert per a representar* (6 singers, flute, clarinet, trumpet, trombone, percussion, bass, and tape, 1964), *Triptic carnavalesc* (soprano, the same winds, percussion, and piano, 1966), *Suite bufa* (dancer, mezzo-soprano, piano, and electronic sound, 1966), and *Homenaje a Joan Prats* (6 actors, electronics, string quartet, and winds). Other works include *Digodal* (strings, 1963); *Ibemia* (chamber orchestra, 1969); *Double Concerto* (ondes martenot, percussion, and orchestra); the ballets *Roba i ossos* (1961), *Petit diumenge* (1962), and *Vegetació submergida* (1962); chamber music, with and without electronics; sonatas for piano (1957) and organ (1960).

Metastasio, Pietro [Trapassi, Antonio Domenico Bonaventura] (b. Rome, 3 Jan. 1698; d. Vienna, 12 Apr. 1782). Librettist. Antonio Trapassi was adopted as a child by Gian Vincenzo Gravina, who renamed the boy Pietro Metastasio and encouraged him to enter the legal profession. Gravina died in 1718, leaving Metastasio enough money to become financially independent; he decided to become a poet and began in the early 1720s to write wedding serenatas and other poems for members of the aristocracy. His first original operatic libretto, *Didone abbandonata,* was performed in Naples in 1724 with music by Sarro; its success quickly established his reputation throughout Italy. He resided in Rome and Venice from 1724 until 1730, turning out several librettos of importance including *Ezio* (1728), *Semiramide* (1729), and *Alessandro nell'Indie* (1729; rev. 1753–54).

In 1729 Metastasio was invited by the Austrian court to succeed Apostolo Zeno as court poet; his first Viennese opera, *Demetrio* (1731), was written for the name day of Emperor Charles VI. The period from 1731 until 1740 was perhaps his most productive, as Charles VI would frequently require the composition of a new oratorio or opera for ceremonial occasions; Charles's successor, the Empress Maria Theresa, was less demanding. Metastasio wrote librettos for 27 3-act heroic operas, many set to music by the leading composers of the time including Handel, Gluck, Mozart, Hasse, and Porpora; there are over 800 settings of his librettos. He was thus the principal exponent of the genre that came to be called opera seria (published at the time, however, with the titles *dramma* or *dramma musicale*). Other librettos include *Catone in Utica* (1728), *Adriano in Siria* (1732), *La clemenza di Tito* (1734), *Il re pastore* (1751).

Bibl.: Charles Burney, *Memoirs of the Life and Writings of the Abate Metastasio* (London, 1796; R: New York, 1973). Raymond Monelle, "The Rehabilitation of Metastasio," *ML* 57 (1976): 268–91. Piero Weiss, "Metastasio, Aristotle, and the *Opera Seria,*" *JM* 1 (1982): 385–94. Gianfranco Folena, ed., *Metastasio e il mondo musicale* (Florence, 1986).

Metheny, Pat [Patrick Bruce] (b. Lee's Summit, Mo., 12 Aug. 1954). Jazz guitarist, composer, and bandleader. He joined Gary Burton's group (1974–77). Having first recorded as a leader in 1975, from 1977 he formed his own groups, playing in a style combining elements of jazz, rock, country, and Latin music. His albums include *The Pat Metheny Group* (1978), *Offramp* (1981), and *Still Life (Talking)* (1987). He has also been devoted to Ornette Coleman's music; he worked with Coleman's former sidemen, including a trio with Charlie Haden and Billy Higgins (from 1983), and in 1985 recorded the free jazz album *Song X* with Coleman himself. Metheny composed the soundtrack for the film *The Falcon and the Snowman* (1985); a song from it, "This Is Not America," became a rock hit in a subsequent collaboration with David Bowie.

Metner [Medtner], **Nikolay Karlovich** (b. Moscow, 5 Jan. 1880; d. London, 13 Nov. 1951). Composer and pianist. After studying piano with his mother and uncle he entered the junior classes of the Moscow Conservatory at age 12; there he studied with Galli, Pabst, Sapelnikov, and Safonov. He was largely self-taught as a composer, but studied with Arensky and, outside the conservatory, with Taneyev. Although he graduated with a gold medal for piano playing in 1900, he decided to concentrate on composition. He taught piano at the Moscow Conservatory (1909–10, 1914–21) before following Rachmaninoff and other compatriots into exile; apart from a concert tour in 1927, he never returned to Russia. He eventually settled near Paris in 1925, finding Parisian musical life unappealing; he expressed his reservations about contemporary music in *The Muse and the Fashion* (Paris, 1935; trans. Eng., 1951). His works did not find favor in Paris, but were widely acclaimed elsewhere in Europe, the U.S., and Canada. In 1935 he settled in London, where he had a small following. Aside from about 100 songs and a few chamber works, he wrote exclusively for the piano; his piano writing owed much to Schumann and Brahms.

Bibl.: Collected edition, *N. Metner: Sobraniye sochineniy* (Moscow, 1959–63). Cenieth C. Elmore, "Some Stylistic Considerations in the Piano Sonatas of Nikolai Medtner" (diss., Univ. of North Carolina, 1972). Malcolm Boyd, "Metner and the Muse," *MT* 121 (1980): 22–25. Terence Kelly, "The Songs of N. Medtner" (diss., Univ. of Maryland, 1988). Barrie Martyn, *Nicolas Medtner: His Life and Music* (Aldershot, 1995).

Métra, (Jules Louis) Olivier (b. Le Mans, 2 June 1830; d. Paris, 22 Oct. 1889). Composer. Son of an actor; himself a child actor, having music lessons from a player in the Théâtre Comte orchestra; 1849–54, student, Paris Conservatory; then a theater orchestra and dance hall conductor. The first of his waltzes, 1856, was a success, and he became noted for them, especially *La vague* and *Les roses* and other dance music. He conducted balls at the Opéra-comique (1871) and La Monnaie, Brussels (1874–76), later Paris Opéra; 1872–77, conductor, Folies-Bergères, for which he composed many operettas and ballets; also *Yedda,* a ballet for the Opéra (1879).

Metzger, Ambrosius (b. Nuremberg, 31 Jan. 1573; d. there, 1632). Composer and Meistersinger. By 1604 he had earned a master's degree from the university at Altdorf; then a schoolmaster at St. Egidien, Nuremberg. Wrote 2 volumes of polyphonic songs (*Venusblümlein,* Nuremberg, 1611–12); because of encroaching blindness turned to poetry and monophonic melodies. He claimed to have written some 3,000 poems and 340 melodies, of which 1 book, a psalter, was printed.

Meulemans, Arthur (b. Aarschot, 19 May 1884; d. Brussels, 29 June 1966). Conductor and composer. He studied at the Lemmens Institute in Mechelen (1900–1906) and taught there until 1914; from 1916 to 1930 he directed the organ and song school at Harselt, after which he was a conductor and director for Belgian Radio. His works are influenced by French impressionism and by Flemish nationalist sentiment. They include 3 operas; the *Peter Breugel Suite* (orchestra, 1952) and several concertos (3 for violin; 2 for cello; 2 for piano; and 1 each for viola, harp, 2 violins, harpsichord or piano, and organ); chamber and piano music;

Sanguis Christi (solo voices, chorus, and orchestra, 1938), which is performed every five years in Bruges; other choral music and songs; a *Serenata* for carillon (1950).

Meyer, Ernst Hermann (b. Berlin, 8 Dec. 1905; d. there, 22 Oct. 1988). Composer and musicologist. As a child he played violin and piano and was composing by the age of 7; after a brief career in business he studied musicology at the Univ. of Berlin; in 1930 he received the D.Phil. in musicology from the Univ. of Heidelberg, where he studied with Besseler; his dissertation dealt with the 17th-century German ensemble sonata. His composition teachers included Eisler and Hindemith. When the Nazis came to power in 1933 he emigrated to England, where he taught, composed music for documentary films, and conducted choirs. In 1948 he returned to Berlin as professor and director of the Institute for Musicology at Humboldt Univ. He continued to be active as a musicologist, especially in the sociology of music from a Marxist standpoint. His much-revised compositions show a respect for the Baroque and classical traditions; some works were published under the pseudonym Peter Baker. As a member of the Central Committee of the Communist party, he had great influence over the organization of the musical life of the former German Democratic Republic.

Works: an opera, *Reiter der Nacht* (1970–71; Berlin Staatsoper, 1973), and a ballet; Symphony for Strings (1947; rev. 1957–58), Violin Concerto (1963–64), and other orchestral music; 4 string quartets (1956–75) and other chamber and piano music; cantatas (*Lenin hat gesprochen,* voices and orchestra, 1970) and other choral music (*Hütet nun ihr der Weisenschaften Licht,* Brecht, 1960); 7 published collections of songs; arrangements and editions of folk songs and 16th- and 17th-century instrumental music.

Meyer, Krzysztof (b. Kraków, 11 Aug. 1943). Composer. Following composition lessons with Stanislaw Wiechowicz, he studied with Penderecki (composition) and Fraczkiewicz (theory) at the State College of Music in Kraków; he was a faculty member there from his graduation in 1966 until 1987. In 1964, 1966, and 1968 he studied with Nadia Boulanger in Paris. From 1965 to 1967 he was pianist with the contemporary music ensemble MW-2. In 1987 he joined the faculty of the Musikhochschule in Cologne. His compositions have been strongly influenced by Lutosławski and Penderecki. Works include *Cyberiada* (comic opera, 1967–70); *The Countess* (ballet, 1980); *Klonowi bracia* [The Klonowi Brothers] (opera, 1990); *Concerto da camera* (flute, percussion, strings, 1964); 6 symphonies (1964, 1967, 1968, 1975, 1978–79, 1982); *Concerto da camera* (oboe, percussion, strings, 1972); *Concerto da camera* (harp, cello, strings, 1986); concertos for violin, for cello, for trumpet (1975); *Fireballs* (orchestra, 1976); *Lyric Triptych,* tenor and orchestra (1976); *Polish chants,* soprano and orchestra (1977); *Songs of Resignation and Denial* (soprano, violin, piano, 1963); *Quartettino* (soprano, flute, cello, piano, 1966); *5 Chamber Pieces* (soprano, clarinet, violin, viola, 1967); *9 Epigrams* (soprano and piano, 1979); *Quattro colori* (clarinet, trombone, cello, piano, 1970); *Hommage à Nadia Boulanger* (flute, viola, harp, 1971); *Concerto retro* (flute, violin, cello, harpsichord, 1976); 7 string quartets (1963, 1969, 1971, 1974, 1977, 1981, 1985); 5 piano sonatas (1962, 1963, 1967, 1969, 1975).

Giacomo Meyerbeer.

Meyerbeer, Giacomo [Jakob Liebmann] (b. Vogelsdorf, near Berlin, 5 Sept. 1791; d. Paris, 2 May 1864). Composer. He was from a wealthy Jewish family named Beer (he received a large inheritance on the condition that he add "Meyer" to the family name), whose home was a meeting place for Berlin intellectuals. Early showing musical aptitude, he had piano lessons, playing in public from 1800; 1805–7, studied theory and composition with Zelter and then with B. A. Weber. His one-act ballet *Der Fischer und das Milchmädchen* was given at the Opera on 26 March 1810. A few days later he went to Darmstadt to study with Weber's teacher, Abbé Vogler. Something of Vogler's teaching of Meyerbeer can be seen in his treatise *System für den Fugenbau,* written in 1811, based on a critical analysis and reworking of a student fugue by Meyerbeer. Under him Meyerbeer advanced as both pianist and composer, having an oratorio performed by the Berlin Singakademie in 1811. At the end of 1811 he went to Munich for nine months and then to Vienna until November 1814. In spite of Vogler's obtaining for him (12 Feb. 1813) the largely honorific title of court composer to the Grand Duke of Hesse, his attempts to establish himsef as a composer were largely unsuccessful. An opera, *Jephtas Gelübde,* aroused no interest in Munich (Dec. 1812) and a singspiel, *Wirth und Gast,* was unsuccessful at Stuttgart in 1813 and in a revised, retitled version at Vienna in 1814. He was much more successful as a virtuoso pianist and improviser, which he still considered making his principal career.

In late 1814 Meyerbeer went to Paris, but was unable to get an opera commission and in 1816 went to Italy to learn the Italian art of vocal writing. Meyerbeer absorbed the Italian operatic manner so thoroughly that he was able to compose opere serie that completely captured Italian audiences: *Romilda e Costanza* (Padua, 1817), *Semiramide riconosciuta* (Turin, 1819), *Emma di Resburgo* (Venice, 1819), very widely performed in Italy and beyond, similarly *Margherita d'Anjou* (Milan, 1820), *L'esule di Granata* (Milan, 1821), and—after three years in which he had a serious illness (his health was to remain delicate throughout his life, and he was to spend much time at spas)—one of the most successful and widely performed operas of the period, *Il crociato in Egitto* (Venice, 1824). In 1825 he produced *Il crociato* at the Théâtre-Italien, Paris. Having decided to establish himself in Paris, he next produced a French version of *Margherita d'Anjou* (1826); a project to turn *Il crociato* into a French grand opera for the Opéra was scrapped when far advanced, Meyerbeer deciding that he should make his debut there with a new work reflecting the latest developments, using a reworking of an opéra comique libretto, *Robert le diable,* that Scribe had given him in 1827. Its premiere only on 21 November 1831 perhaps reflects Meyerbeer's perfectionism and some self-doubt; he was further delayed by personal troubles (married to a cousin in 1826, he had two children die in 1827 and 1829) and by the restless traveling across Europe that was a lifelong pattern. *Robert le diable*'s success was one of the greatest in opera history, repeated all over Europe and beyond.

In 1832 Meyerbeer and Scribe contracted for the opera eventually known as *Les huguenots.* Meyerbeer obligated himself to an unrealistic deadline of December 1833, and when he failed to meet it (because, he said, of having to take his wife to Italy for her health), the Opéra claimed its contractual indemnity of 30,000 francs, which Meyerbeer paid. When it became apparent that the Opéra would not be given the new opera, the money was returned, and the Opéra's director was forced to resign. Ultimately *Les huguenots* (Opéra, 29 Feb. 1836) was an even greater success than *Robert le diable.* In 1837 Meyerbeer and Scribe settled on *L'africaine* as their next opera, but after Mlle. Falcon, intended for the title role, lost her voice, it was shelved and in 1838 *Le prophète* substituted. Because of the lack of a suitable tenor at the Opéra Meyerbeer refused to produce it until his admiration for the contralto Pauline Viardot caused him to rework it for her; its premiere (Opéra, 16 Apr. 1849) was another triumph.

He had been appointed *Generalmusikdirektor* in Berlin in 1842. For the opening of the new opera house there he composed *Ein Feldlager in Schlesien* (1844), which he reworked as *Vielka* (Vienna, 1847), both productions starring Jenny Lind, and used some of its music in his opéra comique *L'étoile du nord* (Opéra-comique, 1854). His direction of the Berlin Opera was marked by conflicts with the intendant and by dissatisfaction over his frequent absences, and he was removed in 1848, remaining director of court music and court composer. He took part in court concerts as conductor and accompanist and composed occasional music of various sorts.

The success of *L'étoile du nord* was followed by that of *Le pardon de Ploërmel* (Paris, Opéra-comique, 1859), but the major work of this period was his last grand opera, *L'africaine,* to which he returned intensively in the 1860s, completing it just before his death. It was seen through rehearsals by Fétis and proved a final triumph (Opéra, 28 Apr. 1865), like its three predecessors remaining in the repertory until the 20th century.

Meyerbeer for a long time was considered to manifest various artistic and moral failings. One source of this was his willingness to use his large personal fortune to advance his career, although the extent to which he actually made payments to journalists or other influential people is now difficult to determine, and in any case his great popular success was impossible to buy. Through his internationalism he became suspect to German nationalism, with its scorn of Italian and French music, the very success of his absorption of these styles being regarded as artistic apostasy by his friend and former fellow student Weber, later by Schumann and especially Wagner, whose excesses of vituperation were strongly tinged with anti-Semitism. Even Meyerbeer's careful craftsmanship and slowness in composition were often interpreted as symptoms of a lack of spontaneity and inspiration, signs that his music consisted only of effect for effect's sake. With the triumph of Wagnerism and the passing of Meyerbeer's operas from the repertory, this view alone tended to survive, and only recently has it begun to be reconsidered.

Bibl.: Heinz Becker, ed., *Giacomo Meyerbeer: Briefwechsel und Tagebücher* (Berlin, 1960–). Karin Pendle, *Eugène Scribe and French Opera of the 19th Century* (Ann Arbor, 1979). Jane Fulcher, "Meyerbeer and the Music of Society," *MQ* 67 (1981): 213–29. Sieghart Döhring, "Die Autographen der vier Hauptopern Meyerbeers: Ein erster Quellenbericht," *AfMw* 39 (1982): 21–63. Heinz and Gudrun Becker, eds. *Giacomo Meyerbeer: A Life in Letters* (Portland, Ore., 1989). Sergio Segalini, *Meyerbeer: Diable ou prophète?* (Paris, 1985). Reiner Zimmermann, *Giacomo Meyerbeer: Eine Biographie nach Dokumenten* (Berlin, 1991).

Meyerowitz, Jan [Hans-Hermann] (b. Breslau, 23 Apr. 1913). Composer, pianist, and conductor. He studied at the Hochschule für Musik in Berlin and from 1933 at the Accademia di S. Cecilia in Rome with Respighi, Casella, and Molinari. After the war he emigrated to the U.S., becoming a citizen in 1951. He taught at the Berkshire Music Center (1948–51), Brooklyn College (1954–61), and City College in New York (1962–80). His works are tonal, influenced by Italian neoclassicism and occasionally by Schoenberg and Berg; his operas are indebted to the 19th-century styles of Meyerbeer and Verdi. Works include 8 operas composed since 1946 (*The Barrier,* Langston Hughes, 1950; revived Naples, 1971); orchestral and band music (Concerto for Oboe, 1962); chamber and piano music; *Missa Rachel plorans* (soprano, tenor, chorus, and organ ad libitum, 1962), Hebrew Service Music (tenor, mezzo-soprano, chorus, organ, 1962), and other choral music and songs.

Miaskovsky, Nicolai. See Myaskovsky, Nikolay.

Michael, David Moritz (b. Künhausen, near Erfurt, 21 Oct. 1751; d. Neuwied, near Koblenz, 26 Feb. 1827). Composer, violinist, and wind player. After attending school at the gymnasium in Erfurt, around 1775 he became a military musician in the Hessian army. He joined the Moravian church in 1781; his music teaching took him to various schools in small Saxon towns. In 1795 the Moravians sent him to the U.S., where he taught at a boys' school in Nazareth, Pa., and founded a concert series there. In 1808 he was made superintendant of the unmarried brethren in Bethlehem, Pa. There he also led a collegium musicum, which in 1811 presented what was probably the first American performance of Haydn's *Creation.* In addition to conducting, he also played violin and several wind instruments. His works are preserved in the archives of the Moravian Church, Bethlehem, and in the Moravian Foundation in Winston-Salem. He composed *Parthien* for winds, two "water-music" suites, anthems, and other choral works. He returned to Germany around 1815, retiring from his church duties.

Bibl.: Albert George Rau and Hans T. David, *A Catalogue of Music by American Moravians, 1742–1842* (Bethlehem, Pa., 1938; R: New York, 1970). Dale Alexander Roberts, "The Sacred Vocal Music of David Moritz Michael: An American Moravian Composer" (diss., Univ. of Kentucky, 1978).

Michelangeli, Arturo Benedetti (b. Brescia, 5 Jan. 1920; d. Lugano, Switzerland, 12 June 1995). Pianist. Studied with Giuseppe Anfossi at the Milan Conservatory, from which he graduated in 1933; won the Geneva International Piano Competition in 1939 and became professor of piano at the Martini Conservatory, Bologna. Resumed his concert appearances after the war, making his London debut in 1946 and quickly establishing himself as a leading pianist of his generation. After a number of successful concert tours he founded the International Pianists' Academy in Brescia in 1964, and in 1973 began teaching at the Villa Schifanoia near Florence.

Mignone, Francisco (Paulo) (b. São Paulo, 3 Sept. 1897; d. Rio de Janeiro, 18 Feb. 1986). Composer. Studied at the São Paulo Conservatory. Traveled to Europe in 1920, studying with Ferroni at the Verdi Conservatory, Milan, until 1925; he wrote his first operas, *O contratador de diamantes* (premiered 1924) and *L'innocente* (premiered 1928), around this time. Taught at the São Paulo Conservatory, 1928–33, and at the National School of Music, Rio de Janeiro, 1933–67, serving also as official conductor at the latter. Toured Europe in 1937–38 and the U.S. in 1942 as a conductor, leading the NBC and CBS orchestras in performances of his music, and later held a variety of important official and artistic positions in Brazil. As a composer he initially wrote in a Romantic vein before turning to Brazilian nationalism (with some popular models) in the late 1920s, following, along with Guarnieri and Villa-Lobos, the aesthetic precepts of Mário de Andrade. He moved away from the nationalist posture in the late 1950s and 1960s, cultivating a broad array of approaches, including atonality.

Works: operas (in addition to those cited) *O chalaça* (1973) and *O sargento de milícias* (1978); ballets, including *Maracatu de chico rei* (1933), *Leilão* (1941), and *O guarda chuva* (1933); orchestral music, including *Suite campestre* (1918), *Elegia* (1924), 4 *Fantasias brasileiras* with piano (1929–36), 4 *Amazônicos* (1942), *Sinfonia tropical* (1956), and *Sinfonia transamazônica* (1972); concertos for piano (1958) and violin (1961, 1975), concertinos for clarinet and bassoon (both 1957), and various multiple concertos; chamber music; choral music; piano pieces; songs.

Migot, Georges (b. Paris, 27 Feb. 1891; d. Levallois, near Paris, 5 Jan. 1976). Composer and writer on music. He studied organ, composition, and orchestration at the Paris Conservatory (with Guilmont and Gigout, Widor, and d'Indy); his serious wounds in the First World War required a long convalescence. Early in his career he won three prizes for composition (1918–20), and in 1921 was awarded the Blumenthal Foundation Prize for French Thought and Art. Exhibitions of his paintings were held in Paris in 1917 and 1919; he was a published essayist (*Essais pour une esthétique générale,* 1920) and poet (*Poèmes,* 2 volumes, 1950–51). The essays marked the beginning of his struggle against the French neoclassicist aesthetic dominant between the wars. From 1936 to 1939 he gave a series of radio lectures on French music history; he was curator of the Museum of Instruments at the Conservatory in Paris from 1949 to 1961. His compositions reflect his interest in Asian music and French medieval polyphony.

Works: *Mystère orphique* (polyphonie choréographique, 1948) and other stage works; 6 oratorios; 13 symphonies (1919–66) and other orchestral music (*D'un cercle de l'Enfer du Dante,* 1966); *Le livre des danceries* (flute, violin, and piano, 1929), 3 string quartets and various other quartets (4 saxophones, 1955; flute, violin, cello, and piano, 1960), *Le mariage des oiseaux* (28 pieces for flute, 1970), and other chamber music; piano (Sonata no. 2, D'Octaves, 1951–52) and organ music (*Premier livre,* 1937; *Deuxième livre,* 1954–71); *De Christo* (baritone, chorus, flute, organ, 1971–72) and other choral music; songs with piano or instrumental ensemble.

Bibl.: *Catalogue des oeuvres de Georges Migot,* ed. Marc Honegger (Strasbourg, 1977).

Miguez, Leopoldo (Américo) (b. Niterói, Rio de Janeiro, 9 Sept. 1850; d. Rio de Janeiro, 6 July 1902). Composer. Lived in Spain and Portugal, aged 2 to 21. From 1877 to 1881 he was associated with Artur Napoleão in a music firm; then turned exclusively to composition and performing, studying in Europe (mainly Brussels) in 1882–84, returning to Brazil a strong Wagnerian. He conducted opera companies (in 1886 Toscanini began his career substituting for him); 1890–1902, director of the new National Institute of Music. He composed 2 Portuguese operas, a symphony (1882), symphonic poems, chamber and piano works.

Mihalovich, Ödön Péter József de (b. Feričance, Slovenia, 13 Sept. 1842; d. Budapest, 22 Apr. 1929). Composer and educator. He worked in Pest with Mosonyi and in 1865 went to Leipzig and studied with Hauptmann; completed his education the following year in Munich with Peter Cornelius. He returned to Pest and in 1872 became president of the Wagner Society; in 1887 he succeeded Liszt as head of the Academy of Music in Budapest, a post he held for over 40 years. Although his own compositions are firmly in the German tradition—Wagner remained a central influence throughout his life—Mihalovich supported the efforts of the younger generation, including Bartók, Kodály, and Weiner, to find a distinctive national voice. Compositions include opera (*Hagbart und Signe,* Dresden, 1882; *Wieland der Schmied,* 1876–78; *Toldi szerelme* [Toldi's Love], Budapest, 1893), 4 symphonies (1879–1902), choral works, chamber music.

Mihalovici, Marcel (b. Bucharest, 22 Oct. 1898; d. Paris, 12 Aug. 1985). Composer. His earliest studies were in Bucharest; he took private lessons with Cuclin in harmony, with Bernfeld in violin, and with Cremer in counterpoint. He went to Paris in 1919 and remained there, becoming a French citizen in 1955. From 1919 to 1925 he studied violin with Lejeune, Gregorian chant with Gastuoé, harmony with Saint-Réquier, and composition with d'Indy at the Schola cantorum. Mihalovici was part of a loose association of emigrants called the École de Paris, which included Martinů, Tcherepnin, Tansman, and Spitzmueller. Mihalovici's musical style was the dissonant impressionism of France and eastern Europe, usually drawing on the standard forms taught at the Schola. He wrote several ballets (his first was *Une vie de Polilichinelle,* 1922) and operas (e.g., *Les Jumeaux,* based on Rostand, 1962); orchestral music (*Caprice romanien,* 1936; *Overture tragique,* 1957). His chamber music includes sonatas and sonatinas; 3 string quartets (1923, 1931, 1946); a ricercar (piano, 1941); *Cantus firmus* (2 pianos, 1970); and *Passacaille* (piano, 1975).

Mihály, András (b. Budapest, 7 Nov. 1917; d. 19 Sept. 1993). Composer. He studied cello (Schiffer) and chamber music (Waldbauer and Weiner) at the Budapest Academy of Music, then studied composition privately with Kadosa and Strasser. During World War II he joined the illegal Communist party, directing workers' choirs and championing new music. His activities in the Resistance movement led to his arrest in 1944. After the war he was solo cellist at the State Opera, and served as general secretary of the Philharmonia Society and of the State Opera (1948–50). In 1950 he joined the faculty of the Budapest Academy; from 1962 he was music adviser to Hungarian broadcasting. In 1968 he founded the Budapest Chamber Ensemble to perform new works. He was director of the Hungarian State Opera from 1978 until 1987. His works include the opera *Együtt és egyedül* [Together and Alone] (1964–65); 3 symphonies; a piano concerto (1954); a violin concerto (1959); *Monodia* (1970); *3 Movements* (ensemble, 1969); 2 string quartets; vocal music.

Mikhashoff, Ivar (b. Troy, N.Y., 8 Mar. 1944; d. Buffalo, 12 Oct. 1993). Pianist and composer. He studied at Eastman and with Beveridge Webster at Juilliard, then with Nadia Boulanger in Paris (1968–69). He received a D.M.A. in composition from the Univ. of Texas in 1973. He taught at SUNY–Buffalo, and at the Tanglewood Institute, beginning in 1981. In his repertory were many works by 20th-century composers including Copland, Foss, and Ives. His compositions include chamber music and a piano concerto.

Miki, Minoru (b. Tokushima, Shikoku, 16 Mar. 1930). Composer. His earliest musical influence was the Japanese musical culture in which his family was active. Beginning in 1950 he studied Western music theory and piano literature. From 1951 until 1955 he took composition lessons with Ifukube and Ikenouchi at the National Univ. of Fine Arts and Music. After graduating, he wrote music for educational and documentary films while exploring composition for larger Western orchestras. In the early 1960s he developed an interest in choral composition as well as in composition for traditional Japanese instruments. In 1964 he helped organize Ensemble Nipponia, a group that performed on traditional Japanese instruments. Also in 1964 Minoru became a teacher at the Tokyo College of Music. He toured in Europe both with the choral ensemble Tokyo Liedertafel and with Ensemble Nipponia, establishing his reputation abroad. His style shows the influence of his background with Western as well as with Japanese musical traditions. He moved increasingly closer to techniques and styles idiomatic to Japanese instruments, producing music with highly varied use of rhythm and special sensitivity to timbre. Works include 9 operas and musicals; orchestral music (*Joya,* [New Year's Eve], 1960); choral music (*Awa Kitobun I, II, III,* 1981); and chamber music. The choral music draws on Japanese lore and poetry. The early chamber works were mostly for Western instruments (Sextet, winds, piano, 1965); the later works gradually incorporated more percussion and Japanese instruments (*Totsu* [Complexity], 3 Japanese ensembles, percussion,

1970; *Sahonokyoku* [The Venus in Spring], koto, 1971; *Yui II,* koto, cello, 1983; *Symphony for Two Worlds,* orchestra, 16 players of Japanese instruments, 1981), though they also include a piano trio (1986).

Milán, Luis [Luys] **de** (b. ca. 1500; d. after 1561). Composer and writer. His many and varied books were all published in Valencia, probably his lifelong home. They include a depiction of courtly life at Valencia, *El cortesano* (1561), and, most important, the tutor *Libro de música de vihuela de mano intitulado El maestro* (1536; ed. and trans. Eng., Charles Jacobs, University Park, Pa., 1971). *El maestro* contains not only verbal instruction but also a large quantity of original music in vihuela tablature. Over 40 instrumental pieces (fantasias, *tientos,* and pavans) are supplemented by a number of accompanied songs *(villancicos, romances, sonetos)* in various languages. Many of the songs are given in 2 versions, one simple and to be ornamented using vocal techniques described but not notated, the other more complex, especially in the vihuela part, and to be performed without additional musical elaboration.

Milano, Francesco Canova da. See Francesco Canova da Milano.

Milanov [née Kunc; Ilić], **Zinka** (b. Zagreb, 17 May 1906; d. New York, 30 May 1989). Soprano. She studied at the Zagreb Academy of Music and with Milka Ternina, Maria Kostrenčić, and Fernando Carpi, making her operatic debut in 1927 in Ljubljana; from 1928 to 1935 she appeared with the Zagreb Opera. In 1937 she was soloist in the Verdi Requiem under Toscanini in Salzburg; made her Metropolitan Opera debut the same year (as Leonora in *Il trovatore*), beginning an association with that house that lasted until 1966. Best known for principal roles in the Verdi operas, though she also sang Donna Anna, the title role in *La gioconda,* and Tosca. She taught at Indiana Univ. (1966–67) and joined the faculty at Curtis in 1977.

Mildenburg, Anna. See Bahr-Mildenburg, Anna.

Milder-Hauptman, Pauline Anna (b. Constantinople, 13 Dec. 1785; d. Berlin, 29 May 1838). Singer. Of Austrian parentage, she began as a chambermaid for a Viennese noblewoman; Emmanuel Schikaneder heard her voice and arranged for instruction with Salieri and Tomaselli. After her debut in the role of Juno in Süssmayr's *Der Spiegel von Arkadien* (1803), she rapidly became a leading singer at the Viennese court theater. Beethoven composed for her the title role of the 1805 *Leonore;* she also sang leading roles in Cherubini's *Faniska* (1806) and Joseph Weigl's *Die Schweizerfamilie* (1809). In 1812 she was acclaimed in Berlin for her role in Gluck's *Iphigénie en Tauride.* Schubert composed his *Der Hirt auf dem Felsen* for her, and in 1829 she sang in Mendelssohn's revival of Bach's St. Matthew Passion. Later she toured Europe and Russia.

Miley, Bubber [James Wesley] (b. Aiken, S.C., 3 Apr. 1903; d. New York, 20 May 1932). Jazz trumpeter. He accompanied Mamie Smith (1921, 1923) and then joined the Washingtonians (1923), which developed into Duke Ellington's orchestra. He remained until 1929, and his plunger-muted, growling solos best defined Ellington's "jungle" style, as on recordings such as "East St. Louis Toodle-oo" (1926) and "Black and Tan Fantasy" (1927). He joined Noble Sissle, playing in Paris (1929), and Zutty Singleton, and later led his own band. He died of tuberculosis, though by 1929 alcoholism had already caused his playing to decline.

Milford, Robin (Humphrey) (b. Oxford, 22 Jan. 1903; d. Lyme Regis, Dorset, 29 Dec. 1959). Composer. He was a student at the Royal College of Music in London, taking composition lessons under Holst, Vaughan Williams, and R. O. Morris. His musical language was conservative and used traditional genres and forms. He found early success, primarily through his choral, chamber, and vocal music (as in *A Book of Songs,* 1926). He also wrote in larger genres, such as oratorio (*A Prophet in the Land,* 1931), concerto (violin concerto, 1937), and opera (*The Scarlet Letter,* 1958–59). But many of his larger works (including the last two named) have received little attention and remain in manuscript form.

Milhaud, Darius (b. Aix-en-Provence, 4 Sept. 1892; d. Geneva, 22 June 1974). Composer, conductor, and pianist. As a child he played the violin and composed; studied at the Paris Conservatory (with Leroux, Dukas, Gédalge, and Widor) and subsequently at the Schola cantorum (d'Indy). He had many contacts in the literary and artistic community and in 1916 went to Brazil as secretary to Claudel, who had been appointed the French ambassador. Works that reflect the music he heard there include *Saudades do Brasil* (1920–21). He returned to Paris in 1918 and by 1920 was known as one of "Les six," the group of composers around Cocteau. His public image during these years was not an especially positive one: works such as the *Cinq études* (piano and orchestra, 1920) were not welcomed by concert audiences. In the 1920s and 1930s he composed prolifically while lecturing, conducting, and playing his own works in Europe, Russia, and the U.S. His first exposure to jazz in London and then in the U.S. (1920–22) is reflected in *La création du monde* (ballet, Cendrars, 1923) and in the *Trois rag caprices* (piano, 1922). He continued to write ballets and chamber operas as well as larger stage works (*Christophe Colomb,* 1928, after Claudel; a grand opera with 45 vocal soloists, offstage orchestra, nonsinging actors, large chorus, and film inserts; staged in Berlin, 1930); in addition he wrote scores for children and amateurs (*Un petit peu de musique,* 1932) and for films (Renoir's *Madame Bovary,* 1933).

Milhaud emigrated to the U.S. in 1940, immediately accepting a position at Mills College. He returned to Europe to live in 1947, but continued to teach at Mills and at the Paris Conservatory in alternate years until his retirement in 1971; in 1949 helped to found the Aspen Music Festival, with which he was long associated. Oliveros, Reich, and Subotnik were among his American students; he received commissions from the Coolidge Festival, the Chicago Symphony (Second Piano Concerto, 1941, which he premiered as soloist), and other major institutions. Several works have obvious American associations: *Music for San Francisco* (1971, concerto for orchestra with audience participation); *Meurtre d'un grand chef d'état* (1963), premiered within a week of the assassination of John F. Kennedy. Many other works have a descriptive element: of 12 symphonies, no. 3 (Te Deum, 1946) is a choral hymn of thanksgiving; no. 8 (1957) a portrait of the Rhône. His Jewish heritage is also of significance, for example, in *Poèmes juifs* (1916); the *Service sacré* (1947); *David* (opera, Armand Lunel, 1952), written for the Festival of Israel in honor of the 3,000th anniversary of King David and the founding of Jerusalem. He was sympathetic to European expressionism (and was among the first to champion Schoenberg's *Pierrot lunaire*); but he felt strong links with the French musical tradition, especially as represented by Couperin, Rameau, Berlioz, Bizet, and Chabrier.

Milhaud saw polytonality as a "tonal, melodic antidote to the disintegration of the diatonic system," but he retained references to the "academic" treatment of tonal harmony even as he explored the polytonal. Polytonality is important as early as 1915 (*Les choëphores,* incidental music for Claudel's translation of Aeschylus); one of the *5 Études* (1920) consists of four simultaneous fugues (in A for winds, in D♭ for brass, in F for strings, and one for piano based on notes common to the other three tonalities). *Essai poétique* (tape, 1954) expands this layering technique in a montage constructed from seven tapes. Six are separate recordings of solo instrumentalists, each repeating a single phrase different in length and tempo from the others; the seventh tape is for two saxophones, mezzo-soprano, and reciter; the final tape for radio simply combines these seven sound patterns. *Les Choéphores* is notable also for its treatment of text and singers: words and sentences are fragmented; two scenes incorporate percussion and a female narrator who declaims strictly; but the chorus whistles, groans, and shrieks. His contrapuntal skill is conclusively demonstrated in two (1948) string quartets that are playable separately or together.

He was among the most prolific of 20th-century composers (there are 441 opus numbers); but it has been suggested that his best work was completed before World War II cut him off from Provence (his bias toward popular and folk music of that area was lifelong). Despite his many years in the Parisian world of Cocteau and Stravinsky, he has been described as a folklorist who crossed between pop culture and high art. In 1956 he was made president of the Académie du disque français; and in 1966 he received the Légion d'honneur. Although he suffered even in the late 1920s from severe rheumatoid arthritis, which eventually confined him to a wheelchair, he continued teaching and composing through his 70th year.

Works: 15 operas (*Bolivar* op. 236, 1943); 17 ballets; a large amount of incidental music; many film (*Gauguin* op. 299, Resnais, 1950) and radio scores, and other dramatic works; orchestral music, including 11 symphonies, concertos, and pieces with descriptive titles (*Les charmes de la vie (Hommage à Watteau)* op. 360, 1957); a few pieces for brass band; 18 numbered string quartets (1912–50) and other chamber and solo instrumental music; accompanied and unaccompanied choral music; many cantatas (*Adieu* op. 410, Rimbaud; voice, flute, viola, and harp, 1964), song cycles, and songs for solo voice and ensemble or piano.

Writings: *Études* (Paris, 1927). *Notes sur Erik Satie* (New York, 1946). *Notes sans musique* (Paris, 1949); rev. and enlarged as *Ma vie heureuse* (1974; R: 1987); trans. Donald Evans et al., *My Happy Life* (London, 1995). *Notes sur la musique: Essais et chroniques* (Paris, 1982).

Bibl.: Christopher Palmer, *Milhaud* (London, 1976). Madeleine Milhaud, *Catalogue des oeuvres de Darius Milhaud* (Geneva, 1982). Paul Collaer, *Darius Milhaud* (Geneva, 1982) [includes catalogue of works, editions, discography, and writings]. E. Hurard-Vittard, *Le Groupe de six; ou, Le matin d'un jour de fête* (1987). Jeremy Drake, *The Operas of Darius Milhaud* (New York, 1989).

Millán, Francisco (fl. early 16th cent.). Composer. A member of the chapel of Queen Isabella in 1501 and 1502. The second most prominent composer in the *Cancionero musical de Palacio* (after Encina), with about two dozen *villancicos,* all secular and most with texts in the tradition of courtly love. The great majority of these seem to be for solo voice with instrumental accompaniment; a few are texted in all voices.

Bibl.: Ed. in *MME* 5 (1947), 10 (1951).

Millard, Harrison (b. Boston, 27 Nov. 1830; d. there, 10 Sept. 1895). Composer. As a boy he sang in Boston church choirs and the Handel and Haydn Society; became a tenor, studying in Italy in 1851–54; in Boston (1854–56), then in New York as singer, teacher, composer. His song "Viva l'America" (1859) was his first big success. He was very well known (musical societies were named after him) as song composer (ca. 350 of his own, ca. 400 foreign-language adaptations); also composed church music.

Miller, Dayton C(larence) (b. Strongsville, Ohio, 13 Mar. 1866; d. Cleveland, 22 Feb. 1941). Flutist and acoustician. Studied and taught at Princeton, then was head of the physics department at the Case School of Applied Science, Cleveland. He wrote about the flute and gathered an important collection of flutes (now in the Library of Congress); designed many concert halls and charted instrument waveforms. He wrote *The Science of Musical Sounds* (1916) and *Anecdotal History of the Science of Sound* (1935).

Miller, Edward J. (b. Miami, 4 Aug. 1930). Composer. He studied at the Univ. of Miami (B.M.) and the Hartt College of Music (M.M.). In 1955 and 1958 he studied at Tanglewood with Carlos Chávez and Boris

Blacher. From 1956 to 1958 he studied in Berlin with Blacher and Josef Rufer. He taught at Hartt College from 1959 until 1971, when he joined the composition faculty at Oberlin Conservatory. He has written works for orchestra and wind ensemble, as well as chamber music and pieces for mixed media. Works include *Seven Sides of a Crystal* (piano and tape, 1984); *Going Home* (clarinet, 1985); *Beyond the Wheel* (solo violin, 11 instrumentalists, 1987); *Piece for Clarinet and Tape* (1967; rev. 1982); *Quartet Variations* (percussion, 1971); *The Folly Stone* (brass quintet, 1966).

Miller, (Alton) Glenn (b. Clarinda, Iowa, 1 Mar. 1904; d. between London and Paris, 15? Dec. 1944). Jazz and popular bandleader, arranger, and trombonist. He joined Ben Pollack (1926–28), then worked as a freelance in New York. He helped Ray Noble organize a big band (1935–36) before forming his own (1937, 1938). In the period 1939–42 it was the most popular band of the swing era, appearing in the films *Sun Valley Serenade* (1941) and *Orchestra Wives* (1942) and recording "Moonlight Serenade," "In the Mood" (both 1939), "Tuxedo Junction," "Pennsylvania 6-5000" (both 1940), "Chattanooga Choo Choo," and "A String of Pearls" (both 1941). After enlisting in the Army Air Force, he led a big band in the U.S. and England. He disappeared during a flight to Paris. A succession of memorial Glenn Miller orchestras has continued to play his music.

Bibl.: John Flower, *Moonlight Serenade: A Bio-Discography of the Glenn Miller Civilian Band* (New Rochelle, N.Y., 1972). George T. Simon, *Glenn Miller and His Orchestra* (New York, 1974).

Miller, Mitch(ell William) (b. Rochester, N.Y., 4 July 1911). Oboist, record producer, and conductor. He studied oboe at the Eastman School and played with numerous orchestras; from 1950 he was principal talent developer for Columbia Records, discovering artists such as Tony Bennett. Between 1958 and 1962 he produced a series of highly successful "Sing Along" albums, featuring popular songs rendered by male chorus; later he turned to classical conducting.

Miller, Robert (b. New York, 5 Dec. 1930; d. Bronxville, N.Y., 30 Nov. 1981). Pianist. He studied with Mathilde McKinney and Abbey Simon before attending Princeton (B.A., 1952); graduated from Columbia Law School in 1957, the same year as his Carnegie Recital Hall debut, and subsequently practiced law and taught piano for a time at Princeton. Miller gave the premiere performance of literally hundreds of compositions; Babbitt, Crumb, and Davidovsky, among many others, wrote works for him.

Miller, Roger (Dean) (b. Fort Worth, Tex., 2 Jan. 1936; d. Los Angeles, Calif., 25 Oct. 1992). Country singer, songwriter, and instrumentalist. He played drums, guitar, and fiddle in bands in Oklahoma and with the army in Korea; after the war he worked as a studio musician in Nashville. His songs were used by artists including Ernest Tubb ("Half a Mind," 1958); from 1960 he made his own recordings. The songs "Chug-a-lug," "Engine #9," and "King of the Road," from 1964–65, achieved crossover success with popular audiences; later efforts include "I Love a Rodeo" (1970) and "Everyone Gets Crazy Now and Then" (1981).

Millet, Luis (b. Masnou, 18 Apr. 1867; d. Barcelona, 7 Dec. 1941). Composer. Student of Vidiella and Redall; founded Orfeó Català, a renowned choral organization, in 1891 and was eventually succeeded by his son as conductor. Also served as director and composition teacher at the Municipal Music School, Barcelona. Works include orchestral folk song adaptations and choral pieces, as well as writings on Catalan folk music.

Millöcker, Karl (b. Vienna, 29 Apr. 1842; d. Baden, near Vienna, 31 Dec. 1899). Composer. Flute student, 1855–58, Vienna Conservatory; then player in theater orchestras. Encouraged by Suppé, who helped get him started as theater conductor; 1864–65, in Graz, where his first 2 1-act operettas were produced in 1865; from 1866 again in Vienna theaters (1868, theater conductor in Budapest, where his first 3-act operetta was not a great success); 1869–83, assistant conductor, Theater an der Wien; 1873, first 3-act operetta for Vienna. His second there, *Das verwunschene Schloss* (1878) was his first big success, followed by *Gräfin Dubarry* (1879), *Der Bettelstudent* (1883), one of the most widely performed Viennese operettas of the time, and *Gasparone* (1884). Of his later ones, *Der arme Jonathan* (1890) was most successful. He traveled widely to conduct his works.

Mills, Charles (Borromeo) (b. Asheville, N.C., 8 Jan. 1914; d. New York, 7 Mar. 1982). Composer. Musically self-taught, he played saxophone, clarinet, and flute in jazz bands from age 17. In 1933 he studied composition with Max Garfield in New York; he later studied with Copland (1935–37), Sessions (1937–39), and Harris (1939–41). He was radio critic of *Modern Music* for eight years, then headed the composition department of the Manhattan School (1954–55). His music was influenced by the spirituals and folk songs he heard in the Carolinas, and by jazz. His works include 6 symphonies; a piano concerto (1948); ballets and film scores; *Concertino* (oboe, strings, 1957); *In a Mule Drawn Wagon* (strings, 1969); 5 string quartets; 6 violin sonatas; piano works; vocal works.

Mills, Kerry [Frederick Allen] (b. Philadelphia, 1 Feb. 1869; d. Hawthorne, Calif., 5 Dec. 1948). Popular composer and publisher. He was trained as a violinist and taught briefly; from 1895 he wrote piano pieces and songs mainly in ragtime styles. Like his contemporary Charles Harris, he founded a private publishing firm to ensure income from his compositions; his most popular works were "At a Georgia Camp Meeting" (1897) and "Meet Me in St. Louis, Louis" (1904).

Mills Brothers: Herbert (b. Piqua, Ohio, 2 Apr. 1912; d. Las Vegas, 12 Apr. 1989), **Harry** (b. Piqua, 19 Aug. 1913; d. Los Angeles, 28 June 1982), and **Donald** (b. Piqua, 29 Apr. 1915). Popular vocal trio. After performances in vaudeville and on radio in Cincinnati, from 1930 they worked in New York. Their recordings included "Tiger Rag" (1931), "The Glow Worm" (1952), and "Cab Driver" (1968); "Paper Doll" (1943) is considered a central work in the shift from big band to vocal dominance of popular music.

Milner, Anthony (Francis Dominic) (b. Bristol, 13 May 1925). Composer. He attended the Royal College of Music in London, studying piano under Fryer and composition under R. O. Morris; concurrently took private composition lessons with Seiber. Beginning in 1947 he served on the faculty at Morley College and in 1954 became a lecturer at London Univ. During this time he worked with Tippett in the performance of early choral music. Beginning in 1962 he served as professor of composition at the Royal College of Music, and in 1971 he became a senior lecturer at Goldsmith's College. Much of his music is choral, using religious texts and drawing on techniques of musical symbolism from the traditions of sacred music as well as on styles such as chant and counterpoint. His music is tonal yet forward-looking, as in the serial treatment of the Medieval Advent hymn "Es ist ein Ros' entsprungen" in the Variations for Orchestra (1958). His choral output also includes large cantatalike settings (*Cantata for Christmas 'Emanuel,'* 1974–75) and solo songs (*Our Lady's Hours,* soprano, piano, 1957). Other works include 3 symphonies (1972, 1978, 1986) and a concerto for string orchestra (1982).

Bibl.: James Siddons, *Anthony Milner: A Bio-Bibliography* (New York, 1989).

Milnes, Sherrill (Eustace) (b. Hinsdale, Ill., 10 Jan. 1935). Baritone. He studied with Andrew White at Drake Univ. and with Hermanus Baer at Northwestern; joined Goldovsky's New England Opera Company in 1960 and toured with that organization in the role of Masetto. He received a prize in the American Opera Auditions competition of 1964, the same year that saw his New York City Opera debut as Valentin in *Faust;* his Metropolitan Opera debut took place a year later in the same role. Milnes's repertory included the leading baritone roles in the Verdi operas as well as Scarpia, Escamillo, and Don Giovanni; he recorded widely.

Milstein, Nathan (Mironovich) (b. Odessa, 31 Dec. 1904; d. London, 21 Dec. 1992). Violinist. He studied with Pyotr Stolyarsky and with Auer at the St. Petersburg Conservatory; made his debut in Odessa in 1920 and often appeared in joint recitals with Vladimir Horowitz. In 1925 both musicians left the Soviet Union on a concert tour and decided to remain abroad; at times they joined forces with Piatigorsky and performed as a trio. Milstein made his American debut with the Philadelphia Orchestra in 1929 and decided to remain in the U.S., becoming an American citizen in 1942. He enjoyed a highly successful career as soloist and recording artist; celebrated the 50th anniversary of his American debut by making a number of solo appearances.

Milton, John (b. Stanton St. John, near Oxford, ca. 1563; d. London, buried 15 Mar. 1647). Composer. An amateur musician and father of the poet. Resident in Oxford from 1572, at first as a chorister at Christ Church. Moved to London in 1585, eventually becoming a member of the Scriveners' Company. He composed madrigals, one printed in *The Triumphes of Oriana* (1601), anthems, Psalm settings, a motet, and some consort music (including a 6-part *In nomine*).

Mimaroğlu, Ilhan (Kemaleddin) (b. Istanbul, 11 Mar. 1926). Composer. He studied law at Ankara Univ. and worked as a music critic and broadcaster before traveling to the U.S. in 1955 on a Rockefeller fellowship. In 1959 he settled in New York, studying at Columbia with Ussachevsky, Beeson, Chou, Lang, and Wolpe; he also received advice from Varèse. In 1963 he began an association with the Columbia–Princeton Electronic Music Center. Taught at the Columbia Teachers College in 1970–71. He composed works for orchestra, including a clarinet concerto (1950), *Metropolis* (1955), and *September Moon* (1967); chamber music, including *Parodie sérieuse* (string quartet, 1947), *Pièces futiles* (clarinet, cello, 1958), *Cristal de Bohème* (percussion ensemble, 1971); a piano sonata (1964), *Valses ignobles et sentencieuses* (piano, 1984); *Epicedium* (voice, ensemble, 1961); *2 x e.e.* (vocal quartet, 1963); electronic works, including *Le tombeau d'Edgar Poe* (1964), *Anacolutha* (1965), *Wings of the Delirious Demon* (1969), *Music Plus One* (violin, tape, 1970), *To Kill a Sunrise* (1974), *Immolation Scene* (voice, tape, 1983).

Mingus, Charles (Jr.) (b. Nogales, Ariz., 22 Apr. 1922; d. Cuernavaca, Mexico, 5 Jan. 1979). Jazz double bass player, composer, and bandleader. He joined the big bands of Louis Armstrong (ca. 1943) and Lionel Hampton (1947–48), Red Norvo's trio with Tal Farlow (1950–51, including the recording *Move,* 1950), and Bud Powell's trio (1953). He formed Debut Records (1952–57); its issues include a bop concert he gave with Charlie Parker and Dizzy Gillespie (1953). He founded in 1955 his Jazz Workshop, which achieved a sophisticated balance between composition and improvisation. Varying from 4 to 11 pieces, the group included at various times Eric Dolphy, John Handy, Roland Kirk, Jimmy Knepper, Jaki Byard, and the drummer Dannie Richmond. Its bop-inspired repertory consisted mainly of pieces by Mingus drawing upon New Orleans jazz, blues, and African American gospel music, and Mingus's arrangements of music associated with Duke Ellington; in the 1970s he turned increasingly to jazz-rock. His compositions include "E's flat, ah's flat too," "My Jelly Roll Soul," "Wednesday Night Prayer Meeting" on the album *Blues and Roots* (1959), "Fables of Faubus," "Goodbye Pork Pie Hat" on *Mingus Ah Um* (1959), "The Black Saint and the Sinner Lady" (1963), and "Praying with Eric" (the first in a series of *Meditations,* on *Town Hall Concert,* 1964). In performance Mingus demonstrated facility in maintaining a bass line while adding inner harmonies and improvised countermelodies, as in his version of "Stormy Weather" on the album *Mingus!* (1960); his ability to create conversational effects is heard on "What Love" on the album *Charles Mingus Presents Charles Mingus* (1960).

Writings: *Beneath the Underdog,* ed. Nel King (New York, 1971).

Bibl.: Brian Priestley, *Mingus: A Critical Biography* (London, 1982).

Minkus, Léon [Alois; Aloysius Ludwig] (b. Vienna, 23 Mar. 1826; d. there 7 Dec. 1917). Composer. Little is known of his early life; 1846, collaborated with Deldevez on the ballet *Paquita* in Paris; from 1853, directed Prince N. B. Yusupov's serf orchestra in St. Petersburg; from 1855, a violinist in the Bolshoi Theater orchestra, Moscow, meanwhile contributing music to Paris ballets, including *La source* (1866) in collaboration with Delibes. His first ballet for Moscow was the very successful and still-performed *Don Quixote* (1869); from August 1870, ballet composer to the imperial theaters of St. Petersburg, associating with Petipa and others on many ballets, including the still-performed *La bayadère* (1877); retired November 1886, but occasionally composed music for Russian ballets into the 1890s, finally returning to Vienna; also a violin teacher (Moscow Conservatory, 1866) and chamber player.

Mintz, Shlomo (b. Moscow, 30 Oct. 1957). Violinist. He grew up in Israel, where he studied with Ilona Feher; made his New York debut at Carnegie Hall in 1973; subsequently settled in the U.S. and studied at Juilliard (diploma, 1979). Music adviser to the Israel Chamber Orchestra from 1989. His recordings include concertos of Mendelssohn, Bruch, and Prokofiev in addition to the Bach sonatas and partitas.

Miroglio, Francis (b. Marseilles, 12 Dec. 1924). Composer. He studied at the conservatories in Marseilles (1954–57) and Paris (with Milhaud, 1951–52); worked in the electronic music studio of the ORTF in Paris (1959–61), and attended the Darmstadt courses in the 1960s; he was awarded the Gaudeamus Prize in 1960. In 1965 he founded (and until 1971 directed) the summer festival Nuits de la Fondation Maeght at St. Paul de Vence. He wrote for the stage (*Il faut rêver dit Lenine,* opera, Avignon, 1972) and for films; orchestral and chamber music, often involving tape, variable instrumentation, and mobile forms (*Masques,* 3–9 winds, 1971). *Projections* (1966–67) calls for string quartet and slides of paintings by Miró.

Mischakoff [Fischberg], **Mischa** (b. Proskurov, Ukraine, 16 Apr. 1896; d. Petoskey, Mich., 1 Feb. 1981). Violinist. Studied with Korguyev and Auer at the St. Petersburg Conservatory and made his debut in Berlin in 1912. Settled in the U.S. in 1921 and served as concertmaster with the New York Symphony (1924–27), Philadelphia Orchestra (1927–30), Chicago Symphony (1930–37), NBC Symphony (1937–52), and Detroit Symphony (1952–68), in addition to summers as concertmaster of the Chautauqua Symphony (1925–65). He taught at Juilliard (1941–52) and at Wayne State Univ. in Detroit (from 1952), and led the Mischakoff String Quartet.

Misón [Missón], **Luis** (bapt. Mataró, Barcelona, 26 Aug. 1727; d. Madrid, 13 Feb. 1766). Composer. Worked for the royal chapel in Madrid as a flutist and oboist from 1748, and as a conductor from 1756; also employed by the Teatro del Buen Retiro. Previously credited with inventing the *tonadilla* (more than 80 of his works in this genre survive), it now appears that Misón at most standardized its solo form. Other works include the intermezzo *La festa chinese* (1761) and 12 sonatas for flute, viola, and bass.

Mitchell, Howard (b. Lyons, Nebr., 11 Mar. 1911; d. Ormond Beach, Fla., 22 June 1988). Conductor and cellist. While studying cello at the Curtis Institute (1930–35) with Felix Salmond, he became principal cellist of the National Symphony in Washington. He remained with that orchestra as assistant (1945), associate (1948), and finally principal conductor (1949–69), leaving as music director emeritus to become principal conductor of the radio orchestra (SODRE) in Montevideo, Uruguay.

Mitchell, Joni [Anderson, Roberta Joan] (b. McLeod, Alberta, 1 Nov. 1943). Folk and rock singer and songwriter. After briefly studying commercial art, in the mid-1960s she performed in folk clubs in Toronto, Detroit, and New York. In 1967 she moved to Southern California and released albums of original folk material (including *Clouds,* 1969; *Blue,* 1971); later she integrated popular and rock styles and met with more commercial success (*Court and Spark,* 1974). She also experimented with jazz, recording with Jaco Pastorius (*Hejira,* 1976) and Mingus (1978). Her albums include also *Chalk Mark in a Rain Storm* (1988).

Mitchell, Red [Keith Moore] (b. New York, 20 Sept. 1927; d. Salem, Ore., 8 Nov. 1992). Jazz double bass player. After mastering the piano, he took up double bass during military service and played both in bands of the late 1940s. Between 1949 and 1954 he played bass with Charlie Ventura, Woody Herman, Red Norvo, and Gerry Mulligan. In the 1950s and 1960s he was prominent in Los Angeles as bandleader, collaborator, and studio bassist for MGM. In 1968 he settled in Stockholm, continuing to work prominently. Noted for his strong, clean soloistic sound, he pioneered expanded double bass techniques and tuning in fifths (C_1 G_1 D A).

Mitropoulos, Dimitri (b. Athens, 1 Mar. 1896; d. Milan, 2 Nov. 1960). Conductor, composer, and pianist. At the Athens Conservatory (1910–19) he studied piano with Ludwig Wassenhowen, composition with Armand Marsick. His opera *Soeur Béatrice* (1919) was seen by Saint-Saëns, who enabled him to study composition in Brussels with Paul Gilson (1920–21), in Berlin with Ferruccio Busoni (1921–24). Répétiteur at the Berlin Staatsoper, 1922–24; conductor of the Athens Symphony, 1924–37; professor of composition at Athens Conservatory from 1930. Achieved widespread notice when in Berlin 1930 he substituted for the pianist he was to conduct in Prokofiev's Third Concerto. Conductor of Monte Carlo Opera, 1934–37. U.S. debut with Boston Symphony, 1937. Music director of the Minneapolis Symphony, 1937–49. Co-conductor of the New York Philharmonic, 1949; conductor, 1950–57. While chief conductor of the New York Metropolitan Opera, 1954–60, he led the premiere of Barber's *Vanessa.* Endowed with a prodigious memory, he rehearsed even works such as *Wozzeck* without a score; his recording of this opera remains his outstanding legacy. His temperament suited him particularly well for interpreting scores of the late 19th and early 20th centuries. He died of a heart attack while rehearsing Mahler's Symphony no. 3. His own compositions include *La mise en tombeau de Christ* (1916), *Fête crétoise* (1928), and Concerto Grosso (1930) for orchestra; chamber and solo piano music.

Bibl.: Stathis A. Arfanis, *The Complete Discography of Dimitri Mitropoulos* (Athens, 1990).

Mitsukuri, Shūkichi (b. Tokyo, 21 Oct. 1895; d. Chigasaki, 10 May 1971). Composer. Educated in chemistry at the Imperial Univ. in Tokyo; after graduating in 1921, he traveled to Berlin, where he studied harmony privately with Georg Schumann. Back in Tokyo, he took composition lessons with Ikenouchi, Koenig, and Rosenstock in 1925. He then served as an engineering officer in the Imperial Navy. In 1930 he helped to form the Shinkō Sakkyokuka Renmei. Throughout the late 1930s he pursued the study of science, earning a doctorate in 1939, but by the mid-1940s he had turned solely to music. The lush tonality and late Romanticism of his musical language show the influence of his Germanic training, though his music occasionally incorporates melodic scales, such as the pentatonic, that are more typical of Japanese musical traditions. His orchestral music includes 2 symphonies (1949, 1963) and a concertino (piano, orchestra, 1953). Works also include chamber music and songs.

Miyagi [Wakabe; Suga], **Michio** [Nakasuga Kengyō] (b. Kobe, 7 Apr. 1894; d. Kariya, 25 June 1956). Composer and performer of the zoku-sō (13-string koto). Blind by the age of 7, he began to study the koto with Nakajima Kengyō II of the Ikunta school and in 1903 gave his first public solo performance. In 1907 he went to Korea to teach koto and the shakuhachi at Jinsen in Inchon and in Keijō in Seoul. By 1909 he had begun composing for the koto and in 1920 formed the Shin Nihon Ongaku (New Japanese Music Movement) with Seifū Yoshida. Together they worked toward integrating Western music concepts with composition for native Japanese instruments. By 1917 he had returned to Tokyo, where his music began to be performed publicly. He taught at the Tokyo Music School from 1930 through the war and, after the war, continued teaching at the National Univ. of Fine Arts and Music. His music integrates forms and genres from European music into the Japanese musical traditions that serve as his compositional foundation. He has also experimented with the construction of Japanese instruments, creating 17-string and 80-string variants of the koto. His works include some choral music for voices and various kinds of accompaniment. He wrote primarily solo vocal and chamber music; the former usually involved accompaniment by Japanese instruments (*Yamato no haru* [Spring in Yamato], voice, koto, ensemble, 1940).

Miyoshu, Akira (b. Tokyo, 10 Jan. 1933). Composer. A prodigious pianist as a child, he studied composition with Kōzaburō Hirai and Ikenouchi. He then went to Paris where, with the aid of a French government scholarship, he studied composition at the Paris Conservatory with Challan and Gallois-Montbrun from 1955 to 1957. He returned to Tokyo Univ. to study French literature, graduating in 1960. In 1965 he became a lecturer at the Toho Gakuen School of Music in Tokyo. His music is influenced in choice of genres and instruments by European traditions. His dramatic music includes 2 poetic dramas (*Happy Prince,* 1959; *Oudine,* 1959). He wrote orchestral music (symphonies; concerto for piano, 1962; concerto for violin, 1965) and chamber music (sonata for flute, cello, piano, 1955). Later he began incorporating percussion and Japanese instruments into chamber works (*IV,* string quartet, 4 Japanese instruments, 1972) and occasionally used electronics (*Transit,* electronic and concrete sounds, percussion, keyboard instruments, 1969). He utilized unusual combinations of instruments (*Odes métamorphosées,* marimba, vibraphone, cello, piano, harp, orchestra, 1968). In addition, his vocal music uses varied combinations of voices and ensemble accompaniment (*Torse II,* chorus, piano, tape, 1961; *Duel,* soprano, orchestra, 1964).

Mizelle, (Dary) John (b. Stillwater, Okla., 14 June 1940). Composer. He studied trombone at California State Univ. in Sacramento and composition at the Univ. of California Davis and San Diego campuses, where his teachers included Gaburo, Oliveros, and Stockhausen. He taught at the Univ. of South Florida (1973–75) and Oberlin College Conservatory (1975–79), then served as technical director for Sonavera Studio of Sonic Arts (Hawthorne, N.Y., 1979–80); on the faculty of SUNY–Purchase from 1990. His works employ live electronics and variable instrumentation; are often minimalist and influenced by Eastern music and thought; frequently they require improvisation. They include *Polyphonies I, II, III* (electronics, shakuhachi, dancer, and actress, 1975); *Polytempus II* (marimba, tape, 1980); *Genesis* (orchestra, 1985); *Blue* (orchestra, 1986); *Fossy: A Passion Play* (music theater, 1987); *Chance Gives Me What I Want* (dance piece, 1988).

Mizler, Lorenz Christoph (b. Heidenheim, 25 July 1711; d. Warsaw, March 1778). Mathematician and writer on music. At the Ansbach Gymnasium he studied singing and keyboard instruments; from 1731 he was a student of theology at the Univ. of Leipzig, where he received a master's degree in 1734. He was a friend of J. S. Bach and a close associate of Mattheson, who published Mizler's autobiography in *Grundlage einer Ehren-Pforte* (Hamburg, 1740). From 1737 he taught at the Univ. of Leipzig, and he began compiling his *Neu eröffnete musikalische Bibliothek* (1739–54). From 1743 he served as librarian and mathematician for the Polish Count Malachowski. In 1752 he became court physician at Warsaw. He published widely, including works in mathematics, theology, philosophy, law, and music. He also annotated and translated Fux's *Gradus ad Parnassum* into German in 1742.

Bibl.: Franz Wöhlke, *Lorenz Christoph Mizler: Ein Beitrag zur musikalischen Gelehrtengeschichte des 18. Jahrhunderts* (Würzburg, 1940).

Mizuno, Sūhkō (b. Tokushima, 24 Feb. 1934). Composer. From 1958 to 1963 he studied composition with Shibata and Hasegawa at the National Univ. for Fine Arts and Music. During this time he explored improvisatory techniques; he used improvisation in his pieces and in 1958 helped create the Group Music improvisatory ensemble. Taught at Chiba Univ. from 1968 until 1971, when he became lecturer at the National Univ. for Fine Arts and Music. He continued to explore avant-garde techniques such as sound clusters, aleatoric devices, and graphic notation. Jazz also serves as musical stimulus. Works include *Remote Control* (tape, 1962); *Dies Irae* (chorus, electronics, 1972); *Jazz Orchestra '73* (1973); *Tenshukaku Monogatari* (opera, 1977).

Młynarski, Emil (b. Kibarty, near Suwałki, 18 July 1870; d. Warsaw, 5 Apr. 1935). Composer. From 1880 until 1889 he attended the St. Petersburg Conservatory, studying violin with Auer, piano with Rubinstein, and composition with Lyadov. In 1894 he traveled to Odessa to teach at the music school of the Imperial Music Society. He went back to Warsaw in 1898 and there established a career as a conductor. He was active in the creation of public orchestral concerts. From 1904 through 1907 he was director of the Warsaw Conservatory; conducted the Scottish Symphony, 1910–16. Through 1917 he conducted at the Bolshoi Theater in Moscow. During the 1920s he was again based in Warsaw. From 1929 to 1931 he taught at the Curtis Institute in Philadelphia but returned to Warsaw because of ill health. His music was late Romantic in style, occasionally using folk elements. His dramatic music included an opera (*Noc letnia* [Summer Night], 1914), and his orchestral music included a symphony (1910) and 2 violin concertos (1897, 1914–17). He also composed chamber music.

Mockridge, Cyril (John) (b. London, 6 Aug. 1896; d. Honolulu, 18 Jan. 1979). Composer. He studied at the Royal Academy of Music in London but moved to the U.S. in 1922, working on Broadway as a rehearsal pianist and arranger. In 1932 he joined the Fox Film Corporation as a composer and director of film music; in that position and as a free-lance composer (from 1960) he contributed to over 200 film scores, including *The Ox-Bow Incident* (1943) and *Donovan's Reef* (1963). He also wrote music for television series.

Mocquereau, André (b. La Tessoualle, Maine-et-Loire, 6 June 1849; d. Solesmes, 18 Jan. 1930). Scholar. Entered the abbey of Solesmes in 1875; took his vows in 1877; became a priest in 1879; prior of Solesmes, 1902–8, going to the Isle of Wight on the expulsion of the order from France in 1903, later returning to Solesmes. He was a student of and then assistant to Joseph Pothier in his scholarly work on plainchant, succeeding him in 1889 as abbey choirmaster and becoming an important influence on the formulation of the Solesmes style of chant performance, especially through his theories of plainchant rhythm; founder (1889) and editor of the first 13 volumes of *Paléographie musicale;* 1904, member of the Vatican commission for a new official edition of the chant.

Bibl.: P. Combe, "Bibliographie de Dom André Mocquereau," *Études grégoriennes* 11 (1957): 189–203.

Moderne, Jacques (b. Pinguente, ca. 1495–1500; d. Lyons, 1562 or later). Printer. Of Italian origin but resident in Lyons by 1523. His press issued books of many sorts but concentrated from 1532 on music. For years he and Pierre Attaingnant, whose first book came out in 1528, were the only music printers active in France. Moderne concentrated on newly composed music and thus produced the first (and in many cases only) prints of the majority of the roughly 800 pieces he published. His output, though predominantly of music by French or Franco-Flemish composers, was notably more cosmopolitan than that of Attaingnant. His best-known publications are the *Motteti del fiori* (4 vols.) and *Le parangon des chansons* (11 or more vols.), but additional books of motets, chansons, Masses, noëls, and instrumental music also came from his press.

Bibl.: Samuel F. Pogue, *Jacques Moderne: Lyons Music Printer of the Sixteenth Century* (Geneva, 1969). Id., "A Sixteenth-Century Editor at Work: Gardane and Moderne," *JM* 1 (1982): 217–38.

Mödl, Martha (b. Nuremberg, 22 Mar. 1912). Soprano and mezzo-soprano. She was working as an accountant when in 1940 she entered the Nuremberg Conservatory to study voice; further studies with Otto Mueller in Milan. Debut as a mezzo-soprano at the Remscheid Stadttheater in 1943 as Humperdinck's

Hänsel. While singing mezzo roles at the Düsseldorf Opera, 1945–49, she grew into a dramatic soprano. Joined the Hamburg Opera, 1949. Covent Garden debut as Carmen, 1949. Sang Kundry and Gutrune at Bayreuth at its reopening in 1951; thereafter appeared annually throughout the 1950s, usually as Isolde or Brünnhilde. New York Metropolitan Opera debut, 1956. Sang Strauss's Clytemnestra, a mezzo role, at Covent Garden, 1966. Created characters in Wolfgang Fortner's *Elisabeth Tudor* in Berlin, 1972; in Friedrich Cerha's *Baal* at Salzburg, 1981.

Moeran, E(rnest) J(ohn) (b. Heston, Middlesex, 31 Dec. 1894; d. near Kernmare, Ireland, 1 Dec. 1950). Composer. His father was a clergyman, and his first musical influence was sacred music. He studied violin at Uppingham School, then at the Royal College of Music, London, in 1913. He served in the British army in World War I but was wounded and discharged. He returned to London to study composition with Ireland from 1920 to 1923 and developed an interest in folk songs, collecting them in Norfolk. This interest was felt in the rhythms and melodies of his compositional style and in his arrangements of folk songs. His early music was much influenced by Delius and Ireland. Through the 1920s his music began to receive public performances. His orchestral music includes a Symphony in G minor (1934–37), many one-movement descriptive works (*Whythorne's Shadow,* 1931) and rhapsodies (*Rhapsody,* piano, orchestra, 1943), and a violin concerto (1945). His chamber music includes programmatic pieces (*Bank Holiday, Summer Valley,* piano, 1923) as well as examples of traditional genres.

Bibl.: Geoffrey Self, *The Music of E. J. Moeran* (London, 1986).

Moeschinger, Albert (b. Basel, 10 Jan. 1897; d. Thun, 25 Sept. 1985). Composer. He studied in Bern, Leipzig, and Munich (1917–23) and taught piano and theory at the Bern Conservatory (1937–43), after which he retired from teaching in order to compose. He was primarily influenced by Reger and Debussy, but wrote some twelve-tone works beginning in the mid-1950s. His compositions include a ballet and a radio opera; 5 symphonies, 5 piano concertos, and other orchestral works (*Blocs sonores,* 1977); string quartets, wind trios, and other chamber music; piano and organ works; and choral and solo vocal music (*Miracles d'enfance,* mezzo-soprano, 2 flutes, 2 clarinets, oboe, harp, double bass, and percussion, 1961).

Moevs, Robert (Walter) (b. La Crosse, Wis., 2 Dec. 1920). Composer and pianist. He graduated from Harvard before serving in the Air Force during the Second World War; from 1947 to 1951 he studied in Paris with Boulanger, then returned to Harvard to work toward a master's degree under Piston (1952). He won the Rome Prize and spent three years at the American Academy in Rome, then taught at Harvard (1955–63) and Rutgers (from 1964), returning to Rome as composer-in-residence at the American Academy in 1960–61. Works include the ballet *Endymion* (1948); Concerto Grosso (piano, percussion, orchestra, 1960–68); *Symphonic Piece* no. 5 (1984); *Pandora: Music for Small Orchestra, II* (1986); *Dark Litany* (wind ensemble, 1987); *Crystals* (solo flute, 1979); *Paths and Ways* (dancer and saxophone, 1970); a woodwind quintet (1988); String Quartet no. 2 (1989); piano and organ music; sacred choral works (*A Brief Mass,* choir, organ, vibraphone, guitar, double bass, 1968); songs.

Moffo, Anna (b. Wayne, Pa., 27 June 1932). Soprano. Studied voice with Euphemia Giannini-Gregory at the Curtis Institute; after 1953 with Luigi Ricci and Mercedes Llopart in Perugia and Rome. Debut in 1955 at the Spoleto Festival as Norina *(Don Pasquale).* La Scala and Salzburg Festival debuts in 1957 as Nannetta *(Falstaff).* New York Metropolitan debut in 1959 as Violetta *(Traviata).* Covent Garden debut in 1964 as Gilda *(Rigoletto).* With the Met she sang Pamina *(Zauberflöte),* Verdi's Luisa Miller, Gounod's Juliette, Debussy's Mélisande, and other French and Italian roles. In 1974–75 she experienced serious vocal problems. She returned to the stage to sing in *Thaïs* (Seattle, 1976), *Adriana Lecouvreur* (Parma, 1978), and *The Taming of the Shrew* (Vienna, Va., 1979).

Mohaupt, Richard (b. Breslau, 14 Sept. 1904; d. Reichenau, Austria, 3 July 1957). Composer. He studied music in Breslau at the university, then worked as a vocal coach and opera conductor; toured as a pianist and conductor in eastern Europe and Asia; and composed and played film music in Berlin before moving to New York in 1939. (He is apparently the author of an article "Inside Germany," on the Nazi debasement of German culture, published in *Modern Music* shortly after his arrival in New York.) He composed much light and film music as well as 4 operas (*Double Trouble,* 1954) and 5 ballets; orchestral music (*Stadtpfeifermusik,* 1939; rev. for winds, 1953); chamber and piano music; vocal and choral music with orchestra; songs and children's songs. He returned to Europe in 1955.

Moiseiwitsch [Moyseivich], **Benno** (b. Odessa, 22 Feb. 1890; d. London, 9 Apr. 1963). Pianist. Studied with Klimov at the Imperial Music Academy, Odessa, and won the Rubinstein Prize at the age of 9. Continued his studies in Vienna with Leschetizky; made his debut in Reading, England, in 1908. He embarked on a number of concert tours beginning in 1919 and was particularly acclaimed for his performances of Rachmaninoff. He took British nationality in 1937.

Mole, Miff [Irving Milford] (b. Roosevelt, N.Y., 11 Mar. 1898; d. New York, 29 Apr. 1961). Jazz trombonist and bandleader. During the 1920s he pioneered a light, precise, swing-style technique that established a new soloistic role for the trombone in Dixieland and innovative jazz. He associated with Bix Beiderbecke, Red Nichols, and the Memphis Five in the 1920s; with NBC studios and Paul Whiteman in the 1930s; and with Benny Goodman in 1943. Thereafter he led his own combos in New York and Chicago, often teaming with cornetist Mugsy Spanier. A hip operation in 1954 reduced his activities.

Molinari, Bernardino (b. Rome, 11 Apr. 1880; d. there, 25 Dec. 1952). Conductor. Graduated in 1902 from the Liceo di S. Cecilia in Rome, where his teachers included Renzi and Falchi; served as artistic director of the Augusteo Orchestra in Rome (1912–43) and taught at the Accademia di S. Cecilia (from 1936). He frequently performed works by a number of modern Italian composers including Alfano, Perosi, and Respighi, as well as other contemporaries such as Strauss and Stravinsky.

Molinaro, Simone (b. ca. 1565; d. Genoa, 1615). Composer. *Maestro di cappella* of S. Lorenzo, Genoa, by 1602. A connoisseur of contemporary Italian music; editor of madrigals by Gesualdo and compiler of 2 volumes of sacred *contrafacta* of other madrigals. His knowledge of these works is evident in both the form and the musical language of his own compositions, written for lute (dances, fantasias, and intabulations of vocal works) or for voices (especially motets and madrigals).

Molique, (Wilhelm) Bernhard (b. Nuremberg, 7 Oct. 1802; d. Cannstadt, near Stuttgart, 10 May 1869). Violinist and composer. Son and pupil of a Nuremberg town musician, learning several instruments, principally the violin; at 14 studied in Munich with Rovelli; 1817–20, played in the Theater an der Wien orchestra; then succeeded Rovelli as concertmaster of the Munich orchestra; 1822, began to tour Germany as soloist; 1826–49, concertmaster, Stuttgart court orchestra; 1849, settled in London as chamber musician, teacher, and composer; 1861, professor of composition, Royal Academy of Music; 1866, retired to Cannstadt. Composed 6 violin concertos, notably no. 5 in A minor, op. 21; a well-known cello concerto, op. 45; an oratorio, *Abraham* (Norwich, 1860); chamber music.

Mollenhauer, Emil (b. Brooklyn, 4 Aug. 1855; d. New York, 10 Dec. 1927). Violinist and conductor. Studied violin with his father, Friedrich Mollenhauer, and played in Booth's Theater and in the Theodore Thomas Orchestra while still a teenager; also played with the New York Symphony Society. In 1884 he joined the Boston Symphony, but left with George W. Stewart in 1889 to form the Boston Festival Orchestra, serving as concertmaster and conductor there for over 20 years. Mollenhauer also conducted the Boston Municipal Band and the Handel and Haydn Society (1899–1927).

Moller, John Christopher [Möller, Johann Christoph] (b. Germany, 1755; d. New York, 21 Sept. 1803). Composer, organist, and concert organizer. Little is known of his early life or training. He was in London during the late 1770s, but moved to the U.S. around 1785. He began in New York; later (during the 1790s) he became a central musical figure in Philadelphia. He was organist at Zion Lutheran Church and in 1793 established, with Henri Capron, a music press; it was one of the first American presses exclusively for music. From 1796 he managed the New York City Concerts. Among his works are a number of pieces published during his London years (mostly chamber music); also a sinfonia (ed. in W. Thomas Marrocco, *Music in America,* New York, 1964); a cantata (*Dank und Gebet,* 1794); piano works.

Bibl.: Ronald D. Stetzel, "John Christopher Moller (1755–1803) and His Role in Early American Music" (diss., Univ. of Iowa, 1965).

Molnár, Antal (b. Budapest, 7 Jan. 1890; d. there, 7 Dec. 1983). Composer. From 1907 to 1910 he studied violin and composition with Herzfeld at the Budapest Academy. He played viola with the Waldbauer String Quartet, 1910–13, and with the Dohnányi–Hubay Piano Quartet, 1917–19. During this time he also collected folk songs and taught music history. From 1919 until 1959 he served on the faculty of the Budapest Academy of Music. He was instrumental in the establishment of musicology in Hungary, writing insightfully about contemporary music, especially Bartók and Kodály, as well as about the aesthetics and teaching of music. He wrote primarily chamber music (3 string quartets, 1912, 1926, 1928), keyboard works, songs, and folk song arrangements.

Molter, Johann Melchior (b. Tiefenort, near Eisenach, 10 Feb. 1696; d. Karlsruhe, 12 Jan. 1765). Composer. Around 1717 he entered the service of the Margrave Carl Wilhelm of Baden-Durlach (who resided in Karlsruhe) as a violinist; was sent to Venice and Rome (1719–21) to study the Italian style; appointed Kapellmeister upon his return. Later served Duke Wilhelm Heinrich of Saxe-Eisenach in the same capacity (1734–41) and made a second trip to Italy (1737–38). From 1747 until his death Molter served Carl Wilhelm's grandson Margrave Carl Friedrich. He composed in all contemporary genres; his music is notable for its experimentation with timbre, especially with wind instruments such as the clarinet and flauto d'amore.

Momigny, Jérôme-Joseph de (b. Philippeville, Namur, 20 Jan. 1762; d. Charenton, near Paris, 25 Aug. 1842). Music theorist and composer. He studied organ and served in church posts in St. Omer and (from 1785) in Lyons. An enemy of the Jacobins, he fled to Switzerland during the French Revolution, returning to Lyons to found a music publishing enterprise in 1800. After publishing more than 700 works, the firm went bankrupt in 1828. In his later years he received a pension, and he died in an asylum. He proposed a fresh theoretical system that included a theory of rhythm based on the principle that all music proceeds from an upbeat to a downbeat and a harmonic theory that accepted the enharmonic equivalents as having equal importance to the seven diatonic pitch classes. Among his writings are a *Méthode de piano* (Paris, 1802); *Cours complet d'harmonie et de composition* (Paris, 1803–6); and *La seule vrai théorie de la musique* (Paris, 1821). He also composed operas, chamber music, and songs.

Mompou, Federico (b. Barcelona, 16 Apr. 1893; d. there, 30 June 1987). Composer. He studied the piano at the Conservatorio del Liceo, then went to Paris and studied piano with Ferdinand Motte-Lacroix and Isidore Philipp and harmony with Marcel Samuel-Rousseau. His extreme shyness prevented him from pursuing a concert career, so he decided to devote himself to composition. In 1914 he returned to Barcelona, but in 1921 went back to Paris, where the critic Vuillermoz championed his music. From 1941 he lived in Barcelona; he was elected a member of the Royal Academy of San Jorge in Barcelona and of San Fernando in Madrid. Debussy and the new French school had strong influences on his music. The influence of Satie in particular can be seen in his ideal of primitivism; he adopted popular themes while shunning modulation and development.

Works: For piano: *Impresiones íntimas* (1911–14); *Pessebres* (1914–17); *Suburbis* (1916–17); *Scènes d'enfants* (1915–19); *Cants magics* (1917–19); *Fêtes lointaines* (1920); *Charmes* (1920–21); *Dialogues* I–IV (1923–44); *Cançons i dansas* I–XII (1921–62); *Preludes* I–X (1927–51); *Souvenirs de l'exposition* (1937); *La canción que más amaba* (1944); *Canción de cuna* (1951); *Variaciones sobre un tema de Chopin* (1938–57); *Paisajes* (1942–60); *Música callada* (1959–67). Also choral works; songs; *Suite compostelana* (guitar, 1963); *Perlimplinada* (ballet, with Montsalvatge, 1956)

Bibl.: Santiago Kastner, *Federico Mompou* (Madrid, 1946). Antonio Iglesias, *Federico Mompou* (Madrid, 1977). Cara Janés, *Federico Mompou: Vida, textos, documentos* (Madrid, 1987).

Monasterio, Jesús (b. Potes, near Santander, Spain, 21 Mar. 1836; d. Casar del Periedo, 28 Sept. 1903). Violinist. A child prodigy; 1843, played for the queen, who became his patron; studied in Madrid, then at the Brussels Conservatory with Bériot; 1854, honorary violinist, Spanish Royal Chapel. From 1857 he taught at the Madrid Conservatory, director in 1894–97; 1861, toured Belgium, Holland, Germany. He was a leading figure in Madrid musical life, founding the Quartet Society (1863) and conducting the Sociedad de conciertos (1869–76); published violin pieces *(Adiós a la Alhambra)* and etudes.

Moncayo García, José Pablo (b. Guadalajara, 29 June 1912; d. Mexico City, 16 June 1958). Composer. Studied under Huízar and Chávez at the Mexico City Conservatory, while he formed the "Group of Four" with Galindo, Ayala, and Contreras. Served as pianist and percussionist, and later as artistic director, of the Mexican Symphony (1932–47), and also led the National Symphony (1949–52). Works include the acclaimed opera *La mulata de Córdoba* (1948); *Huapango,* a folk dance adaptation for orchestra (1941); *Homenaje a Cervantes,* 2 oboes and strings (1947); choral works; and piano compositions.

Monckton, (John) Lionel (Alexander) (b. London, 18 Dec. 1861; d. there, 15 Feb. 1924). Composer. Educated at Charterhouse and Oxford; became a lawyer, also drama and music critic for London newspapers. He composed songs, some of which became popular, for musical comedies, eventually whole shows, especially *The Arcadians* (1909; collaboration with Talbot) and *The Quaker Girl* (1910).

Mondonville, Jean-Joseph Cassanéa de (b. Narbonne, bapt. 25 Dec. 1711; d. Belleville, 8 Oct. 1772). Violinist and composer. Published his first opus, a volume of instrumental music, in Paris (*Sonates,* 1733). In 1734 he appeared as a violinist at the Concert spirituel, then took a post with the Concert de Lille. He returned to Paris in 1739, became a violinist of the royal chapel and chamber and performed in approximately 100 concerts; some of his *grands motets* were also performed that year to considerable acclaim. He was appointed *sous-maître* (1740) and then intendant (1744) of the royal chapel, produced operas and *grands motets* for the Opéra and Concert spirituel, respectively, and was associated with the Théatre des Petits-Cabinets; he maintained his career as a violinist throughout the 1740s. Mondonville is best known today for his *Pièces de clavecin en sonates* (op. 3, 1734) and *Pièces de clavecin avec voix ou violon* (op. 5, 1748). His operas were quite successful in their time; they include *Le carnaval du Parnasse* (Paris, 1749), *Titon et l'Aurore* (Paris, 1753), and *Thésée* (1765). The introduction to his sonatas *Les sons harmoniques* op. 4 (Paris and Lille, 1738) includes the first manual on playing violin harmonics.

Bibl.: Edith Borroff, "The Instrumental Style of Jean-Joseph Cassanéa de Mondonville," *RMFC* 7 (1967): 165-204.

Moniuszko, Stanislaw (b. Ubiel, near Minsk, 5 May 1819; d. Warsaw, 4 June 1872). Composer. In 1827 his family moved to Warsaw, where he studied the piano with August Freyer, and in 1830 to Minsk, where he went to school and began to compose; October 1837–June 1839, studied with Rungenhagen in Berlin, publishing 3 songs there in 1838; then returned to Poland. From 1840 to 1858, organist at St. John's in Vilnius, also active there as a teacher, conductor, composer (operettas, sacred music, cantatas, and especially some 360 Polish songs, which he published in 1842–59 in the 6 installments of his *Home Song Book*). His first opera, *Halka,* was given in concert there in 1848 and staged in 1854. A revised, expanded version was produced in Warsaw in 1858 and hailed as the prototype for a Polish opera. Another opera, *Flis,* was also successful in Warsaw in 1858. Now an important musical personage, he moved to Warsaw in 1859, becoming conductor at the Grand Theater and from 1864 teaching harmony and counterpoint at the conservatory (publishing a harmony text in 1871). Through 1869 he produced 4 more operas with less success, and his last stage work, *Beata,* an operetta (1872), was a fiasco.

Bibl.: W. Rudzinski, ed., *Dzieła* [Works] (Kraków, 1965–). Z. Jachimecki, "Stanislaus Moniuszko," *MQ* 14 (1928): 54–62. B. M. Maciejewski, *Moniuszko, Father of Polish Opera* (London, 1979).

Monk, Meredith (Jane) (b. Lima, Peru, 20 Nov. 1942). Composer and singer. She was raised in New York and Connecticut and attended Sarah Lawrence College (B.A., performing arts, 1969). In 1968 she founded the Meredith Monk Vocal Ensemble, performing in the U.S. and Europe. Her vocal music involves extended vocal techniques and piano accompaniments influenced by minimalism and popular music; her choice of accompanying instruments varies (flute, guitar, dulcimer, accordion, percussion, harmonium, cello, synthesizer, and bagpipes). Active as filmmaker, choreographer, and director of her numerous theater pieces. Works include *Juice* (theater cantata, 85 solo voices, 85 jew's harps, and 2 violins, 1969); *Turtle Dreams* (cabaret, 4 solo voices and 2 electronic organs, 1983); *Book of Days* (film score, 10 voices, cello, shawm, synthesizer, hammered dulcimer, bagpipe, hurdy-gurdy, 1988); *Atlas* (opera, 1991); *Engine Steps* (tape collage, 1983); *Book of Days* (5 solo voices and electronic organ, 1985); *Our Lady of the Late* (voice, wineglass, 1972–73; arranged with percussion, 1974).

Monk, Thelonious (Sphere) [Thelious Junior] (b. Rocky Mount, N.C., 10 Oct. 1917; d. Weehawken, N.J., 17 Feb. 1982). Jazz pianist, composer, and bandleader. In New York he played in bop jam sessions at Minton's Playhouse (early 1940s), recorded with Coleman Hawkins (1944), and briefly joined Dizzy Gillespie's big band (1946). From 1947 his reputation derived mainly from his own recordings, especially after a false drug conviction led to the revocation of his New York cabaret card in 1951. With its return he led quartets including tenor saxophonists John Coltrane (1957), Johnny Griffin (1958), and Charlie Rouse (1959–70). In 1971–72 he toured with the Giants of Jazz, a sextet including Gillespie and Art Blakey (Monk's sideman on many recordings from 1947 to 1957). Characteristic of Monk's unique piano playing were the simultaneous sounding of semitones (to simulate blue notes), unpredictable rhythmic placement, whole note runs, sparse but colorful voicings of chords, recurring references to thematic material, and motivic development; examples include the unaccompanied albums *Thelonious Himself* (1957) and *Solo Monk* (1964). Many of these elements went into his compositions. His recordings of his compositions include "Well You Needn't," "'Round about Midnight" (both 1947), "Misterioso" (1948), "Criss Cross" (1951), "Bemsha Swing" on the album *Miles Davis All Stars* (1954), and the title tracks of his albums *Brilliant Corners* (1956) and *Straight, No Chaser* (1966–67).

Monk, William Henry (b. London, 16 Mar. 1823; d. there, 1 Mar. 1889). Organist and editor. From 1841, an organist, choirmaster, teacher, and lecturer in London and elsewhere; an advocate of the reform of Anglican church music; best known as first editor of *Hymns Ancient and Modern* (1861) and a participant in later editions; composed hymns and other church music.

Monk [Mönch] **of Salzburg** (fl. late 14th cent.). Poet and composer. Author of both words and music for almost 50 sacred and over 55 secular songs, transmitted in manuscripts of the 15th century and later. His patron was the politically active Archbishop of Salzburg, Pilgrim II. Most of the sacred songs are linked to the liturgical year; all are monophonic. The secular songs range widely in lyric genre; a few are polyphonic, the earliest such pieces from Germany to survive.

Monn [Mann], **Matthias Georg** [Georg Matthias] (b. Vienna, 9 Apr. 1717; d. there, 3 Oct. 1750). Composer and organist. He was a chorister in the monastery of Klosterneuburg (ca. 1731), and around 1738 he was appointed organist at the Karlskirche in Vienna. He remained in that post for most of his life; he became well known at court, where his works were performed frequently. He was also prominent as pedagogue; Albrechtsberger was among his pupils. Today he is hailed as a pioneering early symphonist; more than 20 of his symphonies are extant, as well as concertos, chamber works (including 6 string quartets), keyboard music, and vocal works. He wrote a *Theorie des Generalbasses in Beispielen ohne Erklärung,* which remains in manuscript. One of his works is often cited as the first known 4-movement symphony with a third-movement minuet. A number of his works are edited in *DTÖ* 31 and 39. *DTÖ* 39 contains a partial thematic catalog of works by him and by his brother Johann Christoph (1726–82).

Monnikendam, Marius (b. Haarlem, 28 May 1896; d. Amsterdam, 22 May 1977). Composer. Studied composition with Dresden and organ and piano with de Pauw at the Amsterdam Conservatory of music. He traveled to Paris in 1925 and studied composition with Aubert and d'Indy at the Schola cantorum. He taught music in Rotterdam and Amsterdam and was also an influential music critic. His music was in a conservative academic style. He wrote orchestral music and many sacred works, using styles and techniques such as plainchant that he had learned at the Schola. Yet his music often used expanded harmonic resources or extramusical dimensions (*Via sacra,* speaker, chorus, organ, percussion, projector, 1969). He also wrote many works for organ, among them the Toccata no. 2 (1971) and Toccata Concertante (1976).

Monod, Jacques-Louis (b. Asnières, near Paris, 25 Feb. 1927). Conductor, pianist, and composer. He attended the Paris Conservatory and took composition with René Leibowitz (1944–50), continuing his studies at Juilliard with Wagenaar (composition) and at Columbia with Rudolf Thomas (conducting); made his piano debut in Paris in 1949, and in 1951 directed the first all-Webern concert ever given. Monod played or conducted the premieres of several works by the New Viennese school and recorded much 20th-century music. Taught at a number of American institutions including the New England Conservatory, Princeton, and Columbia.

Monosoff [Pancaldo], **Sonya** (b. Cleveland, 11 June 1927). Violinist. After studying at the Juilliard School, she became a founding member of the New York Pro Musica under Noah Greenberg; in 1963 she founded the Baroque Players of New York; she was among the first in the U.S. to record works of Biber, Bach, Geminiani, and Corelli on the baroque violin. From 1972 she taught at Cornell, and played in the Amadé Trio with Bilson and Hsu from 1974; recorded Mozart sonatas with Bilson. In 1988 she held a Fulbright award for lectures and performances in Australia.

Monpou, (François Louis) Hippolyte (b. Paris, 12 Jan. 1804; d. Orléans, 10 Aug. 1841). Composer. From the age of 5 a choirboy in Paris; from 1817 a pupil at Choron's church-music school; from 1825 a church musician in Paris, also working in 1828–30 as accompanist at the school, on the closing of which in 1830 he sought and found success as a composer, first of romances (establishing his popularity with a setting of Musset's *Andalouse*), then of opéras comiques (8 produced, 1835–40); died of ailments exacerbated by overwork on his first Scribe libretto, *Lambert Simnel,* completed by Adam.

Monroe, Bill [William] **(Smith)** (b. near Rosine, Ky., 13 Sept. 1911). Country singer, songwriter, and mandolin player. A founder of bluegrass music. After early performances with brother Charlie (1903–75), in 1938 he formed the Blue Grass Boys, who joined the Grand Ole Opry in 1939. Particularly with the addition in 1945 of guitarist Lester Flatt and banjo player Earl Scruggs, this group established the classic bluegrass sound, featuring Monroe's high harmony singing and a string texture of mandolin, guitar, banjo, and fiddle. It also served as a training ground for many later bluegrass artists including Vassar Clements, Chubby Wise, and Byron Berline. Monroe's compositions include "Mule Skinner Blues" (1940), "Blue Moon of Kentucky" (1947) and "Cheyenne" (1955).

Monsigny, Pierre Alexandre (b. Fauquembergues, 17 Oct. 1729; d. Paris, 14 Jan. 1817). Composer. He was educated by the Jesuits at St. Omer; moved to Paris in 1749 to begin working to support his family as a clerk in the office of the Comptes de Clergé. He was largely self-taught in music, though he had some lessons in harmony and counterpoint with a bassist in the Opéra, Gianotti, whose teachings were based on the theoretical works of Rameau. Monsigny's first opera, *Les aveux indiscrets,* was a huge success at its 1759 performance at Paris's Foire St.-Germain Theater; it sparked 2 more operas for that stage, *Le maître en droit* (1760) and *Le cadi dupé* (1761). He collaborated with librettist Sedaine throughout the 1760s, beginning with *On ne s'avise jamais de tout* in 1761. In 1768 he received a post as *maître d'hôtel* for the Duke of Orleans; he remained until 1784, when the duke died and the post was dissolved. From 1799 he received a pension, and in 1800 he became Inspector of Musical Education, succeeding Piccinni. Around 1810 his works became popular again; his fame continued to grow during the first part of the century. Other operas include *Le roy et le fermier* (1762); *Rose et Colas* (1764); *Aline, reine de Golconde* (1766); *Philémon et Baucis* (1766); *L'isle sonnante* (1767); *Le déserteur* (1769); *Le faucon* (1771); *Félix ou L'enfant trouvé* (1777).

Bibl.: Arthur Pougin, *Monsigny et son temps* (Paris, 1908). Paule Druilhe, *Monsigny, sa vie et son oeuvre* (Paris, 1955).

Montagnana, Antonio (b. Venice; fl. 1730–50). Bass. He may have studied with Porpora and was a member of Handel's company at the King's Theatre (1731–33). In 1731 he performed in *Admeto, Giulio Cesare,* and the first productions of *Ezio* and *Sosarme;* Handel composed the part of Abner in *Athalia* for him. In 1733 Montagnana joined the Opera of the Nobility, remaining with the company through their four London seasons; he also appeared with Heidegger's company at the King's Theatre (1737–38) and the royal chapel at Madrid (1740–50).

Montagnana, Domenico (b. Lendinara, ca. 1687; d. Venice, 7 Mar. 1750). String instrument maker. He went to Venice before 1700 and became a pupil of Goffriller; opened his own shop around 1711, though few extant instruments date from before 1720. Only one viola has been attributed to him, the famous "Tertis" model adopted by modern makers. Montagnana is especially known for his cellos, whose sound quality and volume rival the great Cremonese instruments.

Montague, Stephen (Rowley) (b. Syracuse, 10 Mar. 1943). Composer and pianist. He studied at Florida State Univ., taught at Butler Univ. (1967–69), then studied further at Ohio State Univ. (D.M.A., 1972). In 1972 he held a Fulbright award in Warsaw at the electronic music studio of Polish Radio; in 1974 moved to England, where he founded the Electronic-Acoustic Music Association of Great Britain (1980). His work is strongly influenced by minimalism. One of many dance scores, *Median* (orchestra, 1984), was commissioned by the Sadler's Wells Royal Ballet. Other works include *Sound Round* (orchestra and tape delay, 1973); *Sotto voce* (graphic score for chorus and electronics, 1976); *Paramell III* (piano and audience drone, 1981); a concerto for piano and chamber orchestra (1988); *In memoriam* (string quartet with electronics, 1989).

Montanos, Francisco de (b. ca. 1528; d. after 1592). Theorist. *Maestro de capilla* in Valladolid from 1551. His treatise *Arte de musica theorica y pratica* (Valladolid, 1592) covers both plainchant and mensural music, with numerous original musical examples, and served as a major source for the later theorist Cerone.

Its section on plainchant remained in use for over a century.

Bibl.: Dan Murdock Urquhart, "Francisco de Montanos's *Arte de musica theorica y pratica:* A Translation and Commentary" (diss., Univ. of Rochester, 1969).

Monte, Philippe de [Filippo di, Philippus de] (b. Mechlin, 1521; d. Prague, 4 July 1603). Composer. Prolific and highly esteemed, especially for his secular works. Although born and probably trained in the North (modern-day Belgium), he seems to have spent most of his young adult life in Italy (1542–68; chiefly in Naples and Rome), with one brief interlude (1554–55) in Antwerp and England. From 1568 until his death he was Kapellmeister to the Habsburg court (under Maximilian II and Rudolf II) in Vienna and Prague. Additional income came from two benefices at Cambrai Cathedral, neither requiring his residence there. His friends included Lassus and William Byrd, his students Macque and Regnart.

Although his compositions appeared throughout his career, the vast majority were published after 1568, the year of his move to the Habsburg court. His secular works include a few chansons (under 50, most with texts by Ronsard) but far more madrigals. About 35 complete books and a number of anthologies, dating from 1554 until the start of the 17th century, together contain over 1,100 secular madrigals. There are also 5 books of similarly constructed spiritual madrigals. His sacred works include some 40 Masses (parodies of motets, madrigals, and chansons) and about 260 other pieces, mostly motets. They incorporate cantus firmus construction, canons, imitative textures, polychoral writing, and even techniques such as ostinato figures.

Bibl.: *Opera,* ed. Charles van den Borren, Georgius van Doorslaer, and Julius van Nuffel (Bruges, 1927–39; R: 1965). *New Complete Edition,* ed. René Bernard Lenaerts et al. (Louvain, 1975–). Brian Mann, *The Secular Madrigals of Filippo di Monte, 1521–1603* (Ann Arbor, 1983).

Montéclair, Michel Pignolet [Pinolet] **de** (b. Andelot, bapt. 4 Dec. 1667; d. Aummont, 22 Sept. 1737). Composer and theorist. Studied under Moreau at the choir school of the Cathedral of Langres; made a journey to Italy, about which little is known, and ended up in Paris in 1687. Montéclair performed on the *basse de violon* in the Paris Opéra orchestra around 1699; he was one of the first (along with Fedeli) to introduce the instrument (which he probably encountered in Italian orchestras) into the Opéra. He was highly esteemed as a teacher, and his pupils included Couperin's daughters.

Montéclair is acknowledged as one of the most important composers of the post-Lully generation; his stage works, which premiered at the Opéra (*Les festes de l'été,* 1716; *Jephté,* 1732), influenced Rameau's dramatic music. Other compositions include over 20 cantatas and some instrumental music. He published the first French violin method, *Méthode facile pour apprendre à jouer du violon* (Paris, 1711–12) and several practical theory books, including *Principes de musique* (Paris, 1736; R: Genève, 1972; trans. Eng., Constance Barbara Keffer, thesis, Univ. of Arizona, 1977), a valuable source of information about French vocal ornamentation.

Montella, Giovanni Domenico [Mico] (b. Naples, ca. 1570; d. there, before 2 July 1607). Composer. A student of Giovanni de Macque; lutenist in the service of Don Fabrizio Gesualdo; from 1591 lutenist and later also organist in the Spanish viceregal chapel in Naples. His works, most written between 1600 and 1607, include 14 books of madrigals and *villanelle,* a few *laude,* and several books of motets and other sacred vocal music.

Montemezzi, Italo (b. Vigasio, near Verona, 31 May 1875; d. there, 15 May 1952). Composer. Against his father's wish that he study engineering, Montemezzi entered the Milan Conservatory (diploma, 1900) and subsequently taught harmony there for one year. His one-act opera *Bianca* won a contest at the conservatory. His *Giovanni Gallurese* (Turin, 1905) encouraged the publishing firm of Ricordi to commission two other operas, *Hellera* (Turin, 1909) and *L'amore dei tre re* (Milan, 1913). The success of the latter effectively launched a career that enabled him to devote himself to composition. He lived in California from 1939, but made frequent trips to Italy and returned permanently in 1949. His later works did not achieve success equal to that of *L'amore dei tre re,* although the patriotic *La nave* (Milan, 1918) was well received and was presented under the composer in Chicago the following year. In the first two decades of the century, Montemezzi was seen as a native composer who combined traditional Italian lyricism with a Wagnerian approach to the use of the opera orchestra as a continuous texture and with a sensitivity to instrumental color influenced by the works of Debussy. At the close of the Romantic period in Italian opera, Montemezzi was in tune with the turn-of-the-century internationalism and eclecticism of Italian composers, but after 1918 his style remained conservative and somewhat out of touch with the growing Italian interest in forms beyond opera and more avant-garde approaches. Other works include *La notte di Zoraima* (Milan, 1931); *L'incantisimo* (NBC radio, 1943; staged Verona, 1952); and a few orchestral, chamber, and choral pieces (*Italia mia, nulla fermerà il tuo canto,* symphonic poem, 1944).

Monteux, Pierre (b. Paris, 4 Apr. 1875; d. Hancock, Maine, 1 July 1964). Conductor. Studied at the Paris Conservatory from age 9; conducted an orchestra for the first time at age 12. Played second violin at the Folies-Bergère (1889–92), viola in the orchestra of the Concerts Colonne (1893–1912), participating in the premiere of Debussy's *La mer.* Graduated from the Conservatory in 1896, receiving first prize for violin. Founding conductor of the Concerts Berlioz (1910). Diaghilev noticed him and invited him to become conductor of the Ballets russes. With that ensemble (1911–

14 and 1917), he led premieres of Ravel's *Daphnis et Chloé,* Debussy's *Jeux,* Stravinsky's *Petrushka, Rite of Spring,* and *Rossignol.* In the U.S. he conducted the Ballets russes (1916–17), the New York Metropolitan Opera (1917–19), and the Boston Symphony (1919–24). Returning to Europe, he became associate conductor of the Amsterdam Concertgebouw Orchestra (1924–34). Founding conductor of the Orchestre symphonique de Paris (1929–38). Organized and led the NBC Symphony Orchestra (1937). During his tenure as music director of the San Francisco Symphony (1935–52) he became a U.S. citizen (1942). Family members who remained in France, being Jews, were liquidated during World War II. Guest conductor of the Boston Symphony (1949–62), at the Met (1954–58). Chief conductor of the London Symphony (1961–64). Monteux was adamant about fidelity to the composer's score long before this became common practice.

Monteverdi [Monteverde], **Claudio (Giovanni** [Zuan] **Antonio)** (bapt. Cremona, 15 May 1567; d. Venice, 29 Nov. 1643). Composer. He studied under Marc'Antonio Ingegneri, *maestro di cappella* of Cremona Cathedral, and published collections of motets, canzonettas, and sacred madrigals while still in his teens. In 1587 his first book of secular madrigals appeared, followed by a second book in 1590. He visited Milan in 1589, and probably performed for the Gonzaga family at Mantua; by 1592 he had obtained an appointment as *suonatore di vivuola* (viol and/or violin player) to Duke Vincenzo I of Mantua. Monteverdi's third book of madrigals, published in 1592, reveals the strong influence of the court *maestro di cappella,* Giaches de Wert. Monteverdi accompanied the duke on a foray against the Turks in Austria and Hungary in 1595, and to Flanders in 1599, where the duke went for a cure. Despite the increasing importance at court that these journeys reveal, he was passed over in 1596 to succeed to Wert's post in favor of Benedetto Pallavicino. Monteverdi married the court singer Claudia de Cattaneis in 1599 and had two sons, Francesco (Baldassare) (bapt. 27 Aug. 1601) and Massimiliano (Giacomo) (bapt. 10 May 1604); a daughter Leonora (Carulla) died in infancy.

In 1600 G. M. Artusi published his *L'Artusi, overo Delle imperfettioni della moderna musica ragionamenti dui,* which attacked the contrapuntal licences taken by some of Monteverdi's then-unpublished madrigals; Monteverdi's fifth book of madrigals, which appeared in 1605, included a reply to Artusi which was later amplified by Monteverdi's brother Giulio Cesare in the *Dichiaratione* of the *Scherzi musicali* (Venice, 1607; trans. Eng. in *SR,* 1968). His first opera, *L'Orfeo,* was produced in Mantua in 1607, the same year he was elected to the Accademia degli animosi, Cremona, where part of *L'Orfeo* may have been performed at one of the meetings. At first reluctant to return to Mantua after his wife's death in September 1607, Monteverdi relented in order to supervise the production of his second opera, *L'Arianna,* performed in 1608 to celebrate the homecoming of Francesco Gonzaga with his bride, Margaret of Savoy. He composed two other works for wedding celebrations, the prologue to the pastoral play *L'Idropica* and the French-style ballet *Il ballo delle ingrate.*

Exhausted after this intense period of work, he returned to Cremona and spent over a year in a state of depression. His father's request that he be released from the Gonzaga family service was denied, motivating a bitter letter from the composer himself listing his grievances with the Mantuan court. He journeyed to Rome in 1610, apparently in search of a new position, and visited Venice as well. After Duke Vincenzo's death, Monteverdi was dismissed by his successor, Francesco, in July 1612. With the death of the *maestro di cappella* of St. Mark's, he was invited to compete for the post in 1613, and was appointed later that year at an annual salary of 300 ducats.

In addition to composing some large-scale works, Monteverdi's duties at St. Mark's included reorganizing the *cappella,* finding new singers, and purchasing music. He received some commissions from Mantua, Duke Francesco having been succeeded by his brother Ferdinando, with whom Monteverdi was well acquainted. His ballet *Tirsi e Clori* was performed in Mantua in 1616; two other dramatic works, *Le nozze di Tetide* and *Andromeda,* were begun in 1616 and 1618, respectively, but left unfinished. Monteverdi's seventh book of madrigals appeared in 1619, and the following year he refused an offer to return to Mantuan service, alluding to all his old complaints against the Gonzaga household. In 1624 his dramatic dialogue *Combattimento di Tancredi e Clorinda* was staged at the home of a Venetian nobleman; plans for a full-length opera for Mantua in 1627, *La finta pazza Licori,* were eventually dropped after he had composed most of the first act. In 1630 Monteverdi set Strozzi's drama *Proserpina rapita;* an attack of plague in Venice in 1630–31 and the cessation of commissions from Mantua led to the slackening of his compositional activities. He took holy orders in 1632 and published a small collection of vocal music under the title *Scherzi musicali* the same year. With the opening of public opera houses in Venice in 1637, a new outlet appeared for his dramatic works. *L'Arianna* was revived in 1640, followed by three new works: *Il ritorno d'Ulisse in patria* (1640), *Le nozze d'Enea con Lavinia* (1641, lost), and *L'incoronazione di Poppea* (1643); the ballet *La vittoria d'Amore* (lost) was commissioned by Pincenza and performed there in 1641. A retrospective collection of his secular music was published in 1638, with a similar volume of church music appearing in 1641. Monteverdi died at the age of 76, shortly after returning to Venice from a trip to Cremona, and was buried in the Church of the Frari.

In the exchanges with Artusi, both Monteverdi and his brother Giulio Cesare refer to a second, modern method of composition, the *seconda prattica,* distinguished from the traditional *prima prattica* as taught by Zarlino. As Giulio Cesare defined it, the guiding principle of the *seconda prattica* was that the words should govern the music; this justified the freer dissonance treatment that the reactionary Artusi attacked. The *seconda prattica* was viewed as a resurrection of the principles of music as taught by classical antiquity, rediscovered by Peri, Wert, and Monteverdi himself, among others. This modern approach is clearly evident for the first time in the third book of madrigals (1592), with its extensive use of dissonance and attention to individual words. Also of importance is the invention Monteverdi defined as *stile concitato,* the use of short notes repeated on a single pitch (generally played by string instruments) to express anger and warfare.

Monteverdi was perhaps the first composer to envision opera as a drama in music, a depiction of human psychology; this approach is clearly evident from his correspondence regarding the opera *La finta pazza Licori.* The great collection of sacred music published in 1610 includes a Mass written in the *prima prattica* as well as vesper Psalms and motets written in a more modern style.

Works: *Dramatic. Endimion* (Mantua, 1604–5, lost); *L'Orfeo* (Mantua, 1607); *L'Arianna* (Mantua, 1608, most music lost); *Il ballo delle ingrate* (Mantua, 1608); prologue to *L'Idropica* (Mantua, 1608, music lost); *Tirsi e Clori* (Mantua, 1616); *Le nozze di Tetide* (begun 1616, not completed, lost); *Andromeda* (begun 1618, not completed, lost); intermezzos for *Le tre costanti* (1622, music lost); *Combattimento di Tancredi e Clorinda* (Venice, 1624); *Armida* (1624–27, music lost); *La finta pazza Licori* (begun 1627, not completed, lost); *Gli amori di Diana e di Endimione* (Parma, 1628, music lost); *Mercurio e Marte* (Parma, 1628, music lost); *Proserpina rapita* (Venice, 1630, most music lost); *Volgendo il ciel* (Vienna, 1636?); *Adone* (1639, music lost); *Il ritorno d'Ulisse in patria* (Venice, 1640); *Le nozze d'Enea con Lavinia* (Venice, 1641, music lost); *La vittoria d'Amore* (Piacenza, 1641, music lost); *L'incoronazione di Poppea* (Venice, 1643); prologue to *La Maddalena* (1617).

Sacred vocal. Sacrae cantiunculae . . . liber primus (Venice, 1582); *Madrigali spirituali* (Brescia, 1583); *Musica tolta da i madrigali di Claudio Monteverde* . . . (Milan, 1607); *Il secondo libro della musica di Claudio Monteverde* . . . (Milan, 1608); *Il terzo libro della musica di Claudio Monteverdi* . . . (Milan, 1609); *Sanctissimae virgini missa* . . . (Venice, 1610); *Selva morale e spirituale* (Venice, 1640); *Messa* (Venice, 1650); Latin Masses, other sacred works in Italian and German.

Secular vocal. Canzonette (Venice, 1584); *Il primo libro de madrigali* (Venice, 1587); *Il secondo libro de madrigali* (Venice, 1590); *Il terzo libro de madrigali* (Venice, 1592); *Il quarto libro de madrigali* (Venice, 1603); *Il quinto libro de madrigali* (Venice, 1605); *Musica tolta da i madrigali di Claudio Monteverde* . . . (Milan, 1607); *Scherzi musicali di Claudio Monteverde* . . . (Venice, 1607); *Il secondo libro della musica di Claudio Monteverde e d'altri autori* . . . (Milan, 1608); *Il terzo libro della musica di Claudio Monteverde* . . . (Milan, 1609); *Il sesto libro de madrigali* (Venice, 1614); *Concerto: Settimo libro de madrigali, con altri generi de canti* (Venice, 1619); *Scherzi musicali cioè arie* . . . (Venice, 1632); *Madrigali guerrieri et amorosi* . . . (Venice, 1638); *Madrigali e canzonette . . . libro nono* (Venice, 1651). His best-known madrigals include "A quest'olmo, a quest'ombre" (1619); "Con che soavità" (1619); "Cruda Amarilli" (1605); "Ohimè dov'è il mio ben?" (1619); "Ohimè, se tanto amate" (1603); "Hor che'l ciel e la terra" (1638); "Non si levav'ancor" (1590); "O come sei gentile, caro augellino" (1619); "Tempro la cetra" (1619); "Vattene pur, crudel, con quella pace" (1592); "Zefiro torna" (1632).

Bibl.: *Claudio Monteverdi: Tutte le opere,* ed. G. Francesco Malipiero (Asolo, 1926–42; 1968). *Claudio Monteverdi: Opera Omnia,* ed. Fondazione Claudio Monteverdi (Cremona, 1970–). Leo Schrade, *Monteverdi, Creator of Modern Music* (London, 1950; R: 1979) *C. Monteverdi: Composizioni vocali profane e sacre,* ed. Wolfgang Osthoff (Milan, 1958). Denis Stevens, *Monteverdi: Sacred, Secular and Occasional Music* (Rutherford, 1978). Anna Amalie Abert, *Claudio Monteverdis Bedeutung für die Entstehung des musikalischen Dramas* (Darmstadt, 1979). Claudio Gallico, *Monteverdi: Poesia musicale, teatro e musica sacra* (Turin, 1979). Denis Stevens, ed. and trans., *The Letters of Claudio Monteverdi* (London, 1980). Denis Arnold, *Monteverdi Church Music* (London, 1982). Denis Arnold and Nigel Fortune, eds., *The New Monteverdi Companion* (London, 1985). Paolo Fabbri, *Monteverdi* (Turin, 1985); trans. Eng. Tim Carter (Cambridge, 1994). Gary Tomlinson, *Monteverdi and the End of the Renaissance* (Berkeley, 1987). K. Gary Adams and Dyke Kiel, *Claudio Monteverdi: A Guide to Research* (New York, 1989). Denis Arnold, *Monteverdi,* 3rd rev. ed. (London, 1990). Leopold Silke, *Monteverdi: Music in Transition,* trans. Anne Smith (Oxford, 1991). Eric Thomas Chafe, *Monteverdi's Tonal Language* (New York, 1992). Iain Fenlon and Peter N. Miller, *The Song of the Soul: Understanding Poppea* (London, 1992). Annibale Gianuario, *L'estetica di Claudio Monteverdi attraverso quattro sue lettere* (Sezze Romano, 1993). Silke Leopold, *Claudio Monteverdi und seine Zeit* (Laaber, 1993). Suzanne G. Cusick, "Gendering Modern Music: Thoughts on the Monteverdi–Artusi Controversy," *JAMS* 46 (1993): 1–25.

Monteverdi, Giulio Cesare (b. Cremona, bapt. 31 Jan. 1573; d. Salò, 1630 or 1631). Composer and writer. Claudio Monteverdi's younger brother. Entered the service of the Duke of Mantua in 1602. He composed music for the fourth intermedio of Guarini's play *L'Idropica* in 1608, and his opera *Il rapimento di Proserpina* was given in Casa Monferrato in 1611. In 1620 he became *maestro di cappella* of Salò Cathedral. A collection of 25 motets was published under the title *Affetti musici* (Venice, 1620), and he contributed two pieces to his brother's *Scherzi musicali* (Venice, 1607). He is best known for editing this volume, including a *Dichiaratione* (trans. Eng. in *SR,* 1968) in which he defended his brother at length against the attacks of Artusi.

Montgomery, Wes [John Leslie] (b. Indianapolis, 6 March 1923; d. there, 15 June 1968). Jazz guitarist. He toured with Lionel Hampton (1948–50) and between 1955 and 1962 played in several groups with his brothers, the electric bass guitarist Monk (b. 1921) and the vibraphonist and pianist Buddy (b. 1930). While also working with his own organ and drum trio (1959–60, 1963–64) and as a sideman with John Coltrane (1961–62), he made a series of jazz albums, including *The*

Incredible Jazz Guitar of Wes Montgomery (1960). He worked with Wynton Kelly's group, recording *Smokin' at the Half Note* (1965), but from 1964 concentrated on pop-oriented albums with orchestral accompaniment, including *Goin' Out of My Head* (1965) and *A Day in the Life* (1967). He effortlessly played wide-ranging improvised melodies in octaves, using his thumb (rather than a plectrum) to achieve a mellow timbre.

Bibl.: Adrian Ingram, *Wes Montgomery* (Gateshead, England, 1985).

Montoya, Carlos (b. Madrid, 13 Dec. 1903; d. Wainscott, N.Y., 3 Mar. 1993). Guitarist, principally in the flamenco style. Began to play the guitar when he was 8; soon performed professionally with various dance groups, and embarked on a tour with the dancer La Argentina (Antonia Merce), later touring Europe singly. Gave solo recitals and improvised a number of works, including *Suite flamenca* for guitar and orchestra (1966); recordings include *Carlos Montoya: Flamenco Direct,* vols. 1 and 2.

Montsalvatge, Xavier (b. Gerona, 11 Mar. 1912). Composer. He studied at the Barcelona Conservatory with Millet, Morera, Costa, and Pahissa (1923–36). His close association with the Goubé–Alexander ballet company led to the composition of 20 ballets. In 1942 he became music critic of the Barcelona weekly *Destino,* and in 1962 began to write for the *Vanguardia española.* He held teaching positions in Barcelona at the San Jorge Academy (from 1962), the Destino Seminary (from 1969), and the conservatory (from 1970). Among the major influences on his work were Stravinsky, the composers of "Les six," and West Indian music.

Works: *Operas. El gato con botas* (1948); *Una voce in off* (1961); *Babel 46* (1967). *Ballets. La muerte enamorada* (1943); *Manfred* (1945); *La Venus de Elna* (1946); *Perlimplinada* (with Mompou, 1956). *Orchestra. Poema concertante* (violin, orchestra, 1951); *Concierto breve* (piano, orchestra, 1953); *Partita 1958* (1958); *Danzas concertantes* (1962); *Desintegración morfológica de la Chacona de Bach* (1962; rev. 1972); *Laberinto* (1971); *Concerto capriccio* (harp, orchestra, 1975); *Sortilegis* (1992); *Bric-à-brac* (1993). *Vocal. 5 Canciones negras* (voice, piano, 1945), orchestra version (1946); *Canciones para niños* (1953); *Cinco Invocaciones al Crucificado* (soprano, ensemble, 1969); *Sinfonía de réquiem* (soprano, orchestra, 1985). *Instrumental. Cuarteto indiano* (string quartet, 1952); *Self-paráfrasis* (clarinet, piano, 1953); *Spanish Sketch* (violin, piano, 1972).

Bibl.: Manuel Valls, *X. Montsalvatge* (Barcelona, 1969). Enrique Franco, *Xavier Montsalvatge* (Madrid, 1975).

Moody, James (b. Savannah, 26 Feb. 1925). Jazz tenor and alto saxophonist, flutist. He joined Dizzy Gillespie's big band (1946–48) and worked in Europe (1948–51), mainly playing tenor saxophone, although his most popular recording was as an alto saxophonist on "I'm in the Mood for Love" (1949). He led groups (1951–62), also playing flute from 1956. After a brief period with Gene Ammons and Sonny Stitt, he rejoined Gillespie (1962–68), then worked as a leader, recording the album *Feelin' It Together* (1973). A period of work in bands in Las Vegas (1974–80) interrupted his jazz career, which resumed with a tour with Gillespie (1980).

Moog, Robert A(rthur) (b. Flushing, N.Y., 23 May 1934). Engineer and inventor. He studied physics at Queens College, N.Y. (1952–55), electrical engineering at Columbia (1955–57), and engineering physics at Cornell (1957–65). In 1954 he founded the R. A. Moog Co. in Trumansburg, N.Y., to manufacture theremins. From 1965 the company focused on producing synthesizers. In 1971 the firm merged with MuSonics to form Moog Music, Inc., and moved to Williamsville, N.Y.; it became a subsidiary of Norlin Industries in 1973. Since 1964 the composer Wendy (formerly Walter) Carlos has worked with Moog on the design of the equipment. In 1969 Carlos earned considerable success with her recording *Switched-On Bach,* which used a 5 1/2 octave Moog synthesizer. Among other composers who have worked with Moog are Vladimir Ussachevsky, Lejaren Hiller, John Cage, David Tudor, John Eaton, Richard Teitelbaum, Emmanuel Ghent, and David Borden. In 1984–89 Moog worked with Kurzweil Music Systems of Boston.

Moór, Emanuel (b. Kecskemét, 19 Feb. 1863; d. Mont Pélerin, Switzerland, 20 Oct. 1931). Composer and pianist. He studied organ locally and in Prague, then studied in Budapest and Vienna. After teaching and conducting light opera in Szeged, he toured in Europe and the U.S. as pianist, conductor, and accompanist to Lilli Lehmann and others; in the U.S. he was director of the Concerts artistiques. He went to England in 1888, then settled in Switzerland, where he wrote music for Henri Marteau, Casals, Ysaÿe, and Flesch. After 1923 he was mainly concerned with the Emanuel Moór Pianoforte, a double-keyboard piano of his own invention. His works include 5 operas, 8 symphonies, 4 violin concertos, 2 string quartets, 12 violin sonatas, and many songs.

Moore, Carman (Leroy) (b. Lorain, Ohio, 8 Oct. 1936). Composer and writer on music. He studied at Oberlin College Conservatory and Ohio State Univ.; played horn in the Columbus Symphony; and then studied composition in New York (with Overton, Persichetti, Berio, and Wolpe). He cofounded the Society of Black Composers; taught at various institutions in the New York area; wrote on contemporary concert music and on popular music for the *Village Voice* and the *New York Times.* His style is eclectic, influenced by jazz, gospel music, rock, and the avant-garde; in 1978 a festival of his music was held at La Guardia College, CUNY. His works include *The Illuminated Working Man* (mixed media, 1975); *Concerto for Blues Piano* (1982); *Gospel Fuse* (soprano, 4 voices, saxophone, piano, electronic organ, and orchestra, 1974); *Sky Dance* (2 synthesizers, 7 instruments, and tape, 1984); a concerto for jazz violin and orchestra (1987); *Para-*

dise Re-Lost (music theater, 1987); *Franklin and Eleanor* (musical, 1989); *Mass for the 21st Century* (1994). His writings include a biography of Bessie Smith (1970) and a textbook on teaching popular music (1980).

Moore, Dorothy Rudd (b. New Castle, Del., 4 June 1940). Composer, poet, and singer. She studied at Howard Univ. and then with Boulanger (1963) and Chou Wen-chung (1965); has taught at the Harlem School of the Arts, New York Univ., and Bronx Community College, CUNY; she was a cofounder of the Society of Black Composers (1968). In addition to composing, she is a published poet and professional singer; counterpoint is the dominant element of her musical style. Her works include an opera (*Frederick Douglass,* 1979–85) on her own libretto; a symphony; *In Celebration* (baritone, chorus, and piano, 1977); chamber music (mainly for strings); piano works; and many songs and song cycles with piano or other instrumental accompaniment.

Moore, Douglas S(tuart) (b. Cutchogue, N.Y., 10 Aug. 1893; d. Greenport, N.Y., 25 July 1969). Composer. He studied at Yale (B.A. in music and philosophy, 1915; B.M., 1917); served in World War I; and then remained in Paris to work with Boulanger, d'Indy, and Tournemire (organ). He returned to become assistant curator and then curator of music at the Cleveland Museum of Art (1921–25); he was also organist at Western Reserve Univ. (1923–25) and studied with Block in this period. The Pulitzer Traveling Fellowship (*4 Museum Pieces,* organ, 1922) permitted another year of study in Paris, after which he was appointed to teach at Columbia. He was chairman of the music department from 1940, and retired in 1962 as professor emeritus. He received numerous awards: election to the National Institute of Arts and Letters (1941; president, 1946–52) and to the American Academy (1951; president, 1960–62); the Pulitzer Prize (1951, for the opera *Giants in the Earth*); the New York Music Critics' Circle Award (1958, for the opera *The Ballad of Baby Doe*).

Moore's gifts as a composer lay in his lyric writing for the voice, his unforced prosody, and his sense of musical and dramatic timing and characterization. He used extreme registers and dissonance only for dramatic necessity; the language is tonal, with sudden modulations to remote keys accomplished by means of chromatic or enharmonic pivots; the rhythmic patterns are those of American musical comedy, folk song, ragtime, waltz, and other early 20th-century genres, juxtaposed to recitativelike speech rhythms. The influences on his operatic and vocal music were primarily American and French rather than German.

Works: 12 operas (including, in addition to those mentioned, *The Devil and Daniel Webster* (Benét after Irving's *The Legend of Sleepy Hollow,* 1938); *Puss in Boots* (children's operetta, Abrashkin, after Perrault, 1949), a ballet, incidental music, 3 film scores, and other dramatic music; *The Pageant of P. T. Barnum* (orchestral suite, 1924), Symphony no. 2 (1945), and other orchestral music; chamber music (Clarinet Quintet, 1946); organ and piano works; choral music; songs.

Writings: *Listening to Music* (1932; rev. 1963); *From Madrigal to Modern Music: A Guide to Musical Styles* (1942; rev. 1963); articles.

Moore, Gerald (b. Watford, 30 July 1899; d. Buckinghamshire, 13 Mar. 1987). Pianist. Studied in Watford with Wallis Bandey, in Canada with Michael Hambourg, and later in England with Hambourg's son Mark. In 1925 he served as accompanist to John Coates; from that time until his retirement over 40 years later, Moore appeared in recital with numerous important solo singers of the time. His performances with Fischer-Dieskau and Schwarzkopf, especially in the lieder of Schubert and Wolf, became legendary and elevated the role of accompanist in the public mind to that of artistic collaborator. Moore lectured widely and published a number of musical studies (*The Schubert Song Cycles,* 1975) and memoirs.

Moore, Grace (b. Nough, Tenn., 5 Dec. 1901; d. Copenhagen, 26 Jan. 1947). Soprano and actress. In 1919 she ran away from the Wilson-Greene School of Music in Chevy Chase, Md., to start a career in New York. Discovered by George M. Cohan while singing at the Black Cat Café in Greenwich Village. Her stage debut in *Suite Sixteen* led to six years on Broadway. In Paris (1926–27), studied with Richard Barthélemy, then joined the New York Metropolitan Opera, making her debut in 1928 as Mimi *(Bohéme).* At the same time appeared in eight films, beginning with *A Lady's Morals* (1930) and including *One Night of Love* (1934), Charpentier's *Louise* (1936), and *I'll Take Romance* (1937). Debuts as Mimi at the Paris Opéra-comique in 1928, at Covent Garden in 1935. Published an autobiography, *You're Only Human Once* (1944). Died in a plane crash while on tour.

Moore, Mary (Louise) Carr (b. Memphis, 6 Aug. 1873; d. Inglewood, Calif., 9 Jan. 1957). Composer and singer. She studied voice and composition in San Francisco (the latter with J. H. Pratt); after giving up her singing career in 1895, she taught in Lemoore (Calif.), Seattle (1901), San Francisco (1915), and in Los Angeles at the Olga Steeb Piano School (1926–43) and at Chapman College (1928–47). In 1909 she established the American Music Center in association with Farwell's National Wa-Wan Society; in the 1930s she cofounded the Colorado Society of Composers and the Society of Native American Composers. Her opera *Narcissa, or the Cost of Empire* (1910–11; Seattle, 1912; revived in San Francisco, 1925, and Los Angeles, 1945) received the David B. Ispham Memorial Medal in 1930; she conducted its first performance in Seattle. She was an Americanist, but was influenced by French and German compositional models; her operas and songs were indebted not only to Debussy but also to Puccini. Her works include 10 operas; a piano concerto (1933–34) and a few other orchestral pieces; 2

string quartets, 3 piano trios, and about 24 other chamber pieces; many piano works; 57 choral pieces; a song cycle (*Beyond These Hills,* 4 solo voices and piano, 1923–24) and about 250 songs.

Bibl.: Catherine Parsons Smith and Cynthia S. Richardson, *Mary Carr Moore, American Composer* (Ann Arbor, 1987).

Moore, Thomas (b. Dublin, 28 May 1779; d. Sloperton Cottage, near Devizes, 25 Feb. 1852). Poet. He was a performer from childhood, reciting poetry and singing songs, without much of a voice, but with a highly expressive delivery; from 1794, a student at Trinity College, Dublin; from 1799, a singer in London salons, publishing songs, glees, and poetry, some of which became popular. He was not a trained musician, although he played the piano a little; many of his melodies were adapted from or modeled on existing tunes, and he required help in anything involving technical skill, such as harmonization or the making of accompaniments. His *Irish Melodies,* published in 10 installments (1808–34), had a tremendous vogue; also wrote opera librettos, and his oriental poem *Lalla Rookh* (1817) was used by several composers. His poetry was popular among Continental composers, including Berlioz and Schumann.

Moore, Undine Smith (b. Jarratt, Va., 25 Aug. 1905; d. Petersburg, Va., 6 Feb. 1989). Composer. She studied piano and organ with Alice M. Grasso at Fisk Univ., then won a scholarship to Juilliard; further study was at the Manhattan School, Columbia, and the Eastman School. She taught public school in North Carolina, and in 1927 joined the faculty of Virginia State College, where she cofounded and directed the Black Music Center (1969–72). Most of her works are tonal with a strong contrapuntal interest, but she also wrote a few twelve-tone pieces. Works include the oratorio *Scenes from the Life of a Martyr* (narrator, chorus, and orchestra, 1982); *Afro-American Suite* (flute, cello, and piano, 1969); *Variations on Nettleton* (organ, 1976) and a few piano works; choral music and songs; arrangements of choral music.

Moorman, (Madeline) Charlotte (b. Little Rock, Ark., 18 Nov. 1933; d. New York, 8 Nov. 1991). Cellist and video and performance artist. Studied at Centenary College, Louisiana (B.M., 1955), and with Horace Britt at the Univ. of Texas, Austin; further studies with Leonard Rose at Juilliard (1957–58). After hearing music of Cage and Toshi Ichiyanagi, she founded the Annual New York Avant Garde Festival in 1963 and worked closely with performance artist Nam June Paik. In 1967 she was arrested for indecent exposure while performing Paik's *Opéra sextronique,* which called for her to perform nude from the waist up.

Morales, Cristóbal de (b. Seville, ca. 1500; d. Málaga?, between 4 Sept. and 7 Oct. 1553). Composer. His works were of the highest repute throughout Europe and even in the New World both during his lifetime and for several decades after his death. After studies of music and of the other liberal arts in Seville, he became *maestro de capilla* at Avila (from 1526), then at Plasencia (from 1528). Having left Plasencia in 1530 (official resignation in late 1531), he went to Italy, probably first to Naples; in 1535 he joined the papal choir in Rome. His association with this organization lasted until 1545. Included in his duties and privileges were a number of trips in the papal retinue (to southern France, northern and central Italy) and a paid leave for a visit to Spain in 1540–41. The last years of his life were spent in his native country, as *maestro de capilla* in Toledo (1545–47), Marchena (1548–51), and Málaga (from 1551). Although ill health, financial problems, and various difficulties with the demands of certain jobs hampered his activity, his compositional output was considerable from the start of his tenure in the papal choir. His works achieved exceptionally wide dissemination, and theorists continued to cite them as models for at least a century.

His compositions include nearly two dozen Masses, about 20 Magnificats and Lamentations, and many motets. He produced only a few secular works, including one madrigal and a small number of occasional motets.

Bibl.: *Opera omnia,* ed. Higinio Anglès, *MME* 11, 13, 15, 17, 20, 21, 24, 34 (1952–). *AnM* 8 (1953) [special Morales number]. Robert Stevenson, *Spanish Cathedral Music in the Golden Age* (Berkeley and Los Angeles, 1961). Samuel Rubio, *Cristóbal de Morales: Estudio crítico de su polifonía* (El Escorial, 1969).

Morales, Melesio (b. Mexico City, 4 Dec. 1838; d. there, 12 May 1908). Composer. Studied music in Mexico City and had 2 Italian operas performed there: *Romeo e Giulietta* (1863) and *Ildegonda* (1865). In Europe, 1865–68. The successful production of *Ildegonda* in Florence in 1868 made him a leading figure on his return to Mexico City as composer, conductor, and teacher (organizing and heading a composition department at the conservatory); produced several further Italian operas, orchestral pieces, and other works.

Moran, Peter K. (b. Ireland; d. New York, 10 Feb. 1831). Composer, organist, violinist, and cellist. Little is known of him before his arrival in New York in 1817; he was organist at local churches (Grace Episcopal, St. John's Chapel) and for the New York Handel and Haydn Society. Both he and his wife, who was a singer, became central figures in the city's musical life. Moran also played violin or cello in several orchestras, including that of the García Opera Company (in 1825) and the Philharmonic Society. In 1823 he opened a music store, and in 1828 he published *Moran's New Instructions for the Piano Forte.* Best known for his piano pieces, he also composed songs ("The Carrier Pigeon," 1822) and collections of anthems, Psalms, and hymns.

Moran, Robert (Leonard) (b. Denver, 8 Jan. 1937). Pianist and composer. He studied in Vienna with Apostel, at Mills with Berio and Milhaud (M.A., 1963), and then in Vienna with Haubenstock-Ramati. Between 1959 and 1972 he often directed the New Music Ensemble at San Francisco State Univ.; composer-in-residence at Portland State in Oregon (1972–

74) and at Northwestern Univ. (1977–78); in 1984–85 he and Glass were composers-in-residence at the Third Street Music School Settlement in New York, which resulted in their collaborative children's opera *The Juniper Tree* (1985). His works are often aleatory and improvisatory, requiring audience participation. They include stage and mixed-media works (*Erlösung dem Erlöser,* music drama dealing with the death of Wagner, tape loops and performers, 1982; *Desert of Roses,* opera, 1990; *From the Towers of the Moon,* opera, 1992); works for one or more orchestras (*The Eternal Hour,* orchestras and choruses, 1974); "city pieces" (*Hallelujah,* 20 bands, 40 choruses, organ, carillon, 1971, for Bethlehem, Pa.); and *L'Après-midi du Dracula* (any instruments, 1966).

Moravec, Ivan (b. Prague, 9 Nov. 1930). Pianist. Studied piano with A. Grünfeldova at the Prague Conservatory (1946–50) and with I. Štěpánova-Kurzová at the Prague Academy of the Arts (1950–51). Worked on interpretation with Arturo Benedetti-Michelangeli (1957–58). Based at the Prague Academy of the Arts, he toured Europe and North America infrequently, his repertory ranging from Mozart to Debussy. U.S. debut with the Cleveland Orchestra under George Szell (1964).

Morawetz, Oskar (b. Světlá nad Sázavou, Czechoslovakia, 17 Jan. 1917). Composer. He was raised in Prague from age 8, where he studied piano and was offered a conducting post at the opera by Szell; he fled the Nazis, however, at first to Vienna and Paris, and in 1940 to Toronto. Studied piano with Alberto Guerrero at the Toronto Conservatory; D.Mus. at the Univ. of Toronto (1953); but as a composer essentially self-taught. He won awards from the Composers, Authors, and Publishers Association of Canada for two early works (the First String Quartet, and the *Sonata Tragica* for piano); his Piano Concerto no. 1 won a Montreal Symphony competition in 1962; the *Sinfonietta for Winds* (1965) won the Critics' Award at the International Composers Competition in Italy (1966). His compositions are neo-Romantic and even expressionistic, accessible to a wide audience, and are often responses to events of World War II or to contemporary tragedies (*Memorial to Martin Luther King,* cello and orchestra, 1968). *From the Diary of Anne Frank* (soprano and orchestra, 1970) was recognized as a major contribution to Canadian Jewish music by the Segal Foundation of Montreal (1971). Other works include *Carnival Overture* (1946) and *The Railway Station* (1980) for orchestra; a concerto for clarinet and chamber orchestra (1989); 5 string quartets, *3 Improvisations* (brass quintet, 1977), and other chamber music; piano music (*10 Preludes,* 1966); choral music and many songs, often orchestrated.

Moreau, Jean-Baptiste (b. Angers, 1656; d. Paris, 24 Aug. 1733). Composer. He served as *maître de musique* at the cathedrals of Langres (ca. 1681–82) and Dijon; went to Paris in 1686 and was appointed by Louis XIV *musicien ordinaire* at the royal school of St. Cyr. He composed recitatives and choruses for Racine's *Esther* (1689) and *Athalie* (1691), the latter especially pleasing the king; also set Racine's *Cantiques spirituels* (Paris, 1695) for performance at St. Cyr. Public success came with music for Laînez's *Zaïre* (lost), but the king disapproved of the verse and Moreau fell from royal favor, spending his final years teaching singing at the Jesuit convent of St. Sulpice.

Moreira, Airto (Guimorva) (b. Itaiópolis, Brazil, 5 Aug. 1941). Brazilian jazz percussionist. In the U.S. from 1968, he joined a succession of leading jazz fusion groups: Miles Davis's band (1970), Weather Report (1971, including the album *Weather Report*), and Chick Corea's Return to Forever (1972–73, including the album *Light as a Feather,* 1972). From 1973 he led groups and accompanied his wife, the Brazilian singer Flora Purim (b. 1942). He also joined Al DiMeola's group in the mid-1980s. Self-taught on a vast array of homemade and Brazilian instruments, including the cuíca and berimbau, he brought Latin American rhythms to prominence in jazz fusion.

Moreira, António Leal (b. Abrantes, Portugal, 1758; d. Lisbon, 21 Nov. 1819). Composer. From 1766 he studied with João de Sousa Carvalho at the Lisbon Seminário Patriarcal; in 1777 he entered the Brotherhood of S. Cecilia. He composed his first stage works for the royal court at Lisbon: a serenade *Bireno ed Olimpia* (1782) and an opera seria, *Siface e Sofonisba* (1783). In 1787 he was appointed *mestre de capela* at the Capela Real. During the 1780s and 1790s he composed oratorios (*Ester,* 1786), serenatas (*Ascanio in Alba,* 1785), and comic and serious operas in both Italian and Portuguese (some of the first). Operas include *Artemisia, regina di Caria* (Ajuda, 1787), *Gli affetti del genio lusitano* (Ajuda, 1789), *Raollo* (Lisbon, 1793), *La serva riconoscente* (Lisbon, 1798), and *Il disertore francese* (Turin, 1800).

Morel, (Joseph Raoul) François (d'Assise) (b. Montreal, 14 Mar. 1926). Composer. He studied with Champagne at the Montreal Conservatory (1944–53) and with Varèse in New York (1958). With Garant he founded Musique de notre temps (1958) to promote contemporary music; composed much incidental music while employed by the CBC (1956–70) and also wrote for the National Film Board. He was director of the Académie de musique de Québec (1972–78) and then taught orchestration and composition at the universities of Montreal and Laval (Quebec City). In his early works he adopted models from Debussy, Ravel, Stravinsky, Bartók, and Messiaen; serial principles and Varèse were major influences on works from the 1960s (*L'étoile noire,* 1962), and a freer approach to serialism characterizes later compositions. Works include orchestral music (*Jeux,* 1976); *Prisme anamorphoses* (winds, harp, celesta, piano, and percussion, 1967) and other chamber music; solo instrumental works for piano, guitar, flute, and organ; a few songs.

Morel, Jean (b. Abbeville, France, 10 Jan. 1903; d. New York, 14 Apr. 1975). Teacher and conductor. Studied with Isidore Philipp (piano), Noël Gallon (theory), Maurice Emmanuel (music history), and Gabriel Pierné (composition); taught at the American Conservatory in Fontainebleau (1921–36), Brooklyn College (1940–43), and from 1949 until his retirement in 1971 at Juilliard, where his students included James Levine and Leonard Slatkin. Also made a number of appearances (from 1956) with the Metropolitan Opera.

Morel Campos, Juan (b. Ponce, Puerto Rico, 16 May 1857; d. there, 12 May 1896). Composer. Studied music with M. G. Tavárez; became church organist, player in and then director of military and dance bands in Ponce and elsewhere in Puerto Rico; conductor of a zarzuela company that toured South America; composed 3 zarzuelas, sacred and orchestral music, but best known for his nearly 300 *danzas,* mostly for piano.

Moreno Torroba, Federico (b. Madrid, 3 Mar. 1891; d. there, 12 Sept. 1982). Composer. Initially schooled by his father, José Moreno Ballesteros, a professor at the Madrid Conservatory; later studied composition under del Campo. Though he produced both orchestral music (*Cuadros castellanos,* ca. 1920) and large operas (*La virgen del Mayo,* 1925; *María la tempranica,* 1930; *El poeta,* 1980), he is best known for his many zarzuelas, including *La pastorela* (1947), *Luisa Fernanda* (1932), *Maravilla* (1941), *Orgullo de Jalisco* (1947), and *Maria Manuela* (1953); he gained renown also with music for guitar, both unaccompanied and with orchestra, written in a manner evocative of Castilian folk music.

Morera, Enrique (b. Barcelona, 22 May 1865; d. there, 12 Mar. 1942). Composer. Moved with his family to Argentina in 1867, where he studied organ, violin, and trumpet; after short stays back in Barcelona (1883–86, studying piano with Albéniz), Argentina (1886–88), and Brussels (1888–93), he finally settled in Barcelona, forming the Catalunya nova choral organization (1895) and the Teatre liric català (1901). Established a conservatory in Argentina during a sojourn in 1909–11, then returned to his native city as Municipal Conservatory deputy director. His music is often strongly nationalist in character; works include some 50 stage pieces (operas, zarzuelas, incidental music, lyric scenes) as well as symphonic poems (*Introducció a l'Atlántida,* 1893), a violin concerto (1917), chamber music, piano works, choral compositions, and songs.

Morgan, Justin (b. West Springfield, Mass., 28 Feb. 1747; d. Randolph, Vt., 22 Mar. 1798). Composer. Self-taught in music, he settled in Vermont in 1788 but traveled extensively as an itinerant singing master. His 9 surviving works show him to be an accomplished composer; he is known especially for the fuguing tune "Montgomery." His works appeared in *Federal Harmony,* ed. Asahel Benham (1790).

Bibl.: Betty Bandel, *Sing the Lord's Song in a Strange Land: The Life of Justin Morgan* (Rutherford, N.J., 1981).

Morgan, Lee (b. Philadelphia, 10 July 1938; d. New York, 19 Feb. 1972). Jazz trumpeter and bandleader. He joined Dizzy Gillespie's big band (1956–58) and recorded the album *Blue Train* with John Coltrane (1957). He was twice a member of Art Blakey's Jazz Messengers (1957–61, 1964–65). In the interval and afterward he generally led his own hard bop groups until his murder in a New York nightclub. His albums as a leader include *The Sidewinder* (1963) and *Cornbread* (1965).

Morin, Jean-Baptiste (b. Orléans, 1677; d. Paris, 1754). Composer. He served the royal family of Orléans for his entire professional life, primarily as *ordinaire de la musique* to Philippe III, Duke of Orléans. His most important and influential compositions are his 18 cantatas, which combine French and Italian styles (Paris: bk. 1, 1706; bk. 2, 1707; bk. 3, 1712). Morin was best known in his time for his vividly pictorial *divertissement La chasse du cerf* (1708).

Morini (Siracusano), Erica [Erika] (b. Vienna, 5 Jan. 1904; d. New York, 1 Nov. 1995). Violinist. Studied with Ševčík at the Vienna Conservatory, making her Viennese debut in 1916 and subsequently performing with the Berlin Philharmonic and Leipzig Gewandhaus orchestras. In 1921 she made her American debut at Carnegie Hall under Bodansky and gave a number of recitals that were well received. She left Austria and settled in New York, appearing with most of the principal orchestras in the U.S.; became an American citizen in 1943.

Morlacchi, Francesco (Giuseppe Baldassare) (b. Perugia, 14 June 1784; d. Innsbruck, 28 Oct. 1841). Composer. From a family of musicians; studied music in Perugia, then with Zingarelli in Loreto (1803–4) and Mattei in Bologna (1805); quickly successful as an opera composer; 1810, assistant director, Italian Opera, Dresden; 1811, succeeded Schuster as Kapellmeister for life; produced 7 new operas in Dresden in 1811–29 while also working in major Italian houses. A skilled musician, but remembered mainly for his rivalry with Weber as Kapellmeister of German opera in Dresden (1817–26); he is often presented in an excessively negative way in the Weber literature as little more than an Italian intriguer. Also composed oratorios and much sacred music.

Bibl.: *Francesco Morlacchi e la musica del suo tempo (1784–1841),* Atti del Convegno internazionale di studi (Florence, 1986).

Morley, Thomas (b. Norwich, 1557 or 1558; d. London, Oct. 1602). Composer, theorist, and editor. Concerned with many aspects of music but particularly influential in the field of the English madrigal. It was largely through his efforts as an editor and as a composer that the Italian madrigal came to be well known in Elizabethan England and that features of that genre were incorporated into English music. A student of Byrd, Morley began his career as master of the choristers and organist at Norwich Cathedral from 1583. He received the B.Mus. from Oxford in 1588, then apparently moved to London, where he was organist at St. Giles, Cripplegate, by 1589 and at St. Paul's by 1591. His first book of compositions appeared in the year after he became a Gentleman of the Chapel Royal in 1592. His work as an editor and translator began by 1595; from 1598 he possessed a monopoly over printing music (held until 1596 by Byrd) and was quite active as a printer and publisher.

Morley's compositions can be divided by style into English and Italian works. The English style group reflects Byrd's influence on his pupil. It includes a few keyboard works, about 10 complete Latin motets, and a much larger body of English sacred music (services, anthems, Psalms). The English group is completed by Morley's *First Booke of Consort Lessons* (1599; 2nd ed., 1611), a collection of arrangements for broken consort of English popular music.

The Italian style group contains the English madrigals, canzonets, and songs for which Morley is chiefly known (most ed. in *EMS* 1–4, 1913, rev. 1956–66, and *ELS* 33, 1970). His acquaintance with Italian music seems to date from early in his career—even before his brief tenure at St. Paul's. Among his first publications of secular music are anthologies or books of arrangements of popular light Italian pieces, some issued in both Italian and English editions. As early as 1593, however, certain of his collections are entirely original, a designation that includes some thorough reworkings of borrowed material. Lute accompaniments make their appearance in a book of canzonets for 5 or 6 voices published in 1597. The *First Booke of Ayres* (1600) is a collection of original lute songs. A number of additional madrigals are printed in his treatise *A Plaine and Easie Introduction to Practicall Musicke* (London, 1597; facs., London, 1937; ed., R. Alec Harman, New York, 1952). Various purely instrumental pieces also survive, a few in manuscript, others printed alongside light vocal works. At the end of his career Morley compiled and published *The Triumphes of Oriana* (1601), an anthology of English madrigals by 23 composers, including Morley himself, who contributed 2 items.

Bibl.: Martina Rebmann, *Zur Modusbehandlung in Thomas Morleys Vokalwerk* (Frankfurt am Main, 1994).

Mornington, Garret Wesley (b. Dangan, Ireland, 19 July 1735; d. Kensington, 22 May 1781). Composer. He studied at Trinity College in Dublin (1751–57) and became a baron upon his father's death in 1758. In 1764 he became the Univ. of Dublin's first professor of music, a post in which he served until 1774. He composed prizewinning catches and glees ("Come, fairest nymph," "Here in a cool grot"); also a cantata, *Spartacus,* as well as madrigals and odes.

Moroi, Makoto (b. Tokyo, 17 Dec. 1930). Composer. He studied composition with his father, Saburō Moroi, and with Ikenouchi at the Tokyo Academy of Music. From 1948 to 1952 he studied medieval, Renaissance, and Baroque music with Anouilh and Eta Harich-Schneider. He won an International Society for Contemporary Music prize in 1953 and again in 1955. In 1955 he spent eight months working in the electronic music studio in Cologne. From 1957 to 1963 he worked closely with Mayuzumi and in conjunction with the Institute for Twentieth-Century Music, organizing performances of new music. During the 1960s he developed an interest in the shakuhachi as well as in other Japanese instruments. From 1968 he taught at the Osaka Univ. of Art and Science. His music uses electronics, serialism, and traditional Japanese styles and instruments in a broad eclectic mix; it is frequently lyrical as well as virtuosic. The pieces written for stage are primarily music dramas, often utilizing tape (*Gyosha Paeton* [Phaeton the Charioteer], solo voices, chorus, orchestra, tape, 1965). His orchestral music uses Western genres and forms (Piano Concerto no. 1, 1966; Symphony, 1968) as well as Japanese instruments (*3 Movements,* shakuhachi, strings, percussion, 1970). His chamber music more consistently involves Japanese instruments, and his solo music uses both Japanese and Western instruments.

Moroi, Saburō (b. Tokyo, 7 Aug. 1903; d. there, 24 Mar. 1977). Composer. From 1926 to 1928 he studied literature at Tokyo Univ. From 1932 to 1934 he pursued composition with Trapp and Schrattenholz, orchestration with Gmeindl, and piano with Schmidt at the Hochschule für Musik in Berlin. Directed the Tokyo Metropolitan Symphony from 1965 to 1966 and from 1967 directed the Senzoku Gakuen Academy of Music in Tokyo. His orchestral music includes 5 symphonies (1934–70) and concertos (piano concertos, 1933, 1977; violin concerto, 1939). He also wrote chamber music; his songs and choral works tend to draw more on Japanese culture than do his other works (*Taiyō no otozure* [A Visit of the Sun], fantasy oratorio, baritone, female voices, orchestra, 1968).

Moross, Jerome (b. Brooklyn, 1 Aug. 1913; d. Miami, 25 July 1983). Composer. He studied at Juilliard and New York Univ. (graduating in 1932); successes with stage (*Parade,* revue, 1935; *Frankie and Johnny,* ballet, 1937–38) and orchestral music (*Paens,* 1931) preceded his move to Hollywood in 1940, where he worked for a decade as an orchestrator of film scores (Copland's *Our Town*) while continuing to compose concert music (Symphony no. 1, 1943). He composed film scores from 1948 to 1969; in the 1950s these scores began to receive attention sufficient for him to stop his commercial arranging (*When I Grow Up,* 1950); his film score *The Big Country* (1958) was nominated for an Academy Award. He also wrote music for a few television series *(Wagon Train).* Both popular and folk elements of the American vernacular are prominent in his style. Works include 3 operas (*Sorry, Wrong Number!,* 1977); 3 ballets (*The Last Judgement,* 1953), and 4 ballet-operas; numerous film scores; a few orchestral pieces (*Music for the Flicks,* suite based on film scores, 1952–65) and chamber music (concerto for flute and string quartet, 1978; sonata for piano 4-hands and string quartet, 1975; 4 *Sonatinas for diverse instruments,* no. 1 clarinets, no. 2 double bass and piano, no. 3 brass quintet, no. 4 wind quintet, 1966–70).

Morris, Harold (b. San Antonio, 17 Mar. 1890; d. New York, 6 May 1964). Composer and pianist. He studied at the Univ. of Texas and the Cincinnati Conservatory with Scalero and others; toured as a solo pianist in North America; taught at Juilliard (1922–39) and Columbia Univ. Teachers College (1935–46). He composed in a neo-Romantic idiom, influenced not only by impressionism but also by southern folk music and African-American rhythms. Works include 3 symphonies (1925–46), the *Piano Concerto on 2 Negro Themes* (1927), another piano concerto, a violin concerto, and *Passacaglia, Adagio, and Finale* (orchestra, 1955); 2 string quartets, piano trios, and quintets; piano music.

Morris, Joan (Clair) (b. Portland, Ore., 10 Feb. 1943). Mezzo-soprano. Studied at Gonzaga Univ. and with Frederica Schmitz-Svevo, and gave her debut recital at Brooklyn College in 1973. A celebrated interpreter of American popular song and art song; often performed with her husband, William Bolcom, and the two made a number of recordings together. From 1981, a faculty member of the Univ. of Michigan.

Morris, Kenneth (b. New York, 28 Aug. 1917). Composer, pianist, and publisher. He studied piano in New York and was active as a performer in jazz ensembles until 1935; then worked for the publisher Lillian E. Bowles as a staff arranger and writer of gospel songs. In 1940 he and Sallie Martin founded Martin and Morris Music Company in Chicago, which published gospel songs including those of untrained composers. Morris composed over 300 gospel songs, including "Just a Closer Walk with Thee."

Morris, R(eginald) O(wen) (b. York, 3 Mar. 1886; d. London, 14 Dec. 1948). Composer and writer. Studied music with Charles Wood at the Royal College of Music in London and subsequently taught there. In 1926 he became the head of the theory department at Curtis Institute in Philadelphia and in 1928 returned to the Royal College of Music. He published textbooks in harmony and counterpoint (among them, *Foundations of Practical Harmony and Counterpoint,* 1925). His compositions reflect his intimate and thorough knowledge of contrapuntal procedures and include orchestral works and concertos (violin, 1930), solo songs, folk song settings, and works for choral ensemble (*6 English Folksongs,* 6 voices, 1929).

Morris, Robert (Daniel) (b. Cheltenham, England, 19 Oct. 1943). Composer and theorist. He studied at the Eastman School and the Univ. of Michigan (D.M.A., 1969); taught at Yale (1972–77), the Univ. of Pittsburgh (1977–80), and the Eastman School (from 1980). His compositions combine twelve-tone methods, medieval isorhythmic procedures, and interests in the songs of Stephen Foster and Korean court music; his writings concentrate on formulations employing set theory. Works include *Hagoromo* (soprano, bass, male voices, 2 flutes, 3 violins, double bass, and bells, 1977); orchestral works (*Just Now and Again,* 1987; *Clash,* 1988); *Piano in the Winds* (piano, wind ensemble, 1988); many chamber works (*Inter Alia,* flute, oboe, and cello, 1980; *Arci,* string quartet, 1988); piano music; electronic music; choral pieces and songs; and incidental music.

Bibl.: Robert D. Morris, *Composition with Pitch Classes: A Theory of Compositional Design* (New Haven, 1987).

Morrison, Jim (b. Melbourne, Fla., 8 Dec. 1943; d. Paris, 3 July 1971). Rock songwriter and singer. In 1965 he formed with keyboardist Ray Manzarek (b. 1935) The Doors, a leading psychedelic band; their hits included "Light My Fire" (1967) and "Hello, I Love You" (1968). Morrison also authored 2 volumes of poetry (*An American Prayer,* 1970; *The Lords and New Creatures,* 1971) and directed films.

Morrison, Van [George Ivan] (b. Belfast, 13 Aug. 1945). Popular singer and songwriter. After performing in Europe with groups including Them, from 1966 he worked in the U.S. His style mixes elements of blues, soul, and rock; he is known for a virtuosic vocal technique, particularly well-evidenced on the live album *It's Too Late to Stop Now* (1974). Other albums include *Astral Weeks* (1968), *Moondance* (1970), *Into the Music* (1979), and *Poetic Champions Compose* (1987).

Mortari, Virgilio (b. Passirana di Lainate, Milan, 6 Dec. 1902; d. Rome, 5 Sept. 1993). Composer and pianist. He studied with Bossi and Pizzetti and graduated in piano and composition from the conservatory in Parma (1928). After an early career as a pianist, he taught at the conservatories of Venice (1933–40) and Rome (1940–73). His piano trio won first prize in the initial competition of the Italian Society for Contemporary Music (1924); in 1980 he was the first Italian to win the Montaigne Prize. He was consistently an active promoter of contemporary music, but his own style remained simple and accessible. Works include operas and ballets; orchestral music (*Prospettive,* 1986; and many concertos); choral and solo vocal music; editions of early Italian operas and other vocal music. He coauthored *La technica dell'orchestra moderna* (2nd ed., 1950).

Mortelmans, Lodowijk (b. Antwerp, 5 Feb. 1868; d. there, 24 June 1952). Composer and conductor. After study at the Conservatory of Music in Antwerp he won the Belgian Prix de Rome (1893); from 1902 he taught counterpoint and fugue at the conservatory and later was appointed its director (1924–33). He was an enthusiastic supporter of Flemish culture; some of his songs are settings of Flemish poetry by Gezelle (d. 1899); he made arrangements of numerous Flemish folk songs; served as president of the Society of Flemish Composers. Works include an opera (*De kinderen der zee,* Antwerp, 1915); symphonic poems and other orchestral music (*Homeric Symphony,* before 1900); chamber and piano music; songs and choral pieces.

Mortensen, Finn (Einar) (b. Oslo, 6 Jan. 1922; d. there, 21 May 1983). Composer. In Oslo he studied harmony with Eken in 1942 and vocal polyphony with Egge in 1943; later took composition lessons with Bentzon in Copenhagen (1956). He taught music theory at the Norwegian Correspondence School from 1948 to 1966. From 1970 through 1973 Mortensen served on the faculty of the Oslo Conservatory and then of the Oslo Musikkhøgskolen. He succeeded Egge as chairman of the Norwegian Society of Composers, serving from 1972 to 1974. His early works, basically diatonic, show the heavy influence of Egge. Later works reveal exploration of twelve-tone techniques. The orchestral works from the late 1960s utilize aleatoric devices. Mortensen wrote much chamber music, using traditional genres as well as less standard forms and instrumentation (*Constellations* op. 34, accordion, guitar, percussion, 1971). Works also include vocal and piano music (several sonatas; Nocturne op. 22, 1968).

Morthenson, Jan W(ilhelm) (b. Örnsköldsvik, 7 Apr. 1940). Composer. He studied composition with Mangs, Lidholm, and Metzger. In Cologne he studied electronic music with Koenig, and in 1963 he participated in the Darmstadt summer festival. His pieces reflect his basic philosophy, presented in his book *Nonfigurative Musik* (Stockholm, 1966), that momentum in music has become impossible since the disintegration of tonal hierarchy and its concomitant forms and thematic development. Morthenson has pursued static forms in his works, stressing musical aspects such as timbre (*Coloratura II-IV,* 1962–64). Many of his pieces have been comments on the traditions of certain genres: for example, requiems in *Farewell* (1970) and orchestra music in *Colassus,* the latter also serving as an example of his incorporation of electronic and mixed media into standard ensembles (harp, piano, percussion, orchestra, tape, slides, film, 1970). His works include orchestral (*Paraphonia,* 1987), vocal, and chamber music (*Once,* clarinet, cello, piano, 1988), as well as pieces for organ and for videotapes (*Ionosphères I,* 1969).

Morton, Jelly Roll [Lemott [La Menthe, La Mothe], Ferdinand Joseph] (b. New Orleans, 20 Oct. 1890; d. Los Angeles, 10 July 1941). Jazz composer, bandleader, and pianist. He performed throughout the U.S. for nearly two decades before making his first recordings in 1923, including solo versions of his own "King Porter–A Stomp" [King Porter Stomp] and "New Orleans Joys" [New Orleans Blues]. These reveal a ragtime-based style infused with jazz improvisation and swing, and a technical command rivaling that of any other early jazz pianist. His reputation as the first great jazz composer rests on a series of recordings made in Chicago by his Red Hot Peppers, including "Black Bottom Stomp," "The Chant," "Dead Man Blues," "Grandpa's Spells" (all 1926), and "The Pearls" (1927). In these he successfully integrated the spirit and looseness of collective jazz improvisation into a carefully controlled framework involving frequent changes of texture and timbre among the seven to eight players. He moved to New York in 1928 and formed a touring band, briefly maintaining his popularity, but by 1930 his career was declining, as he was unwilling to abandon New Orleans jazz for swing. In 1938 he made an extensive collection of recordings for the Library of Congress, speaking and playing piano; part insightful history and part fantasy, these offer unparalleled examples of the musical foundations of early jazz. He made new recordings in 1939–40.

Bibl.: Alan Lomax, *Mister Jelly Roll: The Fortunes of Jelly Roll Morton, New Orleans Creole and "Inventor of Jazz"* (New York, 1950). Laurie Wright, *Mr. Jelly Lord* (Chigwell, England, 1980).

Morton, Robert (b. ca. 1430; d. 1475 or later). Composer. Of English origin but active on the Continent, in the Burgundian court chapel from 1457 to 1475. The contemporary fame of his music, of which only a few secular rondeaux survive, was considerable. Hothby and Tinctoris mention him as a composer of the first rank. Two of his pieces, "Le souvenir" and "N'aray je jamais," enjoyed unusually wide distribution and were used as the basis of many works by later composers.

Bibl.: Ed. Allan Atlas, *MMR* 2 (1981).

Moryl, Richard (b. Newark, N.J., 23 Feb. 1929). Composer and conductor. He attended Montclair State College (B.A., 1957) and Columbia Univ. (M.A., 1959) and studied with Boris Blacher at the Berlin Hochschule für Musik (1963–64) and with Arthur Berger at Brandeis (1970); taught at Western Connecticut State College (1960–70 and from 1973) and at Smith College (1970–72). In 1970 Moryl founded the New England Contemporary Music Ensemble, serving as director for many years; also founded and directed the Charles Ives Center for American Music, devoted to the study and performance of American music. His own compositions are eclectic in nature; *Atlantis* (1976), a mixed-media piece for mime, English horn, amplified piano, percussion and tape, quotes from both Lassus and Varèse.

Moscheles, Ignaz (Prague, 23 May 1794; d. Leipzig, 10 Mar. 1870). Teacher, pianist, composer. From 1804 to 1808, studied music in Prague with B. D. Weber and from 1808 in Vienna with Albrechtsberger and Salieri, supporting himself with piano lessons and becoming acquainted with Beethoven, whose music he greatly admired; 1814, commissioned by the publisher Artaria to make the piano vocal score of *Fidelio.* He became known as a piano virtuoso, first locally, from 1816 through German tours; 1820–25, toured more widely to Paris (from 1820) and London (from 1821), where he settled in 1825 after marrying, becoming a leading figure in its musical life as fashionable salon pianist, composer, piano teacher (Royal Academy of Music), conductor (including the Philharmonic Society, of which he was co-director, 1832–41). His virtuosity was of a pre-Lisztian sort, notable for clarity, elegance, and precision, and he gradually withdrew in the face of the flashier bravura of the younger generation, from 1837 giving "historical recitals" that reflect his interest in older music and prefigure the modern piano recital; after 1840 he did not play in public. He was also a renowned improviser. A close friend of Mendelssohn's from 1824; 1835, soloist in Mendelssohn's first Gewandhaus concert; 1846, at Mendelssohn's invitation, moved to Leipzig to teach the piano at the new conservatory, of which he became a leading figure with many distinguished pupils. Published much piano and salon music; also 6 sonatas (2 for 4-hands); etudes; works for piano and orchestra, including 8 concertos, 1819–38 (no. 3 in G minor, op. 60, 1820); a symphony op. 81 (1829); concert overture op. 91 (1835); chamber music with piano; songs. His wife, Charlotte, published a biography, *Aus Moscheles' Leben* (Leipzig, 1872; trans. Eng. 1873, ed. O. E. Coleridge as *Recent Music and Musicians Described in the Diaries and Correspondence of Ignaz Moscheles;* R: 1970).

Bibl.: *Thematisches Verzeichnis im Druck erschienener Compositionen von Ignaz Moscheles* (Leipzig, 1885; R: 1966). Emil Smidak, *Isaak-Ignaz Moscheles: The Life of the Composer and His Encounters with Beethoven, Liszt, Chopin, and Mendelssohn* (Aldershot, 1989).

Mosolov, Alexandr Vasil'yevich (b. Kiev, 29 July/11 Aug. 1900; d. Moscow, 12 July 1973). Composer. He had music lessons from his mother and attended a Moscow high school until 1917. From 1918 to 1920 he fought in the civil war. He studied privately with Glier in 1922, then attended the Moscow Conservatory (1922–25), where he studied harmony and counterpoint with Glier, composition with Myaskovsky, and piano with Prokofiev and Igumnov. He worked as a concert pianist in Moscow until 1937. The condemnation of his music by the Russian Association of Proletarian Musicians during the period 1927–31 led to a simplification of his style. He lived in Moscow from 1939 until his death. During this time he collected folk music in the Turkmen and Kirghiz republics; also in the Kuban and Stavropol regions, and in northern Russia. In the 1960s he worked with the Northern Folk Choir.

Works include the operas *Geroy* [The Hero] (1927), *Plotina* [The Dam] (1931), *Maskarad* (1944); the oratorios *Goroda-geroy* [Town Hero] (1945), *Slava Moskve* [Hail Moscow] (1967), *Narodnaya oratoriya* [People's Oratorio] (1970); 6 symphonies; *Sumerki* [Twilight] (symphonic poem, 1925?); *Zavod* [The Foundry], episode from ballet *Stal* (1926–28); 2 piano concertos (1927, 1932); a harp concerto (1939); a cello concerto (1945); *Elegicheskaya poem* (cello, orchestra, 1961); *Legenda,* cello, piano (1924); String Quartet no. 2 *Na patrioticheskie temï 1812* (1963); 5 piano sonatas; choruses; songs.

Mosonyi, Mihály [Brand, Michael] (b. Boldogasszonyfalva, Hungary [now Frauenkirchen, Austria], 4 Sept. 1815; d. Pest, 31 Oct. 1870). Composer. Picked up music in his native village and from 1829 in Magyaróvár, where he worked as a church officer; from 1832 studied music in Pressburg (Bratislava) with Károly Turányi; 1835–42, piano teacher to family of Count Péter Pejachevich (spending summers in Rétfalu, winters in Pressburg and Vienna), teaching himself composition and producing the first 4 of his 7 string quartets, a Mass, concert overture, etc. From 1842 he lived in Pest, teaching the piano and theory, playing the contrabass, and becoming locally known as a composer. From 1856 friendly with Liszt, and from 1857 increasingly focused on developing a native style for Hungarian music, changing his German name to a Hungarian one in 1859 (German was his principal language, his writings being translated into Hungarian); 1860–65, a frequent contributor to the first Hungarian music periodical, *Zenészeti Lapok.* His music divides into two periods, separated by 1845–56, in which he composed relatively little: 3 operas (only 1 performed in his lifetime, without much success), 2 symphonies (1844, 1856), a piano concerto (1844), 5 Masses and other sacred works, cantatas, choral works, piano pieces, and songs. It is the music of the second, nationalistic period that has mainly interested Hungarian historians.

Moss, Lawrence K(enneth) (b. Los Angeles, 18 Nov. 1927). Composer. He studied at UCLA, Eastman, and the Univ. of Southern California (Ph.D., 1957) with Dahl and Kirchner. Taught at Mills College (1956–59), Yale (1960–68), and the Univ. of Maryland (from 1969). His works often combine electronic music and conventional instruments (*Auditions,* wind quintet and tape, 1971) and include several multi-media pieces involving dancers, actors, and lights (*Unseen Leaves,* soprano, oboe, tape, slides, lights, 1975; *Blackbird,* clarinet, mime/dancer, tape, 1987). Other works include the opera *The Queen and the Rebels* (1989), a symphony for brass quintet and chamber orchestra (1977), *Portals* (tenor, flute, clarinet, percussion, violin, viola, and cello, 1983), *Various Birds* (woodwind quintet, 1987), and *Violaria, una dramma per musica* (viola, tape, 1988).

Mosto, Giovanni Battista (b. Udine, Italy; d. Karlsburg, June 1596). Composer. Pupil of Claudio Merulo. From 1568, worked in Munich at the Bavarian court, in Udine at the court of Prince Sigismond Bathory of Transylvania, and in Padua (*maestro di cappella* at the cathedral from 1580 to 1589 and from 1595 until his death). His output consists entirely of madrigals in a Venetian style, including 4 books published in Venice and many other pieces published in anthologies.

Moszkowski, Moritz (b. Breslau, 23 Aug. 1854; d. Paris, 4 Mar. 1925). Composer and pianist. Studied at the Dresden Conservatory, then in Berlin at the Stern Conservatory and Kullak's school, where he later taught; concert debut, Berlin, 1873; toured as pianist and conductor, his career interrupted in the 1880s by an arm complaint; retired to Paris in 1897. His piano music was enormously popular, especially his *Spanische Tänze* op. 12, originally for 4-hands; also *Album espagnol* op. 21 (1879), *Gondoliera* op. 41; also violin pieces (especially op. 16), an opera, Piano Concerto op. 59 (1898). Brother of the writer Alexander Moszkowski (1851–1934).

Moten, Bennie [Benjamin] (b. Kansas City, Mo., 13 Nov. 1894; d. there, 2 Apr. 1935). Jazz bandleader and pianist. By 1918 he was leading a trio, which through the 1920s gradually expanded into a big band. Between 1929 and 1931 it absorbed members of Walter Page's Blue Devils, including Count Basie (who replaced Moten as the group's pianist), Hot Lips Page, Jimmy Rushing, and Page himself. With Ben Webster added, the group traveled to the New York area in 1932 and made seminal recordings in the Kansas City jazz style, including "Toby" and "Moten Swing." With George E. Lee he co-led a big band in Kansas City and then reestablished his own, which after his death eventually formed the nucleus of Count Basie's orchestra.

Motte, Diether de la (b. Bonn, 30 Mar. 1928). Composer. He studied piano, conducting, and composition in Detmold (1946–50) and attended the Darmstadt courses of Leibowitz, Krenek, Fortner, and Messiaen; from 1950 he taught in Düsseldorf and served as music critic there; worked briefly for Schott in Magonza (1959–62); and then taught at the Musikhochschule in Hamburg. In 1972 he became vice-president of the Freie Akademie der Künste in Hamburg. His interests range from gamelan to Gregorian chant to gesture or "visible music"; his opera *So oder so* (1975) uses episodes of pantomime. Other works include 2 concertos for orchestra (1963, 1980); *Klänge fur zwei Orchester* (1981); *Fünf Charaktere* (violin, horn, and piano, 1977); vocal, choral, and tape pieces. Also wrote books on form and analysis.

Mottl, Felix (Josef) (b. Unter-St. Veit, near Vienna, 24 Aug. 1856; d. Munich, 2 July 1911). Conductor. Boy soprano in Vienna, then a student at the conservatory (theory with Bruckner); early a passionate Wagnerian; 1872, a founder of the Vienna Wagner Society and conductor of its concerts; 1876, helped prepare first Bayreuth Festival, becoming part of the Wagner inner circle. Liszt got his opera *Agnes Bernauer* performed at Weimar in 1880; 1881–1903, conductor, Karlsruhe Opera and (to 1892) Philharmonic (from 1893 as *Generalmusikdirektor*), bringing them to a high degree of excellence; from 1886 conducted much at Bayreuth; from 1903, conductor, Munich Opera and director of the conservatory; 1904–7, also conductor, Vienna Philharmonic. Identified with Wagner but broad in his tastes (for example, championing Chabrier, to Cosima Wagner's disgust); 1903, prepared Metropolitan Opera production of *Parsifal* but withdrew because of Wagner family opposition.

Moulu, Pierre (b. ca. 1480–90; d. ca. 1550). Composer. Ronsard called him a student of Josquin. Texts of certain works suggest a close association with the French royal chapel in the first quarter of the 16th century. He composed Masses, chansons, and over 20 motets.

Mouret, Jean-Joseph (b. Avignon, 11 Apr. 1682; d. Charenton, 20 Dec. 1738). Composer. He moved to Paris around 1707 and became *Surintendant de la musique* at the court of Sceaux in 1708 or 1709. He directed the orchestra of the Paris Opéra (1714–18), became composer/director of the New Italian Theater (1717–37) and director of the Concert spirituel (1728–34). Stage works include *Le mariage de Ragonde* (Sceaux, 1714); *Les fêtes ou Le triomphe de Thalie* (Opéra, 1714); *Pirithous* (Opéra, 1723); *Le temple de Gnide* (Opéra, 1741). Mouret also composed motets, airs, and instrumental music.

Bibl.: Renée Viollier, *Jean-Joseph Mouret, le musician des grâces* (Paris, 1950).

Mouton, Jean [Jehan] (b. Holluigue [now Haut-Wignes], near Samer, ca. 1459; d. St. Quentin, 30 Oct. 1522). Composer. Known particularly for his motets. A singer in Nesle from 1477, *maître de chapelle* there from 1483; subsequently active in Amiens (from 1500), then in Grenoble (from 1501). From 1502 associated with the French royal court, at first serving Queen Anne of Brittany, then François I. Many of his motets are occasional works, clearly written by the official court composer for significant events in the life of the royal family. He may have edited the Medici Codex, an official gift from François I to Lorenzo, Duke of Urbino. He derived some income from benefices at St. André in Grenoble and, late in life, St. Quentin. His compositions were among the favorites of Pope Leo X, who appointed Mouton an apostolic notary. Adrian Willaert was his student.

Mouton's music includes about 20 chansons, 15 Masses, several Magnificats, and, his most important works, over 100 motets. Petrucci issued one book of the Masses (1515) and Le Roy & Ballard a posthumous book of motets (1555). Other works were printed in anthologies or survive in manuscript. These compositions show an impressive mastery of contrapuntal techniques, especially canon, and a predominance of contrapuntal textures. Many pieces employ borrowed material of some sort, whether used as a cantus firmus, paraphrased, or parodied; a few are freely composed.

Bibl.: Andreas C. Minor, ed., *CMM* 43/1–4 (1967–74)

[Masses only]. Edward E. Lowinsky, ed., *The Medici Codex of 1518, MRM* 3–5 (1968).

Moyzes, Alexander (b. Kláštor pod Znievom, Slovakia, 4 Sept. 1906; d. Bratislava, 20 Nov. 1984). Composer. Son of composer Mikuláš Moyzes. Studied conducting with Ostrčil, composition with Karel and Aín and organ with Wiedermann at the Prague Conservatory, 1925–28. He then continued his studies there until 1930 with Novák. Moyzes taught at the Bratislava Academy of Music and Drama, then at the College of Musical Arts in Bratislava in 1949, serving as director from 1965 to 1971. From 1937 to 1948 he was head of the music division of Bratislava Radio. Through his many activities he had a significant impact on Slovak music. His Symphony no. 1 was the first national Slovak symphony. Progressively through his career his music synthesized nationalistic elements such as Slovak folk songs with international avant-garde techniques. He wrote much orchestral and vocal music as well as some chamber works and music for film and radio.

Mozart, (Maria) Constanze (b. Zell, 5 Jan. 1762; d. Salzburg, 6 Mar. 1842). Soprano. Wife of W. A. Mozart. Her father, Fridolin Weber, was a music copyist and theater prompter; as a girl Constanze Weber took lessons in voice and clavier. The family moved to Vienna in 1779; two years later Mozart lodged with them, having met them in Mannheim in 1777. (Initially he had courted Constanze's sister, the soprano Aloysia.) In 1782 Mozart and Constanze were married. After the composer's death in 1791, Constanze organized concerts of her husband's music; in 1799 she negotiated a sale of his remaining manuscripts to the publisher André. Later she married Georg Nikolaus Nissen, the Danish diplomat whose *Biographie W. A. Mozarts nach Originalbriefen* (Leipzig, 1828) she helped complete. They lived first in Copenhagen (from 1810), then in Salzburg (after 1821).

Bibl.: Arthur Schurig, ed., *Konstanze Mozart: Briefe–Aufzeichnungen–Dokumente, 1782–1842* (Dresden, 1922).

Mozart, Franz Xaver Wolfgang ["Wolfgang Amadeus"] (b. Vienna, 26 July 1791; d. Carlsbad, 29 July 1844). Composer and pianist. Youngest son of Wolfgang Amadeus and Constanze Weber Mozart. As a youth he lived with the Dušek family in Prague, where he studied clavier with Franz Niemetschek. Later he also took instruction with Salieri, Hummel, Vogler, and Albrechtsberger in Vienna. He became an excellent pianist, and in 1807 he settled in Lemberg (Lwów), where he served in several posts as music teacher in noble households. Between 1819 and 1822 he toured extensively through Russia, Scandinavia, and Continental Europe. He returned to Lemberg during the 1830s, but in 1838 he settled in Vienna, where in 1841 he was made honorary Kapellmeister of the Dom-Musik-Verein. He composed cantatas, songs, symphonies, chamber works, and many piano works (Sonata op. 10; polonaises, variations, marches).

Bibl.: Walter Hummel, *W. A. Mozarts Söhne* (Kassel, 1956).

Mozart, (Johann Georg) Leopold (b. Augsburg, 14 Nov. 1719; d. Salzburg, 28 May 1787). Composer, violinist, and writer on music. Received his education from the Jesuits in Augsburg, first at the Gymnasium (from 1727), then at the Lyceum (from 1735). After the death of his father, he entered the Benedictine university in Salzburg (in 1737); he was expelled two years later for excessive absences. He took a post as house musician for the Count of Thurn-Valsassina und Taxis in Salzburg; during this period he published his first compositions, a set of six trio sonatas. He was appointed violinist to the Salzburg court chapel in 1743, and by 1763 had advanced to the position of Vice-Kapellmeister. His two surviving children, Maria Anna ("Nannerl") and Wolfgang Amadeus, were born to him and his wife Anna Maria (née Pertl) in 1751 and 1756, respectively. Also in 1756 Leopold published his *Versuch einer gründlichen Violinschule* (Augsburg, 1756; expanded ed., 1770; 3rd rev. ed., 1787; R: Frankfurt, 1976); translated almost immediately into Dutch and French, it was one of the most significant and widely used treatises of the second half of the 18th century.

After about 1760 Leopold devoted much of his energy to his children's musical education. Both Wolfgang and Nannerl were prodigies on the clavier, and beginning in 1762 Leopold took them on extensive, exhausting tours of the major musical centers of Europe. Though he is often criticized as an exploiter of his own children, Leopold felt it his mission to reveal to the world the "miracle that God allowed to be born in Salzburg." He must be given credit for giving his son a broad exposure to international musical styles, which was later to prove essential to his musical development. He took Wolfgang on tours of Austria, Germany, Holland, England, and France; he also served as the boy's stringent teacher of counterpoint and composition. After Wolfgang settled in Vienna, his father's time was increasingly occupied with teaching. Father and son became distant; Leopold made his last trip to Vienna in 1785 and died only partially satisfied with Wolfgang's successes. Among Leopold's own extensive oeuvre is a large number of sacred works (cantatas, oratorios, Masses, litanies, Magnificats, Psalms); many symphonies (a number of which have occasionally been attributed to Wolfgang), including the Symphony in D (De gustibus non est disputandum) and the Symphony in G (Sinfonia da caccia); serenades and divertimentos (incl. "Die Bauernhochzeit," D major, and "Die musikalische Schlittenfahrt," F major); concertos; chamber and keyboard music.

Bibl.: Georg Schünemann, "Leopold Mozart als Komponist," *AMz* 26 (1909): 1039ff. Otto Erich Deutsch and Bernhard Paumgartner, *Leopold Mozarts Briefe an seine Tochter* (Salzburg and Leipzig, 1936). Ludwig Wegele, ed., *Leopold Mozart, 1719–1787: Bild einer Persönlichkeit* (Augsburg, 1969). Adolf Layer, *Eine Jugend in Augsburg: Leopold Mozart*

Wolfgang Amadeus Mozart at the piano with his sister, Nannerl, and his father. Winter 1780–81.

1719–1787 (Augsburg, 1976). Cliff Eisen, "The Symphonies of Leopold Mozart and Their Relation to the Early Symphonies of Wolfgang Amadeus Mozart" (diss., Cornell Univ., 1986).

Mozart, (Johann Chrysostom) Wolfgang Amadeus (b. Salzburg, 27 Jan. 1756; d. Vienna, 5 Dec. 1791). Composer. He and his elder sister Maria Anna ("Nannerl") were the only surviving children of Johann Georg Leopold Mozart and Anna Maria Mozart; Leopold was violinist and composer at the court of the prince-bishop of Salzburg. Wolfgang demonstrated his musical ability at the age of 4, playing pieces from his sister's clavier lessons. Leopold began instructing him in keyboard and violin. The boy's earliest known compositions date from 1761; his first public performance occurred the same year, at the Univ. of Salzburg. In 1762 Leopold took the children on the first of a succession of concert tours; the first appearance abroad was at Munich, where they performed at the elector's court. Back in the imperial capital in late 1762, they appeared in homes of Viennese nobility and twice before Maria Theresia at the imperial court.

After a brief return to Salzburg in early 1763, in June they began a three-year tour of the musical centers of Europe, with Paris and London as chief goals. They traveled through Frankfurt, Munich, Augsburg, Bonn, Mainz, and Cologne before reaching Paris in November 1763. There they played for Louis XV. Wolfgang's first publications also appeared in Paris: four Sonatas for Violin and Clavier (K. 6–9). In April 1764 they traveled to London, where they stayed for more than a year; Wolfgang composed his first symphonies there and became acquainted with J. C. Bach. The family returned to Salzburg in late 1766, embarking for Vienna again in September 1767. They arrived in January 1768, after stops in Brünn and Olmütz. Court intrigues prevented the performance of Wolfgang's first opera buffa for Vienna, *La finta semplice,* but the singspiel *Bastien und Bastienne* was performed at the home of Franz Mesmer.

Upon the family's return to Salzburg in January 1769, the archbishop announced Wolfgang's appointment to the post of *Konzertmeister.* In late 1769 father and son embarked on an Italian tour. In Milan they met G. B. Sammartini and Niccolò Piccinni; the latter arranged for Mozart to compose an opera (*Mitridate, rè di Ponto,* performed in Milan in Dec. 1770). In Bologna Mozart was elected to the Accademia filarmonica, and in Rome he was made a Knight of the Golden Spur

(Oct. 1770). It was on this trip that Mozart allegedly copied out Allegri's *Miserere* after hearing it only once, at the Sistine Chapel.

The next five years were occupied with trips to Italy (1772), where *Lucio Silla* was performed in Milan, and Vienna (1773–74), where Mozart heard comic operas of Piccinni and Galuppi and where he apparently made the acquaintance, if not of Joseph Haydn himself, of that composer's string quartets opp. 9, 17, and 20. Leopold's hopes of a position at the imperial court for his son came to nothing. Early in 1775 father and son traveled to Munich to oversee performances of *La finta giardiniera.* The years 1775–77, spent in Salzburg, saw the composition of the violin concertos and the first sonatas for clavier.

In September 1777 Mozart embarked with his mother on his most important musical tour to date. In Mannheim he sought, in vain, a position at the elector's court; there he also made the acquaintance of the Weber family and fell in love with 16-year-old daughter Aloysia. Mother and son continued to Paris in 1778, where Mozart composed works for the Concert spirituel including a *sinfonia concertante* that was never performed (K.Anh. 9/297B; now lost). In July 1779 Anna Maria fell ill and died. Returning to Salzburg in January 1780, Mozart assumed his newly assigned duties as court organist. In the summer of 1780 he received a commission from the Elector of Bavaria to compose a serious opera for Munich. *Idomeneo,* Mozart's most ambitious serious opera, was performed to notable acclaim in January 1781.

In March of that year his employer, the Archbishop Colloredo, called him from Munich to Vienna, where the Salzburg entourage was residing during coronation ceremonies for the new emperor, Joseph II. There relations between composer and employer worsened, and in May 1781 Mozart petitioned to be released. The request was granted; for the first time he was a "free" composer in the imperial capital. The Weber family, having relocated to Vienna, took him in as a boarder; he began earning a small income teaching piano. He soon received an operatic commission from the imperial court, and *Die Entführung aus dem Serail,* first performed in 1782, became one of the few lasting successes of Joseph II's "National Singspiel" company.

Aloysia Weber had married by this time; Mozart instead grew close to her sister Constanze, and in August 1782 the two were married at St. Stephen's. Mozart pledged membership to a Viennese Masonic lodge and continued to teach and give concerts of his own works. During the early 1780s he composed numerous piano concertos for himself and his pupils. Late in 1785 he and librettist Lorenzo da Ponte began work on an operatic version of Beaumarchais's *Le nozze di Figaro.* Despite cabals against it, the opera was a success at its first performance at the Burgtheater in May 1786.

In May 1787 Leopold fell ill and died. During this time Mozart was composing *Don Giovanni* for a Prague commission; he traveled there for the opera's first performance on 29 October. Returning to Vienna, he accepted a position at court as *Kammermusikus* at a salary of 800 gulden per year. Despite this appointment and the large fees he received for his operas, he continued to borrow money, especially from his friend Michael Puchberg. Nevertheless, his growing family maintained a decent standard of living.

In 1789 Mozart traveled with Prince Karl Lichnowsky to Potsdam, Dresden, Leipzig, and Prague. In Leipzig he played the organ at the Thomaskirche. In Berlin King Friedrich Wilhelm II, a cellist, commissioned him to compose a set of string quartets; Mozart completed three (the Prussian quartets). Soon after his return to Vienna in June 1789 he began *Così fan tutte,* which was performed at the imperial court in January 1790. In February 1790 Joseph II died. Mozart traveled to Frankfurt in October for the crowning of the new emperor, Leopold II; nothing came of his hopes of a better position under the new administration. Back in Vienna in December, he met with Haydn shortly before the latter's departure for England.

Despite illness, Mozart was productive during his last year. With Emanuel Schikander he began work on a new singspiel, and in July he received an operatic commission from Prague. *La clemenza di Tito,* composed with great speed, was performed there on 6 September. Later that month *Die Zauberflöte* was performed at the Theater auf der Wieden, where it was applauded even by Salieri. In November Mozart fell ill. As his condition worsened, he struggled to complete the Requiem, which had been commissioned by a certain Count Walsegg-Stuppach with the intention of presenting the work as his own. Mozart died before finishing the work, but reportedly left instructions with his friend Franz Süssmayr as to its completion. A portion of the work was performed at Mozart's funeral Mass. After his death Constanze was granted a pension from the imperial court.

Works: [Initial "K" nos. are from Köchel, 6th ed.; those in parentheses are from the original edition of 1862.] Major stage works (dates are of first performance): *Apollo et Hyacinthus* (intermezzo, Salzburg, 1767); *La finta simplice* (opera buffa, Salzburg, 1769); *Bastien und Bastienne* (singspiel, Vienna, 1768); *Mitridate, rè di Ponto* (opera seria, Milan, 1770); *Lucio Silla* (opera seria, Milan, 1772); *La finta giardiniera* (opera buffa, Munich, 1775); *Il rè pastore* (*dramma per musica,* Salzburg, 1775); *Zaide* (singspiel, Salzburg, 1779–80); *Idomeneo, rè di Creta* (opera seria, Munich, 1781); *Die Entführung aus dem Serail* (singspiel, Vienna, 1782); *Der Schauspieldirektor* (singspiel, Schönbrunn, 1786); *Le nozze di Figaro* (opera buffa, Vienna, 1786); *Il dissoluto punito, ossia Il Don Giovanni* (opera buffa, Prague, 1787); *Così fan tutte, ossia La scuola degli amanti* (opera buffa, Vienna, 1790); *Die Zauberflöte* (singspiel, Vienna, 1791); *La clemenza di Tito* (opera seria, Prague, 1791). Numerous scenes and concert arias for voice and orchestra; songs and vocal canons.

Oratorios: *Die Schuldigkeit des ersten Gebots* (Salzburg, 1767); *La Betulia liberata* (Salzburg, 1771); *Davidde penitente* (Vienna, 1785).

Sacred music (dates are of composition): *Missa* in C, K. 257

(Credo, 1776); *Missa brevis* in C, K. 259 (Organ, 1776); *Missa brevis* in B♭, K. 272b (275) (1777); *Missa* in C, K. 317 (Coronation, 1779); *Missa solemnis* in C, K. 337 (1780); *Missa* in C minor, K. 417a (427) (1782–83); *Requiem* in D minor, K. 626 (1791; completed by Joseph Eybler and F. X. Süssmayr); litanies, vespers, and other sacred works, incl. *Regina coeli* in B♭, K. 127 (1772); *Exsultate, jubilate* in F, K. 158a (165) (1773); *Ave verum corpus* in D, K. 618 (1791); church sonatas (2 violins, bass, organ).

Symphonies: K. 45a (A221) in G (Lambach, 1765–66); no. 12 in G, K. 75b (110) (1771); no. 24 in B♭, K. 173dA (182) (1773); no. 25 in G minor, K. 173dB (183) (1773); no. 29 in A, K. 186a (201) (1774); no. 28 in C, K. 189k (200) (ca. 1773–74); no. 31 in D, K. 300a (297) (Paris, 1778); no. 33 in B♭, K. 319 (1779); no. 34 in C, K. 338 (1780); no. 35 in D, K. 385 (Haffner, 1782); no. 36 in C, K. 425 (Linz, 1783); no. 38 in D, K. 504 (Prague, 1786); no. 39 in E♭, K. 543 (1788); no. 40 in G minor, K. 550 (1788); no. 41 in C, K. 551 (Jupiter, 1788).

Concertos: 27 for piano and orchestra, incl. nos. 1–4, K. 37, 39–41 (1767; arr. from works by H. F. Raupach, L. Honauer, C. P. E. Bach); no. 9 in E♭, K. 271 (1777); no. 10 in E♭ (2 pianos), K. 316a (365) (1779); no. 11 in F, K. 387a (413) (1782–83); no. 12 in A, K. 385p (414) (1782); no. 14 in E♭, K. 449 (1784); no. 17 in G, K. 453 (1784); no. 18 in B♭, K. 456 (1784); no. 19 in F, K. 459 (1784); no. 20 in D minor, K. 466 (1785); no. 21 in C, K. 467 (1785); no. 22 in E♭, K. 482 (1785); no. 23 in A, K. 488 (1786); no. 24 in C minor, K. 491 (1786); no. 25 in C, K. 503 (1786); no. 26 in D, K. 537 (Coronation, 1788); no. 27 in B♭, K. 595 (1791); 5 for violin and orchestra, including K. 216 in G (1775), K. 218 in D (1775), and K. 219 in A (1775); *Sinfonia concertante* in E♭, violin, viola, orchestra, K. 364 (1779); Rondo in C, violin, orchestra, K. 373 (1781); 4 concertos for horn, orchestra, including K. 386b (412) in D (1791), K. 417 in E♭ (1783), K. 447 in E♭ (1787?), K. 495 in E♭ (1786); a concerto for clarinet and orchestra in A, K. 622 (1791); a concerto for bassoon and orchestra in B♭, K. 186e (191) (1774); a concerto for flute and orchestra in G, K. 285c (313) (1778).

Cassations, divertimentos, and serenades, incl. *Serenata notturna* in D, K. 239 (1776); *Maurerische Trauermusik* in C minor, K. 479a (477) (1785); *Ein musikalischer Spass* in F, K. 522 (1787); *Eine kleine Nachtmusik* in G, K. 525 (1787); serenades for wind ensemble; marches, minuets, *Ländler,* and contredanses, for various instrumental ensembles.

Chamber music: String quintets include K. 516 in G minor (1787) and K. 614 in E♭ (1791); Quintet in A, clarinet and strings, K. 581 (1789); Quintet in E♭, piano and winds, K. 452 (1784); Quartets for piano and strings in G minor, K. 478 (1785) and E♭, K. 493 (1786); Quartet in F, oboe and strings, K. 368b (370) (1781). String quartets include 6 dedicated to Haydn: K. 387 in G (1782), K. 417b (421) in D minor (1783), K. 421b (428) in E♭ (1783), K. 458 in B♭ (Hunt, 1784), K. 464 in A (1785), and K. 465 in C (Dissonant, 1785); also K. 575 in D, K. 478 in B♭, and K. 590 in F (the Prussian quartets, 1789–90). Piano trios include K. 502 in B♭, K. 564 in G. More than 30 sonatas for clavier and violin; sonatas and variations for clavier solo (most for fortepiano), including K. 300d (310) in A minor (1778), K. 300h (330) in C (1783), K. 300i (331) in A (1783), K. 315c (333) in B♭ (1783–84), K. 457 in C minor (1784), K. 570 in B♭ (1789), and K. 576 in D (1789).

Bibl.: Editions: *W. A. Mozarts Werke: Kritisch durchgesehene Gesamtausgabe,* ed. Ludwig Köchel, Johannes Brahms, et al., 24 series (Leipzig, 1876–1905). *Wolfgang Amadeus Mozart: Neue Ausgabe sämtlicher Werke,* ed. Internationale Stiftung Mozarteum, Salzburg (Kassel, 1955–). Most of the *Neue Ausgabe* also appears in *Wolfgang Amadeus Mozart: Werkausgabe in 20 Bänden* (Kassel, 1991).

Catalogs: Ludwig Ritter von Köchel, *Chronologisch-thematisches Verzeichnis sämtlicher Tonwerke Wolfgang Amade Mozarts* (Leipzig, 1862; 2nd ed., Paul Graf von Waldersee, 1905; 3rd ed., Alfred Einstein, Leipzig, 1937, R: with suppl. by Einstein, Ann Arbor, 1947; reprints of 3rd ed., 1958 ["4th ed."] and 1963 ["5th ed."]; extensively rev. 6th ed., Franz Giegling et al., Wiesbaden, 1964; R: 1965).

Franz Xavier Niemetschek, *Leben des K. K. Kapellmeisters Wolfgang Gottlieb Mozart, nach Originalquellen beschrieben* (Prague, 1798; enl. 2nd ed., 1808); trans. Eng., Helen Mautner (London, 1956). Georg Nikolaus Nissen, *Biographie W. A. Mozarts nach Originalbriefen* (Leipzig, 1828; R: Hildesheim, 1964; 1972; 1984). Otto Jahn, *W. A. Mozart* (Leipzig, 1856; 2nd ed., 1867; 3rd ed., Hermann Deiters, Leipzig, 1889–91; 4th ed., Leipzig, 1905–7); trans. Eng., 1882; rev. ed. of orig. by Hermann Abert as *W. A. Mozart: Neu bearbeitete und erweiterte Ausgabe von Otto Jahns 'Mozart'* (Leipzig, 1919–21; 3rd ed., 1955–66). Edward J. Dent, *Mozart's Operas: A Critical Study* (London, 1913; 2nd ed., London, 1947; R: Oxford, 1991). Emily Anderson, ed., *The Letters of Mozart and His Family* (London, 1938; 3rd ed., New York, 1985; R: rev., New York, 1989). Alfred Einstein, *Mozart: His Character, His Work* (New York, 1945). Arthur Hutchings, *A Companion to Mozart's Piano Concertos* (London and New York, 1948; 2nd ed., 1950). H. C. Robbins Landon and Donald Mitchell, eds., *The Mozart Companion* (London, 1956; 2nd ed., 1965; rev. ed., New York, 1969). Eva and Paul Badura-Skoda, *Mozart-Interpretation* (Vienna and Stuttgart, 1957; trans. Eng., New York, 1962, as *Interpreting Mozart on the Keyboard*). Paul Nettl, *Mozart and Masonry* (New York, 1959). Otto Erich Deutsch, *Mozart: Die Dokumente seines Lebens, gesammelt und erläutert* (Kassel, 1961); trans. Eng., Eric Blom et al. (London and New York, 1965; 2nd ed., 1977; supp. 1978). Wilhelm A. Bauer, Otto Erich Deutsch, and Joseph Heinz Eibl, eds. *Mozart: Briefe und Aufzeichnungen,* 7 vols. (Kassel, 1962–75). Paul Henry Lang, ed., *The Creative World of Mozart* (New York, 1963). Rudolph Angermüller and Otto Schneider, *Mozart-Bibliographie (bis 1970)* (Kassel, 1976); *1971–1975* (Kassel, 1978); *1976–1980* (Kassel, 1982); and *1981–1985* (Kassel, 1987). Karl Gustav Fellerer, *Die Kirchenmusik W. A. Mozarts* (Laaber, 1985). Frederick Neumann, *Ornamentation and Improvisation in Mozart* (Princeton, 1986). Alan Tyson, *Mozart: Studies of the Autograph Scores* (Cambridge, Mass., 1987). H. C. Robbins Landon, *Mozart's Last Year: 1791* (New York, 1988). Jean-Pierre Marty, *The Tempo Indications of Mozart* (New Haven, 1988). Baird Hastings, *Wolfgang Amadeus Mozart: A Guide to Research* (New York, 1989). Neal Zaslaw, *Mozart's Symphonies: Context, Performance Practice, Reception* (New York, 1989). Daniel Heartz, *Mozart's Operas* (Berkeley, 1990). H. C. Robbins Landon, *The Mozart Compendium* (London, 1990). Neal Zaslaw with William Cowdery, eds., *The Compleat Mozart: A Guide to the Music Works of Wolfgang Amadeus Mozart* (New York, 1990). Cliff Eisen, *New Mozart Documents: A Supplement to O. E. Deutsch's Documentary Biography* (Stanford, 1991). Id., ed., *Mozart Studies* (Oxford and New York, 1991). R. Larry Todd and Peter Williams, eds., *Perspectives on Mozart Performance* (New York, 1991). Robert L. Marshall, ed., *Mozart Speaks: Views on Music, Musicians, and the World* (New York, 1991). Christoph Wolff, *Mozart's Requiem* (Munich, 1991; Eng. ed., Berkeley, 1994). Neal Zaslaw and Fiona Morgan Fein, *The Mozart Repertory: A Guide for Musicians, Programmers, and Researchers* (Ithaca, N.Y., 1991). Peter Clive, *Mozart and His*

Circle: A Biographical Dictionary (London, 1993). Elaine Sisman, *Mozart, The "Jupiter" Symphony* (Cambridge, 1993). Nicholas Till, *Mozart and the Enlightenment: Truth, Virtue, and Beauty in Mozart's Operas* (New York, 1993). Maynard Solomon, *Mozart: A Life* (New York, 1995).

Mravinsky, Evgeny (Alexandrovich) (b. St. Petersburg, 4 June 1903; d. Leningrad, 19 Jan. 1988). Conductor. Studied conducting with Gauk at the Leningrad Conservatory and took composition with Shcherbachov; served as conductor of the Leningrad Academic Opera and Ballet Theater (1932–38) and in 1938 was appointed principal conductor of the Leningrad Philharmonic. Best known for his interpretations of Soviet composers, including Prokofiev, Khachaturian, and Kabalevsky; premiered a number of symphonies by Shostakovich, including nos. 5, 6, and 8.

Mshvelidze, Shalva Mikhaylovich (b. Tbilisi, 28 May 1904; d. there, 4 Mar. 1984). Composer. Studied at the Tbilisi Conservatory with Bagrinovsky and at the Leningrad Conservatory with Shcherbachov, Tyulin, Shteynberg, and Ryazanov. In 1927 he undertook ethnomusicological expeditions. Graduated from the Tbilisi Conservatory in 1930, then had further study with Shcherbachov. He taught at the conservatory from 1929, becoming professor in 1942. His works include the operas *Ambavi Tarielisa* [The Legend of Tariel] (1946) and *Didostatis mardzhvena* [The Hand of a Great Master] (1961); the oratorio *Vekam v predan'ye* [The Legend to Survive the Centuries] (1970); 5 symphonies; *Zviadauri,* symphonic poem (1940); chamber music; choruses; and songs.

Muck, Carl [Karl] (b. Darmstadt, 22 Oct. 1859; d. Stuttgart, 3 Mar. 1940). Conductor. Pursued academic subjects at the Univ. of Heidelberg and Leipzig; conducted at a number of theaters in Salzburg, Graz, and Brünn, and in 1886 became Kapellmeister at the Deutsches Landestheater in Prague. Named principal Kapellmeister (1892) and then general music director (1908) of the Berlin Opera, where his performances of Wagner were particularly well received; conducted Wagner at Covent Garden (1899) and led *Parsifal* at Bayreuth (1901). Muck also served as director of the Boston Symphony (1906–8, 1912–18), although his second tenure was cut off abruptly as a result of anti-German sentiment, and in March 1918 he was arrested and interned for the duration of the war. Returned to Germany in 1919 and conducted the Hamburg Philharmonic (1922–33) and *Parsifal* at Bayreuth until 1930. His recordings are important documents of Wagnerian performance practice.

Muczynski, Robert (b. Chicago, 19 Mar. 1929). Composer. He studied piano and composition with Tcherepnin at DePaul Univ.; in 1955 wrote a piano concerto for the Louisville Orchestra; and in 1958 made his piano debut at Carnegie Hall in a concert of his own works (many of which he recorded). Taught piano at Loras (Iowa) College (1956–59) and at the Univ. of Arizona (1965–88); from 1959 to 1962 he worked with the Ford Foundation Young Composers Project. Works, in a restrained neoclassic style, include a concerto for saxophone and orchestra (1981); much chamber and keyboard music (*Time Pieces,* clarinet and piano, 1983; *Dream Cycle,* piano, 1983; *Profiles,* harpsichord, 1982); choral works; and documentary film scores.

Mudarra, Alonso (b. ca. 1508; d. Seville, 1 Apr. 1580). Composer. Brought up in noble households in Guadalajara. From 1546 connected with the cathedral in Seville, taking an ever larger role in musical activities there until his death. His *Tres libros de musica en cifras para vihuela* (1546; ed. *MME* 7 [1949]) includes over 70 compositions for vihuela, guitar, harp, organ, or voice and vihuela. These encompass fantasias, *tientos,* dances, variation sets, and intabulations of Mass sections and motets, as well as accompanied songs with Spanish, Galician, Italian, and classical Latin texts.

Muddy Waters [Morganfield, McKinley] (b. Rolling Fork, Miss., 4 Apr. 1915; d. Downers Grove, Ill., 30 Apr. 1983). Blues singer, guitarist, and bandleader. After recording for the Library of Congress as a down-home blues musician (1941–42) he moved to Chicago (1943), where he began singing in a forceful manner and playing electric guitar, using a traditional bottleneck technique. His band, including Little Walter from 1948, came to epitomize the Chicago blues style: recordings such as "I'm Your Hoochie Coochie Man" (1954) and "Got My Mojo Working" (1956) were characterized by a rough, amplified sound, a heavy beat, and brashly sexual lyrics. He played with Chris Barber in England in 1958 and toured widely from the mid-1960s, as he became recognized for his influence on the development of rock.

Mueller, Johann Christoph (b. Württemberg, 1777; d. Bridgewater, Pa., 1845). Pianist, violinist, and flutist. He studied botany and medicine in Germany, then emigrated to the U.S. with the minister Johann Georg Rapp in 1803. Together they formed the Harmony Society, a religious colony in rural Pennsylvania. As music director for the colony, and for another similar group in Indiana (New Harmony), Mueller compiled, copied, and printed hymns, waltzes, overtures, and other music by European and American composers. He also formed an orchestra, which after 1827 gave regular concerts in Economy, Pa.

Bibl.: Richard D. Wetzel, "The Music of George Rapp's Harmony Society, 1805–1906" (diss., Univ. of Pittsburgh, 1970).

Muffat, Georg (b. Mégève, Savoy, bapt. 1 June 1653; d. Passau, 23 Feb. 1704). Composer. As a boy he studied in Paris with Lully and others in 1663–69; he was appointed organist at Molsheim Cathedral in 1671, then went to Ingolstadt to study law. He later traveled to Vienna but could not obtain an official appointment and subsequently appeared in Prague (1677), ultimately finding a position in Salzburg in the service of

Archbishop Max Gandolf, a post he held for over ten years. He was given leave to travel in the 1680s and studied in Rome with Pasquini; some of his compositions were performed in Corelli's house. From 1690 until his death he was Kapellmeister to Johann Philipp von Lamberg, Bishop of Passau.

Muffat was instrumental in bringing the French and Italian styles into German-speaking countries; prefaces to his published works provide details about Lully's and Corelli's practice for his German audience (trans. Eng. in *SR* 1968 and *MQ* 1967). His *Armonico tributo* (Salzburg, 1682; ed. in *DTÖ* 89), with its careful use of the letters *T* and *S* to indicate tutti and solo passages, belongs to the early history of the concerto grosso; these compositions later appeared in modified form in *Ausserlesene Instrumental-Music* (Passau, 1701; ed. in *DTÖ* 23 and 89). The 2 volumes of orchestral suites (*Suavioris harmoniae instrumentalis hyporchematicae florilegium primum,* Augsburg, 1695, ed. in *DTÖ* 2; *Florilegium secundum,* Passau, 1698, ed. in *DTÖ* 4) are particularly fine examples of French influence on a German composer; Muffat (along with Kusser) was one of the first to incorporate the French overture into the German suite.

Bibl.: Kenneth Cooper and Julius Zsako, "Georg Muffat's Observations on the Lully Style of Performance," *MQ* 53 (1967): 220–45. Walter Kolneder, *Georg Muffat zur Aufführungspraxis* (Strasbourg, 1970). Simon Harris, "Lully, Corelli, Muffat, and the Eighteenth-Century String Body," *ML* 54 (1973): 197–202. Inka Stampfl, *Georg Muffat: Orchesterkompositionen* (Passau, 1984).

Muffat, Gottlieb [Theophil] (b. Passau, bapt. 25 Apr. 1690; d. Vienna, 9 Dec. 1770). Composer and organist. Georg Muffat's son; studied with Fux in Vienna from 1711, was appointed court organist in 1717, and assisted in the performance of Fux's opera *Costanza e fortezza* in Prague. His students included several young members of the royal family, among them the future empress Maria Theresia; he was promoted to second organist in 1729 and first organist in 1741 and apparently stopped composing music after this final promotion.

Muffat's output is confined almost entirely to keyboard music, all within traditional Baroque genres (toccata, *ciaccona,* etc.). His ability as a contrapuntist is evident in the fugues of the *72 Versetlsammt 12 Toccaten* (Vienna, 1726; facs. *MMML* 1/18, 1967), often cited in fugal treatises. His second publication, *Componimenti musicali per il cembalo* (Augsburg, ca. 1739; facs. *MMML* 1/8, 1967) includes an explanatory table of ornamentation symbols. Many of Muffat's compositions remained unpublished, raising questions of chronology and authenticity; a few of his works were previously attributed to Handel and Frescobaldi.

Bibl.: Bernd Baselt, "Muffat and Handel: A Two-Way Exchange," *MT* 120 (1979): 904–7. Susan Wollenberg, "The Keyboard Suites of Gottlieb Muffat (1690–1770)," *PRMA* 102 (1975–6): 83–91.

Mugnone, Leopoldo (b. Naples, 29 Sept. 1858; d. there, 22 Dec. 1941). Conductor and composer. He studied at the Naples Conservatory, composed a number of light operas while still in his teens, and made his conducting debut in comic opera at the Teatro La Fenice in Naples. Appointed conductor of the Teatro Costanzi in Rome, Mugnone led the premieres of Mascagni's *Cavalleria rusticana* (1890) and Puccini's *Tosca* (1900); he also appeared in Paris and at Covent Garden and conducted *Nabucco* at La Scala in 1913. In addition to Italian stage works Mugnone performed a number of French operas in Italy, including works of Bizet and Massenet, and conducted *Götterdämmerung* while on a South American tour.

Mühlfeld, Richard (Bernhard Herrmann) (b. Salzungen, 28 Feb. 1856; d. Meiningen, 1 June 1907). Clarinetist. Son of a musician, who taught him and his three brothers; from 1873, violinist in Saxe-Meiningen court orchestra, and from 1876, clarinetist (at which he was self-taught); from 1890, also music director of the court theater; 1884–96, first clarinetist, Bayreuth Festival. He is best known for his associations with Brahms, who in 1891 was led by his playing to compose the Trio op. 114 and Quintet op. 115 (Mühlfeld played their premieres in Berlin, 12 Dec. 1891) and in 1894 the 2 sonatas op. 120, which he premiered in Vienna on 7 Jan. 1895.

Mul, Jan (b. Haarlem, 20 Sept. 1911; d. Overveen, near Haarlem, 30 Dec. 1971). Composer. Studied with Andriessen and at the Roman Catholic School of Church Music in Utrecht. He later took lessons with Dresden at the Amsterdam Conservatory. From 1931 to 1960 he served as organist and conductor in Overveen. He was also music editor of the Amsterdam daily newspaper *De Volkskrant.* His music was influenced by contemporary French composition. He wrote 2 short operas and much choral music, including several Masses. Works also include orchestral music (Piano Concerto, 1938), chamber music (Quintet, clarinet, bassoon, violin, viola, cello, 1957), and keyboard music (Organ Sonata, 1942; Piano Sonata, 1940; Piano Sonatinas, 1928, 1942).

Muldowney, Dominic (b. Southampton, 19 July 1952). Composer. He studied composition at Southampton Univ. and later with Birtwistle in London and Rands and Blake at York Univ. From 1974 to 1976 he was composer-in-residence to the Southampton Arts Association; from 1976 resident composer at the National Theatre in London. Influenced by Weill and Brecht. Although his early music was somewhat severe, his later music moves away from an avant-garde language toward one that is more accessible. He composed the music for a BBC production of Brecht's play *Baal;* conducted and arranged 2 recordings (1981, 1984) of settings of Brecht's writings by Weill, Eisler, and Dessau. Muldowney also wrote 3 of his own cycles using Brecht's texts; the third, *Duration of Exile*

(1983), uses popular elements integrated with twelve-tone techniques. Jazz has also served as a musical resource (Saxophone Concerto, 1984). Other works include a piano trio (1980); a piano concerto (1983); a sinfonietta (1986); *A First Show* (percussion, tape, 1979); *Two from Arcady* (basset-horn, tuba (1979); film music for Michael Radford's *1984.*

Mulè, Giuseppe (b. Termini Imerese, near Palermo, 28 June 1885; d. Rome, 10 Sept. 1951). Cellist, conductor, and composer. He studied at the conservatory in Palermo, which he later directed (1922–24); then directed the Conservatory of Saint Cecilia in Rome (1925–43). As a young man he was active as cellist and conductor and composed operas in the verismo tradition (*La baronessa di Carini,* Palermo, 1912); many of his works show the influence of Sicilian folk song and landscapes, especially those written to accompany classical plays presented at the open-air theater in Syracuse. From 1929 to 1933 he served as secretary of the Sindacato dei musicisti and was its representative in parliament under the Fascists. Other works include *Tema con variazioni* (cello and orchestra, 1940); a string quartet and other chamber music for violin and cello; songs; and film music.

Müller, Adolf [Schmid, Matthias] (b. Tolna, Hungary, 7 Oct. 1801; d. Vienna, 29 July 1886). Composer. Orphaned young; raised in Brno by an aunt married to a dramatist; became a singing actor in Prague, Lvov, Brno, and (from 1823) Vienna; in 1826 engaged at the Kärntnertor Theater, but soon gave up this career because of his success as a theater composer, beginning with the first of his many operatic parodies, *Die Schwarze Frau* (1826). As music director at the Theater an der Wien or Leopoldstadttheater, he was for 50 years a dominant figure in Viennese musical theater, composing for around 680 productions of all sorts and collaborating with Nestroy and other leading figures. Also wrote 400 songs, church music, chamber pieces, singing and accordion methods. His son Adolf (1839–1901) was also a theater conductor (Theater an der Wien) and composer of operas and operettas.

Müller, August Eberhard (b. Nordheim, near Hannover, 13 Dec. 1767; d. Weimar, 3 Dec. 1817). Organist, composer, and conductor. His father, Matthäus, taught him organ and clavier; August also studied with J. C. F. Bach. After studying law briefly he settled in Magdeburg, where he was organist at the Ulrichskirche (from 1789). Moving to Leipzig, in 1800 he was made assistant to J. A. Hiller at the Thomaskirche; in 1804 he assumed Hiller's post as Kantor. Six years later he was appointed music director of the Weimar court, where he earned the praise of Goethe. He authored several influential teaching treatises, including the *Anweisung zum genauen Vortrage der Mozartschen Clavier-Concerte* (1796) and the *Klavier- und Fortepiano-Schule* (Jena, 1804; publ. as the 6th ed. of Löhlein's *Clavierschule).* He also composed a singspiel, *Der Polterabend* (Weimar, ca. 1813); flute concertos and keyboard works.

Bibl.: Nathan Broder, "The First Guide to Mozart," *MQ* 42 (1956): 223–29.

Müller, Georg Gottfried [George Godfrey] (b. Gross Hennersdorf, 22 May 1762; d. Lititz, Pa., 19 Mar. 1821). Composer, violinist, and minister. After emigrating to the U.S. in 1784, he served as minister to Moravian congregations in Lititz and in Beersheba, Ohio. Eight of his anthems survive.

Müller, Wenzel (b. Trynau [Trnava], Moravia, 26 Sept. 1767; d. Baden, near Vienna, 3 Aug. 1835). Composer. He studied music under the Benedictines in Raiger [Rajhrad] near Brno and began composing church music while still in his teens. Traveling to Johannisberg (Silesia) with the local prelate Ottmar, he met Dittersdorf, who gave him further instruction in music. In 1782 he joined the theater orchestra of the Waizhofer company in Brno (as violinist); during this period he composed his first singspiel, *Das verfehlte Rendezvous.* In 1786 he was hired in Vienna as Kapellmeister at Marinelli's Leopoldstadt-Theater, and during the next four decades he contributed more than 200 theater works to that stage. His biggest successes were *Das Sonnenfest der Braminen* (1790); *Das Neusonntagskind* (1793); *Die Schwester von Prag* (1794); and *Die Teufelsmühle am Wienerberg* (1799). Except for a brief stint as Kapellmeister at the German Theater in Prague (1807–13), he remained at his duties in the Leopoldstadt-Theater until his final years.

Bibl.: Walter Krone, *Wenzel Müller: Ein Beitrag zur Geschichte der komischen Oper* (Berlin, 1906).

Mulligan, Gerry [Gerald Joseph; Jeru] (b. New York, 6 Apr. 1927; d. 20 Jan. 1996). Jazz baritone saxophonist, arranger, and bandleader. He arranged for Gene Krupa (1947) and helped found Miles Davis's cool jazz nonet (1948–50), for which he composed "Jeru" and arranged "Godchild" (both recorded in 1949). In 1952 he formed a "pianoless" quartet, engaging in contrapuntal improvisations with Chet Baker on recordings such as "Bernie's Tune" and "Line for Lyons" (both 1952). He led quartets (to 1960s), a sextet, a ten-piece group (both mid-1950s), and the thirteen-piece Concert Jazz Band (1960–64), all without chordal instruments, except when Mulligan played piano. Albums from this period include *The Paris Concert* (1954, with Bob Brookmeyer) and *The Concert Jazz Band* (1960, with Zoot Sims and Brookmeyer). He worked as a free-lance, joined Dave Brubeck (1968–72), then led diverse bands and toured as a soloist. Mulligan showed throughout his career an irrepressible enthusiasm for jam sessions in styles ranging from Dixieland to bop.

Bibl.: Raymond Horricks, *Gerry Mulligan's Ark* (London, 1986).

Mumma, Gordon (b. Framingham, Mass., 30 Mar. 1935). Composer and performer of electronic music.

He studied piano and French horn in Detroit (1949–52) and at the Univ. of Michigan (1952–53). Active at the Cooperative Studio for Electronic Music in Ann Arbor (1958–66); Space Theater (1957–64); ONCE Group (1960–68); the Merce Cunningham Dance Company (1966–74); and from 1966 at the Sonic Arts Union (formed to promote his own electronic and theater music and that of Lucier, Behrman, and Ashley). In order to achieve "cybersonic music"—in which modification and production of sounds is controlled by signals automatically derived from the sounds or motions performers make—Mumma constructed special electronic equipment for each composition. Thus in *Mesa* (bandoneon and electronics, 1965) the circuitry transforms sounds and changes their apparent position, source, and size; in *Hornpipe* (1967) the performer wears an analog computer console that reacts to the resonances produced in particular surroundings by the instrumental sounds as the performer systematically probes the aural environment; in *Beam* (1969) the violinist and violist wear special sleeves that transmit information about the position of the performer's bow arm which serves as the basis for controlling electronic processing of the sounds they make. He collaborated with Tudor, Cage, and Oliveros; fulfilled commissions for the Merce Cunningham Dance Company and the Venice Bienniale (1964) and other groups. Some works are characterized by open form (*Some Voltage Drop,* variable-duration theater piece, 1974) or audience participation (*Cybersonic Cantilevers,* 1973); others are for tape alone (*Dresden Interleaf, 13 February 1945,* 1965; *Pontpoint,* 1980) or for unusual sound sources (*Schoolwork,* crosscut saw, psaltery, piano, melodica, 1970). Other works include *Aleutian Displacement* (chamber orchestra, 1987), *Ménage à deux* (violin, piano, vibraphone, marimba, 1989).

Munch [Münch], Charles (b. Strasbourg, 26 Sept. 1891; d. Richmond, Va., 6 Nov. 1968). Conductor and violinist. Studied violin at the Strasbourg Conservatory and with Carl Flesch and Lucien Capet; taught violin at Strasbourg and Leipzig; served as concertmaster of the Strasbourg orchestra and then of the Gewandhaus under Furtwängler (1926–33). Made his conducting debut in 1932 in Paris and in 1938 became conductor of the Société des Concerts du Conservatoire de Paris. Made his American debut in 1946 with the Boston Symphony and subsequently succeeded Koussevitzky as principal conductor (1949–62); in 1967 he helped found the Orchestre de Paris and was on tour with that ensemble when he died. During his tenure with the Boston Symphony, Munch, like Monteaux before him, introduced a number of modern French compositions into the American repertory, including works of Roussel, Milhaud, and Honegger, in addition to works of Americans such as Barber, Schuman, and Piston.

Münchinger, Karl (b. Stuttgart, 29 May 1915; d. there, 13 Mar. 1990). Conductor. Studied composition and choral conducting at the Stuttgart Musikhochschule, conducting with Hermann Abendroth in Leipzig and Clemens Krauss in Salzburg. Conductor of the Lower Saxony Orchestra in Hannover, 1941–43. After war service he founded the Stuttgart Chamber Orchestra in 1945 to perform Baroque music, especially that of Bach, on modern instruments. They won great success through meticulous recordings of that repertory, later adding works by Mozart, Grieg, Dvořák, Hindemith, Honneger, and others. In 1966 he founded the Stuttgart Classical Philharmonia.

Mundy [Munday], **John** (b. ca. 1555; d. Windsor, 29 June 1630). Composer. Son of William Mundy. A highly esteemed musician, organist at St. George's Chapel, Windsor, for most of his professional life; B.Mus. (1586) and D.Mus. (1624) from Oxford. A book of both sacred and secular compositions, *Songs and Psalms* (London, 1594), was his only published work. Manuscripts preserve some English anthems, Latin motets, keyboard pieces (in the Fitzwilliam Virginal Book), and compositions for instrumental ensemble (including 5 In Nomines).

Mundy [Munday], **William** (b. ca. 1529; d. London?, 1591?). Composer. Father of John Mundy. A chorister at Westminster Abbey by 1543; then held positions in a number of other churches before becoming a Gentleman of the Chapel Royal in 1564. His compositions include at least 4 services, about a dozen English anthems (most full), 2 Mass settings, much other Latin sacred music (including Magnificats and votive antiphons), and 1 In Nomine. Many more pieces, especially services and anthems, may be by either William or John Mundy.

Munrow, David (John) (b. Birmingham, 12 Aug. 1942; d. Chesham Bois, Buckinghamshire, 15 May 1976). Performer on early winds. After teaching in South America he attended Pembroke College, Cambridge (1961–64), and studied 17th-century music at Birmingham Univ.; lectured at Leicester Univ. and taught recorder at the Royal Academy of Music, London. In 1967 he formed the Early Music Consort of London, an ensemble that brought performances of medieval and Renaissance music to an increasingly receptive audience. Munrow took his own life in 1976.

Munz, Mieczyslaw (b. Kraków, 31 Oct. 1900; d. New York, 25 Aug. 1976). Pianist. Studied piano and composition at the Vienna Academy of Music and with Busoni at the Berlin Hochschule für Musik; made his debut with the Berlin Symphony in 1920, performing the Liszt and Brahms concertos and the Franck Symphonic Variations on a single program. In 1922 made his American debut at New York's Aeolian Hall; subsequently appeared with a number of American orchestras and toured as a soloist. Taught at the Curtis Institute (1941–63) and Juilliard (from 1963).

Muradeli, Vano Il'ich (b. Gori, Georgia, 6 Apr. 1908; d. Tomsk, 14 Aug. 1970). Composer. He studied composition at the Tbilisi Conservatory with Barchudarian and Bagrinovsky, graduating in 1931. He then studied composition with Shekhter and Myaskovsky at the Moscow Conservatory (1934–38). During World War II he led the central song ensemble of the Soviet navy. His 1947 opera *Velikaya druzhba* [The Great Friendship] inspired the Central Committee resolution of 10 February 1948, which led to official sanctions against composers such as Myaskovsky, Prokofiev, Shebalin, and Shostakovich. He is best known for his choral music and nationalist songs; the song "Bukhenval'dskiy nabat" [The Buchenwald Alarm] became internationally famous. His other works include the opera *Oktyabr'* (1961); 2 symphonies (1938, 1975); *Put' pobedï* [The Way of Victory] (symphonic poem, chorus, orchestra, 1950); the cantatas *Naveki vmeste* [Forever Together] (1959) and *S nami Lenin* [Lenin is with us] (1960); and more than 200 songs.

Murail, Tristan (b. 1947). Composer and ondes martenot performer. He studied with Messiaen and Boulez. In 1984 he founded the performing ensemble Itinéraire. His works emphasize pure sonority by means of repetitive processes, live electronics, and the concept of harmonicity (the use of fundamentals and reinforcement of the harmonics belonging to those pitches) and its opposite (the introduction of tones foreign to the harmonic spectrum); often not only the details but also the formal structure is derived from the characteristics of the harmonic series (*Memoire/Erosion,* horn and 9 instruments). In composing he focuses on the microscopic level, analyzing "the inner structure of sound" by electro-acoustic means; his approach involves some microtonal tuning and microphonics. Several works were presented at Darmstadt in 1980 (*Territories de l'oubli,* piano), and the theory of *microphonie* was presented by Gérard Grisey, with whom Murail has been associated. Earlier works usually exploit continuous transformation processes, but *Time and Again* (orchestra and synthesizer, 1985) uses flashbacks and pre-echoes inspired by the idea of time travel (the work was loosely based on a science fiction novel of Clifford D. Simak). Other works include several for ondes martenot (*Mach 2.5; Nuages de Magellan,* 2 ondes martenot, electric guitar, percussion; *Tigres de verre,* piano and ondes martenot) and a piano sonata (1989).

Muris, Johannes de. See Jehan des Murs.

Murphy, Turk [Melvin Edward Alton] (b. Palermo, Calif., 16 Dec. 1915; d. San Francisco, 30 May 1987). Jazz trombonist and bandleader. As a sideman in Lu Watter's band throughout the 1940s, he helped revive interest in traditional jazz. He began leading bands in 1947, and from the 1950s into the 1980s was a central figure in traditional jazz on the West Coast, playing mainly at Earthquake McGoon's in San Francisco from 1960.

Bibl.: Jim Goggin, *Turk Murphy: Just for the Record* (San Leandro, Calif., 1982).

Murray, David (b. Berkeley, Calif., 19 Feb. 1955). Jazz tenor saxophonist and bandleader. A member of the World Saxophone Quartet (from 1976), Jack DeJohnette's Special Edition (from 1979), and—playing bass clarinet—John Carter's Clarinet Summit (from 1981). Also led groups, including an octet that recorded the albums *Homes* (1981) and *Murray's Steps* (1982). Achieved a successful synthesis of wild free jazz playing, bop lines, and earthy blues and gospel riffs.

Murray, Sunny [James Marcellus Arthur] (b. Idabel, Okla., 21 Sept. 1937). Jazz drummer. He played in the U.S. and Europe with Cecil Taylor (1959–64, including the album *Live at the Cafe Montmartre,* 1962) and Albert Ayler (1964–ca. 1966, including the album *Spiritual Unity,* 1964). Utterly rejecting timekeeping, he continually varied pitch, texture, pulse, dynamics, and timbre. Based in France (1968–71) and then in Philadelphia, he mainly led groups, rejoining Taylor briefly in 1980.

Murrill, Herbert (Henry John) (b. London, 11 May 1909; d. there, 25 July 1952). Composer. From 1925 to 1928 he studied at the Royal College of Music in London with Bowen, Marchant, and Bush; from 1928 to 1931, studied organ at Worcester College in Oxford under Walker and Allen. He became musical director in 1930 for the Group Theatre of the Westminster Theatre in London and from 1936 worked with the BBC. He taught composition at the Royal College of Music, 1933–52. During World War II he served in the intelligence corps; afterwards he returned to the BBC as assistant head of the music division, becoming head in 1950. His musical style, which drew on contemporary resources, was neoclassic in its orientation. He wrote orchestral music (including 2 cello concertos, 1935 and 1950), solo piano works, and solo songs. He also used elements of jazz (*Man in Lage,* jazz opera, London, 1930).

Murschhauser, Franz Xaver Anton (b. Zabern, Alsace, bapt. 1 July 1663; d. Munich, 6 Jan. 1738). Composer and theorist. He received music lessons from Kerll in Munich and took a position there as music director of the Church of Our Lady in 1691, where he remained for the rest of his life. His compositions include 2 published volumes of organ music, but he is best known as the author of the very conservative treatise *Academia musico-poetica bipartita* (Augsburg, 1721), derived in large part from 17th-century concepts of sacred music. The work was attacked by Mattheson with such devastating effect that the second volume was never published.

Bibl.: Martin Vogeleis, "F. X. A. Murschhauser," *KmJb* (1901): 1–14.

Muset, Colin (fl. ca. 1200–1250). Trouvère and jongleur. Nothing is known of his life besides what is stated or implied in his poetry. Unfortunately, the texts that allude to identifiable persons and places are all of doubtful authorship. But several works of unquestioned authenticity mention instruments and their use, showing clearly that Muset was a jongleur. Of his poems (12 authentic, about 10 doubtful), nearly half survive with their melodies.

Musgrave, Thea (b. Barnton, Midlothian, Scotland, 27 May 1928). Composer and conductor. She studied at the Univ. of Edinburgh and privately with Hans Gál and Mary Grierson; privately and at the Paris Conservatory with Boulanger (1950–54); in 1959 on a scholarship to the Berkshire Music Center studied with Copland and met Babbitt and studied the music of Ives. From 1958 to 1965 she was a lecturer in the Extramural Department of London Univ. in Teddington. Taught at the Univ. of California, Santa Barbara (1970–78). In 1987 she became Distinguished Professor at Queens College, CUNY. Among the ensembles with which she conducted her own compositions are the New York City Opera, the Scottish and San Francisco spring opera companies, the Scottish Ballet, the BBC Symphony, the London Symphony, the San Francisco Symphony, the English Chamber Orchestra, the Los Angeles Chamber Orchestra, the St. Paul Chamber Orchestra, the London Royal Philharmonic, and the Philadelphia Orchestra.

Works: Operas: *The Decision* (1964–65); *The Voice of Ariadne* (1972–73); *Mary, Queen of Scots* (1975–77); *A Christmas Carol* (1978–79); *An Occurrence at Owl Creek Bridge,* radio opera (1981); *Harriet, the Woman Called Moses* (1982–84); *Simón Bolívar* (1993). Orchestral music: *Obliques* (1958); *Nocturnes and Arias* (1966); Concerto for Orchestra (1967); Clarinet Concerto (1967); *Night Music* (1969); *Memento vitae* (1970); Horn Concerto (1971); Viola Concerto (1973); *Peripeteia* (1981); Variations (brass band, 1984); *Moving into Aquarius* (with Richard Rodney Bennett, 1985); *The Seasons* (1988); *Rainbow* (1990); *Autumn Sonata* (Concerto for Bass Clarinet and Orchestra, 1994). Vocal music: *Triptych* (tenor, orchestra, 1959); *Sir Patrick Spens* (tenor, guitar, 1961); *Primavera* (soprano, flute, 1971); *O caro m'é il sonno* (chorus, 1978); *The Lord's Prayer* (chorus, organ, 1983); *For the Time Being: Advent* (narrator, chorus, 1986); *Rorate coeli* (chorus, 1987). Instrumental music: Piano Sonata no. 2 (1956); String Quartet (1958); *Colloquy* (violin, piano, 1960); Trio (flute, oboe, piano, 1960); Chamber Concerto nos. 1 and 2 (1966); *Music for Horn and Piano* (1967); *From One to Another* (viola, tape, 1970); *Space Play* (wind quintet, string quartet, 1974); *Orfeo I* (flute tape, 1975); *Orfeo II* (flute, strings, 1975); *Fanfare* (brass quintet, 1982); *Narcissus* (flute with digital delay, 1988).

Bibl.: Donald L. Hixon, *Thea Musgrave: A Bio-Bibliography* (Westport, Conn., 1984).

Musin, Ovide (b. Nandrun, near Liège, 22 Sept. 1854; d. Brooklyn, N.Y., 24 Nov. 1929). Violinist. From 1863, studied with Léonard, Liège Conservatory (gold medal, 1869); then with Léonard in Paris; 1874–82, toured Europe; from 1883, frequently in the U.S.; 1892, toured Australia, New Zealand; 1896–97, Japan, China, Philippines; 1897–1908, taught at the Liège Conservatory and in New York; then full-time in New York (Belgian School of Violin). He published violin music and didactic works, also *My Memories* (New York, 1920).

Modest Mussorgsky.

Mussorgsky [Moussorgsky, Musorgsky], **Modest Petrovich** (b. Karevo, Pskov district, 21 Mar. 1839; d. St. Petersburg, 28 Mar. 1881). Composer. According to Mussorgsky, his early exposure to Russian folktales inspired him to improvise music even before undertaking formal study. He received his first piano lessons from his mother, and by the age of 7 was already playing short pieces by Liszt; he later studied piano with Anton Herke (1849–54). In 1852 he entered the Cadet School of the Guards in St. Petersburg, where he sang in the school choir, studied early 19th-century Russian church music, and began to compose, despite having had no training in harmony or composition. He left the Cadet School in 1856 and entered the Preobrazhensky Regiment of Guards.

In the autumn of 1857 Mussorgsky met Dargomïzhsky and César Cui, who introduced him to Balakirev and Stasov. He received from Balakirev lessons in musical form, based on works by Beethoven, Schubert, Schumann, and Glinka. During this period he wrote piano works, songs, and an introduction to an opera (*Edip v Afinakh* [Oedipus in Athens], later abandoned). In 1858 he resigned his commission after experiencing a nervous crisis. The emancipation of the serfs in March 1861 required Mussorgsky to spend much of the next two years helping his brother manage the family estate in Karevo. Nevertheless, he was able to produce several songs and begin work on the opera *Salammbô* (1863–66), based on Flaubert's book and inspired by Serov's opera *Judith.* His financial troubles required him to join the Ministry of Communications in December 1863; he remained there in various positions until his dismissal in 1867. Also in 1863 he settled in St.

Petersburg, where he joined a commune. His mother's death in 1865 led to his first serious bout of alcoholism, requiring him to leave the commune and stay with his brother. In 1866 Mussorgsky wrote several songs that were his first essays in musical naturalism and realism: "Svetik Savishna" [Darling Savishna], "Akh tï, p'yanaya teterya!" [You Drunken Sot!], and "Seminarist" [The Seminarist]. During the summer of 1867 he wrote several orchestral works, including *Ivanova noch' na Lïsoy gore* [St. John's Night on the Bare Mountain].

He returned to St. Petersburg in the fall of 1867 and, like other composers in the Balakirev–Stasov circle (dubbed the "Moguchaya Kuchka" [Mighty Handful] of Balakirev, Borodin, Cui, Mussorgsky, and Rimsky-Korsakov), took an interest in the compositions of Dargomïzhsky. In 1868 Mussorgsky embarked on the opera *Boris Godunov,* the original seven-scene version of which was completed by the end of the year. In 1869 he joined the forestry department of the Ministry of State Property. While arranging in 1870 for a production of *Boris,* Mussorgsky wrote and published the song cycle *Detskaya* [The Nursery]. In February 1871 the Mariinsky Theater rejected the opera, prompting the composer to make extensive alterations to the score. The second version, finished in the summer of 1872, had a prologue and four acts. It was initially rejected as well, but excerpts from it were performed in 1873. The entire opera was given a successful production at the Mariinsky Theater in February 1874.

During this period Mussorgsky began work on another historical opera, *Khovanshchina,* with which he was periodically occupied until August 1880. His drinking had worsened to the point that he was at this time incapable of engaging in prolonged periods of work. In 1874 he composed the bitter song cycle *Bez solntsa* [Sunless] and the set of piano pieces *Kartinki s vïstavki* [Pictures at an Exhibition], inspired by the drawings, stage designs, and paintings of his friend Victor Hartmann, who had died in 1873. During 1875 and 1876 Mussorgsky began work on the song cycle *Pesni i plyaski smerti* [Songs and Dances of Death] and a comic opera based on Gogol's story *Sorochinskaya yarmarka* [Sorochintsky Fair]. In both this opera and *Khovanshchina* he attempted a synthesis of lyrical melody and natural declamation.

In 1879 Mussorgsky undertook a three-month concert tour of the Ukraine, central Russia, and the Crimea with the contralto Darya Leonova. He finally had to leave the government service in January 1880. Rushing to his aid, one group of friends guaranteed him a pension of 100 rubles a month to complete *Khovanshchina,* and another offered him 80 rubles a month to complete *Sorochintsky Fair;* neither opera was finished. He continued to appear as Leonova's accompanist and took a job at her music school in St. Petersburg. In late February 1881 recurrent fits of alcoholic epilepsy required him to be admitted to the Nikolayevsky Military Hospital, where he died a month later.

Works: Operas: *Han d'Islande* (projected 1856); *Edip v Afinakh* [Oedipus in Athens] (projected 1858–60); *Salammbô* (1863–66, incomplete); *Zhenit'ba* [The Marriage] (1868, act 1 only); *Boris Godunov* (1868–69; 2nd version, 1871–72); *Bobil'* [The Landless Peasant] (projected 1870); *Mlada* (opera-ballet, with Rimsky-Korsakov, Borodin, Cui; projected 1872); *Khovanshchina* (1872–80, completed and orchestrated by Rimsky-Korsakov); *Sorochinskaya yarmarka* [Sorochintsky Fair] (1874–80, completed and orchestrated by Lyadov, V. G. Karatïgin, and others); *Pugachovshchina* (projected 1877). Orchestral works: Scherzo (1858); *Alla marcia notturna* (1861); Symphony (projected 1861–62); *Ivanova noch' na Lïsoy gore* [St. John's Night on the Bare Mountain] (1867); *Intermezzo symphonique in modo classico* (1867); *Podibrad Cheshskiy* (symphonic poem, projected 1867). Choral music: *Marsh Shamilya* [Shamil's March] (tenor, bass, chorus, orchestra, 1859); *Porazheniye Sennakheriba* [The Destruction of Sennacherib] (1866–67; rev. 1874); *Lisus Navin* [Jesus Navin] (alto, bass, chorus, 1874–77). Songs: "Gde tï, zvezdochka?" [Where art thou, little star?] (1857); "Otchevo, skazhi" [Tell me why] (1858); "Pesn' startsa: Stanu skromno u poroga" [Old Man's Song] (1863); "Tsar' Saul" [King Saul] (1863); "Svetik Savishna" [Darling Savishna] (1866); "Akh tï, p'yanaya teterya!" [You drunken sot!] (1866); "Seminarist" [The Seminarist] (1866); "Hopak" (1866); "Evreyskaya pesnya" [Hebrew Song] (1867); "Ozornik" [The Ragamuffin] (1867); *Detskaya* [The Nursery] (song cycle, 1870, 1872); *Bez solntsa* [Sunless] (song cycle, 1874); *Pesni i plyaski smerti* [Songs and Dances of Death] (song cycle, 1875, 1877); "Pesnya Mefistofelya o blokhe" [Mephistopheles' Song of the Flea] (1879). Piano pieces: *Souvenir d'enfance* (1857); 2 Scherzos (1858); *Impromptu passionné* (1859); *Intermezzo in modo classico* (1860–61); *Iz vospominaniy detstva* [From Memories of Childhood] (1865); *Kartinki s vïstavki* [Pictures at an Exhibition] (1874); *Na yuzhnom beregu Krïma* [On the Southern Shore of the Crimea] (1880).

Bibl.: Paul Lamm with B. V. Asaf'yev, eds., *M. P. Musorgsky: Polnoye sobraniye sochineniy* [Complete Collection of Works] (Moscow, 1928–34; R: 1969). G. Sviridov and E. Levasheva, eds., *Polnoe Akademicheskoe sobranie sochinenia M.P. Musorgskogo v tridtsat dvukh tomakh* [Complete Works of M. P. Musorgsky in 32 volumes] (Moscow, 1989–). Michel D. Calvocoressi, *Moussorgsky* (Paris, 1908; rev. 1911); trans. Eng. (1919). Nicolay Rimsky-Korsakov, ed., *M. P. Musorgskiy: pis'ma i dokumentï* [Letters and Documents] (Moscow and Leningrad, 1932). Jay Leyda and Sergei Bertensson, eds., *The Musorgsky Reader: A Life of M. P. Musorgsky in Letters and Documents* (New York, 1947; R: 1970). Edward R. Reilly, *A Guide to Mussorgsky: A Scorography* (New York, 1980). Malcolm H. Brown, ed., *Musorgsky: In Memoriam, 1881–1981* (Ann Arbor, 1982). Aleksandra A. Orlova, *Musorgsky's Days and Works: A Biography in Documents* (Ann Arbor, 1983). Caryl Emerson, *Boris Godunov: Transpositions of a Russian Theme* (Bloomington, Ind., 1986). Aleksandra A. Orlova, ed., *Musorgsky Remembered* (Bloomington, Ind., 1991). Michael Russ, *Musorgsky, Pictures at an Exhibition* (Cambridge, 1992). Richard Taruskin, *Musorgsky: Eight Essays and an Epilogue* (Princeton, 1993). Caryl Emerson, *Modest Musorgsky and Boris Godunov: Myths, Realities, Reconsiderations* (Cambridge, 1994).

Mustel, Victor (b. Le Havre, 13 June 1815; d. Paris, 26 Jan. 1890). Instrument maker. Orphaned at 12; became a shipwright, but in 1844 moved to Paris with his wife and two sons and learned to make instruments by working for several manufacturers, principally Alexandre. In 1854 he opened his own shop, making harmoniums, winning a prize in 1855 for an improved model and others in 1862 (London) and 1867 (Paris). The firm was carried on by his sons Charles and Auguste (1842–1919), who in 1886 patented the celesta, based on a prototype, called the typophone, invented by Victor.

Muti, Riccardo (b. Naples, 28 July 1941). Conductor. Studied piano at the Naples Conservatory and conducting (with Antonino Votto) at the Milan Conservatory; attended a conducting seminar with Franco Ferrara in Venice in 1965. Won the Guido Cantelli conducting competition in 1967 and was appointed music director of the Maggio musicale in Florence (1969–82) and principal conductor of the Florence Teatro comunale (from 1970). Made his American debut in 1972 with the Philadelphia Orchestra, became principal guest conductor there in 1975, and succeeded Ormandy as music director in 1980, a post he held until 1992, when he was named conductor laureate; also served as music director of the New Philharmonia (later renamed the Philharmonia), London (1978–82). Muti is equally renowned as an opera conductor, appearing at La Scala (music director from 1986), Covent Garden, the Salzburg Festival, and in Munich, Vienna, and Paris in this capacity.

Mutter, Anne-Sophie (b. Rheinfelden, 29 June 1963). Violinist. Studied violin with Erna Honigberger from age 5. In 1970 won first prizes in violin and (with her brother Christoph) 4-hand piano at Germany's Federal Music Competition for Young People. In 1974 she captured another first prize there. Upon the death of her teacher she entered the Winterthur Conservatory to work with Aïda Stucki. She came to worldwide notice in 1977 when Herbert von Karajan invited her to perform and record with the Berlin Philharmonic. Engagements with orchestras under Dohnányi, Sawallisch, and Mehta followed. In 1986 taught a course for young violinists at the Royal Academy of Music in London. The same year soloed with the Collegium musicum Zürich under Paul Sacher in the premiere of Lutosławski's *Chain 2.* Formed a trio with Bruno Giuranna (viola) and Mstislav Rostropovich (cello).

Muzio, Claudia [Claudina] (b. Pavia, 7 Feb. 1889; d. Rome, 24 May 1936). Soprano. Her father was a stage manager at Covent Garden in London and at the New York Metropolitan Opera; her mother sang in the Met chorus. Studied voice in Turin with Annetta Casaloni, in Milan with E. Callery-Viviani. Debut, 1910, at the Teatro Petrarca in Arezzo as Puccini's Manon. Later the same year she sang Violetta *(Traviata)* in Messina and made her first recording. At La Scala in Milan in 1913–14 she sang Desdemona *(Othello)* and Fiora *(L'amore dei tre ré).* Sang Manon at Covent Garden in 1914 and in Havana in 1915. At the Met (1916–22) she created Puccini's Giorgietta in 1918 as well as leads in several U.S. premieres. Although much of her career was spent in Italy from 1926, she sang with the Chicago Lyric Opera, 1922–32, returning briefly to the Met in 1934.

Myaskovsky, Nikolay Yakovlevich (b. Novogeorgiyevsk, 20 Apr. 1881; d. Moscow, 8 Aug. 1950). Composer. Following his mother's death in 1890, he was brought up by an aunt who encouraged his interest in music. He was given a military education at the cadet schools of Nizhny-Novgorod (1893–95) and St. Petersburg (1895–99) and at the Academy of Military Engineering (1899–1902). He continued to study music, playing piano and violin and composing. He studied privately with Glier in Moscow (1902–3) and with Kriïzhanovsky in St. Petersburg (1903). He resigned from the army to enter the St. Petersburg Conservatory (1906–11), where he studied with Lyadov and Rimsky-Korsakov. At this time he joined a circle of progressive musicians that included Prokofiev. He was mobilized during World War I, spending time at the Austrian front and at Reval; from 1917 to 1921 he served in the Red Army. Upon his demobilization in 1921 he became professor of composition at the Moscow Conservatory, a position that he retained until his death; among his pupils were Kabalevsky, Khachaturian, and Shebalin. By the 1920s he had developed a style that gained him both national and international renown. Although he won three Stalin Prizes (for Symphony no. 21, the Cello Concerto, and posthumously for Symphony no. 27) and the title of People's Artist (1946), he was accused of "formalism" during the cultural purge of 1948.

His works include 27 symphonies; *Molchaniye* [Silence] (symphonic poem, 1909); *Sinfonietta* (1910; rev. 1943); *Alastor* (symphonic poem, 1912–13); *Lyric Concertino* (1928–29); Violin Concerto (1938); *Privetstvennaya uvertyrua* [Salutation Overture] (1939); Cello Concerto (1944–45); *Slavonic Rhapsody* (1946); *Divertissement* (1948); *Kirov s nami* [Kirov Is with Us] (cantata, 1942); 13 string quartets; 2 cello sonatas; 9 piano sonatas; other piano pieces; songs.

Bibl.: Alekseï Ikonnikov, *Miaskovsky: His Life and Work* (New York, 1946). George Foreman, "The Symphonies of N. Myaskovsky" (diss., Univ. of Kansas, 1980).

Mysliveček, Josef (b. Horní-Šárka, near Prague, 9 March 1737; d. Rome, 4 Feb. 1781). Composer. He was schooled at the Dominican school of St. Jilgí and later at the Jesuit Gymnasium; then he studied philosophy at the Univ. of Prague. His father was a miller; Josef returned home after his studies and became a master miller in 1761. This he gave up in favor of music. In 1760 he had begun studying composition and counterpoint with František Habermann, and he played violin in a church orchestra in Prague until 1763. At this time he traveled to Venice to continue his studies with Giovanni Pescetti. In 1766 his *Il Bellerofonte* was performed at Naples, and its success drew commissions from a number of other Italian theaters; by the mid-1770s he was venerated throughout Italy. In 1777 he visited Munich for performances of his opera *Ezio* and the oratorio *Abramo ed Isacco.* There he drew great acclaim, including the praise of Mozart (in a letter of 11 Oct. 1777). Ill with syphilis, he returned to Italy and died at the age of 43. Among his operas are *Montezuma* (Florence, 1771); *Il Demetrio* (Pavia, 1773); *Romolo ed Ersilia* (Naples, 1773); and *Il Demofoonte* (Naples, 1775). He also composed oratorios (*La Passione di Gesù Cristo,* 1773); cantatas (*Il tempio d'eternita,* 1777); symphonies, concertos, and chamber works. Mozart recommended Mysliveček's keyboard sonatas for his sister, calling the pieces "very effective."

Bibl.: Rudolf Pečman, *Josef Mysliveček und sein Opernepilog* (Brno, 1970).

N

Nabokov, Nicolas [Nikolay] (b. Lyubcha, near Minsk, 17 Apr. 1903; d. New York, 6 Apr. 1978). Composer and writer. He studied composition in Yalta and St. Petersburg (1913–20), Stuttgart (1920–21), and Berlin (with Juon and Busoni, 1921–23); then took a degree in literature at the Sorbonne. He taught composition, languages, and literature privately in Paris and Germany (1926–33), then emigrated to the U.S. where he taught at several institutions including Wells College, St. John's College, and the Peabody Conservatory. From 1944 to 1947 he was cultural adviser to the American ambassador in Berlin; then editor in chief for the Russian section of the Voice of America; during the 1950s he lived mainly in Paris, but was active in organizing festivals internationally; cultural adviser to the mayor of West Berlin (1960–63); composer-in-residence at the Aspen Institute (1970–73). Works include 2 operas (*The Holy Devil,* Louisville, 1958) and 5 ballets (*Union Pacific,* Philadelphia, 1934); several orchestral pieces (Symphonic Variations, 1967); a string quartet, 1 work for violin and piano, a bassoon sonata; 3 marches for band; a piano sonata (1940); oratorios and cantatas (*Symboli chrestiani,* baritone, orchestra, performed 1956); and songs. Writings include *Old Friends and New Music* (1951); *Igor Stravinsky* (1964); *Bagázh: Memoirs of a Russian Cosmopolitan* (1975).

Naderman, (Jean-)François Joseph (b. Paris, 1781; d. there, 3 Apr. 1835). Harpist and composer. Son of Jean-Henri Naderman, publisher and harp maker. Studied harp with Krumpholtz. Appointed harpist to the royal chapel in 1815, first professor of harp at the Conservatoire in 1825. His music for harp includes 7 sonatas, variations, 2 concertos, 2 quartets for 2 harps, violin, and cello. His etudes are still used today.

Writings: *Ecole ou Méthode raisonnée pour la harpe* (Paris, ca. 1832); *Dictionnaire des transcriptions pour s'exercer dans l'art de préluder et d'improviser tant sur la harpe que sur le piano* (Paris, 1834).

Nägeli, Hans Georg (b. Wetzikon, near Zurich, 26 May 1773; d. Zurich, 26 Dec. 1836). Composer, publisher, and writer on music. He studied music with his father, then opened a music shop and publishing house during the 1790s. In 1803 he founded *Répertoire des Clavecinistes,* a series of first editions of keyboard works by Clementi, Cramer, and Beethoven (including Beethoven's op. 31). In Zurich he founded two Sängervereine and published extensively on music pedagogy and aesthetics. He composed keyboard works and songs, including "Freut euch des Lebens"; also published *Vorlesungen über Musik mit Berücksichtigung der Dilettanten* (Stuttgart, 1826) and *Musikalisches Tabellwerk für Volksschulen* (1828).

Bibl.: Ulrich Asper, *Hans Georg Nägeli: Réflexions sur le choeur populaire, l'éducation artistique et la musique de l'église* (Baden-Baden, 1994).

Nancarrow, Conlon (b. Texarkana, Ark., 27 Oct. 1912). Composer. He played jazz and classical trumpet; then studied at the Cincinnati College-Conservatory (1929–32) and in Boston with Slonimsky, Piston, and Sessions (1933–36). After fighting in the Spanish Civil War he returned to New York (1939) but soon moved to Mexico City; became a Mexican citizen in 1956. He wrote a few works for traditional instruments, but after the late 1940s composed only for one or more player pianos, the hammers of which are modified to give more incisive attacks. Having acquired a machine in 1947 that permitted him to compose directly on paper rolls, he explored rhythm and its relation to pitch in a series of studies for his pianos; he was influenced in part by Cowell's discussion of temporal dissonance (1930). His works employ canon and other symmetrical devices; tonality is retained in most works, but temporal aspects of his style can be quite complex. Each voice not only moves at its own rate but also may accelerate or decelerate at independent rates; tempo ratios between voices are specified very exactly. Widely spaced chords, extreme speed, and large leaps often create an effect of virtuosity beyond the capability of a human performer. He received little attention except from John Cage until the 1970s, when publication and recording began. In 1982 he was awarded a MacArthur Foundation fellowship. Early works include his Suite for orchestra (1943), string quartet (1945), and a few piano pieces; later works include Studies for player piano(s) (No. 27 Canon–5%/6%/8%/11%; No. 30 for Prepared Player Piano), chamber music (String Quartet no. 3, 1987), piano music (*Prelude and Blues for Acoustic Piano,* 1984).

Bibl.: Philip Carlsen, *The Player-Piano Music of Conlon Nancarrow: An Analysis of Selected Studies* (Brooklyn, 1988).

Nance, Ray [Willis] (b. Chicago, 10 Dec. 1913; d. New York, 28 Jan. 1976). Jazz trumpeter, cornetist, violinist, singer, and dancer. He worked principally as a trumpeter with Earl Hines (1937–38) and Horace Henderson (1939–40) before joining Duke Ellington (1940–63), who utilized all his talents. Recordings with Ellington include the widely copied trumpet solo on *Take the "A" Train* (1940), a violin solo on *Moon Mist* (1942), and the comedy song *Tulip or Turnip* (1946).

He switched from trumpet to cornet in 1961. From 1964 he worked with lesser-known bands and as a leader. His own albums include *Body and Soul* (1969).

Nanino, Giovanni Bernardino (b. Vallerano, ca. 1560; d. Rome, 1623). Composer. Brother and pupil of Giovanni Maria Nanino. Chorister at the Cathedral of Vallerano; then active in Rome, probably as *maestro di cappella* at S. Maria de' Monti (after 1588), certainly maestro at S. Luigi dei Francesi (1591–1608) and S. Lorenzo in Damaso (from 1608). At S. Luigi, teacher of many choirboys who later became influential Roman musicians. His compositions include madrigals (3 books, plus many in anthologies), most written in the late 16th century; and many sacred works, especially motets, published in 1610 or later and incorporating musical innovations typical of the early Baroque in Rome.

Nanino, Giovanni Maria (b. Tivoli, 1543 or 1544; d. Rome, 11 Mar. 1607). Composer. Brother and teacher of Giovanni Bernardino Nanino. Chorister at the Cathedral of Vallerano; a pupil of Palestrina, and his successor, probably in 1567, as *maestro di cappella* at S. Maria Maggiore, Rome; *maestro di cappella* at S. Luigi dei Francesi in Rome from 1575 until joining the papal choir in 1577; from 1591, helped his brother with the teaching of the choirboys of S. Luigi. His influence as a teacher of composition was extensive and was often acknowledged on title pages of prints of his students' work. Contemporaries ranked him as one of the best Roman composers of the late 16th century, rivaling or even eclipsing Palestrina. His varied and highly original music includes madrigals, canzonettas, and a quantity of sacred works, especially motets. Publications of the late 16th or early 17th centuries contain all of the secular pieces but only a small part of his output of sacred works, most of which survive only in manuscript.

Nanton, Tricky Sam [Joe; Irish, Joseph N.] (b. New York, 1 Feb. 1904; d. San Francisco, 20 July 1946). Trombonist. He spent his career with Duke Ellington's orchestra (1926–46), in which he adapted to the trombone Bubber Miley's growling and plunger-muted techniques. Recordings with Ellington include *East St. Louis Toodle-oo* (1926), *Black and Tan Fantasy* (1927), and *Ko-Ko* (1940).

Napoli, Jacopo (b. Naples, 25 Aug. 1911; d. Ascea Marina [Salerno], 20 Oct. 1994). Composer. He studied piano, organ, and composition with his father and others at the Naples Conservatory. Directed various conservatories (Naples, 1954–62; Milan, 1962–72; Rome, 1972–76); and was artistic director of the Rome Opera (1975) and at Teatro San Carlo in Naples (1976). In 1972 he founded a music school in Cremona. His compositions are conservative. They include 12 operas (*Il malato immaginario,* Ghisalberti after Molière, Naples, 1939; *A San Francisco,* Naples, 1982); oratorios and cantatas; 6 orchestral pieces (*Ciaccona,* 1981); piano and chamber music; choral pieces; and songs. He also wrote didactic material dealing with composition and music education.

Nápravník, Eduard (Francevič) (b. Býšť, near Hradec Králové, 24 Aug. 1839; d. Petrograd, 23 Nov. 1916). Conductor and composer. Studied music at home in Prague and with Kittl. Engaged in 1861 to lead a private orchestra in St. Petersburg; became a répétiteur at the imperial orchestra in 1863, second conductor in 1867. In 1869 he succeeded Liadov as director of the imperial theaters and Balakirev as conductor of the St. Petersburg branch of the Russian Musical Society. He conducted the premiere of *Boris Godunov* (1874). His Piano Trio op. 24 won a prize at the 1876 Russian Musical Society Competition. Composed 5 Russian operas, 4 symphonies, chamber music, other pieces. His *Dubrovsky* (1895) is still performed.

Bibl.: V. Walther, *Eduard Franzewitsch Naprawnik* (St. Petersburg, 1914). L. M. Kutateladze and I. Keldïsh, eds., *E. F. Napravnik: avtobiograficheskiye tvorcheskiye materialï, dokumentï, pis'ma* (Leningrad, 1959).

Nardini, Pietro (b. Livorno, 12 Apr. 1722; d. Florence, 7 May 1793). Violinist and composer. Studied with Tartini at Padua from the age of 12; returned to Livorno in 1740 and enjoyed considerable success as a performer and teacher. He became solo violinist and leader of the court orchestra in Stuttgart (1762–65), then rushed to Padua in 1769 to care for Tartini during his former teacher's final illness; after Tartini's death (Feb. 1770) he accepted a position as music director of the court orchestra in Florence, where he remained for the rest of his life. Nardini was noted for cantabile playing and purity of sound, especially in adagio movements, rather than for virtuosic pyrotechnics; Burney, Schubart, and Leopold Mozart all praised his beautiful tone quality. Works include 6 violin concertos op. 1 (Amsterdam, ca. 1765), and 6 sonatas op. 2 (Amsterdam, 1770).

Bibl.: Clara Pfäfflin, *Pietro Nardini: seine Werke und sein Leben* (Stuttgart, 1930) [includes thematic index].

Nares, James (b. Stanwell, Middlesex, bapt. 19 Apr. 1715; d. London, 10 Feb. 1783). Composer and organist. His first instruction came from Johann Christoph Pepusch; he held the post as deputy organist at St. George's Chapel, Windsor, and from 1735 as organist at York Minster. In 1756 he was appointed organist of the Chapel Royal; a year later made Master of the Children there. He received a doctorate of music from Cambridge in 1757. Nares composed an ode (*The Royal Pastoral,* soloists, chorus, and orchestra); much sacred music, including 4 services and some 50 anthems (a few appear in Samuel Arnold's *Cathedral Music,* London, 1790); he also published *A Collection of Catches, Canons and Glees* (1775) and instructional works, including *A Treatise on Singing* (London, ca. 1780).

Narváez, Luys [Luis] **de** (b. Granada; fl. 1530–50). Composer. A musician in the service of the Spanish royal court. Wrote 2 motets but is best known for his music for vihuela, all published in his *Los seys libros del delphin* (Valladolid, 1538; ed. Emilio Pujol, *MME* 3 [1945]; facs., Geneva, 1980). This collection includes excellent fantasias, sets of variations *(diferencias),* songs *(villancicos, romances),* a *basse danse* setting, and intabulations of vocal works by Josquin, Richafort, and Gombert.

Nasco, Jan [Gian, Giovanni] (b. ca. 1510; d. Treviso, 1561). Composer. Of Flemish origin, active in Italy. Not to be confused with Maistre Jhan. From 1547 to 1551 musical director of the Accademia filarmonica of Verona; then *maestro di cappella* of the cathedral in Treviso, although still closely associated with the academy. His letters provide useful information about performance practice, especially the use of instruments with voices. Works include sacred pieces in all forms (most destroyed in World War II), many madrigals, canzoni, and other secular compositions.

Nasidze, Sulkhan (b. Tbilisi, 17 Mar. 1927). Composer. Studied at the Tbilisi Conservatory, completing the program in piano under Svanidze in 1950 and composition studies under Tuskiia in 1955. From 1963 taught composition at Tbilisi Conservatory. Became artistic adviser of the Georgian State Philharmonic in 1974; has also been active in the Georgian Composers' Union. Recipient of numerous awards including the Georgian State Prize (1978) and the USSR State Prize (1986). His music—including a ballet, 7 symphonies, concerti, chamber music, incidental and film scores—is infused with the spirit of Georgian folk traditions.

Nassare [Nasarre], **Pablo** (b. Aragon, mid-17th century; d. Saragossa, 1730). Theorist and composer. Blind from infancy, he entered the Franciscan order and served as organist at the Saragossa monastery of S. Francisco. His *Fragmentos músicos* (Saragossa, 1683; 2nd ed., 1700), written in dialogue form, discusses plainsong, mensuration, counterpoint, and dissonance treatment. Nassare's second treatise, *Escuela música* (Saragossa, 1723–74), is a comprehensive work of over 1,000 pages whose topics range from musical definitions and description of instruments to free composition and ornamentation.

Bibl.: Almonte C. Howell, Jr., "Pablo Nasarre's *Escuela música:* A Reappraisal," in *Studies in Musicology: Essays . . . in Memory of Glen Haydon* (Chapel Hill, 1969).

Naudot, Jacques-Christophe (b. ca. 1690; d. Paris, 26 Nov. 1762). Composer and flutist. Naudot was well known in Paris as a player and teacher, though exactly where he performed is unknown. His compositions consist mostly of flute concertos or sonatas for 1 or 2 flutes and continuo, nearly all published in Paris between 1726 and 1740.

Bibl.: T. Jervis Underwood, "The Life and Music of Jacques-Christophe Naudot" (diss., Texas State Univ., 1970).

Naumann, Johann Gottlieb (b. Blasewitz, near Dresden, 17 Apr. 1741; d. Dresden, 23 Oct. 1801). Composer. He studied at the Dresden Kreuzschule. In 1757, at the age of 16, he traveled to Italy with violinist Anders Wesström; there Tartini, Hasse, and Padre Martini all gave him instruction and counsel. His first stage work, the intermezzo *Il tesoro insidiato,* was performed in Venice in 1762. Two years later he was given a post as court composer at Dresden, on Hasse's recommendation; by 1765 he was chamber composer, and by the following year Kapellmeister. In 1767 he was called to Stockholm, where he spent the next decade at Gustav III's operatic establishment; his operas *Cora och Alonzo* (1782) and *Gustav Wasa* (1786) were great successes. After one season in Copenhagen (1785–86) he returned to Dresden, where he remained as *Oberkapellmeister* for the rest of his life; later he also visited Berlin, where he composed 2 opere serie for Friedrich Wilhelm II (*Medea in Colchide,* 1788). Among his nearly 30 operas are *Solimano* (Venice, 1773); *Armida* (Padua, 1773); *Elisa* (Dresden, 1781); *Orpheus og Eurydike* (Copenhagen, 1786); *Protesilao* (Berlin, 1789); and *La dama soldato* (Dresden, 1791). He also composed oratorios (*Davide in Terebinto,* 1794), sacred cantatas, Masses, lieder, symphonies, chamber works (6 quartets for clavier, flute, violin, and bass, op. 1, publ. Berlin and Amsterdam, 1786), and 12 sonatas for glass harmonica (publ. Dresden, 1786–92).

Bibl.: Richard Engländer, *Johann Gottlieb Naumann als Opernkomponist* (Leipzig, 1922; R: Farnborough, 1970). Reiner Zimmermann, ed., *Johann Gottlieb Naumann* (Dresden, 1991).

Navarro, Fats [Theodore] (b. Key West, Fla., 24 Sept. 1923; d. New York, 7 July 1950). Jazz trumpeter. He played in the big bands of Andy Kirk (1943–44) and Billy Eckstine (1945–46), then worked mainly in bop combos in New York until his death from tuberculosis, accentuated by drug addiction. His many recordings include sessions with Kenny Clarke, Coleman Hawkins, Bud Powell (*Wail,* 1949), Charlie Parker, and most often Tadd Dameron (*Our Delight,* 1947; *Jahbero,* 1948).

Navarro, Juan (1) (b. Seville or Marchena, ca. 1530; d. Palencia, 25 Sept. 1580). Composer. Active from 1549 as a singer, then *maestro de capilla* at many places including Marchena (under Morales), Málaga (1553–55), Avila (from 1563), Salamanca (from 1566), and Palencia (from 1578). At Salamanca he collaborated with the theorist Francisco de Salinas. Works include much widely popular sacred music, especially the posthumously published *Psalmi, hymni ac Magnificat totius anni* (Rome, 1590); a few secular songs.

Navarro, Juan (2) (b. Cádiz, 1550; d. Mexico?, after 1604). Composer. A Spanish Franciscan monk serving in Mexico. He composed plainchant-like settings for 4 Passions, 8 Lamentations, and the Prayer of Jeremiah, printed in Mexico City in 1604.

Naylor, Bernard (b. Cambridge, 22 Nov. 1907; d. Keswick, Cumbria, 20 May 1986). Composer. Took composition lessons from 1924 to 1926 at the Royal College of Music with Vaughan Williams, Ireland, and

Holst. From 1927 to 1931 he conducted the Oxford Univ. Opera Club; conducted the Winnipeg Symphony Orchestra, 1932–36; served as director of music at Queen's College in Oxford, 1936–39; from 1942 to 1947 in Montreal as conductor of the Little Symphony Orchestra. From 1950 to 1959 he was on the faculties of Oxford, then Reading Univ. He returned to Canada, where he remained. His music is predominantly sacred choral music in the tradition of the English polyphonists. He also wrote some solo vocal works, including several song cycles with varied accompaniment.

Naylor, Edward (Woodall) (b. Scarborough, 9 Feb. 1867; d. Cambridge, 7 May 1934). Composer. First studied composition with his father, John Naylor, and then at the Royal College of Music, 1888–92, and at Emmanuel College in Cambridge through 1897. He worked as an organist at St. Mary's, Kilburn (through 1898) and, after 1908, played and lectured at Emmanuel College. He also published on the subject of Elizabethan music. His works include much sacred choral music, frequently for male chorus, as well as some chamber music.

Nazareth (Nazaré), **Ernesto (Julio de)** (b. Rio de Janeiro, 20 Mar. 1863; d. there, 4 Feb. 1934). Composer and pianist. Early exposure to Chopin shaped his musical outlook. A polka of his was published in 1877; worked for the publisher Carlos Gomez from 1921; played alongside the cellist Villa-Lobos at the Odeon cinema, 1920–24. He gained a broad following in the 1920s, and made successful tours throughout Brazil, but died deaf and penniless; still, his 200-odd tangos, waltzes, polkas, and other dance compositions, entirely for piano, made him the most important Brazilian popular composer of his day; his music still enjoys wide popularity.

Bibl.: Gerard Béhague, "Popular Musical Currents in the Art Music of the Early Nationalistic Period in Brazil, ca. 1870–1920" (diss., Tulane Univ., 1966). *Composers of the Americas* 10 (Washington, D.C., 1964), pp. 42–60 [includes work list].

Neate, Charles (b. London, 28 Mar. 1784; d. Brighton, 30 Mar. 1877). Pianist and cellist. Studied piano with James Windsor and Field, cello with William Sharp, composition with Wölfl. In 1800 performed in Covent Garden Lenten Oratorios. His first composition, Piano Sonata in C minor, was published in 1808. Founding member of the Philharmonic Society (1813). Traveled in 1815 to Vienna and met Beethoven, with whom he was for a time in close contact; acted as Beethoven's agent in England.

Nebra (Blasco), José (Melchor de) (b. Calatayud, bapt. 6 Jan. 1702; d. Madrid, 11 July 1768). Composer. In 1724 he became principal organist of the Descalzas Reales convent and the royal chapel in Madrid; was named deputy music director and head of the royal choir school in 1751. During the years 1723–30 and 1737–51 Nebra composed nearly 60 stage works (to secular and sacred librettos) that were performed to critical acclaim in Madrid and Lisbon; all include spoken dialogue. He was commissioned (along with Literes) to compose sacred music when the archives of the royal chapel were destroyed by fire in 1734, contributing 7 Salve Regina settings, 19 Masses, and 14 orchestral Lamentations, among other works. In 1758 he composed a Requiem Mass with strings and flutes for Queen Maria Bárbara.

Bibl.: Nicolás A. Solar-Quintes, "El compositor español José de Nebra: Nuevas aportaciones para su biografia," *AnM* 9 (1954): 179–206.

Nedbal, Oskar (b. Tábor, Bohemia, 26 Mar. 1874; d. Zagreb, 24 Dec. 1930). Composer, conductor, and violist. Studied with Bennewitz (violin), Knittl and Stecker (theory), and Dvořàk (composition) at the Prague Conservatory (1885–92). Performed as violist, and at times pianist, with the Czech Quartet (1891–1906); conducted the Czech Philharmonic (1896–1906), Vienna Tonkünstler Orchestra (1906–18), Šak Philharmonic (1920–1), and later served as director of the Slovak National Theater and of Bratislava Radio. As a composer he was best known for his operettas to Viennese librettos, which included *Die keusche Barbora* (1911), *Polenblut* (1913), *Die Winzerbraut* (1916), and *Die schöne Saskia* (1917).

Neefe, Christian Gottlob (b. Chemnitz, 5 Feb. 1748; d. Dessau, 26 Jan. 1798). Composer. After early music instruction from Chemnitz organist Wilhelmi and from C. G. Tag, he went to Leipzig in 1769 to study law. There he also studied with Johann Adam Hiller, whom he replaced in 1776 as director of the Seyler opera troupe. He traveled to Bonn in 1779, where he became Beethoven's instructor in clavier and composition. In 1782 he was appointed court organist there for Elector Max Friedrich; the 12-year-old Beethoven often served as his deputy organist. Upon the elector's death Neefe entered a period of precarious finances; finally in 1796 he was made director of the theater in Dessau. He is remembered chiefly for his role as Beethoven's teacher, but also for his highly popular singspiels, which included *Die Apotheke* (Berlin, 1771); *Amors Guckkasten* (Leipzig, 1772); *Zemire und Azor* (Leipzig, 1776); *Adelheit von Veltheim* (Frankfurt, 1780); *Der neue Gutsherr* (1783–84); and 10 songs in Hiller's *Der Dorfbarbier* (Leipzig, 1771). He also arranged early vocal scores of Mozart's operas for publication.

Bibl.: Alfred Becker, *Christian Gottlob Neefe und die Bonner Illuminaten* (Bonn, 1969).

Neel, (Louis) Boyd (b. Blackheath, Kent, 19 July 1905; d. Toronto, 30 Sept. 1981). Conductor. Studied medicine at Cambridge before musical studies at the Guildhall School of Music. In 1932 he founded the Boyd Neel Orchestra, a small ensemble which included some of the finest string players in the country; the group toured widely, performing (and recording) a large number of Baroque string compositions in addition to works of Britten, Holst, Vaughan Williams,

Stravinsky. Neel conducted at the Sadler's Wells Opera (1945–46) and served as dean of the Royal Conservatory of Music, Toronto (1953–70); in 1953 he formed the Hart House Orchestra, a Canadian counterpart of his earlier ensemble.

Bibl.: Boyd Neel, *My Orchestras and Other Adventures: The Memoirs of Boyd Neel* (Buffalo, 1985).

Neidhart [Neidhardt] **von Reuental** [Reuenthal] (b. ca. 1180; d. after 1237). Minnesinger. Served a Duke of Bavaria in Landshut and later a Bishop of Salzburg; participated in a Crusade; from 1232 lived in Austria, first in Melk, then in Lengenbach bei Tulln. Of his poems 68 survive, 17 with music; 38 pieces (words and music) in direct imitation of his work are also extant, suggesting that his songs were highly popular in their time.

Editions: Wolfgang Schmieder, *DTÖ* 71/37 (1930) [facs. and transcription]. Friedrich Gennrich, *Summa Musica Medii Aevi* 9 (Langen bei Frankfurt, 1962).

Neikrug, Marc (Edward) (b. New York, 24 Sept. 1946). Composer and pianist. Studied with Giselher Klebe at the Nordwesdeutsche Musikakademie, Detmold (1964–68), and at SUNY–Stony Brook (M.M., composition, 1971). In 1978 appointed consultant on contemporary music to the St. Paul Chamber Orchestra. His best-known work is *Through Roses* (1979–80), a theater piece about Jewish violinists in a concentration camp; other works include the opera *Los Alamos* (1988), a piano concerto (1966), a violin concerto (1982), a flute concerto (1989), 2 string quartets (1969, 1972), *Sonata concertante* (1994), and numerous instrumental works. As a pianist Neikrug has performed with violinist Pinchas Zukerman.

Nelhýbel, Václav (b. Polanka nad Odrou, Czechoslovakia, 24 Sept. 1919). Composer and conductor. He studied classics and musicology at the university in Prague, and composition and conducting at the conservatory; in 1942 he began to study musicology at Fribourg Univ., where he later taught theory. He conducted the orchestra of Radio Prague and the City Theatre in Prague (1939–42), and the Czech Philharmonic (1945–46); then conducted for Swiss Radio (1946–50) and Radio Free Europe (1950–57). In 1957 he emigrated to the U.S., where he supported himself as a guest conductor, free-lance composer, and lecturer; he became a citizen in 1962. His works for wind band and those aimed at children have been particularly popular. Works include 3 operas (1954–78); 3 ballets (1942–46); *Slavonic Triptych* (1976); *Polyphonies* (orchestra, 1972); Clarinet Concerto (symphonic band, 1982); Toccata (harpsichord, winds, and percussion, 1972); *Sinfonia resurrectionis* (band, 1980); 2 string quartets, 2 brass quintets, 3 wind quintets, and other chamber music (*Oratorio* no. 2, organ and string trio, 1979); piano and organ music; *Let There Be Music* (baritone, chorus, and orchestra, 1982); *Dies ultima* (3 solo voices, chorus, jazz band, and orchestra, 1967); anthems for choir; songs.

Nelson [née Manes], **Judith (Anne)** (b. Chicago, 10 Sept. 1939). Soprano. Studied at St. Olaf College, Minnesota, and sang with early music ensembles at Univ. of Chicago and Univ. of California, Berkeley. Made her operatic debut as Roberto *(Griselda)* in Berkeley in 1976; performed with the Academy of Ancient Music, the London Sinfonietta, Les Arts Florissants, and the American Bach Ensemble, including a number of recordings. Best known as a performer of 18th-century works, although she has recorded Schubert songs.

Nelson, Oliver E. (b. St. Louis, Mo., 4 June 1932; d. Los Angeles, 27 Oct. 1975). Composer and saxophonist. He played professionally (piano, saxophone) as a youth; then studied at Washington Univ. and privately in New York and Los Angeles (George Tremblay). In the 1950s and 1960s he played saxophone in jazz orchestras; went to Hollywood in 1967, where he wrote for films and television. Works include *Berlin Dialogues* (orchestra, played at the Berlin Jazz Days, 1970); Divertimento (10 winds, 1962); *Soundpiece* (contralto and string quartet, 1963) and other vocal music (*Jazzhattan Suite,* 1967); film and television scores *(Ironsides; The Six-Million-Dollar Man).*

Nelson, Ron(ald Jack) (b. Joliet, Ill., 14 Dec. 1929). Composer. He studied at the Eastman School (1948–56) and at the École Normale in Paris (1954–55); taught at Boston Univ. from 1956 (chairman of the music department 1963–73). His compositions are characterized by melodic inventiveness and formal clarity; his interest in non-Western cultures and meditation are important influences; controlled aleatoric procedures affect the length of some works. Works include 2 operas (*Hamaguchi,* 1981); *Savannah River Holiday* (orchestra, 1953; arr. band, 1973); *Medieval Suite* (band, 1983); *5 Pieces after Paintings by Andrew Wyeth* (1 voice, rock and jazz ensembles, 1976); *Te Deum Laudamus* (chorus, wind ensemble, 1985); *Elegy* (strings, 1988); *Morning Alleluias for the Winter Solstice* (wind ensemble, 1989); choral music (often on biblical texts) and songs; film scores.

Nelson, Willie (Hugh) (b. Abbot, Tex., 30 Apr. 1933). Country singer, songwriter, and guitarist. After working as a disc jockey in Texas and on the West Coast, from 1960 he wrote songs in Nashville; they were recorded by artists such as Faron Young ("Hello Walls," 1961). In 1971 he moved to Austin, where with Waylon Jennings he developed a rock-influenced style later termed "Redneck Rock"; it became popular through his annual picnic music festivals and numerous recordings including the album *Redheaded Stranger* (1975, including "Blue Eyes Cryin' in the Rain"). Several of his songs were associated with films in which he also appeared, including "Mamas, Don't Let Your Babies Grow Up To Be Cowboys" (in *Electric Horseman,* 1979), and "On the Road Again" (in *Honeysuckle Rose,* 1980).

Nelsova [Katznelson], **Zara** (b. Winnipeg, 23 Dec. 1918). Cellist. She studied with Dezso Mahalek and in

London with Herbert Walenn, received some additional lessons from Casals. Made her London debut in 1932; formed the Canadian Trio with her sisters (a violinist and a pianist), touring through England, Australia, and South Africa. Made her American debut in Town Hall (New York, 1942) and became an American citizen in 1955. Often appeared in recital with her pianist husband, Grant Johannesen.

Nenna, Pomponio (b. Bari, near Naples, ca. 1550–55; d. Rome?, by late Oct. 1613). Composer. Little is known of his life. From about 1594 to 1599 he served Gesualdo in Naples, and many of his works, chiefly madrigals (8 books for 5 voices [2 lost] and 1 for 4), incorporate features probably borrowed from the music of that composer. By 1608 he was in Rome. Neapolitan idioms play a reduced role even in some works published before this date, and later works include certain specifically Roman characteristics. Other compositions include 2 books of responsories, a Psalm, and a few more secular pieces (villanellas, ricercares, madrigals).

Nepomuceno, Alberto (b. Fortaleza, Brazil, 6 July 1864; d. Rio de Janeiro, 16 Oct. 1920). Composer. Studied first with his father, then at Recife; moved to Rio in 1884 and taught piano; attended prestigious music schools in Rome, Berlin, and Paris during an 1888–95 sojourn. Returning to Brazil, he taught organ at the National Institute (from 1895) and served twice as director of the same school (1902, 1906–16); as a conductor he led the Sociedade de concertos populares from 1896, and conducted his own music and that of other Brazilians at the Brussels Fair and at Paris and Geneva in 1910. A major champion of nationalism in Brazilian music, he encouraged the use of native folk materials in concert works and supported performances of popular music. His own music shows nationalist traits from the early Quartet no. 3 (1891), the *Série brasileira* (1892), and the last of *Quatro peças lyricas* (1894) onward. Other works include operas (*Abul,* 1899–1905; *A cigarra,* 1911), chamber music, sacred choral works, and songs.

Bibl.: Sergio Alvim Corrêa, *Alberto Nepomuceno: Catálogo general* (Rio de Janeiro, 1985).

Neri [Negri], **Massimiliano** (b. Brescia?, 1615?; d. Bonn, 1666). Composer and organist. He was first organist of St. Mark's, Venice, from 1644 to 1664; also served as organist at SS. Giovanni e Paolo (1644–46, 1657–64). He became *maestro di musica* at an orphanage in Venice in 1655, then served as Kapellmeister to the Elector of Cologne from 1664. Neri's few extant compositions include *Sonate da sonarsi* op. 2 (Venice, 1651) for 3–12 instruments.

Neruda, Wilma [Vilemína (Maria Franziška) Nerudová; Wilhelmina Neruda; Wilma Norman-Néruda; Lady Hallé] (b. Brno, 21 Mar. 1838?; d. Berlin, 15 Apr. 1911). Violinist. Studied violin with her father, organist Josef Neruda, and in Vienna with Leopold Jansa. Performed with her sister, pianist Amálie. Appointed chamber virtuoso in 1863 by King of Sweden. Professor of violin at Stockholm Conservatory (1867–70). In 1888 married pianist-conductor Sir Charles Hallé. In 1901 given title Violinist to the Queen.

Nessler, Viktor E(rnst) (b. Baldemheim, near Schlettstadt, Alsace, 28 Jan. 1841; d. Strasbourg, 28 May 1890). Composer. Studied theology at Strasbourg Univ.; was expelled because of his musical activities. Produced his first opera, *Fleurette,* in 1864. He moved to Leipzig, studied with Hauptmann. Conductor of several male choral societies, and wrote part songs for them. In 1870 he was appointed conductor of the Caroltheater; produced *Der Rattenfänger von Hameln* in 1879. *Der Trompeter von Säckingen* (1884) was the most successful of his 11 operas.

Nesterenko, Evgeny (Evgenyevich) (b. Moscow, 8 Jan. 1938). Bass. Studied at the Leningrad Conservatory with Lukanin and sang at the Maly Theater (1963–67) and the Kirov Opera (1967–71) before joining the Bolshoi Theater in 1971; taught at the Moscow Conservatory beginning 1975. Best known for his performances of Boris Godunov, Dosifei, Ferrando *(Il trovatore),* and Mephistopheles; has appeared at La Scala, the Vienna State Opera, the Metropolitan, and Covent Garden.

Nešvera, Josef (b. Praskolesy, near Hořovice, 24 Oct. 1842; d. Olomouc, 12 Apr. 1914). Composer. Attended teacher training college in Prague, studying piano, organ, and theory with Krejčí, Josef Bohuslav Foerster, and František Blažek. He became director of church music in Beroun in 1868; took the same position at the cathedral in Hradec Králové in 1878. Director of music at cathedral in Olomouc from 1884 until his death. He wrote primarily sacred music.

Neubauer [Neubaur], **Franz Christoph** (b. Melník, 21 Mar. 1750; d. Bückeburg, 11 Oct. 1795). Composer and violinist. He studied music first with a local schoolmaster in Hőrin, then in Prague. Traveled to Munich, Zurich, and Vienna; in Vienna he met Haydn and Mozart. His opera *Fernando und Yariko* was produced in Munich in 1784. In 1790 he was awarded the post of Kapellmeister for the Prince of Weilburg; when the French invaded he went to Minden, then to Bückeburg, where he succeeded J. C. F. Bach as Kapellmeister in 1795. He composed sacred works (including a Requiem and 14 Masses), symphonies, string quartets and other chamber music, songs.

Neuhaus, Max (b. Beaumont, Tex., 9 Aug. 1939). Composer and percussionist. He studied jazz percussion with Krupa, then attended the Manhattan School (M.A., 1962) and had an active career as an avant-garde percussionist, playing under Boulez and Stockhausen. In 1968 he abandoned that career and began to compose electronic music; he was artist-in-residence at the Univ. of Chicago, Bell Telephone Laboratories, the Walker Art Center in Minneapolis, and Artpark in Lewiston, N.Y.; in 1977 he was in Berlin supported by the Deutscher Akademischer Austauschdienst. His works are sound installations (for example in New York, Buffalo, Toronto, Lewiston, Kassel, Chicago, Minnesota, and Pistoia); swimming pool pieces (*Water Whistle Series,* 1970–75, and *Underwater Musics,* 1975–78); participatory radio pieces in which listeners call in material which is then combined in a fluid collage.

Bibl.: Calvin Tomkins, "Onward and Upward with the Arts: Hear," *New Yorker,* Oct. 24, 1988, pp. 110–20.

Neukomm, Sigismund Ritter von (b. Salzburg, 10 July 1778; d. Paris, 3 Apr. 1858). Composer and pianist. First training was with the organist Weissauer; later studied theory with Michael Haydn. Studied philosophy and math at Salzburg Univ. Honorary organist at the university church in 1792; in 1796, became chorusmaster at the court theater. Taught singing and piano in Vienna; among his students was the young Mozart. Kapellmeister at the German Theater in St. Petersburg (1804–9). Moved to Paris in 1809. Introduced music of Haydn and Mozart to South America (1816–21). Arranged many of Haydn's works including *The Creation* and *The Seasons.* Among his own works are the Quintet for clarinet and string quartet op. 8; organ voluntaries; 10 operas; incidental music to 4 plays; 48 Masses; 8 oratorios; motets and other small vocal works; various piano pieces; some 200 songs.

Bibl.: Gisela Pellegrini, *Sigismund Ritter von Neukomm: Ein vergessener Salzburger Musiker* (Salzburg, 1936). Luiz Heitor Corrêa de Azevedo, "Sigismund Neukomm, an Austrian Composer in the New World," *MQ* 45 (1959): 473–83.

Neumann, Václav (b. Prague, 29 Oct. 1920; d. Vienna, 2 Sept. 1995). Conductor. Studied violin with Josef Micka and conducting with Dědeček and Doležil at the Prague Conservatory (1940–45); served as first violinist and then violist of the Smetana Quartet. Conducted orchestras in Karlsbad and Brno, appeared with the Berlin Komische Oper (1956–64), and was appointed Gewandhaus-Kapellmeister in Leipzig; resigned that post after the Soviet invasion of the CSSR, in which the East German government participated; became chief conductor of the Czech Philharmonic (1968–89) and music director of the Stuttgart Staatsoper (1970–73). In 1985 he made his debut at the Metropolitan Opera conducting *Jenůfa.*

Neusidler [Newsidler], **Hans** (b. Pressburg, ca. 1508–9; d. Nuremberg, 2 Feb. 1563). Composer and lutenist. Father of Melchior Neusidler. One of the most important early German lutenists. His 8 lute books, dated 1536–49, include a highly varied repertory, much of it chosen and arranged for teaching. The first book has a didactic introduction on lute playing and many fingering indications. These volumes contain arrangements of German, French, and Italian sacred and secular vocal works; German and Italian dances; and some original preludes. Most common are 2-voice textures for beginners, 3-voice textures (often with virtuoso passage work) for more advanced players.

Neusidler [Newsidler], **Melchior** (b. Nuremberg, 1531; d. Augsburg, 1590). Composer and lutenist. Son of Hans Neusidler. Active chiefly as a performer. Patrons included Octavian II Fugger of Augsburg and Archduke Ferdinand II (Innsbruck, 1580–81). Of his 3 lutebooks, 2 were issued in Venice in 1566, the third in Strasbourg in 1574. These contain arrangements of sacred and secular vocal works, Italian and German dances, and a few original ricercars.

Nevin, Arthur (Finlay) (b. Edgeworth, Pa., 27 Apr. 1871; d. Sewickley, Pa., 10 July 1943). Composer, educator, and conductor. Younger brother of Ethelbert Nevin. Studied at New England Conservatory (1889–93) and for four years in Berlin; his teachers included Klindworth, Boise, and Humperdinck. During the summers of 1903 and 1904 he lived among the Blackfoot Indians in Montana; lectured and published an article as a result ("Two Summers with Blackfeet Indians of Montana," *MQ* 2 [1916]: 257–70). Named head of choral department of the Univ. of Kansas at Lawrence, 1915. Directed orchestras in Memphis, Tenn., 1920–22. Works include operas, piano pieces, chamber pieces, 2 cantatas, 2 orchestral suites.

Nevin, Ethelbert (Woodbridge) (b. Edgeworth, Pa., 25 Nov. 1862; d. New Haven, 17 Feb. 1901). Composer. Brother of Arthur Nevin. Took singing and piano lessons with Böhme in Dresden (1877–78). Studied in Boston (1881–83), where his teachers included B. J. Lang and Emery, and in Berlin (1884–86) with Klindworth. He taught, studied, and composed in Boston and Europe for much of the first half of the 1890s. Concentrated on composing short pieces; his songs "The Rosary" and "Mighty Lak' a Rose" have remained popular.

Bibl.: Virgil Thompson, *The Life of Ethelbert Nevin* (Boston, 1913).

Newlin, Dika (b. Portland, Oreg., 22 Nov. 1923). Musicologist and composer. She studied musicology at Michigan State, UCLA, and Columbia (Ph.D., 1945); composition teachers included Farwell, Schoenberg, and Sessions. She taught at Western Maryland College (1945–49), Syracuse Univ., Drew Univ. (1952–65), North Texas State (1965–73), and Virginia Commonwealth Univ. (from 1978); composed electronic and computer music, mixed-media works, and experimental music theater; wrote *Bruckner, Mahler, Schoenberg* (1947; rev. 2nd ed. 1978), and *Schoenberg Remembered: Diaries and Recollections* (1938–76, 1980). Compositions include 3 operas, a Piano Concerto; Trio (piano and strings, 1948) and *Second-Hand Rows* (violin and piano, 1977–78); *Machine Shop* (gamelan, 1978); piano and vocal music.

Newman, Alfred (b. New Haven, 17 Mar. 1900; d. Los Angeles, 17 Feb. 1970). Composer and conductor. He studied piano in New York with Goldmark and George Wedge and composition with Schoenberg in California. He played in Broadway theaters and in vaudeville to support himself; then studied conducting and conducted on Broadway from 1920. In 1930 he went to Hollywood as music director for United Artists; from 1940 to 1960 he was head of the music division of 20th Century Fox. He worked on more than 230 films (*Street Scene,* 1931; *The Robe,* 1953; *Airport,* 1969), for which he received 9 Academy Awards. He established the Romantic symphonic style in Hollywood and developed a system for synchronizing music and film which was widely used.

Newman, Anthony (b. Los Angeles, 12 May 1941). Harpsichordist, organist, conductor, and composer. Studied at the École Normale de Musique with Cochereau and Boulanger; pursued organ at Mannes (B.S., 1962) and Boston Univ. (D.M.A., 1966) and composition with Berio and Kirchner at Harvard (M.A., 1963). Taught at Juilliard (1968–73), SUNY–Purchase (1968–75), and Indiana Univ. (1978–81). As a recitalist and recording artist Newman specializes in Baroque repertory, in particular the keyboard works of J. S. Bach. His compositions include works for organ, piano, orchestra, and various instrumental ensembles; he is the author of *Bach and the Baroque: A Performing Guide with Special Emphasis on the Music of J. S. Bach* (1985).

Newman, Randy (b. Los Angeles, Calif., 28 Nov. 1943). Popular singer, songwriter, and pianist. He studied music theory at UCLA and worked as a songwriter for Metric in Los Angeles. His songs were successful in recordings by Peggy Lee, Judy Collins, and Three Dog Night; from 1968 he recorded his own material, albums including *Randy Newman* (1968) and the highly successful *Little Criminals* (1977). He also wrote film scores (*Ragtime,* 1981).

Niblock, Phill (b. Anderson, Ind., 2 Oct. 1933). Composer and filmmaker. He studied economics at Indiana Univ., but then moved to New York as a filmmaker and composer of electronic music. Beginning in the 1960s he taped long lines played by conventional instruments (cello, double bass, flutes, oboe, English horn, clarinet, tuba, trombone, saxophone, harmonica) and composed by splicing out the attacks and decays in order to achieve extremely high levels of continuity in the sound; his films and music were often presented together, but with no attempt to correlate them. In 1976 he began to teach at the College of Staten Island, CUNY. Works, all for tape, include *A Third Trombone* (1979); *Who Can Think of Good, Cute Titles for Every Tune* (taped clarinet, 1977).

Niccolò da [Nicolaus de] **Perugia** (fl. Florence, 2nd half of 14th cent.). Composer. Virtually nothing is known of his biography. His approximately 15 madrigals, most for 2 voices, show direct influence of the works of Giovanni da Cascia and especially Jacopo da Bologna. Other extant music includes about 20 *ballate* (1 monophonic, the rest for 2 voices) and 4 3-voiced *cacce.*

Edition: W. Thomas Marrocco, *Italian Secular Music,* Polyphonic Music of the Fourteenth Century, 8 (1972).

Nichelmann, Christoph (b. Treuenbrietzen, 13 Aug. 1717; d. Berlin, 1761 or 1762). Composer. He entered the Leipzig Thomasschule in 1730, coming into contact there with J. S. Bach. Studied composition and keyboard with W. F. Bach; left for Hamburg in 1733 and studied theater music under Telemann, Mattheson, and Keiser. He moved to Berlin in 1739, studying with Quantz and Graun, and in 1745 became (along with C. P. E. Bach) court harpsichordist; he left the royal establishment in 1756. Nichelmann is best known for his keyboard works, especially his sonatas (1745–74) and concertos (1740–59).

Bibl.: Douglas A. Lee, *The Works of Christoph Nichelmann: A Thematic Index* (Detroit, 1971). Douglas A. Lee, "Christoph Nichelmann and the Early Clavier Concerto in Berlin," *MQ* 57 (1971): 636–55.

Nicholas, Albert (b. New Orleans, 27 May 1900; d. Basel, 3 Sept. 1973). Jazz clarinetist. During the first half of his career he also played saxophone. He joined King Oliver in Chicago (1924–26). He performed in China, Egypt, and France (1926–28), then returned to the U.S., where he twice joined Luis Russell (1928–33 and, under Louis Armstrong's leadership, 1937–39). He also worked with Chick Webb (1934) and Zutty Singleton (1939–40), recorded widely (including *High Society* from his sessions with Jelly Roll Morton, 1939–40), and led bands. After a break from music, he participated in the New Orleans jazz revival from 1945, appearing as a soloist and leading groups in Europe from 1953.

Nicholl, Horace (Wadham) (b. Tipton, Engl., 17 Mar. 1848; d. New York, 10 Mar. 1922). Composer and organist. Studied music with his father and organist Samuel Prince. Became organist at a church near Birmingham. Took position as organist at St. Paul's Cathedral in Pittsburgh in 1871. Moved to New York in 1878, where he was organist at several churches and editor for the firms of Schuberth and G. Schirmer. Contributed regularly to the *Musical Courier.* Taught harmony and counterpoint privately. The conductor Seidl and pianist William Sherwood strongly promoted Nicholl's works, which include 4 oratorios (*Adam, Abraham, Isaac,* and *Jacob*), cantatas, 2 symphonies, an orchestral suite, anthems, a cello sonata, chamber music, and piano pieces.

Nichols, Red [Ernest Loring] (b. Ogden, Utah, 8 May 1905; d. Las Vegas, 28 June 1965). Jazz cornetist and bandleader. From 1926 to 1928 he made a series of influential Dixieland recordings, leading his Five Pennies and working under various pseudonyms or as a sideman with his most frequent colleague, Miff Mole. Jimmy Dorsey, Eddie Lang, Adrian Rollini, Pee Wee Russell, and Joe Venuti contributed to these sessions, which included *That's No Bargain* (1926), *Imagination, Feelin' No Pain* (both 1927), and *Shim-me-sha-*

wabble (1928). Except for a period leading a swing big band (mid-1930s), he led small groups, endeavoring to recapture his early success. He regained some prominence after the appearance in 1959 of the semifictional biographical film *The Five Pennies.*

Nicholson, George (b. Great Lumley, 24 Sept. 1949). Composer. He studied composition with Rands and Blake at York Univ. After teaching at King's College, London, and at Guildhall School of Music and Drama, he joined the faculty at Morley College. Frequent performances as pianist with soprano Jane Ginsborg and clarinetist Philip Edwards. *The Convergence of the Twain* (chamber orchestra, 1978) uses standard orchestration and is constructed in two sections which employ striking contrasts and dramatic color and texture in a large-scale narrative unfolding. Other works include orchestral pieces (Chamber Concert, 1984; *Blisworth Tunnel Blues,* soprano, chamber orchestra, 1986-87), dramatic choral works (*The Arrival of the Poet in the City,* 1983), chamber music (*Newly Minted,* brass ensemble, 1983; String Quartet no. 2, 1985; *Sea-Change,* 14 strings, 1988), and solo works (*The Seventh Seal,* viola, 1981; Piano Sonata, 1983; *All Systems Go,* piano, 1989).

Nicholson [Nicolson], **Richard** (fl. 1595; d. Oxford, 1639). Composer. He was appointed *Informator choristarum* at Magdalen College in 1595, receiving a B.Mus. degree at Oxford the following year; was Master of Music Praxis at the university from 1626 until his death. Nicholson's few extant compositions include a consort anthem with viol accompaniment, *When Jesus Sat at Meat,* as well as a full anthem and a handful of madrigals. His madrigal cycle *Joan, Quoth John, When Will It Be* sets episodes in the Elizabethan romance of Joan and John in 11 distinct sections.

Bibl.: *Madrigals,* ed. John Morehen, *EMS* 37 (1976). *Consort Songs,* ed. Philip Brett, *MB* 22 (1967).

Nicodé, Jean Louis (b. Jercik, near Poznań, 12 Aug. 1853; d. Langebrück, near Dresden, 5 Oct. 1919). Composer, pianist, and conductor. Studied piano with Kullak, harmony with Wüerst, and composition with Kiel at the Neue Akademie der Tonkunst in Berlin (1869). Taught piano at the Dresden Conservatory (1878-85). Established the Nicodé Concerts (1893), Nicodé Chorus (1896). Compositions include the symphonic ode *Das Meer* op. 31 (1880); the symphonic poem *Maria Stuart* (1880); *Gloria! ein Sturm- und Sonnenlied* op. 5 (1905); Piano Sonata op. 19; other orchestral and vocal works; chamber music; piano pieces.

Bibl.: Thomas Schäfer, *Jean-Louis Nicodé. Ein Versuch kritischer Würdigung und Erläuterung seines Schaffens* (Berlin, 1907).

Nicolai, Otto (Ehrenfried) (b. Königsberg [Kaliningrad], 9 June 1810; d. Berlin, 11 May 1849). Composer, conductor. His father tried to make a child prodigy of him, treating him badly in the process; a runaway at 16, taken in by a kindly music lover who in 1827 sent him to study in Berlin with Zelter and (1828-30) at the Institute for Church Music with Klein; 1830-33, music teacher, Berlin. He began to compose sacred words and a symphony which he conducted in Leipzig in 1831. Organist, 1833-36, at the Prussian embassy chapel, Rome, becoming a figure in Roman society as a salon pianist and teacher. Drawn to the theater but unable to get an opera commission in Italy, he went to Vienna, where he taught singing and had a one-year appointment (1837-38) as conductor at the Court Opera. He returned to Italy and had quick success with *Enrico II* (Trieste, 1839) and especially *Il templario* (Turin, 1840), which was widely performed; they were followed by two others less successful. He produced *Il templario* at Vienna Opera (1841) and was reengaged as chief conductor; 1842, began concerts that eventually became the Philharmonic. When his last and only originally German opera, *Die lustigen Weiber von Windsor,* was rejected there, he resigned (1847). Kapellmeister, Berlin Opera and at the cathedral, 1848. His opera was successfully produced there (9 Mar. 1849) and is still given in Germany and occasionally elsewhere. Other works include part songs, songs, piano pieces; diaries (ed. B. Schröder, Leipzig, 1892, and W. Altmann, Regensburg, 1937); essays and music criticism (collected by G. R. Kruse, Regensburg, 1913). Several volumes of his letters have also been published.

Bibl.: Ulrich Konrad, *Otto Nicolai, 1810-1849: Studien zu Leben und Werk* (Baden-Baden, 1986).

Nicolau, Antonio (b. Barcelona, 8 June 1858; d. there, 26 Feb. 1933). Composer. Studied with Balart and Pujol. Moved to Paris, where he directed an orchestra and composed. He returned to Barcelona in 1886. Appointed director of the Barcelona Municipal Music School in 1896. Compositions include the operas *Costanza* (1878), *El Rapto* (1887), *La tempestad* (1877); symphonic poems *Ipes* and *El triunfo de Venus* (both 1882); choral works; songs; and other pieces.

Nicolini [Grimaldi, Nicolo] (b. Naples, bapt. 5 Apr. 1673; d. there, 1 Jan. 1732). Alto castrato. Studied under Provenzale and was appointed to the Cappella del Tesoro di S. Gennaro in 1690 and the royal chapel in the following year. He sang in operas at the S. Bartolomeo theater and the royal palace, appearing in many works of A. Scarlatti; he also performed in Rome, Bologna, and Venice in 1699 and 1700. Sang in London at the Queen's Theatre (1708-12); created the title roles in Handel's *Rinaldo* (1711) and *Amadigi* (1715).

Niedermeyer, (Abraham) Louis (b. Nyon, 27 Apr. 1802; d. Paris, 14 Mar. 1861). Composer. Studied with Moscheles (piano) and Foerster (composition) in Vienna; with Fioravanti in Rome; and with Zingarelli in Naples. Lived in Geneva during 1822-23, and composed many songs. Settled in Paris in 1823, where he wrote 4 operas: *La casa nel bosco* (1828), *Stradella*

(1837), *Marie Stuart* (1844), and *La fronde* (1853). Turned to composition of sacred music; reopened the church music school of Choron, renaming it École Niedermeyer; Saint-Saëns was on the faculty, Fauré was one of its first students. Founded *La Maîtrise,* a church music journal, with d'Ortigue, with whom he later (1856) published *Méthode d'accompagnement du plainchant.*

Bibl.: Louis Alfred Niedermeyer, *Vie d'un compositeur moderne, 1802–1861* (Fontainebleau, 1892). Maurice Galerne, *L'École Niedermeyer* (Paris, 1928).

Niedt, Friedrich Erhard (b. Jena, bapt. 31 May 1674; d. Copenhagen, Apr. 1708). Theorist. Little is known of his life. Self-described as a notary public residing in Jena, he moved to Copenhagen, where his 1704 application to become organist at the church of St. Nicolas was rejected. His thoroughbass method, *Musicalische Handleitung* (1700), contains a lengthy satire on the ultraconservative German music instruction of his time; the second part of the method, *Handleitung zur Variation* (Hamburg, 1706), treats the practice of improvising over a thoroughbass. Niedt's writings were highly regarded: J. S. Bach borrowed from his method to teach his pupil Kellner, and Mattheson revised part 2 and published part 3 in 1717.

Bibl.: Friedrich Erhard Niedt, *The Musical Guide,* trans. Pamela L. Poulin and Irmgard C. Taylor (Oxford, 1989).

Nielsen, Carl (August) (b. Nörre-Lyndelse, near Odense, 9 June 1865; d. Copenhagen, 3 Oct. 1931). Composer. Studied violin and trumpet as a child and began composing in his youth. His music was heavily modeled on classical forms and genres and his first efforts gained him entrance to the Royal College in Copenhagen in 1884. Until 1886 he took composition lessons there with Rosenhoff, violin lessons with Tofte, and studied music history with Gade; around 1870 he traveled to Germany to study the music of Wagner. He also felt the influence of Brahms, whom he met while traveling in 1894. Nielsen first worked as a violinist with the Royal Chapel Orchestra. His renown had been steadily growing, and in 1901 he was awarded an annual governmental pension to support his composing. After 1908, when he accepted the position of conductor at the Royal Theater, his career as a conductor gained momentum, equaling the demands for new compositions. In 1914 he resigned from the Royal Theater and in 1915 took a position on the governing board of the Copenhagen Conservatory. In addition, he lectured there from 1916 to 1919 in music theory and composition. From 1915 to 1927 he was head of the Music Society in Copenhagen, meanwhile touring as a conductor in the Netherlands, Germany, Finland, and Sweden. He was named director of the Royal Conservatory in Copenhagen shortly before he died of heart disease in 1931.

Nielsen's early music used as its point of departure the contemporary late Romantic style, touched with the nationalism of Grieg. Around the early 1900s he began to concretize his own style, based in his early classical models, drawing on the late Romantic idiom, and merging with current trends in orchestration, chromaticism, and atonality. The music of this period encompassed all genres, including chamber music (String Quartet in E♭ op. 14, 1897–98), vocal works (Six Songs op. 10, 1894), and piano works (*Festpraeludium "Ved Aarhundredskiftet"* op. 24, 1900). His music increasingly evinced a highly articulate dramatic character in works ranging from his opera *Maskarade* (1904–6) to smaller genres (String Quartet in F op. 44, 1906).

From the 1910s forward, the solo song in a simple folklike setting recurred throughout Nielsen's works. These songs were linked with his continuing interest in music education and convictions about a relationship between music and social use. He composed hymn tunes; with his associate Laub he compiled Danish songs between 1914 and 1917 and again on his own in the early 1920s. This period also saw Nielsen's successful wielding of large, dense forms such as the symphony (Symphony no. 5, 1921–22) and complex piano works (Theme and Variations op. 40, 1917). His conceptions became increasingly linear. His development of form in the symphonic works reflects this linear orientation, moving away from sonata processes, which are fundamentally harmonic, toward structures created by larger cyclic interrelationships, using a large-scale nonfunctional tonality as itself a linear, cohering factor.

The last decade of his life witnessed a focus on the scope and forms of chamber music, as in the Wind Quintet of 1922. His late works refer frequently to historical musical traditions. His only organ compositions date from this period (29 Little Preludes op. 51, 1929; 2 Preludes, 1930; *Commotio* op. 58, 1931), engaging the linear textures as well as the formal processes characteristic of the German organ tradition.

His works include 2 operas (*Saul og David* [Saul and David], 1898–1901; *Maskarade,* 1904–6) and music for 14 incidental plays. He wrote 6 symphonies between 1891 and 1925. Some bear descriptive subtitles (Symphony no. 2, De fire temperamentes [The 4 Temperaments], 1901–2). Also among his orchestral compositions are numerous one-movement works which are sometimes programmatic and concerti (Violin Concerto, 1911; Flute Concerto, 1926). His vocal works include 10 ceremonial cantatas, pieces for chorus and orchestra, as well as a cappella works and solo songs. Among the chamber works are 4 string quartets (1888–1906), pieces for various combinations of instruments, and pieces for solo instruments, including piano and organ. He recorded his childhood memories in the notable volume *Min Fynsky bardom* (originally pubished in Copenhagen, 1927; published in English as *My Childhood,* London, 1953).

Bibl.: Dan Fog and Torben Schousboe, *Carl Nielsen: Kompositioner: en bibliografi* (Copenhagen, 1965). Claus Fabricius-Bjerre, *Carl Nielsen: A Discography* (Copenhagen, 2/1968). Robert Simpson, *Carl Nielsen, Symphonist* (New

York, 1979). Mina Miller, *Carl Nielsen: A Guide to Research* (New York, 1987). Jean-Luc Caron, *Carl Nielsen: Vie et oeuvre, 1865–1931* (Lausanne, 1990). Mogens Rafn Mogensen, *Carl Nielsen: Der dänische Tondichter: Biographischer Dokumentationsbericht* (Arbon am Bodensee, 1992).

Nielsen, Riccardo (b. Bologna, 3 Mar. 1908; d. Ferrara, 30 Jan. 1982). Composer. He studied with Gatti and received his diploma from the conservatory in Bologna in 1931; from 1946 to 1950 he was superintendent of the Teatro Communale there; in 1952 he was made director of the conservatory in Ferrara. His works from the 1930s were influenced by Stravinsky's neoclassicism; in the 1940s he studied the works of Schoenberg, a study reflected in his expressionist monodrama *L'incubo* (1948). *La via di Colombo* (radio opera, 1953) won the Italia Prize. Other works include 2 symphonies and other orchestral, chamber, and piano music; *Requiem nella miniera* (soloists and chorus, 1958) and other vocal music. He wrote *Le forme musicali* (Bologna, 1948; 2nd ed., 1961).

Niemann, Albert (b. Erxleben, near Magdeburg, 15 Jan. 1831; d. Berlin, 13 Jan. 1917). Tenor. Debut at Dessau in 1849. Studied with Schneider and Nusch. Engaged at Halle in 1852. Studied in Berlin; engaged at the Opera (1866–88), and sang in the first local performances of *Die Meistersinger, Aida,* and *Tristan und Isolde.* Sang Siegmund in first complete performance of *The Ring* at Bayreuth. Sang at the Metropolitan Opera in New York (1886–88); took part in the American premieres of *Tristan* and *Götterdämmerung.*

Nietzsche, Friedrich (Wilhelm) (b. Röcken, near Leipzig, 15 Oct. 1844; d. Weimar, 25 Aug. 1900). Philosopher, writer on music. Professor of classical philology at Univ. of Basel (1869–76). Fell under the spell of Wagner; wrote *Die Geburt der Tragödie aus dem Geiste der Musik* (1872) and *Richard Wagner in Bayreuth* (1876). Later turned against Wagner, aligned himself with Bizet in *Der Fall Wagner* (1888) and *Götzendämmerung* (1889). An amateur composer, he wrote pieces for piano solo, piano duet, and 17 songs with piano accompaniment.

Bibl.: Hansell Baugh, "Nietzsche and His Music," *MQ* 12 (1926): 238–47. Luisa Moradei, *La musica di Nietzsche: Proposte di analisi* (Padua, 1983).

Nigg, Serge (b. Paris, 6 June 1924). Composer. He studied with Messiaen and Plé-Caussade at the Paris Conservatory until 1945, then explored twelve-tone music with Leibowitz. In 1949 he was a cofounder of l'Association française des musiciens progressistes; he won the Blumenthal (1950), Chabrier (1953), and Italia prizes (1959, for the ballet *L'étrange aventure de Gulliver à Lilliput*). Works include several radio operas, 2 ballets; *Le Chant du dépossédé* (Mallarmé; baritone, narrator, and orchestra, 1944) and other oratorios and cantatas; *Jérôme Bosch-Symphonie* (1960), *Millions d'oiseaux-d'or* (1980–81), and other orchestral music; piano music; songs.

Birgit Nilsson as Isolde in *Tristan und Isolde.*

Nikisch, Arthur (b. Lébényi Szent Miklós, 12 Oct. 1855; d. Leipzig, 23 Jan. 1922). Conductor. Attended Vienna Conservatory, studied with Dessoff and Hellmesberger. Played violin under Wagner at the laying of the cornerstone at Bayreuth (1872). Won prizes for piano, violin, and composition. He joined the Vienna Court Orchestra in 1874. Became second conductor at Leipzig Theater in 1878, first conductor in 1882. Conductor of Boston Symphony Orchestra, 1889–93. Musical director of Budapest Opera, 1893–95. Later conducted Leipzig Gewandhaus and Berlin Philharmonic. Director of Leipzig Conservatory (1902–7), Stadttheater (1905–6).

Bibl.: Wolfgang Stresemann, *The Berlin Philharmonic from Bülow to Karajan* (Berlin, 1979).

Niles, John Jacob (b. Louisville, Ky., 28 Apr. 1892; d. near Lexington, Ky., 1 Mar. 1980). Folksinger, song collector, and composer. He studied at the Cincinnati Conservatory (1919) and in France; had a brief career as an opera singer; taught at Curtis, Eastman, and Juilliard. He had collected Appalachian songs from his teens, and spent most of his career as a folksinger, song collector, and composer of folklike songs ("I Wonder as I Wander"). Collections of folk songs were published in 1934, 1935, and 1961 *(The Ballade Book).* Many of his own songs were published in a collection in 1975.

Nilsson [Svennsson], **(Märta) Birgit** (b. Västra Karups, Sweden, 17 May 1918). Soprano. Studied with Joseph Hislop at the Royal Academy of Music, Stockholm; made her debut in 1946 at the Royal Opera as Agathe *(Der Freischütz),* sang Electra *(Idomeneo)* at

Glyndebourne (1951), and Brünnhilde in Munich (1954–55) in the complete *Ring.* Nilsson made her debut at Bayreuth as Elsa *(Lohengrin)* in 1959, and returned regularly until 1970, performing Isolde, Sieglinde, and Brünnhilde. In 1956 she made her American debut with the San Francisco Opera and in 1959 debuted at the Metropolitan Opera as Isolde; other roles included Elisabeth *(Tannhäuser),* Beethoven's Leonore, Turandot, Strauss's Elektra and Salome. Widely regarded as the finest Wagnerian soprano of her time, she retired from the stage in 1984.

Bibl.: Birgit Nilsson, *My Memoirs in Pictures* (New York, 1981).

Nilsson, Bo (b. Skellefteaa, Sweden, 1 May 1937). Composer. Self-taught in composition, he experimented early with European avant-garde techniques such as serialism and electronic music; also influenced in his youth by his experience as a jazz pianist. Later he studied music in Cologne and at the Darmstadt summer festival. Through the 1960s Nilsson widened his range of compositional options as he wrote in a more tonal, conservative style for film and television. At the same time he utilized electronic media (*Séance,* orchestra, tape, 1963) and amplified and jazz-influenced material (*Nazm,* 1973). Much of his music is for chamber ensembles, usually for unusual combinations of instruments and often involving percussion (*Kreuzungen* [Crossings], flute, vibraphone, guitar, xylophone, 1957; *Reaktionen,* 1–4 percussionists, 1960) or brass ensemble (*Wendepunkt,* brass, live electronics, 1981; *Carte postale à Sten Frykberg,* brass quintet, 1985). He has also written for orchestra, usually in combination with other sound sources, whether traditional acoustical instruments (*Szenes I–IV: IV,* saxophone, orchestra, chorus, 1974–75) or electronic media (*Entrée,* tape, orchestra, 1963; *Exit,* tape, orchestra, 1970). His autobiography, *Spaderboken,* was published in Stockholm in 1966.

Nilsson, Christine [Törnerhjelm, Kristina] (b. Sjöabol, near Växjö, 20 Aug. 1843; d. Stockholm, 22 Nov. 1921). Soprano. Studied with Berwald in Stockholm; with Wartel, Masset, and Delle Sedie in Paris. Stage debut in 1864 as Violetta in *La traviata* at Theátre-Lyrique. Engaged at Opéra (1868–70); sang often in London. Toured U.S. under Strakosch (1870–72). Sang every season at Drury Lane, 1872–77. She sang in the premiere of Thomas's *Hamlet* (1868); first New York performance of *Mignon* (1871); inaugural performance of *Faust* during opening season at the new Metropolitan (1883); first London performances of *Mignon* (1870) and *Mefistofele* (1880).

Nin (y Castellanos), Joaquín (b. Havana, 29 Sept. 1879; d. there, 24 Oct. 1949). Composer and pianist. He studied in Spain as a child, and then at the Schola cantorum in Paris (1902), where he taught piano from 1905 to 1908. In 1910 he returned to Havana to live and toured Europe and South America as a pianist; the main influences on his own compositions (for piano, violin and piano, and voice) were the Spanish Baroque music that he edited and included on concert programs and French impressionism. His writings published in 1919 and 1912 are contained in *Pro arte e ideas y comentarios* (Barcelona, 1974).

Nin-Culmell, Joaquín (María) (b. Berlin, 5 Sept. 1908). Composer and pianist. Of Cuban origin. He studied with Dukas at the Paris Conservatory (1932–35) and in summers with de Falla in Granada; piano study was with Cortot and Ricardo Viñes. He made his debut as a pianist in Madrid (1931) and in 1938 emigrated to the U.S. He taught at Williams College (1940–50), and then at Univ. of California, Berkeley, from which he retired as professor emeritus in 1974. Spanish influences are clear in his works, which include *La Celestina* (opera, 1965–80), *Le rêve de Cyrano* (ballet, San Francisco, 1978), and other stage works; *Diferencias* (orchestra, 1962); *The Ragpicker's Song* (men's chorus, piano, 1988); chamber, piano, and guitar music (*Tornadas I–IV,* piano, 1956–61; *Doce danzas cubanas,* piano, 1984); 2 Masses, Spanish songs, and other vocal and choral music. He edited *The Spanish Choral Tradition* (1975).

Ninot le Petit [Johannes le Petit; Johannes Baltazar] (d. Rome, by 16 June 1502). Composer. Of northern origin but known through his activity in Italy, where he was singer in the Sistine Chapel from 1488. His works include a few motets, a Mass, and a *lauda.* Most important, however, are his over 15 chansons, of which the majority are 4-part arrangements of popular tunes.

Edition: Barton Hudson, *CMM* 87 (1979).

Nivers, Guillaume Gabriel [Guilaume] (b. Paris?, ca. 1632; d. there, 30 Nov. 1714). Composer and organist. He was organist of St. Sulpice from the early 1650s until his death; named as an organist of the royal chapel (1678) and master of music to the queen (1681), and was music director of the convent school Maison Royale de St. Louis from 1686. His 3 *Livres d'orgue* (Paris, 1665, 1667, 1675) consist of versets that combine sacred and secular styles; their publication helped establish the style of the French organ school of the period.

Bibl.: *Guillaume Gabriel Nivers: Cent préludes,* ed. C. Vervoitte and Norbert Dufourcq (Paris, 1963). *Guillaume Gabriel Nivers: Deuxième [Troisième] livre d'orgue,* ed. Norbert Dufourcq (Paris, 1956 [1958]).

Nixon, Marni [McEathron, Margaret Nixon] (b. Altadena, Calif., 22 Feb. 1930). Soprano. Studied with Carl Ebert at the Univ. of Southern California, with Jan Popper at Stanford, and with Goldovsky and Caldwell at the Berkshire Music Center. A versatile performer, Nixon appeared as recitalist and opera singer, performed with major orchestras, dubbed singing voices for Hollywood, recorded a number of 20th-century compositions, and starred in the children's television program *Boomerang.*

Noble, Ray(mond Stanley) (b. Brighton, 17 Dec. 1903; d. London, 2 Apr. 1978). Popular arranger, songwriter, and bandleader. He recorded with the London Mayfair Orchestra and vocalist Al Bowlly until 1934; later he moved to the United States on the invitation of Glenn Miller. His renditions of "Isle of Capri" (1934) and "Linda" (1947) were very popular, as were his own "Goodnight, Sweetheart" (1931) and "Love Is the Sweetest Thing" (1932).

Noble, (Thomas) Tertius (b. Bath, 5 May 1867; d. Rockport, Mass., 4 May 1953). Composer. Beginning in 1886 he attended the Royal College of Music, where he studied organ with Parratt and music theory with Bridge and Stanford. He worked as a church organist in Cambridge and Colchester. He helped to form the York Symphony Orchestra in 1898 and conducted it until 1912, when he moved to New York City; became organist at St. Thomas's Episcopal Church, overseeing the building of a new organ and the establishment of a choir school. Noble published on the subject of sacred music education. His music is predominantly for the Anglican service, and also includes some orchestral and chamber music.

Nobre, Marlos (b. Recife, 18 Feb. 1939). Composer. He studied piano and theory at the Pernambuco Conservatory (1946–55) and the Ernani Braga Institute (graduating in 1959), then studied composition with Kroellreutter in Rio de Janeiro (1960) and with Guarnieri in São Paulo (1961–62). In 1962 he was appointed artistic supervisor of Radio Ministério da Educaçõ e Cultura (MEC) in Rio de Janeiro. A fellowship to the Torcuato Di Tella Institute in Buenos Aires enabled him to study with Ginastera (1963–64). He studied electronic music with Asuar and at Columbia with Ussachevsky (1969), but made little use of electronic methods. From 1971 to 1976 he was music director of the National Symphony of Brazil.

Works: Orchestral: *Concertino,* piano, strings (1959); *Divertimento,* piano, orchestra (1963); *Convergencias* (1968); *Desafio,* viola strings (1968); *Concerto breve,* piano, orchestra (1969); *Ludus instrumentalis,* chamber orchestra (1969); *Biosfera,* string orchestra (1970); *Mosaico* (1970); *In Memoriam* (1973); Concerto, string orchestra (1975–76); Guitar concerto (1980); Concerto no. 2, string orchestra (1981). Vocal: *Ukrinmakrinkrin,* soprano, ensemble (1964); *Modinha,* voice, flute, viola (1966); *O canto multiplicado,* voice, string orchestra (1972). Instrumental: Piano Trio (1960); Solo Viola Sonata (1963); *Rhythmetron,* percussion (1968); *Tropicale,* piccolo, clarinet, piano, percussion (1968); *Sonancias,* piano, percussion (1972); *Sonata on a Theme of Bartók,* piano (1980).

Bibl.: *Marlos Nobre: Catologo classificado cronológico* (n.p., 1978).

Noda, Ken (b. New York, 5 Oct. 1962). Pianist and composer. A child prodigy; studied piano with Adele Marcus and composition with Sylvia Rabinof and Thomas Pasatieri before attending Juilliard. A one-act opera, *The Canary,* was performed in 1973 and won first prize in the National Federation of Music Clubs Young Composers' Contest; he wrote a second short opera the next year; received an N.E.A. grant to compose *The Rivalry,* an opera based on the life of Andrew Jackson. He made his professional piano debut in Minnesota in 1977 and played with major orchestras in St. Louis, New York, and Baltimore. Other compositions include piano works and 3 song cycles (1977).

Noehren, Robert (b. Buffalo, 16 Dec. 1910). Organist, organ builder, and composer. He studied with Dethier at the Institute of Musical Art, New York, and with Franam at Curtis (1930–31); after the war attended Univ. of Michigan (B.M., 1948) and joined the faculty there (1949–76). Built organs for churches in Milwaukee, San Francisco, and Buffalo; performed widely as organist and composed a number of organ sonatas.

Nola, Giovanni [Giovan] **Domenico del Giovane da** (b. Nola, ca. 1510; d. Naples, May 1592). Composer. *Maestro di cappella* at SS. Annunziata, Naples, from 1563. Known compositions include 2 books of motets; a number of light vocal works of considerable popularity *(villanesche, mascherata*s, *napolitane);* and many madrigals, including over two dozen settings of texts by Petrarch.

Nono, Luigi (b. Venice, 29 Jan. 1924; d. there, 8 May 1990). Composer. He graduated in law from the Univ. of Padua (1946), but had also attended classes with Malipiero at the Accadèmia Benedetto Marcello (1941–46); from 1946 to 1950 he studied with Maderna, and in 1948 investigated twelve-tone technique with Scherchen. Several early works were presented at Darmstadt *(Variazioni canoniche sopra una serie di Schoenberg)* and Donaueschingen in 1950, bringing him immediate recognition. In 1955 he married Schoenberg's daughter, Nuria, whom he had met at the world premiere of *Moses und Aaron* in Hamburg. He lectured at Darmstadt (1957–60) and at Dartington (after 1959); and taught in eastern Europe and Latin America.

He was long active in the Italian Communist party, and maintained a close relation between his art and his politics. The texts he used in the 1950s and 1960s deal with the European postwar situation, as in the libretto of *Intolleranza* (opera, 1960), which equates resistance to wartime fascism with the class struggle of the 1960s. His exotic uses of the voice, political texts (*Il canto sospeso* uses letters of condemned anti-fascists), and concrete sounds (factory noises in *La fabbrica illuminata,* market cries and bells in *Contrappunto dialettico*) reflect his political view and his turn away from the music of the European elite. He also used titles, dedications, texts, and program notes to emphasize the political messages of his works.

His early works (1950–55) consisted primarily of instrumental music in which he developed an idiomatic approach to serialism. *Incontri* (1955) is constructed with bands of sound which change in quality as pitches enter and leave; he used all-interval series and mirror forms, but no other sophisticated serial procedures. *Varianti* (violin, winds, strings, 1957) was his only attempt at total serialism, abandoned in later works; and his 1959 Darmstadt lecture ("Presenza storica . . .") had shown a lack of sympathy for what was then seen as the alternative, the chance procedures of Cage.

From 1956 to 1963 vocal music was more prominent than instrumental music in his works; in *Il canto sospeso* (1955–56) texts are fragmented into words, sounds, and phonemes and allowed to wander from voice to voice. In 1960 he began to explore electronic possibilities at the Milan radio studio; *Omaggio a Emilio Vedova* (1960) was his first electronic work. Much of the electronic music from 1964 was based on sung and spoken vocal material. In the 1980s he made increasing use of electronics to modify the sounds made by live performers; most of these works were produced in Freiburg at the studios of the Southwest German Radio.

Works: 3 operatic works (*Prometeo: Tragedia dell'ascolto,* opera, Venice, Church of S. Lorenzo, 1984); a ballet and incidental music for the play *Die Ermittlung* by P. Weiss (Berlin, 1965; tape); orchestral music (2 piano concertos; *Per Bastiana Tai-Yung-Cheng: L'oriente è rosso,* orchestra and tape, 1967; *A Carlo Scarpa architetto,* 1984); chamber music (*Incontri,* 24 instruments, 1955; *Fragmente-stille, an Diotima,* string quartet, 1980); accompanied choral music (*Ein Gespenst geht um in der Welt,* soprano, chorus, and orchestra, 1971; *Caminantes . . . Ayacucho,* alto, flute, chorus, orchestra, and electronics, 1986–87); unaccompanied vocal music (*Siamo la gioventù del Vietnam,* unison voices, 1973); works for solo voice (*Risonanze erranti,* mezzo-soprano, flute, tuba, 5 percussionists, and electronics, 1986); electronic music (*Contrappunto dialettico alla mente,* 1967–68).

Bibl.: E. Restagno, ed., *Luigi Nono* (Turin, 1987). Jurg Stenzl, *Luigi Nono: Texte: Studien zu seiner Musik* (Zurich, 1975). Gundaris Poné, "Webern and Luigi Nono: The Genesis of a New Compositional Morphology and Syntax," *PNM* 10 (1972): 111–19. Bernd Riede, *Luigi Nonos Kompositionen mit Tonband: Ästhetik des Musicalischen Materials, Werkanalysen, Werkverzeichnis* (Munich, 1986). Friedrich Spangemacher, *Luigi Nono, die elektronische Musik: historischer Kontext, Entwicklung, Kompositionstechnik* (Regensburg, 1983). Otto Kolleritsch, *Die Musik Luigi Nonos* (Vienna, 1991). Mateo Taibon, *Luigi Nono und sein Musiktheater* (Vienna, 1993).

Noone, Jimmie [Jimmy] (b. Cut Off, near New Orleans, 23 Apr. 1895; d. Los Angeles, 19 Apr. 1944). Jazz clarinetist and bandleader. In New Orleans he worked with Freddie Keppard (1913–14) and Buddy Petit (1916). After touring with Keppard (1917–18), he settled in Chicago, joining Doc Cook's orchestra (1920–26) before founding his Apex Orchestra, a small group including Earl Hines (1926–28), which recorded *I Know That You Know, Apex Blues,* and *Sweet Lorraine* (all 1928). Unusually for its time, the group had no trumpeter; Noone or his reed-playing sideman took the melody lines. He continued leading small groups for the remainder of his life, though he also played with Kid Ory's band after moving to California in 1943.

Nordal, Jón (b. Reykjavík, 6 Mar. 1926). Composer. He studied composition at the Reykjavík School of Music with Thórarinsson and Kristjánsson; then went to Zurich, working with Burkhard from 1949 to 1951; and then to Paris, Rome, and Darmstadt (1955–57). He returned to teach at the Reykjavík School of Music and became its director in 1959. Member of the avant-garde group Music Nova. His early music was influenced by French harmonic and orchestration techniques, with some reference to native folk music; later music, influenced by serialism, became atonal. His works are mainly orchestral (Concerto Grosso, 1950; *Adagio,* flute, harp, piano, string orchestra, 1965; *Choralis,* orchestra, 1982; Cello Concerto, 1983) and chamber music (*Schnitte,* clarinet, piano, 1985).

Nordheim, Arne (b. Larvik, 20 June 1931). Composer. From 1948 to 1952 he studied piano and organ as well as music theory at the Oslo Conservatory; also took composition lessons with Andersen, Baden, Brustad, and Holmboe. Until 1968 he worked as a music critic and subsequently toured throughout Europe and the U.S. as a performer of electronic music. His early works are in the colorful chromatic idiom of Bartók. From there, Nordheim freely experimented with timbre and atonality, and his music frequently combines standard instruments with electronic sound; for example, *Respons I* (2 percussion groups and tape, 1966–67) uses acoustic instruments, tape, and the theatrical and acoustical potential of physical space. He has also written music for tape alone: *Solitaire* (1968), based on Baudelaire's texts from *Les fleurs du mal,* uses a tape manipulation of a human voice; *Warszawa* (1967–68) is for 4-track tape. Other works include *Sturm* (ballet, 1979); *Aurora* (4 soloists, chorus, 2 percussionists, tape, 1984); *Varder* (trumpet, orchestra, 1986); *Rendez-vous* (string orchestra, 1987); *Creo* (orchestra, 1989).

Nordica [Norton], **Lillian** [Lilian] (b. Farmington, Maine, 12 May 1857; d. Batavia, Java, 10 May 1914). Soprano. Studied with John O'Neill at the New England Conservatory. Concert debut in 1876 in Boston. Studied in Milan with Antonio Sangiovanni. Operatic debut (1879) as Donna Elvira at Manzoni Theater in Milan. Debut at Covent Garden as Violetta in 1887; at New York Metropolitan in 1890 as Leonora in *Il trovatore.* Performed mostly Wagner after 1895. Beginning 1909, made extensive concert tours.

Nordoff, Paul (b. Philadelphia, 4 June 1909; d. Herdecke, Germany, 18 Jan. 1977). Composer and music therapist. After studying piano at the Philadelphia Conservatory and composition with Goldmark at Juilliard, he had a teaching career (Philadelphia Conservatory, 1938–48; Michigan State College, 1945–49; Bard College, 1948–59). During that period he wrote 6 operas and ballets as well as orchestral (*Winter Symphony,* 1954), chamber, and vocal music (several song cycles). In 1960 he received the Bachelor of Music

Therapy degree from Coombs College, subsequently writing several books with Clive Robbins (*Creative Music Therapy: Individualized Treatment for the Handicapped Child,* 1977) and composing music for performance by handicapped children.

Nordraak [Nordraach], **Rikard** (b. Christiania [now Oslo], 12 June 1842; d. Berlin, 20 Mar. 1866). Composer. Studied with Herman Neupert; took lessons with Gerlacher in Copenhagen; studied in Berlin with Kullak and Kiel (1859). Returned after six months to Christiania, where he studied with Rudolph Magnus and came under the influence of the nationalist movement. Returned to Berlin in 1861 and to Copenhagen in 1864. Helped found the music society Euterpe with Grieg and others. He wrote the Norwegian national anthem (1863–64).

Nørgård, Per (b. Gentofte, near Copenhagen, 13 July 1932). Composer. He studied piano as a child, then began taking private composition lessons with Holmboe; subsequently entered the Copenhagen Conservatory, where from 1952 to 1956 he studied music theory with Homboe, Høffding, and Hjelmborg; 1956–57 studied composition in Paris with Boulanger. On the faculty at the Odense Conservatory from 1958 to 1960, at the Copenhagen Conservatory from 1960 to 1965, and then at the Århus Conservatory. His early works were in the tradition of Sibelius. Increasingly he incorporated elements of the European avant-garde eclecticism, including serialism, coloristic pointalism, quarter tones, metric modulation, and graphic notation. This exploration was systematically manifest in the series *Fragmenter* (1960–61); he also started here to develop a way of establishing a tonal hierarchy in the absence of functional tonality, which he termed "the infinite series." This approach is found in his popular ballet *Den unge mand skal giftes* [The Young Man Is To Marry] (after Ionesco, 1964; Danish television performance, 2 Apr. 1965; first stage performance, Copenhagen, 15 Oct. 1967). He wrote 4 operas (including *The Divine Tivoli,* chamber opera, 1982), 3 ballets, and 3 oratorios. His orchestral music includes 4 symphonies, as well as various descriptive works (*Voyage into the Golden Screen,* chamber orchestra, 1968; *Jousting,* small orchestra, 1975). His chamber music is written for standard groupings (*Inscape,* String Quartet no. 3, 1969; *Syn,* brass quintet, 1988; *Lin,* clarinet, cello, piano, 1986) and for less usual combinations (*Waves,* percussion, 1969; *Hut ab,* 2 clarinets, 1988; *King, Queen, and Ace,* harp, chamber ensemble, 1989). Vocal works are for various combinations of voices and accompaniment (*Libra,* tenor, soprano, chorus, guitar, 2 vibraphones, 1973; *Entwicklung,* alto, chamber ensemble, 1986) as well as for solo voice.

Nørholm, Ib (b. Copenhagen, 24 Jan. 1931). Composer. Studied at the Copenhagen Conservatory with Holmboe, Hjelmborg, Bentzon, and Høffding; he passed examinations in music theory and history (1954), organ (1955), and church music (1956). He worked as organist at the Elsinore Cathedral from 1957 and as a part-time lecturer at the Copenhagen Conservatory from 1961; served on the faculty of the Odense Conservatory from 1967 to 1973, when he returned to teach full-time at the Copenhagen Conservatory. His early works captured the lyricism of Nielsen. Nørholm then felt the influence of avant-garde techniques in western Europe as he came into contact with the musics of Webern, Boulez, and Stockhausen. He attended summer courses at Darmstadt in 1962 and 1963. During this time he worked more thoroughly with serialism (*Fluctuations* op. 25, 1962) and later continued to explore additional dimensions in composition, such as theatrics in *Direction inconnue* op. 26 (1962–64). Works include 5 operas (*Sandhedens haevn* [Truth's Revenge], 1985); 7 symphonies (1959–83); vocal music (*Lux secunda,* soprano, baritone, chorus, small orchestra, 1984; *6 Short Motets,* 1986).

Norman, Barak (b. ca. 1670; d. London, ca. 1740). English string instrument maker. He may have worked under Thomas Urquhart or Richard Meares. His workshop was located in St. Paul's churchyard; sometime around 1715 he formed a partnership with Nathaniel Cross, the two working together on some instruments. Norman is prized for his lutes and viols (particularly bass viols), though he made some violins and is credited as one of the first English makers of cellos.

Norman, Jessye (b. Augusta, Ga., 15 Sept. 1945). Soprano. She worked with Carolyn Grant at Howard Univ. and Pierre Bernac at the Univ. of Michigan in addition to studies at the Peabody Conservatory; won the Munich International Music Competition in 1968 and made her opera debut at the Berlin Deutsche Oper the following year as Elisabeth *(Tannhäuser).* After appearing at La Scala in 1972, made her recital debuts in London and New York in 1973 and her Metropolitan Opera debut in 1983 (as Cassandra in *Les troyens*). In addition to her opera performances, she has achieved considerable success as a recitalist; recordings include lieder of Schubert and Mahler.

Norrington, Roger (Arthur Carver) (b. Oxford, 16 Mar. 1934). Conductor. Attended Clare College, Cambridge, and studied conducting at the Royal College of Music with Boult. Performed as a professional tenor (1962–70) and conducted the Heinrich Schütz Choir and the Heinrich Schütz Chorale. Norrington first appeared at Sadler's Wells in 1971, and served as musical director of the Kent Opera (1969–84) and principal conductor of the Bournemouth Sinfonietta (1985–89); in 1984 he formed the Early Opera Project with his wife, choreographer Kay Lawrence. With the London Baroque and the London Classical Players he conducted a large repertory of period instrument performances; his recordings on period instruments include the complete Beethoven Symphonies and the Berlioz *Symphonie fantastique.*

North, Alex (b. Chester, Pa., 4 Dec. 1910; d. 8 Sept. 1991). Composer and conductor. He studied at Curtis and Juilliard and at the Moscow Conservatory (1933); was director of the German Theater Group of the Latvian State Theater; and belonged to the Union of Soviet Composers. In 1935 he returned to the U.S., teaching music and dance at Bennington and elsewhere. Benny Goodman's New York performance of his *Revue* (clarinet and orchestra, 1946) and his incidental music for Arthur Miller's *Death of a Salesman* (1949) brought him public recognition. He composed music for 11 documentary films (1936–50) and went on to write more than 50 film scores (*A Streetcar Named Desire,* 1951; *Prizzi's Honor,* 1985; *The Dead,* 1987; *Good Morning, Vietnam!,* 1988) and music for television. Other works include incidental music, ballets, children's works for narrator and orchestra; and a few cantatas and songs.

North, Roger (b. Tostock, Suffolk?, ca. 1651; d. Rougham, Norfolk, 1 Mar. 1734). Writer. He was a member of Parliament and Queen's Attorney General under James II; retired after the Revolution of 1688 and wrote a series of essays on music and other subjects. North's *The Musicall Grammarian* (1728) and *Theory of Sounds* (1726, 1728) include a short history of music as well as discussions of musical aesthetics and performance practice.

Bibl.: John Wilson, ed., *Roger North on Music* (London, 1959).

Northcott, Bayan (Peter) (b. Harrow-on-the-Hill, 24 Apr. 1940). Music critic and composer. He attended University College, Oxford (B.A., Dip. Ed.), and the Univ. of Southampton (B.Mus.); served as music critic for *New Statesman* (1973–76) and the *Sunday Telegraph* (1976–86); from 1987 music critic for the *Independent.* Northcott's compositions include Fantasia for Guitar (1982; rev. 1983), *Hymn to Cybele* (1983), and a sextet (1985); he also edited *The Music of Alexander Goehr* (London, 1980).

Norvo, Red [Norville, Kenneth] (b. Beardstown, Ill., 31 Mar. 1908). Jazz xylophonist, vibraphonist, and bandleader. Playing xylophone, he joined Paul Whiteman (early 1930s). He often worked in swing groups with Mildred Bailey (his wife from 1933 to 1945), including a small orchestra (1936–39) which recorded "Remember" (1937). Upon joining Benny Goodman's sextet (1944) he concentrated on vibraphone, played without vibrato (like a xylophone). He brought together swing and bop musicians in recordings with Charlie Parker, Dizzy Gillespie, and Teddy Wilson (1945) and again in the 1950s, when he led trios; the first, with Tal Farlow and Charles Mingus, recorded cool jazz pieces such as "Move" (1950). He rejoined Goodman (1959, 1961), but mainly worked in California and Nevada until the 1980s, when he toured Europe regularly.

Noskowski, Sigismund (Zygmunt von) (b. Warsaw, 2 May 1846; d. there, 23 July 1909). Composer. He was a student at the Warsaw Music Institute and was subsequently active in music education for the blind, creating a music notation for blind students. He went to Berlin to study with Kiel and from 1881 to 1892 he directed the Music Society in Warsaw. He joined the faculty at the Warsaw Conservatory in 1888 and was also active as a conductor with the Warsaw Opera and the Warsaw Philharmonic Society. He collected 2 editions of folk melodies. His music includes 3 operas, 3 symphonies (1875–1903), and symphonic poems.

Notker (Balbulus) (b. near St. Gall, ca. 840; d. St. Gall, 6 Apr. 912). Author. Best known as a writer of sequence texts, preserved in the *Liber hymnorum* of 884. The preface to this book describes the incident that gave Notker the idea of writing such texts and his subsequent efforts to do so. The 40 poems, constructed with great attention to classical literary values, are of considerable importance as a source of information about the early sequence. Notker's other works include histories of Charlemagne and of St. Gall, a *Martyrologium,* some letters (one of which mentions the *litterae significativae,* or St. Gall or Romanian letters), and a few other poems.

Notker Labeo (b. ca. 950; d. St. Gall, 29 June 1022). Theorist, translator, and monk. Translated many nonmusical works from Latin into Old High German; probably wrote 5 short essays in German on musical topics—the 8 notes, the 8 modes, the monochord, the tetrachords, and the measurement of organ pipes. Of these writings, all but that on the modes seem to be intended for elementary music instruction.

Nottebohm, (Martin) Gustav (b. Lüdenscheid, Westphalia, 12 Nov. 1817; d. Graz, 29 Oct. 1882). Musicologist and composer. Studied in Berlin with Berger and Dehn (1838–39), in Leipzig with Mendelssohn and Schumann (1840–45), and in Vienna with Sechter (1846). Taught theory and piano and composed; later focused on scholarly activities. Named director of the archives of the Gesellschaft der Musikfreunde (1864).

Writings: *Ein Skizzenbuch von Beethoven* (Leipzig, 1865); *Thematisches Verzeichniss der im Druck erschienenen Werke von Ludwig von Beethoven* (Leipzig, 1868); *Beethoven Studien* (Leipzig, 1873); *Thematisches Verzeichniss der im Druck erschienenen Werke Franz Schuberts* (Vienna, 1874); *Mozartiana* (Leipzig, 1880); *Beethoveniana* (Leipzig, 1872); *Ein skizzenbuch von Beethoven aus dem Jahr 1803* (Leipzig, 1880); Eusebius Mandyczewski, ed., *Zweite Beethoveniana* (Leipzig, 1887).

Nourrit, Adolphe (b. Montpellier, 3 Mar. 1802; d. Naples, 8 Mar. 1839). Tenor. Eldest son of tenor Louis Nourrit. Studied with Manuel García. Made debut at Opéra (1821) in Gluck's *Iphigénie en Tauride.* Succeeded his father in 1826 as leading tenor of the Opéra. Sang world premieres of many works including revised version of *Moïse* (as Amenophis, 1827), Auber's *La Muette de Portici* (1828), *Guillaume Tell* (as Arnold, 1829), *Robert le Diable* (1831), *La Juive* (as Eleazar, 1835), *Les Huguenots* (as Raoul, 1836). Appointed professor of declamation at Paris Conservatory (1827). Left Opéra in 1836; went to Italy, sang Neapolitan premieres of *Il giuramento* (1838), *Norma* (1839). Vocal problems and illness led to depression; committed suicide by jumping off his lodging.

Novães [Pinto], **Guiomar** (b. São João da Boa Vista, Brazil, 28 Feb. 1895; d. São Paulo, 7 Mar. 1979). Pianist. Studied with Chiafarelli in São Paulo; with financial support from the Brazilian government took part in an entrance competition for the Paris Conservatoire, in which the jury (which included Debussy and Fauré) awarded her first prize. Studied at the Conservatoire with Isidor Philipp, graduated in 1911, and embarked on a highly successful solo career; made her recital debuts in Paris (1911, before she graduated), London (1912), and New York (1915), and was particularly celebrated for her performances of Schumann and Chopin. In 1922 she married the composer Octavio Pinto.

Novák, Jan (b. Nová Říše, 8 Apr. 1921; d. Ulm, 17 Nov. 1984). Composer. Studied composition at the Brno Conservatory with Petrželka, 1940–46; with Bořkovec at the Prague Academy of Music, 1946–47. Traveling to the U.S., he worked with Copland at Tanglewood in 1947 and with Martinů in New York the following year. After staying briefly in Czechoslovakia, he escaped the political turmoil to live first in Denmark and after 1970 in Rovereto, Italy. His orchestral music includes concertos (oboe, 1952; *Capriccio for Cello and Orchestra,* 1958). His one oratorio was *Dido* (1967). His vocal works are for nonstandard combinations of voice and accompaniment, as in *Orpheus et Eurydice* (soprano, viola d'amore, piano, 1971) or *Ioci vernalis* (bass, 8 instruments, bird songs on tape, 1964). Chamber music includes *Quartet* (1960; premiere 1985); *Quadricinium fidium* (string quartet, premiered 1985); *Sonata Phantasia* (cello, bassoon, piano, premiered 1984).

Novák, Vítězslav [Viktor], (Augustín Rudolf) (b. Kamenice nad Lipou, Czechoslovakia, 5 Dec. 1870; d. Skuteč, 18 July 1949). Composer. He studied in Jindřichův Hradec with Vilém Pojman; won an academic scholarship to study law at Prague Univ. but devoted most of his time to musical training at the Prague Conservatory, where his teachers included Jiránek (piano), Knittl (harmony), and Stecker (counterpoint); he also attended some of Dvořák's master classes, where he met Suk and Reissig. When touring Moravia and Slovakia in 1896 he began to collect folk music. Initial experimentation with folk song quotation and folklike melodies (Piano Quintet in A minor, 1897; *Písničky na slova lidové poesie moravské* [Songs on Moravian Folk Texts], 1897–98) led to the orchestral works that first brought him recognition. His lifelong preoccupation with nature manifested itself in *V Tatrách* [In the Tatra Mountains] (1902) and *Slovácká svita* [Slovak Suite] (1903). Another popular orchestral work from this time is *O věčné touze* [Eternal Longing] (1903–5). His reputation was further enhanced with a 5-movement tone poem for piano, *Pan,* and the cantata *Bouře* [The Storm], both from 1910. After World War I Novák's popularity declined as he began to be overshadowed by Janáček as well as by the newer compositional styles emerging in Europe; his later works on patriotic themes, however, including *Podzimní symfonie* [Autumn Symphony] for male and female chorus and orchestra (1931–34) and *Jihočeská svita* [South Bohemian Suite] (1936–37), brought him additional recognition. In 1945 he was honored with the title of National Artist of the Czech Republic; the first volume of his autobiography, *O sobě a jiných,* was published in Prague in 1946. Other works include opera (*Zvíkovský rarášek* [The Imp of Zvikov], Prague, 1913–14; *Karlštejn,* Prague, 1914–15; *Lucerna* [The Lantern], Prague, 1919–22; *Dědův odkaz* [Old Man's Bequest], Brno, 1922–25); ballet pantomimes (*Signorina Gioventu,* 1926–28; *Nikotina,* 1929); orchestral music (*Maryša,* overture, 1898; *De profundis,* 1941; *Svatováclavský triptych* [St. Wenceslas Triptych], 1941); choral works (*Svatební košile* [The Wedding Shift], solo voices, chorus, orchestra, 1912–13; *Májová symfonie* [May Symphony], solo voices, chorus, orchestra, 1943; *Píseň zlínského pracujícího lidu* [Song of the Zlín Working People], 1948); chamber music (3 string quartets, 1899, 1905, 1938); piano music (*Sonata eroica,* 1900); songs and folk song arrangements.

Novello, Clara (Anastasia) (b. London, 10 June 1818; d. Rome, 12 Mar. 1908). Soprano. Daughter of Vincent Novello. Studied at York and the Paris Conservatory. Gave numerous performances in England in the early 1830s. Invited by Mendelssohn to sing at the Gewandhaus, Leipzig (1837). Operatic debut in Padua (1841) as Semiramide. Took part in the first Italian performance of Rossini's *Stabat Mater* the next year. Married in 1843 and retired until 1850, when she began a second career in opera and concert stage (primarily in oratorios). Retired in 1860. Her memoirs were published in 1910.

Bibl.: Averil Mackenzie-Grieve, *Clara Novello, 1818–1908* (New York, 1980).

Novello, Ivor [Davies, David Ivor] (b. Cardiff, 15 Jan. 1893; d. London, 6 Mar. 1951). Composer. Son of singer and choral conductor Clara Novello-Davies. Studied piano and voice at the Magdalen College School, Oxford. Studied theory with Brewer and began writing songs in the 1910s. His song "Till the Boys Come Home [Keep the Home Fires Burning]" saw widespread popularity during World War I. He went on to write music for stage productions. By 1930 he had devoted himself to acting and writing plays. Music for stage works include *King's Rhapsody* (Manchester, 1949) and *Gay's the Word* (Manchester, 1950). He wrote around 100 songs.

Novello, Vincent (b. London, 6 Sept. 1781; d. Nice, 9 Aug. 1861). Organist, conductor, composer, and publisher. Studied organ with Samuel Webbe. Organist at Portuguese embassy, 1797–1822. Founded Novello and Company (1811). Original member of the Philharmonic Society. He examined the collection of music bequeathed to Cambridge University (1816) published as *The Fitzwilliam Music* (1825). Published 5 volumes of Purcell's music (1829); manuscripts he copied were destroyed the following year by a fire in York Minster. When he retired to Nice in 1847, his son (Joseph) Alfred Novello (1810–96) took over the publishing firm.

Bibl.: Mary Cowden-Clarke, *Life and Labours of Vincent Novello* (London, 1862). Michael Hurd, *Vincent Novello . . . and Company* (New York, 1981).

Nowak, Lionel (b. Cleveland, 25 Sept. 1911). Pianist and composer. He performed as a pianist at age 4 and was an organist and choirmaster in his teens; studied at the Cleveland Institute with Elwell, Sessions, and Quincy Porter (1936). He taught at Fenn College (1932–38), Converse College (1942–46), Syracuse Univ. (1946–48), and Bennington College (from 1948); from 1938 to 1942 he was music director for the Doris Humphrey–Charles Weidman Modern Dance Company; and was active as a music educator representing the Association of American Colleges in lectures and performances (1945–63). In the 1950s he began to use serial techniques. Works include orchestral music (*Concert Piece,* timpani and strings, 1961); chamber and piano music (*Games,* suite for 4 flutes, 1984; Suite, flute, harpsichord, 1989); and songs.

Nucius [Nux, Nucis], **Johannes** (b. Görlitz, Silesia, ca. 1556; d. Himmelwitz [now Strzelce], Poland, 25 Mar. 1620). Theorist and composer. Studied composition with Winckler; around 1586 took holy orders at the monastery of Rauden, becoming deacon there in 1591 and abbot at the monastery of Himmelwitz the same year. Nucius's counterpoint treatise *Musices poeticae* (Neisse, 1613) was known to Praetorius and Mattheson; he was the first theorist after Burmeister to use the terminology of rhetoric to illustrate compositional procedure.

Bibl.: Fritz Feldmann, "Das *Opusculum bipartitum* des Joachim Thuringus (1625), besonders in seinen Beziehungen zu Joh. Nucius (1613)," *AfMw* 15 (1958): 123–42.

Nunó, Jaime (b. San Juan de las Abadesas, Gerona, 8 Sept. 1824; d. Bayside, N.Y., 18 July 1908). Composer and conductor. Choirboy in Barcelona (1833–40); studied with Mercadante in Italy. Conducted local orchestras, composed church and dance music. He went to Havana in 1851 as army bandmaster. Named general band inspector in Mexico (1853). Became one of the directors of the National Conservatory in Mexico City. Composed the national anthem of Mexico (1854). He moved to the U.S. in 1855; continued to tour Mexico and Cuba as conductor.

Nyiregyházi, Ervin (b. Budapest, 19 Jan. 1903; d. Los Angeles, 13 Apr. 1987). Pianist and composer. Began to play piano at the age of 2, and by 6 was performing publicly and composing; his precociousness was the subject of a scientific study. Took lessons with Frederick Lamond and Ernö Dohnányi, and made a highly successful New York debut in 1920 at Carnegie Hall. His solo career failed to develop, however, and he eventually worked for film studios in Los Angeles; in the mid-1970s he performed in public again and made a few recordings.

Nystedt, Knut (b. Christiania [now Oslo], 3 Sept. 1915). Composer. He was a student at the Oslo Conservatory from 1931 to 1943, studying organ with Sandvold, conducting with Fjeldstad, and composition with Steenberg and Brustad. Traveling to the U.S. in 1947, he took organ lessons from E. White and composition lessons with Copland. He was appointed organist at the Torshov Church in Oslo and organized and toured with the Norwegian Soloist Choir. He returned to the U.S. to work, first in Long Beach, California, in 1962; in Minneapolis in 1964; at Berea College, Kentucky, in 1968; and at Augsburg College, Minnesota, in 1969. His music is in a late Romantic style and often contains nationalistic references. He wrote mostly orchestral and choral works. The orchestral works include standard forms (Concerto Grosso, 3 trumpets, strings, 1946) and some descriptive pieces. His choral music includes the popular hymn "De Profundis" (1964) as well as a Stabat Mater (1986) and a setting of *The Lamentations of Jeremiah* (1985). He also wrote chamber works, including *Pia memoria,* Requiem (9 winds, 1971); String Quartet no. 5 (1988).

Nystroem, Gösta (b. Silvberg, Dalarna, 13 Oct. 1890; d. Särö, 9 Aug. 1966). Composer. His father was a painter and musician and heavily influenced his son in both arts. From 1913 to 1914 he studied composition privately with Hallén at the Stockholm Conservatory. For the next four years he studied painting and composition in Copenhagen. Lived in Paris, 1920–32. He studied composition and instrumentation with d'Indy and Sabaneyev and conducting with Chevillard; was active in French artistic circles. Nystroem returned to Sweden in 1932, where he was an influential music critic. Though he continued to compose, his primary pursuit was painting, as he toured the Mediterranean, Paris, and the Netherlands. He wrote an opera and a ballet, 2 suites, and much incidental music. Orchestral music includes symphonies and concertos. He also wrote some chamber music and many solo songs.

O

Oakeley, Herbert (Stanley) (b. Ealing, London, 22 July 1830; d. Eastbourne, 26 Oct. 1903). Composer. Studied at Oxford, receiving B.A. (1853) and M.A. (1856). Studied in Leipzig with Plaidy, Moscheles, and Pappeitz; in Dresden with Johann Schneider; in Bonn with Breidenstein. Held the Reid Chair of Music at Edinburgh Univ., 1865–91, and was knighted in 1876. Works include *Suite in the Olden Style* op. 27 (1893); songs, hymns, piano pieces.

Bibl: Edward Murray Oakeley, *The Life of Sir Herbert Stanley Oakeley* (London, 1904).

Oberlin, Russell (Keys) (b. Akron, Ohio, 11 Oct. 1928). Countertenor. Studied at the Juilliard School. In 1952 a founding member of the New York Pro Musica with Noah Greenberg, becoming one of the foremost exponents of early music. He appeared with numerous opera companies, orchestras, and ensembles, and gave many recitals. In the 1960s he gave lectures and master classes at colleges and universities throughout the U.S.; appointed professor of music at Hunter College in 1971.

Oborin, Lev (Nikolayevich) (b. Moscow, 11 Sept. 1907; d. there, 5 Jan. 1974). Pianist. Studied in Moscow at the conservatory and the Gnesin Music School; made his debut in 1924. In 1927 he won the first Warsaw International Chopin Competition, then toured widely. A specialist in Soviet music, he played with David Oistrakh and Svyatoslav Knushevitsky. Taught at Moscow Conservatory from 1928; his pupils included Vladimir Ashkenazy.

Obradović, Aleksandar (b. Bled, 22 Aug. 1927). Composer. Through 1952 he studied composition at Belgrade Academy of Music with Logar. Studied with Berkeley in London, 1959–60, and worked in New York, 1966–67, in the electronic music studio at Columbia Univ. He returned to Belgrade, where he joined the faculty at the Academy of Music in 1954. Obradović's music is mostly in classical forms and genres; it is tonally based yet flexibly utilizes varying modes and may incorporate dodecaphonic techniques or use electronic media. Works include 1 ballet and 6 symphonies (1952–78) as well as works for voice and orchestra; also chamber works and electronic pieces (Symphony no. 3 [*Mikrosimfonija*], orchestra, tape, 1967).

Obrecht [Hobrecht], **Jacob** (b. Bergen op Zoom? or Sicily?, 22 Nov. 1450 or 1451; d. Ferrara, 1505). Composer. One of the foremost figures of his time, particularly noted for his sacred music. Nothing is known of his education. It must have included studies that prepared him to become a priest, as he had done by 1480. Early activities also surely encompassed some musical endeavors, for Tinctoris ranks him as early as about 1475 along with masters of composition such as Dufay, Dunstable, Ockeghem, and Busnois. From 1476 various churches employed him, usually as a singing master, but he seldom stayed long in any one place. He held posts in Utrecht (1476–78); in Bergen op Zoom at the Church of St. Gertrude (1479–84 and 1496–97); in Cambrai (1484–85); in Bruges at St. Donatian (1486–91, with an interruption in 1487–88 for a trip to Ferrara, from which he returned by way of Bergen op Zoom; and 1499–1500); in Antwerp at Notre Dame (perhaps a position unconnected with music; records attest to his association with this church in 1494–95 and in 1498). His career ended with a second trip to Ferrara (1504–5), where he died of the plague. His excellence as a composer earned him a high degree of respect, although there is no indication of special distinction as a teacher, performer, or choir director.

Of Obrecht's compositions the Masses are the most numerous (29 known) and the most distinguished. All are based on preexisting material, which ranges from Gregorian chant to popular tunes to melodies drawn from other composers' motets or chansons. The tenor is usually a long-note cantus firmus, based on the borrowed material, perhaps ingeniously manipulated. Other voices, too, may contain borrowed melodies. Often two or more bits of preexisting material, sometimes from altogether different sources, are quoted simultaneously: several different chant melodies, or a chanson melody and a chant, or phrases of a single monophonic melody combined in counterpoint, or material drawn from various voices of a polyphonic model but combined in new ways.

Obrecht's motets are only marginally fewer in number than the Masses. Many have cantus firmi; few use imitation as a major structural device. Moreover, close links between text and music are uncommon. Certain pieces are exceptional in each of these respects, however.

About the same number of secular works as motets survive. The majority are based on popular tunes, and in contrast to the sacred works many make considerable use of imitation. Most often no more than a text incipit (usually Dutch) survives. Some pieces are fully texted (in Dutch, French, or, in one instance, Italian) or are textless and thus perhaps conceived as instrumental compositions. Three are known only through organ or lute intabulations.

Despite the composer's considerable contemporary

fame his works were not widely disseminated, nor did he have much influence on later composers. The devices he cultivated soon were rejected in favor of the new ideas championed by Josquin.

Bibl.: Works ed. Johannes Wolf (Amsterdam and Leipzig, 1908–12; R: Farnborough, Hants., 1968). *Van Ockeghem tot Sweelinck,* ed. Albert Smijers, 2nd ed. (Amsterdam, 1949–56) [selected compositions]. Works ed. Albert Smijers and Marcus van Crevel (Amsterdam, 1953–64) [incomplete]. Works ed. Chris Maas (Utrecht, 1983–). L. G. van Hoorn, *Jacob Obrecht* (The Hague, 1968). Martin Picker, *Johannes Ockeghem and Jacob Obrecht: A Guide to Research* (New York, 1988). Barton Hudson, "Two Ferrarese Masses by Jacob Obrecht," *JM* 4 (1985–86): 276–302. Rob C. Wegman, *Born for the Muses: The Life and Masses of Jacob Obrecht* (Oxford, 1994).

O'Brien, Eugene (b. Paterson, N.J., 24 Apr. 1945). Composer. He studied at the Univ. of Nebraska, the Cologne Hochschule für Musik (1969), and Indiana Univ. (with Eaton and Xenakis, 1970–71); in 1971 he won the Rome Prize (*Elegy for Bernd Alois Zimmermann,* soprano and chamber ensemble). Taught at the Cleveland Institute (1973–85), the Catholic Univ. of America (1985–87), and the Indiana Univ. School of Music (from 1987). O'Brien employs some aleatoric procedures and has an idiomatic approach to the use of electronics in his compositions. Works include 2 concertos for cello and percussion (1967–71, 1983); *Allures* (percussion, 1979); *Ambages* (piano 4-hands, 1972); *Lingual* (soprano, flute, and cello, 1972); *Close Harmonies* (2 pianos, 1986); *Mysteries of the Horizon* (11 instruments, 1987); Concerto for Alto Sax (1989). Many early works have been withdrawn by the composer.

Obouhov, Nicolas [Obukhov, Nikolay] (b. Kursk, Russia, 22 Apr. 1892; d. Paris, 13 June 1954). Composer. He studied with Shteynberg and Tcherepnin at the St. Petersburg Conservatory; in 1918 he emigrated with his family to Paris, where he met Ravel. With Pierre Dauvillier he constructed the electric "croix sonore" (similar to the ondes martenot) and used the instrument repeatedly in his own compositions. Beginning in 1914 he experimented with a twelve-tone method of composition, devising a special notation system for the purpose employing crosses to indicate sharps and flats. Throughout his life he worked on his magnum opus, the stage work *Le livre de vie* for solo voices, piano 4-hands, and orchestra; the score includes some special vocal effects such as shouting and sighing. His theories of music are discussed in his *Traité d'harmonie tonale, atonale et totale* (Paris, 1946).

Ochsenkun [Ochsenkhun], Sebastian (b. Nuremberg, 6 Feb. 1521; d. Heidelberg, 20 Aug. 1574). Lutenist. He served Count (later Elector) Palatine Ottheinrich at Neuburg an der Donau in 1543–44. By 1552 he followed the court to Heidelberg and remained in service there after Ottheinrich's death in 1559. He published a *Tabulaturbuch* for lute in Heidelberg (1588) dedicated to the elector; it intabulates 29 motets (by Josquin and other Netherlands composers), 38 sacred and secular German songs (by Senfl and lesser Palatinate composers), and a few madrigals and chansons.

Ockeghem, Johannes [Jean] (b. ca. 1410–20; d. Tours, 6 Feb. 1497). Composer. All details of his early life are uncertain. His surname is found in Termonde, in East Flanders, by 1400, but a younger contemporary, the poet Jean Lemaire from the province of Hainaut, refers to him as a countryman; the city of Mons in Hainaut has recently been mentioned as his possible birthplace. From 24 June 1443 to that date a year later he served as singer at Notre Dame in Antwerp. From 1446 to 1448 he was a member of the chapel of Charles I, Duke of Bourbon; the Duke's brother-in-law was Charles the Bold, Duke of Burgundy, through whom Ockeghem could have become familiar with music at the Burgundian court. He was in the service of Charles VII of France as early as 1450, first appearing in the chapel accounts in 1453; he is referred to as first chaplain from 1454, and in 1459 was appointed treasurer of the Abbey at St. Martin of Tours. In 1460 he composed a *déploration* on the death of Binchois, suggesting some personal link with the slightly older composer. Continuing in the employ of Charles's successor, Louis XI (1461–83), he served as a canon at Notre Dame, Paris, from 1463 to 1470. During this period he may have visited Cambrai as a guest of Dufay. In addition, Busnois was likely a student at this time, his motet *In hydraulis* in praise of Ockeghem dating from no later than 1467. He visited Spain in 1470, and corresponded with Galeazzo Maria Sforza of Milan in 1472; although there is no evidence of an Italian journey, Ockeghem could have met the duke previously in France. He apparently retained his posts during the reign of Charles VIII (1483–98), though many records regarding court music during this period are missing. A trip to Bruges and Dammes in Flanders in 1484 is noted in the court archives. In 1487 he made a will leaving his estate to the Chapter of St. Martin; upon his death Crétin and Molinet wrote poetic tributes, the latter of which was set by Josquin.

Ockeghem was a famous bass singer, and was praised universally by contemporary musicians and writers; still, for such a lengthy career he seems to have written relatively little music. The bulk of his work consists of 14 Mass cycles. Of these the *Missa prolationum* (a series of mensuration canons) and the *Missa cuiusvis toni* (capable of being sung in any mode) were often cited by 16th-century theorists. Other Masses include those based on his chansons *Au travail suis, Fors seulement,* and *Ma maistresse,* and on Binchois's *De plus en plus;* 2 chant paraphrase Masses (*Missa Caput* and *Missa Ecce ancilla Domini*); a *L'homme armé* Mass; the *Missa mi-mi;* and the earliest surviving polyphonic Requiem setting. Four other masses mentioned by Zacconi and Tinctoris are lost. There are about 10 motets, including *Alma Redemptoris mater,*

Ave Maria, and 2 settings of *Salve Regina* for 4 voices, and *Gaude Maria, virgo* and *Intemerata Dei mater* (the bass part of which descends to two octaves below middle C) for 5 voices. Among some 20 chansons (mostly rondeaux, along with 4 bergerettes) are *L'aultre d'antan, Ma bouche rit,* and *Prenez sur moi* à 3, and *Petite camusette à 4.*

Bibl.: *Johannes Ockeghem: Collected Works,* ed. Dragan Plamenac and Richard Wexler (New York, 1947–59). Dragan Plamanac, "Johannes Ockeghem als Motetten- und Chansonkomponist" (diss., Univ. of Vienna, 1925). Manfred Bukofzer, "Caput: A Musico-Liturgical Study," in *Studies in Medieval and Renaissance Music* (New York, 1950), pp. 216–30. Marianne Henze, *Studien zu den Messenkompositionen Johannes Ockeghems* (Berlin, 1968). Edward F. Houghton, "Rhythmic Structure in the Masses and Motets of Johannes Ockeghem" (diss., Univ. of California, Berkeley, 1971). Craig Wright, "Dufay at Cambrai: Discoveries and Revisions," *JAMS* 28 (1975): 175–229. Leeman Perkins, "Musical Patronage at the Court of France under Charles VII and Louis XI," *JAMS* 37 (1984): 507–66. David Fallows, "Johannes Ockeghem: The Changing Image, the Songs and a New Source," *EM* 12 (1984): 218–30. Martin Picker, *Johannes Ockeghem and Jacob Obrecht: A Guide to Research* (New York, 1988) [includes works list]. Andrea Lindmayr, *Quellenstudien zu den Motetten von Johannes Ockeghem* (Laaber, 1990). Wolfgang Thein, *Musikalischer Satz und Textdarbietung im Werk von Johannes Ockeghem* (Tutzing, 1992). Clemens Goldberg, *Die Chansons Johannes Ockegehms: Ästhetik des musicalischen Raumes* (Laaber, 1992).

O'Day, Anita [Colton, Anita Belle] (b. Kansas City, Mo., 18 Oct. 1919). Jazz singer. She sang with the big bands of Gene Krupa (1941–43, 1945–46, including the recording *Let Me Off Uptown,* 1941) and Stan Kenton (1944–45), then worked as a soloist. Drug addiction interrupted her career, which was revived by her exuberant performance at the Newport Jazz Festival (preserved in the film *Jazz on a Summer's Day,* 1958). She toured Japan periodically from 1964, in 1972 formed her own record company (including the album *Live at the City,* 1979), and gave a concert at Carnegie Hall celebrating her fiftieth year in jazz (1985).

Writings: with George Eells, *High Times, Hard Times* (New York, 1981).

Odington, Walter [Walter Evesham] (fl. 1298–1316). Theorist. His identity and the dating of his works have been the subject of much speculation. He wrote treatises on many aspects of the quadrivium, including astronomy, arithmetic, geometry, and alchemy, as well as music. His *Summa de speculatione musice* (ed. Frederick F. Hammond, *CSM* 14 [1970]) is an exceptionally systematic and comprehensive work, in which discussion of the mathematical bases of music (drawing heavily on statements of authorities such as Boethius, Isidore of Seville, and Cassiodorus) leads to sections on chant, including a tonary, and on discant, especially modal rhythm and the genres of polyphonic music (such as organum purum, motet, conductus, and copula).

Jacques Offenbach.

Odo of Arezzo (fl. Arezzo, late 10th cent.). Theorist. Wrote a tonary and prefatory treatise in the late 10th century. This work influenced 11th-century Italian theory and practice both through direct dissemination and through the adoption of its principles by others. Parts of it were incorporated into the anonymous *Dialogus* on music (*GS* 1:252–64). Perhaps most important, Guido of Arezzo based his theories in part on Odo's ideas.

Odo of Cluny (b. the Maine, 878/79; d. Tours, 18 Nov. 942). Abbot of Cluny from 927. Wrote 3 hymns and, for the monastic office of St. Martin, a dozen antiphons (ed. G. M. Dreves, *Analecta hymnica* 1, Leipzig, 1907, pp. 264ff.), as well as sermons and biblical commentaries. He has often been confused with Odo of Arezzo and other medieval musicians named Odo. Neither the *Dialogus* on music attributed to him by Gerbert (*GS* 1:252–64) nor any tonary is his work.

Offenbach, Jacques (b. Cologne, 20 June 1819; d. Paris, 5 Oct. 1880). Composer. Son of Isaac Eberst, who moved from Offenbach am Main to Deutz, then to Cologne, where he became known as Offenbach and worked as a bookbinder, but primarily in music, becoming cantor at a Cologne synagogue; Jacob, one of 10 children, learned the violin and, principally, the cello and with a brother Juda (later called Jude and in

France Jules) and sister played as a trio in local taverns. In 1833 their father took the two boys to Paris, and Jacques, as he was thenceforth known, was admitted to the conservatory as a cello student; he remained only a year, as he could not pay the tuition, becoming then an orchestral cellist in Paris theaters (1835–38, Opéra-comique), picking up occasional lessons on his instrument from Louis Norblin and from 1835 in composition from Halévy, who became a friend and protector. Around 1838 Offenbach formed a cello-piano duo with Flotow, which gave him entree to the salons, composing songs and dances that were well received and sometimes published. In 1839 he composed a one-act vaudeville that aroused little attention; in the 1840s he worked as solo cellist, also taught, composing songs and cello pieces, including operatic potpourris, some larger works such as the *Prière et Bolero* op. 21 for cello and orchestra (1840), and didactic music. In May 1844 Offenbach played in England, a visit probably arranged by an English concert agent, whose stepdaughter he married in August 1844 after converting to Catholicism (five children).

A set of six fables of La Fontaine, heard in Paris in 1842, and a duo burlesquing Hugo's *Notre Dame de Paris,* heard in 1843, seem to prefigure the later Offenbach, but he was unable to get a commission for a complete stage work of any kind and was obliged to give his one-act *L'alcôve* in concert performance in 1847. During the 1848 Revolution he took his family to Cologne, returning to Paris in 1849. He finally gained entrance to the theater world by becoming conductor at the Théâtre-Français in 1850, for which he composed incidental music. He produced the one-act *Pépito* at the Variétés in 1853 and the very successful *Oyayaie* at Hervé's Folies nouvelles in June 1855. On 5 July, during the Paris Exhibition, he opened his own theater, a small wooden one on the Champs-Elysées, calling it the Bouffes Parisiens, presenting one-act works for two or three characters, to which he was restricted by his license until 1858, by himself (22 of them until 1858) and others. A great popular success from the start, he eventually settled in more substantial quarters. With *Orphée aux enfers* (1858) he increased his scope to two- and three-act works: *La belle Hélène* (1864), *Barbe-Bleu* (1866), *La vie parisienne* (1866), *La Grande Duchesse de Gérolstein* (1867), *La Périchole* (1868).

Critics had been appalled by Offenbach's popular success, his operettas being regarded as frivolous and flimsy, but the support of the emperor and the public overcame all obstacles, and in the 1860s his popularity spread to England (where he visited with his company in 1857) and central Europe (he visited Vienna in 1864, producing a comic opera at the Opera, and two German operettas in 1872), helping to stimulate a vogue for operetta across Europe. From 1862 he produced a series of small operettas at the summer resort of Bad Ems in Germany. After the events of 1870–71, which he spent mostly out of France, French taste changed, and Offenbach's operettas, which he continued to produce until his death, were less popular generally, although including some notable successes. His management of the Théâtre de la Gaîté in 1873–75 was a financial disaster, from which he tried to recoup by composing a musical comedy for London (*Whittington,* 1874) and by conducting concerts in New York and Philadelphia during the U.S. centenary celebrations of 1876. His *Offenbach en Amérique: Notes d'un musicien en voyage* (Paris, 1877; trans. 1958 as *Orpheus in America*) derives from this trip. From 1877 to his death his principal concern was his opéra comique *Les contes d'Hoffmann,* which he had completed in vocal score at his death. Ernest Guiraud completed the orchestration, added recitatives, and revised the work considerably for its premier (Opéra-comique, 10 Feb. 1881). It became his only work to remain in the regular opera repertory, although occasional revivals of his operettas are often successful.

Bibl.: Peter Gammond, *Offenbach: His Life and Times,* ed. Winfried Kirsch and Ronny Dietrich (Speldhurst, 1980). Alex Faris, *Jacques Offenbach* (New York, 1981). *Jacques Offenbach, Komponist und Weltbürger: ein Symposion in Offenbach am Main* (New York, 1985). Claude Dufresne, *Jacques Offenbach, ou, La gaîté parisienne* (Paris, 1992). Robert Pourvoyeur, *Offenbach* (Paris, 1994).

Ogdon, John (Andrew Howard) (b. Mansfield Woodhouse, 27 Jan. 1937; d. London, 1 Aug. 1989). Pianist and composer. He studied piano at the Royal Manchester College of Music with Iso Elinson; later he had lessons with Claud Biggs, Denis Matthews, Egon Petri, Gordon Green, and Ilona Kabos. He studied composition with Richard Hall, Thomas B. Pitfield, and George Lloyd. While a student, he joined the Manchester New Music Group, with which he gave first performances of works by Goehr, Maxwell Davies, and himself. In 1958 he made his London debut at the Henry Wood Proms. In 1961 he won the Liszt Prize in Budapest, and the following year shared first prize in the Moscow Tchaikovsky Competition with Vladimir Ashkenazy. Formed a piano-duo partnership with Brenda Lucas, whom he married in 1960. His compositions include piano concertos. From 1976 to 1980 he taught at Indiana Univ.

Bibl.: B. Ogdon and M. Kerr, *Virtuoso: The Story of John Ogdon* (London, 1981).

Ogdon, Will [Wilbur Lee] (b. Redlands, Calif., 19 Apr. 1921). Composer and theorist. He received a B.Mus. at the Univ. of Wisconsin (1942), then studied with Krenek at Hamline Univ. (M.A., 1947) and with Sessions at Berkeley. He held a Fulbright Award to study with Honegger and Leibowitz in Paris (1952–53); then attended Indiana Univ. (Ph.D., 1955). Taught at the Univ. of Texas (1947–50), Illinois Wesleyan Univ. (Bloomington, Ill., 1956–64), and the Univ. of California, San Diego. His compositions employ serial techniques. Ogdon wrote about atonal music; in 1974 he collaborated with Krenek and J. Stewart on a book about Krenek *(Horizons Circled).* His opera *The Awakening of Sappho* was completed in 1980; other works include *By the Czar* (soprano, alto flute, and double bass, 1969); *5 Preludes* (violin, chamber orchestra, 1985); *Hurricane* (soprano, baritone, percussion, 1985); *Serenade* (wind quintet, 1986–87).

Ogiński, (Prince) Michał Kleofas (b. Guzów, near Warsaw, 25 Sept. 1765; d. Florence, 15 Oct. 1833). Composer, diplomat, and politician. His uncle was the musician-poet Michał Kazimierz Ogiński (1728–1800). Young Michał Kleofas first studied music in Guzów with Józef Kozłowski (from 1773); several years later he had further violin lessons from Viotti and Baillot. After 1790 he occupied bureaucratic positions in Holland, London, Warsaw, Constantinople, and elsewhere. By 1815 he was in Italy. He composed an opera, *Zélis et Valcour ou Bonaparte au Caïre* (1799); but he is best known for his piano music, which includes some 20 polonaises.

Ogiwara [Ogihara], **Toshitsugu** (b. Osaka, 6 June 1910). Composer. He studied composition at Nihon Univ. with Matsudaira and worked privately with Tcherepnin. In 1952 he organized his performance group, the Jiyū Sakkyokuka Kyōkai. His music uses largely classical forms and genres and is influenced by the Parisian trends of the 1920s and 1930s. Works include 1 ballet (*Springtime,* 1973), symphonies, concertos (2 violin concertos, 1962, 1963), and much chamber music (4 string quartets, 1940, 1949, 1953, 1969; Piano Quintet, 1970; *Serenade,* cello, violin, clarinet, 1972; *Suite,* flute, piano, 1984; *Fantasia,* piano, 1984).

Ogura, Roh (b. Kitakyūshū, 19 Jan. 1916). Composer. He studied early with Fukai and Sugawar; later his most important teachers were Ikenouchi and Rosenstock. His music is in the traditional style of European forms and genres, especially influenced by specifically French trends. Works include 1 opera (*Neta,* 1957), symphonic works (Symphony in G, 1968), concertos (Piano Concerto, 1946; Violin Concerto, 1950), and chamber works (*Divertimento,* 7 winds, 1964; *Divertimento,* 8 winds, 1972).

Ohana, Maurice (b. Casablanca, 12 June 1914; d. Paris, 13 Nov. 1992). Composer and pianist. He studied piano as a child in Bayonne; continued his piano study in Paris (where he had intended to train in architecture); and began a career as a performer in Spain and England. In 1937 he studied counterpoint with Daniel-Lesur at the Schola cantorum; served in the British army; and went to Italy for more piano study with Casella (1944–46). Returning to Paris in 1947, he worked with Schaeffer and Dutilleux and taught counterpoint at the École normale; he won the Italia Prize in 1969. Avoiding both diatonicism and serialism, he was most influenced by Debussy and Falla. Works include opera (*Célestine,* 1988), radio music, film scores; an oratorio (*Llanto per Ignacio Sanchez Mejias,* Lorca, 1950); instrumental music (*Signes,* flute, piano, zither in one-third tones, percussion, 1965; String Quartet no. 2, 1980; Cello Concerto no. 2, 1988–89); piano music (*24 Preludes,* 1973); and vocal music (*Cantigas,* soprano, mezzo-soprano, and ensemble, 1953–54; *Lux Noctis–Die Solis,* 4 choral groups, 2 organs, 1981–88; *Swan Songs,* 12 voices, 1988).

Ohlssohn, Garrick (Olof) (b. Bronxville, N.Y., 3 Apr. 1948). Pianist. Studied at the Westchester Conservatory, then at the Juilliard School with Sascha Gorodnitzki and Rosina Lhévinne. Won the Busoni Piano Competition and the Montreal International Piano Competition in 1966; was the first American to win the Warsaw International Competition (1970). Has made frequent tours of Poland, and has appeared with major orchestras in Europe, the U.S., Japan, and New Zealand. He became known as a Chopin specialist but has a broad repertoire, especially favoring the music of Scriabin. His recordings include music of Brahms, Liszt, Chopin, and Scriabin. In 1984 he gave the premiere of Wuorinen's Third Piano Concerto.

Oistrakh, David (Fyodorovich) (b. Odessa, 30 Sept. 1908; d. Amsterdam, 24 Oct. 1974). Violinist. Studied at the Odessa Conservatory; made his debut in Leningrad in 1928. Won first prizes in the Ukrainian Contest (1930) and the All-Soviet Contest (1935), second prize in the Wieniawski Contest (1935), and first prize in the Ysaÿe Concours in Brussels (1937). Played at the front during the war, then gave concerto programs in 1946–47. Made debuts in London and Paris in 1953, and in New York in 1955. Was the dedicatee and first performer of both Shostakovich violin concertos (1955 and 1967). Taught at the Moscow Conservatory from 1934; his pupils included his son Igor. Received the Lenin Prize in 1960.

Bibl.: Viktor Jusefovich, *David Oistrakh: Conversations with Igor Oistrakh* (London, 1979).

Oistrakh, Igor (Davidovich) (b. Odessa, 27 Apr. 1931). Violinist. Studied privately and at Moscow Conservatory with his father, David Oistrakh, and at the Central Music School in Moscow. He won first prizes at the International Festival of Democratic Youth in Budapest (1949) and at the Wieniawski Contest in Poznań (1952). In 1958 he joined the staff of the Moscow Conservatory, and became a lecturer there in 1965. He performed duets and double concertos with his father.

Ōki, Masao (b. Iwata, Shizuoka, 3 Oct. 1901; d. Kaurakura, 18 Apr. 1971). Composer. Originally studied chemistry at the Osaka Institute of Engineering. Largely self-taught in composition, he studied privately with Ishikawa and saw public success during the 1930s, at which point he focused primarily on the pedagogy and composition of music. His musical style was that of late Romanticism, infused with his socialist political ideals and with melodic characteristics related to Japanese traditions. Works include 6 symphonies, 2 of which bear political titles (Symphony no. 5 [*Atomic*

Bomb], 1953; Symphony no. 6 [*Vietnam*], 1970). He also wrote choral works, including a cantata (*Take Back the Human,* 1961–63).

Olah, Tiberiu (b. Arpăşel, Romania, 2 Jan. 1928). Composer. From 1946 to 1949 he studied at the Cluj Conservatory with Mureşianu and Eisikovits (theory) and Halmoş. From 1949 through 1954 he studied at the Moscow Conservatory, and in 1954 joined the staff of the Bucharest Conservatory. In addition, Olah attended summer courses at Darmstadt, 1966–69. His music is characterized by linear textures and is broadly atonal with the incorporation of some serialistic devices; it utilizes standard forms and genres. Olah's main focus was film music, incorporating folklike elements and liberal use of percussion into carefully balanced, thoroughly dramatic scores. Works also include symphonic poems (*Masa tăcerii* [Table of Silence], 1967–68) and other descriptive pieces; chamber works (Sonata for solo clarinet, 1963; *Spaiţu şi ritm* [Space and Rhythm], etude for 3 percussion groups, 1964; Sonata for violin and percussion, 1985; Sonata for saxophone and tape, 1986).

Oldberg, Arne (b. Youngstown, Ohio, 12 July 1874; d. Evanston, Ill., 17 Feb. 1962). Composer. He studied piano (with A. Hyllested) and composition (with Middelschulte) in Chicago; then studied in Vienna (Leschetizky) and Munich (Rheinberger). In 1899 he was appointed to teach at Northwestern Univ.; he remained there until his retirement in 1941. His second Concerto for piano and orchestra won the Hollywood Bowl Prize in 1932. Works include 5 symphonies (no. 5, 1950) and several concertos (organ, violin, horn, 2 for piano); *S. Francis of Assisi* (baritone and orchestra, 1954); chamber music (2 piano quintets, Quintet for piano and winds, String Quartet); and piano music.

Oliveira, Elmar (b. Waterbury, Conn., 28 June 1950). Violinist. Studied at the Hartt School of Music and at the Manhattan School of Music. Made his solo debut with the Hartford Symphony in 1964, and his New York recital debut in 1973. Won the Naumburg Award in 1975, and in 1978 was the first American violinist to win a gold medal at the Tchaikovsky Competition in Moscow; won the Avery Fisher Prize in 1983. Has played with the Chamber Music Society of Lincoln Center, and has taught at SUNY–Binghamton, and at the Manhattan School of Music (from 1990).

Oliveira, Jocy de (b. Curitiba-Parana, Brazil, 11 Apr. 1936). Composer. She studied piano with J. Kliass in São Paulo and with Marguerite Long in Paris. Following study at Washington Univ. in St. Louis, she appeared as a piano soloist with several major orchestras in Europe and the U.S. Her compositions include *Probabilistic Theater I, II,* and *III* (musicians, actors, dancers, television, traffic conductor); *Polinteracões I, II, III.* Other works include sambas as well as a fantasy novel and a play.

Oliver, Henry Kemble (b. Beverly, Mass., 24 Nov. 1800; d. Salem, 12 Aug. 1885). Organist and composer. Organist at several churches in Boston and Salem. Graduated from Dartmouth in 1818; awarded B.A., M.A. from Harvard in 1862; Mus.D. from Dartmouth in 1883. He wrote many hymns.

Bibl.: Frank J. Metcalf, *American Writers and Compilers of Sacred Music* (New York, 1925; R: 1967), pp. 230–33.

Oliver, King [Joe] (b. in or near New Orleans, 11 May 1885; d. Savannah, Ga., 8 or 10 Apr. 1938). Jazz cornetist and bandleader. He played in New Orleans (from about 1907) and Chicago (from 1918), where he formed his own band in 1920. The group worked in California (1921–22) before returning to Chicago to begin an engagement at Lincoln Gardens as King Oliver's Creole Jazz Band (1922–24). With Louis Armstrong and Baby and Johnny Dodds among his sidemen, Oliver made recordings in 1923, including *Chimes Blues, Snake Rag, Dipper Mouth Blues,* and *Riverside Blues.* These demonstrate the ensemble's skill at collective playing in the New Orleans style, Oliver and Armstrong's "breaks" for two cornets, and Oliver's influential use of muted effects (especially a "wahwah") in solos. He led a 10-piece band, the Dixie Syncopators (1925–27), including Barney Bigard, Albert Nicholas, Kid Ory, and Luis Russell, and continued recording regularly (to 1931), but his tours became increasingly chaotic and unsuccessful. By 1937 he was obliged to retire from music.

Bibl.: Laurie Wright et al., *Walter C. Allen and Brian A. L. Rust's "King" Oliver* (Chigwell, England, 1987).

Oliver, Stephen (b. Liverpool, 10 Mar. 1950; d. London, 29 Apr. 1992). Composer. He studied at Oxford Univ. with Kenneth Leighton and Robert Sherlaw Johnson (1968–72), then taught for two years at the Huddersfield School of Music.

Works: For the theater: *The Duchess of Malfi* (1971); *The Three Wise Monkeys* (1972); *Three Instant Operas* (1973); *Tom Jones* (1974–75); *The Girl and the Unicorn* (1978); *Nicholas Nickelby* (1980); *Euridice* (1981); *Blondel* (1983); *Britannia Preserv'd, Beauty and the Beast, The Ring* (1984); *Waiting* (1985). Vocal: *Sirens,* baritone, piano (1972); *Magnificat, nunc Dimitis* (1976); *A String of Beads,* chorus, orchestra (1980); *Trinity Mass, Namings,* cantata (1981); *Seven Words,* cantata (1985). Orchestral: *The Boy and the Dolphin* (1974); *Luv* (1975); Symphony (1976). Instrumental: *Music for the Wreck of the Deutschland,* piano quintet (1972); *Ricercare,* clarinet, violin, cello, piano (1973); *The Key to the Zoo,* speaker, 2 oboes, bassoon, harpsichord (1980); string quartet (1992).

Oliver, Sy [Melvin James] (b. Battle Creek, Mich., 17 Dec. 1910; d. New York, 27 May 1988). Jazz arranger and trumpeter. He joined Jimmie Lunceford (1933–39), whose big band recordings include Oliver's composition "For Dancers Only" (1937) and his arrangements of "Organ Grinder's Swing" (1936) and "'Tain't What You Do" (1939). He also arranged for Benny Goodman (1934–39). After ceasing to play trumpet he joined Tommy Dorsey, worked as a free-lance arranger, and then served as a music director for several recording companies. In the 1970s and 1980s he played trumpet once again, leading a nonet which played reduced versions of his big band material.

Olivero, Magda [Maria Maddalena] (b. Saluzzo, near Turin, 25 Mar. 1913 or 1914). Soprano. She studied in Turin with Luigi Gerussi, Simonetto, and Ghedini, and made her debut there in 1933. She then sang in Parma, Rome, Naples, Florence, and Venice. She had great success as Cilea's Adriana, and was the composer's favorite interpreter of the role. She retired in 1941, then returned to the stage in 1951. She made her London debut in 1952, her U.S. debut in 1967 (Dallas), and her Metropolitan debut in 1975.

Oliveros, Pauline (b. Houston, 30 May 1932). Composer and performer. She studied composition with Paul Koepke at the Univ. of Texas (1949–52) and with Robert Erickson in San Francisco (1954–60). With Subotnick and Sender she was a cofounder of the San Francisco Tape Music Center in 1961, later becoming its director at Mills College (1966–67). From 1967 until 1981 she taught electronic music at the Univ. of California at San Diego, where she founded an ensemble of women musicians and performers that toured with her compositions; in 1981 became consulting director of the Creative Music Foundation (West Hurley, N.Y.).

Her many compositions include theater and ceremonial pieces; film scores; music for acoustic instruments (*To Valerie Solanas and Marilyn Monroe in Recognition of Their Desperation,* orchestra or chamber ensemble, 1970) and voices; and electronic works. *Duo for Bandoneon and Accordion* (with possible mynah bird obbligato, seesaw version) was performed in 1964 with Tudor, Oliveros, and a live bird in a set designed by Elizabeth Harris. In 1966 she studied electronic music briefly with Hugh LeCaine at the Univ. of Toronto, but she was already beginning to combine taped material with live performers, film, and lighting in an attempt to avoid the "visual vacuum" of tape music (*Pieces of Eight,* wind octet and tape, 1965). By 1967 she had begun to concentrate on meditative and ceremonial pieces. The *Sonic Meditations* (voices, instruments, and performers, 1971–72) focus on drones and extreme prolongation of sounds, along with directions for other physical activities and some audience participation. In *Rose Moon* (ceremonial piece for chorus and percussion, commissioned by Wesleyan Univ. in 1977) the participants (identified as cloth people, runners, or lunatics) engage in a detailed ritual involving processions, chants, coordinated breathing, and sparse percussion accompaniment. Other works include *The Mandala* (4 clarinets, 8 crystal glasses, bass drum, finger cymbals, "timeless date of composition"); *The Wheel of Times* (string quartet, electronics, 1982).

Her awards include the Pacifica Foundation National Prize (1961) for *Variations for Sextet* (flute, clarinet, horn, trumpet, cello, and piano); the Gaudeamus Prize (1962, at Bilthoven, Holland) for *Sound Patterns* (chorus); and the Beethoven Prize from the City of Bonn (1977) for *Bonn Feier* (theater piece for actors, dancers, and performers).

Writings: *Pauline's Proverbs* (1976); *Software for People: Collected Writings, 1963–1980* (1984).

Bibl.: Heidi von Gunden, *The Music of Pauline Oliveros* (Metuchen, N.J., 1983).

Olmstead [Olmsted], **Timothy** (b. Hartford, Conn., 13 Nov. 1759; d. Phoenix, N.Y., 15 Aug. 1848). Composer and tunebook editor. During the Revolutionary War he played the fife in his Connecticut regiment; after the war he played in a corps band until 1780, then took up the itinerant life of a singing master in Connecticut schools. He is best known for the compilation *The Musical Olio* (Northampton, Mass., 1805), which contains 25 pieces of his own, and *Martial Music* (Albany, N.Y., 1807), a collection of regimental pieces.

Bibl.: Henry King Olmsted and G. K. Ward, *Genealogy of the Olmsted Family in America* (New York, 1912; R: Evansville, Ind., 1978).

Olsen, Poul Rovsing (b. Copenhagen, 4 Nov. 1922; d. there, 2 July 1982). Composer. Originally studied law, graduating from the University of Århus in 1942 and from the University of Copenhagen in 1948. He took organ lessons while at Århus. From 1943 to 1946 he studied composition with Jeppesen at the Copenhagen Conservatory and from 1948 through 1949 with Boulanger in Paris. Through the mid-1960s he was active as an ethnomusicologist, traveling to and researching the music of parts of the Middle East and Greenland. Through 1960 he also worked as a copyright lawyer for the Danish Ministry of Education. From 1967 to 1969 he lectured in Sweden at the Univ. of Lund and then at the Univ. of Copenhagen. His early works were within a neoclassic framework, experimenting with techniques such as serialism, as well as with styles and rhythmical concepts associated with the musics that he studied. He wrote 2 operas, 4 ballets, and many orchestral works, including concertos (Piano Concerto, 1953–54) and descriptive pieces (*Au fond de la nuit,* chamber orchestra, 1968). Works also include pieces for voice and orchestra (*Kejseren* [The Emperor], tenor, male chorus, orchestra, 1963) and much chamber music, often for unusual instrumentation (*How To Play in D Major without Caring about It,* fantasy, 2 accordions, 1967).

Ondříček, František [Franz] (b. Prague, 29 Apr. 1857; d. Milan, 12 Apr. 1922). Violinist and composer. Studied with Antonín Bennewitz at the Prague Conservatory (1873–76). Supported by Wieniawski during his study with Massart (1879–81). Gave first performances of Dvořák's Violin Concerto (Prague, 14 Oct. 1883; Vienna, 2 Dec. 1883). Wrote some pieces, paraphrased others for violin. Appointed *Kammervirtuos* (1888) in Vienna. Taught at New Vienna Conservatory, 1909–12. Co-wrote with physician Mittelmann *Neue*

Methode zur Erlangung der Meistertechnik des Violinspiels auf anatomisch-physiologischer Grundlage (Vienna, 1909).

Onegin [née Hoffmann], **(Elisabeth Elfriede Emilie) Sigrid** [Hoffmann, Lilly] (b. Stockholm, 1 June 1889; d. Magliaso, Switzerland, 16 June 1943). Contralto and mezzo-soprano. Studied in Frankfurt, Munich, and Milan. Made concert appearances in 1911 as Lilly Hoffmann, then sang at the Stuttgart Opera, creating the role of Dryad in the world premiere of *Ariadne auf Naxos* (1912). Married Baron Onégin in 1913; thereafter used the professional name Sigrid Onegin. Sang at the Munich Opera (1919–22). Made her Metropolitan Opera debut in 1922, and her Covent Garden debut in 1927. Sang in Berlin (1926–31), Zurich (1931–35), Salzburg (1931–32), and Bayreuth (1933–34). Also concertized extensively. Notable roles included Fricka, Brangäne, and Gluck's Orpheus.

O'Neill, Norman (Houstoun) (b. London, 14 Mar. 1875; d. there, 3 Mar. 1934). Composer and performer. From 1890 to 1893 he studied with Somervell in London and from 1893 through 1897 worked with Knorr in Frankfurt. Back in London he became music director of the Haymarket Theatre beginning in 1908, briefly serving at St. James' Theatre, 1919–20. He wrote incidental music for the productions and conducted performances at these theaters. From 1924 he lectured in harmony and composition at the Royal Academy of Music. His incidental music includes *The Pretenders* op. 45 (Ibsen; London, 1913); *Measure for Measure* (Shakespeare; London, 1929); *Henry V* (Shakespeare; London, 1933). He also wrote several descriptive orchestral pieces (*Humoresque* op. 47, 1913) as well as vocal and chamber works.

Onslow, (André) Georges (Louis) (b. Clermont-Ferrand, 27 July 1784; d. there, 3 Oct. 1853). Composer. Studied piano in London with Dussek and Cramer, in Paris with Reicha. Produced 3 comic operas in Paris: *L'Alcalde de la Vega* (1824), *Le Colporteur* (1827), *Le Duc de Buise* (1837). Other works include 34 string quintets; 35 string quartets; music for piano 4-hands, including *Grand Duo* op. 7; chamber music with and without piano; orchestral works. Became deaf in one ear when stray bullet from a hunt became lodged in the ear. String Quintet op. 38, subtitled Le Quintette de la balle, was a result of this incident.

Bibl.: Jacques François-Fromental Halévy, "Notice sur Onslow" (Paris, 1855); reprinted in *Souvenirs et portraits* (Paris, 1861). William S. Newman, *The Sonata since Beethoven* (New York, 1983), pp. 475–78.

Oppens, Ursula (b. New York, 2 Feb. 1944). Pianist. Studied at Radcliffe College, then at the Juilliard School. Won the Busoni International Piano Competition (1969) and the Avery Fisher Prize (1976). Has performed widely as a soloist and recitalist. A founding member of Speculum musicae. Has also performed with the Chamber Music Society of Lincoln Center, the Group for Contemporary Music, and the Center for Creative and Performing Arts. Carter, Nancarrow, Rzewski, and Wuorinen, among others, have composed works for her.

Orbison, Roy (Kelton) (b. Vernon, Tex., 23 Apr. 1936; d. Hendersonville, Tenn., 6 Dec. 1988). Rock-and-roll singer, songwriter, and guitarist. Early performances with bands in Texas; joined Sun Records in Memphis in 1956; from 1960, released several highly successful singles in Nashville, including "Only the Lonely" (1960) and "Oh, Pretty Woman" (1964). The elaborate arrangements he used were a major influence on 1970s rock artists such as Bruce Springsteen; also famous was his trademark falsetto singing. He regained popularity in the period around his death through the album *The Traveling Wilburys* (1988), a collaboration with Bob Dylan and George Harrison, and a new solo album (*Mystery Girl,* 1989).

Orbón (de Soto), Julián (b. Avilés, Spain, 7 Aug. 1925; d. Miami Beach, 20 May 1991). Composer. Son of a pianist; driven by the Civil War to Cuba, where he studied with Ardevol; in 1946 he received instruction from Copland at Tanglewood. Directed his father's Orbón Conservatory in Havana, 1946–60; taught at the National Conservatory in Mexico City, 1960–63. He moved to the U.S. in 1964, settling in New York; taught at Columbia Univ. Much of his music is neoclassical (Symphony in C, 1945; Concerto, 1958); elsewhere he draws on archaic materials or folk elements. He composed music for orchestra, chamber ensemble, chorus, and solo piano and guitar.

Bibl.: Velia Yedra, *Julián Orbón: A Biographical and Critical Essay* (Coral Gables, Fla., 1990).

Ordonez, Carlo d' (b. Vienna, 19 Apr. 1734; d. there, 6 Sept. 1786). Composer and violinist. His parents were Spanish nobility; as a young man Carlo held a bureaucratic position in Vienna, and he established good ties with important persons in government and at court. He began composing as early as the 1750s; by the 1770s he was known in Viennese musical circles for his violin playing. His first stage work was *Alceste* (Esterháza, 1775), a parody of Gluck's work of the same title, composed for Haydn's marionette theater. His biggest operatic success was *Diesmal hat der Mann den Willen* (1778), which opened the second season of Joseph II's national singspiel series. Ordonez was pensioned in 1780. He is best known as a composer of symphonies; more than 70 are known, including a *Sinfonie périodique* (1764) and the *Sinfonia solenne,* a "church symphony." He also was an important composer of string quartets (some 35 are known), as well as concertos, more than 20 trios, and many other chamber works. He composed a cantata, *Der alte Wienerische Tandelmarkt* (1779).

Bibl.: A. Peter Brown, *Carlo d'Ordonez (1734–1786): A Thematic Catalogue* (Detroit, 1978). Id., "The Symphonies of Carlo d'Ordonez," *Haydn Yearbook* 12 (Cardiff, 1981): 5–

121. David Young, "Karl von Ordonez (1734–1786): A Biographical Study," *RMARC* 19 (1983–85): 31–56.

Orff, Carl (b. Munich, 10 July 1895; d. there, 29 Mar. 1982). Composer and music educator. As a child he played piano, organ, and cello, and composed a few songs (published in 1911) and music for puppet plays; until 1914 he studied at the Munich Academy of Music; thereafter he held positions as Kapellmeister in Munich, Mannheim, and Darmstadt (1915–19, except for a period of military service in 1917–18). At the Munich Kammerspiele he acted as conductor and composer; the other appointments were at operatic institutions for which he directed productions and wrote operas influenced by Debussy and Strauss. At age 26 he studied for a year with Heinrich Kaminsky, becoming especially interested in reviving early music in modern arrangements and performances. In Munich Orff with Dorothee Günther founded the Güntherschule for gymnastics, music, and dance (1924), at which he taught until it was disbanded in 1943. He taught master classes in composition at the Staatliche Hochschule für Musik between 1950 and 1960.

In the 1930s Orff began to revise his earlier works (cantatas, operas, theater scores, and instrumental music), and withdrew them completely after the successful performance of his dramatic cantata *Carmina burana* in 1937. From 1930 to 1933 he had been conductor of the Munich Bach Society, a group for which he continued to make arrangements of earlier music. (His arrangements of Monteverdi's "Lamento d'Arianna," *Orfeo,* and *Ballo delle ingrate* were completed by 1925; he revised *Orfeo* for the Munich group in 1931 and made further revisions to all three works in 1940.) *Carmina burana* stressed the rhythmic aspects of music; Stravinsky's *Oedipus rex* and *Les noces* are the primary influences. His aim in theatrical compositions was to produce works unified in word, sound, scenic design, stage action, and music; his model for the tragedy was in ancient Greek drama. The emphasis on spectacle and decoration, as well as the practice of including deities and mythological beings among the characters, Orff apparently drew from his familiarity with Baroque opera. He was a frequent attendee at Bayreuth after 1951, but his ideas of unified music drama are unlike those of Wagner. The emphasis on driving rhythm and extensive use of percussion instruments remained central to his compositional style; other elements of the music are kept extraordinarily simple. Pedal points and ostinatos are common; polyphony and significant thematic development are lacking.

Orff's interest in elementary music education was parallel to his work in the theater: in both cases he aimed for a unification of music, speech, and movement. His view that musical improvisation and composition need not be dependent on prior attainment of advanced instrumental and notational skills led him to design a variety of simple percussion instruments—some based on those of the Indonesian gamelan, and some more familiar in jazz and orchestral groups—for use with children. Orff and his assistants notated student improvisations at the Güntherschule and published them in the *Schulwerk* volumes (1930); the system of guided improvisation is highly dependent on pentatonic scales and emphasizes instrumental color and rhythmic contrasts, often cast in rondo forms. Pedals and ostinatos are frequently employed. Orff produced educational radio broadcasts for five years from 1948 and published a revised *Schulwerk* collection in 1950–54 (in collaboration with Hans Bergese and Gunild Keetman). The five volumes have been translated and the content adapted for use in many other countries. Adoption of this system for aural training and improvisation by the Salzburg Mozarteum in 1951 and subsequent establishment of the Orff Institute there (1961) further increased its international currency among music educators.

Works include *De temporum fine comoedia* (stage work, Orff; Salzburg, 1973; rev. 1980) and many other dramatic works; *Dithyrambi für gemischten Chor und Orchester* (1981; revision of 2 earlier choral works, *Nänie und Dithyrambe* and *Die Sänger der Vorwelt,* both 1956) and other choral works; arrangements of earlier music (*Entrata,* orchestra in 5 groups, after Byrd's *The Bells*).

Bibl.: Andreas Liess, *Carl Orff: Idee und Werk* (Zurich, 1955; rev. 2nd ed., 1977; trans. Eng., 1966, 2nd ed. 1971). Id., *Zwei Essays zu Carl Orff: "De temporum fine comoedia"* (Vienna, 1981). Udo Klement, *Das Musiktheater Carl Orffs* (Leipzig, 1982). Horst Leuchtmann, *Carl Orff: ein Gedenkbuch* (Tutzing, 1985). Werner Thomas, *Das Rad der Fortuna: ausgewählte Aufsätze zu Werk und Wirkung Carl Orffs* (Mainz, 1990). Alberto Fassone, *Carl Orff* (Lucca, 1994).

Orgad, Ben-Zion (b. Gelsenkirchen, 21 Aug. 1926). Composer. In Palestine in 1933 and again from 1940 to 1946, when he studied composition with Ben-Haim and violin with Kinari and Bergman at the Rubin Academy of Music in Jerusalem. He visited the U.S., studying at Tanglewood with Copland during the summers of 1949, 1952, and 1961 and at Brandeis Univ. with Fine and Shapiro from 1960 to 1962. Returning to Jerusalem, he was employed by the Ministry of Education and Culture. His music, basically tonal, often utilizes Jewish religious texts and exploits the vocal traditions of Judaism. His orchestral music frequently involves a combination of voices and instrumental groupings (*Melodic Dialogues on Three Scrolls,* violin, oboe, percussion, string quartet, string orchestra, 1969). Works also include chamber music (*Min He'afar* [Out of the Desert], quintet, voice, flute, bassoon, viola, cello, 1956; Duo, violin and cello, 1973; *She'arim,* brass orchestra, 1986); choral music (*Sh'ar Larashut,* 1988).

Ó Riada, Seán [Reidy, John] (b. Cork, 1 Aug. 1931; d. London, 3 Oct. 1971). Composer. From 1948 through 1952 he studied with Fleischmann at the University College in Cork. He was music director of the

Abbey Theatre in Dublin from 1955 to 1962, then taught at the University College in Cork until 1971. He was very active throughout his career with the performance of Irish folk music, which had little evident effect on his own compositions. His style was based in serialism and sometimes included quotations of musical styles from the past. His works include 2 ballets and orchestral music (*Nomos* no. 4, piano, orchestra, 1957–58). He also wrote choral music (*Nomos* no. 2, Sophocles, baritone, chorus, orchestra, 1963), chamber and keyboard works, and songs.

Bibl.: Bernard Harris and Grattan Freyer, *The Achievement of Seán O Riada: Integrating Tradition* (Chester Springs, Pa., 1981).

Orlandini, Giuseppe Maria (b. Florence, 19 Mar. 1675; d. there, 24 Oct. 1760). Composer. He was probably *maestro di cappella* to Prince Giovanni Gastone of Tuscany by 1711; named to the same post at the Florence Cathedral (1732) and S. Michele in Florence (1734). Orlandini was extremely popular as a composer of dramatic music; his works include comic intermezzos, oratorios, and nearly 40 operas which premiered in Bologna, Milan, Venice, Naples, and elsewhere. His intermezzo *Il marito giocatore* (Venice, 1719; facs., New York, 1984), also known as *Serpilla e Bacocco,* was one of the most frequently performed musical dramas of the 18th century.

Ormandy, Eugene [Blau, Jenö] (b. Budapest, 18 Nov. 1899; d. Philadelphia, 12 Mar. 1985). Conductor. Studied at the Budapest Royal Academy, becoming professor of violin there at 17. In 1921 he moved to New York, where he played with and later conducted the Capitol Theater Orchestra. Conducted the Philadelphia Orchestra during summer concerts in 1930. Was conductor of the Minneapolis Symphony (1931–36) before sharing the conducting duties of the Philadelphia Orchestra with Stokowski (1936–38); was appointed sole music director in 1938, and held the post until 1980, when he became conductor laureate. Toured extensively with the orchestra, and guest-conducted all over the world. In 1973 the Philadelphia Orchestra, under his direction, became the first American orchestra to tour the People's Republic of China. Conducted the first performances of Rachmaninoff's *Symphonic Dances,* Bartók's Piano Concerto no. 3, and Britten's *Diversions* for left hand; also works by Barber and Sessions.

Ornithoparchus [Vogelhofer], **Andreas** (b. Meiningen, ca. 1490; d. Münster, ca. 1535). Theorist. Studied in Saxony and at various universities, most notably those of Rostok (from 1512) and Tübingen (1515). Among the works of this humanist and follower of Erasmus, the most important is *Musicae activae micrologus* (Leipzig, 1517; trans. Dowland, London, 1609; R: New York, 1973 [both the original and Dowland's translation]). This treatise covers practical aspects of plainsong and mensural music, and reveals the author's extensive acquaintance with contemporary music and performance practice. Popular and widely reprinted (sometimes as *De arte cantandi micrologus*), the book was long used for teaching and was known to J. G. Walther and to Hawkins.

Ornstein, Leo (b. Kremenchug, Ukraine, 2 Dec. 1892). Composer and pianist. The son of a cantor, he was a child prodigy who performed in the salons of Petrograd; the family moved to the U.S. in 1907 to avoid the persecution of Jews; Ornstein studied at the Institute of Musical Art in New York with Bertha Fiering Tapper, who was a major influence on his career. He made his professional debut in 1911, and had soon toured Europe twice; he made few later appearances as a performer owing to his extreme nervousness. From 1920 he was head of the piano department at the Philadelphia Music Academy, then founded the Ornstein School of Music, from which he retired in 1940; he received an award from the National Institute of Arts and Letters in 1975. Some early compositions for piano (*Suicide in an Airplane,* ca. 1913) were marked by such dissonance, polytonality, and polyrhythm that he was quickly labeled a futurist; his later style was more conservative. Works include a Piano Concerto (1923); chamber music (string quartets; *Poem,* flute and piano, 1979); many piano pieces (*2 Legends,* 1982); and songs.

Bibl.: Terence J. O'Grady, "A Conversation with Leo Ornstein," *PNM* 23/1 (1984): 126–33.

Orr, Charles Wilfred (b. Cheltenham, 31 July 1893; d. Stroud, Gloucestershire, 24 Feb. 1976). Composer. Originally engaged in a military career, he withdrew because of medical problems. In London he studied at the Guildhall School of Music under Morgan beginning in 1917. He wrote songs within the European art-song tradition, especially influenced by Delius and Wolf; a small but coherent output, significant in the art-song repertoire. He used English texts, 24 of the 35 settings being poems by Housman. Though tonally centered, his songs used chromaticism expressively and colorfully. Works include "Silent Moon" (1921), "In Valleys Green and Still" (1952), and "Since Thou, O fondest and truest" (1957).

Orr, Robin [Robert] **(Kemsley)** (b. Brechin, Scotland, 2 June 1909). Composer. He played organ as a child. From 1926 through 1929 he studied at the Royal College of Music in London and from 1929 to 1932 at Cambridge, taking lessons in organ, piano, and composition. He also studied with Dent at Pembroke College, Cambridge, through 1938; with Casella in Siena; and Boulanger in Paris. He worked as organist at St. John's College in Cambridge from 1938 to 1950; from 1965 to 1976 he taught at Cambridge. His music was influenced by the neoclassicism of Stravinsky and Bartók. Works include opera (*Full Circle,* 1968; *Hermiston,* 1975; *On the Razzle,* 1988), orchestral music (*Symphony in 1 Movement,* 1963), chamber music, and much music for the Anglican service. Orr served as chairman of the Scottish Opera (1962–76) and director of the Welsh National Opera (1977–83).

Orrego-Salas, Juan (b. Santiago, 18 Jan. 1919). Composer. Studied history at the Liceo Alemán (to 1935) and architecture at the Catholic Univ. (to 1943), studying concurrently with Spikin (piano) and Allende and Santa Cruz (composition) at the National Conservatory. Later studied in the U.S. with Lang and Herzog (musicology) and Thompson and Copland (composition). Joined the music faculty at the Univ. of Chile in 1947; served as editor of the *Revista musical chilena* (1949–61), also writing criticism for *El mercurio* from 1950. He taught composition at Indiana Univ. (1961–87), where he founded and directed the Latin American Music Center; in 1971 he was elected to the Chilean Academy of Fine Arts. His vocal pieces sometimes draw on traditional Iberian and Latin American music. The instrumental works often use Baroque or classical forms; his melodic, harmonic, and motivic processes recall the neoclassical works of composers such as Hindemith and Stravinsky.

Works include operas (*El retablo del rey Pobre,* 1950–52; *Windows,* 1990); oratorio (*The Days of God,* 1976); ballets, film scores, and incidental music; orchestral works, including 4 symphonies, a piano concerto, the *Serenata concertante* (1954), and the *Varaciones serenas* (strings, 1971); chamber works, including a violin sonata (1945; rev. 1964), *Concierto da camera* (1952), *Sextet* (piano, clarinet, string quartet, 1954), 2 divertimentos (wind trio, 1956), Concertino (brass quintet, 1963), *Edgewood Sonata* (flute, oboe, harpsichord, bass, 1964), *Presencias* (flute, oboe, clarinet, string trio, harpsichord, 1972), *Balada* (cello, piano, 1983), *Glosas* (violin, guitar, 1984); vocal works, including *Canciones Castellanos* (soprano and chamber orchestra, 1948), *Ash Wednesday* (3 songs for mezzo-soprano, string orchestra, 1984), cantatas, songs with piano accompaniment, and choral pieces; and works for solo instruments such as piano and guitar.

Bibl.: Juan Orrego-Salas, "Presencia de la Arquitectura en mi Música," *Revista Musical Chilena* 170 (1988): 5–20. "Catálogo de la Obra Musical de Juan Orrego-Salas: 1979–1988," *Revista Musical Chilena* 170 (1988): 21–26. Luis Merino, "Visión del compositor Juan Orrego-Salas," *Revista Musical Chilena* 142–44 (1978): 5–105 [with works list].

Ørsted Pedersen, Niels-Henning (b. Osted, Denmark, 27 May 1946). Jazz double bass player. From 1962 he played at the Montmartre Jazzhus in Copenhagen, accompanying bop musicians such as Bud Powell, Dexter Gordon, and (from 1966) pianist Kenny Drew. He toured briefly with Bill Evans. Later he joined Oscar Peterson (ca. 1972–87), while also working with Joe Pass, including the duo album *Chops* (1978), which captures his lightning speed, clean articulation, and full-bodied timbre. Among his other albums are pianist Tete Montoliu's *Catalonian Fire* (1974) and sessions in all-star groups led by Count Basie.

Orthel, Léon (B. Roosendaal, North Brabant, 4 Oct. 1905; d. The Hague, 6 Sept. 1985). Composer. In his youth he studied composition with Wagenaar and then from 1928 to 1929 at the Berlin Musikhochschule with Juon and Sachs. He taught piano on the faculty of the Conservatory of The Hague (1941–71) and composition at the Amsterdam Conservatory (1949–1971). His music is tonally centric and often characterized by dramatic contrasts and striking lyricism. He wrote primarily orchestral and chamber works, the former including 6 symphonies (1931–61) and concertos (Trumpet Concerto op. 68, 1973–74), and the latter including sonatas for solo instruments (viola, op. 52, 1965; organ, op. 66, 1973).

Ortiz, Diego (b. Toledo, ca. 1510; d. Naples?, after 1570). Composer. Resident in Naples by 1553; *maestro de capilla* of the Spanish viceregal chapel there from 1558. His sacred music (Psalms, hymns, motets, etc.) was printed as *Musices liber primus* (Venice, 1565; ed. Paul Gene Strassler, "Hymns for the Church Year: Magnificats and Other Sacred Choral Works of Diego Ortiz," diss., Univ. of North Carolina at Chapel Hill, 1966). His secular music, all involving bowed stringed instruments, was published in his *Trattado de glosas* (Rome, 1553; issued simultaneously in Spanish and Italian versions; R: Florence, 1984 [Italian edition]), which is both an ornamentation manual and a collection of compositions incorporating the recommended ornaments.

Orto [Dujardin], **Marbrianus [Marbriano, Mabriano] de** (b. diocese of Tournai?, ca. 1460; d. Nivelles, Feb. 1529). Composer. A singer in the papal chapel from 1483 until 1499 or later. Associated with the Church of St. Gertrude in Nivelles from sometime between 1489 and 1496 until his death, although only intermittently resident there. From 1505 a member of the Burgundian chapel, traveling with Philip the Fair to Spain the next year; soon after Philip's death (1506), went to the Netherlands as a singer for Philip's son Charles (the future Emperor Charles V), whom he was still serving in 1522. Also held canonicates in Antwerp (from 1510) and in Brussels (from 1513). Wrote 5 cantus firmus Masses, a few motets and chansons, and a setting of a text by Virgil.

Orton, Richard (Henry) (b. Derby, 1 Jan. 1940). Composer. Studied composition at the Birmingham School of Music with Mellers and with Ridout at St. John's College in Cambridge. In 1967 he became lecturer at the Univ. of York, overseeing the electronic music studio there. He was influenced by the work of Stockhausen. Highly creative with electronic sources, both as a composer (*Kiss,* tape, 1968) and in improvised performance. His works include music for theater (*Concert Music 7,* rope event, 1975), vocal music for various combinations of voices and instruments, chamber music, and live electronic and tape music (*For the Time Being,* 1972; *Ambience,* 6 trombones, tape, 1975).

Ory, Kid [Edward] (b. La Place, La., 25 Dec. 1886; d. Honolulu, 23 Jan. 1973). Jazz trombonist and bandleader. He led bands in New Orleans (1912–19) and California (1919–25), where he recorded *Ory's Creole Trombone* (1922). Moving to Chicago, he joined King Oliver (1926–27) and recorded with Louis Armstrong's Hot Five (1925–27, including one of Ory's classic jazz compositions, *Muskrat Ramble,* 1926), Jelly Roll Morton's Red Hot Peppers (1926), and the New Orleans Wanderers (1926). He returned to Los Angeles (1930), retired from music (1933–42), but then became active in the traditional jazz revival, leading bands until he retired to Hawaii in 1966. His later albums include *Henry Red Allen Meets Kid Ory* (1959).

Osborne, George Alexander (b. Limerick, 24 Sept. 1806; d. London, 16 Nov. 1893). Pianist and composer. Self-taught pianist; guest of the Prince of Chimay in Belgium, where he learned the classical repertoire (1825). Moved to Paris in 1826, where he studied piano with Pixis, harmony and counterpoint with Fétis. Later studied with Kalkbrenner. Befriended Chopin, Berlioz, Hallé, Bériot. Compositions include transcriptions and fantasias from operas of Auber, Donizetti, Rossini, and Verdi.

Osborne, Nigel (b. Manchester, 23 June 1948). Composer. He studied composition at Oxford University with Leighton and Wellesz, graduating in 1970. From 1970 to 1971 he studied composition in Poland under Rudziński and at the Polish Radio Experimental Studio in Warsaw. His music is highly dramatic, utilizing detailed, complex structures and incorporating serialism, electronics, and microtones. Orchestral works include the Cello Concerto (1977). He wrote much chamber music using varying instrumentation, some works bearing descriptive titles (*After Night,* guitar, 1977; *Kerenza at the Zawn,* oboe, tape, 1978; *Mythologies,* trumpet, violin, cello, flute, clarinet, harp, 1980), some based on traditional genres (Chamber Concerto, flute, 1980). Other works include opera (*Hell's Angels,* 1986; *The Electrification of the Soviet Union,* 1987; *Terrible Mouth,* 1992), orchestral music (*Sinfonia I,* 1982; *Sinfonia II,* 1983; *Stone Garden,* small orchestra, 1988); and vocal music with various types of accompaniment (*The Sickle,* soprano, orchestra, 1975; *Under the Eyes,* voice, flute, oboe, percussion, piano, 1979; *Pornography,* mezzo-soprano, ensemble, 1985).

Bibl.: Niall O'Loughlin, "The Music of Nigel Osborne," *MT* 121 (1980): 307–11.

Osiander, Lucas [Lukas] (b. Nuremberg, 15 or 16 Dec. 1534; d. Stuttgart, 17 Sept. 1604). Theologian and composer. A Protestant cleric from about 1555 in Göppingen, Blaubeuren, Stuttgart, and Esslingen. Published *Fünffzig geistliche Lieder und Psalmen* (Nuremberg, 1586; ed. Friedrich Zelle, Berlin, 1903), the first book of German chorales in cantional style, that is, homophonic settings with the chorale melody in the soprano.

Osten, Eva von der (b. Heligoland, 19 Aug. 1881; d. Dresden, 5 May 1936). Soprano. Studied in Dresden; made her debut in 1902 at the Dresden Hofoper, where she sang until her retirement in 1927. Created the role of Oktavian in *Der Rosenkavalier* in 1911. Sang at Covent Garden (1913–14), and toured the U.S. with the German Opera Company (1922–24). After retiring from the stage she was an assistant producer at the Dresden Staatsoper, where she was stage manager for the first performance of *Die schweigsame Frau.*

Osterc, Slavko (b. Veržej, Slovenia, 17 June 1895; d. Ljubljana, 23 May 1941). Composer. He first studied with Beran, a pupil of Janáček, and then at the Prague Conservatory (1925–27) with Novák, Jivák, and Hába. He taught at the conservatory and the academy in Ljubljana. His music employs twelve-tone and quarter-tone techniques. Works include operas (*Krst pri Savici* [Baptism at the Savica], 1921; *Iz komične opere,* 1928; *Krog s Kredo* [The Chalk Circle], 1928–29; *Salome,* 1919–30; *Medea,* 1930; *Dandin v vicah* [Dandin in Purgatory], 1930); ballets (*Iz Satanovega dnevnika,* 1924; *Maska rdeče smrti,* 1930; *Illusions,* 1938–40); works for orchestra (bagatelles, 1922; Symphony, 1922; Suite, 1929; Concerto for Orchestra, 1932; *Ouverture classique,* 1932; Concerto, 1933; *Passacaglia and Chorale,* 1934; *Danses,* 1935; *Mouvements symphoniques,* 1936; *4 pièces symphoniques,* 1938–39; *Mati,* symphonic poem, 1940). He also wrote vocal, chamber, and piano music.

Ostrčil, Otakar (b. Smichov, near Prague, 25 Feb. 1879; d. Prague, 20 Aug. 1935). Composer and performer. From 1897 through 1901 he studied philology at the Univ. of Prague; concurrently took private music lessons with Mikeš (piano) and Fibich (piano, composition). He conducted with Prague's Orchestral Association, 1908–22, also conducting at the National Theater and the Prague Vinohrady Theater. He served as head conductor of the Prague Opera, 1920–35, and from 1925 to 1929 taught at the Prague Conservatory. Cofounded the Society for Modern Music in 1924; as a conductor he always supported contemporary music. His own music used a late Romantic style as a point of departure; by the late 1920s it was showing the influence of the dramatic chromaticism and vivid instrumentation of expressionism. His music contains occasional references to folklike material. His complex polyphonic textures became increasingly linear over the course of his career. Works include 5 operas (*Honzovo království* [Honza's Kingdom], Brno, 1934); orchestral music (*Symfonietta* op. 20, 1921); vocal music, including 2 melodramas, 2 ballads, and a cantata.

Oswald von Wolkenstein (b. Schöneck in Pustertal, the Tirol, ca. 1377; d. Merano, 2 Aug. 1445). Poet and composer. Spent most of his life in extensive travel in Europe and the Near East and in political activities, including service to King (later Emperor) Sigismund, attendance at important councils in Germanic cities, and involvement in local issues. His poetry treats themes of many sorts. Nearly 100 poems with monophonic melodies survive and about 40 more with polyphonic settings, some of them *contrafacta.* His greatest importance lies in his evident concern for close text-music relationships.

Edition: Josef Schatz and Oswald Koller, *DTÖ* 18 (1902).

Otaka, Hisatada (b. Tokyo, 26 Sept. 1911; d. there, 16 Feb. 1951). Composer and performer. He first studied music as a youth in Vienna, then back in Tokyo with Pringheim. Again in Vienna in 1931, he worked with Stöhr and Marx, and studied conducting with Weingartner. After 1940 in Japan he became conductor of the Japan Symphony Orchestra. His music, bearing the influence of his Viennese teachers, was in the style of late German Romanticism. There were occasional references to traditional Japanese musical culture. He wrote only instrumental works, including *2 Japanese Suites* (1936, 1937), Symphony (1948), 2 string quartets (1938, 1943), and a Piano Trio (1941).

Otescu, Ion Nonna (b. Bucharest, 15 Dec. 1888; d. there, 25 Mar. 1940). Composer. From 1903 to 1907 he studied at the Bucharest Conservatory, taking theory lessons with Kiriac and composition lessons with Castaldi; 1908–11, studied composition in Paris at the Schola cantorum with d'Indy and at the conservatory with Widor. From 1913 to 1940 he taught at the Bucharest Conservatory, serving as head of the conservatory after 1918. He helped found the journal *Muzika* in 1916; also helped to organize the Romanian Opera and Romanian Composers' Society, and was resident composer of the Bucharest Symphony. His own works show the influence of his French training, drawing on Romantic genres and French coloristic harmonies. His music often contains references to Romanian folk culture and music. He wrote primarily dramatic music and programmatic orchestral works (*Les enchantements d'Armide,* violin, orchestra, 1915).

Othmayr, Caspar (b. Amberg, 12 Mar. 1515; d. Nuremberg, 4 Feb. 1553). Composer. Studied at the Univ. of Heidelberg (1533–36); by 1545, resident in Heilsbronn, remaining associated with the monastery there for the rest of his life. From 1547 was a canon, and later provost, at the monastery of St. Gumbertus in Ansbach. The foremost German composer of the generation after Senfl and a Lutheran, he wrote about 230 pieces, all but two vocal, in most sacred and secular genres of his time except the Mass. Most of his works are based on preexisting melodies.

Bibl.: Edition, Hans Albrecht, *EDM* 16 (1941; R: 1962), 26 (1956). Id., *Caspar Othmayr, Leben und Werk* (Kassel, 1950) [includes works list].

Otis, Johnny (b. Vallejo, Cal., 28 Dec. 1921). Rhythm-and-blues drummer, vocalist, composer, bandleader, and producer. Born of Greek parents (named Veliotes) in a black neighborhood, he quickly absorbed blues and big band styles. During the late 1940s he led the West Coast rhythm-and-blues movement; he topped the charts in 1950 with several hits. In the late 1950s he moved into rock-and-roll with hits such as "Willie and the Hand Jive." He was a prominent show host on radio and television from the 1950s to the 1970s and produced artists such as Big Mama Thornton, Hank Ballard, and Johnny Ace.

Otterloo, (Jan) Willem van (b. Winterswijk, Netherlands, 27 Dec. 1907; d. Melbourne, 28 July 1978). Conductor and composer. He made his conducting debut with the Concertgebouw Orchestra in 1932 and was appointed assistant conductor (1933–37) and then chief conductor (1937–49) of the Utrecht Symphony. From 1949 to 1973 he served as conductor of The Hague Residentie Orchestra, raising its standards to an international level; he also served as *Generalmusikdirektor* of the Düsseldorf Symphony (1974–77) and as chief conductor of the Sydney Symphony (from 1973).

Oudrid y Segura, Cristóbal (b. Badajoz, 7 Feb. 1825; d. Madrid, 12 Mar. 1877). Composer and conductor. Studied with his father. Went to Madrid (1844); took a few lessons with Saldoni, director of the Teatro español. There he had several works premiered. Wrote many songs, piano music; his 88 zarzuelas were his most successful compositions. Conducted the Italian Opera in Madrid (1867). Named director of Teatro real in 1870.

Bibl.: Emilio Cotarelo y Mori, *Historia de la zarzuela* (Madrid, 1934).

Ouseley, Frederick Arthur Gore (b. London, 12 Aug. 1825; d. Hereford, 6 Apr. 1889). Organist, pianist, and composer. Studied at Oxford; received B.A. (1846), M.A. (1849), D.Mus. (1854). Ordained as priest in 1849. Succeeded Henry Bishop as professor of music at Oxford (1855–89), where he established definite standards and examinations for degrees in music. Founded St. Michael's College, Tenbury. Works include services; cantatas; oratorios; anthems; 1 opera (*L'isola disabitata,* 1834); songs; chamber music; organ preludes and fugues; piano songs without words. Published in London treatises on *Harmony* (1868), *Counterpoint* (1869), *Canon and Fugue* (1869), *Form and General Composition* (1875).

Bibl.: John Stainer, "Character and Influence of Sir Frederick Gore Ouseley," *PRMA* 16 (1889–90): 25–39. Frederick Wayland Joyce, *The Life of the Rev. Sir F. A. G. Ouseley, Bart.* (London, 1896).

Overton, Hall (b. Bangor, Mich., 23 Feb. 1920; d. New York, 24 Nov. 1972). Composer and jazz performer and arranger. He studied with Persichetti at Juilliard (1947–51) and privately with Riegger and Milhaud; served in the U.S. Army; after the war played in prominent jazz

Seiji Ozawa.

groups and arranged for Thelonious Monk. He taught at Juilliard (1960–71), the New School (1962–66), and Yale (1970–71); won two Guggenheim awards (1955, 1957), the B.M.I. Award (1962), and a joint award from the American Academy and National Institute of Arts and Letters (1964). His works include the opera *Huckleberry Finn* (1971) and other stage music; 2 symphonies and other orchestral music (*Pulsations,* chamber orchestra, 1972); chamber music (*Fantasy,* brass quintet, piano, percussion; 1957); piano pieces; and songs.

Owens, Buck [Alvis Edgar, Jr.] (b. Sherman, Tex., 12 Aug. 1929). Country singer, guitarist, and songwriter. Worked as an instrumentalist on radio in Arizona and in studios in Bakersfield and Los Angeles; from 1957, recorded his own material. Successful songs included "Under Your Spell" (1958), "Excuse Me (I Think I've Got a Heartache)" (1960), and "I've Got a Tiger by the Tail" (1965). In the 1970s he served as host of the country music television show *Hee Haw;* he began recording and touring again in the late 1980s.

Ozawa, Seiji (b. Fenytien [now Shenyang, Liaoning, China], 1 Sept. 1935). Conductor. Studied at the Toho School in Tokyo, then conducted the NHK Orchestra and the Japan Philharmonic. Went to Europe and won the Besançon International Conductors' Competition. Following study at the Berkshire Music Center, where he won the Koussevitzky Prize, and with Karajan in Berlin, he became assistant conductor of the New York Philharmonic under Bernstein (1961–65). Music director of the Ravinia Festival (1964–68) and of the Toronto Symphony (1965–69), then music adviser to the Japan Philharmonic (1968). Music director of the San Francisco Symphony (1970–76); appointed artistic director of the Berkshire Music Festival in 1970. In 1972 he became music adviser of the Boston Symphony, and in 1973 was appointed music director of the orchestra. Has conducted opera companies at Salzburg, Covent Garden, La Scala, Vienna, and the Paris Opéra, where he conducted the premiere of Messiaen's *Saint François d'Assise* in 1983.

P

Pablo, Luis de (b. Bilbao, 28 Jan. 1930). Composer. Earned a law degree at the Univ. of Madrid in 1952, studying music independently. Had contact with Boulez and Messiaen in Paris; cofounded the Grupo nueva música in 1957, and was prime mover behind the ensemble Tempo y música (established in 1959); in 1958 he attended the Darmstadt summer courses. Served as president of the Spanish Jeunesses musicales, 1960–62; directed the Madrid Conservatory Music Biennale in 1964. Tempo y música dissolved in 1964; the following year Pablo formed the group Alea in its place, becoming involved in electronic music around the same time; in 1968 Alea integrated live electronic music into its activities. A 1969 recording of his *Tombeau* and *Iniciativas* for orchestra (1963, 1966), *Ejercicio* for string quartet (1965), and *Modulos III* for Alea (1967) won the Grand Prix du Disque. He has also taught at the Madrid Conservatory. Pablo's early musical outlook was shaped by Falla, Stravinsky, and Bartók; he broke with the so-called Spanish tradition in 1953, embracing serialism and experimental timbres.

Works: opera (*Kiú,* 1983; *El viajero indiscreto,* 1990), music theater works (*Protocolo,* 1968), choral music (*Escena,* chorus, strings, percussion, 1964), orchestral music (Concerto for Harpsichord, 1956; 4 *Invenciones,* 1959; *Modulos II,* 1966; *Imaginario II,* 1967; *Quasi una fantasia,* 1969; *Oroïtaldi,* 1971; *Elephants ivres I–IV; Heterogeneo,* speakers and orchestra, 1968; *Senderos dell aire,* 1988), chamber music (*Sinfonias,* brass, 1954–66; clarinet quintet, 1954; string quartet, 1957; *Glosa,* with soprano, 1961; *Cesuras,* 1963; *Módulos I, IV,* 1964, 1967; *Cinco meditaciones,* 15 instruments, 1983–84; *Fragmento,* string quartet, 1985); piano and vocal music (*Malinche,* soprano, piano, 1985–86; *Surcar vemos,* soprano, 1985–86); and electronic works.

Bibl.: José Luis García del Busto, *Escritos sobre Luis de Pablo* (Madrid, 1987).

Paccagnini, Angelo (b. Castano Primo, Milan, 17 Oct. 1930). Composer and writer. He studied clarinet, organ, and composition at the Milan Conservatory (1949–55); attended the summer courses in Darmstadt; until 1960 worked with Berio at the electronic music studio in Milan (director, 1968–70); taught electronic music and founded an early music ensemble at the Milan Conservatory (1969–80); and directed the conservatories in Mantua (1980–83) and Verona. Employed serial procedures; and many works contain strong ideological messages. He won the Premio Italia (1964) for *Il Dio di oro* (soloists, chorus, and orchestra). Works include operas; music for orchestra (*Flou VII,* flute, harpsichord, and strings, 1981), chamber ensemble, chorus and solo voice, tape. His several books include *Musica che fa festa* (1976) and *La musica e Virgilio* (with W. R. Zanetti, 1981).

Pacchiarotti, Gasparo (b. Fabriano, bapt. 21 May 1740; d. Padua, 28 Oct. 1821). Castrato soprano. In Venice he studied with Ferdinando Bertoni at St. Mark's. In 1765 he was made principal soloist there. He traveled to London in 1778, where he received much acclaim for his roles at the King's Theatre. During the 1770s and 1780s he sang in theaters throughout France, Italy, and England. In 1791 he sang Haydn's cantata *Arianna a Nasso* in London, with the composer at the keyboard. He spent his last decades in retirement in Padua. He was one of the last of the great castratos, with a range of B♭–c‴.

Pacheco, Johnny [John] (b. Dominican Republic, 25 Mar. 1935). Jazz and salsa flutist, percussionist, and bandleader. He moved to the United States in 1952, where he played percussion and from 1960 flute; from 1961 led his own bands. He made many popular recordings, including those with vocalist Celia Cruz, and in the 1970s was active in the salsa record label Fania.

Pachelbel, Carl Theodorus [Charles Theodore] (b. Stuttgart, bapt. 24 Nov. 1690; d. Charleston, S.C., 14 Sept. 1750). Organist. Younger son of Johann Pachelbel. He emigrated to Boston in the 1730s, becoming organist at churches in Newport, R.I., and Charleston, S.C.; gave two concerts in New York in 1736. His only known composition is an eight-part Magnificat composed before he left Germany.

Pachelbel, Johann (b. Nuremberg, bapt. 1 Sept. 1653; d. there, buried 9 Mar. 1706). Composer and organist. He studied music with Heinrich Schwemmer and G. C. Wecker, attended lectures at the Auditorium aegidianum and entered the university at Altdorf in 1669, where he also served as organist at the Lorenzkirche. He was forced to leave the university after less than a year owing to lack of funds, and became a scholarship student at the Gymnasium poeticum at Regensburg, taking private instruction under Kaspar Prentz. In 1673 Pachelbel went to Vienna and became deputy organist at St. Stephen's Cathedral; in 1677 he became court organist at Eisenach, where he served for slightly over a year. He became organist at the Protestant Predigerkirche at Erfurt in 1678, where he established his reputation as organist, composer, and teacher. He was a friend of the Bach family and taught music to Johann Christoph (the Ohrdruf Bach), who later was Johann Sebastian's instructor. Pachelbel left Erfurt in 1690, became musician and organist for the Württemberg court at Stuttgart (1690–92), then town organist at Gotha (1692–95). He was invited to succeed Wecker as organist of St. Sebald, Nuremberg, after his former teacher's death in 1695; he obtained his release from Gotha that same year and remained at St. Sebald until his death.

Pachelbel was a prolific composer whose output consists of works for organ, harpsichord, and chamber ensembles as well as sacred concertos, motets, and other vocal works. He was one of the greatest composers of organ chorales; his *Acht Choräle zum Praeambulieren* (Nuremberg, 1693) is particularly noteworthy for its use of "old" prototypes such as the bicinium. In nonliturgical organ music his masterpiece is the *Hexachordum Apollinis* (Nuremberg, 1699), a group of 6 arias with variations for organ or harpsichord, which includes a dedication to Buxtehude and F. T. Richter. His vocal music has generally received less attention, although the sacred concertos and particularly his 11 concertato settings of the Magnificat demonstrate his mastery of choral writing and permutation fugues. Pachelbel is best known to today's concertgoer as the composer of the *Canon and Gigue* in D for 3 violins and basso continuo which has been published in many arrangements for different groups of instruments.

Bibl.: *Orgelkompositionen von Johann Pachelbel,* ed. Max Seiffert, *DTB* 6 (1903). *Klavierwerke von Johann Pachelbel,* ed. Max Seiffert and Adolf Sandberger, *DTB* 2 (1901). *Johann Pachelbel: Ausgewählte Orgelwerke,* ed. Karl Matthaei et al. (Kassel, 1974). Ewald V. Nolte, "The Instrumental Works of Johann Pachelbel" (diss., Northwestern Univ., 1954).

Pachelbel, Wilhelm Hieronymus (b. Erfurt, bapt. 29 Aug. 1686; d. Nuremberg, 1764). Composer and organist. Elder son of Johann Pachelbel. He served as organist at Fürth and at the Predigerkirche in Erfurt, then at the Jakobikirche in Nuremberg (1706), at St. Egidien the same year, and was finally appointed to his father's old post at St. Sebald from 1719 until his death. His few surviving compositions are for keyboard.

Bibl.: *Wilhelm Hieronymus Pachelbel: Gesamtausgabe der erhaltenen Werke für Orgel und Clavier,* ed. Hans Joachim Moser and Traugott Fedtke (Kassel, 1957).

Pachman [Pachmann], **Vladimir de** (b. Odessa, 27 July 1848; d. Rome, 7 Jan. 1933). Pianist. Studied at the Vienna Conservatory with Dachs (1866–68), winning a gold medal. Debut at Odessa in 1869; retired for eight years. Played at Berlin, Leipzig, retired again for two years. Made first U.S. tour, 1891. One of a group of pianists who played primarily the music of Chopin.

Bibl.: Harold Schonberg, *The Great Pianists* (New York, 1963).

Pacini, Andrea (b. Lucca, ca. 1690; d. there, Mar. 1764). Alto castrato. Sometimes called "il Lucchesino," he made his debut in Albinoni's *Astarto* in Venice (1708), and appeared in Naples, Turin, Genoa, and Bologna during the years 1713–22. Pacini sang in London during the 1724–25 season, appearing in Handel's *Tamerlano* and in the 1725 revival of *Giulio Cesare* (as Ptolemy); he became a priest in later life.

Pacini, Giovanni (b. Catania, Sicily, 17 Feb. 1796; d. Pescia, 6 Dec. 1867). Composer. Son of an opera singer; studied music in Bologna (1808) and with Furlanetto in Venice (1809–12); in 1814 began career as opera composer, proving extremely prolific, first in opera buffa, from 1817 also opera semiseria, from 1818 opera seria. From 1824 he worked much at the San Carlo, Naples, with such success that he was given Rossini's former post of music director there in 1825. He was less able to compete with the vogue of Donizetti and Bellini in the 1830s, in 1833–39 producing only one new opera (1855), which was a failure. He established a music school in Viareggio; from 1837, ducal music director in Lucca, moving his school there; in 1842 it was absorbed into the new Istituto musicale (Conservatory), of which he was the first director. In 1839 he returned to opera; his second of this period, which is usually considered to have included his best work, was *Saffo* (San Carlo, 1840), his best known. He continued to produce operas until his death, at a slowing rate in the 1850s and only intermittently in the 1860s. By then, with the rise of Verdi, he was an old-fashioned composer. Other works include much sacred music, oratorios, secular cantatas; *Sinfonia Dante* (piano and orchestra, 1863); chamber music; songs. Memoirs: *Le mie memorie artistiche* (Florence, 1865).

Pacius, Fredrik [Friedrich] (b. Hamburg, 19 Mar. 1809; d. Helsinki, 8 Jan. 1891). Composer. Studied in Kassel with Spohr (violin) and Hauptmann (composition). Violinist in the court orchestra in Stockholm, 1828–34. Named lecturer in music at Univ. of Helsinki (1835), professor (1860); given honorary doctorate (1877). He wrote the first Finnish opera, *Kung Karls jakt* (1852). Author of the Finnish national anthem, *Vårt land* (1843; translated into Finnish 1848). Other works include a violin concerto, songs, orchestral pieces, cantatas.

Bibl.: Otto E. Andersson, *Den unge Pacius* (Helsinki, 1938).

Paderewski, Ignacy Jan (b. Kuryłówka, Poland, 18 Nov. 1860; d. New York, 29 June 1941). Pianist, composer, premier. His father was an estate steward, his mother, who died shortly after his birth, a professor's daughter; 1872–78, student, off and on, at the Warsaw Conservatory, also making a Russian concert tour with a violinist. Piano teacher, 1878–83, at the conservatory; 1881–82, studied polyphonic composition with Kiel in Berlin, returning in 1883–84 to study orchestration with Urban; began to publish piano pieces. He went to Vienna in 1884 to study the piano with Leschetizky, who at first advised him not to attempt a concert career; 1885–86, taught piano and composition, Strasbourg Conservatory, then returned to Leschetizky, making what he considered his real concert debut in Vienna in

Ignacy Jan Paderewski, 1923.

1888 and beginning to tour (Paris, 1888; London, 1890). On 17 November 1891 made his U.S. debut at Carnegie Hall, followed by a 6-month, 117-concert tour of the U.S. and Canada, under the auspices of Steinway.

Perhaps even more than in Europe, Paderewski's charismatic personality, his elegantly if idiosyncratically dressed and handsome figure (and especially his large mop of golden hair), and his electrifying presence (although his movements were restrained when he played) captured the American public's fancy and made him one of those artists whose appeal far surpasses the merely musical. Further U.S. tours in 1892–93, 1895–96, 1900–1901, 1901–2, 1907–8, 1913–14; he also toured South America, Australia (1904), South Africa (1912).

Paderewski was noted for generosity with his time and money. In 1896 he provided $10,000 to establish the Paderewski Fund awarding triennial prizes to American composers. In 1915–16 he made a concert tour of the U.S. to raise money for the Polish Victims' Relief Fund, then abandoned concerts to lecture and lobby in support of Polish independence. At war's end he went to Poland and in January 1919 was chosen premier and foreign minister of the new Polish state, which he represented at the Versailles Peace Conference; in December 1919 he resigned both posts and in 1922 returned to concert touring. In 1940 he was made president of the parliament of Polish government in exile and began a tour of U.S. to raise support for Poland, during which he died.

The piano pieces for which he was best known as a composer were composed and published in the 1880s, including the celebrated Minuet (op. 14, no. 1); from this period also date a Violin Sonata op. 13 and Piano Concerto op. 17. In the 1890s and early 1900s he spent his summers composing larger works at his Swiss villa, including the *Fantaisie polonaise* op. 19 for piano and orchestra; *Manru,* an opera widely performed immediately after its premiere (Dresden, 1901); Piano Sonata op. 21 (ca. 1903); Variations and Fugue for piano op. 23 (ca. 1903); Symphony in B minor op. 24, premiered by the Boston Symphony in 1909, which has a Polish subject, the third (final) movement being concerned with the rebellion of 1863–64.

Bibl.: Ignace Paderewski and Mary Lawton, *The Paderewski Memoirs* (New York, 1938). Janina W. Hoskins, *Jan Ignacy Paderewski, 1860–1941: A Biographical Sketch and a Selective List of Reading Materials* (Washington, D.C., 1984).

Padilla, José (b. Almeria, Spain, 28 May 1889; d. Madrid, 25 Oct. 1960). Composer. Studied at the Madrid Conservatory; led zarzuela performances in Spain and Argentina; produced some 60 works for the musical theater as well as songs for several top Parisian entertainers, among them Josephine Baker, Maurice Chevalier, and Mistinguett; lived in Italy, 1930–34; achieved a final Parisian success with *Symphonie portugaise* (1949). Among his several hundred songs are "Princesita," "El relicario," "Valencia," and "Ça c'est Paris."

Padilla, Juan Gutiérrez de (b. Málaga, ca. 1590; d. Puebla, Mexico, before 22 Apr. 1664). Composer. By 1613 he had become *maestro de capilla* at Jérez de la Frontera; sometime before 1616 he became a priest and was named *maestro de capilla* of Cádiz Cathedral from that year until at least 1620. He went to New Spain, becoming a singer at Puebla Cathedral in 1622 and *maestro de capilla* there from 1629 until his death; his responsibilities included directing a large and well-trained choir. One of the most important Spanish-born composers of his time; Padilla's output includes 2 parody Masses on his own motets, *Ave Regina* and *Joseph fili David,* as well as a large number of vernacular *chanzonetas* and *villancicos.* He liked to use cyclic subjects and head motifs in his Masses, and frequently employed antiphonal effects with double choirs.

Padovano, Annibale (b. Padua, ca. 1527; d. Graz, 15 Mar. 1575). Organist and composer. An organist at St. Mark's, Venice, from 1552 until 1565. From 1566 in Graz as organist and later director of music at the court of Archduke Karl II of Austria. His organ ricercars and toccatas, his most important works, influenced the development of these genres. Also wrote motets, Masses, and madrigals.

Paer, Ferdinando (b. Parma, 1 June 1771; d. Paris, 3 May 1839). Composer. His early study of music was with cellist Gaspare Ghiretti at the Parma court; he was also a pupil of Fortunati. His first known stage work was *Orphée et Euridice,* composed in 1791 for the court theater at Parma. This was followed by the successful *Circe,* performed in Venice in 1792; the same year he was appointed honorary *maestro di cappella* at

Niccolò Paganini. Drawing by Ingres, 1819.

the Parma court. His activity as an opera composer during the 1790s culminated when he moved to Vienna in 1797 to assume the directorship of the Kärntnertortheater; there he composed *Camilla, ossia Il sotterraneo* (1799), his most lasting success. In 1804 he was called to the Dresden court, where he served as theater composer and Kapellmeister until 1806, the year that he followed Napoleon to Warsaw and Poznań (Posen). Settling in Paris, he was appointed *maître de chapelle* and became Empress Marie-Louise's music instructor. Later he was director of the Théâtre-Italien (1812–27) and of the chapel of Louis Philippe (1832). Among his other operas are *Le astuzie amorose* (Parma, 1792); *Una in bene e una in male* (Rome, 1794); *L'intrigo amoroso* (Venice, 1795); *Griselda* (Padua, 1798); *Achille* (Vienna, 1801); *Sargino* (Dresden, 1803); *Leonora, ossia L'amore conjugale* (Dresden, 1804); *Sofonisba* (Bologna, 1805); *Agnese* (Parma, 1809). He also composed cantatas, oratorios, symphonies, concertos, orchestral marches, and chamber music.

Paganini, Niccolò (b. Genoa, 27 Oct. 1782; d. Nice, 27 May 1840). Violinist, composer. First music lessons from his father, from 1791 with a theater orchestra violinist, already having begun to compose; later, composition lessons from the opera composer Gnecco; 1794–95, studied with Genoa's leading violinist, Giacomo Costa. However, he was already original in his technique (although he admitted to modeling some aspects on that of the touring violinist Duranowski, also known as Durand) and liked to regard himself as essentially self-taught, this being part of the legend he created around himself. Studied in Parma, 1795–96 (composition with Paer, counterpoint with Ghiretti), composing much and giving a concert. September 1801–December 1809 he was based in Lucca, as first violinist of the state orchestra, also teaching and composing. Lucca coming under the rule of Napoleon's sister Elise and her husband, Felix Baciocchi (an amateur violinist), Paganini became second violinist in the new court orchestra, the prince's teacher and quartet partner, and eventually court soloist.

From 1810 to 1828 Paganini was a soloist in Italy (Milan, 1813; Venice, 1816; Rome, 1818; Naples, 1819, remaining in the South until fall 1821, also visiting Palermo in 1819–20), establishing himself as Italy's greatest violinist, at least in regard to technique, although this virtuosity was often used in ways offensive to the musically high-minded, such as playing complicated pieces entirely on one or two strings (e.g., his Napoleon Sonata of 1807, composed for the G string) and the imitation of animals and other natural sounds. In 1822, his declining health diagnosed as the result of long-standing syphilis, he began a long, brutal, and unsuccessful treatment with mercury and opium that transformed him into the gaunt figure that later audiences found so romantic. He returned to concertizing early in 1827, receiving the Order of the Golden Spur from the Pope (the attendant title of cavaliere meant a great deal to him). In March 1828 he made his long-planned and astoundingly successful appearance in Vienna.

By most accounts his playing had now matured so that expressivity was equal to technique. With few exceptions Vienna's extraordinary reception was repeated everywhere; 1829–31, toured Germany; March–April 1831, first Paris appearance, then playing in London and touring Britain, which he did frequently through 1834 with occasional returns to Paris. Eventually his vogue seemed to weaken, with audiences declining and criticism rising, less of his art than of his character, especially his avarice (although this was balanced by acts of generosity, such as his commissioning of *Harold in Italy* from the impoverished Berlioz and a later gift of 20,000 francs). He returned to Italy in 1834, settling in Parma. His health continued to decline, and he lost his voice in 1838. He spent his last years mainly in Nice.

Paganini composed mostly for his own use, publishing little in his lifetime, most notably the 24 capricci op. 1 (published 1820, composed years earlier); nos. 1 and 2 of the 6 surviving concertos were published in 1851; some works are still unpublished, others lost or incompletely preserved.

Bibl.: Alan Kendall, *Paganini: A Biography* (London, 1982). Alberto Cantù, *I 24 capricci e i 6 concerti di Paganini: Guida e analisti* (Turin, 1980).

Page, Hot Lips [Oran Thaddeus] (b. Dallas, 27 Jan. 1908; d. New York, 5 Nov. 1954). Jazz trumpeter, singer, and bandleader. He was a soloist with Walter

Page (1928–31; they are not related), Bennie Moten (1931–35, including the recording *Milenbery Joys,* 1932), and briefly Count Basie (1936). Except for periods with Bud Freeman, clarinetist Joe Marsala (both 1940), and Artie Shaw (1941–42, including the recording *St. James Infirmary,* 1941), from 1937 he led swing big bands and combos, and often played in jam sessions. His recordings as a leader include *Pagin' Mr. Page* (1944) and a rhythm-and-blues pairing with Pearl Bailey, *The Hucklebuck/Baby It's Cold Outside* (1949). He performed at the Paris Jazz Fair (1949) and later toured Europe (1951, 1952).

Page, Jimmy [James], **(Patrick)** (b. Middlesex, 9 Jan. 1945). Rock guitarist and songwriter. After work as a studio musician in London and with Jeff Beck in the Yardbirds, in 1968 he formed Led Zeppelin with singer Robert Plant (b. 1947), bassist-keyboardist John Paul Jones (b. 1946), and drummer John Bonham (1947–80). Performing songs authored mainly by Plant and Page, the band established a hard rock sound which served as the model for the heavy metal movement; their popular recordings included "Stairway to Heaven" (1971) and the soundtrack to *The Song Remains the Same* (1976). After the group's dissolution in 1980, both Page (*Outrider,* 1988) and Plant (*Now and Zen,* 1988) released solo albums.

Page, Patti [Fowler, Clara Ann] (b. Tulsa, Okla., 8 Nov. 1927). Popular singer. She began performing on radio in Oklahoma, then on *The Breakfast Club* and in nightclubs in Chicago. From 1948 she made recordings; her early hits were country songs (most notably Pee Wee King's "Tennessee Waltz," 1950), while later she turned to popular material (including "How Much Is That Doggie in the Window," 1953; "Hush, Hush, Sweet Charlotte," 1965).

Page, Walter (Sylvester) (b. Gallatin, Mo., 9 Feb. 1900; d. New York, 20 Dec. 1957). Jazz double bass player and bandleader. While also playing tuba, he led the Blue Devils from 1925 until Bennie Moten hired his sidemen, including Count Basie, Hot Lips Page, and Jimmy Rushing. Walter Page himself joined Moten (1931–34) and Basie (1934, 1936–42, 1946–49). *Swinging at the Daisy Chain,* recorded by Basie's big band, exemplifies Page's firm walking double bass lines. Occasionally he played solos, as on *Pagin' the Devil,* recorded by the Kansas City Six (1938). He accompanied Hot Lips Page (1949) and Rushing (1951), then worked mainly as a free-lance in New York.

Pahissa, Jaime (b. Barcelona, 7 Oct. 1880; d. Buenos Aires, 27 Oct. 1969). Composer. Trained as an architect; studied composition with Morera. Gave a concert of his works in 1905; the opera *La presó de Lleida* was staged the following year and ran for 100 performances. Taught conducting and composition at the Municipal Music School, Barcelona. He emigrated to Argentina in 1937, continuing there his activities as a teacher and composer. His works include about a dozen operas, many of which date from after his move to Latin America; overtures, tone poems, and other orchestral music, often based on Catalan folk material; incidental music; chamber works; piano pieces; and songs. He also published several books, the best known of which is his biography of Manuel de Falla (1947; trans. English, 1954).

Paik, Nam June (b. Seoul, 20 July 1932). Composer. He studied at the Univ. of Tokyo (1952–56), the Univ. of Munich (1956–57), with Fortner at the Freiburg Hochschule für Musik (1957–59), and at the Univ. of Cologne (1958–62). He worked at the Cologne electronic music studios and attended the summer courses in Darmstadt (1957–59). From 1961 until 1964 he was associated with the group Flexus after which he moved to the U.S. Taught at SUNY–Stony Brook (1968), worked for WGBH-TV in Boston (1970), and taught at the California Institute of the Arts in Los Angeles (from 1970). Self-proclaimed influences on his work include Bartók, Schoenberg, Stockhausen, Cage, Schwitters, Marcel Duchamp, and Flexus. Some of his works involve aggressive and even dangerous acts: in *Hommage à John Cage* (2 pianos, 3 tape recorders, projections, live actions with eggs, toy cars, etc.; Düsseldorf, 1959), the 2 pianos are destroyed during the performance; in *Performable Music* (Los Angeles, 1965) the performer must make an incision in his left forearm at least 10 centimeters in length. Other pieces offer less aggressive examples of "action music": in *Variations on a Theme by Saint-Saëns* the pianist plays Saint-Saëns's *Le Cygne* while the cellist dives into an oil drum filled with water. Some works aim at the "sexual emancipation" of music. Some explore the possibilities of television as an art medium: in *TV Bra for Living Sculpture* (1969) the images on miniature television sets (placed over Charlotte Moorman's breasts) vary with the notes she produces on the cello.

Bibl.: John G. Hanhardt, *Nam June Paik* (New York, 1982).

Paine, John Knowles (b. Portland, Maine, 9 Jan. 1839, d. Cambridge, Mass., 25 Apr. 1906). Composer, teacher. Studied music in Portland with a German émigré, Kotzschmar; 1858–61, student, Berlin Hochschule für Musik, with Haupt, Teschner, Wieprecht, Fischer, becoming an accomplished organist and beginning to compose. He settled in Boston, attracting attention with organ recitals and lectures, which led to his appointment as Harvard organist (1862–82) and more significantly to the establishment in 1862 (over much opposition) of the Harvard music department, of which he was the first instructor (professor from 1876, the first in the country). As a composer, he emphasized large, serious genres, including a Mass in D op. 10, whose premiere he conducted with the Berlin Singakademie in 1867, and the oratorio *St. Peter,* whose premiere he conducted in Portland in 1873. He was seen in his own time as having had "classical" and "Romantic" phases as a composer, the latter beginning with his Trio op. 22

and emphasizing the large orchestral and chamber forms. His 2 symphonies (no. 1 in C minor, op. 23, premiered by Theodore Thomas, 1876; no. 2, *In the Spring,* in A, op. 34, 1880) were considered landmarks in American absorption of the high European tradition; also a concert overture *As You Like It* op. 28 (1876), a symphonic poem *The Tempest* op. 31 (1876?), 2 piano trios, and a violin sonata. His incidental music to *Oedipus Rex* (1880–81), especially the prelude, was another high point in his work. His later years were taken up largely with the composition of a grand opera, *Azara* (1886–1900), which he never succeeded in having staged in an opera house. His lectures on music history were published posthumously, ed. Albert A. Howard, as *The History of Music to the Death of Schubert* (Boston, 1907; R. 1971).

Paisiello, Giovanni (b. Roccaforzata, near Taranto, 9 May 1740; d. Naples, 5 June 1816). Composer. He studied at the Jesuit school in Taranto and at the Conservatorio di S. Onofrio, Naples (1754–63). In 1776 became *maestro di cappella* to Catherine II of Russia; in St. Petersburg he composed the court's theater music and directed the court orchestra until 1784, when he left for Naples. In December 1783 he had been nominated as *compositore della musica de' drammi* by Ferdinand IV of Naples. During several months in Vienna he composed his comic opera *Il re Teodoro in Venezia* (given at the Burgtheater in August 1784). Soon after his arrival in Naples his *Antigono,* an opera seria, was given at the Teatro S. Carlo (January 1785). When republican forces captured Naples in 1799, Paisiello was made *maestro di cappella nazionale.* Napoleon Bonaparte, a great admirer of Paisiello's music, made him director of chapel music in Paris from 1802 to 1804. In Naples he was director of sacred and secular music at the courts of Joseph Bonaparte (1806–8) and Joachim Murat (1808–15). Also director (1807–13) of the state college of music founded in Naples by Joseph. When Ferdinand returned to power in 1815, Paisiello was pardoned and retained his court posts.

Paisiello wrote over 80 operas, including *Il duello* (Naples, 1774); *La frascatana* (Venice, 1774); *Demofoonte* (Venice, 1775); *La discordia fortunata* (Venice, 1775); *L'amor ingegnoso* (Padua, 1775); *Socrate immaginario* (Naples, 1775); *Le due contesse* (Rome, 1776); *Gli astrologi immaginari* (St. Petersburg, 1779); *Il matrimonio inaspettato* (Ostrov, 1779); *Il barbiere di Siviglia, ovvero La precauzione inutile* (St. Petersburg, 1782); *Il mondo della luna* (Kammenïy Ostrov, 1782); *La grotta di Trofonio* (Naples, 1785); *Olimpiade* (Naples, 1786); *Le gare generose* (Naples, 1786); *Pirro* (Naples, 1787); *La modista raggiratrice* (Naples, 1787); *L'amor contrastato* (Naples, 1789); *Nina, o sia La pazza per amore* (Caserta, 1789); *I zingari in fiera* (Naples, 1789); *Le vane gelosie* (Naples, 1790); *La locanda* (London, 1791); *Didone abbandonata* (Naples, 1794); *L'inganno felice* (Naples, 1798); and *Proserpine* (Paris, 1803). He also composed cantatas (*Amore vendicato,* Naples, 1786; *Silvio e Clori,* Naples, 1797); oratorios (*La passione di Gesù Cristo,* St. Petersburg, 1783). Also several oratorios, a number of sacred and secular cantatas, several Masses, other liturgical pieces, various occasional works, concertos, 9 string quartets, and violin sonatas.

Bibl.: Michael Robinson, with Ulrike Hoffmann, *Giovanni Paisiello: A Thematic Catalogue of His Works* (Stuyvesant, N.Y., 1991–94). Michael Robinson, *Naples and Neapolitan Opera* (Oxford, 1972). J. L. Hunt, *Giovanni Paisiello: His Life as an Opera Composer* (New York, 1975).

Paix, Jakob (b. Augsburg, 1556; d. after 1623). Composer. Organist from 1576 in Lauingen an der Donau, from 1609 until 1617 at the court in Neuburg an der Donau. His most important works are for keyboard. The majority are intabulations of vocal pieces (motets, songs, etc.), a few by himself but most by other composers, including Palestrina and Lassus. His books also include intabulations of a large number of dances.

Pakhmutova, Alexandra Nikolaievna (b. Beketovka, near Stalingrad, 9 Nov. 1929). Composer. She studied with Shebalin at the Moscow Conservatory, graduating in 1953. Best known for her urban ballads, including "Songs of Turbulent Youth" (1961), "Cuba, My Love" (1962), "A Coward Will Not Play Hockey" (1968), "Sport Heroes" (1972), and "Hope" (1974); other works include a concerto for orchestra (1971) and a trumpet concerto (1955).

Paladilhe, Émile (b. near Montpellier, 3 June 1844; d. Paris, 8 Jan. 1926). Composer. He entered the Paris Conservatory in 1853, where he studied with Halévy (composition), Marmontel (piano), and Benoist (organ), and won first prize for piano. Won the Prix de Rome in 1860 for the cantata *Le Czar Ivan IV.* Succeeded Ernest Guiraud at the Institut de France in 1892. He composed 4 comic operas, *Le passant* (1872), *L'amour africain* (1874), *Suzanne* (1878), and *Diana* (1885); 1 grand opera, *Patrie* (1886); sacred music, including motets, a Stabat Mater (1905), *Messe solenelle de la Pentecôte* (1889), and *Messe de St. François d'Assise* (1905); songs; piano pieces; organ works; 1 symphony.

Palau (Boix), Manuel (b. Alfara de Patriarca, Spain, 4 Jan. 1893; d. Valencia, 18 Feb. 1967). Composer. Studied at the Valencia Conservatory and later, in France, with Koechlin and Bertelin, also having contact with Ravel. Returned to Valencia in 1932 to teach at the conservatory, taking over as director in 1952; also active both as a conductor and as director of the Valencia Institute of Musicology. His compositions show many influences, from impressionism to folk music and atonality, twice winning the National Prize (1927 and 1947). Orchestral works include *Homenaje a Debussy* (1929), 3 symphonies (1945, 1946, 1950), *Concierto dramatico* (with piano; 1948) and *Concierto Levantino* (with guitar); he also wrote chamber works, local-color piano pieces, and songs.

Palazzotto e Tagliavia [Palazotto Tagliavia, Pallazzotti, Palazzotti] **Giuseppe** (b. Castelvetrano, Sicily, ca. 1587; d. after 1633). Composer. He was studying with Antonio Il Verso by 1603; in 1617 he traveled to Naples with the court of the Duke of Osuna, then went to Palermo (1620) and Messina (1631). One of the finest madrigal composers of his time, Palazzotto was influenced by Gesualdo's chromaticism and Monteverdi's *seconda prattica;* published works include 3 books of madrigals (Naples, 1617; Palermo, 1620; Naples, 1632).

Palester, Roman (b. Śniatyñ, 28 Dec. 1907; d. Paris, 25 Aug. 1989). Composer. Studied piano at the Lwów Conservatory with Sołtyosowa and composition at the Warsaw Conservatory with Sikorski after 1925. He earned diplomas in composition and theory there in 1931. Until World War II he worked alternately in Warsaw and Paris. After 1945 he joined the faculty at the Warsaw Conservatory. He moved to Paris in 1948, where he stayed until the end of his life. Through World War II his music showed the influence of Hindemith and current French trends. His often urgent and dramatic language was occasionally infused with elements of Polish folk music (*Kołacze* [Country Cakes], 1942). Through the mid-1950s he grappled with new trends in art music, exploring the principles and devices of serialism. Works during this period indicated a shifting, somewhat more understated sense of drama (*Sonette an Orpheus,* 1951). After the late 1950s Palester's musical style became more individual, exploring texture and color through careful orchestration. Works include 1 opera and 2 ballets. His orchestral music includes concertos (violin, 1941; piano, 1942), symphonies, and one-movement works; a striking early work, *Muzyka symfoniczna* (1930), was lost during the war. His chamber music encompasses standard forms and genres (Divertimento, 1949; *Duo,* 2 violins, 1972). He also wrote choral and solo vocal music; theater and radio music.

Palestine, Charlemagne [Martin, Charles] (b. Brooklyn, N.Y., 15 Aug. 1945). Composer, pianist, video artist, and sculptor. He attended Mannes College (1967–69) and studied electronic music with Subotnick in New York and California; in 1971 he studied gamelan in Indonesia. Drones (perhaps from his experience as a bell ringer at St. Thomas Church, New York, 1962–70) and vocal improvisation similar to that of Indian music form part of his usual style; piano works often require a unique strumming technique; minimalism and the performance art of LaMonte Young also influence his style. Works include a series of *Meditative Sound Environments* (e.g., organ, voice, piano, 1970); *Strumming Music* (piano, 1972–73); other instrumental, vocal, and electronic music.

Palestrina, Giovanni Pierluigi da (b. probably Palestrina, near Rome, between 3 Feb. 1525 and 2 Feb. 1526; d. Rome, 2 Feb. 1594). Composer. A manuscript eulogy gives his age as 68 at the time of his death. It has been suggested that he was born or at least lived from early in life in Rome; a 1537 document at S. Maria Maggiore there includes one "Giovanni da Palestrina" among the choirboys. In 1544 he was installed as organist at S. Agapito Cathedral in Palestrina. He was married in 1547; the couple had three sons, two of whom had pieces printed among their father's works.

With the election of S. Agapito's cardinal as Pope Julius III in 1550, Palestrina was drawn permanently to Rome. He was elevated to maestro at the Capella Giulia in 1551, succeeding Robin Mallapert, a former master from his choirboy years at S. Maria Maggiore. His first publication, a collection of Masses, was issued in 1554; the same year a madrigal of his circulated in a Venetian anthology. In 1555 he joined the papal choir by direct edict of Julius III, but was dismissed several months later on account of being married. The same year he was named *maestro di cappella* of St. John Lateran, a post Lassus had held briefly in 1553; he resigned in 1560 in a dispute over finances for service music, and was engaged at S. Maria Maggiore, where he remained until 1566. In 1564 he led the summer music at the villa of Cardinal Ippolito II d'Este; between 1567 and 1571 he was fully in the employ of Ippolito, teaching also at the Seminario romano during this period. In 1568 he was considered for the chapelmaster's position at Vienna, and the same year began a running exchange on musical matters with Guglielmo Gonzaga, Duke of Mantua; the duke commissioned works from him for his chapel, and on occasion asked for Palestrina's critique of music he himself had written. A bid of employment at Mantua was extended in 1583, but terms were not agreed to.

Palestrina succeeded Animuccia as maestro at the Capella Giulia in 1571, a post he held for the remainder of his life. He lost his wife, two sons, and a brother to the plague between 1572 and 1580; he thought of becoming a priest, but in 1581 married the widow of a Roman furrier. In a 1584 dedication to Pope Gregory XIII of his Song of Songs settings, Palestrina repented for his use of secular texts in earlier madrigals. In 1593 he considered moving back to his native town as maestro, but the plan came to naught.

A 1592 collection of Psalm settings by several prominent composers dedicated to him is evidence of the honor he received while still alive. The years after his death would see his renown expand still further. Theorists such as Artusi and Cerone set him up as a model; the expression "stile del Palestrina" is used by Marco Scacchi in his 1635 defense of the new style currents of the 17th century to denote the *stile antico* as a whole. Fux lauded the composer in his *Gradus ad Parnassum* (1725), while Baini's 1828 biography presents a romanticized image of Palestrina as revered artist. The best-known Palestrina legend, current at least since Agazzari (1607), credits the *Missa Papae Marcelli* with saving church polyphony during the Counter-Reformation; although a movement in this period toward intelligible texts in church music has been documented in some detail, the story can be neither confirmed nor refuted.

Palestrina's works are mainly sacred. There are 104 Masses; parody Masses make up roughly half the total, with his polyphonic models divided evenly between his own compositions and those of other composers. In addition, he composed at least 250 motets (with perhaps 100 more attributed to him in some fashion), 68 offertories, some 65 hymns, 35 Magnificat settings, and several each of Lamentation settings and Litanies. Six books of Masses (containing a total of 41 cycles) and 7 volumes of motets (with 177 works) were printed during his lifetime, while 7 more volumes of Masses were issued between his death and 1601. Individual publications of the offertories and hymns arranged according to the church year appeared late in his life, as did editions of the Magnificats, Lamentations, and Litanies. He also wrote some 140 madrigals, some of which gained considerable renown; there are 2 books for 4 voices (1555 and 1586, the first of these enjoying several reprints) and 2 for 5 voices (1581 and 1594; the latter is a collection of spiritual madrigals). Many other madrigals are scattered about various anthologies.

Bibl.: *G. P. da Palestrina: Werke,* ed. Franz. X. Haberl et al., 33 vols. (Leipzig, 1862–1907). *G. P. da Palestrina: Le opere complete,* ed. Raffaele Casimiri, 32 vols. (Rome, 1939–65, 1973–). Herbert K. Andrews, *An Introduction to the Technique of Palestrina* (London, 1959). Jerome Roche, *Palestrina* (London, 1971). Lewis Lockwood, Introduction to Palestrina, in *Pope Marcellus Mass* (New York, 1975). Alberto Cametti, *Palestrina* (New York, 1979). Karl Gustav Fellerer, *Palestrina-Studien* (Baden-Baden, 1982). Lino Bianchi and Giancarlo Rostirolla, eds., *Convegno internazionale di studi palestriniani* (Palestrina, 1991). Jean-François Gautier, *Palestrina, ou, L'esthétique de l'âme du monde* (Arles, 1994). Michael Heinemann, *Giovanni Pierluigi da Palestrina und seine Zeit* (Laaber, 1994).

Pallavicino, Benedetto (b. Cremona, 1551; d. Mantua, 26 Nov. 1601). Composer. Active by 1584 at the Gonzaga court in Mantua, as *maestro di cappella* from 1596. His numerous and widely popular madrigals often show a close relationship between text and music. Other works include Masses, polychoral motets, Psalm settings.

Bibl.: Edition, Peter Flanders and Kathryn Bosi Monteath, *CMM* 89 (1982–). Peter Flanders, *A Thematic Index to the Works of Benedetto Pallavicino,* Music Indexes and Bibliographies, no. 11 (Hackensack, N.J., 1974).

Pallavicino [Pallavicini], **Carlo** (b. Salò, Lake Garda; d. Dresden, 29 Jan. 1688). Composer. He was *organista ai concerti* at S. Antonio, Padua, 1665–66; his first 2 operas, *Demetrio* and *Aureliano,* were produced in Venice at this time. He was appointed Vice-Kapellmeister at the electoral court in Dresden in 1667 under Schütz's direction, becoming Kapellmeister in 1672 but leaving the following year to become *maestro dei concerti* at S. Antonio. In 1674 he became *maestro di coro* of the Ospedale degli incurabili, Venice, returning to Dresden as court Kapellmeister in 1685. Pallavicino was one of the most popular opera composers in Venice from about 1675 to 1685; his *Vespasiano* (Venice, 1678) was a particular favorite.

Palm, Siegfried (b. Wuppertal, 25 April 1927). Cellist. Studied under his father, and later with Enrico Mainardi; played in the Lübeck city orchestra (1945–47) and with the radio symphonies of Hamburg (1947–62) and Cologne (1962–67). Taught from 1962 at the Cologne Hochschule, serving as director from 1972; from 1976 to 1981 he acted as administrator of the Deutsche Oper, Berlin. Known as a soloist and chamber player in performances of avant-garde music.

Palma, Athos (b. Buenos Aires, 7 June 1891; d. Miramar, 10 Jan. 1951). Composer. Studied at the National Conservatory; lived from 1904 to 1914 in Europe; returning to Argentina, studied medicine as well as letters before focusing on composition and teaching. Served as professor at the National Conservatory and as an official with both the Teatro Colón and the National Council of Education. Works include the operas *Nazdah* (1924) and *Los hijos del sol* (1928; based on Inca myth); the tone poems *Jardines* and *Los hijos del sol;* a string quartet (1915); sonatas for violin and cello (1924, 1912); and songs. He also wrote 2 music texts, the 5-volume *Teoria razonada de la música* and the *Tratado completo de armonia.*

Palmer, Horatio R(ichmond) (b. Sherburne, N.Y., 26 Apr. 1834; d. Yonkers, N.Y., 15 Nov. 1907). Composer, educator, and conductor. Taught at the Rushford Academy in New York (1855–65), where he had been a student. Moved to Chicago, and directed the Second Baptist Church choir. He published the monthly magazine *Concordia.* Compiled *The Song Queen* (1867), which was very successful and resulted in other compilations, including *The Song Monarch* (1874), *The Choral Union* (1884). Returned to New York in 1881. Director of music at Chautauqua, 1888–1901. Composed much music; only 2 hymns, "Yield Not to Temptation" (1868) and "Vincent" (1887), achieved popularity.

Bibl.: William Smythe Babcock Mathews, ed., *A Hundred Years of Music in America* (Chicago, 1889; R: 1970).

Palmer, Robert (Moffat) (b. Syracuse, N.Y., 2 June 1915). Composer. He studied piano and then composition at the Eastman School under Rogers; further work in composition was under Copland, Harris, and Quincy Porter. After a few years at the Univ. of Kansas (1940–43), he taught until retirement at Cornell (1943–80). His compositions have been commissioned by the Koussevitzky Foundation (String Quartet no. 2, 1942), the Elizabeth Coolidge Sprague Foundation (Piano Quintet, 1950), and the Lincoln Center (*Centennial Overture,* orchestra, 1965). The music of Bartók was especially influential on his developing style, along with that of Hindemith and Milhaud; his experience as a jazz pianist is also reflected in his works (for example, in the *Toccata ostinato* for piano in 13/8 time, but inspired by boogie-woogie). Other works include 2 symphonies and a concerto (2 pianos, 2 percussionists, strings, and brass, 1984); *Choric Song and Toccata* (band, 1968); sonata for trumpet and piano (1972), 2 sonatas for cello (1978, 1983), and other chamber music; preludes, sonatas, and other piano music; *Nabuchodonosor* (tenor, bass, male choir, woodwinds, percussion, and 2 pianos, 1964), *Carmina amoris* (soprano, clarinet, viola, and piano, 1951), and other vocal music.

Palmgren, Selim (b. Björneborg [now Pori], 16 Feb. 1878; d. Helsinki, 13 Dec. 1951). Composer. From 1895 to 1899 he studied piano and composition with Wegelius, Petzet, Melcer, and Ekman at the Helsinki Conservatory. Subsequently he went to Germany and Italy, studying with Ansorge, Berger, and Busoni. He returned to Finland and conducted the Finnish Students' Choral Society and the Åbo Musical Society. Beginning in 1912 he earned his living as a composer and pianist. After touring in Europe and the U.S., he accepted a position on the faculty at the Eastman School of Music in 1923. From 1936 to 1951 he served on the faculty at the Sibelius Academy in Helsinki. His style is tonally centered and lyrical, often making dramatic use of contrasts. Many pieces are miniatures, in a descriptive or melodic style. His works include 1 opera, 5 piano concertos (1904–40), a violin concerto (1945), and other one-movement works. Some 260 pieces for piano include the *Fantasy* op. 6 and *24 Etudes* op. 77. He wrote around 200 songs for solo voice or combinations of voices.

Palmieri, Eddie [Eduardo] (b. New York City, 1936?). Salsa bandleader and pianist. In the 1950s he played with bands including that of Tito Rodriguez; from 1961 to 1968 led La Perfecta, one of the most successful salsa bands. In the 1970s he experimented with rhythm-and-blues and jazz idioms; his popular recordings include "Muñeca" (1965), *Justicia* (1969), and *Sun of Latin Music* (1974).

Palombo, Paul (Martin) (b. Pittsburgh, 10 Sept. 1937). Composer. After study at Indiana Univ. of Pennsylvania, Peabody Conservatory, and the Eastman School (Ph.D., 1969, under Barlow and Rogers), he taught at the Cincinnati College-Conservatory, where he founded and directed the electronic music studio (1969–78). In 1978 he became director of the school of music at the Univ. of Washington in Seattle; and in 1981 dean of the college of Fine Arts at the Univ. of Wisconsin (Stevens Point). Among his works are the ballet *Morphosis* (tape, 1970); *Metathesis* (flute, oboe, double bass, and harpsichord, 1970); and *Moody, Moody Blues* (voices and dance band, 1981).

Paniagua y Vasques, Cenobio (b. Tlalpujahua, 30 Oct. 1821; d. Córdoba, Veracruz, 2 Nov. 1882). Composer. Violinist in Morelia Cathedral orchestra, which his uncle conducted. Moved with his uncle to Mexico City; joined the orchestra of the metropolitan cathedral. His first opera, *Catalina de Guisa* (composed in 1845), was first performed in 1859 in Mexico City. Though sung in Italian, it was the first Mexican opera ever performed, establishing a school of operatic composition in Mexico. Composed one other opera (*Pietro d'Abano,* 1863), much sacred music, including about 70 Masses.

Bibl.: Robert Murrell Stevenson, *Music in Mexico* (New York, 1952; 2nd ed., 1971).

Panizza, Ettore (Héctor) (b. Buenos Aires, 12 Aug. 1875; d. Milan, 27 Nov. 1967). Composer and conductor. Studied at the Verdi Conservatory, Milan; made his conducting debut at Rome in 1899; later led opera performances throughout Europe. Conducted at La Scala during 1921–29 (as Toscanini's assistant), 1930–32, and 1946–48. Appeared frequently at the Teatro Colón in Buenos Aires (where his father had been cellist) from 1921, and also in Chicago (1922–24), New York (1934–42), and Berlin (1938). He composed several operas, including *Il fidnazato del mare* (1897), *Aurora* (1908), and *Bisanzio* (Genoa, 1939), as well as orchestral works, chamber music, and songs; he also translated Berlioz's *Traité d'instrumentation* into Italian (1912) and wrote a 1952 autobiography.

Panufnik, Andrzej (b. Warsaw, 24 Sept. 1914; d. Twickenham, 27 Oct. 1991). Composer. His father was a Polish violin maker and his mother was an English violinist. Under the tutelage of his mother, he composed his first works before he was 10 years of age. From 1932 through 1936 he went on to study composition at the Warsaw Conservatory with Sikorski. He traveled to Vienna and studied conducting with Weingartner from 1937 to 1938. Through 1939 he also spent time in Paris, working with Gaubert there, and in London. He returned to Warsaw, appearing as conductor of the Warsaw Symphony. During the Nazi occupation he was part of underground concerts. After the war he conducted the Kraków Philharmonic and the Warsaw Philharmonic. In 1954 he moved to England and in 1961 became a nationalized British citizen, working there both as composer and conductor; he was knighted in 1991.

His early music explored avant-garde techniques such as serialistic treatment of motives (*Krąg kwintowy* [Circle of 5ths], later renamed *12 Miniature Studies,* 1947) and the use of quarter tones and graphic notation. His music before 1944 was lost during the political turmoil of that year, though he reconstructed the Piano Trio (1934), the *5 Polish Peasant Songs* (1940), and the *Uwertura tragiczna* (Tragic Overture, 1942). After 1948 his compositional style saw decreased experimentation. From 1954 through the early 1960s he did little composing, working primarily as a conductor and revising some of his earlier works. By the mid-1960s, though, Panufnik's musical language evidenced a renewed vigor as devices he had cultivated earlier, such as motivic development and proportionate formal designs, reemerged in his works.

He wrote 1 ballet and much orchestral music (*Sinfonia votiva,* 1981; Symphony no. 9, 1987; Symphony no. 10, 1988), including many programmatic or descriptive pieces (*Sinfonia rustica,* 1948, rev. 1955; *Autumn music,* 1962, rev. 1965; *Sinfonia mistica,* 1977) as well as concertos (piano, 1962, recomposed 1972; *Concertino,* percussion, strings, 1980; bassoon concerto, 1985; cello concerto, 1991). His choral music is for various combinations of voice and instruments (*Winter Solstice,* soprano, baritone, chorus, 3 trumpets, 3 trombones, timpani, glockenspiel, 1972). He also composed chamber works (String Quartet no. 1, 1976; no. 2, 1980; no. 3, Wycinanki, 1990; string sextet, 1988), piano music (*Pentasonata,* 1984).

Bibl.: Andrzej Panufnik, *Composing Myself* (London, 1987).

Paolo da Firenze [Paolo Tenorista, Paulus de Florentia] (d. Arezzo, Sept. 1419). Composer. His surviving works reveal an awareness of both Italian and French styles and are sometimes traditional, sometimes more progressive. Many pieces are stylistically similar to the works of Landini. Extant are 11 madrigals, over 35 *ballate* (15 of doubtful authenticity), and 2 sacred compositions.

Bibl.: *Polyphonic Music of the Fourteenth Century,* 9 (1975) [authentic secular works], 12 (1976) [sacred works]. B. Brumana, G. Ciliberti, "Nuove fonte per lo studio dell'opera di Paolo da Firenze," *RIM* 22 (1987): 3–33.

Papaioannou, Yannis Andreou (b. Cavala, 6 Jan. 1911; d. Athens, 11 May 1989). Composer. His formal training in music included piano lessons with Laspopoulou and composition lessons with Kontis at the Hellenis Conservatory from 1922 to 1934. He received a UNESCO fellowship in 1949 and traveled to music centers throughout Europe (studying, for instance, with Honegger in Paris). In 1953 he joined the faculty at the Hellenic Conservatory, teaching counterpoint and composition. He was an influential figure among young composers through his own exploration and advocacy of recent trends in western Europe. His early music bore the influence of his study in France in its careful use of orchestral colors and movement away from functional tonality. His works frequently included references to native folk music. By the late 1940s his music had come under the influence of serialism. He also began to experiment with sound clusters and quarter tones. He wrote much orchestral music, including concertos (Concerto for piano, 1950; Concerto for violin and chamber orchestra, 1971; Concerto for violin, piano, and orchestra, 1979) and descriptive pieces (*Koursarikoi horoi* [Corsair Dances], 1952). He also wrote chamber music and many vocal pieces, among them works for chorus and orchestra as well as for chamber ensemble and solo voice (*To kardhiochtypi* [The Heartbeat], 1959).

Papandopulo, Boris (b. Bad Honneft am Rhein, 25 Feb. 1906; d. Zagreb, 16 Oct. 1991). Composer. Studied composition at the Zagreb Academy of Music with Bersa and conducting at the New Vienna Conservatory under Fock. He then worked as a conductor in Zagreb, Rijeka, Sarajevo, and Split, primarily with opera, though occasionally in orchestral settings. His music often incorporates elements of folk song (*Muka gospodina našega Isukrsta* [The Passion of Our Lord Jesus Christ], oratorio, 1935). His compositional choices remained eclectic throughout his career, drawing easily from different musical styles. Beginning in the late 1940s he focused on vocal works and explored serialism somewhat (*Dodekafonski concert,* 2 pianos, 1961). His music includes stage works (ballets and operas), concertos (harpsichord, 1962; 4 timpani, 1969; Concerto grosso, 1971), chamber music, and vocal pieces.

Papineau-Couture, Jean (b. Montreal, 12 Nov. 1916). Composer. Grandson of the Montreal composer and conductor Guillaume Couture (d. 1915). He studied in Montreal and graduated in 1941 from the New England Conservatory, where his teachers included Quincy Porter; subsequently he studied with Boulanger at the Longy School (Cambridge, Mass.), in Wisconsin, and in California; he had contact with Stravinsky in the mid-1940s while a guest with other Boulanger pupils at the ranch of an American patron (Arthur Sachs). He taught piano at the College Jean de Brébeuf in Montreal in 1943, and in 1945 became director of piano studies there; in addition he taught at the provincial conservatory in Montreal (1946–63) and the Univ. of Montreal (from 1951; dean from 1968 to 1973). He was active in many organizations promoting music education and contemporary music (president of the Montreal Center of Jeunesse Musicales, 1956–64; founding member and president of the Société de musique contemporaine de Québec, 1966–72; founding member and later president of the Canadian Music Center). His early works were tonal and neoclassical (Concerto for violin and chamber orchestra, 1951–52); later he explored atonality (the Suite for solo violin, 1956, is one of the few serial works), Stravinsky's rhythmic language, and Varèse's approach to timbre. He also wrote music for pantomimes and puppet shows; more than 20 orchestral works, including *Clair-obscur* (commissioned by the Montreal Symphony, 1986); chamber music (*Le débat du coeur et du corps du Villon,* speaker, cello, and percussion; 1977); piano and harpsichord pieces; choral music and songs.

Paradies [Paradisi], **(Pietro) Domenico** (b. Naples, 1707; d. Venice, 25 Aug. 1791). Composer. He reportedly studied with Porpora. His early operas were *Alessandro in Persia* (Lucca, 1738) and *Il Decreto di Fato* (Venice, 1740). He tried his fate in London (from 1746), but his opera *Fetone* was a failure. During the 1750s he composed songs for pasticcios; he also gradually became known as a leading teacher of voice, keyboard, and harmony. He is remembered chiefly for his harpsichord works, especially the 12 *Sonate di gravicembalo* (London, 1754; ed. in *Le trésor des pianistes* 14, Paris, ?1870). He also composed concertos and variations for keyboard. He returned to Italy shortly before his death.

Paradis [Paradies], **Maria Theresia von** (b. Vienna, 15 May 1759; d. Vienna, 1 Feb. 1824). Composer, pianist, and singer. She was blinded as a child, and later received instruction in piano from Leopold Kozeluch and in composition from Antonio Salieri and Abbé Vogler. After 1774 she received a pension from the imperial court; from 1783 to 1786 she made concert tours that included London, Salzburg, Frankfurt, Berlin, Prague, and Paris. Mozart probably composed his K. 456 piano concerto for her. In Paris she appeared both as pianist and as singer at the Concert spirituel in 1784. She composed 3 German operas (*Rinaldo und Alcina,* Prague, 1797 [lost]); several cantatas (a lost *Trauerkantate auf Leopold den Gütigen,* Vienna, 1792); songs; and instrumental music. She was a prominent teacher of keyboard and singing, and founded a school of music.

Bibl.: Heinrich Ullrich, "M. T. Paradis: Werkverzeichnis," *BzMw* 5 (1963): 117–54.

Paray, Paul (M. A. Charles) (b. Le Tréport, 24 May 1886; d. Monte Carlo, 10 Oct. 1979). Conductor and composer. Studied organ as a youth; enrolled at the Paris Conservatoire in 1904, winning the Prix de Rome in 1911. He served as assistant conductor of the Concerts Lamoureux (1920–23), then as director (1923–28), later leading the Monte Carlo Orchestra (1928–33) and the Concerts Colonne (1933–40, 1944–52). Conducted the Detroit Symphony from 1952 to 1963, and was active as a guest conductor up to the time of his death. His compositions include a Mass for the 500th anniversary of the death of Joan of Arc (1931; revived 1956); 2 symphonies (1935, 1940); the ballet *Artemis troublée* (1922); chamber music; and piano works.

Parepa(-Rosa), Euphrosyne [De Boyescu, Parepa] (b. Edinburgh, 7 May 1836; d. London, 21 Jan. 1874). Soprano. Debut in 1855 as Amina in *La sonnambula.* First London performance as Elvira in *I puritani* (1857). Tour of U.S. with Carl Rosa (1865), whom she married in February 1867. Together they formed an opera company (1867) in which she sang leading roles.

Parish Alvars, Elias [Parish, Eli] (b. Teignmouth, 28 Feb. 1808; d. Vienna, 25 Jan. 1849). Harpist and composer. Early teachers were Dizi and Bochsa; later studied with Labarre. After 1834, spent most of his time in Vienna. Embarked on a long concert tour of the Far East (1838–42). Appointed chamber musician to the emperor in Vienna (1847). Was associated with Mendelssohn; Berlioz and Liszt were enthusiastic about his playing. Compositions include 1 symphony, 2 piano concertos, 2 harp concertos, many other pieces.

Parisot, Aldo (Simoes) (b. Natal, Brazil, 30 Sept. 1920). Cellist. Studied cello and architectural engineering at Rio; enrolled at Yale in 1946, and was a soloist with the Boston Symphony at Berkshire in 1947; served as principal cellist of the Pittsburgh Symphony in 1949 and 1950. He taught at Yale from 1958, and at Mannes College (1962–66), the New England Conservatory (1966–70), and at Banff (1981–83); then on the faculty at the Manhattan and Juilliard schools. Renowned for his work in both the standard repertory and in new music. In 1977 he established a cello competition in Brazil.

Parkening, Christopher (William) (b. Los Angeles, 14 Dec. 1947). Guitarist. Studied at the Univ. of Southern California and with Segovia, Castelnuovo-Tedesco (whose Second Concerto he premiered in 1966), and Pepe and Celedonio Romero; made his debut in 1963, and performed with the Los Angeles Philharmonic in 1964. He later taught at USC. He has made numerous recordings and has toured extensively; several of his guitar transcriptions have been published.

Parker, Charlie [Charles, Jr.; Bird; Yardbird] (b. Kansas City, Kans., 29 Aug. 1920; d. New York, 12 March 1955). Jazz alto saxophonist and bandleader. He toured as a soloist in the big bands of Jay McShann (1940–42), Earl Hines (1942–43), and Billy Eckstine (1944) while also playing in New York in jam sessions from which the bop style emerged. He worked in bop combos as a leader and a sideman with Dizzy Gillespie (1945–46) before suffering a breakdown resulting in part from alcoholism and heroin addiction. He resumed working in 1947, principally leading small groups; among his sidemen were Miles Davis, Kenny Dorham, Red Rodney, Al Haig, John Lewis, and Max Roach. His hedonistic life-style, leading to an early death, became legendary, and it is portrayed in the movie *Bird* (1988), which largely ignores Parker's intellectual and musical brilliance. Basing his performances on standard chord progressions, Parker invented endlessly changing melodies which expressed the subtlest nuances of accentuation, implied harmony, and rhythmic placement. His melodic materials were largely of his own invention, but drew in part from blues-based Kansas City jazz; he also wittily inserted quotations from completely unrelated genres. His recordings with Gillespie include *Groovin' High, Shaw 'Nuff, Salt Peanuts, Hot House* (all 1945); as a leader, *Billie's Bounce, Now's the Time, Koko* (all 1945), *Yardbird Suite, Ornithology, A Night in Tunisia* (all 1946), *Donna Lee, Embraceable You, Klactoveedsedstene, Scrapple from the Apple* (all 1947), *Bloomdido* (1950), *Au Privave, Blues for Alice* (both 1951); with Jazz at Massey Hall, *Quintet of the Year* (1953).

Bibl.: Robert Reisner, *Bird: The Legend of Charlie Parker* (New York, 1962; R: 1975). Ross Russell, *Bird Lives: The High Life and Hard Times of Charlie "Yardbird" Parker* (New York, 1973). Thomas Owens, "Charlie Parker: Techniques of

Improvisation" (diss., UCLA, 1974). Gary Giddins, *Celebrating Bird: The Triumph of Charlie Parker* (New York, 1987).

Parker, Horatio (William) (b. Auburndale, Mass., 15 Sept. 1863; d. Cedarhurst, N.Y., 18 Dec. 1919). Composer, teacher. At 14 had piano and organ lessons from his mother, then studied in Boston with Chadwick (composition), Orth (piano), and Emery (theory); 1880–82, church organist, Dedham, Mass.; began to compose at 15; 1882–85, student, Munich Conservatory, with Rheinberger (organ, composition) and Abel (conducting); he began to compose sizable choral works and orchestral pieces, several of which were performed there. From 1886 to 1893, in New York City, where he taught at several schools and was church musician at several churches; continued to produce cantatas and other choral works, including considerable church music, winning a prize from the National Conservatory (1893), where he taught counterpoint, for *The Dream King and His Love* (1891). His best-known work, the oratorio *Hora novissima* (to an English text by his mother, based on Latin poems), was premiered under his baton in New York in 1893 and widely performed. Organist and choirmaster, Trinity Church, Boston, 1893–1902; from 1894, professor of music theory, and from 1904 dean, School of Music, Yale; 1895–1918, conducted the newly organized New Haven Symphony; 1903–14, conducted the New Haven Choral Society; 1902–10, organist and choirmaster, St. Nicholas's, New York. The successful performance of *Hora novissima* that he conducted at the Three Choirs Festival (Worcester, 1899) led to the festival's commissioning of *A Wanderer's Psalm,* whose premiere he conducted at Hereford (1900); for the Norwich Festival he composed *A Star Song* (1902). He reached a second peak of attention with his two operas, both of which won $10,000 prizes and productions: *Mona* from the Metropolitan Opera (4 performances, 1912) and *Fairyland* from the National Association of Music Clubs (6 performances, Los Angeles, 1915). His arduous professional activities (he did much of his composing while commuting by train among his various posts) exacerbated his poor health; he died of pneumonia as he was beginning a trip to the West Indies for his health. He composed only a few orchestral and chamber works after his student days, including his Organ Concerto (1902), but published much organ music, songs, hymns. He is now chiefly remembered as Charles Ives's academic teacher.

Bibl.: George W. Chadwick, *Horatio Parker* (New Haven, 1921; R: 1971). William Kearns, *Horatio Parker, 1863–1919: His Life, Music, and Ideas* (Metuchen, N.J., 1990).

Parratt, Walter (b. Huddersfield, 10 Feb. 1841; d. Windsor, 27 Mar. 1924). Organist. Studied with his father; at age 11, became organist at Armitage Bridge. Succeeded Stainer at Magdalen College, Oxford (1872); succeeded Elvey at St. George's Chapel, Windsor (1882). Received B.Mus. from Oxford (1873). Named chief professor of organ at the Royal College of Music when it opened in 1883. Knighted in 1892; Master of the Queen's Musick, 1893. Succeeded Parry as Chair of Music at Oxford (1908–18). Dean of music at London Univ., 1916.

Bibl.: Donald Francis Tovey and Geoffrey Parratt, *Walter Parratt, Master of Music* (London, 1941).

Parris, Robert (b. Philadelphia, 21 May 1924). Composer. He first studied music education at the Univ. of Pennsylvania; turned to composition at Juilliard under Mennin and Bergsma (1945–48); and had further work with Copland and Ibert at the Berkshire Music Center (1950–51) and with Honegger in Paris (1952–53). He taught briefly at Washington State College (1948–49) and the Univ. of Maryland (1961–62), and at the George Washington University (from 1963). He wrote music criticism for Washington, D.C., newspapers intermittently from 1958 to 1978. His works are often expressionistic and highly chromatic; he has also employed serial procedures. He wrote concertos (7 for piano; *The Phoenix,* for timpani, commissioned by the Detroit Symphony in 1969) and other orchestral music (*Chamber Music for Orchestra,* 1984); some 50 chamber works (*The Book of Imaginary Beings II,* clarinet, violin, viola, cello, and 2 percussionists, 1983; 3 duets for electric guitar and amplified harpsichord, 1984); choral music; and songs with ensemble or piano.

Parrott, Andrew (b. Walsall, England, 10 Mar. 1947). Conductor. Studied at Oxford Univ.; founded the Taverner Choir in 1973, soon thereafter adding the Taverner Consort and Players. He has specialized in historical performance, presenting London's first period instrument B minor Mass and attempting liturgical reconstructions of Monteverdi's Vespers; his ensembles have recorded music ranging from Machaut to Bach. In 1989 he was appointed artistic director of the Kent Opera.

Parrott, (Horace) Ian (b. London, 5 Mar. 1916). Composer. From 1932 to 1934 he studied at the Royal College of Music in London and from 1934 to 1937 at New College, Oxford. In 1940 he earned the D.Mus. from Oxford. He lectured in music in 1937 and 1939 at Malvern College and in 1947 at Birmingham Univ. From 1950 to 1983 he held the honorary Gregynog Chair of Music at the University College of Wales, Aberystwyth. He was active in the study and performance of Welsh music. His own music is tonally centered and sometimes includes aspects of Welsh folk music. His works include 4 operas (*The Black Ram,* Welsh folk opera, 1951–53); ballet music; 5 symphonies (1946–79), concertos (piano, 1948; English horn and orchestra, 1956; 2 guitars, 1973) and much chamber music (Septet, flute, clarinet, string quartet, piano, 1962; *Fantasia,* organ, 1974; *Kaleidescope,* piano trio, 1985).

Parry, (Charles) Hubert (Hastings) (b. Bournemouth, 27 Feb. 1848; d. Rustington, near Littlehampton, 7 Oct. 1918). Composer, teacher. From 1861 a student at Eton, where he had music lessons from George Elvey of St. George's Chapel, Windsor, composing Anglican church music, chamber pieces, piano pieces, and earning his B.Mus. from Oxford at 18 while still at Eton. From 1866, published part songs, solo songs, etc.; then at Oxford, studying with Bennett, Macfarren, and Pierson, continuing to compose and publish; B.A., 1870; then for three years a clerk for Lloyd's of London, also studying with Edward Dannreuther, composing and publishing only sporadically in the early 1870s. His work took on a new impetus around 1878, and his first major orchestral work, the Piano Concerto in F♯ minor (1878–79), brought him public attention when premiered by Dannreuther at the Crystal Palace in 1880. His *Scenes from Shelley's Prometheus Unbound* was not a success at the Gloucester Festival (1880), but initiated a long series of works for the festivals, including his oratorios *Judith* (Birmingham, 1888; to his own libretto), *Job* (Gloucester, 1892), *King Saul* (Birmingham, 1894), cantatas and odes (*L'allegro ed il penseroso,* Norwich, 1890), and orchestral works (First Symphony, Birmingham, 1882; Suite Moderne, Gloucester, 1886). The 1880s and 1890s were the period of his greatest creativity: 4 symphonies, 1878–89; Symphonic Variations, 1897; incidental music; an opera, *Guinevere,* not performed; many choral works (*Blest Pair of Sirens,* 1887); solo songs. From its opening in 1883 he taught at the Royal College of Music, becoming its second director in 1894 until his death; from 1883 also choragus at Oxford and professor there, 1900–1908; 1898, knighted; 1903, after composing for the coronation of Edward VII, made a baronet. After 1900 he produced less music, mostly choral works and in his last years some organ pieces. He published *Studies of the Great Composers* (1886), the widely read *The Art of Music* (1893; expanded 2nd ed., 1896, as *The Evolution of the Art of Music*), *The Music of the Seventeenth Century* (1902) in the Oxford History of Music, a book on J. S. Bach (1909), and *Style in Musical Art* (1911).

Bibl.: Jeremy Dibble, *C. Hubert H. Parry: His Life and Music* (Oxford, 1992).

Parry, John (1) (b. Bryn Cynan [northern Wales], ca. 1710; d. Ruabon, 7 Oct. 1782). Harp player and poet. Blind from birth, at an early age he became a virtuoso on the Welsh triple harp. In 1734 he became Sir Watkin Williams Wynn's harper; later he also served his son, W. W. Wynn III. Handel reportedly praised his playing, as did the Prince of Wales (later King George III). With Evan Williams he published what was probably the first collection consisting entirely of Welsh melodies: *Antient British Music, or, A Collection of Tunes . . .* (London, 1742).

Bibl.: *Welsh National Music and Dance* (London, 1932).

Parry, John (2) (b. Denbigh, 18 Feb. 1776; d. London, 8 Apr. 1851). Instrumentalist and composer. Proficient on many instruments, including clarinet and harp. Moved to London in 1807, where he taught the flageolet. Treasurer of the Royal Society of Musicians. Nicknamed "Bardd Alaw" (master of song). Wrote a book on the harp. Composed theater music; collected and published Welsh melodies (*The Welsh Harper,* 1839–48); incidental music to plays; songs; 5 operatic farces; other pieces.

Parry, John Orlando (b. London, 3 Jan. 1810; d. East Molesey, Surrey, 20 Feb. 1879). Singer. Son of John Parry (2). Studied harp with Bochsa. Known primarily as a baritone and entertainer. Went to Italy in 1833, where he worked with Lablanche. The success of his *Buffo Trio Italiano* (1837) and *Wanted, a Governess* (1840) led him to give up serious singing and turn to comic performance. Retired from public performance in 1853.

Bibl.: Cyril Bruyn Andrews and John A. Orr-Ewing, *Victorian Swansdown: Extracts from the Early Travel Diaries of John Orlando Parry* (London, 1935).

Parry, Joseph (b. Merthyr Tydfil, 21 May 1841; d. Penarth, 17 Feb. 1903). Composer. Family emigrated to Danville, Pa., in 1854; Parry returned frequently to Wales. Won several Eisteddfod prizes in both countries. Entered the Royal Academy of Music (1868), studying with Bennett, Garcia, and Steggall. Received a Mus.B. (1871), Mus.D. (1878) from Cambridge. Professor of music at the Univ. of Wales, 1873–77. Lecturer at the University College of South Wales and Monmouthshire in Cardiff, 1888–1903. Composed 5 operas, 2 oratorios, 5 cantatas, piano music, songs, some orchestral works.

Parsch, Arnošt (b. Bučovice, Moravia, 12 Feb. 1936). Composer. He first studied composition as a youth with Jaromír Podešva. He then studied at the Brno Academy with Ištvan in composition and with Kapr, Kahoutek, and Piňos in music theory. In 1967 he cofounded a young composers' group in Brno. He first explored the compositional possibilities inherent in serialism, retaining motivic techniques but rejecting the dogmatic systematic application of dodecaphony. By 1970 he had also begun to explore and incorporate aleatoric devices in the context of nondevelopmental forms often inspired by visual designs. His works are for a range of genres and ensembles, often including electronic media (*Transposizioni I,* wind quintet, 1967; *Poetica no. 3,* electronics, 1967; *Polyphonie no. 1,* bass clarinet, piano, tape, ca. 1970; *Metamorphoses of Time,* electroacoustic, 1989), as well as for more traditional forces (*Invocation of Love,* 5 songs for tenor and piano, 1987; Concerto, bass clarinet, piano, and orchestra, 1989).

Parsley, Osbert (b. 1511; d. Norwich, 1585). Composer. Spent about 50 years as a singer at Norwich Cathedral. His sacred works include both Latin (Catholic) and English service music. Of these, the Latin compositions are decidedly better. A number of instrumental compositions also survive, including 5 *In Nomines.* One instrumental canon on a plainsong is printed in

Morley's *A Plaine and Easie Introduction to Practicall Musicke* (London, 1597).

Parsons, Robert (b. ca. 1530; d. Newark-upon-Trent, 25 Jan. 1570). Composer. A Gentleman of the Chapel Royal from late 1563 until his premature death by drowning. His works encompass Latin and English sacred music, a few songs with lute or viol accompaniment, and a quantity of instrumental music, most for viol consort (including 5 *In Nomines*). Of the vocal works, the Latin compositions are especially fine.

Pärt, Arvo (b. Paide, 11 Sept. 1935). Composer. From 1958 through 1967 he was employed at Estonian Radio, during which time he pursued composition. He graduated in 1963 from the Tallinn Conservatory, where he studied with Elier. In 1982 he moved to West Berlin. His early music used Prokofiev as a model. Eventually he incorporated serialistic techniques (*Perpetuum mobile,* orchestra, 1963). He freely quoted from specific works of past composers or from past musical styles (Symphony no. 2, 1966). From 1970 his music went even further in this regard, drawing concepts as well as forms from medieval music (*Laul armastatule* [Song for the Beloved], cantata, 1973). He also explored aleatoric devices. His works include orchestral pieces (3 symphonies, 1964, 1966, 1971; *Collage teemal BACH,* 1964; Cello concerto, 1983; *Festina lente,* string orchestra, 1989; *Silovans Song,* string orchestra, 1991), choral music (*Credo,* chorus, piano, orchestra, 1968; *Johannespassion,* 1981; *Psalmen,* voices, instruments, 1984; *Te Deum,* chorus, orchestra, 1985; *7 Magnificat-Antiphones,* chorus, 1988; *Litany,* soloists, chorus, orchestra, 1994), and chamber works (*Kriips ja punkt* [Dash and Dot], chamber ensemble, 1967).

Partch, Harry (b. Oakland, Calif., 24 June 1901; d. San Diego, 3 Sept. 1974). Composer, instrument maker, and performer. He played a variety of instruments while growing up in Arizona as the child of missionary parents. As a composer he was self-taught; developed particular interests in alternate tuning systems and the construction of instruments (mainly idiophones and chordophones) on which his tunings could be conveniently employed; and trained various ensembles (including the Gate 5 Ensemble) to play the music he composed for these instruments and tunings. His theories of tuning (based on the just intonation available in a scale with 43 pitches to the octave) are presented in *Genesis of a Music,* which was first drafted in 1928 but not published until 1949. In about 1930 he destroyed several early works (including some 50 songs, orchestral music, and a string quartet in just intonation); the first work in his mature idiom was *17 Lyrics by Li Po* (voice and adapted viola, 1930–33). In his surviving works he drew on American folklore, immigrant culture, and Christian hymns; African and eastern culture; and music of the Yaqui Indians. His influence extends not only to microtonal composers such as Johnston but also to composers of mixed-media works and to the minimalists. Some works combine his invented instruments with traditional ones (*The Bewitched,* dance satire for soprano and ensemble, 1955); others use only his original instruments (*Oedipus,* dance music after Sophocles, 10 solo voices and instrumental ensemble, 1951; rev. 1952–54). In addition to dance scores he wrote music for films (*The Dreamer That Remains: A Study in Loving,* 1972). Most works involve actors and dancers as well as musicians (*Delusion of a Fury: A Ritual of Dream and Delusion,* Partch, after Japanese and African traditional literature; large ensemble, 1955–56; performed Los Angeles, 1969).

Bibl.: Thomas McGeary, *The Music of Harry Partch: A Descriptive Catalogue* (Brooklyn, N.Y., 1991). Harry Partch, *Bitter Music: Collected Journals, Essays, Introductions, and Librettos,* ed. Thomas McGeary (Urbana, Ill., 1991).

Parton, Dolly (b. Locust Ridge, Tenn., 19 Jan. 1946). Country singer and songwriter. After performing on local television shows in Tennessee, in 1964 she moved to Nashville; from 1967 to 1974 she appeared on Porter Wagoner's television show. She has authored the majority of her best-known recordings, including "Joshua" (1970), "Coat of Many Colors" (1971), and "9 to 5" (1980); from 1977 ("Here You Come Again," by Barry Mann and Cynthia Weil) she has achieved success with popular audiences. She has acted in a number of films.

Partos, Oedoen [Ödön] (b. Budapest, 1 Oct. 1907; d. Tel Aviv, 6 July 1977). Composer. He studied violin at the Budapest Academy from the age of 8 (1918–24); also studied composition with Kodály. From 1924 to 1926 he conducted the Lucerne Stadtsorchester and, from 1926 to 1927, the Budapest Konzertorchester. He then moved to Germany until 1933, where he played at the Jewish Cultural Center. Returning to Hungary he taught violin and composition at the Baku Music Conservatory in 1935 and in 1937 returned to the Budapest Konzertorchester. Frequently toured as a violinist, performing solo repertoire (often 20th-century music) or in ensembles. He became director of the Tel Aviv Academy of Music in 1951, serving as professor there from 1961.

His early music was heavily influenced by Bartók. The rhythms and melodic contours of Jewish folk music pervaded many of the compositions of the 1940s and 1950s (*Yizkor* [In Memoriam], strings, 1947). The early 1960s saw his experimentation with serialism (*Dmuyot* [Images], 1960; *Arpiliyot* [Nebulae], 1966). But by 1970 serialism and other avant-garde techniques had become flexible options, though not compositional dictates. His works include much orchestral music (*Tehilim* [Psalms], chamber orchestra, 1960; *Arabesque,* oboe, chamber orchestra, 1975) and concertos. He also wrote many chamber works (*Iltur* [Improvisation], 12 harps, 1960; *Metamorphoses,* piano, 1973) and vocal music.

Pasatieri, Thomas (b. New York, 20 Oct. 1945). Composer. He entered Juilliard at age 16 on scholarship and received his doctorate in 1969, having studied composition with Giannini and Persichetti; he also studied with Milhaud at the Aspen summer festival in Colorado. His style is conservative and neo-Romantic; the emphasis in his works is on vocal music in the tradition of Puccini and Menotti. Three early operas were produced in workshops on college campuses (1965–67), and his one-act opera *Calvary* (1971) has been especially widely produced in churches. *The Trial of Mary Lincoln* was broadcast on National Educational Television in 1972. Subsequently he received commissions from the Houston Grand Opera (*The Seagull,* performed 1974), the Baltimore Opera (*Inez de Castro,* 1976), the Michigan Opera Theater (*Washington Square,* 1976), and the Univ. of Arizona (*Maria Elena,* 1983). In addition to operas Pasatieri has written a large amount of vocal music, including over 400 songs (*3 Poems of James Agee,* 1974); cantatas (*Permit Me Voyage,* soprano, chorus, and orchestra, 1976); and a Mass (4 solo voices, chorus, and orchestra, 1983). Other works include *Invocations* for orchestra (1968) and piano music.

Pasdeloup, Jules Étienne (b. Paris, 15 Sept. 1819; d. Fontainebleau, 13 Aug. 1887). Conductor. Son of François Pasdeloup, conductor of the Opéra-comique. Won first prize for solfège (1832) and piano (1834) at the Paris Conservatory; studied piano with Laurent and Zimmerman. Taught solfège, piano, vocal ensemble (1855–68) at the Conservatory. Organized concerts of the Société des jeunes élèves du Conservatoire (1853), which became Société des jeunes artistes du Conservatoire impérial de musique (1856). Organized Concerts populaires de musique classique, 1861. Shared with Bazin the directorship of Paris Orphéon. Founded Paris Oratorio Society, 1868.

Pashchenko, Andrey Filippovich (b. Rostov-on-Don, 3 Aug. 1885; d. Moscow, 16 Nov. 1972). Composer. He studied composition with Shteinberg and Vītols at the St. Petersburg Conservatory. With Glazunov and Findeizen he established the Society for the Promotion of Contemporary Russian Music in 1923. He was one of the first composers to feature revolutionary and Soviet topics. His compositions include 17 operas (*The Eagle Revolt,* 1925), cantatas, 16 symphonies, 4 sinfoniettas, 8 symphonic poems, 5 overtures, concertos for violin and cello, 9 string quartets, more than 70 romances, choral music, incidental music, and film scores.

Pashkevich, Vasily (Alexeyevich) (b. ca. 1742; d. St. Petersburg, 9/20 Mar. 1797). Composer and violinist. From 1753 he was violinist in the second orchestra at the St. Petersburg court; in 1783 he began playing with the first orchestra, and in 1789 he was appointed its concertmaster. He composed several theater works for the court; in 1786 he wrote on commission an opera, *Fevey,* with a libretto by Catherine II and others. He is best known for 2 collaborations, one with Canobbio and Sarti on *Nachal'noye upravleniye Olega* [The Early Reign of Oleg] (1790), and another with Martin y Soler on *Fedul s det'mi* [Fedul and the Children] (1791). Other operas include *Skupoy* [The Miser] (after Molière, 1782); *Sanktpeterburgskiy gostiniÿ dvor* [The St. Petersburg Bazaar] (1782); and *Pasha tunisskiy* [The Pasha of Tunis] (1783).

Pasquini, Bernardo (b. Massa da Valdinievole [now Massa e Cozzili], Lucca, 7 Dec. 1637; d. Rome, 21 Nov. 1710). Composer and keyboard player. He was in Rome by 1650, studied with Antonio Cesti and Loreto Vittori, and became organist of S. Maria Maggiore (around 1663), S. Maria in Aracoeli (1664 until his death), and the Oratory of SS. Crocifisso (1664–85); at some point around 1670 he entered the employ of Prince Giambattista Borghese as harpsichordist and music director. Famous in his time as an outstanding keyboard virtuoso, Pasquini frequently performed with Corelli; the two became members, along with A. Scarlatti, of the Arcadian Academy in 1706. He was renowned as a teacher; his students included Francesco Gasparini, Georg Muffat, and possibly D. Scarlatti. He composed a considerable amount of vocal music (much of it lost), including about 17 oratorios, 14 operas, and over 50 cantatas, but his present reputation rests on his keyboard works, especially his suites and variations, most unpublished during his lifetime.

Bibl.: *Bernardo Pasquini: Collected Works for Keyboard,* ed. Maurice Brooks Haynes, *CEKM* 5/1–7 (1964–68). Gordon F. Crain, "The Operas of Bernardo Pasquini" (diss., Yale Univ., 1965). Maurice Brooks Haynes, "The Keyboard Works of Bernardo Pasquini" (diss., Indiana Univ., 1960).

Pasquini, Ercole (b. Ferrara, mid-16th century; d. Rome, between 1608 and 1619). Composer. He studied with Alessandro Milleville, moved to Rome in 1597, and was appointed organist of the Cappella Giulia at St. Peter's (1597–1608) and the Santo Spirito in Saxia (1604). Pasquini's keyboard works (all in manuscript) include toccatas, canzonas, and the earliest known examples of *correntes* in Italy.

Bibl.: *Ercole Pasquini: Collected Keyboard Works,* ed. W. Richard Shindle, *CEKM* 12 (1966).

Pass, Joe [Passalaqua, Joseph Anthony Jacobi] (b. New Brunswick, N.J., 13 Jan. 1929; d. Los Angeles, 24 May 1994). Jazz guitarist. He emerged from an early career marred by drug addiction to record the album *Sounds of Synanon* (1961) and then worked as a studio musician. The unaccompanied album *Virtuoso* (1973) brought widespread recognition; he then toured as a member of Oscar Peterson's groups, an accompanist to Ella Fitzgerald (including the duo album *Take Love Easy,* 1973) and Sarah Vaughan, and a soloist. He also played occasionally in Count Basie's small groups. Pass preferred to play popular songs, endlessly varying their texture and inventing new harmonizations.

Passereau, Pierre (fl. 1509–47). Composer. Little is known of his life, except that in 1509 he was a singer in the chapel of the Duke of Angoulême (later François I). His works include 1 motet and 25 chansons, most published by Attaingnant. The majority of the chansons are lively, freely imitative settings of unsophisticated texts; some were widely popular and were much reprinted and their musical material often reused.

Bibl.: Ed. Georges Dottin, *CMM* 45 (1967).

Pasta [née Negri], **Giuditta (Maria Costanza)** (b. Saronno, near Milan, 28 Oct. 1797; d. Blevio, Como, 1 Apr. 1865). Soprano. Studied with Lotti in Como, with Asioli at the Milan Conservatory. Debuted unsuccessfully in Brescia in 1815, London in 1817. Returned to Italy to study with Scappa; debuted in Venice (1819) with success. Sang first Paris performance of Rossini's *Otello* (as Desdemona); first performances of *La sonnambula* (as Amina, 1831), *Norma* (1831), *Beatrice di Tenda* (1833), and *Anna Bolena* (1830). Known for her exceptional dramatic powers.

Bibl.: Maria Ferranti Giulini, *Giuditta Pasta e i suoi tempi* (Milan, 1935).

Pastorius, Jaco [John Francis, III] (b. Norristown, Pa., 1 Dec. 1951; d. Fort Lauderdale, Fla., 21 Sept. 1987). Jazz electric bass guitarist. His first album as a leader, *Jaco Pastorius* (ca. 1975), demonstrated skilled technique and a new approach to electric bass guitar; his timbre was nearly as broad as that of a double bass and he made harmonics an integral part of his playing. He soon joined the jazz-rock group Weather Report (1976–81, including the album *Heavy Weather,* 1977). He toured with his own group, Word of Mouth (1980–83), but drug abuse increasingly interfered with his career. He died after a brawl at a nightclub.

Pastrana, Pedro de (b. ca. 1480; d. after 1559). Composer. His many positions in Spain included service to Ferdinand the Catholic from 1500, to Charles V from 1527 until 1541 and from 1548, and concurrent service as *maestro de capilla* for Prince Philip from 1547. He was also abbot of the monastery of S. Bernardo from 1529 and *maestro de capilla* to the Duke and Duchess of Calabria in Valencia from about 1533. Works, generally short and simple, include a Mass, Magnificats, motets, Psalms, sacred and secular *villancicos.*

Patiño, Carlos (b. S. Maria del Campo, Cuenca; d. Madrid, 5 Sept. 1675). Composer. In 1628 he became chaplain and *maestro de capilla* of the Monasterio de la Encarnación, Madrid, becoming *maestro de capilla* in the royal chapel in 1633; was appointed to a similar position at the Royal Cloister of the Incarnation in 1660. An important composer of sacred works, especially of polyphonic music for large forces (8–12 voices), he also helped establish a specifically Spanish (rather than Italian) madrigal style.

Patterson, Paul (b. Chesterfield, 15 June 1947). Composer. He studied at the Royal Academy of Music from 1964 to 1968, taking composition lessons with Stoker; then took lessons independently with Bennett until 1970. In 1972 he returned to the Royal Academy of Music as Manson Fellow and helped to organize the Contemporary Music Group there, eventually serving as head of Composition and Contemporary Music Studies. His early works were serial and especially influenced by Bennett. He has visited Poland often; in his spatial use of sound and texture Patterson has been influenced by composers there. From 1970 he utilized more electronic sound sources and felt the impact of Ligeti's music on his own. He has written orchestral music: *Sinfonia* (1983) is in 3 movements and suggests the prototypical early classical sinfonia. Also concertos (trumpet, 1968; horn, 1971; clarinet, 1976; harmonica, 1986; violin, 1992). His choral music includes *Mass of the Sea* (1986), which uses the structure of the Mass, integrated with poetry by Tim Rose Price, and *Te Deum* (1988). Works also include much chamber music (*Rebecca,* speaker, 1 woodwind, trombone, violin, cello, piano, percussion, 1965; *At the Still Point of the Turning World,* chamber ensemble, 1980; string quartet, 1986).

Patti, Adelina [Adela] **(Juana Maria)** (b. Madrid, 19 Feb. 1843; d. Craig-y-Nos, near Brecon, Wales, 27 Sept. 1919). Soprano. Daughter of tenor Salvatore Patti (1800–1869) and soprano Caterina Chiesa Barilli-Patti (d. 1870), sister of soprano Carlotta Patti (1835–89). Family moved to New York when Adelina was a child. Took her first singing lessons with her half-brother Ettore Barilli. She made her debut in New York in 1859, operatic debut in 1859 as Lucia. European debut at Covent Garden (1861) as Amina in *La sonnambula.* First London Aida, 1876. Returned to U.S. in 1881. Sang much with the tenor Nicolini, whom she married in 1886. Retired from the stage in 1895. Farewell concert at Albert Hall, 1 December 1906. She was the highest-paid singer of her time.

Bibl.: F. Hernández Girbal, *Adelina Patti: La reina del canto* (Madrid, 1979).

Patton, Charlie (b. Edward, Miss., 1887; d. Indianola, Miss., 28 April 1934). Blues singer, guitarist, composer. Possessed of a charismatic personality and penchant for excess, he dominated the first generation of Mississippi blues singers. His recordings for Paramount (1929–30) and Vocalion (1934) show his driving, gruff vocal delivery wedded to skillful guitar work, including traditional and bottleneck techniques. He influenced later artists such as Tommy Johnson and Howlin' Wolf, and has been covered by Muddy Waters, Eric Clapton, and others.

Bibl.: Stephen Calt and Gayle Wardlow, *King of the Delta Blues: The Life and Music of Charlie Patton* (Newton, N.J., 1988).

Pauer, Jiří (b. Kladno-Libušín, Bohemia, 22 Feb. 1919). Composer. His first composition lessons came from Šín. From 1943 through 1946 he studied at the

Prague Conservatory with Hába and from 1946 to 1950 at the Prague Academy with Bořkovec. From 1951 to 1952 he worked with the Ministry of Education, Sciences, and Arts in Prague and with Czech Radio. He conducted the National Theater Opera (1953–55, 1965–67, 1979–89), and was director of the Czech Philharmonic (1958–80). During the 1950s he exhibited his socialist political sympathies in the composition of workers' songs. He wrote many stage works; his orchestral pieces include descriptive works (*Furiant,* wind orchestra, 1974). Also wrote opera (*Zuzana Vojířová,* 1958; rev. 1978), chamber music (sonata for violin and piano, 1987; *Nonet no. 2,* 1988–89).

Paul, Les [Polfus, Lester] (b. Waukesha, Wis., 9 June 1915). Popular guitarist, inventor. His performing career included country, jazz, and popular recordings, and his work with his wife, Mary Ford (including "How High the Moon," 1951), met with some success. He is best known, however, for technical innovations which revolutionized the music industry: he invented the solid-body electric guitar and several forms of electric guitar pickup, and pioneered multitrack recording and overdubbing.

Paulus, Stephen (Harrison) (b. Summit, N.J., 24 Aug. 1949). Composer. He studied at the Univ. of Minnesota (Ph.D., 1978) with Paul Fetler and Dominick Argento; founded the Minnesota Composers Forum with Libby (Brown) Larsen in 1973; won a Guggenheim Award in 1982; and has been composer-in-residence with the Minnesota Orchestra and the Atlanta Symphony. His opera *The Postman Always Rings Twice* was composed for the St. Louis Opera Theater (1982) and was later presented at the Edinburgh International Festival (1983). Works include other operas (*The Woodlanders,* 1985; *Harmoonia,* 1991; *The Woman at Otowi Crossing,* 1995); orchestral music (Concerto, violin and orchestra, 1987; *Night Speech,* 1989; *Concertante,* 1989; *Street Music,* 1990; Concerto, violin, cello, and orchestra [The Veil of Illusion], 1994; Concerto, string quartet and orchestra [Three Places of Enlightenment], 1995); instrumental chamber music (*American Vignettes,* cello, piano, 1988); choral music (*Letters for the Times,* based on 17th-century American newspapers and diaries, chorus and chamber ensemble, 1980; *Voices,* chorus, orchestra, 1988; *Whitman's Dream,* chorus, brass, timpani, 1995); songs and song cycles (*Letters from Colette,* soprano, string quartet, piano, percussion, 1986).

Pauman, Conrad [Konrad] (b. Nuremberg, ca. 1410; d. Munich, 24 Jan. 1473). Organist, lutenist, and composer. Blind from birth; his musical training, which led to mastery of many instruments, was sponsored by Ulrich Grundherr and later his son Paul Grundherr. By 1446 he was organist at St. Sebald in Nuremberg, from 1447 town organist. From 1450 he resided in Munich, first serving Duke Albrecht II of Bavaria, from 1460 Duke Sigmund, from 1467 Albrecht IV. Extensive travels after 1450 brought his playing to the attention of many other European rulers, some of whom tried in vain to attract him to their own courts.

Although he left few compositions, these are excellently crafted and were widely known and admired even several centuries after his death. They include 1 Tenorlied and about 7 instrumental pieces, including 4 didactic *fundamenta* for organ. Virdung credited him with the invention of German lute tablature.

Paumgartner, Bernhard (b. Vienna, 14 Nov. 1887; d. Salzburg, 27 July 1971). Composer, conductor, and musicologist. The child of musicians, he took a doctorate in law (1911) before studying musicology with Adler and working as a conductor in Vienna. During the First World War he collected songs of soldiers. Directed the Salzburg Mozarteum (1917–38; 1945–59), where he conducted the Salzburg Mozart Orchestra and founded the Camerata academica; was associated with the Salzburg Festival from its outset and served as president from 1960 to 1971. Among his musicological writings are a history of instrumental ensemble music and several biographies; he edited works of Haydn, Mozart, and Corelli; translated opera librettos and plays (Goldoni, Molière). His compositions include 7 operas and ballets; incidental music; orchestral music; and songs.

Paur, Emil (b. Czernowitz, Bukovina, 29 Aug. 1855; d. Mistek, Moravia, 7 June 1932). Violinist, conductor. Studied at the Vienna Conservatory with Hellmesberger (violin) and Dessofl (1866–70). Named conductor of the Leipzig Stadttheater (1891) after similar appointments in Kassel, Königsberg, and Mannheim. Succeeded Nikisch as conductor of the Boston Symphony Orchestra (1893). Conducted New York Philharmonic Society, 1898–1902. Succeeded Dvořák as director of the National Conservatory in New York (1898–1902). Conductor of the Pittsburgh Symphony (1904–10).

Pavarotti, Luciano (b. Modena, 12 Oct. 1935). Tenor. Worked as a schoolteacher before beginning his vocal studies; trained under Arrigo Pola and Ettore Campogalliani; made his debut at Reggio Emilia in 1961, and his international debut at Amsterdam in 1963, thereafter making numerous appearances throughout Europe. He first sang both at La Scala and in the U.S. in 1965; in 1967 he participated in the centenary celebration of Verdi's Requiem, and in 1968 made his Metropolitan Opera debut. His operatic repertory consists mainly of Italian works, a wide variety of which have been issued on record. Apart from opera he has also gained immense popular appeal through recordings of Italian songs, Christmas carols, and other light repertory, and has appeared often on television and at gala events. He published an autobiography in 1981, and a 1984 documentary on his visit to China won several awards; in 1989 he directed *La favorite* at La Fenice. The 1994 telecast of the second "Three Tenors" concert (with Carreras and Domingo) was seen by over a billion people worldwide.

Bibl.: Luciano Pavarotti with William Wright, *Pavarotti, My Own Story* (Garden City, N.Y., 1981). Martin Mayer, *Grandissimo Pavarotti* (Garden City, N.Y., 1986).

Payne, Anthony (b. London, 2 Aug. 1936). Composer. He studied at the Univ. of Durham. A music critic for the *Daily Telegraph.* He began to focus on composing in the mid-1960s. His works, often bearing evocative, descriptive titles, are for ensembles of varying instrumentation (*The Stones and Lonely Places Sing,* flute, clarinet, piccolo, bass, clarinet, horn, piano, violin, viola, cello, 1979; *The Song of the Clouds,* oboe, 2 horns, piano, strings, 1979–80; *Echoes of Courtly Love,* horn, trumpet, flugelhorn, trombone, tuba, 1987; *Sea Change,* flute, clarinet, harp, string quartet, 1988). Choral music includes *A Little Ascensiontide Cantata* and *A Little Whitsuntide Cantata* (both 1977); *Alleluias and Hockets* (chorus and 10 instruments, 1987); *Hoquetus David* (after Machaut, chorus, orchestra, 1987).

Paz, Juan Carlos (b. Buenos Aires, 5 Aug. 1901; d. there, 25 Aug. 1972). Composer. Studied in his home city with Nery (piano), Beyer (organ), and Gaito and Fornarini (composition), and later with d'Indy at the Schola cantorum, Paris. Established the Grupo renovación in 1929 with Juan José and José María Castro, Gilardi, and Ficher, remaining active in it until 1937; later founded the concert series Nueva música with several other local composers, and was involved with other new-music performing groups. As a composer, Paz initially allied himself to neoclassicism. He turned to twelve-tone composition in the mid-1930s, but later abandoned it. He ceased composing in 1964. He was also a distinguished author; among his several books are *Introduccion de la música de nuestro tiempo* (Buenos Aires, 1952), *Schoenberg, o el fin de la era tonal* (Buenos Aires, 1954), and a compilation of reflections and observations, *Alturas, tensiones, ataques, intensidades* (Buenos Aires, 1972).

Works: *Movimento Sinfónico* (1930), a suite for Ibsen's *Juliano Emperador* (1931), *Passacaglia* (1936; rev. 1953), *Música* (1940), *Rítmica constanta* (1952), *Continuidad* (1960), and *Música para piano y orquestra* (1964), for orchestra; chamber music, including *Tema y transformaciones,* 11 winds (1929), a wind octet (1930), 2 concertos for winds and piano (1932, 1935), 3 *Composiciones dodecaphónicas* (1934, 1935, 1937), 2 string quartets (1938, 1943), *Continuidad 1953,* percussion, *Invención,* string quartet (1961), and *Concreción 1964,* winds; piano works, including 3 sonatas (1923, 1925, 1935), *Tres movimientos de jazz* (1932), *Diez piezas sobre una serie dodecafónica* (1936), and *Núcleos* (1962–64); the song "Abel" (1929) is his only vocal composition.

Bibl.: Jacobo Romano, *Juan Carlos Paz: Tribulaciones de un músico* (Buenos Aires, 1970). Michelle Tabor, "Juan Carlos Paz: A Latin American Supporter of the International Avant-Garde," *Latin American Music Review* 9 (1988): 207–32.

Peacock, Gary (b. Burley, Idaho, 12 May 1935). Jazz double bass player. He joined Bill Evans's trio (1962–63) and Albert Ayler's group, in the latter carrying free jazz bass playing to a logical extreme, utterly abandoning timekeeping in favor of improvised melody on albums such as *Spiritual Unity* (1964). After studying medicine and biology and living for a period in Japan, he toured Japan in 1976 with pianist Paul Bley (an intermittent associate since the early 1960s) and in 1977 began recording as a leader. He formed a trio with Keith Jarrett and Jack DeJohnette in 1983, recording the album *Standards.*

Pears, Peter (Neville Luard) (b. Farnham, 22 June 1910; d. Aldeburgh, 3 Apr. 1986). Tenor. Began his career as an organist and music teacher; attended the Royal College of Music (1933–34), then sang with the BBC Chorus and Singers (1934–38). He first performed to Britten's accompaniment in 1937; it was the start of a close personal and musical relationship, with Britten writing the principal tenor roles in many operas for him and often appearing with him in recital. Pears toured the U.S. with the New English Singers between 1936 and 1938, returning with Britten between 1939 and 1942. He made his operatic debut in London in 1942, and joined the Sadler's Wells opera troupe in 1943, premiering the title role of *Peter Grimes* in 1945. He cofounded the English Opera Group in 1946, and the Aldeburgh Festival in 1948; apart from Britten's music and other operatic roles, he is renowned for his interpretations of German lieder and of the part of the Evangelist in Bach's Passions. He was knighted in 1978.

Bibl.: Marion Thorpe, ed., *Peter Pears: A Tribute on His 75th Birthday* (Boston, 1985).

Pearsall, Robert Lucas (b. Clifton, 14 Mar. 1795; d. Wartensee, Switzerland, 5 Aug. 1856). Composer. Studied law and music in Bristol. After a slight stroke (1825), gave up law, moved to Mainz; studied with Joseph Panny (1825–29). Returned to England (1829), leaving his family behind; lived in Karlsruhe, 1830–42. Learned to transcribe early music notation from Kaspar Ett (1832). After 1834, he composed more frequently, including orchestral works, anthems, services, other vocal pieces. Original member of the Bristol Madrigal Society, for which he wrote numerous madrigals.

Bibl.: Julian Marshall, "Pearsall: A Memoir," *MT* 23 (1882): 375–76. Vernon Opheim, "The English Romantic Madrigal" (diss., Univ. of Illinois, 1970).

Pedreira, José Enrique (b. San Juan, 2 Feb. 1904; d. there, 25 Dec. 1959). Composer. Studied piano as a child with Rosa and Ann Sicardo and Ann Tavárez; played for theater and dance companies before studying with Stojowski (a Paderewski pupil) in New York, 1928–32; after a series of concerts began a highly successful teaching career in San Juan, also accompanying visiting artists in recital. Works, primarily for solo piano and Romantic in conception, include 2 sonatas, waltzes, a *Capricho ibérico,* many *danzas* (a native dance form), the ballet *Jardin de piedra,* a piano concerto, works for violin and cello with piano, and songs.

Bibl.: Amaury Veray, "La obra pianística y la mision pedagógica de J. E. Pedreira," *Revista del Instituto de Cultura Puertorriqueña* 3/9 (Oct.–Dec. 1960): 21–24.

Pedrell, Felipe (b. Tortosa, Spain, 19 Feb. 1841; d. Barcelona, 19 Aug. 1922). Scholar, composer. Choirboy at the cathedral; largely self-taught in music, beginning to compose and becoming a Wagnerian; 1873, moved to Barcelona as assistant director of a light opera company; there published a monograph on Beethoven's piano sonatas (1874) and produced 2 operas (1874–75); 1876–77, a government scholarship gave him a year's study in Rome. His resulting research in Roman libraries and archives helped define his life's work: revitalizing Spanish musical tradition by bringing to light its past achievements, collecting and studying Spanish folk and popular music, and encouraging contemporary composition of a recognizable Spanish character. His most important composition, the operatic trilogy *Los Pirineos,* was composed in 1890–91 (premiere, Barcelona, 1902), but he came to regard his own music as secondary to his research. He was prolific in scholarly editions, including sacred music, keyboard, song. His writings include biography, a major collection of Spanish folk songs, specialized historical studies, critical essays on contemporary music and folk music, and 2 volumes of memoirs. From 1894 to 1904, lived in Madrid, where he was professor of choral music at the conservatory (1895–1903); also lectured on music history at the Ateneo, returning then to Barcelona. He is regarded as a central figure in Spanish musical nationalism and as the founder of Spanish musicology.

Pedrotti, Carlo (b. Verona, 12 Nov. 1817; d. there, 16 Oct. 1893). Composer and conductor. Studied with Domenico Foroni. His third opera, *Lina,* was performed successfully in Verona in 1840, followed by *Clara di Mailand* (1841). Conductor of Italian Opera in Amsterdam (1841–45); produced 2 more operas there. Returned to Verona, teaching, coaching opera, and conducting at Teatro filarmonico and Teatro nuovo (1845–68). His first major success was *Fiorina* (1851). Founded weekly series Concerti popolari. Directed Liceo musicale, Teatro regio in Turin (1868). Produced much Wagner, premiered numerous works by other composers there. Appointed first director of Liceo musicale, Pesaro (1882). He composed 19 operas, of which *Tutti in maschera* (1856) was the most successful. Committed suicide, suffering from acute nervous depression.

Bibl.: Tancredi Mantovani, *Carlo Pedrotti* (Pesaro, 1894).

Peerce, Jan [Perelmuth, Jacob Pincus] (b. New York, 3 June 1904; d. there, 15 Dec. 1984). Tenor. In earlier years he was active as both violinist in dance bands and singer on popular Radio City Music Hall broadcasts; made his debut as tenor with Toscanini and the NBC Symphony in Beethoven's Ninth Symphony (1938), and his stage debut the following year. He joined the Metropolitan Opera in 1941, remaining there until 1968; sang with many other U.S. and European companies as well; made the first Western postwar appearance with the Bolshoi Opera, Moscow, in 1956. He took the role of Tevye in *Fiddler on the Roof* on Broadway in 1971.

Peerson [Pearson], **Martin** (b. probably March, Cambridgeshire, between 1571 and 1573; d. London, buried 15 Jan. 1651). Composer. Early in his career he came under the patronage of the poet Fulke Greville. He earned a B.Mus. at Oxford in 1613, and was probably the "Martin Pearson" who was sacrist at Westminster Abbey from 1623 to 1630. In 1624 or 1625 he became almoner and master of the choristers at St. Paul's Cathedral; later he may have become a petty canon there. His works include secular vocal music, a number of verse and full anthems, motets, virginal music, and consort music.

Bibl.: *English Ayres: Elizabethan and Jacobean,* ed. Peter Warlock and Philip Wilson (London, 1927–31). Audrey Jones, "The Life and Works of Martin Peerson" (diss., Cambridge, 1957).

Peeters, Flor (b. Tielen, near Antwerp, 4 July 1903; d. Antwerp, 4 July 1986). Composer and organist. He studied at the Lemmens Institute and had further work in organ with Dupré and Tournemire in Paris. In 1921 he became substitute organist at the Cathedral of Mechelen; in 1925 was named organist there and succeeded his teacher (Depuydt) as organ professor at the institute. Later he taught at the Conservatory of Ghent (1931–48), the Tilburg Conservatory of the Netherlands (1935–48), and the Antwerp Conservatory (director, 1952–68). He gave many master classes in the U.S. and from 1968 annually in Mechelen; as a performer he toured Europe, the U.S., Africa, and Asia. He published many didactic organ works, including *Ars organi* (3 vols., 1952–54) and an accompaniment method for Gregorian chant (1943). His compositional style was influenced by his intimate knowledge of chant, as well as by early Flemish polyphony and Flemish folk song. Although he employed polyrhythm and polytonality as well as dissonant harmonies, he preferred classical forms; organ pedal parts can be virtuosic. His devotion to the works of Bach and his interest in tracker-action instruments are apparent in works from the 1970s. Works include a few orchestral pieces with organ; *Concertino for Positive Organ and Harpsichord* op. 122 (1973); preludes, sinfonias, fantasies, miniatures, and other works for organ (*Hymn Preludes for the Liturgical Year,* 24 vols., 1959–64); some piano and chamber music; and choral music (primarily unaccompanied motets and works with organ or other instruments).

Peiko, Nikolay Ivanovich (b. Moscow, 12 Mar. 1916). Composer. He studied at the Moscow Conservatory with Myaskovsky (composition) and Rakov (orchestration). From 1942 to 1959 he taught at the conservatory, and from 1954 at the Gnesin Institute. In 1944 he became assistant to Shostakovich. His music shows the influence of Myaskovsky, Prokofiev, Shostakovich, and Stravinsky, as well as his interest in folk traditions. His compositions include operas, ballets, 8 symphonies, other orchestral works, chamber music, vocal works, incidental music, and film and radio scores.

Peixinho, Jorge (Manuel Rosado Marques) (b. Montijo, Portugal, 20 Jan. 1940). Composer and pianist. He studied at the Lisbon Conservatory (1951–58), at the Accademia di S. Cecilia (1960–61), and at the Basel Academy of Music (1962–63), where his teachers included Boulez, Stockhausen, and Koenig. He also studied with Nono in Venice, attended Darmstadt summer courses, and studied electronic music in Bilthoven. In 1970 he founded the Grupo de música contemporânea de Lisboa. He taught at the Oporto Conservatory in Brazil and at the New University of Lisbon. Works include *Recitativo II* (music theater, 1966–70); *Poliptico* (chamber orchestra, 1960); *Sobreposições* (orchestra, 1960); *Diafonia 2* (harp, harpsichord, piano, celesta, percussion, 12 strings, 1963–65); *Kinetofonias* (25 strings, 3 tape recorders, 1965–69); *Sucessões simétricas II* (orchestra, 1971); also many vocal, chamber ensemble, and piano pieces.

Pelham, Peter, III (b. London, 9 Dec. 1721; d. Richmond, Va., 28 Apr. 1805). Organist and composer. His father was an engraver who emigrated from England in 1726. The family settled in Boston; from 1732 Peter studied composition with Carl Theodore Pachelbel (son of Johann Pachelbel), whom he followed from Boston to Rhode Island and then to Charleston, S.C. He taught clavier in Charleston (1740–42), then in 1743 was appointed organist at Trinity Church in Boston. From 1755 he lived in Williamsburg; there he served in civic positions, including that as organist at Bruton Church. He also performed solo concerts and accompanied a theater company. A minuet by him is in J. S. Darling's *A Little Keyboard Music* (Williamsburg, Va., 1972).

Pelissier, Victor (b. ?Paris, ca. 1750; d. prob. New Jersey, ca. 1820). Composer and horn player. He moved to the U.S. sometime before 1792, when he first appeared as a horn virtuoso in Philadelphia. He joined the Old American Company in New York in 1793, playing horn and serving as composer and arranger for the troupe. Back in Philadelphia, in 1811–12 he published a set of songs and instrumental tunes arranged for piano, 12 volumes called *Pelissier's Columbian Melodies.* Other works include stage music (*Edwin and Angelina,* New York, 1796; *Sterne's Maria, or the Vintage,* New York, 1799); pantomimes; melodramas (*Ariadne Abandoned by Theseus in the Isle of Naxos,* New York, 1797 [lost]); also dances, variations, and other pieces for instruments.

Pellegrini, Vincenzo (b. Pesaro; d. Milan, ca. 1631–32). Composer. He was priest and possibly organist at Pesaro Cathedral from 1594, then was appointed *maestro di cappella* of the cathedral at Milan in 1611. The year of his death is suggested by the fact that his successor in Milan was elected in 1631; Pellegrini may have died during a plague epidemic. A number of his sacred works were published in Venice, including *Missarium liber primus* (1603) and *Sacri concentus* (1619).

Pelletier, (Louis) Wilfrid (b. Montreal, 20 June 1896; d. New York, 9 Apr. 1982). Conductor and pianist. Played percussion in various bands; played piano for the National Theater (1910) and the Montreal Opera Company (1911–13); later studied in Paris (1916–17) before settling in New York. With the aid of Pierre Monteux he joined the Metropolitan Opera as pianist, later serving as assistant conductor (1922–29) and regular conductor (1929–50). Cofounded the Montreal Symphony in 1934 and the Quebec Conservatoire in 1942.

Peñalosa, Francisco de (b. Talavera de la Reina, ca. 1470; d. Seville, 1 Apr. 1528). Composer. A singer in the chapel of Ferdinand V from 1498. A canon, at first in absentia, at the Cathedral of Seville in 1505–6, 1510–11, 1516–17, and 1521 to his death. Also served as *maestro de capilla* to Prince Ferdinand (grandson of Ferdinand V) in Burgos from 1511 to 1516, and as a member of the papal chapel from 1517 to 1521. His compositions are of the highest quality. They include Masses, Magnificats, motets, hymns, and a few secular vocal works, all of which survive in manuscript only.

Penderecki, Krzysztof (b. Dębica, 23 Nov. 1933). Composer. He first took private composition lessons with Skołyszewski. In 1955 he entered the Kraków Conservatory and studied composition with Malawski and Wiechowicz, graduating in 1958. He stayed on as a lecturer and in 1972 became rector. From the 1960s his music was internationally commissioned and performed, and by the mid-1970s he was touring as a conductor of his own works.

His early works illustrate his experimentation with sound blocks and colors (*Wymiary czasu i ciszy* [Dimensions of Time and Silence], chorus, ensemble, 1960) and, especially, texture to create formal structures (*Threnody,* string, 1960). He felt the influence of Stravinsky and then of Schoenberg and Webern. Penderecki identified his own first stylistic period as beginning around 1960 *(Anaklasis)* and running through 1974 (Magnificat). During this time he explored ritualistic traditions such as religious services. For example, *Utrenia* (1970–71) uses the text and format of the Orthodox Christian rite dealing with burial and resurrection. The *Stabat Mater* (1962) is based on Renaissance Netherlandish composers in its typical liturgical text and use of a unifying chantlike theme. His opera *Paradise Lost* (Chicago, 1979) was similar to Renaissance ecclesiastical plays. He experimented with serialism (*Passio et mors domini nostri Jesu Christi secundum Lucam,* 1963–65) and with electronic sound production. He also developed new forms of graphic notation to accommodate the sound effects he wanted.

From 1974 (*The Awakening of Jacob,* chamber orchestra and 12 ocarinas) Penderecki moved into a new stylistic phase, characterized by a rich lyricism and Romantic orchestration, moving toward modality and tonal centricity and away from serialistic devices. This period includes the Concerto for Cello and Orchestra no. 2 (1982), written for Rostropovich and the 100th anniversary of the Berlin Philharmonic. This work, and the Concerto for viola and orchestra (1983), exploits the dramatic contrasts possible between the two personalities of solo instrument and orchestra. In 1992 the Adagio from his Symphony No. 4 (1989) received the Grawemeyer Award for Music Composition.

Other works include the operas *Diabły z Loudun* [The Devils of Loudun] (1969); *Paradise Lost* (1978); *Die schwarze Maske* (1984–86); *Ubu Rex* (1990–91); choral music, including *Dies Irae* (solo voices, chorus, orchestra, 1967); *Utrenia: 1 Złożenie do grobu* [The Laying in the Tomb], *2 Zmartwychwstanie* [The Resurrection] (solo voices, 2 choruses, orchestra, 1971–72); Magnificat (boys' voices, bass solo, chorus, orchestra, 1974); *Lux aeterna* (soloists, chorus, orchestra, 1983); *Veni creator; Song of Cherubim* (chorus, 1987); instrumental works, including *Trenofiarom Hiroszimy* [Threnody for the Victims of Hiroshima] (strings, 1960); 2 symphonies (1973, 1980); cello concerto (1983); *Passacaglia and Rondo* (orchestra, 1988); *Sinfonietta* (1991); chamber works (*Die unterbrochene Gedanke,* string quartet, 1988), and works for electronic tape.

Bibl.: Wilfram Schwinger, *Krzysztof Penderecki, His Life and Works: Encounters, Biography, and Musical Commentary,* trans. William Mann (London, 1989).

Penna, Lorenzo (b. Bologna, 1613; d. there, 31 Oct. 1693). Composer and theorist. He became *maestro di cappella* at S. Illario, Casale Monferrato, in 1656 and received a doctorate of theology from Ferrara in 1665. He was named *maestro di cappella* at the Cathedral of S. Cassiano at Imola (1667–69) and at the Carmelite Church in Parma (1672–73) before returning to Bologna. Penna published a number of sacred works in the style of Palestrina and a well-known treatise, *Li prima albori musicali* (Bologna, 1672).

Pennario, Leonard (b. Buffalo, 9 July 1924). Pianist. Taken to California as a child; studied with Guy Maier and Isabella Vengerova; performed with the Dallas Symphony at age 12, and with the Los Angeles Philharmonic at age 15; attended the Univ. of Southern California. He made a famous set of chamber music recordings with Piatigorsky and Heifetz, and Miklós Rozsa wrote a concerto for him; he toured and recorded extensively as both recitalist and orchestral soloist, playing a very wide repertory.

Penniman, Richard. See Little Richard.

Pentland, Barbara (b. Winnipeg, 2 Jan. 1912). Composer and pianist. She studied piano and composition as a child; studied organ, piano, and theory while at school in Montreal (1927–29); in Paris (1929–30) studied composition with Cécile Gauthier, a pupil of d'Indy; in 1936 went to Juilliard, where she studied counterpoint with Jacoby and composition with Wagenaar; further study with Copland at the Berkshire Music Center (summer, 1941 and 1942). The Piano Variations of 1942 illustrate the neoclassicism she learned from Copland. By 1942 she was in Toronto, teaching theory and composition at the conservatory (from 1943), and beginning to explore more radical approaches to composition. The Wind Octet of 1948 is her first serial work. In 1955 she attended the Darmstadt lectures and began to be influenced by Webern's music (*Symphony for Ten Parts,* 1957). From the 1960s she retained her interest in free serialism and added aleatoric procedures and microtones to her style. Taught at the Univ. of British Columbia from 1949 to 1963, when she resigned to compose.

Works include a chamber opera and a ballet, incidental music, radio and film scores; 4 symphonies (1945–59) and other orchestral music; a piano quintet (1983), *Tides* (violin, marimba, and harp, 1984); piano music; a few unaccompanied choral pieces; *Disasters of the Sun* (mezzo-soprano, 9 instruments, and tape, 1976), a song cycle, and several songs.

Bibl.: Sheila Eastman and Timothy McGee, *Barbara Pentland* (Toronto, 1983).

Pépin, (Jean-Josephat) Clermont (b. St. Georges-de-Beauce, Quebec, 15 May 1926). Composer and pianist. A child prodigy, he went to Montreal in 1937 for study with Champagne and Arthur Letondal (piano); some early works for piano were orchestrated and performed in Montreal and Quebec City (1938–39); he then attended the Curtis Institute (1941–45), where his teachers were Scalero and Jeanne Behrend. He returned to Montreal and to Toronto for further work in the conservatories, and soon won (as a pianist) the Prix d'Europe from the Quebec Academy of Music, which allowed him to study with Jolivet, Honegger, and Messiaen in Paris. By the mid-1950s his earlier imitations of Franck had given way to serialism (String Quartet no. 2, 1955–56); titles of works from the 1960s reflect his continuing interest in the sciences (Symphony no. 3, *Quasars,* 1967) as well as his commitment to serialism. He taught composition at the Quebec Conservatory in Montreal (1955–64) and later directed that institution (1967–72); from 1969 to 1972 he was national president of Jeunesses musicales; in 1970 he won the Calixa–Lavallée Prize for composition. Works include ballets and incidental music; *Guernica* (symphonic poem, 1952), symphonies (no. 4, *La Messe sur le monde,* calls for speaker, chorus, and orchestra, 1975); 5 string quartets, *Nucléé* (percussion, 1977), and *Pièces de circonstances* (children's choir and school instrumental ensemble, 1967); piano music; and vocal music (*Trois Incantations,* voice, piano, 1987; *Paysage,* soprano, clarinet, cello, piano, 1987).

Pepper, Art [Arthur Edward, Jr.] (b. Gardena, Calif., 1 Sept. 1925; d. Panorama, Calif., 1 June 1982). Jazz alto saxophonist. He joined the big bands of Benny Carter (1943) and Stan Kenton (1943, 1946–51). Problems stemming from narcotics addiction interrupted his career over the next 25 years, but he nonetheless was a leading soloist in the West Coast jazz style. Later he recorded the album *Art Pepper Meets the Rhythm Section* with Miles Davis's hard bop sidemen (1957). From 1977, when he returned to prominence, his bop soloing incorporated elements of free jazz playing for expressive effect, as on the album *Saturday Night at the Village Vanguard* (1977).

Writings: with Laurie Pepper, *Straight Life: The Story of Art Pepper* (New York, 1979).

Pepping, Ernst (b. Duisburg, 12 Sept. 1901; d. Berlin, 1 Feb. 1981). Composer. He studied at the Berlin Hochschule for Music with Gmeindl; in 1926 won the Mendelssohn Prize; worked as an arranger of film scores and a free-lance musician. From 1934 he taught at the Spandau Church Music School (Berlin) and later at the Berlin Hochschule as well (1953–68). His many prizes include the Bavarian Academy of Fine Arts Prize (1964) and the Berlin Kunstpreis for music (1948); he was admitted to the Berlin and the Munich academies of fine arts. His interest in the musical styles of the past is reflected not only in his use of Baroque and classical formal models in his own works, his emphasis on counterpoint, and use of a cantus firmus, but also in his 2 books (*Stilwend der Musik,* 1934; *Der polyphone Satz,* 2 parts, 1941–42 and 1957). Much of his music was intended for use in the German Protestant church, such as the *Spandauer Chorbuch,* which originally consisted of 20 volumes of music in 3–6 voice parts (1934–41; revised version in 4 vols., 1962), and the *Grosses Orgelbuch* (3 vols., 1939). Other works include 3 symphonies (1939–44) and a Piano Concerto (1950); 2 string quartets and a few other chamber works; piano music; a large amount of organ music (preludes, 2 concertos, fugues), some of which is based on chorale tunes (*Partita 3. Mit Fried und Freud,* 1953); sacred and secular choral music (Te Deum, solo voices, chorus, and orchestra, 1956); some 70 songs arranged in cycles (1945–46).

Pepusch, Johann Christoph [John Christopher] (b. Berlin, 1667; d. London, 20 July 1752). Composer. He studied theory under Klingenberg and organ under Grosse; served the Prussian court from 1681, then traveled through Holland sometime late in the century, settling in London by 1704. He was employed as a violist and harpsichordist at Drury Lane, received a D.Mus. from Oxford in 1713, and became organist and composer to James Brydges, later the Duke of Chandos. In 1710 he founded with others the Academy of Ancient Music, then reorganized it as a musical seminary for young boys in 1735. In addition to the enormously successful *Beggar's Opera* (1728), for which Pepusch supplied the basses and an overture, other stage works (nearly all performed at Drury Lane or Lincoln's Inn Fields) include *Venus and Adonis* (1715), *Myrtillo* (1715), and *The Death of Dido* (1716). He composed a large number of instrumental works, heavily influenced by Corelli; church music for the Duke of Chandos, including a Magnificat (before 1721) and the cantata *See from the Silent Groves [Alexis]* (London, 1710). Published a *Treatise on Harmony* (London, 1730, rev. 1731; facs. *MMML* 28, 1966).

Peragallo, Mario (b. Rome, 25 Mar. 1910). Composer. He studied with Casella; served as artistic director of the Accademia filarmonica romana from 1950 to 1954; and was active in the Italian section of the ISCM (president, 1956–60; 1963–85). His first opera (*Ginevra degli Almieri,* 1937) is in the verismo tradition, but after the war he became interested in serialism; his *Emircal* (soloists, orchestra, and tape, 1980) was composed as a requiem after the death of Dallapiccola (the title is a retrograde of "Lacrime"). Works include other operas (*La Parrucca dell'imperatore,* Spoleto, 1959); orchestral music; string quartets; piano and organ music; *In memoriam, corale, e aria* (chorus and orchestra, 1955); songs.

Perahia, Murray (b. New York, 19 Apr. 1947). Pianist and conductor. Graduated from Mannes College in 1969; made debut with the New York Philharmonic in 1972, and the same year won the Leeds International Piano Competition; shared the 1975 Avery Fisher Prize with Lynn Harrell, and became an artistic director at the Aldeburgh Festival in 1982. He has made frequent recital, solo, and chamber appearances, and is perhaps best known for his renditions of Mozart piano concertos, many of which he conducts from the keyboard.

Peranda [Perandi, Perande], **Marco Gioseppe** (b. Rome or Macerata, ca. 1625; d. Dresden, 12 Jan. 1675). Composer. He may have studied with Carissimi in Rome; traveled with Bernhard to Dresden between 1651 and 1656, becoming Vice-Kapellmeister at the court chapel there (1661), then Kapellmeister (1663), and finally first Hofkapellmeister (1672–75) after Schütz's death. Peranda is noted for his sacred music, primarily his sacred concertos, no doubt more representative of Dresden court music after 1660 than Schütz's compositions.

Pérez, David [Davide] (b. Naples, 1711; d. Lisbon, 30 Oct. 1778). Composer. His parents were Neapolitans of Spanish descent. After study at the Conservatorio di S. Maria di Loreto (1722–33), he composed an opera, *Le nemica amante,* for Naples's Teatro S. Bartolomeo in 1735. Through the 1730s and 1740s he established himself as a composer of operas in Naples, Milan, Palermo, Rome, and Vienna. From 1738 he served the Royal Chapel at Naples, becoming *maestro di cappella* in 1741. From 1752 he was in Lisbon, serving as maestro and family music teacher for King José I. There he continued composing Italian operas, mostly Metastasian opere serie, including *Demofoonte* (1752), *L'Olimpiade* (1753); *Solimano* (1757); *L'isola disabitata* (1767); and *Creusa in Delfo* (1774). He remained at that court until his death. Also composed secular serenatas and cantatas; sacred works (including 8 Masses); and an oratorio, *Mattutino de' morti* (London, 1774).

Bibl.: Paul J. Jackson, "The Operas of David Perez" (diss., Stanford Univ., 1967).

Pergament, Moses (b. Helsinki, 21 Sept. 1893; d. Gustavsberg, near Stockholm, 5 March 1977). Composer and critic. Born in Finland, he became a Swedish citizen in 1918. He was trained as a violinist and as an opera conductor. He studied violin in St. Petersburg and in Berlin at the Stern Conservatory; played in the Helsinki Philharmonic Society for four years. He settled in Stockholm, where he worked as a composer, critic, and conductor. He was interested in Russian music, particularly Mussorgsky, and later in French music, particularly "Les six." Some of his works reflect his Jewish heritage; *Rapsodia ebraica* (orchestra, 1935) was written in protest of Nazi massacres. Other major works include *Den judiska sången* (choral symphony, 1944); *Krelantems och Eldeling* (ballet, 1920–21); *Himlens hemlighet* (chamber opera, 1953). He composed other choral works, concertos, chamber music, and many songs, and published 4 books on music.

Pergolesi, Giovanni Battista (b. Iesi, Marche, 4 Jan. 1710; d. Puzzuoli, near Naples, 16 Mar. 1736). Composer. He probably studied with the *maestro di cappella* at Iesi, Francesco Santi, and took violin with Francesco Mondini. Sometime after 1720 he was sent to the Conservatorio dei Poveri di Gesù Cristo in Naples, where he studied composition with Gaetano Greco, Leonardo Vinci, and Francesco Durante; he also performed as a choirboy and violinist. While still a student, his *dramma sacro Li prodigi della divina* (1731) was performed at the monastery of S. Agnello Maggiore. His first commissioned opera, *Salustia* (Naples, 1732), a revision of Zeno's *Alessandro Severo,* was probably written in haste and enjoyed little success. Pergolesi was appointed *maestro di cappella* to Prince Ferdinando Colonna Stigliano in 1732, and the same year his *commedia musicale Lo frate 'nnamorato* was quite successful. After Naples experienced earthquakes in November and December 1732, he composed some works to celebrate the festival of St. Emidius (protector against earthquakes), which apparently included a Mass for double chorus and the Psalms *Dixit Dominus, Laudate* (not extant), and *Confitebor.* In 1733 he was commissioned to write an opera for the empress's birthday; the result, *Il prigionier superbo,* included the intermezzo *La serva padrona,* which would become one of his most celebrated works. In May 1734 his Mass in F was presented in the Church of S. Lorenzo in Lucina, Rome, to an audience that included the Duke of Maddaloni; subsequently Pergolesi entered his service as *maestro di cappella,* returned with the duke to Naples in 1734, and composed an opera on Metastasio's *Adriano in Siria* in the same year. He was commissioned to set Metastasio's *L'Olimpiade* for the Teatro Tordinona in Rome, where the work premiered in 1735; it appears to have been a failure, although a few years later it was produced in Venice and Turin. His last success was the *commedia musicale Il Flaminio* (Naples, 1735); a wedding serenata, *Il tempo felice* (1735, lost), was completed by Niccolò Sabbatino because of Pergolesi's poor health. In 1736 he moved into a Franciscan monastery in Puzzuoli, where during his final illness he composed the cantata *Orfeo,* his *Stabat Mater,* and the *Salve Regina.*

Pergolesi's fame spread rapidly after his death. Four of his cantatas were published posthumously, and traveling troupes of players began to perform his comedies, especially *La serva padrona.* In 1752 the tremendous success of this work in Paris, staged there for the second time, initiated the *querelle des bouffons.* The sacred music enjoyed considerable success as well, the *Stabat Mater* becoming a particular favorite of the 18th century. The enthusiasm for Pergolesi's works caused a considerable number of misattributions, which still cause confusion; Stravinsky's *Pulcinella* made use of material ascribed to Pergolesi, but in fact almost none of the works he selected are by the composer.

Works: Dramatic: *Salustia* (1732); untitled intermezzo, performed with *Salustia* (music lost); *Lo frate 'nnamorato* (1732); untitled introduction and *balli,* performed with *Lo frate* (lost); *Il prigionier superbo* (1733); *La serva padrona,* performed with *Il prigionier; Adriano in Siria* (1734); *La contadina astuta,* performed with *Adriano; L'Olimpiade* (1735); *Il Flaminio* (1735); *Il tempo felice* (with N. Sabbatino, 1735, lost). Sacred dramas and oratorios: *Li prodigi della divina grazia nella conversione di San Guglielmo Duca d'Aquitania* (1731); *La fenice sul rogo, ovvero La morte di San Giuseppe* (1731, authencity questionable). Sacred vocal: Mass (Kyrie-Gloria) in D (1732; also 2 other versions); Mass (Kyrie-Gloria) in F (1734; also 3 other versions); Confitebor (1732); Credo in D; Deus in adjutorium (1732); Dixit Dominus (1732); In coelestibus regnis; In hac die quam decora (incomplete); Laudate pueri (late); Salve Regina (1736); Stabat Mater (1736). Chamber cantatas: *4 cantate da camera . . . di G. B. Pergolesi, raccolte di Gioacchino Bruno, op. 2* (Naples, ca. 1736); *Lontananza, L'addio, Segreto tormento, Orfeo; Ritorno* (1731); *Della città vicino.* Other vocal: Solfeggi; solfeggi, harpsichord acccompaniment. Instrumental: Violin Concerto in B♭; Concerto in C for 2 harpsichords; Organ Sonata in F; Sinfonia in F (cello, basso continuo); Violin Sonata in G; Trio in B♭ (2 violins, basso continuo).

Bibl.: *Giovanni Battista Pergolesi: Complete Works,* ed. Barry S. Brook et al. (New York, 1986–). *Opera omnia di Giovanni Battista Pergolesi,* ed. Francesco Caffarella (Rome, 1939–42). Marvin E. Paymer, *G. B. Pergolesi: A Thematic Catalogue of the Opera Omnia* (New York, 1976). Frank Walker, "Two Centuries of Pergolesi Forgeries and Misattributions," *ML* 30 (1949): 297–320. A. E. Cherbuliez, *G. B. Pergolesi: Leben und Werk* (Zurich and Stuttgart, 1954). *Pergolesi Studies,* ed. Francesco Degrada (Stuyvesant, 1986). Francesco

Degrada, *Pergolesi* (Naples, 1986). Marvin E. Paymer and Hermine W. Williams, *Giovanni Battista Pergolesi: A Guide to Research* (New York, 1989).

Peri, Jacopo ["Zazzerino"] (b. Rome, 20 Aug. 1561; d. Florence, 12 Aug. 1633). Composer and singer. He moved to Florence while still young, studied with Cristofano Malvezzi, and was appointed organist at the Badia (1579) and singer at S. Giovanni Battista (1586); he probably participated in discussions of the "Camerata" during the 1580s at Bardi's house. In 1583 he worked with Malvezzi and others in composing music (no longer extant) to Fedini's comedy *Le due Persilie,* and performed his own aria in the fifth *intermedio* for Bargagli's comedy *La pellegrina* in 1589. He collaborated with Corsi and the librettist Rinuccini on the short pastoral *Dafne* (earliest performance 1598), and worked again with Rinuccini on the opera *Euridice* (Florence, 1600; facs., New York, 1973; R: *RRMBE* 36 and 37, 1981), in which Peri probably performed the role of Orpheus. During the 1610s he composed a number of dramatic works, including *intermedi* and ballets, often collaborating with other Florentine composers such as Gagliano and Caccini; most of this music has been lost. Peri worked with the librettist Cini on *Tetide,* planned for the wedding festivities of 1608 in Mantua but rejected in favor of Monteverdi's *Arianna; Adone* (1611, libretto by Cicognini) was similarly intended for Mantua but not performed there. He collaborated with G. B. da Gagliano on 3 oratorios (*La benedittione di Jacob* and *Il gran natale di Christo salvator nostro,* 1622; *La celeste guida,* 1624), all lost, and with Marco Gagliano on 2 operas on Salvadori texts, *Lo sposalizio di Medoro e Angelica* (1619) and *La Flora* (1628). Peri also composed a large number of songs, some published in *Le varie musiche* (Florence, 1609), as well as a few instrumental ricercars.

Peri presumably composed 4 of the 6 excerpts from *Dafne* that survive in Florentine manuscripts; his music for Ovid's prologue was later adapted for the prologue to *Euridice.* His most innovative work in *Euridice* can be found in the recitatives between choral numbers, which he described as representing "an intermediate course, lying between the slow and suspended movements of song and the swift and rapid movements of speech." In addition to unprepared dissonances and unusual harmonic progressions, the continuous recitatives are noteworthy for their imitations of vocal rhythms and pitch inflections, with an accompaniment that closely follows the principal words of the text.

Bibl.: William V. Porter, "Peri's and Corsi's *Dafne:* Some New Discoveries and Observations," *JAMS* 18 (1965): 170–96. Tim Carter, "Jacopo Peri's *Euridice* (1600): A Contextual Study," *MR* 43 (1982): 83–103. Tim Carter, *Jacopo Peri, 1561–1633: His Life and Works* (New York, 1989).

Perkins, Carl (b. Lake City, Tenn., 9 Apr. 1932). Rock-and-roll and country singer, songwriter, and guitarist. In 1955 he began recording for Sun Records in Memphis; his "Blue Suede Shoes" (1956) joined the recordings of Elvis Presley and Jerry Lee Lewis in establishing rock-and-roll. This popularity ended with a severe automobile accident in 1956; later (1965–76) he toured with Johnny Cash, appearing on his television show; from 1976 he recorded as a solo artist again.

Perkins, John MacIvor (b. St. Louis, Mo., 2 Aug. 1935). Composer. He studied at Harvard and the New England Conservatory of Music; in Paris with Boulanger; in London with Rubbra and Gerhard (1958–59); and at Brandeis (M.F.A., 1962). Taught at the Univ. of Chicago (1962–65), Harvard (1965–70), and Washington Univ. (St. Louis, from 1970). His compositions use serial procedures; often have virtuosic instrumental parts. In 1966 he received an award from the National Institute of Arts and Letters. Works include a chamber opera (1958); *Music for Orchestra* (1964); *Music for 13 Players* (mezzo-soprano and chamber ensemble, 1964–66); and *Caprice* (piano, 1963).

Perkinson, Coleridge-Taylor (b. New York, 14 June 1932). Composer and conductor. He studied at the Manhattan School with Giannini and Charles Mills and at Princeton with Earl Kim; his training as a conductor was at the Berkshire Music Center, in Salzburg (summer 1960), and at the Netherlands Radio Union in Hilversum (summers 1960, 1962, 1963). He was cofounder and conductor of the Symphony of the New World (1965–75), and has composed dance scores for Jerome Robbins and Alvin Ailey. His style is accessible, fusing classical traditions and black musical styles. Works include ballets (*To Bird with Love,* Ailey, 1984); incidental music, film, and television scores; *Lamentations: A Black Folk Song Suite* (cello, 1973); *The Legacy* (narrator, solo voice, chorus, orchestra, 1982).

Perkowski, Piotr (b. Oweczacze, 17 Mar. 1901; d. Otwock, near Warsaw, 12 Aug. 1990). Composer. From 1923 to 1925 he studied at the Warsaw Conservatory, taking composition lessons with Statkowski. He then worked independently with Szymanowski and traveled to Paris, where from 1926 through 1928 he studied composition with Roussel. While in Paris he founded the Association of Young Polish Musicians. From 1936 to 1939 he was head of the Toruń Conservatory and from 1945 to 1949 served as president of the Polish Composers' Union. He taught at the Warsaw Conservatory and the Wrocław Conservatory. His music is largely tonal and often incorporates elements of Polish folk music. Of his orchestral music several works were lost during the war; one, the Violin Concerto no. 1 (1938), was reconstructed, 1947–48. He also wrote several ballets, choral and chamber music, and many songs.

Perle, George (b. Bayonne, N.J., 6 May 1915). Composer and theorist. He studied with LaViolette at De Paul Univ. (1934–38) and with Krenek in the early 1940s; Ph.D. from New York Univ. in 1956. Taught at the Univ. of Louisville (1949–57), the Univ. of California at Davis (1957–61), and Queens College (1961–84); also held visiting professorships at Yale (1965–66), the Univ. of Southern California (1965), SUNY–Buffalo (1971–72), the Univ. of Pennsylvania (1976, 1980), and Columbia Univ. (1979, 1983). In the 1930s he became interested in the music of the Second Viennese School; in 1939 began to develop an approach to twelve-tone composition that would incorporate hierarchic relations among pitch classes and chords analogous to those found in tonal music. This theory of twelve-tone composition is described in his book *Twelve-Tone Tonality* (Berkeley, 1977). His study of the music of Schoenberg, Berg, and Webern (*Serial Composition and Atonality,* 1962; 5th ed., 1981) is a standard introduction to that repertory; he also wrote more extensively on the compositional procedures of Berg (*The Operas of Alban Berg: Wozzeck,* 1980; *Lulu,* 1985). In several articles and in his 1977 book he argues that his compositional theory has historical bases in the works of Berg, Bartók, Stravinsky, and Scriabin.

A prolific composer, most of whose works reflect his theory of twelve-tone tonality. Some earlier pieces were more freely or intuitively conceived (including the first three wind quintets, the 1958 String Quintet, and several works for solo instruments). Several works composed before the early 1970s were withdrawn, individual movements often reused in new compositions. Despite the complexity of his theory, his works sound relatively straightforward. His awards include election to the Institute of the American Academy and Institute of Arts and Letters (1978), the Pulitzer Prize (for the Wind Quintet no. 4), and selection as a MacArthur Fellow (both in 1986). From 1989 to 1991 he was composer-in-residence for the San Francisco Symphony.

Works include orchestral music (*Three Movements for Orchestra,* 1960; Cello Concerto, 1966; Concertino for piano, wind, and timpani, 1979; *A Short Symphony,* 1980; *Serenade no. 3,* piano and chamber orchestra, 1983; *Sinfonietta,* 1988; *Sinfonietta II,* 1990; Piano Concerto no. 1, 1990; Piano Concerto no. 2, 1992); a large amount of chamber music (4 wind quintets, 1949–84; cello sonata, 1985; Sonata a cinque, bass trombone, clarinet, violin, cello, and piano, 1987; String Quartet no. 8, 1988; sextet for piano and winds, 1988); piano music (*6 New Etudes,* 1984; *Sonatina,* 1986); *13 Dickinson Songs* (1979) and other vocal and choral music.

Bibl.: George Perle, *The Listening Composer* (Berkeley, 1990).

Perlemuter, Vlado (Kaunas, Lithuania, 26 May 1904). Pianist. Taken to Paris as a youth; studied with Moszkowski and Cortot; had extensive personal contact with Ravel, recording all of his piano music and becoming an authoritative commentator on it. He became professor at the Paris Conservatoire in 1950; he also gained renown as an interpreter of Chopin.

Bibl.: Vlado Perlemuter and Heléné Jourdan Morhange, *Ravel d'après Ravel* (Paris, 1953; trans. Frances Taylor, London, 1980).

Perlman, Itzhak (b. Tel Aviv, 31 Aug. 1945). Violinist. Stricken by polio at age 4; still, he concertized and played on broadcasts in Israel from an early age. An appearance on the *Ed Sullivan Show* in 1958 introduced him to the U.S. public; he settled in New York, studying at Juilliard with Ivan Galamian and Dorothy DeLay. Making his professional debut in 1963, he won the Leventritt Prize in 1964, later touring widely as orchestral soloist and in recital. Celebrated television and concert appearances with Stern, Zuckerman, and others have broadened his U.S. popularity; also played numerous times at the White House. In addition to the concert repertoire, he has made forays into jazz and ragtime. Teaches at Brooklyn College and at the City Univ. of New York.

Perosi, Lorenzo (b. Tortono, 21 Dec. 1872; d. Rome, 12 Oct. 1956). Composer and church musician. He studied at the conservatories in Rome and Milan, then with Haberl in Regensburg. In 1894 he was appointed choirmaster of San Marco (Venice), and was ordained the next year. In 1898 he became music director of the Sistine Chapel, but he had to leave the post in 1915 as a result of severe psychological problems for which he was institutionalized in 1922; he resumed his position the following year but never achieved his former stature as musician and composer. He wrote over 20 oratorios, most of which were published, in an eclectic style combining influences from Gregorian chant and 16th-century polyphony to Wagner (*L'entrata di Cristo in Gerusalemme,* 1900). Other works include several Masses and some 350 other sacred pieces; about 25 orchestral pieces; a large amount of chamber music (18 string quartets, 1928–29); and organ music.

Pérotin [Perotinus Magnus] (fl. Paris, ca. 1200). Composer. Known through references by the theorists Anonymous IV and Johannes de Garlandia (both mid-13th century). These men described his accomplishments, and Anonymous IV also named a few compositions. Thus, although no musical sources include attributions to Pérotin, it is possible to identify a small number of his works. He is said to have revised the *Magnus Liber* of Léonin, both abbreviating it and writing improved clausulas. He also wrote 3- and 4-voiced organum, a major advance over the earlier 2-voiced organum. In fact, Anonymous IV singles out the 4-voiced *Viderunt omnes* and *Sederunt principes* and the 3-voiced *Alleluia, Pascha nostrum* and *Alleluia, Posui adiutorium.* The theorist also ascribes to him 3 conductus. A number of other 3-voiced organa and some clausulas can be attributed to him on stylistic grounds. In addition, a set of about 150 short clausulas clearly suit the purpose of abbreviating the *Magnus Liber.* Thus, the total number of pieces that are possibly by Pérotin is large; the attributions are far from solid, however. For the most part we cannot be sure exactly which extant compositions are his.

Bibl.: *Die drei- und vierstimmige Notre-Dame-Organa,* ed. Heinrich Husmann, Publikationen ältere Musik, 11 (Leipzig, 1940; R: 1967). *The Works of Perotin,* ed. Ethel Thurston (New York, 1970). Hans Tischler, "Pérotin and the Creation of the Motet," *MR* 44 (1983): 1–7.

Perrin, Pierre (b. Lyons, ca. 1620; d. Paris, buried 26 Apr. 1675). Poet and librettist. In 1669 he received a 12-year privilege to establish "académies d'opéra" after convincing the king's minister that France should have its own opera; *Pomone,* the inaugural production by Perrin and Cambert (1671), did quite well, but Perrin was swindled out of the money and went to debtors' prison. He eventually surrendered his privilege to Lully in 1672, receiving a pension to pay off his debts.

Bibl.: Louis E. Auld, *The Lyric Art of Pierre Perrin, Founder of French Opera* (Henryville, Penn., 1986).

Perrin d'Angicourt (fl. 1245–70). Trouvère. Probably closely associated with Arras. Several of his poems have dedications to French or Flemish royal or noble figures. About 26 surely authentic poems with music survive; another 9 (2 without music) are probably of joint authorship or are doubtful. Some of his works have been transmitted in an unusually large number of sources, and a few seem to be in modal rhythm.

Perry, Julia (Amanda) (b. Lexington, Ky., 25 Mar. 1924; d. Akron, Ohio, 24 Apr. 1979). Composer. She studied voice and composition at the Westminster Choir College, the Juilliard School (1950), and with Boulanger and Dallapiccola. Taught (1967–69) at Florida A.&M. (Tallahassee) and at Atlanta Univ.; from 1951 until 1959 she lived in Europe, and lectured widely for the USIS. Won 2 Guggenheim Awards (1954, 1956) and an award from the National Institute of Arts and Letters (1965). She wrote in a neoclassical style and employed black folk idioms in some of her later works; a series of strokes partially incapacitated her after 1973 but she continued to compose. Her works include 3 operas and an opera-ballet; 12 symphonies (1959–72), 2 piano concertos, and other orchestral works; several pieces for voices and orchestra (*Frammenti dalle lettere de Santa Caterina,* 1 voice, chorus, and orchestra); *Homunculus C. F.* (harp and 10 percussionists, 1960) and other chamber music; songs and arrangements of spirituals.

Persiani, Fanny. See Tacchinardi-Persiani, Fanny.

Persichetti, Vincent (b. Philadelphia, 6 June 1915; d. there, 15 Aug. 1987). Composer. As a child he studied several instruments (piano, organ, double bass) and theory and composition (Russell King Miller, 1924–36) at the Coombs Conservatory in Philadelphia; further work in composition under Roy Harris in Colorado. After graduating from Coombs (1936), he was made head of its theory and composition departments and studied piano (Samaroff) and composition (Nordoff) at the Philadelphia Conservatory (D.Mus., 1945); also studied conducting with Reiner at the Curtis Institute. In 1947 he joined the faculty of the Juilliard School, where he taught for the next forty years (chairman of the composition department from 1963). His own book *Twentieth-Century Harmony* is the best guide to his compositional procedures. The number of keyboard, chamber, and band works he has produced for beginners or amateurs is striking.

Works: a one-act opera, *The Sibyl (Parable XX)* (Persichetti, after the fable Chicken Little, 1976; performed Philadelphia, 1985); 9 symphonies (1942–70), Serenade no. 5 (1950), Piano Concerto (1962), *Night Dances* (1970), Concerto for English horn (1977), and other orchestral music; chorale preludes (*O God Unseen,* 1984); chamber music including Serenades (no. 3, violin, cello, and piano; no. 10, flute and harp; no. 14, oboe, 1984), Parables (I, flute, 1965; X, String Quartet no. 4, 1972; XXIII, violin, cello, and piano; 1981), and the *Little Recorder Book* (1956); at least 12 piano sonatas as well as serenades, parables, and other works for 1 or 2 pianists (*Little Mirror Book,* 1978); organ works including *Dryden Liturgical Suite* (1980) and *Do Not Go Gentle* (organ pedals, 1974); at least 8 harpsichord sonatas (the first in 1951, the others after 1980) and other works for harpsichord; choral music including *Hymns and Responses for the Church Year* (Auden and others, 1955), an unaccompanied Mass (1960), *Stabat Mater* with orchestra (1963), and settings of texts by Cummings and Whitman (*Flower Songs,* Cantata 6, chorus and strings, 1983), as well as an oratorio, *The Creation,* on his own text (4 soloists, chorus, and orchestra, 1969); *Harmonium* (Stevens, song cycle for soprano and piano, 1951) and other songs (Frost, Dickinson, Cummings, Sandburg, Japanese, Chinese, and 17th-century English texts).

Bibl.: Walter G. Simmons, *The Music of Vincent Persichetti* (New York, 1985). Donald L. Patterson and Janet L. Patterson, *Vincent Persichetti: A Bio-Bibliography* (New York, 1988).

Persinger, Louis (b. Rochester, Ill., 11 Feb. 1887; d. New York, 31 Dec. 1966). Violinist and pianist. Attended the Leipzig Conservatory from 1900 to 1904; while based in Brussels between 1904 and 1907, he toured and studied with Ysaÿe and Thibaut. Made U.S. debut in 1912; was concertmaster of the Berlin Philharmonic (1914–15) and the San Francisco Orchestra (1915–17) before forming his own quartet and becoming director of the Chamber Music Society of San Francisco. He later taught at the Cleveland Institute (1929–30) and Juilliard (1930 to his death); Menuhin was one of his pupils.

Pert, Morris (b. Arbroath, Scotland, 8 Sept. 1947). Composer. A virtuoso percussionist, Pert has performed with the Cirencester School Percussion Ensemble. Beginning in the late 1960s active with new music written for small unusual ensembles, often involving a range of percussion instruments, electronic sources, improvisation, and styles from rock and jazz. He founded the group Come to the Edge in the early 1970s with Andrew Powell and Robin Thompson. After working with the Japanese percussionist Stomu Yamash'ta, the group moved toward the performance of their own music, developing an improvisatory, interactive style that strove to communicate with a wide audience. Concurrently, Pert explored his own compositional techniques, writing mostly for small, often nonstandard ensembles. He frequently writes for his group Suntreader, with which he also performs on piano. Works include *4 Japanese verses* op. 2, soprano and piano (1969); *Luminos* op. 16a, basset-horn, piano (1972); *Chromosphere,* 5 instruments and tape (1973); Symphony no. 2, op. 36 (premiered March 1979).

Perti, Giacomo Antonio (b. Bologna, 6 June 1661; d. there, 10 Apr. 1756). Composer. He studied music with his uncle Lorenzo Perti and with Rocco Laurenti, later studying counterpoint with Petronio Franceschini. His Mass was performed at S. Tomaso al Mercato in 1678, and he contributed the third act to the opera *Atide* the following year; in 1689 his operas *Dionisio Siracusano* and *La Rosaura* (facs., New York, 1982) were produced in Parma and Venice, respectively. He succeeded his uncle as *maestro di cappella* at the Cathedral of S. Pietro in Bologna in 1690, then became *maestro di cappella* at S. Petronio (where his application had been turned down earlier) from 1696 until his death; he held similar posts at S. Domenico (1704–55) and S. Maria in Galliera (1706–50). He was admitted to the Accademia filarmonica, made censor in 1719, and continued his studies a few months after that in Parma with Giuseppe Corso. Perti's pupils included Giuseppe Torelli and G. B. Martini. He is noted principally for his sacred vocal music, most of it composed for S. Petronio; these are mainly festive works with strings and, on occasion, trumpets, and include numerous Masses, Psalms, motets, hymns, antiphons, and Magnificat settings. He composed some 26 operas, most of which have been lost, as well as some 20 oratorios.

Bibl.: Jean Berger, "The Sacred Works of Giacomo Antonio Perti," *JAMS* 17 (1964): 370–77. Marcello Di Angelis, "Il Teatro di Pratolino tra Scarlatti e Perti. Il carteggio di G. A. Perti con il principe F. de' Medici," *NRMI* 21 (1987): 605–40.

Pertile, Aureliano (b. Montagnana, 9 Nov. 1885; d. Milan, 11 Jan. 1952). Tenor. Student of Orefice and Bavagnola; made his debut in Vicenza in 1911, and his La Scala debut in 1916; toured South America in 1918, and was engaged at the Metropolitan Opera in 1921 and 1922. He sang regularly at La Scala (1922–37), Covent Garden (1927–31), and other European theaters until his 1946 retirement; he also taught in Rome from 1940, and in Milan from 1946. Noted roles include those of Verdi (Otello and Radames) and Wagner (Lohengrin).

Pescetti, Giovanni Battista (b. Venice, ca. 1704; d. there, 20 Mar. 1766). Composer and keyboardist. He studied under Antonio Lotti and from 1725 to 1732 composed operas for Venetian theaters, sometimes collaborating with his friend Baldassare Galuppi. He was in London in 1736 as a harpsichordist and succeeded Popora as director of the Opera of the Nobility later that year, contributing some operas and pastiche arias for London. By 1747 he was back in Venice as an opera composer, and received an appointment as second organist at St. Mark's in 1762. A number of his operas are based on Metastasio's works, including *Siroe re di Persia* (Venice, 1731); *Alessandro nelle Indie* (Venice, 1732); *Demetrio* (Florence, 1732); *Il Farnaspe* (Siena, 1750); *Artaserse* (Milan, 1751); and *Zenobia* (Padua, 1761).

Bibl.: Francesco Degrada, "Le sonate per cembalo e per organo di Giovanni Battista Pescetti," *Chigiana* 23 (1966): 89–108.

Pesenti [Vicentino], **Michele** (b. Verona?, ca. 1475; d. after 1524). Composer. A priest about whose life virtually nothing definite is known. Aside from 2 motets, he wrote 36 frottole of considerable importance to the early history of this genre. Most were published by Petrucci; Antico issued the others. Some of the frottole were printed with text in all voices, suggesting fully vocal performance, a previously unknown practice in Italian Renaissance music. Popular texts and melodies are often present, although certain pieces incorporate no preexisting material.

Peter, Johann Friedrich [John Frederik] (b. Heerendijk, Holland, 19 May 1746; d. Bethlehem, Pa., 13 July 1813). Composer. After studying in Dutch and German Moravian schools and in the theological seminary of the church at Barby, Saxony, he was sent to America in 1770. There he worked in the Moravian communities of Nazareth, Bethlehem, and Lititz, Pa. In 1780 he was transferred to the community of Salem, N.C., where he became musical director of the congregation. In 1790 he was again transferred, serving successively at Graceham, Md.; Hope, N.J.; and Bethlehem. He remained concerned with music, although his position was usually that of schoolteacher, clerical assistant, or diarist. When he left for America he took with him an extensive manuscript collection of instrumental and vocal works which he had copied at the seminary. He probably learned more from studying these works than from his teachers, who must have included the Moravian composers Johann Daniel Grimm (1719–60) and Christian Gregor (1723–1801). His works include 105 concerted anthems and solo songs as well as 6 quintets (Salem, 1789), which are the oldest surviving chamber music composed in America.

Bibl.: Albert G. Rau, "John Frederick Peter," *MQ* 23 (1937): 306–13. W. E. Schnell, "The Choral Music of Johann Friedrich Peter" (diss., Univ. of Illinois, 1973). J. Ingram, "A Musical Pot-Pourri: The Commonplace Book of Johann Friedrich Peter," *Moravian Foundation Bulletin* 24 (1979). C. Daniel Crews, *Johann Friedrich Peter and His Times* (Winston-Salem, N.C., 1990).

Peters, Carl Friedrich (b. Leipzig, 30 March 1779; d. Sonnenstein, Bavaria, 20 Nov. 1827). Music publisher. In 1814 he bought Kühnel's and Hoffmeister's Bureau de Musique; the firm became known as Bureau de Musique C. F. Peters. The business suffered because of the Battle of Leipzig (1813) and Peters's bouts of depression, which required his committal to an asylum.

In 1828 the firm was taken over by the manufacturer Carl Gotthelf Siegmund Böhme (1785–1855), who brought out works by J. S. Bach. After Böhme's death the Leipzig town council ran the firm as a charity foundation. In 1860 the firm was bought by the Berlin book and music seller Julius Friedländer, who took Max Abraham (1831–1900) into partnership in 1863. Abraham became sole owner in 1880 and built a worldwide reputation for C. F. Peters by publishing first editions of important works, launching Edition Peters (1867), opening the Musikbibliothek Peters to the public (1894), and publishing the *Jahrbuch der Musikbibliothek Peters* from 1895.

Peters, Roberta (b. New York, 4 May 1930). Soprano. Studied with William Hermann; made her Metropolitan Opera debut in 1951 as an understudy Zerlina, and remained with the company through 1985, appearing also in concert and musical theater, on radio and television (as both singer and actress), and as a guest at other opera houses, including Covent Garden (from 1951) and the Vienna Staatsoper (from 1963). She sang Violetta in a celebrated 1972 performance at the Bolshoi Opera.

Peterson, Oscar (Emmanuel) (b. Montreal, 15 Aug. 1925). Jazz pianist. He performed with Jazz at the Philharmonic from 1949. In 1951 he formed a trio with double bass (until 1966, Ray Brown) and guitar (including Barney Kessel, 1952–53, and Herb Ellis, 1953–58). Albums from this period include *The Oscar Peterson Trio at the Stratford Shakespearian Festival* (1956). In 1959 drums replaced the guitar, by the 1970s his trio using either instrument. Among his sidemen have been Niels-Henning Ørsted Pedersen (ca. 1972–87) and Joe Pass (from 1973). He recorded a series of duos with trumpeters, including Dizzy Gillespie and Roy Eldridge, in 1974–75. Having recorded the album *My Favorite Instrument* (ca. 1967), he began performing regularly as an unaccompanied soloist in the 1970s. In 1991 he was named chancellor of York Univ. in Toronto.

Bibl.: Richard Palmer, *Oscar Peterson* (New York, 1984). Gene Lees, *Oscar Peterson: The Will To Swing* (Rocklin, Calif., 1990).

Peterson-Berger, (Olaf) Wilhelm (b. Ullånger, Ångermanland, 27 Feb. 1867; d. Östersund, 3 Dec. 1942). Composer. From 1886 through 1889 he studied organ and composition with Dente and Bolander at the Stockholm Conservatory. He then traveled to Dresden and studied orchestration with Kretzschmar and piano with Schultz, 1889–90, returning to teach there from 1892 to 1894. He worked as a music critic for *Dagens nyheter* in Stockholm, 1896–1930; worked briefly with the Stockholm Opera from 1908 to 1910. He translated the writings of Wagner and Nietzsche, among others. His own music was in a late Romantic style, infused with nationalism. He was influenced by Wagner and wrote a set of music dramas (*Arnljot,* 1907–9) in the style of Wagner's trilogy. His dramatic music includes 5 operas, the final one being *Adils och Elisiv* (1921–24). His orchestral music was often programmatic (Symphony no. 3, "Same-Ätnam" [Lapland], 1913–15; *Earina* [Spring], 1917; Symphony no. 5, Solitudo, 1932–33; *Törnrosasagan* [The Tale of Sleeping Beauty], 1934). Composed many choral pieces, some of which he also wrote the texts for (*Sveagaldrar,* cantata for soloists, chorus, orchestra, 1897), and much music for men's quartets. Also wrote many songs, again some to texts of his own (*Jämtlandsminnen* [Jämtland Memories] op. 4, 1893; *2 Romantiska visor,* texts by Goethe and Bergman, 1932), and piano music, much of it programmatic (*Färdminnen* [Travel Memories], 1908; På fjället i sol [On the Field in Sunshine], 1932).

Petit, Buddy [Crawford, Joseph] (b. White Castle, La., ca. 1897; d. New Orleans, 4 July 1931). Jazz cornetist and bandleader. He co-led a band with Jimmie Noone (1916), worked in California with Jelly Roll Morton (1917), then returned to lead bands in the New Orleans area. Although he never recorded, he was reputedly one of the finest early jazzmen and a rival of Louis Armstrong.

Petrassi, Goffredo (b. Zagarola, near Palestrina, Italy, 16 July 1904). Composer. In Rome with his family from 1911, Petrassi served as a choirboy in the Church of San Salvatore in Lauro. From 1919 he studied scores in the music store where he worked; had piano and harmony lessons; and attended the Conservatory of S. Cecilia (1928–32) as a composition (Bustini) and organ student (Germani). He was appointed to the chair in composition at the conservatory in 1939 and to the more prestigious chair at the academy in 1960; he taught there until his retirement in 1978. He taught as well at summer courses at the Salzburg Mozarteum (1951), the Berkshire Music Center (1956), and the Accademia Chigiana in Siena. He was superintendent of the Fenice di Venezia (1937–40); artistic director of the Accademia filarmonica romana (1947–50); and served as president of the ISCM (1954–56). As a conductor he toured in the U.S. (1955, 1956), Latin America (1953), and Japan (1959) as well as in Europe.

Early recognition came with Casella's presentation of his *Partita* for orchestra at the Amsterdam ISCM meeting (1933), and in Moscow and Leningrad (1935). His first instrumental music was composed within the neoclassical traditions of Hindemith and Stravinsky, but his large choral (*Salmo IX,* 1934) and dramatic (*Il Cordovano,* 1944–48; revived 1988, Dortmund) works draw heavily on models in Italian Baroque music. Beginning with the third concerto (*Récréation concertante,* 1953) he employed serial devices; in the next three (1954–64) motivic fragmentation and a dynamic structure based on free association of related sounds replace thematic development.

Works: 2 operas (*Morte dell'aria,* 1948), ballets, and incidental music; 8 concertos (1934–72), and other orchestral music; *Salmo IX* (chorus and orchestra, 1934), *Noche oscura* (1951), and other works for voices and orchestra; *Sonata da camera* (harpsichord and 10 instruments, 1948), *Sestina d'autunno* "Veni, creator Igor" (viola, cello, double bass, guitar, mandolin, and percussion, 1982), *Romanzetta* (flute, piano, 1980), and other chamber music; a few piano pieces; choral music (*Tre cori sacri,* 1983); solo vocal music; film scores.

Bibl.: Claudio Annibaldi, ed., *Catalogo bibliografico delle opere di Goffredo Petrassi* (Milan, 1971). Edizioni Suvini Zerboni, *Goffredo Petrassi: Catalogo delle opere* (Milan, 1984). John S. Weissmann, *Goffredo Petrassi* (Milan, 1957; rev. 1980). Luca Lombardi, *Conversazioni con Petrassi* (Milan, 1980). Enzo Restagno, ed., *Petrassi* (Turin, 1986).

Petrella, Errico (b. Palermo, 10 Dec. 1813; d. Genoa, 7 Apr. 1877). Composer. Studied with Giovanni Furno, Costa, Ruggi, Zingarelli, and Bellini at the Naples Conservatory. Accepted a commission in 1829 for his first opera, *Il diavolo;* expelled from the conservatory as a result. Composed four more comedies at the Teatro Nuovo during the next nine years. Turned to teaching singing (1839). Appointed musical director at the Teatro Nuovo (1851) and returned to composition with *Le precauzione. Elena di Tolosa* (1852) was so successful that it was transferred after nine days to the Teatro S. Carlo. Produced his first serious opera, *Marco Visconti,* in 1854. His most successful and best-known work, *Jone,* followed in 1858. Collaborated with Ghislanzoni on *I promessi sposi* (Lecco, 1869). Public career ended in 1874. Completed 23 operas in all.

Bibl.: Alfredo Colombani, *L'opera italiana nel secolo XIX* (Milan, 1900). Gino Negri, *L'opera italiana* (Milan, 1985).

Petri, Egon (b. Hannover, 23 March 1881; d. Berkeley, Calif., 27 May 1962). Pianist. Initially studied violin with his father. Busoni, a family friend, became Egon's mentor; the two played joint recitals and collaborated on Busoni's Bach editions. He taught at Royal Manchester College (1905–11) and the Berlin Hochschule (1921–26), also touring in Europe and the Soviet Union; his U.S. debut came in 1932. He fled his Polish vacation home during the 1939 invasion and moved to the U.S., where he taught at Cornell (1944–46), Mills College (1947–57), and the San Francisco Conservatory (1957 to his death).

Petrić, Ivo (b. Ljubljana, 16 June, 1931). Composer. From 1950 through 1958 he was enrolled at the Ljubljana Academy of Music, taking composition lessons with Lucijan Škerjanc and conducting lessons with Danilo Švara. He created a new music group called the Slavko Osterc Ensemble in 1962 with which he performed his and other composers' new works. From 1969 he was active with the Union of Slovenian Composers. From 1972 he was editor of the publishing division of the Association of Slovene Composers, Edicije Društva Slovenskih Skladateljev. His early works are in a neoclassical tradition. He began to incorporate more virtuosity into his writing, exploring the capacities of individual instruments (*Croquis Sonores,* harp, bass clarinet, horn, piano, double bass, percussion, 1963), inspired by the immediate forum that his ensemble offered him. Composed a ballet, *Odisej 67* (1967). His orchestral music includes works that refer to standard forms or genres (Symphony no. 1, Goga, 1954; Divertimento, winds, percussion, 1956; *Dialogues concertantes,* cello, orchestra, 1972; trumpet concerto, 1986) but also, increasingly, descriptive pieces (*Integrali v barvi* [Integrals in Colors], 1968; *3 Images,* violin, orchestra, 1973; *Tako je godel kurent* [This Is the Way To Do the Kurent], viola, orchestra, 1976). His chamber music includes traditional forms (Sonata, clarinet, piano, 1961; *Petit Concerto de Chambre,* oboe, English horn, bass clarinet, horn, harp, string trio, double bass, 1966; *Quatuor 1985,* string quartet, 1985) and works with evocative titles (*Nuances en couleurs,* flute, bassoon, piano, harp, cello, 1966; *Fantasies and Nocturnes,* clarinet, violin, piano, 1986).

Petridis, Petros (John) (b. Nigde, Turkey, 23 July 1892; d. Athens, 17 Aug. 1977). Composer. From 1906 to 1911 he studied in Constantinople at the American Robert College with Hegey and Selvelli. He also studied political science and law at the Univ. of Paris. After the Balkan war he returned to Paris to study theory only briefly with Wolff and Roussel. In 1939 he went back to Athens. He wrote much music criticism for both Greek and British journals and newspapers. He was in London, 1918–19, lecturing on Greek music at King's College. The remainder of his career was split between Athens and Paris. His early music incorporated elements of Greek folk songs. The textures were contrapuntal, the harmony modal or chromatic. He became increasingly influenced by Byzantine music, often employing more than one mode or utilizing traditional forms and genres. He wrote much orchestral music, including concertos (Piano Concerto no. 1, 1934; Cello Concerto, 1936, lost; Piano Concerto no. 2, 1937; Violin Concerto, 1972) and symphonies (no. 1, "Greek," 1928–29; no. 2, "Lyric," 1941; no. 4, "Doric," 1941–43; no. 3, "Parisian," 1944–46; no. 5, "Pastoral," 1949–51, rev. 1972–73). His dramatic music includes the opera *Zefyra* (1923–25; rev. 1958–64) and the oratorio *Hayos Pavlos* (1950).

Petrillo, James C(aesar) (b. Chicago, 16 Mar. 1892; d. there, 23 Oct. 1984). Labor leader. Active as trumpeter before joining the labor movement; became president of the American Musicians' Union in 1914; after an unsuccessful reelection effort in 1917, he joined the American Federation of Musicians, eventually serving as national president (1940–58). He was a central figure in a landmark dispute between musicians and record companies over income from recordings that led to a 1942 strike.

Petrov, Andrei Pavlovich (b. Leningrad, 2 Sept. 1930). Composer. Studied composition with O. Evlakhov at the Leningrad Conservatory, 1949–54; taught composition there, 1961–63. Has received many awards and honors, including USSR State Prizes (1967, 1976), the Order of the Red Banner (1967), the Order of Lenin (1983). Well known as a composer of popular songs and film scores; his music for the concert hall, though largely traditional in form, often reveals the inflections of jazz and popular styles. Works include ballets (*The Creation of the World,* 1971; *Pushkin,* 1978), operas (*Peter the First,* 1975; *Mayakovsky Begins,* 1985); symphonic works (*The Master and Margarita,* 1985); a Violin Concerto (1983); chamber music.

Petrov, Osip (Afanas'yevich) (b. Elizavetgrad [now Kirovograd], 15 Nov. 1806 or 1807; d. St. Petersburg, 12 Mar. 1878). Bass-baritone. Joined Zhurakhovsky's troupe, ca. 1826. Took lessons with Cavos (singing) and Hunke (theory). Was heard singing in Kursk in 1830 and invited to St. Petersburg by Lebedev; debut 1830. Recognized for his dramatic power. Many roles were written for him including Glinka's *A Life for the Tsar* (1836) and *Ruslan* (1842); Ivan the Terrible in Rimsky-Korsakov's *The Maid of Pskov* (1873); Varlaam in Mussorgsky's *Boris Godunov* (1874); the Mayor in Tchaikovsky's *Vakula the Smith* (1876); and Leporello in Dargomïzhsky's *The Stoned Guest* (1872).

Petrovics, Emil (b. Nagybecskerek [now Zrenjanin], 9 Feb. 1930). Composer. He traveled to Budapest and from 1949 to 1951 studied music at the Budapest Conservatory with Sugár, 1951–52 with Viski, and 1952–57 with Farkas. He served as music director at the Petröfi Theater, 1960–64. After 1964 he joined the faculty of the Academy of Dramatic Arts in Budapest; also served as director of the Hungarian State Opera (1986–90). His early music was influenced by French trends as well as by Falla. Many subsequent works developed a highly dramatic musical language, especially visible in the operas *C'est la guerre* (1960–61), *Lysistrate* (1962; rev. for stage 1971), and *Bün és bünhödés* [Crime and Punishment] (1969). His music comfortably moved between serialistic techniques and folklike modality. His works include choral pieces, solo songs and folk song arrangements, and chamber music (*Passacaglia in Blues,* bassoon, piano, 1964; Wind Quintet, 1964; *Nocturne,* cimbalom, 1972; *Rhapsody no. 2,* viola, 1983).

Petrucci, Ottaviano (dei) (b. Fossombrone, 18 June 1466; d. Venice, 7 May 1539). Printer. Developed and put into execution the first method of printing polyphonic music from movable type. His books were of an excellence seldom matched, although his method involved the complex and error-prone device of multiple impression. (Attaingnant's slightly later method required only a single impression.) Resident in Venice from about 1490, he issued his first book in 1501. A collection of chansons entitled *Harmonice musices odhecaton A* (ed. Helen Hewitt, Cambridge, Mass., 1942; R: 1978; facs., *MMML* 1/10, 1973), this began a series that was continued by his *Canti B* (Venice, 1501/2; facs., *MMML* 1/23, 1975; facs., New York, 1976) and *Canti C* (Venice, 1503/4; facs., *MMML* 1/25, 1978). Other publications included collections of frottolas, Masses, and motets, and books in lute tablature. Volumes devoted to the works of single composers (e.g., Josquin, Pierre de la Rue, Obrecht, Agricola, Isaac) appeared alongside many anthologies. Reprints were frequent. Petrucci printed music in Venice until 1509, in Fossombrone from 1511 until 1536. The influence of Petrucci's work was immense, not least because it made possible a far wider dissemination of polyphonic music than could have been achieved previously.

Bibl.: Claudio Sartori, *Bibliografia delle opere musicali stampate da Ottaviano Petrucci* (Florence, 1948). G. Gallico, "Dal laboratorio di Ottaviano Petrucci: Immagine, trasmissione e cultura della musica," *RIM* 17 (1982): 187–206.

Petrus de Cruce [Pierre de la Croix] (fl. ca. 1290). Theorist and composer. Although his only surviving treatise, *Tractatus de tonis* (ed. Denis Harbinson, *CSM* 29, 1976), deals exclusively with the modes, his contribution to the development of mensural notation is well attested by other writers, among them Robert de Handlo, Hanboys, and Jacques de Liège. Petronian notation adheres in most respects to the principles laid out by Franco of Cologne; however, it allows the value of a perfect breve to be subdivided into as many as seven equal semibreves. Jacques de Liège praises his compositions in general and cites two particular motets as examples. Other motets in Petronian notation may also be his work.

Pettersson, (Gustaf) Allan (b. Västra Ryd, Uppsala län, 19 Sept. 1911; d. Stockholm, 20 June 1980). Composer and violist. He studied with Olsson and Blomdahl at the Stockholm Conservatory (1930–39); won a scholarship to study with Vieux in Paris, but the war forced his premature return, and he worked as a violist in the Stockholm Philharmonic (1939–51). In 1951 he returned to Paris and worked with Honegger at the Conservatoire and in twelve-tone theory with Leibowitz. He first attracted attention with a 1968 performance of his Symphony no. 7 by the Stockholm Philharmonic under Dorati, who continued to champion his music. In some respects Pettersson's music resembles Mahler's in both large-scale design and passionate, painful emotional content. Most of the symphonies are in a single extended movement, with frequent shifts of mood, tempo, and meter.

Works: symphonies (no. 1, n.d.; no. 2, 1953; no. 3, 1955; no. 4, 1959; no. 5, 1962; no. 6, 1966; no. 7, 1967; no. 8, 1968–69; no. 9, 1970; no. 10, 1970–72; no. 11, 1973; no. 12, *De döda på torget* [The Dead in the Square], 1974; no. 13, 1976; no. 14, 1978; no. 15, 1978); 3 concertos for string orchestra (1949–50, 1956, 1956–57); Concerto no. 1, violin, string quartet, orchestra (1949); *Symphonic Movement* (1976); violin concerto (1979); viola concerto (1988); *Vox humana* (soloists, chorus, string orchestra, 1973–74); *2 Elegies* (violin, piano, 1934); *Fantasy Piece* (viola, 1936); *4 Improvisations* (violin, viola, cello, 1936); *Andante espressivo* (violin, piano, 1938); *Romanza* (violin, piano, 1942); Fugue in E (oboe, clarinet, bassoon, 1948); 7 sonatas, 2 violins (1951–52); 6 songs (1935); *24 Barfotasånger* [24 Barefoot Songs] (1943–45).

Pettiford, Oscar (b. Okmulgee, Okla., 30 Sept. 1922; d. Copenhagen, 8 Sept. 1960). Jazz double bass player and bandleader. In 1943 he toured with Charlie Barnet's swing band to New York, where he joined Roy Eldridge and recorded an expressive solo on Coleman Hawkins's "The Man I Love." Concurrently active in bop, he played with Thelonious Monk at Minton's Playhouse, then co-led a pioneering group with Dizzy Gillespie (1943–44). He joined the big bands of Duke Ellington (1945–48) and Woody Herman (1949); while with Herman he began using amplified cello as a solo instrument. In the mid-1950s he led bop combos and with a large ensemble recorded 2 albums entitled *The Oscar Pettiford Orchestra in Hi-Fi* (1956–57). He moved to Europe in 1958.

Petyrek, Felix (b. Brno, 14 May 1892; d. Vienna, 1 Dec. 1951). Composer. At the Univ. of Vienna he studied piano with Goldowsky and Sauer, composition with Schreker, and musicology with Adler, graduating in 1919. From 1919 to 1925 he taught piano at the Salzburg Mozarteum and from 1921 to 1925 at the Berlin Hochschule für Musik. During the 1930s he lived and taught in Stuttgart and through 1949 in Leipzig. From 1949 until his death he taught at the Vienna Music Academy. His music is late Romantic in style, especially influenced by Mahler. Like Mahler, Petyrek set images and themes from folk culture into dramatic programmatic pieces. Unlike Mahler, however, he thoroughly incorporated elements of folk music and experimented with current trends in atonality. His works include dramatic music; orchestral and chamber pieces; and many works for piano solo (*Variationen über ein Thema von Verdi,* 2 pianos, 1941; 5 Sonatas for Piano, 1956).

Petzoldt, Johann Christoph. See Pezel, Johann Christoph.

Peuerl [Peyerl, Bäuerl], **Paul** (b. Stuttgart?, bapt. 13 June 1570; d. after 1625). Composer and organ builder. He was an organist at Horn, Lower Austria, from 1602 and at the church of the Protestant school at Steyr, Upper Austria, from 1609. He also built or renovated the organs in these locations as well as in Enns and Wilhering, Upper Austria, though none of these instruments has survived. Peuerl is acknowledged as the originator of the German variation suite, as demonstrated in his *Newe Padouan, Intrada, Däntz und Galliarda* (Nuremberg, 1611).

Bibl.: *Paul Peuerl and Isaac Posch: Instrumental- und Vokalwerke,* ed. Karl Geiringer, *DTÖ* 70, 36/2.

Pevernage, Andreas [Andries, André] (b. Harelbeke, near Courtrai, 1543; d. Antwerp, 30 July 1591). Composer. Choirmaster at St. Salvator, Bruges, in 1563; from later that year until 1578 and again briefly in 1584, at Notre Dame, Courtrai; from 1585 at Notre Dame, Antwerp. Works include Masses, motets, elegies, and secular and spiritual chansons.

Bibl.: Ed. Gerald R. Hoekstra, *RRMR* 60, 61 (1983).

Pezel [Petzel, Petzoldt, Pecelius, Bezel(d), Bezelius], **Johann Christoph** (b. Glatz, Silesia, 5 Dec. 1639; d. Bautzen, 13 Oct. 1694). Composer. He was appointed fourth *Kunstgeiger* in the Leipzig town band (1664) and later promoted to *Stadtpfeifer* for life (1670). He applied unsuccessfully for a position as Kantor of the Thomaskirche, Leipzig, and member of the Dresden *Ratsmusiken* corps. Pezel published 2 collections of music for 5-part cornet and trombone ensembles, *Hora decima musicorum* (Leipzig, 1670) and *Fünff-stimmigte blasende Music* (Frankfurt, 1685).

Bibl.: Elwyn A. Weinandt, *Johann Pezel (1639–1694): A Thematic Catalogue of His Instrumental Works* (New York, 1983). *Johann Christoph Pezel: Turmmusiken und Suiten,* ed. Arnold Schering, *DDT* 63.

Pfitzner, Hans (Erich) (b. Moscow, 5 May 1869; d. Salzburg, 22 May 1949). Composer, conductor, and writer. At his birth his father was working as a violinist in Moscow, but thereafter returned to Frankfurt as music director of the Stadttheater. He studied at the conservatory in Frankfurt (1866–90) with Kwast (theory) and Knorr (piano); remained active as a conductor and accompanist throughout his career. He taught at the Stern Conservatory in Berlin; directed the conservatory and conducted both orchestra and opera in Strasbourg (1908–17); directed a master class in composition at the Prussian Academy of Arts (from 1920); and taught at the Academy of Music in Munich (1920s–early 1930s). Although he had received many honors and was named a *Reichskultursenator* by the Third Reich, he was relieved of his Munich position in 1934 because of his lack of sympathy for the Nazis; he spent the next years as a conductor and accompanist. After the war he was destitute and received support from friends and the Vienna Philharmonic.

Pfitzner achieved early success with his first operas, which were later dismissed as passé; his masterpiece is considered to be the opera *Palestrina* (1912–15), for which he wrote the libretto after extensive study of the events surrounding the Council of Trent. Ostensibly about Palestrina's role in "saving" polyphonic music in the church, it makes a more general statement about the role of the aging artist who fears the loss of his creative power and his sense of belonging. He wrote many polemical articles in response to the views of Busoni (on the contemporary composer's relation to the past), Berg (on the nature of musical inspiration), and others. He was a defender of 19th-century musical values. Although he himself employed dissonant counterpoint and occasional nontriadic harmonies, he remained utterly opposed to atonality.

Works: 5 operas (1891–1931); incidental music; 3 symphonies (1 based on a string quartet), concertos (piano, 1922; violin, 1923; and cello, 1944), and other orchestral music; 3

string quartets, a piano trio and quintet, other chamber and piano music; *Von deutscher Seele* (cantata, Eichendorff; baritone, male voices ad lib.; 1915–16) and other vocal music and songs.

Writings: *Gesammelte Schriften* (Augsburg, 1926–29). *Über musikalische Inspiration* (Berlin, 1940). *Hans Pfitzner: Reden-Schriften-Briefe,* ed. Walter Abendroth (Berlin, 1955). *Hans Pfitzner Sämtliche Schriften,* ed. Bernhard Adamy (1987).

Bibl.: Bernhard Adamy, *Hans Pfitzner: Literatur, Philosophie, und Zeitgeschehen in seinem Weltbild und Werk* (Tutzing, 1980). Peter Franklin, "*Palestrina* and the Dangerous Futurists," *MQ* 70 (1984): 499–514. Reinhard Ermen, *Musik als Einfall: Hans Pfitzners Position in aesthetischen Diskurs nach Wagner* (Aachen, 1986). Elisabeth Wamlek-Junk, *Hans Pfitzner und Wien* (Tutzing, 1987). John Williamson, *The Music of Hans Pfitzner* (New York, 1992).

Phalèse, Pierre (b. Louvain, ca. 1510; d. there?, 1573–76). Music publisher. After five years as a bookseller in Louvain, he began in 1551 to produce high-quality prints of music from movable type. His output includes Masses, motets, and chansons (many by Clemens non Papa and other composers of the Low Countries, as well as Lassus and Rore), Magnificats, and pieces in French lute tablature (solos, accompanied songs, and works for more than one lute). A partnership with Jean Bellère, a printer active in Antwerp, was undertaken in 1570 in order to ensure a wider audience and perhaps to forestall unwanted competition from Plantin, the inheritor of Susato's printing materials.

Bibl.: H. Vanhulst, "Edition comparative des instructions pour le luth, le cistre et la guitarre publiées à Louvain par Pierre Phalèse (1545–1570)," *RBM* 34–35 (1980–81): 81–105.

Phelps, Lawrence Irving (b. Somerville, Mass., 10 May 1923). Organ builder. He studied conducting and organ at the New England Conservatory of Music; worked for five years with G. Donald Harrison at the Aeolian-Skinner Organ Company in Boston and later with Walter Holtkamp. Beginning in 1949 Phelps began working as a consultant, his biggest project being the instrument designed for the First Church of Christ Scientist in Boston. From 1958 to 1972 he served as director of the Quebec firm of Casavant Frères and subsequently operated his own company in Erie, Pennsylvania.

Philidor [Filidor], **François-André Danican** (b. Dreux, 7 Sept. 1726; d. London, 31 Aug. 1795). Composer. He was the youngest son of André Danican Philidor *l'aîné* (b. Versailles, ca. 1647; d. Dreux, 11 Aug. 1730), composer and music librarian, and half-brother of Anne Danican Philidor (b. Paris, 11 April 1681; d. there, 8 Oct. 1728), composer and founder of the Concert spirituel. As a pageboy in the royal chapel at Versailles he studied music with André Campra and learned to play chess. In 1740 he went to Paris, where he earned a living by copying and teaching. But he was more interested in chess; he studied with and defeated France's best player, Légal. After a concert tour of the Netherlands with Geminiani and Lanza was abruptly canceled in 1745, Philidor traveled to London. He was soon recognized as the leading chess player of central and northern Europe; he published a chess treatise in 1749. In 1754 he returned to Paris and applied unsuccessfully for the post of court composer at Versailles. Rebel considered his Italianate style unsuitable for the Opéra, but between 1759 and 1765 Philidor produced 11 opéras comiques, including *Le Maréchal ferrant* (1761), *Le Sorcier* (1764), and *Tom Jones* (1765). After 1771 he spent much of his time in London, where he gave seasonal lectures and demonstrations to the St. James Chess Club in 1771 and 1773, and from 1775 to 1792. Also in London he produced his major choral work, the *Carmen saeculare* (1779). Philidor continued to teach music and compose for the French stage and the Concert spirituel, although his later tragedies, including *Persée* (1780) and *Thémistocle* (1785), were not well received.

Bibl.: C. M. Carroll, "François-André Danican Philidor: His Life and Dramatic Art" (diss., Florida State Univ., 1960). Julian Rushton, "Philidor and the Tragédie Lyrique," *MT* 117 (1976): 734–37.

Philipp, Isidor (b. Budapest, 2 Sept. 1863; d. Paris, 20 Feb. 1958). Pianist. Student of Mathias at the Paris Conservatoire; later studied with Heller, Ritter, and Saint-Saëns; joined the Conservatoire faculty in 1893, remaining there until 1934. He moved to the U.S. in 1941, teaching in New York and Montreal, and returned to France after a 1955 farewell concert. He played chamber music as well, and published many 2-piano arrangements.

Philippot, Michael Paul (b. Verzy, 2 Feb. 1925). Composer. He studied with Dandelot at the Paris Conservatory (1946–48) and also with Leibowitz (1948–50). Beginning 1949 associated with ORTF in Paris (as head of the Groupe de recherches musicales; director of the music division; and science and culture adviser to the director). In 1970 he became professor of composition at the Paris Conservatory and later dean of the new music faculty at the Univ. of São Bernardo do Campo in Brazil. Author of 3 books (*La Musique et la Radio diffusion,* 1965). His compositions employ serial procedures; they include both electronic music and pieces for traditional instruments and voices (*Commentariolus Copernicae,* 9 instruments, 1973; Quintet, strings and piano, 1986). His Concerto for viola and violin was premiered in Paris (10 Sept. 1987).

Philippus de Caserta [Philipoctus, Filipoctus] (fl. ca. 1370). Theorist and composer. Resident at the papal court in Avignon in the late 14th century. His *Tractatus de diversis figuris* (*CS* 3:118) describes many new note shapes for rhythmic values not easily expressed in ordinary *ars nova* notation. Some of these note forms, although not many, appear in his extant secular compositions (6 ballades, plus 1 rondeau of doubtful authenticity; ed. Willi Apel, *French Secular Compositions of the Fourteenth Century, CMM* 53/1, 1970). Also wrote 1 Credo.

Philips, Peter (b. London?, 1560–61; d. Brussels, 1628). Composer. After leaving his native England in 1582 for religious reasons, he became organist at the English College in Rome. From 1585 to 1589 he traveled through Europe in the service of Lord Thomas Paget, who settled in Brussels. After his patron's death, Philips moved to Antwerp in 1590, remaining there until assuming a post in Brussels as an organist in the chapel of Archduke Albert (soon to be a coregent of the Spanish Netherlands) in 1597. His earliest works are for keyboard, many included in the Fitzwilliam Virginal Book. He also wrote several books of conservative Italian madrigals. The yet more numerous motets are highly varied in style and range from fully choral (even polychoral) works to pieces for one voice and continuo. Some instrumental ensemble music and other sacred pieces also survive. His compositions were often reprinted and were known throughout Europe except in Italy.

Phillips, Burrill (b. Omaha, 9 Nov. 1907; d. Berkeley, 22 June 1988). Composer and pianist. He studied at the Denver College of Music (1928–31) and the Eastman School (under Hanson and Rogers; M.M., 1933); taught at Eastman (1933–49), the Univ. of Illinois (1949–64), and briefly at Juilliard and Cornell. Awards include 2 Guggenheim Fellowships (1942, 1961); received several prestigious commissions (*The Return of Odysseus,* baritone, narrator, chorus, and orchestra; commissioned by the Fromm Foundation in 1956). In the 1960s he began to use serial procedures. Works inlcude an opera (*The Unforgiven,* 1981), ballets and incidental music; orchestral, chamber, organ, and piano music; and vocal music (*Canzona III,* soprano, flute, piano, and percussion, 1964).

Phillips, Harvey (Gene) (b. Aurora, Mo., 2 Dec. 1929). Tuba player. Played the sousaphone in high school; after a short period at the Univ. of Missouri he joined the Ringling Brothers band. He studied at Juilliard and the Manhattan School (1950–54, 1956–58). Taught at the Univ. of Hartford (1962–64), Mannes College (1964–65), and Indiana Univ. (from 1971). He performed in many ensembles and in solo recital, has founded innovative programs for tuba players.

Phinot [Finotto], **Dominique** [Domenico, Dominicus] (b. ca. 1510; d. ca. 1555). Composer. Of Franco-Flemish origin but active chiefly in Italy; perhaps resident briefly in Lyons (late 1540s). The many publications of his works and laudatory mentions by theorists (Hermann Finck, Domenico Cerone) confirm his excellent reputation among his contemporaries. Works include Masses, Magnificats, motets (several books), Psalms, and chansons.

Bibl.: Ed. Janez Höfler, *CMM* 59 (1972–82).

Piaf [Gassion], **Edith (Giovanna)** (b. Paris, 19 Dec. 1915; d. there, 11 Oct. 1963). Popular singer and songwriter. From 1930 she performed in nightclubs in Paris, and in 1935 opened at Gerny's as "La môme Piaf"; later she appeared at the A.B.C., the Européen, and Bobino's. After World War II she became known internationally through recordings and films; among her popular recordings were those of her own songs, including "La vie en rose" (1950). She authored 2 books of memoirs (*Au bal de la chance,* 1958; *Ma vie,* 1964).

Bibl.: Monique Lange, *Piaf* (New York, 1981). Auguste Le Breton, *La môme Piaf* (Paris, 1980).

Piatigorsky, Gregor (b. Ekaterinoslav, Ukraine, 17 Apr. 1903; d. Los Angeles, 6 Aug. 1976). Cellist. Entered Moscow Conservatory at age 9; joined the Imperial Opera orchestra and the Lenin Quartet in 1919. Left Russia in 1921, staying in Warsaw, then Leipzig, before Furtwängler engaged him as first cellist for the Berlin Philharmonic in 1924. He began a solo career in 1928, playing with the New York Philharmonic in 1929 and entertaining at the White House. He lived in Paris from 1937 until the war began, when he emigrated to the U.S.; in addition to concertizing, he taught at the Curtis Institute (1942–44) and gave master classes at the Univ. of Southern California (from 1962). He was famed for his chamber music playing, forming trios with Schnabel and Flesch in Berlin, Heifetz and Rubinstein in the U.S.; among his premieres were concertos of Hindemith (1941) and Walton (1957).

Piatti, Alfredo (Carlo) (b. Bergamo, 8 Jan. 1822; d. Crocetto di Mozzo, 18 July 1901). Cellist and composer. Son of Antonio Piatti, director of Bergamo orchestra. Studied cello with Zanetti; attended the Milan Conservatory, 1832–37, where he studied with Merighi. Studied composition with Molique. Debut in Milan, 1837, playing his own concerto; Paris and London debuts, 1844. After 1846, lived in London; joined Italian Opera. Gave concerts there every year to 1898. Professor at the Royal Academy of Music, where the Piatti Prize for cellists was established in his memory. Wrote many pieces for cello, including 12 caprices op. 25 (1875) and 2 concertos (1874, 1877).

Bibl.: Morton Latham, *Alfredo Piatti* (London, 1901).

Piave, Francesco Mario (b. Murano, 18 May 1810; d. Milan, 5 Mar. 1876). Poet and librettist. Began studies for the priesthood, then studied rhetoric and philosophy. During his 20s, published translations and short stories. Put in touch with Verdi in the early 1840s. Wrote libretti for works by Mercadante, Pacini, Ponchielli, and 10 of Verdi's operas: *Ernani* (1844), *I due Foscari* (1844), *Macbeth* (1847), *Il corsaro* (1848), *Stiffelio* (1850), *Rigoletto* (1851), *La traviata* (1853), *Aroldo* (1857), *Simon Boccanegra* (1857), *La forza del destino* (1862).

Bibl.: Guido Antonio Quarti, *Francesco Mario Piave poeta melodrammatico* (Rome, 1939). Ulderico Rolandi, *Libretti e librettisti verdiani* (Rome, 1941).

Picchi, Giovanni (fl. 1600–1625). Composer. He was organist of the Cà Grande, Venice, by 1615, and became organist of the Scuola di San Rocco, Venice, in 1623. His published works include 8 keyboard dances which appeared in *Intavolatura di balli d'arpicordo*

(Venice, ca. 1618; 2nd ed., 1621; facs., Milan, 1934; R: Bologna, 1968), as well as canzonas and sonatas in partbook form in *Canzoni da sonar* (Venice, 1625).

Bibl.: *Collected Keyboard Works: Giovanni Picchi,* ed. J. Evan Kreider, *CEKM* 38 (1977).

Piccinini, Alessandro (b. Bologna, 30 Dec. 1566; d. there?, ca. 1638). Composer and lutenist. He went with his family (also lutenists) to the Este court at Ferrara, remained there until 1597, then entered the service of Cardinal Pietro Aldobrandini. He published 2 volumes, *Intavolatura di liuto, et di chitarrone . . .* (Bologna, 1623; facs., Bologna, 1962) and *Intavolatura di liuto, nel quale si contengano toccata . . .* (Bologna, 1639). In the preface to the earlier volume he claims to have invented a type of archlute (now thought to be a bass lute); the preface also contains interesting performance practice instructions.

Piccinni [Piccini], **(Vito) Niccolò** [Nicola] **(Marcello Antonio Giacomo)** (b. Bari, 16 Jan. 1728; d. Passy, near Paris, 7 May 1800). Composer. From 1742 to 1754 he studied with Leo and then Durante at the S. Onofrio Conservatory in Naples. He then embarked on a successful operatic career, writing serious and comic operas for Naples. His first opera seria, *Zenobia* (1756), was given at the Teatro S. Carlo. In 1758 he received an operatic commission from Rome; his second opera for Rome, *La Cecchina, ossia La buona figliuola* (1760) was a great success and established him as the favorite of the Roman public. From this time on he became known for his fertility as a composer. Sacchini, reported by Burney, claimed Piccinni had written 300 operas, while La Borde and Ginguené gave the more accurate figure of 130. From 1758 to 1773 Piccinni produced over 30 operas in Naples, over 20 in Rome, and others in all the major Italian cities. In Naples he was second *maestro di cappella* at the cathedral, taught singing, and was organist at various convents. In 1771 he became second organist at the royal chapel. From 1773 Piccinni became overshadowed in Rome by Anfossi, but maintained his reputation in Naples with his second setting of *Alessandro nelle Indie* (1774) and the comedy *I viaggiatori* (1775). In 1776 he accepted an offer from the French court to move to Paris. There he was able to transcend the bickering of the "Gluckists" and the "Piccinnists" and successfully adapted his style to the French stage; his *Roland* (1778) was well received. In 1778–79 he directed a troupe of Italians in performances of opere buffe at the Académie-royale. Later he directed the singing instruction at the École royale de musique et de déclamation. Despite the disappointment of having the premiere of his *Iphigénie en Tauride* (1781) delayed until two years after Gluck's, Piccinni had notable success in 1783 with *Didon,* a revival of *Atys* (1780), and *Le faux lord.* During that year he was granted a pension by the French court. But his position deteriorated rapidly from 1784: he faced serious competition from Sacchini and Salieri and saw the failure of several of his operas, including the premiere of *Pénélope* in 1785. In 1791, following the withdrawal of his pension because of the Revolution, he left Paris for Naples. As the result of his daughter's marriage to a French Jacobite, he was placed under house arrest in 1794; he remained there until returning to France in 1798. In Paris his pension was only partially restored, and by the time he was appointed sixth inspector at the Conservatoire, he was already too ill to carry out his duties.

Bibl.: A. dalla Corte, *Piccinni: Settecento italiano* (Bari, 1928). N. Pascazio, *L'uomo Piccinni e la "Querelle célébre"* (Bari, 1951). Julian Rushton, "'Iphigénie en Tauride': The Operas of Gluck and Piccinni," *ML* 53 (1972): 411–30. Id., "The Theory and Practice of Piccinnisme," *PRMA* 98 (1971–72). G. Allroggen, "Piccinnis *Origille,*" *AnMc* 15 (1975): 258–97. Mary Hunter, "The Fusion and Juxtaposition of Genres in Opera Buffa, 1770–1800: Anelli and Piccinni's 'Griselda,'" *ML* 67 (1986): 363–80.

Pichl [Pichel], **Václav** [Venceslaus; Wenzel] (b. Bechyně, near Tábor, Bohemia, 25 Sept. 1741; d. Vienna, 23 Jan. 1805). Composer and violinist. He attended the Jesuit College at Březnice (1752–58) and served as a violinist at St. Venceslaus' seminary in Prague. In 1765 Dittersdorf hired him as a violinist for the orchestra of Bishop Adam Patachich at Nagyvárad, Grosswardein; in 1770 he was appointed first violinist at the Vienna court theater. Pichl served as music director and *Kammerdiener* (valet) to Archduke Ferdinando d'Este, the Austrian governor of Lombardy, first in Milan (1777–96) and then in Vienna, remaining in the archduke's service until his death. Surviving compositions include a large body of chamber music, sacred music, and symphonies similar in style to those of Dittersdorf.

Pick-Mangiagalli, Riccardo (b. Strakonice, Bohemia, 10 July 1882; d. Milan, 8 July 1949). Composer and pianist. His family was in Milan by 1884, and he studied at the conservatory there (1896–1903). Had a career as a pianist, sometimes performing with his brother Roberto (a violinist); after 1914 devoted himself to composition and teaching. He succeeded Pizzetti as director of the Milan Conservatory (1936–49). His most popular works were 12 light operas and ballets (*Il carillon magico, commedia mimo-sinfonico,* Milan, 1918). He also wrote some 17 orchestral pieces, 1914–44 (*Notturno e rondò fantastico,* 1914); chamber music; pieces for piano and for harp; choral music and songs; and 2 film scores.

Picker, Tobias (b. New York, 18 July 1954). Composer and pianist. In his teens he was a pianist at the Martha Graham School; studied with Wuorinen at the Manhattan School and with Carter at Juilliard (M.M., 1978). He received a Rockefeller Foundation Award in 1979 and a Guggenheim Fellowship in 1981; in 1985 he was composer-in-residence with the Houston Symphony. His works include a violin concerto (1981) and 2 concertos for piano (1980, 1983) as well as a symphony (1982); *Encantados* (Melville, narrator and orchestra,

1983); chamber music (*New Memories,* string quartet, 1987), piano, and vocal music; and piano pieces for students.

Pickett, Wilson (b. Prattville, Ala., 18 Mar. 1941). Soul singer and songwriter. After singing with gospel groups in Detroit and the South, in 1959 he joined the Falcons, singing lead on their 1962 success "I Found a Love." His subsequent solo recordings are considered seminal to the history of soul music; they include "It's Too Late" (1963), "Land of 1,000 Dances" (1966), and "Don't Knock My Love, Pt. 1" (1971).

Pierce, Webb (b. near West Monroe, La., 8 Aug. 1926; d. Nashville, Tenn., 24 Feb. 1991). Country singer, songwriter, guitarist, and publisher. Began performing on radio in Louisiana; joined the Louisiana Hayride in 1950 and the Grand Ole Opry in 1952. He was one of the most popular country recording artists of the 1950s; his records (including "Wondering," 1952; "More and More," 1954) introduced the pedal steel guitar to country music. In 1972 he founded the Nashville publishing firm Cedarwood; later projects included a duet album with Willie Nelson (1982).

Pierné, (Henri-Constant-) Gabriel (b. Metz, 16 Aug. 1863; d. Ploujean Finestère, 17 July 1937). Composer and conductor. He lived in Paris from the age of 17 and studied with Franck and Massenet at the Conservatory; in 1882 his cantata *Edith* won the Prix de Rome. He succeeded Franck as organist at Ste. Clothilde (1890–98); was deputy and then principal conductor (1910) of the Concerts Colonne (1903–34), for which he prepared almost weekly concerts. In 1900 he was made a chevalier of the Légion d'honneur, and in 1925 was admitted to the Academie des Beaux-Arts. He wrote at least 10 dramatic works (*Fragonard,* Paris, 1934); ballets, pantomimes, and incidental music; 4 oratorios, cantatas, and other works for voices and instruments; orchestral music (*Fantaisie basque,* with solo harp, 1927); chamber and piano music; choral pieces and songs. He transcribed and arranged works of Rameau, Gluck, Schumann, and others.

Pierson [Pearson], **Henry Hugo** [Hugh] (b. Oxford, 12 Apr. 1815; d. Leipzig, 28 Jan. 1873). Composer. Early studies were with Attwood. Studied at Trinity College, Cambridge (1836), in Germany with Rinck and Reissiger, and with Tomašek in Prague. He knew Mendelssohn, Schumann, Spohr, and Meyerbeer. Elected Reed Professor of Music at Edinburgh, 1844. Used the pen name Edgar Mansfeldt for his published compositions. Compositions include 99 songs (1839–ca. 1875); incidental music to Goethe's *Faust,* pt. 2 (1854); 4 operas (*Der Elfenseig,* 1845; *Leila,* 1848; *Contarini, oder Die Verschwörung zu Padua,* 1853; *Fenice,* 1883); the oratorio *Jerusalem* (1852); overtures; short choral works.

Bibl.: H. G. Sear, "Faust and Henry Hugh Pierson," *MR* 10 (1949): 183–90.

Pietrobono (b. Ferrara?, ca. 1417; d. there, 20 Sept. 1497). Lutenist and singer. Spent most of his career at the ducal court in Ferrara. His excellence as a performer, especially on the lute, earned him the praise of many contemporary writers, including Tinctoris and the poet Antonio Cornazano. Medals honoring him were made as early as 1452.

Pijper, Willem (b. Zeist, 8 Sept. 1894; d. Leidschendam, 18 Mar. 1947). Composer. From 1911 to 1916 he studied composition in Utrecht with Wagenaar. He then wrote music criticism, often controversial, in Utrecht, 1918–30. Taught theory and then composition at the Amsterdam Conservatory from 1918 to 1930. From 1930 until his death he was head of the Rotterdam Conservatory. His early works use a German late Romantic style as a point of departure (Symphony no. 1, 1917). He was also influenced by turn-of-the-century French composers such as Fauré (*Romances sans paroles,* Verlaine, 1916). Through the 1920s he increasingly explored chromaticism, multiple tonal centers, and the development of his "germ cell" approach to composition, by which a motive is unfolded on local and large scales over the course of a composition (Septet, wind quintet, piano, double bass, 1920; *Heer Halewijn,* chorus, 1929). His orchestral works through the 1920s showed experimentation of a wide range of sonorous and formal possibilities. His Second Symphony (1921) was scored for an unusually large and diverse ensemble (including 3 pianos, organ, celeste, and 6 mandolins) and used evocative textures and musical styles to create an overall binary structure. The Third Symphony (1926) was more similar to its Austro-Germanic antecedents in orchestration and in its almost cyclic development of motives over its contrasting 5 movements. The Piano Sonata from 1930 used a chord as a "tonic" point of reference, deriving its motivic "germ cells" from patterns implicit in the chord. His last large work was the opera *Halewijn* (1933), which also drew on the "germ cell" principle.

Bibl.: W. C. M. Kloppenburg, *Thematisch bibliografische catalogus van de werken van Willem Pijper* (Assen, 1960).

Pilkington, Francis (b. ca. 1570; d. Chester, 1638). Composer. He received the B.Mus. at Lincoln College, Oxford, in 1595 and became a lay clerk (1602) and minor canon (1612) at Chester Cathedral. He took holy orders, becoming a "full minister" in 1614 and precentor in 1623 and was active in the cathedral choir; he also held a number of curacies in Chester, including his main charge at St. Bridget's. Pilkington is best known as the composer of 2 books of madrigals, *The First [Second] Set of Madrigals and Pastorals* (London, 1613–14 [1624]; R: 1923, 1959) as well as a volume of lute songs, *The First Booke of Songs or Ayres . . .* (London, 1605; facs., *ELS* 8/34, 1969); most of his pieces for solo lute (all in Jeffery; see below) are probably early compositions.

Bibl.: Brian Jeffery, *Francis Pilkington: Complete Works for Solo Lute* (London, 1970).

Pimsleur, Solomon (b. Paris, 19 Sept. 1900; d. New York, 22 Apr. 1962). Composer and pianist. His family moved to New York in 1903; he studied at Columbia with Daniel Gregory Mason, at Juilliard with Goldmark, and at the Mozarteum in Salzburg. He was active as a pianist and lecturer; operated an artists' agency and production company with his sister Susan Pimsleur Puma; and wrote over 120 instrumental and vocal works (*Heart Rending Sonata for String Sextet* op. 77). He left incomplete an opera based on the *Diary of Anne Frank.* Papers are at Columbia and in the Moldenhauer Archive in Spokane.

Pini-Corsi, Antonio (b. Zara, Dalmatia, 19 June 1858; d. Milan, 22 Apr. 1918). Baritone. Debut in Cremona (1878) as Dandini in *La Cenerentola.* Specialized in comic roles of Rossini and Donizetti. Performed *Rigoletto* at La Scala (Jan. 1893). Created the role of Ford in *Falstaff* (9 Feb. 1906). Sang in first performances of Giordano's *Siberia* (1903), Franchetti's *La figlia di Jorio* (1906), Happy in Puccini's *La fanciulla del West* (1910). Sang at the Metropolitan Opera (1909–14). Last performance, 1917, at Teatro dal Verme.

Pinilla, Enrique (b. Lima, 3 Aug. 1927). Composer. Studied in Lima with Málaga, Sas, and Holzmann; in Paris with Koechlin and Honegger; and in Madrid with del Campo, Arias, and Otero, graduating from the Royal Conservatory, Madrid, in 1958. Studied electronic music with Ussachevsky at Columbia Univ. in 1966–67. Taught ethnomusicology and music history at the National Conservatory, Lima, from 1961, and later at the Univ. of Lima. As a composer he uses a variety of approaches, from folk idioms to atonality and serialism; works include *Festejo* (1965); *Evoluciones* (1967); chamber works; music for theater, film, and television; piano and vocal pieces.

Bibl.: *Composers of the Americas* 11 (Washington, D.C., 1965), pp. 85–90 [includes works list].

Pinkham, Daniel (Rogers, Jr.) (b. Lynn, Mass., 5 June 1923). Composer, organist, and harpsichordist. He studied composition at Harvard with Merritt, Piston, and Copland (1940–44), at the Berkshire Music Center with Honegger and Barber, and with Boulanger. He was an organ pupil of Biggs (1947), and a harpsichord pupil of Putnam Aldrich (1941–42) and Landowska (1946). He taught at Simmons College, Boston Univ., and Harvard before being appointed to teach composition and early music performance at the New England Conservatory (1959); also director of music at King's Chapel (Boston) beginning 1958. In the early 1950s he performed widely in the U.S. and Europe as a harpsichordist, giving lecture-recitals at the summer courses at Dartington Hall (England) in 1954. During that same decade he explored the use of serial procedures in his compositions (which had earlier been in a neoclassical style); in the 1970s he began to combine electronic music with that for live performers. His language became increasingly chromatic, though forms and textures remained influenced by his wide acquaintance with Baroque music.

Works: *The Dreadful Dining Car* (Pinkham, after Twain; mezzo-soprano, actors, soloists, chorus, and 7 instruments; 1982) and 2 other stage works; 3 symphonies (1961, 1963, 1985), *To Troubled Friends* (string orchestra and tape, 1972), *Signs of the Zodiac* (David McCord; optional narrator and orchestra, 1965), and other orchestral music; about 20 film scores; *Toccatas for the Vault of Heavens* (organ and tape, 1972), a Brass Quintet (1985), Sonata da chiesa (viola and organ, premiered 1988) and other chamber and keyboard music; more than 60 choral pieces (*Lauds,* 2 voices, 2 horns, double bass, organ, and percussion, 1984); and solo vocal music (*The Witch of Endor,* alto, harpsichord, and percussion, 1981; *4 Marian Antiphons,* tenor and organ, premiered 1988).

Bibl.: Kee DeBoer and John B. Ahouse, *Daniel Pinkham: A Bio-Bibliography* (New York, 1988).

Pinnock, Trevor (b. Canterbury, 16 Dec. 1946). Harpsichordist and conductor. Attended the Canterbury Cathedral Choir School, and from 1966 to 1968 studied at the Royal College of Music. He was a member of the Galliard Harpsichord Trio from 1966 to 1971, and founded the period instrument ensemble The English Concert in 1972. Among his recordings are Rameau's complete keyboard music, Bach's Goldberg Variations, and orchestral music of J. S. Bach, Handel, Vivaldi, and C. P. E. Bach. He was artist-in-residence at Washington Univ. in 1976, 1978, and 1981.

Piňos, Alois Simandl (b. Vyškov, 2 Oct. 1925). Composer. He initially studied forestry, graduating from the Univ. of Brno in 1953. He went on to study music at the Brno Conservatory, 1948–49, with Petrželka and from 1945 to 1953 at the Janáček Academy with Kvapil and Schaeffer; also studied briefly at Darmstadt and in Munich. He became a professor at the Janáček Academy in 1953. His early music was influenced by Bartók and, to some degree, by Janáček. By the 1960s he began to incorporate serialism and some aleatoric devices (coinciding with his study at Darmstadt), as well as the use of electronic media. His works include orchestral music (*Concerto on BACH,* bass clarinet, piano, cello, orchestra, 1968), chamber music (String Quartet, 1962; *Composition for 3,* flute, clarinet, marimba, marimbaphone, 1975). He also wrote vocal and electronic music.

Pinto, George Frederick (b. Lambeth, England, 25 Sept. 1785; d. Chelsea, 23 Mar. 1806). Composer and violinist. He started violin while very young, becoming a student of Salomon's in 1793 and making his debut three years later at a benefit. Between 1798 and 1803 he concertized widely in London, also becoming an accomplished pianist; in 1800 he performed with John Field. Pinto's early death cut short what would no doubt have been a notable career as a composer; his piano works, including the 2 Grand Sonatas op. 3 (1803), are especially distinguished.

Pinza, Ezio (Fortunato) (b. Rome, 18 May 1892; d. Stamford, Conn., 9 May 1957). Bass. After an unsuccessful career as a bicycle racer, he studied voice at the

Ravenna and Bologna conservatories; made his debut in 1914; sang after World War I in Florence, Rome, and Milan, and was a fixture at the Metropolitan Opera between 1926 and 1948, singing also in San Francisco, Chicago, London, and Vienna. He took roles as diverse as Don Giovanni and Boris Godunov; later scored a major success on Broadway in *South Pacific,* and appeared in films.

Pipelare, Matthaeus (b. ca. 1450; d. ca. 1515). Composer. Active in Antwerp before moving to 's-Hertogenbosch as master of the choirboys of the Marian Brotherhood (1498–1500). His compositions are highly diverse in style and include almost a dozen Masses, a "Credo de Sancto Johanne evangelista," about 10 motets, and slightly fewer chansons (most with Flemish texts, a few French).

Bibl.: Ed. Ronald Cross, *CMM* 34 (1966–67).

Pipkov, Lubomir (b. Lovec, 19 Sept. 1904; d. Sofia, 9 May 1974). Composer. From 1923 to 1926 he studied piano at the Sofia Music Conservatory; then traveled to Paris, where he studied with Boulanger and, between 1926 and 1932, with Dukas and piano with Léfébure. Back in Sofia he worked with the National Opera from 1932 until 1947 and served as president of the Bulgarian Composers' Union, 1947–54. His music is highly influenced in structure, melody, and harmony by Bulgarian folk music. His works include operas, orchestral works (4 symphonies, 1937–70), and concertos (piano op. 48, 1954; clarinet op. 70, 1969). He also wrote chamber and vocal music (*Oratoriya za nasheto vreme* [Oratorio for Our Time] op. 61, 1959).

Pires, (Luis) Filipe (b. Lisbon, 26 June 1934). Composer and pianist. From 1946 to 1954 he studied at the Lisbon Conservatory; his teachers included Mendes (piano) and Crouer de Vasconcelos (composition). He also attended Darmstadt summer courses. Pires taught at the Oporto Conservatory (1969–72) and then at the Lisbon Conservatory, where he also directed the electronic music studio. Works include 2 ballets (*Instantâneo,* 1962–64; *Namban,* tape, 1970); *Regresso eterno* (R. Cinatti, baritone/speaker, orchestra, 1961); *Akronos* (orchestra, 1964); *Perspectives* (3 groups, 1965); *Portugaliae genesis* (baritone, chorus, orchestra, 1968); *Mobiles* (chamber orchestra, piano, 1968–69); *Sintra* (orchestra, 1969); other choral, chamber, and piano music, and pieces for electronic tape.

Pironkov, Simeon (b. Lom, 18 June 1927). Composer. He graduated from the Bulgarian State Academy of Music in Sofia in 1952, where he had taken conducting lessons with Dimitrov and composition lessons with Stoyanov and Hadjiev. He went on to write film music and to serve as head of the National Youth Theater, both of which provided inspiring forums for his growth as a composer. His compositions include opera (*O, moya mechta* [Oh, My Dream], 1987), orchestral works (*Ballet Music in Memoriam Igor Stravinsky,* 1972; flute concerto, 1987), chamber music (*Thema con variazioni,* violin, piano, 1985), a large body of piano music (16 Preludes, 1969), and choral works (*Jitie i stradanie greschnago Sofronija* [The Life and Sorrows of the Guilty Sofronii], solo voices, chorus, orchestra, 1976).

Pisador, Diego (b. Salamanca, ca. 1509; d. after 1557). Vihuelist and composer. Took minor orders in 1526. Published a book in vihuela tablature, *Libro de música de vihuela agora nuevamente compuesta* (Salamanca, 1552; facs., Geneva, 1973). This collection includes some original fantasias but is made up chiefly of intabulations of Masses by Josquin, motets, Spanish and Italian songs, *romances, villanesche,* and madrigals. Although works by a number of major composers appear, Pisador expressed in a preface particular esteem for the music of Josquin.

Pisano [Pagoli], **Bernardo** (b. Florence, 12 Oct. 1490; d. Rome, 23 Jan. 1548). Composer. *Maestro di cappella* at the Cathedral of Florence; from 1514 resident in Rome as a singer in the chapel of the Medici popes. Works include responsories for Holy Week, settings of strophic canzonettas and *ballate,* and some of the earliest true 16th-century madrigals.

Bibl.: Frank A. D'Accone, ed., *Music of the Florentine Renaissance, CMM* 32/1 (1966).

Pisendel, Johann Georg (b. Cadolzburg, 26 Dec. 1687; d. Dresden, 25 Nov. 1755). Violinist and composer. He studied violin with Torelli, singing with Pistocchi, and composition with Heinichen. He was a chorister in Ansbach (1697 or 1698) and became a violinist in the court orchestra several years later. In 1709 he met Bach in Weimar then settled in Leipzig, where he served as director of the Collegium musicum and opera orchestra in 1710. He was a violinist with the Dresden court orchestra from 1712, becoming *Konzertmeister* in 1728; during a visit to Italy (1716–17) he studied with Vivaldi and Montanari. Pisendel was perhaps the greatest German violinist of his time, and several composers, including Vivaldi, Albinoni, and Telemann, dedicated works to him; his own compositions include 7 violin concertos and a solo violin sonata.

Pisk, Paul Amadeus (b. Vienna, 16 May 1893; d. Hollywood, 12 Jan. 1990). Composer, musicologist. He studied with Schreker and Schoenberg and took a doctorate in musicology at the Univ. of Vienna (1916); then taught theory, edited periodicals, and directed the music department of the Volkhochschule (1922–34). He emigrated to the U.S. in 1936 and taught at the Univ. of the Redlands (1937–51), the Univ. of Texas (Austin), and Washington Univ. (1963–72). His works are atonal but do not use twelve-tone methods. He wrote ballets, orchestral (*3 Ceremonial Rites* op. 90, 1958) and chamber music; choral music and over 150 songs. With Homer Ulrich he wrote *A History of Music and Musical Style* (New York, 1963).

Pistocchi, Francesco Antonio Mamiliano ["Il Pistocchino"] (b. Palermo, 1659; d. Bologna, 13 May 1726). Singer and composer. A child prodigy, he published his first work, *Capricci puerili* (Bologna, 1667), at the age of 8, and sang on occasion at S. Petronio, Bologna, from 1670, receiving a regular position there in 1674. After ten years of performing as a contralto on Italian and German stages, he served the court of Parma (1686–95), became Kapellmeister at Ansbach to the Margrave of Brandenburg (1696), and *virtuoso di camera e di cappella* to Prince Ferdinando of Tuscany (1702). His pupils included Antonio Bernacchi and G. B. Martini.

Piston, Walter (Hamor, Jr.) (b. Rockland, Maine, 20 Jan. 1894; d. Belmont, Mass., 12 Nov. 1976). Composer and teacher. He learned to play violin and piano as a child in Boston, where his family had moved by 1905. In 1916 graduated from the Massachusetts Normal Art School after studying architectural drawing. During the First World War he played saxophone in the navy band (having taught himself to play the instrument from a textbook); while at the Normal School he had also continued formal study of violin and piano; following the war he supported himself by playing in dance halls, hotels, and restaurants. In 1919 he entered Harvard as a special student in music, and after graduation in 1924 went to Paris for further study with Boulanger and Dukas. On his return to the U.S. he was appointed to the Harvard faculty, where he taught until 1960. As a teacher he influenced many well-known American musicians (Bernstein, Carter); his several textbooks carried this influence far beyond Cambridge (*Principles of Harmonic Analysis,* 1933; *Harmony,* 1941; *Counterpoint,* 1947; *Orchestration,* 1955). His harmony text in particular was widely adopted.

That so much of Piston's compositional effort was expended on orchestral music may be related to his early success in pieces written for the Boston Symphony: Symphonic Piece (1927), Suite no. 1 (1929), and the Concerto for Orchestra (1933) were all premiered by that orchestra with the composer conducting; his association with the Boston Symphony and Koussevitzky continued throughout his career as the orchestra premiered several more of his works. Piston consistently wrote one or two major works each year over a fifty-year creative life; of these only one work is for the stage (the ballet *The Incredible Flutist,* 1938) and only two include voices. Most of the pieces were written on commission for performers whose abilities Piston knew; even the orchestral works were aimed at particular groups. He received numerous prizes: a Guggenheim Fellowship (1935); 3 New York Critics Circle Awards (1945, 1959, 1964); 2 Pulitzer Prizes (1948, 1961); a Naumburg Award (1953).

Works: 41 orchestral works including 8 symphonies (1937–65), several concertos (orchestra, viola, 2 pianos, violin, clarinet, flute, and string quartet), suites, fantasies, and *Three New England Sketches* (1959); a few works for band or brass and percussion; 13 chamber works for 4 to 9 instruments including 5 string quartets, Wind Quintet (1956), Piano Quartet (1964), Divertimento (flute, oboe, clarinet, bassoon, string quartet, and double bass, 1946), and String Sextet (1964); 18 chamber works for 1 to 3 instruments (*Interlude,* viola and piano, 1942; *Partita,* violin, viola, and organ, 1944; *Improvisation,* piano, 1945); *Carnival Song* (male voices and 11 brass, 1938) and 2 Psalm settings for chorus and instruments (1958).

Bibl.: Howard Pollack, *Walter Piston* (Ann Arbor, 1981) [includes catalogue and discography].

Pitfield, Thomas B(aron) (b. Bolton, 5 April 1903). Composer. Beginning in 1924 he was enrolled at the Royal Manchester College of Music. He went on to study art at the Bolton School of Art, graduating in 1934. From 1947 through 1973 he served on the faculty at the Royal Manchester College of Music, teaching composition. His musical works are in a conservative tradition, utilizing standard forms. He is also known for his paintings and handmade books. His works include Concertino for Percussion and Full Orchestra (published 1972) and *Adam and the Creatures: Morality with Music,* speaker, chorus, organ, percussion (1965). He wrote many songs and chamber works and also arranged many folk songs.

Pitoni, Giuseppe Ottavio (b. Rieti, 18 Mar. 1657; d. Rome, 1 Feb. 1743). Composer. He studied in Rome with Francesco Foggia and sang at S. Giovanni dei Fiorentini and SS. Apostoli. At the age of 16 he became *maestro di cappella* at Monterotondo, then held the same title at Rieti Cathedral (1676) and at the Church of S. Marco in the Palazzo Venezia, Rome (1676 until his death). He was also employed by S. Lorenzo in Damaso, St. John Lateran, and the Cappella Giulia at St. Peter's. A prolific composer of church music, mostly in the style of Palestrina, Pitoni is noted for his brilliant contrapuntal writing and polychoral style; he also wrote *Notitia de contrapuntisti e de compositori di musica* (MS, ca. 1725), an important volume of music lexicography.

Bibl.: Siegfried Gmeinwieser, *Giuseppe Ottavio Pitoni, Thematisches Werkverzeichnis* (Wilhelmshaven, 1976).

Pitt, Percy (b. London, 4 Jan. 1869; d. there, 23 Nov. 1932). Conductor and composer. He studied in Leipzig with Reinicke and Jadassohn and in Munich with Rheinberger; became accompanist for the Queen's Hall concerts in 1896. In 1902 he was appointed musical adviser, and later musical director (1907–24), of the Grand Opera Syndicate at Covent Garden; was artistic director of the British National Opera Company (1922–24), and musical adviser (1922) and then director (1924–30) of the BBC. His reputation as a composer stems mainly from his earlier years. He composed a song, "Sérénade du passant," for Tetrazzini, a Ballade for violin and orchestra for Ysaÿe, a clarinet concerto, and stage music.

Pixis, Johann Peter (b. Mannheim, 10 Feb. 1788; d. Baden-Baden, 22 Dec. 1874). Pianist and composer. Son of Friedrich Wilhelm Pixis, Sr. He settled in Munich in 1809, moving to Paris in 1823 and to Baden-Baden in 1840. He studied with Albrechtsberger in Vienna, where he met Beethoven, Meyerbeer, and Schubert. He held a prominent position in musical circles in Paris. Most of his compositions are for the piano, including a concerto, sonata, and many smaller pieces. Along with Chopin, Liszt, Czerny, Thalberg, and Herz, he contributed to a set of variations on a theme from *I puritani.*

Bibl.: Lucian Schiwietz, *Johann Peter Pixis: Beiträge zu seiner Biographie, zur Rezeptionshistoriographie seiner Werke und Analyse seiner Sonatenformung* (Frankfurt am Main, 1994).

Pizzetti, Ildebrando (b. Parma, 20 Sept. 1880; d. Rome, 13 Feb. 1968). Composer, conductor, and writer on music. Entered the Parma Conservatory in 1895, where he studied harmony and counterpoint with Telesforo Righi and was introduced to Italian Renaissance music by Giovanni Tebaldini. He graduated in 1901, worked as a substitute conductor at the Teatro Regio in Parma, and taught privately while making several attempts to write an opera. In 1905 D'Annunzio asked him to provide incidental music for *La nave* (1905–7); their continued collaboration resulted in the successful opera *Fedra* (1909–12; Milan, 1915). By then Pizzetti was teaching composition at the conservatory in Parma (1907); from there he moved to the Florence Conservatory (1908) as teacher of harmony and counterpoint. He directed the Florence Conservatory from 1917 to 1924; moved to Milan to direct its conservatory in 1924; and finally succeeded Respighi as professor of composition at the Academy of S. Cecilia in Rome (1936–58). He had some ties with the more forward-looking Italian composers during his years in Florence, but by 1932 he had removed himself from those circles sufficiently to sign a manifesto with Respighi and others recommending a return to tradition. He was active as a music critic in Florence, writing for the periodicals *La voce* and *Il marzocco,* and for newspapers. He continued writing in the 1930s and 1940s for *La rassegna musicale* and later for the *Corriere della sera.*

His major compositional efforts were directed at operas and choral music. By 1908 he had developed an operatic style based on the avoidance of the self-sufficient lyricism of his Italian predecessors; his operas move along in an arioso style indebted to the sensitive text setting of the Florentine monodists of the early 17th century and to Debussy's procedures in *Pelléas et Mélisande.* His choral writing reflects his knowledge of vocal polyphony of the Renaissance. Pizzetti provided his own librettos for 9 of his 15 mature operas.

Works: several operas including *Debora e Jaele* (Pizzetti, 1915–21), *Assassinio nella cattedrale* (Eliot, trans. A. Castaldi, abridged by Pizzetti, 1957), and *Ifigenia* (radio opera in 1 act, Pizzetti, 1950); incidental music (*La sacra rappresentazione di Abram e d'Isaac,* 1915–17); a few film scores; Cello Concerto (1933–34), Violin Concerto (1944), Symphony (1940), and a few other orchestral pieces; works for voices and orchestra including *Cantico di gloria 'Attollite portas'* (3 choruses, 22 winds, 2 pianos, percussion, 1948); some chamber and piano music; unaccompanied choral music (*Missa di Requiem,* 1922) and songs.

Bibl.: Bruno Pizzetti, ed., *Ildebrando Pizzetti: Cronologia e bibliografia* (Parma, 1980). Gian Paolo Minardi, *Ildebrando Pizzetti, La giovinezza* (Parma, 1980).

Plançon, Pol (Henri) (b. Fumay, Ardennes, 12 June 1851; d. Paris, 11 Aug. 1914). Bass. He studied voice with Duprez and Sbriglia. His opera debut was in 1877 in Lyons; three years later he made his Paris debut. In June 1883 he appeared in Gounod's *Faust* as Mephistopheles, the role in which he was best known. His first London appearance occurred in 1891 at Covent Garden in *Faust.* He returned to Covent Garden every year from 1891 to 1904. Debuted at the Metropolitan Opera in New York in 1893, and was part of the company there until his retirement in 1908.

Planquette, (Jean) Robert (b. Paris, 31 July 1848; d. there, 28 Jan. 1903). Composer. Studied at the Paris Conservatory with Duprato; won first prize for solfège (1867), second prize for piano (1868). His early compositions include songs, marches, and piano reductions of operas. He is best known for his 20 operettas, including *Les cloches de Corneville* (1877), *Le Chevalier Gaston* (1879), *Rip van Winkle* (1882), *Surcouf* (1887), *Panurge* (1895), and *Mam'zelle Quat'sous* (1897).

Plantin, Christopher [Christophe] (b. Tours?, ca. 1520; d. Antwerp, 1 July 1589). Printer. Active in Antwerp. Music books made up only a small part of his output but were excellently produced (the first in 1578) and widely disseminated, in part through the Frankfurt book fairs. His firm's large collection of typefaces included many for music, including ones obtained from the estate of Susato and from Phalèse.

Platania, Pietro (b. Catania, 5 Apr. 1828; d. Naples, 26 Apr. 1907). Composer, conductor, and theorist. Studied with Raimondi at Palermo. Wrote treatises on canon and fugue (Milan, 1871), harmony (1872). *Maestro di cappella* of Milan Cathedral, 1882; director of the Naples Conservatory, 1885–1902. Invited to contribute to a Requiem in honor of Rossini. Composed a Requiem (1878), 2 solemn Masses (1883), other sacred pieces; songs; 2 string quartets (1868); 8 operas; symphonies in memory of Meyerbeer, Rossini, and Pacini; other orchestral pieces.

Platti, Giovanni Benedetto (b. Padua, 9 July 1697; d. Würzburg, 11 Jan. 1763). Composer. He probably studied music in Venice. From 1722 to at least 1761 he served at the court of the Würzburg bishops as a singing teacher, composer, tenor, and virtuoso on the oboe, violin, cello, harpsichord, and flute. His works reflect a shift in style from Baroque to *galant.* In addition to a number of vocal compositions, Platti wrote about 120 instrumental works including 57 sonatas for various instruments.

Playford, John (b. Norwich, 1623; d. London, Nov. 1686). Music publisher and bookseller. He was apprenticed to a London publisher, John Benson, from 1639/40 to 1647, then opened his own shop in the porch of the Temple Church; he also served as clerk to the church from 1653. He published political tracts before turning to music publication, his output including lesson books, collections of songs and instrumental works, and hymns; 1651–84, he dominated the music publishing trade. *The English Dancing Master* (1651; facs., London, 1957) is his best-known work; other publications include *A Musicall Banquet* (1651), *Catch that Catch Can* (1652), and *A Breefe Introduction to the Skill of Musick* (1654). He retired in 1684 and was succeeded by his son Henry.

Plaza-Alfonso, Juan Bautista (b. Caracas, 19 July 1898; d. there, 1 Jan. 1964). Composer. Studied in Caracas, then in Rome (1920–23); later became choirmaster and organist at the Metropolitan Church of Caracas (1923–47), also teaching at the National School of Music (1924–28, 1931–62) and conducting. Managed Venezuela's colonial music archives, 1936–44, writing articles about the subject and editing the 12-volume *Archivo de Música Colonial Venezolana* (Montevideo, 1943). Served in the Ministry of Education, 1944–46, founding (and later directing) the Escuela preparatoria de musica. Though primarily a choral composer, he also wrote tone poems, chamber music, works for organ and piano, and songs.

Bibl.: J. B. Plaza, "Music in Caracas during the Colonial Period (1770–1811)," *MQ* 29 (1943): 198–213. *Composers of the Americas* 9 (Washington, D.C., 1963), pp. 107–21 [includes works list]. Casa de Bello, *Juan Bautista Plaza: Homenaje en el vigésimo aniversario de su muerte* (Caracas, 1985).

Pleskow, Raoul (b. Vienna, 12 Oct. 1931). Composer. He emigrated to the U.S. in 1939, becoming a naturalized citizen in 1945; attended Juilliard (1950–52) and studied composition with Rathaus at Queens College (B.M., 1956) and with Luening at Columbia (M.M., 1958). In 1959 he joined the faculty of C. W. Post College on Long Island. His early works, such as *Movement for Nine Players* (1966), are in an atonal style; later compositions, including his well-known Four Bagatelles for Orchestra (1981), freely combine tonal and atonal elements.

Pleyel, (Joseph Stephen) Camille (b. Strasbourg, 18 Dec. 1788; d. Paris, 4 May 1855). Composer and pianist. Son of Ignace Pleyel. Studied with Desormuy, Dussek, and Steibelt. Became a partner in his father's piano manufacturing firm in 1815; took over the firm in 1824. He performed in France throughout 1813–14. Was a close friend of Chopin's. Wrote a number of compositions for piano, most of which are character pieces and other shorter works.

Pleyel, Ignace Joseph [Ignaz Josef] (b. Ruppersthal, Austria, 18 June 1757; d. Paris, 14 Nov. 1831). Composer, music publisher, and piano maker. He may have studied with Vanhal as a boy, and from about 1772 he studied and lodged with Haydn in Eisenstadt. Shortly after his puppet opera *Die Fee Urgele* was performed at Esterháza (1776) and the Vienna Nationaltheater, Pleyel became Kapellmeister to Count Ladislaus Erdödy. During the early 1780s he traveled in Italy; his opera *Ifigenia in Aulide* was premiered in Naples in 1785. In about 1784 he became assistant to the Kapellmeister of Strasbourg Cathedral, and succeeded to the post in 1789. During the 1791–92 season he conducted the Professional Concerts in London, where he renewed his friendship with Haydn. In 1795 he settled in Paris and opened a music shop and a publishing house, the Maison Pleyel. In 1801 Pleyel issued a complete edition of Haydn's string quartets, and in 1802 issued the first miniature scores in a series entitled Bibliothèque musicale. The Parisian piano firm he founded in 1807 prospered for over 150 years. During the 1820s Maison Pleyel turned increasingly to popular genres, and in 1834 it closed. Among Pleyel's works, which were extremely popular during his lifetime, are about 45 symphonies, a number of concertos and *symphonies concertantes,* 16 string quintets, over 70 string quartets, and numerous trios and duos.

Bibl.: Rita Benton, *Ignace Pleyel: A Thematic Catalogue of His Compositions* (New York, 1977). Rita Benton with Jeanne Halley, *Pleyel as Music Publisher* (New York, 1989). Geneviève Honegger, "Pleyel à Strasbourg durant la Terreur," *RdM* 73 (1987): 113–20.

Pleyel, (Camille) Marie (Denise) Moke (b. Paris, 4 Sept. 1811; d. St. Josse-ten-Noode, near Brussels, 30 Mar. 1875). Pianist, composer. Wife of Camille Pleyel. Studied with Jacques Herz, Moscheles, and Kalkbrenner. Was engaged to Berlioz but married Pleyel in 1831; they separated in 1835, after which time she embarked on a long tour of Europe. Chopin dedicated his op. 9 Nocturnes (1833) to her. From 1848 to 1872 she was professor of piano at the Brussels Conservatory. She also composed some piano pieces.

Plishka, Paul (Peter) (b. Old Forge, Penn., 28 Aug. 1941). Bass. He began singing lessons while at Montclair State College, then sang with the Paterson Lyric Opera in New Jersey. In 1965 he joined the Metropolitan Opera National Company, joining the parent company in 1967. He eventually took on leading roles in both the serious and comic repertories, appearing with major American opera houses and orchestras.

Plummer [Plourmel, Polumier], **John** (b. ca. 1410; d. in or after 1484). Composer. A member of English royal chapels from at least 1441 until 1484 at London or Windsor. Among his positions were Gentleman of the Chapel Royal (listed as such as late as 1467), Master of the Chapel Children (1444–55), and verger of St. George's Chapel, Windsor (ca. 1458–84). He certainly wrote 3 votive antiphons, a motet, and 2 Mass movements; 2 cyclic Masses may also be his.

Podešva, Jaromír (b. Brno, 8 Mar. 1927). Composer. He first studied music with his father, who was a violin maker. He then went on to study at the Brno Conservatory in 1946, taking composition lessons with Kvapil; from 1947 to 1955 he studied at the Janáček Academy of Music. He was active with the Union of Czechoslovak Composers from 1956. During the early 1960s he traveled to Paris, London, and the U.S., where he studied with Copland. From 1969 he served on the faculty of the Ostrava Conservatory. His early works were modeled on those of Janáček and were tonal. Throughout the 1960s he incorporated twelve-tone techniques into his music. He also composed political songs during the 1950s in accordance with his political beliefs. His works include 2 operas, 6 symphonies (1951–73), and chamber music (5 string quartets, 1948–65).

Poglietti, Alessandro [Boglietti, Alexander de] (b. Tuscany?, 1st half of the 17th century; d. Vienna, July 1683). Composer and teacher. He was probably trained in Rome or Bologna, then settled in Vienna, where he was organist and Kapellmeister to the Jesuits at the Kirche zu den neun Chören der Engel in 1661; in the same year he was appointed court and chamber organist in the Kapelle of Emperor Leopold I. He was highly regarded as a teacher, and his *Compendium oder kurtzer Begriff, und Einführung zur Musica* (1676) offers instruction in keyboard playing and composition. Poglietti's keyboard works, particularly his 12 ricercars, are an important link between the generation of Frescobaldi and that of Bach; he also experimented with imitation of natural sounds such as birdcalls.

Pohl, Carl Ferdinand (b. Darmstadt, 6 Sept. 1819; d. Vienna, 28 Apr. 1887). Musicologist, organist, and composer. Compositions, which are primarily songs and keyboard pieces, date from the early years. Jahn and Köchel were among those who used their influence to have Pohl named archivist and librarian at the Gesellschaft der Musikfreunde in Vienna (1866–87). Published pamphlet on the history of the glass harmonica in 1862; researched Haydn and Mozart in London, 1863–66; wrote *Mozart und Haydn in London* (Vienna, 1867). Worked on a large 3-volume biography of Haydn (vols. 1–2 published 1875–82); last volume published after his death (1927).

Poissl, Johann Nepomuk, Freiherr von (b. Haukenzell, Lower Bavaria, 15 Feb. 1783; d. Munich, 17 Aug. 1865). Composer. Studied at the Univ. of Landshut (1800). From 1805 he resided in Munich. Studied with Danzi and Abbé Vogler. Produced his first comic opera, *Die Opernprobe,* in 1806. Composed 12 operas in all, including *Aucassin und Nicolette* (singspiel, 1813), *Antigonus* (seria, 1808), *Athalia* (grand opera, 1814). His *Die Prinzessin von Provence* (magical opera, 1823) is still performed. Also wrote incidental music to 4 plays, 2 oratorios, 2 cantatas, 3 Masses.

Bibl.: Erich Reipschläger, *Schubaur, Danzi und Poissl als Opernkomponisten* (Berlin, 1911).

Pokorny [Pokorn, Pockorný], **Franz** [František] **Xaver (Thomas)** (b. Mies, Bohemia, 20 Dec. 1729; d. Regensburg, 2 July 1794). Composer. He studied with Riepel at Regensburg, then went to Mannheim at the behest of Count Philipp Karl of Oettingen-Wallerstein to study with Stamitz, Richter, and Holzbauer; in 1754 he returned to Wallerstein but failed to achieve the post of choral director that he desired; in 1766 he joined the Kapelle of the court of Thurn and Taxis at Regensburg. Some 100 symphonies have been attributed to Pokorny, but conflicting attributions exist for over half this number; other works include approximately 50 harpsichord concertos and some chamber music.

Bibl.: J. Murray Barbour, "Pokorny Vindicated," *MQ* 49 (1963): 38–58.

Poldini, Ede (Eduard) (b. Budapest, 13 June 1869; d. Corseaux, Vaud, 28 June 1957). Composer. He studied at the Budapest National Conservatory with Tomka. Traveled to Vienna, where he worked with Mandyczewski in music theory and with Epstein in piano. In 1908 he moved to Bergeroc, Vevey, where he remained until his death. His works were influenced by contemporary French trends. He only superficially incorporated folk elements into his style. His music includes many works for stage, for which he was perhaps best known (*Hochzeit im Fasching,* Budapest, 1924; *Himfy,* Budapest, 1938); also wrote piano works, choral music, and songs.

Poldowski [Irene Regine Wieniawska; Lady Dean Paul] (b. Brussels, 18 Mar. 1879; d. London, 28 Jan. 1932). Composer. The daughter of violinist Henry Wieniewsky, she studied at the Brussels Conservatory with Tordeus and Gevaert (1892–94). She also studied piano with Storck and traveled to Paris to study with d'Indy and Gedalge. She composed under the pen name "Poldowski" rather than that of her father or of her husband (Sir Aubrey Edward Henry Dean Paul). She wrote principally songs and chamber works. Her music was influenced by contemporary French trends, using the centricity yet chromaticism of impressionism. Her songs were in the highly expressive tradition of Fauré, and she set 21 texts for Verlaine. Works include *Dimanche d'avril* (published 1911), *Colombine* and *Mandoline* (both published 1913).

Polin, Claire (b. Philadelphia, 1 Jan. 1926). Flutist and composer. She studied flute with William Kincaid and composition with Persichetti; also worked with Peter Mennin at Juilliard, and Roger Sessions and Lukas Foss at Tanglewood. Taught flute and composition at the Philadelphia Musical Academy (1949–64) and at Rutgers (from 1958). Polin's career as a flutist included performances in Russia, Israel, and Japan. Her compositions often rely on modal systems; works include 2 symphonies (no. 1, 1961; no. 2, "Korean," 1976), chamber music (3 string quartets, 1953, 1959, 1969; *Res naturae,* woodwind quintet, 1982; *Regensburg,* flute, guitar, dancer, 1989), vocal music (*Isaiah Syndrome,* chorus, 1980).

Pollack, Ben (b. Chicago, 22 June 1903; d. Palm Springs, Calif., 7 June 1971). Jazz bandleader and drummer. He joined the New Orleans Rhythm Kings in 1923. From 1926 through the 1930s he led big bands, although he ceased playing drums on a regular basis late in 1928. His sidemen included Benny Goodman, Glenn Miller, Jimmy McPartland, Bud Freeman, Jack Teagarden (all 1920s); other sidemen (early 1930s) formed what was to become the Bob Crosby orchestra. Among recordings made under his name are *My Kinda Love* (1929) and *Two Tickets to Georgia* (1933).

Pollarolo, Carlo Francesco (b. ca. 1653; d. Venice, 7 Feb. 1723). Composer. He served as organist at the Congregazione dei Padri della Pace in Brescia by 1676, then succeeded his father as organist at the Cathedral of SS. Nazaro e Celso later that year. He was named *capo musico* there in 1680 and accepted a similar position at the Accademia degli Erranti in 1681. His first oratorio (1680) and first opera (1685) were written for Brescia, and from 1686 onward his operas and oratorios were performed regularly in Venice. He became second organist at St. Mark's, Venice, in 1690 and was promoted to vice-*maestro di cappella* two years later; he also served as musical director of the Ospedale degli incurabili. Pollarolo's output includes approximately 85 operas and 13 oratorios, which declined in popularity after his death.

Pollikoff, Max (b. Newark, N.J., 30 Mar. 1904; d. New York, 13 May 1984). Violinist. In 1917 he was awarded a scholarship to study violin with Auer; made his New York debut in 1923 at Aeolian Hall, and subsequently embarked on a successful career as a concert artist. He was associated with the Bennington Composers and Chamber Music Conferences (1953–73) and in 1954 established the Music in Our Time chamber music concerts at the 92nd Street Y in New York. During its two decades the series presented some 250 works by a wide variety of contemporary composers.

Pollini, Maurizio (b. Milan, 5 Jan. 1942). Pianist. Made first public appearance at age 9; attended the Milan Conservatory; won the 1960 Warsaw Chopin competition, and subsequently performed and recorded solo piano music and works with orchestra. His repertory extends from Bach to 20th-century compositions.

Pololáník, Zdeněk (b. Brno, 25 Oct. 1935). Composer. From 1952 to 1957 he studied organ at the Brno Conservatory of Music with Černocký. From 1957 until 1961 he studied composition at the Brno Academy of Music with Petrželka and Schaefer. He joined the avant-garde performance group Tvůrčí Skupina A (Creative Group A). His own works have been associated with the avant-garde trends prevalent elsewhere in western Europe, yet have remained freely eclectic. His music ranges from modal to serial and draws on electronic resources as well as elements of popular music. It includes dramatic works (Silák Hungerfield [Hungerfield the Strong Man), opera, 1975) and orchestral works (symphonies and concertos); chamber and vocal works (*Cantus psalmorum,* male solo, harp, organ, percussion, 1966; *Rytmická mše* [Rhythmic Mass], 1973).

Ponce, Manuel (María) (b. Fresnillo, Zacatecas, 8 Dec. 1882; d. Mexico City, 24 Apr. 1948). Composer. Moved to Aguascalientes as an infant; studied piano from childhood. Became assistant organist of S. Diego, Aguascalientes, in 1895, and head organist in 1897. Studied in Mexico City, 1900–01. Traveled to Europe in 1904, studying at Bologna (with Bossi and Torchi) and Berlin (with Krause), also giving recitals. Became piano teacher at the Mexico City Conservatory in 1909; conducted the National Symphony, 1917–19. Lived in France, 1925–33, studying with Dukas and editing the *Gaceta musical;* rejoined the conservatory faculty in 1933. Ponce's style moved from a Romantic orientation to a more neoclassic one. He was among the most popular of Mexican composers. His songs and piano music were widely published; his guitar music is part of the standard repertory; and the song "Estrellita" (1914) was one of Latin America's best-known compositions.

Works: the opera *El patio florido* (1913); vocal-orchestral pieces; orchestral music, including *Estampas nocturnas* (1923), *Poema elegíaco* (1935), *Instantáneas mexicanas* (1938), and *Ferial* (1940); 2 concertos for piano and 1 each for guitar (1941) and violin (1943); *Balada mexicana,* piano and orchestra (1914); chamber music, including *Trio romántico* (1911), 2 violin sonatas, a cello sonata (1922), and a string trio (1933); guitar music, including *24 preludios fáciles* and 5 sonatas; piano music; and songs and folk song arrangements.

Bibl.: *Composers of the Americas* 1 (Washington, D.C., 1955), pp. 60–70 [includes works list]. Pablo Castellanos, *Manuel M. Ponce: Ensayo* (Mexico City, 1982). Corazón Otero, *Manuel M. Ponce and the Guitar* (Shaftesbury, 1983).

Ponchielli, Amilcare (b. Paderno Fasolaro [now Paderno Ponchielli], near Cremona, 31 Aug. 1834; d. Milan, 16 Jan. 1886). Composer. At Milan Conservatory, 1843–54, studying composition under Frasi (to 1851) and Mazzucato (after 1851) and beginning to compose, including a *Scena campestre* for orchestra (1852). He was well regarded as a student but spent his early career in obscurity; from 1854, church organist and music teacher in Cremona, from 1855 also assistant music director at Cremona's Teatro Concordia, where in 1856 his first opera was given, a version (by the composer and some friends) of Alessandro Manzoni's novel *I promessi sposi.* It was not performed elsewhere. In 1858 his *Bertrando dal Bormeo* reached rehearsal at the Teatro Carcano, Milan, but was not performed, apparently because Ponchielli did not like the singers; 1860, he conducted at the Teatro Carcano and in Alessandria; January 1861, his third opera, *La savoiarda,* was performed in Cremona; in May he was appointed conductor of the Piacenza National Guard Band; 1863, his fourth opera, *Roderico re dei goti,* was a failure (1 performance) at the Piacenza theater; 1864, on the expiration of his Piacenza contract he returned to Cremona as conductor of the band, and the following Carnival had a ballet, *Grisetta,* performed at the theater, where he also conducted.

His aspirations to break out of this local sphere to wider recognition were thwarted for years. In 1870 he competed for the professorship of counterpoint and fugue at the Milan Conservatory, but, although successful in the competition, did not receive the appointment. The situation changed only in 1872 with the very successful production of a much-revised version of *I promessi sposi* at the Teatro dal Verme, Milan. This brought him the powerful support of the Ricordi publishing house. A ballet, *Le due gemelle,* was given at La Scala in 1873, and his opera *I lituani* was successful there in 1874. His career reached its zenith with *La gioconda* (libretto by Boito) at La Scala (8 Apr. 1876), which gradually spread through Italy and beyond (London, New York, 1883), becoming his only work to remain in the standard repertory, although suffering much from criticism of its supposed vulgarity and crudeness. His last operas, *Il figliuol prodigo* (La Scala, 1880) and *Marion Delorme* (La Scala, 1885), were well received but did not sustain themselves. From 1880 he was professor of composition, Milan Conservatory (pupils included Puccini, Mascagni); from 1881 also music director, S. Maria Maggiore, Bergamo, for which he composed much sacred music. Other works: occasional cantatas, band pieces, ballets, songs.

Bibl.: Nino Albarosa, *Amilcare Ponchielli, 1834–1886: Saggi e ricerche nel 150 anniversario della nascita* (Casalmorano, 1984). Giampiero Tintori, ed., *Amilcare Ponchielli* (Milan, 1985).

Poné, Gundaris (b. Riga, Latvia, 17 Oct. 1932; d. Kingston, N.Y., 15 Mar. 1994). Composer and conductor. In 1944 he and his family left Latvia for Germany, and in 1950 he emigrated to the U.S. He studied violin and composition at the Univ. of Minnesota (B.A., 1954; Ph.D., 1962) and subsequently made a number of conducting appearances in both the U.S. and Europe. In 1963 he was appointed to the faculty of SUNY–New Paltz, and in 1974 founded the Poné Ensemble for New Music there; he was appointed music director of the Music in the Mountains Festival in 1981. Many of Poné's compositions are for orchestra or large chamber ensemble. *Diletti dialettici* for 9 virtuosi (1973) was performed at the Berkshire Music Center in 1980; the orchestral work *La serenissima* (1979–81) received the Whitney Prize of the Louisville Orchestra in 1984, and *Avanti* for orchestra (1975) was selected in 1982 by the Kennedy Center Friedheim Award as the best new American orchestral work.

Poniridis, Giorgios [Poniridy, Georges] (b. Constantinople, 8 Oct. 1892; d. Athens, 29 Mar. 1982). Composer. He studied violin at the Brussels Conservatory, 1910–12; also studied violin with Ysaÿe and harmony and counterpoint with Gilson. He traveled to Paris, where he was a student at the Schola cantorum. He took composition lessons from d'Indy and Roussel and studied Gregorian chant with Gastoué. Through the 1950s he worked in western Europe as a composer and conductor of new music. In 1954 he became head of the Music Division of the Greek Ministry of Education in Athens. His music was highly influenced by his French models and also drew from traditional Greek and Byzantine music. His late works incorporated serial techniques. Works include *Triptyque symphonique* (premiered Athens, 1937), Symphony no. 2 (premiered Athens, 1948), and many arrangements of Greek folk songs.

Pons, Lily (Alice Joséphine) (b. Draguigon, near Cannes, 12 Apr. 1898; d. Dallas, 13 Feb. 1976). Soprano. Entered the Paris Conservatory at age 13, first studying piano, then voice; appeared in 1924 at the Paris Théâtre des Variétés; made operatic debut in 1927 at Mulhouse; sang in the provinces, then made a 1931 debut as Lucia at the Metropolitan Opera, remaining with the company until 1961, also singing elsewhere in the Americas and in Europe. Renowned for her coloratura singing, she made many recordings and appeared in films.

Ponselle, Rosa (b. Meriden, Conn., 22 Jan. 1897; d. Baltimore, 25 May 1981). Soprano. Began as vaudeville singer alongside her sister Carmela (1892–1977); made her Metropolitan Opera debut opposite Caruso in 1918. She remained the foremost prima donna there until 1937, when she resigned; retiring from the stage, she sang in public again only at President Eisenhower's 1953 inauguration, and made a recording the following year. She was active as a teacher, with Sherrill Milnes and William Warfield among her students; from 1950 she also directed the Baltimore Civic Opera Company. Her voice was regarded as one of the best of the century, with extraordinary range, flexibility, and intonation. She also had a career as recitalist and radio performer.

Pontio [Ponzio], **Pietro** (b. Parma, 25 Mar. 1532; d. there, 27 Dec. 1595). Theorist and composer. *Maestro di cappella* at S. Maria Maggiore, Bergamo (1565–67), Madonna della Steccata, Parma (1567–69 and 1582–92), and Milan Cathedral (1577–82); from spring 1592 associated with the Cathedral of Parma. Composed chiefly sacred music in a conservative style. More important are his 2 theoretical treatises, *Ragionamento di musica* (Parma, 1588; facs., *DM* 1/16, 1959) and *Dialogo* (Parma, 1595). These works reveal a wide-ranging knowledge of 16th-century music and of relevant music theory. Among the topics given particular attention are text-music relationships and characteristics of particular musical forms.

Ponty, Jean-Luc (b. Avranches, France, 29 Sept. 1942). Jazz violinist and bandleader. Initially he pursued a career in classical music, winning a premier prix at the Paris Conservatory and playing for three years with the Concerts Lamoureux orchestra. From 1964 he devoted himself to jazz. He recorded the swing album *Violin Summit* with the violinists Svend Asmussen, Stephane Grappelli, and Stuff Smith (1966); traveled to Los Angeles to record an album of Frank Zappa's jazz-rock compositions (*King Kong,* 1969); and returned to France to lead a free-jazz group (ca. 1970–72). After joining John McLaughlin's Mahavishnu Orchestra (1974–75), he formed a jazz-rock group ; his albums include *Imaginary Voyage* (1976). In addition to the conventional instrument, he plays electric violin and synthesizer.

Poole, Geoffrey (b. 1949). Composer. He studied at the Univ. of East Anglia and then at Southampton from 1970 to 1971 with Goehr and Harvey. From 1977 on the faculty at Manchester Univ. He initially apprenticed himself to serialism but quickly moved away from its strictures and severity, his music then becoming highly expressive and dramatic, often concerned with or stimulated by current social and political events. Works include *Harmonice mundi* op. 15 (1977–78), which draws its shape from the program of the drama that it conveys. Similarly, Yeats's poem "The Second Coming" served as a formal and dramatic inspiration for the Chamber Concerto op. 17 (1979). Other works include *Visions* op. 6 (1974–75), as well as *TEN* op. 19 (1981), in which numerology figures in the formation of its structure.

Poot, Marcel (b. Vilvoorde, near Brussels, 7 May 1901; d. Brussels, 12 Jan. 1988). Composer. His father, Jan Poot, was director of the Royal Flemish Theatre in Brussels. He studied harmony and piano at the Brussels Conservatory, where his teachers included Sevenants, Lunssens, and de Greef, and then counterpoint and fugue at the Royal Flemish Conservatory. He studied composition and orchestration with Paul Gilson (1916). Along with Bernier, de Bourguignon, Brenta, de Joncker, Otlet, Schoemaker, and Strens, he formed the association of pupils of Gilson known as the Synthétistes (1925). At the same time, Poot and Gilson cofounded *La Revue musicale belge.* In 1930, having won the Rubens Prize, Poot went to Paris to work with Dukas at the École Normale de Musique. He returned to Belgium to teach, and in 1938 joined the faculty at the Brussels Conservatory; he was its director from 1949 to 1966. A member of the Royal Flemish Academy.

Early in his career Poot was interested in cinema; *Charlot,* 3 symphonic sketches of 1926, were influenced by Chaplin's films. He wrote a great deal of music for silent films. His ballet, *Paris in verlegenheid* (1925), reflects his interest in jazz.

Works: *Stage. Het ingebeeld eiland* (opera, 1925); *Paris in verlegenheid* (ballet, 1925); *Het vrouwtje van Stavoren* (operetta, 1928); *Moretus* (chamber opera, 1944); *Pygmalion* (ballet, 1951). *Oratorio. Le dit du routier* (1943); *Icare* (1947). *Orchestra. Variations in the Forms of Dances* (1921); *Charlot* (1926); 5 Symphonies (1929, 1938, 1952, 1972, 1974); *Fugato* (1932); *Jazz Music* (1933); *Rondo* (piano, orchestra, 1935); *Vrolijke ouverture* (1935); *Symphonisch triptiek* (1938); *Ballad* (string quartet, orchestra, 1939); *Konzertstück* (cello, orchestra, 1942); *Fantasia* (1944). *Chamber music.* Piano Quartet (1932); 3 Pieces in Trio (piano trio, 1935); 5 Bagatelles (string quartet, 1939); Wind Quintet (1959); Concertino (4 saxophones, 1962); Horn Quartet (1965); Musique de chambre (piano trio, 1972); Impromptu (brass quintet, 1975); many pieces for duos and solo piano.

Popov, Gavriil Nikolayevich (b. Novocherkassk, 12 Sept. 1904; d. Repino, 17 Feb. 1972). Composer. He studied at the conservatory in Rostov-on-Don (1917–22), then at the Leningrad Conservatory (1922–30) with Shcherbachov (composition) and Nikolayev (piano). After graduating, he concertized as a pianist and taught. His compositions include works for the stage, 7 symphonies, over 40 choral works, a septet, chamber music, songs, and film scores.

Popp, Lucia (b. Uhorská Vez, Czechoslovakia, 12 Nov. 1939; d. Munich, 16 Nov. 1993). Soprano. After an early film career, she studied at the Bratislava Academy (1959–63); made her debut there in 1963 as the Queen of the Night, also appearing the same year at Vienna and Salzburg. She made her Covent Garden debut in 1966, and her first Metropolitan Opera appearance in 1967; sang throughout Europe.

Popper, David (b. Prague, 9 Dec. 1843; d. Baden, Vienna, 7 Aug. 1913). Cellist and composer. Studied with Julius Goltermann at the Prague Conservatory. First tour in 1863. Met Bülow, who later accompanied and arranged concerts for him. Appointed *Kammervirtuos* at Löwenberg court chapel. Member of Hellmesberger Quartet. First cellist of Vienna Court Orchestra (1868–73). Married to pianist Sophie Menter (1872–86). Taught at the Budapest Conservatory (1896–1913). Wrote character pieces for cello and piano (opp. 3, 11, 50, 64, 68, and others); String Quartet op. 74 (1905); 4 cello concertos op. 8 (1871), op. 24 (1880), op. 59 (1990), op. 72 (1900); Requiem op. 66 (3 cellos and orchestra, 1891); other orchestral and chamber works.

Porena, Boris (b. Rome, 27 Sept. 1927). Composer. He earned diplomas in piano (1948) and composition (1953) in Rome at the conservatory under Petrassi and graduated in literature from the university (1957). He also attended Darmstadt summer courses (1957–60). Taught an experimental course in composition at the Rome Conservatory starting in 1972. His works include many pieces for orchestra (*Musica per orchestra no. 1,* 1963; *no. 2,* 1966) as well as for chorus (*Der Gott und die Bajadere,* Goethe, soprano, baritone, chorus, orchestra, 1957; *Cantata,* Gryphius, 3 female voices, chorus, orchestra, 1959–61; *Cantata da camera,* Trakl, 1959–64; *Über aller dieser deiner Trauer,* Celan, N. Sachs, soprano, baritone, chorus, orchestra, 1965). Also vocal music (*Vor einer Kerze,* mezzo, instruments, 1958; *Lieder aus dem Barock,* soprano, horn, piano, 1959) and chamber music (*Neumi,* flute, marimba, vibraphone, 1963; *Musica per quartetto,* 1967).

Porpora, Nicola (Antonio) (b. Naples, 17 Aug. 1686; d. there, 3 Mar. 1768). Composer and singing teacher.

He entered the Conservatorio dei Poveri di Gesù Cristo in Naples at the age of 10 and studied there for approximately a decade; his first opera, *Agrippina,* was performed in the Neapolitan Royal Palace in 1708. It appears he held title of *maestro di cappella* to the Prince of Hessen-Darmstadt from 1711 until 1725, during which time his second and third operas, *Flavio Anicio Olibrio* (1711) and *Basilio re d'oriente* (1713), were produced in Naples. In 1714 he composed *Arianna e Teseo* to fulfill an operatic commission from the Viennese court, and *Temistocle* was premiered at the Hoftheater in Vienna in 1718; other works dating from this time include 2 serenatas, *Angelica* (1720) and *Gli orti esperidi* (1721), with texts by the young Metastasio. Between 1715 and 1721 Porpora served as a teacher of singing and composition at the Conservatorio di S. Onofrio in Naples and became famous as a singing instructor; his pupils included Farinelli, Caffarelli, and Salimbeni. His first opera for Rome, *Berenice regina d'Egitto* (1718), was written with Domenico Scarlatti, followed by Porpora's own Roman operas *Eumene* (1721) and *Adelaide* (1723) as well as his first opera to a libretto by Metastasio, *Didone abbandonata* (Reggio, 1725). He settled in Venice in 1726 and became maestro at the Ospedale degli incurabili until 1733.

Porpora was invited to London by a group of noblemen who were organizing the Opera of the Nobility (in competition with Handel); the company opened its season with *Arianna in Nasso* (1733), and Porpora composed 4 more operas for London before leaving in 1736 for Venice, where he took up his old post at the Incurabili the following year. He moved to Naples and was appointed *maestro di cappella* at the Conservatorio di S. Maria di Loreto (1739–41) before returning to Venice and becoming *maestro di coro* at the Ospedale della Pietà (1742–43) and the Ospedaletto. From 1747 until 1751 he was in Dresden as the singing teacher to Princess Maria Antonia, composing the opera *Filandro* (1747) for her birthday. His position in Dresden (he was made Kapellmeister in 1748) brought him into conflict with Hasse (who was named *Ober*-Kapellmeister in 1749), and in 1751 or 1752 Porpora moved to Vienna, where he gave singing lessons; he also taught composition to the young Haydn, who in exchange became his valet and keyboard accompanist. He returned to Naples in 1758, where he served again at the Loreto and the Conservatorio di S. Onofrio; his last opera, *Il trionfo di Camilla* (Naples, 1760), was a revision of a work of the same name given in 1740. Porpora's output includes over 40 operas, a large number of solo cantatas and oratorios, as well as some Masses and a few instrumental works.

Bibl.: Everett Lavern Sutton, "The Solo Vocal Works of Nicola Porpora: An Annotated Thematic Index" (diss., Univ. of Minnesota, 1974).

Porsile, Giuseppe (b. Naples, 5 May 1680; d. Vienna, 29 May 1750). Composer. He studied with Ursino, Giordano, and Greco at the Conservatorio dei Poveri di Gesù Cristo in Naples, and was named vice-*maestro di cappella* at the Spanish chapel in Naples. He was called to Spain in 1695 by Charles II to organize the music chapel at Barcelona, and remained there under Charles III; Charles was named Charles VI, Holy Roman Emperor, in 1711, and Porsile followed him to Vienna in 1713, becoming court composer in 1720. The bulk of Porsile's output consists of over 20 secular dramatic works and 13 oratorios, most premiered in Vienna.

Porta, Costanzo (b. Cremona, 1528–29; d. Padua, 19 May 1601). Composer. A member of the Franciscan Minorites, which he served in various musical capacities throughout his adult life. After studies with Willaert, he became *maestro di cappella* of Osima Cathedral in 1552. Similar positions followed at Padua (1565–67 and 1589 until his death), Ravenna (1567–74 and 1580–89), and Loreto (1574–80). In the 1580s he also visited the Este court at Ferrara and the Gonzaga court at Mantua. His contemporaries, including the theorists Artusi and Zacconi, praised his excellence as a composer, and his many surviving works bear out this judgment. The majority are sacred, particularly motets, written in well-crafted, often imitative polyphony. Many madrigals in a less contrapuntal and highly expressive idiom are also extant.

Bibl.: Ed. Syri Cisilino (Padua, 1964–70; 2nd ed., 1971–).

Porter, Cole (Albert) (b. Peru, Ind., 9 June 1891; d. Santa Monica, Calif., 15 Oct. 1964). Popular songwriter and lyricist. As a child he studied piano and violin; he began writing songs while at the Worcester Academy and Yale, including the Yale fight song "Bulldog" (1911). Later he received training in music theory at Harvard (from 1915) and in Paris after his move there in 1917. From 1915 he placed songs in shows in New York and Paris; his first complete show was *See America First* (1916), and his first successes *Fifty Million Frenchmen* (1929) and *Anything Goes* (1934, including "You're the Top"). He returned to the U.S. in 1935, at first writing for films in Hollywood (*Rosalie,* 1937), and later for Broadway. His two most successful musicals were *Kiss Me, Kate* (1948, including "Wunderbar") and *Can-Can* (1953, including "I Love Paris"); other popular songs were "Night and Day" (1932) and "In the Still of the Night" (1937). Porter's extensive theoretical training made him comfortable with unusually chromatic and extended song structures ("Begin the Beguine," 1935).

Bibl.: George Eells, *The Life That Late He Led: A Biography of Cole Porter* (New York, 1967) [includes works list]. Robert Kimball and Brendan Gill, *Cole* (New York, 1971). David Grafton, *Red, Hot, and Rich!: An Oral History of Cole Porter* (New York, 1987). Jean Howard, *Travels with Cole Porter* (New York, 1991).

Porter, (William) Quincy (b. New Haven, 7 Feb. 1897; d. Bethany, Conn., 12 Nov. 1966). Composer. Attended Yale (B.A. 1919, B.Mus. 1921), where he studied composition with Horatio Parker and David Stanley Smith. In 1920 he went to Paris, where he studied violin with Capet and composition with d'Indy. On his return to the U.S. he studied with Ernest Bloch in New York, earning his living as a violinist in theater orchestras. He joined the Ribaupierre Quartet as violist in 1922 and taught theory at the Cleveland Institute of Music (1923–28; 1931–32). He returned to Paris in 1928 on a Guggenheim fellowship, writing his Violin Sonata no. 2 and String Quartet no. 3, which won awards from the Society for the Publication of American Music. In 1932 he joined the faculty at Vassar College; in 1938 became dean of New England Conservatory; taught at Yale, 1946–65. His *Concerto concertante* for 2 pianos and orchestra won the 1954 Pulitzer Prize.

Works: *Incidental music. A Midsummer Night's Dream* (1926); *The Sunken Bell* (Hauptmann, 1926); *Sweeney Agonistes* (Eliot, 1933); *Anthony and Cleopatra* (1934); *Song for a Broken Horn* (H. M. Hill, 1952); *The Merry Wives of Windsor* (1954); *The Mad Woman of Chaillot* (Giraudoux, 1957); *Music for an Elizabethan Masque at Yale* (1959). *Orchestra.* 2 Symphonies (1934, 1962); *Dance in Three-Time* (1937); *2 Dances for Radio, Four- and Five-Time* (1938); *Music for Strings* (1941); *A Moving Tide* (1944); concertos for viola (1948), cello (1950), harpsichord (1959); *The Desolate City* (baritone, orchestra, 1950); *New England Episodes* (1958). *Chamber.* 9 String Quartets (1923, 1925, 1930, 1931, 1935, 1937, 1943, 1950, 1958); 2 Violin Sonatas (1926, 1929); *In Monasterio* (string quartet, 1927); Piano Quintet (1927); Clarinet Quintet (1929); Piano Sonata (1930); *Lonesome* (piano, 1940); Horn Sonata (1946); String Sextet on Slavic Folk Tunes (1947); *4 Pieces* (violin, piano, 1947); *Divertimento* (2 violins, viola, 1949); *Juilliard Pieces for Strings* (1949); Duos for violin and viola (1954) and viola and harp (1957); *Day Dreams* (piano, 1957); *Divertimento* (wind quintet, 1960); Quintet (harpsichord, strings, 1961); Variations (violin, piano, 1963); Oboe Quintet (1966). He also wrote many songs.

Porter, Walter (b. ca. 1587 or ca. 1595; d. London, buried 30 Nov. 1659). Composer. He was a chorister at Westminster Abbey and sang tenor in a Whitehall masque in 1612; became a Gentleman of the Chapel Royal in 1617. He claimed to have studied with Monteverdi, perhaps between 1612 and 1615. He sang and played theorbo in Shirley's masque *The Triumph of Peace* in 1634, and became master of the choristers of Westminster Abbey in 1639. Published *Madrigales and Ayres* (London, 1632) and *Mottets of Two Voyces* (London, 1657).

Portugal [Portogallo], **Marcos Antônio (da Fonseca)** (b. Lisbon, 24 Mar. 1762; d. Rio de Janeiro, 7 Feb. 1830). Composer. From 1771 he studied composition with João de Souza Carvalho at the Seminário patriarchal in Lisbon. In 1783 he was admitted to the brotherhood of S. Cecilia, the records of which describe him as singer and organist of the Seminário patriarchal chapel. He became conductor of the Teatro do Salitre in 1785, then successfully produced 6 Portuguese comic operas, including *A castanheira* (1787). With royal protection and a government pension he went to Naples for additional study in 1792; he produced a series of 21 operas, both seria and buffa, at all the major Italian centers during the next eight years. Among the most popular were *Le confusioni* (Florence, 1793), *Demofoonte* (Milan, 1794), *Le Donne cambiate* (Venice, 1797), and *Fernando nel Messico* (Venice, 1798). In 1800 he returned to Lisbon and became *mestre de capela* of the royal chapel and director of the S. Carlos Opera, where he remained when the court transferred to Rio de Janeiro preceding the French invasion of 1807. In 1811 he went to Rio de Janeiro to serve as *mestre* of the royal chapel and master of music to the future John VI; there he remained active until about 1820. Two apoplectic fits in 1811 and 1817 forced him to remain in Brazil when the court returned to Lisbon in 1821. In a catalog of his own works Portugal lists 35 Italian operas, 21 Portuguese comic operas, and over 100 pieces of sacred music.

Bibl.: M. Pereira Peixoto d'Almeida Carvalhães, *Marcos Portugal na sua música dramática* (Lisbon, 1910; suppl. 1916).

Poston, Elizabeth (b. near Walkern, Hertfordshire, 24 Oct. 1905; d. Highfield, Hertfordshire, 18 Mar. 1987). Composer. She studied composition at the Royal Academy of Music and also took piano lessons with Samuel. Her works first began to be published in the 1920s. During the 1930s she traveled often, spending time collecting folk songs. From 1939 until 1945 she worked for the BBC, directing music during the war for the European Service. Her music is in a neoclassical vein, and she was much inspired by Elizabethan music. She wrote film music (*Howards End,* 1970) and choral and chamber music. In addition, she edited collections of folk songs and carols.

Pothier, Joseph (b. Bouzemont, Vosges, 7 Dec. 1835; d. Conques, Belgium, 8 Dec. 1923). Editor of Gregorian chant. Ordained in 1858, took vows as a Benedictine monk in 1860. Abbot of Solesmes, 1898–1923. Moved to Belgium when religious orders were banished from France. Appointed president of publication committee of Editio Vaticana by Pope Pius X (1904). Responsible for publication of *Les mélodies grégoriennes d'après la tradition* (Tournai, 1880; 2nd ed., 1890); *Liber gradualis* (Tournai, 1883; 2nd ed., 1895); *Processionale monasticum* (Solesmes, 1888); *Variae preces* (Solesmes, 1888); *Liber antiphonarius* (Solesmes, 1891); *Liber responsorialis* (Solesmes, 1895); and *Cantus mariales* (Paris, 1903; 2nd ed., 1924).

Potter, A(rchibald) J(ames) (b. Belfast, 22 Sept. 1918; d. Greystone, 5 July 1980). Composer. He studied at the choir school of All Saints in London with W. S. Vale (1929–33); at Clifton College in Bristol with D. G. A. Fox (1933–36); with Vaughan Williams at the Royal College of Music (1936–38). He completed his studies at Dublin Univ. (D.Mus. 1953). Joined the faculty of the Royal Irish Academy of Music in Dublin in 1955, was active as a broadcaster, and arranged many Irish folk songs. One of his most popular works is *Sinfonia de profundis* (orchestra, 1968). He wrote numerous works for orchestra, a television opera, 4 ballets, many choral works, chamber music and songs.

Potter, (Philip) Cipriani (Hambly) [Hambley] (b. London, 3 Oct. 1792; d. London, 26 Sept. 1871). Composer and pianist. Studied with his father, flutist and violinist Richard Huddleston Potter; later with Attwood, Callcott, and Crotch. Debut as a pianist at the Philharmonic Society of London (1816). Went to Vienna in 1817 to study with Foerster; was advised there by Beethoven. Returned to London in 1821 after traveling to Germany and Italy. Taught piano at the Royal Academy of Music (beginning 1822), director of orchestra (1827), principal (1832–59). Conductor of Madrigal Society, 1855–70. Introduced Beethoven's Piano Concertos nos. 1, 3, and 4 to England. Member of the Bach Society (1849). Virtually stopped composing after 1837. His compositions include 9 symphonies; overtures; marches; *Bravura variations on a theme by Rossini,* piano and orchestra (1827); at least 3 piano concertos; piano sonatas, toccatas, variations; other miscellaneous pieces.

Bibl.: Philip Henry Peter, "The Life and Work of Cipriani Potter (1792–1871)" (diss., Northwestern Univ., 1972).

Poulenc, Francis (Jean Marcel) (b. Paris, 7 Jan. 1899; d. there, 30 Jan. 1963). Composer. He was educated at Lycée Condorcet and learned music from his mother, who was a pianist. At 16 he studied piano formally with Ricardo Viñes, an established performer of modern French music. In 1917 and 1918 he met Auric, Honegger, and Milhaud, the composers with whom he, and two others, Durey and Tailleferre, were as a group deemed "Les six" by critic Henri Collet. At this time he also met Satie, to whom he dedicated his first published composition, *Rapsodie nègre* (1917).

Following military service (1918–21) Poulenc wanted formal study in composition, and found a useful teacher in composer Charles Koechlin, his teacher for three years. In 1924 his ballet *Les biches* was successfully produced by Diaghilev and the Ballets russes. Two events of 1935, the death of a friend in a car accident and a visit to Notre Dame de Rocamadour, caused Poulenc to return to Catholicism, the tradition of his deeply religious paternal family. He soon produced *Litanies à la vierge noire* (1936), the first of many religious choral works. At this time he also met the singer Pierre Bernac, with whom he established a long-standing association. Poulenc accompanied Bernac, often in premieres of his own songs. In 1948 they toured the U.S.

Poulenc is perhaps best known for his vocal music. He wrote hundreds of songs, choral works, and three operas. His interest in the poetry of Eluard spanned many years and led to the cycle of love songs *Tel jour, telle nuit* (1936–37) and to *Le travail du peintre* (1956), a set based on poems Poulenc himself commissioned from Eluard. His first opera, *Les mamelles de Tirésias,* an opéra bouffe after Apollinaire (1947), was a great success. *La voix humaine* (1958) is a 40-minute solo scena based on text by Cocteau, which portrays one side of a telephone conversation between a woman and the lover who is abandoning her. Poulenc was at work on an opera based on Cocteau's *La machine infernale* when he died suddenly of a heart attack in 1963.

He also wrote a great deal of piano music, much of it from the 1930s, and characterized by its use of the sustaining pedal. He asserted that his most inventive writing for the piano was to be found in his songs, but also that his favorite piano pieces were the *15 Improvisations* (1932–59). One of his most popular chamber works is the Sextet for piano and winds (1932–39). He was somewhat uncomfortable writing for strings; he destroyed 2 violin sonatas (1919, 1924) and a string quartet (1947). His compositional style is characterized by the importance given to melody, and by its basically diatonic harmony, occasionally enriched by chromaticism.

Works: the operas *Les mamelles de Tirésias* (after Apollinaire, 1944), *Dialogues des carmélites* (after Bernanos, 1953–56), *La voix humaine* (after Cocteau, 1958); ballets (*Les biches,* 1923; *Aubade,* 1929; *Les animaux modèles,* after La Fontaine, 1940–41); incidental music to works by Cocteau, Shakespeare, Anouilh, Molière, and others; orchestral works (*Concert champêtre,* harpsichord, orchestra, 1927–28; Concerto in D minor, 2 pianos, orchestra, 1932; Piano Concerto, 1949); choral works (Mass in G major, 1937; Gloria, 1959); numerous songs for voice and piano; chamber music; piano pieces.

Writings: *Emmanuel Chabrier* (Paris, 1961); trans. Eng. (1981). *Moi et mes amis,* ed. Stephane Audel (Paris, 1963). *Journal de mes mélodies* (Paris, 1964).

Bibl.: George Russell Keck, *Francis Poulenc: A Bio-Bibliography* (New York, 1990). Wilfrid Howard Mellers, *Francis Poulenc* (Oxford, 1993).

Poulton, (Edith Eleanor) Diana (Chloe) (b. Storington, Sussex, 18 Apr. 1903). Lutenist and writer. Attended the Slade School of Fine Art (1919–23); studied lute with Dolmetsch. A charter member of the Lute Society (est. 1956). She wrote a biography of Dowland (London, 1972; 2nd ed., 1982) and many articles on his music.

Pound, Ezra (Loomis) (b. Hailey, Idaho, 30 Oct. 1885; d. Venice, 1 Nov. 1972). Poet and amateur composer. As a student Pound became interested in the Provençal troubadours. With the help of George Antheil he composed the opera *The Testament of François Villon* (Paris, 1926), which combines troubadour monody with precise rhythmic notation designed to reflect word rhythms; the work was followed by a similar one, *Cavalcanti* (1932). Pound also reviewed London concerts in *New Age* (1917–20) and wrote an idiosyncratic *Treatise on Harmony* (Paris, 1924, R: 1968).

Bibl.: *Ezra Pound and Music: The Complete Criticism,* ed. R. Murray Schafer (London, 1978).

Pousseur, Henri (Léon Marie Thérèse) (b. Malmédy, Belgium, 23 June 1929). Composer. He studied at the Liège Conservatory (1947–52), where he was associated with the "Variations" group of composers, and was introduced to the music of Webern (whose influence is apparent in *Trois chants sacrés,* 1951). At the Brussels Conservatory (1952–53) studied with André Souris. He met Boulez in 1951 and had contact with Stockhausen in Cologne in 1954. His first electronic pieces, *Seismogrammes* (1954), were composed entirely from sine waves at the Cologne studios and demonstrate the influence of Stockhausen. He worked with Berio and Maderna in Milan in 1957. From 1950 to 1959 he taught music in Belgian schools. He was founder and director of the Studio de musique électronique in Brussels (1958). He gave seminars at Darmstadt (1957–67) and at Cologne (1963–68); was professor at the Basel Conservatory (1963–64) and at the Boston Academy of Music (1964); lectured throughout the U.S. and Europe. He became professor at Liège Conservatory in 1970 and was appointed director in 1975.

His long association with Michel Butor (b. 1926) began in 1960. The 1965 version of *Répons* (1960) includes a text by Butor to be spoken by an actor. Butor's use of literary excerpts inspired Pousseur's interest in quotation (*La chevauchée fantastique* from *Miroir de Votre Faust,* 1965). Pousseur's many writings on music deal with his own compositional philosophy (*Musique, sémantique, société,* Paris, 1972) as well as musical problems that concerned him.

Works: *Sept versets des psaumes de la pénitence* (chorus, 1951); *Symphonies à 15 soloistes* (1954–55); *Quintette à la mémoire d'Anton Webern* (clarinet, bass clarinet, violin, cello, piano, 1955); *Exercices* (piano, 1956); *Scambi* (2-track tape, 1957); *Mobile* (2 pianos, 1956–58); *Rimes pour différentes sources sonores* (3 orchestral groups, 2-track tape, 1958–59); *Electre* (ballet, 2-track disc, 1960); *Ode* (string quartet, 1960–61); *Caractères* (piano, 1961); *Trois visages de Liège* (2-track tape, 1961); *Trait* (strings, 1962); *Votre Faust* (Butor, voices, 5 actors, 12 instruments, tape, 1960–67); *Caractères madrigalesques* (oboe, 1965); *Apostrophe et six réflexions* (piano, 1964–66); *Phonèmes pour Cathy* (voice, 1966); *Couleurs croisées* (orchestra, 1967); *Les éphémérides d'Icare II* (piano, 18 instruments, 1970); *Icare apprenti* (any instruments, 1970); *Invitation à l'utopie* (Butor, speaker, soprano, mezzo, chorus, piano, 18 instruments, 1970); *Ex-dei in machinam memoria* (melody instruments, electric instruments, 1971); *L'effacement du Prince Igor* (orchestra, 1971); *Stravinsky au futur* (1971); *Vue sur les jardins interdits* and *Deuxième vue sur les jardins interdits* (both for organ, 1973–74); *Schönbergs Gegenwart* (actors, singers, instruments, 1974); *La seconde apotheose de Rameau* (orchestra, 1981); *Agonie* (electronically distorted vocal and percussive sounds, 1981); *Sixième vue sur les jardins interdits* (string trio, 1983); *Nacht der Nächte oder die sehende Schlaflosigkeit des Herrn Goldberg* (orchestra, 1985); *Traverser la forêt* (cantata, narrator, vocal soloists, chorus, instruments, 1987); *Ode no. 2, Mnemosyne (doublement obstinée,* soprano, string quartet, 1989).

Bibl.: Heinz-Klaus Metzger and Rainer Riehn, *Henri Pousseur* (Munich, 1990).

Powell, Bud [Earl] (b. New York, 27 Sept. 1924; d. New York, 1 Aug. 1966). Jazz pianist. He joined Cootie Williams's big band (1942–44). Despite suffering a head injury in 1945 which exacerbated lifelong psychological problems, he worked regularly in bop groups in New York (late 1940s to mid–1950s). Having toured Europe in 1956, he moved to Paris in 1959, playing in a trio with Kenny Clarke (to 1962), then returned in 1964 to the U.S. Powell's playing defined the bop piano style: he executed single lines (mainly with the right hand) with dazzling speed (as on *Bud's Bubble,* recorded with his trio in 1947) and altered the role of the left hand, playing stabbing chordal punctuations. Other recordings include *Dance of the Infidels* in a quintet with Sonny Rollins and Fats Navarro (1949) and *Hallucinations,* an unaccompanied performance (1950).

Powell, John (b. Richmond, Va., 6 Sept. 1882; d. there, 15 Aug. 1963). Pianist and composer. He attended the Univ. of Virginia (B.A. 1901) and then studied in Vienna with Leschetizky (piano) and Navrátil (composition). He toured Europe as a pianist before World War I, and continued to perform in the U.S. after 1912. He was very active in musical life in Virginia, particularly the White Top folk music and Virginia State Choral festivals. In 1918 he premiered his *Rapsodie nègre* op. 27 (piano, orchestra, 1918; arr. 2 pianos, 1922) with the Russian Symphony Orchestra. He collected songs from the rural South; many of his later pieces make use of folk idioms. Works include orchestral music (*A Set of 3,* 1935; Symphony in A, 1945; "Virginia" Symphony, 1951); vocal music (*The Babe of Bethlehem,* chorus, 1934; *The Deaf Woman's Courtship,* mezzo, tenor, chorus, 1934; *5 Virginia Folk Songs,* baritone, piano, 1938); chamber and piano music (*Sonata psychologique,* 1905; *Sonata teutonica,* 1913).

Powell, Maud (b. Peru, Ill., 22 Aug. 1868; d. Uniontown, Pa., 8 Jan. 1920). Violinist. Toured with the Chicago Ladies' Quartet at age 9; studied in Leipzig (1881–82) and Paris (1882–83), and with Joachim at the Berlin Hochschule (1883–85), performing with the Berlin Philharmonic before returning to the U.S. She formed the Maud Powell Quartet in 1894, and later a trio. She toured the world, introducing concertos of Dvořák, Sibelius, and many others to U.S. audiences, and was among the first violinists to record for Victor Talking Machine Co.

Bibl.: Karen A. Schaffer and Neva Garner Greenwood, *Maud Powell: Pioneer American Violinist* (Arlington, Vt., 1988).

Powell, Mel (b. New York, 12 Feb. 1923). Composer. At age 14 he played as a jazz pianist with Benny Goodman's band. Later played in the Army Air Force Band led by Glenn Miller. At Yale (B.M. 1952) he studied composition with Hindemith. Taught at Mannes College and Queens College, CUNY, until he joined the faculty at Yale in 1957, where he was director of one of the first electronic music studios in the U.S. In 1969 became dean of the School of Music at the California Institute of the Arts. His composition makes use of twelve-tone and quasi-improvisational techniques, as well as pitch sets, a method also apparent in his electronic music. His concerto for 2 pianos and orchestra, *Duplicates,* won the 1990 Pulitzer Prize in music.

Works: *Orchestra. Cantilena concertante* (English horn, orchestra, 1948); Symphonic Suite (1949); Capriccio for Concert Band (1950); *Intrada and Variants* (1956); *Stanzas* (1957); *Setting,* cello and orchestra (1961); *Immobiles I–IV* (1967); *Settings,* jazz band (1982); *Modules,* intermezzo, chamber orchestra (1985).

Vocal. 6 Choral Songs (1950); *Sweet Lovers Love the Spring* (women's voices, piano, 1953); *Haiku Settings* (soprano, piano, 1961); *Letter to a Young Composer* (soprano, 1987). Voice and ensemble: *2 Prayer Settings* (1963); *Cantilena* (1969); *Settings* (1979); *Little Companion Pieces* (1979); *Die Violine* (1987).

Chamber. Beethoven Analogs (string quartet, 1949); String Quartet (1982); Harpsichord Sonata (1952); Trio for Piano, Violin, and Cello (1954); Divertimento (violin, harp, 1954); Divertimento (5 winds, 1955); Quintet for Piano and String Quartet (1956); Miniatures for Baroque Ensemble (1958); *Filigree Setting* (string quartet, 1959); *Improvisation* (clarinet, viola, piano, 1962); *Nocturne* (violin, 1965; rev. 1985); *Cantilena* (trombone, tape, 1981); Woodwind Quintet (1984–85); *Setting* (guitar, 1986); *Invocation* (cello, 1987); *Amy-abilities* (percussion, 1987); 3 Madrigals for Flute (1988); *Intermezzo* (piano, 1984); Piano Preludes (1987).

Electronic. Electronic Setting (1958); *2nd Electronic Setting* (1961); *Events* (1963); *Analogs I–IV* (1963); *3 Synthesizer Settings* (1970–80); *Inscape* (ballet, 1976); *Variations* (1976); *Strand Settings: Darker* (soprano, electronics, 1983); *Computer Prelude* (1988).

Bibl.: Reid Robbins, "An Interview with Mel Powell," *MQ* 72 (1986): 476–93.

Power, Leonel [Lionel, Lyonel, Leonelle] (d. Canterbury, 5 June 1445). Composer. An approximate contemporary of Dunstable, with whom he shared a preeminent position among English composers in the first part of the 15th century. His earliest known position was in the chapel of Thomas, Duke of Clarence (brother of Henry V). From 1423 he was associated with Christ Church, Canterbury, where from at least 1439 until 1445 he directed the Lady Chapel choir.

His works, all sacred, include Mass cycles, Mass movements, and settings of other liturgical texts (all Marian). Isorhythm appears in the Mass music but not elsewhere. Many pieces incorporate chant melodies, which may act as cantus firmi or may be less evident, having been paraphrased or used quite freely and only intermittently.

Power is traditionally said to have been the first to write paired Mass movements and Mass cycles unified throughout by musical means. Both Power and Dunstable wrote such works, however, and uncertainties about the dates and attributions of some works make it impossible to establish clear priority.

The extent of Power's compositional output has not been established beyond all doubt. While undisputed attributions to him survive for about 40 compositions, nearly another 20 carry his name in at least one source or have been pointed out as stylistically consistent with the surely authentic works; doubtless there exist yet more anonymous works that may be his. Yet attributions on stylistic grounds are problematic, as he is known to have been a teacher and surely influenced other composers.

Power's music ranges from very simple discant settings to highly elaborate contrapuntal pieces for as many as 5 voices. Three-voiced settings, often with frequent or extended duets, are the most common. Musical style evolves over time in the direction of ever greater refinement and subtlety. From the beginning, though, full sonorities, a relatively low tessitura, sequences, and asymmetry are frequent. Many works incorporate considerable rhythmic complexity, including syncopation and conflicting time signatures. Text-music relationships receive little apparent attention.

Many of his earlier compositions are preserved in the Old Hall manuscript (ed. Alexander Ramsbotham, Nashdom Abbey, Burnham, Bucks., 1933–38; ed. Andrew Hughes and Margaret Bent, *CMM* 46, 1969–72). The later works are known from Continental manuscripts. In addition to the music, a short practical treatise on the sights of discant also survives (ed. S. B. Meech, "Three Fifteenth-Century English Musical Treatises," *Speculum* 10 [1935]: 242–58).

Bibl.: Ed. Charles Hamm, *CMM* 50 (1969–76). Roger Bowers, "Some Observations on the Life and Career of Lionel Power," *PRMA* 102 (1975–76): 103–27.

Pownall, Mary Ann (b. London, Feb. 1751; d. Charleston, S.C., 11 Aug. 1796). Singer and composer. Known first as Mrs. James Wrightson, she made her debut in *The Recruiting Officer* in London in 1770. From 1776 to 1788 she was a favorite at Vauxhall. In 1792 she moved to the U.S. and sang in Boston (with the Old American Company), New York (in subscription concerts and with John Henry's Company), Philadelphia, and Charleston. She was among the first women to have her songs published in the U.S.

Pozdro, John (Walter) (b. Chicago, 14 Aug. 1923). Composer. He studied piano with Nina Shafren, and attended the American Conservatory in Chicago and Northwestern Univ.; at Eastman (Ph.D. 1958), studied composition with Howard Hanson and Bernard Rogers. Taught at the Univ. of Kansas in Lawrence, where he became director of theory and composition in 1961; chairman of the Annual Symposium of Contemporary American Music there, 1958–68. Compositions include 2 stage works, *Malooley and the Fear Monster* ("family opera," 1976) and *Hello, Kansas!* (musical play, 1961); 3 symphonies (1949, 1957, 1960); piano music (6 sonatas; *Four Preludes*); chamber and vocal music; pieces for carillon.

Pozo, Chano [Pozo y Gonzales, Luciano] (b. Havana, 7 Jan. 1915; d. New York, 2 Dec. 1948). Cuban jazz conga player and singer. As a member of Dizzy Gillespie's big band for a brief period (1947–48) before he was murdered, Pozo brought authentic Afro-Cuban rhythms into jazz. His recordings include *Cubana Be/Cubana Bop* and *Manteca* with Gillespie (1947) and *Jahbero* with Tadd Dameron (1948).

Prado, Pérez (b. Mantanzas, Cuba, 1922; d. Mexico City, 15 Sept. 1989). Popular pianist and bandleader. After early performances as a pianist in Cuba and Mexico, from 1951 he made a series of highly successful recordings which popularized the Latin mambo sound in the United States. These included "Anna" (1953), "Cherry Pink and Apple Blossom White" (1955), and "Patricia" (1958).

Praetorius [Schulz, Schulze], **Hieronymus** (b. Hamburg, 10 Aug. 1560; d. there, 27 Jan. 1629). Composer and organist. Probably the most important north German composer of the early 17th century. Son of Jacob Praetorius (1); father of Jacob Praetorius (2). Organist at Erfurt (1580–82), then at Hamburg until his death. Wrote Masses, Magnificats (most for organ), and about 100 motets (the great majority in Latin and approximately half polychoral). Also compiled books of church music.

Praetorius [Schulze], **Jacob** [Jacobus] (1) (b. Magdeburg, ca. 1530; d. Hamburg, 1586). Organist and editor. Father of Hieronymus Praetorius. By 1550 associated with St. Jacobi at Hamburg. Compiled books of monophonic (1554) and polyphonic (1566) sacred music.

Praetorius [Schulz], **Jacob** [Jacobus] (2) (b. Hamburg, 8 Feb. 1586; d. there, 21 or 22 Oct. 1651). Organist and composer. Son of Hieronymus Praetorius. Studied with Sweelinck. Organist at St. Petri, Hamburg, from 1603. Works, many incorporating chorale melodies: sacred and secular vocal pieces; organ compositions.

Praetorius [Schultheiss], **Michael** (b. Creuzburg an der Werra, near Eisenach, 15 Feb. 1571; d. Wolfenbüttel, 15 Feb. 1621). Composer and theorist. An exceptionally prolific composer, especially of works based on Protestant hymn tunes, most published in collections that betray some systematic plan, often liturgical.

Praetorius was educated in Torgau, from 1582 until 1584 at the Univ. of Frankfurt an der Oder, and at Zerbst, Anhalt. After playing organ at St. Marien in Frankfurt an der Oder for several years beginning in 1587, he moved to Wolfenbüttel, eventually becoming organist (from 1595), then also court Kapellmeister (from 1604) to Duke Heinrich Julius of Brunswick-Wolfenbüttel. This duke died in 1613; Praetorius retained the same position under his successor until 1620 but was seldom present. He spent much time in Dresden, where he met Schütz and became acquainted with contemporary Italian music, and also visited or worked in Magdeburg, Halle, Sondershausen, Kassel, Leipzig, Nuremberg, and Bayreuth.

His only extant secular works are the instrumental dances published as *Terpsichore* (Wolfenbüttel, 1612). Of his sacred compositions all but a few are based on Protestant hymns (including the tunes) or Lutheran liturgical texts in Latin. The vast majority are vocal, ranging in scope from bicinia to polychoral works, either with or without continuo. There are also 8 chorale settings for organ solo. The preexisting melodies are sometimes deployed as cantus firmi or appear consistently in the top voice; often, however, bits of the borrowed tune are used in each voice, and the whole is nowhere stated intact. The approximately 20 published volumes of such pieces, containing over 1,000 works, are particularly valuable for the insight they provide into Lutheran liturgical practice of Praetorius's day. Individual compositions and collections tend to reflect and thus to illuminate the use to which they were to be put in church services. Furthermore, instructions printed along with the music often clarify any practical details that might not be evident otherwise.

Late in life Praetorius undertook the writing of a comprehensive treatise on music theory and practice. Three of a projected 4 volumes were published as *Syntagma musicum* (Wolfenbüttel, 1614–20; facs, *DM* 1/14–15, 21 [1958–59]; vol. 2 trans. Harold Blumenfeld, 3rd ed., New York, 1962; R: 1980; trans. David Z. Crookes, Oxford, 1986). The second volume, which describes and pictures in a supplement *(Theatrum instrumentorum)* the instruments in use at that time, is perhaps the most valuable.

Bibl.: Ed. Friedrich Blume et al. (Wolfenbüttel, 1928–60). Kurt Gudewill and Hans Haase, *Michael Praetorius Creutzbergensis 1571 (?–1621): zwei Beiträge zu seinem und seiner Kapelle Jubilaumsjahr* (Wolfenbüttel, 1971). Siegfried Vogelsänger, *Michael Praetorius beim Wort genommen: zur Entstehungsgeschichte seiner Werke* (Aachen, 1987). Siegfried Vogelsänger, *Michael Praetorius, "Diener vieler Herren": Daten und Deutungen* (Aachen, 1991). Dietlind Möller-Weiser, *Untersuchungen zum I. Band des Syntagma Musicum von Michael Praetorius* (Kassel, 1993).

Pran Nath (b. Lahore, India [now Pakistan], 3 Nov. 1918). Classical Indian vocalist and composer. The leading modern exponent of the Kirana style of north Indian singing, he studied for twenty years with its greatest master, Ustad Abdul Waheed Khan. He built his reputation through All India Radio performances from 1937; from 1960 he taught at Delhi Univ. In 1971 he became a U.S. resident and established the Kirana Center for Indian Classical Music in New York. He taught at the Univ. of California, San Diego, and Mills College; his disciples included Terry Riley and LaMonte Young. He also produced innovations in instrumental design, notably for the classical tambūrā (drone lute).

Pratella, Francesco Balilla (b. Lugo di Romagna, 1 Feb. 1880; d. Ravenna, 17 May 1955). Composer.

Studied with Mascagni at the Pesaro Liceo musicale. He directed the Licei musicali of Lugo di Romagna (1910–29) and Ravenna (1927–45). Became associated with the futurist movement in 1910, writing *Manifesti dei musicisti futuristi* (Milan, 1910), *Manifesto tecnico della musica futurista* (Milan, 1911), and *La distruzione della quadratura* (Bologna, 1912). He gradually abandoned futurism and became deeply interested in Italian folk music. Composed 7 operas, including *La Sina 'd Vargöun,* (1906–8) and *L'aviatore Dro* (1911–14); operettas; incidental music; film scores; orchestral music (*Romagna,* 5 symphonic poems, 1903–4), chamber music (Trio, violin, cello, piano, 1919), and many songs (*I canti del cammino* op. 52, voice, piano trio, 1958).

Bibl.: Alba Ghigi, *Francesco Balilla Pratella* (Ravenna, 1930) [includes works list, writings, and bibliography].

Pratt, Silas Gamaliel (b. Addison, Vt., 4 Aug. 1846; d. Pittsburgh, 30 Oct. 1916). Composer. His parents became Illinois farmers when he was a child. Taught himself the piano and began to compose in 1861; 1868–71, studied in Berlin, but a wrist injury prevented a concert career, and he turned to composition, producing as student works an opera, *Antonio* (1870–74), a symphonic poem, *Magdalene's Lament* (1870), and his first symphony (1871). In 1872, returned to Chicago where he served as a church organist; 1874, concert performance of *Antonio;* 1875–77, studied with Dorn in Berlin, supporting himself as consular clerk; visited Bayreuth and Weimar, meeting Liszt; 4 July 1876, conducted his *Centennial Ode* in Berlin (and later at the Crystal Palace, London). From 1877 to 1888 he was in Chicago; his second opera, *Zenobia* op. 41, was staged there with moderate success in 1883, and his first (revised as *Lucille*) in 1887. From 1888 to 1902, taught in New York (from 1890 as piano teacher, Metropolitan Conservatory; from 1895, principal, West End Music School); 1906, founded Pratt Institute of Music and Art, Pittsburgh. He also composed symphonies, including *The Prodigal Son* (1876) and *Lincoln;* symphonic poems; many songs, choruses, and piano pieces; a cantata, *The Inca's Downfall,* 1879. His Columbian festival allegory, *The Triumph of Columbus* in 5 acts, was performed at the Metropolitan Opera in 1892.

Pratt, Stephen R. S. (b. Liverpool, 15 June 1947). Composer. From 1965 through 1968 he studied at Christ's College of Education in Liverpool and then at the Royal Manchester College of Music; from 1969 to 1971 at Reading Univ. and after 1971 at Liverpool Univ. with Wood. Then became a lecturer at Christ's College. He was much inspired by Messiaen. He worked initially with serialistic devices, first in the manner of Schoenberg and then of Berg and Boulez. In 1976 he helped found an ensemble, Chronos, which performed his and other composers' new works. His style has become increasingly flexible, using serial techniques freely to explore all the possibilities inherent in a row. He has used standard forms as a point of reference (e.g., the concerto grosso form in *Some of Their Number,* orchestra, 1979). Other works include Piano Sonata (1974–75); Nonet (1976); *Strong Winds, Gentle Airs* (1978); *The Fruits of the Ground* (1982).

Bibl.: Andrew Burn, "Stephen Pratt's Music," *MT* 121 (1980): 173–74.

Prausnitz, Frederik [Frederick] **(William)** (b. Cologne, 26 Aug. 1920). Conductor. Moved to the U.S. as a child; studied at Juilliard, later teaching there (1947–61) and at the New England Conservatory (1961–69), where he conducted the orchestra; served as music director of the Syracuse Symphony, 1971–74, and joined the Peabody faculty in 1976. He wrote a book on conducting (*Score and Podium,* New York, 1983).

Presley, Elvis (Aaron) [Aron] (b. East Tupelo, Miss., 8 Jan. 1935; d. Memphis, Tenn., 16 Aug. 1977). Rock-and-roll singer and guitarist, actor. In 1954 he made his first recordings with Sam Philips at Sun Studios in Memphis, achieving popularity among country audiences with songs such as "Mystery Train" (1955). In 1955 "Colonel" Tom Parker became his manager and he moved to R.C.A. records; his first successful rock-and-roll recordings were "Heartbreak Hotel," "Don't Be Cruel," "Love Me Tender" (all 1956), and "Jailhouse Rock" (1957). After serving in the army, 1958–60, in the 1960s he experimented with other popular styles, becoming famous for lyrical songs such as "Are You Lonesome Tonight" (1960); in the late 1960s he returned to rock-and-roll ("In the Ghetto," 1969). From 1956 he appeared in numerous musical films. The most successful solo singer of the 1950s and 1960s, he was the first prominent white artist to incorporate black idioms such as blues and gospel into his style. Through aggressive and sexually suggestive stage behavior he was also the first artist to associate rock-and-roll with rebellious, counterestablishment feelings among American youth; both of these innovations were seminal to the rise of rock in the early 1960s.

Bibl.: John A. Whisler, *Elvis Presley: Reference Guide and Discography* (Metuchen, N.J., 1981). Wendy Sauers, *Elvis Presley, A Complete Reference: Biography, Chronology, Concerts List, Filmography, Vital Documents, Bibliography, Index* (Jefferson, N.C., 1984). Howard F. Banney, *Return to Sender: The First Complete Discography of Elvis, Tribute and Novelty Records* (Ann Arbor, 1987). Kevin Quain, ed., *The Elvis Reader: Texts and Sources on the King of Rock 'n' Roll* (New York, 1992). David Stanley, *The Elvis Encyclopedia* (Los Angeles, 1994).

Presser, Theodore (b. Pittsburgh, 3 July 1848; d. Philadelphia, 27 Oct. 1925). Publisher. Studied music at New England Conservatory with Emery, Whiting, Parker, and Lang. Attended the Leipzig Conservatory, where he studied with Zwintscher and Jadassohn. In 1833, founded the publication *Etude,* and was editor until 1907. Established the publishing firm Theodore Presser Company in 1833 in Philadelphia; in 1906, established the Presser Home for Retired Music Teachers; in 1916, created the Presser Foundation to support the Presser Home and provide institutional scholarships.

Bibl.: Chris Yoder, "Theodore Presser, Educator, Publisher, Philanthropist" (diss., Univ. of Illinois, 1978).

Pressler, Menahem (b. Magdeburg, 16 Dec. 1923). Pianist. Emigrated to Palestine as a child. In 1955 he cofounded the Beaux Arts Trio, touring and recording with them and as a soloist. A faculty member of Indiana Univ. from 1955.

Preston, Simon (b. Bournemouth, 4 Aug. 1938). Organist. Received degrees from King's College, Cambridge (Mus.B., 1962; M.A., 1964); made his Festival Hall debut in 1962; held posts at Westminster Abbey (1962–67), St. Alban's Abbey (1967–68), and Oxford Univ. (1970–81) before becoming organist and chorusmaster at Westminster in 1981; during his sojourn in Oxford he also conducted the Bach Choir there.

Prêtre, Georges (b. Waziers, France, 14 Aug. 1924). Conductor. Studied at the Douai and Paris conservatories, with Cluytens as a conducting teacher. Directed opera at Marseilles, Lille, and Toulouse (1946–55), at the Opéra-comique in Paris (1955–59) and at the Paris Opéra (from 1959), serving as director general at the Opéra in 1970 and 1971. He made his U.S. debut in 1959, and appeared at the Metropolitan Opera during the 1964–65 season; also conducted in houses throughout Europe.

Previn, André (b. Berlin, 6 Apr. 1929). Conductor, pianist, and composer. He entered the Berlin Hochschule at age 6; forced to flee Germany in 1938, the family first went to Paris, then to Los Angeles. He studied with Castelnuovo-Tedesco, and began work at MGM Studios at age 16 as composer, arranger, and conductor, eventually winning several Academy Awards. He studied conducting with Monteux while in San Francisco in 1951 during military service; around 1960 he turned to it in earnest, leading various minor orchestras before garnering a record contract in 1964. He later took positions with the Houston Symphony (1967–69), the London Symphony (1969–79), the Pittsburgh Symphony (1976–84), the Royal Philharmonic (from 1985), and the Los Angeles Philharmonic (1985–89). A skilled jazz pianist, he recorded 20th-century solo piano music; on occasion he conducted Mozart concertos from the piano. Apart from film scores, his works include concertos for piano, cello, and guitar, chamber music, the Broadway musical *Coco* (1969), and songs.

Bibl.: Martin Bookspan and Ross Yockey, *André Previn: A Biography* (Garden City, N.Y., 1981).

Prévost, André (b. Hawkesbury, Ontario, 30 July 1934). Composer. He studied composition with Clermont Pépin at the Montreal Conservatory. In 1960 he went to Paris to study with Messiaen at the Paris Conservatory and with Dutilleux at the École Normale. He studied electronic music with Michel Philippot, and also attended Tanglewood, where his teachers included Copland, Kodály, Schuller, and Carter. He taught composition and analysis at Montreal Univ. In 1964 his orchestral piece *Fantasmes* (1963), which had been commissioned by the Montreal Symphony, won its annual prize. Other works include, for orchestra: *Scherzo* (1960); *Pyknon* (pièce concertante, violin, orchestra, 1966); *Diallile* (1968); *Evanescence* (1970); *Hommage* (chamber orchestra, 1971); choral: *Terre des hommes* (cantata, M. Lalonde, solo voices, 3 choruses, 2 orchestra, 1967); *Psalm cxlvii* (200 voices, 4 trumpets, 4 trombones, organ, 1971); also chamber music.

Prévost, Eugène-Prosper (b. Paris, 23 Apr. 1809; d. New Orleans, 19 Aug. 1872). Composer and conductor. Studied at the Paris Conservatory with Le Sueur (1827); colleague of Berlioz. Placed second in Prix de Rome with the cantata *La mort de Cléopâtre* (1829), first prize for *Bianca Capello.* Conductor at Le Havre (1835–38), at New Orleans (1838–62). Taught singing in Paris 1862–67. Produced 10 comic operas, including *Le grenadier de Wagram* and *L'hôtel des princes* (both 1831). Also composed sacred music and orchestral pieces.

Prey, Hermann (b. Berlin, 11 July 1929). Baritone. Studied at the Berlin Hochschule with Prohaska, Baum, and Gottschalk; made his recital debut in 1951, operatic debut the following year; joined the Hamburg Opera in 1953, also appearing regularly at Vienna and Berlin from 1956 and at Munich and Cologne from 1959. He sang at the Salzburg and Bayreuth festivals, and with the Metropolitan Opera and other U.S. companies. A much-admired interpreter of lieder, he made many recordings.

Bibl.: Hermann Prey, *First Night Fever: The Memoirs of Hermann Prey* (New York, 1986).

Price [née Smith], **Florence Bea(trice)** (b. Little Rock, Ark., 9 Apr. 1888; d. Chicago, 3 June 1953). Composer. Studied with Chadwick, Converse, and Cutter at the New England Conservatory of Music, graduating with degrees in organ and piano in 1906; taught at Shorter College in Little Rock, then was named head of the music department at Clark Univ. in Atlanta in 1910. In 1912 she married Thomas J. Price, and in 1927 the family moved to Chicago, where she studied with Sowerby and Busch. Recognition came when her Symphony no. 1 in E minor (1931–32) won first prize in the Wanamaker Competition in 1932, which led to a performance of the work by the Chicago Symphony and subsequent performances of her compositions. The first black woman to attain recognition as a symphonic composer, she is best known today for her songs, including "Songs to the Dark Virgin" (1941)

Leontyne Price as Leonara in Verdi's *Il trovatore.*

on a text by Langston Hughes; these draw on traditional black melodies and rhythms.

Price, (Mary Violet) Leontyne (b. Laurel, Miss., 10 Feb. 1927). Soprano. Graduated in 1949 from Central State College, Wilberforce, Ohio; also studied with Florence Kimball at Juilliard (1949–52), appearing in *Falstaff* there. Virgil Thomson selected her for a 1952 revival of *Four Saints in 3 Acts;* immediately thereafter a two-year period with a new production of *Porgy and Bess* established her reputation. Appearances as Tosca on NBC Television and as Aida at San Francisco followed; she repeated the latter role in Vienna and London (1958) and at La Scala (1960). She made her Metropolitan Opera debut in 1961, singing there often until her final performance as Aida in 1985. In 1966 she created Cleopatra in Barber's *Antony and Cleopatra.* Also performed widely in recital and with orchestras.

Price, Lloyd (b. New Orleans, La., 9 Mar. 1933). Rhythm-and-blues singer and songwriter. He began performing and recording in New Orleans, and his "Lawdy Miss Clawdy" (1952) was very popular. After singing in a service band in Korea and Japan, 1952–54, he made recordings successful with both rhythm-and-blues and popular audiences (including "Stagger Lee," 1958; "Personality," 1959); he also operated record companies and a nightclub.

Price, Margaret (b. Blackwood Mon. [now Gwent], Wales, 13 Apr. 1941). Soprano. Studied at Trinity College, London; performed in recital with her coach, James Lockhart; made her operatic debut with the Welsh National Opera in 1962; appeared at Covent Garden in 1963, becoming a permanent member of the company in 1970, and joined the Munich Opera in 1975 after a 1971 German debut at Cologne; in 1985 she made her Metropolitan debut as Desdemona. She has a wide repertory, though she is most renowned for her Mozart roles.

Price, Ray (Noble) (b. near Perryville, Tex., 12 Jan. 1926). Country singer and guitarist. He joined the Grand Ole Opry in 1952, and was closely associated with Hank Williams, whose band formed the core of Price's own Cherokee Cowboys. His early recordings (including "Crazy Arms," 1956; "Heartaches by the Numbers," 1959) are in traditional country styles; later he experimented with popular idioms. Other successes included "For the Good Times" (1970), and the album *San Antonio Rose* (with Willie Nelson, 1980).

Prigozhin, Lyutsian Abramovich (b. Tashkent, 15 Aug. 1926). Composer. He studied at the Leningrad Conservatory with Kochurov, Shcherbachyov, and Yevlakhov, then taught theory and composition. His compositions include an opera, children's operas, cantatas, 4 symphonies, orchestral suites, violin sonatas, string quartets, other chamber music, choral music, songs, and scores for stage, radio, and television.

Primrose, William (b. Glasgow, 23 Aug. 1903; d. Provo, Utah, 1 May 1982). Violist. Studied violin with Ritter in Glasgow and Ysaÿe in Belgium (1925–27); joined the London String Quartet as violist in 1930, staying until 1935; after a series of tours as a virtuoso, he led the viola section of the NBC Symphony from 1937 to 1942, teaching also at the Curtis Institute; founded the Primrose Quartet in 1939, playing concerts on radio. He joined the Festival Piano Quartet in 1956, and later taught at the Univ. of Southern California (1962–65), Indiana Univ. (1965–72), and Brigham Young Univ. (1979 to his death), participating also in the Heifetz–Piatigorsky Concerts of the early 1960s. Among the composers who wrote concertos for him are Bartók, Britten, Milhaud, and Rochberg.

Bibl.: William Primrose, *Walk on the North Side: Memoirs* (Provo, Utah, 1978).

Prince [Nelson, Prince Rogers] (b. Minneapolis, 7 June 1958). Soul and rock singer, instrumentalist, songwriter, and producer. Prolific and multitalented, he was born into a family of pop musicians. Early albums (*Dirty Mind,* 1980) were sexually explicit. He rose to prominence with the album *1999* (1982, including "Little Red Corvette") and the album and film *Purple*

Rain (1984, including "When Doves Cry"). A succession of further albums (*Lovesexy,* 1988), soundtracks (*Batman,* 1989), films, and producing efforts followed. In 1994 he changed his name to a combined male/female symbol with a horn.

Pringsheim, Klaus (b. Feldafing, near Munich, 24 July 1883; d. Tokyo, 7 Dec. 1972). Composer and conductor. He studied piano and composition in Munich before he went to Vienna as assistant conductor of the Court Opera. There he developed a long-standing relationship with Mahler, who instructed him in both conducting and composition. He conducted the German Opera in Prague (1909–14) and the Bremen Opera (1915–18), and was director of the Max Reinhardt theaters in Berlin (1918–25). He taught at the Imperial Academy of Music in Tokyo (1931–37). Following brief stays in Thailand and California he returned to Japan, where he was director of the Musashino Academy of Music. Works include Concerto for Orchestra (1935); *Yamada Nagasama* (Japanese Radio Opera, 1953); Concertino for Xylophone and Orchestra (1962).

Printz, Wolfgang Caspar (b. Waldthurn, Upper Palatinate, 10 Oct. 1641; d. Sorau, Lower Lusatia [now Żary, Poland], 13 Oct. 1717). Composer and theorist. He studied in Weiden under Wolfgang Altus and Johann Conrad Merz, and entered the Univ. of Altdorf in 1659 as a theology student. Lack of funds forced him to return home in 1661, and he became a tenor in the court chapel in Heidelberg that year before embarking on a lengthy journey through Italy. He met Kircher in Rome and became interested in studying music theory. He was named court composer to Count Leopold of Promnitz in Sorau, then served as Kantor at Triebel (1664) and later at Sorau (1665). Only 6 of Printz's 22 treatises are extant. His *Historische Beschreibung* (Dresden, 1690; facs., Graz, 1964) is regarded as the first significant German history of music; *Phrynis Mitilenaeus, oder Satyrischer Componist* (Dresden and Leipzig, 1696), an extensive 3-volume treatise on music theory, includes satirical narratives and dialogues.

Prioris, Johannes (b. Brabant?, ca. 1445; d. ca. 1514). Composer. *Maistre de la chapelle* at the French royal court by 1503; highly regarded by his contemporaries and successors; a follower of Ockeghem in contrapuntal style, and perhaps his successor at the French court, where Ockeghem worked until 1497. Wrote Masses, including a Requiem; motets; Magnificats; chansons.

Bibl.: Ed. T. Herman Keahey and Conrad Douglas, *CMM* 90 (1982–85).

Pritchard, John (Michael) (b. London, 5 Feb. 1921; d. Daly City, Calif., 5 Dec. 1989). Conductor. Studied with his father; led Derby Orchestra from 1943 to 1951; first worked at the Glyndebourne Opera in 1947, later serving as chorusmaster (from 1949) and musical director (1969–77); also led the Royal Liverpool Philharmonic (1957–63) and the London Philharmonic (1962–66) and appeared with the Royal Philharmonic. Beginning in 1982 he conducted the BBC symphony, subsequently appeared at the Cologne Opera (from 1978), the Belgian National Opera (from 1981), and the San Francisco Opera (from 1986). He was knighted in 1983.

Prokofiev, Sergei Sergeievich (b. Sontsovka, near Ekaterinoslav, Ukraine, 27 [not 23] April 1891; d. Moscow, 5 March 1953). Composer and pianist. The son of an agricultural manager of a large steppe estate, he received his earliest musical training from his mother, a well-educated pianist. From the age of 5 he wrote piano pieces; at 9 he had an original children's opera, *Velikan* [The Giant], performed. His mother took him annually to Moscow to play for Taneyev, who arranged for Glier to tutor him at Sontsovka during the summers of 1902–4. Further early operatic projects adumbrated his lifelong predilection to compose for the stage.

From 1904 to 1914 Prokofiev attended St. Petersburg Conservatory, studying piano with Anna Esipov, harmony and counterpoint with Liadov, orchestration with Rimsky-Korsakov, and conducting with Nicolas Tcherepnin. Precociously prolific, experimentative, and youthfully arrogant, he chafed at academic studies; but he gained ready entrance to the Evenings of Contemporary Music produced by the city's avant-garde elite, among whom lasting alliances were made. On his father's death in 1910 he made St. Petersburg his home and began to support himself with concerts and publications. New works included the Straussian opera *Maddelena,* two symphonic poems, many piano pieces, and his first two piano concerti. At his 1914 graduation he won the Anton Rubinstein performance prize for playing, unorthodoxly, his own First Piano Concerto.

In the summer of 1914 Prokofiev went to London to meet Diaghilev; there Stravinsky's ballets impressed him strongly. Diaghilev commissioned *Ala i Lalli* [Ala and Lalli], a primitivistic ballet resembling Stravinsky's *Rite of Spring;* he eventually rejected Prokofiev's score, but the composer made it into a successful concert work, *Scythian Suite.* In 1915 Diaghilev commissioned a comic ballet, *Chout* or *Skazka pro shuta* [The Tale of the Buffoon], but the war prevented its production until mid-1921. Prokofiev composed an opera for Petrograd based on Dostoevsky's *Igrok* [The Gambler], but production was aborted in the wake of political events in early 1917. In 1917 he also wrote a primitivistic cantata, *Semero ikh* [They Are Seven], and two major concert works: the First Symphony [Classical Symphony], which endows Haydnesque forms with modern harmonic idioms, and the First Violin Concerto.

Shortly after the 1917 October Revolution Prokofiev left Russia to tour Japan and America; he gave his first piano recital in New York in late 1918. The Chicago opera commissioned a comic opera for the 1919 season, *Lyubov' k tryom apelsinam* [Love for Three Oranges]; its production was postponed for two years for internal reasons. In financial straits, Prokofiev visited Paris to expedite Diaghilev's production of *Chout.* In December 1921 he returned to Chicago for the opera premiere; he also introduced the Third Piano Concerto, a product of several years' work.

From 1922 to 1936 Prokofiev resided primarily in Paris and gave frequent European concert tours. In 1927 he married the Spanish singer Lina Llubera; his sons Sviatoslav and Oleg were born in 1924 and 1928. In 1925 a new ballet, *Trapetsiya* [Trapeze], was staged in Berlin. Diaghilev commissioned and staged two more ballets: *Pas d'acier* or *Stal'noy skok* [The Steel Step] (1926) and *L'Enfant prodigue* or *Bludnïy sïn* [The Prodigal Son] (1929). Since 1919 Prokofiev had been working on a large uncommissioned opera, *Ognennïy angel* [The Fiery Angel], which he now tried to produce, obtaining a partial reading by Koussevitzky in 1928; it was staged only in 1954. The 1920s saw Symphonies nos. 2, 3, and 4 (the latter two based on *Pas d'acier* and *L'Enfant prodigue,* respectively), the Fifth Piano Sonata, a revision of the opera *Igrok* staged in Brussels (1929), and the ballet *Na Dnepre* or *Sur le Borysthène* [On the Dniepr] (1931) for the Paris Opéra. An American tour in 1925 yielded a commission from the Library of Congress for the First String Quartet; a tour to the USSR in 1927 strongly revived the composer's personal ties to his homeland.

During the early 1930s Prokofiev gradually shifted his attention from the West back to his native land, feeling keen competition from émigré compatriots Stravinsky in Europe and Rachmaninoff in America. Major Soviet commissions came forth: the film score *Poruchik Kizhe* [Lieutenant Kijé] (1933) and the ballet *Romeo and Juliet.* The latter project was initiated in 1934 by Leningrad's Kirov Theater, transferred to Moscow's Bolshoi, then aborted; the work was finally staged in Brno in 1938. Concurrent Western commissions included the Fourth Piano Concerto (commissioned by Austrian left-hand virtuoso Paul Wittgenstein, who never played it) and the Second Violin Concerto (commissioned by the French violinist Robert Soetans); the Fifth Piano Concerto and Cello Concerto also date from these years.

In 1936 Prokofiev settled permanently in Moscow, a date that coincided with preparations for the 20th anniversary of the Revolution in 1937. For this event he composed a cantata for some 500 forces, but performance never took place; his Western tendencies aroused political suspicion. (Stalin's party had already censured Shostakovich in early 1936.) He received commissions for incidental music to three plays of Pushkin, the centennial of whose death fell in 1937, but the productions were aborted. A more modest project of 1936 found greater success: the narrated orchestral folk tale *Petya i volk* [Peter and the Wolf], one of a series of children's pieces from the late 1930s.

Prokofiev toured Europe and America twice in late 1936 and early 1938, taking time to study film scoring in Hollywood. This led to an epochal collaboration with Soviet film maker Sergei Eisenstein on the 1938 film *Alexander Nevsky.* He also collaborated with V. E. Meyerhold, director of Moscow's Stanislavsky Theater, on a socialist-realistic opera, *Semyon Kotko;* it was staged in 1940, but only after Meyerhold's execution (on political grounds). The opera *Obrucheniye v monastïre* [Betrothal in a Monastery] followed in 1941. This period also saw the Piano Sonata no. 6, and work on nos. 7 and 8.

The war years brought great upheaval. In early 1941 Prokofiev suffered a heart attack. The outbreak of war in June forced his temporary evacuation to southern Soviet states. He separated from his wife (whose foreign sympathies led later to her arrest) and formed a liaison with the young Mira Mendelson, whose advantageous political ties aided his circumstances. Still his output remained steady. A second collaboration with Eisenstein yielded the epic *Ivan Groznïy* [Ivan the Terrible], part 1, in 1942. Wartime sentiment encouraged his operatic setting of Tolstoy's *Voyna i mir* [War and Peace]. At first the Moscow Arts Committee accepted the opera, albeit with substantial revisions, but later canceled the production; further revisions occupied Prokofiev for the rest of his life, but the work was not staged until 1957. The war years also saw the completion of the Piano Sonatas nos. 7 and 8, the Second String Quartet (on Kabardinian folk tunes), the Flute Sonata, and the Fifth Symphony (1944). The last received a triumphant Moscow premiere in early 1945, but shortly afterward a bad fall and concussion further weakened the composer's health.

The end of the war expedited the completion of two large projects: part 2 of *Ivan Groznïy* and the ballet *Zolushka* [Cinderella], begun in 1940. Moving in 1946 to a quiet manor at Nikolina Gora outside Moscow, he composed the Sixth Symphony, the last piano sonata (no. 9), two large works for the 1947 anniversary of the Revolution, and a second socialist-realistic opera, *Povest' o nastoyashchem cheloveke* [Story of a Real Man] (staged in 1960).

In 1948 Stalin's party strongly tightened its cultural grip with the "Zhdanov purge," criticizing Prokofiev and banning many of his works. Despite his subsequent receipt of various official commissions (on ideological themes), his spirit and health declined rapidly. The main works of his last years were the ballet *Skaz o kammenom tsvetke* [Tale of the Stone Flower] (1948–50; staged in 1954), the Unaccompanied Violin Sonata, and the Seventh Symphony; for Rostropovich he wrote the Cello Sonata, and the Symphony-Concerto and Concertino for cello and orchestra. Prokofiev and Stalin died on the same day.

Works not mentioned above include numerous early piano pieces, among them *Navazhdeniye* or *Suggestion diabolique* (1908), *Toccata* (1912), *Sarcasms* (1912–14), and *Mimolyotnosti* or *Visions fugitives* (1915–17); and early orchestral works, among them the Sinfonietta

(1909). Mature orchestral works include the Divertissement (1925–29) and the Soviet-inspired *Tridtsat' let* [Thirty Years] (1947), and *Vstrecha Volgi s Donom* [The Meeting of the Volga with the Don] (1951). Many orchestral works were unpublished, including several film scores from the war years. Late Soviet-inspired works include numerous choral pieces with and without orchestra. He wrote over 50 songs with piano, among them *Gadkiy utyonok* [The Ugly Duckling] (1914) and many settings of poems of Balmont. He made numerous arrangements, orchestrations, and reductions of his own works. He left several projects uncompleted on his death.

Bibl.: S. I. Shlifshteyn, ed., *S. S. Prokof'yev: materialï, dokumentï, vospominaniya* [Materials, Documents, Reminiscences] (Moscow, 1956); trans. Eng. (1960; R: 1968). I. V. Nest'yev, *Prokof'iev* (Moscow, 1957; R: 1973); trans. Eng. (1961). S. I. Shlifshteyn, *Notograficheskiy spravochnik S. S. Prokof'ieva* [Thematic Catalogue of Works] (Moscow, 1962). I. V. Nest'yev and G. Y. Edelman, ed., *Sergey Prokof'iev: stat'i i materialï* [Articles and Materials] (Moscow, 1965). Rita McAllister, "The Operas of Sergei Prokofiev" (diss., Univ. of Cambridge, 1970). Vladimir Blok, ed., *Sergey Prokof'iev: Materialï, stat'i, interv'yu* [Materials, Articles, Interviews] (Moscow, 1978); trans. Eng. (1978). David H. Appel, ed. *Prokofiev by Prokoviev: A Composer's Memoir* (Garden City, N.Y., 1979). Victor Ilyitch Seroff, *Sergei Prokofiev, A Soviet Tragedy: The Case of Sergei Prokofiev, His Life and Works, His Critics, and His Executioners* (New York, 1979). Harlow Robinson, *Sergei Prokofiev* (New York, 1987). Oleg Prokofiev, ed., *Soviet Diary, 1927* (Boston, 1992). Klaus Wolfgang Niemöller, ed., *Internationale Symposion "Sergej Prokofjew, Aspekte seines Werkes und der Biographie"* (Regensburg, 1992).

Prosdocimus de Beldemandis (b. ca. 1380; d. Padua, 1428). Theorist. Studied at the universities of Bologna and Padua, receiving degrees in arts and medicine. Taught at Padua. Wrote music treatises, revising most at least once, beginning in 1404. On the whole he approved of earlier theory (that of Franco of Cologne and Jehan des Murs) and practice (such as Italian trecento notation) and disapproved of contemporary developments and, most emphatically, Marchetto da Padova's fivefold division of the tone.

Writings: *Expositiones tractatus pratice cantus mensurabilis magistri Johannis de Muris,* ed. F. Alberto Gallo (Bologna, 1966). *Tractatus pratice cantus mensurabilis, CS* 3:200–228. *Contrapunctus,* ed. and trans. Jan Herlinger (Lincoln, 1984). *Tractatus plane musice; Tractatus pratice cantus mensurabilis ad modum ytalicorum,* ed. and trans. Eng., Jay A. Huff, *MSD* 29 (1972). *Brevis summula proportionem quantum ad musicam pertinet* and *Parvus tractatulus de modo monochordum dividendi,* ed. and trans. Jan Herlinger (Lincoln, 1987). *Tractatus musicae speculative,* ed. D. Rafaelo Baralli and Luigi Torri, *RIM* 20 (1913): 707–62.

Prout, Ebenezer (b. Oundle, 1 Mar. 1835; d. Hackney, 5 Dec. 1909). Scholar and editor. Received B.A. from London in 1854. Entered the musical profession in 1859; taught at the National Training School for Music (1876–82) and at the Royal Academy of Music (1879–1909). Appointed professor of music at Trinity College in Dublin in 1894. Editor of the *Monthly Musical Record* (1871–75). Critic for *The Academy* (1874–79) and *The Athenaeum* (1879–89). Edited Handel's *Samson* (1880) and *Messiah* (1902). Composed many works including several cantatas, an organ concerto, 4 symphonies, church music. Wrote several treatises: *Instrumentation* (London, 1876); *Harmony: Its Theory and Practice* (London, 1889; rewritten 1903); *Counterpoint, Strict and Free* (London, 1890); *Double Counterpoint and Canon* (London, 1891); *Fugue* (London, 1891); *Fugal Analysis* (London, 1892); *Musical Form* (London, 1893); *Applied Forms* (London, 1895); and *The Orchestra* (London, 1897).

Bibl.: "Ebenezer Prout," *MT* 40 (1899): 225–30.

Provenzale, Francesco (b. Naples, ca. 1626; d. there, 6 Sept. 1704). Composer. His first opera, *Il Ciro,* was presented in Naples around 1653; 2 further operas in Naples, *La Cloridea* (1660) and *La Bisalva, ovvero Offendere chi più s'ama* (1667–68), have been attributed to Provenzale on circumstantial evidence. From 1663 he was appointed chief maestro at the Conservatorio S. Maria di Loreto in Naples, then headed the staff at S. Maria della Pietà dei Turchini from 1675 until 1701. He was *maestro di cappella* at S. Gennaro (1686–99) but was passed over in favor of Alessandro Scarlatti for a similar post at the viceregal court; he did serve the court, however, as *maestro di cappella di camera* in 1688 and from 1690 served during Scarlatti's absences. Provenzale is regarded as one of the founders of the Neapolitan opera school. Only 2 operas with music entirely by Provenzale have survived, *Il schiavo di sua moglie* (Naples, 1671; facs., New York, 1979) and *La Stellidaura vendicata* (Naples, 1674); he stopped writing stage works after 1678.

Pryor, Arthur (Willard) (b. St. Joseph, Mo., 22 Sept 1870; d. West Long Branch, N.J., 18 June 1942). Trombonist and bandleader. Mastered the trombone as a youth, joining the Liberati Band in 1888; directed the Stanley opera company from 1889 until 1892, when he joined Sousa's band. He served as Sousa's assistant conductor until 1903, when he formed his own band, touring (1903–9), making hundreds of recordings, and playing a regular schedule in New Jersey and Florida until he retired in 1933. Pryor wrote several hundred pieces, including marches and rags (often trombone showpieces), songs, and piano music.

Bibl.: Daniel E. Frizane, "Arthur Pryor (1870–1942): American Trombonist, Bandleader, Composer" (diss., Univ. of Kansas, 1984).

Ptaszyńska, Marta (b. Warsaw, 29 July 1943). Composer and percussionist. Studied at the Warsaw Lyceum and Academy of Music, where she earned degrees in theory (1967), percussion (1967), and composition (1968); in 1969 studied with Nadia Boulanger in Paris; in 1972 traveled to the U.S. to study percussion at the Cleveland Institute of Music. She taught percussion at Bennington College (1974–77),

Giacomo Puccini.

then composition at the Univ. of California, Berkeley; also taught at Indiana Univ. Composed a television opera, *Oscar from Alva* (1972); an oratorio, *Chant for All the People on Earth* (1969); and *Helio, centricum, musicum,* a multimedia spectacle (1973). More recent works include Marimba Concerto (1985); *La novella d'inverno* (string orchestra, 1984); *Holocaust Memorial Cantata* (1992); *Fanfare for Peace* (1994); saxophone concerto (*Charlie's Dream,* 1995).

Ptolemy, Claudius (b. Ptolemais?, after 83 C.E.; d. 161). Theorist. Although known chiefly for his work on mathematics and astronomy, he also wrote a 3-volume treatise on music theory, the *Harmonika* (Harmonics). The emphasis is on music as number, but some weight is given to the evidence of the senses. Many Pythagorean or Aristoxenian theories are rejected on mathematical or acoustical grounds. The treatise was never lost: it was the subject of a commentary by Porphyry (3rd century) and was later translated into Arabic (9th century) and edited by Byzantine scholars (14th century). Yet it was known to the West in the Middle Ages chiefly through Boethius.

Puccini, Giacomo (Antonio Domenico Michele Secondo Maria) (b. Lucca, 22 Dec. 1858; d. Brussels, 29 Nov. 1924). Composer. Expected to follow family tradition and become organist and choirmaster at S. Martino, he received his earliest instruction from his uncle Fortunato Magi. He then studied with Carlo Angeloni, director of the Istituto musicale Pacini. At age 10 he joined the choirs at S. Martino and S. Michele; at age 14 he became organist at these and several other churches around Lucca. His earliest compositions were organ pieces. A performance of *Aida* in 1876 inspired him to become an opera composer, and after graduating from the Istituto musicale Pacini (1880) he entered the Milan Conservatory with the aid of a scholarship from Queen Margherita, studying with Antonio Bazzini and Ponchielli.

In 1883 Puccini wrote his first opera, *Le villi,* to a libretto by Ferdinando Fontana. The opera failed to win a competition, but was performed at the Teatro del Verme in Milan after Giulio Ricordi and Arrigo Boito heard Puccini sing through it at the piano. *Le villi* was published by Ricordi, who commissioned the opera *Edgar.* This work, first given at La Scala in 1889 and coolly received, has not survived. Puccini's next opera was *Manon Lescaut,* the libretto for which was a collaboration among five different authors. Following the work's premiere at Turin in 1893 Puccini won international fame; the opera was produced in London in 1894. In 1891 he bought a house at Torre del Lago on the lake at Massaciuccoli, where he lived until 1921. *La bohème,* first produced at Turin in 1896 under Toscanini, was not immediately successful. The libretto was adapted by Illica and Giacosa from Henry Murger's autobiographical *Scènes de la vie de Bohème.* With *Tosca* Puccini scored a notable success, although following the Roman premiere (Teatro Costanzi, 1900) the critics attacked the opera for the cruelty and brutality of the action. The audience whistled and shouted during the first performance of *Madama Butterfly* at La Scala in 1904. This disturbance, apparently designed by Puccini's rivals, forced the composer to withdraw the opera immediately and make cuts to both text and music; the revised version was enthusiastically received at Brescia the following year.

In the next several years Puccini's creative energies were sapped by a domestic squabble that resulted in the suicide of his servant Doria Manfredi in 1909 and a much-publicized lawsuit involving his jealous wife, Elvira. Inspired by a production of Belasco's *The Girl of the Golden West,* which he saw in New York in 1907, Puccini engaged Carlo Zangarini and Guelfo Civinni to write a libretto. The opera was first given at the Metropolitan Opera in 1910, with Caruso as Johnson and Emmy Destinn as Minnie. It was a success with the public, but elicited a guarded response from the critics. In 1913 Puccini accepted a commission from the directors of the Vienna Karltheater to write an operetta; the result was *La rondine,* premiered at Monte Carlo in 1917.

His next works for the stage were a series of one-act operas, known collectively as *Il trittico* and including *Il tabarro* (libretto by Adami), *Suor Angelica* (libretto by Giovacchino Forzano), and the comedy *Gianni Schicchi* (also Forzano). The operas were first produced at the Metropolitan Opera in 1918; a performance in Rome followed in 1919. In his final years Puccini worked with Simoni and Adami on a setting of Gozzi's *Turandotte.* The composition of this opera, which lay unfinished at his death, caused Puccini great difficulty, even anguish. In 1921 he moved to Viareggio. In late 1923 he began having pain in his throat, and in autumn 1924 he was diagnosed as having cancer. X-ray treatments at the clinic La Couronne in Brussels led to his death on 29 November. The sketches he left for the final two scenes of *Turandot* were used by Franco Alfano to complete the opera, and the first production was given at La Scala in 1926 under Toscanini's direction. Aside from his 12 operas, Puccini wrote sacred vocal music, songs, several orchestral works, music for string quartet, a violin sonata, and several keyboard works.

Bibl.: Cecil A. Hopkinson, *Bibliography of the Works of Giacomo Puccini, 1858–1924* (New York, 1968). William Ashbrook, *The Operas of Puccini* (New York, 1968; rev. 1985). Charles Osborne, *The Complete Operas of Puccini* (London, 1981). Mosco Carner, *Tosca* (Cambridge, 1985). Arthur Groos and Roger Parker, *Giacomo Puccini: "La Bohème"* (Cambridge, 1986). Michael Kaye, *The Unknown Puccini: A Historical Perspective on the Songs, including Little-Known Music from "Edgar" and "La Rondine," with Complete Music for Violin and Piano* (Oxford, 1987). Michele Girardi, *Puccini: La vita e l'opera* (Rome, 1989). Gianfranco Musco, *Musica e teatro in Giacomo Puccini* (Cortona, 1989). William Ashbrook and Harold Powers, *Puccini's Turandot: The End of the Great Tradition* (Princeton, 1991). Karl Georg Berg, *Giacomo Puccinis Opern: Musik und Dramaturgie* (Kassel, 1991). Mosco Carner, *Puccini: A Critical Biography* (New York, 1992). Giorgio Magri, *L'uomo Puccini* (Milan, 1992).

Puente, Tito [Ernest Anthony] (b. New York, 20 Apr. 1923). Jazz and salsa percussionist, vibraphonist, and bandleader. Studied music at Juilliard and the New York School; formed his own band, The Piccadilly Boys, in 1947; later worked with small jazz groups. With Pérez Prado and Tito Rodríguez he helped popularize the mambo in the 1950s with recordings such as *Dance Mania* (1958); he continued to record Latin and jazz; won Grammys in 1978, 1983, 1985, and 1990.

Pugnani, (Giulio) Gaetano (Gerolamo) (b. Turin, 27 Nov. 1731; d. there, 15 July 1798). Violinist and composer. He studied with G. B. Somis, a Corelli pupil, and at age 10 was allowed to play with the Teatro Regio as a second violinist, although his official membership in the ensemble did not begin until 1748. A royal stipend allowed him to study composition in Rome with Ciampi (1749–50), and he achieved fame through the 1754 performance of one of his own concertos at the Concert spirituel in Paris. Pugnani served as conductor of the King's Theatre in London (1767–69), composing for the theater the first of his operas, *Nanetta e Lubino* (1769). In 1770 he was appointed first violinist of the King's Music in Turin, which included the leadership of the Teatro Regio; subsequently named general director of instrumental music (1776) and supervisor of military music (1786). During this time he continued his career as both an opera composer and a violin soloist, and from 1780 to 1782 he toured Europe with his pupil Viotti; other students included Conforti, Bruni, and Polledro. Pugnani may have consulted with the Parisian bowmaker Tourte and his younger son, François, and thus influenced the development of the modern bow. In addition to works for violin solo and a handful of operas, surviving compositions include chamber music, trio sonatas, and 7 symphonies.

Pugni, Cesare (b. Genoa, 31 May 1802; d. St. Petersburg, 26 Jan. 1870). Composer. Studied violin with Rolla, composition with Asioli at the Milan Conservatory. Composed the ballet *Elerz e Zulmida* (1826) and the opera *Il disertore svizzero* (1831) in Milan. *Maestro di cembalo* and music director at La Scala (1832–34). He began a collaboration with the choreographer Jules Perrot in London in 1843. Named ballet composer to the imperial theaters in St. Petersburg in 1851. Works include 40 Masses; as many as 300 ballets; 5 Italian operas; hymns; symphonies; piano pieces.

Bibl.: Cyril William Beaumont, *A History of Ballet in Russia (1613–1881)* (London, 1930).

Pugno, (Stéphane) Raoul (b. Montrouge, near Paris, 23 June 1852; d. Moscow, 3 Jan. 1914). Pianist and composer. Studied in Paris with Niedermeyer. Entered the Paris Conservatory in 1866, studied piano with Mathias, composition with Thomas. Won first prize for piano (1866), harmony (1867), and organ (1869). He was named musical director of the Paris Opéra in 1871. Choirmaster at St. Eugène Church (1888–92). Taught harmony at the Conservatory, 1892–96; professor of piano there, 1896–1901. He gave frequent recitals with Ysaÿe from 1896. Toured England in 1894, the U.S. 1897–98. Composed 4 comic operas, operettas, ballets and pantomimes, incidental music, an oratorio (*La résurrection de Lazare,* 1879), Piano Sonata in D minor (1873), songs.

Pujol, Juan (Pablo) (b. Barcelona, ca. 1573; d. there, May 1626). Composer. He was *maestro de canto* at Tarragona Cathedral in 1593 and organist at Nuestra Señora del Pilar, Saragossa, in 1596. He became a priest in 1600, and from 1612 until his death he served as choirmaster at Barcelona Cathedral. A prolific composer of sacred music; most of his extant compositions (including 13 Masses, 8 Magnificats, and 9 motets) date from his Barcelona period.

Bibl.: *Juan Purol: Opera omnia,* ed. Higinio Anglès (1926, 1932).

Pujol (Vilarrubí), Emilio (b. Granadella, 7 Apr. 1886; d. Barcelona, 16 Nov. 1980). Guitarist, vihuelist, and musicologist. Played bandurria in Paris at age 12; studied guitar with Tárrega (1902–9); made his concert debut in 1912. He premiered Falla's *Homenaje a Debussy* in 1922, and toured Europe, South America, and Australia. Combining performance with historical research into guitar and vihuela, he taught at the Lisbon Academy (1946–69) and in Siena and Paris. He wrote and arranged music for guitar as well.

Pulgar Vidal, Francisco Bernardo (b. Huánaco, Peru, 12 Mar. 1929). Composer. Studied with Sas in Lima and Duque in Bogotá; graduated from the National Conservatory, Lima, and took both a law degree and a doctorate in art and literature from the National Univ. of San Marcos. Served as humanities professor at Jorge Tadeo Lozano Univ., Bogotá. His cantata *Apu Inqa* won the competition celebrating the 150th anniversary of Peru's independence. Works include *Suite mística* (1956), *Taki Núm. 1* (1960; adapted from a 1956 piano piece), and *Chulpas (7 Estructuras Sinfónicas)* (1968) for orchestra, along with compositions for chamber ensemble, piano, chorus, and solo voice.

Punto, Giovanni [Stich, Johann Wenzel (Jan Václav)] (b. Zehušice, near Čáslav, 28 Sept. 1746; d. Prague, 16 Feb. 1803). Horn player, violinist, and composer. After studying horn in Prague, Munich, and Dresden, he served Count Thun for three years and then ran away, crossing the border into the Holy Roman Empire, where he served the Prince of Hechingen and at the Mainz court (1769–74). In Paris in 1778 Mozart was impressed with his playing. He joined the Prince-Archbishop of Würzburg's band (1781), then served the Count of Artois in Paris (1782) before appearing in the London Pantheon concerts (1788). In Paris (1789–99) he was violinist-conductor at the Théâtre des variétés amusantes. In Vienna in 1800 Beethoven composed the Horn Sonata op. 17 for him. He toured with J. L. Dussek in 1802 before returning to Prague. Most of Punto's works, including concertos and chamber music, are for the horn.

Purcell, Daniel (b. London, ca. 1660; d. 12 Dec. 1717). Composer. Brother of Henry Purcell. He is mentioned in 1679 as a chorister of the Chapel Royal. While organist of Magdalen College, Oxford (1688–95), he wrote anthems and an ode for St. Cecilia's Day. He also wrote a number of songs and supplied music for the final masque of his brother's *The Indian Queen.* Between 1696 and 1707 he supplied incidental music for more than 40 plays by Dryden, D'Urfey, Cibber, Motteux, Farquhar, and others. In 1700 he was awarded third prize in a competition for setting Congreve's masque *The Judgment of Paris.* In 1713 he became organist of St. Andrew's, Holborn, London. Other compositions include 11 solo anthems, 6 cantatas, court odes, and a few instrumental works.

Purcell, Henry (b. London, ca. 1659; d. Westminster, London, 21 Nov. 1695). Composer. Little is known of his life, and his parentage remains unclear, although it is certain that he had three brothers: Edward, Daniel, and Joseph. As a boy Henry was a chorister in the Chapel Royal, where he presumably studied with Cooke, Humfrey, and Blow; at the age of 8 he contributed a three-part song to Playford's *Catch That Catch Can.* A second early work, written in 1670 and now lost, was recorded as an "Address of the Children of the Chapel Royal to the King, and their master, Captain Cooke . . . composed by Master Purcell, one of the Children of the said Chapel." After his voice broke in 1673 he became assistant to John Hingeston, who was in charge of keeping the royal instruments in repair. Purcell became the organ tuner at Westminster Abbey (1674–78), succeeded Matthew Locke as composer-in-ordinary for the violins in 1677, and was appointed organist of Westminster Abbey in 1679. In 1682 Purcell succeeded Edward Lowe as an organist at the Chapel Royal, and the following year, after Hingeston's death, was appointed organ maker and keeper of the king's instruments. Purcell's funeral took place in Westminster Abbey on 26 Nov. 1695.

Purcell is one of the greatest of all English composers and an outstanding figure of the Baroque period. He first became involved with the theater in 1680, most of his dramatic music consisting of overtures, entr'actes, dances, and songs; five works constitute what have been designated "semi-operas," with more substantial amounts of music. *Dido and Aeneas* is exceptional in that the libretto is set to music throughout; it was written for a boarding school at Chelsea in 1689. Purcell's first court odes and welcome songs also date from 1680, and continue throughout his career; best described as cantatas for solo voices, chorus, and orchestra, they represent some of his finest music. As a chorister he was acquainted with the previous generation of church music, as well as the modern anthem style with extensive solo verses and string accompaniment; he probably was writing anthems for the Chapel Royal as early as 1679, and after his 1682 appointment abandoned the full anthem in favor of the verse form. Purcell's secular vocal output is immense and includes, in addition to the nearly 150 songs from dramatic works, an additional 100 works (many published in contemporary songbooks) as well as numerous duets and catches. His instrumental music includes works for harpsichord and organ, as well as chamber music for viol consort or the more modern combination of two violins, bass viol, and keyboard continuo. Aside from Purcell's contributions to anthologies and some popular songs from stage works, few of his compositions were published during his lifetime. The most notable exception is the *Sonnata's of III Parts: Two Viollins and Basse: to the Organ or Harpsecord* (London, 1683; 2nd ed., 1684), which includes a portrait of the composer. In 1697 his widow published the *Ten Sonata's in Four Parts.*

Works: Operas and semi-operas: *Dido and Aeneas* (London, 1689); *The Prophetess, or The History of Dioclesian* (London, 1690); *King Arthur, or The British Worthy* (London, 1691); *The Fairy Queen* (London, 1692); *The Indian Queen* (final masque by D. Purcell; London, 1695); *The Tempest, or The Enchanted Island* (London, ca. 1695). Plays with incidental music and song: Over 40 works, including *Theodosius, or The Force of Love* (1680); *The Double Marriage* (1682–85?); *A Fool's Preferment, or The Three Dukes of Dunstable* (1688); *The Gordian Knot Unty'd* (1691); *The Wives' Excuse, or Cuckolds Make Themselves* (1691); *Oedipus* (1692?); *Timon of Athens* (1694); *Bonduca, or The British Heroine* (1695); *The Rival Sisters, or The Violence of Love* (1695). Other secular music includes over 100 solo songs, over 50 songs for 2 or more voices and continuo, over 50 catches. Anthems and services: Over 60 works, including "Behold, I bring you glad tidings" (1687); "Blessed are they that fear the Lord" (1688);

"Hear my prayer, O God" (before 1683); "In thee, O Lord, do I put my trust" (ca. 1682); "In the midst of life" (2 versions, before 1682); "I will love thee, O Lord"; "My beloved spake" (before 1678); "My heart is inditing" (1685); "O God, thou art my God" (ca. 1680–82); "O sing unto the Lord" (1688); "Who hath believed our report?" (ca. 1679–80). Other sacred works: Approximately 40 works for various vocal combinations, including "Ah! few and full of sorrow" (ca. 1680); "Awake, ye dead" (1693); "Great God and just" (1688); "Lord, what is man?" (1693); "Miserere mei" (1687); "O Lord our governor" (ca. 1680); "With sick and famish'd eyes" (1688). Numerous odes and welcome songs: Instrumental music, including fantasias, overtures, pavans, harpsichord suites, airs, hornpipes, overtures.

Bibl.: *The Works of Henry Purcell* (London, 1878–1965). Franklin B. Zimmerman, *Henry Purcell (1659–1695): An Analytical Catalogue of His Music* (London, 1963). J. A. Westrup, *Purcell* (London, 1980). Arthur Hutchings, *Purcell* (London, 1982). Franklin B. Zimmerman, *Henry Purcell (1659–1695): His Life and Times* (Philadelphia, 1983). Curtis Alexander Price, *Henry Purcell and the London Stage* (New York, 1984). Margaret Campbell, *Henry Purcell: Glory of His Age* (London, 1993). Peter Holman, *Henry Purcell* (Oxford, 1994). Martin Adams, *Henry Purcell: The Origins and Development of His Musical Style* (Cambridge, 1995). Curtis Price, ed., *Purcell Studies* (Cambridge, 1995).

Pustet, Friedrich (b. Hals, near Passau, 25 Feb. 1798; d. Munich, 6 Mar. 1882). Publisher. He founded the Pustet music publishing firm in Regensburg in 1826, focusing on the publication of church music. Appointed "Typographus S. Sedis Apostolicae" by Pope Pius IX in 1862. Pustet's publications of liturgical books were considered the authoritative editions until the publication of the Roman Editio Vaticana in the early 1900s. Also published the writings of Riemann, Kroyer, Peter Wagner, Weinmann, Haberl, Gottron, Johner, and Proske.

Puyana, Rafael (b. Bogotá, 14 Oct. 1931). Harpsichordist. Attended the New England Conservatory and the Hartt School of Music, then studied under Landowska (1951–57); made his New York debut in 1957, and subsequently toured Europe and the Americas and released recordings. Settling in Paris, he built a collection of period keyboard instruments.

Pyamour, John (fl. ca. 1418; d. 1431). Composer. A member of the English Chapel Royal by 1419–20, when he became Master of the Chapel Children under Henry V. From 1427 served John, Duke of Bedford, Regent of France (uncle of Henry VI). The style of his single extant composition (*Quam pulchra es,* 3 voices) suggests that he was a contemporary of Dunstable.

Pygott, Richard (d. after Jan. 1552). Composer. By 1516 associated with the household chapel of Cardinal Thomas Wolsey as Master of the Children. From 1524 a Gentleman of the Chapel Royal and recipient thereafter of many honors and payments stemming from his connection with the English royal house. His few known compositions, most incomplete, are of notably high quality.

Pylkkänen, Tauno (Kullervo) (b. Helsinki, 22 Mar. 1918; d. there, 13 Mar. 1980). Composer. He studied at the Helsinki Academy of Music from 1937 until 1940, taking composition lessons from Madetoja, Palmgren, and Ranta. He went on to study musicology at the Helsinki Univ., graduating in 1941. He worked for the Finnish Broadcasting Company until 1961 and as music critic for the daily *Uusi Suomi* from 1941 until 1969. During the 1960s he served as artistic director for the Finnish National Opera. From 1967 he lectured at the Helsinki Academy. His academic interest was opera, as was his compositional strength. His musical style is that of late Romanticism; his works are tonal and use relatively conventional orchestration. This dramatic ability was also present in his songs. Works include *Varjo* [The Shadow] op. 52 (1952) and *Tuntematon stilas* [The Unknown Soldier] op. 73 (1967).

Quagliati, Paolo (b. Chioggia, ca. 1555; d. Rome, 16 Nov. 1628). Composer. He settled in Rome about 1574 and entered the service of Cardinal Odoardo Farnese (1605–8); also was organist of S. Maria Maggiore. Later in life he was employed by the Ludovisi family, serving as private chamberlain when Cardinal Alessandro Ludovisi became Pope Gregory XV in 1621. Quagliati's compositions include *Carro di fedeltà d'amore* (Rome, 1611; R: Northampton, 1957), an early music drama containing monodies and ensemble numbers for up to 5 voices, and *La sfera armoniosa* (Rome, 1623; R: Northampton, 1957), a collection of pieces for 1 or 2 voices and violin.

Quantz, Johann Joachim (b. Oberscheden, Hannover, 30 Jan. 1697; d. Potsdam, 12 July 1773). Flutist and composer. He was apprenticed to his uncle Justus Quantz and served J. A. Fleischhack as a journeyman until 1716, studying many string and wind instruments and taking harpsichord lessons from Kiesewetter. He joined the Dresden town band in 1716, studied counterpoint in Vienna under J. D. Zelenka the following year, and in 1718 was appointed oboist in the Polish chapel of Augustus II; he also continued to play in Dresden. Finding little opportunity for advancement as an oboist, he took up the flute, studying for four months with P. G. Buffardin. Quantz traveled to Italy in 1724 and studied counterpoint with Gasparini; he also journeyed to Paris (1726–27), where he added a second key to his flutes, and to England in 1727, where he met Handel. Upon his return to Dresden he was made a member of the court Kapelle. From 1728 he instructed Prince Frederick on the flute, and moved to Berlin in 1741 after Frederick became King of Prussia. In Berlin, Quantz was exempt from playing in the opera orchestra; instead, his duties revolved around the king's private evening concerts, where the repertoire (at least in later years) consisted primarily of works by Quantz and Frederick himself. His compositions include over 200 flute sonatas and 300 flute concertos, in addition to trio sonatas and some vocal music; few of his works were published after he moved to Berlin. Quantz is best known for his treatise *Versuch einer Anweisung die Flöte traversiere zu spielen* (Berlin, 1752; trans. New York, 1966), an exhaustive work that discusses nearly all aspects of performance, from ornamentation and accompaniment to criteria for evaluating compositions and musicians; despite its title less than a third of the book is intended specifically for flutists. Quantz also was a flute maker; examples of his instruments can be found in Berlin and Washington, D.C.

Bibl.: *Johann Joachim Quantz: Thematisches Verzeichnis der Musikalische Werke,* ed. Horst Augsbach (Dresden, 1984). Edward R. Reilly, *Quantz and His Versuch: Three Studies* (New York, 1971). Charles Walthall, "Portraits of Johann Joachim Quantz," *EM* 14 (1986): 500–19.

Queler, Eve (b. New York, 1 Jan. 1936). Conductor. Studied at Mannes College; her conducting teachers included Joseph Rosenstock, Walter Susskind, Leonard Slatkin, and Herbert Blomstedt. Worked with the New York City Opera and the Metropolitan; formed the Opera Orchestra of New York (1968), which she directed in a number of rarely performed operas including Puccini's *Edgar* and Boito's *Nerone.* Served as associate conductor of the Fort Wayne Philharmonic (1970–71) and became the first woman to conduct a number of symphony orchestras, including those of Philadelphia, Cleveland, and Montreal.

Quilter, Roger (b. Brighton, 1 Nov. 1877; d. London, 21 Sept. 1953). Composer. He studied at the Hock Conservatory in Frankfurt with Knorr. Quilter was primarily a composer of salon-style songs. Several popular singers incorporated his works into their programs and he quickly became well known. His orchestral music was similarly popular (*A Children's Overture* op. 17, 1919), though his one opera saw less success (*Julia,* London, 1936). Works include *Three Shakespeare Songs: Come Away Death, O Mistress Mine, Blow, Blow Thou Winter Wind* op. 6 (1905); *Three Songs of William Blake: Dream Valley, The Wild Flower's Song, Daybreak* op. 20 (1917).

Bibl.: Trevor Hold, *The Walled-In Garden: A Study of the Songs of Roger Quilter (1877–1953)* (Rickmansworth, 1978).

Quinault, Philippe (b. Paris, bapt. 5 June 1635; d. there, 26 Nov. 1688). Dramatist, librettist, and poet. He was educated by the poet Tristan l'Hermite; his first comedy, *Les rivales,* was performed in 1653. In 1671 he was asked, along with Molière and Corneille, to supply text for Lully to set for the divertissement *Psyché,* thus beginning a 15-year collaboration with the composer; the subject matter for his *livrets* derives from mythology or legends of chivalry. His librettos set by Lully include *Les fêtes de l'Amour et de Bacchus* (1672); *Cadmus et Hermione* (1673); *Alceste* (1674); *Thésée* (1675); *Atys* (1676); *Isis* (1677); *Proserpine* (1680); *Le triomphe de l'amour* (1681); *Persée* (1682); *Phaëton* (1683); *Amadis* (1684); *Roland* (1685); *Le temple de la paix* (1685); *Armide* (1686).

Quinet, Marcel (b. Binche, 6 July 1915; d. Woluwé-St. Lambert, Brussels, 16 Dec. 1986). Composer. From

Mons Conservatory he transferred to the Brussels Conservatory, where he won prizes in harmony, counterpoint, fugue, and piano. His teachers there included Léon Jongen, Marcel Maas, and Raymond Moulaert. He studied composition privately with Jean Absil and won the Belgian Prix de Rome in 1945 for *La vague et le sillon* (cantata, 1945). He taught at the Brussels Conservatory (1943–79) and at the Chapelle musicale Reine Elisabeth (from 1956). Works include *Les deux bavards,* chamber opera (1966); *La nef des fous,* ballet (1969); 3 piano concertos (1955, 1964, 1966); Sinfonietta (1953); Variations, orchestra (1956); Symphony (1960); Viola Concerto (1962–63); also chamber music (Wind Quintet, 1949; Sonata, 2 violins, piano, 1964; *Pochades,* 4 saxophones, 1967).

Quintanar, Héctor (b. Mexico City, 15 Apr. 1936). Composer. Studied in his home city with Galinde, Rodolfo Halffter, and Mabarak; joined the Composition Workshop of Carlos Chávez in 1960, serving as its director, 1965–72. Studied electronic music at Columbia Univ. with Richter in 1964, and *musique concrète* in Paris with Etienne-Marie in 1968; established the Mexico City Conservatory electronic music facility in 1970. Works include *Sinfonía modal* (1961–62), *Galaxias* (1968), and *Sideral II* for orchestra; *Aclamaciones,* orchestra, chorus, and tape (1967); assorted chamber music; *Sideral I,* tape (1968); *Símbolas,* 8 instruments, tape, slides, and lights; and *Diágolos,* piano and tape.

Bibl.: *Composers of the Americas* 15 (Washington, D.C., 1969), pp. 178–80 [includes works list].

Quintón, José Ignacio (b. Caguas, Puerto Rico, 1 Feb. 1881; d. Coamo, Puerto Rico, 19 Dec. 1925). Composer and pianist. Born into a musical family, he was largely home-educated in music. He spent most of his career in Coamo, where he taught at the Municipal Academy of Music and directed municipal ensembles. His works include a Requiem and 10 Salve Reginas for chorus and orchestra, several chamber works, and numerous piano pieces.

R

Raaff, Anton (b. Gelsdorf, near Bonn, bapt. 6 May 1714; d. Munich, 28 May 1797). Tenor. He studied in Munich and Bologna while serving the Elector of Cologne. After singing in Italy he returned to the Elector in Bonn (1741–42), then sang in Vienna, Italy, Lisbon, Madrid, and Naples (1759–70). In 1770 he joined Elector Carl Theodor's court in Mannheim. Mozart wrote the role of Idomeneo and the aria "Se al labbro mio" (K. 295) for him.

Bibl.: H. Freiburger, *Anton Raaff (1714–1797): Sein Leben und Wirken* (Cologne, 1929). Perluigi Petrobelli, "The Italian Years of Anton Raaff," *MJb* (1973–74): 233–73.

Rääts, Jaan (b. Tartu, Estonia, 15 Oct. 1932). Composer. Studied composition with Heino Eller at the Tallinn Conservatory, 1952–57; taught composition there, 1968–70 and from 1978. From 1955 to 1966 worked as sound engineer at Estonian Radio; 1966–74, musical director of Estonian Television. Awards include the Order of the Red Banner (1970) and the Estonian State Prize (1972). His music is noted for its use of rhythm as an expressive device. Works include 8 symphonies, 2 concertos for chamber orchestra (1961, 1987), concertos for piano (1971, 1983), violin (1963, 1979), 2 pianos (1986); chamber music; 9 sonatas and other music for piano.

Rabaud, Henri (Benjamin) (b. Paris, 10 Nov. 1873; d. there, 11 Sept. 1949). Composer and conductor. Studied at the Paris Conservatory with Gédalge and Massenet. His cantata *Daphné* won the Premier Grand Prix de Rome in 1894. In 1908 he became conductor of the Paris Opéra and the Opéra-comique; later director (1914–18). He was also director of the Paris Conservatory (1922–41). He wrote 8 operas: *La fille de Roland* (1904); *Le Premier Glaire* (1908); *Mârouf, savetier du Caire* (1914, perhaps his most successful); *Antoine et Cléopâtre* (after Shakespeare, 1916–17); *L'appel de la mer* (1924); *Le miracle des loups* (1924); *Rolande et le mauvais garçon* (1934); *Le jeu de l'amour et du hasard* (1948). Orchestral and choral works include 2 symphonies (1893, 1900); *L'été* (soprano, alto, choir, orchestra); *La procession nocturne* (symphonic poem, 1899); *Divertissement sur les chansons russes* (1899); *Lamento* (1930); Prelude and Toccata (piano, orchestra, 1945); *Job* (oratorio, 1900); *Hymne à la France éternelle* (chorus, 1916). Also chamber music (*Solo de concours,* clarinet, piano, 1901; string quartet, 1898); piano pieces, songs, and film scores.

Rachmaninoff, Sergei (Vassilievich) (b. Semyonovo, 1 Apr. 1873; d. Beverly Hills, 28 Mar. 1943). Composer, pianist, and conductor. He had his first piano lessons from his mother at the family estate at Oneg near Novgorod. In 1822 the estate was sold as a result of his father's lavish spending habits, and the family moved to St. Petersburg; Rachmaninoff attended the conservatory there (1882–85), studying piano with Vladimir Demyansky and harmony with Alexander Rubets. Perhaps because of his parents' decision to separate, Rachmaninoff's performance at the conservatory was poor, although his musical gifts were obvious. In 1885, acting on the advice of the piano virtuoso Ziloti, his mother enrolled him in the class of Nikolai Zverev at the Moscow Conservatory; Rachmaninoff and two other pupils, Maximov and Presman, lived with Zverev, and received from him a thorough grounding in piano technique and the fundamentals of music. In 1888 he transferred to the senior department of the conservatory to study piano with Ziloti and also studied counterpoint with Taneyev and harmony with Arensky. The following year, when he became increasingly interested in composition, Zverev dismissed him abruptly from his household. In the spring of 1891 Rachmaninoff graduated with honors in piano and completed his First Piano Concerto in F♯ minor (1890–91; rev. 1917); he remained at the conservatory for an additional year to earn a diploma in composition, astonishing the committee by completing an opera score, *Aleko* (1892), in 17 days. He graduated with a gold medal, awarded only twice before in the history of the conservatory, and soon afterward completed his Piano Prelude in C♯ minor (1892), one of his best-loved works.

In 1893 *Aleko* was premiered at the Bolshoi and received enthusiastic reviews; other compositions from this time include the two-piano *Fantasie-tableaux* (1893), the orchestral fantasy *Utyos* [The Rock] (1893), and *Trio élégiaque* for piano trio (1893; rev. 1907, 1917), dedicated to the memory of Tchaikovsky, who died that winter. In 1895 Rachmaninoff began work on his Symphony no. 1 in D minor. The premiere in 1897 under Glazunov's direction was a disaster, however, and it destroyed Rachmaninoff's confidence to such an extent that he was unable to compose for three years. An alternate career began with his engagement as a conductor for the 1897–98 season of the Moscow Private Russian Opera, and Rachmaninoff soon established himself as one of the great conductors of the day; in 1899 he made his London debut at the Queen's Hall conducting a concert of his own works. Still struggling to compose, he sought help from Dr. Nikolai Dahl, a specialist in treatment by hypnosis. Extended sessions apparently restored his confidence, for in the summer of 1901 in Italy he composed the anthem *Panteley the Healer* and the love duet from *Francesca da Rimini.* He also began work on what would become his most popular composition, the Piano Concerto no. 2 in C minor (1900–1901), performing the second and third movements on 15 December 1900 and premiering the completed concerto on 9 November 1901. This marked the beginning of an especially prolific period of composition which produced the Cello Sonata (1901) and the cantata *Vesna* [Spring] (1902); Rachmaninoff also continued to concertize extensively.

In the spring of 1902 he married his cousin Natalie Satina, and following a long honeymoon in Europe he began work on his opera *Skupoy rïtsar'* [The Miserly Knight] and continued work on *Francesca da Rimini.* Both operas were premiered at the Bolshoi in 1906—Rachmaninoff had been appointed conductor there in 1904—but political unrest in the country led him to resign his post and flee first to Italy and then to Dresden. Although he returned to Russia not long afterward, Dresden remained an important refuge: he spent part of each of the next few years there, completing his Second Symphony in E minor (1906–7), the First Piano Sonata (1907), and the symphonic poem *The Isle of the Dead* (1909). In 1909 he made his first American tour, performing, among other works, the Third Piano Concerto in D minor (1908). He declined many offers for the following season in order to return to Russia (1910), where he concertized widely as a pianist and continued composing; works from this time include the cantata *The Bells* (1913) and the *All-Night Vigil* (1915). With the Bolshevik Revolution of 1917 he left Russia, never to return.

He went first to Stockholm and then settled in Copenhagen. He declined an offer to become conductor of the Boston Symphony but nevertheless decided that opportunity awaited him in the U.S. and arrived in New York in November 1918. Between 1918 and 1939 he concertized extensively in the U.S. and Europe, gaining an international reputation as a virtuoso pianist; he also signed a recording contract with the Victor Talking Machine Company. Although the demands of his performing career left him less time for composition, he did complete a number of substantial works, including *Three Russian Folk Songs* for chorus and orchestra (1926), the Fourth Piano Concerto (1926; rev. 1941), Piano Sonata no. 2 (1931), and Variations on a Theme of Corelli for piano (1931). In 1934 he built a home in Lucerne; it was here that he composed the Rhapsody on a Theme of Paganini for piano and orchestra (1934) and the Third Symphony in A minor (1935–36; rev. 1938). With the outbreak of World War II he returned to America, where he composed his *Symphonic Dances* (1940). He gave his last recital on 17 February 1943 and died of cancer four days before his 70th birthday. In 1973 RCA marked the centenary of his birth by releasing *The Complete Rachmaninoff,* a 15-disk set of recordings made between 1919 and 1942. In addition to a substantial body of solo piano music (10 Preludes op. 23, 1903; 13 Preludes op. 32, 1910; *Moments musicaux* op. 33, 1911; *Études-tableaux* op. 39, 1916–17), Rachmaninoff composed a number of solo songs on texts of Pushkin, Polonsky, Tyutchev, and other Russian Romantics.

Bibl.: Robert Threlfall and Geoffrey Norris, *A Catalogue of the Compositions of S. Rachmaninoff* (London, 1982). Robert Palmieri, *Sergei Vasil'evich Rachmaninoff: A Guide to Research* (New York, 1985). Barrie Martyn, *Rachmaninoff: Composer, Pianist, Conductor* (Aldershot, 1990). Maria Biesold, *Sergej Rachmaninoff, 1873–1943: Zwischen Moskau und New York, eine Künstlerbiographie* (Weinheim, 1991). Geoffrey Norris, *Rachmaninoff* (New York, 1994).

Raeburn, Boyd [Raden, Boyde Albert] (b. Faith, S.D., 27 Oct. 1913; d. Lafayette, La., 2 Aug. 1966). Jazz bandleader and saxophonist. After leading dance bands from 1933, he formed in 1944 a big band which played jazz for listeners rather than dancers. Dizzy Gillespie occasionally worked with the group and is the composer, arranger, and principal soloist on Raeburn's recording of "Interlude" [A Night in Tunisia] (1945). The group began playing pieces juxtaposing elements of bop and of European art music; examples include "Dalvatore Sally" and "Boyd Meets Stravinsky," both recorded in 1946. In the late 1940s Raeburn returned to a conventional big band style.

Raff, (Joseph) Joachim (b. Lachen, near Zurich, 27 May 1822; d. Frankfurt am Main, 24 or 25 June 1882). Composer. Schoolteacher in Rapperswil, 1840–44; largely self-taught as musician and composer. In 1843 he sent piano pieces to Mendelssohn, on whose recommendation Breitkopf & Härtel published them; on the strength of this he moved to Zurich, where he eked out a living until Liszt befriended him in 1845, getting him a job in a Cologne music firm and later one as arranger with the Hamburg music publisher Schuberth; 1850, Liszt invited him to Weimar as his paid amanuensis. (The degree of his creative participation in the production, especially the orchestration, of Liszt's music of this period has been much discussed, some maintaining that Raff exaggerated his contributions.) He eventually felt both used and artistically overwhelmed in this relationship and in 1856 moved to Wiesbaden as a piano teacher, partly in pursuit of an actress, Doris Genast (1826–1912), whom he married in 1859; from 1877, director and composition teacher, Frankfurt Conservatory (pupils included MacDowell). An extremely prolific composer (216 opus numbers), judged uneven in quality even by his admirers, he had little success. Works include an oratorio, sacred music, male part songs, solo songs; 11 symphonies, some of which—especially no. 3, *Im Walde* op. 153 (1869) and no. 5, *Lenore* op. 177 (1872)—were very popular; also concertos, orchestral pieces, much chamber music, many piano pieces. In his lifetime he was considered a major figure but disappeared quickly thereafter.

Bibl.: A. Schafer, *Chronologisch-systematisches Verzeich-*

nis der Werke Joachim Raffs (Weisbaden, 1888; R: 1974). Markus Römer, *Joseph Joachim Raff (1822–1882)* (Wiesbaden, 1982).

Raimbaut de Vaqeiras [Vaqueiras] (b. ca. 1155; d. Greece?, 4 Sept. 1207?, or later in Provence). Troubadour. Although probably born in Provence, he spent most of his adult life in the service of the Marquis of Monferrat (Italy), with an interruption from about 1183 to 1192, when the old marquis died and his son Boniface assumed the title. He is known to have written 35 poems, of which 7 (including the *estampida Calenda maya*) survive with music.

Raimon de Miraval (fl. 1180–1215). Troubadour. Until either 1209 or 1211 possessed with his brothers a castle at Miraval, near Carcassonne. His 48 known poems mention various French and Spanish nobles, including his patrons. Melodies survive for 22 songs, more than for any other contemporary figure except Guirart Riquier.

Bibl.: Margaret L. Switten, *The Cansos of Raimon de Miraval: A Study of Poems and Melodies* (Cambridge, Mass., 1985) [includes music]. Jaume Pomar, *Raimon* (Madrid, 1983).

Raimondi, Pietro (b. Rome, 20 Dec. 1786; d. there, 30 Oct. 1853). Composer. Studied at Naples Conservatory with La Barbara and Tritto. Produced his first opera ca. 1807 in Genoa. Returned to Naples in 1811. Appointed director of the royal theaters of Naples in 1824. Taught composition at the Naples Conservatory (1824–32), Palermo Conservatory (1832–52). Appointed *maestro di cappella* at St. Peter's in Rome in 1852. Known as a fine contrapuntalist, he composed fugues for 4, 5, 6, 8, 16, 20, and 64 voices. Among his compositions are 3 oratorios (*Putifar, Giuseppe,* and *Giacobbe*) which are intended to be performed simultaneously on a tripartite stage. Also composed 62 operas, sacred music, ballets.

Bibl.: Filippo Cicconetti, *Memorie intorno a Pietro Raimondi* (Rome, 1867). Cecil Gray, "Pietro Raimondi," *MR* 1 (1940): 25–35.

Rainey, Ma [Gertrude Pridgett] (b. Columbus, Ga., 26 Apr. 1886; d. Rome, Ga., 22 Dec. 1939). Blues singer. From 1904 into the mid-1930s she toured the South and Midwest as a singer. Although her performances in circuses and minstrel and vaudeville shows embraced a wide range of songs, she was recognized as the first great blues singer of the early decades of the century. Most of her recordings (1923–28) are blues, including "Bo-weavil Blues," "Barrelhouse Blues," and "Moonshine Blues" (all 1923). Among her accompanists on subsequent recordings were Louis Armstrong, Fletcher Henderson, and Coleman Hawkins.

Bibl.: Derrick Stewart-Baxter, *Ma Rainey and the Classic Blues Singers* (New York, 1970). Sandra R. Lieb, *Mother of the Blues: A Study of Ma Rainey* (Amherst, Mass., 1981).

Rainier, Priaulx (b. Howick, Natal, 3 Feb. 1903; d. Besse-en-Chandesse, Auvergne, 10 Oct. 1986). Composer. She studied violin at the South African College of Music in Cape Town, after which she traveled to London in 1920 to study with McEwen at the Royal Academy of Music. In 1939 she worked with Boulanger in Paris and subsequently focused primarily on composing rather than on performing. She returned to England and served on the faculty of the Royal Academy of Music, 1943–61, teaching composition. Her own works were influenced by the Zulu music from her home region. Repetitive rhythmic contours are characteristic of her music. After the early 1960s her harmonic language became increasingly dissonant, though she never fully engaged serialism. Her works include orchestral music (violin concerto, 1974–77; Concertante for Two Winds and Orchestra, oboe, clarinet, orchestra, 1977–80), vocal music (Requiem, tenor, chorus, 1955–56), and chamber music (Grand Duo for Cello and Piano, 1980–82).

Raisa, Rosa [Burschstein, Raisa; Rose] (b. Białystok, Poland, 23 May 1893; d. Los Angeles, 28 Sept. 1963). Soprano. Studied with Barbara Marchisio in Naples; made her concert debut in Rome in 1912 and her American debut in Philadelphia the following year (Queen Isabella in Franchetti's *Cristoforo Colombo*). She sang Aida in Chicago in 1913, and after appearing at Covent Garden returned to Chicago (1916–32, 1933–36). She created Puccini's Turandot at La Scala. In 1937 she opened a singing school in Chicago with her husband, baritone Giacomo Rimini.

Raison, André (b. before 1650; d. Paris, 1719). Composer. He studied at the seminary of the abbey of Ste. Geneviève at Nanterre, was organist of the royal abbey of Ste. Geneviève in Paris (from about 1666) and at Jacobins de St. Jacques; he was Clérambault's teacher. He published 2 volumes of organ music, *Livre d'orgue contenant cinq messes* (Paris, 1688) and *Second livre d'orgue* (Paris, 1714).

Bibl.: *André Raison: Livre d'orgue,* ed. A Guilmant and A. Pirro (Paris, 1899; R: 1972). *Premier livre d'orgue,* ed. Norbert Dufourcq (Paris, 1963). *Second livre d'orgue,* ed. Jean Bonfils (Paris, n.d.).

Raitio, Väinö (b. Sortavala, 15 Apr. 1891; d. Helsinki, 10 Sept. 1945). Composer. From 1911 through 1916 he studied at the Helsinki Conservatory with Melartin and Furnhjelm and from 1916 to 1917 in Moscow with Ilyinsky; went on to study in Berlin in 1925 and in Paris, 1925–26. He taught briefly at the Viipuri Music Institute and, after 1932, lived primarily as a composer. His early music was late Romantic in style, but by the late 1910s he had come under the influence of French and Russian orchestral and nontonal tendencies (*Fantasia estatica,* 1921), showing the impact of Scriabin. He wrote primarily orchestral music (*Puistokuja* [The Avenue] op. 29, soprano, orchestra, 1926) through the early 1930s, when his operas became the focus of his compositional innovations. Works include operas (*Lyydian kuningas* [The King of Lydia], 1938) and orchestral music (*Kuutamo Jupiterissa* [Moonlight on Jupiter] op. 24, 1922).

Raksin, David (b. Philadelphia, 4 Aug. 1912). Composer. Wrote mainly film scores, including the theme song "Laura," the success of which led to more than 300 versions. He learned woodwind instruments from his father and studied piano. Attended the Univ. of Pennsylvania (1931) and studied composition privately with Isadore Freed (1934–35). In 1935 he worked with Charlie Chaplin on the music for the film *Modern Times.* He also studied privately with Schoenberg. Starting in 1956 he taught composition at the Univ. of Southern California, where he joined the faculty of the School of Public Administration in 1968. He also taught film and television composition at UCLA. He wrote symphonic suites based on his film music, and incidental music for the theater. At Stravinsky's request he did a band instrumentation of *Circus Polka* for Balanchine's production with the Barnum and Bailey Circus; wrote *Oedipus memneitai* (1986) on an Elizabeth Sprague Coolidge Commission from the Library of Congress.

Rameau, Jean-Philippe (b. Dijon, bapt. 25 Sept. 1683; d. Paris, 12 Sept. 1764). Composer and theorist. He probably received his earliest musical instruction from his father, an organist at St. Etienne, Dijon; attended the Jesuit Collège des Godrans, and at 18 went to Milan for a few months. In January 1702 he was temporarily appointed *maître de musique* at the Cathedral of Notre Dame des Doms, Avignon; by May he had begun a long-term contract as organist at Clermont Cathedral. He moved to Paris by 1706, published his *Premier livre de pièces de clavecin* (Paris, 1706) and was organist at the Jesuit College in the rue Saint-Jacques and at the Mercederians of rue du Chaume. He returned to Dijon in 1709 to succeed his father at Notre Dame; by 1713 he was organist at the Jacobins in Lyons, and finally returned to Clermont Cathedral in 1715. In 1722 or 1723 he went to Paris for the second time, publishing his second and third harpsichord books (1724 and 1728) there as well as his *Traité de l'harmonie* (1722; trans., New York, 1971) and *Nouveau système de musique théorique* (1726; trans. Chandler, diss., Indiana Univ., 1975). By 1732 he was organist at St. Croix-de-la-Bretonnerie and in 1736 at the Jesuit novitiate.

The two theoretical works, along with some polemical exchanges in the *Mercure de France* (the other participant probably being Montéclair), established his reputation as a theorist, but Rameau also wanted to write for the stage. His operatic debut took place during his 50th year: *Hippolyte et Aricie* was given at the Opéra in 1733. Rameau began working with Voltaire on *Samson,* but the project was abandoned. In 1735 his opera-ballet *Les Indes galantes* was performed, followed in 1737 by his masterpiece *Castor et Pollux;* his major theoretical work dating from this time was the *Génération harmonique* (Paris, 1737; trans. Hayes, diss., Stanford Univ., 1968), submitted to and favorably received by the Académie royale des Sciences. From 1745 on, more than half of Rameau's stage works were written for court premieres. In 1745 alone three of Rameau's compositions were written for the court, including two collaborations with Voltaire (*La princesse de Navarre* and *Le temple de la Gloire*); 1750 saw the publication of his *Démonstration du principe de l'harmonie,* written in collaboration with Denis Diderot (Paris, 1750; trans., Briscoe, diss., Indiana Univ., 1975). After 1752 his operatic activity, apart from the major works *Les Paladins* and *Les Boréades,* slackened; at the same time he produced some important theoretical works, including the *Observations sur notre instinct pour la musique.* His theories became widely disseminated with the publication of D'Alembert's lucid book *Éléments de musique théorique et pratique* (1752), translated into German by Marpurg (1757).

Rameau is regarded, along with Lully and Gluck, as one of the principal masters of pre-Revolutionary French opera. His stage works comprise many genres, including the *tragédie lyrique,* the *comédie lyrique,* the *opéra-ballet,* the *comédie-ballet,* the *pastorale,* the *acte de ballet,* and the *divertissement,* as well as incidental music. His harpsichord publications are particularly fine and circulated widely in the 18th century. No less important are his theoretical works, in which he attempted to reduce music to a science. He argued that all music is founded on harmony, and that all chords can be derived from the perfect triad (major or minor, the source of consonance) or the 7th chord (the source of dissonance); in addition, he formulated the idea of harmonic inversion and invented the concept of a fundamental bass, a sequence of roots, present or not, that are distinct from the thorough bass.

Works: Dramatic. *Hippolyte et Aricie* (1733); *Les Indes galantes* (1735); *Castor et Pollux* (1737); *Les fêtes d'Hébé, ou Les talents lyriques* (1739); *Dardanus* (1739); *La princesse de Navarre* (1745); *Platée* (1745); *Les fêtes de Polymnie* (1745); *Le temple de la Gloire* (1745); *Les fêtes de l'Hymen et de l'Amour, ou Les dieux d'Egypte* (1747); *Zaïs* (1748); *Pigmalion* (1748); *Les surprises de l'Amour* (1748); *Naïs* (1749); *Zoroastre* (1749); *La guirlande, ou Les fleurs enchantées* (1751); *Acante et Céphise, ou La sympathie* (1751); *Daphnis et Eglé* (1753); *Les sibarites* (1753); *La naissance d'Osiris* (1754); *Anacréon I* (1754); *Anacréon II* (1757); *Les Paladins* (1760).

Cantatas. *Thétis* (ca. 1715–18); *Aquilon et Orithie* (ca. 1715–19); *L'impatience* (ca. 1715–22); *Les amants trahis* (by 1721); *Orphée* (by 1721); *Le berger fidèle* (by 1728); *Cantate pour le jour de la [fête de] Saint Louis* (ca. 1745); *Médée* (ca. 1715–22).

Solo keyboard. *Premier livre de pièces de clavecin* (Paris, 1706); *Pièces de clavessin avec une methode pour la mechanique des doigts* (Paris, 1724); *Nouvelles suites de pièces de clavecin* (Paris, ca. 1729–30); *Les Indes galantes* (Paris, ca. 1736); five pieces arranged for solo harpsichord in *Pièces de clavecin en concerts* (Paris, 1741); *La Dauphine* (1747?); *Les petits marteaux* (before 1754?). Other instrumental. *Pièces de clavecin en concerts,* harpsichord, violin/flute, bass viol/cello (Paris, 1741).

Bibl.: *Jean-Philippe Rameau: Oeuvres complètes,* ed. C.

Saint-Saëns and others (Paris, 1895–1924; R: 1969). *The Complete Theoretical Writings of Jean-Philippe Rameau,* ed. Erwin R. Jacobi (n.p., 1967–72). Cuthbert Morton Girdlestone, *Jean-Philippe Rameau: His Life and Work* (New York, 1957; 2nd rev. ed., 1969). *Jean-Philippe Rameau: Colloque international organisé par la Société Rameau, 1983* (Paris, 1987). Donald H. Foster, *Jean-Philippe Rameau: A Guide to Research* (New York, 1989). Sylvie Bouissou, *Jean-Philippe Rameau, Les boréades* (Paris, 1992). Thomas Street Christensen, *Rameau and Musical Thought in the Enlightenment* (Cambridge, 1993).

Ramey, Samuel (Edward) (b. Colby, Kans., 28 Mar. 1942). Bass-baritone. Studied with Arthur Newman at Wichita State Univ. and with Armen Boyajian in New York. Made his New York City Opera debut in 1973 (Zuniga in *Carmen*) and his Metropolitan debut in 1984 (Argante in Handel's *Rinaldo*); performed at most of the leading opera houses in roles including Don Giovanni, Leporello, Figaro, Mephistopheles (Gounod's *Faust*), and Philip II (Verdi's *Don Carlos*). His command of florid singing has made him a leading figure in the revival of Handel and Rossini operas.

Ramin, Günther (b. Karlsruhe, 15 Oct. 1898; d. Leipzig, 27 Feb. 1956). Organist, choral conductor, and composer. Sang in the Leipzig Thomanerchor and studied organ with Karl Straube before succeeding him as organist of the Thomaskirche in 1918; in 1920 became organist for the Gewandhaus concerts and taught at the Leipzig Conservatory. Conducted the Leipzig Lehrergesangverein (1922–35), the Gewandhaus Choir (1933–34 and 1945–51), and the Berlin Philharmonic Choir (1935–43) before succeeding Straube again in 1940, this time as Kantor of the Thomaskirche.

Ramírez, Luis Antonio (b. San Juan, 10 Feb. 1923). Composer. Studied with Romero in San Juan (1954–57), and with Cristóbal Halffter and Bravo at the Madrid Conservatory (1957–60). Later served as Professor of Music at the Univ. of Puerto Rico. Works include *Sonata elegíaca,* cello and piano (1970); *Tres piezas breves,* brass, piano, percussion, and strings (1972); *Fragmentos,* orchestra (1973).

Ramos de Pareja [Ramis de Pareia], **Bartolomeo** [Bartolome] (b. Baeza, ca. 1440; d. 1491 or later). Theorist. Taught at Salamanca and later (after about 1472) Bologna; after 1484 went to Rome. His treatise *Musica practica* (Bologna, 1482; facs., *BMB* 2/3, 1969; excerpt trans. *SR,* pp. 200–204) is highly original, rejecting as no longer practical much of the technical apparatus of music of his day and many ideas propounded by earlier theorists. Ramos advanced a new system of solmization to replace that of Guido and suggested revisions to the tuning scheme set forth by Boethius. His ideas sparked vigorous and long-lasting controversy in which his student Giovanni Spataro played an important part.

Bibl.: Francisco José León Tello, "Contribución de Ramos de Pareja y Francisco Salinas a la formación de la escala musical europea," *Revista de musicología* 5 (1982): 287–96.

Ramovš, Primož (b. Ljubljana, 20 Mar. 1921). Composer. Studied at the Ljubljana Academy of Music, 1935–41, taking composition lessons with Osterc; also in Siena with Frazzi in 1941, and in Rome with Casella and Petrassi, 1941–43. In 1945 he took a position in the library of the Slovene Academy of Sciences and Art and became its director in 1952. From 1948 to 1964 he taught at the Ljubljana Conservatory. His early works were heavily influenced by neoclassicism. He then incorporated other avant-garde techniques, including serialism. Works include 4 symphonies (1940, 1943, 1948, 1968), *Kolovrat* for string orchestra (1986), and concerto or concertato-like works (*Contrasts,* flute, orchestra, 1966; *Syntheses,* horn, 3 groups, 1971; *Concerto profano,* organ, orchestra, 1984; trumpet concerto, 1985). He also composed chamber music (*Tryptychon,* string quartet, 1969; *3 Nocturnes,* double bass, 1972; *Improvisations,* harp, 1973) and film music.

Rampal, Jean-Pierre (Louis) (b. Marseilles, 7 Jan. 1922). Flutist. Studied at the Marseilles and Paris conservatories; joined the Vichy Opéra Orchestra (1946–50) and the Paris Opéra (1956–62), and in 1968 was appointed professor at the Paris Conservatory. A highly successful solo flutist, beginning 1947 Rampal toured and made many recordings; his love of chamber music led him to found the Quintette à vent française (1945) and the Ensemble baroque de Paris (1953). A number of composers, including Poulenc and Jolivet, have written works for him.

Ran, Shulamit (b. Tel Aviv, 21 Oct. 1949). Composer. She studied composition with Alexander Boskovich and Paul Ben-Haim, and piano with Miriam Boskovich and Emma Gorochov, before coming to the U.S. on an America–Israel Cultural Foundation scholarship to attend the Mannes School of Music (1962–67). Studied composition with Norman Dello Joio and piano with Nadia Reisenberg and Dorothy Taubman; also composition with Ralph Shapey. As a pianist she toured Europe and the U.S., including a 1967 performance of her own Capriccio for piano and orchestra (1963) with Bernstein and the New York Philharmonic. She was artist-in-residence at St. Mary's Univ. in Halifax, 1972–73, and became composer-in-residence with the Chicago Symphony in 1991. Her Symphony no. 1 won the 1991 Pulitzer Prize for music. Works include *Capriccio* (piano, orchestra, 1963); *Symphonic Poem* (piano, orchestra, 1967); *10 Children's Scenes* (1970, arranged from piano piece); *Concert Piece* (piano, orchestra, 1971); Piano Concerto (1977); Concerto for Orchestra (1986); Symphony no. 1 (1990); *Yearnings* (violin, string orchestra, 1995); Quartet (flute, clarinet, cello, piano, 1967); *Double Vision* (woodwind quintet, brass quintet, piano, 1976); *A Prayer* (clarinet, bass clarinet, bassoon, horn, timpani, 1981); *Invocation* (horn, chimes, timpani, 1995); and compositions for piano.

Randall, James K(irtland) (b. Cleveland, 16 June 1929). Composer. He first studied at the Cleveland

Institute of Music, and then earned degrees at Columbia (B.A., 1955), Harvard (M.A., 1956), and Princeton (M.F.A., 1958). His composition teachers included Herbert Elwell, George Thaddeus Jones, Sessions, and Babbitt. He joined the faculty at Princeton in 1958, where he was involved in the development of the Music IV facility. Also taught at the U.S. Naval School of Music. His compositions utilize computer-synthesized sounds. Works include *Slow Movement,* piano (1959); *Improvisation on a Poem by e. e. cummings,* voice, chamber ensemble (1960); electronic compositions (*Lyric Variations,* violin, computer, 1967; *Quartet in Pairs,* 1964); also music for the film *Eakins* (1972).

Randegger, Alberto (b. Trieste, 13 Apr. 1832; d. London, 18 Dec. 1911). Composer and conductor. Studied piano with Lafont, composition with Luigi Ricci. From 1852 to 1854 he was music director at Fiume, Sinigaglia, Brescia, and Venice. Moved to London in 1854, where he taught singing, conducted, and composed. His first English opera (third opera overall), *The Rival Beauties,* was produced at Leeds in 1864. Appointed professor of singing at the Royal Academy of Music and Royal College of Music; directed at Covent Garden and Drury Lane (1887–98). Wrote a textbook on singing (London, 1893). Promoted Wagner's early works. Composed operas and other vocal works.

Rands, Bernard (b. Sheffield, 2 Mar. 1934). Composer. He studied music and English literature at the Univ. of Wales, Bangor (B.M., 1956; M.M., 1958), then worked with Roman Vlad in Rome and with Luigi Dallapiccola in Florence (1958–60). In the early 1960s he attended conducting and composition seminars taught by Pierre Boulez and Bruno Maderna at Darmstadt and had further lessons with Luciano Berio in Milan. Rands served as composer-in-residence at Princeton, the Univ. of Illinois, and York Univ. in England (1968–74); taught at the Univ. of California, San Diego (from 1975), as well as at the California Institute of the Arts in Valencia (1984–85), Boston Univ., Juilliard, and Harvard. In 1984 he was awarded the Pulitzer Prize for *Canti del sole,* and in 1989 he became composer-in-residence of the Philadelphia Orchestra.

Works include orchestral music (*Per esempio,* 1968; *Wildtrack 1,* 1969; *Agenda,* 1969–70; *Mésalliance,* piano, orchestra, 1972; *Ology,* jazz ensemble, 1973; *Aum,* harp, orchestra, 1974; *Madrigali,* 1977; *Le tambourin,* suites nos. 1 and 2, 1984; *Ceremonial 1,* 1985; *. . . Body and Shadow . . . ,* 1988; *Tre canzoni senza parole,* orchestra, 1992; *. . .where the murmurs die. . . ,* orchestra, 1993; Symphony, 1994; *Canzoni per orchestra,* 1995). Also chamber music: *Obbligato–Memo 2C* (trombone, string quartet, 1980); *Serenata 85* (flute, harp, string trio, 1986); *. . . In the Receding Mist . . .* (flute, harp, string trio, 1988); String Quartet no. 2 (1994). Music for voice: *Serena* (voice, mime, tape, 1972); *Ballad 3* (soprano, tape, 1973); *Wildtrack 3* (soprano, mezzo, chorus, narrator, orchestra, 1975); *Canti lunatici* (soprano, orchestra, 1980); *Canti del sole* (tenor, orchestra, 1982); *Flickering Shadows* (2 sopranos, mezzo, tenor, bass, 1983–84); *Requiescant* (soprano, chorus, orchestra, 1985); *. . . Among the Voices . . .* (chorus, harp, 1988); *Canti d'eclisse* (voice, orchestra, 1993).

Rangström, (Anders Johan) Ture (b. Stockholm, 30 Nov. 1884; d. there, 11 May 1947). Composer. He studied, 1905–7, in Berlin, taking voice lessons with Hey. He went on to study composition in Stockholm with Lindegren and in Munich with Pfitzner. He worked as a music critic for several papers. He conducted the Göteborg Symphony, 1923–25, and then was press adviser to the Stockholm Opera; also taught singing. His early music was in a late Romantic Scandinavian tradition. As his language matured, it became characterized by homophonic textures and balanced, symmetrical forms. He was especially known for his songs, which exhibited what he referred to as "speech melody," in which the melody paralleled the inflections of the spoken text. Works include dramatic music; orchestral (4 symphonies, including Symphony no. 4, *Invocatio',* 1936); chamber and vocal works, including around 250 songs.

Rankl, Karl (b. Gaaden, near Vienna, 1 Oct. 1898; d. Salzburg, 6 Sept. 1968). Conductor and composer. Studied with Schoenberg and Webern in Vienna; served as conductor at the Kroll Opera in Berlin (1928–31) and the German Theater in Prague (1937–39) before taking refuge in England at the outbreak of war. Served as music director at Covent Garden (1946–51) and conductor of the Scottish Orchestra (1951–56); in 1958 he was named director of the proposed Sydney Opera. His compositions include the opera *Deirdre of the Sorrows* and 8 symphonies.

Ranta, Sulho (b. Peräseinäjoki, 15 Aug. 1901; d. Helsinki, 5 May 1960). Composer. He studied with Melartin at the Helsinki Conservatory from 1921 through 1924, with Willner in Vienna and then in Paris in 1930. From 1934 to 1956 he taught at the Sibelius Academy in Helsinki. He edited a biographical dictionary of Finnish composers (Helsinki, 1945) and one of performers (Helsinki, 1947). His music was much influenced by French trends and by the exoticism that was also current in France. His style was lyrical and expressive, occasionally using chromaticism. Works include orchestral music (4 symphonies, 1929–47), concertos (Concertino no. 2, flute, harp, viola, strings, 1934), vocal music (*Oratorio volgare,* soloists, chorus, orchestra, 1951), and chamber works (*Suite symphonique,* flute, clarinet, horn, string quartet, piano, 1926–28).

Raphael, Günter (Albert Rudolf) (b. Berlin, 30 Apr. 1903; d. Herford, Germany, 19 Oct. 1960). Composer. He studied at the Berlin Hochschule für Musik (1922–25), where his teachers included Max Trapp (piano), Walter Fischer (organ), and Robert Kahn (composition). He then taught theory and composition in

Leipzig at the State Conservatory and the Kirchenmusikalisches Institut. His works were banned by the Nazis, which led him to resign his teaching post and move first to Meiningen and then to Sweden. In 1949 he returned to teaching at the Duisburg Conservatory. He later taught at the Mainz Conservatory (1956–58) and at the Cologne Hochschule für Musik (from 1957).

His early music is in a late Romantic style. The influence of earlier composers, such as Bach and Schütz, is evident in his sparser, middle-period music; late music incorporates twelve-tone technique. His many orchestral works include 5 symphonies (1926, 1932, 1942, 1942–47, 1953) and 2 violin concertos (1929, 1960). He also wrote many vocal pieces (*Geistliche Chormusik,* 12 motets, 1938; *Busskantate,* chorus, orchestra, 1952). Chamber music includes 4 string quartets (1926, 1926, 1930, 1945); also piano and organ music.

Bibl.: Elisabeth Schmiedeke, *Günther Raphaels Chormusik: Versuch einer kritischen Wertung* (Kassel, 1985).

Rasbach, Oscar (b. Dayton, Ky., 2 August 1888; d. Pasadena, Calif., 24 Mar. 1975). Composer. He studied piano in Los Angeles with José Anderson; traveled to Vienna in 1909, where he studied piano with Theodor Leschetizky and harmony with Hans Thornton; also studied with Julius Jahn, A. J. Stamm, and Ludwig Thomas. He wrote many songs, including a setting of Joyce Kilmer's poem "Trees," which became very popular; also 2 operettas, *Open House* and *Dawn Boy,* as well as small piano pieces. He taught piano throughout his life.

Rascher, Sigurd (Manfred) (b. Elberfeld [now Wuppertal], Germany, 15 May 1907). Saxophonist. Studied at the Stuttgart Musikhochschule and taught saxophone in Copenhagen and Sweden in the 1930s; made his American debut in 1939 with the Boston Symphony and performed as soloist with many orchestras in the U.S. and Europe. In 1969 he founded the Rascher Saxophone Quartet. Ibert, Hindemith, Martin, and Glazunov are among the composers who wrote works for him.

Raselius [Raesel], **Andreas** (b. Hahnbach, near Amberg, ca. 1563; d. Heidelberg, 6 Jan. 1602). Composer and theorist. From 1581 studied and then taught at Heidelberg. From 1584 worked in Regensburg, returning to Heidelberg in 1600 as court Kapellmeister to Friedrich IV, Elector Palatine. His didactic theoretical works, *Hexachordum seu Questiones musicae practicae . . .* (Nuremberg, 1591) and *Dodechachordi vivi . . .* (manuscript, 1589), are notable particularly for their many excellent music examples. His compositions, all sacred, include collections of chorale settings designed for congregational use; and motets, some polychoral. Most texts are in German.

Rasi, Francesco (b. Arezzo, 14 May 1574; d. Mantua, by 9 Dec. 1621). Composer and tenor. During the 1590s he performed in Rome to great success under the patronage of Grand Duke Ferdinando I of Tuscany, then entered the service of Gesualdo (1594), and finally served the Duke of Mantua (1598). He sang in the first performances of Peri's *Euridice* and Caccini's *Il rapimento di Cefalo* in 1600, and in 1607 almost certainly created the title role in Monteverdi's *Orfeo.* He traveled to Austria in 1612 and dedicated a manuscript of sacred and secular songs to the Prince-Archbishop of Salzburg; in 1617 he composed an opera, *Cibele, ed Ati* (music not extant). He published 2 collections of monodies, *Vaghezze di musica per una voce sola* (Venice, 1608) and *Madrigali di diversi autori* (Florence, 1610).

Bibl.: Carol MacClintock, "The Monodies of Francesco Rasi," *JAMS* 14 (1961): 31–36.

Raskin, Judith (b. New York, 21 June 1928; d. there, 21 Dec. 1984). Soprano. Studied with Anna Hamlin. Joined the NBC Opera in 1957, then made her New York City Opera debut as Despina (1959) and her Metropolitan debut as Susanna (1962); also sang at Glyndebourne and in Santa Fe and Chicago. Raskin performed in a number of Baroque stage works, including various Handel operas, Monteverdi's *Orfeo,* and Rameau's *Les Indes galantes;* her recordings include Anne Trulove under Stravinsky in *The Rake's Progress* and Mahler's Fourth under Szell. She taught at the Manhattan School of Music, the 92nd Street Y, and Mannes College.

Rasmussen, Karl-Aage (b. Kolding, Denmark, 13 Dec. 1947). Composer and conductor. He attended the Academy of Music in Århus, where he studied composition with Per Nørgård and earned degrees in history, theory, and composition (1971). He began to teach there in 1970, and also at the Royal Academy in Copenhagen in 1980. He became director of the Elsinore Players in 1975, and director of the NUMUS Festival in 1978. He founded the Danish Piano Theater (1986) and was chairman of the Danish Arts Foundation (1987–90). Works include opera (*Crapp's Last Tape,* 1967; *Jephta,* 1977; *Majakovskij,* scenic concert piece, 1978; *The Story of Jonah,* radio play, 1981; *Our Hoffmann,* 1986); orchestral music (*Symphony for Young Lovers,* 1966; *Recapitulations,* 1967; *Symphonie classique,* 1968; *Anfang und Ende,* 1972; *Contrafactum,* cello, orchestra, 1979; *A Symphony in Time,* 1982; *Movements on a Moving Line,* 1987); also chamber music.

Rathaus, Karol (b. Tarnopol, 16 Sept. 1895; d. New York, 21 Nov. 1954). Composer. He studied composition with Schreker at the Vienna Academy of Music; he was also a student at the Univ. of Vienna (Ph.D., 1922). He served in the Austrian army in World War I, and then in 1919 premiered his Variations on a Theme by Reger in Vienna. He went to Berlin in 1920 to continue studying with Schreker at the Hochschule für Musik. Several of his works were premiered in Berlin during this period, among them Overture (op. 22, Berlin Philharmonic, Furtwängler, 1928), *Der letzte Pierrot* (ballet, 1927), and *Fremde Erde* (opera, 1930). In 1932 he went to Paris, and then in 1934 to London. The Ballets russes performed *Lelion amoureux* at Covent Garden (1937). He moved to the U.S. in 1938 and became a U.S. citizen in 1946. In 1940 he became professor of composition at Queens College.

Works: *Orchestra.* 3 symphonies (1921–22, 1923, 1942–43); Suite (violin, chamber orchestra, 1929); Suite (1930); *Serenade* (1932); *Contrapuntal Triptych* (1934); *Jacob's Dream* (nocturne, 1938); Piano Concerto (1939); Music for Strings (1941); *Polonaise symphonique* (1943); *Vision dramatique* (1945); *Salisbury Cove Overture* (1949); *Sinfonia concertant* (1950–51); *Louisville Prelude* (1953). *Vocal. Song without Words: Fugue* (chorus, chamber orchestra, 1928); *3 Calderon Songs* (low voice, orchestra or piano, 1931); *XXIII Psalm* (tenor, women's chorus, orchestra or piano, 1945); *O Juvenes* (academic cantata, 1947); *Diapason* (after Dryden and Milton, baritone, chorus, orchestra, 1950). *Chamber.* 5 string quartets (1921, 1925, 1936, 1946, 1954); 2 violin sonatas (1924, 1938); Clarinet Sonata (1927); *Little Serenade* (clarinet, bassoon, trumpet, horn, piano, 1927); Trio (violin, clarinet, piano, 1944); *Rapsodia notturna* (viola or cello, piano, 1950); *Trio Serenade* (piano trio, 1953); 4 piano sonatas (1920, 1920–24, rev. 1928, 1927, 1946). He also wrote film music, including the score for *The Brothers Karamazov* (1931).

Rattle, Simon (Denis) (b. Liverpool, 19 Jan. 1955). Conductor. Studied piano, percussion, and conducting at the Royal Academy of Music (1971–74); won the John Player International Conductors' Competition in 1974 and was named assistant conductor of the Bournemouth Symphony and Bournemouth Sinfonietta. In 1976 he became associate conductor of the Royal Liverpool Philharmonic and assistant conductor of the BBC Scottish Symphony, and conducted at Glyndebourne the following year; subsequently appointed principal conductor of the City of Birmingham Symphony (1979) and principal guest conductor of the Los Angeles Philharmonic (1981).

Bibl.: Nicholas Kenyon, *Simon Rattle: The Making of a Conductor* (London, 1989).

Rautavaara, Einojuhani (b. Helsinki, 9 Oct. 1938). Composer. He studied with Merikanto, 1948–54, at the Sibelius Academy in Helsinki, then musicology at Helsinki Univ.; in the U.S., 1955–56, studied composition with Copland, Persichetti, and Sessions; worked with Vogel in 1957 and in Cologne with Petzold in 1958. Beginning 1966 he taught at the Sibelius Academy. His music incorporates European avant-garde trends. His early works are in the neoclassical tradition; after working with Vogel, he incorporated elements of serialism into his style (Wind Quintet, 1964). Works include operas (*Kaivos* [The Mine] op. 15, television opera, 1963; *Thomas,* 1982–85; *Vincent,* 1987–88), 1 ballet, orchestral and chamber works and choral music (*The Water Circle* op. 65, piano, chorus, orchestra, 1972).

Rauzzini, Venanzio (b. Camerino, near Rome, bapt. 19 Dec. 1746; d. Bath, 8 Apr. 1810). Male soprano, composer, and harpsichordist. After study in Rome, he sang in Venice and entered the service of the Elector Max Joseph III at Munich (1766–72), where he composed operas, including *Piramo e Tisbe* (1769). After singing in Italy, where he was *primo uomo* in Mozart's *Lucio Silla* (1772) and the inspiration for the motet *Exsultate, jubilate* (K. 165/158a), he moved to England. In London (1774–77) he sang at the King's Theatre and composed chamber music, arias for pasticcios, and operas. In 1777 he moved to Bath and managed concerts, although he remained active as a performer in London. Among his pupils were Nancy Storace and Michael Kelly.

Ravel, (Joseph) Maurice (b. Ciboure, Basses Pyrénées, 7 March 1875; d. Paris, 28 Dec. 1937). Composer. Born to a Swiss father and a Basque mother, Ravel grew up in Paris. At age 7 he was given piano lessons with Henri Ghys. At age 12 he studied harmony with Charles-René, a student of Delibes. Two years later, after studying with Emile Descombes as well, he was admitted to Eugène Anthiôme's piano class at the Paris Conservatory. Two years after that he graduated to the class of Charles de Bériot, and studied harmony with Emile Pessard. Musical influences from this time include Javanese gamelan music, heard at the 1889 World Exhibition in Paris, as well as the music of Rimsky-Korsakov. He developed a friendship with Ricardo Viñes, a fellow student in de Bériot's class, with whom he shared an interest in contemporary music.

Ravel left the Conservatory in 1895, having composed the *Menuet antique* for piano, *Habanera* for 2 pianos, and the song "Un grand sommeil noir." He produced little music the following year, but then in 1897 returned to the Conservatory to study composition with Fauré. He also studied counterpoint and orchestration with André Gédalge. The year 1899 saw performance of his very popular *Pavane pour une infante défunte* for piano as well as the premiere of his overture *Schéhérazade,* which he conducted in Paris.

Fauré was an important and sympathetic teacher for Ravel; *Jeux d'eau* and the string quartet of 1903 are both dedicated to Fauré. Ravel did not excel, however, in meeting the academic requirements of the Conservatory, especially in fugue writing. He attempted to win a Prix de Rome each year from 1900 to 1903. Although he had won a second prize in 1901 with his cantata *Myrrha,* he failed to win a Grand Prix, with the result that in 1905 (he did not enter in 1904), when his last entry did succeed beyond the preliminaries, a controversy ensued over the fact that all 6 prizes were given to pupils of Lenepveu. (At this time Ravel was already well established as a composer outside the Conservatory.) This controversy was made public and eventually the director of the Conservatory, Théodore Dubois, resigned, to be replaced by the less conservative Fauré.

The years that followed were productive ones. Among the works Ravel wrote were *Rapsodie espagnole* (1907–8) and his first opera, *L'heure espagnole*

Maurice Ravel.

(1907–9). He worked on *Daphnis et Chloé* for three years (1909–12), a piece commissioned by Diaghilev, and around this time he met Stravinsky, whose ballet *The Firebird* was about to be produced. In 1913 Ravel went to Switzerland to collaborate with Stravinsky on a version of Mussorgsky's *Khovanshchina.*

Ravel became frustrated with the extent to which critics insisted on associating him with Debussy, and in 1906 he wrote a letter to the critic Pierre Lalo pointing out what he saw as the originality of his piano piece *Jeux d'eau* and claiming its independence from the influence of Debussy. This letter was published in 1907 in the midst of a heated controversy over the issue, when Lalo again insisted on the influence of Debussy, this time in Ravel's cycle *Histoires naturelles* (1906).

Ravel's music was becoming quite popular. The String Quartet (1902–3) was often performed; *Daphnis et Chloé* became part of the repertory of the Ballets russes. He traveled to Great Britain in 1909 and 1911, and to Vienna in 1920; his music continued to take him all over Europe throughout the 1920s; in 1928 he toured America. Perhaps his most popular piece, *Boléro,* was written for the dancer Ida Rubenstein and premiered at the Paris Opéra on 22 November 1928. He never taught for any school, and taught very few pupils privately (among the few were Vaughan Williams and Roland-Manuel). Ravel's health began to fail seriously in 1932. As time went on he had increasing difficulties with muscular coordination. He died after unsuccessful brain surgery in December 1937.

Ravel was a perfectionist in his compositional process, paying scrupulous attention to detail. Stravinsky described him as a "Swiss watchmaker." In a sense he was detached from his music; he employed exotic scales and modes, and composed in imitative veins, evoking the past with Baroque gestures or adopting a Spanish style. The repetition of a single accompaniment figure or a single note is highly characteristic; his skill as an orchestrator is renowned. His propensity for a kind of objective precision would later influence composers such as Ligeti and Riley.

Works: Orchestral works include *Une barque sur l'océan* (1906; rev. 1926); *Pavane pour une infante défunte* (1910); *Valses nobles et sentimentales* (1912); *Alborada del gracioso* (1918); *Le tombeau de Couperin* (1919); *La valse* (1919–20); *Fanfare* (1927); Piano Concerto for the left hand (1929–30); Piano Concerto in G (1929–31).

Vocal. *Alcyone,* cantata (1902); *Alyssa,* cantata (1903); *Don Quichotte à Dulcinée* (1932–33); *Ronsard à son âme* (1935). Voice with ensemble: *Trois poèmes de Stéphane Mallarmé* (1913); *Chansons madécasses* (1925–26). Numerous works for voice with piano.

Chamber music. Sonata, violin, piano (1897); *Introduction et allegro,* harp, flute, clarinet, string quartet (1905); Piano Trio (1914); *Le tombeau de Claude Debussy,* violin, cello (1920); Sonata, violin, cello (1920–22); *Berceuse sur le nom de Gabriel Fauré,* violin, piano (1922); *Tzigane,* violin, piano (1924); Sonata, violin, piano (1923–27). For piano: *Sérénade grotesque* (1893); *Sites auriculaires,* 2 pianos (1895–97); *Sonatine* (1903–5); *Miroirs* (1904–5); *Gasparde de la nuit* (1908); *Menuet sur le nom d'Haydn* (1909); *Ma mère l'oye,* 4 hands (1908–10); *Valses nobles et sentimentales* (1911); *A la manière de . . .* (1913); *Prélude* (1913); *Frontispice,* 2 pianos, 5 hands (1918).

Bibl.: *Catalogue de l'oeuvre de Maurice Ravel* (Paris, 1954). *Catalogue de l'exposition Ravel* (Paris, 1975). Roger Nichols, *Ravel* (London, 1977). Burnett James, *Ravel: His Life and Times* (New York, 1983). Theo Hirsbrunner, *Maurice*

Ravel: Sein Leben, sein Werk (Laaber, 1989). Arbie Orenstein, ed., *A Ravel Reader* (New York, 1990; trans. of *Ravel: Correspondance, écrite et entretiens,* Paris, 1989).

Ravenscroft, John (d. not later than 1708). Composer. English, but resided in Italy; the little that is known of his life is derived from copies of his works. His opus 1, 12 trio sonatas, was published in Rome under the name Giovanni Ravenscroft; it includes a dedication (dated 1695) to Prince Ferdinando of Tuscany, perhaps his patron. His second opus, 6 sonatas for 2 violins, was published in London in 1708. It seems likely that Ravenscroft studied with Corelli, whose style he imitated in his works.

Bibl.: William S. Newman, "Ravenscroft and Corelli," *ML* 38 (1957): 369–70.

Ravenscroft, Thomas (b. ca. 1582?; d. ca. 1635). Composer and editor. He was a chorister at Chichester Cathedral from 1594 as well as at St. Paul's Cathedral under Thomas Giles. He wrote some music for the St. Paul's child actors and served as music master at Christ's Hospital (1618–22). In 1609 he edited *Pammelia* (facs., Philadelphia, 1961), the earliest English printed collection of rounds and catches. Ravenscroft's *A Briefe Discourse* (London, 1614; facs., *MMML* 22, 1976) includes some of his own compositions, as does *The Whole Booke of Psalmes* (London, 1621), an important psalter of the period.

Bibl.: David Mateer, "A Critical Study and Transcription of 'A Briefe Discourse' by Thomas Ravenscroft" (diss., Univ. of London, 1970). Ian Payne, "The Sacred Music of Thomas Ravenscroft," *EM* 10 (1982): 309–17. Linda Phyllis Austern, "Thomas Ravenscroft: Musical Chronicler of an Elizabethan Theater Company," *JAMS* 38 (1985): 238–63.

Rawsthorne, Alan (b. Haslington, Lancaster, 2 May 1905; d. Cambridge, 24 July 1971). Composer. In 1925 entered the Royal Manchester College of Music, where he studied piano with Merrick and cello with Fuchs; studied piano in Berlin, 1930–31, with Petri. In 1932 he returned to England to teach at the Dartington Hall School. Beginning in the late 1930s he worked primarily as a composer. His early compositions drew on standard forms and genres; his musical language was influenced by Hindemith and Walton (*Theme and Variations,* 2 violins, 1937). Through the 1950s Rawsthorne made use of a lyricism that he explored more in some works (often in conjunction with the use of singers, as in *Four Romantic Pieces,* 1953) than in others (Piano Concerto no. 2, 1951). By the early 1960s his works frequently incorporated vocal lines with facility and fluidity (*Carmen vitale,* soprano solo, chorus, orchestra, 1963). Concurrently he was experimenting with the implementation of serialistic devices (Oboe Quartet, 1970). Compositions inlcude 1 ballet; orchestral music (Symphony no. 2, Pastoral Symphony, soprano, orchestra, 1959; Piano Concerto no. 1, 1939, no. 2, 1951; Violin Concerto no. 1, 1948; *Concertante pastorale,* flute, horn, strings, 1951; Cello Concerto, 1965); choral works (*A Canticle of Man,* baritone, chorus, flute, strings, 1952); dramatic vocal works (*Practical Cats,* speaker, orchestra, 1954); songs; and chamber works.

Raxach, Enrique (b. Barcelona, 15 Jan. 1932). Composer. Studied composition and theory with Nuri Aymerich. In 1958 he went to Paris, Munich, and Zurich; attended summer courses given by Boulez, Messiaen, Maderna, and Stockhausen at Darmstadt, 1959–64. He settled in the Netherlands in 1962, where he became a citizen in 1969. Works for orchestra: *Polifonias* (string orchestra, 1953–54); *Metamorphose I, II, and III* (1956, 1958, 1959); *Prometheus* (1957); *Fluxion* (1962–63); *Syntagma* (1964–65); *6 Movements* (1965); *Textures* (1965–66); *Equinoxial* (1967–68); *Inside Outside* (1969); *Sine nomine* (soprano, orchestra, 1973); *Figuren in einer Landschaft* (1974); *Ad marginem* (1975); *Erdenlicht* (1975); *Soirée musicale* (clarinet, women's chorus, orchestra, 1978); *Am Ende des Regenbogens* (1980); *Opus incertum* (1985); *Calles y sueños—in Memoriam Federico García Lorca* (1986). Also wrote chamber music and songs.

Read, Daniel (b. Attleboro, Mass., 16 Nov. 1757; d. New Haven, Conn., 4 Dec. 1836). Composer. He may have studied singing with Andrew Law in Providence in 1772 or with Billings there in 1774; in any case he was composing by 1774. In 1782 he settled permanently in New Haven, where he ran a general store, taught singing, composed, and compiled collections of music. With *The American Singing Book* (New Haven, 1785) he became the first American musician since Billings to publish a collection devoted to his own works. His tunes appeared in a number of collections including *The Worcester Collection* (Worcester, Mass., 1786), *The American Harmony* (Philadelphia, 1793), and *The Village Harmony* (Exeter, N.H., 1795); several of his tunes, including "Calvary," "Greenwich," "Judgment," "Lisbon," "Russia," "Windham," and "Winter," quickly became fixtures in the American psalmody repertory. Most of Read's published works, numbering over 80, were written during the 1780s and early 1790s; his output slowed after 1795. Although he was one of the first composers to develop an American musical idiom, he turned in later years increasingly to European-style harmonies and voice-leading. His other publishing ventures included *The Columbian Harmonist* (New Haven, 1793–95), a collection of Psalm tunes, anthems, and set pieces; *An Introduction to Psalmody* (New Haven, 1790), containing instructional dialogues without music; and *American Musical Magazine* (New Haven, 1786–87), the first American music periodical.

Bibl.: Irving Lowens, "Daniel Read's World: The Letters of an Early American Composer," *Notes* 9 (1951–52): 233–48; rev. in *Music and Musicians in Early America* (New York, 1964). Richard Crawford, "Connecticut Sacred Music Imprints, 1778–1810," *Notes* 27 (1970–71): 445–52, 671–79. V. C. Bushnell, "Daniel Read of New Haven (1757–1836): The Man and His Musical Activities" (diss., Harvard, 1979).

Read, Gardner (b. Evanston, Ill., 2 Jan. 1913). Composer. He studied at Northwestern Univ. (1930–32) and then at Eastman (B.M., 1936; M.M., 1937), where his teachers included Howard Hanson and Bernard Rogers; also studied with Ildebrando Pizzetti in Rome (1938–39) and with Copland at the Berkshire Music Center (1941). He taught at the St. Louis Institute of Music (1941–43), the Kansas City Conservatory (1943–45), the Cleveland Institute of Music (1945–48), and Boston Univ. (1948–78). He was editor of the Birchard–Boston University Contemporary Music Series (1950–60).

Works: An opera, *Villon* (1965–67). Orchestra music: 4 symphonies (1936, 1942, 1948, 1951–59); *Sketches of the City* (1933); *Fantasy* (viola, orchestra, 1935); *Prelude and Toccata* (1936–37); *Suite* (strings, 1937); *Pan e Dafni* (1940); Overture no. 1 (1943); Cello Concerto (1945); *Quiet Music* (strings, 1946); *Partita* (1946); *Bell Overture* (1946); *Pennsylvania* (1946–47); *The Temptation of St. Anthony* (1947); *Arioso elegiaca* (strings, 1951); *Toccata giocosa* (1953); *Vernal Equinox* (1955); *Night Flight* (1961); *Sonoric Fantasia no. 2* (violin, chamber orchestra, 1965); *Sonoric Fantasia no. 3* (winds, percussion, 1971); Piano Concerto (1977). Choral music: *A Merry Madrigal* (1934–35); *The Magic Hour* (1934); *To a Skylark* (1939); *Jesous Ahatonhia* (1950); *The Golden Harp* (1952); *Though I Speak with the Tongues of Men* (1960); *The Prophet* (chorus, orchestra, 1960); *Chants d'Auvergne* (1962); *By-Low My Babe* (1978–79). Also many songs; chamber music; piano and organ music.

Writings: *Thesaurus of Orchestral Devices* (New York, 1953; rev. 1969). *Music Notation: A Manual of Modern Practice* (Boston, 1964; rev. 1972). *Contemporary Instrumental Techniques* (New York, 1976). *Modern Rhythmic Notation* (Bloomington, Ind., 1978). *Style and Orchestration* (New York, 1979).

Reading, John (b. ca. 1685 or 1686; d. London, 2 Sept. 1764). Composer and organist. He was educated by Blow at the Chapel Royal until his voice broke in 1699. Served as organist at Dulwich College (1700–1702), and as master of the choristers (1703) and singing teacher (1704) at Lincoln Cathedral; also organist of St. John's, Hackney (1708–27), and of St. Mary Woolnoth and St. Mary Woolchurch Haw. A composer mostly of church music; his works were influenced by the Italian style. Published compositions include *A Book of New Songs . . . with Symphonies* (London, ca. 1710) and *A Book of New Anthems . . . with Proper Ritornels* (London, ca. 1715). He is sometimes confused with his father, also named John (ca. 1645–92), who was a composer and was employed for a time by Lincoln Cathedral.

Rebel, François [le fils] (b. Paris, 19 June 1701; d. there, 7 Nov. 1775). Composer and violinist. Son of Jean-Féry Rebel. In 1714 he entered the orchestra of the Académie royale, and three years later earned the right to succeed his father in the 24 Violons. He collaborated with his close friend François Francoeur on the opera *Pirame et Thisbé* (1726), followed by 17 other jointly written stage works. Rebel also served as *surintendant* and *maître* of the royal chamber music (from 1733), director of the Concert spirituel (1742), and *inspecteur général* (1743–53) and co-director (1757–67) of the Académie royale de musique.

Rebel, Jean-Féry [Jean-Baptiste-Ferry, le père] (b. Paris, bapt. 18 Apr. 1666; d. there, 2 Jan. 1747). Violinist and composer. Father of François Rebel. By 1699 he was first violinist of the Académie royale de musique, journeyed to Spain the following year, and was given a place in the 24 Violons on his return in 1705. He served as court composer, *maître de musique* at the Académie, and director of the Concert spirituel. Compositions include choreographed "symphonies"; the work entitled *Les élémens* (1737) contains a depiction of chaos.

Reber, (Napoléon-) Henri (b. Mulhouse, 21 Oct. 1807; d. Paris, 24 Nov. 1880). Composer. Studied with Reicha and Le Sueur at the Paris Conservatory (1828). Appointed professor of harmony at the Conservatory in 1851; succeeded Halévy as professor of composition in 1871. Wrote *Traité d'harmonie* (Paris, 1862). After the successful performance of his opera *Le père Gaillard* (1852), he virtually gave up composing for the theater. Works include the ballet *Le diable amoureux* (1840); comic operas *La nuit de Noël* (1848) and *Les dames-capitaines* (1857); cantata *Roland* (1887); 55 *mélodies* (1863, 1880); 18 vocalises (1845); 4 symphonies (1858); *Suite de morceaux* (1878); String Quintet (ca. 1835); String Quartets opp. 4, 5; 7 piano trios; Piano Quartet (1866); character pieces and dances for piano.

Rebikov, Vladimir Ivanovich (b. Kresnoyarsk, Siberia, 31 May 1866; d. Yalta, 4 Aug. 1920). Composer. Studied at Moscow Conservatory with Klenovsky and in Berlin. Lived in Odessa, 1894–98; first opera, *V grosu,* performed there in 1894. Moved to Kishinev; organized a branch of the Imperial Russian Musical Society. Music ca. 1900 uses whole-tone techniques. Works include operas *Snow-White* (1909) and *Narcissus* (1913); musico-psychological drama *Alfa i omega* (1911); *Mélomimiques* opp. 11, 15, 17, voice and piano; many short piano pieces; some liturgical music; orchestral works.

Bibl.: William H. Dale, "A Study of the Musicopsychological Dramas of Vladimir Ivanovich Rebikov" (diss., Univ. of Southern Calif., 1955).

Reda, Siegfried (b. Bochum, 27 July 1916; d. Mülheim, 13 Dec. 1968). Composer. He studied first in Dortmund and then in Berlin at the Spandau Church Music School, where his teachers included Pepping and Distler. He became director of the Institute for Evangelical Church Music at the Essen Folkwangschule in 1946, where he also taught composition and organ. In 1953 he became director of church music for Mülheim. He wrote a great deal of organ music and was influential in the development of Protestant church music. *Requiem* (1963) is considered his most important work. Other works include *Choralkantate "Fröh-*

lich soll mein Herze springen" (1946); *Chormusiken nach chinesischen Dichtungen* (1947); *Chormusik für das Jahr Kirche* (1947–58); *Evangelienmusik "Die beiden Schächer"* (1948); *Te Deum* (1950); *Ostergeschichte* (1950); *Amor Dei* (1952); *Das Göttliche Spiel* (1952); *Weihnachtskyrie* (1954); *Altchristlicher Hymnus* (1955); *Psalm viii* (1964); *Psalmus morte servati* (1966). Also many works for organ, including 3 concertos (1947–48); *Prelude, Fugue, and Quadruplum* (1957); Sonata (1960).

Bibl.: Siegfried Reda, "Reda, Siegfried," in *Rheinische Musiker,* 5, ed. K. G. Fellerer (Cologne, 1967) [includes works list].

Redding, Otis (b. Dawson, Ga., 9 Sept. 1941; d. near Madison, Wis., 19 Dec. 1967). Soul singer and songwriter. Through soul artist Johnny Jenkins he met producer Jim Stewart of Stax Volt Records in 1963; their recordings of Redding's songs helped establish a "Memphis" soul sound distinct from that of Berry Gordy's Motown productions. Among his popular songs were "These Arms of Mine" (1963), "I've Been Loving You Too Long" (1965), and "(Sittin' on) The Dock of the Bay" (1967). He became popular with rock audiences through an appearance at the Monterey Pop Festival of 1967, and later his songs were recorded by numerous rock groups including the Rolling Stones.

Redford, John (b. ca. 1485; d. London, late 1547). Composer and organist. In 1534 he was a vicar-choral at St. Paul's Cathedral and at his death almoner and master of the choristers there. Doubtless he also served as organist. The vast majority of his compositions are for organ solo; many are preserved in the Mulliner Book (ed. Denis Stevens, *MB* 1, 1951; rev. 2nd ed., 1954). These works, designed for use in church services, are written examples of what had previously been an improvised art form: instrumental settings of plainsong melodies, to be used in alternation with sung chants. Occasionally the faburden to the chant is used instead of the chant itself.

Redman, Don(ald Matthew) (b. Piedmont, W. Va., 29 July 1900; d. New York, 30 Nov. 1964). Jazz arranger, composer, bandleader, and alto saxophonist. Studied music at Storer College. He joined Fletcher Henderson's band (1924–27) and arranged most of its repertory, including pioneering examples of big band jazz such as "Go 'long Mule," "Shanghai Shuffle," and "Copenhagen" (all recorded in 1924). He was the music director of McKinney's Cotton Pickers (1927–31); under that same name an all-star group recorded Redman's song "Gee, Ain't I Good to You?" (1929). He formed his own big band (1931–40) and also worked as a free-lance arranger (1930s–40s). From 1951 he was Pearl Bailey's music director.

Reed, Alfred (b. New York, 25 Jan. 1921). Composer and conductor. Grew up playing trumpet; studied theory and harmony with John Sacco and Paul Yartin. He worked for the Radio Workshop in New York as a composer, arranger, and conductor (1938–42). During World War II he enlisted in the U.S. Air Force and was associate conductor of the Air Force Band. He attended Juilliard as a student of Vittorio Giannini. Became conductor of the orchestra at Baylor Univ. (1953), where he then earned a B.M. (1955) and an M.M. (1956). Worked as an editor at Hansen Publications in 1955, and joined the faculty of the Univ. of Miami in 1966. Wrote many pieces for band, including *Greensleeves, Fantasia* (1962) and *Russian Christmas Music* (1968).

Reed, H(erbert) Owen (b. Odessa, Mo., 17 June 1910). Composer. He studied at the Univ. of Missouri (1929–33), Louisiana State Univ. (B.M., 1934; M.M., 1936), and then with Howard Hanson and Bernard Rogers at Eastman (Ph.D., 1939); also with Roy Harris, and with Copland and Bernstein at Tanglewood. He explored the folk music of Mexico, the Caribbean, and Scandinavia. Taught at Michigan State Univ. (1939–76). Compositions include *The Masque of the Red Death,* ballet-pantomime (1936); *Peter Homan's Dream,* opera (1955); 3 chamber dance-operas (*Earth Trapped,* 1960; *Living Solid Face,* 1974; *Butterfly Girl and Mirage Boy,* 1980); Symphony (1939); other orchestral and band works. Writings include *Basic Music* (Melville, N.Y., 1954); with Paul Harder, *Basic Contrapuntal Technique* (Melville, N.Y., 1969); with Robert Sidwell, *The Materials of Music Composition,* 3 vols. (Reading, Mass., 1978).

Reed, Lou [Louis Alan] (b. Brooklyn, N.Y., 2 Mar. 1942). Rock singer, songwriter, and guitarist. Studied creative writing at Syracuse Univ.; worked as a songwriter for Pickwick Studios. In 1964 formed with violist and keyboardist John Cale the experimental rock group The Velvet Underground, which was associated with Andy Warhol. From 1970 he recorded as a solo artist; his "Walk on the Wild Side" (1972) was very popular, as were several albums in the 1980s, including *Blue Mask* (1982) and *New York* (1989).

Reeve, Stephen (b. London, 15 March 1948). Composer. Studied with Pousseur at the Liège Conservatory (1971–72). Received commissions from IRCAM (1980) and the London Institute of Contemporary Art (1985), among others. Works include *Colour Music,* woodwind quartet (1970); *Poème: Couleurs de Spectre,* orchestra with optional light projection (1972–73); *Summer Morning by a Lake Full of Colors,* expansion of Schoenberg's *Farben,* large orchestra (1974); *Aux régions éthérées,* 3 chamber groups (1975–76); *Grande thèse de la petite-fille de Téthys,* ethnic encyclopedia for solo cello (1980–87); *La rêverie de St-Estephe,* computer-realized tape, ensemble (1980–87); *L'Oracle de Delphes,* music theater for brass quintet (1985); *Strophe,* solo rock guitar, 4 classical guitars (1985–86); *O que Zeus apparaisse à l'horizon,* gamelan ensemble, tape (1989–90).

Reeve, William (b. London, 1757; d. there, 22 June 1815). Composer. After serving as organist at Totnes in Devon during the early 1780s he came to London, where he wrote operas, pantomimes, and music for plays and ballets for Astley's Amphitheatre, Royalty Theatre, Lyceum Theatre, and Covent Garden (1791–1806). From 1808 until his death he wrote almost all the music for Sadler's Wells. Not a talented composer, though many of his songs and overtures (in piano arrangement) were published.

Reeves, David Wallis (b. Owego, N.Y., 14 Feb. 1838; d. Providence, R.I., 8 Mar. 1900). Composer, bandmaster, cornetist. Joined municipal band in Owego. Became an apprentice to Thomas Conlan, his teacher, and moved to Elmira. Returned to Owego in 1857 to lead the band there. Moved to New York to play with Dodworth Orchestra. Went to England, where he learned double and triple tonguing; introduced the techniques to U.S. when he returned in 1862. Led the American Band in Providence, 1866–92. Leader of the Gilmore Band in 1892; returned to Providence in 1893. Wrote over 100 marches.

Bibl.: F. Marciniak and J. Lemons, *Strike Up the Band* (Providence, 1979).

Reeves, Sims (John) (b. Shooters Hill, 26? Sept. 1818; d. Worthing, 25 Oct. 1900). Tenor. Studied piano with Cramer, harmony with Callcott. Debut as baritone at Newcastle-upon-Tyne, 1838. Studied in Paris with Bordogni, in Milan with Mazzucato. Appeared at La Scala as Edgardo in *Lucia di Lammermoor* (1846). Returned to London in December 1846. Sang first English performance of *La damnation de Faust* (Feb. 1848) with Berlioz conducting. From 1848, appeared in many oratorio festivals. Farewell performance in Albert Hall, 1891.

Bibl.: Henry Sutherland Edwards, *The Life and Artistic Career of Sims Reeves* (London, 1881). Charles E. Pearce, *Sims Reeves: Fifty Years of Music in England* (New York, 1980).

Refice, Licinio (b. Patrica, near Rome, 12 Feb. 1885; d. Rio de Janeiro, 11 Sept. 1954). Composer and conductor. He studied composition and organ at Liceo di Santa Cecilia in Rome, where he earned a diploma in 1910, the same year he was ordained. He taught at the Scuola pontificia di musica sacra (1910–50) and was *maestro di cappella* at S. Maria Maggiore (1911–47). He wrote two religious operas, *Cecilia* (1922–23) and *Margherita da Cortona* (1938). Other works include oratorios, cantatas, over 40 Masses, hymns, motets, and Psalms, as well as some secular songs and instrumental pieces.

Regamey, Constantin (b. Kiev, 28 Jan. 1907; d. Lausanne, 27 Dec. 1982). Composer and pianist. Born to a Russian mother and a Swiss father, he studied piano in Warsaw with Turczyński (1921–25) as well as linguistics at the Univ. of Warsaw, earning a doctorate in 1936. He was deported by the Germans during World War II, but escaped to Switzerland in 1944. While appointed to teach oriental and Slavonic languages at the Univ. of Lausanne, he also pursued his career in composition. His etudes for female voice and piano were premiered in 1955 at Donaueschingen. He was co-editor of the *Revue musicale de Suisse Romande* (1954–62), and president of the Association of Swiss Composers (1963–68) and the Swiss Council of Music. He wrote 2 operas, *Don Robott* (1970) and *Mio, mein mio* (1973), and many pieces for voices and orchestra. His last work, *Visions* (1978–79), was orchestrated by Jean Balissat. He also wrote orchestra and chamber music.

Bibl.: Nicole Loutan-Charbon, *Constantin Regamey, compositeur* (Yverdon, 1978).

Reger, (Johann Baptist Joseph) Max(imilian) (b. Brand, Bavaria, 19 Mar. 1873; d. Leipzig, 11 May 1916). Composer. Son of a musically inclined schoolteacher (from 1874 in Weiden, where Reger grew up), who played several instruments and published a harmony textbook. From 1884 he had music lessons with an organist, Adalbert Lindner, whose book *Max Reger* (Stuttgart, 1922; 3d ed., 1938) is an important biographical source. At 15 he visited the Bayreuth Festival and had an overture played by the local orchestra. Reger entered Weiden Teachers' College to train as a schoolteacher, but Lindner secretly sent some of his compositions to Hugo Riemann, who took him as a composition pupil in 1890, briefly at Sondershausen and then in his new post at the Wiesbaden Conservatory, where Reger eventually became his teaching assistant, remaining until 1896, when he did his year of military service, also in Wiesbaden.

From 1890 Reger produced the first works to which he gave opus numbers and which were published. These included chamber music, a genre in which he composed much throughout his career; lieder, in which he was also very prolific; and piano pieces. Between 1898 and 1905 he produced most of his organ works, a genre in which he was particularly successful, being himself a highly regarded organist. Although a Catholic, he worked much with Lutheran chorales in the Bach tradition. From 1901 to 1907 he lived in Munich as a performer (1905–6, taught counterpoint at the conservatory) and composer, producing his first important orchestral works, including the Sinfonietta op. 90 (1904–5) and the Serenade op. 95 (1905–6), as well as chamber music, piano pieces including the Variations and Fugue on a Theme of J. S. Bach op. 81 (1904), and songs.

His music began to arouse some international attention, and he traveled to perform it (St. Petersburg, 1906). From 1907 he was professor of composition and (1907–8) music director, Leipzig Univ.; in 1909, participated in concerts of his music in the Netherlands, Brussels, and London. Among works of this period are Violin Concerto op. 101 (1907–8); Piano Concerto op. 114 (1910); chamber and choral works. From 1911 he was conductor of the Meiningen court orchestra, continuing to teach one day a week in Leipzig; 1912, toured with the orchestra. From 1915 he lived in Jena, continuing to compose prolifically and to perform. He died of a heart attack returning from concerts in the Netherlands. Among his later works is his best-known orchestral piece, Variations and Fugue on a Theme of Mozart op. 132 (1914). Both influential and controversial when new, its individual combination of progressive and conservative elements falling into no easily defined musical niche, Reger's music has remained current in Germany, as reflected in a large literature devoted to it and to him.

Bibl.: *Sämtliche Werke* (Weisbaden, 1954–). F. Stein, *Thematisches Verzeichnis der im Druck erscheinen Werke von Max Reger einschliesslich seiner Bearbeitungen und Ausgaben* (Leipzig, 1953). H. Rösner, *Max-Reger-Bibliographie* (Bonn, 1968). Helmut Wirth, *Max Reger in Selbstzeugnissen und Bilddokumenten* (Reinbek bei Hamburg, 1982). Susanne Popp and Susanne Shigihara, eds., *Max Reger: Am Wendepunkt zur Moderne: Ein Bildband mit Dokumenten aus den Beständen des Max-Reger-Instituts* (Bonn, 1987). Rainer Cadenbach, *Max Reger und seine Zeit* (Laaber, 1991). Helmut Brauss, *Max Reger's Music for Solo Piano: An Introduction* (Edmonton, 1994).

Regino of Prüm (b. near Ludwigshafen, ca. 842; d. Trier, 915). Theorist. From 885 provost, from 892 abbot of the monastery of Prüm; from 899 abbot of St. Martin at Trier. His treatise *Epistola* (*GS* 1:230–47; abbreviated in the 11th century as *Breviarium de musica*) deals with the question of correct intonations for certain types of Mass and Office chants. He also left an extensive tonary, which covers much of the plainchant repertory of the 9th century.

Regis, Johannes (b. ca. 1430; d. Soignies?, ca. 1485). Composer. Nominal *magister puerorum* at Cambrai Cathedral in 1460; in 1463 at Notre Dame, Antwerp; from perhaps 1464 to 1474, secretary to Dufay in Cambrai; later a canon and scholasticus in Soignies. Tinctoris mentions Regis in two treatises, taking him to task for a notational fault in the first but in the second bestowing upon him high praise and ranking him among the finest composers of his time. His works include Masses, motets, and a very few secular songs.

Bibl.: Ed. Cornelis Lindenburg, *CMM* 9 (1956).

Regnart, Jacob [Jacques] (b. Douai, ca. 1540; d. Prague, 16 Oct. 1599). Composer. From 1557 served the Habsburgs in Prague and Vienna, with an interruption from 1568 to 1570 for study in Italy. By 1579 he was Vice-Kapellmeister in Prague, but by 1582 was in Innsbruck as Vice-Kapellmeister (later Kapellmeister) under Archduke Ferdinand. In 1596 he returned to his earlier post in Prague. His works include much sacred music (especially Masses and motets) and also a number of highly popular secular songs, many in light Italian styles but with German texts.

Bibl.: Ed. Walter Pass, *CMM* 62 (1972–75). Id., *Thematischer Katalog sämtlicher Werke Jacob Regnarts,* Tabulae musicae Austriacae, 5 (Vienna, 1969).

Rehfuss, Heinz (Julius) (b. Frankfurt am Main, 25 May 1917; d. Rochester, N.Y., 27 June 1988). Bass-baritone. He was raised in Neuchâtel, Switzerland, and studied singing with his father, Carl Rehfuss. Made his debut at Biel-Solothurn (1938), then appeared at the Stadttheater in Lucerne (1938–39) and at the Zurich Opera (1940–52); subsequently performed at a number of European houses in roles including Don Giovanni and Boris Godunov. Rehfuss taught at the Montreal Conservatory, the Eastman School, and SUNY–Buffalo.

Reich, Steve [Stephen] **(Michael)** (b. New York, 3 Oct. 1936). Composer. He took piano lessons, and studied drumming at age 14 with Roland Kohloff, a member of the New York Philharmonic. Studied philosophy at Cornell (B.A., 1957) and then composition in New York, privately with Hall Overton and at Juilliard with William Bergsma and Vincent Persichetti (1958–61); at Mills College (M.A., 1963) studied with Milhaud and Berio and became interested in Balinese and African music as well as electronic music.

In 1966 he founded an ensemble (Steve Reich and Musicians) for the performance of his own music, which toured extensively, including a 1986 world tour, and made several recordings. Taught at the New School for Social Research from 1969 to 1971. He studied drumming at the Institute for African Studies at the Univ. of Ghana in the summer of 1970; gamelan in Seattle and Berkeley (1973–74); Hebrew cantillation in 1976 in Jerusalem.

Reich's early works *It's Gonna Rain* (1965) and *Come Out* (1966) make use of spoken text recorded on tape, which is looped for infinite repetition and played back on separate tape recorders with a time delay, producing a kind of counterpoint known as "phasing." Phasing, combined with constant, steady pulse, is the central principle in most of Reich's composition. In *Violin Phase* (1967), two violins begin a repeated six-bar phrase in unison. One accelerates until it is an eighth note ahead of the other, then two more violins enter, highlighting elements of the repeated phrase. This extreme reduction of musical elements, involving repeated rhythmic patterns and harmonic stasis, led to Reich's reputation as one of the chief proponents of musical minimalism, a term first applied in the early 1970s. Later compositions expand this minimalist style (the phrase "pulse music" has also been applied) to include harmonic modulation. *The Desert Music* (1983) incorporates melodic, harmonic, and instrumental writing of increased importance.

Works: *Pitch Charts,* any instruments (1963); *Plastic Haircut,* film score, tape (1963); *Music for Three or More Pianos or Piano and Tape* (1964); *Oh Dem Watermelons,* film score (1965); *Melodica,* tape (1966); *Reed Phase,* soprano saxophone, tape (1966); *My Name Is,* tape recorders, performers, audience (1967); *Piano Phase,* 2 pianos, 2 marimbas (1967); *Slow Motion Sound,* tape (1967); *Pendulum Music,* microphones, amplifiers, loudspeakers (1968); *Four Log Drums,* phase-shifting pulse gate, 4 log drums (1969); *Pulse Music,* phase-shifting pulse gate (1969); *Four Organs,* 4 electric organs, maracas (1970); *Phase Patterns,* 4 electric organs (1970); *Drumming,* 2 female voices, piccolo, 4 pairs tuned bongo drums, 3 marimbas, 3 glockenspiels (1971); *Clapping Music,* 2 performers (1972); *Music for Mallet Instruments, Voices, and Organ* (1973); *Music for Pieces of Wood,* 5 paris tuned claves (1973); *Six Pianos* (1973); *Music for 18 Musicians* (1976); *Octet* (1979); *Variations for Winds, Strings, and Keyboard* (1979); *My Name Is,* tape (1980); *Music for a Large Ensemble* (1980); *Tehillim,* voices, winds, strings, percussion, 2 electric organs (1981); *Vermont Counterpoint,* piccolo, flute, alto flute, tape (1982); *Sextet,* percussion, 2 pianos (1984–85); *Impact,* dance music (1985); *New York Counterpoint,* clarinet, bass clarinet, tape (1985); *3 Movements,* orchestra (1985–86); *The Four Sections,* orchestra (1987); *Electric Counterpoint,* guitar, tape (1987); *Different Trains,* string quartet, tape (1988); *The Cave,* music theater collaboration with Beryl Korot, (1990–93; premiered Vienna, 1993); *Duet,* 2 solo violins, string ensemble (1993); *Nagoya Marimbas,* 2 marimbas (1994); *City Life,* 18 players (1995); *Proverb,* 3 sopranos, 2 tenors, 2 vibraphones, 4 synthesizers (1995).

Bibl.: K. Robert Schwarz, "Steve Reich: Music as a Gradual Process," *PNM* 19 (1980–81): 373–94; 20 (1981–82): 225–87. Steve Reich, *Writings about Music* (New York, 1974).

Reicha [Rejcha], **Antoine(-Joseph)** [Antonín, Anton] (b. Prague, 26 Feb. 1770; d. Paris, 28 May 1836). Composer and theorist. After his father's death he was adopted by his uncle, Josef Reicha, a cellist, concert director, and composer. In 1785 the family moved to Bonn, where Antoine played the violin and flute in the Hofkapelle alongside Beethoven and C. G. Neefe, both of whom may have given him composition lessons. After attending Bonn Univ., he moved to Hamburg to teach and compose. In Paris (1799–1801) operatic success eluded him, although several of his orchestral works were well received. Upon moving to Vienna in 1801, he cultivated friendships with Haydn and Beethoven and took lessons from Albrechtsberger and Salieri. He moved to Paris in 1808, and was appointed professor of counterpoint and fugue at the Conservatoire in 1818. Around this time he began publishing treatises, which ensured the broad dissemination of his theories: the *Traité de mélodie* (1814) was followed by the *Cours de composition musicale* (about 1816–18), a classroom harmony textbook that stresses a knowlege of contemporary usage. His most important treatise, *Traité de haute composition musicale* (1824–26), is a sequel to the earlier treatises; its praise of invertible counterpoint and practical music at the expense of simple counterpoint and "school music" provoked a controversy at the Conservatoire. Both Berlioz and Liszt began studying with Reicha in 1826. In 1833 Reicha published his *Art du compositeur dramatique,* a guide to writing opera and description of performing practice. In 1835 he succeeded Boieldieu at the Académie and took on César Franck as a pupil. His works include a number of operas, sacred and secular choral works, works for solo voices, symphonies, overtures, concertos, and many chamber works for winds and strings.

Bibl.: O. Šotolová, *Antonín Rejcha* (Prague, 1977) [with thematic catalog]. Michael Bulley, "Reicha's 13th Fugue," *MR* 46 (1985): 163–69.

Reichardt, Johann Friedrich (b. Königsberg, 25 Nov. 1752; d. Giebichenstein, near Halle, 27 June 1814). Composer and writer. He studied with his father, the lutenist Johann Reichardt (ca. 1720–80), and became a proficient lutenist, violinist, and singer; other teachers included J. F. Hartknoch, the organist C. G. Richter, and the violinist F. A. Veichtner. Reichardt enrolled at Königsberg Univ. (1768–71), then traveled widely, meeting, among others, J. A. P. Schulz, Franz Benda, C. P. E. Bach, Lessing, and Klopstock; he also had lessons with Kirnberger in Berlin and with Homilius, a Bach pupil, in Dresden. He returned to Königsberg in 1774 with a number of compositions and later that year published his *Über die deutsche komische Oper* as well as travel diaries and letters in *Briefe eines aufmerksamen Reisenden die Musik betreffend* (vol. 1, Frankfurt and Leipzig, 1774; vol. 2, Frankfurt and Breslau, 1776).

In 1775 he entered the service of Frederick the Great, succeeding Agricola as Kapellmeister to the Royal Berlin Opera. The position allowed him to continue his travels, which now included trips to Weimar, Venice, Vienna, Paris, Italy, and England; his circle of friends widened to include Goethe, Galuppi, and Gluck, as well as other leading artists and intellectuals; in 1783 he founded the Berlin Concert spirituel, and in 1789 collaborated with Goethe on the singspiel *Claudine von Villa Bella.* His sympathy for the French Revolution led to his dismissal from his post (1794), and he settled in Giebichenstein, near Halle. With the French invasion in 1806 Reichardt fled with his family to north Germany; the following year Jérome Buonaparte appointed him *Directeur général des théâtres et de son orchestre* in Kassel, but Reichardt renewed his travels in 1808. In 1809 he returned to Biebichenstein, where he made a meager living writing and composing. He is best known today for some 1,500 songs written in a variety of styles, from folklike strophic settings to through-composed dramatic scenes; he was perhaps the most versatile composer of lieder before Schubert. He also composed singspiels, including the popular *Die Geisterinsel* (after Shakespeare's *The Tempest,* Berlin, 1798).

Bibl.: Paul Sieber, *Johann Friedrich Reichardt als Musikästhetiker, seine Anschauungen über Wesen und Wirkung der Musik* (Baden-Baden, 1971). Händel-Haus Halle, *Johann Friedrich Reichardt (1752–1814): Komponist und Schriftsteller der Revolutionszeit* (Halle an der Saale, 1992). Dietrich Fischer-Dieskau, *Weil nicht alle Blütenträume reiften: Johann Friedrich Reichardt, Hofkapellmeister dreier Preussenkönige* (Stuttgart, 1992).

Reichardt, Louise (b. Berlin, 11 Apr. 1779; d. Hamburg, 17 Nov. 1826). Composer. The daughter of Johann Friedrich Reichardt, she settled by 1813 in Hamburg, where she taught singing and directed a women's chorus that became the core of the Hamburg Singverein

(1816). Known for her productions of Handel oratorios, she translated the texts and prepared the choruses for performances conducted by male colleagues. She composed over 90 songs and choruses, both sacred and secular, to Romantic texts.

Reiche, Gottfried (b. Weissenfels, 5 Feb. 1667; d. Leipzig, 6 Oct. 1734). Trumpeter. He moved to Leipzig in 1688, where he was named *Kunstgeiger* (1700), city piper (1706), and senior city piper (1719); from 1723 until 1734 he played all of J. S. Bach's first trumpet parts. His compositions include *Vier und zwantzig neue Quatricinia* (1696; R: Berlin, 1958).

Reicher-Kindermann, Hedwig (b. Munich, 15 July 1853; d. Trieste, 2 June 1883). Soprano. Father was baritone August Kindermann (1817–91). Sang in the chorus of the Munich Court Opera in 1870. Debut at Karlsruhe, 1871; at Berlin, 1874, as Pamina in *Die Zauberflöte* and Agatha in *Der Freischütz.* Sang at the opening of Bayreuth (1876) in first complete performance of *The Ring.* Joined Angelo Neumann's company in 1880, performing many Wagner roles throughout Europe. Final performance at age 29 as Brünnhilde in *Götterdämmerung.*

Reimann, Aribert (b. Berlin, 4 March 1936). Composer and pianist. He studied at the Hochschule für Musik in Berlin (1955–59), where his teachers included Blacher (composition), Pepping (counterpoint), and Rausch (piano). In 1958 he also studied musicology in Vienna. He performed frequently as an accompanist with singers, including Fischer-Dieskau. Taught at the Hamburg Hochschule für Musik from 1974 to 1983, when he joined the faculty at the Berlin Hochschule für Künste. His early music is influenced by Webern; in 1967, however, he abandoned serialism. Works include the operas *Ein Traumspiel* (1964), *Melusine* (1970), *Lear* (1976–78), *Die Gespenstersonate* (1983), *Troades* (1985), *Das Schloss* (1992); 2 ballets; orchestral music (Violin Concerto, 1959; 2 piano concertos, 1961, 1972; *Requiem,* soloists, chorus, orchestra, 1980–82; Double Concerto for Cello and Orchestra, 1986; *Fragmente für Orchester,* 1988; Nine Pieces for Orchestra, 1994); vocal music (*Impression IV,* soprano, piano, 1985; *Denn Bleiben ist nirgends, Sprechstimme,* orchestra, 1986); chamber music (Solo for Cello, 1982).

Bibl.: Georg Borchardt, "Hin zu hellem, lichtem Ton- Ein Blick in die Werkstatt des Komponisten Aribert Reimann," *NZfM* (1988): 22–28.

Reinagle, Alexander (b. Portsmouth, bapt. 23 Apr. 1756; d. Baltimore, 21 Sept. 1809). Composer. He studied with his father, Joseph Reinagle (d. ca. 1775), and with Raynor Taylor in Edinburgh. By 1778 he was teaching harpsichord in Glasgow. He traveled to London in 1783, to Hamburg in about 1784 (visiting C. P. E. Bach), and to Lisbon with his brother Hugh (ca. 1764–85) during 1784–85. In 1786 he arrived in New York, then soon settled in Philadelphia. There he revived the defunct City Concerts for the 1786–87 season and was in demand as a music teacher. He gave many concerts in Philadelphia, New York (1788–89), Baltimore (1791), and Boston (1792). From 1790 or 1791 Reinagle was a partner with the English actor Thomas Wignell and Wignell's successors in the New Company, a theatrical company that performed spoken and musical works (English light opera and ballet) in Philadelphia and Baltimore. Reinagle directed the orchestra from the piano and composed or arranged the music for the company. Almost all this music, for hundreds of productions, was lost in the fire that destroyed the Philadelphia New Theater in 1820. In 1803 he moved permanently to Baltimore. His most significant surviving works are 4 piano sonatas written in Philadelphia about 1790; they are the earliest piano pieces written in the U.S. He also wrote various choral pieces and songs, including *A Collection of . . . Scots Tunes with Variations* (London, ca. 1782), the first publication in the U.S. devoted entirely to secular music; orchestral music (all lost), various keyboard pieces, and 6 violin sonatas (London, 1783).

Bibl.: C. A. Horton, "Serious Art and Concert Music for Piano in America in the 100 Years from Alexander Reinagle to Edward MacDowell" (diss., Univ. of North Carolina, 1965). A. Krauss, "Alexander Reinagle, His Family Background and Early Professional Career," *American Music* (1986).

Reincken [Reinken, Reinike], **Johann Adam** [Jan Adams] (b. Wildeshausen, near Bremen, 27 Apr. 1623; d. Hamburg, 24 Nov. 1722). Composer and organist. He moved to Hamburg in 1654 and studied with Heinrich Scheidemann, was appointed organist of the Berghkercke in Deventer in 1657, then returned to Hamburg as Scheidemann's assistant (1658) and successor (1663). Famous in his time as an organist; in addition to organ music his compositions include a set of suites for strings, *Hortus musicus* (Hamburg, 1687; R: Amsterdam, 1886), from which J. S. Bach made keyboard arrangements (BWV 954, 965, 966).

Bibl.: *Johann Adam Reincken: Sämtliche Orgelwerke,* ed. Klaus Beckmann (Wiesbaden, 1974). *Collected Keyboard Works [of] Adam Reincken,* ed. Willi Apel, *CEKM* 16 (Rome, 1967).

Reinecke, Carl (Heinrich Carsten) (b. Altona, 23 June 1824; d. Leipzig, 10 Mar 1910). Teacher, composer. Son and pupil of music theorist and teacher Rudolf Reinecke (1795–1883). From 1843, active in Germany and Scandinavia as soloist and accompanist, with periods in Copenhagen, where he was court pianist (1846–48); Leipzig, where he was friendly with Mendelssohn and the Schumanns; and Paris, where he gave lessons to Liszt's daughters. From 1851 to 1854, taught piano and composition, Cologne Conservatory; 1854–59, music director in the town of Barmen; from 1860, conductor of the Gewandhaus Orchestra, Leipzig (to 1895), and professor of piano and free composition at the conservatory (director of studies from 1897 to his retirement in 1902), becoming one of the dominant figures and most sought-after teachers there. He maintained, even intensified the conservatory's reputation for musical conservatism, and had many noted pupils, including Grieg, Kretzschmar, Muck, Riemann, Sinding, Svendsen, Weingartner; also continued to tour as a pianist. A prolific composer, with 288 opus numbers, ranging from operas, an oratorio, and cantatas to 3 symphonies, concert overtures, concertos, including 4 for piano; much chamber music, songs, piano pieces, including sonatas, sonatinas, variations; piano method and studies; many piano editions and arrangements; especially noted for his music for children (*Kinderlieder* op. 37, 63, 75, 91, 135, 138, 154b, 196; Toy Symphony op. 239). He wrote many essays and books, including little books on Mozart's piano concertos (1891) and Beethoven's sonatas (1893, much republished) and sketches of musical figures he had known, *Gedenkblätter an berühmte Musiker* (Leipzig, 1900; 2nd. enlarged ed., 1910).

Bibl.: F. Reinecke, *Verzeichnis der Kompositionen von Carl Reinecke* (Leipzig, 1889).

Reiner, Fritz (b. Budapest, 19 Dec. 1888; d. New York, 15 Nov. 1963). Conductor. Studied composition with Koessler and piano with Thomán and Bartók at the Liszt Academy of Music, Budapest, and conducted the People's Opera, Budapest (1911–14), and the Dresden Hofoper (1914–22). After guest appearances in Europe Reiner settled in the U.S., becoming an American citizen in 1928; he served as music director of the Cincinnati Symphony (1922–31) and taught at the Curtis Institute (1931–41), where his pupils included Leonard Bernstein and Lukas Foss. Reiner conducted opera in Philadelphia (1932–33), San Francisco (1936–38), and at the Metropolitan Opera (1948–53), in addition to an appearance at Covent Garden (1936–37); in 1938 he began a ten-year tenure as music director of the Pittsburgh Symphony, then was appointed music director of the Chicago Symphony (1953–62); under his leadership it became one of the most distinguished of American orchestras.

Bibl.: Arthur J. Helmbrecht, *Fritz Reiner: The Comprehensive Discography of His Recordings* (n.p., 1978).

Reiner, Karel (b. Žatec, 27 June 1910; d. Prague, 17 Oct. 1979). Composer and performer. His father was a municipal cantor. Reiner studied law at the German Univ. in Prague (graduating in 1933); musicology at the Univ. of Prague; microtonal composition under Hába at the Prague Conservatory (1934–35). During the late 1930s he worked with the improvisational theater in Prague headed by Burian. After the war, during which he was sent to both the Dachau and Auschwitz concentration camps, he continued to be active as a performer of new music and as a composer. He also wrote music criticism and articles for *Rytmus,* 1935–38 and 1945–47. He first began composing in an atonal system and explored the microtonal techniques he had learned with Hába. He experimented with traditional forms (Concerto, bass clarinet, strings, percussion, 1965; Concertino, bassoon, winds, percussion, 1969) but eventually returned to techniques of the European avant-garde. Works include 1 opera (*Zakletá píseň* [Enchanted Song], Prague, 1951); orchestral works (*Promluvy* [Utterances], chamber orchestra, 1975; *Diptych,* 1977); and chamber and film music.

Reinhardt, Django [Jean Baptiste] (b. Liberchies, near Luttre, Belgium, 23 Jan. 1910; d. Fontainebleau, 16 May 1953). Jazz guitarist. With Stephane Grappelli he formed a string band, the Quintette du Hot Club de France (1935–39, 1946–49); their recordings include "Lady Be Good" (1934), "Djangology" (1935), and "Limehouse Blues" (1936). During the war years he led the quintet with a clarinetist replacing Grappelli (as on the recording "Nuages," 1940), and later a drummer replaced one of the three guitarists. Before rejoining Grappelli he worked briefly with Duke Ellington in the U.S. (1946). A fire in 1928 had mutilated two fingers of his left hand, but this in no way hindered his ability to provide a buoyantly swinging chordal accompaniment (as on Coleman Hawkins's recording "Crazy Rhythm," 1937) or to execute complex improvised phrases of breathtaking length. He brought Gypsy guitar traditions into jazz and also wrote music, including Gypsy waltzes, for guitar.

Bibl.: Charles Delaunay, *Django Reinhardt* (New York, 1982).

Reinken, Johann Adam. See Reincken, Johann Adam.

Reisenberg (Sherman), Nadia (b. Vilnius, Lithuania, 14 July 1904; d. New York, 10 June 1983). Pianist. Studied with Leonid Nikolayev at the St. Petersburg Conservatory; moved to the U.S. in 1922, where she continued her studies with Alexander Lambert and Hofmann, making her American debut the same year with the City Symphony of New York. She appeared frequently with the New York Philharmonic and performed chamber music with the Budapest Quartet; her performances on radio included the complete piano concertos of Mozart in 1939. She taught at the Curtis Institute, Queens College, CUNY, Mannes College, and the Juilliard School.

Bibl.: Robert Sherman and Alexander Sherman, *Nadia Reisenberg: A Musician's Scrapbook* (College Park, Md., 1986).

Reissiger, Karl Gottlieb (b. Belzig, 31 Jan. 1798; d. Dresden, 7 Nov. 1859). Composer and conductor. Student at the Thomasschule in Leipzig (1811–18), studied piano with Schicht. Began theology studies at Univ. of Leipzig; left to pursue music composition and singing. Studied theory with Salieri in Vienna (1821), composition and singing with Winter in Munich (1822). His first opera, *Didone abbandonata,* was performed successfully in Dresden, 1824. Given funds to study music education in France and Italy; returned to Berlin (1825) as champion of German opera. Named *Hofkapellmeister,* 1828; directed first performance of *Rienzi.*

Composed over 60 songs, 9 operas, 1 oratorio *(David)*, Requiem, 9 Latin Masses, 4 German Masses, other sacred works; chamber music, piano works.

Bibl.: Kurt Kreiser, *Carl Gottlieb Reissiger: sein Leben nebst einigen Beiträgen zur Geschichte der Konzertwesens in Dresden* (Dresden, 1918).

Reizenstein, Franz (Theodor) (b. Nuremberg, 7 June 1911; d. London, 15 Oct. 1968). Composer and pianist. He studied at the Hochschule für Musik in Berlin (1930–34) with Leonid Kreutzer (piano) and Hindemith (composition). When the Nazis came to power he went to London, where he studied with Lambert and Vaughan Williams at the Royal College of Music (1934–36); studied piano privately with Solomon. Taught piano at the Royal Academy of Music (1958–68) and the Royal Manchester College of Music (1962–68). Performed his own and many of Hindemith's pieces. His choral work *Voices of Night* (1951) was quite successful. He wrote 2 radio operas, *Men against the Sea* (1949) and *Anna Kraus* (1952); an oratorio, *Genesis* (1958); 2 piano concertos (1941, 1956–61), a cello concerto (1936), a violin concerto (1953), other orchestral music, and many pieces of chamber and piano music.

Rellstab, Johann Carl Friedrich (b. Berlin, 27 Feb. 1759; d. there, 19 Aug. 1813). Music publisher and composer. He performed in student concerts at the Joachimsthal Gymnasium (1768–75) and studied keyboard with J. F. Agricola (from 1773) and composition with C. F. C. Fasch (1776–78). In 1779 he inherited his father's printing firm and expanded the business, adding a publishing firm and music shop; he established a lending music library (1783) and issued music prints (from 1785). In 1787 he instituted a series of subscription concerts. After the press shut down in 1812, he taught singing, keyboard, and composition. From 1808 to 1813 he was critic for the *Vossische Zeitung*. His compositions include a singspiel, cantatas, songs, and instrumental music. His son **(Heinrich Friedrich) Ludwig Rellstab** (b. Berlin, 13 Apr. 1799; d. there, 27 Nov. 1860) was an important music critic and poet; Schubert set 7 of his poems in his *Schwanengesang* cycle.

Remacha, Fernando (b. Tudela, 15 Dec. 1898). Composer. Received initial instruction in his hometown and at Pamplona; later enrolled at the Madrid Conservatory. As Prix de Rome recipient for 1923, he went to Italy as a student of Malipiero; joined the Madrid Symphony as violist in 1928; received the National Music Prize in 1932. The Civil War drove him back to his home, where he remained until becoming director of the Pamplona Conservatory from 1957; received an honorary doctorate from the Univ. of Navarre in 1973. His music includes the oratorio *Jesucristo en la cruz*, soprano, tenor, chorus, and orchestra, his acknowledged masterpiece; Guitar Concerto (1955); *Rapsodia de Estella*, piano and orchestra (1958); and some chamber works.

Reményi [Hoffmann], **Ede** [Eduard] (b. Miskolc, 17 Jan. 1828; d. San Francisco, 15 May 1898). Violinist. Studied at Vienna Conservatory with Joseph Böhm, 1842–45. Debuted at Pest in 1846, at London in 1848. Exiled for political reasons; lived in U.S., 1848–52. Toured Europe, 1852–53, with Brahms. Court violinist to Queen Victoria, 1854–59. Granted amnesty and named Austrian court violinist in 1860. Settled in Paris (1875), in London (1877). Returned to U.S. in 1878. World tour, 1887. Died while playing a concert.

Remington, Emory (b. Rochester, N.Y., 22 Dec. 1891; d. there, 11 Dec. 1971). Trombonist. He studied with Gardell Simons, Edward Llewellyn, and Ernest Williams; played first trombone in the Rochester Philharmonic (1923–49), and taught at the Eastman School from 1922 until his death; best known as an influential teacher.

Renaud, Maurice (Arnold) (b. Bordeaux, 24 July ?1861; d. Paris, 16 Oct. 1933). Baritone. He studied in Paris and Brussels and sang at the Théâtre de la Monnaie, Brussels (1883–90), the Opéra-comique, Paris (1890–91), and the Opéra (1891–1902); performed at Covent Garden a number of times from 1897, and sang with the Manhattan Opera (1906–7, 1909–10), the Metropolitan (1910–12), and in Chicago and Boston. A versatile performer, Renaud's many roles included Don Giovanni, Rigoletto, Athanaël *(Thaïs)*, Escamillo, Nevers *(Les Huguenots)*, and Coppelius, Dapertutto, and Miracle *(Les contes d'Hoffmann)*.

Bibl.: Jacques Erwarn, *Renaud* (Paris, 1982).

Renié, Henriette (b. Paris, 18 Sept. 1875; d. there, 1 Mar. 1956). Harpist and composer. Studied at the Paris Conservatory with Alphonse Hasselmans, also taking lessons with Lenepveu and Dubois in harmony and composition; performed her own harp concerto at the age of 18; other compositions for harp and orchestra include *Pièce symphonie* and *Légende et Danse caprice*, in addition to solo and chamber works for harp. Taught for a number of years at the conservatory.

Resinarius [Harzer], **Balthazar** (b. Tetschen, ca. 1485; d. Leipa [now Česká Lípa], 12 Apr. 1544). Composer. Studied under Isaac; attended Leipzig Univ. from 1515, returning to Tetschen in 1523, where he converted to Lutheranism, eventually becoming bishop of nearby Leipa. His compositions, all published by Rhau, are designed for use in Lutheran church services. Numerous later manuscript copies attest to their considerable popularity.

Resnik, Regina (b. New York, 30 Aug. 1922). Soprano, mezzo-soprano. Studied with Rosalie Miller and in 1942 sang Lady Macbeth with the New Opera Company, New York. After appearances the following year in Mexico City she joined the Metropolitan, making her debut in 1944 as Leonora *(Il trovatore)*; other roles included Donna Anna, Donna Elvira, Leonora *(Fidelio),* Alice *(Falstaff),* and Sieglinde, a role she also performed at Bayreuth in 1953. In 1955, as her voice changed, she began to take on mezzo-soprano roles, including Princess Eboli *(Don Carlos)* and Mistress Quickly *(Falstaff).* Resnik has performed at many leading houses including those at Covent Garden, Salzburg, and Vienna.

Reson [Rezon], **Johannes** (fl. ca. 1425–35). Composer. The only source of information about his life is the text of one possibly autobiographical rondeau, from which, however, only vague generalities can be inferred. A few pieces carry his name in manuscript copies; clear musical links with these form the basis of modern ascriptions of a small number of others. He wrote a cyclic Mass, several other sacred compositions, and two rondeaux.

Respighi, Ottorino (b. Bologna, 9 July 1879; d. Rome, 18 Apr. 1936). Composer. He studied with Torchi and Martucci at the Liceo musicale in Bologna (1891–1901). He visited Russia twice, during 1900–1901 and 1902–3, playing viola in the Imperial Opera Orchestra in St. Petersburg and studying with Rimsky-Korsakov, who had great influence on his orchestration. From 1903 to 1908 he was active as a string player and a pianist. During 1908–9 he was in Berlin. In 1913 he became professor of composition at the Liceo (later Conservatorio) di S. Cecilia; he was appointed director in 1924 but retired in 1926 in order to devote himself to composing and conducting. He toured the U.S. in 1925–26 and in 1932 as a pianist and conductor. He also accompanied his wife, Elsa Olivieri-Sangiacomo Respighi (b. 1894), a singer and composer who published a biography of her husband in 1954.

Respighi's best-known works are *Fontane di Roma* (1916) and *Pini di Roma* (1924), two symphonic poems notable for the colorful orchestration that was perhaps his most characteristic musical trait. He was increasingly drawn to opera during the last decade of his life. *La bella dormente nel bosco* was originally written for marionettes (Rome, 1922) and then for child mimes (Turin, 1934) and is among his most successful works. Respighi was elected to the Reale Accademia d'Italia in 1932.

Works: *Opera. Re Enzo,* comic opera (1905); *Semirama* (1910); *Marie-Victoire* (1913–14); *Scherzo veneziano* (1913–14); *La bella dormente nel bosco* (1916–21); *Belfagor* (1921–22); *La campana sommersa* (1923–27); *Belkis, regina di Saba,* ballet (1930–31); *Maria Egiziaca* (1929–32); *La fiamma* (1930–33); *Lucrezia* (1935; completed by Elsa Respighi, 1936). *Orchestra. Piano Concerto* (1902); *Suite* (1902–5); *Sinfonia drammatica* (1913–14); *Fontane di Roma* (1914–16); *Ballata delle Gnomidi* (1918–20); *Adagio con variazioni,* cello, orchestra (1920); *Concerto gregoriano,* violin, orchestra (1921); *Pini di Roma* (1923–24); *Concerto in modo misolidio,* piano, orchestra (1925); *Poema autunnale,* violin, orchestra (1920–25); *Trittico botticelliano* (1927); *Impressioni brasiliane* (1928); *Feste romane* (1928); *Metamorphoseon modi XII* (1929–30); *Concerto a 5,* oboe, trumpet, piano, violin, double bass, strings (1933); other orchestral pieces.

Vocal. With ensemble: *Aretusa,* mezzo, orchestra (1910); *La sensitiva,* mezzo, orchestra (1914); *Il tramonto,* voice, strings (1914); *La primavera,* soloists, chorus, orchestra (1918–19); *Lauda per la Natività del Signore,* soloists, chorus, woodwinds, 2 pianos (1928–30). Voice and piano: *Nebbie, Nevicata, Stornellatrice, 5 canti all'antica* (1906); *6 melodie* (1909); *6 liriche* (1909); *6 liriche* (1912); *4 rispetti toscani* (1914); *Deità silvane* (1917); *5 liriche* (1917); *E se un giorno tornasse* (1919); *4 liriche* (1920); *4 liriche su parole di poeti armeni* (1920); *3 vocalizzi* (1933).

Chamber music. 2 string quartets (1907, 1924); Sonata, violin, piano (1916–17); other smaller pieces as well as organ and piano music.

Bibl.: Elsa Respighi, *Ottorino Respighi: Dati biografici ordinati* (Milan, 1954); trans. Eng., abridged (1962). Elio Battaglia, *Ottorino Respighi* (Turin, 1985). Pierluigi Alverà, *Respighi* (New York, 1986). David Bryant, ed., *Il Novecento musicale italiano: tra neoclassicismo e negoticismo* (Florence, 1988).

Rethberg, Elisabeth [Sattler, Lisbeth] (b. Schwarzenberg, Germany, 22 Sept. 1894; d. Yorktown Heights, N.Y., 6 June 1976). Soprano. Studied at the Dresden Conservatory and with Otto Watrin; sang with the Dresden Opera (1915–1922), then made her Metropolitan Opera debut in 1922 as Aida. She remained with the Metropolitan for twenty seasons but also performed frequently at Covent Garden, Salzburg, and the principal Italian houses. Rethberg was best known for her performances of the Mozart and Verdi heroines, and the Wagnerian roles of Elsa, Eva, Sieglinde, and Elisabeth.

Reubke, (Friedrich) Julius (b. Hausneindorf, near Quedlinburg, 23 Mar. 1834; d. Pillnitz, near Dresden, 3 June 1858). Composer, pianist, and organist. Son of organ builder Adolf Reubke (1805–75). His early training was with Hermann Bönicke. Later he studied with Kullak and Adolf Bernhard Marx at the Berlin Conservatory (1851), where he was awarded high honors. In 1856 he went to Weimar, where he studied with Liszt. There he completed his Piano Sonata in B♭ and Organ Sonata in C minor on the 94th Psalm in 1857. His other works include solo compositions for piano and organ.

Reusner [Reussner], **Esaias** (b. Löwenberg, Silesia [now Lwówek Śląski, Poland], 29 Apr. 1636; d. Cölln, Berlin, 1 May 1679). Composer and lutenist. He served as lutenist to Georg III, Duke of Silesia (1654–72), and as a chamber musician in Berlin at the court of the Elector Friedrich Wilhelm of Brandenburg (1674–79). His 2 collections of lute suites, *Delitiae testudinis* (n.p., 1667) and *Neue Lauten-früchte* (Berlin, 1676), are early examples of a German composer employing the French lute style.

Reutter, (Johann Adam Joseph Karl) Georg (von) (b. Vienna, bapt. 6 Apr. 1708; d. there, 11 Mar. 1772). Composer. He studied with his father and took composition from Caldara; went to Italy in 1729 or 1730, and was appointed court composer on his return in 1731. He took on the duties of Kapellmeister at St. Stephen's Cathedral from about 1736, succeeding his father officially in the post in 1738; he also was appointed second court Kapellmeister (1747) and later first Kapellmeister (1769). In 1739–40 he engaged the young Haydn as a chorister at St. Stephen's. A prolific composer whose output includes a large number of operas, all premiered in Vienna, as well as numerous sacred works.

Reutter, Hermann (b. Stuttgart, 17 June 1900; d. there, 1 Jan. 1985). Composer. Studied at the Munich Academy of Music (1920–23), where his teachers included Walter Courvoisier (composition), Franz Dorfmüller (piano), Karl Erler (voice), and Ludwig Mayer (organ). He established himself as a composer and a pianist; toured the U.S. seven times as an accompanist with singer Sigrid Onegin. He taught composition at the Stuttgart Musik Hochschule (1932–36) and then became director of the Berlin Staatliche Hochschule für Musik (1936–45). From 1952 he taught composition and lieder classes at the Staatliche Hochschule für Musik in Stuttgart, where he became director in 1956. He also taught at the Munich Academy of Music, and as a visiting professor in the U.S. and Japan. Although he composed in virtually every genre, he is perhaps best known as a composer of songs. He was influenced by Hindemith early on but then adopted a more simplified late Romantic style, discarding the notion of experiment in music.

Works: *Opera. Saul* (1928; rev. 1947); *Der verlorene Sohn* (1929; rev. as *Die Rückkehr des verlorenen Sohnes* (1952); *Doktor Johannes Faust* (1934–46; rev. 1955); *Odysseus* (1940–42); *Der Weg nach Freundschaft* (1948); *Don Juan und Faust* (1950); *Die Witwe von Ephesus* (1953; rev. 1966); *Die Brücke von San Luis Rey* (1954); *Hamlet* (1980). *Orchestra.* 3 piano concertos (1925, 1929, 1944); Violin Concerto (1930); Concerto for 2 Pianos and Orchestra (1949); Symphony for Strings (1960). Also 2 ballets, choral music, numerous songs, chamber and piano music.

Bibl.: Heinrich Lindlar, ed., *Hermann Reutter: Werk und Wirken: Festschrift der Freunde* (Mainz, 1965).

Revelli, William D(onald) (b. Spring Gulch, Colo., 12 Feb. 1902). Band director. He studied at the Chicago Musical College (1918–22) and the Columbia School of Music in Chicago (1922–25); in 1925 became supervisor of music in Hobart, Ind., where he organized a band that achieved national prominence. In 1935 he was appointed band director and chairman of the wind department at the Univ. of Michigan, remaining there until his retirement in 1971; during his tenure the university symphonic band embarked on a number of tours, notably in 1961 to the Soviet Union, eastern Europe, and the Middle East.

Revueltas, Silvestre (b. Santiago Papasquiaro, Durango, 31 Dec. 1899; d. Mexico City, 5 Oct. 1940). Composer and violinist. Began violin studies in Colima in 1907, continuing at the Instituto Juarez, Durango, in 1911; 1913–16, studied at Mexico City with Rocabruna (violin) and Tello (composition). Traveling to the U.S., he attended St. Edward College in Austin, 1916–18, then the Chicago Musical College, 1918–20 and 1922–24, where he first was the pupil of Sametini (violin) and Borowski (composition), then of Kochansky and Sevlik. In the intervening two years and from 1924 to 1926 he concertized widely in Mexico, often accompanied by Chávez at the piano. Returning to the U.S. in 1926, he played in and directed orchestras in San Antonio and Mobile; in 1929 Chávez named him assistant conductor of the Mexico Symphony, a post he held until 1935, when he formed the short-lived National Symphony. A 1937 Spanish tour brought him into contact with the Republican government there, which he served as a cultural official for a short time. After his return to Mexico his life crumbled into dissoluteness, poverty, and alcoholism; he died on the day of the belated premiere of his ballet *El renacuajo paseador* (1933).

Revueltas' style is a distinctive mix of folk elements such as the mariachi band tradition with fragmentary, if tuneful, thematic material and a dissonant harmonic language. He often added an infusion of sharp wit (as in the tone poems *Janitzio,* 1933, and *Caminos,* 1934) or focused on lively rhythmic interplay and complex meters (as in the tone poem *Sensemayá,* 1937–38, his best-known work).

Works: symphonic poems, including *Cuauhnahuac* (1930), *Esquinas* (1930), *Ventanas* (1931), *Alcancías* (1932), and *Colorines* (1932); ballets, including *La coronela* (incomplete); *8 x Radio* (1933), *Planos* (1934), *Homenaje a Federico García Lorca* (1935), *Troka* (1940), and *Tres sonetos* (1940) for small orchestra; *La noche de los Mayas* (1939), *Itinerarios* (1940), and *Paisajes* (1940) for orchestra; vocal/orchestral works, including *Ranas* (1931), *El Tecolote* (1931), and *Parias* (1940); music for films *Redes* (1935), *Vámonos con Pancho Villa* (1936), *El Indio* (1938), *Ferrocarriles de Baja California* (1938), *Los de Abajo* (1939), and *Bajo el signo de la muerte* (1939); chamber music, including 3 string quartets (1930–32) and 3 *piezas serias,* woodwind quintet (1940); songs.

Bibl.: *Composers of the Americas* 1 (Washington, D.C., 1955), pp. 71–83 [includes works list]. Silvestre Revueltas, *Silvestre Revueltas por él mismo: Apuntes autobiográficos, diarios, correspondencia y otros escritos de un gran músico* (Mexico, 1989).

Rey, Cemal Reşit (b. Jerusalem, 24 Sept. 1904; d. Istanbul, 7 Oct. 1985). Composer. At age 9 he went to Paris to study piano with Marguerite Long. He later studied composition with Raoul Laparra and Fauré, and conducting with Henri Derosse. He returned to Istanbul to teach at the conservatory in 1923. His subsequent appointments included music director of Radio Ankara (1938), conductor of the Istanbul City Orchestra (from 1945), and music director of Radio Istanbul (1949–50). His compositional style is influenced by traditional Turkish music; many of his pieces are on Turkish subjects. His works include the operas *Vann Marek* (1922); *Sultan Cem* (1923); *Zeybek* (1926); *Tchelebi* (1945); *Benli Hürmüz* (1965). For orchestra: 3

symphonies (1941, 1950, 1968); *Scènes turques* (1928); *Karagöz* (1931); Violin Concerto (1939); Piano Concerto (1948); 4 symphonic poems. Also wrote chamber music (string quartet, 1935); piano and choral music.

Reyer [Rey], **(Louis-Etienne-) Ernest** (b. Marseilles, 1 Dec. 1823; d. Le Lavandon, Var, 15 Jan. 1909). Composer. He was sent to Algiers in 1839 to work as a civil servant with his uncle Louis Farrenc. There he composed primarily smaller works. In 1847 he composed *Messe pour l'arrivée du Duc d'Aumale à Alger.* The following year he moved to Paris to pursue a musical career. Although he was an ardent fan of the music of Wagner, his own music is more classical in style. His compositions include 5 operas, cantatas, other smaller vocal pieces, and piano works. Music critic of *Journal des débats;* contributed articles to *Revue française, La presse, Moniteur universal, Courrier de Paris.* His travel journals, *Notes de musique,* detailing his trips through Germany (1863) and to Cairo (1871), were published in 1875; also wrote essays on Wagner and Berlioz (collected and published in 1909 as *Quarante ans de musique*).

Bibl.: Henri de Curzon, *Ernest Reyer: Sa vie et ses oeuvres* (Paris, 1923).

Reynolds, Roger (Lee) (b. Detroit, 13 July 1934). Composer. He studied at the Univ. of Michigan, where he first took a degree in engineering (1957) and then studied composition with Finney and Gerhard. He was one of the founders of the avant-garde ONCE festival in Ann Arbor. In 1962–63 he worked at the Cologne electronic music studios. From 1966 to 1969 he was in Japan as a Fellow of the Institute of Current World Affairs. Returned to the U.S. in 1969 to join the faculty of the Univ. of California, San Diego, where he was founder and director of the Project for Music Experiment (1972–77).

Reynolds's music calls on a wide range of resources, including traditional instruments, electronic and computer-generated sounds, serial techniques, graphic notation, and musical quotation. His theater piece *The Emperor of Ice Cream* (1962) reveals his long-term interest in the combination of the musical with the extramusical. Many of his pieces are based on text: *Whispers Out of Time* (1988), winner of the 1989 Pulitzer Prize, is based on John Ashberry's poem "Self-Portrait in a Convex Mirror." He has published two books, *Mind Models: New Forms of Musical Experience* (New York, 1975) and *A Searcher's Path: A Composer's Ways* (Brooklyn, 1987).

Other works include, for the stage, *I/O: A Ritual for 23 Performers* (1970); for orchestra, *Graffiti* (1964); *Threshold* (1967); *Between,* with electronics (1968); *Archipelago,* chamber orchestra, computer (1982); *Transfigured Wind II,* flute, orchestra, computer (1984); also many pieces of chamber music and vocal music.

Bibl.: Gilbert Chase, *Roger Reynolds: Profile of a Composer* (New York, 1982).

Reynolds, Verne (Becker) (b. Lyons, Kans., 18 July 1926). Horn player and composer. He studied violin, piano, and horn before enrolling at the Cincinnati Conservatory of Music (B.M., 1950); subsequently worked with Cecil Burleigh at the Univ. of Wisconsin (M.M., 1951) and with Herbert Howells at the Royal College of Music. Reynolds taught at the Univ. of Wisconsin (1950–53) and Indiana Univ. (1954–59) before joining the faculty of the Eastman School of Music in 1959 as a horn instructor; from 1959 to 1968 he served as principal horn with the Rochester Philharmonic. Compositions include *Horn vibes* (horn, vibraphone, 1986); *Songs of the Seasons* (soprano, horn, piano, 1988); Divertimento (oboe, horn, piano, 1989).

Rezniček, E(mil) N(ikolaus) von (b. Vienna, 4 May 1860; d. Berlin, 2 Aug. 1945). Composer and conductor. Studied law at Graz and music with Wilhelm Mayer. At the Leipzig Conservatory he studied with Reinecke and Jadassohn. Court conductor at Mannheim, 1896–99. Settled in Berlin in 1902; conducted the Comic Opera, 1909–11. Taught theory at the Berlin Conservatory (from 1906). Director of Warsaw Opera and Philharmonic Orchestra, 1907–9. Taught at Hochschule für Musik, 1920–26. Compositions include 4 symphonies; the operas *Donna Diana* (1894), *Till Eulenspiegel* (1902); the operetta *Die Angst vor der Ehe* (1914); Violin Concerto (1925); organ works; piano pieces; songs.

Bibl.: Richard Specht, *Emil Nikolaus von Rezniček: Eine vorläufige Studie* (Vienna, 1923).

Rhau [Rhaw], **Georg** (b. Eisfeld an der Werre, Suhl, 1488; d. Wittenberg, 6 Aug. 1548). Publisher, composer. He earned a B.A. at Wittenberg (1512–14), then worked in his uncle's publishing firm there until 1518. He then served two years as Kantor of the Thomaskirche in Leipzig; for the 1519 Luther–Eck disputations there he composed a twelve-voice Mass. After teaching briefly in Eisleben and Hildburghausen, he returned in 1523 to publishing in Wittenberg; his firm became central to the Reformation movement. His publications include many first editions of writings by Luther, Melanchthon, and others; an original *Enchiridion* on musical theory; many theoretical works of Agricola, Johann Walter, and others; and 15 major musical collections ranging from contemporary polyphony to Reformed church songs.

Rheinberger, Joseph (Gabriel) (b. Vaduz, Liechtenstein, 17 Mar. 1839; d. Munich, 25 Nov. 1901). Teacher, composer, organist. Beginning music lessons at 4, he showed great aptitude as organist and composer; from 1851 lived in Munich, first as a student at the conservatory (to 1854), also having private lessons with Franz Lachner, earning his living as church organist and teacher, and composing prolifically, beginning to publish his work in 1859. From 1859 he taught at the conservatory, first piano, then (1860–65) theory and composition; from 1867, professor of organ and composition at the new conservatory, becoming one of the most sought-after composition teachers of the time, of a rigorously classical, conservative character (pupils included Humperdinck, Wolf-Ferrari, Horatio Parker, Furtwängler). His music, also of a classical, conservative tendency, includes operas, incidental music, 2 symphonies, and other orchestral pieces; many chamber works; 4 piano sonatas and other pieces; 13 Masses, 3 Requiems, and other sacred works; many secular choral works and partsongs; some 70 solo songs. But it is primarily for his organ music, especially some of his 20 sonatas and his 2 concertos, that he is still remembered. He held many musical posts in Munich, most notably director of the court chapel from 1877 with title of court Kapellmeister.

Bibl.: H. J. Irmen, *Joseph Rheinberger: Thematisches Verzeichnis seiner Kompositionen* (Regensburg, 1975).

Rhodes, Harold (b. 1910). Piano maker. Around 1930 he established the Harold Rhodes School of Popular Piano, a chain of schools in the U.S. During World War II he taught piano to his fellow servicemen, and invented the 29-note Air Corps Piano (1942), which could be played by bedridden hospital patients. With the guitar builder Leo Fender he developed an electric piano, and in the late 1950s and early 1960s built the Rhodes electric piano.

Rhodes, Phillip (Carl) (b. Forest City, N.C., 6 June 1940). Composer. He earned a B.A. at Duke Univ. (1962), where he studied composition with Iain Hamilton, and then an M.M. at Yale (1963), where his teachers included Donald Martino, Mel Powell, Gunther Schuller, and George Perle. He served on the faculties of Amherst College (1968–69), the Univ. of Louisville (1969–72), and Carleton College (1974–); was composer-in-residence in Cicero, Ill. (1966–68). Works include 2 operas: *The Gentle Boy* (1979–80; rev. 1987; Tallahassee, 12 June 1987); *The Magic Pipe* (1989); 1 ballet: *About Faces* (1970); orchestra music: *4 Movements* (1962); *3 B's* (1971); Concerto for Bluegrass Band and Orchestra (1974); other orchestral pieces; also works for band, chamber music (string quartet, 1973; Quartet, flute, harp, violin, cello, 1975); and vocal music, including a cantata, *On the Morning of Christ's Nativity* (1976).

Riadis [Eleftheriadis; Khu], **Emilios** (b. Salonica, 13 May 1885; d. there, 17 July 1935). Composer. He originally studied in Salonica with Dimitrios Lalas, who had worked with Wagner. He then studied in Munich from 1908 to 1910 with Mottl, Walbunn, and Mayer-Gschrey. He traveled to Paris in 1910, where he worked primarily as a composer, studying there with Charpentier and Ravel. He then returned to Salonica, where in 1915 he joined the faculty at the conservatory. He was mainly a composer of songs in a lyrical style that bore the inflections of Greek folk music. His music was tonal and occasionally impressionistic, without being as thoroughly chromatic as that of his peers in western Europe. Works include dramatic pieces (the opera *La route verte* from around 1914 exists in sketches) and instrumental music, many movements of which are undated or missing. There are, however, many published songs.

Ricci, Federico (b. Naples, 22 Oct. 1809; d. Conegliano, near Treviso, 10 Dec. 1877). Composer. Entered the Naples Conservatory in 1818, studying with Zingarelli, Raimondi, his brother Luigi, and Bellini. There he composed 2 Masses and a symphony. He left in 1829 to follow his brother to Rome. First opera was a collaboration with his brother, *Il colonello* (1835), the first of four collaborations between the two; the most famous of these was *Crispino e la comare* (1850). Ricci completed 18 operas, the most successful of which were *La prigione di Edimburgo* (1838); *Un duello sotto Richelieu* (1839); *Luigi Rolla* (Florence, 1841); *Corrado d'Altamura* (1841), based on the same plot as Verdi's *Oberto;* and the French opéra bouffe *Une folie à Rome* (1869). Other compositions include 2 Masses, 3 cantatas, smaller sacred pieces, songs.

Ricci, Luigi (b. Naples, 8 June or 8 July 1805; d. Prague, 31 Dec. 1859). Composer. Brother of Federico Ricci, with whom he collaborated on 4 operas. Entered Naples Conservatory in 1814, studied the violin, later keyboard and composition. Teachers included Furno, Zingarelli, and Generali. His first opera, *L'impresario in angustie,* was produced in 1823. His debut at the Teatro nuovo in Naples came with *La cena frastornata* (1824). After a series of failures (1829–31), the semiseria *Chiara di Rosembergh* was well received (1831). Appointed *maestro di cappella* at Trieste in 1836. Gave up composing opera from 1838–45, concentrating on sacred music. Directed the premiere of Verdi's *Il corsaro* at the Teatro grande; directed the 1844–45 season at Odessa and 1847–48 at Copenhagen with the twins Franziska and Ludmilla Stolz. Beset by mental illness, he died in an asylum. Compositions include 30 operas, more than 20 Masses, other sacred music, songs, duets.

Ricci, Ruggiero [Roger; Rich, Woodrow Wilson] (b. San Bruno, Calif., 24 July 1918). Violinist. He studied with Persinger and made his debut in San Francisco at the age of 10; the following year he performed the Mendelssohn concerto in New York and gave his Carnegie Hall debut. Ricci continued his studies with Michel Piastro, Georg Kulenkampff, and Paul Stassevitch, and embarked on a highly successful European tour in 1932, subsequently touring the Soviet Union a number of times and completing his first world tour in 1957. His extensive repertory included all the concertos of Paganini; he premiered the rediscovered Fourth Concerto in 1971, as well as concertos of Ginastera, Gottfried von Einem, and Gerard Schurmann. Taught at Indiana Univ. and the Juilliard School.

Rice, Edward Everett (b. Brighton, Mass., 21 Dec. 1848; d. New York, 16 Nov. 1924). Composer. Could not read or write musical notation. Compositions are burlesques and vaudevilles; the best known are *Evangeline* (1874), *Hiawatha* (1880), *Adonis* (1884), *The Corsair* (1887), *1492* (1893), and *Excelsior, Jr.* (1895). Directed Rice's Extravaganza Combination and Rice's Surprise Party, which introduced new burlesques in Boston and later revived his music.

Bibl.: Deane L. Root, *American Popular Stage Music, 1860–1880* (Ann Arbor, 1981).

Rice, Thomas Dartmouth ("Daddy") (b. New York, 20 May 1808; d. there, 19 Sept. 1860). Minstrel performer. The first solo blackface performer. Created his famous "Jim Crow" act ca. 1828 in Louisville. The song was the first American song to become an international hit; this created a new genre of entertainment, "Ethiopian opera," featuring blackface performers and songs. Other hit shows included *Oh! Hush or the Virginny Cupids* (1883), *Jumbo Jum* (1838), and *Otello* (1845), a parody on Shakespeare.

Bibl.: Robert C. Tell, *Blacking Up: The Minstrel Show in Nineteenth-Century America* (New York, 1974).

Rich, Buddy [Bernard] (b. New York, 30 June 1917; d. Los Angeles, 2 Apr. 1987). Jazz drummer and bandleader. A professional tap dancer and drummer from early childhood, he joined the clarinetist Joe Marsala's swing combo (1937–38) and then big bands, including those of Harry James (1938–39, 1953–54, 1956–57, 1961–66), Artie Shaw (1939), and Tommy Dorsey (1939–42, 1944–45, 1954–55). He toured with Jazz at the Philharmonic from 1947 and recorded with Charlie Parker (1949–50). He led groups regularly from 1966 until his death, including a big band that recorded the album *Mercy, Mercy* (1968). An irrepressibly energetic drummer, Rich demonstrated his dexterity on the album *Buddy Rich vs. Max Roach* (1959).

Bibl.: Doug Meriwether, Jr., *We Don't Play Requests: A Musical Biography-Discography of Buddy Rich* (Chicago, 1984). Mel Tormé, *Traps, the Drum Wonder: The Life of Buddy Rich* (New York, 1991).

Richafort, Jean (b. probably in Hainaut, ca. 1480; d. ?Bruges, ca. 1548). Composer. From 1507 until 1509 *maître de chapelle* at St. Rombaud of Mechelin. Was somehow associated with the French royal chapel in succeeding years, traveling with it to Italy in 1516. From 1542 to 1547 was *maître de chapelle* at St. Gilles in Bruges. His stature can be deduced from the many surviving sources of his music (including a posthumous print of 19 motets), frequent borrowings from his compositions, and statements by figures such as Glarean and Ronsard. Works include Masses (parodies); Magnificats; motets (one of which is the basis for the earliest known full-fledged parody Masses, by Divitis and Mouton); chansons; 2 secular Latin motets.

Bibl.: Ed. Harry Elzinga, *CMM* 81 (1979–).

Richard I, Coeur de Lion (b. Oxford, Sept. 1157; d. Limoges, 11 Apr. 1199). King of England (1189–99), trouvère poet and composer. Son of Henry II of England and Eleanor of Aquitaine; lived principally in Aquitaine. An apocryphal story of his rescue from captivity in Austria (1192–94) makes note of his artistic abilities. Two of his poems survive, both of a political nature, of which one *(Ja nus hons pris)* has an extant musical setting.

Richard [Richards], **Keith** (b. Dartford, Kent, 18 Dec. 1943). Rock guitarist and songwriter. In 1962 he formed with singer Mick Jagger The Rolling Stones, serving as lead guitarist and coauthor of the majority of their songs; he is credited as the principal architect of the Stones' distinctive hard rock sound. After their initial disbandment, he achieved some success with his solo album *Talk Is Cheap* (1988; released under the name Richards).

Richter, Ernest Friedrich (Eduard) (b. Gross-Schönau, Lausitz, 24 Oct. 1808; d. Leipzig, 9 Apr. 1879). Composer and theorist. Entered the Univ. of Leipzig in 1831; taught harmony and counterpoint at the Leipzig Conservatory, beginning 1843. Organist at several churches; Kantor of Thomasschule (1868). Composed a cantata, cello sonata, string quartet, keyboard pieces, sacred music, songs. Wrote *Lehrbuch der Harmonie* (Leipzig, 1853; translated into English, Swedish, Polish, Italian, French, Spanish, Dutch); *Lehrbuch der Fuge* (Leipzig, 1859; translated into English and French); *Lehrbuch des einfachen und doppelten Kontrapunkts* (Leipzig, 1872; translated into Russian and English).

Richter, Franz Xaver (b. Holleschau?, 1 Dec. 1709; d. Strasbourg, 12 Sept. 1789). Composer and singer. Of Moravian-Bohemian descent; little is known about his youth. In 1740 he became Vice-Kapellmeister to Prince-Abbot Anselm von Reichlin-Meldegg in Kempten, Allgäu. By 1747 Richter was a court musican of the Elector Palatine Carl Theodor in Mannheim, and he probably performed as a singer at the Mannheim court opera. He wrote a composition treatise, *Harmonische Belehrungen oder gründliche Anweisung zu der musikalischen Ton-Kunst oder regulären Komposition* (MS, ed. and trans. C. Kalkbrenner as *Traité d'harmonie et de composition,* Paris, 1804), and embarked on a number of concert tours, first at the Oettingen–Wallerstein court (1754), and subsequently in France, the Netherlands, and England. Around 1768 the elector appointed him chamber composer; in 1769 he succeeded Joseph Garnier as Kapellmeister at Strasbourg Cathedral.

Burney considered Richter one of the best of the Mannheim composers; his contrapuntal writing, though somewhat conservative, was particularly admired, and his symphonies (approximately 80 are extant; thematic catalog in *DTB* 4, 3/1 [1902]), string quartets (thematic catalog to the chamber music in *DTB* 28, 16 [1915]), and sacred music (including 39 Masses) are generally well crafted. His pupils included J. M. Kraus, Ferdinand Fränzl, and Carl Stamitz.

Bibl.: Jochen Reutter, *Studien zur Kirchenmusik Franz Xaver Richters (1709–1789),* 2 vols. (Frankfurt, 1993) [including thematic catalog of sacred music].

Richter, Hans (b. Raab, 4 Apr. 1843; d. Bayreuth, 5 Dec. 1916). Conductor. Attended Vienna Conservatory (1860–65), studying violin, harmony, theory, and piano. Played horn at the Kärntnertor Theater (1862–66). Went to Tribschen to prepare a fair copy of *Die Meistersinger.* Later assisted Wagner in preparing the score of *The Ring* (1870) and conducted the first complete *Ring* cycle at Bayreuth (1876). Worked under Bülow as conductor of Munich Opera. Principal conductor at Pest (1871–75). Played trumpet for first performance of *Siegfried Idyll* (1876). Visited England regularly after 1877: conductor of Birmingham Festival (1885–1909), Hallé Orchestra (1897–1911), London Symphony Orchestra (1904–11). Led first performances of Bruckner's symphonies 1, 3, 4, 8; introduced Dvořák's music to England.

Richter, Karl (b. Plauen, 15 Oct. 1926; d. Munich, 15 Feb. 1981). Organist, harpsichordist, and conductor. Studied in Leipzig with Rudolf Mauersberger, Karl Straube, and Günther Ramin; became choirmaster of the Christuskirche, Leipzig (1946), and then organist of the Thomaskirche (1947). He began to teach at the Hochschule für Musik, Munich, in 1951, and founded the Munich Bach Orchestra in 1953; recorded and toured extensively with the Munich Bach Orchestra and Choir.

Richter, Marga (b. Reedsburg, Wis., 21 Oct. 1926). Composer. She went to the MacPhail School of Music in Minneapolis; then studied at Juilliard (B.S., 1949; M.S., 1951) with Tureck (piano), Persichetti and Bergsma (composition). She taught at Nassau Community College in New York (1971–73) and co-directed with Herbert Deutsch the Long Island Composers' Alliance. Works include 4 ballets (*Abyss,* 1964; *Bird of Yearning,* 1967); orchestral pieces (*Music for Three Quintets and Orchestra,* 1980; *Landscapes of the Mind I,* piano concerto no. 2, 1975; Düsseldorf Concerto, 1982; *Blackberry Vines and Winter Fruit,* 1976); also band music, chamber music (Concerto, piano, violas, cellos, double bass, 1977), piano music (*Landscapes III,* 3 performers, 1979), and vocal music (*Do Not Press My Hands,* mixed chorus, 1981; *Sieben Liedes nach Texten von Franzisko Tanzer für Sopran und Orchester,* 1985).

Richter, Sviatoslav (Teofilovich) (b. Zhitomir, Ukraine, 20 Mar. 1915). Pianist. Received some musical training from his father, an organist; at 15 became accompanist to the Odessa Opera and at 18 chief assistant conductor. Formal training began with Neuhaus at the Moscow Conservatory; in 1949, two years after his graduation, he was awarded the Stalin Prize; subsequently performed extensively in the Soviet Union and eastern Europe, followed by concert tours including China (1957) and the U.S. (1960). He also appeared at the music festivals of Aldeburgh and Spoleto, and at the Fêtes musicales near Tours. One of the leading pianists of his generation, acclaimed for his virtuosity and stylistic command; also noted as a chamber pianist (he made a number of recordings with Oistrakh and Rostropovich) and a vocal accompanist.

Ricordi, Giovanni (b. Milan, 1785; d. there, 15 Mar. 1853). Publisher. Early training was as a violinist. Started a copying establishment (ca. 1803) in Milan; official copyist to Teatro Carcano (1804–7), Teatro del Lentasio (1807). Went to Leipzig in 1807 to study publishing techniques at Breitkopf and Härtel. Formed a partnership with the engraver Felice Festa in January 1808 which was terminated in June 1808, and at that time he founded his own shop. Named publisher to the Milan Conservatory in 1811. Exclusive copyist to La Scala (1814), Teatro Re (1816); extended to all opera houses in Venice and Naples during the 1830s and 1840s. Established Casa Ricordi next to La Scala in 1844. Founded *Gazzetta musicale di Milano* in 1845. Giovanni's son Tito (1811–88) opened independent branches in Florence (1865), Naples (1860), Rome (1871), London (1875), Palermo, and Paris (both 1888). Publisher for Verdi and Puccini. Grandson Giulio (1840–1912) and great-grandson Tito (1865–1933) in turn took over the publishing house.

Bibl.: Giuseppe Adami, *Giulio Ricordi e i suoi musicisti* (Milan, 1933). Claudio Sartori, *Casa Ricordi* (Milan, 1958).

Řídký, Jaroslav (b. Liberec, 25 Aug. 1897; d. Poděbrady, 14 Aug. 1956). Composer. From 1919 to 1923 he studied at the Prague Conservatory with Jirák, Foerster, and Křička. He played harp with the Czech Philharmonic from 1924 to 1938, and from 1925 to 1930 conducted the Czech Philharmonic choir. From 1928 to 1949 he was a professor of music theory at the Prague Conservatory and in 1948 joined the faculty at the Prague Academy of Music, where he taught composition until his death. His music, influenced by Dvořák, was tonal and lyrical, and tended to utilize traditional forms and genres. Řídký's music also contains references to Czech folk music traditions. Works include 7 symphonies (1924–55) and concertos (Violin Concerto, 1926; Cello Concertos, 1930, 1940); 2 cantatas (*A Winter Fairytale,* 1936; *To My Fatherland,* 1941) and chamber works (5 string quartets, 1926–37).

Ridout, Alan (John) (b. West Wickham, Kent, 9 Dec. 1934). Composer. In 1951 he enrolled in the Royal College of Music. There he was a composition student of Jacob and Howells, and studied privately with Fricker and Tippett. He traveled to the Netherlands in 1957 to work with Badings. In 1960 he joined the faculty at the Royal College of Music and taught at Cambridge Univ., 1963–75. As a result of his association with Canterbury Cathedral, he frequently wrote sacred music. His eclectic style draws from techniques as diverse as serialism, modality, and microtonality (*Partita,* cello solo, 1959). Works include operas (*The White Doe,* church opera, 1987); 6 symphonies; concertos; and much vocal music (6 cantatas; Christmas

Oratorio; *12 Melodramas with Narrator; 14 Stations of the Cross, 1978).*

Ridout, Godfrey (b. Toronto, 6 May 1918; d. there, 24 Nov. 1984). Composer. After studying at the Toronto Conservatory and the Univ. of Toronto, he taught at both institutions, at the conservatory from 1940 and at the university from 1948. He is known for his reconstruction of *Colas et Colinette,* the earliest known North American comic opera, composed by Joseph Quesnal in 1788. Works include *The Lost Child,* television opera (1975); *Exile,* melodrama (1984); *La Prima Ballerina,* ballet (1966). Orchestra: *Ballade I* (1938); *Ballade II* (1980); *Festal Overture* (1939); *Comedy Overture* (1941); *Dirge* (1943); *2 Etudes* (1946; rev. 1951); *Music for a Young Prince* (1959); *Fall Fair* (1961); *Jubilee* (1973); Concerto grosso (1974). For voices and orchestra: *Esther,* soprano, baritone, chorus, orchestra (1952); *Cantiones mysticae: No. 1,* after Donne, soprano, orchestra (1953); *No. 2, The Ascension,* soprano, trumpet, strings (1962); *No. 3, The Dream of the Rood,* baritone or tenor, chorus, orchestra, organ (1972); *4 Sonnets* (1964); *In Memoriam Anne Frank,* soprano, orchestra (1965); *When Age and Youth Unite* (1966); *4 Songs of Eastern Canada* (1967). Also composed band music, chamber and vocal music.

Riegel. See Rigel.

Riegger, Wallingford (Constantin) (b. Albany, Ga., 29 Apr. 1885; d. New York, 2 Apr. 1961). Composer. His first formal training in music was undertaken at the Institute of Musical Art in New York in 1900, where he studied composition with Percy Goetschius; he had played piano and violin earlier and took up the cello to complete a family string quartet. After graduating in 1907, he continued his studies in Germany with Robert Haussmann and Anton Hekking (cello), and Max Bruch and Edgar Stillman-Kelley (composition). Cellist with the St. Paul Symphony (1911–14); conducted the Blüthner Orchestra in Berlin, first in 1910 and then in 1916–17, as well as at the Stadttheater of Würzburg (1914–15). He returned to the U.S. in 1917 to teach cello at Drake Univ. in Iowa.

His first major composition, the Piano Trio, appeared in 1920. Active in the Pan-American Association of Composers, which included Varèse, Ives, Cowell, and Ruggles. Perplexed by what he saw as a conflict between the old and the new, he composed nothing between 1923 and 1926. He then embarked on a new style, apparent in both *Study in Sonority* (1926–27), a highly dissonant piece for ten violins, and *Dichotomy* (1931–32). From 1933 to 1941 he focused his compositional energy on music for modern dance; he wrote for Martha Graham, José Limon, Doris Humphrey, and Hanya Holm, among others. After 1941 he returned to chamber and orchestral music, the start of what would prove to be his most productive period. Perhaps his best-known work is his Symphony no. 3 (1946–47), which was chosen by the N.Y. Music Critics' Circle in 1948.

Works: *Orchestra. Rhapsody* (1924–26); *Holiday Sketches* (1927); *Fantasy and Fugue* (1930–31); *Scherzo* (1932); *New Dance* (1940; also for band); *Canon and Fugue* (1942); 4 symphonies (1944, withdrawn; 1945, withdrawn; 1946–47; 1956); *Music for Brass Choir* (1949); *Suite for Younger Orchestras* (1953); *Dance Rhythms* (1954); *Festival Overture* (1957); *Variations,* violin, orchestra (1958); *Quintuple Jazz* (1959); *Introduction, Scherzo, and Fugue* (1960); *Duo,* piano, orchestra, 1960). *Chamber. 3 Canons for Woodwinds,* flute, oboe, clarinet, bassoon (1931); *Scherzo,* 2 pianos (1932; chamber orchestra version, 1932); 2 string quartets (1938–39; 1948); Nonet, brass (1951); *Canon on a Ground Bass of Purcell,* strings (1951); woodwind quintet (1952); Concerto, piano and woodwind quintet (1953); *Variations,* violin, viola (1957); other pieces. *Vocal music. Eternity,* women's voices, 4 instruments (1942); *Who Can Revoke?* (1948); *In Certainty of Song* (1950); *Non vincit malitia: Evil Shall Not Prevail* (1951); *A Child Went Forth,* 4 voices, oboe (1953); *A Shakespeare Sonnet,* baritone, chorus, chamber orchestra (1956); other pieces.

Bibl.: Stephen Spackman, *Wallingford Riegger: Two Essays in Musical Biography* (Brooklyn, 1982). Stephen Spackman, "Wallingford Riegger and the Modern Dance," *MQ* 71 (1985): 437–67.

Riemann, (Karl Wilhelm Julius) Hugo (b. Gross-Mehlra, near Sondershausen, 18 July 1849; d. Leipzig, 10 July 1919). Musicologist. His father taught him music; studied at the Gymnasiums in Sonderhausen and Arnstadt. Entered Univ. of Berlin in 1868 to study law, philology, and history. Studied at Leipzig Conservatory and Univ. of Leipzig (1871) with Jadassohn and Reinecke. Received a Ph.D. from Göttingen (diss., "Über das musikalische Hören"). Lecturer at Univ. of Leipzig (1878); taught in Bromberg, where he began his *Musik-Lexikon;* taught piano and theory at Hamburg Conservatory (1881–90), Wiesbaden Conservatory (1890–95). Appointed director of Collegium musicum in Leipzig (1908); director of Forschungsinstitut für Musikwissenschaft (1914). Writings include pedagogical works on composition, figured bass, fugue, piano, orchestration, tonality; *Handbuch der Musikgeschichte* (Leipzig, 1904); *Präludien und Studien: Gesammelte Aufsätze zur Ästhetik, Theorie und Geschichte der Musik,* 3 vols. (1895–1901); *Grosse Kompositionslehre,* 3 vols. (1902–13).

Bibl.: William Cooper Mickelsen, "Hugo Riemann's History of Harmonic Theory with a Translation of *Harmonielehre*" (diss., Indiana Univ., 1970).

Riepel [Ipleer, Leiper, Perile], **Joseph** (b. Hörschlag, Upper Austria, 22 Jan. 1709; d. Regensburg, 23 Oct. 1782). Theorist. He studied at the Lateinschulen in Linz and Graz, and philosophy at the Univ. of Graz; as a musician he was self-taught. He lived in Dresden (1740–45), then from 1751 held posts as a violinist, composer, and music director in the chapel of the Count of Thurn and Taxis at Regensburg. The 5 treatises of his *Anfangsgründe* (1752–68) deal with the theory of composition; their examination of phrase syntax and structure, using the minuet and symphony as basic formats, point to late 18th-century style.

Bibl.: Wilhelm Twittenhoff, *Die musiktheoretischen Schriften Joseph Riepels* (Berlin, 1935; R: 1971). Nola Reed Knouse, "Joseph Riepel and the Emerging Theory of Form in the Eighteenth Century," *CM* 41 (1986): 47–62.

Ries, Ferdinand (b. Bonn, bapt. 28 Nov. 1784; d. Frankfurt am Main, 13 Jan. 1838). Pianist and composer. He studied piano and violin with his father, Franz (Anton) Ries, and cello with B. H. Romberg. In 1801 he went to Vienna and studied piano with Beethoven and composition with Albrechtsberger. He left Vienna for Koblenz and Paris in 1805, then returned to Vienna in 1808. While on tour (1809–13) he visited Kassel, Hamburg, Copenhagen, Stockholm, St. Petersburg, and much of Russia. In 1813 he settled in London, where he and his works appeared in the Philharmonic Concerts. In 1824 he retired to Godesberg and then Frankfurt am Main, though he continued to conduct and compose. With F. G. Wegeler he wrote *Biographische Notizen über Ludwig van Beethoven* (Koblenz, 1838), an important early biography of Beethoven. Among his compositions are several operas, symphonies, concertos, a number of quartets and trios, and many works for solo piano.

Bibl.: Cecil Hill, *The Music of Ferdinand Ries: A Thematic Catalogue* (Armidale, New South Wales, 1977). Alan Tyson, "Ferdinand Ries (1784–1838): The History of His Contribution to Beethoven Biography," *19th-Century Music* 7/3 (1984): 209–21.

Ries, Franz (Anton) (b. Bonn, 10 Nov. 1755; d. Godesberg, 1 Nov. 1846). Violinist. He studied violin with J. P. Salomon. Although successful as a solo violinist and quartet player in Vienna (1779), he remained in Bonn. There he taught Beethoven and received an appointment from Elector Maximilian on 2 May 1779. After the court was dissolved in 1794, he held minor positions and taught. He received the Order of the Red Eagle and an honorary doctorate from Bonn Univ. His eldest son was Ferdinand Ries.

Ries, (Pieter) Hubert (b. Bonn, 1 Apr. 1802; d. Berlin, 14 Sept. 1886). Violinist and composer. Son of Franz (Anton) Ries (1755–1846). Studied with his father, Spohr, and Hauptmann. Settled in Berlin in 1824; member of the Königstadt Theater Orchestra and court. Named director of Berlin Philharmonic Society, 1835. Taught at Royal Orchestra School, 1851–72. Composed 2 violin concertos, string quartets, etudes, exercises, and duets. Author of *Violinschule* (1873).

Rieti, Vittorio (b. Alexandria, Egypt, 28 Jan. 1898; d. New York, 19 Feb. 1994). Composer. Of Italian descent. He studied in Milan with Giuseppe Frugatta (1912–17), concurrently earning his doctorate in economics at the Univ. of Milan; following war service in the Italian army he studied with Casella and Respighi in Rome (until 1920). In the early 1920s he belonged to a group that called itself "I tre," in imitation of the French composers known as "Les six"; from 1925 to 1940 Rieti worked in both Rome and Paris, writing ballet music for Diaghilev (including the popular *Barabau,* 1925) and incidental music for Louis Jouvet's theater. In 1940 he moved to the U.S. and worked with Balanchine. He taught composition at the Peabody Conservatory (1948–49), the Chicago Musical College (1950–53), Queens College (1955–60), and the New York College of Music (1960–64). Following early experimentation with atonality, Rieti employed a lyrical, neoclassical idiom for most of his long career. In addition to operas and ballets, works include orchestral music (Serenata, violin, chamber orchestra, 1931; Symphony no. 4, Sinfonia tripartita, 1942; Concerto, 2 pianos, 1951; Harpsichord Concerto, 1952–55); instrumental works (Partita, flute, oboe, string quartet, harpsichord, 1945; Sonata breve, violin, piano, 1967; piano trio, 1972); piano music (*Second Avenue Waltzes,* 2 pianos, 1942); choral music; songs.

Bibl.: Franco Carlo Ricci, *Vittorio Rieti* (Naples, 1987). Suzannah Lessard, "Vittorio Rieti: A Kind of Dancer," *New Yorker,* 9 Jan. 1989, pp. 32–50.

Rietz, (August Wilhelm) Julius (b. Berlin, 28 Dec. 1812; d. Dresden, 12 Sept. 1877). Cellist, composer, and conductor. Brother of violinist and conductor Eduard (Theodor Ludwig) Rietz (1802–32). Studied cello with Franz Schmidt, B. H. Romberg, and Moritz Ganz. He joined the orchestra of Königstadt Theater in 1829. Assistant director to Mendelssohn at Düsseldorf in 1834; became city's music director. Succeeded Stegmayer as conductor of Leipzig Opera and Singakademie. Secretary of Bach Gesellschaft; edited the B minor Mass and St. Matthew Passion. Music director of city of Dresden in 1860. Composed incidental music, symphonies, a cello concerto, lieder.

Rigel [Riegel], **Henri-Jean** (b. Paris, 11 May 1772; d. Abbeville, 16 Dec. 1852). Pianist and composer. Son of Henri-Joseph Rigel. Entered the École royale de chant in 1784. Debut as a composer in 1787. First published work, *Trois sonates pour fortepiano,* appeared in 1794. Taught at Paris Conservatory, 1795–97. He took part in Napoleon's expedition to Egypt; member of Egyptian Institute for Science and Arts; appointed director of French Theater there. Returned to France, 1800; taught piano. He composed operas, 4 piano concertos, violin sonatas, other chamber music, solo music for piano and harp.

Rigel, Henri-Joseph (b. Wertheim, 9 Feb. 1741; d. Paris, 2 May 1799). Conductor and composer. He studied with Jommelli in Stuttgart (according to La Borde), then settled in Paris in 1767. There he wrote many instrumental works (sonatas, quartets, symphonies, and concertos), and had great success with his oratorios *La sortie d'Egypte* (1774) and *La déstruction de Jéricho* (1778). Between 1778 and 1799 he composed all of his 14 operas for prominent Parisian theaters. He was *chef d'orchestre* of the Concert spirituel from

1783, and was associated with the Paris Opéra. At the Conservatory he was *maître de solfège* and, later, professor for piano.

Bibl.: R. Sondheimer, "Henri-Joseph Rigel," *MR* 17 (1956): 221ff.

Righini, Vincenzo (b. Bologna, 22 Jan. 1756; d. there, 19 Aug. 1812). Composer. He was a choirboy at S. Petronio in Bologna and was trained in the Bologna school of singing. He made his debut as a tenor in Parma (1775), then joined the Bustelli opera troupe in Prague (1776). In 1780 he went to Vienna, where he became singing master to Princess Elisabeth of Württemberg and director of the Italian Opera. In 1787 he was appointed Kapellmeister at the electoral court in Mainz. He went to Berlin in 1793 to become court Kapellmeister and director of the Italian Opera. He remained there after the Italian opera was disbanded in 1806; in 1811 he became Kapellmeister of the court theater. His works include operas, sacred works, songs, and instrumental music.

Bibl.: Konrad-Jürgen Kleinicke, *Das kirchenmusikalische Schaffen von Vincenzo Righini: Beiträge zur Biographie des Komponisten* (Tutzing, 1984).

Rihm, Wolfgang (Michael) (b. Karlsruhe, 13 March 1952). Composer. He attended the Hochschule für Musik in Karlsruhe (1968–72), where he studied with Eugene Velte and Humphrey Searle; later studied with Stockhausen in Cologne and with Klaus Huber in Freiburg. He taught at the Karlsruhe Hochschule (1973–78).

Works: 6 operas, *Deploration* (1974); *Faust und Yorick* (1977); *Jakob Lenz* (1978); *Hamlet-Machine* (1986); *Oedipus* (1987); *Die Eroberung von Mexico* (1987–89). Orchestral music includes 3 symphonies (1969, 1975, 1976); also *Trakt* (1971); *Morphonie, Sektor IV,* string quartet, orchestra (1972); *Magma* (1974); *Dis-kontur* (1974); *Sub-kontur* (1974–75); *Cuts and Dissolves,* 29 players (1976); *Nachtordnung* (1976); *Lichtzwang,* violin, orchestra (1975–76); *La musique creuse le ciel,* 2 pianos, orchestra (1977–79); *Abgesangsszene nos. 1–5* (1979, 1979, 1980, 1979–80, 1979); *Walzer* (1979–81); *Doppelgesang no. 1* (1980); *No. 2* (1981–83); *Tutugurie I–VII* (1981–82); Viola Concerto (1980–83); *Chiffre I* (1982) and *II, Silence To Be Beaten* (1983); *Gebild* (1983); *Monodram,* cello, orchestra (1983); *Schattenstück* (1982–85); *Spur* (1984–85); *Umriss* (1985); *Ritualtänze* (1988); piano concerto (1988); *Gesungene Zeit,* violin, orchestra (1991–92). For voices and orchestra: *Konzertarie* (1975); *O Notte* (1975); *Hölderlin-Fragmente* (1977); *Lenz-Fragmente* (1980); *Wölfli-Liederbuch* (1981–82); *Dies* (1984). Also chamber music, including 8 string quartets (1968, 1970, 1976, 1979–81, 1983, 1984, 1985, 1988), *Fremde Szene I–III* (piano trio, 1982, 1983, 1983); *Verzeichnung-Studie* (viola, cello, string bass, 1986) and works for mixed ensembles (*Gejagte Form,* 11 instruments, 1989), as well as songs, piano and organ music.

Bibl.: Reinhold Urmetzer, *Wolfgang Rihm* (Stuttgart, 1988).

Riisager, Knudåge (b. Port Kunda, Estonia, 6 Mar. 1897; d. Copenhagen, 26 Dec. 1974). Composer. From 1916 through 1921 he studied political science at the Univ. of Copenhagen; also took private lessons in theory and composition with Gram and Malling between 1915 and 1918 and on violin with Møller; in Paris 1923–24 studied with Roussel and LeFlem; again studied composition in 1932 with Grabner in Leipzig. He was employed by the civil service from the time of his graduation from the Univ. of Copenhagen through 1950. Head of the Copenhagen Conservatory, 1956–67. His early works were in the style of French neoclassicism (Trumpet Concertino op. 29, 1933). His large-scale textures were frequently polyphonic and his harmony often drew on polytonality. He wrote several ballets for which he was particularly known abroad. Works include 1 opera (*Susanna* op. 49, Copenhagen, 1950), ballets (*Fruen fra havet* op. 59, New York, 1960; *Galla-variationer,* Copenhagen, 1967), and orchestral music (5 symphonies: no. 1 op. 8, 1925; no. 2 op. 14; no. 3 op. 30, 1935; no. 4, Sinfonia gaia, op. 38, 1940; no. 5, Sinfonia serena, op. 52, 1949–50; and concertos: Violin Concerto op. 54, 1950–55). He also wrote chamber music (6 string quartets, 1918, 1920, 1922, 1925–26, 1932, 1942–43) and music for film.

Riley, Dennis (Daniel) (b. Los Angeles, 28 May 1943). Composer. He earned a B.M. in piano performance at the Univ. of Colorado in 1965 then studied composition at the Univ. of Illinois (M.M., 1968) and the Univ. of Iowa (Ph.D., 1973). His composition teachers included George Crumb, Thomas Frederickson, Ben Johnston, Richard Hervig, and Donald Jenni. He was composer-in-residence in Rockford, Ill., from 1965 to 1967. Taught at California State Univ., Fresno (1971–74), and Columbia Univ. (1974–77). Works include 2 operas, orchestral music (Symphony, 1983), and choral music (Cantata II, III, and IV, 1966, 1968, 1979–80); also chamber music (*Concertante Music nos. 1–4,* 1970, 1971–72, 1972, 1977–78) and vocal music (*Summer Music,* alto, flute, guitar, 1979).

Riley, Terry (Mitchell) (b. Colfax, Calif., 24 June 1935). Composer and performer. He studied piano with Duane Hampton and composition with Erickson at San Francisco State College (1955–57), continuing his composition studies at Berkeley with Seymour Shifrin and William Denny (M.A., 1961). Beginning in 1963 he worked at the ORTF recording studios in Paris; compositions from this time include *Mescalin Mix* and *Keyboard Studies,* both of which experiment with evolving rhythmic and stress patterns in a repeated phrase. *In C* (1964), for any combination of melodic instruments, features a series of motifs that the performers gradually work through (and repeat freely) against a steady piano pulse; this work established Riley's reputation as a "minimalist" composer, an approach explored by others including Glass, La Monte Young, and Palestine. In 1970 Riley studied raga singing with Pran Nath, and the influence of Indian music is evident in his work: he experimented with raga-related scales, combined Indian instruments (sitar, tablā) with more traditional forces, and retuned his keyboard instruments to just intonation. Taught at Mills College, 1971–80.

Works: *Tape and instrumental.* Trio, violin, clarinet, cello (1957); *Spectra,* 3 wind, 3 string instruments (1959); *Concert,* 2 pianos, tape (1960); *Earpiece,* 2 pianos, tape (1960); String Quartet (1960); String Trio (1961); *I Can't Stop No* and *She Moves,* both for tape (1962–63); *Cadenza on the Night Plain,* string quartet (1984).

Improvisational works. Dorian Reeds, wind, brass, strings, unspecified instruments, tape loops (1964); *Olson III,* voices, instruments (1967); *Poppy Nogood and the Phantom Band,* soprano sax, electric keyboard, tape delay (1967); *A Rainbow in the Curved Air,* electric keyboard, dumbak, tambourines (1968); *Persian Surgery Dervishes,* electric keyboard (1971); *Happy Ending,* piano, electric keyboard, soprano sax, tape delay (1972); *Descending Moonshine Dervishes,* electric keyboard (1975); *Shri Camel,* electric organ, tape delay (1976); *Do You Know How It Sounds?,* voice, piano, tablā (1983).

Works with synthesizer (many with Indian instruments). *Chorale of the Blessed Day* (1980); *Eastern Man* (1980); *Embroidery* (1980); *Song from the Old Country* (1980); *G-Song* (1981); *Remember This Oh Mind* (1981); *Sunrise of the Planetary Dream Collector* (1981); *The Ethereal Time Shadow* (1982); *Offering to Chief Crazy Horse* (1982); *Rites of the Imitators* (1982); *The Medicine Wheel* (1983); *Song of the Emerald Runner* (1983).

Bibl.: Wim Mertens, *American Minimal Music: La Monte Young, Terry Riley, Steve Reich, Philip Glass,* trans. J. Hautekiet (London, 1983).

Rimonte [Ruimonte, Ruymonte], **Pedro** (b. Zaragoza?, ca. 1570; d. after 1618). Composer. He served the Spanish court in Brussels as choirmaster and, from 1604, master of chamber music. His principal works, all published in Antwerp, include a set of 5 Masses and a Requiem (1604); a set of 12 motets and a Lamentations (1607); and *El Parnaso español,* a set of 17 madrigals and *villancicos* (1614).

Rimsky-Korsakov, Nikolay Andreyevich (b. Tikhvin, Novgorod govt., 18 Mar. 1844; d. Lyubensk, St. Petersburg govt., 21 June 1908). Composer. He took piano lessons from age 6, and continued them while at the College of Naval Cadets in St. Petersburg (1856–62). His interest in music grew, and in 1861 he met Cui, Mussorgsky, and Balakirev, who took the young composer under his wing. Graduating as a midshipman in 1862, Rimsky-Korsakov embarked on a two-and-a-half-year cruise to Gravesend, the Baltic, New York, Rio de Janeiro, and the Mediterranean. When he returned to Russia in May 1865, he renewed his contact with Balakirev and finished the symphony that he had started several years before. Balakirev gave the first performance on 31 December at the Free School of Music at St. Petersburg. During the next few years Rimsky-Korsakov spent an increasing amount of time composing, moving in a social circle that included Borodin and Dargomïzhsky. His orchestral works from this period (including the programmatic symphony *Antar* of 1868) earned him a reputation as an excellent orchestrator; Dargomïzhsky entrusted him with scoring *The Stone Guest.*

From 1868 to 1872 he was occupied with his first opera, *Pskovityanka* [The Maid of Pskov], which was premiered at the Mariinsky Theater in 1873. Despite his technical deficiencies, he accepted an invitation in 1871 to become professor of practical composition and instrumentation and director of the orchestral class at the St. Petersburg Conservatory. The following year he married the pianist Nadezhda Purgold, who exerted a strong influence on him. In 1873 he became Inspector of Naval Bands, a post that was created for him. After his Third Symphony, completed that year, he turned away from composition for several years and instead took up a practical study of instruments, and taught himself harmony and counterpoint. In 1875 he succeeded Balakirev as conductor of the Free School concerts. His studies of folk music and Glinka's orchestration (in preparation for a new edition of the composer's operas) led him in 1878 to begin an opera, *Mayskaya noch'* [May Night], based on Gogol's story "Vecheri na khutore bliz Dikan'ki" [Evenings on a Farm at Dikanka]. It was first produced at the Mariinsky Theater on 21 January 1880. Another opera soon followed: *Snegurochka* [Snow Maiden], based on Ostrovsky's fantastic play, was finished in April 1881.

For the next several years Rimsky-Korsakov focused his energies on activities other than composition. When his friend Mussorgsky died in March 1881, he set himself the task of sorting his manuscripts and preparing them for publication. This involved "correcting" harmony, melody, and part writing. The opera *Khovanshchina* and *Night on the Bare Mountain* proved to be the most difficult in this respect. In 1883 he became assistant musical director of the imperial chapel. Following Borodin's death in 1887, Rimsky-Korsakov collaborated with Glazunov on completing and orchestrating *Prince Igor.* His next major works, the last of his important orchestral compositions, were brilliant essays in orchestration: *Kaprichchio na ispanskiye temï* [Spanish Capriccio], 1887, the symphonic suite *Scheherazade* (1888), and *Svetlïy prazdnik* [Russian Easter Festival], an "overture on liturgical themes."

In 1889 and 1890 he composed another opera, *Mlada,* and conducted in Paris and Brussels. When the opera failed to achieve lasting success after its 1892 premiere, he became disheartened and convinced that his career was coming to an end. During this time family crises and the deterioration of his health contributed to his depression. Following the death of Tchaikovsky in 1893, he conducted a memorial Russian Symphony Concert and then conducted the rest of the season's concerts. His interest in composition now stimulated, he wrote several new operas: *Noch' pered Rozhdestvom* [Christmas Eve], 1894–95, *Sadko* (1894–96), and *Bagdadskiy borodobrey* [Barber of Baghdad], 1895. The next few years were extremely productive; he wrote 40 songs (1896–97), a setting of Pushkin's *Mozart and Salieri* (1897), chamber music, and full-length operas: *Tsarskaya nevesta* [The Tsar's

Bride], 1898, and *Skazka o Tsare Saltane* [The Tale of Tsar Saltan], 1899–1900. His next operas were an attempt to get away from Russian subjects or local coloring: *Serviliya* (1900–1901), *Kashchey bessmertnïy* [Kaschchey the Immortal], 1901–2, and *Pan Voyevoda* (1902–3). With *Kitezh* (1903–5) he returned to a Russian subject.

In 1905 Rimsky-Korsakov's involvement with the political unrest that culminated in "Bloody Sunday" led to his dismissal from the conservatory and the temporary banning of performances of his music. That summer he went to his country home in Vechasha and continued work on his autobiography (St. Petersburg, 1909) and his book on orchestration, *Osnovï orkestrovki* (St. Petersburg, 1913). His last major work was the opera *Zolotoy petushok* [The Golden Cockerel], based on Pushkin's fairy-tale satire. Although Rimsky-Korsakov had little difficulty with the composition of the opera, the libretto caused trouble with censors, which probably aggravated the heart trouble of which he died on 21 June 1908. Among his students were Lyadov, Glazunov, Myaskovsky, Stravinsky, Prokofiev, and Respighi.

Bibl.: Vasilii Yastrebtsev, *Reminiscences of Rimsky-Korsakov,* 2 vols. (Leningrad, 1959, 1960); trans. Eng., Florence Jonas (New York, 1985). Steven Griffiths, *A Critical Study of the Music of Rimsky-Korsakov* (New York, 1989). Gerald R. Seaman, *Nikolay Andreyevich Rimsky-Korsakov: A Guide to Research* (New York, 1988).

Rinaldo di [da] **Capua** (b. Capua or Naples, ca. 1705; d. Rome?, ca. 1780). Composer. Little is known about his life; he was active chiefly in Rome, where nearly all his operas were given. His first opera for Rome (title unknown) was produced in 1737, followed the same year by *Ciro riconosciuto,* an opera seria on Metastasio's text. His satirical opera *La commedia in commedia* (1738) was so successful that it was staged in Florence, London, Venice, and Munich; *Vologeso re de' Parti* (1739) and *La libertà nociva* (1740) were similarly well received. He composed some opera serie for the Rua dos Condes Theater in Lisbon (1740–42) before returning to Rome. *La donna superba* was performed in Paris in 1752, and *La zingara* the following year; the latter, greatly successful, played an important role in the *querelle des bouffons.*

Rinck, Johann Christian Heinrich (b. Elgersburg, Thuringia, 18 Feb. 1770; d. Darmstadt, 7 Aug. 1846). Organist and composer. After study with Abicht, J. A. Junghanss, H. C. Kirchner, and Bach's pupil J. C. Kittel in Erfurt (1786–89), he became organist at Giessen (1790). In 1805 he moved to Darmstadt, where he was organist and teacher at the music school, and organist and *Kammermusiker* to the Grand Duke Ludwig I. He was an influential teacher and made successful tours. He wrote organ works and sacred music.

Rinuccini, Ottavio (b. Florence, 20 Jan. 1562; d. there, 28 Mar. 1621). Librettist and poet. He began writing verses for court entertainments in Florence. In 1589 he provided the text for an *intermedio* depicting Apollo's combat with the dragon; this was expanded in his *Dafne,* set to music by Peri and Corsi and performed in 1598. Peri also set Rinuccini's *Euridice,* performed in 1600; in the preface the two commented on their work (trans. *SR,* 1968). Rinuccini's next libretto, *Arianna* (1608), was set by Monteverdi, the two collaborating once again on the *Ballo delle ingrate* (1608), but his final libretto, *Narciso* (date uncertain), did not attract potential composers.

Ripa (da Mantova), Alberto da [Rippe, Albert de] (b. Mantua, ca. 1500; d. Paris, 1551). Lutenist and composer. Served Cardinal Ercole Gonzaga of Mantua before 1529, then entered the French court under François I. There he enjoyed great favor; he vied in reputation with Francesco da Milano. His works, published posthumously in 6 volumes, include fantasias, dances, and intabulated chansons and motets.

Riquier (de Narbona), Guiraut (b. Narbonne, ca. 1230; d. Rodez, 1292). Troubadour poet, composer, singer. He served Alfonso X the Wise, King of Castile, from 1269 to 1279, then Henry II, Count of Rodez. The last of the true Provençal langue d'oc troubadours, he documented their decline in status. Of his 89 extant poems, fully 48 survive with melodies; 15 of his letters also survive.

Risset, Jean-Claude (b. Le Puy, 13 March 1938). Composer. Before 1963 he studied piano with Robert Trimaille, harmony with Suzanne Demarques, and composition with Jolivet. He then moved to New York, where he became acquainted with Varèse, and explored computer sound with Mathews (they later did research at Bell Laboratories). He taught at Stanford and at the Centre universitaire de Marseille-Luminy, before directing the Institut de recherche et de coordination acoustique/musique in Paris. Works include *Prelude,* orchestra (1963); *Instantanés,* piano (1965); *Neiz radenn,* English horn, piano (1966); *Little Boy,* incidental music, orchestra, tape (1968); *Updown/Bell Sirens,* tape (1968); *Mutations I,* tape (1969); *Mutations II,* 4 instruments, tape (1973); *Sketches: Duet for One Pianist* (1989).

Rist, Johann (b. Ottensen, near Hamburg, 8 Mar. 1607; d. Wedel, 31 Aug. 1667). Poet and composer. He studied theology, poetry, and law at the universities in Rinteln and Rostock before becoming a pastor at Wedel in 1635. He was made poet laureate in 1644, and founded a poets' academy, the Elbschwanenorden, in 1660. Rist wrote poems, both sacred (including Bible translations) and secular, set to music by himself and other composers of his day, including Hammerschmidt, Heinrich Pape, and Thomas Selle. Most of Rist's poems are strophic with regular meters.

Ristori, Giovanni Alberto (b. Bologna?, 1692; d. Dresden, 7 Feb. 1753). Composer. His first opera, *Pallide trionfante in Arcadia,* premiered in Padua in 1713;

he moved to Dresden in 1715, working there with his father, Tommaso, at the Italian comic theater; also served as director of the *cappella polacca,* Warsaw. His comic opera *Calandro,* written in 1726 for Dresden, is considered the first Italian opera buffa written in Germany; in 1731 and 1732 Ristori was in Russia, where a revival of *Calandro* was staged. He served the Polish court (1734–36) before returning to Dresden by 1744, where he was appointed court *Kirchenkomponist* (1746) and Vice-Kapellmeister (1750). His output, in addition to opera, includes a large number of sacred vocal works.

Ritchie, Stanley (John) (b. Yenda, New South Wales, 21 Apr. 1935). Violinist. His teachers included Florent Hoogstoel, Jean Fournier, Sandor Vegh, Joseph Fuchs, Oscar Shumsky, and Samuel Kissell. Ritchie served as concertmaster at the New York City Opera (1963–65), associate concertmaster at the Metropolitan (1965–70), member of the New York Chamber Soloists (1970–73), a founder of Aston Magna (1974), and first violinist of the Philadelphia String Quartet (1975–81). He came to specialize in 18th-century repertory on period instruments, and beginning in 1974 performed with his wife, the harpsichordist and fortepianist Elizabeth Wright, as Duo Geminiani.

Ritter, Alexander [Sachsa] (b. Narva, Estonia, 27 June 1833; d. Munich, 12 Apr. 1896). Composer and violinist. Family moved to Dresden in 1841. He studied violin with Franz Schubert (the second *Konzertmeister* of court orchestra), and at Leipzig Conservatory (1849–51) with Ferdinand David and E. F. Richter. Second *Konzertmeister* of Weimar Orchestra; conductor of Stettin Opera (1856–58). Played violin under Bülow in Meiningen (1882–86). He wrote 2 operas, tone poems, string quartet, piano pieces, songs.

Ritter, Frédéric Louis (b. Strasbourg, 22 June 1826; d. Antwerp, 4 July 1891). Composer, conductor, and writer on music. Studied in Paris with George Kastner and in Germany. Settled in Cincinnati in 1856; organized the orchestra there. He left for New York in 1861; directed the Sacred Harmonic Society, 1862–70. Author of the first music history written in the U.S. (*A History of Music in the Form of Lectures,* Boston, 1883); also *Music in America* (New York, 1883). Composed 3 symphonies, violin and piano concertos, songs, choruses, other instrumental works.

Ritter, Hermann (b. Wismar, Mecklenberg, 16 Sept. 1849; d. Würzburg, 22 Jan. 1926). Violist and instrument maker. Studied at Hochschule in Berlin and Heidelberg Univ. Created a large viola, the "viola alta," played by five of his students at Bayreuth; arranged much music for the instrument. Taught viola and music history in Würzburg from 1879. Formed the Ritter Quartet in 1905. Wrote *Die Geschichte der Viola alta und die Grundsätze ihres Baues* (Leipzig, 1877). Other writings discuss aesthetics, harmony, and music history.

Ritter, Peter (b. Mannheim, 2 July 1763; d. there, 1 Aug. 1846). Composer. He studied composition with G. J. Vogler, then became cellist in the Mannheim Theater Orchestra (1783); from 1801 until his retirement in 1823 he was its *Konzertmeister.* From 1803 he was also Kapellmeister of the orchestra of the Grand Duchy of Baden. There he directed the operas, conducting from his raised cello desk. In 1833 he became chairman of the Mannheim Society of Arts. His works include operas and singspiels, sacred music, concertos, and chamber music.

Ritter, Tex [Woodward Maurice] (b. Murvaul, Tex., 12 Jan. 1905; d. Nashville, Tenn., 2 Jan. 1974). Country singer and songwriter. He collected cowboy songs while a student at the Univ. of Texas, and began singing them on radio in Houston and New York in 1929. From 1933 he made recordings and from 1936 appeared in western films, helping establish the "singing cowboy" character; his popular recordings included "I'm Wasting My Tears on You" (1944) and "Do Not Forsake Me" (in *High Noon,* 1952). Later he hosted country radio shows and appeared on the Grand Ole Opry (from 1965).

Rivé-King, Julie (b. Cincinnati, 30 Oct. 1854; d. Indianapolis, 24 July 1937). Pianist. She studied with William Mason and S. B. Mills in New York, then went to Europe in 1874 to continue her studies with Carl Reinecke and Liszt. Made her debut in Leipzig in 1874 and her American debut the following year with the New York Philharmonic; subsequently performed frequently in the U.S. and embarked on a number of concert tours, often playing her own compositions; taught at the Bush Conservatory, Chicago (1905–36).

Rivers, Sam [Carthorne] (b. El Reno, Okla., 25 Sept. 1930). Jazz tenor saxophonist. He joined Miles Davis's quintet in 1964, recording the album *Miles in Japan.* He played free jazz with Cecil Taylor (ca. 1967–71). In New York in 1970 he and his wife, Bea, founded Studio Rivbea, which became a center for free jazz performances throughout the decade. He played on Dave Holland's album *Conference of the Birds* (1972) and later worked in duos and trios with Holland (1976–80). Having already doubled on several reed instruments in the mid-1960s, he also played piano and sang blues while with Holland.

Rivier, Jean (b. Villemomble, Seine, 21 July 1896; d. La Penne sur Huveaune, 6 Nov. 1987). Composer. During army service in World War I his health was severely damaged as a result of mustard gas. After a lengthy convalescence he entered the Paris Conservatory in 1922, where he studied with Caussade and graduated in 1926 with a premier prix in counterpoint and fugue. His string quartet of 1924 earned him early notice; he was part of the Groupe du Triton, among other new music societies. Taught at the Paris Conservatory (1947–66) and also worked at the ORTF. His better-known works include the Piano Concerto (1940) and the Concerto for Brass, Timpani, and Strings (1963). Other works include an opera, *Vénitienne* (Paris, 8 July 1937); 7 symphonies (1933, 1937, 1937, 1947, 1951, 1958, 1962); concertos for violin (1942), saxophone and trumpet (1954), flute (1955), clarinet (1958), bassoon (1965), oboe (1968), trumpet (1971); other orchestra pieces (*Climats,* celesta, vibraphone, xylophone, piano, strings, 1968). Also chamber music (2 string quartets, 1924, 1940; woodwind quintet, 1970; brass septet, 1970; *Brillance,* 7 woodwinds (1971), choral music, piano music (*Sonata,* 1969), songs, and scores for radio.

Roach, Max [Maxwell] (b. Elizabeth City, N.C., 10 Jan. 1924). Jazz drummer and bandleader. He recorded with Coleman Hawkins (1943) and joined the bop combos of Dizzy Gillespie (1944) and Charlie Parker (1945, including the recording "Ko-Ko"; 1947–49; 1951–53). He played in Miles Davis's cool jazz nonet (1948–50). With Clifford Brown he founded in 1954 a hard bop quintet which recorded the album *At Basin Street* (1956); with Sonny Rollins (then their sideman) Roach recorded the album *Saxophone Colossus* (1956), which demonstrates his characteristic use of not only rhythmic but also pitch and timbral variation in his solos. After Brown's death he led groups which from the late 1950s became active in artistic contributions to the civil rights movement, including the album *We Insist! Freedom Now Suite* (1960). He also composed for musicals, films, television, and symphony orchestra, and later recorded duos with Abdullah Ibrahim (1977), Anthony Braxton (1978–79), Archie Shepp, and Cecil Taylor (both 1979). In the 1970s and 1980s he led the percussion group M'Boom Re: Percussion and his quintet, while teaching at the Univ. of Massachusetts.

Robbins, Marty [Robinson, Martin David] (b. near Glendale, Ariz., 26 Sept. 1925; d. Nashville, Tenn., 8 Dec. 1982). Country music and pop singer, songwriter, and guitarist. After early work in Phoenix he landed a record contract with Columbia in 1951; his first hit song was "I'll Go on Alone" (1952). Beginning in the late 1950s he tried to broaden his appeal with rockabilly, rhythm-and-blues ("Singing the Blues," 1956), and pop numbers ("A White Sport Coat," 1957). His biggest success was "El Paso" (1959), but he produced hit songs throughout his long career.

Robert de Handlo (fl. early 14th century). Music theorist. Active in England. His only extant work, which survives in an 18th-century transcription, is entitled *Regule cum maximis Magistri Franconis cum additionibus aliorum musicorum compilate a Roberto de Handlo* (*CS* 1, 383–403). Completed ca. 1326, the *Regule* is a collection of maxims and rules assembled primarily from the teachings of Franco of Cologne, Johannes de Garlandia, Petrus de Cruce, Petrus Le Viser, Admetus de Aureliana, and Jacobus de Navernia. The treatise is an important source for understanding late developments in Franconian notation.

Roberts, (Charles) Luckey (Luckeyeth) (b. Philadelphia, 7 Aug. 1887; d. New York, 5 Feb. 1968). Ragtime, musical theater, and jazz pianist and composer. A vaudeville performer from childhood, he played in and wrote *My People* (1911), the first of his 14 musical comedies. He composed "Junk Man Rag" (published in 1913) and "Ripples of the Nile" (popularized by Glenn Miller as "Moonlight Cocktail"). Despite his reputation as one of the finest stride pianists, he seldom recorded. He led lucrative society orchestras in the 1920s and 1930s and gave a concert at Carnegie Hall in 1939. Played from 1940 to 1954 at his own bar in Harlem; participated in the radio series *This Is Jazz* (1947).

Robertson, Leroy (J.) (b. Fountain Green, Utah, 21 Dec. 1896; d. Salt Lake City, 25 July 1971). Composer. He studied with Chadwick and Converse at the New England Conservatory (diploma, 1923), and with Ernst Toch, Ernest Bloch, and Hugo Leichtentritt in Europe; completed his studies in the U.S. at the Univ. of Utah (M.A., 1932) and with Schoenberg at the Univ. of Southern California (Ph.D., 1954). He served as professor and chairman at Brigham Young Univ. (1925–48) and department chairman at the Univ. of Utah (1948–63). Compositions include symphonic works (*Trilogy,* 1947); an oratorio (*The Book of Mormon,* 1953); chamber music (piano quintet, 1933; string quartet, 1940).

Robertson, (Jaime) Robbie (b. Toronto, Ont., 5 July 1944). Rock guitarist, songwriter, and singer. From the late 1950s he performed with drummer Levon Helm (b. 1942), bassist Rick Danko (b. 1943), and pianist Richard Manuel (1945–86)—all also singers—and keyboardist Garth Hudson (b. 1942); they acccompanied Ronnie Hawkins and Bob Dylan, and released their first albums in 1969 as The Band. Their music, an increasing amount of which was authored by Robertson, incorporated many American popular and traditional styles: this is especially evident on *The Band* (1969) and *Northern Lights, Southern Cross* (1975). Their final concert was the subject of a film (*The Last Waltz,* 1978); in 1987 Robertson released a solo album.

Robeson, Paul (b. Princeton, N.J., 9 Apr. 1898; d. Philadelphia, 23 Jan. 1976). Bass-baritone and actor. He attended Rutgers and law school at Columbia before beginning an acting career in 1921; gave his first concert in 1925, in which his singing of spirituals attracted attention, and embarked on a tour of the U.S. the following year. Appeared in London in *Show Boat* (1928) and as Shakespeare's Othello (1930); his films include *The Emperor Jones* (1933), *Sanders of the River* (1935), *Show Boat* (1936), and *The Proud Valley* (1939). His American career ended in the 1940s with his espousal of communism following a tour of the Soviet Union, but he continued to perform elsewhere.

Bibl.: Charlotte Turner Bell, *Paul Robeson's Last Days in Philadelphia* (Bryn Mawr, Pa., 1986).

Robinson, Anastasia (b. Italy, ca. 1692; d. Southampton, Apr. 1755). Soprano, contralto. She studied music with Croft and singing with Sandoni; sometime around 1718 or 1719 her voice dropped from soprano to contralto owing to an illness. Handel composed the soprano part in his *Ode for Queen Anne's Birthday* for her, and she enjoyed considerable success performing in many Handel operas, including *Rinaldo* (1714), *Amadigi* (creating the part of Oriana, 1715), *Floridante* (1724), and *Giulio Cesare* (1724).

Robinson, Earl (Hawley) (b. Seattle, 2 July 1910; d. there, 20 July 1991). Composer. He earned a B.M. and a teaching diploma at the Univ. of Washington in 1933, where he studied with George McKay. He then studied in New York with Copland and Eisler. He joined a Workers' Theater Project there during the 1930s. His *Ballad for Americans* was recorded by Paul Robeson and the American People's Chorus, a group Robinson conducted (1937–43). He wrote 2 folk operas, musicals, and orchestral pieces (*To the Northwest Indians,* narrator, folk instruments, orchestra, 1974), as well as film scores and songs. His song "The House I Live In" (1942) won him an Academy Award in 1947.

Robinson, Smokey [William] (b. Detroit, Mich., 19 Feb. 1940). Soul singer, songwriter, and record producer. He formed the vocal group The Miracles while in high school. With songs written and produced by Robinson and Berry Gordy, Jr., they became Motown Records' first success ("Shop Around," 1960; "Tears of a Clown," 1970); Robinson also produced groups such as The Temptations. From 1972 he made many solo recordings, including "Cruisin'" (1979) and "Being with You" (1981).

Robledo, Melchior (b. in or near Tarragona, ca. 1515; d. Zaragoza, before 7 Apr. 1587). Composer. He was schooled in Tarragona and served as *maestro de capilla* at the cathedral in 1549. He spent some time as a singer at the papal chapel in Rome, then in 1569 became *maestro de capilla* at La Seo, the main cathedral of Zaragoza. His works include 6 Masses and many other sacred works: Mass sections, Magnificats, motets, Psalms, etc.

Rocca, Lodovico (b. Turin, 29 Nov. 1895; d. there, 25 June 1986). Composer. He studied at the Milan Conservatory with Giacomo Orefice. His best-known work is *Il Dibuk* (1928–30), his third opera. He wrote many works for voices with ensembles of somewhat unusual instrumentation (*Proverbi di Salomone,* tenor, female chorus, flute, bassoon, horn, trumpet, harp, 2 pianos, organ, 14 percussion, double bass, 1933). Was director of the Turin Conservatory from 1940 to 1966. Other works include operas (*Monte Ivnor,* 1936–38; *L'uragano,* 1942–51) and orchestra music, including suites from the operas; vocal music (*Salmodia,* baritone, chorus, ensemble, 1934; *Schizzi francescani,* tenor, ensemble, 1939); chamber music and songs.

Rochberg, George (b. Paterson, N.J., 5 July 1918). Composer. He attended Montclair State Teachers College before going to Mannes College, where he studied with Hans Weisse, George Szell, and Leopold Mannes (1939–42). After serving in the military during World War II, he returned to study at the Curtis Institute (B.M., 1947), where his teachers included Rosario Scalero and Gian Carlo Menotti. After earning an M.A. in 1948 from the Univ. of Pennsylvania, he joined the faculty at Curtis (1948–54).

His early compositions are influenced by Stravinsky and Bartók (String Quartet, 1952). A stylistic change took place when he met Dallapiccola in 1950 while in Rome on Fulbright and American Academy fellowships. This meeting fueled his interest in Schoenbergian serialism, a style he fully embraced and explored in works such as the Chamber Symphony (1950), Symphony no. 2 (1955–56), and the Second String Quartet (1959–61).

Rochberg became a music editor with the Presser Company in 1951, a position he held until 1960, when he became chairman of the music department at the Univ. of Pennsylvania. He was Annenberg Professor of the Humanities there from 1979 to 1983. In the early 1960s he began to pull away from serialism (his last serial piece is the Piano Trio, 1963) and to move toward the incorporation of an earlier, traditional musical idiom. His works also employed direct musical quotation; *Contra mortem et tempus* (1965) quotes Boulez, Berio, Varèse, and Ives, and exemplifies the early stages of this stylistic transition. The Third String Quartet (1972), a Naumburg Chamber Music Award Composition, shows its further development with its evocations of Beethoven and Mahler. His later compositional style goes beyond return to a traditional tonal idiom and attempts to draw together a broad spectrum of styles. Authored a book, *The Hexachord and Its Relation to the Twelve-Tone Row* (Bryn Mawr, Pa., 1955). A collection of his writings, *The Aesthetics of Survival: A Composer's View of Twentieth-Century Music,* edited by William Bolcom, was published in 1984 (Ann Arbor).

Works: *Phaedra,* monodrama, mezzo, orchestra (1973–74); *The Confidence Man,* opera (1982; Santa Fe, 31 July 1982). For orchestra: Symphony no. 1 (1948–57, in 3 movements; rev. 1971–77, in 5 movements; 2nd movement: *Night Music,* 1948; 3rd movement: *Capriccio,* 1949); Symphony no. 2 (1955–56); *Time-Span I* (1960); *Time-Span II* (1962); Symphony no. 3, chamber chorus, double chorus, orchestra (1966–69); *Imago mundi* (1973); Violin Concerto (1974); *Transcendental Variations,* strings (1975; based on 3rd movement of Third String Quartet); Symphony no. 4 (1976); Oboe Concerto (1983); Symphony no. 5 (1984–85); clarinet concerto (1996). Chamber: 7 string quartets (1952, 1959–61 with soprano, 1972, 1977, 1978, 1978, 1979); Cheltenham Concerto, winds, strings (1958); *Elektrikaleidoscope,* ensemble (1972); String Quintet (1982); *Muse of Fire,* flute, guitar (1991). Keyboard music and vocal pieces.

Bibl.: Jay Reise, "Rochberg the Progressive," *PNM* 19 (1981–82): 395–407. Joan DeVee Dixon, *George Rochberg: A Bio-Bibliographic Guide to His Life and Works* (Stuyvesant, N.Y., 1992).

Rochlitz, (Johann) Friedrich (b. Leipzig, 12 Feb. 1769; d. there, 16 Dec. 1842). Music critic and editor. He studied with J. F. Doles at the Thomasschule in Leipzig, then studied theology before becoming a writer. In 1798 he became editor of the newly founded journal *Allgemeine musikalische Zeitung;* he resigned in 1818, but remained a contributor until 1835. He was also a director of the Leipzig Gewandhaus Orchestra.

Rockefeller, Martha Baird (b. Madera, Calif., 15 Mar. 1895; d. New York, 24 Jan. 1971). Philanthropist and pianist. Attended Occidental College and the New England Conservatory, continuing her studies with Schnabel in Berlin; toured with Nellie Melba in 1918 and enjoyed a successful career as soloist and recitalist until her retirement in 1931. Married John D. Rockefeller, Jr., in 1951 and established the Martha Baird Rockefeller Fund for Music in 1962, which over a twenty-year period was responsible for approximately $9 million of funding to musicians and music-related organizations and research.

Rode, (Jacques) Pierre (Joseph) (b. Bordeaux, 16 Feb. 1774; d. Château de Bourbon, near Damazon, 25 Nov. 1830). Violinist and composer. He studied violin with André-Joseph Fauvel and with Viotti in Paris. He made his Paris debut in 1790, and played in the orchestra of the Théâtre de Monsieur (1789–92). In 1795 he became professor of the violin at the Conservatory, then gave concerts in Holland, Germany, and London. Upon returning to Paris in 1799 he resumed his Conservatory post and served as solo violinist at the Opéra. During that year he visited Madrid and met Boccherini. In Paris (1800) he became solo violinist to First Consul Buonaparte. From 1804 to 1808 he was solo violinist to the tsar in St. Petersburg, and in 1812 arrived in Vienna, where he gave the premiere of Beethoven's Violin Sonata op. 96. After a period in Berlin (1814–18) he settled in Bordeaux. Although he abandoned the violin, he continued to compose. Among his works, mainly for the violin, are 13 concertos, 12 string quartets, 24 duos for 2 violins, 24 caprices, and *airs variés.*

Rodeheaver, Homer A(lvan) (b. Union Furnace, Ohio, 4 Oct. 1880; d. Winona, Ind., 18 Dec. 1955). Composer and music publisher. He worked with the evangelist Billy Sunday on his tours (1910–30); composed gospel songs, including "Then Jesus Came," and in 1910 cofounded the Rodeheaver–Ackley Company (later Rodeheaver Hall–Mack Company), a leading publisher of gospel music. Rodeheaver established Rainbow Records, one of the first labels devoted solely to gospel recordings, and compiled and edited many collections of gospel songs.

Rodgers, Jimmie [James Charles] (b. Meridian, Miss., 8 Sept. 1897; d. New York, 26 May 1933). Country singer, songwriter, and guitarist. He performed at fairs and picnics in the South while working as a railroadman, and began recording in 1927. He was the first hillbilly singer to achieve national fame, and a major influence on most subsequent country singers; he is often referred to as the "Father of Country Music." Much of his repertory was written with his sister-in-law Elsie McWilliams; particularly popular were his "blue yodels" ("T for Texas," 1928), and the songs "Waiting for a Train" (1929) and "Roll Along, Kentucky Moon" (1932).

Bibl.: Mike Paris and Chris Comber, *Jimmie the Kid: The Life of Jimmy Rodgers* (New York, 1981).

Rodgers, Richard (Charles) (b. Hammels Station, N.Y., 28 June 1902; d. New York City, 30 Dec. 1979). Popular songwriter. He met lyricist Lorenz Hart in 1918, and they began to collaborate while Rodgers attended Columbia and the Institute of Musical Art. They contributed to college and Broadway shows, first achieving success with *The Garrick Gaieties* (1925, including "Manhattan"). Subsequently they wrote several extremely popular musicals, including *Babes in Arms* (1937, including "The Lady Is a Tramp") and *Pal Joey* (1940, "Bewitched"). After Hart's death in 1943 Rodgers worked with Oscar Hammerstein II; their collaborations included *Oklahoma!* (1943, including "Oh, What a Beautiful Mornin'," "Surrey with the Fringe on Top"), *Carousel* (1945, "June Is Bustin' Out All Over"), *South Pacific* (1949, "Bali Ha'i," "Some Enchanted Evening"), *The King and I* (1951, "Hello, Young Lovers") and *Sound of Music* (1959, "My Favorite Things," "Climb Every Mountain"). Rodgers was among the most exclusively Broadway-oriented of American songwriters, writing songs for film only during the brief period 1930–34. He also wrote symphonic music and the instrumental score for the World War II documentary *Victory at Sea* (1952).

Bibl.: Richard Rodgers, *Musical Stages: An Autobiography* (London, 1975). Stanley Green, *Rodgers and Hammerstein Fact Book* (New York, 1980; includes Hart productions). Steven Suskin, *Richard Rodgers: A Checklist of His Published Songs* (New York Public Library, 1984). Ethan Mordden, *Rodgers & Hammerstein* (New York, 1992).

Rodney, Red [Robert Chudnick] (b. Philadelphia, 27 Sept. 1927; d. Boynton Beach, Fla., 27 May 1994). Jazz trumpeter and bandleader. He played in the big bands of Gene Krupa (1946), Claude Thornhill (1947), and Woody Herman (1948–49), then joined Charlie Parker's bop quintet (1949–51, including the recording "Blues for Alice," 1951). Drug addiction ruined his career during the 1950s. He played in show bands in Las Vegas (1960–72). Subsequently he led bop groups, including a quintet with multi-instrumentalist Ira Sullivan which recorded the album *Live at the Village Vanguard* (1980). In the 1980s he made frequent world tours.

Rodolphe, Jean Joseph [Rudolph, Johann Joseph] (b. Strasbourg, 14 Oct. 1730; d. Paris, 12 or 18 Aug. 1812). Horn player, violinist, and composer. He studied with his father and with J. M. Leclair in Paris; by 1754 he was in Parma as violinist in the ducal orchestra, and he received counterpoint lessons from Traetta (from 1758). Around 1760 he joined the court orchestra in Stuttgart, completing his studies with Jomelli; with the choreographer J. G. Noverre he produced several ballets in Stuttgart, Ludwigsburg (*Médée et Jason,* 1763), and Paris. In 1764 he appeared as a horn virtuoso at the Concert spirituel in Paris, and in 1767 joined Prince Conti's orchestra, subsequently playing violin and horn in the Opéra orchestra. He was a composition teacher at the École royale de chant et de déclamation (from 1784), and after the Revolution taught solfège at the Conservatoire (1798–1802). Rodolphe befriended Mozart during the composer's 1778 visit to Paris.

Rodrigo, Joaquín (b. Sagunto, Spain, 22 Nov. 1901). Composer. Blind from childhood, he studied in Valencis with Ribes and Antioch. His *Cinco piezas infantiles* for orchestra won the 1925 National Prize. Enrolled in the Schola cantorum in 1927, studying with Dukas; he also grew close to de Falla. Returned to Spain in 1934, but upon reception of the Conde de Cartagena grant spent two more years in Paris, studying music history with Emmanuel and Pirro. Lived in northern Europe during the Civil War, moving to Madrid in 1939; the 1940 premiere of *Concierto de Aranjuez* for guitar and orchestra, his most famous work, propelled him to the forefront of Spanish music. A Manuel de Falla Chair was created for him at the Madrid Conservatory in 1947. His music offers a stylized view of the Spanish musical heritage in a lyrical, retrospective idiom, with some French elements.

Works: several concertos following the formula of his *Aranjuez* concerto, including *Concierto heroico* with piano (1942), *Concierto de Estío* with violin (1943), *Concierto en modo galante* with cello (1949), *Concierto serenata* with harp (1952), and others with guitar (*Fantasia para un gentilhombre,* 1954; *Concierto Andaluz,* 4 soloists, 1967; *Concierto madrigal,* 2 soloists, 1968; *Concierto para una fiesta,* 1982); orchestral music, including *Juglares* (1924), *Per la flor del lliri blau* (1939; incorporates Catalán and Valencian folk songs), *Soleriana* (1953), *Música para un jardin* (1957), and *Palillos y panderetas* (1982); stage music, including *Pavana real* (ballet, 1955), *El hijo fingido* (zarzuela, 1964), and *La azuzena de Quito* (opera, 1965); *Ausencias de Dulcinea* (1948) and *Rosalina* (1965), vocal soloists and orchestra; chamber and piano music; and songs.

Bibl.: Victoria Kamhi de Rodrigo, *Hand in Hand with Joaquin Rodrigo: My Life at the Maestro's Side,* trans. Ellen Wilkerson (Pittsburgh, 1992).

Rodrigues Coelho, Manuel (b. Elvas, ca. 1555; d. probably Lisbon, ca. 1635). Organist, composer. He studied at Elvas Cathedral; served as organist at Badajoz, 1573–77, at Elvas until 1602, and at the Lisbon court until retirement in 1633. He published the first extant volume of printed keyboard music in Portugal, *Flores de musica pera o instrumento de tecla & harpa* (Lisbon, 1620), containing 24 large *tientos* and over 100 shorter works. His style reflects influences of both Cabézon and the English-Dutch virginalists.

Rodríguez (Amador), Augusto (Alejandro) (b. San Juan, Puerto Rico, 9 Feb. 1904). Chorusmaster, conductor, and composer. Attended the Univ. of Puerto Rico (1920–21) and New York Univ. (1921–22), continuing his studies at Harvard and the New England Conservatory with Edward Burlingame Hill, Leichtentritt, and Piston; established the Midnight Serenaders (1925) and the Puerto Rico Philharmonic (1932) and joined the faculty of the Univ. of Puerto Rico in 1934. In 1936 he organized the Univ. of Puerto Rico Chorus and toured with that ensemble. Composed over 100 choral and some orchestral works.

Rodríguez, Robert Xavier (b. San Antonio, Tex., 28 June 1946). Composer. He studied at the Univ. of Texas (B.M., 1967; M.M., 1969) with Hunter Johnson and Kent Kennan, and at the Univ. of Southern California (D.M.A., 1975) with Halsey Stevens and Ingolf Dahl. Other teachers include Nadia Boulanger, Bruno Maderna, Elliott Carter, and Jacob Druckman. He taught at the Univ. of Southern California (1973–75) and, from 1975, at the Univ. of Texas, Dallas. He was composer-in-residence with the Dallas Symphony (1982–85). Works include *Le diable amoureux,* opera (1978); *Estampie,* ballet (1980); *Suor Isabella,* opera (1982); *Tango,* chamber opera (1985). Orchestra: *Adagio* (1967); *Lyric Variations* (1970); Concerto III, piano, orchestra (1974); Sinfonia concertante (1974); *Oktoechoes* (1983); *Trunks,* narrator, orchestra (1983); *A Colorful Symphony,* narrator, orchestra, optional visual effects (1988). Also chamber and vocal music.

Rodríguez de Hita, Antonio (b. ca. 1724; d. 21 Feb. 1787). Composer and theorist. He was *maestro de capilla* at both Palencia Cathedral (ca. 1740–ca. 1757) and the Madrid Convento real de la Encarnación. From 1768 he collaborated with the dramatist Ramón de la Cruz on a number of zarzuelas. His many choral works consist of liturgical Latin works, Spanish *villancicos,* and other part songs. In his *Diapasón instructivo* (Madrid, 1757) he reacted against the conservative musical style still prevalent in Spain. He proposed adherence to the new homophonic style and stressed simpler rules and greater freedom.

Bibl.: F. Bonastre, "Estudio de la obra teórica y prática del compositor Antonio Rodríguez de Hita," *Revista de musicologica* 2 (1979): 47–86.

Rodríguez de Ledesma, Mariano (b. Saragossa, 14 Dec. 1779; d. Madrid, 28 Mar. 1847). Composer. Studied with García and Palomar. Appointed conductor of opera company of Seville in 1800. Emigrated to London in 1811; named honorary member of Philharmonic Society. Returned to Spain in 1814; named first tenor of the royal chapel. Wrote *40 ejercicios de vo-*

calizacíon (Madrid, 1820). Returned to England, 1823–31; member of the Royal Academy of Music.

Bibl.: Rafael Mitjana y Gordon, *El maestro Rodríguez de Ledesma y sus Lamentaciones de Semana Santa: Estudio crítico biográfico* (Málaga, 1909).

Rodzinski, Artur (b. Spalato, 1 Jan. 1892; d. Boston, 27 Nov. 1958). Conductor. Of Polish descent; studied law in Vienna, simultaneously taking composition with Joseph Marx and Franz Schreker, conducting with Franz Schalk, and piano with Emil Sauer and Georg Lalewicz. After conducting appearances in Warsaw he was appointed guest conductor (1925) and then assistant conductor (1926) of the Philadelphia Orchestra under Stokowski, and joined the faculty of the Curtis Institute. He became conductor of the Los Angeles Philharmonic in 1929 and in 1933 began a ten-year tenure as conductor of the Cleveland Orchestra, during which time it became one of the premiere ensembles in the U.S. Rodzinski was appointed music director of the New York Philharmonic in 1943, but management disputes forced him to resign four years later; his tenure as music director of the Chicago Symphony (1947–48) was even briefer owing to similar problems with management. Subsequently he moved to Europe, conducting frequently in concert and opera (including the western stage premiere of Prokofiev's *War and Peace*).

Rogatis, Pascual de. See De Rogatis, Pascual.

Rogel, José (b. Orihuela, 24 Dec. 1829; d. Cartagena, 25 Feb. 1901). Composer. He studied piano and theory with Joaquin Cascales, organist of Orihuela Cathedral, then law at Valencia (1845–51), where he also took composition lessons from the cathedral organist Pascual Pérez Gascón. In 1852 he went to Madrid and taught piano and singing, arranged zarzuelas for piano, and published some of his works. From 1854 to 1875 he wrote 81 zarzuelas, the most successful of which was *El joven Telémaco* (1865).

Roger, Estienne (b. Caen, 1665 or 1666; d. Amsterdam, 7 July 1722). Music printer. He moved to Amsterdam with his family by 1686, entered the printing trade soon after, and by 1697 he was publishing music and other books under his own name. Roger used his elder daughter's name, Jeanne, on his publications from 1716, leaving the business to her on his death; the firm eventually passed to an employee, Gerrit Drinkman, and then Roger's son-in-law Michel-Charles Le Cène, who maintained it until his own death in 1743. Between 1696 and 1743, 600 titles were printed by the firm, many direct copies from foreign publishers; Roger's stock was particularly strong on Italian composers, including Vivaldi, Corelli, Albinoni, and Marcello. He had an impressive network of distributing agents in many major cities, and was the first printer to use publishers' numbers.

Roger, Gustave-Hippolyte (b. Paris, 17 Dec. 1815; d. there, 12 Sept. 1879). Tenor. Studied with Blès Martin at the Paris Conservatory beginning in 1836; won first prize for singing (1836) and opéra comique (1837). Debuted in 1838 at the Opéra-comique in Halévy's *L'éclair;* premiered many roles by Halévy, Auber, and Thomas. Sang in the first performance of *La damnation de Faust* (as Faust, 1848). Moved to the Opéra in 1849; premiered Meyerbeer's *Le prophète* (as Jean de Leyde, 1849). An accidental shooting forced the amputation of his right arm; he used a mechanical arm after this. Retired in 1861. Taught singing at the Paris Conservatory, 1868–79. Published his autobiography *(Le carnet d'un)* in 1880.

Roger, Victor (b. Montpellier, 22 July 1853; d. Paris, 2 Dec. 1903). Composer. Studied at the École Niedermeyer. Composed songs and operettas for the Eldorado music hall. Critic for *La France;* edited theatrical entries in *Petit journal.* He composed over 25 operettas including *Mademoiselle Louloute* (1882), *Joséphine vendue par ses soeurs* (1886), *Le Fétiche* (1890), and *Miss Nicol-Nick* (1895).

Roger-Ducasse, Jean (Jules Aimable) (b. Bordeaux, 18 Apr. 1873; d. Taillan-Médoc, Gironde, 19 July 1954). Composer. He studied at the Paris Conservatory with Fauré, Pessard (harmony), Gédalge (counterpoint), and de Bériot. In 1910 he was appointed inspector general of singing in schools in Paris; later he joined the faculty of the Paris Conservatory, teaching compsition from 1935 to 1940. His early music is influenced by Fauré and Debussy (String Quartet, 1909) as well as by an attempt to establish a more individual path. His four-act opera *Cantegril* was successfully produced in Paris in 1931. Other works include *Orphée,* monodrama, libretto by the composer (1914). For orchestra: *Au jardin de Marguerite,* soloists, chorus, orchestra (1901–5); *Suite française* (1907); *Nocturne de printemps* (1920); *Epithalame* (1923). Also chamber and keyboard music (*Six préludes,* piano, 1908; *Pastorale,* organ, 1909).

Rogers, Benjamin (b. Windsor, bapt. 2 June 1614; d. Oxford, June 1698). Organist and composer. He was a chorister at St. George's Chapel, Windsor; became organist of Christ Church Cathedral, Dublin, 1638; then returned to Windsor as a lay clerk, 1641. He served as organist of Eton College (1660–64) and was again appointed lay clerk at St. George's in 1662; from 1664 to 1686 he served as organist and *informator choristarum* of Magdalen College, Oxford. His compositions include anthems and some instrumental works.

Rogers, Bernard (b. New York, 4 Feb. 1893; d. Rochester, N.Y., 24 May 1968). Composer. He had piano lessons starting at age 12; at 15 he left school to work for an architecture firm in New York, and also spent time painting. His musical training continued in study with Hans van den Berg (theory), Farwell (composition), and Bloch (harmony, composition). In 1921 he entered the Institute of Musical Art to study with Goetschius. He later studied with Frank Bridge in England

and with Boulanger in Paris. He taught at the Cleveland Institute (1922–23), at the Hartt School of Music (1926–27), and at Eastman (1929–67). Among his students were the composers Mennin, Argento, Diamond, and Ussachevsky. Known for his delicate orchestral colors, he published *The Art of Orchestration* in 1951 (R: 1970). His orchestra piece *To the Fallen* (1918) helped earn him a Pulitzer Traveling Scholarship. His operas *The Marriage of Ande* (1931) and *The Warrior* (1944) were quite successful. Other works include the operas *The Veil* (1950) and *The Nightingale* (1954). For chorus with orchestra: *The Raising of Lazarus* (1929); *The Exodus* (1931); *The Passion* (1942); *A Letter from Pete* (1947); *The Light of Man* (1964). Also 5 symphonies (1926, 1928, 1936, 1940, 1959) and other orchestral works; chamber music (2 string quartets, 1918, 1925); and songs.

Rogers [née Barnett], **Clara Kathleen** [Doria, Clara] (b. Cheltenham, England, 14 Jan. 1844; d. Boston, 8 Mar. 1931). Soprano and composer. Daughter of composer John Barnett. She was the youngest student ever accepted at the Leipzig Conservatory (1856); studied piano there with von Bülow. Studied singing in Berlin and Milan. Debuted at Turin as Isabella in Meyerbeer's *Robert le diable* (1861 or 1862). American debut in Balfe's *Bohemian Girl.* Married lawyer Henry Munroe Rogers in 1878 and ended her performing career. Named professor of singing at New England Conservatory in 1902. Wrote a violin sonata (1888), string quartet (1866), Scherzo op. 15, piano (1883), cello sonata, many songs.

Rogers, Shorty [Rajonsky, Milton M.] (b. Great Barrington, Mass., 14 Apr. 1924; d. Van Nuys, Calif., 7 Nov. 1994). Jazz composer, arranger, trumpeter, flügelhorn player, and bandleader. He joined Woody Herman (1945–49), wrote for Stan Kenton (1950–51), and then became active in West Coast jazz, playing in Howard Rumsey's Lighthouse All Stars and leading groups. His albums included *Cool and Crazy* (1953) and *The Swinging Mr. Rogers* (1955). He contributed arrangements to the sound tracks of the films *The Wild One* (1954) and *The Man with the Golden Arm* (1955), and from the 1960s has composed for film and television. He resumed playing jazz in the mid-1980s.

Rogier, Philippe (b. Arras, ca. 1561; d. Madrid, 29 Feb. 1596). Composer. In 1572 he came from Flanders to the Madrid court, under Philip II, as a boy chorister. There he remained in service, becoming in 1584 *vice-maestro de capilla* (second to de la Hèle), and in 1586 maestro. He was prolific in his short career and widely admired. His only works to survive (mostly in published form) are 7 Masses, 18 motets, and 4 chansons.

Rogowski, Ludomir Michel (b. Lublin, 3 Oct. 1881; d. Dubrovnik, 14 Mar. 1954). Composer. He studied composition with Noskowski and conducting with Młynarski at the Warsaw Conservatory. Traveled to Leipzig to study with Nikisch and Riemann in 1906, returning to Poland in 1909. In 1910 he organized the Vilnius Symphony and served as its first conductor. Throughout the 1910s he toured western Europe as a conductor, moving permanently to Dubrovnik in 1926. His music was characterized by unusual scalar bases for harmony and melody, such as Persian scales, the "Slavonic" scale, and the whole-tone scale. His music contained references to folk music and utilized traditional forms and genres. Works include operas and ballets; 7 symphonies (1926–51); vocal music (*Fantasmagorie,* voice, orchestra, 1920; cantatas); and chamber music.

Roig, Gonzalo (b. Havana, 20 July 1890; d. there, 13 June 1970). Composer and conductor. Worked as a violinist in theater orchestras before founding the Orquesta sinfónica de la Habana in 1922. His song "Quiéreme mucho" (1912) enjoyed widespread popularity; he also was active as a zarzuela composer.

Roland-Manuel [Lévy, Roland Alexis Manuel] (b. Paris, 22 Mar. 1891; d. there, 2 Nov. 1966). Composer. Studied with Roussel at the Schola cantorum in Paris and later privately with Ravel. He joined the faculty of the Paris Conservatory in 1947. Became well known through his founding of a radio show, *Plaisir de la musique,* which appeared in book form (Paris, 1947–55). He was active as a writer on music and as an administrator. His compositional style was definitively anti-Romantic and marked by the restraint and refinement of Ravel's music. He wrote 3 books on Ravel: *Maurice Ravel et son oeuvre* (Paris, 1914); *Maurice Ravel et son oeuvre dramatique* (Paris, 1929); *Maurice Ravel* (Paris, 1938, 2/1948); trans. Eng. (1947). He also wrote on Satie and de Falla. Compositions include 5 operas (*Isabelle et Pantalon,* 1920; *Le diable amoureux,* 1932), ballets (*L'écran des jeunes filles,* 1928), orchestral music (Piano Concerto, 1938), choral and chamber music, and songs.

Bibl.: Robert Craft, "Roland-Manuel and the Poetics of Music," *PNM* 21 (1982–83): 487–505.

Roldán, Amadeo (b. Paris, 12 July 1900; d. Havana, 2 Mar. 1939). Composer. His parents were Cuban. Studied with Hernández (theory) and Soller and Bordas (violin) at the Madrid Conservatory, graduating in 1916 and taking the Saraste Prize; later took private composition lessons with del Campo and Sanjuan and performed on the violin throughout Spain. Moved to Havana in 1921, becoming concertmaster, assistant conductor, and in 1932 music director of the Havana Philharmonic. Initially playing viola in the Philharmonic's chamber music society, in 1927 he founded the Havana String Quartet, giving periodic contemporary concerts. He founded the Escuela nacional de música in 1931; from 1935 to his death he taught at the Havana Conservatory, directing it from 1936 to 1938. He was the leading Cuban musical figure of his day; as a composer he was the first to integrate Afro-Cuban elements into European-oriented concert music, and among the first to compose works for percussion only.

Works: *La Rebambaramba* (1928) and *El milagro de Anaquillé* (1929), ballets; *Obertura sobre temas cubanas* (1925), *Tres pequeños poemas* (1926), *Tres toques* (1931), and *Marcha solemne* (1936) for orchestra; chamber music, including 6 *Rítmicas* (1930), I–IV for wind quintet, V–VI for percussion ensemble; vocal works, including *Danza negra* (1928) and *Motivos de son* (1934), both for voice and 7 instruments; and piano music.

Bibl.: *Composers of the Americas* 1 (Washington, D.C., 1955), pp. 77–83 [includes works list].

Rolla, Alessandro (b. Pavia, 6 Apr. 1757; d. Milan, 15 Sept. 1841). Violinist, violist, and composer. He probably studied in Milan, then became first violist (later first violinist) at the ducal court in Parma (1782–1802). He was first violinist and director of the orchestra at La Scala in Milan (1803–33), and first professor of violin and viola at Milan Conservatory (1808–35). A prolific composer for the violin and viola, he wrote concertos, chamber music, and pedagogical pieces.

Bibl.: Luigi Inzaghi and Luigi Alberto Bianchi, *Alessandro Rolla: Catalogo tematico delle opere* (Milan, 1981).

Rolle, Johann Heinrich (b. Quedlinburg, 23 Dec. 1716; d. Magdeburg, 29 Dec. 1785). Composer. He served as organist in Magdeburg from 1732, left for Leipzig in 1736, and ended up in Berlin, where he served as violinist and violist in Frederick the Great's court orchestra (1741–47). He returned to Magdeburg as organist at the Johanniskirche, and after his father's death in 1751 succeeded him as city music director. He was best known in his time as a composer of dramatic oratorios, 12 of which were published in keyboard reductions; *Der Tod Abels* (1769) was a particular favorite.

Rolli, Paolo Antonio (b. Rome, 13 June 1687; d. Todi, 20 Mar. 1765). Poet and librettist. He studied with Gian Vincenzo Gravina, and was invited to England in 1715 by the Earl of Pembroke or the Earl of Stair; he remained in London for 29 years, where he taught Italian, published poems and translations, and served as Italian secretary to the Royal Academy of Music (1719–22). A number of his librettos or adaptations were set by Handel (*Floridante, Scipione, Alessandro, Riccardo Primo,* and *Deidamia*) as well as other composers, including Bononcini and Galuppi.

Rollini, Adrian (b. New York, 28 June 1904; d. Homestead, Fla., 15 May 1956). Jazz instrumentalist. Principally a bass saxophonist, he also played goofus (a keyboard harmonica), hot fountain pen (a miniature clarinet), and vibraphone. From 1922 into the 1930s he recorded with the California Ramblers, Miff Mole ("Feelin' No Pain," 1927), Bix Beiderbecke ("At the Jazz Band Ball," 1927), Joe Venuti, and many others including his own groups. He interrupted this studio work in New York to join a dance orchestra in London (1927–29). From around 1934, when he founded the nightclub Adrian's Tap Room in New York, he led groups and concentrated on playing vibraphone. His brother Art (Arthur) Rollini (b. 1912) played tenor saxophone in several of the same bands and also with Benny Goodman (1934–39); his autobiography *Thirty Years with the Big Bands* (London, 1987) is the standard source on both brothers.

Rollins, Sonny [Theodore Walter; Newk] (b. New York, 7 Sept. 1930). Jazz tenor saxophonist and bandleader. From 1949 to 1954 he recorded with J. J. Johnson, Charlie Parker, Fats Navarro, Bud Powell, Max Roach, Art Blakey, Thelonious Monk, the Modern Jazz Quartet, and (most frequently) Miles Davis, whose album *Miles Davis Quintet* (1954) includes Rollins's own bop themes "Airegin," "Doxy," and "Oleo." Successfully overcoming drug addiction, he joined the Clifford Brown–Max Roach Quintet (1955–56, including his album *Sonny Rollins Plus 4,* 1956), remaining after Brown's death until 1957, when he briefly rejoined Davis. He subsequently led groups, apart from a tour with the Milestone Jazzstars (including Ron Carter and McCoy Tyner) in 1978. His great strengths were as a bop soloist (the albums *Worktime,* 1955; *Tenor Madness,* 1956; *Way Out West,* 1957) and in a fusion of bop with calypso music ("St. Thomas," on the album *Saxophone Colossus,* 1956). In the mid-1960s he turned toward free jazz (initially in a group with Don Cherry and Billy Higgins) and began to focus on unaccompanied performance. From 1972 he often joined his bop-inspired improvising to rhythm sections oriented toward African American dance music.

Bibl.: Charles Blancq, *Sonny Rollins: The Journey of a Jazzman* (Boston, 1983).

Rolón, José (b. Jalisco, 22 June 1883; d. Mexico City, 3 Feb. 1945). Composer. He first studied music with his father; then went to Paris to study with Moszkowski (piano) and Gédalge (fugue) from 1903 to 1907. He returned to Mexico to found and direct a music school until 1927, when he returned to Paris to study with Boulanger and Dukas. He taught at the Mexican National Conservatory (1930–38). His ballet *El festín de los enanos* is based on his native folk idiom. Other works include the symphonic *Cuauhtémoc* (1929), a piano concerto (1935), a piano quartet (1912), and other chamber music and songs.

Roman, Johan Helmich (b. Stockholm, 26 Oct. 1694; d. Haraldsmåla, near Kalmar, 20 Nov. 1758). Composer. He served the royal chapel from 1711 and traveled to England in 1715, where he probably studied with Pepusch and came into contact with Geminiani and Handel. On his return to Sweden in 1721 he was appointed deputy master of the chapel, becoming chief master in 1727 until his retirement in 1745. A second journey took place in 1735–37, with stops in Germany, Austria, England, France, and Italy. Perhaps the foremost Swedish composer of his time. Roman's instrumental works are stylistically similar to those of Handel and Geminiani; his most famous composition is the orchestral suite *Drottningholmsmusiquen* (1744; R: Stockholm, 1958).

Bibl.: Ingmar Bengtsson, *Mr. Roman's Spuriosity Shop: A Thematic Catalogue of 503 Works . . . from ca. 1680–1750* (Stockholm, 1976).

Romani, Felice (b. Genoa, 31 Jan. 1788; d. Mareglia, 28 Jan. 1865). Librettist. Studied at the Univ. of Pisa. Taught in Genoa, then traveled to and settled in Milan. Wrote libretti for nearly 100 operas, among them operas by Mayr (including *La rosa bianca e la rosa rossa,* 1813), Rossini (including *Il turco in Italia,* 1814), Donizetti (including *Anna Bolena,* 1830; *L'elisir d'amore,* 1832; *Ugo, conte di Parigi,* 1832), Bellini (including *Il pirata,* 1827; *La sonnambula,* 1831; *Norma,* 1831), Verdi (*Un giorno di regno,* 1840), Meyerbeer (*Margherita d'Anjou,* 1820; *L'esule di Granata,* 1822), Mercadante, and Pacini.

Romanos the Melode (b. Emesia?, Syria, late 5th century; d. Constantinople, after 555). Hymn writer. He was a deacon in the Church of the Resurrection in Beirut; from around the end of the century he served in the Church of the Virgin in the Kyrou quarter of Constantinople. The chief Byzantine hymnist of his era, he allegedly wrote 1,000 *kontakia,* about 60 of which are extant in words; none of his melodies survives.

Romberg, Andreas Jakob (b. Vechta, near Münster, 27 Apr. 1767; d. Gotha, 10 Nov. 1821). Violinist and composer. After studying violin with his father, he and his cousin Bernhard Heinrich Romberg embarked on concert tours to Frankfurt am Main (1782) and Paris (1784 and 1785). The cousins then joined the electoral orchestra in Bonn (1790) and the opera orchestra of the Ackermann Theater in Hamburg (1793). In 1795 they toured Italy and in 1796 visited Vienna, where they met Haydn and played with Beethoven. They returned to Hamburg that year; apart from a trip to Paris in 1801, Andreas remained there. He turned to composing, later becoming *Hofkapellmeister* in Gotha. His works include operas, choral music (*Das Lied von der Glocke,* Schiller), 10 symphonies, 30 concertos, 19 string quartets, and other chamber music.

Romberg, Bernhard Heinrich (b. Dinklage, Oldenburg, ?11 Nov. 1767; d. Hamburg, 13 Aug. 1841). Cellist and composer. After studying cello with his father, he pursued the identical performing career as his cousin Andreas Jakob Romberg. He toured Spain on his own (1801) before teaching at the Conservatory in Paris. In 1805 he joined the Berlin royal court orchestra, then made lengthy concert tours. From 1816 until 1819 he was *Hofkapellmeister* in Berlin. He then lived in Hamburg (1820), later returning to Berlin (1826–31). His compositions include operas, symphonies, concertos, and chamber music.

Romberg, Sigmund (b. Nagy Kaniga, Hungary, 29 July 1887; d. New York, 9 Nov. 1951). Composer, conductor. Trained in engineering in Vienna, he came to New York in 1909 and found work as a café pianist, bandleader, and songwriter. From 1913 he worked as chief house composer for the Shubert brothers, writing musical reviews. From 1915 to the depression he composed Viennese-style operettas on the model of Lehar and Friml. Notable successes included *Maytime* (1917), *Blossom Time* (1921, using melodies of Schubert), *The Student Prince* (1924), *Desert Song* (1926), and *New Moon* (1928). During the 1930s he wrote Hollywood film scores; in the 1940s he toured with his own orchestra. His later shows (including *Up in Central Park,* 1945; *The Girl in Pink Tights,* 1954) adapted newer Broadway styles. Among his popular songs are "When Hearts Are Young," "Deep in My Heart," and "Lover, Come Back to Me."

Romero. Family of guitarists. Celedonio Romero (b. Málaga, Spain, 2 Mar. 1918) and his three sons, Celín (b. Málaga, 23 Nov. 1940), Pepe (b. Málaga, 8 Mar. 1944), and Ángel (b. Málaga, 17 Aug. 1946), formed the guitar quartet Los Romeros. A guitar soloist in Spain, Celedonio taught his sons the guitar from an early age; all three sons made their debuts by age 7. Because it was difficult to accept foreign engagements while in General Franco's Spain, the family moved to Portugal and then to California in 1958. In 1961 they toured the U.S. and played in New York at Town Hall and Carnegie Hall. They subsequently appeared with many of the leading orchestras in the U.S., performed abroad, and made numerous recordings. Their repertory includes the family's own flamenco arrangements and classical transcriptions, as well as works by Joaquín Rodrigo, Francisco de Medina, and Federico Moreno Torroba. Pepe and Ángel Romero also maintained solo careers.

Romero, Mateo [Rosmarin, Mathieu] (b. Liège, 1575 or 1576; d. Madrid, 10 May 1647). Composer. He served as a royal choirboy in Madrid from 1586 to 1593 before joining the Flemish chapel, where he became *maestro de capilla* (1598–1634). He was ordained a priest in 1609 and served as chaplain to Philip III in 1605, and also held a nonresidential post of chaplain to the court of John IV of Portugal from 1644. Romero was highly regarded in his time as a composer of sacred and secular vocal music; many of his works are no longer extant.

Ronald [Russell], **Landon** (b. London, 7 June 1873; d. there, 14 Aug. 1938). Conductor and composer. He studied at the Royal College of Music with Parry and Stanford. His appointment as a guest conductor of the London Symphony (1904–7) led to engagements in 1908 in Berlin, Vienna, Leipzig, and Amsterdam. He conducted the New Symphony (1909–14) and the Scottish Orchestra (1916–20), and served as principal of the Guildhall School of Music (1910–38). Perhaps his most important role was as musical director for the

HMV label in its early years. Works include an operetta, a ballet, orchestral music, and about 300 songs.

Ronger, Florimond. See Hervé.

Ronstadt, (Maria) Linda (b. Tucson, Ariz., 15 July 1946). Popular singer. From 1964 performed with country-rock groups including the Stone Poneys in Los Angeles; from 1974 released solo recordings. Particularly popular were her renditions of rock-and-roll era songs, including Buddy Holly's "That'll Be the Day" (1976) and Roy Orbison's "Blue Bayou" (1977); she also produced 2 albums of Tin Pan Alley standards with Nelson Riddle and an album of Mexican ballads (*Canciones di mi Padre,* 1988).

Röntgen, Julius (b. Leipzig, 9 May 1855; d. Bilthoven, near Utrecht, 13 Sept. 1932). Composer, conductor, and pianist. Son of Engelbert Röntgen (1829–97). Studied with Friedrich Lachner, Hauptmann, E. F. Richter, Louis Plaidy, and Reinecke. Taught in Amsterdam (1877–1925); conductor of Society for the Promotion of Music (1886–98). Cofounder of Amsterdam Conservatory, 1884; director, 1914–24. Conductor of Amsterdam Toonkunstkoor (1886–98). Accompanied Messchaert and Casals. Formed piano trio with his sons Julius (1881–1951) and Engelbert (1886–1958). Composed 21 symphonies, 7 piano concertos, 2 violin concertos, 2 cello concertos, piano trios, piano quintets, cello sonatas, viola sonatas, violin sonatas, oboe sonata.

Rooley, Anthony (b. Leeds, 10 June 1944). Lutenist. He studied the guitar with Hector Quine at the Royal Academy of Music (1965–68); on the lute he is self-taught. He founded the Consort of Musicke, a group specializing in Renaissance music, with James Tyler in 1969. Beginning in 1972 Rooley became the sole director of the ensemble. He has concertized extensively in Europe and the U.S. with sopranos Emma Kirkby and Evelyn Tubb, alto Mary Nichols, tenors Andrew King and Paul Agnew, and bass David Thomas.

Root, George Frederick (b. Sheffield, Mass., 30 Aug. 1820; d. Bailey Island, Maine, 6 Aug. 1895). Composer. Had first formal music lessons at age 18 with Artemas Nixon Johnson (piano) and George James Webb (singing) in Boston. Assistant at Lowell Mason's public school music classes. Taught in New York at several institutions including Union Theological Seminary. Studied with Alary and Potharst at Paris Conservatory (1850–51). Composed several cantatas including *The Young Ladies' Choir* (1846), *The Pilgrim Fathers* (1854), *Belshazzar's Feast* (1860), *The Haymakers* (1857). Critic for *New York Musical Review and Choral Advocate.* Published songs during the 1850s and 1860s under the pseudonym G. Friedrich Wurzel. Published his autobiography, *The Story of a Musical Life* (Cincinnati, 1891).

Rootham, Cyril Bradley (b. Bristol, 5 Oct. 1875; d. Cambridge, 18 Mar. 1938). Composer and organist. Studied classics and music at St. John's College, Cambridge; then studied at the Royal College of Music with Stanford, Parratt, and Barton. From 1902 until his death he served at St. John's as organist; also conducted its musical society and lectured there. He is known primarily for his vocal and symphonic works, both of which were usually for large forces. Compositions include 1 opera (*The Two Sisters,* 1920); orchestral music (Symphony no. 1, 1932); vocal music (*Ode on the Morning of Christ's Nativity,* solo voices, chorus, orchestra, 1928; Symphony no. 2, Revelation, female voices, orchestra, 1938; *Full Fathom Five,* unaccompanied female voices, 1937).

Ropartz, Joseph Guy (Marie) [Guy-Ropartz, Joseph] (b. Guingamp, Brittany, 15 June 1864; d. Lanloup, Brittany, 22 Nov. 1955). Composer and conductor. He studied at the Paris Conservatory with Dubois and Massenet, then privately with César Franck, to whose school he adhered. He directed the Nancy Conservatory (1894–1919) and the Strasbourg Municipal Orchestra (1919–29). His music draws often upon Breton-Celtic imagery, lore, and landscape. He composed an opera, *Le pays* (1910); ballets and incidental scores; 5 symphonies; 8 symphonic poems *(La cloche des morts,* 1887, *La chasse du Prince Arthur,* 1912); *Rapsodie,* cello and orchestra (1928); 6 string quartets; violin sonatas; cello sonatas; many piano pieces, organ pieces, songs.

Rore, Cypriano de (b. Machelen, Flanders, Mechelen, or Ronse, 1515 or 1516; d. Parma, Sept. 1565). Composer. A plaque in the Parma Cathedral gives his age as 49 at the time of his death. Details concerning his early years and schooling are lacking; his pupil Luzzaschi indicated in 1606 that Rore had composed a certain Miserere in "Flanders when he was young." Bernhard Meier posits that he served Margaret of Parma before her 1536 marriage to Alessandro de' Medici. His First Book of Madrigals (1542) contains dense, erudite 5-part settings of Petrarchan verse, indicating a close association with Willaert and his circle in Venice. References to Rore in the correspondence of Ruberto Strozzi, discovered by Richard Agee, show his presence at Brescia from 1541, a year in which he visited Venice, through 1545; Ruberto bought several of Rore's works during this time. Rore was *maestro di cappella* to Ercole II of Ferrara from at least November 1546 until the duke's death in 1559, when he was released from the court establishment. He had visited his parents in the North in 1558. He served Margaret of Parma at Brussels during 1560 and her husband, Ottavio Farnese, at Parma from 1561 until 1563, when he was named Willaert's successor at St. Mark's in Venice. The position was a disappointment; he returned to Parma the following year. Many later musicians acknowledged deep debts to him, including Monteverdi, who named Rore as the founder of the *seconda prattica* on the basis of his chromatic madrigals.

His works include 5 Masses; a St. John Passion; 3

Cypriano de Rore.

books of 5-voice motets (1544, 1545, 1549) and 1 for 4 voices (1563); 4 books of 5-voice madrigals (1542, 1544, 1548, and 1557, the last shared with several composers) and 2 books for 4 voices (1550 and 1557, the latter shared with Palestrina). Another collection was published posthumously, with a glowing dedication by Gardane; a 1577 edition in score of 4-voice madrigals for instrumental use or for study was brought out by the same publisher.

Bibl.: *Cypriano de Rore, opera omnia,* ed. Bernhard Meier (Rome, 1959–). Jessie Ann Owens, "The Milan Partbooks: Evidence of Cypriano de Rore's Compositional Process," *JAMS* 37 (1984): 270–98. Edward E. Lowinsky, *Cipriano de Rore's Venus Motet: Its Poetic and Pictorial Sources* (Provo, Utah, 1986). Stefano La Via, "Cypriano de Rore as Reader and Read: A Literary-Musical Study of Madrigals from Rore's Later Collections (1557–1566)" (diss., Princeton Univ. 1991).

Rorem, Ned (Richmond, Ind., 23 Oct. 1923). Composer, pianist, and author. Received early training from Leo Sowerby in Chicago. He attended Northwestern Univ. (1940–42), Curtis Institute (1942–43), and the Juilliard School, where he took a B.A. and an M.A. (1946, 1948); studied privately with Virgil Thomson, whose special influence he acknowledges, and Aaron Copland. He lived briefly in Morocco (1949–51), then in Paris under the patronage of the Vicomtesse Marie Laure de Noailles. After returning to America in 1959 he held teaching posts at the Univ. of Buffalo (1959–60), Univ. of Utah (1966–67), and Curtis Institute (1980–86). He distinguished himself especially as a composer for the voice and is widely considered preeminent among American art song writers; nevertheless, an instrumental work *(Air Music,* for the U.S. Bicentennial) won a Pulitzer Prize. His idiom is economical and rooted in diatonicism.

Works: song cycles with piano or small ensemble *(Flight for Heaven,* 1952; *14 Songs on American Poetry,* 1958; *Poems of Love and the Rain,* 1965; *War Songs,* 1971; *Last Poems of Wallace Stevens,* 1974; *Women's Voices,* 1979; *Santa Fe Songs,* 1980; *The Nantucket Songs,* 1981; *Songs of Sadness,* voice, guitar, cello, clarinet, 1994); vocal works with orchestra *(Sun,* 1969; *Swords and Plowshares,* 4 solo voices, orchestra, 1990; *More Than a Day,* voice, orchestra, 1995); over 80 individual songs; over 50 choral works (some with orchestra); 11 operas; 25 orchestral works, including symphonies, concertos, and tone poems *(Eagles,* 1959; *Air Music,* 1975; violin concerto, 1985; *Goodbye My Fancy,* orchestra, 1990; Concerto, left-hand, 1991; *Triptych,* chamber orchestra, 1992; English horn concerto, 1993); chamber works (*Scenes from Childhood,* oboe, horn, string quartet, piano, 1985; string quartet no. 3, 1990; string quartet no. 4, 1995); piano, harpsichord, and organ pieces.

Writings: *The Paris Diary of Ned Rorem* (1966; R: 1983). *The New York Diary* (1967; R: 1983). *The Final Diary: 1961–72* (1974; R: 1983 as *The Later Diaries*). *The Nantucket Diary of Ned Rorem: 1973–1985* (1987). *Settling the Score* (1988). *Knowing When To Stop: A Memoir* (New York, 1994). Other books.

Bibl.: Arlys McDonald, *Ned Rorem: A Bio-Bibliography* (New York, 1989).

Rosa [Rose], **Carl (August Nikolaus)** (b. Hamburg, 22 Mar. 1842; d. Paris, 30 Apr. 1889). Violinist and conductor. Toured England, Denmark, and Germany as a violinist in 1844. Studied at the conservatories in Leipzig and Paris. *Konzertmeister* in Hamburg, 1863–65. During a tour of the U.S., he met the soprano Euphrosyne Parepa, whom he married in 1867. The two formed an opera company in which she sang all the leading roles. Toured England in 1871; visited Egypt for health reasons. Opened an opera company in London (1875) that performed operas in English.

Rosa, Salvator [Salvatore] (b. Arenella, Naples, 21? July 1615; d. Rome, 15 Mar. 1673). Painter and poet. He went to Rome, then lived in Florence from 1640 to 1649; returned to Rome in 1649, where he stayed for the rest of his life. Contrary to Burney's claim, it appears that Rosa did not compose any music, although his friend Antonio Cesti provided musical settings of some of Rosa's poems. Rosa is principally known as the author of *La musica,* a satire that was distributed widely in the 18th century; Mattheson criticized it in his *Mithridat* (1749).

Rosales, Antonio (b. Madrid, ca. 1740; d. there, 1801). Composer. In 1769 he became *músico secundario* of the Madrid theater company. His popular one-act zarzuela *El licendiado Farfulla* had its premiere at the Teatro del Príncipe. About 1787 he became *maestro de capilla* of the Encarnación convent at Madrid, succeeding Rodríguez de Hita. His compositions include at least 150 *tonadillas, entremeses,* and *sainetes.*

Rosbaud, Hans (b. Graz, 22 July 1895; d. Lugano, 29 Dec. 1962). Conductor. He studied piano with Alfred Hoehn and composition with Bernhard Sekles at the Hoch Conservatory in Frankfurt. In 1921 he became director of the Städtische Musikschule at Mainz. As musical director of Frankfurt Radio (1928–37) he conducted the premieres of Schoenberg's *Four Songs with Orchestra* op. 22 (1932) and Bartók's Piano Concerto no. 2 with the composer as soloist (1933). After serving as *Generalmusikdirektor* at Münster (1937–41) and Strasbourg (1941–44), and of the Munich Philharmonic (1945–48), he was principal conductor of the Southwest German Radio Orchestra at Baden-Baden and the Zurich Tonhalle Orchestra. In 1954 and 1957 he conducted the radio and stage premieres of Schoenberg's *Moses und Aron.*

Bibl.: Joan Evans, *Hans Rosbaud: A Bio-Bibliography* (New York, 1992).

Rosé, Arnold (Josef) (b. Iaşi, Romania, 24 Oct. 1863; d. London, 25 Aug. 1946). Violinist. After study with Heissler at the Vienna Conservatory, he made his debut at a Leipzig Gewandhaus concert in 1879. From 1881 to 1938 he was leader of the Vienna Court Opera (later Staatsoper) orchestra and of the Vienna Philharmonic; he often led the orchestra at the Bayreuth Festival. In 1882 he founded the Rosé Quartet, which toured widely and was recognized as one of the finest quartets of its time. The quartet gave premieres of works by Brahms, Pfitzner, Reger, and Schoenberg. Rosé taught at the Vienna Academy of Music from 1893 to 1924. He left Vienna in 1938 and played chamber music in England until 1945.

Rose, Fred (Knols) (b. Evansville, Ind., 24 Aug. 1897; d. Nashville, Tenn., 1 Dec. 1954). Country and popular songwriter and publisher. Began writing popular songs ("Red Hot Mama," 1924); from 1940, collaborated with Gene Autry on songs for musical westerns; in 1942, founded the first country publishing house with Roy Acuff in Nashville. There he developed talent (Hank Williams) and wrote country songs, many of which have become standards ("Blue Eyes Cryin' in the Rain," 1945).

Rose, Leonard (Joseph) (b. Washington, 27 July 1918; d. White Plains, N.Y., 16 Nov. 1984). Cellist. He studied with Felix Salmond at the Curtis Institute (1934–38); was principal cellist of the Cleveland Orchestra (1939–43) and played with the New York Philharmonic (1943–51), then toured as a soloist and organized a trio with Isaac Stern and Eugene Istomin. He taught at the Cleveland Institute, the Juilliard School, Oberlin College, and the Curtis Institute; among his pupils were Lynn Harrell and Yo-Yo Ma.

Roseingrave, Thomas (b. Winchester, 1688; d. Dunleary, 23 June 1766). Organist and composer. He went to Dublin as a boy, where his father, Daniel (d. 1727), served as organist at Christ Church Cathedral and St. Patrick's. Thomas journeyed to Italy in 1709 and befriended Domenico Scarlatti in Venice; he returned to England in 1714 or 1715, produced Scarlatti's opera *Amor d'un'ombra* under the title *Narciso* in 1720, and in 1739 his edition of Scarlatti's 42 sonatas appeared. He served as organist of St. George's, Hanover Square, from 1725, eventually retiring to Dublin, where his opera *Phaedra and Hippolitus* was produced in 1753. Roseingrave's compositions include keyboard works, cantatas, and anthems, although he was recognized in his own time as a keyboard virtuoso rather than as a composer.

Roseman, Ronald (Ariah) (b. Brooklyn, 15 Mar. 1933). Oboist and composer. He studied oboe with Abe Klotzman, Lois Wann, and Harold Gomberg; studied composition with Elliott Carter, Karol Rathaus, and Ben Weber. Performed widely as a solo recitalist or guest artist and was principal oboist with the New York Woodwind Quintet, the Bach Aria Group, and the New York Pro Musica. Founding member of Musica Sacra and the "Y" Chamber Symphony.

Rosen, Charles (Welles) (b. New York, 5 May 1927). Pianist and writer on music. He started piano lessons as a child and studied at Juilliard from the ages of 7 to 11; continued his musical studies with Moriz Rosenthal and Hedwig Kanner-Rosenthal, and took theory and composition from Weigl. In 1951 he earned his Ph.D. in Romance languages at Princeton, and the same year began his career as a concert pianist with a New York debut and a recording of Debussy's Études. His performance and recorded repertory ranges from Bach to Elliott Carter and Boulez. In 1971 he began teaching at SUNY–Stony Brook; subsequently joined the faculty of the Univ. of Chicago. In 1976–77 served as Ernest Bloch Professor of Music at Univ. of California, Berkeley; and in 1980–81 was Charles Eliot Norton Lecturer at Harvard. Rosen's book *The Classical Style* (New York, 1971) won the National Book Award; other books include *Arnold Schoenberg* (New York, 1975), *Sonata Forms* (New York, 1980; 2nd ed., 1988), and *The Romantic Generation* (Cambridge, Mass., 1995).

Rosen, Jerome (William) (b. Boston, 23 July 1921). Composer and clarinetist. He attended New Mexico State College, UCLA, and Berkeley (M.A., 1949), where he studied with Denny and Sessions; also worked with Milhaud in Paris (1949–50). In 1952 he was appointed to the faculty of the Univ. of California, Davis; retired in 1988. In addition to his career as a composer, Rosen performed as a clarinetist with the San Francisco Composers' Forum, and made a number of recordings, including one of his own sonata for clarinet and cello (1950).

Rosenberg, Hilding (Constantin) (b. Bosjökloster, Ringsjön Skåne, 21 June 1892; d. Stockholm, 19 May 1985). Composer. Served as a church organist in his youth. In 1915 he became a student at the Royal Academy of Music in Stockholm, where he studied conducting and was also a composition student of Elberg and Stenhammar. During the early 1920s he traveled throughout western Europe, encountering avant-garde trends; he returned to Stockholm and took counterpoint lessons with Stenhammar. In 1932 he served as assistant conductor of the Royal Opera in Stockholm, moving into the position of head conductor in 1934.

His early music was lyrical and richly chromatic (First String Quartet, 1920), occasionally making references to Scandinavian folk music. Beginning in 1926, when he first worked with the theatrical producer Per Lindberg, Rosenberg composed music for plays. The highly dramatic, expressive musical language that was given free rein in this forum was developed further in ballets. In addition, many of his concert works took on the large-scale drama of opera (Christmas oratorio *Den Heliga Natten* [The Holy Night], 1936; Symphony no. 4, Johannes uppenbarelse [The Revelation of St. John], 1940). He continued his development of choral-orchestral dramatic works throughout his life; his late works also incorporated some use of serialism. Works include operas (*Josef och hans bröder* [Joseph and His Brothers], opera-oratorio, 1946–48; *Hus med dubbel ingång* [The House with Two Doors], 1969); ballets; vocal music, for which Gullberg was frequently his librettist (*Prometheus och Ahasverus,* melodrama, 1941; Cantata to the National Museum, 1942; *Hymnus,* oratorio, 1965); orchestral music (8 symphonies) and concertos (Viola Concerto, 1942; Piano Concerto, 1950). He composed several song cycles and much chamber music. Works also include film music (*The World of Beauty,* 1960) and incidental music for some 40 plays.

Rosenboom, David (b. Fairfield, Iowa, 9 Sept. 1947). Composer; designer and maker of electronic instruments. He studied at the Univ. of Illinois (1965–67), where his teachers included Binkerd and Martirano (composition) and Hiller (electronic and computer techniques); also studied theory, physics, computer science, and experimental psychology. Served as guest lecturer at New York Univ. (1968–70) and director of computer and electronic media research at York Univ. in Toronto (1970–77); in 1979 he joined the faculty of Mills College. Rosenboom's interests include the relationship between aesthetics and information processing in the brain; in 1975 he published *Biofeedback and the Arts: Results of Early Experiments.* He served as artistic director of the Electric Circus in New York (1967–68) and founded the Neurona Co., a firm that explores relationships between electronics and the arts. He has developed a programming language for interactive computer music systems and, along with D. Buchla, designed the Touché, a computerized keyboard instrument. Some of his compositions employ brain waves to generate sounds.

Rosenman, Leonard (b. Brooklyn, 7 Sept. 1924). Composer. After war service he studied composition with Schoenberg, Sessions, and Luigi Dallapiccola, and piano with Bernard Abramowitsch. He was composer-in-residence at the Berkshire Music Center in 1953, and from 1962 to 1966 lived in Rome, where he acquired conducting experience. Taught at the Univ. of Southern California; musical director of the New Muse, a chamber orchestra specializing in the performance of contemporary music. Among his compositions are several important film scores: *East of Eden* (1954), *Rebel without a Cause* (1955), and *The Chapman Report* (1959).

Rosenmüller, Johann [Rosenmiller, Giovanni] (b. Oelsnitz, near Zwickau, ca. 1619; d. Wolfenbüttel, buried 12 Sept. 1684). Composer. He studied music at the Lateinschule at Oelsnitz and theology at the Univ. of Leipzig. In Leipzig he taught music at the Thomasschule as an assistant from 1642, becoming first assistant in 1650. In 1651 he became organist of the Nikolaikirche, and in 1654 became director of music in absentia to the Altenburg court. His career was interrupted by his arrest and imprisonment on suspicion of homosexuality. In 1658 he was a trombonist at St. Mark's, Venice, and soon became established as a composer there. From 1678 to 1682 he also held the post of composer at the Ospedale della Pietà. His last years were spent as court Kapellmeister at Wolfenbüttel. Many of Rosenmüller's published instrumental works are dance suites, including *Paduanen* (1645), *Studenten-Music* (1654), and *Sonate da camera* (1667). His vocal music, nearly all of it sacred, includes 2 published collections of small sacred concertos, *Kern-Sprüche* (Leipzig, 1648) and *Andere Kern-Sprüche* (Leipzig, 1652–53).

Rosenthal, Manuel [Emmanuel] (b. Paris, 18 June 1904). Conductor and composer. He studied at the Paris Conservatory and with Ravel. He was co-conductor of the French Radio Orchestra from 1934 and chief conductor, 1944–47. From 1948 he taught composition at the College of Puget Sound. Conductor of the Seattle Symphony Orchestra in 1949–51, and thereafter conducted internationally. In 1962 he became professor of conducting at the Paris Conservatory, and conducted the Liège Symphony Orchestra, 1964–67. Starting in 1981 conducted occasionally at the Metropolitan Opera. As conductor and composer he championed the French neoclassical school. His compositions include several stage works (the ballet *Gaîté parisienne,* 1938, on Offenbach's melodies), and many orchestral pieces, chamber pieces, choral works, and songs. He authored *Satie, Ravel, Poulenc: An Intimate Memoir* (New York, 1987).

Rosenthal, Moriz (b. Lemberg, 17 Dec. 1862; d. New York, 3 Sept. 1946). Pianist. Studied with Mikuli at the Lemberg Conservatory (1872–75); moved to Vienna in 1875 to study with Joseffy; recital debut in 1876. Met Liszt in 1877 and studied with him from 1876 to 1878 in Weimar and Rome. Toured the U.S., 1888–89, sharing part of the tour with Kreisler. Collaborated with

Schytte on a piano method, *Schule des höheren Klavierspiels* (Berlin, 1892). Taught at the Curtis Institute of Music, 1928–29.

Rosetti [Rösler, Rosety, Rossetti, Rössler], **(Francesco) Antonio** [Franz Anton, František Antonín] (b. Leitmeritz [now Litoměřice], ca. 1750; d. Ludwigslust, 10 June 1792). Composer and double bass player. He has been confused with Franz Anton Rössler, a cobbler, and with 5 other musicians named Antonio Rosetti. He studied in Prague, at the Jesuit College at Kuttenberg (1763–69), and at the seminaries in Znaim (Znojmo) and Olmütz (Olomouc). He became double bass player to Kraft Ernst, Prince of Oettingen-Wallerstein, in 1773, later becoming deputy Kapellmeister (1780) and Kapellmeister (1785). In Paris (1781) he met Gluck and Piccinni. He made a concert tour in 1783, then became Kapellmeister to the Duke of Mecklenburg-Schwerin (1789). He was a prolific composer of orchestral and chamber music.

Bibl.: Sterling E. Murray, "The Rösler–Rosetti Problem: A Confusion of Pseudonym and Mistaken Identity," *ML* 57 (1976): 130–43.

Rosing, Vladimir (b. St. Petersburg, 23 Jan. 1890; d. Los Angeles, 24 Nov. 1963). Tenor. He studied with Jean de Reszke, making his St. Petersburg debut in 1912 and his London concert debut in 1913. A series of recitals in London and elsewhere (1916–21) led to a tour of the U.S. in 1922. He directed the opera department at the Eastman School of Music from 1923, and founded and directed the American Opera Company (1927–29). He became artistic director of the Southern California Opera Association in 1939.

Roslavets, Nikolay Andreyevich (b. Dushatino, Chernigov region, Ukraine, 5 Jan. 1881; d. Moscow, 23 Aug. 1944). Composer. He studied at the Moscow Conservatory (1902–12) with Hřimalý (violin), Il'insky (counterpoint), and Vasilenko (composition and orchestration). By 1915 he had developed a twelve-tone system that utilized aspects of twelve-tone serialism. His system has a number of features in common with Schoenberg's, whose work he did not encounter until 1923. In 1922 he was temporary director of the Khar'kov Conservatory, then worked as an editor at the Moscow State Music Publishing House and served on the board of the Association for Contemporary Music. His views on new music led to conflicts with the Association of Proletarian Musicians. During the 1930s he worked in Tashkent, but after 1930 his name no longer appeared in concert programs and Soviet dictionaries. His compositions include orchestral music, string quartets, piano trios, other chamber music, piano pieces, choral music, and songs.

Rosolino, Frank (b. Detroit, 20 Aug. 1926; d. Los Angeles, 26 Nov. 1978). Jazz trombonist. He played in army bands from the age of 18 and then with a series of big bands, including those of Glen Gray (1947), Gene Krupa (1948–49), and Stan Kenton (1952–54). Thereafter he worked principally in California, often as a studio musician, but toured occasionally in the U.S., Europe, and Japan.

Rospigliosi, Giulio, Pope Clement IX (b. Pistoia, 28 Jan. 1600; d. Rome, 9 Dec. 1669). Librettist. He went to Rome and served the Barberini family, where most of his librettos' settings were performed; he became a cardinal in 1657 and was elected to the papacy in 1667. Rospigliosi created the genre of sacred opera and wrote librettos for some of the earliest comic operas. Important librettos include *Il Sant'Alessio* (1632); *Erminia sul Giordano* (1633); *Chi soffre speri* (1639); *Il palazzo incantante* (1642); *Dal male il bene* (1653); *La vita humana* (1656); *La comica del cielo, ovvero La Baltasara* (1668).

Ross, Diana (b. Detroit, Mich., 26 Mar. 1944). Soul and popular singer. In high school she formed the vocal group The Supremes with Florence Ballard (1943–76) and Mary Wilson (b. 1944); from 1961 to 1969 they made many successful recordings, including "Baby Love" (1964) and "Reflections" (1968). From 1970 she recorded as a solo artist, successes including "Ain't No Mountain High Enough" (1970) and "Upside Down" (1980); she also sang with Lionel Ritchie on the immensely popular "Endless Love" (1981). She was associated with several prominent soul songwriters, including the Motown group of Lamont Dozier and Eddie and Brian Holland, and later Nickolas Ashford and Valerie Simpson.

Ross, Walter (Beghtol) (b. Lincoln, Nebr., 3 Oct. 1936). Composer. He studied at the Univ. of Nebraska (M.Mus., 1962), at Cornell Univ. with Robert Palmer and Karel Husa (D.M.A., 1966), and in Buenos Aires with Alberto Ginastera (1965). From 1967 taught at the Univ. of Virginia. His works include concertos for various instruments, other orchestral pieces, and many chamber works for brass and other ensembles.

Rossellini, Renzo (b. Rome, 2 Feb. 1908; d. Monte Carlo, 14 May 1982). Composer, critic. He studied in Rome with Settaccioli, Sallustio, and Molineri. He taught composition at the Rome Conservatory from 1940; from 1973 he was artistic director of the Monte Carlo Opera. He wrote several operas, film scores (some for his brother, film maker Roberto Rossellini), and orchestral and chamber works. As a critic for the Rome *Messaggero* he stood for conservatism; he also authored *Pagine di un musicista* (Bologna, 1964) and *Addio del passato* (Milan, 1968).

Rosseter, Philip (b. 1567 or 1568; d. London, 5 May 1623). Composer and theater manager. Half of his *Book of Ayres* (London, 1601; R: London, 1966) are songs by Thomas Campion, and it is probable that Rosseter, like Campion, was under the patronage of Sir Thomas Monson. In 1603 he was appointed lutenist at the court of James I; his collection of arrangements for broken consort of his own and others' compositions,

Lessons for Consort (London, 1609), survives incomplete. In 1609 he helped manage a company of boy actors known as the Children of the Whitefriars; the group was renamed Children of the Queen's Revels and presented several plays at court before being disbanded in 1617.

Bibl.: Robin Headlam Wells, "Ars amatoria: Philip Rosseter and the Tudor Court Lyric," *ML* 70 (1989): 58–71.

Rossetto [Rossetti], **Stefano** (b. Nice, ca. 1520; d. Munich, after 1580). Composer. He served the Giustiniani family on the isle of Chios in 1559; he was briefly *maestro di cappella* at San Gaudenzio, Novara. In 1564 he came to Florence and in 1566–67 served Cardinal Ferdinando de' Medici. In 1579–80 he was organist at the court of Munich. He published 3 books of madrigals, the madrigal cycle *Il lamento di Olimpia,* and a book of motets.

Rossi, Lauro (b. Macerata, 19 Feb. 1812; d. Cremona, 5 May 1885). Composer and conductor. Studied until 1829 at Naples Conservatory with Furno, Zingarelli, and Crescentini. Produced his first opera *(Le contesse villane)* in 1829 in Naples. Collaborated with Raimondi in 1830 on *Costanza e Oringaldo.* Assistant director of Teatro Valle, Rome (1831–33). Moved to Mexico in 1835 to compose for and conduct an Italian opera troupe. When it folded, he established a new troupe in 1837, with which he toured (Havana, 1840; New Orleans, 1842). Returned to Italy in 1843. Appointed director of the Milan Conservatory in 1850; succeeded Mercadante as director of the Naples Conservatory (1870–78). Produced 29 operas in all; also composed cantatas, 1 Mass, an oratorio, fugues.

Bibl.: Francesco Florimo, *La scuola musicale di Napoli* (Naples, 1880–82; R: Bologna, 1909).

Rossi, Luigi (b. Torremaggiore, ca. 1597; d. Rome, 20 Feb. 1653). Composer. He studied with Giovanni de Macque in Naples from about 1608, then moved to Rome, where he entered the service of the Borghese around 1621; he also served as organist of S. Luigi dei Francesi from 1633. In 1641 he left the Borghese family to enter the service of Cardinal Antonio Barberini, in whose theater Rossi's first opera, *Il palazzo incantato* (1642; facs., New York, 1977), enjoyed considerable success. He arrived in Paris in 1646 on the personal invitation of Jules Mazarin; his second opera, *Orfeo* (1647), was produced there for the court and was a sensational success. After returning to his post at S. Luigi dei Francesi, he was once again called to Paris by Mazarin, but no Italian theater spectacles were produced during his second French sojourn (1648–49). He returned to Italy around 1650. In addition to his operas, he was highly regarded in his time as a composer of cantatas, of which approximately 300 survive.

Bibl.: Eleanor Caluroi, *The Cantatas of Luigi Rossi: Analysis and Thematic Index* (Ann Arbor, 1981). Pasquale Ricciardelli, *Repertorio bibliografico-storico delle composizioni del musicista Luigi Rossi* (Torremaggiore, 1988). Patrizia Bassi, *Luigi Felice Rossi* (Turin, 1994).

Rossi, Michelangelo [Michel Angelo del Violino] (b. Genoa, 1601 or 1602; d. Rome, buried 7 July 1656). Composer, violinist, and organist. He assisted his uncle, Lelio Rossi, at the Cathedral of S. Lorenzo, Genoa. He moved to Rome by 1624 and entered the service of Cardinal Maurizio of Savoy, where he met Sigismondo d'India; he also studied with Frescobaldi around this time. His opera *Erminia sul Giordano* was performed in the theater of the Palazzo Barberini in 1633 and published four years later; a second opera, *Andromeda* (1638, music lost), was produced in Ferrara. Rossi was famous in his time as a virtuoso violinist; his surviving keyboard music, especially his toccatas, are stylistically close to Froberger and Frescobaldi.

Bibl.: Catherine Moore, *The Composer Michelangelo Rossi: A "Diligent Fantasy Maker" in Seventeenth-Century Rome* (New York, 1993).

Rossi, Salamone [Salomone, Salamon de', Shlomo] (b. Mantua?, 19 Aug.? 1570; d. there?, ca. 1630). Composer. Little is known of his life; his first published work, *Il primo libro delle canzonette* (1589; R: Tel Aviv, 1975), was dedicated to Duke Vincenzo Gonzaga, though Rossi's exact position with the Gonzaga court is unclear. Of his 5 books of 5-part madrigals (Venice, 1600–1622), particular attention has been devoted to the second book (1602), the first published examples of continuo madrigals. Rossi's *Il primo libro delle sinfonie e gagliarde* (Venice, 1607) is acknowledged as the earliest published trio sonatas; in addition to 3 other books of instrumental sinfonias and dances (1608–23), his compositions include a collection of 33 polyphonic settings of Hebrew Psalms, hymns, and synagogue songs, *Hashirim asher lish'lomo* [The Songs of Solomon] (Venice, 1623).

Bibl.: *Salamone Rossi: Cantiques,* ed. S. Naumbourg and Vincent d'Indy (Paris, 1877). *Sinfonie, Gagliarde, Canzone,* ed. Joel Newman and Fritz Rikko (1965–). Joel Newman and Fritz Rikko, *A Thematic Index to the Works of Salamon Rossi* (Hackensack, N.J., 1972).

Rossi-Lemeni, Nicola (b. Istanbul, 6 Nov. 1920; d. Bloomington, Ind., 12 Mar. 1991). Bass. He studied with Carnevali-Cusinati in Italy before making his debut at La Fenice, Venice, in 1946. From 1947 to 1960 he sang at La Scala and appeared at all the major theaters in Italy; also at Buenos Aires (1949), San Francisco (1951–53), Covent Garden (1952), and the Metropolitan Opera (1953–54). Late in his career he sang in many modern operas such as *Wozzeck,* Bloch's *Macbeth,* and *Billy Budd.* Beginning in 1980 taught at Indiana Univ.

Rossini, Gioachino (Antonio) (b. Pesaro, 29 Feb. 1792; d. Passy, near Paris, 13 Nov. 1868). Composer. His father (1758–1839) was a horn and trumpet player; his mother had a small career in secondary opera roles, which she learned by ear; 1802, they moved to Lugo, where he had music lessons; 1802 or 1803, moved to Bologna, his mother retiring from the stage because of a throat condition. Rossini himself was a good singer

Gioachino Rossini. Lithograph, 1828.

in churches and at least twice appeared in minor opera roles in Ravenna and Bologna; he also began to compose, a set of six *sonate a quattro* (ca. 1804) being one of his earliest extant works. In Bologna he studied with Padre Angelo Tesei and is said to have had singing lessons from the celebrated tenor Babbini; 1806, admitted to the Accademia filarmonica; 1806–10, a student at the conservatory, teachers including Padre Mattei (counterpoint) and Gibelli (singing). His compositions include two Masses and other sacred works, a cantata sung at a school concert, and instrumental pieces; also the set pieces for an opera, *Demetrio e Polibio,* for the tenor Mombelli and his small opera company, though Mombelli did not perform it until 1812.

His actual debut opera was *Il cambiale di matrimonio,* a one-act *farsa* (the lightest of the Italian genres), given at the Teatro San Moise, Venice, on 3 Nov. 1810 and a success with 13 performances. In fall 1811 he was keyboardist for an opera season at a Bologna theater, composing for it the comic *L'equivoco stravagante* (26 Oct.), which had only three performances because the subject was considered indecent. Rossini's rise to domination of Italian opera, which was eventually to drive many old school composers into retirement, was swift but not without setbacks and failures. It could hardly be otherwise with the rate of production he now undertook. In 1812 he had five new works performed, including three one-act *farsa* for the Teatro San Moise, especially *L'inganno felice* on January 8, a great success, widely performed. His other great success of this year was the two-act comic opera *La pietra del paragone,* his debut opera at La Scala, Milan (Sept. 26). To keep up this pace, which lasted through 1819, Rossini composed very quickly, giving rise to the notion that he worked in a slapdash way, a belief reinforced by the air of witty insouciance that he projected; he frequently reused the better material from unsuccessful or unfamiliar operas. In 1813–14 he composed six new operas for Venetian theaters and La Scala, including two of his greatest successes, the opera seria *Tancredi,* his first work for Venice's principal theater, La Fenice (6 Feb. 1813), and the two-act comic opera *L'italiana in Algeri* (Venice, Teatro San Benedetto, 22 May 1813), thus demonstrating mastery of the two principal genres of Italian opera and abandoning the slight one-act *farsa;* however, the opere serie *Aureliano in Palmira* (La Scala, 26 Dec. 1813) and *Sigismondo* (La Fenice, 26 Dec. 1814) and the comic *Il turco in Italia* (La Scala, 14 Aug. 1814) were less successful, although *Il turco* became popular in later productions.

In spring 1815 he first visited Naples, where he contracted with the impresario Barbaja to become music director of the San Carlo and Fondo theaters and to compose two operas a year there. From 1815 to 1822 he produced ten new operas in Naples, as well as staging others first produced elsewhere. Eight of these were opere serie with the Spanish soprano Isabella Colbran as prima donna: *Elisabetta, regina d'Inghilterra* (4 Oct. 1815), *Otello* (4 Dec. 1816), *Armide* (11 Nov. 1817), *Ricciardo e Zoraide* (3 Dec. 1818), *Ermione* (27 Mar. 1819), *La donna del lago* (24 Sept. 1819), *Maometto II* (3 Dec. 1820), and *Zelmira* (16 Dec. 1822). One was among his most popular works, the sacred opera *Mosè in Egitto* (5 Mar. 1818). During this period he also produced, mostly in the comic and semiserious genres, five new operas in Rome, two in Milan, and one in Venice, including two of his best known: *Almaviva, ossia L'inutile precauzione,* better known as *Il barbiere di Siviglia* (Rome, 20 Feb. 1816), his most popular opera, and *La Cenerentola* (Rome, 21 Jan. 1817), his last comic opera produced in Italy.

In March 1822 he left Naples with Colbran, and on March 16 they were married, she having been his mistress for an unknown period. She was seven years older than Rossini, and her voice had been in decline all during their Naples years. Later that month they arrived in Vienna, his only visit there, to begin to take advantage of the Rossini mania that had swept Europe. Between April and July five of his operas were given there with Colbran as principal prima donna. From October to December 1822 Rossini was in Verona for the international congress, composing several occasional cantatas. At Carnival 1823 they were both engaged at La Fenice, where Rossini staged *Semiramide* (3 Feb. 1823), his last opera composed for Italy. In October they left Italy and, after being feted in Paris, arrived in December in London, both engaged at the King's Theatre. Colbran's voice soon proved to have deteriorated to such a degree that she had to retire. Eight Rossini operas were given with varying success, but a promised new opera, although partially composed, was never produced, in part because the theater manager was overextended and could not make the required payments. Rossini made a great deal of money, capitalizing on his lionization by English high society by charging large fees for singing lessons and for appearances at society musicales.

In July 1824 he returned to Paris, having contracted to compose for the Opéra and Théâtre-Italien. In fall 1824 he was made codirector of the Théâtre-Italien with the existing director Paer. On 19 June 1825 he presented there an *oeuvre de circonstance,* a one-act, three-hour Italian opera (his last), *Il viaggio a Reims,* celebrating the coronation of the new king. He did not allow other productions of this work but used material from it in *Le comte Ory.* He presented his *Semiramide* (1825) and *Zelmira* (1826), both new to Paris, at the Théâtre-Italien, but he was carefully preparing a move into French opera, studying French declamation and establishing singers at the Opéra capable of doing justice to his music. In October 1826 he resigned his post at the Théâtre-Italien, where his influence was to remain great, and in November was appointed First Composer to the King and Inspector General of Singing in France, sinecures that paid him 25,000 francs a year.

His next step was to present at the Opéra French versions of two of his Italian operas, extensively revised. *Le siège de Corinthe* (1826), derived from *Maometto II,* and *Moïse et Pharaon* (1827) from *Mosè in Egitto.* Both were successful. On 20 August 1828 he presented the premiere of his French comic opera *Le comte Ory* (libretto by Scribe and Delestre-Poisson); it was a critical success and became moderately popular. This progression was capped by his French grand opera *Guillaume Tell* (libretto by Jouy, revised by Bis), which Rossini, who had long wished to retire, apparently conceived of as his final opera, although in May 1829 he contracted to compose four more French operas over the next decade. Composed—for him—slowly and carefully, *Guillaume Tell* was a success (3 Aug. 1829), though not an extraordinary one, remaining in the standard repertory through the 19th century. The Rossinis then returned to Italy, living a leisurely life in their fine house in Bologna and summer villa at nearby Castenaso. Isabella in middle age, her career long over, became extravagant (mainly through gambling), spiteful, and ailing. When a lifetime pension guaranteed him by his last contract was broken off after the July Revolution, Rossini returned to Paris without her, not returning to Italy, apart from one short visit, until 1836.

From about 1832 his health turned poor, perhaps partly the result of a long-standing gonorrheal infection that at times required him to be catheterized daily, but his mental state was even worse, including periods of extreme anxiety and depression. In Paris he formed a relation with Olympe Pélissier (1797–1878), who took care of him and regulated his life. In fall 1836 he returned to Bologna, legally separated from Colbran, and summoned Pélissier. They married in 1846, after Colbran's death. He composed very little in this period, a few songs and one major work, the *Stabat Mater* (1832–41). From 1839 he was consultant to the Bologna Conservatory, being in effect its acting director until 1842. In 1848, frightened by revolutionary activity in Bologna, he moved to Florence, also spending long periods at spas fruitlessly seeking alleviation of his condition. In 1855 the Rossinis moved to Paris, where he soon improved to an extraordinary degree, recovering his spirits and even his creativity, producing the large collection of songs and piano pieces he called *Péchés de vieillesse* (1857–68), many composed for his celebrated salon and mostly unpublished until the 1950s, unlike his late major work, the *Petite Messe solennelle* (1863), published in 1869.

Mstislav Rostropovich.

Bibl.: Stendhal, *Vie de Rossini* (Paris, 1824); trans. Eng. (1956; 2nd ed., 1970). E. Michotte, *Souvenirs personnels: La visite de R. Wagner à Rossini (Paris, 1860)* (Paris, 1906); trans. Eng. (1968). Herbert Weinstock, *Rossini* (New York, 1968). Nicholas Till, *Rossini: His Life and Times* (New York, 1983). Richard Osborne, *Rossini* (London, 1986). Adriano Bassi, *Gioacchino Rossini* (Padua, 1992). Alan Kendall, *Gioachino Rossini: The Reluctant Hero* (London, 1992). Wilhelm Keitel, *Gioachino Rossini* (Munich, 1992). Jean-Marie Bruzon, *Rossini et Paris* (Paris, 1993).

Rössler, Anton. See Rosetti, Antonio.

Rostropovich, Mstislav (Leopoldovich) (b. Baku, Azerbaidjan, 27 Mar. 1927). Cellist, conductor. He entered the Moscow Conservatory in 1943, studying cello with Semyon Kozolupov and composition with Shostakovich and Vissaryon Shebalin. He toured extensively in the 1950s, and became cello professor at the Moscow Conservatory in 1956. Shostakovich, Britten, and Prokofiev, among others, wrote works for him. As a pianist he accompanied his wife, soprano Galina Vishnevskaya, in song recitals. He made his conducting debut in 1968 with *Eugene Onegin* at the Bolshoi Theater; from 1977 to 1996 served as music director of the National Symphony (Washington, D.C.); regularly guest-conducted the London Philharmonic. Because of his public opposition to the USSR's restriction of cultural freedom, he was stripped of his Soviet citizenship in 1978; this was restored in 1990. He organized the Rostropovich International Cello Competition in Paris in 1981, and in 1983 founded the Rostropovich Festival in Snape, England.

Rosvaenge [Roswaenge], **Helge** (b. Copenhagen, 29 Aug. 1897; d. Munich, 19 June 1972). Tenor. He studied engineering before turning to singing. Following his debut at Neustrelitz in 1921, he sang at Altenburg, Basel, Cologne (1927–30), and the Berlin Staatsoper, where he was leading tenor (1930–44). He also appeared in Vienna, Munich, Salzburg, Covent Garden, and Bayreuth. His roles in the Italian repertory won him the most praise; in his prime his bel canto was compared with Caruso's, but he sang only in German, which restricted his career outside central Europe.

Rota [Rinaldi], **Nino** (b. Milan, 3 Dec. 1911; d. Rome, 10 Apr. 1979). Composer. The grandson of a composer-pianist (Giovanni Rinaldi, d. 1895); he studied piano with his mother, began to compose by the age of 8, and had his first oratorio performed (in Lille and Milan) in 1923. From that year he attended the Milan Conservatory (studying with Orefice, Delache, and Bas); then studied privately with Pizetti (1925–26) and Casella; he graduated from the San Cecilia Academy (Rome) in 1929. He spent two years (1930–32) at the Curtis Institute as a student of Scalero, Beck, and Reiner before completing an arts degree at the Univ. of Milan (1937). He taught theory at the Liceo musicale di Taranto (1937–38) and from 1939 at the Liceo musicale di Bari, which he later directed (1950–77). He composed numerous film scores, especially for Fellini. Works include 11 operas (*Il cappello di paglia di Firenze,* 1946; staged in Palermo, 1955), some of them initially for the radio; 4 ballets (*Le Molière imaginaire,* Béjart, Paris, 1976); incidental music; and some 80 film scores for Visconti, Zefirelli (*Romeo and Juliet,* 1968), Coppola (*The Godfather,* 1972), Fellini (*La dolce vita,* 1960; *Otto e mezzo,* 1963; *Satyricon,* 1969; *Amarcorde,* 1973), and others; 3 symphonies (1939–57), concertos (harp, piano, trombone, cello, bassoon); oratorios and cantatas (*Rabelaisiana,* 1978); chamber and piano music (15 Preludi, 1966); 3 Masses and other sacred choral music; and songs.

Bibl.: Pier Marco De Santi, *La musica di Nino Rota* (Rome, 1983).

Rothmüller, (Aron) Marko (b. Trnjani, near Brud, Croatia, 31 Dec. 1908; d. Bloomington, Ind., 20 Jan. 1993). Baritone. After studies in Zagreb and Vienna with Berg, Regina Weiss, and Franz Steiner, he made his debut at Hamburg-Altona at the Schiller Theater in 1932. At the Zurich Opera (1935–47) he sang in the premiere of Hindemith's *Mathis der Maler* (1938). He then sang at the Vienna Staatsoper (1946–49), Covent Garden (1948–52), Glyndebourne (1949–55), and the Metropolitan Opera (1959–61, 1964–65). He taught at Indiana Univ. from 1962.

Rotten, Johnny [John Lydon] (b. London, 1958). Rock singer and songwriter. In 1975 he formed the Sex Pistols with bassist Sid Vicious (John Ritchie, 1958–79); they were the most influential band of the punk movement, achieving prominence through performances in clubs in London, a tour of the United States in 1977–78, and the album *Never Mind the Bollocks, Here's the Sex Pistols* (1977). After their dissolution in 1978 Rotten (using his original name) formed the rock band Public Image, Ltd., which released several successful albums including *Metal Box* (in the U.S. *Second Edition,* 1979) and *This Is What You Want . . . This Is What You Get* (1984).

Rouget de Lisle [l'Isle], **Claude-Joseph** (b. Lons-le-Saunier, 10 May 1760; d. Choisy-le-Roi, 26 or 27 June 1836). Poet and composer. He entered the École royale du génie at Mézières in 1782, achieving the rank of lieutenant by 1790. In 1791 he was stationed in Strasbourg and the following year wrote the words and music of the "Chant de guerre pour l'armée du Rhin," which later became known as the *Marseillaise.* Much of his later life was spent in poverty.

Rouse, Christopher (Chapman) (b. Baltimore, 15 Feb. 1949). Composer. He attended Oberlin College Conservatory (B.M., 1971), studied privately with Crumb (1971–73), and then with Husa and Palmer at Cornell Univ. (D.M.A., 1977). In 1978 he began teaching at the Univ. of Michigan, which he left in 1981 for the Eastman School. His style is percussive and coloristic, influenced by Crumb, Varèse, Messiaen, and Orff. Commissions include *Phaeton Overture* for the Philadelphia Orchestra, 1986; the Double Bass Concerto for the Minnesota Orchestra, 1985. Composer-in-residence with the Indianapolis Symphony (1985–87) and the Baltimore Symphony (1986–89). In 1981 he won the League of Composers Award (*The Infernal Machine,* orchestra), and in 1988 the Friedheim Award (Symphony no. 1); his trombone concerto (1991) was awarded the 1993 Pulitzer Prize. Other works include *The Surma Ritornelli* (11 players, 1983); *Ku-Ka-Ili-moku* (percussion ensemble, 1978); *Morpheus* (cello, 1975); *Bonham* (8 percussionists, 1988); *Karolju* (chorus, orchestra, 1990); concertos for violin (1992), cello (1992–93), flute (1994); Symphony no. 2 (1994).

Roussakis, Nicolas (b. Athens, 10 June 1934; d. New York, 23 Oct. 1994). Composer and clarinetist. Before his arrival in the U.S. at age 15, he lived in Estonia and Switzerland; he became a U.S citizen in 1956. Studied at Columbia with Luening, Beeson, Ussachevsky, and Cowell (B.A., 1956; M.A., 1960; D.M.A., 1975) and in Europe with Jarnach, Stockhausen, Boulez, Ligeti, and Berio (1961–63); also had contact with Weber and Shapey, and attended the Darmstadt classes in 1962 and 1963. He taught at Columbia (1968–77) and at Rutgers (from 1977). As a clarinetist he taught and performed both contemporary and older repertory. As a composer his style is characterized by a commitment to serial procedures and is influenced by the melodies and rhythms of Greek folk dance; later works combined elements of tonal and serial music as well as chance. Works include *Ode and Cataclysm* (orchestra, 1975); *Ephemeris* (string quartet, 1977–79); *Fire and Earth and Water and Air* (orchestra, 1980–83); *Voyage* (after Baudelaire, "L'invitation au voyage," soprano, alto, tenor, bass, 1980); *Pas de deux* (violin and piano, 1985); *God Abandons Antony* (cantata, narrator, chorus, orchestra, 1987); *Hymn to Apollo* (small orchestra, 1989).

Rousseau, Jean-Jacques (b. Geneva, 28 June 1712; d. Ermenonville, 2 July 1778). Philosopher, author, and composer. Most of his musical training was through self-instruction, which included reading Rameau's treatise on harmony and copying music. He devised a simplified method of musical notation which was rejected by the Académie des sciences in 1742; he defended the system the following year in his *Dissertation sur la musique moderne* (Paris, 1743). In 1743 he traveled to Venice, where he was captivated by Italian opera; he returned to Paris in 1744, continued working on the text and music to his *opéra-ballet Les muses galantes,* and completed the work in 1745. Meanwhile his revision of Rameau's *La princesse de Navarre,* under the title *Les fêtes de Ramire,* was staged at Versailles in 1745 and enjoyed some success. *Les muses galantes* was eventually withdrawn by Rousseau after reaching the rehearsal stage, but his *intermède Le devin du village* (Fontainebleau, 1752) was an overwhelming success, and remained in the repertoire in France for some 60 years. His principal contribution to the *querelle des bouffons* (in which he sided with Grimm as a partisan of Italian opera buffa) was his *Lettre sur la musique française* (Paris, 1753; partly trans. Eng. *SR,* 1968), a scathing attack on French opera; in his articles for the *Encyclopédie,* later incorporated into his *Dictionnaire de musique* (Paris, 1768; facs., Hildesheim, 1969; trans. New York, 1975), he concluded that opera was not possible in the French language. This opinion led to the experimental *Pygmalion* (Lyons, 1770), a spoken monodrama with text and two andantes by Rousseau and an introductory symphony and musical interludes by Horace Cognet; it was widely imitated in Germany during the 1770s. Rousseau's pastoral opera *Daphnis et Chloé* was left incomplete when he died.

Bibl.: John F. Strauss, "Jean Jacques Rousseau: Musician," *MQ* 64 (1978): 474–82. Peter Gülke, *Rousseau und die Musik, oder, von der Zuständigkeit des Dilettanten* (Wilhelmshaven, 1984). R. Cotte, *Jean-Jacques Rousseau, le philosophe musicien* (Braine-le-Comte, 1976). Stephen Blum, "Rousseau's Concept of *Sistême musical* and the Comparative Study of Tonalities in Nineteenth-Century France," *JAMS* 38 (1985): 349–61.

Roussel, Albert (Charles Paul Marie) (b. Tourcoing, 5 Apr. 1869; d. Royan, 23 Aug. 1937). Composer. After completing two years at Collège Stanislas, he entered the École navale as a cadet (1887). He left the college as a midshipman in 1889, was commissioned, and saw service on a number of vessels before deciding in 1894 to pursue a career in music. He studied for the next ten years with Gigout and then with d'Indy at the new Schola cantorum; taught counterpoint from 1902 until 1914 (Satie was among his students); and by 1908 was becoming known as a composer in Paris. His Piano Trio (1902) had been performed in 1904; the First Symphony *(Le poème de la forêt),* which was begun in March 1904, was presented in Brussels in 1908 and the following February in Paris. These and other early works reflected the teaching at the Schola, especially in their cyclic forms. At that point Roussel and his new wife set off on an extended tour of Europe, North Africa, and Southeast Asia. Shortly after his return to Paris he composed a ballet presented at the Théâtre des arts; *Le festin de l'araignée* was written in three months (1913). He served as a transport officer during the war, and completed *Padmâvatî* (an opera-ballet based on a Hindu legend and using Hindu scales) in 1918 while convalescing from an illness. Its production in June 1923 caused a sensation among the critics and musical community: the composers Dukas, Messager, Milhaud, and Auric all found much to praise; critics were somewhat divided but on the whole admitted its importance. Having now left impressionism behind, he aimed to achieve music "divorced from any illustrative or descriptive elements." He produced a series of neoclassical orchestral and chamber works as well as several ballets.

The Société musicale indépendente, in which he had been active since its formation in 1910, sponsored a concert of his music in October 1925; a Roussel Festival in honor of his sixtieth birthday was held in Paris in 1929; he visited the U.S. for the Boston Symphony's performance of his Third Symphony and London for that of his *Psalm 80* (1931).

Works: an opera, several ballets (*Bacchus et Ariane,* 1930), and incidental music; orchestral music including 4 symphonies and concertos for piano (1927) and cello (1936); *Evocations* (soloists, chorus, and orchestra, 1910–11); chamber music (*Divertissement,* wind quintet and piano, 1906); music for solo piano, harp, and guitar; choral music and songs.

Bibl.: *La revue musicale* devoted 2 issues to Roussel, 10 (1929) and 178 (1930). *Cahiers Albert Roussel* (1978–). Julien Tiersot, *J. J. Rousseau* (New York, 1978). Nicole Labelle, ed., *Lettres et écrits d'Albert Roussel* (Paris, 1987). Basil Deane, *Albert Roussel* (Westport, Conn., 1980). Robert Follet, *Albert Roussel, A Bio-Bibliography* (New York, 1988). Nicole Labelle, *Catalogue raisonné de l'oeuvre d'Albert Roussel* (Louvain-La-Neuve, 1992).

Rowicki, Witold (b. Taganrog, 26 Feb. 1914; d. Warsaw, 1 Oct. 1989). Composer and performer. He graduated from the Kraków Conservatory in 1938 with a specialization in violin, having taken violin lessons with Malawski and composition lessons with Piotrowski and Wallek-Walewski. During World War II he took conducting lessons in Germany with Rudolph Hindemith, brother of Paul Hindemith. Rowicki returned to Poland and founded the Polish Radio Symphony in 1945. In 1950 he helped to reorganize the National Philharmonic in Warsaw, which he conducted on tours throughout Europe. Also toward rebuilding Poland's musical establishments in the wake of the war, he assisted in the construction of the Philharmonic concert hall in Warsaw. He wrote in standard forms and genres, emphasizing orchestral music. Works include Symphony (1957) and Concerto for Orchestra (premiered in Warsaw, 1976).

Rowley, Alec (b. London, 13 Mar. 1892; d. Weybridge, Surrey, 11 Jan. 1958). Composer. He attended the Royal Academy of Music, where he was a student of Corder. Beginning in 1920 he served on the staff of Trinity College of Music. He also published monographs on pedagogy and musicianship. His music included orchestral works (*Rhapsody,* viola, orchestra, premiered 1936); concertos (Piano Concerto no. 2, premiered 1938); chamber and vocal pieces.

Roxburgh, Edwin (b. Liverpool, 6 Nov. 1937). Composer. He studied in London at the Royal College of Music and in Cambridge at St. John's College. While traveling throughout Europe, he studied composition with Nono, Boulanger, and Dallapiccola. On the staff of the Royal College of Music beginning in 1967, specializing in 20th-century music. He also worked as a performer on oboe of 20th-century music and conducted the 20th-Century Ensemble of London. All of his works from before 1961 have been withdrawn. His music written after that year is characterized by an eclectic use of techniques such as serialism that allowed him to explore freely the construction of different textures. Works include orchestral (*Montage,* 1977); vocal (*Recitative after Blake,* alto, strings, 1961; *A Mosaic for Cummings,* 2 narrators, orchestra, 1973; *et vitam venturi saeculi,* chorus, 1983); and chamber music (*Voyager,* 3 oboes, 3 English horns, 3 bassoons, 1989).

Royer, Joseph-Nicolas-Pancrace (b. Turin, ca. 1705; d. Paris, 11 Jan. 1755). Composer. He moved to Paris in 1725, where he taught singing and harpsichord; he was *maître de musique* at the Opéra (1730–33) and lessee and director of the Concert spirituel from 1748. In 1753 he bought from Rebel and Bury the reversion of the post of *maître de musique de la chambre du roi,* and was appointed in the same year composer and leader of the orchestra of the Opéra. Royer's stage works include *Pyrrhus* (Opéra, 1730); *Almasis* (Versailles, 1748); *Myrtil et Zélie* (Versailles, 1750).

Rozhdestvensky, Gennady (Nikolayevich) (b. Moscow, 4 May 1931). Conductor. He studied at the Moscow Conservatory with his father, Nikolay Anosov (conducting), and Lev Oborin (piano). At the age of 20 he made his debut at the Bolshoi Theater; he was conductor (1951–61), then principal conductor (1964–70), at the Bolshoi. From 1961 he was permanent principal conductor and artistic director of the Symphony Orchestra of All-Union Radio and Television. In 1974 he became artistic director of the Stockholm Philharmonic, and from 1978 to 1981 he was chief conductor of the BBC Symphony. In 1981 he was appointed chief conductor of the Vienna Symphony. He championed the music of many 20th-century composers, including works by young Soviet composers.

Rózsa, Miklós (b. Budapest, 18 Apr. 1907; d. Los Angeles, 27 July 1995). Composer. As a child he studied the violin and composed; then attended the Leipzig Conservatory, where his teachers included Hermann Grabner and Karl Straube. By 1931 he was living in Paris, from which he went to London (1935) and then to the U.S. (1940). It was in London that he began to write film music, eventually as staff composer for Alexander Korda, for whom he wrote 9 film scores. He settled in Hollywood as a free-lance composer and then as a staff composer for MGM (1948–62); taught at the Univ. of Southern California (1945–65); and continued to free-lance as a film composer after retirement (by 1980 he had written or orchestrated approximately 80 films in the U.S.). His scores drew heavily on Hungarian folk song style, but he avoided borrowing actual melodies; his many concert works have been performed by the Philadelphia, Chicago, Los Angeles, and other major symphonies and at the Berlin Festival, often with the composer as conductor. His autobiography (*A Double Life,* 1982) lists his complete works and discography. Works include concertos for cello (1971), viola (1979), and piano (1966) and *Nottorno ungherse* op. 28 (orchestra, 1964); 2 string quartets (no. 2, op. 38, 1981); *Bagatellen* op. 12 (piano, 1932); *To Everything There Is a Season* op. 21 (8 voices, organ ad lib., 1945).

Różycki, Ludomir (b. Warsaw, 6 Nov. 1884; d. Katowice, 1 Jan. 1953). Composer. He studied at the Warsaw Conservatory, taking piano lessons with Zawirski and composition lessons with Noskowski; studied at the Berlin Academy with Humperdinck, 1905–8. In 1907 he became the opera conductor at the Lwów Conservatory, teaching piano there as well. He again returned to Berlin in the late 1910s and in 1920 was appointed the chief conductor of the Warsaw Opera. He established the Polish Composers' Union in 1926 and served as its first president. Settled in Katowice in 1945, where he taught at the conservatory. His works are, in general, programmatic, with frequent references to Polish folk traditions and history; the late style became increasingly less experimental and exploratory. His works include several operas and ballets (*Casanova,* 1922, reorchestrated 1948); orchestral, vocal, and chamber music.

Rubbra, (Charles) Edmund (b. Northampton, 23 May 1901; d. Gerrard's Cross, 13 Feb. 1986). Composer. During his youth he developed a strong interest in the music of Debussy and Cyril Scott, becoming a student of the latter in composition as well as in piano; also studied composition with both Ireland and Goossens. In 1921 began study at the Royal College of Music; while there, he took composition lessons with

Holst, harmony and counterpoint with R. O. Morris, and piano with Evlyn Howard-Jones. He taught music at Oxford from 1947 to 1968 and after 1961 at the Guildhall School of Music, concurrently writing symphonic, vocal, and chamber music. His early music reflects the influence of Holst in Rubbra's exploration of expressive lyricism in combination with developmental forms. Tonal centricity was the basis of his musical language but did not act as a formal determinant; his orchestration is frequently conservative. Works include orchestral music (11 symphonies: no. 1, op. 44, 1935–57; no. 2, op. 45, 1937; no. 3, op. 49, 1939; no. 4, op. 53, 1941; no. 5, op. 63, 1947–48; no. 6, op. 80, 1954; no. 7, op. 88, 1957; no. 8, op. 132, 1966–68; no. 9, Sinfonia sacra, op. 140, 1971–72; no. 10, Sinfonia da camera, op. 145, 1974; no. 11, op. 153, 1978–79); choral works (*Songs of the Soul* op. 78, chorus, harp, timpani, strings, 1953); chamber music, usually utilizing traditional forms (4 string quartets, 1933, 1952, 1962–63, 1976–77); and vocal works.

Bibl.: *A Complete Catalogue of Compositions of Edmund Rubbra to June 1971* (S. Croydon, England, 1971). Ralph Scott Grover, *The Music of Edmund Rubbra* (Aldershot, 1993).

Rubens, Paul A. (Alfred) (b. Bayswater, London, 29 Apr. 1875; d. Falmouth, 5 Feb. 1917). Composer. He studied law at Oxford, where he was a member of the University Dramatic Society and often helped with and provided some music for the productions. He wrote almost exclusively operettas, which include *Miss Hook of Hooland* (1907), *Tonight's the Night* (1915), *Dear Little Denmark* (1909). Contributed to the musical revue *Floradora* (1899).

Rubini, Giovanni Battista (b. Romano, near Bergamo, 7 Apr. 1794; d. there, 3 Mar. 1854). Tenor. First public operatic performance was in a female role in Romano. Violinist and chorister in Bergamo. Joined a Piedmont touring company as a chorister. In 1814, made his professional debut in Pavia, Neapolitan debut in 1815 as Lindoro in Rossini's *L'italiana in Algeri.* Visited Paris in 1825, performing in *La Cenerentola, Otello,* and *La donna del lago.* Created the leading roles in *Bianca e Gernando* (1826), *Il pirata* (1827), *Anna Bolena* (1830), *La sonnambula* (1831), *I puritani* (1835), and *Marin Faliero* (1835). From 1831 to 1843, performed regularly in Paris and London. Toured with Liszt in Germany and Holland in 1843. Wrote *12 Lezioni di canto moderno per soprano o tenore* (Milan, n.d.).

Bibl.: Agostino Locatelli, *Cenni biografici sulla straordinaria carriera teatrale percosa da Giovanni Battista Rubini* (Milan, 1844).

Rubinstein [Rubinshteyn], **Anton (Grigor'yevich)** (b. Vikhvatinets, Podolia, 28 Nov. 1829; d. Peterhof, near St. Petersburg, 20 Nov. 1894). Pianist and composer. Brother of Nikolay Rubinstein. His mother gave him his earliest musical instruction; in 1836 he began studying with Alexandre Villoing, his only piano teacher. He toured Europe with Villoing (1840–43), including Paris (where he met Chopin and Liszt), the Netherlands, London, Germany, and Austria. In 1844 the Rubinstein brothers settled in Berlin, where Anton received counterpoint lessons from Siegfried Dehn. He moved to Vienna and taught piano for several years, then returned to Russia in 1848 and settled in St. Petersburg, where he enjoyed the patronage of the Grand Duchess Elena Pavlovna.

In 1854 Rubinstein embarked on a successful concert tour of Europe; he founded the Russian Musical Society in 1859, and the St. Petersburg Conservatory in 1862, serving as director until 1854, when he embarked on another European tour. He conducted the Philharmonic Concerts in Vienna (1871–72), and toured America during the 1872–73 season both as a soloist and with Wieniawski. From 1887 until 1891 he resumed his directorship of the St. Petersburg Conservatory. In 1890 he established the Rubinstein Prize, an international competition for piano performance and composition.

At his death Rubinstein was considered one of the foremost pianists of his day, with Liszt his only rival. Many of his compositions were popular at the time (e.g., Symphony no. 2 in G, Ocean, 1851, rev. 1863, 1880; Piano Concerto no. 4 in D minor, 1864) but have since disappeared from the concert stage; most of his Russian operas enjoyed little success. His greatest legacy was his improvement of performance standards in Russia, most notably through the introduction of European teaching methods to Russian conservatories.

Bibl.: *Autobiography of Anton Rubinstein, 1829–1889* (St. Petersburg, 1889); trans Eng. (1890, R: 1969). Anton Rubinstein, *A Conversation on Music* (New York, 1982). Jeremy Norris, "The Piano Concertos of Anton Rubinstein," *MR* 46 (1985): 241–83.

Rubinstein, Artur [Arthur] (b. Łódź, 28 Jan. 1887; d. Geneva, 20 Dec. 1982). Pianist. After lessons in Łódź and Warsaw he went to Berlin, where his musical education was supervised by Joachim. Following his debut in Berlin under Joachim in 1900, he made appearances in Germany and Poland and studied with Paderewski. In 1904 he went to Paris, where he met Ravel, Dukas, Thibaud, and Saint-Saëns. Made his New York debut at Carnegie Hall in 1906; his subsequent American tour was only moderately successful. Appearances in Austria, Italy, and Russia preceded his London debut in 1912; during World War I he lived mainly in London, accompanying Ysaÿe. In 1916–17 he toured Spain and South America, developing an enthusiasm for the music of Granados, Albéniz, Villa-Lobos, and Falla. In 1932 he withdrew from concert life for several years to work on his technique and restudy his repertory; during his American tour of 1937 he was recognized as one of the great players of the century. He spent World War II in the U.S., becoming an American citizen in 1946. His chamber music partners included Heifetz, Feuermann, Piatigorsky, Kochanski, Szeryng, and the

Guarneri Quartet. He retired from the stage in 1976, as his eyesight was rapidly deteriorating.

Bibl.: Artur Rubinstein, *My Many Years* (New York, 1980).

Rubinstein, Beryl (b. Athens, Ga., 26 Oct. 1898; d. Cleveland, 29 Dec. 1952). Pianist and composer. He studied piano with Alex Lambert before touring the U.S. (1905–11). After his formal debut in New York in 1916, he studied in Berlin with Busoni and José Vianna da Motta. In Cleveland he formed a two-piano team with Arthur Loesser and taught at the Cleveland Institute from 1921, becoming its director in 1932. His compositions include an opera, *Sleeping Beauty* (1938); a piano concerto; other orchestral works; and many pieces for solo piano.

Rubinstein [Rubinshteyn], **Nikolay (Grigor'yevich)** (b. Moscow, 14 June 1835; d. Paris, 23 Mar. 1881). Pianist, composer, and conductor. Brother of Anton Rubinstein. Studied in Berlin (1844–46) with Kullak and Dehn (counterpoint). Studied medicine at Moscow Univ., graduating in 1855. Studied with Villoing in Moscow. Founded the Moscow Conservatory in 1866, and was director to 1881. Premiered Balakirev's *Islamey* in 1869; a strong proponent of music of the new nationalist Russian school during the 1860s and 1870s.

Bibl.: Olga Bennigsen, "The Brothers Rubinstein and Their Circle," *MQ* 25 (1939): 407–19.

Ruckers, Hans (b. Mechelen, ca. 1540 or 1550; d. Antwerp, 1598). Harpsichord and organ maker. He was acquainted with the builder Marten van der Biest and possibly studied with him. Ruckers's two sons, Joannes [Hans, Jan] Ruckers (1578–1643) and Andreas [Andries] Ruckers (1579–1645), as well as his grandson Andreas [Andries] Ruckers (1607–ca. 1667) were also harpsichord and organ builders; the elder son, Joannes, was particularly celebrated for his craft. The few surviving instruments of the eldest Ruckers are mostly virginals from the 1580s and 1590s; he also built organs, although no known examples survive.

Bibl.: J. Lambrechts-Douillez, *Hans en Joannes Ruckers* (Antwerp, 1983). Grant O'Brien, *Ruckers: A Harpsichord and Virginal Building Tradition* (New York, 1990).

Rudd, Roswell (Hopkins, Jr.) (b. Sharon, Conn., 17 Nov. 1935). Jazz trombonist and bandleader. After playing in Dixieland groups, he joined Steve Lacy in a quartet devoted to Thelonious Monk's music (1961–64). He played free jazz with the trumpeter Bill Dixon and Archie Shepp (1962), the New York Art Quartet (1964, including John Tchicai), Shepp (1965–67, including the album *Live in San Francisco,* 1966), Charlie Haden's Music Liberation Orchestra (1969), Gato Barbieri (1970–71), and his own groups. He wrote for the Jazz Composer's Orchestra (the album *Numatik Swing Band,* 1973) and recorded again with Lacy (the album *Regeneration,* 1982). He taught improvisation at the Univ. of Maine at Augusta and Orono from 1976 to 1981.

Rudel (de Blaja), Jaufre (fl. mid-12th century). Troubadour poet-composer. Perhaps a prince of Blaja near Bordeaux, he took part in the second Crusade (1147) and possibly died in its course. His poems' frequent mention of an *amor de lonh* (distant love) may have prompted the medieval legend that he traveled to offer his love to the Countess of Tripoli, only to die in her arms on arrival. Seven poems are ascribed to him, four with music.

Rudel, Julius (b. Vienna, 6 Mar. 1921). Conductor. He studied briefly at the Vienna Academy of Music before immigrating to the U.S. in 1938. He continued his studies at the Mannes College of Music, then became a rehearsal pianist with the New York City Opera in 1943. In 1944 he made his conducting debut there, and later became the company's director (1957–79). From 1971 to 1975 he was music director of the Kennedy Center, and from 1979 to 1985 music director of the Buffalo Philharmonic.

Ruders, Poul (b. Ringsted, 27 Mar. 1949). Composer. Studied in Copenhagen at the Royal Danish Music Conservatory (organ with Reiff and composition with Nørholm). He worked as a church organist. His musical language is fundamentally an eclectic one, occasionally part of a neo-Baroque tradition and sometimes using folk music as a resource. His works may alternate rich, complex textures with minimalistic ostinati, processing material less through its development and more through its representation. His works include opera (*Tycho Brahe,* 1985–86); orchestral music (*Etudes,* 1974; *Recitatives and Arias,* piano, orchestra, 1978; *Corpus cum figuris,* chamber orchestra, 1984; clarinet concerto, 1985); chamber pieces (*Regime,* 3 percussionists, 1984); *Dramaphonia* (chamber ensemble, 1988); vocal and organ works.

Rudhyar, Dane [Chennevière, Daniel] (b. Paris, 23 Mar. 1895; d. Palo Alto, 13 Sept. 1985). Composer and writer. He studied at the Sorbonne, and at the Paris Conservatory (1912–13), but much of his musical education was self-directed. He moved to the U.S. in 1916, settling in southern California in 1919, and became an American citizen in 1926. His adoption of a Hindu name reflects his commitment to theosophy. While still in France he wrote a book on Debussy on commission from the publisher Durand (1913); in the U.S. he painted and wrote several books on astrology and other subjects (*Art as a Release of Power,* 1930), but was active also in the Composers Guild and the California New Music Society; he began to compose prolifically and to write about music again after 1970 (*Culture, Crisis, and Creativity,* 1977; *The Magic of Tone and the Art of Music,* 1982; *The Rhythm of Wholeness,* 1983). His compositional style was influenced by Scriabin and by his appreciation of Asian music; it is dominated by melody, often treated sequentially, and lacks sharply stated rhythmic figures.

Works: orchestral music including Sinfonietta (1928), *Cos-*

mic Cycle (1977), and *Encounter* (with solo piano, 1977); string quartets (*5 Stanzas,* 1928; *Advent,* 1978; *Crisis and Overcoming,* 1979); piano music (*Paens,* 1927; *Transmutation,* 1976); and a few songs.

Bibl.: J. Shere, *Dane Rudhyar: A Brief Biography with a Listing of Works* (1972).

Rudolf, Max (b. Frankfurt am Main, 15 June 1902; d. Philadelphia, 28 Feb. 1995). Conductor. He studied at Frankfurt Univ. and the conservatory there. After his conducting debut in 1923 in Freiburg, he held posts there and in Darmstadt and Prague. In 1940 he came to the U.S., conducting the Metropolitan Opera (1945–58) and the Cincinnati Symphony (1958–70) as well as making guest-conducting appearances with several major American orchestras. He taught at the Cleveland Institute (1970–73) and the Curtis Institute, and is the author of *The Grammar of Conducting* (1950).

Rudolph (Johann Joseph Rainer) (b. Florence, 8 Jan. 1788; d. Baden, near Vienna, 24 July 1831). Archduke of Austria and composer. He settled in Vienna in 1790, and in 1803 became Beethoven's pupil, eventually becoming the composer's friend and greatest patron. In 1809 Rudolph signed an agreement with Prince Kinsky and Prince Lobkowitz to make annual payments to Beethoven if he remained in Vienna. Rudolph's compositions include a clarinet sonata and sets of piano variations.

Bibl.: Susan Kagan, *Archduke Rudolph, Beethoven's Patron, Pupil, and Friend: His Life and Music* (New York, 1989).

Rudziński, Witold (b. Siebież, 14 Mar. 1913). Composer. From 1931 to 1936 he studied at the Univ. of Vilnius, then from 1928 to 1936 at the conservatory there, where his composition teacher was Szeligowski; also studied piano with Kaduszkiewiczowa and Szeligowski; composition lessons in Paris with Boulanger and Koechlin, 1938–39. Taught at the Vilnius Conservatory from 1939 to 1942 and the Łódź Conservatory, 1945–47. Served as head of the Polish Ministry of Culture, 1947–48, and during the following year was conductor of the Warsaw Opera and Warsaw Philharmonic. His music is late Romantic in its harmonic and melodic tendencies. Works include operas, choral works, orchestral and chamber music, and songs.

Rudziński, Zbigniew (b. Czechowice, 23 Oct. 1935). Composer. He studied at the Warsaw Conservatory from 1956 to 1962, taking composition lessons with Perkowski; studied in Paris, 1965–66. Head of the music division of the Warsaw Documentary Film Studio, 1960–67. The musical style of his compositions is fundamentally tonal, though at times highly, expressively chromatic. Works include operas (*Antigone,* chamber opera, 1979–82; *Manekiny* [Mannequins], 1981); orchestral pieces (*Moments musicaux,* 1965–68; *Allegro giocoso,* 1969); vocal music (Requiem, speaker, chorus, orchestra, 1971; *To nie sa sny* [These Are Not Dreams], 6 songs, mezzo-soprano, piano, 1987); and chamber works (*Impromptu,* 3 cellos, 2 pianos, 3 percussion, 1966; *Campanella,* percussion, 1977).

Rue, Pierre de la. See La Rue, Pierre de.

Ruffo, Titta [Titta, Ruffo Cafiero] (b. Pisa, 9 June 1877; d. Florence, 6 July 1953). Baritone. After study with Venceslao Persichini, Senatore Sparapani, and Lelio Casini, he made his debut in Rome in 1898. Appearances followed in Rio de Janeiro, Vienna, Paris, London, and all the principal Italian theaters. He made his U.S. debut in Philadelphia in 1912, then spent two seasons with the Chicago–Philadelphia Grand Opera Company in both cities. Following military service in World War I, he rejoined the company, appearing until 1926. From 1922 to 1929 he sang with the Metropolitan Opera. He appeared in several early sound films before his retirement in 1931; he last appeared in the U.S. at the opening of Radio City Music Hall in 1932.

Bibl.: Andrew Farkas, ed., *Titta Ruffo: An Anthology* (Westport, Conn., 1984).

Ruffo, Vincenzo (b. Verona, ca. 1508; d. Sacile, near Pordenone, 9 Feb. 1587). Composer. He was trained at Verona Cathedral and ordained there in 1531. In 1542–46 he was a court musician to Marquis Alfonso d'Alvalos in Milan. From 1547 to 1563 he was back in Verona, becoming *maestro di musica* of the amateur Accademia filarmonica in 1551, and *maestro di cappella* at the cathedral in 1554. During his early years he composed sacred works in conservative style, and some 260 madrigals. From 1563 to 1572 Ruffo was maestro at Milan Cathedral, now writing only sacred works that adhered to the dictate of clarity newly prescribed by the Counter-Reformation (particularly its chief architect, Cardinal Borromeo, Archbishop of Milan). After 1572 Ruffo held lesser posts at Pistoia, Verona, and Sacile. His works include 5 books of Masses, 9 books of other sacred music, 9 books of madrigals, and a book of instrumental *capricci.*

Ruggles, Carl [Charles] **(Sprague)** (b. East Marion, Mass., 11 Mar. 1876; d. Bennington, Vt., 24 Oct. 1971). Composer. As a youth he studied violin and played in theater orchestras; in 1890 moved to East Boston and began to play with members of the symphony in chamber groups. He had composition lessons with John Knowles Paine and theory with Joseph Klaus, worked as an engraver for a Boston music publisher, performed, and gave music club lectures before leaving Boston for Winona, Minnesota, in 1907. There he taught at the Mar d'Mar Music School and founded an orchestra; the orchestra's concertmaster, Christian Timner, coached him in conducting. He returned to New York in 1917, where he was associated with Varèse, Cowell, and Ives. Several works were performed and printed at the time (*Toys,* voice and piano, 1919; *Vox clamans in deserto,* soprano and small orchestra, 1923; *Portals,* 13 strings, 1925); his largest extant work, *Sun Treader,* was premiered by Slonimsky in Paris in 1932 (the Boston Symphony presented the American premiere in 1966 in a Ruggles Festival at Bowdoin College). Many of Ruggles's compositions exist in several versions; he orchestrated almost all his works. His main emphases were on line and polyphony; the presence of some twelve-tone groups, retrograde procedures, and his settings of texts by English and American Romantic poets are also notable. From 1924 he summered and eventually lived year-round in Arlington, Vt., supported in part by a lifetime annuity from a New York patron, Harriet Miller. He taught at the Univ. of Miami (1938–43), but completed few works after the 1930s other than *Exaltation* (unison voices and organ, 1958), composed as a memorial to his wife. He had taken up painting in 1935 and devoted most of his energy to it from the 1950s (works hang in the Brooklyn and Whitney museums). Many compositions were left unfinished, and his early Romantic works were destroyed.

Bibl.: Marilyn J. Ziffrin, *Carl Ruggles: Composer, Painter, and Storyteller* (Urbana, Ill., 1994).

Ruimonte, Pedro. See Rimonte, Pedro.

Rummel, Christian (Franz Ludwig Friedrich Alexander) (b. Brickenstadt, Bavaria, 27 Nov. 1787; d. Wiesbaden, 13 Feb. 1849). Composer and conductor. Studied in Mannheim with Heinrich Ritter and Karl Jakob Wagner. Director of a military band beginning 1806. Director of court orchestra at Wiesbaden, 1815–42. Composed concertos, chamber music, piano works.

Rush, Loren (b. Los Angeles, 23 Aug. 1935). Composer. He studied in Los Angeles with Erickson (1954–60), and then at San Francisco State (B.A., 1957), Berkeley (M.A., 1960), and Stanford (D.M.A., 1960). From 1957 to 1960 he was associate music director for radio station KPFA in San Francisco; in 1966 he founded and directed the San Francisco Conservatory Artists Ensemble and was chairman of the composition department there (1967–69). As recipient of the Rome Prize he was at the American Academy in Rome, 1969–71; in 1971 he also won a Guggenheim Fellowship. In 1975 he became associate director of the Center for Computer Research at Stanford. His works reflect his appreciation of Webern and of earlier French composers; some employ open form (*Hexahedron,* piano, 1962–63); several use the computer to refine recorded sounds (*The Digital Domain,* tape, 1983). Other works include *Soft Music, Hard Music* (3 amplified pianos, 1969–70) and *Nexus 16* (chamber ensemble, 1964).

Rushing, Jimmy [James Andrew; Mr. Five by Five] (b. Oklahoma City, 26 Aug. 1903; d. New York, 8 June 1972). Blues and jazz singer. He joined Walter Page's Blue Devils (1927–29), Bennie Moten (1929–35), and Count Basie (1939–50), with whom he recorded "Evenin'" (1936), "Good Morning Blues" (1937), and "Sent for You Yesterday and Here You Come Today" (1938). He led a band (1950–52), then worked as a free-lance, making international tours with Benny Goodman, Buck Clayton, Eddie Condon, and Basie, and recording as a leader, including the album *Listen to the Blues* (1955). Principally a blues shouter, he also sang popular songs.

Russell, (George) Alexander (b. Franklin, Tenn., 2 Oct. 1880; d. Dewitt, N.Y., 24 Nov. 1953). Organist and composer. At Syracuse Univ. he studied organ with George A. Parker and Henry Vibbard. He taught at Syracuse (1902–6), then studied abroad with Godowsky, Widor, and Harold Bauer; he studied composition with Edgar Stillman Kelley. He toured the U.S. as a pianist and organist (1908–10) before becoming organist, music director, and manager of musical activities at the Wanamaker department stores in New York and Philadelphia (1910–52). Russell was director of music at Princeton Univ. (1917–35), where he lectured and performed and oversaw the design of the Skinner organ in the university chapel, constructed in the 1920s. His compositions include songs, piano pieces, and a series of organ pieces, the *St. Lawrence Sketches.*

Russell, Anna [Russell-Brown, Claudia Ann] (b. London, 12 Dec. 1911). Contralto and comedienne. She studied at the Royal College of Music with Ralph Vaughan Williams, then moved to Canada in 1939. In 1944 she presented her satiric version of highlights from Wagner's *Ring.* She took her one-woman show of parodies of serious music and musicians to Carnegie Recital Hall in 1947, then built an international career, appearing on Broadway, with major American orchestras, and on television. After 70, she made several farewell tours.

Bibl.: Anna Russell, *I'm Not Making This Up, You Know: The Autobiography of the Queen of Musical Parody* (New York, 1985).

Russell, George (Allan) (b. Cincinnati, 23 June 1923). Jazz composer, performer, and theorist. From the early 1940s to the early 1950s he wrote scores for Earl Hines, Dizzy Gillespie, Buddy de Franco, Lee Konitz, and others. He studied composition with Stefan Wolpe and in 1953 published *The Lydian Chromatic Concept of Tonal Organization,* an early cornerstone of jazz theory. Subsequent scores established him as an outstanding postwar jazz composer. He taught at the Lenox, Mass., School of Jazz (1959–60); the Univ. of Lund, Sweden (1963); and the New England Conservatory (from 1969). In the 1960s, 1970s, and early 1980s he performed and recorded widely as pianist with his own sextet and as leader of his own big band.

Russell, Henry (b. Sheerness, 24 Dec. 1812; d. London, 8 Dec. 1900). Singer, organist, and composer. Studied singing in Italy, composition with Rossini and Bellini. In 1834 or 1835 he moved to Canada, where he gave numerous solo recitals. He toured the U.S., both as a soloist and accompanist to William Vincent Wallace, 1837–41. Organist of the First Presbyterian Church of Rochester, N.Y., 1833–41. Returned to England in 1844 or 1845. Popular as a song composer.

Father of the impresario Henry Russell (1871–1937) and the composer-conductor Landon Ronald (1873–1938).

Russell, Luis (Carl) (b. Careening Cay, near Bocas del Toro, Panama, 6 Aug. 1902; d. New York, 11 Dec. 1963). Jazz bandleader, arranger, and pianist. In Chicago he joined King Oliver (1925–27), who brought him to New York. There he eventually took over a big band which included several of Oliver's sidemen, but played in a style that looked forward to swing. The group accompanied Louis Armstrong in 1929 and toured under Armstrong's name from 1935 to 1943. Pops Foster and drummer Paul Barbarin were long-standing sidemen; among Russell's soloists were Henry Allen, J. C. Higginbotham, Albert Nicholas, and trombonist Jimmy Archey. Typical of the band's forceful rhythm section and developing soloists are "Feelin' the Spirit" and "Jersey Lightning" (both 1929). Russell ceased leading big bands in 1948.

Russell, Pee Wee [Charles Ellsworth] (b. St. Louis, 27 March 1906; d. Alexandria, Va., 15 Feb. 1969). Jazz clarinetist. He played with Jack Teagarden in Texas (1924) and Bix Beiderbecke in St. Louis (1925) before settling in New York, where he recorded with Red Nichols (1927–29). He recorded "Home Cooking" with Eddie Condon (1933) and from 1937 to 1967 played intermittently with Condon. He joined Bobby Hackett (recording "A Ghost of a Chance," 1938), Bud Freeman (1939–40), and many other Dixieland and traditional musicians. From 1962 he also explored newer styles and the following year played at the Newport Jazz Festival with Thelonious Monk. His terse clarinet phrases and vocal tone gave his playing considerable individuality.

Russo, Bill [William Joseph] (b. Chicago, 25 June 1928). Composer, arranger, and trombonist. He studied jazz with Lennie Tristano, 1943–47, and classical composition with John J. Becker and Karel B. Jirák in the mid-1950s. In 1947–50 he led the rehearsal band Experiment in Jazz; 1950–54, was trombonist and chief composer-arranger for Stan Kenton's band. He led his own jazz quintet and jazz orchestra in the mid-1950s. He taught at the Lenox (Mass.) School of Jazz, 1957–60, and the Manhattan School of Music, 1959–61; and led the London Jazz Orchestra, 1962–65. From 1965 to 1975 he directed the Center for New Music at Columbia College (Chicago), also teaching at Peabody Conservatory in 1969–71, and Antioch College in 1971–72. Following a period (1975–76) as city composer-in-residence for San Francisco, he worked briefly in film and television; he returned to teach at Columbia College in 1979.

His compositions include numerous operas, cabaret operas, rock operas, rock cantatas, ballets, and theater pieces; also concert works for orchestra, jazz orchestra, concert band, and chamber ensembles. He has recorded extensively and authored 3 books on composition.

Russolo, Luigi (b. Portogruaro, 30 Apr. 1885; d. Cerro di Laveno, Varese, 4 Feb. 1947). Composer, inventor, painter. He was associated with the Italian futurist movement first as a painter (1911–13) and then as signer of the manifesto *L'arte dei rumori* (11 Mar. 1913; a book with the same title appeared in 1916), a more radical statement of the role of music in the futurist movement than had been made by Pratella. He advocated music made by machines, with sounds related to those of daily life; invented numerous machines (intonarumori, scoppiatori, ronzatore, rumorarmonio) for futurist music, which were demonstrated in Modena, Milan, Genoa, and London (1913–14). From 1927 to 1932 he lived in Paris, inventing and refining his machines and composing; all of his Paris manuscripts were lost during the Second World War. His music for machines was a precursor of *musique concrète;* composers whose interest was aroused included Ravel, Honegger, Milhaud, Varèse, and Stravinsky. His final years were devoted to study of the occult and a return to painting.

Rust, Friedrich Wilhelm (b. Wörlitz, near Dessau, 6 July 1739; d. Dessau, 28 Feb. 1796). Composer, violinist, and pianist. In Halle (1758–62) he studied law and was a pupil of W. F. Bach, then served Prince Leopold II of Anhalt-Dessau. In 1763–64 moved to Potsdam and studied violin with Franz Benda and composition with C. P. E. Bach. After traveling to Italy with Prince Leopold (1765) he returned to Dessau, where he promoted public concerts and founded a theater for opera and spoken drama (1774); he became court music director in 1775. His works include chamber music and keyboard pieces. His son Wilhelm Karl Rust (1787–1855) was a pianist and organist; and his grandson Wilhelm Rust (1822–92) was an editor, composer, and keyboard player.

Rutini, Giovanni Marco [Giovanni Maria, Giovanni Placido] (b. Florence, 25 Apr. 1723; d. there, 22 Dec. 1797). Composer. He attended the Conservatorio della Pietà dei Turchini in Naples, then went to Prague (1748 and 1753), where he was under the protection of the Electress of Saxony, Maria Antonia. After visits to Dresden (1754), Berlin (1756), and St. Petersburg (1758), he settled permanently in Florence (1761), where he wrote at least 14 operas. In 1769 he became *maestro di cappella* to the Duke of Modena. He published harpsichord music in Florence and Bologna, and from 1780 wrote several oratorios.

Ruyneman, Daniel (b. Amsterdam, 8 Aug. 1886; d. there, 25 July 1963). Composer. He studied composition at the Amsterdam Conservatory with Zweers; also studied piano with DeJong. He quickly became known as part of the young, experimental avant-garde, helping to organize the Nederlandsche Vereeniging voor Moderne Scheppende Toonkunst in 1918, which became a subsection of the ISCM. He cofounded and directed the Dutch Society for Contemporary Music and the Foundation for Internal Exchange Concerts. His own music shares in contemporary trends, including neoclassicism, serialism, and the exploration of vocal and timbral capabilities. Works include operas, orchestra music, chamber music (*Réflections I-IV,* various instruments, 1958–61); choral and solo vocal music.

Ruzicka, Peter (b. Düsseldorf, 3 July 1948). Composer. He studied piano, oboe, and counterpoint at the conservatory in Hamburg (1963–68), and law and musicology at the universities of Munich and Hamburg. He has been active as a conductor in Hamburg; beginning 1988 served as intendant at the Hamburg State Opera. As a composer he is allied with Henze and Hans Olte in combining free and strict compositional procedures; many of his works are for large orchestra. Prizes include the Förderpreis (Stuttgart, 1969), the UNESCO Prize (Paris, 1971), and the Bartók Prize (Budapest, 1970). Works include *Esta noche* (for Vietnam war victims; alto, flute, English horn, viola, and cello, 1967); *Introspezione* (string quartet, 1970); *Metastrofe* (87 instruments, 1971); *Annäherung und Stille* (piano, 42 strings, 1981); 7 Preludes (piano, 1987); *Drei Bruchstücke für grosses Orchester* (1986); *Fünf Bruchstücke für grosses Orchester* (1988); pieces for tape.

Rysanek, Leonie (b. Vienna, 14 Nov. 1926). Soprano. After studies at the Vienna Conservatory with Alfred Jerger and later with Rudolf Grossmann, she made her debut at Innsbruck in 1949. She then sang at Saarbrücken and Munich. Her London debut was at Covent Garden in 1953, and her U.S. debut was with the San Francisco Opera in 1956; her Metropolitan Opera debut came in 1959. She has appeared at many leading opera houses, winning special praise for her roles in the operas of Verdi, Wagner, and Strauss.

Rzewski, Frederic (Anthony) (b. Westfield, Mass. 13 Apr. 1938). Composer and pianist. He studied with Thompson and Piston at Harvard (B.A., 1958) and with Sessions and Babbitt at Princeton (M.F.A., 1960); then with Dallapiccola in Florence on a Fulbright grant (1960–61). In the 1960s he remained in Europe, active as a pianist in performances and recordings of contemporary music by Boulez, Eisler, and himself; held a Ford Foundation grant to study with Carter in Berlin (1963–65); taught at the contemporary music courses in Cologne (1963, 1964, 1970); and cofounded Musica elettronica viva (Rome, 1966) with Curran and Teitelbaum. He returned to New York in 1971, but five years later went back to Rome and Liège; he was appointed professor of composition at the Royal Conservatory of Belgium in 1977; in 1984 he was visiting professor at Yale. His *Work Songs* (1967–69) draw on his experience in collective improvisation; later works incorporate folk and popular music influences and often demand considerable virtuosity. Works include *Chains* (for the ensemble RELACHE; 3 short television operas, female vocalist and instrumental ensemble; premiered Mar. 1987); *The Price of Oil* (2 speakers, winds, and percussion, 1980); other works for orchestra and jazz band; *Attica* (text from a letter of an inmate at Attica prison; speaker, alto saxophone, trombone, viola, double bass, synthesizer, piano, and vibraphone, 1972); *Moutons de Panurge* (any ensemble, 1969); *Whang Doodles* (violin, piano, percussion, 1990); several mixed-media works and tape works from the 1960s.

S

Sabbatini, Galeazzo (b. Pesaro?, 1597; d. there, 6 Dec. 1662). Composer and theorist. He studied with Vincenzo Pellegrini, a canon of Pesaro Cathedral, before being elected to this position himself in 1626. From 1630 to 1639 he was *maestro di cappella* to the Duke of Mirandola, and from 1641 again served as a canon at Pesaro Cathedral. As a theorist he produced a treatise on continuo playing (1628) and a method of tuning. His compositions consist mainly of motets and madrigals.

Sabbatini, Luigi Antonio (b. Albano Laziale, near Rome, 24 Oct. 1732; d. Padua, 29 Jan. 1809). Composer and theorist. In Bologna he studied with Martini and entered the St. Francis monastery. Became *maestro di cappella* at the Basilica of S. Barnaba in Marino (1767) and at the Franciscan Basilica of the Twelve Holy Apostles in Rome (1772). He held this post at the Basilica of S. Antonio in Padua from 1786 until his death. All of his surviving music is sacred. He was one of the leading theorists of the Paduan school. His most important treatise, *Trattato sopra le fughe* (Venice, 1802), is an analysis of Vallotti's fugues. *Elementi teorici della musica* (Rome 1789–90) is a method for teaching musical beginners.

Sacchini, Antonio (Maria Gasparo Gioacchino) (b. Florence, 14 June 1730; d. Paris, 6 Oct. 1786). Composer. He attended the Naples Conservatorio S. Maria di Loreto and studied with Durante; there he became *mastricello* (1756), *maestro di cappella straordinario* (1758), and *secondo maestro* (1761). In 1761 his first opera seria, *Andromaca,* was performed at the Teatro S. Carlo. In Venice (1762–63) he composed his operas *Alessandro Severo* and *Alessandro nell'Indie.* Following his success with *Olimpiade* (Padua, 1763) and with other operas in Rome, Naples, and Florence, he abandoned his conservatory post. In Rome (1765–68) he composed comic operas for the Teatro Valle. In 1768 he moved to Venice and became director of the Conservatorio dell'Ospedaletto, where his singing pupils included Nancy Storace. He moved to London in 1772, enjoying success with *Il Cid* and *Tamerlano* (both 1773). When his licentious life-style led to legal difficulty in 1781, he left England for Paris, where he was already well known. There he won the favor of Marie Antoinette and composed for the Opéra. With the failure of his first opera, *Renaud* (1783), the initial support given to him by the Piccinnists quickly disappeared, and a rivalry with Piccinni followed. His next opera, *Chimène* (1783), secured for Sacchini a large royal pension. The delay until 1787 of the premiere of his most successful opera, *Oedipe à Colone* (1785), was a major disappointment to him; the opera remained part of the standard repertory until 1830. His last opera, *Arvire et Evelina,* completed by Rey, the conductor of the Opéra orchestra in 1788, was performed in Paris until 1827. In addition to over 40 operas, Sacchini wrote oratorios, numerous sacred vocal pieces, and a small amount of chamber music.

Bibl.: U. Prota-Giurleo, *Sacchini a Napoli* (Naples, 1956). Id., *Sacchini fra Piccinisti e Gluckisti* (Naples, 1957). E. A. Thierstein, "Five French Operas of Sacchini" (diss., Univ. of Cincinnati, 1974). Wolfgang Hochstein, "Musik am Ospedaletto zu Venedig zur Zeit von Antonio Sacchini," *Mf* 40 (1987): 320–37.

Sacher, Paul (b. Basel, 28 Apr. 1906). Conductor. Studied with Weingartner and Nef in his home city; formed the Basel Chamber Orchestra in 1926, adding a chamber choir to it in 1928. He founded the Schola cantorum basiliensis in 1933; in 1954 it merged with the Basel Conservatory and Musikschule to become the Musikakademie, which Sacher directed until 1969. Though specializing in historical performance, his ensembles also premiered works by Bartók, Hindemith, Honegger, Stravinsky, and Britten. He commissioned new works, including Bartók's *Music for Strings, Percussion, Celesta;* Stravinsky's Concerto in D. Established the Sacher Foundation, acquiring important musical source material (Stravinsky's *Nachlass;* Webern estate).

Sachs, Hans (b. Nuremberg, 5 Nov. 1494; d. there 19 Jan. 1576). Meistersinger and poet. After schooling he apprenticed as a shoemaker and joined the Meistersinger guild; he traveled throughout Germany, 1511–16. Becoming a master shoemaker in 1520, he quickly took a leading role in the Nuremberg Meistersingers, making the guild a model for others in Germany. He devised 13 *Töne* or *Weisen* (melodic formulas for singing Meisterlieder), among them the *Silberweise* (1513). His 6,000 poetic works include 4,300 Meisterlieder as well as didactic poems and plays.

Bibl.: Barbara Könneker, *Hans Sachs* (Stuttgart, 1971). Niklas Holzberg, *Hans-Sachs-Bibliographie* (Nuremberg, 1976). Klaus Wedler, *Hans Sachs* (Nuremberg, 1976).

Sadai, Yizhak (b. Sofia, 13 May 1935). Composer. With his family he emigrated to Israel in 1949. From 1951 to 1956 he studied at the Tel Aviv Academy of Music with Boskovich. He subsequently studied with Haubenstock-Ramati, and taught at the music academies in Jerusalem and Tel Aviv. His early music used

Germanic expressionism as a point of departure. He then embraced serialism (*Impressions d'un chorale,* piano, 1960). His music explores the manipulation of timbre in the projection of melodic material and also contains elements of Middle Eastern musical traditions (*Hazvi Israel,* cantata 1960). Phenomenology and linguistic structuralism were important influences in his work from the mid-1960s, and some works make use of electronic media (*Anagram,* chamber orchestra, tape, 1973). Other works include *Reprises* (nonet, 1986); *Canti fermi* (orchestra, synthesizer, 1986); *Antiphonies* (chamber ensemble, 1986).

Saeverud, Harald (Sigurd Johan) (b. Bergen, 17 Apr. 1897; d. 27 Mar. 1992). Composer. He began composing at a young age. From 1915 to 1920 he studied at the Bergen Conservatory with Holmsen, then traveled to Berlin to study with Koch at the Berlin Musikhochschule. He was active with the Norwegian Composers' Association and in 1953 received the Norwegian State Salary of Art, which subsequently supported him. His early music used a late Romantic, highly chromatic idiom as a point of departure, then incorporated the principles of atonality (Cello Concerto, 1931). Through the 1930s he moved back toward a tonal orientation, this time within the context of neoclassicism. His later music became more freely eclectic, exhibiting polyphonic textures, motivic processes, and occasional incorporation of elements of Norwegian folk music. His output, primarily symphonic, includes 9 symphonies (no.1, op. 2, 1916–19; no. 9, op. 45, 1966), concertos (Piano Concerto op. 31, 1948–50), and descriptive pieces and incidental music (*Romanza* op. 23, violin, orchestra, 1942; *Peer Gynt* op. 28, 1947; *Entrata regale* op. 41, 1960). He also wrote chamber music (*6 Sonatiner* op. 30, piano, 1948–50).

Safonov, Vasili (b. near Itsyursk, Terek, Caucasus, 6 Feb. 1852; d. Kislovodsk, Caucasus, 27 Feb. 1918). Pianist and conductor. Studied at St. Petersburg Conservatory with Leschetizky, later with Zaremba (theory) and Brassin (piano); graduated in 1880. Taught there until 1885. Professor at the Moscow Conservatory; director, 1889–1905. Principal conductor, Russian Musical Society (Moscow), 1889–1905, 1909–11; guest conductor, New York Philharmonic Society, 1904; principal conductor, 1906–9. Wrote a book on piano technique (*Novaya formula,* 1916).

Sahl, Michael (b. Boston, 2 Sept. 1934). Composer. He studied at Amherst College and Princeton (M.F.A., 1957) with Sessions and Babbitt; with Citkowitz, Foss, and Copland; and with Dallapiccola, supported by a Fulbright Grant in Florence. In 1965 he became a Creative Associate at SUNY–Buffalo; in 1968–69, pianist and music director for Judy Collins; then worked at radio station WBAI-FM in New York (music director, 1972–73). He has written concert music (5 symphonies, 1972–83), electronic music (*A Mitzvah for the Dead,* violin and tape, 1966), opera (*Dream Beach,* 1988) and other theater pieces (*Civilization and Its Discontents,* in collaboration with Eric Salzman, won the Italia Prize in 1980). Many of his compositions are intended for nontraditional performing mileux (*Dances of Glass,* Corning Glass Museum, 1980). He collaborated with Salzman on *Making Changes: A Practical Guide to Vernacular Harmony* (1977).

Saint-Georges [Saint-George], **Joseph Boulogne, Chevalier de** (b. near Basse Terre, Guadeloupe, ca. 1739; d. Paris, 9 or 10 June 1799). Composer and violinist. He was an expert in fencing, riding, dancing, swimming, and skating. Little is known of his musical training, but he made his debut as a violinist with the Paris Concert des Amateurs in 1772; in 1773 he became musical director and leader of the Amateurs. From 1777 he composed several operas for the Comédie-Italienne. In 1781 he founded the Concert de la Loge Olympique, the ensemble for which Haydn's Paris symphonies were commissioned. Following trips to London (1785–87 and 1789–90), he moved to Lille (1791), where he was captain of the National Guard and formed a corps of light troops. After living with the horn player Lamothe for several years, he returned to Paris (about 1797), where he directed the Cercle de l'harmonie. His works include symphonies, *symphonies concertantes,* violin concertos, and string quartets.

Bibl.: Ellwood Derr, *Joseph Boulogne, Chevalier de Saint-Georges: Black Musician and Athlete in Galant Paris* (Ann Arbor, 1972).

Saint-Lambert, Michel? de (fl. ca. 1700). Composer and theorist. Very little is known of his life, and Fétis is the only source for the name Michel. Saint-Lambert's fame rests principally on 2 treatises: *Les principes du clavecin* (1702), containing useful information on ornaments, and *Nouveau traité de l'accompagnement du clavecin* (1707), in which a revision of minor key signatures is proposed. His only surviving compositions are a minuet and a gavotte in the *Principes.*

Saint-Marcoux, Micheline Coulombe (b. Notre Dame-de-la-Doré, Quebec, 9 Aug. 1938; d. Montreal, 2 Feb. 1985). Composer. She studied with François Brassard in Jonquière and in Montreal with Champagne, Tremblay, and Pépin; in Nice with Tony Aubin (1965); and in Paris with Pierre Schaeffer and others (1969). In 1967 she had received a Premier Prix in composition from the Montreal Conservatoire and the Prix d'Europe for *Modulaire,* an orchestral piece. The Montreal Symphony commissioned *Hétéromorphie* (1970), which uses clusters, glissandi, and some aleatory sections in a manner similar to that of Ligeti; *Arksalalartôq* (tape, 1971; commissioned by the Groupe de Recherches Musicales) combines live and electronic source material. She taught at the Conservatoire in Montreal.

Saint-Saëns, (Charles) Camille (b. Paris, 9 Oct. 1835; d. Algiers, 16 Dec. 1921). Composer. Only child of a government clerk; as a child he showed perfect pitch and strong aptitude as a pianist and composer, beginning to play in public in 1840; piano lessons from 1843 with Camille Stamaty, a Kalkbrenner pupil, and composition with Pierre Maleden, later organ with Boëly, accompaniment with Franchomme, singing with Delsarte. He made his official debut recital at Salle Pleyel (offering to play any Beethoven sonata from memory as an encore) in 1846; from 1848 he was at the Paris Conservatory, studying the organ with Benoist (first prize, 1851), then composition with Halévy, competing unsuccessfully for the Prix de Rome in 1852 and 1864. From 1849 he was a friend of Pauline Viardot, becoming a frequenter of her salon and eventually many others, including Rossini's, emerging as a leading figure in Parisian musical society, displaying considerable wit and volubility in conversation and, being a bit of a polymath, a fund of information on astronomy, classical antiquity, and the natural sciences, on all of which he was to publish; he also published a volume of poems in 1890. His somewhat acerbic personal charm is still evident in his witty, graceful writing. From the 1870s he published many musical essays, some of them collected in books; also a book of philosophical musings, *Problèmes et mystères* (Paris, 1894; enlarged, 1922, as *Divagations sérieuses*), and memoirs, *École buissonnière* (Paris, 1913; abridged Eng. trans., 1919, R: 1969); also edited works of Rameau, Gluck, and others.

Saint-Saëns's powers of musical assimilation, memory, and inventiveness were legendary, making him an extraordinary sight-reader (Wagner, whom he met in 1859, was astonished by his ability to read and then remember his own complicated scores), improviser (from 1853 he held church organist posts, most notably that of the Madeleine, 1857–76, in which his abilities as improviser found full use), and a facile and prolific composer. Reflecting his deep devotion to the German classics, especially Mozart and Beethoven, as well as to Schumann, then hardly known in France, his early work gives a much more central place than was then usual to instrumental music, ignoring opera. In the 1850s he produced three symphonies (one unnumbered), the First Piano Concerto, the first two violin concertos, an unpublished Piano Quartet, a Piano Quintet, and sacred works (Mass; Oratorio de Noël; motets). In the 1860s he made his first attempts at opera, but had little luck with opera-house managers. *Le timbre d'argent,* begun in the mid-1860s for the Théâtre-lyrique, was not staged until 1877, when it was unsuccessful; and *Samson et Delila,* his only popular opera, begun in 1867, was not performed until 1877, and then only at Weimar through his friend Liszt's influence. Although a success there and elsewhere, it was not staged in France until 1890.

In the War of 1870 Saint-Saëns helped defend Paris in the National Guard, but during the ensuing Commune fled to London, where he became popular as composer and performer, by this time having achieved considerable renown throughout Europe. In 1871 he became a founder and first vice president of the Société nationale de musique, designed to foster new French music. The period 1872–77 saw the composition of his four symphonic poems, as well as the First Cello Concerto (1872), the Fourth Piano Concerto (1875), and several large chamber works; his most important piano work, the Variations on a Theme of Beethoven for two pianos (1874); and the oratorio *Le déluge* (1875). In 1875 he married, rather impulsively, the 19-year-old sister of one of his pupils; the marriage was never happy, and in 1881 he suddenly abandoned his wife while they were on holiday together. The 1880s were a crucial period for Saint-Saëns. They marked the high point of his achievement as an orchestral composer with the Third Symphony (1886), which he regarded as completing what he had to say in this sphere thereafter producing only the Fifth Piano Concerto (1896) and Second Cello Concerto (1902) and various small pieces. He remained more productive in chamber music, including two string quartets (1898, 1918); the Second Piano Trio (1892); Second Violin Sonata (1896); Second Cello Sonata (1905); and the sonatas for oboe, clarinet, and bassoon, composed just before his death and thought by some to show a return of creative vitality, which is generally considered to have ebbed in this period.

Very little of Saint-Saëns's later music is ever performed, especially the operas that were the focus of his later work: *Henry VIII* (1883), *Ascanio* (1890), *Les barbares* (1901), all for the Opéra; *Proserpine* (1887) and *Phryné* (1893) for the Opéra-comique; three operas for Monte Carlo in the early 1900s; also two works for the amphitheater at Béziers; incidental music; a ballet; even a film score. None of these had more than a succès d'estime, reflecting his immense prestige in his later years, which brought him countless official honors, including election to the Academy (after having earlier been beaten out by Massenet, of whom he nourished a lifelong jealousy because of Massenet's theatrical successes). In 1886 he lost a power struggle for control of the Société nationale de musique with D'Indy and the Franckists, signaling his lack of touch with current trends in French music. He was even less sympathetic to Debussy and the later French avant-garde, although ironically he had much in common with some of its members, as reflected in Ravel's admiration and use of his works as models. In 1888 his mother—a dominant figure in his life—died; thereafter he traveled frequently, making long trips throughout the world, including visits to the U.S. in 1906 and 1915, no longer maintaining a permanent home. He made his last concert appearance in 1920.

Bibl.: J. Bonnerot, *Camille Saint-Saëns: Sa vie et son oeuvre* (Paris, 1914; 2nd ed., 1922). James Harding, *Saint-Saëns and His Circle* (London, 1965). J. M. Nectoux, ed., *Camille Saint-Saëns et Gabriel Fauré: Correspondance* (Paris, 1973). Camille Saint-Saëns, *Musikalischen Reminiszenzen* (Wilhelmshaven, 1979). Michael Stegemann, *Camille Saint-Saëns and the French Solo Concerto from 1850–1920* (Portland, 1991).

Sala, Nicola (b. Tocco-Caudio, near Benevento, 7 Apr. 1713; d. Naples, 31 Aug. 1801). Composer and writer. He studied with Nicola Fago and Leo at the Naples Pietà dei Turchini Conservatory (1732–40), where he taught for most of his life, eventually becoming *secondo maestro* (1787) and *primo maestro* (1793–99). In 1744 he applied unsuccessfully to succeed Leo as *primo maestro* of the royal chapel. During the 1760s he wrote 3 operas and several occasional works for the S. Carlo theater; apart from these, he wrote sacred vocal music. His most important didactic publication is the *Regole del contrappunto pratico* (Naples, 1794), a thorough course in counterpoint stressing practical demonstration.

Salabert, Francis (b. Paris, 27 July 1884; d. in an airplane accident near Shannon, Ireland, 28 Dec. 1946). Music publisher. From his father, Edouard (1838–1903), he took over the Salabert firm, founded in 1886, already a major publisher of popular and light classical music. Francis expanded the catalog to include classics and bought numerous smaller firms representing modern composers such as Honegger, Milhaud, Poulenc, and Satie. Under his widow's direction the Salabert firm continued to support serious modern music.

Salas y Castro, Esteban (b. Havana, 25 Dec. 1725; d. Santiago de Cuba, 14 July 1803). Composer. He was *maestro de capilla* of Santiago de Cuba Cathedral (1764–1803), where he established a conservatory. He conducted Cuba's first chamber ensemble, and taught philosophy, theology, and ethics following his ordination (1790). The first Cuban composer of art music, he wrote sacred works, *tonadillas,* and 30 *villancicos.*

Bibl.: P. Hernández Balaguer, *Obras de Esteban Salas* (Santiago de Cuba, 1960).

Salazar [Zalazar], **Antonio de** (b. ca. 1650; d. Mexico City, before 27 May 1715). Composer. After serving as a prebendary in Seville, he traveled to Mexico and was appointed *maestro de capilla* of Puebla Cathedral on 11 July 1679. He was appointed *maestro de capilla* of Mexico City Cathedral on 3 September 1688. Apparently highly regarded as a composer of *villancicos* and *chanzonetas,* he also wrote Magnificats, hymns, and responsories among other sacred choral works.

Salieri, Antonio (b. Legnago, 18 Aug. 1750; d. Vienna, 7 May 1825). Composer. He studied violin and harpsichord with his brother Francesco, and violin with the Legnago organist Giuseppe Simonie. After becoming orphaned in 1765, he was taken to Venice, where he studied thoroughbass with Giovanni Pescetti, the deputy *maestro di cappella* of St. Mark's, and singing with Ferdinando Pacini, a tenor there. In 1766 Florian Gassmann took him to Vienna, where he continued his studies and met Metastasio and Gluck. There his *Armida* (1771) was a great success. After Gassmann's death in 1774, Salieri became court composer and conductor of the Italian opera; in 1788 he succeeded Giuseppe Bonno as court Kapellmeister. Receiving a two-year leave of absence from Joseph II in 1778, he traveled to Milan, Venice, Rome, and Naples. His greatest successes were at the Paris Opéra, most notably with *Tarare* (1787); the opera was subsequently recomposed and the libretto translated by Da Ponte for a 1788 production at the Vienna Burgtheater under the title *Axur, Re d'Ormus.* From 1788 to 1804 Salieri wrote 16 operas, of which only *Palmira, Regina di Persia* (1795) had international success. He cited a distaste with modern trends for his abandonment of dramatic music after 1804. After the death of Joseph II in 1790, he successfully petitioned Leopold II for his release from the direction of the opera, although he retained his post as court Kapellmeister. An excellent administrator at court, Salieri also served as president of the Tonkünstler-Sozietät (1788–95), drafted the statutes of the Imperial State Conservatory (1810–20), and directed the musical program of the Congress of Vienna. Among his pupils were Beethoven, Schubert, Czerny, Hummel, Liszt, and Moscheles. Salieri's posthumous reputation has suffered from the unsupported charge that he felt animosity toward Mozart; there is no foundation for the rumor that he poisoned the younger composer. In addition to over 40 operas, Salieri wrote oratorios, Masses, other sacred vocal music, a large body of vocal chamber music, several concertos, and chamber music.

Bibl.: Edward Elmgren Swenson, "'Prima la musica e poi le parole': An Eighteenth-Century Satire," *AnMca* 9 (1970): 112–29. Rudolph Angermüller, *Antonio Salieri: sein Leben und seine weltlichen Werke unter besonderer Berücksichtigung seiner "grossen" Opern* (Munich, 1971–74). Id., "Salieris Gesellschaftsmusik," *AnMca* 17 (1976): 146–93. Julian Rushton, "Salieri's *Les Horaces:* A Study of an Operatic Failure," *MR* 37 (1976): 266–82. Jane Shatkin Hettrick, "A Thematic Catalogue of Sacred Works by Antonio Salieri: An Uncatalogued Holograph of the Composer in the Archive of the Vienna Hofkapelle," *FAM* 3 (1986): 226–35. Volkmar Braunbehrens, *Salieri: ein Musiker im Schatten Mozarts* (Munich, 1989); trans. Eng. (New York, 1992).

Salinas, Francisco de (b. Burgos, 1 Mar. 1513; d. Salamanca, 13 Jan. 1590). Organist and theorist. Blind from childhood, he was trained in organ and languages; he studied humanities at Salamanca Univ. In 1538 he traveled with Cardinal Pedro Sarmiento de Salinas to Rome, where, at the behest of Pope Paul III, he was ordained and given an abbacy. He held organ posts for the Viceroy of Naples (1553–58, under Diego Ortiz), Sigüenza Cathedral (1559–63), and León Cathedral (1563–67); he taught at Salamanca Univ. (1567–87). His *De musica libri septem* (1577; facs., *DM* ser. 1, no. 13; trans. Spanish, Ismael Fernández de la Cuesta) treats proportions, intervals, modes, and tones drawing on both classical and modern theorists; it discusses rhythm and meter with many unique and valuable examples of Spanish and Italian folk melody. He inspired Fray Luis de León's *Oda a Salinas.*

Sallinen, Aulis (b. Salmi, 9 Apr. 1935). Composer. From 1955 to 1960 he was a student at the Sibelius

Academy in Helsinki, a pupil of Merikanto and Kokkonen. From his graduation until 1970 he served as head manager of the Finnish Radio Symphony; concurrently lecturer in theory and composition (1963–76) at Sibelius Academy. Appointed arts professor, 1976–81, by the Finnish state. His early music utilized serial techniques. Toward the end of the 1960s he used tonal references, both melodic and harmonic, in the context of atonal structures. He also incorporated material from Finnish folk music into his works (String Quartet no. 3, *Aspekteja Peltoniemen Hintrikin surumarssista* [Aspects of Peltoniemi Hintrik's Funeral March], 1969). In particular, his operas combined dramatic development with coherent structural principles (*Punainen viiva* [The Red Line], 1977–78; *The King Goes Forth to France,* 1987; *Kullervo,* 1988); other stage works include a number of ballets (*Variations sur Mallarmé,* 1967; *Midsommernatten,* 1984; *Himlens hemlighet* [Secret of Heavens], 1986). His orchestral works include descriptive music (*Kaksi myytillistä kuvaa* [Two Mystical Scenes], 1956) and use traditional genres (Concerto, chamber orchestra, 1959; Violin Concerto, 1968; Cello Concerto, 1986; Symphony no. 1, 1970–71; *Symphony Dialogue* [Symphony no. 2], percussion, orchestra, 1972; Symphony no. 3, 1974–75; Symphony no. 4, 1979; Symphony no. 5, *Washington Mosaics,* 1985; Symphony no. 6, *From a New Zealand Diary,* 1989–90). He also composed vocal and chamber music (String Quartet no. 5, 1983).

Salmanov, Vadim (Nikolayevich) (b. St. Petersburg, 4 Nov. 1912; d. Leningrad, 27 Feb. 1978). Composer. He was guided into music from childhood. After a brief career in geology, he studied composition at Leningrad Conservatory under Gnesin, 1936–41. After wartime service he taught at the Gnesin Institute and from 1946 at the Leningrad Conservatory, becoming professor in 1965. From 1968 he was secretary of the RSFSR (Russian State) Composers' Union. His works range from folkloristic and pictorial symphonic poems, songs, and choral pieces to more formalized symphonies (3) and string quartets (6). His choral concerto *Lebyodushka* [The Hen Swan] won the state Glinka Prize in 1970.

Bibl.: M. Aranovsky, *V. N. Salmanov* (Leningrad, 1961).

Salmenhaara, Erkki (Olavi) (b. Helsinki, 12 Mar. 1941). Composer. He graduated in 1963 from the Sibelius Academy in Helsinki where he had been a composition student of Kokkonen; also studied in Vienna with Ligeti; returning to Helsinki studied musicology with Tawaststierna at the university, writing his dissertation on the works of Ligeti. He served as music critic for the newspaper *Helsingin Sanomat* from 1963 to 1973. Also beginning in 1963 he taught at Helsinki Univ. His music was heavily influenced by the avant-garde trends, and especially those associated with Cage, prevalent in western Europe. Yet through the late 1960s Salmenhaara began freely to incorporate tonality into his eclectic compositional palette so that his mature style became a highly expressive and individual one. Works include operas, orchestral music (*Le bateau ivre,* 1966; Symphony no. 4, *Nel mezzo del cammin di nostra vita,* 1971; *Sinfonietta per archi,* 1985; cello concerto, 1983–87). He has also composed vocal and chamber music (Introduction and Allegro, clarinet or viola, violin, piano, 1985).

Salmond, Felix (b. London, 19 Nov. 1888; d. New York, 19 Feb. 1952). Cellist. Attended the Royal College of Music (1905–9); made his debut in 1909. He introduced several of Elgar's works, including the Cello Concerto (1919); his U.S. debut came in 1922, and he subsequently toured widely. He taught at Juilliard from its inaugural year of 1924 and at the Curtis Institute between 1925 and 1942, with Leonard Rose as one of his students.

Salò, Gasparo da. See Gasparo da Salò.

Salomon, Johann Peter (b. Bonn, bapt. 20 Feb. 1749; d. London, 28 Nov. 1815). Violinist, impresario, and composer. In 1758 he became a musician at the Bonn court, then went on tour (1761 or 1762). By 1764 he was in Rheinsberg serving as musical director to Prince Heinrich of Prussia. Probably in 1780 he left Rheinsberg to settle in London, where he made his debut at Covent Garden in 1781. After establishing himself as a violin virtuoso, he turned to conducting and promoting concerts. From 1783 he promoted subscription concerts; he secured Haydn's visits to London (1790–91 and 1794–95), for which the "London" symphonies were written. He was a founder and member of the Philharmonic Society, and conducted its first concert in 1813. His works include operas, other vocal music, several violin concertos, and chamber music.

Bibl.: Hubert Unverricht, "Die Kompositionen Johann Peter Salomons: ein Überblick," in *Studien zur Musikgeschichte des Rheinlands,* 3 (Cologne, 1965), p. 35.

Salzedo [Salzédo], **Carlos (León)** (b. Arcachon, France, 6 Apr. 1885; d. Waterville, Maine, 17 Aug. 1961). Composer and harpist. He was a child prodigy pianist, studying at the Bordeaux Conservatory from 1891 to 1894; he took up the harp at age 11, graduating from the Paris Conservatoire in 1901. He played both instruments on tour in Europe, and was harpist at Monte Carlo (1905–9) and the Metropolitan Opera, New York (1909–13), before focusing on a career as a virtuoso, forming the Trio de Lutèce with Georges Barrère (flute) and Paul Kéfer (piano). After French Army service in World War I, he returned to the U.S., founding the Salzedo Harp Ensemble in 1917, and toured with his wife, harpist Marjorie Call. He established a summer harp program in Camden, Maine, and taught at Juilliard and the Curtis Institute. His own works include the tone poem *The Enchanted Isle* (1919), a Concerto for harp and 7 wind instruments (1925–26), and *Préamble et Jeux* for harp and chamber orchestra (1928–29), along with many harp solos; with Edgard Varèse, he formed the International Composers' Guild in 1921.

Salzman, Eric (b. New York, 8 Sept. 1933). Composer and writer on music. Studied at Columbia with Beeson, Luening, and Ussachevsky; at Princeton with Babbitt and Sessions. A Fulbright grant enabled him to study in Europe (1955–58) with Petrassi, Scherchen, Stockhausen, and Nono. On returning to the U.S. he wrote music criticism for the *New York Times* (1958–62), the *New York Herald Tribune* (1963–66), and *Stereo Review;* in 1969 he was awarded the Sang Prize for Criticism in the Fine Arts; he was editor of *Musical Quarterly* (1984–91). Taught at Queens College (1966–68), the Institute for Studies in American Music (Brooklyn College), and New York Univ. (from 1982). He founded the Quog Music Theater, a group of singers, dancers, and instrumentalists which emphasized improvisation, for which he wrote mixed-media and music theater pieces; in 1983 he cofounded the American Music Theater Festival in Philadelphia. One of several collaborations with Michael Sahl *(Civilization and Its Discontents)* won the Italia Prize in 1980. Other works include *Toward a New American Opera* (mixed media, 1985) and *Larynx Music* (soprano, guitar, and tape, 1966–67).

Samaroff [née Hickenlooper], **Olga** (b. San Antonio, Tex., 8 Aug. 1882; d. New York, 17 May 1948). Pianist. Studied at the Paris Conservatoire and at Berlin; made her U.S. debut with Damrosch and the New York Symphony in 1905, subsequently touring as soloist and chamber musician (teaming with Kreisler and Zimbalist). She was married to Stokowski between 1911 and 1923. A 1925 hand injury forced her to retire; she taught at Juilliard from 1925 to her death, and from 1928 to 1938 in Philadelphia. She also lectured, contributed to the *Saturday Evening Post* (1926–28), and authored several books.

Samazeuilh, Gustave (b. Bordeaux, 2 June 1877; d. Paris, 4 Aug. 1967). Composer and writer on music. He studied law at the École des haute études and music with Chasson, d'Indy, Bordes (all at the Schola cantorum, 1900–1906), and privately with Dukas. His writings include criticism in French and foreign publications; translations of texts in works by Strauss, Schumann, Schubert, and Liszt; and books on Dukas (1913) and Chasson (1947). He also edited the writings of Dukas (1948). His own works are similar to the early compositions of Debussy and Ravel; they include orchestral (*Le cercle des heures,* women's voices and orchestra, 1933), chamber, and piano music, and songs.

Saminsky, Lazare (b. Vale-Hotzulovo, Ukraine, 8 Nov. 1882; d. Port Chester, N.Y., 30 June 1959). Composer, conductor, and writer on music. At St. Petersburg Univ. he studied mathematics and philosophy (1906–9); was trained in music at the conservatories in Moscow and St. Petersburg by Liadov and Rimsky-Korsakov. He collected traditional chants of the Transcaucasian Jews (1913) and wrote a book on Jewish music (*Music of the Ghetto and the Bible,* 1934); had conducted in Tbilisi, Paris, and London (1915–20) before coming to New York (1920), where he was music director of Temple Emanuel (1924–56). His compositions include operas and opera-ballets; 5 symphonies (1914–32); Hebrew service music and several large choral works (*By the Rivers of Babylon,* soprano, baritone, chorus, and instruments, 1926); chamber and piano music. Other writings include *Physics and Metaphysics of Music and Essays on the Philosophy of Mathematics* (1957) and a conducting textbook (1958).

Sammartini [St. Martini, San Martini, San Martino, Martini, Martino], **Giovanni Battista** (b. 1700 or 1701; d. Milan, 15 Jan. 1775). Composer. Born probably in Milan, he played oboe in the orchestra of the Teatro Regio Ducal in 1720. In 1728 he became *maestro di cappella* at S. Ambrogio and of the Congregation of the Jesuit Church of S. Fedele; he held the latter post for most of his life. In 1775 he was reported to be *maestro di cappella* for 11 churches, including the ducal chapel S. Gottardo, where he became director in 1768. From 1730 he taught at the Collegio de' Nobili, where his pupils included Gluck (probably 1737–41). By the early 1730s his symphonies had placed him at the forefront of the first symphonic school in Europe. Sammartini was active in all spheres of Milan's musical life: he wrote operas, composed and conducted music for various religious and state occasions, presented concerts, and was a founder of a philharmonic society (1758). During the 1750s and 1760s he met J. C. Bach, Boccherini, and the Mozarts (1770). Many of his works were published in Paris and London, where they gained great popularity; his music also had notable success in Vienna and Prague. In addition to 3 operas, Sammartini wrote sacred and secular vocal music, 68 symphonies, 10 concertos, and over 200 chamber and solo works, including string quintets, flute and string quartets, trios, duets, and sonatas.

Bibl.: Newell Jenkins and Bathia Churgin, *Thematic Catalogue of the Works of Giovanni Battista Sammartini: Orchestral and Vocal Music* (Cambridge, Mass., 1976). Henry Mishkin, "Five Autograph String Quartets by Giovanni Battista Sammartini," *JAMS* 6 (1953): 136–47. Bathia Churgin, "The Symphonies of G. B. Sammartini" (diss., Harvard, 1963). Newell Jenkins, "The Vocal Music of Giovanni Battista Sammartini," *Chigiana* 24 (1977): 277–309. M. Marley, "The Sacred Cantatas of Giovanni Battista Sammartini" (diss., Univ. of Cincinnati, 1978).

Sammartini [S. Martini, St. Martini, San Martini, San Martino, Martini, Martino], **Giuseppe** [Gioseffo] **(Francesco Gaspare Melchiorre Baldassare)** (b. Milan, 6 Jan. 1695; d. London, ? between 17 and 23 Nov. 1750). Composer. He was the brother of Giovanni Battista Sammartini. In 1720 he played oboe in the orchestra of the Milan Teatro Regio Ducal. Probably in 1728 he left Italy to settle permanently in London, where he gained instant recognition as a virtuoso oboist and played in the opera orchestras of Bononcini and Handel. From 1736 he was music master to the family of

Frederick, Prince of Wales. His compositions, which were admired only after his death, include 24 concerti grossi, 5 solo concertos, 16 overtures, solo and trio sonatas, and duets.

Bibl.: George Houle, "The Oboe Sonatas of Giuseppe Sammartini," *JM* 3 (1984): 90–103.

Sammons, Albert (Edward) (b. London, 23 Feb. 1886; d. Southdean, Sussex, 24 Aug. 1957). Violinist and composer. Essentially self-taught, he was engaged in 1908 as leader of the Beecham Orchestra; was concertmaster of the Philharmonic Society Orchestra (from 1913) and the Ballets russes Orchestra (from 1911); led the London String Quartet (1907–16), and taught at the Royal College of Music. He introduced much new British music, including works of Delius and Elgar; a muscle disease eventually forced him to retire.

Samuel, Gerhard (b. Bonn, 20 Apr. 1924). Conductor. Attended the Eastman School, also playing violin in the Rochester Philharmonic (1941–45); later studied with Hindemith at Yale (to 1947) and assisted Koussevitzky at Tanglewood. He was active on Broadway, and held posts with the Minneapolis Symphony (assistant conductor, 1949–59), the Oakland Philharmonic (conductor, 1959–70), and the Los Angeles Philharmonic (associate conductor, 1970–73); served as music director of Pacific Northwest Ballet (from 1982) and chief guest conductor of the Oakland Ballet (from 1984). He joined the faculty of the Univ. of Cincinnati in 1976.

Samuel, Harold (b. London, 23 May 1879; d. there, 15 Jan. 1937). Pianist. Attended the Royal College of Music beginning in 1896; after many years of appearances as an accompanist, a week of Bach recitals in 1921 established his reputation, and thereafter he toured frequently in Britain and the U.S. as an orchestral soloist, as a chamber musician, and in recital. He later taught at the Royal College.

Sanborn, David (William) (b. Tampa, Fla., 30 July 1945). Rhythm-and-blues alto saxophonist and bandleader. He toured with Paul Butterfield's blues band (1967–71), Stevie Wonder (1971–73), David Bowie (1974), and the Brecker Brothers (1975). He also was a soloist with Gil Evans's big band (1973 to mid-1980s). From 1976 he led groups and was in demand as a studio musician, owing to his distinctive, heart-wrenching timbre on alto saxophone. His albums include *Voyeur* (ca. 1980).

Sánchez de Fuentes, Eduardo (b. Havana, 3 Apr. 1874; d. there, 7 Sept. 1944). Composer. Student of I. Cervantes and Anckermann; also schooled as a lawyer. An important educator, he encouraged music study in the public schools. Works include several operas, for one of which (*Doreya,* 1918) the composer said he drew upon the pentatonic materials of indigenous Caribbean music; orchestral music, including the 1928 tone poem *Anacaona* and *Bocetos cubanos* (1922) with soprano solo and women's chorus; piano pieces; and songs, among which "Tú" (1892) achieved widespread popularity.

Sánchez Málaga, Carlos (b. Arequipa, Peru, 8 Sept. 1904). Composer. Received early training in Arequipa, then entered musical theater as accompanist and director. Taught solfège and choral singing at the National Conservatory, La Paz, 1923–29, and at the National Conservatory, Lima, after 1929, also teaching piano at the Instituto Bach in Lima and leading classes at other schools as well. As a composer he looked to the mestizo folk tradition of Peru, rather than to that of Inca culture; he cultivated smaller genres almost exclusively, with many character pieces for piano as well as songs, choral pieces, and the 1928 *Romanza* for viola and piano.

Bibl.: *Composers of the Americas* 13 (Washington, D.C., 1967), pp. 114–15 [includes works list].

Sancta Maria, Thomas de. See Santa María, Tomás de.

Sanderling, Kurt (b. Arys, 9 Sept. 1912). Conductor. Active at the Berlin City Opera from 1931 until 1936, when he fled to the USSR; there he led the Moscow Radio Symphony (1935–41) and the Leningrad Philharmonic (1941–60). He returned to Germany to conduct the (East) Berlin Symphony between 1960 and 1977, also directing the Dresden Kapelle from 1964 to 1967.

Sanders, Pharoah [Farrell] (b. Little Rock, Ark., 13 Oct. 1940). Jazz tenor saxophonist and bandleader. He unofficially joined John Coltrane's group (1965–67), playing with a shrieking violence on albums such as *Ascension* (1965) and *Live at the Village Vanguard Again* (1966). In his own groups from 1969 into the 1970s, free-jazz improvisatory techniques were contrasted with tuneful melodies and serene ostinatos, as on the album *Karma* (1969). After briefly turning toward disco (1977–78), he led stylistically wide-ranging jazz groups.

Sanders, Robert Levine (b. Chicago, 2 July 1906; d. Delray Beach, Fla., 26 Dec. 1974). Composer. He studied at the Bush Conservatory in Chicago; from 1925 to 1929 he was at the American Academy in Rome, where he studied with Respighi. In Chicago he conducted the Conservatory Orchestra and the Civic Orchestra (1933–36), and served as organist and choirmaster at the First Unitarian Church (1930–38). Beginning 1938 he was dean of the School of Music at Indiana Univ.; chaired the music department at Brooklyn College (1947–54), where he taught until retirement (1972). His neoclassical and dissonant compositions include the Symphony in A (1954–56) and *Song of Myself* (Whitman; reciter, soprano, choir, brass, and percussion, 1966–70).

Sanders, Samuel (b. New York, 27 June 1937). Pianist. Made many concert appearances in his teens; studied at Hunter College (B.A., 1959) and at Juilliard

(M.S., 1961). He won a prize for accompanying at the 1966 Tchaikovsky Competition, and appeared in such a role with Perlman, Rostropovich, Sills, Norman, and many others; also a chamber music performer. He joined the Juilliard faculty in 1963, teaching at the Peabody Conservatory as well. In 1980 he founded the Cape and Islands Chamber Music Festival, and in 1983 the Musica Camerit of New York Hebrew Arts School.

Sanderson, Sibyl (b. Sacramento, Calif., 7 Dec. 1865; d. Paris, 15 May 1903). Soprano. Studied with Massenet, Sbriglia, and Mathilde Marchesi at the Paris Conservatory beginning in 1885. Debuted under the name Ada Palmer at The Hague in 1888 as Manon. Made her Metropolitan Opera debut in 1895 and toured the U.S., 1901–2, but her reception in the U.S. was often not favorable. Known for her large vocal range (g to g′′′). Several works were written for her, including Massenet's *Esclarmonde* (1889), *Le Mage* (1891), *Thaïs* (1894), and Saint-Saëns's *Phryné* (1893).

Sandi, Luis (Mexico City, 22 Feb. 1905). Composer. Studied violin and composition at the National Conservatory, where he directed the choral groups from 1929, founding the well-known Coro de madrigalistas in 1938. Served in the Ministry of Education (1946–51) and at the National Institute of Fine Arts (1959–63), and wrote Latin America's most popular secondary-school music text, the *Introducción al estudio de música,* of which the 23rd edition appeared in 1956. He also was active as a critic. Works include the operas *Carlota* (1949) and *La señora en su balcón* (1964); ballets, film music, and other orchestral pieces, including the tone poem *América* (1968); chamber music; songs; and numerous choral compositions and arrangements.

Sándor, György (b. Budapest, 21 Sept. 1912). Pianist. Attended the Liszt Conservatory in his home city (Bartók and Kódaly were teachers); made his debut there in 1930, and then toured Europe. He moved to the U.S. in 1939, and premiered Bartók's Third Concerto in 1946. He later toured in Asia and Australia, and taught at the Univ. of Michigan; subsequently joined the Juilliard faculty. Particularly well known for his interpretations of Bartók and Prokofiev.

Sandrin [Regnault, Pierre] (b. St. Marcel?, near Paris, ca. 1490?; d. Italy?, after 1561). Composer. He may have acted in early years, taking his sobriquet from a farcical stage character who spoke in chansons. In 1539 he was a dean at St. Florent-de-Roye, Picardy, from 1543 to 1560 a singer and canon in the French Chapel Royal, and simultaneously *maestro di cappella* to Ippolito d'Este, Cardinal of Ferrara, the French ambassador to the Vatican. He published 50 chansons (and 1 madrigal) that were widely reprinted, intabulated, and adapted to sacred parody. In his late chansons the simple Parisian style is embellished with Italianate madrigalisms such as imitation and word painting.

Sandström, Sven-David (b. Motala, 30 Oct. 1942). Composer. Enrolled at Stockholm Univ. from 1963 to 1967; then attended the Royal Academy, studying composition with Lindholm, 1968–72; also studied compositional techniques with Nørgård and Ligeti. He was appointed to the faculty of the State College of Music in Stockholm in 1980. His music utilizes serialism, microtonality, and occasionally aleatoric devices, sometimes in the context of sadistic or pornographic images or texts. His works include a chamber opera (*Hasta o älskade brud* [Hasta, O Beloved Bride], 1978) and a music drama (*Kejsaren Jones* [Emperor Jones], 1980). He has also composed ballets (*Admorica,* 1985; *Den elfte gryningen,* 1988), a cantata (*Drömmer,* 1988); orchestral music (*To You,* 1970; *Con tutta forza,* 1976; alto sax concerto, 1987; *Invigningsfanfar,* 1988), vocal music (*Visst?,* soprano, 2 choruses, violins, orchestra, 1971), and chamber music (*Just a Bit,* bassoon, violin, harp, 1973; *Effort,* cello, 1977; *The Slumberous Mass,* 4 trombones, 1987; *Dance III,* 3 cellos, 1988).

Sanjuán, Pedro (b. San Sebastián, 15 Nov. 1886; d. Washington, D.C., 18 Oct. 1976). Composer. Composition student of Turina; went to Havana, where he established the Havana Philharmonic and taught many of Cuba's leading composers, including Roldán. After a period back in Spain (1932–36) and a second tour as Havana Philharmonic director (1939–42), he joined the faculty at Converse College (Spartanburg, S.C.), becoming a U.S. citizen in 1947. Works include the *Rondo fantástico* (1926), the suite *Castilla* (1947), the "ritual symphony" *Macumba* (1951), and the Symphonic Suite (1965), in addition to vocal works and piano compositions.

Sankey, Ira David (b. Edinburgh, Pa., 28 Aug. 1840; d. Brooklyn, N.Y., 13 Aug. 1908). Singer and composer. At age 17 he directed a choir in New Castle, Pa. Dwight L. Moody noticed his talents in 1870 at a YMCA convention; they formed a 30-year partnership. He was instrumental in the popularization of gospel music in the U.S. and abroad. He composed about 1,200 songs and collected many more gospel hymns; some were published in *Sacred Songs and Solos* (London, 1873) and are still available. From 1895 to 1908 he was president of the publishing firm Biglow and Main. He retired in 1903. His autobiography, *My Life and the Story of Gospel Hymns,* was published in New York and Philadelphia in 1906.

Bibl.: Charles Ludwig, *Sankey Still Sings* (Anderson, Ind., 1947).

Sanromá, Jesús María (b. Carolina, Puerto Rico, 7 Nov. 1902; d. San Juan, 12 Oct. 1984). Pianist. Studied in his hometown, then at the New England Conservatory (1917–20), making his solo debut in Boston in 1924; served as pianist of the Boston Symphony between 1926 and 1944, also receiving lessons from Schnabel and teaching. He returned to Puerto Rico as a professor at the University and joined the Puerto Rico Conservatory faculty upon its founding in 1959. He was an advocate of 20th-century music, premiering Hindemith's Concerto in 1947.

Santa Cruz, Domingo (b. La Cruz, Valparaiso, Chile, 5 July 1899; d. Santiago, 6 Jan. 1987). Composer. Studied with Soro and Santiago, also taking a law degree from the Univ. of Chile in 1921. Studied with del Campo while on diplomatic assignment in Spain (1921–24); left the Foreign Service in 1927 to concentrate on music. His Bach Society (founded in 1917) became a major force in Chilean musical life after his return from Spain in 1924, performing extensively, opening a conservatory, and publishing a magazine. Charged by the secretary of education in 1928 to reform the National Conservatory, Santa Cruz drew it under the aegis of the Univ. of Chile in 1930; in addition to teaching at the conservatory, 1928–53, he served it as dean, 1932–51 and 1962–68. During this time he founded several arts organizations, including the National Association of Chilean Composers (1936) and the Instituto de Extensión musical (1941), as well as 2 journals, the *Revista de arte* (1934–42) and the *Revista musical chilena* (beginning 1945) and the radio station IEM (1967). Santa Cruz's music is neoclassical in nature, contrapuntally active, with melodic dissonance and periodic dramatic harmonic gestures; it depends little on Chilean folk materials.

Works: *Cantata de los rios de Chile* (1941), *Egloga* (1949), and *Oratio Ieremiae prophetae* (1970), chorus and orchestra; 4 symphonies (1946, 1948, 1968, 1968); orchestral music, including *Variaciones* (1943, with piano solo), *Sinfonia concertante* (1945, with flute solo), *Cinco piezas* (1937), and *Preludios dramáticos* (1946); chamber music, including *Endechas,* tenor and 7 players (1960), a wind quintet (1960), 3 string quartets (1930, 1947, 1959), and *Tres piezas,* violin and piano (1937); piano music, including *Cinco poemas trágicos* (1929) and *Viñetas* (1925–27); choral music; and songs, including *Canciones del Mar* (1952, texts by the composer).

Bibl.: *Composers of the Americas* 1 (Washington, D.C., 1955), pp. 84–94 [includes works list]. Carmen Peña Fuenzalida, "Bibliografía de los escritos de Don Domingo Santa Cruz," *Revista Musical Chilena* 167 (1987): 16–21.

Santa María, Tomás de [Sancta Maria, Thomas de] (b. Madrid, ca. 1510–20; d. Ribadavia, northwest Spain, 1570). Organist, composer, and theorist. A Dominican friar, he was organist at St. Pablo monastery, Valladolid. He devoted most of his career to writing the *Libro llamado Arte de tañer fantasía* (Valladolid, 1565; facs., London, 1972), an early practical keyboard treatise made in consultation with Antonio and Juan de Cabezón; it is contemporary with Bermudo's *Declaración.* Santa María treats (in book 1) notation, keyboard technique, performance, and chant; (in book 2) harmony and counterpoint. His compositions, besides some illustrative fantasias in the treatise, include *tientos,* versos, and *fabordones.*

Santley, Charles (b. Liverpool, 28 Feb. 1834; d. London, 22 Sept. 1922). Baritone. Studied in Milan with Gaetano Nava (1855). Debuted at Pavia in 1857 as Dr. Grenvile in *La traviata.* He then returned to England, where he studied with Manuel García. His London debut was as Adam in Haydn's *Creation* at St. Martin's Hall in 1857. Sang in many oratorio and concert performances. Stage debut in 1859 in Meyerbeer's *Dinorah* at Covent Garden. Sang Valentin in the English premiere of Gounod's *Faust* (1863), for which occasion the composer added the aria "Even bravest heart may swell" ("Avant de quitter ces lieux"). Joined Carl Rosa's company in 1875. Composed some songs under the name Ralph Betterton. Wrote *Student and Singer* (London, 1892), *The Singing Master* (London, 1900), *The Art of Singing and Vocal Declamation* (London, 1908). Santley was knighted in 1907, and published his autobiography in 1909 (R: 1977).

Santoliquido, Francesco (b. San Giorgio a Cremano, Naples, 6 Aug. 1883; d. Anacapri, 26 Aug. 1971). Composer. Studied with W. Setaccioli and S. Falchi at the Conservatory of S. Cecilia in Rome, graduating in 1908; went to Tunisia, where he founded a concert society in 1912 and in 1927 a music school under the Dante Alighieri Society. In 1928 he was elected to the Academy of S. Cecilia and in 1933 moved to Anacapri, where he continued to compose. His works include 4 operas (*La porta verde,* Bergamo, 1953); 2 symphonies and other orchestral music (*Il profumo delle oasi sahariane,* 1915); choral music (*Messa facile ad uso dei conventi,* with orchestra, 1925); chamber and piano music and songs.

Santoro, Claudio (b. Manáos, Brazil, 23 Nov. 1919; d. Brasilia, 27 Mar. 1989). Composer. Studied at the Rio de Janeiro Conservatory (to 1936) and with Koellreutter (from 1938). Helped found the Brazilian Symphony, playing violin (1941–47), then studied with Boulanger in France. Attended the 1948 Prague Congress of Progressive Composers; back in Brazil, he worked as a radio director (1951–53 and from 1956) and taught at Santos Conservatory (1953–56). Joined the faculty at the Univ. of Brasilia in 1962; worked in Heidelberg as director of folk music research (1967–68) and as university professor (1970–78), later returning to Brazil. His music evolved from dodecaphony (before 1947) to a socialist-realist style reminiscent of Shostakovich and Prokofiev, though with Brazilian national elements (1947 to mid-1960s), then to serialism, with aleatory ideas and graphic notation. Works include 8 symphonies (1940–63); several ballets; concertos for violin (1951, 1958), piano (1953, 1959, 1960), and cello (1961); chamber music, including 7 string quartets, 4 violin sonatas, and pieces for ensemble and tape; vocal works, including *Cantata elegíaca* (1970) and *Cantate* (1987); and piano music.

Bibl.: *Composers of the Americas* 9 (Washington, D.C., 1963), pp. 126–43 [includes works list].

Sanz, Gaspar (b. Calanda, Aragon, mid-17th century; d. early 18th cent.). Composer and guitarist. After receiving a Bachelor of Theology degree from the Univ.

of Salamanca he traveled to Italy, where he studied music. Upon his return to Spain he published his *Instrucción de música sobre la guitarra española* (1674), a detailed treatise for a 5-course guitar tuned a/a–d′/d′–g/g–b/b–e′. Included are an introductory tutor, an essay on figured bass accompaniment for guitar, and 90 pieces which range in difficulty and are mostly based on dance forms, such as the *folia, canario,* and *españoleta.* The popularity of Sanz's work continued well into the 18th century and inspired several similar works in Spain.

Sanzogno, Nino (b. Venice, 13 Apr. 1911; d. Milan, 4 May 1983). Conductor and composer. Graduated from the Liceo musicale, Venice, in 1932; directed the Grupo strumentale italiano, the Milan Radio Symphony, and at the Teatro La Fenice; made his La Scala debut in 1939, serving as resident conductor there from 1962 to 1965; in 1955 he opened the Piccola Scala. His repertory extended from the Baroque to the 20th century; his own works include the symphonic poem *I quattro cavalieri dell'Apocalisse* (1930), concertos for viola (1935) and cello (1937), and chamber music.

Saporiti [Codecasa], **Teresa** (b. 1763; d. Milan, 17 Mar. 1869). Soprano. She sang in Leipzig, Dresden, and Prague with Pasquale Bondini's company. Despite unfavorable reviews of her singing, Mozart wrote difficult music for her when she created the role of Donna Anna in *Don Giovanni* (1787). She then appeared in operas in Venice, Milan, Bologna, Parma, and Modena. In 1795 she became *prima buffa assoluta* in Gennaro Astarita's company at St. Petersburg, singing in operas by Astarita, Cimarosa, and Paisiello.

Sapp, Allen Dwight (b. Philadelphia, 10 Dec. 1922). Composer. Received his B.A. from Harvard (where his teachers included Piston, Davison, and Thompson) and studied with Copland and Boulanger (1942–43). After war service he returned to Harvard as a student (M.A., 1949) and then as a teacher (1950–58). Subsequently he taught at Wellesley College (1958–61), SUNY–Buffalo (1961–75), Florida State Univ. (1976–78), and the Cincinnati College-Conservatory (dean, 1978–80, then professor of composition). Works include *Imaginary Creations* (harpsichord and orchestra, 1980); 4 string quartets (1951; nos. 2–4 in 1981); 7 sonatas for piano (1941–80); 5 toccatas (harpsichord, 1981); *The Companion of Sirius: The Serious Companion,* tuba, piano (1984); choral and solo vocal music.

Saracini, Claudio (b. Siena, 1 July 1586; d. there?, after 1649). Composer. He was born into a musical family belonging to the nobility of Siena, and claimed that from his youth he had visited many foreign countries, which probably included Germany and several southeastern European states. A prolific composer. Practically all of his surviving music is monodic; the 129 solo songs which are extant include examples of every kind of solo song known in his day. Saracini often set madrigals by Marino, whose erotic and intensely emotional verses were ideally suited to his bold harmonies and word painting. His strophic songs tend to be more tonally stable, have a clearer sense of form, and often suggest the influence of folk music.

Bibl.: Eva Pintér, *Claudio Saracini: Leben und Werk* (Frankfurt am Main, 1992).

Sárai, Tibor (b. Budapest, 10 May 1919). Composer. He was a composition student of Pál Kadosa. In 1949 he served as chief of the music division of the Ministry of Culture and from 1950 to 1953 as head of music at Hungarian Radio. He taught at the Budapest Conservatory from 1953 to 1959 and then at the Budapest Academy of Music. His early works drew heavily on traditional Hungarian art and folk music. His later work incorporated more expansive and colorful use of dissonance. Works include orchestral music (Symphony no. 2, soprano, orchestra, 1972–73); vocal music for chorus and/or soloists (*Diagnosis '69,* tenor, orchestra, 1969); and chamber music (Autumn Concerto, trumpet, horn, violin, cello, orchestra, 1984).

Sarasate (y Navascuéz), Pablo (Martín Melitón) de (b. Pamplona, 10 Mar. 1844; d. Biarritz, 20 Sept. 1908). Violinist. Son of a military bandmaster; a violin prodigy. After first public concert at 8 in La Coruña, he was given the means to study in Madrid, where he was heard by the queen, who gave him a Stradivarius, which he played throughout his career, and helped send him to the Paris Conservatory, 1856–58. There he studied with Alard, winning first prize (1857), and with Reber for harmony (first prize, 1859); then began concert tours, including North and South America (1867–71; again in 1889–90, with D'Albert). His great celebrity from the 1870s on is reflected in works composed for or dedicated to him by Lalo, Saint-Saëns, Bruch, and others; historically a new type of player, fascinating audiences with a dazzling virtuoso technique (in spite of small hands), noted for his beautiful singing tone and elegance, but less nuanced in expression than the German manner represented by Joachim and therefore sometimes judged more superficial; also a devoted chamber player, taking part in quartet recitals. Published 54 opus numbers, mostly concert show pieces for violin, many being arrangements of national airs, especially Spanish ones, others operatic potpourris. His *Zigeunerweisen* op. 20 (1878) is still often performed, his *Carmen Fantasy* op. 25 (?1883) occasionally.

Bibl.: G. Wooley, "Pablo de Sarasate: His Historical Significance," *ML* 36 (1955): 237–52.

Sargent, (Harold) Malcolm (Watts) (b. Ashford, Kent, 29 Apr. 1895; d. London, 3 Oct. 1967). Conductor. Trained as an organist; received bachelor's and doctoral degrees from Durham Univ. (1914, 1919). He made his conducting debut in 1921 in his own *Impressions on a Windy Day;* he joined the Royal College faculty in 1923, took over the Robert Mayer Children's Concerts in 1924, and appeared with the Royal Philharmonic Orchestra in 1925. He later held posts with the Hallé Orchestra, Manchester (1939–42), the Liverpool Philharmonic (1942–48), and the BBC Symphony (1950–57), and conducted the Promenade concerts in London from 1947 to his death. He appeared often with the London Symphony, leading the premiere of Martinů's Quartet for Strings and Orchestra with them in 1932; other composers whose works Sargent introduced include Walton (*Belshazzar's Feast,* 1932; *Troilus and Cressida,* 1954), Vaughan Williams (Oboe Concerto, 1946; Ninth Symphony, 1958), and Bloch (Sinfonia breve and Concerto grosso no. 2, 1953). He was knighted in 1947.

Sarro [Sarri], **Domenico Natale** (b. Trani, Apulia, 24 Dec. 1679; d. Naples, 25 Jan. 1744). Composer. He studied at the Neapolitan conservatory S. Onofrio, and in 1704 was appointed *vicemaestro di cappella* of the Neapolitan court. As a result of the Austrian invasion of Naples, he lost this position in 1707. In 1720 he was promised two posts when they became vacant: *maestro di cappella* to the city of Naples, which he obtained in 1728; and vice-*maestro di cappella* at court, which he regained in late October 1725. At Mancini's death in 1737 he was appointed *maestro di cappella* at court. Primarily a composer of operas; his most significant works were produced between 1718 and 1725. *Didone abbandonata* (1724) is particularly noteworthy because it is the earliest setting of Metastasio's first major libretto. During his time Sarro's fame was limited abroad because he confined his activities to Naples. His reputation as an innovator has suffered from seemingly unfounded accusations that he copied Vinci's style.

Sarti [Sardi], **Giuseppe** (b. Faenza, bapt. 1 Dec. 1729; d. Berlin, 28 July 1802). Composer. He studied with Valotti in Padua and Padre Martini in Bologna, then was organist of Faenza Cathedral (1748–52) and directed the theater in Faenza, for which he wrote his first opera, *Pompeo in Armenia* (1752). In 1753 he conducted Pietro Mingotti's opera company on its visit to Copenhagen, where he later became court Kapellmeister (1755), director of the Italian Opera, and director of court music (1763). After three years in Italy, during which he was *maestro di coro* at the Pietà Conservatory in Venice (1766–67), he returned to Copenhagen to direct the royal chapel and court theater (1770–75) and serve as the king's singing teacher. In 1775 he was dismissed as a result of political intrigues. After he became *maestro di cappella* of Milan Cathedral in 1779, his *Le gelosie villane* (1776) was successfully produced at La Scala in Milan. The operas that followed gained popularity throughout Europe and won him many pupils, including Cherubini. In 1784 he became director of the imperial chapel in St. Petersburg. On the way there he stopped in Vienna, where he was received by Joseph II and met Mozart. In St. Petersburg Sarti had his greatest success with the comic opera *I finti eredi* (1785), the opera seria *Armida e Rinaldo* (1786), and the Russian opera *The Early Reign of Oleg* (1790). Court intrigue led to his banishment to a Ukrainian village, where he founded a singing school. Reinstated in 1793, he became director of a conservatory. When the emperor died in 1801, he decided to return to Italy by way of Berlin, where he died. In addition to over 70 dramatic works, Sarti wrote sacred vocal works, symphonies, and sonatas.

Bibl.: C. Rivalta, *Giuseppe Sarti, musicista faentino del sec. XVIII* (Faenza, 1928). H. O'Douwes, "De russische jaren van Giuseppe Sarti," *Mens en melodie* 12 (1957): 146. R. Jones, "A Performing Edition and Discussion of G. Sarti's *Te Deum* in D" (diss., Stanford, 1966). Mario Baroni and Maria Gioia Tavoni, eds., *Giuseppe Sarti musicista faentino: Atti del convegno internazionale: Faenza, 25–27 Novembre 1983* (Modena, 1986).

Sartorio [Sertorio], **Antonio** (b. Venice, 1630; d. there, 30 Dec. 1680). Composer. Nothing is known of his life until the production of his first opera, *Gl'amori infruttuosi di Pirro,* at the Teatro SS. Giovanni e Paolo, Venice, on 4 Jan. 1661. In 1666 he was named Kapellmeister to Duke Johann Friedrich of Brunswick-Lüneburg, who resided in Hannover. During his time in Hannover (1666–75) Sartorio made several visits to Venice during the winters, composing operas for Carnival and enlisting musicians to serve at court. Poor health and the invitation to write an opera for the S. Luca Carnival prevented a return to Hannover in the spring of 1672 and led to the productions of his operas *L'Orfeo* (1672) and *Massenzio* (1673). Sartorio left Hannover for good in April 1675, settling in Venice, where on 7 May 1676 he was appointed vice-*maestro di cappella* of St. Mark's. From then until his death, he completed 5 operas and began a sixth, *La Flora.* Besides operas, he composed cantatas, sacred vocal works, and arias.

Sáry, Lázló (b. Györ, 1 Jan. 1940). Composer. He studied at the Budapest Academy of Music from 1961 through 1966 with Szervánszky. Sáry was active within the trends associated with Boulez and Stockhausen. He joined the Budapest New Music Studio and helped to form a group improvisatory ensemble. After attending Darmstadt in 1972, he was much inspired by the thinking of Cage that he had encountered there. In general, his works involve nonstandard instrumentation that varies from piece to piece. The music often incorporates some degree of chance. Works include *Sonanti:* no. 1 (harpsichord, 1969); no. 2 (flute, percussion, 1970); no. 3 (cimbalom, 1970); *Psalmus* (soprano, 2 zithers, 1972); *Sunflower* (at least 3 performers, 1973); *Hommage à Olivier Messiaen* (orchestra, 1977); *Hölderlin tornya* [Holderlins' Tower] (chamber ensemble, 1985); *Polyphonie* (18 strings, 10 winds, 1986); Variations (string quartet, 1986–88).

Sas (Orchassal), Andrés (b. Paris, 6 Apr. 1900; d. Lima, 25 July 1967). Composer. Studied chemical engineering, then music, at Brussels; named teacher of violin and chamber music at the Lima Academy in 1924. After a sojourn back in Belgium (1928–29), he returned to Lima in 1930 and established the Sas-Rosay Academy with his wife, pianist Lily Rosay.

Published research on the microtonal system of the coastal Nazca tribe and on other topics; served also as editor of several Peruvian journals, including one, *Antara,* which he himself founded in 1930; continued to teach composition until 1966. His music mixes impressionist and indigenous Peruvian pentatonic elements; works include several ballets as well as chamber music, choral and piano pieces, and songs.

Bibl.: *Composers of the Americas* 2 (Washington, D.C., 1956), pp. 116–25 [includes works list].

Satie, Erik [Eric] **(Alfred Leslie)** (b. Honfleur, 17 May 1866; Paris, 1 July 1925). Composer, pianist, and writer. He was the eldest of three children born to a French shipbroker and his Scottish wife; they moved to Paris in 1871, but on the death of the mother (1873) the children were sent back to the grandparents in Honfleur. Erik was particularly influenced there by his uncle Adrien, a dreamer and aficionado of the theater; and studied with a local organist-composer. In 1878, his father having remarried, he went back to Paris; the next year he was sent to the Paris Conservatory, but was dismissed in 1882; later was readmitted to study piano with Mathias (1885–86). He served briefly in the army, then began to make his way as a composer, with songs and piano pieces published by his father. From 1888 he played the piano at Le Chat Noir, a café and focal point for the arts in Montmartre; became the official composer for the Rosicrucian society; then withdrew to form his own religion. In 1898 he moved from Montmartre to the working-class suburb of Arceuil-Cachan where he lived in poverty for the next fifteen years.

In the 1890s Satie had little official recognition (he suffered three rejections to his appeals for membership in the Academie des Beaux-Arts); perhaps in response to criticism of his piano and cabaret songs, he studied counterpoint at the Schola cantorum (1905–8). But in 1911 Ravel played Satie's *3 Sarabandes* (1887) at the Société musicale indépendante (the program note called the composer an "inspired forerunner"); Debussy orchestrated and conducted two of the *Gymnopédie* (originally for piano); and Ecorcheville, Calvocoressi, and Roland-Manuel all published articles about him. His collaboration with Cocteau, Picasso, and Massine in *Parade* (1917) confirmed his leadership of the musical avant-garde. He broke with Debussy and Ravel and enjoyed the admiration of "Les six" while denying in print the possibility of a "School of Satie"; Cocteau's *Le coq et l'arlequin* codified his aesthetic aims. By the time of the scandal surrounding the Dadaist ballet *Relâche* (with Francis Picabia and Jean Börlin, 1924), he had broken with most of "Les six"; meanwhile Milhaud had encouraged the new École d'Arcueil to form around him. His influence not only on Debussy and Ravel but also on later composers via Varèse and Cage make his efforts as innovative composer and writer particularly significant. He wrote about 70 works, all relatively short, about half for piano, and usually with programmatic titles. Despite admirers and influence, he remained apart from any school or group. As Roland-Manuel declared (1929): "Satie was against Wagner in 1885, against Debussy in 1905, against Ravel during the war, against the 'Six' just before his death."

Works: 4 ballets (*Uspud,* 1892; *Mercure,* 1924) and other stage music (*Geneviève de Brabant,* puppet play, 1899); instrumental music *3 morceaux en forme de poire* (piano 4-hands, 1890–1903), and *Musique d'ameublement* (with Milhaud; piano, 3 clarinets, trombone, 1920); many piano pieces (*3 Gymnopédies,* 1888; *Sonatine bureaucratique,* 1917; *5 nocturnes,* 1919); *Socrate* (*drame symphonique,* Plato, trans. V. Cousin; voice(s) and piano/orchestra, 1918); songs.

Bibl.: *The Writings of Erik Satie,* ed. and trans. Nigel Wilkins (London, 1976). Pierre-Daniel Templier, *Erik Satie* (New York, 1980). Marc Bredel, *Erik Satie* (Paris, 1982). Alan W. Gillmor, *Erik Satie* (Boston, 1988). Robert Orledge, *Satie the Composer* (Cambridge and New York, 1990). Nancy Lynn Perloff, *Art and the Everyday: Popular Entertainment and the Circle of Erik Satie* (Oxford, 1991). Grete Wehmeyer, *Erik Satie: Bilder und Dokumente* (Munich, 1992). Ornella Volta, *Satie-Cocteau: Les malentendus d'une entente* (Paris, 1993).

Sauer, Emil von (b. Hamburg, 8 Oct. 1862; d. Vienna, 27 Apr. 1942). Pianist. He studied with Nicolai Rubinstein in Moscow, 1879–81; later studied with Liszt and Deppe. He toured the U.S., 1898–99, and again in 1908. Professor at the Meisterschule für Klavierspiel in Vienna, 1901–7, and from 1915. He retired in 1936. He composed 2 piano concertos, 2 piano sonatas, etudes; also edited the piano works of Brahms, and pedagogical works by Pischna, Kullak, and Plaidy.

Sauget [Poupard], **Henri (-Pierre)** (b. Bordeaux, 18 May 1901; d. Paris, 22 June 1989). Composer and organist. He studied piano and organ as a child; worked as an organist and studied further with Jean-Fernand Vaubourgoin and Joseph Canteloube. In 1920 he founded "Les trois" in imitation of the group "Les six" in Paris; began to study the works of Stravinsky and Satie; moved to Paris at Milhaud's suggestion and became a student of Koechlin. He was a member of the École d'Arcueil around Satie (1922) and began in the 1920s to receive performances and commissions, especially for ballets (*Les roses,* 1924). In 1975 he was elected to the Académie des Beaux-Arts. In addition to more than 25 ballets, he wrote operas (*La chartreuse de Parme,* 1927–36); film, radio, and television scores; 4 symphonies (1945–71, some with soloists and choruses); *The Gardener's Concerto* (harmonica and chamber orchestra, 1970); chamber music, including 3 string quartets, and *Oraisons* (4 saxophones and organ, 1976); solo works for piano, organ, accordion, harpsichord, and guitar; choral music and many song cycles.

Bibl.: Henri Sauguet, *La musique, ma vie* (Paris, 1990). David L. Austin, *Henri Sauguet: A Bio-Bibliography* (New York, 1991).

Sauret, Émile (b. Dun-le-Roi, 22 May 1852; d. London, 12 Feb. 1920). Violinist and composer. Debut in 1862. Possibly studied with Vieuxtemps, Charles de Bériot, and Wieniawski, though there is no hard evidence for this. U.S. tour, 1872. Taught at Chicago Mu-

Tenor saxhorn designed by Adolphe Sax.

sical College, 1903–6. Married to pianist Teresa Carreño, 1873–76. Professor at the Royal Academy of Music, 1890–1903; professor at Trinity College of Music in London, 1908. Composed rhapsodies for violin and orchestra, a violin sonata, violin concerto, smaller pieces for violin and piano.

Sauter, Eddie [Edward Ernest] (b. New York, 2 Dec. 1914; d. Nyack, N.Y., 21 Apr. 1981). Arranger and composer. He studied at Juilliard and in 1935 joined Red Norvo's band as a trumpet player; soon afterwards he became Norvo's full-time arranger. Beginning in 1939 he did free-lance work for a number of bandleaders, including Benny Goodman and Artie Shaw. In the mid-1950s he teamed up with Bill Finegan to form the Sauter–Finegan Orchestra; their hits included "Doodletown Fifers" and "Midnight Sleigh Ride" (both 1952). Sauter also collaborated with Stan Getz on Getz's album *Focus* (1961).

Sauveur, Joseph (b. La Flèche, 24 Mar. 1653; d. Paris, 9 July 1716). Acoustician. His election to membership of the Académie des sciences in 1696 led to the development of his interest in acoustics. He gained an understanding of frequency through the study of beats, and introduced the terms acoustics, harmonic sound (overtone), node, and loop. His writings include *Principes d'acoustique et de musique* (1701; R: 1973) and papers in the *Mémoires de l'Académie royale des sciences [1701–13]* (1704–16).

Savart, Felix (b. Mézières, 30 June 1791; d. Paris, 16 Mar. 1841). Scientist. He studied medicine, graduating in 1816. Pursuing his interest in acoustics, he went to Paris where he studied with Biot. In 1820 he was named professor of natural philosophy; he was elected to the Académie in 1827. His name is given to a system of measuring intervals according to which 301 savarts equals 1 octave.

Sawallisch, Wolfgang (b. Munich, 26 Aug. 1923). Conductor and pianist. Attended the Munich Academy; from 1947 worked at the Augsburg Opera, and was active also at Aachen (1953–58), Wiesbaden (1958–60), and Cologne (1960–63). He led the Vienna Symphony (1960–70), the Hamburg Philharmonic (1961–73), and the Suisse Romande Orchestra (1972–80), serving also as the music director of the Bavarian State Opera, Munich (1971–92), and music director of the Philadelphia Orchestra (1993–94). Appeared as a pianist in chamber music and lieder recitals.

Bibl.: Hanspeter Krellmann, ed., *Stationen eines Dirigenten, Wolfgang Sawallisch* (Munich, 1983).

Sax, Adolphe [Antoine Joseph] (b. Dinant, Belgium, 6 Nov. 1814; d. Paris, 4 Feb. 1894). Instrument maker. Eldest son of the 11 children of the Belgian instrument maker Charles Joseph Sax (1791–1865), in whose shop he early learned the crafts of the trade and whose inventiveness he inherited; also became an accomplished flutist (studying at the Brussels Conservatory) and clarinetist. To 1842 he worked in his father's shop, also making improvements of the clarinet and bass clarinet; 1842, set up shop in Paris, supported by leading French musicians, including Berlioz (who wrote in his favor), Halévy, and Kastner, developing and patenting families of new instruments: the saxhorns (1845), saxotrombas (1845), which survived only briefly, and saxophones (1846). Seeing an opportunity in the then-poor state of French military bands, he proposed to the government a complete reorganization, incorporating his new instruments and eliminating French horns and bassoons. A celebrated open-air test on 22 April 1845 before 20,000 people was decided in his favor, and he was granted a virtual monopoly, naturally resulting in opposition from French makers, who organized to destroy him through, so Sax's supporters claimed, industrial sabotage and by attacking the legitimacy of his patents. Litigation continued for many years, undermining the financial soundness of his firm, which went bankrupt in 1856 and 1873, and perhaps his own health (in 1853–58 he had lip cancer, from which his recovery was deemed miraculous). His business was continued by his sons. Taught the saxophone at the Paris Conservatory, 1857–71; published a *Méthode complète pour saxhorn et saxtromba.*

Bibl.: A. Remy, *La vie tourmentée d'Adolphe Sax* (Brussels, 1939). M. Haine, *Adolphe Sax: Sa vie, son oeuvre, ses instruments de musique* (Brussels, 1980).

Saxton, Robert (b. London, 8 Oct. 1953). Composer. Studied composition at Bryanston and subsequently with Lutyens and Berio. He was a student of Holloway at Cambridge (1974–75), and of Johnson at Oxford (1975–76). Taught at Goldsmith's College and, beginning 1984, Bristol Univ. Early on, he was very taken with the music of Stravinsky, Berg, and Bartók, as well as of Bach and Mahler. He was particularly influenced by Britten, Boulez, and Webern. His first works are generally for smaller forces (*Reflections of Narziss and Goldmund,* 2 small wind and string ensembles, piano, harp, 1975), but by the late 1970s he had begun to employ larger resources and forms (*Choruses to Apollo,* orchestra, 1980; *Traumstadt,* 19 instruments, 1980). His musical style includes serial techniques, often related to Messiaen's approach. Works include *Ritornelli and intermezzi,* piano (1972); *Brise Marine,* soprano, tape, piano (1974); *The Rim of Eternity,* chamber orchestra (1983); *The Sentinel of the Rainbow,* 6 instruments (1984); Concerto for Orchestra (1984); *Circles of Light,* 15 instruments (1985); *In the Beginning,* orchestra, 1988; *Caritas,* chamber opera, 1991. In 1990 he became head of composition at the Guildhall School of Music.

Sayão, Bidú [Balduina] **(de Oliveira)** (b. Rio de Janeiro, 11 May 1902). Soprano. Studied in Rio, Bucharest, and Nice; made opera debut in 1926 at Rio, singing at Rome the same year; made first La Scala appearance in 1930, and bowed at Paris in 1931; sang also at the Metropolitan Opera (1937–51), Chicago (1941–45), and San Francisco (1946–52), retiring in 1958. She often sang in concert with Toscanini; at the opera, she focused on Italian roles.

Saygun, Ahmet Adnan (b. Izmir, 7 Sept. 1907; d. Istanbul, 6 Jan. 1991). Composer and ethnomusicologist. He studied by himself and then at Italian conservatories (1926–28) and the Schola cantorum in Paris (1928–31) with Le Flem and d'Indy. He returned to Ankara and Istanbul to make a career as a conductor and composer; his writings concentrated on Turkish popular music. He taught composition at the conservatory in Ankara from 1946, and in 1950 and 1958 made study trips to the U.S. His compositions include the opera *Köroğlu* (1973); the *ballet-féerie Gilgames* for soloists, chorus, and orchestra; 4 symphonies (1953–73); piano (1952) and violin (1967) concertos; chamber music; oratorios, cantatas, and songs.

Saylor, Bruce (Stuart) (b. Philadelphia, 24 Apr. 1946). Composer. He studied composition at Juilliard, with Petrassi in Rome (1969–70), and with Perle at the CUNY Graduate School (Ph.D., 1978). Taught at Queens College (1970–76 and from 1979) and New York Univ. (1976–79). He employs twelve-tone procedures that accommodate focal "tonics." Works include an opera (1976); several dance scores (*Wildfire,* 1979); *Paeans to Hyacinthus* (orchestra, 1980); chamber music (trio, clarinet, viola, piano, 1989); pieces for piano, organ, and carillon; *The Waves* (Woolf, for mezzo-soprano, flute, clarinet, viola, and cello; 1981). In 1992 he was appointed resident composer to the Chicago Lyric Opera.

Sbriglia, Giovanni (b. Naples, 23 June 1829; d. Paris, 20 Feb. 1916). Tenor. He studied with De Roxas. Debuted at Naples in 1853, New York in 1860. He toured the U.S., Mexico, and Havana in 1865. Settled in Paris in 1875 and taught singing. Among his students were Nordica, Sibyl Sanderson, Plançon, and Jean de Reszke.

Scacchi, Marco (b. Gallese, near Viterbo, ca. 1600; d. there, between 1681 and 1687). Composer and theorist. He was a student of Giovanni Francesco Anerio, who probably took him to Warsaw in the mid-1620s. There he was a royal musician in 1626, and from 1628 to 1649 he served as choirmaster. His output as a composer includes Masses in the *stile antico,* 10 operas (now lost), sacred concertos, and madrigals with continuo. Scacchi is most famous for his defense of modern music against the conservative Paul Siefert; his *Breve discorso sopra la musica moderna* (1649) was a call for greater tolerance toward a variety of styles. His identification of 3 main classes of music (church, chamber, and scenic or theatrical) proved influential.

Scala, Francis (Maria) (b. Naples, ca. 1820; d. Washington, D.C., 18 Apr. 1903). Composer and conductor. He studied the clarinet at the Naples Conservatory. Enlisted on the frigate *Brandywine* in 1841 as a musician third class and traveled to the U.S. He joined the Marine Corps in 1842; was named fife major in 1843 and was bandleader, 1855–71. He arranged many works for band. Many of his manuscripts are housed in the Library of Congress.

Scalero, (Bartolomeo Melchiorre) Rosario (b. Moncalieri, near Turin, 24 Dec. 1870; d. Settimo Vittone, Ivrea, 25 Dec. 1954). Composer. He studied in Turin; began a concert career as a violinist (1889), studying in London with Wilhelmj; taught in Lyons (from 1896); then studied in Vienna with Mandyczewski. In 1908 he was appointed to teach theory at the Academy of S. Cecilia in Rome. In 1919 he moved to the U.S., where he taught at the David Mannes School (1919–1928) and the Curtis Institute (1924–33, 1935–46). Among his students at Curtis were Barber, Foss, Menotti, and Rota. His works include orchestral music (*La divine foresta* op. 32, symphonic poem, 1933); chamber (*12 Preludi,* violin and piano) and piano music; songs; and transcriptions of earlier music.

Scandello, Antonio [Scandellus, Antonius] (b. Bergamo, 17 Jan. 1517; d. Dresden, 18 Jan. 1580). Composer. He studied in Bergamo and played cornet at S. Maria Maggiore; in 1547 he entered the service of Cardinal Christoph Madruzzi in Trent and two years later was engaged by Elector Moritz of Saxony. After the elector's death in 1553 Scandello converted to Protestantism, and in 1566 he became assistant to Le Maistre, the Kapellmeister of Dresden; he succeeded him in

1568. Scandello was renowned in his day as a cornetist and sackbut player, as well as for his leadership of the Dresden chapel.

Scarlatti, (Pietro) Alessandro (Gaspare) (b. Palermo, 2 May 1660; d. Naples, 22 Oct. 1725). Composer. The second of eight children of Pietro Scarlatti; at age 12 he was sent to Rome with his two sisters (June 1672). His early musical education remains obscure; he may have received instruction from his father or some other relative. It is possible, as tradition has it, that he studied briefly with Carissimi in Rome until the elder composer's death in January 1674. In any case, Scarlatti must have gained an impression of the music of his time by hearing music in private theaters, the two public opera houses, oratories, churches, and academies of Rome. Among those composers whose works he could have heard are Cesti, Stradella, Pasquini, and Sartorio. On 12 April 1678 he married Antonia Anzalone, a native of Rome; they had seven sons and three daughters, but apparently only five of their children survived to maturity.

Scarlatti's first known activity as a composer was the writing of an oratorio in early 1679 for the Arciconfraternità del SS. Crocifisso. His earliest known opera, *Gli equivoci nel sembiante* (1679), was successful in Rome and was also heard in Bologna, Naples, Palermo, and elsewhere.

By 1680 Scarlatti was *maestro di cappella* to Queen Christina of Sweden (since 1655 a patron of the arts in Rome), a post which he held until his departure for Naples in 1684. In Rome he enjoyed the protection of two cardinals, Benedetto Pamphili and Pietro Ottoboni, enthusiastic patrons of the arts.

At the invitation of the Viceroy of Naples, Scarlatti left Rome to become the viceroy's *maestro di cappella* in February 1684. It is unclear why Scarlatti left his favorable circumstances in Rome, but a scandal there involving one of his sisters may have made his situation uncomfortable. Despite another, more notorious scandal at the start of his tenure in Naples, he retained his post with the viceroy until 1702. During this 18-year period in Naples, Scarlatti's operas accounted for the majority of the new operas produced in the city. If he was correct in stating that *Lucio Manlio* (1705) was his 88th opera, then only half of his operas of 1684–1702 survive. At this time Scarlatti was also active in Rome, often supervising performances of his operas, oratorios, and cantatas; in 1690 both *La Statira* and *Gli equivoci in amore* marked important occasions there. In the 1690s Scarlatti wrote increasing numbers of operas and serenatas for Naples, many of which were also heard in other Italian cities and abroad. His *Il Pirro e Demetrio* (1694) achieved a rare international success with performances in Rome, Siena, Florence, Milan, Brunswick, and probably Mantua and Leipzig; it even ran for 60 performances (1708–17) in London in a partial English translation. *La caduta de' Decemviri* (1697) earned Scarlatti similar acclaim.

By the turn of the century Scarlatti had tired of the great demands placed upon him by his position at Naples. This, coupled with his dissatisfaction with Neapolitan musical tastes and his increasingly unstable social position as a result of the War of the Spanish Succession, led to his departure for Florence with his son Domenico in June 1702. While there, Scarlatti hoped to enter the service of Prince Ferdinando de' Medici, an illustrious patron of music who had previously promoted a dozen of Scarlatti's operas. No position was offered to him, and he left Florence in October 1702 for Naples and Rome, accepting the position of assistant music director at S. Maria Maggiore in Rome in late 1703. Because the public theaters in Rome had been closed since 1700, Scarlatti now concentrated on oratorios, serenatas, and cantatas written for various patrons, including Cardinals Ottoboni and Pamphili and Prince Francesco Maria Ruspoli. In 1706 Scarlatti was elected to the Arcadian Academy, and during the following year was promoted to *maestro di cappella* at S. Maria Maggiore. Perhaps because of financial difficulties Scarlatti accepted an offer in late 1708 from Cardinal Grimani, the new Austrian Viceroy of Naples, to resume his former duties there.

During the next ten years in Naples Scarlatti composed 11 operas, the most famous of which was *Il Tigrane* (1715). In 1716 he was granted a patent of nobility from Pope Clement XI. Scarlatti now became interested in comic opera and instrumental music. His comic opera *Il trionfo dell'onore* (1718) followed experiments with writing comic arias and intermezzi, while his orchestral and keyboard music probably dates from about 1715 on. Supported by his Roman patrons, Scarlatti presented some of his last operas in Rome: *Telemaco* (1718), *Marco Attilio Regolo* (1719), and *La Griselda* (1721), his last surviving opera. Scarlatti composed few works in his final years at Naples (1722–25). He was buried in the Cecilia Chapel at S. Maria di Montesanto.

Works: about 115 operas (many now lost); over 600 cantatas (100 others less reliably attributed to him), mostly for solo voice (usually soprano) accompanied by continuo alone; serenatas; oratorios; numerous Masses, Mass movements, motets, and other sacred and liturgical works (including the Messa di S. Cecilia, Rome, 1720; the Concerti sacri, 1707–8; and the St. John Passion, ca. 1680); madrigals; orchestral works (including 12 Sinfonie de concerto grosso, 1 June 1715–?); chamber sonatas; keyboard pieces (including toccatas and variations on "La follia," 1715).

Bibl.: *The Operas of Alessandro Scarlatti,* ed. Donald Jay Grout et al. (Cambridge, Mass., 1974–). Edward J. Dent, *Alessandro Scarlatti: His Life and Works* (London, 1905; R: 1960). Donald Jay Grout, *Alessandro Scarlatti: An Introduction to His Operas* (Berkeley, 1979). Frank A. D'Accone, *The History of a Baroque Opera: Alessandro Scarlatti's "Gli equivoci nel sembiante"* (New York, 1985). Carole Franklin Vidali, *Alessandro and Domenico Scarlatti: A Guide to Research* (New York, 1993).

Scarlatti, (Giuseppe) Domenico (b. Naples, 26 Oct. 1685; d. Madrid, 23 July 1757). Composer. He was the

Alessandro Scarlatti.

sixth of ten children of Alessandro Scarlatti and Antonia Anzalone. Nothing is known of his musical training; while he profited from the study of compositions by Gasparini, Greco, Pasquini, and the elder Scarlatti, it is not certain that any of them were his actual teachers. His name does not appear on any conservatory rosters. On 13 September 1701 he was appointed *organista e compositore di musica* of the Naples royal chapel, of which his father was maestro. What the younger Scarlatti's official duties were remains obscure, and none of his compositions from the period of his employment at the Neapolitan court appear to be extant. In 1702 father and son left for Florence on a four-month leave of absence. There Domenico may have met the keyboard instrument maker Bartolomeo Cristofori, who was then experimenting with the hammer action of his gravicembalo col piano e forte.

Alessandro soon left for Rome, while Domenico returned to Naples and assumed his father's duties there for the 1703–4 season. Two operas, *L'Ottavia ristituita al trono* and *Il Giustino* (both 1703), probably marked the 18-year-old's debut as an opera composer. But any hopes Alessandro may have had that his son would succeed him as *maestro di cappella* in Naples were not realized; Domenico soon resigned his post and joined his father in Rome. In May 1705, in an effort to secure a post for his son, Alessandro sent Domenico to Venice through Florence in the company of the famous castrato Nicolo Grimaldi, known as "Nicolino" or "Nicolini." Nothing is known of Domenico's stay in Venice except that there he probably became acquainted with Gasparini, Vivaldi, and Handel; by January 1708 he had returned to Rome. Scarlatti's alleged second encounter with Handel presumably took place in 1708 or early 1709. This was the famous contest in virtuosity, at which Handel is said to have prevailed at the organ while Scarlatti held his own on the harpsichord; but the event is reported only in Mainwaring's biography of Handel, written many years later. At the weekly concerts established by Cardinal Pietro Ottoboni, Scarlatti met virtuosos and composers including Corelli and the young Thomas Roseingrave, who was to play an active role in disseminating Scarlatti's music in England and Ireland. In 1709 Scarlatti entered the service of Queen Maria Casimira of Poland, living in self-imposed exile in Rome. In the libretto of his opera *L'Orlando* (1711) he is named as the queen's *maestro di cappella.* By the time she left for France in 1714, she had received from Scarlatti at least one cantata, one oratorio, and at least seven operas.

On 19 November 1713 Scarlatti was named assistant *maestro di cappella* of the Cappella Giulia at St. Peter's; he succeeded to the senior post at the death of Tommaso Baj on 22 December 1714. Earlier that year Scarlatti had been appointed *maestro di cappella* to the Marques de Fontes, Portuguese ambassador to the Vatican. Despite his growing success, Domenico had been unable to free himself from his father's control. Finally, on 28 January 1717 he was granted legal independence from Alessandro.

In August 1719 Scarlatti resigned his positions at Rome and went to Palermo, where a "Dominicus Scarlatti" was admitted to the Unione di Santa Cecilia on 16 April 1720; he remained there until at least 9 December 1722. By about 1723 he was in Lisbon, serving as *mestre de capela.* The following year he traveled to Rome, where he met Quantz and possibly the great castrato Carlo Broschi, better known as Farinelli. He returned there in 1728 to marry 16-year-old Maria Catarina Gentili. While at Lisbon he was responsible for the musical training of King John V's daughter, the Infanta Maria Barbara, and her younger brother, Don Antonio. Scarlatti's relationship with the former resulted in the creation of his most important compositions, 555 single-movement "sonatas" in binary form for unaccompanied keyboard. In the principal manuscript sources most of these movements, though separately titled, form pairs based on their key; there is still disagreement among scholars regarding the extent to which these works were intended by Scarlatti as two-movement cycles. The movements themselves are characterized by unconventional features, which include eccentric gestures, irregular phrases or groups of phrases, extensive use of the acciaccatura, and unusual modulations. Scarlatti also explored virtuoso technique in these sonatas, employing devices such as frequent crossing of the hands, runs in thirds and sixths, leaps wider than an octave, rapid arpeggio figurations, and rapid repeated notes.

In 1728 Maria Barbara married the Spanish Crown Prince Fernando and moved to Madrid. Scarlatti followed her and remained in her service, spending the last 28 years of his life at the Spanish court. There he was for a time alone in the musical spotlight; when Farinelli arrived in 1737 the composer's position must have changed to some degree. On 21 April 1738 knighthood was conferred on Scarlatti by his former patron, King John V of Portugal. The following year on 6 May his wife died; sometime before 1742 he married Anastasia Maxarti Ximenes, the mother of his last four children.

Works: operas (mainly lost); oratorios (lost); serenatas (lost); cantatas (50 firmly authenticated; 12 for which Scarlatti's authorship is less certain); Masses, motets, and other sacred vocal works (most employing the *stile antico,* and including the *Stabat Mater* and the *Salve Regina* [A], 1756–57); 17 sinfonias; 555 "sonatas" for solo keyboard.

Bibl.: *Domenico Scarlatti: Complete Keyboard Works in Facsimile,* ed. Ralph Kirkpatrick (New York, 1971). *Domenico Scarlatti: Sonates,* ed. Kenneth Gilbert (Paris, 1971–84). Sacheverell Sitwell, *A Background for Domenico Scarlatti, 1685–1757* (London, 1935; R: 1970). Ralph Kirkpatrick, *Domenico Scarlatti* (Princeton, 1953). Malcolm Boyd, *Domenico Scarlatti—Master of Music* (New York, 1987). Carole Franklin Vidali, *Alessandro and Domenico Scarlatti: A Guide to Research* (New York, 1993).

Scarlatti, Giuseppe (b. Naples, ca. 1718, or 18 June 1723; d. Vienna, 17 Aug. 1777). Composer. Nephew of Domenico Scarlatti. His first composition, an oratorio *La SS. Vergine Annunziata,* was performed in Rome in 1739. From that year until 1741 Scarlatti probably lived in Rome; from there he went to Florence and Lucca, where he was in residence by 1744. He visited his uncle in Spain before 1755 and settled in Vienna by 1757. After success with two opere buffe, Gluck helped him to obtain employment as a ballet composer at the Vienna Kärntnerthor-Theater. In the 1760s he may have been in the service of Prince Schwarzenberg. During his career Scarlatti received commissions for at least 32 operas.

Scelsi, Giacinto (b. La Spezia, 8 Jan. 1905; d. Rome, 8 Aug. 1988). Composer. He studied in Rome, in Geneva, and in Vienna (twelve-tone methods with Walter Klein, 1935–36). At first his principal activity was in France, where he published 3 volumes of poetry, and edited *La Suisse contemporaine* (1943–45). In 1951 he settled in Rome, and became associated with the group Nuova consonanze. While early works were freely atonal, his interest in Zen and in Eastern musics began to manifest itself in the 1960s, for instance, in the use of micro intervals in pieces for strings (*Xnoybis,* violin, 1964; *Natura renovatur,* strings, 1967). Other works include *Krishna e Rada* (flute and piano, 1986); *Pfhat* (chorus, orchestra, organ, and bells, 1974); several string quartets (1944, 1961, 1963, 1964, 1985).

Bibl.: Adriano Cremonese, *Giacinto Scelsi: Prassi compositiva e riflessione teorica fino alla metà degli anni '40* (Palermo, 1992).

Schack [Cziak, Schak, Žák, Ziak], **Benedikt (Emanuel)** (b. Mirotice, 7 Feb. 1758; d. Munich, 10 Dec. 1826). Tenor and composer. He studied at Staré Seldo, Svatá, and Prague, then studied medicine, philosophy, and singing in Vienna. In 1780 he became Kapellmeister to Prince Heinrich von Schönaich-Carolath in Silesia. In 1786 he joined Schikaneder's theatrical company; after the company settled in Vienna, he became principal tenor at the Freihaus-Theater auf der Wieden (1789). He was a close friend of Mozart, who contributed numbers for Schack's theatrical works and wrote the part of Tamino for him. Schack later moved to Graz (1793) and to Munich (1796), where he sang at the Hoftheater until 1814. He wrote a number of singspiels and sacred music.

Schaeffer, Pierre (b. Nancy, 14 Aug. 1910; d. 19 Aug. 1995). Composer, theorist, and writer. His parents were musicians, but he intended a career in engineering and studied at the École polytechnique from 1929; he worked briefly in the telecommunications industry in Strasbourg before joining Radiodiffusion française in 1936. He wrote essays and novels as well as music, and in 1941 founded the group Jeune France (concerned with developing French music, theater, and visual arts). During the war he helped to establish the Studio d'essai, the center of the Resistance movement in French radio, and began to experiment with the concepts leading to *musique concrète* in which all sounds are considered as appropriate for composition independent of their acoustic or abstract notational source. Schaeffer is credited with originating *musique concrète* in 5 works for tape alone performed in Paris on 5 October 1948 (among them *Étude violette* and *Aux chemins de fers*); in 1951 he founded the Groupe de recherche de musique concrète, then worked in the overseas broadcasting section of the ORTF (1953–57), returning in 1958 to the renamed Groupe de recherches musicales. All of his works are for tape alone, and many were produced in collaboration with other composers and used as ballets or as film scores. Schaeffer was appointed to teach electronic composition at the Paris Conservatory in 1968. He wrote several volumes and articles on *musique concrète* (*Traité des objets musicaux,* 1966; *A la recherche d'une musique concrète,* 1952). Compositions include *Orphée 53* (an opera in collaboration with Pierre Henry, 1953); *Phèdre* (1961); String Quartet (1968); *La course au kilocycle* (radio score, 1950; collaboration with Henry); and *Masquerage* (film score, directed by M. De Haas, 1952).

Bibl.: Michel Chion, *Guide des objets sonores: Pierre Schaeffer et la recherche musicale* (Paris, 1983).

Schäfer, Dirk (b. Rotterdam, 23 Nov. 1873; d. Amsterdam, 16 Feb. 1931). Composer and performer. He studied piano at the Rotterdam Music School beginning in 1888, then traveled to Cologne to study piano with Pauer and composition with Wüllner. He toured frequently throughout western Europe as a performer, especially of 19th- and 20th-century works. His own compositions, mainly for piano, show the influence of Chopin in particular. Works include 2 orchestral pieces; chamber music (4 sonatas for violin and piano op. 4, 1901; String Quartet op. 14, 1922); vocal music; and piano works (8 Etüden op. 3, 1896; 6 Klavierstukken op. 12, 1893–1915).

Schafer, R(aymond) Murray (b. Sarnia, Ont., 18 July 1933). Composer and writer on music. Studied at the Toronto Conservatory; lived in Europe from 1956 to 1961 as a free-lance journalist and interviewer for the BBC. He was artist-in-residence at Memorial Univ. (Newfoundland, 1963–65); taught at Simon Fraser Univ. (1965–75); then retired to a farmhouse in Monteagle Valley (Ontario), from which he published his own music and writings (Arcana Editions). Recognition includes a Guggenheim Fellowship (1974); the Jules Leger Prize for New Chamber Music (1976); Canadian Composer of the Year Award (1977).

He was influenced by the neoclassicism of Stravinsky and by "Les six," and explored serialism; but his mature works avoid ready-made systems. In 1972 Schafer founded the World Soundscapes Project with UNESCO and Donner Foundation support. His view of the acoustic environment led to works such as *Music for Wilderness Lake* (12 trombones, small lake, 1979) and *The Princess of the Stars* (ritual drama, performers and canoeists, 1981), in which the audience must travel to the appropriate environment (a lake at dawn).

Works include *Loving* (television opera, 1965); *Ra* (overnight celebration of the legend of the Egyptian sun god, 33 performers and audience, 1983); orchestral music (*Son of Heldenleben,* 1968; *Arcana,* voice and orchestra, 1972; flute concerto, 1985); chamber music (*Five Studies on Texts by Prudentius,* soprano and 4 flutes, 1962; String Quartet no. 3, 1981; String Quartet no. 4, 1989); choral music (*Apocalypsis,* 12 choirs, brass, percussion, homemade instruments, and tape; 1977); pieces for students and amateurs (*Jonah,* 1979, composed for and with the Maynooth Community Choir). *Patria V: The Crown of Ariadne,* the fifth in a projected series of 12 full-length dramatic works, was premiered in 1992.

Writings: *E. T. A. Hoffmann and Music* (1975). *Ezra Pound and Music* (1977). *The Tuning of the World* (1977). *R. Murray Schafer on Canadian Music* (1984). *The Thinking Ear* (1986). *Smoke: A Novel* (1976). *The Sixteen Scribes* (1981). *Ariadne* (1985).

Bibl.: Stephen Adams, *R. Murray Schafer* (Toronto, 1983).

Schäffer, Bogusław (b. Lwów, 6 June 1929). Composer and theorist. He studied violin in Opole, and took composition from Malawski at the Kraków Conservatory; also studied musicology with Jachimecki at Jagiello Univ. (1949–53), and had lessons with Luigi Nono (1959). From 1953 to 1959 Schäffer worked as a music critic, and in 1967 he founded the new-music periodical *Forum musicum.* He taught composition at the Kraków Conservatory (from 1963), and was associated for a time with the Experimental Studio of Polish Radio in Warsaw (1965–68); beginning in 1986 taught at the Salzburg Mozarteum.

Schäffer's early piano works (19 mazurkas, 1949) draw on Polish folk idioms. In 1953 he composed the first Polish twelve-tone work for orchestra, *Music for Strings: Nocturne.* His 12-tone serial compositions from this time (*Scultura,* 1960; *Musica ipsa,* 1962) are individual in style, and show careful attention to tone color. As early as the mid-1950s he was elaborating the concept of incompletely composed music, an idea that reached fruition with his first work of "instrumental theater," *TIS MW2* (1963). Schäffer's interest in microtonal composition also manifested itself early in his career: *Three Short Pieces for Orchestra* (1951) and *Music for String Quartet* (1954) both employ 23 different microtonal intervals within a 24-tone row. Some of his scores employ graphical notation and contain elements of indeterminacy. Also a prolific writer on music; his books include the influential theoretical treatise *Nowa muzyka* (Kraków, 1958; enlarged, 1969).

Works: Stage and action music, including Non-Stop (piano, 1960); *TIS GK* (ensemble, 1963); *Quartet* (4 actors, 1966); *Monodrama* (1968); *Dreams of Schäffer* (ensemble, 1972); *Twilight* (1972); *Negative Music* (1972); *Hommage à Irzykowski* (1973). Orchestral music, including *6 Movimenti* (piano and orchestra, 1957); *Concerto breve* (cello, orchestra, 1959); *Topofonica* (40 instruments, 1960); *Musica* (harpsichord, orchestra, 1961); symphony in 9 movements (1973); Te Deum (voices, orchestra, 1979); Stabat Mater (soprano, alto, choir, strings, organ, 1983); Concerto (organ, violin, orchestra, B-A-C-H, 1984); saxophone concerto (1986); Sinfonia (1993); concertos for 1, 2, and 3 pianos, and violin concertos.

Ensemble and piano music, including Sonata (solo violin, 1955); *Study in Diagram* (1955–56); *Permutations* (10 instruments, 1956); *6 Models for Piano* (1954–93); *Extremes* (10 instruments, 1957); 8 pieces for piano (1954–58); *Monosonata* (6 string quartets, 1959); *Equivalenze sonore* (percussion, chamber orchestra, 1959); Concerto for String Quartet (1959); 4 pieces (string trio, 1962); *Expressive Aspects* (soprano, flute, 1963); *S'alto* (saxophone, chamber orchestra, 1963); *Collage* (chamber orchestra, 1964); *Decet* (harp, 9 instruments, 1966); *Variants* (wind quintet, 1971); *Gravesono* (wind instruments, percussion, 1977); *Gasab* (Gasab-violin, piano accompaniment, 1983). Electronic and tape music, including *Missa elettronica* (boys' choir, tape, 1975); *Maah* (orchestra, tape, 1979); Open Music nos. 2, 3, and 4 (piano, tape, 1983); *Teatrino fantastico* (actor, violin, piano, multimedia, tape, 1983); *Kwaiwa* (violin, computer, 1986); *Acontecimiento* (3 pianos, computer, 1988).

Bibl.: Bohdan Pociej, "The Art of Boguslaw Schaeffer," *Polish Perspectives* 14 (1971): 85–94. Stefan Maria Ehrenkreutz, "The Fundamental Underlying Determinants of Boguslaw Schäffer's Musical Practice and 20th-Century Musical Function" (diss., Univ. of Michigan, 1984). Ludomira Stawowy, *Boguslaw Schaeffer: Leben, Werk, Bedeutung* (Innsbruck, 1991) [includes works list].

Schalk, Franz (b. Vienna, 27 May 1863; d. Edlach, 2 Sept. 1931). Conductor. Studied with Bruckner at the Vienna Conservatory. Was conductor at Liberec (1888), Graz (1889–95), Prague (1895–98), New York Metropolitan Opera House (1898–99), Berlin (1899–1900), Vienna Court Orchestra (1900), Covent Garden (1898, 1907, 1911). Co-conductor with Richard Strauss at Vienna Opera, 1918–24; principal conductor to 1929. Cofounded the Salzburg Festival. Championed the works of Wolf and Bruckner. Responsible for the spurious first editions of Bruckner's Symphonies nos. 4 and 5.

Scharwenka, (Ludwig) Philipp (b. Samter, 16 Feb. 1847; d. Bad Nauheim, 16 July 1917). Composer. Studied at the Kullak Academy of Music, Berlin, and taught there from 1868. Joined with his brother Xaver on the founding of the Scharwenka Conservatory in Berlin, which later merged with the Klindworth Conservatory (1893). Composed primarily instrumental music including symphonic poems; overtures; 1 piano quintet (1910); 2 string quartets opp. 117, 120; 1 piano trio; 2 violin sonatas opp. 110, 114; viola sonata op. 106; cello sonata op. 116; choruses and songs.

Scharwenka, (Franz) Xaver (b. Samter, 6 Jan. 1850; d. Berlin, 8 Dec. 1924). Pianist and composer. Studied at the New Academy of Music, Berlin, with Kullak (1865). Debuted at the Singakademie, 1869. Toured Europe in 1874, later the U.S. and Canada. Cofounded a series of concerts at the Singakademie. Opened a conservatory in Berlin, 1881 (Scharwenka Conservatory). During an 1886 tour, conducted the works of Liszt and Berlioz, played his own works with Richter and Joachim. Opened a branch of his conservatory in New York (1891). Founded the Music Teachers' Federation in Germany (1900). Works include 1 opera (*Mataswintha,* 1896); Symphony in C minor op. 60 (1885); 4 piano concertos op. 32 (1876), op. 56 (1881), opp. 80 and 82 (1908); Piano Quintet op. 37 (1877); 2 piano sonatas (1872, 1878); Violin Sonata op. 2 (1872); Cello Sonata op. 46; other chamber pieces; shorter piano works. Wrote *Methodik des Klavierspiels* (Leipzig, 1907).

Bibl.: Franz Xaver Scharwenka, *Klänge aus meinem Leben: Erinnerungen eines Musikers* (Leipzig, 1922).

Schat, Peter (b. Utrecht, 5 June 1935). Composer. Studied composition at the Utrecht Conservatory, 1952–58, under Van Baaren; in London, for a year, with Seiber; and in Basel with Boulez, 1960–62. In 1967 he began working with the Studio voor Electro-Instrumentale Muziek in Amsterdam; subsequent compositions were influenced by his access to those facilities. In the same year he visited Cuba and was moved to help organize the Political-Demonstrative Experimental Concerts in 1968, as well as to incorporate social criticism into some of his works. In 1973 he organized the Amsterdam Electrisch Circus, a performing group that created multimedia events. His early works made thorough use of serialism (Concerto da camera, 2 clarinets, piano, percussion, strings, 1960). He then began to wield elements of chance in the form of controlled improvisation and stage directions for the performers (*Improvisations and Symphonies,* wind quintet, 1960). *Clockwise and Anticlockwise* (1967) utilizes the concept of a clock face for placing the 12 performers and for presenting a synopsis of musical style of the past four centuries. By the late 1960s Schat was exploring electronic media (*To You,* 9 electric guitars, 4 electric pianos, 2 electric organs, 6 electric humming tops, 1972). Works include Septet, flute, oboe, bass clarinet, horn, piano, percussion, cello (1957); *Inscripties,* piano (1959); *Entelechie I,* 5 instrumental groups (1961), *Entelechie II,* 11 instruments (1961); *Labyrinth,* opera (1966); *Reconstructie,* opera, collaboration with Andriessen, de Leeuw, Mengelberg, Vlijmen (1969); *Houdini,* circus opera (1976); *I Am Houdini,* ballet, tenor, chorus, 2 piano (1976); Symphony no. 1 (1978); *Aap verslaat de Knekelgeest* [Monkey Subdues the White-Bone Demon], cartoon opera (1980); *Symposion,* opera after Plato (1982–89); *Symposium,* opera (1994).

Scheel, Fritz (b. Lübeck, 7 Nov. 1852; d. Philadelphia, 13 Mar. 1907). Violinist and conductor. Studied with Ferdinand David in Leipzig, 1864–67. Conducted at Bremenhaven, Schwerin, Bremen, and Chemnitz (1869–90). Was associated with von Bülow at Hamburg in 1890. Emigrated to the U.S., 1893. Set up the San Francisco Symphony Society (1895–1906). First director of Philadelphia Orchestra, 1900. Conducted the Orpheus and Eurydice Choruses in Philadelphia.

Scheibe, Johann Adolph (b. Leipzig, 3 May 1708; d. Copenhagen, 22 Apr. 1776). Composer and theorist. After studying law at Leipzig Univ., he taught himself music. In 1736 he moved to Hamburg, becoming established as a music critic and composer; from 1737 to 1740 his *Critischer Musikus* appeared. In his autobiography he claimed to have produced a large output of music: 150 church pieces, 150 flute concertos, over 30 violin concertos, and many other instrumental and vocal works; most of his music has been lost. In 1739 he was named Kapellmeister to Margrave Friedrich Ernst of Brandenburg-Culmbach; he was Kapellmeister to the Danish court from 1740 to 1747 and again after 1766. His writings display his originality and progressiveness as a music theorist.

Bibl.: George Buelow, "In Defence of J. A. Scheibe against J. S. Bach," *PRMA* 101 (1974–75): 85–100.

Scheibler, Johann Heinrich (b. Montjoie [now Monschau], 11 Nov. 1777; d. Krefeld, 20 Nov. 1837). Theorist. A silk manufacturer in Krefeld, he studied with J. N. Wolff and mastered many instruments. Though possessing no scientific knowledge, he built a tonometer, consisting of 56 tuning forks, in order to create an equally tempered scale. His experiments are described in his *Der physikalische und musikalische Tonmesser* (Essen, 1834). In 1834 at Stuttgart he proposed the "Stuttgart pitch," a′=440.

Scheidemann, Heinrich (b. Wöhrden, Holstein, ca. 1595; d. Hamburg, early 1663). Composer. He studied with Sweelinck in Amsterdam from 1611 to 1614. From 1629 until his death he was organist at the Catharinenkirche in Hamburg; from 1633 he was also clerk to the church. There he came into contact with

Praetorius. Almost all his works are for organ and represent the first peak of the north German organ school. He extended Sweelinck's keyboard style into an organ idiom, and helped develop the monodic organ chorale and the virtuosic chorale fantasia.

Bibl.: *Heinrich Scheidemann: Orgelwerke,* ed. Gustav Fock and Werner Breig (1967–71). Werner Breig, *Die Orgelwerke von Heinrich Scheidemann* (Wiesbaden, 1967).

Scheidt, Samuel (b. Halle, bapt. 3 Nov. 1587; d. there, 24 Mar. 1654). Composer. He was instructed in music at the local Gymnasium, and by December 1604 had become organist at the Moritzkirche; he remained there until at least April 1607. About this time he studied with Sweelinck in Amsterdam. By the end of 1609 he was back in Halle as court organist to the new administrator, Margrave Christian Wilhelm of Brandenburg. There Scheidt was responsible for playing the organ during services and providing secular keyboard music. Later, he was able to work with Praetorius, Kapellmeister in absentia, and also with Schütz. In late 1619 or early 1620 he was appointed court Kapellmeister, retaining his position as organist. From 1620 to 1625 Scheidt enlarged the court musical establishment to 10 instrumentalists and 5 vocal soloists and published a collection of motets (*Cantiones sacrae,* 1620); 3 volumes of instrumental ensemble music (*Ludi musici,* 1621, 1622, 1624); 1 volume of large-scale vocal concertos (*Concertus sacri,* 1622); and the most important collection of his keyboard music, the 3-volume *Tabulatura nova* (1624). It was also during this period that Scheidt gained a reputation as an expert in organ construction; throughout his life he was often called upon to inspect new instruments.

When the margrave left Halle for Denmark in 1625 to support the Protestant cause in the Thirty Years' War, Scheidt was able to keep his position without pay. During the next several years he made his living primarily by teaching; his most famous pupil was Adam Krieger. The city of Halle created the post of *director musices* for Scheidt in 1628, which carried the responsibility of supplying music for the Marktkirche, the city's most important church. He lost this post in 1630 as the result of a dispute with Christian Gueinz, *Rektor* of the Gymnasium. In 1636 the plague hit Halle, claiming the lives of his four surviving children. Despite these unfortunate events, Scheidt continued to publish music: the fourth and final volume of his *Ludi musici* appeared in 1627, the *Liebliche Krafft-Blümlein* was brought out in 1635, and 4 volumes of *Geistliche Concerte* were published between 1631 and 1640. Peace returned to Halle in 1638, and Scheidt fully resumed his position as court Kapellmeister. In 1642 he offered to Duke August of Brunswick a collection of more than 100 sacred madrigals for 5 voices (now lost) and a number of instrumental sinfonias designed as preludes to vocal music. His last publication, the so-called *Görlitzer Tabulatur-Buch* (1650), contains 100 organ chorales in 4-part harmonizations.

Bibl.: *Samuel Scheidt: Werke,* ed. Gottlieb Harms and Christhard Mahrenholz, 1–13 (Hamburg, 1923–62), 14–16 (Leipzig, 1971–81). Christhard Mahrenholz, *Samuel Scheidt: Sein Leben und sein Werk* (Leipzig, 1902; R: 1965). Erika Gessner, *Samuel Scheidts geistliche Konzerte: Ein Beitrag zur Geschichte der Gattung* (Berlin, 1961).

Schein, Johann Hermann (b. Grünhain, near Annaberg [now Annaberg-Bucholz], 20 Jan. 1586; d. Leipzig, 19 Nov. 1630). Composer. Upon his father's death in 1593, Schein's family moved to Dresden, where he entered the Hofkapelle of the Elector of Saxony as a boy soprano. There he also received instruction in music from the Kapellmeister, Rogier Michael, and was exposed to much secular and sacred choral music in Latin, German, and Italian. After a brief time at the Univ. of Leipzig, he continued his studies in music at Schulpforta, an electoral school near Naumberg, from 18 May 1603 to 26 April 1607; his teachers there were Bartholomäus Scheer and Martin Roth. In 1608 Schein received an electoral scholarship to study law and the liberal arts at the Univ. of Leipzig, where he remained until 1612. The following year Schein assumed the position of house music director and tutor to the children of Gottfried von Wolffersdorff. On 21 May 1615 he was appointed Kapellmeister to Duke Johann Ernst the Younger at Weimar. The following year he auditioned successfully for the position of *Thomaskantor* at Leipzig, succeeding Calvisius. There his duties included directing the choral music in the Thomaskirche and the Nicolaikirche, and teaching 14 hours a week of Latin and singing in the Thomasschule; his most famous pupils were the poet Paul Fleming and the composer Heinrich Abert. Schein suffered from poor health, and illness restricted his activities during the last several years of his life. He established friendships with Scheidt and Schütz. Primarily a composer for the voice, Schein was one of the earliest composers to combine elements of the Italian madrigal, monody, and vocal concerto with traditional Lutheran music.

Works: Sacred vocal. *Cymbalum Sionium* (1615); *Opella nova* (1618, 1626); *Fontana d'Israel* (1623); *Cantional oder Gesangbuch Augspurgischer Confession* (1627, 1645). Secular vocal (all texts by Schein). *Venus Kräntzlein* (1609); *Musica boscareccia* or *Wald-Liederlein* (1621, 1626, 1628); *Diletti pastorali* or *Hirten Lust* (1624); *Studenten-Schmauss* (1626). Occasional music; instrumental music (*Banchetto musicale,* 1617).

Bibl.: *Johann Hermann Schein: Neue Ausgabe sämtlicher Werke,* ed. Adam Adrio (Kassel, 1963–). Walther Reckziegel, *Das Cantional von Johann Hermann Schein: Seine geschichtlichen Grundlagen* (Berlin, 1963). F. Ellsworth Peterson, "Johann Hermann Schein's *Cymbalum Sionium:* A Liturgico-Musical study" (diss., Harvard, 1966). Ferdinand Conrad, "Johann Hermann Schein und sein *Banchetto musicale,*" in *Heinrich Schütz e il suo tempo,* ed. Giancarlo Rostirolla (Rome, 1981), pp. 90–102.

Schelle, Johann (b. Geising, Thuringia, bapt. 6 Sept. 1648; d. Leipzig, 10 Mar. 1701). Composer. In 1655 he entered the choir of the Dresden electoral chapel, which was directed by Schütz. In 1657 he went to Wolfenbüttel, where he joined the choir of the ducal court. When his voice broke in 1665, he entered the Thomasschule in Leipzig under Knüpfer; he later attended the university. In October 1670 he became Kantor at Eilenburg, and on 31 January 1677 obtained the same post at the Thomaskirche in Leipzig. There he introduced into the Protestant liturgy the Gospel cantata and the chorale cantata. Almost all of Schelle's compositions are sacred works, most of them to German texts. Not many of his works are extant, and few were published in his lifetime.

Schelling, Ernest (Henry) (b. Belvidere, N.J., 26 July 1876; d. New York, 8 Dec. 1939). Composer, conductor, and pianist. He performed in Philadelphia at the age of 4; studied at the Paris Conservatory (1882–85), in Basel and Vienna, and later with Paderewski (1898–1902). He settled in the U.S. in 1905 and was elected to the National Institute of Arts and Letters in 1913. In later years he concentrated on composing and conducting. In 1924 he founded and conducted the Young People's concerts of the New York Philharmonic; he conducted the Baltimore Symphony from 1936 to 1938. His works include *A Victory Ball* (premiered by the Philadelphia Orchestra, 1923) and *Impressions from an Artist's Life* (variations for piano and orchestra, 1913).

Schenk, Johann Baptist (b. Wiener Neustadt, 30 Nov. 1753; d. Vienna, 29 Dec. 1836). Composer. He studied with Anton Stoll, choirmaster at Baden, then went to Vienna to study with Wagenseil (1773–77). During the 1780s he composed singspiels for several Viennese theaters, including Schikaneder's Freihaus-Theater auf der Wieden. His symphonies also met with success during this time. In the mid-1790s he was Kapellmeister to Prince Auersperg and wrote for the court theaters; his singspiel *Der Dorfbarbier* (1796) was his greatest success. After 1802 he wrote no further stage works, concentrating instead on teaching and composing vocal and choral works. In 1793 Beethoven, then a formal pupil of Haydn, took lessons in counterpoint and composition from Schenk.

Schenker, Heinrich (Wisniowczyki, Galicia, 19 June, 1868; d. Vienna, 13 Jan. 1935). Theorist. He was born in Poland of Austrian parents; he studied piano with Karl Mikuli. Sent to Vienna on an imperial scholarship, he studied composition at the conservatory (with Bruckner) and law at the university. He remained in Vienna as a private teacher of piano and theory, working also as editor, critic, chamber music performer, and accompanist (notably for baritone Johannes Messchaert). His compositions attracted favorable notice from Brahms and Busoni. His students included Ernst Oster, Wilhelm Furtwängler, Anthony van Hoboken, Oswald Jonas, and Felix Salzer.

Schenker's theories show that in a well-composed tonal work, overall structural-harmonic design can be analyzed contrapuntally at various levels of complexity *(Schichten)*. The simplest, most fundamental level *(Ursatz)* consists of a melodic stepwise descent to the tonic note *(Urlinie)* supported by a bass I–V–I arpeggiation *(Baßbrechung)*. Other harmonic and melodic features of the work are hierarchically subordinate elaborations or "diminutions" that arise from a "composing-out" *(Auskomponierung)* of the *Ursatz*. Schenker devised an elaborate musicographical system to represent these concepts visually.

Traditional principles of form and vertical harmony play a lesser role in Schenker's analysis. He applied his theories mainly to music of the period from Bach to Brahms (ca. 1700–1900); later adherents have extended its application. His thought won particular favor in America, influencing major texts of Felix Salzer (*Structural Hearing*, New York, 1952), Edward Aldwell and Carl Schachter, and others.

Schenker's principal theoretical work was the multivolume *Neue musikalische Theorien und Phantasien*, including (1) *Harmonielehre* (Stuttgart, 1906), (2/1) *Kontrapunkt* (1910), (2/2) *Kontrapunkt* (1922), and (3) *Der freie Satz* (1935). Several parallel publications supported this work: *Beethovens Neunte Sinfonie* (1912); *Der Tonwille*, 10 issues (1921–24); *Beethovens Fünfte Sinfonie* (1925); *Das Meisterwerk in der Musik*, 3 vols. (1925–30); *Fünf Urlinie-Tafeln* (1932). All but the first were published in Vienna; most have been translated into English. He edited J. S. Bach's *Chromatic Fantasia*, Handel's organ concerti, C. P. E. Bach's keyboard works, and Beethoven's piano sonatas.

Bibl.: Larry Laskowski, *Heinrich Schenker: An Annotated Index to His Analyses of Musical Works* (New York, 1978). Allen Forte and Steven Gilbert, *Introduction to Schenkerian Analysis* (New York, 1982). Oswald Jonas, *Introduction to the Theory of Heinrich Schenker*, trans. and ed. John Rothgeb (New York, 1982). David Beach, ed., *Elements of Schenkerian Theory* (New Haven, 1983).

Scherchen, Hermann (b. Berlin, 21 June 1891; d. Florence, 12 June 1966). Conductor. Self-taught in music, he played viola in the Blüthner Orchestra (1907) and Berlin Philharmonic (1907–10). He began a conducting career as Schoenberg's assistant for the premiere of *Pierrot lunaire* in 1912. In 1914 he conducted the Riga Symphony Orchestra; during World War I he was interned in Russia. Returning to Berlin in 1918, he devoted himself largely to new music: lectured at the Musikhochschule and founded the Neue Musikgesellschaft, the Scherchen Quartet, and the journal *Melos*. He conducted the Leipzig Konzertverein (1921), Frankfurt Museumskonzerte (1922–23), Winterthur Abonnementskonzerte (intermittent, 1922–47), concerts of the International Society for Contemporary Music (from its founding, 1923), and East German Radio Orchestra of Königsberg. Fleeing Germany in 1933, he settled in Switzerland; he conducted the Zürich Radio Orchestra from 1933 and founded the journal *Musica viva* (Brussels, 1933–36) and the Ars Viva Orchestra (1939). After World War II he conducted the Beromünster Radio Orchestra (1944–50) and founded the Ars Viva edition (1939), the Gravesano electro-acoustic research studio (1954), and its organ the *Gravesaner Blätter.* Throughout his career toured widely as conductor and teacher; he authored 3 books on conducting and interpretation. He was considered a model conductor of works of Schoenberg, Berg, Webern, Dallapiccola, Hindemith, Prokofiev, and Stravinsky.

Schermerhorn, Kenneth (de Witt) (b. Schenectady, N.Y., 20 Nov. 1929). Conductor. He studied conducting at New England Conservatory and the Tanglewood Berkshire Music Center. He conducted the American Ballet Theater of New York (1957–67) and was an assistant conductor of the New York Philharmonic (1960–61); musical director of the New Jersey Symphony (1963–68), Milwaukee Symphony (1968–80), American Ballet Theater (from 1982), Nashville Symphony (1983–88), and Hong Kong Philharmonic (1984–88).

Schibler, Armin (b. Kreuzlingen, Lake Constance, 20 Nov. 1920; d. Zurich, 7 Sept. 1986). Composer and writer on music. He studied piano and composition in Zurich and worked with Rubba and Tippett in England (1946); attended the Darmstadt summer courses given by Fortner, Leibowitz, Krenek, and Adorno (1949–53). He taught at the cantonal school in Zurich from 1944; wrote *Neue Musik in dritter Generation* (1953) as well as a book on Mahler (1955), and one on contemporary opera (1956). He explored twelve-tone procedures in the 1950s, but was also influenced by Stravinsky's rhythmic language, jazz, and popular music. Works include the 1986 opera trilogy *Amadeus und der graue Bote, Königinnen von Frankreich, Schlafwagen Pegasus;* music theater pieces and ballets; choral works (*Enkidus Tod,* tenor, baritone, 3 speakers, speaking chorus, orchestra; 1972); 3 symphonies; chamber music (*4 Stücke für Violine und Schlagwerk,* 1986); piano music; songs; film scores, and educational music.

Bibl.: Hans-Rudolf Metzger, *Armin Schibler, 1920–1986* (Zurich, 1990).

Schicht, Johann Gottfried (b. Reichenau, near Zittau, 29 Sept. 1753; d. Leipzig, 16 Feb. 1823). Composer. He studied with the organist Johann Trier at Zittau. While studying law at Leipzig Univ., he played in the Grosses Concert and the Musikübende Gesellschaft, both under Hiller. From 1781 he played violin in the Gewandhaus concerts, whose director he became in 1785. He also held other Leipzig musical posts, including Kantor of the Thomasschule (from 1810). He wrote sacred and secular vocal works and the *Allgemeine Choralbuch* (Leipzig, 1819).

Schickele, Peter (b. Ames, Iowa, 17 July 1935). Composer and writer. Attended Swarthmore College (B.A. 1957) and the Juilliard School (M.S. 1960), studying with Harris, Persichetti, and Milhaud. He composed for the Los Angeles Public Schools in 1960 and 1961, taught at Juilliard from 1961 to 1965, and formed the contemporary ensemble Open Window in 1967. He is the creator of P. D. Q. Bach, complete with "biography" (New York, 1976) and a satirical oeuvre that blends primarily 18th-century concert music with elements of present-day culture; P. D. Q. Bach's many "works" include the operas *Iphigenia in Brooklyn* (1965), *The Abduction of Figaro* (1984), *Oedipus Tex* (1988), and *Prelude to Einstein on the Fritz* (1989). Under his own name Schickele has also composed orchestral works (*Thurber's Dogs,* 1994; oboe concerto, 1995), film music (*Silent Running,* 1972), chamber music, and popular songs.

Schidlowsky, León (b. Santiago, 21 July 1931). Composer. Studied piano at the National Conservatory as a youth; studied psychology and philosophy at the Univ. of Chile, 1948–52; pursued music concurrently under Allende and Focke, and studied in Europe, 1952–55. Returning to Chile, he taught at the Hebrew Institute, Santiago (1955–61), and participated in the Agrupación Tonus ensemble. Took over the archive at the Instituto de Extensión musical in 1961, directing the institute, 1962–66; taught at the Univ. of Chile and the National Conservatory, 1962–68. Lived in Germany in 1968, after which he emigrated to Israel, becoming professor at the Rubin Academy in 1970. His earlier music is freely atonal, while later works use serialism with varying degrees of control, graphic notation, and aleatory techniques. Much of his music (*La noche de cristal,* 1961; *Invocación,* 1964) commemorates the Holocaust. Other works include a string quartet and piano quartet (both 1988), *Laudatio* (orchestra, 1988); *Chanson* (voice, tam-tam, 1988).

Works: *Die Menschen,* opera (1970); works for solo singers or narrators and orchestra, including *Requiem* (1954), *Oda a la tierra* (1960), *Amatorias* (1963), *De profundis* (1963), and *Amereida* (1965–72); choral-orchestral works, including *Jeremias* (1964), *Deutsches Tagebuch* (1966), *Rabbi Akiba* (1972), *Massada* (1972), *Akiva ben Josef* (1972), and *Hommage à Neruda* (1975); orchestral works, including *Triptico* (1959), *Nueva York* (1965), and *Kaddish* (1967, with cello solo); choral music; chamber music; and tape compositions.

Bibl.: William Elias, *León Schidlowsky* (Tel Aviv, 1978).

Schiff, Andras (b. Budapest, 21 Dec. 1953). Pianist. Attended the Liszt Academy; won the 1974 Tchaikovsky Competition in Moscow. Thereafter pursued a career as recitalist and soloist, performing a repertory ranging from Bach to 19th-century composers.

Schifrin, Lalo [Boris] (b. Buenos Aires, 21 June 1932). Composer and jazz pianist. He studied with Messiaen at the Paris Conservatory. After moving from Buenos Aires to New York in 1958, he joined Dizzy Gillespie's quintet (1960–62). Thereafter he concentrated on composing for television, including the series *Mission Impossible* (1966–73), and films, including *The Fox, Cool Hand Luke* (both 1967), *Bullitt* (1968), and *Dirty Harry* (1971). In 1988 he became music director of the Paris Philharmonic; the same year composed his *Songs of the Aztecs* for soloist and orchestra.

Schikaneder, Emanuel (Johann Joseph [Baptist]) (b. Straubing, 1 Sept. 1751; d. Vienna, 21 Sept. 1812). Writer and composer. After studies at the Jesuit Gymnasium at Regensburg, he became an actor with F. J. Moser's troupe (1773 or 1774). As director of the troupe (from 1778), he appeared with it at Ulm, Stuttgart, Augsburg, Nuremburg, Rothenburg, Ljubljana, Klagenfurt, Linz, and Salzburg, where he met the Mozarts. He leased the Kärntnerthortheater in Vienna (1783–85), then joined the National Theater (1785) and formed a new company (1786) while his wife ran the troupe. After directing the court theater in Regensburg, he took over the troupe (now at the Freihaus-Theater auf der Wieden, Vienna) with his wife in 1789, commissioning settings of his texts by Mozart (*Die Zauberflöte,* with Schikaneder as Papageno), Wölfl, Winter, and others. In 1801 he opened the new Theater an der Wien, for which he wrote plays and librettos. After directing the Brno Theater (1806–9), he returned to Vienna (1809), where his mental health declined and he died in poverty. He wrote about 100 librettos and plays, and composed several theater scores.

Bibl.: Kurt Honolka, *Emanuel Schikaneder, Man of the Theater in Mozart's Time* (Portland, Ore., 1990).

Schildt, Melchior (b. Hannover, 1592–93; d. there, 18 May 1667). Composer. He was first instructed by his father and Andreas Crappius; from 1609 until the end of 1612 he studied with Sweelinck in Amsterdam. He was organist at the Hauptkirche in Wolfenbüttel (1623–26) before becoming court organist to King Christian IV in Copenhagen (1626–29). In 1629 Schildt succeeded his father as organist of the Marktkirche in Hannover, where he remained until his death. A founder of the so-called north German organ school, Schildt was also one of its most original composers. Practically all of his surviving music is for keyboard, most of it consisting of chorale-based organ works. The innovative chorale concerto *Ach mein herzliebes Jesulein* is his only extant vocal work.

Schillinger, Joseph (Moiseyevich) (b. Kharkov, Russia, 31 Aug. 1895; d. New York, 23 Mar. 1943). Composer and theorist. He studied mathematics and music in St. Petersburg (1914–18); taught and conducted in Moscow, Kharkov, and Leningrad while composing chromatic but traditional works. He moved to New York in 1928 (U.S. citizen in 1936) and taught music, math, and art history at the New School for Social Research, New York Univ., and Columbia Univ. Teachers College. He developed his own theories of harmony and rhythmic design and experimented with complex rhythms on the rhythmicon designed by Lev Terman. Among his private students in New York were Tommy Dorsey, George Gershwin, and Glenn Miller. His compositions include *North-Russian Symphony* (1930) and *The People and the Prophet* (ballet, 1931). His writings include *The Schillinger System of Musical Composition,* ed. Lyle Dowling and Arnold Shaw (1941); *Kaleidophone: New Resources of Melody and Harmony* (1940); *The Mathematical Basis of the Arts* (1948); and *Encyclopedia of Rhythm* (1966).

Schillings, Max von (b. Düren, 19 Apr. 1868; d. Berlin, 24 July 1933). Composer and conductor. While a student at the Gymnasium in Bonn he studied violin, theory, and piano and as a young composer had frequent performances; at the Univ. of Munich he studied law, philosophy, literature, and art history but finally turned to music under the influence of Strauss and others. In 1892 he was assistant stage conductor at Bayreuth; in 1902 was named chorusmaster. After Strauss left for Berlin in 1898, Schillings was regarded as the leader of the Munich School of composers; Strauss continued to promote his music in the festivals of the Allgemeiner Deutscher Musikverein (Schillings was president of the organization from 1910 to 1920). In 1903 he had been appointed Königlicher Professor at Munich, but in 1908 left for Stuttgart where he was assistant to the intendant at the Royal Opera House; he became general music director there in 1911, conducting not only operas but also concerts with the court orchestra; his own opera *Mona Lisa* was premiered there in 1915. He resigned in 1918 and became intendant at the Berlin Opera, where he remained until 1925. As a conductor he toured the U.S. and Europe and made many recordings with the Berlin State Opera orchestra. He won the Beethoven Prize and the Goethe Medal. His works include 6 operas (*Der Pfeiffertag,* 1899; rev. 1931); Violin Concerto (1910); Piano Quintet (1917); choral music and songs.

Schindler, Anton Felix (b. Meedl, Moravia, 13 June 1795; d. Bockenheim, near Frankfurt, 16 Jan. 1864). Violinist, conductor, writer on music. Began studying law in Vienna in 1813; in 1814 he met Beethoven, becoming his secretary in 1820. He conducted in Vienna at the Josephstadt Theater (1822), the Kärntnerthor Theater (1825). Under Beethoven's supervision he conducted all 9 symphonies, 1823–24. Choirmaster at Münster Cathedral (1831–35); music director and choirmaster at Aachen (1835–40). Published a biography of Beethoven (Münster, 1840; trans. and ed. Donald MacArdle as *Beethoven As I Knew Him,* London, 1966).

Bibl.: Donald W. MacArdle, "Anton Felix Schindler, Friend of Beethoven," *MR* 24 (1963): 50–74.

Schindler, Kurt (b. Berlin, 17 Feb. 1882; d. New York, 16 Nov. 1935). Composer, conductor, and editor. He studied in Berlin and Munich; was assistant at the Berlin Opera in 1904 and at the Metropolitan Opera from 1905. In New York he founded the MacDowell Chorus (later Schola Cantorum) which he conducted until 1926. From 1907 he worked as reader, editor, and critic for G. Schirmer and later for Oliver Ditson; was music director of Temple Emanuel from 1912 to 1925; was active as a collector of Spanish folk melodies (1930–33); and chaired the music department at Bennington College (from 1933). He edited 3 volumes of Russian art and folk song, 1 of songs from Louisiana (1921), and 1 of *Folk Music and Poetry of Spain and Portugal* (1941). Works include *The Mummers' Revel and the Masque of the Apple* (1934) and songs.

Schiøtz, Aksel (b. Roskilde, 1 Sept. 1906; d. Copenhagen, 19 Apr. 1975). Tenor. Attended Copenhagen Univ.; made his concert debut in 1938 and opera debut in 1939; gave clandestine concerts during the German Occupation. Soon after the war a brain tumor disabled him; he returned to the stage as a baritone after a 1947 operation, but never fully recovered. He later taught at the Univ. of Minnesota (1955–58), the Univ. of Toronto (1958–61), and the Univ. of Colorado (1961–68). Renowned for his lieder interpretations, he alternated with Peter Pears in the 1946 premieres of Britten's *The Rape of Lucretia.*

Schipa, Tito (b. Lecce, Italy, 2 Jan. 1888; d. New York, 16 Dec. 1965). Tenor. Trained at Milan; made his debut in 1910 at Vercelli; after singing throughout Italy and at Buenos Aires, bowed at La Scala in 1915; created Ruggiero in Puccini's *La rondine* in 1917. He sang at Chicago (1919–32), San Francisco (1925–40), and the Metropolitan Opera (1932–35, 1941), also appearing throughout Italy between 1929 and 1949; he appeared again at Buenos Aires in 1954, and toured the USSR in 1957.

Bibl.: Renzo D'Andrea, *Tito Schipa: Nella vita, nell'arte, nel suo tempo* (Fasano di Puglia, 1981).

Schippers, Thomas (b. Kalamazoo, Mich., 9 Mar. 1930; d. New York, 16 Dec. 1977). Conductor. Studied organ and piano, finishing high school at age 13; entered the Curtis Institute in 1945; made his conducting debut in 1948. From 1950 he worked closely with Menotti, conducting the televised premiere of *Amahl and the Night Visitors* in 1951 and directing the Spoleto Festival from 1958 to 1975. He made his Metropolitan Opera and La Scala debuts in 1955, and his Bayreuth debut in 1963. He led the premieres of Barber's *Antony and Cleopatra* (New York, 1966) and the stage version of Falla's *Atlántida* (La Scala, 1963). From 1970 to his death from cancer he led the Cincinnati Symphony, also teaching at the Cincinnati Conservatory from 1972.

Schirmer, Ernest Charles (b. Mount Vernon, N.Y., 15 Mar. 1865; d. Waban, Mass., 15 Feb. 1958). Publisher. Son of Gustav Schirmer; left the family firm in New York to work at the Boston Music Company, then founded his own publishing house in Boston in 1921 (E. C. Schirmer). His son E. C. Schirmer, Jr., took over until his death in 1966. His firm's publications include the music of many contemporary American composers, among them Copland, Felciano, Moore, Piston, Pinkham, and Thompson.

Schirmer, Gustav (b. Königsee, Germany, 19 Sept. 1829; d. Eisenach, 5 or 6 Aug. 1893). Music publisher. Son and grandson of piano makers in Sondershausen; 1840, emigrated with his family to U.S.; briefly apprenticed to a cabinetmaker, then employed by music dealers Scharfenberg and Luis. In 1854, manager of Kerksieg & Bruesing; 1861, in partnership with Bernard Beer acquired the firm; 1866, bought out Beer and established the firm as G. Schirmer. The business was carried on by his sons: Rudolph Edward (1859–1919), a graduate of Princeton and Columbia Law School, became president; Gustave (1864–1907), who had in 1885 moved to Boston, and founded the Boston Music Co., returned as secretary (Boston Music Co. affiliated with G. Schirmer from 1891). A third son, Ernest C. (1865–1958), after employment by G. Schirmer and Boston Music Co., founded (1921) his own firm, E. C. Schirmer.

Schiske, Karl (Hubert Rudolf) (b. Raab, Hungary, 12 Feb. 1916; d. Vienna, 16 June 1969). Composer. He was in Vienna from 1923, where he studied piano, composition, and musicology (D.Phil., 1942); professor of composition at the Vienna Music Academy from 1952. He was visiting professor at the Univ. of California (Riverside), 1966–67, and won the Austrian State Prize on his return to Vienna. Influenced by Hindemith, Schoenberg, and Stravinsky, his style is also indebted to his study of Netherlands polyphony. Works include 5 symphonies (1942–62) and a violin concerto (1952); oratorios and cantatas; 2 string quartets (1936, 1945) and a wind quintet (1945); piano and organ music; Psalm settings and a Mass (1954); and 3 volumes of songs.

Schlesinger, Maurice [Moritz Adolf] (b. Berlin, 3 Oct. 1797; d. Baden-Baden, 25 Feb. 1871). Publisher. Son of the publisher Adolf Martin Schlesinger (1769–1838). He worked for his father for a while before starting his own business in Paris in 1821. He published the works of Meyerbeer, Donizetti, Chopin, and Halévy. Wagner worked for the firm, 1840–42. In 1846 the firm was sold to Brandus. Founded the *Gazette musicale de Paris* (1834), which later joined with the *Revue musicale.*

Schlick, Arnolt (b. Heidelberg?, ca. 1460; d. there?, after 1521). Organist and composer. Blind from youth, he was court organist to the Count Palatine in Heidelberg; in artistic stature he ranked with Paul Hofhaimer of the imperial court. He is known to have played for the 1486 coronation of Maximilian I at Frankfurt, the 1495 Diet of Worms, and possibly the 1520 coronation of Charles V at Aachen. He tested and consulted on organs widely: Strasburg Cathedral (1491, 1512), Haguenau (1503, 1510, 1520, 1521), Speyer Cathedral (1505, 1513), the Torgau Saxon court (1516 with Hofhaimer), and elsewhere. He wrote the first printed German treatise on organ building, *Spiegel der Orgelmacher und Organisten* (Speyer, 1511; facs. and Eng.

trans., ed. E. B. Barber, Buren, 1978), and first printed German organ tabulature, *Tabulaturen etlichen lobgesang und lidlein* (Mainz, 1512; facs. 1977; ed. G. Harms, Hamburg, 1924, 1957). Among other extant works is a unique 10-voice (6 manual, 4 pedal) antiphon *Ascendo ad patrem meum* dedicated to Charles V. His organ style, though derived from vocal models, is notably idiomatic for its time.

Schlicker, Herman Leonhard (b. Hohentrüdingen, Bavaria, 31 Jan. 1902; d. Buffalo, N.Y., 4 Dec. 1974). Organ builder. After an apprenticeship and early work in Europe, he emigrated to the U.S. in 1925, where he worked first for Wurlitzer, then Tellers (Erie, Pa.). In 1932 he established his own company in Buffalo; it rose quickly in size and prominence. In 1963 he became the first major U.S. builder to adapt to the trend of classical reform; at his death nearly half the company's production was in mechanical action organs. The firm passed to his widow, Alice Hagman Schlicker, and son-in-law Rolfe Dinwoodie; in 1981 it was bought by Conrad and Theresa Van Viegen.

Schlippenbach, Alex [Alexander von] (b. Berlin, 7 Apr. 1938). Jazz pianist, composer, and bandleader. He studied with Zimmermann and Petzold at the Staatliche Hochschule für Music, Cologne. He joined the free-jazz groups of vibraphonist Gunter Hampel (1963–65) and trumpeter Manfred Schoof (1965–68). From 1966 he led the Globe Unity Orchestra, a big band performing conventional jazz themes, European folk tunes, and compositions by its members, and engaging in collective improvisation. Penderecki composed "Actions" for the group, whose albums include *Globe Unity* (1966) and *Improvisations* (1977). Schlippenbach also performed as a soloist and in duos and small groups with European free-jazz musicians.

Schlusnus, Heinrich (b. Braubach am Rhein, 6 Aug. 1888; d. Frankfurt, 18 June 1952). Baritone. Made his debut in 1915 at Hamburg; after a period at Nuremberg (1915–17) he joined the Berlin Staatsoper, remaining until 1945; he also appeared in recital and at opera houses in Europe, South America, and the U.S., and made many recordings. His operatic farewell took place at Koblenz in 1951. A Verdi specialist, he was known for his strong upper register.

Schmelzer [Schmeltzer, Schmelzer von Ehrenruef], **Johann Heinrich** (b. Scheibbs, Lower Austria, ca. 1620–23; d. Prague, between 29 Feb. and 20 Mar. 1680). Composer. It is not known who gave him his musical training or when he arrived in Vienna, but he began his service at the court chapel there (probably as a violinist) in 1635–36. On 1 October 1649 he officially became a violinist in the court orchestra. He was appointed Vice-Kapellmeister at the imperial court on 13 April 1671; on 24 November 1679 he became Kapellmeister. Schmelzer was influential in the development of the suite, and his *Sonatae unarum fidium* (1664) is the earliest publication in the German-speaking countries to contain exclusively sonatas for violin and continuo.

Schmidt, Franz (b. Pressburg, 22 Dec. 1874; d. Perchtoldsdorf, near Vienna, 11 Feb. 1939). Composer, conductor, pianist, and cellist. By 1888 when the family had moved to Vienna he was sufficiently advanced to earn his living as a pianist in dance schools; studied piano (with Leschetizky) and cello at the Vienna Conservatory. He was cellist in the Vienna Court Opera orchestra (1896–1911); taught cello at the Gesellschaft der Musikfreunde (1901–8); from 1914 taught piano (and later composition) at the Vienna Staatsakademie; directed the Staatsakademie (1925–27) and the Musikhochschule (1927–31). He retired from teaching and performing in 1937. Among his awards are the Beethoven Prize from the Prussian Academy in Berlin. He destroyed most of his youthful compositions and was known primarily as a symphonist; chamber and organ works are similar to those of Reger; other marked influences include Hungarian and Slovak elements, Austrian Baroque styles, and Brahms's variation technique. Works include 2 operas and an oratorio; 4 symphonies; Piano Concerto (left-hand, 1934); chamber, piano, and organ music.

Bibl.: Norbert Tschulik, *Franz Schmidt: A Critical Biography* (London, 1980). Harold Truscott, *The Music of Franz Schmidt* (London, 1984). Thomas Bernard Corfield, *Franz Schmidt, 1874–1939: A Discussion of His Style* (New York, 1989).

Schmidt-Isserstedt, Hans (b. Berlin, 5 May 1900; d. Holm-Hostein, near Hamburg, 28 May 1973). Conductor. Studied in Berlin; held posts at Wuppertal (to 1928), Rostock (1928–31), and Darmstadt (1931–33); led the Hamburg Opera between 1935 and 1942, and the Berlin State Opera from 1943 to 1945. He directed the Hamburg Radio Symphony from its 1945 inception until 1971, also conducting the Stockholm Philharmonic between 1955 and 1964 and making frequent guest appearances. Though an advocate of 20th-century music, he was a Mozart specialist, writing a dissertation on his operas (Münster, 1923).

Schmitt, Florent (b. Blamont, Meurthe-et-Moselle, 28 Sept. 1870; d. Neuilly-sur-Seine, Paris, 17 Aug. 1958). Composer. He studied at the conservatories in Nancy and Paris (with Dubois, Lavignac, Gédalge, Massenet, and Fauré) and won the Prix de Rome in 1900. In several early works he attempted to depict his travels in Europe, for example, in *Musiques de plein air* (suite for orchestra op. 44, 1897–99) and the piano duets *Feuuilets de voyage* and *Reflets d'Allemagne.* His reputation as a composer was formed by 3 early works: *Psalm 47* (1904), the Piano Quintet (1902–8), and *La tragédie de Salomé* (ballet, 1907; rev. as symphonic poem, 1910); all employ tonal harmonies, give principal position to rhythm events, and are cast in conventional forms. "La danse de l'effroi" from *La tragédie de Salomé* presages Stravinsky's *Rite of*

Spring in its rhythms and orchestration. Although his style changed little, in some later works such as the *Sonate libre en deux parties enchaînées* (violin and piano, 1918–19) Schmitt began to experiment with novel formal designs and occasionally to abandon his full orchestral keyboard style in favor of a sparer treatment. He was director of the Lyons Conservatory (1922–24) and wrote music criticism for *Le temps* (1929–39); was associated with the Société musicale indépendante from 1909, and became president of the Société nationale de musique in 1938.

Works: 3 ballets, incidental music, and film scores; orchestral music including the Symphonie concertante (with piano, op. 82, 1928–31), *Introit, récit et congé* (with cello, op. 113, 1951–52), and Symphony no. 2 (op. 137, 1958); 8 works for voices and orchestra; chamber music including *A tour d'anches* (op. 97, oboe, clarinet, bassoon, and piano, 1939–43), and *Pour presque tous le temps* (op. 134, flute and piano trio, 1956); piano and organ music; choral music and songs.

Bibl.: Y. Hucher and M. Raveau, *L'oeuvre de Florent Schmitt* (Paris, 1960).

Schnabel, Artur (b. Lipnik, Austria, 17 Apr. 1882; d. Axenstein, Switzerland, 15 Aug. 1951). Pianist. Moved to Vienna at age 7, studying with Hans Schmitt and Theodor Leschetizky and meeting Brahms and other leading Viennese figures; made his debut in 1890. He was based in Berlin between 1900 and 1933, appearing with the contralto Therese Behr, whom he married in 1905. He toured Europe, playing both solo and chamber music (Karl Flesch was a notable collaborator), and made his U.S. debut in 1921. He also composed, and in 1925 began a teaching career. In 1927 and 1928 he presented the entire piano sonata cycles of Beethoven and Schubert, respectively, in honor of the centenaries of their deaths. A 1930 appearance with Koussevitzky and the Boston Symphony established his U.S. reputation; between 1931 and 1935 he became the first pianist to record the complete Beethoven sonatas. After the rise of the Nazis he settled in London, teaching at Tremezzo during the summers; he teamed with Hindemith, Casals, and Huberman in a 1933 Brahms centenary cycle. He moved to the U.S. in 1939, and taught at the Univ. of Michigan between 1940 and 1945, but still his U.S. acclaim never rivaled that which he received in Europe. Cataracts slowed him in later life; his final performance took place at New York in early 1951. He created editions of Beethoven's sonatas (for which interpretation he was most renowned) and Diabelli Variations; as a composer he adopted the most progressive 20th-century idioms.

Bibl.: Artur Schnabel, *My Life and Music* (New York, 1988).

Schnebel, Dieter (b. Lahr, Baden, 14 Mar. 1930). Composer, writer on music, and theologian. He studied music at the Musikhochschule (1949–52), musicology and theology at the university (1952–55) in Tübingen. From 1955 to 1963 he worked as a curate and vicar in Kaiserlautern, and then taught religious studies in Frankfurt (1963–70) and Munich (from 1970). He wrote several volumes on contemporary music, including *K. Stockhausen: Texte* (Cologne, 1963–71) and *Mauricio Kagel* (Cologne, 1970); his collected essays are in *Denkbare Musik,* ed. Hans Rudolf Zeller (Cologne, 1971). His dissertation dealt with the music of Schoenberg, and his *Versuche I–III* (including *Compositio* for orchestra, 1955–64) are rooted in the serial procedures of Schoenberg, Webern, and Stockhausen. Later works began to challenge commonly held ideas about music, as in *für stimmen für,* in which texts are fragmented and overlaid to the point of incomprehensibility in order to free their primary meanings and expression (for example, helplessness or shrieking). The performer in *réactions 1* (instrument and audience, 1960–61) reacts to sounds made by the audience; the series *visible music* (I: Duo. conductor and instrumentalist, 1960–62; II: *nostalgie.* solo for conductor, 1962) removes organized sound itself from the concert situation; *ki-no* (night music for projectors and listeners) and *mo-no, musik zum lesen* (1968–69) define music only in verbal or graphic terms. *Mundstücke* (mouths and electronics, 1972) is an illustration of Schnebel's concern not only with vocal sounds but also with the human vocal apparatus itself. In addition, he made arrangements of works of Bach, Webern, Beethoven, and Wagner and wrote pieces for educational use (*Übungen und Klängen,* 1974–). Other works include *Missa: Dahlemer Messe* (4 soli, 2 choruses, orchestra, organ, 1984–87); *Mahler-Moment* (strings, 1985); *Raumklang X* (orchestra, 4 instrumental groups, 1987–88); *Zeichen-Sprache* (music theater work, 1989); *Chili "Music and Pictures on Kleist"* (3 narrators, 4 singers, instruments, 1989–91).

Bibl.: Werner Grünzweig, Gesine Schröder, Martin Supper, eds., *Schnebel 60* (Hofheim, 1990).

Schneider, (Abraham) Alexander (b. Vilnius, 21 Oct. 1908; d. New York, 2 Feb. 1993). Violinist. Studied in his home city (from 1918) and in Frankfurt (from 1924), and served as concertmaster of the Frankfurt Museum Orchestra; active also at Saarbrücken and Hamburg. He was second violinist in the Budapest Quartet from 1932 to 1944, settling in the U.S. in 1938. He played chamber music with various leading figures, then rejoined the Budapest Quartet between 1955 and 1967. In addition, he organized concert series; made guest appearances with U.S. orchestras; taught at the Univ. of Washington, the Royal Conservatory in Toronto, and at festivals.

Schneider, (Johann Christian) Friedrich (b. Alt-Waltersdorf, near Zittau, 3 Jan. 1786; d. Dessau, 23 Nov. 1853). Composer and conductor. Studied piano with his father, Johann Gottlob Schneider (1753–1840), later with Schönfelder and Unger at the Zittau Gymnasium. In 1804 his 3 piano sonatas were published. Entered Univ. of Leipzig in 1805. Named organist at St. Thomas's Church, Leipzig, in 1812. Conducted at Dessau in 1821. He may have premiered Beethoven's Piano Concerto no. 5 (Leipzig, 1811). Composed 7 operas, 4 Masses, 6 oratorios, 25 cantatas, 23 symphonies, 7 piano concertos, violin sonatas, flute sonata, cello sonata, miscellaneous sacred works, solo and part songs, shorter piano works.

Schneiderhan, Wolfgang (Eduard) (b. Vienna, 28 May 1915). Violinist. Studied with Ševčik and Winkler, playing the Mendelssohn Concerto at age 10 in Copenhagen; served as the Vienna Symphony's first concertmaster (1933–37), then moved to the Vienna Philharmonic (1937–41); also formed his own quartet. He taught at the Salzburg Mozarteum (1938–56), the Vienna Academy (1939–50), and the Lucerne Conservatory (from 1949), founding the Lucerne Festival Strings in 1956.

Schneitzhoeffer, Jean (b. Toulouse, 13 Oct. 1785; d. Paris, 4 Oct. 1852). Composer. He studied at the Paris Conservatory. Performed as timpanist at the Paris Opéra, 1815–23, and later was named *chef du chant* there. Taught choral classes at the conservatory, 1831–50; wrote a singing method. He composed some Masses and a number of ballets, including *Claire et Mectal* (1818), *Les Filets de Vulcain* (1826), *Le Sicilien ou l'Amour peintre* (1827), and his most successful work, *La sylphide* (1832). Many of his ballets were written for the dancer Tagliani.

Schnitger, Arp (b. Schmalenfleth, Oldenburg, 2 July 1648; d. Neuenfeld, 24 July 1719). Organ builder. He was apprenticed to his cousin Berendt Huess at Glückstadt in Holstein. He completed Huess's organ at St. Wilhadi, Stade, after the latter's death in 1676. From 1682 to 1687 he built his greatest organ at St. Nicolai, Hamburg. Two of his sons became organ builders: Johann Georg (Jürgen) (bapt. 4 Sept. 1690; d. after 1733), and Franz Caspar (bapt. 15 Oct. 1693; d. Netherlands, 1729). With his sons and assistants Schnitger built about 150 organs of all sizes throughout north Germany and the Netherlands; he also enlarged and rebuilt existing organs.

Bibl.: Gustav Fock, *Arp Schnitger und seine Schule* (Kassel, 1975).

Schnittke [Shnitke], **Alfred (Garrievich)** (b. Engels, near Saratov, Russia, 24 Nov. 1934). Composer and theorist. Began piano lessons while living with his family in Vienna, 1946–48; continued studies in the choral conducting department at a specialized music school in Moscow. At the Moscow Conservatory, studied counterpoint and composition with E. Golubev and orchestration with N. Rakov, 1953–58; in 1961, completed graduate studies under Golubev. From 1962 to 1972, taught theoretical subjects at the Moscow Conservatory. Elected to membership in the West Berlin Academie der Künst in 1981; Akademie der Künste of the German Democratic Republic and the Bayerische Akademie der Schönen Künste in Munich in 1986; Swedish Royal Academy of Music in 1987. Familiar to a broad spectrum of the Russian public as a composer of music to more than 60 films in addition to his serious compositions, Schnittke inherited the musical and moral stature of Shostakovich. In the 1960s he was among the first Soviets to experiment with serial, electronic, and other formerly forbidden techniques. By the beginning of the 1970s he had discarded strict serialism in favor of an original synthesis of historical styles for which he used the term "polystylistics." Taught at Hamburg Conservatory from 1989.

Works: Ballets *Labyrinths* (1971), *Sketches* (1985), *Peer Gynt* (1986); *Der gelbe Klang,* scenic composition after Kandinsky (1973–74); operas (*Zhizn's idiotom* [Life with an Idiot], 1992; *Gesualdo,* 1993–4; *Historia von D. Johann Fausten,* 1995); 8 symphonies and other orchestral music (*For Liverpool,* 1994; *Symphonic Prelude,* 1994); 6 concerti grossi (1979, 1981–82, 1985, 1988, 1991, 1993); violin concertos, piano concertos (concerto for piano 4-hands, 1989), cello concertos (no. 2, 1990), a viola concerto, and a triple concerto (1994); works for soloists and chorus (including the cantata "Seid Nüchtern und Wachet . . . ," 1983, and Concerto for Mixed Chorus, 1984–85); string quartets (no. 4, 1989), a string trio, a piano quintet, 2 violin sonatas and other chamber music; music for piano (Piano Sonata no. 2, 1990; no. 3, 1992); film music.

Bibl.: Tamara Burde, *Zum Leben und Schaffen des Komponisten Alfred Schnittke* (Kludenbach, 1993).

Schnorr von Carolsfeld, Ludwig (b. Munich, 2 July 1836; d. Dresden, 21 July 1865). Tenor. Studied with Julius Otto and at the Leipzig Conservatory. First solo appearance at Karlsruhe Opera in 1855 in *Norma* and *Der Freischütz.* Married the soprano Malvina Garrigues in 1860. Moved to Dresden, where he was the leading tenor until his death. Sang lieder, oratorios, and opera. Known especially for his performances of Tannhäuser and Lohengrin. He and his wife sang the first performance of *Tristan und Isolde* (10 June 1865).

Bibl.: Carl Henri Nicolai, *Ein ideales Sängerpaar, Ludwig Schnorr von Carolsfeld und Malwine Schnorr von Carolsfeld* (Copenhagen, 1937).

Schobert, Johann [Jean] (b. Silesia?, ca. 1735; d. Paris, 28 Aug. 1767). Composer. Nothing is known of his early life; he was in Paris by 1760 or 1761 and was employed in the service of the Prince of Conti. During the following several years he published his instrumental music at his own expense. In 1767 his comic opera *La garde-chasse et le braconnier* met with no success. During the 1760s Schobert had a significant influence on the young Mozart. The D major sonata of op. 3 seems greatly to have impressed the 7-year-old composer, who imitated it and others of Schobert in his Parisian and English sonatas. Mozart's earliest piano concerto drew on material from Schobert's sonatas, and in 1778 Mozart taught his Parisian students these works. Schobert's music is remarkable for its forward-looking formal and stylistic features, found especially in the keyboard music with accompanying instruments.

Bibl.: *Johann Schobert: Ausgewählte Werke,* ed. Hugo Riemann, *DDT* 39 (Leipzig, 1909; R: 1958).

Schoeck, Othmar (b. Brunnen, 1 Sept. 1886; d. Zurich, 8 Mar. 1957). Composer, conductor, and pianist. The son of a painter, he spent his childhood near Lake Lucerne; attended Zurich Industrial College; then after a brief period as an art student he went to the Zurich Conservatory to study music; later studied in Leipzig with Reger (1907–8). He began to write songs and operatic pieces as a student and had successful performances; when he returned to Switzerland he conducted various choruses in Zurich (1909–17) and then was appointed to conduct the orchestral concerts at St. Gall, from which he retired in 1944. He composed nearly 400 songs, often using texts by Eichendorff, Mörike, Hesse, and Goethe. His early Romanticism gave way after the First World War to a more expressionist stance; he often used instrumental ensembles with piano in his lieder and wrote linking interludes for the instruments.

Works: 5 operas (*Penthesilea,* Schoeck, after Kleist; 1924–25; Dresden, 1927) and other stage works; a few orchestral works including *Concerto quasi una fantasia* (violin and orchestra, 1911–12), cello and horn concertos (1947, 1951); chamber music including 2 string quartets (1912, 1923); a few piano pieces; choral music (Cantata, Eichendorff, baritone and male chorus, and piano or brass, piano, and percussion; 1933); and many songs (*Das Wandsbecker Liederbuch* op. 52, Claudius, cycle of 17 songs, 1936; *Das stille Leuchten* op. 60, Meyer, cycle of 28 songs, 1946; *Das holde Bescheiden* op. 62, Mörike, cycle of 36 songs, ca. 1950).

Bibl.: Derrick Puffett, *The Song Cycles of Othmar Schoeck* (Bern, 1982).

Arnold Schoenberg.

Schoenberg, Arnold (b. Vienna, 2 Sept. 1874; d. Los Angeles, 13 July 1951). Composer and theorist. His parents were of Hungarian Jewish origin, but Schoenberg (Schönberg) was raised as a Catholic in Vienna. He began violin lessons at age 8 and soon began to compose and arrange music for violin duet. After his father died (1890), he left school to clerk in a bank for five years but continued to study music, literature, and philosophy on his own; during that period he also taught himself the cello in order to play quartets with friends. He played in an amateur orchestra led by Alexander von Zemlinsky, who gave him his only formal instruction and criticized early works. In 1898 his String Quartet in D major was successfully performed before the members of the Wiener Tonkünstlerverein, to whom Zemlinksky had proposed it. In 1901 Schoenberg and his wife (Zemlinsky's sister) moved to Berlin, where he continued to arrange and conduct operettas and cabaret songs for a living until Strauss helped him to obtain the Liszt stipend and a post as composition teacher at the Stern Conservatory. He returned to Vienna after a year and a half, having composed the *Gurrelieder* (not yet orchestrated) and the tone poem *Pelleas und Melisande.* For one year he taught harmony and counterpoint at a new school organized by Dr. Eugenie Schwarzwald, and by 1904 had a nucleus of private pupils including Berg, Webern, and Egon Wellesz. By 1904–5 the Ansorge Verein had sponsored performances of several works, including songs, *Verklärte Nacht,* and *Pelleas und Melisande;* Mahler in particular was impressed. In October 1910 Schoenberg mounted a one-man exhibition of his paintings, which resulted in his lasting friendship with Kandinsky.

During the early period Schoenberg composed within the German Romantic tradition influenced by both Brahms (in his dependence on traditional forms) and Wagner (in his use of chromaticism and his intense subjectivity). The Chamber Symphony (8 winds, horns, and string quintet; op. 9, 1906) he considered the climax of his first period. By 1907 he was ready to abandon tonality and with it development in terms of thematic ideas. *Das Buch der hängenden Gärten* (op. 15, 1908–9) and the 3 Pieces for piano (op. 11, 1909) are composed around short intervallic series rather than around thematic material, so that progression of musical ideas from bar to bar is increasingly unclear; like the other works of this period it avoids key centers. The monodrama *Erwartung* (op. 17, 1909) exemplifies this expressionist period in its exploration of the psychological reality of its single female character reacting to her lover's murder. In *Pierrot lunaire* (op. 21, 1912) emotional subjectivity has reached an extreme; the singer employs *Sprechstimme,* abandoning the notated pitch immediately after it has been sung and sliding to the next. Many of the works of these years are miniatures (*6 Little Pieces* for piano op. 19, 1911); but in less than a decade the unfinished oratorio

Die Jakobsleiter (begun in 1917) was planned for large orchestra, small offstage orchestras and chorus, and a main chorus of hundreds in the tradition of Mahler and Strauss.

To ensure an income Schoenberg took on a heavy teaching schedule; in 1910 he taught composition at the Vienna Academy, but seeing little prospect for a professorship he moved once again to Berlin. He taught again at the Stern Conservatory, published his harmony textbook, and began to have successful performances (of *Pierrot lunaire, Gurrelieder,* and the *Five Orchestral Pieces*) in Vienna, Berlin, London, and elsewhere. His success in Vienna proved to be short-lived. A Viennese audience halted a concert of works by Schoenberg, Berg, and Webern only a few weeks after they had applauded the *Gurrelieder,* and "ever since that day the scandal has never ceased." In the next few years he conducted in several European cities, and had the support of a Viennese patron, Frau Lieser. He served briefly in the army, then returned to teach composition at the Schwarzwald school; most important, he formed with the help of some of his students the Society for Private Musical Performances. It functioned from 1919 to 1921, giving performances at which the press was not welcome, applause was banned, seats cost only what one could afford, and programs were not announced in advance. At 117 concerts 154 different works were presented, often in reductions for piano or chamber ensemble. Schoenberg conducted many of the performances himself. The war, his extensive concert activities, teaching commitments, and his need for a new method of composition all help to explain the silence (in terms of published works) from the *Four Orchestral Songs* (op. 22, 1916) to the *Five Piano Pieces* (op. 23, 1923).

The twelve-tone method he saw as an inevitable historical development. First, tonality had been replaced by extended tonality (Wagner) and impressionism (Debussy), in which harmonies no longer had clear constructive meanings: "In this way tonality was already dethroned in practice, if not in theory. This alone would perhaps not have caused a radical change in compositional technique. However, such a change became necessary when there occurred simultaneously a development which ended in what I call the emancipation of the dissonance" *(Style and Idea).* The ordering of a set of the twelve chromatic pitch classes, all of which were to be stated before any could be repeated, and systematic application of the processes of inversion, transposition, and retrogression to that set was fully developed by the early 1920s. It was first employed by Schoenberg in three pieces composed between 1920 and 1923 (the Piano Pieces op. 23, Serenade op. 24, and the Suite for Piano op. 25). He revealed the method to his students only in 1923, after Hauer had published details of his own method based on *Tropen,* or unordered hexachords. Schoenberg found the ideas of chromatic completion and the ordering of pitches missing in Hauer's formulation and so continued to claim priority for his own method. Along with the development of the twelve-tone method, by 1923 expressivity had given way to objectivity and classicism: the Suite for piano (op. 25, 1921–23) consists of prelude, gavotte with musette, intermezzo, minuet and trio, and gigue. The Third String Quartet, commissioned by Elizabeth Sprague Coolidge (op. 30, 1927), has the structure of classical symphony (sonata-allegro, set of variations, scherzo with trio, rondo), but forms are defined by repetition of thematic material rather than by tonality. In 1930 he began work on the opera *Moses und Aron,* to be based on a single tone row; the composer's libretto bears some similarity to that of a Wagnerian music drama. It remained unfinished at his death.

In the early 1920s he had conducted frequently outside Vienna and lectured in music theory in Amsterdam. His first wife died in the fall of 1923, but within a year he had remarried and soon moved back to Berlin to teach at the Prussian Academy of Arts, succeeding Busoni. The Nazis forced his dismissal from the academy in 1933; he left Berlin for France and immediately reconverted to Judaism. By October 1933 the family was in Boston, where Schoenberg taught at the Malkin Conservatory until May; the climate caused his health to deteriorate, and in the fall of 1934 they moved to California. He composed (another string quartet, the violin and piano concertos, *Ode to Napoleon*), taught privately, lectured at the Univ. of Southern California (1935–36), and then taught at UCLA until his health forced him to retire in 1944 (Kim and Cage were among his many U.S. students). He continued to teach privately, and for a brief period at the Univ. of Chicago; but a heart attack in 1946 further restricted his activities. The subject matter of the late vocal works indicates a new social consciousness, and many of his last works were religiously inspired. He simplified his style and allowed tonal implications in some passages; some works have traditional key signatures (*Kol Nidre* is in G minor; *Ode to Napoleon* makes use of tonal triads within the twelve-tone method).

Schoenberg's music is not easy to appreciate. He expected listeners to hear every complexity of the score, as they did in tonal music. Berg compared Schoenberg's position to that of Bach, as a transitional figure who reconciled the opposing characteristics of two musical styles. While conservatives attacked him for turning his back on the music of tonality, Schoenberg was criticized by the avant-garde serialists for not carrying far enough the implications of his method. Boulez's article "Schoenberg Is Dead" (*Score,* 1952) in particular argued that serialists had now to go beyond this method, and should reject Schoenberg's Romantic aesthetic and his dependence on classical forms. His pupils Berg and Webern were the most heavily influenced by his method, which spread rapidly after Webern's death in 1945. Among the many who adopted it are Boulez, Babbitt, and Nono; Stravinsky and Copland explored it as well. That no contemporary student of composition can ignore it perhaps says enough about the importance of Schoenberg's works and theories, however unreceptive audiences may be to performances.

Works: *Erwartung* (op. 17, monodrama, 1909; Prague, 1924), *Die glückliche Hand* (op. 18, drama with music, 1910–13; Vienna, 1924), *Von heute auf morgen* (op. 32, opera, 1928–29; Frankfurt, 1930), and *Moses und Aron* (opera, inc., 1930–32; acts 1–2 staged Zurich, 1957); orchestral music including *Pelleas und Melisande* (op. 5, symphonic poem, 1902–3), Chamber Symphony no. 1 (op. 9, 1906, arranged full orchestra, 1922), *Five Orchestral Pieces* (op. 16, 1909); Variations (op. 31, 1926–28), Violin Concerto (op. 36, 1935–36), Chamber Symphony no. 2 (op. 38, 1906–16), Piano Concerto (op. 42, 1942); chamber music including *Verklärte Nacht* (op. 4, string sextet, 1899), 4 string quartets (1905–1936), Serenade (op. 24, clarinet, bass clarinet, mandolin, guitar, violin, viola, cello, bass, 1920–23), Wind Quintet (op. 26, 1923–24), Suite in E flat (op. 29, clarinet/flute, clarinet, bass clarinet/bassoon, piano, violin, viola, cello, 1925–26), String Trio (op. 45, 1946); Phantasy (op. 47, violin and piano, 1949); piano and organ music; *Kol Nidre* (op. 39, speaker, chorus, orchestra, 1938), *A Survivor from Warsaw* (op. 46, narrator, male voices, orchestra, 1947), and other choral music; *Das Buch der hängenden Gärten* (op. 15, song cycle, 1909), *Dreimal sieben Gedichte aus Albert Girauds Pierrot lunaire* (op. 21, speaker, flute and piccolo, clarinet and bass clarinet, violin and viola, cello, piano, 1912), *Ode to Napoleon* (op. 41, reciter, piano, string quartet/strings, 1942), other songs with piano or orchestra; canons and arrangements.

Writings: *Style and Idea* (London, 1950); *Harmonielehre* (Vienna, 1911). *Structural Functions of Harmony* (completed 1948; New York, 1954).

Bibl.: R. Wayne Shoaf, *The Schoenberg Discography* (Berkeley, 1986). "Current Bibliography" in *Journal of the Arnold Schoenberg Institute* (1976–). Egon Wellesz, *Arnold Schönberg* (Vienna, 1921); trans., Eng., rev. (1925). René Leibowitz, *Schönberg et son école* (Paris, 1947); trans., Eng. (New York, 1949). Willi Reich, *Schoenberg: A Critical Biography,* trans. Leo Black (London, 1971). Alan Lessem, *Music and Text in the Works of Arnold Schoenberg* (Ann Arbor, 1970). Hans H. Stuckenschmidt, *Schönberg: Leben, Umwelt, Werk* (Zurich, 1974); trans. Eng. (1977). Charles Rosen, *Arnold Schoenberg* (New York, 1975). Martha M. Hyde, *Schoenberg's Concept of Multi-Dimensional Twelve-Tone Music* (Ann Arbor, 1982). Walter Baily, *Programmatic Elements in the Works of Schoenberg* (Ann Arbor, 1983). Jelena Hahl-Koch, ed., *Arnold Schoenberg/Wassily Kandinsky: Letters, Pictures, Documents,* trans. J. C. Crawford (London, 1984). Joan Allen Smith, *Schoenberg and His Circle: A Viennese Portrait* (New York, 1986). Carl Dahlhaus, *Schoenberg and the New Music* trans. Derrick Puffett and Alfred Clayton, (Cambridge and New York, 1987). Arnold Schoenberg, *Arnold Schoenberg Self-Portrait: A Collection of Articles, Program Notes, and Letters by the Composer about His Own Works* (Pacific Palisades, Calif., 1988). Ethan Haimo, *Schoenberg's Serial Odyssey: The Evolution of his Twelve-Tone Method, 1914–1928* (New York, 1990). Alexander L. Ringer, *Arnold Schoenberg—The Composer As A Jew* (New York, 1990). Silvina Milstein, *Arnold Schoenberg: Notes, Sets, Forms* (Cambridge, 1992). Walter Frisch, *The Early Works of Arnold Schoenberg, 1893–1908* (Berkeley, 1993). Mathias Hansen, *Arnold Schönberg, ein Konzept der Moderne* (Kassel, 1993). Colin C. Sterne, *Arnold Schoenberg: The Composer as Numerologist* (Lewiston, Me., 1993).

Schönbach, Dieter (b. Stolp-Pommern, 18 Feb. 1931). Composer. He studied composition in Detmold and Freiburg (1949–59) with Bialas and Fortner; then conducted the municipal theater in Bochum (1959–72), after which he moved to Basel. Active also as a pianist and as organizer of contemporary music concerts, Musica Viva. He was primarily influenced by post-Webern serialism, but turned in the 1960s toward the theatricalization of music. Works include *Farben und Klänge* (orchestra, in memory of Kandinsky, 1958); *Wenn die Kälte in die Hütten tritt, um sich bei den Frierenden zu wärmen, weiss einer "Die Geschichte von einem Feuer"* (multimedia opera, Kiel, 1968); *Hymnus 2* (multimedia, Munich, 1972); and liturgical cantatas with Latin texts.

Schorr, Friedrich (b. Nagyvárád, Hungary, 2 Sept. 1888; d. Farmington, Conn., 14 Aug. 1953). Baritone. He studied law at the Univ. of Vienna and singing with Adolf Robinson in Brno. In 1912 he made his debut in Graz as Wotan, beginning a career as the leading Wagnerian bass-baritone of his era. After Graz (1912–16) he sang at Prague (1916–18), Cologne (1918–23), the Berlin State Opera (1923–31), Bayreuth (1925–31 as a regular Wotan), Covent Garden (1925–33), and the Metropolitan (1924–43). Moving to the U.S. after the rise of the Nazis, he later taught at the Univ. of Hartford and was active as an adviser to the New York City Opera. His major roles included Wagner's Wotan, Hans Sachs, and the Dutchman, Beethoven's Pizarro, and Strauss's Orestes.

Schott, Bernhard (b. Eltville, 10 Aug. 1748; d. Sandholf, near Heidesheim, 26 Apr. 1809). Music publisher. In 1770 he founded a firm in Mainz that was carried on as B. Schotts Söhne by his sons Johann Andreas Schott (1781–1840) and Johann Joseph Schott (1782–1855). The firm published major late works of Beethoven (*Missa solemnis,* Ninth Symphony, quartets) and late operas of Wagner *(The Ring, Die Meistersinger, Parsifal).*

Schrader, Barry (b. Johnstown, Pa., 26 June 1945). Composer. He studied at the Univ. of Pittsburgh (B.A., 1967; M.F.A., 1970) and with Subotnick at the California Institute of the Arts, where he began teaching in 1971. He won an award in the first International Electronic Music Competition in Bourges, France (1973). Works include *Bestiary* (tape, 1972–73) and *Lost Atlantis* (tape, 1977); *Elysium* (harp, dancers, lights, tape, 1971); *Moon-Whales and Other Moon Songs* (soprano, tape, 1982–83); several film scores (*Death of the Red Planet,* 1972; *Mobiles,* 1978); and an outdoor sound environment for Otto Piene's *Sky Ballet* (1970).

Schreier, Peter (b. Meissen, 29 July 1935). Tenor. Studied in Dresden, singing in the Kreuzchor from 1945; made his opera debut in 1961; later sang throughout Germany, at La Scala, and with the Metropolitan Opera. He is best known for his interpretations of lieder and of the Evangelist's roles in Bach's Passions; also pursued conducting. His operatic roles range from Mozart to Loge in Wagner's *Das Rheingold.*

Bibl.: Peter Schreier, *Aus meiner Sicht: Gedanken und Erinnerungen* (Vienna, 1983).

Schreiner, Alexander (b. Nuremberg, 31 July 1901; d. Salt Lake City, 15 Sept. 1987). Organist. Moved to the U.S. in 1912; settled in Salt Lake City, studying with Mormon Tabernacle organist J. J. McClellan. He studied in Paris, 1924–26, and held a post at UCLA in the 1920s; 1939–77 he was head organist at the Mormon Tabernacle. He composed and arranged much music for his instrument, and in 1984 published a volume of reminiscences.

Schreker, Franz (b. Monaco, 23 Mar. 1878; d. Berlin, 21 Mar. 1934). Composer and conductor. He studied violin and composition at the Vienna Conservatory (1892–1900), a period during which various of his student works were performed and attracted attention (*Love Song,* strings and harp, London, 1896; *Abiturienarbeit,* female chorus and orchestra, Vienna, 1900; *Flammen,* 1-act opera, Vienna, 1902). His ballet *Der Geburtstag der Infantin* was a major success in Vienna in 1908; the reception of his first major opera, *Der ferne Klang* (1901–12), in its premiere in Frankfurt am Main (1912) led to his appointment as a teacher of composition at the Music Academy in Vienna. He founded in 1912, and conducted until 1920, the Philharmonic Choir, which gave many premieres (including that of Schoenberg's *Gurrelieder*). In 1920 Schreker left Vienna to become head of the Berlin Hochschule für Musik, but the rise of the Nazis effectively ended his career after little more than a decade. He was compelled to resign as head of the Hochschule in 1932; taught briefly at the Prussian Academy of Arts; after his dismissal in 1933 he suffered a heart attack from which he did not recover. In *Die ferne Klang* and *Das Spielwerk und die Prinzessin* he drew on French impressionism to create a nonfunctional and coloristic harmony; 2 subsequent operas (*Die Gezeichneten,* 1918; *Der Schatzgräber,* 1920) reverted to a more Wagnerian harmonic language. In later operas, however, he employed bitonality and polytonality and a more dissonant harmonic language stemming from a greater emphasis on linear counterpoint. Works include 9 operas and other stage music; orchestral music including a Chamber Symphony (23 instruments, 1916); *Schwanengesang* (chorus and orchestra, 1902) and other choral music; a few chamber and piano works, mainly unpublished; and songs.

Bibl.: Friedrich C. Heller, ed., *Der Franz-Schreker-Fonds in der Musiksammlung der Österreichischen Nationalbibliothek: Katalog* (Vienna, 1975). Eckhardt van den Hoogen, *Die Orchesterwerke Franz Schrekers in ihrer Zeit: werkanalytische Studien* (Regensburg, 1981). Peter Franklin, "Style, Structure and Taste: Three Aspects of the Problem of Franz Schreker," *PRMA* 109 (1982–83): 134–46.

Schröder, Jaap (b. Amsterdam, 31 Dec. 1925). Violinist. Trained in his home city and in Paris; later played in the Hilversum Radio Chamber Orchestra and the Netherlands String Quartet. From 1975 to 1981 he led the authentic-instrument Quartetto Esterhazy, and then became a major figure in the Academy of Ancient Music, London, with which he made many recordings. Since 1982 has performed with various ensembles at the Smithsonian Institution.

Schröder-Devrient, Wilhelmine (b. Hamburg, 6 Dec. 1804; d. Coburg, 26 Jan. 1860). Soprano. Daughter of baritone Friedrich Schröder (1744–1816). Debut in Vienna in 1821 as Pamina in *Die Zauberflöte.* Sang Leonore in *Fidelio* in Vienna in 1822, catapulting her to international fame. Appeared at Dresden (1823–47), Paris (1830–32), London (1832, 1833, 1837). Created 3 Wagner roles: Adriano in *Rienzi* (1842), Senta in *Der fliegende Holländer* (1843), and Venus in *Tannhäuser* (1845). Schumann dedicated "Ich grolle nicht" (1840) to her. Known especially for her roles as Donna Anna, Euryanthe, Rienzi, Norma, Romeo, Valentine, and Desdemona (in Rossini's *Otello*). Dubbed the "Queen of Tears" for her dramatic power. Schumann claimed she was the only singer who could survive Liszt as an accompanist. She retired in 1847.

Bibl.: Alfred von Wolzogen und Neuhaus, *Wilhelmine Schröder-Devrient* (Leipzig, 1863). Carl Hagemann, *Wilhelmine Schröder-Devrient* (Berlin, 1904; 2nd ed., 1947).

Schröter, Christoph Gottlieb (b. Hohnstein, Saxony, 10 Aug. 1699; d. Nordhausen, 20 May 1782). Composer, theorist, and instrument maker. Following early training from his father, he was sent in 1706 to Dresden, where he sang soprano at the royal chapel and studied keyboard with J. C. Schmidt, the Kapellmeister. In 1710 he and C. H. Graun became town descantists. When his voice broke he continued his studies with Schmidt at the Kreuzschule. After studying theology at Leipzig in 1717, he returned to Dresden the following year and became music copyist to Antonio Lotti. From 1719 to 1724 he traveled to the Netherlands, England, and various German courts in the service of an unidentified baron. In 1724 he gave lectures at Jena Univ. and formed a collegium musicum there, becoming one of the first in Germany to return music to the university curriculum. He became organist at Minden in 1726, and in 1732 obtained a similar position at Nordhausen, remaining there for the following 50 years, composing sacred music and producing many theoretical books and essays. Schröter claimed that his compositions, none of which were published or survive, included 5 cantata cycles, 4 Passions, a *Sieben Worte Jesu,* and numerous instrumental works. His most important writing is the thoroughbass treatise *Deutliche Anweisung zum General-Bass* (1772), which had been completed in 1754. Although he stated that he had invented the piano in 1717, Cristofori's work (of which he seems to have been unaware) predates his.

Schröter, Corona Elisabeth Wilhelmine (b. Gruben, 14 Jan. 1751; d. Ilmenau, 23 Aug. 1802). Singer and composer. She studied with her father, the oboist Johann Friedrich Schröter, then with J. A. Hiller in Leipzig, where she appeared in Hiller's Grand Concerts from 1765 and became prominent in musical circles. In 1776 Goethe arranged her appointment to the court of Duchess Anna Amalia in Weimar, where she created many of the leading roles in his early dramas. From 1783 to 1788 she gradually withdrew from the court, taking up poetry, drawing, and painting, and befriending Schiller. She wrote and published 2 collections of lieder in 1786 (with the first setting of Goethe's "Der Erlkönig") and 1794.

Bibl.: Marcia J. Citron, "Corona Schroter: Singer, Composer, Actress," *ML* 61 (1980): 15–27.

Schubart, Christian Friedrich Daniel (b. Obersontheim, Swabia, 24 Mar. 1739; d. Stuttgart, 10 Oct. 1791). Composer. After studying music with his father and G. W. Gruber in Nuremburg, he entered Erlangen Univ. (1758). He then held organ posts at Geisslingen (1763–69) and Ludwigsburg (from 1769), where he was also harpsichordist at the Duke of Württemberg's court opera house. Banished from Württemberg because of his licentious life-style (1773), he moved to Augsburg (1774) and established his periodical *Deutsche Chronik;* continued publication from Ulm (1775–77). His political criticism of the Catholic church and various courts angered the nobility. In 1777 he was imprisoned by Duke Carl Eugen of Württemberg for ten years, during which time he wrote his autobiography (Stuttgart, 1791–93), his *Ideen zu einer Ästhetik der Tonkunst* (Vienna, 1806), and many compositions. In 1787 he became court and theater poet in Stuttgart and resumed publication of his periodical. He wrote many lieder, most set to his own texts. Schubert set his poems "Die Forelle" and "An mein Klavier."

Schubert, Franz (b. Dresden, 22 July 1808; d. there, 12 Apr. 1878). Violinist and composer. He studied with his father, Franz Anton Schubert, and with C. P. Lafont in Paris. He joined the Royal Orchestra at Dresden in 1823. In 1861 he was appointed leader of the Dresden Orchestra. His wife was the singer Maschinke Reval (1815–82). He was a friend of Chopin. His compositions include works for violin and piano.

Schubert, Franz Peter (b. Vienna, 31 Jan. 1797; d. there 19 Nov. 1828). Composer. His father, Franz Theodor Florian Schubert, born in Moravia, was a teacher who emigrated to Vienna, where in 1785 he married Maria Elisabet Vietz. Franz Peter was the youngest of the couple's four surviving sons; he and his brothers assisted their father in schoolteaching duties. Schubert's father was his first violin instructor, his

Franz Schubert.

brother Ignaz his first piano teacher. Parish organist Michael Holzer taught him counterpoint, singing, and organ. In 1808 Schubert was admitted into the choir of the imperial chapel, also becoming a student of the K. K. Stadtkonvikt school. There he met Josef von Spaun, eight years his senior, and joined the student orchestra Spaun had formed. He quickly advanced to the head of the first violin section; he also conducted the orchestra on occasion, gaining an acquaintance with symphonic works of Haydn and Mozart. Schubert and Spaun formed an intricate friendship, the first of a number of close relationships with poets and artists that the composer was to maintain throughout his life.

Around 1810 imperial composer Antonio Salieri took charge of Schubert's advanced musical instruction. In 1811 the youth attended an opera for the first time, Joseph Weigl's popular *Schweizerfamilie.* Schubert's studies at the Stadtkonvikt ceased around 1812, but he continued counterpoint lessons with Salieri until about 1816. Late in 1813 he entered a teachers' training school, possibly against his own will, and the following year he was already teaching elementary pupils at his father's school. His own first setting of the Mass, D. 105, was performed in 1814 as part of the celebrations for the Congress of Vienna. That year he also composed his first important Goethe songs, including "Gretchen am Spinnrade." During 1815 he completed symphonies 2 and 3, several chamber and choral works, and more than 100 songs (including "Rastlose Liebe" and "Erlkönig"), while supporting himself as a full-time teacher. He also composed four dramatic works in

1814–15 (including *Des Teufels Lustschloss*), none of which, however, was to reach the stage until after the composer's death. In 1816 Schubert, not yet 20, initiated his first attempt to survive on his own and make a living as a musician: he moved in with the mother of his friend Franz von Schober and began seeking a position as music instructor. That year he met Spaun's friend Josef Witteczek, in whose home the famous Schubertiade concerts were later to take place. Also that year Spaun sent to Goethe a collection of his friend's settings of Goethe's verse; the poet sent them back. During 1817 Schubert composed the Symphony no. 6 and many songs, including "Der Tod und das Mädchen."

In 1818 Schubert was finally offered the post he sought, as music master for Count Johann Esterházy's daughters. He resigned his post at the Rossau school, where he and his father had begun teaching the year before, and moved to the count's summer palace at Zseliz. Late that year he composed his *Deutsches Requiem* D. 621 for his brother Ferdinand, who tried to pass the work off as his own. He returned to Vienna with the Esterházy family in late 1818; shortly afterward he moved in with the poet Johann Mayrhofer. During the summer of 1819, which he spent with baritone Johann Michael Vogl in the idyllic village of Steyr, he began the Trout Quintet. (It was Vogl who programmed a number of Schubert's songs in his concerts in Vienna.) Late 1819 and early 1820 was an especially productive period: he completed the A♭ Mass D. 678, began the oratorio *Lazarus* (which remained incomplete), and prepared *Die Zwillingsbrüder* for production. The latter was his first opera to reach the stage, at the Kärntnertortheater; it was performed only five times, however, beginning June 14. Two months later the melodrama *Die Zauberharfe* was performed at the Theater an der Wien; it too was received coolly.

Late in 1820 Schubert composed one movement (Quartettsatz D. 703) of a Quartet in C minor; the piece manifests for the first time the full maturity of his instrumental style. In 1821 the firm of Cappi & Diabelli published 20 of the composer's best-known songs, which sold prodigiously. At the same time, Schubert collaborated with Schober in what is perhaps his best opera, *Alfonso und Estrella;* the work's completion coincided with a change in the management of the Kärntnertortheater, however, and *Alfonso* had to wait until long after Schubert's death for its first performance (Leipzig, 1854). In 1821 Schubert also made the acquaintance of Moritz von Schwind, the painter who was later to create the famous depiction of Schubert's circle of friends, *Schubert-Abend bei Joseph von Spaun.* The following year Schubert, now lodging with Schober, composed the first two movements of a symphony that he was never to complete (the Unfinished, no. 8 in B minor). That year he also composed the Mass in A♭, D. 789, the Wanderer Fantasy in C, and a number of songs to Goethe's verse, including "Am Flusse" D. 766. During the second half of 1822, or possibly somewhat earlier, Schubert first became aware of a serious illness, possibly (though not certainly) syphilis. His final years comprised a succession of illnesses. Yet despite his first severe attack, which struck in 1823, he began work on *Die schöne Müllerin* and on the opera *Fierabras.* The latter was rejected by the management of the Kärntnertortheater. The composer's incidental music to the stage drama *Rosamunde* was performed in late 1823, using the overture to *Alfonso.* (*Rosamunde* was later published with that overture, which as a result mistakenly came to be called the *Rosamunde* Overture.)

Schubert spent the summer of 1824 again in the employ of the Esterházy family. In 1825 he moved to Wieden to be near Schwind. The composer's last years, during which he was frequently quite ill, were occupied with the song cycle *Die Winterreise,* the last three piano sonatas, and Symphony no. 9 (the "Great"), the last probably having been begun in 1825 in Gmunden. In March 1828 he presented a concert of his own works before an appreciative Viennese audience. As his health continued to fail, he moved in with his brother Ferdinand. In August he completed his final group of songs, published posthumously as *Schwanengesang,* just three months before finally succumbing (apparently) to symptoms of tertiary syphilis.

Works: Stage works include *Des Teufels Lustschloss* (singspiel, text by August von Kotzebue, 1811–12); *Die Freunde von Salamanka* (singspiel, Johann Mayrhofer, 1815); *Die Zwillingsbrüder* (singspiel, Georg von Hofmann, 1819); *Die Zauberharfe* (melodrama, Georg von Hofmann, 1820); *Alfonso und Estrella* (opera, Franz von Schober, 1821–22); *Die Verschworenen* (singspiel, Ignaz F. Castelli, 1823); *Fierabras* (opera, Josef Kupelwieser, 1823). Sacred music includes 6 Masses; *Deutsches Requiem* in G minor D. 621 (1818); *Deutsche Messe* in F D. 872 (2 vers., 1827); *Lazarus, oder Die Feier der Auferstehung,* oratorio, fragment (1820); Salve Regina in F D. 223 (2 versions, 1815 and 1823); Six Antiphons, Palm Sunday, D. 696 (1820). Secular choral music, including some 40 pieces for SAT and SATB, with and without piano; more than 100 works for male voices (TTB and TTBB) and more than 20 for female voices. Ten symphonies, including no. 8 in B minor ("Unfinished," 1822); no. 9 in C ("Great," 1825–28). Chamber music, including 17 string quartets; Piano Quintet in A (Die Forelle [Trout]) D. 667 (1819); Piano Trios in B♭ D. 898 and in E♭ D. 929 (both probably 1828); Fantasy in C D. 934 (1827); Octet in F D. 803 (string and winds, 1824); Introduction and Variations on "Trockne Blumen" D. 802 (flute and piano, 1824). More than 600 songs, including song cycles *Die schöne Müllerin* D. 795 (20 songs, 1823) and *Winterreise* D. 911 (24 songs in 2 books, 1827); *Schwanengesang* D. 957 (14 songs in 2 books, 1828).

Piano music: 18 complete sonatas for solo piano and numerous incomplete ones; Fantasy in C D. 760 (Wandererfantasie, 1822); Moments musicals (6) D. 780 (1823–28); Impromptus; dances for piano (ländler, deutsche, ecossaises, minuets); works for piano 4-hands.

Bibl.: *Franz Schuberts Werke: Kritisch durchgesehene Gesamtausgabe,* ed. Johannes Brahms et al., 21 ser. (Leipzig, 1884–97; R: 19 vols., New York, 1965). *Franz Peter Schubert: Neue Ausgabe sämtlicher Werke,* ed. Internationale Schubert-Gesellschaft (Kassel & New York, 1964–). Otto Erich Deutsch and Donald R. Wakeling, *Schubert: A Thematic Catalogue*

(London, 1951); trans. Ger., rev. and enl., Walther Dürr et al., as *Franz Schubert: Thematisches Verzeichnis seiner Werke* (in *Neue Ausgabe sämtlicher Werke* 8/4, Kassel, 1978; also "kleine Ausgabe" Kassel & Munich, 1983) (=D). Otto Erich Deutsch, ed., *Franz Schubert: die Dokumente seines Lebens* (Munich, 1914; enl. 2nd ed., Kassel, 1964, as *Neue Ausgabe sämtlicher Werke,* 8/5); trans. Eng., Eric Blom, as *Schubert: A Documentary Biography* (London, 1946; American ed. *The Schubert Reader,* New York, 1947). Eva Badura-Skoda and Peter Branscombe, eds., *Schubert Studies: Problems of Style and Chronology* (Cambridge, 1982). Walter Frisch, ed., *Schubert: Critical and Analytical Studies* (Lincoln, Neb., & London, 1986). John Reed, *Schubert* (London, 1987). Ernst Krenek, *Franz Schubert: Ein Porträt* (Tutzing, 1990). Elizabeth Norman McKay, *Franz Schubert's Music for the Theatre* (Tutzing, 1991). Walther Dürr and Arnold Feil, *Franz Schubert* (Stuttgart, 1991). Richard Kramer, *Distant Cycles: Schubert and the Conceiving of Song* (Chicago, 1994). Marcel Schneider, *Schubert* (Paris, 1994).

Schuch, Ernst (Edler) von (b. Graz, 23 Nov. 1846; d. Kötzschenbroda, near Dresden, 10 May 1914). Conductor. Studied at Graz, Vienna, and Breslau. Debut as a conductor in Breslau in 1867; director Dresden Court Opera, 1872–1914. Directed the premieres of Strauss's *Feuersnot* (1901), *Salome* (1905), *Elektra* (1909), and *Der Rosenkavalier* (1911). Directed first Dresden performances of *Das Ring, Tristan und Isolde, Die Meistersinger,* many of the operas of Puccini, and *Cavalleria rusticana.* From 1877 he conducted the Königliche Kapelle concerts, performing many of the works of Mahler, Reger, Pfitzner, Ravel, Elgar, and Debussy. Married to the soprano Clementine Schuch-Proska (1850–1932).

Bibl.: F. von Schuch, *Richard Strauss, Ernst von Schuch und Dresdens Opera* (Dresden, 1952).

Schuëcker, Edmund (b. Vienna, 16 Nov. 1860; d. Bad Kreuznach, 9 Nov. 1911). Harpist and composer. Studied with Zamara at the Vienna Conservatory (1871–77). Solo harpist in Park Orchestra, Amsterdam (1877–82); Parlow Orchestra, Hamburg (1882–83); Dresden Staatskapelle (1883–84); Chicago Symphony Orchestra (1891); Pittsburgh Symphony Orchestra (1903–4); Philadelphia Orchestra (1904–9). Taught at Leipzig Conservatory (1884–91). Composed much music for solo harp, including etudes and transcriptions from operas. His brother Heinrich Schuëcker (1867–1913) was harpist for the Boston Symphony Orchestra beginning 1885. His son Joseph E. Schuëcker (1886–1938) was solo harpist for the Pittsburgh Symphony and Philadelphia Orchestra.

Schulhoff, Erwin (b. Prague, 8 June 1894; d. Wülzbourg, 18 Aug. 1942). Composer and performer. From 1904 through 1906 he studied at the Prague Conservatory with Kaan. Then he traveled to Vienna to study with Thern and to Leipzig (1908–10) and Cologne (1911–14). After the war he settled in Germany, 1919–23, and was active there within the circles of young artists. Back in Prague in the late 1920s he taught at the university from 1929 to 1931. From 1935 through 1938 he was a performer for Czech Radio, first in Ostrava and then in Brno. Concurrently he performed both jazz and new music on the piano, being the first to introduce the quarter-tone works of Hába. He eventually became a Soviet citizen, which, in combination with his Jewish background, led to his imprisonment and death in a German concentration camp. His music drew on contemporary avant-garde trends of western Europe, including serialism, the highly expressive chromaticism of Schoenberg, as well as folk elements and Soviet currents of socialist realism in art. His works include 1 ballet; 1 opera; orchestral works (6 symphonies and a Concerto for String Quartet and Winds, 1930); vocal music (*HMS Royal Oak,* jazz oratorio, 1930); and chamber music (2 string quartets, 1924, 1925; 2 sonatas for piano, 1924, 1926).

Bibl.: Gottfried Eberle, ed., *Erwin Schulhoff: Die Referate des Kolloquiums in Köln am 7. Oktober 1992* (Hamburg, 1993).

Schuller, Gunther (b. New York, 22 Nov. 1925). Composer, conductor, author, educator. Educated at the St. Thomas Choir School and the Manhattan School of Music, he was a precocious performer on the French horn. He became first horn with the Cincinnati Orchestra in 1943. In 1945 he joined the Metropolitan Opera Orchestra in New York, where he remained until 1959. During this period he became involved in the New York jazz scene, playing horn in ensembles and on recordings with Miles Davis, John Lewis, and others. He had begun composing as a teenager. In the late 1940s his compositions fell under the influence of Schoenberg and twelve-tone music on the one hand and modern jazz on the other. This dual influence is heard in works such as *Twelve by Eleven* (1955) written for the Modern Jazz Quartet, *Transformation* (1956) for small ensemble, Woodwind Quintet (1958), and Concertino for Jazz Quartet and Orchestra (1959). In a 1957 lecture he coined the term "Third Stream" to refer to such efforts at creating a musical middle ground between jazz and "classical" music. Other works of this period—for example, the String Quartet no. 1 (1958), *Seven Studies on Themes of Paul Klee* (1957) for orchestra, and *Spectra for Orchestra* (1958)—contain less overt jazz influence.

In 1959 Schuller resigned from the Metropolitan Opera orchestra to devote more time to composing. The next few years saw a great number of new works, notably *Variants for Jazz Quartet and Orchestra* (1960), *Music for Brass Quintet* (1961), *Meditation* (1963) for concert band, *American Triptych: A Study in Textures* (1965) for orchestra, and *The Visitation* (Hamburg, 1966), an opera based on Kafka's *The Trial,* but with the action moved to the American South. Schuller also became active as a teacher and administrator. In 1963 he was appointed composition teacher at the Berkshire Music Center (Tanglewood), where he subsequently became director (1974–84). He also taught composition at the Yale School of Music (1964–67). In 1967 he became president of the New England Conservatory of Music, a position he retained until 1977. As an administrator and as a conductor, Schuller worked to promote modern music in general, the works of young American composers, and the acceptance of jazz into the musical mainstream. As founder of the New England Conservatory Ragtime Ensemble, he participated in the ragtime revival of the 1970s. Compositions from these years include *Museum Piece* (1970) for Renaissance instruments with modern orchestra, *Deai (Encounters)* (1978) for 3 orchestras and 8 voices, *Eine kleine Posaunenmusik* (1980), trombone and wind ensemble, and *In Praise of Winds—Symphony for Large Wind Orchestra* (1981). In 1991 he was awarded a MacArthur Foundation Grant, and in 1994 received a Pulitzer Prize for the orchestral work "Of Reminiscences and Reflections."

Schuller is the author of a *History of Jazz,* of which the first 2 volumes are *Early Jazz: Its Roots and Development* (London and New York, 1968) and *The Swing Era: The Development of Jazz, 1930–1945* (London and New York, 1988), and also of *Horn Technique* (London and New York, 1962).

Bibl.: Norbert Carnovale, *Gunther Schuller, A Bio-Bibliography* (New York, 1987). Gunther Schuller, *Musings: The Musical Worlds of Gunther Schuller* (New York, 1986).

Schulz [Schultz]**, Johann Abraham Peter** (b. Lüneburg, 31 Mar. 1747; d. Schwedt an der Oder, 10 June 1800). Composer. He received his education in Lüneburg at the Lateinschulen but also had musical instruction with the town organist. In 1765 he went to Berlin to study with Kirnberger; in 1768 he became teacher and accompanist to the Polish princess Sapieha Woiwodin von Smolensk, with whom he traveled through France, Italy, Austria, and Poland. After returning to Berlin in 1773, he was involved with J. G. Sulzer's *Allgemeine Theorie der schönen Künste,* for which he wrote all of the music articles from S to Z. He also began composing more regularly at this point: his first opera, *Clarissa, oder Das unbekannte Dienstmädchen,* was produced in Berlin in 1775. He was named musical director to the Berlin French theater in 1776, Hofkapellmeister in Rheinsburg in 1786–87 and in Copenhagen in 1787–95. He is best known for his numerous collections of lieder; the first collection, *Gesänge am Clavier,* was published in 1779, the first volume of the second, *Lieder im Volkston,* in 1782. He wrote several stage works, oratorios, cantatas, other sacred and secular vocal pieces, and some instrumental pieces. His writings include (with Kirnberger) *Die wahren Grundsätze zum Gebrauche der Harmonie* (1773), *Entwurf einer neuen und leichtverständlichen Musiktablatur* (1786), and *Über den Choral und die ältere Literatur desselben* (2nd ed., 1872).

Bibl.: Bathia Churgin, "The Symphony as Described by J. A. P. Schulz (1974): A Commentary and Translation," *CM* 29 (1980): 7–16.

Schuman, William (Howard) (b. New York, 4 Aug. 1910; d. New York, 16 Feb. 1992). Composer, educator, administrator. Largely self-taught as an instrumentalist, he organized a jazz band in high school and wrote popular songs to lyrics by his friends Edward Marks, Jr., and Frank Loesser. In 1930 he heard his first orchestral concert: Toscanini conducting Wagner, Kodály, and Schumann at Carnegie Hall. The experience was decisive. Schuman withdrew from New York Univ., where he was studying business, and undertook to study composition, first with Max Persin, then with Charles Haubiel, later with Roy Harris. He also attended Columbia Univ. Teachers College, receiving a B.S. in 1935. That year he started teaching music at Sarah Lawrence College, where he remained until 1945. Meanwhile he began to establish himself as a composer. A symphony (1936), a quartet (1936), and a cantata (*Pioneers,* 1937) were all withdrawn soon after their first performances. Symphony no. 2 (1938), though it too was later withdrawn, received a performance by the Boston Symphony Orchestra under Koussevitzky and attracted much critical attention, largely unfavorable. *American Festival Overture* (1939; composed on commission from Koussevitzky), String Quartet no. 3 (1939), and Symphony no. 3 (1941) were more successful. With Symphony no. 5 (Symphony for Strings) (1943), *A Free Song,* a cantata on texts by Whitman (1942; Pulitzer Prize, 1943), and *Circus Overture* (1944), Schuman's reputation was secure.

In 1945 Schuman was appointed president of the Juilliard School of Music. There he introduced a new curriculum, revived the school's opera department, and created a dance division. He established the Juilliard String Quartet as quartet-in-residence at the conservatory, a pioneering example of what has become a familiar institution. Compositions from this period include *Night Journey,* a ballet composed for Martha Graham (1947); Symphony no. 6 (1948); *Judith,* another ballet for Graham (1949); String Quartet no. 4 (1950); *New England Triptych* (1956), an orchestral suite based on tunes by William Billings; and *Carols of Death* (1958) for unaccompanied chorus. He also composed his only opera, *The Mighty Casey* (Hartford, Conn., 1953), based on Ernest L. Thayer's poem "Casey at the Bat" (revised in 1976 as a concert piece for chorus and orchestra).

In 1962 Schuman left his job at Juilliard to become president of Lincoln Center, just being built as a center for the performing arts. Besides moving the Juilliard School to Lincoln Center, he brought the New York City Ballet and the New York City Opera there, created the Chamber Music Society of Lincoln Center, and initiated summer events such as the Mostly Mozart series. The pressures of his very public position left Schuman less time to compose. Symphony no. 8 (1962) was premiered by the New York Philharmonic during its first season at Lincoln Center. Symphony no. 9 *(Le Fosse Ardeatine)* was finished in 1968. Schuman's orchestration of Charles Ives's *Variations on America* (1963) was also composed during this period. In 1968, after a mild heart attack, Schuman resigned from Lincoln Center. Freed of his administrative duties, he composed more: *In Praise of Shahn (Canticle for Orchestra)* (1969); Symphony no. 10 (1975); *The Young Dead Soldiers,* chorus and orchestra (1975); *American Hymn,* brass quintet (1980); *A Question of Taste,* opera (1981); *On Freedom's Ground,* baritone, chorus, and orchestra (1985).

Bibl.: Flora Schreiber and Vincent Persichetti, *William Schuman* (New York, 1954). William Schuman and Christopher Rouse, *William Schuman Documentary (Biographical Essay, Catalogue of Works, Discography and Bibliography)* (New York, 1980).

Schumann [née Wieck], **Clara (Josephine)** (b. Leipzig, 13 Sept. 1819; d. Frankfurt am Main, 20 May 1896). Pianist, composer. First child of Friedrich Wieck, who intended her to be a concert pianist, giving her almost no general education but a rigorous musical training. In 1824 her mother left; Clara seldom saw her thereafter during childhood. Gewandhaus debut in 1830 and first tour, 1830–32, through Germany to Paris. From 1830 Robert Schumann lived with the Wiecks. His affectionate, playful, idealistic (though ultimately unstable) nature contrasted with Friedrich Wieck's harsh rigidity; by 1835 he and Clara were romantically involved. Her father's vehement opposition led to a three-year battle and recourse to the courts before they could marry (12 Sept. 1840). In the meantime, through her concerts and tours (especially to Vienna in 1837–38, where she created a furor), Clara had become established as a great artist. Her marriage markedly reduced her freedom to play, tour, and compose. Between 1841 and 1854 she bore eight children, resuming concerts when she was able, partly for financial reasons and rather against Schumann's inclinations, although she was a major factor in his growing reputation as a composer.

Robert Schumann was always introverted and depressive, and his mental health gradually worsened; his confinement to an asylum in 1854–56 resulted in a full resumption of Clara's career to support her family until age and ill health forced her retirement. She toured frequently, mostly in Germany, central Europe, the Low Countries, and England (19 visits between 1856 and 1888); she gave her last public recital in 1891. She was also a distinguished teacher, privately and, from 1878 to 1892, at the Hoch Conservatory, Frankfurt. The full extent of her relations with Brahms (whether they were ever lovers as well as the closest of friends) has been much discussed but not determined. Her compositions, piano pieces, songs, a Concerto, and Piano Trio (1846) were mostly produced before she was 20, and her compositional talent was never fully developed.

Bibl.: Joan Chissell, *Clara Schumann, A Dedicated Spirit: A Study of Her Life and Work* (New York, 1983). Nancy B. Reich, *Clara Schuman: The Artist and the Woman* (Ithaca, N.Y., and London, 1985). Eva Weissweiler, *Clara Schumann: eine Biographie* (Hamburg, 1990). Beatrix Borchard, *Clara Schumann: ihr Leben* (Frankfurt am Main, 1991). Paul-August Koch, *Clara Wieck-Schuman, (1819–1896): Kompositionen: eine Zusammenstellung der Werke, Literatur und Schallplatten* (Frankfurt am Main, 1991).

Schumann, Elisabeth (b. Meeresburg, 13 June 1888; d. New York, 23 Apr. 1952). Soprano. Schooled in Dresden, Berlin, and Hamburg; made her debut at Hamburg in 1909, remaining there until 1919; sang at the Vienna Opera from 1919 to 1937. She also appeared at the Metropolitan Opera (1914–15), Salzburg (1922–35), and Covent Garden (1924–31), and toured the U.S. with Richard Strauss in 1921. She moved to the U.S. in 1938, teaching at the Curtis Institute and continuing her concert career.

Schumann, Robert Alexander (b. Zwickau, 8 June 1810; d. Endenich, near Bonn, 29 July 1856). Composer. His father, Friedrich August, was a publisher and bookseller whose nervous system was subject to a persistent ailment. Schumann grew up with a strong knowledge of literature and, apparently, an inherited defect that played a conspicuous and tragic role in his adult life. In 1816 he entered the school of Archdeacon Döhrner. The next year he began instruction in music with the organist J. G. Kuntzsch, and from 1820 to 1828 he attended the Zwickau Lyceum. Schumann's interest in the piano had been enhanced when he heard Moscheles play in 1819, and by 1821 he was able to perform at a Lyceum concert. In 1823 he began listening to chamber music at the home of Carl Carus, a wealthy manufacturer; the next year he started participating. At this time he was also performing regularly in musical soirees given at the Lyceum (making his best effect with music by Moscheles). By 1825 Schumann's interest in composition was such that his father tried (unsuccessfully) to arrange composition lessons with Weber. In 1826 Schumann's sister, Emilie, then 19 and plagued by mental and physical problems, drowned herself in a lake; Schumann's father succumbed to his nervous disorder shortly afterwards. The following year Schumann left home for the first time, visiting friends in Colditz, Leipzig, and Dresden. His earliest surviving compositions, four songs, date from this period.

In March 1828 Schumann matriculated at the Univ. of Leipzig to study law (in accordance with his mother's wishes), then immediately set off on a tour of Bavaria. In Munich he met Heine. Back in Leipzig he skipped classes and began studying piano with Friedrich Wieck, whose 9-year-old daughter, Clara, was already a remarkable pianist and a budding composer. In May 1829 he moved to Heidelberg and during the summer attended lectures in law. After a tour of Switzerland and Italy he returned to Heidelberg, again skipping classes to practice piano. Following a well-received performance in February 1830, he traveled to Frankfurt to hear Paganini. Returning to Leipzig, he obtained from his mother, with Wieck's help, permission to devote himself officially for one term to becoming a virtuoso. Schumann lived in the Wieck household under his teacher's watchful eye; the proximity proved less than fortuitous. After two years on his own Schumann had become accustomed to making promises to his widowed mother that he had no intention of keeping, and to spending the money she sent for his studies on champagne and cigars. Wieck was clearly impressed by the young man's talent but not by his character. For his part Schumann resented Wieck's absences, which lasted for months at a time, while Clara was on tour. In those intervals Schumann busied himself by composing, by writing music reviews for *Der Komet* and the *Leipziger Tageblatt* and, beginning in June 1831, by studying thoroughbass under Heinrich Dorn, a young conductor at the Leipzig theater who had already shown himself ready to support local talent by bringing out several of Wagner's early overtures. The same summer Schumann penned for the *Allgemeine Musikalische Zeitung* the famous review of Chopin's op. 2 that begins, "Hats off, gentlemen, a genius!"

Despite Schumann's hard work at composition and pianism, the events of 1832 were discouraging. In April his lessons with Dorn were discontinued; in June voluntary movement of two fingers on his right hand became impaired (apparently permanently); in November the first movement of his G minor symphony was poorly received in his hometown of Zwickau. Still, Schumann pressed on, revising and reorchestrating his symphony (achieving a success when the first movement was given in Leipzig in March 1833) and beginning several ambitious works for the piano. After a prolonged illness during the late summer of 1833, Schumann was deeply depressed in the autumn by news of a sister-in-law's death; on 17 October he attempted suicide, leaping from his fourth-floor window. In November his brother Julius died. Schumann was brought out of his depression largely through the ministrations of a new friend, Ludwig Schunke. Schunke died in 1834, but otherwise the year was one of new beginnings. Since the previous June, Schumann and his friends had been exploring the possibility of launching a new music journal. The result was the twice-weekly *Neue Zeitschrift für Musik,* the first issue appearing on 3 April. No sooner had Schumann launched his career as editor and journalist than he fell in love. The girl was a new piano student of Wieck's, Ernestine von Fricken, the pretty, gifted, but illegitimate daughter of Captain Baron von Fricken. Schumann, ignorant of her parental status, proposed to her in July and began a series of variations (op. 13) on a theme by her father as well as a series of short pieces (op. 9) on the letters/notes A, S (E flat), C, H (B natural), common both to the von Frickens' hometown of Asch and to Schumann's surname. After the families had interviewed each other, the baron quietly adopted his daughter—but to no avail. When in August 1835 Schumann learned the secret of Ernestine's birth, he did not take it well. That autumn he began courting Clara, now 15, in the pages of the *Neue Zeitschrift,* and at the end of the year he formally broke his engagement to Ernestine.

The year 1835 was one of accomplishment for Schumann as journalist and composer; at the Wiecks' he met Chopin, Moscheles, and Mendelssohn. Late in the year Wieck was alarmed to learn that Clara reciprocated Schumann's feelings. He had raised his daughter to be a great pianist. He wanted her to compose. In his view she could never realize her potential were she married to a man whose financial prospects were uncertain, whose family was prone to nervous and mental disorders, who drank to excess, who had attempted suicide, and who had sometimes shown himself to be less than honorable in his dealings with women. By the end of 1835 Clara had been removed to Dresden. In February 1836, after attending his mother's funeral in Zwickau, Schumann visited Clara. Wieck learned of this, broke with Schumann, and brought Clara home. Shortly before her 18th birthday, in 1837, Schumann formally proposed. Wieck, now the estranged rather than merely protective father, opposed the engagement in every way he could, and when, in 1840, his last legal strategem failed and the couple married (12 Sept.), he disowned Clara. Marie, the first of eight children, was born the next year.

Robert and Clara Schumann, 1850. After daguerreotype taken in Hamburg.

Clara expected great things of her husband. Schumann, conscious of the limitations of his craft, systematically, year by year, took on the challenge of mastering established media and genres: the lied in 1840, orchestral music in 1841, chamber music in 1842, oratorio in 1843, canon and fugue in 1845, a cappella choral music in 1846–47, stage music in 1847–49. By the beginning of the 1850s Schumann could move freely between genres as the need or desire arose. Once Schumann had gotten his bearings in a compositional area, he wrote with great concentration, typically completing the first version of a large work in two to six weeks. He might then shelve the work for several months or even several years before giving it its final form. Though Schumann wrote prolifically and well, it cost him dearly in strain to his nervous system. At the start of 1843, exhausted from overwork, he briefly quit composing. Later that year he obtained the coveted post of professor of composition at the new Leipzig Conservatory. Whatever his foibles, he could now hardly be considered a debauched bohemian and in December Wieck attempted a reconciliation. The next month Schumann accompanied Clara on her concert tour of Russia. After their return in August, he had a serious breakdown. Giving up his professorship and his editorship of the *Neue Zeitschrift,* he moved his family in October to Dresden (where Wieck had just relocated) to try his luck as a conductor. The withdrawn and taciturn composer proved singularly unequipped for such duties; moreover, as leader of a Dresden choral society he worked not merely in Wagner's circle but in Wagner's shadow. In 1847 he had another serious breakdown. Much of his professional life in Dresden and, after 1850, as an unloved music director in Düsseldorf was spent in discontent. Meanwhile, between 1845 and 1850 a considerable number of his most successful works were published, and for the first time reviews appeared that named him the successor to Beethoven.

In the large vocal and choral works written from 1847, Schumann struck out in a new direction, motivated in part by his interest in literature, in part by the call—widely articulated, and nowhere more clearly than in the pages of the *Neue Zeitschrift*—for an intrinsically German dramatic music. At first he sought, like Wagner, to emancipate music drama from the received Italian model of recitative and aria. But he also moved—especially after the mixed reception of his opera *Genoveva* in 1850—toward the consolidation of a new hybrid genre, the ballad for soloists, chorus, and orchestra. Inspired by Mendelssohn's ballade *Die erste Walpurgisnacht* (and preceded by his own choral ballads of 1849), this genre, in Schumann's hands, continued the trend toward continuous musical fabric seen in his opera and in *Die Paradies und die Peri.* Also new in Schumann's late output were the melodrama, or accompanied recitation (*Manfred;* three ballads, opp. 106, 122), the programmatic overture (opp. 100, 115, 128, 136; "Faust"), and what might be termed the cultivation of the heroic (the change of tone is immediately evident in such instrumental works as the Third Symphony and the Violin Concerto). At the same time, the syntax of his music was changing, perhaps in part as a result of his determined effort in the late 1840s to compose away from the keyboard. Schumann's earlier amalgamation of Germanic *Volkston* with a freely modulating style is echoed in music by dozens of composers writing during the third quarter of the nineteenth century. But aside from Brahms, a Schumann protégé, few composers were able to come to grips with his late style.

From at least the mid-1840s Schumann's ailment had included long periods of ringing in his ears. In early February 1854 this returned with great intensity, accompanied later in the month by hallucinations. On 26 February he begged to no avail for removal to a sanatorium. The next morning he tore half naked through the rain and leaped into the Rhine. After being placed in a sanatorium, he returned, haltingly, to the musical interests of his youth: piano music, Paganini, variations. During his last year he made alphabetical lists of lands and cities.

Works: *Orchestra.* Symphonies: no. 1 in B♭ (*Spring,* 1841); no. 2 in C (1845–46); no. 3 in E♭ (*Rhenish,* 1850); no. 4 in D minor (1841–51). Piano Concerto in A minor (1841–45); Introduction and Allegro Appassionato, *Conzertstück* (1849); *Manfred* Overture and incidental music (1848–49); Cello Concerto in A minor (1850); *Fantasie* (violin and orchestra, 1853); Introduction and Allegro (piano and orchestra, 1853); Violin Concerto in D minor (1853).

Chamber music. 3 string quartets op. 41 (1842); 3 piano trios (1847, 1847, 1851); 3 violin sonatas (1851, 1851, 1853); a piano quintet (1842); a piano quartet (1842); Adagio and Allegro (horn, piano, 1849); *Phantasiestücke* (clarinet, piano, 1849); *Phantasiestücke* (violin, cello, piano, 1842); *3 Romanzen* (oboe, piano, 1849); *5 Stücke im Volkston* (cello, piano, 1849); *Märchenbilder* (viola, piano, 1851); *Märchenerzählungen* (clarinet, viola, piano, 1853).

Songs for voice and piano. Liederkreis (9 songs on texts of Heine, 1840); *Liekderkreis* (12 songs on texts of Eichendorff, 1840); *Frauenliebe und -leben* (8 songs on texts of Chamisso, 1840); *Dichterliebe* (16 songs on texts of Heine, 1840); numerous collections and individual songs.

Piano. Abegg Variations (1829–30); *Papillons* (1829–31); *Davidsbündlertänze* (1837); *Carnaval* (1833–35); Sonata no. 1 in F♯ minor (1832–35); *Phantasiestücke* (1837); Symphonic Etudes (1834–37); *Kinderszenen* (1838); *Kreisleriana* (1838); *Phantasie* in C (1836–38); *Arabeske* in C (1838); *Humoreske* in B♭ (1838); *8 Novelletten* (1838); Sonata no. 2 in G minor (1833–38); *Faschingsschwank aus Wien* (1839–40); *Album für die Jugend* (1848); *Waldscenen* (1848–49); *Bunte Blätter* (1852); many other pieces and sets of pieces, some for pedal piano.

Genoveva (opera, 1847–49); works for chorus and orchestra; part songs with accompaniment and without.

Bibl.: *Werke,* 31 vols., ed. Clara Schumann and Johannes Brahms (Leipzig, 1879–93). *Neue Gesamtausgabe,* 41 vols. (projected), ed. A. Mayeda and Klaus Niemöller (Düsseldorf, 1986–). *Klavier-Urtextausgabe,* ed. Wolfgang Boetticher (Monaco, 1976–). *Gesammelte Schriften über Musik und Musiker,* 5th ed., 2 vols. (Leipzig, 1914). Kurt Hoffmann and Siegman Keil, *Thematisches Verzeichnis sämtlicher im Druck erschienenen musikalischen Werke,* 5th ed. (Hamburg, 1982). Alan Walker, *Robert Schumann: The Man and His Music,* 2nd ed. (London, 1976). Peter Sutermeister, *Robert Schumann: eine Biographie nach Briefen, Tagebüchern und Erinnerungen von Robert und Clara Schumann* (Tübingen, 1982). Peter F. Ostwald, *Schumann: Music and Madness* (Boston, 1985). Udo Rauchfleisch, *Robert Schumann: Leben und Werk: eine Psy-*

chobiographie (Stuttgart, 1990). Markus Waldura, *Monomotivik, Sequenz und Sonatenform im Werk Robert Schumanns* (Saarbrücken, 1990). Eric Sams, *The Songs of Robert Schumann*, rev. and enlarged 3rd ed. (Bloomington, Ind., 1993). R. Larry Todd., ed., *Schumann and His World* (Princeton, 1994).

Schumann-Heink, Ernestine [née Rössler] (b. Lieben, near Prague, 15 June 1861; d. Hollywood, 17 Nov. 1936). Contralto. Studied with Marietta von Leclair at Graz, and with Franz Wüllner and G. B. Lamperti. First public performance (1876) at Graz in Beethoven's Ninth Symphony. Operatic debut in 1878 at Dresden as Azucena in *Il trovatore.* Engaged at Hamburg, 1883–97; at Bayreuth, 1896–1914. London debut in 1892 with Mahler conducting. Metropolitan Opera debut, 1899. Sang Clytemnestra in the premiere of *Elektra* (Dresden, 1909). Her career continued until the 1930s, encompassing opera, oratorio, operetta, recitals, film, and radio; her last operatic appearance was at the Met in 1932, as Erda in *Siegfried.*

Schuppanzigh, Ignaz (b. Vienna, 20 Nov. 1776; d. there, 2 Mar. 1830). Violinist, violist. Friend of Beethoven's. In 1794 he became first violinist in the string quartet that played for Prince Lichnowsky. He took part in many first performances of Beethoven's works; in 1808 he formed a private string quartet for Prince Razumovsky which featured Beethoven's quartets as well as those of Haydn and Mozart. His appointments as conductor included leadership of the Augarten concerts (from 1795) and directorship of the German opera (from 1828).

Bibl.: Donald W. MacArdle, "Beethoven and Schuppanzigh," *MR* 26 (1965): 3–14.

Schuricht, Carl (b. Danzig, 3 July 1880; d. Corseaux-sur-Vevey, Switzerland, 7 Jan. 1967). Composer and conductor. Studied with von Mannstaedt at Wiesbaden, Humperdinck at Berlin, and Reger at Leipzig; after periods at various theaters, in 1912 he was named musical director at Wiesbaden, remaining there until fleeing to Switzerland in 1944. He hosted annual festivals at Wiesbaden, conducting both new music and cycles of the standard repertory, and between 1930 and 1939 led summer concerts at Scheveningen, Holland. After the war he was a frequent guest conductor with European orchestras. His own works include orchestral compositions, piano music, and songs.

Schurmann [Schürmann], **(Eduard) Gerard** (b. Kertosono, Indonesia, Jan. 1924). Composer and conductor. Educated in England, he studied piano with Kathleen Long, composition with Alan Rawsthorne, conducting with Franco Ferrara. His first compositions—songs, piano pieces, and works for smaller ensembles—date from the early 1940s. From the late 1940s through the mid-1960s he was active as a pianist, conductor, and composer of film scores, but published few compositions; subsequently more prolific. In 1981 Schurmann moved to the U.S. Works include *Six Studies of Francis Bacon* (1968), an interpretation for orchestra of 6 paintings by the English artist; *Piers Plowman* (1980), an opera-cantata; *Chuench'i* (1966), a song cycle on translations from Chinese texts (orchestrated 1967); *The Double Heart* (1976), a cantata for unaccompanied voices; a piano concerto (1973) and a violin concerto (1978).

Schürmann [Schurmann, Scheuermann], **Georg Caspar** (b. Idensen, near Hannover, 1672 or 1673; d. Wolfenbüttel, 25 Feb. 1751). Composer. He began his career in Hamburg, where he sang alto at the opera and in churches. Conradi, Kusser, and Keiser were involved with the opera at this time: their music was performed in addition to works by Steffani and others. In 1697 Duke Anton Ulrich of Brunswick-Lüneburg made Schürmann solo alto to his Brunswick court and a conductor for the opera and court church. Except for a brief period of study in Venice (1701–2) and a period as Kapellmeister and composer at the court of Meiningen (1702–6), Schürmann remained in Brunswick for the rest of his life. Of his more than 40 operas only 3 survive complete, in addition to excerpts from another 9.

Schuster, Joseph (b. Dresden, 11 Aug. 1748; d. there, 24 July 1812). Composer. He studied music with his father, a court musician, and also with J. G. Schürer. He undertook several trips to Italy: during the first (1765–68) he took lessons with Girolamo Pera, and during the second (1774–77) he studied with Padre Martini, as well as composing some operas for Naples and Venice. He wrote more operas during a trip there in 1778–81. He was named Dresden church composer in 1772 and Kapellmeister in 1787 (both of which were simultaneous appointments with Franz Seydelmann). His compositions include about 20 operas, oratorios, Masses, cantatas, symphonies, and other vocal and instrumental pieces.

Bibl.: Richard Engländer, "Die Opern Joseph Schusters (1748–1812)," *ZfMw* 10 (1927–28): 257–91.

Schütz, Heinrich [Henrich] [Sagittarius, Henricus] (b. Köstritz [now Bad Köstritz], near Gera, bapt. 9 Oct. 1585; d. Dresden, 6 Nov. 1672). Composer. Born into a family of innkeepers, Schütz was first educated by his father, Christoph. When his family moved to Weissenfels in 1590, he received instruction in music from both the local Kantor, Georg Weber, and the organist, Heinrich Colander. In 1598 Landgrave Moritz of Hessen-Kassel, while staying at Christoph Schütz's inn, heard young Heinrich sing and was so impressed that he asked to be entrusted with the boy's education. Schütz arrived at Moritz's court at Kassel in August 1599 and served as a choirboy while pursuing his education at the Collegium Mauritianum. There he distinguished himself as a student, particularly of languages; he received his musical training from Georg Otto, Moritz's Kapellmeister. When his voice changed, he set out for the Univ. of Marburg, matriculating on 27 Sept. 1608. There he elected to study law and soon won distinction. In 1609, at the urging of Moritz, Schütz accepted a two-year grant from the landgrave to study with Giovanni Gabrieli in Venice, where he received a solid training in composition and became proficient at the organ. His progress was swift, and he was close to Gabrieli until the elder composer's death in 1612. A book of five-voice madrigals by Schütz, dedicated to Landgrave Moritz, appeared in 1611. In it Schütz demonstrated his thorough assimilation of the Italian madrigal style. He returned to Germany in 1613 and resumed his duties at Moritz's court as second organist.

In 1614 the Elector Johann Georg I of Saxony requested and received permission from Moritz to employ Schütz at Dresden for a few months; Praetorius was occasionally employed there at this time. The following year the elector obtained the composer's services for two years. Although he was not given the title, Schütz was in effect the elector's Kapellmeister. In 1616 Moritz requested that Schütz return to Kassel, but the elector refused to release the composer. Despite the landgrave's efforts, Schütz remained at the Saxon court and was formally given the title of Kapellmeister by 25 January 1619; from 1618 he received an annual salary of 400 florins. His duties included composing music for major court ceremonies, ensuring that the Kapelle was well staffed and that its members had proper living conditions, and supervising the choirboys' musical education. Over the years Schütz's pupils included his cousin Heinrich Albert, Christoph Bernhard, Johann Klemm, Johann Theile, and Matthias Weckmann. Because of the prestige of his position, Schütz was soon able to extend his activities beyond the confines of Dresden: he was called to oversee the reorganization of musical activities in Reuss and in Magdeburg.

In the spring of 1619 he published his first collection of sacred music, the *Psalmen Davids sampt etlichen Moteten und Concerten* (SWV 22–47). On 1 June 1619 he married Magdalena Wildeck, the 18-year-old daughter of a court official in Dresden. In spring 1623 Schütz published the *Historia der . . . Aufferstehung . . . Jesu Christi* (SWV 50), and in 1625 a volume of motets, the *Cantiones sacrae* (SWV 53–93). Perhaps the nadir of his personal life came on 6 September 1625, when his wife died. Schütz entrusted the care of his two daughters to their maternal grandmother. Contrary to custom, he remained a widower for the rest of his life. For over a year after the loss of his wife, Schütz concentrated his efforts on the Becker Psalter (SWV 97a–256a), which appeared early in 1628. On 13 April 1627, during a court visit to the castle of Hartenfels at Torgau, Schütz produced the first German opera, *Dafne,* set to Martin Opitz's translation and adaptation of the libretto written by Rinuccini for Peri's opera.

Because of economic pressures brought about by the Thirty Years' War in the late 1620s, Schütz decided to pay another visit to Italy in 1628. In Venice he found a musical life vastly different from what he had encountered there during his youth. Monteverdi guided his study of the new developments, and of dramatic monody in particular. Schütz's own comment that the dramatic style was then unknown in Germany suggests that *Dafne* did not employ true recitative. Toward the end of his Venetian period he published his *Symphoniae sacrae* (SWV 257–76), which made use of the "fresh devices" found in the latest Italian music.

By 20 November 1629 Schütz had returned to the Dresden court. In January 1631 he published a motet (SWV 277) in memory of Johann Hermann Schein, which had been requested by Schein when Schütz visited him at his deathbed. In autumn 1631 Saxony entered the Thirty Years' War, placing the Dresden court chapel under financial strain. When Crown Prince Christian of Denmark asked Schütz to direct the music at his wedding in Copenhagen, the composer eagerly accepted the invitation. Although the offer was extended in February 1633, Schütz did not arrive in Denmark until early in December of that year, at which time he was appointed Kapellmeister to King Christian IV, effective December 10 at an annual salary of 800 reichsthaler. Schütz remained in Denmark until 1635. Back in Dresden, he composed his *Musicalische Exequien* (SWV 279–81) for the interment of Prince Heinrich Posthumus in 1636, and in autumn of that year he published part one of his *Kleine geistliche Concerte* (SWV 282–305). In order to protect his compositions from unauthorized reprints in the Holy Roman Empire, Schütz petitioned for and received a five-year copyright privilege from Ferdinand III in 1637. On 20 November 1638 his opera-ballet *Orpheus und Euridice,* only the text of which survives, was performed to celebrate the marriage of Prince Johann Georg and Princess Magdalena Sybilla of Brandenburg. The publication of the second part of *Kleine geistliche Concerte* followed in the spring of 1639. A few months later Schütz took a leave of absence from the electoral court to become Kapellmeister to Georg of Calenberg, then living in Hildesheim. When he returned to Dresden at the beginning of 1641 he found the Kapelle to be in total disarray: the ensemble had been drastically reduced in number and was not being paid. From 1642 until April 1644 he was again Kapellmeister at Copenhagen. From then until the spring of 1645 he lived mostly in the city of Brunswick and was active at the Wolfenbüttel court of Duke August the Younger of Brunswick-Lüneburg.

In a letter of 21 May 1645 Schütz asked Elector Johann Georg to allow him to retire with an annual pension of 200 thalers along with the right to keep his title of Kapellmeister and occasionally direct the Kapelle. He had hoped to spend the remainder of his life at Weissenfels, completing the musical works he had begun. Although the elector did let Schütz spend almost every autumn or winter in Weissenfels for the next decade, he refused to allow the composer to retire altogether. In the spring of 1647 Schütz brought out his *Symphoniarum sacrarum secunda pars* (SWV 341–67), and the following spring he published his *Geistliche Chor-Music* (SWV 369–97). In 1650 his *Symphoniarum sacrarum tertia pars* (SWV 398–418) appeared, a collection that he apparently considered to be the culmination of his career in Dresden. Along with this collection, Schütz presented to Johann Georg a petition dated 14 January 1651, in which he renewed his plea to be pensioned. The elector ignored this and subsequent petitions as well as the deteriorating condition of the Kapelle. To make matters worse, Schütz had still not received his salary, with the result that his financial assets were becoming severely depleted. Some relief came in 1655 in the form of an appointment as absentee Kapellmeister to Duchess Sophie Elisabeth of Brunswick-Lüneburg. With the death of Johann Georg on 8 October 1656, Johann Georg II became elector and allowed Schütz to retire as chief or senior Kapellmeister with a pension. Schütz continued to compose works for special occasions, and maintained some authority at court, but probably did not conduct the Kapelle again. Neither Schütz's reserve of earlier works nor the few compositions from his last years (including the Passions) were published in his time. Johann Theile, Schütz's last pupil, went to Weissenfels to study with the aged composer around 1667. About 1670 Schütz left Weissenfels and moved to Dresden, where he remained until his death.

Works: *Il primo libro de madrigali* [op. 1] (1611); *Die Wort Jesus Syrach . . . auff hochzeitlichen Ehrentag des . . . Herrn Josephi Avenarii* (1618); *Concert mit 11 Stimmen: auff des . . . Herrn Michael Thomae . . . hochzeitlichen Ehren Tag* (1618); *Psalmen Davids sampt etlichen Moteten und Concerten* [op. 2] (1619); *Der 133. Psalm . . . auff die hochzeitliche Ehrenfrewde Herrn Georgii Schützen* (1619); *Syncharma musicum* (1621); *Historia der frölichen und siegreichen Aufferstehung unsers einigen Erlösers und Seligmachers Jesu Christi* [op. 3] (1623); *Kläglicher Abschied von der churfürstlichen Grufft zu Freybergk* (1623); *Cantiones sacrae* [op. 4] (1625); *De vitae fugacitate: aria . . . bey Occasion des . . . Todesfalles der . . . Jungfrawen Anna Marien Wildeckin* (1625); *Ultima verba psalmi 23 . . . super . . . obitu Jacobi Schultes* (1625); *Psalmen Davids, hiebevorn in teutzsche Reimen gebracht, durch D. Cornelium Beckern, und an jetzo mit ein hundert und drey eigenen Melodeyen . . . gestellet* [op. 5] (1628; rev. and enlarged 3rd ed. as [op. 14], 1661); *Symphoniae sacrae* [op. 6] (1629); *Verba D. Pauli . . . beatis manibus Dn. Johannis-Hermanni Scheinii . . . consecrata* (1631); *An hoch printzlicher Durchläuchtigkeit zu Dennenmarck . . . Beylager: Gesang der Venus-Kinder in der Invention genennet Thronus Veneris* (1634); *Musicalische Exequien . . . dess . . . Herrn Heinrichen dess Jüngern und Eltisten Reussen* [op. 7] (1636); *Erster Theil kleiner geistlichen Concerten* [op. 8] (1636); *Anderer Theil kleiner geistlichen Concerten* [op. 9] (1639); *Symphoniarum sacrarum secunda pars* op. 10 (1647); *Danck-Lied: für die hocherwiesene fürstl. Gnade in Weymar* (1647); *Musicalia ad chorum sacrum, das ist: Geistliche Chor-Music . . . erster Theil* op. 11 (1648); *Symphoniarum sacrarum tertia pars* op. 12 (1650); *Zwölff geistliche Gesänge*, op. 13 (1657); *Canticum B. Simeonis . . . nach dem hochseligsten Hintritt . . . Johann Georgen* (1657); *Historia, der freuden- und gnadenreichen Geburth Gottes und Marien Sohnes, Jesu Christi* (1664); *Die sieben Wortte unsers lieben Erlösers und Seeligmachers Jesu Christi* (date not determined); *Historia des Leidens und Sterbens unsers Herrn und Heylandes Jesu Christi nach dem Evangelisten S. Matheum, 1666* (perf. Dresden, 1 Apr. 1666); *Historia des Leidens und Sterbens . . . Jesu Christi nach dem Evangelisten St. Lucam* (perf. Dresden, 8 Apr. 1666); *Historia des Leidens und Sterbens . . . Jesu Christi nach dem Evangelisten St. Johannem* (perf. Dresden, 13 Apr. 1666); *Königs und Propheten Davids hundert und neunzehender Psalm . . . nebenst dem Anhange des 100. Psalms . . . und eines deutschen Magnificats* (1671); also numerous lost sacred and secular vocal works including the opera *Dafne* (perf. Torgau, 13 Apr. 1627).

Bibl.: *Heinrich Schütz: Sämtliche Werke,* ed. Philipp Spitta et al. (Leipzig, 1885–94, 1909, 1927; R: 1968–73). *Heinrich Schütz: Neue Ausgabe sämtlicher Werke,* ed. Werner Bittinger et al. (Kassel, 1955–). *Heinrich Schütz: Sämtliche Werke in quellenkritischer Neuausgabe,* ed. Günter Graulich et al. (Stuttgart, 1971–). *Schütz-Werke-Verzeichnis (SWV): Kleine Ausgabe,* ed. Werner Bittinger (Kassel, 1960). Articles in *Schütz-Jahrbuch,* ed. Werner Breig et al. (Kassel, 1979–). Allen B. Skei, *Heinrich Schütz: A Guide to Research* (New York and London, 1981). Martin Gregor-Dellin, *Heinrich Schütz: Sein Leben, sein Werk, seine Zeit* (Munich, 1984). Dietrich Berke et al., *Heinrich Schütz: Texte—Bilder—Dokumente* (Kassel, 1985). *Heinrich Schütz in seiner Zeit,* ed. Walther Blankenburg (Darmstadt, 1985). Basil Smallman, *The Music of Heinrich Schütz* (Leeds, 1985). *Heinrich Schütz: A Bibliography of the Collected Works and Performing Editions,* comp. D. Douglass Miller and Anne L. Highsmith (Westport, Conn., 1986). Gina Spagnoli, *Letters and Documents of Heinrich Schütz, 1656–1672: An Annotated Translation* (Ann Arbor, 1990).

Schuyler, Philippa Duke (b. New York, 2 Aug. 1931; d. Danang, Vietnam, 9 May 1967). Pianist, composer, author. She began performing publicly at age 6; at 7 she published several sets of piano pieces; at 15 she made her debut with the New York Philharmonic. As a teenager she toured extensively outside the U.S., particularly in Latin America and Africa. She became increasingly involved in social and political issues, writing newspaper reports, essays, and books on a variety of topics. She was killed in a helicopter crash while working as a war correspondent. Most of her compositions remain unpublished.

Bibl.: Kathryn Talalay, "Philippa Duke Schuyler, Pianist, Composer, Writer," *The Black Perspective in Music* 10 (1982): 43–68.

Schwantner, Joseph (b. Chicago, 22 Mar. 1943). Composer. Studied with Bernard Dieter at the Chicago Conservatory College (B.M., 1964), then with Anthony Donato and Alan Stout at Northwestern (D.M.A., 1968). Several works composed during his student days received prizes, notably *Diaphonia Intervallum,* alto saxophone, flute, piano, and strings (1965). In 1970 he became professor of composition and theory at the Eastman School of Music. Schwantner's works from the 1970s tended to be for small ensembles. They often combined twelve-tone techniques with a search for new, delicate sonorities and textures, for example, *Consortium II* (chamber ensemble, 1972) and *In Aeternum* (cello and chamber ensemble, 1973). From the mid-70s on his works became more tonal, and many of them were for larger ensembles: *And the Mountains Rising Nowhere* (band, 1977), *Aftertones of Infinity* (orchestra, 1978; Pulitzer Prize, 1979), *Distant Runes and Incantations* (orchestra, 1983). In addition he composed several sets of songs, mainly with instrumental accompaniment, including *Wild Angels of the Open Hills,* for soprano, flute, and harp on texts by Ursula Le Guin (1974) and *Sparrows* for soprano and chamber ensemble (1979), a setting of 15 Japanese haiku. Other works include *Freelight* (orchestra, 1989); *A Play of Shadows* (flute, orchestra, 1990); *Through Interior Worlds* (ballet, 1992); percussion concerto (1995); *Evening Land Symphony* (soprano, orchestra, 1995).

Schwartz, Arthur (b. Brooklyn, N.Y., 25 Nov. 1900; d. Kintnersville, Pa., 3 Sept. 1984). Popular songwriter. He studied English and law at Columbia Univ. and New York Univ., and directed a legal firm in New York from 1924 to 1928. From 1929 he collaborated on revues and musicals with lyricist Arthur Dietz (*The Little Show,* 1929, including "I Guess I'll Have To Change My Plan"; *The Band Wagon,* 1931 and 1951 film, including "That's Entertainment"; *Inside U.S.A.,* 1946; *The Gay Life,* 1961), and from 1936 on songs for films with lyricists including Johnny Mercer, E. Y. Harburg, and Sammy Cahn; he also wrote musicals with Dorothy Fields (*Stars in Your Eyes,* 1939; *By the Beautiful Sea,* 1954).

Schwartz, Elliott (Shelling) (b. Brooklyn, 19 Jan. 1936). Composer. As a teenager he studied piano with Alton Jones at Juilliard. After undergraduate study at Columbia Univ. (B.A., 1953), he took graduate degrees in music education at Columbia Teachers College, where he studied with Otto Luening and Jack Beeson (M.A., 1958; Ed.D., 1962). From 1960 to 1964 he taught music at the Univ. of Massachusetts in Amherst; in 1964 he was appointed professor of music at Bowdoin College; subsequently taught at Ohio State Univ. (1985–86, 1989–91). Starting in the mid-1960s many of Schwartz's compositions involved tape and electronic media, usually combined with traditional instruments, for example, *Music for Prince Albert* (piano and 2 tapes, 1969), *Mirrors* (piano and tape, 1973), *Extended Oboe* (oboe and tape, 1974), *Cycles and Gongs* (organ, trumpet, tape, 1975). Some works involve theatrical devices and audience participation, for example, *Magic Music* (1968) for piano and orchestra, where orchestra members take turns exploring the piano, and *Music for Soloist and Audience* (1970), in which the audience has its own conductors. Other works include *4 Ohio Portraits* (orchestra, 1986); *Palindromes* (cello, percussion, 1989). He is the author of *The Symphonies of Ralph Vaughan Williams* (Amherst, Mass., 1964), *Electronic Music: A Listener's Guide* (New York, 1973; rev. 1976), *Music: Ways of Listening* (New York, 1982).

Schwartz, Francis (b. Altoona, Pa., 10 Mar. 1940). Composer. Attended Juilliard, where he studied piano with Lonnie Epstein, composition with Vittorio Giannini (B.S., 1961, M.S., 1962). In 1965 he joined the faculty of the Univ. of Puerto Rico. He has composed many large-scale pieces combining various media in a theatrical setting: *Auschwitz,* tape, lights, odors, and movement (San Juan, 1968), and *Time Sound, and the Hooded Man,* actors, tape, and videotape (Buenos Aires, 1975). Also composed many smaller pieces for guitar (*Amistad 1 & 2,* 1979; *Bato,* 1986) as well as chamber music (*Trio para Edgar Allan Poe,* violin, cello, piano, 1988; *El sueño de Bolívar,* soprano, clarinet, piano, violin, 1988).

Schwarz, Gerard (b. Weehawken, N.J., 19 Aug. 1947). Trumpeter and conductor. Studied at the Juilliard School (B.S. 1972); played with the American Brass Quintet, 1965–73. He succeeded his teacher William Vacchiano at the New York Philharmonic in 1973, leaving the orchestra in 1977; served as director of the Los Angeles Chamber Orchestra (1978–86) while making guest appearances elsewhere. In 1984 he was appointed music director of the Mostly Mozart Festival, and in 1985 became principal conductor of the Seattle Symphony. Schwarz has commissioned many trumpet works, and has recorded widely.

Schwarzkopf, Elisabeth (b. Jarotschin, Poland, 9 Dec. 1915). Soprano. Studied at the Musikhochschule, Berlin, from 1934, training initially as an alto; made her opera debut in 1938 at the Charlottenburg Opera, Berlin. After study with Maria Ivogün, she gave an acclaimed recital in 1942 at Vienna, and was subsequently engaged by Karl Böhm for the Vienna Staatsoper, an association cut short by illness and the bombing of the opera house. A 1946 recital reestablished her fame; she rejoined the Staatsoper, touring with it to Covent Garden in 1947. She sang with the Covent Garden company itself between 1947 and 1953, created the role of Anne Trulove in Stravinsky's *The Rake's Progress* (Venice, 1951), and appeared also at Salzburg (1947–64) and La Scala (1948–63). From 1955 to 1964 she sang with the San Francisco Opera; her onetime Nazi sympathies delayed her U.S. debut until 1953. Her last operatic performance was as the Marschallin (a role for which she was famed) at Brussels in 1972, and in 1975 she made a farewell recital tour.

Bibl.: Sergio Segalini, *Elisabeth Schwarzkopf* (Paris, 1983).

Schweitzer, Albert (b. Keysersberg, Alsace, 14 Jan. 1875; d. Lambaréné, Gabon, 4 Sept. 1965). Organist, Bach scholar, theologian, physician, and humanitarian. He was born into a family of Lutheran clergymen, organists, and teachers. Early organ studies with Eugen Münch of Mulhouse fostered his love of Bach; Wagner also won his early admiration. He continued organ studies with Ernst Münch of Strasbourg and attended the Univ. of Strasbourg from 1893, earning doctorates in philosophy (1899) and theology (1900). During these years he studied organ with Widor in Paris, played organ continuo for Münch's Strasbourg Bach Concerts, pursued scholarly studies in Paris and Berlin, and established friendships with the Wagner family at Bayreuth.

From 1902 he taught theology at Strasbourg Univ. while pursuing a doctorate in medicine there (awarded 1912) and serving as a local Lutheran pastor; these years saw his most important musical activities. From 1905 he was organist for the Paris Bach Society. At Widor's instigation he wrote *J. S. Bach, le musicien-poète* (Leipzig, 1905), a ground-breaking investigation of Bach's musical word-painting and symbolism; this Wagnerian analysis countered the prevailing Spitta-based view of Bach as an absolute composer. He nearly doubled the length of the book for its German version, *J. S. Bach* (Leipzig, 1908; trans. Eng., Leipzig, 1911). In 1906 he issued his polemical *Deutsche und französische Orgelbaukunst und Orgelkunst* (Leipzig), criticizing the German Romantic orchestral organ building style in favor of the more classical French style of Cavaillé-Coll; this led to a special session at the 1909 Vienna Congress of the International Musical Society at which his views were officially espoused, giving birth to the modern German *Orgelbewegung* or organ reform. Widor and Schweitzer co-edited most of Bach's organ works for G. Schirmer of New York: *J. S. Bach, Complete Organ Works: A Critico-Practical Edition* (vols. 1–5, 1912–14); the remainder were edited by Schweitzer and Edouard Nies-Berger (vols. 6–8, 1954–67).

From 1913 onward Schweitzer served as a pioneering medical missionary at Lambaréné, Gabon, French Equatorial Africa; he made periodic European organ concert tours to help fund his efforts. For this humanitarian work he won the Nobel Peace Prize in 1952.

Bibl. Charles Rhind Joy, *Music in the Life of Albert Schweitzer: Selections from His Writings* (New York, 1951; rev. 1953). Michael Murray, *Albert Schweitzer, Musician* (Aldershot, 1994).

Schweitzer, Anton (b. Coburg, bapt. 6 June 1735; d. Gotha, 23 Nov. 1787). Composer. While in the employ of the Duke of Hildburghausen (as a violist, *Kammermusicus,* and Kapellmeister) he studied with Kleinknecht in Bayreuth (1758) and Italy (1764–66). In 1769 he became Kapellmeister to the Seyler theater company, for which he wrote incidental music, ballet music, and singspiels. In 1771 the company settled in Weimar, where he wrote his popular singspiel *Die Dorfgala* (1772); the first German melodrama, *Pygmalion* (text by Rousseau, 1772; now lost); and the serious opera *Alkeste* (1773; libretto by Wieland). The company moved to Gotha in 1774, and Schweitzer succeeded Georg Benda as director of the ducal chapel there in 1778. In addition to over 20 dramatic works (many lost), he wrote 46 ballets.

Schwindl [Schwindel] **Friedrich** (b. 3 May 1737; d. Karlsruhe, 7 Aug. 1786). Composer and violinist. He composed most of his works between 1760 and 1780. These include symphonies, 28 of which were published; chamber works; and several choral works. He was appointed *Konzertmeister* to the Margrave of Wied-Runkel during the 1760s and, later, *virtuoso di camera* to the Count of Colloredo. During 1770 he was employed by the Zurich Musiksaalgesellschaft as a violinist. He was appointed *Konzertmeister* to the Margrave of Karlsruhe in 1780 and held this position until his death.

Sciarrino, Salvatore (b. Palermo, 4 Apr. 1947). Composer. Largely self-taught, he began composing at the age of 12. He came to public attention in 1965 at the Palermo Festival with *Atto II* for speaker, 3 trumpets, and percussion, a work that he soon withdrew. *Quartetto II* for string quartet (1967) marked the beginning of a new direction. Thereafter he wrote pieces for a great variety of instrumental and vocal combinations. Taught composition at the conservatories of Milan (1974–82), Perugia (1983–86), and Florence (beginning 1987).

Works include *Arabesque* (2 organs, 1971); *Amore e Psiche* (chamber opera, Milan, 1973); *Capricci* (solo violin, 1976); *Il paese senz'alba* (chamber orchestra, 1977); *Aspern* (opera, 1978); *L'addio a Trachis* (harp, 1980); *Autoritratto nella notte* (orchestra, 1983); *Lohengrin* (chamber opera, Milan, 1983); *Morte di Borromini* (narrator, orchestra, 1988); *Perseo e Andromeda* (opera, 1991).

Scimone, Claudio (b. Padua, 23 Dec. 1934). Conductor. A pupil of Ferrara, Mitropoulos, and Zecchi, he formed I soloisti veneti in 1959, with whom he performed in over 50 countries and at major festivals of 18th-century music. As a teacher he held posts at conservatories in Venice (1961–67), Verona (1967–74), and Padua (1974–83); also led the Chamber Orchestra of Padua from 1968, and made guest appearances elsewhere in Europe.

Sciutti, Graziella (b. Turin, 17 April 1927). Soprano. Studied at Rome; made her debut at Aix-en-Provence in 1951, appearing there until 1954, in which year she also sang at Glyndebourne and Naples and created the title role in Sauget's *Les caprices de Marianne.* She participated in the opening of the Piccola Scala, Milan, in 1955, appeared at Covent Garden in 1956, and made her U.S. debut at San Francisco in 1961. Her chief roles included Mozart's soubrette parts. Beginning in 1986 she ran her own music academy in Florence.

Scott, Cyril (Meir) (b. Oxton, Cheshire, 27 Sept. 1879; d. Eastbourne, 31 Dec. 1970). Composer. A child prodigy, he traveled to Frankfurt when he was 11 years old and studied at the Hoch Conservatory with Uzielli and Humperdinck. He returned briefly to Liverpool to study with Stendner-Welsing, then went back to France in 1895 to take composition lessons with Knorr. He settled in Liverpool in 1898 to compose and teach. His music became well known during the first two decades of the century through public debuts, publication, and Scott's own concert appearances, though he eventually withdrew many of his early works. By the 1920s he had developed an interest in Eastern Indian philosophy and occultism and published his own writings on these and related subjects. He also wrote poetry and plays. In general his music was influenced by the highly colorful and expressive orchestration and harmony of Russian and, especially, French trends, using unresolved chromaticism and whole-tone scales. He was particularly popular for his descriptive piano works and songs, of which there were some 100. Works include 3 operas, for which he was his own librettist (*Maureen O'Mara,* 1946); the oratorio *Hymn of Unity* (1947); orchestral music (3 symphonies and several concerti, overtures, and suites); and chamber music (4 string quartets, 1920, 1958, 1960, 1968); 3 piano sonatas (1910, 1932, and 1956).

Scott, James (Sylvester) (b. Neosho, Mo., 12 Feb. 1885; d. Kansas City, Kans., 30 Aug. 1938). Ragtime composer and pianist. The son of former slaves, Scott studied with John Coleman and worked in a local music store, the Dumars Music Company; in 1903 Dumars published 2 of his rags, "A Summer Breeze" and "The Fascinator." He met Scott Joplin in St. Louis in 1906; later that year Joplin's publisher, John Stark, issued Scott's "Frog Legs Rag," and in 1909 "Grace and Beauty," perhaps his finest work, appeared. He moved to Kansas City, Kans., in 1920 and began teaching; his last rag was issued in 1922. Though little recognized during his lifetime, Scott is now considered one of the greatest of ragtime composers.

Bibl.: Marvin L. VanGilder, "James Scott," in *Ragtime: Its History, Composers, and Music,* ed. John Edward Hasse (New York, 1985), pp. 137–45.

Scotti, Antonio (b. Naples, 25 Jan. 1866; d. there, 26 Feb. 1936). Baritone. Studied in his home city, making his debut there in 1889, then sang elsewhere in Italy and in Spain, Russia, and Buenos Aires; made his La Scala debut in 1898, and Metropolitan and Covent Garden debuts in 1899; appeared at the Met until 1933. A touring company he led between 1919 and 1922 met with financial ruin. A fine actor, he was a famous Scarpia; other roles included Rigoletto, Iago, and Don Giovanni.

Scotto, Girolamo [Gerolamo] (b. ca. 1505; d. Venice, 3 Sept. 1572). Printer, bookseller, and composer. With his brother Ottaviano Scotto (fl. 1489–1552) he inherited the publishing firm of his uncle, also Ottaviano Scotto (b. Monda; d. Venice, 24 Dec. 1498), which had issued a number of impressive missals with black musical notation and red 4-line staves. Girolamo first obtained a printing privilege in 1536 and, like his uncle, printed a number of nonmusical books, including Bibles and books on medicine and philosophy. His music books were printed using movable type and in a single impression; these included Jhan Gero's *Madrigali italiani* (1541), Pietro Aaron's *Lucidario* (1545–47), and Antonfranceso Doni's *Dialogo della musica* (1544). He also published madrigals of his own composition.

Scotto, Renata (b. Savona, 24 Feb. 1934). Soprano. Studied in Milan, and made her formal debut there in 1953. After various appearances in Italy, she understudied Callas at Edinburgh during a La Scala tour in 1959. She made debuts at Chicago in 1960, Covent Garden in 1962, and the Metropolitan Opera in 1965, remaining with the Met company until 1987. Made many recordings, chiefly of Italian opera.

Bibl.: Bruno Tosi, *Renata Scotto: Voce di due mondi* (Venice, 1990).

Scriabin, Alexander Nikolaevich (b. Moscow, 6 Jan. 1872; d. Moscow, 27 Apr. 1915). Composer. Born into an aristocratic family of military background. His mother, a noted professional pianist, died in his second year, and his father, a lawyer, remarried and lived abroad. He was raised by his paternal grandmother, great aunt, and young aunt Lyubov, who gave him his first music lessons. After military schooling, he entered the Moscow Conservatory in 1888, studying theory with Taneyev and Arensky, and piano with Safonov; on graduating in 1892 he won the second gold medal in piano (his classmate Rachmaninoff won first). Though his hands were small (as his stature was slight), he launched a successful concert career, notably as a performer of his own music and that of Chopin, to which his own was initially indebted. He became known for his fastidious manner.

In 1894 Scriabin became a protégé of the St. Petersburg music publisher and impresario Belyayev, whose copious patronage and guidance advanced his career decisively. In 1895–96 he toured Europe; in 1897 he married Vera Isaakovich, a brilliant pianist and exponent of his music; and from 1898 he taught at the Moscow Conservatory. Works of this early period include the Piano Concerto (op. 20, 1896), Piano Sonatas nos. 2 and 3 (opp. 19, 1892–97; 23, 1897–98), the orchestral *Reverie* (op. 24, 1898), symphonies nos. 1 and 2 (opp. 26, with choral finale, 1899–1900; 29, 1901), and many short piano pieces, notably 24 Preludes (op. 11, 1888–96).

Between 1901 and 1904 Scriabin underwent an artistic and personal reorientation. He became attracted to mystical philosophy, first that of Trubetskoy, then, through a growing obsession with Wagner, that of Nietzsche. His style became increasingly centered on an idiosyncratic palette of chromatic procedures. His principal project was a philosophically programmatic Third Symphony, *Le divin poème* (op. 43, 1902–4). He quit the conservatory in 1903 and wrote much piano music to support himself, notably the Fourth Sonata (op. 28, 1903) and the *Poème satanique* (op. 36, 1903). On the death of Belyayev that year, he came into a generous annuity from a former student, M. K. Morozova (who financed the premiere of *Le divin poème* in Paris, 1905). In 1904 he moved to Switzerland (later to Brussels), abandoning Vera and his four children; he formed a permanent liaison with a young admirer, Tatyana Shletser (Tatiana de Schloezer), niece of Vera's former teacher at the Moscow Conservatory.

About 1905 Scriabin zealously embraced Blavatsky's "theosophy," which inspired a large orchestral work, *Le poème de l'extase* op. 54 (Poem of ecstasy, 1905–8) and a companion Piano Sonata no. 5, op. 53 (1907). He projected an ambitious philosophical opera, but it did not come forth. In 1906–7 he toured briefly in the U.S. at the invitation of Russian émigré conductor Modest Altschuler (who premiered *Le poème de l'extase* in New York in 1908). Diaghilev programmed Scriabin's orchestral music prominently in his first Paris season in 1907.

In 1908 Scriabin found a new patron and publisher: the conductor Koussevitzky and his Édition russe de musique. Koussevitzky engineered Scriabin's return to Russia in early 1909, generating intense public enthusiasm. Now he projected an extravagant work, *Mysterium,* a mystical fusion of arts and senses culminating in spiritual catharsis. As a first step he wrote *Prométhée, le poème de feu* op. 60 (Prometheus: Poem of Fire, 1908–10), for large orchestra with piano, wordless chorus, and keyboard colored-light projector. Koussevitzky premiered it in Moscow in 1911 with Scriabin as pianist (Altschuler gave the first performance with colored light); but its reception was poor, and relations cooled between the two. In the wake of *Prométhée* Scriabin composed his last five piano sonatas, nos. 6–10 (opp. 62, 64, 1911; opp. 66, 68, 70, 1913). From 1910 he lived permanently in Russia.

Scriabin's style from 1908 is centered on novel harmonic procedures. Instead of dominant-tonic relationships, he favored pairs of unresolved dominant 7ths and 9ths a tritone apart (as found in Mussorgsky, Rimsky-Korsakov, and early Stravinsky), which he modified with a chromatically lowered 5th (providing another tritone factor) and an added major 6th. This "mystic" chord, often arranged in fourths (for example, C-F♯-B♭-e-a-d′), generates much of the substance of *Prométhée* and the late sonatas.

In 1914 Scriabin toured to England and continued to plan his ultimately unrealized *Mysterium.* His few piano pieces of 1914 show new stylistic directions, notably *Vers la flame* (Toward the Flame, op. 72) and the 5 Preludes (op. 74). Of the *Mysterium* itself, only sketches for an *Acte préalable* (Prefatory Rite) were completed, containing twelve-tone chords and other harmonic experiments. Scriabin died of sudden blood poisoning stemming from a boil that turned to a carbuncle under his mustache.

Scriabin's output consists, apart from the orchestral works mentioned, almost entirely of piano music. His pre-1900 "Chopinesque" oeuvre includes some 50 preludes, 12 etudes, numerous mazurkas, waltzes, impromptus, nocturnes, fantasies. After 1900 his works were more diverse, including many "poems" and pieces with impressionistic titles. He wrote a few vocal and chamber pieces early in his career. He penned much poetry and kept journals.

Bibl.: Boris de Schloezer, *Alexander Skryabin* (Berlin, 1923); trans. Eng. Nicholas Slonimsky as *Alexander Scriabin: Artist and Mystic* (Berkeley, 1987). Faubion Bowers, *Scriabin* (Palo Alto, 1969; 2nd. ed., 1970), and *The New Scriabin: Enigma and Answers* (New York, 1973). Gottfried Eberle, *Zwischen Tonalität und Atonalität: Studien zur Harmonik Alexander Skrjabins* (Munich, 1978). Hugh Macdonald, *Skryabin* (London, 1978). Otto Kolleritsch, ed., *Alexander Skryabin* (Graz, 1980). Manfred Kelkel, *Alexandre Scriabine* (Paris, 1984). Luigi Verdi, *Aleksandr Skrjabin, tra musica e filosofia* (Florence, 1991).

Scribe, (Augustin) Eugène (b. Paris, 24 Dec. 1791; d. there, 20 Feb. 1861). Librettist. Studied at the Collège Ste.-Barbe in Paris. Began his career writing vaudevilles and comedies. One of the most prolific librettists of his day. Because of the extreme demand for his works, he often collaborated on the writing of libretti. His works include libretti for operas by Adam, Auber (38 works), Bellini (including *La sonnambula,* 1831), Boildieu (*La dame blanche,* 1825), Cherubini, Donizetti (5, including *L'elisir d'amore,* 1832; *La favorite,* 1840), Gounod, Halévy (6, including *La Juive,* 1835), Hérold, Meyerbeer (5, including *Les Hugenots,* 1836; *Le prophète,* 1849; *L'Africaine,* 1865), Offenbach, Rossini (*Le Comte Ory,* 1828), Suppé, and Verdi (*Les vêpres siciliennes,* 1855).

Scruggs, Earl (Eugene) (b. Flint Hill, N.C., 6 Jan. 1924). Bluegrass and country banjo player, songwriter, and singer. After playing in bands and on radio in the Carolinas, in 1945 he joined Bill Monroe's Bluegrass Boys. In 1948 he left with guitarist Lester Flatt to form the Foggy Mountain Boys, which became one of the most popular country groups of the 1960s through recordings such as "Foggy Mountain Breakdown" (1949) and "The Ballad of Jed Clampett" (1962). After their dissolution in 1969 he performed country and rock with his sons as the Earl Scruggs Revue. He is credited with introducing the 3-finger banjo-picking technique characteristic of bluegrass music.

Sculthorpe, Peter (Joshua) (b. Launceston, Tasmania, 29 Apr. 1929). Composer. He graduated from the Univ. of Melbourne Conservatory of Music in 1950; traveled to England to study with Wellesz and Rubbra from 1958 to 1960 at Wadham College, Oxford; returned to Australia in 1961 and in 1963 joined the music staff at the Univ. of Sydney; served as composer-in-residence at Yale, 1965–67, and visiting professor at the Univ. of Sussex, 1971–72. Although his first compositional efforts, dating from the early 1950s, were influenced by western European composers such as Varèse and Schoenberg, Sculthorpe quickly came to reject the dominant European avant-garde trends and moved instead toward what he felt to be a more naturally Australian style of composition. Cycles of movements such as *Irkanda I, II, III, IV* (1955, 1959, 1961, 1961) and *Sun Music I, II, III, IV* (1965, 1969, 1967, 1967) evidence such "Australianism." For example, the name "Irkanda" is from Tasmanian aboriginal culture and is associated with moods and sounds created within and among the pieces. Sculthorpe expanded his musical interests to include the music of eastern Asia and the experimentation with timbres and sounds to create textures (String Quartet no. 7, "Red Landscape," 1966). He was especially influenced in this regard by Penderecki and explored techniques such as note clusters and harmonics. *Rites of Passage* (1972–74), his first opera, integrates Australian aboriginal culture with ritualistic theater and highly dramatic music. His works also include radio scores (*The Fifth Continent,* narrator, orchestra, 1963); orchestral music (*Rain,* 1970; *Love 201,* vocal band, chamber orchestra, 1971; *Child of Australia,* soprano, narrator, chorus, orchestra, 1988); and chamber music (*Nourlangie,* guitar, percussion, strings, 1989; *Sun Song,* percussion ensemble, 1989).

Bibl.: Michael Hanna, *Peter Sculthorpe: His Music and Ideas, 1929–1979* (New York, 1982). Deborah Hayes, *Peter Sculthorpe: A Bio-Bibliography* (Westport, Conn. 1994).

Searle, Humphrey (b. Oxford, 26 Aug. 1915; d. London, May 12, 1982). Composer. He studied from 1928 to 1933 at Winchester and then at Oxford Univ., where from 1933 to 1937 he was a student of classics; pursued music at the Royal College of Music under Jacob, Ireland, and R. O. Morris in 1937; traveled to Vienna, where he took composition lessons at the New Vienna Conservatory as well as privately with Webern. Appointed a producer at the BBC in 1938; in 1951 became musical consultant with Sadler's Wells Ballet; joined the faculty at the Royal College of Music in 1965. His music bears the influence of the Second Viennese composers, especially Webern. Yet such serialistic premises are developed in the context of a dramatic and expressive language characterized by a lyricism not found in Webern, as in Searle's Second Piano Concerto op. 27 (1955). By the early 1950s he began expanding his use of serialism to encompass larger-scale works, as in the Piano Sonata op. 21 (1951). Form in Searle's works tends toward balance and symmetry and may or may not have been derived from a serial set. The motivicism typical of serial composition often underlay his formal processes. His works include 3 operas (*Hamlet* op. 48, 1965–68), for which he fashioned his own libretti from original texts; orchestral music (including 5 symphonies as well as concerti); chamber music; and vocal music for varying combinations of voices and accompaniment (*The Shadow of Cain* op. 22, speakers, male chorus, orchestra, 1951; *Ophelia* op. 50, voice and piano, 1969; *Dr. Faustus* op. 69, soloists, choir, orchestra, 1977).

Sebastiani, Johann (b. near Weimar, 30 Sept. 1622; d. Königsberg [now Kaliningrad], spring 1683). Composer. He may have studied in Italy before settling in Königsberg sometime around 1650. In 1661 he became the Kantor at the cathedral, and in 1663 the Elector of Brandenburg made him court Kapellmeister. He was pensioned in 1679. Of his many sacred and occasional compositions the most famous is the large-scale St. Matthew Passion (repr. in *DDT* 17). Composed no later than 1663, it includes a 5-part chorus and an ensemble of 6 instruments. The musical style is conservative, although the influence of contemporary Italian opera is perceivable. Sebastiani's is the earliest extant Passion to include simple chorales in the score.

Sechter, Simon (b. Friedberg, Bohemia, 11 Oct. 1788; d. Vienna, 10 Sept. 1867). Teacher, theorist. Music lessons from the village schoolmaster-organist; 1803, studied to be a schoolteacher at normal school in Linz; from 1804 in Vienna, first as a private tutor, studying music on his own, having some lessons from Kozeluch and Hartmann, from 1808 as a music teacher. From 1810 to 1825 he was singing and piano teacher (with salary from 1812), Vienna Institute for the Blind; 1824, assistant court organist; from 1825, court organist but best known as a teacher. He was highly regarded in Vienna for his learning. Schubert decided to study counterpoint with him (taking one lesson), and he led Bruckner through a long and rigorous course of study. Professor of figured bass and counterpoint, 1851–67, Vienna Conservatory (succeeded by Bruckner). He published works on figured bass, an edition of Marpurg's treatise on fugue, and, most notably, 3 volumes of *Die Grundsätze der musicalischen Komposition* (Leipzig, 1853–54); memoirs, "Einiges über mich selbst," in *Wiener allgemeine Musikzeitung* 153–54 (1845): 619. Composition seems to have been an obsession with him, and he would apparently set any text at hand when the need was upon him, including whole newspapers and chapters of textbooks. His output was therefore huge, embracing nearly every vocal and instrumental genre, including opera (of which only one was ever performed) but not the symphony. Most of this was unpublished and unperformed, although some of his large output of sacred music did have some currency, and 12 of his Masses were published.

Bibl.: Walter Zeleny, *Die Historischen Grundlagen des Theoriesystems von Simon Sechter* (Tutzing, 1979). Alfred Mann, "Schubert's Lesson with Sechter," *19th-Century Music* 6 (1982): 159–65.

Seckendorff, Karl Siegmund (Freiherr) von (b. Erlangen, 26 Nov. 1744; d. Ansbach, 26 Apr. 1785). Composer and writer on music. He studied literature and law at Erlangen Univ. Served as an officer from 1761 in the Austrian army, and 1765–74 in Sardinia. In 1775–84, he was chamberlain and steward in Weimar, where he helped introduce Handel's music to Weimar. He wrote works for the stage, string quartets, lieder, smaller instrumental works.

Secunda, Sholom (b. Alexandria, Russia, 4 Sept. (n.s.) 1894; d. New York, 13 June 1974). Composer. Moved to the U.S. with his family in 1907 and studied at Cooper Union (1912–13), Columbia Univ. (1913–14), and the Institute of Musical Art (1914–19). The bulk of Secunda's output consists of Yiddish-language operettas. He also composed *3 Symphonic Sketches* for orchestra, *If Not Higher* (oratorio, 1964), *Yizkor, In Memory of the Six Million* (oratorio, 1967), a string quartet

(1945), and much Jewish liturgical music. He was a founder of the Society of Jewish Composers, Publishers, and Songwriters and music critic for the Yiddish-language daily *Vorwärts*. His most famous song is "Bei mir bist du schoen" from the operetta *I Would If I Could* (1933).

Bibl.: Victoria Secunda, *Bei Mir Bist Du Schön: The Story of Sholom Secunda* (Weston, Conn., 1982).

Seefried, Irmgard (b. Köngetried, 9 Oct. 1919; d. Vienna, 24 Nov. 1988). Soprano. Studied with her father, and later at Augsburg; made her debut at Aachen under Karajan in 1940; joined the Vienna Opera in 1943, singing in a performance of Strauss's *Ariadne auf Naxos* for the composer's 80th birthday in 1944. She appeared on tour at London in 1947; also sang at the Metropolitan Opera (1953–54), La Scala (from 1949), and Covent Garden (from 1948). She made frequent recital appearances, premiering Henze's *Ariosi* (1964) and Martin's *Magnificat* (1968); her operatic roles ranged from Mozart to Berg.

Seeger, Charles (Louis, Jr.) (b. Mexico City, 14 Dec. 1886; d. Bridgewater, Conn., 7 Feb. 1979). Musicologist, composer, folklorist. Graduating from Harvard Univ. in 1908 with a B.A., he went to Europe to study composition, conducting, and musicology (1908–1911). He returned to the U.S. in 1912 to become chairman of the music department at the Univ. of California, Berkeley (1912–19), where he gave the first musicology courses in the U.S. He finished a violin sonata during this period and also a number of songs. Other compositions were lost in a fire in 1926. In 1921 he moved to New York to teach at the Institute of Musical Art (1921–33) and the New School for Social Research (1931–35). During the 1930s he became active in the left-wing Composers Collective of New York and (under the pseudonym Carl Sands) wrote music criticism for the Communist party's *Daily Worker*. In 1935 he went to work for the federal government in Washington, D.C., first in the Resettlement Administration (1935–38), then as deputy director of the Federal Music Project of the WPA (1938–41), finally as chief of the music division of the Pan-American Union (1941–45). During this period he became deeply involved in folk music research, collecting and analyzing American tunes, promoting the study of North and Latin American folklore, and arguing for the expansion of the scope of musicology beyond Western art music. In 1957 he joined the faculty of UCLA, where he helped found the Institute of Ethnomusicology, the pioneer academic ethnomusicology program in the U.S. He retired from UCLA in 1970 but remained active as a writer and lecturer until his death. Seeger's second wife was the composer Ruth Crawford; his children are the singers and folklorists Pete Seeger, Mike Seeger, and Peggy Seeger.

Writings: with E. G. Stricklen, *Harmonic Structure and Elementary Composition* (Berkeley, 1916). *Studies in Musicology, 1935–75* (Berkeley, 1977) [a collection of Seeger's major essays plus bibliography].

Andrés Segovia.

Seeger, Pete(r R.) (b. Patterson, N.Y., 3 May 1919). Folk singer, songwriter, banjo player, and guitarist. Son of Charles Seeger. He formed the Almanac Singers with Lee Hays and Woody Guthrie in 1941, and the Weavers with Hays and Ronnie Gilbert in 1948; through recordings such as "Goodnight Irene" (1951), the Weavers were the first folk group to achieve wide national success. Several songs which he wrote or co-wrote were prominent in the 1960s folk revival, including "We Shall Overcome" (1960) and "Where Have All the Flowers Gone" (1961). His liberal political advocacy caused his blacklisting in the McCarthy era and the consequent demise of the Weavers; later he was active in environmental issues.

Bibl.: David King Dunaway, *How Can I Keep from Singing: Pete Seeger* (New York, 1990).

Seeger, Ruth Crawford. See Crawford, Ruth.

Segni, Julio [Julio da Modena, Biondin] (b. Modena, 1498; d. Rome, 23 July 1561). Organist and composer. He studied in Modena with Giacomo Fogliano. In 1530–33 he was one of 2 organists at St. Mark's, Venice. Thereafter (from 1534?) he served the Cardinal of Santa Fiore, Guido Ascanio Sforza, in Rome, where he was considered the greatest organist of his time. His 13 extant ricercars form the bulk of *Musica* *nova* (Venice, 1540); 12 more ricercars exist in secondary lute intabulations, and 1 as a keyboard piece.

Segovia, Andrés (b. Linares, 21 Feb. 1893; d. Madrid, 2 June 1987). Guitarist. He pursued music against his family's wishes; basically self-taught, he made his debut at Granada in 1909. He toured throughout Spain, then visited Latin America in 1919; he made debuts in London in 1923 and in Paris in 1924, with Dukas and Falla in the latter audience. He toured throughout Europe, and made his U.S. debut in 1928; in the ensuing years he built a worldwide following and recorded extensively. He left Spain for Uruguay in 1936, premiering Ponce's *Concierto del Sur* there in 1941. Eventually he moved to New York, then finally back to Spain, continuing to concertize into his 90s. A renowned teacher for many decades, he conducted classes at Santiago de Compostela, Siena, Berkeley, and Los Angeles, with John Williams, Christopher Parkening, and Oscar Ghiglia among his pupils. He almost singlehandedly raised the guitar to the status of concert instrument, commissioning works by Falla, Turina, Roussel, Villa-Lobos, Castelnuovo-Tedesco, and others, and arranging for guitar music from the Renaissance to Romantic eras.

Bibl.: Graham Wade, *Segovia: A Celebration of the Man and His Music* (New York, 1983).

Seguin, (Arthur) Edward (Shelden) (b. London, 7 Apr. 1809; d. New York, 9 Dec. 1852). Bass. Studied at the Royal Academy of Music. Sang at the Exeter Festival in 1829, and in London in 1831 as Polyphemus in *Acis and Galatea.* Appeared at Covent Garden, 1833–34. New York debut in 1838. Formed the Seguin English Opera Troupe, which toured the U.S. and Canada performing operas in English. Among the troupe's accomplishments was the first performance of Fry's *Leonora,* the first opera written by a native American. His brother William Henry Seguin (1814–50) was a bass. Elizabeth Seguin (1815–70), his sister, was a singer and the mother of Euphrosyne Parepa. Married soprano Anne Childe (b. ca. ?1809–14, d. 1888), who also studied at the Royal Academy of Music and sang at the King's and Drury Lane theaters. Their son Edward (S. C.) Seguin was also a singer, and a member of Carl Rosa's company.

Seiber, Mátyás (György) (b. Budapest, 4 May 1905; d. Kruger National Park, South Africa, 24 Sept. 1960). Composer. He studied cello with Shiffer and composition with Kodály at the Budapest Academy of Music, 1919–24. After some time teaching and traveling as a performer, he joined the faculty of the Hoch Conservatory in Frankfurt, 1928–33, teaching jazz theory among other subjects. He settled in England in 1935, working there at various times as composer of film music and of concert music, as a lecturer (Morley College), and as a conductor. He was an active supporter of contemporary music, helping to establish the Society for the Promotion of New Music. Seiber toured as a lecturer in South Africa in 1960, where he died in an automobile accident. As a composer he embraced genres from opera to popular song. His greatests musical influences were Bartók and Schoenberg. Jazz and folk music are discernible elements of his style. His works include those for the stage (operas, satires, ballet, radio scores), orchestral works (often involving concerto principle, as in the *Elegy,* viola, strings, 1953, and Fantasia Concerto, violin, strings, 1943–44), vocal music (*Ulysses,* tenor, chorus, orchestra, 1946–47; *Three Fragments,* speaker, choir, ensemble, 1957), and chamber music (3 string quartets).

Seidl, Anton (b. Pest, 7 May 1850; d. New York, 28 Mar. 1898). Conductor. Studied at the Leipzig Conservatory, 1870–72. Went to Bayreuth (1872) to assist Wagner in preparing the score for *The Ring.* Succeeded Damrosch at the Metropolitan Opera in 1885; succeeded Theodore Thomas at the New York Philharmonic in 1891. Conducted American premieres of many of Wagner's works, including *Die Meistersinger* (1886), *Tristan und Isolde* (1886), and *Siegfried* (1887). Conducted world premiere of Dvorák's New World Symphony (Carnegie Hall, 1887).

Seixas, (José António) Carlos de (b. Coimbra, 11 June 1704; d. Lisbon, 25 Aug. 1742). Composer. He succeeded his father as organist at Coimbra Cathedral in 1718. From 1720 until his death he was organist at the royal chapel in Lisbon; in 1738 he was granted knighthood by John V of Portugal. Of the 700 keyboard sonatas that Seixas reportedly wrote, only 88 survive. Similarly, the 8 extant choral works must represent only a portion of his output. Although he and Domenico Scarlatti were both at Lisbon, Seixas's style does not reflect the influence of the older composer. In the sonatas he employed a variety of styles and experimented with motivic development.

Bibl.: Macario Santiago Kastner, *Carlos Seixas* (Coimbra, 1947).

Sekles, Bernhard (b. Frankfurt, 20 Mar. 1872; d. Frankfurt, 8 Dec. 1934). Composer, conductor, teacher. Studied at the Hoch Conservatory in Frankfurt, later with Humperdinck. Opera conductor in Heidelberg (1893–94) and Mainz (1895–96). He returned to the Hoch Conservatory in 1896 to teach theory and composition and was director of the conservatory from 1923 to 1933. Works include *Volkspoesien aus dem Rumänischen* (1900); *Scheherazade* (opera, Mannheim, 1917); string quartet (1923); *Die zehn Küsse* (opera, Frankfurt, 1926); *Der Dybuk* (prelude for orchestra, 1928); Symphony no. 1 (1930).

Selby, William (b. England, ca. 1738; d. Boston, 12 Dec. 1798). Composer and organist. He held appointments in England at the London Holy Sepulchre Church and at Magdalene Church before emigrating to America in 1771. At this time he was named organist at King's Chapel in Boston; he held a similar position at Trinity Church in Newport, R.I., during 1773–74, and resumed the King's Chapel position when he returned to Boston. He published some music during the 1760s while still in England, and he continued composition once in America. His compositions include both sacred and secular choral works, and keyboard pieces.

Bibl.: David McKay, "William Selby, Musical Émigré in Colonial Boston," *MQ* 57 (1971): 609–27.

Selika, Marie [née Smith; Williams, Mrs. Sampson] (b. Natchez, Miss., ca. 1849; d. New York, 19 May 1937). Soprano. Possibly born a slave; a wealthy white family in Cincinnati acted as her patron, sending her to study with Bianchi in San Francisco (1873). After her debut in 1876, she went to Chicago, where she studied with Antonio Farini. Settled in Boston in 1878, adopting the stage name Selika (probably from the protagonist of Meyerbeer's *L'africaine*). She studied and performed in England in 1882. She was nicknamed "The Queen of Staccato." Her husband was tenor Signor Velosko (Sampson Williams).

Selle, Thomas (b. Zörbig, near Bitterfeld, 23 Mar. 1599; d. Hamburg, 2 July 1663). Composer. He may have attended the Thomasschule in Leipzig before beginning studies at the university in the summer of 1622. While in Leipzig he may have studied with Seth Calvisius, the Thomaskantor. His appointments included Kantor at Heide (1624), rector at Wesselburen (1625), Kantor at Itzehoe (May 1634) and at the Johanneum in Hamburg (12 Aug. 1641). He was also civic director of church music in Hamburg. Schelle wrote vocal music exclusively, though in a wide variety of forms and styles. Schein, Scheidt, and Praetorius seem to have been significant influences on him. His Johannespassion (1641) is the first Passion to include instrumental interludes.

Selmer, Henri (b.?; d.?). Clarinetist and instrument maker. Formed Henri Selmer & Cie. in Paris, 1885. By 1904 the company produced reeds and mouthpieces for clarinets. Alexandre Selmer, Henri's younger brother, was a clarinetist in the Boston Symphony Orchestra. He opened an import shop in New York, and returned in 1918 to Paris to work with his brother. The American distribution center was sold to George M. Bundy. The company soon expanded by producing other woodwind instruments and saxophones, and by 1927 they added trumpets and trombones. The Selmer Company moved in 1927 to Elkhart, Indiana.

Sembrich, Marcella [Kochańska, Prakseda Marcelina] (b. Wiśniewczyk, Galicia, 15 Feb. 1858; d. New York, 11 Jan. 1935). Soprano. She played violin and piano as a child. At age 11 she studied at the Lemberg Conservatory with Wilhelm Stengel (1846–1917), whom she married in 1877. Also studied with Viktor von Rokitansky and G. B. Lamperti the younger. Debut in Athens (1877) as Elvira in *I puritani,* taking her mother's maiden name as her stage name. Studied the German repertoire with Richard Lewy in Vienna. Appeared at Dresden in 1878, at Covent Garden in 1880, at the Metropolitan Opera in 1883. Engaged at the Met, 1898–1909. Gave recitals until 1917. Head of the voice department at Curtis Institute of Music. At a benefit concert she played two movements of a Bériot violin concerto and a Chopin mazurka, and sang the part of Rosina in excerpts from Rossini's *Il barbiere di Siviglia.*

Bibl.: H. Goddard Owen, *A Recollection of Marcella Sembrich* (New York, 1982).

Semkow, Jerzy [Georg] (b. Radomsko, 12 Oct. 1928). Conductor. Studied in Kraków; later served as an assistant at Leningrad; also conducted at the Bolshoi Theater, Moscow. He later studied with Serafin at Rome and Walter at Vienna, and held opera posts at Warsaw (1959–62) and Copenhagen (1966–71), making guest appearances elsewhere in Europe and in the U.S. He led the St. Louis Symphony (1976–79), the Rome Radio Symphony (1979–83); served as music adviser and principal conductor of the Rochester (N.Y.) Philharmonic (1985–89).

Senaillé [Senallié, Senaillié, Senallier, Senaillier]**, Jean Baptiste** (b. Paris, 23 Nov. 1687; d. there, 15 Oct. 1730). Composer. His first teacher was probably his father, Jean Senaillé, a violinist in the 24 Violons du Roi. He may also have studied with G. A. Piani and Jean Baptiste Anet; reports that he studied with T. A. Vitali are unsubstantiated. In January 1713 he replaced his father in the 24 Violons du Roi, and following a trip to Italy (1717–19) rejoined it permanently in 1720. From 1728 to 1730 Senaillé was a soloist at the Concert spirituel. His 50 sonatas for violin and continuo, published between 1710 and 1727, reveal him to be among the earliest French violinist-composers to combine Italian and French instrumental styles.

Sender, Ramon (b. Madrid, 29 Oct. 1934). Composer. In New York he studied piano with George Copeland and theory with Elliott Carter; attended the San Francisco Conservatory (1959–62), where he studied composition with Robert Erickson. With Morton Subotnick he founded the San Francisco Tape Music Center (1961–66) and later the Mills (College) Tape Music Center. Most of his compositions from this period combine tape and other electronic devices with live performance—for example, *Thrones* (1963) for tape and colored lights, and *Desert Ambulance* (1964) for amplified accordion and tape. After 1966 he turned to composing chants for paraprofessional performers, with the aim of engendering spiritual community and spiritual change. Composed the choral work *I Have a Dream* (1984).

Senesino [Bernardi, Francesco] (b. Siena, ca. 1680; d. there?, by 27 Jan. 1759). Alto castrato. He was called Senesino after his birthplace. From 1707 to 1716 he sang in Venice, Bologna, Genoa, and Naples, playing parts in operas by Caldara, Lotti, and Alessandro Scarlatti, among others. After a time in Dresden (1717–20), he was engaged for the Royal Academy in London, with which he sang from September 1720 to June 1728. From 1730 to 1733 he sang with the second academy, then joined the rival Opera of the Nobility (1733–36). After singing for a time in Florence (1737–39), he ended his career in Naples in 1740. Senesino was extremely popular throughout his career, especially in London. He sang 20 roles in Handel operas, 17 of which were written for him.

Senfl [Sennfl, Sennfli], **Ludwig** (b. Basel?, ca. 1486; d. Munich, between 2 Dec. 1542 and 10 Aug. 1543). Composer. From 1496 he was a chapel singer and copyist in the imperial court of Maximilian I at Augsburg and Vienna, serving under Heinrich Isaac from 1497. He was Isaac's amanuensis from at least 1507 and helped Isaac compose the collection *Choralis constantinus* for the Konstanz Cathedral in 1508–9. A lied by Senfl appeared in the first printed German musical anthology (Augsburg, 1512). From 1513 he deputized for Isaac (who was living in Florence) at the court, succeeding him as *maestro di cappella* in 1517. In 1519 on the accession of Charles V the court chapel was disbanded and replaced with Spanish musicians. Senfl brought out the first German anthology of motets, *Liber selectarum cantionum* (Augsburg, 1520), including 7 of his own works, as part of an unsuccessful bid for reappointment by Charles V.

In 1523 Duke Wilhelm IV of Bavaria reinstated many former imperial musicians, with Senfl as leader, at his own court in Munich, thereby creating the finest chapel in Germany. Senfl began to exhibit sympathies with the Reformation in his correspondence with Duke Albrecht of Prussia and with Martin Luther; the latter commissioned 2 motets from him. In 1529 Senfl gave up customary religious orders and married; but his courtly status remained secure. In his last decade he composed and edited several more printed collections, including the collaborative *Harmoniae poeticae* (Nuremberg, 1539) with Paul Hofhaimer, and a posthumous edition of *Choralis constantinus* (Nuremberg, 1550–55). His works include 300 motets (some in German), 6 or 7 Masses, 8 Magnificats, 40 Latin classical odes, and nearly 300 German lieder ranging from the sacred to the broadly popular. He was widely regarded as the greatest German musician of his time.

Bibl.: Martin Bente, *Neue Wege der Quellenkritik und die Biographie Ludwig Senfls* (Wiesbaden, 1968).

Serafin, Tullio (b. Rottanova di Cavarzere, near Venice, 1 Sept. 1878; d. Rome, 2 Feb. 1968). Conductor. Studied at the Milan Conservatory, also playing violin and viola at La Scala; made his professional conducting debut at Ferrara in 1900; after appearing in several Italian locales he became principal conductor at La Scala in 1909, though continuing to tour. Later engagements included those at the Metropolitan Opera (1924–34) and the Teatro reale, Rome (1934–43); he returned to the U.S. after the war, conducting in New York (1952) and Chicago (1956–58) before assuming the artistic directorship of the Teatro dell'Opera, Rome, in 1962. He was influential in the revival of 19th-century Italian opera, and aided the careers of many singers, including Ponselle, Callas, and Sutherland.

Bibl.: Teodoro Celli and Giuseppe Pugliese, *Tullio Serafin: Il patriarca del melodramma* (Venice, 1985).

Serafino de' Ciminelli dall'Aquila [Serafino Aquilano] (b. Aquila, 6 Jan. 1466; d. Rome, 10 Aug. 1500). Poet and musician. In 1478 he became a page in the Count of Potenza's court; he returned to Aquila in 1481 and three years later entered the service of Cardinal Ascanio Sforza in Rome, where he met Josquin and Andrea Coscia. By 1491 Serafino was in Naples, where he was well regarded as an *improvvisatore.* He entered the service first of Beatrice d'Este (until 1497) and then of Cesare Borgia in Rome (1499). Renowned in his time as a composer of both *strambotti* and sonnets; Serafino's verse is full of Petrarchan conceits and draws freely on Tebaldeo and the classics.

Bibl.: Antonio Rossi, *Serafino Aquilano e la poesia cortigiana* (Brescia, 1980).

Serebrier, José (b. Montevideo, 3 Dec. 1938). Composer, conductor. Studied at the Montevideo Conservatory, then at the Curtis Institute in Philadelphia (1956–58). At the Berkshire Music Center (Tanglewood) he studied composition with Copland, conducting with Monteux and Dorati. His Symphony no. 1 (1956) was introduced by Stokowski in 1957. Serebrier was associate conductor of the American Symphony Orchestra (1962–67), composer-in-residence with the Cleveland Orchestra (1968–70), and conductor of the Cleveland Philharmonic (1968–71). During the 1970s and 1980s, he made frequent guest appearances and recordings with major orchestras; in 1984 he founded the International Festival of the Americas and became its first artistic director. Works include Partita, orchestra (1963); Saxophone Quartet (1969); *Colores mágicos,* harp, chamber orchestra, and lights (1971); Symphony for percussion (1972).

Serkin, Peter (b. New York, 24 July 1947). Pianist. Son of Rudolf Serkin. Performed regularly as a youth, attending the Curtis Institute from age 12; at 14 played a Mozart 2-piano concerto with his father at Cleveland. He co-founded the chamber ensemble Tashi in 1973, performing both new music and the standard repertory. Recorded sonatas and the Diabelli Variations of Beethoven, Mozart piano concertos, Schubert works, and 20th-century music. On the faculties of the Juilliard School and Mannes College.

Serkin, Rudolf (b. Eger, Bohemia, 28 March 1903; d. Guilford, Vt., 8 May 1991). Pianist. Studied with Richard Robert (piano) and Schoenberg (composition) in Vienna, appearing with the Vienna Symphony in 1915; from 1920 he was associated with the violinist Adolf Busch, with whom he played sonata recitals for many years and made his American debut in 1933. Serkin and the Busch family settled near Basel in 1927; in 1935 Serkin married Busch's daughter Irene. In 1936 he played a Mozart concerto with the New York Philharmonic under Toscanini, earning acclaim. He moved to the U.S. at the outset of World War II; taught at the Curtis Institute from 1938, directing it between 1968 and 1975; in 1949 he was a co-founder of the Marlboro School, and in 1950 established the Marlboro Festival.

Serly, Tibor (b. Losonc, Hungary, 25 Nov. 1901; d. London, 8 Oct. 1978). Violist, composer, conductor. His parents, both musicians, brought him to the U.S. as a child in 1904. He studied violin and composition at the Institute of Musical Art in New York. In 1922 he returned to Hungary to the Royal Academy of Music in Budapest, where he studied violin with Jenö Hubay and composition with Kodály. Returning to the U.S. in 1925, he played viola in the Cincinnati Symphony (1927–28), the Philadelphia Orchestra (1928–37), and the NBC Symphony (1937–38), after which he retired from orchestral playing in order to compose, conduct, and write. His early works, such as the Viola Concerto (1929) and *Six Dance Designs* (1933), are strongly influenced by Hungarian folk song. Between 1940 and 1945 he devoted himself to the person and the career of Bela Bartók, who had just arrived in the U.S. as a refugee. Upon Bartók's death in 1945, Serly completed the final measures of the Third Piano Concerto, then undertook a reconstruction of Bartók's Viola Concerto from sketches (1950). During the 1940s Serly worked out a harmonic theory he called "Modus Lascivus"; from 1945 through the 1970s he composed many works using this system—for example, Piano Sonata (1947), *Lament* (string orchestra, 1955–58)—as well as other works using traditional harmony.

Bibl.: Tibor Serly, *A Second Look at Harmony* (New York, 1964). *Modus Lascivus = The Road to Enharmonicism: A New Concept in Composition* (Ann Arbor, 1975). David Dalton, "The Genesis of Bartók's Viola Concerto," *ML* 57 (1976): 117–29.

Sermisy, Claudin [Claude] **de** (b. ca. 1490; d. Paris, 13 Oct. 1562). Composer. He served as a cleric at the Saint-Chapelle in Paris and as a singer in the private chapel of Louis XII, and he may well have traveled with the king on his journeys to Bologna in 1515 and Boulogne-sur-Mer in 1532. After serving as a canon at Notre-Dame-de-la-Rotonde in Rouen, he went to the parish church of Cambron in the Amiens diocese in 1524. In 1532 he returned to Paris as *sous-maître*—essentially music director—at the royal chapel. He was nominated to the 11th canonry of the Sainte-Chapelle in 1533, and in 1554 was given a prebend at Ste. Catherine, Troyes. Sermisy's reputation was high during his lifetime—Jean Daniel grouped him together with Févin, La Rue, Josquin, Prioris, and Janequin—and extended well beyond France. His chansons, mostly in 4 voices, are more syllabic, homophonic, and folklike than those of the previous generation of chanson composers. The substantial body of sacred music includes a number of parody Masses and a St. Matthew Passion.

Bibl.: *C. de Sermisy: Opera omnia,* ed. Gaston Allaire and Isabelle Cazeaux (1970–86). Isabelle Anne-Marie Cazeaux, "The Secular Music of Claudin de Sermisy" (diss., Columbia Univ., 1964).

Serocki, Kazimierz (b. Toruń, 3 Mar. 1922; d. Warsaw, 9 Jan. 1981). Composer. He studied piano with Szpinalski and composition with Sikorski at the Łódź Conservatory. After graduating in 1946 he traveled to Paris, where he studied for a year with Boulanger and Levy. During the late 1940s he toured Europe as a concert pianist, concentrating on composition by the early 1950s. He served as an officer for the Polish Composers' Union, 1954–55. Although some of his music employed dodecaphonic techniques (*Suita preludiów,* piano, 1952), his musical language was eclectic in its use of various avant-garde trends such as unusual instrumentation, graphic notation, and theatrical use or placement of players, with careful attention to the setting of texts. Works include orchestral (*Segmenti,* 1961; *Freski symfoniczne,* 1964; *Pianophonie,* piano, electronics, orchestra, 1976–78), vocal (*Nioke,* male speaker, female speaker, choir, orchestra, 1966), and chamber music.

Serov, Alexander (Nikolaievich) (b. St. Petersburg, 23 Jan. 1820; d. there, 1 Feb. 1871). Composer and critic. He studied at the School of Jurisprudence in St. Petersburg; became a functionary in the Ministry of Justice (1840–45) and presided over the Appeals Court in Simferopol in the Crimea (1845–48) before taking a similar post in Pskov (1848–51). In 1851 he abandoned government work and began writing music criticism, becoming editor of the *Musical and Theatrical Monitor* in 1856. In 1858 and 1859 he undertook two trips to Germany, meeting Wagner on the second journey; he became both an ardent admirer of Wagner's music and an important polemicist for his ideas back in Russia. Serov started composition late in life, and aside from some correspondence courses in counterpoint with Joseph Hunke was entirely self-taught. His 5-act opera *Judith* was performed in St. Petersburg in 1863 to great acclaim; a second opera, *Rogneda,* followed in 1865. He was awarded a pension by the czar, which allowed him to turn down a teaching post at the Moscow Conservatory (the position eventually went to Tchaikovsky). Serov was at work on a third opera, *Vrazhya sila* [Malevolent Power], when he died suddenly from a heart attack; the work was completed by his widow and Soloviev and produced in St. Petersburg in 1871. The style of *Judith* is somewhat reminiscent of Meyerbeer; *Rogneda* and *Vrazhya sila* both make use of Russian folk idioms. His operas were an important influence on Mussorgsky, Tchaikovsky, and Rimsky-Korsakov, and they continue to be performed in Russia.

Bibl.: Gerald Abraham, "The Operas of Serov," in *Essays Presented to Egon Wellesz,* ed. Jack Westrup (Oxford, 1966), pp. 171–83. Richard Taruskin, "Opera and Drama in Russia: The Case of Serov's *Judith,*" *JAMS* 32 (1979): 74–117.

Serrano (Simeón), José (b. Sueca, Valencia, 14 Oct. 1873; d. Madrid, 8 Mar. 1941). Composer. Received initial training from his father; later studied at the Valencia Conservatory with Giner and at Madrid with

Bretón and Chapí. Primarily a theater composer; his *El motete* (1900) brought him his first triumph. He composed a total of about 100 zarzuelas, including *Moros y cristianos* (1905), *Alma de Dios* (1907), *El carro del sol* (1911, in collaboration with Vives), *Los de Aragón* (1927), and *La dolorosa* (1930); the opera *La venta de los gatos* was first performed posthumously in 1943. Other compositions include a Mass and other sacred music as well as songs and keyboard pieces.

Serrano y Ruiz, Emilio (b. Vitoria, 13 Mar. 1850; d. Madrid, 8 Apr. 1939). Composer. He studied at Madrid Conservatory with Arrieta and Eslava; also taught there until 1920. He founded the Madrid Fine Arts Circle Concerts. He composed 5 operas, including *Mitrídates* (1882) and *La maja de numbo* (1910). He collaborated with F. Alonso on the zarzuela *La bejarana,* and also composed many songs.

Sessions, Roger (Huntington) (b. Brooklyn, 28 Dec. 1896; d. Princeton, N.J., 16 Mar. 1985). Composer. Taught piano by his mother, he showed early promise on that instrument. He entered Harvard in 1911 at the age of 14, graduating with a B.A. in 1915. He then went to the Yale School of Music, where he studied with Horatio Parker and received a B.M. in 1917. From 1917 to 1921 he taught music at Smith College, meanwhile studying composition in New York with Ernest Bloch, who was teaching at the Mannes School. When Bloch moved to the Cleveland Institute of Music in 1921, Sessions went with him, working as his assistant and teaching music theory. During this time Sessions composed incidental music for a Smith College production of *The Black Maskers,* a play by the Russian dramatist Leonid Andreyev. Later arranged as a suite, *The Black Maskers* became one of Sessions's most frequently performed works. When, in 1925, Bloch left the Cleveland Institute, Sessions went to Europe to compose. He lived in Florence (1926–27), Rome (1928–31), and Berlin (1931–33). His First Symphony, written in Italy, was performed by the Boston Symphony under Koussevitzky in April 1927. It was received as a "neoclassical" piece in the style of Stravinsky. Sessions's First Piano Sonata (1928–30), by contrast, had moved far enough away from Stravinsky's manner for Aaron Copland to remark on the "universality" of its style and to call it "a cornerstone upon which to base an American Music." Sessions and Copland worked together to produce the Copland-Sessions Concerts of Contemporary Music, a series of eight concerts in New York and one in Paris between April 1928 and March 1931. Intended to present works by the younger generation of American composers, these concerts brought many subsequently well-known composers to greater public attention. During the 1930s Sessions tended to be seen as the representative of an internationalist strain in American music, a characterization that he endorsed.

With the rise to power of Hitler in 1933, Sessions, who was outspokenly opposed to Nazism, returned to the U.S. He took a series of teaching jobs, culminating in a faculty appointment at Princeton Univ., where he remained until 1944, when he moved to the Univ. of California at Berkeley. In 1935 he finished his Violin Concerto, a giant work which was not performed with orchestra until 1940. In 1936 came the String Quartet no. 1, in which twelve-tone elements began to be heard. This direction was confirmed in *Pages from a Diary* (1939; rev. 1940), a suite of piano pieces, the Piano Sonata no. 2 (1946), and the Symphony no. 2, which was premiered by the San Francisco Symphony in January 1947. Many of his works from the 1950s and 1960s employ twelve-tone techniques—for example, the Violin Sonata (1953), the *Idyll of Theocritus* (soprano and orchestra, 1954), or the String Quintet (1958)—yet Sessions always insisted that dodecaphony should be not a mechanical application of rules but a means that the composer may choose toward a "concrete musical result" that he has in mind (*Questions,* pp. 116–17). Another work using serialism in a personal manner was *Montezuma* (1963), a full-scale opera, first produced in Berlin in 1964.

Sessions had returned to Princeton in 1953. During the 1960s and 1970s he occupied himself mainly with orchestral works: Symphonies no. 5–9 (1964, 1966, 1967, 1968, and 1978), Rhapsody for Orchestra (1970), Concerto for Violin, Violoncello, and Orchestra (1971), and Concerto for Orchestra (1981). Dense scores, written in a highly personal idiom and demanding much of the listener, these works were received with enthusiasm and respect but were not performed frequently during the composer's lifetime. *When Lilacs Last in the Dooryard Bloom'd* (1970), a cantata for soloists, chorus, and orchestra, composed on a text by Walt Whitman and dedicated to the memory of Martin Luther King, Jr., and Robert F. Kennedy, drew a more emotional reception and was performed more. Both through his compositions and through his teaching, Sessions exercised considerable influence over a generation of American composers. After retiring from Princeton in 1965, he was Ernest Bloch Professor at Berkeley for a year (1966–67) and then Charles Eliot Norton Professor at Harvard (1968–69). He continued to teach composition on a part-time basis at Juilliard until 1983. Other works: *On the Beach at Fontana,* soprano and piano (1930); *The Trial of Lucullus,* 1-act opera (Berkeley, 1947); Piano Concerto (1956); Symphony no. 3 (1957); Symphony no. 4 (1958); Six Pieces for Violoncello (1966); Five Pieces for Piano (1975); Waltz for Piano (1978).

Writings: *The Musical Experience of Composer, Performer, Listener* (Princeton, 1950). *Harmonic Practice* (New York, 1951). *Reflections on the Music Life in the United States* (New York, 1956). *Questions about Music* (Cambridge, Mass., 1970). *Roger Sessions on Music—Collected Essays* (Princeton, 1979).

Bibl.: Aaron Copland, "Contemporaries at Oxford," *MM* 9 (1931): 17–23. Henry Cowell, ed., *American Composers on American Music* (Palo Alto, 1933). Benjamin Boretz and Edward Cone, eds., *Perspectives on American Composers* (New York, 1971). Edward Cone, "In Defense of Song: The Contribution of Roger Sessions," *Critical Inquiry* 2 (1975): 93–112.

Carol J. Oja, "The Copland–Sessions Concerts and Their Reception in the Contemporary Press," *MQ* 65 (1979): 212–229. "In Memoriam Roger Sessions" [articles by many contributors], *PNM* 23 (Spring–Summer, 1985): 110–65. Andrea Olmstead, *Roger Sessions and His Music* (Ann Arbor, 1985).

Seter, Mordecai (b. Novorossiysk, 26 Feb. 1916; d. Tel Aviv, 8 Aug. 1994). Composer. He traveled to Palestine, where he studied piano with Weinberg and Burstein-Arber; in Paris studied with Dandelot and Levy in 1932; later studied composition with Dukas, Boulanger, and Stravinsky. Returning to Palestine, he became engaged in the local folk music. In the late 1950s he was active with the Inbal Dance Theater and eventually received commissions from Martha Graham as well. His early music bore the influence of French impressionism. His style then incorporated elements of dance and folk song. He experimented with serialism, initially in a strict manner and then with increasing freedom. His musical language was highly dramatic.

Ševčík, Otakar (b. Horaždovice, 22 Mar. 1852; d. Písek, 18 Jan. 1934). Violinist. Studied with Bennewitz at the Prague Conservatory, 1866–70. Led orchestras of Salzburg and Vienna. Concertized in Prague and Vienna. Professor of violin at the Imperial Music School, Kiev, 1875–92, and at the Prague Conservatory, 1892–1906. Wrote many pedagogical works for the violin, including numerous etudes and exercises.

Séverac, (Marie-Joseph-Alexandre) Déodat de (b. St. Félix de Caraman en Laurangais, 20 July 1872; d. Céret, 24 Mar. 1921). Composer. Born in the southwestern corner of France, he remained devoted to the music of his native region. He studied at Toulouse Conservatory (1893–96), then at the Schola cantorum in Paris (1896–1907). His teachers were d'Indy and Albéric Magnard in composition, Charles Bordes in choral conducting, Blanche Selva and Albéniz in piano. During this time he wrote much piano music, of which the suite *En Languedoc* (1903–4) is the best known. He returned to his native province in 1907, establishing himself at Céret. Many of Séverac's works are based on regional themes, for example, the opera *Héliogabale* (Béziers, 1910), which adds folk instruments from the Catalan *cobla* band to the orchestra. He completed Albéniz's *Navarra* after that composer's death in 1909. Other works: *Le coeur du moulin* (opera, Paris, 1909); *Helène de Sparthe* (incidental music, Paris, 1912); *Le chant de la terre* (piano suite, 1901); *Le soldat de plomb* (piano 4-hands, 1905); *Baigneuses au soleil* (piano, 1980); *En vacances* (piano suite, 1921).

Bibl.: Blanche Selva, *Déodat de Séverac* (Paris, 1930); Elaine Brody, "Déodat de Séverac: A Mediterranean Musician," *MR* 29 (1968): 172–83. Déodat de Séverac, *Écrits sur la musique* (Liège, 1993).

Seydelmann [Seidelmann], **Franz** (b. Dresden, 8 Oct. 1748; d. there, 23 Oct. 1806). Composer. He received early musical education from composers J. G. Schürer and J. G. Naumann in Dresden, where his father was a court musician. Between 1765 and 1768 he accompanied Naumann and fellow pupil Joseph Schuster to Italy on a study tour. Together with Schuster he was granted appointment as Dresden court church composer in 1772 and as Kapellmeister in 1787. He composed operas; *Il mostro ossia Da gratitudine amore* (1785) and *Il turco in Italia* (1788) were quite successful. He also wrote other vocal music and chamber music.

Seyfried, Ignaz (Xaver) von (b. Vienna, 15 Aug. 1776; d. there, 27 Aug. 1841). Composer. He studied keyboard with Mozart and Kozeluch, composition with Albrechtsberger and Winter. A conductor in Schikaneder's theater, 1797–1801, and at the Theater an der Wien, 1801–27; both theaters performed many of his works. *Der Wundermann am Rheinfall* (Vienna 1799), on Schikaneder's text, was one of his more frequently performed works. He wrote many operas, singspiels, incidental music, instrumental works, and later in his career Masses, chamber music, and church music. A friend of Beethoven's, he conducted the premiere of *Fidelio.* He contributed to *Neue Zeitschrift für Musik, Allgemeine musikalische Zeitung,* and *Cäcilia* and published theoretical works of other writers.

Bibl.: Bettina von Seyfried, *Ignaz Ritter von Seyfried: thematische-bibliographisches Verzeichnis: Aspekte der Biographie und des Werkes* (New York, 1990).

Seymour, John Laurance (b. Los Angeles, 18 Jan. 1893; d. San Francisco, 1 Feb. 1986). Composer. Studied music and Slavic languages at the Univ. of California, Berkeley (B.A., 1917; M.A., 1919), then went to Italy and France to study composition (1923–28). Taught at Berkeley, then at Sacramento Jr. College. His opera *In the Pasha's Garden* was staged by the Metropolitan Opera in New York (1935). Other operas are *Ramona* (Provo, Utah, 1970) and the Spanish-language *Ollanta, el Jefe Kolla* (1977). He also wrote several operettas, among them *Bachelor Belles* (1922) and *Hollywood Madness* (1936).

Sgambati, Giovanni (b. Rome, 28 May 1841; d. there, 14 Dec. 1914). Pianist, composer, and conductor. Studied with Barbieri from the age of 5; public debut the next year. Joined a church choir, directed a small orchestra, and wrote some sacred music. Studied with Natalucci to 1860, when he embarked on a career as a pianist. He studied a bit with Liszt in Rome, and promoted Liszt's music throughout his life. In 1866, organized a series of concerts in Rome which promoted symphonic repertoire, including Liszt's Dante-Symphony and Beethoven's Eroica Symphony. Upon the recommendation of Wagner, Sgambati's 2 piano quartets were published by Schott in 1876 and 1877. Conducted his First Symphony in Paris, 1886, and his Second Symphony in 1887 in Cologne. Toured Russia and major cities in northern Europe in 1903. Founded with Ettore Pinelli the Liceo musicale di S Cecilia. Com-

Ravi Shankar.

posed 2 symphonies, overtures, Requiem, piano concerto, string quartet, piano pieces, sacred music, and songs.

Bibl.: A. Casella, "Giovanni Sgambati," *ML* 6 (1925): 304–13.

Shankar, Ravi (b. Varanasi, Uttar Pradesh, India, 7 Apr. 1920). Sitar player and composer. Studied with his brother Uday, a dancer, and from 1936 with Ustad Allauddin Khan; led the instrumental ensemble of All-India Radio from 1949 to 1956; toured the U.S. and Europe during 1956 and 1957, also appearing at a UNESCO concert at Paris in 1958 and at the 1963 Edinburgh Festival. His collaborations with Yehudi Menuhin and George Harrison broadened his popularity and that of Indian music generally in the West; he performed with Harrison at the Woodstock Festival in 1969 and at the Concert for Bangladesh in 1971. He founded a music school in Bombay in 1962, and a short-lived annex to it at Los Angeles in 1967. His compositions include ballet and film music, 2 sitar concertos (1971, 1976), and many ragas. He also wrote an autobiography, and the biographical film *Raga* appeared in 1972.

Shapero, Harold (Samuel) (b. Lynn, Mass., 29 April 1920). Composer, pianist. As a teenager he studied piano with Eleanor Kerr and composition with Nicholas Slonimsky and Ernst Krenek. He also played in dance bands and later worked as an arranger for Benny Goodman. He attended Harvard Univ. (1937–41), where he studied with Piston. Beginning in his college years and continuing through the 1940s he composed many works in a tonal framework and classicizing style, for example, the Trumpet Sonata (1940), 3 Sonatas for Piano (1944), and the Symphony for Classical Orchestra (1947). In 1952 he joined the faculty of Brandeis Univ. He experimented with twelve-tone techniques (Partita in C, piano and small orchestra, 1960), electronic instruments (Three Studies in C#, synthesizer and piano, 1969), and jazz-derived idioms (*On Green Mountain,* jazz ensemble, 1957). Other works: *3 Pieces for 3 Pieces* (flute, clarinet, bassoon, 1938); String Trio (1938); *Nine-Minute Overture* (orchestra, 1940); String Quartet (1941); Violin Sonata (1942); Concerto for Orchestra (1950; rev. as Credo for Orchestra, 1955); *American Variations* (piano, 1950); *2 Psalms* (unaccompanied chorus, 1952); *Four Pieces in B♭,* synthesizer and piano (1970); Symphony for Classical Orchestra (1995).

Shapey, Ralph (b. Philadelphia, 12 Mar. 1921). Composer and conductor. A precocious musician, he studied violin with Emanuel Zetlin and composition with Stefan Wolpe. At age 17 he was assistant conductor of the National Youth Symphony. He had no university or conservatory training, but started composing chamber music while in the army during World War II. His second String Quartet (1949) was performed by the Juilliard Quartet; his Concerto for clarinet and chamber ensemble (1954) was introduced by the New York Philharmonic Chamber Society. Three orchestral works of the late 1950s—*Ontogeny* (1958), *Invocation* (violin and orchestra, 1959), and *Rituals* (1959)—established Shapey's reputation and marked the emergence of his mature style. Taught at the Univ. of Chicago, 1964–91. In Chicago he founded the Contemporary Chamber Players. In 1969 Shapey announced that he was withdrawing all of his compositions from performance and that he had ceased to compose new works. In fact, he kept on composing but did not release any new works. He maintained his moratorium until 1976, when friends prevailed upon him to resume public performances with *Praise* (1971), an oratorio on biblical texts, dedicated to the State of Israel. He was awarded a MacArthur fellowship (1982); Fromm award for outstanding contribution to 20th century music (1993). Other works: String Quartet no. 7 (1972); *31 Variations* (Fromm Variations, piano, 1973); *Songs of Eros* (soprano, orchestra, tape, 1975); *The Covenant* (soprano, tape, chamber ensemble, 1977); *Song of Songs I, II, III* (soprano, bass, tape, chamber ensemble, 1979–80); Concerto grosso (woodwind quintet, 1981); Double Concerto (violin, cello, orchestra, 1983); *Variations* (organ, 1985); *Concerto fantastique* (orchestra, 1991); String Quartet no. 8 (1994).

Shaporin, Yuri (Alexandrovich) (b. Glukhov, Ukraine, 8 Nov. 1887; d. Moscow, 9 Dec. 1966). Composer. He studied philology at Kiev Univ. (1906–8) and took composition with Lyubomirsky; attended the Univ. of St. Petersburg as a law student before enrolling at the St. Petersburg Conservatory (1913–18), where his teachers included Sokolov, Steinberg, and Cherepnin. In 1919 he was a cofounder of the Grand Drama Theater and eventually served as its music director; he was also a founder-member of the Association for Contemporary Music (1926–30), which helped promote closer ties to the West. In 1939 he was appointed professor of instrumentation at the Moscow Conservatory, becoming professor of composition after the war; his students included Shchedrin, Volkonsky, and Khachaturian. His life's work was the opera *The Decembrists* (1920–53), which remains in the Russian repertory; it is often compared to Borodin's *Prince Igor.*

Shavers, Charlie [Charles James] (b. New York, 3 Aug. 1917; d. New York, 8 July 1971). Jazz trumpeter. He joined John Kirby's swing sextet (1937–44), for which he composed "Undecided" (recorded in 1938). From 1945 to 1956 he played intermittently with Tommy Dorsey's big band. He also led groups (including a sextet with Louie Bellson, 1950), toured with Jazz at the Philharmonic, and joined Benny Goodman (1954). With an impromptu group called the All Stars he recorded the album *Session at Riverside* (1956). Exciting muted solos and a driving lead are characteristic of his playing.

Shaw, Artie [Arthur Jacob Arshawsky] (b. New York, 23 May 1910). Jazz and popular clarinetist and bandleader. After leading an unusual 12-piece group incorporating a string quartet (1936–37), he formed a conventional swing big band (1937–39, including the recording "Begin the Beguine," 1938). Billie Holiday sang with the group (1938); Buddy Rich played drums (1939). The success of his recording "Frenesi" (1940) led to the formation of a big band enlarged by 9 strings; simultaneously he founded the Gramercy Five, a swing combo which recorded "Summit Ridge Drive" (1940) and pursued further experiments, such as Johnny Guarnieri's harpsichord playing. Shaw led a big band including Hot Lips Page (1941), another for the navy (1942–43), and one including Roy Eldridge (1944–45). He continued leading big bands and Gramercy Fives until 1954. He never played again, but beginning in 1983 directed a big band. He published *The Trouble with Cinderella: An Outline of Identity* (New York, 1952).

Bibl.: Charles Garrod and William Korst, *Artie Shaw and His Orchestra* (Zephyrhills, Fla., 1986).

Shaw, Martin (Fallas) (b. London, 9 Mar. 1875; d. Southwold, 24 Oct. 1958). Composer and performer. He studied composition at the Royal College of Music. Was active with theatrical productions after his graduation, working with Gordon Craig and Isadora Duncan. He then was employed as organist at St. Mary's, Primrose Hill, from 1908 to 1920 and at St. Martin-in-the-Fields from 1920 to 1924. He founded the Purcell Operatic Society. His own works were mostly vocal, whether dramatic, religious, or solo vocal. He also composed music for the Anglican rite.

Shaw, Oliver (b. Middleborough, Mass., 13 Mar. 1779; d. Providence, R.I., 31 Dec. 1848). Singer, composer, and publisher. An accident in his youth eventually led to blindness. Studied with John L. Berkenhead, Gottlieb Graupner, and Thomas Granger. From 1805, taught organ and piano in Dedham, Mass. Organist at First Congregational Church in Providence, 1809–32. Helped found the Boston Handel and Haydn Society, 1815. Collected hymns and songs; composed marches, songs, piano pieces.

Bibl.: B. Degen, "Oliver Shaw: His Music and Contributions to American Society" (diss., Univ. of Rochester, 1971).

Shaw, Robert (b. Red Bluff, Calif., 30 Apr. 1916). Conductor. Attended Pomona College (A.B., 1938), leading the glee club; formed the Fred Waring Glee Club (in association with the Pennsylvanians) in 1938, the Collegiate Chorale, New York (1941), and the Robert Shaw Chorale (1948). He made his orchestral debut at Naumburg in 1946, also appearing with the NBC Symphony that year. In 1950 he studied with Monteux and Rodzinski; he later held posts with the San Diego Symphony (1953–58), the Cleveland Orchestra as Szell's associate (1956–67), and the Atlanta Symphony (1967–88). Considered the dean of U.S. choral conductors; his ideas on choral development have been widely adopted.

Shaw, Woody [Herman, II] (b. Laurinburg, N.C., 24 Dec. 1944; d. New York, 10 May 1989). Jazz trumpeter and bandleader. He recorded with Eric Dolphy (1963) and Chick Corea (1966). Mainly playing hard bop, he joined Horace Silver (1965–66), Max Roach (1968–69), Joe Henderson (1970), and Art Blakey (1971–72). He was a member of the Louis Hayes–Junior Cook Quintet (1975), which became the Woody Shaw–Louis Hayes Quintet and accompanied Dexter Gordon on his return to the U.S. (1976, including the album *Homecoming*). From 1977 to 1987 he led groups; his many albums included *Lotus Flower* (1982). He also played in saxophonist Nathan Davis's Paris Reunion Band (ca. 1985–87). Deteriorating eyesight and narcotics addiction ended his career.

Shchedrin, Rodion Konstantinovich (b. Moscow, 16 Dec. 1932). Composer and pianist. Began music lessons at an early age; from 1944 to 1950 studied at the Moscow Choral School. Attended Moscow Conservatory, 1950–55, where he studied composition with Shaporin and piano with Flier; completed graduate work there under Shaporin in 1959. Taught composition at the Moscow Conservatory, 1965–69; from 1973, head of the Union of Composers of the Russian Federation. Received many awards, including Order of the Red Banner (1971), USSR State Prize (1972), Order of Lenin (1982), Lenin Prize (1984); named honorary corresponding member of Bayerische Akademie der Schönen Künste in 1976. Came to public attention early as performer and composer with the premiere of the First Piano Concerto in 1954. Here and in many subsequent works he incorporated strains of popular folk ditties and demonstrated a dazzling facility with the orchestra. He developed a close working relationship with the Bolshoi Theater, where his 2 operas and 5 ballets all received their premieres.

Works: operas *Not Love Alone* (1961; rev. 1971), *Dead Souls* (1976); ballets *The Little Humpbacked Horse* (1955), *Carmen-Suite* (1967), *Anna Karenina* (1971), *The Seagull* (1979), *The Lady with a Dog* (1985); 2 symphonies and other works for orchestra (including *Naughty Limericks,* concerto for orchestra, 1963); 3 piano concertos; trumpet concerto (1994); vocal-symphonic music; chamber works (*Geometry of Sound,* 18 soloists, 1987); music for piano; incidental and film music.

Bibl.: M. Tarakanov, *Tvorchestvo Rodiona Shchedrina* (Moscow: Sovetskii kompozitor, 1980).

Shcherbachov, Vladimir Vladimirovich (b. Warsaw, 25 Jan. 1889; d. Leningrad, 5 Mar. 1952). Composer. Born into a musical family, he studied with Liadov and Steinberg at St. Petersburg Conservatory (1908–14); simultaneously he worked as a pianist for Diaghilev's ballet company and as a theory teacher. After wartime service he became active in Soviet musical administration; he taught at Leningrad Conservatory, 1923–31 and 1944–48, and elsewhere. His works include 5 symphonies (no. 4, History of the Izhorsky Factory, 1932–34; no. 5, "Russian," 1942–48), symphonic poems, film scores, the opera *Anna Kolosova* (1939), smaller theater pieces, songs, and piano works.

Bibl.: Genrich Orlov, *Vladimir Vladimirovich Shcherbachov* (Leningrad, 1959).

Shearer, Allen (b. Seattle, 5 Oct. 1943). Composer, baritone. He attended the Univ. of California, Berkeley, where his teachers were Andrew Imbrie and Seymour Shifrin (B.A., 1965; M.A., 1970; Ph.D., 1973). He also studied voice in Salzburg with Ludwig Weber and Heinrich Pflanzl (1967–68) and composition in Paris with Max Deutsch (1974). He taught briefly at the Univ. of British Columbia (1974–76), then abandoned his academic career to concentrate on composing, supporting himself by giving voice lessons. His music, though it recalls postwar serialism in its rhythms and textures, relies on traditional counterpoint and on tonal centers. Works include *Fantasy* (cello and piano, 1974); Symphony (chorus and orchestra, 1977); *Variations on Sumer is icumen in* (orchestra, 1979); *Five Poems of Wallace Stevens* (voice and piano, 1980); *Ages of Day* (chorus, 1987); *We Three* (flute, cello, piano, 1989).

Shearing, George (Albert) (b. London, 13 Aug. 1919). Jazz pianist and bandleader. After emigrating to the U.S. in 1947 he led quintets (1949–67) characterized by two sounds: Shearing's use of block chords; and vibraphone doubling the melody in his right hand and guitar—an octave lower—doubling his left. His recordings include "Sorry, Wrong Rhumba" (1949) and his composition "Lullaby of Birdland" (1952). Among his sidemen were Cal Tjader and Joe Pass. Later he worked in trios and duos. Beginning in the 1980s he also accompanied Mel Torme.

Shebalin, Vissarion Yakovlevich (b. Omsk, 11 June 1902; d. Moscow, 28 May 1963). Composer. He studied with Miaskovsky at the Moscow Conservatory (1923–28) and was subsequently appointed to its faculty, becoming director in 1942. He was deposed in 1948 during the Stalin–Zhdanov musical purge but reinstated in 1951. His students included Khrennikov. His works include 2 operas (*Solntse nad stepiu* [Sun over the Steppes], 1939–59; *Ukroshcheniye stroptivoy* [The Taming of the Shrew], 1946–56), ballets, numerous scores for theater, film, and radio; 5 symphonies, 3 orchestral suites; violin concerto, cello concerto, violin concertino, horn concertino; several overtures and descriptive orchestral works, some with chorus; numerous choral works, songs, folk song arrangements; 9 string quartets, chamber works for strings and piano; piano pieces; guitar pieces.

Bibl.: Igor Fedorovich Belza and Vladimir Vasilievich Protopopov, *Vladimir Yakovlevich Shebalin: stat'i, vospominaniya, materialï* (Moscow, 1970).

Shelley, Harry Rowe (b. New Haven, Conn., 2 June 1858; d. Short Beach, Conn., 12 Sept. 1947). Organist and composer. Studied at Yale with Stoeckel, in New York with Buck and Dvořák. Organist at the Church of the Pilgrims in Brooklyn, 1878–81, and after 1887. Organist at Plymouth Church, 1881–87. Organist at Fifth Avenue Baptist Church, New York, 1899–1914. Taught harmony and counterpoint at the Metropolitan College of Music and the American Institute of Applied Music. Composed 4 operas, symphonies, cantatas, a violin concerto. Edited several collections of organ music.

Shepherd, Arthur (b. Paris, Idaho, 19 Feb. 1880; d. Cleveland, 12 Jan. 1958). Composer, conductor, teacher. A musically promising child, he was sent at age 12 to the New England Conservatory in Boston, where he studied piano with Carl Faelten, composition with Percy Goetschius and George Chadwick. He graduated in 1897 at the age of 17 and moved to Salt Lake City, where he conducted and gave music lessons. During this period he became associated with Arthur Farwell and Henry Gilbert in the American Music Society. Several early works—*Five Songs on Poems of James Russell Lowell* (1909) and the First Piano Sonata (1907)—reflect this influence. He returned to Boston and in 1909 began teaching at the New England Conservatory. His most significant composition from this period is the *Overture to a Drama* (1919) for orchestra. In 1920 he moved to Cleveland, first as assistant conductor of the Cleveland Orchestra (1920–26), then as professor at Case Western Reserve Univ. (1927–50). Here he composed works in many genres, all in a firmly tonal idiom enriched by modal and chromatic inflections. Notable works from this period include *Triptych* (soprano and string quartet, 1925), the Second Piano Sonata (1930), and 4 string quartets (1933, 1936, 1944, 1955).

Bibl.: Richard Loucks, *Arthur Shepherd, American Composer* (Provo, Utah, 1980); [includes facs. of songs and piano pieces]. Frederick Koch, *Reflections on Composing—Four American Composers* (Pittsburgh, 1983).

Shepp, Archie [Vernon] (b. Fort Lauderdale, 24 May 1937). Jazz tenor saxophonist and bandleader. After studying dramatic literature at Goddard College (B.A., 1959) he played free jazz with Cecil Taylor (1960–62), the trumpeter Bill Dixon (1962–63), and the New York Contemporary Five, co-led by Don Cherry, John Tchicai, and Shepp (1963–64). Thereafter he led groups. His albums include *Fire Music* (1965) and *Archie Shepp Live in San Francisco* (1966). Beginning in the mid-1960s his repertory gradually expanded to embrace marches, blues, ballads, rhythm and blues, and bop. He taught at SUNY–Buffalo (1969–74) before joining the faculty of the Univ. of Massachusetts.

Sheppard [Shepherd], **John** (b. ca. 1515; d. London?, 1559 or 1560). Composer. He served as *informator choristarum* at Magdalen College, Oxford, 1543–48, and was a Gentleman of the Chapel Royal from at least 1552 (possibly earlier). He took part in the coronation of Elizabeth I in January 1559, but died before September 1560. His music shows a predilection for rich, sonorous counterpoint for 5, 6, and 7 voices. His works include both Latin service music (5 Masses, 2 Magnificats, over 60 motets—mostly Office Psalms, hymns, and responsories) and post-Reformation English music (3 services, canticles for Mass and Office, 15 anthems, 41 Psalm tunes).

Sheriff, Noam (b. Tel Aviv, 7 Jan. 1935). Composer. As a youth he studied piano and horn; he also studied composition with Zeev Priel and Ben Haim. He played with and conducted the Israel Army Band. After meeting with international success in the late 1950s and early 1960s, he traveled to Berlin to study composition with Blacher. Returning to Israel in 1963, he continued to work alternately as composer, conductor, and teacher. His music combines western European genres and forms with elements of traditional Jewish liturgical music. He has also worked with electronic media. His works include *Fest-prelude* (1957), *Song of Degrees* (1960), *Ashrei (Psalms)* (1961), *2 Epigrams* (1968), *A Stone in the Tower of David* (1970), String Quartet (1973), *La Follia* (orchestra, 1984), *A Little "Ligur"* (partita for violin and cello, 1984); *Mechaye Hametin* [Wiederbelebung der Toten] (tenor, baritone, men's chorus, boys' choir, large orchestra, 1987).

Sherman, Russell (b. New York, 25 Mar. 1930). Pianist. A student of Edward Steuermann from 1941, he made his debut at Town Hall in 1945. He attended Columbia Univ. (B.A., 1949), and later taught at Pomona College (1959–62), the Univ. of Arizona (1962–67), the New England Conservatory, and Juilliard (from 1986). His 1972–73 recordings of Liszt's *Transcendental Etudes* brought him recognition; he subsequently appeared in recital and with U.S. and European orchestras.

Sherry, Fred (Richard) (b. Montrose, N.Y., 27 Oct. 1948). Conductor and cellist. Attended the Juilliard School from 1965, making his recital debut in 1969; cofounded the contemporary ensemble Speculum Musicae in 1971, sharing conducting duties until 1978; also cofounded the ensemble Tashi in 1973. A strong advocate of new music. Wuorinen and Davidovsky have dedicated pieces to him, and he has appeared with Chick Corea. From 1980 associated with the Chamber Music Society of New York, serving as its artistic director 1989–91.

Shibata, Minao (b. Tokyo, 29 Sept. 1916). Composer. He studied science at Tokyo Univ., graduating in 1943. During this time he also studied composition with Saburō Moroi and, from 1939 to 1941, played cello with the Tokyo String Orchestra. Together with Irino and Miyagi he organized the group Shinsei Kai in 1946. He taught at the Tōhō Gakuen School of Music, 1942–55, and from 1952 to 1959 at the Ockanomizu Women's College. From 1959 to 1969 he served on the faculty of the National Univ. of Fine Arts and Music in Tokyo. He also wrote about Western art music. His own music is strongly rooted in European traditions. His early works were in the style of late Romanticism; some works from the late 1940s and early 1950s are neoclassical in orientation. Beginning about the mid-1950s, serialism became the dominant technical source for his music (*Sinfonia,* orchestra, 1960). He also experimented with electronic media and aleatoric devices, quarter tones, and theatrical directions for performers. Works include orchestral and chamber, which often utilize Japanese instruments; vocal and solo vocal; and tape music.

Shield, William (b. County Durham, 5 Mar. 1748; d. London, 25 Jan. 1829). Violinist and composer. He studied with Charles Avison in Newcastle. While in Scarborough as a violinist he was heard by Giardini, who counseled him to move to London where he joined the King's Theatre orchestra (about 1773). His first opera, *The Flitch of Bacon* (1778), was very successful; he subsequently wrote about 40 operas, some of which were pastiches. He also wrote pantomimes, afterpieces, songs, and some instrumental works. He was named composer to Covent Garden, 1778–91 and 1792–97, and Master of the King's Music in 1817. He published *An Introduction to Harmony* (1800) and *The Rudiments of Thoroughbass* (1815).

Bibl.: George Haugher, "William Shield," *ML* 31 (1950): 337–42.

Shifrin, Seymour (b. Brooklyn, 28 Feb. 1926; d. Boston, 26 Sept. 1979). Composer. He studied privately with William Schuman (1942–45), then at Columbia Univ. with Otto Luening (B.A., 1947; M.A., 1949). Early works include *Music for Orchestra* (1948) and the First String Quartet (1949). From 1952 to 1966 he taught composition at the Univ. of California, Berkeley. Although greatly impressed and strongly influenced by

Schoenberg and Schoenberg's American followers, he eschewed any straightforward application of twelve-tone principles, and his works from the 1950s remained in some sense tonal—for example, the *Cantata to Sophoclean Choruses* (chorus and orchestra, 1957–58) and *Three Pieces for Orchestra* (1958). The Second String Quartet (1962) and the *Satires of Circumstance* (1964) for mezzo-soprano and chamber ensemble initiated a new phase, in which harmonies are less tonal, textures are sparser, and contrasts are vivid. String quartets nos. 4 (1967) and 5 (1972) and *In Eius Memoriam* (1960) for flute, clarinet, violin, cello, and piano provide examples of these traits. In 1966 Shifrin moved to Brandeis Univ., where he taught composition until his death. Other works include *Trauermusik* (piano, 1956); *The Modern Temper* (piano 4-hands, 1959); *Duo* (violin and piano, 1969); *Chronicles* (vocal soloists, chorus, and orchestra, 1970); *A Renaissance Garland* (soprano, tenor, lute, recorders, bass viol, percussion, 1975); *Five Last Songs* (soprano and piano, 1979).

Shimizu, Osamu (b. Osaka, 4 Nov. 1911; d. Tokyo, 29 Oct. 1986). Composer. As a youth he learned both traditional Japanese instruments (his father was a performer of the gagaku) and western European instruments. He studied at the Tokyo Music School from 1936 to 1939, taking composition lessons with Hashimoto and Hosokawa. Shimizu was associated with Tokyo Radio. His music is primarily vocal and has combined western genres and forms with more typically Japanese instruments, texts, and melodic characteristics. Works include operas (*Shuzenji monogatari* [Tale of Shuzenji], Tokyo, 1954); ballets (*Ai no shishō* [Love Poems], Japanese instruments, strings, 1966); orchestral and chamber works; and choral music (*Yama ni inoru* [The Prayer to the Mountains], reciter, male chorus, orchestra, 1960; *Shi no fuchi yori,* chorus, string trio, 1975).

Shimoyama, Hifumi (b. Aomoriken, Japan, 21 June 1930). Composer. He studied violin with Hiroshi Narita and composition with Yoritsune Matsudaira; from 1956 to 1962 he belonged to the new-music organization "Group 20.5." Compositions include orchestral works (*Fumon,* chamber orchestra, tape, 1974; *Yugenism,* 1988); chamber music (violin sonata, 1956; string quartet, 1959; *Zone,* 16 strings, 1970; *Landscape,* organ, 1983; *Emanation,* alto saxophone, percussion, 1986).

Shinohara, Makoto (b. Osaka, 10 Dec. 1931). Composer. He studied at the Tokyo National Univ. of Fine Arts and Music, where from 1952 to 1954 he took composition lessons with Ikenouchi, piano lessons with Yasukawa, and conducting lessons with Watanabe. From 1954 to 1960 he studied in Paris with Messiaen; then in Cologne, with Zimmerman at the Hochschule für Musik (1962–64) and with Stockhausen (1964–65). He worked with electronic music studios at Utrecht Univ. and, 1971–72, at the Columbia–Princeton Electronic Music Studio in New York City. Returning to Japan, he became associated with Tokyo Radio. His works make use of various avant-garde techniques, including extensive use of electronic media. Works include *Alternance* (percussion ensemble, 1962); *Vision* (tape, 1965); *Consonance* (6 instruments, 1967); *Rencontre* (percussion, tape, 1972); *Kyūdō* (shakuhachi, harp, 1973); *Equalization* (25 instruments, 1976); *Tabiyuki* (chamber ensemble, 1984); *Evolution* (cello, 1986).

Shirley, George (Irving) (b. Indianapolis, 18 Apr. 1934). Tenor. Attended Wayne State Univ., Detroit; studied with Thelmy Georgi (Washington, D.C.) and Cornelius Reid (New York); made his debut at Woodstock, New York, in 1959, and his Metropolitan Opera debut (as Ferrando) in 1961, singing there until 1974. He sang Tamino at Glyndebourne in 1966, and Don Ottavio at Covent Garden in 1967. At the Santa Fe Opera he sang in the American premieres of Henze's *Lula* (1963) and *König Hirsch* (1965). He created Romilayu in Kirchner's *Lily* at the New York City Opera (1977).

Shirley-Quirk, John (b. Liverpool, 28 Aug. 1931). Baritone. Studied with Roy Henderson; made operatic debut at Glyndebourne in 1962; became member of the English Opera Group in 1964; created roles in Britten's *Owen Wingrave* (1971) and *Death in Venice* (1973); sang at the Metropolitan Opera from 1974 to 1976. Also an active concert performer in oratorio and song, and made many recordings.

Shnitke, Alfred. See Schnittke, Alfred.

Shore, Dinah [Frances Rose] (b. Winchester, Tenn., 1 Mar. 1917; d. Beverly Hills, 24 Feb. 1994). Popular singer. As a college student in Nashville she hosted a local radio show whose theme song "Dinah" provided her stage name. In New York from 1939 she recorded and broadcast with Xavier Cugat, Ben Bernie, Eddie Cantor, and the Chamber Music Society of Lower Basin Street. From 1941 she hosted a radio show and recorded hits such as "Yes, My Darling Daughter," "Blues in the Night," and "Buttons and Bows." Later she hosted a television variety show (1951–61) and talk shows (1970s–80s).

Shorter, Wayne (b. Newark, N.J., 25 Aug. 1933). Jazz tenor and soprano saxophonist, composer, and bandleader. He studied music at New York Univ. (B.M.E., 1956). He joined Art Blakey's hard bop group (1959–64), becoming its music director. As a member of Miles Davis's group (1964–70), he composed "E.S.P." (1965), "Nefertiti" (1967), and "Sanctuary" (1969). His albums with Davis include *Live at the Plugged Nickel* (1965). With Joe Zawinul he led the jazz-rock group Weather Report (1970–85) while also touring with Herbie Hancock's group V.S.O.P. (1976–77). He performed in the film *Round Midnight* (1986) and co-led a band with Carlos Santana (1988). As a saxophonist he is noted for the terseness of his improvisations and for his haunting timbre on the soprano instrument.

Shostakovich, Dmitri Dmitrievich (b. St. Petersburg, 25 Sept. 1906; d. Moscow, 9 Aug. 1975). Composer. He was born into a family of the bourgeois intelligentsia with a history of political activism and revolutionary sympathies. His father was a government technical engineer, his mother a professional pianist. His adolescence was marked by exposure to civil upheaval and tsarist brutality, and his health was often poor. His mother gave him his first piano lessons at age 9; he became quickly absorbed in playing and composing. In 1919 Glazunov admitted him at age 13 as the youngest student in the Petrograd Conservatory; there he completed courses in piano under Leonid Nikolaev (1923) and composition under Steinberg (1925). After his father died in 1922, Dmitri worked as a cinema pianist to support his further education.

His first brilliant success came with his graduation piece, the First Symphony (op. 10, 1925), premiered by the Leningrad Symphony Orchestra in 1926; within a year it was conducted by Walter in Berlin and Stokowski in New York. The work exhibits hallmarks of Shostakovich's style: a personal, chromatic-modal brand of tonality, a facility in orchestration, and a gift for sustained irony, tragedy, and lyricism. He achieved success as a pianist also, winning honorable mention in the First International Chopin Competition in Warsaw in 1927.

From 1925 to 1930 Shostakovich pursued postgraduate work at the conservatory. During these years he wrote his symphonies nos. 2 and 3 (To October op. 14, 1927, and First of May op. 20, 1929), both conceived along Soviet-inspired programmatic lines and ending with choral finales. He composed his first theatrical pieces: an opera on Gogol's *Nos* ([The Nose] op. 15, 1927–28), a satirical ballet *Zolotoi vek* ([The Golden Age] op. 22, 1927–30), and incidental music to Mayakovsky's *Klop* ([The Bedbug] op. 19, 1929). His first film score, *Noviÿ Vavilon* ([New Babylon] op. 18, 1928–29), was deemed unplayable at the time, but it inaugurated a long career in film work, with some 35 scores over the next 40 years. The early 1930s saw two more ballets: *Bolt* (op. 27, 1930–31) and *Svetlïy ruchei* ([The Limpid Stream] op. 39, 1934–35). He also wrote his First Piano Concerto (op. 35, 1933), Cello Sonata (op. 40, 1934), and First String Quartet (op. 49, 1935). In 1932 he married the physicist Nina Varzar.

Shostakovich's greatest theatrical success came with his next opera, the controversial *Ledi Makbet Mtsenskovo uyezda* ([Lady Macbeth of Mtsensk District] op. 29, 1930–32). It enjoyed 180 performances in Leningrad and Moscow until its sudden denunciation in *Pravda* (28 Jan. 1936), a severe Stalinist exercise in cultural control. Shostakovich responded by withdrawing his new, extravagant Fourth Symphony (op. 43, 1935–36) from rehearsal (it was not performed until 1961) and writing a sober, grandly conciliatory Fifth Symphony (op. 47, 1937) for the 20th anniversary of the Russian Revolution; the work renewed both his artistic and his political standing.

Shostakovich began to receive official recognition: he was made professor at the Leningrad Conservatory (1939), was awarded cultural prizes (Red Banner of Labor for film music, 1940; Stalin Prize in 1941 for the Piano Quintet op. 57, 1940), and was given honorary incremental administrative ranks. His unorthodox Sixth Symphony (op. 54, 1939) won little notice; but during the war his programmatic Seventh Symphony ("Leningrad" op. 60, 1941) became an internationally adopted emblem of Soviet Russian resistance against Nazism. Two more war symphonies, nos. 8 and 9, (opp. 65, 1943; 70, 1945) proved even more profoundly his capacity for tragedy and ironic humor, but met with less critical success.

In 1943 Shostakovich took a professorship at the Moscow Conservatory, and in 1946 he received the Order of Lenin. But 1948 brought another severe blow from the Stalin administration: a decree of 10 February censured Shostakovich, Prokofiev, and other prominent Soviet composers for "formalistic perversions and anti-democratic tendencies." This temporarily cost Shostakovich his professorship; he resorted to performing, touring, and recording to support himself.

From the war years until Stalin's death (1953) Shostakovich turned increasingly to smaller forms: he wrote the Piano Trio no. 2 in memory of Ivan Sollertinsky (op. 67, 1944), string quartets nos. 2–5 (opp. 68, 1944; 73, 1946; 83, 1949; 92, 1952), 24 Preludes and Fugues inspired by the Bach bicentennial (op. 87, 1950–51), and several song cycles, including *Six Romances on Verses by English Poets* (op. 62, 1942; orchestrated as op. 140, 1971) and *Iz evreiskoi narodnoi poezii* ([From Jewish Folk Poetry] op. 79, 1948). He withheld the last work, as well as his Fourth Quartet and his First Violin Concerto for Oistrakh (op. 77, 1947–48; rev. as op. 99, 1955), from the public eye until after Stalin's death.

From 1953 Shostakovich was the most internationally prominent musical figure in the Soviet Union. From 1957 he was secretary of the USSR Composers' Union, and from 1962 a member of the Supreme Soviet. He traveled widely within and outside the USSR, including four trips to Britain (1958, 1962, 1972, 1973) and three to the U.S. (1949, 1959, 1973). The death of his wife in 1954 was followed by a brief marriage to Margarita Kainova from 1956 to 1960, and a lasting one to Irina Supinskaya from 1962.

Upon Stalin's death Shostakovich produced a Tenth Symphony (op. 93, 1953) that aroused official controversy for its dark summation of the Stalinist era; he signed the work with a recurring motive D–D–E♭–C–B (German D–D–S–C–H) symbolizing his initials, D. D. Sch. He followed it with a trilogy of programmatic symphonies: nos. 11 and 12 ("1905" and "1917" opp. 103, 1957; 112, 1961) having ideological Soviet-inspired themes, but no. 13 ("Babi Yar" op. 113, 1962) countering the establishment by setting five controversial poems of Yevtushenko. In 1962 *Lady Macbeth* (revised as *Katerina Ismailovna* op. 114) was at last officially rehabilitated to international acclaim.

He continued extensively to cultivate the string quartet with nos. 6–11, (opp. 101, 1956; 108, 1960; 110, 1960; 117, 1964; 118, 1964; 122, 1966); no. 8 is overtly autobiographical, quoting earlier works. Other compositions of 1953 to 1966 include a setting of Yevtushenko's revolutionary *Kazn' Stepana Razina* ([The Execution of Stepan Razin] op. 119, 1964); a Second Piano Concerto for his son Maxim (op. 102, 1957); two cello concertos (opp. 107, 1959; 126, 1966) and a reorchestration of Schumann's cello concerto (op. 125, 1966) for Rostropovich; and orchestrations of Mussorgsky's opera *Khovanshchina* (op. 106, 1959) for film and *Songs and Dances of Death* (1962) for soprano Galina Vishnevskaya.

Following a heart attack in May 1966, Shostakovich's health declined; the works of his last years reflect a preoccupation with mortality. The impassioned Symphony no. 14 (op. 135, 1969) sets 11 poems on death by various authors; it is dedicated to Britten, who provided close friendship during his last decade. The final symphony, no. 15 (op. 141, 1971), opens flamboyantly but progresses to a distant, introspective finale, quoting the "fate" motive from Wagner's *Ring*. Other late works include song cycles on poems of Blok, Tsvetayeva, Michelangelo, and Dostoyevski (opp. 145, 1974; 143, 1973; 127, 1967; 146, 1975); string quartets nos. 12–15 (opp. 133, 1968; 138, 1970; 142, 1973; 144, 1974), no. 15 consisting of six consecutive adagios; the Second Violin Concerto for Oistrakh (op. 129, 1967), the Violin Sonata for Oistrakh and Richter (op. 134, 1968), and the Viola Sonata (op. 147, 1975). He suffered a second heart attack in 1971 and was treated for lung cancer in 1972–73. His right hand was paralyzed during his last months; he wrote the Viola Sonata with his left.

In addition to works mentioned, Shostakovich composed much occasional music: film scores; incidental scores for plays, including *Hamlet* (op. 32, 1931–32) and *King Lear* (op. 58a, 1940); a musical comedy, *Moskva, Cheryomushki* (op. 105, 1958); Soviet-inspired orchestral works, including *Festive Overture* (op. 96, 1954), *Overture on Russian and Khirgiz Folk Themes* (op. 115, 1963), and *Oktyabr* ([October] op. 131, 1967); Stalinist choral pieces, including *Poema o rodine* ([Poem on the Homeland] op. 74, 1947), *Pesn' o lesakh* ([Song of the Forests] op. 81, 1949), *Nad rodinoy nashey solntse siyayet* ([The Sun Shines upon Our Native Land] op. 90, 1952). He wrote a few chamber works and songs in his early years, notably the First Piano Trio (op. 8, 1923), *Two Pieces for String Octet* (op. 11, 1924–25), and *Six Japanese Songs* (orchestrated, op. 21, 1928–32). He also wrote much piano music, including 2 sonatas (opp. 12, 1926; 61, 1942), 24 Preludes (op. 34, 1932–33), Concertino for 2 pianos (op. 94, 1953), many early pieces, and pieces for children.

Shostakovich signed frequent articles in the official Soviet press: a complete list to 1964 is in Sadovnikov (2nd ed., 1965); many are collected and translated in Grigorev and Platek (1981). A volume of his memoirs was edited by Volkov (1979), though this edition's authenticity has met with skepticism.

Bibl.: E. L. Sadovnikov, *D. D. Shostakovich: Notografi-cheskiy spravochnik* [Thematic Catalogue] (Moscow, 1961; 2nd ed., 1965). Boris Schwarz, *Music and Musical Life in Soviet Russia* (London, 1972; 2nd ed., Bloomington, Ind., 1983). Malcolm MacDonald, *Dmitri Shostakovich: A Complete Catalogue* (London 1977; 2nd ed., 1985). Roy Blokker and Robert Dearling, *The Music of Dmitri Shostakovich: The Symphonies* (London, 1979). Solomon Volkov, ed., *Testimony: The Memoirs of Shostakovich* (New York, 1979). L. Grigorev and Ya. Platek, eds., *Dmitri Shostakovich: About Himself and His Times* (Moscow, 1981). Derek C. Hulme, *Dmitri Shostakovich: Catalogue, Bibliography, and Discography* (private publ.: 1982; 2nd ed., Oxford, 1991). Christopher Norris, ed., *Shostakovich: The Man and His Music* (London, 1982). Dimitri Dimitrievich Shostakovich, *Testimony: The Memoirs of Dimitri Shostakovich* (New York, 1984). Ian MacDonald, *The New Shostakovich* (London, 1990). Günter Wolter, *Dmitri Schostakowitsch, eine sowjetische Tragödie: Rezeptionsgeschichte* (Frankfurt am Main, 1991). Elizabeth Wilson, *Shostakovich: A Life Remembered* (Princeton, 1994). David Fanning, ed., *Shostakovich Studies* (Cambridge, 1995).

Shostakovich, Maxim (b. Leningrad, 10 May 1938). Conductor and pianist. Son of Dmitri Shostakovich. He studied at the Leningrad and Moscow Conservatories. Served as assistant conductor of the Moscow Symphony (from 1964) and the USSR State Symphony (from 1966). He made his Western debut at London in 1968, subsequently touring the U.S. with the State Symphony in 1969; he directed the USSR State Radio Orchestra from 1971 until his defection in 1981 during a West German tour; subsequently served as principal conductor of the Hong Kong Philharmonic (1983–85), artistic director of the Hartford Symphony (1985–86), and music director of the New Orleans Symphony (1986–91).

Shtogarenko, Andrei Iakovlevich (b. Novye Kaidaki, 15 Oct. 1902). Composer. Studied composition with S. Bogatyrev at the Kharkov Conservatory, 1930–36. Worked as an administrator in various capacities in the Union of Composers; head of the Ukrainian Union from 1968. Served as rector of the Kiev Conservatory from 1954 to 1968; from 1960, professor of composition there. His music, which is accessible and often programmatic, evokes a strong sense of Ukrainian nationalism. Works include 6 symphonies; symphonic poems, suites, and other symphonic music; cantatas and other vocal-symphonic works; a violin concerto and other concerted works; chamber music; choral music; songs; incidental and film music.

Bibl.: N. Borovik, *Andrei Shtogarenko; zhizn', tvorchestvo, cherty stilia* (Kiev, 1984).

Shudi [Schudi, Tschudi, Tshudi], **Burkat** [Burkhardt] (b. Schwanden, canton of Glarus, 1702; d. London, 19 Aug. 1773). Harpsichord maker. He migrated to England in 1718, and worked for H. Tabel. In 1739 he moved to Meard Street, Soho, in London, and in 1742 he moved to Great Pulteney Street. John Broadwood began working for him in 1761, and in 1769 Shudi made Broadwood a partner. Shudi's "Venetian swell," a device operated by louvres that varied volume, was patented in 1769. In 1771 he retired, and upon his death his son Burkat took his place in the partnership; Broadwood became owner of the firm when Burkat died in 1803. Shudi was one of the most important English harpsichord makers of his time; his instruments were owned by Frederick the Great, Haydn, and Handel.

Shumsky, Oscar (b. Philadelphia, 23 Mar. 1917). Conductor and violinist. A pupil of Auer and Zimbalist, he performed with the Philadelphia Orchestra at age 8; attended the Curtis Institute from 1928 to 1936; appeared with the NBC Symphony; joined the Primrose Quartet in 1939, continuing a solo career as well. He made his conducting debut in 1959, later making appearances with several orchestras. He taught at the Curtis Institute, the Peabody and Juilliard Schools, and Yale before retiring in 1981.

Sibelius, Jean [Johan] **(Julius Christian)** (b. Hämeenlinna, 8 Dec. 1865; d. Järvenpää, 20 Sept. 1957). Composer. His family, though they lived in the southern part of Finland, spoke Swedish, and Sibelius learned Finnish at primary school while retaining his fondness for and familiarity with Swedish lore and poetry. Owing to his father's early death, he was raised by his mother and grandmother. He began composing and playing the violin as a child, becoming increasingly proficient in both during his adolescence. He began to perform publicly in chamber music ensembles, and chamber music dominated his compositional efforts too. A particular influence was A. B. Marx's composition treatise, which presented classical formal models interpreted as primarily melodic processes.

When he first went to the Univ. of Helsinki in 1885, Sibelius pursued law. Within a year, however, he changed his course of study to music and began composition lessons with Wegelius, a Wagnerian. During his years at the university Sibelius also continued to study and play the violin in chamber and orchestral settings. In addition, he developed a close relationship with Busoni. In 1889 he traveled first to Berlin, to study with Becker, and then to Leipzig with Busoni. In 1890 he went to Vienna, hoping to study with Brahms, but, upon the refusal of the elder composer, he worked with Goldmark and Fuchs. It was during this time that Sibelius began to concentrate on orchestral music, for which he quickly developed remarkable facility and insight. After returning to Finland in 1891, he premiered *Kullervo* op. 7 (1892), a five-movement orchestral and choral symphony, which met with great success and established his future as a composer. The same year as the premiere he married Aino Järnefelt, whose nationalistic family drew Sibelius even further into the developing fervor for Finnish independence from tsarist Russia. Pieces from the 1890s, such as the orchestral suite *Lemminkäis-sarja* op. 22 (written 1893–95 and subsequently revised), demonstrated Sibelius's increasingly dramatic musical language as well as his nationalistic inspiration.

The first decade of the twentieth century saw both fame and financial difficulties for Sibelius. He began to travel internationally as a composer and a conductor, encountering Dvořák in Prague in 1901. Despite some patronage, however, he developed a substantial debt. In 1904 he built a home at Jäarvenpää, where he found solace throughout his personal and professional unrest. Under the stress of his schedule and of heavy drinking and smoking, he developed symptoms of throat cancer in 1908 and underwent corrective surgery. He continued to travel and compose up until World War I. After the war Sibelius did relatively little composing; among the works he did write were Symphony no. 6, Symphony no. 7, and the tone poem *Tapiola,* which was written in 1926.

Sibelius's early chamber works, as well as his later orchestral works, were influenced by Tchaikovsky and Wagner in their careful use of instrumental color and extended tonal techniques. He used traditional formal schemes such as sonata form in his early works, and throughout his career he worked creatively with processes such as the continuous unfolding of thematic development, as in Symphony no. 7 (1924). Subsections, often delineating a basically simple form and distinguished by varying tempos, became blended together in seamless textures and an organic development typical of late German Romanticism. During the first decade of the twentieth century his music, while exploring these formal tendencies, moved toward a neoclassical orientation. Sibelius did not use literal folk song quotations, nor did he thoroughly research native folk music. Nonetheless, melodic characteristics of Finnish folk song became part of his creative repertoire.

Sibelius's chamber music, written for the most part before the turn of the century and after 1915, shows his understanding of string instruments. His stage music consists largely of incidental music written for plays and displays a facility with dramatic music. His songs, written throughout his career, serve as settings for both Finnish and Swedish texts. His piano pieces were written primarily for amateur rather than concert situations and are neither as idiomatic nor as representative of his musicality as were his symphonic and chamber works.

For the last 30 years of his life Sibelius lived in relative isolation. He ceased to compose; Olin Downes reports the composition of an eighth symphony, but if completed, it was apparently destroyed.

Works: Stage works include *Peléas et Mélisande,* incidental music (1905); *Scaramouche,* music for a pantomime (1913); *Jokamies* [Everyman], incidental music (1916); *The Tempest,* incidental music (1925). Orchestral music includes Lemminkäis-sarja (1893–95; subsequently rev.); *Finlandia* (1899; rev. 1900); Symphony no. 1 (1899); Symphony no. 2 (1901–2); Violin Concerto (1903; rev. 1905); Symphony no. 3 (1907); Symphony no. 4 (1911); *Barden* [The Bard], tone poem (1913; rev. 1914); Symphony no. 5 (1915; rev. 1916, 1919); Humoresques nos. 1–2, violin, orchestra (1917); Humoresques nos. 3–6, violin, orchestra (1917); Symphony no. 6 (1923); Symphony no. 7 (1924); *Tapiola,* tone poem (1926). Choral works include *Kullervo* (1892); *Sandels,* improvisation, male chorus, orchestra (1898; rev. 1915); *Vapautettu kuningatar* [The Liberated Queen], cantata, chorus, orchestra (1906); *Väinön virsi [Väinö's Song],* chorus, orchestra (1926). Songs include *Seven Songs of Runeberg* (1891–92); *Two Songs* op. 35 (1907–8), including "Jubal"; *Six Songs* op. 36 (1899), including "Svarta rosor" [Black Roses]; *Five Songs* op. 37 (1898–1902), including "Var det en dröm?" [Was It a Dream?]; and *Five Songs* op. 38 (1902–4), including "På verandan vid havet" [On a Balcony by the Sea].

Bibl: Robert Layton, *Sibelius* (London, 1979). Erich Brüll, *Jean Sibelius* (Leipzig, 1986). Fabian Dahlstrom, *The Works of Jean Sibelius* (Helsinki, 1987). Tim Howell, *Jean Sibelius: Progressive Techniques in the Symphonies and Tone Poems* (New York, 1989). James A. Hepokoski, *Sibelius, Symphony no. 5* (Cambridge, 1993).

Sicilianos, Yorgo (b. Athens, 29 Aug. 1922). Composer. He studied harmony with Varvoglis and Sklavos in Athens, going on to study counterpoint with Sklavos at the Athens Conservatory, 1944–49. He then traveled to Rome where he studied with Pizzetti, 1951–53, and to Paris, studying there with Milhaud, Aubin, and Messiaen. With the aid of a Fulbright Fellowship he studied in the U.S. with Piston, Blacher, and Persichetti. Upon his return to Greece he immediately became active in the promotion of new music, also serving briefly as head of the music division of the National Broadcasting Institution (1960–61, 1979). His music incorporated both native folk elements and, later, serialism into a broadly polyphonic style and balanced forms. Works include ballets, orchestral music (*I apokalypsi tis pemptis sfragidas* [The Revelation of the Fifth Seal] op. 7, symphonic poem, 1952; Concerto for Orchestra op. 12, 1954), vocal music (*Epitaphion: In Memoriam Nikos Marangopoulos* op. 31, choirs, children's choir, narrator, orchestra, 1971), and chamber music.

Siefert [Syfert, Sivert, Sibert], **Paul** (b. Danzig, 28 June 1586; d. there, 6 May 1666). Composer. After studying with Sweelinck in Amsterdam (1607–9), he returned to Danzig and was appointed assistant organist at the Marienkirche. From 1611 to 1616 he was in Königsberg as organist of the principal church in the old city; following this he was court organist at Warsaw. In 1623 he became principal organist at the Marienkirche in Danzig, remaining there until his death. Siefert was often involved in disputes with others, perhaps the most famous of which was his feud with Marco Scacchi. He was accused by Scacchi of mixing different genres in his *Psalmen Davids* (1640), a collection including 12 Psalm settings and 2 vocal concertos.

Siegmeister, Elie (b. New York, 15 Jan. 1909; d. Manhasset, N.Y., 10 Mar. 1991). Composer. Studied composition with Seth Bingham at Columbia Univ. (B.A., 1927) and privately with Wallingford Riegger. In 1927 he went to Paris, where he studied at the École normale de musique (diploma, 1931) and also with Nadia Boulanger. Returning to the U.S. in 1932, he involved himself in left-wing musical circles, first in the Young Composers Group, later in the Composers Collective of New York. Initially his musical language was astringent and dissonant, as in the *Theme and Variations* (1931) for piano and the song "The Strange Funeral in Braddock" (1933). Searching for an idiom that might appeal more to the working class, he turned to American folk songs, which he began to collect, perform, and integrate into his own works. This direction can be heard in *Abraham Lincoln Walks at Midnight,* chorus and orchestra (1937), *Ozark Set,* orchestra (1943), and *Western Suite,* orchestra (1945). Performed by major orchestras, these works were greeted with critical praise. During this period he also conducted the American Ballad Singers, one of the first American "folk music" ensembles, and published many arrangements of traditional songs. In the 1950s Siegmeister moved toward a more complex and more personal style, for example, in Symphony no. 3 (1957) and the String Quartet no. 2 (1960). This direction continued in works such as *I Have a Dream,* cantata (1967) and *Shadows and Light,* orchestra (1975). He also assimilated jazz influences, as in Clarinet Concerto (1956), the song cycle *Madam to You* (1964), and the Double Concerto, violin, piano, orchestra (1976). He wrote several operas, including *Darling Corie* (Hempstead, N.Y., 1954), *The Plough and the Stars* (Baton Rouge, 1969), and *The Lady of the Lake* (New York, 1985); other works include *Theme and Variations no. 5* (piano, 1987); *Figures in the Wind* (orchestra, 1990); *Four Langston Hughes Songs* (1990).

Siems, Margarethe (b. Breslau, 30 Dec. 1879; d. Dresden, 13 Apr. 1952). Soprano. Studied in her home city; appeared with Caruso at Prague in 1902; joined the German Opera there the same year, remaining until 1908; subsequently sang at Dresden (1908–20) and at the Berlin Staatsoper (1920–26), also teaching at the Berlin Conservatory. She returned to Dresden in 1926, teaching there and in Breslau while continuing to sing in concert. She created the Marschallin in Strauss's *Der Rosenkavalier* in 1911, as well as Strauss's Chrysothemis and Zerbinetta.

Siepi, Cesare (b. Milan, 10 Feb. 1923). Bass. Studied in his own city, making his debut at Schio in 1941; sang at La Scala (1946–50, 1955–58) and at the Metropolitan Opera (1950–74), with Don Giovanni and Figaro his most frequent roles; appeared also at Salzburg (from 1953), San Francisco (from 1954), and Covent Garden (from 1962), and sang at Seattle in 1984 and Parma in 1985. Among his recordings are the Mozart operas and a 1951 Verdi Requiem with Toscanini.

Sigurbjörnsson, Thorkell (b. Reykjavík, 16 July 1938). Composer. He studied at the Reykjavík College of Music, taking lessons in piano, violin, organ, and theory. He traveled to the U.S., where he entered Hamline Univ. in Minnesota and studied with Harris, graduating in 1959. He went on to study with Gaburo and Hiller at the Univ. of Illinois; also studied conducting at Nice and Darmstadt. Subsequently taught at the Reykjavík College of Music and performed, founding the new-music group Musica nova; in addition, he was associated with the Iceland State Broadcasting Service. His works are written for a variety of situations, including children's operas (*Rabbi,* 1968) and television ballet (*Thorgeirsboli* [The Bull Man], 1969). Other works include orchestral music (Flute Concerto, 1977), choral music (*Solstice,* voices, flute, marimba, double bass, 1976), and chamber music (*Hoquetus Minor* [Minor Hiccups], harpsichord, percussion, 1987; *6 Icelandic Folk Songs,* flute, violin, cello, 1988).

Sikorski, Kazimierz (b. Zurich, 28 June 1895; d. Warsaw, 23 June 1986). Composer. He studied as a youth at the Chopin Music High School, taking composition lessons from Szopski; then went on to study philosophy at Warsaw Univ., graduating in 1921. Concurrently he studied musicology with Chybiński. He traveled to Paris, studying there 1925–27 and 1930. He taught in Łódź and Warsaw, becoming head of the Warsaw State College in 1957; served as president of the Polish Composers' Union, 1954–59. His early works are in a post-Romantic style which, over time, became increasingly clear and balanced while remaining highly expressive. Works include orchestral music, which was often based on the concerto principle (4 symphonies, 1919, 1921, 1953, 1969; Clarinet Concerto, 1947; Flute Concerto, 1957–61; *Concerto Polyphonique,* bassoon, orchestra, 1965; Trombone Concerto, 1973), and vocal and chamber music.

Sikorski, Tomasz (b. Warsaw, 19 May 1939). Composer and performer. Son of Kazimierz Sikorski; studied composition with his father and piano with Drzewiecki. He became known as a performer of new music. His own compositions were part of western European avant-garde trends, especially in terms of the treatment of dissonance. Some of his later works moved closer to minimalist concepts. His music includes the radio opera *Przygody Sindbada Zeglarza* [The Adventures of Sinbad the Sailor] (1971); *Antifony,* soprano, piano, horn, percussion, tape (1963); *Architectures,* piano, winds, percussion (1965); *Music from Afar,* chorus, orchestra (1974); *Das Schweigen der Sirenen,* cello (1986); *Omaggio per quattro pianoforti ed orchestra in memoriam Borges* (1987).

Silbermann. Family of organ builders and instrument makers. (1) **Andreas Silbermann** (b. Kleinbobritzsch, near Frauenstein, Saxony, 16 May 1678; d. Strasbourg, 16 Mar. 1734). After training with Daniel Übermann, he was employed by Eugen Casparini and Friedrich Ring. He was in Strasbourg from 1712 until 22 April 1704, when he left for Paris to work for François Thierry; he returned to Strasbourg on 3 May 1706. Among his pupils were his sons Johann Andreas and Johann Daniel (1717–66). His 34 organs reflect the influence of Parisian instruments. (2) **Gottfried Silbermann** (b. Kleinbobritzsch, 14 Jan. 1683; d. Dresden, 4 Aug. 1753). He learned organ building from his brother Andreas in Strasbourg; later he worked with him as a partner. He settled in Freiburg in 1711. His most important pupil was Zacharias Hildebrandt, who worked with him on the last of his 47 organs, that in the Catholic Hofkirche in Dresden. Also an accomplished maker of clavichords, Gottfried invented the *cembal d'amour,* an improved clavichord, by 1721, and before 1736 began building pianos modeled on Cristofori's. (3) **Johann Andreas Silbermann** (b. Strasbourg, 26 May 1712; d. there, 11 Feb. 1783). Son of Andreas. His father introduced him to organ building; in 1741 he toured Germany to study organs. His 54 organs are in Alsace, Lorraine, Baden, and Switzerland. He was associated with Prince Abbot Martin Gerbert of St. Blasien and Abbot Preiss of Marburg. Among his pupils were Konrad Sauer, Johann Andreas Stein, and Ludwig Geib.

Silja, Anja (b. Berlin, 17 Apr. 1935). Soprano. A pupil of her grandfather, Egon van Rijn, she sang in public at 10 and made her operatic debut at 16 at the Berlin City Opera. She later appeared at Brunswick (1956–58) and Stuttgart (1959), making her Bayreuth debut in 1960; she also sang at Covent Garden (from 1967), Chicago (from 1968), and the Metropolitan Opera (from 1972). Her roles include Berg's Marie and Lulu, Isolde and other Wagner parts, and Beethoven's Leonore.

Sills, Beverly [Silverman, Belle] (b. Brooklyn, 25 May 1929). Soprano. She sang on radio as a child; a student of Estelle Liebling, she made her operatic debut at Philadelphia in 1946. Sang on tour with the Charles Wagner Company, and in 1953 at San Francisco. In 1955 she joined the New York City Opera; after 25 years with the company as leading soprano she served as director from 1979 to 1989. A 1966 performance as Cleopatra in Handel's *Julius Caesar* gained wide acclaim, showcasing her skill in coloratura singing. She subsequently appeared at Vienna (1967), La Scala (1969), and Covent Garden (1970). Her formal debut with the Metropolitan Opera took place only in 1975; she sang there for 5 seasons. Among her roles are several Donizetti heroines and Mozart's Constanze and Queen of the Night; she also created the title role in Menotti's *La loca* (San Diego, 1979). She recorded widely, appeared on network television as both performer and personality, and penned an autobiography, *Bubbles: A Self-Portrait* (New York, 1976); also *Bubbles: An Encore* (New York, 1981).

Bibl.: Bridget Paolucci, *Beverly Sills* (New York, 1990).

Silva, Francisco Manuel da (b. Rio de Janeiro, 21 Feb. 1795; d. there, 18 Dec. 1865). Composer and conductor. Studied with José Maurício Nunes Garcia.

Sang in the choir of the royal chapel at Rio de Janeiro in 1809; later played cello in the orchestra. Studied counterpoint and composition with Sigismund Neukomm when he visited, 1816–21. In 1833 he founded the Sociedade beneficência musical. In 1847, founded the conservatory in Rio de Janeiro. When Emperor Dom Pedro I abdicated, he wrote *Hino ao 7 de Abril;* in 1889 the text was changed and it was adopted as the Brazilian national anthem.

Bibl.: Ayres de Andrade, *Francisco Manuel da Silva e seu tempo* (Rio de Janeiro, 1967).

Silver, Horace (Ward Martin Tavares) (b. Norwalk, Conn., 2 Sept. 1928). Jazz pianist, composer, and bandleader. He joined Stan Getz (1950–51) and Art Blakey, with whom he led the hard bop group the Jazz Messengers (1953–55). From 1956 he led his own groups. Recordings of his compositions include "Opus de Funk" (1953), "The Preacher" on the album *Horace Silver and the Jazz Messengers* (1955), "Señor Blues" on the album *Six Pieces of Silver* (1956), and the title track of the album *Song for My Father* (1964). He continued to tour thereafter, playing both his funky hard bop repertory and newer compositions with lyrics concerned with spiritual awareness.

Silverstein, Joseph (b. Detroit, 21 Mar. 1932). Conductor and violinist. Attended the Curtis Institute (1945–50); became a member of the Boston Symphony in 1955, moving to concertmaster in 1962 and to assistant conductor in 1971 after his podium debut the previous year. He led the Worcester Symphony from 1980 and was principal guest conductor of the Baltimore Symphony (1981–83) before taking over the Utah Symphony in 1983; in 1987 he was appointed music director of the Chautauqua Symphony. Active as chamber player and soloist; taught at Yale, Boston Univ., and the Univ. of Utah.

Silvestrov, Valentin Vasilevich (b. Kiev, 30 Sept. 1937). Composer. Began piano lessons at the age of 15, at first privately and later at an evening music school from which he graduated with a gold medal in 1955. In 1955 entered the Kiev Institute of Construction Engineering. From 1958 to 1964 studied composition with Boris Liatoshinsky, harmony and counterpoint with Lev Revutsky at the Kiev Conservatory. Taught at various music schools in Kiev, 1963–70. In the 1960s he was one of the pioneers in contemporary Ukrainian music, exploring serial, aleatoric, and other techniques. His inherently lyrical style later unfolded by means of a mystical, almost minimalistic diatonicism. Works include 5 symphonies; works for solo instrument and orchestra; choral works; vocal works (including *Quiet Songs,* voice and piano, 1974–75); chamber music (including *Drama,* violin, cello, and piano, 1970–71; String Quartet, 1974); piano works; film scores.

Simandl, Franz (b. Blatna, 1 Aug. 1840; d. Vienna, 13 Dec. 1912). Double bass player and composer. From 1869 to 1904 he was a double bass player in the Vienna Court Opera orchestra and the Vienna Philharmonic. From 1869 he also taught at the Vienna Conservatory. He published a *Neueste Methode des Kontrabass-Spiels, 30 Etüden für Kontrabass,* and *Die hohe Schule des Kontrabass-Spiels.* His works include a *Konzertstück, Konzert-Etude,* a concerto, fantasias, and other pieces for double bass. The German-style bow for the double bass, which is held with the palm upward, is named for him.

Simionato, Giulietta (b. Forlì, Italy, 12 May 1910). Mezzo-soprano. Trained at Rovigo and Padua; made debut at Montagnana in 1928, and appeared regularly at La Scala between 1936 and 1966. She sang also at Covent Garden (1953, 1963–65) and the Metropolitan Opera (1959–63), and appeared at Edinburgh (1947), San Francisco (1953), Lisbon (1954), Chicago (1954–61), Vienna (from 1956), and Salzburg (1957–63).

Simmons, Calvin (b. San Francisco, 27 Apr. 1950; d. Lake Placid, N.Y., 21 Aug. 1982). Conductor and pianist. Sang from age 11 in the San Francisco Boys' Choir; attended the Univ. of Cincinnati (1968–70) and the Curtis Institute (1970–72); became pianist and then assistant conductor of the San Francisco Opera between 1968 and 1975, making his podium debut in 1972. He moved to the Los Angeles Philharmonic as assistant conductor in 1975, and from 1979 to his death in a boating accident served as music director of the Oakland Symphony.

Simon, Abbey (b. New York, 8 Jan. 1922). Pianist. Studied at the Curtis Institute (1932–41); began a concert career in 1940, eventually appearing on 6 continents; recorded the complete Chopin and Ravel oeuvre and music of several 19th-century composers. Taught at Indiana Univ., 1966–74, and subsequently at Juilliard and the Univ. of Houston.

Simon, Paul (b. Newark, N.J., 13 Oct. 1941). Folk and rock songwriter, singer, and guitarist. He began working with vocalist Art Garfunkel in high school; from 1964 their recordings of Simon songs such as "Sounds of Silence" (1965), "Parsley, Sage, Rosemary, and Thyme" (1966), "Mrs. Robinson" (1968), "Bridge over Troubled Water" (1970), and "Cecilia" (1970) were very popular. He released his first solo recording in 1972 and achieved intermittent success in the 1970s (including "Loves Me Like a Rock," 1973; "50 Ways To Leave Your Lover," 1975); he returned to prominence with the album *Graceland* (1986), recorded with South African musicians including the vocal group Ladysmith Black Mambazo. He made soundtracks for *The Graduate* (with Garfunkel, 1968), *Shampoo* (1975), and *One Trick Pony,* in which he starred (1980).

Bibl.: Patrick Humphries, *Paul Simon: Still Crazy after All These Years* (New York: 1989).

Simoneau, Léopold (b. Quebec, 3 May 1918). Tenor. Studied at Montreal and New York; made his debut in 1941. He appeared at Paris in 1948, singing also at Glyndebourne (from 1951), La Scala (1953), Salzburg (1956), and the Metropolitan Opera (1963); he retired from opera in 1964, but continued to sing in concert until 1970. He was active in the formation of the Opéra du Québec; joined the faculty of the San Francisco Conservatory in 1972.

Simonov, Yuri (b. Saratov, 4 Mar. 1941). Conductor. Studied viola and conducting at the Leningrad Conservatory (1956–68), winning the Accademia S. Cecilia conducting competition in 1968; directed the Kislovodsk Philharmonic between 1967 and 1969, and was assistant conductor of the Leningrad Philharmonic in 1968 and 1969 before becoming director of the Bolshoi Theater (1970–85), with which he toured Europe, the U.S., and Japan. He has taught at the Moscow Conservatory, and has been an advocate of young Soviet composers.

Simpson [Sympson], **Christopher** (b. Westonby?, near Egton, Yorkshire, ca. 1605; d. Holborne?, London, between 5 May and 29 July 1669). Composer, theorist, and viola da gamba player. He fought on the Royalist side in the English Civil War (1643–44), and later was employed by Sir Robert Bolles. His tutoring of Sir Robert's son John (b. 1641) occasioned the writing of *The Division-Violist* (London, 1659; 2nd ed., 1665), praised by Jenkins, Coleman, and Locke; its practical approach to instruction is reflected in the titles of its three sections: "Of the Viol it self, with Instructions how to Play upon it," "Use of the Concords, or a Compendium of Descant," and "The Method of ordering Division to a Ground." About 1663 he bought an estate near Egton. Another of Simpson's pupils, Sir John St. Barbe, inspired *The Principles of Practical Musick* (London, 1665), which became the *Compendium of Practical Musick* (London, 1667). Simpson's instrumental works are all for viol, with or without other instruments, and vary in difficulty.

Simpson, Robert (Wilfred Levick) (b. Leamington, 2 March 1921). Composer. Originally studied medicine, then pursued music, taking harmony and counterpoint with Howells from 1942 until 1946 in London. He earned a D.Mus. from Durham Univ. and from 1951 to 1980 worked for the BBC. He published monographs on Nielsen, Bruckner, Sibelius, and Beethoven. His own music is similar to Nielsen's and Sibelius's in its symphonic processes. Simpson's symphonies utilize tonal centricity yet may not have one tone as functionally predominant in any movement as a whole. He indicated that certain of his symphonic movements were representative of psychological states. His string quartets, too, exemplify these same characteristics of concept and process. Works include 10 symphonies (1951, 1956, 1967, 1971–72, 1972, 1976, 1977, 1981, 1985, 1988) and chamber music (12 string quartets; Clarinet Quintet, 1968; Trio, violin, cello, piano, 1988–89).

Simpson, Thomas (b. Milton-next-Sittingbourne [now Milton Regis], Kent, bapt. 1 Apr. 1582; d. probably after 1630). Composer. He was employed at the courts of the Elector Palatine at Heidelberg (1608–10), Count Ernst III of Holstein-Schaumburg at Bückeburg (1615–21), and King Christian IV of Denmark (1622–25). He probably returned to England in the late 1620s. His instrumental music reveals a strong Italian influence, and he himself influenced the instrumental music of the north German composers.

Simrock, Nikolaus (b. Mainz, 23 Aug. 1751; d. Bonn, 12 June 1832). Music publisher. Founded a publishing house in Bonn (1793). He played horn in the electoral orchestra in Bonn, and by 1780 was dealing in printed music and instruments. He was succeeded in business by his son Peter Joseph Simrock (b. Bonn, 18 Aug. 1792; d. Cologne, 13 Dec. 1868), who published Brahms's early works. He in turn was followed by his son Friedrich August Simrock (b. Bonn, 2 Jan. 1837; d. Duchy, 20 Aug. 1901), who relocated the firm to Berlin (1870), and he was followed by nephew Johann Baptist Simrock (b. Cologne, 17 Apr. 1861; d. Berlin, 26 July 1910), who expanded the company to include international branches. He was followed by Fritz Auckenthaler, a nephew of Friedrich (b. 17 Nov. 1893; d. Basel, 19 Apr. 1973). The firm was sold out of the family in 1929.

Bibl.: Walther Ottendorf-Simrock, *Das Haus Simrock* (Ratingen, 1954).

Sims, Ezra (b. Birmingham, Ala., 16 Jan. 1928). Composer. Studied with Quincy Porter at the Yale School of Music (B.M., 1952) and with Leon Kirchner and Darius Milhaud at Mills College (M.A., 1956). He also studied mathematics and Asian languages. His early works were in a twelve-tone idiom, though often with imaginative twists. For example, in *Chamber Cantata on Chinese Poems* (1954) the rise and fall of the vocal line mirrors the pitch inflections of the Chinese text, and in *Grave Dance* (1958) for piano, which is a serial rendition of the cowboy ballad "Streets of Laredo." Sims began to use quarter tones in his String Quartet (1959) and continuing in the *Sonate concertante* (1961). From there he worked out a more complicated microtonal system based on scales with 18 notes to the octave. Most of his microtonal works are designed to be sung and played on traditional instruments, for example, String Quartet no. 2 (1974) for flute, clarinet, violin, viola, cello and the *Elegie nach Rilke* (1976) for soprano, flute, clarinet, violin, viola, and cello. Sims also composed a good deal of electronic tape music, beginning with *Sakoku* (1963), composed in Tokyo where he was visiting on a Guggenheim Fellowship. Many of his tape pieces are for dance performances, for example, *Two Toby Minutes, I, II, III* (1971), *Collage XIII: The Inexcusable* (1977). Other works include String Quartet no. 4 (1984), and the string trio *This Way to the Egress—or—Manners Makyth Man* (1984).

Sims, Zoot [John Haley] (b. Inglewood, Calif., 29 Oct. 1925; d. New York, 23 Mar. 1985). Jazz tenor saxophonist. He joined Bill Harris's combo (1944) and the big bands of Benny Goodman (1943, 1946–47) and Woody Herman (1947–49), playing on the latter's recording "Four Brothers" (1947) and thus forming a part of the first saxophone section known by that name. He rejoined Goodman intermittently (1950s–70s), worked with Stan Kenton (1953) and Gerry Mulligan (1954–56; 1960, including the album *Concert Jazz Band*), and co-led a quintet with tenor saxophonist Al Cohn (1957–early 1980s). He also led groups, toured with Jazz at the Philharmonic (1967, 1975), and recorded with Count Basie the album *Basie and Zoot* (1975).

Bibl.: Arne Astrup, *The John Haley Sims (Zoot Sims) Discography* (Lyngby, 1980).

Sinatra, Frank [Francis Albert] (b. Hoboken, N.J., 12 Dec. 1915). Popular singer, actor. After singing in clubs and on radio in New Jersey and New York, in 1939 he joined the Harry James Band. In 1940 he was hired by Tommy Dorsey and sang on several successful recordings (including "I'll Never Smile Again," 1940; "In the Blue of the Evening," 1942); his first solo recordings were made with Alex Stordahl (including "Oh! What It Seemed To Be," 1946; "Mam'selle," 1947). His career underwent a major shift in the 1950s, when he began working with arrangers Billy May, Gordon Jenkins, and Nelson Riddle: with them he produced a series of hits which established him as the most popular male vocalist in the U.S. (including "Young at Heart," 1954; "Strangers in the Night," 1966; the signature "My Way," 1969). His "bel canto" vocal style, influenced by the phrasing of jazz instrumentalists and singers such as Mabel Mercer, was imitated by many later popular artists. He also appeared in numerous movies, winning an Oscar for his performance in *From Here to Eternity* (1953). His 1993 album *Duets,* in which various artists "phoned in" their contributions, attracted attention for its innovative use of technology.

Bibl.: Will Friedwald, *Sinatra! The Song Is You: A Singer's Art* (New York, 1995).

Sinclair, George Robertson (b. Croydon, 28 Oct. 1863; d. Birmingham, 7 Feb. 1917). Organist and conductor. Studied at St. Michael's College, Tenbury, and at the Royal Irish Academy of Music, Dublin. Named assistant organist at Gloucester Cathedral in 1879. Organist and choirmaster at Truro Cathedral in 1880. From 1889 to 1917, organist at Hereford Cathedral. Conducted Birmingham Festival Choral Society, 1899–1917. He is portrayed in the eleventh variation of Elgar's *Enigma Variations.*

Sinding, Christian (August) (b. Kongsberg, Norway, 11 Jan. 1856; d. Oslo, 3 Dec. 1941). Composer. Apprenticed in a piano factory; 1874–77, 1878–79, student, Leipzig Conservatory, his inclination changing from performing to composition; 1882–84, studied in Munich, Berlin, Dresden. Beginning 1880, he was for most of his life subsidized by the Norwegian government, allowing him to devote himself primarily to composition; also conducted, mostly his own music. He lived much in Germany, spending summers in the Norwegian seacoast village of Äsgårdsstrand; 1921–22, visiting professor of theory and composition, Eastman School (substituting for Sibelius, who backed out after accepting); 1924, the government gave him a house in the castle park, Oslo. He began to be known as a composer with the performance of his Piano Quintet op. 5 in 1889 by the Brodsky Quartet and Busoni; very prolific up to about World War I (less so thereafter), especially in songs and piano pieces. The once popular *Rustles of Spring* is no. 3 of his *6 Pieces* op. 32 (1896); also composed a German opera (unsuccessful at Dessau in 1914), 4 symphonies, 3 violin concertos, a piano concerto, chamber music, 4 violin sonatas, 4 violin suites, cantatas, part songs.

Singher, Martial (b. Oloron Ste. Marie, France, 14 Aug. 1904; d. Santa Barbara, Calif., 9 Mar. 1990). Baritone. Studied at the Paris Conservatory from 1927, making his opera debut in 1930 at Amsterdam; sang in Paris from 1930 to 1934, when he left for the U.S.; made his Metropolitan Opera debut in 1943, singing 12 seasons between then and 1959. He sang also at Buenos Aires (1936–43), Chicago (1944–45), and San Francisco (1947). He was on the faculty of Mannes College (1951–62), the Curtis Institute (1955–68), and the Music Academy of the West, San Bernardino, Calif. (1962–81).

Singleton, Zutty [Arthur James] (b. Bunkie, La., 14 May 1898; d. New York, 14 July 1975). Jazz drummer and bandleader. After working in New Orleans and on Mississippi riverboats, he moved to Chicago, joining Jimmie Noone (1927) and recording with Louis Armstrong (1928–29, including "Muggles," 1928) and Jelly Roll Morton (1929, including "That's Like It Ought To Be"). He led or joined many Dixieland, traditional, and swing bands, working with Roy Eldridge (1936–37), Sidney Bechet (1938), Morton (recording in 1939–40), Fats Waller (including the recording "Moppin' and Boppin'," 1943), Eddie Condon (1948), Hot Lips Page, Bill Coleman (both in Europe, 1952–53), and Max Kaminsky (1969–70).

Sinigaglia, Leone (b. Turin, 14 Aug. 1868; d. Turin, 16 May 1944). Composer. Studied at the Turin Conservatory with Giovanni Bolzoni, then in Vienna with Mandyczewski (1893–1900) and in Prague with Dvořák (1900–1901). Under Dvořák's influence he became interested in the folk songs of his native Piedmont, and upon his return to Turin in 1901 he embarked on a project of collection, documentation, and arrangement that culminated in the 6-volume *Vecchie canzoni popolari del Piemonte* (1914–1927). Like Dvořák, he also undertook orchestral arrangements of folk materials, for example, *Danze piemontesi* (1901) and *Piemonte* (1909). He retained his commitment to the harmonic vocabulary of Dvořák and Brahms well into the 20th century. A Jew, he died after being arrested by the Fascist police in 1944. Works include Violin Concerto (1900); *Rapsodia piemontese* (violin and orchestra, 1904); *Le baruffe chiozzotte* (overture, 1908); String Quartet (1902); Cello Sonata (1923); violin sonata (1936).

Bibl.: *Leone Sinigaglia, Torino, 1868–1944,* ed. C. Mosso and E. Bassi (Turin, 1968).

Sinopoli, Giuseppe (b. Venice, 2 Nov. 1946). Composer and conductor. He took a medical degree at the Univ. of Padua and studied composition with Stockhausen, Maderna, and Donatoni. Moving to Vienna in 1972, he studied conducting with Swarowsky; he formed the Bruno Maderna Ensemble in 1975 and taught at Darmstadt in 1976. Sinopoli made his operatic conducting debut in 1978 in Venice, later appearing at Covent Garden, Hamburg, Bayreuth, and the Metropolitan Opera. He served as principal conductor of the Philharmonia Orchestra (1983–95), leading also the St. Cecilia Orchestra, Rome (1983–87), and the Dresden Staatskapelle (1991–92). Works include the opera *Lou Salome* (1981); *Opus Daleth* and *Opus Ghimel,* orchestra (1971); a piano concerto (1974); chamber and choral works; and electronic music.

Siqueira, José (de Lima) (b. Conceição, Paraiba, Brazil, 24 June 1907; d. Rio de Janeiro, 22 Apr. 1985). Composer. Studied saxophone and trumpet as a youth; attended the National Music Institute, Rio, from 1926, studying with Silva and Braga, and teaching there from 1935. Founded the Brazilian Symphony in 1940, leading it until 1948; in 1949 he established the Rio Symphony as well, and in 1960 helped in the creation of a musicians' union. He conducted throughout the Americas and in Europe, and authored several theory texts. Whereas his early compositions are in a neoclassical vein, in the 1940s he embraced musical nationalism, developing modal systems based on his fieldwork with the indigenous peoples of northeast Brazil. Works include ballets; symphonies; 3 piano concertos and 2 violin concertos; the tone poem *Alvorada brasileira* (1946); several *Danças brasileiras;* works for voices and orchestra, including the cantata *Xangô* (1955) and the oratorio *Candomblé* (1958), as well as the comic opera *A Compadecida* (1961); chamber music for various instrumental ensembles; solo music; and songs.

Bibl.: *Composers of the Americas* 16 (Washington, D.C., 1970), pp. 130–44 [includes works list].

Sissle, Noble (Lee) (b. Indianapolis, 10 July 1889; d. Tampa, 17 Dec. 1975). Popular lyricist, composer, singer, and bandleader. From 1915 he worked in bands, vaudeville shows, and musicals with Eubie Blake. They wrote "Shuffle Along" (1921) and "The Chocolate Dandies" (1924). In addition to Blake he collaborated with other songwriters and as a singer led bands (1928–1960s), initially working in Europe with such jazzmen as Sidney Bechet and Buster Bailey.

Bibl.: Robert Kimball and William Bolcom, *Reminiscing with Sissle and Blake* (New York, 1973).

Sitsky, Larry (b. Tientsin, China, 10 Sept. 1934). Composer and pianist. Studied piano at the New South Wales and San Francisco conservatories; held faculty posts at Queensland State Conservatory (1961–65) and Australian National Univ. (from 1966). Busoni was a focus of his research and pianistic efforts, and he wrote extensively on new music as well. Compositions include the operas *Fall of the House of Usher* (1965) and *Lenz* (1972); the ballet *The Dark Refuge* (1964); concertos for wind quintet and for violin with women's chorus (both 1971); a guitar concerto (1984); String Quartet no. 1 (1969) and no. 2 (1989); the children's opera *Three Scenes from Aboriginal Life* (1989) and a cantata for soprano, flute, cello, piano, and percussion (*Deep in My Hidden Country,* 1983–84).

Sivori, (Ernesto) Camillo (b. Genoa, 25 Oct. 1815; d. there, 19 Feb. 1894). Violinist and composer. Studied with Paganini for a short time in 1824, and with Restano, Giacomo Costa, and Agostino Dellepiane. Debut in 1827 at the Teatro Falcone; a tour followed. Paganini composed for and dedicated to him a concertino and 6 sonatas for violin, viola, cello, and guitar. Studied composition with Giovanni Serra in 1829. His compositions include 2 concertos (1841), etudes, many fantasias, variations.

Sjören, (Johann Gustaf) Emil (b. Stockholm, 16 June 1853; d. there, 1 Mar. 1918). Composer. Studied at Stockholm Conservatory, 1869–75, with Thegerström (piano), Mankell (organ), and Berens (harmony). Studied composition with Kiel and organ with Haupt in Berlin, 1879–80. He was named organist at French Reformed Church in Stockholm, 1881; organist at Johanneskyrka, 1891–1918. His compositions include 2 piano sonatas, 5 violin sonatas, cello sonata (1912); Fest-polonaise op. 5, piano 4-hands (1881); piano works; songs. A complete edition of his songs was published in Stockholm (1916).

Skaggs, Ricky (b. Cordell, Ky., 18 July 1954). Country singer, guitarist, fiddler, and mandolin player. He played with Ralph Stanley and numerous bluegrass bands including Country Store, The New South, and Boone Creek, and achieved prominence as a sideman in Emmylou Harris's Hot Band. He made his first solo recording in 1979; with John Anderson he has been associated with the 1980s traditionalist movement in country music.

Skalkottas [Scalcotas], **Nikolaos** [Nikos, Nicos] (b. Halkis, Evia, 8 Mar. 1904; d. Athens, 19 Sept. 1949). Composer. He moved to Athens as a child, where he studied the violin, graduating from the Athens Conservatory in 1920. He then traveled to Berlin, where he continued his study of the violin with Hess at the Hochschule für Musik. While there he began to study composition with Juon and Kahn and, during the late

1920s, Schoenberg and Weill. He returned to Athens in 1933, where he worked as an orchestral violinist. His music, most of which was written during the last decade of his life, was within the modern neoclassical trends; his pieces frequently refer to forms or genres of the classical era and utilize standard instrumentation. His early music was tonal, an orientation that recurs in some of his very late works (*Sixteen Songs* op. 80). Subsequently his musical language spanned both atonal and serial styles, the latter being more fully worked out in late works such as the Fourth String Quartet (1940) and the Third Piano Concerto (1938–39). His textures were contrapuntal and his formal processes were highly motivic. Works include Concertino op. 20, 2 pianos, orchestra (1935); Violin Concerto op. 22 (1937–38); *I Epistrophi tou Odysseus* [The Return of Ulysses], overture (1942–43); 4 string quartets; 4 piano suites.

Skilton, Charles Sanford (b. Northampton, Mass., 16 Aug. 1868; d. Lawrence, Kans., 12 Mar. 1941). Composer. After receiving a B.A. from Yale Univ. in 1889, he studied in New York with Dudley Buck and then in Berlin with Bargiel at the Hochschule für Musik (1891–93). Returning to the U.S., he taught at the Salem Academy, N.C. (1893–96), and the Trenton State Normal School, N.J. (1897–1903), then from 1903 at the Univ. of Kansas, where he remained. In 1915 he became acquainted with students at the Haskell Institute, a national school for American Indians in Lawrence, Kans., and he came to know Native American music and musicians. All of his best-known works are adaptations and orchestrations of Native American songs and dances: *Kalopin* (opera, 1927); *The Sun Bride* (opera, 1930); *Suite Primeval* (orchestra, 1920); *3 Indian Sketches* (piano, 1919); *Shawnee Indian Hunting Dance* (piano, 1929).

Bibl.: John Tasker Howard, *Charles Sanford Skilton* (New York, 1929).

Skinner, Ernest M. (b. Clarion, Pa., 15 Jan. 1866; d. Duxbury, Mass., 27 Nov. 1960). Organ builder. After working for Ryder (Reading, Mass.) and Hutchings (Boston), he founded the E. M. Skinner Co., Boston, in 1901. He excelled in developing imitative orchestral stops and improving the standard "Pitman" windchest. In 1931 he merged with the organ division of the Aeolian Co. to form the Aeolian-Skinner Co.; from 1933 its director was G. Donald Harrison (1889–1956), a former director of the Willis Co., London. Harrison reoriented the company toward more classical (nonorchestral) design, making it the most admired and successful American organ company of its era. Skinner lessened his activity in the company from 1936; it closed in 1971.

Bibl.: Dorothy J. Holden, *The Life and Work of Ernest M. Skinner* (Richmond, Va., 1985).

Skowroneck, (Franz Hermann) Martin (b. Berlin-Spandau, 21 Dec. 1926). Harpsichord maker. As a recorder student in the late 1940s he made instruments for himself and others. (He qualified as a flute and recorder teacher, Bremen, 1950.) In 1952 he restored a war-damaged clavichord, copied it for himself, and took to studying and copying other historical keyboard instruments. From the 1960s Gustav Leonhardt and other European harpsichordists championed his pioneering work in historically informed design.

Skrowaczewski, Stanislaw (b. Lwów, 3 Oct. 1923). Conductor and composer. Composed as a child, and in 1936 led a performance of Beethoven's Third Concerto from the piano; graduated from the Univ. of Lwów in 1945; having injured his hands during a bombing raid, he turned to conducting. He led the Wrocław Philharmonic in 1946 and 1947, then studied in Paris with Boulanger and Kletski; returning to Poland, he held posts with the orchestras of Katowice (1949–54), Kraków (1954–56), and Warsaw (1956–59). After a 1958 U.S. debut, from 1960 to 1979 he was music director of the Minneapolis Symphony, and from 1984 to 1991 he conducted the Hallé Orchestra, Manchester. He introduced many important Polish works to U.S. audiences, including Szymanowski's Second Symphony, Lutosławski's *Funeral Music,* and Penderecki's St. Luke Passion. His own works include 4 symphonies; concertos for English horn (1969), clarinet (1980), and violin (1985); *Ricercari notturni,* saxophone and orchestra (1978); Concerto for Orchestra (1985); film music; chamber and piano music; and songs. During the 1990s he resumed composing after a 10-year period of inactivity.

Skryabin, Alexander. See Scriabin, Alexander.

Slatkin, Felix (b. St. Louis, 22 Dec. 1915; d. Los Angeles, 8 Feb. 1963). Conductor and violinist. Attended the Curtis Institute; joined the St. Louis Symphony in 1931, and was named assistant concertmaster in 1933; moved west in 1937, becoming concertmaster of the 20th-Century Fox studio orchestra. From 1947 to 1961 he led the Hollywood String Quartet, in which his wife, Eleanor Aller, was cellist; he also worked as a freelance studio musician.

Slatkin, Leonard (b. Los Angeles, 1 Sept. 1944). Conductor. Son of Felix Slatkin. Studied at Indiana Univ., Los Angeles City College, and the Juilliard School between 1962 and 1968, making his conducting debut in 1966. He first served with the St. Louis Symphony as assistant conductor (1968–71), later becoming associate (1971–74) and finally music director (1979–96), after a period with the New Orleans Symphony. He led the Minneapolis Orchestra's summer concerts in 1979 and 1980, and in 1982 and 1983 was associated with the Oakland Symphony; he has served as music director of the Great Woods Performing Arts Center (summer home of the Pittsburgh Symphony) from 1990 and of the Blossom Music Center (summer home of the Cleveland Orchestra) from 1991. In 1996 he succeeded Rostropovich as music director of the National Symphony Orchestra. Slatkin is an advocate of American composers and has himself composed many works, including *Dialogue* for 2 cellos and orchestra, *The Raven* for narrator and orchestra, and 4 string quartets.

Slavenski [Stolzer, Štolcer, Štolcer-Salvenski]**, Josip** (b. Čadovec, 11 May 1896; d. Belgrade, 30 Nov. 1955). Composer. He studied composition with Kodály and Siklós at the Budapest Conservatory of Music beginning in 1913. He served in World War I and only in 1921 was again able formally to study music, this time with Novák at the Prague Conservatory. He returned to Zagreb to teach in 1923 and beginning in 1924 settled in Belgrade, where he eventually taught at the academy from 1937 to 1945. His music was influenced by the native musics of his natal region, leading him to polytonality and polyrhythms in the style of Bartók. His music also anticipated aleatoric and other avant-garde techniques of midcentury composers; consequently his work was little understood or appreciated during his lifetime. His music includes orchestral works *(Balkanophonia,* 1927; *Simfonijski epos,* 1944–46), chamber music (4 string quartets), and piano and choral music.

Slavík, Josef (b. Jince, near Příbram, Bohemia, 26 Mar. 1806; d. Budapest, 30 May 1833). Violinist and composer. Joined an amateur quartet in 1815. Studied at Prague Conservatory, 1816–23, under patronage of Count Eugen z Vrna. His teachers included Pixis and Bedřich Diviš. Taught violin in Vienna beginning in 1826. Schubert dedicated his *Fantasia in C* D. 934 (1827) to Slavík, who premiered the work in January 1828. Appointed to Viennese Hofkapelle, 1829. Most of his compositions are for violin; few survive.

Bibl.: Stanislav Klíma, *Josef Slavík* (Prague, 1956).

Slezak, Leo (b. Schönberg, Moravia, 18 Aug. 1873; d. Egern am Tegernsee, Bavaria, 1 June 1946). Tenor. Made his debut at Brno in 1896 as Lohengrin; sang in Berlin (1898–99) and Breslau (1900–1901), then was engaged by Mahler at Vienna, singing there regularly until the mid-1920s. He made frequent guest appearances elsewhere, including the Metropolitan Opera from 1909 to 1913; retiring from the stage in 1933, he then became a popular comedian in films. Several volumes of memoirs reveal his wit. A specialist in German heldentenor roles, he scored successes in Verdi's *Otello* as well.

Slick, Grace (Wing) (b. Chicago, 30 Oct. 1939). Rock singer and songwriter. She sang with Great Society before joining the Jefferson Airplane in 1966, and with guitarist Paul Kantner helped re-form the group as the Jefferson Starship in 1974. She wrote or co-wrote several of their songs, including "White Rabbit" (1967) and "Fast Buck Freddie" (1975). After a brief solo career in the early 1980s she rejoined, recording with vocalist Mickey Thomas the successful "We Built This City" (1986).

Slobodskaya, Oda (b. Vilnius, 28 Nov. 1888; d. London, 29 July 1970). Soprano. Schooled in Leningrad, making her debut there in 1919; created Parasha in Stravinsky's *Mavra* (Paris, 1922), singing also at La Scala (1933) and Buenos Aires (1936). Settling in London during the 1930s, she sang in operas and recitals, performed on radio, and made recordings. A major figure in the interpretation of Russian song, she continued to perform into her 70s, also teaching at Guildhall School in London.

Bibl.: Maurice Leonard, *Slobodskaya: A Biography of Oda Slobodskaya* (London, 1979).

Slonimsky, Nicolas (b. St. Petersburg, Russia, 27 Apr. 1894; d. Los Angeles, 25 Dec. 1995). Conductor and writer on music. He studied piano and composition at the Petersburg Conservatory. Leaving Petersburg in 1918, he journeyed by way of Kiev, Yalta, and Istanbul to Paris, where he worked as accompanist for Koussevitzky. In 1923 he moved to the U.S. to be an accompanist and vocal coach at the newly founded Eastman School of Music. Moving to Boston, he conducted the Harvard Univ. Orchestra (1927–30) and the Boston Chamber Orchestra (1927–34) and made guest appearances with several other ensembles, conducting mainly modern music. His first musico-literary project was *Music since 1900,* a chronology of important events and persons in 20th-century music, which was published in 1937 and updated several times thereafter. In 1939 he became associate editor of Thompson's *International Cyclopedia of Music and Musicians,* which he saw through 4 editions (1946–58). Spurred on by his passion for discovering and correcting the errors of received opinion, he took over as editor-in-chief of *Baker's Biographical Dictionary of Musicians,* and produced its 5th (1958), 6th (1978), 7th (1984), and 8th (1992) editions. He is also the author of *Thesaurus of Scales and Melodic Patterns* (1947), *Lexicon of Musical Invective* (New York, 1952; rev. 1965), and an autobiography, *Perfect Pitch* (Oxford, 1988).

Slonimsky, Sergei Mikhailovich (b. Leningrad, 12 Aug. 1932). Composer. Studied at the Leningrad Conservatory with B. Arapov and O. Evlakhov (composition) and V. Nilsen (piano), 1950–56; pursued graduate work there in musicology, 1956–58, defending a thesis on the symphonies of Prokofiev in 1963. Beginning in 1959, taught composition at the Leningrad Conservatory. Participation in collecting expeditions deepened his interest in Russian folklore which is reflected in many works, particularly in the melodic writing. In the late 1960s and early 1970s he experimented with serial, aleatoric, and other advanced techniques; subsequently he relied on more traditional stylistic means.

Works: operas *Virineia* (1967; rev. 1976), *Master and Margarita* (completed 1973; 1st perf. 1989), *Mary Stuart* (1980); the ballet *Icarus* (1971); 9 symphonies (no. 9, 1989); Concerto buffo for chamber orchestra (1966) and other symphonic music; a violin concerto (1983); cantatas; chamber music; choral works; vocal music.

Bibl.: A. Milka, *Sergei Slonimskii: monograficheskii ocherk* (Leningrad: Sovetskii kompozitor, 1976).

Smallens, Alexander (b. St. Petersburg, 1 Jan. 1889; d. Tucson, 24 Nov. 1972). Conductor. Brought to the U.S. as a youth; studied in New York and at the Paris Conservatory; conducted at the Boston Opera between 1911 and 1914, then toured with the Pavlova dance company; later directed the Chicago Opera (1919–23) and the Philadelphia Civic Opera (1924–31), also assisting the Philadelphia Orchestra (1927–34). He led the premiere of Gershwin's *Porgy and Bess* at Boston in 1935; subsequently he conducted at Philadelphia and New York, and from 1947 to 1950 was associated with the Radio City Music Hall.

Smalley, Roger (b. Swinton, Manchester, 26 July 1943). Composer. He studied from 1961 to 1965 at the Royal College of Music with Fricker and White, the latter being a particular influence on Smalley. In the early 1960s he studied with Goehr, focusing on the music of Boulez, Maxwell Davies, Schoenberg, and then Stockhausen, performing many of these composers' works. In 1967 Smalley became composer-in-residence at King's College, Cambridge, and in 1970 organized, with Souster, the controversial new-music group Intermodulation. He left England for Australia in 1976, where he joined the research faculty at the Univ. of Western Australia. His early compositions reflected the more cerebral tendencies of influences such as Boulez and Schoenberg; beginning with his chorus *The Crystal Cabinet* of 1967, based on Blake, he began incorporating more improvisation, electronic media, and quotation, as well as popular musical style in *Beat Music* (1971). His *Impulses,* premiered in 1988, utilized minimalistic devices. He has also published critical essays on contemporary music in British music journals. Works include *Missa brevis* (16 solo voices, 1966–67); *Missa parodia I* (piano, 1967); *Missa parodia II* (piano, flute, oboe, clarinet, horn, trumpet, trombone, violin, viola, 1967); *Melody Study I* (4 or more players, 1970); *Zeitebenen* (ensemble, tape, for West German radio, 1973); Symphony in One Movement (orchestra, 1981); *The Narrow Road to the Deep North* ("journey" for baritone, 6 players, 1983); *Wind Chimes for Tape* (tape, 1987).

Smareglia, Antonio (b. Pola, Istria, 5 May 1854; d. Grado, Istria, 15 Apr. 1929). Composer. Studied mathematics at Graz Polytechnic; later (1873–77) attended Milan Conservatory, studying with Faccio. After becoming blind, he was appointed honorary artistic director of the Tartini Conservatory in Trieste in 1921. Composed 9 operas, including *Der Vasall von Szigeth* (1889), *Cornil Schut* (1893), *Nozze Istriane* (1895), and *L'abrisso* (1914). Other works include *Inno a Tartini,* voices and band (1896); a few orchestral works; piano music; some vocal pieces.

Smart, George (Thomas) (b. London, 10 May 1776; d. there, 23 Feb. 1867). Organist, composer, and conductor. One of the founders of the Philharmonic Society of London, 1813; one of its conductors, 1813–44; introduced many works of Beethoven and Schumann. Named organist at Chapel Royal, 1822. Introduced Mendelssohn's oratorio *St. Paul* to England, 1826. Knew Beethoven, and many of their conversations survive; Weber died in his house. Conducted first English performance of Beethoven's Ninth Symphony, 1826; conducted many festivals at Liverpool, Manchester, Dublin, Cambridge, Bath, and other cities. He edited Gibbons's madrigals, 1841; published a collection of glees and canons, 1863. His compositions are primarily small sacred pieces. His brother was the violinist Henry Smart (1778–1823).

Smetana, Bedřich (b. Litomyšl, Bohemia, 2 Mar. 1824; d. Prague, 12 May 1884). Composer. Eldest son of the manager of the town brewery and his third wife; attended schools in various towns; 1839, sent to high school in Prague, but soon dropped out, spending much of his time in musical activities. Liszt's Prague recitals in 1840 were a crucial experience, stimulating his own aspirations as a pianist; 1840–43, completed his schooling in Plzeň. Then determining to become a professional musician, although his father, now in reduced circumstances, could give him no further help, and drawn by the presence there of a Plzeň girl with whom, without much encouragement, he had fallen in love, he moved to Prague; 1843–47, studied theory and composition with Jozef Proksch, who got him a job (from Jan. 1844) as music teacher to the five children of Count Thun. In 1847 he resigned to begin a piano tour of Bohemia, but his first concert was a financial failure, and he returned to Prague, eking out a living by teaching. Wanting to open a music school but having no money to do so, in 1848 he composed his op. 1, *Six Characteristic Pieces* for piano, and sent it with a dedication to Liszt asking for help. Liszt gave him no money but got the work published at Leipzig (1851). Later in 1848 he did open a music school, which slowly established itself (partly because of aristocratic support and Smetana's nationalist sympathies, expressed through music written during the 1848 Revolution). In August 1849 he finally married his longtime beloved.

Smetana's first large orchestral work, an overture, was composed in 1848–49; 1853–54, composed the Triumphal Symphony, incorporating the Austrian Hymn and dedicated to the emperor's marriage, but never acknowledged; its premiere, at a concert he organized in February 1855, attracted little notice. Three of his four daughters died, 1854–55, including his favorite; he composed the Piano Trio in G minor as an expression of his grief. It premiered in December 1855 without much response. Depressed and frustrated, in October 1856 he left Prague for Göteborg, Sweden, where he opened a music school, conducted a choral society, and organized chamber concerts, all with success. In September 1857 he brought over his wife, long a consumptive, now in the final stages; her health was not improved by the climate, and she did not take to her new surroundings. Meanwhile, Smetana carried on an affair with a married student. At Weimar he had heard the premieres of Liszt's Faust Symphony and the tone poem *Die Ideale,* and his earlier attraction to the avant-garde music of Liszt, Wagner, and Berlioz now became a strong commitment, stimulating his own creativity: 1857, composed a tone poem for piano, *Cid and Ximene;* 1857–58, orchestral tone poem *Richard III;* 1858–59, *Wallenstein's Camp;* 1858–59, *Macbeth and the Witches,* for piano. His hope for a Weimar performance of the orchestral pieces was not realized, Liszt not being sufficiently impressed. In April 1859 his wife fell desperately ill and died. Visiting friends in the country that summer, he fell in love with their 19-year-old daughter, whom he married in summer 1860; they returned for a final year in Sweden, when Smetana composed the orchestral tone poem *Hakon Jarl* on a Norwegian subject.

In May 1861 Smetana returned permanently to Prague. In fall 1861 he made an unsuccessful piano tour of Germany and Holland. Two concerts of his music were also unsuccessful in Prague early in 1862. Over the next few years he worked to become a significant figure in Prague musical life, his growing nationalism reflecting the temper of the times. His hopes of becoming conductor at the opera (the Provisional Theater) in 1862 and director of the conservatory in 1863 were disappointed, but in 1863 he was elected head of the music section of the new Society of Arts, organizing and appearing in its concerts. In 1863, with the birth of a daughter, he reopened his music school to increase his income; from 1864 published music criticism. Also in 1863 he completed his first opera, *Braniboři v Čechách* (The Brandenburgers in Bohemia) as his entry in a Czech opera competition; it was premiered at the Provisional Theater on 3 January 1866 under Smetana; it was a success and won the prize.

On 30 May 1866 he premiered his second opera, the comedy *Prodana nevěsta* (The Bartered Bride); it was a failure, achieving success only in 1870 after several revisions, eventually overshadowing his other works, rather to his disgust. His resulting stature in Prague was reflected by his appointment as conductor at the Provisional Theater in September 1866. With his next opera, *Dalibor* (16 May 1868), however, he began to have opposition. Its premiere, for the laying of the cornerstone of the new National Theater, was a success, but there were few further performances in his lifetime, the opera becoming popular only after his death. He was accused of Wagnerism, and this charge of musical radicalism was reinforced by his association with the more extreme wing of Czech nationalism. From about 1870 there were continuing attacks designed to drive him from his post at the theater; these failed but soured his life. His next opera to be performed, *Dvě vdovy* (The Two Widows, 1874) was a success. It was the advanced stages of syphilis that ended his conducting career. On 20 October 1874, after months of hearing problems, he became completely deaf. He was forced to resign, giving up performing rights in his existing operas in exchange for a pension, which was not always paid, creating great hardship and eventually forcing him and his family to live with his married daughter in the country. His wife was not able to accept his condition with charity or forgiveness, and their relations became increasingly bitter.

In spite of extreme depression and physical discomfort, he composed some of his most important works in this period: the first four tone poems of the *Má vlast* (My Fatherland) cycle were written in 1874–75, the final two in 1878–79. In 1875–76 he wrote the opera *Hubička* (The Kiss), which was also a success, and in October–December 1876 his most important chamber work, the String Quartet in E minor (From My Life). *Tajemství* (The Secret), composed in 1877–78, premiered in 1878, was not a success. In 1881 his patriotic, pageantlike opera *Libuše,* composed in 1869–72 but reserved for a great national occasion, inaugurated the National Theater. His last completed opera, *Čertove stěna* (The Devil's Wall), composed in 1879–82, premiered in 1882, was a failure, increasing the bitterness of his last years. It was one of several late works, including the Second String Quartet (1882–83) and the orchestral piece *Prague Carnival* (1883), that were composed in great suffering and that some have thought to reflect his mental and physical deterioration, which included hallucinations, paranoia, and violent outbursts. Three weeks before his death he had to be taken to the Prague insane asylum. He left unfinished his last opera, *Viola,* based on *Twelfth Night.*

Bibl.: F. Bartoš et al., eds., *Studijni vydáni děl Bedřicka Smetany* [Collected Works] (Prague, 1940–). B. Large, *Smetana* (London and New York, 1970). J. Clapham, *Smetana* (London, 1972). Guy Erismann, *Smetana, l'éveilleur* (Arles, 1993).

Smirnov, Dmitry Nikolaevich (b. Minsk, 2 Nov. 1948). Composer. Studied at the Moscow Conservatory, 1967–72, with Nikolai Sidelnikov (composition), Yuri Kholopov (analysis), and Edison Denisov (orchestration). From 1973 to 1980 he worked as an editor at the publisher Sovetskii kompozitor. The works of William Blake have been a significant source of inspiration and provided the subjects for his 2 operas, *Tiriel* (1983–85) and *The Lamentations of Thel* (1985–86). Other works include Symphony no. 1, (The Seasons, 1980), Symphony no. 2 (soloists, mixed chorus, and orchestra, on poems of Hölderlin, 1982), and other symphonic music; 2 piano concertos, a clarinet concerto and a triple concerto for alto saxophone, piano, and double bass (1977); works for voice and ensemble; much music for chamber ensembles; piano works; choral and vocal works; film music.

Smit, Leo (b. Philadelphia, 12 Jan. 1921). Pianist and composer. He studied piano with Isabella Vengerova at the Curtis Institute in Philadelphia (1930–32); also studied piano with José Iturbi and composition with Nicholas Nabokov. He worked as an accompanist at Balanchine's American Ballet (1936–37), then at various universities; from 1962 to 1984 he taught at SUNY–Buffalo. As a pianist he became known especially for the performance of modern repertory. His compositions from the 1940s are Americanist in flavor, for example, *Virginia Sampler,* ballet (1947), and *Seven Characteristic Pieces,* piano (1949). Much of his music from the mid-50s on is consciously neoclassical, often borrowing themes from the music of the past, as in *Capriccio,* string orchestra (1958), *American Graffiti,* voice, clarinet, cello, piano, percussion (1959), and Concerto for Orchestra and Piano (1968). Other works include the operas *The Alchemy of Love* (1969) and *Magic Water* (1978), and a sonata for piano 4-hands (1987).

Smith, Bessie (b. Chattanooga, Tenn., 15 Apr. 1894; d. Clarksdale, Miss., 26 Sept. 1937). Blues singer. From 1912 until her death in an automobile accident she toured in minstrel and vaudeville shows. Her greatest success came in the 1920s, when she recorded widely, including "Down-Hearted Blues" (1923), The "St. Louis Blues" (1925, with Louis Armstrong), "Back Water Blues" (1927, with James P. Johnson), and "Empty Bed Blues" (1928, with trombonist Charlie Green). She operated within a narrow range of pitch, subtly manipulating blue notes, phrasing, and timbre (including growls for expressive effect). She preferred slow tempos and bawdy lyrics. Although this style fell out of fashion, she starred in the pioneering African American film *St. Louis Blues* (1929) and continued recording, including "Gimme a Pigfoot" (1933, with Jack Teagarden, Benny Goodman, and Chu Berry).

Bibl.: Chris Albertson, *Bessie: Empress of the Blues* (New York, 1972). Elaine Feinstein, *Bessie Smith* (New York, 1985).

Smith, Craig (b. Lewiston, Idaho, 31 Jan. 1947). Conductor and pianist. Attended Washington State Univ. and the New England Conservatory. Became music director at Emmanuel Church, Boston, in 1970, where he established chamber ensembles and the Liederkreis vocal quartet, and where he has performed a wide variety of music (including the complete Bach cantatas) at Sunday services. Beginning in 1980 he teamed with Peter Sellars in new stagings of operas by Handel, Mozart, and others.

Smith, David Stanley (b. Toledo, 6 July 1877; d. New Haven, 17 Dec. 1949). Composer, conductor, educator. He attended Yale Univ. (B.A., 1900; B.M., 1903), where he was a favorite student of Horatio Parker. He also studied briefly in Europe (1901–2). Appointed to the faculty at Yale in 1903, he remained there for his entire career, serving from 1925 to 1946 as dean of the School of Music. He composed a good deal of instrumental music in a harmonically conservative style, including 5 symphonies, 2 violin concertos, several overtures, 10 string quartets, and sonatas for various instruments.

Smith, "Father" (Bernard) [Schmidt, Bernhard] (b. ca. 1630; d. London, 20 Feb. 1708). Organ builder. He trained in Germany and worked in Holland before moving to England in 1666; he was "the King's organ maker" in 1671. In 1676 he was elected organist of St. Margaret's, Westminster; he formally became King's Organ Maker in 1681. Smith introduced several stops to English organ building and improved unequal temperament. He worked on more than 700 organs, some of which were rebuilds; almost all have been altered.

Smith, Gregg (b. Chicago, 21 Aug. 1931). Conductor and composer. Attended UCLA, studying composition with Leonard Stein and Lukas Foss; formed the Gregg Smith Singers in 1955, with whom he has made many recordings and toured widely; participated in the premiere of Stravinsky's *Requiem Canticles* in 1966. He taught at Ithaca College, SUNY–Stony Brook, and the Peabody Conservatory, and has edited much choral music; his own works include 2 operas, pieces for chamber orchestra, and hundreds of choral settings for varying forces.

Smith, Hale (b. Cleveland, 29 June 1925). Composer. As a youth he studied classical piano and also accompanied jazz singers in nightclubs. He attended the Cleveland Institute of Music (B.M., 1950; M.M., 1952), then moved to New York, where he worked as a music editor for various publishers and as an arranger for jazz musicians such as Chico Hamilton, Abbey Lincoln, and Eric Dolphy. At the same time he was composing concert music. *In Memoriam Beryl Rubinstein,* chorus and chamber orchestra (1953), and *Contours,* orchestra (1961), were performed by several orchestras and recorded. From 1970 to 1984 Smith was professor of music at the Univ. of Connecticut. In some of his works—for example, the jazz cantata *Comes Tomorrow* (1972; rev. 1976)—the influence of traditional jazz is overt; other works, such as *Rituals and Incantations,* orchestra (1974), use serial techniques.

Bibl.: Hansonia Caldwell, "A Man of Many Parts—Conversation with Hale Smith," *Black Perspective in Music* 3 (1975): 58–76. David N. Baker, Lida M. Belt and Herman C. Hudson, eds., *The Black Composer Speaks* (Metuchen, N.J., 1978), pp. 313–336 [interview and works list].

Smith, Jabbo [Cladys] (b. Pembroke, Ga., 24 Dec. 1908; d. St. Louis, 16 Jan. 1991). Jazz trumpeter and singer. He recorded with Duke Ellington (1927) and joined James P. Johnson in the revue *Keep Shufflin'* (1928). In Chicago in 1929 he recorded his own compositions; his daring solos on pieces such as "Jazz Battle" and "Ace of Rhythm" presented a flamboyant challenge to Louis Armstrong's preeminence among jazz trumpeters. He joined Claude Hopkins (1936–38), but otherwise from the 1930s to the 1970s worked in Chicago, New York, and Milwaukee with lesser-known players. He performed in the show *One Mo'*

Time (1978 to early 1980s) and sang, accompanied by Don Cherry (1986).

Smith, Jimmy [James Oscar] (b. Norristown, Pa., 8 Dec. 1925). Jazz organist and bandleader. From 1955 to 1975 he led groups which included guitar and drums (sometimes augmented by saxophone and trumpet), establishing a widely imitated model. Adapting the hard bop style to the Hammond electric organ, he combined walking pedal bass lines and chordal accompaniments with bop and blues solos, and he obtained timbres deeper, more cutting, and less sentimental than those of earlier jazz organists. Among his albums are *The Sermon* (1957–58) and *The Unpredictable Jimmy Smith: Bashin',* including a version of "Walk on the Wild Side" with a big band (1962). After running his own nightclub in Los Angeles, he resumed touring in the 1980s.

Smith, Joe [Joseph C.] (b. Ripley, Ohio, 28 June 1902; d. New York, 2 Dec. 1937). Jazz trumpeter. He toured with Ethel Waters and Mamie Smith in 1922 and made recordings accompanying these and many other singers, notably Bessie Smith (1924–27, including "Money Blues," 1926). He played in Eubie Blake and Noble Sissle's show *In Bamville* (1924), then joined Fletcher Henderson's big band (1925–28), with which his recorded solos include "Fidgety Feet" and "Swamp Blues" (both 1927). He was a member of McKinney's Cotton Pickers (1929–30, 1931–32). His brother Russell (1890–1966) also played trumpet in big bands.

Smith, John Christopher [Schmidt, Johann Christoph] (b. Ansbach, 1712; d. Bath, 3 Oct. 1795). Composer and organist. He was the son of Johann Christoph Schmidt, who moved to London in 1716 to serve as Handel's treasurer and principal copyist. Both father and son used the name John Christopher Smith. The younger Smith moved to London in 1720 and was taught principally by Thomas Roseingrave. He teamed with Arne in the 1730s to produce all-sung English operas in the Italian style; his *Ulysses* (1733) was a failure, as were 2 Shakespearean operas (1755 and 1756). In 1754 he became organist at the Foundling Hospital, where he directed performances of *Messiah* (1759–68). His oratorio *Paradise Lost* (1757–58) was a modest success.

Bibl.: William Coxe, *Anecdotes of George Frederick Handel and John Christopher Smith, with Selected Pieces of Music by J. C. Smith Never Before Published* (New York, 1979).

Smith, John Stafford (bapt. Gloucester, 30 Mar. 1750; d. London, 21 Sept. 1836). Composer. He studied with his father, an organist, as well as with William Boyce in London. In 1761 he joined the Chapel Royal as a chorister. He established a reputation as composer of catches and glees and is thought to be the composer of the song "To Anacreon in Heaven," an adaptation of which is the tune to "The Star Spangled Banner." Considered one of the earliest English musicologists, he acquired a collection of early music including the Old Hall MS.

Smith, Julia (Frances) (b. Denton, Tex., 25 Jan. 1911; d. New York, 27 Apr. 1989). Pianist and composer. She studied at North Texas State Univ., then at Juilliard (1932–39), and at New York Univ. (M.A., 1933; Ph.D., 1952). Much of her music is based on American folk materials—for example, *American Dance Suite,* orchestra (1936; rev. 1963), *Folkways Symphony* (1948), and the opera *Cynthia Parker* (Denton, Tex., 1939). Other works, such as the *Characteristic Suite* (1949) for piano, which uses a twelve-tone row, and the String Quartet (1964), are more abstract. Smith involved herself for years in efforts to gain recognition and performances for women composers. She is the author of *Aaron Copland: His Work and Contribution to American Music* (New York, 1955) and editor of *Directory of American Women Composers* (1970).

Smith, Kate [Kathryn] **(Elizabeth)** (b. Greenville, Va., 1 May 1907; d. Raleigh, N.C., 17 June 1986). Popular singer. After appearing in musicals in New York, from 1931 she sang on radio, eventually becoming the most popular radio singer of the 1930s and 1940s. She also made many successful recordings, including "When the Moon Comes over the Mountain" (1931), "God Bless America" (1938), and "Don't Fence Me In" (1945).

Bibl.: Michael R. Pitts, *Kate Smith: A Bio-Bibliography* (New York, 1988).

Smith, Leland (Clayton) (b. Oakland, 6 Aug. 1925). Composer and teacher. He studied with Milhaud at Mills College (1941–43, 1946–47), then with Sessions at the Univ. of California (M.A., 1948), and in Paris with Messiaen (1948–49). He taught at the Univ. of Chicago (1952–58) and Stanford Univ. (beginning 1958). Many of Smith's compositions from the 1950s are based on serial techniques. As director of the computer music center at Stanford beginning in the late 1960s he was a leader in the field of computer music, developing software for both composing and printing music. He is the author of numerous articles on computer music. Compositions include 6 Bagatelles for piano (1965) and *Machines of Loving Grace,* narrator, bassoon and tape (1970).

Smith [née Robinson]**, Mamie** (b. Cincinnati, 26 May 1883; d. New York, ?30 Oct. 1946). Blues and vaudeville singer. Having begun as a dancer, she sang in New York theaters and clubs from 1913. Her recording "Crazy Blues" (1920) unexpectedly sold a million copies and thereby initiated the craze for female blues singers, though Smith herself was inclined toward a semioperatic delivery of vaudeville songs. She toured theaters with her Jazz Hounds, which early on included Bubber Miley, Coleman Hawkins, Joe Smith, and Sidney Bechet. Late in her career she sang in several films.

Smith, Pine Top [Clarence] (b. Troy, Ala., 11 June 1904; d. Chicago, 15 March 1929). Boogie-woogie pianist and singer. He toured as a pianist, singer, comedian, and tap dancer (1920–28) before settling in Chicago, where he recorded "Pine Top's Boogie Woogie"

(1928), a piano blues with Smith's spoken instructions to dancers. He was accidentally shot dead at a Masonic lodge where he was performing.

Smith, Russell (b. Tuscaloosa, Ala., 23 Apr. 1927). Composer. He began composing while still in high school. At Columbia Univ. he studied with Luening (B.S., 1951; M.A., 1953). He also worked with Copland at Tanglewood and with Varèse. In 1957 his comic opera *The Unicorn in the Garden,* based on the story by Thurber, was performed in Hartford, Conn. *Tetrameron* for orchestra and Piano Concerto no. 2 date from the same year. He was composer-in-residence with the Cleveland Orchestra (1966–67) and the New Orleans Philharmonic (1969–71). In 1975 he moved to Germany, where he continued to compose; works include Percussion Concerto (1979), Piano Sonata (1981), Symphony (1982).

Smith, Stuff [Hezekiah Leroy Gordon] (b. Portsmouth, Ohio, 14 Aug. 1909; d. Munich, 25 Sept. 1967). Jazz violinist and bandleader. He joined Alphonso Trent (1926–30), leaving briefly to join Jelly Roll Morton (1928). Thereafter he led small swing groups, including a sextet with Jonah Jones (1936–40), which recorded "I'se a Muggin'" and "After You've Gone" (both 1936) and played at the Onyx Club in New York. He recorded albums regularly from 1957, including *Violin Summit* with violinists Svend Asmussen, Stephane Grappelli, and Jean-Luc Ponty (1966), made in Europe, where he often toured in the 1960s.

Smith, William (Overton) (Bill) (b. Sacramento, 22 Sept. 1926; d. Havertown, Pa., 24 Mar. 1993). Composer and clarinetist. A jazz clarinetist since his teens, he studied at the Juilliard School of Music (1945–46), then with Milhaud at Mills College (1946–47) and with Sessions at the Univ. of California, Berkeley (M.A., 1952). During this period he performed with the Dave Brubeck Octet. He taught at the Univ. of Southern California (1958–60), and later at the Univ. of Washington (beginning 1966). Many of his compositions are for jazz groupings, for example, Concertino (trumpet and jazz ensemble, 1948), *Elegy for Eric* (1964), and *Quiet Please* (jazz orchestra, 1982). Others integrate jazz elements into traditional ensembles: Concerto for Jazz Soloist and Orchestra (clarinet and orchestra, 1962), *Theona* (jazz ensemble and orchestra, 1975). He also wrote numerous works for unaccompanied clarinet, among them *Five Pieces* (1959) and *Fancies* (1969), as well as *Musings* for 3 clarinets and 3 dancers (1983).

Smith, Willie [William McLeish] (b. Charleston, S.C., 25 Nov. 1910; d. Los Angeles, 7 Mar. 1967). Jazz alto saxophonist. He joined the swing big bands of Jimmie Lunceford (1929–42, including the recording "Uptown Blues," 1939), Harry James (1944–51, 1954–64), and Duke Ellington (1951–52), replacing Johnny Hodges, whose smooth ballad style was further refined by Smith. In 1953 he toured Europe with Jazz at the Philharmonic.

Smith, Willie "the Lion" [William Henry Joseph Bonaparte Bertholoff] (b. Goshen, N.Y., 24 Nov. 1897; d. New York, 18 Apr. 1973). Jazz pianist and composer. He spent most of his career as a solo pianist in New York, though he also recorded with traditional and swing groups (including sessions with Mamie Smith, 1920, and Sidney Bechet, 1941) and later toured Europe and performed at many jazz festivals. Although known as a stride pianist, he demonstrated a wider-ranging style in his finest compositions, recorded unaccompanied in 1939. Pieces such as "Echoes of Spring," "Fading Star," and "Rippling Waters" include stride playing, Alberti bass figurations, a lilting swing, and rhapsodic rubato passages.

Writings: with George Hoefer, *Music on My Mind: The Memoirs of an American Pianist* (Garden City, N.Y., 1964; R: New York, 1978).

Smith Brindle, Reginald (b. Bamber Bridge, 5 Jan. 1917). Composer. His early training was in architecture; after World War II he entered University College of North Wales in Bangor as a music student and went on to study composition with Pizzetti and Dallapiccola in Italy. In 1967 he joined the faculty at University College in Bangor and in 1970 became a professor at the Univ. of Surrey. His early compositions were in the serial style of Dallapiccola. Subsequently his works became more exploratory in terms of the creation of unique textures, especially through the use of electronic media and percussion instruments (on which he wrote the book *Contemporary Percussion,* London, 1970). He also wrote on contemporary music (*The New Music: The Avant-Garde since 1945,* London, 1975, 1987) and composition (*Musical Composition,* Oxford, 1986; *Serial Composition,* London, 1966). Works include *Antigone* (chamber opera, 1969); orchestral music (*Variations on a Theme of Dallapiccola,* 1955; *Cosmos,* 1959; *Homage to H. G. Wells,* 1960; *Interface,* 1972); chamber and vocal works, and works for solo guitar and guitar ensemble (*Poems of Garcia Lorca,* 1975; *Guitar Cosmos,* 1976).

Smyth, Ethel (Mary) (b. Marlebone, 22 Apr. 1858; d. Woking, 9 May 1944). Composer. In 1877 she entered the Leipzig Conservatory, studying with Reinecke and Jadassohn, and later with Heinrich von Herzogenberg; also met various luminaries, including Grieg, Joachim, Clara Schumann, and Brahms. She returned to England in 1888, where her Serenade for Orchestra and the overture *Antony and Cleopatra* were premiered in 1890; it was the performance of her Mass in D at the Albert Hall (1893) that first brought her acclaim, however.

She now turned to the theater. Her first opera, *Fantasio,* was premiered in Weimar in 1898; this was followed by *Der Wald* (Berlin, 1902), both written to her own German librettos; the latter was produced at Covent Garden in 1902 and by the Met the following year. Her greatest work, however, was *The Wreckers,* originally written to a French libretto as *Les nau-*

frageurs and premiered in Leipzig in 1906 as *Strandrecht.*

Smyth became identified with the cause of women's suffrage in England, for which she composed *March of the Women* (1911), the battle song of the Women's Social and Political Union; in her later years she wrote a number of autobiographical works that were quite popular. In 1922 she was made a Dame of the British Empire. Other theater works include *The Boatswain's Mate* (London, 1916), *Fête galante* (Birmingham, 1923), and *Entente cordiale* (Bristol, 1926).

Bibl.: Ethel Smyth, *Impressions That Remained* (New York, 1981).

Snow, Hank [Clarence Eugene] (b. Liverpool, Nova Scotia, 9 May 1914). Country singer, songwriter, and guitarist. He began singing on radio in Canada and gained a recording contract with R.C.A. in 1936; his early records were in the "blue yodeling" style of Jimmie Rodgers. He moved to the U.S. in 1944 and joined the Grand Ole Opry in 1950; many of his subsequent recordings became country standards, including "I'm Movin' On" (1950), "I Don't Hurt Anymore" (1954), and "I've Been Everywhere" (1962).

Sobolewski, (Johann Friedrich) Eduard [Edward] (b. Königsberg, 1 Oct. 1804; d. St. Louis, Mo., 17 May 1872). Violinist, composer, and conductor. Studied with Zelter in Berlin and with Weber in Dresden (1821–24). Appointed director of music at the Königsberg Theater in 1830. Founded and conducted Philharmonische Gesellschaft in 1838. Critic for *Ostpreussische Zeitung* and *Neue Zeitschrift für Musikwissenschaft.* Music director of theater in Bremen from 1854. Settled in Milwaukee in 1859. There he staged his first opera, *Mohega,* based on a tale of the American Indians (October 1859). Founder and conductor of Milwaukee Philharmonic Society Orchestra. Moved to St. Louis as conductor of Philharmonic Society, 1860–66. Professor of vocal music at Bonham's Female Seminary, 1869–72. Compositions are primarily for solo voice or chorus.

Söderman, Johan August (b. Stockholm, 17 July 1832; d. there, 10 Feb. 1876). Composer. Son of conductor and composer Johan Wilhelm Söderman (1808–58). Studied at the Stockholm Conservatory, 1847–50. Music director for the theater troupe of Stjernström, 1851–56. Moved to Leipzig in 1856 to study counterpoint with E. R. Richter; there he wrote a number of songs. Appointed chorusmaster and assistant conductor at the royal chapel, Stockholm, 1860. Compositions include operettas (*Urdur, eller Neckensdotter,* 1852); incidental music; Piano Quintet in E minor (1856); choral works; and Spiritual Songs, soprano, mixed chorus, and organ.

Söderström, Elisabeth (b. Stockholm, 7 May 1927). Soprano. Studied in her home city; made debut there in 1947, joining the Royal Opera in 1949; sang also at Salzburg (from 1955), Glyndebourne (from 1957), and the Metropolitan Opera (1959–63 and 1983–87). She sang in the premiere of Ligeti's *Le grand macabre* (Stockholm, 1978); other roles range from Nero in *L'incoronazione di Poppea* to the Marschallin in *Der Rosenkavalier* and Marie in *Wozzeck.* In 1990 she became artistic director of the Drottningholm Court Theater.

Sojo, Vincente Emilio (b. Guatire, Venezuela, 8 Dec. 1887; d. Caracas, 11 Aug. 1974). Composer. Student of Lugo in Guatire and Moschini at the Academy of Fine Arts, Caracas (from 1906). Taught at the academy from 1921 until 1936, when he became director of the Escuela superior de musica in Caracas; named composition professor there, 1937. In 1930 he helped found the Venezuela Symphony, leading it for over 20 years; also established the Lamas Singing Society and directed the Tribuna musical at Caracas Cathedral. Most of Venezuela's leading composers were among his pupils. The influence of Venezuelan traditional music is strong in Sojo's works; his output consists mainly of sacred vocal music, along with some organ and guitar pieces. In addition, he collected and arranged for chorus hundreds of folk songs.

Bibl.: Eduardo Lira Espejo, *Vicente Emilio Sojo* (Los Teques, 1987).

Sokoloff, Nikolai (b. near Kiev, 28 May 1886; d. La Jolla, Calif., 25 Sept. 1965). Conductor and violinist. Moved to the U.S. at age 12; studied at Yale before joining the Boston Symphony in 1903; after additional study in Europe, he became concertmaster of the Russian Symphony in New York. He directed the San Francisco Philharmonic (1914–18) and the Cleveland Orchestra (1918–33), and later led the Federal Music Project of the W.P.A. (1935–38) and the Seattle Symphony (1938–40) before moving to La Jolla in semiretirement.

Solage (fl. 1370–90). Composer. He wrote 10 chansons (7 ballades, 2 virelays, 1 rondeau) that are preserved in the Chantilly manuscript, Musée Condé 564. One ballade is dedicated to Jean, Duke of Berry, and 2 others refer to the marriage of Jean's son in 1386; Solage was perhaps active in the ducal court. His style in 4 voices resembles that of Machaut, but his 3-voice writing exhibits rhythmic and harmonic complexities of the *ars subtilior.*

Solares, Enrique (b. Guatemala City, 11 July 1910). Composer and pianist. Studied piano in his home city as well as in San Francisco, Prague, and Rome, also studying composition in the latter two places (under Krioka and Casella, respectively) as well as in Brussels with Joseph Jongen and Raymond Moulart. Taught piano in Guatemala from 1943 before becoming a diplomat, serving in Rome, Brussels, Madrid, and Paris. Much of his music uses Baroque and classical formal procedures, while later pieces show some ventures into serial composition. Works include orchestral works such as the *Divertimento* (1945), the *Fantasia sin-*

fonica (1947), and 2 partitas (1947, 1949–59); the *Capricho* for piano and orchestra (1951); chamber music including suites and a *Cuarteto breve* for strings; ricercares (including 1 on B-A-C-H), toccatas, preludes, and other piano works (*7 Traversuras,* 1969; *12 Microtransparenias,* 1970) and songs.

Bibl.: *Composers of the Americas* 4 (Washington, D.C., 1958), pp. 155–64 [includes works list].

Soler (Ramos), Antonio (Francisco Javier José) (bapt. Olot Gerona, 3 Dec. 1729; d. El Escorial, 20 Dec. 1783). Composer. He received early instruction in organ and composition while a student at the choir school of the Monserrat monastery. He became *maestro di capilla* at Lérida around 1750, and at El Escorial in 1757. He took holy orders at El Escorial in 1752 and then joined the Jieronymite monks. Between 1752 and 1757 he was able to study in Madrid with Domenico Scarlatti, who was part of the court entourage there. Later Soler taught keyboard to the Prince Gabriel, for whom he wrote several of his compositions. He is remembered mainly for his keyboard works: these include 120 sonatas; 6 double organ concertos; 6 quintets for organ, 2 violins, viola, and cello; and various liturgical organ works. His other compositions include: 9 Masses, 5 Requiems, 136 *villancicos,* numerous other sacred vocal works (Psalms, hymns, responsaries). Soler also wrote a theoretical treatise, *Llave de la modulación (1762),* which created some controversy. He wrote formal rebuttals to some of the critical reviews in *Satisfacción a los reparos precisos* (1765) and *Carta escrita a un amigo. . .* (1766).

Bibl.: Frank Carroll, "An Introduction to Antonio Soler" (diss., Univ. of Rochester, 1960). Samuel Rubio, *Antonio Soler, Catalogo Critico* (Cuenca, Spain, 1980). Alicia Muniz Hernández, *El teatro lírico del P. Antonio Soler* (Madrid, 1981). Paulino Capdepón Verdú, *Die Villancicos des Padre Antonio Soler (1729–1783)* (Frankfurt am Main, 1994).

Sollberger, Harvey (b. Cedar Rapids, Iowa, 11 May 1938). Flutist, composer, conductor. After receiving a B.A. at the Univ. of Iowa, he studied flute in New York with Samuel Baron and Betty Mather. At Columbia Univ. he studied composition with Jack Beeson and Otto Luening (M.A., 1964). In 1962, with Charles Wuorinen, he founded the Group for Contemporary Music, which he conducted and in which he played flute. He also taught at Columbia (1965–83) and at the Manhattan School of Music (1972–83). He was a pioneer in the development of "extended" techniques for the flute, and many of his own compositions feature these techniques, for example, *Divertimento* (flute, cello, piano, 1970), *Angel and Stone* (flute, piano, 1981), and the series *Riding the Wind I-IV* (1973–74) for flute and various instruments. In 1983 he moved to Indiana Univ. to teach composition. Other works include *Persian Golf* (string orchestra, 1987); *Quodlibetudes* (flute, 1988).

Solomon [Cutner, Solomon] (b. London, 9 Aug. 1902; d. there, 2 Feb. 1988). Pianist. Pupil of Mathilde Verne, herself a student of Clara Schumann; made his debut at age 8. After study in Paris and a time away from the piano, he resurfaced in 1923, continuing his concert career until a 1956 stroke forced him into retirement. He established a reputation as a fine player who disdained flamboyant mannerisms.

Solomon, Izler (b. St. Paul, Minn., 11 Jan. 1910; d. Fort Wayne, Ind., 6 Dec. 1987). Conductor and violinist. Made concert debut as violinist in 1925, and as conductor in 1931; later directed the Michigan W.P.A. music program (to 1936), the Illinois Symphony (1936–41), and the Columbus Philharmonic (1941–49). He led the Indianapolis Symphony (1956–76), and directed at the Aspen Festival (1956–61). An advocate of contemporary music; his programs included music by Sessions, Cowell, Harris, Schuman, and many others.

Solti, Georg (b. Budapest, 21 Oct. 1912). Conductor. Made his debut at the piano at age 12; attended the Liszt Academy, Budapest, a pupil of Bartók and Dohnyáni in piano and Kodály in composition; graduated 1930. He served as coach and accompanist for the Budapest State Opera, then as Toscanini's assistant during the 1936 and 1937 Salzburg festivals; his conducting debut took place at Budapest in 1938. He was in Switzerland when World War II broke out; unable to secure a work permit as a conductor, he turned back to the piano, winning the 1942 Geneva International Competition. In 1944 he conducted Swiss Radio Orchestra concerts at Ansermet's request; invited to Munich by the U.S. Army occupation authorities, he led a production of *Fidelio* and was appointed music director at the Bavarian State Opera, moving to Frankfurt as music director in 1952. In 1961 he took over at Covent Garden, continuing as music director until 1971; he eventually took British citizenship, and was knighted in 1972. He served as music director of the Chicago Symphony from 1969 to 1991, also holding similar posts with L'Orchestre de Paris (1972–75) and the London Philharmonic (1979–83); in 1992 he became artistic director of the Salzburg Music Festival. His recordings are extensive, including the first complete *Ring* cycle (Covent Garden, 1966) and much of the standard orchestral and operatic repertoire.

Bibl.: Paul Robinson, *Solti* (Toronto, 1979).

Somers, Harry (Stewart) (b. Toronto, 11 Sept. 1925). Composer. He began learning piano in 1939, studying with Reginald Godden (1942–43) and Weldon Kilburn (1945–48); studied composition with John Weinzweig in Toronto (1941–49). Many of his works from the 1940s are for piano, and in the late 1940s he gave several recitals featuring his works and those of other Canadian composers. In 1948, however, he gave up performing on the piano in order to devote himself to composition. *North Country* (1948) for string orchestra, String Quartet no. 2 (1950), and Symphony no. 1 (1951) were early fruits of this decision, followed by

Passacaglia and Fugue (orchestra, 1954), and *Five Songs for Dark Voice* (alto and chamber orchestra, 1956). During the 1950s he began to work with serial techniques, sometimes mixing them with tonal passages, as in the ballet *The Fisherman and His Soul* (1956), occasionally using an exclusively twelve-tone idiom, as in *12 x 12: Fugues for Piano* (1951). In the opera *Louis Riel* (Toronto, 1967) he mixes serial techniques not only with tonal writing but with folk song–derived melodies and electronic music. During the late 1960s Somers turned his attention increasingly to the possibilities of the voice, using novel vocal techniques in *Voiceplay* (1971) for a solo singer-actor. In *Kyrie* (soloists, choir, chamber ensemble, 1972) he explores the phonetic possibilities of a traditional text. Other works include the opera *Mario and the Magician* (1992) after Thomas Mann's story.

Bibl.: Brian Cherney, *Harry Somers* (Toronto, 1975).

Somervell, Arthur (b. Windermere, 5 June 1863; d. London, 2 May 1937). Composer. In 1883 he took a degree in classics at King's College in Cambridge. He went on to study music at the Royal College of Music with Stanford and, after two years at the Hochschule für Musik in Berlin, with Parry. He became a lecturer at the Royal College of Music in 1894, and an inspector of music for the Board of Education 1901–28; in 1929 he was knighted. His music is predominantly vocal, including a substantial output of song cycles and choral works in the style of the German romantic composers. He published in the field of music education. His works include the song cycles *Maud* (1898), *The Shropshire Lad* (1904), and *A Broken Arc* (1923); vocal works (Passion of Christ, 1913) and orchestral music (*Symphonic Variations 'Normandy'*, 1912).

Somis, Giovanni Battista (b. Turin, 25 Dec. 1686; d. there, 14 Aug. 1763). Composer and violinist. He was taught the violin by his father, and became a violinist in the Turin ducal orchestra by 1699. He studied with Corelli in Rome (1703–6) and may have received instruction from Vivaldi in Venice. In 1707 he rejoined the Turin chapel as solo violinist and leader, remaining there for the rest of his life. In 1733 he made successful appearances as soloist at the Concert spirituel in Paris. Somis had a considerable influence on contemporary violin playing; his pupils included Leclair, Guillemain, Guignon, and Pugnani. He is reputed to have composed over 150 concertos and 75 violin sonatas; only the sonatas were published in his time, and most of his music has not survived.

Sommer, Vladimír (b. Dolní Jiřetín, near Most, 28 Feb. 1921). Composer. From 1942 to 1946 he studied composition with Janeček at the Prague Conservatory of Music and from 1946 to 1950 with Bořkovec at the Prague Academy of Music. Just after the war he worked with choral groups and gave instrumental instruction. He subsequently worked for Radio Prague and for the Czech Composers' Union. From 1960 he served on the music faculty of Prague Univ. His vocal music, a significant part of his output, reflects his socialistic concerns and includes popular and workers' songs. His instrumental music, influenced by Prokofiev, is broadly tonal, though it frequently uses dramatic chromaticism. Works include the orchestral music *Antigone* (prelude, 1956–57) and Violin Concerto (1977).

Sondheim, Stephen (Joshua) (b. New York City, 22 Mar. 1930). Popular composer and lyricist. He studied music at Williams College and with Milton Babbitt, and wrote songs and lyrics under the direction of Oscar Hammerstein II. He rose to prominence with his lyrics for Leonard Bernstein's *West Side Story* (1957) and Jule Styne's *Gypsy* (1959), and wrote his first score for *A Funny Thing Happened on the Way to the Forum* (1962). In the 1970s he collaborated with director Hal Prince on a series of works which experimented with various parameters of the Broadway musical: *Company* (1970) is plotless; *Pacific Overtures* (1976) incorporates Japanese Kabuki drama; *Sweeney Todd* (1979) is scored for nearly its entire length. They also produced *A Little Night Music* (1972, including "Send in the Clowns"). His *Sunday in the Park with George* (1984, with James Lapine) won a Pulitzer Prize for drama; other works include *Into the Woods* (1987), *Assassins* (1990), and *Passion* (1994, with James Lapine). During his long career in the theater Sondheim has been the recipient of numerous Tony Awards.

Bibl.: Craig Zadan, *Sondheim and Co.* (New York, 1986). Stephen Banfield, *Sondheim's Broadway Musicals* (Ann Arbor, 1993).

Sonneck, Oscar George Theodore (b. Lafayette [now Jersey City], N.J., 6 Oct. 1873; d. New York, 30 Oct. 1928). Musicologist. He was raised in Germany and attended Heidelberg and Munich universities. He studied music privately and wrote orchestral, chamber, and piano pieces, and songs; also published 2 books of German poetry. Returning to the U.S. in 1899, he did extensive research in American musical life before 1800. In 1902 he became the first head of the Library of Congress Music Division; he built the collection into one of the world's finest, especially in the field of opera. From 1915 he was founding editor of G. Schirmer's *Musical Quarterly;* he was a director of Schirmer from 1917 and vice president from 1921. In his honor the Sonneck Society was founded in 1975 for research in American music.

Bibl.: H. Wiley Hitchcock, *After 100 (!) Years: The Editorial Side of Sonneck* (Washington, D.C., 1974) [includes complete bibliography of his works]. Oscar Sonneck, *Oscar Sonneck and American Music* (Urbana, Ill., 1983).

Sonnleithner, Joseph (b. Vienna, 3 Mar. 1766; d. there, 25 Dec. 1835). Librettist and archivist. He was taught by his father, Christoph, a composer. From 1794 to 1796 he was the editor of the *Wiener Theater-Almanach* and from 1804 to 1814 was secretary to the court theaters. He gave his instrument collection as well as his books and musical archives to the Gesellschaft der Musikfreunde, of which he was a founder, in 1812. He wrote opera librettos and adapted others, including *Fidelio* for Beethoven. His nephew **Leopold** (b. Vienna, 15 Nov. 1797; d. there, 4 Mar. 1873) helped Schubert, a friend, to publish his first song, "Erlkönig." Leopold was a member of the Gesellschaft der Musikfreunde, to which he gave his musical papers. Several of Schubert's works were performed in musical evenings at his house, including "Prometheus" and "Gesang der Geister über den Wassern."

Sontag [Sonntag]**, Henriette (Gertrud Walpurgis)** (b. Koblenz, 3 Jan. 1806; d. Mexico City, 17 June 1854). Soprano. Daughter of Franziska Sonntag [née Martloff] (1798–1865). Entered Prague Conservatory, 1815; teachers included Anna Czegka (voice), Josef Triebensee (theory), and Pixis (piano). Sang in Vienna (1822); sang in premiere of *Euryanthe* (1823), Beethoven's *Missa solemnis* and Ninth Symphony (both May 1824). Paris debut, 1826; London, 1828. Goethe wrote *Neue Siren* after hearing her sing in Weimar. Secretly married Count Carlo Rossi, 1828. She left the stage in 1830, gave some concerts; returned to the stage in 1849. Toured Mexico, 1854.

Bibl.: Frank Russell, *Queen of Song: The life of Henriette Sontag, Countess de Rossi* (New York, 1964).

Sor [Sors]**, (Joseph) Fernando (Macari)** (bapt. Barcelona, 14 Feb. 1778; d. Paris, 10 July 1839). Composer and guitarist. He received musical instruction at the monastery in Montserrat, 1790–95, then went to military academy in Barcelona, where his opera *Telemaco nell 'isola de Calipso* (1797) was performed. He relocated to Paris in 1813, London in 1815, and was in Moscow during 1823–26, after which he returned to Paris. He composed extensively for the guitar, including many solo pieces (sonatas, divertimentos, variations, waltzes, fantasias, studies) and many *seguidillas* and boleros for (1–3 voices with guitar or piano accompaniment. He also wrote ballets, ariettas for voice and piano, songs, duets, other vocal and some instrumental works. Published a guitar method in 1830.

Bibl.: Brian Jeffery, *Fernando Sor: Composer and Guitarist* (London, 1977). Id., ed., *Complete Works for Guitar: Fernando Sor* (New York, 1977). William G. Sasser, "The Guitar Works of Fernando Sor" (diss., Univ. of North Carolina, 1960). Bernard Piris, *Fernando Sor: Une guitare à l'orée du Romantisme* (Paris, 1989).

Sorabji, Kaikhosru Shapurji [Leon Dudley] (b. Chingford, 14 Aug. 1892; d. Dorchester, England, 15 Oct. 1988). Composer and performer. He grew up in England and, with the exception of some early harmonic studies, was self-taught as a musician. He toured in the early 1920s as a pianist and worked as a music critic, writing often controversial pieces about composers who, at the time, saw little popularity. His own compositions are in an eclectic and highly individual style. In 1940 he issued a ban on the performance or publication of his music; some early works had already been published, though, and were furtively performed. During the 1960s he recorded some of his own performances of his works and by the mid-1970s allowed performances by the pianists Michael Habermann and Yonty Solomon. Most of his music still remains in manuscript form. He composed works for orchestra (Piano Concerto no. 1, 1917, rev. 1918; Piano Concerto no. 2, 1920; *Symphonic Variations,* piano, orchestra, 1951–55; *Opus Clavisymphonicum,* piano, orchestra, 1957–59; *Opusculum Claviorchestrale,* piano, orchestra, 1973–75) and for piano (100 *Transcendental Studies,* 1940–44; 7 piano symphonies), as well as songs.

Bibl.: Kaikhosru Shapurji Sorabji, *Around Music* (Westport, Conn., 1979). Kaikhosru Shapurji Sorabji, *Mi contra fa: The Immoralisings of a Machiavellian Musician* (New York, 1986). Paul Rapoport, ed., *Sorabji: A Critical Celebration* (Aldershot, 1992).

Sorge, Georg Andreas (b. Mellenbach, Schwarzburg, Thuringia, 21 Mar. 1703; d. Lobenstein, Thuringia, 4 Apr. 1778). Composer and theorist. He studied with Caspar Tischer, court organist at Schney (Franconia), and from 1716 with Pastor Johann Wintzern. In 1722 he became court and civic organist at Lobenstein, where he also taught in the local school; he remained there for the rest of his life. In 1747 he was elected into Mizler's Societät der Musikalischen Wissenschaften. His theoretical writings include the *Vorgemach der musicalischen Composition* (1745–47), which applies the principles of harmony to composition, and the *Anleitung zur Fantasie* (1767), a guide to keyboard improvisation. His keyboard music includes sonatas, preludes, toccatas, and fugues.

Soriano [Suriano, Suriani, Surianus]**, Francesco** (b. Soriano, nr. Viterbo, Italy, 1548 or 1549; d. Rome, 1621). Composer. He was a choirboy at St. John Lateran, Rome; his teachers included Annibale Zoilo, Bartolomeo Roy, G. B. Montanari, and Palestrina. In 1580 he became *maestro di cappella* of S. Luigi dei Francesi, Rome, and was subsequently appointed director of music at the Gonzaga court in Mantua (1581–86). He returned to Rome and remained there for the rest of his life, serving as *maestro di cappella* at S. Maria Maggiore (1587–99 and 1601–3), St. John Lateran (1599–1601), and the Cappella Giulia, St. Peter's (1603–20). In 1611 he and Felice Anerio were appointed by papal commission to complete the revision of chant books begun in 1577 by Palestrina and Zoilo; the *Editio medicaea* was completed the following year but published only in 1614. Soriano is considered one of Palestrina's most distinguished successors, a master of contrapuntal writing and of the Roman polychoral style; his secular music includes several books of madrigals.

Soro, Enrique (b. Concepción, Chile, 15 July 1884; d. Santiago, 2 Dec. 1954). Composer. Studied with his father, José Soro Sforza, then from 1898 to 1904 at

John Philip Sousa and his band. Detail of souvenir picture, 1924.

Milan, receiving the composition award upon graduation. After a major concert tour through Italy and France, he came back to Chile in 1905, joining the piano and composition faculty at the National Conservatory in 1906; he later served there as assistant director (1907–19) and director (1919–28). He toured throughout the Americas, and from 1942 until his death he worked as a director of the Instituto de Extensión musical. His *Sinfonia romántica* of 1920 was the first full-scale symphonic work composed in Chile; other works include the *Suites sinfónicas* nos. 1 and 2 (1918, 1919); 3 *Preludes sinfónicas* (1936), and the *Suite en estilo antiguo* (1943), all for orchestra; *Impresiones líricas* and a Gran concerto, piano and orchestra (1919); chamber music, including 2 violin sonatas, 2 cello sonatas, a string quartet, and a piano trio and quintet; much piano music, including 3 sonatas (1920, 1923, 1942); and songs.

Bibl.: *Composers of the Americas* 1 (Washington, D.C., 1955), pp. 97–103 [includes works list].

Soto de Langa, Francisco (b. Langa, Soria, Spain, 1534; d. Rome, 25 Sept. 1619). Singer, editor, and composer. He was a member of the Papal Choir in Rome (1562–1611) and of the oratory of St. Filippo Neri (1566–75); became a priest in 1575 and went to S. Maria in Vallicella. In 1590 he served as interim *maestro di cappella* of the papal choir, and in 1611 became patron to S. Giacomo degli Spagnoli. Five important anthologies of *laude spirituali* (1583–98) may have been edited by him.

Souris, André (b. Marchienne-au-Pont, Belgium, 10 July 1899; d. Paris, 12 Feb. 1970). Composer, conductor, teacher, musicologist. He studied violin, harmony, counterpoint, and music history at the Brussels Conservatory (1911–18); later studied composition with Paul Gilson and conducting with Hermann Scherchen. His early works were much influenced by Debussy, but around 1923 he became involved with the group of surrealist writers and artists led by Paul Nougé in Brussels. His work of this period is often deliberately banal, as in *Musique* (1925), a collage for orchestra, or parodistic, as in *Les dessous des cartes* (1926). From the late 1920s through the 1930s many of his works had political themes (*Homage à Babeuf,* woodwinds, 1934; *Hourra l'Oural,* incidental music to a play by Aragon, 1934). He also wrote scores for many movies. Taught harmony at the Charleroi Conservatory (1925–37), later at the Brussels Conservatory (1948–64). From 1937 to 1946 he conducted the orchestra of Radio Belgium. At the same time he pursued musicological research, particularly into the lute repertory of the Renaissance, editing several collections and writing on source problems and the realization of tablature.

Bibl.: Jean-Pierre Muller, *André Souris, essai biographique* (Brussels, 1982).

Sousa, John Philip (b. Washington, D.C., 6 Nov. 1854; d. Reading, Pa., 6 Mar. 1932). Composer, conductor. His father played in the Marine Band; 1864–67, studied the violin and other instruments at John Esputa's music school in Washington; 1867–74, an apprentice member of the Marine Band, also studying theory and composition with a local orchestra leader and playing, mostly as violinist, in local theater orchestras and other ensembles. Played in or conducted theater orchestras, 1874–76, including two touring companies; in 1876 played under Offenbach in the American Centenary celebration in Philadelphia, composing the *International Congress Fantasy* for the July 4 performance. Remained in Philadelphia, 1876–80, playing in theater orchestras, also composing and teaching; 1879–80, conducted operetta companies, also composing his first operettas. He was conductor of the Marine Band, 1880–92, making it and himself renowned. The sobriquet "The March King" dates from this period, during which he composed some of the best known of his 136 marches *(Semper Fidelis, The Washington Post).* He then formed Sousa's Band (1892), which became a leading American institution, touring the U.S. and Canada yearly; also very popular in Europe, touring there in 1900, 1901, 1903, 1905; world tour, 1910–11; made many recordings. Also composed operettas, especially *El capitan* (1896); many songs in various genres; band fantasias and suites; dance music; many band arrangements.

Bibl.: J. R. Smart, *The Sousa Band: A Discography* (Washington, D.C., 1970). Paul E. Bierley, *John Philip Sousa: American Phenomenon* (New York, 1973). Paul E. Bierley, *John Philip Sousa: A Descriptive Catalogue of His Works* (Urbana, Ill., 1973). John Newsom, ed., *Perspectives on John Philip Sousa* (Washington, D.C., 1983).

Souster, Tim(othy Andrew James) (b. Bletchley, Buckinghamshire, 29 Jan. 1943; d. 12 Mar. 1994). Composer. He studied music theory at Oxford through 1965, working with Rose, Lumsden, Wellesz, and Bennett. He was also influenced by Berio and Stockhausen at Darmstadt during the summer of 1964. He continued to work with representatives of the avant-garde while associated with the BBC from 1965 to 1967, and in 1971 he became Stockhausen's assistant in Cologne. He also worked in Berlin and Keele, and helped Smalley to found the electronic new-music group Intermodulation in 1969. When it disbanded in 1976, he assembled the group OdB. His own music employs avant-garde techniques such as electronics, serialism, and aleatory. Works include *Tsuwanonodomo,* soprano, 3 choirs, 3 orchestras, piano, prepared piano, harp (1968); *Pelvic Loops,* tape (1969); *Spectral,* viola, tape delay system, 3 synthesizers (1971–74); *Song of an Average City,* small orchestra, tape (1974); *Surfit,* tape, electric organs, percussion, electronics (1976); *Hambledon Hill,* amplified string quartet (1985); concerto for trumpet, live electronics, orchestra (1988).

Souzay [Tisserand], **Gérard (Marcel)** (b. Angers, 8 Dec. 1920). Baritone. A pupil of Bernac, and also of Croiza, Marcoux, and Lotte Lehmann; beginning in 1940 attended the Paris Conservatory, making his recital debut in 1945; toured widely in the postwar years, singing in the 1956 Venice premiere of Stravinsky's *Canticum sacrum.* His operatic debut was as Monteverdi's *Orfeo* in 1960; in 1965 sang Count Almaviva in *Nozze di Figaro* at the Metropolitan Opera. He was artist-in-residence at the Univ. of California, Davis, in 1984; taught at Indiana University and at the Univ. of Texas, Austin (from 1986).

Sowerby, Leo (b. Grand Rapids, 1 May 1895; d. Port Clinton, Ohio, 7 July 1968). Composer and organist. As a teenager in Chicago he studied piano with Calvin Lampert and Percy Grainger, theory with Arthur Olaf Andersen. His First Violin Concerto (1913; rev. 1925) was performed by the Chicago Symphony when he was 18 years old. A Piano Concerto (1916; rev. 1919) and a Cello Concerto (1916) were also premiered by the Chicago Symphony, as well as the orchestral scherzo *Comes Autumn Time* (1916; rev. 1920). In 1920 he won the newly established American Prix de Rome, and the years 1921–1924 were spent at the American Academy in Rome. Several of his compositions from the 1920s are based on traditional American tunes; others have a jazz flavor, such as *Syncopata* (1924) and *Monotony* (1925), both of which were written for Paul Whiteman and his orchestra; still others (Symphony no. 2, 1927) are in a lyrical Romantic idiom. From 1927 until 1962 Sowerby was organist and choirmaster at St. James Episcopal Cathedral in Chicago, a position for which he wrote a considerable amount of ecclesiastical music, notably the cantata *The Canticle of the Sun* (1944), which won a Pulitzer Prize. In 1932 Sowerby joined the faculty of the American Conservatory in Chicago, where he taught until 1962. A flexible composer and in many respects a traditionalist, he produced many works on commission during the 1940s and 1950s: Symphony no. 3 (1940) for the Chicago Symphony, *Fantasy Portraits* (orchestra, 1953) for the Indianapolis Symphony, and *The Throne of God* (chorus and orchestra, 1957) for the National Cathedral. Many of his works are for organ, including Symphony in G major (1930), Toccata (1941), Ballade (English horn and organ, 1949), and preludes on various hymn tunes. In 1962 Sowerby moved to Washington, D.C., where he was a dean at the National Cathedral and a founding director of the College of Church Musicians (1962–68).

Spalding, Albert (b. Chicago, 15 Aug. 1888; d. New York, 26 May 1953). Violinist. Admitted to the Bologna Conservatory at age 14; made debut at Paris in 1905, later touring the French provinces, London, and Vienna. His U.S. debut came at Carnegie Hall in 1908, after which he toured Europe. He served in the army during World War I, after which he resumed a heavy concert schedule, also giving master classes at the Juilliard School and performing on radio; in World War II he directed Radio Rome. He was one of the first Americans to build an international reputation; his playing was praised by Saint-Saëns, Ysaÿe, and Joachim. He composed 2 concertos and much other music for the violin, as well as works for orchestra, string quartet, piano, and voice; in addition, he wrote a 1943 autobiography and a 1953 novel about the composer Tartini.

Spanier, Muggsy [Francis Joseph] (b. Chicago, 9 Nov. 1906; d. Sausalito, Calif., 12 Feb. 1967). Jazz cornetist and bandleader. While working in Chicago he recorded with his Bucktown Five (1924) and the Chicago Rhythm Kings (1928). He joined the big bands of vaudeville clarinetist Ted Lewis (1929–36) and Ben Pollack (1936–38). His Ragtime Band (1939) made Dixieland revivalist recordings, including "At the Jazz Band Ball" and his composition "Relaxin' at the Touro"; these display his powerful plunger-muted style, closely modeled on that of King Oliver. He briefly rejoined Lewis twice (1939–40, 1944), joined Bob Crosby (1940), and formed his own big band (1941–43). Thereafter he led small Dixieland groups, also working with Earl Hines during the 1950s.

Spataro, Giovanni (b. Bologna, late 1548?; d. Bologna, 17 Jan. 1541). Theorist and composer. He studied in 1482 with Ramos de Pareja, who published his *Musica practica* in Bologna that year. When Niccolo Burzio attacked Ramos's forward-looking theories, Spataro responded with *Honesta defensio* (1491). From 1505 he functioned as *maestro di canto* at San Petronio Cathedral in Bologna, being formally installed as such in 1512. He copied choirbooks containing extensive repertory of the era from Dufay to Willaert. Again he defended Ramos against Gaffurius's *Apologia* (1520) in 2 publications of 1521; he published a *Tractato di musica* in 1531. Many of his compositions are lost; 6 motets and a *laude* are extant.

Bibl.: F. Tirro, "La stesura del testo nei manoscritti di Giovanni Spataro," *RIM* 15 (1980): 31–70.

Speaks, Oley (b. Canal Winchester, Ohio, 28 June 1874; d. New York, 27 Aug. 1948). Composer and singer. As a young man in Columbus he studied the piano, sang in local churches, and began to write and publish songs. He moved to New York in 1898, where he was baritone soloist at various churches. He also studied voice with Emma Thursby and composition with Will C. MacFarlane and Max Spicker. He wrote well over 100 songs, of which many became widely popular. These include "On the Road to Mandalay" (1907), "Morning" (1910), "Sylvia" (1914), and "The Lord Is My Light" (1914).

Spector, Phil (b. New York, 25 Dec. 1940). Popular songwriter and record producer. His recording with the Teddy Bears of "To Know Him Is To Love Him" (1958) was very popular, though in the 1960s he worked principally as a producer for his label Philles. He established the dominant artistic position of the producer on popular recordings and developed a heavily orchestrated "wall of sound" which influenced many rock recordings of the 1970s: it is typified on songs such as the Crystals' "Da doo ron ron" (1963) and Ike and Tina Turner's "River Deep, Mountain High" (1966).

Speer, Daniel (b. Breslau, 2 July 1636; d. Göppingen, 5 Oct. 1707). Composer and theorist. He entered the Maria-Magdalenen-Gymnasium, Breslau, in 1644. Following a period of travel across southeast Europe, during which he gained musical experience, Speer became a town and church musician in Stuttgart (1664–66). After a short time as a schoolteacher and church musician at Göppingen (1667–68), he moved first to Gross Bottwar, where he married in 1669, and then to Leonberg. His first publication, *Musicalisches ABC,* appeared in 1671. In 1673 he resumed his duties at the Lateinschule in Göppingen. During the 1680s he published 14 works, including church music, quodlibets, novels, and political writings. His most significant work is the *Grund-richtiger . . . Unterricht der musicalischen Kunst, oder Vierfaches musicalisches Kleeblatt* (Ulm, 1687; rev. and enlarged in 1697). A treatise on practical music making, it includes numerous pieces of instrumental music designed as exercises and examples.

Spelman, Timothy (Mather) (b. Brooklyn, 21 Jan. 1891; d. Florence, Italy, 21 Aug. 1970). Composer. Attended Harvard Univ. (B.A., 1913), where he studied with Albert Spalding and Edward Hill. From 1913 to 1915 he studied in Germany with Walter Courvoisier at the Munich Conservatory. After the end of World War I he settled in Florence, where, except for the period 1935–47, he spent the rest of his life. Works include *La magnifica* (music drama, 1920); *The Sunken City* (opera, 1930); *The Courtship of Miles Standish* (opera, 1943); *Pervigilium veneris* (soprano, baritone, chorus, orchestra, 1929); *Saints' Days* (orchestral suite, 1925); *Jamboree* (pocket ballet, 1945); *Barbaresques* (piano, 1922).

Spendiaryan, Alexander Afanasii [Spendiarov, Alexandr Afanasevich] (b. Kokhovka, Crimea, 1 Nov. 1871; d. Yerevan, 7 May 1928). Composer and conductor. Born of a cultured Armenian family, he took a law degree at the Univ. of Moscow, 1895; he then studied composition privately with Rimsky-Korsakov (1896–1900). From 1900 he served as a conductor and musical educator in the Crimea; he conducted widely within the USSR and abroad. From 1924 he taught at Yerevan Conservatory. His music weds the Russian nationalistic style with Crimean and Armenian folk elements. His works include the opera *Almast* (1916–28); several descriptive orchestral pieces (*Krïmskiye eskizï I, II* [Crimean Sketches], 1903, 1912; *Tri pal'mï* [3 Palm Trees], 1905); choral works and songs with orchestra; chamber and piano music.

Sperger, Johannes (b. Feldsburg, 23 Mar. 1750; d. Ludwigslust, 13 May 1812). Composer and double bass player. Thought to have studied with Albrechtsberger in Vienna. In 1778 he premiered one of his symphonies and a double bass concerto at the Tonkünstler Sozietät. As a renowned double bass player he received appointments in various courts, including those of Pressburg (1777–83) and Fidisch Burgenland (1783–86), and in 1789 accepted a position with the Duke of Mecklenburg at Ludwigslust. His works include 45 symphonies, 18 double bass concertos, other solo concertos, chamber music.

Bibl.: Adolf Meier, *Thematisches Werkverzeichnis der Kompositionen von Johannes Sperger* (Michaelstein, 1990).

Sperontes [Scholze, Johann Sigismund] (b. Lobendau bei Liegnitz, Silesia, 20 Mar. 1705; d. Leipzig, 27 Sept. 1750). Poet. He was educated in Liegnitz and went to Leipzig in the 1720s to study law. In 1749 he wrote a singspiel, *Der Frühling,* with music by J. G. A. Fritzsch. His most important work is the *Singende Muse an der Pleisse* (1736–45), a collection of strophic songs. The work eventually included 250 poems with 248 musical settings; Sperontes added his verse, aimed at the German middle classes, to popular instrumental and vocal compositions. The lieder are in the *galant* style by virtue of Sperontes's preference for the latest dance forms. The *Singende Muse* inspired both a revival of the song in Germany and theoretical discussions of the genre.

Speyer [Speier], **Wilhelm** (b. Offenbach, 21 June 1790; d. there, 5 Apr. 1878). Violinist and composer. Studied law at Heidelberg. From 1811 to 1813, studied violin in Paris with Baillot. In 1818 he took over his father's banking business in Frankfurt, where he became friendly with Liszt, Mendelssohn, Spohr, Weber, Hauptmann, Meyerbeer, Pixis, and Mayr. Wrote articles for *Allgemeine musikalische Zeitung.* He was a prolific composer. Many of his compositions are for violin; other works include chamber music and choral pieces. He was known during his day primarily as a composer of songs. His son Eduard (1839–1934) was a businessman in England and an organizer of many concerts there.

Spialek, Hans (b. Vienna, 17 Apr. 1894; d. New York, 20 Nov. 1983). Arranger. He studied at the Vienna Conservatory. During World War I he was taken prisoner on the eastern front. In Russia he organized an orchestra that played for the troops; after the Revolution he worked at the Bolshoi Theater (1918–20), then as a conductor in Nizhny Novgorod (1920–22). In 1924 he emigrated to the U.S., where he settled in New York and found work as an arranger for Chappell, the music publishing firm. He orchestrated many Broadway shows, including George Gershwin's *Strike Up the Band* (1930), Cole Porter's *DuBarry Was a Lady* (1939), and several Rodgers and Hart shows, among them *On Your Toes* (1936), *The Boys from Syracuse* (1938), and *Pal Joey* (1940). He also did arrangements for film scores and radio shows.

Spiegel, Laurie (b. Chicago, 20 Sept. 1945). Composer. After receiving a B.A. at Shimer College in Mt. Carroll, Ill., she studied at Juilliard (1969–72) and with Jacob Druckman at Brooklyn College (M.A., 1975). Her early compositions were for guitar, her own instrument, but from about 1970 on she became increasingly involved with electronic and computer music. Working with microcomputers and synthesizers, she created pieces such as *The Orient Express* (1974), *The Expanding Universe* (1975), and *Voices Within* (1979). Also composed works using videotape, both in conjunction with music, as in *Voyages* (1978), and without music, as in *A Living Painting* (1979). Other works include *Passage* (electronics, 1987); *3 Movements for Harpsichord, Returning East, After the Mountains* (all 1990).

Bibl.: Laurie Spiegel, "Macromusic from Micros." *Creative Computing* 7 (May 1981): 68–74; "Sonic Set Theory: A Tonal Music Theory for Computers," in *Proceedings, 2nd Symposium on Small Computers in the Arts* (Los Angeles, 1982).

Spiegelman, Joel (Warren) (b. Buffalo, 23 Jan. 1933). Composer, pianist, harpsichordist. A piano prodigy, he played with the Buffalo Philharmonic at the age of 11. He received a B.A. from the Univ. of Buffalo (1953) and an M.A. from Brandeis Univ. (1956), where he studied with Arthur Berger, Harold Shapero, and Irving Fine. He then studied at the Paris Conservatory with Nadia Boulanger (1956–60). From 1961 to 1966 he taught at Brandeis and at other schools in the Boston area, and played harpsichord in several ensembles. His compositions from this period have been characterized as neoclassical. In 1965 he visited the Soviet Union to study and perform. Returning to the U.S., he played concerts of 18th-century Russian harpsichord music and avant-garde Russian piano music. *Kousochki* [Morsels] (1966) for piano 4-hands reflects his Russian experience. He also involved himself in electronic composition, using both tapes and synthesizers. *Sacred Service,* cantor, choir reader, and tape (1970), and *Midnight Sun,* oboe and tape (1976), are examples of this direction. At the same time he composed works for conventional instruments, including *Astral Dimensions,* violin, viola, cello, piano, percussion (1973), and *A Cry, a Song, and a Dance,* string orchestra (1978), as well as works involving non-Western instruments, such as *Cicada Images: Moltings,* soprano, flute, piano, pipa, erhu, percussion (1983). Taught at Sarah Lawrence College beginning in 1966.

Spies, Claudio (b. Santiago, Chile, 26 Mar. 1925). Composer, theorist. He moved to the U.S. in 1942 and studied at the New England Conservatory, then at Harvard with Walter Piston and Irving Fine (B.A., 1950; M.A., 1954). He taught at Swarthmore College (1958–1970), then at Princeton Univ. (beginning 1970). From the 1960s on his compositions were based on serial procedures, for example, *Impromptu,* piano (1963), *Anima, vagula, blandula,* vocal quartet (1964), and *Five Sonnet Settings,* vocal quartet and piano (1977). In his teaching and his writing he explicated and expounded the principles of serialism.

Spinacino, Francesco (b. Fossombrone, Italy, fl. 1507). Lutenist and composer. Renowned in his day as a virtuoso of the lute; his only surviving publications are the *Intabulatura de lauto libro primo* and *libro* *secondo* (both Venice, 1507; facs., Geneva, 1978), the first printed lute music. Approximately a third of the contents of the *libro primo* are drawn from the *Odhecaton;* ricercars are grouped together at the end of each volume.

Bibl.: Henry Louis Schmidt, "The First Printed Lute Books: Francesco Spinacino's Intabulatura de lauto, libro primo and libro secondo (Venice; Petrucci, 1507)" (diss., Univ. of North Carolina, 1969).

Spisak, Michał (b. Dąbrowa Górnicza, 14 Sept. 1914; d. Paris, 29 Jan. 1965). Composer. He studied violin and composition at the Katowice Conservatory, graduating in 1937. Concurrently he traveled to Warsaw and studied composition with Sikorski. In 1937 he moved to Paris, studying composition there with Boulanger and working with the Association of Young Polish Musicians in Paris. He stayed in Paris for the remainder of his life. His music is predominantly instrumental and was influenced by Stravinskian neoclassicism. His forms are usually simple and sectional. Works include *Serenade* (orchestra, 1939); *Melos* (ballet, 1951); *Concerto giocoso* (orchestra, 1957); *Improvvisazione* (violin, piano, 1962).

Spitta, Julius August Philipp (b. Wechold, near Hoya, 27 Dec. 1841; d. Berlin, 13 Apr. 1894). Musicologist. Son of theologian Philipp Spitta (1801–59). Studied at Göttingen from 1860 to 1864 and received a Ph.D. in classical philology. He taught at Reval, where he began his work on Bach; later taught at Sonderhausen and Leipzig. Appointed professor of music history at Univ. of Berlin and director of Hochschule für Musik in 1875. Edited Buxtehude's organ music (1876–77), music of Schütz (1885–94) and of Frederick the Great (1889). With Chrysander and Adler he founded *Vierteljahrsschrift für Musikwissenschaft.* His *Johann Sebastian Bach* was published 1873–80; the first English translation appeared 1884–85.

Spivakovsky, Tossy (b. Odessa, 4 Feb. 1907). Violinist. Studied under Willy Hess at the Berlin Hochschule, making his debut there in 1917; pursued a European concert career until 1933, when he went to Australia, moving to the U.S. in 1940. He appeared often with U.S. orchestras, introducing Bartók's Second Violin Concerto to the U.S. in 1943; he is also known for inventing new bowing techniques that ignited debates in the postwar years. He joined the Juilliard School faculty in 1974.

Spivey, Victoria (Regina) (b. Houston, 15 Oct. 1906; d. New York, 3 Oct. 1976). Blues singer and pianist. The unaccompanied "Black Snake Blues" (1926) was the first of her many blues recordings. Subsequently her sidemen included Lonnie Johnson (T. B. Blues, 1926), Louis Armstrong, and Henry Allen (both 1929). She performed in King Vidor's film *Hallelujah!* (1929). She toured with Armstrong (mid-1930s) and sang in the show *Hellzapoppin'* (1938–early 1940s). Active from 1960 in the blues revival in the U.S. and Europe, she founded the Spivey Record Company in 1962; its issues include her album *The Queen and Her Knights* with Johnson, Memphis Slim, and Little Brother Montgomery (1965).

Spohr, Louis [Ludwig] (b. Brunswick, 5 Apr. 1784; d. Kassel, 22 Oct. 1859). Composer, violinist. From 1797, studied the violin and briefly theory during schooling in Brunswick; from 1799, the protégé of the Duke of Brunswick, who made him his chamber musician; from 1802, pupil of the famous violinist Franz Eck, who in 1802–3 took him on a tour as far as Russia, during which he composed his first concerto op. 1 and his duets op. 3. Returned to his Brunswick post, but his own German concert tour in 1804–5 established him as a virtuoso and composer, leading to his appointment, 1805–12, as concertmaster in Gotha. During this period he composed his first three operas, the third, a three-act singspiel, *Der Zweikampf mit der Geliebten,* having a modest success at Hamburg in 1811. In 1806 he married a Gotha harpist, Dorette Scheidler (1787–1834); his two concertos and six sonatas for violin and harp were written for their joint concerts; from 1807 they toured in Germany and to Vienna. Spohr conducted the festivals at Frankenhausen (1810–11) and Erfurt (1811–12), premiering his second clarinet concerto (1810), First Symphony (1811), and first oratorio, *Das jüngste Gericht* (1812).

His great concert successes in Vienna, where he had a celebrated artistic confrontation with Rode, led to his engagement in 1813–15 as conductor at the Theater an der Wien (with Dorette as harpist). There he composed some notable chamber works—string quartets and, especially, his Nonet op. 31 and Octet op. 32 and his first important opera, *Faust* (1813), premiered by Weber at Prague in 1816. The Spohrs made a concert tour through Germany to Italy in 1815–17; at La Scala (27 Sept. 1816) he premiered his eighth and perhaps best-known and most original concerto, op. 47, in the form of an operatic scene to appeal to Italian taste. He went on to successes in Venice, Florence, Rome, and Naples. In late 1817–19 he became music director of the Frankfurt theater, producing there his *Faust* and a very successful new opera, *Zemire und Azor* (1819). Resigning because of differences with the management, he resumed touring, making his first visits to Paris, where he was at first not very well received, and London, where he was, playing with the Philharmonic (1820). In 1822 he was appointed Kapellmeister at Kassel (from 1847 *Generalmusikdirektor*). There he directed the opera, which until 1832 was well supported, producing his own *Jessonda* (1823), his most popular opera; *Der Berggeist* (1825); *Pietro von Abano* (1827); *Der Alchymist* (1830). Also conducted orchestral concerts and organized a choral society. He retired in 1857. Spohr was venerated as an old master in his later years; also popular in Britain, especially for his oratorios (*Die letzten Dinge,* 1826; *Des Heilands Letzte Stunde,* 1835; *Der Fall Babylons,* 1840), which he conducted there on several visits. He continued occasionally to appear as violinist, sometimes with his second wife (from 1836), Marianne Pfeiffer (d. 1892), a pianist; also a violin teacher with many distinguished pupils; published an important violin method (1832). In 1847 he began his memoirs *(Selbstbiographie);* unfinished, this was posthumously published in an abridgment (Kassel and Göttingen, 1860–61); trans. Eng. (1865; R: 1969); full ed. by F. Göthel (Tutzing, 1968).

Bibl.: Folker Göthel, *Thematisch-Bibliographisches Verzeichnis der Werke von Louis Spohr* (Tutzing, 1981). H. Homburg, *Louis Spohr: Bilder und Dokumente seiner Zeit* (Kassel, 1968). Dorothy Moulton Mayer, *The Forgotten Master: The Life and Times of Louis Spohr* (New York, 1981). Henry Pleasants, ed., *The Musical Journeys of Louis Spohr* (New York, 1987). Helmut Peters, *Der Komponist, Geiger, Dirigent und Pädagoge Louis Spohr (1784–1859) mit einer Auswahlbibliographie zu Leben und Schaffen* (Braunschweig, 1987).

Spontini, Gaspare (Luigi Pacifico) (b. Maiolati, near Iesi, Italy, 14 Nov. 1774; d. there, 24 Jan. 1851). Composer. From a poor family; 1793–96, student, Pietà dei Turchini conservatory, Naples, leaving without graduating, possibly also apprenticing with Cimarosa. He produced at least ten operas, mostly comic, in Italy (including 1800–1801 in Palermo) before emigrating to Paris in 1802. There, supported by Empress Josephine, began to make himself known by giving one of his Italian operas at the Théâtre-Italien, followed by three opéras comiques; the first, *La petite maison* (1804), caused a riot and was suppressed, but *Milton* (1804) and *Julie, ou Le pot de fleurs* (1805) were reasonably well received. Josephine seems to have been instrumental in the difficult business of getting his serious opera *La vestale* (libretto by Jouy) accepted and staged at the prestigious Paris Opéra (15 Dec. 1807). It became the most successful French opera of its time and made Spontini famous, although he was never completely accepted by the French musical establishment, which impugned his professional competence. His next, *Fernand Cortez* (libretto by Jouy), was not a success (Opéra, 28 Nov. 1809; 24 performances), but this may have been partly for political reasons.

In 1810 he married a daughter of the wealthy instrument manufacturer Erard; 1810–12, music director of the Théâtre-Italien, directing an ambitious schedule of productions, but his overbearing personality and lack of tact probably contributed to his dismissal. On the Restoration he courted Bourbon favor with occasional works (the opera *Pélange,* 1814; the opéra-ballet *les dieux rivaux,* 1816, of which he was one of four composers). He was rewarded with the directorship of the king's private music (1814), the directorship of the Théâtre-Italien (1814), which he sold, and a pension (1818). He maintained his operatic position with a new version of *Fernand Cortez* (Opéra, 8 May 1817), which won popularity nearly equal to that of *La vestale;* his monumental opera *Olimpie,* however, four years in gestation and the object of much public anticipation, was a complete failure (Opéra, 22 Dec. 1819; 6 performances). From 1820 to 1841 he was *Generalmusikdirektor,* Berlin. This post, one of great power, began propitiously with the very successful staging of a revision of *Olimpie* (in German as *Olympia,* 14 May 1821), but a month later came the phenomenal reception of Weber's *Der Freischütz,* embroiling Spontini as the symbol of foreignness in a powerful current of German nationalism, Spontini's autocratic and disagreeable personality making it easy to depict him as an arrogant, deceitful Italian intriguer. His kind of opera was increasingly outmoded, and his later works, the operas *Nurmahal* (1822), *Alcidor* (1825), and *Agnes von Hohenstaufen* (final version, 1837), were never performed outside his own theater. He survived, increasingly bitter, through the king's support, but after the latter's death in 1840 his career ended ignominiously with a public demonstration when he tried to conduct at the Opéra and a conviction for lèse-majesté for statements he had made in the press. Pardoned by the new king, he left Berlin in 1842, retiring to Paris and, just before his death, to his birthplace.

Bibl.: Paolo Fragapane, *Spontini* (Florence, 1983).

Spratlan, Lewis (b. Miami, 5 Sept. 1940). Composer. An oboist since his teens, he attended Yale Univ. (B.A., 1962) and the Yale School of Music (M.M., 1965), where he studied with Gunther Schuller and Mel Powell. Taught at Amherst College from 1970. Among his works are *Two Pieces for Orchestra* (1971); Woodwind Quintet (1971); *Three Ben Jonson Songs* (soprano, flute, violin, cello, 1974); *Life Is a Dream* (opera, 1977); *Cornucopi* (piano, 1980); String Quartet (1982); *Celebration* (chorus, orchestra, 1984); *Apollo and Daphne Variations* (orchestra, 1987); *Wolves* (soprano, flute, clarinet, piano, 1988); *A Fanfare for the Tenth* (string quartet, 1988).

Springsteen, Bruce (b. Freehold, N.J., 23 Sept. 1949). Rock singer, songwriter, and guitarist. After performing in bands in New Jersey, in 1973 he released his first recordings with the E Street Band. He first achieved prominence with the album *Born To Run* (1975, including "Thunder Road"), and became extremely popular upon the release of *Born in the U.S.A.* (1984, including title song, "Glory Days," "Dancing in the Dark") and accompanying music videos. He is a consciously traditional artist who increasingly employed simple rock song structures and instrumentation; his lyrics mainly address American economic, social, and personal issues. Other recordings include *The River* (1980, including "Hungry Heart"), *Nebraska* (1982), and *Tunnel of Love* (1988, including "Brilliant Disguise"); live performances are preserved on *Live 1975/85* (1986).

Squarcialupi, Antonio (b. Florence, 27 Mar. 1416; d. Florence, 6 July 1480). Organist. He served at Orsanmichele, Florence, from 1431, and at the Cathedral of Santa Maria del Fiore from 1432. He was widely considered the greatest organist of his time. He associated with the Medici court of Lorenzo the Magnificent and with Dufay; both voiced a high opinion of him. The *Squarcialupi Codex,* a great 14th-century manuscript of Italian polyphony, takes its name from his inscription of ownership.

Stabile, Mariano (b. Palermo, 12 May 1888; d. Milan, 11 Jan. 1968). Baritone. A pupil of Cotogni at Rome; made his debut at Palermo in 1909; appeared in Italy, Spain, and Latin America before Toscanini cast him as Falstaff for the 1921 reopening of La Scala, a role he sang more than 1,000 times to 1961. In 1923 he created the title role in Respighi's *Belfagor;* later he performed at Chicago (1924–29), Covent Garden (1926–31), Salzburg (1931–39), Glyndebourne (1936–39), and again in London after the war; he sang at La Scala until 1955. He was a fine actor, with exceptional enunciation.

Stade, Frederica Von. See Von Stade, Frederica.

Staden, Johann (b. Nuremberg, bapt. 2 July 1581; d. there, buried 15 Nov. 1634). Composer. By age 18 he was active as an organist in Nuremberg, and by 16 April 1604 he was appointed court organist at Bayreuth. When Margrave Christian moved his court to Kulmbach in 1605, Staden apparently followed and published both his *Neue teutsche Lieder* and *Neue teutsche geistliche Gesäng* there in 1609. By the beginning of 1611 he was back in Nuremberg, and on 20 June he became organist at the Spitalkirche; he assumed the same position at St. Lorenz on 19 November. In 1618 Staden obtained the position of organist at St. Sebald, where he remained for the rest of his life. Among his pupils were Kindermann and his son, Sigmund Theophil. Staden was the founder of the so-called Nuremberg school of the 17th century. His *Harmoniae sacrae* (1616) is notable for including some of the earliest sacred concertos in Germany, and his instrumental music is among the most important produced in Germany during his lifetime.

Staden, Sigmund Theophil [Gottlieb] (b. Kulmbach, bapt. 6 Nov. 1607; d. Nuremberg, buried 30 July 1655). Composer. He made such rapid progress in his lessons with his father, Johann Staden, that in December 1620 the Nuremberg town council funded his lessons with Jakob Paumann in Augsburg. When he returned to Nuremberg in 1623, he was granted an expectant's salary and became a city instrumentalist. In 1634 he was given the additional appointment of organist of St. Lorenz; he retained these two posts in Nuremberg for the rest of his life. Staden published only 2 books of vocal music, comprising 47 works, and a number of strophic songs. His singspiel *Seelewig* (1644; ed. in *MfMg* 13 [1881]), is the earliest extant example of the genre.

Stadler, Anton (Paul) (b. Bruck an der Leitha, 28 June 1753; d. Vienna, 15 June 1812). Clarinetist and basset horn player. He is remembered particularly for his association with Mozart. It was for his "basset clarinet," a clarinet with a downward extension, that Mozart's Quintet K.581 and Concerto K.622 were written. Stadler and his brother Johann, also a clarinetist, first performed for the Vienna Tonkünstler Sozietät in 1773, became members of the imperial wind band in 1782, and became the court orchestra's first regular clarinetists in 1787. Anton also composed several chamber pieces for clarinet.

Bibl.: Pamela L. Poulin, "The Basset Clarinet of Anton Stadler," *CMS* 22/2 (1982): 67–82.

Stadler, Maximilian [Johann Karl Dominik] (b. Melk, 4 Aug. 1748; d. Vienna, 8 Nov. 1833). Composer, keyboard player, and music historian. He received musical instruction as a child. In 1772 he was ordained as a Benedictine priest; he became prior of Melk in 1784, abbot of Lilienfield in 1786, abbot of Kremsmünster in 1789; he settled in Vienna in 1796. As a composer he wrote mainly vocal music, much of it sacred; his oratorio *Die Befreyung von Jerusalem* (Vienna, ca. 1813) was quite successful. He also wrote chamber music and keyboard pieces. He wrote several articles and a history of music in Austria, *Materialen zur Geschichte der Musik unter den österreichischen Regenten.* He was a friend of Mozart's, whose widow he advised. Together with Georg Nissen, he catalogued Mozart's manuscripts.

Bibl.: Karl Wagner, *Abbé Maximilian Stadler* (Kassel, 1974).

Stadlmayr [Stadlmair, Stadelmaier, Stadelmayer, Stadelmeyer]**, Johann** (b. Freising?, Bavaria, ca. 1575; d. Innsbruck, 12 July 1648). Composer. In 1603 he was employed by Archbishop of Salzburg; in 1604 he became Kapellmeister there. He left for Innsbruck in 1607 to assume a similar position at the court of the Habsburg Archduke Maximilian II of the Tirol. Well known across Europe in his time; his compositions consist almost exclusively of Catholic church music and reflect both 16th- and 17th-century styles.

Staempfli, Edward (b. Bern, 1 Feb. 1908). Composer. He studied with Philipp Jarnach in Cologne, then with Paul Dukas in Paris. His earlier works are lyrical and tonal, for example 4 Concertante Symphonies (1931–34) and *Liberté,* vocal soloists, chorus, winds, piano (1944). From the early 1950s on, he wrote twelve-tone music almost exclusively. Examples include *Epitaphe pour Paul Eluard,* orchestra (1954); *Ornamente,* 2 flutes, percussion, celeste (1960); *L'avventura d'un povero christiano,* oratorio (1972). In 1951 he moved to Heidelberg, in 1954 to Berlin. Later works include *Sextett für Bläser* (1980); *Duo für Altoflöte und cello* (1987).

Stagliano, James (b. Catanzaro, Italy, 7 Jan. 1912; d. Boynton Beach, Fla., 11 Apr. 1987). Horn player. Growing up in the U.S., he joined the Detroit Symphony at age 14, subsequently playing with the St.

Louis Symphony (1934–36), the Los Angeles Philharmonic (1936–44), the Cleveland Orchestra (1944–45), and the Boston Symphony (1946–71), appearing often as soloist. He formed a record company in 1951; among its releases were his performances of music from the Baroque era to Brahms and Britten. He helped found the Opera Company of Boston in 1958.

Stainer, Jacob [Jakob] (b. Absam, near Hall, Tirol, 14 July 1617?; d. late Oct. or early Nov. 1683). Violin maker. He was apprenticed in Italy to a German violin maker; there is no evidence to support the claim that he worked in Cremona. In 1656 he entered the service of Prince Ferdinand Karl of Tirol at Absam. By this time Stainer was receiving commissions from all over Europe. In his later years, despite suffering from bouts of temporary insanity, he produced his best instruments. He also made tenor viols, cellos, and double basses. Many, including Hawkins, preferred his violins to those made in Cremona.

Bibl.: Walter Senn, *Jakob Stainer, der Geigenmeister zu Absam* (Innsbruck, 1951). Walter Senn and Karl Roy, *Jacob Stainer, Leben und Werk des Tiroler Meisters, 1617–1683* (Frankfurt, 1986).

Stainer, John (b. London, 6 June 1840; d. Verona, 31 Mar. 1901). Musicologist and composer. Blinded in one eye by an accident as a child. Chorister at St. Paul's Cathedral, 1849. Organist at College of St. Michael, Tenbury; later at Christ Church, Oxford (1859), where he received a B.Mus. (1860), B.A. (1864), D.Mus. (1865), and M.A. (1866). Founded Oxford Philharmonic Society, 1866. Organist at St. Paul's, 1872; assisted in reforms there. Named organist and principal at National Training School for Music, 1881. Knighted in 1888; professor of music at Oxford from 1889. Compositions include the oratorios *The Crucifixion* (1887) and *The Story of the Cross* (1893), services, songs, anthems. Did several editions of sacred music. Wrote several texts, including *A Theory of Harmony* (1871) and *Music in Relation to the Intellect and Emotions* (1892).

Bibl.: Peter Charlton, *John Stainer and the Musical Life of Victorian Britain* (North Pomfret, Vt., 1984).

Stainov, Petko (b. Kazanluk, 1 Dec. 1896; d. Sofia, 25 June 1977). Composer. He was almost entirely blinded as a child, but began to play the piano by ear. He went on to study music theory at the Dresden Conservatory with Münch from 1920 to 1924. In 1926 he returned to his native Bulgaria, where from 1922 to 1944 he served on the faculty as a piano teacher at the State Institute for the Blind in Sofia. In 1967 he was appointed head of the National Council of Amateur Art and Music. His own compositions are in a late Romantic style and include *Thracian Dances for Orchestra* (1925–26), *Legend* (symphonic poem, premiered 1928), *Balkan* (1936), 2 symphonies (1945, 1948), and vocal music.

Stamitz, Anton (Thadäus Johann Nepomuk) (b. Německý Brod, 27 Nov. 1750; d. Paris or Versailles, between 1796 and 1809). Composer, violinist, and violist. Son of Johann Stamitz. He studied with his brother Carl and with Christian Cannabich, becoming a violinist with the Mannheim orchestra in 1764. In 1770 he went with his brother Carl to Paris, where they played together at the Concert spirituel in 1772. He played in the Royal Chapel Orchestra in Versailles, 1782–89. Among his compositions are 12 symphonies, 2 *symphonies concertantes,* 5 keyboard and over 20 violin concertos, other solo concertos, over 50 string quartets, and numerous other chamber works.

Stamitz, Carl (Philipp) (bapt. Mannheim, 8 May 1745; d. Jena, 9 Nov. 1801). Composer, violinist. Son of Johann Stamitz. He studied with his father and also with Christian Cannabich, Ignaz Holzbauer, and Franz X. Richter. He joined the Mannheim orchestra in 1762 and went to Paris with his brother Anton in 1770, where they performed together at the Concert spirituel for the first time in 1772. He traveled widely as a virtuoso on the violin viola, and viola d'amore during the 1770s and 1780s. He wrote more than 50 symphonies; at least 38 *symphonies concertantes;* and more than 60 concertos for violin, viola, viola d'amore, cello, clarinet, flute, and other instruments. He also wrote a good deal of chamber music for various combinations.

Bibl.: Friedrich C. Kaiser, "Carl Stamitz (1745–1801): Biographische Beiträge, das symphonische Werk, thematischer Katalog der Orchesterwerke" (diss., Univ. of Marpurg, 1962). Michael Jacob, *Die Klarinettenkonzerte von Carl Stamitz* (Wiesbaden, 1991).

Stamitz, Johann (Wenzel Anton) (bapt. Německý Brod, 19 June 1717; d. Mannheim, buried 30 Mar. 1757). Composer and violinist. He received his formal education in Jihlava at the Jesuit Gymnasium and was in Prague at the university during 1734–35. He arrived in Mannheim probably by 1741 and was employed by the court. He was "first violinist" by 1743, became *Konzertmeister* in 1745 or 1746 and director of instrumental music in 1750. In Paris 1754–55, he appeared at the Concert spirituel. His music was published in Paris, London, and Amsterdam. Today Stamitz is regarded as one of the foremost early classical symphonists. His contributions include regular use of the 4-movement cycle (instead of 3) in his symphonic works and a transfer of features of Italian opera-overture style, including the crescendo, to the symphony. Under his direction the Mannheim orchestra became one of the most renowned in Europe. He was also well regarded as a teacher; among his pupils who went on to achieve success were his own sons Carl and Anton, Christian Cannabich, Ignaz Fränzl, and Wilhelm Cramer.

Precise enumeration of Stamitz's works is made difficult by the fact that several other composers shared some form of his surname, as well as by a lack of autograph manuscripts. He is best known for his symphonies, of which nearly 60 are extant (many others are lost), and his 10 orchestral trios. He wrote many solo concertos, including at least 15 for violin, 11 for flute, 1 for oboe, 1 for clarinet, and several for keyboard. Other extant works include a Mass, liturgical vocal music, and chamber works.

Bibl.: *DTB* 3/1 (1902), 7/2 (1906), 16 (1915), ed. Hugo Riemann. Eugene K. Wolf, *The Symphonies of Johann Stamitz: A Study in the Formation of the Classic Style* (Utrecht, 1981) [with Thematic Catalogue of the Symphonies and Orchestral Trios]. Peter Gradenwitz, *Johann Stamitz: Leben, Umwelt, Werke* (Wilhelmshaven, 1984). Eugene K. Wolf and Jean K. Wolf, eds., *The Symphony at Mannheim: Johann Stamitz, Christian Cannabich,* ser. C, vol. 3 of *The Symphony 1720–1840,* ed. Barry S. Brook et al. (New York, 1984).

Standage, Simon (b. High Wycombe, Buckinghamshire, 8 Nov. 1941). Violinist. Attended Cambridge Univ.; from 1967 to 1969 studied in New York with Ivan Galanian; joined the London Symphony and the English Chamber Orchestra, eventually becoming the leading player of the English Concert. He formed the Salomon Quartet in 1981, joined the faculty of the Royal College in 1983, and became concertmaster of the City of London Sinfonia. A period instrument specialist, he has been soloist on many recordings.

Standford, Patric [Gledhill, John Patrick Standford] (b. Barnsley, 5 Feb. 1939). Composer. He studied composition with Rubbra at the Guildhall School of Music, then traveled to Italy to study with Malipiero; subsequently studied with Lutosławski, 1964–6g5. He returned to the Guildhall School of Music in 1967 as a faculty member. His works are stylistically diverse, ranging from tonality to tone clusters. They include *Epigrams* op. 3, chamber orchestra (1964); *Saracinesco* op. 10, poem for orchestra (1966); *Nocturne* op. 12, orchestra (1967); *Notte* op. 18, chamber orchestra (1968); *How Amiable Are Thy Dwellings* op. 24, anthem (1969); *Christus-Requiem* op. 41 (1972); Piano Concerto (1979); Symphony no. 5 (1986); piano quartet (1988); *Mass of St. Rochus and Our Lady,* chorus (1988).

Bibl.: Leslie East and Denys Corrigan, *Patric Standford: A Profile of the Composer* (London, 1985).

Standfuss, J(ohann?) C. (d. after ca. 1759). Composer. From about 1750 to 1756 he was with G. H. Koch's theater company as a violinist and répétiteur. His singspiel *Der Teufel ist los, oder Die verwandelten Weiber* (perf. Leipzig, 6 Oct. 1752) was based on Charles Coffey's *The Devil To Pay, or The Wives Metamorphos'd* (London, 1731). The work was influential and inspired his *Der lustige Schuster, oder Der zweyte Theil vom Teufel ist los* (perf. Lübeck, 18 Jan. 1759), based on Coffey's *The Merry Cobbler* (London, 1735). None of his music survives.

Stanford, Charles Villiers (b. Dublin, 30 Sept. 1852; d. London, 29 Mar. 1924). Composer, teacher. Son of a lawyer with musical interests; early showed musical talent, having lessons in the piano, organ, violin, and theory; from 1870, student at Cambridge, distinguishing himself as organist of Trinity College (1873–82), conductor of musical societies, and composer, taking his B.A. in 1874, his M.A. in 1877; 1874–76, also studied in Leipzig and Berlin. Began to publish in 1875 (piano Suite op. 2, piano Toccata op. 3); 1876, incidental music for Tennyson's *Queen Mary* in London; 1877, overture played at the Gloucester Festival. His compass then broadened to include opera (the first of 10, *The Veiled Prophet of Khorossan,* composed in 1877, was produced at Hannover in 1881 and once at Covent Garden in 1893) and Anglican church music (the first of his 6 morning, Communion, and evening services dates from 1879); also began his large production of chamber music. In 1882 he settled in London, in 1883 becoming first professor of composition and orchestra conducting at the new Royal College of Music; 1885–1902, conductor, London Bach Choir; 1887–1924, professor, Cambridge Univ. (retaining his Royal College posts); 1901–10, conductor, Leeds Festival, also conducting at many other festivals. He was knighted in 1902.

A highly prolific composer; his music was much respected in Britain, although little of it was popular or regularly performed, and it grew increasingly old-fashioned after the turn of the century because of his resistance to new musical developments. Most of his operas had few performances, except *Shamus O'Brien* (50 performances, London, 1896). Irish or Celtic subjects are also found in several of his many choral works, his 6 Irish Rhapsodies for orchestra, the Irish Symphony (3rd of 6) op. 28 (1887); also 3 piano concertos, 2 violin concertos, clarinet concerto; piano and organ pieces; many part songs and solo songs. Only some of his Anglican church music is performed today. He had more lasting influence as a teacher (students included Vaughan Williams, Holst, Bridge, Bliss, Benjamin). Published many essays, some collected in *Studies and Memories* (London, 1908) and *Interludes, Records, and Reflections* (London, 1922); also memoirs, *Pages from an Unwritten Diary* (London, 1914), a book on Brahms (London, 1912), and a textbook, *Musical Composition* (London, 1911; 6th ed., 1950).

Bibl.: J. F. Porte, *Sir Charles V. Stanford* (London, 1921; R: 1976). H. Plunket Greene, *Charles Villiers Stanford* (London, 1935). F. Hudon, "A Revised and Extended Catalogue of the Works of Charles Villiers Stanford (1852–1924)," *Music Review* 37 (1976): 106.

Stanley, John (b. London, 17 Jan. 1712; d. there, 19 May 1786). Composer and organist. Despite an early accident which left him blind, he began musical studies and became organist at the Church of All Hallows, Bread Street, London, before he was 12. He followed William Boyce as Master of the King's Band of Musicians in 1779. He composed some stage music, including the full-length opera *Teraminta* and oratorios patterned on those of Handel, with whom he was friendly. He also wrote cantatas, court odes, sacred vocal music, concertos, organ voluntaries, and songs.

Bibl.: Alfred G. Williams, "The Life and Works of John Stanley (1712–86)" (diss., Univ. of Reading, 1977). A. Glyn

Williams, "The Concertos of John Stanley," *MR* 42 (1981): 103–15.

Stanley, Ralph (b. Stratton?, Va., 25 Feb. 1927). Bluegrass banjo player, singer, and songwriter. **Stanley, Carter (Glen)** (b. McClure?, Va., 27 Aug. 1925; d. Bristol, Va., 1 Dec. 1966). Bluegrass guitarist, singer, and songwriter. They played together from 1946 as the Stanley Brothers, later forming the Clinch Mountain Boys. They performed mainly traditional country songs as well as compositions by both brothers. Their popular songs include "Molly and Tenbrooks" (1948), "Little Glass of Wine" (1948), and "Train 45" (1958). After Carter's death Ralph continued to perform and record with the Clinch Mountain Boys.

Bibl.: John Wright, *Ralph Stanley and the Clinch Mountain Boys: A Discography* (Evanston, Ill., 1983). Ralph Stanley, *It's the Hardest Music in the World To Play: The Ralph Stanley Story in His Own Words* (Chimacum, Wash., 1988).

Starer, Robert (b. Vienna, 8 Jan. 1924). Composer. He entered the Vienna State Academy at age 13 and studied briefly with Victor Ebenstein, but with the German–Austrian Anschluss he fled to Palestine. He studied at the Jerusalem Conservatory with Joseph Tal, Odeon Partos, and Solomon Rosowsky (1938–43). After serving in the British Air Force in World War II, he moved to the U.S. in 1947 and studied at Juilliard with Frederick Jacobi, supporting himself as a vocal accompanist. He was introduced as a composer by New York performances of his First Piano Concerto (1947), followed by *Prelude and Dance,* orchestra (1949), and *Kohelet (Ecclesiastes),* soloists, chorus, orchestra (1952). He taught at Juilliard from 1949 to 1974, at Brooklyn College (CUNY) beginning 1963. Composed in a variety of genres, including symphonies, concertos, ballets, chamber music, band music, songs, and several operas. Most of his music is based on tonal principles, although in the mid-60s he experimented with serialism in several works, notably the Trio for clarinet, cello, and piano (1964) and *Mutabili Variants for Orchestra* (1965). Many of his works are based on traditional organizational schemes such as concerto or rondo form. Works include *Pantagleize* (opera, 1967; Brooklyn, 1974); *The Last Lover* (opera, New York, 1985); *Samson Agonistes* (ballet, 1961), *Holy Jungle* (ballet, 1974); 3 symphonies (1950, 1951, 1969), 3 piano concertos (1947, 1953, 1972); *Prelude and Rondo giocoso* (orchestra, 1953); Violin Concerto (1980); Cello Concerto (1988); *Symphonic Prelude,* orchestra (1984); Duo, violin and piano (1988); 2 piano sonatas (1949, 1965); *Fantasia Concertante* (piano 4-hands, 1959).

Bibl.: Robert Starer, *Continuo: A Life in Music* (New York, 1987).

Starker, Janos (b. Budapest, 5 July 1924). Cellist. Studied at the Liszt Academy under Cziffer from age 7; played in the Budapest Philharmonic in 1945 and 1946, then left Hungary. Settling in the U.S., he was principal cellist of the Dallas Symphony (1948–49), the Metropolitan Opera orchestra (1949–53), and the Chicago Symphony (1953–58). He joined the faculty of Indiana Univ. in 1958, continuing to perform as chamber musician and orchestral soloist. He was cellist in the Roth Quartet (1950–53) and the Suk, Starker, and Katchen Trio (1967–69), performing in concert and on record. He prepared editions of the Bach cello suites and Beethoven cello sonatas, and published *An Organized Method of String Playing* (New York and Hamburg, 1985).

Starokadomsky, Mikhail Leonidovich (b. Brest-Litovsk, 13 June 1901; d. Moscow, 24 April 1954). Composer. He studied composition with Miaskovsky and organ with Aleksandr Goedicke at the Moscow Conservatory (degree, 1928); he remained there as professor of orchestration. His works include the opera *Sot* (1933), several operettas, orchestral works, incidental and film music, choral works, chamber music, and songs, especially children's songs.

Starr, Ringo [Starkey, Richard] (b. Liverpool, England, 7 July 1940). Rock drummer, singer, and songwriter. In 1962 he replaced Pete Best as the Beatles' drummer; his songwriting contributions included "Octopus's Garden" (1969). He released his first solo album in 1970 *(Sentimental Journey);* the later *Ringo* (1973), which featured performances by all of the former Beatles as well as songs co-written with George Harrison, was very popular. He continued to record and produce records, also appearing in films. In 1994 he reunited with the other surviving Beatles to record some new music based on tapes made by John Lennon before he was murdered.

Bibl.: Alan Clayson, *Ringo Starr: Straight Man or Joker* (New York, 1992).

Starzer, Josef (b. 1726 or 1727; d. Vienna, 22 Apr. 1787). Composer. He was a violinist in the orchestra of the Viennese Burgtheater. As an established composer of ballets, ca. 1759–60 he followed the Viennese choreographer Hilverding to St. Petersburg, where he became concertmaster and court composer. He eventually returned to Vienna (ca. 1768), where he continued to write ballets. Among the most successful of this period were *Roger et Bradamante* (1771), *Adèle de Ponthieu* (1773), and *Gli Orazi e gli Curiazi* (1774). He helped to found the Viennese Tonkünstler Sozietät in 1771 and was one of its "Seniores." Much of Starzer's music was performed at the society's concerts; the first one opened with one of his symphonies. In addition to more than 30 ballets, he wrote a singspiel, *Die drei Pächter;* an oratorio; symphonies, concertos, string quartets and trios; and wind chamber music.

Bibl.: Lisbeth Braun, "Die Ballettkomposition von Joseph Starzer," *Studien zur Musikwissenschaft* 13 (1926): 38–56.

Stebbins, George C. (Coles) (b. East Carlton, N.Y., 26 Feb. 1846; d. Catskill, N.Y., 6 Oct. 1945). Evangelistic singer and composer. He moved to Rochester, where he studied singing and sang in a church choir. Moved to Chicago, 1870. Music director of Baptist church in Chicago and Boston (1874). Worked with Dwight L. Moody beginning in 1876. Arranged many gospel hymns for men's chorus. Collaborated with Sankey and McGranahan in 1877 on vols. 3–6 of *Gospel Hymns and Sacred Songs*. His son George Waring Stebbins (1869–1920) was cofounder of the American Guild of Organists.

Steber, Eleanor (b. Wheeling, W. Va., 17 July 1916; d. Langhorne, Pa., 3 Oct. 1990). Soprano. Studied at the New England Conservatory and in New York, making her debut at Boston in 1936; after winning the Metropolitan Opera radio auditions, she appeared there from 1940 to 1966, specializing in Mozart roles but also singing Verdi, Wagner, Strauss, and Berg; created the lead role in Barber's *Vanessa* (1958). She taught at the Cleveland Institute from 1963 to 1972, and from 1971 to her retirement also at the Juilliard School and the New England Conservatory. In 1963 she became the first American to appear at Bayreuth after the war, singing elsewhere in Europe as well; her concert career continued into the 1970s.

Štědroň, Miloš (b. Brno, 9 Feb. 1942). Composer. He studied musicology at Brno Univ. from 1959 to 1964, then composition with Racek, Vysloužil, and Bohumír Štědroň, his uncle, at the Brno Academy of Music. He worked as a music researcher on Janáček's music from 1963 to 1972 for the Moravian Museum in Brno. In 1972 he began teaching music theory at Brno Univ. His studies of Janáček's music influenced his own compositions, which utilize a folk-derived modality. Other influences are: jazz, the use of electronic instruments, and popular media such as film and television. Works include dramatic music (*Apparat* [The Apparatus], opera, 1967–69; *Chameleon aneb Joseph Fouché* [The Chameleon, or Joseph Fouché], opera, 1984); chamber music (*Utis II,* bass clarinet, tape, 1967; *Free Laudino Jazz,* bass clarinet, piano, 1968; *Danze, canti e lamenti,* string quartet, 1986); vocal music (*Agrafor,* madrigal choir, Renaissance instruments, jazz ensemble, 1968; *Mourning Ceremony,* cantata, 1969, performed on Czech Radio 21 Feb. 1969; *Omaggio a Gesualdo: Death of Dobrovsky,* cantata-oratorio for 2 solo voices, chorus, orchestra, 1988).

Steel, (Charles) Christopher (b. London, 15 Jan. 1939; d. 1992). Composer. He attended the Royal College of Music where, from 1957 to 1961, he studied with Gardner. Then he traveled to Munich to work with Genzmer. In 1968 he became head of the music department at Bradford College in Reading. His music is largely tonal, with passages of nonfunctional tonality, chromaticism, and occasional use of serialism (as in Symphony no. 3, *Shakespeare Symphony*).

Steffani [Staffani, Steffano, Stefani, Stephani], **Agostino** (b. Castelfranco, near Venice, 25 July 1654; d. Frankfurt am Main, 12 Feb. 1728). Composer. He probably attended a municipal school in Padua, and may have learned to sing at an early age. He studied organ in Munich with J. K. Kerll, the Kapellmeister (1668–71), and composition in Rome with Ercole Bernabei, *maestro di cappella* at St. Peter's (1672–74). After his return to Munich in July 1674, Steffani became court organist. On a trip to Paris in 1678 or 1679 he probably heard Lully's opera *Bellérophon.* On 1 January 1681 Elector Maximilian II Emanuel made him director of chamber music; in February his first opera, *Marco Aurelio,* was performed. He left Munich in summer 1688 to become Kapellmeister to Duke Ernst August of Hannover. In Hannover he composed 8 works (including *Henrico Leone,* 1689) for the newly established opera company. During the 1690s Steffani was preoccupied with diplomatic activities. From March 1703 until 1709 he was employed by the Elector Palatine Johann Wilhelm at Düsseldorf. From this period until his last years he essentially abandoned music in favor of furthering his political and ecclesiastical careers. Among his compositions, most of which are vocal, his operas and chamber duets were most influential.

Bibl.: *Agostino Steffani: Ausgewählte Werke,* ed. Alfred Einstein, Adolf Sandberger, and Hugo Riemann, *DTB* 6/2 (1905); 11/2 (1911); 12/2 (1912).

Steibelt, Daniel (b. Berlin, 22 Oct. 1765; d. St. Petersburg, 20 Sept. 1823). Composer and pianist. Studied piano and theory with Kirnberger; joined the Prussian army but deserted by 1784 and spent the next several years in transit. During 1790–96 he lived in Paris, where he wrote his first opera, *Roméo et Juliette* (1793). He spent the next years in London with trips to Hamburg, Prague, Berlin, Vienna, and Paris. He fled Paris and his creditors in 1808 and settled in St. Petersburg; in 1810 he became *maître de chapelle* to the Czar Alexander I. Some of his works that were performed in St. Petersburg include the operas *La princesse de Babylon* (ca. 1812), *Sargines* (ca. 1810), and *Cendrillon* (1810) and the ballets *La fête de L'Empereur* (1809) and *Der blöde Ritter* (ca. 1810). His other compositions include piano concertos, a harp concerto, string quartets, keyboard music, songs. He also wrote a piano method (pub. 1805).

Bibl.: Gottfried Müller, *Daniel Steibelt: Sein Leben und seine Klavierwerke* (Leipzig and Zurich, 1933; R: 1973). Karen A. Hagberg, "*Cendrillon* by Daniel Steibelt: An Edition with Notes on Steibelt's Life and Operas" (diss., Univ. of Rochester, 1975).

Steiger, Rand (b. New York, 18 June 1957). Composer and conductor. He studied composition and percussion, earning a B.Mus. from the Manhattan School of Music (1980) and an M.F.A. from the California Institute of the Arts (1982). Taught at Cal Arts (1982–87) and Univ. of California at San Diego (from 1987), and was the first Composer-Fellow of the Los Angeles Philharmonic (1987–88). He has conducted new music ensembles including SONOR (UCSD), the Los Angeles Philharmonic's New Music Group, and the California E.A.R. Unit (Cal Arts). His works include numerous pieces for experimental chamber and orchestral groups, often employing electronic or computerized elements.

Stein, Johann Andreas (b. Heidelsheim, 6 May 1728; d. Augsburg, 29 Feb. 1792). Maker of keyboard instruments. He apprenticed during 1748–49 in the shop of J. A. Silbermann in Strasbourg; in 1750 he established himself in Augsburg, where he constructed the organ of the Barfüsserkirche and became organist. He built various types of keyboard instruments; among those he created were the "Poli-Toni-Clavichordium" (1769), the "Melodika" (?1772), a "vis-à-vis Flügel," and the "Saitenharmonika" (1789). He was succeeded in business by his son Andreas and his daughter Nanette, who later married J. A. Streicher.

Bibl.: Eva Hertz, *J. A. Stein: Ein Beitrag zur Geschichte des Klavierbaues* (Würzburg, 1937).

Stein, Leon (b. Chicago, 18 Sept. 1910). Composer and teacher. He attended DePaul Univ. in Chicago (M.M., 1935; Ph.D., 1949) and studied privately with Leo Sowerby and Eric DeLamarter. He spent his entire teaching career at DePaul (1931–78), serving as dean of the School of Music from 1966 to 1976. He composed 4 symphonies (1940, 1942, 1951, 1974); concertos for violin (1939), cello (1988), and clarinet (1970); 4 string quartets (1933, 1962, 1964, 1965) and other works for various instrumental combinations, including several featuring the saxophone, such as the Quintet for alto saxophone and string quartet (1961) and the Suite for saxophone quartet (1967). He is the author of *Structure and Style: The Study and Analysis of Musical Forms* (Evanston, Ill., 1962; rev. 1979).

Stein, Richard Heinrich (b. Halle, Germany, 28 Feb. 1882; d. Santa Brigida, Canary Islands, 11 Aug. 1942). Composer and theorist. He studied at the Univ. of Erlangen (D.Phil., 1911), meanwhile composing music in an avant-garde style. His *2 Konzertstücke,* cello and piano (1906), are said to be the earliest published examples of quarter tone music. He also devised a quarter tone clarinet. During World War I he lived in Spain. From 1920 to 1932 he lived in Berlin, where he was music director at Radio Berlin and also gave lessons in piano and composition. After Hitler's rise to power in 1933, Stein lived in exile in the Canary Islands.

Steinberg, Maximilian (Osseievich) (b. Vilna, 4 July 1883; d. Leningrad, 6 Dec. 1946). Composer. He graduated in 1907 from St. Petersburg Univ. and the following year from St. Petersburg Conservatory, where his teachers included Rimsky-Korsakov (composition), Lyadov (harmony), and Glazunov (orchestration). In 1908, the same year as his marriage to Rimsky-Korsakov's daughter, he began teaching theory and composition at the conservatory. He edited a number of his father-in-law's compositions for posthumous publication (including the operas *May Night* and *Boyarinya Vera Sheloga,* and the orchestral suite from *The Golden Cockerel*), and completed Rimsky's *Principles of Orchestration* (St. Petersburg, 1913); in 1939 he edited and completed Spendiaryan's *Almast.* Many of his works employ folk material, including Kirghiz and Uzbek idioms. Compositions include ballet music (*Metamorphoses,* 1914; *Till Eulenspiegel,* 1936); orchestral music (Symphony no. 4, "Turksib," 1933; *In Armenia,* symphonic picture, 1940); choral music; chamber music; songs.

Steinberg, William [Hans Wilhelm] (b. Cologne, 1 Aug. 1899; d. New York, 16 May 1978). Conductor. A child prodigy on piano and violin, he conducted his own works at age 13; by 1924 he was principal conductor of the Cologne Opera, having been Klemperer's assistant there from 1920. He conducted at the German Opera, Prague (1925–29), and the Frankfurt Opera (1929–33); dismissed by the Nazis, he led a Jewish orchestra until 1936, when he emigrated to Palestine, helping to found the Palestine Symphony. In 1938 he became Toscanini's assistant with the NBC Symphony. He later directed the Buffalo Symphony (1945–52) and the Pittsburgh Symphony (1952–76), appearing also with the London Philharmonic (1958–60), the New York Philharmonic (1966–68), and the Boston Symphony (1969–72).

Steiner, Max (Maximilian Raoul Walter) (b. Vienna, 10 May 1888; d. Beverly Hills, 28 Dec. 1971). Composer and conductor. A musically precocious child, he studied at the Imperial Academy in Vienna and, at age 15, composed an operetta which ran for a year in Vienna. He moved to the U.S. in 1916 and worked in New York as an arranger and conductor in the American musical theater. In 1929 he moved to Hollywood, just as sound was transforming the film industry; he continued writing for the movies well into the 1960s. Among his most famous scores are *Symphony of Six Million* (1932), *King Kong* (1933), *Gone with the Wind* (1939), *Casablanca* (1943), *Mildred Pierce* (1945), *The Big Sleep* (1946) and *A Summer Place* (1959).

Bibl.: Max Steiner, "Scoring the Film," in *We Make the Movies,* ed. Nancy Naumburg (New York, 1937), pp. 216–380: Claudia Gerbman, *Unheard Melodies: Narrative Film Music* (Bloomington, Ind., 1987), pp. 70–98.

Steinway, Henry E. [Steinweg, Heinrich Engelhardt] (b. Wolfshagen, Germany, 15 Feb. 1797; d. New York, 7 Feb. 1871). Piano maker. Apprenticed to an organ builder in Goslar, eventually opening his own shop. In 1849 his son Charles moved to the U.S.; Henry Sr. followed in 1850 with his wife, three daughters, and sons Henry, William, and Albert. From 1850 to 1853, father and sons worked in different piano firms around New York learning the American way of business; then with his sons Henry established his own business, which grew rapidly. In 1865 the deaths of Henry Jr., who had made several innovations in design, and Charles caused the eldest son C(hristian) F(riedrick) Theodore (1825–89), who had remained in Germany,

Henry E. Steinway, 1862.

building up his own business there, to emigrate. He took over research and development, being largely responsible for the innovations that enabled the firm to dominate the U.S. (and to a considerable extent foreign) markets, essentially resulting in the modern grand piano. William handled the business and marketing side with equal brilliance. The business was carried on largely by descendants and relatives. Charles's son Charles H(erman) (1857–1919) succeeded William as president (he was also a composer), and was succeeded by his brother Frederich Theodore (1860–1927), followed by William's sons Theodore Erwin (1883–1957), Henry Ziegler (b. 1915), and John Howland (1917–89). In 1972 the company became a subsidiary of CBS, and in 1985 it was bought by the Birmingham Brothers of Boston.

Bibl.: Theodore E. Steinway, *People and Pianos* (New York, 1953; 2d ed., 1961). Cynthia Adams Hoover, "The Steinways and Their Pianos in the Nineteenth Century" *JAMS* 7 (1981). Ronald V. Ratcliffe, *Steinway and Sons* (San Francisco, 1989).

Steinweg. See Steinway.

Stenhammar, (Karl) Wilhelm (Eugen) (b. Stockholm, 7 Feb. 1871; d. there, 20 Nov. 1927). Composer. From an early age Stenhammar played piano, sang, and composed on his own. During his adolescence he studied piano with Andersson and theory with Dente, Sjögren, and Hallén. Beginning in 1897 he performed as a conductor and subsequently held posts with the Stockholm Philharmonic Society, the Royal Opera, the New Philharmonic Society, and the Göteborgs Orkesterförening, where he was active both with Nielsen and Sibelius. Beginning in 1902 he also toured as a concert pianist. His own music was highly influenced by the late Romanticism of Wagner and Liszt as well as by Scandinavian folk and art music traditions. Over the course of his career his music continued to incorporate folk elements, though integrated with frequent modality and colorful orchestration. Works include opera and stage music; orchestral music (2 piano concertos, 1903, 1904–7; 2 symphonies, 1902–3, 1911–15), choral works (*Ett Folk,* cantata, 1904–5), and many songs.

Bibl.: Bo Wallner, *Wilhelm Stenhammar och hans tid* (Stockholm, 1991).

Štěpán [Steffan, Stefani, Stephen, Stephani]**, Josef Antonín** (bapt. Kopidlno, Bohemia, 14 Mar. 1726; d. Vienna, 12 Apr. 1797). Composer and keyboard player. He arrived in Vienna in 1741 and studied composition and harpsichord with Wagenseil. In 1766 he became piano teacher to the princesses Marie Antoinette (later the Queen of France) and Carolina (later the Queen of Naples). By this time he had established himself as a composer and performer in Vienna. He is remembered for his lieder; he published the first volume of *Sammlung deutscher Lieder* in 1778. He also wrote a good deal of keyboard music throughout his life. His divertimenti op. 1 were published in Vienna in 1750. He wrote a singspiel, *Der Doktor Daunderlaun;* a Stabat Mater, Masses, symphonies, keyboard concertos, sonatas, chamber works.

Bibl.: Howard Picton, "The Life and Works of Joseph Anton Steffan (1726–1797)" (diss., Univ. of Hull, 1976).

Stephănescu, George (b. Bucharest, 13 Dec. 1843; d. there, 25 Apr. 1925). Composer. Studied at Bucharest Conservatory with Wachmann (1864–67); at Paris Conservatory (1867–71) with Réber (harmony), Auber and Thomas (composition), Delle (singing), and Marmontel (piano). Taught singing and opera at Bucharest Conservatory (1872–1904). Director of Bucharest National Theater, 1877. Wrote the vocal method *Despre mecanismul vocal* (Bucharest, 1896). Composed the first Romanian symphony, 1869. Other works include 3 operettas, other stage music, symphonic poems, piano sonata (1863), cello sonata (1863), string quartet (1870?). His music uses original folk themes and harmonizations.

Steptoe, Roger (Guy) (b. Winchester, Hampshire, 25 Jan. 1953). Composer. Served as composer-in-residence at the Charterhouse School from 1976 to 1979. His opera *King of Macedon* (premiered 1979) was written for that situation and met with critical success. The texts Steptoe sets are frequently by Ursula Vaughan Williams, the widow of Ralph Vaughan Williams. Steptoe's music is characterized by the use of tonal centers without the necessary implication of functional tonality. He makes comfortable use of traditional forms and genres, as in the constructs that underlie the opera or the Piano Sonata (premiered 1979). In general, his writing is idiomatic and highly lyrical. Works include *The Looking Glass* (soprano, oboe, piano, premiered 1980), *Equinox* (piano, 1981), Sonata (flute, piano, premiered 1984), Concerto (tuba and strings, premiered 1986), *In Winter's Cold Embrace Dye* (cantata, mezzo-soprano, tenor, chorus, orchestra, 1987), Second Piano Sonata (premiered by Steptoe in Portugal in 1988), and Five Rondos (soprano, baritone, piano, premiered 1989).

Sterkel, Johann Franz Xaver (b. Würzburg, 3 Dec. 1750; d. there, 12 Oct. 1817). Composer and pianist. He was ordained as a priest in 1724. In 1778 he became court chaplain and organist in Mainz; he traveled through Italy, 1779–82. While in Naples he wrote his only opera, *Il Farnace,* performed at S. Carlo in 1782. Upon his return to Mainz he was made canon; he was Kapellmeister, 1793–97. He then went to Würzburg, where he wrote a good deal of his sacred music, and then to Regensburg (ca. 1802), where he opened a choir school. He was named music director to the Grand Duke of Frankfurt in 1810 and returned to Würzburg when the court disbanded. He wrote more than 20 symphonies, 6 piano concertos, Masses, 2 Te Deums, overtures, a piano quartet, over 40 piano trios, sonatas, other chamber works, arias, songs.

Bibl.: August Scharnagl, *Johann Franz Sterkel: Ein Beitrag zur Musikgeschichte Mainfrankens* (Würzburg, 1943).

Stern, Isaac (b. Kremnets, Ukraine, 21 July 1920). Violinist. Brought to the U.S. as an infant; performed with the San Francisco Symphony at age 11, studying also at the conservatory there (1930–37); made his New York debut in 1937, then pursued further training with Persinger and Blinder. He played U.S.O. concerts in 1943 and 1944; after the war he began to tour in earnest, making his European debut in 1948, playing at the Casals Festival between 1950 and 1952 and touring the USSR in 1956. He formed an acclaimed trio with Istomin and Rose in 1961, and toured and recorded very extensively both as chamber musician and soloist. A major figure in Israeli musical life, he encouraged various U.S.–Israeli student exchanges, and conceived the idea of the Jerusalem Music Center (opened 1975); in the U.S. he was involved with saving Carnegie Hall and in establishing the National Endowment for the Arts.

Stern, Julius (b. Breslau, 8 Aug. 1820; d. Berlin, 27 Feb. 1883). Violinist, composer, and conductor. Studied in Berlin, Dresden, and Paris. Founded the Sternscher Gesangverein in Berlin, 1847. With Kullak and Marz he founded a conservatory in Berlin (now called the Stern Conservatory) in 1847. Conducted the Berlin Sinfonie-Kapelle (1869–71). Wrote primarily songs and choruses.

Sternberg, Erich Walter (b. Berlin, 31 May 1891; d. Tel Aviv, 15 Dec. 1974). Composer. He originally studied law at Kiel Univ., then pursued music, taking composition lessons with Leichtentritt. He went on to have his music performed publicly in Berlin. In 1932 he emigrated to Palestine, teaching at the Tel Aviv Conservatory. With Huberman he established the Palestine Symphony Orchestra (now the Israel Philharmonic). He wrote predominantly vocal music, and though he frequently used biblical texts and occasionally used folk music references, his musical style, reflecting his training, was one of late German Romanticism. Works include stage music, orchestral music (*Shema Israel* [Hear, O Israel], 1947), and many vocal works (*Ha'orev* [The Raven], baritone, orchestra, 1949).

Steuermann, Edward (b. Sambor, near L'vov, 18 June 1892; d. New York, 11 Nov. 1964). Pianist and composer. He studied piano with Vilem Kurz in L'vov, then with Busoni in Berlin. In 1912 he met Schoenberg, who was living in Berlin and with whom he took composition lessons (1912–14). Steuermann became an important member of Schoenberg's circle, playing piano at the premieres of many works, including Schoenberg's *Pierrot lunaire* in 1912, Berg's Piano Sonata in 1911, and several pieces by Webern. During the 1920s and 1930s he toured widely in Europe, and was known particularly as a performer of new music. In 1936 he emigrated to the U.S., where he became known as a performer of both traditional and modern repertory. He taught piano at the Juilliard School (1952–64) and at the Darmstadt summer courses (1954, 1957, 1958, 1960). Most of own compositions are atonal and/or serial. Works include *Variations* (orchestra, 1958), Suite for Chamber Orchestra (1964), *Seven Waltzes* (string quartet, 1946), *Diary* (string quartet, 1961), Piano Sonata (1926; rev. 1954); Piano Suite (1952).

Bibl.: Gunther Schuller, "A Conversation with Steuermann," *Perspectives of New Music* 3 (1964): 22–35. Edward Steuermann, *The Not Quite Innocent Bystander: Writings of Edward Steuermann* (Lincoln, Nebr., 1989).

Stevens, Bernard (George) (b. London, 2 March 1916; d. London, 2 Jan. 1983). Composer. He studied piano in his youth with Harold Samuel, then went to Cambridge (1934–37), where he studied with Cyril Rootham and Edward Dent, and to the Royal College of Music (1937–40), where his teachers were R. O. Morris, Arthur Benjamin, Gordon Jacob, and Constant Lambert. *A Symphony of Liberation* (1945), introduced immediately after World War II, first brought him to public notice. As a Marxist he took a resolute stand against elitist, avant-garde tendencies in modern music, trying instead to compose music that was serious in purpose yet genuinely popular. Beginning in 1948, taught composition at the Royal College of Music. Other works include Cello Concerto (1952); *The Harvest of Peace,* cantata (1957); *Dance Suite,* orchestra (1957); String Quartet no. 2 (1962); *Variations and Fugue on a Theme of Giles Farnaby,* orchestra (1972).

Bibl.: Bertha Stevens, *Bernard Stevens and His Music: A Symposium* (London, 1989).

Stevens, Halsey (b. Scott, N.Y., 3 Dec. 1908; d. Long Beach, Calif., 20 Jan. 1989). Composer and musicologist. Studied music at Syracuse Univ.—piano with George Mulfinger, composition with William H. Berwald (B.M., 1931; M.M., 1937). He also studied with Ernest Bloch (1944). Held a series of university posts—Dakota Wesleyan (1937–41), Bradley Univ. (1941–43), Univ. of Redlands (1946)—until he was appointed to the faculty at the Univ. of Southern California, where he stayed for the remainder of his career. Most of his works from the 1930s and early 1940s were withdrawn, but his Quintet for flute, piano, and string trio (1945) received a prize, and his First Symphony (1945) was premiered by the San Francisco Symphony in 1948. During the late 1940s and early 1950s he devoted much effort to a study of the life and works of Bartók, culminating in a book, *The Life and Music of Béla Bartók* (New York, 1953; rev. 1963). Bartók's influence can be heard in works in which Stevens uses eastern European materials (*12 Slovakian Folk Songs,* 2 violins, 1962; *Eight Yugoslavian Folk Songs,* piano, 1966). Of Stevens's works from the 1950s, the sonatas for horn (1953), trumpet (1956), and cello (1958) were widely performed. Other notable works include *Sinfonia breve* (1957, commissioned by the Louisville Orchestra), *The Ballad of William Sycamore,* chorus and orchestra (1955, commissioned by U.S.C.), and *Symphonic Dances* (1958, commissioned by the San Francisco Symphony). All these works are firmly tonal, use conventional resources and sonorities, and are organized according to traditional schemes. Works from the 1960s and 1970s in a similar vein include Cello Concerto (1964), Trombone Sonata (1965), *Threnos, in Memoriam Quincy Porter* (orchestra, 1968), Clarinet Concerto (1969), *Dittico* (alto sax and piano, 1972), Viola Concerto (1975).

Stevens, Richard John Samuel (b. London, 27 Mar. 1757; d. there, 23 Sept. 1837). Composer. He was appointed organist of St. Michael, Cornhill, in 1781 and held similar posts at Temple Church (from 1786) and at the Charterhouse (from 1796). He was named Gresham Professor of Music in 1801 and music master at Christ's Hospital in 1808. His most important works were glees, some of them on Shakespearean texts. He also composed songs, hymns, and keyboard sonatas.

Bibl.: R. J. S. Stevens, *Recollections of R. J. S. Stevens: An Organist in Georgian London,* ed. Mark Argent (Carbondale, 1992).

Stevens [Steenberg], **Risë** (b. New York, 11 June 1913). Mezzo-soprano. Studied with Anna Schoen-René at the Juilliard School, making her debut in 1931; after study in Europe, appeared at Prague in 1936 and made her Metropolitan Opera debut in 1938, remaining there until 1961; sang also at Chicago, San Francisco, Paris, London, and Milan. In the film *Going My Way* she performed "Habanera" from *Carmen,* a part she played dozens of times. From 1965 to 1967 she was co-director of the Metropolitan Opera's National Company, and from 1975 to 1978 was president of Mannes College.

Stevenson, Ronald (b. Blackburn, 6 Mar. 1928). Composer and performer. He played piano and composed as a youth; studied composition at the Royal Manchester College. In 1955 he studied in Rome at the Accademia di Santa Cecilia; then joined the faculty at Edinburgh Univ. From 1963 to 1965 he taught at the Univ. of Cape Town; subsequently lived in Scotland, working as a performer and composer. His music, influenced by his own scholarly research in counterpoint, contemporary music, and folk musics, is highly eclectic, drawing on musical styles from different cultures. Music includes *Passacaglia on DSCH* (1960–62) and *Peter Grimes Fantasy on Themes from Britten* (1971), both for piano, as well as many keyboard transcriptions of 19th- and 20th-century compositions.

Bibl.: Malcolm MacDonald, *Ronald Stevenson: A Musical Biography* (Edinburgh, 1989).

Stewart [Stark], **Humphrey John** (b. London, 22 May 1856; d. San Diego, 28 Dec. 1932). Organist, composer, and conductor. Studied at Oxford, receiving a B.Mus. in 1876. Organist in London to 1886, when he changed his name and moved to San Francisco. Given the Clemson Medal by the American Guild of Organists in 1899. Moved to San Diego in 1915. Maintained a huge concert schedule. Compositions include the oratorio *The Nativity* (1910), Masses (1910, 1912), Requiem (1931), the orchestral suite *Montezuma* (1903), incidental music, choral works, songs, and organ music.

Stewart, Reginald (b. Edinburgh, 20 Apr. 1900; d. Montecito, Calif., 8 July 1984). Conductor and pianist. Studied in Toronto and Paris; taught at the Canadian Academy of Music from 1921 to 1924, playing also in the Five Piano Ensemble before founding the Toronto Bach Society in 1933. As a leading musical citizen of Toronto, he had a lively rivalry with Toronto Symphony conductor Ernest MacMillan. Continuing to tour North America and Britain as conductor and pianist, he founded and led the Promenade Concerts in Toronto from 1934 to 1941, when he became conductor of the Baltimore Symphony (to 1952) and director of the Peabody Conservatory (to 1958). In 1962 he joined the faculty of the Music Academy of the West in Santa Barbara, Calif.

Stewart, Rex (William, Jr.) (b. Philadelphia, 22 Feb. 1907; d. Los Angeles, 7 Sept. 1967). Jazz cornetist. Among the many big bands he joined were those of Fletcher Henderson (intermittently 1926–33, including the recording "The Stampede," 1926) and Duke Ellington (1933–45, including the recordings "Boy Meets Horn," 1938, demonstrating his novel use of half-valve effects, and "Morning Glory," 1940). Thereafter he led bands and starred as a soloist, touring Europe (1947–49) and Australia (1949). In 1957–58 he led Henderson reunion bands.

Writings: *Jazz Masters of the Thirties* (New York, 1972; R: New York, 1980).

Stewart, Rod [Roderick David] (b. London, 10 Jan. 1945). Rock singer and songwriter. After singing in rhythm-and-blues bands in London, in 1968 he joined the Jeff Beck Group. From 1969 to 1975 he sang with the band Faces and began recording as a solo artist (including "Maggie May," 1971; "You Wear It Well," 1972). A turn from blues-oriented material to a more popular idiom in the mid-1970s yielded critical derision but greater popularity; later hits included "Tonight's the Night" (1976) and "Da Ya Think I'm Sexy?" (1978). His more recent work includes the album *A Spanner in the Works* (1995).

Stewart, Slam [Leroy Elliott] (b. Englewood, N.J., 21 Sept. 1914; d. Binghamton, N.Y., 10 Dec. 1987). Jazz double bass player. He formed a novelty group, Slim and Slam, with singer and multi-instrumentalist Slim Gaillard (b. 1916), recording "The Flat Foot Floogie" in 1938. He accompanied Fats Waller in the film *Stormy Weather* (1943), joined Art Tatum's trio (intermittently 1943 to early 1950s), Red Norvo (1944–45), and Benny Goodman (1945), while also leading groups from 1944, with Erroll Garner and Billy Taylor among his sidemen. He rejoined Tatum (early 1950s), joined Roy Eldridge (1953), and later toured with Goodman (1973–75). From 1971 he taught at SUNY–Binghamton. Throughout his career he was noted for solos in which he bowed a melody while humming it an octave higher; countless recorded examples include a duo with Don Byas, "I Got Rhythm" (1945).

Stewart, Thomas (James) (b. San Saba, Tex., 29 Aug. 1926). Baritone. Studied at Juilliard with Mark Harrell; made his debut in the North American premiere of Strauss's *Capriccio* in 1954. After marrying soprano Evelyn Lear in 1955, he moved to Europe, studying at the Berlin Hochschule (1957–58) and singing at the Berlin City Opera (from 1957) and at Bayreuth (1960–75). He appeared also at the Metropolitan Opera, the Berlin State Opera, and Covent Garden, and in eastern Europe.

Stich, Johann. See Punto, Giovanni.

Stich-Randall, Teresa (b. West Hartford, Conn., 24 Dec. 1927). Soprano. Attended the Hartford Conservatory and Columbia, appearing in the premieres of Thomson's *The Mother of Us All* (1947) and Luening's *Evangeline* (1948); sang with Toscanini and the NBC Symphony in 1949 and 1950, and made debuts in Florence, Vienna, and Salzburg in 1952. She first appeared at Chicago in 1955, and at the Metropolitan Opera in 1961; she also sang in recital and with orchestras, focusing on the Baroque and classical repertory.

Stiedry, Fritz (b. Vienna, 11 Oct. 1883; d. Zurich, 8 Aug. 1968). Conductor. Attended the Vienna Academy; Mahler aided him in obtaining a post at Dresden (1907–8); later conducted the Berlin State Opera (1914–23), the Vienna Volksoper (1924–25), and the Berlin City Opera (1928–33). After the rise of the Nazis he worked in Leningrad and Moscow, then moved to the U.S. in 1938, conducting the New Friends of Music Orchestra (New York) and later at Chicago (1945–46) and the Metropolitan Opera (1948–60). He specialized in Wagner and Verdi.

Stignani, Ebe (b. Naples, 10 July 1903; d. Imola, 5 Oct. 1974). Mezzo-soprano. Studied with Agostino Roche in her home city, making her debut at the Teatro S. Carlo in 1925; brought to La Scala by Toscanini in 1926, she appeared there until 1956. She sang often at Covent Garden between 1937 and 1957, performing also throughout Italy and at Paris, Buenos Aires, New York, and San Francisco. She was a leading Italian mezzo-soprano in the interwar years.

Still, William Grant (b. Woodville, Miss., 11 May 1895; d. Los Angeles, 3 Dec. 1978). Composer. As a child in Little Rock, Ark., he learned to play the violin. He went to Wilberforce Univ. in Ohio to study medicine (B.S., 1915), but he continued his musical studies as well, learning the oboe and clarinet and arranging music for the college band. He studied music at Oberlin College (1917–18, 1919–21), then went to New York, where he played oboe in the orchestra for *Shuffle Along,* Sissle and Blake's Broadway hit, and worked as a conductor and arranger for a record company. Meanwhile he studied composition with George W. Chadwick and later with Edgard Varèse. His early compositions, in a modernist idiom, were performed at International Composers' Guild concerts: *From the Land of Dreams* (3 voices and chamber orchestra, 1924) in 1925, *Darker America* (chamber orchestra, 1924) in 1926. In the mid-20s Still began to turn away from the avant-garde musical idiom to search for a self-consciously African American style of composition. *Levee Land* (soprano and chamber ensemble, 1925) incorporated jazz elements and was premiered at an I.C.G. concert by Florence Mills, a jazz singer. *From the Black Belt* (orchestra, 1926) was based on African American folk material, *Sahdji* (choral ballet, 1930) on an African subject. The success of his *Afro-American Symphony* (1930), whose melodic materials were drawn from the blues, established Still as a significant American composer and an important voice in African American culture. Several other works of the 1930s and 1940s pursued this same direction: *Kaintuck'* (piano and orchestra, 1935), *Lenox Avenue* (ballet, 1937), *Symphony in G minor (Song of a New Race)* (1937), and 2 operas, *Troubled Island* (1938; first produced New York, 1949) and *A Bayou Legend* (1940; produced Jackson, Miss., 1974). Other works, such as *Plain-Chant for America* (baritone, orchestra, organ, 1941), *Festive Overture* (1944), and *Danzas de Panama* (string quartet, 1948), were less specifically African American in character. In 1934 Still moved to Los Angeles, where he lived for the remainder of his life. Notable works from his later years include *Songs of*

Separation (voice and piano, 1949), *Ennanga* (harp and orchestra, 1956), *The Peaceful Land* (orchestra, 1960), *Highway 1, USA* (1-act opera, 1962).

Bibl.: *William Grant Still and the Fusion of Cultures in American Music,* ed. Robert Bartlett Haas (Los Angeles, 1972); *The Black Perspective in Music* 3/1 (Spring 1975) [special issue on Still]. Verna Arvey, *In One Lifetime* (Fayetteville, Ark., 1984).

Sting [Gordon Sumner] (b. Walksend, England, 2 Oct. 1951). Rock singer, songwriter, bass guitarist, and keyboardist. After early performances in small jazz groups in England, in 1975 he formed The Police with drummer Stewart Copeland (b. 1952; guitarist Andy Summers joined in 1977). Their style incorporated elements of jazz and reggae into rock; among their successful recordings were "Don't Stand So Close to Me" (1980), "Every Little Thing She Does Is Magic" (1981), and "Every Breath You Take" (1983). After their dissolution in 1984 Sting appeared in movies and released a number of solo albums, including *Dream of the Blue Turtles* (1985), *Nothing Like the Sun* (1987), *Bring On the Night* (1988), *The Soul Cages* (1990), *Mercury Falling* (1996).

Stitt, Sonny [Edward] (b. Boston, 2 Feb. 1924; d. Washington, D.C., 22 July 1982). Jazz alto and tenor saxophonist and bandleader. Having rapidly assimilated Charlie Parker's style, he played the alto instrument in Billy Eckstine's bop big band (1945) and Dizzy Gillespie's sextet and big band (1945–46). He co-led groups with Gene Ammons (1950–52, including the recording "Blues Up and Down," 1950; 1960–62), concentrating on the tenor and, less often, baritone instruments. Apart from periods with Gillespie (late 1950s) and Miles Davis (1960) and a tour with the Giants of Jazz (including Gillespie, Thelonious Monk, and Art Blakey, 1971–72), he led bop groups; among his scores of albums is *Stitt Plays Bird* (1963).

Stock, David (Frederick) (b. Pittsburgh, Pa., 3 June 1939). Composer and conductor. He studied composition at Carnegie-Mellon with Nikolai Lopatnikoff and Alexei Haieff (B.F.A., 1962; M.F.A., 1963), then at Brandeis with Arthur Berger (M.F.A., 1973). Of his early works, *Serenade* (1964) and *Quintet* (clarinet and strings, 1966) were performed several times and recorded. *Scat* (soprano and chamber ensemble, 1971) was based on jazz techniques. Other works include *Inner Space* (orchestra, 1973); *The Body Electric* (double bass, winds, and percussion, 1977); *A Joyful Noise* (orchestra, 1983); *Sunrise Sarabande* (recorder quartet, 1988); *Fast Break* (orchestra, 1988); *The Winds of Summer* (sax, band, 1989). From 1987 to 1988 he served as composer-in-residence to the Pittsburgh Symphony.

Stock, Frederick [Friedrich August] (b. Jülich, Germany, 11 Nov. 1872; d. Chicago, 20 Oct. 1942). Conductor. Studied violin and composition at the Cologne Conservatory (1886–91) and was active there as a violinist before joining the Theodore Thomas Orchestra (later the Chicago Symphony) in 1895; became assistant conductor in 1899 and conductor in 1903, holding the latter position until his death. An advocate of new music, he programmed works by Debussy, Mahler, Ravel, Schoenberg, and Hindemith; Prokofiev premiered his Third Piano Concerto with him in 1921. The Chicago Symphony under Stock issued some of the earliest commercial orchestral recordings. As a composer, his works include 2 symphonies and a violin concerto.

Stockhausen, Julius (Christian) (b. Paris, 22 July 1826; d. Frankfurt am Main, 22 Sept. 1906). Baritone and conductor. Son of harpist Franz (Anton Adam) Stockhausen (1789–1868) and soprano Margarethe Stockhausen (1803–77). Worked in Paris with Mathhäus Nagiller (harmony) and Manuel García (voice). First concert success in performance of *Elijah* in Basel (1848). Gave public premiere of *Die schöne Müllerin* (Vienna, 1856). At the Opéra-comique, Paris, 1856–59. Founded choral society in 1858 which focused on Bach cantatas. Director of Hamburg Philharmonic Concerts and Choir, 1863–67. Taught at Hoch Conservatory, Frankfurt, 1878–80, 1883–84. Wrote a 2-volume singing method, *Gesangsmethode* (Leipzig, 1884). Sang in the premiere of Brahms's German Requiem (1884); *Magelone Lieder* was written for him.

Stockhausen, Karlheinz (b. Mödrath, Germany, 22 Aug. 1928). Composer. He learned piano, oboe, and violin as a child. Orphaned during World War II, he graduated from secondary school in 1944 and worked at a variety of jobs: in a military hospital, as a farmhand, as a dance accompanist, as a jazz pianist. In 1947 he entered the Hochschule für Musik in Cologne. There he studied piano with Hans Otto Schmidt-Neuhaus, harmony with Hermann Schroeder, and for a short time composition with Frank Martin. Through Herbert Eimert he began working as a commentator at Radio Cologne; the first public performance of his music was a radio broadcast in 1951 of the Sonatine for violin and piano. Eimert also invited him to attend the summer courses for new music in Darmstadt. There, in 1951, he heard a recording of Olivier Messiaen's "Mode de valeurs et d'intensités" from *Quatre études de rhythme.* Messiaen's piece made an immense impression on Stockhausen, and he began at once to compose *Kreuzspiel* (oboe, bass clarinet, piano, and percussion, 1951), a work in which pitch, rhythm, and register are organized as part of a single serial process. *Kreuzspiel* was introduced at Darmstadt in 1952 but was not particularly successful, and Stockhausen withdrew it temporarily (until 1959).

Early in 1952 Stockhausen went to Paris to study with Messiaen. There he composed *Spiel* (orchestra, 1952; rev. 1973), *Schlagquartett* (piano and timpani, 1952, rev. 1973 as *Schlagtrio*), *Punkte* (1952; rev. 1962), *Kontra-punkte* (1952; rev. 1953), and *Klavierstücke I–IV* (1952–53). In these works he extended the

Karlheinz Stockhausen, 1985.

ultraserial procedures he had broached in *Kreuzspiel.* In Paris he also became involved in the new field of electronic music. He met Pierre Schaeffer, the apostle of *musique concrète,* and worked as an apprentice in the electronic studios of the French radio (ORTF) studying instrumental timbres and their transformations.

In 1953 he returned to Cologne to work at the electronic music studio that Eimert had set up at North German Radio. Here he produced two short electronic studies (*Elektronische Studie I,* 1953; *Elektronische Studie II,* 1954), then *Gesang der Jünglinge* (1956), a studio-produced work in which electronically generated sounds are combined with the human voice. The text, drawn from the biblical story of the three youths in the fiery furnace (Daniel 3), is sung by a boy soprano, but the voice is processed in the studio to such a degree that it can be mixed freely into the texture of electronic sounds. Premiered in Cologne in 1956 and released as a record in 1958, *Gesang der Jünglinge* became one of the first widely popular pieces of electronic music. During the same period (1953–57) Stockhausen composed several instrumental pieces: *Klavierstücke V–VIII* (1954–55), *Zeitmasze* (oboe, flute, English horn, clarinet, bassoon, 1955–56), *Gruppen* (3 orchestras, 1955–57). In these works Stockhausen extended serial control over more and more musical parameters (pitch, register, rhythm, tempo, timbre) while at the same time leaving room for a certain amount of free choice on the part of composer and performers.

By 1957 Stockhausen had established himself as a leading figure in the European avant-garde. His new works were promptly performed and recorded; articles and interviews in which he explained his intentions and his methods were widely discussed. He gathered around himself in Cologne a loyal group of students, performers, and collaborators who helped him realize his projects. He visited the U.S. in 1958 and again in 1962 to lecture and to perform. His works from the late 1950s and the mid-60s extend his previous ideas in several directions. Many use the spatial arrangement of the performers as significant musical aspect. In *Carré* (1959–60) four orchestras and four choirs are placed on four separate stages. In *Kontakte* (1960) for electronic tape, piano, and percussion, four tape tracks are played over widely spaced speakers. Although Stockhausen's works of this period remain serial, the serial operations are no longer performed on single notes but rather on larger units that are defined by timbre, register, instrumentation, and gesture more than by pitch. *Momente* (soprano, 4 choirs, chamber ensemble, 1964) is an assay in this technique. During this period Stockhausen also began to leave much discretion to the performers and to chance. In *Zyklus* (1959) for solo percussion, the percussionist may start at any point in the score and in his circle of instruments and proceed in either direction until he has completed the circle. The score for *Klavierstück XI* (1956) consists of 19 fragments scattered over a large page. The pianist is instructed to let his eye wander over the score and begin with the first fragment that catches his eye, proceeding from fragment to fragment until he has played them all. Also during this period Stockhausen began to experiment with mixing human players and electronics in live performance. For example, in *Mikrophonie I* (1964) a single tam-tam is played by 2 players, while 4 more musicians move microphones around the instrument and process the sounds through filters.

From the late 1960s on Stockhausen's music tended toward ever-increasing grandeur, both of scale and of ideological ambition. In *Hymnen* (1967) he processed and combined the national anthems of various countries in a giant electronic collage, which aims to express and promote universal brotherhood. *Aus den Sieben Tagen* (1968) is a series of 15 pieces for various combinations, with a score consisting of nothing but verbal instructions toward realizing spiritual states in the music, for example, "Play the rhythm of the universe." *Sternklang* (1971), designed for outdoor performance, uses five groups of singers and instrumentalists, all intoning the names of the constellations of the zodiac. From 1978 on Stockhausen worked on the *Licht* series, a succession of large-scale stage works that combine elements of opera, dance, and ritual. He wrote his own scenarios and texts, basing them on myths and religious beliefs from around the world. His grand design aimed at a *Licht* event for each day of the week, with scenes and excerpts available for independent performance as they were composed. *Donnerstag aus Licht* was first performed in its entirety at

La Scala in Milan in 1980, *Samstag aus Licht* at Milan in 1984, *Montag aus Licht* at Cologne (concert version) and Milan (stage version) in 1988. Other works include *X i für Flöte* (1987); *Drachenkampf und Argument* (trumpet, trombone, synthesizer, tenor, bass, 2 dancers, percussion, 1987); *Eva's Erstgeburt* (1988); *Mädchenprozession und Zweitgeburt* (1988); Helicopter Quartet (string quartet, 4 helicopters, 1995).

Writings: *Texte I–III* (Cologne, 1963, 1964, 1971). ". . . How Time Passes . . . ," *Die Reihe* 3 (1957): 10–40. "The Concept of Unity in Electronic Music," *PNM* 1 (Fall 1962): 39–48. "Two Lectures—1. Electronic and Instrumental Music, 2. Music in Space," *Die Reihe* 5 (1959): 59–82.

Bibl.: Jonathan Harvey, *The Music of Stockhausen* (Berkeley, 1975). Robin Maconie, *The Works of Karlheinz Stockhausen* (London, 1976). Mya Tannenbaum, *Conversations with Stockhausen* (Oxford, 1985). *Stockhausen on Music: Lectures and Interviews,* ed. Robin Maconie (London, 1989). Hermann Conen, *Formel-Komposition: zu Karlheinz Stockhausens Musik der siebziger Jahre* (Mainz, 1991). Michael Kurtz, *Stockhausen: A Biography,* trans. Richard Toop (London, 1992).

Stoessel, Albert (Frederic) (b. St. Louis, 11 Oct. 1894; d. New York, 12 May 1943). Violinist, conductor, and composer. He studied violin as a child in St. Louis, then with Willi Hess at the Hochschule für Musik in Berlin, where he also studied composition and conducting. After touring in the U.S. as a violin soloist for several years, he succeeded Walter Damrosch as conductor of the Oratorio Society of New York in 1921. He served as head of the music department at New York Univ. from 1923 to 1930, director of the opera and orchestra departments at the Juilliard Graduate School from 1927 to 1943. He is the author of *Technic of the Baton* (1920; rev. 1928). Works include *Garrick,* opera (New York, 1937); *Cyrano de Bergerac,* orchestra (1922); Concerto grosso, piano and string orchestra (1935); *Flitting Bats,* violin and piano (1925).

Stoker, Richard (b. Castleford, Yorkshire, 8 Nov. 1938). Composer. He studied composition at the Royal Academy of Music with Fenby and Berkeley, then traveled to Paris to continue his study with Boulanger, who had a strong influence on him. He returned to England and in 1963 joined the faculty at the Royal Academy of Music. His music is in a serialistic style which utilizes a tonal centricity derived from functional tonality. Stoker frequently writes music for use in daily situations such as for theater or for children or amateurs. Served as editor of the new-music journal *Composer.* Works include *Petite Suite* op. 1 (1962), *Antic Hay* op. 2 (1962), 3 string quartets (op. 4, 1960; op. 9, 1966; op. 36, 1969), and several operas (*Chinese Canticle* op. 68, 1991).

Stokes, Eric (b. Haddon Heights, N.J., 14 July 1930). Composer. He studied at Lawrence College (B.Mus., 1952), New England Conservatory (M.Mus., 1956), and the Univ. of Minnesota (Ph.D., 1964); he went on to teach there, becoming professor in 1977. His works, often humorously experimental and iconoclastic, include 6 operas and other theater pieces, numerous orchestral and choral-orchestral works, chamber pieces (often using taped or live *concrète* sounds), and songs.

Stokowski, Leopold (Anthony) (b. London, 18 April 1882; d. Nether Wallop, Hampshire, 13 Sept. 1977). Conductor. Admitted to the Royal College of Music at age 13, he studied piano, organ, and composition (diploma, 1900). He also studied at Oxford (B.Mus., 1903). From 1902 to 1905 he was organist at St. James, Piccadilly; he also conducted small orchestras in London. In 1905 he moved to New York as organist and choir director at St. Bartholomew's Church on Madison Avenue. After conducting debuts in Paris and London, he was engaged in 1909 by the Cincinnati Symphony and became an immediate and overwhelming success. In 1912 he left Cincinnati and moved to the Philadelphia Orchestra, remaining in Philadelphia for 25 years, turning the orchestra into a world leader in the quality of its players, the character of its sound, and the diversity of its repertory. Beginning in Philadelphia and continuing throughout his career, he went to great lengths to find and to program new music. He recognized early the role that recordings could play in musical life, and he recorded prolifically; he also made himself into a public figure of great popularity and notoriety—America's first star conductor. Resigning from Philadelphia in 1938, he involved himself in new projects, including the Disney movie *Fantasia* (1940), the All-American Youth Orchestra (1940–41), the NBC Symphony (1941–44) and the New York City Symphony Orchestra (1944–45), and the Hollywood Bowl Concerts (1945–46). From 1955 to 1960 he was principal conductor of the Houston Symphony. In 1962 in New York he organized the American Symphony Orchestra, an orchestra primarily of young musicians, which he conducted until 1972. During all this period, despite his advanced age, he traveled widely, making guest appearances with major orchestras in Europe and the U.S. He continued to conduct until 1975 and to record until 1977.

Writings: *Music for All of Us* (New York, 1943).

Bibl.: Oliver Daniel, *Stokowski: A Counterpoint of View* (New York, 1982). Preben Opperby, *Leopold Stokowski* (New York, 1982). William Ander Smith, *The Mystery of Leopold Stokowski* (Rutherford, N.J., 1990).

Stoltz, Rosine [Noël, Victoire] (b. Paris, 13 Feb. 1815; d. there, 28 July 1903). Mezzo-soprano. Used the concert name Rose Niva in early career. Stage debut as Victoire Ternaux, 1832, in Brussels. Later used the name Heloise Stoltz. Paris Opéra debut, 1837, in *La juive* as Rosine Stoltz; remained at Opéra until 1847, resigning in a scandal as mistress of Léon Pillet, director of Opéra.

Stoltzer, Thomas (b. Schweidnitz, Silesia, ca. 1475; d. near Znaim, Moravia, early 1526). Composer. He may have studied with Finck. From 1519 he served as parish priest and cathedral vicar in Breslau. From 1522 he was *magister cappellae* to the Hungarian royal court at Ofen under Ludwig II. He drowned in the Taja River. His music circulated in print and manuscript widely throughout Germany from the 1520s through the 1570s. His 150 extant works include 4 Masses, 5 Magnificats, 18 Psalm motets (4 in German), many shorter motets and hymns, a few German sacred and secular lieder, and a set of 8 fantasias.

Stoltzman, Richard (b. Omaha, 12 July 1942). Clarinetist. He studied with his father as a child; he took degrees in music from Ohio State Univ. (1964) and Yale (1967). He became associated with the Marlboro Festival and cofounded the chamber ensemble Tashi with Peter Serkin. After teaching at California Institute of the Arts (1970–75), he pursued an international concert career, maintaining a wide repertory of classical music and jazz including many transcriptions and commissions.

Stolz, Robert (Elisabeth) (b. Graz, Austria, 25 Aug. 1880; d. Berlin, 27 June 1975). Composer and conductor. The son of a conductor and a concert pianist, he studied at the Vienna Conservatory, then with Humperdinck in Berlin. Beginning in 1898 he conducted in a series of theaters, including the Theater an der Wien in Vienna (1905–12). Beginning with *Studentenulke* (Marburg, 1899), he turned out a string of operettas, of which *Der Tanz ins Gluck* (1921) was perhaps the best known. In 1924 he went to Berlin, where he composed music for film musicals. *Zwei Herzen im Dreivierteltakt* (1930) became an international hit. Fleeing Berlin in 1936, he went to Vienna, Paris, and finally to the U.S. (1940–46), where he wrote for Hollywood films. Returning to Austria in 1946, he continued to compose operettas and to conduct.

Bibl.: Othmar Herbrich, *Robert Stolz, König der Melodie* (Munich, 1975). Aram Bakshian, ed., *The Barbed Wire Waltz: The Memoirs of the Last Waltz King* (Melbourne, 1983).

Stolz [Stolzová], **Teresa** [Teresina, Terezie] (b. Elbekosteletz [Kostelec nad Labem], 5 June 1834; d. Milan, 23 Aug. 1902). Soprano. Studied at Prague Conservatory. Operatic debut, 1857, at Tbilisi. A favorite of Verdi; she was the first Italian Aida (1872). Toured in Verdi's Requiem (1874). After 1872, sang almost exclusively Verdian roles.

Stölzel [Stöltzel], **Gottfried Heinrich** (b. Grünstädtel, near Schwarzenberg, Erzgebirge, 13 Jan. 1690; d. Gotha, 27 Nov. 1749). Composer and theorist. He studied in Schneeberg with the Kantor Christian Umlaufft, and later attended the Gymnasium in Gera. He then went to Leipzig Univ. in 1707, studying with Melchior Hofmann. From 1710 to 1712 he taught singing and keyboard in Breslau. Following some time in Italy and Prague, he became Kapellmeister at the Gera (1718) and Saxe-Gotha (1720) courts, remaining at the latter for the rest of his life. Stölzel wrote a treatise on canon (1725), and his *Abhandlung vom Recitativ* is the earliest treatise on recitative. Besides operas, he wrote sacred and secular vocal works as well as many pieces of chamber music.

Stölzel [Stoelzel], **Heinrich** (b. Scheibenberg, Saxony, 1772; d. Berlin, 1844). Instrument maker. He began manufacturing brass instruments before retiring in 1829 from the Royal Opera Orchestra in Berlin. Little is known of his career. He produced the first satisfactory piston valves on brass instruments.

Stone, Sly [Stewart, Sylvester] (b. Dallas, 15 Mar. 1944). Rock singer, songwriter, and instrumentalist. In 1968 he formed Sly and the Family Stone; they became popular through an appearance at Woodstock and several successful recordings (including "Dance to the Music," "Everyday People," both 1968; "Family Affair," 1971). Their style, which mixed elements of soul with psychedelic rock, was an important precursor of 1970s funk.

Stoquerus, Gaspar (fl. ca. 1570). Theorist. He was born of German lineage, probably as Caspar Stocker. He apparently lived briefly in Venice, then in Salamanca, where he studied with Salinas at the university. He authored a unique treatise on polyphonic text underlay, *De musica verbali libri duo,* an expansion of Zarlino's *Le istitutioni harmoniche,* bk. 4, chap. 33, which illuminates the practices of Willaert and the previous (Josquin's) generation.

Storace, Nancy [Ann Selina; Anna] (b. London, 27 Oct. 1765; d. there, 24 Aug. 1817). Soprano. Sister of composer Stephen Storace. She studied with Sacchini and Rauzzini in London. She sang in Florence, Milan, Parma, Vienna (from 1783 to 1787); returned to London in 1787. Mozart wrote the role of Susanna in *Le nozze di Figaro* for her; earlier she had portrayed Rosina in Paisiello's *Il barbiere di Siviglia.*

Storace, Stephen (John Seymour) (b. London, 4 Apr. 1762; d. there, 19 Mar. 1796). Composer. Son of Stephen Storace (b. Torre Annunziata, ca. 1725; d. ca. 1781), a double bass player. He studied with his father and, later, at the Conservatorio S. Onofrio in Naples. He joined his sister Nancy in Vienna, and 2 of his comic operas were produced there: *Gli sposi malcontenti* (1785) and *Gli equivoci* (1786). During this time he became friendly with Mozart. In 1787 he returned to London; he continued to write operas, including *La cameriera astuta* and *Dido, Queen of Carthage* (performed at the King's Theatre in 1788 and 1792, respectively). *The Haunted Tower* (Drury Lane, London, 1789) enjoyed great success. He wrote several other operas, adaptations of operas by other composers; other vocal works including *Lamentation of Marie Antoinette on the Morning of Her Execution* (voice, strings, and bassoon); a ballet, *Venus and Adonis;* chamber works.

Bibl.: Roger Fiske, "The Operas of Stephen Storace," *PRMA* 86 (1959–60): 29–44. Jane C. Girdham, "Stephen

Storace and the English Opera Tradition of the Late Eighteenth Century" (diss., Univ. of Pennsylvania, 1988).

Storchio, Rosina (b. Venice, 19 May 1876; d. Milan, 24 July 1945). Soprano. Attended the Milan Conservatory; made her debut in *Carmen* in 1892, her La Scala debut in 1895. She created roles in premieres of operas by Leoncavallo, Mascagni, and Puccini, among them the title role of *Madama Butterfly* in 1904. She also sang at Barcelona (1898–1923), Buenos Aires (1904–14), and Chicago (1921).

Stout, Alan (b. Baltimore, 26 Nov. 1932). Composer. He studied simultaneously at Johns Hopkins Univ. (B.S., 1954) and at the Peabody Conservatory, where he was a pupil of Henry Cowell. He also studied privately with Wallingford Riegger, with Vagn Holmboe in Copenhagen, and with John Verrall at the Univ. of Washington (M.A., 1959). During the 1950s he supported himself by working intermittently as a music librarian, meanwhile composing 10 string quartets (1953–1962), several songs (*Die Engel,* soprano and chamber ensemble, 1957; *Ariel Songs,* soprano and chamber ensemble, 1957), and his First Symphony (1959). He also began work on several other pieces, including his Second and Third symphonies and a Passion. The Third Symphony (soprano, male chorus and orchestra) was finished in 1962, along with the *Movements* for violin and orchestra, *Canticum canticorum* for soprano and chamber ensemble, and the *George Lieder* for baritone and orchestra. In 1963 Stout moved to Chicago to teach at Northwestern Univ. In 1966 he completed his Second Symphony (begun in 1951), which was premiered by the Chicago Symphony in 1968 and attracted attention for its novel orchestral textures and complex rhythms. His Passion was finished in 1975 and performed by the Chicago Symphony in 1976. Other works include Clarinet Quintet (1958); Cello Sonata (1966); *Nocturnes* (narrator, contralto, and chamber ensemble, 1970); *Suite* (saxophone and organ, 1973); Sonata for 2 Pianos (1975); *Nimbus* (string orchestra, 1978); Brass Quintet (1984).

Stoyanov, Veselin (b. Shumen, 20 Apr. 1902; d. Sofia, 29 June 1969). Composer. He came from a musical family; his brother Andrei was a pianist who, with Veselin, studied at the Bulgarian State Conservatory in Sofia. Veselin then went on, after graduating in 1926, to study with Marx and Schmidt in Vienna. He returned to Sofia and in 1937 joined the faculty at the conservatory there. He served as its head, 1943–44 and 1956–62. His compositions are in a post-Romantic extended tonal style, with lush orchestration and traditional formal processes. Early in his career Stoyanov utilized quotations from folk song and, later, more germanely incorporated characteristics of that music. Works include stage music (*Hitar Peter* [Cunning Peter], premiered 1958) and orchestral music (3 piano concertos, 1942, 1953, 1966; Symphony no. 2, *Welikii Preslaw* [The Great Preslaw], 1969).

Strada del Pò, Anna Maria (fl. 1720–40). Soprano. A native of Bergamo, she was briefly in the service of Count Colloredo, governor of Milan (1720–21). During that season she sang in operas at Venice, including Vivaldi's *La verità in cimento.* From 1724 to 1726 she sang at Naples in operas by Vinci, Porta, Leo, and Porpora. Handel heard her in 1729 and engaged her for London; from then until 1 June 1737 she was his principal soprano, singing roles in 24 of his operas in addition to serenatas and oratorios.

Stradella, Alessandro (b. Nepi, ca. 1639; d. Genoa, 25 Feb. 1682). Composer. Before 1664 he studied in Bologna, although with whom and for how long is not known. He probably left Nepi for good in 1664, and was in Rome by 1667. During this time he wrote stage works, oratorios, prologues and intermezzos to operas, and motets. Because he came from a noble family, he was not dependent on any patron or institution; his compositions were written on commission. In 1669 Stradella was involved in an attempt to embezzle funds from the church; he left Rome for a time to let the scandal quiet down. About 1670–72, his *Il Biante,* an *azione drammatica,* was performed in honor of Pope Clement X. In 1677 Stradella again fled Rome after angering Cardinal Alderan Cibo. He went to Venice, where he taught music to Alvise Contarini's mistress. Stradella and the lady absconded to Turin, where they were tracked down by Contarini and his "relatives and thugs." The composer escaped to Genoa, narrowly avoiding death at the hands of Contarini's assassins. There his comic opera *Il Trespolo tutore* (ca. 1677) was performed, and was followed by productions of *La forza dell'amor paterno* (1678) and *Le gare dell'amor eroico* (1679). In 1681 his oratorio *Susanna* was heard at Modena. Following an intrigue with a married woman in the Lomellini family of Genoa, Stradella was murdered by a hired assassin. His vocal works include 7 operas, prologues, intermezzos, a Mass, motets, cantatas, arias, and canzonettas. Most of his 27 instrumental works are *sonate da chiesa.* The Sonata di viole is the earliest known concerto grosso.

Bibl.: Carolyn Gianturco and Eleanor McCrickard, *Alessandro Stradella (1639–1682): A Thematic Catalogue of His Compositions* (New York, 1989). Eleanor McCrickard, "Temporal and Tonal Aspects of Alessandro Stradella's Instrumental Music," *AnMca* 19 (1979): 186–243. Articles in *Alessandro Stradella e Modena: Atti del Convegno internazionale di studi,* ed. Carolyn Gianturco (Modena, 1985). Carolyn Gianturco, *Alessandro Stradella (1639–1682): His Life and Music* (Oxford, 1994).

Stradivari, Antonio (b. Cremona?, 1644; d. there?, 18 Dec. 1737). Instrument maker. He may have been apprenticed as a woodcarver before becoming a pupil of Nicolo Amati in Cremona by 1666. In July 1667 he married Francesca Feraboschi; two of their six children, Francesco (b. 1 Feb. 1671; d. 11 May 1743) and Omobono (b. 14 Nov. 1679; d. 8 June 1742), became Antonio's co-workers. Before 1680 Stradivari probably produced other instruments in addition to violins: harps, lutes, mandolins, guitars, and a tromba marina. Of these only two guitars and the neck of a third survive. In 1680 he and his family moved to the Piazza S. Domenico, where he remained for the rest of his life. Around this time he began to distance himself from Amati's style, and increased his output of violins and cellos. Following Amati's death in 1684, Stradivari's fame spread beyond Cremona. After 1690 he further refined his style and devised the "Long Strad" design. He is generally considered to have produced his greatest instruments in the period from about 1700 to 1720. Around this time he began making smaller cellos in response to the emergence of the virtuoso cellist; these have served as models for makers since the early 19th century. Stradivari continued to make violins until his death.

Bibl.: William H., Arthur F., and Alfred E. Hill, *Antonio Stradivari: His Life and Work* (London, 1902; 2nd ed., 1909; R: 1963). Isaak Vigdorchik, *The Acoustical Systems of Violins of Stradivarius and Other Cremona Makers* (Westbury, N.Y., 1982). Elia Santoro, *Antonius Stradivarius* (Cremona, 1987).

Strang, Gerald (b. Claresholm, Alberta, 13 Feb. 1908; d. Loma Linda, Calif., 2 Oct. 1983). Composer, acoustician. He grew up in Great Falls, Montana, where he took lessons on piano, organ, and violin. He studied at Stanford Univ. (B.A., 1928), then went to the Univ. of California, Berkeley, to study composition. In 1935 he became acquainted with Schoenberg, serving first as his teaching assistant at UCLA (1936–38), then as his editor and factotum (1938–50). Strang's works from the 1940s and 1950s, though heavily influenced by Schoenberg and twelve-tone techniques, still contain many references to tonal harmonies, for example, in Symphony no. 1 (1954), Concerto grosso (orchestra, 1950), and the Cello Concerto (1951). During the 1950s and 1960s he also worked as an acoustical consultant, contributing to the design of many auditoriums, studios, and other music facilities. He was on the faculty at UCLA (1969–74). In 1963 Strang stopped composing for traditional instruments and turned to electronic and computer music exclusively, calling his computer pieces *Compusitions,* his synthesized tape pieces *Synthions.*

Bibl.: Leonard Stein, "Gerald Strang (1908–1983)," *Journal of the Arnold Schoenberg Institute* 7 (1983): 255–62.

Strange, (John) Allen (b. Calexico, Calif., 26 June 1943). Composer. He studied with Donal Michalsky at California State Univ., Fullerton (B.A., M.A., 1967), then at the Univ. of California, San Diego, with Robert Erickson, Kenneth Gaburo, and Pauline Oliveros. In 1970 he became professor of music and director of the electronic music studio at San Jose State Univ. Most of his works involve electronics, often in combination with traditional (though amplified) instruments. Sometimes the electronics are live (i.e., generated in performance), as in *Western Connection* (orchestra and electronics, 1972) and *Soundbeams* (chamber ensemble and electronics, 1977); sometimes they are taped, as in *The Hairbreath Ring Screamers* (flutes and tape, 1969) and *Velocity Studies* (violin and tape, 1983). He is the author of *Electronic Music: Systems, Techniques and Controls* (Dubuque, Iowa, 1972; rev. 1983).

Stransky, Josef (b. Humpolec, Bohemia, 9 Sept. 1872; d. New York, 6 Mar. 1936). Conductor. Originally a medical student, he made his professional conducting debut at the German Theater, Prague, in 1898; conducted the Hamburg Opera (from 1903) and the Blüthner Orchestra at Berlin (from 1910); succeeded Mahler with the New York Philharmonic in 1911, remaining until 1923; conducted the New York State Symphony until 1924, when he left music for a career as an art merchant.

Stratas, Teresa [Strataki, Anastasia] (b. Toronto, 26 May 1938). Soprano. Sang Greek popular music as a teen; studied at the Royal Conservatory, Toronto, from 1954 to 1958, making her debut in the latter year; performed frequently at the Metropolitan Opera from 1959; sang in the posthumous premiere of Falla's *Atlántida* at La Scala in 1962, and appeared with major orchestras and at festivals. She took the title role in the 1979 premiere of the 3-act version of *Lulu,* played Violetta in Franco Zeffirelli's film of *La traviata,* and in 1991 created the role of Marie Antoinette in *The Ghosts of Versailles.*

Straube, Karl (b. Berlin, 6 Jan. 1873; d. Leipzig, 27 Apr. 1950). Organist. Studied with his father and with Heinrich Reimann, serving the latter as assistant at a Berlin church from 1895 to 1897, when he moved to Wesel as organist. At the Thomaskirche, Leipzig, as organist (from 1902) and Kantor (1918–38). He formed the Kirchenmusikalisches Institut at the Leipzig Conservatory in 1919. A close associate of Reger, he conducted a great deal of Bach's music.

Bibl.: Günter Hartmann, *Karl Straube und seine Schule: "Das Ganze ist ein Mythos"* (Bonn, 1991).

Straus, Oscar (b. Vienna, 6 Mar. 1870; d. Bad Ischl, Austria, 11 Jan. 1954). Composer. He studied composition with Hermann Grädener in Vienna, then with Max Bruch in Berlin. From 1893 to 1899 he conducted theater orchestras in various Austrian and German cities, at the same time composing songs and piano music. In 1900 he went to work as the pianist and resident composer at the Überbrettl, the famous Berlin cabaret. Returning to Vienna, he composed a string of operettas, of which *Ein Walzertraum* (1907), *Der tapfere Soldat* (1908), *Der letzte Walzer* (1920), and *Drei Walzer* (1935) were particularly successful. He fled Vienna in 1939, going first to France, then to the U.S., where he lived in New York and Hollywood. He returned to Austria in 1948, settling in Bad Ischl.

Bibl.: Bernard Grün, *Prince of Vienna: The Life, Times, and Melodies of Oscar Straus* (London, 1955). Franz Mailer, *Weltbürger der Musik: eine Oscar-Straus-Biographie* (Vienna, 1985).

Strauss, Eduard (b. Vienna, 15 Mar. 1835; d. there, 28 Dec. 1916). Composer and conductor. Youngest son of Johann Strauss, Sr. His elder brother Johann Jr. influenced his decision to turn to music. Studied theory with Gottfried Preyer and Simon Sechter, violin with Amar, harp with Parish-Alvars and Zamara. Debuted as a composer and conductor in Dianabad-Saal, 1862. Replaced Johann Jr. as conductor on a tour of Russia in 1865. Co-conducted the Strauss Orchestra with brother Josef until 1870. From 1872 to 1878 he was Director of Court Balls. Toured London in 1885, the U.S. in 1890. Composed over 300 waltzes and polkas.

Strauss, Franz Joseph (b. Parkstein, 26 Feb. 1822; d. Munich, 31 May 1905). Horn player and composer. Principal horn of Munich Court Opera Orchestra, 1847–89. Taught at Munich Academy beginning 1896. Wrote horn concertos, pieces for horn and piano; Theme and Variations op. 13, harp and piano. Though he did not care for Wagner's music, he played the premieres of *Tristan* (1865), *Die Meistersinger* (1868), and *Parsifal* (1882).

Strauss, Johann (Baptist), Sr. (b. Vienna, 14 Mar. 1804; d. there, 25 Sept. 1849). Composer, dance orchestra director. Apparently largely self-taught as a musician; played the violin in his father's saloon, later the viola in Pamer's well-known dance orchestra. In 1819 he joined a small ensemble headed by Lanner, which grew to a full dance orchestra, then in 1824 divided into two orchestras with Strauss violinist-director of the second, becoming independent of Lanner in 1825 after quarrels. By 1826 he had begun to compose waltzes and galops, publishing them from 1827, adding to the quickly growing popularity of his orchestra. From 1832 also music director of a local regiment, for which he composed marches. From 1833 to 1838, toured much with his orchestra: Budapest (1833), Austria-Germany (1834–35), Germany, Holland, Belgium (1836), Paris (1837–38), where he was warmly received, Great Britain (1838), taking part in the coronation festivities; but he collapsed on the podium at Calais on the return trip and afterward made only brief tours. It was the fire, piquancy, and precision of his orchestra that impressed his audiences as much as his compositions, which in the 1840s expanded to include the newly popular polkas and quadrilles, which Strauss brought back from Paris and made popular in Vienna. In 1846 he was given the newly created title Director of Music for Court Balls. He died of scarlet fever. His compositions run to 250 opus numbers, the majority being waltzes. His most famous composition is, however, a march: the *Radetzky-Marsch,* still played at every Vienna Philharmonic New Year's Concert.

Strauss, Johann (Baptist), Jr. (b. Vienna, 25 Oct. 1825; d. there, 3 June 1899). Composer, dance orchestra director. Son of Johann Strauss, Sr., who wanted him to go into business. With his mother's connivance he had secret music lessons from the first violinist of his father's orchestra, openly studying the violin and theory after his father left the family in 1842 to live with another woman. In 1844, organized his own 15-man dance orchestra; it and the waltzes he composed for it quickly won him popularity rivaling his father's, whose orchestra was combined with his after the elder man's death.

Somewhat ironically for one who is often regarded as embodying the spirit of imperial Vienna, during the 1848 Revolution Strauss composed marches with titles suggesting liberal sympathies (*Revolutions-Marsch* op. 54, *Studenten-Marsch* op. 56), which he hastened to counteract after the Revolution's failure (*Kaiser Franz Joseph Marsch* op. 67), but he only slowly won favor at court. From 1853 he directed the music of court balls but was not given his father's old title of Director of Music for Court Balls until 1863. From 1846, toured with his orchestra (Styria and Hungary); 1847, Serbia, Romania; 1851, Prague, Germany, Warsaw; then much of western Europe; from 1855, spent 16 lucrative summers at a resort near St. Petersburg.

His health suffering from the orchestra's arduous activity, in 1853 he was joined as co-director by his brother Josef and in 1862 by their youngest brother, Eduard; on receiving his court title in 1863, he gave up an active part in the family orchestra. By 1860 he had published over 200 waltzes, polkas, quadrilles, marches. The 1860s began the period of his great symphonic waltzes, including most of those still heard. After resigning his court post in 1871, he capitalized on his great international celebrity by guest-conducting concerts of his music throughout Europe. In 1872, took part in Gilmore's mammoth International Peace Jubilee in Boston; after 1870, composed relatively few instrumental dances, though some of his best-known waltzes (*Wiener-Blut* op. 354, 1873; *Frühlingsstimmen* op. 410, 1883; *Kaiser-Waltz* op. 437, 1889). Devoting himself mainly to operetta, he produced 15 (13 at the Theater an der Wien), a new one every year or two from 1871 through 1887, with varying success, fewer thereafter. His most enduring, *Die Fledermaus* (1874), was coldly received in Vienna, beginning its rise to worldwide popularity in Berlin and Paris. Only *Der Zigeunerbaron* (1884) has also kept a hold on the standard repertory, although to a lesser degree, Strauss's music in this genre often having dramatically inept librettos. He also attempted a fully composed comic opera for the Vienna Opera, *Ritter Pázmán,* a failure (1892; 9 perfomances). He died from complications of a cold caught while conducting.

Bibl.: *Strauss-Elementar-Verzeichnis (SEV): thematisch-bibliographischer Katalog der Werke von Johann Strauss (Sohn)* (Tutzing, 1990–). A. Weinmann, *Verzeichnis sämtlicher Werke von Johann Strauss Vater und Sohn* (Vienna, 1956). J. Pastene, *Three-Quarter Time: The Life and Music of the Strauss Family of Vienna* (New York, 1951). J. Wechsberg, *The Waltz Emperors* (London, 1973). Norbert Linke, *Johann Strauss (Sohn) in Selbstzeugnissen und Bilddokumenten dargestellt* (Reinbek bei Hamburg, 1982). Franz Mailer, *Leben und Werk in Briefen und Dokumenten Johann Strauss (Sohn)* (Tutzing, 1983). Marcel Prawy, *Johann Strauss* (Vienna, 1991).

Strauss, Johann (Maria Eduard) (b. Vienna, 16 Feb. 1866; d. Berlin, 9 Jan. 1939). Composer and conductor. His father was Eduard Strauss. He left his job as an accountant to enter the field of music. Served as Director of Court Balls, 1901–5, then moved to Berlin. Compositions include the operetta *Katze und Maus* (1898); the "polka schnell" *Schlau-Schlau* op. 6; other dance pieces.

Strauss, Josef [Joseph] (b. Vienna, 22 Aug. 1827; d. there, 21 July 1870). Composer and conductor. Son of Johann Strauss, Sr. Studied with Franz Dolleschal and Franz Amon. Composed a set of waltzes, conducting the premiere in 1853. Co-conductor of the Strauss Orchestra. Frequently served as guest conductor, traveling to many European cities. He collaborated with his brother Johann Jr. on a few works. Composed over 200 waltzes and polkas, 8 marches, 11 quadrilles.

Strauss, Richard (Georg) (b. Munich, 11 June 1864; d. Garmisch-Partenkirchen, Bavaria, 8 Sept. 1949). Composer. Son of Franz Joseph Strauss. He studied piano and violin from an early age and took lessons in theory, harmony, and instrumentation. In 1874 he entered the Ludwigsgymnasium in Munich and in 1877 joined his father's semiprofessional orchestra as a violinist, gradually moving up to the front desks. He was already composing and had several works performed in Munich during March 1881. The following year his Violin Concerto was performed in Vienna, and his Serenade in E♭ for 13 wind instruments was performed in Dresden. He entered Munich Univ. in 1882 but left in 1883 to concentrate on music. During the winter of 1883–84 he went to Berlin, where he heard operas, wrote a symphony, and met Hans von Bülow, then conductor of the Meiningen Court Orchestra. Von Bülow was impressed with Strauss's Serenade, which he performed in Berlin, and invited the composer to write a piece for Meiningen. The result was the Suite in B♭, first performed in Munich in November 1884 by the Meiningen Orchestra, with Strauss conducting.

Between 1881 and 1885 Strauss worked productively, composing the Horn Concerto no. 1, the Cello Sonata, the Piano Quartet, *Wanderers Sturmlied* for chorus and orchestra, the Symphony no. 2 in F minor (premiered in New York), and nine songs ("Zueignung," "Die Nacht," and "Allerseelen"). In the summer of 1885 he accepted von Bülow's offer to become assistant conductor at Meiningen. That fall Strauss succeeded von Bülow as conductor and became third conductor at the Munich Court Opera; he left Meiningen in April 1886 and stayed in Munich for three years, during which time he composed the symphonic fantasy *Aus Italien* (1886) and the symphonic poems (or tone poems, as he called them) *Macbeth* (1886–88) and *Don Juan* (1888–89). In the summer of 1889 Strauss worked as a répétiteur at Bayreuth.

At Weimar the first performance of *Don Juan* on 11 November 1889 marked his most important triumph to date; he was now hailed as the greatest German composer since Wagner. In 1890 he conducted the first performances of his *Burleske* for piano and orchestra and the tone poem *Tod und Verklärung* at an Eisenach concert. During the winter of 1892–93 he went to Egypt to recover from a serious illness; there he completed his first opera, *Guntram*. In 1894 he declined an offer by the Berlin Philharmonic to take over von Bülow's concerts and instead went back to Munich as associate to Hermann Levi. With Levi ailing, he was able to conduct operas by Wagner and Mozart.

For the next five years Strauss was remarkably prolific, composing many lieder and some of his most popular orchestral works: *Till Eulenspiegels lustige Streiche* (1894–95), *Also sprach Zarathustra* (1895–96), *Don Quixote* (1896–97), and *Ein Heldenleben* (1897–98). But conducting remained his primary activity: in 1896 he became chief conductor of the Munich Opera, and the following year guest-conducted his own works in Holland, Spain, France, and England. In 1898 he became chief conductor of the Royal Court Opera in Berlin. Following the satirical opera *Feuersnot* (libretto by Ernst von Wolzogen, 1900–1901), Strauss increasingly turned his attention to writing operas. His next major work, however, was the Symphonia domestica, a work that Strauss premiered in New York in 1904. The opera *Salome* (1903–5), a setting of a German translation of Oscar Wilde's play, caused an uproar and considerable censorship trouble. But the shocking subject matter ensured the opera's success following its Dresden premiere on 9 December 1905; Strauss built a villa at Garmisch with his royalties.

Elektra (1906–8) marked the start of his association with the Austrian poet and dramatist Hugo von Hofmannsthal, and it received its first performance at Dresden under Ernst von Schuch on 25 January 1909. With *Der Rosenkavalier* (1909–10) Strauss had his greatest public success, although some lamented his retreat from the boldness of the two preceding operas. His next opera was the first version of *Ariadne auf Naxos* (1911–12), which was coupled in performance with Molière's *Le bourgeois gentilhomme* with incidental music by Strauss. The second version of the opera (1916), with a sung prologue substituting for the play, was scarcely more successful than the first. While in England in 1914 for a performance of his ballet *Josephs-Legende* (written for Diaghilev, 1912–14), Strauss received an honorary D.Mus. from Oxford Univ. By this time he was already at work on another opera, *Die Frau ohne Schatten* (1914–18). When the outbreak of war interrupted his progress, Strauss finished scoring his tone poem *Eine Alpensinfonie* (1911–15). His idea for a "realistic domestic and character comedy" based on a misunderstanding between his wife, Pauline, and himself did not appeal to Hofmannsthal, who suggested Hermann Bahr as a librettist. In the end, it was Strauss who wrote the libretto of *Intermezzo,* completing it in 1917. The music, however, was not completed until 1923.

In 1918 he ended his eight-year association with the Berlin opera as guest conductor and entered a five-year contract with the Vienna Staatsoper. Despite his considerable artistic success in Vienna, Strauss's uneasy relationship with co-director Franz Schalk and the management of the Staatsoper led to his resignation in 1924. The failure of his next opera, *Die ägyptische Helena* (1923–27), did little to help his reputation among the critics; he was increasingly viewed as a composer with nothing left to say. While at work on the libretto of *Arabella,* Hofmannsthal died of a stroke (1929). Strauss nevertheless resolved to compose the music, finally completing the opera in 1932.

In 1931 Strauss had found a new librettist, novelist and biographer Stefan Zweig. Their first project was an adaptation of Ben Jonson's *Epicene, or The Silent Woman,* which became *Die schweigsame Frau* (1933–34). When the National Socialists came to power in Germany in 1933, they were quick to use Strauss as a propaganda tool: Goebbels appointed him president of the state music bureau, the Reichsmusikkamer, without consulting the composer. Meanwhile, Zweig (a Jew) had gone to Zurich, where he was to take on the secret role of consultant and supervisor to Strauss. When Strauss insisted that Zweig be given credit on posters and programs for *Die schweigsame Frau,* the composer was ordered to resign his presidency of the Reichsmusikkammer.

The librettos for Strauss's next three operas were written by the Viennese theatrical archivist Josef Gregor: *Friedenstag* (1935–36), based on an episode in the Thirty Years' War; *Daphne* (1936–37), intended to be performed with *Friedenstag;* and *Die Liebe der Danae* (after a Hofmannsthal scenario, 1938–40). The conductor Clemens Krauss wrote the libretto for Strauss's last opera, *Capriccio* (1940–41).

In 1941 Strauss and his family were allowed to move back to their home in Vienna, where he wrote his Horn Concerto no. 2 and the First Sonatina for wind instruments. In 1945 he wrote the Oboe Concerto and the elegiac *Metamorphosen* for strings. In October that year he and his wife went to Switzerland in order to avoid a denazification tribunal. Beecham organized a Strauss festival in London in 1947, and the composer spent most of October there. After a serious operation, Strauss returned to Garmisch in May 1949, his name having been cleared by the denazification board in 1948. His last work was the four songs with orchestra (1948), published posthumously as *Vier letzte Lieder.* Soon after the Munich celebrations of his 85th birthday his heart began to fail, and he died on 8 September 1949.

Bibl.: Erich Hermann Mueller von Asow, *Richard Strauss: Thematisches Verzeichnis,* 3 vols. (Vienna, 1954–74). Franz Trenner, *Richard Strauss Werkverzeichnis* (Vienna, 1985). Donald Daviau and George Buelow, *The "Ariadne auf Naxos" of Hugo von Hofmannsthal and Richard Strauss* (Chapel Hill, 1975). Alan Jefferson, *Richard Strauss* (London, 1975). Michael Kennedy, *Richard Strauss* (London, 1976). Barbara Peterson, *Ton und Wort: The Lieder of Richard Strauss* (Ann Arbor, 1979). Rudolf Hartmann, *Richard Strauss: The Staging of His Operas and Ballets* (Oxford, 1982). R. Schlötter, *Musik und Theater im "Rosenkavalier" vom Richard Strauss* (Vienna, 1985). G. Splitt, *Richard Strauss, 1933–35: Ästhetik und Musikpolitik zu Beginn der nationalsozialistischen Herrschaft* (Pfaffenweiler, 1987). Charles Osborne, *The Complete Operas of Richard Strauss* (London, 1988). Kurt Wilhelm, *Richard Strauss: An Intimate Portrait* (New York, 1989). David B. Greene, *Listening to Strauss Operas: The Audience's Multiple Standpoints* (New York, 1991). Bryan Gilliam, *Richard Strauss's "Elektra"* (Oxford, 1991). Bryan Gilliam, ed., *Richard Strauss and His World* (Princeton, 1992). Bryan Gilliam, ed., *Richard Strauss: New Perspectives on the Composer and His Music* (Durham, N.C., 1992). John Williamson, *Strauss, "Also sprach Zarathustra"* (Cambridge, 1993).

Stravinsky, Feodor (b. Voviy Dvor, Minsk, 20 June 1843; d. St. Petersburg, 4 Dec. 1902). Bass. He studied law, but left to embark on a singing career. Entered St. Petersburg Conservatory with Camille Everardi, 1869–73. He was engaged at Kiev until 1876. Had a repertory of over 60 roles, including many Russian roles, and created roles in Tchaikovsky's *Mazeppa* and Rimsky's *Sadko.*

Bibl.: V. M. Bogdanov-Berezovsky, *Fyodor Stravinsky* (Moscow and Leningrad, 1951).

Stravinsky, Igor Fyodorovich (b. Oranienbaum, near St. Petersburg, 17 June 1882; d. New York, 6 Apr. 1971). Composer. Descended from the noble Polish Sulima-Strawinski family, Igor was the third of four sons of Feodor Stravinsky, the eminent operatic bass, and grew up in musical and theatrical surroundings. From age 9 he studied piano, later harmony and counterpoint. Having poor health, from age 14 he spent much time at the Volhynia (Ukraine) estate of his uncle Gabriel Nossenko in Ustilug near Vladimir Volynsk. From 1901 to 1905 he studied law at St. Petersburg Univ.; from 1902 he sought private musical instruction from Rimsky-Korsakov. After his father's death in late 1902, Igor became increasingly attached to Rimsky's circle; under him he wrote piano pieces (Sonata in F♯ minor, 1903–4) and songs, and studied orchestration.

From 1905 Stravinsky intensified his studies with Rimsky-Korsakov, who arranged a court performance of his Symphony in E♭ (1905–7). He wrote a song cycle on Pushkin's *Favn' i pastushka* [Faun and Shepherdess] (1906), the beginning of the short opera *Solovei,* or *Le rossignol* [The Nightingale] (1908–9), and the *Scherzo fantastique* (1907–8) and *Feu d'artifice* [Fireworks] (1908) for orchestra. The last was a nuptial gift for Rimsky's daughter in 1908, but Rimsky died just before its completion. In 1906 Stravinsky married Katerina Nossenko, his first cousin; they had four children, Fyodor (Theodore) in 1907, Ludmila in 1908, Sviatoslav Sulima (Soulima) in 1910, and Maria Milena in 1914.

In early 1909 the successful premiere of *Scherzo* and *Fireworks* under Siloti prompted impresario Sergei Diaghilev (Stravinsky's distant maternal cousin) to engage Stravinsky as musical partner and orchestrator for his upcoming June theatrical season in Paris, the first for his new Ballets russes. For the coming 1910 season he commissioned a Russian fairy-tale ballet, *Zhar'-ptitsa,* or *L'oiseau de feu* [The Firebird] (1909–10). Stravinsky fulfilled the commission with extraordinary skill and flair; the premiere of *Firebird* in June 1910 brought him immediate acclaim as Russia's most promising young nationalistic composer.

Settling in Switzerland, he composed another Russian folk-tale ballet, *Petrushka* (1910–11), for the 1911 season. It commanded equal success, though in style it far overtook Rimsky-Korsakov, incorporating vivid polytonality and asymmetrical rhythm. He wrote a few songs, notably a large choral-orchestral setting of Balmont's *Zvezdoliki* [King of the Stars] (1911–12), and *3 Japanese Lyrics* (1912–13) with scoring influenced by Schoenberg's *Pierrot lunaire* of 1912.

Stravinsky's next ballet, the epochal *Vesna sviashchennaia,* or *Le sacre du printemps* [The Rite of Spring] (1911–13), was begun before *Petrushka* but matured more slowly. Densely polytonal, rhythmically asymmetrical and driving, extravagantly orchestrated with quintuple winds and percussion, it depicted savage, primitive Russian rituals with heavy, stylized choreography by Nijinsky. Its premiere in Paris on 29 May 1913 incited one of the most colorful riots in musical history and propelled Stravinsky to the summit of celebrity.

For the 1914 season Stravinsky completed his opera *The Nightingale* after a four-year hiatus. Planning for 1915, he immersed himself in Russian folklore to prepare the elaborate vocal-orchestral ballet *Svadebka,* or *Les noces* [The Wedding], but the outbreak of war postponed its production indefinitely. Between 1914 and 1917 he wrote several sets of folkloristic songs and the fable-pantomime *Baika,* or *Renard* (1915–16). He also wrote chamber music (*3 Pieces for String Quartet,* 1914) and children's songs and piano pieces (*Pièces faciles,* 1914–15 and 1916–17). He completed a short score of *The Wedding* in late 1917, just before the November Bolshevik coup cut off his estate interests in Ustilug and made return to Russia impossible.

Henceforth Stravinsky turned to frugally conceived works and eschewed Russian nationalism for its own sake. He devised a theater piece for small forces, *L'histoire du soldat* [The Soldier's Tale] (1918, text by C. F. Ramuz), that played in Lausanne. He also conceived compact concert works: *Ragtime* (1918) for 11 instruments, *Piano-Rag-Music* (1919), Concertino (1920) for string quartet, and Symphonies of Wind Instruments (1920) for 24 winds. The lean style of this period still draws upon the tonal and rhythmic innovations of the prewar works.

After the war Stravinsky moved to France (to Brittany in mid-1920, Biarritz in 1921, Nice in 1924, and

Igor Stravinsky, 1923.

Voreppe near Grenoble in 1930); he kept a Paris studio at the Pleyel Company. Diaghilev, who had moved his company to London, commissioned the ballet *Pulcinella* (1919–20) for small orchestra and singers, based on music attributed to Pergolesi (as he had commissioned similar medleys of Scarlatti's and Rossini's music from Tommasini and Respighi). Inspired by the brush with European 18th-century music, Stravinsky wrote for Diaghilev's 1922 season the short opera buffa *Mavra* (1921–22, based on Pushkin's *Domik v Kolomne*). In 1923 Diaghilev at last produced *The Wedding,* for which Stravinsky reduced the forces to four pianos, percussion, and singers.

In the wind Octet (1922–23) Stravinsky embraced explicit elements of 18th-century musical form and manner, beginning the evolution of a neoclassical style that was to inform his works through the early 1950s. With the Octet's premiere he began appearing as conductor of his own music, likewise as pianist with his Concerto (1923–24) for piano and winds; he toured to the U.S. in 1925. Works written for his concerts over the next decade include the Sonata (1924) and Serenade in A (1925) for piano, the *Capriccio* (1928–29) for piano and orchestra, the *Duo concertant* (1931–32) for himself and violinist Samuel Dushkin, and the two-piano Concerto (1935) for himself and his son Soulima. He also wrote the Violin Concerto in D (1931) for Dushkin.

During these years he created a series of austere but imposing theatrical and vocal works: the uncommissioned opera-oratorio *Oedipus rex* (1926–27, text by Jean Cocteau, whose *Antigone* he admired); the ballet *Apollon musagète,* or *Apollo* (1927–28), for the U.S. Library of Congress (per Elizabeth Sprague Coolidge; its simultaneous Paris production was the first of many collaborations with choreographer George Balanchine); the ballet *Le baiser de la fée,* or *The Fairy's Kiss* (1928, based on music of Tchaikovsky), for Ida Rubinstein; the choral-orchestral *Symphony of Psalms* (1930) for Serge Koussevitzky and the Boston Symphony; and the choral-orchestral melodrama *Perséphone* (1934, text by André Gide) for Ida Rubinstein. Along with stylistic conservatisms, these works show a reactionary though profound concern with classical and sacred subject matter; similarly the liturgical *Pater noster* (1926), *Credo* (1932), and *Ave Maria* (1934) manifest spirituality. In 1934 Stravinsky took French citizenship and moved to Paris. In 1935 he futilely sought election to the Institut de France; that year he authored his autobiography, *Chroniques de ma vie.*

American tours in 1935–36 brought a new impulse of recognition and commissions: the witty ballet *Jeu de cartes* [The Card Party] (1935–36) for the American Ballet (per Lincoln Kirstein), the chamber Concerto in E♭ ("Dumbarton Oaks," 1937–38) for Mr. and Mrs. Robert Woods Bliss, the Symphony in C (1938–40) for the Chicago Symphony. Between late 1938 and mid-1939 his elder daughter, wife, and mother died. Stravinsky traveled to America in autumn 1939 to deliver the Charles Eliot Norton lectures at Harvard; there in early 1940 he married Vera de Bosset Sudeikina, who had been his companion since 1921. That summer they filed for citizenship (granted in 1945) and settled in Hollywood.

In the early 1940s Stravinsky took many small American commissions: *Circus Polka* (1942) for band; film music (*Four Norwegian Moods,* 1942, and *Ode,* 1943); jazz band pieces (*Scherzo à la russe,* 1943, and *Ebony Concerto,* 1945); and a short cantata, *Babel* (1944). Larger commissions included *Danses concertantes* (1941–42) for the Werner Janssen Orchestra and *Scènes de ballet* (1944) for a Billy Rose revue; in Europe Paul Sacher commissioned the string Concerto in D (1946). But Stravinsky's major works of the 1940s were the Symphony in Three Movements (1942–45) for the New York Philharmonic, the ballet *Orphée,* or *Orpheus* (1947), for Ballet Society of New York (Lincoln Kirstein), and the uncommissioned Mass (1944–47) for choir and winds; they crown his neoclassical symphonic, balletic, and liturgical oeuvres, respectively.

Stravinsky now conceived his largest work, a comic opera in English, *The Rake's Progress* (1948–51), with a libretto by W. H. Auden and Chester Kallman based on pictures by Hogarth, using the classical conventions of recitative, aria, duo, and chorus. *The Rake* showed enormous musical vigor and won wide acclaim. His acceptance of Venice's bid for the 1951 premiere of this uncommissioned work rejuvenated his standing in Europe.

From 1948 Robert Craft functioned as Stravinsky's amanuensis and increasingly close family member. In 1951 both Craft's interests and Schoenberg's death prompted Stravinsky to study serialism, especially that of Webern. His compositions after *The Rake* show a growing concern with serial techniques, though still with an ear to tonal implications. Many of these works are miniatures, albeit densely wrought: *3 Songs from William Shakespeare* (1953), *In memoriam Dylan Thomas* (1954, text by Thomas), *Epitaphium* for Max Egon (1959), *Anthem, "The Dove Descending"* (1962, text by T. S. Eliot), *Elegy for J.F.K.* (1964, text by Auden), and *Fanfare for a New Theatre* (1964) for New York's Lincoln Center. Larger works include the mostly tonal Cantata (1952, on English Renaissance verses); the partly serial Septet for winds, strings, and piano (1952–53); the partly serial last ballet *Agon* (1953–57) for the New York City Ballet; the *Movements* for piano and orchestra (1958–59); and the orchestral *Variations (Aldous Huxley in memoriam)* (1963–64).

In these years he also wrote a notable body of choral-orchestral sacred works: *Canticum sacrum* (1955, on New and Old Testament texts) for the 1956 Venice Biennale, *Threni* (1957–58, on the Lamentations of Jeremiah) for the North German Radio (at the 1958 Venice Biennale), *A Sermon, a Narrative, and a Prayer* (1960–61, on New Testament and liturgical texts) for Paul Sacher, the musical play *The Flood* (1961–62, on Genesis and other texts) for CBS Television, and the ballad *Abraham and Isaac* (1962–63, on the Hebrew text of Genesis) for the 1964 Israel Festival.

From 1951 Stravinsky maintained a rigorous schedule of international conducting and recording engagements, increasingly with Craft's aid. In 1957 Craft collaborated in a series of interview-memoirs that were published first as articles, then as books (in divergent New York and London editions): *Conversations with Igor Stravinsky* (1959), *Memories and Commentaries* (1960), *Expositions and Developments* (1962), *Dialogues and a Diary* (1963), *Themes and Episodes* (New York, 1966), and *Retrospectives and Conclusions* (New York, 1969); the last two were combined and revised as *Themes and Conclusions* (London, 1972). On the occasion of his 80th birthday in 1962, the USSR Composers' Union feted Stravinsky with concerts in Moscow and Leningrad, bringing about his only visit to Russia after 1914.

Stravinsky's last works (apart from arrangements) were two choral-instrumental settings of Requiem texts, *Introitus (T. S. Eliot in memoriam)* (1965) and *Requiem Canticles* (1966), commissioned by Princeton Univ., and the song "The Owl and the Pussy-Cat" (1966, text by Edward Lear) for his wife, Vera. From 1967 his health declined; from 1969 he lived in New York. He was buried in Venice.

Writings: *Chroniques de ma vie* (Paris, 1935–36; 2nd ed., 1962); trans. as *An Autobiography* (1936; R: 1975). *Poétique musicale* (Cambridge, Mass., 1942); trans. as *Poetics of Music* (1947).

Bibl.: Eric Walter White, *Stravinsky* (London, 1966; 2nd ed., 1979). Benjamin Boretz and Edward T. Cone, *Perspectives on Schoenberg and Stravinsky* (Princeton, N.J., 1968; rev. 1972). Robert Craft, *Stravinsky: Chronicle of a Friendship* (New York, 1972; rev. and expanded ed., 1994). Mikhail Druskin, *Igor' Stravinsky* (Leningrad, 1974; rev. 1979); trans. Eng. (Cambridge, 1983). Vera Stravinsky and Robert Craft, *Stravinsky in Pictures and Documents* (New York, 1978). André Boucourechliev, *Igor Stravinsky* (Paris, 1982); trans., Eng. (New York, 1987). Clifford Caesar, *Igor Stravinsky: A Complete Catalogue* (San Francisco, 1982). Robert Craft, ed., *Stravinsky: Selected Correspondence,* 3 vols. (New York, 1982–85). Pieter van den Toorn, *The Music of Igor Stravinsky* (New Haven, 1983). Louis Andriessen and Elmer Schönberger, *Het apollonisch uurwerk: over Stravinsky* (Amsterdam, 1983); trans. as *The Apollonian Clockwork: On Stravinsky* (Oxford, 1989). Jann Pasler, ed., *Confronting Stravinsky* (Berkeley, 1986). Ethan Haimo and Paul Johnson, eds., *Stravinsky Retrospectives* (Lincoln, Nebr., 1987). André Boucourechliev, *Stravinsky* (New York, 1987). Steven Walsh, *The Music of Stravinsky* (London, 1988). Philip Stuart, *Igor Stravinsky: A Comprehensive Discography* (New York, 1991). Paul Griffiths, *Stravinsky* (New York, 1992). Robert Craft, *Stravinsky: Glimpses of a Life* (New York, 1993).

Stravinsky, Soulima (b. Lausanne, 23 Sept. 1910; d. Sarasota, Fla., 28 Nov. 1994). Pianist and composer. Son of Igor Stravinsky. A pupil of Isidore Philipp and Boulanger at Paris, he later played in concert with his father and edited some of his works. His own compositions include a string quartet and a suite for the right hand.

Strayhorn, Billy [William; Swee' Pea] (b. Dayton, Ohio, 29 Nov. 1915; d. New York, 31 May 1967). Jazz composer, arranger, and pianist. From 1939 until his death he joined Duke Ellington, collaborating so sympathetically that their individual contributions often cannot be identified. Strayhorn wrote for Ellington's orchestra and many recording sessions led by Ellington's sidemen, often playing piano in these groups. Although he wrote the orchestra's theme "Take the 'A' Train" (first recorded in 1941), he is especially associated with harmonically sophisticated ballads, including "Lush Life," "Passion Flower," and "Chelsea Bridge."

Street, Tison (b. Boston, 20 May 1943). Composer and violinist. He studied violin in Boston with Einar Hanson, then composition at Harvard with Leon Kirchner and David Del Tredici (B.A., 1965; M.A., 1971). At the same time he played violin in various ensembles. His best-known works are his String Quartets (1972, 1984) and a String Quintet (1974).

Streicher, Johann Andreas (b. Stuttgart, 13 Dec. 1761; d. Vienna, 25 May 1833). Piano builder. He married Nanette Stein, daughter of piano builder Johann Andreas Stein. They established their own firm in 1802 after Nanette stopped making pianos with her brother Matthaäs Stein, and it became one of the most prominent shops in Vienna. Beethoven was friendly with them and admired their pianos. Streicher wrote a manual specifically for the owners of their fortepianos: "Kurze Bemerkungen über das Spielen, Stimmen und Erhalten den Fortepiano, welche von Nanette Streicher geboren Stein in Wien verfertiget werden" (trans. and ed. by Preethi di Silva, 1983).

Bibl.: Richard A. Fuller, "Andreas Streicher's Notes on the Fortepiano," *EM* 12 (1984): 461–70.

Streicher, Theodor (b. Vienna, 7 June 1874; d. Wetzelsdorf, near Graz, 28 May 1940). Composer. Great-grandson of Viennese piano builders Johann Andreas Streicher and Nanette Stein Streicher. Trained for the stage, he was largely self-taught in music. He achieved great success with *Aus "Des Knaben Wunderhorn,"* 30 lieder (1903), written in the style of Hugo Wolf; among his numerous other songs are *12 Michelangelo-Lieder* (1922). He also wrote choral music (*Wanderers Nachtlied,* 1908, after Goethe; *Szenen und Bildern aus Goethes Faust,* 1913) and a string sextet (1912).

Streisand, Barbra (Joan) (b. Brooklyn, 24 Apr. 1942). Popular singer, actress. She performed in nightclubs in New York and on Broadway, and from 1963 released recordings of popular and, later, rock songs (including "People," 1964; "Evergreen," 1976; "Woman in Love," 1980). She has appeared in both musical (*Hello, Dolly,* 1969) and nonmusical (*Yentl,* 1983) films. In 1994 she embarked on a highly successful concert tour of London and the U.S.

Strepponi, Giuseppina [Clelia Maria Josepha] (b. Lodi, 8 Sept. 1815; d. Sant'Agata, near Busseto, 14 Nov. 1897). Soprano. Entered Milan Conservatory, where she studied piano and singing, 1830–34. May have made stage debut in 1834. First success at Trieste (1835); La Scala debut, 1839. Donizetti wrote *Adelia* (1841) for her. Created the role of Abigaille in *Nabucco* in 1842. Retired in February 1846; went to Paris in October 1846, where she taught and sang a few concerts. Verdi joined her there July 1847; they were legally married in 1859.

Bibl.: Mercede Mundula, *La moglie di Verdi: Giuseppina Strepponi* (Milan, 1938). Frank Walker, *The Man Verdi* (London, 1962).

Strickland, Lily (Theresa) (b. Anderson, S.C., 28 Jan. 1887; d. Hendersonville, N.C., 6 June 1958). Composer. She began to compose as a teenager and received a scholarship to the Institute of Musical Art in New York, where she studied piano and composition. Several of her early works, such as the songs "Pickaninny Sleep Song" (1911) and "Honey Chile" (1922), reflect her southern heritage; others are inspired by American Indian music, for example, *Laughing Star of Zuni,* operetta (1946). From 1920 to 1929 she lived in India, where her husband had business. Her fascination with India and the Middle East is heard in works such as *Two East Indian Nautches,* piano (1930); *From a Sufi's Tent,* vocal soloists and chorus (1923).

Bibl.: Ann Howe, *Lily Strickland—South Carolina's Gift to American Music* (1970).

Striggio [Strigi, Strigia], **Alessandro** (1) (b. Mantua, ca. 1540; d. there, 29 Feb. 1592). Composer and instrumentalist, father of Alessandro Striggio (2). By the 1560s he was the principal composer at the court of Cosimo I de' Medici, Duke of Florence; his responsibilities included writing *intermedi* for important state occasions, including the marriage of Joanna of Austria and Francesco de' Medici (1565) and the visit of Archduke Karl of Austria (1569). His activities during the 1570s are unclear; in 1579 he composed music for the entertainment in honor of the Grand Duke Francesco's wedding and for the anthology *Trionfo di musica di diversi.* In 1584, at Alfonso II d'Este's invitation, he traveled to Ferrara; later that year he returned to Mantua, where he was employed at the Gonzaga court as a supernumerary musician, although he continued to compose *intermedi* for the Medici. He was much admired in his own time as a performer (probably of the *lirone,* a bass *lira da braccio*) as well as a composer. Striggio's music for *intermedi* typically contains a mixture of homophony and counterpoint, and many of the works feature impressive antiphonal effects. Some of his later madrigals are progressive in style, perhaps owing to his contacts with Ferrara.

Bibl.: David Butchart, "The Festive Madrigals of Alessandro Striggio," *JRMA* 107 (1980–81): 46–59. David Butchart, "Musical Journey of 1567: Alessandro Striggio in Vienna, Munich, Paris and London," *ML* 63 (1982): 1–16.

Striggio, Alessandro [Alessandrino] (2) (b. Mantua, 1573?; d. Venice, 15? June 1630). Librettist and viol player. Son of Alessandro Striggio (1). In 1589 he played at the wedding of Grand Duke Ferdinand I in Florence. He studied law in Mantua. In 1596–97 he published the last 3 books of his father's madrigals. Wrote the libretto of Monteverdi's *Orfeo* (Mantua, 1607) and probably that of *Tirsi e Clori* (1615); also the lost *Lamento d'Apollo.* Gagliano set libretti by him as well.

Stringfield, Lamar (Edwin) (b. Raleigh, N.C., 10 Oct. 1897; d. Asheville, N.C., 21 Jan. 1959). Flutist and composer. Studied flute with George Barrere and composition with Nadia Boulanger. He played flute with the New York Philharmonic and the New York Chamber Music Society. His compositions reflect his southern mountain heritage in their themes and melodic materials, for example, *Mountain Echoes,* flute and harp (1921); *From the Southern Mountains,* orchestra (1927); *From the Blue Ridge,* orchestra (1936).

Stringham, Edwin John (b. Kenosha, Wis., 11 July 1890; d. Chapel Hill, N.C., 1 July 1974). Composer and teacher. He studied at Northwestern (B.M., 1914), then at the Cincinnati Conservatory of Music (D.Ped., 1922). Later he studied in Rome with Ottorino Respighi (1929). He taught music at Denver College of Music (1920–29), then in New York at Columbia University Teachers College (1930–38), the Juilliard School of Music (1930–45), Union Theological Seminary (1932–38), and Queens College (1938–46). Works include *The Ancient Mariner,* orchestra (1927); Symphony no. 1 (1929); *Nocturnes* (no. 1, orchestra, 1931; no. 2, winds and harp, 1935; no. 3, orchestra, 1939); *Fantasy on American Folk Tunes* (violin and orchestra, 1941).

Stroe, Aurel (b. Bucharest, 5 May 1932). Composer. He attended the Bucharest Conservatory (1951–56). Taught composition at Bucharest Conservatory (1962–85) and at the Univ. of Mainz (from 1988). His early works, such as Piano Sonata (1955) and *Uvertura burlesca* (orchestra, 1961), are in a folkloristic vein. During the 1960s he turned toward the western European avant-garde, particularly after 1966, when he attended the Darmstadt summer courses (1966–69), studying with Ligeti, Kagel, and Stockhausen. *Laudes I* (strings, 1966) and *Canto I, II* (12 instrumental ensembles, 1967, 1971) are examples of this change in direction. Many of his later pieces involve electronic instruments or tape, for example, *Laudes II* (12 ensembles and 2 ondes martinots, 1968), *Il giardino delle strutture + Rime di Michelangelo* (baritone, trombone, violin, viola, cello, harpsichord and tape, 1975), *10 pizzi pastorali* (clavichord and electronic organ, 1978); other works include the opera *Eumenides* [Orestia III] (1986).

Strong, George Templeton (b. New York, 26 May 1856; d. Geneva, 27 June 1948). Composer. His father was president of the New York Philharmonic Society, 1870–74. Studied oboe as a child; studied at Leipzig (1879) with Jadassohn (counterpoint), Hofmann (orchestration), and Grempert (horn). Moved to Frankfurt in 1881, then to Weimar, where he knew Liszt, Szigeti, and Raff. He dedicated his symphonic poem *Undine* op. 14 (1882–83) to Liszt. He went to Wiesbaden in 1886, where he became friends with MacDowell. Taught at New England Conservatory, 1891–92, then returned to Europe. Founded the Société Vaudorse des Aquarellistes. Compositions include 7 symphonic poems; Suite for cello and orchestra (1923); Berceuse, string trio and orchestra (1923); cantata; choral works; chamber works; piano pieces; songs. Many of his manuscripts are housed in the Library of Congress.

Strouse, Charles (Louis) (b. New York, 7 June 1928). Composer. He attended the Eastman School of Music, then studied with Aaron Copland at Tanglewood and Nadia Boulanger in Paris (1951). Returning to the U.S., he worked as a rehearsal pianist in the New York musical theater and collaborated with Lee Adams on a number of off-Broadway reviews. *Bye Bye Birdie* (1960), their first Broadway show, was a success, as were *Golden Boy* (1964) and *Applause* (1970). He collaborated with Martin Charnin in *Annie* (1977).

Strozzi, Barbara (b. Venice, 6 Aug. 1619; d. there?, 1664 or later). Composer and singer. She was an adopted daughter of Giulio Strozzi and a pupil of Cavalli. She commissioned the first 2 sets of Nicolò Fontei's *Bizzarrie poetiche* (1635, 1636), and was praised as a singer by him. Principal singer at the Accademia degli Unisoni, which met at Giulio Strozzi's residence. Her style as a composer reveals the influence of Cavalli. *Il primo libro de madrigali* (1644) was followed by other madrigals and ariettas, which display her imaginative handling of melody, rhythm, and form.

Bibl.: Ellen Rosand, "Barbara Strozzi, *Virtuosissima cantatrice:* The Composer's Voice," *JAMS* 31/2 (1978): 241–81.

Strozzi, Giulio [Zorzisto, Luigi] (b. Venice, 1583; d. there, 31 Mar. 1652). Librettist, poet, and dramatist. Barbara Strozzi was his adopted daughter, and he was related to Piero Strozzi. He received his early education in Venice and studied law at the Univ. of Pisa. After working in Rome, Padua, and Urbino, he settled in Venice around the early 1620s. His literary output includes orations, plays, poetry, and descriptions of Venetian ceremonies. As a librettist, he collaborated with Monteverdi on the projected opera *La finta pazza Licori* (1627) and on *Proserpina rapita* (Venice, 1630); Monteverdi also set some of his sonnets. Strozzi's libretti were influential in the early stages of Venetian opera; his last libretto, *Veremonda,* was set by Cavalli in 1652.

Strozzi, Gregorio (b. S. Severino, southern Italy, ca. 1615; d. probably Naples, after 1687). Composer. He studied with Giovanni Maria Sabino in Naples and became second organist at SS. Annunziata, Naples, in 1634. In 1645 he was appointed a chaplain in Amalfi. After 1655 he became a doctor of canon and civil law at the Univ. of Naples. He wrote a collection of choral works for Holy Week, and the *Capricci da sonare* (Naples, 1687), which contains 29 pieces for harpsichord or organ.

Strozzi, Piero (b. Florence, ca. 1550; d. there, after 1 Sept. 1609). Composer. He was related to Giulio Strozzi. A member of Count Giovanni de' Bardi's Camerata, he played a leading role in its discussions on music; and as a member of Jacopo Corsi's circle he heard Peri demonstrate the *stile rappresentativo.* He wrote music for the celebration of Francesco I de' Medici's marriage in 1579, and in 1600 composed music for Caccini's *Il rapimento di Cefalo.* Only 3 of his compositions survive.

Strube, Gustav (b. Ballenstedt, Germany, 3 Mar. 1867; d. Baltimore, 2 Feb. 1953). Violinist, composer, conductor, teacher. Taught a variety of instruments by his father, a provincial conductor, he studied violin, piano, and composition at the Leipzig Conservatory (1883–86); played violin in the Leipzig Gewandhaus orchestra and at the Municipal Opera House under Nikisch. Nikisch moved to the U.S. in 1889 to conduct the Boston Symphony and the next year invited Strube to join him. From 1890 to 1913 Strube played in the Boston Symphony; from 1989 to 1912 he conducted the Boston Pops. For this orchestra he composed many waltzes, marches, and lighter works; for the Boston Symphony he wrote 2 symphonies (1896, 1909) and the overture *Puck* (1910). In 1913 he moved to Baltimore to conduct and teach music theory at the Peabody Conservatory of Music, where he remained until 1946. He also conducted the Baltimore Symphony from 1916 to 1930. His compositions from the Baltimore period include *Symphony in G* (Lanier) (1924), 2 Sinfoniettas (1922, 1938), *Americana* (symphonic fantasy, 1930), *Elegy* (viola, string orchestra, harp, 1935), 2 concertos for violin (1924, 1930); sonatas for violin (1923), viola (1924), and cello (1925); 2 string quartets (1922, 1936).

Bibl.: Gustav Klemm, "Gustav Strube: The Man and the Musician," *MQ* 28 (1942): 288–301.

Strungk [Strunck], **Nicolaus Adam** (b. Brunswick, bapt. 15 Nov. 1640; d. Dresden, 23 Sept. 1700). Composer, violinist, and organist. He was his father's assistant organist at St. Magnus's Church, Brunswick, before attending Helmstedt Univ. He became a first violinist at the Wolfenbüttel court chapel in 1660. From 1661 to 1665 he was at the court of Emperor Leopold I in Vienna, and was subsequently employed by Elector Johann Friedrich at Hannover. From 1678 to 1682 he was director of music at Hamburg; there his operas *Esther* and *Semiramis* (1681) were heard. He later held positions at Hannover and Dresden before founding an opera company in Leipzig (1693). Besides operas, Strungk wrote secular and sacred vocal works as well as instrumental compositions.

Stuart, Leslie [Barrett, Thomas Augustine] (b. Southport, 15 Mar. 1864; d. Richmond, Surrey, 27 Mar. 1928). Composer. Organist at Salford Cathedral, 1879–86, then for seven years at Manchester, where he taught and composed music. He also conducted an orchestra there. In 1895 he moved to London. He composed music for the theater, especially popular theater. The revue *Floradora* (1895) was his most successful work.

Stucky, Steven (b. Hutchinson, Kans., 7 Nov. 1949). Composer. He studied at Baylor Univ. with Richard Willis (B.M., 1971), then at Cornell Univ. with Robert Palmer and Karel Husa (M.F.A., 1973; D.M.A., 1978). At Cornell he wrote a book on Witold Lutosławski (*Lutosławski and His Music,* New York, 1981), whose influence may be heard in the textures and tonal procedures of some of his early works. In *Dreamwaltzes,* commissioned by the Minnesota Orchestra in 1986, he turned to the music of the past, working snatches of famous 19th-century waltzes into a kaleidoscopic orchestral texture. Concerto for Orchestra (1986) and *Son et lumière* (1988) do not use direct quotes, but continue to evoke the atmosphere of the 19th century in their orchestration and their Romantic gestures. Taught at Lawrence Univ. in Wisconsin (1978–80), then at Cornell (beginning 1980). He has been composer in residence and new-music adviser with the Los Angeles Philharmonic (1988–91). Other works include *Kennigar* (Symphony no. 4) (1978); *Sappho Fragments* (mezzo-soprano and chamber ensemble, 1982); Double Concerto (violin, oboe, chamber orchestra, 1985; rev. 1989); *Threnos* (wind ensemble, 1988); *Angelus* (orchestra, 1990); woodwind quintet (1990); *Fanfares and Arias* (1995); Concerto for 2 flutes and orchestra (1995); *Fanfare for Cincinnati* (1995).

Sturgeon, N(icholas?) (d. between 31 May and 8 June 1454). Composer. In 1399 he was elected a scholar of Winchester College; held a number of canonries, including one at St. Paul's (from 1432; precentor from 1442), and served as a member of the Royal Household Chapel. Sturgeon's 7 surviving compositions, including the isorhythmic motet "Salve mater Domini," are known only from the Old Hall Manuscript.

Stürmer, Bruno (b. Freiburg im Breisgau, 9 Sept. 1892; d. Bad Homburg, 19 May 1958). Composer. He studied piano at the Karlsruhe conservatory, then organ and composition at Heidelberg. He also studied musicology and fine arts at the Univ. of Munich. During the 1920s he taught piano and conducted in various theaters. From 1925 on he conducted choral societies in Duisburg, Homburg, Kassel, and elsewhere. After 1945 he lived in Darmstadt and Frankfurt. He wrote works for many combinations but is best known as a choral composer. His works include *Wanderers Nachtlied* (male chorus, 1918); *Die Messe des Maschinenmenschen* (baritone, male chorus, orchestra, 1931); *Das Ludwigsburger Te Deum* (chorus and brass band, 1954).

Sturzenegger, (Hans) Richard (b. Zurich, 18 Dec. 1905; d. Bern, 24 Oct. 1976). Cellist, composer, and teacher. He studied cello with Reitz at the Zurich Conservatory, then in Paris with Alexanian and Casals. He also studied composition in Paris with Nadia Boulanger and in Berlin with Ernst Toch. In 1935 he returned to Switzerland, to Bern, where he played in the Musikgesellschaft orchestra and in the Bern String Quartet and taught at the conservatory. He became director of the conservatory in 1963. He wrote 4 cello concertos (1933, 1937, 1947, 1974), works for a variety of instrumental combinations, and many choral works including *Acht Texte Michelangelos* (baritone and string quartet, 1944), *Drei geistliche Lieder* (chorus, 1969), and *Passion nach dem Evangelisten Lukas and Johannes* (5 voices a cappella, 1975).

Bibl.: Ervin Hochuli, ed, *Variationen: Festgabe für Richard Sturzenegger zum 70. Geburtstag* (Bern, 1975) [includes bibliography and works list].

Stutschewsky, Joachim [Yehoyachin] (b. Romny, Ukraine, 7 Feb. 1892; d. Tel Aviv, 14 Nov. 1982). Composer. He studied cello as a child, then attended the Leipzig Conservatory (1909–12), where he studied with Klengel, Paul, and Sitt. He was active first in Jena as a performer, then performed, taught, and composed in Zurich (1914–24) and Vienna (1924–38). He was involved in both the performance of new music and the support of specifically Jewish music. After 1938 he settled in Palestine. His early music was in the style of contemporary modern trends, but he made increasing use of elements of Jewish music and traditions. He published many studies for the cello. Works include orchestral music (*Israel,* symphonic suite, 1964), cantatas (*Yemama bashimsha* [From Dawn to Dawn], narrator, soprano, tenor, ensemble, 1960), chamber music (*Imaginations,* flute, piano trio, 1971), and vocal music (*T'hina* [Supplication], 1953; *Kaddish,* 1957).

Bibl.: *Seventieth Anniversary Catalogue: Works of Joachim Stutschewsky* (Tel Aviv, 1961).

Styne, Jule [Stein, Julius] (b. London, 31 Dec. 1905; d. New York, 20 Sept. 1994). Composer. His family moved to Chicago in 1914, and he won quick recognition as a child prodigy pianist, playing with the Chicago and Detroit Symphony Orchestras before he was 11. He studied briefly at the Chicago College of Music but turned increasingly toward popular music during the 1920s, playing in dance bands and writing songs. In 1937 he moved to Hollywood, where, with lyricist Sammy Cahn, he wrote songs such as "I've Heard That Song Before," "I'll Walk Alone," and "Time After Time," many of them performed by Frank Sinatra. His first Broadway show was the very successful *High Button Shoes* (1947), followed by *Gentlemen Prefer Blondes* (1949), and *Two on the Aisle* (1951), his first collaboration with the lyricists Betty Comden and Adolph Green. With them, Styne composed several more hit shows, including *Bells Are Ringing* (1956), *Gypsy* (1959), *Do Re Mi* (1960), and *Funny Girl* (1964).

Bibl.: Theodore Taylor, *Jule* (New York, 1979).

Subotnick, Morton (b. Los Angeles, 14 Apr. 1933). Composer. As a young man he studied the clarinet, first with Franklin Stokes (1947–51), then with Mitchell Lurie (1953–54). He also started composing, more or less on his own. He studied composition for a year with Leon Kirchner at the Univ. of Southern California (1951), then, after a stint in the army and a B.A. in literature from the Univ. of Denver, he studied again with Kirchner and Milhaud at Mills College (M.A., 1959). His early works were serialist, but he soon abandoned the serial idiom for electronics. Teaching at Mills College (1959–66) and working at the San Francisco Tape Music Center (1961–65), which he founded and co-directed, he composed pieces in which traditional instruments were combined with electronic tape. Several of these works—for example, the series *Play! 1–4*—expanded the traditional performance context with light shows, improvisation, pantomime, and audience participation.

In 1967 Subotnik moved to New York, where he taught at New York Univ. Working with a Buchla synthesizer, he produced a series of all-electronic pieces composed not for live performance but expressly for recordings. *Silver Apples of the Moon* (1967), a tuneful and accessible work, was a commercial success and was followed by *The Wild Bull* (1967), *Sidewinder* (1970), and *Four Butterflies* (1971). In 1969 he returned to California to teach composition at the California Institute of the Arts. His music of the 1970s tended to move back toward live performance, using electronic processing to alter the sounds of the human voice and of traditional instruments, as in *Before the Butterfly* (1975) for orchestra and electronics. He also developed what he called "ghost" pieces, in which a computer program (the "ghost") directs the processing of a live performance. Examples of this technique are *Liquid Strata* (piano, electronics, 1977); *Parallel Lines* (orchestra, electronics, 1978); *The Wild Beasts* (trombone, piano, electronics, 1978); *Ascent into Air* (instrumental ensemble, electronics, 1981). Other works include *The Double Life of Amphibians* (theater piece, 1984); *In Two Worlds* (concerto, sax, electronic wind controller, orchestra, 1987–88); *And the Butterflies Began To Sing* (YCAMS, chamber ensemble, 1988); *A Desert Flowers* (orchestra, 1989); *Jacob's Room* (opera, Philadelphia, 1993).

Bibl.: Harold W. Whipple, "Beasts and Butterflies: Morton Subotnick's Ghost Scores," *MQ* 69 (1983): 425–41.

Sucher [née Hasselbeck], **Rosa** (b. Velburg, 23 Feb. 1849; d. Eschweiler, 16 Apr. 1927). Soprano. Sang solos in a church in Velburg. Engaged in Munich at the Court Opera (1871), in Berlin (1875), in Danzig (1876), and in Leipzig (1877). Married conductor Josef Sucher (1843–1908) in 1877. In 1879 she and her husband were engaged by the Hamburg Opera. London debut in 1882; sang at Bayreuth, 1886–96. Retired in 1903; moved to Vienna in 1908 and taught singing. Published her autobiography in 1914 in Leipzig *(Aus meinem Leben).*

Suchoň, Eugen (b. Pezinok, Slovakia, 25 Sept. 1908; d. Bratislava, 5 Aug. 1993). Composer. Beginning in 1927 he studied composition and piano at the Bratislava School of Music with Kafenda. He went on to study composition in Novák's master classes at the Prague Conservatory from 1931 to 1933; subsequently taught at several schools including the Bratislava Academy, Bratislava School for Education, and, from 1959 to 1974, Bratislava Univ. He served composers' organizations in Czechoslovakia. His early works showed exploratory shifts between late Romantic styles and more modern contrapuntal processes. He utilized both tonal chromaticism and folk-derived modality, which he eventually brought together with Slovakian folk themes into an individual and influential musical language. During the late 1950s he experimented with serialism. Works include stage music (*Krútňava* [The Whirlpool], 1949), orchestral music (*Symfonická fantázia na BACH,* organ, strings, percussion, 1971), and vocal works (*O človeku* [On Man], 1962).

Suderburg, Robert (b. Spencer, Iowa, 28 Jan. 1936). Composer. He studied at the Univ. of Minnesota (B.A., 1957), the Yale School of Music (M.M., 1960), and the Univ. of Pennsylvania (Ph.D., 1966), where he studied with George Rochberg. He taught at the Univ. of Washington (1966–74), where he also conducted the school's contemporary music ensemble. From 1974 to 1984 he was chancellor of the North Carolina School of the Arts; beginning 1985, taught at Williams College. His works include *Orchestra Music I–III* (1969, 1971, 1973); *Within the Mirror of Time* (piano concerto, 1974); *Chamber Music IV* (percussion ensemble, 1979); *Chamber Music V* (voice, string quartet, tape, 1976); *Solo Music* (violin, 1972).

Sugár, Rezső (b. Budapest, 9 Oct. 1919; d. Budapest, 22 Sept. 1988). Composer. He studied at the Budapest Academy of Music from 1937 to 1942 with Kodály; subsequently taught at the Municipal High School for Music, 1946–49. He went on to teach at the Béla Bartók Conservatory in Budapest until 1968, when he joined the faculty at the Budapest Academy of Music. His music was influenced by Bartók's use of form and incorporated elements of Hungarian folk music and lore. Works include orchestral music (*Concerto in memoriam Béla Bartók,* 1962; *Epilógus,* 1973), vocal music (*Kőmíves Kelemen* [Kelemen the Mason], soprano, baritone, chorus, orchestra, 1958), and chamber music.

Suggia, Guilhermina (b. Oporto, Portugal, 27 June 1888; d. there, 31 July 1950). Cellist. Studied with her father, and from 1940 at Leipzig with Julius Klengel; appeared with the Gewandhaus Orchestra in 1905. She was Casals's companion from 1906 to 1912; after the relationship ended she settled in London, appearing regularly in concert. A famous 1923 portrait of her by Augustus John hangs in the British Embassy, Athens.

Suk, Josef (1) (b. Křečovice, 4 Jan. 1874; d. Benešov, near Prague, 29 May 1935). Composer. He studied piano, violin, and organ with his father, who was a village choirmaster; went on to study violin and theory at the Prague Conservatory from 1885 to 1891 and stayed on to work with Wihan and Dvořák. With Wihan, Suk played in the Bohemian String Quartet, which quickly met with great critical success and was in existence through 1933. Suk continued to study composition with Dvořák, establishing a personal as

Scene from W. S. Gilbert and Arthur Sullivan's *Pirates of Penzance.*

well as professional relationship with his teacher and in 1898 married Dvořák's daughter Otilie. The deaths of Dvořák in 1904 and Otilie in 1905 had a great emotional impact on Suk, affecting his compositional explorations as well. In 1922 he joined the faculty at the Prague Conservatory, teaching composition, and served as its head, 1924–26 and 1933–35. His own compositions were highly influenced by Dvořák and were primarily instrumental. His early works were in a late Romantic style, a tonally based chromaticism seen as successive to Dvořák's music. Suk utilized traditional forms and genres (such as symphony, fantasy, and piano miniatures), incorporating a modal poignancy that intensified and transformed in later compositions written after his wife's death. Suk's musical language became increasingly self-referential and complex. He moved close to atonality in the context of thick textures that obscured a sense of symmetry. Although elements of folk music were subtle parts of his compositional idiom, he never used folk song quotations or even surface allusions in his compositions. He did, however, quote from some of his own works. Works include *Serenade* (strings, 1892); *Pohádka* [Fairytale] (suite from "Radúz a Mahulena," 1899–1900); *Asrael* (symphony, 1905–6); *Zrání* [The Ripening] (symphonic poem, 1912–17); *Epilog* (symphonic piece, soprano, baritone, bass, 2 choirs, orchestra, 1920–29); *Sousedská* (chamber ensemble, 1935).

Suk, Josef (2) (b. Prague, 8 Aug. 1929). Violinist. Grandson of the composer Josef Suk (1). A pupil of Jaroslav Kocian, he also studied at the Prague Conservatory and Academy (to 1953), then led the Prague National Theater orchestra (1953–55). He was a member of the Prague Quartet from 1951 until 1952, when he founded the Suk Trio. He toured with the Czech Philharmonic beginning in 1959, making his U.S. and U.K. debuts in 1964. Other chamber music partnerships included that with Starker and Katchen (1967–69). His recordings are extensive, ranging from Bach unaccompanied works to 20th-century music and Czech compositions. He taught at Vienna during 1979 and 1980.

Šulek, Stjepan (b. Zagreb, 5 Aug. 1914; d. there, 16 Jan. 1986). Composer. He studied violin with Huml at the Zagreb Academy of Music and pursued composition largely on his own. In 1945 he began teaching composition at the Zagreb Academy of Music. He also served as conductor of the Zagreb Radio Chamber Orchestra. His own music was Romantic in style in its lush orchestration and drama, yet was underlined by a classical balance and symmetry of formal design. Works include operas, for which Šulek served as his own librettist (*Koriolon,* premiered Zagreb, 1958; *Oluja* [The Tempest], premiered Zagreb, 1969); orchestral music (6 symphonies, concertos for piano, cello, violin, bassoon, viola, clarinet, horn, and organ); vocal and piano music.

Sullivan, Arthur (Seymour) (b. London, 13 May 1842; d. there, 22 Nov. 1900). Composer. Son of Thomas Sullivan (1805–66), a London theater clarinetist. From his father he learned to play many wind instruments; 1852–57, chorister of the Chapel Royal, where at least two anthems by him were performed. In 1856 he was awarded first Mendelssohn Scholarship, using it to study at the Royal Academy of Music, 1856–58 (teachers included Bennett and Goss), and the Leipzig Conservatory, 1858–60 (teachers included Hauptmann, Rietz, David, Moscheles), remaining a third year paid for by his father and George Smart. The graduation concert of April 1861 included his music to *The Tempest.* Returning to London, he worked as a teacher, accompanist, and church organist (1862–72). In April 1862 the *Tempest* music was performed very successfully at the Crystal Palace, making him one of the rising stars of English music; a ballet, *L'île enchantée,* aroused little attention at Covent Garden in 1864; the masque *Kenilworth* was the first of many compositions for the provincial festivals (Birmingham, 1864); a visit to Ireland in summer 1864 led to his Irish Symphony, very successfully premiered at the Crystal Palace in 1866, also the year of the premiere of a Cello Concerto, the overture *In memoriam* composed in memory of his father, and his first venture into operetta, the three-character, one-act *Cox and Box* composed for private amateur performance. In 1867 published a set of piano pieces, *Daydreams,* and had his overture *Marmion* performed. Apart from the *Overture di ballo* (Birmingham Festival, 1870), his only instrumental piece still occasionally performed, he composed very little instrumental music after this. From the mid-1860s through the 1870s he produced most of his solo songs ("The Lost Chord," 1877), part songs, and hymns ("Onward Christian Soldiers," 1872). He composed the oratorio *The Prodigal Son* for the Worcester Festival (1869) and *The Light of the World* for Birmingham (1873); the cantata *On Shore and Sea* was premiered at the Albert Hall in 1871.

Sullivan composed incidental music for three Shakespeare plays, 1871–77; the 1869 revival of *Cox and Box* was a great success (300 performances), but his first collaboration with W. S. Gilbert, the comic opera *Thispis* (1871), caused little stir; it was their one-act *Trial by Jury* (25 Mar. 1875) that had an extraordinary success, leading Richard D'Oyly Carte in 1876 to form a company and lease a theater (the Opera Comique) to produce further collaborations. These began with *The Sorcerer* (17 Nov. 1877), which had a six-month run, but it was the phenomenal reception of *H.M.S. Pinafore* (25 May 1878) that began the transmuting of the collaboration into a national institution. Their success was as great in the U.S. and Australia, and to try to gather some of the profits lost through pirated performances Gilbert, Sullivan, and Carte traveled to the U.S. in November 1879, where Sullivan was lionized (thereby perhaps planting seeds of the resentment that was to lead to the souring and eventual rupture of the collaboration). They staged *The Pirates of Penzance* in New York on 31 December 1879 (for copyright reasons it had an obscure premiere in Devon one day earlier, not reaching London until April 1880). It was followed by *Patience* (London, 23 Apr. 1881), which on 10 October inaugurated the new Savoy Theatre, which Carte had built for them, *Iolanthe* (25 Nov. 1882), *Princess Ida* (5 Jan. 1883), *The Mikado* (14 Mar. 1885), *Ruddigore* (22 Jan. 1887), and *The Gondoliers* (7 Dec. 1889).

The large fortune that resulted allowed Sullivan to indulge his penchants for travel (he spent much time on the Continent, especially in Paris, Switzerland, and Monte Carlo), gambling, racing, and moving in high society. Because of a painful kidney ailment his health was increasingly poor as he grew older. Apart from the operettas, he composed little in these years; notable exceptions are the oratorios *The Martyr of Antioch* (1880) and *The Golden Legend* (1886), both premiered at the triennial Leeds Festival, which he conducted 1880–98. In 1890 the collaboration came to open rupture, with Gilbert going to court against Carte, causing a messy public scandal with Sullivan caught in the middle. This, however, freed him to pursue his ambition to compose grand opera. His *Ivanhoe* was premiered on 31 January 1891 in the Royal English Opera House, built by Carte for this purpose, a glittering occasion with much of the royal family present. The opera had 160 performances but did not establish itself. Sullivan returned to musical comedy, including an anticlimactic reconciliation with Gilbert (*Utopia Unlimited,* 1893; *The Grand Duke,* 1896). He was knighted in 1883; at the queen's command he was buried in St. Paul's.

Bibl.: H. Sullivan and N. Flower, *Sir Arthur Sullivan: His Life, Letters, and Diaries* (London, 1927; 2nd ed., 1950). Percy Young, *Sir Arthur Sullivan* (New York, 1971). Thomas F. Dunhill, *Sullivan's Comic Operas: A Critical Appreciation* (New York, 1981). Philip H. Dillard, *How Quaint the Ways of Paradox!: An Annotated Gilbert and Sullivan Bibliography* (Metuchen, N.J., 1991). Michael Ffinch, *Gilbert and Sullivan* (London, 1993). Arthur Jacobs, *Arthur Sullivan: A Victorian Musician* (Oxford, 1994).

Sullivan, Joe [Joseph Michael] (b. Chicago, 4 Nov. 1906; d. San Francisco, 13 Oct. 1971). Jazz pianist. He recorded with Chicago, Dixieland, and swing groups, including sessions with McKenzie and Condon's Chicagoans ("China Boy," 1927), the Chicago Rhythm Kings (1928), Red Nichols (1929–30), and Billy Banks (the first version of "Oh Peter," 1932). He joined Bob Crosby in 1936 and again, after recovering from tuberculosis, in 1939. He recorded with Lionel Hampton and Billie Holiday (both 1939) and into the 1940s led bands, initially heading a racially integrated swing group in New York (1939–40). Having recorded as an unaccompanied stride and blues soloist from 1933 (including "Little Rock Getaway," 1935), he increasingly worked alone, holding a long residency at the Club Hangover in San Francisco from 1955.

Sullivan, Maxine [Williams, Marietta] (b. Homestead, Pa., 13 May 1911; d. New York, 7 Apr. 1987). Jazz singer. A swing version of *Loch Lomond,* recorded in 1937, typecast her as a singer of folk material, and with John Kirby's group (1938–42) she continued in this vein while also singing popular swing tunes, which she preferred. She performed in musicals and at the Cotton Club with Louis Armstrong (1938–40) and toured with Benny Carter (1941). After working as a soloist she retired from music, but later joined the World's Greatest Jazz Band (1969–ca. 1976) and sang at many jazz festivals. Her albums include *The Great Songs from the Cotton Club* (1984).

Sulzer, Salomon (b. Hohenems, 30 Mar. 1804; d. Vienna, 17 Jan. 1890). Cantor and composer. *Obercantor* in Vienna, 1826–81. His voice was admired by scholars and musicians as well, including Schumann, Liszt, and Meyerbeer. In 1868 he was made Knight of the Order of Franz Joseph. He composed music, arranged for solo cantor and men's chorus, for services throughout the year, which was published as *Schir Zion* in 2 volumes (1838–40; 1855–66). His son Julius Salomon Sulzer (1834–91) was a violinist and director of the Hofburgtheater in Vienna (1875–91).

Bibl.: Hanoch Avenary, ed., *Kantor Salomon Sulzer und seine Zeit: eine Dokumentation* (Sigmaringen, 1985).

Sumac, Yma (b. Ichocan, Peru, 10 Sept. 1927). Soprano. Renowned for the astounding range of her voice. Moved from the Andes to Lima as a youth; formed the Inca Taky Trio with her husband and a cousin, touring South America between 1942 and 1946, when she traveled to the U.S.; there she recorded a best-selling album, *Voice of the Xtabay,* and performed her husband's arrangements of South American music. She made a Broadway appearance in *Flahooley* (1951); after a hiatus of many years, she sang again in 1975 at New York.

Sumera, Lepo (b. Tallinn, 8 May 1950). Composer. Graduated from Tallinn Conservatory in 1973, where he studied composition with Heino Eller and Heino Jürisalu. Served as a consultant to the Estonian Composers Union, 1978–86. Beginning 1986, taught composition at the Tallinn Conservatory. In 1989, appointed minister of culture of Estonia; in 1985, received Estonian State Prize. Works include the theater piece *Saare Piiga laul merest* [The Island Maiden] (1989); 3 symphonies (1981, 1984, 1988) and other symphonic music, ballets, works for chorus and orchestra, chamber music, works for piano.

Summer, Donna [Gaines, LaDonna Andrea] (b. Boston, 31 Dec. 1948). Popular singer and songwriter. She sang in musical theater in Europe; from 1975 the success of her singles released in the U.S. made her the most prominent exponent of disco (including "Love To Love You Baby," 1975; "Bad Girls," 1979). After 1980 she turned to more mainstream popular music but remained very successful through songs such as "Love Is in Control" (1982).

Sun Ra [Blount, Herman ("Sonny"); Le Sony'r Ra] (b. Birmingham, Ala., May 1914; d. there, 30 May 1993). Jazz bandleader, composer, and keyboard player. In Chicago in 1953 he founded a band later known as his Myth-Science (or Solar) Arkestra. Initially it was oriented toward hard bop, although Sun Ra experimented with electric keyboards, as on the album *Angels and Demons at Play* (1955–57). After moving to New York (1960) he recorded free-jazz albums such as *The Magic City* (?1965) and *The Heliocentric Worlds of Sun Ra* (1965). The Arkestra, based in Philadelphia beginning in the 1970s, toured the U.S. and Europe. The film *Sun Ra: A Joyful Noise* (1980) presented his "Egyptian-galactic" costumed performances, ranging from simple dance riffs to wildly virtuosic free-jazz improvising (notably by Sun Ra himself and his saxophonists, including John Gilmore and Marshall Allen).

Supervia, Conchita (b. Barcelona, 9 Dec. 1895; d. London, 30 Mar. 1936). Mezzo-soprano. Attended Colegio de los Damas negras, Barcelona; made her debut at Buenos Aires in 1910; sang Octavian in the Rome premiere of *Der Rosenkavalier* in 1911, and appeared at Chicago in 1915 and 1916; made her La Scala debut in 1926. Known for a powerful, ingratiating stage personality, she gained acclaim for her rendition of Carmen and her performances in Rossini operas, many of which were little known at the time. Sang at Covent Garden in 1934 and 1935. She died in childbirth.

Suppé [Suppè], **Franz (von)** [Francesco Ezechiele Ermenegildo Cavaliere Suppé Demelli] (b. Spalato, Dalmatia, 18 Apr. 1819; d. Vienna, 21 May 1895). Composer. His early musical talent was encouraged by the bandmaster Ferrari and the cathedral choirmaster Cigalla. He studied law in Padua, but made trips to Milan, where he met and heard the operas of Rossini, Donizetti, and Verdi. In 1835 he accompanied his mother to Vienna, where he studied music with Seyfried and Sechter. In 1840 he took the unpaid post of third Kapellmeister at the Theater in der Josefstadt. From 1841, when his comedy *Jung lustig, im Alter traurig, oder Die Folgen der Erziehung* was first performed, to 1845 he wrote over 20 theatrical scores for the Theater in der Josefstadt. These included *Marie, die Tochter des Regiments* and *Ein Morgen, ein Mittag und ein Abend in Wien* (both 1844), and music for *A Midsummer Night's Dream.* Between 1845 and 1862 he was Kapellmeister at the Theater an der Wien, where he wrote scores and conducted numerous significant operatic performances. Suppé's *Das Pensionat* (1860) was the first successful Viennese operetta, modeled after the French works that had become popular in Vienna's theaters. He moved to the Kaitheater (1862), then to the Carltheater (1865, formerly the Theater in der Leopoldstadt), all the while composing overtures and incidental music to operettas, opera parodies, and operas. His most successful scores were *Gervinus* (1849), *Flotte Bursche* (1863), *Fatinitza* (1876), and *Boccaccio* (1879). His invitation to the first Bayreuth festival in 1876 was followed by invitations to Paris, Brussels, Germany, and Italy. In 1881 he was given the freedom of the city of Vienna. After his retirement from the Carltheater in 1882 he continued to compose and successfully conducted his operetta *Die Afrikareise* in Germany in 1883. Aside from over 200 stage works, his compositions include sacred and secular vocal music, symphonies, overtures (*Poet and Peasant, Light Calvary,* and *Morning, Noon, and Night in Vienna*), songs, dances, and string quartets.

Surdin, Morris (b. Toronto, 8 May 1914; d. Toronto, 19 Aug. 1979). Composer and conductor. In Toronto he studied violin with Louis Gesensway and conducting with César Borré. He later studied composition with Henry Brant in New York. Beginning in 1939 and intermittently throughout his career, he worked as a conductor and composer of incidental music for the CBC. From 1949 to 1954 he conducted and composed for CBS in New York. He is credited with over 2,000 scores for radio, television, and films. He also composed concert music, notably 2 concertos for accordion and string orchestra (1966, 1976), a concerto for viola and orchestra (1978), the ballet *The Remarkable Rocket* (1961), and a musical, *Wild Rose* (1967).

Suriano, Francesco. See Soriano, Francesco.

Surinach, Carlos (b. Barcelona, 4 Mar. 1915). Composer and conductor. He studied piano and music theory in Barcelona with José Caminals (1929–36), then composition with Enrique Morera (1936–39). In 1940 he went to Germany to study, first at the Robert Schumann Conservatory in Düsseldorf, then at the Academy of Fine Arts in Berlin with Max Trapp. He returned to Barcelona in 1942 to conduct opera and orchestral concerts. From 1947 to 1950 he lived in Paris, conducting in France and elsewhere in Europe. In 1950 he moved to the U.S. He conducted in New York and elsewhere and began to establish himself as a composer, particularly for the dance. For Martha Graham he wrote *Embattled Garden* (1958), *Acrobats of God* (1960), and *The Owl and the Pussycat* (1978). He also wrote for the José Limón Company, the Joffrey Ballet, the Paul Taylor Dance Company, and others. Much of his music reflects his Spanish heritage, and particularly the flamenco tradition. This is heard in the themes, tunes, rhythms, and scales of pieces such as Symphony no. 2 (1949), *Feria mágica* (orchestra, 1956), Concertino for Piano and Strings (1957), *Symphonic Variations* (1963), *Melorhythmic Dances* (orchestra, 1966).

Surman, John (Douglas) (b. Tavistock, England, 30 Aug. 1944). Jazz baritone and soprano saxophonist. While with composer Mike Westbrook (1958–68), Surman adapted John Coltrane's free-jazz style to the baritone instrument. His recordings include John McLaughlin's jazz-rock album *Extrapolation* (1969) and the unaccompanied album *Westering Home* (1972), incorporating folk themes. He led a trio with double bass and drums (1969–72), formed the saxophone trio SOS, in which each man also played synthesizer (1973–75), and played with double bassist Miroslav Vitous (1979–82) and Gil Evans (1983, 1986–87). He also played for a dance company at the Paris Opera (1974–79) and wrote church, ballet, and brass band music.

Susa, Conrad (b. Springdale, Pa., 26 Apr. 1935). Composer. He attended Carnegie–Mellon Univ. in Pittsburgh, studying with Nicholas Lopatnikoff, then went to Juilliard, where he studied with William Bergsma and Vincent Persichetti. In 1975 he moved to San Francisco. He is best known for his vocal works, particularly his operas *Transformations* (Minneapolis, 1973) and *Black River* (Minneapolis, 1975) and songs such as *Hymns for the Amusement of Children* (1972); other works include the opera *The Love of Don Perlimplín* (1983) and the chorus *Earth Song* (1988).

Susato, Tylman (b. ca. 1500?; d. Antwerp?, 1561–64). Composer and music publisher. He was a calligrapher at Antwerp Cathedral (1529–30) and then a trumpeter there (1531), subsequently becoming a town musician (1532–49). Beginning in 1543 he worked as a music publisher, first in partnership with others, then from 1543, the year he acquired his own privilege, independently. During his 18 years of activity he issued 25 books of chansons, 3 books of Masses, 19 books of motets, and 11 *Musyck boexken* (Flemish songs, dances, and psalter songs). He also authored 2 books of cantus firmus chansons for 2 or 3 voices (1544, ca. 1552).

Susskind, (Jan) Walter (b. Prague, 1 May 1913; d. Berkeley, Calif., 25 Mar. 1980). Conductor. Served as Szell's assistant at the German Opera, Prague, from 1934 to 1938; later was a member of the Czech Trio in London (1938–41) and directed the Carl Rosa Opera (1943–45). After his 1945 orchestral debut, he led the Scottish Orchestra (1946–52); the Victoria Symphony, Melbourne (to 1955); the Toronto Symphony (1956–65); the Aspen Festival (1962–68); the St. Louis Symphony (1968–75); and the Cincinnati Symphony (from 1978).

Süssmayr, Franz Xaver (b. Schwanenstadt, Upper Austria, 1766; d. Vienna, 17 Sept. 1803). Composer. He studied with his father, a choirmaster. In 1779 he went to Kremsmünster, where he was a student at the monastery school and then at the Ritterakademie; he also continued his musical education. He arrived in Vienna in 1788 and supported himself as a music teacher. Eventually he made the acquaintance of Mozart, with whom he studied. After Mozart's death Constanze engaged him to complete the unfinished Requiem K. 626; scholars have argued ever since about the magnitude of Süssmayr's contributions. Following Mozart's death Süssmayr studied with Salieri; he became Kapellmeister of the German opera at the National Theater in Vienna in 1794 and held this position until his death. He enjoyed success as a composer; Beethoven wrote piano variations on a tune from one of his singspiels. His works include over 20 operas (mostly for Vienna, but several for Kremsmünster); the singspiel *Der Spiegel von Arkadien* (1794) was quite popular; also ballets; a Missa Solemnis, 4 other Masses, 2 Requiems, cantatas, other sacred and secular vocal pieces; 2 symphonies, 1 piano concerto, 2 clarinet concertos, other orchestral pieces; and chamber music.

Bibl.: Johann Winterberger, "Franz Xaver Süssmayr: Leben, Umwelt und Gestalt" (diss., Univ. of Innsbruck, 1946). Henry Hausner, *Franz Xaver Süssmayr* (Vienna, 1964). Walter Włcek, *Franz Xaver Süssmayr als Kirchenkomponist* (Tutzing, 1978).

Suter, Hermann (b. Aargau, Switzerland, 28 Apr. 1870; d. Basel, 22 June 1926). Composer and conductor. He studied in Basel, then at the Stuttgart and Leipzig conservatories. He returned to Switzerland in 1892, working as an organist and as a choral conductor in Zurich, then, from 1902 on, in Basel. From 1918 to 1921 he was director of the Basel Conservatory. The majority of his compositions are for chorus, either unaccompanied or with orchestra, *Le laudi di S. Francesco d'Assisi,* oratorio (1925), being perhaps the best known. He also composed a symphony, a violin concerto (1924), 3 string quartets (1901, 1910, 1921), a string sextet (1920), and several songs.

Bibl.: W. Merian, *Hermann Suter: der Dirigent und der Komponist* (Basel, 1926).

Suter, Robert (b. St. Gall, 30 Jan. 1919). Composer. He studied with Walther Geiser at the Basel Conservatory, receiving his diploma in 1943. His *Musikalisches Tagebuch* (1946), a song cycle for soprano and chamber ensemble written in a style recalling the pre-serial songs of Schoenberg and Webern, brought him to public notice. The *Lyric Suite* (chamber orchestra, 1959) and *Heilige Leier, sprich, sei meine Stimme* (cantata, 1960) continue in this direction. Works from the late 1960s and the 1970s tend toward larger forms and larger ensembles, for example, the Piano Sonata (1967), *Trois nocturnes* (viola, orchestra, 1969), *Musik* (orchestra, 1975). Other works include *Marcia funebre* (1982); *Bhalt du mi Allewyyl lieb* (children's chorus, wind ensemble, 1986); string sextet (1987); *Gruezi* (winds, 1987); *Der abwesende Gott* (chorus, orchestra, 1988).

Bibl.: Dino Larese and Jacques Wildberger, *Robert Suter* (St. Gall, 1967).

Sutermeister, Heinrich (b. Schaffhausen, Switzerland, 12 Aug. 1910; d. Switzerland, 16 Mar. 1995). Originally preparing himself for a career as a schoolteacher, he turned to music in his 20s, studying at the Munich Conservatory with Carl Orff (1932–34). His radio opera *Die schwarze Spinne* (1935) was favorably received; *Romeo und Julia,* a 2-act opera based on Shakespeare, premiered in Dresden in 1940. *Die Zauberinsel* is based on Shakespeare's *Tempest* (1942); *Raskolnikoff* (1948) was perhaps his most durably successful opera. Besides these and other operas, he composed many works for chorus with and without accompaniment, other vocal works (*Sechs Liebesbriefe aus dem 16. und 18. Jahrhundert,* soprano, orchestra, 1980); 3 piano concertos (1943, 1954, 1962), 2 cello concertos (1956, 1971), and several smaller pieces for orchestra, including *Divertimento,* string orchestra (1936), and *Sérénade pour Montreux* (1970), plus many dramatic works for radio and television.

Suthaus, Ludwig (b. Cologne, 12 Dec. 1906; d. Berlin, 7 Sept. 1971). Tenor. Attended the Cologne Hochschule (1922–28); made his debut at Aachen in 1928, remaining there until 1931; later sang at Stuttgart (1932–41) and with the Berlin State Opera (1941–48) and Berlin City Opera (1948–65). He appeared at Covent Garden in 1952 and 1953, making his U.S. debut in the latter year; he also toured the USSR in 1955, and sang at the Vienna Opera from 1957. A favorite of Furtwängler, he was best known for Wagnerian roles.

Sutherland, Joan (b. Sydney, 7 Nov. 1926). Soprano. Studied in her home city, singing in Goosens's *Judith* at the Sydney Conservatory in 1951 before leaving for the Royal College of Music, London, where she was a pupil of Clive Carey; appeared at Covent Garden in *Die Zauberflöte* in 1952, singing there opposite Callas in *Norma* in 1953; also appeared in several new productions of Handel operas with the Handel Society. She gained fame for her portrayal of Lucia at Covent Garden in 1959, and the next year made her French, Italian, and U.S. debuts; in 1961 she began a lasting association with the Metropolitan Opera. She toured Australia with her Sutherland–Williamson Opera Company in 1965, and appeared at Sydney's new opera house in 1974. She excelled in the Italian bel canto and Romantic repertories, often with her husband since 1954, Richard Bonynge, leading the orchestra; her recordings are extensive. She was made a Dame of the British Empire in 1979. She retired in 1991.

Sutherland, Margaret (Ada) (b. Adelaide, 20 Nov. 1897; d. Melbourne, 12 Aug. 1984). Composer. She took piano lessons with Goll and composition lessons with Hart at the Marshall Hall (Melba) Conservatorium and the Melbourne Univ. Conservatorium. In 1923 she traveled to London to study with Bax and then to Vienna, returning to Melbourne in 1925. She continued to work as a pianist, teacher, and composer. Her music was influenced by her teacher Bax, as well as by other European composers such as Bartók and Hindemith. Her style is expressive and flexible, often using standard orchestration (Violin Concerto, 1954) and capable of being both dissonant and lyrical. Works include stage music (*The Young Kabbarli,* opera, 1965), orchestral music (*Haunted Hills,* 1950; Concerto grosso, 1955), vocal music (*Six Australian Songs,* voice, piano, 1967), and chamber music.

Sutton, Ralph (Earl) (b. Hamburg, near St. Louis, 4 Nov. 1922). Jazz pianist. He played stride piano on the radio show *This Is Jazz* (1947) and at Eddie Condon's club in New York (1948–56). He joined the World's Greatest Jazz Band (1968–74), having played with group members since 1965. He then played at clubs and festivals mainly as a free-lance and recorded often, including the unaccompanied album *The Other Side of Ralph Sutton* and duos with Ruby Braff and Jay McShann (all 1980).

Bibl.: James D. Shacter, *Piano Man: The Story of Ralph Sutton* (Chicago, 1975).

Suzuki, Shin'ichi (b. Nagoya, 18 Oct. 1898). Violinist and teacher. Son of Masakichi Suzuki (1859–1944), instrument builder and founder of the Suzuki Seizō Co. Shin'ichi studied violin in Japan and from 1921 to 1929 in Berlin; he founded the Suzuki Quartet with three brothers in 1930, the same year becoming head of the Teikoku Music School; he later formed the Tokyo String Orchestra. Beginning in 1933 he developed a teaching method based on creating a proper learning environment and using a process of repetition; after World War II he set up institutes for general learning and for violin tutelage in particular. He traveled widely, including to the U.S., in order to promulgate his technique.

Bibl.: Clifford Cook, *Suzuki Education in Action: A Story of Talent Training from Japan* (New York, 1970). Shin'ichi Suzuki, *Where Love Is Deep: The Writings of Shin'ichi Suzuki* (St. Louis, 1982). Masaaki Honda, *Shinichi Suzuki: Man of Love* (Princeton, 1984). Craig Timmerman, *Journey Down the Kreisler Highway: Reflections on the Teachings of Shinichi Suzuki* (Memphis, 1987).

Svanholm, Set (Karl Viktor) (b. Västerås, 2 Sept. 1904; d. Saltsjö-Duvnäs, near Stockholm, 4 Oct. 1964). Tenor. Attended the Royal Conservatory, Stockholm, from 1927 to 1929; made his debut in 1930 (as a baritone) at the Royal Opera, continuing to appear there until 1963; first appeared as a tenor in 1936. He sang at Milan and Bayreuth (1942), the Vienna Opera (1938–42), the Metropolitan Opera (1946–56), Covent Garden (1948–57), and elsewhere in Europe and the Americas.

Svendsen, Johan (Severin) (b. Christiania [now Oslo], 30 Sept. 1840; d. Copenhagen, 14 June 1911). Violinist, composer, and conductor. Studied violin, later composition, at the Leipzig Conservatory, 1863–67, where his teachers included Hauptmann, Ferdinand David, E. F. Richter, and Reinecke. He traveled to Paris in 1868, where he performed Grieg's Second Violin Sonata; traveled to London and Weimar in 1870, where he met Liszt. In 1872 he played in the orchestra at the laying of the cornerstone at Bayreuth. From 1872 to 1877 he conducted and taught in Norway; was joint conductor with Grieg of the Music Society concerts; from 1883, court conductor at Copenhagen. He retired in 1908. His compositions include 2 symphonies (op. 4, ca. 1886; op. 15, 1877); violin concerto op. 6 (1864–70); cello concerto op. 7 (1870); string quartet op. 1 (1865); string quintet op. 5 (1867); string octet op. 3 (1865–66); other orchestral and chamber works; a few piano works; songs.

Bibl.: Bjarne Kortsen, *Chamber Music Works by Johan Svendsen* (Bergen, 1971).

Svetlanov, Evgeny (b. Moscow, 6 Sept. 1928). Conductor, composer, and pianist. Attended the Gnessin Institute and the Moscow Conservatory; from 1953 led concerts of the Moscow Radio Symphony; joined the Bolshoi Theater in 1955, serving as principal conductor there from 1962 to 1964; named conductor of the USSR State Orchestra in 1965, and received a Lenin Prize in 1972. His works include a symphony (1956), a piano concerto (1951), the *Fantasia siberiana* for orchestra (1953), and film and piano music.

Sviridov, Georgy Vasilevich (b. Fatezh, near Kursk, 16 Dec. 1915). Composer. Pursued early music studies in Kursk, then studied piano and composition at music school in Leningrad, 1932–36. In 1936 he entered the Leningrad Conservatory, where from 1937 he studied composition with Shostakovich, graduating in 1941. Concertized as a pianist. He is best known as a composer of choral and vocal music, both of patriotic and of folk content. Works include the *Pathetic Oratorio* on texts of Mayakovsky for soloists, mixed chorus, and orchestra (1959), *Kursk Songs,* cantata, mixed chorus and orchestra (1964), *Spring Cantata,* mixed chorus and orchestra (1972), and other vocal-symphonic music; *Concerto in Memory of Alexander Yurlov,* mixed a capella chorus (1973), and much other choral music; many songs and song cycles; chamber music; works for piano; incidental and film music.

Bibl.: D. V. Frishman, ed., *Georgii Sviridov: sbornik statei* (Moscow: Muzyka, 1971). A. A. Zolotov, comp., *Kniga o Sviridove: razmyshleniia, vyskazyvaniia, stat'i, zametki* (Moscow, 1983).

Swados, Elizabeth (b. Buffalo, 5 Feb. 1951). Composer. After receiving a B.A. from Bennington College in Vermont in 1972, she worked with various theater groups, including La Mama Experimental Theater in New York and the International Theater Group. Her musical *Runaways* (1978), a string of songs and sketches using child performers and incorporating a variety of popular music styles, brought her to wider notice. She collaborated with the cartoonist Garry Trudeau in *Doonesbury* (1983) and *Rap Master Ronnie* (1984). She wrote several other musicals; a cantata, *Haggadah* (1980); an oratorio, *Jerusalem* (1984); scores for the theater, dance, and films. She is the author of *Listening Out Loud: Becoming a Composer* (New York, 1988).

Swallow, Steve [Stephen W.] (b. New York, 4 Oct. 1940). Jazz bass player and composer. He joined pianist Paul Bley in 1959; together they joined Jimmy Giuffre, playing free jazz (1961–63). He also recorded George Russell's album *Ezz-thetics* (1961) and played Dixieland, swing, and bop. He joined the Art Farmer–Jim Hall quartet (1963–64), Stan Getz (1965–67), Gary Burton, in whose jazz-rock group he switched from double bass to electric bass guitar (1967–70, from 1973), and Carla Bley (from late 1970s). His compositions include the duo "Hotel Hello" with Burton (recorded in 1974) and a setting of poems, "Home" (recorded in 1980).

Swan, Timothy (b. Worcester, Mass., 23 July 1758; d. Northfield, Mass., 23 July 1842). Composer of hymns. He received minimal musical training except for that at a singing school. His publications include "The Songster's Assistant" (ca. 1800) and "New England Harmony" (1801).

Bibl.: Guy B. Webb, "Timothy Swan: Yankee Tunesmith" (diss., Univ. of Illinois, 1972).

Swanson, Howard (b. Atlanta, 18 Aug. 1907; d. New York, 12 Nov. 1978). Composer. He grew up in Cleveland and attended the Cleveland Institute of Music, where he studied piano and composition (B.M., 1937). In 1938 he won a fellowship to go to the American Academy in Fontainebleau to study with Nadia Boulanger. In 1941 he moved to New York. He became known first as a song composer, particularly with his settings of poems by Langston Hughes—"The Negro Speaks of Rivers" (1942), "Joy" (1946), and "Montage" (1947). His *Short Symphony* (1948), introduced by the New York Philharmonic in 1950, was received enthusiastically and was widely performed. Swanson returned to Europe in 1952 and remained there until 1966, when he returned to the U.S., settling in New York. Of his later works the best known are *Fantasy Piece,* soprano saxophone and string orchestra (1969), *Piano Sonata no. 2* (1972), and *Trio,* flute, oboe, piano (1975).

Bibl.: *The Black Composer Speaks,* ed. David Baker, Lida Belt, and Herman Hudson (Metuchen, N.J., 1978) [includes interview and works list].

Swarowsky, Hans (b. Budapest, 16 Sept. 1899; d. Salzburg, 10 Sept. 1975). Conductor. He studied with Schoenberg, Webern, Weingartner, and Strauss. In the 1930s he conducted at the opera houses of Stuttgart, Hamburg, Berlin, and Zurich. Managed the Salzburg Festival, 1940–44, and conducted the Kraków Polish Philharmonic, 1944. From 1946 he taught at the Vienna Academy of Music (Abbado and Mehta among his pupils) and conducted the Vienna Symphony, 1946–48, and Graz opera, 1947–50. From 1957 he conducted at the Vienna Staatsoper and directed the Scottish National Orchestra. He was a noted interpreter of the Viennese classics as well as Bruckner, Mahler, Strauss, Schoenberg, Berg, and Webern. He authored many articles and German translations of Italian operas.

Swayne, Giles (Oliver Cairnes) (b. Stevenage, 30 June 1946). Composer. A cousin of Elizabeth Maconchy, he studied at Cambridge with Leppard and Maw and at the Royal Academy of Music with Birtwistle, Bush, and Maw. He took classes with Messiaen in Paris (1976–77) and studied African music in Africa. His works range from virtuosic avant-garde writing to carefully structured applications of ethnic-folk, amateur, and student-level techniques. His textless depiction of Creation for 28 voices, *Cry* (1979), has won particular acclaim. Other works include orchestral pieces (*Orlando's Music,* 1974; *Pentecost Music,* 1977; *Naotwala Lala,* 1984; Symphony for Small Orchestra, 1984; *The Song of Leviathan,* 1988); many chamber works for various solo and ensemble forces; the opera *Le nozze di cherubino* (1984); choral works; solo vocal works; piano and organ pieces.

Sweelinck [Swelinck, Zwelinck, Sweeling, Sweelingh, Sweling, Swelingh], **Jan Pieterszoon** (b. Deventer, May? 1562; d. Amsterdam, 16 Oct. 1621). Composer. The elder son of Peter Swybbertszdon and Elske Sweeling, he adopted his mother's family name. The assertion that he studied in Venice with Zarlino is not supported by surviving evidence. His only known teachers besides his father were Jacob Buyck, pastor at the Oude Kerk, Amsterdam, and Jan Willemszoon Lossy, a countertenor and shawm player at Haarlem. By 1580, and possibly as early as 1577, he was organist at the Oude Kerk; his duties there were probably to provide an hour of music twice daily in the church. He became famous for his brilliant improvisations at the organ and harpsichord. From this time onward he left Amsterdam only to inspect new organs and advise on repairs and restorations. As a teacher Sweelinck was influential and sought after, and his pupils were among the most highly regarded musicians of the time; they included Andreas Düben, Peter Hasse, Samuel and Gottfried Scheidt, Paul Siefert, Ulrich Cernitz, Jacob Praetorius, and Heinrich Scheidemann, founders of the so-called north German organ school of the 17th century. Sweelinck's 254 vocal works, which were all printed, include 33 chansons, 19 madrigals, 39 motets (*Cantiones sacrae,* 1619), and 153 Psalm settings. His 70 keyboard works consist mainly of fantasias *(Fantasia chromatica),* echo fantasias, toccatas, and variations.

Bibl.: *Jan Pieterszoon Sweelinck: Werken,* ed. Max Seiffert (The Hague and Leipzig, 1894–1901; R: 1968). *Jan Pieterszoon Sweelinck: Opera omnia, editio altera,* ed. R. Lagas et al. (Amsterdam, 1957–). B. van den Sigtenhorst Meyer, *Jan P. Sweelinck en zijn instrumentale muziek* (The Hague, 1934; 2nd ed., 1946); *De vocale muziek van Jan P. Sweelinck* (The Hague, 1948). Robert L. Tusler, *The Organ Music of Jan Pieterszoon Sweelinck* (Bilthoven, 1958). Alan Curtis, *Sweelinck's Keyboard Music: A Study of English Elements in Seventeenth-Century Dutch Composition* (Leiden and London, 1969; 2nd ed., 1972). Frits Noske, *Sweelinck* (Oxford, 1988).

Sweeney, Joel Walker [Joe] (b. Appomattox, Va., ca. 1810; d. there, 1860). Banjo player and maker. Learned banjo from slaves on his father's farm. He may have transformed the body of the banjo from a gourd-shape into a hoop. He also may have added the fifth string to the instrument; he was certainly instrumental in popularizing this form of the instrument. He was the first known white banjo player. During the 1830s he frequently performed in blackface. He taught the banjo to many minstrel players.

Sweney, John R. (b. West Chester, Pa., 31 Dec. 1837; d. Chester, Pa., 10 Apr. 1899). Evangelistic singer and composer. Taught in Dover, Del. Professor of music at the Pennsylvania Military Academy for 25 years. Composer of more than 1,000 gospel hymns. He also compiled many collections of hymns, some with William J. Kirkpatrick.

Bibl.: Jacob Henry Hall, *Biography of Gospel Song and Hymn Writers* (New York, 1914; R: 1971).

Swieten, Gottfried (Bernhard) van (b. Leiden, 29 Oct. 1733; d. Vienna, 29 Mar. 1803). Patron. Although he composed some music of his own, he was better known in his capacity as musical patron. He came to Vienna in 1745. After completion of his education he joined the civil service, which took him abroad frequently; he was ambassador to Berlin in 1770–77, during which time he commissioned C. P. E. Bach's six string symphonies w.182 (1773). After his return to Vienna in 1777 he was appointed prefect of the imperial library, holding informal meetings and concerts in his rooms there that reflected his enthusiasm for the music of Handel and Bach; these were influential in interesting Mozart, a regular attendee from ca. 1782, in the music of the Baroque. Van Swieten also assembled a group of patrons who sponsored performances of oratorios including Haydn's *The Creation* (1798) and *The Seasons* (1801), for which he apparently translated and adapted the texts, and Mozart's arrangement of Handel's *Messiah* (1789).

Bibl.: E. Otteson, "Gottfried van Swieten, Patron of Haydn and Mozart," *PRMA* 89 (1962–63): 63–74.

Swift, Kay (b. New York, 19 Apr. 1897; d. Southington, Conn., 28 Jan. 1993). Pianist and composer. She learned piano as a child, then studied at the Institute of Musical Art in New York with Bertha Tapper (piano) and A. E. Johnstone (composition). At the New England Conservatory in Boston she continued piano study with Heinrich Gebhard and composition with Charles Loeffler and Percy Goetschius. In the late 1920s she worked as a rehearsal pianist for Broadway shows. With her husband, the banker and diplomat James Warburg, as lyricist she wrote several songs, the best known being "Can't We Be Friends?" (1929), "Can This Be Love?" (1930), and "Up among the Chimney Pots" (1930). She continued composing songs, musicals, ballets, film scores, and piano music well into the 1970s.

Swift, Richard (b. Middlepoint, Ohio, 24 Sept. 1927). Composer. He studied at the Univ. of Chicago with Leland Smith and Grosvenor Cooper (M.A., 1956). In 1956 he joined the faculty at the Univ. of California, Davis. A member of the San Francisco Composers' Forum and the New Music Ensemble. His works include Concerto no. 1 (chamber orchestra, 1961); Violin Concerto (1965); Symphony (1970); Concerto no. 2 (chamber orchestra, 1980); 5 string quartets (1955, 1958, 1964, 1973, 1982); *Summer Notes* (piano, 1965); *Domains I* (baritone, chamber ensemble, 1963); *Specimen Days* (soprano and orchestra, 1977); Piano Trio no. 2 (1988); *A Stitch in Time* (guitar, 1989).

Sydeman, William (Jay) (b. New York, 8 May 1928). Composer. Abandoning his studies in business administration at Duke Univ. in 1944, he went to the Mannes College of Music in New York, where he studied with Felix Salzer and Roy Travis (B.S., 1955). He also studied with Roger Sessions and with Arnold Franchetti at Hartt College of Music (M.Mus., 1958). From 1959 to 1970 he taught composition at Mannes College. His compositions from this period tend to be partially or wholly serial, rhythmically complex, and translucent in texture. Examples are *Orchestral Abstractions,* chamber orchestra (1958); 3 *Studies for Orchestra* (1959, 1963, 1965); 3 Concerti da camera, violin and chamber ensemble (1959, 1960, 1965); Concerto, piano 4-hands; and *In memoriam—John F. Kennedy,* narrator and orchestra (1966). In 1970 Sydeman began a period of travel and philosophical study and reflection. He continued to compose, but for smaller ensembles and in a style that aimed at being more accessible. Works from this period include *18 Duos,* 2 violins (1976); *Duo,* xylophone and vibes (1977); *Songs of Milarepa,* violin, narrator, dancer (1980); *Calendar of the Soul,* chorus (1982).

Sykes, Roosevelt (b. Elmar, Ark., 31 Jan. 1906; d. New Orleans, 11 July 1983). Blues pianist. Orphaned from age 7, he taught himself piano; from age 15 he played clubs in Louisiana and Mississippi, often traveling with Lee Green. His recording career began with the famous "44 Blues," 1929; his pseudonyms were R. S. Bey, Easy Papa Johnson, and Willie Kelly, and his nickname "Honeydripper." From the early 1930s he was a leading soloist and accompanist in Chicago; from 1954 he worked out of New Orleans. He toured and recorded widely through the late 1970s.

Szabelski, Bolesław (b. Radoryż, near Łuków, 3 Dec. 1896; d. Katowice, 27 Aug. 1979). Composer. In 1915 he studied at the Polish Musical Society School with Łysakowski, then went on to study organ under Surzyński and composition under Szymanowski and Statkowski at the Warsaw Conservatory. From 1929 to 1939 and from 1954 to 1967 he taught organ and composition at the Katowice Conservatory. His own compositions reflected his knowledge of formal structures of the 16th and 17th centuries, frequently involving passacaglia, toccata, and fuguelike procedures. His orchestral compositions often evince the concertante principle of Baroque compositions, complex contrapuntal textures, and polymodality. By the late 1950s he had begun experimenting with serialism, producing a strikingly innovative style. His works include 5 symphonies (1926, 1934, 1951, 1956, 1968), concertos, choral and chamber works.

Szabó, Ferenc (b. Budapest, 27 Dec. 1902; d. there, 4 Nov. 1969). Composer. He studied composition with Kodály, Siklós, and Weiner at the Budapest Academy of Music from 1922 to 1926. He subsequently became involved with labor issues, joining the Communist party in 1927. His political sympathies were visible in his compositions for amateur and popular use. He moved in 1932 to the USSR, where he was actively engaged with the principles put forth by the Union of

Soviet Composers. After the war he returned to Hungary and in 1945 joined the faculty at the Budapest Academy, which he headed from 1958 to 1967. His early style was eclectic and highly influenced by Kodály; he moved on to explore complexity of form, texture, and tonality in a sophisticated musical language with popular relevance. Works include stage music; orchestral music (*Lyric Suite,* 1936; *Ludas Matyi,* 1950; *Memento,* 1952); vocal music (*Farkasok dala* [Song of the Wolves], 1929–30; *Föltámadott a tenger* [In Fury Rose the Ocean], oratorio, 1955); and chamber works.

Szalonek, Witold (b. Katowice, 2 Mar. 1927). Composer. He studied composition under Woytowicz at the State College of Music in Katowice from 1949 to 1956. During the summer of 1960 he attended courses at Darmstadt, and from 1962 to 1963 worked with Boulanger in Paris. He joined the faculty at the State College in Katowice and served as its head in 1972. In 1974 he moved to West Berlin, where he taught composition at the Hochschule für Musik. His musical output was eclectic in its utilization of various European avant-garde techniques, ranging from tone clusters to nonfunctional tonality and pointillistic textures. His works include orchestral (*Mutazioni,* chamber orchestra, 1966), vocal (*Suita kurpiowska* [Kurpie Suite], alto, wind quintet, piano, string trio, 1955; *Ziemio miła* [O Pleasant Earth], cantata, voice, orchestra, 1969; folk song arrangements), and chamber music (*Inside? Outside?,* bass clarinet, string quartet, 1988).

Szałowski, Antoni (b. Warsaw, 21 Apr. 1907; d. Paris, 21 Mar. 1973). Composer. As a child, he studied violin with his father. He went on to study composition with Sikorski, as well as conducting and piano, at the Warsaw Conservatory. After graduating in 1930 he traveled to Paris, where he studied with Boulanger. He was active with the Association of Young Polish Composers and settled in Paris for the remainder of his life. His compositions are broadly within the contemporary neoclassical trend, utilizing traditional forms and genres, but with a modal and expressive voice that evokes the eastern European post-Romantic tradition. Works include Overture (1936); Sinfonietta (1940); *Radio Music* (1955); Aria and Toccata, chamber orchestra (1957); *La femme têtue,* radio score, speaker, 15 instruments (1958); *Le merveilleux voyage de Susanne Michel,* radio score (1962); chamber works.

Szamotuł [Szamotulczyk, Szamotulski], **Wacław z** (b. Szamotuły, near Poznań, ca. 1524; d. Pińczów?, near Kielce, 1560?). Composer and poet. He studied at the Collegium Lubranscianum at Poznań and at the Univ. of Kraków; served as secretary to Hieronim Chodkiewicz, the governor of Troki, Lithuania (1545–47). In 1547 he was appointed composer at the court of King Sigismund II August, where his responsibilities included writing music for the chapel choir. Beginning in 1550 he was involved in the Polish Protestant movement; from 1555 until his death he was active at the Calvinist court of the Lithuanian Duke Mikołaj Radziwiłł. His music (much now lost) includes principally sacred polyphony with Latin and Polish texts.

Székely, Endre (b. Budapest, 6 Apr. 1912; d. there, 14 Apr. 1989). Composer. He studied composition at the Budapest Academy of Music with Sikorski from 1933 to 1937. He became involved with labor issues and joined the Communist party, which was illegal at that time. He wrote and conducted workers' music and, after the war, was associated with the Hungarian Musicians' Union. He also edited the Hungarian periodicals *Éneklő nép* and *Éneklő munkás.* After 1960 he served on the faculty of the Budapest Training College for Teachers. His early compositions were influenced by Kodály; his music subsequently evinced Bartókian traits and, by the late 1950s, an intense exploration of the serialism of Schoenberg. He further experimented with avant-garde techniques such as tone clusters and aleatory. He wrote stage, orchestral, and chamber music.

Szelényi, István (b. Zólyom, 8 Aug. 1904; d. Budapest, 31 Jan. 1972). Composer. He studied composition with Kodály as well as piano with Laub and Székely at the Budapest Academy of Music. He worked in Paris and London with a ballet company; by 1945 he had returned to Budapest and joined the faculty at the conservatory. From 1956 to 1976 he also taught theory at the Budapest Academy of Music. His early works were highly controversial in their incorporation of avant-garde techniques; he performed music by European contemporaries such as Schoenberg. Szelényi's later works moved closer to traditional Hungarian symphonic style. Works include pantomimes, orchestral music (*Overture Activiste,* 1931; *Egy gyár szimfóniája* [Symphony of a Factory], 1946; *Hommage à Bartók,* 1947), vocal music (*Pro Pace,* oratorio, 1968), and chamber and piano works.

Szeligowski, Tadeusz (b. Lwów, 13 Sept. 1896; d. Poznań, 10 Jan. 1963). Composer. He studied piano with Kurz from 1910 to 1914 at the conservatory associated with the Polish Musical Society in Lwów; took composition lessons under Wallek-Walewski and Jachimecki in Kraków as well as graduating in law from Kraków Univ. He traveled to Paris and from 1929 to 1931 studied with Boulanger. Returned to Poland, where he taught music; after the war, worked with the Polish Composers' Union. His own compositions are in an eclectic style that draws from very diverse conservatory, historical, and avant-garde styles. Works include stage music (operas, ballets), orchestral music (*Suita lubelske,* small orchestra, 1945), vocal music (*Karta serc* [The Charter of the Hearts], cantata, soprano, choir, orchestra, 1952), and chamber music.

Szell, George (b. Budapest, 7 June 1897; d. Cleveland, 29 July 1970). Conductor. Studied piano at Vienna with Richard Robert, making his debut with the Vienna

Symphony in 1908; attended the Vienna Academy, then was a private pupil of Reger and Prohaska; in 1914 he appeared as conductor and pianist with the Berlin Philharmonic, with a symphony of his own on the program. Strauss hired him as an assistant at the Berlin State Opera in 1915; he later worked at Strasbourg (1917–18), Prague (1919–21), Darmstadt (1921–22), and Düsseldorf (1922–24), returning to Berlin to lead the State Opera and Radio Orchestra (1924–30). He directed the German Opera, Prague, from 1930 to 1936; World War II began while he was on tour. Settling in the U.S., he led radio concerts of the NBC Symphony (1941), conducted at the Metropolitan Opera (1942–46), and served as music director of the Cleveland Orchestra (1946 to his death), molding the ensemble into one of the world's finest.

Szervánsky, Endre (b. Kistétény, 27 Dec. 1911; d. Budapest, 25 June 1977). Composer. As a child he learned to play the clarinet and studied at the Budapest Academy of Music from 1922 to 1927. He subsequently made his living as a performer until, in 1931, he went back to the academy to study composition with Siklós. He worked for Hungarian Radio, orchestrating works for the ensemble there; then from 1942 to 1948 he taught at the National Conservatory. Thereafter he served on the composition faculty of the Budapest Academy. His compositions were influenced by the music of Kodály and Bartók, incorporating structures, rhythms, and modes from native Hungarian folk music. By the late 1950s (*Six Orchestral Pieces,* 1959) Szervánsky had engaged serial techniques, successfully drawing together careful, complex textures with dodecaphony. Works include the Clarinet Serenade (1950), Flute Concerto (1952–53), Concerto for Orchestra (1954), Requiem (1963), and Clarinet Concerto (1965).

Szeryng, Henryk (b. Zelazowa Wola, near Warsaw, 22 Sept. 1918; d. Kassel, Germany, 3 Mar. 1988). Violinist and diplomat. He studied violin from age 7, with Flesch in Berlin from age 10; in 1933 he made debuts in Warsaw, Bucharest, Vienna, and Paris. He studied composition with Boulanger in Paris, 1933–39. During World War II he played over 300 concerts for Allied troops; he also served as translator to the exiled Polish government in London and helped 4,000 Polish refugees resettle in Mexico. He took Mexican citizenship in 1946 and taught at Mexico City Univ., 1948–56. From 1954 he resumed extensive concertizing and recording; he won renown as an interpreter of Bach and Mozart. He promoted musical composition in Mexico; from 1970 he was a Mexican adviser to UNESCO.

Szigeti, Joseph (b. Budapest, 5 Sept. 1892; d. Lucerne, 19 Feb. 1973). Violinist. Entered the Budapest Academy at age 8, making his debut at 11; performed at Berlin in 1905; lived in London from 1906 to 1913, concertizing and coming under the influence of Busoni; toured Europe in 1913 and 1914, after which a bout with tuberculosis confined him until 1917. He taught at Geneva until 1924, then moved to Paris in 1925, also touring throughout the world; with the onset of war he left for the U.S., settling in California. In 1960 he went back to Switzerland. Composers such as Bartók, Busoni, Prokofiev, and Bloch wrote works for him; he recorded extensively, offering interpretations of music from Bach to 20th-century composers.

Bibl.: Joseph Szigeti, *With Strings Attached: Reminiscences and Reflections* (New York, 1979). Joseph Szigeti, *Szigeti on the Violin* (New York, 1979).

Szokolay, Sándor (b. Kúnágota, 30 Mar. 1931). Composer. From 1950 to 1957 he studied composition with Szabó and Farkas at the Budapest Academy of Music. He worked with the music division of Hungarian Radio from 1957 to 1961. In 1966 he became a professor at the Budapest Academy. His compositional predilections moved quickly toward dramatic music. His operas and oratorios, on striking political subjects and frequently involving musical and mythical traditions of non-Western peoples, saw great success. In his works of the late 1960s he freely incorporated serial techniques. His style throughout his career remained vivid and highly expressive. Works include *Az iszonyat balladája* [The Ballad of Horror], ballet (1960); *Istár pokoljárása* [Isthar's Descent into Hell], oratorio (1960); *Vérnász* [Blood Wedding], opera (1962–64); *Hamlet,* opera (1965–68); *Az áldozat* [The Sacrifice], oratorio-ballet (1970–71); *Szávitri,* opera (1987–89); *Ecce homo,* Passion opera (1987).

Szymanowska [née Wołowska], **Maria Agata** (b. Warsaw, 14 Dec. 1789; d. St. Petersburg, 24 July 1831). Pianist and composer. Studied with Antonio Lisowski (1789–1800) and Tomasz Gremm (1800–1804). Debut in Warsaw, 1810. Concertized 1815–28. First pianist to the Russian court, 1822. Cherubini dedicated his Fantasia in C major to her. Compositions include a fanfare, 2 trumpets and 2 horns; waltzes, piano 3-hands; *Sérénade,* cello and piano (1820); mazurkas, exercises, nocturnes, and other solo piano music; songs.

Bibl.: M. Iwanejko, *Maria Szymanowska* (Kraków, 1959).

Szymanowski, Karol (Maciej) (b. Tymoszówska, Ukraine, 6 Oct. 1882; d. Lausanne, 29 Mar. 1937). Composer. The young Karol began to study music early with his father. In 1901 he traveled to Warsaw to continue his pursuit of music and there studied harmony with Zawirski and composition with Noskowski. Owing to the limited opportunities for new music in Warsaw, however, Szymanowski focused his efforts in other European musical centers; in 1905 he helped found the Young Polish Composers' Publishing Company in Berlin. He spent the prewar period in Vienna and Italy, and visiting areas of Africa and the Middle East, fueling his musical imagination as well as his musical technique. In 1917 his family's home was leveled and their possessions lost; Szymanowski and his family settled temporarily in Elisavetgrad. During this time he began work on his opera *Król Roger* [King Roger], based on the story of Roger II of Sicily (first perf. 1926).

By 1920 Szymanowski had returned with his family to Warsaw. The decade of the 1920s saw increasing success for him, in Poland as well as in Europe and the U.S. Szymanowski experienced a deepening fervent nationalism. He became an ardent proponent of a nationalism in the tradition of Chopin. As part of his explorations, Szymanowski spent time beginning in the early 1920s in Zapokane, gaining contact with the native musics of the Tatra people. In 1927 he accepted the position of director of the Warsaw Conservatory of Music and was able to implement his ideas about new music, although he came under fire from conservative critics. A worsening condition of tuberculosis finally forced him to spend a year in a sanatorium in Davos.

In 1930 Szymanowski became head of the Warsaw Academy of Music, though he resigned in 1932 because of resistance to his programs. He resumed composing, but a financially unstable period ensued. His health worsened, and before he could afford to reenter a sanatorium, he died.

Early in his life Szymanowski came under the intoxicating influence of Wagner, which heavily affected the younger composer's early compositional and philosophical aesthetic. His piano works from this period were in the tradition of German Romantic composers such as Chopin and Schumann; the orchestral works reflected Wagner's influence. During the prewar years, however, Szymanowski considered it crucial for new music to move from a Romantic idiom to a modern one. His compositional explorations during World War I brought into focus features such as the use of tonal centers without functional tonality, careful use of timbre to create colorful, expressive textures, and large-scale contrapuntal motion. Although he never favored the literal or superficial use of folk melodies, his contact with the Tatra people's music in combination with his national feelings created a more organic fusion of folklike elements within his own musical language. Form in Szymanowski's works was flexible and exploratory, moving away from sectional symmetry toward motivic processes. Works include dramatic works (*Harnasie,* pantomime-ballet, 1923–31); orchestral works (Symphony no. 4 [Symphony Concertante], piano, orchestra, 1932); chamber and vocal works.

Bibl.: Kornel Michałowski, *Karol Szymanowski, 1882–1937: Thematic Catalogue of Works and Bibliography* (Kraków, 1967). Teresa Chylińska, ed., *Karol Szymanowski: Dziela* (Kraków, 1973). Jim Samson, *The Music of Szymanowski* (New York, 1981). Christopher Palmer, *Szymanowski* (London, 1983).

T

Tabachnik, Michel (b. Geneva, 10 Nov. 1942). Composer and conductor. He studied piano, composition, and conducting at the Geneva Conservatory and attended the Darmstadt summer courses in 1964. From 1966 to 1971 he served as assistant to Pierre Boulez in Paris. His compositions from this period—*Supernovae* (chamber ensemble, 1967), *Frises* (piano, 1968), *Fresque* (chamber ensemble, 1970), *Mondes* (2 orchestras, 1972), *Sillages* (string orchestra, 1972), and others—show considerable affinity for the styles of Boulez and Stockhausen. He was conductor of the Ensemble européen de musique contemporaine in Paris (1976–77), and guest conductor of major European orchestras, mainly for modern works. Other works include *Les imaginaires* (orchestra, 1974); *Les perseides* (1976); *Cosmogonie pour une rose* (1983); *La légende de Hajha* (soli, chorus, orchestra, 1989).

Tabuteau, Marcel (b. Compiègne, 2 July 1887; d. Nice, 4 Jan. 1966). Oboist. In 1900 he enrolled at the Paris Conservatory as a pupil of Georges Gillet and at 17 was awarded a *premier prix.* In 1905 he went to the U.S. and played oboe and English horn with the New York Symphony, subsequently becoming principal oboist of the Metropolitan Opera Orchestra under Toscanini (from 1908) and of the Philadelphia Orchestra under Stokowski (1915–54). Tabuteau was an influential teacher at the Curtis Institute (from 1924).

Tacchinardi-Persiani, Fanny (b. Rome, 4 Oct. 1812; d. Neuilly-sur-Seine, 3 May 1867). Soprano. Daughter of Nicola Tacchinardi. Married the composer Giuseppe Persiani in 1830. Debut at Livorno (1832) in Fournier-Gorrés's *Francesca da Rimini.* Paris debut in 1837; stayed there for 13 years. Sang in London every year, 1838–49. Gave first performances of *Rosmonda d'Inghilterra* (Florence, 1834), *Lucia di Lammermoor* (Naples, 1835), *Pia de' Tolomei* (Venice, 1837). Retired from the stage in 1858 and returned to Paris. Nicknamed "la piccola Pasta."

Taddei, Giuseppe (b. Genoa, 26 June 1916). Baritone. He studied in Rome, making his debut at the Teatro reale dell'Opera in 1936; after the war he appeared at the Vienna Staatsoper (1946–48) and at the Salzburg festival (1948). Subsequently performed at La Scala (1948–51, 1955–61), Covent Garden (1960–67), and in Chicago and San Francisco. Best known for his Verdi (Falstaff, Rigoletto, Iago) and Mozart (Papageno, Figaro, Leporello), as well as some Wagner roles.

Tadolini [née Savonari], **Eugenia** (b. Forlì, 1809; d. Naples after 1851). Soprano. She studied with her husband, composer and singing instructor Giovanni Tadolini (1789?–1872). Debuted at Florence in 1828, Paris in 1830, London in 1848. La Scala debut was in Donizetti's *Il furioso all'isola di San Domingo* (1833). During 1840s, performed primarily the works of Donizetti. Sang first performance (in the title role) of Verdi's *Alzira* (1845). Retired in 1851.

Taffanel, (Claude) Paul (b. Bordeaux, 16 Sept. 1844; d. Paris, 22 Nov. 1908). Flutist and composer. Studied composition with Reber and flute with Dorus, from whom he learned the Boehm flute. With Gaubert he wrote *Méthode complète,* which is still in use. Flutist at Opéra-comique during early 1860s. Joined Opéra in 1864; solo flutist there from 1870; named conductor in 1890. Taught at the Paris Conservatory beginning in 1893.

Tagliaferro, Magda (b. Petropolis, 19 Jan. 1893; d. Rio de Janeiro, 9 Sept. 1986). Pianist. She studied with Cortot and at the Paris Conservatory; in 1908 began a concert career that spanned seven decades. She was appointed to the faculty of the Paris Conservatory in 1937.

Tagliavini, Ferruccio (b. Reggio nell'Emilia, Italy, 14 Aug. 1913; d. Reggio Emilia, 28 Jan. 1995). Tenor. He studied in Parma with Brancucci and in Florence with Amadeo Bassi; made his debut as Rodolfo in Florence in 1938, and performed at La Scala (1942–53). His Metropolitan Opera debut (1947) was also as Rodolfo. He remained at the Met for a number of seasons (1947–54, 1961–62), where his roles included Almaviva, Edgardo, and the Duke of Mantua; also sang in San Francisco (1948–49) and Covent Garden (1950, 1955–56). In 1941 he married the soprano Pia Tassinari.

Tagliavini, Luigi Ferdinando (b. Bologna, 7 Oct. 1929). Organist and musicologist. He studied organ at the Paris Conservatory with Marcel Dupré. In 1951 he received a Ph.D. in musicology at the Univ. of Padua; his dissertation on the cantatas of J. S. Bach was published in 1956. At the Bologna Conservatory he served as both organ professor and librarian (1952–60), was concurrently organ professor at the Monteverdi Conservatory in Bolzano (1954–64), and in 1964 became professor of organ at the Conservatory of Parma. He taught musicology at the Univ. of Bologna from 1959, and in 1965 became director of the Institute of Musicology at the Univ. of Fribourg. His influence as a scholar-performer was felt particularly through his regular participation in the Haarlem Summer Organ Academy, through extensive touring as organist and harpsichordist, and through numerous solo and duo (with Marie-Claire Alain) recordings, as well as through publications and editorial supervisions (including 3 volumes of the *Neue Mozart Ausgabe*). Additionally, he was widely influential in the preservation and restoration of Italian and Swiss organs. Visiting professor at Cornell, 1963, and SUNY–Buffalo, 1969.

Tailleferre, Germaine (b. Parc-Saint-Maur, France, 19 Apr. 1892; d. Paris, 7 Nov. 1983). Composer. She entered the Paris Conservatory at age 12, studying there until 1917; her classmates included Milhaud, Honegger, and Auric. With them she became associated with a group of musicians, artists, and writers who called themselves "Les nouveaux jeunes." Among her compositions from this period was *Jeux de plein air,* 2 pianos (1917). In 1920 the critic Henri Collet bestowed the name "Groupe des six" on the composers in the group. Tailleferre collaborated with the others in the *Album des Six* (1920), a piano collection, and the ballet *Les mariés de la tour Eiffel* (1921). During the same period she composed a *Ballade,* piano and orchestra (1922), a violin sonata (1920), and a piano concerto (1924), which was introduced by Koussevitzky in Paris in 1925. For the Ballets suédois she composed the ballet *Le marchand d'oiseaux* (1923). From the early 1930s come *Fleurs de France,* piano suite (1930), and *Ouverture,* orchestra (1932), plus several film scores. During the late 1930s and 1940s she composed rather little, the war years being spent in the U.S. Compositions from the 1950s include *Il était un petit navire,* opéra comique (1951); *Concertino,* flute, piano, strings (1953); *Parisiana,* ballet (1955); *Concerto des vaines paroles,* baritone and orchestra (1956); and a clarinet sonata (1958) composed in a serial idiom. She remained active as a composer, performer, and public figure throughout the 1960s and 1970s; *Concerto de la fidélité,* soprano and orchestra (1981), premiered in Paris in 1982.

Bibl.: "Mémoires à l'emporte pièce," *Revue internationale de musique française* 19 (Feb. 1986): 6–82. Robert Shapiro, *Germaine Tailleferre: A Bio-Bibliography* (Westport, Conn., 1994).

Tajo, Italo (b. Pinerolo, Piedmont, 25 Apr. 1915; d. Cincinnati, 29 Mar. 1993). Bass. He studied in Turin, making his debut there in 1935 as Fafner; subsequently performed at the Rome Opera and at La Scala (1941–56). He made his American debut in Chicago in 1946 as Ramfis, and appeared with the San Francisco opera (1948–50, 1952–53, 1956) and the Metropolitan Opera (1948–50). His roles have included Leporello, Don Giovanni, Don Pasquale, and Colline *(La bohème);* also appeared in Broadway musicals and in several films. Tajo joined the faculty of the Cincinnati Univ. School of Music in 1966. He returned to the Met (1976–91) to sing character roles.

Takács, Jenő (b. Cinfalva [now Siegendorf], 25 Sept. 1902). Composer. He studied piano with Weingartner and composition with Gál and Marx in Vienna. Taught at the Conservatory of Cairo from 1927 to 1932 and spent the next two years in Manila, teaching at the university there and exploring local tribal music. Returning to Cairo, he was associated with Egyptian Radio and, again, with the conservatory. He subsequently toured Europe and the U.S. as a performer and conductor and taught at various institutions. In 1952 he joined the faculty at the Univ. of Cincinnati. His own compositions draw from the tradition of Hungarian art music influenced by Bartók (whom Takács met in 1932), incorporating folk elements. Works include ballets (*Songs of Silence,* 1967), orchestral music, vocal music (*The Chant of the Creation,* voice, orchestra, 1943–44), and chamber and piano works.

Takahashi, Yuji (b. Tokyo, 21 Sept. 1938). Composer. From 1954 to 1958 he studied composition with Shibata and Ogura at the Toho School. He lived in Berlin from 1963 to 1965, studying with Xenakis; in 1966 he traveled to New York, where he explored computer composition; participated in Tanglewood seminars in the summers of 1966–68. His compositions are heavily influenced by Xenakis and evince stochastic techniques. He also toured as a virtuosic pianist of new music. Compositions include works for orchestra (*Kaga-i,* piano, chamber orchestra, 1971), for chamber settings (*Three Poems of Mao Tse-Tung,* piano, 1979), and for tape (*Ye-guen,* 18-track tape, laser beams, 1970).

Takata, Saburō (b. Nagoya, 18 Dec. 1913). Composer. He studied at the Tokyo Academy of Music with Nobutoki and Pringsheim, graduating in 1939. He served as conductor for the Central Symphony. In 1953 he joined the faculty at the Kunitachi Music College in Tokyo. His compositions are in the late Romantic idiom of European, and especially German, composers. Works include an opera (*Aoki ōkami* [The Dark Blue Wolf], 1970–72), orchestral music, and vocal music (*Mizu no inochi* [The Soul of the Water], chorus, piano, 1964).

Takemitsu, Tōru (b. Tokyo, 8 Oct. 1930; d. Tokyo, 20 Feb. 1996). Composer. He pursued composition largely on his own, supplemented with composition lessons from Kiyose. Takemitsu experimented with Euro-American avant-garde trends including serialism, aleatory, extended instrumental techniques, mixed-media performances, graphic notation, and electronic and tape music. In 1951 he cofounded an experimental laboratory called Jikken Kōbō in Tokyo, in conjunction with which he wrote some of his works such as *Shitsunai Kyōsōkyoku* [Chamber Concerto] (1955). The purpose of the laboratory reflected his interest in bringing together characteristics of native Japanese music with western European trends to create a new sonic world. His compositions create form through the use of blocks and spaces of sound and, furthermore, use silence itself as a compositional and musical feature.

From 1950 to 1952 he worked with Kiyose's group for new-music performance, Shin Sakkyokuha Kyōkai. In the early 1960s Takemitsu began to work with Cage; he also incorporated traditional Japanese instruments into his compositions (*November Steps,* biwa, shakuhachi, orchestra, 1967, commissioned by the New York Philharmonic). *Fantasma/Cantos* (1991) won the 1994 Grawemeyer Award.

Works: *Requiem* (strings, 1957); *Arc* (piano and orchestra); *Pile* (1963); *Solitude* (1966); *Your Love and the Crossing* (1963); *Textures* (1964); *Reflection* (1966); *Coda* (1966); *Eclipse* (biwa, shakuhachi, 1966); *Shūteika* [In an Autumn Garden] (gagaku ensemble, 1973); *Far Calls. Coming Far!* (violin, orchestra, 1980); *Dreamtime* (orchestra, 1981); *A Way A Lone* (string quartet, 1981); *Rain Spell* (flute, clarinet, harp, piano, vibraphone, 1982); *Rain Coming* (chamber orchestra, 1982); *Star-Isle* (orchestra, 1982); *From Far beyond Chrysanthemums and November Fog* (violin, piano, 1983); *Orion* (cello, piano, 1984); *Orion and Pleiades* (cello, orchestra, 1984); *Composition for Large Orchestra* (1985); *Static Relief* (tape, 1985); *All in Twilight* (guitar, 1987); flute concerto (1987); *Handmade Proverbs—4 Pop Songs* (6 male voices, 1987); *Treeline* (orchestra, 1988); viola concerto (1989); *From Me Flows What You Call Time* (percussion quintet, orchestra, 1990); *Fantasma/Cantos* (clarinet, orchestra, 1991); *Fantasma/Cantos II* (trombone, orchestra, 1994); also happenings, film music, television scores.

Bibl.: Noriko Ohtake, *Creative Sources for the Music of Tōru Takemitsu* (Aldershot, 1993).

Taktakishvili, Otar (b. Tbilisi, 27 July 1924; d. there, 22 Feb. 1989). Composer. Studied composition with Sergei Barkhudarian at the Tbilisi Conservatory, 1942–47, where he also completed graduate work in 1950. From 1947, taught choral literature and later counterpoint and orchestration at the conservatory; served as rector of that institution, 1962–65; artistic director of the Georgian State Choral Capella, 1952–56. In 1965 he was appointed minister of culture of the Georgian SSR. The ethnic flavor of Georgian folk styles is characteristic of his music, which includes 5 operas (including *Mindia,* 1959–60); 2 symphonies and other orchestral music; 4 piano concertos, 2 cello concertos, and a violin concerto; the national anthem of the Georgian SSR (1945), patriotic cantatas, and other vocal-symphonic music; choral and vocal music; chamber music; works for piano; incidental and film music.

Bibl.: L. V. Poliakova, *Otar Taktakishvili* (Moscow, 2/1979).

Tal [Gruenthal], **Josef** [Joseph] (b. Pinne, near Poznań, 18 Sept. 1910). Composer. He studied composition with Tiessen and piano with Trapp at the Berlin Hochschule für Musik. In 1934 he emigrated to Palestine and began teaching at the Jerusalem Conservatory of Music (which became the Israel Academy of Music). Beginning in 1950 he taught at Hebrew Univ. and served as head of its musicology department from 1965 to 1971; founded the university's Center for Electronic Music in 1961. In 1971 he was nominated as a member of the Academy of Arts in Berlin. His own compositions draw from European avant-garde trends such as serialism and electronic media. Some works also incorporate Jewish tradition. Works include operas (*Massada 967,* 1972; *Else,* chamber scene, 1975; *Der Garten,* chamber opera, 1987); orchestral music (3 piano concertos, 1944, 1953, 1956; Symphony no. 1, 1953; Symphony no. 2, 1960; *Shape,* chamber orchestra, 1975; *Symphonic Fanfare,* 1986); vocal music (*Exodus,* choreographic poem, baritone, orchestra, 1946; *Na'ari,* soprano, clarinet, 1975; *Laga'at makom,* voice, choir, 1987); chamber music (*Orgelstück,* 1984; *Essay I,* piano, 1987); and music for tape (Piano Concerto no. 4, piano, tape, 1962; *Min hameitzar* [From the Depths], ballet, tape, 1971; *Die Hand,* dramatic scene, soprano, cello, 1987).

Talich, Václav (b. Kroměříž, 28 May 1883; d. Beroun, 16 Mar. 1961). Conductor. Studied with his father, Jan Talich, and with Mařák and Ševčík at the Prague Conservatory (1897–1903). Served as leader of the Berlin Philharmonic and the Municipal Opera in Odessa (1904); conducted the Slovenian Philharmonic in Ljubljana (1908–12), and studied in Leipzig with Reger and Hans Sitt (composition) and Nikisch (conducting). In 1919 Talich was appointed chief conductor of the Czech Philharmonic, a post he held until 1941; in addition, he served as head of opera at the National Theater (1935–44). During his tenure the Czech Philharmonic became a world-class ensemble. Talich taught at the Prague Conservatory Master School and the Bratislava Academy.

Tallis [Tallys, Talles], **Thomas** (b. ca. 1505; d. Greenwich, 23 Nov. 1585). Composer. He was organist at the Benedictine Priory in Dover (1532), then was employed, most likely again as organist, at the Church of St. Mary-at-Hill in London (1537–38). Around 1538 he was associated with Waltham Abbey and subsequently was lay clerk at Canterbury Cathedral (1541–42). By 1543 Tallis was a Gentleman of the Chapel Royal, a position he held until the end of his life; he served during the reigns of Henry VIII, Edward VI, Mary I, and Elizabeth I, and his responsibilities included playing the organ and composing vocal polyphonic music for the royal chapels. In 1575 Queen Elizabeth granted Tallis and Byrd one of the first letters patent to print and publish music; later that year the pair issued 34 *Cantiones quae ab argumento sacrae vocantur, 5 et 6 partium,* with each contributing 17 pieces.

Early works include the votive antiphons of the Virgin Mary, *Salve intemerata virgo, Ave rosa sine spinis,* and *Ave Dei patris filia,* all in 5 parts. One of the first musicians to set English words to music as part of the new Anglican liturgy, Tallis composed more than 20 English anthems (including *Hear the Voice and Prayer, If Ye Love Me,* and *Remember Not, O Lord God,* all ca. 1547–48). The formidable 6-voice antiphon *Gaude gloriosa Dei mater* and the 7-voice Mass *Puer natus est* probably date from the restoration of the Catholic rite during Mary's reign (1553–58), while the more than 50 motets (including *Salvator mundi, Derelinquat impius,* and *In jejunio et fletu*) are Elizabethan works. His most famous composition, the 40-voice motet (for 8 choirs of 5 voices) *Spem in alium,* was perhaps written as part of the 40th birthday celebration for Elizabeth in 1573. Other works include 3 compositions for consort (2 *In nomine* settings and a *Libera nos, salva nos*) as well as keyboard music (many in the Mulliner book; also the 2 treatments of the *Felix namque* plainsong found in the Fitzwilliam Virginal Book, dated 1562 and 1564).

Bibl.: *Thomas Tallis, TCM* 6 (1928). *Complete Keyboard Works,* ed. Denis Stevens (London, 1953). *English Sacred Music,* ed. Leonard Webster Ellinwood, *EECM* 12–13 (1971; rev. 1973–74). *The Mulliner Book,* ed. Denis Stevens, *MB* 1 (1954). Paul Doe, *Tallis* (London, 1968). Davitt Moroney, "Under fower sovereygnes: Thomas Tallis and the Transformation of English Polyphony" (diss., Univ. of California, Berkeley, 1980).

Talma, Louise (Juliette) (b. Arcachon, 31 Oct. 1906). Composer. Born in France to American parents, she was taught piano and solfège by her mother, an opera singer. She studied at the Institute of Musical Art in New York (1922–30). Summers she spent at the American School in Fontainebleau (1926–39), studying piano with Isidore Philipp and composition with Nadia Boulanger. From 1928 on, she was a member of the faculty of Hunter College in New York. Her compositions from the 1930s were modest in scope, mainly songs and piano pieces, and neoclassical in their idiom. *Toccata for Orchestra* (1945), her first piece for large ensemble, was introduced by the Baltimore Symphony in 1946. In the 1950s, partly through her acquaintance with Irving Fine, she became interested in twelve-tone techniques, and most of her music from this point on was serial, although she retained the tonal referents, the lyrical lines, and the neoclassical textures of her earlier works. Piano Sonata no. 2 (1955) combines serial and tonal techniques; *Six Etudes,* piano (1954), is entirely serial. From 1955 to 1958 she worked on an opera, *The Alcestiad,* with a libretto by Thornton Wilder. Its premiere at the Frankfurt Opera in 1962 was a critical success. It was followed by a series of works in a similar style: *All the Days of My Life,* tenor, clarinet, cello, piano, and percussion (1965); *The Tolling Bell,* baritone and orchestra (1969); *Summer Sounds,* clarinet and string quartet (1973); *Voices of Spring,* chorus and string orchestra (1973); and *Diadem,* tenor and chamber orchestra (1979).

Talvela, Martti (Olavi) (b. Hiitola, Finland, 4 Feb. 1935; d. Juva, Finland, 22 July 1989). Bass. He enrolled at the Lahti Academy of Music in 1958 and continued his studies in Stockholm, making his debut at the Stockholm Royal Opera House in 1961 as the Commendatore. The following year he performed Titurel at the Bayreuth Festival and joined the Deutsche Oper in Berlin; subsequently performed at the Metropolitan (debut in 1968) and at Covent Garden (debut in 1970). He was best known for his Wagnerian bass roles and for his Boris. Talvela served as director of the Savonlinna Festival (1972–79) and was appointed general director of the Helsinki National Opera shortly before his death.

Tamagno, Francesco (b. Turin, 28 Dec. 1850; d. Varese, 31 Aug. 1905). Tenor. Studied at the Turin Conservatory with Pedrotti. Solo debut in 1870 in *Poliuto.* By 1874 he was one of the leading tenors in Italy. La Scala debut in 1877. Toured South America in 1880. Sang the title role in the premiere of *Otello* (1887). Sang in Chicago, 1889–90. Appeared in New York at the Metropolitan Opera as Otello (1890) and at Covent Garden in the same role (1895). Sang first performance of Leoncavallo's *I Medici* (1893). Retired in 1902.

Tamberg, Eino (b. Tallinn, 27 May 1930). Composer. Studied composition at Tallinn Conservatory with E. Kapp, 1946–53. Worked as sound engineer at Estonian Radio and as consultant to the Estonian Composers Union. From 1968 taught composition at the Tallinn Conservatory. Works include operas, ballets, 2 symphonies (1978, 1986) and other symphonic works; concertos for trumpet (1972), violin (1981), voice (1985), saxophone (1987); choral works; chamber music.

Tamberlik [Tamberlick], **Enrico** (b. Rome, 16 Mar. 1820; d. Paris, 13 Mar. 1889). Tenor. Studied in Rome, Naples, and Bologna; his teachers included Zirilli, Borgna, Guglielmi, and de Abella. Public debut, 1841, in Bellini's *I Capuleti e i Montecchi* (London debut, 1850); regular appearances at Covent Garden to 1864. Often appeared in St. Petersburg. Sang first performance of *La forza del destino* (1862). Known for his legendary high C.

Tamburini, Antonio (b. Faenza, 28 Mar. 1800; d. Nice, 8 Nov. 1876). Baritone. Debut at Cento in 1818. Appeared at La Scala in 1822 in Rossini's *Matilde di Shabran;* sang first performance of Donizetti's *Chiara e Serafin* that year. Sang in premieres of Donizetti's *L'ajo nell'imbarazzo* (1824), *Alabor di Granata* (1826), *La regina di Golconda* (1828) and in Bellini's *Il pirata* (1827). Premiered 5 more operas of Donizetti from 1828 to 1832, and *Don Pasquale* (1843). Retired in 1855.

Taneyev, Sergei (Ivanovich) (b. Vladimir district, 25 Nov. 1856; d. Dyudkovo, 19 June 1915). Composer, pianist, educator. He entered the Moscow Conservatory at the age of 9 and began piano studies with Eduard Langer a few years later; also studied theory with Nikolai Hubert and composition with Tchaikovsky; beginning in 1871 he worked with Nikolai Rubinstein. In 1875 he made his debut as piano soloist in Moscow performing the Brahms D minor concerto; later that year he graduated from the Moscow Conservatory and premiered Tchaikovsky's First Piano Concerto. Taneyev remained a lifelong friend of Tchaikovsky's, and he premiered all of the latter's works for piano and orchestra. In 1876 he toured Russia with the violinist Leopold Auer and in 1878 succeeded Tchaikovsky at the conservatory, although he consented to direct only the classes in harmony and orchestration. He took over the piano class of Rubinstein in 1881, and in 1885 became director of the conservatory, remaining in the post until 1889. Although his reputation as a composer remains very high in Russia, his works are rarely performed elsewhere. Compositions include *Oresteya* [The Oresteia], (1887–94; opera in 3 acts, St. Petersburg, 1895); symphonies (no. 4, C minor, 1896–97); choral music; chamber music; songs; keyboard music. His students included Scriabin, Rachmaninoff, Lyapunov, and Glier. He published *Podvizhnoy kontrapunkt strogovo pis'ma* [Invertible Counterpoint in the Strict Style] (Leipzig and Moscow, 1909); trans. Eng. (1962).

Tannenberg [Tanneberg, Tanneberger], **David** (b. Berthelsdorf, Upper Lusatia, 21 Mar. 1728; d. York, Pa., 19 May 1804). Organ builder. Migrated to the U.S. in 1749 as a member of the Moravian settlement in Bethlehem, Pa. He became an assistant to Johann Gottlieb Klemm, an organ builder, until Klemm's death in 1762. At this point he established himself in Lititz in 1765 and produced on the average one organ per year for churches in Pennsylvania, New York, Maryland, Virginia, and North Carolina.

Tannhäuser, Der (b. ca. 1205; d. ca. 1270). Minnesinger poet-composer. Of noble birth, probably Bavarian, he served in the 5th Crusade and Cypriot war and spent time at the courts of Austria (Friedrich II) and Bavaria (Otto II). "Der Tannhäuser" was perhaps an assumed name. His extant works, 6 *Leiche* and 10 lieder (melodies lost), attest to a life of travel and adventure. From the 1400s he became identified with the legendary knight Tannhäuser, who courted Venus, repented, and was miraculously absolved.

Tansman, Alexandre (b. Łódź, 12 June 1897; d. Paris, 15 Nov. 1986). Composer. He studied from an early age at the Łódź conservatory, then studied composition with Piotr Rytel and piano in Warsaw. In 1919 he moved to Paris. His works, tuneful and ingratiating, were soon performed: *Intermezzo sinfonico* in 1920, *Danse de la sorcière* (orchestra) in 1924, Piano Concerto no. 1 in 1926. Piano Concerto no. 2 and Symphony no. 1 were introduced during a tour of the U.S. which he undertook in 1927 with Koussevitzky and the Boston Symphony. During World War II he moved to the U.S. and lived in Hollywood, where he wrote music for several films and continued to compose concert music. He returned to Paris in 1946. Other works include *Le serment* (opera, Brussels, 1955); *Sabbatat Lévi, le faux Messie* (opera, Paris, 1961); 7 symphonies (1925, 1926, 1931, 1939, 1942, 1943, 1944); Viola Concerto (1936); Concerto for Orchestra (1954); 8 string quartets (1917–56); 5 piano sonatas; *Sonatine transatlantique* (piano, 1930); *Stèle* (low voice and chamber ensemble, 1972).

Tans'ur [Tansur, le Tansur, Tanzer], **William** (b. Dunchurch, Warwickshire, 1700, bapt. 6 Nov. 1706; d. St. Neots, Huntshire, 7 Oct. 1783). Composer. He traveled across England as a teacher of psalmody before settling at St. Neots, where he worked as a stationer, bookseller, and music teacher. In 1734 he published *A Compleat Melody: or, The Harmony of Scion,* which included metrical Psalms, hymns, and anthems in 2–4 parts without accompaniment. His second psalmody collection, *The Melody of the Heart,* appeared in 1735. A later compilation, *The Royal Melody Compleat* (1754–55), became *The American Harmony* (Newburyport, 1771). Besides 100 Psalm and hymn tunes, Tans'ur's output includes 39 anthems, a Te Deum, 2 Magnificats, and responses and chants.

Tapissier, Johannes [Jean de Noyers] (b. ca. 1370; d. before Aug. 1410). Composer. He served as chamber valet and court composer to Philip the Bold, Duke of Burgundy; in 1391 and 1395 he accompanied the duke and his court on journeys to Avignon. Tapissier maintained an "escole de chant" in Paris; on at least one occasion court choirboys were sent there to learn singing. His extant compositions are a Credo, a Sanctus, and an isorhythmic motet.

Tarchi, Angelo [Angiolo] (b. Naples, ca. 1760; d. Paris, 19 Aug. 1814). Composer. He received musical instruction from Fago and Sala in Naples. Tarchi wrote approximately 50 Italian operas, the first of which, *L'archetiello,* was performed in Naples in 1778. In 1797 he went to Paris, where he wrote several opéras comiques. *Ademira* (Milan, 1783) was his first serious opera. He was named music director and composer at King's Theatre in London in 1787–88 and again in 1789. He apparently partially rewrote the third and fourth acts of Mozart's *Le nozze di Figaro* for a Milan performance in 1787.

Bibl.: Alfred Einstein, "Mozart and Tarchi," *MMR* 65 (1935): 127; R: in *Essays on Music* (New York, 1956), pp. 187–90.

Tarp, Svend Erik (b. Thisted, 6 Aug. 1908). Composer. He studied at the Univ. of Copenhagen with Jeppesen (theory) and Simonsen (music history). Subsequently traveled to Germany, Holland, and Austria to continue his study of composition. Taught at the Copenhagen Conservatory, the Statens Larerhøjskole, and the Univ. of Copenhagen. His compositions are in the neoclassical style prevalent in Denmark after World War I. His style is tonally based, rhythmically powerful, and dramatic. Composed music for some 40 films. Works also include stage works (*Skyggen,* ballet, Copenhagen, 1960), vocal music (*Requiem,* 1980), and orchestral music (7 symphonies: no. 1, Sinfonia divertente, 1945; no. 2, 1949; no. 3, Quasi una fantasia, 1958; nos. 4 & 5, 1976; nos. 6 & 7, 1977).

Tarr, Edward H(ankins) (b. Norwich, Conn., 15 June 1936). Trumpeter and musicologist. He studied trumpet with Voisin in Boston (1953) and with Herseth in

Chicago (1958–59), as well as musicology in Basel under Schrade (1959–64). In 1967 he founded the Edward Tarr Brass Ensemble to perform Renaissance and Baroque music on period instruments. In addition to his solo appearances and recordings, Tarr edited a large repertory of trumpet music, including the complete trumpet works of Torelli, and wrote about the history of the instrument, most notably in his book *Die Trompete* (Basel, 1977). He taught at the Rheinische Musikschule in Cologne (1968–70), the Schola cantorum basiliensis (from 1972), and the Basel Musikakademie (from 1974).

Tárrega (y Eixea), Francisco (b. Villarreal, Castellón, 21 Nov. 1852; d. Barcelona, 15 Dec. 1909). Guitarist and composer. Studied with Julian Arcas from 1862. Acquired in 1869 a guitar (made by Antonio Torres) that was more resonant and with which he began to lay the foundations of what became the dominant modern technique for the classical guitar. He entered the Madrid Conservatory in 1874. From 1877 he concertized and taught guitar. Settled in Barcelona in 1885. Composed works for guitar; transcribed music of Gottschalk, Mendelssohn, Chopin, and Beethoven, as well as Albéniz and Granados. Known as "the Sarasate of the guitar," he was also an especially influential teacher.

Bibl.: Emilio Pujol, *Tárrega: Ensayo biográfico* (Valencia, 1978).

Tartini, Giuseppe (b. Pirano, Istria, 8 Apr. 1692; d. Padua, 26 Feb. 1770). Composer, violinist, and theorist. After receiving his early education from clerics at Pirano and Capodistria, he studied law at Padua Univ. In 1710 his secret marriage to Elisabetta Premazore caused him to incur the wrath of the Bishop of Padua, Cardinal Giorgio Cornaro, forcing him to take refuge in the Franciscan monastery at Assisi. There he is said to have studied with "Padre Boemo," probably the organist Bohuslav Černohorský. By 1714 he was employed in the opera orchestra at Ancona. About 1715 he was pardoned by the cardinal and was reunited with his wife, with whom he lived the following year in Venice and Padua. Probably in July 1716, he heard Veracini play in Venice and was so impressed with the virtuoso's violin technique that he is said to have gone into self-exile to perfect his own playing. By about 1720 he had returned to Venice, and on 16 April 1721 he was appointed "primo violino e capo di concerto" at St. Antonio in Padua; he retained this position until 1765. From June 1723 until 1726 he was employed by Count Kinsky at Prague; he then returned to Padua.

From the 1720s until about 1740, when he injured his arm at Bergamo, Tartini enjoyed remarkable success as a violinist. In 1727 or 1728 he founded his violin "school"; his pupils included J. G. Graun, Nardini, J. G. Naumann, Paganelli, and Pagin. He taught until at least 1767. His treatise on violin playing, *Traité des agréments,* appeared after his death, but it must have originated earlier, since material from it was used by Leopold Mozart in his *Violinschule* (1756). Tartini published his acoustical findings in the *Trattato di musica* (Padua, 1754; R: 1966 and 1973; trans. Eng., 1985). His theoretical system incorporates the differential tone *(terzo suono),* which he claimed to have discovered in 1714. Also in the *Trattato* are discussions of melody, cadence types, dissonance, scale structure and harmonization, and meter. His compositions include a small number of sacred vocal pieces, written in the last year of his life; about 125 violin concertos; concertos for other instruments; numerous trio sonatas; and about 175 violin sonatas, including the "Trillo del Diavolo" [Devil's Trill].

Bibl.: *Le opere di Giuseppe Tartini,* ed. Edoardo Farina and Claudio Scimone (Milan, 1971–). Minos Dounias, *Die Violinkonzerte Giuseppe Tartinis* (Wolfenbüttel, 1935; 2nd ed., 1966). Paul Brainard, *Le sonate per violino di Giuseppe Tartini: Catalogo tematico* (Milan, 1975). Alejandro Planchart, "A Study of the Theories of Giuseppe Tartini," *JMT* 4/1 (1960): 32–61. Pierluigi Petrobelli, *Giuseppe Tartini: Le fonti biografiche* (Vienna, Milan, and London, 1968). Lev Ginzburg, *Giuseppe Tartini* (Moscow, 1969); trans. Eng. (1982). Pierluigi Petrobelli, *Tartini, le sue idee e il suo tempo* (Lucca, 1992). Andrea Bombi and Maria Nevilla Massaro, eds., *Tartini: Il tempo e le opere* (Bologna, 1994).

Taskin, Pascal (-Joseph) (b. Theux, near Liège, 1723; d. Paris, 9 Feb. 1793). Harpsichord maker. He worked for François Étienne Blanchet the younger before taking over his business in 1766. In 1774 he was appointed court instrument maker and Keeper of the King's Instruments. He applied the *peau de buffle* registration, a color or echo effect, to instruments by the Ruckers; the device was operated by knee levers. Besides building new instruments, Taskin also rebuilt and enlarged old Flemish harpsichords and virginals. From 1776 he also built pianos, and inventories show that the firm was prosperous from the 1770s to the 1790s. The deep tone of his instruments, his adoption of the sliding coupler, and his lacquered or decorated casework were influential.

Tate, Phyllis (Margaret Duncan) (b. Gerrards Cross, 6 Apr. 1911; d. London, 27 May 1987). Composer. From 1928 until 1932 she studied composition at the Royal College of Music with Farjeon. She then went on to write primarily for smaller ensembles in various and sometimes unusual instrumentations. Tate's musical language was frequently dissonant and involved complex rhythms. Her works include the opera *The Lodger* (1960); orchestral music (*Song without Words,* orchestra, 1976); vocal pieces (*St. Martha and the Dragon,* narrator, soprano, tenor, chorus, children's choir, chamber orchestra, 1976; *Gaelic Ballads,* voice, piano, 1968); and chamber works (*Sonatina pastorale,* harmonica, harpsichord, 1974).

Tatum, Art (Arthur, Jr.) (b. Toledo, Ohio, 13 Oct. 1909; d. Los Angeles, 5 Nov. 1956). Jazz pianist. Despite near-blindness and limited formal training he had developed by the 1930s a technical command of the instrument, which he often played at lightning speeds.

Because of his inclination to reharmonize popular songs and to vary tempo, he preferred to work unaccompanied, as on his stride and swing recordings of "Tiger Rag" (1933), "Sweet Lorraine" (1940), and "Willow Weep for Me" (1949). But he also led trios from 1943 and in the 1950s made albums with swing musicians such as Benny Carter, Lionel Hampton, and Ben Webster.

Bibl.: James Lester, *Too Marvelous for Words: The Life and Genius of Art Tatum* (New York, 1994).

Tauber, Richard (b. Linz, Austria, 16 May 1891; d. London, 8 Jan. 1948). Tenor. He studied at the Frankfurt Conservatory, making his debut as Tamino in Chemnitz in 1913; subsequently performed at the Dresden Opera, and at houses in Vienna (1922–28, 1932–38) and Berlin (1923–33), where he achieved success in Mozart roles such as Belmonte, Don Ottavio, and Tamino. Beginning in the 1920s he began to appear more frequently in operettas, especially those of Lehár; after the German–Austrian Anschluss he performed at Covent Garden, becoming a British subject in 1940.

Bibl.: Diana Napier Tauber, *Richard Tauber* (New York, 1980).

Taubert, (Carl Gottfried) Wilhelm (b. Berlin, 23 Mar. 1811; d. there, 7 Jan. 1891). Pianist, composer, and conductor. Studied piano with Ludwig Berger and composition with Bernhard Klein. Assistant conductor and accompanist of Berlin court concerts, 1831. Conducted his First Symphony in Berlin, 1831. Music director, Berlin Royal Opera, 1845–48. Also worked under Mendelssohn and Meyerbeer. Court conductor at Berlin, 1845–69. Taught at Royal Academy of the Arts from 1865. Composed 6 operas, incidental music, 4 symphonies, overtures, piano concertos, a cello concerto, 4 string quartets, smaller choral works, piano pieces, and over 300 songs, including *Kinderlieder* opp. 145 and 160.

Tauriello, Antonio (b. Buenos Aires, 20 Mar. 1931). Composer. Studied piano with Spivak and Gieseking and composition with Ginastera. Soon after his 1958 conducting debut he was engaged by the Teatro Colón. Served as assistant director of the Chicago Lyric Opera and led performances for the New York City Opera, the Washington Opera Society, and the American Opera Center. Also active as an orchestral conductor, and served as director of the Argentine percussion group Ritmus. Much of Tauriello's music may be termed avant-garde; works include the *Obertura sinfónica* (1961), the *Ricercosi* (1966), and *Mansión de Tlaloc* (1970) for orchestra; the opera *Escorial* (1966); the piano concerto and *Música III* for piano and orchestra; *Canti,* violin and orchestra; *Impromptus,* chamber ensemble (1980); and chamber music, including *Transparencies,* 6 instrumental groups (1963).

Tausig, Carl [Karol] (b. Warsaw, 4 Nov. 1841; d. Leipzig, 17 July 1871). Pianist and composer. Studied with his father, Aloys Tausig (1820–85). After meeting Liszt in Weimar in 1855, he traveled and studied with him. Debut in 1858. Opened a piano school in Berlin in 1865, which folded a few years later. He was considered to have extraordinary technique, but contemporary opinions about his playing were mixed. He composed a few works, including a number of exercises published as *Tägliche Studien,* and transcriptions of Berlioz, Wagner, Weber, Schubert, Scarlatti, and Beethoven.

Tavárez, Manuel Gregorio (b. San Juan, 28 Nov. 1843; d. Ponce, 1 July 1883). Composer. Studied with José Cabrizan and Domingo Delgado in San Juan. Went to Paris in 1856, where he studied with D'Albert and Auber at the Paris Conservatory. He returned to Puerto Rico after an illness, settling in Ponce. He collected and published 2 collections of Puerto Rican music, *Album filharmónico* (1863) and *El delirio puertorriqueño* (1867–69). His own compositions are primarily short character and salon pieces, including a number of waltzes and marches.

Bibl.: Fernando Callejo Ferrer, *Música y músicos puertorriqueños* (San Juan, 1915; R: 1971).

Tavener, John (Kenneth) (b. London, 28 Jan. 1944). Composer. From 1961 to 1965 he studied with Berkeley at the Royal College of Music, as well as with Lumsdaire. Thereafter worked both as a composer and as a church organist. His compositions have met with critical and popular success, as in the case of the biblical cantata *The Whale* (1965–66), which was recorded in 1970 by Apple Records. His early music was influenced by Stravinsky but quickly developed into an eclectic and highly individual style, frequently combined with his interest in religious subjects and symbolism. *The Protecting Veil* (solo cello, strings, 1989), a paean to the Virgin Mary, vaulted the composer to wide prominence. His works include *Cain and Abel* (cantata, solo voices, chamber orchestra, 1965); *Celtic Requiem* (soprano, children's choir, chorus, orchestra, 1969); *Coplas* (soprano, alto, tenor, bass, chorus, tape, 1970); *In memoriam Igor Stravinsky* (2 alto flutes, organ, bells, 1971); *Little Requiem for Father Malachy Lynch* (chorus, chamber orchestra, 1972); *Requiem for Father Malachy* (6 solo voices, trumpet, trombone, organ, percussion, piano, strings, 1973); *Thérèse* (opera, 1973–76); *Funeral Ikos* (chorus, 1981); *Towards the Son: Ritual Procession* (orchestra, 1983); *Towards the Son* (2 oboes, 2 bassoons, 2 trumpets, 2 bass trombones, percussion, low strings, 3 boys' voices, 1984); *16 Haiku of Seferis* (chorus, timpani, handbells, gongs, strings, 1984); *Ikon of Light* (double choir, string trio, 1984); *Akathist of Thanksgiving: Glory Be to God for Everything* (soli, chorus, orchestra, 1988); *St. Mary of Egypt* (opera, 1991).

Taverner, John (b. near Boston, Lincolnshire, ca. 1490; d. there, 18 Oct. 1545). Composer. In 1525–26 he was a lay clerk (singer) in the collegiate church choir of Tattershall, Lincolnshire. In 1527, at the invitation of the Bishop of Lincoln, he became the first instructor of choristers at Cardinal Wolsey's new Cardinal College (later Christ Church), Oxford. He resigned in 1530, shortly after Wolsey's fall from grace and the choir's loss of funding. He apparently returned to Lincolnshire to instruct the choristers of St. Botolph's parish church, Boston. In the reforms of Henry VIII of 1534–35 the choir lost funding; by 1537 Taverner had apparently retired from music. He was well off and remained prominent in Boston's church and town affairs.

Taverner's works represent the culmination of English late medieval polyphony before the Reformation. They include 8 Masses, 9 Mass segments, Magnificats in 4, 5, and 6 voices, a Te Deum, 6 large 5-voiced motets, about 20 smaller motets and motet segments, 4 secular part songs, and a 6-voiced wordless *Quemadmodum.* Most were probably written during his years at Tattershall and Cardinal colleges, but some (including the *Mean, Plainsong,* and *Western Wind* Masses) show affinities with younger composers' works from after 1530 and may have been written at Boston. The highly melismatic *In nomine* segment of the Mass *Gloria tibi Trinitas* became widespread in textless transcriptions that spawned the English *In nomine* consort genre.

Bibl.: Colin Hand, *John Taverner: His Life and Music* (New York, 1982).

Taylor, Billy [William] (b. Greenville, N.C., 24 July 1921). Jazz pianist, broadcaster, educator, and author. He studied music at Virginia State College (B.Mus., 1942) and the Univ. of Massachusetts (D.M.E., 1975). He worked in New York with Ben Webster, Stuff Smith, and many bop musicians, and in 1951 was the house pianist at Birdland. He led a bop trio from 1952. Taylor also worked in radio and television from the 1960s, directing the National Public Radio show *Jazz Alive* (ca. 1977–80) and contributing to CBS Television's *Sunday Morning* (beginning 1981). In 1965 he helped establish Jazzmobile, an ongoing jazz education project in New York, and in 1994 he was named artistic adviser and spokesman on jazz for the John F. Kennedy Center for the Performing Arts in Washington, D.C. He should not be confused with jazz double bass and tuba player Billy Taylor (1906–86).

Writings: *Jazz Piano: History and Development* (Dubuque, Iowa, 1982).

Taylor, Cecil (Percival) (b. New York, 15 Mar. 1933). Jazz pianist, composer, and bandleader. He juxtaposed bop with a freer manner of playing while leading a quartet at the Five Spot club in New York (1956) and the Newport Jazz Festival (1957). He brought saxophonist Jimmy Lyons (who became a long-standing member of his groups) and Sunny Murray on tour in Scandinavia (1962–63), where Albert Ayler joined them. By this point Taylor was playing in an atonal, out-of-tempo, percussive free-jazz style. Despite critical acclaim, work was scarce, but from the mid-1970s he toured as a soloist and leader with some regularity, especially in Europe. His albums include *Unit Structures* (1966), *Silent Tongues* (1974), and *Three Phasis* (1978).

Taylor, (Joseph) Deems (b. New York, 22 Dec. 1885; d. New York, 3 July 1966). Composer and critic. Except for childhood piano lessons and private study of harmony and counterpoint, he was self-taught as a musician. From 1906 to 1919 he worked as a journalist. His first successful composition was *Through the Looking Glass* (chamber orchestra, 1919; full orchestra, 1922), which was introduced by the New York Chamber Music Society. In 1926 on commission from the Metropolitan Opera he wrote *The King's Henchman* (New York, 1927), a work in traditional Romantic style whose enthusiastic reception prompted a second commission resulting in *Peter Ibbetson* (New York, 1931). As radio commentator for the Metropolitan Opera and New York Philharmonic (1931–43), Taylor was an influential voice in American music. From 1942 to 1948 he served as president of ASCAP.

Taylor, James (Vernon) (b. Boston, Mass., 12 Mar. 1948). Popular singer and songwriter. Began playing in groups with brother Alex and Danny Kortchmar; from 1968 released albums in mixed folk and rock styles; wrote many songs, though his most popular recordings were of songs by other artists. His records include *Sweet Baby James* (1970, including "Fire and Rain"), *Gorilla* (1975, including "How Sweet It Is To Be Loved by You"), *JT* (1977, including "Handy Man"), and *Never Die Young* (1988).

Taylor, Raynor (b. London, ca. 1747; d. Philadelphia, 17 Aug. 1825). Composer and organist. He was a choirboy at Chapel Royal; was named organist at Chelmsford and music director and composer at Sadler's Wells Theatre in 1765. He emigrated to the U.S. in 1792, settling first in Baltimore, then Annapolis, then in Philadelphia, where he was appointed organist at St. Peter's Church in 1793. He also helped found the Musical Fund Society there in 1820. His compositions include an opera, *The Ethiop* (Philadelphia, 1814), vocal works (*Monody of the Death of Washington,* 1799), incidental music, songs, anthems, glees, and keyboard pieces.

Tchaikovsky, Alexander Vladimirovich (b. Moscow, 19 Feb. 1946). Composer. Nephew of Boris Tchaikovsky. Studied at the Moscow Conservatory, graduating from the piano class of Lev Naumov in 1970 and the composition class of Tikhon Khrennikov in 1972; in 1975 completed graduate work there under Khrennikov. Has taught composition at the Moscow Conservatory and, beginning 1986, served on the governing board of the USSR Union of Composers. Came to prominence as a composer with his colorful scores to ballets staged at the Kirov Theater (*The Inspector General,* 1980; *The Battleship Potemkin,* 1986). Has also written 3 operas; a symphony and other orchestral music; concertos for piano, viola, bassoon, violin; chamber music.

Tchaikovsky, Boris Alexandrovich (b. Moscow, 10 Sept. 1925). Composer. Not related to Piotr Ilyich Tchaikovsky. Studied composition at the Moscow Conservatory (1941–48) with V. Shebalin, D. Shostakovich, and N. Miaskovsky; piano with L. Oborin. Without pioneering any new territory, his music forms a natural extension of the best traditions of Russian instrumental music. Works include an opera; 3 symphonies (1947, 1967, 1980); *Theme and Eight Variations* (1973) and other symphonic music; concertos for clarinet (1957), cello (1964), violin (1969), piano (1971); 6 string quartets and other chamber music; vocal music (including *Signs of the Zodiac,* cantata, soprano, harpsichord, and strings, 1974); radio and film music.

Tchaikovsky, Piotr Ilyich (b. Votkinsk, Viatka Province, Western Central Urals, 7 May 1840; d. St. Petersburg, 6 Nov. 1893). Composer. His father, Ilya Petrovich Tchaikovsky, descended from Viatka provincial gentry of Cossack lineage, was chief civil inspector of the Votkinsk iron mines. His mother, Alexandra Andreyevna, neé Assier, Ilya's second wife, was of minor French nobility. Her grandfather the Marquis Michel d'Assier had a nervous disorder resembling epilepsy; from this line the composer inherited a nervous tendency.

Piotr, the third of seven children, was an affectionate, precocious, and extremely sensitive pet of the family. He evolved strong emotional bonds with his mother, his younger sister Alexandra, and his French governess Fanny Dürbach. His youth was beset by upheavals. In 1848 the family moved to St. Petersburg, leaving Dürbach behind. In 1849 they returned to the provinces, but in 1850 Piotr was sent to the St. Petersburg School of Jurisprudence, a training college for members of the elite class entering civil service; the move forced a painful break with his mother. He spent nine years at the school, during which he developed a distinct personal attractiveness and homosexual orientation. He suffered a severe blow at his mother's death in the cholera epidemic of 1854. In response he turned to composing and piano playing; having studied music from early youth, he now embraced it seriously for the first time.

Tchaikovsky graduated in 1859 and entered civil service, continuing to study music on the side. In 1860 his sister Alexandra married Lev Davïdov, heir to a large estate at Kamenka near Kiev; henceforth this became a second home for him. He also became close to his youngest brothers, fraternal twins Anatoly and Modest, ten years his junior. In 1861 he began harmony studies with Nikolai Zaremba of the newly formed Russian Musical Society. In 1862, when the Society became the St. Petersburg Conservatory under Anton Rubinstein, he entered Rubinstein's composition class. In 1863 he resigned from civil service and became a full-time student, supporting himself as a free-lance musician.

Piotr Ilyich Tchaikovsky, ca. 1866.

His student works include an overture based on Ostrovsky's *Groza* [The Storm], two more overtures, a scene from Pushkin's *Boris Godunov,* a piano sonata, and as a final exercise a large setting of Schiller's *An die Freude.* At Rubinstein's behest he translated Gevaert's *Traîté général d'instrumentation.* By gaining a conservatory training he distinguished himself from other leading Russian composers (Glinka and the "Five"), who were self-taught. In 1865 Nikolai Rubinstein opened the Moscow Conservatory and invited Tchaikovsky to teach harmony; he took the position upon his graduation in early 1866.

He found allies in Moscow: as a conductor Nikolai Rubinstein championed his works, and Piotr Jürgenson became his main publisher. His first projects were a symphony, *Zimniye gryozï* [Winter Daydreams, 1866], a Festival Overture (1866) for the tsarevich's marriage, and an opera on Ostrovsky's *Voyevoda* (1867–68); he destroyed the last after its unsuccessful staging in 1869. His music caught the attention of Balakirev in St. Petersburg, and he became friendly with the "Five"; to Balakirev he dedicated the symphonic poem *Fatum* (1868). In late 1868 he was briefly engaged to Désirée Artôt, a singer of noted ability; her decision to break off caused him only brief distress. In late 1869 he composed the Fantasy-Overture *Romeo and Juliet,* a masterpiece of orchestral drama modeled largely on suggestions from Balakirev (rev. 1870, 1880); and the Six Songs op. 6, including *Niet, tol'ko tot, kto znal* [None but the Lonely Heart, from Goethe's "Nur wer die Sehnsucht kennt"].

Having aborted two exotic operas, *Undina* (1869) and *Mandragora* (1870), he achieved his first operatic success in *Oprichnik* (1870–72), set in the time of Ivan the Terrible, reusing much material from *Voyevoda.* In the wake of *Oprichnik* came more nationalistic works: a String Quartet (1871) and Second Symphony (1872), both using Ukrainian folk tunes heard at Kamenka; the latter won acclaim from the leading Petersburg critic, Vladimir Stasov. Then came incidental music for Ostrovsky's *Snegurochka* [The Snow Maiden] (1873), the Symphonic Fantasia *Buria* [The Tempest] (1873) suggested by Stasov, two sets of piano pieces (opp. 19 and 21, 1873) that won Hans von Bülow's esteem, and the Second String Quartet (1874). From 1872 to 1876 he served as critic for the Moscow paper *Russkiye vedomosti.*

His next opera, *Kuznets Vakula* [Vakula the Smith] (1874), epitomized his nationalistic bent and revealed a flair for the fantastic. A competition was held to set a libretto based on Gogol's supernatural tale "Christmas Eve"; Tchaikovsky's score won in 1875 and was staged in 1876. Meanwhile, he conceived his vigorous First Piano Concerto (1874–75), with a solo part cast in a romantically heroic vein. The work met with surprising censure from Nikolai Rubinstein, though it was championed by its dedicatee, von Bülow, who premiered it in Boston in 1875; in Moscow it was premiered by a young confidant of the composer, Sergei Taneyev.

The year 1875 also saw the Third Symphony and a commission from the Moscow Bolshoi Theater for the ballet *Lebedinoe ozero* [Swan Lake]. This Tchaikovsky fulfilled in early 1876 with a masterpiece that raised Russian ballet to new heights; it proved his gift for creating large and varied structures out of vividly picturesque moments. Concurrently he wrote the series of piano miniatures *The Seasons* (1875–76) and the Third String Quartet (1876). In 1876 he traveled to Paris to see *Carmen,* and by official invitation to the first Bayreuth Festival to see the *Ring;* on the latter he reported pithily in *Russkiye vedomosti.* That autumn he produced three orchestral works: the *Slavonic March* to benefit the Russo-Turkish war effort, the symphonic fantasia *Francesca da Rimini* based on verses of Dante's *Inferno,* and *Variations on a Rococo Theme* in A for cello and orchestra, which evinced a sentimental affinity for Mozart.

In December 1876 Nadezhda Filaretovna von Meck (1831–94), a wealthy industrialist's widow of Brailov near Kiev, sent Tchaikovsky a commission for some chamber arrangements; she paid extravagantly and extolled him profusely. More correspondence and commissions followed; by mid-1877 she was providing regular monetary allowances, and he offered her the dedication of his planned Fourth Symphony (1877–78). Thus began an epistolary relationship of composer and benefactress spanning some 14 years and 1,100 letters; they considered their relationship platonic and agreed never to meet face-to-face.

Perhaps by coincidence, in early 1877 Tchaikovsky began an opera on Pushkin's classic romance *Evgeniy Onegin* [Eugene Onegin] (1877–78), starting with the scene of Tatiana's epistolary declaration of love to Onegin. Again by coincidence he received just such a letter in the spring from a conservatory student, Antonina Ivanovna Miliukova. Although he privately admitted his homosexuality, in June he felt compelled to propose, and on 18 July they were married. He immediately sought escape. In August he left for Kamenka but had to return for the school term in September. In early October he attempted suicide by wading into the Moscow River on a frigid night; he became violently ill. His brother Anatoly intervened to procure him a leave from the conservatory and a divorce from his wife. She refused and pursued him for the rest of his life, but he remained estranged.

Mme. von Meck responded by fixing on Tchaikovsky an annuity of twice his conservatory salary. Recuperating in the West in early 1878, he completed the Fourth Symphony and *Evgeniy Onegin;* both rank among his most passionately inspired masterworks. While abroad he composed the Violin Concerto for Yosif Kotek, a former student now in Mme. von Meck's employ. That summer he wrote the piano-violin duo *Souvenir d'un lieu cher* for Kotek, several piano pieces, including a sonata, and the rich choral Liturgy of St. John Chrysostom. Secure in Mme. von Meck's support, he resigned from the conservatory in October.

For seven years, 1877–84, Tchaikovsky was overshadowed by the crisis of his sexuality and consequent publicity over his private affairs. He spent his time largely at Kemenka, Brailov (living apart from Mme. von Meck), and abroad, notably in Florence and Paris. He aged dramatically, and his creativity suffered. He conceived two major operas during this period, *Orleanskaya deva* [The Maid of Orleans] (1878–79), a romanticized story of Joan of Arc, and *Mazepa* (1881–83) on Pushkin's Cossack story "Poltava"; while highly charged, both lacked the careful touch of earlier works. For concerts he fashioned a series of Suites (no. 1, 1878–79; no. 2, 1883; no. 3, 1884) that discarded the formal integrity of the symphony but catered to the ear. For Taneyev he wrote a Second Piano Concerto (1879–80) and a lighter *Concert Fantasy* (1884). Three shorter works of 1880 showed a felicity of inspiration: the *Italian Capriccio,* the *Serenade* for strings, and the Overture *1812,* written for the Moscow Jubilee. The finest work of these years was the poignant Piano Trio on the death of Nikolai Rubinstein in 1881.

Tchaikovsky's reputation grew. In 1881 the new tsar Alexander III commissioned coronation music. On Rubinstein's death, Tchaikovsky was offered the conservatory directorship, though he deferred to Taneyev. From 1881 on *Evgeniy Onegin* had growing success. In 1884 the tsar awarded him the Order of St. Vladimir, and he became head of the Moscow branch of the Russian Musical Society.

He found affection in Alexandra's children at Kamenka; one, Anna, married Mme. von Meck's son Nikolai in 1883; another, Vladimir ("Bob," 1871–1906), became Tchaikovsky's close confidant and eventually his heir. But Alexandra's health declined. In early 1885 Tchaikovsky bought a small country manor at Klin, near Moscow on the rail to St. Petersburg; he successively was to own and occupy three properties at Klin. Here he undertook two retrospective projects, a revision of *Kuznets Vakula* as *Cherevichki* [The Slippers] (1885, also known as Oxana's Caprice); and a four-movement symphonic poem on Byron's *Manfred,* suggested in detail by Balakirev in 1882. The latter he completed in a work of rugged power; it received warm approval from the "Five." For the Moscow premiere of *Cherevichki* in early 1887 the composer took the podium, testing his resolve to face the public. Both opera and conductor succeeded; in March he conducted a concert at St. Petersburg. Meanwhile he completed a new opera, *Charodeika* (The Enchantress, 1885–87), a nationalist response to *Carmen;* but its poor libretto and routine setting destined it to failure. In its wake came two lesser works: a Fourth Suite, "Mozartiana" (1887), orchestrated from pieces by Mozart, and the *Pezzo capriccioso* (1887) for cello and orchestra.

Encouraged by domestic conducting success, Tchaikovsky undertook a concert tour for the 1887–88 season, visiting Berlin, Leipzig, Hamburg, Prague, Paris, and London; he met many musical luminaries including Brahms. In the summer of 1888 he composed a Fifth Symphony, his first in a decade (*Manfred* excepted), and the Fantasy-Overture *Hamlet.* Powerfully atmospheric, both acheived popular success, though the symphony's overblown finale aroused criticism. Armed with these works he made a second tour in early 1889 to Cologne, Frankfurt, Dresden, Berlin, Geneva, Hamburg (where Brahms approved the Fifth Symphony), and London.

He was already absorbed in his next major work, *Spiashchaya krasavitsa* [The Sleeping Beauty] (1888–89), a ballet commissioned by the St. Petersburg Mariyinsky Theater. Its creators, the Mariyinsky's director Ivan Vsevolozhsky and choreographer Marius Petipa, were determined to produce a transcendent spectacle; Tchaikovsky responded with a score that remains the benchmark of large-scale ballet. Two weeks after its premiere (to only tepid applause), he began his last full-length theatrical work, the opera *Pikovaya dama* [The Queen of Spades] (1890), with a libretto by his brother Modest based on Pushkin's ghost story. Its main character, the manic-obsessive Hermann, resonated with Tchaikovsky, who created a masterpiece of fantastic melodrama. Staged at the Mariyinsky in December, it had the greatest initial success of any of his operas. From the same year came his last chamber work, the string sextet *Souvenir de Florence.*

In early October 1890 Mme. von Meck wrote Tchaikovsky suddenly ending their relationship. Her reasons remain obscure, though both her health and her judgment were declining. (She died two months after he did.) He sufferred the deep wound more personally than financially, for by now he was earning substantial income. Bouyed by the success of *Pikovaya dama,* he planned a fairy-tale double bill for the Mariyinsky: a one-act opera, *Yolanta* [Iolanthe] (1891), and a two-act ballet, *Shchelkunchik* [The Nutcracker] (1891–92), based on stories by H. C. Andersen and E. T. A. Hoffmann.

In early 1891 he made his most ambitious tour. In Paris he received the crushing news of Alexandra's death, but he went on to New York, Baltimore, Philadelphia, and Washington, meeting everywhere with overwhelming success. During 1891 he finished *Yolanta* and began *Shchelkunchik.* He also produced the symphonic ballad *Voyevoda,* which fared poorly at its November premiere. In early 1892 he conducted a suite from the nearly finished *Shchelkunchik* to immense applause. In the summer he conceived a symphony, but reworked it as a Third Piano Concerto the following year. In December his fairy-tale double bill met with only scant success.

In mid-1892 he was elected to the Académie française and was offered an honorary doctorate at Cambridge, for which he traveled to England the next summer. During 1893 he composed the Sixth Symphony, which proved to be his final masterpiece. He led its premiere in St. Petersburg on 28 October; the unorthodox work puzzled the public.

Four days later Tchaikovsky grew suddenly ill; he had contracted cholera, then in its first Russian epidemic since the one that had taken his mother. He was buried in St. Petersburg's Nevsky Cemetery. Rumors of suicide circulated immediately and have continued to surface, but none has offered tangible evidence.

In addition to works mentioned, as a student Tchaikovsky composed numerous short orchestral, chamber, and choral works. Throughout his life he produced songs and piano pieces, publishing them in groups of 6 or 12. On commission he wrote occasional pieces, both vocal and instrumental, as well as incidental music and insertions for repertory operas by other composers. He produced a substantial amount of liturgical choral music, mostly from 1881 onward, and a few secular choral pieces.

As a teacher he translated Schumann's *Musikalische Haus- und Lebensregeln* and J. C. Lobe's *Katechismus der Musik.* He wrote 2 pedagogical volumes: *Rukovodstvo k prakticheskomu izucheniyu garmoniy* [Guide to the Practical Study of Harmony]; trans. Eng. (1900, 1976); and *Kratkiy uchebnik garmoniy, prisposoblenniy k chteniyu dukhovno-muzïkal'nïkh sochineniy v Rossiy* [Short Manual of Harmony, Adapted to the Study of Sacred Musical Composition in Russia].

Bibl.: Boris Jürgenson, ed., *Catalogue thématique des oeuvres de P. Tschaikowsky* (Moscow, 1897; R: London, 1965). Modest Tchaikovsky, *Zhizn' Petra Ilyicha Chaikovskogo* [Life of P. I. Tchaikovsky] (Moscow, 1900–1902); abridged trans. Eng. (London, 1906). Vasily Yakovlev, ed., *Dni i godi P. I.*

Chaikovskogo [Days and Years of Tchaikovsky] (Moscow and Leningrad, 1940). *P. Chaikovsky: literaturniye proizvedeniya i perepiski* [Literary Works and Correspondence] (Moscow, 1953–81). G. S. Dombayev, *Tvorchestvo P. I. Chaikovskogo v materialakh i dokumentakh* [Work of Tchaikovsky in Materials and Documents] (Moscow, 1958). David Brown, *Tchaikovsky* (London, 1978–91). Peter Ilich Tchaikovsky, *Letters to His Family: An Autobiography* (New York, 1982). Roland John Wiley, *Tchaikovsky's Ballets* (Oxford, 1985). Henry Zajaczkowski, *Tchaikovsky's Musical Style* (Ann Arbor, 1987). Elizabeth Clark, *Tchaikovsky* (New York, 1988). Alan Kendall, *Tchaikovsky: A Biography* (London, 1988). Alexandra Orlova, *Tchaikovsky: A Self-Portrait* (Oxford, 1990). Alexander Poznansky, *Tchaikovsky: The Quest for the Inner Man* (New York, 1991).

Tcherepnin, Alexander (b. St. Petersburg, 20 Jan. 1899; d. Paris, 29 Sept. 1977). Composer and pianist. Son of conductor and composer Nicholas Tcherepnin, he studied piano as a child with his mother and began composing at an early age. He studied for one year at the Petersburg Conservatory (1917), but with the coming of the Revolution, he fled with his family to Tiflis and then in 1921 to Paris, where he studied composition with Paul Vidal at the Conservatoire and piano with Isidore Philippe. He debuted as a pianist in London in 1922 with a program of his own works. In 1923 he introduced his first piano concerto at Monte Carlo, in 1924 his second concerto in Paris. He composed prolifically, mainly for solo piano, but also for chamber orchestra (*Concerto de chambre,* 1924; *3 Pieces,* 1921–25) and for cello (3 sonatas, 1924–26; *12 Preludes,* 1925–26). In 1927 his First Symphony premiered in Paris. From 1926 through 1933 Tcherepnin toured as a pianist, playing throughout Europe, in the U.S. (1926), and in the Middle East (1931). Interrupting a tour of the Far East in 1934, he remained for three years in China, where he taught at the Shanghai Conservatory. His compositions of this period (e.g., *5 Études de concert,* 1936) explore the possibilities of a piano style based on traditional Chinese pentatonic music. The influence of Chinese music is also heard in later works such as *The Farmer and the Fairy,* opera (Aspen, Colo., 1952), and *The Lost Flute,* narrator and orchestra (1954). Returning to Europe in 1937, Tcherepnin married his former piano student Li Hsien-ming and settled in Paris. He completed Mussorgsky's opera *The Marriage,* composed several ballets including *Trepak* (1938), and enjoyed considerable success with *Suite géorgienne,* piano and string orchestra (1938). In 1949 he moved to the U.S. to teach at De Paul Univ. in Chicago (1949–64). His Second Symphony (1951) was premiered in Chicago in 1952, followed by 2 more symphonies (1953, 1957), 2 more piano concertos (1963, 1965), a Harmonica Concerto (1953), and several more works for solo piano (*12 Préludes,* 1953; Second Sonata, 1961).

Bibl.: Willi Reich, *Alexandre Tcherepnin* (Bonn, 1959; rev. 1970). Alexander Tcherepnin, "A Short Autobiography (1964)," *Tempo* 130 (1979): 12–18. Enrique Alberto Arias, "Alexander Tcherepnin's Thoughts on Music," *PNM* 21 (1982–83): 138–44. Guy S. Wuellner, "A Chinese *Mikrokosmos,*" *College Music Symposium* 25 (1985): 130–43. Enrique Alberto Arias, *Alexander Tcherepnin: A Bio-Bibliography* (New York, 1989).

Tcherepnin, Ivan (b. Issy-les-Moulineaux, nr. Paris, 5 Feb. 1943). Composer. He studied piano with his mother and composition with his father, Alexander Tcherepnin, then attended Harvard Univ. (B.A., 1964; M.A., 1969). He also studied with Stockhausen and Pousseur. Taught at the San Francisco Conservatory of Music, 1969–72, and worked with John Chowning and David Tudor. In 1972 he returned to Harvard to teach electronic music. Most of his works involve electronic instruments, electronic processing, or both—for example, *Watergate Suite,* electronic tape (1973); *Santur Opera,* santur and synthesizer (1977); *Flores musicales,* oboe, violin, cello (optional), psaltery, synthesizer, electronics (1979; rev. 1980). Other compositions include *New Rhythmantics IV* (string quartet, trumpet, electronics, 1987); *Concerto for 2 Continents* (synthesizer, wind orchestra, 1989). His Double Concerto for Violin and Cello won the Grawmeyer Award in 1996.

Tcherepnin, Nicholas (b. St. Petersburg, 14 May 1873; d. Issy-les-Moulineaux, nr. Paris, 26 June 1945). Composer and conductor. He studied with Rimsky-Korsakov at the Petersburg Conservatory (1895–98), then joined the faculty himself, teaching conducting and orchestration (1905–1917). He conducted at the Mariinsky Theater and the Imperial Opera and toured in Europe with Diaghilev and the Ballets russes, which danced his *Pavillon d'Armide* (1907) in 1909 and *Narcisse et Echo* in 1911. Fleeing the Revolution in 1918, he became director of the National Conservatory at Tiflis (1918–21), then emigrated to Paris, where he directed the Russian Conservatory in Paris (1925–29, 1938–45). His works written in exile have a strong flavor of Russian nationalism, particularly his operas *Swat* (1930) and *Vanka* (Belgrade, 1935), his songs, and much Russian Orthodox liturgical music.

Tcherepnin, Serge (b. Paris, 2 Feb. 1941). Composer. He learned violin as a child and studied composition with his father, Alexander Tcherepnin, then at Harvard (B.A., 1964) and in Europe with Karlheinz Stockhausen, Herbert Eimert, and Luigi Nono. He taught electronic music at New York Univ. (1968–70), then at the California Institute of the Arts (1970–75). He is the designer, manufacturer, and marketer of the "Serge," a modular synthesizer. Most of his compositions involve electronics of one sort or another.

Tchicai, John (Martin) (b. Copenhagen, 28 Apr. 1936). Jazz saxophonist. Of Congolese and Danish parentage. He played free jazz in New York and Europe as an alto saxophonist with Don Cherry and Archie Shepp in the New York Contemporary Five (1963) and with Roswell Rudd in the New York Art Quartet (1964–65). He also recorded albums with Shepp (*Four for Trane,* 1964) and John Coltrane (*Ascension,* 1965).

From 1966 he again lived in Denmark. Working most often as a leader or sideman in groups with guitarist Pierre Dørge, Tchicai switched from alto to tenor and soprano instruments.

Teagarden, Jack [Weldon Leo] (b. Vernon, Tex., 29 Aug. 1905; d. New Orleans, 15 Jan. 1964). Jazz trombonist, singer, and bandleader. After playing in southwestern bands he moved to New York, where he joined Ben Pollack (1928–33) and Paul Whiteman (1933–38) and, as the first fully sophisticated jazz trombone soloist, recorded prolifically with musicians such as Eddie Condon ("Makin' Friends," 1928), Louis Armstrong ("Knockin' a Jug," 1929), Benny Goodman, Red Nichols, and Bud Freeman. He led a swing big band (1938–46), then worked with small traditional jazz groups. He joined Armstrong's All Stars (1947–51, including the recording *St. James Infirmary,* 1947). His own bands from 1951 included a group co-led by Earl Hines (1957). He recorded the album *Coast Concert* with Bobby Hackett (1955). His mobile playing and simple singing were informed by a relaxed sense of swing and an affinity for blues. Teagarden's siblings were also jazz musicians: pianist Norma (b. 1915), trumpeter Charlie (1913–84), and drummer Cub (1915–69).

Bibl.: Heiner Mückenberger, *Meet Me Where They Play the Blues: Jack Teagarden und seine Musik* (Gautig, Germany, 1986). Jay D. Smith and Len Guttridge, *Jack Teagarden: The Story of a Jazz Maverick* (London, 1960, rev.; R: New York, 1988). Howard J. Waters, Jr., *Jack Teagarden's Music: His Career and Recordings* (Stanhope, N.J., 1960).

Tebaldi, Renata (b. Pesaro, 1 Feb. 1922). Soprano. She studied with Carmen Melis in Parma (1939–42) and made her debut as Elena (in Boito's *Mefistofele*) at Rovigo in 1944. She performed under Toscanini in the concert for the reopening of La Scala in 1946, and remained with that theater for over a decade. She appeared as Desdemona in both her Covent Garden (1950) and Metropolitan Opera (1955) debuts; her 17 seasons at the Met included roles such as Tosca, Mimi, Gioconda, Manon Lescaut, Violetta, and Leonora *(Forza).* She performed at most of the leading houses and undertook a number of concert tours before her retirement in 1976. She is considered one of the leading sopranos of her generation.

Bibl.: Kenn Harris, *Renata Tebaldi* (New York, 1974).

Teitelbaum, Richard (Lowe) (b. New York, 19 May 1939). Composer. He studied at Yale Univ. (M.M., 1964), then with Luigi Nono and Goffredo Petrassi in Italy. With Frederic Rzewski, Alvin Curran, and other American composers in Rome, he founded Musica elettronica viva, an ensemble for the performance of improvised electronic music. Returning to the U.S. in 1970, he went to Wesleyan Univ., where he studied non-Western music and participated in improvised performances with musicians from diverse cultures. He also studied in Japan and collaborated with Japanese musicians (1976–77). Since 1980 he has worked mainly with computers and synthesizers and computers. Works include *In Tune* (amplified brain waves, heartbeats, breathing, and synthesizer, 1967); *Threshhold Music* (instruments and environmental sounds, 1974); *Blends* (shakuhachi and synthesizers, 1977); *Reverse Polish Notation* (keyboards and computers, 1983).

Te Kanawa, Kiri (b. Gisborne, Auckland, 6 Mar. 1944). Soprano. Studied singing in Auckland and won prizes in New Zealand and Australia before leaving in 1966 for London, where she was a pupil of Vera Rozsa. After joining the Royal Opera Company she made her Covent Garden debut in 1970 as a Flower Maiden. Her successful rendition of Mozart's Countess in *Le nozze di Figaro* in London was repeated in Lyons, San Francisco, and Glyndebourne. Other Covent Garden roles included Donna Elvira, Fiordiligi, Desdemona, and Mimì. Her Metropolitan Opera debut was in 1974 as Desdemona. She has toured widely, made many recordings, and in 1982 was made a Dame Commander of the British Empire.

Bibl.: David Fingleton, *Kiri Te Kanawa* (New York, 1983).

Telemann, Georg Philipp (b. Magdeburg, 14 Mar. 1681; d. Hamburg, 25 June 1767). Composer. He received instruction in Latin, rhetoric, and dialectic at the Altstädtisches Gymnasium and the Domschule in Magdeburg. His music master was the Kantor Benedikt Christian, whose compositions he transcribed; by the age of 10 he had learned to play the violin, the flute, the zither, and keyboard instruments. At the age of 12 he began composing an opera, prompting his mother, who wished him to study law, to forbid him to continue his musical studies. In late 1693 or 1694 he was sent to school at Zellerfeld and placed under the care of the superintendent, Caspar Calvoer. Calvoer instructed Telemann in music theory and approved of the boy's teaching himself composition and thoroughbass. Telemann remained there for four years before moving to the Gymnasium Andreanum at Hildesheim. There he composed incidental songs for Latin school dramas, became involved in performances of German cantatas, and made visits to Hannover and Brunswick, where he became exposed to French instrumental music and Italian opera.

In 1701 he entered Leipzig Univ. with the intent of studying law; he organized a student collegium musicum there in 1702. Also in that year he was appointed music director of the Leipzig Opera, where he used students in productions. In 1704 he became organist at the Neue Kirche, and the following year he was appointed Kapellmeister to the court of Count Erdmann II of Promnitz at Sorau. Several visits to Poland acquainted him with Polish folk music, which he admired greatly. In 1708 or 1709 he moved to Eisenach to assume the duties of *Konzertmeister* and later Kapellmeister. For the orchestra he composed French overtures, concertos, and chamber works; for the *Hofkapelle* he supplied church cantatas and occasional music. It was there that he probably met J. S. Bach; he was godfather to C. P. E. Bach in 1714. In 1709 he married Louise Eberlin; she died in January 1711. The following year he became the city director of music at Frankfurt am Main and Kapellmeister at the Barfüsserkirche. There he trained choristers, wrote at least five cycles of cantatas, and supplied occasional music. He also directed weekly public concerts at which his oratorios and instrumental works were performed. In 1714 he married Maria Katharina Textor, with whom he had eight sons and two daughters. In 1717 he became Kapellmeister at Gotha, and on 16 October 1721 he was appointed Kantor of the Johanneum in Hamburg and music director of the city's five main churches. Although the latter position placed considerable demands on Telemann, he still found time to conduct a collegium musicum in public concerts and take part in operatic productions; from 1722 to 1738 he was music director of the Hamburg Opera. From his time in Frankfurt until 1740 Telemann himself published a great many of his works, including sacred cantatas and the three-part *Musique de table.* In 1737 he went to Paris, probably to prevent pirated editions of his music from being published; his works were performed to great acclaim at court and at the Concert spirituel. Like Handel, he turned in his later years to the oratorio.

Works: Sacred vocal music includes about 50 Passions (mostly lost); oratorios; Masses; about 1,400 cantatas (*Harmonischer Gottes-Dienst,* 1725–26); motets; Psalms; occasional music, consisting mostly of cantatas. Secular vocal: operas (*Der geduldige Socrates,* 1721); intermezzos; about 50 cantatas; serenades; occasional music; about 100 songs. Instrumental: over 100 French overtures (*Don Quixote* and *Hamburger Ebb und Fluht*); 47 solo concertos (21 for violin); 40 concertos for 2 or more instruments; 8 concerti grossi; over 200 solo and trio sonatas (*Sonate metodiche,* 1728, and *Essercizii musici,* 1739–40); quartets and quintets (*Nouveaux quatuors,* 1738); keyboard works (*Fantaisies pour le clavessin,* 1732–33); lute music.

Bibl.: *Georg Philipp Telemann: Musikalische Werke* (Kassel and Basel, 1950–). Werner Menke, *Thematisches Verzeichnis der Vokalwerke von Georg Philipp Telemann* (Frankfurt am Main, 1982–83). Martin Ruhnke, *Georg Philipp Telemann: Thematisch-Systematisches Verzeichnis seiner Werke: Telemann-Werkverzeichnis (TWV): Instrumentalwerke,* vols. 1 and 2 (Kassel, 1984, 1992). Hermann Wettstein, *Georg Philipp Telemann: Bibliographischer Versuch zu seinem Leben und Werk, 1681–1767* (Hamburg, 1981). Kurt Ottzenn, *Telemann als Opernkomponist* (Berlin, 1902). Hans Hörner, *Georg Philipp Telemanns Passionsmusiken* (Leipzig, 1933). Käte Schäfer-Schmuck, *Georg Philipp Telemann als Klavierkomponist* (Borna, 1934; R: 1981). Horst Büttner, *Das Konzert in den Orchestersuiten Georg Philipp Telemanns* (Wolfenbüttel and Berlin, 1935). Werner Menke, *Das Vokalwerk Georg Philipp Telemanns* (Kassel, 1942). Erich Valentin, *Georg Philipp Telemann* (Burg, 1931; 3rd ed., 1952). Articles in *Magdeburger Telemann-Festtage* 1-6 (Magdeburg, 1963–78). Richard Petzoldt, *Georg Philipp Telemann: Leben und Werk* (Leipzig, 1967); trans. Eng. (1974). Adolf Hoffmann, *Die Orchestersuiten Georg Philipp Telemanns* (Wolfenbüttel and Zurich, 1969). Siegfried Kross, *Das Instrumentalkonzert bei Georg Philipp Telemann* (Tutzing, 1969). Mary Adelaide Peckham, "The Operas of Georg Philipp Telemann" (diss., Columbia Univ., 1969). Karl Grebe, *Georg Philipp Telemann in Selbstzeugnissen und Bilddokumenten* (Reinbeck bei Hamburg, 1970). *Georg Philipp Telemann: Briefwechsel,* ed. Hans Grosse and Hans Rudolf Jung (Leipzig, 1972). *Georg Philipp Telemann: Autobiographien—1718, 1729, 1739,* ed. Günter Fleischauer, Walther Siegmund-Schultze, and Eitelfriedrich Thom (Blankenburg, 1977). Erkart Klessman, *Telemann in Hamburg: 1721–1767* (Hamburg, 1980). Walther Siegmund-Schultze, *Georg Philipp Telemann* (Leipzig, 1980). Brian Douglas Stewart, "Georg Philipp Telemann in Hamburg (diss., Stanford Univ., 1985). Wolfgang Hirschmann, *Studien zum Konzertschaffen von Georg Philipp Telemann* (Kassel, 1986). Werner Menke, *Georg Philipp Telemann: Leben, Werk und Umwelt in Bilddokumenten* (Wilhelmshaven, 1987). Annemarie Clostermann, *Georg Philipp Telemanns Hamburger Schaffen (1721–1767): eine Vortragsreihe* (Hamburg, 1990).

Tellefsen, Thomas (Dyke Acland) (b. Trondheim, Norway, 26 Nov. 1823; d. Paris, 6 Oct. 1874). Pianist and composer. Studied at home with his father. Gave his first public concert in Trondheim at age 18. Studied in Paris in 1842 with fellow Norwegian Charlotte Thygeson and with Kalkbrenner. From 1844 to 1847 he had occasional lessons with Chopin. His Paris debut was in 1851; after this he was known as one of the top interpreters of Chopin. After Chopin's death, he took on several of Chopin's students. Toured several Scandinavian cities in the early 1860s. Made frequent trips to London. His compositions include 2 piano concertos (1852, 1854), 2 violin sonatas (1856), mazurkas, Norwegian dances, and other works. Many were published by Richautt in Paris.

Telmányi, Emil (b. Arad, Hungary [now Oradea, Romania], 22 June 1892; d. 12 June 1988). Violinist and conductor. Studied both violin (with Hubay) and composition at the Academy of Music in Budapest, after which he began a performing career as violinist. His conducting debut was in 1919 at Copenhagen. In 1918 he married Anne Marie Nielsen, a daughter of Carl Nielsen, and they settled in Denmark; he premiered some of Nielsen's works. His second marriage, in 1936, was to pianist Annette Schiöler, with whom he made a number of recordings. He arranged works of Brahms, Chopin, and others for violin and created a special curved bow (which became known as the Vega bow) for playing Bach's solo violin music.

Templeton, Alec (b. Cardiff, Wales, 4 July 1909; d. Greenwich, Conn., 28 Mar. 1963). Pianist and composer. Blind from birth, he displayed musical talent at a young age. From 1921 to 1935 he did a series of musical programs for the BBC; he also studied at the Royal Academy of Music and the Royal College of Music. Settled in the U.S. in 1935 and performed widely with orchestras and on the radio. His most famous works include humorous musical sketches and parodies, such as "Mozart Matriculates," "Debussy in Dubuque," and "Bach Goes to Town"; he also wrote serious works, mostly for piano, sometimes with orchestra (*Gothic Concerto,* 1954).

Templeton, John (b. Riccarton, near Kilmarnock, 30 July 1802; d. New Hampton, near London, 2 July 1886). Tenor. Studied in London. Opera debut at Drury Lane, 1831. Sang opposite Malibran on several occasions, causing him to be known as "Malibran's tenor." U.S. tour, 1845–46. Retired in 1852. Repertoire of over 80 roles. Participated in first English performances of Meyerbeer's *Robert le diable* (1832), Auber's *Le cheval de bronze* (1836), Hérold's *Zampa* (1836), Rossini's *Le siège de Corinthe* (1836), Donizetti's *La favorite* (1843), and Mozart's *Die Zauberflöte* (1843). His memoirs, *A Musical Entertainment,* were published in Boston in 1845.

Tenducci, Giusto Ferdinando (b. Siena, ca. 1735; d. Genoa, 25 Jan. 1790). Castrato soprano and composer. In 1758 he went to London, where he sang at the King's Theatre; he paid subsequent visits and performed in Ireland and Scotland and returned to Italy in 1789. He sang in the first performance of J. C. Bach's *Adriano in Siria* in London and was acquainted with Mozart, who wrote for him a *scena* with solo parts for piano, oboe, horn, and bassoon (now lost). He wrote a vocal treatise, *Instruction of Mr. Tenducci to His Scholars* (London, ca. 1785); his compositions include adaptations of operas, all first performed in Dublin, and some songs.

Tenney, James (b. Silver City, N.M., 10 Aug. 1934). Composer, pianist. He studied piano at the Juilliard School, then piano and composition at Bennington College (B.A., 1958), where he was associated with Carl Ruggles, and at the Univ. of Illinois, where he worked with Kenneth Gaburo and Lejaren Hiller (M.Mus., 1961). During the 1960s he lived in New York, where he worked on electronic and computer music at Bell Labs in New Jersey, at Yale Univ., and at the Polytechnic Institute of New York. He also played with the ensembles of Steve Reich and Philip Glass (1967–70). Most of his works from this period were for computer and/or tape. In the 1970s he turned back to traditional instruments, though often tuned in microtonal systems and enhanced by electronics. From 1970 to 1975 he taught at the California Institute of the Arts; beginning in 1977 taught at York Univ. in Ontario. He is the author of *A History of Consonance and Dissonance* (New York, 1988).

Bibl.: *Soundings 13: The Music of James Tenney* (Santa Fe, N.M., 1984) [includes works list]. Larry Polanski and David Rosenboom, eds., "A Tribute to James Tenney," *PNM* 25 (1987): 434–591.

Tennstedt, Klaus (b. Merseburg, 6 June 1926). Conductor. Studied piano and violin at the Leipzig Conservatory; in 1948 named concertmaster at the Halle Municipal Theater, at which he later became conductor. Subsequently conductor of the Dresden opera and the Schwerin orchestra. In 1971, left for Sweden, where he conducted in Göteborg and Stockholm; *Generalmusikdirektor* of the Kiel Opera in 1972. His first appearance in the U.S. was with the Boston Symphony in 1974; chief guest conductor of the Minnesota Orchestra, 1979–83; chief conductor of the Norddeutscher Rundfunk Symphony in Hamburg, 1979–81; principal guest conductor of the London Philharmonic, 1980–83, and principal conductor there, 1983–87; conducted *Fidelio* at the Metropolitan Opera in 1983. His performances of Mahler much admired. In 1994 Tennstedt announced his retirement from public appearances owing to poor health.

Ternina [Trnina], **Milka** (b. Doljnji, Moslavina, 19 Dec. 1863; d. Zagreb, 18 May 1941). Soprano. Studied at Zagreb and Vienna (with Gänzbacher, 1880–82). Opera debut at Zagreb, 1882. Appeared in Leipzig (1883–84), Graz (1884–86), Bremen (1886–89), and Munich (1890–99). London and Covent Garden debuts in 1895; American debut in 1896 in Boston as Brünnhilde with Damrosch's company. First London Tosca (1900); first New York Tosca (1901). Sang at Metropolitan Opera, 1900–1904. Banned from Bayreuth in 1903 after singing *Parsifal* outside Bayreuth. Retired in 1906.

Terradellas, Domingo Miguel Bernabe [Terradeglias, Domenico] (b. Barcelona, bapt. 13 Feb. 1713; d. Rome, 20 May 1751). Composer. After instruction at Barcelona, he moved to Italy in 1732 and enrolled in the music conservatory Poveri di Gesù Cristo in Naples. His oratorio *Giuseppe riconosciuto* (1736) was written while he was still a student there. His first opera, *Astarto* (1739), was produced in Rome, where he later had great success with *Merope* (1743). From 1743 to 1745 he was employed in Padua at the Santiago y S. Ildefonso. In 1746 he went to London, where he wrote 2 operas for the King's Theatre. His last opera, *Sesostri re d'Egitto* (1751), was performed in Rome. In addition to operas, Terradellas composed 2 oratorios and other sacred vocal works.

Terry, Clark [Mumbles] (b. St. Louis, 14 Dec. 1920). Jazz trumpeter, flügelhorn player, and bandleader. He joined Charlie Barnet (1947), Count Basie (1948–51), Duke Ellington (1951–59), and Quincy Jones (1959–60). He worked in New York studios, notably for NBC's *Tonight Show;* led a group with Bob Brookmeyer (1961–66, including the album *The Power of Positively Swinging,* 1964); and formed a big band (1967–mid-1980s). Increasingly he played flügelhorn rather than trumpet. His nickname derives from his hilarious mumbling version of blues scat singing, introduced on the album *The Oscar Peterson Trio Plus One—Clark Terry* (1964). He toured from Egypt to India with a quintet (1978) and led a 9-piece swing band, the Ellington Spacemen, in New York (late 1980s). Headed the Thelonious Monk Institute of Jazz at Duke Univ. from 1990.

Terry, Sonny [Terrell, Sanders] (b. Greensboro, Ga., 24 Oct. 1911; d. Mineola, N.Y., 11 Mar. 1986). Blues singer and harmonica player. Musical from his youth, he was blinded from age 16 in separate accidents to each eye. He teamed with Blind Boy Fuller, 1934–39, and developed an intense vocalized harmonica style. A Carnegie Hall appearance in 1939 brought him prominence. From 1939 onward he teamed with Brownie McGhee, creating a long-lived blues act that was especially acclaimed from the 1960s into the 1980s.

Terterian, Avet (Alfred) (b. Baku, 29 July 1929). Composer. Studied composition at the Yerevan Conservatory, 1952–57, with E. Mirzoian; also pursued graduate studies there, 1963–67, and taught at the conservatory beginning in 1970. Experimented widely with contemporary and extended Armenian folk techniques to create a style often conceptual in origin, marked by a distinctive approach to time and space. Works include the operas *A Fiery Ring* (1967) and *The Earthquake* (1984); the ballet *Monologues of Richard III* (1979); 7 symphonies (1969, 1972, 1975, 1976, 1978, 1981, 1987); vocal-symphonic music; choral and solo vocal music; incidental music.

Tertis, Lionel (b. West Hartlepool, 29 Dec. 1876; d. London, 22 Feb. 1975). Violist. Studied violin at the Hochschule für Musik in Leipzig and the Royal Academy of Music in London. He switched to viola and embarked on a solo career, including concert tours of Europe and the U.S., becoming one of the most renowned players on his instrument. In addition to writing a number of books (*My Viola and I: A Complete Autobiography,* London, 1974), Tertis helped design a large viola (see *ML* 28/3 [1947]: 214–22).

Terzakis, Dimitri (b. Athens, 12 Mar. 1938). Composer. He studied at the Athens Conservatory of Music from 1959 until 1964, taking piano lessons with Thurneissen and composition lessons with Papaioannou. He then traveled to Cologne, where from 1965 to 1969 he studied composition (Zimmermann) and electronic music (Einert) at the Hochschule für Musik. In 1974 he joined the faculty of the Hochschule für Musik in Düsseldorf, teaching theory, composition, and Byzantine music. His early works were in a post-Romantic idiom, with tonally based chromaticism. He subsequently incorporated serialistic techniques as well as microtonal characteristics of traditional Greek music. Other works include opera (*Tomas Torguemade,* 1974–76; *Hermes,* 1983–84) and vocal music (*Liturgia profana,* psaltis, tenor, choir, 2 cellos, santouri, percussion, 1977; *Sappho Fragmente,* soprano, 1978; *Odysee nach Homer,* 3 soloists, speaker, mixed chorus, chamber orchestra, 1977–84; *Das sechste Siegel,* choir, ensemble, 1987); orchestral (violin concerto, 1985–86; *Lachesis. Der Mythos vom Ende,* orchestra, 1986), chamber (String Quartet no. 3, 1982; octet, 1988), and incidental music. Terzakis also composed music for tape (*To alloithoro psari* [The Squint-Eyed Fish], 1974).

Tesi (Tramontini), Vittoria ["La Moretta"] (b. Florence, 13 Feb. 1700; d. Vienna, 9 May 1775). Contralto. She was a pupil of Francesco Redi in Florence and Campeggi in Bologna. In the 1718–19 season she sang in Venice as *virtuosa di camera* to Prince Antonio of Parma. She went to Dresden before traveling across Italy (1721–47); in 1737 she sang at the opening of the Teatro S. Carlo in Naples. She later sang in operas by Gluck and Jommelli. Upon her retirement she devoted herself to teaching.

Tessarini, Carlo (b. Rimini, ca. 1690; d. Amsterdam?, after 15 Dec. 1766). Composer. He was a violinist at St. Mark's in Venice in December 1720. From 1729 he led the concerts of the Venetian conservatory SS. Giovanni e Paolo, and from about 1733 he was at the chapel of Urbino Cathedral. He visited Rome (1740–42), where he styled himself "direttore perpetuo" of the Accademia degli Anarconti of Fano. He then gave concerts in the Netherlands (1747–50), returning to Urbino in 1750. In 1761 he went to Arnheim and probably lived in Holland until his death. His compositions are almost all for strings, and his violin treatise, *Grammatica di musica* (Rome, 1741), contains information on high-position playing and cadenzas.

Tessier [Tessiery, Thessier], **Charles** [Carles] (fl. ca. 1600). Composer. On the title page of his *Premier livre de chansons et airs de cour . . . à 4 et 5 parties* (London, 1597), he is identified as *musitien de la chambre du roy* to Henry IV of France. He may have been employed in England by Lord Salisbury at Hertfordshire. His *Airs et villanelles* for 3, 4, and 5 voices appeared in Paris in 1604. Both publications contain mainly strophic *airs,* which can be performed by voices or solo voice and lute.

Tetrazzini, Luisa [Luigia] (b. Florence, 29 June 1871; d. Milan, 28 Apr. 1940). Soprano. Studied in Florence with Ceccherini, making her debut there in 1890 as Inès *(Africaine);* subsequently toured extensively in South America, eastern Europe, and Mexico. Her Covent Garden debut as Violetta in 1907 caused a sensation, and she appeared at Covent Garden until 1912, performing roles such as Lucia, Gilda, and Rosina. She was then engaged by Hammerstein's Manhattan Opera (1908–10), the Metropolitan Opera (1911–12), and the Chicago Grand Opera (1911–13), where her roles included Elvira *(Puritani),* Annetta *(Crispino),* Marie *(Fille),* and Lakmé. In later years she embarked on a number of concert tours, the last in 1934 in London. Tetrazzini was noted for her coloratura technique and warmth of tone. She taught in Milan in later years and published *My Life of Song* (London, 1921; R: 1977) and *How To Sing* (New York, 1923; R: 1975).

Teyte [Tate], **Maggie** (b. Wolverhampton, 17 Apr. 1888; d. London, 26 May 1976). Soprano. Studied first in England, then in Paris with Jean de Reszke. In 1908 she appeared at Monte Carlo and at the Opéra-comique in Paris. Debussy chose her as successor to Mary Garden for the role of Mélisande; he also accompanied her in recitals, particularly of his songs. She sang with Beecham's Opera (1910–11), the Chicago Grand Opera (1911–14), the Boston Opera (1914–17), the British National Opera (1922–23), and the New York City Opera (as Mélisande, 1948). During the 1920s and 1930s she performed in operettas and musical comedies; during the 1940s she was noted for her recitals of French songs. In 1958 she was named Dame of the British Empire.

Bibl.: Gary O'Connor, *The Pursuit of Perfection: A Life of Maggie Teyte* (New York, 1979).

Thalberg, Sigismond (Fortuné François) (b. Pâquis, near Geneva, 8 Jan. 1812; d. Posillipo, Naples, 27 Apr. 1871). Pianist, composer. From 1822, studied at the Polytechnical School, Vienna, intended for a diplomatic career, but also took music lessons from a bassoonist of the opera orchestra and apparently also from Hummel and Sechter; from 1826 made a name as pianist in Viennese salons; 1828, published first of 82 opus numbers, consisting mostly of operatic potpourris and variations; 1830, first international tour, composing for it his only concerto (op. 5). His arrival in Paris late in 1835 created a sensation and led to a celebrated pianistic duel with Liszt, ending in a draw but providing both with immense publicity. His tours reached Russia (1839), Spain (1845), Brazil (1855), the U.S. (1856–58). In 1844 he married Mme. Boucher, daughter of Lablache; after 1858, lived in semiretirement at his Posillipo villa, emerging occasionally (London, Paris, 1862; Brazil, 1863; Germany, 1866). Thalberg's playing was noted for its elegance, precision, expressiveness, and singing tone. The innovatory qualities that astonished audiences of the 1830s resided principally in his new way of writing for the piano, resulting in a greater volume of sound, new kinds of figuration, and the technique for which he was best known—the division of the melody between the 2 hands while accompanying it both above and below with figuration adroitly calculated to sound as if 3 hands must be playing.

Tharpe, Sister Rosetta [Nubin, Rosetta] (b. Cotton Plant, Ark., 20 March 1915; d. Philadelphia, 9 Oct. 1973). Gospel and jazz singer and guitarist. She was a gospel musician from childhood. In 1938 she performed in the From Spirituals to Swing concert at Carnegie Hall, joined Cab Calloway, and recorded "Rock Me," a worldly version of the gospel song "Hide Me in Thy Bosom." She joined Lucky Millinder's big band (1941–42). She made many recordings accompanied by pianist Sammy Price's trio, including "Strange Things Happening Every Day" (1944) and duos with her mother, Katie Bell Nubin, and with Marie Knight.

Thebom, Blanche (b. Monessen, Pa., 19 Sept. 1918). Mezzo-soprano. Studied in New York with Margarete Matzenauer and Edyth Walker and made her debut as a concert singer in 1941. Her New York Metropolitan Opera debut was in 1944, as Fricka in *Die Walküre,* and she remained with the company until 1967, performing mainly Wagnerian roles. Other roles included Dorabella at Glyndebourne (1950) and Dido at Covent Garden (1957) in the first professionally staged English performance of *Les troyens.* She retired in 1970.

Theile, Johann (b. Naumburg, 29 July 1646; d. there, buried 24 June 1724). Composer. He received instruction from Johann Scheffler, Kantor of Magdeburg, and enrolled in the Univ. of Leipzig in 1666 as a law student. There he was a member of the Collegium musicum. He studied with Schütz sometime between 1666 and 1672. In 1673 he became Kapellmeister at Gottorf. On 2 January 1678 his first opera was performed at the opening of the opera house in Hamburg. From 1685 to 1691 he was Kapellmeister at Wolfenbüttel before becoming employed by Duke Christian I at Merseburg. Known as "the father of contrapuntists" by his contemporaries, Theile wrote operas (lost), Passions, Masses, motets, and secular vocal and instrumental works.

Theodorakis, Mikis (Michael George) (b. Khios, 29 July 1925). Composer. He was a student at the Athens Conservatory. His early compositional experiments were based in traditional Greek folk music. He also wrote for Greek dramas, whether stage or film (he wrote the musical score for the film *Zorba the Greek*). In 1954 he traveled to Paris, where he studied at the Conservatory. He returned to Greece, becoming increasingly and publicly antagonistic to the cultural establishment there. In the 1960s he served both as a member of the Greek parliament and as a member of the Communist party. After the conservative political coup of 1967 he was arrested and his music was banned. He was freed after the international release of the movie *Z,* for which he had written the music and which dealt with the oppression of the political left. He then moved to Paris. His works include dramatic music (*Epiphania Averoff,* oratorio, 1968; *Dionysos,* religious drama, voice, choir, chamber ensemble, 1984; *Zorbas,* opera-ballet, 1988), orchestral music (*Oedipus Tyrannus,* 1946; 7 symphonies, and film music.

Bibl.: Gail Holst, *Theodorakis: Myth and Politics in Modern Greek Music* (Amsterdam, 1981). Mikis Theodorakis, *Meine Stellung in der Musikszene: Schriften, Essays, Interviews, 1952–1984* (Leipzig, 1986).

Thérémin, Léon (b. St. Petersburg, 15 Aug. 1896; d. Moscow, 3 Nov. 1993). Inventor. Thérémin was a Russian of French descent. He studied physics at Petrograd Univ., and in 1919 became director of the Laboratory of Electrical Oscillators there. The following year he gave a demonstration of an electronic instrument (the aetherophone or theremin) that changed pitch and volume based on the proximity of the player's hands to an antenna and a loop on the device. Thérémin traveled to the U.S. in 1927 and gave a number of concert demonstrations; in 1938 he returned to Russia. A documentary film about his life and invention was released in 1994.

Thibaud, Jacques (b. Bordeaux, 27 Sept. 1880; d. Mont Cemet, 1 Sept. 1953). Violinist. At age 13 he enrolled at the Paris Conservatory, where he studied with Martin Marsick and won first prize in 1896. He played at the Café rouge and was heard by Édouard Colonne, who secured him a spot in his orchestra; his solo debut was in 1898. He toured widely in Europe and the U.S. and formed a trio with his brothers, but is better remembered for his collaboration with Casals and Cortot.

Thibaut IV (b. Troyes, 30 May 1201; d. Pamplona, 7 July 1253). Trouvère. Count of Champagne and Brie; became King of Navarre in 1234 after the death of his uncle, Sancho the Strong. In 1239 he left France to head a Crusade; returned the following year, having visited Jerusalem. Nearly 50 of Thibaut's compositions have been identified, including *chansons courtoises, chansons de croisade, jeux-partis, débats,* and religious works.

Bibl.: Yvonne Bellenger and Danielle Quéruel, *Thibaut de Champagne, prince et poète au XIIIe siècle* (Lyons, 1987). Kathleen Brahney, ed. and trans., *The Lyrics of Thibaut de Champagne* (New York, 1989).

Thielemans, Toots [Jean Baptiste] (b. Brussels, 29 Apr. 1922). Jazz harmonica player, guitarist, and whistler. He toured Europe with Benny Goodman (1950) and, after emigrating to the U.S., joined George Shearing (1953–59), also recording his own album, *Man Bites Harmonica* (1957). Later he recorded his bop waltz "Bluesette," playing guitar and whistling (1961). As a studio musician he often recorded with Quincy Jones, including the soundtrack to *Midnight Cowboy* (1969). In the 1970s he resumed playing in jazz groups.

Thierry, Pierre (b. Paris, late 1604; d. there, 28 Oct. 1665). Organ builder. He was apprenticed to Valeran de Héman in 1623; from 1634 to 1636 he worked with Crespin Carlier at St. Nicholas-des-Champs. He then worked on his own at Notre Dame, St. Jean, and St. Gervais, Paris. He did his most important work at the Hôtel-Dieu at Pontoise (1637–41), St. Paul, Paris (1644–46), and Les Mathurins. His greatest organ was that at St. Germain-des-Prés (1661). In 1664 he became *facteur du roi.*

Thomas, (Charles Louis) Ambroise (b. Metz, 5 Aug. 1811; d. Paris, 12 Feb. 1886). Composer. Student, 1828–32, Paris Conservatory (Zimmermann, piano; Lesueur, composition), first prizes in piano (1829), harmony (1830). Prix de Rome, 1832; after returning to Paris from Rome in December 1835 he began to publish songs, church music. Produced a 1-act opéra comique in 1837 that had some success, leading to 3 more at the Opéra-comique in 1838–40; produced 2 works, both failures, at the Opéra, 1841–42; returned to the Opéra-comique with 2 works in 1843. Apart from a ballet for the Opéra in 1846, discouraged by his lack of success, he wrote no more for the stage until 1849 with *Le caïd* (Opéra-comique). The great success of this work, which remained in the theater's repertory until 1866, made him one of the principal figures in French light opera, a position reinforced by his next opéra comique, *Le songe d'une nuit d'été* (Opéra-comique, 1850; though not a version of Shakespeare's *Midsummer Night's Dream,* it is based on Shakespearean motifs, and has Shakespeare and Queen Elizabeth among the characters). This success was reflected in his election to the Académie in 1851 and his appointment as professor of composition at the Conservatory in 1852. Produced 6 more operas at the Opéra-comique, 1851–60, with varying success, none equal to the 2 preceding, and some failures (*Psyché,* 1857; *Le roman d'Elvire,* 1860). As before, he retired from the stage temporarily, returning with his greatest success, *Mignon* (Opéra-comique, 1866; thousandth performance there, 1894), which remained widely popular well into the twentieth century, followed by the grand opera *Hamlet* (Opéra, 1868), one of the most popular works of its day and occasionally revived in recent years as a vehicle for coloratura sopranos, its absurd but not ineffective libretto now relished as a period piece. In 1871 he became director of the Conservatory, though increasingly out of touch and sympathy with the musical atmosphere of Paris in the 1870s and 1880s; his administration of the Conservatory became a symbol of reaction. His last grand opera, *Françoise de Rimini* (1882), and a ballet, *La tempête* (1889), were failures. He received many official honors reflecting his great international reputation, including the Grand Cross of the Legion of Honor in 1894.

Bibl.: Elisabeth Rogeboz-Malfroy, *Ambroise Thomas, ou, La tentation du lyrique* (Besançon, 1994).

Thomas, Arthur Goring (b. Ratton Park, Sussex, 20 Nov. 1850; d. London, 20 Mar. 1892). Composer. Initially he was educated for the civil service. Studied in Paris with Sullivan and Prout, and in Berlin with Bruch (orchestration). Carl Rosa commissioned *Esmeralda* (based on Hugo's *Notre-Dame de Paris,* though with a happy ending) in 1883 and *Nadeshda* in 1885. Thomas completed one more opera; a fourth, *The Golden Web* (1893), was completed by Waddington. Other works include the choral ode *The Sun-Worshippers* (1881); the anthem "Out of the Deep" (1878); works for violin, piano, cello; songs, romances, and lyrics. The cantata *The Swan and the Skylark* was completed and orchestrated by C. V. Stanford. Thomas died insane in an asylum. A scholarship was established in his memory at the Royal Academy of Music in 1893.

Bibl.: John W. Klein, "Tragic, Forgotten Pioneer: Arthur Goring Thomas," *MR* 36 (1975): 180–86.

Thomas, John Charles (b. Meyersdale, Va., Sept. 1891; d. Apple Valley, Calif., 13 Dec. 1960). Baritone. Began his singing career in operettas, studied with

Adelin Fermin, and made his operatic debut in 1924 in Washington, D.C., as Amonasro in *Aida.* Sang with the Théatre de la Monnaie in Brussels (1925–28) and also with the San Francisco Opera and Chicago Opera. His Metropolitan Opera debut was in 1934 as Germont in *Traviata;* he was with that house until 1943. Toured the U.S. giving concerts and occasionally sang on the Bell Telephone radio program.

Thomas, Kid [Valentine, Thomas] (b. Reserve, La., 3 Feb. 1896; d. New Orleans, 16 June 1987). Jazz trumpeter and bandleader. From 1922 he worked in New Orleans. He led his own Algiers Stompers, first recording in 1951. The band toured internationally (1960s–80s), sometimes as the Preservation Hall Jazz Band. His albums include *Kid Thomas Valentine's Creole Jazz Band* (1959). Employing a variety of mutes, he simplified and paraphrased traditional jazz melodies in a sparse, explosive manner.

Thomas, Kurt (Georg Hugo) (b. Tonning, Germany, 25 May 1904; d. Bad Oeynhausen, 31 Mar. 1973). Choral conductor and composer. A student of Karl Straube at the Leipzig Conservatory, he was appointed to the faculty there in 1925. The a cappella performance style of his chamber choir was widely influential, as were his own compositions, such as the Mass in A (1925) and the St. Mark Passion (1926), both for a cappella chorus. Beginning in 1934 he was professor at the Hochschule für Musik in Berlin; he also founded and directed the Musisches Gymnasium in Frankfurt (1939–45). After the war he served as Kantor at the Frankfurt cathedral, then as director of the Thomasschule in Leipzig (1955–61). In 1961 he returned to Frankfurt. His manual *The Choral Conductor* (Leipzig, 1935; rev. 1948; trans. Eng. 1971) became a standard text. Besides a cappella choral works and works for chorus and orchestra, he composed many instrumental works.

Bibl.: Neithard Bethke, *Kurt Thomas: Studien zu Leben und Werk* (Kassel, 1989).

Thomas, (Amos) Leon (Jr.) [Leone] (b. East St. Louis, Ill., 4 Oct. 1937). Jazz singer. He joined Count Basie (1961, 1964–45). His album *Spirits Known and Unknown* and Pharoah Sander's album *Karma* (both 1969) exemplify his scat singing, which incorporates fast bop lines and yodeling, as well as his Eastern-oriented lyrics of peace, delivered in a rich baritone voice. He worked with Sanders's group until 1972 and then as a free-lance, then joined Joe Henderson's group, 1985.

Thomas, Michael Tilson [Tomashevsky] (b. Los Angeles, 21 Dec. 1944). Conductor. Attended the Univ. of Southern California and studied composition with Ingolf Dahl; also studied with harpsichordist Alice Ehlers and pianist John Crown. In 1963–67, conducted the Young Musicians Foundation Debut Orchestra; 1966, attended master classes at Bayreuth; 1967, assisted Boulez at the Ojai Festival. Named assistant conductor of Boston Symphony in 1969, associate conductor in 1970, and was principal guest conductor in 1972–74. Music director of the Buffalo Philharmonic (1971–79), principal guest conductor of the Los Angeles Philharmonic (1981–85), conductor of the London Symphony (1988–95), and music director of the San Francisco Symphony (from 1995).

Thomas, Theodore (Christian Friedrich) (b. Esens, East Friesland, 11 Oct. 1835; d. Chicago, 4 Jan. 1905). Conductor. Family moved to the U.S. in 1845. Solo debut in New York at age 15. Played violin in Jullien's Orchestra, 1853. Played in the New York Philharmonic Orchestra from 1854; elected conductor, 1877–91. With pianist William Mason, founded a monthly matinee chamber series, which lasted from 1854 to 1871; premiered Brahms's Piano Trio in B minor op. 8. Led New York Academy of Music Orchestra, 1856. Formed his own orchestra in 1862; made a major tour in 1869. Director of Philadelphia Centennial Exhibition, 1876. First conductor of the Chicago Symphony Orchestra, 1891–1905. Director of Cincinnati College of Music, 1878–79. Popularized German music from Bach to Strauss, music of Berlioz, Smetana, Dvořák, Franck, Saint-Saëns, and Grieg, and the music of many American composers. *A Musical Autobiography* was published in Chicago (1904; R: 1964).

Bibl.: Theodore Caskey Russell, "Theodore Thomas: His Role in the Development of Musical Culture in the U.S., 1835–1905" (diss., Univ. of Minnesota, 1969). Ezra Schabas, *Theodore Thomas: America's Conductor and Builder of Orchestras, 1835–1905* (Urbana, Ill., 1989).

Thompson, Randall (b. New York, 21 Apr. 1899; d. Boston, 9 July 1984). Composer and educator. As a young man he studied piano, organ, and voice. He attended Harvard Univ., where he studied with Archibald Davison (B.A., 1920; M.A., 1922). He also studied with Ernst Bloch in New York (1920–21). Receiving the Prix de Rome in 1922, he spent three years in Rome, where he composed the *5 Odes of Horace,* male chorus (1924), and several other works including his first symphony. Returning to the U.S. in 1925, he had a critical success with his Second Symphony (1931), which was praised for its skillful assimilation of American popular music elements. His favorite medium, however, was choral music. *Americana,* chorus and piano (or orchestra) (1932), *The Peaceable Kingdom,* chorus a cappella (1936), *Alleluia,* chorus a cappella (1940), and *The Testament of Freedom,* male chorus and piano (or orchestra) (1943), became mainstays of the American choral repertory. He also wrote some instrumental chamber music, including a Suite for oboe, violin, and viola (1940) and his First String Quartet (1941). Thompson taught and conducted choruses at several schools and colleges: Wellesley College (1927–29, 1936–37), Univ. of California, Berkeley (1937–39), Curtis Institute (1939–41), Univ. of Virginia (1941–46), and Princeton Univ. (1946–48). In 1948 he joined the faculty at Harvard Univ., where he stayed for the remainder of his career. After World War II

Thompson continued to concentrate on choral pieces, many of them on sacred subjects, such as *Requiem,* double chorus (1958), *The Nativity According to St. Luke,* a sacred opera (1961), *The Passion According to St. Luke,* oratorio (1965), and *The Place of the Blest,* women's voices and orchestra (1969). Of his secular choral music *A Concord Cantata,* voices and orchestra (1975), is perhaps the best known. Symphony no. 3 (1949) and *A Trip to Nahant,* symphonic fantasy (1954), are his only postwar works for orchestra.

Bibl.: Elliot Forbes et al., "The Choral Music of Randall Thompson," *American Choral Review* 16/4 (1974). Randall Thompson, "On Choral Composition—Essays and Reflections," *American Choral Review* 22/2 (1980). Caroline Cepin Benser and David Francis Urrows, *Randall Thompson: A Bio-Bibliography* (New York, 1991).

Thomson, Virgil (b. Kansas City, Mo., 25 Nov. 1896; d. New York, 30 Sept. 1989). Composer and critic. He studied piano and organ as a teenager, earning money by accompanying singers and playing in church. Envisioning a career as a church organist and choir director, he went to Harvard Univ., where he studied with Edward Burlingame Hill and Archibald Davison. He was active in the Harvard Glee Club, for which he wrote several youthful compositions. Awarded a traveling fellowship, he went in 1921 to Paris, where he studied organ and composition with Nadia Boulanger and became acquainted with Satie, Cocteau, and "Les six." He composed a bit, mainly for piano and organ, and wrote music reviews for a Boston newspaper, a job that gained him entrance to concerts. Returning reluctantly to the U.S., he finished his degree at Harvard in 1923, spent a year in New York studying conducting with Chalmers Clifton and counterpoint with Rosario Scalero and writing for *The American Mercury* and *Vanity Fair.*

In 1925 he returned to Paris, where he resided (with periodic trips to the U.S.) until 1940. Again he studied with Boulanger, writing for her the *Sonata da chiesa,* clarinet, trumpet, horn trombone, and viola (1926; rev. 1973), a work in a neoclassical style considerably influenced by Stravinsky. Through George Antheil, Thomson met Gertrude Stein, whose poetry he had long admired and now began to set to music: *Susie Asado* (voice and piano, 1926), *Preciosilla* (voice and piano, 1927), *Capital Capitals* (men's voices and piano, 1927; rev. 1968). Together they set to work on an opera, *Four Saints in Three Acts,* which Thomson finished in piano score in 1928. The music—unprepossessing and doggedly diatonic—makes frequent allusion to Protestant hymn tunes, popular songs, and social dances. Its performance, in 1934 by an all-black cast, first in Hartford, Conn., then in New York and Chicago, secured Thomson's American reputation. He also wrote instrumental music, which was performed with increasing frequency in both France and the U.S.: Violin Sonata (1930), Serenade for Flute and Violin (1931), and two string quartets (1931, 1932). He began a series of "portraits"—instrumental depictions of his friends and acquaintances, e.g., "Alternations . . . Maurice Grosser" (piano, 1929), "Miss Gertrude Stein as a Young Girl" (violin, 1928), "Alice Toklas" (violin and piano, 1930)—which he continued to compose throughout his life.

Visiting the U.S. for the premiere of *Four Saints,* Thomson was engaged by filmmaker Pare Lorentz to write music for two government-sponsored documentaries: *The Plow That Broke the Plains* (1936) and *The River* (1937). The scores make use of American hymns, ballads, and popular songs, treated in Thomson's characteristically dispassionate manner. *Filling Station,* ballet (1937), commissioned by Lincoln Kirstein, was another evocation of Americana, this time considerably tongue-in-cheek.

Returning to the U.S. in June 1940, Thomson took a job as music critic at the *New York Herald Tribune,* where he remained until 1954. Plainspoken yet elegant, concentrating on the music rather than the performance, raising general issues of musical culture, Thomson's criticism made a strong impression at the time and has been much admired since. New works from this period include *The Mayor La Guardia Waltzes* (orchestra, 1942), *Three Portraits* (orchestra, 1947, 1948, 1952), Cello Concerto (1950), *Five Songs from William Blake* (baritone and orchestra, 1951), Concerto for Flute, Strings, Harp, and Percussion (1954). He continued to write for the movies: *Tuesday in November* (1945), *Louisiana Story* (1948; Pulitzer Prize, 1949). He composed a second opera, *The Mother of Us All* (1946; New York, 1947), once again on a Gertrude Stein text, this one based on the life of Susan B. Anthony.

Resigning from the *Herald Tribune* in 1954, Thomson toured Europe and South America as a conductor and lecturer, then visited a succession of universities on one-year appointments. Larger works from this period include the *Missa pro defunctis* (1960), *Lord Byron* (opera, 1968; New York, 1972), *Cantata on Poems of Edward Lear* (soloists, chamber orchestra, 1973). He also composed incidental music for the stage and continued to add to his by now vast collection of portraits.

Writings: *The State of Music* (New York, 1939). *The Musical Scene* (New York, 1945). *The Art of Judging Music* (New York, 1948). *Music Right and Left* (New York, 1951). *Virgil Thomson* (New York, 1966 [autobiography]). *American Music since 1910* (New York, 1971). *A Virgil Thomson Reader* (New York, 1981). *Music with Words: A Composer's View* (New Haven, 1989).

Bibl.: Kathleen Hoover and John Cage, *Virgil Thomson: His Life and Music* (New York, 1959). Anthony Tommasini, *Virgil Thomson's Musical Portraits* (New York, 1986). Michael Meckna, *Virgil Thomson: A Bio-Bibliography* (New York, 1986).

Thorne, Francis (b. Bay Shore, N.Y., 23 June 1922). Composer and administrator. The child of a wealthy family, he studied music at Yale (B.A., 1942), but was more enthusiastic about playing jazz piano than about his classes with Hindemith. After a stint in the navy, he went to work as a banker in New York (1946–54). In 1955 he quit his job to concentrate on music. He worked as a jazz pianist in New York, then moved in 1958 to Florence, where he studied composition with David Diamond. His first work to achieve recognition was *Elegy for Orchestra* (1963), introduced by the Philadelphia Orchestra in 1964. Returning to the U.S. in 1964, he used family money to set up the Thorne Music Fund (1964–74), which commissioned new works and offered fellowships to composers. He also served as president of the American Composers' Orchestra (beginning 1976) and as executive director of the American Composers' Alliance (beginning 1975). His own music combines jazz rhythms and sonorities with the resources of post-Wagnerian chromaticism.

Works include 5 symphonies (1960, 1964, 1969, 1977, 1984); *Rhapsodic Variations* (piano and orchestra, 1965); *Liebesrock* (3 electric guitars and orchestra, 1969); *Fanfare, Fugue, and Funk* (3 trumpets and orchestra, 1972); 4 string quartets (1960, 1967, 1979, 1983); *Songs and Dances* (cello, keyboard, percussion, 1969); *Pop Partita* (piano, 1978); *Nature Studies* (mezzo-soprano, flute, harp, 1981); Concerto for Orchestra (1981); *Mario and the Magician* (opera, 1994).

Thornhill, Claude (b. Terre Haute, Ind., 10 Aug. 1909; d. Caldwell, N.J., 1 July 1965). Jazz bandleader and pianist. He attended the Cincinnati Conservatory and the Curtis Institute. For Maxine Sullivan he arranged "Loch Lomond" and led recording and touring bands (1937–38). His big band (1940–42, 1946–48) was noted for using orchestral winds. He composed "Snowfall," the band's theme (recorded 1941), but the principal arranger was Gil Evans, who anticipated the cool jazz style in his version of the bop tune "Anthropology," recorded by Thornhill in 1947 with Lee Konitz and Red Rodney. Gerry Mulligan also arranged for the group. Thornhill continued leading bands into the early 1960s.

Thuille, Ludwig (Wilhelm Andreas Maria) (b. Bozen, the Tirol, 30 Nov. 1861; d. Munich, 5 Feb. 1907). Composer. Studied with his father. Moved to Kremsmünster in 1872 after his parents died; studied violin, piano, and organ. Studied at Innsbruck, and with Rheinberger in Munich, 1879–81. Taught at Königliche Musikschule from 1883. Friend of Richard Strauss and Alexander Ritter. Wrote *Harmonielehre* with Rudolf Louis (1907). Compositions include 3 operas, Symphony in F major (1886), Overture op. 16 (1896), Wind Sextet in B♭ op. 6 (1886–88), Piano Quintet in E♭ op. 20 (1897–1901), other chamber pieces, choral pieces, songs.

Bibl.: B. Edelmann et al., *Ludwig Thuille* (Tutzing, 1993).

Tibbett [Tibbet], **Lawrence** (b. Bakersfield, Calif., 16 Nov. 1896; d. New York, 15 July 1960). Baritone. During the early part of his career he performed both as an actor and as a singer. Studied with Basil Ruysdael and Frank La Forge and in 1923 made his Metropolitan Opera debut as Lovitsky in *Boris Godunov.* Achieved great success there in 1925 when he sang Ford in *Falstaff.* He remained at the Metropolitan until 1950 and premiered many baritone roles, including those in Taylor's *The King's Henchman,* Hanson's *Merry Mount,* and J. L. Seymour's *In the Pasha's Garden,* as well as singing in the first Metropolitan performances of *Simon Boccanegra* (in the title role), *Peter Grimes,* and *Khovanshchina.* He also sang the title role in the world premiere of Goossen's *Don Juan de Mañara* at Covent Garden in 1937. He made several films, including *The Rogue Song* and *The New Moon.*

Bibl.: Andrew Farkas, ed., *Lawrence Tibbett, Singing Actor* (Portland, Ore., 1989) [with preface and discography by William R. Moran].

Tichatschek, Joseph (Aloys) [Ticháček, Josef] (b. Ober-Weckelsdorf, 11 July 1807; d. Blasewitz, near Dresden, 18 Jan. 1886). Tenor. Studied with his father; sang in local choir as a youth. Moved to Vienna in 1827 to study medicine; took singing lessons with G. Cicimera. Joined the Kärntnerthor Theater Chorus, 1830. Principal tenor at Graz and Vienna. Debut at Dresden, 1837; sang there to 1872. Created the roles of Rienzi (1842) and Tannhäuser (1845).

Tiessen, Heinz (b. Königsberg, 10 Apr. 1887; d. Berlin, 29 Nov. 1971). Composer and educator. He studied at the Stern Conservatory in Berlin and privately with Wilhelm Klatte. He also wrote music criticism for the *Allgemeine musikalische Zeitung* (1911–17). His compositions from this period are in a traditional Romantic style. After World War I he served as assistant to Richard Strauss at the Berlin Opera, then as composer and conductor at the Berliner Volksbühne and director of the chorus at the Univ. of Berlin. During this period he composed politically conscious music in a simple style, for example, *Aufmarsch,* chorus and winds (1930). He came under attack during the Nazi period (1933–45), but remained in Germany. Afer World War II he served as director of the Berlin Conservatory (1946–49), as professor at the Berlin Hochschule (1949–55), and as director of the West Berlin Academy of Arts.

Bibl.: Hans Tiessen, *Wege eines Komponisten* (Berlin, 1962). Manfred Schlösser, ed., *Für Heinz Tiessen, 1887–1971: Aufsätze, Analysen, Briefe, Erinnerungen, Dokumente, Werkverzeichnis, Bibliographie* (Berlin, 1979).

Tietjens, Therese (Carolina Johanna Alexander) (b. Hamburg, 17 July 1831; d. London, 3 Oct. 1877). Soprano. Studied in Hamburg and Vienna. Opera debut at Altona (1849) as Lucrezia Borgia. Sang at Frankfurt Opera, 1850–56; Vienna, 1856–59. London debut (Covent Garden), 1858. Settled in England. Sang in New York, 1874, 1876; Paris, 1869. First London Marguérite (Gounod's *Faust,* 1863); sang first London performances of *Ballo in maschera* (1861), *La forza del destino* (1867), Gounod's *Mireille* (1864), and Cherubini's *Médée* (1865).

Tinctoris, Johannes (b. Braine l'Alleud, near Nivelles, ca. 1435; d. ca. 1511). Composer and theorist. Served under Dufay at Cambrai as a *petit vicaire* in 1460; received a degree from the Univ. of Orléans in 1462, where he may have matriculated as early as 1457. He was elected procurator of the German nation there in 1463. He later wrote that he had also taught choirboys at Chartres, probably sometime between 1463 and 1472. He joined the court of Ferdinand I of Naples around 1472 as instructor of the king's daughter Beatrice, for whom he probably oversaw the compilation of the Mellon Chansonnier. A journey to Ferrara was recorded in 1479; he was instructed by the king to recruit singers in 1487, but no records of related trips have been located. He praised Pope Alexander VI in a poem of 1492, indicating a sojourn at Rome. No notice of his death has been found, though a prebend of his changed hands in 1511. Among Tinctoris's compositions are 5 Masses (including one based on *L'homme armé*) and several motets and chansons, but he is best known for his voluminous theoretical writings, which encompass a dictionary of musical terms (*Terminorum musicae diffinitorium,* Treviso, 1495); treatises on mensural notation (several, including *Proportionale musices,* ca. 1473–74; trans. Eng., London, 1964), the modes (*Liber de natura et proprietate tonorum,* 1476; trans. Eng., Colorado Springs, 1967, rev. 1976), and counterpoint (*Liber de arte contrapuncti,* 1477; trans. Eng., *MSD* 5 [1961]); and descriptions of practical music making. His writings are filled with references to ancient theorists as well as to contemporary composers and works; in his *Proportionale musices* he credits Dunstable and the English with devising a new art of composition, while at the outset of his counterpoint volume of 1477 he asserts that no music more than 40 years old is worth hearing.

Bibl.: *Opera omnia,* ed. W. Melin, CMM 18 (1976). *Opera theoretica,* ed. Albert Seay, *CSM* 22 (1975). Leeman Perkins and Howard Garey, eds., *The Mellon Chansonnier* (New Haven, 1979). Ronald Woodley, "Iohannes Tinctoris: A Review of the Documentary Biographical Evidence," *JAMS* 34 (1981): 217–48. Sydney R. Charles, "Communication," *JAMS* 35 (1982): 371–73. Allan Atlas, *Music at the Court of Naples* (Cambridge, 1985). Bonnie Blackburn, "On Compositional Process in the 15th Century," *JAMS* 40 (1987): 210–84.

Tinel, Edgar (Pierre Joseph) (b. Sinaai, East Flanders, 27 Mar. 1854; d. Brussels, 28 Oct. 1912). Pianist and composer. Studied at Brussels Conservatory with Brassin and Gevaert. His cantata *Klokke Roeland* won the 1877 Belgian Prix de Rome. Director of Institute for Church Music at Malines, 1881. Named inspector of music education, 1889. Professor of counterpoint and fugue at Brussels Conservatory from 1896. Wrote much sacred music including *Missa in honorem BMV de Lourdes* op. 41 (1905), cantatas, 1 piano sonata, 1 organ sonata, some orchestral works, Psalms, songs.

Tio, Lorenzo, Jr. (b. New Orleans, 21 Apr. 1893; d. New York, 24 Dec. 1933). Jazz and ragtime clarinetist. He played in orchestras and parade and brass bands. After working with Papa Celestin (ca. 1917) he joined violinist A. J. Piron's New Orleans orchestra (1918–28, early 1930s), recording solo breaks on "Bouncing Around" and "New Orleans Wiggle" and a slithering duet with Piron on "Mamma's Gone, Good-Bye" (all 1923). Like his uncle Papa (Luis) Tio (1863–1927) and father, Lorenzo Sr. (1866–ca. 1920), Lorenzo Jr. taught clarinetists, including Barney Bigard, Johnny Dodds, Albert Nicholas, and Jimmie Noone.

Tiomkin, Dmitri (b. Poltava, 10 May 1894; d. London, 11 Nov. 1979). Composer. At the St. Petersburg Conservatory he studied piano with Felix Blumenthal, composition with Alexander Glazunov. After the Russian Revolution he went to Berlin, where he studied with Ferruccio Busoni and Egon Petri. He toured the U.S. as a pianist in 1925 and again in 1928. In 1929 he went to Hollywood, where he composed scores for movie musicals and background music for a series of films while continuing to tour as a concert pianist. The great success of his score to Frank Capra's *Lost Horizon* (1937) and an injury to his right arm committed him to a career as a movie composer. Among his best-known scores are *It's a Wonderful Life* (1947), *High Noon* (1952), *The High and the Mighty* (1954), *The Alamo* (1960). In 1968 he moved to London.

Bibl.: Dmitri Tiomkin and Prosper Buranelli, *Please Don't Hate Me* (Garden City, N.Y., 1959). Christopher Palmer, *Dmitri Tiomkin: A Portrait* (London, 1984).

Tippett, Michael (Kemp) (b. London, 2 Jan. 1905). Composer. Attended the Royal College of Music from 1923 to 1928; studied composition with Wood and Kitson, piano with Raymar, and conducting with Sargent and Boult. He extended his conducting experience during this time by undertaking small choral and operatic productions. From 1930 to 1932 he studied composition with R. O. Morris at the Royal College of Music. By the mid-1930s Tippett was working primarily as a conductor with groups such as the South London Orchestra at Morley College, composed of unemployed performers. In 1940 the group was dissolved, and Tippett replaced Arnold Foster as head of the music department at Morley College; there he fostered a new range of musical activities, including concerts of Renaissance and contemporary music, until his resignation in 1951. He then took a position as a broadcaster with the BBC, and continued to work as a conductor and to compose.

He composed in nearly every genre. His compositional development is frequently referred to as neoclassical because of his use of traditional structures and textures; yet his style is distinct from other early 20th-century neoclassical trends. Late Romantic eastern European symphonic music, as well as native English folk music, affected him. Tippett's early works evinced his interest in classical, symmetrical forms; he used tonally based material without necessarily using functional tonality. By the mid-1940s his musical language began utilizing quartal rather than tertian harmony; melodic lines often projected a modal quality and were highly lyrical. Rhythm became increasingly irregular; counterpoint became more developed, and fugue occurred frequently. Also typical of Tippett was his incorporation of other musics, such as African American spirituals or blues and English folk song, into his own works. For example, the oratorio *A Child of Our Time* (1939–41) uses spirituals in an integrated expression of helplessness in the face of oppression. The opera *The Midsummer Marriage* (1946–52) incorporates dance as an integral part of the expression of drama. Other late works experimented with characteristics typical of avant-garde music, such as tone clusters, extended techniques, and nondevelopmental forms.

Works include music for the stage (*The Midsummer Marriage,* opera, 1946–52; *King Priam,* opera, 1958–61; *The Knot Garden,* opera, 1966–69; *The Ice Break,* 1973–76; *New Year,* opera, 1985–88); vocal music (*The Vision of St. Augustine,* baritone, chorus, orchestra, 1963–65; *Songs for Dov,* tenor, orchestra, 1969–70; *The Mask of Time,* chorus, orchestra, 1981–84); orchestral music (4 symphonies, 1944–45, 1956–57, 1970–72, 1976–77; Concerto, violin, viola, and cello, 1979; *Festal Brass with Blues,* brass band, 1984; *Byzantium,* soloist, orchestra, 1991); and chamber music (*Music for Words Perhaps,* speaker, bass clarinet, trumpet, percussion, piano, violin, cello, 1960; String Quartet no. 5, 1992).

Bibl.: Meirion Bown, *Michael Tippett* (London, 1981). Eric Walter White, *Tippett and His Operas* (New York, 1982). Ian Kemp, *Tippett: The Composer and His Music* (New York, 1984). Nicholas John, *Operas of Michael Tippett* (London, 1985). Gordon Theil, *Michael Tippett: A Bio-Bibliography* (New York, 1989). David Clarke, *Language, Form, and Structure in the Music of Michael Tippett* (New York, 1989). Michael Tippett, *Those Twentieth-Century Blues: An Autobiography* (London, 1991).

Tishchenko, Boris Ivanovich (b. Leningrad, 23 Mar. 1939). Composer. At the Leningrad Conservatory, 1957–63, studied composition with Salmanov, Voloshinov, and Evlakhov, and piano with Logovinsky. Pursued graduate studies in composition with Shostakovich, 1962–65. Beginning 1965, taught composition at the Leningrad Conservatory. Works include ballets (*Yaroslavna,* 1974); 6 symphonies (*The Siege Chronicle,* 1984); concertos (violin, 1958, 1981; piano, 1963; cello, 17 winds, and percussion, 1963; cello, 1969; flute, piano, and string orchestra, 1972; harp, 1977); vocal-symphonic works; 5 string quartets and other chamber music, including *Concerto allamarcia,* 16 performers (1989); 8 sonatas and other piano music; songs and choral works; film and incidental music.

Bibl.: B. Kats, *O muzyke Borisa Tishchenko* (Leningrad, 1986).

Titelouze, Jehan (b. St. Omer, ca. 1562–63; d. Rouen, 24 Oct. 1633). Composer. By 1585 he had entered the priesthood and had performed as substitute organist at St. Omer Cathedral. In that year he became organist at St. Jean, and in 1588 he became organist of the cathedral, at which post he remained for the rest of his life. In 1610 he was made a canon at the cathedral. From 1588 to 1623 he was involved in the installation and renovation of important organs. Besides organ works, he wrote several sacred vocal compositions (lost).

Bibl.: *Jean Titelouze: Oeuvres complètes d'orgue,* ed. Norbert Dufourcq (Paris, 1965–67).

Titov, Alexey [Alexei] **Nikolayevich** (b. St. Petersburg, 23 July 1769; d. there, 20 Nov. 1827). Composer and violinist. He was in the cavalry and became a major general before he retired. He wrote primarily stage music, including operas, ballets, and incidental music, all performed in St. Petersburg; much of it portrays Russian subject matter and utilizes folk tunes. Operas produced in St. Petersburg include *Andromeda and Perseus* (1802); *King Solomon's Judgment* (1803); *Judge Cupid, or The Argument of the Three Graces* (1805); *Yam, or The Post Station* (1805), *The Winter Party, or The Sequel to Yam* (1808); *The Wedding Eve Party, or Filakin's Wedding* (1809); *Polixena* (1809); *The Cossack Woman* (1810); *Maslenitsa* (1813).

Titov, Nicolai Alexeyevich (b. St. Petersburg, 10 May 1800; d. there, 22 Dec. 1875). Composer. Son of violinist and composer Alexei Titov (1769–1827). Held a military position, 1817–67; had no formal training in music. He began composing in 1819. Later advised by Glinka and Dargomyzhsky. He was nicknamed "the father of Russian song." Wrote some 60 songs; also marches and piano music. His uncle Sergei Titov (1770–1825) composed works for the stage. His cousin Nicolai Sergeyevich Titov (1798–1843) also composed songs, some of which have been attributed to him.

Tjader, Cal (Callen Radcliffe, Jr.) (b. St. Louis, 16 July 1925; d. Manila, 5 May 1982). Jazz vibraphonist and bandleader. He mainly played drums in Dave Brubeck's trio (1949–51), doubled on vibraphone in George Shearing's quintet (1953–54), then concentrated on vibraphone in Latin jazz groups which he led from 1954 until his death. His recordings include *West Side Story* (1958), the hit tune "Soul Sauce" (1964), and the Grammy Award–winning salsa album *La onde va bien* (1979).

Toch, Ernst (b. Vienna, 7 Dec. 1887; d. Los Angeles, 1 Oct. 1964). Composer. He taught himself music as a child and a teenager, composing string quartets modeled on those of Mozart. In 1909 while he was a medical student one of his compositions won the Mozart Prize, which provided him with a fellowship at the Frankfurt Conservatory. There he studied piano with Willy Rehberg and composition with Ivan Knorr (1910–13). In 1913, with an already impressive body of compositions to his credit, he was appointed professor of composition at the Musikhochschule in Mannheim. So far his music had been Brahmsian in style, but with the String Quartet no. 9 in 1919 he adopted a dissonant, modernist idiom, which he maintained and intensified in works such as *Burlesques* (piano, 1924) and Piano Concerto no. 1 (1926). In 1929 he moved to Berlin, but as a Jew and a leader of Germany's musical modernists he was forced to emigrate in 1933. In 1934 he arrived in New York to teach at the New School for Social Research; some of his new compositions were performed by American orchestras, for example, *Big Ben* (1934; Boston Symphony, 1934), *Pinocchio: A Merry Overture* (1935; Los Angeles Philharmonic, 1936). In 1936 he moved to Los Angeles, where he wrote scores for movies, including *Peter Ibbetson* (1935) and *Address Unknown* (1944). He also composed chamber music in his characteristically advanced style, including a String Trio (1936) and a Piano Quintet (1938). Disappointed by the indifferent response of American audiences, however, he composed less and less. After the war his productivity resumed. *Hyperion* (orchestra, 1947) was introduced by the Cleveland Orchestra in 1948. Symphonies no. 1 (1949) and no. 2 (1951) were both premiered by the Vienna Philharmonic; Symphony no. 3 (1955) won the 1956 Pulitzer Prize. Works from his later years include Symphonies nos. 4–7 (1957, 1963, 1963, 1964); 2 Sinfoniettas (1964, 1964); String Quartet no. 13 (1954); *Valse* (speaking chorus and percussion, 1961). From 1940 to 1948 he taught composition at UCLA.

Writings: *The Shaping Forces in Music* (New York, 1948). *Placed as Link in the Chain* (Los Angeles, 1971).

Bibl.: Lawrence Wechsler, *Ernst Toch, 1887–1964* (Los Angeles, 1974). Diane Jezic, *The Musical Migration and Ernst Toch* (Ames, Iowa, 1989).

Toda, Kunio (b. Tokyo, 11 Aug. 1915). Composer. As a young man he studied both music and law; graduating from Tokyo Univ. in 1938, he joined the diplomatic corps and was sent to Germany, where he continued his musical studies. Returning to Tokyo in 1941, he studied composition with Saburō Moroi. After the war he became acquainted with the theories of Schoenberg, and he was influential in introducing serialism to Japan. His Violin Sonata (1957; rev. 1959) is a wholly serial work, but several other works of the period mix twelve-tone with tonal elements. He continued his diplomatic career but also taught music at the Tōhō Gakuen College, the Gauken School of Music (1964–76), and Senzoku Gauken College (1977–88). Works include *Akemi,* opera (Tokyo, 1956); *History of the City of Kyara,* opera (Tokyo, 1973); *Salome in Studio,* ballet (1951); Concerto grosso, orchestra (1967); *Fantasy on the Sound of the Koto,* piano (1965); *Song of the River,* mezzo-soprano, baritone, orchestra (1989).

Todi [née d'Aguiar], **Luisa** (Rosa) (b. Setubal, 9 Jan. 1753; d. Lisbon, 1 Oct. 1833). Mezzo-soprano. She made her debut at age 14 as a comic actress. In 1769 she married violinist Francesco Todi, and in 1770 made her first operatic debut in Lisbon in Giuseppe Scolari's *Il viaggiatore ridicolo.* She appeared in London, 1777–78, at the King's Theatre, in Paris, 1778, and in Berlin. On a return engagement to Paris in 1783 she became involved in a famous rivalry with the soprano Elisabeth Maria. She went to St. Petersburg in 1784 and had subsequent engagements in Berlin, Paris, and Venice.

Toeschi, Carl Joseph (bapt. Ludwigsburg, 11 Nov. 1731; d. Munich, 12 Apr. 1788). Composer and violinist. Son of Alessandro Toeschi, a composer and violinist in the Mannheim orchestra. He studied with Johann Stamitz and Anton Fils, joined the Mannheim orchestra as a violinist in 1752 and was made *Konzertmeister* in 1759. He moved to Munich in 1778 with Carl Theodor's entourage. A representative of the second generation of the "Mannheim school," he wrote more than 60 symphonies, many ballets, about 20 flute concertos, over 30 flute quartets, and other chamber works.

Bibl.: Robert Münster, "Die Sinfonien Toeschis" (diss., Univ. of Munich, 1956).

Togni, Camillo (b. Gussago, Italy, 18 Oct. 1922; d. Brescia, 27 Nov. 1993). Composer. He studied piano and composition with Franco Margola (1935–40), composition with Alfredo Casella (1939–42), and piano with Arturo Benedetti Michelangeli (1943–50). His early compositions were neoclassical, but beginning with *7 Serenate,* piano (1940–44), he embraced serial techniques. He continued this direction in *Helian di Trakl,* soprano and piano (1954), and *3 Capricci,* piano (1954–57). Besides *Helian,* he composed several more works on texts by Georg Trakl, including *Gesang zur Nacht,* mezzo-soprano and chamber orchestra (1962), and a short opera, *Blau Bart* (Venice, 1978). In works such as *Rondeaux per 10,* soprano and chamber ensemble (1964), *Aubade,* chamber ensemble (1965), and *Su frammenti di Peire Vidal,* soprano and orchestra (1982), he turned to medieval poets and themes while retaining a serial idiom. Other works include the opera *Barrabas* (1981–85).

Tomášek, Václav Jan Křtitel (b. Skuteč, 17 Apr. 1774; d. Prague, 3 Apr. 1850). Composer. In part self-taught; also studied violin and singing, 1783–85, with the choirmaster from a neighboring town and organ and theory at Jihlava while he was a student there. In 1790 he left for Prague to study law and philosophy at the Gymnasium; he also established himself as a piano teacher at this time. He was music teacher to the family of Count Georg Buquoy from 1806. In 1824 he started his own music school (J. H. Voříšek and E. Hanslick were among his pupils). He met Haydn and Beethoven during his various trips to Vienna; he also knew Hummel, Dussek, and Clementi. His compositions include 2 operas (*Seraphine,* Prague, 1811, and *Alvaro*); several *scenas,* 2 Masses, a coronation Mass, a Requiem, a Te Deum, symphonies, orchestral pieces, 3 string quartets, other chamber works, numerous solo songs. He also wrote a good deal of solo keyboard music including 5 variation sets, 7 sonatas, 42 eclogues, 15 rhapsodies. He wrote an autobiography that was published in the Prague periodical *Libussa* in installments between 1845 and 1850; a modern edition was published in 1941 and excerpts appeared in *MQ* 32 (1946): 244–64.

Bibl.: Marie Tarantová, *Václav Jan Tomášek* (Prague, 1946).

Tomasi, Henri (b. Marseilles, 17 Aug. 1901; d. Paris, 13 Jan. 1971). Composer and conductor. He studied at the conservatory in Marseilles, then at the Paris Conservatory. His early symphonic poem *Tam-tam* (soprano, male chorus, and orchestra, 1932) already displayed the traits that would characterize his music throughout his career: non-European subjects (here African), rhythmic intensity, colorful orchestration, and sympathy with colonial and third world peoples. From 1930 to 1935 he was music director at a radio station in French Indochina. After World War II he established himself as a conductor and as an opera composer with *Atlantide* (Mulhouse, 1954) and *Miguel de Mañara* (Munich, 1956). He also wrote several concertos, including 2 for trumpet (1948, 1966), 1 for trombone (1956), 1 for guitar (1967), and 1 for 2 guitars (1966). Several of his works from the 1960s testify to his political commitment, for example, *Symphonie du Tiers-Monde* (1967) and *Chant pour Vietnam* (symphonic poem, 1968).

Tomasini, Alois Luigi (b. Pesaro, 22 June 1741; d. Eisenstadt, 25 Apr. 1808). Composer and violinist. He became a friend of Haydn (with whom he perhaps studied) while engaged as a violinist in Prince Paul Anton Esterházy's orchestra (1756–90); in 1802 he was named director of chamber music to the Esterházy family. Haydn dedicated violin concertos to him. Besides a few symphonies and violin concertos, he wrote about 30 string quartets, 24 baryton trios (for Prince Anton, a baryton player), *duos concertants* for violin, violin sonatas.

Bibl.: Erich Schenk, ed., *Luigi Tomasini: Ausgewählte Instrumentalwerke,* 124 (1972). Efrim Fruchtman, "The Baryton Trios of Tomasini, Burgksteiner, and Neumann" (diss., Univ. of North Carolina, 1960).

Tomkins, Thomas (b. St. Davids, Pembrokeshire, 1572; d. Martin Hussingtree, Worcester, buried 9 June 1656). Composer. In 1596 he was *instructor choristarum* at Worcester Cathedral. At this time he was active in London: he may have studied with Byrd, and Morley included a madrigal by him in *The Triumphs of Oriana* (London, 1601). By 29 June 1620 he was a Gentleman in Ordinary of the Chapel Royal choir, and in 1621 he became an organist there; with the death of Orlando Gibbons in 1628, he probably became senior organist. Tomkins seems to have retained his royal position into old age and was active at Worcester Cathedral until 1646. He wrote 5 services; over 100 anthems (95 are in *Musica Deo sacra et ecclesiae anglicanae,* London, 1668); madrigals, published in *Songs of 3, 4, 5, & 6 parts* (London, 1622) (including *When David Heard*); and about 70 instrumental works, which include pieces for keyboard and consort music.

Bibl.: Denis Stevens, *Thomas Tomkins* (London, 1957; 2nd ed., 1967). John Irving, *The Instrumental Music of Thomas Tomkins, 1572–1656* (New York, 1989).

Tommasini, Vincenzo (b. Rome, 17 Sept. 1878; d. Rome, 23 Dec. 1950). Composer. He studied violin, piano, and composition at the Liceo di S. Cecilia in Rome and classical philology at the Univ. of Rome. He continued his classical studies in Berlin, also attending the Hochschule für Musik, where he studied with Max Bruch. He became familiar with the music of Debussy, whose influence can be heard in his *Chiari di luna* (orchestra, 1915). *Il beato regno* (orchestra, 1920) is Pre-Raphaelite in flavor and based on Gregorian melodies. During the 1930s he was influenced by the neoclassical movement. He is best remembered for *The Good-Humored Ladies* (1916), a ballet suite arranged from the harpsichord music of Domenico Scarlatti.

Toradze, David Alexandrovich (b. Tbilisi, 14 Apr. 1922; d. there, 7 Nov. 1983). Composer. He studied at the Tbilisi Conservatory with Barkhudarian (composition) and Virsaladze (piano), and at the Moscow Conservatory with Glier; he started teaching at the Tbilisi Conservatory in 1952, becoming a professor there in 1973. Best known for his stage works, many on Georgian themes; these include operas (*Suramis tsikhe* [The Surami Fortress], 1942; *Mtebis dzakhili* [The Call of the Mountains], 1947; *Chrdiloetis patardzali* [Bride of the North], 1958) and ballets (*Gorda,* 1949; *Mshvidobisatvis* [For Peace], 1953; rev. as *Kedukhrelni* [The Unsubdued], 1970).

Torelli, Giuseppe (b. Verona, 22 Apr. 1658; d. Bologna, 8 Feb. 1709). Composer and violinist. He may have received his early musical training from Giuliano Massaroti in Verona. Between 1681 and 1684 Torelli moved to Bologna, where he became a member *(suonatore di violino)* of the Accademia filarmonica on 27 June 1684; probably in 1692 he was elevated to the rank of *compositore.* He studied composition with G. A. Perti and played viola in the regular *cappella musicale* at S. Petronio from 28 September 1686 to January 1696. He may have gone to Ansbach and Berlin before becoming *maestro di concerto* to the Margrave of Brandenburg at Ansbach in 1698. By December 1699 he was in Vienna, where he wrote an oratorio. In 1701 he joined the recently reestablished *cappella* at S. Petronio, where he remained until his death. Torelli's output as a composer consists primarily of chamber and orchestral works, the majority for strings. Torelli's publications include 2 sets of 12 trio sonatas each, *Sonate [da chiesa]* op. 1 (1686), and *Concerti da camera* op. 2 (1687); 12 *Sinfonie* (i.e., *sonate da chiesa*) *a 2–4,* op. 3 (1687); *Sinfonie à tre e Concerti à quattro* op. 5 (1692), containing 6 *sonate da chiesa* and 6 ripieno concertos, the latter the earliest published examples of the genre; *Concerti musicali* op. 6 (1698), containing 10 ripieno concertos and the first 2 published examples of the solo violin concerto (nos. 6 and 12); and *Concerti grossi con una pastorale* op. 8 (1709), 12 concertos for 1 and 2 violins. Torelli also wrote a large number of unpublished sinfonias, concertos, and sonatas for trumpet(s) and strings.

Bibl.: Franz Giegling, *Giuseppe Torelli: Ein Beitrag zur Entwicklungsgeschichte des italienischen Konzerts* (Kassel, 1949). Richard E. Norton, "The Chamber Music of Giuseppe Torelli" (diss., Northwestern Univ., 1967). Eugene J. Enrico, "Giuseppe Torelli's Music for Instrumental Ensemble with Trumpet" (diss., Univ. of Michigan, 1970). Eugene K. Wolf et al., eds., *Antecedents of the Symphony,* ser. A, vol. 1 of *The Symphony, 1720–1840,* ed. Barry S. Brook et al. (New York, 1983).

Tormé [Torme], **Mel** [Melvin Howard] (b. Chicago, Ill., 13 Sept. 1925). Popular singer and songwriter. As a child he sang on radio in Chicago; later he performed with Chico Marx's band and led the vocal group the Mel-Tones. He became successful after World War II with a repertory including both jazz and popular idioms, recordings including "Careless Hands" (1949) and "Bewitched" (1950). He also worked as an arranger and composed many songs, including "The Christmas Song (Chestnuts Roasting on an Open Fire)" (1940) and "County Fair" (1948).

Torri, Pietro (b. Peschiera, Lake Garda, ca. 1650; d. Munich, 6 July 1737). Composer. He was organist and *maestro di cappella* at the court of the Margrave of Bayreuth in 1684. He may have left Bayreuth in that year to travel to Italy. In 1689 he became organist at the court of Max Emanuel II, Elector of Bavaria, in Munich. He remained in the Elector's service until his death, traveling with the court to Brussels (1692–99) and later to Brussels and France (1704–15). Over the years he was given more prominent positions: *maître de chapelle* (1692), director of chamber music (1701), *Hofkapell-Director* (1715), and *Hofkapellmeister* (1732). He was also guest Kapellmeister at the Hannover court (1696) and *maître de chapelle* at Ste. Gudule, Brussels (1704). Torri wrote operas, oratorios, serenatas, Masses, cantatas, chamber duets, sinfonias, and sonatas.

Torroba, Federico Moreno. See Moreno Torroba, Federico.

Tortelier, Paul (b. Paris, 21 Mar. 1914; d. Villarceaux, France, 18 Dec. 1990). Cellist and composer. He studied with Gérard Hekking at the Paris Conservatory, receiving a first prize at the age of 16. Made his debut at the Concerts Lamoureux the following year, then played with the Orchestra of Monte Carlo (1935–37), the Boston Symphony (1937–39), and the Paris Conservatory Orchestra (1946–47). Subsequently embarked on a solo career, making his American solo debut at Carnegie Hall in 1955; in 1957 he was appointed a professor at the Paris Conservatory. He composed a number of works, including several cello concertos and a sonata. He is the author of *How I Play, How I Teach* (London, 1975) and *Paul Tortelier: A Self-Portrait in Conversation with David Blum* (London, 1984).

Tosar, Héctor (b. Montevideo, 18 July 1923). Composer. Studied in his home city, then in the U.S. with Copland and Honegger (1946), and also at the Paris Conservatory with Rivier and Milhaud. His works have been performed elsewhere in the Americas and in Europe; he has toured in Asia, and has also taught at the Montevideo and Puerto Rico conservatories. Works include 3 symphonies (1945, 1950, 1973); *Concertino* (1941) and *Sinfonia concertante* (1957), piano and orchestra; *Aves errantes,* baritone and 11 instruments (1964); *Recitativo y variaciones* (1967) and *A 13* (1970), orchestra; vocal and choral works; chamber music, including violin and clarinet sonatas (1947, 1957); piano pieces; and songs.

Bibl.: *Composers of the Americas* 6 (Washington, D.C., 1960), pp. 101–6 [includes works list].

Toscanini, Arturo (b. Parma, 25 March 1867; d. New York, 16 Jan. 1957). Conductor. He displayed musical talent early and at age 9 was sent to the Parma Conservatory, where he studied cello, piano, and composition and graduated in 1885 with first prize for cello. Before he embarked on his conducting career he was engaged as a professional cellist. His first conducting job, in 1886, was a performance of *Aida* in Rio de Janeiro as replacement conductor while he was on tour. He spent the early years of his conducting career employed at Italian theaters; he was the music director at the Turin Teatro regio during 1895–98. He conducted the premieres of *Pagliacci* in Milan (1892) and *La bohème* in Turin (1896). From 1898 to 1903 Toscani was artistic director at La Scala in Milan; he quit after a disagreement, then returned in 1906–8 and 1920–29, and again in 1946 to conduct the first concert at the restored La Scala. He was in New York from 1908 to 1915 as artistic director of the Metropolitan Opera, during which he gave the world premiere of *La fanciulla del West* and American premieres of *Boris Godunov* and *Armide.* He resigned in 1915, again after a disagreement, and returned to Italy. He was the first non-German to conduct at Bayreuth (1930–31) but subsequently refused to conduct there, as well as at Salzburg, in reaction to Hitler's condemnation of Jewish artists. In 1928 he became conductor of an orchestra that combined forces from the New York Symphony and the New York Philharmonic; this group had a successful European tour in 1930, but Toscanini resigned in 1936. From 1937 to 1954 he directed the NBC orchestra, a group that had been formed especially for him and with which he made most of his recordings. He retired in 1954.

Toscanini's interpretations of Wagner, Verdi, and Beethoven are thought to be among his finest, though he is also highly regarded for his performances of other

Arturo Toscanini.

classical and Romantic composers, of modern Italian composers, and of Debussy, Richard Strauss, and Samuel Barber, whose Adagio for Strings he premiered. Considered one of the greatest conductors of modern times.

Bibl.: Robert Charles Marsh, *Toscanini and the Art of Orchestral Performance* (Philadelphia, 1956). David Ewen, *The Story of Arturo Toscanini* (New York, 1959). Bernard Haggin, *Conversations with Toscanini* (New York, 1959). Id., *The Toscanini Musicians Knew* (New York, 1967). Harvey Sachs, *Toscanini* (Philadelphia, 1978). Joseph Horowitz, *Understanding Toscanini* (New York, 1987). Harvey Sachs, *Reflections on Toscanini* (New York, 1991).

Toselli, Enrico (b. Florence, 13 Mar. 1883; d. there, 15 Jan. 1926). Pianist and composer. Studied piano with Sgambati and composition with Martucci and Grazzini. Toured Italy and the rest of Europe as a concert pianist. He later settled in Florence. Compositions include the operas *La cattiva Francesca* (1912) and *La Principessa bizzarra* (1913), the symphonic poem *Il fuoco,* and several songs.

Toshiko. See Akiyoshi, Toshiko.

Tosi, Pier Francesco (b. Cesena, 13 Aug. 1654; d. Faenza, on or after 16 July 1732). Theorist, composer, singer. He was trained by his father, and embarked on a successful career as a castrato. From 6 April 1693 he sang and taught singing in London. From 1705 to 1711 he worked as a composer at the Viennese court. He later went to Dresden, Bologna, and London again. His treatise on singing, *Opinioni de' cantori antichi e moderni* (1723), contains valuable information on late 17th- and early 18th-century performance practice.

Tosti, (Franceso) Paolo (b. Ortano sul Mare, 9 Apr. 1846; d. Rome, 2 Dec. 1916). Composer and singing teacher. He studied violin with Pinto and composition with Conti and Mercadante in Naples. Princess Margherita of Savoy heard him sing in Rome and appointed him her singing teacher. He visited London in 1875, and settled there in 1880, when he was appointed singing teacher to the royal family. Many of his original songs were highly popular. He was knighted in 1908. Composed many Italian, French, and English songs.

Bibl.: E. A. Mario [pseudonym for Giovanni Gaeta], *Francesco Paolo Tosti* (Siena, 1947). *Francesco Paolo Tosti e il suo tempo* (Milan, 1987). Francesco Sanvitale, ed., *Tosti* (Turin, 1991).

Tough, Dave [David Jaffray] (b. Oak Park, Ill., 26 Apr. 1908; d. Newark, N.J., 6 Dec. 1948). Jazz drummer. He helped formulate the Chicago jazz style before working in Europe (1927–29). In New York he recorded with Red Nichols (1929). He played in many big bands, notably those of Tommy Dorsey (1936–37, 1938–39), Benny Goodman (1938, 1941), Artie Shaw (1941, 1942–43), and Woody Herman (1944–45, including "Caldonia," recorded in 1945). He joined Bud Freeman's swing and Dixieland group (1939–40, including "Prince of Wails," recorded in 1940), a swing combo led by Bill Harris and tenor saxophonist Charlie Ventura (1947), and Muggsy Spanier's traditional jazz band (1947–48).

Tourel [Davidovich], **Jennie** (b. Vitebsk, Belorussia, 22 June ?1900; d. New York, 23 Nov. 1973). Mezzo-soprano. Her early life remains unclear, as she told conflicting versions. Her family probably fled Russia at the time of the Revolution; they eventually settled in Paris, where Jennie studied with Anna El Tour. In 1931 she made her debut in Paris at the Opéra russe; her Metropolitan Opera debut was in 1937. She sang the role of Baba the Turk in the premiere of *The Rake's Progress* in 1951 and premiered several songs of Hindemith and Poulenc.

Tournemire, Charles (b. Bordeaux, 22 Jan. 1870; d. Arcachon, 3 Nov. 1939). Organist and composer. A child prodigy on organ, he studied with César Franck and Charles-Marie Widor at the Paris Conservatory. In 1898 he became organist at Ste. Clothilde in Paris, a position he retained for the rest of his life. From 1919 on he taught at the Conservatory. Although he composed 4 operas, 8 symphonies, and much chamber music, he is best known for his organ works. These include the *Triple Choral* (1910), *7 Poèmes-Chorales* (1935), *Suite évocatrice* (1938) and the massive *L'orgue mystique* (1927–32), a cycle of 51 suites of 5 movements each, based on plainsong melodies and designed to accompany the Mass throughout the liturgical year. His *5 Improvisations for Organ* (1958) were transcribed by his student Maurice Duruflé from a recorded performance by Tournemire.

Bibl.: Joël-Marie Fauquet, *Catalogue de l'oeuvre de Charles Tournemire* (Geneva, 1979).

Tourte, François (b. Paris, 1747; d. there, 26 Apr. 1835). Bow maker. Member of a family of bow makers; François is the most famous and is generally regarded as the "creator" of the design of the modern bow. After an early apprenticeship with a clockmaker, François joined his father and brother in their workshop, probably by the early 1770s. His bow design reached its standard (which bow makers have copied for about 200 years) probably around 1785. In this bow he combined and developed the features in bows of his predecessors, including a concave bowstick and a higher, larger head. Two contributions with which he is credited are a method for obtaining the curvature of the stick by heating and bending it (rather than cutting it initially) and invention of the ferrule, a piece at the end of the frog that spreads the hair and increases the amount of playing surface. He was the first to use pernambuco wood consistently; he standardized the length of the bow; and he derived a mathematical formula for obtaining optimum weight distribution and balance.

Tovey, Donald (Francis) (b. Eton, 17 July 1875; d. Edinburgh, 10 July 1940). Music scholar, composer, and pianist. He studied with Sophie Weisse (piano), Walter Parratt (counterpoint), and James Higgs (composition); attended Balliol College, Oxford, graduating in 1898 in classical honors. In 1894 he began a long association with Joachim, often appearing as pianist with the latter's quartet; performed his own works in London, Vienna, and Berlin, and gave a series of chamber music concerts in London known as the Chelsea Concerts (1906–12). In 1914 he was named Reid professor of music at Edinburgh Univ., and in 1917 he founded the Reid Orchestra; it was for these concerts that his program notes, many later incorporated into *Essays in Musical Analysis,* were written. He continued to concertize (he undertook a U.S. tour in 1927–28); his compositions include a piano concerto (1903), a cello concerto written for Casals (1935), and the opera *The Bride of Dionysus* (1929). Tovey, however, is best known for his analytical writings, which represent some of the best literature on music in the English language, and which remain influential to this day. He was knighted in 1935.

Writings (all published in London): *A Companion to the Art of Fugue* (1931). *Essays in Musical Analysis* (1935–39; R: 1981). *A Musician Talks* (1941). *Essays in Musical Analysis: Chamber Music* (1944; R: 1972). *Musical Articles from the Encyclopaedia Britannica* (1944). *Beethoven* (1944). *A Companion to Beethoven's Piano Sonatas* (1948; R: 1976). *Essays and Lectures on Music* (1949).

Bibl.: M. Grierson: *Donald Francis Tovey* (London, 1952; R: 1970) [includes complete list of publications].

Tower, Joan (b. New Rochelle, N.Y., 6 Sept. 1938). Composer, pianist. She studied piano as a child, attended Bennington College (1958–61), then studied music at Columbia Univ. with Otto Luening and Chou Wen-chung (M.A., 1967; D.M.A., 1978). While in school she organized the Da Capo Chamber Players, a contemporary music ensemble in which she played piano. Most of her early compositions were written for this group, for example, *Hexachords* (flute, 1972), *Breakfast Rhythms I–II* (clarinet and chamber ensemble, 1974–75), *Platinum Spirals* (violin, 1976), *Wings* (clarinet, 1982). *Amazon II* (1979), her first orchestral work, was a revision of an earlier piece for chamber ensemble (*Amazon I,* 1977). *Sequoia* (orchestra, 1981) was performed by the New York Philharmonic in 1982 with considerable success; *Silver Ladders* (orchestra, 1986) won the 1990 Grawemeyer Award. Other works include *Noon Dance* (chamber ensemble, 1982); piano concerto (1985); clarinet concerto (1986); *Island Prelude* (orchestra, 1989); flute concerto (1990); *Fanfare for the Uncommon Woman no. 4* (orchestra, 1990); concerto for orchestra (1991); violin concerto (1993); clarinet quintet (1994); *Night Field* (string quartet, 1994).

Townshend, Pete(r) (b. Chiswick, England, 19 Mar. 1945). Rock guitarist and songwriter. Attended art school in London; from 1964 played with singer Roger Daltrey (b. 1945), bassist John Entwistle (b. 1946), and drummer Keith Moon (1947–78), first as the High Numbers and later as The Who. They were among the most important rock bands of the 1960s and 1970s, and Townshend's guitar style, which combined elements of lead and rhythm playing, influenced many later artists. His songs include "My Generation" (1965), "I Can See for Miles" (1967), and "Who Are You" (1978); he also authored the rock opera *Tommy* (1969; film, 1977) and concept album *Quadrophenia* (1973; film, 1979), and released solo albums (*Empty Glass,* 1980). The Who disbanded in 1983; they played a reunion tour in 1989.

Trabaci, Giovanni Maria (b. Monte Pelusio [now Irsina], ca. 1575; d. Naples, 31 Dec. 1647). Composer. On 1 December 1594 he was appointed a tenor at the Church of the Annunziata, Naples. Later he was appointed organist at the Oratorio dei Filippini, Naples. He became organist at the Spanish viceregal chapel in Naples on 30 October 1601, and was promoted to *maestro di cappella* there on 1 November 1614; he served in this capacity for the rest of his life. Later he was again organist at the Oratorio dei Filippini (1625–30). His compositions include over 200 sacred and secular vocal works and 165 works for keyboard.

Bibl.: Roland Jackson, "The Keyboard Music of Giovanni Maria Trabaci" (diss., Univ. of California at Berkeley, 1964).

Traetta [Trajetta], **Tommaso (Michele Francesco Saverio)** (b. Bitonto, near Bari, 30 Mar. 1727; d. Venice, 6 Apr. 1779). Composer. He studied at the Conservatorio di S. Maria di Loreto, Naples, with Porpora and Durante (1738–48). His first opera, *Il Farnace,* was performed at S. Carlo, Naples, on 4 November 1751. In the early 1750s he worked with Jommelli in Naples and Rome. In 1758 he became *maestro di cappella* to the court of Parma, where his *Ippolito ed Aricia* (1759), inspired by Rameau's *Hippolyte et Aricie,* was produced. From 1760 to 1763 he wrote operas for Turin, Vienna, and Mannheim. Great success came with *Ifigenia in Tauride* (Vienna, 1763), which was indebted to Gluck's *Orfeo ed Euridice.* In 1765 he became director of the Conservatorio dell'Ospedaletto at Venice; there he wrote sacred vocal works. In 1768 he was employed by Catherine II of Russia in St. Petersburg as singing instructor and musical director of the opera. There his greatest opera, *Antigone,* was performed in 1772. After a short time in London, he settled permanently in Venice by 1777. In addition to over 40 operas, Traetta wrote a number of other sacred and secular vocal works.

Bibl.: Franco Casavola, *Tommaso Traetta di Bitonto (1727–1779): La vita e le opere* (Bari, 1957). Domenico Binetti, *Tommaso e Filippo Trajetta nella vita e nell'arte* (Bitanto, 1972).

Trajetta [Traetta], **Filippo** (b. Venice, 8 Jan. 1777; d. Philadelphia, 9 Jan. 1854). Composer. Son of Tommaso Traetta. He studied with Fenaroli and Perillo in Venice and Piccini in Naples. He became a soldier in the patriot army; was eventually imprisoned by the French and escaped to Boston in 1799. He founded the American Conservatorio in Philadelphia in 1822. His works include oratorios, cantatas, songs, instrumental pieces. He also wrote 2 singing tutors, *An Introduction to the Art and Science of Music* and *Rudiments of the Art of Singing* (1841–43).

Trampler, Walter (b. Munich, 25 Aug. 1915). Violist. Received early instruction from his father and later at the State Academy of Music in Munich. His debut was in 1933 in Munich as a violinist in Beethoven's Concerto; two years later, in Berlin, he performed as violist in Mozart's Sinfonia concertante. He played in the orchestra of Radio Deutschlandsender (1935–38) before immigrating to the U.S. He joined the symphony and opera orchestra of the City Center in New York (1946–48); played in the New Music Quartet (1947–55); appeared with the Juilliard, Guarneri, Budapest, and Emerson Quartets and the Beaux Arts Trio. In 1969 he joined the Chamber Music Society of Lincoln Center. He premiered many works, made solo and chamber recordings, and held appointments at Juillard, Yale, and Boston Univ.

Trapp, Max (b. Berlin, 1 Nov. 1887; d. Berlin, 29 May 1971). Composer. At the Hochschule für Musik in Berlin he studied piano with Ernst von Dohnányi, composition with Paul Juon (1905–11). He taught piano at the Berlin Hochschule (1920–34), composition at the Dortmund Conservatory (1924–30), the Prussian Academy (1934–45), and later at the Berlin Conservatory (1950–53). In his musical style he emulated the late Romantic manner of Richard Strauss. Works include *Der letzte König von Orplid* (incidental music, 1922); 7 symphonies; 3 concertos for orchestra (1935, 1938, 1946); concertos for violin (1925), piano (1931), and cello (1938); many songs and piano pieces.

Traubel, Helen (Francesca) (b. St. Louis, Mo., 20 June 1899; d. Santa Monica, 28 July 1972). Soprano. Began study with Vetta Karst in 1912. Her concert debut was in 1923 with the St. Louis Symphony, and her operatic debut was at the Metropolitan Opera in 1937 as Mary in Walter Damrosch's *The Man without a Country.* Later she concentrated on Wagnerian roles, beginning with Sieglinde in 1939. During the 1940s she was regarded as the leading Wagnerian soprano at the Metropolitan, but she left in 1953 after disagreements with the management over her nightclub appearances. She also published several mystery novels.

Bibl.: Helen Traubel, *St. Louis Woman* (New York, 1959).

Travis, Merle (Robert) (b. Rosewood, Ky., 29 Nov. 1917; d. Tahlequah, Okla., 20 Oct. 1983). Country guitarist, singer, and songwriter. He began recording honky-tonk music in California in 1944, including "Divorce Me C.O.D." (1946) and "Nine Pound Hammer" (1947); many of his own songs became country standards, including "Smoke, Smoke, Smoke That Cigarette" and "I Am a Pilgrim" (both 1947). His influential "Travis style" of guitar picking was developed from banjo technique, and featured melody played by the fingers accompanied by a thumbed bass.

Travis, Roy (Elihu) (b. New York, 24 June 1922). Composer. He studied at Columbia Univ. (B.A., 1947; M.A., 1951) and also at the Juilliard School (B.S., 1949; M.S., 1950). After studying for a year in Paris with Darius Milhaud, he taught at Columbia (1952–53) and at the Mannes College of Music (1952–57). His *Symphonic Allegro* (1951) was introduced by the New York Philharmonic in 1952. In 1957 he joined the faculty at UCLA. At the Institute of Ethnomusicology there he became acquainted with African music, which deeply influenced his works from that point on. These include *African Sonata* (piano, 1968), *The Passion of Oedipus* (opera, Los Angeles, 1968), piano concerto (1969), *The Black Bacchants* (opera, 1982), *Switched-on Ashanti* (flute and tape, 1973).

Tremblay, George (Amadée) (b. Ottawa, 14 Jan. 1911; d. Tijuana, 14 July 1982). Pianist and composer. Son of the Canadian organist Amadée Tremblay, he showed precocious ability on the piano. He moved with his family to the U.S., settling eventually in Los Angeles, where he studied privately with David Patterson (1927–32), then with Arnold Schoenberg (1934–36). His early compositions—for example, String Quartet no. 1 (1936) and *Prelude and Dance* (piano 1937)—adopted Schoenberg's methods literally. By contrast, *Modes of Transportation* (string quartet, 1940) applied serial methods to eight-note rather than twelve-note pitch collections. In subsequent works, including Symphony in One Movement (1949), *Serenade* (chamber ensemble, 1955), and Sextet (wind instruments, 1968), he continued to extend and expand serial methods.

Writings: *The Definitive Cycle of the Twelve-Tone Row* (New York, 1974).

Tremblay, Gilles (b. Arvida, Quebec, 6 Sept. 1932). Composer and pianist. He studied at the Montreal Conservatory (1949–54) with Germaine Malépart (piano) and Claude Champagne (composition), then at the Paris Conservatory with Messiaen and Yvonne Loriod (1954–58). He also studied ondes martenot with Maurice Martenot, worked at the RTF with Pierre Schaeffer, and attended the Darmstadt summer courses. His first major work, *Cantique de durées* (1960), reflects these influences, particularly that of Messiaen. Returning to Montreal in 1961, he began to teach at the conservatory in 1962. During the 1960s he explored rhythmic textures and instrumental sonorities in a series of chamber works: *Champs I,* piano and percussion (1965; rev. 1969); *Kékoba,* voices, percussion, ondes martenot (1965; rev. 1967); *Souffles (Champs II),* chamber ensemble (1968); *Vers (Champs III),* chamber ensemble (1969). During the 1970s he composed several large pieces for orchestra, including *Jeu de solstices* (1974) and *Vers le soleil* (1978). Other works include *Un 9,* mime, 2 percussion instruments, 2 trumpets (1987); *Katadrone: Contrecri,* orchestra (1988); *Cèdres en voiles,* cello (1989).

Bibl.: Louise Laplante, *Gilles Tremblay* (Montreal, 1974).

Trent, Alphonso [Alphonse] **(E.)** (b. Fort Smith, Ark., 24 Aug. 1905; d. there, 14 Oct. 1959). Jazz bandleader. His southwestern big band broadcast regularly from Dallas (mid-1920s) and toured widely through 1933. Owing to its location away from major studios, it recorded only 8 sides, including "Black and Blue Rhapsody" (1928) and "After You've Gone" (1930), both with Stuff Smith and trombonist Snub Mosleye as sidemen.

Trimble, Lester (b. Bangor, Wis., 29 Aug. 1920; d. New York, 21 Dec. 1986). Composer. As a teenager in Pittsburgh he learned the violin and began to compose. After World War II he studied composition with Nikolai Lopatnikoff at Carnegie Institute of Technology (B.F.A., 1948; M.F.A., 1949), then in Paris with Honegger, Milhaud, and Boulanger (1951–52). Returning to the U.S., he was hired as music critic at the *New York Herald Tribune,* where he worked until the early 1960s. He had already written a string quartet (1950) and a Symphony in 2 Movements (1952), to which he added a second string quartet (1955), *Closing Piece,* orchestra (1957; rev. as *Sonic Landscape,* 1967), and *Five Episodes,* orchestra (1962). From 1963 to 1968 he taught composition at the Univ. of Maryland, from 1971 on at Juilliard. His Symphony no. 2 (1967) was premiered in 1969. From 1970 to 1976 he composed a series of "Panels" for various ensembles, in which he used a technique of building a piece out of independently composed modules, assembled by the performers. He also composed a violin concerto (1981) and a Symphony no. 3 (1985).

Tristano, Lennie [Leonard Joseph] (b. Chicago, 19 March 1919; d. New York, 18 Nov. 1978). Jazz pianist, teacher, and bandleader. Blind from childhood. He studied at the American Conservatory, Chicago (B.Mus., 1943), thereafter working mainly as a teacher. In New York he led a sextet which included his pupils Lee Konitz, tenor saxophonist Warne Marsh, and guitarist Billy Bauer (1948–49). Proceeding from the bop style, Tristano advocated constructing themes and solos of lengthy, fast-running, lightly articulated phrases emphasizing harmonic rather than timbral variety, as on recordings of "Subconscious-Lee" and "Crosscurrent" (both 1949). This manner of playing cool jazz became identified with him. He was reunited with Konitz and Marsh intermittently from 1958 to 1966.

Tritonius, Petrus [Treybenreif, Peter] (b. Bozen [Bolzano], ca. 1465; d. Hall [Solbad Hall]?, probably 1525). Composer. Of Tirolian background; he studied at Vienna Univ. in 1486 and Ingolstadt Univ. from 1497. There under the humanist Conradus Celtis he composed widely admired 4-voiced syllabic settings of Horatian odes that illustrated classical meters and quantities. After teaching at Brixen Cathedral School and taking a doctorate at Padua in 1502, he taught at Vienna Univ. under Celtis until the latter's death in 1508. He returned to the Tirol, where he taught at Bozen, Schwaz, and Hall. His bilingual Latin-German *Hymnarius* (Schwaz, 1524) is the first-known printed Catholic hymnbook.

Tritto [Tritta], **Giacomo (Domenico Mario Antonio Pasquale Giuseppe)** (b. Altamura, 2 Apr. 1733; d. Naples, 16 or 17 Sept. 1824). Composer. He studied at the Pietà dei Turchini conservatory; later he became "secondo" and then "primo maestro" there. Among his pupils were Bellini, Conti, Mercadante, Spontini, and Meyerbeer. He wrote upwards of 50 operas; the first, *La fedeltà in amore,* was performed in Naples in 1764. He also composed a number of sacred works, including a Mass for double choir with 2 orchestras, 7 other Masses, 2 Passions, 1 Requiem, cantatas, and other small pieces.

Bibl.: Giuseppe de Napoli, *La triade melodrammatica altamurano: Giacomo Tritto, Vincenzo Lavigna, Saverio Mercadante* (Milan, 1931).

Tromboncino, Bartolomeo (b. Verona, ca. 1470; d. Venice?, 1535 or later). Composer. From 1477 his father, Bernardino Piffaro, appears to have served the Gonzaga court in Mantua as a wind instrument player; there Tromboncino was raised and played trombone. He seems to have served the Florentine Medici court, 1489–94, then returned to Mantua. Gonzaga paid him highly and treated him well, but he behaved badly: he fled briefly in 1495, killed his wife for adultery in 1499, and fled permanently in 1501. In February 1502 he was engaged in Ferrara by Lucrezia Borgia to sing *intermedi* (in plays of Plautus) at her wedding to Duke Alfonso d'Este (whose sister Isabella was Gonzaga's wife). He remained in Lucrezia's service until at least 1508 and stayed in Ferrara until at least 1513. From at least 1521 he lived in Venice.

Tromboncino was, with Cara, a great early frottolist. Some 176 frottole are attributed to him; nearly all were in print by 1520. About half are simple *barzellette;* others use a variety of texts, including verses of Petrarch and other Renaissance and classical poets. His sacred works include 13 *laude* (some contrafact frottole), a Lamentations cycle, and a motet, *Benedictus Dominus Deus;* they are mainly homorhythmic.

Troyanos, Tatiana (b. New York, 12 Sept. 1938; d. New York, 21 Aug. 1993). Mezzo-soprano. She was a student at the Juilliard School and received instruction from Hans Heinz. Made her debut in 1963 with the New York City Opera as Hippolyta in Britten's *A Midsummer Night's Dream.* She appeared frequently in Hamburg, where she created the role of Jeanne in Penderecki's *The Devils of Loudun* (1969). She sang at Covent Garden in 1969 and with the Paris Opéra in 1971, also appearing at Salzburg and at the Edinburgh, Munich, and Aix-en-Provence festivals. Sang the title role in Handel's *Ariodante* at the opening of the Kennedy Center in Washington, D.C., in 1971; her Metropolitan Opera debut was in 1976 as Octavian. Some of her other roles include the Composer from *Ariadne auf Naxos,* Poppaea, Jocasta, and Carmen.

Trumbauer, Frankie [Frank; Tram] (b. Carbondale, Ill., 30 May 1901; d. Kansas City, Mo., 11 June 1956). Jazz C-melody and alto saxophonist. In St. Louis his band included Bix Beiderbecke (1925–56). He and Beiderbecke played in the orchestras of Jean Goldkette (1926–67), Adrian Rollini (1927), and Paul Whiteman (from 1927) and also recorded in Dixieland bands (1924, 1927–29), including under Trumbauer's leadership "Trumbology" and "Singin' the Blues" (both 1927). His light-toned C-melody saxophone solo on the latter recording greatly influenced Lester Young. Trumbauer remained with Whiteman until 1936, when he briefly led a band with Jack and Charlie Teagarden. He formed a big band and played in studio groups before working outside music.

Trythall, (Harry) Gilbert (b. Knoxville, Tenn., 28 Oct. 1930). Composer. Brother of Richard Aakre Trythall. He attended the Univ. of Tennessee, where he studied with David Van Vactor (B.A., 1951), then studied at Northwestern with Wallingford Riegger (M.M., 1952) and at Cornell with Robert Palmer (D.M.A., 1960). His Symphony no. 1 (1958; rev. 1961) was introduced by the San Francisco Symphony in 1959. Taught at Knox College (1960–64), George Peabody College for Teachers (1964–75), and West Virginia Univ. (from 1975). The majority of his works from the early 1960s on combine electronics with traditional instruments. Several involve visual media as well. Works include *Entropy* (harp, celeste, piano, brass choir, and tape, 1969); *Surfaces* (wind ensemble, tape, lights, 1962); *Echospace* (brass, tape, film, 1971; rev. 1973); *Luxikon I* (synthesizers, percussion, laser lights, 1978); *The Terminal Opera* (1982); *Mass in English and Spanish* (congregation, organ, descant, 1988).

Writings: *Principles and Practice of Electronic Music* (New York, 1973).

Trythall, Richard Aaker (b. Knoxville, Tenn., 25 July 1939). Composer and pianist. Brother of Gilbert Trythall. He studied with David Van Vactor at the Univ. of Tennessee (B.M., 1961), then with Roger Sessions and Earl Kim at Princeton (M.F.A., 1963) and with Boris Blacher at the Hochschule für Musik in Berlin (1963–64). Receiving a Rome Prize in 1964, he remained in Rome, teaching at St. Stephen's School and serving as music liaison at the American Academy in Rome (from 1974). As a pianist performed his own works and those of other contemporary composers in Italy and in the U.S. Works include *Penelope's Monologue* (soprano and orchestra, 1966); *Coincidences* (piano, 1969); *Omaggio a Jerry Lee Lewis* (tape, 1975); *Variations on a Theme by Haydn* (woodwind quintet and tape, 1976).

Tsintsadze, Sulkhan (b. Gori, Georgia, 23 Aug. 1925). Composer. Studied cello at the Tbilisi Conservatory and played in the Georgian State Symphony Orchestra (1942–44), the Georgian Radio Orchestra (1942–45, 1953–63), and the State String Quartet of Georgia (1943–46). Studied cello with Kosolupov (1948–53) and composition with Bogatyrev (1948–53) at the Moscow Conservatory. Taught orchestration and composition at the Tbilisi Conservatory beginning 1963; in 1965 was made rector of that institution. The flavor of Georgian folk melos infuses his traditionally conceived music. Works include 2 operas; 3 musical comedies; 4 ballets; 5 symphonies; 3 concertos for cello, 2 violin concertos, 2 piano concertos; 11 string quartets and other chamber music; songs and choral music; incidental and film music.

Tsontakis, George (b. New York, 24 Oct. 1951). Composer. He attended Juilliard (1978–86) and studied with Stockhausen in Rome (1981); also worked with Sessions (1974–79). He served as an assistant at the electronic music facilities at Juilliard (1978), and taught at the Brooklyn College Conservatory of Music (1986–87), Bard College, and Sarah Lawrence College (from 1993). Compositions include sacred vocal music (*Saviors,* soprano, chorus, orchestra, 1985; *Stabat Mater,* soprano, chorus, orchestra, 1990); orchestral works (*5 Sighs and a Fantasy,* 1984; *Fantasia Habanera,* 1986; *Overture Vera,* 1988; *To the Sowers of the Seed,* 1989; *The Dove Descending,* orchestra, 1995); chamber music (4 string quartets, 1980, 1984, 1986, 1989;

brass quintet, 1984; *3 Mood Sketches,* wind quintet, 1989; *Heartsounds,* piano quintet, 1990; *Eclipse,* clarinet, violin, cello, piano, 1995).

Tubb, Ernest (Dale) (b. near Crisp, Tex., 9 Feb. 1914; d. Nashville, Tenn., 6 Sept. 1984). Country singer, songwriter, and guitarist. He performed in honky-tonks in Texas, at first imitating Jimmy Rogers; his first recording success came with "Walking the Floor over You" (1941). He joined the Grand Ole Opry in 1943, where he was an early endorser of the electric guitar in country music; further recordings included "Try Me One More Time" (1943) and "Thanks a Lot" (1963). He also recorded duets with Loretta Lynn, and from 1947 hosted the radio show "Midnight Jamboree," which introduced many rock-and-roll artists.

Tucker, Richard [Ticker, Reuben] (b. Brooklyn, 28 Aug. 1913; d. Kalamazoo, 8 Jan. 1975). Tenor. Studied with Paul Althouse. His debut was in 1943 with the Salmaggi Company in New York as Alfredo in *La traviata;* his Metropolitan Opera debut was in 1945 as Enzo in *La Gioconda.* His association with the Metropolitan continued for the rest of his life; he specialized in the Italian repertory and performed as many as 30 roles. He appeared abroad, first at Verona Arena in 1947, also in Milan, Florence, London, Vienna, Buenos Aires. He also appeared in concert with major orchestras.

Bibl.: James A. Drake, *Richard Tucker: A Biography* (New York, 1984) [includes discography].

Tuckwell, Barry (Emmanuel) (b. Melbourne, 5 Mar. 1931). Horn player. He studied with Alan Mann at the Sydney Convervatorium, and performed with the Melbourne and Sydney orchestras. Went to England in 1950, where he met Dennis Brain and joined the Hallé Orchestra in Manchester (1951–53), the Scottish National Orchestra (1953–54), and then, as principal horn, the Bournemouth Symphony (1954–55) and London Symphony (1955–68). After leaving the London Symphony he embarked on a solo career, becoming a leading player of his generation; a number of composers wrote works for him, including Musgrave, Hoddinott, Richard Rodney Bennett, and Don Banks. He founded the Tuckwell Wind Quintet (1968), and served as conductor of the Tasmanian Symphony (1980–83) and music director of the Maryland Symphony (from 1982). He is the author of *Horn* (New York, 1983).

Tudor, David (b. Philadelphia, 20 Jan. 1926). Pianist and composer. As a teenager he studied organ with William Hawke, piano with Josef Martin and Irma Wolpe, composition with Stefan Wolpe. He worked as an organist at St. Mark's Church in Philadelphia (1938–43) and at Swarthmore College (1944–48), meanwhile developing a virtuoso piano technique aimed at the performance of contemporary music. In the early 1950s he began performing works by John Cage and the group of avant-garde composers associated with Cage. His New York performance of Pierre Boulez's Second Piano Sonata (from memory) in 1950 attracted considerable attention, as did his premieres of Cage's *Music of Changes* (1951) and *4′33″* in 1952. In 1953 he began a long association with the Merce Cunningham Dance Company (*Webwork,* 1987; *Vital Focus,* 1990). In 1954 he toured with Cage in Europe, where his performances gained the admiration of the European avant-garde and inspired several pieces, among them Silvano Bussotti's *Five Pieces for David Tudor* (1959) and Karlheinz Stockhausen's *Klavierstück VI* (1955). During the 1960s, along with Cage, he turned toward the live performance of electronic music, helping to conceive, assemble, and perform works such as Cage's *Cartridge Music* (1960), *Variations II* (1961), *Variations III* (1963). He also began to take credit as collaborator in the composition of electronic works (for example, *Reunion,* 1968, with Cage, Lowell Cross, David Behrman, Gordon Mumma, and Marcel Duchamp) and as sole composer (*Rainforest I,* live electronics, 1968; *Toneburst,* live electronics, 1974). Many of his compositions involve multiple media, as in *Bandoneon!* (1966), where the Argentine accordion of that name controls circuits that operate lights and video images, and *Video/Laser I–II* (1969, with Lowell Cross and Carson Jeffries), where electronic sounds drive laser projections.

Tudway, Thomas (b. ca. 1650; d. Cambridge, 23 Nov. 1726). Composer. He was a chorister at the Chapel Royal in 1668. From 1670 he was organist of King's College, Cambridge, and from 1670 to 1680 he was also master of the choristers there. He was later made university organist and organist of Pembroke College. Cambridge Univ. granted him the degrees of Mus.B. (1681) and Mus.D. (1705). Between 1714 and 1720 he assembled a 6-volume anthology of cathedral music. His compositions consist mainly of verse anthems.

Tunder, Franz (b. Bannesdorf, near Burg, Fehmarn, 1614; d. Lübeck, 5 Nov. 1667). Composer. He studied with his father and with Christian Prusse, Kantor of the church in Burg, before becoming court organist at Gottorf in 1632. There he may have studied organ with Johann Heckelauer. On 29 September 1641 he was appointed organist at the Marienkirche, Lübeck, where he remained until his death; his son-in-law Buxtehude succeeded him. In addition to his duties as organist, Tunder arranged evening concerts *(Abendmusiken)* consisting of German organ music and Italian vocal works. His surviving compositions include 17 vocal works (motets, solo and chorale cantatas, sacred arias), 14 organ pieces (preludes, chorale fantasias, chorale variations), and a sinfonia for strings. His chorale cantatas mark the beginning of the Lutheran church cantata's evolution, and his organ preludes (arranged toccata–fugue–postlude) influenced those of Buxtehude.

Bibl.: *Franz Tunder: Kantaten und Chorwerke,* ed. Max Seiffert, *DDT* 3 (Leipzig, 1900; R: 1957). *Franz Tunder: Sämtliche Orgelwerke,* ed. Klaus Beckmann (Wiesbaden,

1974). Kurt Gudewill, *Franz Tunder und die nordelbingische Musikkultur seiner Zeit* (Lübeck, 1967).

Tuotilo (d. St. Gall, 27 Apr. 915). Monastic musician. He studied under Iso, as did Notker Balbulus. According to the 11th-century St. Gall chronicler Ekkehard IV, he was an expert player and teacher of instruments at St. Gall and composer of "matchless and easily recognizable" tunes. Works attributed to him include the well-known Christmas introit trope *Hodie cantandus est* and tropes for several other major feasts. He was also a poet and an artist.

Turchi, Guido (b. Rome, 10 Nov. 1916). Composer, critic, and administrator. He studied piano and composition at the Rome Conservatory (diploma, 1940) and at the Accademia di S. Cecilia with Ildebrando Pizzetti. His works from the 1940s and early 1950s reflect a variety of influences, particularly those of Pizzetti in *Invettiva,* chorus and 2 pianos (1947), Bartók in *Concerto breve,* string quartet (1948), and Hindemith in *Piccolo concerto notturno,* orchestra (1950). From the late 1940s on he played an active part in the musical life of Italy, teaching at the Rome Conservatory (from 1941), directing the Parma Conservatory (1967–69) and the Florence Conservatory (1970–72), and serving as artistic director of the Accademia filarmonica of Rome (1963–66), the Teatro comunale of Bologna (1968–70), the Accademia musicale chigiana (from 1978), and the Teatro angelicum in Milan (from 1988). He also wrote music criticism for the *Corriere della sera.* Other works include: *Cinque commenti alle Baccanti di Euripide* (orchestra, 1952); *Il buon soldato Svejk* (opera, Milan, 1962); *Rapsodia* (orchestra, 1969).

Tureck, Rosalyn (b. Chicago, 14 Dec. 1914). Pianist and scholar. She studied in Chicago with Jan Chiapusso and with Olga Samaroff at Juilliard, graduating in 1935, the same year as her New York recital debut. In 1937 she attracted attention with her series of all-Bach recitals, and is in fact best known for her recitals and recordings of the music of that composer, on the harpsichord, clavichord, and Moog synthesizer as well as the piano. Tureck toured extensively from 1937. She founded the International Bach Institute (1966) and the Tureck Bach Institute (1981), and published a number of articles and the 3-volume anthology *An Introduction to the Performance of Bach* (London, 1960). She taught at the Univ. of Maryland, Mannes, Juilliard, and the Univ. of California, San Diego.

Turetzky, Bertram (Jay) (b. Norwich, Conn., 14 Feb. 1933). Double bass player and composer. He studied with Joseph Iadone and Josef Marx at the Hartt School of Music and with Curt Sachs at New York Univ., and attended the Univ. of Hartford (M.M., 1965). Since his New York debut in 1964 he has given recitals and recorded music for solo double bass, including works written for him by Erb, Perle, Martino, Barney Childs, and Ben Johnston. Some of his own compositions include double bass (e.g., *Reflections on Ives and Whittier,* double bass, tape, 1978–81; *In memoriam Charles Mingus,* 2 singers, 3 jazz groups, double bass choir, tape, film, 1979). He is the author of *The Contemporary Contrabass* (Berkeley, 1974; R: 1989).

Turina, Joaquín (b. Seville, 9 Dec. 1882; d. Madrid, 14 Jan. 1949). Composer. Received initial tutelage in piano and harmony in his home city and made a sensational local debut as a pianist in 1897; he soon went to Madrid, studying piano under Tragó at the conservatory and befriending Manuel de Falla. Moved to Paris in 1905, studying piano with Moszkowsky and also composition with D'Indy at the Schola cantorum, from which he graduated in 1913. Turina performed his Piano Quintet op. 1 in a 1907 concert attended by Falla and Albéniz; in a discussion afterward, the three Spanish composers resolved to write music in a national vein. His 1913 symphonic poem *La procesión del Rocio* was performed by the Madrid Symphony to wide acclaim. He returned to Madrid in 1914, and was later active as a conductor for the Ballets russes and as choirmaster at the Teatro real. Two other major works, *Evangelio de Navidad* (1915) and *Sinfoniá sevillana* (1920), were premiered by the Madrid Symphony, and his opera *Jardin de oriento* (1923) was given at the Teatro real. He joined the faculty at the Madrid Conservatory in 1930; after the Civil War he was admitted to the San Fernando Academy and was named head of the Ministry of Education's general music commission upon its creation in 1941. In addition to his music, he produced 2 significant books, the *Enciclopedia musical abreviada* (1917; with a prologue by Falla) and the *Tratado de composición* (1947), and contributed criticism to *El debate* and *Digame.* In addition to stage and orchestral music, he also composed chamber works, much piano music, and songs.

Bibl.: Linton E. Powell, "The Piano Music of Joaquín Turina" (diss., Univ. of North Carolina, 1974). José Luis García del Busto, *Turina* (Madrid, 1981). Joaquín Turina, *Escritos de Joaquín Turina* (Madrid, 1982). José María Benavente, *Aproximación al lenguaje musical de J. Turina* (Madrid, 1983). Antonio Iglesias, *Joaquín Turina (su obra para piano)* (Madrid, 1989).

Türk, Daniel Gottlieb (b. Claussnitz, near Chemnitz, 10 Aug. 1750; d. Halle, 26 Aug. 1813). Theorist and composer. He studied with G. A. Homilius at the Dresden Kreuzschule and with J. A. Hiller at the Univ. of Leipzig. In 1774 he became Kantor at the Halle Ulrichskirche, in 1779 music director at Halle Univ., and in 1787 music director and organist at the Liebfrauenkirche in Halle. He wrote several important treatises and theoretical works including *Von den wichtigsten Pflichten eines Organisten* (1787), *Klavierschule* (1789), *Kurze Anweisung zum Generalbassspielen* (1791), and *Anweisung zu Temperaturberechnungen* (1808). He composed an opera (now lost), cantatas, about 48 keyboard sonatas, other keyboard pieces, lieder.

Bibl.: Daniel Gottlieb Türk, *School of Clavier Playing,* trans. Raymond H. Haggh (Lincoln, Neb., 1982).

Turner, (Big) Joe [Joseph Vernon] (b. Kansas City, Mo., 18 May 1911; d. Inglewood, Calif., 24 Nov. 1985). Blues, rhythm-and-blues, and jazz singer. He formed a duo with pianist Pete Johnson, working in Kansas City before coming in 1938 to New York, where he sang in the From Spirituals to Swing concert at Carnegie Hall and recorded "Roll 'Em Pete." His blues shouting adapted well to swing groups and boogie-woogie pianists (he continued to work with both into the 1980s) and also to rhythm and blues (in which style he recorded numerous hits during the 1950s). "Shake Rattle and Roll" proved most influential: a cover version by Bill Haley initiated the rock-and-roll era. Turner should not be confused with stride pianist Joe [Joseph H.] Turner (b. 1907).

Turner, Tina [Bollock, Annie Mae] (b. Brownsville, Tenn., 26 Nov. 1939). Popular and rock singer. She began singing with Ike Turner in 1956; they were married in 1958. Until their divorce in 1976 they were among the most successful exponents of rhythm-and-blues, with recordings including "River Deep, Mountain High" (1966), "Proud Mary" (1971), and Tina's "Nutbush City Limits" (1973). She later recorded several successful solo albums, including *Private Dancer* (1984) and *Break Every Rule* (1986), and appeared in films (*Tommy,* 1977).

Turner, William (b. Oxford, 1651; d. London, 13 Jan. 1740). Composer and singer. He was a chorister under Edward Lowe at Christ Church, Oxford, and in the early 1660s at the Chapel Royal. With Humphrey and Blow he wrote "The Club Anthem," *I Will Always Give Thanks* (ca. 1664). He became master of the choristers at Lincoln Cathedral in 1667, and returned to the Chapel Royal in 1669 to sing countertenor. He served as a member of the King's Private Musick from 1672, and appeared in Shadwell's *The Tempest* in 1674. He was later employed at St. Paul's Cathedral (1683) and at Westminster Abbey (1699). Cambridge Univ. granted him the degree of Mus.D. in 1696. Turner's compositions include 40 anthems, odes, a cantata, a motet, services, hymns and chants, and over 50 songs.

Turrentine, Stanley (William) (b. Pittsburgh, 5 Apr. 1934). Jazz tenor saxophonist and bandleader. He toured the South in Lowell Fulson's rhythm-and-blues group, which included Ray Charles, then joined his brother, trumpeter Tommy Turrentine (b. 1928), in groups led by Earl Bostic (1953–54) and Max Roach (1959–60). Through the 1960s he made albums of his own, in hard bop and soul jazz styles, including *A Chip off the Old Block* with organist Shirley Scott (1963). He also played on recordings by Scott and Jimmy Smith. From 1970, when he recorded his composition "Sugar," he reached wider audiences by emphasizing tuneful melodies and glossy arrangements.

Turski, Zbigniew (b. Konstancin, near Warsaw, 28 July 1908; d. Warsaw, 7 Jan. 1979). Composer. He studied composition with Rytel and conducting with Bierdiajew at the Warsaw Conservatory, then served as music producer at Polish Radio from 1936 until 1939. From 1945 to 1946 he conducted the Baltic Philharmonic. He eventually resettled in Warsaw. His compositional style is a blend of modern trends with a post-Romantic lushness that is particularly apt in the context of his dramatic music. Works include stage music (*Rozmówki* [Chats], micro-opera, 1966; *Ndege* [The Bird], choreographic story), vocal and chamber music as well as music for film and theater.

Twitty, Conway [Jenkins, Harold Lloyd] (b. Friars Point, Miss., 1 Sept. 1933; d. Springfield, Mo., 5 June 1993). Country and rock-and-roll singer and songwriter. After playing country music in the South, after World War II he had success with rock-and-roll, particularly the song "It's Only Make Believe" (1958). He returned to country in the late 1960s, becoming one of its most popular male singers; he recorded solo (including "You've Never Been This Far Before," 1973; "Happy Birthday, Darlin'," 1979) and with Loretta Lynn (including "Mississippi Woman, Louisiana Man," 1973).

Tye, Christopher (b. ca. 1505; d. 1572?). Composer. Probably born in the east of England, he took a B.Mus. at Cambridge in 1536; he was a lay clerk at King's College, Cambridge, from 1537 for about a year. He seems to have befriended Dr. Richard Cox, who studied at King's (matriculated 1519). In 1541 Cox became Archdeacon of Ely, and in 1543 Tye became choirmaster at Ely Cathedral. Tye took a Mus.D. at Cambridge in 1545; in 1547 Cox became chancellor at Oxford Univ., and the following year Oxford granted Tye a reciprocal D.Mus. From 1544 to 1550 Cox served as a tutor to Prince Edward (later Edward VI); manuscripts show Tye's music to have enjoyed currency in the Chapel Royal at about this time. In his *Actes of the Apostles* (printed in 1553 and dedicated to Edward) Tye styled himself a Gentleman of the Chapel, but the rolls do not record his membership. In 1558 Cox became Bishop of Ely, and within a year Tye renewed his Ely appointment after a decade's absence. In 1560 Cox ordained Tye as both deacon (in July) and priest (in November). Tye received a generous living at Doddington-cum-Marche, Isle of Ely; his death is not recorded, but the living passed to his successor on 15 March 1573. His Latin church music includes motets, Magnificats, and 3 Masses (one on "Western Wind"); his English church music includes anthems and service music. He also composed over 20 *In nomine*s and other consort music.

Bibl.: *The Latin Church Music,* ed. J. R. Satterfield (Madison, Wis., 1972). *The Instrumental Music,* ed. R. W. Weidner (New Haven, 1976). *The English Sacred Music,* ed. J. Morehen, *EECM* 19 (1977). J. R. Satterfield, "The Latin Church

Music of Christopher Tye" (diss., Univ. of North Carolina, 1962).

Tyler, James (b. Hartford, Conn., 3 Aug. 1940). Lute, cittern, and viol player. Studied at the Hartt School of Music and with Joseph Iadone. Appeared with the New York Pro Musica in 1962. Moved to England in 1969 and joined the Early Music Consort of London and Musica Reservata. With Anthony Rooley, started the Consort of Musicke. Played with the Julian Bream Consort (1974–) and The London Early Music Group, which he founded. Published musical writings, including *The Early Guitar* (London, 1980), *A Brief Tutor for the Baroque Guitar* (1984), and with Paul Sparks *The Early Mandolin* (Oxford, 1989). Began teaching at the Univ. of Southern California in 1986.

Tyner, (Alfred) McCoy [Saud, Sulaimon] (b. Philadelphia, 11 Dec. 1938). Jazz pianist and bandleader. He played hard bop in Art Farmer and Benny Golson's Jazztet (1959–60). As a member of John Coltrane's quartet (1960–65) he developed a new accompanimental style of jazz piano, reiterating rich chordal patterns built largely upon intervals of fourths and fifths. His albums with Coltrane include *Selflessness* (1963, 1965) and *A Love Supreme* (1964). From 1965 he has worked as a leader. He struggled commercially at the start, but he has met great success since the 1970s, recording albums such as *Sahara* (1972) and *Supertrios* (1977) and touring into the 1990s with small groups. He also joined the Milestone Jazzstars, a quartet including Sonny Rollins and Ron Carter (1978).

U

Uccellini, Marco (b. ca. 1603; d. Forlimpopoli, near Forli, 10 Sept. 1680). Composer. He studied in Assisi and settled in Modena before 1639. There he became head of instrumental music at the Este court in 1641, and from 1647 to 1665 was *maestro di cappella* at the cathedral. He then served as *maestro di cappella* at the Farnese court in Parma until his death. His extant compositions, all instrumental, include 7 printed collections. Opp. 2–5 contain sonatas for 1–4 violins; they are virtuosic for the time, extending the range of the violin up to fourth position, and feature chromaticism and the use of unusual keys. Later collections consist of dances and sinfonias.

Ugarte, Floro M(anuel) (b. Buenos Aires, 15 Sept. 1884; d. there, 11 June 1975). Composer. Studied in Argentina, then at the Paris Conservatory with Fourdrain; returned to Buenos Aires in 1913 to teach and compose. He helped form a music curriculum for the newly founded National Conservatory in 1924, later teaching there; he also directed the Teatro Colón and the Buenos Aires Municipal Conservatory. Works include the opera *Saika* (1918); the ballet *El junco* (1944); several nationalistically evocative orchestra pieces (*Entre las montañas,* 1922; the 2 parts of *De mi tierra,* 1923, 1934; *La Rébelión del agua,* based on his own poetry, 1931); a symphony (1946); chamber music; piano works; and songs.

Bibl.: *Composers of the Americas* 1 (Washington, D.C., 1955), pp. 104–10 [includes works list].

Ugolini, Vincenzo (b. Perugia, ca. 1580; d. Rome, 6 May 1638). Composer. He studied with G. B. Nanino from June 1592 to October 1594 at the choir school of S. Luigi dei Francesi, Rome, and was employed there as a bass on 1 May 1600. He was *maestro di cappella* of S. Maria Maggiore, Rome (1603–9), and was employed at Benevenuto Cathedral from 1610. From 1614 he was director of music to Cardinal Arrigoni in Rome, where he served as *maestro di cappella* of S. Luigi dei Francesi from 1616 to 1620, and again from 1631 until his death. He was maestro of the Cappella Giulia at St. Peter's from 1620 to 1626. An advocate of the Palestrina school, Ugolini wrote Masses, motets, Psalms, hymns, antiphons, sacred songs, and madrigals.

Ugolino of Orvieto [Ugolino di Francesco Urbevetano] (b. Orvieto?, ca. 1380; d. Ferrara, 1457). Theorist and composer. A cleric at Forlì from at least 1411, he served at S. Croce as canon from 1415 and archdeacon from 1425. On the rise of Ghibelline factions there he removed to Ferrara, where he was cathedral archpresbyter from the late 1430s to 1448. His 5-volume *Declaratio musice discipline,* completed ca. 1430–35, is among the last metaphysically speculative musical treatises in the medieval scholastic tradition; it enjoyed esteem through the 16th century. Of his reportedly numerous compositions only 3 2-voiced motets survive.

Uhl, Alfred (b. Vienna, 5 June 1909; d. there, 8 June 1992). Composer. He studied with Franz Schmidt at the Hochschule für Musik in Vienna (diploma, 1932), then traveled abroad and composed music for several films. He returned to Austria in 1938, was wounded in World War II, then taught at the Hochschule from 1945 on. His music is tonal, follows classical formal models, and often emphasizes instrumental virtuosity. Works include *Der mysteriöse Herr X* (opera, Vienna, 1966); *Concertante sinfonie* (clarinet and orchestra, 1943); Violin Concerto (1963); *Sinfonietta* (orchestra, 1977); *Humoreske* (wind quintet, 1965); Guitar Sonata (1937); *Eine vergnügliche Spielmusik* (3 violins and cello, 1970); *Commedia musicale* (viola, clarinet, piano, 1982); *Konzertante Musik für Violine und Orchester* (1986).

Bibl.: Alexander Witeschnik, *Alfred Uhl: eine biographische Studie* (Vienna, 1966).

Uhlig, Theodor (b. Wurzen, near Leipzig, 15 Feb. 1822; d. Dresden, 3 Jan. 1853). Violinist, music critic, and composer. He studied with his father, then with Friedrich Schneider in Dessau (1837–40). He was a member of the Dresden Orchestra beginning in 1841. Helped prepare vocal score of *Lohengrin.* He was an early defender of Wagner. Most of his writings were published in 1914 in Regensburg as *Musikalische Schriften* (*Deutsche Musikbücherei* 14). His compositions are numerous, and include symphonies, chamber music, and songs.

Um Kalthoum [Kalthum, Ibrahim Um] (b. Tamayet el Zahayra, Sinbellawein, Egypt, 1898; d. Cairo, 3 Feb. 1975). Singer. From 1922 she worked in Cairo, where she assembled a group of instrumentalists; from 1936 she appeared in many musical films; a major figure in Middle Eastern music in the 1950s and 1960s. She sang a wide repertory of traditional and newly composed music.

Umlauf, Ignaz (b. Vienna, 1746; d. Meidling, 8 June 1796). Composer and violinist. By 1775 he was principal violist in the German Theater Orchestra. He was known mainly as a composer of singspiels; in 1778 he wrote the first work for Joseph II's German National Singspiel in Vienna, *Bergknappen,* which enjoyed great popularity. He was then promoted to Kapellmeister. His other singspiels (all for Vienna) include *Die Insul der Liebe* (ca. 1772), *Die Apotheke* (1778), *Die schöne Schusterin oder Die pücefarbenen Schuhe* (1779), *Das Irrlicht* (1782), *Der Oberamtmann und die Soldaten* (1782), *Die glücklichen Jäger* (1786), and *Der Ring der Liebe* (1786).

Bibl.: Robert Haas, ed., *I. Umlauf: Die Bergknappen, DTÖ* 36, 18/1 (1911/R): ix–xxxiv.

Unger [Ungher], **Karoline** [Caroline, Carolina, Carlotta] (b. Stuhlweissenburg, 28 Oct. 1803; d. Florence, 23 Mar. 1877). Contralto. Studied piano as a child. Later studied voice with Joseph Mozatti and Ugo Bassi, and with Roncini in Milan. Debuted in Vienna in 1824 as Dorabella in *Così fan tutte.* Sang in premiere of Beethoven's Ninth Symphony (1824), and is known as the person who turned the deaf composer to see the applause. Sang in Italy with success from 1825. Went to Paris in 1833. Retired in 1843 when she married. A number of works were written for her, including Donizetti's *Parisiana* (1833), *Belisario* (1836), and *Maria di Rudenz* (1838); Bellini's *La straniera* (1829); Mercadante's *Le due illustri rivali* (1838); and Pacini's *Niobe* (1826).

Urhan [Auerhahn], **Chrétien** (b. Montjoie, near Aix-la-Chapelle, 16 Feb. 1790; d. Paris, 2 Nov. 1845). Violinist, violist, and composer. Studied with Le Sueur in Paris (1804). Joined orchestra of Paris Opéra in 1814. First violin in 1823, violin soloist in 1836; occasionally played viola. In 1827 became organist at St. Vincent. Led Société des Concerts du Conservatoire in 1828. Played in several quartets. Viola soloist in premiere of *Harold in Italy* (1834). Viola d'amore solo in act 1 of *Les Huguenots* was written for him.

Bibl.: Paul Garnault, "Chrétien Urhan," *RdM* 14 (1930): 98–111.

Uribe Holguín, Guillermo (b. Bogotá, 17 Mar. 1880; d. there, 26 June 1971). Composer. Studied as a child at the National Academy, Bogotá, continuing his studies from 1895 with Narciso Garay. Worked in New York as a violinist and arranger, 1904–5, also visiting Mexico; taught back at the National Academy, 1905–7; studied at the Schola cantorum, Paris, under D'Indy and alongside Satie and Turina from 1907. Returning to Colombia, he served as director of the National Conservatory, 1910–35 and again 1942–47. The leading Colombian composer of his time; his earlier works show French traits, while later music is nationalist in tone. Works include 11 symphonies; symphonic poems; 2 violin concertos, viola concerto, many orchestral dances and other nationalist tableaux; 10 string quartets; 7 violin sonatas; the opera *Furatena* op. 76; church music, including a Requiem; hundreds of piano pieces, including some 300 *Trozos en el sentimiento popular;* and songs. He also produced a 1941 autobiography.

Bibl.: *Composers of the Americas* 1 (Washington, D.C., 1955), pp. 111–21 [includes works list].

Urio, Francesco Antonio (b. Milan, 1631? or 1632; d. there, 1719 or later). Composer. He was *maestro di cappella* at Spoleto Cathedral (1679), and at Urbino (1681–83), Assisi, and Genoa (dates unknown). He also held this position at the Basilica de' Santi Dodici Apostoli, Rome (1690), I Frari, Venice (1697), and S. Francesco, Milan (1715–19). Two collections of his compositions were published: *Motetti di concerto* (1690) and *Salmi concertati* (1697). Among his other surviving sacred vocal works are an oratorio and a Te Deum, Urio's most famous composition. Handel may have seen the latter work in Florence and borrowed from it in his *Dettingen Te Deum, Saul, Israel in Egypt,* and *L'allegro ed il penseroso.*

Urreda, Johannes (fl. 1476–81). Composer. He is generally considered identical to "Jo. Wreede brugen" ("of Bruges," hence of Flemish birth), the author of a Kyrie and Gloria in a Sistine Chapel manuscript. In 1476 he sang in the chapel of García Álvarez de Toledo, first Duke of Alba. In 1477 he was *maestro de capilla* to King Ferdinand II of Aragon (later Ferdinand V of Castille), whom he served until at least 1481. His works include sacred works and *canciones;* his 4-voiced setting of the Mozarabic hymn *Pange lingua* and 3-voiced setting of the Duke of Alba's *canción Nunca fue pena mayor* were widely parodied and intabulated both within Spain and abroad.

Urrutia Blondel, Jorge (b. La Serena, Chile, 17 Sept. 1905; d. Santiago, 5 July 1981). Composer. Studied humanities at the Instituto nacional, Santiago, and law at the Univ. of Chile; received musical instruction from Allende and Santa Cruz, and was active with Santa Cruz's Bach Society. Studied with Boulanger, Koechlin, and Dukas in Paris and with Hindemith and Meresmann in Berlin, 1928–31; returning to Chile, became professor at the National Conservatory; also served as a dean at the Univ. of Chile. Contributed many articles on folk topics to the *Revista musical chilena,* and collaborated on a history of music in Chile; his own music shows both Chilean and European features. Works include the ballet *La guitarra del diablo* (1942); *Música para un cuento de antaño,* orchestra (1948); a piano concerto (1950); chamber music, including a piano trio (1933) and a string quartet (1944); choral music; and songs.

Bibl.: *Composers of the Americas* 14 (Washington, D.C., 1968), pp. 160–67 [includes works list]. Mario Silva Solís, "Catálogo de la obra musical de Jorge Urrutia Blondel," *Revista musical chilena* 158 (1982): 11–46.

Ursuleac, Viorica (b. Czernowitz [now Chernovtsy, Romania], 26 Mar. 1894; d. Ehrwald, Austria, 23 Oct. 1985). Soprano. Studied in Vienna; made her debut at Agram in 1922. Sang at Czernowitz (1923–24), the Vienna Volksoper (1924–26), the Frankfurt Opera (1926–30), Vienna (1930–35), and the Munich Opera

(1937–44). Married the conductor Clemens Krauss, and under his direction sang in the premieres of Strauss's *Arabella* (1933), *Friedenstag* (1938), and *Capriccio* (1942). Appeared at the Salzburg Festival and at Covent Garden.

Usandizaga, José María (b. San Sebastián, 31 Mar. 1887; d. there, 5 Oct. 1915). Composer. After initial study in his home city, on the recommendation of Planté he enrolled at the Schola cantorum, Paris, in 1901; there he studied with D'Indy, Grovlez, Trícon, and Séré. Returning to Spain in 1906, he produced music in many genres, generally with a strong Basque nationalist profile. His greatest successes were in opera, with *Mendi mendigan* (1910), *Las golondrinas* (1914), and *La llama* (1915, completed by his brother Ramón). His early death from tuberculosis was mourned throughout Spain. Other works include orchestra and band music, of which there are works from his student tenure in Paris (the tone poem *Dans la mer,* 1904) as well as later Basque pieces (*Irurak bak* and *Bidasoa,* both ca. 1906); chamber music; and sacred and secular vocal pieces.

Usmanbaş, Ilhan (b. Istanbul, 28 Sept. 1921). Composer. He studied cello with Rey at the Istanbul Municipal Conservatory in 1941; went on to study composition with Alnar and piano with Erkin at the Ankara State Conservatory through 1948, at which point he began teaching there. He traveled to the U.S. in 1982 to study with Dallapiccola and again in 1958 for a series of concerts of his own music. In 1963 he returned to the Ankara State Conservatory. His own compositions moved from modernist trends such as neoclassicism and nonfunctional tonality to serialism and aleatory. Works include *On Three Paintings of Salvador Dalí* (strings, 1953), *Un coup de dès* (chorus, orchestra, 1959), *Open Forums* (different groups, 1968), *Little Night Music* (orchestra, 1972), and *Senilikname* (voice, percussion, harp, female chorus, 1970).

Uspensky, Viktor Alexandrovich (b. Kaluga, 31 Aug. 1879; d. Tashkent, 9 Oct. 1949). Composer and ethnomusicologist. He studied composition with Lyadov as well as the harp at the St. Petersburg Conservatory (1908–13); in 1918 he cofounded the Tashkent Conservatory and taught there; also taught at the Uzbek Music Technical School. In the 1920s he conducted ethnomusical research in Turkmenistan and Uzbekistan, publishing with Belyayev in 1928 a study of Turkmenian music. Compositions include *Farkhad i Shirin,* a music drama of 1936 revised as an opera in 1940; it is considered the first national Uzbek dramatic work with actual folk tunes.

Usper [Sponga, Spongia, Sponza], **Francesco** (b. Parenzo, Istria, before 1570; d. Venice, early 1641). Composer. He studied in Venice with Andrea Gabrieli before 1586. From 1596 until his death he served the confraternity of S. Giovanni Evangelista in various capacities. By 1614 he was organist at the Church of S. Salvatore. Later he collaborated with Giovanni Battista Grillo and Monteverdi on a Requiem Mass (lost) for the Medici Grand Duke Cosimo II, performed at SS. Giovanni e Paolo in May 1621. In 1622 and 1623 he was a substitute organist at St. Mark's. Usper's vocal compositions include motets, Psalms, and madrigals; his instrumental music includes some of the earliest Venetian ensemble canzonas as well as sinfonias, capriccios, and a sonata.

Ussachevsky, Vladimir (b. Hailar, Manchuria, 3 Nov. 1911; d. New York, 2 Jan. 1990). Composer. Growing up in a Russian family resident in China, he learned piano from his mother and sang at the Russian church. Moved with his family to the U.S. in 1930 and studied piano with Clarence Mader in Los Angeles. He attended Pomona College (B.A., 1935), then studied at the Eastman School of Music, where his teachers were Bernard Rogers and Howard Hanson (M.M., 1936; Ph.D., 1939). After wartime service in the O.S.S., he was appointed lecturer at Columbia Univ. Up to this point his compositions had been in a neo-Romantic style, influenced by the music of the Russian Orthodox church and by his studies with Hanson. In 1951, with Otto Luening, he began to explore compositional possibilities of tape-recording the sounds of traditional instruments, then altering these by means of filtering, reverb, overdubbing, and mixing, unaware of the parallel experiments of Pierre Schaeffer's *musique concrète* group in Paris. Ussachevsky completed 2 compositions for tape alone: *Transposition, Reverberation, Composition* (1951) and *Underwater Valse* (1951). On 28 October 1952, his *Sonic Contours* was performed at the Museum of Modern Art in New York—the first public performance of electronic music in the U.S. Ussachevsky and Luening also explored the possibilities of combining electronic music on tape with live performance by traditional instruments. Their first work in this genre was *Rhapsodic Variations* for orchestra and tape, commissioned by the Louisville Orchestra and premiered in March 1954. It was followed by *A Poem of Cycles and Bells,* introduced by the Los Angeles Philharmonic in November 1954.

Ussachevsky also combined instrument-derived sounds with environmental sounds and purely electronic sounds, as in *A Piece for Tape Recorder* (1955) and *Studies in Sound Plus* (1958), and he experimented with vocal sounds in *Creation Prologue,* 4 choruses and tape (1961), and other works. His best-known pieces, however, rely on traditional instruments to provide the initial sonic material, for example, *Of Wood and Brass,* tape (1965). In 1959 Ussachevsky, Luening, Milton Babbitt, and Roger Sessions founded the Columbia–Princeton Electronic Music Center in New York. During the late 1960s and 1970s he began to work with computers to generate and combine sounds, as in *Computer Piece no. 1* (1968) and *Conflict* (1971; rev. 1975). He also composed a few pieces for traditional instruments played in traditional ways and for voices, for example, *Missa brevis* (soprano, chorus, brass, 1972); *Triskelion* (oboe and piano, 1982). In 1980 Ussachevsky retired from Columbia, but he continued to teach at the Univ. of Utah.

Ustvolskaia, Galina Ivanovna (b. Petrograd, 17 July 1919). Composer. Studied composition with Shostakovich at the Leningrad Conservatory from 1939 to 1947 with a break during the war. Taught composition at the Leningrad Conservatory preparatory school; her students included Boris Tishchenko. Remained indifferent to contemporary trends and embraced an uncompromising style of obsessive rhythms and expressive contrapuntal dissonance. Works include 5 symphonies (1955, 1979, 1983, 1985–87, 1989–90); a piano concerto (1946); works for instrumental ensemble (Trio, clarinet, violin, and piano, 1949; Octet, 2 oboes, 4 violins, piano, and timpani, 1949–50; Composition no. 1, *Dona nobis pacem,* piccolo, tuba, and piano, 1970–71; Composition no. 2, *Dies irae,* 8 double basses, percussion, and piano, 1972–73; Composition no. 3, *Benedictus qui venit,* 4 flutes, 4 bassoons, and piano, 1974–75); 6 piano sonatas.

Uttini, Francesco Antonio Baldassare (b. Bologna, 1723; d. Stockholm, 25 Oct. 1795). Composer. He studied with Padre Martini and became a member of the Accademia dei filarmonici in Bologna in 1743. In 1752 or 1753 he became the conductor for an Italian traveling opera company for which he wrote his operas *L'olimpiade* and *Zenobia,* both of which were first performed in Copenhagen. With members of his troupe he went to Stockholm in 1755, where he was made Master of the King's Music in 1767. He composed mainly operas; his *Thetis och Pelée* (Stockholm, 1773) was the first large-scale opera set in Swedish. *Aline* (Stockholm, 1776) was also set in Swedish, and he wrote other operas with French and Italian texts. In addition, he composed cantatas, 2 oratorios, 3 symphonies, 6 harpsichord sonatas, arias, trio sonatas.

Bibl.: Einar Sundström, "Francesco Antonio Uttini som musikdramatiker," *STMf* 45 (1963): 33–93.

V

Vaccai, Nicola (b. Tolentino, 15 Mar. 1790; d. Pesaro, 5 Aug. 1848). Composer. Wrote poetry as a youth. Went to Rome (1807) to study law; began counterpoint lessons with Giuseppe Janacconi. Studied at Accademia di S. Cecilia until 1811; studied with Paisiello in Naples. Composed the first of his 17 operas, *I solitari di Scozia* (1815), for the Teatro nuovo, Naples. Less successful in Venice with his next series of operas. Taught singing in Trieste (1821). Moved to Parma in 1823; had some success with operas. Biggest success was *Giulietta e Romeo* (1825). Taught in Paris in 1830, then in England to 1833. Wrote *Metodo pratico di canto italiano per camera* (1832), still in use. Returned to Italy, 1833; taught at Milan Conservatory from 1838. Also composed 5 cantatas, ballets, 1 Mass, other Mass movements, sacred music, arias, songs.

Bibl.: Giulio Vaccai, *La vita di Nicola Vaccai scritta dal figlio Giulio* (Bologna, 1882).

Vaet, Jacobus (b. Courtrai or Harelbeke, ca. 1529; d. Vienna, Jan. 8, 1567). Composer. He was a chorister at Notre Dame in Courtrai from 1543, a student at Louvain Univ. from 1547, and a singer in the imperial chapel of Charles V from 1550. From at least 1554 until his death he was Kapellmeister to Archduke Maximilian of Austria (later Emperor Maximilian II). His works include 9 or 10 Masses; 2 volumes of motets (*Modulationes,* Venice, 1562), and several independent motets; Magnificats, Salve Reginas, and hymns; and a few chansons. His style shows the influence of Josquin and Gombert. He was widely anthologized in print in the 1560s.

Bibl.: Milton Steinhardt, *Jacobus Vaet and His Motets* (East Lansing, Mich., 1951).

Vainberg [Weinberg], **Moisei** [Mieczyslaw] **Samuilovich** (b. Warsaw, 8 Dec. 1919). Composer. Studied piano with Turczyn'ski at the Warsaw Conservatory, 1931–39, composition with V. Zolotarev at the Minsk Conservatory, 1939–41. Lived in Tashkent, 1941–43; in Moscow beginning in 1943. Works include 7 operas (including *Madonna and the Soldier,* 1970; *The Idiot,* 1986); ballets and operettas; 19 symphonies, instrumental concertos, and other symphonic music; 16 string quartets and other chamber music; piano music; vocal music; incidental and film music.

Valcárcel, Edgar (b. Puno, Peru, 4 Dec. 1932). Composer. Nephew of Teodoro Valcárcel. Studied at the Lima Conservatory (with Sas), Hunter College in New York (with Lybbert), the Di Tella Institute in Buenos Aires (with Ginastera, Messiaen, Malipiero, and others), and the Columbia–Princeton Electronic Music Center (with Ussachevsky). Named to the faculty at the Lima Conservatory in 1965; also appeared as a pianist. Works include *Sinfonietta* (1954), *Aleaciones* (1966), Piano Concerto (1968), *Checán II* (1970), and *Sajra* (1974) for orchestra; chamber music for various ensembles (3 *Espectros,* 1964, 1966, and 1974; *Hiwaña uru,* 1967); 2 string quartets (1960, 1963), *Fissions* (1967); works mixing electronic and acoustic media (*Antaras,* 1968); piano pieces (including 2 sonatas, 1963, 1971); and vocal music.

Valcárcel, Teodoro (b. Puno, Peru, 17 Oct. 1900; d. Lima, 20 Mar. 1942). Composer. Uncle of Edgar Valcárcel. Studied in Milan and with Pedrell in Barcelona, 1914–16; returned to Peru, serving as a cultural official; visited Europe again in 1929 as the Peruvian delegate to the Barcelona Ibero-American Music Festival, traveling back to Peru in 1931. His music has a strong nationalist cast, with emphasis on Andean models. Upon his death he left many pieces unfinished; Rodolfo Holzmann orchestrated them, and also compiled a catalog of Valcárcel's compositions. Works include 2 *Suites sinfónicas* (1939), *En las ruinas del Templo del Sol* (1940), and *Concierto indio* (with violin, 1940) for orchestra; *IV canciones incaicas* (1930) and *XXX Cantos de Alma Vernacular,* voice and piano; piano works such as *Fiestas andantinas* (1933); and 3 *ensayos* for indigenous instruments. He also collected many Indian songs.

Valderrábano, Enríquez de (b. Peñaranda de Duero, ca. 1500; d. after 1557). Vihuelist and composer. He served Francisco de Zúñiga, fourth Count of Miranda. He published a 7-volume tabulature for vihuela, *Silva de Sirenas* (Valladolid, 1547; ed. in *MME* 22–23, 1965), containing transcriptions of sacred and secular works of Josquin, Morales, Gombert, Willaert, and others for 1 or 2 vihuelas and voice; fantasias (some original), *sonetos,* and pavans.

Valen, (Olav) Fartein (b. Stavanger, Norway, 25 Aug. 1887; d. Haugesund, 14 Dec. 1952). Composer. As a youth he studied piano and taught himself the rudiments of theory. He studied with Catharinus Elling in Oslo (1906–9), then went to Berlin, where he studied with Max Bruch and Karl Leopold Wolf at the Hochschule (1909–11), remaining for several years thereafter on his own. During this period he published a *Legende* for piano (1909), a Piano Sonata (1912), and a Violin Sonata (1916), all works in the late Romantic tradition. Returning to Norway in 1916, he worked at compositional and contrapuntal exercises but completed few pieces, notably an *Ave Maria,* soprano and orchestra (1921), and a Piano Trio (1924), which uses twelve-note melodies without adopting Schoenberg's twelve-tone principles. Moving to Oslo in 1924, he increased his productivity considerably, completing 2 string quartets (1929, 1931) and several songs including "Mignon," soprano and orchestra (1927), "Drei Gedichte von Goethe," soprano and piano (1927), and "Darest Thou Now o Soul," soprano and orchestra (1928). By the 1930s he had arrived at a novel individual style—atonal but rigorously contrapuntal—which is exemplified in a series of orchestral works: *Nenia* (1932), *Le cimetière marin* (1934), Symphony no. 1 (1939), Violin Concerto (1940), Symphonies nos. 2–5 (1944, 1946, 1949, 1951). Also in the 1930s his music was more favorably received in Norway, beginning with the performance in 1934 of his *Ave Maria* in Oslo. In 1938 he moved out of Oslo to Valevåg, where he lived and composed in relative isolation.

Bibl.: Bjarne Kortsen, *Fartein Valen: Life and Music,* 3 vols. (Oslo, 1965).

Valencia, Antonio Mariá (b. Cali, Colombia, 10 Nov. 1902; d. there, 22 July 1952). Composer. Studied piano with Alarcón at the Bogotá Conservatory (1917–19) and with d'Indy, Falla, and others at the Schola cantorum in Paris (1923–29). Returning to America, he founded the Cali Conservatory in 1933, serving as director until his death; he also spent a short period as director of the Bogotá Conservatory in 1937–38. His output consists of 39 compositions completed between 1925 and 1952, generally cast in a nationalist idiom. Works include *Chirimía y bambuco sotareño* for orchestra (1942), a violin sonata (1926), the wind quartet *Egloga incaica* (1935), and the trio *Emociones caucanas* (1938); sacred and secular choral works, including a Requiem Mass (1943); piano pieces; and songs.

Bibl.: *Composers of the Americas* 4 (Washington, D.C., 1958), pp. 105–10 [includes works list].

Valens, Ritchie [Valenzuela, Richard] (b. Pacoima, Calif., 13 May 1942; d. Mason City, Iowa, 3 Feb. 1959). Rock-and-roll singer, songwriter, and guitarist. He made his first records in 1958, and with the success of "Come On, Let's Go" (1958) and "Donna" (1959) became the first Mexican-American rock-and-roll star; he died in a plane crash. In 1987 he was the subject of a biographical film, *La Bamba.*

Valente, Antonio (fl. 1565–80). Organist and composer. Blind from early childhood, he was organist at S. Angelo a Nido (or Nilo) in Naples, 1565–80. He published an early harpsichord miscellany, *Intavolatura de cimbalo* (Naples, 1576, in Spanish tabulature), and a set of free organ versets, *Versi spirituali* (Naples, 1580, in open score).

Valente, Benita (b. Delano, Calif., 19 Oct. 1934). Soprano. She studied with Lotte Lehmann at the Music Academy of the West and later with Martial Singher at the Curtis Institute, from which she graduated in 1960. That same year she sang in the Marlboro Festival, where with Rudolf Serkin and Harold Wright she recorded Schubert's *Der Hirt auf dem Felsen.* She appeared with the Freiburg Opera, making her debut in 1962, and at Nuremberg. She sang the role of Pamina from *Die Zauberflöte* in her Metropolitan Opera debut in 1973; her other operatic roles include Nannetta, Liù, and Violetta. Also made frequent appearances as a concert artist and gave many lieder recitals.

Valenti, Fernando (b. New York, 4 Dec. 1926; d. Red Bank, N.J., 6 Sept. 1990). Harpsichordist. He studied with Ralph Kirkpatrick at Yale. Undertook a tour of South America in 1946; made his New York and European recital debuts in 1950. The following year Juilliard appointed him the school's first professor of harpsichord; also taught at Baylor, the Cleveland Institute, San Jose State, and Yale. Best known for his interpretations of Domenico Scarlatti; he is the author of *A Performer's Guide to the Keyboard Partitas of J. S. Bach* (New Haven, 1989).

Valentini [Valentino], **Pier** [Pietro] **Francesco** [Pierfrancesco] (b. Rome, ca. 1570; d. there, 1654). Composer and theorist. He was from a noble family. Although he studied with G. B. Nanino, he remained an amateur. His skill as a contrapuntist and theorist was recognized in his time. Among his extant compositions are a Mass, motets, Psalms, madrigals, canzonettas, arias, and many canons (*Canone nel modo Salomonis* for 96 to as many as 144,000 voices). His theoretical works deal with topics such as modal theory *(Duplitonio),* temperament, counterpoint, rhythm, and the beat (*Trattato della battuta musicale,* 1643).

Bibl.: Ludvík Kunz, *Die Tonartenlehre des römischen Theoretikers und Komponisten Pier Francesco Valentini* (Kassel, 1937). Mariella Casini Cortesi, "Pier Francesco Valentini: Profilo di un musicista barocco," *NRMI* 17 (1983): 529–62.

Valenzuela, Pedro [Valenzola, Pietro] (fl. 1569–79). Composer. He served briefly as a salaried maestro of the Accademia filarmonica of Verona in 1569. In 1577–78 he sang at St. Mark's in Venice; there he published *Madrigali, libro primo* (1578) on texts of Petrarch, Ariosto, Parabosco, and others. In 1579 he was a singer at the church of the Annunziata in Naples.

Vallee [Vallée], **Rudy** [Hubert Prior] (b. Island Pond, Vt., 28 July 1901; d. Hollywood Hills, Calif., 3 July 1986). Popular bandleader, singer, saxophonist, publisher. He played in bands while attending the Univ. of Maine and Yale, and many of his later recordings were of college songs. From 1928 he led his own band, The Connecticut Yankees; in 1929 he appeared in the first of several films *(The Vagabond Lover);* from the 1930s he ran Vallee Publications and later Ruval Music. His recordings included "Stein Song" (1930), "Brother, Can You Spare a Dime" (1932), and "As Time Goes By" (1943).

Bibl.: Larry F. Kiner, *The Rudy Vallée Discography* (Westport, Conn., 1985).

Valli [Valley], **Frankie** [Castellucio, Frankie] (b. Newark, N.J., 3 May 1937). Rock-and-roll singer. From 1956 he led the group that became known as The Four Seasons; their hits included "Sherry" (1962) and "Rag Doll" (1964); he recorded with them into the 1970s. From 1966 he made solo recordings as well, achieving success with "Can't Take My Eyes off You" (1967) and the title song to the movie *Grease* (1978).

Vallotti, Francesco Antonio (b. Vercelli, Piedmont, 11 June 1697; d. Padua, 10 Jan. 1780). Composer and theorist. He studied with G. A. Bissone, *maestro di cappella* at St. Eusebius, Vercelli, and joined the Franciscan order in 1716; he was ordained a priest in 1720. After further study he became third organist at S. Antonio in 1722; he became maestro in 1730, and retained the position for 50 years. There he was in charge of a choir and an orchestra with Tartini as leader. Vallotti's major theoretical work is the 4-volume *Della scienza teorica e pratica.* He wrote sacred vocal and instrumental compositions.

Bibl.: *Francescantonio Vallotti: Biografia, catalogo tematico della opere e contributi critici,* ed. Giulio Cattin (Padua, 1981). M. Lindley, "La 'Pratica ben regolata' di Francesco Antonio Vallotti," *RIM* 16 (1981): 45–95.

Valls, Francisco (b. Barcelona, 1665; d. there, 2 Feb. 1747). Composer. He became *maestro de capilla* at Mataró parish church before 1688, and acquired positions at Gerona Cathedral (1688) and S. María del Mar, Barcelona (1696). On 22 December 1696 he became assistant to the *maestro de capilla* at Barcelona Cathedral; he became maestro on 18 February 1709, and retired in 1740. His compositions include 12 Masses, 22 responsaries, 16 Magnificats, 12 Psalms, 2 Misereres, about 35 motets, and about 120 *villancicos.*

Bibl.: Antonio Martín Moreno, "Algunos aspectos del barroco musical español a través de la obra teórica de Francisco Valls (1665?–1747)," *AnM* 31–32 (1976–77): 157–94. Lothar Siemens Hernández, "Contribución a la bibliografía de las fuentes de la cuestión Valls," *AnM* 31–32 (1976–77): 195–224.

Valverde, Joaquín (b. Badajoz, 27 Feb. 1846; d. Madrid, 17 Mar. 1910). Composer. Studied at Madrid Conservatory, receiving first prize for flute (1867) and composition (1870). Wrote first symphony, *Batylo,* 1871. Conducted in various Madrid theaters (1871–91). He composed some 30 zarzuelas, instrumental works, songs. Wrote *La flauta: Su historia, su estudio* (Madrid, 1886). His most successful work was the operetta *La gran via* (Madrid, 1886), which was performed in many Spanish-speaking countries through North and South America, and in England as *Castles in Spain* (1906). His son Quinito [Joaquín] Valverde Sanjuán (1875–1918) was also a composer.

Bibl.: Matilde Muñoz, *Historia de la zarzuela española y del género chico* (Madrid, 1946).

Van Beinum, Eduard (b. Arnheim, 3 Sept. 1900; d. Amsterdam, 13 Apr. 1959). Conductor. He received instruction in viola, piano, and composition. In 1927 he was named conductor of the Haarlem orchestra, and in 1931 was appointed second conductor of the Concertgebouw Orchestra, of which he became conductor in 1945. He also appeared as guest conductor with the London Symphony, the Leningrad Philharmonic, and the Philadelphia Orchestra. In 1956 he was named musical director of the Los Angeles Philharmonic, though he retained his post with the Concertgebouw and returned to Amsterdam in 1959.

Bibl.: Wouter Paap, *Eduard van Beinum: 25 Years Conductor of the Concertgebouw Orchestra* (Amsterdam, 1956).

Vancea, Zeno (Octavian) (b. Bocşa-Vasiova, 21 Oct. 1900). Composer. He studied at the Cluj Conservatory of Music under Dima from 1919 to 1921 and at the Vienna Conservatory with Kanitz, 1921–26 and 1930–31. Vancea taught at and subsequently directed the Tîrgu-Mureş Conservatory, then taught successively at the Timişoara Conservatory (1940–1945) and the Bucharest Conservatory (1949–73). He was active with the Romanian Composers' Union and served as editor of the music journal *Muzica* from 1953 until 1964. His compositions evince the early 20th-century trends of neoclassic forms and textures and the incorporation of folk music elements. Works include 1 ballet (*Priculiciul* [Werewolf], 1935; rev. 1957); orchestral music (Concerto, string orchestra, 1961); and vocal and chamber music, as well as music for film and theater.

Van Hagen. See Hagen, von.

Vanhal [Wanhal], **Johann Baptist** [Jan Křtitel Vaňhal; Jan Ignatius] (b. Nové Nechanice, Bohemia, 12 May 1739; d. Vienna, 20 Aug. 1813). Composer. After early musical study in Bohemia he went with Countess Schaffgotsch in about 1761 to Vienna, where he studied with Dittersdorf. From 1769 to 1771 he traveled in Italy. He never held any formal appointments but supported himself with composing and teaching; Pleyel was one of his students. He was a prolific composer, though problems of attribution prevent an accurate count of his compositions. He wrote 2 operas (lost) and about 60 Masses. There are over 70 authentic symphonies, numerous concertos, orchestral pieces, many string quartets and trios, keyboard quartets and trios, duos, keyboard sonatas, programmatic works, variations, divertimentos, fantasias; songs.

Bibl.: Paul R. Bryan, "The Symphonies of Johann Vanhal" (diss., Univ. of Michigan, 1955). Paul Bryan, ed., *Five Symphonies: Jan Kritel Vanhal,* ser. B, vol. 10 of *The Symphony, 1720–1840,* ed. Barry S. Brook et al. (New York, 1983). Alexander Weinmann, *Themen Verzeichnis der Kompositionen von Johann Baptist Wanhal* (Vienna, 1987).

Van Halen, Eddie (b. Amsterdam, 26 Jan. 1957). Rock guitarist and songwriter. His family moved to California in 1968, where he formed the band Van Halen with brother Alex (b. 1955) and singer David

Lee Roth (b. 1955). The albums *Diver Down* (1982) and *1984 (MCMLXXXIV)* (1984, including "Jump") were among the first heavy-metal recordings to achieve success with popular audiences. After 1984 Sammy Hagar replaced Roth.

Van Heusen, Jimmy [James; Babcock, Edward Chester] (b. Syracuse, 26 Jan. 1913; d. Rancho Mirage, Calif., 6 Feb. 1990). Popular pianist and songwriter, publisher. Wrote for Cotton Club revues and was a pianist and song plugger in New York; composed musicals and songs for films, primarily with lyricists Johnny Burke ("Swingin' on a Star," in *Going My Way,* 1944, and many other Bing Crosby films) and Sammy Cahn ("High Hopes," in *A Hole in the Head,* 1959); won several Oscars.

Van Lier, Bertus (b. Utrecht, 10 Sept. 1906; d. Groningen, 14 Feb. 1972). Composer. He studied at the Amsterdam Conservatory, taking cello lessons with de Castro and composition with Pijper; studied conducting with Scherchen in Strasbourg in 1933. Returning to Utrecht he worked as a composer with the Groningen student orchestra and as a music critic. During the early 1960s he studied music history at Groningen Univ. His own compositions drew on traditional forms and were heavily influenced by Pijper's concepts of motivic "germ cell" processes. Works include orchestral music (*Antigone,* incidental music, 1952; *Concertante muziek,* oboe, violin, orchestra, 1959), vocal music (*Het Hooglied* [Song of Songs], vocal soloists, chorus, orchestra, 1949), and chamber music.

Van Rooy, Anton(ius Maria Josephus) (b. Rotterdam, 1 Jan. 1870; d. Munich, 28 Nov. 1932). Bass-baritone. Studied voice with Julius Stockhausen in Frankfurt. In 1897 was hired to sing at Bayreuth, where he sang Wotan every year until 1902 (and also the Dutchman, 1901–2). From 1898 to 1913 he appeared at Covent Garden, where he performed leading Wagnerian roles; in 1898 he made his Metropolitan Opera debut as Wotan. He occasionally performed other types of roles, including Escamillo and Don Fernando *(Fidelio),* and he sang the role of John the Baptist in the American premiere of *Salome* (1907). In 1908 he joined the Frankfurt opera, where he remained until his retirement in 1913.

Van Vactor, David (b. Plymouth, Ind., 8 May 1906; d. Los Angeles, 24 Mar. 1994). Composer, conductor, flutist. He studied flute and composition at Northwestern Univ. (B.A., 1928), then in Europe. He joined the Chicago Symphony as a flutist in 1931. His compositions of the 1930s, in a conservative style, were promptly performed and favorably received—e.g., Concerto, 3 flutes, harp, and orchestra (1935), Symphony no. 1 (1937), Symphony no. 2 (1943). In 1943 he moved to the Kansas City Philharmonic as flutist and assistant conductor. In 1947 he became conductor of the Knoxville Symphony Orchestra and professor of music at the Univ. of Tennessee, where he taught until 1976. His later works include 3 more symphonies (1959, 1971, 1975); *Economy Band no. 1* (trumpet, trombone, and percussion, 1966); *Economy Band no. 2* (horn, tuba, and percussion, 1969).

Van Vleck, Jacob (b. New York, 1751; d. Bethlehem, Pa., 3 July 1831). Composer. A Moravian clergyman, he was appointed director of the Seminary for Young Ladies in Bethlehem in 1790. He assumed a similar post at the Nazareth Hall Academy in 1800, then succeeded Johannes Herbst as bishop of Salem in 1812 after the latter's death. Van Vleck's works include Moravian hymns and liturgies.

Van Zant, Ronnie (b. Jacksonville, Fla., 1949; d. near McComb, Miss., 20 Oct. 1977). Rock singer and songwriter. In 1966 he formed the band Lynyrd Skynyrd with guitarists Gary Rossington and Allen Collins; by the mid-1970s they were the best-known southern rock group, led by Van Zant's blues-influenced vocal style; particularly popular were their songs "Sweet Home Alabama" and "Free Bird" (both 1974). The group dissolved after a 1977 plane crash killed Van Zant and several other band members.

Varèse, Edgard (Victor Achille Charles) (b. Paris, 22 Dec. 1883; d. New York, 6 Nov. 1965). Composer. He was forbidden to study music by his father, who wanted him to become an engineer. As a teenager he paid out of his own pocket for clandestine lessons in harmony and counterpoint with Giovanni Bolzoni, director of the conservatory in Turin, where the Varèse family then lived. In 1903 he broke irrevocably with his father and moved to Paris. Through the good offices of the pianist Alfred Cortot, his cousin, he was admitted to the Schola cantorum, where he studied with Albert Roussel (composition), Vincent d'Indy (conducting), and Charles Bordes (early music). In 1905 he transferred to the Conservatory and studied composition with Charles-Marie Widor. Feeling stifled by what he saw as the rigid Conservatory instruction and the narrow musical life of Paris, he departed in 1907 for Berlin, where his talent, energy, and commitment to musical change earned him the friendship of Ferruccio Busoni, Richard Strauss, and Hugo von Hofmannsthal. He worked as a copyist, conducted a choir, and composed a good deal, though none of his music from this period survives. His symphonic rhapsody *Bourgogne* (1907) was performed in Berlin in 1910 and provoked a scandal on account of its uncompromising dissonance. A projected European tour as a conductor was interrupted after one concert in 1914 by the First World War. Varèse returned to Paris, served for six months in the army, became ill with pneumonia, and was discharged in 1915.

In December 1915 Varèse departed for the U.S., intending, it seems, to stay for the duration of war; he remained, becoming an American citizen in 1926. He conducted a New York performance of the Berlioz Requiem in 1917, then concerts of modern music in Cincinnati (1918) and New York (1919). In 1921, together with harpist Carlos Salzedo, he founded the International Composers' Guild, an organization for the performance of modern music.

The first piece by Varèse to be heard in the U.S. was *Offrandes,* soprano and chamber ensemble (1921). An atonal setting of surrealist poems, it was performed at an I.C.G. concert in New York in April 1922 and aroused limited but favorable comment. In the same year he finished *Amériques* (1921), an ebullient, somewhat diffuse work exploring the timbral possibilities of an orchestra with a percussion section of 21 instruments including a siren. It was not heard until 1926, when Leopold Stokowski introduced it in Philadelphia and New York. In the meantime Varèse composed and premiered three new works in which his aesthetic and his compositional technique were distilled and embodied. *Hyperprism* (1923) employs an ensemble of 9 winds and 16 percussion instruments. The wind instruments are used not melodically but to establish and prolong areas of pitch, register, and timbre. The result is very far from what American audiences of the time defined as "music," and the work's premiere in March 1923 provoked a vigorous reaction from the audience and the press, adding to Varèse's notoriety and leading to several more performances of the piece. *Octandre,* 7 winds and double bass (1923; first perf., Jan. 1924), and *Intégrales,* winds and percussion (1925; first perf., Mar. 1925), were similar in style to *Hyperprism* and evoked a similar response. Varèse's last work of this period was *Arcana* (1927), a work for large orchestra. Although its thematic and formal procedures are more traditional than those of the preceding works, it was received at its premiere (1927) with hostility.

In 1928 Varèse returned to Paris for a visit which lasted until 1933. He introduced his new works and worked on several projects, of which only two were realized: *Ionisation* (percussion ensemble, 1931) and *Ecuatorial* (bass voice, brass, percussion, and 2 theremins, 1934; rev. 1961). In *Ionisation* 41 percussion instruments, including 2 anvils, bongos, sleigh bells, lions' roar, and 2 sirens, are played by 13 performers. As in his previous works, Varèse uses percussion not to establish periodic patterns or a "beat" but rather to develop timbres, textures, and masses of sound. He became increasingly interested in the possibilities for electronic generation of sounds, working with the inventor Léon Thérémin. Returning to the U.S. in 1933, Varèse hoped to raise interest and money for research into electronic music. Disappointed in this endeavor and frustrated by the nationalism and conservatism of the American new-music scene in the 1930s, he composed very little. Between 1933 and 1954 his only works were *Densité 21.5,* solo flute (1936), and *Étude pour espace,* chorus, percussion, and 2 pianos (1947), both somewhat uncharacteristic works.

With the advent and availability of the tape recorder in the 1950s, Varèse broke out of his creative silence. *Déserts* (1954) is scored for wind instruments, percussion, and a prerecorded 2-channel tape. Electronic and acoustical sounds do not overlap but are arranged in four instrumental segments separated by three taped interpolations. The taped passages were created by the methods of *musique concrète*—recording natural and man-made sounds, then altering, combining, and arranging them on tape. (Varèse revised the tapes several times during the 1960s as new technology became available.) *Déserts* was introduced in Paris in 1954. As with the premiere of *Hyperprism* 30 years earlier, there was a near-riot in the theater, but *Déserts* was soon acknowledged as a masterpiece of electronic music. In 1958, for the Le Corbusier–designed Philips Pavilion at the Brussels World's Fair, Varèse composed *Le poème électronique* for 3-track tape. *Nocturnal,* soprano, bass chorus, and chamber orchestra, remained unfinished at the time of his death and was completed by his student Chou Wen-chung.

Other works include *Un grand sommeil noir* (voice and piano, 1906); *Le prélude à la fin d'un jour* (orchestra, ca. 1905, lost); *Oedipus und die Sphinx* (opera, unfinished, lost); *Dance for Burgess* (chamber orchestra, 1949); *La procession de Vergès* (tape, 1955).

Bibl.: Fernand Ouellette, *Edgard Varèse* (Paris, 1966); trans. Eng. (New York, 1968). Edgard Varèse, "The Liberation of Sound," in *Contemporary Composers on Contemporary Music,* ed. Elliott Schwartz and Barney Childs (New York, 1967). Georges Charbonnier, *Entretiens avec Edgard Varèse* (Paris, 1970). *Perspectives on American Composers,* ed. B. Boretz and E. T. Cone (New York, 1971), pp. 25–58 [articles by Varèse, Babbitt, Chou]. Louise Varèse, *Varèse: A Looking-Glass Diary,* vol. 1, *1883–1928* (New York, 1972). *The New Worlds of Edgard Varèse: A Symposium,* ed. S. van Solkema (New York, 1979). James Siddons, Jeffrey Kresky, and Marion Guck, "Varèse Forum," *PNM* 23/1 (1984): 296–347. Jonathan Bernard, *The Music of Edgard Varèse* (New Haven, 1987). Helga de la Motte-Haber, ed., *Edgard Varèse, die Befreiung des Klangs: Symposium Edgard Varèse Hamburg 1991* (Hofheim, 1992).

Varlamov, Alexander Egorovich (b. Moscow, 27 Nov. 1801; d. St. Petersburg, 27 Oct. 1848). Composer. Joined the court choir at St. Petersburg (1811) and studied with the director Bortniansky. He moved to the adult choir in 1817; left in 1818. Named director of choir in Russian ambassadorial chapel at The Hague, 1819. He returned to St. Petersburg in 1823; taught singing to 1826. Kapellmeister for the imperial theaters in Moscow, 1832–43. Composed, taught privately in St. Petersburg, 1845–48. Wrote incidental music, ballets, piano music, songs. Complete works were published in St. Petersburg as *Polnoye sobraniye sochineniy* (1861–64).

Varnay, Astrid (Ibolyka Maria) (b. Stockholm, 25 Apr. 1918). Soprano. She studied with her mother, Maria Yavor, and with Paul Althouse and the conductor Hermann Weigert, whom she later married. In 1941, substituting for the ailing Lotte Lehmann, she made her Metropolitan Opera debut as Sieglinde, and performed Brünnhilde less than a week later. She remained at the Met until 1956, singing the Wagnerian soprano roles as well as Venus, Kundry, Elektra, Salome, and Amelia *(Boccanegra).* She also appeared at Bayreuth (1951–67), where her roles included Isolde, Ortrud, Senta, and Brünnhilde. Performed at most of the leading houses; returned to the Met in 1974 in mezzo roles, including Strauss's Herodias and Clytemnestra, and Begbick *(Mahagonny).* She was one of the most compelling Wagnerian sopranos of her generation.

Varvoglis, Mario (b. Brussels, 22 Dec. 1885; d. Athens, 30 July 1967). Composer. He originally studied art at the Athens School of Fine Arts, then went to Paris to study law. There he began the pursuit of music; he attended the Paris Conservatory, where he took lessons with Leroux, and the Schola cantorum, where he studied under d'Indy and Bourgault-Ducouday. Varvoglis returned to Greece and taught at the Athens Conservatory of Music from 1920 until 1924 and then at the Hellenic Conservatory. He was also active as a music critic. His compositions reflect his conservative French training in their use of forms and orchestration; they occasionally incorporate aspects of Greek melodic scales. Works include dramatic music (*Tő apóyema tís agápis* [The Afternoon of Love], 1935), orchestral music, vocal music (*Ta sýnnefa* [The Clouds], 1940), and chamber music (*Meditation of Areti,* string quartet, 1929).

Vasilenko, Sergei (Nikiforovich) (b. Moscow, 30 Mar. 1872; d. there, 11 Mar. 1956). Composer. He studied law at Moscow Univ. (1891–96) and had private music lessons with Gretchaninoff (theory) and Conus (composition); attended the Moscow Conservatory (1895–1901), where his teachers included Taneyev (counterpoint), Ippolitov-Ivanov (composition), and Safonov (piano). He joined the faculty of the Moscow Conservatory in 1906, subsequently becoming chair of the composition department there (1907–41; 1943–56); his students included Khachaturian, Polovinkin, and Titov. As a composer he drew inspiration from Russian and Asian folk melodies as well as French impressionism. In 1938 he collaborated with Ashrafi on the first Uzbek opera, *Buran* [The Snowstorm].

Vasks, Peteris (b. Aizpute, Latvia, 16 Apr. 1946). Composer. At the Lithuanian State Conservatory he studied double bass with V. Sereiko (graduated 1970); studied composition at the Latvian State Conservatory with V. Utkins (graduated 1978). Played in various orchestras including the Latvian State Philharmonic, 1963–74. His music has been influenced by contemporary Western developments, including the coloristic textures of the Polish school. Works include symphonic compositions (*Message,* string orchestra, percussion, and 2 pianos, 1983; *Musica dolorosa,* string orchestra, 1983); a concerto for organ; 2 string quartets (1977, 1984), 2 wind quintets (1977, 1981), a piano trio, and much other chamber music; choral music.

Vasquez [Vázquez], **Juan** (b. Badajoz, Spain, ca. 1510; d. Seville? ca. 1560). Composer. He was a singer and *sochantre* at Badajoz Cathedral; in 1539 he was engaged as a singer at Palencia Cathedral. For a brief period he was associated with the Madrid court, but he returned to Badajoz to serve as *maestro de capilla* at the cathedral (1545–50). In 1551 he entered the service of the Sevillian nobleman Don Antonio de Zúñiga, to whom he dedicated his first publication, *Villancicos i canciones,* 3–5 voices (Osuna, 1551); also published *Recopilacion de sonetos y villancicos,* 4–5 voices (Seville, 1556; ed. in *MME* 4, 1946), a compilation of his secular music including pieces first published as vihuela intabulations by Valderrábano (1547) and Pisador (1552). Best known in his day as a composer of *villancicos;* his output also includes a volume of sacred music, *Agenda defunctorum* (1556; ed. Samuel Rubio, Madrid, 1975).

Bibl.: Eleanor Russell, "Villancicos and Other Secular Polyphonic Music of Juan Vasquez: A Courtly Tradition in Spain's Siglo del Oro" (diss., Univ. of Southern California, 1970).

Vaughan, Sarah (Lois) (b. Newark, N.J., 27 Mar. 1924; d. Hidden Hills, 3 Apr. 1990). Jazz singer. As a child she learned piano; she became a church organist at age 12. At 18 (1942) as a singer she won an amateur night at Harlem's Apollo Theater; she soon joined Earl Hines's big band as pianist and vocalist. In 1944–45 she sang with Billy Eckstine's band, where work with Dizzy Gillespie and Charlie Parker made her fluent in bebop-progressive styles. From 1946 she soloed in a variety of jazz and pop-orchestral settings, toured worldwide, and recorded extensively. Through the 1950s and 1960s she worked mainly in commercial popular fields. From about 1970 she embraced jazz more overtly; she appeared at the 1974 Monterey Jazz Festival and recorded with small jazz goups. Through the 1980s she performed with leading jazzmen and major symphony orchestras.

Bibl.: Denis Brown, *Sarah Vaughan: A Discography* (New York, 1991).

Vaughan Williams, Ralph (b. Down Ampney, Gloucestershire, 12 Oct. 1872; d. London, 26 Aug. 1958). Composer. Vaughan Williams's aunt gave him his first music lessons, teaching him piano as well as rudimentary harmony and thoroughbass. He also gained competency on the violin and organ, and attended the Charterhouse School, where he focused on viola. He went on to pursue composition, studying variously with Parry, Wood, and Stanford, first at the Royal College of Music, then at Trinity College in Cambridge, where he studied music and history, then again briefly at the Royal College of Music. In 1897 he traveled to Berlin to work with Bruch and to Paris in 1908 to study under Ravel. During the first decade of the 20th century Vaughan Williams worked alternately as a church organist, music editor, and researcher of folk songs. He wrote some melodies in the style of native folk songs and published his arrangements of traditional songs he had collected. In 1905 he became conductor of the newly established Leith Hill Musical Festival, delivering there his noted performances of Bach's choral works. He served as the conductor of the festival until 1953.

In 1919 he was appointed to the faculty of the Royal College of Music. He also worked with the Bach Choir from 1920 until 1928, as well as with other musical groups, and taught in conjunction with the English Folk Dance and Song Society. His compositions saw increasing performance and popularity, and he frequently served as conductor for his own music. In the late 1930s he began to compose music for film, with *49th Parallel* being his first effort (1940–41).

Vaughan Williams's output, through its fluctuations, is characterized by a subtle but powerful nationalism, manifest in the influence of English folk song and traits of English art music of the past. Like Sibelius, by whom he was influenced and to whom he dedicated his Fifth Symphony, Vaughan Williams utilized styles and techniques from contemporary Continental European music but deployed them in the context of a language born directly from his own cultural experience. He was also influenced by British composers such as Holst and Bax. He avoided Schoenbergian serialism and its consequents. Although some of his textures and structures approached a neoclassicism, it was not that of Stravinsky or Hindemith. He rarely incorporated actual folk songs into his music, yet the harmonic and melodic characteristics of the repertoire were absorbed into his general style.

His Seventh Symphony, *Sinfonia antarctica* (1949–52), written when he was 80 years old, was a development of the musical score he had composed for the film *Scott of the Antarctic* (1948 based on the 1912 expedition to the South Pole). The Eighth Symphony (1953–55; rev. 1956) is less programmatic and more abstract. Yet despite its neoclassical orientation, it is exploratory in its use of percussion instruments such as vibraphone, gong, and bells. The Ninth Symphony (1956–57; rev. 1958) incorporates a trio of saxophones into its instrumentation.

Works: Stage works include *Job,* masque for dancing (1927–30); *The Poisoned Kiss,* romantic extravaganza (1927–29; rev. 1956–57); *Riders to the Sea,* opera (1925–32); *The Pilgrim's Progress* (1949; rev. 1951–52). Orchestral works include *The Wasps,* suite from incidental music (1909); *Fantasia on a Theme by Thomas Tallis,* 2 string orchestras (1910; rev. 1919); A London Symphony, no. 2 (1912–13; rev. 1920, 1933); Pastoral Symphony, no. 3 (1921); *English Folk Song Suite,* band (1923); Piano Concerto (1926–31); *Fantasia on "Greensleeves,"* flute, harp, strings (1934); Symphony no. 4 (1931–34); *Five Variants of "Dives and Lazarus,"* string, harp (1939); Symphony no. 5 (1938–43; rev. 1951); Symphony no. 6 (1944–47; rev. 1950); Bass Tuba Concerto (1954). Choral works include A Sea Symphony, no. 1, soprano, baritone, chorus, orchestra (1903–9; rev. 1923); *Five Mystical Songs,* baritone, chorus, orchestra (1911); *In Windsor Forest,* cantata, chorus, orchestra (1930); *Six Choral Songs To Be Sung in the Time of War,* chorus, orchestra (1940); *Three Shakespeare Songs,* unaccompanied chorus (1951); *O Taste and See,* motet, chorus, organ (1952); *Song for a Spring Festival,* unaccompanied chorus (1955); *The First Nowell,* Nativity play, soloists, chorus, small orchestra (1958, completed by Douglas). Also songs, chamber music, and music for some 11 films (beginning with *49th Parallel,* 1940–41, and ending with *The Vision of William Blake,* 1957), theater, and radio.

Bibl.: Michael Kennedy, *A Catalogue of the Works of Ralph Vaughan Williams* (New York, 1982). Elliott Schwartz, *The Symphonies of Ralph Vaughan Williams* (New York, 1982). Ralph Vaughan Williams, *National Music and Other Essays* (New York, 1987). Wilfrid Howard Mellers, *Vaughan Williams and the Vision of Albion* (London, 1989). Neil Butterworth, *Ralph Vaughan Williams: A Guide to Research* (New York, 1990).

Vecchi, Orazio [Horatio] **(Tiberio)** (b. Modena, bapt. 6 Dec. 1550; d. there, 19 Feb. 1605). Composer. After musical studies in Modena, he traveled to Brescia (1577) and Bergamo (1578). He was *maestro di cappella* of the Salò Cathedral from 1581, of the Modena Cathedral from 1584, and of the Reggio Emilia Cathedral in 1586. He was appointed a canon of the Correggio Cathedral in 1586 and became an archdeacon there in 1591 before returning to Modena as *maestro di cappella* in 1593. It was in Modena during this period that he composed and published a significant number of his most important works, both sacred and secular, including his single most well known work and the best-known work of its kind, *L'Amfiparnaso* (first performed in 1594; published in 1597; ed. in *Capolavori polifonici del secolo XVI* 5, Rome, 1953, and in *Early Musical Masterworks,* Chapel Hill, 1977), a madrigal comedy with a pastoral setting and incorporating characters from the commedia dell'arte, though not intended for staging. Its music draws on both the serious madrigal and the lighter forms of vocal polyphony at which Vecchi excelled such as the canzonetta and the villanella. In 1598 he became maestro of the Este court but continued in his duties at the cathedral until just before his death.

Vecchi's sacred music includes books of motets, hymns, Lamentations, Magnificats, and Masses, much of it in the Venetian style. His secular works include 6 books of canzonette for 3 to 6 voices, 2 books of madrigals, and, in addition to *L'Amfiparnaso,* the large-scale works *Selva di varia ricreatione* (1590, for 2 to 10 voices, sometimes with lute), *Il convito musicale* (1597, for 3 to 8 voices), and *Le veglie di Siena* (1604, employing as its theme the games of the aristocracy).

Bibl.: J. B. Rodgers, "The Madrigals of Orazio Vecchi" (diss., UCLA, 1954). William R. Martin, "The *Convito musicale* of Orazio Vecchi" (diss., Univ. of Oxford, 1964). R. Rüegge, *Orazio Vecchis geistliche Werke* (Bern, 1967).

Vega, Aurelio de la (b. Havana, 28 Nov. 1925). Composer. He studied law in Havana, music privately with Frederick Kramer (1942–46). In 1947–48 he worked as cultural attaché in Los Angeles, where he took composition lessons from Ernst Toch. Back in Cuba he studied with Harold Gramatges (1950–55), and worked as a music critic and as director of the music school at the Univ. of Oriente (1953–59). His compositions of this period were modernist in character (Piano Trio, 1949; *Elegy,* string orchestra, 1954), moving eventually toward serial techniques, as in his String Quartet "In memoriam Alban Berg" (1957) and Symphony in Four Parts (1960). Soon after the Cuban revolution in 1959 he moved back to California, where he taught composition and directed the electronic music studio at San Fernando Valley State College (beginning 1959). His works soon moved away from serialism toward electronics, as in *Para-Tangents* (trumpet, tape, 1973) and aleatoric procedures, as in *Infinite Square* (1974). In some of his later compositions he managed to work Cuban rhythms and fragments of melodies into the modernist texture (*Septicilium,* chamber ensemble, 1974; *Inflorescencia,* soprano, bass clarinet, tape, 1978). Other works include *Olas, ecos* (1983); *Odissea* (orchestra, 1988); *Metamorphoses* (wind ensemble, 1989).

Bibl.: Ronald Erin, "Cuban Elements in the Music of Aurelio de la Vega," *Latin American Music Review* 5 (1984): 1–32.

Vejvanovský, Pavel Josef [Weiwanowski, Wegwanowskij, Paul Josep] (b. Hukvaldy or Hlučín, ca. 1633? or ca. 1639; d. Kroměříž, buried 24 Sept. 1693). Composer. He studied at the Jesuit college at Opava, and was appointed principal trumpeter and Kapellmeister to Prince-Bishop Karl Liechtenstein-Kastelkorn at Kroměříž in 1664. He was also director of the choir at St. Mořice. In his compositions he made extensive use of trumpets and trombones, and was influenced by Moravian folk music. His works include Masses, offertories, motets, vespers, litanies, and many instrumental pieces.

Bibl.: *Pavel Josef Vejvanovský: Composizioni per orchestra,* ed. Jaroslav Pohanka, *MAB* 47–49 (1960–61).

Venegas de Henestrosa, Luis (b. ca. 1510; d. ca. 1557 or later). Composer. He served the Cardinal of Toledo, Juan Tavera (1534 or 1535–45); in 1543 he was a priest in Hontova. In his *Libro de cifra nueva* (Alcalá de Henares, 1557; ed. in *MME* 2, 1944) Venegas used a new type of tablature notation in which the ciphers 1–7 represent diatonic scale degrees, a notation later employed by Antonio de Cabezón and Francisco Correa de Arauxo. The *Libro* includes works by Palero, Soto, and Venegas himself, as well as transcriptions of sacred and secular music by Morales, Josquin, Clemens non Papa, and others.

Vengerova, Isabelle [Isabella Afanasyevna] (b. Minsk, 1 Mar. 1877; d. New York, 7 Feb. 1956). Pianist. Studied in Vienna with Joseph Dachs and in St. Petersburg with Anna Essipoff. She taught at the St. Petersburg Conservatory (1906–20) and then made concert tours before moving to the U.S. in 1923. She was one of the founders of the Curtis Institute and also taught at Mannes College. Some of her better-known students were Samuel Barber, Lukas Foss, Gilbert Kalish, and Leonard Bernstein.

Bibl.: Robert D. Schick, *The Vengerova System of Piano Playing* (University Park, Pa., 1982).

Venuti, Joe [Giuseppe] (b. Lecco, Italy, 16 Sept. 1903; d. Seattle, 14 Aug. 1978). Jazz violinist. From childhood he worked in partnership with Eddie Lang, both men eventually leading bands together, and together joining Adrian Rollini (1927) and Paul Whiteman (1929–30). Venuti was the first inventive, swinging improviser among jazz violinists. His recordings include "Stringing the Blues" (a duet with Lang, 1926) and "Raggin' the Scale" (with their Blue Five, 1933). He led a big band (1935–43), then worked mainly on the West Coast and in Nevada. He returned to prominence from 1968, touring Europe regularly and recording with Zoot Sims (the album *Joe and Zoot,* 1974), Marian McPartland, Earl Hines, Dave McKenna, and others.

Veracini, Francesco Maria (b. Florence, 1 Feb. 1690; d. there, 31 Oct. 1768). Composer. He was instructed in Florence by his uncle Antonio Veracini, and by Giovanni Maria Casini, Francesco Feroci, and G. A. Bernabei. In 1711 and 1712 he played violin in Venice at St. Mark's and S. Maria Gloriosa dei Frari. In spring 1712 his oratorio *Il trionfo della innocenza patrocinata da S. Niccolò* was performed in Florence. From 23 January to 24 December 1714 he was in London, where he played in benefit concerts and as soloist at the Queen's Theatre. After time in Düsseldorf and Venice, he became employed at the Dresden court in 1717. From 1723 to 1733 he was again in Florence. He returned to London in 1733 and gave many concerts; he began playing for the Opera of the Nobility, Handel's rival, which presented his first 3 operas (1735–38). In 1744 he published his greatest violin sonatas, the *Sonate accademiche* op. 2. He returned to Florence in the 1750s, serving as *maestro di cappella* at S. Pancrazio from 1755 until his death. He continued to play violin in his old age. Veracini's compositions include 4 operas, 8 oratorios (lost), Masses, motets, vespers, a Te Deum, cantatas, songs, sonatas, and concertos.

Bibl.: John Walter Hill, *The Life and Works of Francesco Maria Veracini* (Ann Arbor, 1979).

Verdelot, Philippe (b. Verdelot, Les Loges, Seine-et-Marne, between 1470 and 1480; d. before 1552). Composer. Little is known of his early career, which was probably spent in northern France and northern Italy; by 1522 he was in Florence, where he served as *maestro di cappella* at the Baptisterium S. Giovanni (1523–25) and at the Cathedral (1523–27). Between 4 December 1523 and 16 January 1524 Verdelot, along with two other singers, performed for Clement VII in Rome. It is unclear if he was in Florence during the siege (1529–30), and nothing is known of his subsequent fate. The surviving sacred music includes 2 Masses related to Richafort's 4-voice motet *Philomena praevia* as well as nearly 60 motets (parodied by, among others, Arcadelt, Palestrina, Lassus, and Morales). The chansons, relatively few in number, bear a closer stylistic resemblance to those of Josquin and Mouton than to the Parisian chanson. Verdelot was one of the pioneers of the madrigal, many of which he composed in Florence and Rome during the 1520s.

Bibl.: *Opera omnia,* ed. Anne-Marie Bragard, *CMM* 28 (1966–). Donald Lee Hersh, "Verdelot and the Early Madrigal" (diss., Univ. of California, 1963).

Verdi, Giuseppe (Fortunino Francesco) (b. Le Roncole, near Parma, 9 or 10 Oct. 1813; d. Milan, 27 Jan. 1901). Composer. He believed himself born on October 9, but the parish records seem to indicate the 10th. His father and grandfather kept a modest tavern in the tiny village of Le Roncole. He began music lessons at the age of 3 with the village schoolmaster-organist, at 9 succeeding him as organist after his death; November 1823, sent to school in the larger nearby town of Busseto, probably from about 1825 having music lessons from its leading musician, Ferdinando Provesi, and walking to Le Roncole every Sunday to play the organ. He began to compose for local use marches, vocal and instrumental pieces for concerts and church, piano pieces, occasional works. He came to the attention of a rich merchant (supplier of his father's tavern) and music lover, Antonio Barezzi, whose support was a crucial factor in Verdi's early career. From 1831 he lived in Barezzi's house, eventually becoming engaged to his daughter Margherita, his music pupil.

In 1831 Verdi's father petitioned Busseto's Monte di Pietà for one of its four scholarships for poor students to allow Verdi to study at the Milan Conservatory. Since no scholarship was available until 1833, Barezzi undertook to pay for Verdi's first year. In June 1832 Verdi applied for admission; since he was overage, admission depended on the demonstration of exceptional talent. Although the examiners found him talented, they cited deficiencies in his piano playing and he was rejected; that he was a "foreigner" from the Duchy of Parma and that the conservatory was overcrowded were also factors. This rejection was a source of bitterness throughout Verdi's life. He became a private pupil in Milan of Vincenzo Lavigna, an ex-opera composer of the old school and former *maestro al cembalo* at La Scala. Verdi later, with some exaggeration, described Lavigna's teaching as old-fashioned and largely limited to academic counterpoint, canon, and fugue, thus presenting himself as virtually self-taught in practical composition and in writing for the theater. These private studies were more expensive than the conservatory, and Barezzi generously paid, Verdi's scholarship covering only about a third of the cost. After the death of Verdi's old teacher Provesi in 1833, Barezzi expected Verdi to assume his position as choirmaster-organist; despite grander aspirations Verdi went along with his wishes. When in 1834 the church authorities awarded the post to another without holding a promised competition, the resulting controversy between Verdi's supporters and opponents at times threatened to turn into civic strife. In 1836 he became civic music teacher and orchestra conductor at Busseto, and in May of that year he married Margherita Barezzi.

During this period Verdi composed a good deal of music for local use, very little of which seems to be preserved, and in 1836 an opera, *Rocester,* trying unsuccessfully for its production in Milan or Parma. In September 1838 Verdi went to Milan for this purpose and received sufficient encouragement that he resigned his Busseto post and moved his family to Milan. On 17 November 1839 his *Oberto, Conte di San Bonifacio* was produced at La Scala with moderate success (14 peformances). (The musical relation between it and the earlier *Rocester,* or another libretto known only by its title, *Lord Hamilton,* remains largely conjectural.) He began his long association with the Ricordi publishing firm (having already had six *romanze* published by another Milan firm in 1838), and La Scala's impresario Merelli commissioned three more operas for the coming two years. The comic *Un giorno di regno,* however, was a fiasco (one performance, 5 Sept. 1840). During its composition his wife had died (his two children had died in 1838 and 1839, not all three within two months, as he later came to believe). In his grief Verdi resolved to give up music, but the following winter Merelli skillfully manipulated him into composing Solera's libretto *Nabucco,* which had been rejected by Nicolai. Completed in fall 1841, it was a great success (9 Mar. 1842) and was revived for an extraordinary 57 further performances that fall, making Verdi a major figure.

He began to mix with the social and artistic elite of Milan, and entered a period of intense operatic production. During this time Verdi evolved his own style and principles of music drama, learning how to obtain from his librettists a text suited to the kind of opera he envisioned for any particular subject. He dealt shrewdly with impresarios and publishers, beginning to build what was to become a considerable fortune. At the same time, this life was antipathetic to another side of his nature, which was highly sensitive to slights or double-dealing (real or imagined), and he grew to hate the theater and to look forward to withdrawing from it. From 1844 he suffered from throat and stomach complaints, probably partly nervous in origin and usually connected with his work.

In 1843 Verdi went to Vienna to supervise the production of *Nabucco.* Travel for premieres or important productions (for which he was paid) became a central facet of his life, as it was for most opera composers. *Nabucco* was followed by *I Lombardi alla prima crociata* (libretto by Solera; La Scala, 2 Nov. 1843); *Ernani,* his first collaboration with the librettist Piave and the most widely popular of his early operas (Venice, 9 Mar. 1844); *I due Foscari* (Piave; Rome, 3 Nov. 1844); *Giovanna d'Arco* (Scolera; La Scala, 15 Feb. 1845);

Giuseppe Verdi. Photograph taken in 1850s.

Alzira, his first collaboration with the Neapolitan librettist Cammarano and his only real failure in this period (San Carlo, Naples, 12 Aug. 1845; 5 performances); and *Attila,* his last collaboration with Solera, revised by Piave (Venice, 17 Mar. 1846). It is typical of Verdi's character that in spite of what might be considered his debt to Merelli, he took an extremely hard line when he became dissatisfied with the way Merelli produced his operas at La Scala, refusing to compose for that theater after *Giovanna d'Arco* and eventually refusing to enter it, positions he maintained for over 20 years, until several years after Merelli's departure.

Verdi's work was interrupted after *Attila* by a flareup of his gastric ailment, for which his doctors recommended six months' complete rest, causing him to postpone a contracted trip to London to compose an opera. On recovering he had composed part of *I masnadieri* for Florence before learning that his favorite tenor, Fraschini, would not be part of the company; for that reason he changed to *Macbeth* (Piave and Maffei; Florence, 14 Mar. 1847), which he regarded as his best work to date. In 1847 he went to London via Germany, Brussels, and Paris, conducting the premiere of *I masnadieri* (22 July 1847, with Jenny Lind as prima donna) with great success. Back in Paris he renewed acquaintance with the former prima donna Giuseppina Strepponi, now a singing teacher there. Verdi undertook to turn *I Lombardi* into a French opera, *Jérusalem,* for the Paris Opéra (26 Nov. 1847), but his continued postponement of his return to Italy was probably mainly due to his blossoming love affair with Strepponi. A woman of enormous warmth, humor, and intelligence, she exerted a happily moderating influence. Verdi was angry when the publisher Lucca inconveniently held him to a contract to compose an opera at this time; *Il corsaro* was not composed with his usual care, and he did not supervise the rather unsuccessful first production (Trieste, 25 Oct. 1848). In February 1848 he contracted with the Paris Opéra to compose a French grand opera, which eventually became *Les vêpres siciliennes.* It was the uprising against the Austrians in northern Italy in March 1848 that finally drew him home, ecstatic at the prospect of a united, republican Italy—hopes that were gradually crushed by events. During this visit he bought a farm at Sant'Agata, two miles from Busseto, where his father's family had lived in the 17th and 18th centuries, in 1849 installing his parents there.

Returning to Paris in May he composed his patriotic opera *La battaglia di Legnano,* which had an enthusiastic reception in Revolutionary Rome (12 Jan. 1849). Verdi and Strepponi had begun living together in Paris, but when they returned to Italy in August 1849 and established themselves in a house that Verdi had bought in Busseto in 1845, the arrangement proved too much for small-town morality, and they lived largely withdrawn. In spring 1851 they moved to Sant'Agata. Gradually Verdi's operatic output decreased, a reflection of Strepponi's influence (she urged him to compose what pleased him and to be less concerned with money), his often repeated wish to withdraw from the theater, and his increasing involvement with the practical aspects of managing his estate. *Luisa Miller,* sometimes taken as the beginning of a new stage in his artistic development, was a success at Naples (San Carlo, 8 Dec. 1849), where Barezzi accompanied Verdi. After various abortive projects (including the *King Lear* that surfaces several times in his career), he settled on *Stiffelio,* which was not successful (Trieste, 16 Nov. 1850) and began *Rigoletto,* which, after considerable difficulty with the censor, was a great success at Venice (11 Mar. 1851). *Il trovatore,* its composition interrupted by the death of its librettist, Cammarano, was a success at Rome (19 Jan. 1853); but the Venice premiere (6 Mar. 1853) of *La traviata* (libretto by Piave) was, as Verdi had foreseen, a fiasco because of an inadequate cast. It began its rise to popularity only with later productions.

From October 1853 to December 1855 and July 1856 to January 1857 Verdi and Strepponi were in Paris. Verdi composed Scribe's *Les vêpres siciliennes,* mostly in 1854; after months of rehearsals it had a successful premiere (13 June 1855), but it never became popular and remains among the least-performed of Verdi's later works. Returning to Italy he produced the not very successful *Simon Boccanegra* at Venice (12 Mar. 1857; libretto by Piave). Early in 1858 he spent four months in Naples for the rehearsals of *Un ballo in maschera,* but after conflicts with the censor he withdrew the opera; it had its premiere (17 Feb. 1859) at Rome, whose censor was satisfied with a change of the opera's setting from Sweden to Boston. With this opera Verdi ended what might be called the conventional part of his career. He was thereafter to work only intermittently, when he pleased and when the terms suited him. From around the mid-1850s Strepponi had taken the name Verdi and traveled with him as his wife; they were married on 29 August 1859.

The 1859 war that was to lead to the independence and unification of Italy did not affect Verdi directly. He gave up his earlier republican sympathies and supported Victor Emmanuel. In 1861 Verdi accepted a substantial offer to compose an opera for St. Petersburg. *La forza del destino* was largely completed by November 1861, and the Verdis then went to Russia via Paris, but the opera could not be staged because of the prima donna's illness. They returned to Italy via Paris and London, Verdi composing his *Inno delle nazioni* to words by the young Boito for the London Exhibition. In August 1862 they again went to St. Petersburg, where the new opera had its premiere on 10 November, enjoying a succès d'estime; Verdi then supervised its production in Madrid. In winter 1864–65 he revised *Macbeth* for the Théâtre-lyrique, Paris (21 Apr. 1865), and was disappointed by its relative lack of success (14 performances). He did not go to Paris himself for this production, but spent much of the period from November 1865 to March 1867 there because of his contract with the Opéra for *Don Carlos* (mostly composed at Sant'Agata in March–July 1866). In spite of lengthy rehearsals, *Don Carlos* was not a great success in Paris (11 Mar. 1867), but both it and *La forza del destino* received considerable play in Verdi's Italian versions. It was supervising the premiere of the revised *Forza* that brought him back to La Scala (27 Feb. 1869); he had visited Milan itself for the first time in twenty years in 1868 to meet Manzoni. Rossini's death in 1868 led Verdi to propose honoring him with a collective Requiem by eleven Italian composers (reserving to himself the final *Libera me*). A committee was formed and the work composed, but its performance never materialized.

In 1869 Verdi was invited to compose an opera for Cairo to celebrate the opening of the Suez Canal. After first refusing, he accepted in 1870; Ghislanzoni became the librettist of the resulting *Aida,* as Piave had suffered a disabling stroke. Verdi did not go to Cairo for the premiere (24 Dec. 1871), but supervised the European premiere at La Scala and several later productions (including Naples, 1872, where he composed his String Quartet in E minor). The great success of *Aida* was followed by that of his Requiem, conceived as a tribute to Manzoni, its premiere coming in Milan on 22 May 1874, the first anniversary of the writer's death. Verdi then supervised rehearsals for its Paris premiere and in April–July 1875 conducted it in Paris, London, and Vienna. After these crowning successes Verdi seems to have considered himself retired from composition. In spite of his commanding position, his extreme sensitivity led him to feel insufficiently appreciated; he resented as a threat and an implicit criticism the inroads of German music, especially Wagner's, in Italy, and was suspicious of the younger generation. One of these was Arrigo Boito, who had deeply offended Verdi with some sweeping and injudicious statements about the state of Italian music (not naming Verdi and probably not meaning to include him). Therefore, when Giulio Ricordi, trying to coax Verdi back to the theater, attempted to bring him together with Boito—now the most talented Italian librettist—Verdi was highly skeptical. These efforts began in 1871 but came to nothing until 1879, when Ricordi suggested *Otello;* Boito provided a scenario, and Verdi told him to work it into a libretto. Verdi liked the result and bought the libretto (his usual practice), but did not commit himself to composing it. Any doubts he may have had were quieted by the success of the revision of *Simon Boccanegra* on which the two collaborated in 1880–81 (premiere, La Scala, 24 Mar. 1881).

A true friendship and creative relationship with Boito blossomed, but Verdi did not begin composing *Otello* until 1884, completing it in 1886. Its premiere (La Scala, 5 Feb. 1887) was a great musical event, Verdi having by this time attained an almost transcendental status. He was much more open to the idea of *Falstaff,* which Boito wrote in 1889–90. The music was completed in 1892, Verdi working intermittently, his age apparently beginning to become a burden. Its premiere (La Scala, 9 Feb. 1893) was another triumph. Boito suggested a further collaboration, but Verdi felt his strength unequal to another opera. He did compose the Te Deum (1895–96) and Stabat Mater (1896–97). In 1894 he had gone to Paris for the premieres there of *Otello* and *Falstaff,* composing ballet music for *Otello,* but by 1897 he was becoming feeble, his sight and hearing weakening. The death of Giuseppina Verdi that year was another blow. He sent Boito to Paris in April 1898 to supervise the world premieres of these two works and the *Laudi alla Vergine Maria,* composed a few years earlier. They were published in 1898 along with the Ave Maria, not intended for performance, as *Four Sacred Pieces,* his last work. Verdi had built a hospital for Sant'Agata in 1888 and in 1889 began plans for his major philanthropy, a rest home for musicians in Milan, the Casa di Riposo, begun ten years later. He died from a stroke in his Milan hotel.

Bibl.: Cecil Hopkinson, *A Bibliography of the Works of Giuseppe Verdi, 1813–1901* (New York, 1973–78). Martin Chusid, *A Catalog of Verdi's Operas* (Hackensack, N.J., 1974). Gaetano Cesari and Alessandro Luzio, *I copialettere di Giuseppe Verdi* (Milan, 1913; R: 1973); abridged Eng. trans. (1971). Julian Budden, *The Operas of Verdi* (Oxford, 1973–81;

rev. 1992). William Weaver, *Verdi: A Documentary Study* (London, 1977). William Weaver and Martin Chusid, eds., *The Verdi Companion* (New York, 1979). Gabriele Baldini, *The Story of Giuseppe Verdi: "Oberto" to "Un ballo in maschera"* (New York, 1980). David R. B. Kimbell, *Verdi in the Age of Italian Romanticism* (New York, 1981). Frank Walker, *The Man Verdi* (Chicago, 1982). James A. Hepokoski, *Giuseppe Verdi, "Falstaff"* (New York, 1983); *"Otello"* (New York, 1987). Julian Budden, *Verdi* (London, 1985). Charles Osborne, *Verdi: A Life in the Theatre* (New York, 1989). Mary Jane Phillips-Matz, *Verdi: A Biography* (Oxford, 1993). Marcello Conati and Mario Medici, eds., *The Verdi–Boito Correspondence,* trans. William Weaver (Chicago, 1994). Pierluigi Petrobelli, *Music in the Theater: Essays on Verdi and Other Composers* (Princeton, 1994). David Rosen, *Verdi, Requiem* (Cambridge, 1995).

Veress, Sándor (b. Kolozsvár [now Cluj], Romania, 1 Feb. 1907; d. Bern, Switzerland, 4 Mar. 1992). Composer. At the Budapest Academy of Music he studied piano with Bartók and composition with Kodály (1927–32). With László Lajtha at the Ethnological Museum (1929–33) he collected, transcribed, and analyzed Hungarian folk music. He began to attract attention as a composer during the 1930s with his 2 string quartets (1931, 1937) and a *Divertimento* (chamber orchestra, 1935), which was performed by the BBC Orchestra in London in 1939. From 1943 to 1948 he taught at the State Academy of Music in Budapest; a guest lecturership at Bern Univ. took him to Switzerland, where he remained teaching at the Bern Conservatory (1950–68), then at Bern Univ. (from 1968). His ballet *Térszili Katica* (1942) was introduced in Stockholm in 1949 and widely performed thereafter. During the 1950s his music became increasingly influenced by serialism, for example, *Hommage à Paul Klee* (2 pianos, strings, 1952) and Symphony no. 2 (1953). In *Passacaglia concertante* (oboe, strings, 1961) and *Musica concertante* (strings, 1966), he applied serial techniques in a free manner. Other works include a clarinet concerto (1981); *Deux essais* (orchestra, 1986); *Stories and Fairy Tales* (2 percussion, 1987); Concerto (2 trombones and orchestra, 1989); *Concerto Tilinko* (flute, orchestra, 1988–89).

Bibl.: John S. Weismann, "The String Quartets of Sándor Veress," in *Miscellanea del Cinquantenario Suivini Zerboni* (Milan, 1978), pp. 130–45. *Schweizerische Musikzeitung* 122 (1982): 213–78 [special issue on Veress, including works list and bibliography].

Veretti, Antonio (b. Verona, 20 Feb. 1900; d. Rome, 13 July 1978). Composer. He studied at the Bologna Conservatory with Franco Alfano and Guglielmo Mattioli (diploma, 1921). He was active as a composer, pianist, and critic in Milan, with his opera *Il favorito del re* being performed at La Scala in 1932. Moving to Rome, he founded the Conservatorio musicale della gioventù italiana, where he taught until 1943. After the war he directed the conservatories at Pesaro (1950–52), Cagliari (1953–55), and Florence (1956–70). In the 1950s he turned increasingly toward serial techniques, for example, in *I sette peccati,* mystery in music and dance (La Scala, Milan, 1956), and *Prière pour demander une étoile,* chamber chorus (1966; rev. for chorus and orchestra, 1967).

Verrall, John (Weedon) (b. Britt, Iowa, 17 June 1908). Composer. He went to the Minneapolis College of Music (B.M., 1932), then to the Univ. of Minnesota, where he studied with Donald Ferguson (B.A., 1934). During the same period he also studied in London at the Royal College of Music and at the Liszt Conservatory in Budapest with Zoltán Kodaly. From 1934 to 1942 he taught at Hamline Univ. in St. Paul. His Symphony no. 1 (1939) was introduced by the Minneapolis Symphony in 1940. In 1948 he joined the faculty of the Univ. of Washington in Seattle, where he remained until he retired in 1973. Many of his compositions of the period 1948–54 are based on a 9-note scale of his own devising (String Quartet no. 4, 1949; *The Wedding Knell,* opera, Seattle, 1952). Around 1956 he switched to modal harmonies as a basis for his works (String Quartet no. 6, 1956; Nonet, 1970; Flute Sonata, 1972).

Writings: *Fugue and Invention in Theory and Practice* (Palo Alto, 1966). *Basic Theory of Scales, Modes, and Intervals* (Palo Alto, 1969).

Verrett [Carter], **Shirley** (b. New Orleans, 31 May 1931). Mezzo-soprano, later soprano. She studied in Los Angeles with Anna Fitziu and Hall Johnson, and with Marion Székely-Fresski at Juilliard. Made her New York City Opera debut as Irina (Weill's *Lost in the Stars*) in 1958, and her European debut in Cologne the following year in Nabokov's *Rasputins Tod.* She received critical acclaim for her Carmen in Spoleto (1962), and repeated the role at the Bolshoi (1963), the City Opera (1964), La Scala (1966), the Metropolitan Opera (her debut in 1968), and Covent Garden (1973). Beginning in the late 1970s she began to tackle soprano roles, including Tosca and Norma; she also sang Didon *(Troyens),* Léonor *(Favorite),* Gluck's Orpheus, Amneris, Lady Macbeth, and Selika *(L'africaine).*

Verstovsky, Alexei Nikolayevich (b. Seliverstovo, Tambov, 1 Mar. 1799; d. Moscow, 17 Nov. 1862). Composer. Educated at St. Petersburg Institute of the Corps of Engineers to 1817. Studied piano with Steibelt and Field, violin with Franz Böhm and Maurer. Wrote couplets for the vaudeville *Les perroquets de la mère Philippe* (1819). Named inspector of theaters in Moscow, 1825. Director of Moscow theaters, 1842–60. Composed 6 operas, music for more than 30 vaudevilles, incidental music; cantata for the centenary of Moscow Univ. (1855); cantata for the inauguration of the Moscow Society of Lovers of Russian Literature; hymns, choruses, songs. A modern edition of songs and music from vaudevilles was published in Moscow (1971).

Bibl.: Boris Dobrkhotov, *Alexei Nikolayevich Verstovsky* (Moscow, 1949). Gerald Abraham, "The Operas of Alexei Verstovsky," *19th-Century Music* 7 (1984): 326–35.

Veyron-Lacroix, Robert (b. Paris, 13 Dec. 1922; d. there, 2 Apr. 1991). Harpsichordist. He studied with Yves Nat and was awarded the first prize at the Paris

Conservatory; toured widely, often appearing with flutist Rampal, with whom he recorded. He taught at the Paris Schola cantorum, the International Academy, Nice, and at the Paris Conservatory (beginning 1967), and performed with the Ensemble Baroque de Paris.

Viadana [Grossi da Viadana], **Ludovico** (b. Viadana, near Parma, ca. 1560; d. Gualtieri, near Parma, 2 May 1627). Composer. His family name was Grossi, but he adopted the name Viadana when he entered the order of the Minor Observants sometime before 1588. He was *maestro di cappella* at Mantua Cathedral (1594–ca. 1597) and was in Rome at the end of the century. He then held the position of *maestro di cappella* at the convent of S. Luca, Cremona (1602), the cathedral at Concordia, near Venice (1608–9), and Fano Cathedral (1610–12). In 1614 his religious order appointed him *diffinitor* of the province of Bologna. His sacred works include Masses, motets, Psalms, Magnificats, and Lamentations; his *Cento concerti ecclesiastici* op. 12 (1602) is one of the earliest publications of sacred music with basso continuo. His secular works include canzonettas and pieces for 2 instrumental choirs.

Bibl.: *Opere di Lodovico Viadana,* ed. Claudio Gallico, in *Monumenti Musicali Mantovani* (Kassel, 1964–).

Vianna da Motta [Viana da Mota], **José** (b. S. Tomá, 22 Apr. 1868; d. Lisbon, 31 May 1948). Pianist and composer. After early musical instruction in Lisbon he went to Berlin, where he studied piano with Xaver Scharwenka and composition with Philipp Scharwenka. He also studied with Liszt in Weimar (1885) and with Hans von Bülow in Frankfurt (1887). He appeared widely in Europe and South America as a concert artist and later returned to Lisbon to assume directorship of the Lisbon Conservatory (1919–38). He published several of his own compositions including a symphony, a string quartet, piano pieces, and songs.

Viardot, (Michelle Ferdinande) Pauline (b. Paris, 18 July 1821; d. there, 18 May 1910). Mezzo-soprano. Daughter of Manuel García. Her sister was Maria Malibran, her brother Manuel García. Studied piano with Meysenberg and Liszt, composition with Reicha. Concert debut 1837 in Brussels; stage debut 1839 in London, later Paris, as Desdemona (Rossini's *Otello*). Married Louis Viardot, manager of the Théâtre-Italien in Paris, 1840. She sang Fidès in the first performance of Meyerbeer's *Le prophète* (1849). After retiring in 1863, she painted and wrote poetry and music. She gave the first performance of Brahms's *Alto Rhapsody* op. 53 (1869). She also gave the first private performances of numerous works. She taught at the Paris Conservatory from 1871 to 1875. Her compositions include several operettas and vocal transcriptions of Chopin mazurkas.

Bibl.: April FitzLyon, *The Price of Genius: A Biography of Pauline Viardot* (London, 1964). Nicole Barry, *Pauline Viardot* (Paris, 1990).

Vicentino, Nicola (b. Vicenza, 1511; d. Milan, ca. 1576). Composer and theorist. Little is known of his early life, aside from his studies with Willaert; at some point he arrived in Ferrara and entered the service of Cardinal Ippolito II d'Este; he also was musical tutor to members of Duke Ercole II's family. His first book of 5-voice madrigals appeared in Venice in 1546, and he subsequently followed the cardinal to Rome. In 1551 he engaged in a famous debate with the Portuguese musician Vicente Lusitano concerning the ancient Greek genera (diatonic, chromatic, and enharmonic); he lost the debate, but expanded his ideas in his treatise *L'antica musica ridotta alla moderna prattica* (Rome, 1555; facs. *DM* ser. 1, 17, 1959; *RFsC,* p. 47), which gives Pythagorean harmonics derived from Boethius and addresses solmization, modes, and counterpoint in the 3 genera. By 1561 Vicentino had constructed both an arcicembalo and arciorgano, keyboard instruments capable of playing chromatic and enharmonic genera. Around 1563 he left the service of the cardinal to become *maestro di cappella* at Vicenza Cathedral; later he was in Milan.

Bibl.: *Opera omnia,* ed. Henry W. Kaufmann, *CMM* 26 (1963). Id., *The Life and Works of Nicola Vicentino, MSD* 11 (1966). Id., "Vicentino's Arciorgano: An Annotated Translation," *JMT* 5 (1961): 32–53.

Vickers, Jon(athan Stewart) (b. Prince Albert, Saskatchewan, 29 Oct. 1926). Tenor. He was employed as a merchant before his singing career got under way; he eventually attended the Royal Conservatory of Music in Toronto, where he studied with George Lambert. Among his early engagements was an appearance at the 1956 Stratford Festival. In 1957 he became a member of the Covent Garden Opera and established his reputation with his debut in the role of King Gustavus (Riccardo) from *Un ballo in maschera.* Other Covent Garden roles of his early years included Aeneas, Don Carlos, Don José, Radamès. His Metropolitan Opera debut was in 1960 (as Canio in *Pagliacci*). He performed with many of the world's major opera houses; other important roles include Siegmund, Parsifal, and Peter Grimes.

Victoria, Tomás Luis de (b. Ávila, 1548; d. Madrid, 20 Aug. 1611). Composer and organist. After serving as a choirboy at Ávila Cathedral under the *maestros de capilla* Gerónimo de Espinar and Bernardino de Ribera, Victoria went to Rome around 1565 and entered the Jesuit Collegium germanicum; he met Palestrina, who was *maestro di cappella* at the nearby Seminario romano, and may well have studied with him. In 1569 he became a singer and organist at S. Maria di Montserrato, an Aragonese church in Rome; he also officiated at the Church of S. Giacomo degli Spagnuoli. The Collegio germanico hired him in 1571 to teach music, and two years later he was appointed *maestro di cappella* there, a position he held until 1576 or 1577. Ordained a priest in 1575, he joined the Congregazione dei Preti dell'Oratorio, and in 1578 received a chaplaincy at S. Girolamo della Carità, which he held until 1585. During this time he published volumes of motets (*Motecta,* 4–6 and 8 voices, Venice, 1572; *Motecta,* 4–6, 8, and 12 voices, Rome, 1583; *Motecta festorum . . . ,* 4–6, 8 voices, Rome, 1585), Masses (*Liber primus: qui missas, psalmos, Magnificat . . . aliaque complectitur,* 4–6 and 8 voices, Venice, 1576; *Missarum libri duo,* 4–6 voices, Rome, 1583), Magnificat settings (*Cantica beatae virginis vulgo Magnificat, una cum 4 antiphonis beatae virginis per annum,* 4, 5, and 8 voices, Rome, 1581), and hymns (*Hymni totius anni secundum sanctae romanae ecclesiae consuetudinem,* 4 voices, Rome, 1581), as well as music for Holy Week (*Officium Hebdomadae Sanctae,* 3–8 voices, Rome, 1585). The five Spanish benefices conferred by Gregory XIII supplied much of his income.

In 1587 King Philip II of Spain appointed Victoria as chaplain to his sister, the Dowager Empress María, who lived in retirement with her daughter Princess Margarita at the Monasterio de las Descalzas de S. Clara at Madrid; the composer subsequently was appointed maestro of the convent choir and then served as organist until his death. In 1592 he went to Rome to supervise the printing of his *Missae . . . liber secundus;* in 1600 a collection of polychoral Masses, Magnificat settings, motets, and Psalms was issued in Madrid entitled *Missae, Magnificat, motecta, psalmi et alia quam plurima* (3, 4, 8, 9, and 12 voices). The *Officium defunctorum,* in 6 voices (Madrid, 1605), was composed on the death of Empress María. That Victoria succeeded in publishing nearly his entire oeuvre during his lifetime, generally in sumptuous editions, makes clear that he had the support of wealthy patrons. He was the greatest Spanish composer of the Renaissance and wrote some of the finest church music of the time. The motets and the Office for the Dead are generally considered his best works, but the 20 authentic Masses (including the well-known *Missa Papae Marcelli*), the 18 Magnificats, and the hymns and Marian antiphons are equally fine.

Bibl.: *Opera omnia,* ed. Higinio Anglès, *MME* 25–26, 30–31 (1965–68). *Opera Omnia, Nuova edizione pratica* (Padua, 1994–). Thomas Rive, "An Investigation into Harmonic and Cadential Procedures in the Works of Tomas Luis de Victoria, 1548–1611" (diss., Univ. of Auckland, 1963). James Arthur Kriewald, "The Contrapuntal and Harmonic Style of Tomas Luis de Victoria" (diss., Univ. of Wisconsin, 1968). Josep Cerbós and Josep Cabré, *Tomás Luis de Victoria* (Madrid, 1981). Josep Soler, *Victoria* (Barcelona, 1983).

Vidal, Paul (Antonin) (b. Toulouse, 16 June 1863; d. Paris, 9 Apr. 1931). Conductor and composer. He studied at the Toulouse Conservatory, then at the Paris Conservatory with Jules Massenet (1878–83). He conducted at the Paris Opera, beginning in 1889 as chorus director and eventually becoming head conductor. From 1914 to 1919 he was musical director at the Opéra-comique; taught solfège, accompaniment, and composition at the Paris Conservatory. Works include *Eros* (opera, Paris, 1892); *Guernica* (opera, Paris, 1895); *La Burgonde* (opera, Paris, 1898); *La maladetta* (ballet, Paris, 1893); *L'impératrice* (ballet, Paris, 1903); *Le gladiateur* (cantata, 1883).

Vierne, Louis (b. Poitiers, 8 Oct. 1870; d. Paris, 2 June 1937). Organist and composer. Blinded by measles at the age of 6, he learned piano and violin at the Institution nationale des jeunes aveugles. At the Paris Conservatory (1890–98) he studied organ with César Franck, Charles Marie Widor, and Félix Guilmant. In 1900 he was appointed organist at Notre Dame Cathedral, a post he held for his entire life. He enjoyed success during the 1920s and 1930s as an organ recitalist at Notre Dame and on tour in Europe and the U.S. His best-known works are his 6 organ symphonies (1899, 1903, 1911, 1914, 1925, 1931), a violin sonata (1906), a quintet for piano and strings (1918), and many smaller works for organ.

Bibl.: Bernard Gavoty, *Louis Vierne: La vie et l'oeuvre* (Paris, 1943) [includes works list]. Henri Doyen, *Mes leçons d'orgue avec Louis Vierne* (Paris, 1966).

Vieru, Anatol (b. Iaşi, 8 June 1926). Composer. From 1946 until 1951 he was at the Bucharest Conservatory, studying harmony with Constantinescu, orchestration with Rogalski, composition with Klepper, and conducting with Silvestri. From 1947 to 1950 he was conductor at the Bucharest National Theater, and in 1950–51 edited the music journal *Muzica.* He then attended the Moscow Conservatory, where from 1951 to 1954 he studied composition with Khachaturian and orchestration with Rogal-Levitsky. Returning to Bucharest, he taught at the conservatory there. He also taught briefly in the U.S. at Sarah Lawrence College and in 1968 at the Composers' Forum at the Juilliard School of Music. In 1982 and 1983 he traveled to Jerusalem, where he taught at the Rubin Academy for Music and Dance. His compositions combine advanced modern techniques with characteristics of Romanian folk music, such as modality, rhythmic irregularities, and the use of traditional Romanian instruments. His music includes opera (*Iona,* 1976; *Praznicul Calicilor,* 1980); orchestral works (Concerto for Orchestra, 1955; Symphony no. 1, 1966–67; no. 2, 1973; no. 3, 1977–78; no. 5, chorus and orchestra, 1984–85; *Clepsidra I,* 1968); vocal music (*Clepsidra II,* choir, orchestra, 1971; *Quatre angles pour regarder Florence,* voice, keyboard, percussion, 1973); and chamber music (*Tara de piatra* [Land of Stones], tape, 1972; *Narration,* organ, 1975; String Quartet no. 6, 1986).

Vieuxtemps, Henri (b. Verviers, 17 Feb. 1820; d. Mustapha, Algeria, 6 June 1881). Violinist and composer. He studied with Bériot in Paris beginning in 1828. In 1833 he made a tour of Germany, and studied counterpoint in Vienna with Sechter. There he performed Beethoven's Violin Concerto op. 61 in 1834, reviving interest in the work. In 1835 he went to Paris, where he studied composition with Reicha. He toured Russia in 1838, the U.S. in 1844. Court violinist and professor of violin in St. Petersburg, 1846–52; professor of violin at Brussels Conservatory, 1871–73. A stroke in 1873 left him paralyzed. His compositions include 7 violin concertos, of which no. 4, op. 31 (ca. 1850), still receives frequent performances. Other compositions include 2 cello concertos, a violin sonata, 3 piano quartets; 6 *Études de concert* op. 16, violin solo (ca. 1845); many pieces for violin and piano. His two brothers were also musicians: (Jean-Joseph-) Lucien Vieuxtemps (1828–1901) was a pianist, and Jules Joseph Ernest Vieuxtemps (1832–96) was a cellist.

Bibl.: Jean Théodore Radoux, *Henri Vieuxtemps: His Life and Works* (Linthicum Heights, Md., 1983).

Vila, Pedro Alberto. See Alberch Vila, Pere.

Villa-Lobos, Heitor (b. Rio de Janeiro, 5 Mar. 1887; d. there, 17 Nov. 1959). Composer. He received his first instruction from his father, Raul, a senior officer of the Brazilian National Library, an author, and a good amateur musician who adapted a viola to function as a cello for his son. Heitor later also mastered the guitar, and was proficient on clarinet. A childhood sojourn in Brazil's interior gave him his first exposure to the country's traditional music, kindling a lifelong interest of central importance to his music. As a youth he played in the *chôro* ensembles then popular in Rio, in clubs, and as cellist in the Recreio Theatre opera orchestra. Between ages 18 and 25 he traveled throughout Brazil, collecting and studying folk music. He returned periodically to Rio, even enrolling at the National Institute of Music in 1907, though he soon broke off his studies. By 1912 he had established himself back in Rio, and began to devote much time to composing; he wrote his opera *Izaht* (though it was not staged until 1958) and studied carefully d'Indy's *Cours de composition musicale.* A concert of his works on 13 November 1915 (the first of a series) provoked heated debate among critics; some were laudatory, while others condemned his music. He met Milhaud in 1917 when the latter was in Rio on diplomatic assignment, around the same time also meeting Artur Rubinstein, who would become one of his most ardent advocates, not only giving him financial aid but also persuading others to do so. In 1922 a "Week of Modern Art" in São Paulo generated additional interest in his work.

Villa-Lobos left for France in 1923, supported both by a Brazilian government grant (approved after acrimonious debate) and by his wealthy benefactors. Until 1930 he was based in Paris; he traveled back home several times, conducting Brazilian premieres of his own works and those of French composers. A sensationalized account of his youthful journeys in Brazil appeared in Paris in 1924; though denying its veracity, he did admit that it helped draw crowds to his concerts. His circle in France included Prokofiev, d'Indy, Roger-Ducasse, Schmitt, Varèse, and other prominent musical figures, as well as the painters Picasso and Roca. French critics praised his music highly; while controversy was not absent at his initial 1924 Parisian concerts, those given near the end of 1927 were received enthusiastically and cemented his international stature. The 1920s were among his most fruitful periods of composition; he produced the 14 *Chôros* for various forces, from solo instrument to chorus and orchestra (1920–29), as well as the Nonet (1923), the *Rudepoema* for piano (1921–26, dedicated to Rubinstein), and the fantasy *Momoprecoce* for piano and orchestra (1929).

Returning to Brazil in 1930, he became an important official in public education, implementing reforms of music instruction in São Paulo state, 1930–32, and founding the Superintendancy of Musical and Artistic Education in 1932 to accomplish the same goal in Rio de Janeiro. Choral singing was a major part of his program; he produced a *Guia pratico* of folk song arrangements to be used in schools, introduced a chironomic solfège method, and often conducted student festival choirs thousands strong. He founded a Ministry of Education conservatory in 1942, and the Brazilian Academy of Music in 1945. He traveled abroad to lead performances of his works, appearing in Paris (1934), Buenos Aires (1935 and 1940), Uruguay (1940), and Chile (1942), and attended the International Congress for Music Education in Prague (1936). He made his first trip to the U.S. in 1943, receiving an honorary doctorate at New York Univ.; on later visits he conducted in Boston, New York, Chicago, Philadelphia, and Los Angeles. He continued to travel, conduct, record, and compose until his final days.

Works: operas, including *Izhat* (1914, rev. 1932), *Magdalena* (1948), and *Yerma* (1955); ballets, including *Uirapuru* (1917), *Dança da terra* (1939), *Rudá* (1951), *Genesis* (1954), and *Emperor Jones* (1955); 12 symphonies (1916–20 [1–5], 1944–57 [6–12]); 2 sinfoniettas (1916, 1947); symphonic poems, including *Myremis* (1916), *Amazonas* (1917), and *Madona* (1945); 9 *Bachianas brasileiras* for various forces (1932–44); 14 *Chôros;* concertos for cello (1915, 1953), piano (1945, 1948, 1952, 1952–57, 1954), guitar (1951) and harp (1953); fantasias for bassoon (1933), cello (1945), and saxophone (1948) with orchestra, 1 for at least 32 cellos (1958) and 1 for winds (1958); 17 string quartets (1915–17 [1–4], 1931–57 [5–17]); *Sexteto místico* (1917); wind quintet and quartet (1928) and trio (1921); 4 piano trios (1911–18, 1945); *Fantasia concertante,* flute, bassoon, and piano (1953); 4 violin sonatas (1915 [2], 1920, 1923); 2 cello sonatas (1915–16); choral music, including the *Canto orfeónico* (2 vols; 1940, 1950) and much sacred music; *Suite popular brésilienne* (1908–12), 12 Etudes (1929), and 5 Preludes (1940) for guitar; piano music including *Danças características africanas* (1915), *Prole do bebê* (I, 8 pieces, 1918; II, 10 pieces, 1921), *Cirandinhas* (12 pieces, 1925), *Cielo brasileiro* (4 pieces, 1936), *As tres Marias* (1939), and *Hommage à Chopin* (1949); and many songs.

Bibl.: Vasco Mariz, *Heitor Villa-Lobos* (Rio de Janeiro, 1949; 5th ed., 1977); trans. Eng. (Washington, D.C., 1963, 1970). Andrade Muricy, *Villa-Lobos, uma Interpratação* (Rio de Janeiro, 1960) [includes works list]. David P. Appleby, *Heitor Villa-Lobos: A Bio-Bibliography* (New York, 1988). Eduardo Storni, *Villa Lobos* (Madrid, 1988). Lisa M. Peppercorn, *Villa-Lobos* (London, 1989). Radamés Giro, *Heitor Villa-Lobos: Una sensibilidad americana* (Havana, 1990). Simon Wright, *Villa-Lobos* (Oxford, 1992). Gerard Béhague,

Heitor Villa-Lobos: The Search for Brazil's Musical Soul (Austin, 1994). Eero Tarasti, *Heitor Villa-Lobos: The Life and Works, 1887–1959* (Jefferson, 1995).

Vinay, Ramón (b. Chillán, 31 Aug. 1912). Tenor. He began his career as a baritone and later switched to tenor. Studied in Mexico City and made his debut there in 1931 as Alfonso in *La favorite.* His tenor debut was in 1943 as Don José in *Carmen,* also in Mexico City. Was engaged by the Metropolitan Opera, 1946–61. He also sang at Bayreuth, La Scala, Covent Garden, and Salzburg. He returned to baritone roles late in his career.

Vincent, John (b. Birmingham, 17 May 1902; d. Santa Monica, 21 Jan. 1977). Composer and teacher. He studied flute at the New England Conservatory and also composition with Frederick Converse and George Chadwick (diploma, 1927). He also studied with Walter Piston at Harvard (1933–35), with Nadia Boulanger in Paris (1935–37). He taught at Western Kentucky Teachers College (1937–46), then at UCLA (1946–69). His mature works embody a system of "paratonality" in which diatonic elements are employed within an atonal context. Works include Symphony in D (1954; rev. 1956); *Symphonic Poem after Descartes* (1959); *Nude Descending a Staircase* (string orchestra, 1966); *The Phoenix, Fabulous Bird* (symphonic poem, 1966); *Mary at Calvary* (chorus and organ, 1972); 2 string quartets (1936, 1967); *Nacre* (flute and piano, 1925; rev. for band, 1973).

Writings: *The Diatonic Modes in Modern Music* (New York, 1951; rev. 1974).

Vinci, Leonardo (b. Strongoli, Calabria, ca. 1690 or ca. 1696; d. Naples, 27 or 28 May 1730). Composer. He studied with Gaetano Greco at the Conservatorio dei Poveri di Gesù Cristo from 1708. In 1719 he was *maestro di cappella* to the Prince of Sansevero, and from 1725 until his death was *pro-vicemaestro* of the royal chapel. He wrote at least 3 operas a year between 1722 and 1730, and probably traveled to Venice, Parma, Rome, and Naples to direct their premieres. In summer 1728 he became *maestro di cappella* at the Conservatorio dei Poveri di Gesù Cristo, where Pergolesi was one of his pupils. In addition to some 40 operas, Vinci wrote a few cantatas, sonatas, a serenata, and an oratorio. Of the operas, his commedie were composed between 1719 and 1724, and the opere serie date from between 1722 and 1730 (*Le zite 'n galera,* Venice, 3 Jan. 1722; *Silla dittatore,* Naples, 19 Oct. 1723; *L'Astianatte,* Naples, 2 Dec. 1725; *Didone abbandonata,* Naples, 14 Jan. 1726; *La caduta dei Decemviri,* Naples, 1 Oct. 1727; *Artaserse,* Rome, 4 Feb. 1730).

Bibl.: G. Silvestri Silva, *Illustri musici calabresi: Leonardo Vinci* (Genoa, 1935).

Vinci, Pietro (b. Nicosia, Sicily, ca. 1535; d. there or Piazza Armerina, on or after 15 June 1584). Composer. Following travels to Tuscany and Lombardy he was appointed *maestro di cappella* at the Basilica of S. Maria Maggiore in Bergamo (1568–80). Around this time he began an association with the Milanese patron Antonio Londonio, to whom he dedicated several of his books of madrigals. He returned to Sicily to serve as *maestro di cappella* of Nicosia Cathedral (1581–82?); by 1583 he was in the employ of the viceroy Marc'Antonio Colonna. Surviving works include nearly 250 madrigals (over half are settings of Petrarch) and parody and cantus firmus Masses as well as motets. Vinci is regarded as the founder of the Sicilian polyphonic school.

Viñes, Ricardo (b. Lérida, 5 Feb. 1875; d. Barcelona, 29 Apr. 1943). Pianist. He studied with Juan Pujol in Barcelona; in 1887 went to Paris and studied with Bériot (piano), Godard (composition), and Lavignac (harmony), winning first prize in piano at the Paris Conservatory in 1894. With the exception of his extensive concert tours, he remained in Paris for the rest of his life. His friends included Debussy, Ravel, Albéniz, and Séverac, and he premiered many of their works; indeed, he was best known for his playing of contemporary French and Spanish music. Poulenc was among his pupils.

Bibl.: Elaine Brody, "Viñes in Paris: New Light on Twentieth-Century Performance Practice," in *A Musical Offering: Essays in Honor of Martin Bernstein* (New York, 1977).

Viotti, Giovanni Battista (b. Fontanetto da Po, 12 May 1755; d. London, 3 Mar. 1824). Violinist and composer. When he was 11 he went to Turin to the household of Prince Alfonso dal Posso della Cisterna, who provided for his education. While he was there he studied violin with Pugnani. In 1775 he became a member of the court orchestra in Turin and in 1780 joined Pugnani on a concert tour through Switzerland, Germany, Poland, and Russia. Viotti went alone to Paris, where he played at the Concert spirituel in 1782 and achieved immediate popularity. He was employed by Marie Antoinette in 1784 and in 1788 he opened an opera theater, the Théatre de Monsieur (later called the Théatre Feydeau). Because of difficulties caused by the Revolution, Viotti left for London in 1792. He appeared at Salomon's Hanover Square Concert in 1793, was appointed musical director of the Opera Concerts in 1795, and became orchestral director at the King's Theatre in 1797. He was forced to leave England in 1798 owing to government misgivings about his political activities. He went to Germany for a few years but returned to London by 1801 and started a wine business which later failed. He returned to Paris in 1819 and was made director of the Paris Opéra; he resigned in 1821 and returned to England in 1823.

The majority of Viotti's compositions feature the violin. His most influential works are his 29 violin concertos, the first 19 of which were published during his early years in Paris. His other works include 2 *symphonies concertantes,* 15 string quartets, 21 trios (2 violins, cello), around 40 violin duos, 15 violin sonatas, 13 arias (mostly soprano, with piano accompaniment). Many of these works appeared in other arrangements, both by Viotti and others. He also wrote a

Méthode théorique et pratique de violon (Paris, ca. 1835).

Bibl.: Chappell White, *Giovanni Battista Viotti (1735–1824): A Thematic Catalogue of His Works* (New York, 1985). Remo Giazotto, *Giovan Battista Viotti* (Milan, 1956). Chappell White, "G. B. Viotti and His Violin Concertos" (diss., Princeton Univ., 1957).

Virdung, Sebastian (b. Amberg, 19 or 20 Jan. ca. 1465). Theorist and composer. He studied at the Univ. of Heidelberg and took lessons with Johannes von Soest at the Palatine court chapel there, where he served as an alto, Kapellmeister, and chaplain. He was a singer at the Württemberg court chapel in Stuttgart (1506–7) and served as a succentor at Konstanz Cathedral (1507–8); in 1511 he was probably employed in Heidelberg. Virdung's treatise *Musica getutscht* (Basel, 1511; facs., Kassel, 1931; R: 1970; trans. and ed. Beth Bullard, Cambridge, 1993) is the oldest printed manual on musical instruments. The first section of the treatise describes and classifies instrument families, the second addresses notation.

Bibl.: Edwin M. Ripin, "A Reevaluation of Virdung's *Musica getutscht*," *JAMS* 29 (1976): 189–223. Gerhard Stradner, *Spielpraxis und Instrumentarium um 1500: dargestellt an Sebastian Virdung's "Musica getutscht" (Basel 1511)* (Vienna, 1983).

Visée, Robert de (b. ca. 1650; d. ca. 1725). Guitarist, theorbo and viol player, singer, and composer. He may have studied with Corbetta. About 1680 he became a chamber musician to Louis XIV, in which capacity he often performed at court. In 1709 he was appointed a singer in the royal chamber, and in 1719 he formally became guitar teacher to the king. Rousseau stated that he also played the viol at court. Visée's 2 books of guitar music, *Livre di guittarre dédié au roy* (Paris, 1682) and *Livre de pièces pour la guittarre* (Paris, 1686), contain 12 suites between them. He also wrote works for Baroque lute and theorbo.

Bibl.: *Robert de Visée: Oeuvres complètes pour guitare,* ed. Robert Strizich (Paris, 1971).

Vishnegradsky, Ivan. See Wyschnegradsky, Ivan.

Vishnevskaya, Galina (Pavlovna) (b. Leningrad, 25 Oct. 1926). Soprano. She studied in Leningrad with Vera Garina. Her earliest professional engagements were in operetta, in which she made her debut in 1944. In 1952 she became a member of the Bolshoi Theater in Moscow. In addition to those in the Russian repertoire, her roles include Aida, Violetta, Tosca, Cio-cio-san, Leonore *(Fidelio),* and Cherubino. She performed Aida for her debut at the Metropolitan Opera in 1961, as well as at Covent Garden in 1962; her debut at La Scala was in 1964, as Liù. She has toured in Europe, the U.S., Australia, and New Zealand. In 1955 she married the cellist Mstislav Rostropovich, with whom she performed (he on piano). They left the Soviet Union in 1974 and settled in the U.S. In 1987 she directed Rimsky-Korsakov's *The Tsar's Bride* in Washington, D.C. Her 1984 autobiography is titled *Galina: A Russian Story.*

Vitali, Filippo (b. Florence, ca. 1590; d. there?, after 1 Apr. 1653). Composer. Until at least 1631 he was probably in Florence. His opera *Aretusa* (1620) was the first opera performed in Rome. There he was a priest in the services of Cardinal Francesco Barberini and Cardinal Antonio Barberini (1637–42). He was also a singer in the papal choir (1633), and *maestro di cappella* at S. Lorenzo, Florence (1642), and at S. Maria Maggiore, Bergamo (1648–49). He wrote both sacred and secular vocal music.

Vitali, Giovanni Battista (b. Bologna, 18 Feb. 1632; d. there, 12 Oct. 1692). Composer. He was a pupil of Cazzati, *maestro di cappella* of S. Petronio, Bologna, where Vitali worked as a singer and cellist from 1658. He joined the Accademia filarmonica in 1666. He was *maestro di cappella* of S. Rosario, Bologna (1673), and from 1674 *vicemaestro di cappella* to Duke Francesco II at the Este court in Modena; he became the duke's *maestro di cappella* in 1684, but was demoted to *vicemaestro* in 1686. He was also a member of the Accademia dei Dissonati in Modena. His 12 published collections of instrumental music are important in the history of the Baroque sonata. He also wrote sacred and secular cantatas, oratorios, Psalms, and hymns. The 60 instrumental pieces contained in the didactic collection *Artificii musicali* (1689) constitute a contrapuntal tour de force.

Bibl.: John G. Suess, "Giovanni Battista Vitali and the 'Sonata da chiesa'" (diss., Yale Univ., 1963).

Vitali, Tomaso Antonio (b. Bologna, 7 Mar. 1663; d. Modena, 9 May 1745). Composer and violinist. His father, Giovanni Battista Vitali, took him to Modena in 1674 and probably taught him the violin. He studied composition with Pacchioni, and was employed at the Este court orchestra from 1675 to 1742, first as a violinist and later as its leader. Among his pupils were Dall'Abaco and Senaillé. Vitali's works are all instrumental; his solo and trio sonatas reveal the influences of his father and Corelli.

Vitásek [Wittaschek, Wittasek], **Jan (Matyáš Nepomuk) August** [Johann Matthias] (b. Hořín, 23 Mar. 1770; d. Prague, 7 Dec. 1839). Composer. He obtained an early musical education from his father and studied in Prague with F. X. Dušek and J. A. Kozeluch, whom he succeeded as music director at the Cathedral of St. Vitus in Prague in 1814. He spent the remainder of his life in Prague, turning down an offer for the director's position at St. Stephen's in Vienna. In 1830 he was appointed director of the organ school at the Society for the Promotion of Church Music in Bohemia. He wrote the opera *David* (1810), 12 Masses, 7 Requiems, numerous other sacred and secular choral works, symphonies, concertos, chamber music, organ preludes and fugues.

Vītols, Jāzeps (b. Valmiera, 26 July 1863; d. Lübeck, 24 April 1948). Composer. From 1880 until 1886 he studied in St. Petersburg at the conservatory with Rimsky-Korsakov. Vītols taught there after he graduated and took Rimsky-Korsakov's position after 1908. Both Prokofiev and Myaskovsky studied with Vītols. He worked as a critic for the *St. Petersburg Zeitung.* In 1918 he moved to Latvia, where he became a central musical figure until 1944, serving as conductor and pedagogue and establishing the Latvian Conservatory in 1919. He left for Germany when, in 1944, Soviet troops neared Riga. His own compositions were heavily influenced by Rimsky-Korsakov and were in a late Romantic Russian idiom; he frequently incorporated elements of Latvian folk music, and he also wrote arrangements of hymns and folk tunes. His works include *Gaismas pils* [The Castle of Light] (chorus, orchestra, 1899), String Quartet (1899), and *Spriditis,* Latvian fairy tale for orchestra (1908).

Vitry, Philippe de [Vitriaco, Vittriaco] (b. Paris, 31 Oct. 1291; d. there, 9 June 1361). Theorist and composer. He attended the Sorbonne in Paris and was ordained a deacon; held prebends in Cambrai, Clermont, St. Quentin, and elsewhere, and was canon of Soissons and Archbishop of Brie. From 1346 to 1350 he was employed by Duke Jean of Normandy, remaining in his service when the duke became king in 1350. Pope Clement VI appointed him Bishop of Meaux in 1351.

Vitry was known in his lifetime as both a poet and a composer, although little poetry, and only a handful of motets, survive; a number of his early motets appear in the *Roman de Fauvel* (12 motets are in *The Works of Philippe de Vitry,* ed. Leo Schrade, 1956). His fame rests primarily on his treatise *Ars nova* (ca. 1322–23; *CS* 3:13–22; *CSM* 8 [1964]; trans. Leon Plantinga, *JMT* 5 [1961]: 204–23), which established a new theory of mensural notation. In the treatise Vitry recognizes the existence of 5 note values *(duplex longa, longa, brevis, semibrevis,* and *minima),* codifies a system of binary as well as ternary mensuration at 4 levels *(maximodus, modus, tempus, prolatio),* and introduces 4 time signatures. He also discusses the use of red notes to signal both changes of mensural meaning and deviations from an original cantus firmus. The *Ars nova* is transmitted in 4 manuscripts, which appear to represent Vitry's work as formulated by his disciples; only the last 10 of its 24 chapters—those that address mensural rhythm and notation—are original.

Bibl.: Ernest H. Sanders, "The Early Motets of Philippe de Vitry," *JAMS* 28 (1975): 24–45.

Vivaldi, Antonio (Lucio) (b. Venice, 4 Mar. 1678; d. Vienna, 28 July 1741). Composer. His father, Giovanni Battista, was a successful violinist and taught Antonio the instrument from an early age. From 1693 until he was ordained in 1703, Vivaldi prepared for the priesthood at S. Geminiano and S. Giovanni in Oleo; he was called "il prete rosso" (the red priest) because of his red hair. Although he remained a deeply religious man, he stopped saying Mass soon after his ordination; later in life he cited a long-term ailment as the reason for this. From September 1703 to February 1709 he was *maestro di violino* at the Pio Ospedale della Pietà in Venice, an orphanage for girls which offered musical training. In addition to teaching violin, directing, and composing instrumental works, Vivaldi also taught the *viole all'inglese* and was responsible for acquiring and maintaining string instruments for the orchestra. By this time he had begun to establish himself as a composer: his op. 1 trio sonatas appeared in 1705, and his op. 2 violin sonatas were brought out in 1709. In 1711 Étienne Roger of Amsterdam published his *L'estro armonico* op. 3, a collection of concertos for one, two, and four violins. This publication was extremely influential across Europe, and earned Vivaldi great fame; Bach transcribed five of the concertos for keyboard, and other German composers such as Stölzel, Heinichen, and Pisendel visited him in Venice.

Page from the 1709 Italian edition of Antonio Vivaldi's *Violin Sonatas Op. II.*

Vivaldi resumed his post at the Pietà in 1711, and in 1716 was appointed to the more prestigious position of *maestro de'concerti.* He was also given the responsibility of writing sacred music; his oratorio *Juditha triumphans* was performed in November 1716. The twelve concertos of *La stravaganza* op. 4 (ca. 1714), the sonatas and concertos of opp. 5–7 (ca. 1716–17), and several operas for the theaters of S. Angelo and S. Moisè belong to this period. From 1718 to 1720 he was in Mantua as *maestro di cappella da camera* to Prince Philipp of Hessen-Darmstadt. Vivaldi then returned to Venice before spending three Carnival seasons in Rome (1723–25), where he composed operas, played before the pope, and probably associated with Cardinal Ottoboni. He returned to S. Angelo, Venice, as a composer and impresario (1726–28), and traveled from 1729 to 1733, perhaps visiting Prague. His reputation was further spread by the publications of the concertos in *Il cimento dell'armonia e dell'invenzione* op. 8 (ca. 1725) and *La cetra* op. 9 (1727). His flute concerto op. 10 and violin concerto op. 11 appeared ca. 1729–30. After 1735 he confined his operatic activities to Verona, Ancona, Reggio, and Ferrara; from that year until 1738 he was *maestro di cappella* at the Pietà. His popularity in Venice had declined considerably by 1739, and this may have prompted him to travel to Vienna, where he arrived by 28 June 1741. He died there the following month, and was given a pauper's burial at the Hospital Burial Ground.

Vivaldi was most influential as a composer of instrumental music, particularly concertos, in which his regular use of ritornello form in the fast movements and of a three-movement plan were influential. A skillful orchestrator, he favored effects such as muting and pizzicato. A number of his orchestral works are programmatic, the best-known examples being the concertos *Il Gardellino, La tempesta di mare,* and *Le quattro stagione* (The Four Seasons) of op. 8.

Works: *Secular vocal.* Over 40 operas (21 extant, including *Orlando furioso,* Venice, 1727; *La fida ninfa,* Verona, 1732); serenatas *(Mio cor povero cor);* about 40 cantatas (mostly for solo voice). *Sacred vocal.* Masses and Mass movements; oratorios (*Juditha triumphans;* Psalms *(Nisi Dominus);* motets *(Invicti bellate); Magnificat; Stabat mater. Instrumental.* Over 500 concertos, including over 20 "chamber concertos"; about 60 ripieno concertos and sinfonias; about 80 concertos for 2 or more solo instruments; over 230 solo violin concertos; over 110 solo concertos for bassoon, cello, oboe, flute, viola d'amore, recorder, and mandolin; 26 trio sonatas; about 60 solo sonatas for violin, cello, and wind instruments.

Bibl.: *Le opere di Antonio Vivaldi,* ed. Gian Francesco Malipiero et al. (Rome, 1947–72). *Antonio Vivaldi: Edizione critica* (Milan, 1982–). Mario Rinaldi, *Catalogo numerico tematico delle composizioni di Antonio Vivaldi* (Rome, 1945). Marc Pincherle, *Inventaire thématique,* vol. 2 of *Antonio Vivaldi et la musique instrumentale* (Paris, 1948). Instituto italiano Antonio Vivaldi, *Antonio Vivaldi: Catologo numerico-tematico delle opere strumentale* (Milan, 1968; rev. 2nd ed., 1986). Peter Ryom, *Antonio Vivaldi: Table des concordances des oeuvres (RV)* (Copenhagen, 1973). Id., *Verzeichnis der Werke Antonio Vivaldis (RV): Kleine Ausgabe* (Leipzig, 1974; 2nd ed., 1979). *Antonio Vivaldi: Leben und Werk* (Wiesbaden, 1965); trans. Eng. (1970). Remo Giazotto, *Antonio Vivaldi* (Turin, 1973) [with catalogue of works by Agostino Girard and discography by Luigi Bellingardi]. Walter Kolneder, *Melodietypen bei Vivaldi* (Berg am Irchel and Zürich, 1973). Michael Talbot, *Vivaldi* (London, 1978). *Antonio Vivaldi: Dokumente seines Lebens und Schaffens,* ed. Walter Kolneder (Wilhelmshaven, 1979); trans. Eng. (1982). Mario Rinaldi, *Il teatro musicale di Antonio Vivaldi* (Florence, 1979). Eric Cross, *The Late Operas of Antonio Vivaldi, 1727–38* (Ann Arbor, Mich., 1981). *Opera and Vivaldi,* ed. Michael Collins and Elise K. Kirk (Austin, 1984). Michael Stegemann, *Antonio Vivaldi in Selbstzeugnissen und Bilddokumenten dargestellt* (Reinbek bei Hamburg, 1985). Michael Talbot, *Antonio Vivaldi: A Guide to Research* (New York, 1988). Antonio Fanna and Michael Talbot, eds., *Vivaldi, vero e falso: Problemi di attribuzione* (Florence, 1992). H. C. Robbins Landon, *Vivaldi: Voice of the Baroque* (New York, 1993).

Vivanco, Sebastián de (b. Ávila, ca. 1551; d. Salamanca, 26 Oct. 1622). Composer. He served as *maestro de capilla* at Segovia, Ávila, and Salamanca cathedrals following his 1576 dismissal from a similar post at Lérida Cathedral; in 1603 he was appointed a professor of music at Salamanca Univ. One of the leading composers of his day; his sacred music includes the *Liber magnificarum* (Salamanca, 1607), 10 Masses (1608), and 36 motets (1610).

Bibl.: Enrique Alberto Arias, "The Masses of Sebastián de Vivanco" (diss., New York Univ., 1967). Enrique Arias, "Canonic Usage in the Masses of Sebastián Vivanco" *AnM* 41 (1986): 135–46.

Vives, Amadeo (b. Collbató, near Barcelona, 18 Nov. 1871; d. Madrid, 1 Dec. 1932). Composer. Studied with Ribera and Pedrell in Barcelona. Formed the influential chorus Orteó Catalá in 1891 in collaboration with Luis Millet, later supplying it with many compositions and arrangements. Served as organist at a convent, but an ailment cut short his keyboard activities. Moved to Madrid, where he gained fame as a composer of operas and zarzuelas, among them *Maruxa* (1914), *Balada de Carnaval* (1919), *Pepe Conde* (1920), *Doña Francisquita* (1923, considered by many his greatest work), and *La villana* (1927); these were admired by connoisseurs and public alike. He also published a book of essays, and wrote a play, *Jo no sabia que el món era eixi,* staged in 1920. Other compositions include piano pieces and songs.

Bibl.: Angel Sagardiá, *Amadeo Vives: Vida y obra* (Madrid, 1971). Sol Burguete, *Amadeo Vives* (Madrid, 1978).

Vlad, Roman (b. Cernauti, Romania, 29 Dec. 1919). Composer and critic. He studied at the Cernauti Conservatory (diploma, 1933), then in Rome with Alfredo Casella at Santa Cecilia (diploma, 1941). He remained in Italy and became an Italian citizen in 1951. His early compositions drew on his Romanian heritage (*Sinfonietta,* orchestra, 1941), but he experimented with various harmonic idioms, and by the 1950s he had embraced serialism (Cantata III, "Le ciel est vide," choir and orchestra, 1953). His serialism, however, employs forms, techniques, and even melodic reminiscences of 18th- and 19th-century music. He composed scores for many films and wrote extensively about 20th-century music. Other works include *Storia di una mamma* (opera, Venice, 1951); *Il dottore di vetro* (radio opera, 1960); *Il sogno* ("azione musicale," Bergamo, 1973); *Variazioni concertanti su una serie di 12 note dal Don Giovanni di Mozart* (piano and orchestra,

1955); *Musica per archi no. 2* (1988); *Cadenze michelangiolesche* (tenor and orchestra, 1967); *Colinde transilvane* (voice and piano, 1941); *Tre poesie di Montale* (voice and piano, 1976); *Studi dodecafonici* (piano, 1943; rev. 1957).

Writings: *Luigi Dallapiccola* (Milan, 1957). *Storia della dodecafonia* (Milan, 1958).

Bibl.: Ronald Stevenson, "An Introduction to the Music of Roman Vlad," *MR* 22 (1961): 124–35.

Vladigerov, Alexander (b. Sofia, 4 Aug. 1933). Composer and performer. His father was the composer Pantcho Vladigerov. The young Alexander studied composition first with his father, concurrently studying conducting with Simeonov, both at the Bulgarian State Conservatory of Music in Sofia, graduating in 1956. He served as conductor in Ruse and for Bulgarian Radio and Television, and worked as a pianist. His own compositions include the children's opera *Little Red Riding Hood* (1969), Rondo Concerto, violin and orchestra (1955), and *Rumanian Dance,* orchestra (1960).

Vladigerov, Pantcho (b. Zurich, 13 Mar. 1899; d. Sofia, 8 Sept. 1978). Composer. As a child he learned the piano; he also studied composition at the Sofia Music School from 1910 to 1912. He traveled to Berlin where he studied composition under Juon, Gernsheim, and Schumann and piano under Barth and Kreutzer at the Musikhochschule. From 1921 until 1932 he worked with the Deutsches Theater there as conductor and composer. He then went back to Sofia and joined the music faculty at the Academy of Music, teaching there until 1972. His compositional style was rooted in the colorful and expressive late Romantic language of western Europe. Yet he creatively infused much of his music with elements either of specific Romanian folk songs or of that repertoire in general. His music includes stage works (*Tsar Kaloyan,* opera, 1936); orchestral music (2 symphonies, 1940, 1949; 2 violin concertos, 1921, 1968; descriptive suites and tone poems such as *Essenna elegiya* [Autumn Elegy], 1922, and *Deveti septemvri* [September 9], heroic overture, 1949); chamber and vocal pieces.

Vlasov, Vladimir Aleksandrovich (b. Moscow, 7 Jan. 1903; d. there, 7 Sept. 1986). Composer and conductor. He studied with Yampolsky, Katuar, Krylov, and Zhilyayev at the Moscow Conservatory (1924–31); settled in the Kirghiz Republic, where he was founder and director of the Academic Theater for Opera and Ballet (1936–42). From 1943 to 1949 Vlasov directed the Moscow Philharmonic; he collaborated with Fere and Malybayev in the composition of national operas (*Adzhal orduna* [Not Death but Life], 1938; *Aychurek* [The Moonlight Beauty], 1939; *Vedma* [The Witch], 1958) as well as the Kirghiz national anthem.

Vlijmen, Jan van (b. Rotterdam, 11 Oct. 1935). Composer. He studied composition with van Baaren at the Utrecht Conservatory, as well as studying piano and organ there. From 1961 until 1965 he served as head of the Amersfoort Music School and then, through 1967, taught at the Utrecht Conservatory. Vlijmen then became deputy director at the Conservatory of The Hague, succeeding his former teacher as its director in 1971. He began composing in the atonal style of Schoenberg and Berg. By the early 1960s he was exploring serialism as a determinant for parameters of music beyond simply pitch. His music also began incorporating improvisation. Vlijmen's works often used contrast of blocks of sound and timbre to create form. Compositions include *Serie* (piccolo/flute/alto flute, oboe/English horn, clarinet/bass clarinet, bassoon, trumpet, piano, 1960); *Gruppi* (20 instruments, percussion, 1962); *Reconstructie* (opera, collaboration, 1966); *Omaggio a Gesualdo* (violin, 6 instrument groups, 1971); *Axel* (opera, collaboration with de Leeuw, 1975–77); *Un malheureux vêtu de noir* (opera, 1990). Vlijmen has served as general manager of the Netherlands Opera (1985–88); in 1991 he was appointed director of the Holland Festival.

Vogel, Jaroslav (b. Plzeň, 11 Jan. 1894; d. Prague, 2 Feb. 1970). Composer and conductor. At Prague Conservatory he studied violin with Ševčik and composition with Novák. He traveled to Munich to study from 1910 to 1912 and then to Paris, where in 1912–13 he studied with d'Indy at the Schola cantorum. After serving in World War I he returned to Prague, where he completed a degree at the conservatory with Novák. He worked as an opera conductor in Ostrava from 1919 to 1923 and again from 1927 to 1943. From 1949 to 1958 he conducted the National Theater in Prague and from 1959 to 1962 the Brno State Philharmonic.

Vogel, Wladimir (b. Moscow, 29 Feb. 1896; d. Zurich, 19 June 1984). Composer. The son of a German father and a Russian mother, he grew up in Moscow. He left Russia in 1918 and went to Berlin, where he studied with Heinz Tiessen (1919–21) and with Ferruccio Busoni (1922–24). His first important work was *Drei Sprechlieder* (bass and piano, 1922), in which he combined spoken and sung delivery of the text, a technique that he used again and again (*Wagadu's Untergang durch die Eitelkeit,* soloists, chorus, speaking chorus, 5 saxophones, 1930; *Arpiade,* soprano, speaking chorus, chamber ensemble, 1954). He also experimented with serialism, attempting to adapt Schoenberg's theories to traditional techniques, as in *Sinfonia fugata* (orchestra, 1925) and *Epitaffio per Alban Berg* (piano, 1936). In 1933 he fled Berlin and settled in Switzerland, where he lived first in Ascona, then in Zurich.

Bibl.: Hans Oesch, *Wladimir Vogel: sein Weg zu einer neuen musikalischen Wirklichkeit* (Bern, 1967) [including works list].

Vogelweide, Walther von der. See Walther von der Vogelweide.

Vogl, Heinrich (b. Au, near Munich, 15 Jan. 1845; d. Munich, 21 Apr. 1900). Tenor and composer. Studied with Lachner in Munich. Opera debut in Munich (1865) as Max in *Der Freischütz.* Created Loge in *Das Rheingold* (1869) and Siegmund in *Die Walküre* (1870). Sang at Bayreuth, 1876–77. London debut in

1882; New York Metropolitan Opera debut in 1890. Wrote the opera *Der Fremdling* (1889) and sang in the premiere. Known for his great vocal stamina. He was married to soprano Therese Thoma (1845–1921).

Bibl.: Rolf Wünnenberg, *Das Sängerehepaar Heinrich und Therese Vogl: ein Beitrag zur Operngeschichte des 19. Jahrhunderts* (Tutzing, 1982).

Vogl, Johann Michael (b. Ennsdorf, near Steyr, Austria, 10 Aug. 1768; d. Vienna, 19 Nov. 1840). Baritone. Studied law at the Univ. of Vienna; later studied at Kremsmünster, where he was a classmate of Süssmayr. Member of Vienna Court Opera, 1795–1822. Sang in premiere of revised version of *Fidelio* (1814). Traveled with Schubert, with whom he was a close friend, to Upper Austria in 1819, 1823, 1825. He was first to sing the cycle *Winterreise* (1827). He also composed several Masses and many songs.

Vogler, Georg Joseph [Abbé Vogler] (b. Pleichach, near Würzburg, 15 June 1749; d. Darmstadt, 6 May 1814). Composer and theorist. He studied law at the Univ. of Würzburg and theology at the Univ. of Bamberg. Became the Mannheim court chaplain in 1772; the Elector, Carl Theodor, financed his Italian study tour (1773–75), during which Padre Martini was one of his teachers. He was named Vice-Kapellmeister in 1775 when he returned to Mannheim and also started a music school, the Mannheimer Tonschule. In 1784 he was appointed Kapellmeister in Munich and in 1786 in Sweden to King Gustavus III; in 1807 the Grand Duke of Hessen-Darmstadt named him *Hofkapellmeister.* He traveled widely as teacher, performer, and organ reformer during his career. Among his students were Carl Maria von Weber, Giacomo Meyerbeer, Peter Winter, and Joseph Kraus. He wrote a number of theoretical and pedagogical treatises, including *Tonwissenschaft und Tonsetzkunst* (1776) and *Betrachtungen der Mannheimer Tonschule.* He constructed a portable organ, the "orchestrion," and devised a means for simplifying organ construction, described in his *Système de simplification pour les orgues* (1798). His own compositions include several operas, ballets, other incidental stage music, many Masses, Psalms, other sacred vocal pieces, several secular cantatas, 33 symphonies, piano concertos, and chamber music for various combinations.

Bibl.: Floyd Grave, *In Praise of Harmony: The Teachings of Abbé Georg Joseph Vogler* (Lincoln, Neb., 1987).

Voisin, Roger (b. Angers, 26 June 1918). Trumpeter. He left France in 1927 when his family immigrated to the U.S., settling in Boston. He received early instruction on the trumpet from his father, who was himself a distinguished player, and later from Georges Mager and Marcel La Fosse. In 1935 he was named third trumpet in the Boston Symphony. He became first trumpet with that orchestra (1949–67), then returned to third trumpet until his retirement in 1973. He held teaching appointments at Boston Univ., the New England Conservatory, and the Berkshire Music Center.

Volkmann, (Friedrich) Robert (b. Lommatzsch, near Dresden, 6 Apr. 1815; d. Budapest, 29 Oct. 1883). Composer. He studied with his father, music director in Lommatzsch; later studied with Friebel and Anacker in Leipzig (1836), where he met Schumann and Mendelssohn. He taught in Prague (1839–41), in Pest (1841–54), and in Vienna (1854–58); named professor of harmony and counterpoint at the Budapest Academy of Music in 1875. His compositions include an overture and interludes to *Richard III;* 2 Masses; 2 symphonies; a cello concerto; *Conzertstück,* piano; 2 serenades; 6 string quartets; 2 piano trios; piano solos and duets; songs.

Bibl.: Thomas Michael Brawley, "The Instrumental Works of Robert Volkmann" (diss., Northwestern Univ., 1975).

Volkonsky, Andrey Mikhaylovich (b. Geneva, 14 Feb. 1933). Composer, conductor, and harpsichordist. He studied piano with Auber at the Geneva Conservatory (1944–45) and with Boulanger and Lipatti in Paris; moved with his family to the USSR in 1947, studying at the Tambov School and at the Moscow Conservatory with Shaporin. His foreign training was not well received, however, and he was expelled in 1954, a week after a performance of his Concerto for Orchestra. His troubles with the establishment continued after the performance of his first serial work, *Musica stricta* (piano, 1956); he was expelled from the Composers' Union, and the work was criticized by Kabalevsky, Khrennikov, and Shchedrin, among others. After a series of pointillistic works (*Serenade for an Insect,* chamber orchestra, 1958), Volkonsky began experimenting with aleatoric writing with *Games for Three* (flute, violin, harpsichord, 1962). He emigrated in 1973, returning to Switzerland.

Voloshinov, Victor (b. Kiev, 17 Oct. 1905; d. Leningrad, 22 Oct. 1960). Composer. He studied composition with Scherbatchev at the Leningrad Conservatory and later was appointed to the faculty there; well known as a teacher. His works include opera (*Glory,* 1939; *Stronger Than Death,* 1942); symphonic suites; chamber music; songs.

Von Schlippenbach, Alexander. See Schlippenbach, Alex.

Von Stade, Frederica (b. Somerville, N.J., 1 June 1945). Mezzo-soprano. She studied voice with Sebastian Engleberg at the Mannes School in New York. Her Metropolitan Opera debut was in 1970 as one of the three spirits in *Die Zauberflöte;* she quickly worked her way up to more major roles there, including Siebel in Gounod's *Faust,* Cherubino, Lola in *Cavalleria rusticana,* Zerlina, and Suzuki in *Madama Butterfly.* Her renditions of Cherubino, particularly those at Glyndebourne and the Paris Opéra (both in 1973), and Octavian, from *Der Rosenkavalier,* have been especially praised. Made many recordings and appeared as recital and concert artist; a member of the Chamber Music Society of Lincoln Center. She has performed widely in Europe and the U.S.

Von Tilzer, Harry [Gumm, Harold] (b. Detroit, 8 July 1872; d. New York, 10 Jan. 1946). Popular songwriter, publisher. He began as a vaudeville performer in Detroit and New York, and became involved in publishing at the turn of the century, founding his own firm in 1902. He was important to the early Tin Pan Alley music industry; he aided Gershwin and Irving Berlin and helped form ASCAP in 1914. Many of his own songs were very popular, particularly "My Old New Hampshire Home" (1898), "A Bird in a Gilded Cage" (1900), and "Wait 'Til the Sun Shines, Nellie" (1905).

Voormolen, Alexander Nicolas (b. Rotterdam, 3 Mar. 1895; d. there, 12 Nov. 1980). Composer. He began to compose as a youth, then attended the Utrecht School of Music, where he studied composition with Wagenaar and piano with Petri. From 1916 to 1923 he lived in Paris and studied with Ravel and Roussel. Back in The Hague he worked as a music critic, music librarian, and composer. His compositional style bears a marked French influence, displaying in particular neoclassical forms and textures; his music makes frequent and facile use of functional and nonfunctional tonality. He occasionally incorporated elements of native Dutch folk music. Works include music for orchestra (2 *Baron Hop Suites,* 1923, 1931; Oboe Concerto, 1938; *Kleine Haagse Suite,* chamber orchestra, 1939; Chaconne and Fugue, 1958) and chamber ensembles (*Tableaux des Bays-Pas,* 1921, 1926) and vocal music (*Obsession,* voice, piano, 1952; *Aux baigneurs,* chorus, 1967).

Vořišek, Jan Václav [Worzischek, Johann Hugo] (b. Vamberk, northeast Bohemia, 11 May 1791; d. Vienna, 19 Nov. 1825). Composer. He received early musical training from his father. Later went to Prague to attend the university, where he studied law; he also studied composition with Tomášek at this time. Went to Vienna in 1813 and became acquainted with Beethoven, Spohr, and Hummel, studying piano with Hummel. In 1818 he was appointed conductor at the Gesellschaft der Musikfreunde. He worked as a civil servant in Vienna until 1822, when he became assistant court organist (later he was made principal). His works include 1 symphony; 4 orchestral pieces that feature piano; piano rhapsodies, impromptus, and other solo pieces; secular and sacred vocal pieces.

Bibl.: Adrienne Simpson, "A Profile of Jan Václav Vořišek," *PRMA* 97 (1970–71): 125–32.

Vuillaume, Jean-Baptiste (b. Mirecourt, 7 Oct. 1798; d. Paris, 19 Mar. 1875). Violin maker. From a family of violin makers; he went to Paris at age 19 to work for François Chanot and in 1828 established his own business there. He was a pioneer of imitation, and his best violins were modeled on old Italian instruments. When dealer Luigi Tarisio died in 1855, Vuillaume rushed to Italy and bought the collection. His firm made copies of the instruments of Amati, Maggini, and Stradivari. He was also responsible for several innovations in the construction of violin bows, none of which lasted.

Vulpius [Fuchs], **Melchior** (b. Wasungen, near Meiningen, ca. 1570; d. Weimar, buried 7 Aug. 1615). Composer. He studied with Johann Steuerlein at the Wasungen Lateinschule and in 1589 became a supernumerary Latin teacher in Schleusingen; in 1592 he secured a permanent position there and took on the reponsibilities of Kantor. From 1596 until his death he was Kantor and teacher at the Weimar Lateinschule. A prolific composer of sacred music; Vulpius's output includes nearly 200 motets and some 400 hymns, all written for the Lutheran service.

Bibl.: Hans Heinrich Eggebrecht, "Das Leben des Melchior Vulpius," *Festschrift Max Schneider* (Leipzig, 1955), pp. 87–104.

Vycpálek, Ladislav (b. Prague, 23 Feb. 1882; d. there, 9 Jan. 1969). Composer. As a child he learned the violin and piano and was exposed to vocal music through his parents' musical activities. He went on to study literature and philosophy at Prague Univ. from 1901 to 1906, then worked in association with the university library after 1907. Vycpálek began studying composition with Novák in 1908 and continued through 1912, but the friendship ruptured in 1917 because of Vycpálek's criticism of his teacher's work. He established the university's music department in 1922 and served as its head through 1942. He continued composing, though around 1950 the performance of his music underwent a decline when it was criticized by the political establishment. His limited output concentrated on choral music. He was frequently inspired by or used folk music and was most influenced by Novák and, later, d'Indy. Textures are highly contrapuntal, though his music is often tonally centric, making use of modality and chromaticism but not of functional tonality. Works include *Kantáta o posledních věcech člověka* [Cantata of the Last Great Things of Man] (soprano, baritone, chorus, orchestra, 1920–22); *České requiem "Smrt a spasení"* [Czech Requiem "Death and Redemption"] (soprano, alto, baritone, chorus, orchestra, 1940); *Září* [September] (solo voices, chorus, 1951; rev. 1953).

Vyshnegradsky, Ivan. See Wyschnegradsky, Ivan.

W

Waart, Edo de. See De Waart, Edo.

Wacław z Szamotuł. See Szamotuł, Wacław z.

Wadsworth, Charles (William) (b. Newman, Ga., 21 May 1929). Pianist. He studied piano and conducting at Juilliard (B.S., 1951; M.S., 1952), and the song repertoire in Paris and Munich. At Menotti's request he served as director and pianist for chamber music concerts in Spoleto, Italy (1960–77), and in 1977 founded a similar series for the Spoleto Festival in the U.S. In 1969 he helped found the Chamber Music Society of Lincoln Center, and was made artistic director. Appeared in recital with leading artists.

Waelrant [Waelrand], **Hubert** [Huberto] [Waelrandus, Hubertus] (b. between 20 Nov. 1516 and 19 Nov. 1517; d. Antwerp, 19 Nov. 1595). Composer, music editor, and singer. Of Flemish origin, he probably studied in Italy, perhaps with Willaert; subsequently served as a tenor soloist at Antwerp Cathedral (1544–45) and taught at a music school operated by his landlord Gregorius de Coninck (1553–56). Beginning in 1554 he served as music editor for the printer Jean de Laet; together the pair produced 16 volumes of mostly sacred music, including a volume devoted exclusively to Waelrant's own motets (Antwerp, 1556?). The product of their collaboration is notable both for the fine quality of type employed and for Waelrant's attention to details of text underlay and *musica ficta.* Waelrant's surviving compositions also include a volume of 5-part madrigals and chansons (Antwerp, 1558), but it is his motets, somewhat reminiscent of those by Lassus, that are particularly outstanding. He is often credited with extending the hexachord to an octave by adding the syllables *si* and *ut,* as well as with the invention of a solmization system called bocedization.

Bibl.: Walter Piel, *Studien zum Leben und Schaffen Hubert Waelrants unter besonderer Berücksichtigung seiner Motetten* (Marburg, 1969). Robert Lee Weaver, "The Motets of Hubert Waelrant (c. 1517–1595)" (diss., Syracuse Univ., 1971). Id., *Waelrant and Laet: Music Publishers in Antwerp's Golden Age* (Warren, Mich., 1995).

Wagenaar, Bernard (b. Arnhem, Netherlands, 18 July 1894; d. York Harbor, Maine, 19 May 1971). Composer. He studied violin and piano at the Utrecht Conservatory (1909–14), then taught and conducted in the Netherlands. In 1920 he came to the U.S., where he played violin in the New York Philharmonic (1921–23). From 1925 to 1927 he taught composition at the Institute of Musical Arts in New York, remaining at its successor institution, the Juilliard School of Music, until 1968. Willem Mengelberg introduced Wagenaar's First Symphony (1926) with the New York Philharmonic in 1927. Divertimento no. 1 (orchestra, 1927) was premiered by the Detroit Symphony in 1929. Both works are in a late Romantic style derived from Mahler and Richard Strauss. Subsequent works include Symphonies 2–4 (1930, 1936, 1946); *Sinfonietta* (orchestra, 1929); Divertimento no. 2 (orchestra, 1953); Triple concerto (flute, cello, harp, and orchestra, 1935); 3 string quartets (1931, 1936, 1960); Violin Sonata (1925); Piano Sonata (1928); *Four Vignettes* (harp, 1965).

Wagenaar, Johan (b. Utrecht, 1 Nov. 1862; d. The Hague, 17 June 1941). Composer. He studied in Utrecht, taking composition lessons with Hol and organ lessons with de Lange; then in Berlin, composition with Herzogenberg. From 1887 through 1904 he headed the Utrecht Music School and from 1887 to 1919 served as organist at the Utrecht Cathedral. He was director of the Conservatory of The Hague, 1919–37. His own compositions were in a late Romantic Germanic idiom with careful attention to lush, colorful orchestration and chromatic extension of tonality. Works include 2 operas (*De Doge van Venetie,* 1901; *De Cid,* 1915), orchestral music (*Cyrano de Bergerac,* overture, 1905; *Elverhoi,* symphonic poem, 1939), and vocal and organ music.

Wagenseil, Georg Christoph (b. Vienna, 29 Jan. 1715; d. there, 1 Mar. 1777). Composer. His talents as a composer and keyboard performer were recognized by J. J. Fux, who took him on as a pupil in 1735; he also studied at that time with Matteo Palotta. In 1739 he became court composer, holding the position for the rest of his life. In 1749 he was appointed *Hofklaviermeister* to the imperial archduchesses. His music was widely known; a good deal of it was published in Paris. Mozart and Haydn were both familiar with his music. His first opera, *Ariodante,* was produced in Venice in 1745. Some of his own pupils went on to achieve success: F. X. Dušek, Leopold Hoffmann, and J. A. Štěpán. His compositions include several operas, 3 oratorios, Masses, cantatas, other sacred vocal music, symphonies, harpsichord concertos, other solo concertos, chamber music for strings alone or with keyboard or winds, and numerous solo keyboard pieces. He also wrote *Rudimenta panduristae oder Geig-Fundamenta* (Augsburg, 1751), a theoretical treatise.

Bibl.: Helga Michelitsch, *Das Klavierwerk von G. C. Wagenseil: thematischer Katalog* (Vienna, 1966); *Das Orchester- und Kammermusikwerk: thematischer Katalog* (Vienna, 1972). John Kucaba, Jr., "The Symphonies of Georg Christoph Wagenseil" (diss., Boston Univ., 1967). Helga Scholz-Michelitsch, *Georg Christoph Wagenseil: Hofkomponist und Hofklaviermeister der Kaiserin Maria Theresa* (Vienna, 1980). John Kucaba, ed., *Fifteen Symphonies: Georg Christoph Wagenseil,* ser. B, vol. 3 of *The Symphony, 1720–1840,* ed. Barry S. Brook (New York, 1981).

Wagner, Joseph F(rederick) (b. Springfield, Mass., 9 Jan. 1900; d. Los Angeles, 12 Oct. 1974). Conductor and composer. He studied at the New England Conservatory and at Boston Univ. (B.M., 1932). Founded and conducted the Boston Civic Symphony Orchestra (1925–44) and worked in the Boston Public Schools (1923–44). After World War II he conducted the Duluth Symphony (1947–50) and the Orquesta sinfónica nacional de Costa Rica (1950–54). From 1961 to 1974 he taught at Pepperdine College in Malibu, California. Works include *The Birthday of the Infanta* (ballet, 1935); *Hudson River Legend* (ballet, 1941); 4 symphonies (1934, 1945, 1951, 1976); 2 Sinfoniettas (1931, 1941); *Twelve Concert Preludes* (organ, 1974); *Missa sacra* (mezzo-soprano, chorus, and orchestra, 1952).

Wagner, (Wilhelm) Richard (b. Leipzig, 22 May 1813; d. Venice, 13 Feb. 1883). Composer and author. He was the ninth child of Carl Friedrich Wagner (b. 1770), a police actuary, and Johanna Rosine Wagner (b. 1774), former mistress of Constantin, prince of Saxe-Weimar-Eisenach. When Wagner's father died of typhus on 23 November 1813, the infant and his mother had been living for months in Teplitz, Bohemia, with Ludwig Geyer (b. 1780), an actor, playwright, and close family friend. Geyer married Wagner's mother in August 1814. Known as Richard Geyer for his first 14 years and treated as a favorite son, Wagner in his maturity suspected that Geyer was his natural father. He also suspected—wrongly—that Geyer was Jewish. In 1820 Wagner was placed in Pastor Wetzel's school at Possendorf, near Dresden, where he also received instruction in piano. After Geyer's death on 30 September 1821, Wagner's mother settled in Dresden, where Wagner continued piano study with Humann. Equally important to his subsequent development was the residence there of Weber, Spohr, and Marschner, the three chief figures of German Romantic opera. In 1826 his mother and sisters moved to Prague, where Joanna Rosalie (b. 1803) had an offer for the stage. Left behind at school, Wagner began a play, "Leubald und Adelaide," that was, by his own account, a cathartic bloodbath. In 1827 his mother moved to Leipzig, where his sister Luise Constanze (b. 1805) had accepted a stage role; this time circumstances permitted Wagner to follow.

In Leipzig Wagner's first instruction in composition was taken in 1828–31 with Christian Gottlieb Müller. During these years he wrote copiously: piano sonatas in D minor, F minor, and B♭ major (four-hand); an Overture in B♭ major, a *Politische* Overture, an Overture in E♭ major, and an Overture in D minor (Concert Overture no. 1). The first- and last-named overtures were performed under Heinrich Dorn in Yuletide concerts at the Königliches Sächsisches Hoftheater in 1830 and 1831. In 1831–32, while enrolled at the Thomasschule, Wagner took further lessons with Christian Theodor Weinlig, a theorist and composer who was music director at the Thomaskirche. Weinlig's pedagogy seems to lie behind a fugue and a two-hand arrangement of Haydn's Symphony no. 103. Wagner's talent was such that Weinlig refused all payment and arranged to have a Sonata in B♭ published by Breitkopf & Härtel (as op. 1). To this may be added a Fantasie in F♯ minor and a Grosse Sonate in A op. 4 for piano; an overture and incidental music to Ernst Raupach's *König Enzio* (premiered 17 Feb. 1832); an Overture in C major (Concert Overture no. 2); and a Symphony in C major (clearly modeled on Beethoven). A performance of the C major overture by the Musikverein Euterpe in March 1832 marked Wagner's debut as a conductor. Performances of the symphony at the Gewandhaus in Leipzig and the Ständisches Konservatorium in Prague brought him favorable notice as far away as London.

Wagner now turned his attention to opera. While in Prague for the performance of his symphony he began the libretto to *Die Hochzeit;* back in Leipzig in December he began setting the text. In January 1833 Wagner's brother Karl Albert (b. 1799), who sang at the theater in Würzburg, arranged for him to become chorusmaster there. The same month Wagner began drafting a new libretto, *Die Feen* (The Fairies; after Carlo Gozzi's *La donna serpente*). In February *Die Hochzeit* was abandoned and the music for *Die Feen* begun, reaching completion in January 1834, then revised that spring. Although the opera's musical and aesthetic premises are derived from Weber's *Oberon* and Marschner's *Der Vampyr,* they are nonetheless realized with a skill and attractiveness quite exceptional in a young man's first opera.

Wagner's intellectual life had gained a notable stimulus in 1832 when the composer became friends with Heinrich Laube, along with Heine a leading figure in the Young Germans, an informal literary society that rejected the Romantic movement of the century's first decades in favor of a more politically conscious posture. The pages of Laube's *Zeitung für die elegante Welt* provided Wagner with his first forum as a belle-lettrist. In "Die Deutsche Oper," published in June 1834, Wagner began the practice, typical for him but unusual at that time, of working out a specific aesthetic or theory in print before trying it out in music. According to this article, Germans needed to learn from recent achievements in Italian opera. The same month he sketched the story of an opera in which he would heed his own advice, *Das Liebesverbot; oder, Die Novize von Palermo* (The Censure of Love; after Shakespeare's *Measure for Measure*), a *grosse komische Oper* in two acts.

In July Wagner was offered the position of music director with Heinrich Bethmann's theatrical company, based in Magdeburg. The company was failing, and Wagner at first refused the post, then accepted it after meeting one of the troupe's actresses, Christine Wilhelmine "Minna" Planer (b. 5 Sept. 1809). In August he made his debut as an opera conductor with a production of *Don Giovanni,* began a Symphony in E major, and drafted the libretto to *Das Liebesverbot,* completing it in December. The same month he wrote an overture and incidental music to his friend Theodor Apel's *Columbus.* In April 1835 Wilhelmine Schröder-Devrient, famous for the force of her characterizations and for creating Leonore in *Fidelio,* sang with the company; it was the beginning of an association between the diva and the composer that would include premieres of three subsequent operas.

The music to *Das Liebesverbot* was begun in January 1835 and completed in March 1836. In it Wagner does indeed learn from recent scores by Bellini and Rossini—and also by Auber; but the foreign influences, rather than supplanting the native idiom of German Romantic opera, are integrated into it. The premiere on 29 March was so ill prepared that major roles were, in effect, improvised. Shortly afterward the Bethmann company folded. Minna was invited to join the theater in Königsberg. There she campaigned for the conductor's post on Wagner's behalf. Wagner followed, and the two married on 24 November 1836. It took only a few weeks to learn that the marriage would be a stormy one.

After his fiasco with the modest, insolvent Bethmann company, Wagner determined to produce works on a scale that could only be undertaken by major opera companies. French grand opera, especially as typified in the five-act librettos of Scribe, served as his model. Wagner's first attempt was the five-act *Die hohe Braut; oder, Bianca und Giuseppe,* in July (later set by Kittl). He then turned to instrumental genres. An overture, *Polonia* (1836), may have been performed in Königsberg that winter; a new overture, *Rule Britannia,* was given there on 23 March 1837. On 1 April Wagner was appointed conductor. But the Königsberg theater also proved to be on the verge of bankruptcy. Over the summer, with the help of Dorn, Wagner obtained the post of music director at the theater in Riga. He also began his second five-act libretto, *Rienzi, der Letzte der Tribunen* (Rienzi, the Last of the Tribunes; after Edward Bulwer-Lytton), a *grosse tragische Oper.* This work marked the beginning of an interest in historical subjects.

Wagner arrived in Riga on 21 August. For two seasons he conducted opera there as well as occasional orchestral concerts. In summer 1838 he began a singspiel, but quit it to finish the libretto to *Rienzi;* the music to *Rienzi* was begun in August 1838. In March 1839 Wagner learned that his contract was not being renewed; together with Minna he left Riga and his creditors under cover of night, heading for Paris over the stormy Baltic.

The couple arrived in Paris 17 September. As in most political and cultural centers, money and connections

Richard Wagner, 1867.

played an important role in Parisian life. Wagner lacked both, and his two years in Paris turned into a bitterly disappointing experience, all the more so for beginning with great promise. After a chance meeting, Meyerbeer was persuaded to wield his considerable clout on Wagner's behalf; but the doors the older composer opened led to dead ends. Having exhausted his small capital, Wagner eked out something less than a living by making arrangements for the publisher Schlesinger, by writing articles and stories for the Paris *Revue et gazette musicale* and the Dresden *Abend-Zeitung,* and by composing a number of popular *mélodies.*

He managed at the same time to complete *Rienzi* (in November 1840) and to conceive and realize *Der fliegende Holländer* (The Flying Dutchman; after Heine), a *romantische Oper* in three acts. This time text and music were conceived more or less in parallel: the libretto between May 1840 and July 1841, the setting between May 1840 and November 1841. In this work Wagner sought to eliminate the operatic conventions that impeded the unfolding of the drama. The last months of the Wagners' stay in Paris, while no less difficult, were brightened by the news (received June 1841) that *Rienzi* had been accepted for production by the Dresden theater. Wagner sketched two more librettos before leaving Paris, the first for a third five-act grand opera, *Die Sarazenin,* in 1841, the second for a Romantic opera, *Die Bergwerke zu Falun* (after Hoffmann), in three acts, in February and March 1842. Wagner and Minna left Paris for Dresden 7 April.

Rienzi, considered by many today to be Wagner's least convincing opera, was finely gauged for audiences of its era. Its Dresden premiere on 20 October 1842 was a huge success (despite this, the opera was twice revised, in 1843–44 and 1847). In the wake of his triumph Wagner was offered, and accepted, the position of co-music director at the Dresden court. Thus began one of the more stable periods in his life. Material security freed him to pursue even more vigorously new paths in music drama. In the first of the new works, the *Dutchman,* the break with the conventions of number opera was by no means complete, but it was sufficient to challenge its first audiences. After its Dresden premiere, 2 January 1843, Wagner revised the scoring on three occasions (1846, 1852, 1860), partly to expunge traces of grand opera.

The first opera conceived in Dresden, *Tannhäuser und der Sängerkrieg auf Wartburg* (Tannhauser and the Contest of Singers on the Wartburg), a *grosse romantische Oper* in three acts, carried the process further, though its considerable success over the next century was due to the effectiveness of what were, in fact if not in principle, individual numbers. The libretto of *Tannhäuser* was written between June 1842 and April 1843, the music from July 1843 almost up to the premiere, 19 October 1845. Dissatisfied with parts of the opera, Wagner worked at revisions from October 1845 to May 1847 and again in 1851.

In July 1845 Wagner had sketched a prose draft for another three-act historical opera with a song contest, *Die Meistersinger von Nürnberg.* But his earlier discovery of Jacob Grimm's *Deutsche Mythologie* and, subsequently, of the old epics and eddas was inclining him in a different direction. A reading of Wolfram von Eschenbach's *Parzifal* inspired Wagner to make prose sketches for two operas, *Parsifal* and *Lohengrin.* The libretto of the latter was written from August to November 1845, the music from early 1846 through April 1848. In this opera the music of the scenes is much more of a piece. Although not lacking in grandeur, *Lohengrin* is suffused, above all, with an intense lyricism that made it, by the end of the century, Wagner's most-performed opera. The conclusion to act 1 was given in concert September 1848; the premiere of the whole, under Liszt at Weimar, 28 August 1850 (Wagner first heard the opera in 1859).

Wagner next turned to two librettos on figures whose historicity is overshadowed by their mythic dimension: the first a five-act libretto for *Jesus von Nazareth* (for which there are music sketches); the second, in three acts, reflecting his study of Greek drama, *Achilleus.* But revolution came to Dresden in 1849, and Wagner became deeply involved, to the extent of obtaining hand grenades for the fight. When the uprising was crushed by Prussian troops Wagner fled to Weimar, where Liszt arranged for his safe transport to Paris. From there Wagner moved to the safe haven of Zurich. Almost immediately he wrote *Die Kunst und die Revolution* (Art and Revolution), a tract that argues a necessary connection between the two endeavors. Then, in *Die Kunst der Zukunft* (The Artwork of the Future) and *Oper und Drama,* he elaborated at length the cultural, aesthetic, and (for the creator) practical consequences of this position. A number of shorter essays followed, among which the most historically significant has been "Das Judentum in der Musik" (Jewishness in Music), published under the pseudonym K. Freigedank. In all these works Wagner synthesizes ideas that were already abroad.

The same is true of his next and largest operatic project, *Der Ring des Nibelungen.* Heine had selected many of the same mythic elements for his 1839 treatment of the Nibelungs. The philosopher Vischer, in 1844, suggested in his *Äesthetik* that the legend of the Nibelungs would make a suitable subject for German opera. Luise Otto (in 1845) and, more prominently, Franz Brendel (in 1846) advanced the same idea in the pages of the *Neue Zeitschrift für Musik.* Wagner did not pen his first sketch on the topic, "Die Nibelungensage (Mythus)," until March or April 1848, but he later recalled becoming aware of the potential of the Nibelung legends in 1846. He began with a single work, *Siegfrieds Tod,* the text begun in October 1848, the music in 1850. But it soon became clear that more of the story was needed, so he began writing a preliminary opera, *Der junge Siegfried,* in May 1851. By October his overall conception had emerged: an operatic tetralogy. He worked on the texts of all four operas intermittently, completing *Das Rheingold* in November 1852, *Die Walküre* in July 1852, *Der junge Siegfried* (later *Siegfried*) and the revised *Siegfrieds Tod* (later *Götterdämmerung*) in November or December 1852. The musical composition of *Das Rheingold* occupied Wagner from November 1853 to September 1854; that of *Die Walküre* from June 1854 to March 1856; that of *Siegfried* (in short score) from September 1856 to August 1857. Time for creation was gained through the generosity of friends, especially Otto Wesendonck, who advanced Wagner large sums and eventually provided a house for him.

By 1856 Wagner found himself growing tired of the Nibelungs. During his years at this herculean labor he had, under the influence of Schopenhauer, moved beyond the poetic embodied in its conception. Already he had taken time out in January 1855 to revise the *Faust* overture and in May 1856 to make a prose draft (with music sketches) for *Der Sieger.* At the end of 1856 he began musical sketches for a work that would, he confided to Liszt, embody his unfulfilled dreams of love. However metaphysical the scope of these dreams, they were closely connected at the time with the object of his quotidian dreams, Mathilde Wesendonck, wife of Otto. In August and September 1857 he turned in earnest to writing the libretto for the new work, *Tristan und Isolde.* During its composition he also composed the *Fünf Gedichte* (the Wesendonck Lieder) on very

Wagnerian texts penned by Mathilde. Wagner was still in the throes of composition when deteriorating relations between Minna and Mathilde necessitated a move to Venice. *Tristan* was completed there in August 1859 (then touched up in December). The opera, in part because of its chromaticism, became Wagner's most influential and most analyzed work.

Wagner's next project was to conquer Paris, city of his deepest humiliations. This time he had an entrée to the Opéra, and for that stage he made a major revision of *Tannhäuser.* At the opening night, 13 March 1861, and also the second and third performances young aristocrats of the Jockey Club, wishing to humiliate Wagner and his patrons, created constant disturbances that drowned out the opera. *Tannhäuser* was withdrawn, and Wagner hurriedly left Paris (and Minna) for Karlsruhe. There, between November 1861 and January 1862, he took up once again the *Meistersinger* libretto, composing act 2 between April 1862 and September 1864.

The years following the Paris fiasco were difficult ones for Wagner. Not only was he between lovers, but also his friends had drifted away, and with them his lines of credit. In a foreword to the 1863 edition of the *Ring* Wagner wondered if, somewhere, there was a German prince with the means and the vision to support dreams such as his. There was. Upon his accession to the throne in 1864, Ludwig II, King of Bavaria (b. 1846), answered this cry for help and installed Wagner (in May) in a sumptuous villa in Munich. Soon thereafter, Cosima von Bülow (b. 1837), daughter of Liszt and wife of the brilliant Munich music director Hans von Bülow, answered another kind of cry for help by joining Wagner in his villa. Wagner's first project was to work on the libretto to *Parsifal,* but he soon turned to the scoring of *Siegfried,* act 2 (September 1864–December 1865), this being slowed down by the premiere of *Tristan* (June 1865). In January 1866 he returned to *Die Meistersinger,* completing it at his new home at Tribschen, on Lake Lucerne, in October 1867. The Munich premiere, 21 June 1868, was a complete success, and it whetted Ludwig's appetite for more. Against Wagner's better judgment, the king commanded a Munich production of the *Ring*'s first two parts (1869, 1870). Meanwhile, during 1868, Wagner had sketched two new opera librettos: *Romeo und Julie* (April–May) and *Luthers Hochzeit* (August). The next year he returned to *Siegfried,* composing and scoring act 3 (Mar. 1869–Feb. 1871) in alternation with work on *Götterdämmerung* (Oct. 1869–Nov. 1874). He was also producing children with Cosima: Isolde (1865), Eva (1867), and Siegfried (1869). In January 1866 Wagner's wife, Minna, had died in Dresden. In July 1870 Cosima's marriage to von Bülow was annulled; she and Wagner were married in Lucerne 25 August. For Christmas 1870 he wrote the *Siegfried Idyll* for her.

In 1871 Wagner decided to build his long-dreamed-of festival theater in Bayreuth and began trying to raise the necessary capital. The Bayreuth town council favored the idea, land was donated, and in 1872 the Wagners were confident enough to move there. In 1874 King Ludwig "lent" Wagner funds to cover the major expenses. The festival theater finally opened in Bayreuth in summer 1876; it was afterward conceded by all but his most adamant critics that, on the whole, Wagner's achievement had matched his conception. Financially, however, the festival proved a disaster, and Wagner never again heard his tetralogy in Bayreuth.

After a rest Wagner returned to *Parsifal;* he finished the libretto (Feb.–Apr. 1877) and composed the music (Sept. 1877–Jan. 1882). As he conceived this work, the boundary in it between art and religion was so thoroughly dissolved that only a theater "consecrated" for the purpose—that is, only Bayreuth—could mount a production. Such was the respect in which Wagner was held that the atmosphere at the premiere, 26 July 1882, was one of hushed reverence. Less hushed was Cosima's reaction to Wagner's infatuation with one of the opera's Flower Maidens, Carrie Pringle. On 13 February 1883, after learning of the girl's impending visit to their winter quarters in Venice, Cosima confronted her husband; a stormy scene ensued. Hours later Wagner was found slumped over an unfinished essay on the eternal feminine, dead of a heart attack.

Bibl.: *Sämtliche Werke,* ed. Carl Dahlhaus and Egon Voss (Mainz, 1970–). *Gesammelte Schriften und Dichtungen,* 4th ed. (Leipzig, 1907; R: Hildesheim, 1976). Richard Wagner, *My Life,* ed. Martin Gregor-Dellin; trans. Eng. (Cambridge, 1983). Robert Donington, *Wagner's "Ring" and Its Symbols* (London, 1963). Curt von Westerhagen, *Wagner: A Biography,* 2 vols. (Cambridge, 1978). Peter Burbidge and Richard Sutton, eds., *A Wagner Companion* (New York, 1979). Carl Dahlhaus, *Richard Wagner's Music Dramas;* trans. Eng. (Cambridge, 1979). Theodor W. Adorno, *In Search of Wagner* (London, 1981). Richard Wagner, *Richard Wagner on Music and Drama: A Compendium of Richard Wagner's Prose Works* (New York, 1981). John Deathridge and Carl Dahlhaus, *Wagner* (London, 1984). Barry Millington, *Wagner* (London, 1984). Ulrich Müller and Peter Wapnewski, *Wagner Handbook* (Cambridge, Mass., 1992); rev. trans. of *Richard-Wagner-Handbuch* (1986). Elizabeth Magee, *Richard Wagner and the Niebelungs* (Oxford, 1990). Dieter Borchmeyer, *Richard Wagner: Theory and Theatre* (New York, 1991). Ernest Newman, *The Wagner Operas* (Princeton, 1991). Paul Lawrence Rose, *Wagner: Race and Revolution* (New Haven, 1992). Barry Millington and Stewart Spencer, eds., *Wagner in Performance* (New Haven, 1992). Jean Jacques Nattiez, *Wagner Androgyne: A Study in Interpretation,* trans. Stewart Spencer (Princeton, 1993). Marc A. Weiner, *Richard Wagner and the Anti-Semitic Imagination* (Lincoln, Neb., 1995).

Wagner, Roger (Francis) (b. Le Puy, France, 16 Jan. 1914; d. France, 17 Sept. 1992). Conductor. Moved to the U.S. as a child and studied for the priesthood in Santa Barbara. He returned to France and studied organ with Marcel Dupré; in 1937 returned to the U.S., where he was organist and choir director at St. Joseph's in Los Angeles. He studied conducting with Otto Klemperer and Bruno Walter. He founded the Roger Wagner Chorale and the Los Angeles Master Chorale and Sinfonia Orchestra, both of which toured widely.

Wagner, Siegfried (Helferich Richard) (b. Tribschen, near Lucerne, 6 June 1869; d. Bayreuth, 4 Aug. 1930). Composer and conductor. Son of Richard and Cosima Wagner. He studied with Humperdinck as a youth. He then was educated as an architect but turned to music. He was the assistant conductor at Bayreuth, 1892–96. In 1906 he produced *Der fliegende Holländer* at Bayreuth, and was named general director there until his death. He worked on 17 operas of his own, completing 12. Other compositions include a violin concerto (1915), 2 symphonic poems (1895, 1924), Symphony in C major (1925).

Bibl.: Peter P. Pachl, *Siegfried Wagner: Genie im Schatten: mit Opernführer, Werkverzeichnis, Diskographie und 154 Abbildungen* (Munich, 1988).

Wagner-Régeny, Rudolf (b. Szász-Régen, Romania, 28 Aug. 1903; d. East Berlin, 18 Sept. 1969). Composer. He moved to Germany in 1919 to study music in Leipzig, then in Berlin at the Hochschule für Musik. He achieved sudden success with *Der Günstling,* which was introduced in Dresden in 1935. His next opera, *Die Bürger von Calais,* was produced in Berlin (1939) but was criticized because of its subject matter, and *Johanna Balk* (Vienna, 1941) caused a political scandal and was banned. After World War II he turned to twelve-tone methods, which he combined with Boris Blacher's system of "variable meters." Examples of works in this style include *2 Klavierstücke* (1950); *5 französische Klavierstücke* (1951); *Divertimento* (winds and percussion, 1954); *Das Bergwerk zu Falun* (opera, Salzburg, 1961).

Bibl.: Dieter Härtwig, *Rudolf Wagner-Régeny* (Berlin, 1965). Rudolf Wagner-Régeny, *An den Ufern der Zeit: Schriften, Briefe, Tagebücher* (Leipzig, 1989).

Walcha, Helmut (b. Leipzig, 27 Oct. 1907; d. Frankfurt, 11 Aug. 1991). Organist. He studied with Ramin at the Leipzig Conservatory (1922–27); his blindness did not keep him from recording all the organ music of Bach, composing many chorale preludes, and editing works of Bach and Handel. In 1929 he began teaching at the Frankfurt Music Institute; also served as organist at Three Kings Church (from 1981).

Waldteufel [Lévy], **(Charles) Emile** (b. Strasbourg, 9 Dec. 1837; d. Paris, 12 Feb. 1915). Pianist, composer, and conductor. His father, Louis (1801–84), and brother Léon (1832–84) were both violinists and composers. The family moved to Paris in 1842; he studied at the Paris Conservatory. In 1865 he was named court pianist. He appeared at Covent Garden in 1885 and in Berlin in 1889 as a conductor. His first published waltz, *Joies et peines,* was a big success (1859). The majority of his compositions were waltzes; *Les patineurs* (The Skater's Waltz) remains his most famous.

Walker, George (Theophilus) (b. Washington, D.C., 27 June 1922). Pianist and composer. He studied at Oberlin College (B.M., 1941), the Curtis Institute of Music (A.D., 1945), and later at the American School in Fontainebleau and the Eastman School of Music (D.M.A., 1957). His teachers included Clifford Curzon, Rudolf Serkin, and Robert Casadesus for piano, Normand Lockwood, Rosario Scalero, and Nadia Boulanger for composition. He made his debut as a pianist at Town Hall in New York in 1945. His debut as a composer came in March 1947 with a performance by the National Gallery Sinfonietta of *Lyric for Strings* (1946). During the late 1950s he lived in Paris, where he composed a Trombone Concerto (1957) and *Address for Orchestra* (1959). Returning to the U.S. in 1960, he taught at Smith College (1961–68), then at Rutgers Univ. (from 1969). His mature works integrate diverse elements: serial techniques, jazz rhythms, folk-derived melodies. Examples include Cello Sonata (1957); *Perimeters* (clarinet and piano, 1966); *Variations* (orchestra, 1971); Piano Concerto (1975); Piano Sonata no. 3 (1975); *In Praise of Folly* (orchestra, 1980); Cello Concerto (1982). *Lilacs* (1996), a cantata commissioned by the Boston Symphony Orchestra, won the Pulitzer Prize.

Bibl.: David N. Baker et al., *The Black Composer Speaks* (Metuchen, N.J., 1978), pp. 356–78. Dominique-René de Lerma, "The Choral Works of George Walker," *American Choral Review* 23/1 (1981) [special issue including works list].

Walker, T-Bone [Aaron Thibeaux] (b. Linden, Tex., 28 May 1910; d. Los Angeles, 17 Mar. 1975). Blues singer and guitarist. He accompanied Ida Cox and recorded "Wichita Falls Blues" (1929) in the down-home blues style of Blind Lemon Jefferson. After moving to California he took up electric guitar around 1935, but later toured with Les Hite's big band as a singer, recording "T-Bone Blues" in 1940. Thereafter he led bands, visiting Europe regularly from 1962 to 1971. His hit recordings of the late 1940s include an influential guitar solo on the rhythm-and-blues song "Call It Stormy Monday" (1947).

Bibl.: Helen Oakley Dance, *Stormy Monday: The T-Bone Walker Story* (Baton Rouge, 1987).

Wallace, (William) Vincent (b. Waterford, 11 Mar. 1812; d. Château de Haget, Vieuzos, Hautes-Pyrénées, 12 Oct. 1865). Composer and performer. He studied piano and organ as a youth. He made his violin debut in Dublin in 1834. His family moved to Dublin when he was 15; there he played violin in theater orchestras and organ in several churches. In 1835 he emigrated to Tasmania, where he concertized frequently. He opened an academy of music in Sydney with his wife, Isabella Kelly, and his sister-in-law. He later traveled to South America and the U.S.; while in New York he declared his marriage to Kelly invalid and married pianist Helen Stoepel. In 1845 in London he produced his first of 6 completed operas, *Maritana,* which was received with considerable success. His third opera, *Lurline,* was also well received. He also composed songs, duets, and piano solos.

Wallace, William (b. Greenock, 3 July 1860; d. Malmesbury, 16 Dec. 1940). Composer. He originally studied medicine, going into ophthalmology and serving in the Royal Army Medical Corps. He then turned to the study of music and enrolled at the Royal Academy of Music. He was most influenced by late Romantic German music, especially that of Liszt and Wagner. He published monographs on musicality and was active in the establishment of the legal rights of composers in England. Works include symphonic poems (*Passing of Beatrice,* 1892; *To the New Century,* 1901), the symphony *The Creation* (1899), and an orchestral suite based on *Pelléas et Mélisande* (1900).

Wallenstein, Alfred (b. Chicago, 7 Oct. 1898; d. New York, 8 Feb. 1983). Conductor and cellist. He moved with his family to Los Angeles in 1905 and joined the cello section of the San Francisco Symphony (1915) and the Los Angeles Philharmonic (1919); went to Leipzig in 1920 for further study with Julius Klengel. On his return to the U.S. became principal cellist with the Chicago Symphony (1922–29) and the New York Philharmonic under Toscanini (1929–36). With Toscanini's encouragement he began to conduct; in 1933 he founded the Wallenstein Sinfonietta and gave regular Sunday radio concerts, including cycles of Bach cantatas and much contemporary music. He became the first American to be named music director of the Los Angeles Philharmonic (1943–56), and also served as music director at the Hollywood Bowl (1952–56) and the Caramoor Festival (1958–61); he began teaching at Juilliard in 1968.

Waller, Fats [Thomas Wright] (b. New York, 21 May 1904; d. Kansas City, Mo., 15 Dec. 1943). Jazz and popular pianist, organist, singer, bandleader, and composer. He studied piano with James P. Johnson and first worked as a theater organist. By 1923 he was a soloist (recording discs and piano rolls, broadcasting), blues accompanist, jazz composer, songwriter ("Squeeze Me"). He recorded with Fletcher Henderson's big band (including his own composition "Whiteman Stomp," 1927) and with Billy Banks and his Rhythmakers (1932). He composed for and performed in the musical revues *Keep Shufflin'* (1928), *Load of Coal* (1929; including "Honeysuckle Rose"), and *Hot Chocolates* (1929; including "Ain't Misbehavin'," "Black and Blue"). His best-known songs had lyrics by Andy Razaf. His most profound work was as an unaccompanied jazz pianist; from 1929 he recorded versions of his stride piano compositions (including "Handful of Keys," 1929) and popular songs. From 1934 he broadcast, toured, and recorded with a swing combo, Fats Waller and his Rhythm. In this setting he became famous as a singer of material that was joyful, witty, or laced with sarcasm. Among his hit recordings were "I'm Gonna Sit Right Down and Write Myself a Letter" (1935) and "Your Feet's Too Big" (1939). For tours and recordings he occasionally led a big band from 1935. He appeared in several films, including *Stormy Weather* (1943).

Bibl.: Paul Machlin, *Stride: The Music of Fats Waller* (Boston, 1985). Alyn Shipton, *Fats Waller* (Tunbridge Wells, 1988).

Walmisley, Thomas Attwood (b. London, 21 Jan. 1814; d. Hastings, 17 Jan. 1856). Organist and composer. He was the son of Thomas Forbes Walmisley, editor of *Cathedral Music: A Collection of Services and Anthems* (1875). Studied with his godfather, Thomas Attwood. Named organist at Croydon Church in 1830, at Trinity and St. John's Colleges (Cambridge) in 1833. He received a Mus.B. at Trinity in 1833. Named professor of music at Cambridge Univ. in 1836, he continued to study, receiving a B.A. (1838), M.A. (1841), and Mus.D. (1848). He composed 2 symphonies, 4 overtures, an organ concerto, 3 string quartets; anthems, services (including 2 famous services in B flat and D minor), odes, part songs, and solo songs.

Walsh, John (b. 1665? or 1666; d. London, 13 Mar. 1736). Music seller and publisher. He was in London by about 1690, and in 1692 was appointed musical instrument maker in ordinary to William III. In 1695 he began publishing music by English and Continental composers, and soon became the most successful publisher of music in England; in 1711 he published Handel's *Rinaldo.* His son John (b. London, 23 Dec. 1709; d. there, 15 Jan. 1766) took over the business about 1730 and published all of Handel's later works.

Walter, Bruno [Schlesinger, Bruno Walter] (b. Berlin, 15 Sept. 1876; d. Beverly Hills, 17 Feb. 1962). Conductor. After early musical training in Berlin he held his first conducting appointment with the Cologne Opera in 1893. In 1894 he was Mahler's assistant at the Hamburg Opera and in 1901 joined Mahler, again as his assistant, at the Vienna Opera, after having conducted at Breslau, Pressburg, and Riga during the intervening years. He held many positions during his career including those of musical director at the Munich Opera (1913–22), at Covent Garden (1924–31), Charlottenburg Opera, Leipzig Gewandhaus, and Vienna Staatsoper. He appeared widely in Europe and in the U.S. as guest conductor of both operas and orchestras. He settled in the U.S. in 1939, conducting at the Metropolitan Opera and for the Los Angeles Philharmonic, the NBC Symphony, the New York Philharmonic, and the Philadelphia Orchestra. He was an enthusiastic proponent of Mahler's music and conducted the premieres of "Das Lied von der Erde" and of the Ninth Symphony. He is especially renowned for his interpretations of Mozart, Mahler, and Bruckner. His own compositions include orchestral and choral works, chamber music, and songs. His writings include *Von den moralischen Kräften der Musik* (Vienna, 1935); a biography of Mahler (Vienna, 1936, 2nd ed., 1957; trans. Eng., 1937, 2nd ed., 1941, R: 1970); *Von der Musik und vom Musizieren* (Frankfurt am Main, 1957; trans. Eng., 1961); and an autobiography, *Theme and Variations: An Autobiography* (New York, 1947; rev., 1960).

Bibl.: Artur Holde, *Bruno Walter* (Berlin, 1960).

Walter [Walther], **Johann** (b. Kahla, Thuringia, 1496; d. Torgau, 25 Mar. 1570). Composer and poet. He studied at the Univ. of Leipzig (1521–25) and served as a bass in the chapel of the Elector Friedrich the Wise of Saxony. In 1524 he published in Wittenberg the first Protestant collection of choral music, the *Geystliches gesangk Buchleyn,* and the following year Luther summoned him to Wittenberg to assist in the composition of the German Mass. Following the death of Elector Friedrich in 1525 Walter became cantor of the Municipal Latin School in Torgau and director of the Stadtkantorei (1526–48); in 1548 the new Elector of Saxony hired him to organize the court chapel in Dresden. He remained there, serving as Kapellmeister, until 1554, when he retired to Torgau.

Bibl.: *Sämtliche Werke,* ed. Otto Schröder (Kassel, 1953–73). Ulrich Asper, *Aspekte zum Werden der deutschen Liedsätze in Johann Walters Geistlichem Gesangbüchlein (1524–1551)* (Baden-Baden, 1985).

Walther, Johann Gottfried (b. Erfurt, 18 Sept. 1684; d. Weimar, 23 Mar. 1748). Composer and theorist. He entered the lower school of Erfurt in 1691 and studied organ with Johann Bernhard Bach and Johann Andreas Kretschmar. After studying at the Ratsgymnasium he became organist at the Thomaskirche at Erfurt in 1702. He then devoted himself to music, reading the treatises of Werckmeister, Fludd, and Kircher, and studying composition with Buttstett. In 1706 he studied with Wilhelm Hieronymus in Nuremberg, and was appointed organist at the Church of St. Peter and St. Paul, Weimar, in 1707; he remained there until his death. In Weimar he also taught music to Duke Wilhelm Ernst and Prince Johann Ernst and befriended J. S. Bach. In 1721 he joined the duke's court orchestra as *Hof-musicus.* He wrote sacred vocal works and numerous organ pieces, consisting mostly of chorale preludes (published in *DDT* 26–27). His theoretical works include the *Musicalisches Lexicon oder Musicalische Bibliothec* (Lepzig, 1732; R: 1953), the first dictionary of musicians and musical terms, and the *Praecepta der musicalischen Composition.*

Bibl.: Klaus Backmann and Hans-Joachim Schulze, eds., *Johann Gottfried Walther* (Leipzig, 1987).

Walther von der Vogelweide (b. ca. 1170; d. Würzburg?, ca. 1230). Minnesinger. Considered the greatest lyric poet of medieval Germany, he was active at the Vienna court at the time of the Babenbergs Leopold V and his son Friedrich (1190–98); after Friedrich's death Walther spent some two decades wandering through Europe and appearing at the courts of, among others, Philip of Swabia, Wolfger von Ellenbrechtskirchen, Margrave Dietrich von Meissen, Duke Bernhard von Kärten, and the Count of Katzenellenbogen. From 1212 to 1213 Walther was at the court of the German emperor Otto IV; beginning around 1214 he was associated with Friedrich of Sicily (later Emperor Friedrich II), from whom he received a fief near Würzburg around 1220. Walther elevated the *Minnelied* and the *Spruch* to unprecedented heights; although many of his poetic works survive, only a single complete melody, the *Palästinalied,* is extant.

Walton, William (Turner) (b. Oldham, 29 Mar. 1902; d. Ischia, Italy, 8 Mar. 1983). Composer. His father was a choirmaster and his mother a singer; as a child he learned to sing and play the piano and violin. He became a chorister at the Christ Church Cathedral in Oxford in 1912, where he also began to compose and pursued a B.A. degree in music. He subsequently lived in Chelsea with Osbert and Sacheverell Sitwell until the early 1930s, receiving further support from patrons such as Mrs. Samuel Courtauld and Lady Wimborne. When Walton was 46 he married a young Argentinian named Susana Gil Passo; they settled on Ischia, where he was based for the remainder of his life. He toured as both composer and conductor, freqently leading performances of his own works in the U.S., Australia, New Zealand, England, and the USSR. He was knighted in 1951.

His early works were characterized by a lyricism that was to emerge strongly over the course of his output but also bore clearly the imprint of influences such as Schoenberg and postwar French composers. Walton experimented with various musics such as jazz and popular dances, assimilating their general characteristics rather than utilizing specific discernible styles. The international nature of the influences on Walton assisted his international visibility. He was seen by some to be an antidote to conservative English traditionalism in composition, despite his genuine indebtedness to English choral and instrumental traditions as well as to composers such as Sibelius and Hindemith, to whom English composers have typically related. Walton's works came to be performed more and more often through the early 1930s. The 1940s saw the creation of some of his most striking film scores (*Major Barbara,* 1941; *Next of Kin,* 1941; *Went the Day Well?,* 1942; *Henry V,* 1943–44). The music, influenced by that of Elgar, used flexible tonal centers and was highly lyrical. In addition to *Henry V,* Walton worked with Laurence Olivier on the films *Hamlet* (1947) and *Richard III* (1955). During the late 1940s and early 1950s, Walton moved toward a more introspective style. Orchestration was more studied as textures became more open and individual lines exposed. His first opera, *Troilus and Cressida,* dates from 1950–54. It relied heavily on conventions of Italian opera such as stereotypical, almost allegorical, characters and music that supported, but rarely transcended, the plot and character presentation on stage. His other opera, *The Bear* (1965–67), was more neoclassic in spirit and style.

Other works include the ballets *The Wise Virgins* (1940) and *The Quest* (1943); orchestral music (Symphony no. 1, 1932–35; Violin Concerto, 1938–39; *The Wise Virgins,* suite, 1940; Symphony no. 2, 1959–60; *Variations on a Theme by Hindemith,* 1962–63; *Improvisations on an Impromptu of Benjamin Britten,*

1969; *Passacaglia,* cello, orchestra, 1982); choral music (*Belshazzar's Feast,* baritone, chorus, orchestra, 1930–31; *Set Me as a Seal upon Thine Heart,* unaccompanied chorus, 1938; *Missa brevis,* chorus, organ or orchestra, 1966); vocal and chamber music (String Quartet, 1945–47; 5 Bagatelles, guitar, 1972).

Bibl.: Stewart R. Craggs, *William Walton: A Thematic Catalogue* (London, 1977; rev. 1990). Carolyn J. Smith, *William Walton: A Bio-Bibliography* (New York, 1988). Susanna Walton, *William Walton: Behind the Facade* (New York, 1988). Michael Kennedy, *Portrait of Walton* (Oxford, 1989).

Waltz, Gustavus (fl. 1732–59). Bass. He made his earliest known appearances in Arne's English opera season at the Little Haymarket Theatre (1732). In 1733 he had a small part in the premiere of Handel's *Deborah,* and in July of that year he went with Handel to Oxford and sang in oratorios and anthems. He joined Handel's opera company until 1736, singing roles in the revivals of *Ottone, Sosarme, Il pastor fido, Caio Fabricio,* and the first performances of *Arianna in Creta, Il Parnasso in festa, Ariodante, Alcina,* and *Atalanta.* He then sang in theater music by Arne, Lampe, and Purcell. After singing in several Handel oratorios, including the title role in the premiere of *Saul* (1739), he sang in concerts and at Covent Garden, Drury Lane, and the Little Haymarket.

Wanhal, Johann Baptist. See Vanhal, Johann Baptist.

Ward, John (b. Canterbury, bapt. 8 Sept. 1571; d. before 31 Aug. 1638). Composer. He was probably a chorister at Canterbury Cathedral; subsequently moved to London, where he was employed by the office of the Remembrancer of the Exchequer. He served as a household musician to the family of Sir Henry Fanshawe, composing both sacred and secular music for their use. Works include a volume of madrigals dedicated to his patron (London, 1613; ed. in *English Madrigalists* 19, 1922), 22 verse anthems, and music for viol consort (*MB* 67, 1995).

Bibl.: Michael W. Foster, "The Sacred Music of John Ward" (diss., Univ. of Durham, 1971). Helen Wilcox, "'My Mournful Style': Poetry and Music in the Madrigals of John Ward," *ML* 61 (1980): 60–70.

Ward, Robert (Eugene) (b. Cleveland, 13 Sept. 1917). Composer. He studied at the Eastman School of Music with Bernard Rogers, Howard Hanson, and Edward Royce (B.M., 1939), and at the Juilliard School, with Frederick Jacobi and Bernard Wagenaar (1939–41). Several works of his student years were publicly performed, Symphony no. 1 (1941) several times. At first Ward adhered to traditional forms and neo-Romantic harmonies, but in *Jubilation: An Overture* (1946) and Symphony no. 2 (1947) he added jazz inflections and popular dance rhythms. These were followed by Symphony no. 3 (1950), *Sacred Songs for Pantheists* (soprano and orchestra, 1951) and Symphony no. 4 (1954). From 1946 to 1956 he taught at Juilliard; from 1956 to 1967 he was vice president and managing editor of Galaxy Music in New York. Ward achieved wide recognition with his opera *The Crucible,* based on Arthur Miller's play about the Salem witch trials. It was introduced by the New York City Opera in 1961, received a Pulitzer Prize in 1962, and was revived several times. From 1967 to 1972 he was chancellor at the North Carolina School of the Arts; from 1979 to 1987, he taught at Duke Univ. Other works include *He Who Gets Slapped* (opera, New York, 1956; original title: *Pantaloon*); *Claudia Legare* (opera, St. Paul, 1977); *Minutes till Midnight* (opera, Miami, 1982); *Canticles of America* (Symphony no. 5; soprano, baritone, chorus, orchestra, 1976); Piano Concerto (1968); *Sonic Structures* (orchestra, 1980).

Bibl.: Kenneth Kreitner, *Robert Ward: A Bio-Bibliography* (New York, 1988).

Ward-Steinem, David (b. Alexandria, La., 6 Nov. 1936). Composer. He learned piano and clarinet as a child and was already composing in high school. He studied at Florida State Univ. (B.M., 1957), and the Univ. of Illinois (M.M., 1958; D.M.A., 1961), and also in Paris with Nadia Boulanger (1958–59). In 1961 he joined the faculty at San Diego State College. His music of the 1960s emphasizes instrumental colors, for example, *Prelude and Toccata for Orchestra* (1962), *Fragments from Sappho* (soprano, flute, clarinet, piano, 1965), *Song of Moses* (oratorio, 1964). From the 1970s on, most of his works involve electronics, for example, *Antares* (orchestra and electronics, 1971), *Arcturus* (orchestra and electronics, 1972), Sonata for Fortified Piano (1972), *Tamar* (mixed media opera, 1977). Other works include *Children's Corner Revisited* (voice, piano, 1985); *Winging It* (chamber orchestra, 1986); *What's Left* (piano, left-hand, 1987); *Gemini* (2 guitars, 1988); *Cinnabar Concerto* (viola, chamber orchestra, 1993).

Warfield, William (Caesar) (b. Helena, Ark., 22 Jan. 1920). Baritone. Received both undergraduate and graduate music instruction at the Eastman School. During the early part of his career he sang in the theater; his recital debut was in 1950 at Town Hall in New York. Made extensive concert tours, including to Australia, Asia, Africa, Europe, and South America as a soloist, as well as European and American appearances in musicals, including the role of Porgy in Gershwin's *Porgy and Bess* and Joe in Jerome Kern's *Showboat.* From 1952 to 1972 he was married to the soprano Leontyne Price. He became a member of the faculty at the Univ. of Illinois in 1974 and in 1984 was named president of the National Association of Negro Musicians.

Waring, Fred(eric Malcolm) (b. Tyrone, Pa., 9 June 1900; d. State College, Pa., 29 July 1984). Popular songwriter and bandleader, choral teacher, and publisher. He formed a band while at Penn State; from 1923 they had many popular recordings as Fred Waring's Pennsylvanians ("Sleep," 1923; "Laugh, Clown, Laugh," 1928; "Little White Lies," 1930) and later appeared on radio and television. From 1947 he published choral music and led workshops for conductors and singers.

Warlock, Peter [Heseltine, Philip (Arnold)] (b. London, 30 Oct. 1894; d. there, 17 Dec. 1930). Composer. He attended Eton, where he studied music under Colin Taylor. In 1910 the young Heseltine met Delius, and there ensued a relationship that was powerful for both of them. Heseltine then moved decisively toward the pursuit of composition. Although he had worked as a music critic and arranger under his original name, he published all of his musical compositions under the name Peter Warlock. His compositions are primarily vocal, especially focusing on songs for voice and piano. His melodic lines are lyrical, the texture of his music at times almost impressionistic. His many songs include *Lillygay: The Distracted Maid, Johnny Wil the Tye, The Shoemaker, Burd Ellen and Young Tamlane, Rantum Tantum* (1922); *The Lover's Maze* (1927); and *The Frostbound Wood* (1929). His choral works include *Bethlehem Down* (1927). He also wrote chamber music.

Bibl.: Ian Alfred Copley, *The Music of Peter Warlock: A Critical Study* (London, 1979). Barry Smith, *Peter Warlock: The Life of Philip Heseltine* (Oxford, 1994).

Warren, Harry [Guaragna, Salvatore] (b. Brooklyn, 24 Dec. 1893; d. Los Angeles, 22 Sept. 1981). Popular songwriter. He began working as a performer and song plugger in New York and published his first song in 1922. He wrote revues with Billy Rose (*Sweet and Low,* 1930), but from 1930 composed principally for films, working with numerous lyricists including Al Dubin and Mack Gordon. Many of his most popular songs have become standards, including "Absence Makes the Heart Grow Fonder" (1929), "Jeepers Creepers" (1938), "Chattanooga Choo-Choo" (1941), and "On the Atchison, Topeka and the Santa Fe" (1946).

Warren [Warenoff], **Leonard** (b. New York, 21 Apr. 1911; d. there, 4 Mar. 1960). Baritone. Studied in New York with Sidney Dietch; he also belonged to the Radio City Music Hall chorus (from 1935). After winning the Metropolitan Opera Auditions of the Air in 1938 he went to Italy, where he studied with Giuseppe Pais and R. Piccozi. His first Metropolitan Opera appearance was in 1938 in a concert performance of excerpts, but his operatic debut soon followed as Paolo from Verdi's *Simon Boccanegra* in 1939. In addition to other U.S. appearances, he sang in Milan (1953), in the Soviet Union (1958), and in South America. He specialized in and was praised for his Verdi roles. He died on the stage of the Metropolitan while performing Don Carlo from *La forza del destino.*

Warwick(e), (Marie) Dionne (b. East Orange, N.J., 12 Dec. 1941). Popular singer. From 1960 she worked with composer Burt Bacharach and lyricist Hal David; she popularized several of their songs including "Anyone Who Had a Heart" (1963) and "Do You Know the Way to San Jose" (1968). In the 1970s she worked with various artists including the Spinners ("Then Came You," 1974) and Barry Manilow ("I'll Never Love This Way Again," 1979); in 1985 she was successful with "That's What Friends Are For" by Bacharach and Carole Bayer Sager.

Washington, Dinah [Jones, Ruth] (b. Tuscaloosa, Ala., 29 Aug. 1924; d. Detroit, 14 Dec. 1963). Popular singer. After singing gospel and blues in Chicago, in 1943 she joined Lionel Hampton's band. In 1946 she began working as a solo artist, and had many successful blues and rhythm-and-blues recordings, including "Teach Me Tonight" (1954) and "What a Difference a Day Makes" (1959).

Bibl.: James Haskins, *Queen of the Blues: A Biography of Dinah Washington* (New York, 1987).

Waters [née Howard], **Ethel** (b. Chester, Pa., 31 Oct. 1896; d. Chatsworth, Calif., 1 Sept. 1977). Popular singer, actress. She began recording in 1921; "Am I Blue" (1929) and her signature "Stormy Weather" (1933) were very popular. She appeared in Cotton Club revues, musicals (*As Thousands Cheer,* 1933), and drama (*Member of the Wedding,* 1950), and in the 1960s performed with evangelist Billy Graham.

Waters, Muddy. See Muddy Waters.

Watkins, Michael Blake (b. Ilford, Essex, 4 May 1948). Composer. He studied guitar and lute with Michael Jessett (1964–67) and composition with Elisabeth Lutyens (1966–70) and Richard Rodney Bennett (1970–75); from 1981 to 1983 he was an appointed fellow in television composition with London Weekend Television. Compositions include concertos for violin (1977), trumpet (1988), and cello (1992), as well as a string quartet (1979) and a sinfonietta for 12 instruments (1982).

Watson, Doc [Arthel Lane] (b. Deep Gap, N.C., 2 Mar. 1923). Country and folk guitarist and singer. He played with Clarence Ashley in New York in the early 1960s, and became prominent in the folk revival through a performance at the 1963 Newport Folk Festival. His repertory comprised mainly traditional country songs; famous for his brilliant flat-picking acoustic guitar technique.

Watters, Lu(cious) (b. Santa Cruz, Calif., 19 Dec. 1911; d. Santa Rosa, Calif., 5 Nov. 1989). Jazz trumpeter, bandleader, and arranger. From 1940 to 1950 he led the Yerba Buena Jazz Band in the San Francisco Bay area, except for a period in navy bands. The group helped popularize a revival of interest in traditional jazz. In turn many Dixieland bands copied its instrumentation—2 trumpets, trombone (played by Turk Murphy), clarinet, piano, banjo (sometimes 2 banjos), tuba, drums—and its repertory, which centered on recreations of early jazz recordings but also included new pieces by Watters such as "Big Bear Stomp" and "Emperor Norton's Hunch" (both recorded in 1946).

He led another band in the mid-1950s but otherwise worked outside of music.

Watts, André (b. Nuremberg, 20 June 1946). Pianist. His first instruction on the piano came from his Hungarian mother; his father was an American soldier. Once in the U.S. he continued his studies in Philadelphia with Genia Robiner. His public appearances began at age 9 when he played a Haydn concerto at a Philadelphia Orchestra children's concert; when he was 16 he played Liszt's First Piano Concerto at a New York Philharmonic Young People's concert under Bernstein. His first world tour was in 1967, sponsored by the U.S. State Department. Toured and recorded extensively; in 1976 he played the first live network television broadcast of a solo recital.

Waxman [Wachsmann], **Franz** (b. Königshütte, Silesia, 24 Dec. 1906; d. Los Angeles, 24 Feb. 1967). Composer and conductor. After studying at the Dresden Music Academy and the Berlin Conservatory, he worked in the German film industry, first as an orchestrator (*The Blue Angel,* 1930), then as a composer (*Liliom,* 1933). He moved to the U.S. in 1934, where his first project was *The Bride of Frankenstein* (1934). He worked in Hollywood for over 30 years; among his best-known scores are *Rebecca* (1940), *Suspicion* (1941), *Sunset Boulevard* (1950), *The Spirit of St. Louis* (1957). He also composed a number of works for the concert stage, and he conducted frequently in Los Angeles, elsewhere in the U.S., and in Europe.

Webb, Chick [William Henry] (b. Baltimore, 10 Feb. 1909; d. Baltimore, 16 June 1939). Jazz drummer and bandleader. From 1926 he led bands in New York; among early members were Johnny Hodges, Jimmy Harrison, and Benny Carter. During the 1930s his big band was often resident at the Savoy Ballroom in New York, and also toured widely. Ella Fitzgerald joined in 1935, taking over the leadership after Webb's death. Webb's recordings included "Stomping at the Savoy" and "Don't Be That Way" (both 1934; both composed by Edgar Sampson). Although crippled by tuberculosis, Webb was a forceful swing drummer. "Clap Hands! Here Comes Charley" (recorded in 1937) exemplifies his creative solo breaks.

Webbe, Samuel (1) (b. ?London, 1740; d. there, 15 May 1816). Composer. Regarded by some as the leading composer of glees; his first collection of vocal music came out in 1761. In 1776 he was organist at the Portuguese embassy chapel. In 1787 he was the librarian of the Glee Club and from 1794 until his death, the secretary. He won many of this club's prizes for his catches and glees; his "Glorious Apollo" was performed at the opening of each meeting. In addition to his many collections of glees, catches, canons, etc., he wrote keyboard sonatas, both Latin and English sacred vocal music, and organ pieces. He also wrote 3 singing tutors.

Bibl.: J. Merrill Knapp, "Samuel Webbe and the Glee," *ML* 33 (1952): 346–51.

Webbe, Samuel (2) (b. London, ca. 1770; d. there, 25 Nov. 1843). Composer. Son of Samuel Webbe (1). From ca. 1798 to 1817 he was the organist of the Unitarian chapel in Liverpool and from 1817 at the Spanish embassy chapel in London. His works include a musical comedy, *The Speechless Wife* (London, 1794), Masses, motets, many glees and catches, and instrumental music.

Weber, (Maria) Aloysia (Louis Antonia) [Lange] (b. Zell or Mannheim, between 1759 and 1761; d. Salzburg, 8 June 1839). Soprano. She had singing lessons with Mozart during his 1777–78 trip to Mannheim, and she and her father accompanied him on brief concert tours. Mozart was in love with her but eventually married her younger sister Constanze. She went with the court to Munich in 1778, and thence to Vienna, where she sang at the German opera in 1779. Mozart wrote several pieces with her in mind, including several arias and the part of Madame Herz in *Der Schauspieldirektor.* In 1788 she was Donna Anna in the first Viennese production of *Don Giovanni.*

Weber, Ben (William Jennings Bryan) (b. St. Louis, Mo., 23 July 1916; d. New York, 9 May 1979). Composer. He grew up in Chicago and briefly studied voice and piano at De Paul Univ. For the most part he was self-taught as a composer. In 1945 he moved to New York, where he earned his living as a music copyist. His String Quartet no. 2 premiered in New York in 1951, *Two Pieces for String Orchestra* in Boston in 1952; *Prelude and Passacaglia* (orchestra, 1954) was commissioned by the Louisville Orchestra. All these works are in a twelve-tone idiom, but they follow traditional forms and contain a strain of lyrical expression. This combination of the serial and the traditional persisted in Weber's subsequent works, for example, *Rhapsodie concertante* (viola and orchestra, 1957), Piano Concerto (1961), *The Ways* (song cycle for soprano, tenor, and piano, 1964), and *Dolmen* (elegy, winds and strings, 1964). Beginning in 1965 Weber taught composition at New York Univ.

Other works include String Quartet no. 1 (1942); *Concert Aria after Solomon* (soprano and chamber ensemble, 1949); *Sonata da camera* (violin and piano, 1950); Symphony in Four Movements (baritone and chamber orchestra, 1951); Violin Concerto (1954); *The Enchanted Midnight* (orchestra, 1967); *Concert Poem* (violin and orchestra, 1970); *Sinfonia Clarion* (chamber orchestra, 1973); *Capriccio* (cello and piano, 1977).

Weber, Carl Maria (Friedrich Ernst) von (b. Eutin, Germany, ?18 Nov. 1786; d. London, 5 June 1826). Composer. Son of Franz Anton von Weber (?1734–1812), who at his son's birth was a town musician in Eutin, but in 1787 gave that up to organize a touring theatrical company; it was probably he who added the noble *von* to the family name. Franz Anton's brother Fridolin was also a musician and father of the musical Weber sisters, who included Constanze Mozart. Weber was born with a hip deformity which gave him a pronounced limp, and he was never of robust constitution. He traveled with his father's company and had music lessons from age 3; the company's stay in Salzburg in 1797–98 led to lessons from Michael Haydn and his first published compositions, six fughettas (1798). In 1799 the company moved to Munich, where he studied with J. E. Wallishauser (known as Valesi) and J. N. Kalcher, composing his first opera, now lost, and the first version of his Mass in E♭. In 1800 he made a short tour as a pianist (Erfurt, Gotha, Leipzig); composed an opera, *Das Waldmädchen,* performed in Freiberg. By November 1801 he was back in Salzburg, where he composed *Peter Schmoll und seine Nachbarn* (it premiered in 1803, in Augsburg, where his half-brother was theater conductor), revised his Mass, and published piano pieces.

In September 1803 Weber arrived in Vienna, intending to study with Joseph Haydn, but instead became the pupil and disciple of Abbé Vogler, who then recommended him as music director at the Breslau theater. In this post (June 1804–autumn 1806), which exposed Weber to various personal enmities, partly because of his youth, he learned theater conducting and production but had little time to compose, producing only a few numbers for a never-finished fairy opera, *Rübezahl,* to a libretto by the theater manager. An accident—he drank acid, thinking it wine—incapacitated him for two months; his enemies gained the upper hand during his absence and he resigned. From late 1806 to February 1807 he was at the court of the Duke of Württemberg-Öls at Karlsruhe, where he was encouraged to compose, producing his only two symphonies, a horn concertino, and piano variations. After a brief concert tour, in July 1807 Weber became secretary to Duke Ludwig, younger brother of the King of Württemberg, at Stuttgart. In this rather dissolute milieu he found a sympathetic friend in the composer Franz Danzi, engaged in a love affair with the soprano Margarethe (Gretchen) Lang, and composed his opera *Silvana* (1808–10), the cantata *Der erste Ton* (text by Rochlitz), a Piano Quartet (1809), incidental music to Schiller's *Turandot* (1809), piano pieces, and 16 songs. He also began writing (1809) a semi-autobiographical novel, *Tonkünstlersleben,* which he pursued desultorily until 1820 without finishing it, publishing fragments. In 1809 he was joined by his father, who characteristically appropriated a large sum of money that the duke had given Weber to pay for some horses. The resulting financial imbroglio led to an abortive prosecution, Weber's brief imprisonment, and finally the expulsion of both Webers from the kingdom.

He gave two concerts of his music in Mannheim, conducted the premiere of *Silvana* in Frankfurt (16 Sept.), with his future wife, Caroline Brandt, in the title role, and resumed his studies with Vogler, now resident in Darmstadt, renewing or forming friendships with other students, including Meyerbeer. They formed the Harmonische Verein, of which Weber was a leader, to propagate their views and their music, partly through pseudonymous writings. In February 1811 Weber resumed concert tours as a pianist, with longer stays at times; from March to August 1811 he was in Munich, where he conducted the successful premiere of his singspiel *Abu Hassan* (11 June) and formed a fruitful artistic relationship with the clarinetist Heinrich Bärmann. It was for him that Weber composed his two clarinet concertos, the Clarinet Concertino, and later his Clarinet Quintet (1815) and Grand Duo Concertant (1816). With Bärmann he made a concert tour (Prague, Leipzig, Gotha, Weimar, Dresden) in December, ending in Berlin (Feb.–Aug. 1812), where he conducted the successful Berlin premiere of *Silvana* in July. In Berlin he found a congenial atmosphere and made important friends, including the theater intendant Count von Brühl, who over the next years was to make repeated unsuccessful attempts to get Weber a permanent post there. He composed some patriotic part songs, reflective of the nationalistic spirit of Berlin, which he shared, and his first piano sonata. He then spent several months visiting the music-loving Duke of Gotha, where he completed his second piano concerto. In January 1813 he moved on to Prague, where on arriving he was unexpectedly offered and accepted a three-year contract as music director of the Opera. This was a time-consuming post, as the Opera was in decline, and Weber reorganized it completely. Among the new singers was Caroline Brandt (from December 1813), whom he courted with varying success during this whole period. By 1812 he had begun to show signs of consumption, which was to advance for the rest of his life, gradually undermining his physical and emotional stamina. He composed relatively little during this period, completing or revising some earlier works and composing the patriotic cantata *Kampf und Sieg* (1815) and the patriotic song collection *Leyer und Schwert* (1814–16), which strengthened his identification with the cause of German nationalism. From 1815 he published musical essays to educate the Prague public, which had disappointed him with its cool reception of *Fidelio* in 1814.

In October 1816 Weber resigned and went to Berlin, where he completed his second and third piano sonatas; in December he was appointed music director of the new German Opera in Dresden (later made Royal Kapellmeister for life, making him equal to Morlacchi, head of the Italian Opera there). The post was a difficult one, not least because of its involvement in court politics and the inevitable rivalry between the German and Italian operas, almost a paradigm of the general situation in opera. In November 1817 Weber married Caroline Brandt. He composed a good deal in Dresden, including cantatas and other works for court occasions. His friendship with Friedrich Kind led to their collaboration on *Der Freischütz,* a subject to which Weber had been attracted earlier. It was composed in 1817–21, during which time he also produced his Masses in E♭ and G, his *Jübel-Ouvertüre,* his incidental music of P. A. Wolff's Spanish drama *Preciosa* (1820), and his once-popular *Konzertstück* for piano and orchestra, premiered in Berlin on 25 June 1821, four days after the triumphant premiere there of *Der Freischütz.* The success of *Freischütz* made Weber an international celebrity.

In November 1821 the impresario of the Vienna Opera, Barbaia, commissioned a new opera, in which Weber decided to demonstrate his range by treating a subject of greater weight and seriousness; he therefore gave up *Die drei Pintos,* a Spanish comedy on which he had been working since 1820 (it was to be completed by Mahler in 1888). Unfortunately, *Euryanthe* suffered from an inept libretto by the inexperienced Helmina von Chezy, resulting in only a succès d'estime in Vienna (25 Oct. 1823) and elsewhere. After this Weber, his strength ebbing, composed almost nothing until January 1825, when he began work on an English opera for London, *Oberon,* knowing that the trip there would shorten his life but feeling that he must undertake it to provide for his family after his death. He left Dresden in February 1826, going to London via Paris. *Oberon* was a success in London (12 Apr. 1826), but because of the special nature of English opera, it was not to sustain itself on the Continent (German premiere: Leipzig, 23 Dec. 1826). He conducted the first 12 performances and took part in concerts and musicales under great physical strain. He died in his sleep two nights before he was scheduled to leave. In 1844 his remains were returned to Dresden in solemn ceremonies conducted by Wagner.

Bibl.: Friedrich Wilhelm Jähns, *Carl Maria von Weber in seinen Werken: Chronologisch-thematisches Verzeichniss seiner sämmtlicher Compositionen* (Berlin, 1871; R: 1967). John Warrack, *Carl Maria von Weber* (London, 1968; 2nd ed., 1976). John Warrack, ed., *Carl Maria von Weber: Writings on Music,* trans. M. Cooper (Cambridge, 1981). Karla Höcker, *Oberons Horn: Das Leben von Carl Maria von Weber* (Berlin, 1986). Hans Hoffmann, *Carl Maria von Weber: Biographie eines Realistichen Romantikers* (Düsseldorf, 1986). Donald G. Henderson, *Carl Maria von Weber: A Guide to Research* (New York, 1990). Michael Charles Tusa, *"Euryanthe" and Carl Maria von Weber's Dramaturgy of German Opera* (Oxford, 1991).

Weber, (Jacob) Gottfried (b. Freinsheim, 1 Mar. 1779; d. Kreuznach, 21 Sept. 1839). Theorist and composer. His most important work was the treatise *Versuch einer geordneten Theorie der Tonsetzkunst* (Mainz, 1817–21, 3/1832). His other writings include *Über chronometrische Tempobezeichnung* (1817), *Allgemeine Musiklehre zum Selbstunterricht* (1822), and *Generalbasslehre zum Selbstunterricht* (1833). He also composed Masses, 1 Requiem, 1 Te Deum, chamber music, and songs. In 1806 he founded a musical society in Mannheim, and he also founded and edited the magazine *Caecilia* (from 1824).

Webern, Anton (Friedrich Wilhelm von) (b. Vienna, 3 Dec. 1883; d. Mittersill, Austria, 15 Sept. 1945). Composer. Anton Webern spent his formative years (1883–1902) in Klagenfurt, near the family's hereditary estate at Preglhof. He learned piano, cello, and some music theory from Edwin Komauer, a local composer and music teacher. In 1902 he enrolled in the Univ. of Vienna to study musicology with Guido Adler, earning his Ph.D. in 1906 with an edition of part 2 of the *Choralis Constantinus* by the Renaissance composer Heinrich Isaac. He also studied harmony with Hermann Graedener and counterpoint with Karl Navrátil, and he composed several songs, some chamber music, and an orchestral tone poem, *Im Sommerwind* (1904). In 1904, seeking further instruction in composition, he encountered Arnold Schoenberg, who soon became the decisive influence in his music and in his life. With Alban Berg, Egon Wellesz, Heinrich Jalowetz, and a few others, he became part of a small but extraordinarily loyal band of disciples who followed Schoenberg along the path to twelve-tone music and who fought tenaciously for Schoenberg's music and ideas. Under Schoenberg's tutelage Webern composed several chamber music sketches and a one-movement Quintet for piano and string quartet, which was performed in November 1907 in Vienna. The *Passacaglia* for orchestra (1908), which was eventually published as Webern's op. 1, is a late Romantic work in an extravagantly chromatic style reminiscent of Schoenberg's *Verklärte Nacht. Entflieht auf leichten Kähnen* op. 2 for chorus a cappella (1908) is a very nearly atonal double canon that owes as much to Heinrich Isaac as to Schoenberg.

Meanwhile Webern's pursuit of his chosen career as a conductor was proceeding in less than satisfactory fashion. He worked as assistant conductor of the theater orchestra in Bad Ischl (summer 1908), as a replacement in Innsbruck (July 1909), as second conductor in Bad Teplitz (summer 1910), as assistant in Danzig (1910–11) and in Stettin (1912–13). He conducted mainly light opera and operetta, and he complained constantly about the low quality of the repertory, the boorishness of the management, and the philistinism of the public. Each position he left on bad terms. Between engagements he was supported first by an allowance from his father, later by proceeds from the sale of the family estate. At the same time he was composing steadily, working his way, along with Schoenberg and Schoenberg's circle, toward a new musical language free from the constraints of tonality and key. His first efforts were a group of songs written in 1908 and 1909 on texts by Stefan George, of which 10 were eventually published as opp. 3 and 4. They are brief, enigmatic settings, free not only from tonality but from melodic and rhetorical gesture as well. They were followed by *Five Movements,* string quartet op. 5 (1909), and *Six Pieces for Orchestra* op. 6 (1909; rev. 1928). The *Six Pieces* make great use of the coloristic possibilities of the large orchestra, often distributing a motif or a phrase among several instruments in what Schoenberg later termed *Klangfarbenmelodie.* The tendency toward brevity and concision becomes yet more pronounced in Webern's works of the period 1910–14, particularly the *Four Pieces* op. 7 (violin and piano, 1910), *Six Bagatelles* op. 9 (string quartet, 1913), and *Five Pieces for Orchestra* op. 10 (1913). The fourth of the orchestra pieces, for example, is only six measures long. Webern later tried to explain this brevity, which remained a hallmark of his works until the mid-20s, as the consequence of atonality: "With the abandoning of tonality the most important means of building up longer pieces was lost" (Webern, *Path,* p. 54).

Almost all Webern's works between 1914 and 1926 were songs, a genre in which the structure of the text could help give form and duration to the music. *Four Songs* op. 12 (1915–17) were for voice and piano. In the subsequent sets of opp. 13–19 the voice is accompanied by small, carefully chosen instrumental ensembles, for example, violin, clarinet, bass clarinet, and cello in the Trakl songs op. 14 (1917–21). The texts for many of these songs are devotional verses, either from folk sources, as in *Five Sacred Songs* op. 15 (1917–22), or from the liturgy, such as the setting of the Marian antiphon "Ave, Regina coelorum" (*Three Songs* op. 18, violin, E♭ clarinet, and guitar, 1925). The simplicity of syntax and the directness of expression in the texts balance the compression and complexity of the musical language. Webern also uses contrapuntal devices to generate form. "Fahr hin, o Seel'," the last of the *Five Sacred Songs,* is a double canon in contrary motion (trumpet and clarinet play the same melody one measure apart and going in opposite directions while voice and violin do the same with a different melody). *Five Canons on Latin Texts* op. 16 (1923–24) are canonic throughout. Several of the later songs of this period contain traces of the "method of composition with twelve notes related only to one another," which Schoenberg was working out at this time and which he communicated "officially" to his disciples in February 1923. Webern's sketches for "Mein Weg geht jetzt vorüber" (op. 15, no. 4, 1922) show the twelve-tone row, its inversion, retrograde and various transpositions, all neatly labeled.

During the period 1914–24, while Webern was moving from atonal toward twelve-tone composition, he was also beginning to obtain greater professional success. When World War I was over, instead of returning to his career as a theater conductor, he threw himself into the activities of the Society for Private Musical Performances, an organization founded by Schoenberg and devoted to the performance of new music (1918–22). He also found work as a choral conductor with the the Mödling Men's Chorus (1921–34) and the Vienna Singverein (1923–34), a chorus sponsored by the Austrian Social Democratic party, positions that gave him some financial security and enabled him to conduct both choral and orchestral works at the party-sponsored Arbeiter-Sinfonie-Konzerte series. (These appointments do not reflect Webern's personal political views; he was not politically active.) In 1920 Universal Editions started to publish his works, and he began to get performances, particularly of the *Passacaglia* op. 1 and the *Bagatelles* op. 9 for string quartet, but also of newer works. By 1929 Webern was well enough known as a composer and conductor to undertake a concert tour of Germany and England.

With his adoption of the twelve-tone method in the early 1920s Webern felt encouraged to turn once again to instrumental compositions and toward larger forms. He wrote a small piano piece (*Kinderstück,* 1924) and two individual movements for string trio (both 1925). These led to the String Trio op. 20 (1927), a work in which serial pitch organization is combined with traditional formal schemes—the first movement a rondo, the second a sonata-allegro. In a letter Webern expressed satisfaction at having created "more expansive movements of truly symphonic nature" (Moldenhauer, *Webern,* p. 320). The trio was followed by the Symphony op. 21 (1928), the Quartet op. 22 (violin, clarinet, tenor saxophone, and piano, 1930), and a Concerto op. 24 (chamber ensemble, 1934). These works employ an exceedingly high degree of serial organization that now became characteristic for Webern. For example, the second movement of the op. 21 Symphony, a set of variations, is a multiple-level palindrome in which not only the twelve-note row but also the rhythms, the dynamics, and the instrumentation read the same backward and forward. At the same time the row—inverted, played backward, and transposed—accompanies itself in a wealth of canons. Webern compared his techniques in the Symphony to the art of the Renaissance polyphonists: "Greater unity is not possible. Not even the Netherlanders have managed this" (*Path,* p. 56).

For his vocal works of the 1930s, Webern used exclusively texts by his friend Hildegard Jone. In *Three Songs* op. 23 and *Three Songs* op. 25, both for soprano and piano, the high degree of organization is tempered by a search for melodic smoothness and lyrical expression. *Das Augenlicht* op. 26 (chorus and orchestra, 1935) is more contrapuntal; but the slower rhythms required by choral singing and the verbal reinforcement of canonic entrances make the counterpoint more accessible than in the instrumental works. This style was developed further in Cantata no. 1, op. 29 (soprano, chorus, and orchestra, 1939), and Cantata no. 2, op. 31 (soprano, bass, chorus, and orchestra, 1941–43). Instrumental works from the same period include the *Variations for Piano* op. 27 (1936), the string quartet op. 28 (1938), and *Variations* op. 30 (orchestra, 1940).

In March 1938 came the Anschluss: Austria was incorporated into Hitler's German Reich. Webern had already lost his conducting posts in 1934 when the Social Democratic party was outlawed. Now his music was branded by the Nazis as "degenerate art" and banned from performance and publication. He supported himself by teaching and by doing occasional arrangements for Universal Editions. He composed productively, however, finishing opp. 29–31 and beginning a new work. In March 1945, with Russian troops approaching Vienna, he fled with his wife to Mittersill in the Austrian Alps and in the American zone. On 15 September 1945, as an innocent bystander during the breakup of a black market operation, Webern was shot and killed by an American soldier.

Other works published by Webern include *Two Songs* op. 8 (voice and chamber ensemble, 1910; rev. 1925); *Three Little Pieces* op. 12 (cello and piano, 1914); *Three Traditional Rhymes* op. 17 (soprano, clarinet, bass clarinet, violin, viola, 1924–25); *Two Songs* op. 18 (chorus, violin, guitar, clarinet, bass clarinet, and celesta, 1926); *J. S. Bach: Fuga (Ricercata) a 6 voci* [arrangement from Bach's *Musical Offering*] (orchestra, 1935). Works published posthumously include *Eight Early Songs* (voice and piano, 1901–4); 2 movements for string quartet (1905); *Five Songs after Poems by Richard Dehmel* (voice and piano, 1906–8); *Four Stefan George Songs* (voice and piano, 1908–9); *Three Orchestral Songs* (1913–14); *Cello Sonata* (1914).

Bibl.: Hans Moldenhauer and Demar Irvine, eds., *Anton von Webern: Perspectives* (Seattle, 1966). Edward T. Cone, "Webern's Apprenticeship," *MQ* 53 (1967): 39–52. Walter Kolneder, *Anton Webern: An Introduction to His Works* (Berkeley, 1968). George Perle, "Webern's Twelve-Tone Sketches," *MQ* 57 (1971): 1–25. Hans Moldenhauer, *Anton von Webern: Chronicle of His Life and Works* (New York, 1978) [includes works list and bibl.]. Henri-Louis Matter, *Anton Webern: Essai* (Lausanne, 1981). Angelika Abel, *Die Zwölftontechnik Weberns und Goethes Methodik der Farbenlehre* (Wiesbaden, 1982). Arnold Whittall, "Webern and Multiple Meaning," *Music Analysis* 6 (1987): 333–54. Christopher F. Hasty, "Composition and Context in Twelve-Note Music of Anton Webern," *Music Analysis* 7 (1988): 281–312. Kathryn Bailey, *The Twelve-Note Music of Anton Webern: Old Forms in a New Language* (New York, 1991).

Webster, Ben (Benjamin Francis) (b. Kansas City, Mo., 27 March 1909; d. Amsterdam, 20 Sept. 1973). Jazz tenor saxophonist. He joined many big bands, including those of Bennie Moten (1931–33), Andy Kirk (1933), Fletcher Henderson (1934, 1937), and Duke Ellington (1940–43; with whom he recorded "Cotton Tail," 1940). Thereafter he mainly led small groups, although he also rejoined Ellington (1948–49) and toured with Jazz at the Philharmonic (1950s). He made albums with Art Tatum (1956), Coleman Hawkins (1957), Oscar Peterson (1959), Harry Edison (1962), and Don Byas (1968), the last recorded in Europe, where he was based from 1964. "Sleep" and "Memories of You," both recorded in Sid Catlett's quartet (1944), exemplify respectively Webster's propulsive, growling solo style and his breathy, passionate ballad playing.

Webster, Beveridge (b. Pittsburgh, 13 May 1908). Pianist. He studied with his father, founder of the Pittsburgh Conservatory, and with Isidor Philipp and Boulanger in France (1921–26), and later with Schnabel in Berlin. He premiered Ravel's *Tzigane* in Paris (1924); made his American debut in 1934 with the New York Philharmonic. He enjoyed a successful concert career, appearing with numerous orchestras, chamber music groups, and as a recitalist; best known for his playing of American composers and of Debussy and Ravel. He taught at the New England Conservatory (1940–46) and at Juilliard (beginning 1946).

Weckerlin, Jean-Baptiste (Théodore) (b. Gruebwiller, 9 Nov. 1821; d. Trottberg, near Gruebwiller, 20 May 1910). Composer and bibliographer. He studied at the Paris Conservatory with Halévy. Conducted the St. Cecelia Society, 1850–55. From 1876 to 1905 he served as librarian at the Paris Conservatory. He collected folk songs and published many with new harmonizations and piano accompaniment; also edited the works of Lully, Janequin, Gluck, and Cambert. He contributed articles to the supplement of Fétis's *Biographie universelle, Revue et gazette musicale,* and other journals. His compositions, which are virtually unknown, include stage works, music for chorus and orchestra, piano pieces, chamber music, and songs.

Weckmann, Matthias (b. Niederdoria, near Mühlhausen, 1619 or earlier; d. Hamburg, 24 Feb. 1674). Composer. He was a choirboy at the Dresden court chapel (1630–33), where he was a pupil of Schütz and studied organ and singing. In 1633 he went to Hamburg to study with Praetorius. Upon his return to Dresden in 1637 he became organist at the electoral chapel. In 1642 he followed Schütz to Nykøbing, Denmark, and was organist at the chapel there until 1647. After resuming his Dresden duties, he was appointed organist at the Jacobikirche, Hamburg, in 1655; he remained there until his death, founding a collegium musicum in 1660 and composing much of his extant music, which includes cantatas, choral works, canzonas, sonatas, and keyboard music.

Bibl.: *Solokantaten und Chorwerke mit Instrumentalbegleitung,* ed. Max Seiffert, *DDT* 6 (Leipzig, 1901; R: 1957). *Matthias Weckmann: Gesammelte Werke,* ed. Gerhard Ilgner, *EDM,* 2nd ser., 4 (Kassel, 1942).

Weelkes, Thomas (b. Elsted?, Sussex, ca. 1575; d. London, 30 Nov. 1623). Organist and composer. He published his first volume of madrigals in 1597 and spent some time in the service of the courtier Edward Darcye. In 1598 he was appointed organist of Winchester College, and it was during this time that he produced some of his greatest madrigals, which were issued in 2 volumes (1598, 1600). In 1601 or 1602 he joined the choir of Chichester Cathedral as organist and *informator choristarum;* he received the B.Mus. degree from New College, Oxford, in 1602 and produced his fourth and last volume of madrigals in 1608. In 1617, following years of increasingly dissolute behavior, he was dismissed from his post for drunkenness; by 1622 he was again employed as organist, though sporadically, and it appears that he spent much of his time in London, where he made his will. In addition to madrigals and lighter forms of secular vocal music, he composed anthems, services, and a few instrumental pieces.

Bibl.: Madrigals ed. in *EM* 9 (2nd ed., 1967), 11–12 (2nd ed., 1968), and 13 (2nd ed., 1965). *Collected Anthems,* ed. David Brown, Walter S. Collins, and Peter Le Huray, *MB* 23 (1966; 2nd ed., 1975). David Brown, *Thomas Weelkes: A Biographical and Critical Study* (London, 1969).

Weerbeke [Werbeke, Werbeck], **Gaspar van** (b. Oudenaarde, ca. 1445; d. after 1517). Composer. By 1471 he was active at the Sforza court in Milan; in 1472 and 1473 he was in Flanders and Burgundy to recruit singers for Duke Galeazzo Maria Sforza's choir, and upon his return he served as *vice-abbate* to the *cantori de camera* (the other half of the choir, the *cantori de cappella,* included Josquin, Compère, and Johannes Martini). Following the murder of the duke in 1476 Weerbeke went to Rome, where he served in the papal choir (1481–89). He left Rome in 1489, returning to the court of Duke Ludovico Sforza, "il Moro," in Milan; beginning in 1495 he was associated with the court choir of Philip the Fair, although he retained contacts with the Sforza court. He was back in Rome as a papal chorister from 1500 to 1509; in 1517 he was mentioned as canonicus of the Church of S. Maria ad Gradus in Mainz. He composed Masses and motets; 5 chansons of doubtful authenticity have also been attributed to him.

Bibl.: *Gaspar van Weerbeke: Messe e mottetti,* ed. Giampiero Tintori (Milan, 1963). Gerhard Croll, "Gaspar van Weerbeke: An Outline of His Life and Works," *MD* 6 (1952): 67.

Wegelius, Martin (b. Helsinki, 10 Nov. 1846; d. there, 22 Mar. 1906). Composer. He studied in Helsinki, Vienna, and Leipzig. Conductor at the Finnish Opera, 1878–79. Named the first director of the Helsinki Music College, 1882 (his students included Sibelius and Palmgren); named to the Swedish Royal Academy of Music, 1904. Compositions include an overture, cantatas, piano music, and songs. He also authored several texts, including books on theory and analysis (1888–89), history of Western music (1891–93), and composition (1897–1905).

Weigl, Joseph (b. Eisenstadt, 28 Mar. 1766; d. Vienna, 3 Feb. 1846). Composer. Son of Joseph Franz Weigl, a cellist in Prince Esterházy's orchestra. He moved to Vienna in 1769, where he later studied composition with Albrechtsberger and Salieri, and where his first opera, *Die unnütze Vorsicht* (for marionettes), was produced in 1783. He was appointed deputy Kapellmeister to Salieri at the court theater by 1790 and named court Vice-Kapellmeister in 1827. During his career he wrote over 30 operas, of which *La Principessa d'Amalfi* (Vienna, 1794) and *L'amor marinaro* (Vienna, 1797) were particularly successful; 18 ballets; 2 oratorios, 11 Masses, over 20 cantatas; orchestral music, chamber music, lieder.

Bibl.: Franz Grasberger, "Joseph Weigl (1766–1846): Leben und Werk mit besonderer Berücksichtigung der Kirchenmusik" (diss., Univ. of Vienna, 1938).

Weigl, Karl (b. Vienna, 6 Feb. 1881; d. New York, 11 Aug. 1949). Composer. He studied composition with Alexander von Zemlinsky and musicology with Guido Adler at the Univ. of Vienna. Served as an opera coach under Mahler (1904–6). His prewar compositions were in a late Romantic style (e.g., *Rhapsodie,* string orchestra, 1905; *Weltfeier,* soloists, chorus, and orchestra, 1912). He taught at the New Vienna Conservatory (1918–28) and at the Univ. of Vienna (1930–38). After the German–Austrian Anschluss he emigrated to the U.S., where he held a number of teaching posts (Hartt School of Music, 1941–42; Philadelphia Academy of Music, 1948–49). Works include 6 symphonies (1908, 1912, 1931, 1936, 1945, 1947); 2 piano concertos (1925, for left-hand alone; 1931); 8 string quartets (1903–49); 2 violin sonatas (1922, 1937); viola sonata (1939).

Weigl, Vally [Valerie] (b. Vienna, 11 Sept. 1894; d. New York, 25 Dec. 1982). Composer and music therapist. She studied composition with Karl Weigl, whom she married. Together they emigrated to the U.S. in 1938. Her own orthopedic surgery and rehabilitation aroused her interest in music therapy. She trained in the subject at Columbia Univ. (M.A., 1953), and went on to become a leader in the field, working at New York Medical College (1954–64) and teaching at the New School for Social Research (beginning 1975). She continued to compose; indeed, her best-known works date from this later period: *New England Suite* (clarinet, cello, and piano, 1955); *Nature Moods* (tenor, clarinet, and violin, 1956); *Peace Is a Shelter* (soloists, chorus, and piano, 1970); *The People Yes* (chorus, piano, and drums, 1976).

Weill, Kurt (Julian) (b. Dessau, 2 Mar. 1900; d. New York, 3 April 1950). Composer. The son of a synagogue cantor, he learned piano as a child, and by age 15 he was working at the Ducal Theater in Dessau as an accompanist. In 1918 he spent one semester at the Berlin Hochschule für Musik, studying composition with Humperdinck and conducting with Rudolf Krasselt, but, offered a job as chorusmaster and opera coach at the State Theater, he returned to Dessau. In 1919 he obtained a job as head conductor at the municipal theater in the Westphalian town of Lüdenscheid, where he conducted everything from Wagner to operettas. He had already been composing since he was 11, but all that survives from this period are a few songs, a string quartet (1919), and a cello sonata (1920). In 1920 he was accepted into Ferruccio Busoni's master class in composition at the State Academy of the Arts in Berlin. Weill quickly became Busoni's favorite pupil. To the class he brought Symphony no. 1 (1921), Divertimento

Scene from Kurt Weill's *Dreigroschenoper.*

for orchestra and male choir (1922), *Sinfonia sacra* for orchestra (1922), and String Quartet no. 1 (1923), the last of which earned him a contract with Universal Publishers. He also composed a ballet-pantomime, *Die Zaubernacht* (1922), which he later pointed to as the first work in his mature style, and Concerto for Violin and Wind Orchestra (1924), which was widely performed. Weill's first real success came with *Der Protagonist* (1925), a one-act opera written in collaboration with the playwright Georg Kaiser and premiered in Dresden in March 1926. With its stripped-down scoring and sharp textures, *Der Protagonist* immediately gained Weill a place as one of Germany's leading dramatic composers.

A much greater success was *Die Dreigroschenoper* (Three-Penny Opera), which opened on 31 August 1928, in Berlin. Weill's collaborator this time was Bertold Brecht, the communist poet and playwright, with whom he had already written the *Mahagonny-Songspiel* (1927). A very free adaptation of John Gay's *Beggar's Opera* of 1728, *Die Dreigroschenoper* inverted all the conventions of traditional opera. Instead of kings and princes, the characters were prostitutes and thieves; instead of arias and recitatives, they sang songs in the popular style of the 1920s; instead of an orchestral accompaniment, there was an eight-piece jazz band. *Die Dreigroschenoper* was a sensation; within a year, according to one count, it had been performed over 4,200 times in Europe. In the next few years Brecht and Weill collaborated on several more productions, including two cantatas written for radio broadcast (*Das Berliner Requiem,* 1928, and *Der Lindberghflug,* 1929), a school opera (*Der Jasager,* 1929), and *Aufstieg und Fall der Stadt Mahagonny* (1929), a full-scale opera in which the logic of modern capitalism is followed to its horrifying conclusions, accompanied by a score that ranges from popular songs to Wagnerian interludes.

Breaking with Brecht over the Berlin production of *Mahagonny* in 1931, Weill wrote an opera, *Die Bürgschaft* (1931), to a text by Caspar Neher, and incidental music to Georg Kaiser's *Der Silbersee: Ein Wintermärchen* (1932). After Hitler became chancellor of Germany in January 1933 the February opening of *Silbersee* was disrupted in Magdeburg by storm troopers, and in March Weill was warned by a friend that he was about to be arrested by the Gestapo. He fled to Paris, where he remained for two years, composing the ballet with songs *Die sieben Todsünden* (1933), his last work in collaboration with Brecht, plus a second Symphony (1934) and a set of songs for Jacques Deval's play *Marie Galante* (1934).

In September 1935 Weill arrived in New York to work on the production of *The Eternal Road,* a theatrical pageant of Jewish history, written in collaboration with the author Franz Werfel and the director Max Reinhardt. Because of financial problems *The Eternal Road* did not open until 1937. Meanwhile, Weill composed *Johnny Johnson,* a combination of European opera and Broadway musical, with American characters and an antiwar theme. Opening on Broadway in 1936, *Johnny Johnson* was greeted with respect but not enthusiasm. *Knickerbocker Holiday* (1938), however, written in collaboration with Maxwell Anderson, ran for four months and yielded the hit "September Song." *Lady in the Dark* (1941), with lyrics by Moss Hart and Ira Gershwin, enjoyed a Broadway run of almost two years. Weill's work for Broadway retained the progressive politics and the innovative approach to the theater that had marked his European works, but the popular and American elements no longer served the subversive function they had on the European stage, and his music came increasingly to resemble standard musical theater. This trend is evident in *One Touch of Venus* (1943), *Street Scene* (1947), *Love Life* (1948), and *Lost in the Stars* (1949), his last show.

Other works include *Frauentanz* (soprano and chamber orchestra, 1923); *Der neue Orpheus* (cantata, 1925); *Royal Palace* (opera, 1926; Berlin, 1927); *Der Zar lässt sich photographieren* (opera, 1927; Leipzig, 1928); *Kleine Dreigroschenmusik* (wind orchestra, 1928); *Happy End* (opera, 1929); *The Firebrand of Florence* (operetta, 1944; New York, 1945); *Down in the Valley* (school opera, 1948).

Bibl.: Kim Kowalke, *Kurt Weill in Europe* (Ann Arbor, 1979) [works list to 1934]. Ronald Sanders, *The Days Grow Short* (New York, 1980). Douglas Jarman, *Kurt Weill: An Illus-*

trated Biography (Bloomington, Ind., 1982). *A New Orpheus—Essays on Kurt Weill,* ed. Kim Kowalke (New Haven, 1986). David Drew, *Kurt Weill—A Handbook* (Berkeley, 1987) [works list]. Ronald Taylor, *Kurt Weill: Composer in a Divided World* (Boston, 1992). Jürgen Schebera, *Kurt Weill: An Illustrated Life,* trans. Caroline Murphy (New Haven, 1995).

Weinberger, Jaromír (b. Prague, 8 Jan. 1896; d. St. Petersburg, Fla., 8 Aug. 1967). Composer. He studied at the Prague Conservatory (1910–15), then with Max Reger in Leipzig (1916). Rejecting the fashionable styles of the day, he turned to Czech folk tunes harmonized in the tradition of Smetana. His opera *Schwanda, The Bagpiper* (Prague, 1927) enjoyed international success. He continued in a similar vein with *Six Bohemian Songs and Dances* (1930) and *Die geliebte Stimme,* opera (Munich, 1931). With the Nazi takeover of Czechoslovakia imminent, Weinberger emigrated to the U.S., arriving in 1939. Now he turned to American sources in works such as *Prelude and Fugue on "Dixie"* (1939) and *The Legend of Sleepy Hollow,* orchestra (1940). In later works, such as *Preludes réligieuses et profanes,* orchestra (1953), he aimed at a more international style.

Weiner, Lazar (b. Cherkassy, near Kiev, 17 Oct. 1897; d. New York, 10 Jan. 1982). Composer. As a child he sang in a synagogue choir and studied the piano, at first with the cantor, then in the Kiev Conservatory (1910–14). In 1917 his family emigrated to New York, where he worked as a vocal accompanist. In New York he was drawn into the Yiddish cultural revival movement, and he began to set Yiddish poems to music. He continued his musical studies with Frederick Jacobi and Joseph Schillinger, and he also studied eastern European Jewish traditions as a basis for his own compositions. He directed several choirs in New York, most notably the Workman's Circle Chorus (1930–65); he was music director of Central Synagogue in New York (1930–75); and he lectured widely on Jewish music. He wrote several piano pieces, an opera (*The Golem,* 1956; New York, 1981), and assorted instrumental works, but the bulk of his compositions are songs and choral music in Yiddish and liturgical music in Hebrew.

Bibl.: Marsha Edelman, "In Memoriam Lazar Weiner (1897–1982)," *Musica Judaica* 4 (1981–82): 99–112 [including partial works list].

Weiner, Léo (b. Budapest, 16 Apr. 1885; d. there, 13 Sept. 1960). Composer. He played the piano as a child. From 1910 to 1906 he studied composition at the Budapest School of Musical Art with Koessler. During 1908 he traveled to various musical centers in western Europe and then returned to Budapest, joining the faculty at the School of Musical Art, where he was especially known for his work with small ensembles. Meanwhile his own works became known internationally. His compositional language remained in a late Romantic style, heavily influenced by Beethoven and Mendelssohn. The work and nationalistic philosophy of Bartók also affected Weiner's use of native folk music in his own compositions. His works include dramatic music (*Csongor és Tünde,* ballet, Budapest, 1930), orchestral music (*Preludio, notturno e scherzo diabolico,* 1950), and chamber pieces (*Magyar népi muzsika* [Hungarian Folk Music], piano, 1953).

Weingartner, (Paul) Felix, Edler von Münzberg (b. Zara, Dalmatia, 2 June 1863; d. Winterthur, 7 May 1942). Conductor, composer, author. He studied with W. A. Rémy in Graz, and with Reinecke, Jadassohn, and Paul at the Leipzig Conservatory (1881–83). He met Liszt, who recommended that Weingartner's first opera, *Sakuntala,* be produced in Weimar (1884). The same year he accepted a conducting post at the Königsberg Opera, then conducted in Danzig (1885–87), Hamburg (1887–89), and Mannheim (1889–91). In 1891 he was named conductor at the Berlin Opera, and served as director of the Kaim concerts in Munich (1898–1903). He succeeded Mahler at the Vienna Court Opera (1908–11), and remained with the Vienna Philharmonic until 1927. He guest-conducted the Hamburg Opera (1912–14), and served as conductor at Darmstadt (1914–19), director of the Vienna Volksoper (1919–24), and briefly directed the Vienna Opera once again (1935–36); also served as director of the Basel Conservatory (1927–33).

Weingartner made a number of appearances in both England and the U.S., conducting the Royal Philharmonic, the London Symphony, the New York Philharmonic, and the Boston Opera. He composed several operas, of which *Genesius* (Berlin, 1892) was the most successful, and served on the editorial boards for the projected complete works of Berlioz (1899) and of Haydn (1907). But he is best known for his brilliant conducting career and his many fine writings on musical subjects, some of which appear in English in *Weingartner on Music and Conducting* (New York, 1969).

Weinrich, Carl (b. Paterson, N.J., 2 July 1904; d. Princeton, N.J., 13 May 1991). Organist. Studied with Mark Andrews, Marcel Dupré, and Lynnwood Farnam, receiving degrees from New York Univ. (1927) and the Curtis Institute (1930); in 1930 he succeeded Farnham at the Church of the Holy Communion in New York. He taught at Westminster Choir College in Princeton (1934–40), Wellesley (1936–46), and Columbia (1942–52), and served as director of music at Princeton Univ. Chapel (1943–73); he made a number of recordings.

Weinzweig, John (Jacob) (b. Toronto, 11 Mar. 1913). Composer. He learned piano and string bass as a youth; studied at the Univ. of Toronto with Healey Willan and Sir Ernest MacMillan (B.M., 1937), then at the Eastman School of Music with Bernard Rogers (M.M., 1938). Here he became acquainted with twelve-tone theory and practice, which are reflected in the *Suite for Piano* (1939), whose second movement is regarded as the first serial music by a Canadian composer, as well as in a Symphony (1940) and a Violin Sonata (1941).

During the early 1940s he composed in a similar idiom for radio and film; some of this music he later arranged into orchestral suites, for example, *Our Canada* (1943), *Edge of the World* (1946), *Red Ear of Corn* (1949). After World War II his works began to gain international recognition and performance, particularly *Divertimento no. 1* (flute and string orchestra, 1946), String Quartet no. 2 (1946), Cello Sonata ("Israel," 1949), and the Violin Concerto (1954). In Canada he was very influential as a teacher. At the Toronto Conservatory of Music (1939–43, 1945–60) and at the Univ. of Toronto (1951–78) he introduced two generations of Canadian composers to modern music. He also founded the Canadian League of Composers in 1951, serving as its president (1951–57, 1959–63). His later works held to a serial idiom while exploring timbres (e.g., Concerto for Harp and Chamber Orchestra, 1967; *Divertimento no. 4,* clarinet and strings, 1968), jazz rhythms (*Divertimento no. 3,* bassoon and strings, 1960; Piano Concerto, 1966), collage techniques (*Riffs,* flute, 1974), and the relation of sound and silence (*Dummiyah/Silence,* orchestra, 1969).

Bibl.: Elaine Keillor, *John Weinzweig and His Music: The Radical Romantic of Canada* (Metuchen, N.J., 1994).

Weir, Gillian (Constance) (b. Martinborough, New Zealand, 17 Jan. 1941). Organist. She studied with Ralph Downes at the Royal College of Music, London, and with Anton Heiller, Marie-Claire Alain, and Boulanger; in 1964 she won the St. Albans International Organ Playing Competition. Known for her interpretations of contemporary music; a number of works have been composed for her. She played her debut in the Royal Festival Hall in London in 1965. She has made concert tours of Europe, the U.S., Australia, and New Zealand both as organist and as a harpsichordist.

Weir, Judith (b. Cambridge, 11 May 1954). Composer. As a youth she began playing the oboe and composing, studying composition with Tavener at North London Collegiate. She was influenced by Stravinsky as well as by her experience as an orchestral player, and her music immediately began to meet with public performance and success. She worked on computer music under Vercoe at the Massachusetts Institute of Technology and then went on to study at King's College, Cambridge, in 1973. During the summer of 1975 she attended classes at Tanglewood, where she met Gunther Schuller. He proved to be a key influence in the change of direction that ensued as Weir more freely drew on various compositional techniques. In 1976, still at Cambridge, she worked with Holloway and was commissioned by Peter Maxwell Davies to write a work for his group The Fires of London. Weir has also worked with the choreographer Robert Cohan. She served as composer-in-residence for the Southern Arts Association, and from 1979 until 1982 was a Cramb Fellow in composition at Glasgow Univ. Works include *Out of the Air* (flute, oboe, clarinet, bassoon, horn, 1975); *Wunderhorn* (orchestra, 1978); cello sonata (1980); *Ballad* (baritone, orchestra, 1981); *Thread!* (speaker, flute/alto flute/piccolo, clarinet/bass clarinet, string quartet, piano, percussion, 1981); *A Night at the Chinese Opera* (opera, 1987); *Gentle Violence* (piccolo, guitar, 1987); *Narcissus* (flute, digital delay, 1988); *Heaven Ablaze in His Breast* (opera, 1989); *The Vanishing Bridegroom* (1990); string quartet (1990); *Music, Untangled* (orchestral overture, 1991); *Blond Eckbert* (opera, 1994).

Weis, (Carl) Flemming (b. Copenhagen, 15 Apr. 1898; d. there, 30 Sept. 1981). Composer and performer. From 1916 to 1920 he studied at the Copenhagen Conservatory, taking organ and theory lessons with Helsted and composition with Nielsen. In Leipzig he pursued organ with Straube and composition with Graener at the Hochschule für Musik from which he graduated in 1923. Back in Copenhagen he served as organist at Annakirke from 1929 until 1968; also worked as a music critic and as an administrator for musical associations. Weis's harmonic bases ranged from purposeful diatonicism to freely applied serialism. His music includes works for orchestra (Symphony no. 1, 1943, no. 2, 1948; *Femdelt Form no. 3,* 1963; *Sine nomine,* 1972), as well as vocal and chamber pieces (*Femdelt Form no. 1,* piano, 1962; *Femdelt Form no. 2,* string quartet, 1963).

Weisberg, Arthur (b. New York, 4 Apr. 1931). Conductor and bassoonist. He studied at Juilliard with Simon Kovar (bassoon) and Jean Morel (conducting); joined the New York Woodwind Quintet as bassoonist in 1957, and in 1960 founded the Contemporary Chamber Ensemble. The latter group premiered much contemporary music, including Crumb's *Ancient Voices of Children* (1970), and recorded works of Babbitt, Rochberg, Schiller, and others. Weisberg taught at Juilliard (1962–69), at SUNY–Stony Brook, and at Yale (1973–89). He served as chief conductor of the Iceland Symphony (1987–88), and wrote *The Art of Wind Playing* (1973).

Weisgall, Hugo (David) (b. Ivančice, Czechoslovakia, 13 Oct. 1912). Composer. His father was an opera singer, cantor, and composer of synagogue music, who immigrated with his family to Baltimore in 1921. Hugo Weisgall studied at Johns Hopkins Univ. (Ph.D., 1940) and simultaneously at the Peabody Conservatory. He also studied at the Curtis Institute of Music in Philadelphia with Rosario Scalero and Fritz Reiner (1936–39) and privately with Roger Sessions (1933–41). During the 1930s he conducted a synagogue choir and composed songs, liturgical works, and ballets. An orchestral suite from *Quest* (ballet, 1938) was performed by the New York Philharmonic in 1942. During World War II he served as military attaché in London, then as cultural attaché in Prague, making several appearances as a conductor and writing a ballet, *Outpost* (1947), for the National Theater in Prague. Returning to the U.S. in 1948, he wrote 2 one-act operas: *The*

Tenor (1950; Baltimore, 1952) and *The Stronger* (1952; New York, 1955), a "monodrama" for a single soprano plus a silent female role. His first full-scale opera was *Six Characters in Search of an Author* (1956), based on the play by Pirandello and introduced by the New York City Opera in 1959. These 3 operas were in a chromatic but basically tonal idiom. In his subsequent operas he made extensive use of twelve-tone techniques: *Purgatory* (1958; Washington, D.C., 1961); *Athaliah* (1963; New York, 1964); *Nine Rivers from Jordan* (New York, 1968). In the 1970s he turned to song cycles with *Fancies and Inventions* (baritone and chamber ensemble, 1970), *End of Summer* (tenor and chamber ensemble, 1970), *Translations* (mezzo-soprano and piano, 1972). Taught at the Jewish Theological Seminary in New York beginning 1952, at Juilliard 1957–68, and at Queens College 1961–83.

Other works include *The Gardens of Adonis* (opera, 1959; rev. 1981); *Jennie, or The Hundred Nights* (opera, New York, 1976); *One Thing Is Certain* (ballet, 1939); *Four Songs* (voice and piano, 1934); *Soldier Songs* (baritone and orchestra, 1946; rev. 1965); *The Golden Peacock: Seven Popular Songs from the Yiddish* (voice and piano, 1960; rev. 1976); *Lyrical Interval* (voice and piano, 1985); *Will You Marry Me* (opera, 1989); *Esther* (1993).

Bibl.: Bruce Saylor, "The Music of Hugo Weisgall," *MQ* 59 (1973): 239–62 [includes works list to 1972].

Weismann, Julius (b. Freiburg, Germany, 26 Dec. 1879; d. Singen am Hohentweil, 22 Dec. 1950). Composer. He studied piano as a child, then composition with Josef Rheinberger (1892) and with Ludwig Thuille (1899–1902). His orchestral and chamber works of the 1920s and 1930s, in a conservative Romantic style, were widely performed. He also composed several operas, among them *Leonce und Lena* (Mannheim, 1924) and *Die Gespenstersonate* (Munich, 1930). Other works include 2 symphonies; 3 violin concertos (1911, 1929, 1943); 2 piano concertos (1942, 1948); 9 string quartets (1905–47); sonatas for various instruments; and many piano works.

Weiss, Adolph (b. Baltimore, 12 Sept. 1891; d. Van Nuys, Calif., 21 Feb. 1971). Composer and bassoonist. As a child he learned piano, violin, and bassoon, and he worked for many years as a bassoonist in major orchestras, including the New York Symphony and the Chicago Symphony. Meanwhile he studied composition privately. In 1925 he went to Berlin to study with Arnold Schoenberg, who was teaching at the Akademie der Künste (1925–27). He immediately adopted Schoenberg's twelve-tone methods in 2 string quartets (1925, 1926) and a Chamber Symphony (1927), and he continued to write in the serial idiom from then on. His most significant works include *American Life,* orchestra (1928), in which twelve-tone and jazz idioms are mixed; *The Libation Bearers* (1930), a "choreographic cantata"; and *Theme and Variations,* orchestra (1933). He continued to work as a bassoonist in the Hollywood studios and in the Los Angeles Philharmonic.

Weiss, Silvius Leopold (b. Breslau, 12 Oct. 1686; d. Dresden, 16 Oct. 1750). Composer and lutenist. By 1706 he was employed in Breslau by Count Carl Philipp of the Palatinate. He was next in Rome with the Polish Prince Alexander Sobiesky (1708–14); there he probably worked with the Scarlattis. In 1715 he was at the courts of Hessen-Kassel and Düsseldorf; from 1717 he worked at Dresden. A celebrated lutenist, Weiss wrote more music for the lute—almost 600 pieces grouped in sonatas or dance suites—than any other composer in the history of the instrument.

Bibl.: *Silvius Leopold Weiss: [Complete Works],* ed. Douglas Alton Smith (Frankfurt, 1980–).

Weissenberg, Alexis (Sigismund) (b. Sofia, Bulgaria, 26 July 1929). Pianist. He studied with his mother and with Pancho Vladigerov in Bulgaria; fled from Nazi occupation to Palestine; after the war moved to New York, where he attended Juilliard and studied with Schnabel, Samaroff, and Landowska. In 1947 he won the Leventritt International Competition; after a lengthy absence from the stage he resumed his career in 1966. He recorded the Beethoven concertos with Karajan and toured widely with Maazel and the New Philharmonic.

Weldon, John (b. Chichester, 19 Jan. 1676; d. London, 7 May 1736). Composer. He was a chorister at Eton College and studied with the organist John Walter; from 1693 he studied with Purcell. His first appointment was as organist at New College, Oxford (1694–1702). In 1701 he became a Gentleman Extraordinary of the Chapel Royal, and the following year he was appointed organist of St. Bride's, Fleet Street, in London. Weldon later acquired the positions of an organist of the Chapel Royal (1708), organist of St. Martin-in-the-Fields (1714), and second composer to the Chapel Royal (1715). His compositions include several stage works (*The Judgement of Paris,* 1701; *The Tempest,* ca. 1712), anthems, services, odes, songs, and several instrumental works.

Welin, Karl-Erik (b. Genarp, 31 May 1934). Composer, pianist, organist. Studied organ with Alf Linder at the Royal College of Music, Stockholm (1956–61); took composition with Bucht (1958–60) and Lidholm (1960–64), continuing his studies at Darmstadt (1960–62) and with David Tudor. His earliest works, from the late 1950s and early 1960s, were indebted to impressionism in their orchestration; he subsequently moved to an experimental, avant-garde idiom. He worked as organist at St. Johannes Church in Stockholm and was associated with the Swedish experimental group "Fylkingen." At a concert in 1964 he transcended traditional performance boundaries when, in addition to having a pyrotechnical display emerge from the piano, he sawed off the legs of the instrument with a chainsaw (injuring himself). Works include opera (*Dummerjöns*

[Silly Jöns], 1966–67; *Drottning Jag* [I the Queen], 1972); choral (*4 kinesiska dikter,* 1956; *Natalino* [Christmas], 1971; *4 japanska dikter,* 1974; *Viso,* 1975); orchestral (*Pereo,* 35 strings, 1964; *Copelius,* ballet, 1968; *Jeux à l'occasion d'une fête,* chamber orchestra, 1976; Symphony no. 1, 1985–86); solo vocal music; chamber music (String Quartet no. 8, 1986–87; *EssAEG,* 2 pianos, electronics, 1988).

Welitsch [Veličkova], **Ljuba** (b. Borissovo, Bulgaria, 10 July 1913). Soprano. Studied in Vienna with Lierhammer, then performed in Graz (1937–41), Hamburg (1941–42), and Munich (1943–46); joined the Vienna State Opera in 1946, where her roles included Butterfly, Nedda, Elisabeth, Desdemona, and Fiordiligi. But she was best known for her Salome, which she performed under Strauss in 1944, and with which she made her Metropolitan Opera debut in 1949. She also appeared at Glyndebourne and with the Covent Garden company in London.

Welk, Lawrence (b. Strasburg, N.D., 11 Mar. 1903; d. Santa Monica, Calif., 17 May 1992). Popular bandleader and accordionist. He formed his first groups in the 1920s; from 1951 appeared on television. He termed his characteristic sound "Champagne Music"; his repertory featured light classical arrangements and dance music. He published music in California and made several successful recordings ("Calcutta," 1960).

Wellesz, Egon (Joseph) (b. Vienna, 21 Oct. 1885; d. Oxford, 9 Nov. 1974). Composer and musicologist. He studied musicology at the Univ. of Vienna with Guido Adler, concentrating on 17th- and 18th-century opera. At the same time he studied composition privately with Arnold Schoenberg. He remained close to Schoenberg and especially to Anton Webern, although he did not adopt their twelve-tone methods in the 1920s. His early compositions were mainly songs (e.g., *6 George-Lieder,* 1917) and short piano pieces (*Der Abend,* 1910; *Drei Skizzen,* 1911), plus a series of string quartets (1912, 1916, 1918, 1920). He remained active as a scholar, publishing several studies on opera and ballet in 17th-century Venice and Vienna. He followed a similar direction in his own composition in the 1920s with *Die Prinzessin Girnara* (opera, Hannover, 1921), *Achilles auf Skyros* (ballet, Stuttgart, 1926), *Alkestis* (opera, Mannheim, 1924), and several other works that combined Baroque subjects with 20th-century harmonies. Meanwhile his scholarly interests had been drawn toward Middle Eastern and Byzantine music and their relation to Western traditions. His editions of Byzantine sources and his monographs on Byzantine notation and music theory remain classics in the field. In 1929 he became professor of music history at the Univ. of Vienna. Fleeing Austria after the Nazi takeover in March 1938, he went to England, where he taught music history at Oxford (1943–72). He continued to compose a good deal, particularly a series of 9 symphonies (1945, 1948, 1951, 1952, 1956, 1965, 1968, 1970, 1971), an English-language opera, *Incognita* (Oxford, 1951), and several songs in both English and German.

Other works include *Der Opferung des Gefangenen* (opera, Cologne, 1926); *Die Bakchantinnen* (opera, Vienna, 1931); *Persisches Ballett* (Donaueschingen, 1924); *Die Nächtlichen* (ballet, Berlin, 1924); 4 Masses (1934, 1937, 1958, 1963); 10 string quartets (1912–68); Octet (clarinet, horn, bassoon, violin, viola, cello, bass, 1949); 2 violin sonatas (1923, 1953); cello sonata (1920).

Writings: *Arnold Schönberg* (Vienna, 1921); trans. Eng. (1924). *Byzantinische Kirchenmusik* (Breslau, 1927). *Eastern Elements in Western Chant* (Oxford, 1947). *A History of Byzantine Music and Hymnography* (Oxford, 1949; rev. 1963). With Emmy Wellesz, *Egon Wellesz: Leben und Werk* (Vienna, 1981).

Bibl.: Robert Schollum, *Egon Wellesz* (Vienna, 1963; rev. 1985). David Symons, "Egon Wellesz and Early Twentieth-Century Tonality," *Studies in Music* 6 (1972): 42–54. Otto Kolleritsch, ed., *Egon Wellesz* (Vienna, 1986).

Wells, Dicky [William] (b. Centerville, Tenn., 10 June 1907; d. New York, 12 Nov. 1985). Jazz trombonist. He played in the big bands of Benny Carter (1932–33), Fletcher Henderson (1933), Teddy Hill (1934–37), and Count Basie (1938–46, 1947–50). As a soloist in small groups he recorded as a leader (including "Lady Be Good" and "Dicky Wells Blues," both 1937) and sideman (including Basie's "Dickie's Dream," 1939). He joined Jimmy Rushing, toured Europe with Bill Coleman (1952–53), and worked with Earl Hines (1954). He returned to Europe with Buck Clayton (1959, 1961), toured in Ray Charles's band (1961–3), and rejoined former Basie band members in the Countsmen (late 1970s).

Writings: with Stanley Dance, *The Night People: Reminiscences of a Jazzman* (Boston, 1971).

Wells, Junior [Blackmore, Amos, Jr.; Wells, Amos, Jr.] (b. West Memphis, Ark., 9 Dec. 1934). Blues harmonica player and singer. He moved to Chicago in 1946 and formed a band with David and Louis Myers and Fred Below, Jr., called, variously, the Little Boys, Three Deuces, and Four Aces. In 1952 Wells replaced Little Walter in Muddy Waters's group; recordings from around this time include "Eagle Rock" (1953) and "So All Alone" (1954). In the late 1960s Wells began performing and recording with Buddy Guy.

Wells, Kitty [Muriel Ellen Deason] (b. Nashville, 30 Aug. 1919). Country singer and songwriter. After early performances on radio in Nashville, in 1937 she began to tour with her husband, Johnny Wright, and his Tennessee Mountain Boys; they appeared on radio shows including the *Louisiana Hayride* (1947–52) and the Grand Ole Opry (from 1952). She made many successful solo recordings, including "It Wasn't God Who Made Honky-Tonk Angels" (1952), "I Can't Stop Loving You" (1958), and "Heartbreak U.S.A." (1965). The first female singer to achieve success as a soloist in country music, she facilitated the later careers of artists such as Loretta Lynn.

Wenzinger, August (b. Basel, 14 Nov. 1905). Cellist and viola da gamba player. Studied at the Basel Conservatory and later went to Cologne, where he was a pupil of Paul Grümmer and Philipp Jarnach. He was first cellist with the Bremen Orchestra (1929–34) and with the Basel Allgemeine Musikgesellschaft (1936–70), and also played in the Basel String Quartet (1933–47). He learned the viola da gamba and became interested in performing early music on original instruments; he directed several groups, including the West German Radio Orchestra in Cologne (1954–58), Baroque operas in Hannover (1958–66); in 1933 helped to found the Schola cantorum Baseliensis, forming the viola da gamba trio at this institution in 1968. He edited early music, published a viola da gamba tutor, and undertook concert tours through Europe, the U.S., and Asia.

Werckmeister, Andreas (b. Benneckenstein, Thuringia, 30 Nov. 1645; d. Halberstadt, 26 Oct. 1706). Theorist and organist. He studied organ with his uncle Christian, and was educated at Nordhausen and Quedlinburg. He was then organist at Hasselfelde (1664), Quedlinburg (1675), and the Martinkirche, Halberstadt (1696). His treatises were influential; he devised a successful tuning method in the *Orgel-Probe* (Frankfurt and Leipzig, 1681; trans. Eng. 1976). His other writings include *Musicae mathematicae Hodegus curiosus* (Frankfurt and Leipzig, 1686; *Musicalische Temperatur* (Frankfurt and Leipzig, 1686–87? [lost]); *Hypomnemata musica* (Quedlinburg, 1697; R: 1970); *Die nothwendigsten Anmerckungen und Regeln, wie der Bassus continuus oder General-Bass wol könne tractiret werden* (Aschersleben, 1698); *Harmonologia musica* (Frankfurt and Leipzig, 1702; R: 1970); and the *Musikalische Paradoxal-Discourse* (Quedlinburg, 1707; R: 1970).

Werder, Felix (b. Berlin, 24 Feb. 1922). Composer. His father was a Jewish cantor and composer; under his auspices Felix learned the piano, viola, and clarinet. From 1934 to 1941 he lived with his family in England, fleeing the Nazi regime in Germany. After 1941 Werder lived and worked in Australia as a music teacher, a critic for *Age* (1960–77), and a composer. His eclectic language was affected by the melodic patterns of Hebrew chant as well as by contemporary trends such as atonality, quartal harmonies, serialism, electronics, and tonal clusters. The music of Schoenberg and Berg, in particular, influenced Werder's orchestral music, and his development of the string quartet bears the mark of Bartók. His works include operas (*The Agamemnon of Aeschylus,* mime-chant opera; *The Affair,* opera, 1969; *The Vicious Square,* 1971), ballets (*La belle dame sans merci,* 1973), vocal music (*Francis Bacon's Essays,* oratorio, 1971), orchestral music (5 symphonies, 1951–71; concertos), and chamber music.

Werle, Lars Johan (b. Gävle, 23 June 1926). Composer. As a youth he played the piano and headed a jazz band. He studied musicology with Moberg and counterpoint with Bäck at Uppsala Univ. from 1948 to 1951. Beginning in 1958 he worked with the Swedish Broadcasting Corporation; also taught at Stockholm School of Music Drama. His early compositions were serial, progressively becoming more freely eclectic. For example, his first opera, *Drömmen om Thérèse* (1960–64), used prerecorded music. His musical language moves easily between various styles and is generally accessible. Works include stage productions (*Resan* [The Journey], opera, 1969; *Medusan och djävulen* [Medusa and the Devil], lyrical mystery play, 1973; *Lionardo,* opera, 1988; *Väntarna* [The Ones Who Wait], chamber opera, 1990; *Tavlan: en eftermiddag på Prado* [The Painting: An Afternoon at the Prado], chamber opera, 1991); orchestral and vocal music (*Flower Power,* 6 or more voices, instrumental ensemble, 1974); chamber and tape music.

Werner, Gregor Joseph (b. Ybbs an der Donau, 28 Jan. 1693; d. Eisenstadt, Burgenland, 3 Mar. 1766). Composer. He was organist at Melk Abbey from 1715 to 1716 or 1721, and in 1728 became Kapellmeister at the Esterházy court at Eisenstadt. After Haydn became Vice-Kapellmeister there in 1761, Werner, as *Oberhofkapellmeister,* remained in control of sacred music. Werner's bitter resentment of the younger composer is evident in a petition he sent to Prince Nikolaus von Esterházy in October 1765 in which he blames Haydn for the decline of the Esterházy musical establishment. His compositions display a mastery of counterpoint and include Masses (several a cappella), oratorios, smaller sacred vocal works, symphonies, and trio sonatas.

Wernick, Richard (b. Boston, Mass., 16 Jan. 1934). Composer. He attended Brandeis Univ., where he studied with Irving Fine, Arthur Berger, and Harold Shapero (B.A., 1955), then Mills College, where he studied with Leon Kirchner (M.A., 1956). From 1956 to 1958 he lived in Canada, composing and conducting at the Winnipeg Ballet; from 1958 to 1964 he lived in New York, composing music for documentary films and television and also for the public schools. He taught at the Univ. of Chicago (1965–68), then at the Univ. of Pennsylvania (beginning 1968). His best-known works are settings of political and/or religious texts, for example, *A Prayer for Jerusalem* (mezzo-soprano and percussion, 1971); *Kaddish-Requiem, a Secular Service for the Victims of Indo-China* (mezzo-soprano, chamber ensemble, and tape, 1971); *Visions of Terror and Wonder* (mezzo-soprano and orchestra; Pulitzer Prize, 1977). His compositions often use the music of the past; for example, in the *Kaddish-Requiem* he quotes Brahms, Lassus, and Palestrina, while *Introits and Canons,* chamber orchestra (1977), is based on Baroque forms such as canon and passacaglia.

Other works include *Stretti* (clarinet, violin, viola, and guitar, 1964); *Haiku of Bashō* (soprano, chamber ensemble, and tape, 1968); *Moonsongs from the Japanese* (soprano and tape, 1969); *Songs of Remembrance* (mezzo-soprano, shawm, English horn, and oboe, 1974); *A Poison Tree* (soprano and chamber ensemble,

1980); Piano Sonata (1982); *Musica Ptolemeica* (brass quintet, 1986); Symphony no. 1 (1987); String Quartet no. 3 (1988); Concerto for Piano and Orchestra (1989); Symphony no. 2 (1995); *Cassation* (horn trio, 1995); . . . *And a Time for Peace* (mezzo-soprano, orchestra, 1995).

Wert [Vuert, Werth], **Giaches** [Jaches] **de** (b. Weert?, near Antwerp, 1535; d. Mantua, 6 May 1596). Composer. As a child he was brought to Italy to serve as a chorister at the court of Maria di Cardona, Marchese della Padulla, at Avellino, near Naples; little else is known of his early life. By 1558 he was employed by Count Alfonso Gonzaga at Novellara; he may have been a member of the *cappella* at Parma under Rore, and in 1565 he was appointed *maestro di cappella* at the ducal chapel of S. Barbara in Mantua. In addition to his activities at the Gonzaga court, he had considerable contact with the Este court at Ferrara, especially during the 1580s; he had an affair with Tarquinia Molza, niece of the poet Francesco Maria Molza and member of the second Ferrarese *concerto delle donne.* Between 1582 and 1583 and again in 1585 Gastoldi was called upon to serve as *maestro di cappella* while Wert battled attacks of malaria; Gastoldi succeeded him in the post in 1592, although Wert remained active at court until his death. One of the outstanding madrigalists of his day, Wert was praised by, among others, Palestrina, Artusi, and Berard. Monteverdi cited him, along with Rore, Marenzio, Ingegneri, and Luzzaschi, as a composer of the *seconda prattica.*

Bibl.: *Collected Works,* ed. Carol MacClintock and Melvin Bernstein, *CMM* 24 (1961–). Carol MacClintock, *Giaches de Wert, 1535–1596: Life and Works* (Rome, 1966).

Wesley, Charles (b. Bristol, 11 Dec. 1757; d. London, 23 May 1834). Composer, organist. Brother of Samuel Wesley. He studied organ with Joseph Kelway and eventually had a position at St. Marylebone; studied composition with William Boyce. His published compositions include 6 concertos for organ or harpsichord, 6 string quartets, other keyboard music, hymns, anthems, and songs.

Wesley, Samuel (b. Bristol, 24 Feb. 1766; d. London, 11 Oct. 1837). Composer, organist. Younger brother of Charles Wesley. He learned to compose and play violin at an early age; he composed an oratorio, *Ruth,* when he was 8. He was regarded as one of the leading organists of his day, but he held few permanent appointments and spent much of his life close to poverty. He greatly admired Bach's music and figured prominently in the England Bach revival. He wrote Latin sacred vocal music, hymns, anthems, secular vocal pieces, some orchestral and chamber works, and many organ and other keyboard works.

Bibl.: James T. Lightwood, *Samuel Wesley, Musician* (London, 1937). J. Marsh, "The Latin Church Music of Samuel Wesley" (diss., Univ. of York, 1975).

Wesley, Samuel Sebastian (b. London, 14 Aug. 1810; d. Gloucester, 19 Apr. 1876). Composer, organist. Son of Samuel Wesley. His father's pupil in organ and composition; from 1817 a choirboy of the Chapel Royal, also St. Paul's. From 1826 to 1832, church organist and theater conductor in London, beginning to compose church music, songs. Served as cathedral organist at Hereford, 1832–35 (leaving there because of his elopement with the dean's sister); Exeter, 1835–41; Leeds parish church, 1842–49; Winchester, 1845–65, also Winchester College, 1850–65; Gloucester, 1865–76. He had a difficult personality (and was asked to resign from Winchester for neglecting his duties), but was highly regarded for his playing and improvising. From 1850, professor at the Royal Academy; also conducted at provincial festivals. He is best known for Anglican church music (few written organ compositions), especially the Service in E (1841–44) and some of his ca. 38 anthems; he also composed or harmonized many hymns.

Bibl.: Paul Chappell, *Dr. S. S. Wesley* (Great Wakering, 1977).

Westergaard, Peter (Talbot) (b. Champaign, Ill., 28 May 1931). Composer and theorist. He studied at Harvard with Walter Piston (B.A., 1953), at Princeton with Roger Sessions (M.F.A., 1956), and in Freiburg with Wolfgang Fortner (1956–58). His compositions are in a serial idiom and feature delicate timbres, as in *The Plot against the Giant (Cantata I),* female chorus, clarinet, cello, harp (1956), *Mr. and Mrs. Discobbolos,* chamber opera (1966). Taught at Columbia Univ. (1958–66), Amherst College (1967–68), Princeton Univ. (beginning 1968). As a theorist his work is concerned with both tonal and atonal music. Other compositions include *The Tempest* (opera, 1970–90); *Ode* (soprano, 5 instruments, 1989).

Wetz, Richard (b. Gliwice, Upper Silesia, 26 Feb. 1875; d. Erfurt, Germany, 16 Jan. 1935). Composer. He studied at the Leipzig Conservatory, then with Ludwig Thuille in Munich (1899–1900). He moved to Erfurt in 1906, where he conducted and taught at the conservatory. He also taught at the Weimar Musikschule (1916–35). In his compositions and in his teaching he perpetuated the tradition of German Romanticism. His early works were mainly songs, but his *Kleistouvertüre* (1904) for orchestra was introduced by Nikisch in 1908 and often performed thereafter. In orchestral works such as his three symphonies (1916, 1919, 1922), he followed Bruckner closely in form, harmony, and orchestration. Other works include *Das ewige Feuer* (Düsseldorf, 1907); *Requiem* (1925); *Christmas Oratorio* (1929); violin concerto (1933); 2 string quartets (1916, 1923).

Bibl.: Hans Polack, *Richard Wetz* (Leipzig, 1935) [includes works list].

Wetzler, Hermann (Hans) (b. Frankfurt, 8 Sept. 1870; d. New York, 29 May 1943). Organist, conductor, and composer. He spent his childhood in the U.S., but he returned to Germany at the age of 12 to study at the Hoch Conservatory in Frankfurt. Returning to New

York in 1892, he played the organ at Old Trinity Church and conducted the Wetzler Symphony Concerts (1903–5). During the 1910s and the 1920s he conducted opera in Germany and appeared widely in Europe as a guest conductor. In 1940 he returned to New York. Works include *Die baskische Venus* (opera, Leipzig, 1928); *Assisi* (orchestra, 1924); *Symphonie concertante* (violin and orchstra, 1932).

Weyse, Christoph Ernst Friedrich (b. Altona, 5 Mar. 1774; d. Copenhagen, 8 Oct. 1842). Composer. From 1789 he studied with J. A. P. Schulz in Copenhagen. In 1794 he became the principal organist at the Reformed Church and in 1805 at the Cathedral in Copenhagen, a position he held until his death. He was designated court composer in 1819, a position that required him to produce cantatas. Other compositions include several operas, all first performed in Copenhagen; *Miserere,* double chorus, orchestra; symphonies, songs, keyboard pieces.

Bibl.: Dan Fog, *Kompositionen von C. E. F. Weyse: Thematisch-bibliographischer Katalog* (Copenhagen, 1979).

Whettam, Graham (Dudley) (b. Swindon, 7 Sept. 1927). Composer. He at first focused on science, pursuing music largely on his own; then became a music teacher and taught until 1948, when he came to concentrate solely on composition and conducting. The influence of Bartók is visible in his music, which uses colorful, dramatic orchestration and vibrant, emphatic rhythm. He wrote many film scores. His orchestral music includes *The Masque of the Red Death* (orchestral ballet, 1968), *Symphonic Prelude* (premiere 1985); chamber music includes Oboe Quartet (1960), String Quartet no. 1 (1967), and *Partita for Percussion* (premiere 1985). Other works include choral music (*A Mass for Canterbury,* 1986); chamber music (*Ballade,* violin, orchestra, 1988).

White, Clarence Cameron (b. Clarksville, Tenn., 10 Aug. 1880; d. New York, 30 June 1960). Violinist and composer. He played the violin from childhood, studying with Will Marion Cook, then with Joseph Douglass, and playing his first solo recital at age 15 in Washington, D.C. He attended Howard Univ., then Oberlin Conservatory (1896–1901), and later studied with Samuel Coleridge-Taylor in London (1906, 1908–10) and with Raoul Laparra in Paris (1930–32). He toured widely in the U.S. as a violinist and taught at several black schools and conservatories, including the Washington Conservatory of Music (1903–7), West Virginia State College (1924–30), and Hampton Institute (1932–35). Almost all of his mature compositions are based on black folk music. The earlier ones are violin virtuoso pieces (*Bandanna Sketches,* 1918, *From the Cotton Fields,* 1920). His later works include operas (*Ouanga,* 1932; South Bend, Ind., 1949), ballets (*A Night in Sans Souci,* 1929), orchestral pieces (*Kutamba Rhapsody,* 1942; *Elegy,* 1954), and arrangements of spirituals (*40 Negro Spirituals,* 1927; *Traditional Negro Sprituals,* 1940).

Bibl.: Vernon Edwards and Michael Mark, "Clarence Cameron White," *The Black Perspective in Music* 9 (1981): 51–72.

White, Josh(ua Daniel) [Pinewood Tom] (b. Greenville, S.C., 11 Feb. 1915; d. Manhasset, N.Y., 5 Sept. 1969). Blues, gospel, and folk singer and guitarist. As a child he performed with street evangelists and gospel singers and learned to play guitar; at 13 he sang and played guitar with Blind Joe Taggart on "There's a Hand Writing on the Wall" (1928). In 1932 he began a long recording career, which included "Mean Mistreater Mama" (1934, as "Pinewood Tom," with Leroy Carr), "There's a Man Goin' around Taking Names" (1933) and, with his group the Carolinians, "Told My Cap'n" (1940). He performed with Woody Guthrie, Libby Holman, and Paul Robeson, among others.

Bibl.: D. S. Sieger, *The Glory of the Road: The Story of Josh White* (New York, 1982).

White, Maude Valérie (b. Dieppe, France, 23 June 1855; d. London, 2 Nov. 1937). Composer and writer on music. She studied in Torquay and in London at the Royal Academy of Music from 1876 to 1879. She was the first woman to win the Mendelssohn Scholarship there. She traveled to South America, then to Vienna, where she studied with Fuchs in 1883. Illness forced her to travel to better climates; this allowed her to become proficient in many languages. She composed nearly 200 songs in Italian, German, French, and English. Other compositions include incidental music to several scores, the ballet *The Enchanted Heart* (1912–13), and piano music.

White [Whyte], **Robert** (b. ca. 1538; d. London, Nov. 1574). Composer. He served as a chorister and then as a cantor at Trinity College, Cambridge; in 1562 he was appointed master of the choristers at Ely Cathedral, a position previously held by his father-in-law, Christopher Tye. By 1567 he was master of the choristers at Chester Cathedral and two years later held a similar position at Westminster Abbey. He died of the plague. White was one of the first English composers to write fantasias; his hymns served as models for two of Byrd's settings of *Christe qui lux es.*

Bibl.: *Robert White: The Instrumental Music,* ed. Irwin Spector, *RRMR* 12 (1972). Irwin Spector, "The Music of Robert White," *The Consort* 23 (1966): 100–108.

Whitehill, Clarence (Eugene) (b. near Parnell, Iowa, 5 Nov. 1871; d. New York, 18 Dec. 1932). Baritone. Studied in Paris with Giraudet and Sbriglia, making his debut in Brussels in 1898. Subsequently performed at the Opéra-comique, Paris (1899), Bayreuth (1904–9), Covent Garden (1905), and the Paris Opéra (1909); made his Metropolitan Opera debut as Amfortas in 1909, remaining with the Met for 19 seasons; also sang with the Chicago Opera (1911–17). Best known for his Wagnerian roles, which he studied with Cosima Wagner, and for his Golaud.

Whiteman, Paul (b. Denver, 28 March 1890; d. Doylestown, Pa., 29 Dec. 1967). Popular bandleader.

In 1919 he formed a dance orchestra which made such million-selling recordings as "Whispering" (1920) and "Three O'Clock in the Morning" (1922). When the instrumentation grew to include a big band, orchestral winds, and strings, and when jazzmen such as Bix Beiderbecke, Joe Venuti, and Jack Teagarden contributed occasional solos, Whiteman promoted his music as "symphonic jazz" and himself as "king of jazz." The acceptance of these labels hindered an appreciation of New Orleans jazz and obscured Whiteman's contributions to popular and semiclassical music. In addition to recording many hit songs, Whiteman commissioned and first performed Gershwin's *Rhapsody in Blue* (1924) and later commissioned Grofé's *Metropolis* (ca. 1928) and Stravinsky's *Scherzo à la russe* (1942).

Whithorne [Whittern], **Emerson** (b. Cleveland, 6 Sept. 1884; d. Lyme, Conn., 25 Mar. 1958). Composer. As a teenager he showed talent for the piano, and in 1904 went to Europe to study with Theodor Leschetizky, then with Artur Schnabel (1905–7). From 1907 to 1915 he lived in London, where he wrote music criticism, taught piano, and began to make himself known as a composer. Most of his music of this period was exoticist; for example, *The Rain* (orchestra, 1912) used Chinese pentatonic scales, while *Greek Impressions* (string quartet, 1914) was based on Greek folk tunes. Returning to the U.S. in 1915, he found exotic color in American subjects. *New York Days and Nights* (piano, 1922; orchestrated 1923), a suite of portraits of New York scenes, was widely performed and became his best-known work. He turned to Negro spirituals as a source in *Saturday's Child* (mezzo-soprano, tenor, and chamber orchestra, 1926) and *The Grim Troubadour* (voice and string quartet, 1927; also arranged for baritone and piano), to western lore in *El Camino Real* (piano, 1937) and *Sierra Morena* (orchestra, 1938). His 2 symphonies (1929, 1935) and his violin concerto (1931) are less programmatic in character.

Bibl.: John Tasker Howard, *Emerson Whithorne* (New York, 1929).

Whiting, Arthur Battelle (b. Cambridge, 20 June 1861; d. Beverly, Mass., 20 July 1936). Pianist and composer. He studied piano and composition at the New England Conservatory in Boston with William Hall Sherwood and George Chadwick, then at the Munich Conservatory with Joseph Rheinberger (1883–85). He returned to Boston in 1885, then moved to New York in 1895. He was active as a concert pianist, and he also performed on harpsichord along with illustrated lectures. He wrote rather few works, most of them in the style of German Romanticism. Works include *Concert Overture* (1886); Piano Concerto (1888); *Fantasia* (piano and orchestra, 1897); *The Rubaiyát of Omar Kayyám* (baritone and piano, 1901).

Whiting, George E. (Elbridge) (b. Holliston, Mass., 14 Sept. 1842; d. Cambridge, 14 Oct. 1923). Organist and composer. Obtained a position as an organist in Hartford in 1858. There he organized the Beethoven Society. In 1862 he took the position as organist at Tremont Temple and Mount Vernon Church in Boston. He studied briefly in New York with George W. Morgan, then in Liverpool. Returning to the U.S., he held positions in Albany and Boston. In 1874 he moved to Berlin to study with Haupt and Radecke. By 1876 he was back in Boston as organist at the Immaculate Conception Church, a position he held until 1910. He also was head of the organ department at New England Conservatory until 1898. He published several collections of organ music.

Whiting, Richard A. (b. Peoria, 12 Nov. 1891; d. Beverly Hills, 10 Feb. 1938). Popular songwriter. He published his first songs while working for the Remick publishing firm in Detroit (including "It's Tulip Time in Holland," 1915; "Where the Morning Glories Grow," 1917); in 1919 he moved to New York and became a leading figure on Tin Pan Alley. From the late 1920s he composed for films in Hollywood; successes include "When Did You Leave Heaven" (in *Sing, Baby, Sing,* 1936) and "Louise" (in *Innocents in Paris,* 1939).

Whitney, Robert (Sutton) (b. Newcastle upon Tyne, 9 July 1904; d. Louisville, Ky., 22 Nov. 1986). Conductor and composer. He studied piano and composition at the American Conservatory of Music in Chicago. During the 1920s he played piano in Chicago nightclubs and on the radio. He studied conducting with Eric DeLamarter and made his debut with the Chicago Civic Orchestra in 1932. In 1937 he was engaged as conductor of the Louisville Orchestra. Beginning in 1948, with the strong support of orchestra management, Whitney undertook to make the Louisville orchestra a leader in the performance of contemporary music by commissioning a new work for every program. In 1953 the orchestra received a grant from the Rockefeller Foundation to commission and record new music, a project that continued through the 1980s and resulted in over 200 "First Edition" recordings. Whitney retired from the orchestra in 1967. He served as dean of the Univ. of Louisville Music School from 1956 to 1972. His own compositions include Concerto grosso (orchestra, 1934), Symphony in E minor (1936), Concertino (orchestra, 1960).

Whittaker, William (Gillies) (b. Newcastle upon Tyne, 23 July 1876; d. Orkney Isles, 5 July 1944). Composer. He originally studied science at Durham Univ.; he then turned to the study of organ, singing, and conducting and was appointed to the music faculty of Armstrong College at Durham Univ. in 1898. From 1929 to 1938 he was a professor of music at Glasgow Univ. and head of the Royal Scottish Academy of Music from 1929 until 1941. He conducted various choral societies, in particular the Newcastle Bach Choir Society, which he established in 1915 and which focused on historically correct performances. Whittaker published arrangements of English folk song as well as monographs on choral music by Bach, Byrd, Purcell, and Beethoven.

Whittenberg, Charles (b. St. Louis, Mo., 6 July 1927; d. Hartford, 22 Aug. 1984). Composer. He studied at the Eastman School of Music with Burrill Phillips and Bernard Rogers (B.A., 1948). He worked at the Columbia–Princeton Electronic Studios (1962) and later at the Yale Electronic Studio. From 1967 to 1977 he taught composition at the Univ. of Connecticut. His best-known works exploit brass and woodwind textures in a serial idiom. They include *Fantasy* (wind quintet, 1962); *Triptych* (brass quintet, 1962); *Variations for 9 Players* (chamber ensemble, 1964); Concerto for Brass Quintet (1968); *Five Feuilletons* (clarinet, 1976).

Whittern, Emerson. See Whithorne, Emerson.

Whythorne, Thomas (b. Ilminster, England, 1528; d. London 31? July 1596). Lutenist and composer. He attended Magdalen College School, Oxford, and matriculated at Magdalen College. For a time he was servant and scholar to John Heywood; subsequently found employment as a music tutor and was taken into the service of the Duchess of Northumberland. Following several years of travel on the Continent (1553–55) he returned to England and resumed his career as a music tutor. Inspired by the popularity of madrigal books in Italy, he composed *Songes for Three, Fower and Five Voyces* (London, 1571), the first work of its kind published in England; later that year he was appointed master of music at the chapel of Archbishop Parker. The 1955 rediscovery of Whythorne's autobiography (ca. 1576; ed. James M. Osborn, Oxford, 1961) has revealed much about both musical and social practice of the time.

Widmann, Erasmus (b. Schwäbisch Hall, bapt. 15 Sept. 1572; d. Rothenburg ob der Tauber, 31 Oct. 1634). Composer. He attended the Lateinschule at Schwäbisch Hall and the Univ. of Tübingen (1589–90) before obtaining the position of organist at Eisenerz, Styria (1595), and at Graz (1596–98). He later worked at Schwäbisch Hall (1598 or 1599), Weikersheim (1602), and at the Jacobskirche at Rothenburg ob der Tauber (1613). A prolific composer, Widmann wrote motets, Psalms, songs, and dance music.

Bibl.: *Erasmus Widmann: Ausgewählte Werke,* ed. Georg Reichert, *EDM* 3 (Mainz, 1959). Georg Reichert, *Erasmus Widmann: Leben, Wirken und Werke eines württembergisch-fränkischen Musikers* (Stuttgart, 1951).

Widmer, Ernst (b. Aaraca, Switzerland, 25 Apr. 1927). Composer. Graduated from the Zurich Conservatory in 1950; Koellreutter invited him to Brazil in 1956 to teach at his Seminários livres de música in Salvador, Bahia; in 1959 Widmer succeeded Koellreutter as director, serving until 1969; in addition, he was a professor there from 1963. His compositions fluctuate between progressive and retrospective outlooks; works include *Hommages* to Stravinsky, Bartók, and Martin for oboe and strings (1960); *Prismas,* piano and orchestra (1971); *Wettinger Sternsingerspiel* (1968) and *Sinopse* (1970), chorus and orchestra; Wind Quintet no. 1 (1954); *Divertimento III,* "Côco 61," 3 winds, piano, and percussion (1961); *Pulsars,* chamber ensemble (1969); and *Rumor,* narrator, chorus, smetak, orchestra, tape, and audience (1971); *Paisagem Bahiana IV (Lagoa da Abaete)* (flute, violin, viola, cello, 1988).

Widor, Charles Marie (Jean Albert) (b. Lyons, 21 Feb. 1844; d. Paris, 12 Mar. 1937). Organist, composer, teacher. From a family of organists and organ builders; studied at the Brussels Conservatory with Fétis (composition) and Lemmens (organ), from whom he absorbed the Bach tradition, then not widely known in French-speaking regions. From 1860 he was organist at St. François, Lyons, building a reputation by provincial recitals; 1870–1934, organist at St. Sulpice, Paris. From 1890 to 1896 he was organ professor, Paris Conservatory, suceeding Franck; from 1896, composition professor. He had many distinguished pupils (organ: Tournemire, Vierne, Schweitzer, Dupré; composition: Honegger, Milhaud). He was elected permanent secretary of the Académie in 1914 (member from 1910); also a music critic; conducted a choral society, Concordia. He was a noted improviser and a prolific composer; works include 3 operas (especially *Les pêcheurs de Saint Jean,* Opéra-comique, 1905), a ballet and incidental music, 3 numbered symphonies and other orchestral works, much chamber music, piano pieces, sacred works, songs. Best known for his organ music, which remains a basic element of the instrument's repertory, especially the 10 organ symphonies, nos. 1–4 published as op. 13 (1876), nos. 5–8 as op. 42 (?1880), *Symphonie gothique* op. 70 (1895), *Symphonie romain* op. 73 (1900). His writings include *Technique de l'orchestre moderne* (Paris, 1904); trans. Eng. (1905; rev. 2nd ed., 1946).

Bibl.: Andrew Thomson, *Widor: The Life and Times of Charles-Marie Widor* (New York, 1987).

Wiechowicz, Stanisław (b. Kroszyce, 27 Nov. 1893; d. Kraków, 12 May 1963). Composer. He studied music at the Kraków Conservatory, the Dalcroze Institute in Dresden, the St. Petersburg Conservatory, and the Schola cantorum in Paris. He later taught at the Poznan Conservatory and the Kraków Conservatory and served as a music critic for *Muzyka polska.* His own compositions are pervaded by native folk music, whether through the incorporation of specific songs or of characteristics of the repertoire in general. Orchestration is colorful and melodic lines highly lyrical; rhythm in Wiechowicz's music is striking and repetitive. Works include some orchestral pieces and much vocal music (*3 suity ludowe* [3 Folk Suites], solo voices, chorus, orchestra, 1942; *List do Marc Chagalla* [Letter to Marc Chagall], dramatic rhapsody, male and female speakers, 2 solo voices, chorus, orchestra, 1961).

Wieck, Clara. See Schumann, Clara.

Wieck, (Johann Gottlob) Friedrich (b. Pretzsch, near Torgau, 18 Aug. 1785; d. Loschwitz, near Dresden, 6 Oct. 1873). Performer and music teacher. Father of Clara Wieck Schumann. He studied theology at the Univ. of Wittenberg, but abandoned this after passing his exams in 1807 to study music. He was essentially self-taught. In 1816 he settled in Leipzig; two years later he established a piano factory and music lending library. In 1844, moved to Dresden. Wrote *Klavier und Gesang* (Leipzig, 1853; enlarged 3rd ed., 1878; trans. Eng., 1878) as well as some piano studies. A number of articles he wrote under the pseudonyms Raro and Das appeared in *Neue Zeitschrift für Musik* and other journals.

Wiegold, Peter (John) (b. Ilford, Essex, 29 Aug. 1949). Composer. He studied at the University College of Wales in Aberystwyth, and went on to study from 1972 to 1975 at Durham Univ. with Lumsdaire. He served as visiting composer from 1976 to 1978 at the Arnolfini Gallery in Bristol and in 1979 became a teacher at the Univ. of Sussex. His early compositions were within the serial tradition; yet his style progressively broadened into a flexible one that moved easily between tonal and atonal harmonies. Wiegold has worked closely with amateur musicians and also helped to establish the new music group Gemini. Works include *Night Visitors* (ballet, tape, 1975); *And He Showed Me a Pure River of Water of Life* (soprano, 3 clarinets, percussion, 1976); *The Flowers Appear on Earth* (flute/piccolo, clarinet/bass clarinet, harp, guitar, percussion, viola, cello, 1978).

Wielhorski, Count Michal [Viyel'gorsky, Mikhail Yur'yevich] (b. Volhynia, 11 Nov. 1788; d. Moscow, 9 Sept. 1856). Composer and patron. He studied with Martín y Soler, and played both violin and piano. At age 13 he composed some songs with orchestral accompaniment. In 1804 he moved to Riga with his family; there he studied counterpoint and played quartets with his father and two brothers. He studied with Cherubini in Paris (1808). By 1810 he was back in St. Petersburg. There he arranged a number of private concerts of Western music which included Beethoven's symphonies. He was friends with Glinka. His music includes 1 opera (*Tsïgane,* 1838), 3 symphonies (1822, 1822, unfinished), overtures, a string quartet, and a string quintet. His brother Count Mateusz Wielhorski (1794–1860) was a cellist and also a patron of the arts.

Wieniawski, Henryk [Henri] (b. Lublin, Poland, 10 July 1835; d. Moscow, 31 Mar. 1880). Violinist, composer. A child prodigy, he had lessons in Warsaw, then (1843–46) at the Paris Conservatory, from 1844 under Massart (first prize, 1846); 1846–48, continued as private pupil of Massart. In 1848 he gave concerts in Paris, St. Petersburg, Moscow, and Warsaw, but returned to the conservatory in 1849–50 to study harmony. He began to publish virtuoso violin pieces from ca. 1850, some of which became very popular. From 1851 he was a touring virtuoso, his Gewandhaus concert in 1853 establishing him in Germany. From 1860 to 1872 he lived in St. Petersburg, serving as solo violinist to the tsar (1859), concertmaster of St. Petersburg orchestra, and leader of Russian Musical Society quartet. In 1872–74 he toured North America (with Rubinstein the first year, then alone to California); then toured Europe and taught at the Brussels Conservatory (1875–77). He was a charismatic musician, considered one of the great violinists of his time. His virtuoso numbers (especially the 2 polonaises opp. 4, 21 and *Souvenir de Moscou* op. 6) are still occasionally heard, as is his second concerto, premiered in St. Petersburg in 1862; also *L'école moderne,* 10 etudes-caprices, op. 10, and *Etudes-Caprices* op. 18, both still used. Brother of Józef Wieniawski.

Wieniawski, Józef [Joseph] (b. Lublin, 23 May 1837; d. Brussels, 11 Nov. 1912). Pianist and composer. Brother of Henryk Wieniawski. He studied with Zimmermann and Marmontel at the Paris Conservatory in 1847, leaving in 1850. During 1851–53 he concertized with his brother in Russia. He received a scholarship from the tsar in 1855 to study with Liszt in Weimar. In 1856–58 in Berlin he studied theory with Adolf Bernhard Marx. After returning to Paris he moved to Moscow, where he was named to the piano faculty at Moscow Conservatory when it was founded in 1866. In 1878 he became professor of piano at Brussels Conservatory. His compositions include the Symphony in D op. 49, Piano Concerto in G minor op. 20, Violin Sonata op. 24, Cello Sonata op. 26, String Quartet op. 23, Piano Trio op. 40, and many short piano pieces.

Wieprecht, Wilhelm (Friedrich) (b. Aschersleben, 10 Aug. 1802; d. Berlin, 8 Aug. 1872). Instrument maker. Studied in Dresden and Leipzig, and in Berlin in 1824. He had contact with Briesling and Schlott, makers of the first practical piston valves. In 1825 he reorganized a military band in Berlin, introducing valve instruments to the brass players. With Moritz he invented a bass tuba in 1835. He also devised the Bathyphon, a contrabass clarinet for military band. He was invited in 1845 to reorganize the musical division of the Prussian Cavalry Guards.

Wigglesworth, Frank (b. Boston, 3 Mar. 1918). Composer. He was an undergraduate at Columbia Univ. (B.S., 1940) and studied in New York with Otto Luening and Henry Cowell. He later worked with Edgard Varèse (1948–51). Beginning 1954 he taught at the New School for Social Research in New York. His music draws from diverse sources, including American hymnody and French Ars nova, mixing them in a personal idiom that is often polytonal or polymodal, sometimes atonal. Works include *The Willowdale Handcar* (opera, 1969); *Ballet for Esther Brooks* (1961); 3 symphonies (1953, 1958, 1960); New England Concerto (violin and strings, 1941); *Telesis* (orchestra, 1951); Concertino (viola and orchestra, 1965); *Music for Strings* (1981); *Lake Music* (flute solo, 1947); String Trio (1972); Woodwind Quintet (1975); 2 Short Masses (1961, 1970); *Duets* (mezzo-soprano and clarinet, 1978); *The Police Log of the Chronicle* (opera, 1984).

Wihan, Hanuš (b. Police u Broumova, Bohemia, 5 June 1855; d. Prague, 1 May 1920). Cellist. Studied at the Prague Conservatory with František Hegenbarth. From 1880 he was principal cellist in the Munich court orchestra and a cellist in King Ludwig's Quintet. In 1888 he was named professor of cello at the Prague Conservatory. He formed the Bohemian String Quartet in 1871 with some of his students. Dvořák dedicated his Cello Concerto (1895) to Wihan. He retired in 1914.

Wihtol, Joseph. See Vītols, Jāzeps.

Wilbye, John (b. Diss, Norfolk, bapt. 7 Mar. 1574; d. Colchester, between Sept. and Nov. 1638). Composer. By 1598, the year of his first volume of madrigals, he was a musician in the employ of Sir Thomas Kytson at Hengrave Hall, outside Bury St. Edmunds; he remained at Hengrave for nearly three decades, where he served as a domestic musician and gradually amassed a considerable fortune; his only other collection of madrigals appeared in 1609. After the death of Lady Kytson in 1628 he moved to Colchester to spend the final decade of his life with her daughter, Lady Rivers. Wilbye was one of the finest and most expressive of the English madrigalists.

Bibl.: David Brown, *John Wilbye* (London, 1974).

Wild, Earl (b. Pittsburgh, 26 Nov. 1915). Pianist and composer. He studied at Carnegie Technical College (1930–34) and took piano with Selmar Jansen, Egon Petri, and Paul Doguereau. He served as pianist with the NBC Symphony, and in 1942 Toscanini invited him to appear as soloist with that orchestra. He premiered Marvin David Levy's First Piano Concerto and Paul Creston's Piano Concerto op. 43. His own compositions include orchestral music, an oratorio, and many piano transcriptions, but he is best known for his virtuoso performances of much of the Romantic repertory, and as an exponent of Gershwin's music. He taught at Juilliard (from 1977), the Manhattan School (1981–83), and Ohio State Univ. (from 1987); in 1978 he became artistic director of the Wolf Trap Chamber Group.

Wildberger, Jacques (b. Basel, 3 Jan. 1922). Composer. He studied at the Basel Conservatory: piano with Eduard Ehrsam and Paul Baumgartner and composition with Walther Geiser. From 1948 to 1951 he studied privately with Wladimir Vogel, from whom he adopted both serialism and speaking chorus techniques. The former may be heard in *Tre mutazioni,* chamber orchestra (1952), and *In My End Is My Beginning,* soprano, tenor, and chamber orchestra (1964), the latter in *Epitaphe pour Evariste Galois,* soprano, baritone, speaking chorus, orchestra, and tape (1962). Other works include *Konzertante Szenen für einen Saxophonisten und Orchester* (1984). He taught at the Hochschule für Musik in Karlsruhe (beginning 1959), and at the Musikakademie in Basel (beginning 1966).

Bibl.: *Jacques Wildberger: Werkverzeichnis* (Zurich, 1982).

Wilder, Alec [Alexander] **(Lafayette Chew)** (b. Rochester, 16 Feb. 1907; d. Gainesville, Fla., 24 Dec. 1980). Composer. He studied briefly at the Eastman School of Music but was largely self-taught as a pianist and a composer. During the 1930s and 1940s he did arrangements for several bands, and his songs were recorded by Tommy Dorsey ("Who Can I Turn To?" 1941), Mildred Bailey ("It's So Peaceful in the Country," 1941), the Mills Brothers ("I'll Be Around," 1943), Frank Sinatra ("Where Is the One?" 1948), and others. He also experimented with blending popular and classical music in a series of *Octets* for winds, harpsichord, and rhythm section (1939). By the 1950s he had turned primarily to concert music, writing 12 wind quintets, 8 brass quintets, and sonatas for a great variety of wind instruments. He continued to write songs ("Song from Moulin Rouge," 1953), and he wrote several works for the stage: *Kittiwake Island* (1955; New York, 1960) and *The Truth about Windmills* (opera, 1975).

Writings: *The American Popular Song* (New York, 1972). *Letters I Never Mailed* (Boston, 1975).

Bibl.: David Demsey and Ronald Prather, *Alec Wilder: A Bio-Bibliography* (Westport, Conn., 1993).

Wilder, Philip van (b. Flanders, ca. 1500; d. London, 24 Feb. 1553). Lutenist and composer. Around 1520 he entered the service of King Henry VIII and rapidly became one of the king's favorite musicians; by 1528 he was a lutenist with the King's Musick and in the following years frequently performed as a member of the "pryvay Chamber"; he was, in effect, director of the king's private music. From 1537 he taught Princess Mary the lute. Edward VI retained his services and in 1550 commissioned him to find choristers for the king's chapel. Although he was renowned in his day as a lute player, only one of Van Wilder's lute pieces, a 4-part fantasia, is extant; the bulk of the surviving work is vocal, including chansons and sacred vocal music.

Bibl.: *Collected Works,* ed. Jane A. Bernstein, *MMR* 4 (1991). Jane A. Bernstein, "Philip Van Wilder and the Netherlandish Chanson in England," *MD* 33 (1979): 55–76.

Wilding-White, Raymond (b. Caterham, Surrey, 9 Oct. 1922). Composer. He spent his childhood in Europe and in Argentina, then moved to the U.S. to study at the Juilliard School of Music (1947–49). He studied composition with Judd Cooke at the New England Conservatory (B.M., 1951; M.M., 1953) and with Gardner Read at Boston Univ. (D.M.A., 1962). He taught at the Case Institute of Technology in Cleveland (1960–67), then at De Paul Univ. in Chicago (1967–85). He composed works in a variety of genres, some in a neoclassical idiom influenced by Stravinsky (*Paraphernalia,* chorus and chamber ensemble, 1959), several using electronic tape (*Whatzit no. 4,* orchestra and tape, 1969).

Wilhelmj, August (Emil Daniel Ferdinand Viktor) (b. Usingen, 21 Sept. 1845; d. London, 22 Jan. 1908). Violinist. He studied in Wiesbaden in 1849; debuted in 1854. He studied (1861–64) at the Leipzig Conservatory with Ferdinand David (violin), Richter and Hauptmann (counterpoint and harmony). In Frankfurt am Main in 1864 he studied with Raff. He made a world tour, 1878–82. With Rudolf Niemann he founded a violin school. He was concertmaster at Bayreuth in 1876. He was named principal violin professor at the Guildhall School of Music in London in 1894. He composed several works for violin and for string quartet.

Wiłkomirski, Kazimierz (b. Moscow, 1 Sept. 1900). Composer and cellist. His father, Alfred Wiłkomirski, was a violinist and conductor; Kazimierz's siblings and half-siblings became professional musicians as well. Kazimierz studied cello, conducting, and composition at the Moscow Conservatory. He traveled to the Warsaw Conservatory in 1919, where he studied composition with Statkowski and conducting with Młynarski. He taught music beginning in 1917. From 1932 to 1934 he studied conducting with Scherchen in Switzerland and from 1934 to 1939 was head of the Gdynia Conservatory. He subsequently held administrative posts at Łódź State College of Music, the Wrocław Philharmonic, and the Gdańsk Philharmonic. He also taught at music schools in Zopport, Wrocław, and Warsaw and toured with his sisters Wanda and Maria, performing chamber music. His own compositional style was predominantly late Romantic; he was especially known for his book on cello pedagogy.

Willaert, Adrian (b. Bruges or Roulaers, ca. 1490; d. Venice, 17 Dec. 1562). Composer. Zarlino relates that Willaert intended to study law at Paris but instead became a pupil of Jean Mouton and served at the court of Louis XII and Francis I. He may have been in Rome in 1515, where according to Zarlino the papal choir of Leo X mistook his motet *Verbum bonum* for a work of Josquin. From July 1515 he is listed among the retinue of Cardinal Ippolito I d'Este, perhaps residing with the prelate in Hungary from October 1517 until August 1519. He entered the employ of Duke Alfonso upon Ippolito's death in 1520, remaining until 1527, when he was appointed *maestro di cappella* at St. Mark's in Venice; under him the chapel there became one of the most prestigious in Europe. He was an important teacher, whose pupils included Rore, Vicentino, Parabosco, Andrea Gabrieli, Porta, Buus, Barré, and Zarlino, the last of whom lionized him in his treatises as the perfecter of music. A participant in Venetian social and literary circles, he figured in the work of Andrea Calmo, Pietro Aretino, and Antonfrancesco Doni.

An interest in theoretical questions is indicated by references to him in Spataro's correspondence as well as by a composition of his from the time of Leo X, *Quid non ebrietas,* in which the tenor falls through the circle of fifths, ending on a written seventh to be changed by *musica ficta* to an octave. His works include Masses, motets, hymns, Psalms (some using the *cori spezzati* effect then current in the Veneto), madrigals, *villanesche,* chansons, and a lute intabulation of Verdelot's madrigals. His best-known publication is the *Musica nova,* dedicated to Alfonso II d'Este and published in 1559, though the contents probably circulated long before that date as a collection named after the Venetian singer Pulissena Pecorina.

Bibl.: *Opera omnia,* ed. Hermann Zenck and Walter Gerstenberg (Rome, 1950–). Lawrence Bernstein, ed., *La couronne et fleur de chansons à troys* (New York, 1984). Jane Bernstein, ed., *Adrian Willaert: The Complete Five- and Six-Voice Chansons* (New York, 1992). Gioseffo Zarlino, *Le istitutioni harmoniche* (Venice, 1558; R: 1965); pt. 3 trans. Guy Marco as *The Art of Counterpoint* (New York, 1968); pt. 4 trans. Vered Cohen as *On the Modes* (New Haven, 1983). Id., *Dimostrationi harmoniche* (Venice, 1571; R: 1966). Edward Lowinsky, ed., *The Medici Codex, MRM* 2–5 (New York, 1968).

Willan, (James) Healey (b. London, 12 Oct. 1880; d. Toronto, 16 Feb. 1968). Composer and organist. He was educated in St. Saviour's Choir School in Sussex, then studied in London: organ with William Stevenson Hoyte, piano with Evlyn Howard-Jones. Beginning in 1898, he held posts as organist and choirmaster at a series of churches. His organ works of this period combine part writing in the tradition of Bach with Wagnerian harmonies, for example, the *Epilogue* (1908) and the *Prelude and Fugue in C minor* (1908). In 1913 he moved to Canada to teach at the Toronto Conservatory of Music. In addition he became organist at St. Paul's Anglican Church in Toronto, for which he composed his well-known *Introduction, Passacaglia and Fugue in E♭ minor* (1916). In 1921 he moved from St. Paul's to St. Mary Magdalene, a small church where he was free to arrange the service to suit his own Anglo-Catholic beliefs. Over the years he wrote a great deal of liturgical music for Mary Magdalene, including many short Masses and plainsong canticle settings. During the 1920s he also composed songs (*Healey Willan Song Album no. 1,* 1925; *no. 2,* 1926) and a considerable amount of music for the stage, including incidental music for plays such as James Barrie's *Pantaloon* and Shakespeare's *Winter's Tale,* and several ballad operas (*L'ordre de Bon Temps,* 1928). In 1937 Willan moved from the conservatory to the Univ. of Toronto, where he taught until 1950. During the 1930s and 1940s he wrote some concert music, including 2 symphonies (1936, 1941) and a piano concerto (1944; rev. 1949), all in a late 19th-century idiom. He also composed music specifically for radio broadcast, including *Nativity Play* (1940), *Brébeuf* (pageant, 1943), and *Deirdre of the Sorrows* (opera, 1944). *Deirdre,* a full-length neo-Wagnerian opera, was revised for stage production in 1965. After retirement in 1950 Willan worked on many commissions (e.g., *Coronation Suite,* chorus and orchestra, 1953) and composed a good deal more for organ, including *Six Chorale Preludes, Set I* (1950), *Set II* (1953); *Passacaglia and Fugue no. 2* (1959).

Bibl.: Giles Bryant, *Healey Willan Catalogue* (Ottawa,

1972); *Supplement* (1982). F. R. C. Clarke, *Healey Willan: Life and Music* (Toronto, 1983).

Willcocks, David (Valentine) (b. Newquay, 30 Dec. 1919). Composer and organist. From 1929 until 1933 he was in the choir at Westminster Abbey. He then studied music at Clifton College and specialized in organ at the Royal College of Music and King's College in Cambridge. From 1947 to 1950 he was organist at Salisbury Cathedral and from 1950 to 1957 at Worcester Cathedral. He also conducted many choral works in the contexts of festivals and of choral societies. In 1957 he returned to King's College Chapel in Cambridge as organist and choirmaster and gained prominence through his concerts, services, and tours with that choir. Willcocks was appointed conductor of the London-based Bach Choir in 1960 and toured with that group as well. In 1974 he became director of the Royal College of Music. He was knighted in 1977.

Williams, Alberto (b. Buenos Aires, 23 Nov. 1862; d. there, 17 June 1952). Composer. Attended the Colegio S. Martin and the Provincial Music School. Appeared as a pianist in the 1870s; studied at the Paris Conservatory under Franck and Bériot from 1882. On his return in 1889 he performed throughout Argentina, developing at the same time a nationalist composing style based on folk idioms. Founded a conservatory (later named for him) in Buenos Aires in 1893, directing it until 1941; conducted the Berlin Philharmonic in his own works in 1900. His musical language developed from one based on European models (to 1890) to one centered on Argentine nationalism (to 1910); he merged both approaches in later works. Compositions include 9 symphonies, 3 Argentine Suites (1923), *Aires de la Pampa* (1944), and other orchestral music; 3 violin sonatas (1905, 1906, 1907) and other chamber works, all written before 1907; much piano music; choral pieces and songs.

Bibl.: *Composers of the Americas* 2 (Washington, D.C., 1956), pp. 136–55 [includes works list].

Williams, Clarence (b. Plaquemine, La., 8 Oct. 1898; d. New York, 6 Nov. 1965). Jazz pianist and composer. He moved to New Orleans in 1906, eventually settling in New York, where he founded a music publishing firm and a number of music stores; also organized recording sessions for Okeh Records (1923–28). He promoted and published the work of a number of outstanding musicians, including Fats Waller, Spencer Williams, and James P. Johnson. Williams also served as accompanist to Bessie Smith, and frequently performed with his wife, Eva Taylor.

Williams, Cootie [Charles Melvin] (b. Mobile, 24 July 1908; d. Long Island, 15 Sept. 1985). Jazz trumpeter and bandleader. He joined Duke Ellington (1929–40), continuing the growling, plunger-muted style developed by Bubber Miley. This sound contrasts with both straight mute and open playing on Ellington's "Concerto for Cootie," recorded in 1940. He recorded not only with Ellington's big band but also with small groups drawn from it. He joined Benny Goodman's big band and small groups (1940–41). Formed a big band (1941–48) which at times included Charlie Parker, Bud Powell, and Thelonious Monk, whose "Round Midnight" he recorded (1944). He led small groups, recorded with Rex Stewart (1957–58), and rejoined Goodman (1962) before returning to Ellington's orchestra (1962–1970s).

Williams, Grace (Mary) (b. Barry, Glamorganshire, 19 Feb. 1906; d. there, 10 Feb. 1977). Composer. She learned violin as a child and studied composition at University College in Cardiff with Evans, 1923–26; then went to the Royal College of Music, where she studied composition with Vaughan Williams and Jacob; in Vienna she worked with Wellesz, 1930–31. She subsequently taught at the Camden School for Girls and at Southland College of Education and also wrote educational scripts for the BBC. Her music was influenced by Vaughan Williams; it is usually characterized by a diatonic basis, lyrical lines, colorful chromaticism, and some modality. She occasionally used elements of folk music and wrote primarily vocal or dramatic music. Her works include the opera *The Parlour* (1961); orchestral works (*Sea Sketches,* strings, 1944; *Penillion for Orchestra,* 1955; *Ballads for Orchestra,* 1968); choral pieces (*Ye Highlands and Ye Lowlands,* male chorus, piano, 1972); and songs.

Bibl.: Malcolm Boyd, *Grace Williams* (Cardiff, 1980).

Williams, Hank [Hiram] (b. near Georgiana, Ala., 17 Sept. 1923; d. Oak Hill, W.Va., 1 Jan. 1953). Country singer, songwriter, and guitarist. After performing in honky-tonks and on radio in Alabama, from 1946 he worked with songwriter and producer Fred Rose. He made many successful recordings with his band The Drifting Cowboys, particularly "Move It On Over" (1947), "Cold, Cold Heart" (1951), "Hey, Good Lookin'" (1951), and "Your Cheatin' Heart" (1953); he also appeared on the *Louisiana Hayride* (from 1947) and the Grand Ole Opry (from 1949). His music was seminal to the development of country music in the 1950s and 1960s; his songs have also been performed by rock and popular artists.

Bibl.: Hank Williams with Michael Bane, *Living Proof: An Autobiography* (New York, 1979). George William Koon, *Hank Williams: A Bio-Bibliography in Popular Culture* (Westport, Conn., 1983). Colin Escott, *Hank Williams: The Biography* (Boston, 1994).

Williams, Joe [Goreed, Joseph] (b. Cordele, Ga., 12 Dec. 1918). Jazz and blues singer. As a soloist in Chicago he sang with bands led by Jimmie Noone (1937), Coleman Hawkins (1941), and Lionel Hampton (1943). He also toured to New York with Andy Kirk (1946). Having sat in with Count Basie's septet in 1950, he joined the big band (1954–61), recording "Everyday I Have the Blues" on the album *Count Basie Swings & Joe Williams Sings* (1955). He joined Harry Edison's quintet (1961–62), then again worked as a soloist, returning to perform with Basie intermittently into the 1980s. He appeared regularly as an actor on the *Bill Cosby Show* on television. A blues shouter, Williams was equally comfortable singing popular songs in a rich bass-baritone voice.

Bibl.: Leslie Gourse, *Every Day: The Story of Joe Williams* (New York, 1985).

Williams, John (Christopher) (b. Melbourne, Australia, 24 Apr. 1941). Guitarist. He received early instruction from his father, also a guitarist, and he later studied with Segovia in Siena and at the Royal College of Music in London. He made his debut at Wigmore Hall in London in 1958. Toured the U.S., the USSR, Japan, South America, and Europe. His repertoire includes non-Western, jazz, and folk musics, and works by composers such as Takemitsu, André Previn, Leo Brouwer, and Stephen Dodgson written for him.

Williams, John (Towner) (b. New York, 8 Feb. 1932). Pianist, composer, and conductor. The son of a professional drummer, he showed early promise on the piano. He studied in Los Angeles with Bobby van Eps and at Juilliard with Rosina Lhévinne (1954), meanwhile playing in clubs and recording studios in New York and Los Angeles. He also took composition lessons with Arthur Olaf Andersen and Mario Castelnuovo-Tedesco. During the 1960s he composed music for television *(Kraft Suspense Theatre, Gilligan's Island)* and for films (*How To Steal a Million,* 1966; *Valley of the Dolls,* 1967). At the same time he composed concert music (*Essay,* string orchestra, 1966; *Sinfonietta,* winds, 1968). He achieved great success with his scores for *Jaws* (1975), *Close Encounters of the Third Kind* (1977), and George Lucas's *Star Wars* trilogy (1977, 1980, 1983). Williams conducted the Boston Pops from 1980 to 1995; recent works include a cello concerto (1995) written for Yo-Yo Ma.

Bibl.: Irwin Bazelon, *Knowing the Score* (New York, 1975), pp. 193–206 [interview].

Williams, Mary Lou [née Scruggs, Mary Elfrieda] (b. Atlanta, 8 May 1910; d. Durham, 28 May 1981). Jazz pianist, arranger, and composer. She joined Andy Kirk's big band (1929–42); recordings of her compositions include "Walkin' and Swingin'" (1936) and "Mary's Idea" (1938). She also wrote arrangements for Benny Goodman, Earl Hines, Tommy Dorsey, and—after leaving Kirk in 1942 to lead groups—Duke Ellington ("Trumpets No End," recorded in 1946). She wrote the "Zodiac Suite" (recorded in 1945) and began playing with bop musicians during this period. After working in Europe (1952–54), she retired until 1957. Later she concentrated on writing sacred works while maintaining a career as a soloist in styles ranging from blues to bop.

Bibl.: Max Jones, *Talking Jazz* (London, 1987), pp. 178–207.

Williams, Tony [Anthony] (b. Chicago, 12 Dec. 1945). Jazz drummer. He joined Miles Davis (1963–69), forming for much of that period a rhythm section with Herbie Hancock and Ron Carter that was renowned for its flexible, interactive approach. Among his recordings were Davis's albums *My Funny Valentine* (1964) and *Nefertiti* (1967) and Hancock's *Maiden Voyage* (1965). After helping shape Davis's gradual move from hard bop to jazz-rock, Williams left to form his own jazz-rock group Lifetime, initially with John McLaughlin, but the group was not commercially successful. From 1976 Williams occasionally played in groups led by Hancock. He performed in the film *Round Midnight* (1986).

Williamson, John Finley (b. Canton, Ohio, 23 June 1887; d. Toledo, 28 May 1964). Conductor. Studied voice in New York with David Bispham and Herbert Witherspoon, and organ in Leipzig with Karl Straube. He started the Westminster Choir, touring with them, and in 1926 founded the Westminster Choir School (later College), of which he was president until 1958. He was the editor of the Westminster Series of Choral Music.

Bibl.: D. A. Weher, "John Finley Williamson (1887–1964): His Life and Contribution to Choral Music" (diss., Miami Univ., Ohio, 1971).

Williamson, Malcolm (Benjamin Graham Christopher) (b. Sydney, 21 Nov. 1931). Composer. As a child he studied horn and violin, as well as composition with Goossens and piano with Sverjensky, at the Sydney Conservatory. He traveled to London in 1950, where he studied composition with Lutyens and subsequently also with Stein. He focused on the organ as well, making a thorough study of the output of Messiaen, who proved to be an influence on Williamson's works; also explored Messiaen's mysticism. He worked as a church organist from 1955 until 1960. He toured in the U.S. and was composer-in-residence at Westminster Choir College in 1970. In 1977 he became president of the Royal Philharmonic Orchestra.

Williamson's instrumental works through the 1960s and 1970s utilized techniques from serialism or modalism to rhythms not unlike those of Stravinsky. He used standard genres such as concerto (Organ Concerto, 1961) and symphony (Symphony no. 1, *Elevamini,* 1957), as well as, in his chamber music, the serenade (Serenade, flute, piano quartet, 1967) and the sonata (Sonata, 2 pianos, 1967). By the mid-1960s he had begun to explore dramatic music, achieving success with works such as the opera *Our Man in Havana* (1963) and *English Eccentrics* (1964). Also composed semi-dramatic cantatas such as *The Musicians of Bremen* (1972). His choral music ranges from children's dramatic works such as *Dustan and the Devil* (1967) to the larger choral pieces Symphony for Voices (unaccompanied 4-part choir, 1962) and *The Icy Mirror* (1972; libretto by Ursula Vaughan Williams, also known as Symphony no. 3).

Works include *The Violins of Saint-Jacques* (opera, 1966), *The Growing Castle* (chamber opera, 1968), *The Red Sea* (opera, 1972), and the ballet *Perisynthyon*

(1974); orchestral music (Piano Concerto no. 1, 1957–58; no. 2, 1960; no. 3, 1962; Concerto grosso, 1965; Violin Concerto, 1965; Symphony no. 2, 1968–69; Symphony no. 4, 1977; Symphony no. 5, *Aquero,* 1980; Symphony no. 7, 1984; *Three Poems of Borges,* 1985); choral works (*A Young Girl,* chorus, 1964; *The Brilliant and the Dark,* choral-operatic sequence, female chorus, orchestra, 1966; *In Place of Belief,* chorus, piano 4-hands, 1970; *Mass of Christ the King,* chorus, orchestra, 1977); chamber works, songs, and pieces for organ (Symphony, 1960; *Vision of Christ-Phoenix,* 1961; *Elegy—J.F.K.,* 1964; *2 Epitaphs for Edith Sitwell,* 1966; *Peace Pieces,* 1971; *The Lion of Suffolk,* 1977).

Bibl.: *Malcolm Williamson (Born 1931): A Catalogue To Celebrate the Composer's 50th Birthday* (London, 1981). Ernest Bradbury, "Williamson at 50," *MT* 122 (1981): 735–37.

Williamson, Sonny Boy [John Lee] (b. Jackson, Tenn., ca. 1916; d. Chicago, 1 June 1948). Blues singer and harmonica player. He made his first recording, "Good Morning School Girl," in 1937; other recordings included "Big Apple Blues" (1941), "Sloppy Drunk Blues" (1941), and "Mellow Chick Swing" (1947). His distinctive style of harmonica playing was much imitated and was an important influence on Little Walter.

Williamson, Sonny Boy [Miller, Rice; Miller, Alex] (b. Glendora, Miss., 5 Dec. 1897; d. Helena, Ark., 25 May 1965). Blues singer and harmonica player. He began to broadcast for the Interstate Grocer Company in 1941 and recorded fairly late in life; "Eyesight to the Blind" (1951) and "Mighty Long Time" (1952) were followed by the hit "Don't Start Me To Talkin'" (1955), backed by Muddy Waters and his band. Williamson often recorded with the guitarist Robert Lockwood, Jr.; in 1963–64 he undertook a successful concert tour of Europe.

Wills, Bob [James Robert] (b. near Kosse, Tex., 6 Mar. 1905; d. Ft. Worth, 13 May 1975). Country singer, songwriter, fiddler, and bandleader. In 1931 he helped form the Light Crust Doughboys, and in 1934 founded his own Texas Playboys: both were important to the early history of western swing. Among his popular recordings were "Steel Guitar Rag" (1936) and his own "San Antonio Rose" (1938); his repertory included popular and jazz tunes as well as country.

Bibl.: Jimmy Latham, *The Life of Bob Wills: The King of Western Swing* (Odessa, Tex., 1987).

Willson, (Robert Reiniger) Meredith (b. Mason City, Iowa, 18 May 1902; d. Santa Monica, 15 June 1984). Flutist, composer, conductor. He went in 1919 to the Institute of Musical Art in New York, where he studied flute with Georges Barrère and composition with Henry Hadley. He played flute in John Philip Sousa's band (1921–23), then in the New York Philharmonic under Toscanini (1924–29). In 1929 he went to Seattle, where he conducted the Seattle Symphony and did radio work for ABC. In 1932 he became musical director of NBC's Western Division, first in San Francisco, then in Los Angeles. He remained with NBC until 1956, conducting and performing on radio and later television and writing songs, of which "You and I" (1941) and "May the Good Lord Bless and Keep You" (1950) became popular. He also composed some concert music, including 2 symphonies (1936, 1940) and some film scores (*The Great Dictator,* 1940). From 1952 to 1957 Willson worked on the book and the score to a musical based on his Iowa boyhood; *The Music Man* opened on Broadway in December 1957 and logged over 1,300 performances, then toured for almost 4 years and has been revived countless times. Subsequent musicals include *The Unsinkable Molly Brown* (New York, 1960); *Here's Love* (New York, 1963).

Writings: *And There I Stood with My Piccolo* (New York, 1948). *But He Doesn't Know the Territory* (New York, 1959).

Wilson, Brian (b. Hawthorne, Calif., 20 June 1942). Rock singer, songwriter, pianist, and bass guitarist. In 1961 he formed the Beach Boys with his brothers Dennis (1944–83) and Carl (b. 1946), his cousin Mike Love (b. 1941), and Alan Jardine (b. 1942). Their style was similar to early rock-and-roll and featured high vocal harmonies; the preoccupation of Wilson's lyrics with life on Southern California beaches gave rise to its name "surf rock." Among their popular recordings were "Surfin' U.S.A." (1963), "California Girls" (1965), and the album *Pet Sounds* (1966). Psychological problems forced Wilson into retirement from 1967 until 1988, when he released a solo album. The Beach Boys continued to record and perform in his absence. In 1995 he released a new album of Beach Boys and solo songs entitled *I Just Wasn't Made for These Times;* a documentary film about his career appeared under the same title.

Bibl.: Timothy White, *The Nearest Faraway Place: Brian Wilson, the Beach Boys, and the Southern California Experience* (New York, 1994).

Wilson, John (b. Faversham, Kent, 5 Apr. 1595; d. Westminster, London, 22 Feb. 1674). Composer, lutenist, and singer. He was active in London at court and in the theaters from 1614, became a city wait in 1622, and entered the King's Musick among the lutes and voices in 1635. Oxford Univ. granted him the D.Mus. in 1644; he was professor of music there from 1656 to 1661. He became a Gentleman of the Chapel Royal in 1662. Wilson's most notable works are his songs, many of which were written for plays.

Bibl.: Vincent Duckles, "The 'Curious' Art of John Wilson: An Introduction to His Songs and Lute Music," *JAMS* 7.2 (1954): 93–112. Hubert Henderson, "The Vocal Music of John Wilson" (diss., Univ. of North Carolina, 1962).

Wilson, Olly (Woodrow) (b. St. Louis, Mo., 7 Sept. 1937). Composer. He studied piano and clarinet as a child, accompanying gospel choirs and playing in jazz bands. Later he learned bass, which he played professionally. He studied at Washington Univ. in St. Louis (B.M., 1959), the Univ. of Illinois (M.M., 1960), and the Univ. of Iowa (Ph.D., 1964); taught at Florida A & M (1960–65), Oberlin (1965–70), and the Univ. of California at Berkeley (beginning 1970). His music often combines avant-garde instrumental combinations and harmonic procedures with rhythms and sonorities drawn from black traditional and popular music and the music of Africa. Works include *Sinfonia* (orchestra, 1984); *Akwan* (piano and orchestra, 1974); *Expansions II* (orchestra, 1987); *Piece for Four* (flute, trumpet, piano, bass, 1966); *Black Martyrs* (chorus and electronic tape, 1972); *Sometimes* (tenor and tape, 1976); *Cetus* (tape, 1967).

Bibl.: Eileen Southern, "Conversation with Olly Wilson," *Black Perspective in Music* 5 (1977): 90–103; 6 (1978): 57–70.

Wilson, Richard (Edward) (b. Cleveland, 15 May 1941). Pianist and composer. He attended Harvard Univ. (B.A., 1963), meanwhile studying piano with Leonard Shure in New York. After graduation he studied piano with Friedrich Wührer in Munich and composition with Robert Moevse, then composition and theory at Rutgers Univ. (M.A., 1966). Beginning in 1966 he taught music at Vassar College. Works include Violin Concerto (1979); Bassoon Concerto (1983); Symphony no. 2 (1986); *Silhouette* (orchestra, 1988); *Orchesterwerk* (1989); *Articulations* (orchestra, 1989); 3 string quartets (1968, 1977, 1982); *Music for Violin and Cello* (1969); *Figuration* (clarinet, cello, piano, 1980); *Profound Utterances* (bassoon, 1980); *The Ballad of Longwood Glen* (tenor and harp, 1975); *Eclogue* (piano, 1974); Sonata (violin and piano, 1989).

Wilson, Teddy [Theodore Shaw] (b. Austin, 24 Nov. 1912; d. New Britain, Conn., 31 July 1986). Jazz pianist and bandleader. He received widespread publicity as a founding member of Benny Goodman's racially integrated small groups (1936–39); their recordings (1935–39) include "Body and Soul" (1935), which demonstrates his ability to combine an uncluttered striding accompaniment in the left hand with an ornate freely phrased improvised melody in the right. In its reduction of ragtime-based accompaniment and greater emphasis on linear melody, this widely imitated swing style also served as a bridge to the bop piano style. Also from 1935 to 1939 Wilson directed recording sessions featuring Billie Holiday. He led a swing big band (1939–40) and sextet (1940–44), then rejoined Goodman (1944–45). He played in small groups (including the album *Pres and Teddy* with Lester Young, 1956) and unaccompanied (including the album *Striding after Fats,* 1974), frequently making international tours as a soloist and in reunions with Goodman (1950s–80s).

Wilson, Thomas (Brendan) (b. Trinidad, Colorado, 10 Oct. 1927). Composer. He studied with Bullock, Woodham, and Rimmer at Glasgow Univ.; he graduated in 1951 and returned there in 1957 as a teacher. His early works were serial and progressively incorporated other modern techniques such as complex aggregated rhythms. Works include operas (*The Charcoal Burners,* 1968; *The Confessions of a Justified Sinner,* 1976); orchestral music (*Ritornelli per archi,* 1972; Chamber Concerto, premiered 1985; Piano Concerto, premiered 1986); choral, vocal, and chamber music (*Concerto da camera,* flute, oboe, piano, violin, cello, 1965; *Canti notturni,* flute/alto flute, clarinet/bass clarinet, piano, violin, viola, cello, 1972).

Windgassen, Wolfgang (b. Annemasse, Switzerland, 5 Sept. 1914; d. Stuttgart, 5 Sept. 1974). Tenor. He studied with his father, Fritz Windgassen, and with Maria Ranzow and Alfons Fischer at the Stuttgart Conservatory; performed with the Stuttgart Opera (1945–72), gradually making his way into the Wagnerian repertory. He appeared at Bayreuth (1951–70) as Siegfried, Lohengrin, Tannhäuser, Walther, Tristan, Erik, and Loge; also performed at Covent Garden, La Scala, the Paris Opéra, and the Metropolitan Opera, where he debuted in 1957 as Siegmund. Served as director of the Stuttgart Opera, 1972–74.

Bibl.: Berndt W. Wessling, *Wolfgang Windgassen* (Bremen, 1967).

Winding, Kai (Chresten) (b. Ärhus, Denmark, 18 May 1922; d. Yonkers, N.Y., 7 May 1983). Jazz trombonist and bandleader. He joined the big bands of Benny Goodman (1945–46) and Stan Kenton (1946–47); solos he recorded with Kenton include "Willow Weep for Me" (1946). He was a soloist in swing and bop groups, as well as in Miles Davis's cool jazz nonet (1949). With J. J. Johnson he co-led a bop quintet (1954–56) and later recorded the album *The Great Kai and J. J.* (1960). He toured with the Giants of Jazz (a sextet including Dizzy Gillespie, Thelonious Monk, and Art Blakey, 1971–72) and led the group Giant Bones with trombonist Curtis Fuller (1979–80).

Winkelmann [Winckelmann], **Hermann** (b. Brunswick, 8 Mar. 1849; d. Vienna, 18 Jan. 1912). Tenor. He studied at Paris and Hannover with Koch. Debuted at Sondershausen in 1875 in *Il trovatore.* He created the role of Parsifal at Bayreuth in 1882. His London debut came that same year; he was the first London Tristan and Walther. From 1883 to 1906, sang at the Vienna Opera. He appeared in New York, Philadelphia, Boston, Cinncinnati, Chicago, and Bayreuth. He was coached by Wagner himself.

Winner, Septimus [pseudonym Alice Hawthorne] (b. Philadelphia, 11 May 1827; d. there, 22 Nov. 1902). Composer and publisher. He was essentially self-taught, though he had some lessons with Leopold Meignen. In 1845 he went into publishing with his brother Joseph E(astburn) Winner (1837–1918). He played in the Philadelphia Brass Band and the Cecilian Musical Society. A successful composer of popular songs under the name Alice Hawthorne. Among his most popular songs are "Listen to the Mocking Bird" (1855), "Der Deitcher's Dog" (1864), and "Ten Little Injuns" (1868). He also composed under the names Percy Guyer, Mark Masen, and Paul Stenton.

Bibl.: Charles Eugene Claghorn, *The Mocking Bird: The Life and Diary of Its Author Septimus Winner* (Philadelphia, 1937).

Winter [von Winter], **Peter** (bapt. Mannheim, 28 Aug. 1754; d. Munich, 17 Oct. 1825). Composer. He studied briefly with Abbé Vogler and played violin as a young boy in Karl Theodor's orchestra; he was named director of the orchestra when the court moved to Munich in 1778. It was at this point that he began to compose stage music. He became Vice-Kapellmeister in 1787 and court Kapellmeister in 1798. He wrote many operas, the first of which, *Helena und Paris* (Munich, 1782), was not a great success; but *Das unterbrochene Opferfest* (Vienna, 1796) and subsequent operas achieved wide recognition. He wrote operas for Munich, Vienna, Naples, Venice, Milan, Paris, and London. Other compositions include ballets (all for Munich), Masses, cantatas, symphonies, various solo concertos, and chamber music.

Wirén, Dag (Ivar) (b. Striberg, Närke, 15 Oct. 1905; d. Danderyd, 19 Apr. 1986). Composer. From 1926 to 1931 he studied composition with Ellberg at the Stockholm Conservatory. He then traveled to Paris, where from 1932 to 1934 he studied composition with Sabaneyev. Returning to Sweden, he worked as a librarian for the Swedish Composers' Association, as a music critic for *Svenska Morgonbladet,* and with the Swedish Composers' International Music Agency. His early works were in a neoclassical style and developed both a dramatic language, which utilized individualized form for each piece and thematic transformation, and a lighter, more popular idiom. His works include dramatic music (*Oscarbalen* [The Oscar Ball], ballet, 1949; *Hamlet,* incidental music, 1960), orchestral music (Serenade for Strings, 1937; 5 symphonies, 1932–64; concertos); and chamber music.

Wise, Michael (b. Salisbury?, ca. 1647; d. there, 24 Aug. 1687). Composer. Following the Restoration in 1660, he was a chorister at the Chapel Royal under Cooke until 1663. From 1666 to 1668 he was a lay clerk at St. George's Chapel, Windsor, and at Eton College. In 1668 he was appointed organist and instructor of the choristers at Salisbury Cathedral. Later he became a Gentleman at the Chapel Royal (1676) and almoner and master of the choristers at St. Paul's Cathedral (1687). At several times during his career he was involved in disputes with authorities; he met his end during a heated argument with a nightwatchman. His compositions include 4 services, 30 anthems *(The Ways of Sion Do Mourn),* and a few songs and catches.

Wissmer, Pierre (b. Geneva, 30 Oct. 1915). Composer. He studied in Paris at the Conservatory (1935–38) and at the Schola cantorum. He spent the war years in Switzerland, but returned to France in 1949 and became a French citizen in 1958. During the 1950s he worked at Radio Luxembourg. From 1957 he taught at the Schola cantorum, becoming director in 1962; in 1969 he became director of the École nationale de musique in Le Mans. His music, in a mildly dissonant idiom and emphasizing clarity of theme and texture, has been much performed on radio and television. Works include *Marion ou la belle au tricorne* (opera; stage premiere, Paris, 1957); *Léonidas* (1-act opera, Verdun, 1958); *Christine et les chimères* (ballet, French television, 1967); *Le quatrième mage* (oratorio, 1965); 6 symphonies (1938, 1951, 1955, 1962, 1969, 1977); 3 piano concertos (1937, 1948, 1972); 2 violin concertos (1942, 1954); guitar concerto (1957); clarinet concerto (1960); Sonatina (flute and guitar, 1962).

Witt, Franz Xaver (b. Walderbach, Bavaria, 9 Feb. 1834; d. Landshut, 2 Dec. 1888). Composer. He studied science and theology at Regensburg, where he sang in the choir. Was ordained in 1856 and taught Gregorian chant at the seminary at Regensburg. In 1867 he was named inspector of the seminary of St. Emmeram. During 1870–71 director of the choir at the Eichstätt Cathedral. In 1873 he was awarded a D.Phil. by Pope Pius IX. In 1880, named an honorary canon at the cathedral at Palestrina. Instrumental in the move to improve Roman Catholic church music. Works include Masses, motets, litanies, and hymns.

Bibl.: Karl Gustav Fellerer, ed., *Franz Xaver Witt: Ausgewählte Aufsätze zur Kirchenmusik* (Cologne, 1934).

Witt, Friedrich (b. Niederstetten, Württemberg, 8 Nov. 1770; d. Würzburg, 3 Jan. 1836). Composer and cellist. He played in the Prince of Oettingen-Wallerstein's orchestra from ca. 1789; became Kapellmeister for the Prince Bishop of Würzburg in 1802 and held a similar position at the Würzburg theater from 1814, a post he held until his death. He composed symphonies, concertos, oratorios, Masses, cantatas, chamber music. He is remembered today for his Jena Symphony, which was misattributed to Beethoven.

Bibl.: Fritz Stein, "Eine unbekannte Jugendsymphonie Beethovens?," *SIMG* 13 (1911): 127–72. H. C. Robbins Landon, "The Jena Symphony," *MR* 18 (1957): 109–13.

Wittgenstein, Paul (b. Vienna, 5 Nov. 1887; d. Manhasset, N.Y., 3 Mar. 1961). Pianist. Studied piano with Theodor Leschetizky and Malvine Brée and theory with Joseph Labor. Embarked on a performing career but was wounded in World War I and lost his right arm. Nevertheless, he continued his career as a left-hand virtuoso. Several works were written for him, including Ravel's Concerto for the Left Hand, Prokofiev's Concerto no. 4, and Richard Strauss's *Panathenäenzug* and *Parergon zur Symphonia domestica.* He performed widely and published *School for the Left Hand* (London, 1957).

Bibl.: E. Fred Flindell, "Paul Wittgenstein (1887–1961): Patron and Pianist," *MR* 32 (1971): 107–27.

Wizlâv [Wizlaw] **III von Rügen** (b. 1265–68; d. Barth, near Stralsund, Germany, 8 Nov. 1325). Minnesinger, Prince of Pomerania and Rügen (from 1302), brother of Queen Eufemia of Norway. He was a well-known patron of literature; Frauenlob and other poets visited his court. Fourteen *Minnelieder* and 13 *Sprüche* survive; 17 have melodies.

Wolf, Hugo (Filipp Jakob) (b. Windischgratz, Styria, 13 Mar. 1860; d. Vienna, 22 Feb. 1903). Composer. First music lessons from his father; in 1867 the family leather business burned, and money was to be extremely scarce for the rest of Wolf's life. He entered the Vienna Conservatory in September 1875, studying harmony with Fuchs, piano with Schenner, composition with Krenn; he had started to compose piano pieces, songs, choruses, and a violin concerto by 1875. Soon after reaching Vienna he became a fervent Wagnerian; his musical radicalism, accompanied by radical political and social ideas, probably led to dissatisfaction with the conservatism of his schooling, and he left the conservatory toward the end of his second year. He then tried to make a living in Vienna as a private teacher, a calling to which his character was completely unsuited. He never earned enough to support himself, and lived primarily on money from his impoverished father (who was in nearly perpetual exasperation at his mode of life) and on the generosity of his Viennese friends. The charming side of Wolf's personality and his aura of genius attracted many mostly well-to-do members of the middle class, in spite of his mercurial mood shifts and impulsive behavior. His nature was probably aggravated by the burden of illness: he was very likely infected with syphilis by 1878.

In 1884–87 Wolf was music critic for a fashionable Vienna weekly, the *Wiener Salonblatt* (but even his salary in this post was paid by a friend without his knowledge), in which he attracted much attention through his outspoken opinions and particularly his attacks on Brahms. The vehemence of this animosity probably had a personal basis; in 1879 he had taken some of his work to Brahms, who had dismissed him with the advice to study counterpoint with Nottebohm. (Wolf's criticism is collected in *Musikalische Kritiken,* ed. R. Batka and H. Werner, Leipzig, 1911; trans. Eng., 1979.) Wolf's creativity was irregular, alternating between long, more or less sterile periods and unpredictable bursts of inspiration, which he waited for, often in frustration and despair. Periods of inspiration occurred in 1878, including his first burst of song composition (perhaps stimulated by his first serious love affair) and the beginning of the String Quartet (completed in 1884); from December 1882 to May 1883; and from winter 1886 to spring 1887. The period 1888–89 was crucial in Wolf's career: at this time he produced more than half his songs, including the *Mörike Lieder,* most of the *Eichendorff Lieder,* the *Goethe Lieder,* and 26 songs of the *Spanish Songbook* (completed in March–April 1890). This period also represents the beginning of Wolf's public recognition. The first public performance of his songs was on 2 March 1888; on 15 December he first accompanied his songs in public, as he was frequently to do thereafter. In 1888, after years of failure to find a publisher, he brought out two volumes (12 songs). Eventually he was published by Schott, largely because of the advocacy of Humperdinck, Schott's reader.

Wolf's aspirations to compose an opera were a source of continuing frustration in the 1890s, as he was unable to find an acceptable libretto. After composing part of the *Italian Songbook* in 1890–91, he produced virtually nothing in 1892–94. In January 1895 he suddenly decided that the libretto *Der Corregidor,* written for him several years before by Rosa Mayreder, an amateur writer and relative of a friend, which he had then rejected as incompetent, was in fact what he had been looking for. The opera was composed in an intense creative period, March–December 1895. In March–April 1896 he composed the second part of the *Italian Songbook.* His certainty of a tremendous success for the opera, on the basis of which he took an apartment in Vienna, his first permanent home since 1887, was illusory. Its premiere at Mannheim (7 June 1896) was successful because of the presence of part of Wolf's now sizable coterie of admirers, but it did not establish itself. In February 1897 he made his last concert appearance, in March composed the three Michelangelo Songs, his last. In July 1897 he began composition of a new opera, *Manuel Venegas,* but in September had a complete mental collapse, believing himself the director of the Vienna Opera, a delusion probably brought on by a painful scene with the actual director, Mahler, who reneged on an earlier promise to stage *Der Corregidor* there. He was confined in an asylum, improved enough to be discharged in January 1898, but in October had a relapse and never again emerged.

Other works include *Penthesilea,* symphonic poem (1883–85); Italian Serenade, string quartet (1887; arranged for string orchestra, 1892); choral works, especially *6 Geistliche Lieder* (Eichendorff, 1881); *Der Feuerreiter* (arranged from a solo song), incidental music, especially for Ibsen's *Das Fest auf Solhaug* (1890–91).

Bibl.: H. Jancik et al., eds., *Sämtliche Werke* (Vienna, 1960–). Frank Walker, *Hugo Wolf: A Biography* (London, 1951; enlarged 2nd ed., 1968). H. Pleasants, ed., *The Music Criticism of Hugo Wolf* (New York, 1978). Mosco Carner, *Hugo Wolf Songs* (London, 1982). Eric Sams, *The Songs of Hugo Wolf* (New York, 1983). Deborah J. Stein, *Hugo Wolf's Lieder and Extensions of Tonality* (Ann Arbor, 1985). Kurt Honolka, *Hugo Wolf: sein Leben, sein Werk, seine Zeit* (Stuttgart, 1988). David Ossenkop, *Hugo Wolf: A Guide to Research* (New York, 1988). Susan Youens, *Hugo Wolf: The Vocal Music* (Princeton, 1992).

Wolff, Albert (Louis) (b. Paris, 19 Jan. 1884; d. Paris, 20 Feb. 1970). Conductor and composer. He studied at the Conservatory in Paris, at the same time working as an organist and cabaret pianist. In 1908 he joined the Opéra-comique as chorusmaster; in 1911 he was appointed conductor. He was associated with the Opéra-comique for his entire career, serving as music director (1921–24) and as director-general (1945–46). He was also involved as a conductor and/or administrator with the Concerts Pasdeloup (1925–40), the Concerts Lamoureux (1928–34), the Opéra (beginning 1949), the Teatro Colón in Buenos Aires (1911, 1940–45), and the Metropolitan Opera in New York (1919–21). His own compositions include operas (*L'oiseau bleu,* New York, 1919), orchestra music (Symphony in A, 1951), songs, chamber music, and film scores.

Wolff, Christian (b. Nice, 8 Mar. 1934). Composer. He came to the U.S. as a child; attended Harvard Univ., where he studied classics and comparative literature (A.B., 1955; A.M., 1957). He studied piano but had no other formal musical training. Wolff began to compose, however, as a teenager, becoming associated with a group of avant-garde composers in New York that included John Cage, David Tudor, Morton Feldman, and Earle Brown. His earliest published compositions (e.g., *For Prepared Piano,* 1951; *Trio I,* flute, trumpet, cello, 1951; *For Piano 1,* 1952) were atonal but not serial; for the most part they used a severely restricted number of pitches, and they included long periods of silence. Beginning with *Duo for Pianists 1* in 1957, Wolff introduced elements of choice and chance into his music, using a system he called "cuing," in which the notes that one performer plays are determined to a considerable extent by what another performer has just played. Examples of cuing can also be found in *Duo for Pianists 2* (1958) and *Burdocks* (multiple ensembles, 1971). Besides composing, Wolff continued his classical studies at Harvard, receiving a Ph.D. in comparative literature (1963). He taught classics at Harvard (1962–70), then classics and music at Dartmouth College (beginning 1970). From the mid-1960s on much of Wolff's music was explicitly related to left-wing political themes (*Changing the System,* chamber ensemble, 1972; *I Like To Think of Harriet Tubman,* female voice and 3 instruments, 1984), and he continued to develop new ways to leave more scope in his music for the freedom and initiative of the performers.

Wolf-Ferrari, Ermanno (b. Venice, 12 Jan. 1876; d. there, 21 Jan. 1948). Composer. His father, August Wolf, was a Bavarian artist resident in Venice. Ermanno too studied painting, first at the Accademia di Belle Arti in Rome (1891–92), then in Munich (1892). There he transferred to the Akademie der Tonkunst, where he studied counterpoint with Joseph Rheinberger and conducting with Ludwig Abel (1892–95). Returning to Venice in 1895, he appended his Italian mother's maiden name to his father's name. His early works, like *Cenerentola* (opera, Venice, 1900; rev. Bremen, 1902), *Sinfonia da camera* (chamber ensemble, 1901), and *La vita nuova* (cantata, 1901), were in the German Romantic tradition. In *Le donne curiose* (Munich, 1903) and *I quattro rusteghi* (Munich, 1906), both on libretti adapted from Goldoni, he turned to a spare, lively, almost neoclassical style, well suited for the modernization of 18th-century opera buffa. *Il segreto di Susanna* (1-act opera, Munich, 1909), although on a modern subject (Susanna's secret is that she smokes cigarettes), is cast in the same mold and has become perhaps his best-known work. During these years Wolf-Ferrari lived alternately in Venice and in Munich, pursued his career equally in Germany and Italy, and identified spiritually and aesthetically with both cultures. The outbreak of the First World War found him with divided loyalties; he moved to Zollikon near Zurich and composed little. In 1922 he moved back to the Munich area and resumed composing. He continued to write operas, most of them on 17th- and 18th-century subjects, for example, *Sly* (Milan, 1927), adapted from Shakespeare's *Taming of the Shrew,* and *Il Campiello* (Milan, 1936) on another Goldoni libretto. He also composed a good deal of instrumental music, including *Idillio-concertino* (oboe and chamber orchestra, 1933), *Suite veneziano* (chamber orchestra, 1936), Violin Concerto (1946), String Quintet (1942), and *duo,* viola d'amore and viola da gamba (1946).

Bibl.: Alexandra Carola Grisson, *Ermanno Wolf-Ferrari: Autorisierte Lebensbeschreibung* (Regensburg, 1941; rev. 1958). Peter Hamann et al., *Ermanno Wolf-Ferrari* (Tutzing, 1986) [includes works list].

Wölfl [Woelfl, Wölffl], **Joseph** (b. Salzburg, 24 Dec. 1773; d. London, 21 May 1812). Composer and pianist. He studied in Salzburg with Leopold Mozart and Michael Haydn. Visited Vienna in 1790 and made the acquaintance of Mozart, returning there permanently in 1795. He was regarded as an accomplished pianist and was thought by some to be a rival to Beethoven. After a concert tour through Germany he arrived in Paris in 1801, where his reputation preceded him. He moved to London in 1805, where he enjoyed success as a composer and performer. He wrote 7 operas (5 for Vienna and 2 for Paris), 2 ballets (for London), 7 piano concertos, 2 symphonies, chamber music, 30 solo piano sonatas, other keyboard music, and some vocal music.

Bibl.: Richard Baum, *Joseph Wölfl: Leben, Klavierwerke, Klavierkammermusik und Klavierkonzerte* (Kassel, 1928).

Wolkenstein, Oswald von. See Oswald von Wolkenstein.

Wolle, John Frederick (b. Bethlehem, Pa., 4 Apr. 1863; d. there, 12 Jan. 1933). Conductor and organist. He was the grandson of Peter Wolle. Studied with Rheinberger in Munich, 1884–85. From 1885 to 1904 he was the organist at Central Moravian Church in Bethlehem. He conducted the Bethlehem Choral Union from 1885 to 1892; they gave the first complete performance of the St. John Passion (1888) and St. Matthew Passion (1892). A performance of the B minor Mass in 1900 was hailed as the first Bach Festival, and the Bethlehem Bach Choir was formally organized shortly thereafter. He was a founding member of the American Guild of Organists; director of music at the Univ. of California, 1905–11.

Bibl.: Raymond Walters, *The Bethlehem Bach Choir* (Boston, 1918).

Wolle, Peter (b. New Herrnhut, St. Thomas, West Indies, 5 Jan. 1792; d. Bethlehem, Pa., 14 Nov. 1871). Composer. Grandfather of John Frederick Wolle. He moved to Pennsylvania in 1800 and was admitted to the Moravian Theological Seminary at Nazareth in 1806. He was a minister at Nazareth and was made a bishop in 1845. He may have studied composition with David Moritz Michael (1751–1827) and Johannes Herbst (1735–1812), two important composers in the Moravian congregation. He composed a number of anthems and hymns, including "Sing Hallelujah, Christ Doth Live." He also edited the *Moravian Tune Book* (1836).

Wolpe, Stefan (b. Berlin, 25 Aug. 1902; d. New York, 4 Apr. 1972). Composer and teacher. He studied briefly at the Berlin Hochschule für Musik with Paul Juon (1920) and came into contact with a variety of musicans and artists, including Ferruccio Busoni, Hermann Scherchen, the Novembergruppe, and the Bauhaus movement. During 1925–33 he was a member of the Communist party of Germany, and much of his music from these years has political themes and aims at mass accessibility (e.g., "Es wird die neue Welt geboren," 1932). In 1933 he fled Berlin, first to Vienna, where he studied with Anton Webern, then to Palestine, where he taught at the Jerusalem Conservatory (1934–38). In 1938 he emigrated to the U.S. and settled in New York. His works of the late 1930s and early 1940s show the influence of Middle Eastern music (*The Man from Midian,* ballet, 1942; *Two Choral Songs,* soprano and alto, 1944; *Yigdal,* cantata, 1945). At the same time Wolpe engaged in the study of atonal music, particularly the music of Schoenberg and his school. Searching for atonal techniques that would avoid the repetitiveness of serialism, Wolpe wrote many studies and sketches that remained unpublished, arriving by the late 1940s at a style in which motivic cells are varied, elaborated, and superimposed contrapuntally in dramatic fashion. Early examples of this style are *Battle Piece* (piano, 1947) and the Violin Sonata (1949), followed by the more complex *Enactments* (3 pianos, 1953) and Symphony (1956). In the U.S. Wolpe became well known as a teacher in New York, Philadelphia, and at Black Mountain College in North Carolina, imparting to his students—who included Ralph Shapey, Morton Feldman, and David Tudor—a rigorous but nondogmatic approach to pitch organization. Wolpe's later scores, from about 1959 on, continue the nonserial pitch organization and contrasting textures of his earlier works, but they tend to be somewhat simpler, and they allude occasionally to other musical styles or even to specific works. Examples include *Form for Piano* (1959); *Trio in 2 Parts* (flute, cello, and piano, 1964); *Chamber Piece no. 1* (ensemble of 14 instruments, 1964); *Chamber Piece no. 2* (13 instruments, 1967).

Bibl.: Austin Clarkson, *Stefan Wolpe: A Brief Catalogue of Published Works* (Islington, Ont., 1981).

Wonder, Stevie [Judkins, Steveland; Morris, Steveland; Hardaway, Steveland] (b. Saginaw, Mich., 13 May 1950). Soul and popular singer, songwriter, and keyboardist. Blind from birth. He received a contract from Motown Records in 1963 and made successful recordings while a teenager ("Fingertips, Pt. 2," 1963). From 1971 he produced albums of his own songs (*Talking Book,* including "You Are the Sunshine of My Life," 1972; *Songs in the Key of Life,* including "Isn't She Lovely," 1976; *In Square Circle,* 1985). He was one of the first to use electronic synthesizers in popular music.

Bibl.: Jeffrey Peisch, *Stevie Wonder* (New York, 1985). John Swenson, *Stevie Wonder* (New York, 1986).

Wood, Charles (b. Armagh, 15 June 1866; d. Cambridge, 12 July 1926). Composer. Studied with T. O. Marks at Armagh Cathedral, and at the Royal College of Music (1883–87), where he won the Morley Scholarship for composition and studied with Stanford and Bridge. He taught harmony at the Royal College of Music from 1888. Professor of conducting at Cambridge Univ. Music Society, 1888–94; lecturer in harmony and counterpoint at Cambridge, 1897–1924, and professor of music from 1924. Among his compositions are 3 operas (*The Pickwick Papers,* 1922), incidental music, 3 string quartets, anthems, part songs, and solo songs. Also known as the composer of the chimes for the clock at Gonville and Caius Colleges, Cambridge.

Wood, Haydn (b. Slaithwaite, 25 Mar. 1882; d. London, 11 Mar. 1959). Composer. He studied violin as a child, quickly becoming proficient; known as a child prodigy. He studied violin with Arbos and composition with Stanford at the Royal College of Music. He then went to Brussels, where he studied violin with Thomson. Wood was known primarily for some 200 salon songs as well as chamber music. He also wrote dramatic orchestral works and the musical *Cash on Delivery* (1917).

Wood, Henry J(oseph) (b. London, 3 Mar. 1869; d. Hitchin, Hertfordshire, 19 Aug. 1944). Conductor. While still young, gave a number of public performances on the organ; studied with Prout, Steggall, Macfarren, and García at the Royal Academy of Music, and conducted in various theaters, including the Royalty Theatre and New Olympic Theatre. In 1895 he initiated the Queen's Hall Promenade Concerts (the "Proms") with great success; they remained almost exclusively under his direction until 1940, and he continued to conduct there until the year of his death. He founded the Nottingham Orchestra in 1899; served as conductor of the Wolverhampton Festival Choral Society, of the Sheffield Festival, and of the Norwich Festival. Made a number of arrangements under the pseudonym Paul Klenovsky, including Chopin's *Marche Funèbre* and "Purcell's" [actually Clarke's] *Trumpet Voluntary;* in 1923 he was appointed professor of conducting at the Royal Academy of Music. Wood published a number of books, including *The Gentle Art of Singing,* 4 vols. (London, 1927–28); *About Conducting* (London, 1945), and *My Life and Music* (London, 1938). He was knighted in 1911.

Bibl.: Reginald Pound, *Sir Henry Wood: A Biography* (London, 1969).

Wood, Hugh (b. Parbold, Lancashire, 27 June 1932). Composer. He studied harmony and counterpoint with Lloyd Weber, then composition with Hamilton and Seiber, as well as with Milner. From 1956 to 1960 he taught music at London Univ., from 1958 to 1967 at Morley College, and from 1962 to 1965 at the Royal Academy of Music; also taught at Glasgow, Liverpool, and Cambridge universities. Although his early music bore the mark of his English teachers, he quickly came under the influence of Schoenbergian serialism. His works include *Songs to Poems by Christopher Logue* (mezzo-soprano, clarinet, violin, cello, 1961), *Scenes from Comus* (soprano, tenor, orchestra, 1965), *The Horses* (song cycle for high voice, piano, 1967; rev. 1968), String Quartet no. 3 (1978), Piano Trio (1984).

Woodbury, Isaac Baker (b. Beverly, Mass., 23 Oct. 1819; d. Columbia, S.C., 26 Oct. 1858). Composer, editor, and writer on music. Studied in Boston with Lowell Mason from 1832. During 1838–39 he studied in Paris and London. Returned to Boston, where he taught music privately; also held positions as an organist and choral conductor. During the 1840s and 1850s he traveled. Returned to Boston and trained music teachers. Served as corresponding editor of *World of Music* (1846–48), *American Monthly Musical Review* (1850–53), and other journals. In 1849 he settled in New York. Traveled to the Mediterranean and Florida to fight off tuberculosis. With his cousin Benjamin Baker he founded a school, the National Musical Convention. His compositions include 3 oratorios, 4 secular cantatas, choruses, glees, a few piano works, and numerous pedagogical works.

Bibl.: Robert Marshall Copeland, "The Life and Works of Isaac Baker Woodbury (1819–1858)" (diss., Univ. of Cincinnati, 1974).

Woods, Phil (Philip Wells) (b. Springfield, Mass., 2 Nov. 1931). Jazz alto saxophonist and bandleader. While studying clarinet at the Juilliard School, he toured with Charlie Barnet's big band. He worked with bop combos, recording the album *Jimmy Raney Quintet* (1954). Toured Europe with Quincy Jones's orchestra (1959–60) and the USSR with Benny Goodman (1962), and worked as a studio musician. In Paris he founded a quartet, the European Rhythm Machine (1968–72). He returned to the U.S. and in 1973 formed a bop group; its albums include *"Live" from the Showboat* (1976) and *Integrity* (1984). He is the soloist on Billy Joel's hit song "I Love You Just the Way You Are" (1977).

Woodward, Roger (b. Sydney, 20 Dec. 1942). Pianist. Studied with Alexander Sverenksy at the Sydney State Conservatorium (1952–62), continuing his studies with Ilona Kabos in London and with Zbigniew Drzewiecki in Warsaw. He won the International Chopin Festival in Warsaw in 1968, and the International Gaudeamus Competition in the Netherlands in 1970. In addition to concerts and recordings of Russian music and Chopin, Woodward premiered works of contemporaries such as Penderecki, Bussotti, Birtwistle, and Stockhausen.

Wooldridge, David (b. Deal, Kent, 24 Aug. 1927). Composer. His godfather was Rachmaninoff, who briefly gave the young Wooldridge piano lessons; he also studied violin and conducting as a youth. He went to the Univ. of London, then traveled to Vienna, where he studied conducting under Clemens Krauss at the Vienna State Opera and worked briefly as a conductor of the Bavarian State Opera. He toured and conducted in the U.S., in Beirut, and in South Africa, and taught at various colleges in the U.S. His works include dramatic music (*Octet,* ballet, 1958; *The Duchess of Amalfi,* opera, 1978); orchestral music (*Partita,* small orchestra, 1967); and film scores.

Woollen, (Charles) Russell (b. Hartford, 7 Jan. 1923; d. McLean, Va., 16 Mar. 1994). Organist, pianist, composer. He attended St. Mary's Seminary in Baltimore and was ordained as a Catholic priest in 1947. He studied with Walter Piston at Harvard Univ. (M.A., 1954), at the Pius X School of Liturgical Music in New York, and in France with Nadia Boulanger. He taught at Catholic Univ. in Washington, D.C. (1948–64), and performed on organ, piano, and harpsichord in the Washington area. The bulk of his compositions are for the liturgy, though he also composed 2 symphonies (1957, 1961) and other orchestral works, all in a conservative idiom. In 1964 he left the priesthood, eventually becoming organist at a Unitarian church in Arlington, Va., and continuing to write liturgical music in a similar style.

Wordsworth, William (Brocklesby) (b. London, 17 Dec. 1908; d. Kingussie, Scotland, 10 Mar. 1988). Composer. From 1921 to 1931 he studied harmony and counterpoint with Oldroyd. He studied composition at Edinburgh Univ. from 1934 to 1936 with Tovey, who encouraged him. Eventually Wordsworth became active in the establishment of the Scottish Composers' Guild (1966). His musical language is, in general, conservative in its use of a tonal basis and Romantic thematic processes. His works include 8 symphonies, 3 concertos (piano, 1946; violin, 1955; cello, 1962), and chamber music (6 string quartets: 1941, 1944, 1947, 1950, 1957, 1964).

Work, Henry Clay (b. Middletown, Conn., 1 Oct. 1832; d. Hartford, 8 June 1884). Composer. He apprenticed as a printer in Hartford. Published his first song, "We Are Coming, Sister Mary," in 1853. He moved to Chicago in 1855, where he worked as a printer. G. F. Root later saw some of his works and had them published. He worked for the periodical *Song Messenger of the Northwest* (published by Root and Cady). Compositions include over 75 songs, including his most famous Civil War song, "Marching through Georgia" (1865). His best-known song is "Grandfather's Clock" (1876). His songs were edited and published as *Henry Clay Work: Songs* (New York, 1884; R: 1974).

Work, John Wesley (II) (b. Nashville, 6 Aug. 1872; d. Nashville, 7 Sept. 1925). Singer, conductor, musicologist. He attended Fisk Univ. (B.A., 1895, M.A., 1898) and Harvard Univ. (1896–97). From 1898 to 1923 he taught history and Latin at Fisk, at the same time conducting the school choir and touring as a singer with the Fisk Jubilee Quartet. He was active as a collector of black folk songs, particularly spirituals, publishing several collections of arrangements and the scholarly treatise *Folk Song of the American Negro* (Nashville, 1915).

Work, John Wesley, III (b. Tullahoma, Tenn., 15 June 1901; d. Nashville, 17 May 1967). Composer, conductor. Son of John Wesley Work II; he studied piano and sang as a child; attended Fisk Univ. (B.A., 1923), the Juilliard School (1923–24; then called the Institute of Musical Art), Columbia Univ. Teachers College (M.A., 1930), and Yale Univ. (B.M., 1933). Beginning in 1927 and continuing with occasional interruptions, he taught at Fisk. He conducted and sang with various university ensembles, lectured on music, and collected, arranged, and wrote about black folk song. In addition he was active as a composer. Both his choral and his instrumental works are deeply influenced by black folk and traditional music. Works include *Yenvalou* (orchestra, 1946); *The Singers* (cantata, 1941); *Appalachia* (piano, 1954); *From the Deep South* (organ, 1936).

Wormser, André (Alphonse-Toussaint) (b. Paris, 1 Nov. 1851; d. there, 4 Nov. 1926). Composer. He studied with Bazin and Marmontel at the Paris Conservatory. Won the Prix de Rome in 1875 with the cantata *Clytemnestre.* His most successful work was the pantomime *L'enfant prodigue* (1890). Other compositions include several operas, the ballet *L'étoile, Suite tsigane, Diane et Endymion,* choruses, and songs.

Woytowicz, Bolesław (b. Dunajowce, near Uszyca na Podolu, 5 Dec. 1899; d. Katowice, 11 July 1980). Composer, pianist. His grandfather, Mikołaj Woytowicz, taught the child Bolesław composition and keyboard; he went on to study piano with Nowacki and Hanicki from 1913 to 1915 and with Wielhorski from 1916 to 1917. He studied literature, mathematics, and law at university, and from 1920 to 1924 he took piano lessons with Michałowski at the Chopin College of Music in Warsaw. He continued his pursuit of composition with Szopski, Maliszewski, and from 1929 to 1932 with Boulanger. Through the 1930s he taught music, as well as touring as a concert pianist. From 1945 he was a professor at the Katowice Conservatory and from 1963 at the Kraków Conservatory. His own compositions employ serial techniques. Works include orchestral (*Symphonic Sketches,* 1949), vocal, and chamber music.

Wranitzky [Vranický, Wraniczky, Wranizky], **Anton** (b. Nová Říše, Moravia, 13 June 1761; d. Vienna, 6 Aug. 1820). Composer, violinist. Brother of Paul Wranitzky, with whom he studied. He also received instruction from Mozart, Haydn, and Albrechtsberger in Vienna. Some of his various appointments included those of Kapellmeister for the Prince J. F. Maximilian Lobkowitz (1797), orchestral director for the Viennese court theater (1807), orchestral director at the Theater an der Wien (1814). He wrote 15 symphonies, 15 violin concertos, other solo concertos, overtures, serenades, notturnos, a great deal of chamber music, vocal music. He also wrote *Violin Fondament* (Vienna, 1814), a violin tutor.

Wranitzky [Vranický, Wraniczky, Wranizky], **Paul** [Pavel] (b. Nová Říše, Moravia, 30 Dec. 1756; d. Vienna, 26 Sept. 1808). Composer. Brother of Anton Wranitzky. He arrived in Vienna in 1776 to study theology, but also studied music with Joseph Kraus and Haydn. He became a violinist in Prince Esterházy's orchestra at Eisenstadt around 1780, was appointed head orchestral director of the Viennese court theaters about 1790, and joined the Viennese Tonkünstler Sozietät, of which he became secretary. He was well known as a conductor (he directed the first performance of Beethoven's First Symphony) as well as a composer. His singspiel, *Oberon, König der Elfen* (Vienna, 1789), enjoyed great success. His compositions include about 9 other operas (all for Vienna), ballets, 51 symphonies, several solo concertos, many string quartets, quintets, and trios.

Wuensch, Gerhard (b. Vienna, 23 Dec. 1925). Composer and teacher. He studied composition and piano at the State Academy in Vienna (diploma, 1952), then music theory at the Univ. of Texas with Paul Pisk (1954–56). He taught at Butler Univ. in Indianapolis (1956–63) and the universities of Toronto (1964–69), Calgary (1969–73), and Western Ontario (from 1973). He wrote music in a variety of styles, for a great variety of instrumental combinations, most notably accordion (*Music without Pretensions,* accordion and string quartet, 1969; *4 Mini-Suites,* accordion, 1968; *Diversions,* accordion, 1972). Other works include *Serenade for a Summer Evening* (orchestra, 1986); *3 Episodes from St. John* (soli, chorus, organ, 1987).

Wüllner, Franz (b. Münster, 28 Jan. 1832; d. Braunfels, 7 Sept. 1902). Composer and conductor. His son was the singer Ludwig Wüllner (1858–1938). He studied at Brussels, Bremen, Cologne, Leipzig, and Munich; his teachers included Joachim, Brahms, and Jahn. Named professor of piano at the Munich Conservatory in 1856. He became court conductor in 1864; was music director at Aix-la-Chapelle from 1858. In 1871 he succeeded Bülow as director of the Munich Opera. He was director of the Dresden Conservatory from 1877, and of the Cologne Conservatory from 1884. Conducted the premieres of *Das Rheingold* (1869), *Die Walküre* (1870), *Till Eulenspiegel* (1895), and *Don Quixote* (1898).

Wunderlich, Fritz (b. Kusel, Rheinland-Pfalz, 26 Sept. 1930; d. Heidelberg, 17 Sept. 1966). Tenor. Studied at the Freiburg Hochschule für Musik and made his professional debut in 1955 as Tamino *(Die Zauberflöte)* with the Stuttgart Opera. Though especially remembered for his Mozart roles, he premiered the role of Tiresias in Orff's *Oedipus der Tyrann* (1959) and Christoph in Egk's *Die Verlobung in San Domingo.* He was also engaged by the opera companies in Frankfurt (1958–60) and Munich (1960–66).

Wuorinen, Charles (b. New York, 9 June 1938). Composer. He studied piano with Vladimir Ussachevsky and Jack Beeson, and began composing at an early age. As an undergraduate at Columbia Univ. he composed prolifically and had many works performed, including his Second and Third Symphonies (1959, 1959), *Triptych* (violin, viola, and percussion, 1957), and a Piano Sonata (1958). By the early 1960s his music—nondiatonic, sometimes atonal, sometimes serial, emphasizing unusual textures—was receiving considerable attention from the press. Wuorinen received his B.A. from Columbia in 1961, an M.A. in 1963, and he joined the faculty in 1964. With Harvey Sollberger he founded in 1962 the Group for Contemporary Music, a campus-based ensemble dedicated to the performance of new music, in which he played keyboards and conducted.

Beginning in about 1961 Wuorinen sought to base his music on more rigorously serial principles, taking his cue initially from Webern's contrapuntal procedures (e.g., Chamber Concerto, cello and chamber ensemble, 1963), then from Milton Babbitt's methods of serializing non-pitch parameters such as rhythm and dynamics (e.g., Chamber Concerto, flute and chamber ensemble, 1964; Piano Concerto, 1965). By around 1966 he had worked out what he called a "time-point system," in which serial relationships were generalized to include rhythm, pitch, and formal proportion. Works using the time-point system include *Duo* (violin and piano, 1966), *The Politics of Harmony* (masque, New York, 1968), Piano Sonata no. 1 (1969), String Quartet no. 1 (1971). Wuorinen applied the same principles to electronic composition in *Time's Encomium* (1969), produced on an RCA Mark II synthesizer at the Columbia–Princeton Electronic Music Center. This work was awarded the Pulitzer Prize for music in 1970.

Wuorinen was denied tenure at Columbia in 1971; he took the Group for Contemporary Music with him when he left. He taught at the Manhattan School of Music (1972–79), supporting himself in considerable measure from commissions and grants, then in 1984 moved to Rutgers. During the 1970s Wuorinen modified his serial technique, reducing the degree to which details of pitch and rhythm are predetermined by the serial framework. In works such as *Grand Bamboula* (string orchestra, 1971) and *Percussion Duo* (mallet instruments and piano, 1979), a set or group of sets provides the basic materials of pitch, rhythm, and proportion, but the surface of the music is shaped by compositional choices. Some compositions involve preexisting musical materials. The *Bearbeitungen über das Glogauer Liederbuch* (flute, clarinet, violin, bass, 1962) are close rearrangements of Renaissance originals. *A Reliquary for Igor Stravinsky* (orchestra, 1975) is based on fragmentary sketches left by Stravinsky at his death. In the Percussion Symphony (percussion ensemble, 1976), rearrangements for percussion of "Vergine bella" by the Renaissance composer Guillaume Dufay are used as interludes between movements based on serial procedures.

Other works include *The W. of Babylon* ("baroque burlesque," New York, 1975); *Evolutio transcripta* (chamber orchestra, 1961); *Orchestral and Electronic Exchanges* (orchestra and tape, 1965); *Contrafactum* (orchestral arrangement of *Time's Encomium,* 1969); Violin Concerto no. 2 (amplified violin and orchestra, 1972); 3 piano concertos (1965, 1973, 1984; the second for amplified piano); Two-Part Symphony (orchestra, 1978); *Janissary Music* (percussion solo, 1966); String Trio (1968); *Speculum speculi* (chamber ensemble, 1972); *Arabia felix* (chamber ensemble, 1973); Piano Sonata no. 2 (1976); String Quartet no. 2 (1979); *Spinoff* (violin, bass, conga drums, 1984); String Quartet no. 3 (1987); *Miami Bamboula* (orchestra, 1988); *Machault non chou* (1989).

Bibl.: Charles Wuorinen, *Simple Composition* (New York, 1979). Richard D. Burbank, *Charles Wuorinen: A Bio-Bibliography* (Westport, Conn., 1994).

Wurlitzer, Franz Rudolph (b. Schöneck, Saxony, 31 Jan. 1831; d. Cincinnati, 14 Jan. 1914). Instrument maker. He emigrated to Cincinnati in 1853, where he dealt in musical instruments and worked in a bank. He opened a branch of his instrument company in Chicago in 1865. His brother Anton joined with him to form Rudolph Wurlitzer & Brother in 1872 (incorporated in 1890). Rudolph served as president from 1890 to 1912 and chairman, 1912–14. His son Howard Eugene (1871–1928) joined the firm in 1889 and introduced the firm to the automatic instrument trade; he served as president, 1912–27, and chairman, 1927–28. Rudolph's son Rudolph Henry (1873–1948) studied violin with Emanuel Wirth in Berlin in 1891; he returned to Cincinnati in 1894 to develop the company's violin department. He served as president, 1927–32, and chairman, 1932–42. Another son, Farny Reginald (1883–1972), studied in Germany in 1901 and apprenticed with Phillips & Söhne; he returned in 1904 and bought an organ company in Elmira in 1910. He served as president, 1932–41, chairman, 1942–66. In 1957 the name of the firm was changed to the Wurlitzer Company.

Wurm, Marie (b. Southhampton, 18 May 1860; d. Munich, 21 Jan. 1938). Composer and performer. She traveled to Germany, where she studied piano with Raff and Clara Schumann and at the Stuttgart Conservatory. Back in England she studied theory with Stanford and Arthur Sullivan and became known there as a performer. She eventually returned to Germany and worked as a performer and conductor, having organized an orchestra for women in Berlin. She was also known for her improvisation skills. Works include the opera *Die Mitschuldigen* (Leipzig, 1923) as well as symphonic and chamber music.

Wyk, Arnold(us Christian Vlok) van (b. near Calvinia, Cape Province, 26 Apr. 1916; d. Cape Town, 27 May 1983). Composer. From 1936 to 1938 he studied music at the Univ. of Stellenbosch. He then traveled to England to study composition with Holland and piano with Craxton at the Royal Academy of Music. He worked for the Afrikaans division of the BBC during the war. After 1946 he resettled in South Africa to teach, first at the Univ. of Cape Town and then at the Univ. of Stellenbosch. His musical style is generally conservative in its use of traditional forms and genres as well as a tonal basis. Many of his works remain unpublished. They include orchestral, chamber, and vocal (*Vier weemoedige liedjies,* voice, piano, 1934–38; *Van liefde en verlatenheid,* voice, piano, 1953).

Wyner, Yehudi (b. Calgary, 1 June 1929). Pianist and composer. Son of composer Lazar Weiner. He went to Juilliard as a teenager (diploma, piano, 1946), then attended Yale Univ. (B.A., 1950) and the Yale School of Music, where his teachers were Richard Donovan and Paul Hindemith (B.M., 1951; M.M., 1953). In addition he studied with Walter Piston at Harvard (M.A., 1952). During the 1950s he was active as a pianist, composer, and conductor in New York. He returned to Yale in 1963 to teach composition (1963–73); also taught at the Berkshire (Mass.) Music Center (1975–78), and SUNY–Purchase (beginning 1978), where he was dean of music, 1978–82. Most of his instrumental music is for piano and/or chamber ensemble, for example, the Piano Sonata (1954), *Concert Duo* (violin and piano, 1957), *Three Short Fantasies* (piano, 1963), String Quartet (1984–85), *Composition* (viola, piano, 1986), *Sweet Consort* (flute, piano, 1988). He composed several pieces for his wife, soprano Susan Davenny Wyner (b. 1943), including *Intermedio* (soprano and string orchestra, 1974), *Fragments from Antiquity* (soprano and orchestra, 1981), and *On This Most Voluptuous Night* (soprano and chamber ensemble, 1982). Also composed Jewish liturgical music (*Friday Evening Service,* 1963; *Torah Service,* 1966).

Wynette, Tammy [Pugh, Wynette] (b. Itawamba County, near Tupelo, Miss., 5 May 1942). Country singer and songwriter. From 1966 she made numerous successful recordings with producer Billy Sherrill (including "D-I-V-O-R-C-E" and "Stand by Your Man," both 1968). From 1969 she sang duets with husband, George Jones ("Take Me," 1971); she remained among the most popular female country performers throughout the 1970s and 1980s.

Bibl.: Tammy Wynette, *Stand by Your Man* (New York, 1979).

Wyschnegradsky [Vishnegradsky], **Ivan Alexandrovich** (b. St. Petersburg, 16 May 1893; d. Paris, 29 Sept. 1979). Composer. He studied law at the Univ. of St. Petersburg (1911–16), at the same time studying composition with Nicolas Sokoloff. Under the influence of Scriabin he composed an oratorio, *La journée de l'existence* (1917; rev. 1927, 1939), which combined mystical ideas with chromatic harmonies. These led him to explore the possibilities of microtonal intervals, which for him signified "cosmic consciousness." Emigrating from Russia in 1919 and settling in Paris in the early 1920s, he established contact with Alois Hába and other composers interested in quarter tone music, and he attempted unsuccessfully to construct a quarter tone piano. He used quarter tones in his string quartets (1924, 1932), *Ainsi parlait Zarathoustra* (orchestra, 1930), and several other works, always as extensions of traditional chromatic harmony. In the mid-30s he hit upon the system of tuning several pianos at microtonal intervals from one another, so that quarter tone music could be realized on 2 pianos, sixth tone music on 3 pianos. He rearranged several earlier works for these combinations, and composed new works such as the Preludes (2 pianos, 1934) and *Acte chorégraphique* (baritone, chorus, and 4 pianos, 1940).

Writings: *Manuel d'harmonie à quarts de ton* (Paris, 1932). "La musique à quatres de ton et sa réalisation pratique," *ReM* 171 (Jan. 1937): 26–33. "Problèmes d'ultrachromatisme," *Polyphonie* 9–10 (1954): 129–42.

Bibl.: Lucile Gayden, *Ivan Wyschnegradsky* (Frankfurt, 1973). *Revue Musicale* 290–91 (1972) [special issue on Wyschnegradsky].

Wyttenbach, Jürg (b. Bern, 2 Dec. 1935). Composer and pianist. He studied at the Bern Conservatory and at the Paris Conservatory with Lefébure and Calvet, and later with Karl Engel. He has taught at the Biel (1959–67) and the Bern (1962–66) conservatories; in 1967 he joined the Basel Academy. His earlier works show the influence of Stravinsky and Bartók (*Sutil und Laar,* chorus, 2 pianos, 1962–63) and serial techniques (*De metalli,* baritone, orchestra, 1965); he later turned to "instrumental theater" (*Exécution ajournée I, Gesten für 13 Musiker,* 1970; String Quartet [Exécution ajournée II and III], 1970–71, 1973; *Kunststücke die Zeit tot zu schlagen, Hör- und Sehstück für Musiker,* 1972; *Clastrophonic,* 6 players, 1973).

X

Xenakis, Iannis (b. Braila, Romania, 29 May 1922). Composer, architect. Born into a Greek family resident in Romania, he was educated in Greece. His musical education was minimal—piano lessons, singing in the school choir, a few lessons in harmony and counterpoint. At the Polytechnic Institute in Athens he studied engineering. During World War II Xenakis joined the Resistance, and soon entered the Communist party. In 1944 he was severely wounded, leaving him blind in the left eye. He enlisted in the army; then, denounced as a communist, he deserted, living underground in Athens, then escaping in 1947. He arrived in Paris in November of that year. Xenakis found a job as an engineer, working for the architect Le Corbusier; he remained with Le Corbusier until 1959, becoming a trusted assistant. Meanwhile he resumed his study of music, briefly with Arthur Honegger and Darius Milhaud, finally with Olivier Messiaen.

Xenakis focused on finding ways in which mathematical structures or processes could be realized as musical sound. For example, in his first major composition, *Metastasis* (orchestra, 1954), the mathematical models are provided by the Fibonacci series, then mapped onto the score as pitch, register, timbre, and duration. In *Pithoprakta* (orchestra, 1956) the individual instruments of the orchestra are conceived as molecules obeying the Maxwell–Boltzmann law of molecular velocities in a gas. *Metastasis* was introduced in 1955 at the Donaueschingen Festival, where it attracted considerable notice. *Pithoprakta* and *Achorripsis* (chamber ensemble, 1957) were premiered by the conductor Hermann Scherchen in 1957 and 1958, establishing Xenakis as a major figure in the European avant-garde. Resigning from Le Corbusier's firm in 1959, Xenakis supported himself by commissions, grants, and teaching activities. From the 1950s through the 1970s he experimented with *musique concrète* (*Diamorphoses,* 1958), with purely electronic music (*Analogique B,* 1959), with music in which the performance involves elements of performer choice (*Duel,* 2 orchestras, 1959; *Stratégie,* 2 orchestras, 1962), and with music involving space and light as well as sound (*Le diatope,* incandescent light, laser light, tape, 1978). He also began to use computers, first to carry out mathematical calculations (*ST/4,* string quartet, 1962; *ST/48,* orchestra, 1962), later as a means of translating mathematical structures directly into sounding music (*Mycenes Alpha,* 1978).

Works: *Terretektorh* (orchestra, 1966); *Nomos gamma* (orchestra, 1968); *Noomena* (orchestra, 1975); *Jonchaies* (orchestra, 1977); *Horos* (orchestra, 1986); *Oresteia* (incidental music, chorus and orchestra, 1966); *Cendrées* (chorus and orchestra, 1974); *Akrata* (wind ensemble, 1965); *Anaktoria* (chamber ensemble, 1969); *Nuits* (vocal ensemble, 1968); *Herma* (piano, 1964); *Khoaï* (amplified piano, 1976); *Ais* (baritone, percussion, orchestra, 1980); *Mists* (piano, 1981); *Nekuia* (choir, orchestra, 1981); *Pour Maurice* (baritone, piano, 1982); *Chants des soleils* (mixed choir, children's choir, brass, percussion, 1983); *Tetras* (string quartet, 1983); *Shaar* (large string orchestra, 1983); *Lichens I* (orchestra, 1984); *Naama* (amplified piano, 1984); *Thallein* (14 instruments, 1984); *Alax* (orchestra, 1985); *Keqrops* (piano, 92-piece orchestra, 1986); *Horos* (89-piece orchestra, 1986); *Akea* (string quartet, piano, 1987); *Jalons* (orchestra, 1988); *Tracées* (orchestra, 1988).

Writings: *Musiques formelles* (Paris, 1963); trans. as *Formalized Music* (1971). *Musique architecture* (Tournai, 1971; rev. 1976).

Bibl.: Mario Bois, ed., *Iannis Xenakis—the Man and His Music* (London, 1967). Nouritza Matossian, *Iannis Xenakis* (Paris, 1981); trans. Eng. (London, 1984). *Iannis Xenakis,* ed. Heinz-Klaus Metzger and Rainer Riehn (Munich, 1987) [includes works list]. Iannis Xenakis, "Xenakis on Xenakis," *PNM* 25 (1987): 16–63.

Xyndas [Xinta, Xinda, Xinds, Xyntas], **Spyridon** (b. Corfu, 8 June 1812; d. Athens, 12 Nov. 1896). Guitarist and composer. Studied at the Conservatory of S. Pietro a Majella at Naples and in Corfu with Mantzaros. Moved to Athens in 1888, where he died blind and in poverty. Most of his manuscripts were lost during the bombing of Corfu in World War II. His compositions include the first opera written on a Greek libretto (*O ypopsifios vouleftis,* 1867), other operas, choral works, short guitar pieces, keyboard works.

Bibl.: S. Mocenigo, *Neoelliniki mousike* (Athens, 1958).

Y

Yamada, Kōsaku [Kôsçak] (b. Tokyo, 9 June 1886; d. there, 29 Dec. 1965). Composer. From 1904 to 1908 he studied vocal music with Shibata and cello and theory with Werkmeister at the Tokyo School of Music. He then traveled to Berlin; at the Hochschule für Musik he took composition lessons with Bruch and Karl Wolf until 1913. Back in Japan, he established and conducted the Tokyo Philharmonic (predecessor to the later orchestra). Beginning in 1917 he toured the U.S. as a conductor of his own and others' compositions. In Japan he was active with the exploration and performance of vocal music. He established the Japanese Association for Music Drama in 1920, and in 1922 worked with the poet Kitahara to found the journal *Shi to ongaku* [Verse and Music], which dealt with the relationship between poetry and music. His music was influenced by Wagner and, in particular, Strauss, yet he moved toward a more native Japanese aesthetic in the settings and subjects of his vocal works. Works include operas (*Ochitaru tennyo* [The Depraved Heavenly Maiden], 1912; *Kurofune* [The Black Ships], 1939); orchestral music (*Yajin sōzō* [The Creation of the Rustics], dance poem, 1916; *Meiji shōka* [Ode to the Meiji], 1921; *Shukuten jokyoku* [Festival Overture], chorus, orchestra, 1940); choral music (*Tsuki no tabi* [A Journey of the Moon], voices, violin, 1914); chamber music, many songs, and film scores.

Yamash'ta [Yamashita], **Stomu** [Tsutomu] (b. Kyoto, 10 Mar. 1947). Composer and performer. He studied drums and piano as a youth and in 1961 became a percussionist with the Kyoto Philharmonic and the Osaka Philharmonic. He had attended the Kyoto Academy of Music since 1960 and in 1964 traveled to the U.S., where he went to the Interlochen Arts Academy in Michigan and the Berklee School. He became highly successful as a concert performer of jazz, traditional art music, and new music. His own compositions focused on his experimental new-music group Come to the Edge and his forum for experimental theater, the Red Buddha Theatre. His pieces frequently incorporate multimedia sources and improvisation. Works include *Prisms* (solo percussion, 1970), *Man from the East* (theatrical work, 1971), and *Rain Mountain* (theatrical work, 1973), as well as musical scores for Japanese films.

Yancey, Jimmy [James Edwards] (b. Chicago, 20 Feb. 1898; d. there, 17 Sept. 1951). Boogie-woogie pianist. After touring the U.S. and Europe as a vaudeville singer and dancer, he settled in Chicago in 1915 and took up piano. Although he mainly worked as a baseball groundskeeper, he taught Albert Ammons and Meade "Lux" Lewis and was himself invited to record after they had initiated the craze for boogie-woogie in the late 1930s. His recordings include "Yancey Stomp," "State Street Special" (both 1939), and "Yancey's Bugle Call" (1940). He and his wife, singer Mama Yancey, performed at Carnegie Hall in 1948. Despite limited technical ability and a small repertory, he was among the most imaginative boogie-woogie players, particularly in the variety and originality of his left-hand patterns.

Bibl.: Peter Sylvester, *A Left Hand Like God: A Study of Boogie Woogie* (London, ?1988 or 1989).

Yannay, Yehuda (b. Timişoara, 26 May 1937). Composer. He immigrated to Israel in 1951, where he studied (1959–64) with Boscovich at the Rubin Academy in Tel Aviv. He then traveled to the U.S. to study composition with Berger and Shapero at Brandeis Univ., with Schuller at Tanglewood, and at the Univ. of Illinois. He joined the faculty at the Univ. of Wisconsin, where he created the new-music performance group Music from Almost Yesterday Ensemble. His compositions, many of them associated with this ensemble, are avant-garde in form, style, and message, frequently confronting in a theatrical way what Yannay perceived to be bourgeois values. Works include *Incantations* (voices, keyboard, piano interior, 1964), *Per se* (chamber concerto, 1968), *Houdini's 9th* (double bass, escape artist, and 2 hospital orderlies, 1969), *A Noiseless Patient Spider* (women's chorus, 1975), *Celan Ensembles* (tenor, ensemble, 1986); *Jidyll* (film score, 1988).

Bibl.: Yehuda Yannay, "A European Trilogy," *PNM* 26 (1988): 281–99.

Yardumian, Richard (b. Philadelphia, Pa., 5 April 1917; d. Bryn Athyn, Pa., 15 Aug. 1985). Composer. He taught himself piano as a child and music theory as a young man, composing piano pieces and several movements of *Armenian Suite* (orchestra, 1937). His formal training consisted of private study of composition and piano in Philadelphia (1939–41). In 1945 his *Desolate City* was premiered by Eugene Ormandy and the Philadelphia Orchestra. For many years thereafter Ormandy championed Yardumian's music, premiering and programming many works and designating Yardumian as "composer laureate" of the orchestra (1949–64). Yardumian's music is colored by his Armenian heritage and his Swedenborgian religious beliefs. During the 1940s he worked out his own harmonic system, based on superimposed thirds. From the 1950s on his harmonies were also influenced by medieval and Renaissance modality. Works include 2 symphonies (1950, rev. 1961; 1947, rev. 1964); Violin Concerto (1949; rev. 1960); *The Story of Abraham* (oratorio, 1972); *Mass "Come Creator Spirit"* (1966); *Cantus animae et cordis* (string quartet, 1955).

Yashiro, Akio (b. Tokyo, 10 Sept. 1929; d. Yokohama, 9 Apr. 1976). Composer. Studied composition with Saburo Moroi and entered the National Univ. of Fine Arts and Music in Tokyo, graduating in 1949 after study with Hashimoto, Ifukube, Ikenouchi, and Kreutzer; undertook further studies at the Paris Conservatory with Boulanger, Messiaen, Noël Gallon, and de la Presle. Returned to Tokyo and taught at his former school, and at the Tōhō Gakuen School of Music. Most of his works are instrumental and in a lyrical, neoclassical style; they include a String Quartet (1954–55), a Cello Concerto (1960), a Piano Concerto (1967), a Sonata for 2 flutes and piano (1957), and a Symphony (1958).

Yepes, Narciso (b. Lorca, Spain, 14 Nov. 1927). Guitarist and composer. He studied with Vicente Asencio at the Valencia Conservatory. In 1947 he made his debut, in Madrid, playing Rodrigo's *Concierto de Aranjuez.* Continued his studies in 1950 with Gieseking and Enescu in Paris. Yepes toured widely throughout Europe, the Far East, South America, and the U.S. He also wrote film scores, transcribed early music for guitar, and made many recordings, including all of Bach's music for lute.

Yim, Jay Allan (b. St. Louis, Miss., 24 Apr. 1958). Composer. He studied at the Univ. of California (B.A., 1980), at the Royal College of Music, London (M.Mus. 1981), at Tanglewood, and at Harvard. Works include orchestral music (*Askesis,* 1980; *Mille graces,* 1986; *Geometry and Delirium,* 1987); chamber music (*Timescreen no. 2,* piano, 1983; *Furiosamente,* flute, 1985); electronic music (*Kinkakuji,* 1984; *Shiosai,* 1984).

Yoder, Paul V(an Buskirk) (b. Tacoma, 8 Oct. 1908). Bandmaster and composer. He attended the Univ. of North Dakota (B.A., 1930) and Northwestern Univ. (M.M., 1941). He taught public school music (1930–36), then struck out on his own as a composer and arranger. Composed many pieces for band and arranged hundreds more. Among the best known of his original compositions are *Alpha and Omega, Hurricane, La Fonda,* and *Relax.*

Yon, Pietro Alessandro (b. Settimo Vittone, near Turin, 8 Aug. 1886; d. Huntington, N.Y., 22 Nov. 1943). Organist and composer. He studied in Milan with Fumagalli, and at the Accademia di S. Cecilia in Rome with Remigio Renzi and Sgambati, graduating in 1905. Became assistant organist at St. Peter's in Rome, then moved to New York in 1907 and became organist and choir director of St. Francis Xavier Church (1907–19, 1921–26); later served as organist at St. Patrick's Cathedral (1927–43). He became a U.S. citizen in 1921. Of his compositions *Gesù Bambino* (1917) was the most popular; he also wrote an oratorio, *The Triumph of St. Patrick* (1934), and over 20 Masses.

Yonge [Young, Younge], **Nicholas** (b. Lewes?; d. London, buried 23 Oct. 1619). Singer and music editor. He sang in the choir at St. Paul's Cathedral (1594–1618) and served as the editor of 2 anthologies of Italian madrigals published with English texts, both entitled *Musica transalpina* (1588, 1597). The earlier collection, which contains nearly 60 works by 18 composers, was one of the most influential volumes of Italian madrigals to appear in England at the time.

Bibl.: David Scott, "Nicholas Yonge and His Transalpine Music," *MT* 116 (1975): 875–76.

Youmans, Vincent (Millie) (b. New York, 27 Sept. 1898; d. Denver, 5 Apr. 1946). Popular songwriter. He was a song plugger for the Remick firm and composed for the navy in World War I; his first publication came in 1920. Between 1921 and 1927 he wrote 4 successful musicals (*Two Little Girls in Blue,* 1921; *The Wildflower,* 1923; *No, No, Nanette,* 1925; *Hit the Deck,* 1927); while subsequent efforts at musical theater failed, a large number of songs from these and later productions became standards ("Tea for Two," 1925; "Through the Years," 1932). He is credited as a highly original songwriter, standing in neither the Tin Pan Alley nor operetta traditions. He was forced to retire in 1933 because of tuberculosis.

Bibl.: Gerald Bordman, *Days To Be Happy, Years To Be Sad: The Life and Music of Vincent Youmans* (New York, 1982).

Young, Douglas (b. London, 18 July 1947). Composer. He studied at the Royal College of Music from 1966 until 1970, taking composition lessons with Milner and piano lessons with Hopkins. His own compositions met quickly with critical success. In 1973 Young formed the performance ensemble Dreamtiger, with which many of his works were associated. He has experimented with traditional forms and genres as well as with avant-garde trends. Works such as *Dreamlandscapes Book 2* (1979–85), which is part of a larger compositional project, evoke powerful imagery and create form through the use of large-scale rhythmic and textural gestures. Other works include Sonata (string trio, 1967–68), *Charlotte Brontë—Portrait* (ballet, 1971–73), *Landscapes and Absences* (sketches, tenor, English horn, string trio, 1972–73), and *Ludwig—Fragmente eines Rätsels* (premiered Bavarian State Opera, 1986).

Young, La Monte (Thornton) (b. Bern, Idaho, 14 Oct. 1935). Composer and performer. Growing up in Los Angeles he learned the clarinet and saxophone, and performed with a number of jazz musicians; studied at UCLA (B.A., 1958) with Stevenson, and at the Univ. of California, Berkeley (1958–60), with Shifrin and Imbrie; also worked with Leonard Stein, with Maxfield at the New School for Social Research (1960–61), and at Darmstadt. In 1963 he married the artist and illustrator Marian Zazeela, and has collaborated with her in many of his works; in 1970 he began studying Indian classical folk music with Pran Nath. Young served as editor of the highly influential volume *An Anthology* (1963; R: 1970), a major stimulant to the Fluxus movement; in 1969 he published his *Selected Writings.*

Young's interest in organum and in the drones of non-Western music influenced his earliest compositions, which often center on sustained notes, and emphasize stasis and extended duration (*For Brass,* 1957; *For Guitar,* 1958; *Trio for Strings,* 1958); these pieces are considered early examples or forerunners of minimalism. During the early 1960s Young experimented with a series of works that consisted solely of verbal instructions with no musical notes (e.g., the series titled *Composition 1960*). His interest in sustained sounds led him to study intonation systems, particularly just intonation, in which intervals exactly match the ratios in the harmonic series, so that sustained harmonies are free of beats. To perform music in just intonation he founded the Theatre of Eternal Music, for which he began to compose *The Tortoise, His Dreams and Journeys,* a multisectional work in progress in which the performers improvise in just intonation over electronic and acoustic drones. Just intonation is also used in *The Well-Tuned Piano,* another ongoing, multisectional piece (begun in 1964). Compositions include action and text works (*arabic numeral (any integer) to H.F.,* piano or gong, 1960); electronic and mixed media (*The Big Dream,* 1984); works for conventional forces (*For Brass,* 2 horns, 2 trumpets, 2 trombones, 2 tubas, 1957; Trio for Strings, 1958; *For Guitar,* 1958; *Orchestral Dreams,* orchestra, 1985).

Young, Lester (Willis) [Pres; Prez] (b. Woodville, Miss., 27 Aug. 1909; d. New York, 15 March 1959). Jazz tenor saxophonist. After playing in the Southwest with Walter Page (1930), Bennie Moten (1933), and an early Count Basie group (1934), he had a relatively unsuccessful stay in Fletcher Henderson's big band, owing to his refusal to imitate Coleman Hawkins's tenor saxophone style (1934). His own approach—playing with a delicate dry timbre and emphasizing swinging tuneful melodies rather than arpeggiated harmonies—offered the most significant alternative to Hawkins. Young joined Basie (1936–40), recording solos with small groups, including "Shoe Shine Boy," "Lady Be Good" (both 1936), "Lester Leaps In" (1939); and with the big band, including "John's Idea" (1937), "Every Tub," "Jumpin' at the Woodside" (both 1938). He occasionally doubled on clarinet. During this period he also recorded many sympathetic accompaniments to Billie Holiday's singing (1937–41). He led groups and recorded with Nat "King" Cole (1942, including "Indiana"). He rejoined Basie (1943–44), leaving for a disastrous year of army service which culminated in his imprisonment. From 1946 he toured with Jazz at the Philharmonic and led groups. Among his recordings were "These Foolish Things" (1945) and the album *Pres and Teddy* with Teddy Wilson (1956). Young was enormously influential, spawning such direct imitators as Paul Quinichette ("the Vice-Pres") and an entire school of white swing, cool, and bop players (including Stan Getz, Zoot Sims, Al Cohn, Brew Moore).

Bibl.: Lewis Porter, *Lester Young* (Boston, 1985). Frank Büchmann-Möller, *You Got To Be the Original, Man: The Music of Lester Young* (New York, 1990). Frank Büchmann-Möller, *You Just Fight for Your Life: The Story of Lester Young* (New York, 1990).

Young, Neil (b. Toronto, 12 Nov. 1945). Rock singer and songwriter. In 1966 he moved to Los Angeles, where he joined Buffalo Springfield; 1969–71, performed in [David] Crosby, [Stephen] Stills, [Graham] Nash, and Young. From 1969 he released albums of folk- and country-influenced rock songs, principally in collaboration with his band Crazy Horse. Among his best-known recordings are "I Am a Child" (1967), "Helpless" (1970), "Heart of Gold" (1972), "Like a Hurricane" (1977), and "Powderfinger" (1979). In the 1980s he experimented with diverse styles, including electronic techno-pop (*Trans,* 1983), country (*Old Ways,* 1985), and blues (*This Note's for You,* 1988). More recent albums include *Sleeps with Angels* (1994) and *Mirror Ball* (with Pearl Jam, 1995).

Young, Victor (b. Chicago, 8 Aug. 1900; d. Palm Springs, 10 Nov. 1956). Popular songwriter, conductor, and violinist. Trained as a classical violinist, from 1922 he led popular and movie orchestras. He began composing in the late 1920s, and moved to Hollywood in 1935. His works include songs for revues ("A Hundred Years from Today," 1933), musicals, and films ("My Foolish Heart," 1949), many film scores (including *Gulliver's Travels,* 1939; *For Whom the Bell Tolls,* 1943; *Shane,* 1953), and instrumental compositions (mainly excerpted from film scores).

Young [Joungh], **William** (d. Innsbruck, 23 Apr. 1662). Composer and viol player. An Englishman, he was one of the chief transmitters of the English style of viol playing to Continental courts. By 1652 he was employed by Archduke Ferdinand Karl of Innsbruck; he accompanied him to Italy in 1652 and 1654. By the time Queen Christina of Sweden heard him play in Innsbruck in 1655 his reputation had spread across Europe. His compositions, many of which are for lyra-viol, include sonatas, fantasies, and dances.

Yradier, Sebastián de. See Iradier, Sebastián de.

Yriarte [Iriarte], **Tomás de** (b. Puerto de la Cruz de Orotava, Canary Islands, 18 Sept. 1750; d. Santa María, near Cádiz, 17 Sept. 1791). Composer and poet. His career was as a poet, and he held various government posts, but he also was an active amateur musician. He published a long poem, "La Musica" (1779), which became well known, and wrote the libretto to *Guzman el bueno,* a melodrama, as well as orchestral pieces for its production. He supposedly composed other musical works, but they have not been found.

Bibl.: Ralph M. Cox, *Tomás de Iriarte* (New York, 1972).

Ysaÿe, Eugène(-Auguste) (b. Liège, 16 July 1858; d. Brussels, 12 May 1931). Violinist, conductor, and composer. He studied with his father and entered the Liège Conservatory at the age of 8, studying with Heynberg and Rodolphe Massart; later worked with Wieniawski at the Brussels Conservatory and with Vieuxtemps in Paris. In 1879 he became leader of the Bilse orchestra in Berlin, and toured Scandinavia and Russia with Anton Rubinstein a few years later. He spent several years in Paris (1883–86), where he met Franck, Saint-Saëns, Debussy, d'Indy, and Fauré. From 1886 to 1898 he taught at the Brussels Conservatory and initiated a series of concerts called the Concerts Ysaÿe, which was devoted to contemporary Belgian and French music. Ysaÿe enjoyed a highly successful career as soloist and conductor during his many tours of England and the U.S.; in 1918 he began a four-year term as conductor of the Cincinnati Symphony. He turned more to conducting in his later years as ill health plagued him (he was diabetic). Considered by many to be the pioneer of the 20th-century school of violin playing, Ysaÿe also composed a number of works in post-Romantic style, including 8 violin concertos.

Bibl.: A. Ysaÿe and B. Ratcliffe, *Ysaÿe: His Life, Work, and Influence* (London, 1947). Maxime Bennoît-Jeannin, *Eugène Ysaÿe: Le dernier romantique ou le sacre du violon* (Brussels, 1989).

Ysaÿe, Théophile (b. Verviers, 22 Mar. 1865; d. Nice, 24 Mar. 1918). Pianist, composer, and conductor. Brother of Eugène Ysaÿe. He studied at the Liège Conservatory (1876–80), then went to Berlin to join his brother in 1881; there he studied with Kullak at the Neue Akademie der Tonkunst. In 1885 he settled with his brother in Paris, where he studied composition with Franck, and frequently accompanied his brother. Professor of piano at the Geneva Academy of Music, 1889–1900. After returning to Belgium he served as rehearsal conductor for the Concerts Ysaÿe. His compositions include a piano concerto (1909); Symphony no. 1 in F major op. 14 (1908); Requiem Mass (ca. 1906); Piano Quintet op. 20 (1913); Variations op. 10, 2 pianos (ca. 1910).

Yuasa, Jōji (b. Kōriyama, 12 Aug. 1929). Composer. From 1951 to 1957 he worked as a member of the Experimental Workshop in Tokyo, and he began working at Japanese Radio's electronic music studio in 1964. In 1968 Yuasa helped organize the "Crosstalk Festival" of Japanese and American multimedia works in Tokyo and Osaka, and received a Japan Society Fellowship which sponsored a lecture tour in the U.S. and Europe. Many of his works involve multimedia and use *musique concrète.* His compositions include stage works (*Circus Variation,* ballet, 1954; *Aya no tsuzumi* [Music for Noh Play], string quartet, 1955; *Carmen,* ballet, band, 1956; *Aoi no ue* [Music for Noh Play), tape, 1961); orchestral (*Projection for Koto and Orchestra: Hana, tori, kaze, tsuki* [Flower, Bird, Wind, Moon], 1967; *Music for Space Projection,* orchestra, tapes, 1970; *9 Levels by Ze-ami,* orchestra, 4-channel tape, 1988); vocal (*Bashō goku* [Poems by Bashō], voice, jūshichigen, koto, 1978; *Mutterings,* soprano, 7 instruments, 1988); chamber (*Projection for 7 Performers,* flute, oboe, clarinet, horn, trumpet, piano, cello, 1955; Ryō-iki, flute, 1978); vocal works; music for piano; tape; film scores.

Yun, Isang (b. Tongyong, 17 Sept. 1917; d. Berlin, 3 Nov. 1995). Composer. He studied in Korea and Japan; taught music at Seoul Univ., then continued his studies with Revel at the Paris Conservatory (1956–57) and with Blacher, Rufer, and Schwarz-Schilling at the Berlin Hochschule für Musik (1958–59); also attended summer courses at Darmstadt. He settled in Berlin, but his work was interrupted in 1967 when he was abducted and forced to return to Seoul, where he was imprisoned on political charges. After protests from the government of West Germany and from a number of prominent composers, he was granted amnesty and returned to Berlin in 1970. Subsequently taught composition at the Hannover Hochschule für Musik (1970–71) and the Berlin Hochschule (from 1970). Yun's early works were serialist, but beginning in the 1960s he began to combine Korean musical idioms with Western instruments. Beginning in 1964, in works such as *Loyang* and *Garak,* he let finely shaped melodic lines *(Haupttöne)* generate his musical forms.

Works: opera (*Der Traum des Liu-Tung,* 1965; *Die Witwe des Schmetterlings,* 1968; *Geisterliebe,* 1970; *Sim Tjong,* 1972); orchestral (Concerto, cello, orchestra, 1976; Double Concerto, oboe, harp, chamber orchestra, 1977; *Dialogue between Butterfly and Atom Bomb,* violin, orchestra, 1983; Symphony no. 1, 1984; *Festliches Präludium,* violin, orchestra, 1984; Symphony no. 2, 1984; Symphony no. 3, 1985; Symphony no. 5, 1987; Violin Concerto no. 2, 1987); chamber (String Quartet no. 3, 1959; *Loyang,* flute, oboe, clarinet, bassoon, harp, 2 percussion, violin, cello, 1962; *Images,* flute, oboe, violin, cello, 1968; *Octet,* 1978; *Monologue for Bass Clarinet,* 1983; Double Concerto, oboe, cello, string quartet, 1987; *Mugung Dong,* chamber ensemble, 1987; *Distanzen,* winds, string quartet, 1988; *Kammersinfonie I,* 2 oboes, 2 horns, strings, 1988); instrumental (*Gasa,* violin, piano, 1963; *Garak,* flute, piano, 1963; *Tuyaux sonores,* organ, 1967; *Duo,* viola, piano, 1976; *Salomo,* flute, 1978; *Kontraste,* violin, 1987; *In Balance,* harp, 1987); vocal works (*Teile Dich, Nacht,* soprano, orchestra, 1980).

Z

Zabaleta, Nicanor (b. San Sebastián, 7 Jan. 1907; d. Puerto Rico, 31 Mar. 1993). Harpist. Studied in Madrid and in Paris with Marcel Tournier, and undertook a number of concert tours in the U.S., Europe, and South America. He did much to bring solo harp playing before a wide audience, through both his resurrection of previously forgotten works and his performance of new works in recital and at music festivals. Halffter, Krenek, and Tailleferre wrote solo works for him, and Ginastera, Milhaud, Piston, Virgil Thomson, Villa-Lobos, and Josef Tal are among the composers who wrote concertos for his use. He also made a number of recordings.

Zacar [Zacharias, Zachara, Zacharie]. The name of at least two, or perhaps three, musicians who flourished ca. 1400 in Italy; copyists often fail to specify a first name for "Magister Zacharias," making attribution a complicated matter. Nicola Zacharie of Brindisi was a singer and chaplain at S. Maria del Fiore in Florence in 1420, the same year he became a singer in the papal choir; in 1434 he returned to the choir after a 10-year absence. Nothing is known of the life of Antonio Zachara da Teramo. Antonio composed a number of *ballate* that were extremely popular during his lifetime; his sacred music includes Mass pairs and movements. Nicola's output also includes *ballate,* as well as the motet *Argi vices/Com Pilemon.*

Bibl.: Nino Pirrotta, "Zacarus musicus," *Quadrivium* 12 (1971): 153–75.

Zacconi, Lodovico [Giulio Cesare] (b. Pesaro, 11 June 1555; d. Fiorenzuola di Focara, near Pesaro, 23 Mar. 1627). Singer and theorist. He was trained in plainsong and organ at Pesaro, where he became a subdeacon by 1573. In 1575 he was ordained a priest; at this time he was active as a singer and learned to play the harpsichord, lute, and viola da gamba as a means to supplement his income. From 1577 to 1583 he was at the Augustinian convent of S. Stefano in Venice. He sang in the convent choir under Ippolito Baccusi and studied counterpoint in Venice with Andrea Gabrieli. After studying theology in Padua, Zacconi became a singer at the courts of Archduke Karl of Austria in Graz (1584–90) and Duke Wilhelm V of Bavaria in Munich (1590–96). His most important theoretical work, the 2-part treatise *Prattica di musica* (Venice, 1592, 1622; R: 1967), deals with various theoretical topics and provides important information regarding the performance of figured chant and 16th-century polyphonic music.

Zacher, Gerd (b. Meppen, Germany, 6 July 1929). Organist and composer. He studied at the Northwest German Academy of Music in Detmold (1949–52), with Theodor Kaufmann in Hamburg (1952–54), and with Messiaen at the Darmstadt summer courses (1952–53). He was organist at the German church in Santiago, Chile (1954–57), then at the Lutherkirche in Hamburg (1957–70). In 1970 he was appointed professor at the Folkwangschule in Essen. As a performer he became known as an advocate and interpreter of avant-garde music on the organ, introducing works by György Ligeti, Mauricio Kagel, John Cage, Silvio Bussotti, and others. His own compositions make use of many new techniques and sonorities on the organ.

Bibl.: Rudolf Lück, *Werkstattgespräche mit Interpreten neuer Musik* (Cologne, 1972), pp. 129–49 [interview].

Zachow [Zachau], **Friedrich Wilhelm** (b. Leipzig, bap. 14 Nov. 1663; d. Halle, 7 Aug. 1712). Composer. He received his early schooling in Leipzig, and probably studied with Johann Hildebrand in Eilenburg from 1676. From 1684 until his death he was organist at the Marienkirche in Halle, where he took charge of the town choir and instrumentalists and became well known as a teacher; among his pupils were Handel and Johann Gotthilf Krieger. About 30 sacred cantatas as well as numerous chorale preludes and fugues for organ survive.

Bibl.: *Friedrich Wilhelm Zachow: Gesammelte Werke,* ed. Max Seiffert, *DDT* 21–22 (Leipzig, 1905; R: 1957). Günter Thomas, *Friedrich Wilhelm Zachow* (Regensberg, 1966).

Zador, Eugene [Zádor, Jenő] (b. Bátaszék, Hungary, 5 Nov. 1894; d. Hollywood, 4 Apr. 1977). Composer. He learned piano and began composing as a child. He studied at the Vienna Conservatory with Richard Heuberger (1911–12) and with Max Reger in Leipzig (1912–14), and he received a Ph.D. in musicology from the Univ. of Münster (1921). From 1922 to 1928 he taught at the New Vienna Conservatory. Two orchestral works, *Rondo* (1933) and *Hungarian Caprice* (1935), brought him to public attention as a musical traditionalist and a colorful orchestrator in the tradition of Richard Strauss. In 1938, as Hitler entered Austria, Zador emigrated to the U.S. He worked as an orchestrator in New York, then in Hollywood, where he orchestrated over 100 movies. He remained active as a composer, particularly of orchestral music and opera. Works include *The Inspector General* (opera, 1928; Los Angeles, 1971); *Christopher Columbus* (New York, 1939); *The Magic Chair* (Baton Rouge, La., 1955); *The Scarlet Mill* (New York, 1968); *Festival*

Overture (1964); *Variations on a Merry Theme* (orchestra, 1965); Cimbalom Concerto (1969); Accordion Concerto (1971).

Bibl.: Leslie Zador, *Eugene Zador: A Catalogue of His Works* (San Diego, 1978).

Zahortsev, Vladimir Nikolaevich (b. Kiev, 27 Oct. 1944). Composer. Attended the Kiev Conservatory, studying composition with Liatoshinsky and Shtogarenko and graduating in 1968. A member of the Kiev avant-garde in the 1960s. His music has been influenced by serial and aleatoric principles. Works include opera (*Maty,* 1985); 2 symphonies, chamber symphonies, and other symphonic music; chamber music; vocal and choral music.

Zaimont, Judith Lang (b. Memphis, 8 Nov. 1945). Composer. As a teenager she studied piano with LeLand Thompson at the Juilliard School, then with Zaven Khachadourian at the Long Island Institute of Music (diploma, 1966). With her sister Doris she performed and toured as a duo pianist. She studied composition with Hugo Weisgall at Queens College (B.A., 1966), with Jack Beeson and Otto Luening at Columbia Univ. (M.A., 1968) and with André Jolivet in Paris (1971–72). Taught at Adelphi Univ. (1978–80), at Peabody Conservatory (1980–87), then again at Adelphi (beginning 1989). Her compositions are tonal and often Romantic in gesture. Her best-known works are sets of songs and piano pieces (*Songs of Innocence,* soprano, tenor, flute, cello, harp, 1974; *The Magic World,* baritone, piano, percussion, 1979; *A Calendar Set,* piano, 1978; *Nocturne: La fin de siècle,* 1979).

Zajc, Ivan [Zaytz, Giovanni von] (b. Rijeka, 3 Aug. 1832; d. Zagreb, 16 Dec. 1914). Composer. Studied at the Milan Conservatory beginning in 1850; his teachers included Rochetti, Monteviti, Rossi, and Mazzucato. In 1855 he conducted the premiere of his first opera, *La tirolese.* Soon after this he returned home, where he taught music, composed, and conducted. In 1862 he moved to Vienna and was named conductor of the Carltheater. He moved to Zagreb in 1870, where he conducted the opera and composed. His works include 54 operas and operettas; symphonies; 19 Masses, 4 Requiem Masses; cantatas; incidental music to plays; a string quartet; organ preludes; other orchestra, chamber, and keyboard music.

Bibl.: H. Pettan, *Ivan Zajc* (Zagreb, 1971).

Zandonai, Riccardo (b. Sacco di Rovereto, in the Trentino, 30 May 1883; d. Pesaro, 5 June 1944). Composer and conductor. He studied with Pietro Mascagni at the Liceo musicale in Pesaro (1898–1901) and enjoyed operatic success at an early age with *Il grillo del focolare* (Turin, 1908), followed by *Conchita* (Milan, 1911) and *Francesca da Rimini* (Turin, 1914). Vivid operas in the verismo tradition, with elaborate orchestrations and exotic touches, they established Zandonai as Puccini's heir apparent. During World War I he was accused of treason by the Austrians on account of his nationalist agitation in the Trentino. Between the wars he composed several more operas, including *I cavalieri di Ekebù* (Milan, 1925) and *La farsa amorosa* (Rome, 1933), but none became popular outside of Italy. He was active as a conductor, and he composed a good deal of orchestral music, including *Concerto romantico* (violin and orchestra, 1919), *Tra gli alberghi delle Dolomiti* (1922), *Concerto andaluso* (cello and orchestra, 1934), and *Rapsodia trentina* (1936).

Bibl.: Bruno Cagnoli, *Riccardo Zandonai* (Trento, 1983). Renato Chiesa, ed., *Riccardo Zandonai* (Milan, 1984). Adriano Bassi, *Riccardo Zandonai* (Milan, 1989).

Zanella, Amilcare Castore (b. Monticelli d'Ongina, near Piacenza, 26 Sept. 1873; d. Pesaro, 9 Jan. 1949). Pianist and composer. He studied at the Parma Conservatory (diploma, 1891), then toured as a conductor and pianist in South America (1893–1900). His early works are in a conservative Romantic idiom, but piano pieces of 1900–1910 contain radical, sometimes whimsical, touches such as parallel harmonies, long passages without bar lines, and nonsensical titles. Examples are *L'arte del fare il nuovo* (ca. 1902) and *Due Studi (amaritmiche)* (1906). From 1905 to 1940 he directed and taught at the Liceo musicale Gioacchino Rossini in Pesaro. Works include *Aura* (opera, Pesaro, 1910); *Il revisore* (opera, Trieste, 1940); 2 symphonies (1901, 1919); *Elegia e momento frenetico* (string orchestra and xylophone, 1923); 2 string quartets; 2 piano sonatas (1890, 1916).

Bibl.: Arrigo Dioli and Maria Fernanda Nobili, *La vita e l'arte di Amilcare Zanella* (Bergamo, 1941).

Zannetti [Zanetti], **Francesco** (b. Volterra, 27 Mar. 1737; d. Perugia, 31 Jan. 1788). Composer. He displayed musical talent at an early age and was sent to study with G. C. M. Clari in Pisa. He was appointed *maestro di cappella* at Volterra in 1754 and at Perugia Cathedral in 1760. His compositions include 8 operas, the most popular of which were *Le lavanderine* (Rome, 1772) and *Le cognate in contesa* (Venice, 1780); sacred music, other vocal works, and instrumental chamber music.

Zappa, Frank [Francis Vincent] (b. Baltimore, 21 Dec. 1940; d. Los Angeles, 4 Dec. 1993). Rock songwriter and guitarist, composer. His family moved to California in 1950, where he began playing guitar in rock bands in high school. After writing film scores in the early 1960s, in 1964 he joined the band which became known as the Mothers of Invention; he released albums with them from 1966 to the mid-1970s, and under his own name from 1969. Often extremely difficult, his music mainly eschews or parodies normal rock music forms and styles, while his lyrics purposely test the moral tolerance of the popular music industry. Among his better-known recordings are the albums *Freak Out* (1966), *We're Only in It for the Money* (1967, a parody of the Beatles, *Sgt. Pepper's Lonely Hearts Club Band*), and *Joe's Garage* (1980, including

"Why Does It Hurt When I Pee?"), and the singles "Don't Eat the Yellow Snow" (1973) and "Valley Girl" (1982). Beginning around 1980 he became increasingly involved in avant-garde composition and performance; he conducted concerts of Varèse's music and had his works recorded by the Ensemble intercontemporain (*The Perfect Stranger,* 1984). He wrote works for orchestra, orchestra and chorus, synclavier, and various chamber ensembles.

Bibl.: Frank Zappa with Peter Occhiogrosso, *The Real Frank Zappa Book* (New York, 1989). Wolfgang Ludwig, *Untersuchungen zum musikalischen Schaffen von Frank Zappa* (Franfurt am Main, 1992). Ben Watson, *Frank Zappa: The Negative Dialectics of Poodle Play* (New York, 1995).

Zarlino, Gioseffo [Gioseffe] (b. Chioggia, 31? Jan. 1517; d. Venice, 4 Feb. 1590). Music theorist and composer. He was educated by the Franciscans and had some music lessons from Francesco Maria Delfico. He received his first tonsure in 1532, took minor orders in 1537, and was made a deacon in 1539. After service as a singer (1536) and organist (1539–40) at Chioggia Cathedral, Zarlino was elected *capellano* and *mansionario* of the Scuola di S. Francesco in Chioggia. He subsequently went to Venice and continued his musical training with Willaert (1541); in 1565 he succeeded Rore as *maestro di cappella* at San Marco, a position he held until his death. He also served as chaplain of S. Severo (from 1565); his students included Artusi, Vincenzo Galilei, and Claudio Merulo.

Zarlino's significance rests on his theoretical writings, especially *Le istitutioni harmoniche* (1558), a seminal work in the history of music theory. The treatise is divided into four parts: the first classifies music and illustrates its arithmetic basis; the second describes intervals; the third is a study of counterpoint and mensural notation; and the fourth addresses the modal system. Zarlino sought to expand the number of consonant intervals from the perfect intervals recognized by Pythagorean theory to include thirds and sixths; he did so by deriving all but the minor sixth from the division of the string into six equal segments. He codified rules of counterpoint that were widely influential and that would continue to be propagated by his pupil Artusi into the following century; they included the restriction of strong-beat dissonances to those notes held over from a syncopated consonance, and the organization of a composition around a fixed mode. The treatise also gives ten rules for proper syllabification of the text in musical settings. In his *Dimostrationi harmoniche* (Venice, 1571) he renumbered the modes, using as his primary octave C to c rather than A to a of Boethius and his followers. The theoretical foundations of Zarlino's work were attacked by a number of contemporaries, most notably by Galilei in his *Dialogo* of 1581; Zarlino responded with his *Sopplimenti musicali* (Venice, 1588). He also composed motets and madrigals.

Writings: *Le istitutioni harmoniche* (Venice, 1558–59; facs., *MMML* ser. 2/1, 1965, and Ridgewood, N.J., 1966); pt. 3 trans. Guy A. Marco and Claude V. Palisca, *YTS* 2 (1968; R: 1976); pt. 4 trans. Vered Cohen, *YTS* 7 (1983); *SR,* pp. 228–61; *RFsC,* pp. 48–49. *Dimostrationi harmoniche* (Venice, 1571; facs., Ridgewood, N.J., 1966; *MMML* ser. 2/2, 1965). *Sopplimenti musicali* (Venice, 1588; facs., Ridgewood, N.J., 1966).

Bibl.: James Haar, "Zarlino's Definition of Fugue and Imitation," *JAMS* 24 (1971): 226–54. Karol Berger, *Musica Ficta: Theories of Accidental Inflections in Vocal Polyphony from Marchetto da Padova to Gioseffo Zarlino* (Cambridge, 1987). Roberto Airoldi, *La teoria del temperamento nell'età di Gioseffo Zarlino* (Cremona, 1989). Loris Tiozzo, *Gioseffo Zarlino: Teorico musicale* (Conselve, 1992).

Zarzycki, Aleksander (b. Lwów, 21 Feb. 1834; d. Warsaw, 1 Nov. 1895). Pianist and composer. Studied in Berlin. In 1857, moved to Paris, studied with Reber and Reinecke. During 1862–63 he gave a number of concerts in Germany and Austria. In 1871, settled in Warsaw, where he founded and directed the Warsaw Music Society Concerts until 1875. Served as director of the Music Institute, 1879–88. Choirmaster of St. John's Cathedral from 1879. Compositions include Piano Concerto op. 17 (ca. 1859–60), works for violin and piano, solo keyboard pieces, songs.

Zawinul, Joe [Josef Erich] (b. Vienna, 7 July 1932). Jazz keyboard player, composer, and bandleader. Upon immigrating to the U.S. he played piano with Maynard Ferguson (1959) and then joined Dinah Washington (1959–61). He concentrated on electric piano in Cannonball Adderley's group (1961–70), for which he composed the title track of the album *Mercy, Mercy, Mercy* (1966). In 1969–70 he recorded with Miles Davis's jazz-rock groups and composed the title track of Davis's album *In a Silent Way* (1969). Playing synthesizer, he co-led with Wayne Shorter the jazz-rock group Weather Report (1970–85), for which he composed the hit tune "Birdland" (on the album *Heavy Weather,* 1976). Renaming the group Weather Update, Zawinul continued as sole leader, but by 1989 he was leading a new jazz-rock quartet.

Zaytz, Giovanni von. See Zajc, Ivan.

Zbinden, Julien-François (b. Rolle, Switzerland, 11 Nov. 1917). Composer. He studied piano with Ernest Décosterd and Marie Panthès (1940–45), and he attended the conservatory at Lausanne (1934–38). In the late 1930s and 1940s he played jazz piano. Beginning in the early 1950s he worked at Radio Lausanne, from 1965 at Radio Suisse Romande in Lausanne, and many of his works were originally written for broadcast (e.g., *Espéranto,* speaker, soprano, chorus, orchestra, 1961). His early instrumental works were in a neoclassical vein (e.g., *Concerto da camera,* piano and string orchestra, 1951). Several works were explicitly influenced by jazz (*Jazzific 59–16,* jazz band and string orchestra, 1958), others by the early music movement (*Sonate en trio,* 2 violas da gamba and harpsichord, 1969). Other works include 2 symphonies (1953, 1957); violin concerto (1964); *Terra Dei* (oratorio, 1967); *Monophrases* (chorus, 2 pianos, and percussion, 1970); *Jazz Sonatine* (piano, 1955); *La solitude* (soprano, orchestra, 1985).

Bibl.: *Julien-François Zbinden: Liste des Oeuvres* (Zurich, 1974).

Zech, Frederick, Jr. (b. Philadelphia, 10 May 1858; d. San Francisco, 25 Oct. 1926). Pianist, composer, and conductor. Son of piano maker Frederick Zech, Sr. Moved to San Francisco (1860); studied with Reinhard Schumacher and Louis Heckmann. In Berlin his teachers included Kullak and Breslauer. Gave a concert of his own works in San Francisco (the first concert of its kind in that city) in 1882. Taught at the College of Notre Dame in Belmont, Calif. Works include several operas, 5 symphonies, 5 symphonic poems, 4 piano concertos, a violin concerto, cello concerto; sonatas for violin, cello, clarinet, and flute.

Zechlin, Ruth (b. Grosshartmannsdorf, 22 June 1926). Composer and harpsichordist. She studied piano, organ, and composition at the Hochschule für Musik in Leipzig (1943–49). Beginning in 1950 she taught composition at the Berlin Musikhochschule, then from 1975 at the Akademie der Künste in Berlin. Her works of the 1950s and early 1960s employed clear counterpoint in a basically tonal framework (*Lidice-Cantata,* baritone, chorus, and orchestra, 1956; *Sonatine,* flute and piano, 1957). From the late 1960s on her style became less tonal and relied more on timbral effects (Piano Concerto, 1974; *Hommages à PHL,* chamber ensemble, 1974). She performed widely as a harpsichordist. Other works include the operas *Reinecke Fuchs* (1968) and *Die Salamandrin und die Bildsäule* (1989); 3 symphonies (1964, 1965, 1966); *Briefe für Orchester* (1980); *Prager Orgelkonzert* (1987); *Träume* (orchestra, 1988); *Träume für Orchester* (1989); *Apparitions* (women's chorus, 1965); 7 string quartets.

Bibl.: Ruth Zechlin, *Situationen, Reflexionen, Gespräche, Erfahrungen, Gedanken* (Berlin, 1986).

Zeisl, Eric (b. Vienna, 18 May 1905; d. Los Angeles, 18 Feb. 1959). Composer. He studied at the Akademie für Musik und Darstellende Kunst in Vienna with Richard Stöhr (1919–23), and he became known as a song composer with *Mondbilder* (1928), *Kinderlieder* (1931), and several other cycles. When Hitler invaded Austria in 1938, Zeisl fled to Paris, then, in 1939, to the U.S. He moved to Hollywood, where he worked as a film composer for MGM (1941), then taught at Los Angeles City College (1949–59). Many of his later works are based on Jewish subjects and on Jewish melodic and modal practice (*Four Songs for Wordless Chorus,* 1948; *The Vineyard,* ballet, 1953; 3 violin sonatas, 1950, 1950, 1951; String Quartet no. 2, 1953).

Bibl.: Malcolm Cole and Barbara Barclay, *Armseelchen: The Life and Music of Eric Zeisl* (Westport, Conn., 1984).

Zeisler [née Blumenfeld; Bloomfield], **Fannie** (b. Bielitz, Poland, 16 July 1863; d. Chicago, 20 Aug. 1927). Pianist. Her family emigrated to the U.S. in 1865. She studied with her brother Maurice Bloomfield and with Ziehn. Debut in Chicago, 1875. She studied with Leschetizky in Vienna, 1878–83. She made her New York debut, 1884; married lawyer Sigmund Zeisler in 1885. She played the standard repertoire, but also promoted the works of women composers.

Zeitlin, Zvi (b. Dubrovna, 21 Feb. 1923). Violinist. Studied at the Hebrew Univ. in Jerusalem and then at the Juilliard School. His professional debut was with the Palestine Orchestra in 1940. He toured widely, appearing both with major orchestras and in smaller recitals. Known for his support of contemporary music; several composers wrote works for him. He became a member of the faculty of the Eastman School in 1967. Also active in research, he discovered 6 concertos by Pietro Nardini, one of which he edited and published.

Zelenka, Jan Dismas [Johann Dismas, Jan Lukáš] (b. Lounovice, Bohemia, 16 Oct. 1679; d. Dresden, 22 Dec. 1745). Composer. He may have attended the Jesuit college Clementinum in Prague before serving Count Hartig in that city (1709–10). From 1710 he played double bass in the royal orchestra at Dresden. On his way to Italy in 1715, he studied with J. J. Fux in Vienna and A. Lotti in Venice. After a few years in Venice (1717–19) he returned to Dresden, where he stayed for the rest of his life; in 1735 he became *Kirchen-compositeur.* His compositions include Masses, oratorios, cantatas, motets, other sacred vocal works, 6 trio sonatas, and various orchestral works.

Bibl.: Wolfgang Reich, *Jan Dismas Zelenka: Thematisch-systematisches Verzeichnis der musikalischen Werke (ZWV)* (Dresden, 1985). Susanne Oschmann, *Jan Dismas Zelenka: Seine Geistlichen Italienischen Oratorien* (New York, 1986). Wolfgang Reich, *Zwei Zelenka-Studien* (Dresden, 1987). Wolfgang Horn and Thomas Kohlhase, eds., *Zelenka-Dokumentation* (Wiesbaden, 1989).

Żeleński, Władysław (b. Grodkowice, near Kraków, 6 July 1837; d. Kraków, 23 Jan. 1921). Pianist and composer. As a child he studied violin, then piano. Studied composition in Kraków with Mirecki. Studied philosophy and music in Prague, 1859; received Ph.D. in 1862. Studied at Paris Conservatory (1866) with Reber. Returned to Kraków in 1871. He taught harmony at the Warsaw Music Institute beginning in 1872. Director of Kraków Conservatory Music Society concerts from 1881. Composed several operas, 2 symphonies, 3 Masses, cantatas, 3 overtures, 4 string quartets, string sextet, string trio, piano trio, keyboard works, songs.

Bibl.: Zdzisław Jachimecki, *W. Żeleński: życie i twórczość* (Kraków, 1952).

Zeller, Carl (Johann Adam) (b. St. Peter in der Au, 19 June 1842; d. Baden, near Vienna, 17 Aug. 1898). Composer. He studied law at the Univ. of Vienna, where he took composition lessons with Simon Sechter. Received a doctorate in law at Univ. of Graz, 1869. Entered the Ministry of Education and Culture in

1873. Composed 7 light operas, including *Joconde* (1876) and *Der Vogelhändler* (1891).

Zelter, Carl Friedrich (b. Berlin, 11 Dec. 1758; d. there, 15 May 1832). Composer. The son of a mason, he also learned the trade (becoming a master in 1783) but pursued musical activities early, including piano and violin instruction. In 1779 he was a violinist in the Doebblin Theater orchestra; he studied composition with Carl Fasch, 1784–86, and joined his Singakademie in 1791. He took over as director of the group when Fasch died in 1800 and started a companion orchestral ensemble for the Singakademie, the Ripienschule, in 1808. He became a member of the faculty of the Royal Academy of the Arts in Berlin in 1809, the same year that he started the Liedertafel, a men's singing society for which he wrote many choral pieces. In 1822 he established the Royal Institute for Church Music, which he himself directed. Goethe admired Zelter's settings of his poems; the two became friends and established an extensive correspondence. He was a composer primarily of vocal works; it is for his lieder (around 200) that he is remembered today. His first book of lieder was published in 1796, the second in 1801. Several other collections followed, as well as songs published in almanacs. He composed cantatas, various other sacred and secular choral works, a viola concerto, keyboard music. He wrote the pedagogical works *Practische Gesang-Lehre* (MS, 1812) and *Gesang-Übungen sowie 2 und 3 Cursus der Compositionslehre* (MS, 1812). He also wrote an autobiography (ed. W. Rentel, Berlin, 1861).

Bibl.: Raymond Barr, "Carl Friedrich Zelter: A Study of the Lied in Berlin during the Late 18th and Early 19th Centuries" (diss., Univ. of Winconsin, 1968).

Zemlinsky, Alexander (von) (b. Vienna, 14 Oct. 1871; d. Larchmont, N.Y., 15 Mar. 1942). Composer and conductor. He studied piano and composition at the Vienna Conservatory (1887–92) and enjoyed early success with his chamber music (Trio, clarinet, cello, piano, 1896; String Quartet no. 1, 1895). His early works are strongly influenced by Brahms, whom Zemlinsky knew. He also became acquainted with Mahler, who introduced Zemlinsky's opera *Es war einmal* at the Hofoper in 1900, and with Schoenberg. Sponsored by Mahler, Zemlinsky played an increasingly important part in Viennese musical life, as conductor at the Carltheater (1899–1903), the Volksoper (1904–7, 1909–11), and the Hofoper (1907–8). With Schoenberg he founded the Vereinigung Schaffender Tonkünstler to promote new music. In 1911 he moved to Prague as principal conductor of the Deutsches Landestheater. He remained close to Schoenberg and to Viennese contemporary music circles, engaging Schoenberg disciples Heinrich Jalowetz and Anton Webern to conduct at the Landestheater and founding a Prague branch of the Verein für Musikalische Privataufführungen.

As a composer, Zemlinsky moved during the first decade of the 20th century toward a chromatic and intensely lyrical style in which formal organization and harmonies are both derived from thematic content, as in the second string quartet (1914). Zemlinsky's stylistic evolution paralleled that of Schoenberg; indeed the two men were in close communication during the entire period. Zemlinsky, however, declined to follow Schoenberg into atonality. By the time Schoenberg proclaimed the discovery of the twelve-tone method, Zemlinsky had arrived, in the *Lyrische Symphonie* (soprano, baritone, and orchestra, 1922) and the third string quartet (1924), at a style in which tonal centers and traditional forms are restored, though often undermined by contrapuntal virtuosity, expressive outbursts, and references to works by other composers. Zemlinsky moved in 1927 from Prague to Berlin, where he conducted at the Kroll Opera (1927–30) and taught at the Musikhochschule (1927–33). With Hitler's rise to power in 1933, he returned to Vienna; when the German-Austrian Anschluss came in 1938 he fled to the U.S.

Other works include *Sarema* (opera, Munich, 1897); *Der Traumgörge* (opera, 1906; 1st perf., Nuremberg, 1980); *Eine florentinische Tragödie* (opera, Stuttgart, 1917); *Der Zwerg* (opera, Cologne, 1922); 2 symphonies (1892, 1897); *Sinfonietta* (orchestra, 1934); string quartet no. 4 (1936); "Maeterlinck Songs" (mezzo-soprano or baritone and piano, 1913; also orchestrated); *Symphonische Gesänge* (voice and orchestra, 1929).

Writings: *Briefwechsel mit Schönberg, Webern, Berg und Schreker* (Munich, 1982).

Bibl.: Lawrence A. Oncley, "The Works of Alexander Zemlinsky: A Chronological List," *Notes* 34 (1977–78): 291–302. Horst Weber, *Alexander Zemlinsky* (Vienna, 1977). Rudolf Stephan, *Alexander Zemlinsky* (Kiel, 1978). Werner Loll, *Zwischen Tradition und Avantgarde: die Kammermusik Alexander Zemlinskys* (Kassel, 1990).

Zender, Hans (b. Wiesbaden, 22 Nov. 1936). Conductor and composer. He studied piano and conducting at the Frankfurt Musikhochschule (1956–57), then composition at the Freiburg Musikhochschule with Wolfgang Fortner (1957–59). He was assistant conductor in Freiburg (1959–63), then chief conductor at the theaters in Bonn (1964–68) and Kiel (1969–71), conductor of the Radio Orchestra of the Saar (1971–77), and music director at the Hamburg Opera (1977–88). His compositions include *Three Orchestra Pieces* (1955); Piano Concerto (1955); *Schachspiel* (2 orchestras, 1970); *Zeitströme* (orchestra, 1974); *Hölderlin lesen* (string quartet, ad lib *Sprechstimme,* 1979); *Die Wüste hat zwölf Dinge* (mezzo-soprano and orchestra, 1986); *Five Haiku* (flute and strings, 1982); *Mondschaft* (flute solo, 1978); *Happy Band* (trumpet, 1989).

Zeno, Apostolo (b. Venice, 11 Dec. 1668; d. there, 11 Nov. 1750). Librettist. After receiving his education at the seminary of the Somaschi fathers, he was a founder of the Accademia degli Animosi (1691) and the *Giornale dei letterati d'Italia* (1710). His first success as a librettist came in 1700 with *Lucio Vero,* set by C. F.

Pollarolo and performed at the Teatro S. Giovanni Grisostomo in Venice. He later collaborated with Pietro Pariati. He worked as an administrator in Venice from 1711, and from 1718 until his retirement in 1729 he was "poeta e istorico di S. M. Cesarea" in Vienna; he was succeeded there by Metastasio. Zeno wrote about 70 librettos.

Bibl.: Robert Freeman, "Apostolo Zeno's Reform of the Libretto," *JAMS* 21 (1968): 321–41.

Zeuner, Charles (Heinrich Christoph) (b. Eisleben, 20 Sept. 1795; d. Philadelphia, 7 Nov. 1857). Pianist, organist, and composer. Studied with Hummel at Weimar. Court and military musician near his birthplace. Emigrated sometime during the late 1820s or in 1830 to Boston. Organist for the Handel and Haydn Society, 1830; president, 1838–39. Moved to Philadelphia, 1839, and was organist at several churches. Composed oratorios, Masses, cantatas, organ works (including many fugues), band marches, choral works, songs.

Bibl.: William George Biggers, "The Choral Music of Charles Zeuner with a Performance Edition of Representative Works" (diss., Univ. of Iowa, 1976).

Ziani, Marc'Antonio (b. Venice, ca. 1653; d. Vienna, 22 Jan. 1715). Composer. He was probably taught by his uncle Pietro Andrea Ziani. In 1686 he was appointed *maestro di cappella* at S. Barbara, Mantua; he was probably also in the service of the Duke of Mantua. While there he taught Caldara. Later he was in Vienna, Bologna, and Venice, where he became successful as an opera composer in the 1690s. In 1700 he became *vice-Hofkapellmeister* to Emperor Leopold I in Vienna; he was made *Hofkapellmeister* in 1712. Ziani wrote about 45 operas, 16 oratorios, over 20 Masses, 3 Requiem Masses, more than 100 other sacred vocal works, secular cantatas, and arias.

Bibl.: Theophil Antonicek, "Die *Damira*-Opern der beiden Ziani," *AnMca* 14 (1974): 176–207.

Ziani, Pietro Andrea (b. Venice, probably before 21 Dec. 1616; d. Naples, 12 Feb. 1684). Composer. Uncle of Marc'Antonio Ziani. He became a deacon in 1639 and took holy orders the following year. He was organist at S. Salvatore, Venice, and was later *maestro di cappella* at S. Maria Maggiore, Bergamo (1657–59). In 1662 Ziani became vice-Kapellmeister to the Dowager Empress Eleonora in Vienna, and in 1669 succeeded Cavalli as first organist of St. Mark's, Venice. Later he taught at the Conservatorio S. Onofrio, Naples, and was appointed *maestro di cappella* at court (1680). Ziani was one of the most important of the early opera composers in Venice. He wrote about 30 operas, oratorios, other sacred vocal works, madrigals, canzonettas, cantatas, and sonatas.

Ziehn, Bernhard (b. Erfurt, Germany, 20 Jan. 1845; d. Chicago, 8 Sept. 1912). Theorist. He studied in Erfurt, and later taught at Mühlhausen. From 1868 to 1870 he taught mathematics, German, and music theory at a school in Chicago. He wrote many critical essays in which he championed Bruckner and frequently attacked a number of contemporary scholars, including Riemann and Spitta. He wrote a bilingual (German and English) piano method (Hamburg, 1881), which led him to discover the principle of "symmetric inversion." Other bilingual texts include *Five- and Six-Part Harmonies* (Milwaukee and Berlin, 1911) and *Canonical Studies: A New Technic in Composition* (Milwaukee and Berlin, 1912).

Bibl.: Severine Neff, "Otto Luening and the Theories of Bernhard Ziehn," *CM* 39 (1985): 21–41.

Zieleński [Zelenscius], **Mikołaj** (fl. 1611). Composer. He was organist and director of music to Wojciech Baranowski, Archbishop of Gneizno and primate of Poland from 1608. His two publications, the *Offertoria* and the *Communiones* (both Venice, 1611), contain polychoral sacred music as well as the earliest examples of Polish monody, concertato, and music specifically written for instruments.

Zilcher, Hermann (b. Frankfurt, 18 Aug. 1881; d. Würzburg, 1 Jan. 1948). Pianist, composer, and teacher. He studied at the Hoch Conservatory in Frankfurt (1897–1901) with James Kwast (piano) and Iwan Knorr (composition). He toured as a pianist and taught at the Akademie der Tonkunst in Munich (1908–20). From 1920 to 1944 he was director of the Würzburg Conservatory. In his compositions he stuck closely to the traditions of German Romanticism. Works include *Fitzebutze* (opera, Mannheim, 1903); *Doktor Eisenbart* (opera, Mannheim, 1922); 4 symphonies; 2 piano concertos; concertos for 1 and 2 violins; chamber works and many songs.

Zildjian. Family of cymbal makers. The business consists of the Avedis Zildjian Co. of Norwell, Mass., and K. Zildjian of Istanbul. The Zildjians trace their method of treating alloys in the cymbal-casting process to Turkish alchemists of the early 17th century. After centuries of production in Turkey, a foundry was established in North Quincy, Mass., in 1929.

Zillig, Winfried (Petrus Ignatius) (b. Würzburg, 1 Apr. 1905; d. Hamburg, 17 Dec. 1963). Composer and conductor. He studied at the Würzburg Conservatory with Hans Zilcher, then with Arnold Schoenberg (1925–28). As Schoenberg's disciple he adopted twelve-tone techniques, for example, in his first string quartet (1927) and *Serenade no. 1* (1928). Embarking on a career as a conductor, he was Kleiber's assistant at the Berlin Staatsoper (1927–28), vocal coach in Oldenburg, then conductor at Düsseldorf, Essen, and Poznan. After World War II he conducted at Radio Frankfurt (1947–51), at North German Radio in Hamburg (beginning 1959), and elsewhere in Germany. Zillig remained committed to Schoenberg and to twelve-tone music during the Nazi period, and he was an important figure in the revival of modern music in Germany after the war. Works include *Rosse* (opera, Düsseldorf, 1933); *Das Opfer* (opera, Hamburg,

1937); *Das Verlobnis* (opera, Linz, 1963); Concerto for Orchestra (1930); Violin Concerto (1955); many songs.

Writings: *Variationen über neue Musik* (Munich, 1959). "Notes on 'Die Jakobsleiter,'" *Score* 25 (1959): 7–16.

Ziloti (Siloti), Alexander Il'yich (b. near Kharkov, 9 Oct. 1863; d. New York, 8 Dec. 1945). Pianist. Studied with Nikolay Rubenstein, Zverev, and Tchaikovsky in Moscow, and later with Liszt in Weimar. In 1887 he joined the faculty at the Moscow Conservatory, where Rachmaninoff, a cousin, was one of his students. In 1901–2 he conducted the Moscow Philharmonic and the next year he started his own orchestra in St. Petersburg. He moved to the U.S. in 1922 and taught at the Juilliard School. He published his recollections of Liszt (St. Petersburg, 1911).

Zimbalist, Efrem (Alexandrovich) (b. Rostov-na-Donu, Russia, 21 Apr. 1889; d. Reno, 22 Feb. 1985). Violinist and composer. Received early instruction on the violin from his father and later from Leopold Auer at the St. Petersburg Conservatory, from which he graduated with the gold medal in 1907. Following a series of successful European performances he settled in the U.S. after his debut with the Boston Symphony in 1911. He taught at and later became the director of the Curtis Institute (1941–68). He also composed several works including the opera *Landara* (1956); concertos for piano, cello, and violin; several orchestral works; chamber works and solo violin music.

Zimmer, Ján (b. Ružomberk, north Slovakia, 16 May 1926). Composer. He studied at the Bratislava Conservatory through 1948, taking keyboard and composition lessons with Suchoň. He went on to study with Farkas at the Budapest Music Academy and then in Salzburg in 1949. From 1948 through 1952 he was a teacher at the Bratislava Conservatory. His compositional language incorporates native Slovakian folk music, often set within a thick, colorful orchestration. He frequently used traditional forms and genres. Works include the opera *Král' Oidipus* (1967), the television ballet *Herakles* (1970), orchestral music (6 piano concertos; 9 symphonies; *Strečno,* symphonic poem, 1959; *Concerto Polyphonico,* organ, orchestra, 1986; Concerto, viola and chamber orchestra, 1989), vocal music (4 motets, 1967), and chamber music.

Zimmermann, Agnes (Marie Jacobina) (b. Cologne, 5 July 1845; d. London, 14 Nov. 1925). Pianist and composer. Studied with Potter at the Royal Academy of Music. London debut, 1863; Leipzig, 1864. She composed piano sonatas, violin sonatas, songs. Edited piano works of Mozart, Beethoven, and Schumann. First English performance of the piano transcription of Beethoven's Violin Concerto, 1872.

Zimmermann, Bernd Alois (b. Bliesheim, Germany, 20 Mar. 1918; d. Königsdorf, 10 Aug. 1970). As a child he attended a Salvatorian monastery school; religious belief was one of his principal concerns throughout his life. He attended the Univ. of Cologne and the Cologne Hochschule für Musik, where he studied with Heinrich Lemacher and Philipp Jarnach. His works of the late 1940s and early 1950s—for example, *Symphony in One Movement* (1951; rev. 1953)—were influenced on the one hand by the expressionism of Berg and Schoenberg, on the other by Stravinskian neoclassicism. Other works of this period were influenced by non-Western music and American jazz, such as the trumpet concerto (1954), which is based on the spiritual "Nobody Knows the Trouble I Seen." Study with Wolfgang Fortner and René Leibowitz at the Darmstadt summer courses (1948–50) plus intense study of the works of Anton Webern led Zimmermann by the mid-50s toward serialism in works such as the viola sonata (1955), *Perspektiven* (2 pianos, 1956), and the sonata for solo cello (1960). He taught at the Univ. of Cologne (1950–52), and was active at West German Radio in Cologne, composing many radio scores. In 1957 was appointed professor at the Cologne Musikhochschule, where he continued to teach until his death.

The 1965 premiere in Cologne of his opera *Die Soldaten* launched Zimmermann as a composer of international stature. *Die Soldaten* combines strict serialism, expressionistic orchestration, jazz interludes, Bach chorales, Gregorian chant, and still other musical styles in a texture that Zimmermann called "pluralistic." He linked musical pluralism with a philosophical notion of time: references to past pieces and styles express actual simultaneity in the consciousness of composer and performer. In *Requiem für einen jungen Dichter* (speakers, singers, jazz ensemble, orchestra, and electronic sounds, 1969), the idea is applied to create an aural collage of European history from 1920 to 1969.

Other works include *Dialoge* (2 pianos and orchestra, 1960; rev. for 2 pianos solo, 1965); Cello Concerto (1966); *Stille und Umkehr* (orchestra, 1970); *Ich wandte mich und sah an alles Unrecht . . .* (speakers, baritone, orchestra, 1970); violin sonata (1950); *Musique pour les soupers du roi Ubu* (ballet, 1966); *Intercommunicazione* (cello and piano, 1967); *Tratto* (tape, 1966); *Tratto II* (tape, 1969).

Bibl.: Bernd Alois Zimmerman, *Intervall und Zeit: Aufsätze und Schriften zum Werk* (Mainz, 1974). Wulf Konold, *Bernd Alois Zimmermann—Der Komponist und sein Werk* (Cologne, 1986) [including works list]. Klaus Ebbeke, *"Sprachfindung": Studien zum Spätwerk Bernd Alois Zimmermanns* (New York, 1986). Hermann Beyer and Siegfried Mauser, *Zeitphilosophie und Klangestalt: Untersuchungen zum Werk Bernd Alois Zimmermanns* (Mainz, 1986).

Zimmermann [Zimmerman], **Pierre-Joseph-Guillaume** (b. Paris, 19? Mar. 1785; d. there, 29 Oct. 1853). Pianist and composer. Father was a piano maker. Studied piano at the Paris Conservatory with Boieldieu (1798), where he won first prize for piano (1800) and harmony (1802). Later studied with Cherubini. Assisted in piano at the Conservatory in 1811; appointed professor in 1816. Offered professorship, which he refused, of counterpoint and fugue in 1821. His students included Bizet, Gounod, Franck, and Alkan.

Bibl.: Jean Baptiste Labat, *Zimmermann et l'école française de piano* (Paris, 1865).

Zimmermann, Udo (b. Dresden, 6 Oct. 1943). Composer. He studied at the Dresden Hochschule für Musik with Johannes Paul Thilman, then at the Akademie der Künste in Berlin with Günther Kochan. He returned to Dresden in 1970 as composer and producer at the Dresden Opera and at the Studio for New Music (beginning 1974). In 1978 he became professor of composition at the Dresden Hochschule; in 1986 he was appointed director of Dresden Zentrum für Zeitgenössische Musik and artistic adviser to the opera workshop of the Bonn Opera; in 1990 he became intendant for the Leipzig Opera. Many of his works are serial (e.g., *Sonetti amorosi,* alto, flute, and string quartet, 1967; *Mutazione,* orchestra, 1973); some employ aleatory elements.

Works: *Die weisse Rose* (dramatic cantata, 1967); *Musik für Streicher* (1967); *Die zweite Entscheidung* (opera, Magdeburg, 1970); *Ode an das Leben* (mezzo, chorus, orchestra, 1972); *Levins Mühle* (opera, Dresden, 1973); *Der Schuhu und die fliegende Prinzessin* (opera, 1976); Concerto (percussion and orchestra, 1980); *Die wundersame Schusterfrau* (Schwetzingen, 1982); *Mein Gott, wer trommelt denn da?* (orchestra, 1985); *Canticum Marianum* (12 cellos, 1985); *Gib Licht meinen Augen oder ich entschlage des Todes* (soprano, baritone, orchestra, 1986); *Die Sündflut* (1988); Horn Concerto (1987); *Gantebein Gesänge* (baritone, orchestra, 1988); *Nouveau divertissement* (viola concerto, 1988).

Zingarelli, Niccolò Antonio (b. Naples, 4 Apr. 1752; d. Torre del Greco, near Naples, 5 May 1837). Composer. He studied at the Conservatorio Santa Maria di Loreto with Fenaroli, Sacchini, Anfossi, and Speranza. His *I quattro pazzi,* an intermezzo, was performed there in 1768; his first opera, *Montezuma,* was produced in Naples at S. Carlo in 1781. He was named *maestro di cappella* of the Milan Cathedral in 1793, at Loreto in 1794, at St. Peter's in Rome in 1804; in 1813 he took charge of the conservatory S. Pietro a Majella in Naples, and in 1816 became musical director at the Naples Cathedral. Among his more famous pupils were Mercadente and Bellini. He was a prolific composer. He wrote at least 41 operas and a large amount of church music, including the oratorio *La passione di Gesù Cristo* (Milan, 1787) and 7 other oratorios, many Masses, about 55 Magnificats, and 23 Te Deums. The so-called Annuale di Loreto contains 541 Psalms and propers. His secular vocal music includes approximately 20 cantatas. His symphonies (over 50) and sonatas are mostly in one movement. He also wrote string quartets, pastorales for keyboard, several duets.

Bibl.: Rey M. Longyear, "The Symphonies of Niccolò Zingarelli," *AnMca* 19 (1979): 288–319. Maria Caraci, "Niccolò Zingarelli tra mito e critica," *NRMI* 22 (1988): 375–422.

Zinman, David (Joel) (b. New York, 9 July 1936). Conductor. He received formal education at the Oberlin Conservatory and the Univ. of Minnesota. He studied conducting with Pierre Monteux and at the Berkshire Music Center at Tanglewood and made his debut in 1963 at the Holland Festival. Subsequently he held several conducting positions, including those of music director of the Netherlands Chamber Orchestra (1964–77), music director of the Rochester Philharmonic (1974–85), music director of the Rotterdam Philharmonic (1979–82), and principal guest conductor of the Baltimore Symphony (1983–84), for which he became music director in 1985.

Zipoli, Domenico (b. Prato, 16 or 17 Oct. 1688; d. Santa Catalina, near Córdoba, Argentina, 2 Jan. 1726). Composer. He studied with Giovanni Maria Casini in Florence (1707–9), Alessandro Scarlatti in Naples (1709), Lavinio Felice Vannucci in Bologna (1709), and Bernardo Pasquini in Rome (1709–10). In 1715 he was appointed organist at the Jesuit church in Rome. His keyboard collection *Sonate d'intavolatura* was published there in 1716. He settled in Córdoba in 1717, and prepared to enter the priesthood by studying philosophy and theology. His other works include oratorios, Masses, and cantatas.

Bibl.: Susan Erickson-Bloch, "The Keyboard Music of Domenico Zipoli" (diss., Cornell Univ., 1975). Francisco Curt Lange, "Domenico Zipoli: Storia di una riscoperta," *NRMI* 19 (1985): 203–26.

Zoilo, Annibale (b. Rome, ca. 1537; d. Loreto, 1592). Composer and singer. He served as choirmaster of S. Luigi dei Francesi (1561–66) and then held a similar position at St. John Lateran (1567–70); also was employed by Cardinal Guglielmo Sirleto and subsequently joined the choir of the Sistine Chapel (1570–77). In 1577 Pope Gregory XIII appointed Zoilo and Palestrina to prepare a corrected edition of the Roman *Graduale,* but the project was canceled the following year owing to lack of funds. Zoilo was appointed choirmaster of Todi Cathedral in 1581, and from 1584 until his death was choirmaster of the Santa Casa, Loreto. His works are similar in style to those of Palestrina.

Bibl.: Lucia Navarrini, "Nuovi cenni biografici su Anníbale Zoilo," *AnM* 41 (1986): 105–34.

Zöllner, Heinrich (b. Leipzig, 4 July 1854; d. Freiburg, 8 May 1941). Composer and conductor. He was the son of composer Carl Friedrich Zöllner (1800–1860). Studied at Leipzig Conservatory, 1875–77. Conducted Cologne Male Voice Choir, 1875. Lived in U.S., 1890–98. Music director, Leipzig University, 1898; professor of composition, Leipzig Conservatory, from 1902. Conductor at Flemish Opera in Antwerp, 1907–14. He taught at Freiburg, 1914. Served as editor of *Leipzig Tageblatt,* 1903–6. His cantata *Die neue Welt* won a prize at the Cleveland Sängerfest in 1892. Other works include 5 symphonies, overtures, 5 string quartets, solo piano works, piano 4-hand pieces, music for men's chorus, songs.

Zolotarev, Vasili (Andreievich) (b. Taganrog, 7 Mar. 1872; d. Moscow, 25 May 1964). Composer and teacher. He studied violin and music theory at the imperial court chapel in St. Petersburg; took composition lessons with Balakirev and subsequently studied with Rimsky-Korsakov at the St. Petersburg Conservatory (graduated 1900). He was instructor of violin at the Court Chapel (1897–1900) and taught composition at the Rostov Music School (1906–8), the Moscow Conservatory (1908–18), the Ekaterinodar Conservatory (1918–24), the Odessa Conservatory (1924–26), the Kiev Musico-Dramatic Institute (1926–31), the Sverdlovsk Music School (1931–33), and the Minsk Conservatory (1933–41). His pupils included Polovinkin, Dankevich, and Vainberg.

Zoras, Leonidas (b. Sparta, 8 Mar. 1905; d. Athens, 22 Dec. 1987). Composer. He studied law in Athens and concurrently studied conducting with Boutnikoff and Mitropoulos and composition with Lavrangas and Riadis. From 1926 until 1938 he took composition lessons with Kalomiris at the National Conservatory and with Blacher, Grabner, and Höffer at the Berlin Hochschule für Musik. He went on to conduct the Greek National State Opera from 1948 to 1958 and from 1958 to 1968 the Deutsche Oper. At that point he took on the directorship of the Athens National Conservatory. His own compositional language moved from a tonal or modal approach, often involving folk music, to an atonal one. His works include an opera (*Elektra,* 1969), orchestral music (Symphony, 1947; rev. 1950), vocal pieces (*Sti gis afti* [On This Earth], narrator, piano, 1939–48; *14 Cavafy Poems,* baritone, piano, 1955–60).

Zukerman, Pinchas (b. Tel Aviv, 16 July 1948). Violinist, violist, and conductor. He displayed early musical talent and began formal study at the Tel Aviv Academy of Music at age 8; his teacher there was Ilona Feher. He entered the Juilliard School in 1961 upon encouragement from Isaac Stern and Pablo Casals and during his time there also learned the viola. He won the Leventritt Competition in 1967, made his New York debut at Lincoln Center in 1969, and embarked on a successful career as soloist, appearing with American and European orchestras. His conducting debut was in 1974 in London with the Philharmonia Orchestra; since then he has been a frequent guest conductor and was conductor of the St. Paul Chamber Orchestra, 1980–86. Many of his collaborations with orchestras feature him as both soloist and conductor.

Zukofsky, Paul (b. Brooklyn, 22 Oct. 1943). Violinist. A child prodigy, he began playing the violin at age 4 and was a soloist with the New Haven Symphony at age 8. He later studied with Ivan Galamian at the Juilliard School and made his Carnegie Hall debut in 1956. He is particularly recognized for his activity in contemporary music and has given several premieres including those of works by Babbitt, Sessions, Carter, Crumb, and others. He has made many recordings, including an anthology of American violin music written between 1940 and 1970. Taught at the New England Conservatory and SUNY–Stony Brook and elsewhere. Conductor of the Contemporary Chamber Ensemble at Juilliard from 1984, and director of the Arnold Schoenberg Institute from 1992.

Zumaya [Sumaya], **Manuel de** (b. Mexico, ca. 1678; d. Oaxaca, Mexico, between 12 Mar. and 6 May 1756). Composer. He was a choirboy at Mexico City Cathedral, where he studied with Antonio Salazar, the *maestro de capilla,* and Joseph Ydiaquez, the principal organist. He became a priest about 1700, and was an organist at the cathedral by 1708. His opera *La partenope* was performed at the Mexico City palace of the Duke of Linares on 1 May 1711; it was the first full opera heard in North America. After assisting and substituting for Salazar at the cathedral, Zumaya succeeded him as *maestro de capilla* there in 1715. In 1739 he moved to Oaxaca, where he eventually became *maestro de capilla.* His compositions include Masses, motets, hymns, and Spanish *villancicos* and cantatas.

Zumpe, Herman (b. Oppach, 9 Apr. 1850; d. Munich, 4 Sept. 1903). Composer and conductor. Studied at Leipzig Conservatory. Helped prepare the first score of *The Ring,* 1872–76. Conducted at Salzburg, Würzburg, Hamburg Opera (1884–86), Stuttgart (1891–95), Munich (1895, 1900), Covent Garden (1898). He completed 6 operas; another, *Sâwitri* (performed 1907), was completed by Rössler. Other works include a symphony (1868), 2 string quartets (1871, 1891), Psalms, songs.

Bibl.: E. von Possart et al., *Herman Zumpe: persönliche Erinnerungen* (Munich, 1905).

Zumpe, Johannes [Johannes Christoph] (b. in Germany, ca. 1735; d. ca. 1800). Harpsichord and piano maker. Before emigrating to England after the Seven Years' War, he most likely was employed at the Silbermann workshop. Once in London he worked for Burkat Shadi until he opened his own shop at Hanover Square in 1761. Gabriel Buntebart was his partner from 1769 to 1778, when he was joined by C. Meyer. He is known for his square pianos; the earliest extant one dates from 1766. Zumpe built other instruments as well: there is a mandora of his in Glasgow and a guitar in Frankfurt am Main.

Zumsteeg, Johann Rudolf (b. Sachsenflur [Odenwald], 10 Jan. 1760; d. Stuttgart, 27 Jan. 1802). Composer. He studied at the Karlsschule in Stuttgart; also studied cello with Eberhard Malterre. From 1775 he studied with Agostino Poli, the court Kapellmeister, from whom he also learned theory. In 1781 he became a member of the court orchestra; in 1785 a music teacher at the Karlsschule; in 1791 a music director at the court theater; and in 1793 court *Konzertmeister.* Between 1777 and 1792 he composed 10 cello concertos. He composed several operas for Stuttgart, beginning with the singspiel *Das tartarische Gesetz* (1780). He also wrote incidental music (for *Hamlet, Macbeth*) and cantatas. Other surviving instrumental works include a symphony, 2 overtures, flute concertos, pieces for wind instruments, a few chamber pieces. He is remembered chiefly for his songs, of which there are about 300, and he is said to have had an influence on Schubert. Between 1800 and 1805 he published 7 volumes of *Kleine Balladen und Lieder;* his songs were also published in other collections, as well as singly and in periodicals.

Bibl.: Gunter Maier, "Die Lieder Johann Rudolf Zumsteegs und ihr Verhältnis zu Schubert" (diss., Univ. of Tübingen, 1970).

Zupko, Ramon (b. Pittsburgh, 14 Nov. 1932). Composer. He studied at Juilliard with Vincent Persichetti (B.M., 1956; M.M., 1957), then with Karl Schiske at the Vienna Academy of Music (1958–59) and at Columbia Univ., where he worked in the electronic music studios. Many of his works involve electronics either alone or in combination with instruments (*Fluxus I,* tape, 1977; *Fixations,* violin, cello, piano, and tape, 1974). Several works are inspired by American Indian ritual (*Life Dances,* orchestra, 1981; *Earth and Sky,* band, 1984). Beginning in 1971 he taught at Western Michigan Univ. in Kalamazoo. Other works include *Tangents* (brass ensemble, 1967); *Windsongs* (piano and orchestra, 1979); *Noösphere* (string quartet, 1980); *Fluxus II* (piano, 1978); *Fluxus III* (amplified violin, percussion, tape, 1978); *Chorale* (brass quintet, 1989).

Zwilich, Ellen Taaffe (b. Miami, 30 Apr. 1939). Composer. She was trained as a violinist, studying with Richard Burgin in Tallahassee and Ivan Galamian in New York. She attended Florida State Univ. in Tallahassee (B.M., 1956; M.M., 1962), then the Juilliard School, where she studied composition with Elliott Carter and Roger Sessions (D.M.A., 1975). By the mid-70s her works—tonal, lyrical, and formally clear—were getting performances and winning prizes, for example, *Symposium for Orchestra* (1973), which was premiered by Pierre Boulez in 1975, Sonata in Three Movements (violin, 1973), written for her husband, the violinist Joseph Zwilich, and String Quartet (1974), which won the Elizabeth Sprague Coolidge Chamber Music Prize. In 1983 her Symphony no. 1, a Romantic work in the vein of Mahler and Shostakovich, was awarded the Pulitzer Prize for music. Zwilich joined the Juilliard faculty in 1993; in 1995 she became the first composer appointed to Carnegie Hall's Composer's Chair. Other works include Chamber Symphony (1979); *Passages* (soprano and chamber ensemble, 1981); String Trio (1982); *Divertimento* (flute, clarinet, violin, cello, 1983); Double Quartet (2 string quartets, 1984); *Celebration for Orchestra* (1984); Symphony no. 2 (1985); trombone concerto (1988); *Symbolon* (orchestra, 1989); flute concerto (1990); clarinet quintet (1990); Double Concerto (1992); Symphony no. 3 (1993); Concerto for Horn and String Orchestra (1993); *Fantasy* (orchestra, 1994); *A Simple Magnificat* (chorus, organ, 1994); *American Concerto* (trumpet, orchestra, 1994); Triple Concerto (1996).